Central America & Mexico

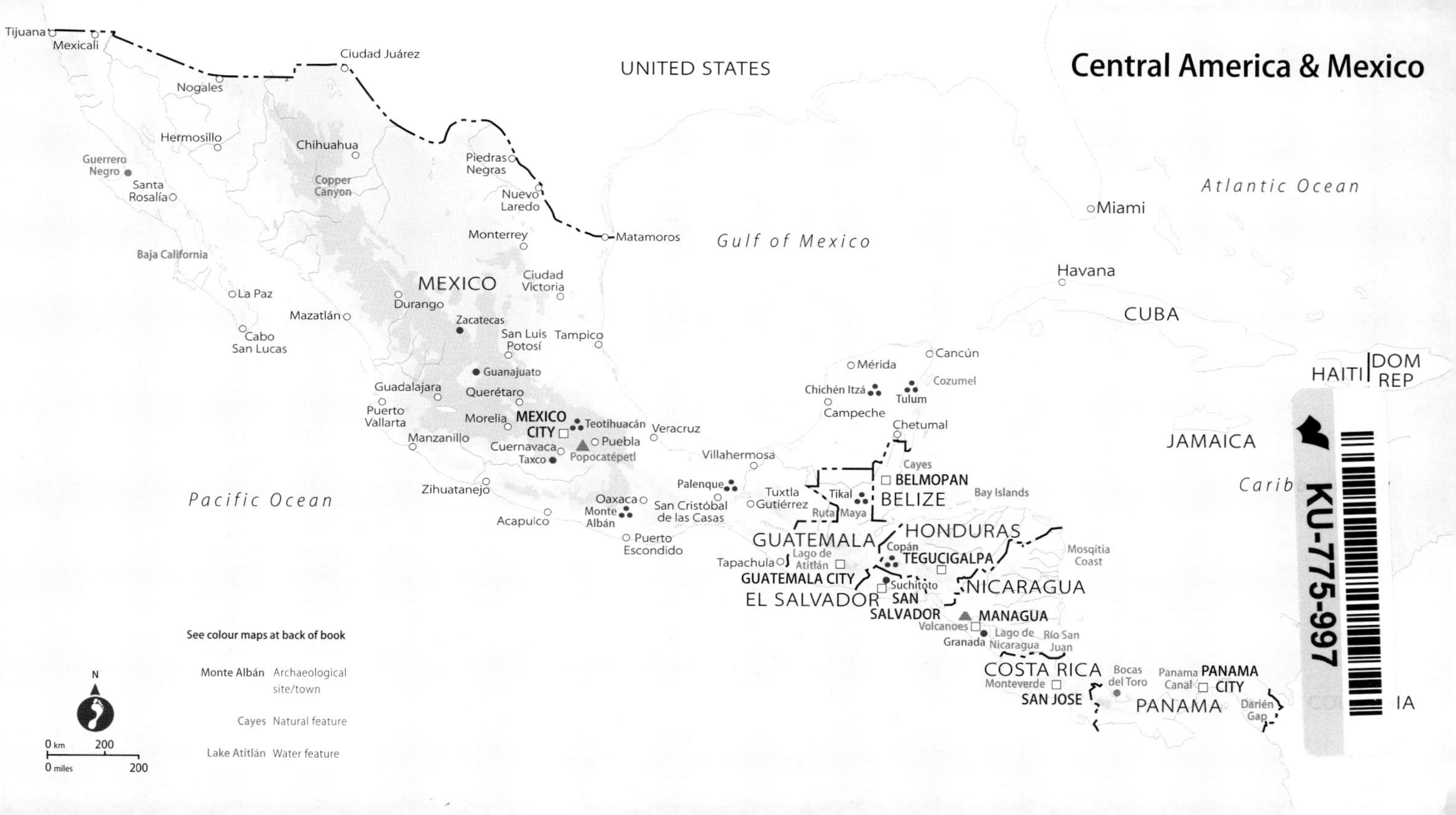

KU-775-997

Atlantic Ocean

Gulf of Mexico

Pacific Ocean

Carib

UNITED STATES

MEXICO

GUATEMALA

BELIZE

HONDURAS

EL SALVADOR

NICARAGUA

COSTA RICA

PANAMA

CUBA

JAMAICA

HAITI

DOM REP

IA

Miami

Havana

Cancún
Cozumel
Tulum
Mérida
Chichén Itzá
Campeche
Chetumal
Cayes

Bay Islands
Mosquitia Coast

BELMOPAN
GUATEMALA CITY
Tikal
Ruta Maya
Copán
TEGUCIGALPA
SAN SALVADOR
Suchitoto
San
MANAGUA
Granada
Lago de Nicaragua
Río San Juan
SAN JOSE
Monteverde
Bocas del Toro
PANAMA CITY
Panama Canal
Darién Gap
Volcanoes

Tuxtla Gutiérrez
Tapachula
Lago de Atitlán

Palenque
San Cristóbal de las Casas
Villahermosa
Veracruz
Puerto Escondido
Oaxaca
Monte Albán
Acapulco
Zihuatanejo
MEXICO CITY
Teotihuacán
Puebla
Popocatépetl
Cuernavaca
Taxco
Morelia
Querétaro
Guanajuato
San Luis Potosí
Tampico
Ciudad Victoria
Matamoros
Nuevo Laredo
Piedras Negras
Monterrey
Zacatecas
Durango
Guadalajara
Puerto Vallarta
Manzanillo
Mazatlán
Chihuahua
Copper Canyon
Ciudad Juárez
Nogales
Hermosillo
La Paz
Cabo San Lucas
Santa Rosalía
Guerrero Negro
Baja California
Tijuana
Mexicali

See colour maps at back of book

Monte Albán Archaeological site/town

Cayes Natural feature

Lake Atitlán Water feature

N

0 km 200
0 miles 200

4

Contents

Footprint

Central America
& Mexico Handbook 2003

Peter Hutchinson

We've got everything God needed to make paradise. Great farming, beaches, mountains, wildlife you wouldn't believe, put a stick in the ground you get a fruit tree, people so beautiful you could cry

John le Carré – The Tailor of Panama

Celebrating 100 years of Panamanian Independence on 3 November 2003

Central America and Mexico Handbook 2003

Thirteenth edition
© Footprint Handbooks Ltd
September 2002

Published by Footprint Handbooks
6 Riverside Court
Lower Bristol Road
Bath BA2 3DZ. England
T +44 (0)1225 469141
F +44 (0)1225 469461
Email discover@footprintbooks.com
Web www.footprintbooks.com

ISBN 1 903471 36 2
ISSN 0965-5492
CIP DATA: A catalogue record for this
book is available from the British Library

Distributed in the USA by
Publishers Group West

Credits

Series editors
Patrick Dawson and Rachel Fielding

Editorial
Editor: Felicity Laughton
Maps: Sarah Sorensen

Production
Page layout: Leona Bailey
Maps: Claire Benison and Robert Lunn
and Leona Bailey
Colour maps: Kevin Feeney
Proof reading: Carol Franklin
Cover: Camilla Ford

Design
Mytton Williams

Photography
Front cover: Robert Harding
Picture Library
Back cover: Jamie Marshall/Tribal Eye
Inside colour section: Jamie
Marshall/Tribal Eye; Robert Harding
Picture Library; Eye Ubiquitous; Pictures
Colour Library; Panos Pictures; South
American Pictures; Jeff Booth; Trip

Print
Manufactured in Italy by LEGOPRINT

Every effort has been made to ensure
that the facts in this Handbook are
accurate. However, travellers should still
obtain advice from consulates, airlines
etc about current travel and visa
requirements before travelling. The
authors and publishers cannot accept
responsibility for any loss, injury or
inconvenience however caused.

Right Fetching wood in the Guatemalan highlands

A foot in the door

Highlights

Mention of Central America and Mexico brings images flowing as freely as tequila in a Mexican *cantina*: colourful Indian markets, chaotic mega-cities contrasting with the calm serenity of rural life, pristine national parks and reserves, and stunning beaches.

Forces of nature

But the activity isn't limited to the surface. Volcanoes and earthquakes have shaped and moulded these mountainous lands for millennia. Active volcanoes are blasting in Mexico, Guatemala, Nicaragua and Costa Rica; earthquakes are recorded annually, in the vast majority of cases without loss of life. But the wreckage left by Hurricane Iris as it swept through Belize, the devastating earthquakes in El Salvador and the impressive eruptions of Popocatépetl are very real reminders of the power of nature and the fragility of life.

While human impact on this land is less dramatic it is equally impressive. Ruined remnants of ancient civilizations litter the region in a density that seems almost unbelievable. City states rose and fell leaving teasing evidence of complex societies that clearly understood the dynamics of life – maybe even up to the point of self-destruction.

Spectacular architecture, civic and religious, ancient and modern, is profuse. The conquistadores barely crossed a river without founding a town and, shortly after, building a church and a plaza. After visiting a few dozen colonial churches architectural fatigue can easily set in, but local peculiarities and subtle influences usually make a short pilgrimage worthwhile. A history of despots and dictators, civil war and revolution has seen architecture undergo a constant evolution of magnificent municipal palaces and plazas and intricate edifices. Each new leader commemorates their power sometimes noting or simply running roughshod over the failures of the old. Such impressive symbols of pomp and ceremony are made more prominent by the hardships of the majority who toil the soil and have unwittingly paid for such flamboyance with their labours.

The power & the glory

From such eclectic forces, it is hardly surprising to find Central Americans equally varied. Hidden in rural pockets, culture and struggle remain resolutely unchanged, living as their forebears have for centuries – with perhaps the exception of a fuzzy black and white TV emitting a dependable hiss. In urban areas, capitalism evolves with a unique local flavour; sadly cultural preservation and Westernization rarely share the same town, let alone the same room.

The old & the new

As signs of wealth range from absent to obscene (and they do), one trait is shared across the board – friendliness and an almost obsessive desire for a damn good fiesta. Whether celebrating a birthday, religious festival, the town's local saint or something seemingly as simple as raising the national flag, every Central American worth their tortilla will have an ornate and detailed plan for celebrating the occasion. Fortune may find you unexpectedly stuck in a small town at fiesta time – experience says there is little in this world to beat a surprise celebration. Lifelong friends, honorary membership of the family and unforgettable memories will travel with you when you, should you, indeed if you eventually move on.

Celebration time

Add to this mixture a weather system that still has a degree of reliability, with fairly dependable seasons, and a region that has enough to keep the mildly curious traveller interested for a long time. If you are genuinely fascinated, obsession is a real risk and you'll be returning for years – and there is more than enough information in the annually updated Central America and *Mexico Handbook* to help. Almost nowhere is off limits to the visitor now. With an appropriate and essential amount of respect for local people you meet and areas you visit, you'll find something of interest everywhere – in fact the main problem you have will be deciding where to spend the time you have.

Spoiled for choice

Left *Teotihuacán, the awe-inspiring City of the Gods, once housed about 250,000 people*

Mexico

Capital gains Encapsulating Mexico is difficult, but imagine countries within countries. Gloriously manic Mexico City is a world away from the serenity of the country's quieter spots. For thousands of years, cultures have fought for domination of these fertile Central Highlands but Cortés finally ended all that back in 1519. Little remains of the island city of Tenochtitlán that ruled this world, but the vast ruins of Teotihuacán stand as monument to the value of this prized land. Today's capital, filled with monumental architecture and sculptures, with sweeping broad boulevards, enlivened by dramatic murals displaying the country's turbulent past, is equally impressive. Struggling to move for congestion, gasping for breath in the pollution, the Federal District is one of the world's great cities, a living, working, still just-breathing celebration of the metropolis – and definitely worth a visit.

Life's a beach The deserts of the north, travelled by road or rail, are endless, interspersed only by towns and cities feigning at best general indifference to the traveller. The working cities of the country are the industrial centres and their concerns rarely cross over with those of the tourist. Likewise, in Tabasco and other sweaty oil centres in the tropical south, you can explore as if you were the first.

But change is a fundamental part of this country. Inland, colonial cities founded on the wealth of silver mines, rest assuredly on their architectural laurels. The Pacific coast from Puerto Vallarta, stretching south to the resorts of Acapulco, Puerto Escondido and beyond provide a fantastic welcome enticing the traveller with glorious beaches. The Yucután Peninsula, jutting out into the Caribbean, is home to mega-resorts and quiet beaches that sit side by side. You can visit one without even noticing the other.

Viva Mexico! In the deep tropical south, the state of Chiapas stands prominent as defender of the rights of some 24 million indigenous peoples that live throughout the country. Southern tropical rainforest hides scores of Mayan temples, from where lost ruins are retrieved at regular intervals from the all-consuming jungle. The cultural heritage is continuously evolving, creating lively markets and colourful fiestas. History continues to impinge on the country's present. What of the future?

As the merits of NAFTA membership are still being assessed, Mexico has entered the new millennium with a quiet revolution. President Vicente Fox, of the centre-right National Action Party is the first non-PRI head of state for over seven decades. After playing host to President Bush and 59 other heads of state in the United Nations' Development Conference in Monterrey, his international profile has been raised, but at home his popularity is slipping as the economy shadows the recent downturn of its northern neighbours. People are beginning to expect change. Viva variety, viva change, viva confusion, viva Mexico!

Guatemala

It's a well-travelled person who would fail to be impressed by Guatemala. The expansive ruins of Tikal symbolize Guatemala, with majestic temples looking out across the endless rainforest canopy of the north. To the south it's altogether far less tranquil. The Maya have not disappeared with the civilizations that once ruled massive cities of stone but live on in hundreds of towns and villages nestled amongst the intensely farmed foothills of scenic mountains and volcanoes, each with its own unique textile and its own fiesta.

Charm offensive The hypnotic beauty of Lake Atitlán draws you in and some just cannot leave. Colourful markets welcome visitors while packed buses ignore your pleas for a ride. But serenity and calm await. Not in the chaos of Guatemala City, but the charm of Antigua – once the capital and now one of Central America's many must-sees. In the mad rush to see the whole country, it's easy to overlook the Atlantic and Pacific coastlines. To the east, trekking and hiking in the lowland sierras and Caribbean beach life; to the west a fledgling tourism interest supports nesting turtles – it's quiet over there, go take a look.

Left Lying back and soaking up Cancún's Caribbean sun
Below A ride in the colourful 'trajineras' of Xochimilco make a great day out from Mexico City

Above And some of the wildlife's pretty colourful, too; scarlet macaws in Guatemala
Left Semana Santa in Zunil, Guatemala

Right *Bringing in the catch, El Salvador*
Below *Off the trail, the hidden beauty of El Salvador*

Above *Caye Caulker's Caribbean paradise, Belize*
Right *Fine stelae at the ruins of Copán, Honduras*

Belize

Compact and easy to move around, this tiny nation often gets overlooked, being more expensive than its immediate neighbours. So why go? Why not? For a start, there's the Mesoamerican Barrier Reef – the longest in the Western Hemisphere – which offers some of the best diving in the world, and a boatload of other watersports worth getting wet for.

The list goes on. Over 35% of the country is protected in national parks and reserves – compared with a mere 25% in Costa Rica – including the world's only jaguar sanctuary at Cockscomb Basin. Settlement Day, one of the great Central American fiestas held around Dangriga and Placencia, celebrates the freedom of the Garífuna peoples. The area was badly damaged by Hurricane Keith in late 2001, but now welcomes visitors with open arms, just as it did before. To the east an intricate system of caves drains the rivers of Mountain Pine Ridge, many of which can be explored by boat, inflated tube or on foot. And in the pine-clad hills to the south, Caracol, the largest and of many ruins, hides unexplored, revelling in the widely believed but little-known fact that it once ruled over nearby Tikal.

Plenty in reserve

El Salvador

Top of the Central America small country list, El Salvador, like Belize, gets short shrift due to the popularity of its neighbours. Barely a decade without civil war, a reputation for crime and violence has hardly helped, but following the massive destruction of a double earthquake in early 2001, the feeling now is one of intense sympathy. The loss of architectural treasures is devastating, the human toll tragic. Could there be a better opportunity to reach out and build new bridges? San Salvador normally evokes a love-hate relationship, and if it's the latter in your case, short trips take you quickly to the Izalco and Santa Ana volcanoes, overlooking the beautiful Lago de Coatepeque and close to the Parque Nacional Cerro Verde.

Near the capital, and further west, there are hot springs and countless waterfalls. Northern towns are currently enjoying a cultural revival moving out from the shadows of civil war, with Suchitoto leading the way, rejoicing in its colonial past. To the south, long sandy beaches secretly prized by surfers for decades stretch along the Costa del Sol to the Gulf of Fonseca, dotted with islets and bays to explore. To the west are coffee plantations and the beauty of the Ruta de las Flores. And who could resist the draw of a national park called *El Imposible* – your mission should you choose to accept it.

Mission unmissable

Honduras

One of Central America's dark horses, Honduras has been pushing for a place in the limelight for years. The Bay Islands off the Caribbean coast are still the cheapest place to learn to dive, and you just can't help but kick back when you arrive. Onshore activities are catching up and the adventure continues with whitewater rafting and, for the more sedate, hiking and bird-watching. The network of roads, routes and paths just invite exploration. Close to the border with Guatemala the spectacular and calming Copán ruins mark the southernmost tip of the Maya Empire.

But if this list is too short, rejoice, there are benefits. The quiet villages are quieter and the hillside paths of the west less travelled, dotted as they are with colonial treasures and Indian communities.

Bearing the brunt of the devastating Hurricane Mitch in late 1998, Honduras quickly repaired its basic infrastructure. Now, the country is very much open for business.

The roads less travelled

Nicaragua

While memories of the 1979 Sandinista Revolution still evoke images of work crews, *comandantes* and communist sympathies, the Nicaragua of today is a very different and rapidly changing place. While the country flirted with a democratic return to power of the Sandinistas, Nicaragua is embracing a deluge of tourist dollars that is set to increase as word gets around – Nicaragua is cool!

Genuine appeal There is a freshness about the country where the smiles are still warm, the questions still honest and the eyes wide open, not dulled by the fatigue of thoughtless travellers. Beautiful sites like Volcán Masaya, the Corn Islands, the island of Ometepe, Río San Juan and the Pacific beaches are matched by some of Central America's oldest towns including Granada and León. It's the contrasts that make Nicaragua; the highlands of the north; the lowlands to the south and east; liberal León and conservative Granada. In part, these differences divide the country, they inspired the Revolution and continue to impact the country today and make it such a pleasure to explore.

Costa Rica

Peaceful, calm and 100% democratic... ah, that'll be Costa Rica. Then start talking about national parks, reserves and biospheres, sprinkled with generous helpings of private reserves and national monuments and you'd think *Ticos* had a monopoly on nature. And they did until the rest of the sub-continent started playing catch-up. What makes the difference in Costa Rica is the sheer variety of what is on offer. Quetzales here, nesting turtles there, big cats at all points of the compass.

Worth waiting for In fact, it's easy to get blasé about the place, and frustration mounts when the small things that creep, crawl, fly and slither don't greet you with a welcome card. There is no substitute for good old-fashioned patience. Or is there? World-class whitewater rafting, surfing and fishing, erupting volcanoes and steaming mud pools, hot-air ballooning, walking, hiking, canoeing or just lazing about; others may do these things, but they won't find them all packed into a bundle as small as Costa Rica. And they don't do it in quite the same way as the laid-back *Ticos* who simply espouse *Pura Vida*.

Panama

There is no escape from the fact that Panama is the crossroads of the world and why should there be? The Panama Canal may not be natural but it is spectacular and 100% Panamanian since the country successfully took control of the world's greatest shortcut from the United States at the end of 1999. Once obsessed purely with banking and jaded by hazy memories of one of the world's most notorious dictators, Panama can be heady stuff.

The final 'fun'tier But there is life beyond Panama City. The autonomous region of the San Blas Islands provides a precious moment of calm and tranquillity. The true wilderness of the Darién still offers one of the great challenges this side of space travel. To the more accessible west, Panamanians and visitors alike are discovering new things to do on the Azuero Peninsula, in the Chiriquí Highlands and around Bocas del Toro. Slowly, and slightly nervously, Panama is exploring this global thoroughfare and finding out what fun can be like.

Left: *You'll see white-faced monkeys and maybe a sloth at Playa Manuel Antonio, Costa Rica*
Below *Herding the cattle; traditions die hard in Nicaragua*
Next page *The mystery and magic of the rainforest – a steaming cocktail of life in the making*

Above *The adrenaline of whitewater – Costa Rica, a growing destination for adventure sports*
Left *Panama Canal, a wonder of the modern world*

Essentials

Essentials

Planning your trip

'Where to go' is perhaps the most frequently asked question about Central America and Mexico, particularly by the first time visitor. Images of Central America and Mexico in travel articles, on television and on the Internet are complemented by tales of friends and family who have passed through one or two countries. The sheer variety of options means that for once the cliché is true – there is something for everyone. It is perhaps the sheer variety of landscapes, cultures and opportunities that excites, entices and to start with bewilders.

The scope for adventurous holidays – at whatever pace – is vast, whether it be branching out from a resort like Puerto Vallarta or climbing a volcano, scuba diving and snorkelling, whitewater rafting or seeking out the elusive quetzal bird from the forests of Guatemala right down to Panama. Equally enticing are the pyramids and sculptures of the Aztecs, Maya and other cultures, the Spanish colonial heritage, from the grandest cathedral to the smallest village church, the flora and fauna of a vast array of habitats, Indian markets, or the mere prospect of lazing at some palm-shaded hideaway fringed with golden sands.

The countries themselves are by no means secret places, we know from your letters that the popularity of the region is already great – it is no longer a lonely planet. The options are limited only by your imagination.

Detailed planning information is given for each country:
Belize, page 697
Costa Rica, page 1017
El Salvador, page 763
Guatemala, page 555
Honduras, page 825
Mexico, page 69
Nicaragua, page 937
Panama, page 1147

Where to go

Choosing which country or countries to visit can be a strangely paralyzing experience. Each is worth visiting on its own merits and deserves time – your dilemma is deciding whether to skim the surface of a few countries or really get to grips with a couple of spots. Here are a few suggested itineraries.

Not long enough to cover the region, but you don't have to do the whole isthmus in one trip. Breaking down the options, three weeks could comfortably be spent exploring Guatemala with a fortnight taking in the essentials of **Antigua**, **Tikal** and **Lake Atitlán**. Spend an extra week in the **Cayo District** of Belize, the **Caribbean** coast of Guatemala crossing into Honduras for a bit of diving in the **Bay Islands** or heading north to the Indian homelands of **Chiapas**, Mexico. The **Ruta Maya**, taking in Guatemala, Belize and southern Mexico is possible in three weeks but doesn't really allow time for deviation.

Three weeks

Another three-week trip could focus on **Costa Rica**, with a great variety of national parks on offer. The particular recommendation will depend on the time of year, but the most popular include **Manuel Antonio National Park**, **Monteverde Cloud Forest Reserve**, **Tortuguero National Park** to the east and **Corcovado National Park** to the south. The explosive **Volcán Arenal** never disappoints unless it is shrouded in cloud. For the active there is whitewater rafting, surfing, horse-riding and trekking.

You could just about manage an overland trip from **Guatemala** through to **Costa Rica** in three weeks. If you're feeling particularly manic, you could even manage a mad dash down the **Pan-American Highway** from **Mexico City** all the way to **Panama City** but you'll see little more than tarmac.

Six to eight weeks is long enough to travel across a few countries without feeling you've rushed too much. Arriving in **Mexico City**, and after a few days' exploring the sights and sounds, the **architecture** ancient and modern, and dodging the traffic, you can head south to the beaches of **Oaxaca**, before making your way east to **Chiapas** and the Maya ruins of **Palenque**. From here continue south to Guatemala or west out to the **Yucatán Peninsula** for the beautiful beaches and more **Maya** ruins. Dropping south, **Belize** is worth some time. **Diving**, though more expensive than Honduras, is some of the best in the world and includes the spectacular **Blue Hole**. Head west for **Guatemala** and the eerie cave and river trips of the **Cayo District** or, to the south, the calm serenity around **Plancencia**, the jaguar sanctuary at **Cockscomb Basin** and the cultural Maya villages close to **Punta Gorda**.

Six to eight weeks

Six weeks is long enough to include a short Spanish language course in **Antigua**,

Essentials

Quetzaltenango or even **Todos Santos** – world famous for its annual festival in November. After Guatemala, **Honduras** draws many to the affordable diving of the **Bay Islands** which need at least a week. Other attractions include whitewater rafting on the **Río Cangrejo** close to **La Ceiba**. Inland, treks and hikes in the quiet hills around **Gracias** go through beautiful scenery and small Indian communities - the very heart of Honduras.

An alternative six-week trip might arrive in **Guatemala City** and head south overland flying out of **San José, Costa Rica**. While experiencing Guatemala and Costa Rica, you can travel at leisure through **Honduras**, dip into the slowly emerging and increasingly appreciated lakes and volcanic beauty of **El Salvador** as it struggles to fight off the devastation of earthquakes in early 2001, and visit **Nicaragua** where revolutionary history merges with colonial legacy and scarred beauty to create one of Central America's most endearing nationalities.

Three months Entering the realms of comfortably travelling from top to bottom, three months is plenty to enter into the classic trip – to follow the **Pan-American Highway** from the Río Grande to the Darién Gap. (Equally you could start at Panama and head north.) You can cross the US-Mexico border at several points. From **Laredo**, the route heads south through **Monterrey** and the port of **Tampico** before veering inland through the silver-mining centre of **Pachuca** and on to **Mexico City**.

From **Ciudad Juárez** on the border, it's a short trip to **Chihuahua**, the vast **Copper Canyon** and the glorious railroad down to the Pacific Ocean. The famous train journey is one of several options for leaving **Chihuahua** on a route that takes in the old silver towns of **Colonial Heartland** of Zacatecas and San Luis Potosí.

On the west coast **Tijuana** offers the simplest route to the rugged desert beauty of the **Baja California Peninsula**, popular for beaches and whale-watching. This is also an alternative (and longer) route to the Copper Canyon via **Los Mochis**. After sweeping the Pacific **Costa Alegre**, head inland for **Guadalajara** and then **Mexico City**.

Head southeast from the Mexican Central Highlands to **Guatemala** and continue the route south, or take in **Belize** after travelling through the **Yucután Peninsula**.

A gentle meander through **Honduras, El Salvador** and **Nicaragua** can involve a switch of coastlines in **Costa Rica**, to the Caribbean coast and take in the idyllic and increasingly popular alternative of the southern beaches and the dive sites of **Bocas del Toro**. Alternatively you can continue south to Costa Rica's **Osa Peninsula** before taking the Pan-American Highway across the final border to **David** and on to **Panama City**. From David, you can blend adventure and beauty with a visit to the **Chiriquí Highlands**. A voyage through the **Panama Canal** would be the ideal way to end a trip of trans-continental travel before heading further south or returning home. The great adventure challenge of the region is still travelling through the **Darién Gap**. On top of the personal strengths and abilities required, you do need plenty of time, cash and good language skills.

Over three months If only we all had so much time…; longer than three months is worth sketching out into some form of plan. In addition to suggestions mentioned above, you might want to consider stopping for **language courses, diving instruction**, or a whole range of **cultural** and **activity** courses available throughout the region – if there's something that happens in Central America that you want to learn, there's someone who runs a course. You can stay in one place or choose to stagger your studies over several countries. **Work**, both voluntary and paid, can also be found if you want to stop moving for a while. Unpacking your bag for more than a few nights can change your perspective on a place dramatically. Spending time in one place means you get to explore much more than just the obvious places of interest. With luck you'll also make some good friends and may be able to contribute something long lasting to the region.

In addition to the suggestions above, if you look at the first pages of each country chapter, you will find an overview to help you start planning what to see and when to go. You will also find important information pertinent to that destination. The suggestions are, of course, not definitive. For some the fascination of travelling is to be able to get away from the crowd and explore off the beaten track, for others, being in a new place, a new culture and enjoying the novelty of the experience is enough.

Essentials

Essentials

 ## Tour operators

In the UK

Bridge the World, T020-7911-0900, www.bridgetheworld.com

Dragoman, Camp Green, Debenham, Suffolk, IP14 6LA, T01728-861133, F01728-861127, www.dragoman.co.uk

Exodus Travels, T020-8772-3822, www.exodus.co.uk

Hayes & Jarvis, 152 King St, London, W6 0QU, T020-8222-7844

Journey Latin America, 12-13 Heathfield Terr, Chiswick, London, W4 4JE, T020-8747-8315, F020-8742-1312, also 12 St Ann's Square (2nd floor) Manchester, M2 7HW, T0161-832-1441, F0161-832-1551, www.journeylatinamerica.co.uk

Last Frontiers, Fleet Marston Farm, Aylesbury, Buckinghamshire, HP18 0QT, T01296-658650, F01296-658651, www.lastfrontiers.co.uk

South American Experience, 47 Causton St, Pimlico, London, SW1P 4AT, T020-7976-5511, F020-7976-6908, www.southamericanexperience.co.uk

Travelbag, T020-7497-0515, www.travelbag.co.uk

Trips Worldwide, 9 Byron Pl, Bristol, BS8 1JT, T0117-311-4400, www.tripsworldwide.co.uk

Tucan Travel, 316 Uxbridge Rd, Acton, London, W3 9RE, T020-8896-1600, F020-8896 1400, www.tucantravel.com

Veloso Tours, 33-34 Warple Way, London, W3 0RG, T020-8672-0616, F020-8762-0716, www.veloso.com

In North America

EXito Latin American Travel Specialists, 1212 Broadway Suite 910, Oakland, CA 94612, T1-800-655-4053; worldwide T510-655-2154, F510-655-4566. www.exito-travel.com

GAP Adventures, 19 Duncan St, Toronto, Ontario, M5H 3H1, T1-800-465-5600 (in the UK: 01373-858956), www.gap.ca

LADATCO Tours, T800-327-6162 (in USA), www.ladatco.com

Mila Tours, 100 S Greenleaf Av, Gurnee, Il 60031, T1-800-367-7378, F847-249-2772. www.MILAtours.com

S&Stours, 3366 E Trevino Dr, Sierra Vista, AZ 85650, T800-499-5685, F520-803-1355, www.ss-tours.com

In South America

Southtrip, Sarmiento 347, Floor No 4, Of 19, Capital Federal, Buenos Aires, Argentina, T/F0054 11 4328 7075, www.southtrip.com

None of the major tourist destinations in Central America is off limits. Travellers can move freely through the region, with a guarantee of finding lodging, food and all necessary services. If you are planning to venture far from the beaten track, it is a good idea to check whether your presence would be an inconvenience to the local inhabitants, although it is more than likely that you will be welcome everywhere.

When to go

If you are not tied to the European or American summer for times when you are able to travel then the best time to go is between October and April, although there are slight regional variations. The rainy season works its way up from the south beginning in May and running through until August, September and even October. This is also hurricane season along the Caribbean. The last few years have produced the devastating storms of Hurricane Mitch and several lesser-known local hurricanes and tropical storms, landfall is relatively rare. Don't be put off by the term 'rainy season' – in most places and in most years, heavy rain falls for an hour or two a day. And given that much of the area is in the tropics you should experience at least one tropical storm.

Fiestas   In terms of events, general regional celebrations are around Easter (*Semana Santa*), the Day of the Dead (2nd November) and Christmas. Beyond that each country will be certain to celebrate wildly on its respective Independence day. Other general fiestas are held throughout the year.

As well as national and regional holidays, August is vacation time for Mexicans and Central Americans and this can make accommodation scarce especially in the smaller resorts.

Tours and tour operators

For some the idea of travelling independently is just too nerve wracking, time consuming or simply not worth the hassle. Cobbling together the bits of knowledge, experience and courage to take the plunge can be tough. And what if you want to travel with people, but your friends just don't have the time? In today's flexible tourist market alternatives now exist. Several tour companies provide overland trips that cover parts or all of the region. The companies are not just for posh backpackers. Neither are they too expensive for the financially challenged (poor!). You can arrange tailored trips or join overland routes that travel on regular schedules. The tours on offer can be just as enjoyable as independent travel, are incredibly flexible and you meet like-minded people.

Essentials

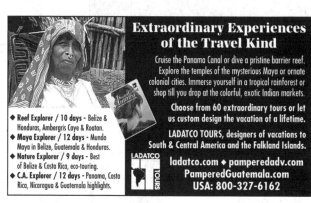

Essentials

Finding out more

Essentials

Many countries have tourist boards working in North America, Europe and other parts of the world

All countries in the region have a tourist board but not all have an international presence. With the advent of the internet it's possible to get the latest information on developments in a country.

At the regional level a group of like-minded obsessives joined together to form the **South American Explorers Club.** Despite the name, the whole of Latin America is covered and members receive help with travel planning as well as informed access on books and maps covering the region. Head Office in the US is at 126 Indian Creek Rd, Ithaca, NY 14850, USA T607-277-0488, F607-277-6122, www.samexplo.org. In Latin America there are offices in Lima (Calle Piura 135, Miraflores, Lima 18. T/F511-445-3306, limaclub@saexplorers.org) and Quito (Jorge Washington 311 y Leonidas Plaza, Apartado 17-21-431, Eloy Alfaro, T/F593-222-5228), neither of which is terribly handy for Central America and Mexico. In the UK the *South American Explorers Club* is represented by *Bradt Travel Guides*, 19 High Street, Chalfont St Peter, Bucks, SL9 9QE, T01753-893444, F01753-892333, www.bradt-travelguides.com

The **Latin American Travel Advisor** is a travel information service offering the most up-to-date detailed and reliable information about 17 South and Central American countries. Public safety, health, weather and natural phenomena, travel costs, economics and politics are highlighted for each nation. You can subscribe to this comprehensive quarterly newsletter (a free sample is available), obtain country reports by email or fax and choose from a wide selection of Latin American maps. Orders may be placed by mail, fax or through the Web; credit cards accepted. Individual travel planning assistance is available for all customers. Contact PO Box 17-17-908, Quito, Ecuador, F593-2-562566 (international), F1-888-215-9511 (USA and Canada toll free), LATA@pi.pro.ec, www.amerispan.com/lata/

If you are *au fait* with the internet you'll already know the joys of search engines. You can put in a country and see what comes up. A few more specific regional websites include **www.spanishconnection.com** which offers a Latin American search engine directory, as well as email, e-commerce and translation services. **www.centralamerica.com** covers Belize, Nicaragua, Costa Rica and Panama. A phenomenal resource which is staggering for its detail on everything from ecotourism and language schools, through to cybercafés is Ron Mader's **www.planeta.com**

www.southtrip.com Site acting as a portal for Latin American specialists (based in Buenos Aires) offering all that is available in this part of the world with the emphasis on tailor-made activity-based trips such as mountain biking, golf, fishing, horse-riding, rafting, bird-watching, etc (including accommodation, flights, tournaments, shopping, and the rest). They are Sarmiento 347, Floor No 4, Office 19, Capital Federal, Buenos Aires, Argentina, T/F0054-11-4328-7075.

For details of national and religious holidays, visit **www.holidayfestival.com** For information on everything from birth rates to natural resources, try **www.odci.gov/cia/publications/factbook/index.html**, and for political updates go to **www.latinnews.conm/newsroom.html**

Central America & Mexico on the web *A list of useful websites for each country is given in the relevant Essentials section*

Essentials

Language

Spanish is spoken throughout Central America and Mexico and while you will be able to get by without knowledge of Spanish you will become very frustrated and feel helpless in many situations. English, or any other language, is absolutely useless off the beaten track (except in Belize). A pocket dictionary and phrase book together with some initial study or a beginner's Spanish course before you leave to get you up to a basic vocabulary of 500 words or so are most strongly recommended: your pleasure will be doubled if you can talk to the locals. If you have the time, booking a week or two of language classes at the beginning of your travels is an excellent use of time. Just remember to be bold, make an attempt and don't take it too seriously. Dialects change from region to region, and when you cross a border you'll often find that even the way people ask for fares on a bus has changed completely.

See Footnotes for a list of useful words and phrases

Some areas have developed a reputation for language classes, for instance Cuernavaca in Mexico, Antigua and Quetzaltenango in Guatemala and San José in Honduras. Many other locations also provide tuition. The merits of a well-known centre normally include a wide-range of cultural activities and supporting options for homestay. But the temptation with other travellers around is to take comfort in your home language. Conversely, seeking out a hidden corner to completely immerse yourself is not suitable or appropriate for everyone. As ever, you choose. For details, see Language schools in the directories of individual towns.

Not all the locals speak Spanish, of course; you will find that some Indians in the more remote areas – the highlands of Guatemala for example – speak only their indigenous languages, although there will usually be at least one person in a village who can speak Spanish.

Arranging language tuition internationally is increasingly popular. One of the most comprehensive options is provided by *AmeriSpan*, Worldwide T215-751-1100, F215-751-1986; USA and Canada, PO Box 40007, Philadelphia, PA 19106-0007, T1-800-879-6640, www.amerispan.com, offers Spanish immersion programmes, educational tours, volunteer and internship positions throughout Latin America.

Women travellers

Some women experience problems, whether accompanied or not; others encounter no difficulties at all. You should be aware that unaccompanied Western women will be subject to close scrutiny and exceptional curiosity. Don't be unduly scared – or flattered. Simply be prepared and try not to over-react. When you set out, err on the side of caution until your instincts have adjusted to the customs of a new culture. On the positive side, if, as a single woman, you can befriend a local woman, you will learn much more about the country.

Essentials

To help minimize unwanted attention, do not wear suggestive clothing. If politeness fails, do not feel bad about showing offence and departing. When accepting a social invitation, make sure that someone knows the address and the time you left. Ask if you can bring a friend (even if you do not intend to do so). A good rule is always to act with confidence, as though you know where you are going, even if you do not. Someone who looks lost is more likely to attract unwanted attention. Do not disclose to strangers where you are staying.

Women travelling alone should take a wedding ring – a fake one if necessary – to prevent being hassled

Essentials

Student travellers

If you are in full-time education you will be entitled to an **International Student Identity Card** (ISIC), which is distributed by student travel offices and travel agencies in 77 countries. ISIC gives you special prices on all forms of transport (air, sea, rail etc), and access to a variety of other concessions and services, and it is worth having. If you need to find the location of your nearest ISIC office contact: The International Student Travel Confederation, Herengracht 479, 1017 BS Amsterdam, The Netherlands, T+31-20-421 2800, F+31-20-421 2810, www.istc.org Student cards must carry a photograph if they are to be of any use for discounts in Latin America.

Teachers may also want to take some form of international identity as discounts afforded students are often extended to teachers.

Gay and lesbian travellers

Most of Latin America is not particularly liberal in its attitudes to gays and lesbians. Even in the cities people are fairly conservative, and more so in provincial towns and rural areas. Having said that, things are changing and you'll find there is a gay scene with bars and clubs at least in most of the bigger cities and resorts.

Disabled travellers

As in most Latin American countries, facilities for disabled travellers are severely lacking. Most airports and hotels and restaurants in major resorts have wheelchair ramps and adapted toilets. While some cities such as San José in Costa Rica are all ramped, in general pavements are often in such a poor state of repair that walking is precarious.

But of course only a minority of disabled people are wheelchair-bound and it is now widely acknowledged that disabilities do not stop you from enjoying a great holiday. Some travel companies are beginning to specialize in exciting holidays, tailor-made for individuals depending on their level of disability. For those with access to the internet, a Global Access – Disabled Travel Network Site, www.geocities.com/Paris/1502, provides travel information for 'disabled adventurers' and includes a number of reviews and tips from members of the public. You might also want to read *Nothing Ventured*, editied by Alison Walsh (Harper Collins), which gives personal accounts of world-wide journeys by disabled travellers, plus advice and listings.

Travelling with children

One of those topics with as many opinions as there are people, but if you're contemplating travelling with children then you're already game. Travel with children can bring you into closer contact with Latin American families and generally presents no special problems – in fact the path is often smoother for family groups. Officials tend to be more amenable where children are concerned and they are pleased if your child knows a little Spanish. Moreover, even thieves and pickpockets seem to have some of the traditional respect for families, and may leave you alone because of it! Always carry a copy of your child's birth certificate and passport-size photos.

For health matters, see page 53

Specifics worth considering. Overland travel in Latin America can involve a lot of time spent waiting for public transport, so make sure you pack enough toys, books and so forth.

Food can be a problem if the children are not adaptable. It is easier to take biscuits, drinks, bread, etc with you on longer trips than to rely on meal stops where the food may not be to taste. A small immersion heater and jug for making hot drinks is invaluable, but remember that electric current varies. Try and get a dual-voltage one (110v and 220v).

Fares On long-distance buses children generally pay half or reduced fares. For shorter trips it is cheaper, if less comfortable, to seat small children on your knee. Often there are spare seats which children can occupy after tickets have been collected. In city and local excursion buses, small children do not generally pay a fare, but are not entitled to a seat when paying customers are standing. On sightseeing tours you should *always* bargain for a family rate – often children can go free. Note that a child travelling free on a long excursion is not always covered by the operator's travel insurance.

All airlines charge a reduced price for children under 12 and less for children under two. Double check the child's baggage allowance – some are as low as 7 kg.

In hotels try to negotiate family rates. If charges are per person, always insist that two children will occupy one bed only, therefore counting as one tariff. If rates are per bed, the same applies. In either case you can almost always get a reduced rate at cheaper hotels. In the better hotels in more commercial resorts, it is quite common for children under 10 or 12 to be allowed to stay for no extra charge as long as they are sharing you room.

Working in Central America and Mexico

Willingness to help others in a voluntary capacity is reasonably popular in Central America and Mexico. Sometimes a willing pair of hands can greatly assist the less fortunate and those in more demanding situations. Two main areas provide opportunities for unskilled volunteers, childcare – often at orphanages or schools – and projects with a nature orientation. But be warned, spontaneous volunteering is becoming more difficult. Organizations that use volunteers have progressed and plan their personnel needs so you may be required to make contact before you visit. A second consideration is that many organizations now 'charge' volunteers for board and lodging, particularly nature projects and the volunteer project will normally be for a minimum of four weeks. Again this needs to be considered before embarking on trip that focuses on volunteering. Skilled volunteers looking for career-enhancing positions should consider making enquiries and arrangements before arriving in a country.

If you are interested, Guatemala and Costa Rica have fairly well-organized volunteer programmes. Instinct suggests that strong hands, a generous spirit and genuine charity will also be much appreciated in El Salvador for several years to come.

Variations on the volunteering programme are to enrol on increasingly popular GAP year programmes. These normally incorporate a period of volunteer work with a few months of free time at the end of the programme for travel. While this may seem like a fairly new development the idea has been around for years. *Experiment in International Living*, T01684-562577, www.eiluk.org is the UK-based element of a US international homestay programme that arranges stays with families in Central America and Mexico with social projects based on the ethos that if you want to live together you need to work together. It's very similar in essence to a GAP year/volunteering programme, but was founded in 1932: an excellent way to meet people and learn the language.

Working in Central America and Mexico is perfectly possible but as with employment at home, if you expect a decent job you will have to go through the normal application procedures. Casual work is likely to be very difficult to find although you may get the opportunity to work somewhere in return for board and lodgings if that appeals and your face fits.

Before you travel

Getting in

Visas, immigration, insurance & documents

All international travel requires that you have at least six months remaining on a valid passport. Beyond a passport, very little is required of international travellers to Central America and Mexico. However, there are a few little tricks that can make your life a lot easier. Latin Americans, especially officials, are very document-minded. You should always carry some form of identification, ideally your passport or even better a plasticated copy of it, in a safe place about your person. If staying in a country for several weeks, it is worth while registering at your embassy or consulate. Then, if your passport is stolen, the process of replacing it is faster and easier. It can also be handy to keep some additional passport-sized photographs together with photocopies of essential documents – including your flight ticket – in a separate place to the originals.

It is your responsibility to ensure that your passport is stamped in and out when you cross borders. The absence of entry and exit stamps can cause serious difficulties: seek out the proper immigration offices if the stamping process is not carried out as you cross. Also, do not lose your entry card; replacing it can cause you a lot of trouble and possibly expense.

If planning to **study** in Latin America for a long period, make every effort to get a **student visa** in advance.

If **driving**, or considering renting, an international driving licence is very useful, although not always essential. Membership of British, European and US motoring organizations can also be useful for discounts off items such as hotel charges, car rentals, maps, and towing charges, etc. Business people should carry a good supply of visiting cards, which are essential for good business relations in Latin America. Identity, membership or business cards in Spanish (or a translation) and an official letter of introduction (also in Spanish) are useful too.

Insurance has to be strongly recommended, although it is not essential. If you have budgetry restraints the most important aspect of any insurance policy is medical care and repatriation. Policies are very reasonable. Accidents do happen and they can become dramas when you have to worry about money as well. Ideally you want to make sure you are covered for personal items too. Make sure you read the small print *before* heading off so you are aware of what is covered and what is not (some policies do not cover items over a certain value unless declared on the policy before travel) so you know what is required to submit a claim (normally a police record from or close to the incident.)

> Essentials

Duty free allowances and export restrictions for each country are listed in the essentials section. It goes without saying that drugs, firearms and banned dead and living animal products should not be traded and certainly not taken across international boundaries.

Customs, duty free & export restrictions

Vaccinations and immunizations are an important part of the pre-trip planning, with some being required several months before you arrive in a country.

Vaccination & immunization

Vaccination against the following diseases is recommended: yellow fever, typhoid, poliomyelitis and tetanus. Hepatitis should also be considered (see Health on page 53).

What to take

Take as little as possible – remember you'll have to carry it everywhere. Take clothes that are quick and easy to wash and dry – the range of goods on the market is such that you no longer have to look the part of an 19th-century explorer. Loose-fitting clothes are more comfortable in hot climates and can be layered if it gets cooler. Sarongs are versatile: they can be used as a towel, a beach mat, a skirt, a sheet, or a scarf, to name but a few. But don't pack too many

A good principle is to take half the clothes and twice the money, that you think you will need

Essentials

clothes; you won't need an extensive wardrobe and you can easily, and cheaply, buy things en route. Four musts are good walking shoes, sun hats, dark glasses, and flip-flops for the hot sandy beaches. It is difficult to obtain shoes over US size nine and a half.

Don't load yourself down with toiletries either. They're heavy and can usually be found cheaply and easily everywhere. Items like contact lens solutions and tampons may be harder to find, but stock up in major cities as you go along and there shouldn't be a problem. Throughout Central America, but not Mexico, lens solution is hard to find. One thing you don't want to get stuck without is **toilet paper**, so keep a stash close by, and **dental floss** which can be useful for backpack repairs as well as its original purpose.

In addition to general advice, any specialist activity would require that you take the appropriate equipment.

There are some items we just can't live without. Probably the most useful single item is a Swiss Army knife (with corkscrew), followed by a money belt, a headtorch/flashlight (not everywhere has 24-hour electricity and for those dark lanes and late-night beach walks), the smallest travel alarm clock you can find and a basic medical kit. Sanity savers include some good books (though don't bring too many as you can always swap with other travellers), a Walkman and tapes/CDs. Also, don't forget to pack photocopies of essential documents like passport, visas and travellers' cheques receipts just in case you lose the originals.

For security a small padlock is useful for locking up your bag, and on the doors of some of the more basic hotels. Finally, a climbing karabiner can be handy for clipping your bag on to something when you don't want to hug it all the time.

Photographers will want to take all the film that they will require for the trip, ideally in a bag that is both water and dust proof. Obtaining film in the region is getting easier, but you may not be able to get the precise film you want when you want it.

It is equally important to mention **what not to take**. Although the vast majority of people travel through Central America and Mexico without losing anything, the possibility always exists. So, just in case your bags do go missing, it is probably best to leave any specially prized or sentimental possessions at home.

Money

While most – but not all – countries in Central America and Mexico have their own currencies, the main currency of the region is the US dollar. Both Panama and El Salvador now use the currency as if it were their own. Consequently that proportion of your money you take in cash and travellers' cheques should be in US dollars. In theory there should be greater support for the Euro than there was for each individual European currency, but to date, few organizations and banks are making any move from the current situation.

How much?
Always take a credit card in case of emergencies or special occasions when you want to splash out

One of the first questions is usually "How much will I need?" to which the immediate answer is "How long is a piece of string?" quickly followed by "...depends what you're doing with it?" Deciding how much to take is very difficult as no two people travel the same. Prices also vary greatly between countries. As a rough calculation budget travellers can get by on US$25-US$30 a day, without getting carried away on every excursion. Plenty of travellers manage on smaller budgets but it's probably better to spend a little longer at home saving up, and then have a good time while you're away, rather than find yourself adding up the small change on a Saturday night to see if you can afford a weekly beer.

The three main ways of keeping in funds while travelling are with US dollars cash, US dollars travellers' cheques (TCs), or plastic (credit cards). It is recommended that you take all three.

Cash
The chief benefit of taking US dollars is that they are accepted almost everywhere – they are used as national currency in El Salvador and Panama – and rates and commissions are more competitive than for other currencies, if other currencies can be changed.

In many countries, US dollar notes are only accepted if they are in excellent condition – no small tears, rips, nicks or holes. When ordering money at home bear this in mind. Try to take

Exchange rates

Country	Unit of currency	Exchange rates/US$
Belize	Belize dollar	2.00
Costa Rica	Colón	372.85
El Salvador*	Colón	8.75
Guatemala	Quetzal	8.12
Honduras	Lempira	17.14
Mexico	Peso	9.86
Nicaragua	Córdoba	13.40
Panama*	Balboa	1.00

US notes and coins are legal tender

Essentials

and accept 'new-style' US dollar bills (US$20, US$50, US$100) with centre thread microprinting and watermarks, as there are countless forged 'old-style' notes in circulation. Take a selection of bills including several low-value US dollar bills (US$5 or US$10) which can be carried for changing into local currency if arriving in a country when banks or *casas de cambio* are closed, and for use in out of the way places when you may run out of local currency. They are very useful for shopping: shopkeepers and bureaux de change (*casas de cambio*) tend to give better exchange rates than hotels or banks (but see below). The better hotels will normally change travellers' cheques for their guests (often at a poor rate).

If your budget is tight it is essential to avoid situations where you are forced to change money regardless of the rate; watch weekends and public holidays carefully and never run out of local currency. Take plenty of local currency, in small denominations, when making trips away from the major towns and resorts.

El Salvador's 'dollarization' in early 2001 has led to much speculation that other countries in Central America will follow suit. Guatemala has liberalized the use of dollar bank accounts, a move which has lead to a flurry of speculation that they will be the next to change. Other countries sporadically explore the idea, but while such a move may be in the minds of political leaders and economists, the opinion on the ground, for the time being at least, is that it would be unacceptable to the broader population.

Travellers' cheques

In Mexico, casas de cambio may be open longer hours than banks, but they do not offer better exchange rates

The appeal of travellers' cheques is obvious, providing reasonably accessible cash with peace of mind against theft. On the downside they can be inconvenient requiring you to wait in long lines in banks as you try to cash them. Denominations of US$50 and US$100 are preferable, with a few of US$20 to increase your options when you only have a short time left in a country or if you want to pay for a trip. Some banks will change the cheques for US dollars cash if you need to top up your supply. **American Express**, **Visa** or **Thomas Cook** US dollar TCs are recommended, but less commission is often charged on **Citibank** or **Bank of America** TCs, if they are cashed at Latin American branches of those banks.

Several banks charge a high fixed commission for changing TCs because they don't really want the bother. *Casas de cambio* are usually a much better bet for this service. Some establishments may ask to see a passport and the customer's record of purchase before accepting. Keep the original purchase slip in a separate place to the travellers' cheques and make a photocopy for security.

Credit cards

Remove your credit card from the machine immediately after the transaction to avoid it being retained – getting it back can be difficult and takes time

It is straightforward to obtain a cash advance against a credit card and even easier to withdraw cash from ATMs (Automatic Telling Machines). There are two acceptance systems, **Plus** and **Cirrus**. Many issuers of debit and credit cards are linked to one or both. Look for the relevant symbol on an ATM and draw cash using your PIN. You may have to experiment to see what combination of options your require. Fortunately, most ATMs give you a 'language' option after you enter your card. The rates of exchange on ATM withdrawals are the best available for currency exchange but your bank or credit card company imposes a handling charge. Obviously you must ensure that the account to which your debit card refers contains

Essentials

 ## Airline and internet travel resources

Most international and several domestic airlines have websites which are useful for gaining information about flights; as yet, you are unlikely to get the best price online, so use the websites in an advisory capacity only.

AeroCaribe *www.aerocaribe.com*
AeroMéxico *www.aeromexico.com*
Air France *www.airfrance.com*
Air Jamaica *www.airjamaica.com*
Alitalia *www.alitalia.it*
American Airlines *ww.aa.com*
Avianca *www.avianca.com.co*
Aviateca *www.flylatinamerica.com/ acc_aviateca.html*
British Airways *www.british-airways.com/ regional*
Canadian *www.cdnair.ca*
City Bird *www.citybird.com*
Condor *www.condor.de*
Continental *www.continental.com*
Copa *www.copaair.com*
Cubana *www.cubana.cu*
Delta *www.delta-air.com*
Grupo Taca *www.grupotaca.com*
Iberia *www.iberia.com*
Japan Airlines *www.japanairlines.com*

KLM *www.klm.com*
Lacsa *www.grupotaca.com*
LanChile *www.lanchile.com*
Lufthansa *www.lufthansa.com*
Martinair *www.marintair.com*
Mexicana *www.mexicana.com.mx/mx2/ english/home.asp*
Northwest *www.nwa.com*
Qantas *www.qantas.com*
Taca *www.grupotaca.com*
United *www.ual.com*
Varig *www.varig.com.br*

www.evasions.com/airlines1.htm *has a full list of airline website addresses. If you want to hear horror stories from fellow travellers about their airline experience, try www.traveldesk.com*

Web resource
www.expedia.com
www.travelocity.com
www.orbitz.com
www.opodo.com (co.uk, .fr, .de)
www.priceline.com
www.lastminute.com

sufficient funds. With a credit card, obtain a credit limit sufficient for your needs, or pay money to put the account in credit. If travelling for a long time, consider a direct debit to clear your account regularly. If you lose a card, immediately contact the 24-hour helpline of the issuer in your home country (keep this number in a safe place).

In an ideal world taking a couple of cards (one Visa and one MasterCard) will make sure you are covered in most options

For purchases, credit cards of the *Visa* and *MasterCard* groups, *American Express* (Amex), *Carte Blanche* and *Diners Club* can be used. Make sure you know the correct procedure if they are lost or stolen. Credit card transactions are normally at an officially recognized rate of exchange; they are often subject to sales tax. In addition, many establishments in Latin America charge a fee of about 5% on credit card transactions; although forbidden by credit card company rules there is not a lot you can do about this, except get the charge itemized on the receipt and complain to the card company. For credit card security, insist that imprints are made in your presence. Any imprints incorrectly completed should be torn into tiny pieces. Also destroy the carbon papers after the form is completed (signatures can be copied from them).

Changing money
When departing by air, don't forget that you will have to pay airport departure tax

Whenever possible change your money at a bank or a *casa de cambio* – black markets have largely disappeared, and you are unlikely to get a significantly better rate. If you need to change money on the street, do not do so alone. If you are unsure about rates of exchange when you enter a country, check at the border with more than one changer, or ask locals or any traveller who may be leaving that country. Whenever you leave a country, sell any local currency before leaving – the further you get away from a country, the less the value of a country's money; in some cases you may not be able to change it at all.

Americans should know that if they run out of funds they can usually expect no help from the US Embassy or Consul other than a referral to some welfare organization. Find out before you go precisely what services and assistance your embassy or consulate can provide if you find yourself in difficulties.

Discount flight agents in the UK and the rest of Europe

In the UK
In addition to tour operators, Journey Latin America and the South American Experience try the following:
Council Travel, *28a Poland St, London, W1V 3DB, T020-7437-7767, www.destinations- group.com*
STA Travel, *6 Wrights Lane, London, W8 6TA, T0870-160-6070, www.statravel.co.uk, with other branches in London, throughout and the country, and a growing international presence. Specialists in low-cost student/youth flights and tours, also good for student IDs and insurance.*
Trailfinders, *194 Kensington High Street, London, W8 7RG, T020-7938-3939, www.trailfinders.com*
In France
Images du Monde , *14 rue Lahire, 75013 Paris, T01-4424-8788, F01-4586-2773,*

www.imagenes-tropicales.com
In Germany
Die Reisegalerie , *Myliusstr 48, 60323 Frankfurt, T069-9720-6000, F069-9720-6002, www.reisegalerie.com*
MD-Tours , *Rathausstrasse 9, D-72810 Gomaringen, T070-7292-0270, F070-7292-0271, www.md-tours.net*
In Holland
Thika Travel , *T03-624-2526, F03-624-2525, www.thika.nl*
In Switzerland
Kundert Travel , *Fähnlibrunnenstrasse 3, 8700 Küsnacht, Zurich, T01-910-9969, F01-910-5585, www.kundert-travel.ch*
Helvetic Tours , *Neuengasse 26, 3001 Berne, T031-329-4242, F031-329-4272, www.helvetictours.ch Good for the last minute and the tour market.*

Essentials

Getting there

All countries in Latin America officially require travellers entering their territory to have an onward or return ticket. In 2001 this regulation was rarely enforced by any country, but it can create problems. In lieu of an onward ticket out of the country you are entering, any ticket out of another Latin American country may suffice, or proof that you have sufficient funds to buy a ticket (a credit card will do).

International air tickets are very expensive if purchased in Latin America

Air

Details of all the main airlines flying to each country are given in the relevant Essentials sections. Fares from Europe and North America to Latin American destinations vary from airline to airline, destination to destination and according to time of year. Peak periods, and higher prices, correspond to holiday season in the northern hemisphere. Check with an agency for the best deal for when you wish to travel. There is a wide range of offers to choose from in a highly competitive environment. Check the lists of discount flight agents for UK and Ireland, North America, and Australia and New Zealand. Also check the list of airline websites here and the list of tour operators in the UK and North America, on page 22.

Certain Central American countries impose local tax on flights originating there. Among these are Guatemala, Costa Rica, Panama and Mexico

Most airlines offer discounted (cheaper than official) fares of one sort or another on scheduled flights. These are not offered by the airlines direct to the public, but through agencies who specialize in this type of fare. The very busy seasons are as follows: 7 December-15 January and July to mid-September. If you intend travelling during those times, book as far ahead as possible.

An indication of cost is difficult to give due to the large number of variables. As an example, a three-month return London-Mexico flying out in in July is about US$600, a six-month return flying out of San José, Costa Rica is roughly US$870. Move that flight to November and both prices drop by about US$150. Prices from Europe are roughly similar.

From the US flight costs are highly variable, seasonal and subject to special offers. Travellers from Australia and New Zealand will struggle to see change out of A$2,500 coming in through Los Angeles.

Essentials

 Discount flight agents in North America

Air Brokers International, 323 Geary St, Suite 411, San Francisco, CA94102, T01-800-883-3273, www.airbrokers.com Consolidator and specialist on RTW and Circle Pacific tickets.
Council Travel, 205 E 42nd St, New York, NY 10017, T1-888-COUNCIL, www.counciltravel.com Student/budget agency with branches in many other US cities.
Discount Airfares Worldwide On-Line, www.etn.nl/discount.htm A hub of consolidator and discount agent links.
EXito Latin American Travel Specialists, 1212 Broadway Suite 910, Oakland, CA 94612, T1-800-655-4053; worldwide T510-655-2154, F510-655-4566.

www.exito-travel.com
International Travel Network/Airlines of the Web, www.itn.net/airlines Online air travel information and reservations.
STA Travel, 5900 Wilshire Blvd, Suite 2110, Los Angeles, CA 90036, T1-800-777-0112, www.sta-travel.com Also branches in New York, San Francisco, Boston, Miami, Chicago, Seattle and Washington DC.
Travel CUTS, 187 College St, Toronto, ON, M5T 1P7, T1-800-667-2887, www.travelcuts.com Specialist in student discount fares, Ids and other travel services. Branches in other Canadian cities.

Other fares fall into three groups, and are all on scheduled services: **Excursion (return) fares**: with restricted validity either 7-90 days, or 7-180 days (Mexico), depending on the airline; 7-90 days (Central America). These are fixed-date tickets where the dates of travel cannot be changed without incurring a penalty. **Yearly fares**: these may be bought on a one-way or return basis, and usually the returns can be issued with the return date left open. You must, however, fix the route. **Student (or Under-26) fares** (there is a wider range of these to Mexico than elsewhere). Some airlines are flexible on the age limit, others strict. One way and returns available, or 'Open Jaws' (see below). There is also a wider range of cheap one-way student fares originating in Latin America than can be bought outside the continent. There is less availability in the busy seasons (see above).

Open Jaw fares For people intending to travel a linear route and return from a different point from that which they entered, there are 'Open Jaw' fares, which are available on student, yearly, or excursion fares. All airlines can provide Open Jaw fares simply calculated on the extra distance travelled.

Flights from Europe
If buying airline tickets routed through the USA, check that US taxes are included in the price

With the promotion of Cancún as a gateway from Europe, there has been an increase in the number of scheduled flights to Mexico, at the expense of charter flights from Britain (for example *Iberia* flies daily Madrid-Miami-Cancún; *Air France/AeroMéxico* twice-weekly Paris-Cancún; *Condor Flugdienst* from Frankfurt to Cancún, Acapulco and Puerto Vallarta – also to San José, Costa Rica). *British Airways* operates a twice weekly flight from London Gatwick to Cancún and three scheduled services a week from London Heathrow to Mexico City. *British Airways'* flights link with *AeroMéxico* and, to a lesser extent, *Mexicana* for access to the rest of the country. If you do not stop over in Mexico City, low-cost add-ons are available to Mexican domestic destinations through *British Airways'* link with the main national airlines.

Between February and June scheduled airfares from Europe to Mexico City can be very low, commensurate with some transatlantic fares (the same does not apply to holiday destinations like Cancún or Acapulco). It is therefore worth considering Mexico City as an entry/exit point for a Mexican trip. For the widest range of options and keenest prices Mexico City is best, but US carriers provide the bulk of access both to Cancún and to the other regional points which have no direct access from Europe (but through fares are available). If flexible on time, you can seek promotional fares on smaller Mexican carriers not represented in Europe when you arrive.

Seasonal charter flights can work out to be very affordable. *Martinair*, a subsidiary of *KLM*, flies Costa Rica-the Netherlands, for around US$500 return. There are several cheap French charters to Mexico and Guatemala. There are a number of 'packages' that include flights from Mexico to Cuba which can be bought locally in Mexico, Guatemala, Costa Rica or in advance.

Discount flight agents in Australia and New Zealand

Flight Centres, 82 Elizabeth St, Sydney, T133-133, www.flightcentre.com.au; 205 Queen St, Auckland, T09-309-6171, www.flightcentre.co.nz. Also branches in other towns and cities.
STA Travel, T1300-360960, www.statravelaus.com.au; 702-730 Harris St, Ultimo, Sydney, toll free on T1-300-60960, and

240 Flinders St, Melbourne. In NZ: 10 High St, Auckland, T09-366-6673. Also in major towns and university campuses.
Travel.com.au, 76 Clarence St, Sydney, T02-924-95232, www.travel.com.au
Trailfinder, 8 Spring St, Sydney, NSW 2000. Offices in Melbourne, Cairns, Brisbane and Perth.

Travellers starting their journey in continental Europe should make local enquiries about charters and agencies offering the best deals. There is no substitute for early enquiry and planning if budgets are important.

Flying to Mexico from the US and Canada offers a very wide range of options. The main US carriers of **American Airlines**, **Continental** and **United** offer flights to many cities throughout Mexico in addition to daily flights to Mexico City, Guadalajara, Cancún, Monterrey and Puerto Vallarta. Direct international flights also serve many other cities in the country, but the main through points are Miami, Dallas/Fort Worth, Los Angeles and San Francisco. From Canada the options are less varied, but regular flights serve the main cities with direct flights from Montreal and Toronto.

Flights from the US & Canada

Flights to Central America from the US and Canada offer fewer options. All capital cities receive a regular service, with connections to regional cities and large towns normally available.

Links throughout the isthmus are provided by *Grupo Taca*, the association of Central American national carriers. Main connections within the region and to other countries in Latin America and the Caribbean are provided through Mexico, San Salvador and Panama City.

Flights from Central & Latin America

Flights to Central America and Mexico from Australia and New Zealand are with *United Airlines* and generally connect through Los Angeles, where the range of flights available to US travellers can be used for connections.

Flights from Australia & New Zealand

Increasing numbers of direct flights are available from Asia with flights from Hong Kong, Shanghai and Tokyo. Most go via Mexico City with just a few heading south.

Flights from Asia

Although it's a little more complicated, it's possible to buy tickets in London and Europe for travel originating in Latin America at substantially cheaper fares than those available locally. This is useful for the traveller who doesn't know where he or she will end up, or who plans to travel for more than a year. But a one-way ticket from Latin America is more expensive than a one-way in the other direction, so it's always best to buy a return (but see Student fares, above).

General hints

If you buy discounted air tickets always check the reservation with the airline concerned to make sure the flight still exists. Also remember that IATA airlines' schedules change in March and October each year, so if you're going to be away a long time it's best to leave return flight coupons open. If you know that you will be returning at the very busy seasons you should make a reservation. In addition, it is vital to check in advance whether you are entitled to any refund or re-issued ticket if you lose, or have stolen, a discounted air ticket.

Weight allowances if going direct from Europe are generally 20 kg for economy and business class or 30 kg for first class. If you have special baggage requirements, check with an agency about anomalies which exist on different weight allowances one way, for example. Certain carriers (for example *Iberia*, *Air France*) offer a two-piece allowance out of the UK only, each piece up to 32 kg. Many people travel to Mexico and Central America via the USA, and all carriers via the USA offer this allowance in both directions. However, weight limits for internal flights are often lower, so it's best to enquire beforehand.

Road

Travel from the USA

There are a multitude of entry points from the US that can be used. These are all covered in detail within the Mexico chapter. Crossing the border is simple and hassle free for foot passengers and reasonably straightforward for people travelling with their own vehicle. All border towns have a bus terminal that offers long-distance bus services.

An alternative is to consider catching a long-distance bus from inside the US. Greyhound and several other companies offer the service from border towns and towns further north such as Arizona, Los Angeles and even as far as Chicago.

If you are thinking of travelling via the USA, or of visiting the USA after Latin America, you are strongly advised to get your visa and find out about any other requirements from a US Consulate in your own country, not while travelling. Although visa requirements for air travellers with round-trip tickets to the USA have been relaxed, it is advisable to have a visa to allow entry by land, or on airlines from South and Central America which are not 'participating carriers' on the Visa Waiver scheme.

Travellers are required to list on the Customs' declaration form any meats, fruits, vegetables, plants, animals, and plant and animal products they are bringing into the country. The US Department of Agriculture places restrictions on agricultural items brought to the United States from foreign countries and it's probably simpler not to carry anything. Inspectors will confiscate illegal items for destruction. Travellers who fail to declare items can be fined up to US$100 on the spot, and their exit from the airport will be delayed. Some items are permitted. Call 301-436-5908 for a copy of the helpful pamphlet, 'Travelers Tips'.

Travel from Colombia

It is not possible to travel from Colombia to Panama by road.

Boat

Details on shipping cars are given in Motoring, below, and in the relevant country sections

Travelling by boat to the region is not cheap and is really only worth considering if you are shipping a vehicle from Europe or the US. Enquiries regarding passages should be made through agencies in your own country, or, **in the UK**, through *Strand Voyages*, who also have information on occasional one-way services to the Gulf of Mexico from Europe: *Strand Voyages*, Charing Cross Shopping Concourse, The Strand, London WC2N 4HZ, T020-7836-6363, F020-7497-0078, www.strandtravel.co.uk   Also in the UK, information can be obtained from *Cargo Ship Voyages Ltd*, Hemley, Woodbridge, Suffolk, IP12 4QF, T01473-736265, F01473-736726, cargovoyager@cargoshipvoyages.com (Panama, Costa Rica, Honduras and Belize – 12 days), and *The Cruise People*, 88 York Street, London W1H 1DP, T020-7723-2450, F020-7723-2486 (reservations 0800-526313), www.cruisepeople.co.uk and in North America at 1252 Lawrence Avenue East, Suite 202, Toronto, Canada, M3A 1C3, T416-444-2410. **In Europe**, contact *Wagner Frachtschiffreisen*, Stadlerstrasse 48, CH-8404, Winterthur, Switzerland, T052-242-1442, F242-1487. **In the USA**, contact *Freighter World Cruises*, 180 South Lake Ave, Suite 335, Pasadena, CA 91101, T1-800-531-7774 or T626-449-3106, www.freighterworld.com, or *Travltips Cruise* and *Freighter Travel Association*, PO Box 580188, Flushing, New York 11358, T1-800-872-8584, www.travltips.com

Sailing your own vessel

Following the coastal route doesn't have to be done from the land side, as thousands of sailors who follow the good-weather sailing around the coast of Mexico and Central America can confirm. Between California, the Panama Canal and Florida dozens of marinas await the sailor looking to see the region from the sea. Mooring up for a while, you can head inland to experience life away from the coast. A guide to the marinas and sailing ports of the region is *Cruising Ports: Florida to California via Panama*, by Capt John Rain, published by Point Loma Publishing in San Diego. Captain Rain is an experienced navigator of Mexican and Central American waters with over 50 Panama transits under his cap (his website is home.san.rr.com/caprains).

Touching down

As a general rule, try to avoid arriving at night and if you can't, have a hotel booked and take a taxi straight there. It may not be the cheapest way out of the airport, but it is the simplest and safest.

Each country in the region charges an airport departure tax - information is given in the Essentials sections for each relevant country.

Essentials

Local customs and laws

There is a natural prejudice in all countries against travellers who ignore personal hygiene and have a generally dirty and unkempt appearance. Most Latin Americans, if they can afford it, devote great care to their clothes and appearance; it is appreciated if visitors do likewise. How you dress is mostly how people will judge you.

Clothing

Remember that politeness – even a little ceremoniousness – is much appreciated. Men should always remove any headgear and say '*con permiso*' when entering offices. Shaking hands is much more common in Latin America than in Europe or North America; always say '*Buenos días*' before midday, '*Buenas tardes*' in the afternoon or '*Buenas noches*' later in the evening, and it's normal to wait for a reply before proceeding further. In shops and markets, saying '*No, gracias*' with a smile is always better than an arrogant dismissal. Remember that travellers from abroad have usually enjoyed greater advantages in life than most minor officials in Latin America, and should be friendly and courteous in consequence. Try not to be impatient and avoid criticizing situations in public; the officials may know more English than you think and gestures and facial expressions are certainly open to interpretation. Be judicious about discussing politics with strangers (especially in Guatemala, Honduras, Nicaragua and El Salvador). In certain situations, however, politeness can be a liability: for example when queuing, as, with the exception of Mexicans, most Latin Americans are disorderly queuers.

Courtesy
Always ask permission before photographing people

Punctuality is more of a concept than a reality in Latin countries. The *mañana* culture reigns supreme and any arrangement to meet at, say 1900, will normally rendezvous about 2100. However Murphy's Law states that the one time you are late to catch a bus, boat or plane, it will leave on time – the rule is hurry up and wait.

Users of **drugs**, even of soft ones, without medical prescription should be particularly careful, as some countries impose heavy penalties – up to 10 years' imprisonment – for even the simple possession of such substances. In this connection, the planting of drugs on travellers, by traffickers or the police, is not unknown. If offered drugs on the street, make no response at all and keep walking. Note that people who roll their own cigarettes are often suspected of carrying drugs and are subjected to intensive searches.

Prohibitions

If you are taking illegal drugs – even ones that are widley and publically used – be aware that numerous traps have been set from time to time. Should you get into trouble, your embassy is unlikely to be very sympathetic.

Responsible tourism

Travel to the furthest corners of the globe is now commonplace and the mass movement of people for leisure and business is a major source of foreign exchange and economic development in many parts of Central America. In some countries (for example Costa Rica) it is probably the most significant economic activity.

The benefits of international travel are self-evident for both hosts and travellers – employment, increased understanding of different cultures, business and leisure opportunities. At the same time there is clearly a downside to the industry. Where visitor pressure is high and/or poorly regulated, adverse impacts to society and the natural environment may be apparent. Paradoxically, this is as true in undeveloped and pristine areas

Essentials

 A few ideas

So how can you actually makes a difference? Make a voluntary contribution to Climate Care to countact the pollution caused by tax-free fuel on your flight. Their projects make savings in carbon dioxide that match your share of the plane's emissions. Find out more at www.co2.org

Where possible choose a destination, tour operator or hotel with a proven ethical and environmental commitment – if in doubt ask; Spend money on locally produced (rather than imported) goods and services and use common sense when bargaining – your few dollars saved may be a week's salary to others.

Use water and electricity carefully – travellers may receive preferential supply while the needs of local communities are overlooked.

Learn about local etiquette and culture – consider local norms and behaviour and dress appropriately for local cultures and situations.

Consider staying in local accommodation rather than foreign-owned hotels – the economic benefits for host communities are far greater – and there are far greater opportunities to learn about local culture.

Protect wildlife and other natural resources – don't buy souvenirs or goods made from these materials unless they are clearly sustainably produced and are not protected under CITES legislation (CITES controls trade in endangered species).

Always ask before taking photographs or videos of people.

(where culture and the natural environment are less 'prepared' for even small numbers of visitors) as in major resort destinations.

The travel industry is growing rapidly and increasingly the impacts of this supposedly 'smokeless' industry are becoming apparent. These impacts can seem remote and unrelated to an individual trip or holiday. But air travel is clearly implicated in global warming and damage to the ozone layer, resort location and construction can destroy natural habitats and restrict traditional rights and activities. With this in mind, individual choice and awareness can make a difference in many instances (see box), and collectively, travellers are having a significant effect in shaping a more responsible and sustainable industry.

In an attempt to promote awareness of and credibility for responsible tourism, organizations such as *Green Globe* (T020-7730-4428, www.greenglobe21.com) and the *Centre for Environmentally Sustainable Tourism* (CERT) (T01268-795772, F01268-759834, www.c-e-r-t.org) now offer advice on selecting destinations and sites that aim to achieve certain commitments to conservation and sustainable development. Generally these are larger mainstream destinations and resorts but they are still a useful guide and increasingly aim to provide information on smaller operations.

Of course travel can have beneficial impacts and this is something to which every traveller can contribute – many national parks are part funded by receipts from visitors. Similarly, travellers can promote patronage and protection of important archaeological sites and heritage through their interest and contributions via entrance fees. They can also support small-scale enterprises by staying in locally run hotels and hostels, eating in local restaurants and by purchasing local goods, supplies and arts and crafts.

In fact, since the Responsible Travel section was first introduced in the 1992 *Mexico and Central American Handbook* there has been a phenomenal growth in tourism that promotes and supports the conservation of natural environments and is also fair and equitable to local communities. This 'eco-tourism' segment is probably the fastest-growing sector of the travel industry and it provides a vast and growing range of destinations and activities Central America. For example, in **Mexico**, cultural heritage is being protected by the *Oaxaca Protection of Archaeological Sites* (52-951-65786, www.antequera.com/muscoax), and in **Costa Rica** (www.puravidaspa.com) and **Belize** (Belize Ecotourism Association, T501-07-22119, www.belizenet.com/beta.html), a range of ecotourism destinations are now being promoted.

While the authenticity of some ecotourism operators' claims need to be interpreted with care, there is clearly both a huge demand for this type of activity and also significant opportunities to support worthwhile conservation and social development initiatives.

Organizations such as **Conservation International** (T1-202-429-5660, www.ecotour.org), the **Eco-Tourism Society** (T1-802-447-2121, www.ecotourism.org), **Planeta** (www2.planeta.com/mader) and **Tourism Concern** (T020-7753-3330, www.tourismconcern.org.uk) have begun to develop and/or promote eco-tourism projects and destinations and their websites are an excellent source of information and details for sites and initiatives throughout South America. Additionally, organizations such as, **Earthwatch** (US/Can1-800-776-0188, in UK on T01865-311601, www.earthwatch.org) and **Discovery International** (T020-7229-9881, www.discoveryinitiatives.com) offer opportunities to participate directly in scientific research and development projects throughout the region.

Central America offers unique and unforgettable experiences – often based on the natural environment, cultural heritage and local society. These are the reasons many of us choose to travel and why many more will want to do so in the future. Shouldn't we provide an opportunity for future travellers and hosts to enjoy the quality of experience and interaction that we take for granted?

Essentials

Safety

Generally speaking, most places in Latin America are no more dangerous than any major city in Europe or North America. In provincial towns, main places of interest, on daytime buses and in ordinary restaurants the visitor should be quite safe. Nevertheless, in large cities (particularly in crowded places such as markets and bus stations) crime exists, mostly of the opportunistic kind. If you are aware of the dangers, act confidently and use your common sense you will lessen many of the risks. The following tips, all endorsed by travellers, are meant to forewarn, not alarm.

Keep all documents secure; hide your main cash supply in different places or under your clothes (extra pockets sewn inside shirts and trousers, pockets closed with a zip or safety pin, moneybelts (best worn below the waist rather than at it or around the neck), neck or leg pouches, and elasticated support bandages for keeping money and cheques above the elbow or below the knee have been repeatedly recommended. Waist packs worn outside the clothes are not safe. Keep cameras in bags (preferably with a chain or wire in the strap to defeat the slasher) and don't wear fancy wrist-watches or jewellery. If you wear a shoulder-bag in a market, carry it in front of you.

When you have all your luggage with you at a bus or railway station, be especially careful: don't get into arguments with any locals if you can help it and lock all the items together with a chain or cable if you are waiting for some time, or simply sit on top of your backpack. Take a taxi between airport/bus station/railway station and hotel, if you can possibly afford it. Keep your bags with you in the taxi and pay only when you and your luggage are safely out of the vehicle (but keep an eye on it!). Avoid night buses unless essential or until you are comfortable travelling in the area; avoid arriving at night whenever possible; and watch your belongings whether they are stowed inside or outside the cabin (rooftop luggage racks create extra problems, which are sometimes unavoidable – many bus drivers cover rooftop luggage, but a waterproof bag or outer sack can be invaluable). Major bus lines often issue a luggage ticket when bags are stored in the hold, generally a safe system. When getting on a bus, keep your ticket handy as you will probably have to show it at some point. Finally, be wary of accepting food, drink, sweets or cigarettes from unknown fellow-travellers on buses or trains; they may be drugged, and you would wake up hours later without your belongings. In this connection, never accept a bar drink from an opened bottle (unless you can see that the bottle is in general use); always have it uncapped in front of you.

Safety on public transport
For specific local problems, see under the individual countries in the text

Ignore mustard smearers and paint or shampoo sprayers, and strangers' remarks like 'what's that on your shoulder?' or 'have you seen that dirt on your shoe?'. Furthermore, don't bend over to pick up money or other items in the street. These are all ruses intended to distract your attention and make you easy for an accomplice to steal from. If someone follows you when you're in the street, let him catch up with you and 'give him the eye'. While you should take local advice about being out at night, do not assume that daytime is any safer. If walking after dark, walk in the road, not on the pavement/sidewalk.

Scams

Be wary of 'plain-clothes policemen'; insist on seeing identification and on going to the police station by main roads. Do not hand over your identification (or money – which he should not need to see anyway) until you are at the station. On no account take them directly back to your lodgings. Be even more suspicious if he seeks confirmation of his status from a passer-by. If someone implies they are asking for a bribe, insist on a receipt. If attacked, remember your assailants may well be armed, and try not to resist.

It is best, if you can trust your hotel, to leave any valuables you don't need in a safe-deposit. Always keep an inventory of what you have deposited. If you don't trust the hotel, lock everything in your pack and secure that in your room (some people take eyelet-screws for padlocking cupboards or drawers). If you do lose valuables, you will need to report to the police for insurance purposes and note details of the report.

Rape This can happen anywhere in the world. If you are the victim of a sexual assault, you are advised in the first instance to contact a doctor (this can be your home doctor if you prefer). You will need tests to determine whether you have contracted any sexually transmitted diseases; you may also need advice on post-coital contraception. You should also contact your embassy, where consular staff are very willing to help in cases of assault.

Police Probably the best advice with regards the police in Mexico and Central America is to have as little to do with them as possible. An exception to this rule are the Tourist Police, who operate in some of the big cities and resorts, and who are there to provide assistance. Whereas in Europe and North America we are accustomed to law enforcement on a systematic basis, in general, enforcement in Latin America is achieved by periodic campaigns.

You may well be asked for identification at any time and if you cannot produce it, you may be jailed. If a visitor is jailed his or her friends should provide food every day. This is especially important for people on a special diet, such as diabetics. If you are jailed, you should contact your embassy or consulate and take advice. In the event of a vehicle accident in which anyone is injured, all drivers involved are automatically detained until blame has been established, and this does not usually take less than two weeks.

Never offer a bribe unless you are fully conversant with the customs of the country. Wait until the official makes the suggestion, or offer money in some form which is apparently not bribery, for example 'In our country we have a system of on-the-spot fines (*multas de inmediato*). Is there a similar system here?' Do not assume that officials who accept a bribe are prepared to do anything else that is illegal. You bribe them to persuade them to do their job, or to persuade them not to do it, or to do it more quickly, or more slowly. You do not bribe them to do something which is against the law. The mere suggestion would make them very upset. If an official suggests that a bribe must be paid before you can proceed on your way, be patient (assuming you have the time) and he may relent.

Bear in mind that by bribing you are participating in a system that, on a different occasion at a customs or check-point for example, may cause you immense frustration.

Where to stay

Hotels The variety of hotels in the region is understandably highly varied. At the top end of the
See box page 43 market, mid- and upper-range hotel chains can be found throughout the region including
and inside front *Holiday Inns, Best Westerns, Intercontinentals* and *Marriotts*. Moving down through the price
cover for hotel brackets the presence of international chains is reduced.
grade price guide

A cheap but not bad hotel might be US$10 a night upwards in Mexico, less in some, but not all, of the Central American countries. In many of the popular destinations, there is often an established preferred choice budget option. The quality of these fluctuates. The good ones stay on top of the game, the mediocre ones fade and bloom with the fashions. For those on a really tight budget, it is a good idea to ask for a boarding house – *casa de huéspedes, hospedaje, pensión, casa familial* or *residencial*, according to country – they are normally to be found in abundance near bus and railway stations and markets. The very cheapest hotels often do not have 24-hour water supplies so ask when the water is available. There are often great seasonal

Hotel prices and facilities

LL (over US$150) to **A** (US$46-65) Hotels in these categories can be found in most of the large cities but especially where there is a strong concentration of tourists or business travellers. They should offer pool, sauna, gym, jacuzzi, all business facilities (including email), several restaurants and bars. A safe box is usually provided in each room. Credit cards are generally accepted and dollars cash changed usually at poor rates.

B (US$31-45) Hotels in this category should provide more than the standard facilities and a fair degree of comfort. Many include a good breakfast and offer extras such as a colour TV, minibar, air conditioning and a swimming pool. They may also provide tourist information and their own transport for airport pick-ups. Service is generally good and most accept credit cards although a lower rate is often offered for cash.

C (US$21-30) and **D** (US$12-20) Hotels in these categories range from very comfortable to functional and there are some real bargains to be had. You should expect your own bathroom, constant hot water, a towel, soap and toilet paper. There is sometimes a restaurant and a communal sitting area. In tropical regions rooms are usually equipped with air conditioning although this may be rather old. Hotels used to catering for foreign tourists and backpackers often have luggage storage, money exchange and kitchen facilities.

E (US$7-11) and **F** (under US$6) Hotels in these categories are often extremely simple with bedside or ceiling fans, shared bathrooms and little in the way of furniture. Standards of cleanliness may not be high and rooms may also be rented to couples by the hour.

Essentials

variations in hotel prices in resorts. In Mexico, couples should ask for a room with *cama matrimonial* (double bed), normally cheaper than a room with two beds. Note that in the text the term 'with bath' usually means 'with shower and toilet', not 'with bath tub'. Hotel rooms facing the street may be noisy; always ask for the best, quietest room. Cheaper hotels don't always supply soap, towels and toilet paper (they may loan you a towel in return for a deposit).

Motels, particularly in northern Mexico, are extremely popular and tend to provide accessible, economic accommodation close to the main roads. Further south, the term 'motel' picks up an altogether seedier interpretation and is used by those with a car who want to get away for an hour or two with their lovers. Voyeurs may enjoy the experience, few others will.

Making reservations is a good idea, particularly at times you know are going to be busy or if you are travelling a long distance and won't have the energy to look around for a room. At the lower end of the market, having reservations honoured can be difficult. Ask the hotel if there is anything you can do to secure the room. If arriving late, make sure the hotel knows what time you plan to arrive.

The *International Youth Hostal Association* has a growing presence in the region with several places in Mexico and Costa Rica. With other affiliated hostals joining it is worth considering getting membership if you are staying in Mexico for a while. While there is no shortage of cheap accommodation in the region, youth hostals do still offer a fairly reliable standard of cleanliness. Members with an identity card normally get a small discount. The simplest way to find out details is on the internet at **www.hostelslatinamerica.org**

Youth hostels

Organized campsites are referred to in the text immediately below hotel lists, under each town. If there is no organized site in town, a football pitch or gravel pit might serve. Obey the following rules for 'wild' camping: (1) arrive in daylight and pitch your tent as it gets dark; (2) ask permission to camp from a person in authority; (3) never ask a group of people – especially young people; (4) try to avoid camping on a beach (because of sandflies and thieves). If you can't get information from anyone, camp in a spot where you can't be seen from the nearest inhabited place and make sure no one saw you go there.

Camping

If taking a cooker, the most frequent recommendation is a multifuel stove (for example *MSR International, Coleman Peak 1*), which will burn unleaded petrol or, if that is not available, kerosene, benzina blanca, etc. Alcohol-burning stoves are simple, reliable, but slow and you

Essentials

have to carry a lot of fuel: for a methylated spirit-burning stove, the following fuels apply, *alcohol desnaturalizado, alcohol metílico, alcohol puro (de caña)* or *alcohol para quemar* (avoid this in Honduras as it does not burn). Ask for 95%, but 70% will suffice. In Mexico fuel is sold in supermarkets; in all countries it can be found in chemists/pharmacies. Gas cylinders and bottles are usually exchangeable, but if not can be recharged; specify whether you use butane or propane. Gas canisters are not always available. Camping supplies are usually only available in larger cities, so stock up when possible.

Hammocks   A hammock can be an invaluable piece of equipment, especially if travelling on the cheap. It will be of more use than a tent because many places have hammock-hooks, or you can sling a hammock between trees, etc. A good tip is to carry a length of rope and some plastic sheeting. The rope gives a good choice of tree distances and the excess provides a hanging frame for the plastic sheeting to keep the rain off. Metal S-hooks can be very useful. Don't forget a mosquito net if travelling in insect-infected areas. Tips on buying a hammock are given in the Mérida (Yucatán) Shopping section. Good hammocks are also sold in Guatamala. If in any doubt about quality or size, seek advice before buying.

Toilets   Almost without exception, used toilet paper should not be flushed down the pan, but placed in the receptacle provided. This applies even in quite expensive hotels. Failing to observe this custom blocks the pan or drain. You will get the hang of it after a while, and may even do it automatically when you return home!

Cockroaches   These are ubiquitous, unpleasant, but not dangerous. Buy some insecticide powder if staying in cheap hotels, trailer parks, etc; *Baygon* (Bayer) has been recommended. Stuff toilet paper in any holes in walls that you may suspect of being parts of cockroach runs.

Getting around

Independent   By far the most popular style of transport for the 'independent' traveller is by public transport.
travel   An excellent network of buses criss-cross Central America and Mexico varying in quality from luxurious inter-city cruisers equipped with a/c, videos and fully reclining seats, to beaten-up US-style school buses. Bus travel is certainly a very good way to get a feel for the countries you are travelling through and to meet people going about their daily lives.

Travelling under your own steam is also very popular and brings with it a freedom to explore that bus travel simply does not allow. Driving your own vehicle – car, camper van, motorbike and bicycle – offers wonderful freedom and may not be as expensive or as bureaucratic as you think. From the letters we receive, the ever-greater co-operation between the nations of Central America is producing dramatic benefits at border crossings for those who decide to go it alone.

With the comprehensive road network it's easy to miss out on other sensible choices. Don't shun the opportunity to take a short flight. While you'll need to enquire for precise costs, the view from above provides a different perspective and the difference in cost may not be as great as you think.

Getting around in Central America is rarely a problem whether travelling by bus, car, bike, in fact almost any mode of transport. In the *Handbook* we try not to tell you where you should go but rather prefer to point out the options – it is after all *your* trip.

There is just one caveat that stands good across all situations: be patient when asking directions. Often Latin Americans will give you the wrong answer rather than admit they do not know. Distances are notoriously inaccurate so, in an ideal world, ask three people and take the majority response.

Air

With the exception of El Salvador, all countries have a domestic flight service. Prices vary dramatically but it is definitely worth considering an aerial 'hop' if it covers a lot of difficult terrain quickly and you get a good view included.

If you know the outline of your itinerary, it may be worth booking internal flights before you arrive in the country. They are usually, but not always, cheaper.

An option worth exploring is the airpass, usually offered by an airline or group of airlines. The standard scheme works on system of vouchers. A voucher would cover a set distance between any two destinations, You simply buy as many vouchers as you want.

Air passes

The only airpass currently in operation in the region is with *Mexicana* and must be purchased in conjuction with an international air ticket. Once *Grupo Taca*, the Central American regional airline who are still getting to grips with the merging of the Central American national flag carriers, have got new systems in place it is quite possible they will introduce an airpass scheme.

Finally, seasonal offers are occassionally introduced. In Costa Rica, *SANSA* offered unlimited flight for two or three weeks for a set price. That offer has finished but after three flights, the offer was very cost effective.

Advice to people travelling on a tight budget in Latin America is to pay for all transport as you go along, and not in advance. This advice does not apply to people on a tight schedule: paying as you go along may save money, but it is likely to waste more time.

Road

There is an extensive road system with frequent bus services throughout Mexico and Central America. Some of these services are excellent. In mountainous country, however, do not expect buses to get to their destination, after long journeys, anywhere near on time. Avoid turning up for a bus at the last minute; if it is full it may depart early. Tall travellers are advised to take aisle, not window, seats on long journeys as this allows more leg room. When the journey takes more than three or four hours, meal stops at country inns or bars, good and bad, are the rule. Often no announcement is made on the duration of the stop: ask the driver and follow him, if he eats, eat. See what the locals are eating – and buy likewise, or make sure you're stocked up well on food and drink at the start. For drinks, stick to bottled water or soft drinks or coffee (black). The food sold by vendors at bus stops may be all right; watch if locals are buying, though unpeeled fruit is of course reliable. (See above for Security in buses.) Make sure you have a sweater or blanket to hand for long bus journeys, especially at night; even if it's warm outside, the air-conditioning is often fierce.

Bus

International buses link the capital cities providing an effective way of quickly covering a lot of ground. However, bear in mind that Panama-Guatemala with *Ticabus* takes about four days and costs around US$100. You may want to consider flying if you need to get through more than one country quickly.

What kind of motoring you do will depend on what kind of car you set out with. Four-wheel drive is not necessary, although it does give you greater flexibility in mountain and jungle territory. Wherever you travel you should expect from time to time to find roads that are badly maintained, damaged or closed during the wet season, and delays because of floods, landslides and huge potholes. Don't plan your schedules too tightly.

Car

The electronic ignition and fuel metering systems on modern emission controlled cars are allergic to humidity, heat and dust, and cannot be repaired by mechanics outside the main centres. Standard European and Japanese cars run on fuel with a higher octane rating than is commonly available in North, South or Central America. Unleaded fuel is now available nearly everywhere. Note that in some areas gas stations are few and far between. Fill up when you see one: the next one may be out of fuel.

Security Spare no ingenuity in making your car secure. Try never to leave the car unattended except in a locked garage or guarded parking space. Remove all belongings and leave the empty glove compartment open when the car is unattended. Also lock the clutch or accelerator to the steering wheel with a heavy, obvious chain or lock. Street children will generally protect your car fiercely in exchange for a tip. Be sure to note down key numbers and carry spares of the most important ones (but don't keep all spares inside the vehicle).

Essentials

Documents A *carnet de passage* is no longer accepted in any country. Land entry procedures for all countries are simple though time-consuming, as the car has to be checked by customs, police and agriculture officials (see, however, Mexico, Getting around by car in Essentials, on regulations). All you need is the registration document in the name of the driver, or, in the case of a car registered in someone else's name, a notarized letter of authorization. Note that Costa Rica does not recognize the International Driving Licence, which is otherwise useful. In Guatemala, Honduras and Costa Rica, the car's entry is stamped into the passport so you may not leave the country even temporarily without it. A written undertaking that the vehicle will be re-exported after temporary importation is useful and may be requested in Nicaragua, Costa Rica and Panama.

Most countries give a limited period of stay, but allow an extension if requested in advance. Of course, do be very careful to keep **all** the papers you are given when you enter, to produce when you leave. (An army of 'helpers' loiters at each border crossing, waiting to guide motorists to each official in the correct order, for a tip. They can be very useful, but don't give them your papers.) Bringing a car in by sea or air is much more complicated and expensive: generally you will have to hire an agent to clear it through. Insurance for the vehicle against accident, damage or theft is best arranged in the country of origin: in Latin American countries it is very expensive to insure against accident and theft, especially as you should take into account the value of the car increased by duties calculated in real (that is non-devaluing) terms. If the car is stolen or written off, you will be required to pay very high duty on its value. A few countries (for example Costa Rica) insist on compulsory third-party insurance, to be bought at the border: in other countries it's technically required, but not checked up on (again, see Mexico, Getting around by car, for details on *Sanborn's* and other insurers, who will insure vehicles for driving in Mexico and Central America). Get the legally required minimum cover – not expensive – as soon as you can, because if you should be involved in an accident and are uninsured, your car could be confiscated. If anyone is hurt, do not pick them up (you become liable). Seek assistance from the nearest police station or hospital if you are able to do so. You may find yourself facing a hostile crowd, even if you are not to blame. Expect frequent road checks by police, military (especially Honduras, where there is a check point on entering and leaving every town), agricultural and forestry produce inspectors, and any other curious official who wants to know what a foreigner is doing driving around in his domain. Smiling simple-minded patience is the best tactic to avoid harassment.

Shipping a vehicle to and beyond Central America Two shipping lines recommended by *South American Explorers* for shipping cars from the US to Panama are ***Wilhelmsen Lines***, World Trade Center, 401E Pratt St, Suite 1400, Baltimore, MD 21202, T410-659-7900, F410-659-7994, www.protos.ca; and ***American Cargo Service Inc***, 2305 Northwest 107 Ave, Box 122, Miami, FL 331720, T305-592-8065, F305-477-3936.

Shipping from Panama to mainland South America is expensive; you must shop around to find the cheapest way. The shipping lines and agents, and the prices for the services from Panama and elsewhere change frequently. Current details and recent recommendations will be found in the Panama chapter under Shipping a vehicle, page 1153.

Car hire While not everyone has the time or inclination to travel with their own car, the freedom that goes with renting for a few days is well worth considering, especially if you can get a group of three or four together to share the cost. The main international car hire companies operate in all countries, but tend to be very expensive, reflecting the high costs and accident rates. Hotels and tourist agencies will tell you where to find cheaper rates, but you will need to check that you have such basics as a spare wheel, toolkit and functioning lights, etc. If you plan to do a lot of driving and will have time at the end to dispose of it, investigate the possibility of buying a second-hand car locally; since hiring is so expensive it may well work out cheaper and will probably do you just as well. For visiting Mexico and beyond, investigate the cost of buying a vehicle in the USA and selling it there at the end of a round trip (do not try to sell a car illegally in Mexico or Central America).

For RV/motorhome users, a surge protector is recommended to prevent damage to electrical equipment. Ground your trailer with a rod and jumper cable/jump lead

Car hire insurance Check exactly what the hirer's insurance policy covers. In many cases it will only protect you against minor bumps and scrapes, not major accidents, or 'natural' damage (for example flooding). Ask if extra cover is available. Also find out, if using a credit card, whether the card automatically includes insurance. Beware of being billed for scratches which were on the vehicle before you hired it. When you return the vehicle make sure you check it with someone at the office and get signed evidence that it is returned in good condition and that you will not be charged.

Motorcycling

People are generally very friendly to motorcyclists and you can make many friends by returning friendship to those who show an interest in you. Buying a bike in the States and driving down works out cheaper than buying one in Europe. In making your choice go for a comfortable bike. The motorcycle should be off-road capable without necessarily being an off-road bike.

Security This is not a problem in most countries. Try not to leave a fully laden bike on its own. An Abus D or chain will keep the bike secure. A cheap alarm gives you peace of mind if you leave the bike outside a hotel at night. Most hotels will allow you to bring the bike inside but it's better to look for hotels that have a courtyard or more secure parking and never leave luggage on the bike overnight or whilst unattended. Also take a cover for the bike.

Documents A passport, International Driving Licence, and bike registration document are necessary. In Mexico and Central America, a *carnet de passages* is not required.

Shipping Bikes may be sent from Panama to Colombia by cargo flight (for example CAC). You must drain the fuel and oil and remove the battery, but it is easier to disconnect and seal the overflow tube. Tape cardboard over fragile bits and insist on loading the bike yourself. The Darién Gap is impossible unless you carry the bike. For details on shipping to and from Panama see page 1153.

Border crossings All borders in Central America seem to work out at about US$20 per vehicle. The exceptions to this are Mexico (see Getting around by car in Mexico Essentials) and Panama (approximately US$4.50). All borders are free on exit, or should be on most occasions. Crossing borders on a Sunday or a holiday normally incurs double the standard charges in Central American countries. It is sometimes very difficult to find out exactly what is being paid for. If in doubt ask to see the boss and/or the rule book.

Cycling

Unless you are planning a journey almost exclusively on paved roads – when a high-quality touring bike such as a Dawes Super Galaxy would probably suffice – a mountain bike is strongly recommended. The good-quality ones (and the cast-iron rule is never to skimp on quality) are incredibly tough and rugged, with low gear ratios for difficult terrain, wide tyres with plenty of tread for good road-holding, cantilever brakes, and a low centre of gravity for improved stability. Although touring bike and to a lesser extent mountain bike spares are available in the larger Latin American cities, remember that in the developing world most locally manufactured goods are shoddy and rarely last. In some countries, such as Mexico, imported components can be found but they tend to be extremely expensive. (Shimano parts are generally the easiest to find.) Buy everything you possibly can before you leave home.

Useful tips Wind, not hills is the enemy of the cyclist. Try to make the best use of the times of day when there is little; mornings tend to be best but there is no steadfast rule. Take care to avoid dehydration by drinking regularly. In hot, dry areas with limited water supplies, be sure to carry an ample supply on the bike. For food, carry the staples (sugar, salt, dried milk, tea, coffee, porridge oats, raisins, dried soups, etc) and supplement these with whatever local foods can be found in the markets. Give your bicycle a thorough daily check for loose nuts, bolts or bearings. See that all parts run smoothly. A good chain should last 2,000 miles/3,200 km or more but be sure to keep it as clean as possible – an old toothbrush is good for this – and to oil it lightly from time to time. Remember that thieves are attracted to towns and cities, so when sightseeing, try to leave your bicycle with someone such as a café owner or a priest. Country people tend to be more honest and are usually friendly and very inquisitive. However, don't take unnecessary risks; always see that your bicycle is secure (most hotels will allow bikes to be kept in rooms). In more remote regions dogs can be vicious; carry a stick or some small stones to frighten them off. Traffic on main roads can be a nightmare; it is usually far more rewarding to keep to the smaller roads or to paths if they exist. Most cyclists agree that the main danger comes from other traffic. A rear-view mirror has frequently been

From Guatemala to Panama, border officials ask for a document of ownership and a frame number for your bicycle. Without these you will have a lot of trouble crossing frontiers

Essentials

recommended to forewarn you of trucks or cars which are too close behind. You also need to watch out for oncoming, overtaking vehicles, unstable loads on trucks, protruding loads, etc. Make yourself conspicuous by wearing bright clothing and a helmet; also, displaying a flag of the country you are travelling through helps to keep truckers patient and prompts encouragement. Most towns have a bicycle shop of some description, but it is best to do your own repairs and adjustments whenever possible.

Recommended reading *Richard's New Bicycle Book* (Pan, £12.99) makes useful reading for even the most mechanically minded. Also recommended are: *Latin America by Bike – A Complete Touring Guide*, Walter Sienko (The Mountaineers, 1993); *Bicycling Mexico*, Erick Weisbroth and Eric Ellman (Hunter Publishing Inc, 1990); *Bicycling Baja*, Bonnie Wong (Sunbelt Publications, 1988).

The **Expedition Advisory Centre**, administered by the Royal Geographical Society, 1 Kensington Gore, London SW7 2AR, 020 7591 3030, www.rgs.org, has published a useful monograph entitled *Bicycle Expeditions*, by Paul Vickers. Published in March 1990, it is available direct from the Centre, price £6.50 plus postage. In the UK there is also the **Cyclists' Touring Club**, CTC, Cotterell House, 69 Meadrow, Godalming, Surrey, GU7 3HS, T0870 8730060, www.ctc.org.uk for touring and technical information.

Hitchhiking

See Essentials sections under the individual countries for local conditions

Hitchhiking in Latin America is reasonably safe and straightforward for males and couples, provided you speak some Spanish. It is a most enjoyable mode of transport – a good way to meet the local people, to improve one's languages and to learn about the country. Truck drivers in particular are often well versed in things of interest one is passing, for example crops and industries. Some trucking companies, though, do not allow their drivers to take hitchhikers. If trying to hitchhike away from main roads and in sparsely populated areas, however, allow plenty of time, and ask first about the volume of traffic on the road. On long journeys, set out at crack of dawn, which is when trucks usually leave. They tend to go longer distances than cars.

However, it should be said that hitchhiking involves inherent risks and should be approached sensibly and with caution.

River, sea and lake

Keeping all options open water transport has to be a consideration – although not a very realistic one in terms of reaching a set destination. Beyond the value of sight-seeing particularly in small, quiet tropical rivers, genuine water transportation is on the decline. You'll find a few regular ferry schedules that avoid circuitous land routes. The main journeys are from the tip of Baja California to the Mexican mainland, between the Cayes of Belize and skipping down the coastline, from the Bay Islands of Honduras to the mainland, across Lake Nicaragua and in Costa Rica, where there are connections between the mainland and the Osa and Nicoya peninsulas on the Pacific Coast. If heading from Panama to South America you can work your way along the Caribbean coastline to Colombia using a number of small sporadically available vessels.

Beyond this functional travel a couple of journeys stand out. Travelling the Panama Canal (as opposed to just seeing it!) and crewing a private yacht. Both of these requiring flexible schedules and good timing, but you might hit lucky and find someone who is doing the full journey from California to Florida and you can help for part of the way. Conditions of 'employment' vary greatly - you may get paid, you may get board and lodgings, you may even have to pay. The days of seeking out a fishing community and just getting a ride are now largely over. Most fishermen have worked out that travellers can pay more than fish.

Train

Trains are like nature – they are treasured when threatened with extinction. Now that the privatization and subsequent closure of train lines in Mexico and Central America is almost complete there is a renaissance of interest in the classic journeys including the **Copper Canyon** in northern Mexico, the **Tequila Express** running from Guadalajara to Tequila, a fledgling tourist service in **Costa Rica** offering a couple of short runs and the **Trans-Isthmus** railroad in Panama. With the exception of the Copper Canyon, none of these are genuine train journeys. Trains do run in a few countries – Mexico and El Salvador – but they are slower than buses and there is no such thing as a scheduled service. They tend to provide finer scenery and you can normally see much more wildlife than from the road – it is less disturbed being used by just one or two trains a day than the more frequent road traffic. Sadly then, it must be said that train travel is not a viable means of transport for the region.

Maps

Maps from the Institutos Geográficos Militares in the capitals are often the only good maps available in Latin America. It is therefore wise to get as many as possible in your home country before leaving, especially if you plan to travel overland. An excellent series of maps covering the whole region and each country is published by *International Travel Maps* (*ITM*), 345 West Broadway, Vancouver BC, V5Y 1P8, Canada, T604-879-3621, F604-879-4521, www.itmb. com, most compiled with historical notes by the late Kevin Healey.

A good source of maps with an international mail order service is *Stanfords*, 12-14 Long Acre, Covent Garden, London, WC2E, 9LP, UK, T020-7836-1321, F020-7836-0189, www.stanfords.co.uk

Essentials

Keeping in touch

Email is becoming more common and public access to the internet is becoming endemic with cybercafés opening in both large and small towns. This is by far the cheapest way to stay in touch, and while some may lament the loss of standing in the queue for Poste Restante, it is also the quickest. We list cybercafés in the text, but obviously these change as new ones open and old ones close. If you can't find the cybercafes listed, just ask someone locally. Three websites which give information on cybercafés are: **www2.planeta.com/mader/ecotravel/ resources/cybercafe.html**, **www.netcafeguide.com** and **www.latinworld.com** (which also gives a directory of internet resources on Latin America and the Caribbean).

Internet

Many of the telecommunications networks have been privatized and prices have fallen considerably and in some areas service has even improved. Consequently keeping in touch by phone is no longer prohibitive. Alternatively international telecom chargecards are useful and available from most countries; obtain details before leaving home. For the US AT&T's 'USA Direct', Sprint and MCI are all available for calls to the USA. It is much cheaper than operator-assisted calls. Communicating by fax is a convenient way of sending messages home. Many places with public fax machines (post offices, telephone companies or shops) will receive as well as send messages. Internet whizz-kids might be able to make internet calls through the Hotmail system if an internet café is set up for calls.

Telephone
See inside front cover for telephone dialling codes

Postal services vary in efficiency from country to country and prices are quite high; pilfering is frequent. All mail, especially packages, should be registered. Check before leaving home if your embassy will hold mail, and for how long, in preference to the Poste Restante/General Delivery (Lista de Correos) department of a country's Post Office. (Cardholders can use American Express agencies.) If there seems to be no mail at the Lista under the initial letter of your surname, ask them to look under the initial of your forename or your middle name. If your name begins with 'W', look for letters under 'V' as well, or ask. For the smallest risk of misunderstanding, use title, initial and surname only.

Post

World Band Radio Latin America has more local and community radio stations than practically anywhere else in the world; a shortwave (world band) radio offers a practical means to brush up on the language, sample popular culture and absorb some of the richly varied regional music. International broadcasters also transmit across Central America in both English and Spanish, these include the **BBC World Service** (www.bbc.co.uk/worldservice/index.shtml for schedules and frequencies, the **Voice of America** (www.voa.gov), and Boston (Mass)-based **Monitor Radio International** (operated by *Christian Science Monitor*, www.csmonitor.com).

Media
Details of the national newspapers, television and radio are given in the Essentials sections of each country

Compact or miniature portable radios are recommended, with digital tuning and a full range of shortwave bands, as well as FM, long and medium wave. A good one will set you back US$200, although you can pick up cheaper, less reliable models in Central America and Mexico.

Food and drink

There is a section on each nation's food under Essentials. We don't attempt to include everywhere listed, but a cross section of the type of places available, and hopefully managing to include the best of what is on offer. Naturally the dining experience varies greatly. An excellent general rule when looking for somewhere to eat is to ask locally at your hotel for example. The staff know the best places with the best food and if you know what you're looking for they'll point you in the right direction.

We are introducing bands of restaurants that aim to help when choosing a restaurant. 'Seriously cheap' restaurants will be no more than US$3, 'cheap' puts the cost somewhere between US$4 and US$8, with the 'mid-range' carrying on up to US$15. Thereafter eating out fall into the 'expensive' category by Central American standards. While the cost of eating out varies greatly across the region, these categories should provide some guidance.

Most restaurants serve a daily special meal, usually at lunchtime called an *almuerzo*, *comida corrida* or *comida corriente*, which works out much cheaper and is usually filling and nutritious. Vegetarians should be able to list all the foods they cannot eat; saying '*Soy vegetariano/a*' (I'm a vegetarian) or '*No como carne*' (I don't eat meat) is often not enough.

Universally the cheapest (and often the most entertaining) place to eat is the local market. If sticking to health rules you should strictly avoid these places at all costs, although some would contend that a popular market vendor is likely to be as clean as any mid-range hotel – food simply doesn't sit around long enough to become unhealthy. Until you're comfortable with spotting what looks like 'dodgy food', only eat where there are a number of people passing through. It's unlikely they would eat there if they regularly get ill.

Shopping

Souvenirs
Shipping items home is a good option

The range of gifts available is daunting. From the fine silver of Mexico's Colonial Heartlands, the tacky T-shirts of the more popular spots, the textiles and clothing of Guatemala, leather goods from Nicaragua and the finely crafted *molas* of Panama, if you were to buy one of everything you would need a second bag by the end of your trip. If buying souvenirs is important to you, the best place to end up without doubt is Guatemala, in particularly the market at Chichicastenango.

But in general few will organize their travels around shopping and you will pick up special items as you travel. We point out the best buys and regional items in each country section. Remember that these can almost invariably be bought more cheaply away from the capital, though the choice may not be as wide. Always make sure you know the price before purchasing an item. Bargaining seems to be the general rule in most countries' street markets, but don't make a fool of yourself by bargaining over what, to you, is a small amount of money.

Buying souvenirs is probably – although not always – best left to the end of your trip. Lugging precious ceramics round for a couple of months is likely to get a bit tedious.

Photography

If photography is important to you you need to plan for your trip before arriving in the region. When shopping for film for the rainforest bare in mind that 400 ASA is impossibly slow. Film prices vary but are not much different from Europe. Film can be bought cheaply in the USA or in the Colón Tax Free Zone (Panama). While print film is readily available (check the expiry date) slide film is difficult to find. *Kodachrome* is almost impossible to buy, and *Fuji* is less easy to find than Kodak in Central America. Some travellers (but not all) have advised against mailing exposed films home; either take them with you, or have them developed, but not printed, once you have checked the laboratory's quality. Note that postal authorities may use less sensitive equipment for X-ray screening than the airports do. Modern controlled X-ray machines are supposed to be safe for any speed of film, but it is worth trying to avoid X-ray as the doses are cumulative. Western camera shops sell double lead-lined bags which will protect new and used film from X-rays.

Developing film in Latin America is often, but not always, a problem. Often it is shoddily machine-processed and the negatives are ruined. If you want to develop the film, try and get a local recommendation. Ask the store if you can see an example of their laboratory's work and if they hand-develop. Exposed film can be protected in humid areas by putting it in a balloon and tying a knot. Similarly, keeping your camera with a sachet of silica gel crystals or in a plastic bag may reduce the effects of humidity.

Essentials

Holidays and festivals

If the time and mood is right, there is little to beat a Latin festival. Fine costumes, loud music, the sounds of firecrackers tipped off with the gentle wafting of specially prepared foods all (normally) lubricated with a drink or two. Whether seeking the carnival or if you happen to stumble across a celebration, the events – big or small – are memorable.

Holidays and festivals are mentioned in the respective countries

If you want to hit the carnivals there are a few broad dates generally significant throughout the region. Carnival is normally the week before the start of Lent. It's more important in Mexico but you'll probably find regional celebrations in most places. *Semana Santa* (Easter Week) is an understandably more spiritual affair. November 2 is *Día de los Muertos* (Day of the Dead), again most popular in Mexico but significant throughout the region when families visit cemeteries to honour the dead. Christmas and New Year result in celebrations of some kind, but not always public.

Public holidays throughout the region lead to a complete shut-down in services. No banks, government offices, usually no shops and often far fewer restaurants and bars. It is worth keeping an eye on the calendar to avoid having to change money or trying to make travel arrangements on public holidays.

Mexico

Here are the region's highlights – holidays and festivals for each country are mentioned in respective countries

Carnival / Mardi Gras   The week before Lent which traditionally throughout Latin America is a time for celebration before the hardships and denials of Lent, but in Mexico is particularly popular in La Paz, south Baja California, and Veracruz.

15 September   Celebrating the Cry for Independence, particularly impressive in Mexico City. **16 September**   Independence Day, with regional festivities and parades.

2 November   Day of the Dead in which the souls of the deceased return to earth and family and friends turn out in costume and festival to meet them – particularly colourful around Lake Pátzuaro.

12 December   The pilgrimage of thousands to the Basílica of Guadalupe, in northeast Mexico City, ot one of the most venerated shrines in Mexico. Well worth a visit if it fits in with your schedule.

Guatemala

Semana Santa   Particularly colourful in Antigua with floats carrying Christ over wonderfully coloured and carefully placed carpets of flowers.

Todos Santos Cuchumatán   in the small town of Todos Santos, a colourful and drunken horse with lots of dancing and antics.

Belize

10 September   St George's Cay Day, with celebrations in Belize City which start with river races up in San Ignacio.

19 November   Settlement Day, celebrating the liberation (or arrival) of the Garífuna from distant shores. Also celebrated in Guatemala and Honduras.

El Salvador

29 November   Big celebrations in San Miguel celebrating Nuestra Señora de la Paz.

Honduras

15 May   San Isidro, La Ceiba's patron saint, followed by a fortnight of celebrations. The highlight is an internatoinal carnival on the third Saturday in May.

Essentials

1-4 February Supaya, southeast of Tegucigalpa, the most important shrine in Honduras with a tiny wooden image of the Virgen de Supaya.

Nicaragua Keep an eye out for patron saints of villages and towns.

Costa Rica **Late January/early February** *Fiesta de los Diablitos* in the small towns of Boruca and Rey Curre, south Costa Rica, symbolic of the fight between indigenous cultures, religion and colonization.
2 August celebrating the Virgin of Los Angeles with mass-pilgrimages to the basilica in Cartago
15 September Independence Day with celebrations and parades in the capital San Jose and throughout the country.
12 October Día de la Raza (Columbus Day) celebrated with gusto in the Caribbean city of Puerto Limón.

Panama **3 November** Independence Day. Expect bigger than usual celebrations in Panama City and throughout the country as 100 years of independence is celebrated in 2003.

Sport and special interest travel

Special interest travel in the region is widespread. Whether seeking cooking courses or specializing in sun-bathing you can find somewhere to do your thing. But some areas in Central America and Mexico have developed reputations for particular activities.

Just one word of advice. Adventure sports tourism tends to develop in correlation with general tourist services. Carrying out a dangerous sport in a location where supporting infrastructure is limited probably indicates that the risks are not worth it. You should always make sure you have the necessary equipment for the activity you are doing. If you have any worries about safety you have a responsibility to yourself and to others who will follow you to speak out and voice your concerns until you are reassured.

Archaeology For both the generalist and the specialist the heartland of the Maya civilization from the Yucután down to northern Honduras is dotted with ruins including Tikal, Chichén Itzá and Palenque. The central region of Mexico also has a host of archaeological sites including the spectacular, and normally busy Teotihuacán to the north of Mexico City and the site of Monte Albán near Oaxaca.

South of Honduras, archaeological sites are significantly fewer and generally require either specialist knowledge or interest.

Bird-watching Central America is home to a spectacular number of bird species. Ornithologists get positively over-excited by the opportunities, and general nature lovers get a sense of the pleasure that bird-watching can bring. From Mexico to Panama there are countless sites. The all-important bird for the novice is the resplendent quetzal, a bird of legend matched only by its beautifully flamboyant tail feather.

Canopy tours Developing like a rash from Costa Rica outwards to Panama and Nicaragua, this is one way of getting up into the forest canopy. The more sedate options follow aerial walkways retaining a degree of quiet and decorum that make bird-watching (and spotting) a possibility. The more popular type is zipping down high-tension cables strung between forest giants. Good fun, big adrenaline rush but no chance of seeing anything that has a choice where it lives!

Canyoning Some options in Mexico but the best caving in the region and the western hemispere is
& caving found in Belize with some of the longest cave systems in the world.

Climbing The main climbing in the region is found in the highlands of Mexico with several peaks over 5,000 m (see page 88). Further south there are several volcanic peaks, active and dormant that give excellent views and a challenging climb all the way through the isthmus down to Panama. Opportunities for rock climbing are still quite undeveloped throughout the region with the exception of the big-wall appeals near Hidalgo, just outside Monterrey in northern Mexico.

Naturally enough many places in the region offer diving. The best diving for safety and opportunity is probably in Belize, especially in the offshore Cayes, but prices tend to be expensive when away for a few days. The cheapest good diving is in Honduras with Bocas del Toro in Panama growing in popularity. Every other country offers diving. Two diving Mecca's are the Blue Hole in Belize and the Cocos Islands off Costa Rica. Neither can be considered affordable to the average person, but any serious diver will put them on their list for future dive spots.

Diving & snorkelling

A network of paths and tracks covers much of Central America and is in constant use by the local people. In Guatemala, which has a large Indian population, you can walk just about anywhere, but in the more 'European' countries, particularly Costa Rica, you must usually limit yourself to the many excellent national parks with hiking trails. Most Central American countries have an Instituto Geográfico Militar which sells topographical maps, scale 1:100,000 or 1:50,000. The physical features shown on these are usually accurate; the trails and place names less so. National Parks offices also sell maps.

Hiking & trekking
For recommended maps, see page 49

Trekking should not be approached casually. Even if you only plan to be out a couple of hours you should have comfortable, safe footwear (which can cope with the wet) and a daypack to carry your sweater and waterproof. At high altitudes the difference in temperature between sun and shade is remarkable. The longer trips mentioned in this book require basic backpacking equipment. Essential items are: a good backpack, sleeping bag, closed cell foam mat for insulation, stove, tent or tarpaulin, dried food (not tins), water bottle, compass, trowel for burying excreta (which can be done after burning toilet paper in the excavated hole – take care fire doesn't spread). Some but not all of these things are available locally.

Hikers have little to fear from the animal kingdom apart from insects (although it's best to avoid actually stepping on a snake), and robbery and assault are very rare. You are much more of a threat to the environment than vice versa. Leave no evidence of your passing; don't litter and don't give gratuitous presents of sweets or money to rural villagers. Respect their system of reciprocity; if they give you hospitality or food, then is the time to reciprocate with presents.

It's a widely held belief that anyone can go mountain biking and to some extent that is true. If you're looking for a challenging ride through interesting scenary and want something more than a bit of exercise on two wheels, it is probably worth seeking out a specialist regional guide.

Mountain biking

Being a potentially dangerous sport, rafting is not as widespread as it could be, but there are many world-class opportunities in the region, including the Rivers Antigua/Pescados and Filo-Bobos near Veracruz, the Cangrejal near La Ceiba in North Honduras, the Reventazón and Pacuare in Costa Rica, and the River Chiriquí in Boquete, Panama. Beginners can probably manage up to Class IV, beyond this you should probably have a natural ability, or the courage to say no thanks.

Rafting

Sea and freshwater fishing are world class with marlin and sailfish in the deep waters off Costa Rica and Mexico, bonefish a little closer to shore on the flats in Belize, while the freshwater dreams of snook and tarpon lurking in tropical streams along the Caribbean. Costs, however, are generally prohibitive running to several hundred dollars for the day.

Sport fishing

It's an endless summer of surfing all the way down the Pacific coast if you want to make that the focus of your trip. Particular hotspots for surfers are mentioned in the text. There are also endless opportunities for learning – probably best in Mexico and Costa Rica – if you fancy trying to get up on a board.

Surfing

Health

Despite their proximity to the United States of America parts of Central America and Mexico remain poor enough that health indicators may be appalling, health services are often basic and communicable diseases an ever-present threat. However, there is a thriving private sector and standards can only go up.

Medical facilities

Essentials

Essentials

Your embassy or consulate should be able to recommend a local clinic or hospital. If you do get ill, and you have the opportunity, you should also ask your medical insurer whether they are satisfied that the medical centre or hospital that you have been referred to is of a suitable standard.

Disease risks The greater disease risk in Central America and Mexico is caused by the greater volume of disease carriers in the shape of mosquitoes and sandflies. The key viral disease is **dengue** fever, which is transmitted by a mosquito that bites during the day (see page 57). Bacterial diseases include **tuberculosis** (TB) and some causes of the more common traveller's **diarrhoea**. The main parasitic disease is **malaria**. Filariasis, leishmaniasis, onchocerciasis, and American trypanosomiasis (Chagas' disease) are insect-carried diseases that also occur in this region, but the risk to travelers is thought to be low. Protecting yourself against insect bites will help to prevent these diseases.

Before you go

Medical checks & travel insurance
Ideally, see your GP or travel clinic at least six weeks before departure for general advice on travel risks, **malaria** and **vaccinations**; get a **dental check** (especially if you are going to be away for more than a month); know your own **blood group** and if you suffer a long-term condition such as diabetes or epilepsy make sure someone knows or that you have a Medic Alert bracelet/necklace with this information on it.

Take out adequate **travel insurance**. Make sure it covers all eventualities, especially evacuation to your home country by a medically equipped plane

Vaccinations
BCG Recommended if staying for more than 1 month.
Hepatitis A Recommended the disease can be caught easily from food/water.
Polio Recommended if nil in last 10 years
Rabies Recommended for most areas.
Tetanus Recommended if nil in last 10 years (but after 5 doses you have had enough for life).
Typhoid Recommended if nil in last 3 years.
Yellow fever Mexico and Central America have no yellow fever and want to keep it that way. That is why if you arrive from Africa or South America they may want to see your yellow fever certificate.

Malaria risk by country
Always check with your doctor or travel clinic for the most up to date advice
Over 80% of the malaria in risk areas of Mexico and Central America is of the kinder (i.e. it does not readily kill you like falciparum) vivax type. However some falciparum does exist. Rural areas are the main or only risk areas for malaria in El Salvador, Guatemala and Honduras. Other countries have mainly rural risk but include other areas also:
Belize: Rural areas at risk, including forest preserves, offshore islands and tourist resorts. However, there's no risk in the central coastal District of Belize.
Costa Rica: Rural areas at risk, including tourist areas. However, no risk in Central Highlands, ie Cártago and San José provinces.
Mexico: Rural areas at risk, including resorts in the rural areas of the following states: Campeche, Chiapas, Guerrero, Michoacán, Nayarit, Oaxaca, Quintana Roo, Sinaloa, and Tabasco. Antimalarial drugs are not recommended for travel to the major resort areas on the Pacific and Gulf coasts, although travellers should use anti-mosquito measures and remember the ABCD of malaria (see below).
Nicaragua: Rural areas at risk, as well as the outskirts of Bluefields, Bonanza, Chinandega, León, Puerto Cabezas, Rosita, and Siuna.
Panama: Rural areas at risk in the eastern provinces (Darién and San Blas), northwestern provinces (Boca del Toro and Veraguas), Lake Boyana area, and Lake Gatún. No risk in Panama City and vicinity.

Put simply for most of the mainly rural risk areas **chloroquine** and **paludrine** would be the first choice recommendation, this also applies to Panama, in the risk areas west of the Panama Canal Zone. However, there is chloroquine resistance requiring either *Mefloquine*,

Doxycycline or *Malarone* in Panama in the risk areas east of the Canal Zone and the San Blas Islands. So take special advice when planning your Panama trip.

Foreign and Commonwealth Office (FCO) **www.fco.gov.uk** is a key UK travel advice site, with useful information on the country, people, climate and lists the UK embassies/consulates. The site also promotes the concept of 'Know Before You Go', and encourages travel insurance and appropriate travel health advice. It has links to the Department of Health travel advice site (see below).

Department of Health Travel Advice (UK) **www.doh.gov.uk/traveladvice** This excellent site is also available as a free booklet, the T6, from UK post offices. It lists the vaccine advice requirements for each country.

Medic Alert (UK) **www.medicalalert.co.uk** This is the website of the foundation that produces bracelets and necklaces for those with existing medical problems. Once you have ordered your bracelet/necklace you write your key medical details on paper inside it, so that if you collapse, a medical person can identify you as someone with epilepsy or allergy to peanuts, etc.

Blood Care Foundation (UK) **www.bloodcare.org.uk** Charity 'dedicated to the provision of screened blood and resuscitation fluids in countries where these are not readily available'. They will dispatch certified non-infected blood of the right type to your hospital/clinic. The blood is flown in from various centres around the world. The Blood Care Foundation order form PO Box 7, Sevenoaks, Kent TN13 2SZ, T44-(0)1732-742427.

Public Health Laboratory Service (UK) **www.phls.org.uk** This site has up-to-date malaria advice guidelines for travel around the world. It gives specific advice about the right drugs for each location. It also has useful information for those who are pregnant, suffering from epilepsy or planning to travel with children.

Centers for Disease Control and Prevention (USA) **www.cdc.gov** This US Government site gives excellent advice on travel health, has useful disease maps and details of disease outbreaks.

World Health Organization **www.who.int** The WHO site has links to the WHO Blue Book (it was Yellow up to last year) on travel advice. This lists the diseases in different regions of the world. It describes vaccination schedules and makes clear which countries have Yellow Fever Vaccination certificate requirements and malarial risk.

Tropical Medicine Bureau (Ireland) **www.tmb.ie** This Irish based site has a good collection of general travel health information and disease risks.

Fit for Travel (UK) **www.fitfortravel.scot.nhs.uk** This site from Scotland provides a quick A–Z of vaccine and travel health advice requirements for each country.

British Travel Health Association (UK) **www.btha.org** This is the official website of an organization of travel health professionals.

NetDoctor (UK) **www.Netdoctor.co.uk** This general health advice site has a useful section on travel and has an 'ask the expert', interactive chat forum.

Travel Screening Services (UK) **www.travelscreening.co.uk** This is the author's website. A private clinic dedicated to integrated travel health. The clinic gives vaccine, travel health advice, email and SMS text vaccine reminders and screens returned travellers for tropical diseases.

Useful websites

Essentials

Travellers' Health: How to Stay Healthy Abroad, by Dr Richard Dawood (ISBN 0-19-262947-6). An excellent book and has at last been updated in 2002.

The Travellers' Good Health Guide by Dr Ted Lankester (ISBN 0-85969-827-0).

Expedition Medicine (The Royal Geographic Society), Editors David Warrell and Sarah Anderson (ISBN 1 86197 040-4).

International Travel and Health, World Health Organization, Geneva (ISBN 92 4 158026 7).

The World's Most Dangerous Places, by Robert Young Pelton, Coskun Aral and Wink Dulles (ISBN 1-566952-140-9).

The Travellers' Guide to Health (T6), can be obtained in the UK by calling the Health Literature Line on T0800-555-777.

Advice for travellers on avoiding the risks of **HIV** and **AIDS** (*Travel Safe*) available from Department of Health, PO Box 777, London SE1 6XH.

Books & leaflets

What to take

Mosquito repellents Remember that DEET (Di-ethyltoluamide) is the gold standard. Apply the repellent every 4-6 hours but more often if you are sweating heavily. If a non-DEET product is used check who tested it. Validated products (tested at the London School of Hygiene and Tropical Medicine) include *Mosiguard*, non-DEET *Jungle formula* and *Autan*. If you want to use citronella remember that it must be applied very frequently (ie hourly) to be effective. If you are popular target for insect bites or develop lumps quite soon after being bitten, carry an *Aspivenin* kit. This syringe suction device is available from many chemists and draws out some of the allergic materials and provides quick relief.

It is risky to buy medicinal tablets abroad because the doses may differ and there may be a trade in false drugs

Anti-malarials Important to take for the key areas. Specialist advice is required as to which type to take. General principles are that all except *Malarone* should be continued for four weeks after leaving the malarial area. *Malarone* needs to be continued for only seven days afterwards (if a tablet is missed or vomited seek specialist advice). The start times for the anti-malarials vary in that if you have never taken *Lariam* (Mefloquine) before, it is advised to start it at least 2-3 weeks before the entry to a malarial zone (this is to help identify serious side-effects early). *Chloroquine* and *Paludrine* are often started a week before the trip to establish a pattern but *Doxycycline* and *Malarone* can be started only 1-2 days before entry to the malarial area.

Insect bite relief If you are prone to insect's bites or develop lumps quite soon after being bitten, carry an Aspivenin kit. This syringe suction device is available in the UK from *Boots Chemists* and draws out some of the allergic materials and provides quick relief.

Sun block The Australians have a great campaign, which has reduced skin cancer. It is called Slip, Slap, Slop. Slip on a shirt, Slap on a hat, Slop on sun screen.

Pain killers Paracetomol or a suitable painkiller can have multiple uses for symptoms but remember that more than eight paracetemol a day can lead to liver failure.

Diarrhoea treatment *Immodium* A great standby for those diarrhoeas that occur at awkward times (ie before a long coach/train journey or on a trek). It helps stop the flow of diarrhoea and in my view is of more benefit than harm. (It was believed that letting the bacteria or viruses flow out had to be more beneficial. However, with Immodium they still come out, just in a more solid form. *Pepto-Bismol* Used a lot by Americans for diarrhoea. It certainly relieves symptoms but like Immodium it is not a cure for underlying disease. Be aware that it turns the stool black as well as making it more solid. *Ciproxin* (Ciprofloaxcin) is a useful antibiotic for some forms of travellers diarrhoea (see below).

First-aid kit including water-sterilizing tablets, plasters/band-aid, antiseptic cream, etc. For longer trips involving jungle treks taking a clean needle pack, clean dental pack and water filtration devices are common-sense measures.

MedicAlert These simple bracelets, or an equivalent, should be carried or worn by anyone with a significant medical condition.

Health care A-Z

Altitude sickness

Symptoms This can creep up on you as just a mild headache with nausea or lethargy during your visit. The more serious disease is caused by fluid collecting in the brain in the enclosed space of the skull and can lead to coma and death. There is also a lung disease version with breathlessness and fluid infiltration of the lungs.

Cures The best cure is to descend as soon as possible.

Prevention Get acclimatized. Do not try to reach the highest levels on your first few days of arrival. Try to avoid flying directly into the cities of highest altitude such as La Paz (4,000 m above sea level). Climbers like to take treatment drugs as protective measures but this can lead to macho idiocy and death. The peaks are still there and so are the trails, whether it takes you a bit longer than someone else does not matter as long as you come back down alive. In Potosí at 4,000 metres even some of the locals suffer a chronic form of mountain sickness.

Dengue fever

Symptoms This disease can be contracted throughout Central America and Mexico and is an increasing problem. In travellers this can cause a severe 'flu-like illness which includes symptoms of fever, lethargy, enlarged lymph glands and muscle pains. It starts suddenly, lasts for 2-3 days, seems to get better for 2-3 days and then kicks in again for another 2-3 days. It is usually all over in an unpleasant week. The local children are prone to the much nastier haemorrhagic form of the disease, which causes them to bleed from internal organs, mucous membranes and often leads to their death.

Cures The traveller's version of the disease is self-limiting and forces rest and recuperation on the sufferer.

Prevention The mosquitoes that carry the dengue virus bite during the day unlike the malaria mosquitoes. Sadly this means that repellent application and covered limbs are a 24-hour issue. Check your accommodation for flower pots and shallow pools of water since these are where the dengue-carrying mosquitoes breed.

Diarrhoea/ intestinal upset

This is almost inevitable. One study showed that up to 70% of all travellers may suffer during their trip

Symptoms Diarrhoea can refer either to loose stools or an increased frequency; both of these can be a nuisance. It should be short lasting but persistence beyond two weeks, with blood or pain, require specialist medical attention.

Cures *Ciproxin* (Ciprofloaxcin) is a useful antibiotic for bacterial traveller's diarrhoea. It can be obtained by private prescription in the UK which is expensive, or bought over the counter in Central America and Mexican pharmacies. You need to take one 500 mg tablet when the diarrhoea starts and if you do not feel better in 24 hours, the diarrhoea is likely to have a non-bacterial cause and may be viral (in which case there is little you can do apart from keep yourself rehydrated and wait for it to settle on its own). The key treatment with all diarrhoeas is rehydration. Try to keep hydrated by taking the right mixture of salt and water. This is available as **Oral Rehydration Salts** (ORS) in ready-made sachets or can be made up by adding a teaspoon of sugar and a half teaspoon of salt to a litre of clean water. Drink at least one large cup of this drink for each loose stool. You can also use flat carbonated drinks as an alternative. *Immodium* and *Pepto-Bismol* provide symptomatic relief.

Prevention The standard advice is to be careful with water and ice for drinking. Ask yourself where the water came from. If you have any doubts then boil it or filter it and treat it. There are many filter/treatment devices now available on the market. Food can also transmit disease. Be wary of salads (what were they washed in, who handled them), re-heated foods or food that has been left out in the sun having been cooked earlier in the day. There is a simple adage that says wash it, peel it, boil it or forget it. Also be wary of unpasteurised dairy products, these can transmit a range of diseases from brucellosis (fevers and constipation), to listeria (meningitis) and tuberculosis of the gut (obstruction, constipation, fevers and weight loss).

Hepatitis

Symptoms Hepatitis means inflammation of the liver. Viral causes of the disease can be acquired anywhere in Central America or Mexico. The most obvious symptom is a yellowing of your skin or the whites of your eyes. However, prior to this all that you may notice is itching and tiredness.

Cures Early on, depending on the type of hepatitis, a vaccine or immunoglobulin may reduce the duration of the illness.

Prevention Pre-travel hepatitis A vaccine is the best bet. Hepatitis B (for which there is a vaccine) is spread through blood and unprotected sexual intercourse, both of these can be avoided. Unfortunately there is no vaccine for Hepatitis C or the increasing alphabetical list of other hepatitis viruses.

Leishmaniasis

Symptoms A skin and a liver/kidney form of this disease occurs in Central America and Mexico. If infected, you may notice a raised lump, which leads to a purplish discoloration on white skin and a possible ulcer. The parasite is transmitted by the bite of a sandfly. Sandflies

Essentials

do not fly very far and the greatest risk is at ground levels, so if you can avoid sleeping on the jungle floor, do so. There is another rarer form which is casued by a sub-species of the parasite, this affects the musocal tissues such as lips and nose. Treatment and mode of transmission are the same.

Cures Several weeks' treatment is required under specialist supervision. The drugs themselves are toxic but if not taken in sufficient amounts, recurrence of the disease is more likely.

Prevention Sleep above ground, under a permethrin treated net, use insect repellent and get a specialist opinion on any unusual skin lesions as soon as you can.

Malaria & insect bite prevention

Symptoms Malaria can cause death within 24 hours. It can start as something just resembling an attack of flu. You may feel tired, lethargic, headachy; or worse, develop fits, followed by coma and then death. Have a low index of suspicion because it is very easy to write off vague symptoms, which may actually be malaria. Whilst abroad and on return get tested as soon as possible, the test could save your life.

Cures Treatment is with drugs and may be oral or into a vein depending on the seriousness of the infection. Remember ABCD: Awareness (of whether the disease is present in the area you are travelling in), Bite avoidance, Chemoprohylaxis, Diagnosis.

Prevention This is best summarized by the B and C of the ABCD, bite avoidance and chemoprophylaxis. Wear clothes that cover arms and legs and use effective insect repellents in areas with known risks of insect-spread disease. Use a mosquito net dipped in permethrin as both a physical and chemical barrier at night in the same areas. Guard against the contraction of malaria with the correct anti-malarials (see above). Some would prefer to take test kits for malaria with them and have standby treatment available. However, the field tests of the blood kits have had poor results: when you have malaria you are usually too ill to be able to do the tests correctly enough to make the right diagnosis. Standby treatment (treatment that you carry and take yourself for malaria) should still ideally be supervised by a doctor since the drugs themselves can be toxic if taken incorrectly. The Royal Homeopathic Hospital in the UK does not advocate homeopathic options for malaria prevention or treatment.

Rabies

Symptoms Most of you will know when you have been bitten. It may take days or weeks before odd tingling sensations occur in the affected part, followed by a fear of drinking water and spasms which lead to death.

Cures There is no cure for rabies once it has hold of the Central Nervous System.

Prevention Avoid getting bitten. Dog lovers have to remember that this is a whole new ball game and you are the ball. A full course of rabies vaccine is 100% effective. If you get bitten you will need more vaccine and if you had no pre-exposure vaccine or an inadequate amount you will also need to be injected with something called immunoglobulin. It is always wise to wash the wound but animal bites should ideally not be stitched up in the early stages.

Sexual health

Unprotected sex can spread HIV, Hepatitis B and C, Gonorrhea (green discharge), chlamydia (nothing to see but may cause painful urination and later female infertility), painful recurrent herpes, syphilis and warts, just to name a few. You can cut down the risk by using condoms, a femidom or avoiding sex altogether.

Underwater health
Make sure you are fit before you dive

Cures Antibiotics for secondary infections. Serious diving injuries may need time in a decompression chamber.

Prevention Protect your feet from cuts, beach dog parasites (larva migrans) and sea urchins. The latter are almost impossible to remove but can be dissolved with lime or vinegar. Keep an eye out for secondary infection.

Check that the dive company know what they are doing, have appropriate certification from BSAC or Professional Association of Diving Instructors (PADI), Unit 7, St Philips Central, Albert Rd, St Philips, Bristol, BS2 0TD, T0117-3007234, www.padi.com, and that the equipment is well maintained.

Sun protection

Symptoms White-skinned people are notorious for becoming red in hot countries because they like to stay out longer than everyone else and do not use adequate sun protection. This can lead to sunburn, which is painful and followed by flaking of skin. Aloe vera gel is a good pain reliever for sunburn. Long-term sun damage leads to a loss of elasticity of skin and the development of pre-cancerous lesions. Many years later a mild or a very malignant form of cancer may develop. The milder basal cell carcinoma, if detected early, can be treated by cutting it out or freezing it. The much nastier malignant melanoma may have already spread to bone and brain at the time that it is first noticed.

Prevention Sun screen. SPF stands for Sun Protection Factor. It is measured by determining how long a given person takes to 'burn' with and without the sunscreen product on. So, if it takes 10 times longer to burn with the sunscreen product applied, then that product has an SPF of 10. If it only takes twice as long then the SPF is 2. The higher the SPF the greater the protection. However, do not just use higher factors just to stay out in the sun longer. 'Flash frying' (desperate bursts of excessive exposure), as it is called, is known to increase the risks of skin cancer.

Essentials

Tuberculosis (TB)

Symptoms Cough, blood in spit, weight loss, fever, night sweats. If you drink unpasteurized milk you can get gut or pelvic TB which can lead to intestinal obstruction and infertility.

Cures At least three drugs are required and the total treatment period is at least 6 months.

Prevention If staying for over one month have a skin test for TB followed by the BCG vaccine. Unfortunately BCG vaccine may not protect against lung TB. The best you can do is avoid unpasteurised dairy products and do not let anyone cough or splutter all over you.

Typhoid fever

Symptoms This a gut infection which can spread to the blood stream. You get it from someone else's muck getting into your mouth. A classic example would be the waiter who fails to wash his hands and then serves you a salad. The fever is an obvious feature, occasionally there is a mild red rash on the stomach and often you have a headache. Constipation or diarrhoea can occur. Gut pain and hearing problems may also feature.

Cures Antibiotics are required and you are probably best managed in hospital.

Prevention The vaccine is very effective and is best boosted every 3 years. Watch what you eat and the hygiene of the place or those serving your food.

Water purification

There are a number of ways of purifying water in order to make it safe to drink. Dirty water should first be strained through a filter bag (camping shops) and then boiled or treated. Bringing water to a rolling **boil** at sea level is sufficient to make the water safe for drinking, but at higher altitudes you have to boil the water for a few minutes longer to ensure that all the microbes are killed. There are **sterilizing** methods that can be used and there are proprietary preparations containing chlorine (for example *Puritabs*) or iodine compounds. Chlorine compounds generally do not kill protozoa (for example giardia). There are a number of water **filters** now on the market available in personal and expedition size. They work either on mechanical or chemical principles, or may do both. Make sure you take the spare parts or spare chemicals with you and do not believe everything the manufacturers say.

Background

History and culture

Pre-Columbian civilizations

The Aztec Empire which Hernán Cortés encountered in 1519 and subsequently destroyed was the third major power to have dominated what is now known as Mexico. Before it, the empires of Teotihuacán and Tula each unified what had essentially been an area of separate Indian groups. All three, together with their neighbours such as the Maya (dealt with below) and their predecessors, belong to a more or less common culture called Mesoamerica.

Despite the wide variety of climates and terrains that fall within Mesoamerica's boundaries, from northern Mexico to El Salvador and Honduras, the civilizations that developed were interdependent, sharing the same agriculture (based on maize, beans and squash) and many sociological features. They also shared an enormous pantheon, with the god of rain and the feathered serpent-hero predominant; the offering of blood to the gods, from oneself and from sacrificial victims usually taken in war; pyramid-building; a game played with a rubber ball; trade in feathers, jade and other valuable objects, possibly from as far away as the Andean region of South America; hieroglyphic writing; astronomy; an elaborate calendar.

The **Mesoamerican calendar** was a combination of a 260-day almanac year and the 365-day solar year. A given day in one of the years would only coincide with that in the other every 52 years, a cycle called the Calendar Round. In order to give the Calendar Round a context within a larger timescale, a starting date for both years was devised; the date chosen by the Classic Maya was equivalent to 3113 BC in Christian time. Dates measured from this point are called Long Count dates.

Historians divide Mesoamerican civilizations into three periods, the **Pre-classic**, which lasted until about AD 300, the **Classic**, until AD 900, and the **Post-classic**, from 900 until the Spanish conquest. An alternative delineation is: Olmec, Teotihuacán and Aztec, named after the dominant civilizations within each of those periods.

Olmecs Who precisely the Olmecs were, where they came from and why they disappeared, is a matter of debate. It is known that they flourished from about 1400 to 400 BC, that they lived in the Mexican Gulf Coast region between Veracruz and Tabasco, and that all later civilizations have their roots ultimately in Olmec culture. They carved colossal heads, stelae (tall, flat monuments), jade figures and altars; they gave great importance to the jaguar and the serpent in their imagery; they built large ceremonial centres such as San Lorenzo and La Venta. Possibly derived from the Olmecs and gaining importance in the first millennium BC was the centre in the Valley of Oaxaca at Monte Albán. This was a major city, with certain changes of influence, right through until the end of the Classic period. Also derived from the Olmecs was the Izapa civilization, on the Pacific border of present day Mexico and Guatemala. Here seems to have taken place the progression from the Olmec to the Maya civilization, with obvious connections in artistic style, calendar-use, ceremonial architecture and the transformation of the Izapa long-lipped god into the Maya long-nosed god.

Teotihuacán Almost as much mystery surrounds the origins of Teotihuacan as those of the Olmecs. Teotihuacán, 'the place where men become gods', was a great urban state, holding in its power most of the central highlands of Mexico. Its influence can be detected in the Maya area, Oaxaca and the civilizations on the Gulf Coast which succeeded the Olmecs. The monuments in the city itself, which still stands beyond the northeastern outskirts of Mexico City, are enormous, the planning precise; it is estimated that by the 7th century AD some 125,000 people were living in its immediate vicinity. Early evidence did not suggest that Teotihuacán's power was gained by force, but research now indicates both human sacrifice and sacred warfare. Again for reasons unknown, Teotihuacán's influence over its neighbours ended around 600 AD. Its glory coincided with that of the Classic Maya, but the latter's decline occurred some 300 years later, at which time a major change affected all Mesoamerica.

Toltecs The start of the Post-classic period, between the Teotihuacán and Aztec horizons, was marked by an upsurge in militarism. In the semi-deserts to the north of the settled societies of central Mexico and Veracruz lived groups of nomadic hunters. These people, who were given the general name of Chichimecs, began to invade the central region and were quick to adopt the urban characteristics of the groups they overthrew. The Toltecs of Tula were one such invading force, rapidly building up an empire stretching from the Gulf of Mexico to the Pacific in central Mexico. Infighting by factions within the Toltecs split the rulers and probably hastened the empire's demise sometime after 1150. The exiled leader Topíltzin Quetzalcóatl (Feathered Serpent) is possibly the founder of the Maya-Toltec rule in the Yucatán (the Maya spoke of a Mexican invader named Kukulcán – Feathered Serpent). He is certainly the mythical figure the Aztec ruler, Moctezuma II, took Cortés to be, returning by sea from the east.

Another important culture which developed in the first millennium AD was the Mixtec, in western Oaxaca. The Mixtexs infiltrated all the territory held by the Zapotecs, who had ruled Monte Albán during the Classic period and had built many other sites in the Valley of Oaxaca, including Mitla. The Mixtecs, in alliance with the Zapotecs successfully withstood invasion by the Aztecs.

Mixtecs

The process of transition from semi-nomadic hunter-gatherer to city and empire-builder continued with the Aztecs, who bludgeoned their way into the midst of rival city states in the vacuum left by the destruction of Tula. They rose from practically nothing to a power almost as great as Teotihuacán in about 200 years. From their base at Tenochtitlán in Lake Texcoco in the Valley of Mexico they extended through aggression their sphere of influence from the Tarascan Kingdom in the north to the Maya lands in the south. Not only did the conquered pay heavy tribute to their Aztec overlords, but they also supplied the constant flow of sacrificial victims needed to satisfy the deities, at whose head was Huitzilopochtli, the warrior god of the Sun. The speed with which the Aztecs adapted to a settled existence and fashioned a highly effective political state is remarkable. Their ability in sculpting stone, in pottery, in writing books, and in architecture (what we can gather from what the Spaniards did not destroy) was great. Surrounding all this activity was a strictly ritual existence, with ceremonies and feasts dictated by the two enmeshing calendars.

Aztecs

It is impossible to say whether the Aztec Empire would have gone the way of its predecessors had not the Spaniards arrived to precipitate its collapse. Undoubtedly, the Europeans received much assistance from people who had been oppressed by the Aztecs and who wished to be rid of them. Within two years Cortés, with his horses, an unknown array of military equipment and relatively few soldiers, brought to an end an extraordinary culture.

The best known of the pre-Conquest Indian civilizations of the present Central American area was the Maya which is thought to have evolved in a formative period in the Pacific highlands of Guatemala and El Salvador between 1500 BC and about 100 AD. After 200 years of growth it entered what is known today as its Classic period when the civilization flourished in Guatemala, El Salvador, Belize, Honduras and Mexico (Chiapas, Campeche and Yucatán).

Maya

The Maya civilization was based on independent and antagonistic city states, including Tikal, Uaxactún, Kaminaljuyú, Iximch, Zaculeu and Quiriguá in Guatemala; Copán in Honduras; Altún Ha, Caracol, Lamanai in Belize; Tazumal and San Andrés in El Salvador; and Palenque, Bonampak (both in Chiapas), Uxmal, Mayapán, Tulum and the Puuc hill cities of Sayil, Labná and Kabah (all on the Yucatán peninsula) in Mexico. Recent research has revealed that these cities, far from being the peaceful ceremonial centres as once imagined, were warring adversaries, striving to capture victims for sacrifice. Furthermore, much of the cultural activity, controlled by a theocratic minority of priests and nobles, involved blood-letting, by even the highest members of society. Royal blood was the most precious offering that could be made to the gods. This change in perception of the Maya was the result of the discovery of defended cities and of a greater understanding of the Maya's hieroglyphic writing. Although John Lloyd Stephens' prophecy that "a key surer than that of the Rosetta stone will be discovered" has not yet been fulfilled, the painstaking decipherment of the glyphs has uncovered many of the secrets of Maya society (see *Breaking the Maya Code* by Michael D Coe, Thames and Hudson).

Alongside the preoccupation with blood was an artistic tradition rich in ceremony, folklore and dance. They achieved paper codices and glyphic writing, which also appears on stone monuments and their fine ceramics; they were skilful weavers and traded over wide areas, though they did not use the wheel and had no beasts of burden. The cities were all meticulously dated. Mayan art is a mathematical art: each column, figure, face, animal, frieze, stairway and temple expresses a date or a time relationship. When, for example, an ornament on the ramp of the Hieroglyphic Stairway at Copán was repeated some 15 times, it was to express that number of elapsed 'leap' years. The 75 steps stand for the number of elapsed intercalary days. The Mayan calendar was a nearer approximation to sidereal time than either the Julian or the Gregorian calendars of Europe; it was only .000069 of a day out of true in a year. They used the zero centuries in advance of the Old World, plotted the movements of the sun, moon, Venus and other planets, and conceived a cycle of more than 1,800 million days.

Their tools and weapons were flint and hard stone, obsidian and fire-hardened wood, and yet with these they hewed out and transported great monoliths over miles of difficult country, and carved them over with intricate glyphs and figures which would be difficult enough with modern chisels. Also with those tools they grew lavish crops. To support urban populations now believed to number tens of thousands, and a population density of 150 per sq km (compared with less than 1 per sq km today), an agricultural system was developed of raised fields, fertilized by fish and vegetable matter from surrounding canals.

The height of the Classic period lasted until AD 900-1000, after which time the Maya concentrated into Yucatán after a successful invasion of their other lands by non-Maya people (this is only one theory: another is that they were forced to flee because of drought and a peasant rebellion). They then came under the influence of the Toltecs who invaded Yucatán; Chichén Itzá is considered to be an example of a Maya city which displays a great many Toltec features. From that time their culture declined. The Toltecs, who had firm control in Yucatán in the 10th century, gradually spread their empire as far as the southern borders of Guatemala. They in turn, however, were conquered by the Aztecs, who did not penetrate into Central America.

Conquest

It was only during his fourth voyage, in 1502, that Columbus reached the mainland of Central America; he landed in Costa Rica and Panama, which he called Veragua, and founded the town of Santa María de Belén. In 1508 Alonso de Ojeda received a grant of land on the Pearl Coast east of Panama, and in 1509 he founded the town of San Sebastián, later moved to a new site called Santa María la Antigua del Darién (now in Colombia). In 1513 the governor of the colony at Darién was Vasco Núñez de Balboa. Taking 190 men he crossed the isthmus in 18 days and caught the first glimpse of the Pacific; he claimed it and all neighbouring lands in the name of the King of Spain. But from the following year, when Pedrarias de Avila replaced him as Governor, Balboa fell on evil days, and he was executed by Pedrarias in 1519. That same year Pedrarias crossed the isthmus and founded the town of Panamá on the Pacific side. It was in April 1519, too, that Cortés began his conquest of Mexico.

Central America was explored from these two nodal points of Panama and Mexico. By 1525 Cortés' lieutenant, Pedro de Alvarado, had conquered as far south as San Salvador. Meanwhile Pedrarias was sending forces into Panama and Costa Rica: the latter was abandoned, for the natives were hostile, but was finally colonized from Mexico City when the rest of Central America had been taken. In 1522-24 Andrés Niño and Gil González Dávila invaded Nicaragua and Honduras. Many towns were founded by these forces from Panama: León, Granada, Trujillo and others. Spanish forces from the north and south sometimes met and fought bitterly. The gentle Bartolomé de las Casas, the 'apostle of the Indies', was active as a Dominican missionary in Central America in the 1530s.

Settlement The groups of Spanish settlers were few and widely scattered, and this is the fundamental reason for the political fragmentation of Central America today. Panama was ruled from Bogotá, but the rest of Central America was subordinate to the Viceroyalty at Mexico City, with Antigua Guatemala as an Audiencia for the area until 1773, thereafter Guatemala City. Panama was of paramount importance for colonial Spanish America for its strategic position, and for the trade passing across the isthmus to and from the southern colonies. The other provinces were of comparatively little value.

The small number of Spaniards intermarried freely with the local Indians, accounting for the predominance of *mestizos* in present-day Central America. In Guatemala, where there were the most Indians, intermarriage affected fewer of the natives, and over half the population today is pure Indian. On the Meseta Central of Costa Rica, the Indians were all but wiped out by disease; as a consequence of this great disaster, there is a buoyant community of over two million whites, with little Indian admixture, in the highlands. Blacks predominate all along the Caribbean coasts of Central America; they were not brought in by the colonists as slaves, but by the railway builders and banana planters of the 19th century and the canal cutters of the 20th, as cheap labour.

Independence and after

in San Salvador, organized a revolt in conjunction with another priest, Manuel José Arce. They proclaimed the independence of El Salvador, but the Audiencia at Guatemala City quickly suppressed the revolt and took Delgado prisoner.

It was the revolution of 1820 in Spain itself that precipitated the independence of Central America. When on 24 February 1821, the Mexican General Agustín de Iturbide announced his Plan de Iguala for an independent Mexico, the Central American *criollos* decided to follow his example, and a declaration of independence, drafted by José Cecilio del Valle, was announced in Guatemala City on 15 September 1821. Iturbide invited the provinces of Central America to join with him and, on 5 January 1822, Central America was declared annexed to Mexico. Delgado refused to accept this decree and Iturbide, who had now assumed the title of Emperor Agustín I, sent an army south under Vicente Filísola to enforce it in the regions under Delgado's influence. Filísola had completed his task when he heard of Iturbide's abdication, and at once convened a general congress of the Central American provinces. It met on 24 June 1823, and established the **Provincias Unidas del Centro de América**. The Mexican Republic acknowledged their independence on 1 August 1824, and Filísola's soldiers were withdrawn.

The congress, presided over by Delgado, appointed a provisional governing *junta* which promulgated a constitution modelled on that of the United States on 22 November 1824. The Province of Chiapas was not included in the Federation, for it had already adhered to Mexico in 1821. No federal capital was chosen, but Guatemala City, by force of tradition, soon became the seat of government.

The first President under the new constitution was Manuel José Arce, a liberal. One of his first acts was to abolish slavery. El Salvador, protesting that he had exceeded his powers, rose in December 1826. Honduras, Nicaragua and Costa Rica joined the revolt, and in 1828 General Francisco Morazán, in charge of the army of Honduras, defeated the federal forces, entered San Salvador and marched against Guatemala City. He captured the city on 13 April 1829, and established that contradiction in terms: a liberal dictatorship. Many conservative leaders were expelled and church and monastic properties confiscated. Morazán himself became President of the Federation in 1830. He was a man of considerable ability; he ruled with a strong hand, encouraged education, fostered trade and industry, opened the country to immigrants, and reorganized the administration. In 1835 the capital was moved to San Salvador.

These reforms antagonized the conservatives and there were several risings. The most serious revolt was among the Indians of Guatemala, led by Rafael Carrera, an illiterate *mestizo* conservative and a born leader. Years of continuous warfare followed, during the course of which the Federation withered away. As a result, the federal congress passed an act which allowed each province to assume the government it chose, but the idea of a federation was not quite dead. Morazán became President of El Salvador. Carrera, who was by then in control of Guatemala, defeated Morazán in battle and forced him to leave the country. But in 1842, Morazán overthrew Braulio Carrillo, then dictator of Costa Rica, and became president himself. At once he set about rebuilding the Federation, but was defeated by the united forces of the other states and was shot on 15 September 1842. With him perished any practical hope of Central American political union.

The separate states Costa Rica, with its mainly white population, is a country apart, and Panama was Colombian territory until 1903. The history of the four remaining republics since the breakdown of federation has been tempestuous in the extreme. In each the ruling class was divided into pro-clerical conservatives and anti-clerical liberals, with constant changes of power. Each was weak, and tried repeatedly to buttress its weakness by alliances with others, which invariably broke up because one of the allies sought a position of mastery. The wars were rarely over boundaries; they were mainly ideological wars between conservatives and liberals, or wars

Essentials

motivated by inflamed nationalism. Nicaragua, for instance, was riven internally for most of the period by the mutual hatreds of the Conservatives of Granada and the Liberals of León, and there were repeated conflicts between the Caribbean and interior parts of Honduras.

Of the four republics, Guatemala was certainly the strongest and in some ways the most stable. While the other states were skittling their presidents like so many ninepins, Guatemala was ruled by a succession of strong dictators: Rafael Carrera (1844-65), Justo Rufino Barrios (1873-85), Manuel Cabrera (1898-1920), and Jorge Ubico (1931-44). These were separated by intervals of constitutional government, anarchy, or attempts at dictatorship which failed. Few presidents handed over power voluntarily to their successors; most of them were forcibly removed or assassinated.

Despite the permutations and combinations of external and civil war there has been a recurrent desire to reestablish some form of **La Gran Patria Centroamericana**. Throughout the 19th century, and far into the 20th, there have been ambitious projects for political federation, usually involving El Salvador, Honduras and Nicaragua; none of them lasted more than a few years. There have also been unsuccessful attempts to reestablish union by force, such as those of Barrios of Guatemala in 1885 and Zelaya of Nicaragua in 1907.

During colonial times the area suffered from great poverty; trade with the mother country was confined to small amounts of silver and gold, cacao and sugar, cochineal and indigo. During the 20th century the great banana plantations of the Caribbean, the coffee and cotton trade and industrialization brought some prosperity, but its benefits have, except in Costa Rica and Panama, been garnered mostly by a relatively small landowning class and the middle classes of the cities. Nicaragua is now a case apart; extensive and radical reforms were carried out by a left-leaning revolutionary government, but protracted warfare and mistakes in economic management have left the country still extremely poor.

Regional integration Poverty, the fate of the great majority, has brought about closer economic cooperation between the five republics, and in 1960 they established the Central American Common Market (CACM). Surprisingly, the Common Market appeared to be a great success until 1968, when integration fostered national antagonisms, and there was a growing conviction in Honduras and Nicaragua, which were doing least well out of integration, that they were being exploited by the others. In 1969 the 'Football War' broke out between El Salvador and Honduras, basically because of a dispute about illicit emigration by Salvadoreans into Honduras, and relations between the two were not normalized until 1980. Despite the handicaps to economic and political integration imposed by nationalist feeling and ideological differences, hopes for improvement were revived in 1987 when the Central American Peace Plan, drawn up by President Oscar Arias Sánchez of Costa Rica, was signed by the Presidents of Guatemala, El Salvador, Honduras, Nicaragua and Costa Rica. The plan proposed formulae to end the civil strife in individual countries, achieving this aim first in Nicaragua (1989), then in El Salvador (1991). In Guatemala, a ceasefire after 36 years of war led to the signing of a peace accord at the end of 1996. After the signing of the peace accords, emphasis has shifted to regional economic and environmental integration. National and international bodies insist that to maintain peace the gulf between rich and poor must be eradicated, including in those countries not previously affected by civil war. Moreover, the indigenous peoples, who are usually at the lowest end of the social scale must be given greater asssistance.

In October 1993, the presidents of Guatemala, El Salvador, Honduras, Nicaragua and Costa Rica signed a new Central American Integration Treaty Protocol, to replace that of 1960 and set up new mechanisms for regional integration. The Treaty was the culmination of a series of annual presidential summits since 1986 which, besides aiming for peace and economic integration, has established a Central American Parliament and a Central American Court of Justice.

Attempts at further economic and regional integration continue. The Plan Puebla is the promotion of an economic corridor stretching from Puebla, west of Mexico City, as far as Panama. The plan, strongly promoted by President Fox as a means for economic development, is seen by some as draining cheap labour resources with little concern for environmental concerns and long-term progress. While the Plan Puebla may continue to simmer on the back burner, the desire for Central American nations to strengthen ties is regularly voiced. Regional meetings occur periodically (or spontaneously in the case of the diplomatic problems between Honduras and El Salvador in mid-2001) to promote and encourage trust and cooperation. While the final destination of such cooperation is far from clear, all are agreed that the Central America of today is far more productive and safer than it was in the 1980s.

The Mundo Maya

Integrated tourism and conservation

First envisaged in the 1980s, this ambitious project aims to tap the tourist potential of southern Mexico and Central America once dominated by the Maya. Involving the co-operation of public and private tourist bodies of Mexico, Guatemala, Belize, El Salvador and Honduras, it is one of the regions of the world with the greatest variety of tourist attractions. As well as the many archaeological sites – both large and small – the various countries share to a greater or lesser degree modern Maya culture, national parks, beaches, lakes, volcanoes and various types of forest. There is still a long way to go before the fully integrated tourist circuit envisaged in the late 1980s comes to fruition, but the whole idea is well established. Government representatives have been meeting since 1988 and the concept was given huge impetus by a feature in the *National Geographic* magazine of October 1989.

Many archaeological sites are already popular tourist attractions, with the accompanying infrastructure (Tikal, Guatemala for example, page 677; Palenque, Chichén Itzá, Mexico, page 453 and page 500; Copán, Honduras page 825). Others, while thoroughly excavated, are less well known and yet others, still under excavation, are becoming part of the tourist route (for example Caracol, Belize page 741; Calakmul, Mexico page 474; Joya del Cerén, El Salvador page 790). As present-day knowledge of the historical Maya grows, so efforts are being made to safeguard the traditions of the Maya peoples living now, traditions which are both centuries old and enmeshed with Catholicism. In the context of the Mundo Maya, such safeguards must include the avoidance of the worst aspects of voyeuristic tourism. Both people and their environment face economic and population pressures. The expansion of natural parks, for instance the enlargement by 55,000 ha of the Montes Azules biological reserve in Lacandonia to include Bonampak and Yaxchilán (Mexico page 458), have been welcomed. Parks in existence cover a wide range of ecological zones including rainforest and cloud forest, the diverse marine and terrestrial environments of Belize, the Caribbean coast of Honduras, the *biotopos* in Guatemala and the waterbird sanctuaries in northern Yucatán, Mexico. Of the landscapes, one can mention the chain of volcanoes extending through Mexico, Guatemala and El Salvador, associated with which are some beautiful lakes, or, offshore, the cayes and reefs of Belize.

The Mundo Maya should prove beneficial in terms of road building, flight links, hotel construction and ease of access between neighbouring countries. One major question surrounds this development, though; is there a danger that the Mundo Maya will isolate this region as a tourist 'hot spot', to the detriment of the region itself (that is as an extension of what is generally accepted to be overdevelopment at Cancún, Mexico, page 508), and to the detriment of other parts of Mexico and the rest of Central America through a lack of comparable funding? Mexican tourism projects are spread over many areas in the country, taking in a wide array of archaeological heritage, both pre-conquest and colonial. Beach developments, such as Huatulco (Mexico see page 415), are taking place concurrently with whatever progress is being made on the Mundo Maya. A colonial cities programme, covering 51 places, has been developed. For both Guatemala and Belize, the Mundo Maya will build on the attractions to which visitors are already drawn. While Copán, Honduras' main Maya connection, may act as an enticement for people to travel to other parts of the country, El Salvador will expect the Mundo Maya to encourage the reemergence of a tourist industry as the country rebuilds after the civil war. Much depends upon how great a percentage of Mundo Maya tourism is concentrated in the package tour market.

Essentials

Two different bodies have been promoting the Maya World, or Maya Route. In Mexico and Central America, the **Organización Mundo Maya** was established in 1990. It coordinates the activities of the five countries and its executive secretariat rotates among the member countries every two years. For information apply to the tourism secretariats or institutes in the member states.

In the USA, the **Ruta Maya Foundation** was set up by Wilbur Garrett, retired editor of *National Geographic* and author of the above-mentioned article. Among other activities the Foundation receives donated or acquire Pre-Columbian artefacts in the USA so they may be returned to museums in Mesoamerica. Fernando Paiz is the current President of the Ruta Maya Foundation and he may be contacted at: 1607 Ponce de León Blvd, Coral Gables, FL 33134-4011, USA. T305-569-0012, F305-448-6778, fpaiz@cidcosa.com

Books

Recommended books for Central America and Mexico are listed under the relevant Books sections of each country. It is worth looking around for a few good books before you leave. Overland travel lends itself well to reading, and a related book will set you off on exactly the right foot. And as you will see when you're looking to swap, the book shops could do with a few healthy contributions – some actually ban romance novels! Books covering the the region looks like a Who's Who of literature with classic contributions from Jack Kerouac (*On the Road*), D H Lawrence (*The Plumed Serpent*), Graham Greene (*The Lawless Road, The Power and the Glory, The Captain and the Enemy* and *Getting to Know the General*), Paul Theroux (*The Old Patagonian Express* and *The Mosquito Coast*), Iain Banks (*Canal Dreams*), Norman Lewis (*The Volcanoes Above Us*) and Aldous Huxley (*Eyeless in Gaza* and *Beyond the Mexique Bay*) and that without even touching on the homegrown talents of Carlos Fuentes, Rubén Darío and Ernesto Cardenal – these are just pointers. Any of these books would make an excellent choice to accompany the start of your travels. A general guide to the literature of the region is Jason Wilson's, *Traveller's Literary Companion, South and Central America* (Brighton, UK: In Print, 1993), which has extracts from works by Latin American writers and by non-Latin Americans about the various countries and has very useful bibliographies.

An excellent overview of the Maya is *The Maya* by Michael D Coe (Thames and Hudson). The same author has written *Breaking the Maya Code* by an indepth account of how the hieraglyphics of the Maya were eventually read.

Nature lovers may want to carry Louise Emmon's *Neotropical Rainforest Mammals: A Field Guide* which will help with identify wildlife. Bird-watchers and keen twitchers will have to choose between *A Guide to the Birds of Mexico and Northern Central America* by Steven Howell or *Field Guide to Mexican Birds* by R Peterson, both excellent bird books.

Mexico

3

Mexico

Essentials

Mexico's size makes it impossible for anyone (unless you have unlimited time) to see it all in one go. Fortunately, with so many attractions, and with relatively good transport links, it is not difficult to select a good variety of options. The Pacific, Gulf of Mexico and Caribbean Sea provide thousands of miles of beaches on either side of the country. The bulk of the interior is made up of mountains and plateaux, in the north predominantly arid, but, in the south, more densely forested and wet.

For those flying in, there are two main ports of entry to Mexico, the capital and Cancún. To the north there is one long and wonderfully permeable border across which most driving traffic arrives.

Planning your trip

Central Mexico One of the world's great capitals, **Mexico City**'s splendour of architecture and vast public plazas survive side by side with the chaos of traffic and 20 million people. It deserves several days' stay just to visit the highlights – the Museum of Anthropology, Centro Histórico, Chapultepec Park, Coyoacán, San Angel and Xochimilco among them. Get a feel for its stirring revolutionary past through the brilliant murals of Orozco, Rivera and Siqueiros, and for its ancient history with the awesome ruins of Teotihuacán, a short trip outside the capital.

A relatively short circuit north of Mexico City, possible in a week, is to the Colonial Heartland, taking in the towns of **Querétaro**, **Guanajuato**, **San Miguel de Allende** and **Dolores Hidalgo**, architectural gems built on silver wealth.

The south A hub for travellers, **Oaxaca City** is worth several days in itself for the colonial architecture and nearby ruins of **Monte Albán**. If you continue east you come to **San Cristóbal de las Casas** with myriad Indian villages in the surrounding hills that are worth exploring for several days. From here you can continue down to Guatemala and sweep back into the Yucatán via Tikal in north Guatemala, through Belize, and on to the **Mexican Caribbean** coast at Quintana Roo. Or you can follow the isthmus to the Yucután before heading to Belize or Guatemala.

The Mayan routes If you like to party, you'll love **Cancún**, a major holiday destination. If you're looking for something a little quieter, a short journey will take you to quiet beaches nearby, where you can snorkel and dive, relaxing in the warm, soothing waters. Cancún is the perfect starting point for the Ruta Maya – a roughly eliptical route that takes in the major Maya ruins in Mexico, Belize, Guatemala and Honduras. Close to Cancún is **Tulum**, while from **Mérida** it's a short trip to **Uxmal**, and **Chichén Itzá** is about halfway between the two. Not far from the fine ruins of **Palenque** are the waterfalls of Misol-Há and Agua Azul. Whichever route you take, it's a gentle lead into the foundation culture of Central America.

Northern Mexico If you're making the full sweep from the US border, the busiest land port of entry is Tijuana and most travellers head down the **Baja California Peninsula** through spectacular desert scenary to lay up at idyllic beach hang-outs such as Playa Santispac on Bahía Constitución and, if you time it right, to watch the migrating whales. Once you hit La Paz or the Cape you are effectively on an island – the ferry to the mainland is an overnighter.

The shortest route from north of the border to the heart of Mexico is down the east coast, staying close to the **Gulf**, but more interesting by far is the route from **Ciudad Juárez** which meanders through the rugged barren lands of the high Sierra Madre, giving access to Chihuahua and the classic rail journey through the **Copper Canyon** to the Pacific. An alternative is down the west coast through the desert lowlands of the state of Sonora and then taking the train from Los Mochis up the railway, seeing the best stretch as far as Creel and then visiting the Copper Canyon at Batópilas en route to Hidalgo del Parral via

Where to go
Picking a spot and covering it well, moving around or doing the big trip from top to bottom, here are a few ideas

Not many buses go this way so add a few days for erratic scheduling

Mexico

Guachochi. Durango is seven hours by road from here and then you are just a few hours from the gems of **Zacatecas**, Guanajuato and other towns of the Colonial Heartland.

When to go If you are not tied to the European or American summer for times when you are able to travel then the best time to go is between October and April when there is virtually no rain. The rainy season works its way up from the south beginning in May and running through until August, September and even October. This is also hurricane season in the Caribbean and on rare occasions the Yucatán and Gulf states get hit. But don't be put off by the term 'rainy season' – most years, the rains only really affect travellers for an hour or two a day. In the northern states of Baja, Sonora, Chihuahua and Coahuila, it can remain very hot and dry.

August is holiday time for Mexicans and this can make accommodation scarce in the smaller resorts and in popular places close to Mexico City. Semana Santa (Easter week), and the Christmas holidays can also affect room availability. Day of the Dead celebrations (at the beginning of November, and particularly around Pátzcuaro) and other important local fiestas also make it advisable to pre-book.

Finding out more

A calendar of fiestas is published by Mexico This Month

Tourist offices overseas **Canada**, 2 Bloor St West, Suite 1801, Toronto, Ontario M4W 3EZ, T416-925-0704. **France**, 4 rue Notre Dame des Victories, 75002 Paris, T331-402-00734. **Germany**, Welsenhuttenplatz 26, D60329 Frankfurt/Main 1, T4969-253413. **Italy**, Via Barberini 3, 00187 Rome, T396-474-2986. **UK**, 41 Trinity Square, London EC3N 1DJ, T020-7488-9392. **USA**, 405 Park Avenue, Suite 1401, New York NY 10022, T212-755-7261.

There are telephone numbers that tourists can call to clarify problems. In Mexico, tourists can call T01-800-00148 and in Mexico City T5604-1240. The *Secretaría de Turismo* has an emergency hotline, open 24 hours a day: T05-5250-0123/0151.

All Mexican Government tourist agencies are grouped in the Department of Tourism building at Avenida Masaryk 172, near the corner of Reforma. See under Mexico City for full details. Many cities and more popular areas run municipal tourist offices to help travellers.

Mexico on the web The Mexico Tourist Board website, **www.visitmexico.com**, is a comprehensive site with many links.

Mexicanwave, **www.mexicanwave.com**, is a well-constructed site updated daily, with current affairs, feature articles and advice on travel in Mexico. Look out for the forum where comments from fellow travellers are exchanged. The *World Travel Guide – Mexico*, **www.wtgonline.com/data/mex/mex.asp**, has an overview of Mexico for travellers, with useful 'Essentials' section with facts on visas, public holidays, money and health. Adventurers can look at *GORP: Basic Mexico* **www.gorp.com/gorp/location/latamer/mexico.htm,** with lots of detailed information including good suggestions and tips on more adventurous travel.

The *US Library of Congress Study: Mexico* at **lcweb2.loc.gov/frd/cs/mxtoc.html** is an excellent starting point for learning about Mexico. *Mexico Reference Desk*, **www.lanic.utexas.edu/la/Mexico/**, is a huge site containing a variety of information about Mexico ranging from anthropology to sport and trade. Rather academic in tone, it is nevertheless an excellent source for background information.

Language The official language of Mexico is Spanish. Outside of the main tourist centres, travelling without some knowledge of Spanish is a major hindrance. Adding to the challenges of communication, there are also some 50 indigenous languages spoken in Mexico, the most common of which are Nahuatl, Maya, Zapotec and Mixtec.

Before you travel

Visas & immigration A passport is necessary, but US and Canadian citizens need only show a birth certificate (or, for US, a naturalization certificate). Tourists need the free tourist card (FM-T), which can be obtained from any Mexican Consulate or Tourist Commission office, at the Mexican airport on entry, from the offices or on the aircraft of airlines operating into Mexico, and at land borders. Ask for at least 30 days (maximum 180 days); if you say you are in transit you may be charged US$8, with resulting paper work. Not all Mexican consuls in the USA are aware of exact entry requirements; it is best to confirm details with airlines that fly to Mexico. Tourist cards are available for citizens of Western European countries (except Cyprus and Malta), the US, Canada, Australia, New Zealand, Hungary, Iceland, Japan, Singapore, South Korea, Argentina, Bermuda, Chile, Costa Rica, Uruguay, Venezuela and Israel. Citizens of other countries need to obtain a visa before travelling. The tourist card is also available at border offices of the American Automobile Association (AAA), which offers this service to members and non-members. There is a multiple-entry card valid for all visits within six months for US nationals. The normal validity for other nationals is 90 days, but sometimes only 15-30 days are granted at border crossings; insist you want more if wishing to stay longer. Although technically you are only supposed to stay 180 days a year on a tourist card, one correspondent lived in Mexico for five years on a tourist card, making short visits to the US three to four times a year, with no problems. Tourist cards are not required for cities close to the US border, such as Tijuana, Mexicali, etc.

Renewal of entry cards or visas must be done at **Servicios Migratorios**, 862 Ejército Nacional. Only 60 days are given, and you can expect to wait up to 10 days for a replacement tourist card; open Monday-Friday 0900-1300, take metro to Polanco then a taxi. There are also immigration offices at international airports and in cities such as Guadalajara, Oaxaca or Acapulco, which can renew tourist cards. To renew a tourist card by leaving the country, you must stay outside Mexico for at least 72 hours. Take travellers' cheques or credit card as proof of finance. The Oaxaca immigration office will renew your tourist card for only 15 days unless you have US$1,000 in cash for one month's stay; credit cards not accepted.

Travellers not carrying tourist cards need visas, multiple entry is not allowed, and visas must be renewed before re-entry (South Africans and those nationalities not listed above need a visa). Business visitors and technical personnel should apply for the requisite visa and permit. For a Visitante Rentista visa (non-immigrant pensioner) for stays over six months (up to two years) the following are required: passport, proof of income from abroad of US$750 per month (or 400 days of the minimum wage), which is reduced by half if you own a house in Mexico, and your tourist card.

At the border crossings with Belize and Guatemala, you may be refused entry into Mexico if you have less than US$200 (or US$350 for each month of intended stay, up to a maximum of 180 days). This restriction does not officially apply to North American and European travellers. If you are carrying more than US$10,000 in cash or travellers' cheques, you must declare it. In most cases on entering Mexico from Belize and Guatemala only 30 days' entry is given, possibly renewable for up to 60 days.

Visas and travelling with children If a person under 18 is travelling alone or with one parent, both parents' consent is required, certified by a notary public or authorized by a consulate. A divorced parent must be able to show custody of a child. (These requirements are not always checked by immigration authorities and do not apply to all nationalities.) Exact details are available from any Mexican Consulate.

The luggage of tourist-card holders is often passed unexamined. If flying into Mexico from   **Customs**
South America, expect to be thoroughly searched (body and luggage) at the airport. US citizens can take in their own clothing and equipment without paying duty, but all valuable and non-US-made objects (diamonds, cameras, binoculars, typewriters, computers, etc), should be registered at the US Customs office or the port of exit so that duty will not be charged on returning. Radios and television sets must be registered and taken out when leaving. Anyone entering Mexico is allowed to bring in: clothing, footwear and up to three litres of wine, beer or spirits; 20 packs of cigarettes, or 20 cigars, or 200 g of tobacco; medicines for personal use. Foreigners who reside legally outside Mexico are also allowed: a portable TV, stereo, 20 records or audio cassettes, a musical instrument, five used toys, fishing tackle, tennis racket, a pair of skis, a boat up to 5 m without an engine, camping equipment, a tent. Those entering by trailer, private plane or yacht may also bring a video-cassette recorder, bicycle, motorbike and kitchen utensils. Anything additional to this list with a value of over US$300, if entering by land, air or sea, is taxable and must be declared as such (for Mexicans returning by land the value is US$50). This stipulation is rarely invoked for those entering by motor home. Goods imported into Mexico

Mexico

with a value of more than US$1,000 (with the exception of computer equipment, where the limit is US$4,000) have to be handled by an officially appointed agent. One recommended agency is Agencia Promoción y Servicio Aduanal, Durango 111, Colonia Peñón de los Baños, T5785-5769, F5785-7476, pysasa@aaadam.com.mx, who will arrange everything, including delivery to one's address.

Vaccinations A vaccination certificate is required for travellers arriving from countries where yellow fever is present. Otherwise no specific vaccinations are needed to enter Mexico. However, before travelling make sure your tetanus and polio vaccinations are up to date. Immunization against hepatitis A and B and typhoid are recommended for people travelling to more remote areas, particularly in the south. See Health on pages 53 and 92.

What to take General advice is given in the What to take in the main Essentials section (see page 31) In the Highlands it can be cold at night especially in winter, and most hotels do not have heating. Cheaper hotels often provide only one blanket and, while they will certainly provide a second if available, a light sleeping bag that packs up small can be useful. This applies in popular tourist centres such as San Cristóbal de las Casas, Oaxaca and Pátzcuaro.

Money

Currency
US$1=$9.86
(Mexican pesos)

The monetary unit is the Mexican peso, represented by '$' – the dollar sign. Hardly surprising therefore that the potential for confusion is great, especially in the popular tourist places where prices are higher and normally quoted in US$. There are notes for 10, 20, 50, 100, 200 and 500 pesos; coins for 5, 10, 20 and 50 centavos and for 1, 2, 5, 10, 20 and 50 pesos. The one- and two-peso coins and the 10- and 20-peso coins are similar in size; check the number on the coi

Cash Dollars are easily changed in all cities and towns at banks and *casas de cambio* and in the more popular places can sometimes be used if you're running short of pesos. Take a mix of large and small denominations – you don't want to get stuck trying to change a US$100 bill in a dusty village in the middle of nowhere.

Travellers' cheques
Casas de cambio may be open longer hours than banks, but they do not offer better exchange rates

The safest way of carrying money is in US$ travellers' cheques, which can be changed at most banks and *casas de cambio*. Fees are not charged although the exchange rate will be lower than it is for cash. You may be asked to show your passport or another form of ID. Denominations of US$50 and US$100 are preferable, though you will need a few of US$20. American Express and Visa US$ travellers' cheques are recommended as the easiest to change and it is also easier to obtain refunds for stolen travellers' cheques with them.

Credit cards
ATMs are now found even in small towns allowing you to travel without carrying large amounts of cash or TCs

American Express, **MasterCard** and **Visa** are generally accepted in Mexico and cash is obtainable with these credit cards at certain banks. Automatic teller machines (ATM, *cajero automático*) of *Banamex* accept Visa, MasterCard and ATM cards of the US Plus and Cirrus ATM networks for withdrawals up to 1,500 pesos. ATM withdrawals on Visa can also be made at branches of *Bancomer* and *Cajeros RED* throughout the country. Many banks are affiliated to MasterCard but locations of ATMs should be checked with MasterCard in advance. Visa is more commonly found. There have been repeated instances of *Banamex* ATMs stating that cash cannot be given, 'try again later', only for the card-holder to find that his/her account has been debited anyway. If you get a receipt saying no cash dispensed, keep it. Emergency phone numbers for MasterCard, T001-800-307-7309, and Visa, T95-800-847-2911, toll free. There is a 6% tax on the use of credit cards.

Exchange In the border states such as Baja California Norte, the most-used currency is the US dollar, although the Mexican peso is often accepted by stores on the US side of the border. Travellers' cheques from any well-known bank can be cashed in most towns if drawn in US dollars; travellers' cheques in terms of European currencies are harder to cash, and certainly not worth trying to change outside the largest of cities. If you are stuck, large branches of BITAL have been known to change sterling cheques. *Casas de cambio* are generally quicker than

Mexico embassies and consulates

Australia, 14 Perth Avenue, Yarralumia, 2600 ACT, Canberra, T61-2-6273-3963, F61-2-6273-1190.

Austria, Türkenstrasse 15, 1090, Vienna, T43-1-310-7383, F43-1-310-7387.

Belgium, Av Franklin Roosvelt 94, 1050 Bruxelles, T32-2-629-0777, F32-2-646-8768.

Canada, 45 O 'Connor Street, Suite 1500 K1P 1A4, Ottawa, Ont, T613-233-8988, F613-235-9123.

Denmark, Strandvejen 64E Hellerup, 2900, Copenhagen, T45-3961-0500, F45-3961-0512

France, 9, Rue de Longchamp, 75116 Paris, T331-5370 2770, F331-4755 6529.

Germany, Klingelhöferstrasse 3, 10785 Berlín, T49-30-269-3230, F49-30-26-9323-700.

Holland, Burgemeester Patijnlaan 1930, 2585 CB La Haya, T31-70-345-2569, F31-70-356-0543.

Ireland, 43 Ailesbury Road, Ballsbridge 4, Dublin, T353-1-260-0699, F353-1-260-0411.

Israel, Trade Tower 25, Hemered St, 5th floor 63125. Tel-Aviv, T972-3-516-3938, F972-3-516-3711.

Italy, Via Lazzaro Spallanzani 16, 00161, Rome, T39-6-440-4400, F39-6-440-3876.

New Zealand, 111-115 Customhouse Quay, 8th floor, Wellington, T64-4-472-5555, F64-4-472-5800.

Norway, Karenslyst Allé 2 - 2 et., 0277 Oslo, T44-2411-7200, F47-2211-7201.

South Africa, 1 Hatfield Square, 3rd Floor, 1101 Burnett Street, Hatfield 0083 Pretoria, PO Box 9077, 0001, T27-12-362-2822, F27-12-362-1380.

Spain, Carrera de San Jerónimo 46, 28014 Madrid, T34-91-369-2814, F34-91-420-2292.

Switzerland, Bernastrasse 57, 3005, Berne, T41-31-351-1875, F41-31-351-3492.

UK, 42 Hertford Street, Mayfair, London W1Y 7TF, T44-20-7499-8586, F44-20-7495-4035.

USA, 1911 Pennsylvania Ave, NW, 20006 Washington DC, T1-202-728-1600, F1-202-728-1698.

There are embassies/consulates in most other European countries, many US cities, throughout the Americas, and selected countries elsewhere. Addresses and email numbers can be found on **www.sre.gob.mx/delegaciones/ embajadas.htm**

Mexico

banks for exchange transactions, and stay open later, but their rates may not be as good. If you need to make a transfer ask your bank if they can transfer direct to a Mexican bank without using an intermediary, which usually results in greater delays. Beware of short-changing at all times. **Western Union**, T1-800-325-4045 (for US only), www.westernunion.com, have outlets throughout Mexico but the service is more expensive than a traditional bank wire

Cost of living

Budget travellers should note that there is a definite tourist economy, with high prices and, on occasion, unhelpful service. This can be avoided by seeking out those places used by locals; an understanding of Spanish is useful. In hotels there are sometimes no single rooms, or they cost 80% of the price of doubles. As accommodation will probably be your main expense this should be built into your budget if travelling singly.

Doctors and dentists can provide good-quality care at high prices (taking appropriate insurance is highly recommended). Film is reasonably cheap, but developing is expensive and often of poor quality.

Student cards

Although an international student (ISIC) card will generally be sufficient for student discounts, only national Mexican student cards permit free entry to archaeological sites, museums, etc, see SETEJ page 93. The surest way to get in free is to go on Sunday, when all such places have no entry charge, but are crowded as a result.

Getting there

Air

If you foresee returning home at a busy time (eg Christmas-beginning of January, August), a booking is advisable on any type of open-return ticket

There are several international airports, the two busiest ones being **Mexico City** and **Cancún**, both of which receive frequent flights from Europe, North and South America and the Caribbean. For cities other than the capital, see text below for details. For information on the reduced fare Mexiplan, see page 78.

From Europe Several airlines have regular direct flights from Europe to Mexico City. From Amsterdam with *KLM*; from Frankfurt with *Lufthansa* and *AeroMéxico* (LTU and *Condor* charter flights from to Mexico City or Cancún); from London and Manchester with *British Airways*; from Barcelona with *Iberia*; from Madrid with *Iberia* and *AeroMéxico*; from Paris with *Air France* and *AeroMéxico*. Most connecting flights in Europe are through Madrid or Gatwick. Fares vary from airline to airline and according to time of year. Check with an agency for the best deal for when you wish to travel.

    Cancún from Europe. From Amsterdam with *Martinair*, Dusseldorf with *LTU*, Frankfurt with *LTU* and *Condor*, Munich with *LTU* and *Condor*; London and Manchester with *British Airways*, Madrid with *Aeromexio* and *Avianca*, Milan with *Lauda Air* and Paris with *American Airlines*.

From US and Canada From the US to Mexico City with a variety of airlines including *American Airlines, AeroMéxico, Delta, Continental, United, Northwest, Taesa* and *Americawest*. Flights leave from Atlanta, Baltimore, Boston, Chicago, Dallas/Fort Worth, Denver, Detroit, El Paso, Fort Myers, Houston, Indianapolis, Laredo, Las Vegas, Los Angeles, Miami, Nashville, New York, Ontario (CA), Orlando, Philadelphia, Phoenix, Portland, Providence (Rhode Island), Sacramento, Salt Lake City, San Antonio (TX), San Diego, San Francisco, San José (CA), Seattle/Tacoma, Tampa and Washington DC.

    From the **US** to Cancún from Albany, Atlanta, Baltimore, Buffalo (New York), Charlotte (NC), Chicago, Dallas/Fort Worth, Detroit, Houston, Indianapolis, Las Vegas, Los Angeles, Memphis, Miami, New Orleans, New York, Philadelphia, Phoenix, Pittsburgh, St Louis, San Francisco, Seattle/Tacoma and Washington DC.

    From **Canada** to Mexico City flights are available from Montreal and Sault Ste Matie with *Mexicana*; from Toronto with *Mexicana* and *United;* and from Vancouver with *Japan Airlines*.

    From **Canada** to Cancún flights are available from Montreal and Vancouver with *Mexicana*.

From Israel Flights with *El Al-Continental* travel via New York.

From Australia and New Zealand From Sydney with *United* and from Auckland with *Air New Zealand*, all flying through Los Angeles.

From the Far East From Beijing with *United*; from Hong Kong with *United* and *Cathay Pacific*; from Osaka with *United*; from Seoul with *United* and *Korean Air;* and Tokyo with *Japan Airlines*.

From Latin America and Caribbean From **Argentina** there are flights from Buenos Aires with *Mexicana* and *Taca*; from Cordoba with *Lan Chile*; Menoda with *Lan Chile*; from **Bolivia** flights from Cochabamba, La Paz, Santa Cruz and Trinidad with *LAB*; from **Guatemala City** with *Mexicana* and *Taca*; from **Brazil** from Rio de Janerio with *Mexicana* and *Varig*; from São Paulo with *Aeromexico, Mexicana* and *Varig*; from **Chile** flights from La Serena with *Lan Chile* and Santiago with *LAB, Lan Chile* and *Mexicana*; from **Colombia** there are flights (all with Avianca unless stated) from Arauca, Armenia *(Aces)*, Barranquilla, Bogota *(Mexicana)*, Bucaramanga, Cali, Cartagena, Manizales *(Aces)*, Medellin *Copa*, Monteria *SAM*, Pasto, Pereira, Santa Maria; from San José (**Costa Rica**) with *Mexicana*; from Havana, **Cuba**, with *Cubana* and *Mexicana*; from **Ecuador** flights from Quayaquil with *Copa*, Quito with *Avianca* and *Copa*; from San Salvador (**El Salvador**) with *Mexicana* and *Taca*; from Tegucigalpa (**Honduras**) with *Taca*, from Kingston, **Jamaica**, with *Air Jamaica*; from Managua, **Nicaragua**, with *Copa*; from Asuncion, **Paraguay**, with *LAB*; from **Panama City** with *LAB*, *Lan Chile* and *Mexicana*; from San Juan (**Puerto Rico**) with *Aeromexico* and *Copa*; from Caracas, **Venezuela**, with *Mexicana*.

General tips Weight allowance is normally 30 kg for first class and 20 kg for business and economy classes. These limits are often not strictly enforced when it is known that the plane is not going to be full. On some flights from the UK there is a two-piece allowance of up to 32 kg per item but check in advance.

Student/youth and discount fares Some airlines are flexible on the age limit, others strict. One way and returns available, or 'Open Jaws' (when you fly into one point and return from another). Do not assume that student tickets are the cheapest; though they are often very flexible.

Check whether you are entitled to any refund or re-issued ticket if you lose, or have stolen, a discounted air ticket. Some airlines require the repurchase of a ticket before you can apply for a refund, which will not be given until after the validity of the original ticket has expired. The Iberia group and Air France, for example, operate this costly system. Travel insurance in some cases covers lost tickets.

From US There are many crossings all along the border with the US. Some are busier than others depending on the number of trucks that pass through. The main crossings are at Tijuana, Mexicali, Nogales, Ciudad Juárez, Piedras Negras, Nuevo Laredo and Matamoros.

Overland

From Guatemala The principal border town is Tapachula, with a crossing over the Talismán Bridge or at Ciudad Hidalgo. A more interesting route is via Ciudad Cuauhtémoc or heading northwest from Santa Elena/Flores towards Tenosique. There are also options for road and river travel from the Yucatán Peninsula.

From Belize The border crossing at Santa Elena is near Chetumal, where public transport can be arranged. See Chetumal for details. A second very quiet crossing is at Blue Creek – good for a challenge but little else.

Touching down

When arriving in Mexico by air, make sure you fill in the immigration document before joining the queue to have your passport checked. If you are not given one on the plane, find one in the arrivals hall. Also at Mexico City airport you may be subject to a brief interview by the Federal District Health Service, in relation to the control of cholera, yellow fever and other diseases.

Airport information & exit tax

Airport departure tax US$17.30 on international flights (dollars or pesos accepted); US$10.50 on internal flights; always check when purchasing if departure tax is included in ticket price.

Sales tax is payable on domestic plane tickets bought in Mexico. Domestic tax on Mexican flights is 15%, on international flights 3.75%.

Clothing Casual clothes are adequate for most occasions although men may need a jacket and tie in some restaurants. Topless bathing is increasingly acceptable in parts of Baja California, but take guidance from others.

Local customs & laws

Complaints If you have any complaints about faulty goods or services, go to the *Procuraduría Federal de Protección del Consumidor* of which there is a branch in every city (head office in Mexico City, José Vasconcelos 208, CP 06720, México DF, T5761-3801/11).

Identification It is becoming increasingly common when visiting offices or tourist sites within government buildings to have to present some form of identification (*identificación* or *credencial*; photocopied passport will usually do), to register one's name, and sometimes to leave the ID with the security guard in exchange for a pass. This can be irksome but remember that the people on the door are only doing their job.

Photography There is a charge of US$4-5 for the use of video cameras at historical sites. If you want to use professional equipment, including a tripod, the fee is US$150 per day.

Mexico

Mexico

Touching down

Official time *US Central Standard Time, six hours behind GMT; Daylight Saving Time, from first Sunday in April to last Sunday in October, five hours behind GMT. Sonora, Sinaloa, Nayarit and Baja California Sur are seven hours behind GMT; Baja California Norte (above 28th Parallel) is eight hours behind GMT (but seven hours behind GMT between 1 April and end October).*
IDD *52.* **Operator** *T020.* **International operator** *T090.* **Directory enquiries** *T040.*
Hours of business *The hours of business in Mexico City are extremely variable. All banks are open from 0900 to 1330 from Monday to Friday, some stay open later, and (main branches only) 0900 to 1230 on Saturday. Business offices usually open at 0900 or 1000 and close at 1300 or 1400. They reopen at 1400 or 1500, but senior executives may not return until much later, although they may then stay until after 1900. Business hours in other parts of the country vary considerably according to the climate and local custom.*
Weights and measures *The metric system is used everywhere.*

Tipping Tipping is more or less on a level of 10-15%; the equivalent of US$0.25 per bag for porters, the equivalent of US$0.20 for bell boys, theatre usherettes, and nothing for a taxi driver unless some kind of exceptional service.

Prohibitions **Drugs** Note that anyone found in possession of narcotics, in however small a quantity, is liable to a minimum prison sentence of 10 years, with a possible one-year wait for a verdict. Narcotics include 'magic mushrooms'.

Smoking Smoking is not allowed on most forms of public transport, including intercity buses, the metro and *colectivos*; there are generally non-smoking areas in the better restaurants. However, the attitude towards smoking is more relaxed than in the US and some other countries.

Safety Mexico is generally a safe country to visit, although crime is on the increase and precautions over personal safety should be taken, especially in Mexico City. Never carry valuables visibly or in easily picked pockets. Leave passports, tickets and important documents in a hotel safety deposit, not in your room. Underground pedestrian crossings are hiding places for thieves; take extra care at night. Cars are a prime target for theft; never leave possessions visible inside the car and at night always park in hotel car parks. There has also been a rapid rise in robbery by taxi drivers in Mexico City, especially after 2200; drivers stop in poorly lit streets where accomplices get in the cab and assault the passenger. Avoid travelling by bus at night particularly in Guerrero, Oaxaca, Veracruz and Chiapas; if at all possible make journeys in daylight. Couples and, even more, women on their own, should avoid lonely beaches. Those on the west coast are gaining a reputation as drug-landing points. The police service has an equivalent to the *Green Angels* (*Angeles Verdes*, see page 81), the *Silver Angels*, who help victims of crime to file a report. US citizens should present this report to the nearest embassy or consulate. Otherwise, it is best to avoid the police if at all possible; they are rarely helpful and tend to make complicated situations even worse. Should you come into contact with them, try to stay as calm and polite as possible. Never offer a bribe unless you are fully conversant with the customs of the country (see Warnings page 82).

Speaking Spanish is a great asset for avoiding rip-offs targeting gringos, especially short changing and overcharging (both rife), and for making the most of cheap *comedores* and market shopping.

Where to stay

Hotel prices in the lower and middle categories are still very reasonable by US and European standards. Prices of top and luxury hotels have risen more steeply as tourism has increased but good discounts are often available in the low season. Ask – politely. English is spoken at the best hotels and increasingly common throughout Mexico. There is a hotel (or *hospedaje*) tax, ranging between 1% and 4%, according to the state, although it is generally levied only when a formal bill is issued.

Hotels & hospedajes
Beware of 'helpfuls' who try to find you a hotel, as prices quoted at the hotel desk rise to give them a commission

Casas de huéspedes are usually the cheapest places to stay, although they are often dirty with poor plumbing. Usually a flat rate for a room is charged, so sharing works out cheaper. Sleeping out is possible anywhere, but is not advisable in urban areas. Choose a secluded, relatively invisible spot. Mosquito netting (*pabellón*) is available by the metre in textile shops and, sewn into a sheet sleeping bag, is adequate protection against insects.

If backpacking, it is best for one of you to watch over bags while the other goes to book a room and pay for it; some hotels are put off by backpacks. During peak season (November-April) it may be hard to find a room. The week after Semana Santa (Easter) is normally a holiday, so prices remain high, but resorts are not as crowded as the previous week. Discounts on hotel prices can often be arranged in the low season (May-October), but this is more difficult in the Yucatán and Baja California. There is not a great price difference between single and double rooms. Rooms with double beds are usually cheaper than those with two singles. Check-out time from hotels is commonly 1400. Always check the room before paying in advance. Also ask if there is 24-hour running water.

Motels and auto-hotels, especially in central and south Mexico, are not usually places where guests stay the whole night (you can recognize them by curtains over the garage and red and green lights above the door to show if the room is free). If driving, and wishing to avoid a night on the road, they can be quite acceptable (clean, some have hot water, and in the Yucatán they have a/c), and they tend to be cheaper than other, 'more respectable' establishments.

Twenty-one *albergues* exist in Mexico, mostly in small towns, www.hostelslatinamerica.org; they are usually good value and clean. While the hostels take YHA members and non-members, members pay a slightly reduced rate and, after about four nights, it normally works out to be cost effective to become a member. You have to pay a deposit for sheets, pillow and towel; make sure that this is written in the ledger or else you may not get your deposit back. Hostels have lockers for valuables; take good care of your other possessions.

Youth hostels

Many towns have a *Villa Deportivas Juvenil*. While these are essentially the Mexican equivalent of a Youth Hostel their main market is for groups of student travelling Mexicans who may be taking part in a regional event for example. It's worth looking out for the option as they are normally very cheap. But while some cater very well for the international traveller, others are barely interested. See text details or ask locally.

Most sites are called Trailer Parks, but tents are usually allowed. For camping and youth-hostel accommodation, see ***Villas Deportivas Juveniles*** page 123. ***Playas Públicas***, with a blue and white sign of a palm tree, are beaches where camping is allowed. They are usually cheap, sometimes free and some have shelters and basic amenities. You can often camp in or near National Parks, although you must speak first with the guards, and usually pay a small fee. Paraffin oil (kerosene) for stoves is called *petróleo para lámparas* in Mexico; it is not a very good quality (dirty) and costs about US$0.05 per litre. It is available from an *expendio*, or *despacho de petróleo*, or from a *tlapalería*, but not from gas/petrol stations. Methylated spirits is called *alcohol desnaturalizado* or *alcohol del 96* and is available from chemists. Calor gas is widely available, as it is throughout Central America. *Gasolina blanca* may be bought in *ferreterías* (ironmongers) or paint shops; prices vary widely, also ask for Coleman fuel. Alcohol for heating the burner can be obtained from supermarkets. Repairs to stoves at Servis-Coleman at Plaza de San Juan 5, Mexico City. Katadyn water-purifying filters can be bought in Mexico City at: Katadyn/Dispel, Distribuidores de Purificadores y Electrodomésticos, Francisco Javier Olivares Muñoz, Sinaloa 19 PB, Colonia Roma, CP 06700, México DF, T5533-0600, F5207-7174, spare parts also available.

Camping

Mexico

Getting around

This may be stating the obvious but Mexico is huge. Travelling Tijuana (top west) to Cancún (far right) without stops by bus and good links would take at least 3 days and cost in the region of US$200. Be realistic about the distances you hope to travel. And, if time is short, think about the options – a short flight might seem like an expensive option if you're on a tight budget but weighing up the benefits of covering a long-distance, the real cost of long-distance bus travel in Mexico vis-à-vis air travel and the benefits of seeing things from a different perspective and it's well worth keeping an open mind.

Air Note that the majority of internal routes involve a change in Mexico City, for example there is no direct flight Acapulco-Cancún. *Mexicana* and *AeroMéxico* combine to offer **MexiPlan** tickets, which are for a minimum of two coupons covering five zones of the country; the pass is eligible only to those arriving on transatlantic flights, valid 3-90 days and must be purchased before arrival in Mexico. Fares range from US$60-150 per coupon; extra coupons may be bought and reservations may be changed. There are several other airlines flying internal routes (a few with international flights as well), for example *Aero California*, *Aeromar*, *Aerolitoral*, *Taesa*, *Saro*, *Aviacsa* and *Aerocaribe*.

Bus Most people in Mexico travel by bus whether by short distances or the long-haul from regional capital to capital. You'll find the full range of characters from smooching young lovers to aspirational business types and more rural characters on the bumpier stretches.

Beware of 'scalpers' who try to sell you a seat at a higher price; you can usually get one stand-by, at the regular price, when somebody doesn't turn up

The Mexican bus system is both complicated and confusing; trying to understand it is impossible. Fortunately you don't really have to and in reality few – including Mexicans – do. The bottom line is that there is normally a bus going from where you are to where you want to go. The problem is trying to locate where that bus leaves from. In some cities there is a central bus terminal (in Mexico City there are four – one at each point of the compass), in others there are a couple – one for first-class buses, one for second, still a third variation is division by companies. At times travelling by bus seems perfectly designed to confuse the independent traveller. The best approach is to take it easy, and take the knocks as they come. You will get the hang of it and while looks can be deceptive, it is actually pretty easy.

Bus services have been upgraded in recent years and are generally clean and prompt. However, the ordinary traveller should not be beguiled into thinking that it is necessary to purchase an expensive ticket in order to travel comfortably. On many routes, the second, or 'normal', class has disappeared.

On daytime journeys consider whether you want to see the scenery or a video. If going on an overnight bus, book seats at the front as toilets get very smelly by morning. Also make sure you have a jacket, jumper or blanket to hand as the air conditioning can be very cold at night. You must book in advance for buses travelling in the Yucatán Peninsula, especially around Christmas, but it is also advisable to book if going elsewhere. Some companies, for example *ADO*, are computerized in main cities, so advance reservations can be made. Bus seats are particularly hard to get during school holidays, August and the 15 days up to New Year when many public servants take holidays in all resorts; transport from Mexico City is booked up in advance and hotels are filled too. If travelling to a popular tourist destination, try to get on the bus at the starting-point of a route; buses are often full at the mid-point of their journeys. Sometimes it helps to talk to the driver, who has two places to use at his discretion behind his seat (don't sit in these until invited). Lock your luggage to the rack with a cycle lock and chain. If protecting luggage with chicken wire it will set off metal detectors used by *Cristóbal Colón* bus line in southern Mexico. Stowing your luggage on the roof is not advisable on night buses as theft can occur. Luggage racks on both classes of long-distance bus are spacious and will take a rucksack with a little persuasion (either of the rucksack itself, or the bus driver). Some companies now provide luggage receipts, which offer a degree of security. But however well organized a company (for example *ADO*), always check that your luggage is on your bus if you are putting it in the hold.

First class is perfectly satisfactory, but there now exist three superior classes, usually called *Primera Plus*, *Futura* and *Ejecutiva*, which offer varying degrees of comfort and some extra

Useful bus links

ADO *www.adogl.com.mx Covers the Yucután Peninsula and southeast Mexico*
Cristóbal Colón *www.cristobalcolon.com.mx South of Mexico City*
ETN *www.etn.com.mx*
Estrella de Oro *www.estrelladeoro.com.mx Mainly southwest of Mexico City*
Estrella Rojo *www.estrellarojo.com.mx East of Mexico City*
Flecha Amarilla *www.flecha-amarilla.com.mx*
Grupo Estrella *www.grupoestrellablanca.com.mx Covers most of Mexico*
Omnibus *www.omnibus.com.mx North of Mexico City*

Mexico

services. Companies offering these services include UNO (recommended) and ETN, as well as the major bus companies. The extras are reclining seats, toilets, drinks, videos, etc. ETN has exceptional buses with very comfortable, extra-wide seats (only three across) but prices are about 35-40% above regular first class. The superior classes are probably best for journeys over six hours.

Second-class buses usually operate from a different terminal from first-class buses and are often antiques (interesting, but frustrating when they break down) although they may be brand new. They call at towns and villages and go up side roads the first-class buses never touch. They stop as often for meals and toilets as their superiors do and, unlike the first-class buses, people get on and off so often that you may be able to obtain a seat after all. Autobuses Unidos (AU) are usually a little cheaper than other services, but they stop more often, including at the roadside when flagged down. They will not stop on curves, so walk until you find a straight stretch. It is not unusual to have to stand on these buses. Some second-class seats are bookable (for example in Baja California), others are not; it depends on the company. In general, it is a good idea to take food and drink with you on a long bus ride, as stops may depend on the driver. When a bus stops for refreshment, remember who your driver is and follow him; also memorize your bus number so you don't miss it when it leaves.

First-class fares are usually 10% dearer than second-class ones and the superior classes are even more. On a long journey you can save the price of a hotel room by travelling overnight, but in many areas this is dangerous and not recommended. Some companies give holders of an **international student card** a 50% discount on bus tickets, especially during the summer holiday period; persistence may be required. Look out for special offers, including discounts at some hotel chains. If making a day trip by bus, do not lose your ticket; you will have to show the driver and operator proof that you have paid for the return. There always seem to be many buses leaving in the early morning. All classes of bus invariably leave on time. Buses are often called *camiones*, hence *central camionero* for bus station. A monthly bus guide is available for US$1 (year's subscription) from Guía de Autotransportes de México, Apartado 8929, México 1, DF.

Car

Permits Vehicles may be brought into Mexico on a Tourist Permit for 180 days each year. The necessary documents are: passport, birth certificate or naturalization papers; tourist card; vehicle registration (if you do not own the car, a notarized letter from the vehicle's owner, be it the bank, company, whoever, is necessary); a valid driver's licence. National or international driving licences are accepted. The original and two photocopies are required for each. It takes 10 days to extend a permit, so ask for more time than you expect to need. Don't overstay; driving without an extension gets a US$50 fine for the first five days and then rises abruptly to half the value of the car! US$16.50 is charged for the permit, payable only by credit card (Visa, MasterCard, American Express or Diners Club), not a debit card, in the name of the car owner, as recorded on the vehicle registration. The *American Automobile Association* (AAA) is permitted to issue Tourist Permits for 'credit card' entry, free to members, US$18 to non-members; in California this service is available only to members. If you do not have a credit card, you have to buy a refundable bond in cash to the value of the vehicle according to its age (a set scale exists), which is repaid on leaving Mexico. The bond is divided into two parts, the bond itself and administration; the latter, accounting for about 43% of the total cost,

Mexico

is retained by the authorities; the bond is refunded. The bond is issued by Afianziadora Mexicana at US/Mexican border crossings, or by *Sanborn's* (see page 80). It may be waived if you are only going to the State of Sonora, under the Sonora Department of Tourism's 'Only Sonora' programme.

English versions of leaflets giving the rules on temporary importation of vehicles state that you must leave at the same crossing by which you entered. The Spanish versions do not say this and in practice it is not so. The temporary importation permit is multiple entry for 180 days; within that period you can enter and leave by whatever crossing, and as often as you like. Remember, though, that you must have a new tourist card or visa for each new entry. The Sanborn's website, **www.sanbornsinsurance.com**, is an excellent source of information

On entry, go to Migración for your tourist card, on which you must state your means of transport. This is the only record of how you entered the country. At the *Banjército* desk sign an *Importación Temporal de Vehículos/Promesa de retornar vehículo*, which bears all vehicle and credit card details so that, if you sell your car illegally, your credit card account can be debited for the import duty. Next you purchase the *Solicitud de importación temporal*, which costs US$12; it bears a hologram that matches the dated sticker, which must be displayed on the windscreen or, on a motorcycle, on some safe surface. Then go to *Copias* to photocopy all necessary documents and papers issued. The sticker and other entry documents must be surrendered on departure. They can only be surrendered at a Mexican border crossing, with date stickers cancelled by Banjército at Immigration. If you neglect to do this, and re-enter Mexico with an expired uncancelled sticker on you car, you will be fined heavily for each 15-day period that has elapsed since the date of expiry. If you intend to return to Mexico within the 180-day period, having surrendered your sticker and documents, keep safe the *Importación Temporal de Vehículos* form, stamped *Cancelado*, as a receipt. If entry papers are lost there can be much delay and expense (including enforcement of the bond) in order to leave the country. *Banjército* (*Banco del Ejército*) offices at borders are open daily, some for 24 hours. Each vehicle must have a different licensed driver (that is, you cannot tow another vehicle into Mexico unless it has a separate driver).

On arrival, you have to find the place where car permits are issued; this may not be at the border. If driving into Mexico from California, Nogales is probably the easiest crossing, which means going first into Arizona. The main car documentation point here is Km 21, south of Nogales. Entering at Tijuana, it seems that car entry permits are given at Mexicali (which means taking the very busy Route 2 through Tecate), or, if you drive through Baja California, at the ferry offices in Santa Rosalía or La Paz. This does not apply if you are not going beyond Baja. In Nuevo Laredo permits are issued at a new complex in town, opposite the train station. If crossing from Brownsville to Matamoros and you intend staying longer than 10 days, send a fax with car details to immigration at the border three days before leaving the country. Before crossing the border, pick up the fax and show it at the US side of the border. Most visitors to Mexico at this border are just crossing for shopping and only need a 10-day visa.

In Mexico foreign insurance will not be honoured; you must ensure that the company you insure with will settle accident claims outside Mexico

Insurance According to latest official documents, insurance for foreign cars entering Mexico is not mandatory, but it is highly recommended to be insured. Arranging insurance when crossing from the USA is very easy as there are many offices at US border crossings. Policy prices vary enormously between companies, according to age and type of vehicle, etc. One example from Sanborn's: Vehicle value US$3,000-10,000, one year including fire, theft, third party liability or US$50,000, US$270.

Sanborn's Mexican Insurance Service, with offices in every US border town, and many more, will provide comprehensive insurance, including full-year cover, within Mexico and other parts of Latin America, and provides free 'Travelogs' for Mexico and Central America with useful tips. Their head office is Sanborn's Insurance, Travco Services Inc, 2009 S 10th Street, McAllen, TX 78503, T956-686-3601, F956-686-0732, toll free 800-222-0158, info@sanbornsinsurance.com, www.sanbornsinsurance.com *Tepeyac,* with offices in most Mexican cities, and towns and at border crossings (including Tapachula), and in US (eg in San Diego, Mexican American Insurance Agency, corner of 6th and A streets, downtown, T233-7767).

Entering Mexico from Guatemala presents few local insurance problems now that *Tepeyac* (see above), has an office in Tapachula, and *Seguros La Provincial*, of Avenida General Utrillo 10A, upstairs, San Cristóbal de las Casas, have an office in Cuauhtémoc, Avenida Cuauhtémoc 1217 ground floor, Sr García Figueroa, T5-604-0500. Otherwise, try *Segumex* in Tuxtla Gutiérrez. In Mexico City, try *Grupo Nacional Provincial*, Río de la Plata 48, T528-67732, who have offices in many towns.

British AA and Dutch ANWB members are reminded that there are ties with the AAA, which extends cover to the US and entitles AA members to free travel information including a very useful book and map on Mexico (note that some AAA offices are not open at weekends or on US holidays). Luggage is no longer inspected at the checkpoints along the road where tourist cards and/or car permits are examined.

Petrol/gasoline All petrol stations in Mexico are franchised by Petróleos Mexicanos (PEMEX) and fuel costs the same throughout the country except near the US border, where it may be a bit cheaper. Roughly US$0.55 a litre. The old leaded *gasolina Nova* is scarce, and impossible to find in big cities, where vehicles must have catalytic convertors. Non-leaded petrol is classified either as *Magna*, from the green pumps, or the more expensive *Premium*, from the red ones. Diesel is also available. Petrol stations are not self-service. Make sure the pump is set at zero before your tank is filled and that your filler cap is put back on before you drive off. Specifiy how much you want either in litres or in money; it is normal to give the attendant a small tip.

All gasolina is now unleaded

Assistance The free assistance service of the Mexican Tourist Department's green jeeps (**Angeles Verdes** patrol most of Mexico's main roads. Every state has an Angeles Verdes Hotline and it is advisable to find out the relevant number when entering each state. The number in Mexico City is T5250-8221. The drivers speak English, are trained to give first aid and to make minor auto repairs and deal with flat tyres. They carry gasoline and have radio connection. All help is completely free, and you pay cost price for the gasoline. Although the idea is great, few Mexicans rely on the service in outlying areas and your best bet is to keep your vehicle in good condition and carry out the usual regular checks.

Parking Multi-storey car parks are fairly common, and parking is often to be found right in city centres under the main square. Whenever possible choose hotels with secure overnight parking. Never leave possessions visible inside a parked car.

Road tolls A toll is called a *cuota*, as opposed to a non-toll road, which is a *vía libre*. There are many toll charges, mostly of US$1 to US$2, on roads and bridges. Some new freeways bypassing city centres charge US$4-12, or more. Because of the high cost of toll roads, they are often quite empty, which means that good progress can be made on them. With the privatization of many freeways, hefty tolls are charged to road-users (double the car fee for trailers and trucks). Some can be avoided if you seek local, or motoring club (see above) advice on detours around toll gates (follow trucks). This may involve unpaved roads, which should not be attempted in the wet. However, the *carreteras libres* are normally perfectly acceptable and more interesting as they often travel through small towns and sometimes beautiful countryside. Two advantages of the expensive *super carretera* toll roads are that they are patrolled and safe, even at night, and drivers are insured against accident or breakdown. Whether you want to travel on a toll road or not, it is easy to end up on one by mistake, particularly in the north, so keep an eye out for signs.

In case of accident Do not abandon your vehicle. Call your insurance company immediately to inform it of the accident. Do not leave Mexico without first filing a claim in Mexico. Do not sign any contract or agreement without a representative of the insurance company being present. Always carry with you, in the insured vehicle, your policy identification card and the names of the company's adjusters (these are the recommendations of Asemex). If, in an accident, bodily injury has occurred or the drivers involved cannot agree who is at fault, the vehicles may be impounded. Drivers will be required to stay in the vicinity in cases of serious accidents, the insured being confined to a hotel (or hospital) until the claim is settled (according to Sanborn's). Should parties to an accident be incarcerated, a bail bond will secure release. A helpline for road accidents is available by phoning 02 and asking the operator to connect you to Mexico City T5684-9715 or 5684-9761.

Warnings On all roads, when two vehicles converge from opposite directions, or when a vehicle is behind a slow cart, bicycle, etc, the driver who first flashes his lights has the right of way. This also applies when a bus or truck wishes to turn left across the opposing traffic: if the driver flashes his lights he is claiming right of way and the oncoming traffic must give way. At *Alto* (Halt) signs, all traffic must come to a complete stop. At a crossroads, however, the first person to come to a complete halt then has precedence to cross. This requires a lot of attention to remember your place in the sequence (this is the same system as in the US). Do not drive at night. Night-time robberies on vehicles are on the increase especially in Guerrero and Oaxaca States. 'Sleeping policemen' or road bumps can be hazardous in towns and villages as often there are no warning signs; they are sometimes marked *zona de topes*, or incorrectly marked as *vibradores*. In most instances, their distinguishing paint has worn away. Don't drive fast; farm and wild animals roam freely.

Roadworks are usually well marked. If your vehicle breaks down on the highway and you do not have a warning triangle or a piece of red cloth to act as a warning, cut branches from the roadside and lay them in the road some distance in front of and behind your vehicle.

Foreigners may be searched for drugs on the west coast. The following precautions should help towards an incident-free passage of a drug search. Carry copies of all prescriptions for medicines (typed). Keep medicines in the original container. Carry a notice of all medical conditions that need a hypodermic syringe or emergency treatment. Never take packages for another person. Never take hitchers across a border. Always cross a border in your own vehicle. Check your vehicle carefully for suspicious packages secreted by someone other than yourself. If you have bodywork done in Mexico, supervise it yourself and keep records, even photos, of the workshop that did it. Prior to inspections, open all doors, hatches, etc. Put away all money and valuables. Offer no drinks, cigarettes or gifts to the inspectors; accept none. When searched, cooperate with narcotics officers (who wear black and yellow, and have an identity number on a large fob attached to the belt); do not intrude, but watch the proceedings closely.

If you are stopped by police in town for an offence you have not committed and you know you are in the right, do not pay the 'fine' on the spot. Take the policeman's identity number, show him that you have his number and tell him that you will see his chief (*jefe*) at the tourist police headquarters instead. It is also advisable to go to the precinct station anyway whenever a fine is involved, to make sure it is genuine. If stopped in a remote area, it is not advisable to get into a dispute with a policeman; drugs may be planted in your vehicle or problems may occur.

Note that cars must by law display a number/licence plate front and back; as this is not the case in some US States, you may have to improvise. Tourists' cars cannot, by law, be sold in Mexico.

If your car breaks down and cannot be repaired, you must donate it to the Mexican people. This is done through the Secretaría de Hacienda. If you have to leave Mexico in a hurry and cannot take the car with you, you have to get permission from the Secretaría de Hacienda, which will keep your car until you return.

Further information A useful source of information and advice (whose help we acknowledge here) is the Recreation Vehicle Owner's Association of British Columbia, Box 2977, Vancouver, BC, V6B 3X4 (members receive RV Times publication; Mexican insurance can be arranged for members). RV tours including Mexico are available from RV Adventuretours, 305 West Nolana Loop 2, McAllen, TX78505, US. Another recommended source of information in Canada is *Mexi-Can Holidays Ltd*, 150-332 Water St, Vancouver, BC, V6B 1B6, T604-685-3375, F604-685-3321. Motorists are referred to: *Clubmex*, PO Box 1646, Bonita, California 91908, US, T619-585-3033, F619-420-8133, which publishes a regular newsletter for its members (annual subscription US$35). The newsletter gives useful information and advice for drivers, specialist trips for sport fishing enthusiasts, and some interesting travel articles. Clubmex also arranges insurance for members. *RVing in Mexico, Central America and Panamá*, by John and Liz Plaxton (Travel 'N Write, Canada, 1996) has been recommended as full of useful information.

Car hire   Car rental is very expensive in Mexico and 15% sales tax is added to rental costs. Rates will vary from city to city. It can be cheaper to arrange hire in the US or Europe, but rentals booked abroad cannot be guaranteed (though usually they are). Proceed with caution. At some tourist resorts, however, such as Cancún, you can pick up a VW Beetle convertible for US$25 per day, which you will not be told about abroad. Renting a vehicle is nearly impossible without a credit card. It is twice as expensive to leave a car at a different point from the starting point than a round trip. See Car hire in Essentials for more information.

Motorcycle   Motorcycling is good in Mexico as most main roads are in fairly good condition and hotels are usually willing to allow the bike to be parked in a courtyard or patio. In the major tourist centres, such as Acapulco, Puerto Vallarta or Cancún, motorbike parts can be found as there are Honda dealers for bike and jet ski rentals. All Japanese parts are sold only by one shop in Mexico City at extortionate prices (but parts and accessories are easily available in Guatemala at reasonable prices for those travelling there).

Cycling   Mexico offers plenty of enjoyable places for riding bicycles. The main problems facing cyclists are the heavy traffic that will be encountered on main roads, the poor condition of these roads and the lack of specialized spare parts particularly for mountain bikes. It is possible to find most bike spares in the big cities, but outside these places it is only possible to find the basics: spokes, tyres, tubes, etc. Traffic is particularly bad around Mexico City and on the road between Mazatlán and Guadalajara. The easiest region for cycling is the Gulf of Mexico coast, however, many of the roads are dead flat, straight and generally boring. The mountains may appear intimidating, but gradients are not difficult as clapped-out buses and trucks have to be able to climb them. Consequently, much of the best riding is in the sierra. If cycling in Baja, avoid riding in mid-summer; even during October temperatures can reach 45°C+ and water is very scarce all the time. Also beware of Mexican bike mechanics who will attempt to repair your bike rather than admit that they don't know what they are doing, particularly when it comes to mountain bikes. The toll roads are generally preferable to the ordinary highways for cyclists; there is less traffic, more lanes and a wide paved shoulder. Some toll roads have 'no cyclists' signs but usually the police pay no attention. If you walk your bicycle on the pavement through the toll station you don't have to pay. If using the toll roads, take lots of water as there are few facilities. Cycling on some main roads can be very dangerous; it is useful to fit a rear-view mirror.

Hitchhiking   Hitchhiking is usually possible for single hikers, but apparently less easy for couples. It is generally quick, but not universally safe (seek local advice). Do not, for example, try to hitch in those parts of Guerrero and Oaxaca States where even driving alone is not recommended, yet in Baja California it is almost the best way to travel. In more out of the way parts, short rides from village to village are usually the rule, so progress can be slow. Getting out of big cities is best done by taking a local bus out of town in the direction of the road you intend to take. Ask for the bus to take the *Salida* (exit) to the next city on that road. From Mexico City to the US border, the route via Tula, Ciudad Valles, Ciudad Victoria and the Sierra Madre Oriental is scenic but slow through the mountains. The quicker route is via Querétaro, San Luis Potosí and Matehuala. Elsewhere, the most difficult stretches are reported to be Acapulco-Puerto Escondido, Santa Cruz-Salina Cruz and Tulum-Chetumal. It is very easy to hitch short distances, such as the last few km to an archaeological site off the main road; offer to pay something, like US$0.50.

Taxis   To avoid overcharging, the government has taken control of taxi services from airports to cities and only those with government licences are allowed to carry passengers from the airport. In some cities you do not pay the driver but purchase a ticket from a booth before leaving the airport. No further tipping is then required, except when the driver handles heavy luggage or provides some extra service for you. The same system has been applied at bus stations but it is possible to pay the driver direct. Avoid flagging down taxis in the street at night in Mexico City. It is safer to phone for a *sitio* taxi from your hotel.

Train
Check locally to find out whether trains are running or at: www.ferrocarriles.com

The railways are in the process of being privatized, with the result that passenger services have been stopped. Apart from the Chihuahua-al-Pacífico, between Los Mochis, Creel and Chihuahua, considered one of the world's greatest routes (see page 233), and the Tequila Express, a rather chitzy way of shifting people from Guadalajara to Tequila so they can drink and not drive, the only services still running are between Mexico City and Querétaro and Apilzalco.

Given that train travel in Mexico was as challenging as it was enjoyable the absence of this service is a great loss. As you travel through Mexico you may well see that as a long cargo trains approaches a station, people appear from nowhere as if attempting to get on the train. Discussion with several station masters and tourist boards has revealed that most trains do still take passengers and still have passenger wagons. The problem with having a public train schedule is that the public then expect the service to arrive and depart roughly on schedule – train travel in Mexico never had such lofty aspirations in the first place.

To repeat, passenger travel and scheduled services do not exist but if you have a great deal of time, patience and are train mad then you will be able to travel through Mexico on trains. The service are said to be ridiculously cheap and stupidly slow – walking may be quicker. Successfully reaching your destination is also likely to be more through luck and persistence than planning. Good luck.

Maps
Internationally, *ITM* (see page 49), www.itmb.com, provide several maps including one covering all Mexico, Mexico City, Baja California, Mexico North West, Mexico South East and Yucutan Peninsula. The Mexican Government Tourist Highway Map is available free of charge at tourist offices (when in stock). If driving from the US you get a free map if you buy your insurance at *Sanborn's* in the border cities.

Guía Roji publish a wide range of regional maps, city plans and gazettes, available at most bookshops. The *Dirección General de Oceanografía*, Calle Medellín 10, near Insurgentes metro station, sells excellent maps of the entire coastline of Mexico. Buy good detailed maps of states of Mexico and the country itself from *Dirección General de Geografía y Meteorología*, Avenida Observatorio 192, México 18 DF, T5515-1527 (go to Observatorio metro station and up Calle Sur 114, then turn right a short distance down Avenida Observatorio). Maps are also available from *Instituto Nacional de Estadística, Geografía e Informática* (*INEGI*), which has branches in Mexico City (see page 93) and in state capitals (US$3 per sheet). Pemex road atlas, *Atlas de Carreteras y Ciudades Turísticas*, US$5 in bookshops (for example *Sanborn's*), has 20 pages of city maps, almost every road one may need, contour lines, points of interest, service stations, etc (it is rarely on sale in Pemex stations), recommended.

Keeping in touch

Internet
A list of useful websites is given on page 70

As in many places nowadays, internet access in Mexico is extensive and often easier and more reliable than the phone. Every major town now has at least one internet café, with more springing up daily. A list of some (but not all) cybercafés in Mexico can be found at the website of the Asociación Mexicana de Cyber Cafés: **www.amcc.org.mx** If money is tight and you have time, look around; prices vary from place to place but are normally between US$1-2 an hour.

Post
Rates are raised periodically in line with the peso's devaluation against the dollar but are occasionally reported to vary between towns. They are posted next to the windows where stamps are sold. Rates in pesos are: within Mexico, letters up to 20 g $2.60, postcards $1.80; to North and Central America and the Caribbean: letters $3.90 (20 g), postcards $2.90; South America and Europe $4.90, postcards $3.50; Asia and Australia $5.50, postcards $4.00.

International service has improved and bright red mailboxes, found in many parts of the city, are reliable for letters. Weight limit 2 kg (5 kg for books) from Mexico to the UK. Surface mail takes about three months to Europe. Small parcel rate is cheaper. Parcel counters often close earlier than other sections of the post office in Mexico. A permit is needed from the Bellas Artes office to send paintings or drawings out of Mexico. Not all these services are obtainable outside Mexico City; delivery times in/from the interior may well be longer than those from Mexico City. Poste Restante ('general delivery' in the US, *lista de correos* in Mexico) functions quite reliably, but you may have to ask under each of your names; mail is sent back after 10 days (for an extension write to the Jefe de la Administración of the post office holding your mail, any other post office will help with this). Address '*Favor de retener hasta llegada*' on envelope.

Telephone

The Mexican telephone system underwent a comprehensive number change *twice* in 12 months, the latest being in November 2001. The predictable confusion ensued but most problems have now been ironed out. Simply put, calls made to Mexican numbers are local, between regions or international. The majority of destinations have a 7-digit number with the exceptions of Mexico DF, Guadalajara and Monterrey, which have 8-digit numbers. The format of a number, depending on the type of call, should be as follows: **local** – use 7- or 8-digit numbers; **between regions** – long-distance access (01) + regional code + 7- or 8-digit number; **international** – international access + country code (52) + regional code + 7- or 8-digit number.

Most public phones take phone cards only (Ladatel) costing 30 or 50 pesos from shops and news kiosks everywhere. AT&T's US Direct service is available, for information in Mexico dial 412-553-7458, ext 359. From LADA phones (see below), dial **01, similar for AT&T credit cards. To use calling cards to Canada T95-800-010-1990. Commercially run *casetas*, or booths (for example Computel), where you pay after phoning, are up to twice as expensive as private phones, and charges vary from place to place. Computel have offices countrywide with long opening hours. The cost of credit card calls is not usually posted but has been quoted as follows: to US US$39 for first eight minutes, then US$2 for each subsequent minute. For the UK, it was US$31 for first five minutes, then US$1 for each subsequent minute. However, it would seem that the charges levied may be much higher, so be wary. It is better to call collect from private phones, but better still to use the LADA system. Reverse-charge (collect) calls on LADA can be made from any blue public phone, say you want to *llamar por cobrar*; silver phones are for local and direct long-distance calls, some take coins. Others take foreign credit cards (Visa, MasterCard, not Amex; not all phones that say they take cards accept them, others that say they don't do).

Transatlantic calls cannot be made on a 25-peso LADA phone card. LADA numbers are: 01 long distance within Mexico, add city code and number (half-price Sunday); 001 long distance to US and Canada, add area code and number; 00 to rest of the world, add country code, city code and number; it is not possible to call collect to Germany, but it is possible to Israel. Cheap rates vary according to the country called. For information dial 07 or 611-1100. Foreign calls (through the operator, at least) cannot be made from 1230 on 24 December until the end of Christmas Day. The Directorio Telefónico Nacional Turístico is full of useful information, including LADA details, federal tourist offices, time zones, yellow pages for each state, sights and maps.

Media

Newspapers The more important journals are in Mexico City. The most influential dailies are: *Excelsior, Novedades, El Día, Uno Más Uno; The News*, in English, now available in all main cities (Grupo Novedades, which comprises *Novedades* and *The News* has a website at www.thenewsmexico.com); *El Universal (El Universal Gráfico); El Heraldo; La Jornada* (more to the left, is on-line at unam.netgate.net/jornada); *La Prensa*, a popular tabloid, has the largest circulation. *El Nacional* is the mouthpiece of the Government.

La Jornada publishes a supplement, Tiempo Libre, on Thursdays, listing the week's cultural activities

In Guadalajara, *El Occidental, El Informador* (www.infored.com.mx) and *Siglo 21*. The *Guadalajara Reporter* is a weekly English-language newspaper. There are influential weekly magazines *Proceso, Siempre, Epoca*, and *Quehacer Político*. The political satirical weekly is *Los Agachados*.

Mexico

Mexico

The New York edition of the *Financial Times* and other British and European papers are available at Mexico City Airport and from the *Casa del Libro*, Calle Florencia 37 (Zona Rosa), Hamburgo 141 (Zona Rosa) and Calle Homero (Polanco).

Food and drink

Cuisine
The best value is undoubtedly in small, family-run places

Food for most Mexicans represents an integral part of their national identity, and this fact is immediately seen in their desire to offer visitors an excess of the most typical dishes and specialities.

Much has been written since the 1960s about the evolution of Mexican food and the manner of its preparation, and experts suggest that there are three important stages: first, the combination of the indigenous and the Spanish; later, the influence of other European cuisines, notably the French in the 19th century; and finally, the adoption, in the 20th century, of exotic oriental dishes and fast-food from the US.

Because of the use of chilli as the principal seasoning in Mexican cooking, it is usually perceived as spicy or hot. However, there is another element that is even more characteristic and which visitors become aware of as they get to know the wide range of Mexican dishes. Maize, or corn, has been a staple crop from oldest times not only in Mexico but in the continent as a whole. Maize can be seen in what is called *antojitos* (light snacks that may be eaten by themselves or as a starter), some of the most common of which are *quesadillas*, *sopes*, *tostadas*, *tlacoyos* and *gorditas*, which consist of various shapes and sizes of *tortillas*, with a variety of fillings and usually garnished with a hot sauce. Tasting such offerings, wrapped in maize, will probably be the visitor's first introduction to Mexican food.

Certain dishes such as *mole* (chicken or turkey prepared in a chilli-based sauce) or *pozole* (a pot-au-feu with a base of maize and stock) are closer to indigenous traditions. Others, however, are of more recent creation, for example the following breakfast dishes, all with eggs: *huevos rancheros* (fried, with spicy sauce on a bed of *tortillas*), *machaca norteña* (scrambled with dried minced beef), *huevos motuleños* (fried with sauce of tomatoes, peas, cheese and fried banana) and *huevos a la mexicana* (scrambled with chilli and tomatoes).

As one travels around Mexico it becomes apparent that in certain provincial cities food takes on a more European aspect, whereas in others it seems to belong to the period when the process of development and integration was still taking place. Furthermore, there are so many regional specialities all over the country that it is difficult to use such a simple term as 'Mexican cooking'.

Usual meals are breakfast (which can consist of several courses), and a heavy lunch between 1400 and 1500. Supper, between 1800 and 2000, is light. Many restaurants give foreigners the menu without the *comida corrida* (set meals), so forcing them to order à la carte at double the price; watch this! Try to avoid eating in restaurants that don't post a menu. Meals in modest establishments cost about US$1.50-2 for breakfast, US$2-3 for set lunch (US$3-5.50 for a special *comida corrida*) and US$5-8 for dinner (generally no set menu). A la carte meals at modest establishments cost about US$7; a very good meal can be had for US$11 at a middle-level establishment. Much higher prices are charged by the classiest restaurants (for example, in Mexico City, US$15-22 medium class, US$30 first class, US$40 luxury). For those who are self-catering, the cost of food in markets and supermarkets is not high. In resort areas the posh hotels include breakfast and dinner in many cases. Check bills and change; even if service is included waiters have been known to deduct a further tip from the change; they will hand it back if challenged. In some restaurants, beer will not be served unless a meal is ordered.

Drink
There are few outdoor drinking places in Mexico except in tourist spots

The beer is good: brands include Dos Equis-XX, Montejo, Bohemia, Sol and Superior. Negra Modelo is a dark beer; it has the same alcohol content as the other beers. Some beer is drunk with lime juice and a salt-rimmed glass, or *michelada* with chilli sauce (both available in Oaxaca). Local wine is cheap and improving in quality; try Domecq, Casa Madero or Santo Tomás; the white sold in *ostionerías*, oyster restaurants, is usually good. Cetto Reisling Fumé has been recommended. The native drinks are *pulque*, the fermented juice of the agave plant (those unaccustomed to it should not over-indulge), *tequila*, made mostly in Jalisco, and *mezcal* from Oaxaca; also distilled from agave plants. *Mezcal* usually has a *gusano de maguey* (worm) in the bottle, considered by Mexicans to be a particular delicacy. Tequila and *mezcal* rarely have an alcoholic content above 40-43%; tequila Herradura, Sauza and Cuervo have been recommended. Also available is the Spanish aniseed spirit, *anís*, which is made locally. Imported whiskies and brandies are expensive. Rum is cheap and good. *Puro de caña* (called *chingre* in Chinanteca and *posh* in Chamula) is distilled from sugar cane, stronger than *mezcal* but with less taste; it is found in Oaxaca and Chiapas.

There are always plenty of non-alcoholic soft drinks (*refrescos*) and mineral water (bottled water is available throughout the country in small bottles or more economical large ones, which are useful to refill small ones). Fresh juices (as long as they aren't mixed with unpurified water) and milk shakes (*licuados*) are good and usually safe. If you don't like to drink out of a glass ask for a straw, *popote*. Herbal teas, for example chamomile and mint (*manzanilla* and *hierba buena*), are readily available.

Mexico

Shopping

Artesanía in Mexico is an amalgam of ancient and modern design. The stronger influence, however, is undoubtedly the traditional popular art forms of indigenous communities the length and breadth of the country, which pour into colonial towns such as Oaxaca, San Cristóbal, Pátzcuaro, and Uruapan. These are convenient market centres for seeing the superb range of products from functional pots to scary masks hanging over delicately embroidered robes and gleaming lacquered chests.

Crafts
Wandering around the colourful markets and artesanía shops is one of the highlights of any visit to Mexico

Weaving and textile design go back a long way in Mexico and the variety on offer is enormous. Textiles can be spun in cotton or wool on the traditional *telar de cintura*, a 'waist loom', or *telar de pie*, a pedal-operated loom introduced by the Spanish. Many woven items are on sale in the markets, from sarapes and *morrales* (shoulder bags) to wall-hangings, rugs and bedspreads. Synthetic fibres are often used too, so make sure you know what you're getting before you buy.

Textiles

Textile art is heavily influenced by religious ritual, particularly dances to master natural forces, but as well as being impressively robed, priests, witches and shamans are often masked in the guise of animals such as eagles, jaguars, goats, monkeys, and coyotes, particularly in the states of Guerrero (for example in Chilapa), Sinaloa, Sonora and Nayarit.

Masks

Ceramics are generally crafted out of baked clay or plaster and are polished or glazed or polychrome. In some parts such as Michoacán men paint the pieces but in the main pot-making is done by women. Some of the best pots have a brilliant glaze such as the Patambán pottery found in Michoacán and on sale in Uruapan. The green finish comes from the oxidization of copper while its fragility comes from 'eggshell' thin clay working. Also outstanding is the *bandera* pottery of Tonalá (Jalisco) decorated in the Mexican national colours.

Ceramics
The variety of wonderful folk art on offer is mindboggling

For silver and gold work, known as *orfebrería*, look under Taxco and the markets in Mexico City. Jade jewellery is made in Michoacán while semi-precious stones such as onyx, obsidian, amethyst and turquoise are found in Oaxaca, Puebla, Guerrero, Zacatecas and Querétaro.

Silver & gold

Holidays and festivals

Sunday is a statutory holiday. Saturday is also observed as a holiday, except by the shops. There is no early-closing day. National holidays are as follows:

New Year: 1 January; Constitution Day: 5 February; Birthday of Benito Juárez: 21 March; Maundy Thursday; Good Friday and Easter Saturday; Labour Day: 1 May; Battle of Puebla: 5 May; *El Informe* (Presidential Message): 1 September; Independence Day: 16 September; *Día de la Raza* (Discovery of America): 12 October; Day of the Revolution: 20 November; Christmas Day: 25 December.

The Mexican calendar of religious fiestas lists over 5,000 each year – roughly 10 pages in this book. The most widely celebrated are: *Santos Reyes*: 6 January; Mother's Day: 10 May; All Souls' Day: 1-2 November; Our Lady of Guadalupe: 12 December.

Sport and special interest travel

Mexico's massive coastline of reefs and swells and expanse of mountain ranges cut by long rivers make it very well suited to outdoor adventure. There is an adventure tourism organization in Mexico City, the Associación Mexicana de Turismo de Aventura y Ecoturismo (AMTAVE), Insurgentes Sur 1981-251, Colonia Guadalupe Inn, Mexico DF.

Aerial sports There are some agencies that specialize in aerial sports. See under 'Specialists in adventure tourism' under the Directory for Mexico City. **Guanajuato**, **Valle de Bravo** (for hang-gliding), and **Hidalgo** state are most often the backdrop.

Canyoning Rappel, or abseiling, is often the only way to reach some sites so canyoning is frequently a part of any trip. Two of the best locations for this new sport are the **Cañadas de Cotlamani**, near Jalcomulco in Veracruz and in the **Cumbres de Monterrey National Park**, the *Recorrido de Matacanes* circuit based on the **Cascada Lagunillas** and a circuit spilling out from the Cascada El Chipitín, known locally as *Recorrido Hidrofobia*.

Caving Caving, or speleology, in Mexico is more than just going down into deep dark holes. Sometimes it is a sport more closely related to canyoning as there are some excellent underground river scrambles. The best of these is probably the 8-km-long Chontalcuatlán, a part of the Cacahuamilpa cave system near Taxco. There is an underground lagoon here in Zacatecolotla cave. Beside the Matacanes river circuit in Nuevo León (see Canyoning) there are some large caves, the *Grutas de La Tierrosa*, *La Cebolla* and *Pterodáctilo*.

For purist potholers there are many vertical caves or *sótanos* (cellars) such as *El Jabalí*, *El Nogal* and *Tilaco* in the Sierra Gorda de Querétaro and *La Purificación* near Ciudad Victoria. The biggest cave systems are in Chiapas especially around Tuxtla Gutiérrez. One of the best elsewhere is the Sótano de las Golondrinas on the Santa María river, San Luis Potosí (see rafting), but perhaps the most challenging is Pozo Verde, 1,070m deep, near Ocotempa, Puebla.

Climbing
Snow climbing is known as 'Alta Montaña' here

The big glaciated volcanoes are within relatively easy reach of Mexico City and climbing them is the best way to get above the throng. Although there are few technical routes, crampons, ice-axe and occasionally rope are required for safe ascents. The season is October to May.

Now that Popocatépetl (5,452 m) and Colima Volcano (3,842 m) are sporadically erupting (although it may still be possible to climb **El Nevado** 4,339 m, behind Colima Volcano), the two remaining high-altitude challenges are **Pico de Orizaba** (Citlatépetl 5,760 m, Mexico's highest volcano) and **Iztaccíhuatl** (5,286 m, the best technical climbing with great views over 'Popo').

Two good acclimatization climbs before attempting these 5,000-m plus peaks are **Cofre de Perote** (Nouhcampatépetl 4,282 m) and **Nevado de Toluca** (Xinantécatl, 4,558 m). Further afield, near Tapachula in Chiapas, **Volcán Tacaná** (4,150 m) is a worthwhile but little-climbed mountain.

Rock climbing is an increasingly popular sport for Mexicans and there is good to great climbing in most parts of the country. Specialist opportunities can be found near Pueblo Viejo and also in the area surrounding Creel, in Chihuahua.

Diving This is practised off most of Mexico's coastline but two regions, **Quintana Roo** and **Baja California** at opposite ends of the country, are particularly noteworthy. The first offers warm water reefs close to the shore and visibility of over 30 m. Southern Baja has adventurous diving in deep waters.

Cozumel, in Quintana Roo, has some of the best diving in the world and there are marine parks at Chankanaab and at Palancar Reef with numerous caves and gullies and a horseshoe-shaped diving arena. Also excellent on the west side of the island are Santa Rosa and sites off San Francisco beach. To the southwest are good sites off Laguna Colombia, while off Punta Sur there is excellent deep diving. There is concern, however, over the damage to the reef inflicted by the new cruise ship pier, and more of these piers are planned. At Isla Mujeres, also in Quintana Roo, the most dived sites include Los Manchones, La Bandera, a shallow dive south of the island, and El Frío, a deep wreck an hour and a half to the north.

The variety in Mexico's rafting rivers opens the activity up to all types of traveller. The attraction is not just the run but the trek or rappel to the start and the moments between rapids, drifting in deep canyons beneath hanging tropical forests, some of which contain lesser-known and quite inaccessible ruins. For sheer thrills many of the best are in the centre of the country. **Rafting**

The most popular is the **Río Antigua/Pescados** in Veracruz. The upper stretch, the Antigua, has some good learning rapids (Grade II) running into Grade III, but, if you have more than one day, the Pescados (the lower Antigua), nearer to Jalcomulco, can give a bigger adrenalin rush with some Grade IV whitewater. The biggest rush in the country, however, is on the **Barranca Grande** and at **Cañón Azul** where there is excellent quality Grade V water – ouch. To complete the pre-eminence of **Veracruz** as a rafting destination is the **Filo-Bobos.** The Alto Filo (Grades IV and V) and the 25-km-long Tlapacoyan to Palmilla stretch, halfway along which the Bobos enters the Filo, are the areas of most interest to rafter-archaeologists.

Rafting in **Chiapas** covers the spectrum from sedate drifting on rivers such as the Lacan-Há through the Lacandón jungle to Grade IV and V rapids on the Río Jataté, which gathers force where the Lacan Tum enters it and gradually diminishes in strength as it nears the Río Usumacinta.

The season for whitewater rafting is generally July to September in the centre, when rivers are fuller, but in Chiapas, January and February are preferred because the climate is cooler.

This requires no special prior expertise and you can usually take off on your own in quiet waters for day trips. The simplest kayaks are more like rafts and have no open compartments that you need to worry about flooding. Agencies will assess your experience when renting out more advanced equipment and for longer periods. **Sea kayaking**

The warm waters of the **Sea of Cortés** off Baja California Sur are kayak heaven. **Isla Espíritu Santo** and **Isla Partida** are easily accessible from La Paz and whether in or out of your kayak you can experience a wild party of stingrays, sea-lions, dolphins, porpoises and occasionally grey whales and hammerheads.

Another good spot for kayaking is in the **Bahía de Sayulita** just north of Puerto Vallarta and around the nearby **Islas Marietas**.

There are resort-based sports fishing fleets along much of Mexico's Pacific coast, from **Acapulco** to **Bahía Kino**, where there is a tournament at the end of June-beginning of July. There is also a tournament in **Manzanillo** in February. **Sports fishing**

Some of the world's most exhilarating surfing can be experienced along Mexico's Pacific coast. The highlights are the huge Hawaiian-size surf that pounds the **Baja** shoreline and the renowned **'Mexican Pipeline'** at **Puerto Escondido**. There are numerous possibilities, ranging from developed beaches to remote bays accessible only by four-wheel drive vehicles. Many are to be found at the estuaries of rivers where sandbars are deposited and points are formed. It is impossible to name all the good beaches; the following is a selection starting in the north. **Surfing**

The alleged longest break in the world is at Bahía de Matanchén beside San Blas

Isla de Todos Santos in front of Ensenada has big swells. It is much frequented by US surfers and is best in winter. A wetsuit is usually necessary when surfing in Baja.

Mazatlán is the point on the mainland where currents escape the shielding effects of the peninsula and surfing is possible. As the geographical centre point on Mexico's surfing coast it has been chosen as home to the Surfing Association, PO Box 310. In front of the town Isla de la Piedra is good along with Playa Cerritos just north of the town and also **El Caimanero** and near **Teacapan**, 100 km to the south. **San Blas** is an excellent learning centre. The waves are normally not too big and there are few rocks or dangerous currents. Surfing is best in the spring and summer, particularly between July and October.

Trekking   The **Copper Canyon** is a vast wilderness for trekking. Creel is the obvious base but an excellent trek is from Batópilas to Urique – three days in the heat of the *barranca*, through Tarahumara lands – no better way to experience the abyss after you have spent a day or two wondering, from a *mirador* on its rim, what it is like down there. Be careful about where you camp. Ask landowners' permission and don't slow down too much should you stumble across a marijuana plantation.

Best trekking within easy reach of a major city is from Monterrey, particularly in the **Cumbres de Monterrey National Park**. There are several organizations in Mexico City that arrange weekend mountain hiking excursions.

One of the attractions of more remote trekking – in the states of **Oaxaca** and **Nayarit**, for example – is to visit indigenous communities such as Cora and Huichol villages. However, one should be sensitive to local reaction to tourist intrusion. Baja California's petroglyph cave sites can often only be visited on foot, which adds to the mystical experience, but here too remember that most sites are sacred and you should be accompanied by a guide. Seek advice before trekking in **Chiapas** and **Guerrero**, both hideouts for rebel groups, with the hefty military presence that goes with them.

National parks

Mexico is the world's third most biologically diverse country, behind only Brazil and Colombia. It boasts between 21,600 and 33,000 of the 250,000-odd known species of higher plants (including 150 conifers, and around 1,000 each of ferns, orchids, and cacti), 693-717 reptiles (more than any other country), 436-455 mammals (second only to Indonesia), 283-289 amphibians (fourth in the world), 1,018 birds, 2,000 fish, and hundreds of thousands of insect species. Five Mexican vertebrates (all birds) have become extinct in the 20th century, and about 35 species are now only found in other countries; 1,066 of around 2,370 vertebrates are listed as threatened.

This is of course an immense country, with an immense range of habitats and wildlife; the far south is in the Neotropical kingdom, with a wealth of tropical forest species, while the far north is very much part of the Nearctic kingdom, with typically North American species, and huge expanses of desert with unique ecosystems. The greater part of the country is a transition zone between the two kingdoms, with many strange juxtapositions of species that provide invaluable information to scientists, as well as many endemic species. Many of these sites are now protected, but are often of little interest except to specialists; what's more Mexico's National Parks per se were set up a long time ago primarily to provide green recreation areas for city dwellers; they are generally small and often now planted with imported species such as eucalyptus, and thus of no biological value. However the country does also have a good number of Biosphere Reserves, which are both of great biological value and suitable for tourism.

Starting in the far south, in Chiapas, **El Triunfo Biosphere Reserve** protects Mexico's only cloud forest, on the mountains (up to 2,750 m) above the Pacific coast; the main hiking route runs from Jaltenango (reached by bus from Tuxtla) to Mapastepec on the coastal highway. Groups need to book in advance through the state's Institute of Natural History, on Calzada de Hombres de la Revolución, by the botanical garden and Regional Museum (Apdo 391, Tuxtla 29000; T(961) 612-3663, F(961) 612-9943, ihnreservas@laneta.apc.org).

From Jaltenango you need to hike or hitch a ride about 29 km to Finca Prusia and then follow a good muletrack for three hours to the El Triunfo campamento (1,650 m). There are endemic species here, including the very rare azure-rumped tanager; the horned guan is found here and across the border in the adjacent mountains of Guatemala. Other wildlife includes the quetzal, harpy eagles, jaguars, tapirs, and white-lipped peccary.

Turn left in the clearing for the route down to Tres de Mayo, 25 km away; this is an easy descent of five hours to a pedestrian suspension bridge on the dirt road to Loma Bonita. From here you should take a pick-up to Mapastepec, 25 km away.

Also in Chiapas is the immense **Selva Lacandona**, supposedly protected by the Azules Biosphere Reserve but in reality still being eaten away by colonization and logging. New plant species and even families are still being discovered in this rainforest, best visited either from the Bonampak and Yaxchilán ruins, or by the road/boat route via Pico de Oro and Flor de Café to Montebello.

In the Yucatán the **Sian Ka'an Biosphere Reserve** is one of the most visited in Mexico, being just south of Cancún; it's a mixture of forest, savanna and mangrove swamp, best visited on a day-trip run by Los Amigos de Sian Ka'an at Av Cobá 5, third floor, offices 48-50, Apdo 770, Cancún T(998) 884-9583, F(998) 887-3080, sian@cancun.rce.com.mx. *Sian Ka'an Information Centre* in Tulum (Av Tulum between Satelite and Geminis, T/F(984) 871-2363, siankaan_tours@hotmail.com), has information about visiting the reserve and several other areas of interest. It is also well worth visiting the **Río Lagartos** and **Río Celestún** reserves on the north and west coasts of Yucatán, well known for their flamingos. The **Calakmul Biosphere Reserve** is important mainly for its Mayan ruins, seeming to the layman more like scrub than forest.

Across the country's centre is the Transversal Volcanic Belt, one of the main barriers to Nearctic and Neotropic species; it's easiest to head for the **Parque Nacional Izta-Popo** (from Amecameca), the **Parque Nacional Zoquiapan** (on the main road to Puebla) or the **Parque Nacional El Tepozteco** (on the main road to Cuernavaca), and naturally the volcanoes themselves are well worth climbing.

Only small areas of the northern deserts and sierras are formally protected. The most accessible areas are in Durango state, including **La Michilía Biosphere Reserve**, with pine, oak and red-trunked Arbutus and Arctostaphylus trees typical of the Sierra Madre Occidental. A daily bus runs to San Juan de Michis, and you should get off at a T-junction 2 km before the village and walk west, first getting permission from the Jefe de Unidad Administrativo, Instituto de Ecología, Apdo 632, 34000 Durango T(618) 812 1483; their offices are at Km 5 on the Mazatlán highway. The **Mapimí Biosphere Reserve** covers an area of desert matorral (scrub) that receives just 200 mm of rain a year; it lies to the east of Ceballos, on the Gómez Palacio-Ciudad Jiménez highway. In addition to many highly specialized bushes and cacti, this is home to giant turtles, now in enclosures at the Laboratory of the Desert.

There is a great variety of protected areas in Baja California, all of considerable biological value: the highest point (3,000 m) is the **Sierra de San Pedro Mártir**, in the north, which receives plenty of precipitation and has largely Californian fauna and flora. A dirt road starts at the Puente San Telmo, on the main road down the west coast, and leads almost 100 km to an astronomical observatory. Desert environments are, of course, unavoidable here, with 80 endemic cacti: the **Gran Desierto del Altar** is a dry lunar landscape, best seen from the main road along the US border, while the **El Vizcaíno Biosphere Reserve** protects a huge area of central Baja, characterized by agaves and drought-resistant scrub. However the main reason for stopping here is to see the migration of the grey whale to its breeding grounds. In the far south, the **Sierra de La Laguna** boasts a unique type of cloud forest, with several endemic species; to get here you have to cross about 20 km of desert from just south of Todos Santos to La Burrera, and then follow a trail for 11 km to a rangers' campamento at about 1,750 m.

Limited information on National Parks and Biosphere Reserves can be had from SEDESOL (Ministry of Social Development), Av Revolución 1425, Mexico DF (Barranca del Muerto metro), where you'll also find the National Institute of Ecology (INE), for more general information on conservation; their publications are stocked by the Librería Bonilla, nearby at Francia 17.

Non-governmental conservation organizations include Naturalia (Apdo Postal 21541, 04021 México DF; T(55) 5674-6678, F(55) 5674-5294), and Pronatura (Asociación Mexicano por la Conservación de la Naturaleza, Av Nuevo León 144, Col Hipódromo Condesa, México DF, T(55) 5286-9642).

Mexico

Health

The Social Security hospitals are restricted to members, but will take visitors in emergencies; they are more up to date than the Centros de Salud and Hospitales Civiles found in most centres, which are very cheap and open to everyone. There are many homeopathic physicians in all parts of Mexico. You are recommended to use bottled or mineral water for drinking, except in hotels, which normally provide purified drinking water free.

Advisable to vaccinate against hepatitis, typhoid, paratyphoid and poliomyelitis if visiting the low-lying tropical zones, where there is also some risk of malaria. Dengue fever is spreading in Mexico so seek advice on where the Aedes mosquito is present and protect yourself against being bitten. Note also that cholera is on the rise. Hepatitis is a problem in Mexico and, if you have not been vaccinated, gamma globulin is available at better pharamacies/chemists. Locals recommend *Imecol* for 'Montezuma's Revenge' (the very common diarrhoea).

Mexico City

Colour map 3, grid B4
Population:
approx 20 mn
Altitude: 2,240 m

Although very little remains of the ancient Aztec capital, the island city of Tenochtitlán that ruled the Central Highlands for a couple of hundred years, the city that has replaced it is equally impressive. Founded by the Spaniards in 1521, Mexico City is colourful, bawdy, gaudy, vibrant, cultured, noisy, sometimes dangerous, and always fascinating – a celebration of humanity, good and bad.

One of the largest cities in the world, the Ciudad de México, Distrito Federal, or DF as it is often called, needs some time to do it justice, especially the Centro Histórico. Monumental architecture, magnificent church interiors, museums and vibrant pulsating murals full of the optimism of the post-Revolution period, invite you to drift around savouring the delights (and unfortunately, the pollution) of this vast metropolis. There is music, dance and theatre in parks and plazas round every corner and, beyond the city centre, you can explore San Angel, Coyoacán, Xochimilco and the Villa de Guadalupe.

Ins and outs

Getting there
See also Transport, page 130

Mexico City is well served by air and road. The airport is 13 km east of the city centre. For details of international scheduled flights see Essentials, page 74, and for airport information see page 133. Domestic flights go to all major towns in Mexico. There are 4 long-distance bus terminals, north, south, east and west, divided, more or less, according to the regions they serve. The railway station is fairly central but there are currently no scheduled services.

Getting around

Traffic is congested and driving is best avoided if you have the option. The metro is straightforward, cheap and the most convenient form of public transport, see page 130. It is also less polluted than the alternatives, such as buses and taxis. The Centro Histórico is best managed on foot and most other sights are within easy walking distance of a metro station.

Orientation You will find, as you explore the city, that you use two thoroughfares more than any others. The most famous is **Paseo de la Reforma**, with a tree-shaded, wide centre section and two side lanes. From the west it skirts the north edge of the Bosque de Chapultepec and then runs diagonally northeast past the Centro Histórico and on towards the Basílica de Guadal0upe, still fairly wide but without side lanes. The other thoroughfare is **Av Insurgentes**, a diagonal north-south artery about 35 km long. Reforma and Insurgentes bisect at a *glorieta* (roundabout) with a statue of Cuauhtémoc, the last of the Aztec emperors. Other important thoroughfares are the **Eje Central** (**Lázaro Cárdenas**), which runs south to north only from the Circuito Interior (near the Olympic swimming pool) via Bellas Artes and the Latin American Tower, through Tlatelolco, past the Terminal del Norte (North Bus Terminal) and beyond; the **Calzada de Tlalpan**, which runs north-south from near the city centre, past the Terminal del Sur (South Bus Terminal) and leads out of the city towards Cuernavaca; the **Circuito Interior**, which encircles most of the city at an average distance of about 5 km from the centre; further out is the **Periférico**; and crossing from the east, near the airport, and joining the Periférico in the west is the **Viaducto Miguel Alemán**.

Maps Until they run out there is an excellent free pocket map available from Tourist Information booths – there's one on the northwest corner of the Zócalo. Good maps of the city from *Guía Roji* (an excellent A to Z, US$14), *Ciudad de México, mapa turístico* (Quimera Editores, 1999, 1:10,000, US$8.75), and *Trillas Tourist Guide* (US$6.50, recommended). Street vendors on Zócalo and in kiosks sell a large city map for US$3.

Metro stations have useful large-scale wall maps of the immediate vicinity

Specialized maps can be obtained from the Instituto Nacional de Estadística Geografía e Informática (INEGI), which sells maps and has information. You'll find it in the arcade below the traffic roundabout at Insurgentes (where the metro station is), all maps available, including topographical maps for trekking. ■ *Mon-Fri 0800-2000, Sat 0800-1600. La Rosa de los Vientos*, on Higuera, Coyoacán, in the south of the city, sells maps of all parts of the country.

Climate Spring is the hottest time of year, but because of the high altitude, the climate is usually mild and exhilarating save for a few days in mid-winter, when it can get quite cold. Even in summer the temperature at night is rarely above 13°C and in winter there can be sharp frosts. Despite this, central heating is not common. The normal annual rainfall is 660 mm and most of it falls, usually in the late afternoon, between May and Oct.

Students SETEJ (Mexican Students' Union), Hamburgo 301, Zona Rosa, metro Sevilla, issues student cards, required to buy hostel cards, T5211-0743 or 5211-6636, and deals with ISIS insurance. To obtain a national student card you need 3 photos, passport, confirmation of student status and US$7. ■ *Mon-Fri 0900-1800, Sat 0900-1400*. Most museums are free to students and teachers with ID.

Tourist offices The *Mexican Secretariat of Tourism* (Secretaría de Turismo) is at Masaryk 172, 5th floor, between Hegel and Emerson, Colonia Polanco (reached by bus No 32), T5250-8555, ext 116, F5254-2636, emergency hot line T5250-0123/0151, www.mexicocity.gob.mx The amount and quality of printed information available varies enormously, although it is possible to book hotels in other parts of the country.

Better information is available at tourist information centres operated by the Mexico City Government at several places throughout the city. There office is at Nuevo León 56, 9th floor, 06100. You may refer complaints here, or to the tourist police, in blue uniforms, who are reported to be very friendly. Bus and metro maps available. Information bureau outside Insurgentes metro station and on Juárez, just east of Paseo de la Reforma (closed Sun). Tourist information can be dialled on T5525-9380 between 0800 and 2000 (bilingual operator). For problems, eg theft, fraud, abuse of power by officials, call Protectur, T5516-0490. Also try the *Agencia Especializada en Asuntos de Turista*, Florencia 20, Col Juárez, English spoken, very helpful.

Safety, traffic and pollution As with any large city there are grounds for caution at times. Take care in the centre at quiet times (eg Sun afternoon) and in Chapultepec, where Sun is the safest day. At night you are advised to phone for a taxi.

The city lies in the Valley of Mexico, a huge basin roughly 110 km long by 30 km wide. Rimming this valley is a sentinel-like chain of peaks of the Sierra Nevada mountains. About one in five of Mexico's population live in this city, which has over half the country's manufacturing employment and much of the nation's industrial smog (the worst months being Dec-Feb). Closing a huge Pemex refinery has reduced lead and sulphur dioxide emissions to acceptable levels, but ozone levels are occasionally dangerous. Common ailments that creep up over hours or days are a burning sensation in the eyes (contact-lens wearers take note) and nose, and a sore throat. Citizens are advised by local authorities not to smoke and not to take outdoor exercise. The English-language daily *The News* gives analysis of air quality, with warnings and advice.

Mexico City

Mexico City

The city suffers from a fever of demolition and rebuilding, especially since the heavy damage caused by the 1985 earthquake. This was concentrated along the Paseo de la Reforma, Avenida Juárez, the Alameda, and various suburbs and residential districts. About 20,000 people are believed to have lost their lives, largely in multi-storey housing and government-controlled buildings, including 3,000 fatalities in Hospital Juárez.

Mexico City orientation

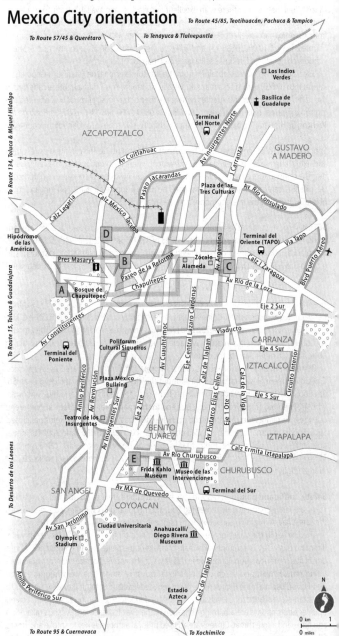

Related maps
A *Bosque de Chapultepec & Polanco*, page 108
B *Reforma & the Zona Rosa*, page 104
C *Centro Histórico: Zócalo & Alameda*, page 100
D *City Centre*, page 96
E *Coyoacán*, page 115

Mexico City has long burst its ancient boundaries and spread; some of the new residential suburbs are most imaginatively planned, though there are many appalling shanty-towns. Like all big centres it is faced with a fearsome traffic problem, despite the building of inner and outer ring roads (the Circuito Interior and the Periférico), and a nine-line metro service.

Central Mexico City

Starting at the Zócalo (main square) and the streets around it, and moving in the general direction of the west, to the Palacio de Bellas Artes, through the Alameda Central, down Reforma, skirting the Zona Rosa, the following route will eventually lead you Chapultepec Park, and, to the north of the park, the fashionable area of Polanco.

Sightseeing in and around the city can easily take up 10 days

Centro Histórico

Much of the Historical Centre has been refurbished; this is roughly a rectangle from Alhóndiga/Santísma, east of the Zócalo, to Guerrero, west of the Alameda; República de Honduras by Plaza Garibaldi, north of the Alameda, to Arcos de Belén/Izazaga south of the Alameda and Zócalo. Calle Tacuba is especially fine; street vendors have been banished from it. The *Guía Peatonal* of Sacbé (US$1.15) is recommended, giving eight suggested walking routes, all starting from metro stations. Two ways of familiarizing oneself quickly with the Centro Histórico are to take a trip (US$5 for 45 minutes) on a 1910-type street car (every 30 minutes from the Museo de la Ciudad de México, Pino Suárez, or from in front of the Palacio de Bellas Artes), or to ride on a form of rickshaw (*bici-taxi*) from the Zócalo, US$1.65 for 30 minutes.

Most museums and galleries are closed on Mondays

For details of museums and sights away from the centre, see pages 111-120

The great main square, or Plaza Mayor, centre of the oldest part, is always alive with people and often vivid with official ceremonies and celebrations, also with demonstrations and marches. The flag in the centre of the square is raised at 0600 (0500 in winter), and taken down, with ceremony, at 1800 (1700 in winter) on most days. On the north side, on the site of the Great Teocalli or temple of the Aztecs, is the cathedral.

Zócalo

This is the largest and oldest cathedral in Latin America. It was first built in 1525 and rebuilding began in 1573; it was consecrated in 1667 and finished in 1813. It is singularly harmonious considering the many architects employed and time taken to build it. Restoration work on the exterior has been completed but work continues inside. The cathedral has been subject to subsidence over many years and a lengthy programme of work is under way to build new foundations. A plumb line hanging from the cupola and a notice board by the west entrance give some idea of the extent of the problem. The massive scaffolding inside the cathedral serves as a preventive measure. There is an underground crypt reached by stairs in the west wing of the main part of the building (closed for restoration since 1993). Next to the cathedral is the **Sagrario Metropolitano**, 1769, with fine churrigueresque façade. Unlike the cathedral, it was built on the remains of an Aztec pyramid and is more stable than the former. ■ *Tourist information booth on northwest corner of Zócalo, with free city maps.*

Cathedral

To the side of the cathedral are the Aztec ruins of the **Templo Mayor** or *Teocalli*, which were discovered in 1978 when public works were being carried out. They make a very worthwhile visit, especially since the Aztecs built a new temple every 52 years, and seven have been identified on top of each other. The **Museo Arqueológico del Sitio** was opened in 1987 behind the temple to house various sculptures found in the main pyramid of Tenochtitlán and six others, including a huge, circular monolith representing the dismembered body of Coyolxauhqui, who was killed by her brother Huitzilopochtli, the Aztec tutelary god, and many other objects. The Templo Mayor and museum are at Seminario 4 y Guatemala, entrance in the northeast corner of the Zócalo. There is a café, bookshop and left-luggage

Templo Mayor

Mexico City

office. ■ *0900-1700 daily except Mon, last tickets at 1630, museum and temple US$2.20, free Sun, US$1.25 to take photos, US$3.00 to use video camera; guided tours in Spanish Tue-Fri 0930-1800, Sat 0930-1300, in English Tue-Sat 1000 and 1200, US$0.85 per person (sometimes cancelled at short notice), T5542-4784.*

Palacio Nacional The National Palace takes up the whole of the eastern side of the Zócalo. Built on the site of the Palace of Moctezuma and rebuilt in 1692 in colonial baroque, it has a façade of the red volcanic stone called *tezontle*; the top floor was added by President Calles in the 1920s. It houses various government departments. Over the central

Mexico City centre

door hangs the Liberty Bell, rung at 2300 on 15 September by the President, who commemorates Mexican Independence from Spain and gives the multitude the *Grito* – '¡Viva México!'

The staircase leading to the first floor of the inner courtyard and two of the walls of the first floor are decorated with frescoes by Diego Rivera. The right-hand panel on the staircase (1929) depicts pre-Hispanic Mexico; the large central panel (275.17 sq m and started 1929, finished 1935) shows the History of Mexico from 1521 to 1930 and the panel on the left is known as *El mundo de hoy y de mañana* (The

Mexico City

Related maps

Los Tres Grandes

The story of muralism in Mexico has largely been that of 'Los Tres Grandes', Diego Rivera, Jose Clemente Orozco and David Alfaro Siqueiros, although there were many other artists involved from the start. In 1914 Orozco and Siqueiros were to be found in the Carranza stronghold of Orizaba fomenting social and artistic revolution through the mouthpiece of the pamphlet La Vanguardia. Seven years later, out of the turmoil and divisiveness of the Revolution emerged a need for a visual expression of Mexican identity (mexicanidad) and unity, and in 1921 Orozco and Siqueiros answered the call of the Minister of Education, José Vasconcelos, to provide a visual analogue to a rapidly changing Mexico. Rivera was brought onto the team that in buildings like the National Preparatory School and the Ministry of Education, attempted to produce a distinctly Mexican form of modernism, on a monumental scale, accessible to the people. These were ideas forged in Orizaba and later clarified in Europe (where Rivera and Siqueiros saw Italian frescoes) but which derived their popular form from paintings on the walls of pulquerías and in the satirical broadsheet engravings of José Guadalupe Posada. Themes were to include

Pre-Columbian society, modern agriculture and medicine and a didactic Mexican history pointing to a mechanized future for the benefit of all. Siqueiros in particular was keen to transform the working practice of artists who would henceforth work as members of co-operatives.

The 'movement' fell apart almost from its inception. There were riots objecting to the communist content of murals and the beginnings of a long ideological and artistic disagreement between Siqueiros and Rivera, which would culminate on 28 August 1935 at the Palacio de Bellas Artes with Rivera, brandishing a pistol, storming into a Siqueiros lecture and demanding a debate on what the Mexican Mural Renaissance had all been about! The debate ensued over several days before they agreed to disagree.

Despite the failings of the 'movement' many outstanding murals were painted over a long period. With Siqueiros frequently off the scene, in jail or in exile, Los Tres Grandes became the big two; Rivera carving up much of Mexico City as his territory and Orozco taking on Guadalajara. However, Siqueiros outlasted both of them and carried the torch of Muralism and Revolution into the early 1970s. See also Mural sites, page 110.

World Today and Tomorrow, 1934). The first fresco (4.92 x 9.71 m) on the first floor is known variously as *La Gran Tenochtitlán* and *El mercado de Tlatelolco* (1945), and shows the market of Tlatelolco against a background of the ancient city of Tenochtitlán. There follow representations of various indigenous cultures – Purépecha, Mixteca-Zapoteca, Totonaca and Huasteca (the last showing the cultivation and worship of maize), culminating in the final fresco, which shows in narrative form the arrival of Hernán Cortés in Veracruz. These murals were done between 1942 and 1951. There are knowledgeable guides who speak English. They also sell postcards of the murals, but much better reproductions of the same works are available in most museums in the city. The Juárez Museum, which used to be on the first floor, has been moved to Avenida Higalgo 79.

On the first and second floors of the Palacio Nacional, on the left as one enters the great courtyard, an area formerly occupied by government offices has been transformed into elegant galleries open to the public housing temporary exhibitions. Across from the main entrance and beyond the courtyard is a pleasant open-air area that the public can also visit. **Museo de las Culturas**, Moneda 13, beind the Palacio Nacional holds exhibitions from countries worldwide and also has some historical information. ■ *Tue-Sun 1000-1700, closed Mon, free.*

The **Suprema Corte de Justicia de la Nación**, opposite Palacio Nacional, on the southeast corner of the Zócalo, has frescoes by Orozco (*National Riches* and *Proletarian Struggle*). ■ *Closes at 1400.* The ornate building in the southwest corner of the Zócalo is the **Antiguo Ayuntamiento** (City Hall), which is now used for ceremonial purposes and is where visiting dignitaries are granted the Keys of the City.

On the west side of the Zócalo are the Portales de los Mercaderes (Arcades of the Merchants), which have been very busy since they were built in 1524. North of them, opposite the cathedral, is the **Monte de Piedad** (National Pawnshop), established in the 18th century and housed in a 16th-century building. Prices are government controlled and bargains are often found. Auctions are held each Friday at 1000 (first, second and third Friday for jewellery and watches, fourth for everything else), US dollars accepted.

On Calle Justo Sierra, north of cathedral between Guatemala and San Ildefonso, is the **Mexican Geographical Society** (No 19), in whose courtyard is a bust of Humboldt and a statue of Benito Juárez, plus a display of documents and maps (ask at the door to be shown in); opposite are the **Anfiteatro Simón Bolívar**, with murals of his life in the lobby and an attractive theatre, and the former **Colegio San Ildefonso**, built in 1749 as the Jesuit School of San Ildefonso in splendid baroque style (it later became the Escuela Nacional Preparatoria). There are important frescoes by Orozco (including *Revolutionary Trinity* and *The Trench*) and, in the Anfiteatro Bolívar, by Diego Rivera (*Creation*) and Fernando Leal, all of which are in excellent condition. There is another Leal mural, *Lord of Chalma*, in the stairwell separating the two floors of Orozco works, as well as Jean Charlot's *Massacre in the Templo Mayor*. In a stairwell of the Colegio Chico there are experimental murals by Siqueiros. The whole interior has been magnificently restored. There are occasional important temporary exhibitions. More Orozco frescoes can be seen at the Biblioteca Iberoamericana on Cuba between República de Brasil and Argentina (for more information on the muralists and their work, see pages 98 and 110). Just along the road is the **Museo de la Caricatura**, Calle de Donceles 97. Housed in the former Colegio de Cristo, this collection includes works by contemporary cartoonists as well as the influential artist José Guadalupe Posada, famous for using skeletal images in his caricatures. ■ *Tue-Sun 1000-1800, US$0.70.*

North of the Zócalo

Mexico City

The **Secretaría de Educación Pública**, on Argentina 28, three blocks from the Zócalo, was built in 1922. It contains frescoes by a number of painters and includes some of Diego Rivera's masterpieces, painted between 1923 and 1928, illustrating the lives and sufferings of the common people, as well as satirising the rich. Look out for *Día de Muertos* (Day of the Dead) on the ground floor (far left in second courtyard) and, on the first floor, *El pan nuestro* (Our Daily Bread) showing the poor at supper, *El banquete de Wall Street* (The Wall Street Banquet), and the splendidly restored *La cena del capitalista* (The Capitalist's Supper). ■ *Daily 1000-1730, free.* A long passageway connects the Secretaría with the older Ex-Aduana de Santo Domingo where there is a dynamic Siqueiros mural, *Patriots and Parricides.* ■ *Mon-Sun 1100-1800, except Wed 1100-2100, US$2, Sun US$1.30.*

Plaza Santo Domingo, two blocks north of the cathedral, is an intimate little plaza surrounded by fine colonial buildings. There is the Antigua Aduana (former customs house) on the east side; the Portales de Santo Domingo, on the west side, where public scribes and owners of small hand-operated printing presses still carry on their business; the church of Santo Domingo, in Mexican baroque, 1737, on the north side (note the carving on the doors and façade); and the old Edificio de la Inquisición, where the tribunals of the Inquisition were held, at the northeast corner. By standing on tiptoe in the men's room one can see – if tall enough – through the window into the prison cells of the Inquisition, which are not yet open to the public. It became the Escuela Nacional de la Medicina and is now the **Museo de la Medicina Mexicana**, Brasil 33. There is a remarkable staircase in the patio and it also has a theatre.

Two blocks east of Santo Domingo are the church and convent of **San Pedro y San Pablo** (1603), both massive structures and now turned over to secular use. A block north is the Mercado Rodríguez, a public market with striking mural decorations.

The **Church of Loreto**, built 1816 and now tilting badly, but being restored, is on a square of the same name, surrounded by colonial buildings. Its façade is a remarkable example of 'primitive' or 'radical' neoclassicism.

La Santísima Trinidad (1677, remodelled 1755), a little further south, on Moneda, should be seen for its fine towers and the rich carvings on its façade. **Museo José Luis Cuevas**, Academia 13, in a large colonial building, houses a permanent collection of paintings, drawings and sculptures (one is two storeys high) by the controversial, contemporary Cuevas (**NB** the Sala Erótica), and temporary exhibitions. ■ *Tue-Fri 1000-1830, Sat-Sun 1000-1730, US$1.*

La Merced The **Mercado Merced** (metro Merced), said to be the largest market in all the Americas, dates back over 400 years. Its activities spread over several blocks and it is well worth a visit. In the northern quarter of this market are the ruins of La Merced monastery; the fine 18th-century patio is almost all that survives; the courtyard, on Avenida Uruguay, between Calle Talavera and Calle Jesús María, opposite No 171, is nearly restored. **Museo Legislativo** is inside the Palacio Legislativo on Avenida Congreso de la Unión 66, entrance in Sidar y Rivorosa, Metro Candelaria east of La Merced. It shows the development of the legislative processes in Mexico from

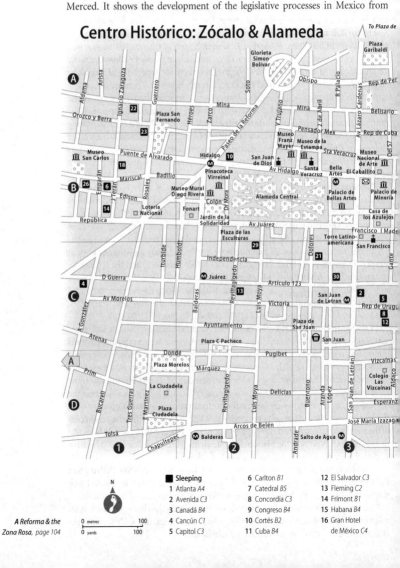

Centro Histórico: Zócalo & Alameda

A Reforma & the Zona Rosa, page 104

0 metres 100
0 yards 100

N

■ Sleeping	6 Carlton *B1*	12 El Salvador *C3*
1 Atlanta *A4*	7 Catedral *B5*	13 Fleming *C2*
2 Avenida *C3*	8 Concordia *C3*	14 Frimont *B1*
3 Canadá *B4*	9 Congreso *B4*	15 Habana *B4*
4 Cancún *C1*	10 Cortés *B2*	16 Gran Hotel
5 Capitol *C3*	11 Cuba *B4*	de México *C4*

pre-Hispanic times to the 20th century. ■ *1000-1800, closed Mon, free.*

Heading back towards the centre the oldest hospital in continental America, **Jesús Nazareno**, is at 20 de Noviembre 82. It was founded in 1526 by Cortés and was remodelled in 1928, save for the patio and staircase. Cortés's bones have been kept since 1794 in the adjoining church, on the corner of Pino Suárez and República de El Salvador, diagonally opposite the Museo de la Ciudad.

Museo de la Ciudad, on Avenida Pino Suárez and República de El Salvador, two blocks south of the Zócalo, shows the geology of the city and has life-size figures in period costumes showing the history of different peoples before Cortés. It also has a photographic exhibition of the construction of the metro system. The permanent exhibition is sometimes inaccessible during temporary shows. In the attic above the museum is the studio of Joaquín Clausell, with walls covered with impressionist miniatures. ■ *Tue-Thu, free.* Two blocks south of this museum at Mesones 139 is the **Anglican (Episcopal) Cathedral**, called the Catedral de San José de Gracia. Built in 1642 as a Roman Catholic church, it was given by the Benito Juárez government to the

Mexico City

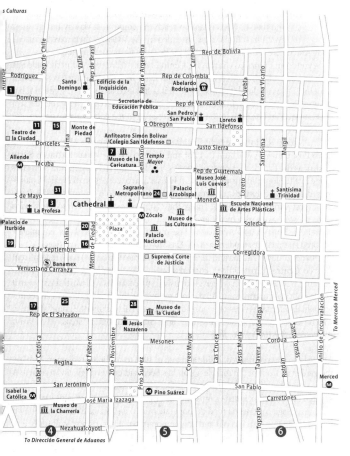

Episcopal Mission in Mexico. Juárez himself often attended services in it.

Further south, **Museo de la Charrería**, on Isabel la Católica and José María Izazaga, is close to metro Isabel la Católica. It is small, with interesting artefacts and history of the *charro*(Mexican cowoy). Information labels are in Spanish, English and French. ■ *Free.*

Zócalo to Alameda

Avenida Madero leads from the Zócalo west to the Alameda. On it is the late 16th-century **La Profesa** church with a fine high altar and a leaning tower. The 18th-century **Palacio de Iturbide**, Avenida Madero 17, once the home of Emperor Agustín (1821-23), has been restored and has a clear plastic roof. Wander around, it is now a bank head office. The **Museo Serfín**, Madero 33, displays indigenous costumes in two rooms. ■ *Tue-Sun 1000-1700. Free.*

The 16th-century **Casa de los Azulejos** (House of Tiles) is near the Alameda on Avenida Madero. It is brilliantly faced with blue and white 18th-century Puebla tiles. Occupied by the Zapatista army during the Revolution, it is now home to *Sanborn's Restaurant.* The staircase walls are covered with an Orozco fresco *Omniscience* (1925). Opposite is the **Church of San Francisco**, founded in 1525 by the 'Apostles of Mexico', the first 12 Franciscans to reach the country. It was by far the most important church in colonial days, attended by the Viceroys themselves. Cortés's body rested here for some time, as did the body of 'Emperor' Iturbide.

Beyond San Francisco church, Eje Central Lázaro Cárdenas, formerly Calle San Juan de Letrán, leads south towards **Colegio Las Vizcaínas**, at Plaza Las Vizcaínas, built in 1734 as a school for girls; some of it is still used as such, but some of it has become slum tenements. In spite of neglect, it is still the best example of colonial secular baroque architecture in the city. ■ *Not open to the public; permission to visit sometimes given.*

The **Museo Nacional de Arte**, Tacuba 8, is opposite Palacio de Minería, near the main Post Office. It was built in 1904 and designed by the Italian architect, Silvio Contri, as the Palacio de Comunicaciones. The building has magnificent staircases made by the Florentine firm Pignone. It houses a large collection of Mexican paintings, drawings, sculptures and ceramics dating from the 16th century to 1950. It has the largest number of paintings (more than 100) by José María Velasco in Mexico City, as well as works by Miguel Cabrera, Gerardo Murillo, Rivera, Orozco, Siqueiros, Tamayo and Anguiano. The museum building has been completely restored and facilities modernized. ■ *Tue-Sun 1030-1730. US$2, Sun free.*

On the corner of Tacuba and the Eje Central (Lázaro Cárdenas) is the magnificent **Correo Central** (Post Office), commissioned 1902, completed 1907. The whole building, inside and out, has been gloriously restored, and is well worth a visit even if you are not posting anything. Apart from examining the headings above each counter (which refer to services of bygone days) do not fail to climb the grand staircase, which leads to the postal museum and other exhibition areas. ■ *Mon-Fri 0900-1800, Sat 1000-1400, free.*

Palacio de Bellas Artes

The fresco by Rivera is a copy of the one rubbed out in disapproval at Radio City, New York

The Palacio was refurbished, inside and out, in 1994 to celebrate its diamond jubilee; the garden in front of the marble apron has been laid out as originally designed. A large, showy building, interesting for Art Deco lovers (see the fabulous stained-glass skylight in the roof), it houses a museum, theatre, a *cafetería* at mezzanine level (light, serving average continental food at moderate prices) and an excellent bookshop on the arts. The museum has old and contemporary paintings, prints, sculptures, and handicrafts. There are spirited Riveras in the room of oils and watercolours. Other frescoes are by Orozco, Tamayo and Siqueiros. ■ *Tue-Sun 1000-1800, closed Mon, US$2, free Sun and with ISIC.* There are also prestigious temporary fine art exhibitions (no extra charge). On the top floor is a museum of architecture, which holds temporary exhibitions and and shows the building's history. The most remarkable thing about the theatre is its glass curtain designed by Tiffany. It is solemnly raised and lowered before each performance of the Ballet Folclórico de México. The Palacio is listing

badly, for it has sunk 4 m since it was built. Operas are performed and there are frequent orchestral concerts. ■ *Performances by the **Ballet Folclórico de México** are on
Sun 0930 and 2030, and on Wed at 2030 (check press for details or call T5521-9251); you
must book in advance. Tickets US$22 on the balcony, US$33 and US$39 (cheap balcony
seats have blocked views). Tickets are on sale from 1100; hotels, agencies, etc only sell the
most expensive; cheaper tickets only at the theatre. Concessions of 50% are available for
students and teachers (show documents at counter on right before going to the box office).
There are cheap concerts at 1200 on Sunday.*

Across the road is the **Torre Latinoamericana**, which has a viewing platform with
telescopes on the 44th floor. ■ *0930-2230, US$4.50 to go up.* This great glass tower
dominates the gardens of the **Alameda Central**, once the Aztec market and later the
place of execution for the Spanish Inquisition. Beneath the broken shade of eucalyptus, cypress and ragged palms, wide paths link fountains and heroic statues. It
became a popular area for all social classes to stroll casually in the 19th century. It is
now much more a common thoroughfare, with many temporary stalls at certain festive times of year. On Sunday afternoons it is a popular walking-place for young
women in domestic service. The park is illuminated at night. There is much rebuilding going on in this area, which was badly affected by the 1985 earthquake.

The Alameda

Along the south side of the Alameda runs Avenida Juárez, a broad street with a
mixture of old and new buildings. Opposite the Palacio de Bellas Artes is a building
known as **La Nacional**, which was Mexico City's first skyscraper in the 1930s. Look
carefully at its perpendicularity, a result of the 1985 earthquake.

Also on the south side of the Alameda is the **Hemiciclo a Juárez**, designed by
Guillermo de Heredia in white marble, inaugurated in 1910 to mark the centenary of
Independence. Opposite, the colonial church of Corpus Christi is used to display and
sell folk arts and crafts. Further west a sunken section of the pavement shelters the
Plaza de las Esculturas (1998), with 19th-century sculptures. A stroll down Calle
Dolores, a busy and fascinating street, leads to the market of San Juan. Three blocks
west, on Plaza Ciudadela, is a large colonial building, **La Ciudadela**, dating from 1700.
It has been used for all kinds of purposes but is now a library. On the other side of the
Plaza, the **Mercado de la Ciudadela** sells crafts from all over Mexico.

Diego Rivera's huge (15 m by 4.80 m) and fascinating mural, the *Sueño de una
Tarde Dominical en la Alameda Central*, was removed from the earthquake-dam-
aged *Hotel del Prado* on Avenida Juárez in 1985 and now occupies its own purpose-built museum, the **Museo Mural Diego Rivera**, on the north side of the Jardín
de la Solidaridad at the west end of the Alameda Central. One of Rivera's finest
works, it presents a pageant of Mexican history from the Conquest up to the 1940s
with vivid portraits of national and foreign figures, heroes and villains as well as
characters from everyday life. It is highly recommended. ■ *Tue-Sun 1000-1800,
US$1, free for students with ISIC card.*

Around the corner from the Museo Mural, on Dr Mora, 7, is the **Pinacoteca
Virreinal**, in the former church of San Diego (1621), a gallery containing colonial
and religious paintings of the 16th-18th centuries. ■ *Tue-Sun 1000-1800. Free.*

On the northern side of the Alameda, on Avenida Hidalgo, is the Jardín Morelos,
flanked by two old churches: **Santa Veracruz** (1730) to the right and **San Juan de
Dios** to the left. The latter has a richly carved baroque exterior; its image of San
Antonio de Padua is visited by those who are broken-hearted from love. The **Museo
Franz Mayer** is located next to this church, in the former Hospital de San Juan de
Dios, which was built in the 17th century. Recently rebuilt and exquisitely restored,
it houses a library and an important decorative arts collection of ceramics, glass, silver, timepieces, furniture and textiles, as well as Mexican and European paintings
from the 16th-20th centuries. Its cloister, with a pleasant *cafetería*, is an oasis of
peace in the heart of the city. ■ *1000-1700 Tue-Sun; US$1.50 (US$0.30 if only visiting the cloister), T5518-2265.* On the same side of Hidalgo, next to the Franz Mayer,
is the **Museo de la Estampa** (Museum of Engraving). ■ *1000-1700 (closed Mon),*

Mexico City

US$1.50. A little further west, just before Metro Hidalgo, is the former Augustine Hospice (1780) of Santo Tomás de Villanueva, now the **Hotel Cortés**.

North of the Alameda

Plaza Garibaldi

On one side of Plaza Garibaldi is a gigantic and very entertaining eating hall; different stalls sell different courses

About four blocks north of the post office off Eje Central Lázaro Cárdenas is Plaza Garibaldi, a must, especially on Friday and Saturday night, when up to 200 *mariachis* in their traditional costume of huge sombrero, tight silver-embroidered trousers, pistol and *sarape*, will play your favourite Mexican serenade for US$5 (for a bad one) to US$10 (for a good one). If you arrive by taxi you will be besieged. The whole square throbs with life and the packed bars are cheerful. The **Lagunilla** market is held about four blocks northeast of the plaza, a hive of activity particularly on Sundays.

Plaza de las Tres Culturas

Take Metro line 3 to Tlatelolco

You may want to combine this with a visit to the Basílica de Guadalupe, see page 119, just a bit further north

Further north still Lázaro Cárdenas leads to Santa María la Redonda, at the end of which is Plaza Santiago de Tlaltelolco, next oldest plaza to the Zócalo. Here was the main market of the Aztecs, and on it, in 1524, the Franciscans built a huge church and convent. This is now known as the Plaza de las Tres Culturas, which shows elements of Aztec, colonial and modern architecture. The Aztec ruins have been restored and the magnificent Franciscan church of Santiago Tlaltelolco, completed 1609, is now the focus of the massive, multi-storey Nonoalco-Tlatelolco housing scheme (heavily damaged in the 1985 earthquake), a garden city within a city, with pedestrian and wheeled traffic entirely separate. In October 1968, the Plaza de las Tres Culturas was the scene of serious disturbances between the authorities and

Reforma & The Zona Rosa

Related maps
A Centro Histórico: Zócalo & Alameda, page 100
B Bosque de Chapultepec & Polanco, page 108

0 metres 200
0 yards 200

■ **Sleeping**
1 Casa González *B3*
2 Imperial *A6*
3 María Cristina *B4*
4 Suites Amberes *D3*

5 Suites Havre *C4*
6 Uxmal *A5*
7 Viena *C5*

Mexico City

students, in which a large number of students were killed (see *The Other Mexico* by Octavio Paz, or *La Noche de Tlatelolco* by Elena Poniatowska, Biblioteca Era, 1971 – *Massacre in Mexico* in English – and the very readable, and startling, *68* by Paco Ignacio Taibo II, 1991, in Spanish).

From Plaza de las Tres Culturas return south along Reforma. At the corner of Juárez and Reforma is the Lotería Nacional building. Draws are held three times a week, at 2000: an interesting scene, open to the public. Also at this site is a large yellow sculpture known as **El Caballito** after the original equestrian statue that stands in front of the Palacio de Minería.

West of the Alameda

Beyond Plaza de la Reforma is the **Monumento a la Revolución**, a great copper dome, soaring above supporting columns set on the largest triumphal arches in the world. Beneath the monument is the **Museo Nacional de la Revolución**, which deals with the period 1867-1917, is very interesting and has lots of exhibits, original photographs and videos. ■ *Tue-Sun 1000-1700, US$1.50.*

The Museo de San Carlos, Puente de Alvarado 50 (Metro Revolución), a 19th-century palace, has fine Mexican colonial painting and a first-class collection of European paintings. It is the former home of Señora Calderón de la Barca who wrote *Life in Mexico* while living there. ■ *Closed Tue, US$2.* It can be reached by crossing Reforma near Metro Hidalgo.

Santa María la Ribera & San Cosme

These are two wards north of Metro San Cosme, which became fashionable residential areas in the late 19th century, and many elegant, if neglected façades are to be seen. On the corner of Ribera de San Cosme and Naranjo next to San Cosme metro note the **Casa de los Mascarones**. Built in 1766, this was the country house of the Conde del Valle de Orizaba, later the Escuela Nacional de Música. Recently restored, it now houses a university computer centre. The **Museo Universitario del Chopo**, Enrique González Martínez 10 is between Metro San Cosme and Av Insurgentes Norte. It holds contemporary international photography and art exhibitions in a church-like building designed by Eiffel. ■ *Wed-Sun 1000-1400, 1600-1900.* In the pleasant **Alameda de Santa María**, between Pino and Torres Bodet, stands an extraordinary Moorish pavilion designed by Mexicans for the Paris Exhibition in 1889. On its return to Mexico, the *kiosko* was placed in the Alameda Central before being transferred to its present site in 1910. On the west side of this square, on Torres Bodet, is the **Museo del Instituto Geológico**; apart from its collection of fossils and minerals (and magnificent early 20th-century showcases), the

Mexico City

building itself (1904) is worth a visit for its swirling wrought-iron staircases and unusual stained-glass windows of mining scenes by Zettler (Munich and Mexico). ■ *Tue-Sun 1000-1700, free.*

Parque Sullivan Popularly known as Jardín del Arte, Parque Sullivan is reached by going up Paseo de la Reforma to the intersection with Insurgentes, and then west two blocks between Calle Sullivan and Calle Villalongín. Here, each Sunday afternoon, there is a display of paintings, engravings and sculptures near the Monumento a La Madre, packed with sightseers and buyers; everything is for sale.

Paseo de la Reforma

The wide and handsome Paseo de la Reforma continues to the Bosque de Chapultepec. It is lined with shops, offices, hotels, restaurants and some striking modern buildings: the *Hotel Crowne Plaza*, the Mexican Stock Exchange (*Bolsa de Valores*) and the *Hotel María Cristina*, as well as a red-and-black cuboid office structure on the left. Along it are monuments to Columbus, Cuauhtémoc and, at the intersection with Tiber/Florencia, a 45-m marble column supports the golden form of a female angel representing Independence. Known as 'El Angel' or 'El Angelito' to the Mexicans, the statue fell to the ground in the 1956 earthquake. This is a favourite spot for demonstrations, sporting and national celebrations. One block north of Reforma, the **Museo Carranza**, Lerma y Amazonas, is a museum with items linked to the life of this revolutionary and constitutionalist, and to the Revolution itself. Worth a visit. And, just south of Reforma, the **Museo de Cera de la Ciudad de México** (Wax Museum) is in a remarkable house at Londres 6. ■ *1100-1900 daily.*

Zona Rosa The famous **Zona Rosa** (Pink Zone) lies to the south of Reforma, bounded approximately by Reforma, Sevilla, Avenida Chapultepec and Insurgentes Sur. This was formerly the setting for Mexico City's most fashionable stores, restaurants and nightclubs. It suffered considerable damage in the 1985 earthquake, and subsequently lost ground to Polanco (see below). In recent times it has seen a revival, and is once again a very pleasant area in which to stroll, shop (or window-shop) and dine, as there are many open-air or half-covered restaurants. **Casasola Archive**, Praga 16, T5564-9214, holds amazing photos of the revolutionary period, with reproductions for sale. Be careful, though, as thieves operate in this area, particularly with foreign tourists in their sights, and it is not to be recommended late at night especially at the weekends.

Bosque de Chapultepec and Polanco

The park, with its thousands of *ahuehuete* trees (so sacred to the Aztecs), is beautiful and is now being kept litter-free and well policed (park closes at 1700). The best day to visit is Sunday when it is all much more colourful (and more crowded). The park is divided into three sections: the first, the easternmost, was a wood inhabited by the Toltecs and Aztecs. Most of the interesting sites are in this section (see below).

The second section, west of Boulevard Manuel Avila Camacho, was added in 1964. It has a large **amusement park**. There is a wonderful section for children and another for adults and huge roller-coasters including the *Montaña Rusa*, one of the world's largest, bridle paths and polo grounds. ■ *Wed, Fri and weekends 1030-2000, US$1. Montaña Rusa Sat and Sun only, US$0.40.* Diego Rivera's famous fountain, the **Fuente de Tláloc**, is near the children's amusement park. Close by are the Fuentes de las Serpientes (Snake Fountains). There are two museums in this section: the **Museo Tecnológico** is free; it is operated by the Federal Electricity Commission with touchable exhibits that demonstrate electrical and energy principles. It is located beside the roller coasters. The **Museo de Historia Natural** is beside the Lago Menor of the second section. ■ *Tue-Sun, 1000-1700.* Both the Lago Menor and Lago Mayor are popular for boating; on the shore of each is a restaurant.

The third section, which was added in 1974, stretches a long way beyond the Panteón Civil de Dolores (cemetery), and has little to interest the tourist.

The first section contains a maze of pathways, the **Plaza del Quijote** and **Monumento a los Niños Héroes** (frequently visited by foreign heads of state, a large lake and a smaller one (with an outdoor theatre used for performances of *Swan Lake* and similar), shaded areas, and stalls selling snacks of all kinds, especially at weekends. There is also a **zoo** with giant pandas and other animals from around the world; it is well laid out, the cages are spacious and most animals seem content. ■ *Free, closed Mon, shuts 1630.* The official residence of the President, **Los Pinos**, is also situated in the first section.

At the top of a hill, and visible from afar (a long climb on foot; train to the top US$0.20, return journey) is the imposing **Castillo de Chapultepec**, with a view over the Valley of Mexico from its beautiful balconies – a total refurbishment was completed in 2000. It now houses the **Museo Nacional de Historia** but its rooms were once used by the Emperor Maximilian and the Empress Carlota during their brief reign. There is an impressive mural by Siqueiros, *From the Dictatorship of Porfirio Díaz to the Revolution* (in Sala XIII, near the entrance) and a notable mural by O'Gorman on the theme of Independence as well as several by Camarena. ■ *0900-1700, US$2.50, free on Sun; long queues on Sun, closed Mon.* Free classical music concerts are given on Sunday at 1200 by the Bellas Artes Chamber Orchestra; arrive early for a seat.

Halfway down the hill is the **Galería de Historia**, which has dioramas, with tape-recorded explanations of Mexican history, and photographs of the 1910 Revolution. Just below the castle are the remains of the famous Arbol de Moctezuma, known locally as *El Sargento*. This immense tree, which has a circumference of 14 m, was about 60 m high before it was cut down to 10 m.

Also in the first section of the Bosque de Chapultepec and on the same side of Reforma as Chapultepec Castle, is the **Museo de Arte Moderno**, which has a permanent collection of modern Mexican art and regularly stages temporary national and international exhibitions. It consists of two circular buildings pleasantly set among trees with sculptures in the grounds. The temporary exhibitions are usually held in the smaller of the two buildings; entrance through the larger one. The delightfully light architecture of the larger building is balanced by a heavy, marble staircase, with a curious acoustic effect on the central landing under a translucent dome, which must have been unplanned. There is a good bookshop, gift shop and an open-air cafeteria behind the first building. A free galleries map and monthly calendar of exhibitions is available here and at other museums and galleries. ■ *1000-1700 daily except Mon. US$1.50, free with ISIC card.*

The **Museo Rufino Tamayo** (on the other side of Reforma, cross near the Museo de Arte Moderno, on the way to the Anthropological Museum) has a fine collection of works by Rufino Tamayo and shows contemporary Mexican and other painters. The interior space of the museum is unusual in that it is difficult to know which floor one is on. Very pleasant restaurant. ■ *1000-1800, closed Mon, US$1.70, free to students with ISIC card.*

The crowning glory of Chapultepec Park was built by architect Pedro Ramírez Vásquez to house a vast collection illustrating pre-Conquest Mexican culture. It has a 350-m façade and an immense patio shaded by a gigantic concrete mushroom measuring 4,200 sq m, the world's largest concrete and steel expanse supported by a single pillar. The largest exhibit (8½ m high, weighing 167 tonnes) is the image of Tlaloc, the rain god, removed (accompanied by protesting cloudbursts) from near the town of Texcoco to the museum. Upstairs is a display of folk costumes, which may be closed Sunday. Attractions include *voladores* and Maya musicians. After more than 10 years, 140 invaluable objects have been returned to the museum; they had been stolen by some rich young people and had been kept in a cupboard in their parents' house in downtown Mexico City.

Museo Nacional de Antropología
Nearest metro
Auditorio

Mexico City

Allow enough time to do justice to the museum; it is huge and exhausting

The museum is very well organized; each major culture that contributed to the evolution of Mesoamerican civilization is well represented in its own room or *Sala*: Pre-Classic, Teotihuacán, Toltec, Aztec, Oaxaca, Gulf Coast, Maya, Northwestern and Western Mexico. It might be an idea to leave your visit until after you have seen as many of the archaeological sights as possible. You will then understand how each item functioned within the specific culture. Two areas are often missed by visitors: the Torres Bodet Auditorium where visiting archaeologists, art historians, anthropologists, etc, give seminars, often in English and usually free; the Temporary Exhibitions Hall is also worth checking out; it can make a pleasant change when they offer an exhibition unrelated to pre-Hispanic culture.

The Biblioteca Nacional de Historia y Antropología is upstairs; access is by means of a staircase to the left as you enter the foyer. It contains a wealth of pre-Hispanic and early-colonial documents. Although admittance is not always possible, those with a special interest in ancient documents (see the facsimile of the Dresden Codex) could ask to speak with the senior librarian, who is charming and probably the most knowledgeable person in this field in Mexico. ■ *Tue-Sun 0900-1900 (library 0900-2130). US$4 except Sun (free, and very crowded; arrive early). Free to those with Mexican student card. With written explanations in Spanish and English. An audio guide available in English, US$4, describes 130 of the exhibits. Guided tours in English or Spanish free with a minimum of 5 people. Ask for the parts you want to see as each*

Bosque de Chapultepec & Polanco

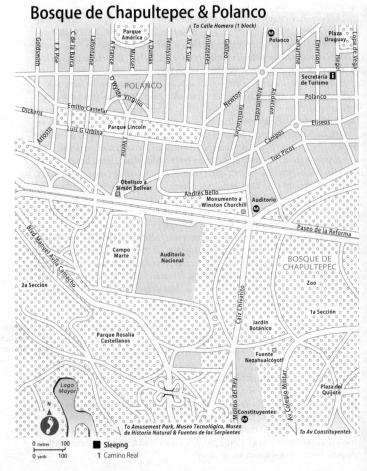

■ **Sleepng**
1 Camino Real

tour only visits 2 of the 23 halls. Excellent audio-visual introduction free (lasts 1 hr, includes 3D models). If you want to see everything, you need at least 2 days. Permission to photograph (no tripod or flash allowed) *US$1, US$5 for video camera. On sale are English and Spanish books plus a few in French and German, and guides to Mexican ruins including maps. Guide books of the museum itself cost US$10-12. Cafetería on site is good, recommended, particularly for the soup, but pricey with long queues at times.*

The **Auditorio Nacional** (beyond the Museo de Antropología), on the left of Reforma, is a vast modern concert hall. At the rear there are various theatres, and at the far side is the Campo Marte, a large green sports area, where Prince Charles has played polo.

To the right of this section of Reforma, and behind the Museo de Antropología, lies the luxury residential area area known as Polanco, which has many interesting art galleries and shops. It does not suffer from the tourists that crowd the Zona Rosa and other so-called chic areas. Many of the old houses have carved stone façades, tiled roofs and gardens, especially on Calle Horacio, a pretty street lined with trees and parks. Polanco also contains some of the most modern (and conspicuous) hotels in the city, eg the *Nikko, Presidente* and *Camino Real*, which are at least worth a walk-in visit. Also here are exclusive private residences, commercial

Polanco

Mexico City

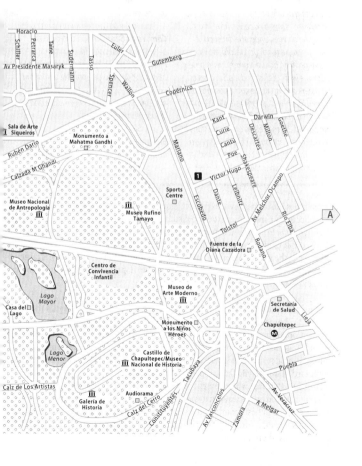

Mural sites

Apart from the main centres of mural painting already listed geographically in the text (Palacio Nacional, Suprema Corte de Justicia, Palacio de Bellas Artes, Museo Mural Diego Rivera, Escuela Nacional Preparatoria-San Ildefonso, Secretaría de Educación, Castillo de Chapultepec and below Polyforum Cultural Siqueiros), there are other sites well worth visiting that all lie within walking distance or short metro ride from the centre. Some of these are functioning workplaces, so tact should be shown when visiting: ask permission before heading off into labyrinthine buildings and always check about photo restrictions (invariably flash is prohibited).

Mercado Abelardo Rodríguez, on Venezuela four blocks northeast of Zócalo, main entrance on Rodríguez Puebla, is fascinating as one of the only examples of a concerted attempt by a cooperative of artists of varying abilities, under the direction of Diego Rivera, to teach and record the workers' revolution in an actual workers' environment. Today the work of this food market goes on, but the murals, at all the entrances, are largely ignored by traders and tourists alike. Perhaps the most emblematic is The Markets by Miguel Tzab on the ceiling above the stairs at the northwest entrance, while Ramón Alva Guadarrama's The Labours of the Field, at the southeast corner, reflects the market's agricultural base. Most elaborate are the murals of the American Greenwood sisters, Marion and Grace, showing Industrialization of the Countryside and The Mine, on the stairs either side of the main entrance. Opposite, upstairs, is a relief mural by Isamu Noguchi. For permission to take photos go to the market office behind the restaurant at the southwest entrance.

In the theatre foyer is Antonio Pujol's Problems of the Worker, much praised at the time of its completion in 1936. In the cloisters of the confusingly named Patio Diego Rivera, behind the ticket office, is Pablo O'Higgins's tirade against international fascism, The Fight of the Workers Against the Monopolies. A location plan of the murals is available at the tourist agency on Venezuela 72, beside the Teatro del Pueblo attached to the market.

Next to the Museo Nacional de Arte is the **Cámara de Senadores**, Hipoteca Beride between Donceles and Tacuba, metro Allende or Bellas Artes, which has a violent mural (1957) by Jorge González Camarena on the history of Mexico, starting with the pre-Cortesian battles between eagle and jaguar warriors.

The **Sindicato Mexicano de Electricistas**, Antonio Caso 45 (west of Cristóbal Colón monument on Reforma), T5535-0386, has one of Siqueiros' most

art galleries, fashion stores, expensive restaurants and other establishments that are collectively a monument to the consumer society; one glaring example of this is the huge *Palacio de Hierro* department store and offices along Mazaryk. There are also a couple of fairly unremarkable modern churches and, in fact, little of cultural value, with the exception of the **Sala de Arte Siqueiros** (Tres Picos 29). Traffic is frequently very congested; avoid taking a taxi if possible; metro Polanco on Horacio is centrally situated.

Beyond the Auditorio Nacional, Reforma continues southwest towards the area known as **Lomas de Chapultepec** (or simply 'Lomas'), which gradually rises through broad tree-lined avenues to an altitude that leaves most of the pollution behind. It is mostly residential, with large properties, including many embassies or ambassadorial residences. To the north, taking a right at the Fuente de Petróleos up Boulevard Manuel Avila Camacho, one comes to the modern office and commercial area of **Las Palmas**, while straight ahead, some 8 km further beyond Lomas de Chapultepec and on the way out towards Toluca, lies the district of **Santa Fe** perched on some of the highest ground and therefore in one of the least polluted areas in the city with some extraordinary, futuristic architecture: offices, hotels, banks, university buildings, shopping malls and apartment blocks.

Mexico City

important murals Portrait of the Bourgeoisie *(1939-40), located up the second floor stairwell to the left of the entrance. It depicts the revolutionary struggle against international fascism and is considered a seminal work for its use of cinematic montage techniques and viewing points. Before taking photos ask permission in the secretaría office on the right at the end of the corridor on the second floor.*

A 15-minute walk away at Altamirano 118, Colonia San Rafael, T5535-2246, is the **Teatro Jorge Negrete**, *in the foyer of which is a later Siqueiros mural,* Theatrical Art in the Social Life of Mexico *(1957), precursor in its expression of movement to his mural in Chapultepec Castle. Ask permission to see it in the office at No 128. No photos (nearest metro San Cosme).*

At the **Hospital de La Raza** *in what was once an outer entrance hall (but is now at the centre of the building) is Rivera's* History of Medicine *(1953) and to the left of the main entrance, in a naturally lit theatre foyer (usually locked but you can see it through the large frontal windows if there is nobody about with keys), is Siqueiros'* For the Complete Safety of All Mexicans at Work *(1952-54). Ask a security guard or at main reception for directions to the murals. Take metro La Raza and from the station head south along the right side of Insurgentes*

Norte, cross the railway, go straight ahead and then cross the freeway by the footbridge to the hospital. For permission to take photos here and at other medical centres you must ask at the Sede IMSS, Hidalgo 230, Metro Bellas Artes.

Another hospital with a relevant themed mural is the **Centro Médico Nacional**, *Avenida Cuauhtémoc, where Siqueiros'* Apology for the Future Victory of Medicine over Cancer *(1958) has been restored following damage in the 1985 earthquake. Since 1996 it has been on display in the waiting area of the oncology building beyond the main entrance building on the right. At the entrance, as you come up the stairs from the metro station Centro Médico, is a mural by Chávez Morado commemorating the rebuilding of the hospital in which many died during the earthquake.*

Before or after visiting the mural sites we recommend one or more of the following: The Murals of Diego Rivera, *by Desmond Rochfort, London, 1987;* Mexican Muralists, *same author, New York, 1984.* Dreaming with his Eyes Open, *by Patrick Marnham, New York and London, 1998, is an immensely readable though not entirely scholastic biography of Diego Rivera, which deals with Orozco, Siqueiros and the other muralists as well as Rivera. See also box, page 98*

Transport To visit the area from Chapultepec Park take the metro to Chapultepec station. For the Museo de Antropología, use metros Chapultepec/Auditorio, or *colectivo* down Reforma marked 'Auditorio'. For Polanco, take a *colectivo* marked Horacio from Metro Chapultepec or Metro Polanco. For 'Las Palmas', take a *colectivo* or bus marked Las Palmas from Antropología. For Lomas de Chapultepec, take a bus marked 'Km 15' or 'Cuajimalpa' from Antropología. These buses start from the bus station by the exit from metro Chapultepec. To get to Santa Fe, take a *colectivo* marked 'Centro Comercial Santa Fe' from Antropología or a bus from metro Chapultepec bus station.

Beyond the city centre

When you have exhausted the centre of Mexico City, or perhaps when it has exhausted you, the surrounding areas have much to offer in the way of museums, colonial architecture, markets, shops, restaurants and parks. At Xochimilco you can float in a colourful boat and enjoy a picnic on the banks of the chinampas, or floating gardens. At La Villa you can visit Mexico's most venerated shrine. The enormous university should not be missed, nor should the botanical gardens. Visit the Saturday bazaar in San Angel, try a glass of pulque or take in a theatrical performance at Coyoacán.

Insurgentes Sur Heading out of the city centre along Insurgentes towards the delightful suburbs, or *colonias*, of San Angel and Coyoacán, there are several sites that should not be missed. A little to the west of where Insurgentes crosses Chapultepec, and on Avenida Chapultepec itself between Calle Praga and Calle Varsovia, are the remains of the old aqueduct built in 1779. The **Polyforum Cultural Siqueiros** on Insurgentes Sur includes a handicraft shop and an art museum, with huge frescoes by Siqueiros, one of the largest in the world, inside the ovoid dome. ■ *Closed for lunch. Frescoes US$0.40; 1000-1900.* Next door is the *Hotel de México* skyscraper, which is now Mexico's **World Trade Centre**.

A little further south is the **Plaza México**, the largest bullring in the world, with capacity for some 55,000 spectators. It is situated in the **Ciudad de los Deportes**, just off Insurgentes Sur, metro San Antonio or *colectivo* to junction of Insurgentes Sur with Eje 5. The apprentice season (*temporada chica*) runs from May-October, and the *temporada grande*, from November-April. There are bullfights at 1600 or 1630 most Sundays. The 'México' is one of the world's three most important bullfighting venues. As virtually every great matador comes to fight in Mexico in the winter months, the chances of seeing an important event are high. Useful introductory reading to bullfighting includes Hemingway's *Death in the Afternoon*; Lapierre and Collins' *I'll Dress you in Mourning*; and *Matador* magazine. ■ *US$1-18 in the cheaper sol (sun) half of the Plaza (binoculars almost essential in the upper rows and recommended in any case); seats in the sombra (shade) are more expensive, up to US$35 in the barreras. Best to buy tickets, especially for important fights, early on Sat morning from the taquillas at the Plaza. Details of what's on from the Plaza itself, T5563-1659, or in the newspaper Ovaciones.*

Besides the Bullring, the Ciudad de los Deportes includes a football stadium with 50,000 capacity, a boxing ring, a cinema, a frontón court for jai-alai, a swimming pool, restaurants and hotels.

Further south still on Avenida Insurgentes Sur at the corner of Mercaderes is a remarkable building by Alejandro Prieto: the **Teatro de Los Insurgentes**, a theatre and opera house seating 1,300 people. The main frontage consists of a high curved wall covered with mosaic decoration, the work of Diego Rivera.

Eating *New York Deli and Bagel, Av Revolución 1321, just south of metro Barranca del Muerto, 0800-0100. Good coffee and full meals available.*

San Angel

Thirteen kilometres southwest of the centre, Villa Obregón, popularly known as San Angel, has narrow, cobblestone streets, many old homes, huge trees, and the charm of an era now largely past. Most of the distinguished architecture is of the 19th century. See the triple domes of its Iglesia del Carmen, covered with coloured tiles, and of the former Convento del Carmen, now the **Museo Colonial del Carmen**, which houses 17th- and 18th-century furniture and paintings. In the crypt, several mummified bodies are displayed in glass-topped cases. ■ *1000-1700.* See also the beautifully furnished and preserved old house, **Casa del Risco**, near the Bazar del Sábado, on Callejón de la Amargura. ■ *Photographic ID required for entry, Tue-Sun 1000-1700, free.* Also worth a visit is the church of San Jacinto, once belonging to a Dominican convent (1566). The **Museo de Arte Carrillo Gil**, Avenida Revolución 1608, has excellent changing exhibits and a permanent collection including paintings by Orozco and Siqueiros as well as several Diego Rivera Cubist works. There is a good bookshop and cafetería. ■ *US$3.35.*

The **Museo Estudio Diego Rivera** (Avenida Altavista y Calle Diego Rivera, opposite Antigua Hacienda de Goicochea - now *San Angel Inn*) is where Rivera and Frida Kahlo lived and worked. It contains several works by Rivera, as well as belongings and memorabilia. The building was designed by Juan O'Gorman. Many tourists come to San Angel on a Saturday to visit the **Bazar del Sábado**, a splendid folk art and curiosity market. Reach San Angel by bus from Chapultepec Park or by metro Line 3 to Miguel Angel de Quevedo. There are some excellent restaurants: the *San Angel Inn* is first class; good *panadería* by the post office (which is no good for letters abroad). Between San Angel and Coyoacán is the monument to Obregón on the spot where he was assassinated in 1928 (by the junction of Avenida Insurgentes Sur and Arenal). ■ *0900-1400.* The **Centro Cultural San Angel** (on Revolución opposite Museo del Carmen) stages exhibitions, concerts, lectures, etc; **La Carpa Geodésica**, Insurgentes Sur 2135, has theatre of all types from works for children to the very avant-garde; the **Centro Cultural Helénico**, Insurgentes 1500, metro Barranca del Muerto, always has a lively and diversified programme of drama, music and dance.

Mexico City

Coyoacán

The oldest part of Mexico City, Coyoacán is the place from which Cortés launched his attack on the Aztec city of Tenochtitlán. It is also one of the most beautiful and best-preserved parts of the city, with hundreds of fine buildings from the 16th-19th centuries, elegant tree-lined avenues and carefully tended parks and, in the Jardín Centenario and the Plaza Hidalgo, two very attractive squares. There are no supermarkets, no high-rise buildings, no hotels, no metro stations (see transport below), making it an area best explored on foot.

An excellent postcard-cum-pedestrian map of the centre of Coyoacán can be found in local book and gift shops

It is culturally one of the most lively parts of Mexico City and with its attractive cafés and good shops it is much frequented by the inhabitants of the capital, particularly at weekends. From San Angel, one can reach Coyoacán via a delightful walk through Chimalistac, across Avenida Universidad and down Avenida Francisco Sosa; or one can take a bus or *pesero* marked 'Tasqueña' as far as Caballocalco.

From the city centre, it is easiest to take the metro to Viveros, Miguel Angel de Quevedo or General Anaya. Alternatively, take the metro to Coyoacán then *colectivo* for Villa Coapa, which drops you in the historic centre. If coming from metro Viveros (a large park in which trees are grown for other city parks) or Miguel Angel de Quevedo it is worth making a slight detour in order to walk the length of **Francisco Sosa**, said to be the first urban street laid in Spanish America. At the beginning of this elegant avenue is the 18th-century church of **San Antonio Panzacola** by the side of Río Churubusco; nearby, on Universidad, is the remarkable, beautiful (and modern) chapel of **Nuestra Señora de la Soledad**, built in the grounds of the 19th-century ex-hacienda El Altillo. A little way down, in Salvador Novo, is the **Museo Nacional de la Acuarela** (National Watercolour Museum). The terracotta-fronted residence at No 383 is said to have been built by Alvarado. ■ *Tue-Sun, free. Courtyard and garden may be visited 0900-1600 Mon-Fri, no*

Sights

For Eating and Shopping in Coyoacán, see pages 125 and 127

Frida Kahlo

The life of Frida Kahlo was not a very happy one; she questioned her European and Mexican roots, very much like the artists of an earlier era who were infuenced by styles and subjects originating in the Old World, which they attempted to express in New World terms. Frida suffered greatly because her treatment after an accident when she was young went terribly wrong, added to which she and her spouse, Diego Rivera, were not the most compatible of couples. Her anguish is expressed in many of her paintings on display at the Museo Frida Kahlo, in Coyoacán.

Frida's life is now the subject of a big budget Hollywood biopic, filmed on location in San Luis Potosí and due for release in October 2002.

charge, *enquire at entrance*. Many fine houses follow, mostly built in the 19th century. **Santa Catarina**, in the square of the same name, is a fine 18th-century church; on Sunday, at about one o'clock, people assemble under the trees to tell stories (all are welcome to attend or participate). In the same square, the **Casa de la Cultura Jesús Reyes Heroles** should not be missed, with its delightful leafy gardens. Just before arriving at the **Jardín Centenario**, with its 16th-century arches, is the 18th-century **Casa de Diego Ordaz**.

The centre of Coyoacán is dominated by the 16th-century church of **San Juan Bautista**, with later additions and a magnificent interior. Jardín Centenario was once the atrium of this 16th-century Franciscan monastery, which now houses the *Delegación*. On the north side of Plaza Hidalgo, the **Casa de Cortés** was in fact built 244 years after the Conquest, on the site of Cortés' house. The beautiful 18th-century church of **La Conchita** in a pretty square of the same name is reached by taking Higuera from Plaza Hidalgo; the interior, especially the altarpiece, is magnificent, but the church is normally open only on Friday evenings and Sunday mornings. On the corner of Higuera and Vallarta is what is reputed to be the **Casa de La Malinche**, Cortés' mistress and interpreter.

Admirers of Frida Kahlo will want to visit the **Museo Frida Kahlo**, or Casa Azul, Allende and Londres 247. Two rooms are preserved as lived in by Frida Kahlo and her husband Diego Rivera, and the rest contain drawings and paintings by both. She was very interested in folk art, an interest that is illustrated by the small collection of regional costumes on display. ■ *Tue-Sun 1000-1800, US$1.50, no photos*. In the **Jardín Cultural Frida Kahlo**, near Plaza de La Conchita, there is a striking bronze statue of Frida by the contemporary Mexican sculptor Gabriel Ponzanelli.

La Casa de Trotsky is at Río Churubusco 410, between Gómez Farías and Morelos. This is where the Russian revolutionary lived before he was murdered in the study here in 1940. The house is dark and sombre. There is a tomb in the garden where his ashes were laid. ■ *Tue-Sun 1000-1700, US$1.50, half-price with ISIC card, US$1.50 to take photos*. Also in Coyoacán are the **Museo del Retrato Hablado**, Universidad 1330-C, the **Museo Geles Cabrera**, Xicoténcatl 181, T5688-3016, which has sculpture (prior appontment needed); and the **Museo del Automóvil**, División del Norte 3752.

To reach the centre of Coyoacán from Metro General Anaya, there is a pleasant walk along Héroes del 47 (one block along on the left is the 16th-century church of **San Lucas**), across División del Norte and down Hidalgo (one block along on the left, and two blocks down San Lucas is the 18th-century church of **San Mateo**). The **Museo Nacional de Culturas Populares** is on Avenida Hidalgo, just off Plaza Hidalgo, and should be seen. It houses permanent and temporary exhibitions, cinema-cum-auditorio and a good bookshop on Mexican culture and folklore. ■ *Tue-Sun 1000-1600, free*.

Coyoacán has several **theatres**, medium and small, and similar establishments, for example the *Coyoacán* and *Usigli* theatres (Eleuterio Méndez, five blocks from Metro General Anaya), the *Foro Cultural de Coyoacán* (Allende;

most events free of charge), the *Museo Nacional de Culturas Populares* (Hidalgo), the *Foro Cultural Ana María Hernández* (Pacífico 181), the *Teatro Santa Catarina* (Plaza Santa Catarina), the *Rafael Solana* theatre on Miguel Angel de Quevedo (nearly opposite *Caballocalco*), the *Casa del Teatro*, Vallarta 31 and *Foro de la Conchita*, Vallarta 33. Also note *El Hábito* (Madrid) and *El Hijo del Cuervo* (Jardín Centenario) for avant-garde drama and cabaret, *Los Talleres de Coyoacán* (Francisco Sosa) for dance and ballet, *CADAC* (Centenario) for traditional and experimental drama. On the edge of the Delegación Coyoacán (southeast corner of Churubusco and Tlalpan, Metro General Anaya) is the *Central Nacional de las Artes*, a huge complex of futuristic buildings dedicated to the training and display of the performing and visual arts. It has a good bookshop, library and cafeterías. Details can be found in *Tiempo Libre* and local broadsheets. At weekends there are many open-air events especially in Plaza Hidalgo. Also at weekends is the *artesanía* market, in a site off Plaza Hidalgo, which is well worth a visit. Prices are reasonable and there is lots of potential for bargaining; with the best deals to be had either early or late in the day.

Transport The *pesero* from metro General Anaya to the centre of Coyoacán is marked 'Santo Domingo', alight at Abasolo or at the Jardín Centenario; it also goes past the Mercado (Malintzin). Alternatively, get off the metro at Ermita and get a *colectivo* 'Santo Domingo' from Pirineos, on the west side of Tlalpan just north of the metro station. The *colectivo* passes in front of the Frida Kahlo museum.

Ciudad Universitaria The world famous University City, 18 km from the centre via Insurgentes Sur on the road towards Cuernavaca highway, was founded in 1551. Perhaps the most notable building is the 10-storey **Biblioteca** (library), by Juan O'Gorman, its outside walls iridescent with mosaics telling the story of scientific knowledge, from Aztec astronomy to molecular theory.

The **Rectoría** has a vast, mosaic-covered and semi-sculpted mural by Siqueiros. Across the highway is the **Estadio Olímpico**, with seats for 80,000, in shape, colour and situation a world's wonder, but now closed and run down. Diego Rivera has a

Mexico City

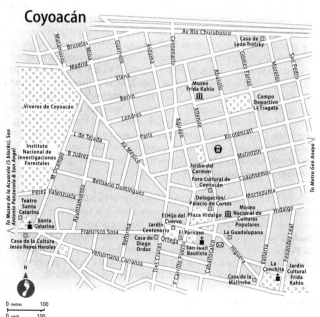

Coyoacán

sculpture-painting telling the story of Mexican sport. A new complex has been completed beyond the Ciudad Universitaria, including the newspaper library (the **Hemeroteca Nacional**), **Teatro Juan Ruiz de Alarcón**, **Sala Nezahualcóyotl** (concerts, etc), bookshop and post office; also the **Museo Universitario Contemporáneo de Arte** and the extraordinary **Espacio Escultórico**, a large circular area of volcanic rock within a circle of cement monoliths; on the opposite side of the road is another large area with many huge sculptures; stick to the path as it is possible to get lost in the vegetation. In the University museum there is an exhibition of traditional masks from all over Mexico. Beyond the Olympic Stadium is the **Jardín Botánico Exterior**, which shows all the cactus species in Mexico. ■ *0700-1630, 30-min walk, ask directions.*

Transport Take a bus marked CU, along Eje Lázaro Cárdenas; also bus 17, marked Tlalpan, which runs the length of Insurgentes, about 1 hr journey. Another way to the university is on metro Line 3 to Copilco station (20 mins' walk to University) or to Universidad station (30 mins' walk). At the University City free buses ferry passengers to the different areas of the campus.

Further east, off División del Norte, is **Anahuacalli**, Museo 150, T5617-4310, which is usually called the **Diego Rivera Museum**. Here is a very fine collection of pre-Columbian sculpture and pottery, effectively displayed in a pseudo-Mayan tomb purpose-built by Diego Rivera. There is a big display here for the Day of the Dead at the beginning of November. ■ *Tue-Sun 1000-1400, 1500-1800, closed Holy Week, US$1.70, free Sun. The museum is reached by Combi 29 from the Taxqueña metro station to Estadio Azteca, or take the bus marked División del Norte from outside Salto del Agua metro.*

Churubusco Situated 10 km southeast is Churubusco, which is reached from the Zócalo by Coyoacán or Tlalpan buses, or from General Anaya metro station. The picturesque and partly ruined convent (1762), at General Anaya y 20 de Agosto, is now the **Museo Nacional de las Intervenciones**. It has 17 rooms filled with mementoes, documents, proclamations and pictures recounting foreign invasions, incursions and occupations since Independence and also holds temporary exhibitions. The site of the museum was chosen because it was the scene of a battle when the US Army marched into Mexico City in 1847. This was where the San Patricios, the famous Saint Patrick's Brigade who fought as volunteers on the Mexican side, were captured by the US Army. ■ *0900-1800, closed Mon, US$3.35, free Sun and holidays.* Next door is the 16th-century church of San Diego, with 17th- and 18th-century additions. Near the church, on the other side of Calzada General Anaya, is the delightful Parque de Churubusco. One block from Tlalpan along Héroes del 47, to the left, is the 18th-century church of San Mateo. There is a golf course at the Churubusco Country Club. Churubusco was for many years the home of Mexico's most important film studios; a smaller-scale operation now exists, devoted to post-production. The new Olympic swimming pool is here. It is near enough to Coyoacán (see page 113) to walk there.

Tlalpan A further 6 ½ km, or direct from San Angel (see page 112), is this suburb with colonial houses, gardens, and near the main square, Plaza de la Constitución, the early 16th-century church of San Agustín with a fine altar and paintings by Cabrera. It can be reached by bus or trolley bus from the Taxqueña metro station. The suburb of **Peña Pobre** is 2½ km west, near which, to the northeast, is the **Pyramid of Cuicuilco**, believed to be the oldest in Mexico. The pyramid dates from the fifth or sixth century BC; it is over 100 m in diameter but only 25 m high. There is an archaeological museum on site, on Insurgentes Sur Km 16 at the intersection with Periférico. ■ *0800-1800, closed Mon.*

Xochimilco

Some 20 km to the southeast of the city centre, Xochimilco has many attractions, not *Colour map 3 grid B5* least the fact that it lies in an unpolluted area. Easiest access is by bus, *colectivo* or metro to Metro Tasqueña, then *tren ligero* (about 20 minutes). Get off at the terminal, which is misleadingly named 'Embarcadero' (there are several *embarcaderos*, see map and below).

Meaning 'the place where flowers grow', Xochimilco was an advanced settlement long before the arrival of the Spaniards. Built on a lake, it developed a form of agriculture using *chinampas*, or 'floating gardens'; the area is still a major supplier of fruit and vegetables to Mexico City. The Spaniards recognized the importance of the region and the need to convert the indigenous population; evidence of this is the considerable number of 16th- and 17th-century religious buildings in Xochimilco itself and in the other 13 *pueblos* that make up the present-day *delegación*, or municipality.

Xochimilco is famous for its canals and colourful punt-like boats, *trajineras*, which bear girls' names. There are seven landing-stages, or *embarcaderos*, in the town, the largest of which are Fernando Celada and Nuevo Nativitas (the latter is where most coachloads of tourists are set down, large craft market). All are busy at weekends, especially Sunday afternoon. Official tariffs operate, although prices are sometimes negotiable; a boat taking six passengers costs US$5.75 per hour (a trip of at least 1½ hours is desirable); floating *mariachi* bands will charge US$3.50 per song, marimba groups US$1.50. There are reasonably priced tourist menus (lunch US$2) from passing boats; good, clean and cheap restaurants opposite Fernando Celada (for example *Beto's*, US$2 for lunch); first-rate cheap lunch (US$2) at *Restaurante Del Botas*, Pino, to the left of the cathedral; more expensive restaurants are opposite Nuevo Nativitas.

The indisputable architectural jewel of Xochimilco is the church of **San Bernardino de Siena** (begun in 1535, completed 1595; magnificent Renaissance-style altarpiece, 1580-90) and its convent (circa 1585). The oldest Spanish-built religious edifice is the tiny chapel of **San Pedro** (1530). Also worthy of mention are **Nuestra Señora de los Dolores de Xaltocán** (17th-century façade, 18th-century retable), **Santa Crucita Analco** and **San Juan Tlaltentli**. All are within walking distance of the centre of Xochimilco.

For those who have an interest in **church architecture** there is a rich range in the villages to the west, south and east of Xochimilco. The main constraining factor for most travellers will be time (and the pronunciation of some of the names). Churches include **Santa María Tepepan** (1612-21), with a unique decorated earthenware font dated 1599; *tren ligero* Tepepan, walk up 5 de Mayo; **Santiago Tepatcatlalpan** (1770); **San Lucas Xochimanca** (16th century); **San Francisco Tlanepantla** (small 17th-century chapel), village right in the country, superb views; the 16th-century **San Lorenzo Atemoaya**. After **Santa Cruz Acalpixca**, 16th century with a 17th-century façade; near a mediocre Archaeology Museum, are the imposing **San Gregorio Atlapulco** (17th century; 16th-century font), the tiny chapel of **San Luis Tlaxiatemalco** (1633) and the enormous, late 18th-century **Santiago Tulyehualco**. Finally, beyond the boundary of the Delegación Xochimilco, is the church of **San Andrés Míxquic** (second quarter of 16th century; façade 1620; many alterations), built on the site of an earlier temple using some of the original blocks, which bear traces of pre-Hispanic designs; it is much-frequented around *Día de los Muertos* (Day of the Dead). All of these villages may be reached by *colectivo* from the centre of Xochimilco, and there is also a bus to Tulyehualco (30 minutes). Eating options are generally limited to stalls with tortas, tacos and occasional spit-roasted chicken.

To the north of the town is the **Parque Ecológico**, an extensive area of grassland, lagoons and canals, with not much shade, but lots of birdlife. One can walk beyond the asphalt paths along the canal banks. There is also a punt station. ■ *Daily 1000-1800, 1000-1700 winter months, US$1.50, children free, over-60s US$0.75.*

Mexico City

Access from Mexico City: bus, colectivo or tren ligero *to the Periférico, then colectivo to Cuemanco; from Xochimilco, bus or colectivo to Periférico, then likewise.*

Museo Dolores Olmedo Patiño, Avenida México 5843, on corner with Antiguo Camino a Xochimilco, one block southwest from La Noria *tren ligero* station, is set in eight acres of beautiful garden and grassland on the site of an old estate, probably dating from the 16th century. Rare Mexican hairless dogs and peacocks parade. It houses 137 works by Diego Rivera, 25 by Frida Kahlo, and an important collection of drawings by Angelina Beloff. There are also pre-Hispanic artefacts, 19th-century antiques and Mexican folk art. Highly recommended. ■ *1000-1800 Tue-Sun, US$1.50, students US$0.75, T5555-1016.* There is a very pleasant open and covered café and **D** *Hotel Plaza El Mesón*, Avenida México 64, T5676-4163. Mixed reports, noisy. Tourist office at Pino 36, open 0800-2100.

Ajusco Another excursion can be made to Ajusco, about 20 km southwest of Mexico City. Catch a bus from Estadio Azteca on Calzada Tlalpan direct to Ajusco. From the summit of the extinct **Volcán Ajusco** (3,929m) there are excellent views on a clear day, but a stroll through the foothills is also pleasant. The way up is 10 km west of the village, 400m west of where the road branches to Xalatlaco (there is a hut south of the road where the path goes to the mountain).

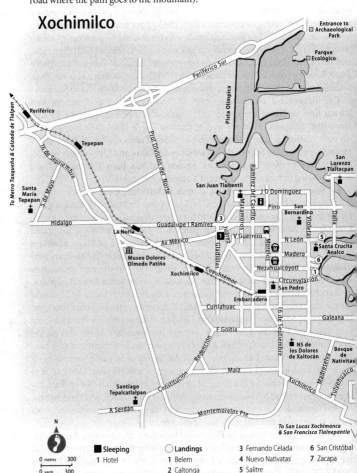

Xochimilco

■ **Sleeping**	○ **Landings**	3 Fernando Celada	6 San Cristóbal
1 Hotel	1 Belem	4 Nuevo Nativatas	7 Zacapa
	2 Caltonga	5 Salitre	

0 metres 300
0 yards 300

Northern suburbs

In the northern suburbs of Mexico City is the Basílica de Guadalupe, often called La **Basílica de** Villa de Guadalupe and the most venerated shrine in Mexico. It was here, in Decem- **Guadalupe** ber 1531, that the Virgin appeared three times in the guise of an Indian princess to the Indian Juan Diego and imprinted her portrait on his cloak. The cloak is pre- served, set in gold, but was moved into the new basilica next door as a massive crack had appeared down the side of the old building. Visitors stand on a moving platform behind the altar to view the cloak. The huge, modern basilica is impressive and holds over 20,000 people (very crowded on Sunday). Pope John Paul II held Mass here when visiting Mexico in 1999, and an estimated 20 million pilgrims visit the shrine every year. The original basilica has been converted into a museum. It still houses the original magnificent altar, but otherwise mostly representations of the image on the cloak, plus interesting painted tin plates offering votive thanks for cures, etc, from about 1860. ■ *US$3.* A chapel stands over the well that gushed at the spot where the Virgin appeared. The great day here is **12 December**, the great night the night before: Indian dance groups provide entertainment in front of the Basílica. There are, in fact, about seven churches in the immediate neighbourhood, including one on the hill above (Iglesia del Cerrito - excellent view of the city, especially at night, free access); most of them are at crazy angles to each other and to the ground, because of subsidence; the subsoil is very soft. The **Templo de los Capuchinos** has been the subject of a remarkable feat of engineering in which one end has been raised 3.375 m so that the building is now horizontal. There is a little platform from which to view this work. Buses marked 'La Villa' go close to the site, or you can go by metro to La Villa (Line 6).

The pyramid of Tenayuca, 10 km to the **Tenayuca** northwest of the city centre, is about 15 m high and the best preserved in Mexico. The Aztecs rebuilt this temple every 52 years; this one was last reconstructed about 1507 and is well worth seeing, for it is surrounded with serpents in masonry. ■ *1000-1645, US$1.50.* The easiest way to get there by car from Mexico City cen- tre is to go to Vallejo, 11 km north of the intersection of Insurgentes Norte and Río Consulado. By metro, take the line to the Terminal de Autobuses del Norte (see page 132), La Raza, and catch the bus there. By bus from Tlatelolco, ask the driver and passengers to advise you on arrival as the site is not easily visible. An excursion to Tula (see page 144) may go via Tenayuca. It is not far from the old town of **Tlalnepantla**: see the ancient convent (ask for the *Catedral*) on the Plaza Gustavo Paz, and the church (1583), which contains the first image, a Christ of Mercy, brought to the New

Mexico City (vertical, right margin)

World. The smaller pyramid of **Santa Cecilia Acatitlán**, which is interesting for its restored sanctuary is 2½ km to the north. It is difficult to find; head for the church tower visible from the footbridge over the highway. ■ *US$1.50.*

Los Remedios, a small town 13 km northwest of Mexico City, has in its famous church an image, 30 cm high, adorned with jewels. See the old aqueduct, with a winding stair leading to the top of two towers. It can be reached by car or by taking the Los Remedios bus at Tacuba metro station. The local fiesta starts on 1 September and runs until its climax on 8 September.

At **Naucalpan**, northwest of the city just outside the city boundary on Boulevard Toluca, pre-Classic Olmec-influenced figurines can be seen in the **Museo de la Cultura de Tlatilco**, opposite the *Hotel Naucalpan* on Vía Gustavo Paz. ■ *Closed Mon.* This is said to be the oldest settlement in the Cuenca de México.

Iztapalapa At the foot of the Cerro de la Estrella, whose top is reached by a paved road or a path through some ruins, is a small museum, a good view of volcanoes and two interesting churches. The Santuario del Calvario (1856) and San Lucas (1664) have original roof timbers restored in the 19th century, with a main door embodying Aztec motifs and a fine interior. The most spectacular of Mexican passion plays begins at Iztapalapa on Holy Thursday.

Essentials

Sleeping

■ on maps
Price codes: see
inside front cover

Prices of the more expensive hotels do not normally include 15% tax; service is sometimes included. Always check in advance. Reductions are often available; breakfast is rarely included in the room price. There are fair hotel reservation services at the railway station and at the airport; also services for more expensive hotels at bus stations.

Near the airport Several airport hotels. **AL** *JR Plaza*, Blvd Puerto Aéreo 390, T5785-5200, F5784-3221. Free airport transport, expensive restaurant, quiet, good rooms with solid furniture, close to metro.

In & around the city centre
Many of the expected chains are here including Camino Real, Fiesta, Four Seasons, and Intercontinental

LL *Gran Hotel de México*, 16 de Septiembre 82 (Zócalo), T/F5510-4040 to 47, www.granhotel.com.mx Has an incredible foyer, 30's style, 4th floor restaurant and balcony good for Zócalo-watching, especially on Sun morning (breakfast buffet US$10). **LL** *Imperial*, Reforma 64, T5705-4911. Very good, restaurant, café, bar, 24-hr service, all business facilities. **LL** *Krystal*, Liverpool 155, T5228-9928, F5511-3490. Good hotel, aimed at the North American business traveller. Recommended. **LL** *Presidente Intercontinental*, Campos Elíseos 218, overlooking Chapultepec Park, T5327-7700, F5327-7730, www.interconti.com, ideal hotel for business and pleasure. **LL** *Royal Zona Rosa*, Amberes 78, T5228-9918, F5514-3330, reservaciones zr@hotelesroyal.com.mx A good Spanish hotel with fine suites ideal for business people and holiday-makers alike.

AL *Cortés* (Best Western), Av Hidalgo 85, T5518-2181, F5512-1863, www.hotelcortes.com.mx This is the only baroque-style hotel in Mexico City, a former pilgrims' guesthouse, with a pleasant patio, TV, good bathroom, no a/c or pool, quiet, good yet touristy floor show, good food. **AL** *Majestic* (Best Western), Madero 73 on Zócalo, T5521-8609, F5512-6262. Interesting rooms, lots of tiles, carved wooden beams, large beds, quiet rooms overlook courtyard, magnificent breakfast in 7th floor restaurant with excellent views of centre. **AL** *María Cristina*, Lerma 31, T5566-9688, F5592-3447. Attractive colonial-style, comfortable, helpful, safe parking. Recommended (book well in advance). **A** *Viena*, Marsella 28 (close to Juárez market and Cuauhtémoc metro), T5566-0700. Quiet, Swiss decor, garage, dining room. Recommended.

B *Brasilia*, near Terminal del Norte bus station, on Av Cien Metros 48-25, T5587-8577, F5368-2714. Excellent modern hotel, king-size bed, TV. 24-hr traffic jam in front. **B** *Cancún*,

Donato Guerra 24, T5566-6083, F5566-6488. Restaurant, safe, noisy. Recommended. **B** *Catedral*, Donceles 95, T5518-5232, F5512-4344, behind cathedral. Clean, spacious, good service. Recommended. **B** *Fleming*, Revillagigedo 35, T5510-4530. Good value, central. **B** *Jena*, Jesús Terán 12, T5566-0277. New, central. Recommended (but not the travel agency on the premises). **B** *Mayaland*, Maestro Antonio Caso 23, T5566-6066. Very clean rooms, with bath, good value, good restaurant. Recommended. **B** *Palace*, Ignacio Ramírez 7, T5566-2400. Very friendly, good restaurant. **B** *Premier*, Atenas 72, T5566-2700. Good location, clean, front rooms noisy, will store bags. **B** *Prim*, Versalles 46, T5592-4600, F5592-4835. Clean, good in all respects. **B** *San Francisco*, Luis Moya 11, T5521-8960, F5510-8831, just off Alameda. Great views, friendly, excellent value, takes credit cards, good set meals.

C *Canadá*, Av 5 de Mayo 47, T5518-2106, F5521-1233, closest metro station Allende. With bath, hot water, TV, collect calls can be made for US$1, good value, friendly, helpful, no restaurant. **C** *Capitol*, Uruguay 12, T5518-1750, F5521-1149. Attractive lobby, recently remodelled, TV, bath, clean, friendly, don't miss the restaurant in the same building: *El Malecón*. **C** *Casa González*, Lerma y Sena 69 (near British Embassy), T5514-3302. Full board available, shower, clean, quiet and friendly, English spoken by Sr González, no credit cards. Recommended. **C** *Congreso*, Allende 18, T5510-9888. With bath, hot water, good, central, clean, quiet, TV, garage. **C** *Gilbert*, Amado Nervo 37, Col Buenavista, Mex 4 DF, T5547-9260. Good location but a bit spooky at night. **C** *Gillow*, 5 de Mayo e Isabel la Católica 17, T5518-1440, F5512-2078. Central, large, clean, best rooms on 6th floor, many services, attractive, hospitable, good value, mediocre restaurant. **C** *Marlowe*, Independencia 17, T5521-9540, F5518-6862. Clean, modern, finished to a high standard, safe parking, lift, restaurant good but service is slow (tourist office at airport refers many travellers here – if this one is too expensive, the cheaper *Concordia*, see below, is round the corner). **C** *Nueva York*, Edison 45. Large, clean rooms, expensive restaurants. **C** *Parador Washington*, Dinamarca 42 y Londres. With bath, clean, safe area, café next door. **C** *Uxmal*, Madrid 13, quite close to Zona Rosa. Clean rooms, same owner as more expensive *Madrid* next door (**AL**). With access to their better facilities. Recommended.

D *Atlanta*, corner of Blvd Domínguez and Allende, T5518-1201. Good, clean, quiet if you ask for a room away from street, friendly, luggage store. **D** *Avenida*, Lázaro Cárdenas 38 (San Juan de Letrán metro), T5518-1007. With bath, central, friendly, will store luggage, good value, cheapest hotel that can be booked at airport. Recommended. **D** *Buenos Aires*, Av 5 de Mayo. Safe, friendly, TV, stores luggage, hot water. **D** *Florida*, Belisario Domínguez 57. TV, shower, clean. Recommended. **D** *Lafayette*, Motolinia 40 and 16 de Septiembre. With bath, and TV, good, clean, quiet (pedestrian precinct), but check rooms, there's a variety of sizes. **D** *Principal*, Bolívar 29. With bath, central, OK, friendly owner. **D** *San Antonio*, 2nd Callejón, 5 de Mayo 29, T5512-9906. Clean, pleasant, popular, friendly, TV in room. Recommended. **D** *Toledo*, López 22 (Bellas Artes Metro), T5521-3249. With bath, TV. Warmly recommended. **D-E** *Cuba*, on Cuba 69, T5518-1380. With bath, TV, good beds but sheets too small, noisy. **D-E** *Habana*, República de Cuba 77 (near metro Allende), T5518-1589. Spacious rooms, huge beds, renovated, very clean, phone, TV, friendly and helpful staff. Highly recommended. **D-E** *Isabel la Católica* on street of the same name, No 63, T5518-1213, F5521-1233. Pleasant, popular, clean, helpful, safe (taxi drivers must register at desk before taking passengers), roof terrace, large shabby rooms with bath and hot water (some without windows), central, a bit noisy, fax service, quite good restaurant, luggage held, rooms on top floor with shared bathroom are cheaper. Recommended. **D-E** *Washington*, Av 5 de Mayo 54. Clean, small rooms, cable TV.

E *La Marina*, Allende 30 y Blvd Domínguez. Clean, comfortable, safe, friendly, TV, hot water, will store luggage. Recommended. **E** *Rioja*, Av 5 de Mayo 45, next door to *Canadá*, see above. T5521-8333. Shared or private baths, reliable hot water, clean, popular, luggage store, well placed. Normally recommended, but we have received a report of theft from rooms in the hotel. Opposite are **E** *Juárez*, in small alley on 5 de Mayo 17, 1-min walk from Zócalo, T5512-6929. Ask for room with window, safe, clean, with marble (!) bathrooms, phone, radio, TV. Will hold bags, try to book in advance as often full. Great location near the Zócalo. Highly recommended. **F** *Pensión del Centro*, Cuba 74, apt 203 y Chile, Centro Histórico,

Near Metro Allende

The best of the cheaper hotels are in the old part of town between the Zócalo and the Alameda

Mexico City

T5512-0832, paic@data.net.mx Laundry, luggage store, email service, 4-bed dorms. **F** *Princess*, Cuba 55. With bath, good value, TV, fairly secure, front rooms noisy. **F** *República*, Cuba 57, T5512-9517. With bath, hot water, rooms upstairs quieter, 3 blocks from Bellas Artes. Recommended. **F** *Zamora*, Av 5 de Mayo 50. Clean, cheap, hot water, OK.

North of the Zócalo **C** *La Villa de los Quijotes*, Moctezuma 20, near Basílica de Guadalupe (Metro La Villa), T5577-1088. Modern, quiet, clean, expensive restaurant. **D** *Hostel Catedral*, Guatemala 4, T5518-1726, F5510-3442, www.remaj.com New hostel just behind the cathedral, 209 beds (private rooms and dorms), restaurant, kitchen, laundry, internet centre, secure storage, travel agency has booking service. **D-E** *Hostal Moneda*, Moneda 8, one block east of the cathedral, T5522-5821, F5522-5803, www.hostalmoneda.com.mx Clean, friendly, safe and very good location. Happening meeting place, rooftop terrace used for serving great inclusive breakfasts with a beautiful view of the cathedral and other surrounding buildings. Add 10 minutes of free internet and it's recommended. **E** *Tuxpan*, on Colombia, near Brasil. Modern, clean, TV, hot shower. **E** *Azores*, Brasil 25, T5521-5220. Large rooms, TV, a/c. **F** *Río de Janeiro*, on Brasil, near Colombia. Dirty, noisy.

North of Metro Hildago **D** *Managua*, on Plaza de la Iglesia de San Fernando. With bath, phone, TV, good location, car park, very friendly, run down. **D** *Mina*, José T Salgado 18, esq Mina, T5703-1682. Modern, clean, TV, large beds. **D** *Monaco* opposite, Guerrero 12, T5566-8333. Comfortable, TV, modern, good service. Almost behind is **D** *La Fuente*, Orozco y Berra 10, T5566-9122. Bath, TV, garage, bar (noisy bar opposite). **D** *Detroit*, Zaragoza 55, T5591-1088. Hot shower, central, clean, has parking. **D** *Savoy*, Zaragoza 10, T5566-4611, near Hidalgo metro. Convenient for Zócalo, with bath and hot water, clean, phone, TV, modernized, good value.

North of Plaza de la República **C** *Oxford*, Ignacio Mariscal 67, T5566-0500. Very clean, radio and satellite TV, helpful, but short stay. **C** *Texas*, Ignacio Mariscal 129, T5564-4626. With bath, clean, hot water, small rooms, good breakfasts. **D** *América*, Buena Vista 4 (near Revolución metro). With bath, hot water, TV, good service. Recommended. **D** *Frimont*, Jesús Terán 35, T5705-4169. Clean, central. **D** *Royalty*, Jesús Terán 21, opposite *Hotel Jena*. With bath, TV, clean, very quiet, near Hidalgo metro. **E** *Carlton*, Ignacio Mariscal 32-bis, T5566-2911. Getting rough around the edges, small rooms but some with fine views, rooms at front noisy, good restaurant. Recommended. **E** *El Paraíso*, Ignacio Mariscal 99, T5566-8077. Hot water, clean, private bath, TV, phone, recently renovated. Friendly. **E-F** *Casa de los Amigos*, Ignacio Mariscal 132. T5705-0521, near train and bus station (metro Revolución). In dormitory, **D-E** in double room, pay 2 nights in advance, use of kitchen, recommended, maximum 15-day stay, separation of sexes, run by Quakers for Quakers, or development-work related travellers, other travellers taken only if space is available, good information on volunteer work, travel and language schools, breakfast US$2.50 (weekdays only) and laundry facilities on roof, safe-keeping for luggage, English library, references or advance booking recommended.

Near the train station **D** *Encino*, Av Insurgentes, 1 block from the railway station. Clean, private bath. **D** *Pontevedra*, Insurgentes Norte opposite railway station. Bath, hot water, TV, clean, helpful, will store luggage. **D** *Santander*, Arista 22, not far from railway station. With bath, good value and service, clean. **D** *Nueva Estación*, Zaragoza opposite Buenavista station. With bath, clean, quiet, friendly, colour TV. **D** *Yale*, Mosqueta 200, 5 mins' walk from Buenavista station. Showers, toilet, large room with TV and phone, very good value. Recommended. **E** *Atoyac*, Eje de Guerrero 161, Col Guerrero, 200 m from metro. Clean, friendly, safe.

South of the Zócalo **D** *El Roble*, Uruguay y Pino Suárez. Bath, TV, restaurant closes early. Recommended. **D** *El Salvador*, República de El Salvador 16, T5521-1247, near Zócalo. Modern, clean, laundry, safe, parking, good value. **D** *Monte Carlo*, Uruguay 69, T5518-1418/5521-2559/ 5521-9363 (D H Lawrence's hotel). Elegant, clean, friendly owner (also suites), with bath, hot water, good about storing luggage, safe car park inside the hotel premises, US$3.45, rooms in front noisy, even rooms at the back vibrate with noise from disco 2230-0300 Wed-Sat, can make collect calls abroad from room. Refuses to take bookings without payment in advance, also has mosquito-net problems. **E** *San Pedro*, was Mesones 126 and Pino Suárez, but reports say it has moved one block back! With bath, TV, tiny rooms, clean (but the occasional cockroach) and friendly. Good value.

D *Danky*, Donato Guerra 10, T5546-9960/61. With bath, central, hot water, phone, clean, easy parking. Recommended. **E** *Fornos*, Revillagigedo 92, near Balderas metro, 10 mins' walk to Alameda. Extremely clean, bathroom, TV, radio, smarter bigger rooms for **D**, restaurant, large, indoor car park, friendly staff, Dutch-speaking, Spanish owner, very good value. Highly recommended. **E** *Meave*, Meave 6, esq Lázaro Cárdenas, T5521-6712. Bath, TV, clean, quiet, very friendly, ground floor rooms rented by hour, but very discreet. Recommended.

South of the Alameda

B *Suites Quinta Palo Verde*, Cerro del Otate 20, Col Romero de Terreros (México 21 DF) T5554-3575. Pleasant, diplomatic residence turned guesthouse, near the University; run by a veterinary surgeon, Miguel Angel, very friendly, speaks English and German, but the dogs are sometimes noisy. *Suites Amberes*, Amberes 64, Zona Rosa, T5533-1306, F5207-1509. Kitch-enette, good value (US$150 per day and the equivalent of US$105 a day, for a week's stay). Recommended. *Suites Havre*, Havre 74, T5533-5670, near Zona Rosa. 56 suites with kitchen, phone and service. Recommended for longer stays.

For longer stays

Campo Escuela Nacional de Tantoco, Km 29.5 on road Mexico City to Toluca, T5512-2279. Cabins and campsite. The Dirección de Villas Deportivas Juveniles, T5665-5027, same address as Condep (see below), has details of campsites throughout the country. They have either camping, or camping and dormitory accommodation on sites with additional facili-ties, including luggage lockers; ask in advance what documentation is required. The nearest trailer park is *Pepe's* in Tepotzotlán, 43 km north of the capital (address: Eva Sámano de López, Mateos 62, T5876-0515/0616, in Mexico City, or contact *Mallorca Travel Service,* Paseo de la Reforma 105, T5705-2424, F5705-2673); it costs about US$12 a night, 55 pads with full hook-ups, very friendly, clean, hot showers, Canadian run. Recommended (owner has a hotel in Mexico City if you want to leave your trailer here and stay in the capital). You could try camping in the parking lot of the Museo de Antropología.

Campsites

Asociación Mexicana de Albergues de la Juventud, Madero 6, Oficina 314, México 1, DF. Write for information. There is a similar organization, *Comisión Nacional del Deporte* (Condep), which runs the *Villas Deportivas Juveniles* (see above); information office at Glorieta del Metro Insurgentes, Local C-11, T5525-2916/5533-1291. Condep will make reser-vations for groups of 10 or more; to qualify you must be between 8 and 65 and have a *Tarjeta Plan Verde* membership card, US$6, valid for 2 years, obtainable within 24 hrs from office at Tlalpan 583, esq Soria, metro Xola, or a IYHF card. See also SETEJ, below, for information on hotels and other establishments offering lodging for students.

Youth hostels

Eating

Bar La Opera, 5 de Mayo near Bellas Artes. Good atmosphere, expensive, see Pancho Villa's bullet hole in ceiling. Cocktails made with foreign spirits are 3 times as expensive as tequila. A very old restaurant with stunning tile décor and not touristy is the *Café Tacuba*, Tacuba 28. It specializes in Mexican food, very good *enchiladas*, excellent meat dishes, *tamales* and fruit desserts, good ser-vice, live music, very popular with local business people. It's also where renowned Mexican politi-cian, Danilo Fabio Altamirano, was assassinated in 1936. Highly recommended. *Cardenal*, Palma 23. Food, service and music (from 1530) is outstanding, 1930s ambience. *Casa Neri*, Bélgica 211, Col Portales. Excellent authentic cooking, Oaxacan specialities, huge *comida corrida* for US$4. *Casa Zavala*, Bolívar y Uruguay. Cheap, large selection of dishes. *Club de Periodistas de México*, Mata 8, near 5 de Mayo, open to public. OK. *Don Albis*, Tomás Edison 100. Delicious, large, cheap meals, popular with office workers. *Doneraky*, Nuevo León y Laredo, Col Condesa. Good tacos. Recommended. *El Huequito*, Bolívar 58. Casual, friendly, cheap meals for US$2. *El Perro de Enfrente*, Copenhaguen. Excellent food and service. Recommended. *El Refugio*, Liv-erpool 166. Tourist-oriented, good desserts, check bill carefully. *Focolare*, Hamburgo 87. Swanky

Mexican food
All the best hotels have good restaurants. The number and variety of eating places is vast; this is only a small selection

Mexico City

and expensive. *Fonda del Recuerdo*, Bahía de las Palmas 39A, México 17 DF. Excellent *mole poblano*, with music. *Hotel Majestic's* Mexican breakfast, Sat and Sun till 1200, excellent, go to terrace on seventh floor, otherwise food mediocre, live music. *Hostelería Santo Domingo*, Belisario Domínguez, 2 blocks west of Plaza Santo Domingo. Good food and service, excellent music, the oldest restaurant in the city. *La Plancha Azteca*, Río Lerma 54. Good tacos and tortas, moderate prices. *La Puerta del Angel*, Varsovia y Londres. Local food and specializing in American cuts, very good. *Los Girasoles*, corner of Tacuba and Gante. Mexican cuisine, makes a cover charge of US$1.20, which is not mentioned in the menu. Reasonable food. *La Casa de las Sirenas*, Tacuba y Seminario, behind the cathedral. Mexican menu. Excellent food and service. Recommended. *La Luna*, Oslo y Copenhaguen, Zona Rosa. Mostly Mexican, good breakfasts. *La Lupe*, Industria, Metro Coyoacán. Leafy patio, good and cheap, open till 1800. *México Viejo*, Tacuba 87 (near Zócalo). Excellent breakfast, not touristy, pricey. *Nadja*, Mesones 65, near Pino Suárez. Typical food, set menu for US$1.30, large portions, friendly. Recommended.

In Polanco For tacos and other tortilla-based dishes: *Los Tacos*, Newton just south of Horacio. Inexpensive. *Chilango's*, Molière between Ejército Nacional and Homero. Good value and service, MTV videos. Recommended. *El Tizoncito*, south of Ejército Nacional just west of Pabellón Polanco mall. Very popular at lunchtime. *El Jarocho*, Homero between Emerson and Hegel. Informal, eat-at-counter place, inexpensive.

International **Spanish** *Centro Castellano*, on Uruguay. Excellent, cheap, try the steaks. *Centro Catalán*, Bolívar 31, open 1100-1700 only. Excellent paella and other Spanish cuisine (2nd floor). *Del Cid*, Humboldt 61. Castilian with medieval menu. *El Faro*, Belgrado y Reforma, Zona Rosa. Very good, US$25-30 per head, closed in evenings except Thu and Fri, closed Sat. *Mesón del Castellano*, Bolívar y Uruguay, T5518-6080. Good atmosphere, plentiful and not too dear, excellent steaks. Highly recommended. *Mesón del Perro Andaluz*, Copenhaguen 26, and Luis P Ogazón 89. Very pleasant.

Oriental *Chen Wan*, Bolívar 104. Large portions, set meal US$2-3. *Dinastía Lee*, Independencia y Dolores. Reasonable Chinese food, open 0800-2400. *Mr Lee*, Independencia 19-B. Chinese, seafood, good food, value and service. Many Chinese restaurants are on or around the street of Dolores, near the Alameda.

US *Sanborn's* (known as the foreigners' home-from-home) has 36 locations, soda fountain, drugstore, restaurant, English, German and Spanish-language magazines, handicrafts, chocolates, etc, try their restaurant in the famous 16th-century *Casa de los Azulejos*, the 'house of tiles' at Av Madero 17, poor service, but many delicious local dishes in beautiful high-ceilinged room, about US$10-15 per person without wine (also has handicraft shops in basement and 1st floor). Almost everywhere are American-style restaurant chains, eg *Vips*, *Toks*, *El Portón* and *Lyni's*, offering Mexican and international food, clean and reliable, but by no means cheap by local standards (breakfast US$3.50, lunch US$7).

Many US chain fast-food restaurants (eg *Burger Boy* for good value breakfasts, *McDonalds* and *Dunkin Donuts* on Madero). Also Argentine, *Esquina La Pibe*, 2 locations just off Madero, OK. *El Patio del Gaucho*, Uruguay. Moderate prices, attentive service, good *asado*. Recommended.

Other *Andreson's*, Reforma 400. Very good atmosphere, excellent local menu, not cheap. *Delmonico's*, Londres 87 and 16 de Septiembre 82. Elegant. *Jena*, Morelos 110. Deservedly famous, *à la carte*, expensive. *La Cava*, Insurgentes Sur 2465. Excellent food and steaks, lavishly decorated as an old French tavern, moderate. *Keops*, Hamburgo 146, near Amberes in Zona Rosa, T5525-6706. Reasonable food, good live music. Also in Zona Rosa are *La Calesa de Londres*, Londres 102. Good meat. *Carousel Internacional*, Hamburgo and Niza. Very popular drinking-hole for smartly dressed Mexicans, resident *mariachi*, food not gourmet but fun atmosphere, about US$15 per person. *Trevi*, Dr Mora y Colón (west end of Alameda). Italian/US/Mexican, reasonable prices. *Milomita*, Mesones 87, Centro, 0800-2000. Specializes in American cuts of meat. *Café El Popular* next door to *Hotel Zamora* on 5 de Mayo.

French cuisine at *Le Gourmet*, Dakota 155. Said to be the most expensive restaurant in Mexico, and also said to be worth it! Others include *Ambassadeurs*, Paseo de la Reforma 12. Swanky and high priced. *Bellinghausen*, Londres y Niza. Excellent food, lunch only. *Café Konditori*, Génova 61. Danish open sandwiches. *Casa Bell*, Praga 14, T5511-5733. Smaller, identical menu, old house, elegant. Recommended. *Chalet Suizo*, Niza 37. Very popular with tourists, specializes in Swiss and German food, moderate. *Grotto Ticino*, Florencia 33. Swiss food. Recommended. *Les Moustaches*, Río Sena 88 (second most expensive in town, probably). *Rivoli*, Hamburgo 123. A gourmet's delight, high-priced. *Sir Winston Churchill*, Avila Camacho 67. Serves British food, expensive, smart, popular.

In Polanco (in the lower price ranges): *La Parrilla Suiza*, Arquimedes y Presidente Masaryk. For grilled meats, *alambres*, *sopa de tortilla* and other meat-and-cheese dishes, very popular, especially 1400-1600, service fair, moderately priced. *The City Bistro*, Lope de Vega 341, north of Horacio. Serves finest English and international cuisine, also stunningly inventive dishes, moderately priced. *El Buen Comer Marcelín*, Edgar Allan Poe 50, T5203-5337. Mainly French, very good. *Cambalache*, Arquimedes north of Presidente Masaryk. Argentine steakhouse, good steaks, wide selection of wines, cosy atmosphere, not as expensive as *El Rincón Argentino*, Presidente Masaryk 181, which is very expensive. *Embers*, Séneca y Ejército Nacional. 43 types of excellent hamburger, good French fries. Recommended.

La Costa Azul, López 127 y Delicias. Central, good, stark lighting, reasonable prices. **Seafood**
Marisquito, near Congress on Donceles 12. Very good. *Sushi Roll*, corner of 5 de Mayo and Filomeno Mata, about 5 blocks west of the Zocalo. Large selection of sushi rolls, very good.

Chalet Vegetariano, near Dr Río de la Loza. *El Bosque*, Hamburgo 15 between Berlín and **Vegetarian**
Dinamarca. Recommended. Vegetarian restaurant at Motolinia 31, near Madero, is open *The best place to buy* Mon-Sat 1300-1800. Reasonably priced. *Karl*, on Amberes near junction Londres. Excellent *natural products is in* buffet lunch and dinner. *Restaurante Vegetariano*, Filomeno Mata 13, open until 2000, Sun *the San Juan market* 0900-1900. Good *menú del día* US$3. *Saks*, Insurgentes Sur 1641, close to Teatro Insurgentes. *(see Markets page* Very good. *Super Soya*, Tacuba, metro Allende. Good juices and fruit salads, health food *129), including tofu* shop. *Yug*, Varsovia 3. Cheap, vegetarian, 4-course set lunch US$3.50. Health food shop, *(queso de soya)* *Alimentos Naturales*, P Arriaga, close to metro Revolución. Health food shops in other metro stations.

Coyoacán There are several pleasant *cafeterías* in the Jardín Centenario, some of which **Eating beyond** serve light snacks and *antojitos*; the best known is *El Parnaso*, adjacent to the bookshop of **the centre** the same name. Two of the best-known cantinas in Mexico are *La Guadalupana* (Higuera) and the *Puerta del Sol* on Plaza Hidalgo. No shortage of restaurants with *comida corrida*, though prices tend to be higher than in other parts of the city (US$1.75-US$2.50). Very good value are: *Rams*, Hidalgo, almost opposite Museo Nacional de las Culturas Populares, excellent fish; *Fabio's*, overlooking Plaza Hidalgo and the Delegación, credit cards accepted; *Rincón Oaxaqueño*, Carrillo Puerto 12, US$1.75. Good value, too, in the *Mercado*, between Malintzin and Xicoténcatl. Possibly the most exquisite *quesadillas* in the whole of Coyoacán are found at Local 31 (outside the market, opposite Jardín del Carmen, closed Wed); stall holders are very friendly and fruit and vegetable sellers are ready to explain the names and uses of their goods; frequent musical entertainment particularly lunchtime and weekends. The *Restaurante Vegetariano*, Carranza y Caballocalco, offers an excellent US$5 buffet lunch; *El Morral*, Allende 2, set lunch US$3, double at weekends, no credit cards, quieter upstairs, palatial lavatories. Highly recommended. *Caballocalco*, Plaza Hidalgo. Expensive, but very good, especially for breakfast. There is a *Sanborn's* on Jardín Centenario, near *El Hijo del Cuervo*. *Hacienda de Cortés*, Fernández Leal 74, behind Plaza de la Conchita. Exceptionally pleasant surroundings, large, shaded, outdoor dining area, excellent breakfast, good value, *comida corrida* US$5, try the *sábana de res con chilaquiles verdes*. Tucked away down Higuera, opposite the post office, is *El Jolgorio*, excellent lunch menu, reasonable set meal prices, good salads and vegetarian dishes. If you are lucky - they don't always open - you may find the same menu (same management), as well as breakfasts, in *Los Talleres*, in Francisco Sosa, with a delightful tranquil patio. *Pacífico*, Av Pacífico, in restored 19th-century

Mexico City

residence. Specialities include pre-Hispanic dishes, not cheap but good value. *Villa Cristal*, Allende. Excellent *comida corrida*. *La Doña*, Héroes del 47, No 141. Elegant restaurant, good value. Very fine home-made pastries at *Como a La Antigua*, Allende 14, just past the Foro Cultural Hugo Argüelles and before a Jarocho coffee shop.

Cafés Many economical restaurants on 5 de Mayo, eg *Café La Blanca* at No 40. Popular and busy atmosphere, good expresso coffee, open for Sun breakfast and early on weekdays. Recommended. *Torta Brava*, near Zócalo. Good *comida*, friendly. *París*, No 10. Good breakfast and dinner. *Popular*, No 52 between Alameda and Zócalo, on corner of alley to *Hotel Juárez*. Cheap, rushed, 24 hrs, meeting place. *Gili's Pollo*, opposite *Hotel Rioja*. Excellent chicken, eat in or takeaway. *El 20 de Bolívar*, Bolívar 20. Excellent service and highly recommended for breakfasts. *Klein's*, Av Madero with Simón Bolívar. Buffet US$3.30. *Comida Económica Verónica*, República de Cuba, 2 doors from *Hotel Habana* (No 77). For tasty breakfasts and set *comida corrida*, very hot *chilaquiles*, good value and delightful staff. Recommended. *La Rosita*, 2a Callejón de Allende 14-C. Cheap and good. *El Reloj*, 5 de Febrero 50. Good *comida* and *à la carte*. *Rex*, 5 de Febrero 40, near Zócalo. Good *café con leche* and cheap *comidas*. *Shakey's*, Monte de Piedad (at the Zócalo). Self-service, large helpings of pizza and chicken. *Pastelería Madrid*, 5 de Febrero 25, 1 block from *Hotel Isabel la Católica*. Good pastries and breakfasts. *Bamerette*, Av Juárez 52 (*Hotel Bamer*). Excellent breakfast. Good small restaurants on Uruguay, near *Hotel Monte Carlo*. The *Maple*, next to *Hotel Roble* at No 109, has been recommended for its *comida*, and *Pancho* (No 84), for its breakfasts, cheap meals and service. *Flor*, San Jerónimo 100, near *Hotel Ambar*. Recommended for breakfast, non-touristy atmosphere, cheap. *Tic Tac*, Av Balderas. Very good *comida corrida*. *La Habana*, Bucareli y Morelos. Not cheap but good food and excellent coffee. Another centre for small restaurants is Pasaje Jacarandas, off Génova 44: *Llave de Oro* and many others. *La Casa del Pavo*, Motolinia near 16 de Septiembre. Clean, courteous, excellent *comida corrida*. Also Motilinia between 5 de Mayo and Tacuba. Cheap *cafeterías* on Belisario Domínguez. *Gaby's*, Liverpool y Nápoles. Excellent Italian-style coffee, décor of old coffee machines, etc. *Duca d'Este*, Av Florencia y Hamburgo. Good coffee and pastries. *Il Mangiare*, opposite Poliforum Cultural Siqueiros (see page 112). Very good sandwiches. *El Núcleo*, Lerma y Marne. Excellent fruit salads, breakfasts and lunches, closes 1800 and all day Sun. *Zenón*, corner of Madero 65 and Palma. Trendy décor, average Mexican food, *comida corrida* US$1.50-US$3.50. *Enanos de Tapanco y Café*, Orizaba 161, between Querétaro and San Luis Potosí. Great coffee, warm friendly atmosphere. Good breakfasts can be had at *Woolworth*, 16 de Septiembre. *Dulcería de Celaya*, 5 de Mayo 39. Good candy store and lovely old premises. Good bakeries on 16 de Noviembre, near Zócalo. Also *Panadería La Vasconia*, Tacuba 73. Good, also sells cheap chicken and fries. *Jugos California* on Guerrero by Hidalgo metro. Good juices. *Roxy*, Montes de Oca y Mazatlán, Col Condesa. Good ice cream. Good juices and sandwiches at the *Juguería* on 5 de Mayo, next to *Hotel Rioja*. *El Sol*, Gómez Farías 67, Col San Rafael. Frequented by journalists, superb Mexican cuisine, *comida corrida* US$2. See Internet page 135, for cybercafés.

Bars *Bar Jardín*, in the *Hotel Reforma*. *El Morroco*, Conjunto Marrakesh, Florencia 36. *Casino*,
There are many Isabel la Católica, near *Sanborn's*. Superb painted glass doors and lavish interior, also has
safe gay bars in the Spanish restaurant. *Abundio*, Zaragoza y Mosqueta. Very friendly, free food. *Yuppies*
Zona Rosa in the *Sports Bar*, Génova. Expensive but good atmosphere. *Guadalupana*, near Plaza Hidalgo,
area between Niza Coyoacán.
and Florencia,
north of Londres

Nightclubs *El Patio*, Atenas 9. *Passepartout*, Hamburgo. *La Madelón*, Florencia 36. *Brasileirinho*, León 160. There are many discos in the better hotels and scattered throughout town.

Entertainment

In a city the size of Mexico DF you have the chance to do, try and test things that maybe you haven't had the chance to experience before. Step out and give it a go.

A number show non-Hollywood films in original language (Spanish subtitles); check *Tiempo Libre* magazine, or *Mexico City News* for details. Some recommended cinemas are: *Cineteca Nacional*, Metro Coyoacán (excellent bookshop on the cinema and related topics, library). *Cinematógrafo del Chopo*, Dr Atl, non-commercial films daily 1700 and 1930, US$1; good cinema in Ciudad Universitaria; *Cine Latino*, Av Reforma between the statue of Cuauhtémoc and El Angel. *Cine Versalles*, Versalles (side street off Av Reforma, near statue of Cuauhtémoc). *Cine Electra*, Río Guadalquivir (near El Angel). *Cine Diana*, Av Reforma, at the end where Parque Chapultepec starts. *Cine Palacio Chino*, in the Chinese *barrio* south of Av Juárez (also interesting for restaurants). The sound is often very low on subtitled films, only option is to sit near speakers at front. Most cinemas, except *Cineteca Nacional*, offer reduced prices on Wed.

A fine place for light refreshments and music is the *Hostería del Bohemio*, formerly the San Hipólito monastery, near Reforma on Av Hidalgo 107, metro Hidalgo: poetry and music every night from 1700 to 2200, light snacks and refreshments US$4 minimum, expensive but no cover charge.

Charreadas (cowboy displays) *Rancho Grande de la Villa*, at very top of Insurgentes Norte (from metro Indios Verdes, walk north beyond bus station and keep asking), Sun 1100-1500, US$1.30.

Football Sun midday, Aztec and Olympic stadia (former has a great atmosphere at football matches, latter has a Rivera mural of the history of Mexican sport); also Thu (2100) and Sat (1700). Tickets from US$3.35 at Olympic Stadium. To Aztec Stadium take metro to Taxqueña terminus, then tram en route to Xochimilco to Estadio station; about 75 mins from Zócalo. To Olympic Stadium take bus down Insurgentes marked 'CU' (Ciudad Universitaria), or metro to Universidad terminus, then local bus (US$0.35) or taxi (US$1); leave Zócalo at 1045 for 1200 kick-off.

Horse races *Hipódromo de las Américas*, west of Blvd Manuel Avila Camacho, off Av Conscriptos. Beautiful track with infield lagoons and flamingos, and plenty of atmosphere.

Palacio de Bellas Artes (for ballet, songs, dances, also concerts 2-3 times a week, see page 102), *Fábregas*, *Lírico*, *Iris*, *Sullivan*, *Alarcón*, *Hidalgo*, *Urueta*, *San Rafael* and *Insurgentes* in town and a cluster of theatres around the Auditorio Nacional in Chapultepec Park (check at tourist office for details of cheap programmes). Also in Chapultepec Park is the Audiorama (behind the Castle on the Constituyentes side) where one may listen to recorded classical music in a small open amphitheatre in a charming wooded glade. A request book is provided, for the following day. There may be a free performance of a play in one of the parks by the Teatro Trashumante (Nomadic Theatre). Variety show nightly with singers, dancers, comedians, magicians and ventriloquists, very popular with locals, at *Teatro la Blanquita*, on Av Lázaro Cárdenas Sur near Plaza Garibaldi. The *Teatro de la Ciudad*, Donceles 36 (T5510-2197 and 5510-2942), has the Ballet Folklórico Nacional Aztlán, US$3-US$15 for tickets, very good shows Sun morning and Wed.

Festivals

The largest is the Independence celebration on **15 Sep**, when the President gives the *Grito*: 'Viva México' from the Palacio Nacional on the Zócalo at 2300, and rings the Liberty Bell (now, sadly, electronic!). This is followed by fireworks, and on **16 Sep** (0900-1400) there are military and traditional regional parades in the Zócalo and surrounding streets – great atmosphere. Also definitely worth a visit if you're in town on **12 Dec** is the *Guadalupana* at the Basílica de Guadalupe (see page 119).

Shopping

Mexican **jewellery** and hand-made **silver** can be bought everywhere. Among the good silver shops are *Sanborn's*, *Calpini*, *Prieto*, and *Vendome*. *Joyería Sobre Diseño* (Local 159) at the Ciudadela Market is helpful and will produce personalized jewellery cheaply. There are

Cinemas
For all cultural events, consult Tiempo Libre, every Thursday from news stands, US$1, or monthly programme pamphlets from Bellas Artes bookshop

Folk music

Spectator sports

Theatres
Spectaculars (eg presidential inauguration) are often staged in the Auditorio Nacional itself

Just as much fun, and probably safer, is the Grito that takes place at the same time in the Plaza in Coyoacán

Mexico City

also good buys in perfumes, quality leather, and suede articles. *De Sol* on 16 de Septiembre, and on Periférico Sur, T5806-8427, for cheap food, drinks, clothes, domestic goods, etc. With the extension of the ringroads around the city, **hypermarkets** are being set up: there are two, *Perisur* in the south of the city (with *Liverpool, Sears, Sanborn's* and *Palacio de Hierro*), open Tue-Fri 1100-2000, Sat 1100-2100; and *Plaza Satélite* in the north (with *Sumesa, Sears* and *Liverpool*), open on Sun. There is an ISSSTE supermarket in Tres Guerras, 2 blocks from metro Balderas and 1 block from Bucareli. At Pino Suárez metro station are several shops selling *charro* clothing and equipment (leggings, boots, spurs, bags, saddles, etc), eg *Casa Iturriaga*. Recommended. Many small **tailors** are found in and around República de Brasil; suits made to measure in a week or less at a fraction of European prices. Guatemalan Refugee shop, Yosemite 45, Col Nápoles, off Insurgentes Sur, T5523-2114. **Art supplies** *Casa Bernstein*, República de El Salvador 66.

Books & music Many good ones in the city centre, especially along Av Juárez, Madero and Donceles, also along Miguel Angel de Quevedo (Coyoacán/San Angel – Metro Miguel Angel de Quevedo). Good chain of literary and art bookshops called *Libros y Arte* in the Palacio de Bellas Artes, the airport (area D), the Centro Nacional de Las Artes, the Cineteca Nacional, Coyoacán (Av Hidalgo), Museo del Carmen (San Angel) and the Museo Nacional de las Culturas (Moneda 13, Centro). Several shops belonging to the *Gandhi* chain (large selection, keen prices), two large branches on Miguel Angel de Quevedo, another opposite Palacio de Bellas Artes. Good range of **music** CDs and tapes at *Gandhi Discos*, Carrillo Puerto 6, excellent prices. One of the most famous bookshops is *El Parnaso*, Jardín Centenario, Coyoacán (its coffee is equally well known). Others include *Librería Británica*, Serapio Rendón 125 (near Parque Sullivan, west of Monumento Cuauhtémoc on Reforma), also Madero 30-A (limited range of titles in English). The *American Bookstore* (Madero 25, also on Revolución – 5-min bus ride south from metro Barranca del Muerte), is much better in this and other respects – large stocks of Penguins and Pelicans, low mark up. For inexpensive editions in Spanish look out for branches of the *Librería del Sótano* (Av Juárez, Antonio Caso, Miguel Angel de Quevedo), and of the *Fondo de Cultura Económico* (Miguel Angel de Quevedo). *Librería Madero*, Madero 12, good, also stocks antiquarian books. *Nueva Librería Francesa*, Hamburgo 172, T5525-1173. *Librería Italiana*, Plaza Río de Janeiro 53, Col Roma, T5511-6180. The *Sanborn's* chain has the largest selection of English-language magazines in the country, also stocks some best-selling paperbacks in English. *Casa Libros*, Monte Athos 355, Lomas, large stock of second-hand English books, the shop is staffed by volunteers, gifts of books welcome, all proceeds to the American Benevolent Society. *Libros y Discos*, Madero 1. Plenty of Spanish bookshops on Argentina and many open-shelf bookstores in the underpass between metros Zócalo and Pino Suárez appropriately called the Paseo por los Libros. *UNAM* bookshop has a comprehensive range. Second-hand book market on Independencia just past junction with Eje Lázaro Cárdenas has some English books; also Puente de Alvarado, 100 m from Metro Hidalgo, and Dr Bernard 42, metro Niños Héroes. Second-hand Spanish and antiquarian booksellers on Donceles between Palma and República de Brasil, about 1½ blocks from Zócalo. *La Torre de Papel*, Filomeno Mata 6-A, in Club de Periodistas, sells newspapers from all over Mexico and US. See also Newspapers, page 85.

Cards & posters Diego Rivera posters and postcards are available from *Mexport UK*, T5658-5376, wwwjohngibbs.com, at museums throughout Mexico City. International trade enquiries welcome.

Cycle shops *Tecno-Bici*, Av Manuel Acuña 27 (Camarones metro station, line 7), stocks almost all cycle spares, parts, highly recommended. *Benolto*, near Polanco metro, stocks almost all cycle spares. Another good shop is between San Antonio and Mixcoac metro stations. The Escuela Médico Militar, near Pino Suárez metro station, has a very good shop, stocking all the best-known international makes for spare parts. The best **cycle repair** in Mexico City is *Hambling González Muller*, Ezequiel Ordóñez 46-1, Col Copilco el Alto, Coyoacán, T/F5658-5591, builds wheels and frames for Mexican racers, reasonable prices, highly recommended.

Fonart, Fondo Nacional para el Fomento de las Artesanías, a state organization founded in 1974 in order to rescue, promote and diffuse the traditional crafts of Mexico. Main showroom at Av Patriotismo 594 (Metro Mixcoac), T5598-1666, and a branch at Av Juárez 89 (metro Hidalgo). Competitive prices, superb quality. *The Mercado de Artesanías Finas Indios Verdes* is at Galería Reforma Norte SA, González Bocanegra 44 (corner of Reforma Norte, near statue of Cuitláhuac, Tlatelolco); good prices and quality but no bargaining. For onyx, *Müllers*, Londres y Florencia, near Insurgentes metro, good chess sets. For Talavera pottery from Puebla, *Uriarte*, Emilio Castelar 95-E, Polanco, T5282-2699, and Pabellón Altavista, Calzada Desierto de los Leones 52 D-6, San Angel, T5616-3119, www.talavera.com There is an annual *national craft fair* in Mexico City, first week in December. There are many gift shops in Coyoacán, in the south of the city: *Etra*, on corner of Francisco Sosa opposite Jardín Centenario, offers good taste and prices; *Mayolih*, Aldama with Berlín, 2 blocks from Museo Frida Kahlo; and *La Casita* on Higuera.

Mercado San Juan, Ayuntamiento and Arandas, near Salto del Agua metro, good prices for handicrafts, especially leather goods and silver (also cheap fruit and health food); open Mon-Sat 0900-1900, Sun 0900-1600 (but don't go before 1000). The *Plaza Ciudadela* market (Mercado Central de Artesanías, open 1100-1800 weekdays, Sun 1100-1400), beside Balderas 95 between Ayuntamiento y Plaza Morelos, government-sponsored, fixed prices, good selection, reasonable and uncrowded, is cheaper than San Juan, but not for leather; craftworkers from all Mexico have set up workshops here (best for papier maché, lacquer, pottery and Guatemalan goods) but prices are still cheaper in places of origin. *Mercado La Lagunilla* near Glorieta Cuitláhuac (take *colectivo* from metro Hidalgo) is a flea market where antique and collectable bargains are sometimes to be found, also a lot of rubbish (open daily, but Sun best day). The market, which covers several blocks, now has all sorts of merchandise, including a wider range of non-silver jewellery; good atmosphere. Mercado Insurgentes in Calle Londres, Zona Rosa, good for silver, but other things expensive, stallholders pester visitors, only place where they do so. There is a market in every district selling pottery, glassware, textiles, *sarapes* and jewellery. Try also *San Angel Bazar del Sábado*, (see page 113), although expensive, many items are exclusive to it; good leather belts, crafts and silver; open Sat only from about 1100. Mexican tinware and lacquer are found everywhere. Vast fruit and veg market, *Mercado Merced* (see page 100), metro Merced. A few blocks away on Fray Servando Teresa de Mier (nearest metro Fray Servando) lies the fascinating *Mercado Sonora*: secret potions and remedies, animals and birds as well as *artesanías*. *Buena Vista craft market*, Aldama 187 y Degollado (nearest metro Guerrero), excellent quality (open 0900-1800, Sun 0900-1400). Also on Aldama, No 211, between Sol and Luna, the *Tianguis del Chopo* is held on Sat 1000-1600, selling clothes, records, etc, frequented by hippies, punks, rockers, and police. You can bargain in the markets and smaller shops. *Mercado Jamaica*, Jamaica metro, line 4, has a huge variety of fruits and vegetables, also flowers, pottery, and canaries, parrots, geese, and ducks, indoor and outdoor halls.

Kodak film (Ektachrome, not Kodachrome) is produced in Mexico and is not expensive. Imported film is also available. Cheapest film reported to be on Av Madero, but shop around. The price for slide film does not include processing. Small shops around República de Chile and Tacuba are cheaper than larger ones south of Av 5 de Mayo, but it may be worth paying more for good quality prints. Special offers abound, quality is good, prints normally ready in 45 mins (no express charge), slides up to 48 hrs. *Laboratorio Mexicano del Imagen*, Carlos B Zetina 34, Col Hipodromo Condesa, T5515-5540, excellent quality, fast service, normal prices. Several shops sell slide and print film (Fuji and Kodak) on Donceles, near Zócalo. **In Coyoacán**, rapid **film** developing and printing at *Foto Coyoacán*, Francisco Sosa 1, opposite the Arches. English, French, German spoken. **Camera repairs** *Vanta*, Gabriel Barreda 93, Col San Rafael, metro San Cosme, T5566-5566. Mon-Fri 1000-1400 and 1530-1730.

Sports

At *Chapultepec Golf Club* and *Churubusco Country Club*. These are private clubs, open to visitors only if accompanied by a member. Green fees are US$20 upwards.

Handicrafts

Markets

Photography

Golf

Mexico City

Hiking Every weekend with the Alpino and Everest clubs. *Club de Exploraciones de México*, Juan A Mateos 146, Col Obrero (Metro Chabacano), DF 06800, T5578-5730, 1930-2400 Wed or Fri, organizes several walks in and around the city on Sat and Sun, cheap equipment hire, slideshow Wed. *Club Alpino Mexicano*, Córdoba 234, Col Roma (Metro Hospital General), T/F5574-9683, open Mon-Fri 1000-2000, Sat 1000-1500, small shop (if club door is closed ask here for access). José María Aguayo Estrada, club president, very helpful; also arrange (free) mountain hiking at weekends, run ice climbing courses. **Equipment suppliers** *Vertimania*, Federico I de la Chica 12, Plaza Versailles, Local 11-B, Col Satélite, T/F5393-5287. More central is *Deportes Rubens*, Venustiano Carranza 17, T5518-5636, F5512-8312. **Stove repair** *Servicio Coleman*, Marqués Sterling 23.

Climbing/ *Rocadromo*, climbing wall, Lindavista, T5752-5674. Further reading: *Iztaccíhuatl, Toluca and*
abseiling *Colima*, by Alfredo Careaga Pardave; *Mexico's Volcanoes*, by R Secord.

Swimming Agua Caliente, Las Termas, Elba, Centro Deportivo Chapultepec and others.

Transport

Local **Car hire** *Budget Rent Auto*, Reforma 60; *Hertz*, Revillagigedo 2; *Avis*, Medellín 14; *VW*, Av
See also Ins and Chapultepec 284-6; *National Car Rental*, Insurgentes Sur 1883; *Auto Rent*, Reforma Norte
outs, page 92 604; quick service at Av Chapultepec 168, 15533-5335 (5762-9892 airport); *Pamara*,
Hamburgo 135, T5525-5572, 200 km free mileage; *Odin*, Balderas 24-A; and many local firms,
If you want to which tend to be cheaper. It is generally cheaper to hire in the US or Europe. **NB** When driv-
bring your car into ing in the capital you must check which *día sin auto hoy no circula* applies to your vehicle's
the city, find a cheap number plate; if your car is on the street when its number is prohibited, you could be fined
hotel where you US$80. This should not apply to foreign-licensed cars. The regulation covers the State of
can park and leave México as well as the Distrito Federal. The ban applies to the last digit of your number plate:
it, while you explore Mon 5, 6; Tue 7, 8; Wed 3, 4; Thu 1, 2; Fri 9, 0. Occasionally, when contamination levels are
the city by bus, even worse than usual, the programme runs at weekends too: Sat, all even numbers and 0;
metro or on foot Sun, all odd numbers. Normally, you can drive freely in 'greater' Mexico City on Sat, Sun and
between 2200 and 0500 all week.

City buses Buses have been coordinated into one system: odd numbers run north-south, evens east-west. Fares on large buses, which display routes on the windscreen, are US$0.15, exact fare only. There are 60 direct routes and 48 feeder (SARO) routes. Thieves and pickpockets haunt the buses plying along Reforma and Juárez. A useful route for tourists (and well known to thieves, so don't take anything you don't require immediately) is No 76, which runs from Uruguay (about the level of the Juárez Monument at Parque Alameda) along Paseo de la Reforma, beside Chapultepec Park. A *Peribus* service goes round the entire Anillo Periférico. Trolley buses also charge US$0.15. **Colectivos** run on fixed routes, often between metro stations and other known landmarks; destination and route displayed on the windscreen. Fares are US$0.20 up to 5 km, US$0.25 up to 10 km and US$0.35 beyond. If a bus runs on the same route, it may be preferable as it has fixed stops.

Beware of pick- **Metro** An efficient, modern system and the best method of getting around the city, espe-
pocketing at any cially when the pollution is bad. Trains are fast, frequent, clean and quiet although over-
time on the metro; crowded at certain times. Pino Suárez, Hidalgo and Autobuses del Norte are particularly
the police are infamous for thieves. Between 1800 and 2100 men are separated from women and children
not as helpful as at Pino Suárez and certain other central stations. Two pieces of medium-sized luggage are
the vigilancias permitted. Music is played quietly at the stations. Tickets cost 2 pesos, buy several to avoid queuing, check train direction before entering turnstile or you may have to pay again. Lines 1, 2, 3 and A open 0500-0030 Mon-Fri, 0600-0130 Sat and 0700-0030 Sun and holidays; the other lines open 1 hr later on weekdays (same hours on weekends and holidays). Do not take photos or make sound-recordings in the metro without obtaining a permit and a uniformed escort from metro police, or you could be arrested. For lost property enquire at Oficina de Objetos Extraviados at Chabacano (intersection of lines 2, 8 and 9), open Mon-Fri only.

There is a metro information service at Insurgentes station on the Pink Line 1, which dispenses maps, and most interchange stations have information kiosks. The *Atlas de Carreteras*, US$1.65, has a map of Mexico City, its centre and the metro lines marked. *Pronto's* map of the metropolitan area displays the metro clearly. Good metro and bus maps at the Anthropology Museum, US$1.25. *Guía práctica del Metro*, US$9, explains all the station symbols; also *Guía cultural del Metro*, US$3, both for sale at Zócalo station. All the stations have a symbol, eg the grasshopper signifying Chapultepec and there is a detailed local street map of the immediate vicinity – *planos de barrio* – at every station.

There are 9 lines in service. **Line 1** (pink) from **Observatorio** (by Chapultepec Park) to **Pantitlán** in the eastern suburbs. It goes under Av Chapultepec and not far from the lower half of Paseo de la Reforma, the Mercado Merced, and 3 km from the airport. **Line 2** (blue) from **Cuatro Caminos** in the northwest to the Zócalo and then south above ground to

Mexico City metro

Mexico City

Taxqueña. **Line 3** (olive) from Indios Verdes south to the University City (free bus service to Insurgentes). **Line 4** (turquoise) from **Santa Anita** on the southeast side to **Martín Carrera** in the northeast. **Line 5** (yellow) from **Pantitlán**, via Terminal Aérea (which is within walking distance of gate A of the airport, but some distance from the international gates – opens 0600), up to **Politécnico** (if using La Raza to connect with Line 3, note that there is a long walk between Lines 5 and 3, through the Tunnel of Knowledge). **Line 6** (red) from **El Rosario** in the northwest to **Martín Carrera** in the northeast. **Line 7** (orange) from **El Rosario** in the northwest to **Barranca del Muerto** in the southwest. **Line 8** (green) runs from **Garibaldi** (north of Bellas Artes, Line 2), through Chabacano (Line 9) and Santa Anita (Line 4), to **Constitución de 1917** in the southeast. **Line 9** (brown) parallels Line 1 to the south, running from **Tacubaya** in the west (where there are interesting paintings in the station) to **Pantitlán** in the east.

In addition to the numbered lines: running southeast from Pantitlán, Line A, the *metro férreo* goes as far as La Paz, 10 stations in all. From Taxqueña the *tren ligero* goes as far as Xochimilco, a very convenient way to this popular destination. Line B, from Buenavista to Ciudad Azteca in Ecatepec, north of the city, is now partially open and should be completed by the end of 2000.

At the Zócalo metro station there is an interesting permanent exhibit about the city. At Pino Suárez, the station has been built around a small, restored Aztec temple. *Art in the metro*: Line 1, Pino Suárez and Tacubaya; Line 2, Bellas Artes and Panteones; Line 3, La Raza, scientific display in the Tunnel of Knowledge, and south of Coyoacán; Line 4, Santa Anita; Line 5, Terminal Aérea; Line 6, all stations, Line 7, Barranca del Muerto; Line 9, Mixuca.

Taxis There are 3 types: *1) Turismo taxis*, which operate from first-class hotels, the Museo Nacional de Antropología, etc – are the most expensive. *2) Taxis from sitios (fixed ranks)*, from bus terminals, railway station and other locations; no meters. About double the normal price but safer. You pay in advance at a booth (check your change); they charge on a zone basis, US$4.60 for up to 4 km, rising to US$22 for up to 22 km (the same system applies at the airport – see below). *3) Taxis on unfixed routes are green* (lead-free petrol) and can be flagged down anywhere; tariffs US$0.35 plus 5 cents for each 250 m or 45 seconds; between 2200 and 0600 they charge 20% extra. They have meters (check they are working properly and set at zero); if you do not bargain before getting in, or if the driver does not know the route well, the meter will be switched on, which usually works out cheaper than negotiating a price. Some drivers refuse to use their meter after 1800. Note that radiotelephone taxis and those with catalytic converters have a basic fee of 2.50 pesos. Drivers often do not know where the street you want is; try to give the name of the intersection between two streets rather than a number, because the city's numbering can be erratic. A tip is not normally expected, except when special help has been given. For information, or complaints, T5605-5520; if complaining, make sure you take the taxi's ID number. Another type of taxi travel, the tricycle, is now being encouraged to counter exhaust pollution, and is a good way to see the architecture of the centre.

Warning Lone travellers, especially female, are advised to take only official *Sitio* taxis (not VW ones) from hotels or ordered by phone, particularly at night. Tourist police advise that you make note of registration and taxi numbers before getting in.

Long distance

See also Transport, page 130

See map on page 94, for location of terminals

For details of bus services, see destinations in text

Buses At all bus stations there are many counters for the bus companies, not all are manned and it is essential to ask which is selling tickets for the destination you want (don't take notice boards at face value). On the whole, the bus stations are clean and well organized. Book ahead where possible. Buses to destinations in north Mexico, including US borders, leave from **Terminal del Norte**, Av Cien Metros 4907, which has a *casa de cambio*, 24-hr cafés, left luggage, pharmacy, bakery and phone offices for long-distance calls (often closed and poorly informed, very high charges). The bus station is on metro line 5 at Autobuses del Norte. City buses marked Cien Metros or Central del Norte go directly there. **Terminal del Sur**, at corner of Tlalpan 2205 across from metro Taxqueña (line 2), serves Cuernavaca, Acapulco and Zihuatanejo areas. Direct buses to centre (Donceles) from Terminal del Sur, and an express bus connects the Sur and Norte terminals. It is difficult to get tickets to the south, book as soon as possible; the terminal for the south is chaotic. The **Terminal Poniente** is situated opposite the Observatorio station of line 1 of the metro, to serve the west of Mexico. You can go to the centre by bus from the *urbano* outside the bus station, Terminal Poniente (US$0.10). The **Terminal Oriente**, known as **TAPO**, Calzada Ignacio Zaragoza (Metro San Lázaro, Line 1) for buses to Veracruz, Yucatán and southeast, including Oaxaca and Puebla (2 hrs). It has a tourist information office open from 0900; luggage lockers, US$2.65 per day, key is left with guard; post office, *farmacia* changes travellers' cheques. To **Guatemala**, from TAPO, take a bus to Tapachula, Comitán or Ciudad Cuauhtémoc, pesos only accepted.

There are also buses departing from Mexico City airport (outside Sala D), to Puebla, Toluca, Cuernavaca and Querétaro, very convenient. Buy ticket from driver.

All bus terminals operate taxis with voucher system and there are long queues (check change carefully at the taxi office). It is much easier to pay the driver, although beware of extra charges. In the confusion at the terminals some drivers move each other's cabs to get out of the line faster and may take your voucher and disappear. Fares are given under Taxis above. The terminals are connected by metro, but this is not a good option at rush hours, or if carrying too much luggage. Advance booking is recommended for all trips, and very early reservation if going to fiestas during Holy Week, etc. At Christmas, many Central American students return home via Tapachula, and buses from Mexico City are booked solid for 2 weeks before, except for those lines that do not make reservations. You must go and queue at the bus stations, which can involve a long wait, sometimes 2-2½ hrs. Even if you are travelling, you may sometimes be required to buy a *boleto de andén* (platform ticket) at many bus stations. Note that many bus companies require luggage to be checked in 30 mins in advance of departure.

Bus companies (tickets and bookings) **Going north**: *Transportes del Norte*, at Av Insurgentes Centro 137, near Reforma, T5587-5511/5400; depart from Terminal del Norte. *Omnibus de México*, Insurgentes Norte 42, at Héroes Ferrocarrileros (T5567-6756 and 5567-5858). *Greyhound* bus, Reforma 27, T5535-2618/4200, F5535-3544, closed 1400-1500 and all day Sun; information at Terminal del Norte from *Transportes del Norte* (*Chihuahuenses*) or *Tres Estrellas* bus counters, prices only, no schedules. **Going to central states**: *Autobuses Anáhuac*, Bernal Díaz 6, T5591-0533; Terminal del Norte departures. **Going northwest**: *ETN*, Terminal del Norte, T5567-3773, or Terminal Poniente, T5273-0251; *Tres Estrellas de Oro*, Calzada Vallejo 1268 Norte, Col Santa Rosa, T5391-1139/3021, Terminal del Norte. **Going northeast**: *ADO*, Av Cien Metros 4907, T5567-8455/5322. Beware of *ADO* selling tickets for buses and then not running the service. Although the ticket will be valid for a later bus, there are then problems with overbooking (your seat number won't be valid). **Going south** (including Guatemala): *Cristóbal Colón*, Blvd Ignacio Zaragoza 200, T5542-7263 to 66; from Terminal de Oriente; also *ADO*, Buenavista 9 (T5592-3600 or 5542-7192 at terminal). **Going southwest**: *Estrella de Oro*, Calzada de Tlalpan 2205 (T5549-8520 to 29).

Air The airport terminal is divided into sections, each designated by a letter. A row of shops and offices outside each section contains various services. **Section A: national arrivals**; post office, city of Mexico tourist office, exit to taxis and metro, INAH shop, telecommunications office. Between **A** and **B**: *AeroMéxico*; *Bancomer* ATM. Outside **Section B**: *Banamex*. Between **B** and **C**: entrance to *Continental Plaza* hotel, *casa de cambio*. **Section C**: *Mexicana*; map shop. Ladatel phones just after C (Ladatel cards are sold at many outlets in the airport). Between **C** and **D** is the Exposición Diego Rivera exhibition hall. **C-D**: Other national airline offices; bookshop. **Section D: national and international departures**; *cambio* opposite. By D are more national airline desks, long-distance phones, a bar and restaurant. From D you have to leave the building to get to **Section E: international arrivals**; car hire offices, exchange (Banamex), 24-hr luggage lockers (US$2.50 per day). **F: international check-in**; banks. Upstairs at **E-F** are shops, fast-food restaurants (mostly US-style), exchange and phones. **Money exchange** Pesos may be bought at any of the bank branches liberally spread from **A-F**. Most foreign currencies or travellers' cheques accepted, also most credit cards. The rate can vary considerably, so shop around. When buying dollars (and other 'hard' currency, when available), *Coberturas Mexicanas* almost always offers the best rates (Local 1, section

Mexico City

D and Local 8/9, section E). Only US$500 may be changed back into dollars after passing through immigration and customs when leaving. Exchange facilities in E or F (particularly on the upper floor) are less crowded. Banks and *casas de cambio* between them provide a 24-hr service. **Telephones** Phone calls from the airport may be made at many locations, but you have to keep trying all the phones to find one in operation that will accept the method of payment you wish to use. Look for the Lada *multitarjeta* phones. There is a phone office at the far end of section F, which accepts Amex and, in theory, Visa, MasterCard and other cards. It is very expensive though.

From the airport Fixed-price **taxis** by zone, buy tickets from booths at exits by Sections A, E and F; you can buy tickets before passing customs but they are cheaper outside the duty free area; rates range from US$5 upwards, according to distance (per vehicle, not per person), drivers may not know, or may be unwilling to go to, cheaper hotels. For losses or complaints about airport taxis, T5571-3600 Ext 2299; for reservations T5571-9344/5784-8642, 0800-0200. The fixed-price taxi system is efficient and safe. A cheaper alternative (about 50%) if one doesn't have too much luggage is to cross the Blvd Puerto Aéreo by the Metro Terminal Aérea and flag down an ordinary taxi outside the *Ramada* hotel. There are regular **buses** from the city centre to the airport (eg No 20, along north side of Alameda), but the drawback is that you have to take one to Calzada Ignacio Zaragoza and transfer to trolley bus at the Boulevard Puerto Aéreo (ie at metro Terminal Aérea). Buses to airport may be caught every 45 mins until 0100 from outside *Hotel de Carlo*, Plaza de la República 35. It takes 1 hr from downtown (and, in the rush hour, most of the day, it is jam-packed), but you can take baggage if you can squeeze it in. To get to the airport cheaply, take **metro** to Terminal Aérea and walk, or take metro to Blvd Puerto Aéreo and then a *pesero* marked 'Oceanía', which will leave you at the Terminal metro station. There are airport information kiosks at *Salas* A, D, E and F. There is a hotel desk before passing through customs. The tourist office at A has phones for calling hotels, no charge, helpful, but Spanish only. The travel agency at east exit will book hotels or reconfirm flights, charges 5 pesos. For air freight contact the Agencia Aduanales, Plazuela Hermanos, Colima 114, Mon-Fri 0900-1700, US$5.75 per kilo.

For information on any services that may be available, call T5547-1084/1097

Trains The main railway station, Buenavista, on Insurgentes North, nearest metro Revolución, is now almost a complete ghost terminal. There are just two passenger services still running, to Querétaro and Apizalco three days a week, and these services – each very slow – are run principally to justify keeping Buenavista open. Train travel, unfortunately, has virtually died out.

Directory

Airline offices

See page 34 for web addresses

The majority are on **Paseo de la Reforma**: *Aero California*, No 332, T5207-1392. *Alitalia*, No 390-1003, T5533-5590. *American Airlines*, No 314, T5208-6396, airport T5571-3219. *Avensa*, No 325, T5208-4998. *Avianca*, No 195, T5566-8588. *Canadian Airlines*, No 390, T5207-6611. *Delta*, No 381, T5525-4840, airport T5762-3588. *Iberia*, No 24, T5566-4011, airport T5762-5844. *Japan Airlines*, No 295, T5533-6883, airport T5571-8742.

On **Hamburgo**: *Air Canada*, No 108, p 5, T5511-2004. *Alaska Airlines*, No 213-1004, T5533-1747. *Ecuatoriana de Aviación*, No 213, T5533-4569, airport T5762-5199. *SAS*, No 61, T5533-0098, airport T5511-9872. *Swissair*, No 66, T5533-6363.

Others include: *Aeroflot*, Insurgentes Sur 569, T5523-7139. *Aeromar*, Sevilla 4, T5133-1111. *AeroMéxico*, Insurgentes Sur 724, T5133-4010. *Air France*, Edgar Allan Poe 90, T5627-6000, airport 5571-6150. *British Airways*, Jaime Balmes 8, Los Morales, T5387-0310. *Continental*, Andrés Bello 45, T5546-9503, airport T5571-3661. *Cubana*, Temístocles 246, Polanco, T5255-0646. *El Al*, Paseo de las Palmas, T5735-1105. *Icelandic Airlines*, Durango 103, T5514-0159. *KLM*, Paseo de las Palmas 735, T5202-4444. *Lufthansa*, Paseo de las Palmas 239, T5202-8866. *Mexicana*, Xola 535, Col del Valle, T5660-4433, airport T5762-4011. *Northwest Airlines*, Reforma y Amberes 312, T5511-3579, Reforma 300, T5525-7090. *Taca*, Morelos 108, Col Juárez, T5546-8807. *United Airlines*, Leibnitz 100, loc 23-24, T5250-1657.

Mexico City

Always see if there is a special counter where currency transactions can be effected to avoid standing in long queues. It often happens when you are queuing up that bank employees ask you what you are wishing to do (*¿Qué operación quiere hacer?*). This is not a nosey inquiry, but rather a desire to be of assistance. Branches of all major Mexican banks proliferate in most parts of the city. Cash advances on credit cards are easy with good rates. TCs in most major currencies can be cashed at any branch of Bancomer or Banca Serfín without undue delay. Banks do not charge commission for changing TCs. The exchange of foreign currency notes, other than dollars, can be difficult apart from at the airport and main bank branches in the city centre. There are 2 *casas de cambio* at the airport that specialize in obscure currencies. Before buying or selling currency, check the day's exchange rate from a newspaper and then shop around. There is often a great disparity between different banks and *casas de cambio* particularly in times of volatile currency markets. Hotels usually offer very poor rates. *Banco de Comercio* (Bancomer, Visa agent), head office at Av Universidad 1200, also Venustiano Carranza y Bolívar, good quick *cambio*, same rate for cash and TCs. *Banco Nacional de México (Banamex)*, Palmas, Banamex's offices nearby, at Av Isabel la Católica 44, are in a converted baroque palace, ask the porter for a quick look into the magnificent patio. Another worthwhile building is the bank's branch in the Casa Iturbide, where Agustín de Iturbide lived as emperor, at Madero 17 with Gante. *Banco Internacional* recommended, they deal with MasterCard (Carnet) and Visa (usually quicker than Bancomer or Banamex for cash advances against credit card), also *Banca Serfín*, corner of 16 de Septiembre y Bolívar, or Madero 32, near Bolívar. *Citibank*, Paseo de la Reforma 390, for Citicorp TCs, they also give cash advances against credit cards with no commission. *American Express* emergency number, T5326-2626, platinum, T5326-2929; also office at Reforma 234 esq Havre, T5533-0380, will change cheques on Sats 0930-1330, also open Mon-Fri until 1800 (there are 5 other Amex offices in Mexico City, including Campos Elíseos 204, Local 5, Polanco; Centro Comercial Perisur). For more details on Visa and Master Card, see **Credit cards**, page 72. There are many *casas de cambio*, especially on Reforma, Madero and in the centre. Their hours may be more convenient, but their rates can be poor. *Central de Cambios (Suiza)*, Madero 58, west of Zócalo and *Casa de Cambio Plus*, Av Juárez, have been recommended for rates. The Perisur shopping centre, Insurgentes and Periférico Sur, has a *casa de cambio* (T5606-3698), which is usually open until 1900, with a better exchange rate in the morning. See also **Airport** above.

Banks

0930-1700 Mon-Fri, 0900-1300 Sat, although some branches open earlier and close later

Internet General opening hours Mon-Sat 1000-2200, with some variations. Rates US$2-3/hr. Currently one of the handiest non-hotel options is *Lafoel Internet Service*, just a couple of blocks north of the northwestern corner of the Zócalo, at Donceles 80 y Brasil, 1st floor, T5512-3584. Ask in your hotel for the closest. Rates about US$2/hr, opens at 0800. Others include *Café Java Chat*, Génova 44 K, T5525-6853, Zona Rosa (metro Insurgentes). Mon-Fri 0900-2200, Sat-Sun 1000-2200, US$3.60 per hour, free coffee and soft drinks. *Café Pedregal*, Av San Jerónimo 630, Col Jardines del Pedregal T5681-6672. *Cafe@Rock Shop*, Belisario Domínguez 17, Coyoacán, T5554-3699. *Cyberpuerto*, Alfonso Reyes 238, Col Hipódromo, T5286-0869. *Interlomas*, Paseo de la Herradura 5, Col Fernando la Herradura, Huixquilucan T5245-0330. *Internet Café* in Plaza Computación at Cárdenas end of Uruguay, US$3.25/hr, free coffee, soft drinks US$0.60. *Internet Station*, Arquímedes 130, Local 20 (metro Polanco) T5280-6091. *Novanet*, Nuevo León 104 y Michoacán, Col Hipódromo (metro Chilpancingo), T5553-7503. *Ragnatel*, Centro Comercial Santa Fé, Local 472, Col Antigua Mina la Totolapa T5258-0782. *Tarea*, Presidente Carranza esq Tres Cruces, Coyoacán, T5659-2420.

Post office Tacuba y Lázaro Cárdenas, opposite Palacio de Bellas Artes, open for letters 0800-2400 Mon-Fri, 0800-2000 Sat, and 0900-1600 Sun. For parcels open 0800-1800 Mon-Fri, Sat 0800-1600. Parcels up to 2 kg (5 kg for books) may be sent. It is an interesting historic building with a stunning interior, worth a visit. Philatelic sales at windows 9 to 13. Mail kept for only 10 days at poste restante window 3, recommended, but closed Sat and Sun (see page 85). If they can't find your mail under the initial of your surname, ask under the initials of any other names you may happen to have. EMS Mexpost, accelerated national and international postage, is available at the Central Post Office, the airport, Zona Rosa, Coyoacán and 13 other post offices in the city; payable by weight. Other post offices (open 0800-1900 Mon-Fri, 0800-1300 Sat), which travellers may find useful: Centre, Nezahualcóyotl 184 and Academia 4; P Arriaga and Ignacio Mariscal, 2 blocks north of Monumento a la Revolución; Zona Rosa, Londres 208; Tlatelolco, Flores Magón 90; San Rafael, Schultz 102; Lomas de Chapultepec, Prado Nte 525; Buenavista, Aldama 216; San Angel, Dr Gálvez 16; Coyoacán, Higuera 23; Iztapalapa, Calzada Ermita Iztapalapa 1033; Xochimilco, Prolongación Pino 10; also at the airport and bus terminals. In all there are 155 branches in the federal capital, so there is no need to go to the Correo Central.

Communications

The symbol @ is called arroba in Spanish

Mexico City

See page 85 for details of the LADA phone system **Telephones** Finding a public phone that works can be a problem. Most now take phone cards (Ladatel), costing 20, 50 and 100 pesos, from shops and news kiosks everywhere. Calls abroad can be made from phone booths with credit cards (via LADA system). International calls can easily be made from the phone office in the Terminal del Oriente bus terminal. There are several places, including some shops, all officially listed, with long-distance phones.

Number changes Don't forgot all Mexican telephone numbers have changed. Most numbers are 7 digit with 3 exceptions. When calling long distance dial 01+ regional code (3 digits) + 7 digit code. Numbers are 8 digit in **Mexico City** (55), **Guadalajara** (33) and **Monterrey** (81). Dial 01+ regional code (2 digits) + 8 digit number.

Cultural centres *American Community School of Mexico*, complete US curriculum to age of 12, Observatorio and Calle Sur 136, T5516-6720. *American Chamber of Commerce*, Lucerna 78. *Benjamin Franklin Library*, Londres 116 (has *New York Times* 2 days after publication). *Anglo-Mexican Cultural Institute* (with British Council Library), Maestro Antonio Caso 127, T5566-6144. *British Chamber of Commerce*, Río de la Plata 30, Col Cuauhtémoc, T5256-0901. *British Council*, Lope de Vega 316, Polanco, T5263-1900, F5263-1910. *Instituto Italiano*, Francisco Sosa 77, Coyoacán, T5554-0044/53, has 3-week intensive yet painless courses in Spanish, 3 hrs a day. *Goethe-Institut*, Tonalá 43 (Metro Insurgentes), 0900-1300, 1600-1930. *Colegio Alemán*, Alexander V Humboldt, Col Huichapan, Xochimilco CP 16030. *Instituto Francés de la América Latina*, Nazas 43, free films every Thu at 2030.

Embassies & consulates *Check location of embassies and consulates; they tend to move frequently. Most take 24 hrs for visas; check to make sure you have a visa and not just a receipt stamp* *Australia*, Plaza Polanco Torre B, Jaime Balmes 11, 10th floor, Col Los Morales, T5395-9988. *Belize*, Bernardo de Gálvez 215, Lomas Virreyes, T5520-1346, F5531-8115, open 0900-1300 Mon-Fri, visa US$10, takes a day. *Canada*, Schiller 529 (corner Tres Picos), near Anthropology Museum, T5724-7900, www.canada.org.mx *Colombia*, Reforma 195, 3rd floor, will request visa from Bogotá by telegram (which you must pay for) and permission can take up to 1 month to come through. *Costa Rica*, Río Póo 113, Col Cuauhtémoc, T5525-7764 (metro Insurgentes). *Denmark*, Tres Picos 43, Col Polanco, Apdo Postal 105, CP 11580, T5255-3405, open Mon-Fri 0900-1300 (nearest metro Auditorio). *Ecuador*, Tennyson 217, T5545-3141. *France*, Havre 15, near the Cuauhtémoc monument, T5533-1360. *Germany*, Byron 737, Col Rincón del Bosque, T5280-5534, open 0900-1200. *Guatemala*, Explanada 1025, Lomas de Chapultepec, CP11000, T5540-7520, F5202-1142, morning only (take No 47 bus from Observatorio to Virreyes, then walk up hill, or No 76 'Km 15.5 por Reforma', or 'por Palmas', or taxi); to visit Guatemala some nationalities (eg Australians and New Zealanders) need a compulsory visa costing US$10 in US$ cash only, others need either a free visa (take a passport photo) or a tourist card (issued at the border). Open 0900-1300 for visas. *Honduras*, Alfonso Reyes 220, T5515-6689 (metro Chilpancingo), visas issued on the spot (no waiting) valid up to 1 year from date of issue, cost varies per nationality, up to US$20 for Australians. *Ireland*, Sylvia Moronadi, San Jerónimo 790a, metro Miguel Angel, T5595-3333, open Mon-Fri 0900-1700. *Israel*, PO Box 25389, T5540-6340, F5284-4825. Sierra Madre 215 (nearest metro Auditorio), open Mon-Fri 0900-1200. *Italy*, Paseo de las Palmas 1994, Col Lomas de Chapultepec, T5596-3655. *Japan*, Apdo Postal 5101, Paseo de la Reforma 395, Col Cuauhtémoc, T5211-0028. *Netherlands*, Monte Urales 635-203 (near Fuente de Petróleos), T5202-8267, F5202-6148. *New Zealand*, JL Lagrange 103, 10th floor, Polanco, T5281-5486, F5281-5212. *Nicaragua*, Payo de Rivera 120, Col Virreyes, Lomas de Chapultepec, T5520-4421 (bus 13 along Reforma, get out at Monte Altai and walk south on Monte Athos), visas for 30 days from date of issue, 1 photograph, US$25, plus US$5 if you want it 'on the spot'. *Panama*, Campos Elíseos 111-1, T5250-4259, near Auditorio metro (visa US$20 for Australians). *El Salvador*, Monte Altai 320, T5202-8250, metro Auditorio. *Sweden*, Paseo de las Palmas 1375. *Switzerland*, Edificio Torre Optima, Paseo de las Palmas 405, 11th floor, Col Lomas de Chapultepec, T5520-8535, open 0900-1200 Mon-Fri. *UK*, Río Lerma 71, T5207-2593 (Apdo 96 bis, México 5), open Mon and Thu 0900-1400 and 1500-1800, Tue, Wed, Fri 0900-1500. Consular Section at Usumacinta 30, immediately behind main embassy building. Reading room in main building; poste restante for 1 month, please address to Consular section, this is not an official service, just a valuable courtesy. *US Embassy*, Reforma 305, Col Cuauhtémoc, T5211-0042, F5511-9980, open Mon-Fri 0830-1730. If requiring a visa for the US, it is best to get it in your home country.

Medical services Hospitals *American British Cowdray Hospital*, (also known as El Hospital Inglés, or ABC), on Observatorio past Calle Sur 136. T5277-5000 (emergency: 5515-8359); very helpful. **Medical services** *Dr César Calva Pellicer* (who speaks English, French and German), Copenhague 24, 3rd floor, T5514-2529. *Dr Smythe*, Campos Elíseos 81, T5545-7861, recommended by US and Canadian Embassies. For any medical services you can also go to the *Clínica Prensa*, US$1.20 for consultation, subsidized medicines. *Hospital de Jesús Nazareno*, 20 de Noviembre 82, Spanish-speaking, friendly, drugs prescribed cheaply. It is a historical monument (see page 101). Most embassies have a list of recommended doctors and dentists who speak languages other than Spanish. **Pharmacies** *Farmacia Homeopática*, Mesones 111-B. *Farmacia Nosarco*, corner of 5 de Febrero and República de El Salvador, stocks wide range of drugs for stomach bugs and tropical diseases, may give 21% discount. *Sanborn's* chain and *El Fénix* discount pharmacies are the largest chains with the most complete selection (the *Sanborn's* behind the post officestocks gamma globulin). Many supermarkets have good pharmacies. **Vaccination centre** Benjamín Hill 14, near Metro Juanacatlán (Line 1). Open Mon-Fri 0830-1430, 1530-2030, avoid last 30 mins, also open on Sat from 0830-1430; typhoid free (this is free all over Mexico), cholera and yellow fever (Tue and Fri only) US$2; will give a prescription for gamma globulin. For hepatitis shots you have to buy gamma globulin in a pharmacy (make sure it's been refrigerated) and then an injection there (cheap but not always clean), or at a doctor's surgery or the ABC Hospital (see above). Gamma globulin is hard to find (see Pharmacies above); try Hospital Santa Elena, Querétaro 58, Col Roma, T5574-7711, about US$50 for a vaccination. Malaria prophylaxis and advice free from San Luis Potosí 199, 6th floor, Col Roma Nte, 0900-1400, or from the Centro de Salud near metro Chabacano, opposite Comercial Mexicano supermarket – no typhoid vaccinations here (ask at Centro de Salud Benjamín Hill, which does not supply malaria pills). It seems that paludrine is not available in Mexico, only chloroquine.

Language schools The UNAM has excellent classes of Spanish tuition and Mexican culture: *Centro de Enseñanza para Extranjeros*, US$200 for 6 weeks, 5 different levels, free additional courses in culture, free use of medical service, swimming pool, library, a student card from here allows free entry to all national monuments and museums and half price on many bus lines (eg *ADO* during summer vacations). See also Learning Spanish, page 27, and Cultural centres above.

Laundry Laundry on Río Danubio, between Lerma and Pánuco and at Chapultepec and Toledo, near Sevilla metro, expensive. *Lavandería* at Chapultepec y Toledo. *Lavandería Automática Edison*, Edison 91 (nearest metro Revolución), between José María Iglesias y Ponciano Arriaga, Col Tabacalera (centre). Mon-Fri 0900-1900, Sat 0900-1800. Has automatic machines, US$1.50 per 3 kg, US$1.50 drying. Also at Parque España 14 and Antonio Caso 82, near British Council, US$4 for 3 kg, quick service. Dry cleaning shops (*tintorerías* or *lavado en seco*) are plentiful. Typical charges: jacket or skirt US$1.10, suit US$2.20, can take up to 48 hrs.

Places of worship **English-speaking** Roman Catholic, St Patrick's, Bondojito 248, Tacubaya, T5515-1993; Evangelical Union, Reforma 1870, Lomas de Chapultepec, T5520-0436; Baptist, Capital City Baptist Church, Calle Sur 138 y Bondojito, T5516-1862; Lutheran, Church of the Good Shepherd, Paseo de Palmas 1910, T5596-1034; Anglican, Mexican Anglican Cathedral, Mesones 139 (see page 101) has services in Spanish, for services in English, Christ Church, Monte Escandinavos 405, Lomas de Chapultepec, T5202-0949 (services at 0800 and 1000, sung Eucharist, take bus Reforma Km 15 or Km 16 to Monte Alti, then down hill off opposite side of the road); First Church of Christ Scientist, 21 Dante, Col Anzures; Jewish, Beth Israel, Virreyes 1140, Lomas Virreyes, Nidche Israel (Orthodox), Acapulco 70, near Chapultepec metro.

Tour operators Use a travel agent that has been recommended to you (if possible), as not all are efficient or reliable. One of the most reliable is *Hivisa Viajes*, Río Támesis 5, Col Cuauhtémoc, T5703-0911, hivisa3@hivisaviajes.com.mx Good for flights to Europe, Central and South America, and for changing flight dates, English spoken, ask for Icarus Monk. *American Express*, Reforma 234 y Havre, T5533-0380, open Mon-Fri 0900-1800, Sat 0900-1300 (charges US$3-4 for *Poste Restante* if you do not have their travellers' cheques and US$1 if no card or cheques are held for other services), service slow but helpful. *Asatej*, Insurgentes Sur 421, Local B.10, Col Hipódromo Condesa, T5574-0899, F5574-3462, ve@ve.com.mx *Corresponsales de Hoteles*, Blvd Centro 224-4, T5360-3356, for hotel reservations (upmarket). *Grey Line Tours*, Londres 166, T5208-1163, reasonably priced tours, car hire, produces *This is Mexico* book (free). *Hadad Viajes*, Torres Adalid 205, Of 602, Col del Valle, T5687-0488. *Humboldt Tours*, José María Velasco 34, San José Insurgentes, T5660-9152, F5660-0735, one of Mexico's leading tour operators, good for individual tours as well as groups, multilingual staff. *Mundo Joven Travel Shop*, Guatemala 4, Colonia Centro, T5518-1726, www.remaj.com, issues ISIC card, agents for International Youth Hostel Federation. *Protures Viajes*, Av Baja California 46, Col Roma Sur, T5264-4497, www.proturs.com.mx Recommended agency for organizing flights to Central and South America and Cuba. *Thomas Cook*, Campos Elíseos 345, Col Polanco, travellers' cheques agency only.

Shop around as prices vary considerably, although deals regularly available in Europe or the US are rare or impossible to find

Mexico City

Mexico City

Turisjoven, Tuxpan 54-903 (metro Chilpancingo). For cheap tickets to Cuba, ask in agencies around Hamburgo. Try *Vacation Planning*, Copenhague 21-203, Zona Rosa, T5511-1604. *Viajes Tirol*, José Ma Rico 212, Depto 503, T5534-5582, English and German spoken, recommended. *Wagons-Lits*, Av Juárez 88, F5518-1180 (reported to be closed all day Sat), also Av de las Palmas 731, T5540-0579, very helpful and knowledgeable. *W Tours and Travel*, T5682-1718, are also recommended. Finding a cheap flight to Europe is difficult.

Specialists in adventure tourism The Asociación Mexicana de Turismo de Aventura y Ecoturismo (AMTAVE) regulates and promotes many of the agencies listed below. Not all areas of adventure sport come under their umbrella, for instance specialist diving agencies remain unattached to any Mexico-based organization, as diving is a mainly regional activity. *Río y Montaña*, Prado Nte 450-T, Lomas de Chapultepec, T/F5520-2041, sea kayaking, rafting (Ríos Pescados-Antigua stretch, Filo Bobos, Usumacinta, Santa María, Río Grande, Jatate); climbing expertise – Alfonso de la Parra, one of the guides, has climbed Everest. *Al Aire Libre*, Centro Comercial Interlomas, Local 2122, Lomas Anáhuac Huixquilucan, T5291-9217, rafting (Ríos Pescados-Antigua, Santa María, Amacuzac), climbing, caving (Chontalcuatlán, Zacatecoltla, La Joya), ballooning, parapenting. *Intercontinental Adventures*, Homero 526-801, Col Polanco, T5225-4400, F5255-4465, email: adventu@mpsnet.com.mx, run by Agustín Arroyo who is president of AMTAVE, operates mainly in Veracruz, historical tours, rafting and sea kayaking, represents *México Verde* agency (see under Guadalajara tour operators) in Mexico City. *Ecogrupos de México*, Centro Comercial Plaza Inn, Insurgentes Sur 197-1251, T5661-9121, F5662-7354, nature tours, eg butterfly habitats.

Useful addresses **Customs** Dirección General de Aduanas, 20 de Noviembre 195, T5709-2900. **Delegation building** Av Central, the Ministry of Public Works is the place to report a theft; take a long book to read. **Immigration** Servicios Migratorios, of the Secretaría de Gobernación, Ejército Nacional 862, between Platón and Séneca. Not so easy to get to. Best take metro to Polanco, then taxi. Mon-Fri 0900-1330. Get there early, usually long queues, little English spoken. Here you can extend tourist cards for stays over 90 days or replace lost cards; new cards can take just a couple of hours, but charges are as high as US$40; you may be given 10 days to leave the country. This is also where you have to come to exchange a tourist card for a student's visa and for any other immigration matter concerning foreigners. It is essential to be armed with a lot of patience, and to attend with a Spanish-speaker if you don't speak the language. The normal procedure is to fill out a form indicating which service you need; you are then given a receipt with a number. See page 70 for more information on visas.

Around Mexico City

Right in the centre of the country, Mexico City is well suited for exploring the colonial towns, villages, national parks, pre-Hispanic sites, volcanoes, caves and hot springs that are within easy reach for a day or weekend trip.

Everyone heads north to see Mexico's most-visited pyramids at the vast and awe-inspiring site of Teotihuacán, 'the place of the gods'. Less crowded are the towering Atlantes at Tula, the Toltec capital, and the pretty villages in the hills near Pachuca where you can eat the Cornish pasties that are a legacy of the English who once mined gold in the region. Head west from the capital on Friday, through cool pine forests, for Toluca's massive street market. Going south, charming Cuernavaca, 'city of eternal spring', is the weekend resort, where everybody goes to get away from the metropolis and relax. Wander through the pretty up-and-down streets of colonial Taxco, wonder at the magnificent Santa Prisca church and stroll around the shops and market stalls seeking bargains in beautifully crafted silver. Snow-capped Popocatépetl, the smoking-mountain warrior, and his princess Iztaccíhuatl rise majestically to the east of the capital en route to Puebla, City of the Angels, or tucked-away Tlaxcala, delightful capital of Mexico's smallest state. Nearby are the dramatic murals of Cacaxtla and Cholula's artificial 'mountain', in fact the largest pyramid in all Mesoamerica.

North of Mexico City

Acolman is 35 km northeast of Mexico City and is easily visited after La Basílica de Guadalupe (see page 119) and on the way to Teotihuacán. It has the formidable fortress-like convent and church of San Agustín. This dates from 1539-60, with much delicate detail on the façade and some interesting murals inside. Note the fine portal and the carved stone cross at the entrance to the atrium. An interesting architectural feature is the open chapel just above and to the right of the main entrance. While Mass was being celebrated inside the monastery for the benefit of the Spaniards, the spiritual needs of the indigenous worshippers were catered for by the friar who celebrated the Mass in this tiny balcony chapel. Acolman can be reached by bus from Indios Verdes metro station, or from the Zócalo.

Teotihuacán

This site has some of the most remarkable relics of an ancient civilization in the world. Thought to date from around 300 BC-AD 600, the builders of Teotihuacán, or 'place of the gods', remain a mystery. Where they came from and why the civilization disappeared is pure conjecture. It seems that the city may have housed 250,000 people who were peace-loving but whose influence spread as far as Guatemala. However, the 'peace-loving' theory is constantly being challenged. There are definite indications that human sacrifice was being practised at Teotihuacán long before the arrival of the Aztecs to the Valley of Mexico. Recent research indicates that an individual from Teotihuacán arrived at Copán in Honduras and usurped the power of the rightful ruler, thus continuing to spread the influence of Teotihuacán throughout the Maya region. Teotihuacán was not just a ceremonial centre; vast areas of enclaves have been excavated showing that, apart from those zones designated as sacred, there were also areas occupied by artisans, labourers, merchants, and representatives of those crafts and professions that contribute to a functioning city. One zone housed merchants from the Maya area, another was occupied by representatives from Monte Albán in Oaxaca. Some time in the seventh century

Colour map 3, grid B4
49 km N of Mexico City

Teotihuacán was ravaged by fire and may also have been looted, causing an exodus of its inhabitants. So completely was it abandoned that it was left to the Aztecs to give names to its most important features. There are many questions still to be answered about Teotihuacán culture; a recent discovery in 1997 of 50 clay figurines is one more piece in the jigsaw.

Ins and outs Reckon on about 5-8 hrs to see the site properly; arrive early before the vast numbers of *ambulantes*, or wandering vendors, and the big tourist groups at 1100. There is a perimeter road with a number of car parking places – go anticlockwise. If short of time, try to get a lift from a tourist bus to the Pyramid of the Moon car park. This is the most interesting

Teotihuacán

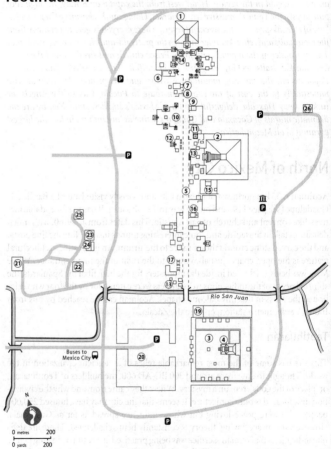

Buses to Mexico City

0 metres 200
0 yards 200

1 Pyramid of the Moon	10 Plaza of the Columns	19 Plaza Two
2 Pyramid of the Sun	11 Palace of the Sun	20 Great Compound
3 Ciudadela	12 Patio of the Four Little Temples	21 Palace of Atetelco
4 Temple of Quetzalcoatl	13 Plaza of the Sun	22 Palace of Tetitla
5 Avenue of the Dead	14 Plaza of the Moon	23 Palace of Zacuala
6 Palaces of Quetzalpapalotl,	15 House of the Priest	24 Patio of Zacuala
Jaguars & Feathered Shells	16 Viking Group	25 Palace of Yayahuala
7 Temple of Agriculture	17 Avenue of the Dead complex with	26 Palace of Tepantitla
8 Mural of the Mythological Animals	'Superimposed Buildings' group	
9 Jaguar Temple & Mural	18 Northwest Cluster	

area. Also take food and water as most of the shops are on the west side and you may be some distance from them. There is a handicraft centre with weavings, obsidian carvings and explanations (and tastings) of the production of tequila and mescal.

Sights

There are three main areas: the **Ciudadela**, the **Pyramid of the Sun** and the **Pyramid of the Moon**. The whole is connected by the Avenue of the Dead, which runs almost due north for nearly 4 km. To the west lie the sites of Tetitla, Atetelco, Zacuala and Yayahuala (see below). To the northeast lies Tepantitla, with fine frescoes. The old city is traceable over an area of 3½ by 6½ km.

The small pebbles embedded in mortar indicate reconstruction (most of the site apparently!)

Capable of holding 60,000 people, the citadel's main feature is the **Temple of Quetzalcoatl** (the Plumed Serpent, Lord of Air and Wind). Go to the east side of the 1 km square. Behind the largest of the temples (take the right-hand path) lies an earlier pyramid, which has been partially restored. Lining the staircase are huge carved heads of the feathered serpents.

Follow the Avenue of the Dead to the **Plaza of the Sun**. You will pass small grassy mounds, which are unexcavated temples. The Plaza contains many buildings, probably for the priests, but is dominated by the massive **Pyramid of the Sun** (64 m high, 213 sq m at the base) and covering almost the same space as the Great Pyramid of Cheops in Egypt. The sides are terraced, and wide stairs lead to the summit. The original 4 m covering of stone and stucco was removed by mistake in 1910. The view from the top gives a good impression of the whole site. But beware, it is a steep climb.

The car park to the north leads to Tepantitla. The murals here depict the rain god Tlaloc. The **museum** (admission included in price of ticket) now lies south of the Pyramid of the Sun. It is well laid out and contains a large model of Teotihuacán in its heyday as well as many beautiful artefacts, recommended. At the museum there is an expensive restaurant with indifferent service, but it is not always open.

The **Pyramid of the Moon** is about 1 km further north and on your right a tin roof covers a wall mural of a large, brightly coloured jaguar (the **Jaguar Temple**). The plaza contains the 'A' altars – 11 in a peculiar geometric pattern. The Pyramid is only half the size of the Pyramid of the Sun. The best view of the Avenue of the Dead is from the first level of this pyramid – 48 steep steps – well worth the climb.

To the west of the Plaza of the Moon lies the **Palace of Quetzalpapalotl** (Palace of the Precious Butterfly) where the priests serving the sanctuaries of the Moon lived, which has been restored together with its patio. Note the obsidian inlet into the highly decorated carved pillars. Follow the path left under the Palace through the Jaguars' Palace, with catlike murals protected from the sun by green canvas curtains, to the **Temple of the Feathered Shells**. The base of the simple altar is decorated with shells, flowers and eagles.

You will pass several more temples on the west side of the Avenue of the Dead. If you want to visit the temples of Atetelco, go through the car park opposite the Pyramid of the Sun, turn right past *Restaurant Pirámides Charlies* (reputed to be the best on the site) and turn right along a small track. Alternatively, to get to them from the museum, exit west and walk right up to main road, turning left after crossing the stream. They are well worth a visit: **Tetitla**, a walled complex with beautiful frescoes and paintings; **Atetelco** with its three tiny temples and excellent murals; and the abandoned sites of **Zacuala** and **Yayahuala**.

At the spring equinox on 21 March the sun is perfectly aligned with the west face of the Pyramid of the Sun; many ad hoc sun worshippers hold unofficial ceremonies to mark the occasion. This is also Benito Juárez's birthday so entry is free.

Around Mexico City

■ *Daily 0800-1700. If the entrance near the bus stop is not open at 0800 try entrance near the Pyramid of the Moon. US$3.50, free on Sun (extra charge for videos, tripods not permitted). The outside sites may be closed on Mon. Son et lumière display, US$4 per person (good lumière, not so good son); lasts 45 mins, 1900 in Spanish, 2015 in English (Oct-Jun only); take blanket or rent one. Official guidebook US$1, gives a useful route to* *follow. The Bloomgarden guide contains a useful map, good description and is recommended. The guide, Ricardo Cervantes (Gorilla), T614-156-0540, has been recommended. At weekends students give free guided tours, ask at the entrance.*

Sleeping **AL** *Villas Arqueológicas*, San Juan Teotihuacán, T(594) 956-0909, F956-0928. Close to the pyramids, with a pool.

Transport **Buses** From Terminal del Norte, Gate 8, platform 6 (Autobuses del Norte metro), Mexico City; at least 45 mins, US$2 one way (Pirámides buses are white with a yellow stripe). You can also take the metro to Indios Verdes (last stop on line 3), then a public bus (US$2.50) to the pyramids. Bus returns from Door 1 (some others from 2 and 3) at Teotihuacán site, supposedly every 30 mins. Some return buses to the capital terminate in the outskirts in rush hour without warning. You can ride back to town with one of the tourist buses for about US$3. Note that the site is more generally known as 'Pirámides' than as 'Teotihuacán'. If driving, the toll on the Autopista Ecatepec-Pirámides is US$3. Tours to Teotihuacán, picking you up at your hotel and usually including the Basílica de Guadalupe (see page 119), cost US$30-35, with little time at the site.

Pachuca

Phone code: 771
Colour map 3, grid B4
Population: 320,000
Altitude: 2,445 m

94 km northeast of Mexico City

Capital of Hidalgo state (www.hidalgo.gob.mx), Pachuca is also one of the oldest silver mining centres in Mexico. The Aztecs, the Spaniards and more recently the English all mined here leaving the hills honeycombed with old workings and terraced with tailings. The English left a small culinary legacy with a Mexicanized version of a Cornish pasty available in some of the town's cafés.

Although the centre is largely modern, there are a number of colonial buildings among its narrow, steep and crooked streets. These include the treasury for the royal tribute, **Las Cajas Reales** (1670), Venustiano Carranza 106, now used as offices; **Las Casas Coloradas** (1785), on Plaza Pedro María Anaya, now the Tribunal Superior de Justicia; and a former **Convento de San Francisco** (1596) on Arista e Hidalgo next to Parque Hidalgo. **Casa de las Artesanías** for Hidalgo state is at the junction of Avenida Revolución and Avenida Juárez. In the Plaza Independencia is a huge clock with four Carrara marble figures. The modern buildings include a notable **theatre**, the **Palacio de Gobierno** (which has a mural depicting ex-President Echeverría's dream of becoming Secretary-General of the UN), and the **Banco de Hidalgo**. The town centre is partly pedestrianized. *Colectivos* run from Julián Carrillo (very frequent, US$0.40) to the large silver mining camp of Real (or Mineral) del Monte, picturesque and with steep streets. The **tourist office** is on Avenida Revolución 1300, T718-3937, F718-4605.

Museums The **Museo de la Minería** at Mina 110 has an excellent display of the history of mining in Pachuca. ■ *Tue-Sun 1000-1400, 1500-1800. Free.* An industrial heritage programme is under way to restore some of the old mining settlements. Up-to-date information in the musuem. An outstanding **photographic museum** is in the large cloister on the far side of the convent. ■ *Tue-Sun 1000-1800. Free. T714-3653.* The **Museo Regional de Hidalgo**, in the Centro Cultural Hidalgo, displays chronological exhibits of the state's history. In the complex there is a souvenir shop with reproductions of ceramic and metal anthropological items and recordings of indigenous music, a library and exhibition hall. ■ *Tue-Sun 0900-1800, may close early on Sun afternoon.*

Excursions **Real del Monte**, a very interesting and attractive small town, is one of a number of mining centres in the area, most of which are no longer operative. It is particularly noted for its association with Britain and especially Cornwall. Cornish miners were present in large numbers in the second quarter of the 19th century. Traces of their presence can still be seen in blue-eyed inhabitants, surnames and, of course, the pasties or *pastes*. Most of the buildings have sloping roofs or *techos de dos aguas* and are carefully preserved. The **Panteón Inglés** (English cemetery) is on a wooded hill opposite the town; the caretaker will recite stories about families buried there. No accommodation is available at present: take a *colectivo* from Pachuca, 10 mins' drive. **Mineral del Chico** is a beautiful little town 30 km from Pachuca in **Parque Nacional El Chico**. There are huge rock formations covered in pine forests and some splendid walks. But the park campsites are mostly dirty with no facilities and there is no information or maps at the park headquarters. Buses run from Pachuca.

B *Ciro's*, Plaza Independencia 110, T715-5351. Recommended. **C** *De los Baños*, Matamoros 205, T713-0700. Rooms not up to standard of entrance, good, friendly and helpful. Recommended. **C** *El Dorado*, Guerrero 721, T714-2831. Clean, friendly. **C** *San Antonio*, 6 km from Pachuca on road to Mexico City (ask for directions), T711-0599. Spacious rooms, good value, clean, quiet, restaurant. **D** *Grenfell*, Plaza Independencia 116, T715-0277. With bath, clean, friendly, pleasant, good value. Some cheaper rooms (**F**) but undergoing renovation so prices may rise. Bus from bus station passes the door. **D** *Juárez*, Barreda 107. With bath, some rooms without windows, just before Real del Monte, in superb wooded surroundings. **F** *Colonial*, Guerrero 505. Central. **Sleeping**

Casino Español, Blvd Everardo Márquez 202. Old-time favourite serving Mexican, Spanish and international dishes, open all day. *La Blanca*, next to *Hotel de los Baños*. Local dishes. Recommended. *El Buen Gusto*, Arista y Viaducto Nuevo Hidalgo. Clean, good-value *comida corrida*. *El Rinconcito*, on Juárez. Good cheap food. *Paste* is the local survivor from Cornish miners' days; a good approximation of the real pasty, but a bit peppery! *Pastes Pachuqueños*, Arista 1023. Recommended. **Eating**

A 4-lane highway now runs from Mexico City to Pachuca via Venta de Carpio, Km 27, from which a road runs east to Acolman, 12 km, and Teotihuacán, another 10 km. If travelling by bus, there are frequent departures from Terminal del Norte. **Transport**

Buses Terminal is outside town; take any bus marked 'Central'.

Around Mexico City

North and east of Pachuca

North of Pachuca via Atotonilco el Grande, there is a chapel and convent halfway down a beautiful canyon, the impressive **Barranca de Metztitlán**, which has a wealth of different varieties of cacti, including the 'hairy old man' cactus, and a huge 17th-century monastery. The death of Ome Tochtli (Two Rabbit) at the hands of Tezcatlipoca (Smoking Mirror) occurred at Metztitlán. Further north on a difficult road is Molango, where there is a restored convent, Nuestra Señora de Loreto. **San Miguel Regla**, 34 km northeast of Pachuca, is a mid-18th century hacienda built by the Conde de Regla, and now run as a resort, **B** *Hacienda San Miguel Regla*, T(771) 792-0102. It has a fine atmosphere, excellent service, pool, lush gardens, tennis, horse-riding and log fires. Highly recommended. A road continues towards **Tulancingo** on the Pachuca-Poza Rica road, Route 130, with a handful of hotels. **Epazoyucan**, 17 km east of Pachuca, and a further 4 km off Route 130 to the right, is a village with the interesting convent of San Andrés. After Tulancingo, Route 119 branches off to the right to **Zacatlán**, famous for its apple orchards, plums, pears and cider. Its alpine surroundings include an impressive national park, the **Valle de las Piedras Encimadas** (stacked rocks), where camping is possible. Nearby is **AL** *Posada Campestre al Final de la Senda*, a ranch with weekend accommodation, horse-riding and walks. Some 16 km south of Zacatlán and about 1½ hours from Puebla (see page 152) is **Chignahuapan**, a leading producer of *sarapes*, surrounded by several curative spas.

Situated 30 km from Tulancingo on Route 130 is *La Cabaña* restaurant, of log cabin construction; thereafter, the road descends with many bends and slow lorries, and in winter there may be fog. At **Huauchinango** an annual flower fair is held in March; 22 km from here is **Xicotepec de Juárez** with **A** *Mi Ranchito*, T(764) 764-0212, one of the best small hotels in Mexico and **D** *Italia* near the main square.

Along the route are the villages of **Pahuatlán** and **San Pablito**, where sequinned headbands are made, and flattened *amate* bark is used for paintings.

Northwest of Mexico City

Tepotzotlán
Phone code: 55
Colour map 3, grid B4

About 43 km northwest of Mexico City; don't confuse Tepotzotlán with Tepoztlán, which is south of Mexico City, near Cuernavaca

In the town of Tepotzotlán, just off the road to Querétaro, is the splendid Jesuit **Church of San Francisco Javier** in churrigueresque style and with fine colonial paintings in the convent corridors. The old Jesuit monastery has been converted into the **Museo Nacional del Virreinato**, a comprehensive and well-displayed collection covering all aspects of life under Spanish rule. ■ *1000-1700, closed Mon, US$4.35, Sun free.* It is also a tourist centre with restaurants. There is a big market on Wednesday and Sunday when the town gets very congested; there is a good selection of handicrafts and jewellery, as well as meat, cheese and other foods.

In the third week of December, *pastorelas*, or morality plays, based on the temptation and salvation of Mexican pilgrims voyaging to Bethlehem, are held. Tickets are about US$10 and include a warming punch, the play, a procession and litanies, finishing with a meal, fireworks and music. Contact *Viajes Roca*, Neva 30, Colonia Cuauhtémoc, Mexico City, for tickets.

Sleeping and eating **AL** *Tepotzotlán*, Industrias, about 3 blocks from centre. TV, restaurant, swimming pool, good views, secure parking. Highly recommended. **A** *Posada San José*, Plaza Virreinal No 13, T(55) 5876-0835. Nice rooms, but not great value. *Hostería del Monasterio*. Very good Mexican food and a band on Sun; try their *café de olla*, (coffee with cinnamon). *Restaurant Artesanías*, opposite church. Cheap. Recommended. Also good food at *Brookwell's Posada*.

Transport **Buses**: from near El Rosario metro station, US$1.50, 1-hr ride. Many Querétaro or Guanajuato buses from Terminal del Norte pass the turn-off at 'Caseta Tepotzotlán' from where you can take a local bus or walk (30 mins) to the town.

Tula

Phone code: 773
Colour map 3, grid B4
65 km N of Mexico City

A half-day excursion from Mexico City can be made to Tula, thought to be the most important Toltec site in Mexico; two ball courts, pyramids, a frieze in colour, and remarkable sculptures over 6 m high have been uncovered. There are four huge warriors in black basalt on a pyramid, these are the great Atlantes anthropomorphic pillars. One warrior is a reproduction; the original is on display at the Museo Nacional de Antropología, Mexico City. The platform on which the four warriors stand is encircled by a low relief frieze depicting jaguars and coyotes, and Tlaloc masks adorn the walls. Note the butterfly emblem on the chests of the warriors and the *atlatl* (spear-thrower) held by their sides. The butterfly, so important an element in Toltec iconography, was once more to become associated with the warrior class during the Aztec period, when dead warriors became butterflies who escorted the Sun to midday. The museum is well worth visiting and there is a massive fortress-style church, dating from 1553, near the market. **Warning** Assaults have been reported in the ball court; be alert at all times, especially in deserted areas of the site. There are no security guards. ■ *Tue-Sun 0930-1630 (museum open Wed-Sun till 1630). Site and museum, US$2 weekdays, reduction with ISIC card, free Sun and holidays. The small restaurant is not always open. Multilingual guidebooks at entrance, fizzy drinks on sale.* The town itself is pleasant, clean and friendly. If driving from Mexico City, take the turn for Actopan before entering Tula, then look for the Parque Nacional sign (and the great statues) on your left.

Sleeping & eating **B** *Sharon*, Callejón de la Cruz 1, T732-0976. Large clean rooms, secure car parking, restaurant, lift. Recommended. **C** *Catedral*, Zaragoza No 106, T732-0813. Clean, pleasant, TV. *Restaurant la Cabaña*, on main square. Local dishes. Also *Nevería*, with good soup.

Bus Tula can also be reached by 1st class bus, 'Valle de Mesquital', from Terminal del Norte, Av de los Cien Metros, which goes to Tula bus terminal in 2-2½ hrs; US$5 each way, every 40 mins, 0600-2100; Tula bus terminal is 3 km from the site, take a 'Chapantago' bus (every 20 mins) to the entrance, 5 mins (ask where to get off), or a taxi, or walk, turning right out of the bus station. At the main road, cut diagonally left across road and take first right, which will take you to a bridge over an evil-smelling river. Carry on to the main highway, then turn left. Also bus or car from Actopan, on the Pan-American Highway (see page 256). Tula-Pachuca US$3.30; safe to leave belongings at bus station. *Grey Line* excursions from Mexico City have been recommended. | **Transport**

West of Mexico City

Toluca

From Mexico City head towards **Parque Nacional Miguel Hidalgo**, or **La Marquesa**, which has lakes suitable for watersports and other activities such as hiking. Here also is the turn-off for Chalma and Santiago Tianguistenco from Route 15. Occassionlly there are great panoramic views of the city and the Valley of México, smog permitting. Descending into the Basin of Toluca, you can see the proud form of the Toluca volcano dominating the towns and villages that are spread around the base of its piedmont.

Phone code: 722
Colour map 3, grid B3
Population: 600,000
Altitude: 2,639m

64 km west of Mexico City by dual carriageway

Toluca is the capital of the state of México. It is known mostly for its huge Friday market where Indians sell colourful woven baskets, *sarapes*, *rebozos*, pottery and embroidered goods (beware of pickpockets and handbag slashers). The new market is at Paseo Tollocan e Isidro Fabela, spreading over a number of streets, open daily. As well as textiles, the city is famous for confectionery and for *chorizos* (sausages). It is also a centre of chemical industries, which cause pollution. The **tourist office** is at Lerdo de Tejada Pte 101, Edificio Plaza Toluca, 1st floor, T215-0131. It has a free *Atlas Turístico* of the state of México, including street maps of all towns of interest.

The centre of the city is the **Plaza de los Mártires**, a very open space. On its south side is the **cathedral**, begun in 1870, but not completed until 1978. Incorporated in its interior is the baroque façade of the 18th-century church of the Tercera Orden. Also on the south side is the **Church of Veracruz**, housing a black Christ and with a very attractive interior. On three sides of the block containing these two churches are | **Sights**
Look out for an orange liqueur known as moscos, a local speciality

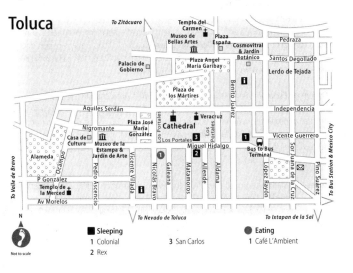

Toluca

N

Not to scale

■ Sleeping	● Eating
1 Colonial 3 San Carlos	1 Café L'Ambient
2 Rex	

Los Portales (Calle Bravo, Calle Hidalgo and Calle Constitución), arcaded shops and restaurants. Northeast of Plaza de los Mártires is a park, Plaza Angel María Garibay, with trees and fountains, on which is the **Museo de Bellas Artes**, formerly the Convento del Carmen, with seven halls of paintings from 18th-century colonial baroque to the 20th century, and temporary exhibitions. A tunnel is said to run from the ex-Convento to all the central churches. ■ *Tue-Sun 1000-1800, US$0.25, concessions half price, booklet US$1.35*. Next door is the **Templo del Carmen**, a neoclassical church with a gold and white interior, and next to that is Plaza España. At the eastern end of Plaza Garibay is the **Cosmovitral** and **Jardín Botánico**. From 1933 to 1975 the building was the 16 de Septiembre market; it was reopened in 1980 as a formal garden in honour of the Japanese Eizi Matuda, who set up the herbarium of Mexico State, with fountains and exhibitions, all bathed in the blues, oranges and reds of the vast stained-glass work of Leopoldo Flores Valdez, a unique sight. ■ *Tue-Sun 0900-1700, US$0.60*. One block west of Plaza Garibay is the **Palacio de Gobierno**. Four blocks west of Los Portales is the **Alameda**, a large park with a statue of Cuauhtémoc and many tall trees; on Sunday morning it is very popular with families strolling among the many stallholders. The entrance is at the junction of Hidalgo and Ocampo. At Ocampo and Morelos is the **Templo de la Merced**. The **Casa de las Artesanías** (Casart), with an excellent display of local artistic products for sale, is at Paseo Tollocán 700. It is more expensive than Mexico City. ■ *Daily 0930-1850*. **Zacango**, 10 km south of the city, is a good zoo.

Excursions   From Toluca take a bus north to the pyramids and Aztec seminary of **Calixtlahuaca**, 2 km off the road to Ixtlahuacan. The pyramids are to Quetzalcoatl (circular) and to Tlaloc. They are situated just behind the village, 10 minutes' walk from the final bus stop. ■ *US$4.35*. Forty-five minutes north of Toluca by car, near the town of Temoaya, is the Centro Ceremonial Otomí, a modern site for cultural events in a beautiful landscape.

From Toluca to the coast at Ixtapa along Route 134 (see page 381) via Tejupilco, Ciudad Altamirano and La Salitrera, the road is paved but deteriorating in parts, traffic is sparse and the landscape hilly and pleasant.

Sleeping
■ *on map page 145*
Price codes: see inside front cover

C *San Carlos*, on Hidalgo at Portugal Madero 210, T214-9422. **C** *Colonial*, Hidalgo Ote 103, T214-7066. Pleasant courtyard with stained glass, with bath, clean, TV, cheap food (good restaurant, closed Sunday). Recommended (bus from Terminal de Autobuses to Centro passes in front). **D** *Rex*, Matamoros Sur 101, T215-9300. With bath, hot water, no restaurant.

On Hidalgo Pte C *La Mansión*, No 408, T215-6578. With hot water, clean, garage, TV, no restaurant. **E** *Maya*, No 413, no check-in before 2000. Shared bath, hot water, clean, small rooms without door locks, towels extra. All the above are in the centre, not many cheap hotels. **D** *Terminal*, adjoining bus terminal, T215-7960 (prices vary according to floor). Restaurant next door.

Motels   AL *Del Rey Inn*, Km 63, Mexico-Toluca Highway, T212-2122, F212-2567. Resort facilities. On same exit road is **A** *Paseo*, T216-5730 (4-star).

Eating
● *on map page 145*

Ostionería Escamilla, Rayón Nte 404. Good fish. *Café L'Ambient*, Hidalgo 231 Pte. Snacks, meals, quite simple; next door are *Son Jei* and *Panadería Libertad* (good pizza takeaway), oriental; opposite, in Los Portales, is *Impala* for *comida corrida*, coffee. Open Sun from 0930 for good set breakfasts. *Fonda Rosita* in Los Portales central avenue going through to Plaza de los Mártires. Also open Sun morning, pleasant, Mexican. *Las Ramblas*, on Constitución side of Los Portales. Mexican food, average.

Transport   **Buses** Bus station is some distance from the centre; information is difficult to gather inside and all is confusion outside – look for a bus marked 'Centro', US$0.15; from centre to terminal buses go from, among other places, Ignacio Rayón Nte and Hidalgo Ote, look for 'Terminal' on window (yellow or orange bus). To Mexico City (Terminal del Occidente, close to Metro Observatorio), US$3.50, 1 hr. Bus to **Pátzcuaro**, 6 hrs, US$23, several daily; to **Taxco**, 4 buses a day, 3 hrs, US$8 with Frontera, a spectacular journey. To **Morelia**, several buses daily with

Herradura de Plata, 4 hrs, US$11. Many buses to **Tenango de Arista** (30 mins, US$1), **Tenancingo**; also regular buses to **Calixtlahuaca** 1 hr, US$3.50 from platform 7.

Nevado de Toluca

A road branches off the Toluca to Valle de Bravo road at Km 75 to the Toluca volcano, *Colour map 3, grid B3*
Nevado de Toluca, or Xinantécatl. At 4,558 m this is the fourth highest mountain in
Mexico. The road climbs to the deep blue lakes of the Sun and the Moon in its two
craters, at about 4,270 m, from which there is a wide and awe-inspiring view. It is 27
km from the turning off the main road to the heart of the craters. During winter it is
possible to ski on the slopes; 2 km from the entrance is an *albergue* with food and cooking facilities. From here it is 10 km to the entrance to the crater, where there is a smaller
albergue (cooking facilities, food sold at weekends only, no bathroom or water, dirty),
and then a further 6 km to the lakes. A short-cut from the small *albergue* takes 20 minutes to the crater; it is not possible to drive. At the third refuge, 21 km from the turn-off
is an attendant. Trips to the volcano are very popular at weekends. You can stay overnight at any of the refuges (**F**), although they are sometimes closed during the week,
and there is a restaurant, but the trip can be done in one day from Toluca. If walking
remember the entrance to the crater is on the far left side of the volcano.

To reach the Toluca volcano take the first bus to Sultepec from Toluca at about
0700, every two hours thereafter. Leave the bus where the road to the radio station
branches off, just after Raíces village (US$1); from there it is about 20 km to the
crater, hitching is fairly easy, especially at weekends. Aim to get to the crater by midday, otherwise clouds will cover everything. Visitors must leave by 1700.

Along Route 55 south of Toluca, or reached from it, are a number of interesting art
and craft producing villages, all with fine old churches. The first village is **Metepec**,
the pottery-making centre of the valley, 1½ km off the road to Tenango. The clay figurines made here, painted bright fuchsia, purple, green and gold, are unique. This is
the source of the 'trees of life and death', the gaudily painted pottery sold in Mexico.
Craft workshops are very spread out. Market day is Monday. A recommended place
to eat is *Las Cazuelitas*, near the main church. Bus Toluca-Metepec US$0.65.

A detour east off Route 55 or south from Route 15, the Toluca-Mexico City highway, *If you're feeling brave*
goes to the town of **Santiago Tianguistenco** (*population* 38,000), where there are *try atepocates; embryo*
good *cazuelas*, *metates*, baskets and *sarapes*. Try *gordas* or *tlacoyos*, blue corn stuffed *frogs with tomato*
with a broad bean paste. Try restaurant *Mesón del Cid*, good regional food, go to *and chillies, boiled in*
kitchen to see choice. Try *sopa de hongos* (mushroom soup). Market day is Wednes- *maize leaves*
day and the town is crowded at weekends.

San Mateo Atenco (*population* 65,000; *altitude* 2,570 m) is situated south of the
Toluca-Lerma 'corridor'. Settled in ancient times, it has featured in several important
historical moments by virtue of occupying a bridge-head between lagoons: Axayácatl,
Hernán Cortés and Hidalgo all passed this way. There is a Franciscan church and
monastery, the earliest parts of which date from 1550. The town is famous for its shoes,
and leather goods of all descriptions. Excellent bargains are to be had. On 25 October
St Crispin, the patron saint of shoemakers, is honoured in the open chapel of the
church in the presence of the local bishop. Market is on Friday and Saturday.

Route 55 descends gradually to **Tenango de Arista**, where there are two hotels with
a car park alongside the main road, where one can walk (20 minutes) to the ruins of
Teotenango. The Toluca-Tenango bus costs US$0.65. Teotenango shows the
Matlazinca culture and is reminiscent of La Ciudadela at Teotihuacán, with five plazas, 10 structures and one ball court. There is an interesting museum by the ruins; to
enter go to the end of town on the right-hand side. If you ask the guard, you can pitch
a tent at the museum inside the gate. ■ *Entry to museum and ruins US$1.*

Tenancingo
Phone code: 714
Altitude: 1,830 m

West of Mexico City, just 48 km south of Toluca, the road descends abruptly through gorges to Tenancingo, which has a soft, warm climate all year round. Thirty minutes by bus to the south along an unpaved road is the magnificent 18th-century Carmelite convent of El Santo Desierto, where they make beautiful *rebozos*. The townspeople themselves weave fine *rebozos* and the fruit wines are delicious and cheap. Overlooking this busy commercial town is a statue of Christ on a hill. The daily market area is two blocks from the bus terminal (continue one block, turn left for two further blocks to the main square); market day is Sunday, with excellent local cheese.

Sleeping and eating Recommended are **D** *Lazo*, Guadalupe Victoria 100, T142-0083 (1½ blocks straight on from market, away from bus terminal). Clean rooms in annex with shower, leafy courtyard, *El Arbol de la Vida* restaurant. **D** *María Isabel*, Nezahualcóyotl 706, T142-0821. Clean, well-lit. **E** *Don Ale*, corner of Insurgentes y Netzahualcoyotl, T142-0516. Good value, with clean rooms, nice balcony and garden and no bugs. Loud TV may annoy some. Good bakery in private house at Guillermo Prieto 302.

Transport Buses: frequent buses to **Toluca**, US$3 with *Tres Estrellas del Centro*, 1 hr; also to **Ixtapan de la Sal** US$1.40 (change here for Taxco US$3), **Malinalco**, US$2.20, and **Chalma**.

Malinalco

Phone code: 714

About 11 km east of Tenancingo is Malinalco, from which a path winds up 1 km, 20 minutes, to the partly excavated Malinalco ruins, dating from 1188, certainly one of the most remarkable pre-Hispanic ruins in Mexico. Here is a fantastic rock-cut temple in the side of a mountain, which conceals, in its interior, sculptures of eagle and jaguar effigies. Apparently, you can feel movement in the rock if you lie on it or lean against it. The staircase leading to the temple has over 430 steps. The site, which shows Matlatzinca culture with Aztec additions, is very small, but in a commanding position over the valley, and overlooks the town and surrounding wooded hills. ■ *Tue-Sun 1000-1630, US$2, Sun free.*

The site is visible from the town as a ledge on the hillside; the walk up passes a tiny, blue colonial chapel. For an even better view of the ruins carry straight on where the path leading to the ruins branches off to the right. This old road is cobbled in places and rises up the mountainside pretty steeply, arriving (after about 1½ hours' walk) at a small shrine with two crosses. It is possible to camp here but there is no water. Breathtaking views can be seen from here off both sides of the ridge. The trail then carries on gently down the other side, past avocado trees, for 20 minutes, to the paved road to Tenancingo, almost opposite a new brick house with arches. It is possible to catch a bus back over the mountains to Malinalco. It would also be much quicker and easier, a downhill walk mostly, to do this whole hike in reverse; catch the bus out, ask for the old road, and walk back.

You should not fail to visit also the Augustinian **Templo y Ex-convento del Divino Salvador** (1552), in the centre of town, the nave of which has a patterned ceiling, while the two-storey cloisters are painted with elaborate, early frescoes. Just below the main square in front of the convent is the market (market day Wednesday). There is a **fiesta** in Malinalco on 6 August.

You can also get to Malinalco from Toluca, or Mexico City, by taking a second class bus to **Chalma**. This is a popular pilgrimage spot. From the bus lot, walk up hill, past the market stalls, to the crossroads where blue *colectivos* leave for Malinalco until 2000 (10 km, 20 minutes, US$1), or take a taxi.

Sleeping
& eating

D *Posada Familiar*, T147-0354. **E** *Santa Mónica*, Hidalgo 109, T147-0031. With bath, pretty courtyard, good value. Cabins for families at north edge of town. *El Paraíso,* opposite the small blue chapel, camping and trailer park, not well named; no facilities other than one dirty toilet. Eating places include *La Playa* on road to ruins, just off square, with garden, nice place;

opposite is *La Salamandra*, good value; trout farm and fishery has a restaurant, superb, bring own supplies of beverages, bread, salad (trout costs US$5-6); also *El Rincón del Convento*, behind the convent on road to square.

A direct road runs from **Tenancingo** to Malinalco, paved to the summit of a range of hills, poor at the summit, then graded to the junction with the Malinalco-San Pedro Zictepec road; pick-up truck or buses run on this direct road hourly, 40 mins, US$3.50 (in Malinalco, bus leaves from corner of Av Progreso and the square). From **Toluca** you can go to Malinalco by leaving the Toluca-Tenancingo road after San Pedro Zictepec, some 12 km north of Tenancingo, which is paved and 28 km long. In Mexico City, buses leave from Terminal del Pte, opposite Observatorio. Buses to Chalma from **Mexico City** leave frequently from Terminal del Pte, 2½ hrs, US$6.50 direct. This is also where you make connections if coming from **Cuernavaca** (take a Cuernavaca-Toluca bus to Santa Marta, then wait for a Mexico City or Toluca-Chalma bus).

Thirty-two kilometres from Tenancingo on Route 55 is Ixtapan de la Sal, a pleasant leisure resort with medicinal hot springs surrounded by forest. In the centre of this quiet whitewashed town is the municipal spa. ■ *US$1.60. 0700-1800, not always open.* At the edge of town is the privately run Parque Los Trece Lagos, which has a train running around it and numerous picnic spots. Private baths charge US$6 for admission only, everything else is extra. For the hedonist there are private 'Roman' baths, for the stiff-limbed a medicinal hot-water pool, mud baths for the vain, an Olympic pool for swimmers, rowing boats and a water slide for the adventurous. The latter is 150 m long (prohibited to those over 40). ■ *US$1.55, US$0.90 for two slides, US$2.20 for slides all day, free midweek 1200-1400.* Market day is Sunday and there is a **fiesta** on the second Friday in Lent.

Ixtapan de la Sal
Phone code: 721
Colour map 3, grid B3

Sleeping AL *Ixtapan*, Blvd Arturo San Román, T143-2440, F143-0856, www.spamexico.com Including food and entertainment. **AL** *Vista Hermosa*, T143-0092. Next door, full board only, good, friendly. **B** *Casablanca*, Juárez 615, T143-0036, F143-1031. **C** *María Isabel*, T143-0102. Good. **D** *Guadalajara*. With bath. **D** *Casa de Huéspedes Margarita*, Juárez. Clean. Recommended. **D** *Casa Guille*, José María Morelos 12, T143-0220. With bath, clean. **E** *Casa Yuyi*. With bath, clean, good; many others.

Eating There are plenty of reasonable restaurants on Av Benito Juárez; most close by 1900. Good value is *Fonda Jardín* on Zócalo.

Transport Car: Ixtapan de la Sal can be reached in about 2 hrs from Mexico City: turn off Route 15, the Toluca highway, at La Marquesa, go through Santiago Tianguistenco and join Route 55 at Tenango. The road goes on to the Grutas de Cacahuamilpa (see page 171), from where you can continue either to Cuernavaca or Taxco. **Buses**: to/from Mexico City every 30 mins from Terminal Oriente, 3 hrs, US$7, every 30 mins from Terminal Oriente; to Toluca every 30 mins, 2 hrs, US$5.80. Also to Taxco, Coatepec, Cuernavaca.

Tonatico, 5 km past Ixtapan de la Sal, is a much cheaper village with a pleasant municipal *balneario* filled with medicinal hot water supposed to help blood circulation, rheumatism and other illnesses. There is also a waterslide, open at weekends only, and a cheap hotel (**D**) at the entrance to the *balneario* with bathroom, T141-0691.

The mountain resort of Valle de Bravo, located on a branch road of Route 134, is a charming old town on the edge of an attractive artificial lake and close to an important Monarch butterfly wintering area. Valle de Bravo's **fiesta** is 26 February-14 March. From Valle del Bravo it's an easy excursion to **Colorines** with six series of rock paintings dating from AD 800. There are two direct buses a day Zitácuaro-Valle de Bravo, 1½ hours, US$4; hourly buses to Toluca and Mexico City; first-class bus to Toluca, US$4.80.

Valle de Bravo
Phone code: 726
Colour map 3, grid B3

This area gets the rich weekend crowd from Mexico City

Sleeping L *Loto Azul Resort*, Av Toluca, T262-0796, F262-2747. 4-star, top quality. **B** *Los Arcos*, Bocanegra 310, T262-0042. Some rooms with excellent view, swimming pool, restaurant (open only at weekends), not very helpful staff (**A** at weekends). **C** *Casa Vieja*, Juárez 101, central. Recommended. **D** *Blanquita's*, opposite church off main plaza. Basic, fairly clean, OK. **D** *Mary*, main plaza. Hot showers. A few cheap *posadas familiares* around the plaza.

Trailer park   Av del Carmen 26, T262-1972. Familia Otero, English spoken, 5 hook-ups, 7 dry camping, 3 rentals, small private grounds. Recommended. **NB** Drivers with trailers must approach Avándaro from the Toluca end, no other way is safe because of the hills, narrow streets and town centre.

Eating   Restaurants are normally cheaper mid-week. *Alma Edith*, on Zócalo. One of the few places to be open for breakfast by 0900. Very good, but slow service, good *comida corrida*. *El Monarca*, Juárez 203. Excellent *comida corrida* just US$1.50. *La Estación*, Bocanegra 318. Recommended. Good, cheap food in the *mercado*. The *cecina* - a variety of salted beef – in this part of the country is magnificent and highly recommended. Restaurants on pier are expensive. *Los Pericos*, Embarcadero Municipal, T262-0558. International menu, specializes in fish dishes, 0900-2000.

Ixtapan del Oro
Population: 20,000

Ixtapan del Oro is a pleasant town in a valley, 70 km southeast of Zitácuaro. It has a few hotels including **E** *Posada Familiar Portal Moreno*, with bath, clean. A road, mostly dirt, runs between Ixtapan del Oro and Valle de Bravo.

East of Mexico City

Popocatépetl and Iztaccíhuatl

Colour map 3, grid B4

See Transport, page 176

At Km 29 on Route 190 is **Ixtapaluca**, where a road heading south leads to the small town of Amecameca, the starting point for exploring Popocatépetl (5,452 m) – smoking mountain in Nahuatl – and Iztaccíhuatl (5,286 m) – the White Woman. On the way to Amecameca, see the restored 16th-century convent and church at **Chalco**, and the fine church, convent and open-air chapel of the same period at **Tlalmanalco**.

Legend has it that a princess was waiting for her warrior lover to return when news came of his death. Overcome with grief, she poisoned herself and when the warrior returned from battle he took her body to the top of Iztaccíhuatl and jumped into its crater. The three summits of Iztaccíhuatl are the head, breasts and knees of the princess. The saddle between the two volcanoes is reached by car via a paved road up to the Paso de Cortés (25 km from Amecameca) and gives particularly fine views.

Amecameca
Phone code: 587
Colour map 3, grid B4
Population: 57,000
Altitude: 2,315 m
60 km to Mexico City

The Amecameca Cholula road through the volcanoes is officially closed due to eruptions

The Zócalo here is pleasant with good taco stands. A road reaches the sanctuary of El Sacromonte, 90 m above the town, with magnificent views, a small and very beautiful church built round a cave once inhabited by Fray Martín de Valencia, a conquistador who came to Mexico in 1524. It is, after the shrine of Guadalupe, the most sacred place in Mexico and has a much-venerated full-sized image of Santo Entierro weighing only 1½ kg. From the Zócalo, take the exit under the arch and head for the first white station of the cross; the stations lead to the top. Market day is Saturday, and there is an excellent non-touristy market on Sunday. The **tourist office** is near the plaza, open 0900-1500. They can provide information and guides for Iztaccíhuatl.

From Mexico City, take the metro to Pantitlán, then a bus or *pesero* to Ixtapaluca. Behind the Mercado Municipal take another *pesero* on the 'Avila Camacho' route and get off at La Vereda (transportation from 0600-2100 daily).

Sleeping and eating The town seems to be suffering as a result of the eruptions. The only hotel, **E** *San Carlos*, Constitución 10, T978-0746, has simple basic rooms. **Camping** Permitted at the railway station, ask the man in the office (leaving town, it's after the road to Tlamacas, on the right, 1-2 km away).

There are several eating places and a good food market. A good-quality *pulque* is available at the *pulquería* on the main plaza. There is also an **internet** café on the main plaza.

Transport Buses: from Mexico City with *Cristóbal Colón*. Los Volcanes 2nd class bus 1-1½ hrs journey, US$2.80, from the Terminal del Oriente; if hitching, take the Calzada Zaragoza, a very dusty road.

Climbing the volcanoes

Popocatépetl has been closed to climbers because of volcanic activity since 1994

In December 2000, Popocatépetl, known familiarly as Don Goyo, had its largest eruption for 500 years. The crater lid, which was in part blown sky-high, had increased, according to experts, to 14 million cubic metres; not only did smoke and ash rise to a height of more than 10 km, but the volcano also threw out incandescent rocks for a radius of up to 2 km. There was another similar eruption less than a month later.

Among the implications of these spectacular events – which could be seen clearly from Mexico City – is that the volcano, which had been moderately active over the previous few years, probably demonstrated the limits of real damage that it is able to inflict; even the villages nearest to the crater experienced – apart from some panic – nothing more than heavy volcanic ash, and the feared lava, and mud from molten glaciers, did not materialize. There were heavy falls of very fine volcanic ash, in Puebla, Amecameca and as far away as Mexico City. It was also demonstrated that the population of some 30 villages deemed to be at risk were able to be evacuated swiftly; that said, most inhabitants returned home equally promptly, fearful of the fate of their livestock and belongings, although there were no reports of looting.

For the foreseeable future it will not be possible to climb, or get close to, Popocatépetl; furthermore, outsiders should exercise discretion about visiting villages in the danger area out of respect for the inhabitants. We suggest that readers seek local up-to-the-minute information and advice before attempting a visit to the National Park.

Iztaccíhuatl From Paso de Cortés a road goes left, north along another dirt road, which leads past a TV station for 8 km to the parking nearest to the summit of Iztaccíhuatl at La Joya. Near the antennae is a *refugio* called Atzomani, which is the safest place to park, and there is a box (*buzón*) for notifying potential rescue groups of your intended route. From there you find various routes to the summit (12-15 hours return) and three to four refuges in which to stay overnight (no furniture, bare floors, dirty). Iztaccíhuatl has been described as 'an exhilarating roller-coaster of successive summits'. To climb **Iztaccíhuatl** take a taxi to La Joya, from there follow the tracks up the grassy hill on the right, four to six hours to first huts. The first two huts are at 4,750 m (places for 30 people), the third at 4,850 m (10-15 people), and the last hut is at 5,010 m (in poor condition, 10-12 people); the Luis Menéndez hut is the most salubrious. From the last hut it is 2½-3 hours to the top, set off at 0400, over two glaciers. Some rock climbing is required, so crampons and ice-picks are necessary and can be hired in Amecameca.

A more technical route starts at the *buzón* and at first descends left into the valley. Walk three to four hours from La Joya to the Ayoloco glacier before which is a *refugio* for 8 to 10 people at 4,800 m; it is three to four hours to the summit from here. Guides are available in Amecameca and Rigoberto Mendoza has been recommended. The cost is about US$110 and worth it, as walking on glaciers without knowing the conditions is hazardous.

Volcanic activity permitting, the best time to climb the volcanoes is between late October and early March when there are clear skies and no rain. From May to October the weather is good before noon only

Around Mexico City

The route to Puebla

Assuming that travellers start the journey from Mexico City, we have suggested an early detour to take in Texcoco and the towns and villages in its environs. There is a steady flow of traffic between the valleys of Mexico and Puebla-Tlaxcala.

Our description involves a trip along the old road, which goes east along the Puebla road, past the airport and swimming pools, and some spectacular shanty towns. At Los Reyes, Km 19, a road runs left into a valley containing the now almost completely drained Lake Texcoco, a valley that was settled early by the conquistadores. Along it you'll come to **Chapingo**, where there is a famous agricultural college with particularly fine frescoes by Rivera in the chapel. ■ *Mon-Fri 0900-1800. Colectivo from General Anaya y San Ciprián or bus from TAPO (Autotransportes Mexico-Texcoco, US$0.70).*

Next is Texcoco, which is a good centre for visiting villages in the area. Bus from Mexico City, from Emiliano Zapata 92, near Candelaria metro station or TAPO. Near Chapingo a road runs right to the village of **Huexotla**, with an Aztec wall, ruined fortifications and pyramid, and the 16th-century Franciscan convent of San Luis Obispo. Another road from Texcoco runs through the public park of Molino de las Flores. From the old hacienda buildings, now in ruins, a road (right) runs up the hill of Tetzcotzingo, near the top of which are the Baños de Nezahualcóyotl, the poet-prince. **San Miguel de Chiconcuac**, on the road to San Andrés and left at its church, 4 km away, is where Texcoco *sarapes* are woven. Tuesday is market day and there is a rousing **fiesta** in honour of their patron saint on 29 September.

Beyond Ixtapaluca, southeast of Los Reyes on Route 190, the road climbs through pine forests to reach 3,196 m, about 63 km from Mexico City, and then descends in a series of sharp bends to the town of **San Martín Texmelucan**, Km 91. The old Franciscan convent here has a beautifully decorated interior, and a former hacienda displays weaving and old machinery. The Zócalo is beautiful, with benches covered in ceramic tiles and a central gazebo. Market day is Tuesday. Recommended hotels are **D-E** *Hotel San José*, Pte 115 and **E** *La Granja*, opposite.

Puebla

Phone code: 222
Colour map 3, grid B4
Population: 1,346,176
Altitude: 2,060m

'The city of the angels', Puebla de los Angeles is one of Mexico's oldest and most famous cities and the capital of Puebla state. It was founded in 1531 by Fray Julián Garcés who saw angels in a dream indicating where the city should be built, hence its name. It is also one explanation of why Puebla wasn't built over Indian ruins like many other colonial cities. Talavera tiles are an outstanding feature of Puebla's architecture and their extensive use on colonial buildings distinguishes it from other colonial cities. Puebla is a charming city, pleasant and friendly, and always popular with travellers.

Getting there Aeropuerto Hermanos Serdán (PBC) has mostly domestic flights. The CAPU bus station is to the north of the city. Taxis from the terminal to the city centre leave from outside the departure terminal. From the centre to the terminal, take any form of public transport marked 'CAPU'. The train station is a long way from the centre, so before going there check at the tourist office to see if passenger services are running. Puebla is on the main Highway 150 from Mexico City to the Gulf Coast, the same *supercarretera* that branches south, beyond Puebla, to Oaxaca. An important commercial centre, Puebla is also the hub of other lesser routes to towns and villages in the surrounding area.

Getting around Although Puebla is a big city, most of the major sites are around the centre, within easy walking distance of each other. City buses, *colectivos* or taxis will take you to any of the more distant sites.

The **tourist office** is at 5 Ote 3, Avenida Juárez behind the cathedral, next to the post office, T246-2044, F242-3161, **www.turismopuebla.com.mx**, closed Sat and Sun.

Sights

The centre, though still beautifully colonial, is cursed with traffic jams and pollution, except in those shopping streets reserved for pedestrians. Puebla is said to have had 365 churches dating from the early colonial period, one for each day of the year. The din from the church bells was so loud that the residents requested that it be toned down a little since they were driven to distraction on Sundays and Feast days. Some of these churches are quite beautiful and should not be missed.

The **Congreso del Estado** in Calle 5 Poniente 128, formerly the Consejo de Justicia, near the post office, is a converted 19th-century Moorish-style town house. The tiled entrance and courtyard are very attractive and it had a theatre inside, shown to visitors on request. It is now the seat of the state government. The **Patio de los Azulejos** should also be visited; it has fabulous tiled façades on the former almshouses for old retired priests of the order of San Felipe Neri. The colours and designs are beautiful. It is at 11 Poniente 110, with a tiny entrance on 16 de Septiembre, which is hard to find. Ring the bell on the top right and you may get a guided tour. Also worth visiting is the **Biblioteca Palafoxiana**, or the library of Bishop Palafox, in the Casa de la Cultura, 5 Oriente 5, opposite the cathedral; it has 46,000 antique volumes. It is in a colonial building with a large courtyard, which also houses paintings and art exhibitions. ■ *Open 1000*. Next door at 5 Oriente 9 is another attractive building, the **Tribunal Superior de Justicia**, built in 1762; you may go in the courtyard.

The Plaza y Mercado **El Parián** is between Avenida 2 y 4 Oriente and Avenida 6 y 8 Norte. On Calle 8 Nte between Avenida 6 Oriente and Avenida 4 Oriente there are many small shops selling paintings. The area is also notable for onyx souvenir shops. Onyx figures and chess sets are attractive and cheaper than elsewhere, but the *poblanos* are hard bargainers. In the adjoining Barrio del Artista the artists' studios are near to *Hotel Latino*. Live music and refreshments at small *Café del Artista*, Calle 8 Norte y Avenida 6 Oriente. Just south at Calle 8 Norte 408 is the *Café Galería Amparo*, which serves light food. The University Arts Centre offers folk dances at various times; look for posters or enquire direct. ■ *Free*.

Also worth seeing are the church and monastery of **El Carmen**, with its strange façade and beautiful tile work. The **Teatro Principal** (1550), Avenida 8 Ote y Calle 6

The very tiny glass animal figures make an attractive buy

Around Mexico City

Puebla centre

Sleeping
1 Colonial
2 Del Portal
3 Royalty

Eating
1 Fonda Sta Clara

Related map
Puebla, page 155

0 metres 200
0 yards 200

Nte, is possibly the oldest in the Americas although it was badly damaged by fire in 1902 and had to be rebuilt. The 17th-century **Academia de las Bellas Artes** has a grand staircase and an exhibition of Mexican colonial painting. The Jesuit church of **La Compañía** on Avenida Don Juan de Palafox y Mendoza y 4 Sur, has a plaque in the sacristy showing where China Poblana is said to be buried. Also worth visiting is the house of **Aquiles Serdán** at 6 Oriente 206, a leader of the Revolution, preserved as it was during his lifetime. It houses the **Museo de la Revolución Mexicana**. ■ *1000-1630, US$1*. The tiled façade of the **Casa de los Muñecos**, 2 Norte 1, corner of the main square, is famous for its caricatures in tiles of the enemies of the 18th-century builder. Inside, in the **Museo Universitario**, some rooms contain old physics instruments, old seismographs, cameras, telescopes, another has stuffed animals, but most rooms contain religious paintings from the 17th and 18th centuries. ■ *US$1*. Avenida Reforma has many fine buildings, for example No 141, *Hotel Alameda*, which is tiled inside and out. The **Palacio Municipal** is on the north side of the Zócalo. To the right of the entrance is the **Biblioteca del Palacio** (opened 1996) with some tourist information and books on the city. To the left is the **Teatro de la Ciudad**, opened 1995, where music and drama are performed. There is also an art gallery in the same building.

The Casa del Dean has been closed and some of the churches are under repair since the earthquake of June 1999. It is to be hoped that the repairs will have been completed by the time this handbook is published

The **Casa del Dean**, 16 de Septiembre y 7 Poniente, was built in 1580. The walls of the two remaining rooms are covered with 400-year-old murals in vegetable and mineral dyes, which were discovered in 1953 under layers of wallpaper and paint. After President Miguel de la Madrid visited in 1984, the house, previously used as a cinema, was taken over by the government and opened to the public. The murals were inspired by the poems of the Italian poet and humanist, Petrarch, and are believed to have been painted by Indians under the direction of the Dean, Don Tomás de la Plaza, whose house it was. The murals contain a mixture of classical Greek, pagan (Indian) and Christian themes. About 40% have been restored. ■ *US$1 plus tip for the guide if wanted. The current guide, Mariano Díaz, has been recommended.*

Churches

There are 60 churches in all, many of their domes shining with the glazed tiles for which the city is famous

On the central arcaded plaza is a fine **cathedral**, one of the most beautiful and interesting anywhere, notable for its marble floors, onyx and marble statuary and gold-leaf decoration. There are statues flanking the altar, which are said to be of an English king and a Scottish queen. The bell tower gives a grand view of the city and snow-capped volcanoes. ■*1030-1230*. In November 1999 it was not permitted to climb the bell tower.

In the **Capilla del Rosario** of the **Church of Santo Domingo** (1596-1659), 5 de Mayo 407, the baroque displays a beauty of style and prodigality of form that served as an exemplar and inspiration for all later baroque in Mexico. The chapel has very detailed gold leaf all over it inside. The altar of the main church is also decorated with gold leaf with four levels from floor to ceiling of life-size statues of religious figures. There is a strong Indian flavour in Puebla's baroque; this can be seen in the churches of Tonantzintla and Acatepec (see below); it is not so evident, but it is still there, in the opulent decorative work in the cathedral. Beyond the church, up towards the Fuerte Loreto (see below), there is a spectacular view of the volcanoes.

Other places well worth visiting are the churches of **San Cristóbal** (1687), 4 Nte y 6 Ote, with modern churrigueresque towers and Tonantzintla-like plasterwork inside as well as the 18th-century **San José**, 2 Nte y 18 Ote, with attractive tiled façade and decorated walls around the main doors and beautiful altarpieces inside. One of the most famous and oldest local churches is **San Francisco** at 14 Ote 1009, with a glorious tiled façade and a mummified saint in its side chapel; see also the pearl divers' chapel, given by the poor divers of Veracruz; the church thought it too great a sacrifice but the divers insisted. Since then they believe diving has not claimed a life. The **Capilla de Dolores**, the other side of Boulevard 5 de Mayo from San Francisco, is small but elaborately decorated. **Santa Catalina**, 3 Nte with 2 Pte, has beautiful altarpieces; **Nuestra Señora de la Luz**, 14 Nte and 2 Ote, has a good tiled façade and so has **San Marcos** at Av Reforma and 9 Nte. The Maronite church of **Belén** on 7 Nte and 4 Pte has a lovely old tiled façade and a beautifully tiled interior. The church **La Puerta del Cielo**, at the top of the Cerro de San Juan in Colonia La Paz, is modern but in classical style, with over 80 figures of angels inside.

The **Museo de Artesanías del Estado** in the ex-Convento de Santa Rosa (3 Nte **Museums** 1203) has a priceless collection of 16th-century Talavera tiles on the walls and ceilings of its kitchen, well worth a visit. It was here that the nuns invented the famous *mole poblano*. The museum has a good display of the many crafts produced in the State of Puebla. ■ *Tue-Sun 1000-1630.*

The fragile-looking and extravagantly ornamented **Casa del Alfeñique** (Sugar Candy House), Av 4 Ote 418, a few blocks from the cathedral is worth seeing, now the Museo Regional del Estado. ■ *US$0.40.*

Museo Bello, Av 3 Pte 302, is the house of the collector and connoisseur Bello who died in 1938. It has good displays of Chinese porcelain and Talavera pottery and is beautifully furnished. ■ *US$1.10, free Tue and Sun, guided tours, closed Mon.* **Museo de Santa Mónica**, 18 Pte 103, is housed in a former convent where generations of nuns hid after the reform laws of 1857 made the convent illegal. This is where the nuns invented *chiles en nogada*. ■ *1000-1800, closed Mon.* **Museo Amparo**, 2 Sur 708, esquina 9 Ote, has an excellent anthropological exhibition with one of the best pre-Hispanic collections in Mexico and audiovisual explanations in Spanish, English, French and Japanese (take your own headphones, or hire them). Colonial art and furniture is on show upstairs. Recommended. ■ *1000-1800, closed Tue, free guided tour 1200 Sun, US$2, students half price.*

The **Cinco de Mayo Civic Centre**, with a stark statue of Benito Juárez, is, among other things, a regional centre of arts, crafts and folklore. It is near the **Museo Regional de Puebla**, which has magnificent collections but little information. ■ *1000-1700.* Also nearby is the **Museo de Historia Natural**, auditorium, planetarium, fairgrounds and an open-air theatre. In the same area, the forts of Guadalupe and Loreto were the scene of the Battle of Puebla, in which 2,000 Mexican troops defeated Maximilian's 6,000 European troops on 5 May 1862 (although the French returned

Around Mexico City

Puebla

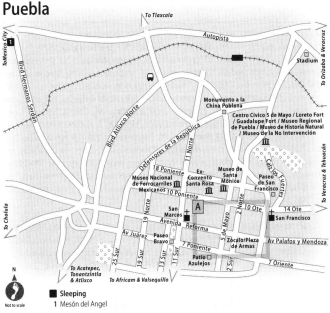

Related maps
A Puebla centre,
page 153

Sleeping
1 Mesón del Angel

victorious 10 days later). This is why 5 May is a holiday in Mexico.Inside the **Fuerte Loreto**, which has views of the city (and of its pollution), is a small museum, **Museo de la No Intervención**, depicting the battle of 1862. ■ *1000-1700, closed Mon, US$1.30.*

For railway enthusiasts there is an outdoor museum, **Museo Nacional de los Ferrocarriles Mexicanos**, displaying old engines and wagons at 11 Nte, between 10 y 14 Pte, in the old Puebla railway station known as El Mexicano.

Essentials

Sleeping
■ *on maps,*
page 155 and below
Price codes:
see inside front cover

L-AL *Camino Real*, 7 Pte 105, T229-0909, F232-9251, www.caminoreal.com/puebla In ex-Convento de la Concepción, built 1593, beautifully restored, all rooms are different, quiet, bar, restaurant, room service, boutiques, dry cleaning. **A** *Del Portal*, Portal Morelos 205, T246-0211, F232-3194. Very good, but ask for room away from Zócalo side (noisy), restored colonial, plain rooms, TV, phone, parking across the street. **A-C** *Aristos*, Av Reforma, esq 7 Sur, T232-0565. Good facilities in rooms and bathrooms, gym with sauna, pool, attractive public areas, restaurant, piano bar, cheaper rates at weekends.

B-C *Royalty*, Portal Hidalgo 8, T242-4740. Pleasant, central, quiet, restaurant good but expensive and service slow, tables outside under the portales where a marimba band sometimes plays. **C** *Colonial*, 4 Sur 105, T246-4199. Across pedestrian street from La Compañía church, old-fashioned and charming, very friendly, colonial style, restaurant, accepts Amex, ask for back room, with bath, TV and phone. **C** *Gilfer*, 2 Ote No 11, T246-0611, F242-3485. Attractive, modern building, large rooms, reasonable restaurant, excellent service; next door is **B-C** *Palace*, 2 Ote No 13, T242-4030, F242-5599. Price depends on number and size of beds, attractive, modern lobby, cafetería, satellite TV, phones, 60 rooms. **C** *Granada*, Blvd de la Pedrera 2303, T232-0966, F232-0424. Very close to bus terminal, bus to centre leaves from front door, quiet, comfortable, restaurant, room service, TV in rooms. Also close to the bus terminal **C** *Imperial*, 4 Ote 212, T242-4980. Good-sized plain rooms with TV and phones, shower, clean, some rooms noisy, laundry, restaurant, gym, parking, 30% discount offered to *Handbook* owners, good value.

D *Alameda*, Reforma 141, close to the Zócalo, T242-0882. Most rooms windowless, parking, TV, phone, bath, very clean, friendly, good value. **D** *Ritz*, 2 Nte 207 y 4 Ote, T232-4457, 2 blocks from Zócalo. Reasonable, drab front rooms with balcony quieter, hot water. **D** *Virrey de Mendoza*, Reforma 538, T242-3903. Old colonial house, plain, fairly basic rooms, high ceilings, TV, bath, beautiful wooden staircase. **D-E** *Santander*, 5 Pte 111, near cathedral, T246-3175, F242-5792. Colonial façade, recently renovated, hot showers, clean, simple, big bright rooms towards street, TV, enclosed parking. Recommended. **D-E** *Teresita*, 3 Pte 309, T232-7072. Small modern rooms, with bath ('comedy showers'), hot water, friendly. **E** *Casa de Huéspedes Los Angeles*, Calle 4 Nte 9. Basic, communal bathrooms, irregular hot water, *comedor*, central. **E** *Latino*, Calle 6 Nte 8, T232-2325, next to Barrio del Artista, basic. **E** *Victoria*, near Zócalo, 3 Pte 306, T232-8992. Clean, quiet, hot showers. Recommended. **E-F** *Avenida*, 5 Pte 336 between 5 and 3 Sur, 2 blocks from Zócalo, T232-2104. Price depends on number of beds and shared or private bathroom, airy rooms (except those without windows), quiet, friendly, clean, hot water morning and evening, drinking water. Recommended. Several basic *casas de huéspedes* near markets. Very cheap hotel (**F**), 2 blocks south of train station, *20 de Noviembre*. Big rooms, no water 2000 to 0700, clean, bus to town.

Motels LL-AL *Mesón del Angel*, Hermanos Serdán 807, T224-8300, F224-8304, www.gruporeal.com.mx, near 1st Puebla interchange on Mexico-Puebla motorway. Possibly best in town, but far from the centre, 192 rooms, a/c, cable TV, conference and banqueting facilities, 2 restaurants, bar, 2 pools, tennis. **B-D** *Panamerican*, Reforma 2114, T248-5466. Restaurant, no bar, parking. Recommended.

Camping Possible on the extensive university grounds about 8 km south of centre.

Local specialities *Mole poblano* (chicken or turkey with sauce of chillies, spices, nuts, chocolate and coconut); best at *La Poblanita*, 10 Nte 1404-B, and *Fonda Santa Clara*, 3 Pte 307. Good for local specialities, very popular, often crowded, very good but expensive, second larger location with parking a couple of blocks west on 3 Pte. *Mixiote is lamb with chilli, wrapped in paper with hot sauce. Chiles en nogada* are *poblano* chillies stuffed with minced meat and almonds and topped with a sweet cream sauce made with ground nuts, then topped with pomegranate seeds, best in Jul-Sep, delicious. Calle 6 Ote specializes in shops selling *dulces* (sweets) and *camotes* (candied sweet potatoes). *Nieves*, drinks of alcohol, fruit and milk, are also worth trying as are the excellent *empanadas* and *quesadillas*.

Eating
The green, white and red colours of chiles en nogada are supposed to represent the Mexican flag

El Vasco, Portal Benito Juárez 105, on Zócalo. Slow service, most dishes US$3, US$6 for *plato mexicano*. Several others to choose from on Zócalo, eg *La Princesa*, Portal Juárez 101. Good variety and good prices, breakfast US$2-3, *comida corrida* US$3. *Mac's*, US-style diner, good variety. Cheap *comidas* at *Hermilo Nevados*, 2 Ote 408, good value. Recommended. Also *Munich*, 3 Pte y 5 Sur. Many cheap places near main square with menus prominently displayed. *Cafetería La Vaca Negra*, Reforma 106, just off Zócalo. Modern, attractive, part of a chain, meals US$2-7. *Hotel Royalty*, Portal Hidalgo 8. Nice restaurant with meals around US$6-7, *platillos poblanos*, tables under the portales, marimba band plays sometimes. *Mesón Sacristía de la Compañía*, 6 Sur 304, T242-3554. In the old sacristy, marvellous patio, lots of plants, very cosy. Reasonable prices. *Bajo el Cielo de Jalisco*, Calle 3 sur 507. Recommended. *Mercado El Alto*, in the San Francisco quarter. Beautiful market covered with *azulejos*, with good local cuisine. Breakfast and lunch, 8 different menus. *Woolworth's*, corner of 2 Pte and 5 de Playo, 1½ blocks from northwest corner of Plaza Mayor, 0800-2200. Good range of cheap, reasonable meals and some expensive dishes. *El Vegetariano*, 3 Pte 525 (near *Hotel San Agustín*). Good, serves breakfast. Recommended. *Super-Soya*, 5 de Mayo. Good for fruit salads and juices. Several other good places for *comidas corridas* on 5 de Mayo. *Librería Cafetería Teorema*, Reforma 540, esq 7 Nte. Café, books and art, live music at night, good coffee and snacks, pastries, *platillos mexicanos*. Recommended. *La Gardenia*, Palafox 416. Local dishes, a bit cramped but very good quality, selection and value. Recommended. Several other reasonably priced places nearby. *Cafetería Tres Gallos*, 4 Pte 110. Good coffee and pastries. *Café Britannia*, Reforma 528. Cheap. Recommended. *Jugos y Licuados*, 3 Nte 412. Recommended. *Tony's Tacos*, 3 Nte and Reforma. Quick and very cheap. *La Super Torta de Puebla*, on 3 Pte. Good sandwich bar. *Tepoznieves*, 3 Pte 150 esq 3 Sur. Rustic Mexican décor, serves all varieties of tropical fruit ice cream and sherbet. *La Pasita*, 5 Ote between 2 y 4 Sur, in front of Plaza de los Sapos. The oldest bar in Puebla, sells a drink by the same name, a local speciality. Recommended. *Al Kalifa*, 2 Sur between 15 y 17 Ote. Cheap tacos, very good *taco arabe*. Recommended.

Feria in mid-Apr for 2 weeks. The *Fiesta Palafoxiana* starts on the last Fri in **Sep** until **Festivals** mid-Nov for 9 weekends of dancing, music, theatre, exhibitions, etc; some free performances.

5 de Mayo is a pedestrian street closed to traffic from the Zócalo to Av 10. The entire block **Shopping** containing the Capilla del Rosario/Templo de Santo Domingo in the southeast corner has been made into a shopping mall (opened 1994), called the Centro Comercial La Victoria after the old La Victoria market. The old market building still exists.

Craft shops sponsored by the authorities: *Tienda Convento Santa Rosa*, Calle 3 Nte 1203, T240-8904. The famous Puebla Talavera tiles may be purchased from factories outside Puebla, or from *Taller Uriarte*, Av 4 Pte 911 (spectacular building, tours Mon-Fri 1000-1200, 1700, Sat 1000-1300, morning best). Recommended. *Talavera de la Reyna*, Camino a la Carcaña 2413, Recta a Cholula. Recommended (also in *Hotel Mesón del Angel*); *Centro de Talavera*, Calle 6 Ote 11; *D Aguilar*, 40 Pte 106, opposite Convento de Santa Mónica, and *Casa Rugerio*, 18 Pte 111. *Margarita Guevara*, 20 Pte 30. **Bookshop**: *Librería Británica*, Calle 25 Pte 1705-B, T240-8549. **Bicycle shops** There are several shops in 7 Nte, north of 4 Pte, with international spare parts. **Food** *Mercado Venustiano Carranza*, 11 Nte and 5 Nte,

Around Mexico City

is good for *mole*. The best shops for the famous local hand-made **sweets** and *rompope* (egg nog) are on Calle 6 Ote.

Sports *Las Termas*, 5 de Mayo 2810, T232-9562, gay bath house, entry US$2.50, steambaths, sauna, gym; ***Lidromasaje***, beer and soft drinks.

Transport **Local Taxis**: radio taxi service, ***Radio Omega***, T240-6299. New Chevrolet cars, 24-hr service, will deliver packages or pick up food or medicine and deliver it to your hotel.

Long distance Air: Hermanos Serdán airport (PBC) has flights to Guadalajara, León, Mexico City, Monterrey and Tijuana.

Buses: new, huge CAPU bus terminal for all buses north of city. From the centre to the terminal, take any form of transport marked 'CAPU', many *colectivos* and buses (route 12) on Av 9 Norte, fare US$1.50 per person flat rate. To the centre from the terminal take Combi No 14, US$0.30, which stops at 11 Nte and Reforma at Paseo de Bravo (make sure it's a No 14 'directo', as there is a No 14 that goes to the suburbs). To reach the terminal, take bus 37 or 21 at Av Camacho. The departure terminal has a banking services (with ATM), and a good practical mix of shops including gift shops, phone booths, food shops and luggage storage. The arrivals terminal has some shops including small grocery, free bathrooms, long-distance pay phones and taxi ticket booth (but you have to take ramp to the departure terminal to get the taxi). Companies ***Autobuses de Oriente (ADO)***, T249-7144. Mercedes Benz buses, 1st class and 'GL' plus service; ***Oro***, T249-7775, *gran turismo* or 1st class service; ***UNO***, T230-4014, luxury service; ***Estrella Roja***, T249-7099, 2nd class, 1st class and *plus* service; ***Cristóbal Colón***, T249-7144 ext 2860, plus service; ***Estrella Blanca***, T249-7561, 1st class, *plus* and *élite* services; ***Autobuses Unidos (AU)***, T249-7366, all 2nd class without toilets.

There are services to most parts of Mexico from Puebla

To **Mexico City**, *ADO* to TAPO (eastern) terminal every 20 mins from 0445 to 2145, US$6.50; to Terminal del Sur every hour from 0635 to 2135, US$6.50; to Terminal del Norte every 20-40 mins from 0520-2150, US$6.50, *Estrella Roja* to Mexico City airport every hour from 0300 to 2000, 2 hrs, US$9. To Mexico City 2nd class every 10 mins, US$5, *plus* service US$5.50; *AU*, every 12 mins from 0510 to 2300.

To **Acapulco**, *Estrella Blanca*, *plus* service, 2200, US$33, 1st class, 1030, 1230, 2130, 2230, 2300, US$28. To **Chetumal**, *ADO*, 1145, US$58. To **Mérida**, *ADO*, 2105, US$59. To **Oaxaca**, all take new *autopista*, 4 hrs; *ADO* 'GL' *plus* service, 2 daily, US$28.25, 1st class, 5 daily, US$17; *UNO* at 1800, US$26. To **Xalapa**, *ADO* 'GL' *plus* service at 0805 and 1700, US$9, 1st class, 8 a day, US$7.50, 4 hrs; *AU*, 2nd class. To **Reynosa**, *ADO* at 1155, US$44. To **San Cristóbal de las Casas**, *Cristóbal Colón*, *plus* service, 1715, 1845, 2215, US$50. To **Tapachula**, *UNO*, 1830, US$71, 16 hrs; *Cristóbal Colón*, *plus* service, 2115, US$46. To **Tehuacán** direct *ADO* every 30-45 mins from 0600-2100, US$5.50. To **Tuxtla Gutiérrez**, *ADO*, 2010, US$42; *UNO*, 2215, US$65, 14 hrs. To **Villahermosa**, *ADO* 'GL' plus service via autopista, 2200, US$38, 1st class, 1900, 2145, US$32; *UNO* at 2100, US$53, 8 hrs.

Directory

For website addresses, see page 34

Airline offices *Aero California*, Blvd Atlixco 2703, Locales B y C, Col Nueva Antequera, T230-4855. ***AeroMéxico***, Av Juárez 1514, Col La Paz, T232-0013. ***Aeromar***, T232-9633. ***Mexicana***, Av Juárez 2312, between Calle 23 Sur and 25 Sur, T248-5600. ***Lufthansa*** and ***LanChile***, at Av Juárez 2916, Col La Paz, T248-4400. **Banks** *Bancomer*, 3 Pte 116, changes TCs 0930-1300, good rates. On the Zócalo are ***Banco Santander Mexicano***; ***Banco Inverlat*** at Portal Benito Juárez 109, changes money 0900-1400; and a *casa de cambio* at Portal Hidalgo 6 next to *Hotel Royalty*. On Av Reforma are: ***Banamex***, No 135; ***Bancomer***, No 113; ***Banco Bital***, across the street. Most banks have ATMs. **Communications Internet**: colonial building with red/orange bricks and blue and white tiles, also has email service for US$3 per ½ hr; at the ***Escuela Sandoval***, on 5 Ote, you can email for US$2 per hr. ***Soluciones Alternativas***, Calle 4 Nte 7, 101, 1st flr, no sign, email service US$2 per hr. At the ***BUAP University***, Av San Claudio esq 22 Sur, T244-4404, open Mon-Fri 0700-2100, Sat, Sun 0800-1800, 48 PCs, but slow, US$2.50 per hr. **Post office**: 5 Ote between 16 de Septiembre and 2 Sur, open Mon-Fri 0800-2000. **Laundry** In large commercial centre on Av 21 Pte and Calle 5 Sur, US$4 wash and dry, 3 hrs. Another on 9 Nte, between 2 and 4 Pte, US$2.80 for good service wash. **Medical services** Dentist: ***Dr A Bustos***, Clínica de Especialidades Dentales, 2 Pte 105-8, T232-4412, excellent service, recommended. **Doctors:** ***Dr Miguel Benítez Cortázar***, 11 Pte 1314, T242-0556, US$15 per consultation. ***Dr Cuauhtémoc Romero López***, same address and phone. **Hospitals:** ***Beneficiencia Española***, 19 Nte 1001, T232-0500. ***Betania***, 11 Ote 1826, T235-8655.

UPAEP, 5 Pte 715, T246-6099, F232-5921. The cheapest is *Universitario de Puebla*, 25 Pte y 13 Sur, T243-1377, where an outpatient consultation is US$5. **Tour operators** *American Express*, Centro Comercial Plaza Dorada 2, Héroes 5 de Mayo, Locales 21 and 22, T237-5558, F237-4221, open Mon-Fri 0900-1800, Sat 0900-1300.

Cholula

This small somnolent town, with the Universidad de las Américas, was once as influential as Teotihuacán. When Cortés arrived, it was a holy centre with 100,000 inhabitants and 400 shrines, or *teocallis*, grouped round the great pyramid of Quetzalcoatl. When razing the shrines, Cortés vowed to build a chapel for each one destroyed; in fact there are 'only' about 70 churches in Cholula.

Phone code: 222
Population: 20,000

The excavated **pyramid**, a man-made mountain, has 8 km of tunnels and some recently discovered frescoes inside; 1 km of tunnel is open to the public, giving an idea of the layers that were superimposed to create the pyramid. The **museum** near the tunnel entrance has a copy of the frescoes (the originals are not open to the public). ■ *1000-1700, US$2 weekdays, free on Sun and holidays, guides charge US$6.50, recommended as there are no signs inside (some guides speak English).* From the Zócalo follow Avenida Morelos and cross the railway. The 16th-century chapel of **Los Remedios** on top of the pyramid gives a fine view. The Franciscan fortress church of **San Gabriel** (1552) is in the plaza. ■ *0600-1200, 1600-1900, Sun 0600-1900.* Next to it is the **Capilla Real**, which has 49 domes. ■ *1000-1200, 1530-1800, Sun 0900-1800.*

Sights

See the Indian statuary and stucco work of the 16th-century church of Santa María de Tonantzintla, or 'the place of our venerable mother', in the neighbouring village of **Tonantzintla**; the church is one of the most beautiful in Mexico. ■ *1000-1800 daily.* It may be reached by paved road from San Francisco **Acatepec**, another village with an equally beautiful, but less ornate 16th-century church, whose interior has been restored following a fire, but whose wonderful tiled façade is still intact. ■ *Supposedly open 0900-1800 daily, but not always so – key is held by José Ascac, ask for his shop.* These two tiny churches are exquisite and should not be missed; they are resplendent with Poblano tiles and their interiors, especially that of Tonantzintla, are a riot of Indian stucco-work and carving. Best light for photography after 1500. Photography *inside* the churches is frowned upon.

Excursions
It seems that regular visiting hours are not strictly observed at Cholula, Acatepec, Tonantzintla or Huejotzingo

You can visit Tonantzintla and Acatepec from Cholula main square with a *pesero* and you might get to see the (real) lion sitting outside the black and white castle-type building en route. Or you can take a combi from Cholula to Acatepec or to Tonantzintla (marked Chilapo or Chipanco, ask which combi goes to the church you want) for US$0.55 from junction of Avenue 5 and Avenue Miguel Alemán. You can walk the 1 km to the other church, and then take a bus or combi back to Cholula or Puebla. Acatepec from CAPU in Puebla, US$0.45, 30 minutes, bus stops outside the church. The villages are off Highway 190 en route from Puebla to Izúcar de Matamoros.

Between Acatepec and Puebla is the superb church of **Tlaxcalantzingo**, with an extravagantly tiled façade, domes and tower.

Huejotzingo, Km 106, has the second-oldest church and monastery in Mexico, which was built in 1529 and is now a museum. Market is held on Saturday and Tuesday. There is a dramatic carnival on Shrove Tuesday, portraying the story of Agustín Lorenzo, a famous local bandit. **D** *Hotel Colonial.* Secure but poor value.

B *Villas Arqueológicas*, 2 Pte 501, T247-1966, F247-1508. Behind pyramid, affiliated to *Club Med*. Heated pool, pleasant garden, tennis, French restaurant, rooms have heating, TV, phone, English and French spoken. **C** *Cali Quetzalcoatl*, on Zócalo, Portal Guerrero 11, T247-4199. Clean. Good restaurant. **D** *Reforma*, near main square, T247-0149. **D** *Super*

Sleeping

Around Mexico City

Motel on the road from Puebla as you enter town. Each room with private garage, very secure, popular with men and their mistresses. **E** *Las Américas*, 14 Ote 6 in the San Andrés part of town, T247-0991. Near pyramid, actually a motel, modern with rooms off galleries round paved courtyard (car park), small restaurant, clean, good value. **E** *Trailer Park Las Américas*, 30 Ote 602. Hot showers, secure, as are the furnished apartments.

Eating Many good restaurants and food stops due to the large number of North Americans in town. *Restaurant Choloyán*, also handicrafts, Av Morelos. Good, clean, friendly. *Pasta e Pizza*, Portal Guerrero 9B, centre. Try *licuados* at market stalls, fruit and milk and 1 or 2 eggs as you wish; *mixiote* is a local dish of lamb or goat barbecued in a bag.

Transport **Buses** Frequent 2nd class *Estrella Roja* buses from **Puebla** to Cholula from 6 Pte y 13 Nte, 9 km on a new road, 20 mins, also 1st and 2nd class *Estrella Roja* buses from CAPU bus terminal hourly (be ready to get out, only a quick stop in Cholula); from Cholula take a 'Pueblo Centro' bus to the city centre, or a 'Puebla-CAPU' bus for the terminal; *colectivos* to Cholula. From **Mexico City**, leave for Cholula from Terminal del Oriente with *Estrella Roja*, every 30 mins, US$4.20, 2½ -3 hrs, 2nd class every 20 mins, a very scenic route through steep wooded hills. Good views of volcanoes.

Directory **Useful services** There is a *casa de cambio* on the corner of the main plaza, and a travel agency in the Los Portales complex on the plaza. **Internet** on 5 de Mayo (San Andrés), US$1.50 per hour.

Tlaxcala

Phone code: 246
Colour map 3, grid B4
Population: 73,184
Altitude: 2,240 m

From Texmelucan a side road leads northeast for 24 km to the once quaint old Indian town of Tlaxcala, with its pleasant centre of simple buildings washed in ochre, pink and yellow, and its vast suburbs. It is the capital of the state of the same name whose ranchers breed fighting bulls, but whose landless peasantry is still poor. The annual fair is held 29 October-15 November each year.

The **tourist office**, Av Juárez y Landizábal, T465-0960, F465-0962, has many maps and leaflets and is very helpful (no English spoken). The official Tlaxcala tourism website is at **www.tlaxcala.gob.mx**

Sights Dating from 1521, the **Church of San Francisco** is the oldest in Mexico, from whose pulpit the first Christian sermon was preached in New Spain (Mexico). Of course, the sermon would have been for the benefit of the Spanish residents; the Indians would have congregated outside at the open chapel. Almost next door is the **Museo del Estado de Tlaxcala**, with two floors of interesting historical and artistic exhibits. In the Palacio de Gobierno on the main square are the extremely colourful murals depicting the indigenous story of Tlaxcala, the history of Mexico and of humankind. ■ *0900-1700, US$1.* The **Museo de Artes y Tradiciones Populares** is a 'living museum' where Otomí Indians demonstrate traditional arts and customs including the sweat bath, cooking, embroidery, weaving and pulque-making. It is highly recommended. ■ *Closed Mon, US$0.60.*

Excursions The **Basílica de Ocotlán** (1541), on a hill in the outskirts of Tlaxcala (a stiff 20-minute climb from Juárez via Guribi and Alcocer), commands a view of valley and volcano. It was described by Sacheverell Sitwell as 'the most delicious building in the world', but others have been less impressed. Nevertheless, its façade of lozenge-shaped vermilion bricks, framing the white stucco portal and surmounted by two white towers with fretted cornices and salomonic pillars, is beautiful. The sumptuous golden interior was worked on for 25 years by the Indian Francisco Miguel.

The ruined pyramid of **Xicoténcatl** at San Esteban de Tizatlán, 5 km outside Tlaxcala, has two sacrificial altars with original colour frescoes preserved under glass. The pictures tell the story of the wars with Aztecs and Chichimecs. Amid the archaeological digs at Tizatlán are a splendid 19th-century church and the

16th-century chapel of San Esteban. To get there, take a *colectivo* to Tizatlán from 1 de Mayo y 20 de Noviembre, Tlaxcala; at the main square, you get out when you see a yellow church dome on the left.

La Malinche Volcano, 4,461m, takes its name from the Nahuatl, *matlalcueye*, meaning the greenish-blue skirt. It can be reached from Tlaxcala or Puebla; buses from the market beside the old railway station, Tlaxcala 1½ hours, US$1, one at 0800 and others, return 1800. You go to La Malintzin Centro de Vacaciones at the base of the volcano, now closed to the public. The hike to the summit takes four hours, the descent 1½ hours (take an ice-axe; altitude is a problem). Alternatively, stay at nearby town of Apizaco. There is a reasonable hotel and restaurant next to the roundabout with a locomotive in the centre and safe parking. It is a good day trip from Puebla. Another route is via Canoa (bus from Puebla, US$0.50). It is a long hike to the top, 10 hours return at a good pace; take warm clothes. Be careful not to be caught on the mountain during an extended rainstorm; it is very easy to lose your way. The volcano could be visited on a two-day trip from Puebla; on the first day reaching the foot of the mountain, where it is possible to set up a tent or rent a four-bed cabaña (US$20 per night, firewood can be bought at the office, kitchen with no utensils, shower). On the second day you could climb the volcano, six to seven hours at an easy pace, before returning to Puebla.

Sleeping **A** *Posada San Francisco* (Club Med), Plaza de la Constitución 17, T462-6022, F462-6818. Lavishly decorated in colonial style, 2 restaurants, good food, secure parking, swimming pool, tennis courts. Highly recommended. **B** *Alifer*, Morelos 11, uphill from plaza, T462-5678. Safe parking. **C** *Albergue de la Loma*, Av Guerrero, T462-0424.

Eating *Los Portales*, main square, popular with regional dishes, mid-price. *Fonda del Convento*, San Francisco 1. Serves excellent 4-course traditional meals in a lovely setting. Set lunch US$8. *Oscar's*, Av Juárez, near corner of Zitlalpopocatl. Excellent sandwiches and juices. *La Arboleda*, Lira y Ortega, near square. Good. *The Italian Coffee Company*, Plaza de la Constitución. Very good coffee.

Entertainment *The Cine American*, on Blvd G Valle (continuation of Av Juárez) has 2 for 1 on Wed.

Transport **Buses** Tlaxcala's bus station is about a 10-min walk from the centre. Frequent *Flecha Azul* buses from **Puebla**, central bus station (platform 81/82) between 0600 and 2130, 45 mins, US$1.50. To **Cacaxtla** US$0.55.

Directory **Communications** Internet: *Café Internet*, Independencia 21, south of Av Guerrero. **Laundry** *Servi-Klim*, Av Juárez, 1½ blocks from plaza, dry cleaners, will launder but at dry cleaning prices. *Lavandería Acuario*, Alonsa Escalona 17, between Juárez and Lira y Ortega, 3 kg US$3, self-service 4 kg US$1, 0830-2000.

Cacaxtla

Colour map 3, grid B4

A remarkable series of pre-Columbian frescoes are to be seen at the ruins of Cacaxtla near San Miguel del Milagro, between Texmelucan and Tlaxcala. The colours are still sharp and some of the figures are larger than life size. To protect the paintings from the sun and rain, a huge roof has been constructed. An easily accessible visitors' centre has been opened. There is disappointingly little published information on the site, however. In theory there is a 'per picture' charge for photography, but this is not assiduously collected although flash and tripod are strictly prohibited. ■ *Tue-Sun 1000-1630, US$2, which also includes access to Xochitecatl. From Puebla take a Flecha Azul bus marked 'Nativitas' from C 10 Pte y C 11 Nte to just beyond Nativitas where a sign on the right points to San Miguel del Milagro and Cacaxtla (US$1). Walk up the hill (or colectivo US$0.20) to a large sign with its back to you, turn left here for the ruins.*

Around Mexico City

Excavations over the past few decades have uncovered some of the most interesting and complex murals ever found in Mesoamerica. Much fascinating material for the art historian has been derived from them, not because the symbolism and iconography is obscure and difficult to understand, but due to the motifs and symbols incorporating images that stem from several cultural traditions.

Huamantla Thirty miles east of Tlaxcala on Route 136 is Huamantla, an attractive little town (*population* 66,000). The **Museo Nacional de Títeres** (puppet museum) is on Parque Juárez. It has nine rooms of puppets from around the world. ■ *Tue-Sat 1000-1400, 1600-1800, US$1, students and children US$0.50. Camera US$2.50. Videos by prior arrangement.* **Parroquia de San Luis Obispo**, Parque Juárez, lots of gold inside. Also on Parque Juárez is the **Templo Franciscano**, with interesting ceiling paintings, side chapels and a high altar screen painted to look like green marble.

The eve of the feast of the Assumption, 14 August, is known locally as *La noche que nadie duerme* (The night when nobody sleeps). Overnight, the people of Huamantla create carpets of flowers and coloured sawdust along 12 km of streets. After a week of festivities there is a **Huamantlada**, a Pamplona-style bull running through the streets of the town.

Cuetzalan

Phone code: 233
Colour map 3, grid B5

It can be very foggy at Cuetzalan, even when it is fine in Puebla

An interesting day trip from Puebla is to Cuetzalan market (via Tetela-Huahuaxtla), which is held on Sunday in the Zócalo (three hours' walk up). In the first week of October each year dancers from local villages gather and *voladores* 'fly' from the top of their pole. Nahua Indians sell cradles (*huacales*) for children, machetes and embroidered garments. Women decorate their hair with skeins of wool. The *Día de los Muertos* (2 November) is interesting here. Big clay dogs are made locally; unique stoves that hold large flat clay plates on which *tortillas* are baked and stews are cooked in pots. Also available in nearby Huitzilán. You can also go via Zaragoza, Zacapoaxtla and Apulco, where you can walk along a path, left of the road, to the fine 35-m waterfall of La Gloria. **C** *Hotel Taselotzin*, a set of cabins, very clean, great views, two beds per cabin, and bathroom (**E** per person per night). Highly recommended. Tourist information is available at Calle Hidalgo y Bravo, helpful, good map.

From Cuetzalan it is a 1½-hour walk to the well-preserved, niched pyramids of Yohualichan (Totonac culture); there are five excavated pyramids, two of them equivalent to that at El Tajín (see page 350), and three still uncovered. There has been earthquake damage, though. Take a bus from Calle Miguel Alvarado Avila y Calle Abosolo, more frequent in morning and market days, to San Antonio and get off at the sign Pirámides Yohualichan (30 minutes, bad road), then walk 2 km to the site. ■ *Closed Mon and Tue, US$2.* In the Cuetzalan area are 32 km of caverns with lakes, rivers and wonderful waterfalls. These include Tzicuilan (follow Calle Emiliano Zapata, east of town) and Atepolihuit (follow Carretera Antigua up to the Campo Deportivo, west of town). Children offer to guide visitors to the ruins and caves.

Sleeping and eating Several cheap, quite clean hotels, eg **E** *Hotel Rivello*, G Victoria 3, T331-0139, 1 block from Zócalo, with bath, **F** without, basic, friendly, clean. **D** *Posada Jackelin*, upper end of plaza, near market behind church, T331-0354, pleasant. *Posada Quetzal*, Zaragoza. Good, cheap restaurant. *Yoloxochitl*, 2 de Abril. Good for breakfasts, huge juices. *Casa Elvira Mora*, Hidalgo 54. Recommended. *Villacaiba* for seafood, Francisco Madero 6. *Café-Bazar Galería*, in centre. Good sandwiches and tea, nice garden, English magazines. Recommended.

Transport Direct buses from Puebla (Tezuitecos line only), 5 a day from 0500 to 1530, US$8.50; quite a few return buses, but if none direct go to Zaragoza and change buses there. There are many buses to Zacapoaxtla with frequent connections for Cuetzalan.

South of Puebla

From Puebla, Route 150 continues to **Amozoc**, where tooled leather goods and silver decorations on steel are made, both mostly as outfits for the *charros*, or Mexican cattlemen. Beyond Amozoc lies **Tepeaca** with its late 16th-century monastery, well worth a visit; its weekly market is very extensive. On the main square is Casa de Cortés, where Hernán Cortés signed the second of five *Cartas de Relación* in 1520. ■ *1000-1700.* An old Spanish tower or *rollo* (1580) stands between Tepeaca's main square and the Parroquia. Beyond Tepeaca, 57 km from Puebla, lies **Tecamachalco** where the vast 16th-century Franciscan monastery church has beautiful murals on the choir vault, in late medieval Flemish style, by a local Indian. Language school Escuela de Español en Tecamachalco, run by Patricia O Martínez, Calle 29 Sur 303, Barrio de San Sebastián, Tecamachalco, CP 75480, Apdo Postal 13, T(249) 422-1121, very good; possible to live with families. There is a good seafood restaurant; enquire at José Colorado's shop near the school.

This charming town, southeast of Puebla, has a pleasant, sometimes cool, climate. Water from the mineral springs is bottled and sent all over the country by Garci Crespo, San Lorenzo and Peñafiel. From the small dam at Malpaso on the Río Grande, an annual race is held for craft without motors as far as the village of Quiotepec. The central plaza is pleasant and shaded. **Museo de Minerológia Romero** is in the ex-Convento del Carmen, Avenida Reforma, 7 Norte 356. It has one room with a good collection of minerals from all over the world, ■ *0900-1200, 1600-1800, mornings only on Sat, free.* The Ayuntamiento on the Zócalo is decorated inside and out with murals and tiles. A short bus ride beyond Peñafiel Spa is the spa of **San Lorenzo** with spring-fed pools surrounded by trees. ■ *US$2 entry.*

Tehuacán

Phone code: 238
Colour map 3, grid C5
Population: 190,000
Altitude: 1,676 m

Around Mexico City

Sleeping A *México*, Reforma Nte and Independencia Pte, 1 block from Zócalo, T382-2419. With garage, TV, restaurant, renovated colonial building, pool, quiet. **B-C** *Bogh Suites*, 1 Nte 102, northwest side of Zócalo, T382-3879. New, businessman's hotel, safe parking. **D** *Iberia*, Independencia Ote 217, T383-1500. With bath, clean, airy, pleasant restaurant, noisy weekends, public parking nearby at reduced fee with voucher from hotel. Recommended. **C** *Inter*, above restaurant of same name, close to bus station (ask there), T383-3620. Hot shower, clean, modern. **E** *Madrid*, 3 Sur 105, T382-0272, opposite Municipal Library. Comfortable, pleasant courtyard, cheaper without bath. Recommended. Several *casas de huéspedes* along Calle 3 (Nte and Sur) but low standards.

Eating Many eating places on Zócalo with reasonable prices (eg on same corner as cathedral, good breakfast). The main meal is served at midday in Tehuacán. Try *Restaurant Santander*. Good but pricey. *Cafetería California*, Independencia Ote 108. Excellent juices and *licuados*. *Pizzería Richards*, Reforma Nte 250. Quite good pizzas, good fresh salads; excellent taco stands.

Transport *ADO* bus station on Av Independencia (Pte). Bus direct to **Mexico City**, 5 hrs, US$13; to **Puebla**, 2½ hrs, US$5.50; to **Oaxaca** (5½ hrs, US$16 *Autobuses Unidos* at 1430, coming from Mexico City, may be full), **Veracruz**, US$11, and the Gulf: *Autobuses Unidos*, 2nd class on Calle 2 Ote with several buses daily to Mexico City and Oaxaca. Local bus to **Huajuapan**, 3 hrs, US$7; from there, frequent buses to Oaxaca.

From Tehuacán there are two paved roads to Oaxaca: one, very scenic, through Teotitlán del Camino (US$1.65 by second class bus), and the other, longer but easier to drive, through Huajuapan (see page 383). Railway junction for Oaxaca and Veracruz; no passenger trains on line to Esperanza. Wild maize was first identified by an archaeologist at Coxcatlán Cave nearby. There is an airport.

Teotitlán del Camino, en route to Oaxaca, is a glaringly bright town with a military base. Vehicles are stopped occasionally; make sure, if driving, that your papers are in order. From Teotitlán it is possible to drive into the hills to the Indian town of **Huautla de Jiménez**, where the local Mazatec Indians consume the hallucinogenic 'magic' mushrooms made famous by Dr Timothy Leary. Huautla has all four seasons of the year in each day: springlike mornings; wet, foggy afternoons; fresh, autumn evenings; and freezing nights. Hiking in the mountains here is worthwhile. There is the hotel *Olímpico*, **E**, above market, with no sign. It is clean, friendly and simple, with small rooms, bath. You cannot buy food in the town after 2000. Several daily buses to/from Mexico City and Oaxaca (US$6.50); children meet buses offering lodging in their homes. There are many police and military. Drivers may be waved down by people in the road up to Huautla; do not stop for them, they may be robbers.

The road from Tehuacán to the Gulf coast soon begins to climb into the mountains. At Cumbres, 2,300 m, there is a wide view: the silvered peak of Citlaltépetl, 'Star Mountain' (or Pico de Orizaba – see page 344) volcano to the northeast, the green valley of Orizaba below. In 10 km the road drops down, through steep curves, sometimes rather misty, to Acultzingo 830 m below. The road joins the main toll road from Puebla to Orizaba at Ciudad Mendoza, where it has emerged from the descent through the Cumbres de Maltrata, which are usually misty and need to be driven with care and patience. The expensive toll road Puebla-Orizaba is a much safer drive than the route described here; it, too, is scenic.

South of Mexico City

Cuernavaca

Phone code: 777
Colour map 3, grid B4
Population: 337,966
Altitude: 1,542 m

The capital of Morelos state, originally Tlahuica Indian territory, is 724 m lower than Mexico City. The Nahuatl name, Cuauhnáhuac, means 'Adjacent to the tree'. The temperature never exceeds 27°C nor falls below 10°C and there is almost daily sunshine even during the rainy season. The city has long attracted visitors from the cooler highlands and Cortés himself, following the custom of the Aztec nobility, had a palace there. Today some of its charm has been swamped; the centre can be crowded and the rapidly growing outskirts are dotted with the ultra-modern walled homes of rich 'capitalinos' and a new industrial area to the south.

Ins & outs

Getting there Buses leave the capital from the Terminal del Sur to one of Cuernavaca's four bus stations, each serving a different bus company (for details see Transport page 167). To drive the 89 km to Cuernavaca, follow Insurgentes Sur all the way south beyond Ciudad Universitaria and then take either the fast *cuota* (toll), or the picturesque *libre*. Beyond Cuernavaca, Route 95 and 95D continue south towards Taxco and Acapulco, or you can head east to Tepoztlán, Cuautla and on to the state of Puebla. There is a small airport at Cuernavaca with some domestic flights.

Getting around Most of the sites in Cuernavaca are near the centre of town, within easy walking distance of each other. Local bus routes can be confusing as they take long, roundabout routes through the *colonias*. Buses marked 'Centro', or 'Buena Vista', all go to the cathedral. Taxis are plentiful and easy to flag down; agree on the price before travelling. The state **tourist office** is at Av Morelos Sur 187m T/F314-3872, **www.morelosvisit.com**

Sights

The centre of the city has two adjacent squares, the larger **Zócalo** and the smaller **Alameda**. At the western end of the Zócalo is the Palacio de Gobierno; north of the Zócalo, east of the Alameda is the Centro Las Plazas shopping mall. Heading north from the Alameda, Calle Vicente Guerrero is lined with shops in arcades. Calle Degollado leads down to the main market in a labyrinth of shops and alleys. There is a tourist kiosk on Vicente Guerrero outside *Posada San Angelo*. For cultural activities, go for information to the university building behind the cathedral on Morelos Sur.

The palace Cortés built in 1531 for his second wife stands at the eastern end of the tree-shaded Zócalo; on the rear balcony is a Diego Rivera mural depicting the Conquest of Mexico. It was the seat of the State Legislature until 1967, when the new legislative building opposite was completed; it has now become the **Museo Regional de Historia Cuauhnáhuac**, showing everything from mammoth remains to contemporary Indian culture, explanations are not very logical and most are in Spanish. ■ *1000-1700, closed Mon, US$1.60.* West of the centre, Calle Hidalgo leads to one of the main areas of historical interest in the city.

The **cathedral**, entrance on Hidalgo, near Morelos, was finished in 1552. Some 17th-century murals were discovered during restoration depicting the martyrdom of the Mexican saint San Felipe de Jesús on his journey to Japan. The scenes show monks in open boats, and mass crucifixions. The interior is bathed in different colours from the modern stained-glass windows. At the west end is a stone font full of water; the east end, painted gold, contains the modern altar. In the entrance to the chapel of the Reserva de la Eucarista is a black and white fresco of the crucifixion. There are also two-storey cloisters with painted friezes and a fragment of massed ranks of monks and nuns. By the cathedral entrance stands the charming small church of the **Tercera Orden** (1529), whose quaint façade carved by Indian craftsmen contains a small

The Sunday morning Mass at 1100 is accompanied by a special mariachi band. Mariachis also perform on Sunday and Wednesday evenings in the cathedral

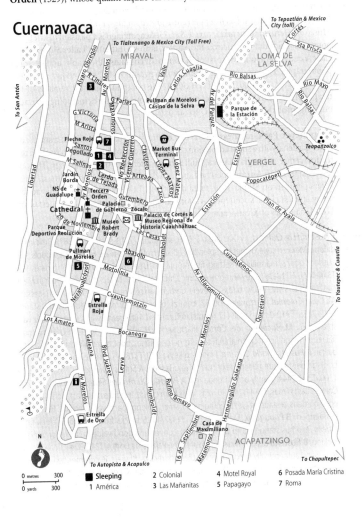

Cuernavaca

Sleeping ■
1 América
2 Colonial
3 Las Mañanitas
4 Motel Royal
5 Papagayo
6 Posada María Cristina
7 Roma

figure suspected to be one of the only two known statues of Cortés in Mexico. The other is a mounted statue near the entrance of the *Casino de la Selva* hotel. The gates to the cathedral and the Tercera Orden are closed each day at 1400. Next to the cathedral, in the Casa de la Torre (Calle Nezahualcoyotl 4), is the **Museo Robert Brady**, housing a collection of paintings by, among others, Diego Rivera, Frida Kahlo, Paul Klee and Francisco Toledo. It also has colonial furniture, textiles, pre-Hispanic objects and African art and ceramics and is well worth a visit. Descriptions are in English and Spanish. ■ *1000 to 1800, closed Mon, US$2, café and shop.* The 18th-century **Jardín Borda** on Calle Morelos was a favourite resort of Maximilian and Carlota. It has been restored and is in fine condition. It holds open-air concerts and there are exhibition rooms, café, good bookshop and museum. ■ *1000-1730, closed Mon, US$10.* Boats can be rented on the small lake, US$1-2 depending on duration. Next to the Jardín Borda is the neoclassical church of Nuestra Señora de Guadalupe. Two kilometres on the right up Morelos (*pesero*), side by side are the churches of San José Tlaltenango (1521-23) and the early 19th-century Nuestra Señora de la Natividad; bazaar on Sunday, second-hand English books.

The weekend retreat of the ill-fated imperial couple, Casa de Maximiliano, in the Acapatzingo district is now the **Herbolario y Jardín Botánico**, with a peaceful and interesting museum, at Matamoros 200, Colonia Acapatzingo. ■ *Daily 0900-1700, free. To get there take a bus from the centre to Acapatzingo and ask the driver for the Museo del Herbolario, or take a taxi, US$1.75.* Acapatzingo is a pleasant place. The house of David Alfaro Siqueiros, the painter, is now a museum. **Taller Siqueiros**, at Calle Venus 7, is a long way east of the centre. It contains lithographs and personal photographs. The very unusual **Teopanzolco** pyramid is to be found just east of the railway station. ■ *1000-1630, US$1.50.* At the pyramid's summit remains of the temple can be seen. Also in the complex are various structures including a circular building, probably dedicated to Quetzalcoatl.

Excursions

Chapultepec Park, southeast of the city centre, has boating facilities, a small zoo, water gardens, with a small admission charge. Also east of the centre is a zoo and recreation centre at **Jungla Mágica**, built around a series of natural springs. The potters' village of **San Antón** is perched above a waterfall a little west of the town, where divers perform on Sundays for small donations. In the vicinity of Cuernavaca are many spas, such as Xochitepec, Atotonilco, Oaxtepec, Temixco, Las Huertas and Los Manantiales at Xicatlocatla.

Sleeping

■ *on map page 165*

Good-value cheap hotels are hard to find – but higher cost hotels are excellent

L *Hostería Las Quintas*, Av Díaz Ordáz 9, Col Cantarranas, T318-3949, F318-3895. Built in traditional Mexican style, owner has splendid collection of bonsai trees, restaurant, 2 pools, spa, outdoor jacuzzi, magnificent setting, fine reputation. **L** *Las Mañanitas*, Ricardo Linares 107, T314-1466, F318-3672, reyl@infosel.net.mx One of the best hotels in Mexico, built in Mexican colonial style, many birds in lovely gardens, excellent food, reservation necessary. **AL** *Casa Colonial*, Netzhualcoyotl 37, central, opposite Pullman de Morelos bus station T312-7033, F310-0395. Small (17 rooms), refurbished 18th-century inn. Comfortable with small pool. **AL** *Hacienda de Cortés*, Plaza Kennedy 90, T315-8844. 16th-century sugar hacienda. Magnificent colonial architecture, garden, suites, pool, excellent restaurant, access by car. **A** *Posada María Cristina*, Francisco Leyva 200, T318-5767, near Zócalo. Restaurant, pool, garden, secure parking, extensively refurbished. **A** *Suites Paraíso*, Av Domingo Díaz 1100, T313-2444. Family accommodation. **A** *Posada Quinta Las Flores*, Tlaquepaque 210, Colonia Las Palmas, T314-1244, 30 mins' walk from centre. Includes breakfast, no TV, helpful, pool, gardens, restaurant (set evening meal), small parking space, very pleasant. Highly recommended. **B** *Papagayo*, Motolinia 13, T314-1711, 5 blocks from Zócalo, 1 block from *Estrella Roja* bus station. 25-m pool, gardens, convenient, good value, suitable for families, parking. **B** *Hostería del Sol*, Hidalgo, close to the Palacio de Cortés, T318-3241. Loaded with charm and authentically Mexican, lots of tiles, courtyards, flowers. Recommended. **C** *Bajo el Volcán*, Humboldt 117, T312-4873. Pool, restaurant, fair. **C** *Las Hortensias*, Hidalgo 22, T318-5265. Takes Visa, pretty courtyard, central, long-distance phone service.

D *Colonial*, Aragón y León 104, T318-6414. Friendly, pleasant courtyard, clean airy rooms. **D-E** *Roma*, Matamoros 405, T312-0787. Hot water morning and evening, noisy. Several cheaper hotels in Aragón y León between Morelos and Matamoros: eg **E** *América*, No 111. Safe, good value but noisy, clean, basic; some rent rooms by the hour.

Motels A *Posada Cuernavaca*, Paseo del Conquistador, T313-0800. View, restaurant, grounds. **B** *El Verano*, Zapata 602, T317-0652. **C** *Royal*, Matamoros 11, T318-6480. Hot water 0700-2300, central, clean. Recommended. *Suites OK Motel* with *Restaurant Las Margaritas*, Zapata 71, T313-1270. Special student and long-term rates, apartments, trailer park, swimming pool and squash courts.

Eating

Hacienda de Cortés (see above); *Las Mañanitas*,(see above) Ricardo Linares 107. Beautiful but expensive, only Amex accepted; also *La India Bonita*, Morrow 20. Excellent Mexican food but expensive. *Sushi Itta*, corner Hidalgo and Blvd Juárez. Japanese. On the Zócalo and Alameda: *Villa Roma, Café/Pastelería Viena* (expensive); *La Parroquia, La Universal* (on corner of Zócalo and Alameda). *Subway* and other fast-food joints on Alameda and in Centro las Plazas. *Parrots*, next to the Museo Regional, opposite which, at Hidalgo y Juárez, are *La Adelita* and *Flash Taco*. *Marco Polo*, opposite cathedral. Good, Italian, good pizzas, popular meeting place. Recommended. *Vivaldi*, Pericón 102, restaurant and *pastelería*. Very reasonable, popular with locals. There are other *cafés* opposite the cathedral. Near the Glorieta Niña in Col Las Palmas, *Los Vikingos*, restaurant and a good *pastelería*. There is also a large *panadería pastelería* on this roundabout. Generally, it is not easy to find good, authentic Mexican cooking at reasonable prices. A major exception is *La Pasadita*, Morelos esq Abasolo. Usually an amazingly wide choice at very good prices, quieter upstairs. Just down from the *Comercial Mexicana* supermarket in Morelos there is a very good branch of the *California* chain; excellent buffet lunches, good price.

Pollo y Más, Galeana. Decent, cheap *comida corrida*. *Malvias*, Matamoros, next to *Motel Royal*. Friendly, good value *comida corrida*. Fruit juices are sold from stalls beneath the bandstand on the Zócalo. *Paletas Cuernavaca*, corner Zócalo and Salazar. Terrace with view on the Zócalo. Large choice of ice creams and yogurt.

Shopping

Bookshop Particularly good on art and history in the Palacio de Cortés, to the left of the main entrance; also at Jardín Borda in Morelos. Another good bookshop, *Gandhi Colorines*, Av Teopanzoclo 401, not far from the archaeological site of the same name. Second-hand English books at *Guild House*, Tuxtla Gutiérrez, Col Chipitlán, T312-5197. **Handicrafts market** behind Palacio de Cortés, moderately priced and interesting silver, textiles and souvenirs.

Transport

Air Flights from Acapulco, Culiacán, Guadalajara, Hermosilla, León, Monterrey, Tijuana and Veracruz with *Aerolíneas Internacionales*.

Buses Each bus company has its own terminal; *Estrella de Oro*, Morelos Sur 900, Col Las Palmas, T312-3055. Local buses from the bus station up Morelos, marked Centro, or Buena Vista, all go to the cathedral. From the centre take bus on Galeana marked Palmas. *Pullman de Morelos* has 2 terminals: at Abasolo 106 y Netzahualcóyotl in the centre, T318-0907, for Mexico City and some local departures to Alpuyeca, Tehuixtla, Zacatepec, Jojutla and Grutas de Cacahuamilpa at 'Casino de la Selva', Plan de Ayala 102, opposite Parque de la Estación, T318-9205, for *Ejecutivo Dorado* to Mexico City and 10 daily buses to Mexico airport. *Flecha Roja* on Morelos Nte 503 y Arista, T312-5797. *Estrella Roja*, Galeana y Cuauhtemotzín, south of the centre.

Many minibuses and second class buses leave from a terminal by the market

To **Mexico City** 1½ hrs, fares US$4.30 ordinary to US$5.50 *Ejecutivo Dorado*: *Pullman de Morelos* is said to be the most comfortable and fastest, from Terminal del Sur, Mexico City every 30 mins.

To **Acapulco**, 4 hrs, *Estrella de Oro*, US$23 (US$27 *plus*). For advance tickets for Acapulco or other points on the Pacific Coast, be at *Estrella de Oro* office between 1645 and 1700, 2-3 days before you want to travel, this is when seats are released in Mexico City and full fare from Mexico City to the coast must be paid. To **Zihuatanejo**, *Estrella de Oro*, 1 a day, US$31.

Around Mexico City

To **Taxco**, *Flecha Roja*, 2nd class buses, hourly on the ½ hr (not recommended), or *Estrella de Oro*, 1st class, US$5.80; to **Puebla**, *Estrella de Oro*, *gran turismo* service, US$7, 1st class hourly, US$5.50, 2 stops; **Cuautla** (page 170) either *Estrella Roja* every 20 mins, US$2.50, or 2nd class or minibus from market terminal, via Yautepec every hour, 1 hr, interesting trip; go there for long-distance buses going south (Puebla buses do not stop at Cuautla).

Warning: luggage theft from waiting buses in Cuernavaca is rife; don't ever leave belongings unattended. Robberies have been reported on the non-toll mountain road to Taxco and on the road to Mexico City. On the toll road between Mexico City and Cuernavaca, at Les Tres Mariás, is a sign to Toluca. Do not be tempted to take this route; it is well-surfaced but narrow over the pass before leading to the lakes at Zempoala, but thereafter it is almost impossible to navigate the backroads and villages to Toluca. Among the problems are livestock on the road, unsigned intersections, signposts to villages not marked on the Pemex atlas, heavy truck traffic, potholes, *topes* and congested village plazas.

Directory **Banks** *Cambio Gesta*, Morrow 9, T318-3750, open 0900-1800. *Divisas de Cuernavaca*, Morrow 12; many banks in the vicinity of the Zócalo.

Communications Internet: *Axon Cyber Café*, Av Cuauhtémoc 129-B. *California Cybercafé*, Lerdo de Tejada 10b, Mon-Sat 0800-2000, Sun 0900-1400. **Post office:** on Hidalgo, just off the Alameda. **Telephone:** Telmex on Hidalgo, just off the Alameda, LADA phones are outside, almost opposite junction of Nezahualcoyotl. There is a telephone office at *Parrots* restaurant and bar on the Alameda, next to the Museo Regional.

Language schools Spanish courses start from about US$100 per week. Staying with a local family will be arranged by a school and costs US$12-20 a day including meals; check with individual schools, as this difference in price may apply even if you stay with the same family. *Cemanahuac*, San Juan 4, Las Palmas, T318-6407, F312-5418, www.cemanahuac.com, claims high academic standards, field study, also weaving classes. *Center for Bilingual Multicultural Studies*, Apdo Postal 1520, T317-1087, F317-0533 or Los Angeles, LA, T800-932-2068, www.bilingual-center.com *Centro de Artes y Lenguas*, Nueva Tabachín 22-A, T317-3126, F313-7352, scale@infosel.net.mx, 5 hrs a day, registration US$100, 1 week minimum, classes US$160, US$300 a week accommodation with families including meals. It's about US$100 a week plus US$60 registration at the *Centro de Lengua, Arte e Historia para Extranjeros* at the Universidad Autónoma del Estado de Morelos, Río Pánuco 20, Col Lomas del Mirador, T316-1626 (accommodation with families can be arranged). Private schools charge US$100-150 a week, 5-6 hrs a day and some schools also have a US$75-125 registration fee. The peak time for tuition is summer: at other times it may be possible to arrive and negotiate a reduction of up to 25. *Cetlalic*, Madero 721, Col Miraval, Cuernavaca, T317-0850, F313-2637, cetlalic@mail.giga.com, themed courses, plus Mexican and Central American history and culture. Non-profit making. Various levels. Small groups (maximum 5 people). Stay with families. Recommended. There is a co-operative language centre, *Cuauhnáhuac*, Morelos Sur 123, T312-3673, F318-2693, www.cuauhnahuac.edu.mx, intensive Spanish 6 hrs a day and flexible private classes, registration US$70, US$200 per week or US$650 per month high season, US$170 per week, US$560 per month low season, family stays US$18 per day shared room with meals or US$25 single room with meals, efficient, helpful. *Cuernavaca Language School*, T317-5151, F316-3546, cls@infosel.net.mx, or PO Box 4133, Windham, New Hampshire, US, T603-437-9714, F603-437-6412. *Encuentros*, Morelos 36, Col Acapantzingo, CP 62440, T312-5088, F312-9800, www.learnspanishinmexico.com *Experiencia*, Leyva, Col Las Palmas, T312-6579, F318-5209, www.experiencia.com free '*intercambios*' (Spanish-English practice sessions) Tue and Wed afternoon, open 5 days a week. *Fenix Language Institute*, Leñeros 128, Col Vista Hermosa, T/F315-4731, www.giga.com/~fenimexic/ *Idel*, Apdo 1271-1, Calz de los Actores 112, Col Atzingo, T/F313-0157, 5 levels of course. *Instituto Chac-Mool*, Privado de la Pradera 108, Col Pradera, T3171163, www.chac-mool.com *Kukulcán*, Manuel Mazari 208, Col Miraval, CP 62270, T312-5279, F313-7453, www.kukulcan.com.mx *Mexican Immersion Centre*, Piñanonas 26, Col Jacarandas, CP 62420, T322-1083, F315-7953, mic@axon.com.mx *Spanish Language Institute* (SLI), Pradera 208, Col Pradera, T311-0063, F317-5294, sli@infosel.net.mx, open 5 days a week, minimum 6 hrs per day, classes start every Mon. *Universal*, JH Preciado 332, Col San Antón, T312-4902 (Apdo Postal 1-1826), 3 levels of language course, tutorials and mini courses on culture.

Laundry On Calle de Galeana, 1½ blocks from the Zócalo.

Tour operators *Marin*, Centro Las Plazas, Local 13, Amex agent, changes Amex travellers' cheques but poorer rate than *casas de cambio*, charges US$1 to reconfirm flights. Also in Centro Las Plazas, *Pegaso*, French, Italian, German, English spoken (the sign says), charges US$2 to reconfirm. *Viajes Adelina*, Pasaje Bella Vista, on Zócalo.

Tepoztlán

Tepoztlán, meaning 'Where copper abounds', is 24 km northeast of Cuernavaca at the foot of the spectacular **El Tepozteco National Park**, with the small Tepozteco pyramid high up in the mountains. The only way into the park is on foot. It takes 40 minutes to one hour to climb from the car park at the end of Avenida de Tepozteco to the pyramid. The pyramid was dedicated to the pulque deity, Tepoztecatl. It is a 2-km strenuous climb uphill; climb up before the sun is too high, although most of the climb is through trees. The trip is well worth it. The altitude at the top of the pyramid is 2,100 m and the view from the top is expansive. Signs remind you on the way that you must pay at the top; five minutes before the entrance a steel ladder has to be scaled. Cold drinks are sold at the entrance for US$1. ■ *Opens any time between 0900 and 1030, officially 1000-1630, US$3, free with student card.*

Phone code: 739
Colour map 3, grid B4
Population: 20,000

The town has picturesque steep cobbled streets, an outdoor market and a remarkable 16th-century church and convent, María de la Natividad. The Virgin and Child stand upon a crescent moon above the elaborate plateresque portal, no tripod or flash allowed. A mural by Juan Ortega (1887) covers the eastern end of the church. There is a small archaeological museum with objects from all over Mexico behind the church. ■ *Tue-Sun 1000-1800, US$0.75.* There is an arts and crafts market on the plaza at the weekend with a good but expensive selection of handicrafts from Mexico, Guatemala and East Asia. In the first week of November, there is an arts festival with films and concerts held outside and in the main church's cloister. This was the village studied by anthropologist Robert Redfield and later by Oscar Lewis.

Sights

Around Mexico City

Sleeping **L-AL** *Posada del Tepozteco*, T395-0010, F395-0323. A very good inn, quiet, old fashioned, with swimming pool, excellent atmosphere and view. Highly recommended. **AL** *Hotel Restaurant Anatlán de Quetzalcoatl*, T395-1880, F395-1952. Pool, children's park, gardens. **A** *Posada Ali*, Nezahualcóyotl 2 'C', off Av del Tepozteco, T395-1971. 4 rooms, 2 family suites (**AL**) breakfast, pool, fine view. **A** *Casa Iccemanyan*, Familia Berlanga, Calle del Olvido 26, T395-0096. With 3 meals, **B** without meals, monthly rates available, 4 cabañas, swimming pool, clothes washing facilities, use of kitchen, laundry, restaurant, English, French and German spoken, beautiful garden. **D** *Mesón del Indio*, Av Revolución 44, no sign, Sr Lara. Basic.

Eating *Los Colorines*, Av del Tepozteco 13-B. Good Mexican vegetarian. Next door is *El Chinelo*. Mexican. *El Jardín del Tepozteco*. Italian, Wed-Sun 1300-2200. *Axitla*, at beginning of path up to Tepozteco, open Fri, Sat, Sun and holidays. *La Costa de San Juan*, by plaza on opposite side of street. Meat and seafood. *Tapatía*, Av Revolución 1910 (just across street from church wall). Good food and pleasant view from 1st floor, takes credit cards. *El Ciruelo*, Zaragoza 17. Quiet, nice décor, popular with wealthy Mexicans.

Transport **Buses** Local bus, *Autobus Verde*, from Cuernavaca market terminal, takes 1 hr to **Mexico City**, US$1 (bus returns to Cuernavaca from the top of the Zócalo); bus to Mexico City, US$4.50 1st class, US$4.80 *primera plus*, hourly. There are buses from Tepoztlán to Yautepec (Marigold Hill).

Directory **Language schools** Tepoztlán is a definite alternative to Cuernavaca. Try *Spanish Communications Institute*, Cuauhtemotzín, T315-1709, USA T956-994-9977, www.spancom.com

Cuautla
Phone code: 735
Colour map 3, grid B4
Population: 153,132

Take Route 160 from Cuernavaca via Yautepec to the semi-tropical town of Cuautla, meaning 'Where trees abound'. This crowded weekend resort for the capital is a popular sulphur spring, known as *aguas hediondas* or stinking waters. The tourist's Cuautla is divided from the local's Cuautla by a wide river and the locals have the best bargain; it is worth crossing the stream. The plaza is pleasant, traffic-free and well maintained. There is a market in the narrow streets and alleyways around 5 de Mayo. The tourist office is opposite *Hotel Cuautla*, on Av Obregón. The **Casa de la Cultura**, three blocks north of the Zócalo, has useful information and maps. There is a museum and ex-convent next door.

Sleeping **C** *Jardín de Cuautla*, 2 de Mayo 94, opposite Colón bus station, T352-0088. Modern, clean, but bad traffic noise, pool. One block from *Jardín de Cuautla* is **C** *Colonial*, José Perdiz 18, T352-0323. Modern, pool. **D** *Hotel Colón* in Cuautla is on the main square. Good, clean; *Hotel-restaurante Valencia*, 4 blocks north of *Cristóbal Colón* terminal. **C-D** *España*, 2 de Mayo 22, 3 blocks from bus station, T352-2186. Very good, clean. Recommended. *Casa de Huéspedes Aragón*, Guerrero 72. Hot water, friendly, basic, clean, good value. Recommended. **Youth hostel** Unidad Deportiva, T352-0218, CP 60040.

Eating Try the delicious *lacroyas* and *gorditas*, *tortillas* filled with beans and cheese. Four good restaurants in main square, all serving cheap *comidas*, try the one in the *Hotel Colón*; good restaurant at *Hotel Granada*, Defensa de Aguas 34.

Transport **Buses**: from **Mexico City** to Cuautla from Terminal del Sur or Terminal del Oriente (Volcanes terminal), 2nd class US$1. Buses from Cuautla at *Cristóbal Colón* terminal, 5 de Mayo and Zavala, to **Mexico City** hourly US$4.50 1st class, US$5.80 *plus*; *Estrella Roja* 1st class, 2nd class buses or minibuses to **Cuernavaca** at least hourly, 1 hr, US$2.60; to **Oaxaca**, US$19, 2 *Cristóbal Colón* buses per day (2nd class 1430 and 1st class 2330), 7-8 hrs, also *ADO*, most overnight and en route from Mexico City so book ahead, also try *Fletes y Pasajes* 2nd class buses, or change twice, at Izúcar de Matamoros and Huajuapan. The 115 road leads to Amecameca (see page 150).

Chalcatzingo This interesting Olmec sanctuary can be reached from Cuautla. It has an altar, a pyramid and rock carvings, one of which depicts a procession of warriors led by a prisoner with a beard and horned helmet (a Viking, some say), while others depict battles between jaguars and men. To get there take Route 160 southeast, direction Izúcar de Matamoros; at Amayuca turn right towards Tepalcingo. After 2 km down this road turn left towards Jonacatepec and it's 5 km to the village of Chalcatzingo (take a guide). There are buses from Puebla to Amayuca. A taxi from Amayuca costs US$5. Near Jonacatepec are the ruins of Las Pilas. Some 7 km further down the road to Tepalcingo is Atotonilco where there is a *balneario* for swimming (bus from Cuautla).

South of Cuernavaca

Alpuyeca, Km 100, has a church with good Indian murals. A road to the left runs to **Lago Tequesquitengo** (*Paraíso Ski Club*) and the lagoon and sulphur baths of **Tehuixtla**. Near the lake a popular resort, with swimming, boating, water skiing and fishing, is **AL** *Hacienda Vista Hermosa*, Hernán Cortés' original *ingenio* (sugar mill), and several lakeside hotels. East of the lake is **Jojutla** and a nearby old Franciscan convent of **Tlaquiltenango** (1540), frequent bus service from Cuernavaca, US$1.75, *Pullman de Morelos*. The route through Jojutla can be used if coming from the coast heading for Cuautla, to avoid Cuernavaca. Enquire locally for road conditions off the major highways.

At 15 km on the westerly road from Alpuyeca is the right-hand turn to the Xochicalco ruins, 36 km southwest of Cuernavaca, topped by a pyramid on the peak of a rocky hill, dedicated to the Plumed Serpent whose coils enfold the whole building and enclose fine carvings which represent priests. The site is large and needs two to three hours to see it properly.

Xochicalco
Colour map 3, grid B4

Xochicalco was at its height between AD 650 and 900. It is one of the oldest known fortresses in Middle America and a religious centre as well as an important trading point. The name means 'Place of the flower house' although now the hilltops are barren. The sides of the Pyramid of the Plumed Serpent are faced with andesite slabs, fitted invisibly without mortar. After the building was finished, reliefs 3-4 in deep were carved into the stone as a frieze. There are interesting underground tunnels; one has a shaft to the sky and the centre of the cave. ■ *1100-1400*. There are also ball courts, an avenue 18.5 m wide and 46 m long, remains of 20 large circular altars and of a palace and dwellings. Xochicalco is well worth the 4-km walk from the bus stop; take a torch for the underground part. There is a new museum about 500 m from ruins, a striking edifice incorporating many ecological principles and housing some magnificent items from the ruins, descriptions in Spanish only. There is also a cafetería. ■ *US$2, free with ISIC card. Tickets must be bought at the museum, which is open 1000-1700.*

It was the meeting place of northern and southern cultures and, it is believed, both calendar systems were correlated here

Transport To get to Xochicalco, take a Pullman de Morelos bus from Cuernavaca en route to El Rodeo (every 30 mins), Coatlán or Las Grutas; alight at the turn-off, 4 km from the site, then take a *colectivo* taxi, US$0.35-US$1.20 per person, or walk up the hill. From Taxco, take bus to Alpuyeca (US$1.60, 1 hr 40 mins) and pick up bus from Cuernavaca to turn-off, or taxi from junction at Alpuyeca directly to ruins (12 km, US$2.50).

From Alpuyeca, a road runs west for 50 km to the Cacahuamilpa caverns known locally as 'Las Grutas'. These are some of the largest caves in North America and are well worth a visit. They have strange stalactite and stalagmite formations; steps lead down from near the entrance to the caverns to the double opening in the mountainside far below, from which an underground river emerges. Guided tours take you 2 km inside; some excursions have gone 6 km; the estimated maximum depth is 16 km. It is worth going with a guided tour, available in Spanish only, as the caves are then lit properly. Don't miss the descent to the river's exit at the base of the cliff, called Dos Bocas, which is tranquil and less frequently visited. ■*1000-1700*,

Cacahuamilpa

US$2.50, children US$1.50, including 2¼-hr tour, every hour on the hour up to 1600 – crowded after 1100 and at weekends, take a torch.

Transport Buses: there are direct *Pullman de Morelos* buses from Cuernavaca at 1030 and 1200, returning 1700 and 1830, 1 hr, US$2; also *Flecha Roja*; usually overcrowded at weekends, enquire about schedules for local buses or buses from Taxco to Toluca, which stop there (from Taxco, 30 km, 40 mins).

Taxco

Phone code: 762
Colour map 3, grid C4
Population: 99,901

Shortly after Amacuzac (Km 121) a branch autopista scales mountainsides with breathtaking views taking you right to the outskirts of Taxco, a colonial gem, with steep, twisting, cobbled streets and many picturesque buildings, now wholly dedicated to tourism.

Ins and outs

Getting there For international flights, Mexico City or Acapulco airports are the closest. Some domestic routes are served by Cuernavaca airport. Buses to Taxco leave from Mexico City's Terminal del Sur. You should book onward or return bus tickets to Mexico City on arrival. Some buses en route to Mexico City drop passengers on the main highway, some way from the centre. Taxco is connected to Mexcio City and Acapulco via Route 95 and the fast supercarretera Route 95D.

Getting around Combis or taxis will take you up the hill from the bus terminal. Taxco is a fairly small town and, although hilly and cobbled, it is best experienced on foot.

The first silver shipped to Spain came from the mines of Taxco. José de la Borda made and spent three fortunes here in the 18th century; he founded the present town and built the magnificent twin-towered, rose-coloured parish church of **Santa Prisca**, which soars above everything but the mountains. There are large paintings about Mexican history at the Post Office. The roof of every building is of red tile, every nook or corner in the place is a picture, and even the cobblestone road surfaces have patterns woven in them. It is now a national monument and all modern building is forbidden. Gas stations are outside the city limits. The plaza is 1,700 m above sea-level. A good view is had from the **Iglesia de Guadalupe**. There are superb views also from the *Teleférico* to Monte Taxco, US$1.50 return, you can return by bus. The *Teleférico* is reached by microbus along the main street from Santa Prisca. The climate is ideal, never any high winds (for it is protected by huge mountains immediately to the north); never cold and never hot, but sometimes foggy. The processions during Holy Week are spectacular. The main central area is full of shops and shopping tourists; the district between the four-storey Mercado and the Carretera Nacional is quieter and free of tourists. Also quieter are those parts up from the main street where the taxis can't go. Wear flat, rubber-soled shoes to avoid slithering over the cobbles. **Tourist office** Avenida de los Plateros 1, T622-2274. ■ *0900-1400 and 1600-2000 every day.* City tours from Tourist Office North, US$35 for up to five people.

Sights

One of the most interesting of Mexican Stone-Age cultures, the Mezcala or Chontal, is found in the State of Guerrero in which Taxco lies. Its remarkable artefacts, of which there are many imitations, are almost surreal. The culture remained virtually intact into historic times. The **Museum of the Viceroyalty** (formerly Casa Humboldt), J Ruiz de Alarcón 12, where Baron von Humboldt once stayed, has been recently renovated; exhibits include beautiful religious art from Santa Prisca and elsewhere. Descriptions are in English and Spanish. ■ *Tue-Sat 1000-1700, Sun 0900-1500, US$1, concessions US$0.50.* **Casa Figueroa**, the 'House of Tears', so called because the colonial judge who owned it forced Indian labourers to work on it to pay their fines, is now a private house. **Museo Guillermo Spratling**, behind Santa Prisca, houses pre-Hispanic artefacts bought by William Spratling, a North American architect who came to Taxco in the 1920s. His designs in silver helped bring the city to world recognition and revived a dwindling industry. On his death bed Spratling donated his collection to the state. ■ *Tue-Sun 1000-1700, US$1.80.* The **Museo de la Platería** is a new museum devoted to modern silverworking, on Plaza

Around Mexico City

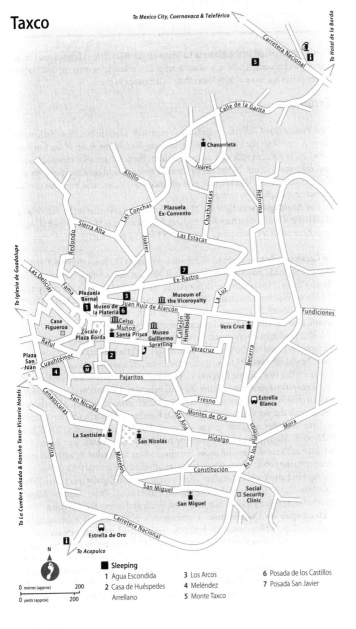

Taxco

Sleeping
1 Agua Escondida
2 Casa de Huéspedes Arrellano
3 Los Arcos
4 Meléndez
5 Monte Taxco
6 Posada de los Castillos
7 Posada San Javier

0 metres (approx) 200
0 yards (approx) 200

Shopping for silver

Silverwork is a speciality and there are important lead and zinc mines. Vendors will bargain and cheap silver items can often be found. Beware of mistaking the cheapish pretty jewellery, alpaca, an alloy of copper, zinc and nickel, for the real stuff. By law, real silver, defined as 0.925 pure, must be stamped somewhere on the item with the number 925, unless the item is very small when a certificate is provided instead. The downtown shops in general give better value than those on the highway, but the best value is among the booth-holders in the Pasaje de Santa Prisca (from the Zócalo). Prices usually drop in the low season. On the second Sunday in December there is a national silversmiths' competition.

Borda 1 ■ *US$0.80*; at the **Platería La Mina** on Avenida de los Plateros you can see mining techniques. There is a silver market at weekends next to the bus station, where prices are around 50% lower than in the shops in town.

Excursions

Visit *Posada Don Carlos*, Bermeja 6, also Ventana de Taxco in *Hacienda del Solar* for view. A combi to the Panorámica leaves every 30 minutes from Plaza San Juan, US$0.20, or you can walk up the steep hill from Plaza San Juan for views of the hills and volcanoes. About 20 km out of Taxco a rodeo is held on some Sundays at El Cedrito, costs about US$4-5, tickets in advance from Veterinario Figueroa on Calle Nueva near *Flecha Roja* terminal.

The **Acuitlapán** waterfalls are 21 km from Taxco; *colectivo* or *Flecha Roja* bus (US$1.20); 4 km along a narrow path (watch out for snakes) from nearest village to large clear pools for swimming. Taxis about US$7.50 per hour.

To **Cacahuamilpa** for caverns, 40 minutes, see page 171. Buses from 0820 but service erratic, US$1.65, *colectivo* van marked No 1, or take a long white taxi marked 'Grutas' from corner of the bus station, US$3.50. Take an Ixtapan bus from opposite the *Flecha Roja* bus terminal, US$1.50, one hour, which passes the turn-off to the site, 1 km downhill; Ixtapan-Taxco buses go to the site car park. Alternatively, to return, take bus coming from Toluca at junction, 500 m from the caves.

Visit the villages where *amate* pictures are painted (on display at Museum of the Viceroyalty/Casa Humboldt and in the market). **Xalitla** is the most convenient as it is on the old Highway 95 to Acapulco, take a second class bus there. Villages near Taxco worth a visit include **Taxco el Viejo** (home of many individual jewellery makers), **Tecapulco** (enormous copper-domed church) and **Tehuilotepec** (or '*Tehui*' – ancient church, fine hillside views; chicken *rosticería* in main square). At Tecapulco, you can visit the workshop and sales room at Rancho La Cascada, which is reported to have on offer original pieces designed by Antonio Castillo, T622-1016, F622-5048. Many pieces are inspired by pre-Columbian motifs. Just beyond the entrance to Taxco el Viejo is Rancho Spratling, where the workshop and sales room are open to the public. The pieces here are reportedly more artistic than those on sale in Taxco but also more expensive. These villages are delightfully quiet after Taxco. *Colectivos* leave from near *Estrella Blanca* bus station. Other villages: Maxela, Ahuelicán, Ahuehuepán and San Juan, past Iguala and before the Río Balsa.

Ixcateopan de Cuauhtémoc (Cuauhtémoc's birthplace), is a beautiful and peaceful village, where most of the buildings, and even the cobblestones, are made of marble. A statue honouring Cuauhtémoc stands at the entrance to the village. To get there, take a *pesero* from the road out of Taxco towards Acapulco, one hour's drive west through beautiful mountain scenery. The old church has been converted into a museum. The skeleton of Cuauhtémoc (Swooping Eagle), the last Aztec Emperor executed by Cortés, is said to rest in the glass-covered tomb, in the place of the altar.

The anniversary of Cuauhtémoc's death, called *Día de la Mexicanidad* is celebrated on 22-23 February. Runners come from Mexico City to Ixcateopan via Taxco, carrying a torch representing the identity of the Mexican people. Aztec dancers (in traditional dress and colourful plumed headdresses) come from all over Mexico to dance all night and most of the following day.

Essentials

AL *De la Borda*, on left as you enter Taxco, T622-0225. Largest, all facilities, great views, most expensive and best. **AL** *La Cumbre Soñada*, 1½ km or so towards Acapulco on a mountain top. Colonial, exquisite. **AL** *Rancho Taxco-Victoria*, Soto la Marina 15, walk to centre. Fantastic view, good restaurant. Recommended. **AL** *Monte Taxco*, on right entering Taxco, T622-1300, F622-1428, www.montetaxco.com.mx Spectacular hilltop setting, pool, horse-riding, golf course, some mosquitoes. **B** *Posada Don Carlos*, Consuelo 8, T622-0075. Converted old mansion, restaurant, good view. **B-C** *Agua Escondida*, near Zócalo at Guillermo Spratling 4, T622-1166. With bath, nice view, rooftop bar, parking, pool. **C** *Posada San Javier*, down a small street opposite Municipalidad, T622-3177. Clean, lovely garden, pool (sometimes dirty), excellent value, no restaurant. **C** *Posada Santa Anita*, Av de los Plateros 106, T622-0752, close to *Flecha Roja* buses. With hot shower and toilet, cheaper without, very clean, basic, overpriced, noisy at night, friendly, secure parking; the cheapest hotels are in this area. **C** *Meléndez*, near Zócalo, T622-0006. Best rooms Nos 1 and 19, superb views. **C-D** *Los Arcos*, Juan Ruiz de Alarcón 2, T622-1841. Reconstructed 17th-century ex-convent, delightful rooftop garden, breakfast available, best rooms for views are 18 and 19, rooms overlooking street are noisy, otherwise recommended. **C-D** *Posada de los Castillos*, Alarcón 7, T622-1396, off main square. Mexican style, friendly, excellent value. These last two are extremely popular: book ahead where possible.

D-F *Casa de Huéspedes Arrellano*, Pajaritos 23, below Santa Prisca and Plaza Borda. Terrace, quiet at night, with bath, basic, old beds, hot water. **D** *Casa Grande*, Plazuela San Juan 7, T622-0969. Pleasant, well-furnished but a bit ramshackle, rooms at the top are better, takes credit cards, good value. **E** *El Jumil*, Reforma 6, near Tourist Office North. Without bath, hot water, basic, friendly, but noisy. **F** *Central*, round the left-hand corner of *Casa de Huéspedes Arrellano*. Shared bath, quite clean, some rooms without windows.

There are many places on the Zócalo: *Alarcón*, overlooking Zócalo. Very good. *Sr Costilla*, next to church on main square. Good drinks and grilled ribs. *Papa's Bar*, on Zócalo. A discotheque and a small pizza place in an arcade. *Bora-Bora*, overlooks Zócalo, Guadalupe y Plaza Borda. Good pizzas. *Pizzería Mario*, Plaza Borda. Beautiful view over city, excellent pizzas, the 1st pizzeria in town, opened 30 years ago, pleasant service. Highly recommended. *La Pagaduría del Rey*, Cerro de Bermeja, T622-0075. Fabulous panoramic view over city, international menu, excellent food but over-priced wine, main course about US$8, closes 2130, closed Mon. *Restaurant La Ventana* in La Hacienda del Solar, T622-0587. Wonderful view of the city, Italian and Mexican menu, main course about US$9. Recommended. *La Parroquia*, Plaza Borda 5. Terrace with excellent views, but indifferent food and poor service. *La Hacienda*, Plaza Borda 4 (entrance is off the square). Excellent Mexican food and wine at reasonable prices, chic décor and a nice atmosphere (sit near the door for the comic view of vehicles navigating a 3-point turn to make the sharp corner just outside), fair prices. Exquisite *quesadillas* in the *nevería* on top of the silver shop *Perlita* looking on to the Plaza Borda.

El Atrio, next to Posada San Javier in front of the old convent, is a little pricey but has good food. *Mi Taverna* next to the Post Office. Excellent Italian food, friendly. *Concha Nuestra*, Plazuela San Juan (above *Hotel Casa Grande*). Mediocre food and poor service, live Latin American music excellent, cheap for breakfasts, other meals pricey. *La Hamburguesa*, off Plaza San Juan. Excellent *comida corrida*, US$1.80, home-cooked food, despite name. *De Cruz*, Veracruz. Good Mexican food at low prices. *Armando*, Av Plateros 205, opposite *Flecha Roja* bus station. Excellent tacos. *Pozolería Betty*, Mora 20 (below bus station). Good food includes the local beetle (*jumil*) sauce. Many small restaurants just near *Hotel Meléndez*.

Sleeping
■ on map, page 173
Price codes:
see inside front cover

Eating
Restaurants tend to be pricey

Around Mexico City

Santa Fe, Hidalgo 2, opposite *Hotel Santa Prisca*, T622-1170. Excellent *comida corrida* (US$6) but disappointing *enchiladas*. Used by locals. Cheap *comida corrida* in market and good cheap restaurants on San Nicolás. **Freddie's**, J Ruiz de Alarcón 8, next to Museo de Arte Virreinal. Excellent coffee and cakes.

Festivals There is much festivity in **Semana Santa** (Holy Week); at this time the price of accommodation rises steeply. At any time it is best to book a room in advance because hoteliers tend to quote inflated prices to those without reservations.

Transport **Buses** Taxco is reached from **Mexico City** from the Terminal del Sur, *Estrella de Oro*, 2½ hrs, luxury US$15, *plus* US$12, non-stop, with video, 3 a day, 1st class US$11, quick, no over-crowding; also *Estrella Blanca*, throughout the day, on the hr US$11, up to 5 hrs. Buses to **Cuernavaca**; 4 1st class buses, 5 2nd class, 1½ hrs US$4. Little 24-seaters, 'Los Burritos' (also called Combis), take you up the hill from the bus terminal on main road, US$0.35, same fare anywhere in town. Spectacular journey to **Toluca**, missing out Mexico City, 2nd class buses only, 3 hrs, US$8, change at Toluca for Morelia. To **Acapulco**, *Estrella de Oro*, or *Estrella Blanca*, 5 hrs, US$15. Other destinations from *Estrella Blanca* terminal include Iguala, Chilpancingo, Iztapan de la Sal and Cuernavaca by old road (via Puente de Ixtla and Alpuyeca).

Directory **Banks** Good rates at *Cambio de Divisar Argentu* on Plazuela San Juan 5. **Bancomer**, between Plazuela San Juan and Plaza Principal, is OK. **Communications** Internet: *Azul Cybercafé*, Hidalgo, near Plaza San Juan, Mon-Sat 0900-2200. **Post office**: on Carretera Nacional about 100 m east of *Estrella de Oro* bus terminal. **Laundry** *Lavandería La Cascada*, Delicias 4.

36 km south of Taxco join the Ruta 95 at **Iguala** (**E** *Hotel Central*, basic. **E** *Pasajero*. **E** *Mary*, OK, enclosed parking. Bus to Taxco US$1, to Cuernavaca US$4.25, to Mexico City from US$9.35 to US$15.35).

Mexico City

Baja California Peninsula

If you're planning the Big Trip you have to start or end at the Mexican border with the US. It's long, stretching from Tijuana on the Pacific Coast east to the outlet of the Río Grande near Matamoros in the Gulf of Mexico

Baja California (Lower California) is that long, narrow appendage that dangles southwards from the US border between the Pacific Ocean and the Gulf of California for 1,300 km. It is divided administratively into the states of Baja California and Baja California Sur, with a one-hour time change at the state line. Rugged and almost uninhabited mountains split its tapering length, which has an average width of only 80 km. The tourist hotspots are found at the far north and south. Bordering the US is the brassy and gaudy Tijuana and nearby northern beaches, and in the far south the up-market resorts of Cabo San Lucas and San José del Cabo of the southern Cape zone or the colourful carnival in La Paz. But others come to the wilderness in between to watch the whales and dolphins at Guerrero Negro or nearby San Ignacio, comb the beaches, explore the national parks, discover the ancient cave paintings, and enjoy the awe-inspiring and ever-changing desert landscapes. For them the Peninsula, with its hundreds of kilometres of virgin coastline, is a magical place of blue skies, fresh air, solitude and refuge from the rat race north of the border.

History Cortés attempted to settle at La Paz in 1534 after one of his expeditions had brought the first Europeans to set foot in Baja, but the land's sterile beauty disguised a chronic lack of food and water; this and sporadic Indian hostility forced the abandonment of most early attempts at settlement. Jesuit missionary fathers arrived at Loreto in 1697 and founded the first of their 20 missions. The Franciscans and then Dominicans took over when the Jesuits were expelled in 1767. The fathers were devoted and untiring in their efforts to convert the peninsula's three ethnic groups, but diseases introduced unknowingly by them and by ships calling along the coasts soon tragically decimated Indian numbers; some Indians remain today, but without tribal organization. Scattered about the *sierras* are the remains of 30 of these missions, some beautifully restored, others no more than eroded adobe foundations.

Today's population of about 2,800,000 has increased by two-thirds in the past decade through migration from Mexico's interior and Central Pacific coast.

The development of agriculture, tourism and industry, together with migrant **Economy** labour from California and the opening of the Transpeninsular Highway, have resulted in an upsurge of economic growth and consequently of prices, especially in areas favoured by tourists.

Food and accommodation tend to be more expensive than they are in the rest of **Essentials** Mexico, but cheaper than in the US. Tijuana, Ensenada and La Paz all have a good range of duty-free shopping. Stove fuel is impossible to find in Baja California Sur. Beware of overcharging on buses and make a note of departure times of buses in Tijuana or Ensenada when travelling south: between Ensenada and Santa Rosalía it is very difficult to obtain bus timetable information, even at bus stations. Don't ask for menus in English if you can help it; prices are often cheaper in the Spanish version. Always check change as overcharging is rife. Note also that hotels have widely divergent winter and summer rates; between June and November tariffs are normally lower than those given in the text below (especially in expensive places). The US dollar is preferred in most places north of La Paz.

Stretching 1,704 km from Tijuana to Cabo San Lucas, Highway 1 is generally in good repair, although slightly narrow and lacking hard shoulders. Roads in the north are more potholed than those in Baja California Sur. Service stations are placed at adequate intervals along the route, but motorists should fill their tanks at every opportunity and carry spare fuel, particularly if venturing off the main roads. Stations in small towns may not have fuel, or may sell from barrels at inflated prices. The same conditions apply for Highway 5 (Mexicali-San Felipe), Highway 3 (Tecate-Ensenada-San Felipe) and Highway 2 (Tijuana 196, Mexicali-San Luis-Sonoyta). Hitchhiking is difficult, and there is very little public transport off the main highway.

There is no immigration check on the Mexican side of the border. The buffer zone **Border** for about 120 km south of the frontier allows US citizens to travel without a tourist **crossing** card. Some have reported travelling in Baja California Sur without a tourist card. If you are bringing in a vehicle you should try to get a tourist card/vehicle permit in Tijuana (see page 180); if you are travelling beyond Baja California, with or without a vehicle, getting a tourist card in Tijuana will save a lot of trouble later. Immigration authorities are also encountered at Mexicali, Ensenada, Quitovac (28 km south of Sonoyta, Sonora on Highway 2), and when boarding the ferries to cross the Gulf of California. Ferries sail from Pichilingüe (north of La Paz) and Santa Rosalía to various places on the mainland. As a car needs an import permit, make sure you get to the ferry with lots of time to spare and preferably with a reservation if going on the Pichilingüe-Mazatlán ferry (see under La Paz below).

Crossing into Mexico: Mexicali

The border is open 24 hours a day for all formalities. Day visitors may prefer to **Calexico/** park on the California side, since the extremely congested Avenida Cristóbal **Mexicali** Colón in Mexicali, which parallels the frontier fence, is the only access to the US port of entry. Southbound flow is generally better than northbound; entering *The new crossing,* Mexico, follow the diagonal Calzada López Mateos, which leads to the tourist *5 km east of the centre,* office and train and bus stations. *is much quicker for northbound traffic*

Pedestrians travelling from Mexicali to Calexico should take the underpass beneath Calzada López Mateos, which passes through the utterly indifferent Mexican immigration office before continuing to the US side.

Highway 2 runs east from Mexicali through San Luis Río Colorado, Sonoyta and Caborca to join the Pacific Highway at Santa Ana; see page 210.

Mexicali
Phone code: 686
Colour map 1, grid A1
Population: 764,902

Capital of Baja California, Mexicali is not as geared to tourism as Tijuana and thus retains its busy, business-like border-town flavour. It is a good place to stock up on supplies, cheap clothing and souvenirs. The new **Centro Cívico-Comercial**, Calzada López Mateos, is an ambitious urban development comprising government offices, medical school, hospitals, bullring, bus station, cinemas, etc.

The **State Tourism Office** is on Calle Comercio, between Reforma and Obregón ('Centro Cívico' bus); better is the **Tourist and Convention Bureau**, Calzada López Mateos y Calle Camelias, helpful, English spoken. ■ *Mon-Fri 0800-1900, Sat 0900-1300.* The Procuraduría de Protección al Turista, which provides legal assistance for visitors, is in the same building as the State Tourism office.

The **City Park**, in the southwest sector, contains a zoo, picnic area and **Museo de Historia Natural**. ■ *Tue-Fri 0900-1700; weekend 0900-1800.* The University of Baja California's **Museo Regional**, Avenida Reforma y Calle L, has interesting exhibits illustrating Baja's archaeology, ethnography and missions. ■ *Tue-Fri 0900-1800, weekend 1000-1500, free.*

Calexico, the much smaller city on the California side of the border, is so thoroughly Mexicanized that it can be difficult to find a newspaper from San Diego or Los Angeles. Mexican shoppers flock here for clothing bargains.

Sleeping B *Del Norte*, Melgar y Av Madero, T552-8102. Some a/c and TV, across from border crossing, pleasant but a little noisy, has free parking for guests and offers discount coupons for breakfast and dinner in its own restaurant. C *Siesta Inn*, Justo Sierra 899, T568-2001. Reasonable, coffee shop. D *Rivera*, near the railway station. A/c, best of the cheaper hotels. D *Las Fuentes*, Blvd López Mateos 1655, T557-1525. A/c and TV but noisy, tolerable if on a tight budget.

Motels B-C *Azteca de Oro*, Industria 600, T557-1433, opposite the train station and only a few blocks from the bus terminal. A/c, TV, a bit scruffy but convenient. Others around town and in Calexico just across the border around east 4th St. B-C *Hotel De Anza*, on the Calexico side. Excellent value for money.

Youth hostel Av Salina Cruz y Coahuila 2050, CP 21050, T555-1230.

Transport Air Airport (MXL) 25 km east, Boulevard Aviación. Flights to Chihuahua, Ciudad Obregón, Guadalajara, Hermosillo, Mexico City, Monterrey and Torreón. **Trains** The railway station to the south is about 3½ km from the tourist area on the border and Calle 3 bus connects it with the nearby bus terminal. There are currently no passenger services. For up-to-date information ask locally or refer to www.trainweb.com/travel **Buses** All trips leave from the new central bus station (Camionera Central) on Av Independencia. 'Central Camionera' bus to Civic Centre and bus station. **Ensenada**: 4 a day, 4 hrs, US$16. **Guadalajara**: 1 service, 34 hrs, US$100. **Hermosillo**: regular service, 10 hrs, US$29. **La Paz**: daily 1630, 24 hrs, US$82. **Mazatlán**: every 30 mins, 24 hrs, US$68. **Mexico City**: 1 a day, 40 hrs, US$120. **San Felipe**: 4 a day, 3 hrs, US$12. **Tijuana**: every 30 mins, 3 hrs, US$12.

Golden State buses from Mexicali to Los Angeles (US$40) tickets available at trailer/kiosk across from *Hotel del Norte*, also with services within Mexico. Greyhound from Los Angeles to Calexico (901 Imperial Avenida), US$33, 6 hrs. San Diego to Calexico via El Centro, US$20, 3 to 4 hrs. The 1200 bus from San Diego connects with the *Pullman* bus to Mazatlán, US$40, 21 hrs. Local buses are cheap, about US$0.55.

Directory Airline offices: *Mexicana*, T553-5402. *AeroMéxico*, T91-800-90999. **Banks**: **all major banks**: currency exchange is only from 0900-1330. *Casas de cambio* in Calexico give a slightly better rate. There are several on López Mateos. **Useful addresses**: *Mexican Consulate* in Calexico: T357-3863.

West of Mexicali

The road from Mexicali west to Tijuana is fast and well surfaced, running across barren desert flats, below sea level and with organ-pipe cacti in abundance, until reaching the eastern escarpment of the peninsula's spine; it winds its way up the Cantú Grade to **La Rumorosa**, giving expansive, dramatic vistas of desert and mountain.

Crossing into Mexico: Tecate

The border crossing is open from 0600-2400. To get to the border immigration facilities, go north three blocks, uphill, from the west side of the Parque. You will pass the theatre. Mexican offices are on the left, Lázaro Cárdenas and Callejón Madero, T654-0280, US on the right. The orderly and friendly Mexican immigration and customs officers will only process vehicle papers between 0800 and 1600; at other hours, continue to Mexicali or Sonoyta. All documents are obtainable at the border. Tourist cards may also be obtained at the bus terminal. Services to the interior resemble those from Tijuana (*Tres Estrellas de Oro* to Mexico City, US$93.50). The Baja California **Secretary of Tourism**, opposite the park at Libertad 1305, provides a useful map of the town and other information, T654-1095. English spoken.

Visitors will find that placid Tecate is more like a Mexican city of the interior than a gaudy border town, perhaps because there is no town centre on the US side. It is a pleasant place to break the journey, especially around the shady Parque Hidalgo. The local tourism website is at **www.tecatemexico.com**

Tecate
Phone code: 665
Colour map 1, grid A1
Population: 77,444

Sleeping and eating **B** *Hotel Hacienda*, Juárez 861, T654-1250. A/c, clean. **D** *Frontera*, Callejón Madero 131, T654-1342. Basic but clean and friendly, is probably a step up in quality (Antonio Moller Ponce, who resides here, is knowledgeable on the area's history and ethno-history). Budget-minded travellers may try **E** *Juárez*, Juárez 230. Rooms with or without bath, hot water, rumoured to be a staging post for unauthorized border crossings. Excellent Mexican and Italian specialities at *El Passetto*, Libertad 200 near Parque Hidalgo. *La Escondida*, 174 Callejón Libertad. Popular with locals. Many other good restaurants.

Crossing into Mexico: Tijuana

The big trip through Mexico and Central America starts at Tijuana, well San Diego in reality. It is worth considering staying in San Diego for a couple of nights, and popping over the border to orientate yourself, check out bus times and so forth without weighty baggage. You can cross the border and return without completing formalities if you stay within a few miles of Tijuana.

San Diego/ Tijuana

A tourist office at the border gives out maps of the border area explaining money changing, buses etc

Arriving in San Diego International Airport bus No 992 stops outside all terminals and gets you from the airport to the downtown Gaslamp district with the **D** *San Diego Downtown Hostel*, 521 Market St, T(619) 525-1531, F(619) 338-0129, hisddwntown@aol.com, with clean, tidy dorm rooms, breakfast included. It's a good spot, also close to the Greyhound station (120 Broadway) with many services to Los Angeles (US$13 one way, T1-800-231-2222, www.greyhound.com). The trolley bus service that covers most of the city goes right to the border at San Ysidro.

Due to the sheer volume of people crossing the border, it is very easy to enter Mexico without completing formalities for foot and vehicle passengers. If travelling on into Mexico, don't follow the crowds who cross without visiting immigration. When you actually leave the US try to complete US exit formalities (difficult – hand your US entry card to the US immigration office where people are entering Mexico) and get a Mexico entry stamp at the border as it will avoid serious problems later on.

If entering without a vehicle, you can get a tourist card from the office just over the pedestrian bridge – the office faces the traffic and you will have to look around. After completing immigration procedures it's a meandering walk over another pedestrian bridge before you get to Tijuana proper where you're greeted by money changers, shops selling various tacky souvenirs and pharmacists selling cut-price medication. From there, it's a short walk to the downtown bus terminal. The main terminal is 5 km southeast of town.

Baja California Peninsula

For drivers US freeways funnelling 12 lanes of traffic into three on the Mexican side means great congestion, particularly at weekends. As for pedestrians there is no passport check at the border for vehicles, so try to deal with US exit formalities and get an entry stamp at the border as it will avoid serious problems later on. Be sure to get an entry stamp on your tourist card as well as your passport. The Migración office is difficult to find: try the right-hand lane marked 'Customs'. When entering with a vehicle or motorcycle you should be able to obtain your tourist card/vehicle permit at this office, then you are supposed to get a stamp from a vehicle registry office about 100 m south. The officials will ask for copies of your documents, including the vehicle permit.

If entering by **bicycle**, go to 'secondary', the immigration area to the right, where an official will process your tourist card to travel beyond Ensenada. Cyclists are not allowed on Highway 1-D (the toll road), so head for Highway 1 (*libre*) to Ensenada. Going into the US, be prepared for tough immigration procedures.

A quieter recommended alternative is the **Otay Mesa** crossing (open 0600-2200) 8 km east of Tijuana, reached from the US side by SR-117. Traffic is less frantic and parking much easier, but car insurance and vehicle permit facilities are no longer available here. From the Mexican side it is harder to find: continue on the bypass from Highway 1-D to near the airport and the 'Garita de Otay' sign.

Tijuana

Phone code: 664
Colour map 1, grid A1
Population: 1,212,232

Sitting on the south side of the River Tijuana 35 million people annually cross the border to Tijuana, fuelling the city's claim to be 'the world's most-visited city'; this is the frontline at which the US and Mexico face up to each other in pleasure and politics. Often criticized as 'not being the real Mexico', it is nevertheless an historic and impassioned place. It came to prominence with Prohibition in the US in the 1920s when Hollywood stars and thirsty Americans flocked to the sleazy bars and enterprising nightlife of Tijuana and Mexicali, both at this time little more than large villages. Today, tourism is the major industry.

Although countless bars and nightclubs still vie for the visitor's dollar, it is the duty-free bargains, horse racing, cheap medicines and inexpensive English-speaking dentists which attract many visitors. Modern Tijuana is Mexico's fourth-largest city and one of the most prosperous. However, a walk along the barrio beside the border (don't go alone) to see the breached fence will demonstrate the difference between the first and third worlds.

Ins and outs

Getting there It is cheaper to fly south from Aeropuerto Rodríguez (TIJ), 17 km (20 mins) from San Diego, CA, than it is from any US airports. For details on destinations and transport to and from the airport, see Transport, page 182. The new bus station is 5 km southeast of the town centre at the end of Vía Oriente (at La Mesa); take any local bus marked 'Central Camionera' or 'Buena Vista'. Local buses marked 'La Línea/Centro' go from the bus station to the border.

Tijuana is at the junction of Highway 1, from the border down to Cabo San Lucas, at the tip of the Baja California Peninsula, and Highway 2, which runs east to Mexicali, San Luis Río Colorado and on to Ciudad Juárez.

Getting around Downtown buses to the border leave from Calle 2 near Revolución. When taking a taxi in Mexico (unless it is a fixed-price airport service), it is often a good idea to agree on a price before travelling (some bargaining may be acceptable).

The main **tourist office** is on Plaza Patria, Boulevard Agua Caliente, T688-0555. ■ *Mon-Fri 1000-1900.* A more convenient office is at the top of Avenida Revolución and Calle 1, T688-1685. Brochures and schematic maps available. English-speaking staff, helpful. ■ *Mon-Fri 0900-1400, 1600-1900; Sat 0900-1300.*

Sights

The main drag, Avenida Revolución, runs directly south from the tourist kiosk on the edge of the red-light district, with many bars and restaurants and souvenir shops (generally open 1000-2100). The **Centro Cultural**, Paseo de los Héroes y Avenida Independencia, contains the excellent **Museo de las Identidades Mexicanas**, which lets visitors know in no uncertain terms that they are in Mexico. There are also handicraft shops, restaurant, concert hall, and the ultra-modern spherical Omnimax cinema, T684-1111, www.cecut.org.mx, where three films are shown on a 180° screen; it is best to sit at the back/top so you don't have to lean too far back. ■ *English performance 1400 daily, US$4.50, Spanish version 1900, US$3.75.* The **Casa de la Cultura** is a multi-arts cultural centre with a 600-seat theatre. There is a small **Wax Museum** at Calle 1 y Madero with historical figures and movie stars. ■ *Daily 1000-1800, US$1.80.* The cathedral of **Nuestra Señora de Guadalupe** is at Calle 2. The **Jai-Alai Palace** (Palacio Frontón) is at Avenida Revolución y Calle 7, T685-2524, but games have stopped and the palace now houses a market of tourist souvenirs. Tijuana has two bullrings: the **Plaza de Toros Monumental** at Playas de Tijuana is the only one in the world built on the sea shore. **El Toreo** bullring is 3 km east of downtown on Bulevar Agua Caliente; *corridas* alternate between the two venues between May and September; Sunday at 1600 sharp. Tickets from US$4.50 in the sun (*sol*) to US$16 in the shade (*sombra*), T680-1808. Horse and dog racing (bet on the horse – every time) is held at the Agua Caliente track, near the Tijuana Country Club. ■ *Horse racing Sat and Sun from 1200; greyhound meetings Wed-Mon at 1945, Mon, Wed, Fri at 1430. Admission US$0.50, reserved seats US$1.* Charreadas take place each Sunday from May to September at one of four grounds, free. Tourism offices will give up-to-date information.

If entering from the US: it is easier to sightsee in Tijuana without luggage, so stay in San Diego and make a day excursion before travelling on

Baja California Peninsula

Tijuana

```
N
0 metres    200
0 yards     200
```

■ Sleeping
1 Adelita
2 Catalina
3 El Rey
4 Lafayette
5 Nelson
6 París
7 San Jorge

● Eating
1 El Torito
2 La Especial
3 Tequila Sunrise
4 Tia Juana Tilly's
5 Tilly's Fifth Avenue

Essentials

Sleeping
■ *on map*
Price codes: see inside front cover

LL *Grand Hotel Tijuana*, Blvd Agua Caliente 4500, T681-7000. Heated pool, suites, etc. First rate. **AL-A** *Lucerna*, Héroes y Av Rodríguez in new Río Tijuana development, T633-3900. A/c, pool, piano bar. Popular with business travellers. **B** *Caesar*, Calle 5 y Av Revolución, T685-1606. A/c, restaurant, decorated with bullfight posters, unique character. Good. **B** *Nelson*, Av Revolución 721, T685-4302, F685-4302. Central, simple clean rooms, coffee shop.

C *Adelita*, Calle 4 between Revolución and Madero, T685-9495. Simple rooms, next door is **C** *El Rey*, Calle 4 8235, T685-1184, which is slightly better. **C** *Lafayette*, Av Revolución 325, between Calle 3 and 4, T685-3940. Clean and safe rooms, and right in the centre of things. **C** *París*, Calle 5, No 8181, T685-3023. Adequate, value-for-money budget hotel. **C** *Catalina*, Calle 5 and Madero, T685-9748. Clean and good for Tijuana. **E** *San Jorge*, Av Constitución 506. Old but clean, basic.

Motels C-D *Suiza*, Av Niños Héroes 924, T685-7947, F685-4016. Simple and basic, no frills.

Eating
Countless restaurants all the way down Revolución

El Torito, Av Revolución between Calle 2 and 3, Mexican diner style, with rock music in the evenings. *La Especial*, Av Revolución 718, T685-6654. Surprisingly authentic Mexican food by Tijuana standards, and reasonably priced. *Tequila Sunrise*, Av Revolución, between Calle 5 and 6. Balcony bar with great opportunity to get your bearings without being hassled on the street. *Tía Juana Tilly's*. Excellent meal, popular local open air spot, reasonably priced. *Tilly's Fifth Avenue*, Revolución and Calle 5, T685-9015. Good lively bar.

Nightclubs
Flamingos, south on old road to Ensenada, and *Chantecler* are both recommended.

Shopping
The Plaza Río Tijuana Shopping Centre, Paseo de Los Héroes, is a new retail development; opposite are the Plaza Fiesta and Plaza del Zapato malls, the latter specializing in footwear. Nearby is the colourful public market. Downtown shopping area is Avs Revolución and Constitución. Bargaining is expected at smaller shops, and everyone except bus drivers is happy to accept US currency.

Transport
Air Aeropuerto Rodríguez (TIJ), T683-2102. Lots of flights to Mexico City, also to Acapulco, Aguascalientes, Cancún, Chihuahua, Ciudad Juárez, Colima, Cuernavaca, Culiacán, Durango, Guadalajara, Hermosillo, La Paz, León, Los Mochis, Mazatlán, Mexico City, Monterrey, Morelia, Oaxaca, Puebla, Puerto Vallarta, Reynosa, Tepic, Torreón, Uruapan, Veracruz and Zacatecas. Also international flights to Las Vegas, Los Angeles in the US and Panama City. Taxi between airport and centre is quoted at US$15.

Buses Downtown buses to border depart from Calle 2 near Av Revolución. Local buses also go to the border from the bus station, every 30 mins up to 2300, marked 'La Línea/Centro', US$0.50.

General information at bus station, T621-2606

There are many services from downtown Tijuana, with the office close to the pedestrian bridge. It is possible to get buses to most destinations from here. There are local buses to Central Camionera, the new bus station 5 km southeast of the centre at the end of Vía Oriente, from Constitución and Calle 3, about US$0.50, taxis ask US$10. Rather disorganized bus station, even more so if this is your introduction to Mexico. Good facilities including *casa de cambio*, ATM machine, pharmacy and a couple of fast food outlets. Services provided by *Estrella Blanca* (T621-2955), *TAP* (T621-3903) and *Transportes del Pacífico* (T621-2606) for services throughout Mexico. For Baja California the main option is ABC (T621-2424).

All services hourly unless stated. **Culiacán**: 22 hrs, US$76. **Guadalajara**: 34 hrs, US$90. **Hermosillo**: 11 hrs, US$35. **Los Mochis**: 19 hrs, US$65. **Mazatlán**: 26 hrs, US$81. **Mexicali**: 2 hrs, US$16. **Mexico City**: 38 hrs, US$135. **Sonoyta**: 2½ hrs, US$33.

Heading down the peninsula from north to south, with ABC departures every 30 mins, the options are: **Ensenada**: 1½ hrs, US$8. **El Rosario**: 6½ hrs, US$23. **Guerrero Negro**: 12 hrs, US$43. **Santa Rosalía**: 17 hrs, US$56. **Mulegé**: 18 hrs, US$62. **La Paz**: 24 hrs, US$90.

From Tijuana bus terminal Greyhound has buses every 2 hrs to San Diego via the Otay Mesa crossing, except after 2200, when it uses the Tijuana crossing; coming from San Diego stay on the bus to the main Tijuana terminal, entry stamp given at border (ask driver to get it for you), or at bus station. Long queues for immigration at lunchtime. Fare San Diego-Tijuana US$12.50, 2 hrs. Walk across *La Línea* (border) and catch a Golden State bus to downtown Los Angeles, US$13 (buy ticket inside *McDonald's* restaurant), 12 a day, or take trolley to downtown San Diego and get a Greyhound, US$20, or Amtrak train, US$25, to Los Angeles. Golden State is the cheapest and fastest; its terminal is about 1 km from Greyhound terminal in downtown LA, but stops first at Santa Ana and elsewhere if requested.

Airline offices *Aero California*, T684-2100. *AeroMéxico*, T685-4401. *Mexicana*, T683-2851. **Banks** Many banks, all dealing in foreign exchange. For Visa TCs, go to *Bancomer*. Better rate than *cambios* but less convenient. Countless *casas de cambio* throughout Tijuana open day and night. Most *cambios* collect a commission (up to 5%), even for cash dollars; ask before changing. **Communications** Internet: down Revolución just beyond Calle 3. Telephones: Computel, Calle 7 y Av Negrete, metered phones, fax, computer facilities. **Embassies and consulates** *Canadian Consul*, Germán Gedovius 5-201, T684-0461. **France:** Av Revolución 1651, T685-7177. **Germany:** Av Sánchez Taboada 9210, T680-1830. **Spain:** Av de los Olivos 305, T686-5780. **UK:** Blvd Salinas 1500, T681-7323. *Mexican Consulate-General*, in San Diego, CA, 549 India St, Mon-Fri 0900-1400, for visas and tourist information. *US Consulate*, Tapachula 96, between Agua Caliente racetrack and the Country Club, Mon-Fri 0800-1630, T681-7400. **Tour operators** *Honold's Travel*, Av Revolución 868, T688-1111, F688-1502, provides all standard services and plane ticketing services. **Useful numbers** Fire: 135. **Police:** 134. **Red Cross:** 132; valid for Tijuana, Rosarito, Ensenada, Tecate, Mexicali and San Luis Río Colorado.

Directory

South of Tijuana

A dramatic 106-km toll road (Highway 1-D) leads along cliffs overhanging the Pacific to Ensenada; the toll is in three sections of US$2 each. There are emergency phones approximately every 2 km on the toll road. This is the safest route between the two cities and 16 exit points allow access to a number of seaside developments and villages along the coast.

Rosarito is variously described as a drab resort strung out along the old highway, or 'a breath of fresh air after Tijuana', with numerous seafood restaurants and curio shops. There is a fine swimming beach; horse-riding on north and south Rosarito beaches. In March and April accommodation is hard to find as college students in great numbers take their holiday here. Of the many things that you could stop to see, an essential for lovers of the big screen is *Foxploration*, 2 km beyond the La Paloma toll. This is where *Titanic* was filmed. ■ *Open daily, US$21.* The **tourist office** is at Quinta Plaza Mall, Benito Juárez 96, T612-0200. ■ *0900-1600 daily.*

Rosarito
Phone code: 661
Colour map 1, grid A1
Population: 63,549

   El Sauzal de Rodríguez, 9 km before Ensenada and now almost a part of the city, is a quieter alternative to staying in the port. Get off the bus at the Pemex gas station in El Sauzal and walk to **D** *Hostal Sauzal* (per person), three blocks from the road, T(646) 174-6381, hostelsauzalbc@hotmail.com Has four-bed dormitory rooms, hot water, storage lockers, use of kitchen and a library of books and maps on Baja – good place to stop, chill, and pick up info before rushing down south. María is very friendly and welcoming and will give you the complete low down on the latest developments throughout Baja. It should almost be compulsory to stop here.

Ensenada

Baja's third city and leading seaport, Ensenada, is a popular place for weekenders from San Diego, situated on the northern shore of the Bahía de Todos Santos. There is a tourist village atmosphere at its centre with a lively and very North American nightclub/bar zone at its northern edge, which caters perfectly to the cruise ships that stop over for a night or two. On the harbour fringe is a good locals' fish market with small, cheaper restaurants. Outside of the waterfront centre the town is more commercial with little of interest for party trippers or travellers – there is no beach in the centre. Sport and commercial fishing, and agriculture (with canning, wineries,

Ensenada
Phone code: 646
Colour map 1, grid A1
Population: 255,700

Baja California Peninsula

olive growing) are the chief activities. The port itself is rather unattractive and the beach is dirty. Out of town, go and see **La Bufadora** blowhole.

The **tourist office** is at Boulevard Costero y Azueta, on the main seafront boulevard. ■ *Open daily 1000-1900.* The Ensenada website is at **www.sdro.com/cotucoeda**

Sights Tourist activity concentrates along Avenida López Mateos and, especially, along its northern section, where most of the hotels, restaurants and shops are located. The twin white towers of **Nuestra Señora de Guadalupe**, Calle 6, are a prominent landmark; on the seafront boulevard is the new **Plaza Cívica**, a landscaped court containing large busts of Juárez, Hidalgo and Carranza. The **Museo Histórico Regional**, on Gastelum, near Calle 1, has an ethnographic collection on peoples of Mesoamerica. ■ *Closed Mon.* A splendid view over the city and bay can be had from the road circling the Chapultepec Hills on the western edge of the business district. Steep but paved access is via the west extension of Calle 2, two blocks from the bus station. The **Bodegas de Santo Tomás**, Avenida Miramar 666, between Calle 6 y 7, T178-2509, is Mexico's premier winery. ■ *Daily tours at 1100, 1300, 1500, US$2. Charreadas* (rodeos) are held on summer weekends at the *charro* ground at Blancarte y Calle 2. A weekend street market is held from 0700-1700 at Avenida Riveroll y Calle 7; the fish market at the bottom of Avenida Macheros specializes in *tacos de pescado* (a fish finger wrapped in a tortilla!).

Highway 1 south from Ensenada passes turn-offs to several beach resorts. Just before the agricultural town of **Maneadero**, a paved highway runs 23 km west on to the Punta Banda pensinsula, where you can see **La Bufadora** blowhole, one of the most powerful on the Pacific, apparently best seen on a rising tide. Air sucked from a sea-level cave is expelled as high as 16 m through a cleft in the cliffs. This is one of the easiest side trips off the length of Highway 1.

Sleeping Some of the larger hotels have different rates for summer and winter; cheaper tariffs are given above, check first! All hotels are filled in Ensenada at weekends, get in early. **LL** *Las Rosas Hotel and Spa*, on Highway 1, 7 km west of town, T/F174-4310. Suites, spectacular ocean views, pool, sauna, restaurant. **AL** *Quintas Papagayo*, 1½ km north on Highway 1, T174-4575. Landscaped beach resort complex with all facilities, Hussong's *Pelícano* restaurant attached, seafood and local specialities, 0800-2300. Best value for an Ensenada 'splurge'. **B** *Bahía*, López Mateos, T178-2101. Balconies, suites, fridges, quiet, clean, parking, a/c, good value, popular.

C *Plaza*, López Mateos 542, T178-2715. Central, plain but clean, rooms facing street noisy. **D** *América*, López Mateos, T176-1333. Basic, hard beds, kitchenettes, good. **D** *Ritz*, Av Ruiz y Calle 4, No 379, T174-0573. Central, a/c, TV, phone, coffee shop, parking.

Several cheaper hotels around Miramar and Calle 3, eg **C** *Perla del Pacífico*, Av Miramar 229. Quite clean, hot water, parking. **D** *Pacífico No 1*, Av Gastelum 235. Communal bath. **D** *Río*, Av Miramar 231 and Calle 2, opposite *Perla*. Basic, but cheapest in town.

Just 9 km north of town *Hostal Sauzal* (see page 183), in El Sauzal de Rodríguez, is a much better deal.

Motels In our **AL-A** ranges: *Ensenada Travelodge*, Av Blancarte 130, T178-1601. A/c, heated pool, whirlpool, family rates available, restaurant. **C** *Balboa*, Guerrero 172 y Cortés, T176-1077. Modern, comfortable, some way east of downtown. **D** *Pancho*, Av Alvarado 211. Shabby but clean rooms, opposite the *charro* ground. Cheapest habitable motel in town.

Trailer parks A great many good trailer parks, eg *Campo Playa RV Park*, Blvd Costero y Agustín Sanginés, south of town, US$8-10 per person.

Eating & Plenty of places to choose from down the Blvd Costero promenade, or the upper section of
drinking Av Lopéz Mateos. *Cantina Hussong's*, Av Ruiz 113. An institution in both the Californias, more of a bar than a restaurant, open 1000-0100. *Cha-Cha Burgers*, Blvd Costero 609. American-style burgers, fish, chicken, fast food 1000-2200. *China Land*, Riveroll 1149

between Calle 11 and 12. *El Pollo*, Macheros y Calle 2. Grilled chicken 'Sinaloa style', fast food 1000-2200 every day of year. *El Rey Sol*, López Mateos 1000 y Blancarte. French/Mexican, elegant, reasonable prices for the style. *Las Brasas*, López Mateos 486, between Ruiz and Gastelum. Barbecue chicken and fish, Mexican specialities, attractive mid-price patio dining, 1100-2200, closed Tue. *La Cochinita*, Macheros and Calle 4, good, cheap, Japanese fast food. *Lonchería La Terminal*, opposite bus station. Cheap and filling *comida*, good but basic. *Mandarin*, López Mateos 2127, between Soto and Balboa (Chinese). Elegant surroundings, good food, expensive, considered to be the best *chifa* in Ensenada. *Mesón de Don Fernando*, López Mateos. Good breakfasts, tacos and seafood, good value. *Muylam*, Ejército Nacional y Diamante. Seafood and Chinese cuisine, 1200-2400. *Pancho's Place* (don't confuse with *Motel Pancho*), Ejército Nacional (Highway 1) y San Marcos. Well-run place, wide menu. Pleasant.

Transport

Buses To **Tijuana**, US$7, 1½ hrs. *ABC* have a service heading south through the peninsula. *Transportes ABC* and *TNS* buses to **San Felipe**, direct, over the mountains, at 0800 and 1800, 3½ hrs, US$13. **Hitching** is a great way to get around the Baja and used by many budget travellers. There seems to be a slightly different approach on the peninsula to the 'mainland'. While hitching out of Tijuana would range between pointless and dangerous, Ensanada would be a good starting point if heading south.

Directory

Communications Internet: *Equinoxio*, Blvd Lázaro Cárdenas 267 in front of Plaza Marina, T179-4646, US$2/hr, with a mighty fine cappuccino served on the side – a rare thing, a true internet café. **Language school** *Baja California Language College* in the east of the town towards San Quintín, PO Box San Diego, CA 92167, T174-5688 or USA 1-877-444-2252, www.bajacal.com Specializes in Spanish immersion for business executives, teachers, travellers and students. **Useful addresses** Immigration Office: beside the shipyard, for tourist entry permits.

Southeast to San Felipe

Highway 3 heading east to San Felipe leaves Ensenada at the Benito Juárez *glorieta* monument on the Calzada Cortés. About 26 km out of Ensenada, an 8-km dirt road branches south for a steep descent to the basic resort of **Agua Caliente** (C *Hotel Agua Caliente*. Restaurant, bar, closed in winter; adjoining is a campground and large concrete pool heated to 38° by nearby hot springs; access road should not be attempted in wet weather).

At Km 39, a paved road leads off 3 km to Ojos Negros, continuing east (graded, dry weather) into scrub-covered foothills. It soon climbs into the ponderosa pine forests of the Sierra de Juárez. The road enters the **Parque Nacional Constitución de 1857** 37 km from Ojos Negros. The jewel of the park is the small Laguna Hanson, a sparkling shallow lake surrounded by Jeffery pines; camping here is delightful, but note that the lake is reduced to a boggy marsh in dry seasons and that the area receives snow in mid-winter.

Highway 3 descends along the edge of a green valley to the rapidly developing town of Valle de Trinidad. A reasonable dirt road runs south into the **Parque Nacional Sierra San Pedro Mártir**. Here, *Mike's Sky Rancho* (35 km) is a working ranch that offers motel-style accommodation, a pool, camping and guided trips into the surrounding mountains; rooms **E**, T681-5514 (Tijuana). Good meals.

After leaving the valley, Highway 3 follows a canyon covered in dense stands of barrel cacti to the **San Matías Pass** between the Sierras Juárez and San Pedro Mártir, which leads on to the desolate Valle de San Felipe. The highway turns east and emerges on to open desert hemmed in by arid mountains; 201 km from Ensenada it joins Highway 5 at the La Trinidad T-junction, 142 km south of Mexicali and 51 km north of San Felipe.

San Felipe
Phone code: 686
Colour map 1, grid A2
Population: 13,000

On weekends it can become overcrowded and noisy

Highway 5 heads south from Mexicali for 193 km to San Felipe, passing at about Km 34 the Cerro Prieto geothermal field. After passing the Río Hardy (one of the peninsula's few permanent rivers) and the **Laguna Salada** (Km 72), a vast, dry alkali flat sometimes turned into a muddy morass by rare falls of rain, the road continues straight across sandy desert until entering San Felipe around a tall, white, double-arched monument. Floods can cut the road across the Laguna Salada; when it is closed, motorists have to use Highway 3 from Ensenada (see above) to get to San Felipe.

San Felipe is a pleasant, tranquil fishing and shrimping port on the Gulf of California with a population of about 13,000. Long a destination for devoted sportfishermen and a weekend retreat for North Americans, San Felipe is now experiencing a second discovery, with new trailer parks and the paving of many of the town's sandy streets. The **tourist office** on Mar de Cortés y Manzanillo, opposite *Motel El Capitán*, T(686) 575-1303, is helpful but has little handout material. ■ *Tue-Sun 0900-1400 and 1600-1800. Navy Day* is celebrated on 1 June with a carnival, street dancing and boat races.

Sleeping **AL** *Castel*, Av Misión de Loreto 148, T577-1282. A/c, 2 pools, tennis, etc. Best in town. **B** *La Trucha Vagabunda*, Mar Báltico, near *Motel Cortés*, T577-1333. Also a few RV spaces and *Restaurant Alfredo* (Italian), seafood, international cuisine. **C** *San Felipe*, 9 km south on the airport road, T577-1455. Isolated, every room has a Gulf view, tennis, pool, restaurant.

Motels **B** *Cortés*, on Av Mar de Cortés, T577-1055. Beachside esplanade, a/c, pool, *palapas* on beach, launching ramp, disco, restaurant. **C** *El Pescador*, T577-1044, Mar de Cortés and Calzada Chetumal. A/c, modest but comfortable.

Camping Many trailer parks and campgrounds in town and on coast to north and south, including **D** *El Faro Beach and Trailer Park*, on the bay 18 km south. **E** *Ruben's*, Golfo de California 703, T577-1442. *Playa Bonita*, Golfo de California 787, T577-1215. *La Jolla*, Playa de Laura and *Mar del Sol*, Av Misión de Loreto, T577-1088, and the more primitive *Campo Peewee* and *Pete's Camp*, both about 10 km north.

Eating *Clam Man's Restaurant*, Calzada Chetumal, 2 blocks west of Pemex station. Used to belong to the late, famous Pasqual 'The Clam Man', oddly decorated, but excellent clams, steamed, fried, barbecued, at budget prices. *El Toro II*, Chetumal. Mexican and American food, popular for breakfasts; *Green House*, Av Mar de Cortés 132 y Calzada Chetumal. Good food, beef or chicken *fajitas* a speciality, friendly service, cheap breakfasts, 'fish fillet for a fiver', 0730-0300 daily. *Las Misiones* in *Mar del Sol* RV park. Small menu, moderately priced, seafood crêpes a speciality, popular with families, good service. *Las Redes*, Mar de Cortés Sur. *Ruben's Place*, Junípero Serra, both favourites for seafood.

Other pleasant places on Av Mar de Cortés: *Corona*, No 348; *El Nido*, No 358, grilled fish and steaks (closed Wed). *George's*, No 336. Steaks, seafood, live music, pleasant, friendly, popular with US residents. Recommended. *Puerto Padre*, Cuban.

Transport **Bus**: *Transportes ABC* and *TNS* buses to **Ensenada**, direct, over the mountains, at 0800 and 1800, 3½ hrs, US$13. Bus to **Mexicali** US$12, 4 a day from 0730, 2 hrs. Hitching to Mexicali is not difficult (much traffic), but beware the desert sun. Bus station is on Mar Báltico near corner of Calzada Chetumal, in town centre.

Directory **Banks**: *Bancomer*, Av Mar de Cortés.

South from Ensenada

Santo Tomás
Colour map 1, grid A1

Chaparal-clad slopes begin to close in on the highway as it winds its way south, passing through the small town of Santo Tomás (**D** *El Palomar Motel*, T/F(646) 178-8002. Adequate but overpriced rooms, restaurant, bar, general store and gas station, RV park with full hook-ups, campsite with swimming pool, clean, refurbished, US$10). Nearby are the ruins of the Dominican Mission of 1791 (local Santo

Baja California Peninsula

Tomás wine is cheaper out of town). A little north of San Vicente a road heads west to **Eréndira**, a beach resort made popular and accessible by **D** *Coyote Cal's*, www.coyotecals.com good range of activities including beaches, surfing, whale watching and hiking. All services you need to relax. **San Vicente** comes next (**E** *Motel El Cammo*, Highway 1, south of town. Without bath, friendly, OK restaurant), with two Pemex stations, cafés, tyre repairs and several stores. **Colonet**, further south, is a supply centre for surrounding ranches with several services. A dry-weather dirt road runs 12 km west to **San Antonio del Mar** where there are many camping spots amid high dunes fronting a beautiful beach renowned for surf fishing and clam-digging.

Seven kilometres south of Colonet a reasonable graded road branches east to San Telmo and climbs into the mountains. At 50 km it reaches the **L-AL** *Meling Ranch* (also called San José), which offers resort accommodation for about 12 guests. About 15 km beyond San José the road enters the **Parque Nacional Sierra San Pedro Mártir** and climbs through forests (four-wheel drive recommended) to three astronomical observatories perched on the dramatic eastern escarpment of the central range. The view from here is one of the most extensive in North America: east to the Gulf, west to the Pacific, and southeast to the overwhelming granite mass of the **Picacho del Diablo** (3,096 m), Baja's highest peak. Turning west off the main road goes to **D** *Campo 4 Casas*, international hostel, T165-0010. Good beach resort with all services and good surfing.■ *Small entrance fee.*

San Quintín, 179 km from Ensenada, is a market town that just hasn't quite managed to escape the 'why-stop' effects of the highway rolling through, and remains a 'strip' plan town – long and not very wide. It is almost joined to Lázaro Cárdenas, 5 km south. There are service stations in both centres and San Quintín provides all services. Rising out of the peninsula west of San Quintín Bay is a line of volcanic cinder cones, visible for many kilometres along the highway; the beaches to the south near Santa María are hugely popular with fishermen, campers and beachcombers.

San Quintín
Phone code: 616
Colour map 1, grid A1
Population: 15,000

Sleeping AL *La Pinta*, T/F165-9008, isolated beachfront location 18 km south of San Quintín then 5 km west on paved road. A/c, TV, balconies, tennis, nearby airstrip, reasonably priced breakfasts, even for non-residents. **C** *María Celeste*, T165-3999, in the centre of town on the main drag. Comfortable, reasonable restaurant next door. Good value. **D** *Hada's Rooms*, just north of Benito Juárez army camp in Lázaro Cárdenas. Cheapest in town, shabby, basic, sometimes closed when water and electricity are cut off.

Motels C *San Carlos*, by *Muelle Viejo* restaurant. Large rooms, friendly, good value. **C** *Chávez*, on highway north of Lázaro Cárdenas. Family-style, clean rooms, TV, plain but good value. **E** *Uruapan*, at northern end of town. Very clean and friendly.

Camping Pabellón RV Campground, 15 km south and 2 km west on coast. Disposal station, toilets, showers, beach access, no electricity, 200 spaces, US$5 per vehicle, great area for clam-digging. *Posada Don Diego*, off highway in Colonia Guerrero (south of town, Km 174). Wide range of facilities, laundry, restaurant, etc, 100 spaces, US$7.

Eating El Alteño, on highway next to the cinema. Bare but clean roadhouse, fresh seafood and Mexican dishes, *mariachi* music, moderate prices. Closed Jul-Sep. Also on highway: *Viejo San Quintín*, central, good seafood. Just south, on opposite side is *Autotransportes de Baja California*, café where the bus company stops for lunch, reasonably priced and sized meals. *Mi Lien* on Highway 1, north end of town. Very good Chinese food.

Festivals 20 Nov *Day of the Revolution*, street parades with school children, bands and the military.

Transport ABC to **Ensenada** 3½ hrs, **Guerrero Negro** 7 hrs, **Santa Rosalía** 9 hrs.

Baja California Peninsula

Baja California Peninsula

El Rosario
Colour map 1, grid B1

After leaving the San Quintín valley the scenary starts to get spectacular, bypassing Santa María (fuel), the Transpeninsular Highway (officially the Carretera Transpeninsular Benito Juárez) runs along the Pacific before darting inland at Rancho El Consuelo. It climbs over a barren spur from which there are fine views, then drops in a succession of tight curves into El Rosario, 58 km from San Quintín. This small, agricultural community has a Pemex station, small supermarket, a basic museum, and meals, including Espinosa's famous lobster *burritos* (expensive and not particularly good) and omelettes. Another 3 km south is a ruined Dominican Mission, founded 1774 upstream, then moved to its present site in 1882; take the graded dirt road to **Punta Baja**, a bold headland on the coast, where there is a solar-powered lighthouse and fishing village.

Sleeping **D** *Motel Rosario*, new motel at south end of town. Small, basic. **D** *Sinai*. Comfortable, very clean, small RV park, friendly owner makes good meals, but beware of overcharging.

Central desert of Baja California

Highway 1 makes a sharp 90° turn at El Rosario and begins to climb continuously into the central plateau; gusty winds increase and astonishingly beautiful desertscapes gradually become populated with many varieties of cacti. Prominent are the stately *cardones*; most intriguing are the strange, twisted *cirios* growing to heights of 6-10 m. They are unique to this portion of Baja California and extend as far south as the Vizcaíno Desert, and to a small area of Sonora state on the mainland. At Km 62, a 5-km track branches south to the adobe remains of **Misión San Fernando Velicatá**, the only Franciscan mission in Baja, founded by Padre Serra in 1769. The highway is now in the **Parque Natural Desierto Central de Baja California** (not yet officially recognized). About 26 km north of Cataviña a strange region of huge boulders begins, some as big as houses; interspersed by cacti and crouching elephant trees, this area is one of the most picturesque on the peninsula.

Cataviña
Colour map 1, grid A2

Cataviña is only a dozen buildings, with a small grocery store/*Café La Enramada*, the only Pemex station on the 227-km stretch from El Rosario to the Bahía de Los Angeles junction (there are in fact two fuel stations, but do not rely on either having supplies), and the attractive **A** *La Pinta Hotel*, T676-2601, F676-3688. Also a couple of **C** motels in the area including Racho Santa Inés. Just 2 km north of Cataviña there are easily accessible cave paintings near Km 170 on the Transpeninsular Highway.

Highway 1 continues southeast through an arid world of boulder-strewn mountains and dry salt lakes. The new graded road to Bahía San Luis Gonzaga (see under South of San Felipe, above) branches off to the east.

Bahía de los Angeles
Colour map 1, grid B2
Population: 1,245

The series of tiny beaches at the foot of Cabañas Díaz are good for swimming, but watch out for stingrays when wading

The side road runs 68 km through *cirios* and *datilillo* cactus-landscapes and crosses the Sierra de la Asamblea to Bahía de los Angeles (no public transport but hitchhiking possible), a popular fishing town, which, despite a lack of vegetation, is one of Baja's best-known beauty spots. The bay, sheltered by the forbidding slopes of Isla Angel de la Guarda (Baja's largest island), is a haven for boating, although winds can be tricky for kayaks and small craft. There is good clamming and oysters. Facilities in town include gas station, bakery, grocery stores, two trailer parks, four restaurants. There is also a modest but interesting museum in town, good for information on the many mines and on mining techniques used in the region around the turn of the 20th century. One such mine is the Mina San Juan, high in the mountains 24 km south-southwest, which had its own 2-ft-gauge railway and wire-rope tramway down to a smelter at Las Flores as early as 1895. The relic steam locomotive and mine car on display beside the airstrip are from this remarkable mine, which returned US$2 mn in gold and silver before closing down in 1910.

There are thousands of dolphins in the bay June-December. Some stay all year. There are large colonies of seals and many exotic seabirds. Fishing is excellent. **La Gringa**, a beautiful beach 13 km north of town, charges a small fee for its many camping sites, pit toilets and rubbish bins.

In July and August you can hear the whales breathe as you stand on shore

Sleeping and eating D *Casa de Díaz*. 15 rooms, restaurant, grocery store, campground, boat rentals, clean but cockroaches, well-run, popular. *Guillermo's Trailer Park*. Flush toilets, showers, restaurant, gift shop, boat ramp and rentals. *Guillermo's* also has a restaurant in a white building on main street, above the gift shop, well-prepared Mexican food, attractive, reservations advised at weekends. *Sal y Mauro*, campsite. First gravel road on left before entering town, friendly. Recommended. *Restaurant Las Hamacas*, on north edge of town. Budget café with bay view, slow service, popular for breakfast.

Baja California Sur

Back on the main route, Highway 1 now runs due south. Before you enter Baja California Sur you pass Rosarito (one store and one restaurant) and go through **Villa Jesús María** (gas station, store, cafés) to the 28th parallel, which marks the state border between Baja California and Baja California Sur (soaring stylized eagle monument and **A** *Hotel La Pinta*, T157-1305. A/c, pool, dining room, bar, trailer park attached, 60 spaces, full hook-ups, US$5, laundry and gasoline at hotel).

Advance clocks one hour to **Mountain time** when entering Baja California Sur, but note that Northern Baja observes **Pacific Daylight Saving Time** from first Sunday in April to last Sunday in October; time in both states and California is thus identical during the summer

Three kilometres beyond the state line and 4 km west of the highway, Guerrero Negro is the halfway point between the US border and La Paz and that, as far as the town goes, is about where its interest starts and ends. There are two gas stations, bank (Banamex, does not change travellers' cheques), hospital, cafés, stores, an airport with scheduled services (just north of the Eagle monument), and the headquarters of Exportadora de Sal, the world's largest salt-producing firm and a cause for much concern among environmentalists.

At the far western end of town is the skeleton of a grey whale, a fitting memorial to a town that is recognized for whale watching. Many hotels and agencies in town thrive or die on the backs of the tourists who migrate to the region from mid-December to mid-March. The alternative base for whale-watching tours is San Ignacio 142 km to the east. See box.

Guerrero Negro
Phone code: 615
Colour map 1, grid B2
Population: 9,000

Sleeping **C** *Malarrimo*, east end of town, T157-0100, www.malarrimo.com Mix of family rooms, cabanas and rooms. Tour operator arranging whale-watching tours, good surf'n'turf restaurant. Very clean, TV, fan, quiet. Good deal overall. **C** *San José*, opposite bus terminal, T157-1420. Clean, will help to organize whale-watching tours. **C-D** *El Morro*, on road into town from highway, T157-0414. Modest, clean. **E** *Las Dunas*, few doors from *El Morro*. Friendly, modest, clean. Recommended.

Eating *Malarrimo Restaurant-Bar* in hotel of the same name. Good fish and steak menu, moderate prices, music, open for breakfast. *El Figón*, next to *Las Dunas*. Good breakfast. *Mario's Restaurant-Bar*, next to *El Morro*. Modest surroundings and fare, disco. Excellent taco stall a few blocks towards town from *El Morro*. Good bakery on main street.

Transport Air: airport (GUB), 3 km from town, very handy if you want to go to Hermosillo and nowhere else. There are regular flights to Isla Cedros and Bahía Tortugas; information from airfield downtown. **Bus: La Paz**: 0030, 0600, 2030, 2100, 11 hrs, US$40. **Mexical**, 0000, 14 hrs, US$60. **Mulegé**: 4½ hrs, US$21. **Santa Rosalía**: 0530, 3 hrs, US$24. **Tijuana**: 0630, 0830, 2030 and 2200, 11 hrs, US$43.

Baja California Peninsula

Desierto Vizcaíno

After Guerrero Negro the highway enters the grim Vizcaíno Desert. A gravel road branches off due east for 42 km to El Arco and other abandoned mining areas. The road then crosses the peninsula to **San Francisquito** on its beautiful bay overlooking the Gulf of California (77 km). It should be stressed that these minor Bajan roads require high-clearance, preferably four-wheel-drive, vehicles carrying adequate equipment and supplies, water and fuel. A new gravel road from Bahía de Los Angeles (135 km) gives easier road access than from El Arco and opens up untouched stretches of the Gulf coast.

Vizcaíno Peninsula
Colour map 1, grid B2

Vizcaíno Peninsula, which thrusts into the Pacific south of Guerrero Negro, is one of the remotest parts of Baja. Although part of the Vizcaíno Desert, the scenery of the peninsula is varied and interesting; isolated fishcamps dot the silent coast of beautiful coves and untrodden beaches. A dry-weather road cuts west through the peninsula to Bahía Tortugas and the rugged headland of Punta Eugenia. It leaves Highway 1, 70 km beyond Guerrero Negro at the Vizcaíno Junction (also called Fundolegal). The new road is paved for 8 km to Ejido Díaz Ordaz. It passes Rancho San José (116 km) and the easily missed turn-off to Malarrimo Beach (where beachcombing is unparalleled). After another bumpy 50 km is **Bahía Tortugas**, a surprisingly large place (*Population*: 3,200) considering its remoteness. Two roads leave the Vizcaíno-Bahía Tortuga road for **Bahía Asunción** (*Population*: 1,600), which has the peninsula's only other gas station. From here there is a coast road south to Punta Prieta, La Bocana and Punta Abreojos (93 km). A lonely road runs for 85 km back to Highway 1, skirting the Sierra Santa Clara before crossing the salt marshes north of Laguna San Ignacio and reaching the main road 26 km before San Ignacio.

San Ignacio
Phone code: 615
Colour map 1, grid B2
Population: 2,200

The Highway continues southeast on a new alignment still not shown on most maps and, 20 km from the Vizcaíno Junction, reaches the first of 23 microwave relay towers that follow Highway 1 almost to the Cape. They are closed to the public but make excellent landmarks and, in some cases, offer excellent views. The turn-off right for the oasis town of San Ignacio, marked by a grey whale skeleton, is at San Lino, 143 km from Guerrero Negro. A road of about 3 km (US$2 in a taxi) leads to a small, attractive town with thatched-roof dwellings, pastel-coloured commercial buildings and a good old mission church; there is limited shopping but several restaurants, and a service station with mechanical assistance. Whale-watching tours can be arranged from here and it's a far more enjoyable place to spend time than Guerrero Negro.

Several tours can be arranged around town, including whale watching and nearby cave paintings. Whale-watching trips are US$30 per person, with transport costs of US$120 per person shared between the number of people travelling. Try *Ecoturismo Kuyima*, on the main plaza, T/F154-0070, kuyimasi@cybermex.net who can organize the trip and other nearby excursions. See below for details of excursions.

Sleeping and eating AL *La Pinta*, on road leading into town, T154-0300. A/c, pool, all facilities, built in mission style. Attractive but overpriced. **D** *Chalita*, south side of the plaza, cheap and cheerful. **D** *La Posada*, on rise 2 blocks from Zócalo, just ask in town, T154-0313. Well-maintained, fans, shower, best value in town, worth bargaining. **Eating** Just walk around the plaza to find somewhere to eat. *Lonchería Chalita*, on Zócalo. Excellent value. *Rice'n'Beans* on the plaza is good and cheap.

Around San Ignacio

A 70-km road from San Ignacio leads to **Laguna San Ignacio**, one of the best whale-viewing sites; mothers and calves often swim up to nuzzle boats and allow their noses to be stroked. The Cooperativa Laguna de San Ignacio, Calle Juárez 23, off the Zócalo in San Ignacio, takes fishermen to the lagoon every day and can sometimes accommodate visitors.

Whale watching

Whale watching is the main attraction on **Laguna Ojo de Liebre**, *usually known as* **Scammon's Lagoon** *after the whaling captain who entered in 1857. California grey whales mate and give birth between end-December and February, in several warm-water lagoons on central Baja's Pacific coast. Most leave by the beginning of April, but some stay as late as May or June. They can be seen cavorting and sounding from the old salt wharf 10 km northwest of Guerrero Negro on the Estero San José, or from a designated 'whale-watching area' with observation tower on the shore of Scammon's Lagoon, 37 km south of town. The access road branches off Highway 1, 8 km east of the junction (if going by public transport, leave*

bus at the turn-off and hitch). There is a small fee for camping at the watching area, which pays to keep it clean. The shores of Scammon's Lagoon are part of the **Parque Natural de la Ballena Gris**. *Pangas are available for hire (US$10 per person), but a more straightforward way of seeing the whales is on one of the daily tours from Guerrero Negro including a 1½-hour boat trip, sandwiches and transport to the lagoon, US$40-45 per person, with departures at 0800 and 1100, between mid-December and mid-March, when as many as 50 whales are in lagoon. One reader saw a dozen on a trip in mid-January. There are also some trips from San Ignacio*

Whale conservation

Mexico was the first country in the world to set aside habitat for whales. In 1971, Scammon's Lagoon was designated a grey whale refuge. A few years later, two more grey whale lagoons were protected – Guerrero Negro and San Ignacio. Whale watching and some fishing is still permitted in the lagoons under special regulations but other industrial activities are prohibited.

In 1988, a new biosphere reserve and world heritage site was created, which included all of Laguna Ojo de Liebre, Laguna Guerrero Negro and Laguna San Ignacio as well as the desert areas all around – a total area of more than 2.5 million hectares. Called the Vizcaíno Desert Biosphere Reserve, it is the largest nature reserve in Latin America. It is definitely worth visiting. Besides whales and dolphins, it is possible to see California sea lions, black and green turtles, osprey, brown pelicans, Caspian terns, great blue herons, great egrets and peregrine falcons.

With such habitat protection, the return of grey whale numbers, and the sightings of more and more humpback, blue, fin and Bryde's whales in the Gulf of California,

Mexico's whales seemed to be in good shape.

In 1995, however, the Mexican government in partnership with Mitsubishi, the Japanese conglomerate, announced plans to build the largest salt mine in the world inside the reserve, greatly expanding existing salt factories. The US$120 million development, which would create 208 permanent jobs in a relatively underdeveloped area, was not part of the management plan for the biosphere reserve and would jeopardize the designation. A substantial percentage of the reserve (as high as 60% by some estimates) would experience direct impact from the construction of salt production facilities, roads, and new settlements, as well as the dramatic increase in barge and other boat traffic. The facility would be located on the shore of Laguna San Ignacio, the most pristine grey whale habitat, and water would be continuously pumped out of the lagoon to make the salt, thereby lowering the temperature and salinity of critical grey whale habitat. Since construction of the plant, there has been considerable national and international outcry led by the Grupo de los Cien (The Group of 100), Mexico's leading environmental organization. The long-term impact remains uncertain.

Baja California Peninsula

There are many cave painting sites around San Ignacio; colourful human and animal designs left by Baja's original inhabitants still defy reliable dating, or full understanding. To reach most requires a trek by mule over tortuous trails; Oscar Fischer, owner of *Motel La Posada*, arranges excursions into the sierras (about US$10 per person to Santa Teresa cave). The cave at the **Cuesta del Palmarito**, 5 km east of Rancho Santa Marta (50 km northwest of San Ignacio), is filled with designs of humans with uplifted arms, in brown and black; a jeep and guide (if one can be found) are required. A better road leads east from the first microwave station past Vizcaíno Junction up to **San Francisco de la Sierra**, where there are other paintings and petroglyphs in the vicinity.

Reserva de la Biósfera El Vizcaíno
Two-and-a-half million hectares of the Vizcaíno Desert are now protected by the Reserva de la Biósfera El Vizcaíno, supposedly the largest in Latin America. It was decreed in November 1988 and has absorbed the **Parque Nacional Ballena Gris**.

Santa Rosalía

Phone code: 615
Colour map 1, grid B3
Population: 14,500

Santa Rosalía's streets are narrow and congested; larger vehicles should park along the highway or in the ferry dock parking lot

Seventy-two kilometres from San Ignacio is Santa Rosalía, squeezed into a narrow bottleneck valley running off the harbour. It was built by the French El Boleo Copper Company in the 1880s, laid out in neat rows of wood-frame houses, many with broad verandas, and there is something intangible about Santa Rosalía that doesn't quite make it French but neither is it Mexican in appearance. The town is along the road with a train engine at the junction, leading away from the coastline.

Up the hill near the *Hotel Francés*, the dusty old street of shaded verandas is split down the middle by half-a-dozen rusting old engines. Subject to the fierce elements their display is both nostalgic and pointless but still good to see. There is a small **museum** off Calle Francisco next to the Impecsa warehouse, with historic exhibits of mining and smelting. The port was one of the last used in the age of sail. The church of **Santa Bárbara**, Obregón y Calle 3, a block north of the main plaza, was built of prefabricated galvanized iron for the 1889 Paris Worlds' Fair from a design by Eiffel. It was then shipped around the Horn to Baja. Also visit the panadería **El Boleo**, which has been baking and selling fresh bread for over 100 years.

A car ferry leaves for the seven-hour trip to Guaymas, from the small harbour (T152-0931, fares are the same as for the La Paz-Topolobampo ferry, see schedule, page 200; tickets sold on day of departure). **Immigration Office** T152-0313.

The Pemex station is conveniently located on the highway, unlike the one at Mulegé (see below), so larger RVs and rigs should fill up here. There is a 24-hour store a couple of hundred yards south.

Excursions from Santa Rosalía
Painted cave sites can be visited from the farming town of **Santa Agueda**. Turn off 8 km southwest of Santa Rosalía then it's rough dirt road for 12 km (four-wheel drive necessary, guide can be arranged at the Delegado Municipal, Calle Madero, Mulegé). The caves are in the San Borjita and La Trinidad deserts; the drawings depict animals, children and, some claim, female sexual organs.

The fishing village of **San Lucas**, on a palm-fringed cove, is 14 km south of Santa Rosalía; camping is good and popular on the beaches to the north and south. *San Lucas RV Park*, on beach, no hook-ups, flush toilets, boat ramp, ice, restaurant, US$5 per vehicle, 35 spaces. Recommended. Offshore lies **Isla San Marcos**, with a gypsum mine at the south end.

Sleeping
A *Francés*, Calle Jean Michel Cousteau up the hill, T152-2052. This two-story French colonial building is a living piece of history – you can visit but there is a charge. A/c, restaurant, bar, pool excellent views overlooking the Gulf, photos of sailing vessels on walls. Charming.
  B-C *Real*, Av Manuel Montoya near Calle 1, T152-0068. Slowly undergoing renovation, similar to *Olvera*. Recommended. **C** *Minas*, Av Constitución and Calle 10, T152-1060. Dark,

modern, large rooms, looks half finished from outside. **C** *Olvera*, on plaza at entrance to town, 2nd floor, T152-0267. A/c, showers, clean, could do with a lick of paint. Good value. **E** *Blanca y Negra*, Calle 3 and Serabia. Basic but clean.

Camping Possible on the beach under *palapas*, access via an unmarked road 500 m south of *El Morro*, free, no facilities, a beautiful spot. Also trailer park *El Palmar*, 3 km south of town. US$5 for 2, showers, laundry, good value.

Balneario Selene, T152-0685, on Highway opposite Pemex. *Panadería El Boleo*, Av   **Eating**
Constitución, widely noted for its delicious French breads.

ABC/Autobus Aguila station (T152-0150) 400 m south of ferry terminal; stop for most   **Transport**
Tijuana-La Paz buses, several per day. To **La Paz**, 1100, US$33. *Tijuana*, US$56.

Banks *Banamex* and *Bancomer*, both with ATMs. **Communications** Internet: *Centcom* is on   **Directory**
Obregón and Calle 9, US$2.30/hr, with another place just behind the main junction entrance to the town. **Post office**: only from here and La Paz can parcels be sent abroad; customs check necessary first, at boat dock. **Laundry** Opposite *Hotel Central*, wash and dry US$2.50 per load.

Mulegé

Baja California Peninsula

Sixty-one kilometres south of Santa Rosalía, is another oasis community, a tranquil retreat outside of spring break, which is an increasingly popular hideaway for retirees from the US and Canada. There are lovely beaches, good diving, snorkelling and boating in the Bahía Concepción. The old Federal territorial prison (La Cananea) has been converted into a museum. It became renowned as the 'prison without doors' because the inmates were allowed out during the day to work in the town. The prison is a short walk from the town centre. A pleasant walk leads for 3 km out of town to the stony beach complete with lighthouse with good views. The tidal lagoons are popular for collecting clams.

Phone code: 615
Colour map 1, grid B3
Population: 5,000

There are no banks in Mulegé, but you can change dollars – make sure you come with cash

Just upstream from the highway bridge on the south side of the river is the Misión de Santa Rosalía de Mulegé, founded by the Jesuits in 1705. Above the mission there is a good lookout point over the town and its sea of palm trees. Looking the other way there is a fine view at sunset over the inland mesas. Locals swim at an excellent spot about 500 m inland from the bridge and to the right of the track to the Mission. Tours to cave painting sites, US$30 per person including drinks; a guide is necessary; recommended is Salvador Castro, ask for him at the taxi rank in the plaza. There is no bank in Mulegé. One Pemex station is in Calle General Martínez, one block before plaza in the centre; not convenient for large vehicles, which also have a one-way system to contend with. But there is another Pemex station 4½ km south of the bridge, on the road out of town towards Loreto, with restaurant and mini-market. There is good free **Tourist Information** in the centre of town, with a handy map.

A *Serenidad*, 4 km south of town near the river mouth on beachside road, T153-0530. Good   **Sleeping**
views over the Gulf and a relaxing away from it all ambience. **B-C** *Las Casitas*, Callejón de los   *Prices change*
Estudiantes y Av Madero 50, T153-0019. Central, a/c, showers, restaurant and bar, shady gar-   *dramatically*
den patio, fishing trips arranged, pleasant older hotel, well-run. **C** *Vieja Hacienda*,   *between high*
Madero 3, T153-0021, F30340. Lovely courtyard, pool, rooms refurbished, bar, trips to cave   *and low season*
paintings offered. Recommended. **D** *Suites Rosita*, Av Madero near main plaza. A/c, kitchenettes, clean and pleasant, hot water, a bit run-down but good value. **D** *Manuelita's*, with a
beautiful patio, basic with private shower. Several **E-F** *Casas de Huéspedes*, on the road into
town *Nachita*, *Canett*, *Sorpresa*. All basic but reasonably clean.

Camping *The Orchard (Huerta Saucedo) RV Park*, on river south of town, partly shaded,
off Highway 1. Pool, free coffee, book exchange, boat ramp, fishing, up to US$10.50 for 2, dis-
count with AAA/AA membership. Recommended. *Villa María Isabel RV Park*, on river and
Highway east of *Orchard*. Pool, recreation area, disposal station, American-style bakery.

Eating *Patio El Candil*, Zaragoza. Simple outdoor dining with good breakfasts. *Jungle Jim*, signed turn-off from Highway, 2 km south. Rustic, Mexican, friendly. *Tandil*, romantic and quiet atmosphere, good. *Equipales*, Zaragoza, upstairs. Recommended for good local cooking and for breakfasts. *Donna Moe's Pizza*, Zaragoza, on corner of Plaza Corona. Pleasant roof-top breakfast patio and bar. Opposite is *El Mezquite*, good burgers, live music. A few bars in town that will offer you the full range of tequilas.

Excursions *Cortez Explorers*, Moctezuma 75 A, T/F153-0500, www.cortez-explorer.com friendly, English spoken, US$60 for 2-tank boat dive including equipment. US$30 snorkelling from boat with minimum for 3 people. Diving is off Punta Concepción or Isla Santa Inés. Best snorkelling from shore is just past the point, opposite way up beach from lighthouse. There is a small sports fishing fleet operating out of the harbour here. Also hires out 4-wheel motorbikes (must be 16 or over), mountain bikes US$15 per day, horse-riding and fishing tours. Bicycle repairs near *Doney's Tacos*, 1 block before Casa de la Cultura, on left.

    Day tips to nearby cave paintings at La Trinidad can be arranged from Mulegé. US$40 per person, slightly less with groups. T/F153-0232 or book through *Hotel Las Casitas*.

Transport Buses to the south do not leave at scheduled times, ask in town as everyone knows when they come through. Allow plenty of time to complete your journey. Bus stop is on highway, north of bridge, at entrance to town. There is an airstrip for private planes beside the currently closed Hotel Vista Hermosa.

Directory **Banks** There are none in town and very few places take TCs. You can change dollars at most stores. **Communications** No internet yet, but certain to arrive soon. **Telephone** and fax abroad at mini-supermarket *Padilla*, 1 block from Pemex station, also from video store, nearby, both on Zaragoza. **Post office** and **police** in old city hall, 1 block up from Pemex. **Laundry** *Claudia*, Zaragoza and Moctezuma, next to *Hotel Terrazas*, self-service and with good information boards.

South of Mulegé

Beyond Mulegé the Highway climbs over a saddle and then runs along the shores of Bahía Concepción for 50 km. This stretch is the most heavily used camping and boating area on the Peninsula; the water is beautiful, swimming safe, camping excellent and there is varied marine life. **Playa Santispac**, in the cove called Bahía Coyote, 23 km south of Mulegé, about a 30-minute ride, is recommended. There are many small restaurants (for example *Ana's*, which sells water and bakes bread, none other available, food good value, and *Ray's*, good food, bit pricey) and *palapas* (shelters) for hire (day or overnight, US$2.50). You can get to Santispac from Mulegé on the La Paz bus. Taxi about US$12. It is also quite easy to hitch. Just south of here, in the next cove, at **Playa Concepción**, tents, *palapas* and kayaks can be hired at Ecomundo, T153-0409, Apartado Aerea 60, ecomundo@aol.com (office in Mulegé at *Las Casitas* hotel). Accommodation is in our **E**, and there is also a bookshop, gallery, bar and restaurant. Idyllic place to hang out, run by an American couple. Further south from El Coyote is **Playa Buenaventura**, which has rooms at **A** *George's Olé*, *palapas* and three cabañas for rent (US$20), and an expensive restaurant serving wine, burgers and spaghetti. From the entrance to the beach at Requesón, veer to the left for Playa La Perla, which is small and secluded.

    A new graded dirt road branches off Highway 1 to climb over the towering **Sierra Giganta**, whose desert vistas of flat-topped mesas and *cardón* cacti are straight out of the Wild West. The road begins to deteriorate after the junction (20 km) to San José de Comondú and limps another 37 km into San Isidro after a spectacular drop into the La Purísima Valley. The road leads on southwards to La Poza Grande (52 km) and Ciudad Insurgentes (85 km); it is now beautifully paved and is probably the fastest stretch of road in Baja.

Loreto

Some 1,125 km from Tijuana, Loreto is one of the most historic places in Baja. Here Spanish settlement of the Peninsula began with Father Juan María Salvatierra's founding of the **Misión de Nuestra Señora de Loreto** on 25 October 1697. It was the first capital of the Californias. Nestled between the slopes of the Sierra Giganta and the offshore Isla del Carmen, Loreto has experienced a tourist revival; fishing here is some of the best in Baja California.

Phone code: 613
Colour map 1, grid C3
Population: 11,787

The Mission is on the Zócalo, the largest structure in town and perhaps the best restored of all the Baja California mission buildings. It has a gilded altar. The **museum** beside the church is worth a visit. ■ *0900-1300, 1345-1800, closed Mon, US$1.80.*

Sleeping **A-B** *La Pinta*, on Sea of Cortés 2 km north of Zócalo, T/F135-0025. A/c, showers, pool, tennis, restaurant, bar, considered by many the best of the original 'Presidente' *paradores*, 30 rooms, fishing boat hire. Recommended. **B** *Junípero*, Av Hidalgo, T135-0122, new. Recommended. **C** *La Siesta Bungalows*. Small, manager owns the dive shop and can offer combined accommodation and diving trips. **Motel C** *Salvatierra*, Salvatierra, on south approach to town, T135-0021. A/c, hot showers but poor water pressure, limited channel cable TV, clean, good value. **D** *Posada San Martín*, 2 blocks from the beach. Clean with small patio and very friendly lady. Laundry service. Recommended. **E** *Motel Davis*, Davis. Friendly.

Camping *Ejido Loreto RV Park*, on beach 1 km south of town. Full hook-ups, toilets, showers, free coffee, laundry, fishing and boat trips arranged, US$5 per person. Butter clams are plentiful in the sand. *El Moro RV Park*, Robles 8, T/F135-0542. Central – 1 block from plaza.

Eating On Playa, *Embarcadero*. Owner offers fishing trips, average prices for food. *El Nido* and *El Buey*. Both good (latter barbecues); several taco stands on Salvatierra. *Playa Blanca*, Hidalgo y Madero. Rustic, American meals, reasonable prices. *César's*, Zapata y Juárez. Good food and service, candle-lit, moderate prices. *Café Olé*, Madero 14. Mexican and fast food, *palapa*-style, open-air breakfasts, budget rates. *La Palapa*, Av Hidalgo, ½ block from seafront. Excellent seafood.

Sport **Diving** Scuba and snorkelling information and equipment booth on municipal beach near the fishing pier; the beach itself stretches for 8 km, but is dusty and rocky. Beware of stingrays on the beach. **Fishing** *Arturos Sports Fishing Fleet*, T135-0409.

Transport **Air** 7 km south of town. Flights to Ciudad Obregón, Guadalajara, Hermosillo, La Paz and internationally to Los Angeles. Other destinations in high season.

Buses Station at Salvatierra opposite intersection of Zapata; to **La Paz** 6 a day, from 0700, US$10.75; to **Tijuana** throughout the day, US$70, 19 hrs. **Mulegé** with Aguila 2½hrs, US$8.

Directory **Bank**: *Bancomer* on southwest corner of plaza. **Communications** **Internet**: at *Gigante*, estate agent above shoe shop, on Salvatierra.

Route south of Loreto

Just south of Loreto a rough road runs 37 km through impressive canyon scenery to the village of **San Javier**, tucked in the bottom of a steep-walled valley; the settlement of some 120 people has only one store but the Misión de San Javier is one of the best preserved in North America; it was founded by the Jesuits in 1699 and took 59 years to complete. The thick volcanic walls, Moorish ornamentation and bell tower are most impressive in so rugged and remote a location. Taxis from Loreto can be arranged at roughly US$65 for the day, but hitching is quite possible. The trip is worth the effort.

The highway south of Loreto passes a picturesque stretch of coast. Fonatur, the government tourist development agency, is building a resort complex at **Nopoló** (8 km), which it was hoped would one day rival its other resort developments at Cancún, Ixtapa and Huatulco. An international airport, streets and electricity were laid out, then things slowed down. Sixteen kilometres further on is **Puerto Escondido**, with a new yacht harbour and marina; although the boat landing and anchoring facilities are operating, the complex is still far from complete, slowed by the same diversion of funds to other projects as Nopoló. There is, however, the *Tripui Trailer Park*, claimed to be the best in Mexico (PO Box 100, Loreto). Landscaped grounds, paved roads, coin laundry, groceries, restaurant and pool, lighted tennis court, playground; 116 spaces (most rented by the year), US$17 for two, extra person US$5 (T706-833-0413). There are three lovely public beaches between Loreto and Puerto Escondido (none has drinking water): **Notrí**, **Juncalito** and **Ligüí**, palm-lined coves, which are a far cry from the bustle of the new resort developments nearby. Beyond Ligüí (36 km south of Loreto) Highway 1 ascends the eastern escarpment of the **Sierra Giganta** (one of the most fascinating legs of Highway 1) before leaving the Gulf to strike out southwest across the Peninsula again to Ciudad Constitución.

Ciudad Constitución

Phone code: 613
Colour map 1, grid C3

The highway passes by **Ciudad Insurgentes**, a busy agricultural town of 13,000 with two service stations, banks, auto repairs, shops and cafés (no hotels/motels), then runs dead straight for 26 km to **Ciudad Constitución**, which is the marketing centre for the Magdalena Plain agricultural development and has the largest population between Ensenada and La Paz (50,000). Although not a tourist town, it has extensive services of use to the visitor: department stores, restaurants, banks, public market, service stations, laundries, car repairs, hospital (see introduction to this section, **Insurance and Medical Services**) and airport (near Ciudad Insurgentes).

Sleeping C *Casino*, Guadalupe Victoria, a block east of the *Maribel*, T132-1415. Quiet, 36 clean rooms, restaurant, bar. **C** *Conchita*, Blvd Olachea and Hidalgo, T/F132-0266. A/c, TV. **C** *Maribel*, Guadalupe Victoria and Highway 1, T132-0155, 2 blocks south of San Carlos road junction. A/c, TV, restaurant, bar, suites available, clean, fine for overnight stop. **D-E** *El Arbolito*, Hidalgo. Basic, clean, central. **E** *Reforma*, Obregón, 2 blocks from the plaza. Basic, with bath. Friendly.

Camping *Campestre La Pila*, 2,500 m south on unpaved road off Highway 1. Farmland setting, full hook-ups, toilets, showers, pool, laundry, groceries, tennis courts, ice, restaurant, bar, no hot water, US$10-13 for 4. *RV Park Manfred*, on left of main road going north into town. Very clean, friendly and helpful, Austrian owner (serves Austrian food).

Eating *Nuevo Dragón de Oro*, Av Olachea with Esgrima, 5 blocks north of plaza. Chinese. *Panadería Superpan*, north of market hall. Excellent pastries.

'Mag Bay' is considered the finest natural harbour between San Francisco and Acapulco

Excursions Deep artesian wells have made the desert of the Llano de Magdalena bloom with citrus groves and a chequerboard of farms growing cotton, wheat and vegetables; this produce is shipped out through the port of **San Carlos**, 58 km to the west on **Bahía Magdalena** (40 minutes by bus from Ciudad Constitución), known to boaters as 'Mag Bay'. Small craft can explore kilometres of mangrove-fringed inlets and view the grey whales that come here in the winter season. The best time to whale-watch is January-March, US$25 per hour for a boat for up to six persons. C *Hotel Alcatraz*. E *Las Palmas*, on same street as bus station. Clean, fan, hot water. E *Motel Las Brisas*, one block behind bus station. Clean, friendly, quiet.

Whales can be seen at Puerto López Mateos further north (access from Ciudad Insurgentes or Ciudad Constitución); no hotel, but ask for house of María del Rosario González who rents rooms (**E**) or take a tent and camp at the small harbour near the fish plant. On **Isla Santa Margarita** are Puerto Alcatraz (a fish-canning community of 300) and Puerto Cortés (important naval base).

La Paz

Capital of Baja California Sur, La Paz is a relaxed modern city, nestled at the southern end of Bahía La Paz (where Europeans first set foot in Baja in 1533). Sunsets can be spectacular. Prices have risen as more tourists arrive to enjoy its winter climate, but free port status ensures that there are plenty of bargains (although some goods, like certain makes of camera, are cheaper to buy in the US). Oyster beds attracted many settlers in the 17th century, but few survived long. The Jesuit mission, founded here in 1720, was abandoned 29 years later. La Paz became the territorial capital in 1830 after Loreto was wiped out by a hurricane. Although bursting with new construction, there are still many touches of colonial grace, arched doorways and flower-filled patios. The early afternoon *siesta* is still observed by many businesses, especially during summer.

Phone code: 112
Colour map 1, grid C3
Population: 168,000

First impressions certainly inspire you to move on fairly promptly, but if you're looking for a challenging way to move on, hang around a while and visit one of the marinas at the northern end of town to see if you can get a crewing job with a boat heading down the coast.

The **tourist office** is on Tourist Wharf at the bottom of 16 de Septiembre. English spoken, will make hotel reservations; they have some literature and town maps. Noticeboard for rides offered, crew wanted, etc. Apparently helpful in high season, neutral at best at other times ■ *Mon-Fri 0800-1500, Sat 0900-1300, 1400-1500, open till 1900 high season.* There's a local tourism website at **www.gbcs.gob.mx**

Sights

The street grid is rectangular; westerly streets run into the Paseo Alvaro Obregón, the waterfront **Malecón**, where the commercial and tourist wharves back on to a tangle of streets; here are the banks, Palacio Municipal, Chinatown and many of the cheaper *pensiones*. The local landmark is Carlos 'n' Charlies restaurant from where you can find most things within a couple of blocks. The more expensive hotels are further southwest. The heart of La Paz is the **Plaza Constitución**, a little east of the main tourist area, facing which are the government buildings and the graceful **Catedral de Nuestra Señora de la Paz**, built in 1861-65 on or near the site of the original mission. The post office is a block northeast at Revolución de 1910 y Constitución. A must is the **Museo Antropológico de Baja California Sur**, Ignacio Altamirano y 5 de Mayo (four blocks east of the Plaza), with a small but admirable display of Peninsula anthropology, history and pre-history, folklore and geology. The bookshop has a wide selection on Mexico and Baja. ■ *Mon-Fri 0800-1800, Sat 0900-1400, free.* **The Museum of the Whale** is at Navarro and Ignacio Altamirano, and a carved mural depicting the history of Mexico can be seen at the **Palacio de Gobierno** on Isabel La Católica, corner of Bravo.

Beaches

There are many beaches around La Paz, the most popular on the Pichilingüe Peninsula; most have restaurants (good seafood restaurant under *palapa* at Pichilingüe). Going north from La Paz to the ferry terminal on Highway 11 you will pass **Palmira**, **Coromuel** (popular with *paceños*), **El Caimancito** (admission fee) and **Tesoro**. Wind surfing and catamaran trips can be arranged. Buses to Pichilingüe run from 1000-1400 and 1600-1730, US$1.30 from station at Paseo Alvaro Obregón and Independencia; 100 m north of ferry terminal is a *playa pública*. **Balandra** (rubbish bins, *palapas*, US$2) and **Tecolote** (same but camping free under *palapas*) are reached by the road beyond the ferry terminal (paved for some distance beyond this point; some buses on this route run beyond the ferry terminal at weekends). The road ends at a gravel pit at **Playa Cachimba** (good surf fishing), 13 km northeast of Pichilingüe; the north-facing beaches are attractive but can be windy, and there are some sandflies. **El Coyote** (no water or facilities), on the east coast, is reached by a road/track from La Paz running inland along the middle of the peninsula. Southwest of La Paz on the bay are the tranquil, no-surf beaches of Comitán and El Mogote. In October (at least) and after rain, beware of stinging jellyfish in the water.

Excursions from La Paz

There are boat tours from the Tourist Wharf on the Malecón around the bay and to nearby islands like Espíritu Santo. Travel agencies offer a daily boat tour to **Los Lobos Islands** ranging from US$40 (basic) to US$80; the tour should include lunch and snorkelling, six hours, you can see pelicans, sea-lions and dolphins, with luck whales, too. About 17 km west of La Paz a paved road branches northwest off Highway 1 around the bay leading to the mining village of **San Juan de la Costa**, allowing a closer look at the rugged coastal section of the Sierra de la Giganta. After San Juan (45 km), the road is passable for medium-size vehicles to Punta Coyote (90 km), closely following the narrow space between mountains and coast with wonderful untouched camping spots. From Coyote to **San Evaristo** (27 km) the track is poor and a rugged vehicle is recommended. San Evaristo is a sleepy fishing village on a delightful cove sheltered on the east by Isla San José. It is an ideal boating area but is as yet undiscovered. This is a rewarding excursion for those with smaller, high-clearance vehicles (vans and pick-ups) for the steep final 20-mile stretch.

State Highway 286 leads southeast out of La Paz 45 km to **San Juan de Los Planes** (*Population*: 1,350), a friendly town in a rich farming region. A fair road continues another 15 km to the beautiful **Ensenada de los Muertos**, where there is good fishing and swimming and 'wild' camping. A further 11 km is the headland of **Punta Arena de la Ventana**, with a magnificent view of the sterile slopes of Isla Cerralvo. (**LL** *Hotel Las Arenas*, resort overlooking Ventana Bay). Six kilometres before Los Planes, a graded road leads to the **Bahía de la Ventana** and the small fishing villages of La Ventana and El Sargento, which have lovely beaches facing Cerralvo Island.

Sleeping
■ *on map*
Price codes:
see inside front cover

AL *Los Arcos*, Paseo Alvaro Obregón 498 at Allende, T122-2744, F125-4313, www.bajahotels.com A/c, pool, restaurant, coffee shop, across the Malecón from the beach, walking distance of centre, fishing trips arranged. Excellent value. **AL-A** *Mediterráneo*, Allende 36, T/F125-1195, www.hotelmed.com Beautiful Greek style hotel with classic standards as you would expect. Great service, outstanding *La Pazta* restaurant with Greek and Italian dishes. Internet access. Owner cut his teeth travelling with the *South American Handbook*. **A** *La Perla*, Obregón 1570, on the water front, T122-0777, F125-5363, perla@lapaz.cromwell.com.mx; clean, a/c, friendly, restaurant expensive, swimming pool, locked garage.

C *Lorimar*, Bravo 110, T125-3822, F125-6387. Hot showers, clean, very helpful, run by a Mexican/American couple, popular, good place to meet fellow travellers, good-value restaurant, can organize trip to Tecolote beach. Best value for money in town by a long shot. Recommended.

D *Posada del Cortez*, Av 16 de Septiembre, T122-8240. Pretty basic uninspiring rooms, but good for the price and safe. **D** *Posada San Miguel*, Belisario Domínguez Nte 45, T122-1802, near Plaza. Colonial-style, bathroom, clean, hot water (limited), quiet. Looks better on the outside than it is inside. Often full and recommended.

E *Hostería del Convento*, Madero 85, T122-3508. Friendly enough but pretty basic, fans, clean, shower, tepid water between 0700 and 0900. Cheapest in town. **E** *Cuartos Jalisco*, Belisario Domínguez 251. Very basic. **E** *Pensión California*, Degollado 209, near Madero, T122-2896. Basic, fan, shower, garden patio, noisy, friendly, weekly deals, not too clean. Good budget choice.

Camping *El Cardón Trailer Park*, 4 km southwest on Highway 1, T124-0078, F40261. Partly shaded area away from beach, full facilities. *Aquamarina RV Park*, 3,500 m southwest, 400 m off Highway 1 at Calle Nayarit, on bay, T122-3761, F125-6228. Nicely landscaped, all facilities, marina, boat ramp, fishing, scuba trips arranged. *La Paz Trailer Park*, 1,500 m south of town off Highway 1, access via Calle Colima, T122-8787, F122-9938. Deluxe, nearest RV Park to La Paz, very comfortable.

Eating Excellent and cheap tacos at a restaurant with no name on Av 16 de Septiembre, near the bus station. Good *lonchería* and juice bars in the market. Superb seafood tacos at stand outside *Pensión California*. and also on the street outside *Posada San Miguel*.

Adriana, on beachfront. Open air, excellent service, mid-price and stylish. *Carlos 'n' Charlies*, right on the seafront. A popular Mexican staple, good to know where it is, but probably not the best food. *El Mesquite*, on Madero between Ocampo and Bravo, is a wicked little streetside burger bar. Cheap, tasty and filling. Evenings only. *El Quinto*, Independencia y Belisario Domínguez. Very good vegetarian with lots of wholesome foodstuffs if you're in need of a few vitamins. *La Fabula Pizza*, on the beach front, good value. *Kiwi*, on the sea front, open 0800-0000, serving a mix of Mex and international dishes. Good prices through the day. *Sushi Express*, Madero and Degollado, good, mid-price sushi eat in or takeaway.

Pre-Lenten Mardi Gras (carnival) in **February or March**, inaugurated in 1989, is becoming one of Mexico's finest. The Malecón is converted into a swirling mass of dancing, games, restaurants and stalls, and the street parade is happy and colourful. **Festivals**

A duty-free port. *Casa de las Artesanías de BCS*, Paseo Alvaro Obregón at Mijares, just north of *Hotel Los Arcos*, for souvenirs from all over Mexico. *Centro de Arte Regional*, Chiapas y Encinas (5 blocks east of Isabel la Católica), pottery workshop, reasonable prices. *Fortunato Silva*, Highway 1 (Abasolo) y Jalisco at south end of town, good quality woollen and hand-woven cotton garments and articles. *Bazar del Sol*, Obregón 1665, for quality ceramics and good Aztec art reproductions. *Solco's*, Obregón y 16 de Septiembre, large selection of Taxco silver, leather, onyx chess sets. The *Mercado Central*, Revolución y Degollado, and another at Bravo y Prieto, have a wide range of goods (clothes, sandals, guitars, etc), plus fruit and vegetables. Tourist shops are concentrated along the Malecón between the Tourist and Commercial Wharves. **Bookshop** at the *Art House*, Belisario Domínguez with Juárez. The *ferretería* across from the main city bus terminal sells white gas stove fuel (*gasolina blanca*). *La Perla de la Paz* department store, Arreola y 21 de Agosto, sells general camping supplies. *CCC Supermarket*, opposite Palacio de Gobierno, is good for supplies. **Shopping**

Diving *Baja Diving and Service*, Obregón 1680, T122-1826, F122-8644. Hires equipment and takes diving trips (US$320 for 4-day PADI course); snorkelling day trip about US$35, very **Sports**

Baja California Peninsula

La Paz

Sleeping	**6** Mediterráneo
1 Del Cortez	**7** Pensión California
2 Hostería del	**8** Posada San Miguel
Convento	
3 La Perla	**Eating**
4 Lorimar	**1** Adriana
5 Los Arcos	**2** Carlos 'n' Charlies
	3 El Mesquite Grill
	4 El Quinto
	5 Kiwi
	6 La Fabula Pizza
	7 Sushi Express

0 metres   200
0 yards   200

Baja California Peninsula

Sematur Ferry Schedule

Route:		La Paz - Mazatlán	Mazatlán - La Paz
Frequency:		*Daily*	*Daily*
Departure time:		*1500*	*1500*
Arrival time:		*0800**	*0800**
Class:	**Salón**	*US$49*	*US$49*
	Turista	*US$111*	*US$111*
	Cabina	*US$135*	*US$135*
	Especial	*US$160*	*US$160*

Fare per person sharing accommodation
Children under 12 half price; under 2 free
No pregnant women allowed on board
* next day
Salón – General seating
Turista – Cabin with bunkbeds and washbasins
Cabina – Cabin with bunkbeds and bathroom
Especial – Cabin with living room, bedroom, bathroom and closet

good. *La Paz BCS Dive Centre*, Esquerro 1560, T/F57048. **Kayaking** *Baja Outdoor Activities*, right on the seafront, T125-5636, www.kayactivities.com Run by Ben and Alejandra Gillam. Simple half-day tours or full trips out to Espíritu Santo Island in the Gulf, also whale watching. Prices start at US$35. Excellent. **Cycling**, *Katun Tours*, 16 de Septiembre 15, across the street from Carlos 'n' Charlies, T123-3009. Hire a bike and head out on your own or take a tour, it's worth the effort.

Transport **Local Buses**: Local buses about US$0.50, depot at Revolución de 1910 y Degollado by the Mercado Central. Central Bus Station (Central Camionera): Jalisco y Héroes de la Independencia, about 16 blocks from centre (taxi US$2). You can get most buses you need from the promenade Aguila terminal on Obregon between Independencia and 5 de Mayo, one block up from Carlos 'n' Charlies.

Cycle hire: *Viajes Palmira*, Av Obregón, opposite *Hotel los Arcos*, T122-4030. Rents cycles and mopeds. **Car Hire:** *Budget, Avis, Hertz, Auto Renta Sol* and *Auto Servitur* booths at airport.

Long distance **Air**: General Manuel Márquez de León International Airport (LAP), 11 km southwest on paved road off Highway 1. Taxi fare US$6, supposedly fixed, but bargain. Flights within Mexico to Chihuahua, Ciudad Obregón, Culiacán, Guadalajara, Hermosillo, Loreto, Los Mochis, Mazatlán, Mexico City, Monterrey, Tijuana. US destinations include Los Angeles and Phoenix. More charter flights in high season. Airline numbers at airport: *Aero California* T125-1023; *AeroMéxico* T122-1636.

Buses heading for the Cape go clockwise or counter clockwise. Head counter clockwise if going for Todo Santos or Cabo San Lucas. Services at 0730, 1030, 1130, 1530 and 1930, 2½ hrs, US$11. Head counter clockwise if going to San José del Cabo. Services at 0800, 1000, 1200, 1430, 1630 and 1830, 3 hrs, US$11. Information T122-7094 ext 111.

For most long-distance journeys you will have to go to the main terminal. **Guerrero Negro**: 6 per day, US$40; **Loreto**: 3 per day, US$20; **Tijuana**: 1300 and 2000, 22 hrs, US$89,

Try to book at least two weeks ahead (six weeks at Christmas, Easter, and in July and August) **Ferry** For schedule to Mazatlán and Topolobampo, see page 200. Modern ferry terminal at Pichilingüe, 21 km north on paved highway. Tickets for the same day are sold at the terminal itself. In advance, tickets may be bought at *Sematur*, c/o *Agencia de Viajes y Expediciones de Puerto*, 5 de Mayo and Guillermo Prieto, T125-2346 and T125-1255. Open 0800-1730 Mon-Fri, 0800-1300 Sat.

La Paz - Topolobampo	Topolobampo - La Paz	Sta Rosalía - Guaymas	Guaymas - Sta Rosalía
Daily	Daily	Tue and Fri	Mon and Thu
2200	2200	2200	1000
0800 *	0800*	0600*	1800
US$38	US$38	US$49	US$49
US$86	US$86	US$111	US$111
US$111	US$111	US$135	US$135
US$135	US$135	US$160	US$160

Sematur Offices:
Central reservations: T01-800-696-9600
www.ferrysematur.com.mx
Tickets also available from Viajes Ahome in Los Mochis, www.viajesahome.com

Arrive early as queues build up and move ridiculously slowly – sort of hurry up and wait. Tourist cards must be valid, allow 2 hrs as there are long queues, trucks have loading priority. It should be noted that many motorists have had difficulty getting reservations or having them honoured. If you have left booking to the last minute, get to the ticket office at 0400 and you may be able to get a cancellation. If cancelling 24 hrs before journey foot passengers are refunded ½ the fare, full refund with more than 48 hrs' notice, ticket non-transferable, check for other types of ticket. Vehicles must have **car permits**, obtainable at ferry terminal and at Sematur, or at Registro Federal de Vehículos in Tijuana; automobile clubs will provide information. Service and conditions on the ferry are reported to be improving. Restaurants on board are reasonably priced and food OK. Bus to Pichilingüe from seafront terminal in La Paz. Reasonable facilities at terminal but crowded; large parking lots, officials may permit RVs to stay overnight while awaiting ferry departures. On all ferry crossings, **delays** can occur from Sep if there is bad weather. Keep a flexible schedule if travelling to the mainland. For further information about schedules and fares try the official site at www.ferrysematur.com.mx or www.trybaja.com/ ferry.html

Airline offices *Aero California*, city office at Malecón y Bravo, T125-1023. *AeroMéxico*, T122-0091. **Directory**
Banks Plenty of banks and ATMs down 16 de Septiembre: *Banamex*, Arreola y Esquerro. 2 *casas de cambio* on 5 de Mayo off Obregón, 0800-2000, better rates than banks. **Communications** Internet: *Espacio Don Tomás*, Obregón between 5 de Mayo and Constitución. Internet access in an art gallery with fine snacks and coffee. **Laundry** *Laundromat Yoli*, 5 de Mayo y Rubio. Also at Marina de La Paz.
Useful addresses Immigration: 2nd floor of large building on Paseo Alvaro Obregón, opposite the pier, reported to be very helpful, possible to extend visa here.

South of La Paz

South of La Paz and the central mountain spine rises again into the wooded heights of the Sierra de la Laguna and bulges out into the 'Cape Region', Baja's most touristically developed area. The highway winds up to El Triunfo, a picturesque village (almost a ghost town) where silver was discovered in 1862. The town exploded with a population of 10,000 and was for a while the largest town in Baja. The mines closed in 1926 but small-scale mining has resumed in places. There is a craft shop at the village entrance where young people make palm-leaf objects.

El Triunfo
Colour map 2, grid C1

Present-day miners are using arsenic in the old mine tailings; these areas are fenced and signed

Eight kilometres further on is the lovely mountain town and farming centre of **San Antonio** (gasoline, groceries, meals), which was founded in 1756 and served briefly as Baja's capital (1828-30) when Loreto was destroyed. Eight kilometres south of San Antonio was the site of Santa Ana, where silver was first discovered in 1748. It was from this vanished village that the Viceroy and Padre Junípero Serra planned the expedition to establish the chain of Franciscan missions in Alta California.

Highway 1 climbs sharply from the canyon and winds past a number of ancient mines, through the peaceful orchard-farming town of San Bartolo (groceries and meals) and down to the coastal flats around **Los Barriles**, a small town with fuel, meals and limited supplies. A number of resort hotels are situated near here along the beautiful **Bahía de Palmas** and at nearby **Buena Vista**; none is in the 'budget' class but all are popular.

The Highway turns inland after Los Barriles (106 km from La Paz). An 'East Cape Loop' turns east off the Highway through La Rivera (E *La Rivera RV Park* in palm grove next to beach. Excellent swimming, hot showers, laundry, friendly. Recommended). A new spur leads towards **Cabo Pulmo**; it is being paved at a rapid rate and will eventually take a slightly inland route paralleling the coast to San José del Cabo. Off Cabo Pulmo, a beautiful headland, is the Northern Pacific's only living coral reef; fishing, diving and snorkelling are excellent (56 km from Los Barriles).

Santiago

Colour map 2, grid C1
Population: 2,000

Santiago is a pleasant, historic little town 3 km off Highway 1 (bus stop at junction, two hours from La Paz, US$3.50 in a taxi from the highway). On the tree-lined main street are a Pemex station, café and stores grouped around the town plaza. The Jesuits built their 10th mission in Santiago in 1723 after transferring it from Los Barriles. The town was one of the sites of the Pericué Indian uprising of 1734. There are hot springs (warm, not hot, some rubbish at site) behind a mini dam, in a pleasant setting, 12 km away along a dirt road at the foot of the mountains. Head towards the village of Aguascalientes (8 km) and the hot springs are 4 km beyond this. You can walk on from the spring to a waterfall (**C** *Palomar*. A/c, hot showers, restaurant, bar, on main street, modest, good meals. Camping in hotel grounds US$5, with cold shower and toilets available).

Some 3.5 km south of the Santiago turn-off, Highway 1 crosses the **Tropic of Cancer**, marked by a large concrete sphere, and runs south down the fertile valley between the lofty **Sierra de la Laguna** (west) and the **Sierra Santa Clara** (east), to Los Cabos International Airport. San José del Cabo is 14 km further south.

San José del Cabo

Phone code: 624
Colour map 2, grid C1
Population: 10,000

The largest town south of La Paz and founded in 1730, San José del Cabo is now essentially a modern town divided into two districts: the very Americanized resort sectors and new Fonatur development on the beach, and the downtown zone to the north, with the government offices and many businesses grouped near the tranquil Parque Mijares. The attractive church on the Plaza Mijares was built in 1940 on the final site of the mission of 1730; a tile mosaic over the entrance depicts the murder of Padre Tamaral by rebellious Indians in 1734.

Sleeping

Several top-quality hotels along the beach front, about 1 km south of town, of varying excellence and seclusion. All are booked as part of resort holidays; some won't even allow passing trade to enter. **LL** *Palmilla*, one of the top resorts in Baja, 8 km west at Punta Palmilla (outstanding surfing nearby). Some a/c, showers, pool, beach, tennis, narrow access road, restaurant, bar, skin diving, fishing cruisers and skiffs for hire (daily happy hour allows mere mortals to partake of *margarita* and appetizers for US$3 and see how royalty and film stars live!).

AL *El Encanto Inn*, C Morales and Alvaro Obregón, T142-0388, F142-4620. Easy Mediteranean feel to the place with stylish decor. Good choice. **A** *Posada Terranova*, on Degollado between Doblado and Zaragoza, T142-0534, F142-0902, www.hterranova.com.mx Pleasant rooms in a quietly professional atmosphere. Fine mid-price restaurant with patio dining. **AL-B** *Señor Mañana*, Alvaro Obregón 1, just off the main square, T/F142-0462, www.srmanana.net   Several options of rooms ranging from basic to quite comfortable. None of the rooms are fantastic, but the small pool, use of kitchen and hammock area make it a good choice for the cheaper rooms. **B** *Collí*, close to the centre, T142-0052. Fans, hot showers, 12 clean and adequate rooms in a family-run hotel.

D *Ceci*, Zaragoza 22, 1 block west of plaza, T142-0041, Central, fans, hot showers (occasionally), cable TV with more channels than much better hotels, basic but clean, good value. **D** *Nuevo San José*, Alvaro Obregón. Clean, quiet, cool, comfortable, ceiling fans. New owners giving the place a face-lift. Good value. **D** *Posada San Rafael*, a basic choice with big rooms, which makes it bearable.

Motel D *Brisa del Mar*, on Highway 1, 3 km southwest of town near *Hotel Nuevo Sol*. 10 rooms, restaurant, bar, pool, modest but comfortable, at rear of trailer park on outstanding beach.

Camping Unofficial camping is possible on those few beaches not fronted by resort hotels. *Brisa del Mar Trailer Park*, 100 RV sites in fenced area by great beach. Full hook-ups, flush toilets, showers, pool, laundry, restaurant, bar, fishing trips arranged, popular, good location. Recommended.

Eating

The town is full of tasty options, many of them courting the dollars of visiting vacationers over travellers on a budget. For more realistic budget options you have to head west of the centre and the numerous places along Manuel Doblado.

If you're looking for a moment to flex the plastic try *Baan Thai*, on Morelos and Comonfort, opposite *Encanto Inn*, T142-3344. Wonderful atmosphere, quiet patio out the back, mid-price. *Damiana*, at the top of Blvd Mijares offers mid-price Mexican and international dishes under the most spectacular bougainvillaea tree. Very romantic. *Casa Natalia*, in the hotel of the same name, offer an equally stylish setting with a more chic approach to romance. Many others in town including *Fandango*, and *Rawhide*, on Alvaro Obregón.

Transport

Air To Los Cabos International Airport (SJD), 14 km, take a local bus, US$3, which drops you at the entrance road to the airport, leaving a 2-km walk, otherwise take a taxi. Airport to San José del Cabo in *colectivo*, US$7. Flights to Chihuahua, Ciudad Obregón, Culiacán, Guadalajara, Hermosillo, Los Mochis, Mazatlán, Mexico City, Monterrey, Puerto Vallarta. In the US: Anchorage, Burbank, Dallas, Denver, Fort Lauderdale, Houston, Los Angeles, New York, Orange County, Phoenix, Portland, San Diego, San Francisco, Seattle, Spokane, Tucson.

Bus Bus station on Valerio González Canseco, about 600 m south of the main road into town. To **Cabo San Lucas** (*Tres Estrellas*) daily from 0700, US$1.25, 30 mins; to **La Paz** daily from 0630, US$9, 3 hrs.

Directory

Airlines *Aero California*, T123-3700. *Mexicana*, T122-2722. **Banks** Several *casas de cambio* around town. There is a branch of *Bancomer* on Zaragoza and a branch of BanCrecer with an ATM, just off the junction of the Transpeninsula Highway and Doblado. **Communications** Internet: several places in town, many asking ridiculous prices (US$7.50/hr). Try *Espacio Café Internet* (US$3/hr with discounts for students) on the 2nd floor opposite the hospital on Doblado. **Post office** is a few blocks from the town centre down Blvd Mijares. **Laundry** *Lavamática San José*, on Valerio Gonzaléz.

From San José del Cabo to Cabo San Lucas the good road is bordered either side with time share apartments, golf courses and exclusive beaches. A regular bus service runs between the two.

Baja California Peninsula

Cabo San Lucas

Phone code: 624
Colour map 2, grid C1

*Everything is quoted
in US dollars and food
is more American
than Mexican*

The resort town of Cabo San Lucas has grown rapidly in recent years from the sleepy fishing village of 1,500 inhabitants it was in 1970. It is now a bustling, expensive international resort with a permanent population of 8,500. The place is fit to bursting with vacationers experiencing a bit of sanitized Mexico. The place is full of neon-signed cafés and restaurants, condominiums, gift shops, discos and a marina to cater for the increasing flood of North Americans who come for the world-famous fishing or to find a retirement paradise.

What a shock it was to the majority when, in 2001, a hurricane swept through, knocked out water and power supplies and telephone communications for several days. As one tour operator said, "Well, this is a third world country"!

Beaches Ringed by pounding surf, columns of fluted rock enclose **Lover's Beach** (be careful if walking along the beach, as huge waves sweep away several visitors each year), a romantic sandy cove with views out to the seal colonies on offshore islets. At the very tip of the Cabo is the distinctive natural arch, **El Arco**; boats can be hired to see it close up, but care is required because of the strong currents. At the harbour entrance is a pinnacle of rock, **Pelican Rock**, which is home to vast shoals of tropical fish; it is an ideal place for snorkelling and scuba diving, and glass-bottomed boats can be rented at the harbour-side (45-minute harbour cruise in glass-bottomed boat to El Arco, Lover's Beach, etc US$5 per person; most hotels can arrange hire of skiffs to enable visits to the Arch and Land's End, about US$5-10 per hour).

Sleeping **L** *Finisterra*, perched on promontory near Land's End, T143-3333, www.finisterra.com A/c, TV, shower, pool, steps to beach, poolside bar with unsurpassed view, restaurant, entertainment, sport-fishing cruisers. **B** *Mar de Cortés*, on Cárdenas and Guerrero in town centre, T143-0032. A/c, showers, helpful, pool, outdoor bar/restaurant, good value. **B** *Marina*, Blvd Marina y Guerrero, T143-0030. Central, a/c, restaurant, bar, can be noisy, pricey. **B-C** *Dos Mares*, Calle Emiliano Zapata, T143-0330. A/c, TV, clean, small pool, parking space. Don't get drunk and fall down the stairs – survival unlikely. Recommended. **C** *San Antonio*, Av Morelos between Obregón and Carranza, 3 blocks back from the main street, T143-7353. Cheapest option in town really, and much better than the rest.

*Cheap
accommodation
simply doesn't exist in
Cabo*

Motel **C** *Los Cabos Inn*, Abasolo y 16 de Septiembre. Central, 1 block from bus station, fans, showers, central, modest, good value. **D** *El Dorado*, Morelos (4 blocks from bus terminal). Clean, fan, hot water, private bath.

Camping *El Arco Trailer Park*, 4 km east on Highway 1, restaurant. *El Faro Viejo Trailer Park*, 1.5 km northwest at Matamoros y Morales. Shade, laundry, ice, restaurant, bar, clean, out-of-town but good.

Eating Many expensive but good eateries around town, particular on the promenade in front of the marina. The *Giggling Marlin* is a landmark used for directions, and a fine place to experience what makes Cabo San Lucas tick. Actually the food is good, the prices reasonable and the self-deprecating humour on the walls refreshing. As alternatives to expensive restaurants, try the 2 pizza places just beyond *Mar de Cortés*, 1 next to the telephone office, the other in the block where the street ends; also *Flor Guadalajara*, Lázaro Cárdenas, on the way out of town a few blocks beyond 'Skid Row'. Good local dishes. *Rays Tequila – The Corner Cafe*, does what is says on the tin – a chap called Ray serving fine tequila. Internet planned. A good budget choice is *Paty's Garden*, an authentic atmosphere, complete with pool table, and tasty as well.

Excursions Absolutely no shortage of activities. The full range includes scuba diving (US$60 for a 2-tank dive), snorkelling (US$35), horse-riding (US$57 for 2 hrs), parasailing (US$35) and so on. Latest craze is personal submarines (US$85 for 30 mins)!

Baja California Peninsula

There are no **ferries** from Cabo San Lucas to Puerto Vallarta. **Buses** Bus station at 16 de **Transport**
Septiembre y Zaragoza, central, few facilities. Regular service to San José del Cabo, 30-45
mins depending on traffic, US$2. **La Paz**: 6 a day from 0630, US$8.

Banks Plenty of branches with ATMs in town. **Communications** Internet: kill 2 birds with one **Directory**
stone, log on while doing your washing at the Laundromat on Leona Vicario and 20 de
Noviembre, 30 mins US$2.40, one load wash and dry US$2.40. Cafés on the main drag are pricey.
Post office: Morelos y Niños Héroes.

Todos Santos

Highway 9, the western loop of the Cape Region, was not paved until 1985 and the *Phone code: 612*
superb beaches of the west coast have yet to suffer the development and crowding of *Colour map 2, grid C1*
the east. The highway branches off Route 1 just after San Pedro, 32 km south of La *Population: 4,000*
Paz, and runs due south through a cactus-covered plain to Todos Santos. This quiet
farming town just north of the Tropic of Cancer is slowly becoming a tourist and
expat centre rather than a working town. There has been a recent influx of expats
from the US and there is a community of artists and craftspeople. There is a Pemex
station, cinema, stores, cafés, galleries, *artesanía* shops, a bank, market, and a Casa
de la Cultura, Calle Topete y Pilar, with a museum.

Sleeping **AL** *Todos Santos Inn*, Calle Legaspi 33, 2 blocks north of Plaza T/F145-0040,
todossantosinn@yahoo.com 19th-century house refurbished in that style, some *en suite*
rooms, very tranquil. Worth splashing out. **B** *Hotel California*, formerly the *Misión de Todos
Santos Inn*, Juárez and Morelos. Historic brick building near town centre, Juárez, a block
north of Highway 9. Fans, showers, pool, a/c, dining room. Closed for renovation in late
2001, reopening in Nov 2002. Opposite is **C** *Motel Guluarte*. Calle Morelos, T145-0006.
Fan, fridge, shower, pool, good value. **C** *Way of Nature*, Bed and Breakfast, along dirt road
signposted at southern end of Juárez, 2 blocks south of Hotel California. Large circular
palapa with rooms. Very quiet. **D-E** *Misión de Pilar*. Clean, good value. **C** *Miramar*, south
end of village. New, with bath, hot water, fan, pool, clean, safe, parking. Recommended.
Camping *El Molino Trailer Park*, off Highway at south end of town, 30 mins from
beach. Full hook-ups, flush toilets, showers, laundry, American owner, very helpful, US$8
for 4. No camping here but apparently OK to use the beach (clean, but look out for dogs –
see below). Several kilometres south is *Trailer Park San Pedrito* (see below), on the beach.
Closed to camping, new hotel being built, full hook-ups, flush toilets, showers, pool, laundry, restaurant, bar, US$12 for RVs. Tent camping **(E)** at *Way of Nature B&B*.

Eating *Café Brown* is a new mid-price Mexican and sandwich bar. On main Plaza is *Café
Santa Fe*. Gourmet Italian food, pricey but very highly rated restaurant. *Las Fuentes*,
where main drag takes a right angle eastwards. Large portions. *Tequila Sunrise*, opposite
the Hotel California, is a colourful spot serving drinks and snacks to those venturing up from
Cabo San Lucas.

Surfing Board hire at Todos Santos surf shop, Rangel and Zaragoza, US$10.50 per day,
US$5.25 for body board. They have kiosk at Playa Los Cerritos beyond El Pescadero. They also
hire out tents (US$5.50 per day) and mountain bikes (US$10) at the main shop.

Transport **Bus**: stop beside park on Juárez.

Directory **Banks** *BanCrecer*, with ATM but doesn't change TCs, *Casa de Cambio* on Colegio Militar
with Hidalgo does. **Communications** Fax from Message Centre on Hidalgo between Juárez and
Centenario. **Laundry** Lavanderia Mision. US$3.50 wash and dry. **Shopping** *El Tecolote Libros* is an
excellent bookshop selling good maps, books, book swap (no romance though!) and excellent general
information on the area.

Baja California Peninsula

West coast beaches Two kilometres from Todos Santos is a stretch of the Pacific Coast with some of the most beautiful beaches of the entire Baja California Peninsula. Nearest to the town is **Playa Punta Lobos** where the local fishermen shore up (the *pangas* come in early afternoon); it is a popular picnic spot, but with too much rubbish and too many unfriendly dogs for wild camping. Next comes Playa Las Palmas, good for swimming. Cleaner for camping is the sandy cove at **Playa San Pedro** (4 km southeast). Backed by groves of Washingtonia fan palms and coconut palms, this is one of the loveliest wild camping spots anywhere; it is also good for surfing. Opposite the access road junction is the **Campo Experimental Forestal**, a Botanical Garden with a well-labelled array of desert plants from all regions of Baja; staff are very informative. Here too is the *Trailer Park San Pedrito* (see above), an open area on the beach and one of the most beautifully sited RV parks in Baja. Eleven kilometres south of Todos Santos is **El Pescadero**, a fast-growing farming town with few facilities for visitors.

The Northwest Coast

The Northwest Coast of Mexico has much to offer the traveller who, with only a few days to spare, can drift through the scenic Sierra de Pintos to the copper-mining centre at Cananea, see the longest sand dunes in North America at Algodones, or brave the desert conditions of the Desierto de Altar. Alternatively, you can enjoy the beaches and watersports of Puerto Peñasco. At the Pinacate Natural Park the moonscape of volcanic craters and lava fields is very impressive and so is the wildlife. With a little more time, you can explore the Kino Missions and enjoy sportfishing at Kino Nuevo, participate in fishing tournaments at La Choya and San Carlos or take a boat excursion from Rocky Point. There are many opportunities to take boat trips to the islands just off the coast and you can take an overnight ferry to Baja California.

Heading south you can make a detour to the beautiful colonial town of Alamos, home of the original Mexican jumping bean. Relax in the streets of Los Mochis and enjoy the music of the roaming mariachis before boarding the famous Copper Canyon train for the journey of a lifetime. The popularity of Mazatlán as a holiday resort is well established; from here, you can travel northeast to Durango and the Colonial Heartland, or southeast to Tepic and Guadalajara, pleasant resting places if you are travelling on to Mexico City.

Nogales to Mazatlán: the Pacific Highway The road along the Pacific Coast gives access to several resorts (for example *Guaymas, Mazatlán* and *Puerto Vallarta*), to ferry terminals for Baja California, and to the Los Mochis end of the Chihuahua al Pacífico railway through the Copper Canyon. From Nogales to Guaymas on the Gulf of California, the road runs along the western slopes of the Sierra Madre, with summits rising to 3,000 m. From Guaymas on to Mazatlán it threads along the lowland, with the Sierra Madre Occidental's bold and commanding escarpment to the east. Like the west coast of all continents between latitudes 20° and 30°, the whole area is desert, but fruitful wherever irrigated by water flowing from the mountains. Summers are very hot, sometimes rainy, winters mild and very dry.

The Pacific Highway down the coast to Acapulco and Salina Cruz is completely paved but has military searches in the State of Guerrero (for narcotics and arms). There are many motels along the whole route, so that each town of any importance has one or more nearby.

Crossing into Mexico: Nogales

Nogales(US)/ Nogales The Nogales crossing is open 24 hours. Walking into Mexico there's no checkpoint on the Mexican side although there is a customs area that is sometimes staffed and sometimes not. If it is staffed, you push a button and if you get a green light you can pass without being inspected; no such luck if you get a red light. After you cross the border, if you keep walking straight ahead about 50 m you'll get to the immigration office (on your right) where you can pick up your tourist card (FM-T).

It is important to get your tourist card validated before you leave the area. Customs agents at the bus station will turn a blind eye if you get on a bus without a tourist card, but if the bus is stopped for routine checks (frequent) you may get sent back to the border.

To avoid the congestion of the downtown route, motorists are generally advised to use the truck crossing (open 0600-2000, currency exchange available), which is reached by the Mariposa Avenida exit from Interstate 19, 4 km north of downtown Nogales, Arizona. Returning from Mexico to the US, follow the sign to the 'Periférico', which avoids the downtown area.

Motor vehicle documents can be obtained at the Mexican Customs Post 21 km south of Nogales, on Highway 15 to Santa Ana, along with US insurance (which may also be obtained at the border proper). There is a tourist office and a *casa de cambio* here. You need to have title to the car with you, ie you can't drive someone else's car into Mexico at least past Km 21. You also need two photocopies of vehicle registration, driver's licence, insurance papers, credit card and visitor's permit (approved); a photocopy machine is available. In the same building as the immigration office on the border is a *Seguros Tepeyac* outlet where you can buy car insurance. If you only want liability, not collison, insurance, they charge US$2.24 per day. To insure a car worth US$7,000 with both liability and collision insurance costs US$5.63 daily. There are also a few other insurance agencies nearby.

Nogales

The City of Nogales lies astride a mountain pass at 1,120 m across from Nogales, Arizona. Population estimates range from the official 160,000 to 240,000, with another 20,000 on the Arizona side. Nogales is the largest town in the Pimería Alta, the area of southern Arizona and northern Sonora occupied by the Pima Indians at the arrival of the Spaniards. The **Pimería Alta Historical Society**, a block from the border in Nogales, Arizona, has excellent exhibits on the history of the region, a valuable library and archives, and also organizes tours to the Sonoran missions. The staff are a good source of information on the Mexican side. ■ *Weekdays 0900-1700, Sat 1000-1600, and Sun from 1300-1600; free.* The **tourist office** is just past the immigration office. The staff are friendly, helpful and have brochures on many parts of Sonora.

Phone code: 631
Colour map 1,
grid A3
Population: 159,103
Km 2,403 from
Mexico City

Sleeping **B** *Fray Marcos de Niza*, Campillo 91, T312-1651. Gaudy but none too good. **C** *Olivia*, Obregón 125, T312-2200. A/c, TV, reasonable. **D** *Miami*, Campillo and Ingenieros, T312-5450. Friendly, good restaurant. Recommended. There is a wide selection of cheaper hotels on Juárez, a 1-block extension of Av López Mateos between Campillo and the border, 2 blocks from the Mexican port of entry.

Eating *El Greco*, upstairs at Obregón and Pierson. Attractive, reasonably priced international menu. Occasionally has live mariachi music. Other recommended restaurants on or near Obregón, including *El Cid* (No 124, good but expensive), *Olivia*, *Casa de María*, *El Toro Steakhouse*. *Café Olga*, Juárez 37 next to bus station. Open all hours. *Elvira's Restaurant*, Obregón 1. Very colourful, relaxed and informal atmosphere. *La Roca*, Elías 91. Secluded, attractive courtyard, live music.

Transport **Buses** Nogales' new bus terminal is 8 km south of the city centre, along the highway to Magdalena and Hermosillo; parking US$1 per hour. Taxis at the border ask US$5 to take you to the bus station, but on the return journey the booth selling taxi vouchers charges less than US$4. A local bus, 1 peso, leaves 1 block from the border. Bus 46 from Juárez goes to the terminal (US$0.25). The bus station has a booth to change money. It also has a Computel outlet with fax and long-distance phone service.

Northwest Coast

There are 3 bus lines that go into Mexico using the terminal: *Norte de Sonora*, *Transportes del Pacífico*, and *Elite*. They all seem to have high-quality buses; *Transportes del Pacífico* also runs 2nd class buses to most of their destinations.

Chihuahua; Elite 0800, 1915, $42. **Ciudad Obregón**: 7 throughout the day, US$27. **Culiacán**, several mid-afternoon departures. **Durango**: 1530, US$72. **Guadalajara**: every couple of hrs, US$110. **Guaymas**: regular hourly service, US$20. **Hermosillo**: hourly, US$13. **Los Mochis**: hourly, US$32. **Mazatlán**: hourly, US$74. **Mexicali**; *Norte de Sonora* US$24.10, hourly, with various route options, US$140. **Puerto Peñasco (Rocky Point)**: 1 bus at 1530. **Tepic**, hourly service, US$90. **Zacatecas**, direct, US$87.

Autobuses Cricero runs buses into the US: **Los Angeles**: US$52.00. **Phoenix**: US$19.00. **Tucson**: US$7.00 There are also links to the Greyhound network in the US.

To get to the US border, turn left as you leave the building and walk to the 1st traffic light and cross the street you can pick up the buses to the border, referred to by the locals as *La Línea*. The buses run down the same street you'd be walking on. Just past that traffic light is a motel called the **B-C** *Motel Campestre*. Just past that is another private bus terminal for the Tufesa line, which run buses down the coast as far as Culiacán (US$33). They have several departures daily and have nice, modern buses.

On the **Arizona** side, 1 block from the port of entry, Citizen Auto Stage Company (T287-5628) runs 10 buses daily between Tucson and Nogales (US$6.50); stops at Tucson airport en route. Stopovers (no additional charge) are possible to visit Tumacacori mission, north of Nogales. US Greyhound is about ¼ block from the border. If you're entering the US from Mexico, you'll see a ramp and stairs on your left on the street after you've crossed the border. The Grehound station is at the top of the stairs, where you can catch buses to Tucson (US$7) and points beyond. Buses leave for Tucson almost hourly from 0630 until 2000. There are smaller vans that leave at 0800, 1200, and 1600. Buses leave for Phoenix, AZ (Arizona's largest city, about 2 hrs north of Tucson) at 0700, 1400, and 1930, US$19.00. They also have buses for **Hermosillo** (US$10) and **Ciudad Obregón** (US$20) that don't require a transfer in Nogales, Sonora, at 0715, 1215, 0230, 0545, and 0945, which stop across the border on the Mexican side to pick up passengers. The Greyhound bus station is a small, 1-room building with restrooms, lockers, pay phones and a few fast food outlets.

Road tolls If driving from Nogales to Mazatlán by the 4-lane, divided toll road (Route 15), there are 12 toll gates. The first is 88 km south of Nogales. No motorcycles, bicycles (but see page 83), pedestrians or animals are allowed on the highway, which is fenced and patrolled. The toll stations are well lit, have good public conveniences, fuel and food. The total distance from Nogales to Mazatlán is 1,118 km; the road is being extended beyond Mazatlán so that about 70% of the entire Nogales-Guadalajara route is now four-lane. It is not possible to list every toll location and every deviation to avoid it. Most deviations are dirt roads and should not be taken in the rainy season. On toll routes and their avoidance, seek advice from US motoring associations and clubs (see page 82) as costs and conditions change rapidly.

Directory **Banks** *Casa de Cambio Money Exchange*, Campillo y López Mateos. *Casa de Cambio 'El Amigo'*, Campillo y López Mateos local No 14. *Compra-venta de Dólares Serfín*, Av López Mateos y Calle Pierson 81, 1st floor. *Casa de Cambio 'Maquila'*, Juárez 74. **Medical services** There's a *Farmacia Benavides* behind the immigration office. They give injections. There are several other pharmacies nearby. According to the tourist office, the best hospital in Nogales (private) is the *Hospital del Socorro*, Dirección Granja, T314-6060. Any taxi driver will know how to get there.

The northwest border

San Luis Río Colorado
Colour map 1, grid A2
Population: 134,000

Route 2 from Tijuana (see page 180) runs close to the border, going through Mexicali (see page 178), San Luis Río Colorado, Sonoyta, and Caborca to Santa Ana, where it joins the West Coast Highway (Route 15) to Mexico City. East of Mexicali the fast four-lane highway crosses the fertile Mexicali valley to a toll bridge over the diminished Colorado River, and continues to San Luis Río Colorado, a cheerfully tourist-oriented border town in the 'free zone' and serving cotton country. There are summer bullfights and small nightlife district like those of the Old West, including a so-called *zona de tolerancia*.

North of San Luis (35 km) is Baja California's last international border-crossing point, the farming town of Algodones. The border is open 0600-2000, but motor vehicle documents are processed weekdays only, 0800-1500. The road north from San Luis skirts the Algodones dunes, the longest in North America. Algodones has one hotel, the rather misnamed **E** *Motel Olímpico*. Mexican car insurance is readily available, and there are several *casas de cambio*.

At Andrade, on the California side, the Quechan Indians from the nearby Fort Yuma Reservation operate an RV park and campground (US$12 per site with electricity, US$8 without; including hot showers and access to laundry room).

Algodones
Colour map 1, grid A2
Population: 12,000

After leaving San Luis Río Colorado, Route 2 crosses the sandy wastes of the Desierto de Altar – Mexico's own mini-Sahara. The road is very narrow in places, watch out for overloaded Mexican trucks. For 150 km there are no facilities (petrol at Los Vidrios), only three houses and an enveloping landscape of sand dunes, cinder cones and a dark lava flow from the Cerro del Pinacate. All the area around the central range is protected by the **Pinacate Natural Park**. A gravel road 10 km east of Los Vidrios gives access to the northern sector of the park, which contains much wildlife, for example puma, deer, antelope, wild boar, Gila monster, wild sheep, quail and red-tailed eagle.

Desierto de Altar
This area was used to train US astronauts during the Moon Missions

After a hot and monotonous 200 km from San Luis, Route 2 reaches the sun-bleached bordertown of **Sonoyta**, a short distance from Lukeville, Arizona. Sonoyta has little of interest itself, but there are several American-style accommodations: Arizona's picturesque Organ Pipe Cactus National Monument is just across the border from Sonoyta.

The border crossing between Lukeville and Sonoyta is open from 0800 to 2400. Camping is possible at developed sites near the visitor centre at Organ Pipe National Monument for US$8 (US$3 visitor permit is valid for 15 days).

Highway 8 goes southwest from Sonoyta through 100 km of sand dunes; a sign, 'Dunas – 10 km', at Km 80, points along a sandy road that leads to dramatic, desolate inland dunes through mountain-rimmed black lava fields; four-wheel drive is recommended.

Lukeville/ Sonoyta
Colour map 1, grid A2

One of the most important shrimping ports on the Gulf; the huge shrimp are too expensive for the US market and are mostly exported to Japan. It is very popular with Arizona and California RV drivers for fishing, surfing and the beach. On the north side of the bay, 12 km, is **La Choya**, largely a *gringo* place, sandy streets, full of trailers and beach cottages, and several fine beaches.

Puerto Peñasco
Phone code: 638
Colour map 1, grid A2
Population: 31,101

Sleeping C *Viña del Mar*, Calle 1 de Junio y Blvd Malecón Kino, T383-3600. Modern resort, cliffside jacuzzi, video-disco, etc, attractive rooms, good value. **D** *Motel Mar y Sol*, Km 94 on road to Sonoyta, T383-3190. Pleasant gardens, restaurant, a/c, friendly. **E** *Motel Davis*, Emiliano Zapata 100, T383-4314. Pleasant.

Camping *Playa de Oro Trailer Resort*, Matamoros 36, T383-2668, 2 km east. Laundry, boat ramp, 200 sites, US$12 for 2. *Playa Bonita RV Park*, on lovely Playa Bonita, T383-2596, 245 spaces, restaurant, shop, laundry.

Eating *Costa Brava Restaurant*, Kino y 1 de Junio. Best in town, modest prices, exotic menu, pleasant. *Café La Cita*, 1 de Junio near the petrol station. Authentic Mexican, budget. *La Curva*, Kino y Comonfort, T383-3470. Americanized menu, popular, budget prices, little atmosphere. *La Gaviota*, coffee shop at *Hotel Viña del Mar*. Good breakfasts and views.

Northwest Coast

Shopping *Jim-Bur Shopping Center*, Benito Juárez near railway crossing, is the main commercial hub. Try *El Vaquero* or *El Gift Shop* for souvenirs and camping supplies. Fresh fish from open-air fish market on the Malecón (old town).

Directory Banks 2 banks. **Laundry** *Laundromat Liz*, Altamirano y Simón Morua.

Recently paved State Highway 37 continues southeast, roughly following the rail line to Caborca (180 km) – an alternative to the inland Highway 2 route.

Caborca
Phone code: 637
Colour map 1, grid A3
Population: 69,359
Altitude: 286 m

Route 2 runs from Sonoyta to Caborca (150 km), passing through a number of small towns (San Emeterio, San Luisito) and a more mountainous but still arid land. There is a Customs and Immigration station near Quitovac (28 km south of Sonoyta).

Caborca lies on the Mexicali-Benjamín Hill railway in the midst of a gently sloping plain. Caborca's restored Church of Nuestra Señora de la Concepción was one of the 25 missions founded by Padre Kino in Sonora and Arizona between 1687 and 1711. Caborca is the best base for exploring the **Kino Missions.**

Sleeping C *Motel San Carlos*, AV 6 de Abril, T372-1300. **D** *Hotel San Francisco*. **D** *Hotel Yaqui*. All clean with a/c, TV, service station and general facilities.

Altar to
Arizona
border
Keep an eye out for
semi-wild longhorn
cattle along the
road to El Sásabe

Highway 2 continues east through **Altar** (café, gas station) to join Highway 15 at Santa Ana (*Population*: 13,534), a small town of little note. The *Fiesta de Santa Ana* is held 17-26 July, with horse racing, fireworks, etc. **B** *Motel San Francisco*, T(641) 324-1380. A/c, shower, baths, restaurant, also **B**. There is a Canadian-Mexican trailer park south of town, on the right going south, space for 9-10 trailers, rustic, useful overnight stop.

El Sásabe
Colour map 1, grid A3

The border at El Sásabe is open from 0800 to 2000, but there is no public transport on either side, nor is there any Mexican automobile insurance agency. For information as to road conditions, phone US Customs (T602-823-4231); although they appear not to encourage traffic over this route.

South of Nogales

Magdalena
Valley

South of the border at Nogales, Route 15 passes through the Magdalena Valley. The Cocóspera mines are near **Imuris** and there are famous gold and silver mines near **Magdalena** (*Hotel El Cuervo*, near plaza, **C** without TV, **B** with), which has a great Indian **fiesta** in the first week of October.

From Imuris, Route 2 heads east (to Naco and Agua Prieta) through the scenic Sierra de Pintos to the historic and still important copper mining centre of **Cananea**. This was the site of a 1906 miners' strike against the American-owned Cananea Consolidated Copper Company, one of the critical events in the last years of the Porfirio Díaz dictatorship. Hundreds of Arizona Rangers crossed the border to join the Sonora militia in putting down the strike, which is commemorated at the Museo de La Lucha Obrera, the former city jail, on Avenida Juárez. Back on Route 15, 120 km from Nogales, is Santa Ana, where the road enters from Tijuana and Mexicali.

Hermosillo

Phone code: 662
Colour map 1, grid B3
Population: 608,697
Altitude: 237 m

Capital of Sonora state, Hermosillo is a modern city, resort town and centre of a rich orchard area. Just east, the Rodríguez Dam captures the fickle flow of the Río Sonora, producing a rich strip of cotton fields, vegetables, melons, oranges and grapes. **Tourist office** Paseo del Canal y Comonfort Edificio Sonora 3rd floor, T/F217-0176. The local Sonora tourism website is at **www.sonoraturismo.gob.mx**

Reminders of an illustrious colonial past can be found around the central Plaza **Sights**
Zaragoza (invaded by noisy birds at sunset): the imposing **Catedral de La Asunción** (1779, neoclassical, baroque dome, three naves), and the **Palacio de Gobierno**, with its intricately carved pillars and pediment, historical murals and grandiose statues amid landscaped gardens.

Not far north of downtown (Rosales y Transversal) is **Ciudad Universitaria** (University City), with its modern buildings of Mexican architecture blended taste-fully with Moorish and Mission influences. There is an active fine arts and cultural life, with many events throughout the year open to visitors (check at the tourist office for details). Two kilometres south of Plaza Zaragoza, near the Periférico Sur, is the wonderful **Centro Ecológico de Sonora**, a botanical garden and zoo displaying Sonoran and other desert flora and fauna in well-cared-for surroundings.

Generally poor standard of hotels, although at the top end is **AL** *Señorial*, Blvd Kino y **Sleeping**
Guillermo Carpena, T215-5613, F215-5093. With a/c, pool, parking, restaurant, bar. **C** *San Alberto*, Serdán y Rosales, T213-1840. With breakfast, a/c, cable TV, pool, good value. **C** *San Andres*, Av Juárez and Oaxaca No 14 Ote, T217-4305. Good new hotel, price includes break-fast. **C** *Monte Carlo*, Juárez y Sonora, T212-3354. With a/c, old, clean, very popular, as is adjoining restaurant. **D** *Washington*, Dr Noriega Pte 68, T213-1183. With a/c, clean, basic rooms off narrow courts, with bath, best budget hotel, parking for motorbikes. **E** *Casa de los Amigos*, contact the Asociación Sonorense de los Amigos, Felipe Salido 32, Col Centro, T/F217-0142. Dormitories, living room, library, garden, laundry and kitchen. Cheap hotels and *casas de huéspedes* can be found around Plaza Zaragoza and along Sonora near Matamoros (red-light activity, choose carefully).

Jardín Xochimilco, Obregón 51, T250-4052, Villa de Seris. Very good beef, not cheap. **Eating**
Mariscos Los Arcos de Hermosillo, Michel y Ocampo (4 blocks south of Plaza), T213-2220. Fresh seafood, attractive and expensive. *Henry's Restaurant*, Blvd Kino Nte, across the road from *Motel Encanto*. Nice old house, good. *San César*, Plutarco Elías Calles 71 Pte. Excellent chop sueys, seafood and expensive *gringo* food.

Air The Gen Pesquira/García airport (HMO) is 12 km from town. Daily flights to Mexico City **Transport**
with *Aero California*, *AeroMéxico* and *Mexicana*. Other domestic flights to Chihuahua, Ciudad Juárez, Ciudad Obregón, Cuernavaca, Culiacán, Guadalajara, Guaymas, Guerrero Negro, La Paz, Loreto, Los Mochis, Mazatlán, Mexicali, Monterrey, Morelia, Oaxaca, Tijuana and Torreón. International flights to Los Angeles, Tucson and Phoenix.

Buses Bus station on Bulevar Transversal 400, north of University. To **Agua Prieta**: 6 a day, 7 hrs, US$18. **Guaymas**: hourly round the clock, 2½ hrs, US$8. **Kino**: 4 a day, 2 hrs, US$4. **Los Mochis**: 7½ hrs through scrubland and wheat fields, US$29. **Mazatlán** 10-12 hrs, US$42. **Nogales**: hourly 0230-1830, 4 hrs, US$14. **Tijuana**: 11 hrs, US$47.

Airline offices *Aero California*, T260-2555. *AeroMéxico*, T216-8206. *Mexicana*, T217-1103. **Directory**
Embassies and consulates *US Consulate*, T217-2375 for appointment, Mon-Fri 0900-1700.

Bahía Kino

A paved 118-km road runs west past the airport to Bahía Kino, divided into the old, *Phone code: 662*
somnolent and somewhat down-at-heel fishing village, and the new **Kino Nuevo**, a *Colour map 1, grid B3*
'winter *gringoland*' of condos, trailer parks and a couple of expensive hotels. Although the public beaches are good, most American visitors come for the sportfishing. The Seri Indians, who used to live across El Canal del Infiernillo (Little Hell Strait) on the mountainous Isla Tiburón (Shark Island), have been displaced by the Navy to the mainland, down a dirt road from Bahía Kino in a settlement at Punta Chueca (no east access). They come into Kino on Saturday and Sunday to sell their ironwood animal sculptures and traditional basketware (not cheap). They may usually be found at the

Northwest Coast

Posada del Mar Hotel. For the visitor interested in exploring nature reserves, **Isla Tiburón** is of especial interest. Protected in the nearly 400 sq m preserve, the population of both the big horn sheep and mule deer has grown enormously. On the south end of the island, water depths of 50 m or more are common. It is an excellent area not only for scuba diving but also for fishing, and **Dog Bay** provides shelter and ideal anchorage for spending the night. **Isla Patos** (Duck Island), 30 minutes north of Isla Tiburón, offers the opportunity to explore the submerged Spanish vessels that once sailed the Sea of Cortés. Other islands worth visiting are **Alcatraz** (also known as Pelican Island), **Turner**, and **San Esteban**. In Kino Nuevo, a fine **Museo Regional de Arte Seri** has opened on Mar de Cortés, the main boulevard.

Sleeping **A** *The Anchor House*. Beautiful bed and breakfast house on the beach, American-run, T242-0141. **C** *Hotel Saro*, Mar de Cortés, between Nueva York and Vancouver, T242-007. 5 rooms, on beach. **Camping** On the beaches is possible with or without tent. Camping at one of the trailer parks costs about US$12 a night (eg *Kino Bay RV Park*, Av Mar de Cortés, T242-0216).

Eating Reasonably priced meals are available in Old Kino at *La Palapa* and *Marlín* restaurants (latter next to *Islandia Marina Trailer Park*). Fresh seafood and snacks. *El Pargo Rojo*. For really good seafood. Recommended.

Directory There is no bank in the area. The nearest is Bancomer in Miguel Alemán, between Kino and Hermosillo, 48 km away.

Guaymas and Bahía San Carlos

Phone code: 622
Colour map 1, grid B3
Population: 130,108

Guaymas acquired the title 'heroic' in 1935, in memory of the valiant defence by its inhabitants during the French Invasion of 1854

At Km 1,867 (from Mexico City) the road reaches the Gulf at the port of **Guaymas**, on a lovely bay backed by desert mountains; excellent deep-sea fishing, and seafood for the gourmet. Miramar beach, on Bocachibampo Bay with its blue sea sprinkled with green islets, is the resort section. The climate is ideal in winter but unpleasant in summer. The 18th-century church of San Fernando is worth a visit; so, too, outside the town, is the 17th-century church of San José de Guaymas. The port area also boasts some worthy buildings, among which are the Templo del Sagrado Corazón de Jesús, the Banco de Sonora, the Palacio Municipal (constructed in 1899), the Ortiz Barracks and the Antigua Carcel Municipal (old Municipal Prison) constructed in 1900.

Fifteen kilometres north of Guaymas (or 12 km from Highway 15) is the **Bahía San Carlos**, very Americanized and touristy, where *Catch-22* was filmed. Above the bay a twin-peaked hill, the Tetas de Cabra, is a significant landmark. There is good fishing with an international tournament each July. North of San Carlos further development is taking place on Sonora Bay. Both Miramar and San Carlos beaches are easily reached by bus. The free beaches are dirty. The **tourist office** at Avenida Serdán has lots of pamphlets.

Sleeping &
eating

Guaymas **B** *Santa Rita*, Serdán and Calle 9. With bath, a/c, clean, good. **F** *Casa de Huéspedes Martha*, Calle 13. With bath, fan, hot water, a little run down. **Motels**: **C** *Malibu*, T226-2244, Carretera Internacional N. **D** *Motel Cominse*, Calle 14. Clean and simple, but a good choice. **Eating** *Cantón*, Serdán between Calle 20 and 21. Good Chinese. *Todos Comen*, on Serdán. Good food at reasonable prices.

Bahía San Carlos Plenty of accommodation out of town including **A-B** *Fiesta San Carlos*, T226-1318. Clean, good food (US$10-15), pool. After 10 km from the Highway a road branches to **C** *Dorada Rental Units*, T226-0307, PO Box 48. On beach, pleasant. **C** *Ferrer Apartments*. Cooking facilities, hot water, pleasant patio, good value. At Km 13 the road forks: left 1 km to 2 secluded bays with limited trailer camping, and right to the *Marina Real* and *Club Mediterranée*, T226-0176, all on Sonora Bay, and beyond a beach with open camping. **Eating** *Piccolo*. Good pasta, salads, good value. Just over 1 km up a dirt track is *Restaurant Norsa*. Good limited menu, no alcohol. Generally, restaurants are overpriced.

Transport   Air: The General José M Yáñez airport (GYM) is 5 km from Guaymas on the way to San Carlos. AeroMéxico (T226-0123) has flights to La Paz, Mexico City and Phoenix.

Buses: 1st class bus to **Hermosillo**: 2½ hrs, US$8; **Mazatlán**: frequent, 12 hrs, US$42; **Tijuana**: 18 hrs, US$62. To **Culiacán**: 9 hrs, US$22. Buses from Empalme to **Los Mochis**/Sufragio with *Autotransportes Tufesa*, 5½ hrs, US$13.

Ferry: Sematur sail from Guaymas to **Santa Rosalía**, Baja California, 7-hr trip, see schedule, page 200, for details.

Directory   7 km from the Highway, behind the shops, are the **post office** and **police station**; the beer depository will sell by the half case. After 10 km are the Pemex station and **bank** opposite the **phone** and fax centre.

From Guaymas to Mazatlán is 784 km. Ciudad Obregón, mainly important as the centre of an agricultural region, is a good place for buying leather goods, such as western boots and saddles.

Ciudad Obregón

Phone code: 644
Colour map 2, grid B1
Population: 180,000

Sleeping and eating **A** *Costa de Oro*, M Alemán 210, T414-1765. Well-kept and pleasant. **C** *San Jorge*, M Alemán 929 Nte, T414-9514, F414-4353. With a/c, TV, restaurant, bar, pool, safe parking, clean, friendly, with colonial Spanish decor; also 2 hotels on street of main bus station (turn right on leaving), 1 block to **D** *La Aduana*. Dirty, cold water.

From Ciudad Obregón to Navojoa is a four-lane highway in poor condition (toll at Navojoa, US$7). Navojoa has the *Motel El Rancho* (T(642) 422-0310) and *Motel del Río* (T(642) 422-0331) and a trailer park in the north of town on Route 15 (run down, shaded, US$10 for full hook-up, US$5 for car or small jeep, dollars preferred to pesos). West of Navojoa, on Huatabampo bay, are the survivors of the Mayo Indians; their festivals are in May. Hourly buses to Alamos.

Navojoa

Phone code: 642
Colour map 2, grid B1
Population: 200,000

Alamos

Fifty-two kilometres into the hills is the delightful old colonial town of Alamos, now declared a national monument. It is set in a once famous mining area fascinating for rock enthusiasts. Although the area was explored by the Spanish in the 1530s, development did not begin for another 100 years when the Jesuits built a mission nearby. With a rich history in silver mining, trips to old mine sites can easily be arranged. The area is also rich in birdlife, with many species arriving to overwinter.

   Another, altogether more lighthearted reason for visiting in June in particular, is to see the jumping beans: a symbiotic relationship between a plant and a moth larvae. The two develop simultaneously giving the impression that the seed pod or bean is actually jumping.

Phone code: 647
Colour map 1, grid C5

The Alamos Music Festival is an annual event held for seven days at the end of January

Sleeping   Several options in town including **B** *Los Portales Hotel*, T428-0111. With beautiful frescoes, on plaza. **D** *Somar*, on the road into Alamos, T428-0125, Madero 110. *El Caracol Trailer Park*. Rustic, good pool, not always open (US$8.50).

Transport   Buses: Navojoa-Alamos every hr on the ½ hr from 0630-1830, 1 hr, US$2, good road. Bus station for Alamos is about 8 blocks from main bus station in Navoja, but you must ask directions because it is a confusing route.

Los Mochis

Los Mochis, in a sugar cane area, is a fishing resort 25 km from the sea with a US colony. The name is derived either from a local word meaning 'hill like a turtle', or possibly, from *mocho*, meaning one-armed, perhaps after a cowboy thus mutilated. The city was founded in 1904 around a sugar mill built by the American, Benjamin

Phone code: 668
Colour map 2, grid B1
Population: 200,000

Northwest Coast

Johnson, and his wife was responsible for building the Sagrado Corazón church. The family lost everything in the Revolution. This is the starting point for the uphill railway journey through the Copper Canyon. Try doing anything else in town, and you'll probably be looked at rather strangely. There are plenty of nightspots and bars visited by roaming *mariachis*, who play excellent music.

Tourist information for Los Mochis and the state of Sinaloa in the municipal building, Marcial Ordoñes and Allende – try to follow the signs, **www.sinaloanorte.com.mx**

Sleeping **AL-A** *Santa Anita*, Leyva and Hidalgo, T818-7046, F812-0046, www.mexicoscoppercanyon.com Comfortable, clean dining-room (good), noisy a/c, stores luggage, mixed reports about *Flamingo* travel agency attached. **A** *El Dorado*, on Gabriel Leyva 525 Nte, 20 mins from centre, T815-1111, F812-0179, www.eldroadomochis.com.mx A/c, pool, friendly, very good. **C** *Beltrán*, Hidalgo 281 Pte, T812-0688, F812-0710. Noisy a/c, TV, has all travel timetables and will make reservations. Recommended. **D** *América*, Allende Sur 655, T812-1355, F812-5983. No hot water in early morning, noisy, a/c, has restaurant with good, cheap sandwiches, enclosed parking. **C** *Fénix*, A Flores 365 Sur, T812-2623, F815-8948, hotelfenix@email.com Safe, clean, wake-up call, very good, credit cards accepted. **C-D** *Hidalgo*, opposite *Beltrán* at No 260 Pte, T/F818-3453. Cheap *cafetería*, friendly, occasionally no hot water. **C-D** *Lorena*, Prieto y Obregón 186 Pte, T/F812-0239. With bath, TV, gloomy, poor value, but good *cafetería*. **C** *Montecarlo*, Independencia y Flores 322 Sur, T812-1818. Clean, a/c, TV, restaurant, parking. **E-F** *Los Arcos*, Allende 524, between Castro and Obregón, T812-3253. Without bath, clean but dingy, fills up quickly, some rooms noisy, more expensive with a/c, but a good deal and the best budget choice. **Motel** **D** *Santa Rosa*, López Mateos 1051 Nte, T812-2918. Modest.

Trailer Park *Río Fuerte Trailer Resort*, 16 km north of Los Mochis on Route 15. Good, heated swimming pool, US$10 per car and 2 people, US$14.50 motor home, offers hunting, shooting, fishing expeditions. Recommended.

Los Mochis

Sleeping
1 América
2 Beltrán
3 Fénix
4 Hidalgo
5 Los Arcos
6 Lorena
7 Montecarlo
8 Santa Anita

Eating
1 Chispa
2 El Delfín
3 El Farallón
4 El Taquito
5 España
6 Mi Cabaña Tacos

El Farallón, Flores and Obregón. Good seafood and service, reasonably priced; opposite, on Obregón, is *España*. Very good, with style and grace. Mid-range *Mochis* in *Hotel Montecarlo*. Recommended. *El Delfín*, on Allende Sur near Obregón. Restaurant and bar, nice atmosphere if a little rough and ready. Get thrown out … through the swing doors. *El Taquito*, Leyva, 1 block from Santa Anita. Open 24 hrs. *Tay-Pak*, near Independencia. Chinese, good clean, reasonably priced. *Chispa*, Leyva Sur 117, near Morelos. Art deco design, clean, good. *Mi Cabaña Tacos*, corner of Obregón y Allende. Popular with locals, friendly. Recommended. *Las Palmeras*. Excellent, reasonably priced. *El Bucanero*. Good seafood.

Eating
Birria is a local beef dish; many places to eat are referred to as a birriería

Air Airport Federal (LMM) is 6½ km from town. Flights to **Chihuahua, Ciudad Obregón, Culiacán, Guadalajara, Hermosillo, La Paz, Los Cabos, Mazatlán, Mexico City, Monterrey** and **Tijuana** with a variety of airlines. Flights to **Los Angeles, Phoenix** and **Tucson** with *AeroMéxico* and *Aero California*.

Transport

Trains For **Creel** and **Chihuahua**, see below. If coming from Chihuahua and you don't want to stay in Los Mochis, assuming the train is not over-delayed, you can take a night bus to Mazatlán at 2200, arriving 0630. Los Mochis station has toilets and local phones; ticket office is open 1 hour before train leaves. The station is 8 km from town; do not walk there or back in the dark. There is a bus service from 0500, US$0.15 from corner of hotels *Hidalgo* and *Beltrán*, otherwise take the 0500 bus from *Hotel Santa Anita*, US$3.50 (for house guests only), or taxi, of which there is any number going into town after the arrival of the Chihuahua train. Taxis in the centre go from Hidalgo y Leyva; fare to station US$5 per car, bargaining not possible, make sure price quoted is not per person, rip-offs are common. Bus to town from corner of 1st junction from station from 0530.

Buses Buses to the train station leave from the corner of Obregón and Zaragoza, first leaves at 0515 in time to get tickets for the train, US$0.40. Local buses to destinations around Sinaloa, eg Topolobampo, Guasave, San Blas (Sufragio) and Culiacán leave from Cuauhtémoc, near the post office.

There is a new bus station in town on the corner of Castro and Constitución, to the south of town, about 10 mins' walk. *Estrella Blanca* group of bus companies (*Futura* and *Elite*) with long-distance services leave from here as well as international services coming down from the US. The terminals of *Norte de Sonora*, T812-1757, *Transporte del Pacífico*, T812-0341 and *Tufesa*, T818-2222 for services along the western coast leave from several terminals clustered together near Degollado and Juárez, to the east of town. Check locally for the best option for your destination if it is slightly unusual. **Ciudad Obregón**, US$29. **Guadalajara**, hourly, 13 hrs, US$43. **Guaymas**, 6 hrs, US$15. **Mazatlán**, hourly, 6 hrs, US$19. **Mexico City**, every couple of hrs, 24 hrs, US$80. **Monterrey**, 0900 and 2000, 24 hrs, US$90. **Nogales**, 1930 and 2030, 12 hrs, US$26. **Tepic**, hourly, 10 hrs, US$38. **Tijuana**, hourly, 20 hrs, US$65.

Airline offices *Aero California*, T818-1616. **Banks** Many banks on Leyva, with ATMs, and a *casa de cambio* open a little longer. **Communications** Internet: *Hugo's Internet Café*, G. Leyva 537, US$1.30/hr, with printers and scanners, same price at *Cyber Más*, Independencia 421. **Post office**: Ordóñez Pte, between Prieto y Zaragoza Sur, south of centre, open Mon-Fri 0900-1400,1600-1800. **Laundry** *Lavamatic*, Allende 218, self-service if you want; *Lavarama* at Juárez 225. **Medical services** *Hospital Fátima*, Loaizo 606 Pte, T815-5703, private, English spoken, maybe a good place to start in an emergency. **Tour operators** *Aracely*, Obregón 471 Pte, T812-5090, F815-8787. American Express agents, and full services with reservations for first-class train. *Viajes Flamingo*, in the lobby of *Hotel Santa Anita*, Leyva and Hidalgo, T812-1613, F818-3393. Bookings for the trains attract a commission of 8%. *Viajes Ahome*, Leyva Sur 121, T815-6120, www.viajesahome.com, for booking tickets on the ferry to Baja California from Topolobampo.

Directory

A side road, running southwest from Los Mochis, crosses the salt flats to Topolobampo (20 km, 30 minutes). The town is built on a number of hills facing the beautiful bay-and-lagoon-indented coast. In the bay, which has many outlets, there are a number of islands; sunsets here are lovely. It's also one option for getting a ferry to La Paz in south Baja California.

Topolobampo
Phone code: 668
Colour map 2, grid B1

Sleeping B *Yacht Hotel*, 3-4 km south of town. Modern, a/c, clean and good food, quiet, good views, but seems to close for the winter. E *Estilo Europeo Poama*, at the ferry terminal, 10 mins' walk from Los Mochis bus; for other accommodation go to Los Mochis.

Ferry Topolobampo-La Paz, Baja California Sur. For schedule, fares and information, see page 200. No reservations, buy ticket in Los Mochis (office Morelos 392, T815-6120) or on day of travel at Muelle Topolobampo office, opens 3 hrs prior to departure (be there at least 2 hrs before sailing), T862-0141.

To Creel and Chihuahua by train

The famous **Chihuahua al Pacífico** train journey shows the spectacular scenery of the Sierra Madre and the Barranca del Urique/Cobre (Urique/Copper Canyon). The *Servicio Estrella* train should leave daily at 0600 (but often at 0700), US$59 to Creel (about nine hours), US$109 to Chihuahua (about 14 hours, but expect delays). For train information, check www.ferromex.com.mx

Bring your own toilet paper, food and drinking water. Tickets must be bought in advance either on morning of departure or, in high season (July-August, New Year, Holy Week), a day or more before. *Estrella* class tickets can be bought from tour operators in Los Mochis, with an 8% surcharge, but they will try to persuade you to book into preferred (expensive) hotels. It may be worth buying tickets from them to avoid long queues at the station. If you are only going as far as Creel buy return tickets as it is impossible to reserve seats from Creel back to Los Mochis. Local buses leave from Los Mochis on Obregón and Zaragoza (US$0.40) for the train station, departing 0515, in time for the queues.

On the *Primera Especial* the windows do not open, so, to take photos, stand between the carriages if you can. Motorists taking the train to Creel have been advised to park in front of the station as there are lights and people at all times. Alternatively, ask for Sr Carlos at the station ticket office, who will guard the car at his home for a modest fee. There is more expensive parking downtown.

The ordinary second class train, *Tarahumara*, aims to leave at 0700, with prices roughly half that of the first class, but it is not possible to reserve seats. Second class trains make many stops but are reasonably comfortable and it is possible to open the windows. On either train, sit on the right for the best views, except when approaching Temoris when it's all jump to the left, then return to the right until the first tunnel after Temoris when the views are good on both sides. For prices and more information see page 233.

El Fuerte
Phone code: 698
Population: 89,556
Colour map 2, grid B1

This town, 1½ hours by train from Los Mochis, has recently been renovated and has interesting colonial architecture in the centre (it was founded in 1564). The station is 10 km from the town; taxis US$4 per person. *Posada del Hidalgo* is a historical mansion, details from *Hotel Santa Anita* in Los Mochis. D *Hotel Oasis*, half a block from Calle Benito Juárez in centre. Not very clean, some rooms better than others, a/c, expensive restaurant. D *Hotel San Francisco*, T893-0055, good value. There is an attractive plaza and good restaurants.

For those travelling on the train, the high, long bridge over the Río Fuerte heralds the beginning of more interesting scenery (this is the first of 37 major bridges); three hours from Los Mochis the first, and longest, of the 86 tunnels is passed, then, 10 minutes later the Chinapas bridge (this is approximately the Sinaloa/Chihuahua border, where clocks go forward an hour).

Culiacán

Phone code: 667
Colour map 2, grid C2
Population: 744,859

Some 210 km beyond Los Mochis, and 1,429 km before Mexico City, Culiacán, the capital of Sinaloa state, was founded in 1531 by Beltrán de Guzmán. It can no longer be called a colonial city, but is attractive and prosperous; it has a university and is an important centre for winter vegetables.

AL-Q *Executivo*, Madero y Obregón, T713-9310, www.executivo.com.mx **C** *San Francisco*, Hidalgo 227, T713-5903. With bath, clean, friendly, free parking. **D** *Louisiana*, Francisco Villa 478, T73-9152. **Motels A** *Los 3 Ríos*, 1 km north of town on highway 15, at Km 1423, T750-5280. Trailer park, US$10, pool, resort-style, good restaurant. *Pizzería Tivoli*. Good, friendly. **C** *Los Caminos*, Blvd Colegio Militar y Blvd Leyva Solano, T715-3300. With a/c, phone, satellite TV, restaurant, pool, nightclub, safe parking, clean rooms.

Sleeping

Air The Aeropuerto Federal de Bachigualato (CUL) is 10 km from centre. *Aero California*, T716-0250; *AeroMéxico*, T715-3772; have flights to Acapulco, Aguascalientes, Chihuahua, Ciudad Obregón, Cuernavaca, Durango, Guadalajara, Hermosillo, La Paz, Los Cabos, Los Mochis, Mexico City, Monterrey, Reynosa, Tijuana, Torreón and Uruapan. International flights to Los Angeles and Tucson.

Transport

Buses Buses to all places along the west coast, including **Guaymas**: 9 hrs, US$32. **Tepic**: 8½ hrs, US$28.

Road North of the city, the north and southbound carriageways are on different levels with no divide (very dangerous). A new toll section of freeway heads nearer to the coast, past Navolata, bypasses Culiacán and rejoins Highway 15 a few km south of that city.

Mazatlán

Beyond the Tropic of Cancer, 1,089 km from Mexico City, is Mazatlán, spread along a peninsula at the foot of the Sierra Madre. It is the largest Mexican port on the Pacific Ocean and the main industrial and commercial centre in the west. The beauty of its setting and its warm winters have made it a popular resort, but unfortunately with expansion it has lost some of its attraction. But while the big developments attract international tourists, in the heart of the old town you can join Mexicans taking their vacations and enjoying the city, without the hard sell. The old town overlooks Olas Altas (High Waves) Bay, which has a very strong current. The area of extensive development called the Zona Dorado stretches for several kilometres to the north of the Old Town. Entering Mazatlán by sea from Baja shows the city at its most impressive – two pyramid-shaped hills, one topped by a lighthouse, the other the 'rock' of Isla Piedra, guards the harbour entrance.

Phone code: 669
Colour map 2, grid C2
Population: 380,265

Northwest Coast

Ins and outs

First class buses go to and from most major cities west and north of the capital, while second class will take you to smaller towns such as San Blas. The main bus station is north of the old town centre, with local buses and taxis providing links to the old town. A ferry service operates between Mazatlán and La Paz, in Baja California (see page 200 for ferry schedules). For drivers, Route 15, the coastal road, heads north to the US border, and south to Tepic then inland to Guadalajara; Route 40 is the picturesque but hair-raising road to Durango. The local airport has flights to Mexico City and destinations in northern and western Mexico and in the US. Planes are met by the usual fleet of fixed-fare taxis and microbuses.

Getting there
See Transport page 220

Most local buses leave from the market. There is an express service (green and white buses), which runs from the centre along the seafront to the Zona Dorada and beyond. Taxis are readily available and *pulmonias*, taxis that looks like golf carts, will ferry you between the bus station and your hotel.
 The **tourist office** is at Edif Banrual 4th floor, Av Camarón Sábalo and Tiburón, at the northern end of Zona Dorada – a long way to go for information easily obtained at any travel agency or hotel information desk, **www.sinaloa.gob.mx**

Getting around

The old part of town is located around **Plaza Machado**, which is on Calle Carnaval. This is far and away the most interesting part of the city. Half a block from the plaza is

Sights

the **Teatro Peralta**, the 17th-century opera house, which has been restored and reopened to the public. The **Aquarium**, Avenida de los Deportes III, just off the beach, behind *Hotel Las Arenas*, is interesting, and includes sharks and blindfish. ■ *0900, US$3, children US$1.50*. The **Museo Arqueológico de Mazatlán**, Sixto Osuna 115, half a block from *Hotel Freeman*, is small, covering the state of Sinaloa. Recommended. ■ *US$1, free gallery in same building*. The **Museo de Arte** has a 20th-century collection. ■ *Closes Sun at 1400, US$0.90*.

Beaches

The lighthouse on El Faro Island is 157 m above sea level

Tourism is now concentrated in the **Zona Dorada**, which includes the beaches of Gaviotas, Los Sábalos, Escondida, Delfín, Cerritos, Cangrejo and Brujas (north of **Playa Brujas** is a rocky area, which is good for snorkelling); the area is built up and accommodation is expensive. The Old Town around Olas Altas bay has a distinctly more relaxing feel with a promenade lined by hotels with a long beach at its foot, curves northwards around the bay, first as Paseo Claussen, then Avenida del Mar, which leads to Avenida Camarón Sábalo in the Zona Dorada (take bus from Juárez – best from in front of market – marked Sábalo Centro US$0.30). The sunsets are superb seen from this side of the peninsula; at this time of day high divers can be watched and the fishermen return to the north beach. There are many good beach bars from which to view the setting sun. Buses from Calle Arriba go to the Zona Dorada for US$0.50.

Mazatlán

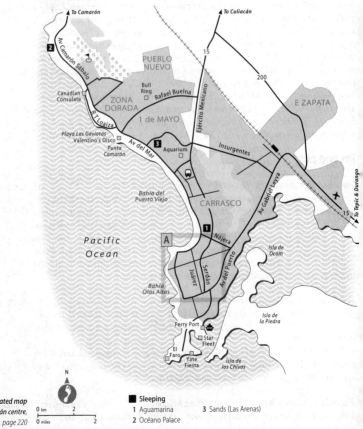

N

0 km   2
0 miles   2

■ **Sleeping**
1 Aguamarina
2 Océano Palace
3 Sands (Las Arenas)

Excursions

To reach **Isla de la Piedra** (which is in fact a peninsula) take a small boat from the south side of town from Armada (naval station near Pacífico brewery, reached by 'Zaragoza' bus from Juárez outside market), regular service, US$1 return ticket. The 30-km beach on the Mazatlán side is now littered but you can walk across the peninsula either side of the hill (10 minutes) to a clean beach where there is good surfing. There is also a ferry that goes from near the lighthouse to the *isla*; runs until 1700. Local *comedores* on the beach provide primitive accommodation, or ask for permission to camp on the beach. Try smoked fish sold on a stick; *Victor's comedor* has been recommended. Beware of sandflies.

Essentials

Along the northern beach on Av Camarón Sábalo or just off it there are many full service resorts **LL-AL** including *Océano Palace*, Av Camarón Sábalo, T913-0666, north end of Zona Dorada, all-inclusive, www.omegaresorts.com   **A** *Las Palmas*, Camarón Sábalo 305, Zona Dorada, PO Box 135, T916-5664, F916-5666. Good value. Recommended. **B** *Azteca Inn*, Camarón Sábalo, T913-4477, F913-7476. Swimming pool.

Along Av del Mar, across the road from the beach (front rooms in all are likely to be noisy) are: **AL-A** *Aguamarina*, No 110, T981-7080, F982-4624. **B-C** *Sands (Las Arenas)*. With swimming pool, a/c, TV, fridge, garden, good restaurant, on beach. Recommended.

Down in the Old Town there are generally better deals. **B** *Belmar*, Belisario Domínguez 166 Sur and Flores, T982-1866, F981-3428. Modernized but old, a bit run-down with a pool – popular with Mexicans and groups. **B-C** *La Siesta*, No 11 Sur, T981-2640, F913-7476. With a/c, clean, friendly, safe, very good, nice patio, restaurant: *Shrimp Bucket*.

Most of the others are in the downtown area away from the beach front: **C** *Del Centro*, J M Canizale 705 Pte and Aquiles Serdán, in the centre of town, pretty dingy but friendly. **C** *San Jorge*, Aquiles Serdán 2710, T981-3695. Quiet spot, tidy rooms close to the beach.

D *Hotel de Río*, Benito Juárez 410 and Alejandro Quijano, neat and tidy. **D-E** *Vialta*, Azueta 2006, 3 blocks from market, T981-6027. With bath and fan, nice central patio, friendly, helpful, comfortable. **E** *San Fernando*, 21 de Marzo 926, T981-7990. With bath, hot water eventually, very basic, very friendly. Recommended. **E** *Lerma*, Simón Bolívar 622 and Aquiles Serdán, near beach, T981-2436. With fan and hot showers, friendly, spotless, simple, but quiet and cool. Shared balconies. Secure parking. A good choice. **E** *México*, México 201 and Aquiles Serdán, T981-3806. Good tidy rooms, basic, but the popular budget option. **E** *Zaragoza*, Zaragoza 917, T912-9275. Old and pretty, with bath, but a bit grubby, free drinking water, parking for motorbikes.

Sleeping
The expensive hotels are in the area known as the Zona Dorada; budget hotels are around the Old Town. Ask taxi drivers for the cheaper places

Camping   North of the city there are undeveloped beaches with free overnight camping; some have camped alone, but it is safer in a group (take bus to Sábalos and get out where it turns round). There are at least 10 trailer parks on Playa del Norte/Zona Dorada and on towards the north.

No shortage of places to eat. A little north of the old town, but many cheap street places selling fruit shakes and simple Mexican dishes at the beach end of Av Manuel G Nájera. A few recommendations: *Mamucas*, Bolívar 404. Seafood expensive. *Shrimp Bucket*, Olas Altas 11 and Av del Mar. Rightly famous for seafood, good environment, popular, good, mid-range. *La Cumbre*, Benito Juárez and Hidalgo. Few seats, very busy, not many tourists, open 1100-1500. Recommended. *El Paraíso*, on beach in Zona Dorada. Recommended. Also nearby is *Panama Joe Oster's Bar* with good music and busy in the tourist season. The best deal is at the market where you can get an excellent fish lunch for US$1.50.

Eating

Joe's Oyster Bar. Very good disco behind *Hotel Los Sábalos*, open-air, US$10 cover charge and open bar. *Edgar's Bar*, Aquiles Serdán. One of Mazatlán's oldest drinking joints.

Entertainment

Northwest Coast

Sports **Fishing** is the main sport (sailfish, tarpon, marlin, etc). Mazatlán's famous fishing tournament follows Acapulco's and precedes the one at Guaymas. In the mangrove swamps are egrets, flamingos, pelicans, cranes, herons, and duck. Nearby at Camarones there is **parasailing**, drawn by motorboats. The northern beach tourist strip offers boat trips to nearby deserted islands, snorkel hire and paragliding. **Bungee jumping** is done at junction Camarón Sábalo y Rafael Buelna opposite *McDonald's*, US$26. Always check with the locals whether **swimming** is safe, since there are strong rip currents in the Pacific, which run out to sea and are extremely dangerous. There are **bullfights** at Mazatlán, good view from general seats in the shade (*sombra*), although you can pay much more to get seats in the first 7 rows – Sun at 1600, very touristy.

Transport **Local** Green and white express buses on the 'Sábalo Centro' route run from Playa Cerritos to the city centre along the seafront road, US$0.35. Taxis charge an average US$3.50-US$5 between Zona Dorada and city centre. From Bahía del Puerto Viejo to centre, taxi US$1, bus US$0.20. **Car hire** all on Camarón Sábalo: *Budget*, No 402, T913-2000. *National*, No 7000, T913-6000, US$280 per week. *AGA*, No 316, T914-4405.

Air Aeropuerto General Rafael Buelna (MZT), 3 km from centre. Domestic flights to Ciudad Juárez, Durango, Guadalajara, Hermosillo, La Paz, Los Cabos, Mexico City, Monterrey, Piedras Negra, Tijuana and Torreón. International connections with San José (Costa Rica), Calgary (Canada), Denver, Houston, Los Angeles, Ontario (Calif), Phoenix, Portland, Salt Lake City, San Francisco, Seattle and Spokane (Washington).

Buses A big central terminal, making travel a bit easier, is just off the Carretera Internacional and Ferrusquilla s/n, about 3 km north of the Old Town, 4 km south of the Zona Dorado. Take 'Insurgentes' bus from terminal to Av Ejército Mexicano for the centre, via

Mazatlán centre

■ **Sleeping**
1 Belmar	4 La Siesta	7 San Fernando	10 Zaragoza
2 Del Centro	5 Lerma	8 San Jorge	
3 Del Río	6 México	9 Vialta	

Related map
Mazatlán, page 218

0 metres 200
0 yards 200

Music in Mazatlán

Firmly rooted and extremely popular in the State of Sinaloa is a type of orchestra known as the Banda Sinaloense orTamborera, which plays 'Chaparral' at almost any time of day or night in restaurants, dance halls, bars, at family parties or on the street. It usually has from 14 to 16 musicians: four saxophones,

four trumpets, clarinets, tuba, 3-4 men on drums and other percussion instruments, including maracas, guiro, and loud, strong voices. It is unabashed, brutal music, loud and lively. One such Banda plays every afternoon at the Chaparral bar, opposite the Conasupo market near the bus station.

market at Aquiles Serdán. *Transporte Norte de Sonora*, T981-2335, *Transportes del Pacífico*, T981-5156, *Estrella Blanca*, T982-1949.

Chihuahua: 1400 and 1800, 16 hrs, US$55. **Durango**: hourly from 0600 to 1900, 7 hrs, US$27. **Guadalajara**: 8 hrs, US$28. **Guaymas**: hourly, 11 hrs, US$36. **Los Mochis** 6 hrs, US$19. **Mexicali**: 24 hrs, US$72. **Mexico City**: 17 hrs, US$65. **Navojoa**: every 1½ hrs, 18 hrs, US$59. **Nogales**: every 1½ hrs, 18 hrs, US$58. **Puerto Vallarta**: 1600, 8 hrs, US$32. **Tepic**: 5 hrs, US$15. **Tijuana**: hourly, 26 hrs, US$82,

All services hourly, 24 hours a day, unless stated

Bus to **Rosario**: US$1.65, you can then (with difficulty) catch bus to Caimanero beach, nearly deserted (see below). Terminal Alamos, Av Guerrero Ote 402, 2 blocks from market, buses to **Alamos** every hr on the ½-hr.

Cycling Beware, the road Mazatlán-Tepic-Guadalajara has been described as 'the most dangerous in the world for cyclists'.

Ferry La Paz (Baja California Sur), see schedule, page 200, for other information see under La Paz, Baja California section. Allow plenty of time for booking and customs procedure. Tickets from *Hotel Aguamarina*, Av del Mar 110, with 10% commission, also from travel agents. Ferry terminal is at the southern end of Av del Puerto, quite a way from the centre (take bus marked 'Playa Sur', which also goes from the street corner opposite ferry terminal to Av Ejército Méxicano near bus station). **Ticket office** for La Paz ferry opens 0830-1300 only, on day of departure, arrive before 0800, unclaimed reservations on sale at 1100. Don't expect to get vehicle space for same-day departure.

Airline offices *Aero California*, T913-2042. *AeroMéxico*, T984-1111. *Mexicana*, T982-7722. **Banks** Many banks in the centre, near the plaza. *Banamex*, Juárez and Angel Flores, also Av Camarón Sábalo 434, 0900-1330, 1530-1730. *Casas de Cambio* on same avenida, Nos 109, 1009 and at junction with Rodolfo T Loaiza; also at R T Loaiza 309. *American Express*, Camarón Sábalo, T913-0600, open Mon-Fri 0900-1700, Sat 0900-1400. **Communications** Internet: *Mail Boxes Etc*, Camarón Sábalo 310, T916-4009, F916-4011, mail boxes, courier service, fax service, US$3.50 per 15 mins, mailboxes@red2000.com.mx; across the street at Centro Comercial Lomas. In the Old Town, a couple of internet cafés on the south side of the main plaza, US$1.50/hr. Also cheap international calls. *Sendnet*, in the bus terminal has aspirations to provide internet (US$1.80/hr) and international calls and faxes Open Mon-Fri 0600-2200, Sat-Sun 0900-1700. Post office: Juárez y 21 de Marzo, opposite Palacio Municipal, T981-2121. DHL is a couple of doors from *Mail Boxes Etc* (see above), Mon-Fri 0900-1330, Sat 1500-1800, 0830-1330. **Telephones**: 1 block from American Express; also 21 de Marzo y Juárez. Computel phone and fax service, Aquiles Serdán 1512, T985-0109, F985-0108. Phone rental, Accetel, Camarón Sábalo 310-4, T916-5056. There are public phones taking international credit cards all along Camarón Sábalo and RT Loaiza in the Zona Dorada for long-distance calls. **Embassies and consulates** *Canada*, Hotel Playa Mazatlán, Rodolfo T Loaiza 202, T913-7320. *France*, Jacarandas 6, T982-8552. *Netherlands*, Av Sábalo Cerritos, T913-5155. *Germany*, Jacarandas 10, T982-2809. *Italy*, Av Olas Altas 66-105, T981-4855. *Norway*, F Alcalde 4, T981-3237. *US*, RT Loaiza, opposite *Hotel Playa Mazatlán*, T/F916-5889, Mon-Fri 0930-1300, T913-4455 ext 285. **Hospitals** *Hospital General*, Av Ferrocarril, T984-0262. *Cruz Roja Mexicana*, Alvaro Obregón 73, T981-3690. There is a free Red Cross treatment station on Camarón Sábalo, opposite the *Beach Man*. **Laundry** *Lavandería*, on Zúñiga and Juárez, near *Hotel Lerma*. **Tour operators** *Explora Tours*, Centro Comercial Lomas, Av Camarón Sábalo 204-L-10, T913-9020, F916-1322, very helpful. Recommended. *Zafari Tours*, Paseo Claussen 25, ferry bookings, helpful. *Hudson Tours*, T913-1764, for mountain biking. **Useful telephone numbers** Emergency: call T06; Red Cross T981-3690; Ambulance T985-1451; Police T982-1867.

Directory

Northwest Coast

Mazatlán to Durango

Travel by day – the views are spectacular

Twenty-four kilometres beyond Mazatlán, the Coast-to-Coast Highway heads east to Durango (a spectacular stretch in good condition – a must see road section) turns off left at Villa Unión. Heading east, the road reaches **Concordia**, a delightful colonial town with a well-kept plaza and a splendid church (two **F** hotels, one at each end of town on the main road), then climbs the mountains past **Copala**, another mining ghost town (basic hotel); *Daniel's Restaurant*, open 0900-1700. On this road, 40 km from Concordia, 3 km before **Santa Lucía**, at La Capilla del Taxte, 1,240m, there is a good German hotel and restaurant, **D**, *Villa Blanca*, T(244) 442-1628. Before reaching **La Ciudad** (one very basic hotel) and the plains, the road goes through a spectacular section, winding through many vertical-sided canyons with partly forested slopes. The road is a phenomenal feat of engineering, as it is cut into the cliff side with steep drops below.

At one point, called **El Espinazo del Diablo** (Devil's Spine), the road crosses a narrow bridge (approximately 50 m long) with vertical drops either side and superb views to the south and north. No signs, just ask on the bus and the locals will tell you when it's coming up. If you're lucky you may be able to get the bus driver to stop. After reaching the high plateau, the road passes through heavily logged pine forests to Durango (see page 243). Cyclists will find this road hard work in this direction, as there are many bends and steep hills. Trucks are frequent but they travel at very reduced speeds.

South of Mazatlán

Route 15 continues south from Villa Unión. At **Rosario**, 68 km south of Mazatlán, an old mining town riddled with underground workings. There is an attractive and generally clean beach at **Playas El Caimanero**, about 45 km southwest of Rosario. Try the fish. Be careful of hiking around the Baluarte River valley as there are *caimanes* (alligators), hence the name of the beach. South of Rosario and several kilometres north of Escuinapa is **B** *Motel Virginia*, Carretera Internacional Km 1107-1108, T(694) 953-2755, good clean, *palapa* restaurant next door, possible trailer parking. There is a good seafood restaurant on the left at the entrance to **Escuinapa** coming from Mazatlán.

Teacapan

In Escuinapa a good road turns off 30 km to the coast at Teacapan. There is a bus that connects the two towns. The fishing is excellent and you can buy fresh fish directly from the fishermen on Teacapan beach. There are fine beaches such as **Las Cabras**, **La Tambora** and **Los Angeles**. Dolphins can be seen at certain times of year. Buses from Escuinapa; tours from Mazatlán US$45. The Institute of Archaeology is excavating a 25-m pyramid about 9.5 km east of Rancho Los Angeles; it is hoped that the site will be open to the public shortly.

Sleeping and eating **A** *Rancho Los Angeles*, Teacapan Ecológico (Las Palmas 1-B, Col Los Pinos, Mazatlán, T/F695-953-2550). Former home of a drug baron (deceased), 16 km north from Teacapan towards Escuinapa, on beach. Good value, luxurious swimming pool. Recommended. **D** *Hotel Denisse*, on square, T/F(695) 954-5266, José Morales and Carol Snobel. Clean, next to phone office, local trips arranged. There are 3 trailer parks (**Oregon**, US$8, no signs, on beach in town, run-down but one of better places to stay, new Mexican hotel next door; *Las Lupitas*. US$8, rustic, run-down; another on bay, take road next to *Las Lupitas*. US$3, primitive, pretty setting). *Sr Wayne's Restaurant*. On beach behind *Palmeras Hotel*. Recommended.

South of Escuinapa the road passes several quaint little towns: **Acaponeta** (turn-off for El Novillero beach, large waves and many sandflies), **Rosamorada**, **Tuxpan** and **Santiago Ixcuintla** (several hotels), all with colonial religious buildings and archaeological museums. Nearby is the tiny island of Mexcaltitán and, further south, the beaches at San Blas (see page 338). After Tepic, Route 15 heads inland to Guadalajara (see page 303).

Northern Highlands

Mexico City

The imposing Sierra Madre highlands of northern Mexico are rarely a destination in their own right. But these vast landscapes, at times barren and monotonous, hold some of Mexico's most spectacular surprises. The most important archaeological site in Northern Mexico is just a couple of hours' drive south of the border at Casas Grandes or Paquimé, a maze of multi-storeyed adobe buildings, once a thriving community with over 3,000 inhabitants. Don't expect to see too many dainty little dogs in Chihuahua; this, Mexico's biggest state, is the rugged land of Pancho Villa and there are museums and memorabilia dedicated to the Bandido-turned-Hero of the Revolution, even the bullet-ridden Dodge car he was finally gunned down in. It's dramatic stuff; and so is the Chihuahua-al-Pacífico, billed as 'the world's most scenic railroad', which wends its way across bridges, through tunnels and over the Sierra Madre down to the Pacific Coast at Los Mochis. It's a journey of a lifetime. Hikers will want to stop off at Creel or Divisadero to absorb the views, discover the awe-inspiring landscapes, strange rock formations and wildlife, visit Mexico's tallest waterfall and penetrate the vertiginous depths of the Barranca del Cobre, the Copper Canyon, bigger than Colorado's Grand Canyon. This is the craggy land of the Tarahumara Indians, and some 60,000 live in the Sierra where you can buy their hand-carved and woven crafts in any of the towns or villages. And if you're still looking for action, why not try some of the Wild-West kind and walk the streets of real Western film sets in the state of Durango.

Crossing into Mexico: Ciudad Juárez

From El Paso you can get on a bus outside Gate 9 of the Greyhound terminal and pay the driver (US$5); as you cross the border he should stop and wait for your documents to be processed. On entry you are automatically given 30 days to stay in Mexico, unless you ask for longer. Trolley buses cross the border for short trips. Alternatively you can walk across (US$0.35 toll per person). Walking from Mexico to the US costs US$0.55 (toll for cars leaving Mexico US$2.05). Border formalities are minimal. If you cross into the US as a non-US citizen and with a view to leaving the US by plane, you must ask for an immigration card for when you do leave. Remember, also, to make sure you have your US visa if you require one.

El Paso/ Ciudad Juárez

There is a new border crossing at Santa Teresa, New Mexico, just west of El Paso. Good for trucks and southbound travellers avoiding the congestion of Ciudad Juárez.

Ciudad Juárez

Crossing the border from El Paso, Texas you'll reach Ciudad Juárez, 1,866 km from Mexico City. Ciudad Juárez and El Paso have over 1.2 million people each; the cross-border industry has made Ciudad Juárez the largest *maquiladora* or workshop city in the world. Twin plant assembly and manufacturing operations now supersede tourism and agriculture in the city.

Phone code: 656
Colour map 2, grid A2
Population: 1,217,818
Altitude: 1,150 m

The Spanish conquistador Cabeza de Vaca discovered the Paso del Norte (Northern Pass) on the Camino Real. The name was retained until 1888 when Porfirio Díaz renamed the city after Benito Juárez. Today four bridges link the two cities.

El Paso is on Mountain Standard Time, which is one hour behind Central Standard Time and General Mexican Time.

The **tourist office** is on the ground floor of the Presidencia Municipal (City Hall), Malecón y Francisco Villa, on the left as you cross the Sante Fe bridge, T615-2301.

In Ciudad Juárez, the **Nuestra Señora de Guadalupe de El Paso del Norte** mission was the first established in the region; the building was completed in 1668. The mission, and the nearby **cathedral**, are two blocks west of Avenida Juárez on 16 de Septiembre. At the junction of Avenida Juárez and 16 de Septiembre is the

Sights
Very few services are open at weekends in El Paso

Northern Highlands

Aduana, the former customs building, now the **Museo Histórico**. In Parque Chamizal, just across the Córdova bridge, are the **Museo de Arte Prehispánico**, with exhibits from each Mexican state, the **Botanic Gardens** and a memorial to Benito Juárez. Continuing south down Avenida Lincoln, you come to the Pronaf area with the **Museo de Arte e Historia**. The University Cultural Centre and the **Fonart** artisan centre, which acts as a Mexican 'shop window', are well worth a look for the uninitiated tourist. The **Plaza Monumental de Toros**, López Mateos y Triunfo de la República, holds bullfights between April and August, and *charreadas* (rodeos) are held at the **Lienzo Charro**, Av del Charro. The main street is Avenida Juárez, on or near which are most of the souvenir shops, hotels, cheap and expensive restaurants, clubs and bars. The bars and other nightlife cater mostly for El Paso high school students who can drink at 18 in Mexico, but not until 21 in El Paso.

To the east of **El Paso**, over the border, the **Ysleta Mission** is the oldest in Texas (1680), built by Franciscan monks and Tigua Indians, who have a 'reservation' (more like a suburb) nearby; the Socorro mission (1681) and San Elizario Presidio (1789, rebuilt 1877-87) are in the same direction. There are a number of museums, including the **Americana Museum** in the Civic Centre (which also houses a performing arts centre, convention centre and tourist office), the **Museum of Art** at 1211 Montana, and the **Fort Bliss Air Defence Museum** of the nearby Air Base. Conducted tours of El Paso (US$10 – same price for Ciudad Juárez) usually take in Fort Bliss, the University, the Scenic Drive and the Tigua Reservation. El Paso **Tourist Office** is in the Civic Centre Plaza, T534-0686; also at the airport.

Ciudad Juárez / El Paso

Sleeping
■ *on map*

AL *Holiday Inn Express*, Paseo Triunfo de la República 8745, T629-6000, F629-6020. **C** *Continental*, Lerdo Sur 112 (downtown), T615-0084. Clean, TV, noisy, friendly, restaurant good. **D** *Correo*, Lerdo Sur 250, just across 16 de Septiembre. **D** *Hotel D'Manely*, close to bus station. Go out of the west (taxi) entrance, walk straight ahead across the parking lot to the street, cross the street, and walk left about 2 blocks. Heating, private bath. **E** *Juárez*, Lerdo Nte 143, close to Stanton St bridge. Comfortable, hot water, good value.

In **El Paso** there are many places to stay, including **B** *International Hotel*, on Oregon. A/c, TV, clean. Recommended. **D** *Gardner*, 311 East Franklin Av, T532-3661. Hot water, shared bath, TV and phone in room, rooms with bath available, also serves as **Youth Hostel**. **D** *Budget Lodge Motel*, 1301 N Mesa St, T915-533-6821. They take Visa, MC, and AmEx.

Eating
Many eating places either side of the border

In Juárez, *Taco Cabaña* on Calle de la Peña, next to *Hotel Continental*, and *El Gordo No 2*, Francisco Madero, ½ block from 16 de Septiembre. Both are good for tacos and

0 metres 500
0 yards 500

■ **Sleeping**
1 Correo   2 Gardner

burritos (about US$2-3). *Plaza Lerdo Café*, Lerdo Sur 285 at Galeana. Good breakfasts. *El Saucito*, Lerdo Sur 263. Popular, good breakfasts. *Florida*, Juárez 301, 2 blocks from *Hotel Impala*. Clean, good food and service. There are plenty of Chinese restaurants.

2-5 May, *Festival de la Raza*; music, dance, cultural events. **5 May** celebrations on Av **Festivals**
Juárez. **15 Sep**, Independence. **Jun-Jul**, *Feria Juárez* in Parque Chamizal.

Local Taxis: in Juárez, charge by zone, from US$2.75 to US$7.25. You can also negotiate **Transport**
with the driver for hourly rates. The going rate about US$20 per hour. Some cabs are allowed
to cross the border and take you to downtown El Paso; US$30.

Long distance Air: Ciudad Juárez's airport, Abraham González (CJS), is 19 km south of
the city (T619-0734); flights with *AeroMéxico, Aerolitoral, Taesa* and/or *Aero California* to Mexico City, Chihuahua, Ciudad Obregón, Culiacán, Durango, Guadalajara, Hermosillo, Ixtapa,
León, Los Cabos, Mazatlán, Monterrey, Torreón, Tijuana and Zacatecas. **El Paso's airport
(ELP)** is near Fort Bliss and Biggs Field military airbase with flights by *American, Delta, America West Airlines* and *Southwest Airlines* to all parts of the US. There are also flights to El Paso
from Chihuahua and Guadalajara. *Colectivo* from Ciudad Juárez airport to El Paso, or El Paso
airport, US$15.50.

Trains: station in Ciudad Juárez is at Eje Vial Juan Gabriel and Insurgentes, a couple of blocks
south of junction of Av Juárez and 16 de Septiembre. There are currently no passenger trains.

Road: *Sanborn's*, for insurance and information, 440 Raynolds, El Paso, T915-779-3538,
F772-1795, open Mon-Fri 0830-1700. AAA office: 916 Mesa Av, El Paso,
www.sanbornsinsurance.com

Buses: terminal is at Blvd Oscar Flores 4010, T613-2083, south of the centre. There is a taxi
information booth, which can give you estimated fares before you approach a driver. From
the terminal to centre or Santa Fe bridge, taxi fare is about US$8. If you walk from the termi-
nal to the highway, take any bus going to the right marked *'Centro'* for US$0.30. Shuttle bus
to **El Paso** Greyhound Terminal, US$5, hourly. The **Greyhound Terminal** is right downtown,
on the corner of San Antonio and Santa Fe streets, and from there you can get buses to
Laredo, Tucson, etc, and other connections in the US. They have buses every hr on the ½ hr to
Ciudad Juárez, from 0630 to 2130 that cost US$5. You can buy your ticket on the bus. It stops
at the Mexican side of the border for customs and immigration where you can pick up your
FM-T (tourist card) there. The Ciudad Juárez Bus Station has good sevices including long-distance telephones, money-changing facilities and left-luggage.

On the west side of the building is a taxi booth (tickets cost US$4.80 to the city centre). Exit
the west side (the same door you use to get taxis) and cross the parking lot to take any northbound bus to the city centre. Ticket counters for the various bus lines are on the north side of
the terminal.

Chihuahua: every ½ hr, 0700- 0200, 4½ hrs, US$20. *Chihuahenses Plus* hourly, 0400-2400.
Turistar Ejecutivo, 3 a day, US$28. **Durango**: every couple of hrs, US$62-51. **Guadalajara**:
1000, 1300 and 2200, US$81. **León**: 5 a day, US$75. **Matamoros**: 1630 and 2145, US$72.
Mexico City: 25 hrs, US$100. **Monterrey**: 1330, 1630 and 2145, US$62. **San Luis Potosí**:
US$72. **Zacatecas**: hourly from 0800-2400, US$62.

You can also buy tickets with *Omnibus de México*, www.omnibus.com.mx, for points in
the US: **Alburquerque, NM**: 1000, 1700, 2000, US$25. **Denver, Colorado**: 1000, 1900,
US$45. **Los Angeles, CA**: 1030, 1600, 1845, US$50. *Greyhound*, El Paso, T532-2365.
Turismos Rápidos, 828 South El Paso, off Santa Fe Bridge, to many US destinations.

Airline offices *Aero California*, T618-3399. *AeroMéxico*, T613-8719. **Banks** In Ciudad Juárez most **Directory**
cambios are on Av Juárez and Av de las Américas; there is also a *cambio* at the bus terminal. Rates vary
little. The best and most convenient exchange houses are in El Paso: *Valuta Corp*, 301 Paisano Drive,
buys and sells all foreign currencies but at poor rates, wires money transfers, open 24 hrs including

Northern Highlands

holidays. *Melek Corp*, 306 Paisano Drive, offers most of the same services as Valuta but only dollars and pesos, not open 24 hrs. If coming from US Immigration, when you reach Paisano Drive/Highway 62, turn east for these places. In El Paso, banks are closed on Sat. **Communications** Post office: on corner of Lerdo Sur and Ignacio de la Peña. **Embassies and consulates** *British*, Fresno 185, Campestre Juárez, T617-5791. *Mexican*, 910, E San Antonio, El Paso, T533-4082. *US*, López Mateos 924, Cd Juárez, T613-4048.

Ciudad Juárez to Chihuahua The road is wide, mostly flat, easy to drive, and not as interesting as the Gulf and Pacific routes. From Ciudad Juárez for some 50 km along the Río Bravo there is an oasis that grows cotton of an exceptionally high grade. The next 160 km of the road to Chihuahua are through desert.

Crossing into Mexico: Ojinaga to Chihuahua

Presidio/ Ojinaga
Phone code: 626
Population: 24,313

Chihuahua may also be reached from the border at Ojinaga, east of El Paso/Ciudad Juárez. This route is recommended not only for the ease of crossing, but also for the spectacular scenery either side of the border.

Crossing the border Follow signs to Ojinaga; pass US immigration on left (if you need to, surrender US visa waiver form here). On the Mexican side, a guard will check your passport. Those with vehicles then park before doing paperwork. Boys selling *chiclets* will look after your car/bike, but you can see it through the office windows. There are separate desks for personal and vehicle papers. Photocopying can be done for US$1. Get insurance before Presidio, no one sells it there, but you could ask Stella McKeel Agency, T915-229-3221/5, www.ridetherio.com/todo!.htm   Full details of entry requirement for drivers is given in Essentials, page 79. The border is open 24 hrs.

Leaving Mexico, note that the bus station is 2 km from the border. Make sure all your papers are stamped correctly.

Sleeping and eating   Ojinaga has 5 hotels, including **C** *Armendariz*, Zaragoza near Zócalo, T453-1198. Clean, safe parking. Cheap meals at *Lonchería Avenida* opposite bus station. **Festivals** 1-4 Jun. **Transport**   Daily buses to/from Chihuahua, US$6.

Directory   Banks: *Bancomer* on Zócalo, changes TCs, no commission; opposite is *Casa de Cambio Allende*, cash only, poorer rates.

Forty-two kilometres from Ojinaga on Route 16 towards Chihuahua is **El Peguis**, overlooking an extraordinary canyon. There is also a *garita*, where vehicle papers are checked.

Crossing into Mexico: Palomas and Agua Prieta

Columbus/ Palomas Route 2 runs west from Ciudad Juárez, roughly parallel with the Mexico-US border. Between Juárez and Janos, at the northern end of lateral Mexico 24, is the dusty border town of Palomas, Chihuahua, opposite Columbus, New Mexico. The modern border facilities are open 24 hours. Palomas itself has few attractions apart from limited duty-free shopping for liquor and pharmaceuticals, but Columbus was the site of Pancho Villa's 1916 incursion into New Mexico, which led to reprisals by the forces of American General John J Pershing. **The Columbus Historical Museum**, on the southeast corner of the highway intersection, contains many old photos of Pancho Villa, a copy of his death mask, and one of his sombreros; it also offers exhibits on Villa's sacking and burning of Columbus. There is a small shelf of books on the history of the town that you can browse through. The father of the museum's curator played a part in the battle. ■ *Daily 1000-1600*.

It's nearly 5 km from Columbus to the border, south on highway 11. Palomas is just across the border, and you park for free in a paved lot just before the border and walk across. The Mexican immigration office is just on the right as you cross the border. If you're driving, there's also a customs checkpoint at the border crossing. The customs' administrative building is about 60 m south of the immigration office.

Sleeping Reasonable accommodation at **D** *Hotel Restaurant San Francisco*, also **E** *Motel Santa Cruz*. Behind seafood restaurant, opposite gas station. Fairly basic. **E** *Hotel García*, Progreso 950. Basic. On the Columbus side, **A** *Martha's Place*, Main and Lima Sts, T505-531-2467, marthas@vtc.net It has a very attractive lobby and an attractive breakfast area. **C** *Motel Columbus*. **C** *Suncrest Inn*, Highway 11, just north of Highway 9. TV and phones in rooms: just ordinary. **Camping** Excellent, well-maintained sites at *Pancho Villa State Park*, opposite the Columbus Historical Museum, for US$7 per night, additional charge for electrical hook-up.

At the intersection of border Route 2 and Chihuahua Route 10 to Nuevo Casas Grandes is **Janos** (*Restaurant Durango*, de facto bus station at the intersection, has good inexpensive food; several others at junction, plus **D** *Hotel Restaurant La Fuente*). The landscape between Ciudad Juárez and Nuevo Casas Grandes (see below) is quite barren and, in the winter months, it can be cold.

Janos
Colour map 2, grid A2

Near Janos are the northernmost **Mennonite colonies** in Mexico; numerous vendors sell Mennonite cheese, which also has a market in upscale restaurants across the border in New Mexico. The German-speaking Mennonites are very conspicuous, the men in starched overalls and the women in long dresses and leggings, their heads covered with scarves.

Northwest of Janos, via border Route 2, are the border crossings of **Agua Prieta** (opposite Douglas, Arizona) and **Naco** (adjacent to its Arizona namesake and a short distance south of the historic, picturesque copper mining town of Bisbee). Agua Prieta is growing rapidly with the proliferation of *maquiladoras* on both sides of the border.

**Douglas/
Agua Prieta**
Phone code: 633
Colour map 2, grid A1
Population: 61,821

Crossing into Agua Prieta on foot, walk on the right-hand side of the road to enter Mexico. There are no obligatory checkpoints if you just want to see Agua Prieta. Otherwise, the **immigration office** for your FM-T (tourist card) is on the right just as you cross the border, and customs is just past it. You also pick up papers for your car here if you're driving, and get auto insurance. If you keep walking straight ahead you'll cross a street, which has buses running to the Agua Prieta bus station. Take buses running east, which have '13-20', 'Ejidal' or 'P Nuevo' on their front windows. Taxis charge US$3 from the border to the bus station, a 5-10- minute ride.

Agua Prieta is 162 km from Janos via Route 2, which crosses the scenic Sierra San Luis, covered by dense oak-juniper woodland, to the continental divide (elevation 1,820 m) at Puerto San Luis, the border between the states of Sonora and Chihuahua. There are outstanding views of the sprawling rangelands to the west. Southbound motorists from the US must present their papers to Mexican customs at La Joya, a lonely outpost 70 km northwest of Janos.

Sleeping **A** *Motel La Hacienda*, Calle Primera and Av 6T338-0621, a few blocks from the border. Best in town. **C** *Motel Arizona*, Av 6 between Calle 17 and 18, T338-2522. With heating, pleasant. **D** *Hotel Yolanda*, corner of Calle 2 and Av 4, T338-1253. Has restaurant. **D** *Hotel Linda*, Calle 4 between Av 7 and 8, T338-1550. Heat and hot water.

In **Naco**, the only formal accommodation is **D** *Motel Colonial*, which is often full, but the manager may tolerate a night's auto camping within the motel compound.

Accommodation is cheaper in **Douglas**, on the Arizona side. The venerable **B** *Gadsden Hotel*, 1046 G Av, T364-4481. A registered historical landmark, has been used as a location for Western films. Fabulous lobby, completely unexpected to find such a place in a border town. Recommended. **Camping** RV parks on the Arizona side charge about US$10 per night for vehicle, US$5 for tent camping: *Double Adobe Trailer Park* off Highway 80, *Copper Horse Shoe R V Park* on Highway 666.

Northern Highlands

Eating Agua Prieta, *El Pollo Loco*, near the plaza, for roasted chicken. 3 seafood restaurants: *Restaurant de Mariscos Hermanos Gómez*, corner of Calle 2 and 6; *Mariscos and Carnes 'La Palapa'*, Calle 6 between Av 11 and 12; and *Mariscos Mazatlán*, corner of Calle 5 and Av 16. **Naco**: *Restaurant Juárez*.

Transport Taxi: Armando Chávez, T335-2162. Recommended. If you are crossing the border, when you come to the first cross street, take a left and the office is just around the corner on the north side of the street.

Buses: the bus station in Agua Prieta is one small room with an adequate restaurant called *Don Camione*, and a Sendetel booth with phone and fax service.

There are services to: **Chihuahua**: every couple of hrs from 0600, US$32. **Ciudad Juárez**: 0900, 0930 and 2230. **Durango**: 1930, US$65. **Hermosillo**: every couple of hrs from 0600-1400, US$18. **Mexico City**: 1700. **Nogales**: every couple of hrs from 0830-1600, US$15. **Phoenix**: every 3 hrs from 0515-1630, US$42. **Tijuana**: *Norte de Sonora*, 2030. **Zacatecas**: *Cabellero Azteca* (all 2nd class), 2130, US$56.

Douglas has a small bus terminal, 538 14th Street, between Avs F and G, T364-2233, operated by *Greyhound* and *Autobuses Crucero*. **Tucson**, US$19. **Phoenix**, US$30. **Los Angeles**: US$65. The schedules for all the buses are the same: 0545, 1145, 1515, and 1715. The terminal closes at 1600 so you'd have to wait outside for the 1715 bus.

During winter **Directory** On the Douglas side, the Chamber of Commerce, T364-2477, at 1125 Pan American has good *Arizona time is the* information on Mexico as well as Arizona, with a wealth of maps (including Agua Prieta) and brochures. *same as Agua Prieta* *Librolandia del Centro*, a bookstore, has a good selection of material on local and regional history. **Medical** *time but during* **services** *Cruz Roja*: corner of Calle 17 and Av 6. From there they can take you to other hospitals. *summer Agua Prieta* **Pharmacies**: Open 24 hrs: 1 on the corner of Calle 3 and Av 8, and another on the corner of Av 5 and 7. *is one hour ahead*

Casas Grandes/Paquimé

Colour map 2, grid A2 The archaeological site of Casas Grandes, or Paquimé, can be reached from Chihuahua, Ciudad Juárez or Agua Prieta, roughly 60 km south of Janos on Route 2. **Nuevo Casas Grandes** is a town built around the railway; it is very dusty when dry, the wind blowing clouds of dust down the streets, and when wet the main street becomes a river. There is not much to do, but there are cinemas that show US and Mexican films.

Casas Grandes/Paquimé was probably a trading centre, which reached its peak between 1210 and 1261. The city was destroyed by fire in 1340. Its commercial influence is said to have reached as far as Colorado in the north and into southern Mexico. At its height, it had multi-storeyed buildings; the niches that held the beams for the upper floors are still visible in some structures. A water system, also visible, carried hot water from thermal springs to the north, and acted as drainage. Most of the buildings are of a type of adobe, but some are faced with stone. You can see a ball court and various plazas among the buildings. The site is well tended. ■ *1000-1700, US$3.50.* To get there take a yellow bus from outside the furniture shop at 16 de Septiembre y Constitución Pte in, US$0.20, 15 minutes. From the square in Casas Grandes village either take Calle Constitución south out of the square past the school, walk to the end of the road, cross a gully, then straight on for a bit, turn right and you will see the site, or take Avenida Juárez west out of the square and turn left at the sign to Paquimé, 1 km.

Paquimé ceramics, copying the original patterns, either black on black, or beige with intricate red and grey designs, are made in the village of **Mata Ortiz**, 21 km southwest of Nuevo Casas Grandes.

Sleeping **B** *Motel Hacienda*, Av Juárez 2603, T694-1046. The best, sometimes has Paquimé ceramics *In Nuevo Casas* on sale. **C** *Paquimé*, Av Benito Juárez, T694-1320. With fan and a/c, clean, large, pleasant. *Grandes only* Recommended. **D** *Juárez*, Obregón 110, between bus companies. Supposedly hot water, *Phone code: 636* some English spoken, friendly, safe parking, basic bathroom.

Northern Highlands

Café de la Esquina, 5 de Mayo y Obregón, near bus offices. Cheap, clean, friendly, popular. **Eating**
Tacos El Brasero, Obregón opposite *Hotel Juárez*. Open 24 hrs. *Dinno's Pizza*, Minerva y
Constitución Ote, opposite Cine Variedades. Fair, takes credit cards.

Buses All bus offices are on Alvaro Obregón. To **Ciudad Juárez**: several daily, 4 hrs, US$15. **Transport**
Chihuahua: 5 hrs, US$18. **Mexico City**: once a day via El Sueco, once via Cuauhtémoc. 3 a
day to **Agua Prieta**. Also 1 service a day to **Cuauhtémoc**, **Hermosillo**, **Madera**, **Monterrey**,
Nogales and **Tijuana**.

Banks Banks on 5 de Mayo and Constitución Ote; *Casa de Cambio California* next to hotel of that **Directory**
name. **Communications** Long-distance telephone: at Rivera bus office, on Alvaro Obregón.

Madera

Madera is in the Sierra Madre, northwest of Chihuahua, surrounded by rugged   *Phone code: 157*
mountain scenery. It is high enough to receive snow in winter (rainy season Septem-   *Colour map 2, grid A2*
ber-March, best time to visit May-August). The region around Madera has ample   *Population: 13,000*
scope for tourism: archaeological sites, bird-watching, hunting, fine landscapes and   *Altitude: 2,100 m*
good infrastructure.

C *Parador de la Sierra*, Calle 3 and Independencia, T572-0277. Clean, heating, discount for **Sleeping &**
more than 1 night, off-street parking, restaurant. **C** *María*, Calle 5 y 5 de Mayo. Cheaper **eating**
rooms available, heating, clean, limited parking, restaurant open 24 hrs. Good. **F** *Motel*
Maras, Calle 5 (1 block south of *Mirmay*). Hot water, noisy, clean apart from dusty rooms.
There are several restaurants in town.

Estrella Blanca bus (T572-0431) to/from Chihuahua every hr, takes 5 hrs, bus stop on Calle 5. **Transport**

Banks Banamex, Bancomer and Banrural with ATMs and will change dollars (possibly TCs). **Directory**

Around Madera

Madera is on an important waterfowl migratory route, with white-fronted, blue and
snow geese, mallard, pintail, teal, widgeon and redhead duck, and sandhill crane
passing through. This does mean that it has become a popular centre for shooting
(season mid-November to February), but bird-watching expeditions can be
arranged at *Motel Real del Bosque*.

    Taking Calle 3 in a northerly direction out of town you come to a signed turning
right to Las Varas, which leads to Casas Grandes (there is another, unsigned turning to Las Varas further on). Straight on is **El Salto**, a 35-m waterfall, best seen after
the spring thaw (March-April). The fall is along a track to the left; to see it you have
to walk round the rim of a little canyon. It is possible to hike down to the river
below (about one hour). Ask at the house on the track to the fall if you want to
camp (no facilities).

    Four kilometres from the turn-off to El Salto is the entrance to **Cuarenta Casas** (40
houses) 1½ hours from Madera. Cuarenta Casas is a series of cave dwellings, inhabited
originally by Indians of the Paquimé culture. Some of the houses have the
palet-shaped windows/doorways also seen at Casas Grandes (called here *La Cueva de*
las Ventanas); some are two storeys high. There is a good view of the cave houses from
the visitors' hut at the entrance. A trail descends to the river before climbing steeply to
the cave, a hike that takes 45 minutes-one hour one way. ■*0900-1600 daily (except 16*
Sep), free. Camping is possible only when personnel are staying the night; there are no
facilities other than water. (Tour from *Motel Real del Bosque*, takes six hours, US$65,
minimum four people; alternatively, hitchhiking is possible.)

    South of Madera is the **Misión Tres Ojitos**, where the Spanish priest, Padre
Espronceda, makes ham. Take the road to La Junta from Madera and at the signpost,

Northern Highlands

turn off right. On the dirt road, take the left fork through the village. Go past the church and on the right the Mission is signed (10 km from Madera).

around madera

In Madera there is a sign indicating **Zona Arqueológica Huapoca**, going west on Independencia. At Km 13 on this good dirt road is **Lago Campo 3**, shallow and marshy, with wildlife. Eighteen kilometres from town you reach an altitude of 2,500 m, with stunning views of the Sierra Madre. Plenty of birdlife can be seen from the road. At Km 41 is the entrance to the **Zona Arqueológica Anasazi**, which contains the **Nido del Aguila** (Eagle's Nest) cave dwellings and the **Cueva del Serpiente** (Serpent's Cave). The 2-km road to the site is terrible and about 300 m are impassable (you have to find somewhere to leave your car before the so-called 'car park'). There is no path to the Nido del Aguila, and a guide is recommended.

Chihuahua

Phone code: 614
Colour map 2, grid B2
Population: 670,208
Altitude: 1,420 m

The capital of Chihuahua state and centre of a mining and cattle area, Chihuahua City is 375 km from the border and 1,479 km from the capital. It is mostly a modern and rather run-down industrial city, but has strong historical connections, especially with the Mexican Revolution. Pancho Villa operated in the surrounding country, and once captured the city by disguising his men as peasants going to market. There are also associations with the last days of Independence hero Padre Hidalgo. Summer temperatures often reach 40°C but be prepared for ice at night as late as November. Rain falls from July to September.

The **tourist offices** in the Libertad 1300, Edificio Agustín Melgar, 1st floor, T/F429-3421, has general information, but not that up to date. ■ *Mon-Fri 0900-1900, Sat-Sun 0900-1400.* The tourism website is at **www.chihuahua.gob.mx**

Sights The old tower of the **Capilla Real** where Hidalgo awaited his execution is now in the **Palacio Federal** (Libertad y Guerrero). The dungeon (*calabozo*) is quite unremarkable and the Palacio itself is very neglected. The **Palacio de Gobierno**, on the other hand, is in fine condition, with a dramatic set of murals by Aaron Piña Morales depicting Chihuahua's history. There are a number of old mansions (see Museums below) and the Paseo Bolívar area is pleasant. Calle Libertad is for pedestrians only from Plaza Constitución to the Palacio de Gobierno and Palacio Federal. Calle 4 and streets that cross it northwest of Juárez are bustling with market stalls and restaurants. Worth looking at is the **cathedral** on Plaza Constitución, begun 1717, finished 1789; its Baroque façade dates from 1738, the interior is mostly unadorned, with square columns, glass chandeliers and a carved altarpiece. In the southeast of the town near Calle Zarco are ancient aqueducts. Walk north along Ocampo and over the river for fine views of the city at sunset.

Museums The **Quinta Luz** (1914), Calle 10 No 3014, where Pancho Villa lived, is now the **Museo de la Revolución**, with many old photographs, the car in which Villa was assassinated (looking like a Swiss cheese from all the bullet holes), his death mask and postcards of the assassinated leader, well worth a visit. ■ *0900-1300 and 1500-1900, US$1.* The **Museo Regional**, in the former mansion Quinta Gameros at Bolívar 401, has interesting exhibits and extremely fine Art-Nouveau rooms: the dining room, the child's room that features Little Red Riding Hood scenes; the bathroom, with frogs playing among reeds, etc, an exhibition of Paquimé ceramics, as well as temporary exhibitions. ■ *Tue-Sun 0900-1300, 1600-1900, US$0.70.* **Museo de Arte e Industria Populares**, Av Reforma 5 (Tarahumara art and lifestyle; shops). ■ *Tue-Sat 0900-1300, 1600-1900, free.* The **Museo Casa Juárez**, Juárez y Calle 5 was once the house and office of Benito Juárez. ■ *Mon-Fri 0900-1500, 1600-1800.*

AL *San Francisco*, Victoria 409, T416-7770. *Degá* restaurant good for steaks. **B** *El Campanario*, Blvd Díaz Ordaz 1405, southwest of cathedral, T415-4545. Good rooms, clean, TV. Recommended. **C** *Del Cobre*, Calle 10A y Progreso T415-1730. With bathroom, hot water, TV, very comfortable, *Bejarano* restaurant good, reasonable laundry. **D-E** *Reforma*, Victoria 809, T410-6848. Also colonial-style (including rooms, some floors look unsafe), friendly, clean, fan, hot water, restaurant, TV in reception, safe, parking next door for cars (US$0.25) or motorbikes in courtyard. Recommended. **D-E** *Cortés*, Gómez Farías 6, near Plaza

Sleeping
■ *on map*
Price codes:
see inside front cover

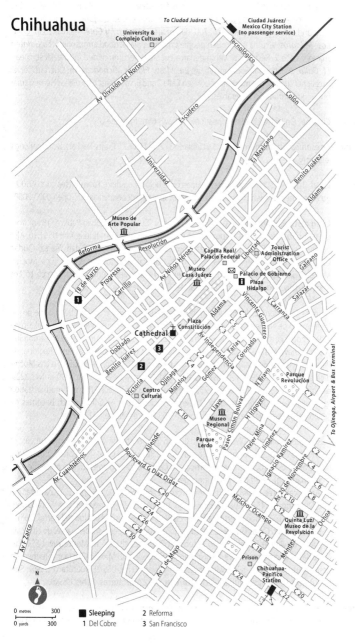

Chihuahua

To Ciudad Juárez

Ciudad Juárez/
Mexico City Station
(no passenger service)

University &
Complejo Cultural

Museo de
Arte Popular

Capilla Real/
Palacio Federal

Tourist
Administration
Office

Museo
Casa Juárez

Palacio de Gobierno

Plaza
Hidalgo

Plaza
Constitución

Cathedral

Centro
Cultural

Museo
Regional

Parque
Revolución

Parque
Lerdo

Quinta Luz/
Museo de la
Revolución

Prison

Chihuahua-
Pacífico
Station

To Ojinaga, Airport & Bus Terminal

0 metres 300
0 yards   300

■ **Sleeping**
1 Del Cobre

2 Reforma
3 San Francisco

Northern Highlands

Constitución, T410-0471. Clean, quiet, big courtyard, pleasant. **E** *San Juan*, Victoria 823, T410-0035. In old colonial house, but rooms (repairs needed, a bit sombre) are in another part, reasonable food, water sometimes scarce, friendly. **E** *Casa de Huéspedes*, Libertad 1405. With bath, basic but clean, several others in the same street. The cheaper hotels are in Juárez and its cross-streets; the cheapest are behind the cathedral.

Eating The smartest and best are in the *Zona Dorada*, northeast of the centre on Juárez, near Colón, eg: *Los Parados de Tomy Vega*, Juárez 3316; *La Calesa*, Juárez y Colón; and *La Olla*, Juárez 3331. Excellent steaks. *La Parilla*, Victoria 450. Recommended. *Quijote's*, Victoria 807. Good food and value, buffet meals till 1700, dinner also, friendly. *Mi Café*, Victoria 1000. Good. *Los Milagros*, Victoria 812. Young people's meeting place, good atmosphere. *La Galatea*, Juárez y Calle 2. Restaurant within department store, recommended for breakfast, cheap. *El Gallo*, on Libertad. Good and cheap breakfasts. *Flor de Michoacán*, on Libertad. Serves excellent *licuados*. The **market** is between Calle 2 and 6, southeast of Av Niños Héroes, small but good for fruit and vegetables.

Entertainment **Cinema** On Universidad near post office, shows films from the US.

Shopping *Artesanías Tarahumaras*, Calle 5 y Doblado 312, T413-0627. Crafts, baskets, wood carvings, jewellery.

Transport **Local Taxis** work on a zone system. Agree price before boarding. **Town buses** cost US$0.20, go everywhere, ask which one to take. **Bicycle spares** Independencia 807, open 0900-2000.

Long distance Air Airport Gen Fierro Villalobos (CUU) on Blvd Juan Pablo II, 18 km from centre on road to Ojinaga. Airport buses collect passengers from hotels, fare US$1.10. Also minibuses. Taxi US$16 (no other transport at night). Flights to Ciudad Juárez, Ciudad Obregón, Culiacán, Guadalajara, Hermosillo, La Paz, Loreto, Los Cabos, Los Mochis, Manzanillo, Mazatlán, Mexico City, Monterrey, Tijuana and Torreón. *AeroMéxico* to Los Angeles daily, and *Aerolitoral* to Dallas and El Paso in the US.

Trains The station for the 631-km Chihuahua-Pacífico railway is 1 block behind the prison (near Av 20 de Noviembre and Blvd Díaz Ordaz – take bus marked Rosario, or walk up Av Independencia, then right along Paseo Bolívar or Av 20 de Noviembre); in the early morning you may have to take a taxi. Information and tickets by post: Departamento Regional de Pasajeros, Apdo Postal 46, Chihuahua, CHIH, México, T415-7756, F410-9059. To Los Mochis daily at 0700, arrives 1950, returns 0600 arrives 2050, also Mon, Wed, Fri at 0800, arrives 2225, returns Tue, Thu, Sat 0700, arrives 2325 (see page 233 for details). There is another station (currently freight only) 3 km along Av Niños Héroes, left at Av Colón, which becomes Av Tecnológico, past the river and right along Av División del Norte, T413-0714.

Buses Bus terminal on Blvd Juan Pablo II, 8 km from centre on way to airport, southeast of town, T420-2286, 20 mins by bus to centre (US$0.30), or taxi US$4 (fixed price). Buses from centre at Niños Héroes between Ocampo and Calle 10. There is an exchange office (beware short-changing), cafetería and left luggage.
  Aguascalientes: US$48. To **Creel**: every couple of hrs from 0600, 4-5 hrs, US$16, paved all the way; **Durango**: US$45. To **Guadalajara**: several, US$57, including *Estrella Blanca*, which also goes to **Acapulco**, US$88, and **Puerto Vallarta**, US$81. 2nd class bus, to **Hidalgo del Parral**: 2½ hrs, US$11. To **Nuevo Casas Grandes**: see above (note that Chihuahua- Madera buses go either via El Sueco, or via the Sierra). **Nuevo Laredo**: at 2030, US$48; also to **Monterrey**: US$44, to **Mazatlán**: 2 companies, US$53, 19 hrs, heart-stopping view; to **Mexico City** (and intermediate destinations): frequent services with several companies, 20 hrs, US$79; **Querétaro**: US$62; **San Luis Potosí**: US$48; and **Saltillo**: US$35. **Torreón**: US$22. **Zacatecas**: 12 hrs, US$48.

Directory **Airline offices** *AeroMéxico*, T415-6303. **Banks** *Bancomer* on Plaza Constitución offers better rates than *Multibanco Comermex* on same square. *Casa de Cambio Rachasa*, Independencia y Guadalupe

Chihuahua-Pacífico Primera Express*

Chihuahua-Los Mochis		Price	Destination	Price
0600		Chihuahua	$109	1950
0815	$22	Cuauhtémoc	$86	1725
1125	$49	Creel	$59	1414
1245 (20-min wait)	$59	Divisadero	$50	1235 (20-min wait)
1320	$60	Posada	$49	1225
1330 (10-min wait)	$61	San Rafael	$47	1205 (10-min wait)
1432	$67	Bahuichivo	$42	1112
1530	$73	Temoris	$36	1011
1815	$95	El Fuerte	$20	0726
1950	$109	Los Mochis		0600

Los Mochis-Chihuahua (read from bottom)
*Económica class tickets are roughly half price, see text for details

Victoria, on Plaza, poorer rates, no commission on cash, 2 on TCs, open Mon-Sat 0900-2100 (also at Aldama 711). Exchange is available in the bus terminal, but rates are slightly better downtown. **Communications** Internet: *Cyber Café Canaco*, Chamber of Commerce, Av Cuauhtémoc 1800, 2nd floor, US$3.75 per hour. **Telephone**: Libertad, in the Palacio Federal. Also in Central Camionera. Credit card phone outside *AeroMéxico* office on Guadalupe Victoria, ½ block from Plaza Constitución (towards Carranza). Main phone office on Av Universidad. **Laundry** Ocampo 1412. Julián Carrillo 402. **Tour operators** *Guillermo Bechman*, T413-0253, arranges stays at cabins above Bahuichivo, near Copper Canyon. *Viajes Flamingo*, Santa Anita Hotel, T412-1613, F418-3393, will book train tickets in advance, no commission charged, English spoken. *Turismo Al Mar*, T416-5950, accommodation and rail packages to Copper Canyon, 5 nights and some meals, US$500 for 2 people.

Route 16 leads west through Ciudad Cuauhtémoc and La Junta to the Basaseachi falls, which, at 311 m, is the highest single-jump waterfall in North America – described by one reader as definitely worth the effort. The top of the falls is 3 km from town (2 km by good dirt road, 1 km by signed trail). A paved road leads to a car park (with taco stalls) and *mirador* 1½ km above the falls. From here a path leads to the top of the falls and continues steeply to the pool at the bottom (best to swim in the morning when the sun still strikes the pool). Hitching is difficult here, better to take a tour (US$16). The falls can also be reached from Creel (see below) via San Juanito along a very rough road. Route 16 goes on through beautiful mountains and forest to **Yepachic**, winding its way through Maycoba, Yécora and **San Nicolás** into Sonora. From San Nicolás the road continues to Hermosillo. The scenery is beautiful, the services in the villages limited, but you will probably not meet another tourist.

Basaseachi Falls
Colour map 2, grid B2
The falls are at their best in July-September

Chihuahua to Los Mochis: the Copper Canyon Railroad

The **Chihuahua al Pacífico** train journey to Los Mochis is spectacular and exciting especially on the descent through the Barranca del Cobre, the Copper Canyon, to the coast beyond Creel: it's lauded as one of the great journeys in the world and with good reason. As a result it's popular and at busy times you will need to book seats in advance. Sit on the left-hand side of the carriage going down to Los Mochis, right-hand side coming up from Los Mochis.

Northern Highlands

Train details The schedule on page 233 is for *Primera* (**first class**). These tickets can be pre-booked at travel agents in Chihuahua, Los Mochis (see page 213) and some stations along the way. The schedule is an approximation of intent, but check details as they are subject to change. On average trains are about one hour late by the time they arrive in Los Mochis. Bring your own drinking water and toilet paper. Do not take large amounts of cash or jewellery, there can be security problems on the railway.

A **second class train** (*mixto* or *clase económica*) also runs but travelling on it is much more difficult. You can only buy tickets in person, they are sold once the first train has left or passed through, the train leaves in theory about one hour after the first class land the timetable is quintessentially latino – the train may be along, it may be along tomorrow. Prices are roughly half that of the first-class train.

The most interesting part of the journey is between Creel and Los Mochis. If wishing to see the best scenery, there is little point in taking the train Chihuahua-Creel-Chihuahua (on this stretch, the cheaper train is just as good as the *Primera Especial*). If planning to spend a few days in Creel, there are frequent buses Chihuahua-Creel. Delays are possible in the rainy season. ■ For enquiries contact the information and reservations office on T01-800-122-4373, or www.ferromex.com.mx

West of Chihuahua are high plains, windy and sparsely populated. From Chihuahua, the railway and road (Route 16, *cuota* and *libre* after Km 45; the latter is good) cross the Sierra of the Tarahumara Indians, who call themselves the *Raramuri* ('those who run fast'). They were originally cave-dwellers and nomads, but now work as day-labourers in the logging stations and have settled around the mission churches built by the Spanish in the 17th century.

Creel

Phone code: 635
Colour map 2, grid B2
Population: 5,000
Altitude: 2,356 m

Creel (very cold in winter) is the commercial centre of the Tarahumara region, important for its timber and as a tourist centre. Creel is easily reached by car from El Paso or Arizona. The town is named after Enrique Creel (1854-1931), economist and entrepreneur, governor of Chihuahua state in 1907, who initiated the building of the railway and planned to improve the Tarahumara's lives by establishing a colony here. His statue stands in the central square, just below the railway. Around the square are two churches (one of which broadcasts classical music in the evening), the Presidencia Municipal (containing the post office; second door inside on right), Banca Serfín and the Misión Tarahumara. The Misión has maps of the region (US$5 for topographical sheets, US$2.50 for simpler ones), a description of the train ride and other good buys (such as excellent photographs, wood carvings, baskets and books). It acts as a quasi-tourist office. ■ *Mon-Sat 0900-1300, 1500-1800, Sun 0900-1300.*

There are several souvenir shops selling Tarahumara weavings, musical instruments, pine-needle baskets, etc. Also on sale are books such as *The National Parks of Northwest Mexico* and *Tarahumara of the Sierra Madre* by John Kennedy (published by AHM, ISBN 0-88295-614-0).

Sleeping
■ *on map*
Make hotel reservations in advance as not many rooms are available

AL *The Lodge at Creel*, used to be *Pensión Creel*, Av López Mateos 61, about 1 km from the plaza and railway station, T456-0071, F456-0082, lodgecreel@ infosel.net.mx Including breakfast and dinner. **B** *Margarita Plaza Mexicana*, Elsido Batista, T456-0245. Including dinner and breakfast, bar. **B** *Parador La Montaña*, Av López Mateos 44, T456-0075, F456-0085 (full board available). Will exchange foreign currency at reasonable rates, TV, clean, quiet, restaurant, bar, organizes excursions, safe parking. **B** *Nuevo*, other side of railway from station, T456-0022, F456-0043. Meals overpriced, but nice and clean, some inside rooms dark. *Parador* and *Cascada* have live music most evenings.

C-D *Korachi*, Francisco Villa 16, T456-0207. Right beside the station, and a good budget choice. **C-E** *Cabañas Berti's*, Av López Mateos 31, T456-0086. Heating, soap and towels, parking, 1 kitchenette, excursions, friendly owner Sr Sergio Arnoldo Rascón plays

Northern Highlands

guitar in local clubs. **C** *Los Piños*, has similar rooms and is a good choice. **D** *Posada de Creel*, 1½ blocks south of station on opposite side of the tracks, T/F456-0142, Apdo Postal 7. Remodelled building, gas fires in rooms, very clean, **E** in room. Not helpful. **F** per person without bath in dormitory. Hot water, helpful, English-speaking managers, coffee served from 0630. Recommended. **F** per person *Casa de Huéspedes Margarita*, López Mateos 11, T456-0045, between the 2 churches on corner of square. Cheapest in dormitory (packed in high season with mattresses on floor) rising to **D**, double with bath, breakfast and dinner included, good communal meals, very popular meeting place (book in advance in high season), Margarita's reps meet arriving train passengers, quite pushy, organizes tours (see below), horses can be hired (US$2.50 per hour with guide, lazy horses). Highly recommended (if full, Margarita's sister will put you up for **E** with dinner and breakfast, enjoyable).

Creel

To Chihuahua
Av Tarahumara
Estrella Blanca
Misión Tarahumara
Town Map
Parroquia
Main Plaza
Zapata
E Creel
Presidencia Municipal
Francisco Villa
Av López Mateos
Oscar Flores
Elfido Batista Caro
Divisadero, Cusárare & Laguna Arareco
To Cerro Chapultepec
Av Cuesta
To Divisadero & Los Mochis
To Cusárare
Comercial de Creel Supermarket

N

metres 50
yards 50

● **Sleeping**
Casa de Huéspedes Margarita

2 Margarita Plaza Mexicana
3 Nuevo
4 Parador La Montaña
5 Posada de Creel

● **Eating**
1 Heladería & Mi Café

There are plenty of eating places in the town, on López Mateos, eg *Verónica*. Good *comida corrida*. *Estela*. Also good, open 0800-2100 and on Sun. *Café El Manzano*, beside railway line. Good food. *Panadería* next to *Estela*. *Bar Plaza Mexicana*, on Elfido Batista Caro, owned by *Margarita's* (see hotels). Recommended. Good ice-cream shop (*heladería*) on López Mateos between Parroquía and Oscar Flores. Next door is *Mi Café*. Good food, cheap, try the apple *empanadas*, friendly. There's a general stores on López Mateos.

Eating
Water shortages are common

Rock climbing *Expediciones Umarike* (see Bicycle hire below), US$50 per ½ day, at Humira (road to Batópilas), Chapultepec rock (in town) abseil at Basaseachi, bouldering. Generally top rope climbing because of loose volcanic rock. Rents out tents (US$6.50 per night), sleeping bags, stoves.

Sport

Trains For schedule see page 233. Station office is open Mon 0800-1000, 1100-1600; Tue-Fri 1000-1600, Sat 1000-1300. From Creel to Los Mochis takes about 8 hrs on the train.

Buses Buses to surrounding villages all leave from outside *Hotel Korachi*, across railway track from square. To **Chihuahua**: every couple of hrs from 0600, US$16, 4-5 hrs. To **Ciudad Juárez**, 0800. To **Cusárare** (see below): at 0700, US$2.50, or lift in *Margarita's* transport US$6, or hitchhike. To **Guachochi**: 1200, 1730, US$4.50. To **San Rafael** via **Divisadero**: at 1030, 1500 and 1830, US$3 to Divisadero.

Transport

Banks *Banca Serfín*, on the square, very friendly, open 0900-1300, changes dollars cash with no commission, but commission charged on TCs (US$1 per cheque), TCs must be authorized by manager, Visa and MasterCard advances, no commission. **Communications** Post office: on

Directory
There is a time change (though generally not recognized locally) between Creel (GMT – 6 hrs) and Los Mochis (GMT – 7 hrs)

Northern Highlands

Tarahumara Indians

This is the country of the long-haired, fleet-footed Tarahumara Indians, able, it is said, to outstrip a galloping horse and to run down birds. A few Indians can be seen in Chihuahua and Nuevo Casas Grandes, mostly women and children and most, sadly, *begging. Tarahumara can be seen in much less unfortunate conditions and in greater numbers in Creel and beyond, but note that the Indians are shy, living in remote ranchos rather than the towns. A Tarahumara festival is held on the 12 December.*

main square in Presidencia Municipal, no sign. **Telephone**: long-distance phone office in *Hotel Nuevo*. **Laundry** Pink house opposite side of tracks from square, US$3 per load, 2 hrs, good, Mon-Sat 0900-2000, restricted hrs on Sun. **Tour operators** Many people hang around the square offering tours in a variety of vehicles, or other means of transport. *Roberto Venegas*, T456-0049, has a van. Recommended. **Horses**: for rent at several locations, eg Rarajipa 18 (near *Expediciones Umarike*), US$4 per hour to Cristo Rey statue above town, US$3.20 per hour for 4-5 hr ride to waterfalls. **Bicycle hire**: *Expediciones Umarike*, Av Ferrocarril s/n, north of tracks west of Plaza, PO Box 61, T/F456-0212. Run by Arturo Gutiérrez and his Welsh wife Audrey, very friendly, open every day, cosy offices with literature and real coffee, US$6.50 for ½ day, US$10.50 whole day, provide map, good bikes, must deposit ID; longer guided tours available on bike or in 4WD, eg to Tararecua Canyon. Bikes from several other places roughly US$13 for the day – look around if you need better bikes.

Excursions from Creel Creel is an excellent centre for trekking and horse-riding. It is also a good centre for reaching several deep canyons, including that of the Río Urique, known as the Barranca del Urique, or del Cobre (the Urique, or Copper Canyon – see below).

From the town, footpaths lead to the Cristo Rey statue, to a viewpoint on Cerro Chapultepec and into the hills around. To see inhabited Tarahumara caves, turn right off the main road south out of town, about five minutes (by car) after the turn-off signed to San Rafael. It seems that visitors are no longer particularly welcome. Further to the south, walk to the San Ignacio Mission, passing the Valle de los Hongos (Valley of the Mushrooms). Continue to **Laguna Arareco** (8 km from Creel), around which one can walk. ■ *US$1.30*. The lake is just off the Creel-Guachochi/Batópilas road. Together these make up the Complejo Ecoturístico Arareko, ■ *Entrance US$1.80 – an easy day ride from Creel*.

Just past Laguna Arareco is an unsigned right turn on to a bumpy track, which leads, in 1½ hours in a hardy vehicle, to the top of the **Recohauta canyon**. A clear path descends, in an hour or so, to a dry river first, and then the Río Tararécua. Follow the path along the river to where hot springs come out of the canyon's side. A pool has been made. Backpacking in the canyon is beautiful and, with a topographical map, original walks are easy to do, as there are more trails than shown on maps.

Cusárare
Colour map 2, grid B2

Twenty kilometres south of Laguna Arareco, is Cusárare ('Place of the eagles'), with a Jesuit church (1767) painted by Indians, and a 30-m waterfall. ■ *US$1*. To get to the falls, continue 100 m after the junction to Cusárare where there is a hotel sign on the right; turn right, pass the hotel and then the bridge, at the junction turn right, about 45 minute's walk; it is not well-signposted. There is very good hiking around Cusárare, but a guide may be necessary. Sr Reyes Ramírez and his son have been recommended for tours to the canyon, US$20 per day for two people, including guide and two pack donkeys. Allow four days to see the canyon properly, tough hiking. The canyon is hot by day and cold by night. Accommodation is extra. The American guide Cristóbal, at *Margarita's*, has also been recommended.

Guachochi
Colour map 2, grid B2

Guachochi, 156 km south of Creel, has a Wild West appearance. There is a bank in town. From Guachochi you can walk four hours to the impressive **Barranca de Sinforosa**. The canyon is not visible until you reach the edge. From a point several hundred metres above the Río Verde you can see an unforgettable

Northern Highlands

extended system of immense canyons, grander (according to some) than you can see from El Divisadero or on crossing the Barranca del Cobre. You can descend to the river on a path.

Sleeping C *Melina*, Belisario Domínguez 14, T30255. Clean, hot water, bar. **D** *Chaparre*, T30001. Overpriced but good restaurant, bath, TV, hot water. **E** *Orpimel*, in same building as bus station.

Buses To Creel twice daily 0730 and 1330, US$4 (check at *Hotel Korachi* for schedule from Creel); also reached from Hidalgo del Parral, bus leaves for Parral at 0800 and 1200, now paved, but not spectacular.

Copper Canyon

The road south out of Cusárare leads eventually to Batópilas, passing a turn-off to El Tejabán above the **Barranca del Urique/Cobre** (this is claimed to be the 'real' Copper Canyon); **Basíhuare** ('Sash') village, surrounded by pink and white rock formations (40 km from Creel); and the Puente del Río Urique, spanning the Urique Canyon. The climate is ideal for camping. At the junction Creel-Guachochi-Bufa, near Samachique, is a small restaurant/hotel, **F** *La Casita*. Very primitive and romantic. The road is paved as far as the junction but is bumpy from then on. Just after the junction, 3 km down into the valley is **Samachique**, where the *rari-pame* race, kicking a wooden ball for 241 km without rest, often takes 2-3 days and nights in September. Stranded travellers can find a room and food at the bus stop (no more than a shack) in Samachique, which is 1 km off the main route to Batópilas (1330 bus from Guachochi arrives at 1500 after Creel bus has gone through). If wishing to hitch to Batópilas (2½-hour drive) take the right fork as you walk back out of Samachique; it rejoins the route at a junction where you can wait for traffic both coming through and by-passing the village. **Quírare**, 65 km from Creel, offers views of the beautiful **Batópilas Canyon**. After Quírare there is an awesome 14-km descent to La Bufa, in the Batópilas canyon, and on to Batópilas, possibly the most scenic road in northern Mexico.

Colour map 2, grid B2

Copper Canyon area

Batópilas

Batópilas, 120 km from Creel, is a little town of 1,100 inhabitants, quiet, palm-fringed, subtropical, delightful and hot, hemmed in by the swirling river and the cactus-studded canyon walls. It is an excellent centre for walking and within easy reach of the Urique Canyon (see box). Europeans arrived here in 1690. The Mina de Guadalupe was discovered in 1780 by Pedro de la Cruz. Batópilas became a thriving silver-mining centre, with mines owned by the Shepard family. Their mansion (near the bridge), abandoned during Pancho Villa's campaign, must be one of the most elaborate adobe houses anywhere, but it is now overgrown and dilapidated. Shepard, whose big strike was La Bufa mine, built houses, bridges and canals around the town.

Northern Highlands

Batópilas to Urique

A three-day hike goes from the Batópilas Canyon to Urique (once known as the Camino Real, or Royal Way), from where you can get a ride to Bahuichivo for a train to Creel or Los Mochis.

Routes Batópilas-Cerro Colorado Piedra Redonda-Cerro El Manzano-La Estación-Los Alisos-Urique. You climb from 500 m, reaching 2,200 m before descending to Urique at 600 m. It can be very hot in the canyons; drink at least four litres of water a day (you can fill up at settlements along the way) and take plenty of sunblock. There are many junctions of paths and so if you are without a guide it is vital to check that you are on the correct route as often as possible (try not to wander into marijuana plantations). One recommendation if you are using the 'Batópilas' survey map (1:50,000 sheet G13A41, covering the entire route, available from the Misión Tarahumara in Creel US$5) is that you take the ridge path (not marked on the 1979 edition) after Cerro El Manzano to La Estación, both for the views and directness.

Horse-riding A recommended guide (not cheap) is Librado Balderrama Contreras who will guide you to Urique or to surrounding attractions such as Mesa Quimoba, Mesa de San José and Monerachi. There are several places in town where you can hire mules (with a handler) for carrying gear.

Sleeping C *Mary*, reservations as for *Parador de la Montaña* in Creel. D *Monse*, on the main plaza, with a few simple rooms and private showers, cheaper for longer stays. D *Juanita*, on central plaza, very clean and recommended. E *Batópilas*. Clean, also *Parador Batópilas*, more expensive, but not too much. E *Chulavista*, on way into town, owned by Don Mario, near bridge at entrance to village. Clean, hot water, tiny rooms. Basic rooms also at F *Restaurant Clarita*.

Eating *La Quinta*, round the corner from the *Hotel Mari*, has been recommended by a couple of readers. *El Puente Colgante*. New, pleasant and friendly, garden, cold beer, bit pricey. Meals at the private house of Sra Enedina Caraveo de Hernández on Plaza Constitución are good and cheap, large portions. *Carolina*, between bridge and centre. Friendly owner. In the village there are only basic supplies in shops. The store on the plaza, *Tienda Grande* (Casa Morales), can change travellers' cheques at a poor rate.

Transport Buses from Creel, Tue, Thu and Sat at 0700, 5-6 hrs (paved as far as Samachique turn-off) depending on weather, US$16, buy ticket the day before, very crowded. Tickets are sold from *Restaurant La Herradura* in the main street. Return to Creel, Mon, Wed, and Fri; it leaves Batópilas at 0500 (have a torch handy as it is very dark). Also a 10-seater van on Mon, Wed and Fri, leaving at 0930, US$17, returns following day at 0500. Supply lorry leaves for Chihuahua Tue, Thu, Sat at 0600, takes passengers.

Directory **Tour operators** Several people in Creel offer trips to Batópilas. A recommended guide is *Pedro Estrada Pérez* (limited English but patient), T456-0079. An overnight trip for 4 (minimum) costs US$60 per person, plus lodging and meals, including trip to Jesuit Mission at Satevo (see below). Many hotels arrange tours including *Hotel Los Pinos*, on Av López Mateos. Some examples: to Cusárare (US$12-15), mission and falls, and Basíhuare; Recohauta hot springs (US$8 plus US$1.50 entrance); San Ignacio, Valle de los Hongos and Laguna Arareco; to Basaseachi (US$58 includes lunch, minimum 4, from *Parador La Montaña*); Divisadero (US$20, minimum 5, from *Margarita's*). These tours are pricey, but good fun and may involve more walking or climbing than advertised.

Excursions from Batópilas The **Porfirio Díaz Mine** above the bridge into town can be explored to about 3 km into the mountain (take torch); as you get into the mine there is the sickly, sweet smell of bat droppings, after about 1 km the air is thick with disturbed bats. **Satevo**, a 7-km walk from Batópilas along the river, a poor place with 15 houses, two of which sell drinks, has a 350-year-old Jesuit Mission whose dome has been repainted and whose interior is under repair. The mission has flattering acoustics for those who like to sing to themselves. The family next door has the key. ■ *US$ donation appreciated*. At **Cerro Yerbanis** there are amazing views of the Batópilas Canyon.

Beyond Creel, the **Chihuahua al Pacífico** train passes its highest point, Los Ojitos and, soon after, the Lazo loop, in which the track does a 360° turn. Pitorreal is 17 km further on. At Divisadero there is an all-too-brief 20-minute stop to view the canyon and buy souvenirs from the Tarahumara women. Five minutes further on, the train comes to *Hotel Posada Barrancas*. See page 233 for schedule.

Divisadero
Colour map 2, grid B2

For those who aren't travelling on the train the Barranca de Urique/Cobre (Urique/Copper Canyon) is quite a long way from Creel. Apart from the access from Batópilas (see box, page 238), or from Bahuichivo (see below), the simplest way to see the canyon is to take a bus or hitch to Divisadero or Posada Barrancas on the rough road, paved halfway from Creel, or else take the train.

Sleeping In Divisadero is the upmarket **L** *Divisadero Barrancas*. 2-3 km by road, 5 mins by train from Divisadero. In **Posada Barrancas** there are more options with the **A** *Posada Barrancas Mirador*, across the tracks from the old *Posada Barrancas*. New hotel has views from every room, full board, free lemonade on arrival and free *margarita* later, book through *Hotel Santa Anita*, Los Mochis, T(668) 818-7046, tours arranged, including hike or horse-riding trip to a Tarahumara village. Recommended.

C *Casa de Huéspedes Díaz*. Rooms with 2 double beds, hot water on request, prepares meals. **D** *Rancho de Lancho*, with a couple of basic rooms, dirty bathrooms, but very helpful with walks and breakfast available. **E** *Cabañas*. And bed and breakfast near church, 2 food shops, or, walk 1½ km down the road, past the 'camping' sign to a hamlet of 3 houses. 1st house on left has a rustic room with earth floor and lantern with a double and a single bed, **F**.

The Balancing Rock is at the edge of the canyon; it wobbles in a stomach-churning way as you stand on it. Reached by *camioneta* from *Hotel Divisadero Barrancas*, or walk 1-2 km from Divisadero (away from Creel) and on the left you will see the wooden entrance gate. From there it is 45 minutes to the rock with stops at the canyon viewing points.

Excursions from Divisadero

The canyon can also be reached on foot from Divisadero or *Posada Barrancas*; from the former it is 6 km (walk or hitch) along the dirt road that runs beside the railway to the house of Florencio Manzinas (at the first group of houses you come to). From there it's a day's hike along narrow, slippery, often steep and sometimes overgrown trails into the canyon, descending from cool pine forest into gradually more subtropical vegetation as you approach the river and the canyon floor. At this point there are mango, orange and banana trees. Take plenty of water for the hike as, after descending the first section following a stream, you have to go over another hill before getting down to the river, which means several hours without access to water.

Twenty-five minutes beyond the *Hotel Posada Barrancas* the Chihuahua al Pacífico reaches **San Rafael**, where there is a 10-minute stop, and then passes the La Laja bridge and tunnel. It is a further 20 minutes to **Cuiteco**, which has the **B** *Hotel Cuiteco*, delightful, with a patio that has an unimpeded view of the mountains, quiet, oil lamps, gas stove in courtyard. Next on the line comes Bahuichivo, **E** *Viajero*, restaurant next door, and a few shops; if you don't want to go all the way to Los Mochis you can return from here (Bahuichivo-Creel, 1st class, US$4, three hours). From Bahuichivo to Los Mochis is five hours on the train.

Bahuichivo
Colour map 2, grid B2

From Bahuichivo, bus and pick-ups make the five-hour journey to Urique, in the heart of the Barranca de Urique. Before the canyon is the town of Cerocahui, on a meander in the river, with a solid red-stone church (one hotel – **LL** *Mission*, full board, book in Flamingo Travel in Los Mochis, T(668) 818-7046). At the lip of the canyon is a *mirador* offering fine views. The road into the canyon is spectacular, only rivalled by the road to Batópilas.

Urique
Colour map 2, grid B2

Northern Highlands

Témoris Near Témoris, the train track enters a tunnel in which the railway turns through 180°. Témoris, an attractive town 11 km above the train station, in the mining and cattle country of the lower western Sierra Madre, is a good base for visiting working ranches, Tarahumara villages, waterfalls and swimming holes, on foot, horse or mountain bike. *Colectivos* make the trip or you may be able to hitch with local merchants. There are three hotels in the area and several cheap restaurants. *Campamento Adame*, a good choice for backpackers, has cabañas, dormitories and tent sites with shower and cooking facilities.

South from Chihuahua

Ciudad Delicias The first major town southeast of Chihuahua on Route 45, Ciudad Delicias, is the
Phone code: 639 centre of a major agricultural area. There is a **Museo de Paleontología**, Avenida Río
Colour map 2, grid B3 Chuvíscar Nte y Círculo de la Plaza de la República, T472-8513, with fossils from the
Population; 116,132 Zona de Silencio (see below) and from the inland sea that covered the area 80 million years ago. ■ *0900-2000, Mon-Sat.*

Sleeping A *Del Norte*, Av Agricultura Nte 5, T472-0200. **B-C** *Baeza*, Calle 2 Nte 309, T472-1000. **D** *Delicias*, near market. Several others of similar quality nearby.

Transport Train station: Av 7 Ote, T472-0834. **Buses**: to/from **Chihuahua** hourly, US$4; *Omnibus de México*, Av 6 y Calle 2 Nte, T472-1020; *Estrella Blanca*, Av 6 Nte 300, T472-1509; *Rápidos Delicias*, Av 5 Nte 301, T472-1030.

Ciudad A small cattle town, Ciudad Camargo is quiet except for its eight days of **fiesta** for
Camargo Santa Rosalía beginning on 4 September, when there are cockfights, horse racing
Phone code: 648 and dancing. **A** *Hotel Santa Fe*, south edge of town on highway, T462-4022. Very
Colour map 2, grid B3 quiet, secure parking, good breakfast, some English spoken. Recommended. **Motel**
Population: 45,830 **C-D** *Victoria*, Comonfort y Jiménez, T462-0801. Clean and cheap.

From **Ciudad Jiménez** (1,263 km from Mexico City, **B** *Motel Florido*, T(629) 542-0400, hot water) there are two routes south to Fresnillo and Zacatecas: the Central Highway through Durango, or a more direct route via Torreón (237 km from Ciudad Jiménez), passing Escalón (restaurant), **Ceballos** (**E** *Hotel San José*, basic), Yermo (restaurants) and Bermejillo (restaurant), on Route 49.

Between Escalón and Ceballos is the **Zona del Silencio** (the Silent Zone), a highly magnetic area where, it is claimed, electrical appliances fall silent, aircraft radar goes haywire, and so on. It inspires much interest and research but as yet no proof.

Torreón

Phone code: 871 Torreón is the principal industrial city of La Laguna cotton and wheat district. It is hot,
Colour map 2, grid B4 polluted and devoid of colonial atmosphere. Here is the **Bolsón de Mayrán**, an oasis of
Population: 529,093 about 28,500 sq km, which might be irrigated, but only about 2,000 sq km has been
Altitude: 1,137 m developed and much of that is stricken with drought. On the opposite side of the mostly dry Río Nazas are the two towns of **Gómez Palacio** (*feria* first half of August) and **Ciudad Lerdo**.

Sleeping **Torreón** A *Río Nazas*, Av Morelos y Treviño, T716-1212. High-rise, very good. **A-D** *Posada de Sol*, Blvd Revolución, T720-2991. Modern motel, secure parking, small restaurant, bar, hot showers, rooms range from basic, windowless, clean cabañas to large, US-style rooms with TV, good value. There are a few decent places to eat in the centre.

Gómez Palacio **B** *Motel La Siesta*, Av Madero 320 Nte, T714-0291. Clean, hot water, safe parking. Good. **D** *Motel La Cabaña*. Hot water.

The assassination of Pancho Villa

The infamous assassination of Pancho Villa took place in the town centre on 20 July 1923. Villa owned a house on Calle Zaragoza (now a shop called Almacenes Real de Villa, *painted bright pink) and was making his way from there to the* Hotel Hidalgo, *which he also owned, when he was ambushed on Av Juárez. The house chosen by the assassins is now the Museo Pancho Villa (Mon-Fri*

0900-2000, Sat 0900-1300.) Twelve of the 100 bullets fired hit Villa, who was taken immediately to the Hotel Hidalgo. *The death mask taken there can be seen in the museum and also in the museum in Chihuahua. His funeral took place the next day and he was buried in the Panteón Municipal; his tomb is still there even though the body has been transferred to Mexico City.*

Air Torreón airport (14½ km from the centre) has domestic services to Chihuahua, Ciudad Juárez, Culiacán, Durango, Guadalajara, Hermosillo, Ixtapa, Mazatlán, Mexico City, Monterrey, Piedras Negras, and Tijuana. International flights to Houston and Los Angeles in the US, Panama City and Sao Paulo, Brazil.

Transport

Buses To **Chihuahua**: 6 hrs, US$24; to **Ciudad Juárez**: US$42; to **Durango**: about 6 a day, 4½ hrs; to **Tepic**: US$42. Gómez Palacio has its own bus station, without a shuttle to the centre. City buses outside have frequent services to all 3 city centres, US$0.33.

Between Gómez Palacio and Zacatecas are **Cuencamé** (**D** *La Posta*, Gral Ceniceros 68 Nt, T(671) 763-0029, hot water, with parking. **Río Grande** and **Fresnillo**. This last town is the birthplace of the artist Francisco Goitia and musician Manuel M Ponce. (**A-C** *La Fortuna*, Panamericana Km 724.3, T(493) 932-5664, comfortable, hot water. **C** *Maya*, Ensaye 9, T(493) 932-0351, good travelling option).

Northern Highlands

Hidalgo del Parral

Connecting to the north through Ciudad Jiménez (77 km) Hidalgo del Parral, or often just Parral, is an old mining town with narrow streets, 1,138 km from Mexico City. In 1629, Juan Rangel de Viezma discovered *La Negrita*, the first mine in the area. Now known as *La Prieta*, it overlooks the city from the top of Cerro la Prieta. Rangel founded the town in 1631 under the name of San Juan del Parral. The mine owners were generous benefactors to the city, leaving many beautiful buildings that still stand. On 8 September 1944, severe damage was caused by a flood. The decrease in population, either through drowning or flight, led to a recession.

Phone code: 627
Colour map 2, grid B3
Population: 100,881

The city's history is split between its mining heritage and the fact that Pancho Villa was assassinated here

Hidalgo del Parral is now a pleasant, safe, affluent city. It has a compact centre with a string of shaded plazas, many bridges over the sinuous, and often dry, Río del Parral, and several churches.

On the Plaza Principal is the **Parroquia de San José**, with a beautiful interior. **Plaza Baca** has a statue to *El Buscador de Ilusiones* (the Dream Seeker), a naked man panning for gold. The **cathedral** is on this square and, on the opposite side, is the **Templo San Juan de Dios** with an exuberant altarpiece, painted gold. Across the road from the cathedral is the former *Hotel Hidalgo* (not in use), built in 1905 by mine owner Pedro Alvarado and given to Pancho Villa in the 1920s. Next door is **Casa Stallforth** (1908), the shop and house of a German family who supplied everything imaginable to the city. It is still a shop, with the original interior. Continuing on Mercaderes, before the bridge, is **Casa Griensen**, now the Colegio Angloamericano Isaac Newton. Griensen, another German, married Alvarado's sister. Behind this house is **Casa Alvarado**, still a private residence, only for viewing from the outside. Crossing the bridge at the end of Mercaderes, you come to the site of Villa's death, on the corner of Plaza Juárez. Also worth seeing is the façade of the **Teatro Hidalgo**

Sights

on Plazuela Independencia. Just off Avenida Independencia is the **Templo de la Virgen del Rayo** (the Virgin of the Lightning).

Excursions Twenty-six kilometres east of Parral on the Jiménez road, a well-signed road leads 5 km south to **Valle de Allende** (*Population*: 4,000). Originally called Valle de San Bartolomé, it was the site of the first Franciscan mission in Chihuahua, founded in the late 16th century by Fray Agustín Rodríguez. The original monastery building still stands on the main square, but it is unused (it has been used as a *refrigeradora* to store apples).

Sleeping **A** *Adriana*, Colegio 2, between Plaza Principal and Plaza Baca, T522-2570, F522-4770. A/c, restaurant, bar, parking. **B** *Acosta*, Agustín Barbachano 3, T522-0221, F522-9555, off the Plaza Principal. Quiet, parking for car or motorbike, rooftop terrace with fine view, laundry facilities, very clean, central, friendly, helpful, hot water, excellent value. Recommended. **C** *San José*, Santiago Méndez 5, near Plaza Principal, T522-2453. With bath, safe parking, clean, central.

D *Chihuahua*, Colón 1, off Jesús García. Clean, simple. **D** *Fuentes*, near Plaza Baca. Dirty, dour rooms, restaurant has cheap *comida corrida*. **E** *Margarita*, near bus station. A bit noisy, but excellent value, well-run with friendly staff and a café next door. 24-hour parking available in supermarket next door. Recommended. **F** *Internacional*, Flores Magón. Basic, friendly, parking, dirty.

Eating *La Parroquia* in *Hotel San José*. Good-value meals, including breakfast. *Morelos*, Plazuela Morelos 22, off Plaza Principal. Clean, rather expensive, open 0700-2300, Friday and Saturday open 24 hrs. *Café Corales*, Flores Magón opposite Buses Ballezano. Good beef sandwiches. On Independencia: *Nutripan*, No 221. Cakes, pastries and bread, including brown; sliced brown bread at *La Patita*, No 60; wide choice of bread and cakes at *El Parralense*, off Independencia on Calle Los Ojitos.

Transport **Buses** The bus station is 20 mins' walk out of town on Av Independencia, east of centre, taxi about US$2. Few bus lines start here so it is difficult to reserve seats. To **Durango**: 6 hrs, US$24. To **Zacatecas**: 9 hrs, US$42. To **Chihuahua**: frequent departures, 2½ hrs, US$11. Also to **Guachochi** (see page 236). Buses Ballezano to Guachochi leave from office on Carlos Fuero y Flores Magón at 0800, 1230, 1545, US$4.

Directory **Banks** *Banco Unión*, in *Hotel Adriana* complex, exchange until 1200, poor rates, similarly at *Banamex* opposite. Good rates at *Bancomer*, Plaza Principal until 1200. Opposite is *Cambios de Oro*, no commission, good rates, open Mon-Fri 0900-1900, Sat until 1400. Also at Gasolinera Palmilla on road to Santa Bárbara, 3 km out of town. **Communications** Post office: on Del Rayo, just over bridge from centre, open 0800-1500.

Hidalgo del Parral to Durango

Route 45, south of Parral, is in good condition all the way to Durango. At Villa de Nieve, 3 km down a winding road, well signed, is Pancho Villa's hacienda, with an excellent museum (give a donation to the man who opens the door). Villa was given the hacienda in exchange for promising to lay down his arms and retire to private life (28 July 1920).

Between Roedo and Durango is the 'Western' landscape beloved of Hollywood film-makers

Cinema enthusiasts can visit the Western serts of *Villa del Oeste* (9 km from Durango) and *Chupaderos* (14 km), both decaying (especially the latter) but smelling authentically of horse. San Juan del Río buses go there or take a taxi, US$14. 4 km east off the road, at **San Juan del Río**, is a Pemex station. Halfway down the side road to San Juan is a signed road to Coyotada, off which is a 4-km road to Pancho Villa's birthplace and museum (modest, a few artefacts and photos). ■ *Free, donation welcome.*

Santiago Papasquiaro is three hours north of Durango on Route 23 (on the way, in Canatlán, are Mennonite colonies), **D** *Hotel División del Norte*, Madero 35,

T(674)- 862-0013, in a former convent; the owner's husband was in Pancho Villa's *División del Norte*. *Restaurant Mirador*, across from the market, good food. There are a number of hot springs in the area; Hervideros is the most popular, take the bus to Herreras, then it's a 30-minute walk. **Tepehuanes**, one hour further on, is a small pleasant town with a couple of hotels. Walk to Purísima and then to a small, spectacular canyon. A dirt road continues to **Guanacevi**, a mining town in the Sierra.

South of Durango on the road to Zacatecas is **Sombrerete**, a small, lively and pretty colonial silver mining town, which at the height of its prosperity at the end of the 17th century rivalled Zacatecas. The town has 10 good churches and the superb, partially restored Franciscan convent San Mateo, 1567. Next door to it is the elliptical Chapel of the Third Order. **Sleeping**: **D** *Avenida Real*, T(433) 935-0266, clean, restaurant. **E** *Real de Minas*, T(433) 935-0340 Clean, comfortable, enclosed parking. **E** *Villa de Llerena*, T(433) 935-0077, on main plaza. Clean but dark rooms. *La Calera* restaurant, good. Seven kilometres north of the Durango road, 12 km before Sombrerete, is the **Sierra de los Organos** or Valley of the Giants, now a national park, where John Wayne made several of his Westerns. It is named after the basalt columns, which are supposed to resemble organ pipes.

Durango

Phone code 618
Colour map 2,
grid C3
Population: 490,524
Altitude: 1,924 m

Northern Highlands

Victoria de Durango, capital of Durango state was founded in 1563 some 260 km southwest of Torreón and 926 northwest of Mexico City. It is a modernizing city but with many beautiful old buildings (see the 18th-century **Casa de los Condes de Suchill**, now *Bancomer*, on 5 de Febrero, and the French-style **Teatro Ricardo Castro**), with wonderfully calming murals in the auditorium, a **cathedral** (1695) and a famous iron-water spring.

The town is all pretty much within a couple of blocks of the main plaza – wander around a little and get the feel of the place, market-style and busy to the southeast of the plaza, a little smarter and more relaxed to the northwest. The main street is Avenida 20 de Noviembre, a wide dominating thoroughfare that reflects the 'Wild West' image of the state of Durango, so often a backdrop to not only Hollywood movies but also the Mexican film industry at its height. Lest you think the city rests

Durango

■ Sleeping		● Eating	
1 Buenos Aires	5 Posada San Jorge	1 Café La Mancha	4 El Zocabón
2 Casa Blanca	6 Reforma	2 El Manjar	5 Gorditas Gabino
3 Gallo	7 Roma	3 El Pastocito	6 La Peña
4 Plaza Catedral		Taquería	7 Los Farolitos

on the laurels that made such classics as *The Wild Bunch* by Sam Peckinpah (1968), modern classics include *The Mask of Zorro I* (1997).

There is a small **Museo de Cine** (Cinema Museum) on Florida 1106, Barrio El Calvario, with a good collection of Mexican film posters plus old cameras. ■ *Tue-Sun 1000-1800, US$0.50*. There is also a **Museo de Cultura Popular**, on the corner of Juárez and Gabino, and the **Museo Arqueológico de las Culturas Prehispánicas**, on Zaragoza, between 5 de Febrero and 20 de Noviembre. Both closed on Mondays. The tourist office is above the Museo de Cine.

Sleeping
■ *on map page 243*
Price codes:
see inside front cover

A *Fiesta Plaza*, 20 de Noviembre and Independencia, T812-1050, F121511. Very pleasant, lots of plants. B *Campo México Courts*, 20 de Noviembre extremo Ote, T818-7744, F818-3015. Good but restaurant service poor. B *Casa Blanca*, 20 de Noviembre 811 Pte, T811-3599, F14704. Nice, big old hotel in the centre, unguarded parking lot. B *Posada San Jorge*, Constitución 102 Sur, T811-3526, F811-6040. Old colonial building, patio, large rooms, friendly, parking. Recommended. C *Plaza Catedral*, Constitución 216 Sur, T813-2660. Great old building oozing bigness. Private bathrooms and parking out back. Good value. C *Roma*, 20 de Noviembre 705 Pte, T/F120122. Clean, comfortable.

D *Gallo*, 5 de Febrero 117, T811-5290. With bath, clean, motorcycle parking. Bit grubby but OK. D *Reforma*, 5 de Febrero y Madero, T813-1622. Authentic 1960s lobby, clean, comfortable rooms, free indoor parking, good restaurant. A little overpriced but you can pay with a credit card. E-F *Buenos Aires*, Constitución 126 Nte, T812-3128. Clean, tidy and very safe. A good budget choice. E *Oasis*, Zarco between 20 de Noviembre y 5 de Febrero. With bath, hot water, rooms on the top floor have a good view.

Out of town opposite the bus station is D *Pancho Villa*, Pino Suárez 206, behind the statue of Pancho, T818-7191. Clean, pretty basic but OK if you're at the station for the night.

Eating

Café La Mancha, 20 de Noviembre 807 Pte. Relaxed, tables outside at back, cheap lunches. *El Manjar*, Negrete and Zaragoza, vegetarian Mexican dishes – open for breakfast. *El Pastorcito Taquería*, divinely tasty kebabs, with a few interesting options. Cheap. *El Zocabón*, on 5 de Febrero, off main plaza. Recommended. *Gardy*, F de Urdiñola 239, Nueva Viscaya, T818-7162. Vegetarian. *Gorditas Gabino*, Constitución 112 Nte. Mexican food in a US-diner style. Cheap, good and central. *La Peña*, Martínez 120 Nte. Friday night is fiesta night with local music and singing, very popular, but possibly closing down. *La Unica*, 20 de Noviembre y Pasteur. Cheap *taquería*. *Los Farolitos*, Martínez and 20 de Noviembre, exquisite tacos and burritos with juice certain to drip down your sleeve. *Samadhi*, a couple of blocks from the cathedral on Negrete 403 Pte. Good-value vegetarian food, delicious soups, popular with locals. *Salum*, 5 de Febrero y Progreso. Good breakfasts, nice.

Transport

Air Guadalupe Victoria Airport (DGO), 12 km from centre (taxi US$8.50). Domestic flights to Chihuahua, Guadalajara, Mazatlán, Mexico City, Monterrey, Tijuana and Torreón. There are international flights to Chicago, El Paso and Los Angeles.

Buses Bus station out of town: minibus No 2 to centre, every 5 mins from 0600 to 2130, US$0.25. Services with *Omnibus de México* and *Estrella Blanca*. Across the Sierra Madre Occidental to **Mazatlán** there are several buses daily, 7 hrs, US$26. The views are fantastic and recommended if you cannot do the Chihuahua-Los Mochis train journey; sit on left side. 2nd class buses for camera buffs stop more frequently, and if you're cheeky enough the bus may even stop for you. **Chihuahua**: several daily, 8 hrs, US$36. **Hidalgo del Parral**: 7 hrs, US$24. **Guadalajara**: 2000 and 2200, 8 hrs, US$40. **Mexico City**: every couple of hours, 12 hrs, US$58. **Zacatecas**: 4½ hrs, US$18.

Directory

Airline offices *Mexicana*, T813-6299, *Aero California*, T817-7177. *AeroMéxico*, next to cathedral, T817-8828. **Banks** *Bancomer*, and many others with ATMs neatly on the west side of the plaza by cathedral. **Communications** Internet: at *Virus Café Internet*, Constitución, 1 block past the cathedral heading north, US$1.30/hr, open 1000-2200. *Enter Zone*, Florida, past the Cinema Museum. Many others in town. **Post office**: Av 20 de Noviembre 500 B Ote.

Northern Highlands

Northeast Mexico

Mexico City

Some of the most crucial battles of the 1846-48 War between Mexico and the United States were fought in the northeast of Mexico. Brownsville and Matamoros experienced the first outbreak of hostilities and it was here that many US troops deserted and joined the Mexican forces, giving rise to the St Patrick's Battalion. Museums in the towns and cities along the way tell this and other stories of the region. On a more contemporary note, the galleries of Monterrey are at the cutting edge of modern Mexican art. Outside the city you can explore Mexico's largest national park, venture into vast caves with stalactites and stalagmites, try rock climbing on mountains that tower above chasms, or set out on a two-day adventure circuit involving river canyoning, abseiling or swimming through tunnels. Further south you can enjoy tropical bird sanctuaries, jungle and even cloud forest and visit archaeological sites of the enigmatic Huastec civilization. You could even take in some deep-sea fishing before finally reaching Tampico and the Gulf Coast or heading inland to the Colonial Highlands.

Laredo to Tampico

The Gulf Route from Laredo (along the Pan-American Highway) takes in the major industrial centre of Monterrey and the port of Tampico. The route passes through the coastal state of Tamaulipas before entering Huastec and Otomí Indian regions. Then there is a choice of either continuing south or heading west to the Central Highlands via the old silver-mining centre of Pachuca.

The first route to be opened was the Gulf Route. Traffic from the central and eastern parts of the US can enter northeast Mexico through five gateways along the Río Bravo; at **Matamoros**, opposite Brownsville; at **Reynosa** opposite McAllen; at **Ciudad Miguel Alemán**, opposite Roma; at **Nuevo Laredo**, opposite Laredo; and at **Piedras Negras**, opposite Eagle Pass. The roads from these places all converge upon Monterrey (a new toll road from Nuevo Laredo is the quickest route, US$12).

Crossing into Mexico

By car, the best way is over the **Colombia Bridge**, north of Laredo: on Interstate 35, take the exit to Milo (the first exit north of the Tourist Bureau, then take Farm Road 1472 west). This crossing has little traffic and friendly staff, but it does involve a 40-km detour (it is well-signposted on the Mexican side). There is a toll on the international bridge. Once in Mexico, you can continue to Monterrey either on Route 85 via Nuevo Laredo, or by following the railway line via Ciudad Anáhuac and Lampazos.

The direct route is on San Bernardo parallel to Interstate 35 on the west; turn west at Washington, south at Salinas, cross about 10 traffic lights and turn east to the **International bridge**. Do not be directed into the narrow columns: after verbal processing, go 3 km to the full vehicle processing location at Avenida Cesar López de Lara 1200, opposite the train station. This entails six steps, including photocopying of documents (keep copies), US$2-3, and the bureaucracy described under **Motoring** in Essentials.

This is the most important town of the eastern border crossings. Nuevo Laredo is a bit of a tourist trap but it is fun to stroll through the souvenir shops.

After 130 km of grey-green desert, the road from Nuevo Laredo climbs the Mamulique Pass, which it crosses at 700 m, before descending to Monterrey. From Laredo to Monterrey there is a toll road (*cuota*) and a non-toll road (*vía libre*). The latter goes through Sabinas Hidalgo (hotels and museum). There is a toll bypass and a free truck route around Monterrey.

Laredo/ Nuevo Laredo
Phone code: 867
Colour map 2, grid B6
Population: 310,277

Northeast Mexico

Sleeping (Laredo) The better of the 2 trailer parks is on the east side of Interstate 35, Main Street exit, 10 mins from border. **(Nuevo Laredo) C** *Alameda*, on plaza, T712-5050. **E** *Calderón*. With bath, hot water, fan, run-down, friendly. Many **F** hotels, none of which have been recommended. **Motels**: **A** *Hacienda*, Prolongación Reforma 5530, T717-0000. **B** *Reforma*, Av Guerrero 822, T712-6250. **Shopping** *Centro Artesanal Nuevo Laredo*, Maclovio Herrera 3030, T712-6399.

Transport Buses: The Nuevo Laredo **bus** station is not near the border; take a bus to the border, then walk across. It is not possible to get a bus from the Laredo Greyhound terminal to the Nuevo Laredo terminal unless you have an onward ticket. Connecting tickets from Houston via Laredo to Monterrey are available, 14 hrs. Some buses to Laredo connect with Greyhound buses in the US.

To **Guadalajara**: 9 a day, 18 hrs, US$72. To **Mexico City** with *Estrella Blanca/Transportes del Norte*: 9 buses a day, 16 hrs, US$65. To **Monterrey**: hourly departures, 4 hrs, US$12. To **San Luis Potosí**: US$52. To **Tampico, Morelia**: 17 hrs, US$56.

Directory Banks: *UNB Convent* and *Matamoros* charges 1% commission on TCs, open 0830-1600, Mon-Fri. *IBC*, no commission under US$500. **Embassies and consulates** *Mexican Consulate*, Farragut and Maine, 4th light on the right after leaving Interstate 35, open Mon-Fri 0800-1400, helpful. **Useful addresses** Car insurance: *Sanborn's* on Santa Ursula (Exit 16 on Interstate 35), a bit more expensive, open 24 hours a day, www.sanbornsinsurance.com *Johnson's Mexico Insurance*, Tepeyac Agent, Lafayette and Santa Ursula (59 and Interstate 35), US$2.60 per day, open 24 hrs, recommended.

McAllen/ Reynosa
Phone code: 899

Opposite McAllen on the border, Reynosa has a population of just over 400,000 but there's not much to see. If you have time to kill, pop in to the **Museo Histórico Reynosa** on Morelos and Hidalgo.

Sleeping If you're in town looking for a bed try the following: **D** *San Carlos*, Hidalgo 970 Nte, T922-1280. Recommended. **E** *Arcade*, corner of Cedar and North 12th St, 2 blocks from Greyhound terminal, south from Valley Transit bus terminal.

Brownsville/ Matamoros
Phone code: 88
Colour map 2, grid B6
Population: 416,428

Matamoros is a town with a bright and unforbidding museum, designed to let prospective tourists know what they can expect in Mexico. Visas can be obtained in **Brownsville** on the US side of the border from the Mexican Consulate at 940 East Washington. Crossing the border by car here is quick and easy; permission is usually granted for six months (multiple entry) for passengers and vehicle, paperwork takes only about 10 minutes if everything is in order.

Sleeping B *Ritz*, Matamoros 612 y Siete, T812-1190. There are 4 motels on the road to the beach, all **B-C**. **Shopping** *Centro Artesanal Matamoros*, Calle 5 Hurtado and Alvaro Obregón, T812-0384. **Transport Buses**: Several lines run 1st class buses to **Mexico City**: 14 hrs, US$54. *Transportes del Norte* to **Ciudad Victoria** regular departures, US$15.50, 4 hrs.

Eagle Pass/ Piedras Negras
Phone code: 878
Colour map 2, grid B5
Population: 127,898
Altitude: 220 m

Piedras Negras, is across the Río Bravo from Eagle Pass, Texas. Beyond Hermanas (137 km), the highway begins to climb gradually up to the plateau country.

Shopping *Centro Artesanal Piedras Negras*, Edif la Estrella, Puerta México, T782-1087, *artesanía* shop. **Trains**: Check locally, all passenger schedules have ceased.

Saltillo

Phone code: 884
Colour map 2, grid B5
Population: 650,000
Altitude: 1,600 m

The capital of Coahuila state is a cool, dry popular resort noted for the excellence of its *sarapes*. Its 18th-century cathedral, a mixture of romanesque, churrigueresque, baroque and plateresque styles, is the best in northern Mexico. College students from the US attend the popular Summer School (T414-9541, F414-9544). The Tourist office is at Bulevar Venustiano Carranza 3206, T/F439-2745.

The **Museo de las Aves** (Bird Museum), on Hidalgo y Bolívar 151 (a few blocks north of *sarape* factory), T140167, contains hundreds of stuffed birds. ■*Tue-Sat 1000-1800, Sun 1100-1800. Small admission charge. Guides available.* The house of the artist Juan Antonio Villarreal Ríos, Boulevard Nazario Ortiz Garza, Casa 1, Manzana 1, Colonia Saltillo 400, T415-2707, has an exhibition in every room of Dali-esque work; visitors are welcome, phone first. ■ *Free.* There are good views from El Cerro del Pueblo overlooking the city. An 87-km road runs east to Monterrey, both toll and *vía libre*. You turn right (southwest) for Mexico City.

Sleeping

Several hotels a short distance from the plaza at the intersection of Allende and Aldama, the main streets. Saltillo is a conference centre with many hotels in the luxury range, several on north end of Boulevard V Carranza north of Boulevard Echeverría Nte, eg: *Holiday Inn Eurotel* and *Imperial del Norte*. In the centre **B** *Rancho El Morillo*, Prolongación Obregón Sur y Echeverría, T417-4376. A converted hacienda, excellent value, meals available. **C** *Jardín*, Padre Flores 211, T412-5916. Basic, cold water, safe motorcycle parking.

D *Hidalgo*, Padre Flores 217, T414-9853. Without bath, not worth paying for bath in room, cold water only (hot baths open to public and guests for small fee). **E** *Brico*, Ramos Arizpe Pte 552, T412-5146. Cheap, noisy, clean, tepid water. **E** *El Conde*, Pérez Treviño y Acuña, T412-0136. Several hotels in front of the bus station. **F** *Bristol Aldama*, near *Hotel San Jorge*. Recommended. **Motels A** *La Fuente*, Blvd Los Fundadores, T430-1599.

Trailer park Turn right on road into town from Monterrey between *Hotel del Norte* and *Kentucky Fried Chicken*. Hook-ups, toilets, basic.

Eating

El Tapanco, Allende 225 Sur. Expensive. *Arcasa*, Victoria. Good local food. *El Campanario Saloon and Grill*, Ocampo, open noon-midnight. Recommended. *Café Plaza*, off Plaza de Armas. Good breakfasts. *Victoria*, Padre Flores 221, by *Hotel Hidalgo*. Has reasonable *comida*. Drinks and night-time view can be had at the *Rodeway Inn* on the north side of town.

Festivals

Local *feria* in 1st half of **Aug**; cheap accommodation impossible to find at this time. Indian dances on **30 May** and **30 Aug**; picturesque ceremonies and bullfights during **Oct** fiestas. *Pastorelas*, the story of the Nativity, are performed in the neighbourhood in Christmas week.

Transport

Air The airport (SLW) is 16 km from town. Flights to Mexico City daily with *Mexicana*. *Aerolitoral* flies to Guadalajara and Monterrey.

Buses Terminal is on Blvd Echeverría, 3 km south of centre (yellow bus marked 'Periférico' from Allende y Lerdo de Tejada in centre); minibuses to Pérez Treviño y Allende (for centre) will take luggage. Bus to **Ciudad Acuña**: 2nd class, 8 hrs, US$23. To **Hidalgo de Parral**: 9 hrs, US$32. To **Mexico City**: 1st class, 11 hrs, US$48. To **San Luis Potosí**: US$20. To **Monterrey** and **Nuevo Laredo** with *Transportes del Norte*. For **Torreón**: 3 hrs, US$16, all buses originate in Monterrey and tickets are only sold when bus arrives; be prepared to stand.

Directory

Banks *Bancomer*, Allende y Victoria. *Banamex*, Allende y Ocampo. **Communications Telephones**: long-distance calls from *Café Victoria*, Padre Flores 221, near market. **Post office**: Victoria 223.

Matehuala

Phone code: 488

From Saltillo, two roads run south: one heads southwest to Zacatecas (see page 278) and the other south to Matehuala and San Luis Potosí (see page 283). Along the Saltillo-Matehuala section the scenery is worthwhile, as the road winds its way up and down through wooded valleys. The final section passes through undulating scrub country to Matehuala, an important road junction with a **fiesta** from **6-20 January**. It's also a good jumping off point to visit the important mining town of Real de Catorce (see page 287). From Matehuala you go via the Colonial Heartland route to Mexico City.

Sleeping A *Trailerpark Las Palmas*, north of town (Km 617), T882-0001. Clean, English spoken and paperbacks sold, bowling alley and miniature golf. **C** *El Dorado*, nearby,

Northeast Mexico

T882-0174. Cheaper. Recommended. **E** *Alamo*, Guerrero 116, T882-0017. Hot showers, clean and very pleasant rooms, safe motorcycle parking, friendly. Recommended. *Restaurant La Fontella* in the centre. Good regional food.

Transport Buses: **Mexico City**: 8 hrs, US$31. **Monterrey**: 4 hrs, US$18. **Real de Catorce**: US$3. **San Luis Potosí**: with *Estrella Blanca*, 2½ hrs, US$8.50.

Monterrey

Phone code: 81
Colour map 2, grid B5
Population: 1,108,499
Altitude: 538 m

Capital of Nuevo León state and third largest city in Mexico, Monterrey is 253 km south of the border and 915 km from Mexico City. The city is dominated by the Cerro de la Silla (saddle) from the east and the Cerro de las Mitras in the west. It is an important cultural centre in Mexico and there are many fine museums to visit.

The city now has a modern and efficient metro system

Monterrey's population continues to grow in spite of its unattractive climate: too hot in summer, too cold in winter, dusty at most times and a shortage of water. Evenings are cool. Its streets are congested, its layout seems unplanned and its architecture uninspiring except in the centre, which has undergone renewal and remodelling in recent years. All of this made it the perfect location for the United Nations Conference on Development in 2001, attended by 58 heads of state from around the world including President George W Bush and President Vicente Fox.

Ins and outs

Getting there
Aeropuerto Internacional General Mariano Escobedo (MTY), 24 km from city centre, has flights to most cities in Mexico and to many in the US, Canada, Caribbean and Latin America. A taxi from the airport to the city centre costs US$10. The vast, long-distance bus terminal is north of the city centre on Avenida Colón (metro Cuauhtémoc). Several major routes converge at Monterrey, connecting the industrial city to the rest of Mexico and to Nuevo Laredo, Reynosa and Matamoros on the US border.

Getting around
For more details, see Transport page 251

The Monterrey metro system now has two intersecting lines, which run north-south and east-west of the city. Urban buses run to all areas within the city; ask at the tourist office for a bus map.

The **State Tourist Office** is on the 3rd floor, of Edif Elizondo Páez, 5 de Mayo 525, T8344-4343, F8344-1169. Large city maps are available free of charge. An easier to find office is at Padre Mier y Dr Coss on the east side of the Plaza. ■ *Tue-Sun 1000-1700, sometimes closes at lunchtime.* The local tourism website is at **www.monterrey-mexico.com**

Sights

The centre lies just north of the Río Santa Catarina. Plaza Zaragoza, Plaza 5 de Mayo, the Explanada de los Héroes and Parque Hundido link with the Gran Plaza to the south to form the **Macro Plaza**, claimed to be the biggest civic square in the world. It runs north-south and is nine blocks long by two blocks wide; its centrepiece is the **Faro de Comercio** (Commerce Beacon). To the east of the Faro is the 18th-century **cathedral**, badly damaged in the war against the US in 1846-47, when it was used by Mexican troops as a powder magazine. Running along the west side of the northern part of the Plaza are the Torre Latina, High Court and State Congress; opposite, on the east side are the Biblioteca and the Teatro de La Ciudad, all modern buildings. The Plaza is bordered at its southern end by the **Palacio Municipal**, and at its northern limit is the **Palacio de Gobierno** looking over the Explanada de los Héroes.

Museums
Calle Morelos is a pedestrian-only shopping centre. Its famous **Instituto Tecnológico**, Avenida Garza Sada 2501, has valuable collections of books on

16th-century Mexican history. The new **Museo de la Historia Mexicana** (Mexican History Museum), Dr Coss 445 Sur, off the north end of the Plaza, T8342-4820, is an excellent interactive museum, good for children. ■ *1100-1900, closed Mon, free Tue.*

The **Museo de Monterrey** is in the grounds of the Cuauhtémoc Brewery, Avenida Alfonso Reyes 2202 Norte (500 m north of Metro Central), T8328-6060. ■ *Tue-Sun 1100-2000, Wed 1000-2000. Visits to brewery Mon-Fri 0930-1530, Sat 0930-1300.*

Museo de Arte Contemporáneo (MARCO), Zua Zua y PR Jardon, T8342-4820, is one of the best modern art galleries in Mexico; it holds temporary shows and has a good bookshop. ■ *Wed and Sun 1100-2100, other days 1100-1900, closed Mon. US$2, free Wed.* Two other art galleries with temporary shows are the **Pinacoteca de Nuevo León**, Parque Niños Héroes, T8331-5462 ■ *Tue-Sun 1000-1800* and **Centro Cultural de Arte**, Belisario Domínguez 2140 Pte, Col Obispado, T8347-1128 ■ *Mon-Fri 0900-1300, 1500-1800.*

Museo de las Culturas Populares, Abasolo 1024, Barrio Antiguo, T8345-6504. ■ *Tue-Sun 1000-1800.* Also in the centre is the **Museo Metropolitano de Monterrey** in the old Municipal Palace building, Zaragoza s/n between Corregidora and Hidalgo, T8344-1971. ■ *Mon-Sun 0800-2000.*

The **Centro Cultural Alfa**, in the Garza García suburb, T8356-5696, has a fine planetarium, an astronomy and a physics section. In a separate building is a Rufino Tamayo stained-glass window. ■ *Tue-Fri 1500-2100, Sat 1400-2100, Sun 1200-2100, closed Mon.* The centre is reached by special bus from the west end of the Alameda, hourly on the hour 1500-2000.

The **Alameda Gardens**, between Avenidas Aramberri and Washington, on Avenida Pino Suárez, are a pleasant place to sit. ■ *1000-1700, closed Tue.*

Northeast Mexico

Monterrey centre

Related map
Monterrey metro
system & main streets,
page 250

Sleeping	Eating
1 Crown Plaza	1 Los Girasoles
	2 Superbom

0 metres 200
0 yards 200

Excursions

In the hills around Monterry is the bathing resort of **Topo Chico**, 6½ km to the northwest; water from its hot springs is bottled and sold throughout Mexico. Reached by a road heading south (extension of Avenia Gómez Morín), is **Chipinque**, an ecological park in the Sierra Madre, with magnificent views of the Monterrey area. It is popular for hiking, mountain biking and climbing, with peaks reaching 2,200 m.

West of Monterrey, off the Saltillo road, are the **Grutas de García** (about 10 km from Villa García, which is 40 km from Monterrey). The entrance to the caves is 800 m up, by cable car, and inside are beautiful stalagmites and stalactites. At the foot of the cable car are a pool and recreational centre. A tour of the caves takes 1½ hours, and it is compulsory to go in a group with a guide. You can take a bus to Villa García, but it is a dusty walk to the caves. On Sunday *Transportes Saltillo-Monterrey* run a bus to the caves at 0900, 1000 and 1100. Otherwise, take an agency tour, for example *Osetur* (details from *Infotur*); book at *Hotel Ancira*. ■ *Tue, US$3.50.*

Hidalgo is a small town 38 km northwest of Monterrey on the Monclova road (Route 53). Dominating the area are the massive limestone cliffs of **Potrero Chico** (4 km west of town, take road leading on from Calle Francisco Villa). The cliffs are a magnet for big-wall climbers, particularly during the US winter, and have some of the hardest pitches in the world (up to 5.12d), including the 650-m long *Sendero*

Monterrey metro system & main streets

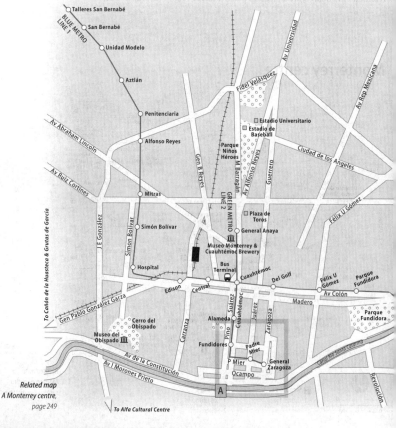

*Related map
A Monterrey centre,
page 249*

Luminoso route on the central pillar of *El Toro*. A sheet guide by Jeff Jackson describing 80 of the best climbs and places to camp is available at the store on the left before you reach the *balneario*. Accommodation **F** at *rancho*. Autobuses Mina leave at hourly intervals from Monterrey bus station to Hidalgo (bus station on plaza). Another excellent rock-climbing area is at the **Cañón de la Huasteca**, near Santa Catarina, 20 km west of Monterrey along Route 40.

Essentials

There are many new hotels in the luxury category in the centre and on radial routes coming into the city (not all listed). Most of the cheap hotels are situated in the area around the bus station (metros Central and Cuauhtémoc).

Sleeping
■ *on map, page 249*
See inside front cover for price codes

L *Crowne Plaza*, Av Constitución 300 Ote, near Plaza Zaragoza, T8319-6000, F8319-6061, www.hotelesmilenium.com Best. **B** *Yamallel*, Zaragoza 912, Norte Madero, T8375-3500, www.hotelyamallel.com.mx Good. **D** *Posada*, Amado Nervo 1138 Nte, T8372-3908. With bath, clean. Recommended. Further down same street at Juan Méndez 1518 Nte y Aquiles Serdán is **B** *Monterrey La Silla*, T/F8375-4141, www.hotellasilla.com TV, and opposite at 1515, **D** *La Silla*, its sister hotel. Clean, friendly. Recommended. **D** *Nuevo León*, Amado Nervo 1007 Nte by Av Madero, T8374-1900. With bath (hot water), dark, seedy, poor value, close to bus station. Many hotels between Colón and Reforma, 2 blocks from the bus station, nothing below US$15.

It can be difficult to get accommodation because so many people are travelling north/south

Motels A *El Paso Autel*, Zaragoza y Martínez, T8340-0690. **C** *Motel/Trailerpark Nueva Castilla*, on Highway 85 before Saltillo bypass. 12 spaces for RVs with hook-up, pool, hot showers, reasonable restaurant, clean but drab; several on Nuevo Laredo highway.

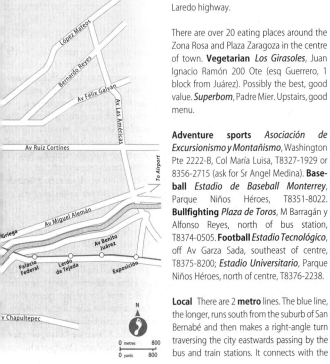

There are over 20 eating places around the Zona Rosa and Plaza Zaragoza in the centre of town. **Vegetarian** *Los Girasoles*, Juan Ignacio Ramón 200 Ote (esq Guerrero, 1 block from Juárez). Possibly the best, good value. *Superbom*, Padre Mier. Upstairs, good menu.

Eating

Adventure sports *Asociación de Excursionismo y Montañismo*, Washington Pte 2222-B, Col María Luisa, T8327-1929 or 8356-2715 (ask for Sr Angel Medina). **Baseball** *Estadio de Baseball Monterrey*, Parque Niños Héroes, T8351-8022. **Bullfighting** *Plaza de Toros*, M Barragán y Alfonso Reyes, north of bus station, T8374-0505. **Football** *Estadio Tecnológico*, off Av Garza Sada, southeast of centre, T8375-8200; *Estadio Universitario*, Parque Niños Héroes, north of centre, T8376-2238.

Sports

Local There are 2 **metro** lines. The blue line, the longer, runs south from the suburb of San Bernabé and then makes a right-angle turn traversing the city eastwards passing by the bus and train stations. It connects with the

Transport

Northeast Mexico

green line (at Cuauhtémoc near the bus station), which runs south into the centre. Tickets bought from machines (2 pesos a ticket, less for more than 1). **Car rental** *Monterrey*, Serafín Peña 740-A Sur, T344-6510. *National*, Escobedo Sur 1011 Local 8, T344-6363.

Air Gen Mariano Escobedo airport (MTY), 24 km from centre. Daily flights from Mexico City take 1 hr 20 mins. Good links to many other Mexican cities and numerous flights to the US and Canada and to Havana, Cuba.

Buses Terminal on Av Colón, between Calzada B Reyes and Av Pino Suárez (metro Cuauhtémoc), T318-3737. To **Santiago**, for Cola de Caballo falls, US$2.20.

To **Mexico City**: US$52, 12 hrs. A more scenic trip is from Mexico City (northern bus terminal) to **Ciudad Valles**: 10 hrs, from where there are many connecting buses to Monterrey. To **Chihuahua**: with *Transportes del Norte*, 8 a day, 12 hrs, US$46. To **Guadalajara**: US$42. To **Matamoros**: *Transportes del Norte*, 4 hrs, US$18. To **Nuevo Laredo**: departures every hr, 4 hrs, US$14. Frequent buses to **Saltillo**, but long queues for tickets. To **San Luis Potosí**: US$26. To **Tampico**, 7-8 hrs, US$26. To **Torreón**, US$20.

NB Motorists if driving Monterrey-Saltillo, there is nothing to indicate you are on the toll-road until it is too late. The toll is US$7. Look for the old road.

Directory **Airline offices** *AeroCalifornia*, T8345-9700. *AeroMéxico*, T8343-5560. *American Airlines*, T8340-3031. *Aviacsa*, T8153-4304. *Mexicana*, T800-715-0220. **Banks** Plenty of ATMs in town. **Communications** Post office: *Palacio Federal*, Av 5 de Mayo y Zaragoza (behind Government Palace), T342-4003.

Embassies and consulates *British* (Honorary), T8333-7598. *Canadian*, T8344-3200, F344-3048. Mon-Fri 0900-1330 and 1430-1730. *French*, T8336-4498. *German*, T8338-5223. *Guatemalan*, T8372-8648. *Israeli*, T8336-1325. *Netherlands*, T8342-5055. *Swedish*, T8346-3090. *Swiss*, T8338-3675. *USA*, T8345-2120. **Medical services** *Hospital General de IMSS*, Pino Suárez y J I Ramón, T8345-5355. *Angeles Verdes*, T8340-2113. **Red Cross**: T8375-1212.

Monterrey to Ciudad Victoria

Heading south from Monterrey, the road threads through the narrow and lovely Huajuco canyon; from Santiago village a road runs to within 2 km of the Cola de Caballo, or Horsetail Falls, in the **Cumbres de Monterrey** national park, the largest in Mexico. There is a first-class hotel on the way, and you can get a *colectivo*, US$1.65, from the bus stop to the falls, and a horse, US$1.65, to take you to the top of the falls. ■ *US$2.40; cost of guide US$5.* Deeper into the park are other waterfalls, the 75-m Cascada El Chipitín and Cascada Lagunillas. There is a two-day circuit, *Recorrido de Matacanes*, starting at Las Adjuntas, taking in both these falls and involving river canyoning, abseiling and swimming through tunnels. Ask at Asociación de Excursionismo y Montañismo in Monterrey (see above).

At **Montemorelos**, just off the highway, 79 km south of Monterrey, a branch road from the Matamoros-Monterrey highway enters. Another 53 km takes you to **Linares** (*Population: 69,000*), a fast-expanding town.

Ciudad Victoria
Phone code: 834
Colour map 2, grid C6
Population: 262,686
Altitude: 336 m

The north-south streets (parallel to the Sierra) have names and numbers, the east-west streets have only names

Capital of Tamaulipas state, at Km 706, Ciudad Victoria is a quiet, clean, unhurried city with a shaded plaza. Here Route 85 from Monterrey meets Route 101 from Matamoros.

The **Parque Siglo 21** is the same end of town as the bus station. The centrepiece is a planetarium, which looks like a huge red ball that landed on the banks of the Río San Marcos. Across the river is the Government Plaza, a 12-storey glass tower, the tallest building in town. Also worth seeing is the state library in a green, tiled, Aztec-style building. The **Centro Cultural Tamaulipas**, Calle 15 and Hidalgo, opposite the Palacio de Gobierno, is a functional, modern building with a library, theatre, art gallery and various cultural functions. The **Museo de Antropología e Historia**, on the plaza, has a good section on the Huastec culture. On top of a hill is a tiny church, the temple of Nuestra Señora de Guadalupe, the patron saint of Mexico.

The **tourist office** is on Calle 8 Anaya y Olivia Ramírez 1287, T/F316-1074, while the state tourism website is at **www.turismo-tamaulipas.gob.mx**

Sleeping **A** *Santorín*, Cristóbal Colón Nte 349, T318-1515, F318-1516. A/c, TV, parking, restaurant. **B** *Sierra Gorda*, Hidalgo 990 Ote, T312-2010. Garage US$0.70 a night. Several **E** hotels by bus station and in the centre. **Motels** **B** *Panorámica*, Lomas del Santuario, T312-5457. **D** *Los Monteros*, Plaza Hidalgo, T312-0300. Downtown. **Trailer Park** *Victoria RV Trailer Park*, Libramiento 101-85, T/F312-4824. Follow signs, good service, electricity, hot showers; owner (Rosie) has travel information.

Eating *Chavos*, Calle 12, Hidalgo y Juárez. All you can eat buffet. *Daddy's* on the plaza. A sort of *Denny's*, with a Mexican touch for the homesick American. Locals congregate at *Café Cantón*, ½ a block from the plaza on Calle 9.

Transport **Train**: check locally whether rail services are available. **Buses**: terminal is on the outskirts near the ring road northeast of the town centre. *Omnibuses Blancos* to **Ciudad Valles** (see below) for US$12. Bus to **Mexico City**: 10 hrs, US$41.

Ciudad Mante

Phone code: 831
Colour map 2, grid C6

After crossing the Tropic of Cancer the road enters the solid green jungle of the tropical lowlands. Ciudad Mante (Route 85), 137 km south of Ciudad Victoria, is almost exactly the mid-way point between Matamoros and Mexico City and makes a convenient stopover place despite being a grubby city. It has a **Museo de Antropología e Historia**, with objects from the Huastec culture.

Excursions Forty-five kilometres north of Ciudad Mante is the village of **Gómez Farías**, an important centre for ornithological research: the highlands above the village represent the northernmost extent of several tropical vegetation formations. Many tropical bird species reach the northern limit of their range. Gómez Farías is reached by turning west off the main highway, 14 km over a paved road to the town plaza. From there, an easy 2-km walk provides excellent views of bird habitats. A one-hour drive from Ciudad Mante, plus a five-hour walk, leads to **El Cielo Biosphere Reserve**, which has four different ecosystems at various altitudes, including tropical jungle and cloud forest (about 200 m to 2,500 m).

South of Ciudad Mante, at Km 548 from Mexico City, is Antiguo Morelos where a road turns off west to San Luis Potosí (see page 283) 314 km, and Guadalajara (see page 303).

Sleeping The best hotel is probably **B** *Mante*, Guerrero 500 Nte, T232-0990. Shaded grounds at north edge of business sector. **C** *Monterrey*, Av Juárez 503 Ote, T232-2712, in old sector. With bath, hot water, a/c, cable TV, helpful manager speaks English, safe parking, restaurant not so good. Recommended. Several hotels a few blocks south of Zócalo.

Tampico

Phone code: 833
Colour map 2, grid C6
Population: 294,789

Fishing (both sea and river) is excellent

Tampico, on the Gulf of Mexico and definitely not a tourist attraction, is reached by a fine road from Ciudad Mante, in a rich sugar-growing area. Tampico was founded in 1522 by Gonzalo de Sandoval but was sacked by pirates in the 17th century and refounded in 1823. It has the faded grandeur of a once prosperous river port and is situated on the northern bank of the Río Pánuco, not far from a large oilfield; there are storage tanks and refineries for miles along the southern bank. The summer heat, rarely above 35°C, is tempered by sea breezes, but June and July are trying. Cold northerlies blow now and again during the winter. There are two pleasant plazas, Plaza de Armas at Colón y Carranza, with squirrels in the trees, and Plaza de la Libertad at Madero y Juárez. There are two interesting buildings on the Plaza de Armas: the **Catedral Santa Iglesia** has an international flavour: a clock from

Northeast Mexico

England, an altar from Carrara in Italy and *swastikas* inlaid into the aisle floor. The former **Palacio Municipal** on the northwest corner (now DIF building) is an Art Nouveau construction. The **tourist office** on 20 de Noviembre 218 is helpful.

Excursions The **Playa de Miramar**, a beach resort, is a tram or bus ride from the city, but is reported dirty. **Laguna del Carpintero**, just north of the centre, is popular for watersports.

Sleeping ■ *on map* **B** *Impala*, Díaz Mirón 220 Pte, T212-0990. **B** *Nuevo León*, Aduana N 107, T124370. With a/c, shower, clean. **B** *Tampico*, Carranza 513, T219-0057. **C** *Ritz*, on Miramar beach (see above). Deserted at night.

Several cheap hotels near Plaza de la Libertad: **E** *América*, T232-3478, near market on Olmos. Dirty but safe and friendly. **E** *Hawaii*, Héroes del Cañonero 609 (2 blocks east of Plaza Libertad), T234-1887. Dark rooms, clean. There are others on this street. RVs can stay in the parking lot of the airport, which has public conveniences, US$15 per vehicle, noisy from traffic.

Eating *Emir*, Olmos between Díaz Mirón and Madero. Good for breakfast. *El Selecto*, opposite market. There are many cheap restaurants in the *Centro Gastronómico Mercado de Comida* east of the market.

Festivals **(Re-)Founders day**, beginning of **Apr**.

Sports **Apr-Aug** is the **Deep-Sea Fishing** competition season, with several big international competitions.

Transport **Air** The Francisco Javier Mina Airport (TAM), T238-0571 is 8 km from the centre. *Mexicana* has daily flights to **Mexico City** and *Aerolitoral* flies to **San Antonio** (Texas), **Ciudad del Carmen, Monclova, Monterrey, Piedras Negras, Poza Rica, San Luis Potosí, Torreón, Veracruz** and **Villahermosa**. *Aero California* flies to **Los Angeles** via **Mexico City, Tepic** and **Tijuana**. *Continental Express* flies to Dallas and Houston.

Bus Bus station is several km from the centre on Av Ejército Mexicano on the far side of Laguna del Carpintero. *Colectivos* to bus station leave from Olmos between market and plaza. To **Ciudad Valles**: US$9. To **Mexico City**: 9 hrs, US$27. To **Monterrey**: 7-8 hrs, US$29. To **San Luis Potosí**: 7 hrs, US$24.

Tampico

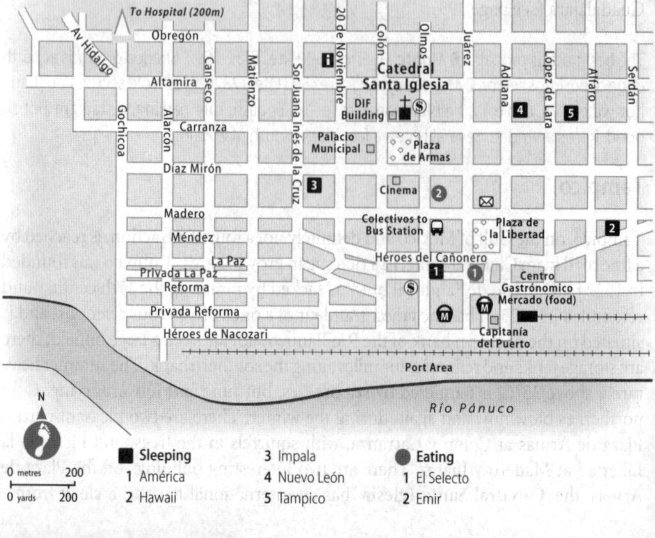

Northeast Mexico

Airline offices *Aero California*, T213-8400. *AeroMéxico*, T217-0939. *Mexicana*, T213-9600. **Directory**
Communications Post office: on Madero 309 Ote, T212-1927. **Embassies and consulates**
German Consul, 2 de Enero, 102 Sur-A, T212-9784. Also deals with British affairs. **Medical**
services Red Cross: T212-1313.

A 145-km paved road west from Tampico through the oil camp of **Ebano** joins the Nuevo **Routes**
Laredo-Mexico City highway further south at Ciudad Valles. There are direct buses to
Brownsville (Texas). South of Tampico a splendid new bridge was opened in 1988 to replace
the ferry to **Villa Cuauhtémoc**. Further south, the coast road, Route 180, enters Veracruz
state, leading to Tuxpan, Poza Rica and Veracruz (see Chapter 5).

Tampico to the Colonial Heartland

Ciudad Valles, on a winding river is a popular stopover with many hotels. **Museo** **Ciudad Valles**
Regional Huasteco, Rotarios y Artes (or Peñaloza), is the centre of archaeological *Phone code: 481*
and ethnographic research for the Huastec region. ■ *Mon-Fri 1000-1200, 1400-1800.* *Colour map 2, grid C6*
Visit the market, which is very busy. There are many cheap places to eat tacos. *Population: 146,411*

Sleeping A *Valles*, T382-0050, with trailer park. Full hook-up, hot shower, a bit run down,
US$10 for 2 in car, on Carretera México-Laredo. **B** *San Fernando*, T382-0184, on main high-
way. Clean, large rooms, a/c, TV, parking. **C** *Condesa*, Av Juárez 109, T382-0015. Clean, basic,
fan, friendly, OK. 11 km south of town is campground *El Bañito*. With warm sulphur pools,
good restaurant, a bit run down.

Transport Buses: *Omnibus Ote* to **San Luis Potosí**, US$11, 4 hrs; **Mexico City**: US$26, 10 hrs.

With riotous tropical vegetation, Tamazunchale is perhaps the most popular of all **Tamazunchale**
the overnight stops on this route. (**B** *Mirador*, good, but passing traffic by night is *Phone code: 483*
noisy. **E** *Hotel OK*, cheapest but not recommended.) The potholed road south of *Colour map 3, grid B4*
here begins a spectacular climb to the highland, winding over the rugged terrain cut *Population: 88,991*
by the Río Moctezuma and its tributaries. The highest point on the road is 2,502 m. *Altitude: 206 m*
From **Jacala**, Km 279 (two very basic hotels, erratic water supply), there is a dizzying
view into a chasm. **Zimapán** (*Posada del Rey*, fascinating but very run down, out on
the highway), with a charming market place and a small old church in the plaza, is as
good a place as any to stay the night. From **Portezuelo** (Km 178 from Mexico City) a
paved road runs west to Querétaro (see page 257), 140 km.

An area of 23,300 sq km north and south of Ixmiquilpan (Km 169 from Mexico **Ixmiquilpan**
City), just off the highway, is inhabited by 65,000 Otomí Indians. The beautifully *Phone code: 759*
worked Otomí belts and bags may sometimes be bought at the Monday market, and *Colour map 3, grid B4*
also in the *artesanía* shop in the main street.
    See early Indian frescoes in the main church, one of several 16th-century
battlemented Augustinian monastery-churches; the monastery is open to the public. At sunset each day white egrets come to roost in the trees outside the church; it's
worth going up on to the battlements to see them swoop down. The church of El
Carmen is worth a visit too; it has a lovely west façade and gilded altars inside. There
is also a 16th-century bridge over the river and a beautiful walk along the
ahuehuete-lined banks.

Excursions Near Ixmiquilpan are several warm swimming pools, both natural and
manmade: San Antonio, Dios Padre, Las Humedades, Tzindejé (about 20 minutes
from town) and near Tephé (the only warm-water bath, clean. ■ *US$0.40*). The
Otomí villages of La Lagunita, La Pechuga and La Bonanza, in a beautiful valley,
have no modern conveniences.
    The **Barranca de Tolantongo**, 37 km northeast of Ixmiquilpan, is about 1,500 m
deep with a waterfall and thermal spring; at weekends there is a small eating place.

Northeast Mexico

■ *US$2, car parking US$2 at entrance to recreational area; camping permitted.* To get there take the road towards El Cardonal, then an unpaved turn-off about 3 km before El Cardonal (there is a bus from Pachuca).

Sleeping C *Hotel Diana*. Rear buildings slightly dearer rooms, safe parking. Recommended. **E** *Hotel/Restaurant Los Portales*, 1 block from main square. Clean, safe parking.

Actopan to Tula

Actopan (Km 119 from the capital) has another fine 16th-century Augustinian church, convent, and an impressive open chapel (**B** *Hotel Rira*). From Actopan a 56-km branch road runs to one of Mexico's great archaeological sites: Tula, capital of the Toltecs (see page 144).

On the way to Tula there is an interesting co-operative village, **Cruz Azul**, where there are free Sunday-morning concerts at 1000 in front of main market. At Colonia (Km 85), a road runs left for 8 km to Pachuca (see page 142). Route 85 continues to Mexico City.

Parque Nacional Sierra de la Laguna

In the rugged interior east of Todos Santos is the **Parque Nacional Sierra de la Laguna** (under threat and not officially recognized). Its crowning peak is the Picacho La Laguna (2,163 m), which is beginning to attract a trickle of hikers to its 'lost world' of pine and oak trees, doves and woodpeckers, grassy meadows and luxuriant flowers; there is nothing else like it in Baja. The trail is steep but straightforward; the panoramic view takes in La Paz and both the Gulf and Pacific coasts. It gets cold at night. The park can be reached from Todos Santos by making local enquiries; three-day guided pack trips are also offered by the *Todos Santos Inn*, US$325 per person. Alternatively, take a taxi from Todos Santos to La Burrera, from where it is eight hours' walk along the littered path to La Laguna.

Colonial Heartland

Mexico City

For centuries, the mines of Central Mexico churned out much of the world's silver and a fair amount of gold and precious stones too. Spanish-style architecture built with the fortunes amassed from silver and gold is at its most opulent and impressive in the magnificent towns and cities of the Colonial Highlands. While the mines of Zacatecas, San Luis Potosí and Guanajuato supplied the precious metal to the Spanish crown, the states of Aguascalientes and Querétaro were important supply centres and stopovers on the silver route to the capital and the port of Veracruz. Mining is still important in this area and many of these old cities are today important modern industrial centres, mostly with sprawling suburbs; but they mostly manage to retain at their core the magnificence of their colonial past. The 'ghost towns' of Pozas and Real de Catorce, once thriving mining centres, have not fared so well, but it is fascinating to wander through their semi-deserted streets. The years of heavy-handed Spanish rule and obvious inequalities led to discontent, and in the early 19th century this region was the Cradle of Independence; nearly every town or village played a part in the break with Spain and many museums and monuments tell the story. Colonial rule relied heavily on the work of the missionaries and a tour of the 18th-century Missions of Querétaro, well off the beaten track, with a stop-off at the thermal baths and opal mines of Tequisquiapan, is well worth the hair-raising journey of 700 curves.

Querétaro

An important industrial centre and state capital, Querétaro is 215 km from the capital and 1,105 km from the US border at Eagle Pass. The city was founded in 1531 and the name means 'Place of Rocks' in Tarascan. Hidalgo's rising in 1810 was plotted here, and it was also here that Emperor Maximilian surrendered after defeat, was tried and shot on 19 June 1867, on the Cerro de las Campanas (the Hill of Bells), outside the city.

Phone code: 442
Colour map 3, grid B3
Population: 639,839
Altitude: 1,865 m

The Central Camionera (bus station) is 5 km southeast of the centre, on the south side of the Mexico City-León highway. There are regular services to Mexico City (Terminal del Norte) and to Mexico City Airport (outside Sala D). For details of other destinations see Transport, page 259. Querétaro is at the crossroads of Route 57 (San Luis Potosí-Mexico City) and Route 45 to Celaya, León and Aguascalientes. There are regular flights from Mexico City and Monterrey.

Getting there

Querétaro centre is reasonably compact and can be managed quite easily on foot; walking tours are very popular. City buses Nos 8 and 19 link the town centre and bus station; make sure they say 'Central Camionera' or 'Terminal de Autobuses'. City buses are quite slow and taxis a not-too-expensive alternative.

Getting around

The **State Tourist Office**, Pasteur Nte 4, is on Plaza Independencia at junction with Libertad, T212-1412, F212-1094. The official tourism website for Querétaro state is at **www.queretaro.gob.mx/turismo**

Sights

In 1810, Doña Josefa Ortiz de Domínguez , wife of the Mayor and prominent member of a group plotting for Independence, got word to Father Hidalgo that their plans for revolt had been discovered. Hidalgo immediately gave the cry (*El Grito*) for Independence. Today, El Grito is given from the balcony of the **Palacio Municipal** (once home of Doña Josefa) every 15 September at 2300 (and is echoed on every civic balcony throughout Mexico). Dona Josefa, or La Corregidora's, home may be visited.

Because of the altitude it can be quite cold at night

Colonial Heartland

The **Santa Rosa de Viterbo** church and monastery was remodelled by Francisco Tresguerras. He also reconstructed the **Templo de Santa Clara**, one of the loveliest churches in Mexico. The 16th-century church and monastery of **Santa Cruz** served as the HQ of Maximilian and his forces and later as the Emperor's prison before he faced the firing squad in 1867. There is a good view from the bell tower. The church of **San Felipe**, recently restored, is now the cathedral. The splendid **Palacio Federal**, once an Augustinian convent with exceptionally fine cloisters, has been restored and houses an art gallery containing some beautiful works. The **Teatro de la República**, by Jardín Obregón, is where Maximilian and his generals were tried, and where the Constitution of 1917 (still in force) was drafted. The **aqueduct**, built in 1726, is very impressive.

Several *andadores* (pedestrian walkways) have been developed, greatly adding to the amenities of the city. ■ *Walking tours can be arranged through the tourist office, daily at 1030 and 1800, 2½ hrs, US$1.80, recommended. City tour plus execution site and Juárez monument, excellent value, from J Guadalupe Velásquez 5, Jardines de Oro, Santa Cruz, T212-1298, daily at 1130, US$12.*

Museums   The important and elegant **Museo Regional** is on the main plaza, known as the Plaza de Armas or as Jardín Obregón (not all its galleries are always open). It contains much material on the Independence movement and the 1864-67 period leading to the imprisonment and death of Maximilian. ■ *0900-1900, closed Mon, free.*

Sleeping   **LL** *La Casa de la Marquesa*, Madero 41, T212-0092. 3 categories of rooms, the cheapest a
■ *on map*   steal at US$180. Very opulent and lovely lobby. Mid-priced rooms equally opulent.
Price codes: see   **AL-A** *Mesón de Santa Rosa*, Pasteur Sur 17, Centro, T224-2781, F212-5522. Small, 300-year
inside front cover   old inn, tastefully modernized, good restaurant with international and Mexican cuisine.
A *Casa Inn*, Constituyentes 69 Pte, T216-0102, F216-0100. 4-star. **A** *Mirabel*, Constituyentes 2, T214-3585, F214-3585. Good, restaurant and parking.

C *Del Marqués*, Juárez Nte 104, T212-0414. TV, phone, clean. **C** *Hidalgo*, Madero 11 Pte, near Zócalo, T212-0081 (English owner, Adrian Leece). With bath, quiet, friendly, excellent

Querétaro

To Railway Station

To San Luis Potosí, Juárez Monument & Cerro de las Campanas
To Celaya
To Mexico City
To Los Arcos

San Felipe Cathedral

Santa Rosa de Viterbo

Alameda

■ **Sleeping**		
1 Hidalgo	3 Mesón de Santa Rosa	6 Posada la Academia
2 La Casa de la Marquesa	4 Mirabel	7 Posada la Colonial
	5 Plaza	8 San Agustín

0 metres   200
0 yards   200

Colonial Heartland

value for 2 or more, not so for singles, has restaurant. **C** *Plaza*, Jardín Obregón, T212-1138. With bath, TV and phone, good location, airy, lovely inner patio, modernized, safe, clean, comfortable. Recommended.

D *San Agustín*, Pino Suárez 12, T212-3919. Small. **D** *El Cid*, Prolongación Corregidora, T214-1165. More of a motel, clean, good value. **D** *Corregidora*, Corregidora 138, T214-0406. Reasonable but noisy. **D** *Posada La Academia*, Pino Suárez 3, just off Plaza Constitución. With bath and TV. Recommended. **D** *Posada La Colonial*, Juárez 19 Sur, T212-0239. Good value (**E** without bath). **D** *Posada Teresa*, Reforma 51 Ote, T212-6180. Basic. **E** *Posada Familiar*, Independencia 22, T212-0584. Basic but OK, courtyard. **E** *Ex-Convento de la Cruz*, Av del Ejército Republicano, T223-1120. Youth hostel, running water morning only.

Motels **L** *Jurica*, Km 229 on road to San Luis Potosí, T218-0022, F218-0136, former hacienda. With gardens, squash, golf course, opulent. **AL** *La Mansión*, 6½ km south of town. Excellent dining facilities, gorgeous grounds. **B** *Flamingo*, on Constituyentes Pte 138, T216-2093, F215-5778. Comfortable.

Eating

Arcangel, Plaza Chica. Pleasant setting, good food. *Bisquetes*, in arcade of old *Gran Hotel* on Zócalo. Good value. Try local Hidalgo Pinot Noir wine. *Café del Fondo*, Pino Suárez 9. Nice coffee house. *Don Juan*, Plazuela de las Casas. Recommended. *Flor de Querétaro*, on Jardín Obregón, Juárez Nte 5. Good but pricey. *La Cocina Mexicana*, Pino Suárez 17, opposite *Hotel San Agustín*. Cheap and good but rather dark, à la carte better value than *comida corrida*. *La Mariposa*, A Peralta 7. Excellent coffee, *tortas* and fruit shakes. *Le Bon Vivant*, Pino Suárez. Cheap, good value. Recommended. *Leo's*, at La Cruz market. Excellent tacos and quesadillas, popular. *Lonergan's*, Plaza de Armas. Pleasant café with small art gallery, magazines in English, French and German. *Los Tacos de mi General*, Av Reforma y Manuel G Nájera. Cheap and good 4-course *comida corrida*. *Mesón de Chucho el Roto* (since 1810), Plaza Independencia. Very popular at night. Serves drinks. Musicians. *Mesón Santa Rosa*, Pasteur 17, in hotel of same name. Good but expensive, restored colonial building. *Ostionería Tampico*, Corregidora Nte 3. Good cheap fish. *Supersoya*, on Corregidora, north of Zaragoza, has a wide selection of vitamins and health food. *Terramar*, where Jardín Obregón and Jardín Corregidora intersect, top floor of 1870 house.

Entertainment

Corral de Comedias, Carranza 39, T212-0765. An original theatre company, colonial surroundings and suppers. *JBJ Disco*, Blvd Zona Dorada, Fracc Los Arcos. *Mariachis* play in the Jardín Corregidora, 16 de Septiembre y Corregidora, in the evenings. The town band plays in the Jardín Obregón on Sun evening, lovely atmosphere.

Festivals

There is a *Feria Agrícola* from 2nd week of **Dec** until Christmas; bull fights and cock fights. On **New Year's Eve** there is a special market and performances are given in the main street.

Shopping

Cheaper than San Juan del Río, but more expensive than Taxco

There are local opals, amethysts and topazes for sale; remarkable mineral specimens are shaped into spheres, eggs, mushrooms, and then polished until they shine like jewels (US$10-30). Recommended is *Joyería Villalón*, Andador Libertad 24a, for fine opals at good prices. **La Cruz market**, 10 mins' walk from the centre, is very well stocked, busy and clean. Open daily, with a street market on Sun.

Transport

Air Flights connecting to Guadalajara, Mexico City, Monterrey and San Luis Potosí.

Trains The station is not far north of the centre, close to Prolongación Corregidora. No passenger trains are running on the Mexico City-Cuidad Juárez line. Check locally for any services that may be running.

Buses The bus station is 5 km southeast of the centre, near Estadio Corregidora. Terminal A, modules 1 and 2, 1st class and *Plus*, Terminal B, modules 3, 4 and 5, 2nd class. Buses aren't allowed in the centre so there are no buses that run from the bus station directly to the centre; the closest you'll get is the south end of Corregidora. There are fixed-cost taxis and buses. The bus station has a place for bag storage, restaurants (with a bar upstairs), travel agency, newsagents and public conveniences. Public phones are available.

Colonial Heartland

Missions of Querétaro

A little-known feature of Querétaro is the existence of 18th-century missions in the far northeast of the state. They were founded by Fray Junípero de la Serra, who later went on to establish missions in California with names like Nuestra Señora de los Angeles and San Francisco de Asís. He is also said to have planted a miraculous tree in the convent of the Santa Cruz in the city of Querétaro by thrusting his staff into the ground. The tree is apparently the only one of its kind in the world to have cruciform thorns.

All five missions, most easily visited from Jalpan, have been restored, and two of them have hotels nearby. The journey itself requires something of a head for heights in that there are said to be 700 curves en route. There is a slightly shorter way, but that has over 1,000.

At least three days should be allowed to enjoy the tour of the missions.

There are good connections with most towns on the US border if you are heading north. Likewise, if heading south, Querétero is a good target to aim for, with good connections. **Acapulco**: *Estrella Blanca*, 2200, 0040, US$42. **Aguascalientes**: *Omnibus de México*, 1315 and 0215, US$19. **Chihuahua**: *Omnibus de México*, 1930, 2030, US$62. **Ciudad Juárez**: 16 a day, US$114. **Durango**: *Omnibus de México*, 1120, 2100, US$36. **Guadalajara**: frequent services, 5 hrs, US$27. **Guanajuato**: 6 a day between 0800 and 1700, 3 hrs, US$9. **León**: every couple of hours, US$11. **Mazatlán**: *Estrella Blanca*, 1000, 1210 and 1830, US$58. **Mexico City**: an endless stream of buses of all classes, 3 hrs, US$14-11. **Monterrey**: *Elite/Futura/Chihuahuenses*, 12 per day, US$33. *Omnibus de México*, 1920, 2115, 2300, US$32.50. **Morelia**: *Servicios Coordinados*, 16 per day, US$9. **Nogales**: *Elite/Futura/Chihuahuenses*, departure time uncertain, US$135. **Piedras Negras**: *Elite/Futura/Chihuahuenses* (US border), 1540, 1900, 1955, US$75. *San Juan del Río*, every 15 mins, 1 hr. **San Luis Potosí**: regular throughout the day, 3 hrs, US$12. **San Miguel de Allende**: roughly hourly, 1 hr, US$5. **Tijuana**: 1000, 1210 and 1830, US$130. **Zacatecas**: almost hourly, US$24.

Directory **Airline offices** *Aeromar*, T220-6936. **Banks** There is a *Banamex ATM* on the Jardín Obregón at Juárez and 16 de Septiembre that accepts Visa and MasterCard. There is a *Banco Inverlat ATM* (that should accept AmEx cards) at Corregidora Norte 60. There is a Casa de Cambio at Corregidora Nte 134. **Communications** Internet outlets: *Café Internet Asodi*, Fco. Márquez 219, Col Las Campanas, T215-2783. *Café Internet Cibers Pace*, Av Universidad 297, Col Las Brujas, T213-7662. *Café Internet Welo*, Ezequiel Montes 67 Sur (close to corner of Constituyentes) T212-7272. **Post office**: Arteaga Pte 5. *DHL*, International courier service, Blvd Zona Dorada 37, Fracc Los Arcos, T214-2526 or 214-5256, open Mon-Fri 0900-1800, Sat 0900-1200. **Language schools** *Centro Intercultural de Querétaro*, Reforma 41, Centro, T/F122831. *FEPE* (*Franco Español para Extranjeros*), Luis Pasteur Nte 29, Col Centro, T212-0819, info@fepe.edu.mx, www.fepe.edu.mx Only Spanish is spoken; no knowledge of English is necessary. Classes have a maximum of 5 students, 25 hrs per week for US$130, 6 proficiency levels, 100 hrs per level, 4 weeks each. Also 1-to-1 tuition at US$12 an hr. 'Spanish for travellers' course is 2 weeks, 5 hrs per day, costs US$265. They offer homestay. A double room costs US$49 per person, a single room costs US$90 per week. Meals are extra: US$2 for breakfast, US$3 for lunch, and US$2 for dinner.

Missions of Querétaro

The road to the **Missions of Querétaro** goes through the small market town of **Ezequiel Montes** (*population:* 5,000), reached either by a road turning northeast from the main highway 21 km east of Querétaro, or by Route 120 from San Juan del Río (see below). Two places of interest off the first-mentioned road are the town of **Colón** (14 km off the road, with 17th-century Templo de Nuestra Señora de los Dolores de Soriana) and **Bernal**, 75 km from Querétaro, a centre for clothing, blankets, wall hangings and carpets made by cottage industry. Near Bernal is the remarkable **Peñón de Bernal**, a massive rocky outcrop 350 m high. On the night before and the day of the spring equinox (21 March) there is a festival held here. Local indigenous people believe the mountain is an energy point, because of its distinctive shape, and come to get energy from the first sun of the year. Of its kind, it is considered third after the Rock of Gibraltar and the Sugarloaf Mountain in Rio de Janeiro.

Forty-eight kilometres from Querétaro is San Juan del Río, near where some of the best fighting bulls are raised; the town is a centre for handicrafts, and also for polishing gemstones: opals and amethysts. *La Guadalupana*, 16 de Septiembre 5, is a friendly shop with reasonable prices. Of the several *balnearios* in San Juan try *Venecia*, which has cold water and is very quiet mid-week (US$1.30).

San Juan del Río
Phone code: 427
Colour map 3, grid B3
Population: 179,300

Sleeping AL *Hotel Mansión Galindo*, T272-0050. Restored hacienda; apparently given by Cortés to his mistress La Malinche, beautiful building. **C** *Layseca*, Av Juárez 9 Ote, T272-0110. Colonial building, large rooms, nice furniture, excellent, car parking, no restaurant; several picturesque hotels, for example, **D-E** *Estancia*, good, enclosed parking.

A branch road runs northeast from San Juan to the picturesque town of Tequisquiapan, with thermal baths, fine climate, watersports, weekend residences and expensive, good hotels. The town is deserted from Monday to Thursday and big reductions in hotel prices can be found. The dam near the town is worth a visit. There is a geyser, at Tecozautla, 1¼ hours from Tequisquiapan.

Tequisquiapan
Phone code: 414
Colour map 3, grid B3
Population 49,910

Sleeping and eating A *El Relox*, Morelos 8, T273-0066. Spa pool, open to non-residents. *Maridelphi*, T273-0052, similar price and services. Restaurant *La Chiapaneca*, Carrizal 19. Centre, opposite craft market, very good, reasonably priced, clean.

Transport Buses: San Juan del Río-Tequisquiapan, regular services, 20 mins, US$1.

North of Tequisquiapan is Cadereyta (Km 75), colonial in style, with two noteworthy churches in the main square, one dedicated to St Peter, the other St Paul. The latter houses an important collection of colonial religious art. Nearby is the Casa de los Alemanes, which has an enormous collection of cacti.

Cadereyta
Phone code: 441
Colour map 3, grid B3
Population 51,688

East of Route 120, there are ruins at San Joaquín (Km 138): **Ranas** and **Toluquilla** have been only partially excavated. The former receives about 200 visitors a month, the latter only 40. You must register upon arriving and a donation is requested. The sites have been attributed to the Toltecs and the Chichimecs. Ranas is a 30-minute walk from the village and has stupendous views from a series of terraced platforms and pyramids (*entry US$1*); Toluquilla lies 10 km from the village (poorly marked road). Although there were only, at most, 200 inhabitants, there are six ball courts. Tarantulas abound! Fifteen minutes' walk from San Joaquín is a beautiful cave (Las Grutas). San Joaquín is famous for the annual Huapango dance festival on 15 April.

San Joaquín
Colour map 3, grid B3

The roads to both ruins are steep and the ruins are often swathed in mist

Sleeping D *Victoria*, halfway up hill, Av Insurgentes. Basic. **D** *Mesón de Joaquín*, T272-5315, next to bus park. Good-value rooms for four and a camp-ground with shelters and barbecue stands on the outskirts above the town. **Transport** San Joaquín can be reached in 3 hours by car or bus on a windy road going through desert and then misty pine forests. *Flecha Amarilla* run 6 buses a day, earliest from Querétaro 0620, last 1620, US$4; *Flecha Azul* also run buses San Joaquín-San Juan del Río.

The bends really start after Vizarrón. Much of the journey from here on is through rather arid and dramatic terrain with gorges and panoramic views. The high point is called la Puerta del Cielo (Door to the Sky), which is apt enough as you can actually look down on the clouds. As the road begins to descend, so the vegetation becomes more tropical and the weather gets much warmer. There is a petrol station at Ahuacatlán (Km 166), before Jalpan.

Colonial Heartland

Jalpan

Phone code 441
Colour map 3, grid B4
Altitude: 700 m

Jalpan, the first of the missions in the region, becomes visible way below in a broad, lush valley. It is the largest of the missions, which are located in valleys that spread out from here. Jalpan was the first to be founded in 1774 and has cloisters as well as the main church. The town itself is picturesque without being spoilt. It makes a good base for day trips to the other missions. Also there are pleasant walks along tree-lined riverbanks. The town museum is worth a visit. ■ *1000-1500, US$0.50.*

The missions in the area (see box) are distinguished by the profusion of baroque carving, their superb location and the care with which they have been conserved. They are all different and all worth the trip: **Landa de Matamoros**, 18 km east of Jalpan; **Tilaco**, 25 km beyond Landa to the east; and **Tancoyol**, 37 km to the north of Landa. The roads are good apart from the last 15 km into Tilaco.

Sleeping and eating C *Posada Fray Junípero*, Ezequiel Montes 124, T412-1241, opposite church. With bath and TV, clean, friendly, credit cards, colonial style, pool, restaurant, good value but noisy because of bus station. **E** *Posada Aurora*. With bath, hot water, fan, clean, friendly. Recommended.

Las Cazuelas, to right of church. Delicious tacos, very clean. *Las Jacarandas*, next to bus station. Good *comida corrida*, reasonably priced, clean. Shrimp cocktails at stalls on plaza.

Transport Buses: To *Mexico City*, 3 direct, 6 hrs, US$18, beautiful trip. *Landa de Matamoros*, hourly, US$0.80, 20 mins. To *Tilaco* and *Tancoyol*, 40-min bus journey to La Lagunita, hourly, then combis (on market day, Sat) or hitchhike. To *Querétaro*, every hr, 5 hrs, US$5. To *Ciudad Valles*, frequent, via Landa de Matamoros and Xilitla.

Concá

Altitude: 500 m

Thirty-eight kilometres northwest of Jalpan is Concá. *Acamaya* (freshwater crayfish), is a local speciality. At the bridge of Concá a hot water river flows into one with cold water. The church is built on a ridge, creating a dramatic skyline when viewed from below. The village is very small with two restaurants and a general store. Hourly bus to Concá from Jalpan, US$1.30.

Xilitla

Phone code: 489
Colour map 3, grid B4

Between Jalpan and Ciudad Valles is the charming village of Xilitla, overlooking a lush tropical valley. Famous for the house (El Castillo) and garden (Las Pozas) of the late Edward James, born 1907, millionaire heir to the Phelps Dodge copper fortune, with connections to the British royal family. Las Pozas is 30 minutes' walk from Xilitla and is fascinating with extravagant concrete structures intertwined with exuberant vegetation, waterfalls, birds and butterflies. **Sleeping and eating** at **A-B** *El Castillo*, T485-2136, F485-0055. Includes breakfast, pool, fine views, run by Avery and Leonore Danzinger. Several smaller hotels too. At *Restaurant Los Cayos* (good view), try *enchiladas huastecas* and local coffee. Buses from Jalpan every hour, US$2.30, 2½ hours.

Querétaro to Mexico City

There is a four-lane motorway (US$3 a car) from Irapuato past Querétaro to Mexico City. The Mexico City motorway passes close to Tula and Tepozotlán (see page 144). There are various country clubs along the road.

Celaya

Phone code: 461
Colour map 3, grid B3
Population: 382,140
Altitude: 1,800 m

Celaya is famous for its confectionery, especially a caramel spread called *cajeta*, and its churches, built by Mexico's great architect Francisco Eduardo Tresguerras (1759-1833), a native of the town. His best is considered to be **El Carmen**, with a fine tower and dome. He also built a fine bridge over the Río de la Laja. Founded on 1 January 1571, the city's prosperity came from the fertile soils of the region, which helped the growing town to develop as an important trade and supply centre for mining communities in the region. The processing role of the city has continued, moving beyond food processing to chemical products. The **tourist office**, Casa del Diezmo, Juárez 204, T/F613-4313, is helpful.

Not surprisingly the appeal of the town lies in the architecture of Tresguerras – if **Sights** churches aren't your thing move on. **Templo del Carmen**, built by Tresguerras in 1802-07, the interior and exterior are neoclassical with a simple elegance, and you can see Tresguerras' own paintings inside. **Convento de San Francisco**, is one of the largest in the country, the interior is 17th-century baroque; the façade of the cloisters was rebuilt by Tresguerras. **Templo de San Francisco** was rebuilt in 1683 after the original chapel was demolished. The façade is neoclassical and was rebuilt, together with the altars, by Tresguerras between 1810-20. **Claustro Agustino** dates from the beginning of the 17th century and was the municipal prison until 1961, but now doubles as the Casa de la Cultura. **Templo de San Agustín** was built in 1609 in the plateresque style. **Templo de la Tercera Orden** is another of Tresguerras' neoclassical works, built in 1820 with marvellous altars. The **Columna de la Independencia** was designed by Tresguerras and was the first monument in the country to celebrate Mexico's freedom in 1828. **Torre Hidráulica**, also known as the **bola de agua** (ball of water), has been adopted as the symbol of the city; it was inaugurated on the centenary of Mexico's Independence from Spain and holds one million litres of water. **Casa del Diezmo**, built at the end of the 17th century, now houses the tourist office. The **Presidencia Municipal** has impressive murals up the stairways in the entrance off the main square, a metamorphosis of people and events in Mexico's history, created in 1980 by local artist Octavio Ocampo González. The **Mausoleo de Tresguerras** is a baroque chapel where the famous architect is buried.

AL *Celaya Plaza*, Blvd López Mateos y Carretera Panamericana, T614-6260, F614-6889. 143 **Sleeping** rooms, tennis, spa, meeting rooms. **B** *Plaza Bajío Inn*, Libertad 133, T613-8600, F613-7353. *There are some 30* 80 rooms, central, restaurant, disco, convention facilities, parking, medical service, laundry. *hotels of different* **C** *Isabel*, Hidalgo 207, T612-2096, F613-3449. Restaurant, bar, laundry, parking. *prices and standards;* **D** *Guadalupe*, Portal Guadalupe 108, T612-1839, F612-9514. Very old hotel with historical *many of the better* connections, central, cheaper rooms without bath. *hotels are outside the centre*

Many restaurants serve steak and others specialize in seafood. *El Caserío*, Blvd López Mateos **Eating** 1302 Pte, T615-5608. Spanish cuisine. *El Mezquital*, Blvd López Mateos 1113 Ote. Meat and traditional barbeque. *La Mansión del Marisco*, Blvd López Mateos 1000, esq Juárez, T615-5262. Fish and seafood, live music at weekends. *Mamma O'Fan*. 3 restaurants, at Benito León 203, Blvd López Mateos 1008 Ote, and Plaza Juárez 127, in Apaseo el Grande. Italian food, pizza, pasta, etc.

10-20 Jan is the fiesta of the appearance of the *Virgin of Guadalupe* in the Tierrasnegras bar- **Festivals** rio, one of the oldest districts of Celaya. There is drama, dancing, fireworks and eating a typical *antojito, gorditas de Tierrasnegras*. **Easter** is marked by visiting several *balnearios* in the area and there are processions through the streets, much eating of local delicacies, and on Easter Sun Judas is burned in many places in the city. The *Virgen del Carmen* is celebrated **16 Jul**.

6 buses a day to **Mexico City** airport with *Primera Plus*. 24-hr pharmacy at the bus station. **Transport**

Irapuato is World Strawberry Capital and is justly noted for the delicious fruit, but don't **Irapuato** eat them unwashed. It is also a prosperous industrial and agricultural town and an *Phone code: 462* important distribution centre. In the town centre, around the **Plaza de los Fundadores** *Colour map 3, grid B3* and the **Jardín Hidalgo**, there is a cluster of historic buildings. The **Templo del Hospi-** *Population: 440,039* **tal** built around 1550, rebuilt 1617, façade completed 1733, is said to have the country's *Route 45, Km 315* largest chandelier. Outside, the **Cruz Monolítica** commemorates the visit of San Sebastian of Aparicio. The façade of the **Templo de San Francisco**, also known as El Convento (1799), is a mixture of baroque and neoclassical. The huge **Parroquia** (parish church) was rebuilt mid-18th century. The **Presidencia Municipal**, 19th century, incorporates a former 18th-century school, the **Colegio de Enseñanza para Niños**. The fountain, **Fuente de los Delfines**, was given to the town by Emperor Maximilian. The **tourist office** is at Escuela Médico Militar 60, Colonia Jardines, T624-7174. The local tourism website is at **www.irapuato.gob.mx** (Spanish only)

Colonial Heartland

Unfortunately, the centre of town has been invaded by unsightly and incongruous modern buildings, but just to the edge is the 16th-century church of **San José**, with fine examples of American indigenous art, and the **Templo of Nuestra Señora de Guadalupe** (1890), with a striking late neoclassical gold-leaf-decorated interior.

Sleeping and eating A *Hotel Real de Minas*, T626-2380. Overpriced, with equally over-priced restaurant, on Portal Carrillo Puerto, quiet rooms on church side. **C** *Kennedy*, Kennedy 830, T627 4110. Simple rooms with TV. *Restaurant El Gaucho*, Díaz Ordaz y Lago.

San Miguel de Allende

Phone code: 415
Colour map 3, grid B3
Population: 134,645
Altitude: 1,850 m

This charming old town on a steep hillside facing the broad sweep of the Río Laja and the distant blue of the Guanajuato mountains is 50 km north of Querétaro by paved road, 90 km from Guanajuato. It was founded as San Miguel in 1542, with Allende added in honour of the independence patriot born there. Its twisting cobbled streets rise in terraces to the mineral spring of El Chorro, from which the blue and yellow tiled cupolas of some 20 churches can be seen. It has been declared a national monument and all changes in the town are strictly controlled.

Ins and outs

Getting there The long-distance bus station is west of the town centre along Calle Canal. The town centre can be reached by taxi or bus. The train station is beyond the bus terminal; no scheduled passenger trains but check locally. The nearest airport is at Silao, close to León, sometimes called the Aeropuerto del Bajío.

Getting around Most places of interest can be reached from the town centre on foot. Walking tours of old houses and gardens leave from the Biblioteca Pública (public library), Insurgentes 25, between Reloj and Hidalgo, T152-0293. ■ *Sun 1215, 4 hours, US$8.*

The **tourist office** is on the Plaza / Jardin Prinicpal, next to the church, helpful with finding hotels, English spoken, US$2 for city map, T152-6565.

Sights

Social life revolves around the market and the Jardín, or Plaza Principal, an open-air living room for San Migueleans. Around it are the colonial **Palacio Municipal**, several hotels, and **La Parroquia** (parish church), adorned in the late 19th century by Zeferino Gutiérrez, an Indian stonemason who provided the austere Franciscan front with a beautiful façade and a Gothic tower. See also the mural in the chapel. The church of **San Felipe Neri**, with its fine baroque façade, is at the southwest end of the market. Notable among the baroque façades and doors rich in churrigueresque details are the **Casa del Mayorazgo de Canal**, and **San Francisco** church, designed by Tresguerras. The convent of **La Concepción**, built in 1734, now houses an art school, the **Centro Cultural Ignacio Ramírez Nigromonte**, locally known as Escuela de Bellas Artes (good *cafetería* in its courtyard). The summer residence of the Condes de Canal, on San Antonio, contains the art school and a language school, the **Instituto Allende**, started by Stirling Dickinson (which has an English-language library and runs Spanish courses). A magnificent view of the city can be gained from the mirador on the Querétaro road.

Excursions

A good all-day hike can be made to the **Palo Huérfano** mountain on the south side of town. Take the road to just before the radio pylon then take the trails to the summit, where there are oaks and pines. Between San Miguel de Allende and

Celaya is **Comonfort** (25 km); from there go 3 km north to Rancho Arias: on a hilltop to the west are pre-Columbian ruins. Cross the river north of the church and climb to the ruins via goat-tracks. **El Charco del Ingenio Botanical Gardens** (reached by taking a bus to El Gigante shopping centre, turn left and continue for 15 minutes, or go up Calle Homobono, a more interesting and attractive route) cover an area of 64 ha with lovely views, a deep canyon, an artificial lake and cacti. ■ *US$1, free on Wed.*

Essentials

AL *Casa Luna B&B*, Pila Seca 11, T/F152-1117, casaluna@unisono.net.mx American-run, excellent breakfast included, beautiful themed rooms, no smoking inside. Highly recommended. **A** *La Hermita*, Pedro de Vargas 64, T152-0777. Attractive suites with fireplaces, pool, gardens, used to belong to the comic actor Cantinflas. **A** *Parador San Miguel Aristos*, at Instituto Allende, Ancha de San Antonio 30, T152-0149. Students given priority, large rooms, some with a fireplace and kitchen, parking US$2. **A** *Posada La Aldea*, Ancha de San Antonio, T/F152-1022. Colonial style, clean, quiet, swimming pool, gardens. **A** *Rincón del Cielo*, Correo 10, next to main plaza, T152-1647. Rooms are very large and have 2 storeys, the bedroom is upstairs with fireplace and huge bathroom with bathtub, living room has wet bar, quite attractive and good value. **AL-B** *Posada Carmina*, Cuna de Allende 7, T152-0458, F152-0135. Colonial building, courtyard for meals. Recommended. Near Jardín, on Vinaron, **B** *La Siesta*, Salidad a Celaya 82, T152-0207, F152-3722. Pool (not in use), fireplaces in rooms (US$34 with breakfast). **B-C** *Vista Hermosa Taboada*, Allende 11, T152-0078, F152-2638. Very popular, nice old colonial building.

C *Monteverde*, Volanteros 2, T152-1814. Clean, hot water. **C** *Posada de las Monjas*, Canal 37, T152-0171. With shower, excellent set meals in restaurant, bar, clean and attractive, very good value, a converted convent, also has a few **D** rooms at back if you ask. **C** *Posada La Fuente*, Ancha de San Antonio 95, T152-0629. Has a few rooms, good food (by arrangement). **C-D** *Hotel Posada 'El Mayorazgo'*, Hidalgo 8, T152-1309, F152-3838. If you stay 6 days, the 7th is free. Also rent by the month for US$250 and have 1-bed apartments with kitchen for US$350 per month. **C-D** *Quinta Loreto*, Loreto 13, T152-0042, F152-3616. TV, clean, quiet, swimming pool, pleasant garden, next to Mercado de Artesanías, hot water problems. Good, cheap food, restaurant closed in evening (beware of mosquitoes). **D** *Casa de Huéspedes*, Mesones 27, T152-1378. Family atmosphere, clean, hot water, popular, roof garden, nice location, good value. **D** *La Huerta*, Callejón de Atascadero 9, T154-4475. Bath, clean, well furnished, quiet, at the bottom of a dead-end street 4 blocks from the market in woodland, dark and unpleasant at night for lone females walking back, free parking, but watch your valuables. **D** *Posada San Sebastián*, Mesones 7, T152-0707, near market. With bath, charming, large rooms with fireplace, clean, car park, noisy at front (most rooms at the back), courtyard. Recommended. **D** *Sautto*, Dr Macías 59, T152-0072. Rooms with fridge, fireplace and bath, new rooms best, rustic, garden, hot water, parking. Recommended. **E-F** *San Miguel International Hostal*, C Jaime Nuno 28, Col Guadalupe (a long way from the centre). Private rooms for 2 people or bed in dorm, cheaper with a youth hostel card. Shared kitchen, friendly. Another cheap *Casa de Huéspedes* on Animas, just past the market building. **F** *El Nuevo Hostal*, Jaime Nuno 28, T152-0674. Shared bath, friendly, cosy, clean, kitchen and laundry facilities available.

Motels AL *Villa del Molino*, on road to Mexico City. **B** *Siesta*, on road to Guanajuato, with trailer park, gardens; *KAO campgrounds* further out on same road. Quiet, grassy site, all facilities, pleasant, Dutch owner.

Casa Mexas, Canal 15. Good American food, clean, popular with gringos. *Eclipse*, Hidalgo 15. Vegetarian, *menú del día* US$4. Recommended. *El Buen Café*, Jesús 23, T152-5807. Good quiche, pies, cakes and juices. *El Infierno*, Mesones, just below Plaza Allende. Excellent *sopa azteca*, good value, *menú del día*, US$2.50. *El Jardín*, San Francisco, close to Plaza. Friendly service, good food, also vegetarian, violinist plays upstairs at weekends for price of a

Sleeping
■ *on map page 266*
Price codes:
see inside front cover

Many weekend visitors from Mexico City: book ahead if you can

A good source of information on inexpensive accommodation is the English language paper published weekly by the Anglo-Mexican Library on Insurgentes

Eating

Colonial Heartland

drink. *El Tomate*, vegetarian restaurant on Mesones, attractive, spotless, excellent food, generous helpings, not cheap. *Mama Mía*, Umarán, west of main square. Main meals good but not cheap, free live folk music or films in the afternoon, excellent cheap breakfasts. *Mesón de San José*, Mesones 38. Mexican and international cuisine, vegetarian dishes, excellent breakfasts, nice setting, German/Mexican owners, open 0800-2200, live music Sun, gift shop. Recommended. *La Princesa*, Recreo 5. Set menu 1300-2000, including glass of wine, live music from 2100, cosy cellar atmosphere. *La Vendimie*, Hidalgo. English proprietor, poetry readings Mon afternoon (must book), occasional fish and chips. *Rincón Español*, opposite Correos. Good *comida corrida*, flamenco at weekends. Recommended. *Tentenpié*, Allende. Pleasant café/*taquería*. Good cheap chicken restaurant on San Francisco between Juárez and Reloj (roast chicken in windows). *Tío Lucas*, Mesones, opposite Teatro Angela Peralta. Very good. Recommended.

Entertainment English-language films at *Villa Jacaranda* hotel video bar. US$5 including alcoholic drink and popcorn. *Teatro Angela Peralta*, Mesones 82, has theatre, musical events and dance. There's a coffee house in the front entrance hall.

Festivals End-Jul to mid-Aug, classical chamber music festival, information from Bellas Artes. Main festivals are *Independence Day* (15-16 Sep); *Fiesta of San Miguel* (28 Sep-1 Oct, with Conchero dancers from many places); *Day of the Dead* (2 Nov); the *Christmas Posadas*, celebrated in the traditional colonial manner (16-24 Dec); the *pre-Lenten carnival*, *Easter Week*, and *Corpus Christi* (Jun). There is a Christmas season musical celebration, started in 1987, which attracts musicians of international level.

Shopping **Bookshop** *El Colibrí*, Diez de Sollano 30, good selection of French and English books. The English-language daily *The News* is sold on the Jardín. **Handicrafts** Pottery, cotton cloth and brasswork. The Mercado de Artesanías tends to sell tacky souvenirs rather than real handicrafts; prices are high and the selection poor. *La Casa del Vidrio*, Correo 11, offers an excellent selection of brown-glass items at fair prices (sale prices in the summer, 40% off).

San Miguel de Allende

	Sleeping	3	Posada Carmina	7	Rincón del Cielo
1	La Huerta	4	Posada La Aldea	8	Sautto
2	Parador San Miguel	5	Posada San Sebastián	9	Vista Hermosa
	Aristos	6	Quinta Loreto		Taboada

Buses The bus station is on the outskirts, regular bus to the centre US$0.25, returns from the market or outside *Posada San Francisco* on the Jardín. A taxi costs about US$1 to the centre. Buses to the centre leave from in front of the terminal.

Transport

Aguascalientes: 1235 and 1435, 2 hr, US$11. **Celaya**: every 15 mins, 1 hr, US$2.60. If there are no buses leaving for Guadalajara from San Miguel at the time you want to go, it's best to go to Celaya and catch a bus from there. **Guadalajara**: 0730, 0930 and 1730, 4 hrs, US$28. **Guanajuato**: 12 a day, US$5. **León**: 0730, 0930 and 1730, US$10. **Mexico City** (northern terminal): 0940 and 1600, US$19, cheaper services every 40 mins from 0520 to 2000, US$15. **Querétaro**: every 40 mins from 0520 to 2000, US$3.50. **San Luis Potosí**: 7 per day, US$9.

International connections: Autobuses Americanos have daily buses to Laredo, Texas, San Antonio and on to Dallas at 1800. Also daily buses to Houston at 1800. Costs US$44.40 to Laredo, Texas and US$67 to Dallas. They also have buses on Wed leaving at 1800 to Chicago for US$116.

Banks *Casa de Cambio Deal* on Correo, opposite post office, and on Juárez. **Communications** Internet: *WWW.Punto*, Canal 120, T152-8124. *La Conexión*, Aldama 1, T/F152-1599; they charge 10 pesos for blocks of 10 mins. *Border Crossings*, Correo 19, phone, fax, and email service. *Estación Internet*, Recreo 11. There is a long-distance phone service at Diez de Sollano 4, just off the plaza. There are *DHL* and *UPS* agencies across the street from the post office. **Embassies and consulates** *US Consular Agent*, Plaza Golondrinas arcade, Hernández Macías, interior 111. T152-2357, emergencies T152-0068, Mon and Wed 0900-1300. **Language schools** Many of the schools demand payment in US dollars (technically illegal) and you may prefer to arrange private tuition for US$3-4/hr. *Academia Hispanoamericana*, recommended for language lessons and sessions on Mexican history, folklore, literature, singing and dancing; very helpful; accommodation with families. *Card Game Spanish*, Pilancón 19, T152-1758, F152-0135, intensive courses for beginners or intermediate, run by Warren Hardy, the inventor of the Card Game method. **Laundry** On Pasaje de Allende, US$3 wash and dry, same day service; unnamed laundry at Correo 42, good. **Libraries** English-language library on Insurgentes has an excellent selection on Mexico; very extensive bilingual library, with computer centre and English-speaking staff. **Tour operators** *Viajes Vertiz*, on Hidalgo, American Express agent, mail collection and cheque cashing available. **Useful addresses** Immigration: 2nd flr Plaza Real del Conde, T152-2542, 0900-1300. For tourist card extensions, etc, take 2 copies of passport, tourist card and credit card or TCs.

Directory

Colonial Heartland

Dolores Hidalgo

The home of Father Hidalgo, 54 km from Guanajuato, is a most attractive, tranquil small town. The main square, or Jardín, is lovely, dominated by a statue of Hidalgo. On one side is the church of **Nuestra Señora de los Dolores** (1712-78) in which Hidalgo gave *El Grito de la Independencia* (the Cry for Independence from Spain); the façade is impressive, and the churrigueresque side altar pieces, one of gold leaf, one of wood, are more ornate than the main altar. It is not always open. Also on the Jardín are many restaurants, cafés and banks.

Phone code: 418
Colour map 3, grid B3
Population: 128,675

Independence celebrations are held on 15 and 16 September

Dolores Hidalgo

Sleeping
1 El Caudillo
2 Posada Cocomacán
3 Posada Dolores
4 Posada Las Campanas

Not to scale

The **tourist office**, on the main square T/F182-1164, can direct you to places making the traditional Talavera tiles, which can be seen all over the town and are available at very good prices.

Sights   The **Iglesia de La Asunción**, Puebla y Sonora, has a large tower at one end, a dome at the other, with extensive murals and a tiled floor inside. Two blocks away, at Puebla y Jalisco, is Plaza de los Compositores Dolorenses with a bandstand. Between these two sites on Puebla is the post and telegraph office. Visit Hidalgo's house, the **Museo Casa Hidalgo**, Morelos y Hidalgo, a beautiful building with a courtyard and wells, memorabilia and one room almost a shrine to the Father of Independence. ■ *Tue-Sat 1000-1800, Sun 1000-1700, US$4.35.* The **Museo de la Independencia**, on Zacatecas, was formerly a jail, but now has displays of striking paintings of the path of Independence. ■ *US$0.70.*

Excursions   About 5 km southeast of town on a dirt track are the ruins of the **Hacienda de la Erre**, Padre Hidalgo's first stop on the Independence Route after leaving Dolores. The standing walls are only 3-4 m high; there are about four rooms with ceilings; the patio, with a lot of litter, is overgrown, but the chapel has been rebuilt. Outside is the huge mezquite tree under which Hidalgo is supposed to have said mass for his insurgent troops ■ *Free entrance to the untended ruins and grounds.* The walk to the ruins (1½-2 hours) starts from the plaza. Take Calle Guerrero to the east, then Tamaulipas to the main road. Turn left for 1 km to a gravel road on the left on a long curve. Follow this to the Hacienda in a fertile area with plenty of trees; in May there is much colour with the cacti in flower.

Sleeping   **B** *Posada Las Campanas*, Guerrero 15, T182-0427. **C** *El Caudillo*, Querétaro 8, just off plaza, opposite the church of Nuestra Señora de los Dolores, T182-0198. Clean, good value. **C** *Posada Hidalgo*, Hidalgo 15, T/F182-0477. Clean, dark rooms, TV. **C** *Posada Cocomacán*, T182-0018, on the Jardín. Pleasant colonial house where Juárez stayed, comfortable, good value, good food, parking. Recommended. **D** *Posada Dolores*, on Yucatán. With bath, clean, OK, small rooms.

Eating   *Caballo Blanco*, on Jardín by corner of Hidalgo and Guerrero. Good value. Excellent ice cream at *Helado Torres*, southwest corner of Jardín. *Fruti-Yoghurt*, Hidalgo y Guerrero, just off Jardín. Delicious yoghurt, wholefood cakes and biscuits.

Shopping   **Market** *Tabasco*, south side, between Jalisco and Hidalgo. Another market, near *Posada Dolores*, on Yucatán. *Artesanías Castillo*, Ribera del Río (between Hidalgo and Jalisco), beautiful ceramics at low prices. Visit to factory can be arranged.

Transport   **Buses** Bus station is at Hidalgo y Chiapas, 5 mins from main square; has restaurant, toilets, left-luggage, local phones. Frequent buses to Guanajuato, Querétaro (US$3.80), León (US$3.65), Mexico City (US$10.50), San Luis Potosí (US$5) and San Luis de la Paz (US$2). To Aguascalientes, US$6.50, 2nd class, via San Felipe.

Guanajuato

Phone code: 461
Colour map 3, grid B3
Population: 141,215
Altitude: 2,010 m

The beautiful university city in the central state of Guanajuato, declared a national monument and Unesco World Heritage Zone, has been important for its silver since 1548. Its name derives from the Tarascan Quanax-Huato, 'Place of frogs'. It stands in a narrow gorge amid wild and striking scenery; the Guanajuato River which cuts through the city has been covered over and several underground streets opened – an unusual, though often confusing system.

Getting there   The international Aeropuerto del Bajío (BJX), some 40 km west of Guanajuato, near the town of Silao, has flights to and from destinations in Mexico and the US. The long-distance bus terminal is on the outskirts southwest of town (for details see Transport page 273); taxis or buses ('Centro') will ferry you into town. There is no train service to Guanajuato at present.

Although there is a lot to see in Guanajuato, many of the interesting places are along and around Juárez and can be visited on foot in a day or two. *Transportes Turísticos de Guanajuato*, underneath the Basílica on Plaza de la Paz, T732-2838, offer guided tours to some of the interesting sites outside the city.

Getting around

Some streets, like Padre Belaunzarán, are not entirely enclosed; others, such as Hidalgo, are, so they fill with traffic fumes. The Túnel Los Angeles leads from the old subterranean streets to the modern roadway that connects with the Carretera Panorámica and the monument to Pípila (see below). Taking traffic underground has not relieved the congestion of the surface streets, which are steep, twisted and narrow, following the contours of the hills. Some alleys and lanes have steps cut into the rock: one, the **Callejón del Beso** (Alley of the Kiss), is so narrow that, according to legend, two lovers kept apart by their families were able to exchange kisses from opposite balconies. Parking for hotels is often a fair distance away. Over the city looms the shoulder of La Bufa mountain. You can hike to the summit up a trail, which takes one hour: from the Pípila monument (see below), follow the main road for about 1 km to the hospital. Walk past the hospital to a power station where the main trail starts; if you pass the quarry, note the quality of the stonemasonry on the mason's shelter.

The **tourist office** is at Plaza de la Paz 14, off to one side of the Basílica, T732-7622, F732-4251, **www.guanajuato.gob.mx**, provides hotel rates (except the cheapest), sells maps and has various booklets and brochures on the city and surrounding areas.

Sights

Guanajuato contains a series of fine museums (see below), as well as the most elegant marble-lined public lavatories in Mexico. The best of many colonial churches are **La Compañía** (Jesuit, 1765, by the University), note the brick ceiling; **San Diego** (1663) on the Jardín de la Unión; the **Parroquia del Inmaculado Corazón de María**, on Juárez, opposite Mercado Hidalgo, has interesting statues on the altar; and the **Basílica** (cathedral, 1693, on Plaza de la Paz), which has a beautiful yellow interior and an ornately painted vaulted ceiling. **San Roque** (1726), on a small park between Juárez and Pocitos (Plazuela de San Roque), also has a pretty vaulted ceiling, reached by a walkway that goes from the northeast side of the Jardín Reforma. The **Templo de San Francisco** (1671), on Sopeña, is also worth visiting.

A most interesting building is the massive **Alhóndiga de Granaditas**, built as a granary, turned into a fortress, and now a museum with artefacts from the pre-Colombian and colonial periods. When Father Hidalgo took the city in 1810, the Alhóndiga was the last place to surrender, and there was a wanton slaughter of Spanish soldiers and royalist prisoners. Later when Hidalgo was himself caught and executed, along with three other leaders, in Chihuahua, their severed heads were fixed, in revenge, at the four corners of the Alhóndiga. ■ *US$1.80.*

Museums

An unusual sight shown to visitors is of mummified bodies in the small **Museo de las Momias** in the Panteón Municipal, above the city off Tepetapa; buses go there ('Momias', signposted Panteón Municipal, 10 minutes, along Avenida Juárez), but you can walk. It's a gruesome and disturbing spectacle, glass cases of naturally mummified bodies. ■ *0900-1800, US$2, US$0.75 to take photos, tip the Spanish-speaking guide, long queues on Sun.* The **Museo Iconográfico del Quijote**, opened in 1987 at Manuel Doblado 1, is highly recommended: paintings, drawings, sculptures of the Don (see **Festivals** below for Festival Cervantino). ■ *Free.* The painter **Diego Rivera** was born at Pocitos 47, now a museum with a permanent collection of his work on various floors, showing his changing styles; on the ground floor are his bed and other household objects; temporary exhibitions also held. ■ *1000, US$1,* recommended. Also on Pocitos, at No 7, just across from the University, is the **Museo del Pueblo** in a beautiful 17th-century mansion; it has one room

Colonial Heartland

of work by the muralist José Chávez Morado, a room of selected items of all Mexican art forms and temporary exhibitions. ■ *Tue-Sun 0900-1900, US$1.* The **Museo Alfredo Dugues**, of natural history, is in the University building. ■ *Mon-Fri 0900-1400, 1630-1900.* The **University** was founded in 1732; its façade of coloured stone, above a broad staircase, glows richly at sunset. Also in the University is the **Sala Hermenegildo Bustos**, which holds art exhibitions. The School of Mining has a **Museo de Minería** on the Carretera Panorámica, north of the city. ■ *Mon-Fri 0900-1300, 1630-1900.*

Excursions

There is a fine view from the **Monument to Pípila**, the man who fired the door of the Alhóndiga so that the patriots could take it, which crowns the high hill of Hormiguera. Look for the 'Al Pípila' sign. A number of cobbled stairways through picturesque terraces such as Callejón del Calvario, leading off Sopeña, go up to the monument. It's a steep but short climb (about 15 minutes). Otherwise take a local bus from Hotel Central, on Juárez. Take a camera for fine panoramic views of the city. The Carretera Panorámica, which encircles the city, passes the Pípila monument. At its eastern end the Panorámica goes by the **Presa de la Olla**, a favourite picnic spot with good cheap meals available from roadside stalls. From the dam, Paseo de la Olla runs to the city centre, passing mansions of the wealthy silver barons and the **Palacio de Gobierno** (note the use of local stone). Also on the east side of the Panorámica is **Casa de las Leyendas**, with entertainment for children.

Tours of the city and outskirts by minibus cost US$6.15, rising to US$18 for tours out of town and US$40 to the south of the state; if you want a guide in English, prices multiply. The splendid church of **La Valenciana**, one of the most impressive in Mexico, is 5 km out of town on the Dolores Hidalgo road; it was built for the workers of the Valenciana silver mine, once the richest in the world. The church, dedicated to

Guanajuato

■ **Sleeping**
1 Casa Kloster
2 Central
3 Hostería del Frayle
4 Posada San Francisco
5 Posada Santa Fe
6 San Diego

0 metres 100
0 yards 100

San Cayetano, has three huge, gilt altars, a wooden pulpit of sinuous design, large paintings and a cupola. The style is churrigueresque, done in grey-green and pink stone; the façade is also impressive.

The **Valenciana mine** (1548) is surrounded by a wall with triangular projections on top, said to symbolize the crown of the King of Spain. The huge stone walls on the hillside, supported by enormous buttresses, created an artificial level surface from earth excavated higher up the slope. The mine is still working with both gold and silver being extracted. With care you can walk freely in the whole area. Guides are available to take you round (about 30 minutes), interesting. ■ *0900-1700, US$1.* A local 'Valenciana' bus starts in front of *Hotel Mineral de Rayas*, Alhóndiga 7, leaving every 30 minutes during the day, US$0.10, 10 minutes' ride; it is a 10-minute walk between church and mine pit-head; don't believe anyone who tells you a taxi is necessary, but don't walk to it along the highway, as it is narrow and dangerous.

At Marfil on the Irapuato road is the former *Hacienda de San Gabriel de Barrera*, now a four-star hotel (**AL**, T732-3980, F732-7460) with 15 patios and gardens, a chapel, museum and colonial furniture (take bus marked 'Marfil' from outside *Hotel Central*, 10 minutes). 30 km west of Guanajuato is **Cerro Cubilete**, with a statue of Christ the King, and spectacular views of the Bajío; local buses take 1½ hours, US$1.15, 0700, 0900, 1100, 1400, 1600 from Guanajuato (also from Silao for US$0.75). Dormitory at the site (US$1.50), food available, but best to take your own, plus drink (and toilet paper); last bus up leaves at 1600 from Silao and Guanajuato. See also the three local silver mines of Rayas, the city's first mine, La Valenciana (see above) and La Cata. All are to the north of the city, reached from the Carretera Panorámica. It is possible to visit the separating plant at **La Cata**, but visitors are not admitted to the mines. At the old site of La Cata mine (local bus near market) is a church with a magnificent baroque façade and the shrine of El Señor de Villa Seca (the patron saint of adulterers) with *retablos* and crude drawings of miraculous escapes from harm, mostly due to poor shooting by husbands.

Fifteen kilometres from Guanajuato on the road to Dolores is **Santa Rosa**; in a storybook setting in the forest is D *Hotel El Crag*, clean; *Restaurant La Sierra* next door (the *Flecha Amarilla* bus stops here on the way to Dolores Hidalgo). There are two or three other places, including *Rancho de Enmiedo*, good dried meat specialities and beautiful scenery. The road corkscrews up in spectacular fashion before winding down through impressive rocky outcrops and ravines to the plain on which Dolores Hidalgo stands. The last 10 km or so are very arid.

Colonial Heartland

Hotel rooms can be hard to find after 1400. For holidays and weekends it is advisable to book ahead. However, there are lots of hotel rooms in the city, and in all price ranges. Hotels seem to be somewhat more expensive than in other parts of Mexico.

Sleeping
■ *on map page 270*
Price codes:
see inside front cover

On Dolores Hidalgo road exit AL *Mission Guanajuato*, Camino Antiguo a Marfil, Km 2.5, T732-3980, F732-6092, www.hotelsmision.com.mx Very large rooms. **AL** *Parador San Javier*, Calle San

Javier 1, T732-0696. Very extensive grounds, some rooms have fireplaces. **AL-A** *Real de Minas*, Nejayote 17, at city entrance, T732-1460, F732-1508 (they will lower their rates if business is slow). Large, attractive rooms and restaurant (prices vary according to time of week). **A** *Posada Santa Fe*, Jardín de la Unión 12, T732-0084, F732-4653. Regular rooms are plain but the suites are very attractive with colonial-style furniture. Good restaurant on open terrace with excellent service. Tables on the plaza for dining. Recommended. **A** *San Diego*, Jardín de la Unión 1, T732-1321, F732-5626. Good bar and restaurant but slow, colonial-style, very pleasant. **B** *Hostería del Frayle*, Sopeña 3, next door to Teatro Juárez, T732-1179. Rooms next to the Teatro are noisy, nice adjoining *Café Veloce*.

On Insurgentes D *Alhóndiga*, No 49, T732-0525. Good, clean, quiet, TV in rooms, parking, restaurant *La Estancia*. **D** *del Conde*, Rangel del Alba 1 (next door to Alhóndiga), T732-1465. TV in rooms, complaints of musty smell in at least one room. With excellent and reasonable restaurant *Mesa de los Reyes* . **D** *Murillo Plaza*, No 9, T732-1884, F732-5913. Hot water, phone and TV. **E** *Posada La Condesa*, Plaza de La Paz 60 (west end of plaza), T732-1462. Small, basic rooms, clean, hot water, drinking water available.

On Alhóndiga C *Socavón*, No 46A, T732-6666. Pretty rest/bar. Colonial décor, attractive interior courtyard, nice rooms for price, with TV and phones. **D** *Dos Ríos*, No 29, T732-0749. TV in rooms, good value, rooms on street noisy. **D** *Mineral de Rayas*, No 7, T732-1967. With bath, clean linen, pool, garage, restaurant, bar and *Danny's Bar*. Recommended.

On Juárez B *Hotel Suites Casa de las Manrique*, No 116 (between the Mercado and the Callejón del Beso), T732-7678, F732-8306. Large, attractive suites, colonial décor, very good value for price. **C** *El Insurgente Allende*, No 226, T732-3192. Pleasant, clean, avoid rooms on 4th floor where there is a disco, good breakfasts. **C** *La Fragua*, at the western end, Very clean, good staff, 5 mins' walk from the centre of town. **D** *Central*, No 111, T732-0080, near Cine Reforma. Friendly, good restaurant but noisy for rooms beside it. **D** *Posada San Francisco*, corner of Gavira, T732-2467, F732 2084. On Zócalo. Good value but outside rooms, noisy, no hot water, lovely inner patio. **E** *Posada Juárez*, T732-2559. Has bathhouse inside (25 pesos). Recommended. **F** *Gran Hotel Granaditas*, No 109, T732-1039. With bath, hot showers, clean, friendly, run-down. Other hotels are mostly in our **C** range. Accommodation in private home, **F** per person *Marilú Ordaz*, Barranca 34, T732-4705. Friendly, 5 mins' walk from market.

Elsewhere B *La Casa del Quijote*, Pocitos 37, T732-3923, next to and over the Túnel Santa Fe de Guanajuato. All rooms are suites and have tiled bathtubs, wet bar, and you can ask for a microwave oven to be put in your room. **D** *Posada Molino del Rey*, Campañero 15, T732-2223, F21040. Simple and quaint. **D-E** *Casa Kloster*, Alonso 32, T732-0088. Book ahead, good location, very friendly, dormitory rooms for 4, a few with private bath, some without windows, clean, very good value. Repeatedly recommended, often full, gardens, no parking (touts in town will say it is shut, but it is not).

Motels Many on Dolores Hidalgo road exit: **A** *Villa de Plata*, T732-1173. Trailer Park 1 km north of *Mineral de Rayas*, there is a sign on the Carretera Panorámica. Hot showers and funky décor. **B** *de Los Embajadores*, Paseo Embajadores, T732-0081. Mexican décor, restaurant, famous Sun lunch. **B** *Guanajuato*, T732-0689. Good pool and food, quiet. Recommended.

Eating Tourists are given the à la carte menu; ask for the *menú del día* or *comida corrida*. Reasonable food, *comida corrida* very good value, at *El Retiro*, Sopeña 12, near Jardín de la Unión. *Pizza Piazza*, Plaza San Fernando and several other locations. Cheap and good. *Cuatro Ranas*, in *Hotel San Diego*, Jardín de la Unión 1. Good location but loud US music and overpriced, reasonable *menú del dia*, US$3. *Valadez* on Jardín de la Unión y Sopeña. On Jardín de la Unión, *Bar Luna* and *El Gallo*. Popular with travellers, good. *La Lonja*, on the corner of the Jardín opposite *Hotel San Diego*. Pleasant and lively bar, beers come with complimentary dish of tacos with salsa. *Mesón de Marco* , Juárez 25, T182-7040. 'Rare' Mexican food, flights in balloon offered at US$100. *La Carreta*, Av Juárez about 200 m up from Mercado Hidalgo. Mostly chicken, fair. Also on Juárez, *Tasca de los Santos*, Plaza de la Paz. Smart. *Diva's*, Plaza de la Paz 62B. Smart. Highly recommended. *El Zaguán*, Plaza de la Paz 48. Very good and cheap food, entertainment inside courtyard. *Café Truco 7*, Callejón Truco, off Plaza de la Paz. Menu of the day US$2-3, relaxed family atmosphere. Theatre in back room Fri and Sat afternoon. Recommended. *La Flor Alegre* (*Casa de pan pizza*), Plazuela de San Fernando 37. Good, clean and cheap. *El Mexicano*, Juárez 214. Good *comida corrida* with dessert and drink. *El Granero*, Juárez 25. Good *comida*, until 1700. *La Mancha*, Galarza 7. Reasonable price. Recommended for *comida corrida*. *Cafetería Nevería*, opposite University. Good, inexpensive. *Vegetariano*, Callejón Calixto 20. Inexpensive, sells wholewheat bread. *Jelly Shot Bar*, below *Hostería del Frayle*. Lovely atmosphere, cheap drinks. Recommended. *El Unicornio Azul* on Plaza Baratillo. Good health food shop, *pan integral*, also sells cosmetic products. Also on Plaza Baratillo is *Café Las Musas*. Good-value breakfast. You can eat well and cheaply in the market (eg *bolillos* – sandwiches, fresh fruit juices) and in the *locales* behind Mercado Hidalgo. Good *panaderías* also, eg *Panadería Internacional*, Contarranas y Sopeña, sells wholewheat bread. *La Infancia*, *panadería y pastelaría*, Contarranas 57. Delicious, freshly made pastries. Dairy products are safe, all coming from the pasteurizing plant at Silao. Also from Silao come strawberries in Dec.

Entertainment Theatre sketches from classical authors out of doors in lovely old plazas from **Apr-Aug**. *Teatro Juárez* on Sopeña (a magnificent French-type Second Empire building, US$0.50 to view, US$0.35 to take photos), shows art films and has symphony concerts, US$1.50. A band plays in Jardín de la Unión (next to the theatre) 3 times a week. The *Teatro Principal* is on Cantarranas, by Plaza Mexiamora. Two nightclubs have been recommended: *Disco El Grill* on Alonso (100 m from *Casa Kloster*) and *Disco Los Comerciales* on Juan Valle.

Festivals Arts festival, the *Festival Cervantino de Guanajuato* (in honour of Cervantes), is an important cultural event in the Spanish-speaking world, encompassing theatre, song and dance. There is a mixture of free, open-air events, and paying events. Internationally famous artists from around the world perform. The festival lasts 2 weeks, is highly recommended and is very crowded; accommodation must be booked in advance (usually held the last 2 weeks in **Oct**, check dates). ■ *T732-0959. Viernes de las Flores* is held on the Fri before Good Friday, starting with the Dance of the Flowers on Thu night at about 2200 right through the night, adjourning at Jardín de la Unión to exchange flowers. Very colourful and crowded. During the **Christmas** period, students dress up in traditional costumes and wander the streets singing carols and playing music. Groups leave from in front of the theatre at 2030.

Shopping *Fonart* shop opposite La Valenciana church (see above) has an excellent selection of handicrafts; high prices but superb quality. Local pottery can be bought in the *Mercado Hidalgo* (1910), in the centre of town, and there is a *Casa de Artesanías* behind the Teatro Juárez (see Entertainment above).

Transport **Trains** Station is off Tepetapa, west of centre, but no scheduled passenger service.

Buses A new bus terminal has opened on the road to Silao, near toll gate, 20 mins from centre by bus, US$0.30. Taxi to centre, US$2.00. Buses leave for the centre from right outside the front of the terminal. Look for 'centro' on the front window of the bus, or the sign above the front window. To get to the bus station from the centre, you pick up buses on Av Juárez in front of the *Hotel Central*, about a block west of the Mercado Hidalgo. The bus stop has a sign saying 'C Camionera'. The bus terminal has a place for storing luggage.

There are several booths in the area behind the terminal, where the buses arrive, where you can buy tickets for tours of the city and outlying areas, such as Dolores Hidalgo and San Miguel de Allende. They also have hotel price lists for hotels costing over 200 pesos, and will phone the hotel for you.

Cuidad Juárez: *Omnibus de México* (1st class) transferring in León 1015, US$105. **Guadalajara**: 19 buses a day between 0900 and 2330, US$22. **Irapuato**: 5 between 0530

Colonial Heartland

and 1830, US$4. **León**: 0830, 1230 and 1730, 45 mins, US$4.50. **Mexico City**: regular service, 4½ hrs, US$26. **Monterrey**: seven all running in the afternoon, US$42. **Morelia**: 0820, 121C and 1620, US$11. **Nuevo Laredo**: 1930, US$67. **Querétaro**: six between 0710 and 1820, US$11. **San Luis Potosí**: 5 through the day, US$13. **San Miguel de Allende**: regular service from 0700 until 1915, 1½ hrs, US$5. **Tijuana:**, *Expreso Futura*, 1800, US$125.

To many destinations it is better to go to León and pick up the more frequent services that go from there (buses every 10 mins Guanajuato-León, US$1.30). *Flecha Amarilla* have more buses, to more destinations, than other companies in this area; it is not the most reliable company and buses tend to leave when full. Set fare for city buses, US$0.25.

Directory **Banks** *Bancomer, Banca Serfin, Banamex*, 0900-1100. **Communications** Internet: on Alonso 70B, 0900-1800, Mon-Sat. **Post office**: corner of Subida San José, by La Compañía church. **Telephone**: international phone calls from phone booths with coins, or collect. Long-distance offices in Miscelánea Unión shop, by Teatro Principal and on Pocitos, opposite Alhóndiga de Granaditas. **Language schools** Spanish courses: for foreigners at the *University*, T732-0006, F732-7253, email, montesa@quijote.ugto.mx Postal address: Centro de Idiomas, Universidad de Guanajuato, Lascuraín de Retana 5, 36000, Guanajuato, Gto, México. Also at *Academia Falcón*, Presa 80, T731-1084, F731-0745, www.institutofalcon.com, good-quality instruction. Also at the University are many US exchange students so you can usually find someone who speaks English. See also Learning Spanish in Essentials, page 27. **Laundry** *Lavandería Internacional*, Alhóndiga 35A, self or service wash, US$3.45. *La Burbuja Express*, Plazuela Baratillo. *Lavandería Automática Internacional*, Manuel Doblado 28, US$3.50; *Lavandería del Centro*, Sopeña 26, US$3.60.

León

Phone code: 477
Colour map 3, grid B2
Population: 1,133,576
Altitude: 1,885 m

In the fertile plain of the Gómez River, León is now said to be Mexico's fifth city. Nuño de Guzmán reached the area on 2 December 1530 and subsequently local farms and estates were granted to the Spaniards. Eventually Don Martín Enríquez de Almanza decreed on 12 December 1575 that a city, called León, would be founded if 100 volunteers could be persuaded to live there for 10 years, or a town if only 50 could be found. On 20 January 1576 a town was founded by Dr Juan Bautista de Orozco, and it wasn't until 1830 that León became a city. The business centre is the delightful **Plaza de la Constitución**.

The **tourist office**, Edificio Cielo 501, López Mateos Poniente and M Alemán, provides helpful but limited information and a good city map is available free at the Palacio Municipal. You can also check out **www.leon-mexico.com**

Sights There is a striking **Palacio Municipal**, a cathedral, many shaded plazas and gardens. The Palacio Municipal is said to have been built as a result of a winning lottery ticket bought by a local doctor! The small **cathedral** was started by Jesuits in 1744, but they were expelled from Mexico in 1767 by Carlos III. It was eventually finished in 1837 and consecrated in 1866. The **Templo Expiatorio** has been under construction for most of the last century; the catacombs are well worth seeing. ■ *1000-1200 closed*

Colonial Heartland

Wed. The **Teatro Doblado**, on Avenida Hermanos Aldama, stages opera, ballet, classical concerts, contemporary theatre and houses art exhibitions. The **Casa de Cultura** also houses exhibitions and is 'buzzing' at night. Also worth seeing is the **Casa de Las Monas** on 5 de Mayo 127-29 where Pancho Villa issued the Agrarian Reform Law on 24 May 1915, and the beautiful **Santuario de Guadalupe**. A new tourist attraction, the **Parque Metropolitano** on Prolongación Morelos, Camino a la Presa, opened in 1995. León is the main shoe centre of the country and is noted for its leather work, fine silver-trimmed saddles, and *rebozos* (shawl).

The **Museo de León**, on Hermanos Aldama, has art exhibitions. ■ *Tue-Sat* **Museums**
1000-1400 and 1630-1930, Sun 1000-1400. The **Museum of Anthropology and History** on Justo Sierra is housed in a beautiful building; the **Explora Science Museum** is on Boulevard Francisco Villa 202, T711-6711.

L *La Nueva Estancia*, A López Mateos 1317 Pte, T637-0000, F716-9900. Restaurant recom- **Sleeping** mended. **A** *Real de Minas*, López Mateos 2211, T710-4090, F771-2400. Recommended. **B** *Condesa*, on Plaza, Portal Bravo 14, T713-1120, F714-8210. 3-star. Restaurant recommended. **C** *Fundadores*, Ortiz de Domínguez 218, T716-1727, F716-6612. Better than similarly priced hotels in centre. **D** *Posada de Fátima*, Belisario Domínguez 205. Clean, central. **D** *Rex*, 5 de Febrero 104, near Plaza, T714-2415. Recommended. **D** *Monte Carlo*, Justo Sierra 432, T713-1597. Clean, friendly, central. **D** *Tepeyac*, Obregón 727, T716-8365. 1-star, OK, rooms a bit dark. Also several cheaper hotels near market.
    At **Silao** (for airport) **B** *Villa Victoria*, Alvaro Obregón 245, T712-1831, F712-2422.

Several in Col Jardines del Moral area in centre, including: *El Jardín de Ling Choy*, López **Eating** Mateos 2105 Pte, T717-7507, also *La Pagoda de Ling Choy*, López Mateos 1501 Ote, T714-9026. Both Chinese. *Kamakura*, Rocío 114, T718-4383. Japanese. *Lupillos*, López Mateos 2003 Ote, opposite stadium, T771-1868. Pasta and pizza; also several branches of the US fast food chains. Many restaurants in the Gran Plaza complex next to Macdonald's. Vegetarian snacks at *GFU*, on López Mateos, near IMSS building. *Cadillac*, ½ block from cathedral on Hidalgo. Good *comida corrida* US$5. *Panteón Taurino*, Calzado de Los Héroes 408, T713-4969. Expensive but worth visiting to see the incredible décor.

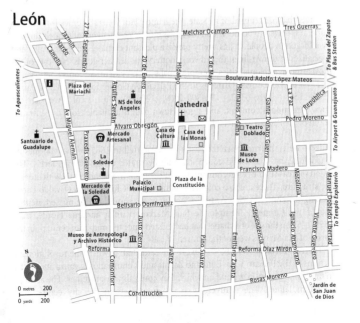

Colonial Heartland

Nightlife   Lots of **bars** including *JJ Sport*, Rocío 115-A, Jardines del Moral. *Pepe's Pub*, Madero 120 Zona Centro. *Fut-bol Bar*, Hidalgo 923-B, T717-8020. **Discos** Including *Domus*, López Mateos 2611 Ote, T711-6614. *Ossy's*, Av Paseo de los Insurgentes, on exit road to Lagos de Moreno, T717-6880. *La Iguana*, Centro Comercial Insurgentes, Local 4 y 5B, T718-1416. **Nightclubs** *Piano Bar Maya*, Prolongación Calzada 112, T716-9734.

Festivals   *Fiesta de San Sebastián*, 19-24 Jan, very crowded, good fun.

Shopping   Several shopping centres: *La Gran Plaza*, Blvd López Mateos 1902 Pte. *Plaza Mayor*, Av de las Torres, corner of Prolongación Morelos. *Plaza León*, Blvd López Mateos 1102 Ote. *Plaza Piel*, Hilario Medina y López Mateos for leather work (also along Belisario Domínguez).

Transport   **Air**   New international airport, del Bajío (BJX), 18 km from León, 6 km from Silao. Domestic connections with Acapulco, Ciudad Juárez, Cuernavaca, Mexico City, Monterrey, Morelia, Puerto Vallarta, Tijuana, Veracruz and Zacatecas. International flights to Chicago, Dallas, Guatemala City, Hong Kong, Houston, Lima, Los Angeles, Memphis, Oakland (Calif), Raleigh/Durham (US), Santiago (Chile), Sao Paulo (Brazil).

   Taxis are expensive to León; either take one to Silao, US$10, and then take a bus to León or Guanajuato, or walk 1½ km to the main road and take a bus from there.

Buses   The terminal has post office, long-distance phones, restaurant and shops (street plan on sale, US$2.75). **Chihuahua**: US$52. Many buses run to **Ciudad Juárez**: US$50. **Durango**: US$16.50. **Guadalajara**: every 30 mins, first at 0600, 4 hrs, US$16. **Guanajuato**: all the time, 40 mins, US$3. **Mexico City**: more buses than you can count, 5 hrs, US$23. **Monterrey**: US$25. **Poza Rica**: US$21. **Querétaro**: hourly, 2 hrs, US$8. **Zacatecas**: 4½ hrs, US$16.

Directory   **Airline offices** *AeroMéxico*, Madero 410, T716-6226. *Mexicana*, Blvd López Mateos 401 Ote, T714-9500. *Continental*, Blvd López Mateos 2307 Pte, T713-5199. **Banks** *Bancomer*, Belisario Domínguez 322, and *Banco Internacional* on the plaza. **Communications** Post office: on Obregón y 5 de Mayo, open Mon-Fri 0800-1900. **Tour operators** *Viajes Sindy de León*, 20 de Enero 319, T713-1224, F716-5080. Recommended. *Jovi de León*, Madero 319 Centro, T714-5094, F716-6217. Recommended.

Aguascalientes

Phone code: 449
Colour map 3, grid B2
Population: 643,360
Altitude: 1,987m

Founded in 1575, capital of its state, the name ('Hot waters') comes from its hot mineral springs. An oddity is that the city is built over a network of tunnels dug out by a forgotten people. It has pretty parks, a pleasant climate, delicious fruits, and specializes in drawn-linen threadwork, pottery and leather goods. Not one of the most attractive colonial cities, shopping malls are as evident as Spanish heritage.

   The **Federal Tourist Office** is in the Palacio de Gobierno on the Plaza Patria, T915-1155, T916-0347. ■ *0800-2000*. There's a local website at **www.turismoags.com.mx**, and a good town plan is available from the entrance booth of the Palacio Municipal.

Sights   **Palacio de Gobierno**, once the castle home, started in 1665, of the Marqués de Guadalupe, has a splendid courtyard, with decorated arches on two levels. The grand staircase in the centre, built in the 1940s, blends in magnificently with the earlier structure. There are also colourful murals by the Chilean artist Osvaldo Barra. Among the churches, **San Antonio**, on Zaragoza, should not be missed, neither should the Carmelite **Templo de San Marcos**, with a baroque façade, built 1655-1765 on the site of a chapel that had existed since the mid-16th century, in the barrio of San Marcos west of the centre.

   Teatro Morelos, T915-0097, next to the cathedral, is where the revolutionary factions led by Pancho Villa, Emiliano Zapata and Venustiano Carranza attempted to find some common ground on which they could all work together. The attempt ended in failure. The **University** is 30 minutes from the city centre. Its administrative offices are in the ex-Convento de San Diego, by the attractive Jardín del Estudiante, and the Parián shopping centre.

South of the centre on Boulevard J M Chávez is an aviary, with 50 species of bird, in the **Parque Héroes Mexicanos**. The market is not far away. There is carp fishing at El Jocoqui and Abelardo Rodríguez. The bullring is on Avenida López Mateos.

Museo de Aguascalientes, Calle Zaragoza 505, by the church of San Antonio, has a collection of contemporary art, including fine paintings by Saturnino Herrán, and works by Orozco, Angel, Montenegro and others. ■ *Daily from 1030, except Sun and Mon.* The **Museo José Guadalupe Posada** is in a gallery by the Templo del Cristo Negro, close to the pleasant Jardín del Encino or Jardín Francisco, on Díaz de León. The museum has a remarkable collection of prints by the artist Posada, best known for his engravings of *calaveras*, macabre skeletal figures illustrating and satirizing the events leading up to the Revolution. There are cultural events in the courtyard on Saturday and Sunday. ■ *Tue-Sun 1030-1900, closed Mon US$.60.* **Museums**

Museo de Arte Contemporáneo, Calle Juan de Montoro, is just east of Plaza. The **Casa de las Artesanías** is also near the main square. The **Casa de la Cultura**, on Venustiano Carranza and Galeana Norte, is a fine colonial building. It holds a display of *artesanía* during the April *feria*. Nearby, on Carranza is the **Museo Regional de Historia**.

Hacienda de San Blas, 34 km away, contains the **Museo de la Insurgencia**, with murals by Alfredo Zermeño. **Excursions**

Balneario Ojo Caliente (thermal baths), towards the east end of town beyond the train station, at the end of Calzada Revolución (Alameda), claims to have been founded in 1808. There are some private baths (US$3.50 per hour) and two public pools. Take bus marked 'Alameda'. There are also saunas, squash and tennis courts on the site. At end of Alameda fork right to Deportivo Ojo Caliente, a large complex with several pools, US$0.65. Twenty kilometres north is a thermal swimming pool at **Valladolid** (camping is permitted in the grounds, secure, night watchman in attendance).

Encarnación de Díaz (**C** *Hotel Casa Blanca*, Anguiano 107 on the plaza, T(475) 953-2007 m hot water, secure parking nearby, reasonable restaurant) is halfway to **Lagos de Moreno** (Km 425), a charming old town with fine baroque churches. The entry over the bridge, with domes and towers visible on the other side, is particularly impressive. See the ex-convent of the Capuchins and the Teatro Rosas Moreno. The *Feria* is during the last week of July and first of August. Lagos de Moreno has several hotels (on the main plaza: **C** *La Traje*; **D** *París*, T(474) 742-0200; **D** *Plaza*, best rooms facing the front, small and dark at the back; just off the plaza is **C** *Colonial*, T(474) 742-0142; **C** *Victoria*, two blocks away, near river, T(474) 742-0620) and restaurants (recommended is *La Rinconada*, colonial building, old photos, on plaza two blocks behind Municipalidad, which is on main plaza, good *enchiladas*). Route 80 heads off right to Guadalajara, 197 km away, and left to Antiguo Morelos via San Luis Potosí. Forty-two kilometres southwest en route to Guadalajara is the colonial town of **San Juan de los Lagos**, a major pilgrimage centre and crowded during Mexican holidays. There is also a fine view on entering this town: as the road descends you see the twin-towered church with its red, blue and yellow tiled dome. San Juan is famous for glazed fruits. There are many hotels in the town.

LL-AL *Gran Hotel Hacienda de la Noria*, Av Héroe de Nacozari Sur 1315, Col La Salud, T918-4343, F918-5150, www.granhotellanoria.com.mx Very comfortable, jacuzzi in all rooms, Mexican, Japanese and international cuisine, gardens, swimming pool. **AL** *De Andrea Alameda*, Alameda esq Av Tecnológico, T970-3800, F970-3757. Old hacienda, large rooms, good restaurant. **B** *Suites Alamo*, Alameda 129, T915-6885, F918-5046. Pool. **Sleeping**
Price codes:
see inside front cover

D *Imperial*, Moctezuma y 5 de Mayo, T915-1650, on plaza. Large, sparse rooms. **D** *Praga*, Zaragoza 214, T915-2357. With TV, OK. **D** *Señorial*, Colón 104, T915-1630. Rooms with phone, helpful lady speaks English. **D-E** *Don Jesús*, Juárez 429, T915-5598, F918-4841. Hot water 3 hrs

Colonial Heartland

morning and evening, good value. **D** *San José*, Hidalgo 207, T915-5130. Friendly. Cheap hotels around Juárez market (Av Guadalupe y Guadalupe Victoria), eg **E** *Brasil*, Guadalupe 110, T915-1106. With bath, quiet. **E** *Casa de Oro*, on Hidalgo 205, next to *San José*. Good. **E** *Maser*, Montoro 303, T915-3562, 3 blocks from cathedral. *Comedor* for breakfast. **E** *Reforma*, Nieta y Galeana, 1 block west of main plaza. Colonial-style, large courtyard, rooms a bit dark, friendly, clean. **F** *Casa Belén*, López Mateos y Galeana, T915-8593. Central, hot water, clean, friendly.

Motels A *El Medrano*, Chávez 904, T915-5500. **B** *La Cascada*, Chávez 1501, T916-1411.

Eating

Lack of conventional facilities, except in some of the more expensive hotels

Try the area around 5 de Mayo for *pollo rostizado*. Good *comida corrida* at *Sanfer*, Guadalupe Victoria 204, and at *Woolworth* restaurant 1 block away. *Jacalito*, López Mateos, also near Plaza Crystal. Cheap *tortas*, clean. *La Mamma*, quite new Italian, 7 blocks south of the plaza where the *mariachis* play, top quality. *Lonchería Gorditas Victoria*, popular with locals especially for tacos. *Mitla*, Madero 220. Good breakfast, moderate prices. *Mexicali Rose*, López Mateos. *Comida corrida*, US$10. Also *Freeday*, near Benito Juárez statue. Video bar and restaurant, lively at weekends. *Café Parroquia* on Hidalgo, 1 block west off Madero. Good, cheap. *Jugos Acapulcos*, Allende 106. Good *comida corrida*.

Festivals

The area is famous for viticulture; the local wine is called after San Marcos, and the *feria* in his honour lasts for 3 weeks, starting in the middle of **April**, with processions, cockfights (in Mexico's largest *palenque*, seating 4,000), bullfights, agricultural shows, etc. The Plaza de Armas is lavishly decorated for the occasion. The *feria*, covered by national TV networks, is said to be the biggest in Mexico. Accommodation can be very difficult and prices double during the *feria*. Bullfight also on **New Year's Day**.

Shopping

Many shops sell boots made to order, eg *Zapatería Cervantes*, Guerrero 101 Sur y Nieto, T915-1943. **Bookshop** *Librería Universal*, Madero 427. **Market** Main one at 5 de Mayo y Unión, large and clean, with toilet on upper floor.

Transport

Air The airport (AGU) is 21 km from the town centre. Domestic flights to Culiacán, Mexico City, Monclova, Monterrey, Puerto Vallarta, Reynosa, San Luis Potosí, Tijuana and Zacatecas with a variety of airlines. US flights to Los Angeles with AeroMéxico.

Buses Bus station about 1 km south of centre on Av Circunvalación Sur with post office and pharmacy, take city bus from Galeana near López Mateos. To **Ciudad Juárez**: US$68. **Chihuahua**: US$88. **Guadalajara**: several through the day 6 hrs, US$18. **Guanajuato**: 5 daily, US$5, 3½ hrs. **León**: 21 a day, 2 hrs, US$9. **Mexico City**: 9 a day, 7 hrs, US$30. **Monterrey**: US$48. **Morelia**: Primera Plus, 4 a day, US$17. **Nuevo Laredo**: US$72. **Puerto Vallarta**: at 2230, US$46. **Querétaro**: 8 a day, 6 hrs, US$21. **San Luis Potosí**: Futura, 16 a day between 0600-2300, US$9. **Tijuana**: 1530 and 2100, US$145. **Zacatecas**: every 30 mins, 2½ hrs, US$6.

Directory

Airline offices *Aero California*, Juan de Montoro 203, T915-2400. *AeroMéxico*, Madero 474, T916-1362. **Banks** On Plaza Inverlat, *ATM* takes AmEx. *Banamex*, ATM. **Communications** Internet: *Sistemas Alt 64*, Vásquez del Mercado 206, T915-7613, US$2.60/ hr, open 1000-1400, 1600-2100 Mon-Sat, closed Sun. *Acnet*, Edificio Torreplaza Bosques 2nd flr, Av Aguascalientes near University, bus from Rivero Gutiérrez. **Post office**: Hospitalidad, near El Porián shopping centre. **Cultural centres** *El Centro Cultural Los Arquitos*, Narcozari y Alameda, T917-0023, formerly a 19th-century bathhouse, restored 1993, museum, bookshop, café. **Medical services** Red Cross: T915-2055.

Zacatecas

Phone code: 493
Colour map 3, grid A2
Population: 123,700
Altitude: 2,495m

Founded 1548, and capital of Zacatecas State, this picturesque up-and-down mining city is built in a ravine with pink stone houses scattered over the hills. The largest silver mine in the world, processing 10,000 tonnes of ore a day or 220 tonnes of silver, is at Real de Angeles. Silver has bestowed an architectural grandeur on Zacatecas to match that of the Guanajuato. You could easily spend three or four days drifting around soaking up the atmosphere. There's also a lively nightlife with bars and discos if that's what you're looking for.

ns and outs

The international Aeropuerto La Calera (ZCL) is 27 km north of the city, with flights to domestic locations and several cities in the US. The new(er) and more commonly used bus terminal is 4 km south of town. Bus No 8 from outside the terminal leaves for the centre of town every 10-15 mins.

Boulevard López Mateos, a busy highway, runs close to the centre of town from the bus station (about 4 km south of town) and down the ravine. Driving can be a nightmare with many one-way systems. The **tourist office**, Av Hidalgo 403, 2nd floor T924-0552, F924-0393, **www.turismozacatecas.gob.mx**, is friendly and helpful, get the right person and the information is staggering; they provide free maps and good hotel information, including cheaper hotels. Ask here about language classes at the University.

Sights

The **cathedral** (1730-52) is the centrepiece of town with a fine Churrigueresque façade; a little south is the **San Agustín** church, with interior carvings, now being restored, and the Jesuit church of **Santo Domingo** has frescoes in the sacristy by Francisco Antonio Vallejo (ask the sacristan to turn the lights on). Also worth seeing are the **Casa Moneda** (better known as the Tesorería), founded 1810, and the **Teatro Calderón**, opposite the cathedral. The **Mina del Edén**, Avenida Torreón y Quebradilla at the western side of town, is an old mine with a short section of mine railway in operation (not a proper train); the tour lasts about one hour, commentary in fast Spanish. ■ *1000-1800, US$2.20.* There is also a disco in the mine. ■ *Thu, Fri and Sat US$5.50, buy ticket before 2030, varied music.* You can leave the mine the way you went in or work your way through to the end and the **teleférico**, which carries you over the city, with predictably spectacular views, to Cerro de la Bufa and the **Capilla de Los Remedios** (1728).

Zacatecas is reckoned by many travellers to be the most pleasant town in this part of Mexico

Close to the centre of town is **Museo Pedro Coronel**, on Plaza Santo Domingo, which houses an excellent collection of European and modern art (including Goya, Hogarth, Miró, Tàpies) as well as folk art from Mexico and around the world (take a guide to make the most of the collections). ■ *1000-1700; closed Thu, US$.2.20.* A couple of blocks to the south is **Museo Zacatecano**, east of San Agustín, which contains religious paintings, Huichol handicrafts and some colonial items. ■ *1000-1700, closed Tue, US$1.20.*

To the north of town the **Museo Rafael Coronel**, housed in the ex-Convento de San Francisco, has a vast collection of masks and puppets, primarily Mexican, and an attractive garden perfect for a small picnic. ■ *US$2.20, closed Tue.*

Heading south near the fine, old **Acueducto El Cubo** is the **Museo Francisco Goitia**, housed in what was once the governor's mansion, by the Parque General Enrique Estrada, Colonia Sierra de Alicia. The museum has modern paintings by Zacatecans, but its main attractions are the paintings of small-town poverty in Mexico by Francisco Goitia. ■ *1000-1700 Tue-Sun, US$2.20.* Behind the museum is the spectacular and modern **Parroquia de Fátima**; built in 1975 it pays good tribute to the heritage of the city.

Up on the hill, best visited after going through Mina El Edén and El Teleférico, is **Museo de la Toma de Zacatecas**, on the Cerro de la Bufa, commemorates Pancho Villa's victory over Huerta's forces in 1914. ■ *1000-1700, US$1.40.* The hill, northeast of the city centre, is recommended for views over the city. It is a pleasant walk though crowded on Sundays. There is also a statue of Villa, an observatory, and the Mausoleo de Los Hombres Ilustres. It's a 10-15 minute walk down the hill, with a small café on the first road you meet with good views over the city.

Beyond Zacatecas to the east lies the **Convento de Guadalupe**, a national monument, with a fine church and convent, which now houses a **Museum of Colonial**

Colonial Heartland

Religious Art. The galleries of the convent are full of paintings covering the life of S• Francis and huge frescoes.The labyrinthine convent is well worth a visit, with the Virgin as a child set in gold held in the church. ■ *Tue-Sun 1000-1700, US$3.45.* Next door is the **Museo Regional de Historia**, under development. Frequent buses, No 13, from López Mateos y Salazar, near old terminal, US$0.15, 20 minutes.

Visit also the **Chicomostoc** ruins (also known as **La Quemada**), 56 km south, by taking the 0800 or 1100 Línea Verde bus from main terminal to Adjuntas (about 45 minutes, US$0.60), on the Villanueva road. Then walk 30 minutes through beautiful, silent, nopal-cactus scenery to the ruins, which offer an impressive view. There is the Palace of the Eleven Columns, a Pyramid of the Sun and other remains on a rocky outcrop, in various stages of restoration. In themselves the ruins are not spectacular, but together with the setting they are worth the trip. A museum is being built. Take water. ■ *US$3.35; no information on site, so ask for explanations.* Women are advised to keep at a distance from the caretaker. For the return from the junction at Adjuntas, wait for a bus (possibly a long wait) or hitch back to Zacatecas.

Jerez is an old colonial town about 65 km from Zacatecas, where the wide-brimmed *sombrero charro* is still worn. It is worth a visit and is becoming popular with tourists. There are two interesting churches in the town: **La Soledad**, begun 1805, completed later that century, has a baroque façade, but most elaborate are the three gateways –

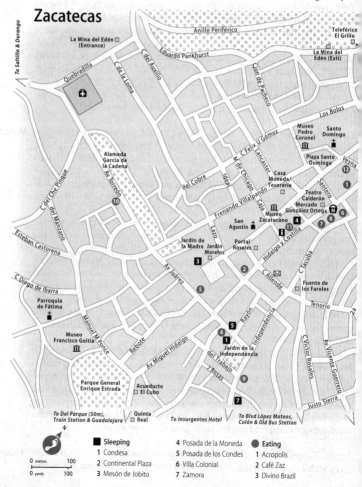

Zacatecas

Sleeping ■
1 Condesa
2 Continental Plaza
3 Mesón de Jobito
4 Posada de la Moneda
5 Posada de los Condes
6 Villa Colonial
7 Zamora

Eating ●
1 Acropolis
2 Café Zaz
3 Divino Brazil

0 metres 100
0 yards 100

composites of all manner of over-the-top classical styles; **La Inmaculada**, also with a baroque façade, has a neo-Romanesque interior. **Sleeping**: B *Posada Santa Cecilia*, Constitución/San Francisco 4, T(494) 945-2412. Old style, pleasant atmosphere. *La Cofradía*, Constitución y San Francisco. Best in town and with moderate prices.

L *Mesón de Jobito*, Jardín Juárez 143, Centro, T924-1722, F924-3500, in heart of Centro Histórico. Small, select and very stylish hotel, attractive restaurant with international and Mexican cuisine. **L** *Quinta Real*, Av González Ortega, T922-9104. Beautiful, built around old bullring (said to be the 2nd oldest in Latin America), aqueduct goes past the front door. Excellent. **AL** *Continental Plaza*, opposite cathedral, on Av Hidalgo, T922-6183 (discount offered for AAA members). Recommended. **AL-B** *María Bonita*, Av López Velarde 319, T922-4545, F922-6645, www.donmiguel.com.mx Hot water, heating, very good.

A *Posada de la Moneda*, near cathedral, Av Hidalgo 413, T922-0881, F922-3693. Nice and clean, but a bit noisy and dark for the price. **B** *Condesa*, opposite *Posada de los Condes*, Av Juárez 102, T922-1160. OK, helpful, some rooms quiet with good views of Cerro de la Bufa, cheap restaurant.

C *Posada de los Condes*, Juárez 107, T922-1093, F924-0072. A bit noisy, rooms darkish except those at front with balconies. **D** *Insurgentes*, Insurgentes 114, off Plaza del Vivar. Without bath, hot showers extra. **D** *Jardín*, on main plaza, T925-2026. **D** *Del Parque*,

Sleeping
■ *on map, page 280*
Price codes:
see inside front cover

4 El Jacalito   8 La Cuija   12 Viva Pizza
5 El Tragedero   9 La Unica Cabaña
6 Gaudi   10 Recovedi
7 La Cantera Musical   11 San Patricio

Colonial Heartland

González Ortega 302, T922-0479. Cheapest in town, bit grubby but clean, fair value. **D** *Zamora*, Plaza de Zamora 303, T922-1200. With bath, central, very basic.

E-F *Hostal Villa Colonial*, T/F922-1980, hostalvillacolonial@hotmail.com, Primero de Mayo y Callejón Mono Prieto, just south of the cathedral. New place – barely open and we're already getting letters – right in the historic centre, shared bath in a mix of dormitories and private rooms. Great views from the rooftop patio. Can provide information on sites and transport. Use of kitchen, internet access. Good deal.

There are a few cheap hotels within 5 mins' walk of the old bus station, to the southeast of town in Barrio La Paz. **C** *Colón*, Av López Velarde 508, T922-8925. Clean, showers. **C-D** *Gami*, Av López Mateos 309, T922-8005. Rooms with TV, OK. **E** *Río Grande*, Calzada de la Paz 217, T922-5349. With bath (**F** without), ask for quiet room on the patio, beautiful view from one side, cleanish, hot water, good value even if the receptionist is a bit surly.

Motels **B-C** *Del Bosque*, T922-0745, Periférico Díaz Ordaz, overlooking the city. Attractive rooms, good food, has camping facilities and hook-ups, showers and toilets, only for small cars and vans.

Youth hostel Parque del Encantado 103, T922-1151, CP 98000, on bus route to centre from bus station, no singles. Also Av de los Deportes beside Estadio Francisco Villa, CP 98064, T922-9377.

Trailer park at Morelos junction, about 20 mins northwest of the city, where Route 54 Saltillo-Guadalajara crosses Route 49. Hook-ups, basic, US$8, behind Pemex.

Eating & drinking Plenty of good places in town. Zacatecas is large enough to offer variety, and small enough for you to never really get lost. *Divino Brazil*, Hidalgo 802, T922-9710. Good Brazilian food with live music in the evenings, open until 0230. *El Jacalito*, Juárez 109. Excellent *comida corrida* and breakfast, open 0800-2230, daily. Further east on Juárez at 232 is *El Tragadero*. Pretty basic café set up but good local Zacatecan dishes, veggie dishes, very friendly, cheap and excellent value. Open 0900-2100, open 365 days a year with special dishes on Christmas Day. *El Paraíso*, Av Hidalgo y P Goitia, corner of market. Bar/restaurant, nice atmosphere, closed Sun. *La Cantera Musical*, Av Tacuba, Mexican. Good atmosphere, poor a/c, good food but drinks limited after 2000. *La Cuija*, in old Centro Comercial on Av Tacuba. Good food, music, atmosphere. *La Unica Cabaña*, Jardín de la Independencia. Cheap, excellent set meals. *Mesonero*, very good food, but pricey. Recommended. *Nueva Galicia*, Plazuela Goitia 102. Wide range of Mexican food, also offers delicious sushi. Recommended. *Recovedi*, facing Plaza Alameda, all you can eat buffets, good veggie options, good wholesome food. Cheap. *Viva Pizza*, Callejón de Veyna, up a small alley almost opposite the cathedral, good pizza, mid-price.

Good cafés include: *Acrópolis*, opposite cathedral. 50-year-old café and diner, good breakfast, slow service. *Café Zaz*, Av Hidalgo 201, reasonably priced in a smart café setting. Several cheap restaurants along Av Independencia. *San Patricio Caffe*, wonderful (and pricey) coffees, where the smart, young and rich visiting Zacatecas hang out.

Plenty of good coffee shops selling real *expresso* coffee. Many good *tamales* sold on the streets. **Health food** Store at Rayón 413, excellent food at reasonable prices.

Festivals Spread over most of **Sep**, a rainy month here. There are bullfights on Sun, but given the growth in popularity of the town you could stumble across an impromtu celebration at any time of year.

Shopping Interesting shops on Independencia selling hats, riding equipment, fruit and other produce, not touristy. Between Hidalgo and Tacuba the elegant 19th-century market building has been converted into a pleasant shopping centre (popular café on balcony, reasonable). The **market** is now dispersed in various locations a few blocks to the southwest. Zacatecas is famous for its *sarapes* and has two delicacies: the local cheese, and *queso de tuna*, a candy made from the fruit of the nopal cactus (do not eat too much, as it has laxative properties).

Air Aeropuerto La Calera (ZCL), 27 km north of city, flights daily to Mexico City, Tijuana, **Transport**
Guadalajara, Ciudad Juárez, Morelia, Aguascalientes. Direct flights to several US cities: Chicago, Denver, Los Angeles, Oakland, California.

Trains Zacatecas is on the Mexico City-Querétaro-Chihuahua line. No scheduled trains running but if a cargo train is passing through there may be a passenger wagon.

Buses New terminal 4 km south of town; taxi US$1.20; red No 8 buses from Plaza
Independencia (US$0.15) or white *camionetas* from Av González Ortega (old bus station on
Blvd López Mateos only serves local destinations). Apart from buses to Mexico City, Chihuahua and a few other major towns, most routes do not have bookable seats. Frequent buses
passing through Jerez back to Zacatecas with *Rojo de Los Altos*, US$2.20.
   Aguascalientes: every 30 mins, 2½ hrs, US$5. **Chihuahua**: via Torreón, 12 hrs, US$45.
Durango: 5 hrs, many throughout the day, US$8 (if continuing to Mazatlán, stay the night in
Durango in order not to miss the views on the way to the coast). **Guadalajara**: hourly, 4 hrs,
US$18. **Hidalgo del Parral**: 10 hrs, US$39. **León**: 3½ hrs, US$11. **Mexico City**: almost hourly,
8 hrs, US$38. **San Luis Potosí**: 7 daily, 2½ hrs, US$8.

Airline offices *Mexicana*, T922-3248. **Banks** *Banamex* recommended. *Bancomer* has a Visa cash **Directory**
dispenser and gives cash (pesos) on Visa cards. Both on Av Hidalgo as are several other banks with
ATMs. **Communications** Internet: *Café @rroba*, Félix U Gómez 520 B, 0900-2200, daily, US$2 per hr,
chmnet@gauss.logicnet.com.mx *Cybertech*, Hidalgo 771, T922-0870. Open Mon-Sat 0930-2130,
US$1.80/hr. Ask around for the latest good place. **Post office**: on Allende between Independencia and
Hidalgo, towards the south of town. **Fax**: service at *Telégrafos*, Av Hidalgo y Juárez. **Cultural
centres** *Alianza Francesa*, Callejón del Santero 111, T924-0348, French film every Tue at 1900 (free).
Language school *Fénix Language Institute*, T922-1643. **Laundry** At the north end of town are
Lavandería El Indio Triste, Juan de Tolosa 828, US$.80 per kg, and *Lavbasolo*, similar prices and times.
Medical services *Santa Elena Clinic*, Av Guerrero, many specialists, consultation, US$15. **Tour
operators** *Cantera Tours*, Centro Comercial El Mercado, Av López Velarde 602-6, Local A-21,
T922-9065. *Operadora Zacatecas*, T924-0050, F924-3676. Offer several interesting tours. *Viajes
Masoco*, Enlace 115, Col Sierra de Alca, T922-5559, tours to Chicomostoc and Jerez, US$15.50.

San Luis Potosí

Lying 423 km from Mexico City, the capital of its state is the centre of a rich mining   *Phone code: 444*
and agricultural area, which has expanded industrially in recent years. Glazed,   *Colour map 3, grid B3*
many-coloured tiles are a feature of the city; one of its shopping streets, the main   *Population: 669,353*
plaza, and the domes of many of its churches are covered with them. It became an   *Altitude: 1,880 m*
important centre after the discovery of the famous San Pedro silver mine in the 16th
century, and a city in 1658. There is a festival in the second half of August.
   The **tourist office**, Obregón 520, T812-9939, is about half a block west of the
Plaza de los Fundadores. It's in a beautiful colonial house with lovely gardens. They
are helpful and have good brochures and maps of the city and places to see in the
state. The local tourism website is at **www.visitasanluispotosi.com**

The **cathedral** is on **Plaza Hidalgo**; fronting the east side. It has a beautiful exterior of **Sights**
pink cantera (a type of local stone), with ornately carved bell towers. The interior is
also very beautiful. There are rows of stone columns running down the length of each
side of the church's interior, each column being about 2 m in diameter. Also on the
east side of the plaza, just the north of the cathedral, is the **Palacio Municipal**. In the
interior, over the double branching staircase, you can admire the glasswork representing the city's coat of arms. In the upper floor, the Cabildo Hall has a ceiling painted by
Italian artist Erulo Eroli, featuring mythological Christian themes. Do not miss the
church of **San Francisco**, which fronts the plaza of the same name. This church is one
of the baroque jewels of the city. The construction dates back to 1686. In that year, the
work of the beautiful pink limestone façade was begun. But it wasn't until the next century that some of its most important features were added, such as the baroque tower

Colonial Heartland

and the main altar. The interior is embellished with wonderful paintings, among which the works by Miguel Cabrera and Antonio Torres are the most outstanding. Worthy of admiration is the sacristy, the most magnificent in San Luis Potosí. The **Templo del Carmen**, in **Plaza del Carmen**, has a grand tiled dome, an intricate façade, and a fine pulpit and altar inside. The room to the left of the main altar (as you face it) has another exquisite, very striking altar covered in gold leaf. The **Teatro de la Paz** is next door. The baroque **Capilla de Aranzazú**, behind San Francisco, inside the regional museum (see below), must not be missed; the carved stone framework of the chapel window is one of the most beautiful pieces of baroque art in the city.

Then there is the **Capilla de Loreto** with a baroque façade; the **Templo de San Miguelito**, in the oldest part of the city; **San Agustín**, with its ornate baroque tower; and the startling modern **Iglesia de la Santa Cruz**, in the Industria Aviación district, designed by Enrique de la Mora. The **Palacio de Gobierno**, begun 1789, contains oil paintings of past governors. There is also the colonial treasury, **Antigua Caja Real**, built 1767. Of great artistic merit are the doors and windows of the chapel, carved in stone in the purist baroque style. Of especial interest is the stairway leading to the first floor. It has very low steps, so that the mules, laden with precious metals, could climb easily. ■ *Some rooms may be visited Mon-Fri 0930-1330.*

Other points of interest are the pedestrian precinct surrounding **Jardín Hidalgo** and the **Caja del Agua** fountain (1835) in Avenida Juárez. **Plaza de San Francisco** is very pleasant. The modern railway station has frescoes by Fernando Leal. The **Teatro Alarcón**, on Calle Abasolo, between Zaragoza and Morelos, is by Tresguerras (see under Celaya, page 262). It is now being used as offices for a miners' union. The **University** was founded in 1804.

San Luis Potosí

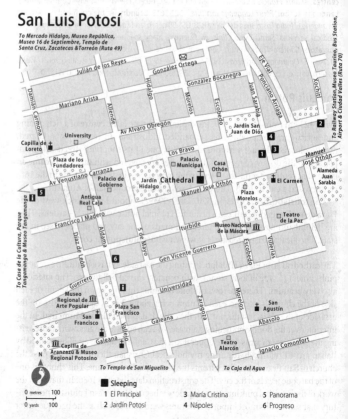

Colonial Heartland

Sleeping

1 El Principal
2 Jardín Potosí
3 María Cristina
4 Nápoles
5 Panorama
6 Progreso

The **Museo Regional de Arte Popular**, next to San Francisco church, is housed in what used to be a private residence. Handicrafts from various parts of the state can be seen, including ceramics, woodwork, *rebozos*, textiles, etc. There are also items for sale. ■ *Tue-Sat 1000-1345, 1600-1745; Sun 1000-1400, Mon 1000-1500.* Nearby is **Museo Regional Potosino**, located in the building that originally was a Franciscan convent. The ground floor has an exhibition of pre-Hispanic artefacts, mainly from the Huastec culture. ■ *Tue-Fri 1000-1300, 1500-1800, Sat 1000-1200, Sun 1000-1300.* **La Casa de la Cultura** on Avenida Carranza, halfway between the centre and university, is a very elegant building, made of limestone in a neo-classic style with large and beautiful gardens. Built in 1919 by the architect Joaquín Meade, it was the first residence of Gerardo Meade until 1970, when the state government acquired it to create the Cultural Centre. Now it has on display a selected collection of art works, archaeological pieces and arts and crafts. ■ *Tue-Fri 1000-1400, 1600-1800, Sat 1000-1400, 1800-2100.* **Museo Nacional de la Máscara**, in what used to be the Palacio Federal, has an excellent collection of masks. The most impressive are the masks used in colonial and pre-Hispanic times in pagan religious ceremonies. ■ *Tue-Fri 1000-1400, 1600-1800, Sat-Sun 1000-1400, US$0.20 plus US$0.20 for use of camera.* In Parque Tangamanga is the **Museo Tangamanga** in an old hacienda, and also a planetarium, observatory and open-air theatre ■ *0600-1800. In Plaza España, next to the Plaza de Toros, is a* **Museo Taurino** (bullfighting museum), east of Alameda on Universidad y Triana. ■ *Tue-Sat 1100-1330, 1730-1930.* **Casa Othón**, Manuel José Othón 225, is the birthplace and home of the poet. ■ *Tue-Fri 0800-1900, Sat and Sun 1000-1300.* **NB** For motorists driving into the centre, parking is very difficult. There is an *estacionamiento* near the police station on Eje Vial, US$1 for 1st hr, US$0.65 for each subsequent hour.

Museums

Hot springs at Ojo Caliente, Balneario de Lourdes and Gogorrón. **Balneario de Lourdes** (B hotel, clean, nice atmosphere, small pool) is south of San Luis Potosí. **Gogorrón** is clean and relaxing, with pools, hot tubs, picnic grounds and campsites. There is a restaurant.

Excursions

B *María Cristina*, Juan Sarabia 110, Altos, T812-9408, F812-8823. Modern, clean, small rooms with phone and TV, with restaurant, good value. **B** *Panorama*, Av Venustiano Carranza 315, T812-1777, F812-4591. Price includes breakfast and a 20% discount on other meals. Large, attractive rooms. Very good views of the city from the rooms on the upper floors. **C** *Nápoles*, Juan Sarabia 120, T812-8418, F812-2260. Good restaurant attached, TV, phones, ceiling fans in rooms. Recommended.

Sleeping
There are many hotels
between the railway
station and
the cathedral

    D *Hotel Anáhuac*, Xochitl 140, about 1 block west of the station, T712-6504, F814-4904. Extra for TV. **D** *Hotel Guadalajara*, Jiménez 253, near train station, T812-4404. Small rooms with TV and phone; has enclosed parking. **D** *Progreso*, Aldama 415, T812-0366, less than a block from the Plaza San Francisco. Attractive colonial façade. Rooms are large but rather dark and a little run down. Not bad for the price. **D** *Universidad*, Universidad 1435, between train and bus station. Clean, friendly, hot showers. **D-E** *Jardín Potosí*, Los Bravo 530, T812-3152. Good, hot water, restaurant. Recommended. **E** *El Principal*, Juan Sarabia opposite *María Cristina*. With bath, OK, loud TV in hall.

    There are several very basic hotels with shared bath by the train station that charge around 35 pesos a night for a double on Jiménez.

Motels Along Highway 57: **A** *Santa Fe*, T813-1207, F811-1415. Parking, pool, restaurant and bar, near University campus. **C** *Mansión Los Arcos*, a few kilometres south of San Luis Potosí, signposted, T824-0530. With restaurant and safe parking.

Café Florida, Juan Sarabia 230; many other reasonably priced eating places at western end of Alameda Juan Sarabia. *Café Pacífico*, corner of Los Bravo and Constitución, a couple of blocks from the train station. Open 24 hrs. Dinner costs around US$5. Good hot chocolate. Nice atmosphere. *La Parroquia*, corner of Díaz de León and Carranza, on the Plaza de los

Eating

Colonial Heartland

Fundadores. In old building but modern inside. Attractive wood panelling. *Comida corrida* costs US$2.70, plus cost of beverage. Good food. *La Posada del Virrey*, on north side of Jardín Hidalgo. The restaurant is in a beautiful covered courtyard of an old colonial building. They also have a dining room facing the plaza. *Los Molinos*, in *Hostal del Quijote*. Excellent, well-served food. *Restaurant de Mariscos El Pacífico*, across the street from the *Café Pacífico*, at Los Bravo 429. *Tokio*, Los Bravo 510. Excellent *comida*.

Shopping Excellent sweet shop at Galeana 430, next to the Museo Regional Potosino. **Markets** Head north on Hidalgo and you come to Mercado Hidalgo, then Mercado República, and Mercado 16 de Septiembre. Locally made *rebozos* (the best are from Santa María del Río) are sold in the markets. 3-storey hypermarket, *Chalita*, on Jardín San Juan de Dios between Av Alvaro Obregón and Los Bravo. **Health food store** *Casa de Nutrición*, 5 de Mayo 325, fairly limited.

Transport **Air** The airport (SLP) is nearly 6 km from the centre. Flights to Chicago, San Antonio (Texas). Many daily to Mexico City, also flights to Aguascalientes, Guadalajara, Monterrey, Tampico.

Buses Bus station on outskirts of town 1½ km from centre. For local buses to the centre, walk out the front door of the terminal and turn right. Walk down the street to the first traffic light. Then take buses heading south on the cross street (ie to your right as you're facing it) marked 'de Mayo' or 'Los Gómez'.

Luggage can be left at the bus terminal (3 pesos per bag per hour). Snack food, magazines, stationery and typical Mexican sweets are avaiable and there is a booth with long-distance and fax service. There is a taxi ticket booth in the centre of the terminal. Taxis to the centre cost about US$2.

Aguascalientes: hourly, 2½ hrs, US$18. **Chihuahua**: 9 buses per day, US$68. **Ciudad Juárez**: 9 buses per day, US$92. **Durango**: 1405, 2045 and 2330, US$29. **Guadalajara**: hourly service, 5 hrs, US$20. **Guanajuato**: regular service, 4 hrs, US$11. **Nuevo Laredo**: 10 hrs, US$45. **Matehuala**: 13 buses per day, 1½ hrs, US$11. **Mexico City**: very regular service, 5 hrs, US$25. **Monterrey**: 14 daily, 6 hrs, US$25. **Morelia**: regular service, US$19. **Querétaro**: hourly from 0900, 2½ hrs, US$13. **San Miguel de Allende**: 6 a day, 3 hrs. **Tijuana**: 1530 and 1830, US$140. **Zacatecas**: 7 buses daily, 2½ hrs, US$8.

Also run other 2nd class buses. *Autobuses Americanos*; two buses daily, stopping at **Laredo**, **San Antonio**, **Dallas**, and **Houston**, in Texas, and **Chicago**.

Directory **Airline offices** *Aeromar*, Av Carranza 1160-2; T911-4671. *Mexicana*, T917-8836. *Aerocalifornia*, T911-8050. *Mexicana de Aviación*, T917-8920. **Communications** Internet: *Café Cibernético*, Av Carranza 416. Post office: Morelos y González Ortega. **Medical services** *Red Cross*, Av Juárez and Diez Gutiérrez, T915-3332. *Hospital Central* (public), Av Carranza 2395, T913-0343. **Private Hospitals** *Sociedad de Beneficios Española*, Av V Carranza 1090, T913-4048. *Hospital de Nuestra Señora de la Salud*, Madre Perla 435, Frac Industrias (4 blocks behind *Holiday Inn Hostal del Quixote*), T924-5424. *Clínica Díaz Infante*, Arista 730, T912-3737.

Pozos
Phone code: 478
Colour map 3, grid B3
Altitude: 2,305 m

South of San Luis Potosí, east of the junction with Route 110, is San Luis de la Paz. Nearby is one of Mexico's mining ghost-towns, Pozos, once one of the most important mining centres of Mexico. First you come to the ruins. It's very silent and a complete contrast to Real de Catorce (see below). Many of the mining shafts still remain pristine and very deep.

Pozos was founded in 1576 when silver was discovered. In the 19th century the population reached 80,000 but following the Revolution most of the foreign (French and Spanish) owners left and the workforce migrated to Mexico City. After the 1985 earthquake, people who had lost their homes in the capital drifted back. The men now work in Querétaro and the women work at home making clothes to sell in local markets. The population has slowly risen to 2,000. The town is very quiet and the whole area was decreed a historical monument in 1982. There are no rooms to let. Pozos can be reached by bus from San Miguel de Allende (change at San Luis de la Paz) or San José Iturbide.

Real de Catorce

Fifty-six kilometres west of Matehuala, an important junction on Route 57, is one of Mexico's most interesting old mining towns, Real de Catorce, founded in 1772. This remarkable city, clustering around the sides of a valley, used to be so quiet that you could hear the river in the canyon, 1,000 m below. It is becoming increasingly popular as a tourist destination and new hotels are being built.

Phone code 488
Colour map 3, grid A3
Altitude: 2,765 m

The first church was the **Virgen del Guadalupe** (1779), a little way out of town. Beautiful ceiling paintings remain, as well as the black coffin used for the Mass of the Cuerpo Presente. Many of the images from this church were moved to the **Church of San Francisco** (1817), which is believed to be miraculous. The floor of the church is made of wooden panels, which can be lifted to see the catacombs below. In a room to one side of the main altar are *retablos*, touchingly simple paintings on tin, as votive offerings to the saint for his intercession. Next to the church is a small but worthwhile museum showing mining equipment, etc. ■ *US$0.10.*

Sights

There are good hikes in the surrounding mountains. Very peaceful. Take good footwear, sun protection and a jumper. A 30-minute walk takes you to the *pueblo fantasmo* (ghost town) from where there are fine views over the town.

B *El Coral del Conde*, Morelos, close to Mesón de la Abundancia, T887-5048. 6 rooms, fine furniture, clean, big bathrooms. **B** *Puesta del Sol*, on way to cemetery from main square, T887-5050. With bath, TV, beautiful views, poor restaurant. Recommended. **D** *Hotel Real*, in a side street. Clean, nice atmosphere, friendly owner, good restaurant. Recommended. **E** *Providencia*, on main street. Hot water, clean, restaurant. Several other hotels, and various restaurants. Accommodation is easy to find: boys greet new arrivals and will guide motorists through the peculiar one-way system (or face a police fine).

Sleeping & eating

El Eucalyptus, on way to Zócalo. Italian-Swiss run. Excellent homemade pasta, vegetarian food, cakes. Pricey but recommended. Many cheap restaurants on main street and stalls selling tacos and hot drinks.

There is a pilgrimage here for *San Francisco* (**4** Oct), on foot from Matehuala, overnight on **3 Oct**. Take the local bus from Matehuala to La Paz and join the groups of pilgrims who set out from early evening onwards. On Good Friday, thousands of visitors gather to watch a lively *Passion play* 'with almost real Roman soldiers and very colourful Jews and apostles'.

Festivals

Trains The station, called Catorce, is 13 km away. There is one hotel or you can stay in private homes. Jeeps collect passengers from the station (US$16.50 per jeep) and follow a more spectacular route than the minibuses. Check locally to find out if any trains are running.

Transport

Buses Many buses a day to Matehuala with *Transportes Tamaulipas*, from the corner of Guerrero and Mendiz, US$2 one-way. A taxi can be hired nearby for US$25, economic for 4 people; local buses from office 1 block north of the Zócalo.

Colonial Heartland

Mexico City

Michoacán

West of Mexico City the State of Michoacán, home to the Purépecha (or Tarascan) Indians, is a country of deep woods, fine rivers and great lakes, with abundant fruit, fish and game. Visitors are drawn by the Tarascan customs, folklore, way of life, craft skills (pottery, wood work and lacquer), music and especially dance. Try to catch one of the festivals. The Day of the Dead, an important date in the Mexican calendar of festivals, is especially prominent in Michoacán, particularly around Pátzcuaro where, on 1 November every village around the lake honours its dead; it is a festive occasion, but also profoundly spiritual.

People flock to El Campanario Ecological Reserve each year to see millions of Monarch butterflies take to the wing, one of the most impressive sights in all of Mexico.

There are many small pre-Hispanic sites to be explored en route, and the open chapel at Cuitzeo should not be missed. As elsewhere in Mexico, the colonial architecture will impress and the natural beauty of Paricutín volcano will bemuse. A few days relaxing on the almost deserted beaches of Playa Azul will prepare you for the next stage of your journey.

Morelia

Phone code: 443
Colour map 3, grid B3
Population: 619,958
Altitude: 1,950 m

Founded in 1541, Morelia, capital of Michoacán state, is a rose-tinted city with grand, attractive colonial buildings, delightful courtyards and shady plazas. It is a quiet, provincial city although the narrow streets suffer from vehicle pollution.

Ins & outs

The airport is about 27 km north of Morelia. Blue-and-white *Aeropuerto* buses will take you to the centre. The train station is about 2 km from town, but there are no scheduled passenger services. The bus terminal is close to the town centre, on Eduardo Ruiz between León Guzmán and Gómez Farías. For details see page 291. Morelia is connected by Route 43 to Salamanca, Route 14 to Uruapan and Route 15 to Zamora and Mexico City.

The **tourist office** is inside Palacio Clavijero (south end), Nigromante 79, T312-3710, F312-9816, **www.michoacan.gob.mx**, and has local hotel information list and map, English spoken. ■ *Mon-Fri 0800-2000, Sat and Sun 0900-1900.* Good city maps are available from *Casa de Cambio Troca Mex*, Melchor Ocampo y I Zaragoza and on Guillermo Preito, just south of the Plaza de las Rosas.

Sights

There are many good language schools in Morelia (see Directory page 291)

The **cathedral** (1640) is set between the two main plazas, with graceful towers and a fine façade, in what is called 'sober baroque' style. The **Santuario de la Virgen de Guadalupe**, east of the aqueduct, has an ornate interior of terracotta garlands and buds, painted in pastels. There are four huge oil paintings of the missionaries 'Christianizing' the Indians. Other important churches are the modernized **Templo de la Cruz** and the 18th-century **Templo de las Rosas** in the delightful plaza of the same name (its ex-Convento now houses the Conservatorio de Música). The oldest of Morelia's churches is the **Templo de San Francisco** of the Spanish Renaissance period, although it lacks many of the decorative features of that style. The **Templo de las Monjas** has an extravagant baroque façade, constructed in 1727. The **Templo de San Agustín** (16th century) has a more Gothic influence but is also imposing.

Even more interesting than the colonial churches are the many fine colonial secular buildings still standing. The Independence hero José María Morelos, the reformer Melchor Ocampo, and the two unfortunate Emperors of Mexico (Agustín de Iturbide and the Archduke Maximilian of Austria) are commemorated by plaques on their houses. **Morelos' birthplace** , at Corregidora 113, is open to visitors, admission free. The **Colegio de San Nicolás** (1540) is the oldest surviving institution of higher education in Latin America. (It has a summer school for foreign students.) Opposite is the **Centro Cultural Universitario**, with many free events. The fine former Jesuit college, now called the **Palacio Clavijero**, corner of Madero and Nigromante, contains government offices and an extensive market selling *artesanía* and sweets in the arcades, with a helpful tourist office on the ground floor. At the east edge of the downtown area, on the road to Mexico City, are the 224 arches of a ruined **aqueduct**, built in 1788 (walk 11 blocks east from cathedral along Avenida Madero). Both Banamex and Bancomer have their offices in magnificent old houses on Madero Poniente, near the Plaza; the patio of the former is especially fine. Also notable are the **Law School**, in the former monastery of **San Diego**, next to the Santuario de la Virgen de Guadalupe, past the aqueduct; the **Palacio de Gobierno** (1732-70), facing the cathedral; the **Palacio Municipal**; and the **Palacio Federal**, built in the 18th century, and formerly a convent. Visit also the churches of **La Merced**, with its lovely tower and strange, bulging *estípites* (inverted pyramidal supports), **Las Capuchinas**, Ortega y Montaño, southeast of the centre, which has some Churrigueresque *retablos*, and **Santa María**, on a hilltop south of the city.

Next to the Plaza de Morelos is the Alameda de Calzones, a shady pedestrianized walkway with restored mansions leading three blocks to the **Fuente Tarasca**, a fountain with three bare-breasted women holding up a giant basket of fruit.

Thursday and Sunday are market days: specialities are pottery, lacquerwork, woodcarving, jewellery, blankets and leather sandals; in this connection see the **Casa de Artesanías de Michoacán**, in the ex-Convento de San Francisco, next to the church of the same name; it is full of fine regional products for sale but they are not cheap. The small shops upstairs, some of which have local artisans at work, have better quality crafts than in the shops downstairs. The masks are particularly fine. ■ *The shop on the ground floor is open Mon-Sat 1000-1500, 1700-2000.*

Museums

Museo de Michoacán, has a collection of objects relating to the history of Michoacán from pre-Hispanic times to the present day. ■ *Daily, 0900-1900, Sun, 0900-1400, US$4.35. Calle Allende 305.* The **Casa de la Cultura**, housed in the ex-Convento del Carmen, has a good collection of masks from various regions, and also of crucifixes. The centre hosts arts workshops (nominal fee), daily music and dance performances, exhibitions, etc. ■ *Daily, free. Av Morelos Norte.* The **Museo**

Michoacán

Morelia

Sleeping	2 Del Matador	4 Los Juaninos	5 Posada de la
1 Catedral	3 Florida		Soledad

del Estado, in the house of Iturbide's wife (Casa de la Emperatriz), southeast corner of Jardín de las Rosas, is well worth a visit. Most of the ground floor is dedicated to Tarascan history and culture, lots of information about Michoacán and, at the front, an old pharmacy with all its bottles, cabinets, scales, etc, intact. ■ *Mon-Sat 0900-1400, 1600-2000, Sun same but closes at 1900, free.* The **Museo Casa de Morelos**, on Morelos Sur, about three blocks south of the cathedral, has exhibits on the Independence movement and its hero, José María Morelos. ■ *0900-1900, US$1.20.* **Museo de Arte Contemporáneo Alfredo Zalce**, Avenida Acueducto, in a 19th-century French-style building, has temporary exhibitions. ■ *Closes for siesta, reopens 1600, closed Mon.* For a guided tour of the city, contact David, front desk, Villa Montaña Hotel, where there are many other tours on offer, including one to the Monarch Butterfly Reserve (see below).

Essentials

Sleeping
■ *on map page 288*

Some of the cheaper hotels may have water only in the morning; check

AL *Los Juaninos*, Morelos Sur 39, T312-0036, juaninos@mich1.telmex.net.mx   At one time the Episcopal Palace (1685), beautifully restored in 1998, rooftop restaurant overlooking Zócalo. Luxurious. **AL** *Posada de la Soledad*, Zaragoza 90 and Ocampo, T313-0627, F312-2111. Off the Plaza de Armas and much quieter. Fine courtyards, converted chapel as dining room, TV and fireplaces in rooms, parking opposite, good value. Recommended. **A** *Catedral*, Zaragoza 37, T313-0783, F313-0467, hote_catedral@infosel.net.mx, close to plaza. Spacious, nice bar, restaurant closes quite early. Recommended. **B** *Florida*, Morelos Sur 165, T312-1819, F312-1038. Clean, good value. **C** *Valladolid*, Portal Hidalgo 241, on main plaza, T312-0027, F312-4663. With bath, good value for its location but a bit drab.

C *del Matador*, E Ruiz 531, opposite bus station, T/F312-4649. Simple, with bath. **D** *Don Vasco*, Vasco de Quiroga 232, T/F312-1484. With shower and hot water, clean, safe, some rooms dingy. Recommended. **C** *Mintzicuri*, Vasco de Quiroga 227 (opposite *Don Vasco*), T312-0590, F312-0664. Clean, small rooms, hot shower, TV, parking, helpful tourist office. **D** *Posada del Cortijo*, E Ruiz 673, T312-9642, F313-1281. Good value, but small rooms, overlooks the Casa de la Cultura, hot water. **D** *Posada de Luz*, Calle de Trabajo 32, T/F317-4878. Single rooms dingy.

Cheap hotels on **Morelos Norte**: **C** *Concordia*, Gómez Farías 328, T312-3052, F324-2949, round corner from bus station. TV and phone in rooms. **D** *Colonial*, corner with 20 de Noviembre 15, T312-1897, F313-1051. Pleasant, lots of hot water, good value. **On Madero Pte**: **C** *San Jorge*, No 719, T312-4610. With hot shower, clean. **D** *Vallarta*, No 670, T312-4095. Fair. **E** *Fénix*, No 537, T312-0512. With bath, noisy, clean, cheap. **E** *Posada Lourdes*, No 340, T312-5603. Basic, clean, quiet, hot water. **F** *Señorial*, Santiago Tapiá 543, 1 block south from bus terminal. Basic, with bath. Cheap *posadas* and *casas de huéspedes* tend to be uninviting, some around the bus station are reported clean and cheap.

On **Santa María hill**, south of the city, with glorious views, are hotels **LL-L** *Villa Montaña*, Patzimba 201, T314-0231, F315-1423, www.villamontana.com.mx   Each room is a house on its own, run by French aristocrats, very expensive but worth it, superb restaurant. **AL** *Villa San José*, Patzimba 77, Col Vista Bella, T/F324-4545, www.villasanjose.com.mx   Rooms have nice views and fireplaces. Reached only by car. **B** *Vista Bella*, Camino a Santa María s/n, T312-0248, F314-0284. Large rooms with wood-burning fireplaces, TVs with VCRs and phones, parking, bar-restaurant, piano bar.

Motels B *Villa Centurión*, on road to Morelos, T313-2272. Good antiques, pool, TV. **C** *El Parador*, Highway 45, with trailer park. **C** *Las Palmas*, on road to Guadalajara, also trailer park. 2 good trailer parks on Route 126 between Morelia and the capital: *Balneario Las Ajuntas*, after Queréndaro; and *Balneario Atzimba*, hot springs at Zinapécuaro.

Youth hostel Known by its initials *IMJUDE*, although some people refer to it as *CREA*, its former initials. At corner of Oaxaca and Chiapas 180, T313-3177, 1 km southwest of bus station (walk west to Cuautla, then south along Cuautla to Oaxaca) **F** per person. Camping possible in a forest about 4 km south of centre on unnumbered road signposted to Pátzcuaro.

Café de Conservatorio, on Plaza de las Rosas (opposite music academy). Not cheap but nice atmosphere and tasty cakes. *Quinta Sol*, Aquiles Serdán 729, 5 blocks east of Morelos. Also vegetarian, good *comida corrida*, US$4, served from 1400; both close daily at 1700 and both closed Sun. *El Viejo Paral*, Madero Ote and Quiroga, for cakes. And *comidas corridas* in an unnamed restaurant on Gómez Farías, on right hand side heading away from bus station, US$1.50. *La Flor de las Mercedes*, León Guzmán. Colonial-style house, beautiful decor, moderate prices. *Woolworth's*, Virrey de Mendoza and Madero. Pretty old building with stone vaulted ceilings. *Viandas de San José*, Alvaro Obregón 263 and Zapata. Good cheap *comida corrida*, excellent service. Recommended. *Los Pioneros*, Aquiles Serdán y Morelos Norte. Cheap, good local food. *La Bodega de la Iguana*, Av Camelinsa 3636, T314-4204. Very good traditional cuisine. Highly recommended. *Boca del Río*, Gómez Farías185. Good fish. *Café del Olmo*, Benito Juárez 95. In a nice colonial building. There is a good café in *Casa de la Cultura*, with delicious home-made cakes. *Café Colón*, Aquiles Serdán 265, good coffee.

Eating
The Mercado de Dulces, on Gómez Farías at the western end of the Palacio Clavijero, is famous for ates (fruit jams), candies and rompope (an alcoholic drink similar to advocaat)

Peña Bola Suriana, Allende 355. Live traditional guitar music, open courtyard, small cover charge. Free weekly concerts are held in the Teatro Municipal.

Entertainment

Air Mexican destinations include Cuernavaca, Leon, Mexico City, Tijuana, Uruapan, Veracruz and Zacatecas. International connections to Chicago, Los Angeles, San Francisco, San José (California).

Transport

Buses The terminal is on Eduardo Ruiz between León Guzmán and Gómez Farías, an easy walk to the town centre. Tourist kiosk, restaurants and left luggage.
    Aguascalientes: 0230, 0805, 1205, 1605, 1705, 7 hrs, US$23. **Celaya**: *Servicios Coordinados* (1st class) 18 per day, US$9. **Colima**: 0740, 1200, US$20. **Guadalajara**: at least hourly, 3-5 hrs, quicker on the autopista, US$23-16. **Guanajuato**: 8 daily from 0650 to 1525, 3½ hrs, US$9. **Leó**: regular throughout the day, 4 hrs, US$12. **Manzanillo**: *ETN* (luxury service) 2230, US$33. **Mexico City**: very regular services, some to the North terminal, some to the West terminal, 4 hrs, US$21. **Monterrey**: *Turistar Ejecutivo* (luxury service) 1700, US$72. **Nogales**: *Transportes del Pacífico* 2000, US$110. **Nuevo Laredo**: *Turistar Ejecutivo* (luxury service) 1700, US$92. **Pátzcuaro**: very regular service, 1 hr, US$4. **Querétaro**: *Flecha Amarilla* 14 per day, US$7. *Primera Plus* 9 per day, US$8.60. *Servicios Coordinados* 15 per day, US$7.70. **San Luis Potosí**: hourly, US$13. **Uruapan**: very regular departures, 2 hrs, US$8.

Airlines *Aeromar*, T312-8545. **Banks** *Bancomer*, Av Madero Oriente, just off main plaza, Visa ATM. There is an ATM just east of the Hotel Casino that accepts Visa and MasterCard. There is a *Banco Inverlat* ATM next to the bus station at the corner of Eduardo Ruiz and Gómez Farías that accepts American Express cards. **Communications** Internet: *Chatroom Cybercafé*, Nigromante 132A, Mon-Sat 0900-2200, Sun 1200-2100, US$1.60 per hr, spacious, tranquil, a real café. *Shareweb Cybercafé*, Av Madero Ote, 573-c, T312-2446. Mon-Sat 0900-2200, Sun 1400-2200, US$2.20 per hr. **Post office**: in Palacio Federal. Long-distance phone and fax; Gómez Farías 113, near the *mercado de dulces*. Another at the corner of Zaragosa and Melchor Ocampo. **Medical services** Dentist: *Dr Leopoldo Arroyo Contreras*, Abraham González 35, T312-0751, near cathedral. Recommended. **Language schools** *Centro Mexicano de Idiomas*, Calz Fray Antonio de San Miguel 173, T312-4596, 313-2796. Intensive weekly classes (US$280 for 1st week); other courses available include handicrafts. Accommodation with families. *Baden-Powell Institute*, Antonio Alzate 565, T312-4070. From US$6.50 per hr to US$8.50 per hr, depending on length of course, lodging US$12 per day, including 3 meals, courses for all levels, plus cultural, social science and extracurricular courses. Highly recommended. (See Learning Spanish in Essentials, page 27) **Laundry** *Lavandería Chapultepec*, Ceballos 881. *Lavandería* on Santiago Tapiá towards bus station.

Directory

Michoacán

East of Morelia

The road east of Morelia soon climbs through 50 km of splendid mountain scenery of forests, waterfalls and gorges, to the highest point (Km 253), Puerto Gartan, and **Mil Cumbres** (2,886 m), with a magnificent view over mountain and valley, and then descends into a tropical valley. A new, four-lane highway avoids the Mil Cumbres pass.

The pavements here are covered in chillies drying in the blazing sun, and all the shops are filled with large bags of chillies in the season

Another alternative to the Mil Cumbres pass is to take Route 126 from Morelia to **Queréndaro** (E *Hotel Imperial*, near church, pleasant rooms and courtyard, hot water, good value. Good tacos on main square). At a junction 10 km short of Zinapécuaro, turn right to join Route 15 (to Toluca and Mexico City) at Huajúmbaro. If, instead of turning right you carry straight on, the road climbs and descends to **Maravatío** (hotel) and then turns south and climbs steeply towards **Tlalpujahua**, an old mining town with a museum, several churches, and cobblestoned streets, very picturesque among forests and hills (*Casa de Huéspedes*). From Maravatío, Route 122 goes south to join Route 15 just east of Ciudad Hidalgo. Also from Maravatío, Route 126 to Toluca has been upgraded to a toll road, renamed 15D and is one hour quicker than Route 15 over the mountains.

Northwest of Maravatío, on the Río Lerma (18th-century bridge), lies the town of **Acámbaro**, founded 1526. It has a Franciscan church of the same date and monastery (finished 1532), with the Capilla de Santa Gracia (mid-16th century) and an ornate fountain. It was the point from which the irrigation system for the whole area was laid out when the town was founded. Acámbaro continues to thrive as an agricultural centre and railway junction. It is also on the main highway from Celaya to Toluca. The mini-diversion from the main route just described can as easily be undertaken starting at Ciudad Hidalgo and ending at Morelia.

Ciudad Hidalgo
Colour map 3, grid B3
Population: 100,000

Worth a glance is the façade of the 16th-century church at Ciudad Hidalgo. The town is also known for its thermal baths. **C** *Morenita*, T(786) 154-0079. **D** *Hotel Fuente*, Morelos 37, T(786) 154-0518. Some rooms have no keys, clean, showers, no water in the afternoon. **E** *Florida*, damp rooms, garage US$0.50 a night. *Restaurant Manolo*. Inexpensive, good. *Restaurant Lupita's*, excellent, family-run. Also see the old colonial bridge and church at **Tuxpan**, halfway between Cuidad Hidalgo and Zitácuaro; **C** *Ojo de Agua*, T/F(786) 154-1588. **F** *Mara*, on main square. Dirty, hot water, wood stove. *Tuxpan*, Miguel Cabrera, T(786) 155-0058. Noisy. Not far from Tuxpan a side road runs south to the spa of **San José Purúa** at an altitude of 1,800m, in a wild setting of mountains, gorges and woods. Trailers can park outside the guarded gate (24 hours, tip the guard for security), small charge for entry to grounds. Alternatively, drive down the steep hill to the river, just over the bridge on the right to **Agua Amarilla**, a spa where you can camp for a small fee, friendly. Smaller, cheaper hotels lie on the road past the spa and in the town of **Jungapeo**.

Zitácuaro
Phone code: 715
Colour map 3, grid B3

Zitácuaro is a small town with a pleasant plaza and a good covered market. The **tourist office** is at Km 4 on the Zitácuaro-Toluca road, T153-0675.

Sleeping A *Villa Monarca Inn*, T153-5346, F153-5350, www.villamonarca.com, on road to Morelia. Has a pool. **B** *Rancho San Cayetano*, 3 km out on Huetamo road, T153-1926. Chalets, friendly, clean. Highly recommended. **B** *Salvador*, Hidalgo Pte 7, T153-1107. Clean and pleasant. **B** *Lorenz*, Av Hidalgo Ote 14, T153-0991. Quiet, clean, TV, friendly, 9 blocks from bus station. **C** *México*, Revolución Sur 22, T153-2811. Clean, large rooms with cable TV, parking, restaurant. Recommended. **D** *Florida*. With bath, clean, garage US$0.50 a night. **D** *Colón*. Reasonable, fan, not very quiet, friendly management, can store luggage. **D** *América*, Revolución Sur 8, 1st block, T153-1116. TV, pleasant, clean. Recommended. **D** *Mary*, Revolución Sur 4, T153-0847. Hot shower, TV, clean. **D** *Posada Michoacán*, 5 de Mayo, main square, T153-0008 TV, clean, friendly, luggage store. **F** *Caroline* is a cheap option one block north of the plaza.

Michoacán

Monarch butterflies

The wintering ground of the Monarch butterfly in El Campanario Ecological Reserve is rightly considered to be one of the natural wonders of the world. Every year millions of the bright orange coloured butterflies gather to enjoy the warm climate having migrated from southeast Canada and northeast US. Huge clusters of butterflies hang from branches, which bow under their weight, eventually rising in a swirling mass of red clouds when warm air blows through the reserve. Most impressive is the sound of their wings, like a strong breeze blowing through the trees. The butterflies arrive between December and March, with the best time of year to visit being January and February. They leave in March, after which there is nothing to see until the following November/December. The reserve is at a high altitude and you need to walk a few kilometres (30 minutes) to see the butterflies. Bring warm clothes. It is very cold at night. It gets very busy at weekends, when all the accommodation will be full; your best bet is to arrive at the sanctuary when it opens at 0900 to avoid the rush of tourists. ■ US$2.50.

*The reserve can easily be visited from the villages of **Angangueo** or **Zitácuaro**, both of which cater for the influx of butterfly-watchers. Alternatively, you can arrange transport from Mexico City or Guadalajara.*

*In Angangueo hotel options include: **C Albergue Don Bruno**, Morelia 92, T60026, good but a little overpriced, nice setting, restaurant. **D Parakata**, Matamoros 7, T80191. **D La Margarita**, Morelia, very clean, highly recommended, owner does tours to butterfly sanctuary. **E Juárez**, Nacional s/n, T80023, friendly, some rooms damp; **E Paso de la Monarca**, Nacional 20, T80187, large comfortable rooms, hot water, friendly, meals, highly recommended. There are several cafés and restaurants near the plaza, wholesome food, but not gourmet. See Zitácuaro for hotel options.*

*Half-hourly local bus (marked Angangueo) from Zitácuaro (Av Santos Degollado Ote, or from bus station on outskirts of town) to Ocampo, one hour, US$1.20, and from Ocampo another local bus via El Rosario (one every hour, 1¼ hours, US$2.80, 12 km on a mountainous dirt road) to the parking lot below the reserve from where it is a 15-minute walk to the Reserve. A truck from Ocampo to the butterfly refuge costs US$17; this can be shared, especially at weekends. All hotels will arrange transport to the Reserve, about US$20 per vehicle, one hour. From Mexico City, **Aguila Tours**, Amsterdam 291-C, Col Hipódromo Condesa, run tours from early December. Day trips cost around US$100-120. There are four direct buses a day to Mexico City, US$11.*

Transport Buses To **Guadalajara**, 11 hrs, US$14.80. To **Mexico City**, 3 hrs, US$9; to **Morelia**, hourly, 3 ½ hrs, US$5.

North of Zitácuaro, a turning off the main road at Angangueo brings you to a unique site, the wintering grounds of the Monarch butterfly in **El Campanario Ecological Reserve**, above the village of El Rosario. Try to form a small group to go round the reserve. There is a visitors' centre and food kiosks near the entrance. ■ *0900-1700, US$2, plus a tip for your guide (only Spanish spoken).*

El Campanario
See box above

North of Morelia

Just north of Morelia there is a good road to two lakeside villages in the neighbouring state of Guanajuato. At **Cuitzeo**, the first one (hotel, *Restaurant Esteban*, by post office), there is a fine Augustinian church and convent (begun in 1550), with a cloister, a huge open chapel, and good choir stalls in the sacristy. The church houses a collection of Mexican graphic art, spanning four centuries, in a gallery in the basement. **Laguna de Cuitzeo**, beside which it stands, is the second largest lake in Mexico; the road crosses it on a causeway. From here one can go through the attractive mountain scenery around **Valle de Santiago** (D *Hotel Posada de la Parroquia*). The second village, 33 km to the north, **Yuriria**, has a large-scale Indian version of the

Michoacán

splendid church and convent at Actopan (see page 256). It is on Laguna de Yuriria, which looks like a grassy swamp. (Between Cuitzeo and Yuriria is Moreleón, the clothing distribution centre of Mexico – buses empty here.)

West of Morelia

Quiroga
Phone code: 454
Colour map 3, grid B3
Population 23,858

Quiroga is a good place to buy cheap leather jackets – most shops in town sell them

Quiroga (Km 357), heart of the Tarascan Indian country, is named after Bishop Vasco de Quiroga, who was responsible for most of the Spanish building in the area and for teaching the Indians the various crafts they still practise: work in wool, leather, copper, ceramics and cane; many Indians, few tourists. There is a fair and craft exhibitions in December. The night-time entertainment seems to be driving through town in a pick-up with blaring speakers in the back.

Sleeping **B** *Misión don Vasco*, Av Lázaro Cárdenas y Guadalupe Victoria, T354-0035. On the main street (Vasco de Quiroga) are **C** *Quiroga*, T354-0035, and **D** *Tarasco*, T354-0100, both modern with parking. The latter is colonial-style, with a courtyard, clean, hot water, pleasant but front rooms noisy. **Trailer park** 3 km north of town. Old summer residence of a former Mexican president, apparently, wonderful view over Lake Pátzcuaro.

Transport **Buses**: from Pátzcuaro station every 15 mins. Bus Quiroga-Mexico City, US$17.

Tzintzuntzan
(pronounced rapidly as sin-sun-san)
Colour map 3, grid B3
Population: 12,419

Tzintzuntzan was the pre-conquest Tarascan capital; the ruins are just behind the village; a Purépecha ceremonial centre, with five pyramids, is across the road and up the hill (10 minutes' walk) from the monastery. ■ *Daily 0900-1700, US$2, Sun free.* The monastery, on Magdalena, was built in 1533 but closed over 250 years ago. It has been restored, but its frescoes have deteriorated badly. The church bells date from the 16th century; a guard will show you round. In the grounds are some very old olive trees which are still bearing fruit, said to have been planted by Vasco de Quiroga. Fortuitously they were missed in a Spanish edict to destroy all Mexican olive trees when it was thought that Mexican olive oil would compete with Spain's. A most interesting Passion play is given at Tzintzuntzan and fiestas, such as El Señor del Rescate on 1 February, are very colourful. Beautiful, hand-painted pottery, displayed everywhere, is very cheap but also brittle. (It is also available in other markets in Mexico.) Other handicrafts on sale include woodcarving, leather and basket-woven Christmas tree ornaments. Good bargaining opportunities.

Transport Bus from Pátzcuaro bus station every 15 mins, US$0.50, same bus as for Quiroga, which is 8 km further on. If taking the route Uruapan-Pátzcuaro-Morelia, Tzintzuntzan and Quiroga come after Pátzcuaro.

Pátzcuaro

Phone code: 434
Colour map 3, grid B2
Population: 78,127
Altitude: 2,110 m

Twenty-three kilometres south of Quiroga, Pátzcuaro (cold in the evenings) is one of the most picturesque towns in Mexico, with narrow cobbled streets and deep overhanging eaves. The houses are painted white and brown. It is built near Lago de Pátzcuaro, about 50 km in circumference, with Tarascan Indian villages on its shores and many islands.

Ins and outs

Getting there

The nearest airports are at Morelia to the east and Uruapan to the west. The bus station is on the outskirts of town. A local bus, *colectivo* or taxi will take you to the centre. Pátzcuaro is connected by Route 14 to Morelia and Uruapan.

Getting around

The Indians used to come by huge dugout canoes (but now seem to prefer the ferry) for the market, held in the main plaza, shaded by great trees. It is a steep 3-km walk uphill from the

Michoacán

lake shore to the plaza; *colectivos* run every few minutes to the Plaza Chica. The **tourist office** is on the north side of the Plaza Grande next to Banca Serfín, friendly, good information. ■ *Mon-Fri 0900-1500, variable in afternoon, usually 1700-1900, Sat-Sun only morning.*

Sights

There are several interesting buildings: the unfinished **La Colegiata** (1603), known locally as La Basílica, with its much venerated Virgin fashioned by an Indian from a paste made with cornstalk pith and said to have been found floating in a canoe. Behind the Basílica there are remains of the pre-Columbian town and of a pyramid in the precincts of the Museo de Artes Populares; the restored Jesuit church of **La Compañía** (and, almost opposite, the early 17th-century church of the **Sagrario**) at the top of Calle Portugal. Behind this street are two more ecclesiastical buildings: the **Colegio Teresiano** and the restored **Templo del Santuario**; on Calle Lerín is the old monastery, with a series of small patios. There are murals by Juan O'Gorman in the **Library**, formerly San Agustín. On Calle Allende is the residence of the first governor. On Calle Terán is the church of **San Francisco**; nearby is **San Juan de Dios**, on the corner of Calle Romero. Visit also the **Plaza Vasco de Quiroga**. Fifteen minutes' walk outside the town is the chapel of **El Calvario**, on the summit of Cerro del Calvario, a hill giving wide views; the views are also good from the old chapel of the **Humilladero**, above the cemetery on the old road to Morelia. This chapel is said to have been built on the spot where the last Tarascan emperor knelt in submission to the Spanish Conquistador, Cristóbal de Olid.

The very well-arranged **Museo de Artes Populares** is in the former Colegio de San Nicolás (1540) and is excellent for seeing regional ceramics, weaving, woodcarving and basketware. ■ *0900-1900 Tue-Sat, 0900-1430 Sun (free), English speaking, friendly guide, US$1.70.* Ask there for the **Casa de los Once Patios**, which contains boutiques selling handicrafts; you can see weavers and painters of lacquerwork in action.

An 'International Hippy Crafts Market' is held every Sat and Sun on the north side of the Plaza Grande

Michoacán

Pátzcuaro

Sleeping
1 El Artillero
2 Gran
3 Los Escudos
4 Mansión Iturbe
5 Mesón del Gallo
6 Misión San Manuel
7 Posada de la Rosa
8 Posada de la Salud
9 Posada La Basílica
10 Posada San Rafael

Eating
1 Cafetería El Buho

0 metres 200
0 yards 200

Excursions

The best-known lake island is **Janitzio**, which has been spoilt by the souvenir shops and the tourists (visit during the week if possible). It is 45 minutes by motorboat; boats leave when full from 0800 onwards, US$2.50 return from Muelle General; cheaper from Muelle San Pedrito, 500 m further on, tickets from office at dock, last boat back (return by any boat) at 2000. It is a 45-minute walk from the centre of Pátzcuaro or take a bus marked 'Lago' from Plaza Bocanegra. There is an unfortunate monument to Morelos crowning a hill on the island, with a mural glorifying Independence inside, which nevertheless affords magnificent views (often queues to climb spiralling stairs inside to the top). ■ *US$0.60*. A circular path goes around the island where there are lots of good restaurants; those on the waterfront charge more than those on the hill, same quality. One hotel **D** *Teru'nukua*, *T313-6152*, 50 m from *muelle*. Winter is the best time for fishing in the somewhat fish-depleted lake, where Indians traditionally threw nets shaped like dragonflies, now a rather rare event. The Government is planning to improve the lake's water quality, but there are still plenty of places selling white fish on the island.

Another island to visit is **Yunuen**, boat from Muelle General, US$2.70. The island is clean and quiet. There is a cabaña (**B**) on the hill with a good restaurant, T312-1072. During the week there are few *lanchas*, so be sure to arrange a return trip unless you want to spend the night. Bring provisions. On a lakeside estate (formerly the country house of General Lázaro Cárdenas) is the Educational Centre for Community Development in Latin America, better known as *CREFAL* (free films every Wednesday at 1930).

For a truly spectacular view of the lake, the islands and the surrounding countryside, walk to Cerro del Estribo; an ideal site for a quiet picnic. It is a 1½-hour walk to the top from the centre of Pátzcuaro. The areas round Pátzcuaro are also recommended for bird-watching.

From Pátzcuaro, you can also visit Tzintzuntzan and Quiroga by regular bus service. Thirty minutes by local bus from Plaza Chica is **Ihuatzio**, on a peninsula 12 km north of Pátzcuaro town, 8 km from Tzintzuntzan. This was the second most important Tarascan city; two pyramids are well preserved and afford good views of the lake. ■ *US$1.10, leaflets in Spanish or English, US$0.40*. The pyramids are signposted, 1 km from the village, but the road is very bad. To get to Tzintzuntzan from Ihuatzio, take bus or hitch back to main road and wait for Pátzcuaro-Quiroga bus.

A good option in the week is **Lago Zirauhen**, reached by a 40-minute bus journey. Fairly quiet in the week when you can stroll along the lake shore and enjoy the natural forest. Several cheap hotels in the **D** range, but prices rise at the weekend.

Essentials

Sleeping
■ *on map*

Rooms in some hotels are reserved four weeks prior to Día de los Muertos, and other hotels do not take reservations, so it is pot luck at this time

In the centre AL-B *Mansión Iturbe*, Portal Morelos 59, T342-0368, F343-4593, www.mexonline.com/iturbe.htm 14 rooms, English, French and German spoken, beautiful restored 1790s mansion on main plaza, breakfast included, nice décor, satellite TV, cold at night, expensive restaurant, *El Gaucho Viejo*, Argentine *churrasco*, open Wed-Sun 1800-2400, folk music, 2 other restaurants. Recommended. **B** *Mesón del Gallo*, Dr Coss 20, T342-1474, F342-1511. 25 rooms, good value, flower garden, tasteful furnishings. **B** *Misión San Manuel*, Portal Aldama 12 on main plaza, T342-1313, F342-1050. Restaurant. Highly recommended. **B** *Posada La Basílica*, Arciga 6, T342-1108, F342-0659. 12 rooms, nice restaurant with good views, central. **B** *Posada San Rafael*, Portal Aldama 15, T342-0770. Safe, average restaurant, parking in courtyard. **C** *Fiesta Plaza*, Plaza Bocanegra 24, T342-2516, F342-2515. Beautiful interior patio, good. **C** *Gran Hotel*, Portal Regules 6, on Plaza Bocanegra, T342-0443, F342-3090. Small rooms, clean, friendly, pleasant, good food. **C** *Los Escudos*, Portal Hidalgo 73, T/F342-1290. 17th-century building (*Baile de los Viejitos* every Sat at 2000), ask for room with fireplace, good food. Recommended.

Michoacán

D *El Artillero*, Ibarra 22, T342-1331. With hot water, bath, gloomy, noisy, not too clean or secure, no drinking water, near Zócalo (discounts for long stays paid in advance). **D** *Imperial*, Obregón 21, T342-0308. Large clean rooms. **C** *Posada de la Salud*, Benigno Serrato 9, T342-0058. Clean, quiet, pleasant, nice garden, excellent value, no hot water during middle of day, some rooms with individual fireplaces. Recommended. **E** *Laguna*, Títere. With bath, cheaper rooms also with bath but no water, buckets outside! **D** *Posada de la Rosa*, Portal Juárez 29 (Plaza Chica), T342-0811. With bath, doors to rooms not very secure, **F** without, parking, colonial style, clean. Also on Plaza Chica is **E** *Posada San Agustín*, T342-0442. Very good value, clean, hot water. **E** *Valmen*, Padre Lloreda 34-A, T342-1151. Good, friendly.

There are many *hospedajes* and hotels near the bus station. **Public baths**, US$0.50.

Towards the lake A *Posada de don Vasco*, Av Lázaro Cárdenas 450, T342-0227, F342-0262. 103 rooms, attractive, colonial-style hotel (halfway between lake and town), breakfast good, other meals poor, presents the Dance of the Old Men on Wednesday and Saturday at 2100 at no charge, non-residents welcome but drinks very expensive to compensate, also mariachi band. **B** *Mesón del Cortijo*, Obregón, just off Américas, T342-1295. Often fully booked at weekends. Recommended. **C** *Apo-Pau*, between lake and town (closest to town of the non-central hotels), T342-0601, F342-4186. Pleasant, friendly.

Motels and camping B *Hostería de San Felipe*, Av Lázaro Cárdenas 321, T/F342-1298. Friendly, clean, fireplaces in rooms, good restaurant (closes 2030). Highly recommended. *Villa Pátzcuaro*, Av Lázaro Cárdenas 506, T342-0767, F342-2984, 1 km from centre. Very quiet, pleasant, hot water, gardens, lots of birds, tennis, also camping and caravan site. *Trailer Park El Pozo*, on lakeside, opposite *Chalamu*, T342-0937. Hot showers am, large, delightful, well equipped, US$10, owner speaks English, also camping.

Eating

Michoacán

Local speciality is pescado blanco (white fish), but it is disappearing from menus as a result of over-fishing and pollution

Several lakeside restaurants serve fish dishes, but it is advisable to avoid locally caught fish. Many places close before 2000. Make sure you don't get overcharged in restaurants. *Comida corrida* at restaurants around Plaza Grande and Plaza Chica costs about US$4 and is usually the same each day. *Los Escudos*, Plaza Quiroga. Open until 2200, popular with tourists, try *sopa tarasca* (a flavoursome soup made with toasted *tortillas*, cream and cheese), which is good value, and coffee. Also on this plaza *La Casona*, reasonable prices (cheapest breakfast in town) and *El Primer Piso*. *Mery Lerín* (opposite Basílica). Cheap local dishes. *Mandala*, on Lerín. Vegetarian. OK. *Gran Hotel*, filling *comida corrida*, excellent *café con leche*. Good chicken with vegetables and *enchiladas* over the market (budget restaurants here, usually open in evening). *Restaurant T'irekua*, Plaza Vasco de Quiroga 29. Beautiful patio, peaceful, good breakfast. Recommended. *Cafetería El Buho*, Tejerías 8. Meals, drinks, slow but very good food, good value, stylish, friendly. Recommended. *Camino Real*, next to Pemex, 100 m from *El Pozo Trailer Park*. Very good *comida corrida*, quick service. *Viejo Sam*, Benito Mendoza 8. Good *tortas*. Excellent *paletería* and ice cream parlour at Codallos 24, also sells frozen yoghurt. Fruit and yoghurt for breakfast at *El Patio*, Plaza Vasco de Quiroga 19, T342-0484. Open 0800-2200, also serves good meals, good service. Recommended. Breakfast available from small stands in the market, usually 0600-0700 (*licuados*, *arroz con leche*, etc). At the Plaza in Erongarícuaro, 17 km clockwise around the lake, is a Hindu vegetarian restaurant at the weekends; also a local crafts fair (take *ADO* bus from bus or rail station, US$0.65).

Festivals

1-2 November: *Día de los Muertos* (All Souls' Day), ceremony at midnight, 1 Nov, at almost every village around the lake; if you are in the region at this time it is well worth experiencing. The ceremony is most touristy on Janitzio island and at Tzintzuntzan, but at villages such as Ihuatzio, Jarácuaro and Uranden it is more intimate. The tourist office has leaflets listing all the festivities. **1 Jan** *Los Viejitos* (Old Men), in Janitzio; **2 Feb** *Los Sembradores* (The Sowers); also in **Feb** is *Carnival* when the *Danza de los Moros* (The Moors) is performed (Lake Pátzcuaro region); *Los Apaches*, **4 Feb** (at the churches); **12 Oct** *Día de la Raza*, when Columbus reached America, there is also a procession with the Virgin and lots of fireworks. **6-9 Dec**, *Virgen de la Salud*, when authentic Tarascan dances are performed in front of the Basílica; and there is an interesting fiesta on **12 Dec** for the *Virgin de Guadalupe*.

Sports **Massage** *Shiatsu Massage*, Stephen Ritter del Castillo, in Tócuaro, 15 minutes by bus or taxi clockwise around the lake about halfway to Erongarícuaro, Mon-Fri 0900-1700, excellent, English/Spanish bilingual. Cost? By donation!

Transport **Buses** New bus station (called Central) out of town, with left luggage office, *colectivo* from centre US$0.30, taxi US$1.70. Bus US$0.20 from Plaza Bocanegra. You can pick up buses from large roundabout 1 km north of centre. Taxi US$1.45.
  Guadalajara: late morning service, 6 hrs, US$15. **Lázaro Cárdenas**: hourly from 0600, 8 hrs, long but spectacular ride through mountains and lakes (police checks likely), US$16. **Mexico City**: regular service through the day, 6 hrs, US$18. **Morelia**: every 30 mins, 1 hr, US$3. **Toluca**: from 0915, 5 hrs, 1st class US$17.50, from 0915, 5 hrs. Local buses from corner of market in town to lakeside (*colectivo* to lakeside US$0.25). **Uruapan**: 1 hr, US$2.50.

Directory **Banks** Four ATMs in the centre. *Banamex*, Portal Juárez 32. *Promex*, Portal Regules 9. *Serfín*, Portal Allende 54. *Bancomer*, Zaragoza 23; *cambio* at Benito Mendoza 7. 4 ATMs in the centre. **Communications** Internet: *México en Línea*, Fed Tena 30-L9, T342-4566, not a café. **Post office:** Obregón, 1 block from Plaza Chica, Mon-Sat 0800-1600, Sat 0900-1300. **Medical services** Dentist: *Dr Antonio Molina*, T342-3032. *Dr Augusto Tena Mora*, T342-2232. Doctor: *Dr Jorge Asencio Medina*, T342-4038. *Dr Javier Hernández* and *Dr Guadalupe Murillo*, T342-1209. Pharmacy: *Gems*, Benito Mendoza 21, T342-0332, open 0900-2100 daily. **Laundry** *Lavandería 'San Francisco'*, Terán 16, T342-3939, Mon-Sat 0900-2000.

Uruapan

Phone code: 452
Colour map 3, grid B2
Population: 265,211
Altitude: 1,610 m

The town suffers badly from traffic fumes

From Pátzcuaro, the road continues southwest to Uruapan, the 'place where flowers are plentiful'. The most attractive of its three plazas is the **Zócalo**, which has the **Jardín de los Mártires** at its west end. Opposite the Jardín is part of the former Collegiate church of San Francisco (17th century with later additions such as an interesting 1960s modern art interior), which houses the attractive **Casa de la Cultura** (small museum upstairs, free, with excellent display of the history of Uruapan). Local crafts can be bought in the *portales* or at the market. At the east end of the Zócalo is the restored hospital, built by Fray Juan de San Miguel in the 16th century; now a ceramics museum, the **Museo La Huatápera**. Adjoining it is a 16th-century chapel now converted into a craft shop. Behind the chapel and museum is the Mercado de Antojitos and, beyond it, the clothes and goods market permanently occupying several streets. The food market has now moved out of the centre to two sites, one at Obregón and Francisco Villa with cheap eateries upstairs, and the other on Calzada Benito Juárez at the end of the goods market that extends up Constitución from the centre.

The **tourist office** is on Ayala, between Independencia and Pino Suárez, T524-7199. ■ *Mon-Sat 0900-1400 and 1600-2000, Sun 1000-1400.*

On M Treviño, between A Isaac and Amado Nervo, there is a house that is just 1½ m wide and several storeys high, possibly the narrowest building in Mexico.

The town is set beside streams, orchards and waterfalls in the **Parque Nacional Eduardo Ruiz**, cool at night, and well worth a visit. Local foods are sold in the Parque. At the entrance to the Parque, on the corner of Independencia and Culver City, 1 km from the town centre, is a good **Mercado de Artesanías** selling wooden boxes and bracelets ■ *US$0.35*. Walk there or catch a bus one block south of the Zócalo marked 'El Parque'.

Excursions It is 10 km through coffee groves and orchards along Río Cupatitzio (meaning Singing River) to the **Tzararacua Falls** ■ *US$0.25*. There are restaurants at the bus stop where you can hire a horse to the falls (US$4 per person); it is not advisable to walk to the falls alone. To extend the trip beyond the falls, cross the stone bridge to the other side of the stream. Take a path to the right, which then switches back and heads up the other side of the gorge. After a while you will reach a plateau at the top of the mountain, with good views all around. A well-worn path/stream leads down the other side of the mountain to a more secluded waterfall, from the top of which are many paths down to the river and lake into which the stream flows (a great spot for a swim). There is good camping some 300 m below the village under the shelter on the top of a rim, with a view down into the valley to the waterfall (1 km away) and a small lake. A bus (marked Tzararacua, or Zupomita, but ask if it goes all the way) will take you from the Zócalo at Uruapan to Tzararacua, US$1 (15-25 minutes), weekends and public holidays only.

Sleeping

AL *Victoria*, Cupatitzio 13, T523-6700, F523-9662. Good, quiet, restaurant and garage. **A-B** *Concordia* on main plaza, T/F523-0400, www.hotelconcordia.com Comfortable rooms and a nice restaurant. **B** *El Tarasco*, Independencia 2, T524-1500. Pool, lovely, good restaurant, moderate prices. **B** *Plaza Uruapan*, Ocampo 64, T523-0333, F523-3980. Good, clean, large rooms. **C** *Villa de Flores*, Emilio Carranza 15, west of centre, T524-2800. Quiet, pleasantly furnished, lovely flowers. Recommended.

C *Atzimbal*, Francisco Villa, T524-4325, F524-4153 (street where the *mariachis* are waiting). Modern. Recommended. On main plaza, **C** *Nuevo Hotel Alameda*, Av 5 de Febrero, T523-4100. With bath, clean, TV, good value. **C** *del Parque*, Av Independencia 124. With bath, very nice, by entrance to national park, clean, quiet, enclosed parking. Recommended. **D** *Acosta*, opposite bus station. Nearby is **E** *Sandy*. With bath, TV, basic and **E** per person *Betty's*. With bath. **D** *Capri*, Portal Santos Degollado, by market. Friendly. **D** *Los Tres Caballeros*, Constitución 50, T524-7170. Walk out front door into market. **D** *Mi Solar*, Juan Delgado 10, T522-0912. Good value, hot water, clean. Recommended. **E** *Moderno*, main plaza. Lovely building, with bath, water spasmodic, friendly, very basic. **E** *Oseguera*, main plaza. Dirty but good hot shower.

Motels A *Mansión del Cupatitzio*, on the road to Guadalajara, T523-2100, www.mansioncupatitzio.com Swimming pool, patio, restaurant, good souvenir shop. Outstanding. **B** *Pie de la Sierra*, Km 4 Carretera a Carapán, on north outskirts, T524-2510. Good moderately priced restaurant. **C** *Paricutín*, Juárez 295, T524-0303. Well maintained.

Eating
● *on map*

Local speciality, cecina, dried meat

La Pérgola, on plaza. Good breakfasts and coffee. Recommended. *Calypso*, Alvaro Obregón 2A. Excellent cakes and hamburgers, ask for local speciality: *agua fresca de rompope*. Locals eat at open-air food stalls under one roof at back of church, very picturesque. *Café El Sol y La Luna*, Independencia between Zócalo and Parque. Arty/student bar, sometimes live music at weekends. *La Puesta del Sol*, supermarket, Juan Ayala. Has good meals. Cheap meals from *comedores* in the *Mercado de Antojitos*.

Festivals

In the 1st week of **Apr** the Zócalo is filled with pottery, which Indians bring from all the surrounding villages. **Jun** *Las Canacuas* (Crown Dance), on Corpus Christi. Around **16 Sep**, in nearby village of San Juan, to celebrate the saving of an image of Christ from the San Juan church at the time of the Paricutín eruption. The 2 weeks either side of **15 Sep** are *feria* in Uruapan, too.

Transport

Air Daily to Mexico City. Also flights from Culiacán, Guadalajara and Tijuana.
    Buses Bus station on the northeast edge of town, necessary to get a city bus (US$0.25) into town, finishing at about 2100, or a taxi to the plaza, US$3. Left luggage, US$0.35 per item for 7 hrs. **Colima**: 6 hrs, US$14. **Guadalajara**: roughly hourly, 4½ hrs, US$18. **Lázaro Cárdenas**: every 30 mins, 6 hrs, US$15. **Mexico City**: more than 1 per hr, 6 hrs, US$28. **Morelia**: every 20 mins, 2½ hrs, US$7. **Pátzcuaro**: frequent, 1 hr, US$3.

Directory

Directory Airlines: *Aeromar*, T523-5050. **Banks** *Banamex*, Cupatitzio y Morelos, visa agent. *Bancomer*, Carranza y 20 de Noviembre. *Serfín*, Cupatitzio. **Communications** Internet: *Logicentro Cyber Café*, Av Juárez 57, T524-9494, US$3.70 per hr, open 0900-1400, 1600-2100 Mon-Sat. Also in computer shop in basement of hotel *Plaza*. **Post office**: Reforma 13. **Telephone and fax**: *Computel*, Ocampo, on plaza, open every day 0700-2200. **Medical services** Red Cross: T524-0300. **Laundry** Carranza 47, open Mon-Sat 0900-1400 and 1600-2000, US$3.20 service wash. *Mujer Santayo Lavandería*, Michoacán 14, T523-0876.

Michoacán

Volcán Paricutín

Colour map 3, grid B2   The volcano of Paricutín can be visited from Uruapan. It started erupting on 20 February 1943, became fiery and violent and rose to a height of 1,300 m above the 2,200-m-high region, and then died down after several years into a quiet grey mountain (460 m) surrounded by a sea of cold lava. The church tower of San Juan, a buried Indian village, thrusting up through cold lava is a fantastic sight. If you are not taking an organized tour (with horses and guides included), Paricutín is best reached by taking a 'Los Reyes' bus on a paved road to Angahuan, 34 km from Uruapan, US$0.85, one hour, nine a day each way (from 0500 to 2000) with Galeana, then hire a horse or mule or walk (one hour). Señores Juan Rivera, Francisco Lázaro (tour is a bit hurried, he lives in the second house on the right, coming from the *albergue*, see below), Atanacio Lázaro and his horse 'Conejo', and Lino Gómez are recommended, but there are a host of other guides at the bus stop. It is definitely worth a guide – essential for the volcano – but it is expensive if you are on your own as you have to pay for the guide's mule too. A full day's excursion with mules to the area costs about US$8-12 per mule, with US$3-4 tip for the guide (six to seven hours); shorter journeys cost less. To go on foot with a guide costs US$10. It is best if you can speak Spanish. It is 3 km from Angahuan to the San Juan ruins, an easy walk: as you enter the village square with the church on the left, turn immediately right and take the first left after you leave the square and follow this cobbled street with telegraph poles on the left-hand side for 750 m to a stone pillared gateway and a sight of the ruins. At the gate, turn right down a dirt path that zig-zags downhill, past a plantation to a three forked junction. Take the centre path that winds through the lava field to the church. Alternatively, start at the new hostel from where you can also see the church. Guide on foot to church US$5 per group.

To the crater of the volcano is 10 km, a long, tough walk (also a long day on horseback for the unaccustomed, especially if you get a wooden saddle). Walk westwards round the lava field, through an avocado plantation. Wear good walking shoes with thick soles as the lava is very rough and as sharp as glass in places (some people find they cannot make the last stretch over the tennis-ball size rocks); bear in mind the altitude too, as the return is uphill. It takes seven to nine hours to the volcano and back. The cone itself is rather small and to reach it there is a stiff 30-minute climb from the base. A path goes around the tip of the crater, where activity has ceased. Take something to drink because it is pretty hot and dusty out on the plains. If going in one day, leave Uruapan by 0800 so that you don't have to rush. Go even earlier in the rainy season as clouds usually build up by midday. Take a sweater for the evening and for the summit where it can be windy and cold after a hot climb. Last bus back to Uruapan at 1900 (but don't rely on it).

Angahuan   Much better, though, is to stay the night in Angahuan, where there is an *albergue*, at the Centro Turístico de Angahuan, T(452) 523-3934 (Uruapan) **B** cabañas, sleep 6, with a log fire, or **E** per person in dormitory with bunk beds (dormitories closed in low season, both have hot showers), meals US$5, restaurant closes 1900 in low season, basic facilities, but clean and peaceful, warm and recommended but service poorer when few people are staying. It can be crowded and noisy at weekends. The *albergue* is signposted from the bus stop and signs are repeated several times en route. It takes about half an hour to walk from the bus stop to the *albergue*. The church ruins can be seen from the *albergue*. To reach them just follow the very dusty road downhill; if ever in doubt follow the route with most hoofprints. It is possible to drive to the *albergue* where they try to charge US$1.60 for the free car park. Camping is possible near the hostel. In the village are shops selling food and drink and there is a good local restaurant in the street behind the church. Two reasonable restaurants are on the road to the *albergue*. There is a water tap near the church; follow the signs. Just outside the village, on the dirt track to the main road, is the cemetery. The local

Tarascan Indians still preserve their language. Angahuan is a Purépecha Indian village and in the evening the local radio station broadcasts in Puripeche over a public tannoy system in the plaza until 2200.

Zamora (58 km east of Jiquilpan) is an agricultural centre founded in 1540. There is a large, interesting Gothic-style church in the centre, the **Catedral Inconclusa**, started in 1898, work suspended during the Revolution, now with a projected completion date of 2000. There are several other, fine churches, and a market on Corregidora. Much of the area around the plaza is pedestrianised. Nearby is tiny Laguna de Camécuaro, with boats for hire, restaurants and wandering musicians; popular at holiday times.

Zamora
Phone code: 351
Colour map 3, grid B2
Population: 161,191

Sleeping A *Fénix*, Madero Sur 401, T512-0266, F512-0150, www.hotelfenix.com Clean, big swimming pool, poor ventilation, pleasant balconies. **C** *Amalia*, Hidalgo 194, T512-1327. Pleasant, some rooms noisy, restaurant OK. **C-D** *Posada Fénix*, Esquina Morelos y Corregidora, 1 block from Zócalo. Rooms of varying quality, nice owner (also owns *Fénix* – see above), good laundry service. **D** *Jasmín*, 2 km on road to Morelia, opposite Pemex. With bath, clean, noisy, used a lot by truckers. **D** *Posada Marena*. Simple, clean; other cheap *hospedajes* near market, none very clean. **E** *Hotel 5 de Mayo*. Cheapest in centre.

Eating *El Campanario*, Nervo 22, off main square. Recommended. *Carnes Toluca*, Madero Sur and Leonardo, and *Antigua Carnes Toluca* over the road. Not much more than meat, but plenty of it.

Transport Bus station at north edge of town, local bus to centre US$0.25, taxi US$3.50, from centre to bus station from 5 de Mayo in front of Catedral Inconclusa. Bus to **Mexico City**: 1st *plus*, US$24, 1st US$14.20. To **Guadalajara**: US$16, and US$15 to **Morelia**. To **Pátzcuaro**: 2½ hrs, with Via 2000. To Tamazula for **Ciudad Guzmán**: 3½-4 hrs, US$9.

Directory **Communications** Internet: In small mall on Morelos, between Colón and Ocampo. **Tourist office** Morelos Sur 76, T512-4015.

Southeast of Zamora, on Route 15, is **Carapán** (**E** *Motel La Hacienda*. Friendly, clean, cold water, good restaurant), a crossroads at which a road goes north to **La Piedad de Cabadas**, a pleasant stopping place on the old toll road between Guadalajara and Mexico City (**D** *Hotel Mansión Imperial*. Parking. **E** *San Sebastián*. Central, hot water, old but nice, parking across the street. **E** *Gran Hotel*. On main street, OK. *Restaurant El Patio*, near church. Very good, dish of the day good value).

At Carapán a branch road runs 32 km south through pine woods to **Paracho**, a quaint, very traditional Indian village of small wooden houses; in every other one craftworkers make guitars, violins and mandolins worth from US$15 to US$1,500. A recommended workshop is that of Ramiro Castillo, Av Independencia 259, Galeana 38, good value, friendly. Bargaining possible in all workshops. On the main plaza is the *Casa para el Arte y la Cultura Purépecha* with information, library, shops, etc. There is a guitar museum and concert hall, main venue for a famous week-long guitar festival in the second week of August (free concerts). There are buses to/from Uruapan US$.80, 45 minutes. Also to Morelia via Pátzcuaro.

Paracho

Sleeping and eating **D** *Hermelinda*, in centre. **E** hotel on main road south of town, hot water morning only. Eating places include *La Casona*, on main Plaza, quiet; *Café D'Gribet*, on main street, cheap and good snacks. Try local pancakes.

Michoacán

The Pacific coast of Michoacán

Playa Azul
Phone code: 753
Colour map 3, grid C2

Beware of the large waves at Playa Azul and of dangerous currents; always check with locals if particular beaches are safe

The Pacific coast of Michoacán is only just coming under development. From Uruapan, Route 37 goes to Playa Azul, 350 km northwest of Acapulco (bus US$12, 10½ hours minimum) and 122 km from Zihuatanejo (see page 379). Playa Azul is a coconut-and-hammock resort (reported dirty and dilapidated) frequented much more by Mexicans than foreigners, with a few large hotels. The town of La Mira, on the main road, is larger than Playa Azul. Forty kilometres of excellent deserted beaches stretch to the north of Playa Azul. At night there is beautiful phosphorescence at the water's edge.

Sleeping and eating A *Playa Azul*, Venustiano Carranza s/n, T536-0088, F536-0090. Has a trailer park with 20 spaces, full hook-up, bathrooms, cold shower, 2 pools, bar and restaurant, US$13 for car and 2 people. Many small fish restaurants along beach, but most close early. **C** *Delfín*, Venustiano Carranza s/n, T536-0007. No a/c, clean, pleasant, swimming pool. **D** *Del Pacífico*, Blvd Francisco Vill, opposite beach, T536-0106. Bath, fan, clean, hammocks on roof, friendly. A bit run down but recommended. **E** *Costa de Oro*, Francisco I Madero s/n, T536-0982. Clean, with fan, safe parking. Recommended. *Martita*. Highly recommended. Tap and shower water seems to smell of petrol.

Transport **Buses**: these ply up and down the coast road, stopping at the road junction 4 km from Plaza Azul. *Colectivos* take you between town and junction. If driving north it is 5 hrs to Tecomán (where the road from Colima comes down to the coast).

Lázaro Cárdenas
Phone code: 753
Colour map 3, grid C3
Population: 170,878

Lázaro Cárdenas is the connecting point for buses from Uruapan, Manzanillo and Zihuatanejo. There is a **tourist office** at Nicolás Bravo 475, T532-1547, in the *Hotel Casablanca* building. **Sleeping** A *De la Curva*, Nicolás Bravo 235, T537-3656, F532-3237. Good services across the board. A *Sol del Pacífico*, Javier Mina 178, T532-0660, F537-0490. **C** *Viña del Mar*, Javier Mina 352, T/F532-0415. Avoid **E** *Hotel Sam Sam*, near terminal; go to *Capri*, Juan Alvarez 237, T532-0551, or *Costa Azul*, 5 de Mayo 276, T532-0780, both **E** with bath, or **E** *Verónica*, Javier Mina 47, T532-3409, 2 blocks on left as you leave bus station. **Transport** Galeana to Manzanillo 7¾ hrs, US$15; to Uruapan, US$16, 6½ hrs; to Guadalajara, US$31 with La Línea; to Mexico City US$43, luxury.

Caleta de Campos
76 km northwest up the coast from Playa Azul. Watch out for elaborate, if dangerous, fireworks at fiesta time

Buses continue along the coast road to La Mira, then a short distance to Caleta de Campos. In this poor village perched above a beautiful bay, there is little to eat other than seafood. **D** *Hotel Yuritzi*. With bath, a/c, TV, **E** without, clean, no hot water, good views from front, changes travellers' cheques at reasonable rates. **E** *Los Arcos*. With bath, good views from most rooms; cabañas with hammock space at US$1 per person, northwest of village, where Río Nexpa reaches the coast. At beach here, five minutes from the village, there are bars and restaurants, popular with surfers. Be careful as there are strong currents. **Fiesta**: 10-13 December; at 0200 on 13 December *El Torito*, a bull mask and sculpture loaded with fireworks, makes its spectacular appearance.

Avoid night-time driving in this area as hold-ups have been reported

Eighty-six kilometres further up the coast, to the northwest, is **Maruata**, unspoilt and beautiful. This is a turtle conservation area. There are floods in the rainy season and the river has washed away some of the beach. There are cabañas for rent (**F**) and *palapas* under which you can camp. For southbound traffic seeking Maruata, road signs are inadequate.

Michoacán

Guadalajara to the Pacific Coast

Mexico City

If it's the Mexican stereotype you're after, get to the State of Jalisco. This is where you'll find the town of Tequila, the lasso-swinging charros, the swirling Jarabe Tapatío (Mexican hat dance), and the romantic mariachis, those roving musicians dressed in fine, tight-trousered gala suits and massive sombreros of early 19th-century rural gentry. All these originated in Jalisco, but there are other attractions worth making a song and dance about.

Guadalajara, the state capital, is today a huge, modern metropolis. But the 'pearl of the west' has a magnificent and elegant Spanish core with shady plazas, impressive colonial architecture, some fine museums and the vast Mercado Libertad. A short visit to the famous craft centre suburbs of Tlaquepaque or Tonalá is relaxing and rewarding, take a boat ride on Mexico's largest lake, Lago de Chapala, go and see the volcanically active Nevado de Colima, cool off in the pine forests around the delightful old town of Tapalpa, or visit one (or all) of the distilleries in Mexico's most famous small town, Tequila.

Jalisco is also gateway to the Pacific Coast and the mega resort of Puerto Vallarta on the vast Bahía de Banderas, one of the largest bays in the world. But there are other beautiful and secluded beaches both north and south of Vallarta. Up the coast, in the neighbouring state of Nayarit, sleepy San Blas is a mecca for surfers and bird-watchers. Away from the resorts, remote in the Sierra Madre Occidental, live the Cora and Huichol Indians, renowned for their stunningly beautiful chaquira beadwork and colourful nierika yarn paintings, as well as for the ancestral ritual that takes them hundreds of miles every year on a pilgrimage to the sacred peyote grounds near Real de Catorce to collect the hallucinogenic cactus.

Guadalajara

Guadalajara, Mexico's second city, founded on 14 February 1542 and capital of Jalisco State, is 573 km from Mexico City, and warmer than the capital. In the Historic Centre, graceful colonial arcades, or portales, flank scores of old plazas and shaded parks. Efforts are being made to preserve the colonial atmosphere and restore noteworthy buildings. At weekends and on public holidays, the town fills with Guadaljarans meandering through the town, taking time to soak up the intense combination of historic heritage and mad, frenetic city life.

Phone code: 33
Colour map 3, grid B2
Population: 5,000,000
Altitude: 1,650 m

The climate is mild, and clear all through the year, although in summer it can be thundery at night. Pollution from vehicles can be bad downtown and the winter is the worst time for smog. However, afternoons are usually clear and sunny and during the rainy summer season smog is no problem. In the past 25 years the city has developed to the west of Avenida Chapultepec, where the best shops and residential neighbourhoods are now located. But for those just passing through the area of greatest interest is the Historic Centre. If you have the time and you're headed this way, it's worth stopping off for a couple of days.

Ins and outs

Frequent flight connections with Mexico City and many other domestic and international **Getting there** destinations arrive at the Aeropuerto Internacional Miguel Hidalgo (GDL) 20 km south of the

Guadalajara to the Pacific Coast

The Cristero War

The 1917 Constitution contained many provisions to curtail the political and economic power of the Roman Catholic Church and the governments of the 1920s were decidedly anti-clerical in their efforts to implement it. Many, including President Plutarco Elías Calles (1924-28), who consolidated the Sonoran Dynasty in power for 15 years after the Revolution, sought to extirpate the Church. Catholic resistance turned to civil war (1926-29), which was most virulent in west-central parts of the country, where many clergy and others lost their lives. The war cry of the Catholic rebels was 'Viva Cristo Rey' (long live Christ the King), which became shortened to Cristero as a nickname for the rebels and their war. The rebels were eventually betrayed by the Vatican and the bishops, who reached a compromise peace settlement with the Government.

city centre. Fixed-rate taxis will take you into the city; no tip necessary. Two local bus routes also service the airport (for details see Transport page 314).

An important commercial centre, Guadalajara is the hub of several major land routes heading south to Ciudad Guzmán, Colima and Manzanillo; north to Zacatecas and beyond; east to Mexico City and the towns of the Colonial Heartland; and west to Tepic, Puerto Vallarta and the Pacific Coast. The appropriately vast bus terminal is 10 km southeast of the centre; allow at least 30 minutes to get there on one of the luxury bus services (Línea Azul and Línea Cardenal). The terminal is a nightmare if you try to understand it, but fortunately that's not important. Simply put, there are seven modules at the terminal, each serving different bus companies rather than towns or regions within Mexico.

The old bus station, a few blocks south of the city centre, serves towns within 100 km of Guadalajara, mainly with second class buses. There is a train station at the south end of Calzada de la Independencia, but apart from the Tequila Express there are currently no passenger services running.

Getting around The most pleasant way of seeing the city is by horse-drawn carriage; these are to be found outside the Museo Regional at the corner of Liceo and Hidalgo and a few other places. US$22 for an hour tour, up to 5 people. More traditionally buses and *colectivos* run to most areas of the city although regular services can be frustratingly bad. Trolley buses and the new luxury buses with guaranteed seats on a few fixed routes are a much better option. Guadalajara also has two metro, or rather *tren ligero* lines, one running north-south and the other from west-east of the city. Taxis tend not to use meters so agree on a price before setting off.

Tourist offices State and Federal tourist office (*Sectur*), Morelos 102, Plaza Tapatía, T3668-1602, has information in German and English including good walking tour map of the historic centre, very helpful. Mon-Fri 0800-2000, Sat and Sun 1000-1600. There are also tourist booths in front of the cathedral and at the eastern end of Plaza Tapatía. *Siglo 21* newspaper has a good entertainments section, *Tentaciones*, on Friday, and music, film and art listings every day.

Sights

Guadalajara is generally a safe city. The centre is not deserted at night and people wander the streets in sociable groups. Normal precautions are required against pickpockets but little more. Much safer than many US cities

The heart of the city is the Plaza de Armas. On its north side is the **cathedral**, begun in 1561, finished in 1618, in a medley of styles; its two spires are covered in blue and yellow tiles. There is a reputed Murillo Virgin inside (painted 1650), and the famous *Virgen del Carmen*, painted by Miguel Cabrera, a Zapotec Indian from Oaxaca. In the dome are frescoes of the four gospel writers and in the Capilla del Santísimo are more frescoes and paintings of the Last Supper. From outside you can see the evening sun's rays streaming through the dome's stained glass. The cathedral's west façade is on Plaza de los Laureles, on the north side of which is the **Palacio Municipal** (1952), which contains murals by Gabriel Flores depicting the city's founding.

Also on the Plaza de Armas is the **Palacio de Gobierno** (1643) where in 1810 Hidalgo issued his first proclamation abolishing slavery. **José Clemente Orozco**'s great murals can be seen on the central staircase; they depict social struggle, dominated by Hidalgo, with the church on the left, fascism on the right and the suffering peasants in the middle. More of Orozco's work can be seen in the **Congreso**, an integral part of the Palacio de Gobierno (entrance free), and in the main **University of Guadalajara** building, on Avenida Juárez y Tolsá (re-named Enrique Díaz de León). Here, in the *Paraninfo* (main hall) is portrayed 'man asleep, man meditating, and man creating'; lie on your back or look in a mirror. The building also houses the **Museo de Arte**. ■ *Small fee, good café*. Other works by this artist can be seen at the University's main Library, Glorieta Normal, and at the massive Hospicio Cabañas near the Mercado Libertad, to the east (visit later) now known as **Instituto Cultural Cabañas**. The ex-orphanage is a beautiful building with 22 patios, which is floodlit at night. The contents of the former Orozco Museum in Mexico City have been transferred here. Look for *Man of Fire* painted in the dome. Also in the Instituto Cabañas are exhibitions of Mexican and international art and other events, listed under Entertainment below. ■ *Tue-Sat 1015-1745, Sun 1015-1445, US$0.80, US$15 to take photos.*

Going east from the cathedral is the Plaza de la Liberación, with a statue of Hidalgo, where the national flag is raised and lowered daily (with much ceremony). On the north side are the **Museo Regional** (see Museums below) and the **Palacio Legislativo** a neoclassical building, remodelled in 1982. ■ *Open to the public 0900 to 1800*. It has a list of the names of all the Constituyentes, from Hidalgo to Otero (1824-57 and 1917). At the eastern end of this plaza is the enormous and fantastically decorated **Teatro Degollado** (1866, see **Entertainment** below), well worth seeing even if you do not go to a performance. ■ *1000-1400.*

Guadalajara

To Old Bus Station, Parque Agua Azul, Museo de Arqueología del Occidente de México, Train Station, Airport & Chapala

To Bus Terminal, Tlaquepaque, Tonalá & Mexico City

0 metres 200
0 yards 200

Sleeping
1 Ana-Isabel
2 Aranzazú
3 Azteca
4 Continental
5 Francés
6 Hamilton
7 Hostal Guadalajara
8 Imperio
9 Internacional
10 Janeiro
11 León
12 Maya
13 México 70
14 Nueva York
15 Plaza Génova
16 Posada San Pablo
17 Posada Tapitía
18 Rotonda
19 Sevilla

Eating
1 Café D'Osio
2 Café Madoka
3 Carnes Asadas Rigo's
4 El Mexicano
5 La Chata
6 La Playita
7 La Rinconada
8 Madrid

Bars
9 Femina La Latina
10 La Jaula
11 La Mansión
12 La Maskara
13 La Maestranzo

Related map
Guadalajara
orientation,
page 306

Guadalajara to the Pacific Coast

A pedestrian mall, **Plaza Tapatía**, has been installed between the Teatro Degollado and the Instituto Cultural Cabañas, crossing the Calzada Independencia, covering 16 blocks. It has beautiful plants, fountains, statuary and a tourist office. Facing the Cabañas, on Morelos, is a sculpture in bronze by Rafael Zamarripa of Jalisco's symbol: two lions supporting a tree. The **Mercado Libertad** (locally known as San Juan de Dios, see **Shopping**) is south of Plaza Tapatía and between the market and the Cabañas is a park, with a fine modern sculpture, *The Stampede*, by Jorge de la Peña (1982). Immediately in front of the Instituto Cultural Cabañas are four bronze seats/sculptures by local artist Alejandro Colunga, which could be regarded as amusing or macabre, depending on your sense of humour. They include skeletons, an empty man's suit topped by a skull, a large pair of ears, etc.

Other sights worth seeing are the **Parque Alcalde**, Jesús García y Avenida de los Maestros, to the north of the centre; the **Plaza de los Mariachis**, Obregón and Leonardo Vicario, near Mercado Libertad; and the **Templo Expiatorio**, Avenida Enrique Díaz de León y Madero, with fine stained glass and intricate ceiling, Gothic style but still unfinished after a century. On the way out of the city going north along Calzada Independencia, near the Barranca de Oblatos, a huge canyon, there is a large **zoological garden** with plenty of Central American animals and aviaries in a delightful atmosphere ■ *US$0.50, Bus 600, 60 and 62 heading north on C Independencía.*. **Selva Mágica** amusement park is inside the zoo; it has a dolphin and seal show three or four times a day. There is also a **Planetarium**.

Guadalajara orientation

Related map
A Guadalajara,
page 305

On Calzada Independencia Sur, a reasonable but interesting walk of about 15 blocks south of the centre at the intersection of Constituyentes and González Gallo is **Parque Agua Azul**. ■ *0800-1900 Tue-Sun, US$0.20*. A park with a good aviary, trees, flowers and fountains, it contains the **Auditorio González Cano**, an outdoor concert bowl with portraits of famous Jalisco musicians, the **Teatro Experimental** and the **Casa de las Artesanías de Jalisco** (see **Crafts** below). On the other side of Calzada Independencia Sur is **Plaza Juárez** with an impressive monument ringed by the flags of other Latin American countries (take bus 52 or 54 up Avenida 16 de Septiembre or 60 or 62 up Calzada Independencia back to centre).

Churches

Other than the cathedral, churches include: **Santa Mónica** (1718), Santa Mónica y Reforma, which is small, but very elaborate with impressive arches full of gold under a clear atrium and a richly carved façade; **La Merced**, Hidalgo y Pedro Loza, has a beautiful interior with a remarkable number of confessional booths; **El Carmen**, Avenida Juárez 638, whose main altar is surrounded by gilded Corinthian columns; **San José**, Alcalde y Reforma, a 19th-century church with a fine gilded rococo pulpit, has eight pillars in a semicircle around the altar, painted deep red and ochre behind, giving an unusual effect, the overall light blue gives an airy feel; in the plaza outside is a statue of Núñez, defender of the Reforma who was killed in 1858; **San Miguel de Belén**, Hospital 290, enclosed in the Hospital Civil Viejo contains three fine late 18th-century *retablos*; behind the hospital is the **Panteón de Belén**, a beautiful old cemetery closed to new burials for many years, entrance at Calle Belén 684 at the corner of Eulogio Parra, open until 1500; **San Agustín**, Morelos y Degollado (16th century), is quite plain, with carved stones, music school next door; and **San Francisco Neri** (1550) a three-tiered altar with columns, a feature repeated on the façade. To the north of this last church is the **Jardín San Francisco** (pleasantly shaded, and the starting point for horse-drawn carriages), and to the west is the old church of **Nuestra Señora de Aranzazú**, with three fantastic churrigueresque altarpieces; equally impressive are the coloured ceilings and the finely carved dado, the only light coming from high-up windows and from the open east door. In the shadow of San Francisco is a modern statue to teachers. **María de Gracia**, Carranza and Hidalgo, is another beautiful church. The **Santuario de Guadalupe**, north of the centre, on the corner of Avenida Alcalde and Juan Alvarez, is lovely inside; outside, in the Jardín del Santuario, fireworks are let off on 12 December, the day of the Virgin of Guadalupe, with musicians, vendors, games and people celebrating in the plaza.

Museums

Museo de Arqueología del Occidente de México, Calzada Independencia Sur y Calzada del Campesino (Plaza Juárez), has a very comprehensive collection of objects

from Jalisco, Colima and Nayarit, including pottery, ornaments, weapons, figures and illustrations of tombs. A small booklet in English is available. ■ *Mon-Fri 1000-1400, 1600-1800, Sat-Sun 1100-1430, US$0.20.* **Museo Regional de Guadalajara**, Liceo 60, between Hidalgo and Independencia (northeast of cathedral), T3614-2227. In an old seminary (1710), with a good prehistoric section (including the complete skeleton of a mammoth found in Jalisco), this museum has an interesting display of shaft tombs, an excellent display of Colima, Nayarit and Jalisco terracotta figures (but less extensive than the Museo de Arqueología), and possibly the finest display of 17th to 18th-century colonial art in Mexico outside the Pinacoteca Virreinal in Mexico City (see page 103). There are also musical instruments, Indian art and one room devoted to the history of Jalisco from the Conquistadores to Iturbide; highly recommended. ■ *Mon-Sat 0900-1745, Sun 0900-1500, US$1.60, free on Sun, Tue, and holidays, free for children and senior citizens.* The **Museo de Periodismo y Artes Gráficas**, Avenida Alcalde 225, between San Felipe and Reforma, T3613-9285/6, restored and opened in 1994; the building is known as the Casa de los Perros because of two large dog statues on the roof. The first printing shop in Guadalajara was here and the first *periódico insurgente* (insurgent newspaper) in the Americas, *El Despertador Americano,* was published here in 1810. The museum contains old printing presses, newspapers, etc. When Avenida Alcalde was widened in 1950, the building's façade was moved back 9 m. ■ *Tue-Sat 1000-1800, Sun 1100-1500, US$0.50, students with ID half price, over 60s free, Sun free.* **Museo de la Ciudad**, Calle Independencia 684, in a pretty colonial building with two columned patios, has information on the city from its founding to the present day, including maps and population statistics. ■ *Wed-Sat 1000-1730, Sun 1000-1430, US$0.30, free Sun and for over 60s.* **Casa Museo López Portillo**, Calle Liceo 177, T3613-2411, formerly the family home of the ex-President, was restored in 1982 when he was in office. It is a colonial house with a large tiled courtyard, and surrounding rooms furnished with 18th and 19th-century Italian and French furniture. It is also used as a cultural centre with classes in music, dance, literature, chess, Indian culture and languages. Across the street at Liceo 166 in another colonial building are the offices of the **Instituto Nacional de Antropología e Historia** (INAH), where there is a library with books on Guadalajara. ■ *1000-1600.* **Casa José Clemente Orozco**, Aurelio Aceves 29, pedestrian street half a block from Los Arcos, was built in the 1940s and donated to the state of Jalisco by the family after the artist's death in 1951. ■ *1000-1600.* Two other museums are the **Museo de Cera**, on the south side of the Plaza de la Liberación, right downtown, on Calle Morelos a couple of doors west of Calle Degollado. The **Casa de la Cultura**, Avenida 16 de Septiembre y Constituyentes, holds contemporary art exhibitions and lectures.

Excursions

A visit to Tequila is an easy day trip from Guadalajara – see page 341

In a northwest suburb of Guadalajara is the **Basílica de Zapopan**, completed 1690, with a miraculous image of Nuestra Señora, known as *La Generala* on the main altar, given to the Indians in 1542. There is a huge **fiesta** for the Virgen de Zapopan on 12 October. Next door is a museum of Huichol Indian art. ■ *Mon-Fri 1000-1400, Sat-Sun 1000-1300.* At one end of the pedestrian street, Paseo Teopitzintli, leading to the plaza and Basílica, is the colonial-style Arco de Ingreso. The **tourist office** is in the Casa de la Cultura, two blocks behind the Basílica, on Guerrero. ■ *Mon-Fri 0900-2100, Sat 0900-1300. T3110-0754. Getting there: bus No 275 along Av Alcalde, or take line 1 of the Tren Ligero to Avila Camacho stop and pick up bus No 175 to Zapopan (there are several different 175s, so check with driver that the bus goes all the way to Zapopan).*

Eight kilometres northeast is the **Barranca de Oblatos**, a 600-m deep canyon. Guides will take you down to see the Río Grande de Santiago cascading at the bottom (except in the dry season). Once described as a stupendous site, it is now rather spoilt by litter and sewage. See especially the Cola de Caballo waterfall and the Parque Mirador Dr Atl. ■ *Getting there: bus La Normal from the centre of town.* **Balneario Los Comachos**, a large swimming pool with diving boards set on one side of the Barranca de Oblatos, has many terraces with tables and chairs and barbecue pits under mango trees; drinks and snacks are on sale. ■ *US$1.50.*

You can also visit the **Barranca de Huentitán**, access via the Mirador de Huentitán at the end of Calzada Independencia Norte, near the zoological gardens, a tremendous natural site, with interesting flora and better views than at Oblatos. It is one hour to the bottom (no guide needed) and the river, which is straddled by the historic bridge of Huentitán. *Getting there: buses Nos 60, 62A, 'Jonilla Centro' from city centre; 44 'Sevilo C Médico', stops 100 m short. All buses cost US$0.25.*

About 7 km southeast of the city centre is the attractive suburb of Tlaquepaque, well worth a visit. Calle Independencia runs from Boulevard Tlaquepaque (the main avenue into Guadalajara) to the main plaza where you can see the restored Parroquia de San Pedro Tlaquepaque and the Basílica La Teranensis. Further on is the **Parián**, a very large, square building occupying most of another plaza, with bars (pretty woodwork and tiling) and kitchens around the perimeter. The rest is an open courtyard. By day Tlaquepaque is a fusion of craft ideas ranging from red-hot and pricey minimalist style through to stack it high and sell it cheap tack (see Shopping below); at night the boulevards and main square fill with diners and and *mariachis,* who play Friday, Saturday, Sunday, 1530 and 2130, also roving *mariachis* play for a fee.

If you're looking to stay a couple of days there is accommodation – see below.

Tlaquepaque
Colour map 3, grid B2

Fifteen kilometres southwest of Guadalajara on the road to Mexico City is **Tonalá**, noted for its Sunday and Thursday markets, where you can pick up bargains in pottery, glass and ceramics. The market is held on the central avenue, where all the buses from Guadalajara stop. Calle Benito Juárez intersects this avenue and is a main shopping street. It runs to the main plaza (where it intersects with Calle Madero, the other main shopping street in the centre) and on another block to the Parroquía de Santiago de Tonalá, a very beautiful church built in the mid-17th century. On the plaza is the cream-coloured Iglesia del Sagrado Corazón. The walls are lined with crucifixion paintings. Also on the plaza are the Presidencia Municipal, a pastel blue-green colonial-style building, and the municipal market (food and crafts). For shopping in the centre of town, *Aldana Luna*, at Juárez 194, T3683-0302, sells wrought-iron furniture; *Plaza Juárez* is a large building at Juárez 141 with several craft shops in it; *Artesanías Nuño*, T3683-0011, at Juárez 59, sells brightly painted wooden animals. On Madero: there is a *casa de cambio* at No 122; *Restaurant Jalapeños* at No 23 serves pizza, beer and regular meals; D *Hotel Tonalá*, opposite, at No 22, is plain but in good shape, some rooms with TV. Another attractive restaurant is *El Rincón del Sol*, at 16 de Septiembre 61, serving steaks and Mexican food.

Tonalá
Colour map 3, grid B2

Four hours north of Guadalajara on the road from Zapopan through San Cristóbal de la Barranca is the small town of **Totatiche** near the Río Tlatenango, founded by the Caxcan Indians but taken over by the Spaniards between 1592-1600. Both Totatiche and neighbouring Temastián were evangelized by Franciscans and the church is in the classical Franciscan style, with a three-tiered tower. In the church is the urn containing the remains of the recently beatified Father Cristóbal Magallanes, who was killed in the Cristero War (see box). Next to the church is the Museo Cristero containing personal effects and furniture. At **Temastián**, 12 km away, the Basílica houses an image of Christ venerated for escaping a lightning bolt, which destroyed the cross it was on, known as *El Señor de los Rayos*. The **fiesta**, on 11 January, is celebrated with dancing, parades and rodeos. ■ *Buses leave from the old bus station.*

Essentials

The smart business hotels are in the modern western part of the city, roughly 2 km west of the historic centre. Many to choose from including **LL** *Presidente Intercontinental*, López Mateos Sur and Av Moctezuma, T3678-1234, F3678-1222. Some deluxe suites with private patio, high-rise tower with built-in shopping centre, cavernous lobby.

Sleeping
Price codes:
see inside front cover

LL *Quinta Real*, Av México 2727 y López Mateos, T3615-0000, F3630-1797. Designed as colonial manor, convenient location, good, 78 large, well-furnished rooms, but original art work, good restaurant.

Centro Histórico **AL** *Plaza Génova* (Best Western), Juárez 123, T3613-7500, F3614-8253, www.hplazagenova.com Including continental breakfast and welcome cocktail, clean, good service, good restaurant, recommended. **AL** *Aranzazú*, Av Revolución 110 Pte, T3613-3232, F3613-6650. Central, very good, full business services – see the bats departing from the top floor roof eaves at dusk. **A** *Plaza Diana*, Av Circunvalación Agustín Yáñez 2760, T/F3615-5510. 126 rooms, many refurbished 1995, a/c, TV, restaurant with low-cal menu. **A** *Francés*, Maestranza 35, T3613-0917, F3658-2831, www.hotelfrances.com Colonial building with central patio, oldest hotel in the city, built in 1610, have a drink there at 'happy hour' 1800-1900, to enjoy the bygone atmosphere, disco and bar music noisy at night, some rooms small but very good-value penthouse suite (**AL**) for 4, with 2 very large bedrooms, living room and kitchen, free parking underneath adjoining Plaza de la Liberación, 3 blocks away. **A** *Internacional*, Pedro Moreno 570, T3613-0330, F3613-2866. Clean, comfortable, safe. Recommended. **A** *Rotonda*, Liceo 130, T/F3614-1017, central, near cathedral. Remodelled 19th-century building, attractive, dining area in courtyard, cheap set lunches, nice public areas, rooms OK, with TV, phones, covered parking. **B** *Hotel Plaza Los Arcos*, Av Vallarta 2456, T3616-3816, F3615-1806. 1-bedroom suites, huge hard bed, sitting room, kitchen, good bathroom, very clean, 2-weekly and monthly rates available.

C *Continental*, Corona 450 and Libertad, T3614-1117. Clean, good spot where it's quiet, but close enough to get to everything. Recommended. **C** *Maya*, López Cotilla 39, T3614-4654. With private bath, blankets, pleasant atmosphere.

D *Posada Tapatía*, López Cotilla 619, T3614-9146. Colonial-style house, 2-3 blocks from Federalismo, one of the better budget places, traffic can be a problem. **D** *Posada San Pablo*, Madero #429 (no sign), T3614-2811. A family home that's been welcoming backpackers for years. No sign, just ring the bell and Lilia will let you in if she thinks you look OK. Quiet, informal and friendly. Use of laundry and kitchen a little more. **D** *Sevilla*, Prisciliano Sánchez 413, T3614-9037. Good (4 blocks south of cathedral), owner speaks English, good restaurant.

E *Hamilton*, Madero 381, T3614-6726. A bit too hotel-like for this price, but clean, friendly, with bath and TV. Good value. **E** *Hostal Guadalajara*, Maestranza 147, close to the centre. A new Youth Hostel-affiliated place in town, with good facilities including kitchen, laundry, internet access, and lounge area. Certain to build on the successes of others throughout Mexico. **E** *Lisboa*, on corner of Grecia and Juárez in precinct, but almost impossible to find. Cheaper with shared bath, noisy, but cheap.

There are cheap hotels along Javier Mina (southside of Mercado Libertad), down Calzada Independencia (very noisy), and around the old bus staion (5 de Febrero). All interesting and lively spots to use as a base, but all with a slightly raw edginess.

Mercado Libertad **D** *Janeiro*, Av Obregón 95, one block south of the market, T3617-5063. Best value in the market area. A few rooms have balconies overlooking the busy market street, close to Plaza de los Mariachis. Ideal for people-watching or insomnia. **D** *México 70*, Javier Mina 230, southside of Mercado Libertad. With bath, clean, TV available. Friendly, aimed at Mexican familes, but welcomes all normal people. Hangover from the Mexico 1970 World Cup – great business planning meant success got out of hand. **C** *Azteca*, Javier Mina 311, 1½ blocks east of Mercado Libertad. Clean, very friendly, some rooms with good views, parking around the corner. **D** *Ana-Isabel*, Javier Mina 164, T3617-7920. Good sized rooms. **D** *Imperio*, next door. Clean, popular and a little noisy.

Independencia **C-D** *Nueva York*, Independencia Sur 43, T/F3618-7095. With bath, hot water. **E** *León*, Independencia Sur 557. Bath, towels, hot water, clean, staff friendly and helpful. **E** *Estación*, Calzada Independencia Sur 1297, T3619-0051, F3619-0534, across the main boulevard beside train station. Quiet, clean, safe, luggage store, hot water, small, limited restaurant. Recommended.

Old bus terminal Several to choose from including **C** *Canadá*, Estadio 77, ½ block west of old bus station, T3619-4014, F3619-3110. All rooms with bath, hot water, some with TV, clean, good value. 3 in a row on 5 de Febrero, southside of the terminal, are: **C** *Emperador*, No 530, T3619-2246. Remodelled, adequate, all rooms have TV and phone, enclosed parking, good public areas. **C-D** *San Jose*, No 116, T/F3619-1153. Simply OK, nothing special. **D-E** *Monaco*, Febrero 152, T3619-0018. Best deal of the 3.

New bus terminal **C** *El Parador*, T3600-0910, F3600-0015. Overpriced because of location (does not take Amex), spartan rooms with TV, expensive laundry, clean, noisy, pool, 24-hr café *El Jardín*.

Tlaquepaque AL *El Tapatío*, Blvd Aeropuerto 4275, T3635-6050, F3635-6664, in Tlaquepaque, nearest hotel to airport. Fine view of city, extensive grounds, very attractive and comfortable rooms. **AL-A** *La Villa del Ensueño*, Florida 305, Tlaquepaque, T3635-8792, aldez@ soca.com 8 rooms, 2 suites, pool, including breakfast, no smoking, English and Spanish spoken.

Worth considering if stocking up on gifts before heading home

   C *La Posada de la Media Luna*, off Juárez 1 block east of the Parián, T3635-6050. Delightful rooms, with private bath, TV and telephone, includes breakfast on colourful patio. Excellent value. Many restaurants and bars to choose from. Banks with ATMs around the Parián.

Motels AL *Las Américas*, López Mateos Sur 2400, T3631-4256, F3631-4415, opposite Plaza del Sol shopping centre. A/c, pool, good. **B** *Del Bosque*, López Mateos Sur 265, T3121-4700, F3122-1955. TV and phone in all rooms. **C** *Isabel*, Montenegro 1572, Sector Hidalgo, T/F3826-2630. Pleasant, pool.

Trailer parks D *La Hacienda*, Circunvalación Pte 66, 16 km out of town, in Col Ciudad Granja, off Av Vallarta on left before you reach *periférico* and head to Tepic, T3627-1724, F3627-1724 ext 117. Shaded, pool, clubhouse, hook-ups.

Youth hostel At Prolongación Alcalde 1360, Sector Hidalgo, T3853-0033, away from centre in a state government complex, entrance gate at intersection of Alcalde and Tamaulipas on east side of Alcalde. Women's and men's dormitories, bunk beds and lockers. Described as a nightmare to get to; buses 52 and 54 along Av Alcalde from the centre pass the hostel, or bus 275 goes as far as La Normal roundabout, from where it is about 2 blocks northeast, buses stop between 2200-2300, a taxi from downtown costs US$2-3 but many people walk, about 30 mins.

As can be expected in a city of this size there is a wide variety of restaurants on offer, look in local tourist literature for the latest in International, Mexican, Spanish, Italian, Argentine, Arab, Chinese, Japanese or German cooking. There are also fast food outlets, *pizzerías* and Mexican *cafeterías* and bars. The cheapest restaurants are in the streets near the old bus station, especially in Calle de Los Angeles, and upstairs in the large Mercado Libertad (San Juan de Dios) in centre, but not always very hygienic here. There are also cheap, and filling, loncherías around town. Try *La Playita*, Av Juárez between Corona and Maestranza, very good, also one at Morelos 99, by the Tourist Office. Try *tortas de lomo doble carne con aguacate* (pork and avocado special).

Eating

   In the cloister of *La Merced* is a fast-food place, popular with young people. *Búfalo*, Calderón de la Barca and Av Vallarta. Tacos and cheap *comida corrida*, very friendly. *Café D'Osio*, around the corner from *Hotel Hamilton*, on corner of Prisciliano Sánchez and Ocampo. Excellent breakfast and delicious tortas, especially the roast pork, not expensive, open 0900-1800. *Café Madoka*, Enrique González Martínez 78, T3613-3134, just south of Hidalgo. Excellent very early breakfasts, well known for the men who play dominoes there. Friendly, a real gem! *Café Pablo Picasso*, Av Américas 1939, T3636-1996. Breakfast, lunch, dinner and *tapas*, *galería*, boutique, decorated with photos of Picasso and his work, smart clientele. Pricey.

   Strictly for carnivores, try delicious *carne en su jugo* (beef stew with potatoes, beans, bacon, sausage, onion and avocado, garnished with salsa, onion and coriander) from **Carnes Asadas El Tapatío** in Mercado Libertad (there are 3), or **Carnes Asadas Rigo's**,

Independencia 584A, popular. Goat is a speciality, roasted each day and served with radish, onion and chilli. *Cortijo La Venta*, Federación 725, T3617-1675, open daily 1300-0100. Invites customers to fight young bulls (calves) after their meal (the animals are not harmed, guests might be), restaurant serves meat, soups, salads.

El Asadero, opposite the Basílica in Zapopán suburb (see Excursions above). Very good. A good place for fish is *El Delfín Sonriente*, Niños Héroes 2293, T3616-0216. Nice, attractive. *El Ganadero*, on Av Américas. Excellent beef, reasonable prices. *El Mexicano*, Plaza Tapatía, Morelos 81. Rustic Mexican décor. Recommended. *Karne Garibaldi*, Garibaldi 1306, J Clemente Orozco, Col Sta Teresita. Nice place, serves *carne en su jugo* (see above). *La Banderillas*, Av Alcalde 831. Excellent food at reasonable prices. *La Bombilla*, López Cotilla y Penitenciaría. Very good for *churros* and hot chocolate. *La Catedral del Antojito*, Pedro Moreno 130, a pedestrian street. Colonial-style house, restaurant upstairs above bridal gown shop, serves tacos, tortas, etc, good meal for under US$2. *La Chata*, Francisco Zarco 2277, and *Gemma*, López Mateos Sur 1800, 2 chains serving Mexican food, are usually quite good (*Gemma* has 8 branches in the city and does Guadalajaran *lonches* and *tortas ahogadas*). A good Mexican restaurant is *La Gorda*, Juan Alvarez 1336, esq Gen Coronado, Col Sta Teresita. *La Pianola*, Av México 3220 and several other locations. Good, reasonable prices, serves *chiles en nogada*. Excellent. *La Rinconada*, Morelos 86 on Plaza Tapatía. A beautiful colonial building, columned courtyard, carved wood doors, entrées at US$4-8 range, open until 2130, separate bar. *La Trattoria*, Niños Héroes 3051. Very good, reasonably priced Italian, very popular (queues form for lunch from 1400). *Madrid*, Juárez 264 and Corona. Poor service, poor selection of dishes, pricey. *Piaf*, Marsella 126. French cuisine, live music, friendly, closed Sun. Excellent. For those so inclined, *Lido*, Colón 294 and Miguel Blanco (Plaza San Francisco), serves *criadillas* (bulls' testicles). Plenty of international fast food places – you can find them.

Bars & nightclubs Easy one to work out, just stroll down Maestranza south of Juárez from about 0830 and listen for the noise. *La Maestranza* is very popular, and brings out the machismo with distinctive themes of the matador. *La Maskara* and *La Jaula* are on the same block, and gay friendly. *La Mansión* is round the corner, and *Femina La Latina* offers an altogether more cultured approach to the whole drinking/socializing malarkey.

Entertainment **Cinema** Average cost of a ticket is US$2. Good quality films, some in English, are shown in the evenings at 1600, 1800, 2000, US$1.25, at the *ciné-teatro* in the *Instituto Cultural Cabañas* (see Sights above), which also has a good *cafetería*.

Music Concerts and theatre in the ex-Convento del Carmen. A band plays every Thu at 1800 in the Plaza de Armas, in front of the Palacio de Gobierno, free. Organ recitals in the cathedral. *Peña Cuicacalli*, Av Niños Héroes almost at corner of Av Chapultepec, T3825-4690, opens 2000, US$5, food and drink available, fills up fast; local groups perform variety of music including Latin American folk music Fri, Sat.

Theatre *Ballet Folclórico de la Universidad de Guadalajara*, every Sun at 1000 in the Teatro Degollado, superb, highly recommended, pre-Hispanic and Mexican-wide dances, and other cultural shows, US$2-10, T3658-3812 (check before you go). The theatre is open to the public from 1000-1300 Mon-Fri just to look inside. The *Grupo Folclórico Ciudad de Guadalajara* performs here every Thu at 2000. The *Ballet Folclórico del Instituto Cultural Cabañas* performs Wed 2030, US$4. The Instituto is also an art school, with classes in photography, sculpture, ceramics, literature, music, theatre and dance.

Festivals **21 March** commemorates Benito Juárez's birthday and everything is closed for the day. In **Jun** the *Virgin of Zapopan* (see Excursions above), leaves her home to spend each night in a different church where fireworks are let off. The virgin has a new car each year but the engine is not started; men pull it through the beautifully decorated streets with ropes. The climax is **12 Oct** when the virgin leaves the cathedral for home, there are great crowds along the route. Throughout the month of **Oct** there is a great fiesta with concerts, bullfights, sports and exhibitions of handicrafts from all over Mexico. **12 Dec**, fiesta in honour of the *Virgin of Guadalupe*; Av Alcalde has stalls, music, fair, etc.

The *Feria Internacional del Libro*, the third largest book fair in the world, is held every year in late November/early December in Guadalajara's Gran Salón de Exposiciones. As well as the usual gathering of publishers, there are round-the-clock readings of poetry and fiction, music, dance, theatre, games, food and drink. For information, write (in English or Spanish) to FIL Guadalajara, Francia 1747, Col Moderna, Guadalajara, Jal 44190, México, T523-8100331, F523-8100379, fil@udgserv.cencar.udg.mx. Or write to FIL New York, c/o David Unger, Division of Humanities NAC 6/293, The City College of New York, NY 10031, USA, T212-6507925, F212-6507912, filny@aol.com

Shopping

The best shops are no longer in the centre, although a couple of department stores have branches there. The best stores are in the shopping centres, of which there are many, small and large, mainly on the west side.

Mercado Libertad (San Juan de Dios) has colourful items for souvenirs with lots of Michoacán crafts including Paracho guitars and Sahuayo hats, leather jackets and *huaraches* (sandals) and delicious food upstairs on the 1st level (particularly goat meat, *birria*, also very sweet coconut called *cocada*), fruit juices and other soft drinks. In **Tonalá** market days are Sun and Thu (see Excursions).

Bookshops English books available at a reasonable mark up, at *Sanborn's*, Av Vallarta 1600 and Gen San Martín, Juárez and 16 de Septiembre, Plaza Bonita and López Mateos Sur 2718 (near Plaza del Sol), also English language magazines. German journals at *Sanborn's*, Av Vallarta branch. *Sandi's*, Av Tepeyac 718, Col Chapalita, T3121-0863, F3647-4600, has a good selection of English language books, including medical textbooks and cards. *Librería México* in Plaza del Sol, local 14, area D, on Av López Mateos side, T3121-0114, has US magazines and newspapers. *El Libro Antiguo*, Pino Suárez 86, open 1000-2000, mostly Spanish but large selection of English paperbacks. *Librería La Fuente*, Medellín 140, near Juan Manuel in the centre, T3613-5238, sells used books and magazines in English and Spanish, interesting to browse in, some items quite old, from 1940s and 1950s. Bookshops can be found on López Cotilla, from González Martínez towards 16 de Septiembre.

Crafts The Museo Regional de la Cerámica is at Independencia 237. For beautiful, expensive furniture go to *Antigua de México*, Independencia 255, lovely building, used to be a convent, the family has branches in Nogales and Tucson so furniture can be shipped to their shops there. *La Casa Canela*, opposite, sells furniture and crafts, don't miss the colonial kitchen at the back of the house. *Adobe Diseño*, also in a colonial house, sells expensive leather furniture. Visit the shop of *Sergio Bustamante*, who sells his own work (good modern jewellery): expensive but well worth a look, a stream runs through this house with a colonial façade at Independencia 236. Some way from the main shopping area is the *Casa de los Telares*, Hidalgo 1378, where Indian textiles are woven on hand looms.

There are two glass factories at **Tlaquepaque**, where the blue, green, amber and amethyst blown-glass articles are made (Bus 275 from the centre goes through Tlaquepaque en route to bus station). Many other crafts available in the suburb. Potters can be watched at work both in Guadalajara and at Tlaquepaque; but you may find better bargains at **Tonalá** (pottery and ceramics, some glass), see Excursions, above, on market days Thu and Sun; take Bus 275 (see local Transport below), bumpy 45-min journey. Overall, Tlaquepaque is the cheapest and most varied source of local crafts, with attractive shops set in old colonial villas; best buys are glass, papier-mâché goods, leather (cheapest in Mexico), and ceramics. See also the *Tienda Tlaquepaque*, at Av Juárez 267-B, in Tlaquepaque, T3635-5663. *Casa de Artesanías de Jalisco*, González Gallo 20, T3619-4664, open 1000-1900 (1400 Sun), in Parque Agua Azul: high quality display (and sale) of handicrafts, ceramics, paintings, handblown glass, dresses, etc (state-subsidized to preserve local culture, reasonably priced but not cheap). There is another shop-cum-exhibition at the *Instituto de Artesanía Jaliscense*, *Casa de Las Artesanías Normal*, Av Alcalde 1221, T3624-4624.

Bullfights Oct-Mar. **Football** a passion throughout year. *Charreadas* (cowboy shows) are held in mid-Sep at Unión de San Antonio; *lienzo charro* near Parque Agua Azul at Aceves

Sports

Guadalajara to the Pacific Coast

Calindo Lienzo, Sun at 1200. **Baseball** Apr-Sep. **Golf** at Santa Anita, 16 km out on Morelia road, championship course; Rancho Contento, 10 km out on Nogales road; San Isidro, 10 km out on Saltillo road, noted for water hazards. **Hiking** club *Colli*, bulletin board Av Juárez 460, details from *Café Madrid*, Juárez 264 or T3623-3318, 617-9248.

Transport
For the Tequila Express, see page 341

Local Horse-drawn carriages US$22 per hr from the Museo Regional de Guadalajara at the corner of Liceo and Hidalgo, or on Independencía just below Plaza Tapatía. **Buses**: Tourist Office in Plaza Tapatía has a full list of local and long distance buses. If in doubt ask bus driver. Regular buses cost US$0.20, *Línea Azul* 'luxury' bus US$0.45. Some useful lines: *No 275*, on 16 de Septiembre and Revolución, from Zapopan – Plaza Patria – Glorieta Normal – Av Alcalde – Av 16 de Septiembre – Av Revolución – Tlaquepaque – new bus station – Tonalá (there are different 275s, from A to F, most follow this route, check with driver). *Route 707* also goes to Tonalá (silver-blue bus with Tur on the side). Bus 60 goes along Calzada de la Independencia from zoo, passing Estadio Jalisco, Plaza de Toros, Mercado Libertad and Parque Agua Azul to the old bus terminal and the railway station (if you are going to Parque Mirador, take bus 62 northbound, otherwise 62 has the same route as 60). There is also a new trolley bus that runs along the Calzada de la Independencia to the entrance to the Mirador, better than 60 or 62. For the old bus station, take minibus 174 south along Calzada de la Independencia from Mercado Libertad, or bus 110 south along Av Alcalde. Bus 102 runs from the new bus terminal along Av Revolución, 16 de Septiembre and Prisciliano Sánchez to Mercado Libertad. No 258 or 258A from San Felipe (north of cathedral) or 258D along Madero go to Plaza del Sol. No 371 runs from Tonalá to Plaza del Sol. A shuttle bus runs between the 2 bus stations. The **Metro**, or *Tren Ligero*, has Línea 1 running under Federalismo from Periférico Sur to Periférico Norte. Línea 2, runs from Juárez station westbound and passes Mercado Libertad. Fare US$0.40, 1-peso coins needed to buy tokens.

Car hire: *Quick*, Av Niños Héroes, esq Manzano, T3614-2247. *Budget*, Av Niños Héroes, esq 16 de Septiembre, T3613-0027. *National*, Main office: Niños Héroes 961, by *Hotel Carlton*, and other offices at the hotels *Fiesta Americana, Holiday Inn Select*, and the airport, T3614-7175. *Avis*, at airport, T3688-5656, toll free within Mexico 800-288-8888. *Hertz*, Office at *Hotel Quinta Real*, other at airport. Others scattered throughout city, T3614-6162.

Taxis: no meters used. A typical ride in town costs US$2-4. From the centre to the new bus station is about US$6, although if the taxi ticket booths are open at the bus station it costs around US$4. A taxi to the airport costs US$10.

Long distance Air: Miguel Hidalgo (GDL), 20 km from town; 3 classes of taxi (*especial*, *semi-especial* and *colectivo*) charge fixed rates for 3 city zones; no tip necessary. Bus No 176 'San José del 15', leaves from intersection of Corona and Calzada de la Independencia every 20 mins, US$0.25, grey bus. *Autotransportes Guadalajara- Chapala* runs 2nd class buses from old bus terminal every 15 mins, 0655-2125, US$0.35, stop at airport on way to/from Chapala.

Many flights daily with connections to most domestic cities and internationally including Atlanta, Auckland (New Zealand), Bakersfield (Calif), Birmingham (Alabama), Bogota, Buenos Aires, Caracas, Chicago, Dallas, Detroit, El Paso, Fresno (Calif), Guatemala City, Havana, Hong Kong, Houston, Las Vegas, Lima, Los Angeles, Miami, New York, Oakland, Oklahoma City, Ontario, Panama City, Phoenix, St Louis, Salt Lake City, San Antonio (Texas), San Francisco, San José (Calif and Costa Rica), Santiago and Sao Paulo.

Buses: The **old bus station**, in the centre of town at Los Angeles and 28 de Enero, serves towns roughly within 100 km of Guadalajara. You have to pay 20 centavos to enter the terminal (open 0545-2215). It has 2 *salas* (wings): A and B, and is shaped like a U. The flat bottom of the U fronts Dr R Michel, where the main entrances are. There is a side entrance to Sala A from Los Angeles and to both A and B from 15 de Febrero via a tunnel. Taxi stands on both sides of the terminal. By the entrances to the *salas* is a Computel outlet with long-distance and fax service. There are lots of Ladatel phones for long distance and local calls outside the main entrance, some take coins and others debit cards, as well as food and magazine stalls (maps available). The shuttle buses to the new bus station leave from here, US$0.20. In Sala A there are 2nd class buses to **Tepatitlán** and **Zapotlanejo** and *'La Penal'* (the prison), with Oriente. 1st class buses to the same destinations leave from the new bus terminal. Buses to **Chapala**

(every 30 mins, 0600-2140, US$1.60) and **Ajijic** (every 30 mins, 0700-2100, US$1.80) leave from here with *Autotransportes Guadalajara-Chapala*. Round trip package to the *balneario* at **San Juan Cosalá**, US$5.25 including admission to the baths. In Sala B, *Omnibus de Rivera* sells tickets to the same *balneario* for US$1.50 and at La Alteña booth for the *balnearios* **Agua Caliente** and **Chimulco**. A Primera Plus/Servicios Coordinados booth sells tickets to places served by the new bus terminal. Buses to **Tequila** every 30 mins, US$3. Both *salas* have several food stands serving *tortas*, etc, and there are toilets, luggage store and magazine stand.

The **new bus station** is 10 km from the centre, near the El Alamo junction; buses 102 and 275 go to the centre, US$0.25, frequent service (see Local Transport above), journey takes at least 30 mins. There is a new luxury bus service (*Línea Azul*) running from Zapopan, along Avila Camacho, past Plaza Patria shopping centre to the Glorieta La Normal, south down Av Alcalde, through Tlaquepaque, to the new bus station and ending in Tonalá. Another luxury bus service to the centre is Línea Cardenal. No buses after 2230.

In the centre of town bus information and tickets are available at 2 offices on Calzada de la Independencia underneath the big fountain on Plaza Tapatía (access from Independencia), open 0900-1400, 1600-1900. Very handy because of the distance from the centre of town although it is worth getting your departure information at the bus station before you go into town. Most services sold are for the higher class travel.

Simply put, the Guadalajara bus terminal is fascinating in an intensely frustrating way. It is devoid of logic; information on timetables and prices is gathered by osmosis – those who have it assume those who don't (ie the international traveller just passing through) are stupid and those who don't have the information are destined to wander round for hours, maybe days, trying to understand what is going on. The purpose of this guide should be to guide you through this chaos – sorry, we can't. But here are a few pointers.

The terminal is in the shape of a big U, with modules 1 to 7 evenly spaced around the outside. Buses enter the U at Module 1, following through to 7 at the other end of the U. (That's where the logic starts and ends.) Different companies have a presence in several modules and while they will sell you a ticket to any destination, you have to get to the correct terminal. So, shop around, preferably without your bag. Most, if not all terminals now have baggage storage, along with telephones, toilets, restaurants, shops and occasionally manned tourist information booths.

There are probably direct buses to every conceivable destination in Mexico. The schedules for the most commonly used are below, with modules. *Acapulco*: 1730 and 1900, 17 hrs, US$57, Mod 7. *Aguascalientes*: hourly 0500-2000, 4 hrs, US$15, Mods 1, 2, 6 and 7. *Barra de Navidad*: every 2 hrs 0700-1500, and 2200 and 0100, 5 hrs, US$18, Mods 1 and 2. *Chihuahua*: 8 between 0600 and 2000, 16 hrs, US$65, Mod 7. *Colima*: hourly, 3 hrs, US$12, Mods 1, 2 and 6. *Guanajuato*: hourly, 4 hrs, US$18, Mods 1, 2 and 7. *Hermosillo*: every couple of hours, 23 hrs, US$76, Mods 3 and 4. *Lagos de Moreno*: very regular, 3 hrs, US$11, Best service from Mod 5. *León*: hourly, 4 hrs, US$15, Mods 1 and 2. *Los Mochis*: almost hourly through the day, 15 hrs, US$60, Mods 3 and 4. *Manzanillo*: hourly, more regular in the afternoon, 6 hrs, US$16, Mods 1, 2 and 3. *Mazatlán*: every hour day and night, 8 hrs, US$32, Mods 3 and 4. *Mexicali*: every hour day and night, 34 hrs, US$109, Mods 3 and 4. *Mexico City (North Terminal)*: every 15 mins, 8-9 hrs, US$33, Most often at Mod 1. *Morelia*: every 2 hrs, 4 hrs, US$16, Mods 1 and 2. *Puerto Vallarta*: every 2 hrs in the morning, 6 hrs, US$27, Mods 1, 2, 3 and 4. *Querétaro*: every 30 mins, 5 hrs, US$21, Most often at Mod 1. *San Luis Potosí*: every 2 hrs, 5 hrs, US$19, Mod 5. *San Miguel de Allende*: 1300 and 1500, 6 hrs, US$26, Mod 1. *Tepic*: every 30 mins, day and night, 3½ hrs, US$15, Mods 3, 4, 6 and 7. *Tijuana*: hourly, day and night, 33 hrs, US$116, Mods 3 and 4. *Uruapan*: every 2 hrs, 4½ hrs, US$13, Mods 1 and 2. *Zacatecas*: roughly every 3 hrs, 5 hrs, US$20, Mods 6 and 7.

Airline offices *Mexicana*, reservations T3678-7676, arrival and departure information T3688-5775, ticket office: Av Mariano Otero 2353, by Plaza del Sol, T3112-0011. *AeroMéxico*, reservations T3669-0202, airport information T3688-5098, ticket offices, Av Corona 196 and Plaza del Sol, Local 30, Zona A. *Delta*, López Cotilla 1701, T3630-3530. *Aero California*, López Cotilla 1423, T3688-8850. On Av Vallarta: *Air France*, No 1540-103 T3630-3707), *American*, No 2440 (T3616-4090 for reservations, T3688-5518 at airport). *KLM*, No 1390-1005 T3825-3261, *Continental*, ticket office Astral Plaza, Galerías del *Hotel Presidente Intercontinental*, Locales 8-9, T3647-4251 reservations, T3688-5141 airport. *United*, Plaza Los Arcos, Av Vallarta 2440, local A13, T3616-9489.

Directory

Guadalajara to the Pacific Coast

Banks There are many *casas de cambio* on López Cotilla between Independencia and 16 de Septiembre and one in Plaza del Sol. Despite what they say, *casas de cambio* close 1400 or 1500 till 1600, not continuously open 0900-1900. *American Express*, Plaza Los Arcos, Local 1-A, Av Vallarta 2440, esq Francisco García de Quevedo, about 5 blocks east of Minerva roundabout, T3630-0200, F3615-7665, open 0900-1800 for the travel agency and 0900-1430, 1600-1800 to change money. Across Prisciliano Sánchez from the Jardín San Francisco is a *Banco Inverlat* with a 24-hr ATM, which gives cash on American Express cards if you are enrolled in their Express Cash programme.

Communications Internet: a couple of places in the centre include *Imprenta Rápida*, Local J in the mall on Juárez 323, T3613-5258, US$2 per hr. *Futurama*, Pedro Moreno 570, Local 1, T3613-7318, US$2/hr. Cyber café is at *López Cotilla*, southwest corner of Parque Revolución, 1st floor, T3826-3771, US$2.50 hr, with free training if you need it, also with pizza, snacks, beer and soft drinks. *Mr Ch@t*,on Madero between Ocampo and Guerra, US$1.50/hr, printers and scanners too. *Arrobba*, Av Lázaro Cárdenas 3286, just west of intersection with López Mateos, open Mon-Sat 1000-2200, internet access US$2.20/ hr, printouts US$0.25, drinks, snacks, salads www.arrobba.com.mx **Post office**: V Carranza, just behind Palacio de Justicia, open Mon-Fri 0800-1900, Sat 0900-1300. There are also branches at the Mercado Libertad (San Juan de Dios) and at the old bus station, convenient for the cheap hotels. To send parcels abroad go to Aduana Postal in same building as main post office, open Mon-Fri 0800-1300, T3614-9002. **FedEx** has 3 outlets: Av Américas 1395, Plaza del Sol Locales 51-55, Av Washington 1129, next to Bolerama 2000, T3817-2502, F3817-2374. **UPS** at Av Américas 981, Local 19, T01-800-902-9200. **Telephone**: international collect calls can be made from any coin-box phone kiosk and direct dial calls can be made from LADA pay phones, of which there are many all over the city. You can also make long-distance calls and send faxes from *Computel* outlets: 1 in front of old bus station, 1 on Corona y Madero, opposite *Hotel Fénix*. Another chain, *Copyroyal*, charges 3 times as much for a fax to USA. *Mayahuel*, Paseo Degollado 55 has long-distance service, fax, sells Ladatel cards, postcards and maps. There is a credit card phone at Ramón Corona y Av Juárez, by cathedral. 2 USA Direct phones, 1 within and 1 beyond the customs barrier at the airport.

Cultural centres *Instituto Goethe*, Morelos 2080 y Calderón de la Barca, T3615-6147, F3615-9717, library, nice garden, newspapers. *Alliance Française*, López Cotilla 1199, Sector Juárez, T3825-2140. *The Instituto Cultural Mexicano-Norteamericano de Jalisco*, Enrique Díaz de León 300, (see below, Language schools).

Embassies and consulates *Australia*, López Cotilla 2030, T3615-7418, F3630-3479, open 0800-1330, 1500-1800. *Austria*, Montevideo 2695, Col Providencia, T3641-1834, open 0900-1330. *Belgium*, Metalúrgica 2818, Parque Industrial El Alamo, T3670-4825, F3670-0346, open Mon-Fri 0900-1400. *Brazil*, Cincinati 130, esq Nueva Orleans, Col La Aurora, next to train station, T3619-2102, open 0900-1700. *Canada*, trade officer and consul, *Hotel Fiesta Americana*, local 31, T3616-5642, F3615-8665 open 0830-1400 and 1500-1700. *Denmark*, Lázaro Cárdenas 601, 6th floor, T3669-5515, F3678-5997, open 0900-1300, 1600-1800. *Ecuador*, Morelos 685, esq Pavo, T3613-1666, F3613-1729, open 1700-2000. *El Salvador*, Fermín Riestra 1628, between Bélgica and Argentina, Col Moderna, T3810-1061, hours for visas 1230-1400, normally visas will be received the same day. *Finland*, Justo Sierra 2562, 5th floor, T3616-3623, F3616-1501, open 0830-1330. *France*, López Mateos Nte 484 entre Herrera y Cairo y Manuel Acuña, T3616-5516, open 0930-1400. *Germany*, Corona 202, T3613-9623, F3613-2609, open 1130-1400. *Guatemala*, Mango 1440, Col del Fresno, T3811-1503, open 1000-1400. *Honduras*, Ottawa 1139, Col Providencia, T3817-4998, F3817-5007, open 1000-1400, 1700-1900. *Israel*, Av Vallarta 2482 Altos, Sector Juárez, T3616-4554, open 0930-1500. *Italy*, López Mateos Nte 790-1, T3616-1700, F3616-2092, open Tue-Fri 1100-1400. *Netherlands*, Lázaro Cárdenas 601, 6th floor, Zona Industrial, T3811-2641, F3811-5386, open 0900-1400, 1630-1900. *Nicaragua*, Eje Central 1024, esq Toreros, Col Guadalupe Jardín, behind Club Atlas Chapalita, T3628-2919, open 1600-1800. *Norway*, Km 5, Antigua Carretera a Chapala 2801, Col La Nogalera, T3812-1411, F3812-1074, in the building Aceite El Gallo, open 0900-1800. *Peru*, Bogotá 2923, between Terranova and Alberta, Col Providencia, T3642-3009, open 0800-1600. *Spain*, Av Vallarta 2185, T3630-0450, F3616-0396, open 0830-1330. *Portugal*, Colimán 277, Ciudad del Sol, T3121-7714, F3684-3925. *Sweden*, J Guadalupe Montenegro 1691, T3825-6767, F3825-5559, open 0900-1400, 1600-1900. *Switzerland*, Av Revolución 707, Sector Reforma, T3617-5900, F3617-3208, open 0800-1400, 1600-1900. *UK*, Eulogio Parra 2539, T3616-0629, F3615-0197, 0900-1500, 1700-2000. *US*, Progreso 175, T3825-2700, F33626-6549.

Language schools *Centro de Estudios para Extranjeros de la Universidad de Guadalajara*, Tomás V Gómez 125, between Justo Sierra and Av México, T3616-4399, registration US$85, US$585 for 5 weeks of 4 hrs per day instruction, US$490 for 5 weeks living with a Mexican family with 3 meals a day. *The Universidad Autónoma de Guadalajara (UAG)*, a private university, offers Spanish classes through their Centro Internacional de Idiomas, T3641-7051, ext 32251, 0800-1800, at Edificio Humanidades 1st floor, on the main campus at Av Patria 1201, Col Lomas del Valle, 3a sección, US$350 for 4 weeks of 4 hrs per day instruction, 5 days a week, 7 levels of instruction, each lasting 4 weeks, US$13 per day accommodation and 3 meals with Mexican family. *The Instituto Cultural Mexicano-Norteamericano de Jalisco*, at Enrique Díaz de León 300, T3825-5838, US$440 for 6 weeks of 3 hrs per day plus 30 mins' conversation, 5 days a week, 5 levels of instruction, cultural lectures on Fri, US$18 per day to live with Mexican family with 3 meals. *Vancouver Language Centre*, Av Vallarta 1151, Col América, T3826-0944, F3825-2051 (T1-604-687-1600-Vancouver), US$150 for 1 week intensive programme. For German and French lessons see Cultural centres, above. See also National Registration Center for Study Abroad under Learning Spanish in Essentials, page 27.

Laundry Aldama 125, US$3.30 per 3 kg load (walk along Independencia towards train station, turn left into Aldama).

Medical services Dentist: *Dr Abraham Waxtein*, Av México 2309, T3615-1041, speaks English. **Doctor:** *Dr Daniel Gil Sánchez*, Pablo Neruda 3265, 2nd floor, T3642-0213, speaks English (1st cosultation, 2½ hrs, including thorough physical, US$50). **Hospitals:** good private hospitals are *Hospital del Carmen*, Tarascos 3435, Fraccionamiento Monraz (behind Plaza México), T3813-0042 (take credit cards). *Hospital San Javier*, Pablo Casals 640 (on the corner of Eulogio Parra and Acueducto), Col Providencia, T3669-0222 (take credit cards). *Hospital Angel Leaño*, off the road to Tesistán, T3834-3434, affiliated with the University (UAG). Probably the best private laboratory is the *Unidad de Patología*, Av México 2341, T3616-5410, takes credit cards. For those who cannot afford anything else there are the *Hospital Civil*, T3614-5501, and the *Nuevo Hospital Civil*, T3618-9362, F3617-7177. For *antirrábico* (rabies), T3643-1917; to receive the vaccine you have to go to Clinic 3 of the Sector Salud, T3823-3262, at the corner of Circunvalación División del Norte and Calzada Federalismo, across the street from a Telmex office, near the División del Norte Station, Line 1, *tren ligero*; you can also get an AIDS blood test here. *Sidatel* (AIDS), T3613-7546. Infectologist: *Dr J Manuel Ramírez R*, Dom Ermita 103126, Col Chapalita, by the intersection of Lázaro Cárdenas and López Mateos, T3647-7161. **Ophthalmologist:** *Dr Virginia Rivera*, Eulogia Parra 2432, near López Mateos, T3616-6637, F3616-4046, English speaking (US$25 for 1st consultation, US$20 for subsequent consultations. Consultations only on Mon, Wed, and Fri between 1600 and 1930). **Pharmacies:** 3 big chains of pharmacies are *Farmacias Guadalajara*, *Benavides* and *ABC*. *Farmacia Guadalajara* at Av Américas and Morelos has vaccines and harder-to-find drugs, T3615-5094.

Tour operators *Expediciones México Verde*, José Ma Vigil 2406, Col Italia Providencia, T/F3641-5598, rafting specialists (Actopan, Jatate, Santa María, Antigua-Pescados, Filobobos and Usumacinta rivers).

Useful services Immigration: Mexican tourist cards can be renewed at the immigration office (1st floor) in the Palacio Federal on Av Alcalde between Juan Alvarez and Hospital, across the avenue from the Santuario de Guadalupe. The Palacio Federal also contains a post office and fax service.

Chapala

Chapala town, 64 km to the southeast of Guadalajara on the northern shore of **Laguna de Chapala** (113 km long, 24-32 km wide), has thermal springs, several good and pricey hotels, three golf courses, and is a popular resort particularly with retired North Americans and Mexican day-trippers. Watch women and children play a picture-card game called *Anachuac*.

Phone code: 376
Colour map 3, grid B2
Population: 43,319

Laguna de Chapala is set in beautiful scenery. There are boats of all kinds for hire, some go to the **Isla de los Alacranes** (restaurant), and there is water-fowl shooting in autumn and winter. Most fish in the lake have been killed by pollution, but the 5-cm 'XYZ' fish, called *charales*, are a delicacy similar to whitebait. Beside the lake, four blocks east of Avenida Madero along Paseo Ramón Corona, **Parque de la Cristinia** is worth a visit, it is popular with families at weekends, and there is a swimming pool. Horses can be hired at bargain prices on the beach by the Parque. There is a market on the east side of the Zócalo with stalls selling handicrafts, places to eat, dirty public conveniences (1 peso); entrance on street behind the market. The regional **tourist office** is at Aquiles Serdán 26, T765-3141.

The water level is low because of irrigation demand, and it is getting smelly and overgrown at the edges

B *Villa Montecarlo*, west edge of town on Av Hidalgo at Calle Lourdes, T765-2120. Family rooms or suites available, beautiful grounds with palms and mangoes, all rooms have phone, bath tub, balcony overlooking lake, pool, tennis, good restaurant, tables outside under

Sleeping

Guadalajara to the Pacific Coast

massive *laurel de la India* tree. **C** *Chapala Haciendas*, Km 40, Chapala-Guadalajara highway, T765-2720. Live music Wed and Sat. Unheated pool. **C** *Nido*, Av Madero 202, close to lake, T765-2116. Brick building, old photos in reception hall, clean, cheaper without TV, accept Visa and MasterCard, good restaurant, swimming pool, parking for motorcycles beside pool. **D** *Casa de Huéspedes Palmitas*, Juárez 531, behind market. TV, hot water, bath, but run down, noisy, cockroaches.

Lots of estate agents on Hidalgo, west of Madero, with house or apartment rentals. *Chapala Realty*, Hidalgo 223, T765-3676, F765-3528. Helpful.

Trailer park 1 km from the lake between Chapala and Ajijic: *PAL*, Apdo Postal 1-1470, Guadalajara, T766-0040. US$13 daily, 1st class, pool, good.

Eating *La Leña*, Madero 236. Open air, serves *antojitos* and steaks, bamboo roof; next door is *Che Mary*. *Café Paris*, Madero 421. Sidewalk tables, popular, *comida corrida* US$3, also breakfast, sandwiches; also on Madero are *El Patio*. Good, cheap, and next door at 405A, *Los Equipales*. Where Madero reaches the lake is a restaurant/bar, *Beer Garden*. Live amplified Mexican music, dancing, tables on the beach. *Bing's* ice cream parlour next door. *La Langosta Loca*, Ramón Corona. Seafood; 1 block further is the bar *Centro Botanero Los Caballos Locos*, and 2 doors down is the *Scotland Café*. In part of a colonial house with tables on the front porch and on the back lawn, as well as inside at the bar, open until 0200 or 0300. Several seafood places close by.

Festivals *Fiesta de Francisco de Asís*, **2-3 Oct**, fireworks and excellent food served in the streets.

Transport **Local Bus**: bus station on Av Madero at corner of Miguel Martínez. Buses from Guadalajara every 30 mins, 0515-2030, 1 hr. 2 blocks south of bus station, minibuses leave every 20 mins for Ajijic, 2 pesos, and San Juan Cosalá, 3 pesos. **Taxi**: stand on Zócalo and at bus station.

Directory **Banks** *Casa de cambio* on Av Madero near *Beer Garden*, open 0830-1700, Mon-Sat. *Banco Bital*, Madero 208, next to *Hotel Nido*, ATM taking Visa, MasterCard, and cards of Cirrus and Plus networks. Nearby is a *Banamex* with ATM. *Bancomer* at Hidalgo 212 near Madero, ATM taking Visa; across the street is a *Banca Serfín*, ATM accepting Visa, MasterCard, Diner's Club, Cirrus and Plus networks. *Lloyds*, Madero 232, is a real estate office, *casa de cambio*, travel agency and *sociedad de inversión*; many Americans keep their money here. **Communications** Postal services: *Mail Box*, *Etc*, Carretera Chapala-Jocotepec 155, opposite *PAL* Trailer Park, T766-0747, F766-0775. Shipping office at Hidalgo 236 uses FedEx and DHL. Just west of it is the post office. At Hidalgo 223 is a UPS office. **Telephones**: Computel on the plaza, long distance and fax, accept Amex, MasterCard, AT&T. Also pay phones for long distance-calls on Zócalo and outside bus station. **Laundry** Zaragoza y Morelos. Dry cleaners at Hidalgo 235A, also repair shoes and other leather items. **Medical services** Clinic: *IMSS* clinic on Niños Héroes between Zaragoza and 5 de Mayo. Centro de Salud at Flavio Romero de V and Guerrero. **Red Cross**: in Parque de la Cristina.

Ajijic
Phone code: 376

Seven kilometres to the west of Chapala, a smaller, once Indian village, has an arty-crafty American colony with many retired North Americans. The village is pleasant, with cobbled streets, a pretty little plaza and many single-storey villas. One block east of the plaza at the end of Calle Parroquia is the very pretty church of San Andrés, started in 1749. On Colón, in the two blocks north of the plaza, are several restaurants, boutiques and galleries. Going south from the plaza, Colón becomes Morelos, crossing Calle Constitución and continuing some five blocks to the lake with lots of restaurants, galleries and shops. The lake shore has receded about 200 m from the original shoreline and is a bit smelly. The Way of the Cross and a Passion Play are given at Easter in a chapel high above the town. House and garden tours, Thursday 1030, 2½ hrs, US$10, in aid of Lakeside School for the Deaf, T766-1881 for reservation. Bus from Chapala or taxi US$3.20.

Sleeping **A** *Danza del Sol*, Av Lázaro Cárdenas 3260, T766-0220, ground floor. Large complex, nice units and gardens, pool. **A** *La Nueva Posada*, Donato Guerra 9, T766-1444,

The Plumed Serpent

In May-July 1923, D H Lawrence lived in Chapala, renting a house called Los Cuentales. The house still stands at Zaragoza 307, although a second floor and some modernization have been added. The church that figures in the final pages of The Plumed Serpent *is on the waterfront, its humble façade and interior now covered by a handsome veneer of carved stone. Lawrence's novel, published in 1926,* *explored Mexican society in the light of the Revolution and there are descriptions of the countryside around Lake Sayula (in reality Lake Chapala) and its 'sperm' coloured, shallow water: "It was a place with a strange atmosphere: stony, hard, broken with round, cruel hills and the many and fluted bunches of the organ-cactus behind the old house, and an ancient road trailing past, deep in ancient dust."*

F766-1344. Breakfast included, vast rooms, Canadian management, horse-riding, golf, tennis, theatre, gardens, swimming pool, restaurant, attractive outdoor seating in garden overlooking lake, colonial décor, delightful. **B** *Los Artistas Bed and Breakfast*, Constitución 105, T766-1027, F766-0066, artistas@acnet.net. 6 rooms, fireplaces, pool, living room, no credit cards, English and Spanish spoken. **C** *Laguna Bed 'n' Brunch*, Zaragoza 29, T766-1174, F766-1188. Good value, clean, comfortable, with bath, parking. **C** *Mariana*, Guadalupe Victoria 10, T766-2221. Breakfast available, weekly and monthly rates, all rooms have cable TV. Furnished apartments, swimming pool. *Mamá Chuy Club*, and *Villa Chello*, on hillside, T763-0013 for both. Good, pools, spacious, monthly rentals, good value.

Eating *Los Telares* on main street. Nice, courtyard garden. Clean *lonchería* on plaza, good simple meals, cheap, grilled chicken, used by locals and Americans. *Ajijic*, pavement café on corner of plaza. Cheap drinks, Mexican snacks, hearty *parrillada* Sat, Sun. *Los Girasoles*, 16 de Septiembre 18. Moderately priced, Mexican food in walled courtyard. *Posada Ajijic*, Morelos, opposite pier, T766-0744. Bar and restaurant, accept credit cards; pier here with fish restaurant at the end, indoor and outdoor seating and bar, used to be over water but stilts are now over dry land. *Bruno's*, on main street. Excellent steaks. Fresh fish shop on plaza and other small food shops.

Directory Medical services Clinics: *Clínica Ajijic*, Carretera Ote 33, T766-0662, with 24-hr ambulance service. **Dr Alfredo Rodríguez Quintana** (home T766-1499). 2 dentists' offices on Colón, just south of plaza. **Banks** Opposite taxi stand at Colón 29 is a *casa de cambio*. On southwest corner of plaza is Banco Promex with 2 ATMs, accept Cirrus, Plus, Visa, MasterCard, Diner's Club. *Ajijic Real Estate* at Morelos 4, T766-2077, is an authorized UPS outlet. *El Ojo del Lago* is a free English-language newspaper, available at hotels and at chapala@infosel.net.mx **Immigration** Castellanos 4, T766-2042. **Communications** On the northwest corner of the plaza is a Computel booth for long-distance phone and fax, open daily, 0800-2100. About ½ block north at Colón 24A is a *lavandería*, US$2 to wash and dry a load. Taxi stand on west side of plaza, next to it is a large map of Ajijic on one side and Chapala on the other, showing businesses and tourist sites. **Useful services** Post office: 1 block south of plaza, corner of Colón and Constitución; newspaper shop near plaza sells *Mexico City Times*; small art gallery but few cultural events advertised.

Beyond Ajijic to the west lies the small town of **San Juan Cosalá**, less prosperous than Ajijic but pleasant, with cobblestone streets and fewer gringos. There are thermal springs (varied temperatures, crowded and noisy at weekends, five pools of different sizes) at **A-B** *Hotel Balneario San Juan Cosalá* (Apdo Postal 181, Chapala, T(376)761-0302, F10222), which has private rooms for bathing with large tiled baths. Sunbathing in private rooms is also possible. Bed and breakfast in clinical modern quarters with bar/restaurant. Rooms to let at **D** *Balneario Paraíso*. Bus service from Chapala. Fish restaurants are squeezed between the carretera and the lake at **Barrenada**, 1 km east of town.

Jocotepec
Phone code 387
Population: 18,000

Beyond San Juan Cosalá at the western end of the lake is the Indian town of Jocotepec, a sizeable agricultural centre, recently invaded by more cosmopolitan types, little budget accommodation. **C** *Posada del Pescador*, cabañas on outskirts, T763-0028. With bedroom, living room, kitchen and bathroom, set in a lovely garden. The other small hotel in town **D** *Quinta*, on Matamoros 87, T763-1400, with bath. There is a local **fiesta** on 11-18 January. Jocotepec can be reached from Ajijic or from the Mexico-Guadalajara highway. Bus Chapala-Jocotepec US$2, every hour in each direction. The Indians make famous black-and-white *sarapes*.

Forty kilometres due south of Lake Chapala is the colonial town of **Mazamitla** (2,200 m), a pleasant place on the side of a range of mountains, but cold at night. It has a charming Zócalo. Hotels, **D** *Posada Alpina*, on square, T(382) 538-0104; **E** *Fiesta Mazamitla*, Reforma, T538-0050. With bath, clean. Recommended. *La Llorona County Club*, in Sierra del Tigre woods, T682-1186. Has cabañas, spa club house and driving range. About 4 km out of town is **Zona Monteverde** with pine forests, small *casitas* for rent, two good restaurants at entrance; steep hills, access only by car or taxi.

Tapalpa
Phone code: 343
Population: 15,402

About 130 km south of Guadalajara off Route 54 to Sayula and Ciudad Guzmán is Tapalpa, a very pretty village indeed. It is a 3½-hour drive from Guadalajara. The bus makes several detours into the hills to stop at small places such as Zacoalco (Sunday market) and Amacueca. The road up to Tapalpa is winding and climbs sharply and the air becomes noticeably cooler. The area is becoming increasingly popular as a place for weekend homes. The town itself, with only 11,000 inhabitants, shows ample signs of this influx of prosperity. There are two churches (one with a curious atrium) and an imposing flight of stone steps between them, laid out with fountains and ornamental lamps. Tapalpa is in cattle country; the rodeo is a popular sport at weekends.

The main street is lined with stalls, selling *sarapes* and other tourist goods on Sunday and fresh food the other days of the week. The local speciality is *ponche*, an improbable blend of tamarind and mezcal, which is sold in gallon jars and recommended only for the curious or foolhardy.

Sleeping and eating The more expensive restaurants have tables on balconies overlooking the square – the *Restaurante Posada Hacienda* (which has a US$1 cover charge) is well placed. Others are the *Buena Vista* (which also has rooms) and *La Cabaña*, and all are visited by the *mariachis*. Less grand is the **D** *Hotel Tapalpa*. With huge holes in the floor, but clean and fairly cheap. Some rooms are for hire at *Bungalows Rosita*, and *Posada Hacienda* has nice bungalows with fireplace and small kitchen.

Ciudad Guzmán
Phone code 341
Colour map 3, grid B2

Route 54 continues south through Ciudad Guzmán (formerly Zapotlán) to Colima. Ciudad Guzmán is a mid-19th-century Republican town with wide streets, a huge square, eclectic European-style architecture and a relaxed atmosphere. There are more arcades here than in most Mexican towns, and a central pedestrianised market area. It is a good base for climbing the volcanoes (see below, **Colima**).

Sleeping B *Posada San José*, M Chávez Madrueño 135, T412-0756. **B** *Tlayolan*, Javier Mina 33, T412-3317. Clean, quiet. **C** *Flamingo*, Federico del Toro 133, near main square, T412-1379. Excellent value, very modern, very clean, and quiet. Recommended. **C** *Hacienda Nuera*, Hidalgo 177, T/F412-1379. Car park. **C** *Reforma*, Reforma 77, T412-4560. **C-E** *Zapotlán*, Federico del Toro 61, on main plaza, T412-0040, F412-4783. Very reasonable, gym, tennis court. Stores luggage. **F** *Morelos*, Refugio B de Toscana 12. Run down.

Eating *Juanito*, on main square. Steak dishes, good service. *Bon Appetit*, upstairs on main square. Views of town, excellent chef called Blas Flores, large servings, Japanese, Greek and continental food. Recommended. *La Flor de Loto*, José Rodón 37C. Vegetarian, cheap soya burgers. *Pilón Burgers* next to *Hotel Flamingo*. On Prisciliano Sánchez there are stalls selling juices, yoghurts and cereals. Good cheap meals in the market (upstairs).

Climbing the volcanoes of Colima

Protected by Parque Nacional Volcán Nevado de Colima, the volcanoes of Colima (3,860 m), which erupted with great loss of life in 1941, and El Nevado de Colima (4,330 m) are to the north of the city of Colima. The former was one of the most exciting climbs in Mexico but in recent years activity has increased dramatically and a curfew radius of 11 km has been put in place, with nearby villages poised for immediate evacuation. In the first half of 2002 reports from the University of Colima said there were slow emissions of lava on the western and southeastern flanks of the volcano. The emissions are part of a period of greater activity that peaked in 1999 with explosions that sent columns of dust 8 km into the sky.

Colima volcano has been erupting periodically for 500 years with over 30 major eruptions dating as far back as 1585. This latest period of activity puts the volcano off limits for the time being – you can check on the current situation on the web at www.ucol.mx/volcan

If the situation changes the best way to tackle the volcanoes is from Ciudad Guzmán, and take a bus to the village of Fresnito (currently off limits). From there you can arrange guiding services with Sr Agustín Ibarra, who will also provide homely accommodation in the village. There are a couple of shops but only limited supplies. In the meantime, the possibility of seeing an active volcano is the main appeal. With the situation changing so quickly your best bet is to ask locally to see if any viewing sites have been set up or are recommended.

Festivals There is a fair for 2 weeks in Oct. On 1st Sun in Oct the *Festival of San José* is cele-brated. Farmers march to the church to give presents to the saint, who they believe will bring rain to help their crops grow. There is bull-running through the streets on the 1st Sat in Oct. Famous Mexican singers perform at the local theatre throughout the month.

Transport Buses to Colima 2 hrs, US$3 (*Flecha Amarilla*); to Uruapan and Morelia involves changes in Tamazula and Zamora. To Tamazula with Trans Tamaz, 1¼ hrs, US$1.40.

Directory Internet: *Podernet*, RB de Toscano 16-A, next to Hotel Morelos, T/F412-7299, 0900-1400, 1600-2000 Mon-Sat.

Colima

The capital of Colima state is a most charming and hospitable town with a 19th-cen-tury Moorish-style arcade on the main square and a strange rebuilt gothic ruin on the road beyond the **cathedral** (late 19th century). Also on the east side of the main square is the **Palacio de Gobierno**, which contains interesting murals of the history of Mexico. Behind them is the Jardín Torres Quintero, another pretty plaza but smaller. Andador Constitución is a pedestrian street, with people selling paintings, several small, attractive restaurants and a state-run artisan's shop at the north end on the corner of Zaragoza. Crossing Zaragoza, Constitución is open to traffic, and one block north on the corner with Vicente Guerrero is the church of **San Felipe de Jesús** (early 18th-century plateresque façade) where Miguel Hidalgo was at one time parish priest. There is a public swimming pool in the Parque Regional Metropolitano on Calle Degollado about five to six blocks from southwest corner of the main plaza. **Teatro Hidalgo** on the corner of Degollado, and Morelos, has a pink colonial façade and large carved wooden doors (only open during functions). Parque Núñez, five blocks east of the plaza is also attractive and twice the size of the plaza. **Tourist office** Hidalgo, on the corner of 27 de Septiembre, T312-4360, F312-8360. Good, but no information on climbing local volcanoes.

Phone code: 312
Colour map 3, grid B2
Population: 129,454
Altitude: 494 m

Museo de las Culturas de Occidente María Ahumada, Calzada Pedro Galván, in the Casa de Cultura complex deserves a visit if only for its ample collection of pre-Hispanic figurines. The region specialized in the production of pottery figures

Museums

concerned with earthly problems and not cosmological events, as in other areas. ■ *Tue-Sun 0900-1300, 1600-1800.* **Museo de la Máscara, la Danza y el Arte Popular del Occidente,** Calle 27 de Septiembre y Manuel Gallardo, exhibits folklore and handicrafts and has items for sale. The **Museo de la Historia de Colima,** on the Zócalo, has a comprehensive collection of pre-Hispanic ceramics; look out for the figurines of dogs, which were clearly being fattened for the supper table. The ceramicists attained a high level of perfection in portraying realistically the facial expressions of people engaged in their daily tasks.

Excursions **El Chanal** is an archaeological site, about 15 km to the north of Colima, which has a small pyramid with 36 sculptured figures, discovered in 1944. Another site, closer by, is **La Campana**, just off Avenida Tecnológico, taxi US$1. These largely unexcavated, extant remains include a ball court and a few temples and platforms aligned with Colima Volcano 30 km to the north. ■ *US$1.30.*

El Hervidero, 22 km southeast of Colima, is a spa in a natural lake of hot springs which reach 25°C.

Comala, a pretty colonial town with whitewashed adobe buildings near Colima, is worth a few hours' visit; bus US$0.25, 20 minutes every half an hour, from Suburbana bus station. The climate in Comala is somewhat cooler and more comfortable than Colima. The surrounding vegetation is lush with coffee plantations. In the town are two popular restaurants, *Los Portales* and *Comala*, with *mariachis* and local specialities; they are open until 1800. If you sit and drink you will usually be brought complementary food until you wilt from *mariachi* overload. Outside the town on the Colima road is the *Botanero Bucaramanga*, a bar with *botanas* (snacks) and more *mariachis*.

Sleeping **A** *Hotel América*, Morelos 162, T312-9596. A/c, cable TV, phone, largest rooms in new section, pretty interior gardens, travel agency, steam baths, good restaurant, central, friendly. **B-C** *Ceballos*, Torres Quintero 16, T312-4449, main square. A fine building with attractive *portales*, some huge rooms with a/c, clean, good food in restaurant (pricey), secure indoor parking, very good value. Highly recommended. **B** *Motel Costeño* on outskirts going towards Manzanillo, T312-1925. Recommended. **C** *Gran Hotel Flamingos*, Av Rey Colimán 18, T412-2526, near Jardín Núñez. Pleasant small rooms with fan, bath, simple, clean, breakfast expensive, disco below goes on till 0300 on Sat and Sun. **C-D** *La Merced*, Hidalgo 188, T312-6969. Pretty colonial house with rooms around patio filled with plants, entrance at Juárez 82 with reception, all rooms same price, TV, bath. Highly recommended for budget travellers. **E** *Núñez*, Juárez 88 at Jardín Núñez, T312-7030. Basic, dark, with bath. **E** *San Cristóbal*, Reforma 98, T312-0515, near centre. Run down. Many *casas de huéspedes* near Jardín Núñez. **E** *San Lorenzo*, Cuauhtémoc 149, T312-2000. Parking.

Eating Several restaurants on the Zócalo serve inexpensive meals. *El Trébol* is probably the best, on southwest corner; opposite, on Degollado 67, is nice open-air restaurant on 2nd floor on south side of plaza, overlooking it. *Los Naranjos*, Gabino Barreda 34, ½ block north of Jardín Torres Quintero. Going since 1955, nice, well known. *Samadhi*, Filomeno Medina 125, T313-2498, opposite *La Sangre de Cristo* church. Vegetarian, good, meal about US$3, good yoghurt and fruit drinks, attractive, large garden with iguanas. *Giovannis*, Constitución 58 Nte. Good pizzas and takeaway. *Centro de Nutrición Lakshmi*, Av Madero 265. Good yoghurt and wholemeal bread run by Hari Krishnas. *La Troje*, T312-2680, on southeast of town heading to Manzanillo. Good, *mariachis*, very Mexican. Try the local sweet *cocada y miel* (coconut and honey in blocks), sold in *dulcerías* (sweet shops).

Festivals *Feria* The annual fair of the region (agriculture, cattle and industry, with much additional festivity) runs from the last Sat of **Oct** until the 1st Sun of **Nov**. Traditional local potions (all the year round) include *jacalote* (from black maize and pumpkin seeds), *bate* (*chía* and honey), *tuba* (palm tree sap) and *tecuino* (ground, germinated maize).

Air Airport (CLQ) 19 km from centre, T314-4160. Flights to Mexico City and Tijuana available. **Buses** 2 bus stations on the outskirts; 'Suburbana' for buses within Colima state – urban buses and combis run to centre, US$0.50, take Routes 1 or 19, or taxi about US$1, and, 'Foránea' for buses out of state, take Route 18 from Jardín Nuñez. If going to **Uruapan** it is best to go to **Zamora** (7-8 hrs, although officially 4) and change there. **Guadalajara**: hourly service, US$12, 2½ -3 hrs, **Manzanillo**: 3 hrs, US$7, **Mexico City**: US$68.

Transport

Airline offices *Aero California*, T314-4850. *AeroMéxico*, T313-1340. *Aeromar*, T313-1340. **Banks** *Banco Inverlat* at Juárez 32 on west side of Jardín Núñez, ATM takes Amex, Visa, Diner's Club. *Casa de cambio* at Morelos and Juárez on southwest corner of same park. *Bancomer* at Madero and Ocampo 3 blocks east of plaza, ATM takes Visa and Plus. *Casa de cambio* across the street. *Banamex* 1 block south on Ocampo at Hidalgo, has an ATM. **Communications** Internet: cyber café in *Plaza Country* on Av Tecnológico, 15 blocks north of centre, Mon-Fri 0900-2200, Sat-Sun 1000-2200, US$1.90 per hr. **Post office:** Av Francisco I Madero and Gen Núñez, northeast corner of Jardín Núñez. **Telecommunication:** Computel at Morelos 234 on south side for long-distance phone and fax, and at bus station, open 0700-2200, accepts Visa, MasterCard, Amex and AT&T cards. Fax not always in use. **Laundry** *Lavandería Shell*, 27 de Septiembre 134, open 0900-2000, inexpensive, quick. **Medical services** Hospital: *Hospital Civil*, T312-0227. **Pharmacy:** *Farmacia Guadalupana* on northeast corner of Jardín Torres Quintero behind cathedral. Another pharmacy on northeast corner of Zócalo. **Red Cross:** T312-1451.

Directory

Manzanillo

A beautiful, three-hour hilly route runs from Colima to Manzanillo, which has become an important port on the Pacific, since a spectacular 257-km railway has been driven down the sharp slopes of the Sierra Madre through Colima. A new fast toll road has been opened between Guadalajara and Manzanillo, good, double-laned in some sections, but total cost US$19 in tolls. The tolls from Mexico City

Phone code: 314
Colour map 3, grid B1
Population: 124,014

Manzanillo centre

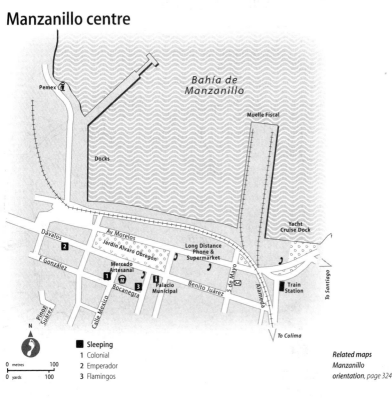

Bahía de Manzanillo

Pemex

Muelle Fiscal

Docks

Yacht Cruise Dock

Dávalos

Av Morelos

F González

Jardín Alvaro Obregón

Long Distance Phone & Supermarket

Mercado Artesanal

Bocanegra

Palacio Municipal

Benito Juárez

5 de Mayo

Alameda

Train Station

To Santiago

Piñoz Juárez

Calle Mexico

N

To Colima

0 metres 100
0 yards 100

Sleeping
1 Colonial
2 Emperador
3 Flamingos

Related maps
Manzanillo
orientation, page 324

Guadalajara to the Pacific Coast

to Manzanillo total US$66. Activities for tourists at Manzanillo, which is not a touristy town, include deep-sea fishing (US$250 to hire a boat for a day, with beer, *refrescos* and *ceviche*), bathing, and walking in the hills. There is a good snorkelling trip starting at the beach of *Club Las Hadas* (see below), US$40 includes soft drinks and equipment. The water is clear and warm, with lots to see. Trips two to three times daily, last one at 1230. There is a bullring on the outskirts on the road to Colima. The best beach is the lovely crescent of Santiago, 8 km north, but there are three others, all of which are clean, with good swimming. **Tourist offices** Boulevard Miguel de la Madrid 4960, T333-2277, F333-1426, halfway along Playa Azul. **Tourist helpline** (*Angeles Verdes*): T336-6600.

Sleeping

■ *on map below*
Price codes:
see inside front cover

LL *Las Hadas Golf Resort and Marina*, Península de Santiago, T331-0101, F331-0121, www.brisas.com.mx A Moorish fantasy ("architecture crowned by perhaps the most flamboyantly and unabashedly phallic tower ever erected, and the palpable smell of money; should on no account be missed"). **AL** *La Posada*, Calz Lázaro Cárdenas 201, T333-1899 near the end of Las Brisas peninsula. English manager, German wife, beautifully designed rooms carved into the very rock of an outcrop. **B** *Las Brisas Vacation Club*, Av Lázaro Cárdenas 207, T333-2716. Some a/c, good restaurant.

At **Santiago beach** **B** *Playa de Santiago*, T333-0055. Good, but food expensive. **C** *Anita*, T333-0161. Built in 1940, has a certain funky charm and it is clean and on the beach. **C** *Marlyn*, T333-0107. 3rd-floor rooms with balcony overlooking the beach, a bargain. Recommended.

At the port **B** *Colonial*, México 100, T332-1080. Good restaurant, friendly, avoid rooms above the record shop (very loud music). **D** *Casa de Huéspedes Posada Jardín*, Cuauhtémoc. Reasonable. **D** *Emperador*, Dávalos 69, T332-2374. Good value, good, cheap

Manzanillo orientation

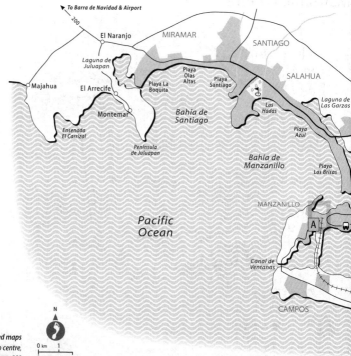

Related maps
A Manzanillo centre,
page 323

restaurant. **D** *Flamingos*, 10 de Mayo and Madero, T332-1037. With bath, quite good. **E** *Casa de Huéspedes Central*, behind bus station. With bath, fan, OK.

Camping At Miramar and Santiago beaches. 4½ km north of Manzanillo is *Trailer Park El Palmar*, T333-5533. With a large swimming pool, run down, very friendly, coconut palms, US$13 for 2. *La Marmota* trailer park, at junction of Highways 200 and 98. Cold showers, bathrooms, pool, laundry facilities, US$8 per car and 2 people.

Willy's Seafood Restaurant, Playa Azul, on the beach. French owner, primarily seafood, **Eating** some meat, very good, 3 courses with wine US$15 per person. *Portofino's*, Blvd M de la Madrid, Km 13. Italian, very good pizza; next door is *Plaza de la Perlita*. Good food, live music; also Italian, *Carlos and Charlie's*, Blvd M de la Madrid Km 6.9, on the beach. Seafood and ribs, great atmosphere. Good but not cheap food at the 2 *Huerta* restaurants, the original near the centre, and *Huerta II* near the Las Hadas junction. *Johanna*, opposite bus station entrance. Good food, cheap.

Local Car hire: *National*, Km 9.5, Carreterra Manzanillo-Santiago, T333-0611. *Budget*, **Transport** same road, T333-1445.

Long distance Air: frequent flights from airport (ZLO) (T333-1119) 19 km from town, to Mexico City and Guadalajara. Other domestic destinations: Chihuahua, Monterrey, Puerto Vallarta and Saltillo. US destinations: Los Angeles.

Buses: to **Miramar**: US$0.50, leave from J J Alcaraz, 'El Tajo'. Several to **Guadalajara**: 6 hrs, US$16. To **Mexico City**: 19 hrs, 35. **Barra de Navidad**, 1½ hrs, US$3.50; **Colima**: 3 hrs, US$7.

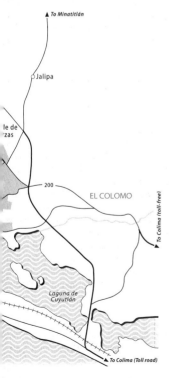

Down the coast to **Lázaro Cárdenas** and crossroads for Playa Azul (see page 302) with Autobus de Occidente or Galeana, 7 hrs. To **Acapulco**: US$11. To **Puerto Vallarta**: 1st class with Trans Cihuatlán at 0800 and 1200, 4½ hrs. Bus terminal in Av Hidalgo outside centre, local buses go there. Taxi to centre US$1.50.

Airlines *Aeromar*, T333-0151; *Aerolitoral*, **Directory** T333-2424; *Mexicana*, T332-1972; *Aero California* (Boulevard Miguel de La Madrid Km 13.5), T334-1414. **Medical services** *Hospital Civil*, T332-4161. **Red Cross**: T336-5770.

Southeast of Manzanillo is **Tecomán** **South of** (Phone code: 313, Population: 99,296), **Manzanillo** which has a delightful atmosphere. **B-C** *Gran Fénix*, Javier Mina 460, T324-0791. Larger rooms have a/c, smaller rooms are noisier but hotel is recommended; **D-E** *Yeza*, Lázaro Cárdenas 59. Very clean, spacious rooms in a quiet spot on the corner from the bus station, the owner's son speaks English; unnamed *pensión* on the corner of the Zócalo, if you face the church it is on your left, east. Try the local deep-fried *quesadillas* (*tortillas* filled with cheese). To the west of Tecomán is the small coastal resort of **Cuyutlán**, on the fast

Guadalajara to the Pacific Coast

highway between Colima and Manzanillo. It has a pleasant, black-sand beach and **C** *Hotel Bucanero*, near the north end of the front, T326-4005. Clean rooms, good restaurant, games room and souvenir shop. Swimming here is excellent and umbrellas and wooden walkways protect feet against the hot sun and sand. The coast road continues southeast to the unspoilt fishing village of **Boca de Apiza** (no hotels but some seafood restaurants). There is abundant bird life at the mouth of the river.

Local police warn against camping in the wild in this area; it is not safe The road continues to Playa Azul, Lázaro Cárdenas, Zihuatanejo and Acapulco: for 80 km beyond Manzanillo it is good, then Route 200, through paved, in some parts is in poor condition and for long stretches you cannot see the ocean. In other places there are interesting coastal spots. About one hour south of Tecomán is the village of **San Juan de Lima**, on a small beach; two or three hotels, the furthest south along the beach is very basic, **D**. There are a couple of restaurants, one unnamed, about 200 m from the hotels, serving excellent red snapper and shrimp dishes. Halfway between Tecomán and Playa Azul is another uncrowded beach, **Maruata**, where you can ask the restaurant owner if you can camp or sling a hammock (see page 302).

Tecolotlán & Autlán Another road to Manzanillo, Route 80, goes from Guadalajara to the coast, passing the outskirts of several pleasant towns with cobbled streets. The road is fairly busy as it plummets from the Sierra Madre to the Pacific. **Tecolotlán**, 200 km northeast of Melaque, is a small town whose Zócalo is 1 km from the highway along rough cobbles. It has a few hotels, eg **D** *Albatros*, one block east of the Zócalo. Modern, clean, with bath, TV. Highly recommended. **Autlán de Navarro**, 115 km from Melaque, is a clean, modern, mid-sized town, with public phones in the Zócalo and several hotels (eg **D** *Palermo*. With bath, pleasant, clean). **Casimiro Castillo**, 74 km from Melaque, is a small town with three hotels, including **E** *Costa Azul*.

Melaque
Phone code: 315
Colour map 3, grid B1

The bay is one of the most beautiful on the Pacific Coast, but San Patricio Melaque is very commercialized, crowded at holiday times and targets long-stay residents. An earthquake in 1994 has left a few modern buildings in ruins. The beach is long, shelving and sandy with a rocky coast at each end and pelicans diving for fish. The waves are not so big at San Patricio beach. The week leading up to St Patrick's Day is **fiesta** time, when there are nightly fireworks, dances, rodeos, etc.

Tourist office Sonora 15, T357-0100, but better to visit Mari Blanca Pérez at *Paraíso Pacífico Tours* in *Hotel Barra de Navidad*, T355-5122, F355-5303, open 0900-1400 May to December and 0900-1800 in winter, very helpful.

Sleeping **L-B** *Villas Camino del Mar*, San Patricio Melaque, T355-5207, F355-5498. Rooms or villas on beach, 2 pools, discounts for long stays, up to 50% for a month, including tax, many US visitors stay all winter. **AL** *Hacienda Melaque*, Morelos 49, T355-5334. Tennis court, kitchen, pool. **B** *Royal Costa Sur*, Bahía de Cuastecomate, 2½ km from crossroads at northern edge of town, T/F355-5085. Tennis court, private beach. **C** *Flamingo*, Vallarta 19. Clean with fan, balconies, water coolers on each floor. Opposite is **D** *Santa María*, T357-0338. Friendly. Recommended. **D** *Posada Pablo de Tarso*, Gómez Farías 408, T357-0117, facing beach. Pretty, galleried building, tiled stairs, antique-style furniture. **D** *San Nicolás*, Gómez Farías 54, T357-0066, beside *Estrella Blanca* bus station. Noisy but clean. Off season, very pleasant. **C** *Monterrey*, Gómez Farías 27, T357-0004, on beach. Clean, fan, bath, parking, superb view. **D** *Hidalgo*, Hidalgo 7 off Gómez Farías, T355-5045. Fan, cheapest. OK. *Trailer Park La Playa*, San Patricio Melaque, T357-0065, in the village, on beach. US$13 for car and 2 people, full hook-up, toilets, cold showers. Follow the 'Melaque' signs and at the end of the main road is a free camping place on the beach at the bay, very good, easily accessible for RVs, popular for vehicles and tents.

Eating *Restaurant Los Pelícanos*, on beach. Overpriced. Many restaurants on beach but most close at 1900. *Koala's at the Beach*, Alvaro Obregón 52, San Patricio, 2 blocks from *Camino del Mar*. Small, good, great food in walled garden compound off dusty street. Canadian/Australian run. *Restaurant Alcatraz*, good food.

Directory Communications *Cybernet* between beachfront and Gómez Farías, near *Hotel Monterrey*.

The village of Barra de Navidad, commercial but still pleasant, has a monument to the Spanish ships that set out in 1548 to conquer the Philippines. Barra is 1½ hours from Manzanillo; the beach is beautiful, very good for swimming, but at holiday times it is very crowded and a lot less pleasant. The Colorín liquor store, opposite *Hotel Barra de Navidad*, changes money, sells stamps and has a mailbox. You can also change money in Cihuatlán (buses every 30 minutes). Bus to Manzanillo, US$2.50, 1½ hours. There is a book exchange on Mazatlán between Sinaloa and Guanajuato. The **tourist office** is at Jalisco 67, T355-5100. ■ *Mon-Fri 0900-1700*.

Barra de Navidad
Phone code: 315
Colour map 3, grid B1

Sleeping B *Tropical*, López de Legazpi 96, T357-0020, on beach. Seedy but pleasant. **B** *Sand's*, Morelos 24, T357-0018 (Barra). Bar, clean, some kitchen units, good value, pool. Opposite is **C** *Delfín*, Morelos 23, T357-0068. Very clean, pool, hot water. Highly recommended. **C** *Hotel Barra de Navidad*, López de Legaspi 250, T357-0122. With balcony on beach, or bungalows where you can cook, pool, very good value. **D** *Hotel Jalisco*, Av Jalisco 91. Hot water, safe but not very clean, and noisy, nightclub next door with music till 0300. **D** *Marquez*, T355-5304. Recommended. **D** *San Lorenzo*, Av Sinaloa 87, T357-0139. Very clean, hot water, friendly staff, good restaurant opposite. **E** *Posada Pacífico*, Mazatlán 136, 1 street behind bus terminal. Clean, fan, friendly, good restaurant opposite. **E** *Casa de Huéspedes Caribe*, Av Sonora. Fan, friendly, family-run. Ask about **camping** on beach.

Eating Fish restaurants, eg *Antonio* on beach. Many good restaurants on the Pacific side, a couple of good restaurants on the lagoon side. *Velero's*. Delicious snapper and good views. *Ambar*, Veracruz 101. Half of menu vegetarian, real coffee, good breakfast and crêpes, closed lunchtime. Highly recommended. *Pacífico*. Very good barbecued shrimp, and good breakfasts. *Seamaster*, on beach. Best ribs. *Cactus Café*. Best burgers. *Paty's*. Good, cheap, especially for barbecued chicken.

Pretty seaside villages near Barra de Navidad include **La Manzanilla**, 14 km north of Routes 200/80 junction (**D** *Posada de Manzanilla*. Nice. Recommended. *Posada del Cazador*, T70330). Camping possible. South of the village at the end of Los Cocos beach is the **B** hotel and RV trailer park, *Paraíso Miramar*, T321-60434. Pool, gardens, palm huts, restaurant, bar. Three kilometres north of the beach is **Boca de Iguanas** with two trailer parks: *Boca de Iguanas*, US$7 per person, vehicle free, hook-ups, cold showers, toilets, laundry facilities, clean, pleasant location; and *Tenacatita*, US$9 with hook-ups, US$7 without, cold showers, toilet, laundry facilities, restaurant. For both places take the unpaved road from Highway 200 to the abandoned *Hotel Bahía de Tenacatita*; at the T-junction, turn right, pass the hotel, and the campsites are about 500 m further on the left. This place is nothing to do with the village of **Tenacatita**, which has a perfect beach complete with palm huts and tropical fish among rocks – good for snorkelling (two sections of beach, the bay and oceanside). **D** *Hotel* (no name) in village near beach, or you can sleep on the beach under a palm shelter, but beware mosquitoes.

Route 200, a little rough in places, links Barra de Navidad with Puerto Vallarta, the second largest resort in Mexico. There are beaches and hotels on this route. In Perula village at the north end of **Chamela** beach, **C** *Hotel Punta Perula*, T(322) 337-0190, on beach, Mexican style; *Villa Polonesia Trailer Park*, US$12 for car and two people, full hook-ups, hot showers, on lovely beach (follow signs from Route 200 on unmade road). Recommended. Restaurant on road to trailer park, clean, good food. Pemex at Chamela is closed, no other for miles. At 103 km south of Puerto Vallarta and 12 km inland, at the town of **Tomatlán** (not to be confused with Boca de Tomatlán, on the coast), are a few modest hotels (eg **E** *Posada Carmelita*, with bath, clean). Two hours south of Puerto Vallarta is the luxury resort **LL** *Las Alamandas*, T(322) 285-5500. Beautiful beach, health club, horse-riding, tennis, etc. The resort is 1 km south of Puente San Nicolás on Route 200, turn left towards

North of Barra de Navidad

Guadalajara to the Pacific Coast

the coast at sign to Quemaro. Owned by Isobel Goldsmith, it is very exclusive, has been featured in several magazines for the clientele it attracts and reservations should be made in advance. The excellent **L** *Hotel Careyes* is en route, and several others, **L** *El Tecuán*, Carretera 200, Km 32.5, T333-70132. Lovely hotel, gorgeous beach, mediocre bar/restaurant, pool. Highly recommended.

Puerto Vallarta

Phone code 322
Colour map 3, grid B1
Population: 183,741

A highly commercialized sun-and-sand holiday resort marred by congestion and widespread condominium developments, Puerto Vallarta also has its advantages. The stepped and cobbled streets of the old centre are picturesque, accommodations and restaurants are varied enough to suit everybody, there is much good hiking in the surrounding hills and watersports and diving are easily accessible. Increasingly it has become a base for excursions and for special interest trips including ornithology and whale-watching.

Ins and outs

Getting there   The Aeropuerto Internacional Ordaz (PVR), 6 km north of the town centre, is served by national and international airlines with flights to destinations in Mexico, the US and Europe (mostly package). The long-distance bus station, almost directly opposite the airport, is a 40-minute ride from town. Puerto Vallarta is on the Carretera Costera, Route 200, which runs south along the Pacific Coast, all the way to the Guatemalan border. If you want to get a taxi into town they're half the price if you get them from across the main road outside the airport.

Getting around   Taxis are expensive in Puerto Vallarta. Local buses and *colectivos* operate on most routes north to Nuevo Vallarta and beyond, and south to Mismaloya and Boca de Tomatlán. Buses marked 'Centro' go through town, while those marked 'Túnel' take the bypass.
   Tourist office   Morelos 28-A; in the government building on the main square, helpful; T223-0744. Tourist news, tribuna@ pnet.puerto.net.mx

Greater Puerto Vallarta is drawn out along some 25 km of the west-facing curve of the deeply incised Banderas Bay. It can be split into six sections: **North Central**, the oldest, with the main plaza, cathedral and seafront Malecón as well as an uninviting strip of pebble/sand beach; **South Central**, across the Río Cuale, is newer but similarly packed with shops and restaurants and bordered by the fine, deep sand of Playa de los Muertos; **South Shore**, where the mountains come to the sea, there are several cove beaches and a scattering of big hotels; **North Hotel Zone**, a long stretch from town towards the cruise ship terminal and the airport, with mediocre beaches, many big hotels and several commercial centres; **Marina Vallarta**, further north, with a dazzling array of craft, a golf course, smart hotels and poor quality beach – you can't walk far because of condominiums built around the marina; **Nuevo Vallarta**, 18 km north of centre, with golf course and marina, in the neighbouring state of Nayarit (time difference), where modern, all-inclusive hotels are strung along miles of white sand beach, far from amenities.

   Most travellers will find the central area the most convenient to stay in; its two halves are divided by the Río Cuale and a narrow island where souvenir shops, cafés and the museum are located. The most dramatic beach in the centre is Playa de los Muertos, apparently named after the murderous activities of pirates in the late 16th century, although the 'dead' tag could apply equally to the fierce undertow or possibly to the pollution that affects this corner of the bay. The authorities are trying to get people to use a sunnier sobriquet: 'Playa del Sol'. Conchas Chinas is probably the best beach close to town, being quiet and clean (at any holiday time, though, every beach is packed); a cobblestone road leads to Conchas Chinas from Route 200, just after *Club Alexandra*.

Excursions

During the rainy season, June-September, some trips are not possible. From November-April, humpback whale watching is organized. A recommended trip including snorkelling is with John Pegueros, who owns the schooner *Elias Mann*. Contact him at Lázaro Cárdenas 27, Apdo Postal 73, Bucerías, Nayarit, CP63732, T(329) 298-0060, F298-0061. Tickets from Marina Vallarta, US$60, includes some meals, starts 0800. See also Tour operators, page 334.

Playa de los Tomates is a 25-minute walk north of the marina, with buses every hour from the marina, where there is good bird-watching, half a dozen beach restaurants and very few tourists. You can hire a boat to go to the mangroves – too peaceful for tour operators to get involved. Forty kilometres northeast of Puerto Vallarta is the inland village of **Las Palmas**, a typical though unremarkable town (buses every

Puerto Vallarta centre

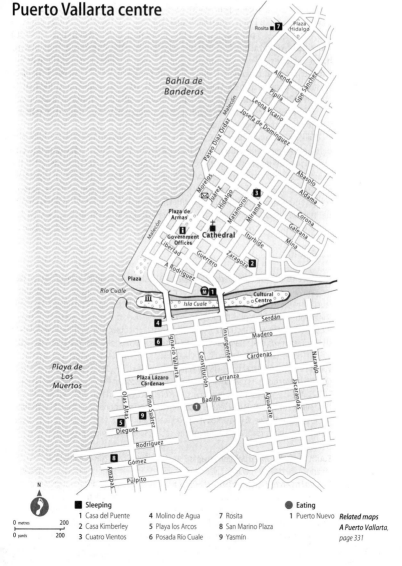

0 metres 200
0 yards 200

N

Sleeping
1 Casa del Puente
2 Casa Kimberley
3 Cuatro Vientos
4 Molino de Agua
5 Playa los Arcos
6 Posada Río Cuale
7 Rosita
8 San Marino Plaza
9 Yasmín

Eating
1 Puerto Nuevo

Related maps
A Puerto Vallarta,
page 331

Guadalajara to the Pacific Coast

30 minutes, takes one hour 10 minutes). On the way is the workers' *pueblo* of **Ixtapa**, established by the Montgomery Fruit Co in 1925. Near here are post-Classic stone mounds scattered over a wide area.

Ten kilometres south of Puerto Vallarta, along the coast road is **Mismaloya**, where John Huston made *Night of the Iguana* with Richard Burton. It is a lovely beach backed by a steep subtropical valley, even though the *La Jolla Mismaloya* hotel looms over the sands. The beach is clean and you can hire umbrellas and chairs for the day, US$1; beware of the undertow at low tide. The film set has been developed as *Iguana Park*. There are many condominiums on the north side. You can go horse-riding up the valley with Victor, of Rancho Manolo, beside the road bridge, T80018. **Boca de Tomatlán**, 4 km further south, is a quaint and rather down-at-heel fishing village at the river estuary. There are apartments to rent, simple restaurants, a dirty beach and a footbridge across the river. Further round the bay is **Yelapa**, an Indian village with a waterfall, now commercialized with entertainment ranging from live music to rodeo. Tourist water taxi from pier (Los Muertos), US$12 return, leaves 1030, 1100. From fisherman's quay on Malecón (by *Hotel Rosita*, opposite *McDonald's*) US$5 one way, leaves 1130. From Boca de Tomatlán (bus, US$0.30) water taxi from beach is US$3.50 one way, leaves 1030. Organized tours may be better value for anyone wanting to combine such activities as snorkelling at Los Arcos en route. **B** *Lagunitas*. Cabin hotel with pool. *Tino's Oasis*. An excellent place to stay, American owned, cheap. Alternatively stay with Mateo and Elenita, **C**, including breakfast, visit their waterfall. Camping available 30 minutes' walk up valley, US$4 per person, in beautiful setting, owners Beto and Felicidad (ask for Felicidad's home-made *tortillas*, 'the best in Mexico').

Walk or mountain bike up the Río Cuale valley, through magnificent hills with dense subtropical vegetation, some bathing pools, many birds, a few *ranchitos* and *pueblecitos*. To begin, walk to the eastern extremity of Lázaro Cárdenas, cross the wide bridge and turn sharp right; walk along cobbled street with river on right. Pass Colonia de Buenos Aires and water purification plant; later cross suspension footbridge and continue up rough track with river on left. Two kilometres later, recross the now crystalline Río Cuale via stepping stones. Go as far as you like. 54 km onward is the rustic, ex-mining (silver, gold) village of **Cuale**, with cobbled streets.

Essentials

Sleeping
■ on maps, page 331 and opposite
Price codes: see inside front cover

North Central L *Casa Kimberley*, Zaragoza 445, T222-1336. Former home of Richard Burton and Elizabeth Taylor, 10 rooms full of memorabilia of the actors, breakfast included, much cheaper in low season. **AL** *Casa del Puente*, by bridge opposite market, T222-0749. Suites with kitchen in a private villa suspended above river, delightful, book months ahead. **B** *Cuatro Vientos*, Matamoros 520, T222-0161. Up steep cobbled street from church, lots of steps, great views, restaurant, plunge pool, breakfast included. **C** *Rosita*, Paseo Díaz Ordaz 901, at north end of Malecón, T223-2000, F32142, hrosita@zonavirtual.com.mx Puerto Vallarta's original holiday hotel (1948) with pool, on town beach, excellent value and location. Recommended. Its sister hotel 2 blocks north is *Pescador*, Paraguay 1117, esq Uruguay T/F222-1884, hpescador@pvnet.com.mx **D** *Hotel Escuela*, Hidalgo 300, corner Guerrero, T222-4910, F223-0294, is where they teach trainee hotel personnel. A bit clinical, with street noise, but good value. **E** unmarked *hospedaje* at Allende 257, esq Guadalupe, T222-0986. US owner, Isabel Jordan, also has rooms and cabañas in Yelapa, more expensive.

South Central L *Meza del Mar*, Amapas 380, T222-4888, F222-2308. Perched high above Los Muertos beach with slow lifts, balconies remain in shade, small pool, all-inclusive packages. **L** *Playa Los Arcos*, Olas Altas 380, T222-0583, F222-2418. Good location for restaurants, undersized pool terrace overflows to Los Muertos beach. **AL** *Buenaventura*, Av México 1301, T222-3737, F222-3546. On shore, fringe of centre, lively holiday hotel. **AL** *Molina de Agua*, Ignacio L Vallarta 130, T222-1957, F222-6056. Cabins in pleasant wooded glade on bank of river, a/c, good service, 2 pools. Recommended. **AL** *San Marino Plaza*, Rodolfo Gómez 111,

T222-3050, F222-2431, sanmarino@omegaresorts.com A/c, pleasant, friendly, standard holiday package, compact pool terrace adjoins Los Muertos beach. **A** *Casa Corazón*, Amapas

Puerto Vallarta

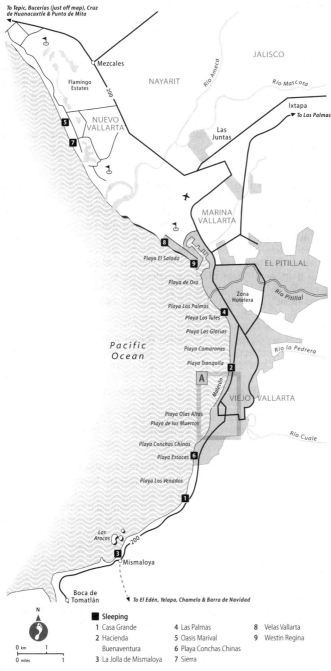

To Tepic, Bucerías (just off map), Cruz de Huanacaxtle & Punta de Mita

Mezcales

JALISCO

NAYARIT

Río Ameca

Río Mascota

Flamingo Estates

200

NUEVO VALLARTA

Las Juntas

Ixtapa
To Las Palmas

MARINA VALLARTA

EL PITILLAL

Playa El Salado

Playa de Oro

Zona Hotelera

Río Pitillal

Playa Las Palmas

Playa Los Tules

Pacific Ocean

Playa Las Glorias

Playa Camarones

Río la Pedrera

Playa Tranquila

Malecón

A

VIEJO VALLARTA

Playa Olas Altas

Playa de los Muertos

Río Cuale

Playa Conchas Chinas

Playa Estacas

Playa Los Venados

200

Los Arocos

Mismaloya

Boca de Tomatlán

To El Edén, Yelapa, Chamela & Barra de Navidad

N

0 km   1
0 miles   1

■ Sleeping
1 Casa Grande
2 Hacienda Buenaventura
3 La Jolla de Mismaloya
4 Las Palmas
5 Oasis Marival
6 Playa Conchas Chinas
7 Sierra
8 Velas Vallarta
9 Westin Regina

Related maps
A Puerto Vallarta
centre, page 329

Guadalajara to the Pacific Coast

326, T/F222-1371. Hard to find, US-owned hideaway on steep slope down to Los Muertos beach, overpriced but 3 big rooms on top terrace with spectacular views worth the premium, including big breakfast. **B** *Gaviotas*, behind *Eloisa*, Madero 154, Parque Lázaro Cárdenas, T222-1500, F222-5516. Faintly colonial, balcony access, glimpses of sea. **B** *Posada Río Cuale*, Aquiles Serdán 242, near new bridge, T/F222-0450. Small pool in front garden, not very private, nice, colonial-style rooms. **C** *Gloria del Mar*, Amapas 115, T222-5143, by Playa de los Muertos. Charmless but clean, convenient holiday base, small rooms.

D *Belmar*, Insurgentes 161, T/F222-0572. Spartan, ill-lit but friendly, on main road near buses. **D** *Yasmín*, Basilio Badillo 168, T222-0087. A claustrophobic courtyard arrangement behind *Café Olla*, good value, noisy till at least 2300. There are several cheaper hotels grouped on Francisco I Madero, west of Insurgentes: **D** *Azteca*, No 473, T222-2750. Probably best of this group. **D** *Villa del Mar*, No 440, T222-0785. Also satisfactory. **D-E**, and within a few doors are: *Cartagena*, No 428, *Lina*, No 376, T222-1661. With bath, no hot water, run down, rooms on street noisy. *Bernal*, No 423, T222-3605. Friendly, large rooms, fan, good showers. Recommended. Cheapest is *El Castillo* at No 273, all convenient for restaurants, a few blocks from long-distance buses.

North Hotel Zone **L** *Las Palmas Beach Resort*, Blvd Medina Ascencio, Km 2.5, T224-0650, F224-0543. Castaway-on-a-desert-island theme, all rooms with sea view. **AL** *Hacienda Buenaventura*, Paseo de la Marina, T224-6667, F224-6242. Modern, with colonial influence, pleasant pool, is nicest in zone but 100 m to beach and on main road, discounts out of season. **AL** *Los Pélicanos*, T224-1010, F224-1111. Small scale, rooms enclose central quadrangle with pool, 100 m to beach. **AL** *Plaza Las Glorias*, T224-4444, F224-6559. Attractive white, low-rise, breezy beachfront location. **AL** *Suites del Sol*, Francia y Liverpool, T224-2541, F224-2213. Above offices at busy junction on wrong side of road for beach, jumbled open-plan public rooms, tiny pool, large rooms. Cheap hotels are scarce here: **C** *Motel Costa del Sol*, T222-2055. 300 m north of *Sheraton* on the opposite side.

Marina Vallarta **LL** *Westin Regina*, T221-1100, F221-1141. Vibrant colours, imaginative lighting, much cascading water, lush gardens. **LL** *Velas Vallarta*, T221-0751, F221-0755. Moorish touches to big, part timeshare hotel with verdant gardens. **LL-AL** *Omega Nautilus and Marina*, T221-1015, F221-8906, nautilus@omegaresorts.com Olympic pool and dive tank in this resort. Most rooms have private balcony or patio. **AL** *Plaza Iguana*, T221-0880, F221-0889. Small pool adjoins marina promenade, 10 mins' walk to beach.

Nuevo Vallarta **LL** *Sierra*, T(322) 297-1300, F(322) 297-0800. Colourful building-block hotel, smart, modern, all-inclusive. **L** *Oasis Marival*, T(322) 297-0100, F(322) 297-0160. More established and sedate than competitors here, all-inclusive.

Southern shore **LL** *La Jolla de Mismaloya*, Km 11.5, T228-0660, F228-0500. Romantic though overdeveloped setting on filmset beach. **L** *Majahuitas Resort*, between Quimixto and Yelapa beaches, T322-15808, run by Margot and Lirio González. Including breakfast and dinner, 3 guesthouses, more planned, on cove, sandy beach, rustic furniture, solar energy, horse-riding and snorkelling available, 30% of profits go to indigenous community of Chacala. **AL** *Casa Grande*, Playa Palo María, T222-1023. Hulking twin towers of all-inclusive fun on crummy beach, 4 km south of centre. **AL** *Playa Conchas Chinas*, Km 2.5 road to Barra de Navidad, T/F221-5770, about 1 km before *Camino Real*, on west side of road. Spacious rooms with kitchenettes and ocean views.

Camping 2 trailer parks: *Tacho*, on road to Pipala, opposite Marina. 60 spaces but spacious, US$14.50. *Puerto Vallarta*, north of centre, just north of bypass then east 2 blocks. Popular. Also at fishing village of Yelapa, best reached by boat from *Hotel Rosita* at 1130: camp under *palapas* (shelters), about US$4 per person.

South Centre *Posada de Roger*, Basilio Badillo 237. Good courtyard dining, mainly Mexican menu, cheapish. *Café Olla*, lower end Basilio Badillo. Good-value Mexican and barbecue in cramped open-fronted dining room, queues wait for more than an hour in high season, demonstrating a lack of imagination rather than discerning palate. *Puerto Nuevo*, on Badillo. Expensive but good food. *Buengusto*, Rodríguez. Excellent home-cooked Mexican meals. *A Page in the Sun* (café), Olas Altas opposite *Los Arcos* hotel on corner. Coffee is excellent, cakes home-made, second-hand bookshop. *Daiquiri Dick's*, Olas Altas 314, T222-0566. Restaurant and bar open for breakfast, lunch and dinner, opposite Los Muertos beach, excellent cooking, classical harp and guitar music Sun 1300-1500, about US$18-20 per person. *Las Palapas*, on the beach near Playa de los Muertos. Good food, service, value, décor and atmosphere. *Felipe's*, Prolongación Insurgentes 466, Colonia Alta Vista, T222-3820. Beautiful view over town from large balcony, good food and service, can share 1 portion between 2. *Los Arbolitos*, east end of Lázaro Cárdenas, 3 balconied floors above river. Mexican, good atmosphere, moderate prices. *El Dorado*, *palapa* restaurant on Playa de los Muertos. Inexpensive and attractive surroundings but touristy and besieged by belligerent *chiclet* vendors, 3rd-rate musicians, etc. *La Fuente del Puente*, riverfront at old bridge, opposite market. Mexican, colourful, good music, good-value meals but drinks expensive. *Jazz Café/Le Bistro*, by the bridge on Insurgentes. Garden, bamboo, beside river, pleasant for coffee and classical music (piano or harp) in morning, crowded and expensive in evening, many vegetarian dishes, clean. *Café Maximilian*, Olas Altas 380-B, rear part of *Playa Los Arcos*, open 1600-2300, closed Sun. Huge Austrian owner, about US$22 per person for meal with wine, clean, efficient, busy, some tables on pavement. Recommended.

North Centre *Pepe's Tacos*, on Honduras, opposite Pemex at northern end of downtown. Cheap, ethnic and delicious in spartan pink/white dining room, open all night. *Juanita's*, Av México 1067. Attracts locals as well as value-seeking gringos, good. *Gaby*, Mina. Small, family-run, eat in garden, excellent food, cheap and clean. *Las Margaritas*, Juárez 512. Forget the queues at the popular gringo restaurants, this one is excellent, moderately priced, cosmopolitan and curiously under-patronized, colonial-style courtyard. Recommended. *Café Amadeus*, Miramar 271, up steps from Guerrero. Classical music, books, board games in delightful whitewashed rooms or balcony perched above old town, coffee, delectable cakes. Recommended. *La Dolce Vita*, midway along Malecón. Hugely popular (queues) Italian and pizza place favoured by package tourists. *Rico Mac Taco*, Av México, corner Uruguay. Busy, cheap and widely popular eatery.

Carlos O'Brian's, Malecón and Andale, Olas Altas. Attracts a motley crowd of revellers and starts hopping after 2200. Martini types head for *Christine*, at *Hotel Krystal*. For spectacular light show, disco, expensive drinks and cover. Many clubs and late bars throughout central area.

Endless opportunities, including armies of non-aggressive beach vendors. The flea market is grossly overpriced; the many shops often better value, but not to any great degree. Guadalajara is cheaper for practically everything. The market, by the bridge at the end of Insurgentes, sells silver, clothes and souvenirs as well as meat and fish. Large, well-stocked supermarket nearby. Jewellery at *Olas de Plata*, Francisco Rodríguez 132. Plaza Malecón has 28 curio shops, restaurant, music, etc. *GR* supermarket, Constitución 136, reasonable for basics. Second-hand books, English and some in German, at *Rosas Expresso*, Olas Altas 399.

Local Buses: Mismaloya to Marina, US$0.24, but complicated routing. The main southbound artery through town is México-Morelos-Vallarta; the main northbound is Juárez-Insurgentes. Plaza Lázaro Cárdenas is the main terminal in south of town and starting point for Mismaloya-Boca buses going south. Buses marked 'Olas Altas' go to South Central, those marked 'Hoteles' or 'Aeropuerto' to North Hotel Zone and beyond. Buses are also marked for 'Marina' and 'Mismaloya/Boca' (Boca de Tomatlán). The ones marked 'Centro' go through town, those with 'Túnel' take the bypass. Buses to outlying villages with Medina bus line, terminal at Brasil, between Brasilia and Guatemala, regular (15-20 mins) service to Nuevo Vallarta,

Eating
● *on map, page 329*

Nightlife

Shopping

Transport

Guadalajara to the Pacific Coast

San José, San Juan, Bucerías, Manzanilla, Punta de Mita and others. Fares from US$0.75-US$1.50. **Car hire**: widely available. **Scooter hire**: opposite *Sheraton*, T222-1765.

Long distance Air: International Ordaz airport (PVR) 6 km from centre, T221-1325. If you walk 100 m to the highway and catch a local bus to town, it will cost far less than the US$10 taxi fare. International flights from Anchorage (Alaska), Austin (Texas), Boston (MA), Burbank (California), Chicago, Dallas, Denver (Colorado), Frankfurt (Germany), Houston, Los Angeles, New York, Phoenix (Arizona), Portland (Oregon), San Diego (California), San Francisco, Seattle and Tampa. Mexican destinations served include Mexico City, Guadalajara, Acapulco, Chihuahua, Ciudad Juárez, Morelia, Querétaro, Tijuana, Aguascalientes, León, Los Cabos, Mazatlán and Monterrey.

Buses: all buses leave from bus station almost opposite the airport (turn left when you exit from arrivals, then it's a short walk), 40 min from centre. Taxis from the airport to the main bus station charge inflated prices. Frequent service to **Guadalajara**: 6 hrs, 8 a day, US$27. **Tepic**: 3 hrs, US$9.50. To **Barra de Navidad** and **Manzanillo** with *Primera Plus* at 0745 and 1200 US$9.50, 4½ hrs and to Barra only with *Elite*, 0800 and 1300, 4 hrs. Other services to Acapulco, Aguascalientes, Ciudad Guzmán, Ciudad Juárez, Colima, León, Mazatlán, Melaque, Mexico City, Monterrey, Querétaro, Tecomán, Tijuana and Zihuatanejo.

Ferry: for Baja California ferry schedules and fares see page 200. Vehicles need to cross at Mazatlán.

Directory **Airline offices** *AeroMéxico*, T224-2777. *Alaska Airlines*, T95-800-426-0333, or 11350. *American Airlines*, T91-800-90460, or 11799. *America West*, T800-235-9292, 800-533-6862, or 11333. *Continental*, T91-800-90050, or 11025. *Delta*, T91-800-90221, or 11032. *Mexicana*, T224-8900. *United*, T911-800-00307, 800-426-5561. **Banks** *Cambios* on nearly every street in tourist areas. Rates inferior to Guadalajara. Check *Bancomer's cambio* at Juárez 450, for good rates. Like most, it is open every day until late. Numerous banks offer slightly better rates (but slower service) and ATMs for Visa, MasterCard. **Communications** Internet: *Net House CyberCafé*, Ignacio L Vallarta 232, T222-6953, open 0700-0200, US$5 per hr, charges by the min. *Eclipse* cybercafé, Juárez 208, US$5 per hr, T222-1755, Mon-Sat 0900-2200, Sun 1000-1400. *Cybercafé*, Juárez 388, US$4.50 per hr, T222-0204, 0900-2300. **Post office**: Mina between Juárez and Morelos. Long-distance **phone** (*casetas*) and **fax** at Lázaro Cárdenas 267, open daily to 2300, also in lobby of *Hotel Eloisa*, both US$3 per min to Europe. Many shops bear *Larga distancia* sign, check tariffs. **Embassies and consulates** *Canada*, Edif Vallarta Plaza, Zaragoza 160, 1st floor, interior 10, T222-5398, F222-3517, open 1000-1400. *US*, T222-0069. **Laundry** Practically 1 on every block in south central; numerous throughout resort. **Medical services** Doctor: *Dra Irma Gittelson*, Juárez 479, speaks French and English, very helpful. **Emergency**: T915-724-7900. **Tour operators** *American Express*, Morelos 660, esq Abasolo, T223-2955, F223-2926, town guide available. *Open Air Expeditions*, Guerrero 339, T222-3310, openair@vivamexico.com, Oscar and Isabel run hiking trips (mountain or waterfall), whale-watching (winter), kayaking, bird-watching and other trips from US$40, knowledgeable guides. *Vallarta Adventure*, Edif Marina Golf, Local 13-C, Marina Vallarta, T/F221-0657, boat trips, whale-watching, Las Marietas (US$50), Sierra Madre expedition (US$60), jeep safari (US$60), dolphin encounter (US$60), Las Caletas by night or by day (US$50), also scuba diving, PADI certification, a 2-tank dive to Las Marietas, or Las Caletas, with lunch costs US$80, 0900-1630. *Mountain Bike Adventures*, Guerrero 361, T223-1834, offer trips for cyclists of varying grades of competence, from local environs up to 3-4 days in old silver towns of Sierra Madre, all equipment provided including good, front-suspension bikes, from US$36. *Sierra Madre*, facing the Malecón near Domínguez, are agents for many tours and some of their own, including a long, all-day truck safari to Sierra Madre mountains. *Rancho El Charro*, T224-0114, horse-riding expeditions to jungle villages, Sierra Madre silver towns. Independent guides and horses congregate at lower end of Basilio Badillo; also occasionally at fisherman's wharf, by *Hotel Rosital* for short beach and mountain trips, agree price beforehand. Many agents and hotel tour desks offer boat trips, car hire and tours at big discounts if you accept a timeshare presentation. Worthwhile savings are to be made for those prepared to brazen out the sales pitch, and many do. **Useful addresses** Immigration: Morelos 600, T221-1380.

North of Vallarta

The coast road continues in a northerly direction from Puerto Vallarta to Las Varas and then veers eastwards to Compostela where it turns north again towards Tepic. From Puerto Vallarta to Las Varas the road passes some very attractive beach resorts, the first of which is **Bucerías** (*Hotel Playa de Bucerías*, and **B** *Marlyn*). **Los Veneros**, between Bucerías and Punta de Mita, T(329) 291-0088, is a pretty cove with fairly safe sea bathing where there is a private beach club reached down a 7-km private road through woods to the beach. Entry includes a margarita or non-alcoholic infusion called *jamaica* made from hibiscus petals. The resort is beautifully designed and clean with two restaurants, bar, café and gardens terraced towards the beach. The food is excellent, no extra charge for sunbeds/umbrellas. Further development is likely and there are plans to introduce horse-riding, mountain bikes, watersports, archaeological trail, guided tour and botanical garden. ■ *Daily 1000-1800, entry US$8, you can take a shuttle bus from Los Veneros bus station.* **Punta de Mita**, a fishing village and beach resort at the tip of a peninsula, has fish restaurants, miles of beach and abundant birdlife; nearby **A** *Hotel and Trailer Park Piedras Blancas*, good, also camping, US$10, hook-ups US$12-14, restaurants. There is an excellent restaurant at Playa Desileteros, not cheap but delicious food; Medina or Pacífico bus from Puerto Vallarta every 15 minutes. There are boat trips to the nearby **Islas Marietas**, where there are caves and birds. Camping is possible on the beach. Simple accommodation available or stay at the attractive **C** *Quinta del Sol* (beach). **Sayulita** is a beach resort with accommodation and restaurants but the beach is littered (*Trailer Park* highly recommended, on beautiful beach, German owner, very friendly, US$10 per day, also has bungalows, Apdo 5-585, CP 06500, Mexico City, T5572-1335, F5390-2750, 2½ km off Route 200; *Tía Adriana's* bed and breakfast, T/F(329) 275-1092, November-June, good, central, good value). Then come **San Francisco** (*Costa Azul Resort*, on beach, delightful, pool, apartments, restaurant), Lo de Marcos and Los Ayala. **Rincón de Guayabitos** is being developed as a tourist resort with hotels, holiday village and trailer park (**C** *Coca*, among several hotels and restaurants on a rocky peninsula to the south of the beach). Further on is **Peñita de Jaltemba** (**C** bungalows at north end of town, with clean rooms and kitchen; **C-D** *Hotel Mar Azul*). Route 200 continues to **Las Varas** (**E** *Hotel Contreras*, with fan and bath, clean, small rooms). Las Varas is connected also by good road to San Blas, north up the coast (see page 338). Beaches on the coast road include **Chacala**, nice free beach lined with coconut palms, good swimming, cold showers (restaurant *Delfín*, delicious smoked fish), and reached by an unsurfaced road through jungle.

Turning east at Las Varas, the road leads to **Compostela** (**F** *Hotel Naryt*, with bath, basic but clean), a pleasant small town with an old church, El Señor de la Misericordia, built 1539. From Compostela one can catch an old bus to **Zacualapan**, 1½ hours over a paved road, to visit a small enclosed park with sculptures that have been found in the area, two blocks from main square. Knock on a door to ask for the caretaker who will unlock the gate to the park. Inside there is a small museum. At Compostela, the road veers north to Tepic.

There is a time change between Nayarit and Jalisco; the latter is 6 hours behind GMT, the former, as with all the Pacific Coast north of Jalisco, 7 hours behind

Tepic

Capital of Nayarit state, Tepic was founded in 1531 at the foot of the extinct volcano of Sangagüey. It is a clean but slightly scruffy town with much rebuilding going on. There are many little squares, all filled with trees and flowers.

The landscape around Tepic is wild and mountainous; access is very difficult. Huichol and Cora Indians live in the region. Their dress is very picturesque; their craftwork – bags (carried only by men), scarves woven in colourful designs, necklaces of tiny beads (*chaquira*) and wall-hangings of brightly coloured wool – is available from souvenir shops. You may see them in Tepic but it is best to let Indians approach you when they come to town if you want to purchase any items.

Phone code: 311
Colour map 3, grid B1
Population: 305,025
Altitude: 900 m

The **tourist office**, Avenida México and Calzada del Ejército, one block from the cathedral, T213-9203, is officially open daily (0900-2000) but in reality this is not so. English spoken, helpful. The Municipal Tourist Office, Puebla and Amado Nervo, T216-5661, F212-6033, is also very helpful. The local tourism website is at www.turismonayarit.com.mx

Sights
The tombs in the cemetery are worth seeing

The **cathedral** (1891), with two fine Gothic towers, on the Plaza Principal, has been restored; it is painted primrose yellow, adorned with gold. Worth seeing are the **Palacio Municipal**, painted pink; the **Casa de Amado Nervo**, Zacatecas Norte 281, the house of the great Mexican poet and diplomat. ■ *Mon-Fri 1000-1400, Sat 1000-1300*; the **Museo Regional de Antropología e Historia**, Avenida México 91 Norte, has a fine collection of Aztec and Toltec artefacts and some beautiful religious paintings from the colonial period. ■ *Mon-Fri 0900-1900, Sat 0900-1500*; **Museo de Los Cuatro Pueblos**, Hidalgo y Zacatecas, exhibits the work of four indigenous ethnic groups. It is worth visiting to see the colourful artwork, textiles and beadwork of the Coras, Nahuas, Huicholes and Tepehuanos. ■ *Mon-Fri 0900-1400, 1600-1900, Sat-Sun 0900-1400;* **Museo Emilia Ortiz**, Calle Lerdo 192 Poniente has works by this local artist. ■ *Mon-Sat 0900-1400*; and the **Museo de Arte Visual 'Aramara'**, Allende 329 Poniente. ■ *Mon-Fri 0900-1400 and 1600-2000, Sat 0900-1400*. **Plaza de los Constituyentes**, México y Juárez, is flanked on the west side by the **Palacio de Gobierno**. On the summit of a hill south of the centre is the **ex-Convento de la Cruz**.

Tepic

Guadalajara to the Pacific Coast

Sleeping		Eating
1 Altamirano	4 Ibarra	1 El Apacho
2 Camarena	5 Real de Don Juan	2 Tiki Room
3 Fray Junípero Serra	6 Sarita	
	7 Sierra de Alicia	

0 metres 100
0 yards 100

To San Blas & Mazatlán   *To Convento de la Cruz*
To Bugam Villas   *To Museo Aramara*   *To Main Bus Station, Airport & Guadalajara*

Sleeping
● *on map*

A *Real de Don Juan*, Av México 105 Sur, on Plaza de Los Constituyentes, T/F216-1888. Parking. **A-B** *Bugamvillas*, Av Insurgentes y Libramiento Pte, T218-0225, F218-0225. Very comfortable rooms with a/c, TV, pool, restaurant with great food and good wine list. **B** *Fray Junípero Serra*, Lerdo Pte 23, T212-2525, main square. Comfortable, big rooms, clean, a/c, good restaurant, friendly, good service. A little noisy with the new road, but still recommended. **B-C** *Ibarra*, Durango Nte 297A, T212-3870. Luxurious rooms, with bath and fan (some rooms noisy), and slightly spartan, cheaper rooms without bath, very clean, DHL collection point. **C** *San Jorge*, Lerdo 124, T212-1324. Very comfortable, good value.

C *Altamirano*, Mina 19 Ote, T212-7131, near Palacio de Gobierno. Parking, noisy but good value. **C** *Santa Fe*, Calzada de la Cruz 85, near Parque La Loma, a few mins from centre, T213-1966. With TV, clean, comfortable, good restaurant. **C** *Sierra de Alicia*, Av México 180 Nte, T212-0322, F212-1309. With fan, tiled stairways, friendly. **D** *Las Américas*, Puebla 317 Nte, T216-3285. Clean, bath, TV, fan, rooms at back quiet. Recommended. **E** *Sarita*, Bravo 112 Pte, T212-1333. Clean, TV, restaurant, parking. Good. **E** *Tepic*, Dr Martínez 438, T213-1377, near bus station outside town. With bath, clean, friendly but noisy. **F** *Pensión Morales*, Insurgentes y Sánchez, 4 blocks from bus station. Clean and friendly, hotel is now closed but family still put up backpackers in what is now a private house. **F** *Camarena*, 4 blocks southeast of Zócalo, San Luis Nte 63. Without bath, clean, friendly.

Motels *Bungalows and Trailer Park Koala*, La Laguna, Santa María del Oro. Has bungalows at US$20, each accommodating up to 4, several trailer sites (US$10) and a large campground. Good cheap meals available. Fishing and waterskiing on nearby lagoon.

Eating
● *on map*

El Apacho, opposite *Hotel Ibarra*. Good *sopes*, cheap. *El Tripol*, in mall, near plaza. Excellent vegetarian. *Danny O*, ice-cream shop next door. *Roberto's* and *Chante Clair*. Both good food and near Parque La Loma, closed Sun. *La Terraza*, Mexican and American food, pies, cakes; good vegetarian restaurant at Veracruz 16 Nte, try the granola yoghurts. *Tiki Room*, San Luis Nte opposite *Hotel Camarena*. Restaurant, art gallery, video bar, fun. Restaurant in bus terminal, overpriced. Lots of fish stalls by market on Puebla Nte. The local *huevos rancheros* are extremely *picante* (hot).

Transport

Air Airport Amado Nervo (TPQ) with flights to Los Angeles, Mexico City, Tampico and Tijuana daily with Aero California, T216-1636 or AeroMéxico, T213-9047.

Trains Station at Prolongación Allende y Jesús García.

Buses Bus station is a fairly short walk from town centre, T213-6747; bus from centre to terminal from Puebla Nte by market. At bus station there are phones, including credit card, post office, left luggage and tourist information (not always open). Bus to **San Blas** from main bus terminal and from local bus station on park at Av Victoria y México, from 0615 every hour US$3.60. To **Guadalajara**: frequent departures, 3½ hrs, US$15, several companies; **Mazatlán**: 4½ hrs, US$10; to **Los Mochis**: US$52; to **Puerto Vallarta**: 3 hrs, US$9.50; **Mexico City**: US$41.

Directory

Banks *Casas de cambio* at México 91 and 140 Nte, Mon-Sat 0900-1400, 1600-2000. **Communications Telephones**: credit card phone at Veracruz Nte y Zapata Pte. **Tour operators** *Viajes Regina*, tours to San Blas, 8 hrs, US$22.50; Playas de Ensueño, Fri, 8 hrs, US$15.50; Tepic city tour, Mon and Sat, 3 hrs, US$7. *Tovara*, Ignacio Allende 30.

Huaynamota

One can visit **Cora** villages only by air, as there are no real roads, and it takes at least two days. However, it is possible to visit **Huichol** villages from the small town of **Huaynamota** in the mountains northeast of Tepic. Huaynamota has become much easier to reach with the opening of the Aguamilpa Dam. Boats leave from the west end of the dam at 0900 and 1400 (US$7), stopping at *embarcaderos* for villages along the way. The valley, despite being flooded, is still beautiful, particularly at the narrower parts of the dam where huge boulders hang precariously on clifftops. The *embarcadero* for Huaynamota is at the end of the dam where the Río Atengo feeds in. A community truck meets the launch (US$1.30). It is 8 km up a dirt road to the

Guadalajara to the Pacific Coast

town, which is half populated by Huichol, some of whose traditional houses can be seen on its fringes. There are no hotels. Ask at church or at store (basic supplies) on long south side of plaza for possible lodging. There is a good view over the river valley from the large boulder beside the road at the edge of town. From Huaynamota ask around for guides to Huichol villages four or more hours away. *Semana Santa* (Easter week) is famous, and many people from surrounding communities converge on Huaynamota at this time. Combis leave for the dam from Tepic at Avenida México just down from Zaragoza, US$3, 1½ hours.

Santa Cruz There are various beaches along the coast west of Tepic. **Santa Cruz**, about 37 km from Tepic, has a rocky beach. No hotels, but there are rental apartments, a camping area and accommodation at *Peter's Shop*, **E**, basic but pleasant and friendly. Simple food available, *Restaurant Belmar*, fish and rice, all reminiscent of the South Seas. There is a shrimp farm nearby. Two buses a day run from San Blas to Santa Cruz, US$1.10, or 2½ hours' ride by open-sided lorry, US$0.75.

San Blas

Phone code: 328
Colour map 3, grid B1
Population 42,741

This old colonial town, built as a fortress against piracy, is 69 km from Tepic and overcrowded during US and Mexican summer holidays. Founded in 1768, little is left of the old Spanish fortress, **Basilio**. It is from here that the Spanish set off to colonize Baja California and North America. Above the town are **La Contaduría** (1773), the Spanish counting house ■ *US$.60*, and **La Marinera**, a ruined church. The views over the town, estuaries and mangrove swamps from beside an incredibly ugly statue on the battlements are superb.

In town, near the harbour, is the old **Customs House** (1781-85) and a stone and adobe church (1808-78) on the plaza. Up to the mid-19th century, San Blas was a thriving port and it still has a naval base and a (smelly) harbour.

There are few tourists early in the year or in August when it becomes very hot and there are many mosquitoes, but not on the beach 2 km from the village (although, there are other biting insects, so take repellent anyway). The two worst bugs are *jejenes* or *no sees* during the dry season, and *sancudos* the big black monsters, during the wet season. But don't be too put off, as they are diminishing year by year, and if you don't linger around vegetation and still water they are not so bad.

Quieter than the town beach (which is dirty) is the extensive and often-deserted **Playa El Rey** on the north side of the estuary of the same name, beyond the light-house. Take a boat across the river from just west of the harbour, US$0.60 each way; the boatman works until 1730, but stops at lunchtime. Best to tell him when you want to return so that he knows to look out for your frantic waving from the other bank. The best beach is **Playa de las Islitas** reached by bus marked 'Las Veras' from the bus station, or 'El Llano' from Paredes y Sinaloa, just off the plaza. There is some threat of resort development here, but no signs of it as yet. At the beach of **Matanchén**, 7 km from San Blas (taxi US$3), there is good swimming but many mosquitoes. Good homemade fruitcakes and bread are sold here. Surfing can be done at these beaches, but rarely at any one time is the surf up at all of them. Check at Juan Bananas (see below, Sports). About three times a year it is possible to surf non-stop for over a mile, from town towards Las Islitas, relaying on a series of point breaks.

Sixteen kilometres south from San Blas is the beautiful **Playa Los Cocos**, which is empty except at weekends. The **tourist office**, Mercado, one block from plaza, T255-0021, has information in English on the history of San Blas as well as a town map. ■ *Mon-Sat 0900-1300, 1800-2000, Sun until 1300*. **NB** Don't wander too far from public beach; tourists have warned against attacks and robberies. The Mexican Navy has a training base in San Blas and there is a strong naval and military presence in town as well as the sound of automatic weapons fire in the afternoon.

Four-hour boat trips to see whales and dolphins are available. Ask at the tourist **Excursions** office. Armando is a good guide; he charges US$52 for three people.

It is possible to take a three-hour jungle trip in a boat (bus to *embarcadero* on Matenchén road) to **La Tovara**, a small resort with a fresh-water swimming hole brimming with turtles and catfish, a restaurant, and not much else. The mangrove swamps can be visited on the way to La Tovara. Tour buses leave from the bridge 1 km out of town and cost US$30 for a canoe with six passengers, but it is cheaper to arrange the trip at *Embarcadero El Aguada*. Official prices are posted but it still seems possible to shop around. Away from the swimming hole there are coatis, raccoons, iguanas, turtles, boat-billed herons, egrets and parrots. Avoid fast motorized boats as the motor noise will scare any animals. Tours on foot are even better. Crocodiles are kept in caves along the route. You have to pay US$2 to see the poor, shabby creatures, not recommended. Twilight tours enable naturalists to see potoos and, if very lucky, an ocelot. La Tovara is crowded at midday during the summer. A cheaper 1½-2-hour cruise is also possible from the *Embarcadero El Aguada* (reached by Las Islitas bus – see above), US$17 per boat, but US$4.25 *each* if more than four people; it goes through a tunnel of mangroves, to the swimming hole 20 minutes away. You can take a bus from San Blas towards Santa Cruz (see page 338) and get off at Matachén beach (see above). From here, a boat for half-day hire includes the best part of the jungle cruise from San Blas.

Just 3 km east of San Blas is **Singayta**, which has a bird sanctuary that is supposed to be particularly impressive in November and December; very popular with birders from the US. Lucio Rodríguez (T255-0537) provides eight-hour tours to see the crater lake at Santa María del Oro; Mexcaltitán and Santiago Ixquintla; the waterfalls at El Cora/Tecuitata; or Ixtlán del Río and Los Toriles. He can be found at the *Bungalows Tesoro* de San Blas.

Accommodation becomes scarce and more expensive around Semana Santa and other holi- **Sleeping** days. A good source of information for alternative rooms and longer stay apartments is Rosa López Castellano who lives at Juárez 5, just off the plaza.

L *Garza-Canela*, Cuauhtémoc Sur 106, T285-0307, F285-0308. Very clean, excellent restaurant, small pool, nice garden. Highly recommended. **A** *Bucanero*, Juárez Pte 75, T285-0101. With bath and fan, frequented by Americans, food good, pool, lizards abound, noisy discos 3 times a week and bar is open till 0100 with loud music. **A** *Posada del Rey*, Campeche, T285-0123. Very clean, swimming pool, excellent value. Recommended. *Posada de Morales*, T285-0023. Also has a swimming pool, more expensive, ½ block from *Posada del Rey*. **B** *Marino Inn*, Batallón, T285-0340. With a/c, friendly, pool, fair food. **C** *Apartamentos Béjar*, Salas 144. Furnished with daily, weekly or monthly rates, hot water problematic, owner, Rafael Béjar speaks English and is friendly. **C** *Posada Portales*, Paredes 118, T285-0386. Rooms with *en suite* dining area and fully equipped kitchen, book exchange. Recommended particularly for longer stays. **C** *María's*, Canalizo s/n (moved from Batallón, same owners as *El Ranchero* and *Morelos*). Fairly clean with cooking, washing and fridge facilities, a bit noisy, no single rooms, friendly. Recommended. **C** *La Quinta California*. Closest to beach, just off Batallón down from *Marino Inn*, T285-0111. Rooms with well-equipped *en suite* kitchen, free freshly ground coffee in morning, pleasant central court, longer stay discounts, book exchange. Recommended. **C-D** *El Tesoro de San Blas*, 50 m south of dock, 5 mins from centre. Rooms and villas, hot water, satellite TV, US owners. **C-D** *El Ranchero*, Batallón 102. With bath, laundry service, kitchen. **D** *Posada Irene*, Batallón 122, four blocks southwest of Zócalo. Basic with a fan, few rooms with a shower and hot water. Kitchen, friendly. **D** *Posada Azul*, Batallón 126, T285-0129, 4 blocks from plaza towards beach. 3-bedded rooms with fan and hot water, **E** for simple 2-bedded rooms without bath, cooking facilities.

Camping No camping or sleeping permitted on beaches but several pay campsites available. **Trailer park** at town beach; all trailer parks in the centre are plagued by mosquitoes. The best trailer park is on Los Cocos beach: *Playa Amor*. Good beach, on a narrow strip of

Guadalajara to the Pacific Coast

land between road to Santa Cruz and cliff, good, popular, 16 km south of town, US$7-10. Next south is **E** *Hotel Delfín*. With bath, balcony, good view; good value; then *Raffles Restaurant* with trailer and camping area attached (no facilities). Last on Los Cocos beach is *Hotel y Restaurante Casa Mañana*, Austrian-run, good food. Many apartments for rent.

Eating   *Amparo*, on main plaza. Cheap and good. *Tumba de Yako*, on way to beach. Yoghurt and health foods, and the original version of *pan de plátano* (banana bread) that is advertised all over town. *Las Islitas,* with a distinctly nautical feel, good-value seafood, also sells banana bread. Recommended. *Tony's 'Islas' restaurant*, good seafood, not cheap, closed Mon. *Cocodrilo's*, on the square with lots of foreigners. Good for dinner if a little pricey. *La Familia*, 2 blocks west of the square. Good for lunch or dinner, moderately priced. Plenty of seafood restaurants on the beach; eg *Las Olas*. Good and cheap. Also on Juárez is *Wala Wala*. Good local dishes. *Lonchería Paz*, Canalizo, ½ block off plaza. Cheap.

On Sun women prepare delicious pots of stew for eating *al fresco* on the plaza.

Shopping   For art of the Huichol Indians try the *Huichol Cultural Community store*, Juárez 64; it claims to be non-profit making. Great freehand beadwork with glass beads, yarn paintings, decorated masks and scented candles.

Sports   **Surfing** *Tumba de Yako* (see above, Eating) rents out boards, US$2.70 per hour, US$8 per day, owner, Juan Bananas, was coach to the Mexican surfing team, gives lessons, speaks English. **Mountain bike** and **kayak** hire (for estuaries) also from *Tumba de Yako*.

Transport   Bus station on corner of Plaza; to **Tepic**, frequent – on hour from 0600, US$3.60, 1½ hrs. To **Guadalajara**, US$16, 8½ hrs.

Directory   **Banks** *Banamex* just off Zócalo, exchange 0830-1000 only. *Comercial de San Blas* on the main square will change money, plus commission. **Laundry** 2 blocks down toward the beach from *La Familia*. Will take your clothes and return them, very clean, later or the next day, US$4.44 for about 1½ loads.

Tepic to Guadalajara

The old Route 15 leaves Tepic for Guadalajara. About 50 km from Tepic, off the Guadalajara road, is an attractive area of volcanic lagoons. Take the bus to **Santa María del Oro** for the lagoon of the same name. On the south side of the toll road is the Laguna Tepetiltic and near Chapalilla is another lake at San Pedro Lagunillas. There is a turn-off at Chapalilla to Compostela and Puerto Vallarta. At **Ahuacatlán**, 75 km from Tepic, the 17th-century Ex-Convento de San Juan Evangelista stands on the Plaza Principal; handicrafts are on sale here. Nearby, the village of **Jala** has a festival mid-August. **E** *Hotel Cambero*. From here the **Ceboruco** volcano can be reached in a day. On the main road a lava flow from Ceboruco is visible (*El Ceboruco*, *Parador Turístico*, with restaurant, information, toilets and shop).

Eighty-four kilometres (1¼ hours by bus) from Tepic is **Ixtlán del Río** (**D** *Hotel Colonial*, Hidalgo 45 Poniente, very friendly, recommended; *Motel Colón*; cheaper hotels round the Zócalo are *Roma* and *Turista*). There are a few souvenir shops, a Museo Arqueológico in the Palacio Municipal, and a *casa de cambio*. Harvest (maize) festival mid-September. Two kilometres out of town are the ruins of **Los Toriles**, a Toltec ceremonial centre on a warm, wind-swept plain. The main structure is the Temple of Quetzalcoatl, noted for its cruciform windows and circular shape. The ruins have been largely restored and some explanatory notes are posted around the site. There is a caretaker but no real facilities. ■ *US$2.35*. Two kilometres beyond the Los Toriles site is *Motel Hacienda*, with pool. The road climbs out of the valley through uncultivated land, where trees intermix with prickly pear and chaparral cactus.

The journey from Tepic to Guadalajara cannot easily be broken at Ixtlán for sightseeing since buses passing through in either direction tend to be full; the bus on to Guadalajara takes three hours, US$4.25. The route enters the State of Jalisco and,

19 km before Tequila, comes to the town of Magdalena (*Hotel Restaurant Magdalena*), congested with traffic. Nearby there is a small lake. As the bus approaches Tequila there may be opportunities to buy the drink of the same name on board. The blue agave, from which it is distilled, can be seen growing in the pleasant, hilly countryside.

Tequila

Tequila, 58 km from Guadalajara, is the main place where the famous Mexican drink is distilled. Tours of the distilleries are available (see box page 342) and stores will let you sample different tequilas before you buy. Often around 20 bottles are open for tasting. The town is attractive, a mix of colonial and more modern architecture. It is a pleasant place to stay but there is not much to do other than tour the distilleries and there is little in the way of nightlife. Of course one option is to spend the evening imbibing the local produce, the following morning recovering. Along Calle Sixto Gorjón, where the arriving buses will drop you, there are several liquor stores selling tequila, restaurants where you can eat for under US$5, pharmacies, doctors, dentists and the Rojo de los Altos bus ticket office at No 126A. In the town centre there are two plazas next to each other. On one is the **Templo de Santiago Apóstol**, a large, pretty, old stone building, with a 1930s municipal market next to it. Behind the church is the *Elypsis* discotheque, open at weekends. Also on this plaza is the post office and *Banamex*. About a block behind *Banamex* where Sixto Gorjón ends is the entrance to the **Jose Cuervo distillery**. Along Calle Ramon Corona is the **Sauza** distillery. Both provide tours – see box. The **Museo Nacional del Tequila** is at Calle Ramon Corona 34. Recently renovated, it's full of the history of tequila, along with the origins, processes, cultivation and distilling of tequila. Full of reassuring facts. Apparently 100% agave tequila blends in well with the human metabolism to the extent that if it's good stuff you don't get a hangover. Years of personal experience suggests otherwise, but buy the best you can. ■ *Tue-Sun 1000-1700, US$1, 50% discount for students.*

The **Municipal** building on the main square puts out a stall by the map, which supposedly offers tourist information. In reality, it just sells tours of the Tequila distilleries, which include trips out to the fields.

Phone code: 374
Colour map 3, grid B2
Population: 35,502
Altitude: 1,300 m

A day trip from Guadalajara is possible

Sleeping **C** *Posada del Agave*, Sixto Gorjon 83, T742-0774. New place in town, excellent value with private bath, TV, very comfortable. **D** *Motel Delicias*, Carretera Internacional 595, T742-1094, on the highway to Guadalajara about 1 km outside Tequila. Best available, TV, off-street parking. **C** *Abasolo*, Abasolo 80, T742-0195. Well (over) decorated, rooms have TV. **E** *Colonial*, Morelos 52, T742-0355, corner of Sixto Gorjón. Characterless, but central, clean and not run-down, some rooms with private bath. A good deal.

Eating *El Callejón*, Sixto Gorjón 105. Rustic Mexican décor, main courses for under US$5, *antojitos* for less than US$3, hamburgers also available. *El Marinero*, Albino Rojas 16B. Nice seafood restaurant with strolling musicians. *El Sauza*, Juárez 45, beside Banamex. Restaurant/bar, Mexican atmosphere.

Transport **Buses** 2nd class from the old terminal, Sala B, in Guadalajara, Rojo de los Altos, every 45 mins, up to 2 hrs, US$2.80. Return from outside Rojo de los Altos ticket office, Sixto Gorjón, 126A, every 20 mins, 0500-1400, then every 30 mins until 2030. **Taxi** to Guadalajara US$19, plus US$9 in tolls if you take the expressway.

Train The *Tequila Express*, T3880-90-99 (Guadalajara), www.mariachi-jalisco.com.mx, is a rather comfortable way of visiting the town from Guadalajara. It's all jazzed up and smart-looking – not how the Mexican rail industry used to be that's for sure – but you spend the day drifing towards the town, exploring one of the plantations and then returning with no fear of driving or being stuck on a bus. Daily (in theory), leaving about 0900, US$60 for adults, US$32 for kids. Book from tour operators in Guadalajara.

Guadalajara to the Pacific Coast

"A field of upright swords" – the making of tequila

The quote from Paul Theroux's *The Old Patagonian Express* describes the swathes of blue agave grown in the dry highlands of the State of Jalisco and a few neighbouring areas. Agave is the raw material for the firewater, tequila, and although there are some 400 varieties of agave, only one, the blue agave, is suitable. After eight years growing in the fields, the spiky leaves are hacked off and the central core, weighing around 45 kg, is crushed and roasted to give the characteristic smell and flavour to the drink. The syrup extracted is then mixed with liquid sugar, fermented for 30-32 hours and then distilled twice. White tequila is the product of a further four months in wooden or stainless steel vats. It can be drunk neat, with a pinch of salt on the back of your hand, followed by a suck on a wedge of lime, or mixed into cocktails such as the famous Margarita. Gold tequila is a blend of white tequila and tequila which has been aged in wooden casks. Añejo, or aged, tequila, is a golden brown from spending at least two years in oak casks. As it ages it becomes smoother and is drunk like a fine brandy or aged rum. Special premium tequila, has no sugar added; it is pure agave aged in wooden casks.

In pre-conquest times, the Indians used the agave sap to brew a mildly alcoholic drink, pulque, which is still drunk today. The Spaniards, however, wanted something more refined and stronger. They developed mezcal and set up distilleries to produce what later became tequila. The first of these was established in 1795 by royal decree of King Charles IV of Spain. It is still in existence today: La Rojena, the distillery of José Cuervo, known by its black crow logo, is the biggest in the country.

In recent years tequila has been strongly marketed to international markets and exports have increased dramatically but not without problems. With the agave plant requiring eight years to reach maturity, demand has oustripped supply – quite simply, not enough blue agave was planted eight years ago. Tequila, like many other spirits, is blended. While the best tequila is 100% puro de agave a couple of distilleries appear to have been blending more than they would like to admit. In 2001 the Consejo Regulador del Tequila, whose job it is to check and monitor standards on the industry, made a couple of surprise calls on well-established distilleries and were denied entry – suggesting strongly they had something to hide. But rest assured if you're in the market to buy, the shock has made the industry realise there is to much to lose if standards are diluted. For the latest tequila news, visit www.donrafael.com

Around the town of Tequila there are 12 distilleries, of which 10 produce 75% of the country's tequila. Tours of the distilleries can be arranged with a free sample at the end, and of course shopping opportunities. ■ Tours hourly between 1000-1400, US$3.50, lasting about one hour. Some tours in English – check locally for precise times. **Tequila Cuervo**, T3634-4170, F3634-8893, in Guadalajara, or T742-0076 in Tequila (contact Srta Clara Martínez for tours). At **Tequila Sauza**, T742-0244, or in Guadalajara on T3679-0600. Dating from 1873, you can see the famous fresco illustrating the joys of drinking tequila. **Herradura**, T3614-9657, F3614-0175, 8 km from Tequila, is in an old hacienda outside the village of Amatitlán, which has adobe walls and cobblestone streets and is worth a visit.

If buying tequila most of the liquor available in town should be drunk quickly and kept off the palette as much as possible. If you're looking for quality there are a few things you can look for. Look for the stamp of CRT (the mark of the Consejo Regulador del Tequila), look for 100% agave and finally for the very best look for reposada (matured). If it has all three, just sip it gently; you won't need the salt and lemon to hide the sharpness.

Directory **Banks** *Banamex*, corner of Sixto Gorjón and Juárez, 24-hr ATM accepts Visa and MasterCard. Many others in town with ATMs. *Casa de cambio*, Sixto Gorjón 73, open 0900-1400, 1600-2000, change cash and TCs.

Guadalajara to the Pacific Coast

Veracruz and the Gulf Coast

Mexico City

Often overlooked by tourists, the State of Veracruz is off the usual beaten track. Maybe it hasn't got the best beaches in Mexico but for almost everything else it's hard to beat. Inland, there's adventure tourism with Mexico's highest mountain, deepest caves and fastest rapids. Temperatures rise as the land drops to the green, fertile coastal plain and the endless plantations. To the south, beyond the plains of the vast Papaloapan River, the Tuxtla mountains, tropical and lush, a bird-watcher's paradise, contrast dramatically with the wilderness of the massive oil refineries at Minatitlán and Coatzacoalcos.

In the north the Huastec people are best known for their traditional huapango music and falsetto singing. In the vanilla-growing Papantla area, the spectacular volador ritual, an example of surviving Totonac traditions, is performed regularly in Papantla and outside the ruins of El Tajín, one of the most magnificent archaeological sites in all America. Xalapa, the lively state capital and an important university city, has one of the best museums in the whole country. But it's the rich cultural mix that makes Veracruz so special. For 300 years, the port was Spain's gateway to the riches of the New World. The arrival of black slaves profoundly influenced the people and culture – most notably the music – of this region. Veracruz is a popular destination for Mexican tourists who enjoy the famous hospitality of the Veracruzanos, known as jarochos, and the eternally festive, tropical-port atmosphere that crescendoes each spring during the liveliest carnival in all Mexico.

Mexico City to Veracruz

Much of the area east of Mexico City constituted the eastern tribute quarter conquered by the Mexica, formerly the Aztecs, who derived great wealth from those subject nations that stretched from the Basin of Mexico to the Guatamalan border. Commodities such as cacao, cochineal (obtained from the red insect that was nourished by cacti), jade jewellery, cloaks and rubber poured into Tenochtitlán from these provinces to the east.

By road, the principal route to the coast from Mexico City is paved all the way, with no Pemex service station on the road between Puebla and Orizaba, a distance of about 150 km. A new *autopista* (motorway) now runs all the way from Mexico City to Veracruz with four tolls that range from US$4.35 to US$9.

The favourite resort of the Emperor Maximilian, on the eastern edge of the mountains, lost much of its charm in the 1973 earthquake, when the bullring, many houses and other buildings were lost, and is now heavily industrialized. The setting, however, is lovely. In the distance is the majestic volcanic cone of Orizaba. The town developed because of the natural springs in the valley, some of which are used by the textile and paper industries and others are dammed to form small pools for bathing beside picnic areas; Nogales is the most popular, Ojo de Agua is another. The **Cerro del Borrego**, the hill above the Alameda Park, is a favourite early-morning climb. On the north side of the Zócalo is the market, with a wide variety of local produce and local women in traditional dress, and the many-domed **San Miguel** church (1690-1729). There are several other interesting churches, and there is an Orozco mural in the neo-classical **Palacio Municipal**, formerly the Centro Educativo Obrero on Avenida Colón. The **ex-Palacio Municipal** is the actual cast-iron Belgian pavilion brought piece by piece from France after the famous 19th-century Paris Exhibition, an odd sight. The **Museo de Arte del Estado**, in the Oratorio de San

Orizaba

Phone code: 272
Colour map 3, grid B5
Population: 118,448
Altitude: 1,283 m

Pico de Orizaba

*Also known as Citlaltépetl, Orizaba is the highest mountain in Mexico (5,760 m). It is not too difficult to climb, although acclimatization to altitude is essential and there are some crevasses to be negotiated. Some people ski on the glacier, but the surface is unpredictable. From **Acatzingo** you can go via a paved road to **Tlachichuca** (35 km, or you can take a bus, every 30 minutes, from Puebla to Tlachichuca). Guides and transport can be arranged: Sr Reyes (F(245) 451-5019), arranges trips in a four-wheel drive up an appalling road to two huts on the mountain, about US$50, including one night at his house, a former soap factory – very clean (**D** full board), his truck leaves at 1200, three-hour journey, and he picks you up at about 1600. Sr Reyes is well-equipped and keen to give ground support to climbers; Sr Canchola Limón, 3 Poniente 3, Tlachichuca, T(245) 451-5082, charges US$30 for transport to the mountain and pick up, registers your climbing intentions, has equipment, and can provide somebody to guard your equipment at the refugio (two days) for US$13; Sr Espinosa Coba, T(245) 451-5103, is another transporter. Alternatively, stay at **E** Hotel Panchita, Av Benito Juárez 5, T(245) 451-5035, hot water, bath, restaurant, friendly; **E** Hotel Gerar, 20 de Noviembre 200, with bath; or **E** Hotel Margarita, no sign, then, early in the morning, hitchhike to the last village, **Villa Hidalgo** at 3,000 m (about 15 km) or take a taxi, US$10. From there it's about 10 km (two hours) to the huts. The huts, one small (sleeps six, water nearby), one larger (sleeps 80, start of north route – normal – or Jamapa glacier route) and colder, are at 4,200 m. There is no hut custodian; it's usually fairly empty, except on Saturday nights. No food or light, or wood; provide your own. Take a good sleeping bag and warm clothes. Water close at hand, but no cooking facilities. Start from the hut at about 0500, first to reach the glacier at 4,700*

m, and then a little left to the rim. There is a hazardous section before you get to the Jamapa glacier where several icy slopes spill down from its lip and have become a bowling alley for dislodged rocks. From the rim the summit, marked with a cross, is 100 m further on and 40 m higher up. Be very careful walking round the rim to the summit. It's about 7-8 hours to the top; the ice is not too steep (about 35-40°), take crampons, if not for the ascent then for the descent, which takes only 2½ hours. At the weekend you're more likely to get a lift back to Tlachichuca. 1:50,000 maps are available from INEGI information and sales office, eg in Puebla (Av 15 de Mayo 2929), Veracruz or Mexico City.

*Volker Huss of Karlsruhe (Germany) informs us of an alternative route up the volcano; this is easier, because there is no glacier and therefore no crevasses, but is best done in the rainy season (April-October), when there is enough snow to cover the loose stone on the final stage. Crampons and ice-axe are necessary. The route is on the south face of the volcano. Stay in **Orizaba** and take a very early bus to **Ciudad Serdán** (depart 0530), or stay in Ciudad Serdán. At Serdán bus station take a bus, US$1.50, to **San Antonio Atzitzintla**, and then taxi US$4 to **Texmalaquila**; the driver will know the way. Five hours from Texmalaquila is the Fausto González hut at 4,760 m (take own food and water). Miguel Quintero in Texmalaquila has mules for luggage transport to the shelter (US$5 per bag). Spend the night there and climb the final 1,000 m early in the morning, about five hours. From the top are fine views, with luck even to Veracruz and Mexico City. In the rainy season the summit is usually free of cloud until midday. The entire descent takes six hours and can be done the same day.*

Felipe Neri, 4 Oriente y 23 Sur, has a delightful collection of colonial to contemporary paintings, including, in Sala 3, foreign artists' impressions of Veracruz. ■ *Tue-Sun 1000-1400, 1600-1900.* The **tourist office** is at Poniente 2, across the river from the Zócalo. Open mornings only.

Sleeping **B** *Aries*, Ote 6, No 263, T725-3520 (nightclub on top floor). **B** *Trueba*, Ote 6 and Sur 11, T724-2930. Resort facilities. **C** *De France*, Ote 6, No 186, T725-2311. US$0.25 for parking in courtyard, charming building, clean, comfortable, shower, friendly, reasonable if uninspiring restaurant. **D** *Vallejo*, Madero Nte 242. Dirty, smelly. **E** *América*, on the main street, No 269. Very friendly and good value.

Eating *Romanchú* and *Paso Real*, on the main street, have excellent cuisine. *Hare Krishna* vegetarian restaurant, *Radha's*, on Sur 4 between Ote 1 and 3. Excellent. The *Indian vegetarian* restaurant on Sur 5, has an excellent *comida corrida*. Highly recommended. *Crazy Foods*, opposite *Hotel de France*, is good and cheap, nice sandwiches. In the **market**, try the local morning snack, *memelita picadita*.

Transport Mérida, 1 bus a day (*ADO*), US$55, 1st class. To **Veracruz**, many buses, 2½ hrs, US$6.

A road leaves Orizaba southwards, up into the mountains of **Zongolica**, a dry, poor and isolated region, cold and inhospitable, inhabited by various groups of Indians who speak Nahuatl, the language of the Aztecs. Zongolica village is a good place to buy *sarapes*; take early bus from Orizaba (ask for direct one) to get clear views of the mountains. Ask about weather conditions before attempting to drive.

South to Zongolica

Beyond Orizaba, en route to the coast, the scenery is magnificent. The road descends to coffee and sugar cane country and a tropical riot of flowers. It is very pleasant except when a northerly blows, or in the intolerable heat and mugginess of the wet season.

This small town is devoted to growing flowers and exporting them. Sometimes Indian women sell choice blossoms in small baskets made of banana-tree bark. Between Orizaba and Fortín there is a viewpoint looking out over a dramatic gorge, the **Barranca de Metlac**, which plunges down to the river in a cascade of flame trees and luxurient vegetation. The *autopista* from Orizaba to Córdoba passes over this deep valley on a concrete bridge. Night trains sound their horns when passing Fortín which can be disturbing

Fortín de las Flores
Phone code: 271
Colour map 3, grid B5
Km 331

Sleeping B *Posada la Loma*, Km 333 Carretera Nte, T713-0658. Very attractive, tropical garden with butterflies, distant view of snow-capped volcano in early morning, moderately expensive. There are others, slightly cheaper, which also offer tropical gardens for relaxation.

Night trains sound their horns when passing Fortín which can be disturbing

Eight kilometres beyond Fortín in the rich valley of the Río Seco, is the old colonial city of Córdoba, which is also crazy with flowers. Its Zócalo is spacious, leafy and elegant; three sides are arcaded; two of them are lined with tables. On the fourth is an imposing church with a chiming clock. There are several hotels in the Zócalo, which is alive and relaxed at night. In **Portal de Zavallos**, General Iturbide signed the Treaty of Córdoba in 1821, which was instrumental in freeing Mexico from Spanish colonial rule. There is a local museum at Calle 3, No 303. ■ *1000-1300, 1600-2000.* Córdoba has the highest rainfall in Mexico, but at predictable times.

Córdoba
Phone code: 271
Colour map 3, grid B5
Population: 176,985
Altitude: 923 m

This is an important coffee-growing area

Sleeping A *Hotel Layfer*, Av 5 between Calle 9 y 11, T714-0099. 4-star hotel, swimming pool, gymnasium, video games room, a/c, secure parking, friendly. Highly recommended. **B** *Mansur*, Av 1, No 301 y Calle 3, T712-6600, on square. Smart. **C** *Hostal de Borreña*, Calle 11 308, T712-0777. Modern, clean, really hot water, some traffic noise but good value. Near the *ADO* terminal is **C** *Palacio*, Av 3 y Calle 2, T712-2188. **C** *Gorbeña*, Calle 11, No 308, between 3 and 5, T712-0777. Large rooms, recommended. **D** *Iberia*, T712-1301, **D** *Trescado*, T712-2366 and *Casa de Huéspedes Regis* are all on Av 2. *Casa de Huéspedes La Sin Rival* and **E** *La Nueva Querétana* are at 511 and 508 of Av 4, respectively (latter is basic but cheap). **F** *Los Reyes*, Calle 3. Shower, hot water, street rooms double-glazed, street parking OK. Recommended.

Eating *Cantábrico*, Calle 3, No 9, T712-7646, 1 block from Zócalo. Excellent meat and fish dishes, fine wines and good service, 'worth a trip from Mexico City!'. Highly recommended.

Veracruz and the Gulf Coast

El Balcón, enter through Hotel Zevallos. Balcony overlooking Zócalo. Recommended. *Brujes*, Av 2, No 306. Good *comida corrida*.

Transport Cars: Nissan, Chevrolet and Dodge dealers, mechanics all on Calle 11. **Trains**: Check locally as train services have dwindled. **Buses**: bus station is at the end of Av 6. Direct services to **Veracruz**, 2 hrs, US$5; **Puebla**, 3 hrs, US$9; **Mexico City**, hourly, 5 hrs, US$14; to **Coatzacoalcos**, US$17; **Oaxaca** and many others.

Directory Banks: *Casa de Cambio* on Av 3 opposite *Bancomer*, recommended.

Córdoba to Veracruz The direct road from Córdoba to Veracruz is lined, in season, by stalls selling fruit and local honey between Yanga and Cuitláhuac. **Yanga** is a small village named after the leader of a group of escaped black slaves in colonial times. A slightly longer but far more attractive road goes from Fortín de las Flores northwards through Huatusco and Totutla, then swings east to Veracruz. For cyclists, the 125 km from Córdoba to Veracruz has no accommodation en route, but is mostly flat, so could be done in a day.

Xalapa

Phone code: 228
Colour map 3, grid B5
Population: 390,058
Altitude: 1,425 m

Capital of Veracruz state since 1885 and 132 km from the port, Xalapa (also spelt **Jalapa**) is in the tierra templada and is a lively town in keeping with its climate. It is yet another 'City of Flowers', with walled gardens, stone-built houses, wide avenues in the newer town and steep, cobbled, crooked streets in the old.

Sights
Look out for Toma Nota, a free sheet advertising what is on, available from the shop in front of Hotel Salmones

A settlement called Xallac (the place of the sandy waters) is known to have existed here in the 12th century. It has always been a good place to break the journey from the coast to the highlands and, in the 18th century, development was helped by the creation of a huge annual trading fair. There was a passion for building and renovation in the flamboyant Gothic style during the first part of the 19th century. The 18th-century **cathedral**, with its sloping floor, has been recently restored.

The excellent, modern **Anthropology Museum**, second only to the one in Mexico City, is in the northern suburbs of Xalapa, on the road out towards Mexico City. The museum concentrates on exhibits from the region's three major pre-Hispanic civilizations, showing treasures of the Olmec, Totonac and Huastec coastal cultures. It has the best collection of Olmec monumental stone sculptures in all Mexico, including several of the magnificent colossal heads from the south of Veracruz and Tabasco, and the exquisite *Señor de las Limas*, unearthed by chance by local children who, thinking it was just a stone, used his smooth jade head, which protruded from the earth, to crack open nutshells. ■ *Tue-Sun 1000-1800, US$1, Tue free, half price for students with ID, guided tours included in fee. To get there take the Tesorería Avila Camacho bus, which stops in front of the museum.*

The **Pinacoteca Diego Rivera**, Herrera 5 (Zócalo), has a small permanent collection of Rivera's paintings as well as temporary exhibitions. ■ *Tue-Sun 1000-1800, free.* Xalapa has a university; you can take a pleasant stroll round the grounds, known as **El Dique**. Pico de Orizaba is visible from hotel roofs or Parque Juárez very early in the morning, before the haze develops.

The **tourist office** is at Blvd Cristóbal Colón 5, T841-8500, a long walk or short taxi ride from the centre.

Essentials

Sleeping **LL** *Misión Xalapa*, Victoria y Bustamante, T818-2222. Good restaurant, excellent bookshop, changes travellers' cheques. **AL** *María Victoria*, Zaragoza 6, T818-0268. Good. **B-C** *Mesón del Alférez*, Zaragoza y Sebastián Camacho, T/F818-6351. Charming, small rooms, free parking opposite, good food. Highly recommended. **C** *Araucarias*, Avila Camacho 160, T817-3433. With balcony and view (**D** without), TV, fridge, good cheap restaurant.

Cheaper hotels are up the hill from the market. Town centre hotels are generally noisy. **C** *Principal*, Zaragoza 28, T817-6400. Good if a bit shabby, safe parking nearby. **C** *Salmones*, Zaragoza 24, T817-5431. Excellent view of Orizaba from the roof, good restaurant. Recommended. **D** *Amoro*, near market. No shower but public baths opposite, very clean. **E** *Limón*, Av Revolución, behind the cathedral, good clean rooms, with hot water bath, some with nice views. **E** *Plaza*, Enríquez, T817-3310. All rooms with private bath and TV, some rooms airless, clean, safe, friendly, will store luggage, good view of Orizaba from the roof. Recommended. **F** *El Greco*, Av Revolución 4 blocks up from the cathedral. With bath, hot water, clean.

La Parroquia, Zaragoza 18, and another one on Av Camacho, same menu and prices as famous restaurant of same name in Veracruz. *La Casona del Beaterio,* Zaragoza 20. Good atmosphere, tastefully restored house with patio and bubbling fountain, good breakfast. *Quinto Reyno*, Juárez 67 close to main plaza. Lunches only. Excellent vegetarian with health food shop, very good service. *La Champion*, Allende, going towards the bus terminal. Vegetation, nice atmosphere, good value *comida corrida* Mon-Sat. *Café Linda*, Primo de Verdad. Good service and good-value *comida corrida* every day, often live music in the evenings. *Estancia*, opposite Barranquilla. Good food. *Aladino*, Juárez, up from ADO. Excellent Mexican food. *La Sopa*, on Diamante, an alleyway just off Enríquez. Great tapas, cheap. Several other small restaurants on Diamante including *La Fonda*, very pleasant upstairs and *El Diamante*. *Fruitlandia* on Abasolo (uphill from cathedral). Wonderful fresh juices. Health food shops, Ursulo Galván, near Juárez, good bread and yoghurt, another opposite the post office on Zamora. Several good cafés on Carrillo Puerto for good value *comida corrida*. *La Churrería del Recuerdo*, Victoria 158. Superb, authentic Mexican food at very reasonable prices. No alcohol. Highly recommended.

Eating

The famous Xalapeño (Jalapeño) chilli comes from this region

Centro de Recreación Xalapeño has exhibitions; live music, films and exhibitions in *El Agora*, underneath Parque Juárez; 10-pin bowling, Plaza Cristal, next to cinema. **Cinemas** There are 2 cinemas next to *Hotel Xalapa*, off Camacho; 3-screen cinema in Plaza Cristal; cinemas in the centre tend to show soft porn and gore. **Theatre** *Teatro del Estado*, Avila Camacho; good Balet Folclórico Veracruzano and symphony orchestra. **Nightclubs** *La Tasca*, good music. Another club is *La Cumbre*, rock.

Entertainment

Crafts *Artesanía* shop on Alfaro, more on Bárcenas, turn off Enríquez into Madero, right again at the top, the owner of *El Tazín* on the corner speaks English. **Books** *Instituto de Antropología*, Benito Juárez, has books in English and Spanish, student ID helps.

Shopping

Local Bus: many of the urban creamy yellow buses are for seated passengers only, so they will not stop if all seats are full. **Taxis** from the bus station to the centre charge about US$1; buses marked 'Centro' will also take you. Buses marked 'Xalapa' or 'Museo' run north to the **Anthropology Museum**. To reach the nearby towns of **Coatepec** and **Xico** take a bus from Av Allende, just west of the city centre. **Car hire**: *Automóviles Sánchez*, Av Ignacio de la Llave 14, T817-9011. Recommended. **Moped hire**: in Camacho US$4-6/hr.

Transport

Long distance Air: there is a small airport serving a few national destinations only, about 15 km southeast of the city, on the Veracruz road.

Buses: a new 1st and 2nd class bus station has been built called CAXA; taxi from centre US$1.75. Taxi ticket office outside terminal on lower level. **Coatzacoalcos**: 8 a day, up to 8 hrs, US$26. **Mexico City**: hourly, 5 hrs, US$25 travelling to the Terminal de Oriente (TAPO). **Puebla**: almost hourly, 4 hrs, US$8. **Veracruz**: every 20 mins 0700-2000, 2½ hrs, US$6. **Villahermosa**: 3 a day, 10 hrs, US$42. Also buses to **Poza Rica** and **Papantla**.

Car: the road from Puebla, Route 140, twists and turns, particularly in the Perote area and is often notoriously foggy; if driving, avoid at night if possible. From Xalapa to the coast and Veracruz, Route 140 is good.

Trains: railway station on outskirts of town with buses leaving from near market to get there No scheduled passenger services at present.

Directory **Banks** *Banca Serfín* on Enríquez will change TCs in dollars and other major currencies; *Santander* on Carrillo Puerto changes dollar TCs. Banks are slow, rates offered are rarely those advertised in the window and money transferred from abroad comes via Mexico City. *American Express* at Viajes Xalapa, Carrillo Puerto 24, T817-6535, in centre, sells cheques against Amex card but does not change them. *Casa de Cambio*, on right side of Zamora going down hill, English spoken. Rates vary enormously, so shop around. Quick service and good rates at *Dollar Exchange*, Gutiérrez Zamora 36. **Communications** Internet: *Serviexpress*, Zaragoza 14B. *Café Chat* on Camacho opposite Parque Bicentenial, another in shopping arcade off Enríquez. Most charge US$2.50/hr. **Post office:** letters can be sent to the *Lista de Correos* on Diego Leño, friendly post office, and another at the bottom of Zamora. **Telephone:** long-distance phone in shop on Zaragoza, with a sign outside, others behind the government palace also on Zaragoza. **Laundry** Several on Allende and Ursulo Galván, all charge by weight, usually US$3 per 3kg, some offer same day service, others up to 3 days. **Medical services** Dentists: there are 2 dentists on Ursulo Galván. **Hospitals:** *Nicolás Bravo*. **Travel agents** 4 on Camacho; the one nearest Parque Juárez is very helpful. Xalapa is a base for whitewater rafting on the Filobobos River.

Excursions Two-and-a-half kilometres along the Coatepec road are lush **botanical gardens**
from Xalapa with a small museum. ■ *US$0.20. Getting there: take bus from the terminal marked Coatepec Briones, 10 mins.*

Coatepec, famous for its ice-cream, fruit liqueurs and orchids, is a pleasant town and an important centre for the surrounding coffee haciendas. A *Posada Coatepec*, Hidalgo 9, Centro, T(228) 816-0544, F816-0040. Tastefully modernized colonial house. Reserve in advance, excellent restaurant with Mexican and international cuisine. Several good cafés and restaurants around the main plaza. Particularly recommended is the seafood at *Casa Bonilla* (Cuauhtémoc 20). ■ *Direct Coatepec bus from Xalapa bus terminal every few mins, US$0.40, 10 mins.*

The **Texolo** waterfalls are some 15 km southwest of Xalapa and 5 km from the pretty village of **Xico**, just beyond the town of Coatepec. There is a deep ravine and an old bridge, as well as a good, cheap restaurant at the falls. The old bridge is still visible but a new bridge across the ravine has been built. It is a pleasant place for a cold swim, bird-watching and walking. The film *Romancing the Stone* used Texolo as one of its locations. ■ *Getting there: US$0.60 by bus from Xalapa every 30 mins.*

Hacienda Casa de Santa Anna was taken over in the Revolution and is now **Museo Lencero**. ■ *US$1, Tue-Sun 1000-1800, no bags allowed inside. Getting there: bus from the centre, take Circunvalación bus to Plaza Cristal shopping centre, cross the road and catch bus to Miradores, ask to be put down near the museum. From the stop (by pedestrian bridge) it is a 7 min walk to the museum.*

Palo Gacho falls are also worth a visit. Take Route 40 from Xalapa, towards Cardel, to Palo Gacho. The waterfalls can be reached on a dirt road next to the church, 4 km steep descent. Avoid weekends.

Naolinco is 30 minutes' ride, 40 km northeast of Xalapa up a winding hilly road. Two waterfalls, with various pools, tumble several thousand feet over steep wooded slopes. *Restaurant La Fuente* serves local food and has a nice garden. *Las Cascadas* has a *mirador* to admire the falls from. Both restaurants are on the way into town. Flocks of *zopilotes* (buzzards) collect late in the afternoon, soaring high on the thermals.

Two hours northwest from Xalapa is the archaeological site of **Filobobos**. It includes El Cuajilote, a 400m-wide ceremonial centre, and Vega de la Peña, an area of basalt rocks decorated with bas reliefs, a ball court and several pyramids by the river banks. Abundant wildlife here includes toucans, parrots and otters. At the end of the Veracruz mountain range is the spectacular Encanto waterfall. ■ *US$2. Getting there: 4WD is recommended for this journey by car: on the outskirts of Tlapacoyan, take the road marked Plan de Arroyas. After ½ hr (many bends and hills) you'll see the sign for Filobobos on the left. This is a 5-km dirt track to a refreshment cabin, from where you can walk for 25 mins to the ruins; follow signs for El Cuajilote.*

Route 140 towards the capital, renowned for being foggy, continues to climb to **Perote**, 53 km from Xalapa. **E** *Hotel Central*, near plaza. Quiet, friendly, with bath, TV. **F** *Gran Hotel*, on plaza. Basic, limited water. The **San Carlos fort** here, now a military prison, was built in 1770-77; there is a good view of Cofre de Perote volcano (known, in Aztec times, as *Nauhtecuhtli*, 'Four Times Lord'). A road branches north to Teziutlán (**D** *Hotel Valdéz*, hot water, car park), with a Friday market, where good *sarapes* are sold. A local fair, *La Entrega de Inanacatl*, is held in the third week in June. The old convent at **Acatzingo**, 93 km beyond Perote on Route 140, is worth seeing. Another 10 km and you join the road to Puebla and Mexico City.

Papantla

Some 40 km inland from Tecolutla is Papantla ('Where banners abound'), built on the top of a hill overlooking the lush plains of northern Veracruz. It was the stronghold of a Totonac rebellion in 1836. Traditional Totonac dress is still seen: the men in baggy white trousers and sailor shirts and the women in lacy white skirts and shawls over embroidered blouses. Papantla is also the centre of one of the world's largest vanilla-producing zones, and the distinctive odour sometimes lingers over the town. Small animal figures, baskets and other fragrant items woven from vanilla bean pods are sold at booths along Highway 180, as well as the essence; packaged in tin boxes, these sachets are widely used to freshen cupboards and drawers. The vanilla is processed in **Gutiérrez Zamora**, a small town about 30 km east (close to Tecolutla), and a 'cream of vanilla' liqueur is also produced. The *Fiesta de la Vainilla* is held throughout the area in early June. The **tourist office** is on the first floor of Palacio Municipal, on the Zócalo, T842-0026 ext 730, F842-0176, helpful, good local information and maps, bus schedules, English spoken. ■ *Mon-Fri 0900-1400 and 1800-2100.*

Phone code: 784
Colour map 3, grid B5
Population: 170,123

Veracruz and the Gulf Coast

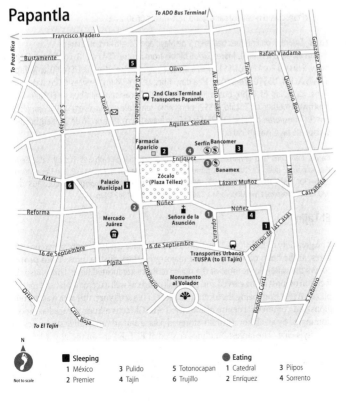

Papantla

Sleeping ■
1 México
2 Premier
3 Pulido
4 Tajín
5 Totonacapan
6 Trujillo

Eating ●
1 Catedral
2 Enríquez
3 Piipos
4 Sorrento

Not to scale

Sights The Zócalo, formally known as **Plaza Téllez**, is bordered by Enríquez on its down-hill north edge; on the south uphill side is the **Catedral de Nuestra Señora de la Asunción** (1700) with a remarkable 50 m-long mural on its northern wall called *Homenaje a la Cultura Totonaca*, by Teodoro Cano García (1979), with the plumed serpent Quetzalcoatl along its entire length. *Voladores* perform each Sunday at 1100 in the church courtyard and as many as three times daily during the colourful 10 days of Corpus Christi (late May or early June), along with games, fireworks, artistic exhibitions, dances and cockfights. For a sweeping view of the area, walk up Reforma to the top of the hill where the giant **Monumento al Volador** was erected in 1988. Murals and mosaic benches in the Zócalo also commemorate Totonac history and their conception of creation. Beside the main plaza is the Mercado Juárez (poultry and vegetables); more interesting is Mercado Hidalgo, 20 de Noviembre, off the northwest corner of the Zócalo, where traditional handmade clothing is sold amid fresh produce and livestock. ■ *Daily 0600-2000.*

Sleeping
■ *on map*

A *Tajín*, Dr Núñez and Domínguez 104, T/F842-0121, F21062. 59 rooms, restaurant with good value breakfast and bar, fairly clean, hot water, phone, TV, parking, reasonable. **B** *Premier*, on Zócalo, T842-4213, F842-1062. 20 rooms, a/c, phone, TV, hot water, fax service, free car wash. Recommended. **C-D** *Totonocapan*, 20 de Noviembre y Olivo, T842-1224, F842-1218. Hot water, TV, a/c, bar/restaurant, good value. **D** *México*, Obispo de Las Casas y Núñez (beyond *Hotel Tajín*, opposite *Cine* Tajín), T842-0086. Basic, cheapest in town. **E** *Pulido*, Enríquez 205, T842-0036. Modern, 23 rooms, hot water, fan, noisy, parking. **E** *Trujillo*, 5 de Mayo 401. Rooms with basin, friendly.

Eating
● *on map*

Las Brisas del Golfo, Dr Núñez. Reasonable prices and very good. *Sorrento*, Zócalo. Covered in decorative tiles, good, cheap. Recommended. *Enríquez*, on Zócalo. Popular, pleasant, not cheap. *Piipos*, Enríquez 100. Speciality paella. *Catedral*, Núñez y Curado, behind cathedral. Plain, clean, cheap breakfasts and good 'fast' meals, 0630-2100.

Transport
Taxis Taxi rank on Enríquez between 5 de Mayo and Zócalo and on Juárez.

Buses *ADO* terminal, Juárez 207, 5 blocks from centre, T842-0218. To **Mexico City**: 4 a day, 5 hrs via Poza Rica, US$12; **Poza Rica**: regular service, 30 mins, US$0.50; to **Xalapa**: 8 daily, 6 hrs, US$10; **Veracruz**: 10 a day, 4 hrs, US$14. Many services to local destinations, including **El Tajín**, buses leave when full. Occasional minibus to El Tajín from southwest corner of Zócalo, US$2, unreliable schedule about every 1-1½ hrs. Other buses (*Transportes Urbano-TUSPA*) for El Tajín leave from office on 16 de Septiembre near Obispo de las Casas (US$0.50).

Directory
Banks *Bancomer* and *Banamex*, on Zócalo, 0900-1300, change cash and TCs till 1200. *Serfín*, between the 2, does not change TCs. **Communications** Post office: Azueta 198, 2nd Floor, Mon-Fri 0900-1300, 1500-1800, Sat 0900-1200. **Medical services** *Farmacia Aparicio*, Enríquez 103, daily 0700-2200. *Hospital Civil*, Madero 518, T842-0094. **Red Cross:** T842-0126.

El Tajín

Colour map 3, grid B5

The great city of El Tajín, 12 km from Papantla, once covered approximately 2,600 acres, at the heart of which are four major groupings of structures: **Tajín proper** covers the valley floor; most of the major temples are located here. This is also the location of most of the carved and plain ball courts as well as ceremonial and market plazas. Apart from being the location of most of the sculpture, this area was the religious and commercial centre of the city. **Tajín Chico** is a huge terraced acropolis dominated by an elaborate multi-storeyed palace and administrative structures for the city's élite. The largest buildings erected at El Tajín are on the upper levels of Tajín Chico. Along with its Annex, the **Building of the Columns** is the greatest architectural complex in the city. It was the special domain of the ruler 13 Rabbit, who governed at the city's zenith. The **West Ridge** is mostly an artificially tiered

The voladores of El Tajín

Traditionally, on Corpus Christi, Totonac rain dancers erect a 30-m mast with a rotating structure at El Tajín. Four voladores (flyers) and a musician climb to the surmounting platform. There, the musician dances to his own pipe and drum music, while the roped voladores throw themselves into space to make a dizzy spiral descent, head down, to the ground.

Voladores are now in attendance every day (during high season, other times just weekends), and fly if and when they think there are enough tourists (donations expected).

natural hill. The structures here are thought to be élite residences, modest temples, and, perhaps, small ball courts. The **East Ridge** is very similar to the West Ridge but with fewer structures.

The suggested time-scale for El Tajín's construction is AD 300-900, with a great surge of energy around AD 600, the time when Teotihuacán and Monte Albán were experiencing collapse and abandonment. Although impressive, the architecture of El Tajín is less informative than the rich corpus of iconography that decorated the Pyramid of the Niches, the North Ball Court, the South Ball Court and the Building of the Columns. Most of the imagery associated with these structures tells of conquest, ball games, the interplay between this existence and that of the gods, the dignified sacrifice of warriors and ball players and the undignified sacrifice of captive enemy lords. But the ball game was the single most important activity expressed in the imagery of El Tajín, as emphasized by the presence of at least 11 ball courts at the site. The obsession with the ball game and its related iconography suggests that the city was an immense academy where young men were trained in the skills and rules associated with the game. As yet, no evidence supports this suggestion, but it is tempting to speculate that the residences on the East and West Ridges were intended to house young trainees.

Associated almost exclusively with the ball game and players, the cult of the maguey, pulque and pulque deities at El Tajín presents a puzzle, perplexing because the maguey will not grow in the general area. The probability is that the city was the creation of a small enclave of Huastecs rather than the Totonacs who then inhabited and still inhabit the region. The maguey proliferates throughout the Highlands, and in the mythology of the Central Highlands it was a Huastec who drank more than the stipulated four cups, became drunk, stripped naked and had to return in disgrace to his homeland.

Pyramid of the Niches The form of the pyramid, one of the earliest structures at El Tajín, is very distinctive, and said to have 365 niches, or one for each day of the year. Dated approximately AD 600, it is crowned with a sanctuary that was lined with engraved panels, one of which shows a cacao plant bearing fruit. Cacao was precious and of great commercial value to the people of the area. There is some evidence that the rulers of Tajín controlled its cultivation in the zones surrounding the site. Another trapezoidal panel depicts a priest or ruler adorned with ballgame accoutrements and holding a knife ready to perform ritual sacrifice, the scene being set within the confines of a ball court. The depiction of a skull at the foot of the executioner indicates sacrifice by decapitation.

North Ball Court The imagery of the North Ball Court is only partially understood. Most of the problems associated with this zone derive from erosion and mutilation of the engravings. Men in bat costumes are a major theme in these panels and suggest influence from the Maya region where men dressed in this way were common images on ceramics of the Classic period. Also present in the North Ball Court is the imagery of the ball game and human sacrifice.

Veracruz and the Gulf Coast

South Ball Court   The South Ball Court offers a fascinating glimpse into the philosophy that underpinned the whole ritual life of El Tajín. Central to the narrative is the role of the ball player who acts as an intermediary between this world and that of the gods. In the engravings, the ball player is presented to the executioner and decapitated while the gods look on. Two of the panels are bordered with the image of a laughing pulque deity with two bodies, there are many Venus symbols, the death god, Mitlantecuhtli, emerges from an urn of pulque, and many of the known gods of the mesoamerican pantheon are represented. In some of the painted books of the Central Highlands, the powerful gods Quetzalcoatl and Tezcatlipoca oppose each other in a ball game; at El Tajín, it is possible that the human players represented the earthly aspects of these gods. The imagery of the engravings of the South Ball Court is extremely complex, but it does imply that through the ball game humans can approach the realm of the gods by means of the decapitation of the principal players.

El Tajín

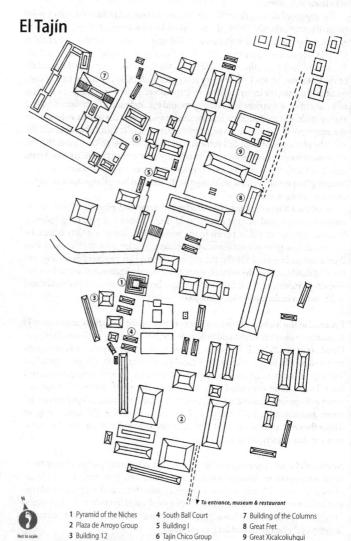

▼ *To entrance, museum & restaurant*

N

Not to scale

1 Pyramid of the Niches	**4** South Ball Court	**7** Building of the Columns
2 Plaza de Arroyo Group	**5** Building I	**8** Great Fret
3 Building 12	**6** Tajín Chico Group	**9** Great Xicalcoliuhqui

Tajín Chico The Building of the Columns (11th century) is another area with a very complex iconographical narrative. However, where the iconography of the South Ball Court expresses a communion between gods and men, the iconography of the Building of the Columns refers to themes that are much more mundane. The focus of attention is the ruler 13 Rabbit, whose glyph is repeated many times on the surface of the column drums, always with the image of a rabbit and the number 13 expressed by two bars, each counting as five, and three dots. 13 Rabbit has clearly been on a conquest campaign because a number of prisoners are lined up in preparation for the decapitation ritual. They have been divested of almost all their clothes and thus divested of their dignity. They are named by glyphs above or near their persons, which indicates that they were chiefs of opposing polities; the common warrior was rarely identified by name. Whereas the warrior/ball player of the South Ball Court approached his death with calm dignity, the prisoners of the Building of the Columns are forced toward the sacrificial block, some held by the hair. Two sacrificial sequences but two very different approaches to death. The narrative of 13 Rabbit is now in the site museum. Although seen and depicted as all-powerful, 13 Rabbit was not omnipotent enough to prevent the destruction of the city and probably the state of El Tajín, which occurred shortly after the engraving of the Building of the Columns was completed. The great centre of the ball game, like so many others, perished, but at whose hands has yet to be discovered.

■ *0800-1800, except mid-Aug 0800-1900. US$2.80, free on Sun. Guidebook US$1.25, available in Museo de Antropología, Mexico City, rarely available on site. There is a small modern museum, a cafetería and souvenir shops. In the wet season beware of a large, poisonous creature like a centipede. El Tajín can be visited either from Papantla or from Poza Rica, the oil town, see below.*

Four kilometres along a road east of the Río Tecolutla bridge (Puente de Remolino), near Paso de Correo (35 km southeast of Papantla, past Chote), are the Totonac ruins of **Cuyuxquihui**, probably founded around AD 1250, shortly after El Tajín's demise, and later taken over by the Aztecs as a garrison. There is a large pyramid, platforms, altars and a ball court. From Papantla take bus marked 'Joloapan' (every hour, on the hour) from 2nd class bus station.

Poza Rica

Sleeping
1 Aurora
2 Berlín
3 Casa Blanca
4 Fénix
5 Nuevo León
6 Poza Rica
7 San Antonio

Eating
1 Café Manolo
2 Lonchería El Petrolero

N
Not to scale

Poza Rica

Twenty-one kilometres northwest of Papantla is Poza Rica, an ugly oil city formed out of four old *rancherías*, which happened to lie on top of the then second largest oil strike in the world. It has an old cramped wooden market and a simple mural by O'Higgins (*From Primitive Pre-Hispanic Agricultural Works to the Present Day Oil Industry Development*, 1959) on the outside of the **Palacio Municipal**. The tourist office is at the back of the Palacio Municipal on the ground floor, T822-1390 ext 129.

Phone code: 782
Colour map 3, grid B5
Population: 152,678

There is little else to recommend Poza Rica, apart from an inordinate number of dentists

Sleeping

A *Poza Rica*, 2 Nte, between 10 and 12 Ote, T822-0134, F823-2032. Experienced for what it offers, friendly, credit cards accepted, fairly comfortable, good *comida corrida* in restaurant. **C** *Nuevo León*, Av Colegio Militar, T822-0528, opposite market. Rooms

Veracruz and the Gulf Coast

quite spacious, fairly clean and quiet. Recommended. **C** *Salinas*, Blvd Ruiz Cortines, 1905, or Cazones road, T822-0706, F823-3525. Good, a/c, TV, restaurant, pool, secure parking.
      D *Berlim*, 2 Ote y 6 Nte, T822-0055. With fan, TV. **D** *Casa Blanca*, Prolongación 20 de Noviembre 49, T823-7798. Bath and TV, cheaper without. **D** *Fénix*, 6 Nte (near Av Central Ote), T822-3572. Basic, but one of the better cheap places, opposite town centre *ADO* ticket office in an express mail company office. **D** *San Antonio*, Prolongación 20 de Noviembre (near Plaza), T823-3784. With bath, fan, friendly. **E** *Aurora*, Bolívar 4. Basic but quiet and fairly clean. **F** *Cárdenas*, Bermúdez y Zaragoza, T822-6610. Basic, not central.

Eating   *Lonchería El Petrolero*, Plaza Cívica 18 de Marzo y Av Central Ote. Excellent bread baked on premises, popular with locals. *Café Manolo*, 10 Ote 60 y 6 Nte. Good breakfast, moderate prices.

Transport   **Air**   Airport El Tajín, 3 km south, T822-2119; several flights daily to Mexico City. **Buses**   All buses leave from new terminal referred to as *ADO*, about 1½ km from centre, take white bus from centre, or taxi, US$1.50. Terminal is divided into *ADO* (T822-0085, also office in centre, 6 Nte opposite Hotel Fénix, open daily, hours vary) and all others, good facilities, tourist office. **El Tajín**: buses leave every 20-30 mins 0700-2000 from behind Monumento de la Madre statue, marked Chote or Chote Tajín. Ask driver for fare to Las Ruinas, US$0.50, 20-25 mins, most go to the entrance.
      Barra de Cazones, *Transportes Papantla* or *Autotransportes Cazones*, 1 hr, US$1.20 (often waits 30 mins in Cazones on way back until bus fills). It is not always necessary to go to bus station to catch your bus: buses to Barra de Cazones leave the terminal but can be picked up as they pass through the centre along Blvd Cortines. **Mexico City** and **Tampico**: every 30 mins, 5 hrs, US$16. **Monterrey**: 4 a day, US$16. **Pachuca**: 4½ hrs, US$6, change in Tulancingo. **Papantla** bus may be caught on Av Central Ote by Plaza Cívico 18 de Marzo. **Tecolutla** (see below): 1¼ hrs, US$2.20. **Veracruz**: almost hourly, 4 hrs, US$12. **Xalapa**: US$11-14.50, up to 5½ hrs, frequent.

Directory   **Airline offices** *AeroMéxico*, Edificio Géminis, Parque Juárez, T822-6142. *Aeromar*, T824-3001. **Banks** *Bancomer*, opposite *Hotel Poza Rica*. *Serfín*, 4 Nte y 2 Ote. **Cultural centres** *Casa de la Cultura*, Guatemala 502, T822-3185. **Laundry** *Yee del Centro*, Prolongación 20 de Noviembre, US$2.50 per 3 kg. **Medical services** Red Cross: Blvd Lázaro Cárdenas 106, T823-6871.

From Poza Rica you can head north to visit the **Castillo de Teayo**, a pyramid with the original sanctuary and interesting carvings on top, buses every 30 minutes, change halfway. **Barra de Cazones** (not to be confused with Cazones, the town you pass on the way) is 25 km along Route 8, with one dirty beach and a less developed, cleaner one on the north side of the river (ferry US$0.25). **B** *Mariner Costa*, on hill above river. Pool, good view over boca. **D** *Estrella del Mar*, north end of south beach.

Tuxpan

Phone code: 783
Colour map 3, grid B5
Population: 126,475

On the north bank of the wide Río Tuxpan, 55 km from Poza Rica, 189 km south of Tampico is Tuxpan, tropical and humid, 12 km from the sea. Essentially a fishing town (shrimps a speciality), it is now decaying from what must have been a beautiful heyday. There's an interesting covered market; fruit sold on the quay. The beach, about 12 km east of town, is at least 10 km long and is reached by taxi or bus from Boulevard Reyes Heroles (marked 'Playa' US$0.50). Few people weekdays, no hasslers, some sand flies; hire deckchairs under banana-leaf shelters for the day (US$2). The **tourist office** is at Av Juárez 20, T834-0177 ext 117.

Sleeping & eating   **B** *Florida*, Av Juárez 23, T834-0222. Clean, hot water. **B** *Plaza Palmas*, on edge of town along bypass route, T834-3535. A/c, tennis, pool, secure parking, clean, boat launch to river, TV, good restaurant. Recommended. **C** *Riviera*, Blvd Reyes Heroles 17a, T834-5349. On waterfront, parking, rooms vary in size so check first. **D** *California*, Arteaga 16, T834-0879. Clean, hot water, good breakfast. **D** *Parroquia*, Médico Militar 4, beside cathedral,

T834-1630. Clean, friendly, hot water, fan, noisy. **E** *Posada San Ignacio*, Melchor Ocampo 29, 1 block north of plaza, T824-2905. Clean, with bath, fan, friendly. Recommended. **E** *Tuxpan*, Juárez and Mina, T824-4110. OK. *Cafetería El Mante*, Juárez beside market. Popular with locals, good *comida corrida*. Also *Bremen*. With a/c, food good and cheap.

Many restaurants line the beach (for example *El Arca*, friendly), with showers for the use of bathers (US$0.35). It is worth asking to hang up a hammock for US$2 per night.

Nightlife *Hotel Teján*, over the river, south side, then about 1 km towards the sea. Very plush, good singers but US$6.50 cover charge. *Acropolis*. Disco, dull, no beer. **Cinema** Just off Blvd Reyes Heroles, 1 block east of plaza. — **Entertainment**

Watersports *Aquasport*, 7 km along road to beach, T827-0259. — **Sports**

Buses *ADO* Terminal, east of market, near north end of bridge. Buses to Mexico City (Terminal del Norte): US$14.80, 6½ hrs via Poza Rica. — **Transport**

Banks *Bancomer*, Juárez y Zapata; opposite is *Serfín*. — **Directory**

The coast road

East of Papantla, a side road branches off the main Route 180 to the coast at Tecolutla, a very popular resort on the river of that name, toll bridge US$2.50. A **fiesta** takes place two days before the carnival in Veracruz. Recommended. — **Tecolutla**

Sleeping and eating C *Playa*, Alvaro Obregón 45, T846-0390. Good. **B** *Tecolutla*, Matamoros, T846-0071, the best in town.

D *Casa de Huéspedes Malena* (pleasant rooms, clean) and **D** *Posada Guadalupe* are on Av Carlos Prieto, near river landing stage. **E** *Los Buhos*, close to the beach. Very good rooms with hot shower and TV.

Other hotels, **D**, on road to Nautla. *Torre Molina* trailer park, 16 km before Nautla on coastal Route 180 (coming from Veracruz). Electricity, water and sewage disposal, hot showers, bathrooms, swimming pool, on beach, US$10 per vehicle with 2 people. Recommended. *Restaurant Paquita*, next to *Hotel Playa*. Recommended.

Forty-two kilometres further south, Route 180 passes through **Nautla** (one hotel **E**, recommended, on main street), a pleasant town. Three kilometres before Nautla, Route 131 branches inland to Teziutlán. — **Nautla & El Pital**

El Pital (15 km in from the Gulf along the Nautla River, 80 km southeast of Papantla), was identified early in 1994 as the site of an important, sprawling pre-Columbian seaport (approximately AD 100-600), which lay hidden for centuries under thick rainforest. Now planted over with bananas and oranges, the 100 or more pyramid mounds (some reaching 40 m in height) were assumed by plantation workers to be natural hills. Little excavation or clearing has yet been done, but both Teotihuacán -style and local-style ceramics and figurines have been found. Archaeologists believe El Pital may mark the principal end point of an ancient cultural corridor that linked the north central Gulf Coast with the powerful urban centres of Central Mexico. As at nearby El Tajín, ball courts have been discovered, along with stone fragments depicting what may be sacrificed ball players.

The ruins of **Cempoala** are 40 km north of Veracruz. The coastal city was conquered by Cortés and its inhabitants became his allies. The ruins are interesting because of the round stones uniquely used in construction. Sundays can be very crowded. It is a pleasant site and setting and *voladores* are often in attendance. From Veracruz take a picnic. ◼ *US$1.40, small museum on site. Take 2nd class bus to Cardel, and then a micro to Cempoala.*

Chachalacas is a beach with a swimming pool and changing facilities (US$1 adults) in an expensive but spotless hotel of the same name. Recommended.

Thatched huts; local delicacies sold on beach, including *robalito* fish. It is worth asking the restaurants on the beach to let you hang up your hammock, most have showers and toilets. They charge US$2 if you agree to eat at their restaurant.

La Antigua, the site of what was thought to be Cortés's house, is 1½ km off the road to Cardel, some 30 km north of Veracruz. Take a Cardel bus from the second-class part of the bus station (US$0.40) and get off at La Antigua Caseta, the first toll booth the bus comes to. It is an easy walk from there, 10-15 minutes. The house is worth the visit to see the large ceiba roots growing all over the walls. There is also an attractive early 16th-century church, the Ermita del Rosario. A small boy at the site gives an excellent tour in Spanish. Boats can be hired on the river. **D** *Hotel Malinche*. Quiet, laid back, peaceful.

Veracruz

Phone code 229
Colour map 3, grid B5
Population: 1,000,000

Veracruz is a mixture of the very old and the new; there are still many picturesque white-walled buildings and winding side streets. The centre is at the back of the harbour and has something of a 1950s feel about it. It is very much a port town, noisy and congested, but lively, full of music and dance, and with a definite Caribbean air.

Ins and outs

Getting there   Aeropuerto Las Bajadas (VER), about 12 km from the city centre, has flights to Mexico City and other domestic destinations, as well as to Havana, Cuba and to Houston and San Antonio in the US. There is an efficient shuttle service into town. The bus terminals (1st and 2nd

Veracruz

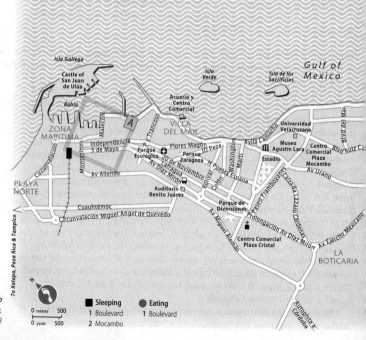

Related map
A Veracruz centre,
page 358

■ Sleeping	● Eating
1 Boulevard	1 Boulevard
2 Mocambo	

0 metres 500
0 yards 500

class) are about 3 km from the town centre, on Av Díaz Mirón (see Transport page 361). High-ways 150 and 150D (*supercarretera*) link Mexico City to the Gulf Coast at the port of Veracruz. Route 180 runs north-south along the coast.

All places of interest are within easy walking distance of the Plaza de Armas. Frequent buses run along the seafront to Mocambo or Boca del Río during the day, but at night you may have to take a taxi. The **tourist office** in the Palacio Municipal on the Zócalo, T932-9942, is helpful but they have no hotel price lists or town maps. The Federal Tourist Office, en route to Boca del Río, T932-1613, has more information.

Getting around

If planning to visit Veracruz or the hills inland (for example Xalapa) between Jul and Sep, check the weather forecast because many tropical storms, known as *nortes*, blow themselves out in this region, bringing heavy rain. From Oct to Jan the weather tends to be changeable, with cold, damp winds from the north. At this time the beaches and Malecón are empty and many resorts close, except over Christmas and New Year when the tourists flood in and all road transport is booked up 5 days in advance. Otherwise it is generally hot.

Best time to visit

Background

The principal port of entry for Mexico lies on a low alluvial plain bordering the Gulf coast. Cortés landed near here at Isla de los Sacrificios on 17 April 1519. The first set-tlement was called Villa Rica de la Vera Cruz; its location was changed several times, including to La Antigua (see above). The present site was established in 1599.

Culturally, Veracruz is a Caribbean city, home to the *jarocho* costume, dance and music, which features harps and guitars. The most famous dances, accompanied by the *conjunto jarocho* dressed in white, are the *bamba* and *zapateado*, with much stamping and lashing of feet related to the flamenco of Andalucía in Spain. Mexico's version of the Cuban *danzón* music and the *música tropical* add to the cultural richness. Many cultural events can be seen at the **Instituto Veracruzano de Cultura**, a few blocks from the Zócalo, with a good, new café and library; a nice place to relax and mingle with students.

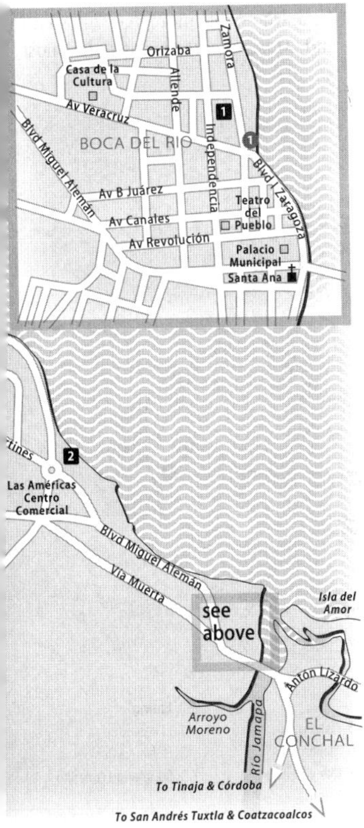

Sights

The heart of the city is the **Plaza de Armas** (Zócalo). The square is white-paved, with attractive cast-iron lampstands and benches, and surrounded by the cathedral (with an unusual cross, depicted with hands), the **Palacio Municipal** and colonial-style hotels. The plaza comes alive in the evenings with an impressive combination of the crush of people, colour and marimba music in the floodlit setting. From 15 July to the end of August there is jazz in the Zócalo from 1900. At night, too, the Malecón (seafront) is very lively, with performers entertaining the public.

Map labels: Orizaba, Zamora, Casa de la Cultura, Attende, Av Veracruz, Blvd Miguel Alemán, BOCA DEL RÍO, Independencia, Blvd Zaragoza, Av B Juárez, Av Canales, Teatro del Pueblo, Av Revolución, Palacio Municipal, Santa Ana, Las Américas Centro Comercial, Blvd Miguel Alemán, Via Muerta, Isla del Amor, see above, Antón Lizardo, Arroyo Moreno, Rio Jamapa, EL CONCHAL, To Tinaja & Córdoba, To San Andrés Tuxtla & Coatzacoalcos

The food is good, the fishing not bad, and the people noisy and welcoming

The city's two most interesting buildings are the very fine 17th-century **Palacio Municipal** (1627), on Plaza de Armas, with a splendid façade and courtyard, and the **fortress of San Juan de Ulúa** (1565), on Gallega Island, now joined by a causeway to the mainland. The fortifications failed to deter the buccaneers and San Juan de Ulúa later became a political prison. Mexico's 'Robin Hood', Chucho el Roto, was imprisoned here, and escaped three times. Benito Juárez was also incarcerated here between 1858 and 1861. In 1915, Venustiano Carranza converted it into a presidential palace. ■ *Take the bus marked Ulúa from Malecón/Av República; it is not advisable to walk there. Tue-Sun 0900-1700 fortress US$1.80.* The **Baluarte de Santiago**, a bastion that once formed part of the city walls, is at Francisco Canal y Gómez Farías and contains a small pre-Hispanic gold collection recovered from a wreck. ■ *Tue-Sun 1000-1630, US$2.10.* The **aquarium** has moved from the harbour breakwater to a new building at Villa del Mar. ■ *Mon-Fri 1000-1900, Sat and Sun 0900-1900, US$4.35.* The market on the Salvador Díaz Mirón triangle (Ignacio Allende/Miguel Alemán/H Cortés) is a fascinating experience.

The **Museo de la Ciudad**, at Zaragoza 397, has a good, well-displayed collection of photographs; it traces the history of Veracruz from the Conquest to 1910. ■ *Mon-Sat 0900-1500, US$0.35, English booklet available.* Plazuela de la Campana, by Serdán and Zaragoza, is an attractive small square. The **Museo Carranza**, on the Malecón, has photos of the Revolution, the life of Carranza and his battles against the Huerta régime. ■ *Tue-Sun 0900-1700, free.* The **Museo Histórico Naval**, Gómez Farías and Morales, has an excellent and extensive collection of naval memorabilia especially 1914 resistance to US invasion. ■ *Mon-Sun 0900-1700, free.*

On the way to Mocambo beach, where the Boulevard Avila Camacho meets Boulevard Ruiz Cortines, is the **Museo Agustín Lara**, *La Casita Blanca*, a must for anyone interested in Mexican popular music. It was the home of the greatest 20th-century Mexican song-writer, Agustín Lara, who wrote more than 700 songs (*Solamente una vez, Veracruz, Granada,* and *María Bonita* among the most

Veracruz centre

Related maps
Veracruz, page 356

0 metres 200
0 yards 200

■ **Sleeping**
1 Amparo
2 Baluarte
3 Colonial
4 Emporio
5 Hatzin
6 Mallorca
7 Mar y Tierra
8 Paloma

● **Eating**
1 El Pescador
2 La Nueva Parroquia
3 Submarino Amarillo

amous), many of which still reverberate around the streets and squares of Veracruz. US$2, free on Sun. A pianist plays and sings Tue-Sat 1100-1400, 1600-1900, and at other times visitors are welcome to play Lara's piano.

The beaches along the waterfront, and the sea, are polluted from the heavy shipping. A short bus ride from the fish market takes you to Mocambo beach, which has a superb, 50 m swimming pool (with restaurant and bar, admission US$3.30), beach restaurants, Caribbean-style beach huts and dirty sand; the water is quite a bit cleaner though still rather uninviting in colour. There are crabs and mosquitoes and much pestering by sellers. The Gulf is even warmer than the Caribbean. The beach is crowded, and at holiday time cars race up and down, there are loud radios, etc. To Mocambo take a bus marked 'Boca del Río' on Avenida Zaragoza.

Beaches
There is a fine, uncrowded beach at Chachalacas, 50 km north (see page 355)

Harbour trips from the Malecón, US$4 per person for 35 minutes, minimum 15 people. On Sunday, to Mandinga for cheap fresh seafood (big prawns), and local entertainment.

Harbour trips
For excursions north of Veracruz, see page 355

Some 6 km to the south of Veracruz (*colectivo* from Av Zaragoza) is Boca del Río, beyond Mocambo, on the left bank of the mouth of Río Jamapa. In 1518, the Spaniard Grijalva gave the already existing settlement the name of Río de Banderas as the inhabitants carried small flags in order to transmit messages. Despite commercial and residential development steadily filling up the space between Veracruz and Boca, the latter guards its own identity, and still has the atmosphere of a small village. Worthy of a visit is the church of Santa Ana (1716). Modern buildings of interest include the Palacio Municipal, Teatro del Pueblo and the Casa de la Cultura, but most people come to Boca del Río to eat at one of its many fish restaurants.

Boca del Río

A 10-minute bus ride from Boca del Río to the other side of the river is **El Conchal**, a small residential development overlooking picturesque lagoons with a number of attractive restaurants. The bus continues along a low sandy spit to Punta Antón Lizardo where there is a small village with a few beach restaurants and good sand and bathing.

Essentials

AL *Hostal de Cortés*, 3-star, Avila Camacho y de las Casas, T932-1200, F931-1209. Convenient for clean beaches, helpful. Recommended. **AL** *Mocambo*, Calzada Ruiz Cortines 4000, T922-0203, F922-0212, south of the port on Mocambo beach. 1930s palace, good service and food. Highly recommended. **A** *Calinda Veracruz*, Av Independencia and Lerdo, near Zócalo, T931-2233, F931-5134, www.hotelescalinda.com.mx Probably the best in the centre. **A** *Emporio*, Insurgentes Veracruzanos 210 y Xicoténcatl, T932-0020, F931-2261. Very good, with bath, swimming pool, inexpensive *comida corrida* and superb buffet breakfast (US$5) Sat-Sun, rather old-fashioned. **B** *Colonial*, on Zócalo, T932-0193, F932-0193. Swimming pool, indoor parking. Recommended. **B** *Hawaii*, Aquiles Serdán 458, T938-0088, F932-5524. 'Funky' architecture, comfortable, quiet.

Sleeping
■ on maps, pages 357 and opposite
Price codes: see inside front cover

Because of the liveliness of the Zócalo at night, hotels rooms overlooking the square can be noisy

  C *Baluarte*, opposite the small fort of Baluarte, Canal 265, T932-6042, F325486. Good, clean. Recommended. **C** *Concha Dorada*, on Zócalo, T/F313246. Very pleasant. **C** *Cristóbal Colón*, Avila Camacho 681, T982-3844. Small, quiet, some rooms with sea-view, balconies, clean. **C** *Mar y Tierra*, Figueroa y Malecón, T/F932-6096. Cheaper in low season, some rooms with balconies overlooking the harbour, restaurant serving good breakfast. **C** *Príncipe*, Collado 195. Some distance from centre, very clean with hot shower and toilet. **C** *Royalty*, Abasolo 34, T932-3988, F932-7096. Average, near beach, 20 mins' walk from Zócalo, but noisy as it caters mainly to student groups. Recommended. **C** *Zamora*, in Boca del Río, comfortable rooms with a/c.

  D *Casa de Huéspedes*, on Morelia, near Zócalo. With bath, hot water, quiet, clean, use of mosquito net needed, economical restaurant next door. **D** *Faro*, 16 de Septiembre 223, near *Hotel Emporio*, T931-6538, F931-6176. Good value. **D** *Impala*, Orizaba 658, T937-0169. With bath, cold water, mosquitoes but clean, near bus station. **D** *Mallorca*, Aquiles Serdán 42 T932-7549. With bath and fan, radio, newly furnished, very clean. Highly recommended **D** *Oriente*, M Lerdo 20, T/F931-2490. Secure parking, clean, friendly, balconies (noisy from street), good fans, some a/c.

E *Amparo*, Aquiles Serdán 482, T932-2738. With fan, insect screens, clean, hot water good value. Recommended. **E** *Casa de Huéspedes La Tabasqueña*, Av Morelos 325. Far new bathrooms, upper rooms less good, front rooms noisy, many others without windows cheap, clean, safe, helpful. **E** *Hatzin*, Reforma 6 and Avlsta. Friendly. Recommended **E** *Paloma*, Av Morales y Reforma, T932-4260. Clean, basic, fan, friendly, good value **E** *Santander*, Landero y Coss 123, T932-4529. With bath and TV, very clean. **F** *Las Nievas* Tenoya, off Plaza Zamora, T932-5748. With bath, fan, dark rooms. Many others in port area, reached by bus from the bus terminal.

Trailer park The only trailer park is behind *Hotel Mocambo* (see above). Dry camping, showers and bathrooms dirty, US$6.50 for vehicle and 2 people.

Eating
● *on maps, pages 357 and 358*

Toritos are the local drinks made of eggs, milk, fruit and alcohol, delicious and potent

La Nueva Parroquia, on Malecón, is famous throughout Mexico (it used to be called *Café La Parroquia*, on Plaza de Armas). 2 coffee houses in same block, very popular, excellent coffee and capuccino, good food and full of atmosphere. In the **main market**, there are inexpensive restaurants in the mezzanine, overlooking the interior (watch out for extras that you did not order). The **fish market** has excellent fish and shrimp cocktails, and opposite are *La Garlopa* and *Doña Paz/ Normita*. Good seafood. Excellent fresh fish at *Tano's* just off the Malecón, Mario Molina 20. Highly recommended. There is a good local fish restaurant, *Olímpica*, Zaragoza 250, near the fish market, 2 blocks from the Zócalo. *El Pescador*, for fish, Zaragoza 335 y Morales (not evenings). Good cheap *comida corrida*; and the steakhouse *Submarino Amarillo*, Malecón 472. *La Carreta*, Mariano Arista 574. Highly recommended. *Karen*, Arista 574 between Landero y Coss and Zaragoza. Good fish restaurant. *Café de la Catedral*, Ocampo y Parque Zamora. Large, local, few tourists, try fish stuffed with shrimps. *El Azteca de Cayetano*, Mario Molina 94. *Mondongos de fruta* (a selection of all the fruits in season, plus fruit-flavoured ice) are prepared on a plate; also *Mondongo de Fruta*, M Molina 88. Not cheap but delicious for fruits, juices and ices. An interesting place is *Tiburón*, Landero y Coss 167, esq Aquiles Serdán, 2 blocks from Zócalo, run by 'Tiburón' González, the 'Rey de la Alegría', or 'Rey Feo' of carnival; the walls are covered in pictures of him and his *comparsas*, dating back to at least 1945. The food is good and inexpensive too. *La Paella*, Plaza de Armas, 138, has its name written into the concrete of the entrance floor as well as a sign. Good *comida corrida*. *Pizza Palace*, Zamora. Buffet 1200-1700, US$5. *Emir Cafetería*, Independencia 1520, near F Canal. Good breakfast. *La Quinta del Son*, on paved side street off Aquiles Serdán. Bar and restaurant, food nothing special but excellent Cuban-style *trova* band in afternoon. *Gran Café del Portal*, opposite cathedral. Traditional (marimba all day), but not cheap. *La Puerta del Sol*, on Molina, 1 block south of the Zócalo. Friendly bar, cheap beer. *El Tranvía*, General Prim esq Rayón, opposite Parque Zamora. For good value unpretentious food (not just fish). *Le Blé*, coffee house, on road parallel to Blvd Avila Camacho, between F Canal and Rayón. Good décor, fine variety of coffees. *Nevería y Refresquería Aparito*, Aquiles Serdán and Landero y Coss, near fish market. Good for fruit and juices, try *mondongo de frutas*.

In Boca del Río *Boulevard*, Blvd I Zaragoza esq Zamora. Expensive. Excellent cheaper restaurants nearby serving large variety of fresh fish. **In El Conchal** *Restaurant El Payán*.

Festivals The *Shrovetide carnival*, 7 weeks before Easter, is said to be Mexico's finest, rivalling those of New Orleans, Brazil and Trinidad. The carnival starts a week before Shrove Tuesday and ends on Ash Wednesday; Sat-Tue are the main days with parades. At this time of year it can be very difficult to find accommodation or transportation.

Shopping The local tortoiseshell jewellery adorned with silver is not commonly found. Remember that tortoises are a protected species and the import of tortoiseshell into the US and many other countries is prohibited.

Air At Las Bajadas (VER), 12 km from the centre, to the capital several flights daily and flights **Transport**
up and down the coast: Monterrey, Tampico, Villahermosa, Ciudad del Carmen, Mérida,
Cancún, Tapachula and Tuxtla Gutiérrez. Flights also to **Houston**, **San Antonio** and
Havana. *AeroMexico*, García Auly esq Simon Bolivar, between bus station and seafront.

Buses The majority of buses are booked solid for 3 days in advance throughout summer
and other holiday periods; at other times queues of up to 2 hrs possible at Mexico City booking offices of bus companies (best company: *ADO*). Book outward journeys on arrival in
Veracruz, as the bus station is some way out of town and there are often long queues.
Referred to as *ADO*, it is divided into 1st and 2nd class; the 1st class part, mostly *ADO* company, is on the main street, Díaz Mirón y Xalapa, T937-6790; *Autobuses Unidos*, mostly 2nd
class, is on Lafragua y Xalapa (2 blocks from *ADO*), T937-2376. For local buses, get accurate
information from the tourist office. Buses to the main bus station along Av 5 de Mayo,
marked *ADO*; and from the station to the centre, blue and white or red and white buses
marked Díaz Mirón; pass 1 block from the Zócalo, US$0.35, or *colectivos*, also US$0.35. Taxi to
ADO terminal from centre, US$1.50.

To **Cempoala** (see page 355): 2nd class buses from *ADO* terminal 30 mins to Cardel then
micro, US$0.40. **Mexico City**: frequent services round the clock, 5 hrs, US$28. **Mérida**: 16 hrs,
US$62. **Oaxaca**: a few services through the day, 7 hrs, US$22. **Puebla**: every couple of hrs, 8 hrs,
US$13; **Villahermosa**: almost hourly, 7 hrs, US$36. To **Xalapa**: frequent departures, 2 hrs, US$4.

Connections with Guatemala There are no through buses to Guatemala, but there are
connecting services. Local bus services run Tapachula-border and border-Guatemala City;
quicker than the much more mountainous route further north. Bus Veracruz-Tapachula 14
hrs, 1½-hr meal stop (at 0230), 4 10-min station stops, US$44, *plus* service US$50, 1900 every
night, 13 hrs, video, reclining seats. Alternatively, take *ADO* bus to **Oaxaca**, then carry on to
Tapachula (12 hrs) by bus. This allows you to stop at intermediate points of your choice.

Airline offices *AeroMéxico*, García Auly 231, T935-0142. *Mexicana*, Av 5 de Mayo y Aquiles Serdán, **Directory**
T932-2242. **Banks** *Bancomer*, Independencia y Juárez has its own *casa de cambio* for dollars and TCs,
good rates, open Mon-Fri 0930-1730, Sat-Sun 1100-1400, also branches at Prim esq Rayón, Blvd Avila
Camacho e Iturbide, Centro Comercial Plaza Cristal, Centro Comercial Las Américas, Blvd Ruiz Cortines
esq Fraccionamiento Costa de Oro. *Banca Serfín*, Díaz Mirón, 2 blocks from bus station, changes US$
cash and TCs. *Banamex* is at Independencia esq Juárez with branches at 5 de Mayo esq Emparán,
Mario Molino and 5 de Mayo, Centro Comercial Las Américas, Plaza Hotel Continental. American
Express agency is *Viajes Olymar*, Blvd Avila Camacho 2221, T931-3406. 2 *casas de cambio*: *La Amistad*,
Juárez 112 (behind the hotels on the Zócalo), rates not as good as the banks but much quicker; *Hotel
Veracruz* changes money at similar rates. **Communications** Internet: *Networld Café*, Callejón
Clavijero 173, near Francisco. *Canal*, Mon-Sat 0900-2100, US$1.25/hr. *Stationet*, 5 de Mayo, between
Lerdo and Zamora, Mon-Sat 0900-2100, US$1/hr. *Micro Café*, Ruiz Cortines, 100 m on from Museo
Agustín Lara, Mon-Sat 1000-2300, US$1.80/hr. **Post offices**: main post office by bridge to San Juan de
Ulúa fortress, a fine building inaugurated in 1902 by Porfirio Díaz, open 0900-1200 Mon-Fri; also at
Palacio Federal, 5 de Mayo y Rayón, 0800-1900. **Embassies and consulates** *US Consular Agency*,
Víctimas del 25 de Junio 388, in centre. **Laundry** Madero 616, US$1.50 per 3 kg, open 0730-2300.

The Papaloapan Region

Route 180 heads southeast from the port of Veracruz along the flat, wet coastal plain
through Alvarado and on the Tuxtla mountains and the Isthmus of Tehuantepec.
An alternative route is to turn inland through the fertile Papaloapan region and on
south into the state of Oaxaca.

Puerto Alvarado is a modern fishing port 1½ hours south from Veracruz by bus, **Puerto**
none too pleasant for women on their own as there are many bars and drunks. **Alvarado**
Sleeping **D** *Hotel Lety*. Reasonable but for grim plumbing system. **D** *Hotel del Pas-* *The people of Alvarado*
tor. Avoid next-door restaurant. **D** *María Isela*. Quiet, clean with fan. Recom- *are notorious*
mended. Exchange services 1000-1200. The local fair/carnival runs from 31 *throughout Mexico for*
March-5 April. *their expletives and*
colourful language

Cross the **Río Papaloapan** (Butterfly River) by a toll bridge (US$1.70) and go along Route 180 into the sugar-cane area around Lerdo de Tejada and Angel R Cavada. At *El Trópico* shop a dirt road turns left to some quiet beaches such as Salinas and Roca Partida. Only at Easter are the beaches crowded; they are normally the preserve of fishermen using hand nets from small boats. In the dry season (December-May) there is a passable road along the coast.

Tlacotalpan
Phone code: 288
Colour map 3, grid C6
Population: 14,492

There is a famous Candelmas fiesta here on 31 January when accommodation is impossible to find

About 15 km from Alvarado a new bridge replaces the old ferry-crossing at Buenavista over the Río Papaloapan, and Route 175 heads southwards to the town of Tlacotalpan where the Papaloapan and San Juan rivers meet. It used to be on an island until the Cabezo and San Cristóbal rivers dried up and it has a secluded feel about it. This small town, once the main town in southern Veracruz, and an important international port in the steamship era, is regarded as the centre of Jarocho culture (an amalgam of Spanish, mainly from Seville, African and indigenous cultures). It has many picturesque streets with one-storey houses all fronted by stuccoed columns and arches painted in various bright colours. There are two churches in the Zócalo, the Parroquia de San Cristóbal and the Capilla de la Candelaria, and a Casa de las Artesanías on Chazaro, 1½ blocks from the Zócalo. The **Museo Salvador Ferrando** contains interesting local 19th-century paintings, furniture, artefacts and Jarocho costume. ■ *US$0.50.* The **tourist office** is on the main plaza, T884-2050. ■ *Mon-Fri 0800-1400, 1500-1900, Sat-Sun 1000-1400.*

Sleeping and eating B *Tlacotalpan*, R Beltrán 35, T/F884-2063. Clean, a/c, restaurant, good value. D *Reforma*, Carranza 2, sometimes known as *Viajero*, T884-2022. Good. C *Posada Doña Lala*, Carranza 11, T884-2580, F42455. With a/c and TV, good restaurant. F *Jarocho*, Carranza 22. Seedy, but large rooms in old house, good view of town from roof. *Restaurant La Flecha*. Excellent *sopa de mariscos* and *jaiba a la tlacotalpina* (crab). Many good fish restaurants with terraces on the riverfront, eg *Brisas de Tlacotalpan*.

Transport Buses to/from Veracruz via Alvarado (Rápidos de Papaloapan US$3.10, 2¼ hrs), to Santiago Tuxtla, San Andrés Tuxtla (Cuenca US$2.50, 1½ hrs) and Villahermosa.

Cosamaloapan
Phone code: 288
Population: 54,059

Cosamaloapan, some 40 km beyond Tlacotalpan on Route 175, is the local market centre with a number of hotels, and the staging point for most bus lines from Veracruz, Orizaba and Oaxaca (bus station 5 blocks from plaza). One of the largest sugar mills in Mexico is situated just outside the town – Ingenio San Cristóbal. From Cosamaloapan to Papaloapan the banks of the river are lined with fruit trees.
Sleeping D *San Martín*, Hidalgo 304, 1 block from plaza towards main highway, T882-0888, F882-0977. Old style, a/c, bar, restaurant. D *Roma*, Carranza 101, T882-1377, F882-1543. Modern. E *Licona*, Carranza, just off plaza. Basic. E *Central*, Morelos 302, on plaza, T882-0108. A/c, restaurant.

Otatitlán

Another 40 km, beyond Cosamaloapan, is a ferry to Otatitlán, also on the east bank of the river (US$0.25, it leaves whenever there are sufficient passengers). The town, also known as El Santuario, dates back to early colonial times, its houses with tiled roofs supported by columns (not as impressive as Tlacotalpan), but most interesting is the church. The padre maintains that the gold-patterned dome is the largest unsupported structure of its kind in Mexico, measuring 20 m wide and 40 m high. El Santuario has one of the three black wooden statues of Christ brought over from Spain for the son of Hernán Cortés. During the anti-clerical violence of the 1930s, attempts to burn it failed, although the original head was cut off and now stands in a glass case. The first weekend in May is the saint's day and fair, for which pilgrims flock in from the *sierra* and from the Tuxtlas, many in local dress. (*Restaurant-Bar Pepe* serves delicious but unusual local food. *Restaurant-Bar Ipiranga III* also offers excellent cooking; both by embarkation point.) To continue on to Tuxtepec either cross back over the river, or take a bus from the plaza to Santa Cruz, where there is a bus station at the junction.

At the town of **Papaloapan** on the eastern bank of the river, Route 145 from Orizaba to Rodríguez Clara and Sayula crosses Route 175, the Alvarado to Oaxaca road. On the west bank is the Santa Cruz bus terminal (almost under the railway bridge) where all second-class buses stop. A passenger ferry may be taken from here to Papaloapan (US$0.50). Although Papaloapan is the route centre for the area, the most convenient centre is Tuxtepec, 9 km further south (see below).

Papaloapan to La Tinaja

In the cane cutting season great care should be taken at night for carts travelling on the road with no lights

Route 145 heads northwest past **Tres Valles** (cheap, good regional food; annual fair mid-November), and on to **Tierra Blanca**, a railway junction on the Tapachula-Veracruz and Mérida-Córdoba-Mexico City lines (Hotels: **D** *Principal*. Own shower and fan, clean, just above bus station, noisy. **E** *Balún Canán*. Cheap, hot. *Bimbis* restaurant by *ADO* bus station, good; shopping centre, market, car repairs, including Volkswagen agent). Route 145 passes under a sign saying 'La Puerta del Papaloapan', to join the main Mexico City with Veracruz road (Route 150) at **La Tinaja**, a second class bus junction, with gasoline, and restaurants (one air-conditioned at service station). Papaloapan to La Tinaja takes about one hour; the road often has a lot of lorries. There are three poorly marked railway crossings on the road, two near La Granja and one near Tierra Blanca. The tarmac is often damaged in the wet season (June-December).

Papaloapan to Sayula

From Papaloapan a paved road runs eastwards to Rodríguez Clara and on to Sayula de Alemán on the Trans-Isthmian road. This road passes through the main pineapple-producing region of Mexico, which has encouraged the development of towns such as **Loma Bonita** (local airstrip, hotels, restaurants and gasoline) and **Villa Isla** (*Hotel La Choca*, restaurant good, railway station, *ADO* bus terminal, and centre for the rich cattle-producing area that surrounds it).

From Villa Isla a good dirt road runs south to **Playa Vicente** (*Population*: 6,974), another ranching town, located beside a wide river (**F** *Hotel Ros Bal*, clean, safe, fan, good); excellent crayfish may be eaten at the *Restaurant La Candileja*, while the café on the central plaza serves tender steaks. A dirt road leaves the Villa Isla-Playa Vicente road for **Abasolo del Valle** (*Population*: 2,000), but only reaches to within 7 km. The last few kilometres can be impassable by vehicle in the wet season. The town is set beside a lagoon and the houses are surrounded by fruit trees (no hotels or restaurants). Gasoline can be bought – ask at a shop who has some to sell.

At the crossroads of the Papaloapan-Sayula road about 80 km from Papaloapan, where the south turn is to Villa Isla, the north turn is a paved road, which in about 30 minutes will take you past two turnings to the Olmec site at Tres Zapotes and up to Santiago Tuxtla (see page 367).

Route 145 continues east to **Rodríguez Clara**, a compact, thriving town, which is reached by branching off south down a dirt road. There are two hotels, the better is in the centre of the town, **D** *Hotel Roa*; *Restaurant La Mexicana*. Recommended.

Tuxtepec

This is the natural place for a stay in the Papaloapan area. It is an important supply centre in the state of Oaxaca, a large commercial city, untouristed and tranquil; prices here are lower than in other parts of Oaxaca. The region has significant agricultural activity, including cattle-raising, sugar cane and pineapple plantations. The local industries are a sugar mill, brewery and paper mill. The city is built on the left bank of the Río Santo Domingo, a tributary of the Papaloapan. Avenida Independencia, the main commercial avenue, runs along the riverfront and has the market and many shops, as well as several *miradores* offering good views. A small ferry crosses the river from below the viewpoint next to *Hotel Mirador*. The people of Tuxtepec consider themselves more *Jarochos* (i.e. from the state of Veracruz) than *Oaxaqueños*; the mixture of the music and exuberance of Veracruz with the food and handicrafts of Oaxaca is fascinating. The **tourist office**, *Cámara Nacional de*

Phone code: 287
Colour map 3, grid C5
Population: 77,500

Watch out for biting gnats near the river

Veracruz and the Gulf Coast

Comercio Serytour, Libertad esq Allende, opposite Parque Juárez, T875-0886 has limited information. ■ *Mon-Fri 0900-1400 and 1700-2000, Sat 0900-1300*.

Parque Benito Juárez, the main plaza, has a monument to the mother and child, an ample Palacio Municipal to the south, and a modern cathedral to the east. Further west is Parque Hidalgo, with a statue of the father of Mexico's independence. The modern **Casa de la Cultura** is on Daniel Soto by Blvd Benito Juárez.

Sleeping **B-C** *El Rancho*, Avila Camacho 435, T875-0722, F875-0641. With a/c, pool, restaurant, evening entertainment, parking, US motel style. Recommended. **C** *Hacienda*, Blvd Benito Juárez 409, T875-1500, F875-1732. With a/c, restaurant, pool, gardens, parking. **C-D** *Playa Bruja*, Independencia 1531, T875-0325. With a/c, pool, cafeteria, parking. **D** *María de Lourdes*, 5 de Mayo 1380, T875-0410, F875-0016. A/c, cheaper with fan, hot water, good parking. Recommended. **D** *Mirador*, Independencia 751, T875-0500. With a/c, hot water, **E** with fan, views of the river, a bit run down but OK, parking. **D** *Sacre*, Libertad 1170 esq Ocampo, T875-0846. With a/c, **E** with fan. Good. **D** *Posada del Sol*, 20 de Noviembre 1103 y Ocampo, T875-3737. With a/c, **F** with fan, opposite Fletes y Pasajes terminal. Noisy. **D** *Tuxtepec*, Matamoros 2 esquina Independencia, T875-0934. With a/c, **E** with fan, hot water, restaurant, good value. Recommended. **E** *Posada la Misión*, Hidalgo 409, T875-2381. With bath, fan. **E** *Posada La Choca*, Independencia 1713, T875-0532. Basic. **E-F** *Casa de Huéspedes Ocampo*, Ocampo 285 y Libertad. With bath, fan, friendly. **F** *Avenida*, Independencia 566, T875-0065. With bath, fan, basic, good value. **F** *Catedral*, Guerrero, near Zócalo, T875-0764. Very friendly, fan and shower.

Eating *Los Caporales*, Independencia 560, 2nd floor. Good value *comida corrida* and à la carte. *El Estero*, Benito Juárez by Independencia. Fish dishes and local cuisine. Excellent. *La Tablita*, Matamoros 2. Good *comida corrida* and à la carte. Long hours. *Mandingo*, 20 de Noviembre. Fish dishes. *Manhattan*, Independencia 49. International food, pricey. *Villa de Carvajal*, Muro Blvd esq Nicolás Bravo, on the riverfront. Seafood and grill. *Taquería Gambrinos*, 5 de Mayo 438, 1½ blocks from Parque Juárez. Excellent tacos, very popular, busy every evening. Recommended. *Pizza Viva*, 5 de Mayo 568. Pizza. *La Mascota de Oro*, 20 de Noviembre 891. Cheap, very friendly. Beer from the barrel can be bought from the bar next to the Palacio Municipal and the best ices are found at *La Movida*.

Sports The Papaloapan River and its tributaries, as well as the Presa Miguel Alemán, offer plenty of opportunities for watersports (see *Excursions* below). **Fishing** The most common species found are *robalo* (sea bass), *mojarra* (carp), and on the Río Tonto (Puente de Caracol), *sábalo* (tarpon). **Boating** Motor boating and rowing is popular on the rivers and artificial lake; popular races are held in the month of May. **Rodeo** Tuxtepec has a *lienzo charro* with capacity for 5,000 spectators, where rodeos are held; this is an important regional tradition.

Festivals The *Fiestas Patronales* in honour of St John the Baptist are held **24** and **25 Jun**. There are fairs, fireworks and dances, including the *flor de piña* folk dance for which the Papaloapan region is well known.

Shopping Tuxtepec is a busy commercial centre, which attracts shoppers from many nearby towns. There are many clothing stores with good prices.

Transport **Air** A new airport was opened in 1999 in Loma Bonita, 36 km to the east on the road to Sayula. Veracruz, 165 km to the north, has the main airport in the area.

Roads The Tuxtepec-Palomares road, Route 147, provides a shortcut to the Transístmica, but armed robberies are a danger along this route day and night. The road via Sayula is 20 km longer, but much safer. *AU* buses covering the route from Tuxtepec to Tehuantepec, Juchitán and Salina Cruz, take only the Sayula road.

Buses There is a joint bus station for *ADO*, *AU* and *Cuenca* at Matamoros by Blvd Avila Camacho. Other 2nd class companies have their own stations. 3 nightly to **Juchitán**, (US$14), **Tehuantepec** (US$15) and **Salina Cruz**: (US$16) with *AU*. To **Oaxaca**: 12 daily, 7½ hrs,

US$10.50. To **Mexico City**: 8 daily, US$26. To **Puebla**: 6 daily, US$20. To **San Andrés Tuxtla**: frequent daily service, US$9. To **Valle Nacional**, every 15 mins from 0500-2199, 1 hr, US$1.60. To **Veracruz**: frequent daily service, US$8.

Banks *Bancomer*, Independencia 437, Cash and TCs, 0900-1400, complicated. *Bital*, Independencia 895, cash and TCs. *Agencia de Divisas Greco*, Independencia 269, cash and TCs, poor rates, Mon-Fri 0900-1800, Sat 0900-1400. **Communications** Internet: *Tuxcom*, Guerrero esq Muro Blvd, by riverfront, Mon-Sat 0800-2100, Sun 0900-1900. US$1.95/hr. *Tux-Net*, Morelos 200, Mon-Sat 0900-2100. US$2.15/hr. **Laundry** *Lava Sec*, Guerrero esq Muro Blvd and Independencia 1683, wash and dry US$3.25 per 4 kg load. **Tour operators** *Sotelo Viajes*, Morelos 118, T875-2656. Primore, Juárez 163, T875-4344.

Directory

The **Presa Miguel Alemán**, a lake formed by the Miguel Alemán and Cerro de Oro dams, is very scenic. There are several points of access, the most widely used being that of **Temascal**, a small town near the Alemán dam, with shops and a few places to eat, but no hotels although there is a woman who offers very basic accommodation. Sunday is the most active day in Temascal. Access is via a paved road off the Tuxtepec-Tierra Blanca road. ■ *There is an hourly bus service from Tuxtepec with AU, 0615-1815, US$2, two hours, last bus back from Temascal at 1800.* At one end of the dam, atop a pyramid, is an imposing monument to Miguel Alemán, former president and promoter of the project. To the right of the monument is a small village along the shoreline with thatched huts serving fish and cold drinks; *mojarra* (carp) is the speciality here, brought in by small fishing craft. The same boats can be hired for touring or fishing for approximately US$1.75 per hour. For swimming best take a boat to the island across the bay. There are a number of settlements around the lake and on some islands; Soyaltepec, on an island of the same name, is the closest to Temascal. A nice trip is from Temascal to **San Pedro Ixcatlán**, a Mazatec village to the south. ■ *One boat at 1100 daily, US$2.20 per person, 1½ hours.* The crossing is lovely, with many cormorants and herons flying by and spectacular views of the mountains rising abruptly behind the lake. There is a large colonial church in San Pedro, a lovely spot set on a hilltop with fine views of the lake. Nearby, across from a school, is **E-F** *Hotel Nanguina*. With bath, fan, clean, comfortable large rooms, good value, nice terrace with views. There are three simple restaurants in town. The *fiestas patronales* are held on **May 14** and **15** when the town gets very crowded. The boat from San Pedro to Temascal goes in the early morning. Shared taxis go from San Pedro along a dirt road to a crossing on the Tuxtepec – Jalapa de Díaz road (30 minutes, US$0.65 per person), from where you can get a pick-up to Jalapa de Díaz (see below, US$0.40 per person) or a bus to Tuxtepec.

Excursions from Tuxtepec

The road west of Tuxtepec towards the state of Puebla is quite scenic; along it are a number of towns and villages that maintain an indigenous flavour, *huipiles* and crafts can be found here, especially on market day. The road is paved as far as Jalapa de Díaz and then continues to San Bartolomé Ayautla and Huautla de Jiménez; there is a bus service with AU between Tuxtepec, Ojitlán and Jalapa de Díaz every 30 minutes, 0430-1800, US$1 to Ojitlán, US$2 to Jalapa de Díaz. **San Lucas Ojitlán** is a Chinantec town, 42 km from Tuxtepec, with a hilltop church dominating the surroundings. It is an important regional centre and its Sunday market gathers many people from the nearby villages; this is the best time to see Chinantec women wearing their *huipiles*. **F** *Hotel Gallegos*, off the main street, enquire at the Farmacia Veterinaria. Very basic, no running water. There are also a few basic eating establishments. The local **fiesta** in honour of Santa Rosa is held the last week in August, when there is much drinking and festivities. **Jalapa de Díaz** (*population* 8,000) is 70 km from Tuxtepec, near the base of Cerro Rabón, a mountain with a spectacular 500 m sheer cliff face. The town is built on several small hills, with the church on the highest. The population is mainly Mazatec; the women wear colourful *huipiles* which may be purchased in shops and private homes. **F** Unnamed hotel near the Palacio Municipal, shared bath, very basic. A couple of simple eating establishments and several well-stocked shops. The local **fiestas** are held in mid-January.

Veracruz and the Gulf Coast

Tuxtepec to Oaxaca

The road from Tuxtepec to Oaxaca, Route 175, is a spectacular steep and winding route, cars need good brakes and it is reported to be difficult for caravans and cyclists; the latter are recommended to take a bus. It is mostly a paved road, but sections near the high passes can at times be badly potholed and rutted. The ride up from Tuxtepec to Oaxaca takes six to seven hours, a bit less in the opposite direction. From Tuxtepec, at 30 m above sea level, the road climbs 30 m gradually to Valle Nacional (see below). Just after crossing the Río Valle Nacional it climbs steeply into the Sierra Juárez, reaching the El Mirador pass (2,900 m) in 2½ hours. The transition from lush lowland forest to pines is splendid, there are lovely views of the ridges and valley far below (sit on the right if travelling south to Oaxaca). At Cerro Machín, just after the pass, is *Restaurant Yoana*. Good. From here the road drops in two hours to Ixtlán de Juárez and San Pablo Guelatao, the birthplace of Benito Juárez (gas station, restaurants, see Excursions northeast of Oaxaca, page 367). The route continues to drop to the dry valley of the Río Manzanillo, at 1,500 m, before climbing again to La Cumbre pass (2,700 m), from which there are fine views of Oaxaca below, one hour further.

Valle Nacional
Population: 6,244
Colour map 3, grid C5
Altitude: 60 m

Set in the beautiful valley of the Río Valle Nacional, 48 km south of Tuxtepec, is the small town of **Valle Nacional**, which sees few visitors, but offers basic services and excellent opportunities for birding and walking in the surrounding hills. The town is laid out lengthwise along the main road, there is a gas station at the Tuxtepec end; tank-up here on the way to Oaxaca. Nearby are several rubber plantations (for example just across the bridge on the road to Oaxaca) and tappers may be seen at work early in the morning, especially in the dry season. This area had a horrific reputation as the *Valle de los Miserables*, in the era of Porfirio Díaz, for political imprisonment and virtual slavery from which there was no escape; a vivid description of this period can be found in John Kenneth Turner's *Barbarous Mexico* (1911). *Fiestas patronales* of nearby San José are held 18-19 March.

Along the scenic Tuxtepec-Valle Nacional road are several recreational opportunities, including **Chiltepec**, a popular bathing spot on the Río Valle Nacional, 22 km from Tuxtepec. Not far from Valle Nacional is a lovely natural spring at **Zuzul**. The setting, by the Soloyapan river and the town of Sola de Vega, is very pretty; although the water is chilly, it is quite pleasant for swimming, free entry, there are a few bars nearby, many people on Sundays and holidays, especially Easter Week. From Valle Nacional, take a Tuxtepec-bound bus as far as La Boca (US$0.33, 20 minutes), then a pick-up truck (US$0.20, 5 minutes) or walk 20 minutes (take the side road right from La Boca, then the first turn-off to the left) to the end of the road at the river's edge, where a motorboat will take you to Zuzul on the other shore (US$0.20). Pick-up trucks also run from La Boca to San Cristóbal and other towns in the valleys to the east of Valle Nacional; you can make some nice day trips in this area.

Sleeping and eating E *Lourdes Sánchez*, near gas station at north end of town. With bath, fan, good restaurant, basic, family run, friendly. E *Valle*, off main street. With bath, fan, cold water, parking, basic, family run, friendly. E Unnamed hotel next door. With bath, cold water, a bit run down. Several simple restaurants and *taquerías* along the main street.

Transport Buses: Oaxaca: 13 daily, 6 hrs, US$8.50. **Tuxtepec**: every 15 mins throughout the day, 1 hr, US$1.10.

In the Sierra Juárez, some 50 km south of Valle Nacional, on the road to Oaxaca is a turn-off west for **San Pedro Yolox**, a peaceful Chinantec village, clustered on the side of the mountain, which lies some 20 minutes' drive from the main road, along a dirt road. About 25 km further south and 90 km from Oaxaca is **Llano de las Flores**, a huge grassy clearing in the pine forest, with grazing animals and cool scented air; nearby are waterfalls. Wood from these forests is cut for the paper mill in Tuxtepec.

Veracruz and the Gulf Coast

As you make the transition from the lowlands to the mountains, the wooden houses with thatched roofs are replaced by adobe or brick homes. At 106 km south of Valle Nacional and 65 km north of Oaxaca is Ixtlán de Juárez and a couple of kilometres further south **Guelatao**, the birthplace of Benito Juárez. At 30 km from Oaxaca is **El Punto**, surrounded by pine and oak forest.

Los Tuxtlas

Back on the coastal Route 180, southeast of Alvarado and the Papaloapan, is Tula where there is a spectacular waterfall, **El Salto de Tula**; a restaurant is set beside the falls. The road then climbs up into the mountainous volcanic area of Los Tuxtlas, known as the Switzerland of Mexico for its mountains and perennial greenness.

This pleasant town of colonial origin is set on a river. In the main square is the largest known Olmec head, carved in solid stone, and also a museum, **Museo Tuxtleco**, containing examples of local tools, photos, items used in witchcraft (*brujería*), the first sugar-cane press used in Mexico, and another Olmec head. ■ *Mon-Sat 0900-1800, Sun 0900-1500, tourist info available here.* There is dancing to *jarana* bands in the Christmas fortnight. In June and July, dancers wear jaguar masks to perform the *danza de los liseres*.

The archaeological site of **Tres Zapotes** lies to the west; it is reached by leaving the paved road south towards Villa Isla and taking either the dirt road at Tres Caminos (signposted) in the dry season (a quagmire from May-December), or in the wet season access can be slowly achieved by turning right at about Km 40, called Tibenal, and following the dirt road north to the site of the museum. ■ *0900-1700, US$1.65. If it is closed, the lady in the nearby shop has a key.* The site, once the centre of the Olmec culture, is 1 km walk (the bus cannot reach Tres Zapotes if rain has swollen the river that the road has to cross). At the museum, there is an Olmec head, also the largest carved stela ever found and stela fragments bearing the New World's oldest Long Count Date, equal to 31 BC. In this region of Mexico are other Olmec sites at Cerro de las Mesas, Laguna de los Cerros and San Lorenzo Tenochtitlán. The other major Olmec site is further east, at La Venta, in the neighbouring state of Tabasco (see page 426).

Santiago Tuxtla
Phone code: 294
Colour map 3, grid C6
Population: 54,433

Travellers with little time to spare may find the trip to Tres Zapotes not worth the effort as there is little to see at the site

Sleeping and eating C *Hotel Castellanos*, on Plaza, T947-0300. Hot shower, clean, swimming pool (US$1 for non-residents). Recommended. **D** *Estancia Olmeca*, No 78 on main highway just north of *ADO* office, T947-0737. Clean, friendly, parking. **E** *Morelos*, Obregón 13 and Morelos, T947-0474. Family run, quiet, nicely furnished.

For eating, try *Chazaro*, near bridge over stream, on other side to Morelos. Small, good seafood especially *sopa de mariscos* and *chucumite* (fish). Inexpensive.

Transport AU bus from **Veracruz**: 2nd class, 3 hrs, US$2.80. **Tlacotalpan**: with Cuenca, 1¼ hrs, US$3. To **Tres Zapotes**: from Morelos (1 block below *ADO*), 0700, 0830, 1130, 1300, 1500, 1630.

Directory Banks: exchange at *Banco Comermex* on Plaza, TCs 0900-1330.

A further 15 km beyond Santiago lies San Andrés Tuxtla, the largest town of the area, with narrow winding streets, by-passed by a ring road. It has a well-stocked market with Oaxacan foods such as *totopos* (nachos), *carne enchilada* (spicy meat), and *tamales de elote* (cakes of maize-flour steamed in leaves). It is the centre of the cigar trade. One factory beside the main road permits visitors to watch the process and will produce special orders of cigars (*puros*) marked with an individual's name.

San Andrés Tuxtla
Phone code: 294
Colour map 3, grid C6
Population: 142,251

Sleeping B *del Parque*, Madero 5, T942-0198. A/c, very clean, good restaurant. **B** *Posada San Martín*, Av Juárez 304, T942-1036. Clean, modern. **C** *Posada San José*, Belisario

Veracruz and the Gulf Coast

Domínguez 10, T942-1010, close to plaza. Run by nice family and staff, restaurant, pick-up truck for excursions, 2nd hotel at Monte Pío. **C** *San Andrés*, Madero 6, just off plaza, T942-0604. Clean, a/c, restaurant, parking, laundry service. **D** *Colonial*, Pino Suárez opposite *Figueroa*, T942-0552. With bath, hot water, clean. **D-E** *Figueroa*, Pino Suárez 10. Hot water, friendly. **D** *Isabel*, Madero 13, T942-1617. A/c, OK. **D** *Zamfer*, ½ block from Zócalo. **E** *Casa de Huéspedes la Orizaba*, in the centre of town. Without bath, clean, hot water, friendly. **E** *Catedral*, Pino Suárez and Bocanegra, near cathedral, T942-0237. Very nice. **E** *Juárez*, 400 m down street from *ADO* terminal (No 417, T942-0974). Clean, friendly.

Eating Near the town centre is the restaurant *La Carreta*, otherwise known as *Guadalajara de Noche*. It appears small from the outside but is large and pleasant inside. Well recommended. Sells *tepache*, a drink made from fermented pineapple, similar in flavour to cider, and *agua de Jamaica*. *La Caperucita*, popular with locals.

Transport **Bus**: *ADO* to **Campeche**: 13 hrs, US$30. **Cancún**: US$56. *AU* to **Catemaco**: frequent, US$0.60. **Frontera**: US$15, **Mexico City**: 9 hrs, US$28. **Tuxtepec**: 13 buses per day, US$4 via Cosamaloapan. **Villahermosa**: regular service, 6 hrs US$14.

Directory **Tourist office**: Palacio Municipal, in office of Secretaría de Relaciones Exteriores. **Communications**: Internet *'Ri' Chat*, Constitución Nte 106, near plaza.

Catemaco

Phone code: 294
Colour map 3, grid C6
Population: 45,289

There are few street name signs

A pleasant town with a large colonial church and picturesque setting on the lake, 13 km from San Andrés Tuxtla (bus service irregular, taxi US$5). There are stalls selling handicrafts from Oaxaca, and boat trips out on the lake to see the shrine where the Virgin appeared, the spa at Coyamé and the Isla de los Monos (boat owners charge US$30-35 per boat). The Isla de los Monos is home to a colony of macaque monkeys introduced from Thailand for the University of Veracruz. Launches to the island charge US$12.50, or you can pay US$3.20 to be rowed there by local fishermen – cheaper and more peaceful. Many feature films have been made on or around the lake, such as *Medicine Man*, with Sean Connery, which was filmed using the **Nanciyaga** ecological park as a 'jungle' backdrop. Catemaco town is famed for its traditional *brujos* (sorcerers), which have become a great tourist attraction.

Excursions The **Reserva Ecológica Nanciyaga**, T943-0808, 7 km round the northern shore of the lake has rainforest with rich birdlife, including toucans.

At Sihuapan, 5 km from Catemaco, is a turning south onto a paved road that leads to the impressive waterfall of **Salto de Eyipantla** (well worth a visit, especially early morning) where there are lots of butterflies. A stairway leads down to the base and a path winds through a small village to the top. Small boys at the restaurant near the falls offer their services as guides. Take second class AU bus Catemaco-Sihuapan; from 1030 buses leave every 30 minutes from Sihuapan to Eyipantla, otherwise it's a 20-minute walk to Comoapan; then take a taxi for US$2. There are also buses from the plaza in San Andrés Tuxtla.

Sleeping **A** *La Finca*, just outside town, T943-0430. Pool, attractive grounds, beautiful setting beside
A number of hotels are situated at the lakeside lake, full at weekends, a/c, comfortable rooms, but poor food and service. **B** *Playa Azul*, 2 km on road to Sontecomapan, T943-0042. Modern, a/c; in a nice setting, comfortable and shady. **B-C** *Juros*, Playa 14, T943-0084. Hot water, café, water-skiing on lake, will allow trailers and use of parking. **C** *Posada Koniapan* (swimming pool and restaurant), T943-0063. Very comfortable. **C** *Catemaco*, T943-0203, F943-0045. A/c, excellent food and swimming pool, and **C** *Berthangel*, T943-0411. A/c, satellite TV, similar prices; both on main square.

D *Del Cid*, 1 block from *ADO* bus terminal. With fan and bath, OK. **C** *Imalca*, Independencia and Ocampo, T943-412. Parking. **D** *Los Arcos*, T943-0003. Clean, fan, good value. **D** *Del Brujo*, Ocampo y Malecón, T943-0071. Fan, a/c, shower, nice clean rooms, balcony overlooking the lake. Recommended. **E-F** *Acuario*, corner of plaza, T943-0418. Hot water, parking next to **E** *Loud Pasc*, T943-0108. **E** *San Francisco*, Matamoros 26, T943-0398. With bath, basic, but good and clean.

Camping *Trailer park* at Solotepec, by the lake on the road to Playa Azul. US$6.50 per vehicle, very clean, hook-ups, bathrooms. Recommended. Also La Ceiba, restaurant and trailer park, Av Malecón, 6 blocks west of Zócalo. By lakeshore, camping and hook-ups, bathrooms with hot water, restaurant and lakeside patio.

On the promenade are a number of good restaurants: *María José*. Best. *Las 7 Brujas*. **Eating**
Wooden restaurant open till 2400, good, try *mojarra* (local fish). Opposite cathedral are *La Pescada*, good fish, US$5 and *Melmar*, popular. *La Ola*, built almost entirely by the owner in local natural materials, and *La Luna*, among others. At the rear of the market, diagonally from the back of *La Luna*, are some inexpensive, good restaurants serving *comida corrida* for US$2-US$2.50, *La Campesina* is recommended. Best value are those not directly on the lake, eg *Los Sauces*, which serves *mojarra*. *Bar El Moreno*, 2 de Abril, at the beach. 'Not too fancy' but good *cuba libres* and live synthesizer music.

Buses Coatzalcoalcos: regular service, 4 hrs, US$8. **Minatitlán:** (US$4.50) (see below). **Transport**
Santiago Tuxtla: regular service, 30 mins, US$0.80. For **Tuxtepec:** change in San Andrés Tuxtla. **Veracruz:** every 10 mins, 4 hrs with many stops, US$8. **Villahermosa:** 6 hrs, US$13.

Banks Bancomer, opposite cathedral, open Mon, Wed, Fri 0900-1400. **Directory**

The Gulf Coast may be reached from Catemaco along a dirt road (often washed out **Catemaco to**
in winter). It is about 18 km to **Sontecomapan**, crossing over the pass at Buena Vista **Playa Hermosa**
and looking down to the *laguna* where, it is said, Francis Drake sought refuge. The
village of Sontecomapan (*population*: 1,465; *Hotel Sontecomapan*) lies on an entry to *For most of the*
the *laguna* and boats may be hired for the 20-minutes ride out to the bar where the *year it is not*
laguna meets the sea (US$10 return). A large part of the lagoon is surrounded by *recommended to*
mangrove swamp, and the sandy beaches, edged by cliffs, are almost deserted except *sleep on the beaches*
for local fishermen and groups of pelicans. There are two good restaurants in *(assaults and*
Sontecomapan. Beaches, such as Jicacal and Playa Hermosa, are accessible to those *robberies), although*
who enjoy isolation. **Jicacal** can be reached by going straight on from the Catemaco- *at Easter time*
Sontecomapan road for 9 km on a good dirt road to La Palma where there is a small *many people from*
bridge that is avoided by heavy vehicles; immediately after this take left fork (poor *the nearby towns*
dirt road, there is a bus) for **Montepío**, a pretty location at the mouth of the river *camp here*
(**D** *Posada San José Montepío*, Playas Montepío, T942-1010. Family run, also basic
rooms to let, **E**, and a restaurant. Recommended). Watch out for a very small sign
marked **Playa Hermosa**, about 2 km, (the road is impassable when wet) and then
continuing for about 4 km from there. Playa Jicacal is long and open, the first you see
as you near the water. The track reaches a T-junction: to the right is Jicacal, to the left
Playa Hermosa, **E** *Hotel* and restaurant.

Coatzacoalcos and Minatitlán

The road from Catemaco heads south to Acayucan then east to Minatitlán and *Phone code:*
Coatzacoalcos. The latter is the Gulf Coast gateway for the Yucatán Peninsula, 1½ *Coatzacoalcos 921,*
km from the mouth of its wide river. Pemex has a huge oil tanker loading port here. It *Minatitlán 922*
is hot, humid and lacking in culture, and there is not much to do save watch the river *Colour map 3, grid C6*
traffic. The river is too polluted for fishing and swimming, and there are less than *Population: 420,020*
salubrious discos on the equally polluted beach by the pier at the river mouth; the
beach is dangerous at nights, do not sleep there or loiter. **Minatitlán**, the oil and pet- *Both cities are*
rochemical centre (*Population*: 145,000; airport), whose huge oil refinery sends its *often under a*
products by pipeline to Salina Cruz on the Pacific, is 39 km up river. The road *pall of smog*
between the two towns carries very heavy industrial traffic. The offshore oil rigs are

serviced from Coatzacoalcos. Sulphur is exported from the mines 69 km away. The air is constantly scented with petrochemical fumes and sometimes ammonia and sulphur compounds. There is a high incidence of lung disease. Not many foreigners visit either town.

Acayucan, at the junction of Highway 180 and 185, makes a great place to stop if you're driving from Mexico City to points south. There's not a great deal to do, apart from wander the streets, watch the municipal game of basketball, log on in an internet café, or watch a movie, but it's a decent town. (**B** *Kinaku*, on the corner of Ocampo and Victoria, T245-0016. Clean, modern rooms, with a/c and TV. Restaurant and pool. A better deal is **C** *Ritz*, many new rooms, with good showers, a/c, TV, very clean, spacious and comfortable. *Soyamar*, Guerrero 23, is a good vegetarian snack option if you're passing through.)

Sleeping in Coatzacoalcos

Hotels are used by oil workers and rooms can be hard to find; prices are double those of hotels elsewhere, but don't spend the night on the street if you can't find lodging

Coatzacoalcos **A** *Enríquez*, Ignacio de la Llave, T212-7700. Good. **C** *Alex*, JJ Spark 223, T212-4137. With bath, fan, clean, safe parking. **D** *Oliden*, Hidalgo 100, T212-0067. With fan, clean, noisy (other similar hotels in this area). **E** *San Antonio*, Malpica 205, near market. With shower. Several others nearby. *Motel Colima* at Km 5, Carretera Acayucan-Coatzacoalcos. May have rooms if none in Coatzacoalcos; it is clean, in a quiet position, but does have a lot of red-light activity.

Minatitlán **B** *Palazzo* on Hidalgo 16, main street. A/c, credit cards accepted. **B** *Tropical*. With bath, no hot water. **C** *Nacional*, opposite *Palazzo*, Hidalgo 16, T223-7639. Luggage store, friendly, with bath, fan, hot water, clean. Recommended.

Eating

Coatzacoalcos *Los Lopitos*, Hidalgo 615. Good *tamales* and *tostadas*. **Mr Kabubu's**. Bar and restaurant, near *Hotel Alex*, good food and drinks. Cheap restaurants on the top floor of the indoor market near the bus terminal. *Cafetería de los Portales*, near main plaza. Very good food and service. By the river here are several cafés, beware of overcharging. **Minatitlán** *El Marino*, behind the colourful church on main plaza. Opens relatively early, very good, clean and friendly service.

Transport

Air Minatitlán airport (MTT), 30 mins from Coatzacoalcos, 10 mins from Minatitlán. Mexicana to Mexico City and Monterrey. **Trains** Railway station is 5 km from town at Cuatro at end of Puerto Libre bus route and on Playa Palma Sola route, smelly and dingy; irregular bus services. But no scheduled passenger train services.

Buses **From Coatzacoalcos** The *ADO* and interurban bus terminal is some way from city centre. Taxi fare about US$1.50 but they will charge more. **Mexico City**: US$38. **Mérida**: US$42. **Veracruz**: 7¼ hrs, US$16. **Xalapa**: 8 hrs or less depending on the number of stops, US$24. **Villahermosa**: US$11.

From Minatitlán Two terminals, 1st class (*ADO*) near town centre, 2 blocks from Hidalgo, clean toilets, left luggage. *ADO* to many destinations. *Cristóbal Colón* buses leave from Sur, not *ADO* terminal, in Minatitlán. Taxi between the 2, US$1.60. All buses originate in Coatzacoalcos and seat availability is assigned to each destination en route. Buses between the 2 town centres are marked *directo*, 40 mins, US$0.60. Those marked *Cantices* go via the airport, 200 m walk from bus stop to terminal, much cheaper than US$15 taxis.

Directory

Communications Post office: Carranza y Lerdo, Coatzacoalcos. Stamps and postage upstairs at post office on Hidalgo, Minatitlán.

About 40 km east of Coatzacoalcos, on a side road off Route 180 is **Agua Dulce**, where there is a campground, *Rancho Hermanos Graham*. Nice location, full hook-up, cold showers, US$6.50 for car and two people.

Further east along the Gulf Coast is **Sánchez Magallanes** (turn off Route 180 at Las Piedras, 70 km from Coatzacoalcos, signposted), a pleasant, friendly town where you can camp safely on the beach.

Guerrero, Oaxaca and the Isthmus

While Acapulco still retains something of its old mystique and promises of exotic encounters, there are many other resorts dotting the coastline of Guerrero and Oaxaca. From Iztapa to Huatulco all the usual beach holiday activities are there for the taking: surfing, water-skiing, parascending and scuba diving or trips in glass-bottomed boats. And if you want to avoid the crowds, there are still many beautiful offbeat beaches well away from the mega resorts. Inland, these states are rugged and remote, until you come to the attractive university city of Chilpancingo, or the lively, colourful and cosmopolitan Oaxaca, where very pleasant evenings can be spent 'people-watching' from the terrace restaurants. Days are filled visiting the magnificent Santo Domingo church and museum, and exploring the austere archaeological site of Monte Albán. Before crossing the Isthmus to Veracruz, allow a little time to explore Tehuantepec, where you can admire the Zapotec dress and the white churches of the early colonial period that dot the landscape.

The journey from Mexico City to Acapulco and the Pacific Coast often includes a stop-off at Cuernavaca, the 'city of eternal spring' (see page 164) and a detour to the silver town of Taxco (see page 172). Further south, beyond the Mexcala River, the road passes for some 30 km through the dramatic canyon of **Zopilote** to reach the university city of Chilpancingo, capital of Guerrero state at Km 302. There is a small but grandly conceived plaza with solid neo-classical buildings and monumental public sculptures commemorating the workers' struggle: *El hombre hacia el futuro* and *El canto al trabajo* by Victor Manuel Contreras. In the **Palacio de Gobierno** there is a museum and murals. The colourful reed bags from the village of Chilapa (see below) are sold in the market. The **Casa de las Artesanías** for Guerrero is on the right-hand side of the old main Mexico City-Acapulco highway. It has a particularly wide selection of lacquer-ware from Olinalá (see below). The local **fiesta** starts on 16 December and lasts a fortnight.

Chilpancingo

Phone code: 747
Colour map: 3, grid C4
Population: 120,000
Altitude: 1,250 m

Excursions Olmec cave paintings can be seen at the **Grutas de Juxtlahuaca** east of Chilpancingo. The limestone cavern is in pristine condition; it has an intricate network of large halls and tunnels, stalagmites and stalactites, a huge underground lake, cave drawings from about AD500, a skeleton and artefacts. Take a torch, food and drink and a sweater if going a long way in. To reach the caves, drive to Petaquillas on the non-toll road then take a side road (paved, but poor in parts) through several villages to Colotlipa (*colectivo* from Chilpancingo, see below, US$1.50, 1½ hours). Ask at the restaurant on the corner of the Zócalo for a guide to the caves. They can only be visited with a guide (three-hour tour US$25).

Chilapa, east of Chilpancingo, is accessible by several local buses and is worth a visit (about one-hour journey US$2). On Sunday there is an excellent craft market that covers all of the large plaza and surrounding streets, selling especially good-quality and well-priced Olinalá lacquer boxes as well as wood carvings, textiles, leather goods, etc; worth a visit even if you don't buy anything. *Hotel Camino Real* on plaza. *Restaurant Casa Pilla* on other side of plaza, local dishes. Recommended. The **Grutas de Oxtotitlán**, with more Olmec cave paintings, are about 18 km north of Chilapa.

Sleeping and eating C-D *La Posada Meléndez*. Large rooms, helpful, swimming pool, cheap *comida corrida* in restaurant. Recommended. **D** *Laura Elena* and *Cardeña*, both on

Guerrero, Oaxaca and the Isthmus

Madero. **D** *El Portal* on Madero on corner of plaza, T50135. **F** *Chilpancingo*, Alemán 8, 50 m from Zócalo. Clean, shower, basic. Small café at back of *Tienda Naturista*, Hidalgo, 2 blocks from plaza. Good yoghurt.

Transport Buses: services north to **Cuernavaca** (hourly, 2 hrs, US$10), **Mexico City** (hourly, 3½ hrs, US$15-18), less regular services to **Taxco** (5 a day, US$7) with *Estrella de Oro* (T472-2130) and *Estrella Blanca* (T472-0634). Services south to **Acapulco** (hourly, 2 hrs, US$5).

Olinalá

Phone code: 747
Altitude: 1,350 m

This small town is known for the beautiful lacquered wooden boxes, chests, screens and other objects made from *lináloe* wood, which gives the objects a gentle fragrance. In an area of mountains, rivers and ravines, access is difficult so the region is visited by few. Most of the population is involved in the production and selling of the lacquer work, which is available from the artisans direct as well as from the more expensive shops on the square. The lacquering technique includes both the scraping away of layers and applying new ones. Other villages in the area similarly devote themselves almost exclusively to their own *artesanías*. The church on the square is decorated inside with lacquer work and a chapel dedicated to Nuestra Señora de Guadalupe crowns a hill just outside the town and offers striking views. The hill is pyramid-shaped and there are said to be tunnels, but to date no archaeological investigations have been carried out. There are three **F** hotels around the square and a restaurant (no name displayed) above the furniture shop on the main square serves exquisite Mexican cooking.

Transport Buses: catch a local bus towards Tlapa from Chilpancingo or Chilapa, from where you can catch a second local bus to the junction for Olinalá. **Road**: there is 1 paved road (1 hr) from the Chilpancingo-Tlapa road; the turning to Olinalá is between the villages of Tlatlauquitepec and Chiepetepec, about 40 km west of Tlapa. There is an unpaved road (4 hrs) from Chiautla to the north, but you have to cross rivers whose bridges are often washed away in the rainy season. A better unpaved road (2½ hrs) from Santa Cruz to the east, near Huamuxtitlán on Route 92, fords the river Tlapaneco, which is feasible for most vehicles except in the rainy season. The scenery is spectacular, with huge bluffs and river valleys, but filling stations are infrequent – fill up when you can.

The four-lane toll freeway from Mexico City runs west of the old highway, bypassing Chilpancingo, continuing as far as Tierra Colorada (where there is an exit), and on to Acapulco. The completion of the highway is the third improvement: the first motor road was pushed over the ancient mule trail in 1927, giving Acapulco its first new lease of life in 100 years; when the road was paved and widened in 1954, Acapulco began to boom.

About 20 km from the coast, a branch road goes to the northwest of Acapulco; this is a preferable route for car drivers because it avoids the city chaos. It goes to a point between Pie de la Cuesta and Coyuca, is signed, and has a drugs control point at the junction.

It takes about 3½ hours to drive from the capital to Acapulco on the 406-km four-lane highway. The total toll for the route at eight booths is US$89.

Warning Do not travel by car at night in Guerrero, even on the Mexico City-Acapulco highway and coastal highway. There are many military checkpoints on the highway. *Guerrilleros* have been active in recent years, and there are also problems with highway robbers and stray animals.

Acapulco

Acapulco is the most popular resort in Mexico, particularly in winter and spring. It does not fit everyone's idea of a tropical beach resort. The town stretches for 16 km in a series of bays and cliff coves and is invading the hills. The hotels, of which there are 250, are mostly perched high to catch the breeze, for by midday the heat is sizzling; they are filled to overflowing in January and February. While the party mood may suit some, with lots more competition along the coast you may find another option more suitable to your tastes.

Phone code: 744
Colour map 3, grid C3
Population: 1,000,000

Ins and outs

Getting there

Aeropuerto Alvarez Internacional (ACA) is 23 km east of Acapulco. The airport bus takes 1 hr to town, US$3.35, and the ticket office is outside the terminal. *Transportaciones de Pasajeros Aeropuerto* shuttle service charge the return trip (*viaje redondo*) when you buy a ticket, so keep it and call 24 hrs in advance for a taxi, US$11.

The long-distance bus terminal is on Av Ejido, reached by bus from Costera Miguel Alemán; allow at least 45 mins during peak time. *Estrella de Oro* buses leave from the bus station on Av Cuauhtémoc. For people travelling by car, Route 95 connects Acapulco with Mexico City along a 4-lane toll road, while Route 200, the Carretera Costera, runs along the coast, west towards Ixtapa-Zihuatanejo and east towards Puerto Escondido, Huatulco and the beaches of Oaxaca.

Getting around

The most useful bus route runs the full length of Costera Miguel Alemán, linking the older part of town to the different beaches and hotels. Bus stops on the main thoroughfare are numbered, so find out which number you need to get off at.

The **tourist office**, at Costera Miguel Alemán 38a, T484-0599 and T484-4416, is helpful and has brochures and maps. You can call them for the information on hotels and telephone numbers. Also try the Hotel Association, T484-2216, or check out the local tourism website at **www.guerrero.gob.mx**

Acapulco has all the paraphernalia of a booming resort: smart shops, nightclubs, red light district, golf club, touts and street vendors and now also air pollution. The famous beaches and expensive hotels are a different world from the streets, hotels and crowded shops and buses of the city centre, which is only two minutes' walk away. The Zócalo is lively in the evenings, but the surrounding streets are grimy.

Guerrero, Oaxaca and the Isthmus

Acapulco centre

Sleeping
1 California
2 Chamizal
3 Colimense
4 Isabel
5 Mama Hélène
6 Misión
7 Sacramento
8 Santa Lucía

Eating
1 El Pulpo
2 Nachos
3 Pipo's

Related maps
Acapulco Bay,
page 374

Acapulco in colonial times was the terminal for the Manila convoy. Its main defence, **Fuerte de San Diego**, where the last battle for Mexican Independence was fought, is in the middle of the city and is worth a visit. ■ *Tue and Sun only 1000-1800, free.*

Beaches

The surf is dangerous on the beach west of the road and the beaches are unsafe at night

A campaign to tidy up the whole city and its beaches is in process. Acapulco was badly hit by storms in 1997; Hurricane Pauline left more than 111 dead along the coast, dozens missing and 8,000 homeless after mudslides swept away poor areas of the city. Now, however, there is almost no evidence of the damage. There are some 20 beaches, all with fine, golden sand; deckchairs on all beaches, US$0.50; parachute skiing in front of the larger hotels at US$12 for five minutes. Every evening, except Monday, there is a water-skiing display opposite Fuerte de San Diego. The two most popular beaches are the sickle-curved and shielded **Caleta**, with its smooth but dirty water yet clean sands, and the surf-pounded straight beach of **Los Hornos**. Swimmers should look out for motor boats close in shore. At **Playa Revolcadero** development is continuing, with new luxury hotels, new roads and landscaping; it is being called Acapulco Diamante.

At **Playa Icacos** there is a marineland amusement park *Ci-Ci*, with a waterslide, pool with wave-machine and arena with performing dolphins and sea-lions (nothing special). ■ *US$5.70 for whole day, 1000-1800.* Pleasant boat trip across beach to **Puerto Marqués**, US$2 return (or 30 minutes by bus); one can hire small sailing boats there, US$12 per hour. Bay cruises, 2½ hours, from Muelle Yates, US$9, including free bar, at 1100, 1630 and 2230. *Yate Bonanza* has been recommended, stops 30 minutes for swim in bay. Visit the island of **La Roqueta**, in a glass-bottomed boat; tours leave at

Acapulco Bay

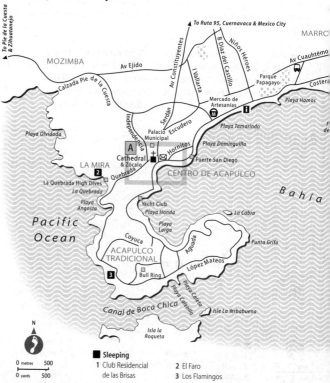

■ Sleeping
1 Club Residencial de las Brisas
2 El Faro
3 Los Flamingos

100 and 1300 from Fuerte San Diego and return at 1500 and 1700, US$4; once on the island follow the path that goes over the hill towards the other side of the island (towards the right) where there is a small, secluded and usually empty bay (about 15 minutes' walk). Take food and drink as it is expensive on the island. Several operators around the bay offer parascending, US$12 for a few minutes. There is an **Aqua Marine Museum** on a little island (Yerbabuena) off **Playa Caleta**, with sharks, piranhas, eels and stingrays in an aquarium, and a swimming pool with water-chute, and breezy bar above. ■ *US$7.*

One sight that should not be missed in Acapulco is that of the amazing cliff divers at **La Quebrada** who plunge 40 m into the water below, timing their dives to coincide with the incoming waves. ■ *Daily, US$1.20, at 1915, 2015, 2115 and 2215.*

Essentials

Acapulco is a full-on commercial resort. In some hotels, a double room can cost up to US$200 a night. There is a good selection of cheaper accommodation. In the high season you should make reservations, at least for 1 night, before arriving, in the low season (May-Nov) you may be able to negotiate discounts for longer stays. For the better hotels you can make reservations at the bus terminal in Mexico City.

For out-and-out luxury try the fabulous **LL** *Club Residencial de las Brisas*, T784-1733, where the services match the astronomical price; it begins at sea-level and reaches up the mountain slope in a series of detached villas and public rooms to a point 300 m above sea-level, each room has own or shared swimming pool, guests use pink jeeps to travel to the dining-room and recreation areas. Another luxury option is **LL** *Villa Vera Raquet Club*, T784-0333, a celebrity spot where Elvis once stayed. **A** *Los Flamingos*, Av López Mateos, T482-0690, F483-9806. One of the finest locations in Acapulco, glorious cliff-top views. In the 1950s it was a retreat for John Wayne, Johnny Weissmuller et al, and the present owner preserves the atmosphere of those days, gardens, pool, restaurant, breakfast included. Highly recommended.

B *Casa Blanca Tropical*, Cerro de la Pinzona, T482-1212. With swimming pool. Recommended. **B** *Real del Monte*, Inalambra, T484-1010. Clean, friendly, on the beach, pool, good food, Playa del Coco opposite new convention centre.

C *Acuario*, Azueta 11, T482-1784. Popular. **C** *Embassy*, Costera Miguel Alemán, T481-0881. Clean, a/c, pool. **C** *Fiesta*, Azueta 16, 2 blocks Zócalo, T482-0019. Clean and nice, with bath, fan. **C** *Misión*, Felipe Valle 12, T482-3643. Very clean, colonial, close to Zócalo. Recommended.

D *Colimense*, JM Iglesias 11, off Zócalo, T482-2890. Pleasant, limited parking. **D** *El Tropicano*, Costera Miguel Alemán 150, on Playa Icacos, T484-1332. Clean, a/c, big garden, 2 pools, bars, restaurant, very friendly and helpful. Recommended. **D** *Isabel*, La Paz y Valle, near Zócalo, T482-2191. With fan. Recommended. **D** *Los Pericos*, Costera Miguel Alemán near Playa Honda, T482-0301. Fan,

Sleeping
■ *on maps, opposite and page 373*

Most cheaper hotels are grouped around the Zócalo, especially on La Paz and Juárez.

To Ruta 95, Cuernavaca & Mexico City

Paseo del Farallón

LAS CUMBRES

ACAPULCO MODERNO

COSTA AZUL

Alemán

Zona Hotelera

Playa Condesa

Convention Centre

Zona Hotelera

La Redonda

ACAPULCO MODERNO

Playa Icacos

Ci/Ci Recreation Centre

A c a p u l c o

COLONIA ICACOS

Naval Base

Punta del Guitarrón

PLAYA GUITARRON

Carretera Escénica

Playa La Paloma

To Puerto Márques, Playa Revolcadero & Airport

1

Guerrero, Oaxaca and the Isthmus

clean, friendly, pool. Recommended. **D** *Mama Hélène*, who owns 2 hotels in same pric⌐ range, and offers laundry service, homemade lemonade. **D** *Olivieda*, Costera Miguel Alemán, block from cathedral. Clean, fan, hot water, great views from top floor rooms. **D** *Sacramento* Carranza y Valle, T482-0821. With bath and fan, no towel, soap or loo paper, friendly, noisy, Ok purified water. **D** *San Francisco*, Costera Miguel Alemán 219, T482-0045, old part of town Friendly, good value, noisy in front. **D** *Santa Lucía*, López Mateos 33, T482-0441. Family owned, will negotiate if not full, good value. **D-E** *California*, La Paz 12, T482-2893, 1½ blocks west of Zócalo. Good value, fan, hot water, pleasant rooms and patio.

E *Aca-Plus*, Azueta 11, T483-1405. With bath and fan, clean, safe. **E** *La Posada*, Azueta 8 near Zócalo, T483-1930. With bath, more expensive in high season. **E** *Paola*, Teniente Azueta, Centro, T480-0651, 2 blocks from Zócalo. Hot shower, fan, roof terrace with pool, free coffee. Highly recommended. **E-F** *Chamizal*, López Mateos 32, close to Zócalo. Shower, OK.

Many cheap hotels on La Quebrada, basic but clean with fan and bathroom, including **D** *Asturia*, Quebrada 45, T483-6548. With bath, no single rooms, clean, friendly, pool, a few cockroaches on lower floor, otherwise recommended. **D** *Beatriz*, 3 blocks from *Flecha Roja* terminal, 2 from beach, T485-3317. With fan, shower and pool, only for 2 nights or more. **D** *Betty*, Belisario Domínguez 4, T483-5092, 5 mins from bus station. With bath, fan, short stay, dirty. Not recommended. Just around corner on same street is **E** *Alberto*, much better. Turn left at *Betty* for several cheap *casas de huéspedes*. **D** *Casa de Huéspedes Aries*, No 30. With bath, older house. **D** *Coral*, No 56, T482-0756. Good value, friendly, reasonably quiet, small pool. **D** *El Faro,* No 83, T482-1365. Clean. **E** *Sagamar*, No 51, T483-5053. With bath, basic, friendly, some English spoken, safe, clean, use mosquito coil.

For longer stays (1 month plus), try **C** *Amueblados Etel*, Av la Pinzona 92 (near La Quebrada), T482-2240. For self-catering apartments, cheap off-season (before Nov), short stays possible in rooms, a/c, fan, hot shower, sundeck, large pool. Recommended. **C** *Apartamentos Maraback*, Costera Miguel Alemán. **D** *Amueblos Caletilla Diamante*, López Mateos 28, Las Playas, T482-7975. Apartments with kitchen, pool, close to beach and market, safe parking.

Camping *Trailer Park El Coloso*, in La Sabana. Small swimming pool. *Trailer Park La Roca* on road from Puerto Márquez to La Sabana. Both secure. *Estacionamiento Juanita* and *Quinta Dora* at Pie de la Cuesta (latter is 13 km up the coast on Highway 200. *Palapas*, bathrooms, cold showers, hook-ups, US\$12 for 2 plus car, US\$4 just to sling hammock). *Casa Blanca*, near military base at Laguna Coyuca, and *U Kae Kim*, all US\$50 a week upwards, but negotiable. *Acapulco West KDA*, on Barra de Coyuca. Opened 1996, beach-front, security patrol, pool, restaurant, hot showers, laundry, store, volleyball, basketball, Spanish classes, telephones.

Eating

■ *on map*

Fish dishes are a speciality of Acapulco

One of the oldest established and best restaurants is *Pipo's*, Almirante Breton 3 (off Costera near Zócalo). Highly recommended, 2 other branches: Costera esq Plaza Canadá; and Calle Majahua, Puerto Márquez. There are a number of variously priced restaurants along and opposite Playa Condesa, including *Embarcadero* on the Costera Miguel Alemán. Thai/Mexican/US food. Extraordinary décor with waterfalls, bridges, bamboo huts and 'a hall of mirrors on the way to the loo', expensive but worth it for the atmosphere. Many cheap restaurants in the blocks surrounding the Zócalo, especially along Juárez, for example, *El Amigo Miguel* (popular), Juárez 9, near Zócalo, Fixed menu lunch, good. *Nachos*, on Azueta, at corner of Juárez. Popular, excellent prawns. *El Pulpo*, Costera Miguel Alemán 183, 1½ blocks from Zócalo. Good filling breakfasts, friendly. By La Diana roundabout is *Pizza Hut*. Reliable, with 'blissful a/c'. *Italianissimo*. Nearby, decent pizza and garlic bread, average price for area. *Parroquia*, on Zócalo. Excellent. *El Zorrito*, opposite *Ritz Hotel*. Excellent local food with live music, average prices, reputedly popular with Julio Iglesias when he is in town. Another group of restaurants along Playa Caleta walkway; better value on Caleta beach itself is *La Cabaña*. Good food, delightful setting. Yet another group with mixed prices on the Costera opposite the *Acapulco Plaza Hotel*. 250 or so to select from. *El Mayab*, Costera Miguel Alemán 151. Good value, set meal. Recommended.

capulco has a superb, varied nightlife at the weekends, and every major hotel has at least 1 disco. Others worth trying include *Baby O*, towards the naval base on Costera Miguel Alemán, *Discoteca Safari*, Costera Miguel Alemán. Free entry, 1 drink obligatory, good ambience; a cheaper option is *Disco Beach*, Costera Miguel Alemán, between the *Diana* and *Hotel Fiesta Americana Condesa* by the beach, informal dress, open till 0500, good.

Bars & nightclubs

Local Taxis: US$9, 1 hr; sample fare: Zócalo to Playa Condesa US$3.50. Taxis more expensive from bus terminal, walk ½ block round corner and catch one on the street. **Buses**: several bus routes, with one running the full length of Costera Miguel Alemán linking the older part of town to the latest hotels, marked 'Caleta-Zócalo-Base', US$0.80, another operating to Playa Caleta. Buses to Pie de la Cuesta, 12 km, US$0,40.

Transport

Long distance Air: Direct international connections with Atlanta, Miami, Chicago, Dallas, Houston, Los Angeles and Tucson by Mexican and US carriers, with many charter flights from Europe and North America. Domestic services to Mexico City, also to Ciudad Juárez, Cuernavaca, Culiacán, Guadalajara, León, Monterrey, Puerto Vallarta and Tijuana. *AeroMéxico*, T484-7009. Flights to Mexico City are worth booking early in high season.

Buses: there are 3 bus terminals. *Grupo Estrella Blanca* is on Av Ejido for Puerto Escondido and coastal destinations. Reached by bus from Costera Miguel Alemán, allow at least 45 mins during peak time. There is a left-luggage office. *Estrella Blanca*'s 1st class terminal is 2 blocks from *Estrella de Oro*'s on Av Cuauhtémoc, with buses for Puebla, Cuernavaca, Guadalajara, Tijuana, Tampico and Mexico City. **Mexico City**: 406 km, 4-5 hrs (1st class or *plus*) – 8 hrs (others); deluxe a/c express buses US$28.35 and super luxury US$36.65; ordinary bus, US$21.65 1st and US$25.65 *plus*, all-day services from Terminal del Sur by the Taqueña metro station, Mexico City, with *Estrella de Oro* (10 a day, 1 stop) or *Flecha Roja* (part of *Líneas Unidas del Sur*, hourly). Taxi to Zócalo, US$5.50; bus, US$0.50. To **Manzanillo**: direct bus US$8.50. Several 1st class buses, *Estrella de Oro*, 5 hrs, and *Flecha Roja* buses a day to **Taxco** US$11. To **Cuernavaca**: with *Estrella de Oro*, 6 hrs, US$14.75-19.50. To **Oaxaca**: no direct bus, change at Puerto Escondido or Pochutla (waiting room and luggage deposit at Pochutla); also via Pinotepa Nacional (at 2100) but worse road. Bus to **Puerto Escondido** every hr on the ½ hr from 0430-1630, plus 2300, 2400, 0200, US$10.50, 9 hrs, and *directo* at 1330 and 2300, US$20, seats bookable, advisable to do so the day before, 7½ hrs, there may be check-points adding up to 2 hours to the journey; *Flecha Roja*, *Transportes Gacela* (US$15.65). To **Tapachula**: take Impala 1st class bus to **Huatulco**, arriving 1930; from there *Cristóbal Colón* at 2030 to **Salina Cruz**, arriving about midnight, then take 1st or 2nd class bus.

Airline offices *AeroMéxico* and *Mexicana* offices in Torre Acapulco, Costera Miguel Alemán 1252, Mexicana T484-1215. **American**, T466-9248. **Delta**, T800-902-2100. *Taesa*, T485-2488. Condor, T800-524-6975. **Communications Post office**: Costera, 2 blocks south of Zócalo. **Telephones**: public offices will not take collect calls; try from a big hotel (ask around, there will be a surcharge). **Embassies and consulates** *Canada*, States of Guerrero and Michoacán, Honorary, Mrs Diane McLean de Huerta, T01-7-484-1305, Local 23, Centro Comercial Marbella, esq Prolongación Farallón y Miguel Alemán. Postal address: Apartado postal 94-C, 39670, Acapulco, Gro. Mon-Fri. 0900-1700. *France*, Av Costa Grande 235, T482-3394. *Germany*, Antón de Alaminos 46, T484-7437. *Holland*, *El Presidente Hotel*, T483-7148. *Norwegian*, *Marilisa Hotel*, T484-3525. *Spain*, Av Cuauhtémoc y Universidad 2, T485-7205. *Sweden*, Av Insurgentes 2, T485-2935. *UK* British Consul (Honorary), Lorraine Bajos, T484-1735. *US*, Alexander Richard, *Hotel Continental Emperial*, T469-0505, 0900 –1400. **Laundry** *Tintorería Bik*, 5 de Mayo. *Lavadín*, José María Iglesias 11a, T482-2890, next to *Hotel Colimense*, recommended. **Useful addresses Immigration**: Juan Sebastián el Cuno 1, Costa Azul el Lado, T484-9021, open 0800-1400, take a 'Hornos Base' bus from Miguel Alemán, US$0.20, 30 mins, visa extensions possible.

Directory

Guerrero, Oaxaca and the Isthmus

Coast northwest of Acapulco

Pie de la Cuesta, 12 km northwest, is preferred by many budget travellers to Acapulco itself, but it is also commercialized. There are several bungalow-hotels and trailer parks (see below), a lagoon (six-hour boat trip US$10), and long, clean, sandy beaches. At Pie de la Cuesta you can swim and fish year round, drink *coco loco* (fortified coconut milk), and watch the sunset from a hammock.

Sleeping: B *Puesta del Sol*, T460-0412. Pool and restaurant, comes recommended. C *Villa Nirvana*. Canadian/Mexican owners (depending on season) with kitchen, clean, pool, good value. Recommended. D *Casa Blanca*. Rooms for 3, management nice, food good.

D *Quinta Dora Trailer Park*. For hammock, managed by American, helpful. The student organization *SETEJ* offers dormitory accommodation, D, if you have a valid international student card, at *Centro Vacacional*, Pie de la Cuesta, 0700-2400.

Laguna Coyuca (also known as La Barra or Laguna Pie de la Cuesta), over 10 km long, 38 km northwest of Acapulco, has interesting birdlife, water hyacinths and tropical flowers and can be explored by motor boat. **Coyuca de Benítez**, near the Laguna Coyuca, is a market town selling exotic fruit, cheap hats and shoes. There is no bank but shops will change US dollars. Take a combi from town to La Barra on the lagoon. Pelicans fly by the lagoons, there are passing dolphins and plentiful sardines, and young boys seek turtle eggs. **Sleeping D** *Parador de los Reyes*. Clean, pool. **E** *Imperial*, off the main square.

El Carrizal One-and-a-half kilometres beyond Coyuca is a turn-off to El Carrizal (7½ km), a delightful village of some 2,000 people, a short distance from a beautiful beach (many pelicans) with a steep drop-off (unsafe for children), dangerous waves and sharks behind them. But it's good for spotting dolphins and, if you are lucky, whales. There are frequent minibuses from Acapulco or Pie de la Cuesta, US$0.55.

Sleeping and eating Good restaurant (opposite *Hotel-Bungalows El Carrizal*), which has 6 rooms with bath and toilet, **E**, closes early (1800 for food), poor food, not very clean. **E** *Aída*, friendly, but little privacy, more expensive rooms more secure and mosquito-proof, all rooms with bath and fan, Mexican food (good fish). Recommended.

El Morro A couple of kilometres southeast of El Carrizal is El Morro on an unpaved road between the ocean and the lagoon. The waves on the ocean side are very strong, while swimming in the lagoon is excellent. El Morro is a small fishing village (carp) reminiscent of African townships as it is constructed entirely of *palapa* (palm-leaf and wood). Every other house is a 'fish-restaurant', the best are 1 km left along the beach to La Ramada; ask for bungalow rental (**F**), no running water but there is a toilet, mosquito nets on request; *El Mirador* (Jesús and Maty), rooms, canoe hire. At El Morro you can rent a canoe for US$2 per hour and sail down river, past El Carrizal; you can also go up river to the lagoon, an all-day trip, very beautiful with plenty of birdlife (beware, strong winds blow around midday off the sea). Minibuses run Coyuca-El Carrizal-El Morro.

Tecpan de Galeana & Cavaquito San Jerónimo, 83 km from Acapulco, has an 18th-century parish church; you can make canoe trips up river to restaurants. Tecpan de Galeana, 108 km from Acapulco, is a fishing village. Ten kilometres beyond Tecpan is a turn-off to another El Carrizal, which is 7 km from the Pacific Highway. There is some public transport from Tecpan, but plenty of cars go there (the road is rough). Very little accommodation, but plenty of hammock space; there is a beautiful beach and lagoon and the place is very friendly. There is a beach further on at Cavaquito where a series of small rivers joins the ocean and there is a large variety of birds and dense vegetation; three restaurants offer fish dishes, there is a reasonable modern hotel, *Club Papanoa*, with lovely views and a camping site; a cheaper, nameless hotel with restaurant on the beach, **E**; and one can also visit the lovely bay of Papanoa.

Zihuatanejo

A beautiful fishing port and expensive, commercialized tourist resort 237 km northwest of Acapulco by the paved Route 200, which continues via Barra de Navidad along the Pacific coast to Puerto Vallarta (see page 328). The road to Ixtapa continues through coconut plantations where the slightly alcoholic drink *tuba*, made from coconut milk fermented on the tree, is for sale.

Phone code: 755
Colour map 3, grid C2
Population: 22,000

Despite being spruced up, 'Zihua', as it is called locally, still retains much of its Mexican village charm. There is an Indian handicraft market by the church, some beachside cafés and a small **Museo Arqueológico**, in the old Customs and Immigration building on Av 5 de Mayo. ■ *US$0.70.* At sunset thousands of swallows

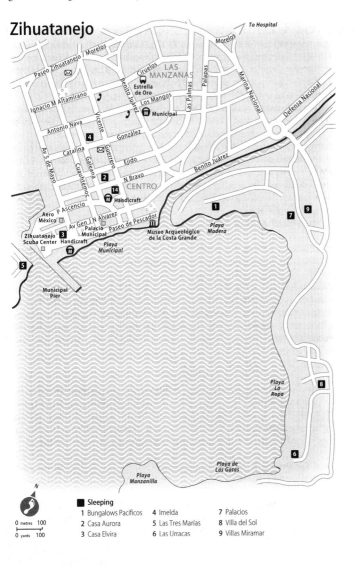

Zihuatanejo

Guerrero, Oaxaca and the Isthmus

0 metres 100
0 yards 100

■ Sleeping

1 Bungalows Pacíficos	4 Imelda	7 Palacios
2 Casa Aurora	5 Las Tres Marías	8 Villa del Sol
3 Casa Elvira	6 Las Urracas	9 Villas Miramar

meet in the air above the local cinema in the centre of town and all settle for the night within the space of one minute on the telephone poles. The **Plaza de Toros** is at the town entrance with seasonal *corridas*. **Tourist information**, with bilingual assistance, is available from the Palacio Municipal, T554-2355. The local tourism website is at **www.ixtapa-zihuatanejo.com**

Beaches There are five beaches in the bay, including **Playa La Madera**, near town and a bit dirty; better is **Playa La Ropa**, 20 minutes' walk from the centre, with the *Sotavento* and other hotels, and some beach restaurants. Also good is **Playa Las Gatas**, secluded, and a haven for aquatic sports. It can be reached by boat from the centre (US$2 return) or a 20-minute walk from La Ropa beach over fishermen-frequented rocks. Off the coast there are rock formations, to which divers go, and **Isla Ixtapa**, a nature reserve with numerous restaurants. **Playa Linda**, to the north, is a beautiful beach (no hotels) easily reached by *colectivo* (30 minutes). The yacht, *Fandango Zihua*, takes bay cruises from the municipal pier.

Sleeping **LL** *Villa del Sol*, Playa La Ropa, T554-2239, F554-4758, Apdo 84. No children under 12 in high
■ *on map* season, very expensive but highly regarded. **AL** *Villas Miramar*, Playa La Madera, T554-2106,
Difficult to find F554-2149. Suites, pool, lovely gardens. **B** *Pacíficos Bungalows*, T554-2112. Advance reserva-
accommodation in tion necessary, huge terrace, good views. Highly recommended. **B** *Las Urracas*, Playa La Ropa,
March and around T554-2049. Cooking facilities, good value. **B** *Palacios*, T554-2055, on Playa La Madera. Good. **C**
Christmas/New Year *Imelda*, Catalina González 11, T43199. Clean, no restaurant. Recommended.
　　D *Casa Aurora*, Nicolás Bravo 27. Clean with bath and fan, not all rooms have hot water.
D *Las Tres Marías*, La Noria 4, T554-2191, cross the wooden footbridge. Very pleasant with large communal balconies overlooking town and harbour, clean but sparely decorated, tiny baths, nice plants, hotel has an annexe at Juan Alvarez 52, part of restaurant, similar rooms and tariffs, best on 2nd floor, note that price doubles during Christmas holidays. **E** *Casa Elvira*, hotel-restaurant, on Juan Alvarez, T554-2061, in older part of town on waterfront. Very basic but clean, fan, with bath (cold water only), the restaurant is on the beachfront (the place to watch the world go by), good and reasonable. **E** *Rosimar*, Ejido, T554-2140. Quiet, hot water, some rooms TV.
　　Youth hostel Av Paseo de las Salinas s/n, CP 40880, T554-4662.

Eating **Playa La Ropa** *La Perla*. Very popular, good food, slow service. *Elvira*, by *Hotel Sotavento*.
Look out for Small, attentive service, good value. *Rossy*. Good, live music at weekends.
cheaper dining
near the market **Zihuatanejo** Many including *El Patio*, 5 de Mayo, beside Catholic church. Excellent food and atmosphere, beautiful patio/garden, live music occasionally. *Il Piccolo*, Nicolás Bravo 22. Restaurant and video bar, excellent value, good pizzas. *Gitano's*. *Coconuts*. Good atmosphere, pricey, dinner only. Recommended. *La Marina*. Popular. Recommended. *Puntarenas*, close to *Hotel Las Tres Marías*. Excellent cooking, friendly, not expensive, popular, slow service. *Stall 27* at marketplace. Very popular, cheap and good, try local lobster for about US$10; most meals cost US$6 or over.

Sports Activities in the region are varied including **sailfishing**, with several operators found by the pier, and **scuba diving**. Hire of all equipment and guide from *Zihuatanejo Scuba Center*, T554-2147, English spoken. Off Playa Las Gatas is an underwater wall built, according to legend, by the Tarascan King Calzonzin, to keep the sharks away while he bathed; the wall is fairly massive and can be seen clearly while scuba diving. US$4 a day for mask, snorkel and fins.

Transport **Local Car hire**: *Hertz*, Nicolás Bravo and airport, T554-3050 or F554-2255; Several others with offices at the airport and in Ixtapa hotels including: *Avis*, *Budget*, *Dollar* and *Economy*.

Long distance Air: Ixtapa-Zihuatanejo international airport (ZIH), 20 km from town, T554-2070. Many direct domestic flights from Mexico City and Guadalajara, with other destinations by connection. International from Houston, Los Angeles, Phoenix, San Francisco and Seattle.

Buses: *Estrella de Oro* operates its own terminal on Paseo Palmar, serving **Mexico City**: with services at 0600, 1130, 2130, 9 hrs, US$35. Services to **Acapulco** (4-5 hrs): calling at Petatlán and Tecpan de Galeana, at 1135 (US$8.50), and 0700, 0800 and 1300 (US$11.50). To **Lázaro Cárdenas**: hourly, 2 hrs, US$5.

The **Central de Autobuses** is on the Zihuatanejo-Acapulco highway opposite Pemex station (bus from centre US$0.20); 3 lines operate from here, all using good, 32-seater buses. The terminal is clean, with several snackbars and services with *Estrella Blanca*, *Blancas Fronteras* and *Cuahtémoc*.

To **Acapulco**: hourly, US$11-8, **Manzanillo**: US$15, 9 hrs. **Mexico City**: almost hourly from 0600-2130, US$31, US$44 direct. **Laredo**: at 1730, 30 hrs, US$65. **Lázaro Cárdenas**: daily, for connections further north and to the interior, US$5.50. **Puerto Escondido** and **Huatulco**: 2130, US$42. Cuauhtémoc serves all towns between Zihuatanejo and Acapulco almost ½-hourly from 0400 to 2000.

The old Central de Autobuses is ½ block from the new; old buses use it, with erratic service to **Mexico City** via the less-used and more dangerous road through Altamirano (to be avoided if possible, robberies).

Road: by car from Mexico City via the Toluca-Zihuatanejo highway (430 km) or via the Acapulco-Zihuatanejo highway (405 km). To Acapulco can be done in 3½ hrs, but sometimes takes 6 hrs. To Lázaro Cárdenas, 103 km, takes 3½ hrs, the road is very bad.

Airlines *AeroMéxico*, T554-2018; *Delta* (airport), T554-3386; *Mexicana*, *Hotel Dorado Pacífico*, Ixtapa, T322-0810. **Banks** *Banca Serfín* will change TCs at lower commission than banks in hotel district. *Banamex*. *Bancomer*. Several *casas de cambio*. **Tourist offices** Tourist Office and Complaints, see under Ixtapa, below. **Useful telephone numbers** Customs at airport: T554-3262. **Immigration**: T554-2795. **Police**: T554-2040. **Red Cross**: T554-2009.

Directory

Ixtapa

From Zihuatanejo it's a short 7-km drive, bus journey (US$0.30 from Paseo Zihuatanejo/Morelos) or taxi (US$5, *colectivo*, US$1) to **Ixtapa**, meaning 'where there are salt lakes'. The resort, developed on a large scale, boasts 14 beaches. There are turtles, many species of shellfish and fish, and pelicans at El Morro de los Pericos, which can be seen by launch. There is an island a few metres off Playa Quieta; boats go over at a cost of US$5. Ixtapa has 10 large luxury hotels and a *Club Méditerranée* (all obtain food supplies from Mexico City making food more expensive, as local supplies aren't guaranteed); there is also a shopping complex, golf course, water-ski/parachute skiing and tennis courts. There is a yacht marina and an 18-hole golf club, Palma Real. **Isla Grande** has been developed as a nature park and leisure resort. The **tourist office** is in Ixtapa Shopping Plaza, T553-1967.

Phone code: 755
Colour map 3, grid C2
Population: 32,000

The beach can be dangerous with a strong undertow; small children should not be allowed in the sea alone. Also, there are crocodiles in the beautiful lagoons at the end of the beach

All in LL-A range *Westin Resort Ixtapa*, T553-2121. Spectacular, in a small jungle. *Krystal*, T553-0333, book in advance. Highly recommended. *Sheraton*, Blvd Ixtapa, T553-1858. With panoramic lift, reductions for AAA members. Recommended. Taxi between centre and main hotels, US$3.

Sleeping

   Camping *Playa Linda Trailer Park*, on Carretera Playa Linda at *Playa Linda Hotel*, just north of Ixtapa. 50 spaces, full hook-ups, restaurant, recreation hall, babysitters, on beach, US$14 for 2, comfortable.

Besides the restaurants in every hotel, there are many others, including *Villa de la Selva*, T30362. Recommended for food and views, book in advance. *El Sombrero*. Mexican, very good. *Montmartre* (French), *Onyx*, *Bogart's* (opposite *Hotel Krystal*), *Gran Tapa*. All more costly than in Zihuatanejo.

Eating

Every hotel without exception has at least 1 nightclub/disco and 2 bars.

Bars & nightlife

Guerrero, Oaxaca and the Isthmus

Road Although paved Highway 134 leads directly from Mexico City and Toluca to Ixtapa, there is no fuel or other supplies after Ciudad Altamirano (188 km, pleasant motel on south-west edge of city, **C** with a/c). This road also runs through remote country, prone to land-slides, and there is occasional bandit activity, with unpredictable army check-points (looking for guns and drugs).

The coastal route continues northwest to Lázaro Cárdenas and Playa Azul in Michoacán (see page 302). The pleasant little beach town of **Troncones**, 20 km north of Ixtapa, has several restaurants and **AL** *Eden* (evandjim@aol.com).

Mexico City to Oaxaca

The express toll road from Mexico City to Oaxaca first runs generally eastwards to Puebla (see page 152), where it turns south to wind through wooded mountains at altitudes of between 1,500 m and 1,800 m, emerging at last into the warm, red-earth Oaxaca valley. It has been described as a stunning bus ride along a new motorway through cactus-filled valleys and plains. The route described here, however, avoids the new motorway in favour of the less sophisticated but equally attractive Route 190, which continues from Oaxaca to Tehuantepec. The road, although paved throughout and in good condition, serpentines unendingly over the Sierras and is quite beautiful. The alternative coastal route is also very attractive and of especial interest to visitors who wish to engage in the many watersports available. Buses on the new express toll road road now take six hours from Mexico City to Oaxaca. Total road toll Mexico City-Oaxaca, US$30.32.

Atlixco
Phone code: 244

Route 190 heads south from Puebla to Izúcar de Matamoros (side road to **Huaquechula**: 16th-century Renaissance and plateresque chapel) via Atlixco ('the place lying on the water'), with interesting baroque examples in the Capilla de la Tercera Orden de San Agustín and San Juan de Dios. The annual **Atlixcayotl festival**, is on San Miguel hill. Nearby are the curative springs of **Axocopán**.

Sleeping and eating **B** *Molina de Herrera*, Km 40 of Puebla-Izúcar de Matamoros road, 15 mins from Atlixco, T445-3034. 50 a/c rooms with satellite TV, pool, restaurant, bar, convention hall for 300 people. **C** *Mansión Atlixco*, T445-0691. Highly recommended. **E** *Hotel Colonial* behind parish church, T445-0697, shared bath. *Restaurant La Taquería*, Avenida Libertad, 1 block from Plaza. Highly recommended.

Izúcar de Matamoros
Phone code: 243
Colour map 3, grid C4
Population: 70,532

After Atlixco, Route 190 continues to the town of Izúcar de Matamoros (from *itzocan*, meaning his dirty face), famous for its clay handicrafts, 16th-century convent of Santo Domingo, and two nearby spas, **Los Amatitlanes** (about 6 km away) and **Ojo de Carbón**.

Sleeping **C** *Premier*, on Zócalo, T436-0241. **D** *Hotel Ocampo*, next to bus station. **D** *Las Fuentes*, Guerrero 46, T436-1052. Bath and hot water, clean, quiet, TV, courtyard. Recommended. **F** *La Paz*, off Zócalo. Friendly, clean, basic rooms, hot water. **F** *Hotel Independencia*, just off Zócalo. OK. *Restaurant Oasis*, Hidalgo, just off Zócalo. Cheap set menu.

A road leads southwest from Izúcar to **Axochiapan**, Morelos state **E** *Hotel Primavera*, bath, hot water, clean, tiny room, leading to a paved road to the village of **Jolalpan** with the baroque church of Santa María (1553). There are very few restaurants in Jolalpan; ask where you can get a meal. The bus from Axochiapan stops in front of the church in Jolalpan. The road (and bus) continues to Atenango del Río in Guerrero state, the last 20-30 km unpaved.

From Izúcar de Matamoros Route 190 switchbacks to **Tehuitzingo**. Then the landscape is fairly flat to **Acatlán**, a friendly village where black and red clay figures, and palm and flower hats are made.

Sleeping C *Plaza*. Clean, hot showers, TV, new, good restaurant. Recommended. **D** *México*, Ricardo Reyes Márquez 3, T(953) 534-0273; *Lux*; *Romano*, both **D**.

Carry on to Petlalcingo (restaurant), then ascend to **Huajuapan de León**, an important centre for palm products. To the southeast (12 km) is the Yosocuta Dam with fish farms and recreational facilities. Second class bus from Oaxaca to Huajuapan, four a day, US$3.50.

Sleeping *Hotel García Peral*, on the Zócalo. Good restaurant. *Hotel Casablanca*, Amatista 1, Col Vista Hermosa. Also good restaurant (just outside Huajuapan on the road to Oaxaca); **C-D** *Plaza de Angel*. Central, nice, clean. **D** *Playa*, El Centro. Hot water, clean, big windows, good value. **D** *Hotel Bella Vista*. **D** *Colón*. Very good.

After Huajuapan de León, Route 125 leads to **Pinotepa Nacional**. The next town on Route 190 is **Tamazulapan** with a 16th-century church and a pink stone arch in front of the city hall.

Sleeping **D** *Gilda*, 1 block south of Highway 190. Central, new, large clean rooms, safe parking. **D** *México*, on highway. Modern, clean, has lush courtyard, balconies, good restaurant with *comida corrida*. **D** *Santiago*, without sign, on Zócalo. **E** *Hidalgo*, behind church; restaurant *Coquiz*, on Highway 190, good.

Yanhuitlán, 72 km northwest of Oaxaca on Route 190, has a beautiful 400-year-old church, part of the Santo Domingo monastery, built on a pre-Hispanic platform; it is considered one of the best examples of 16th-century New World Hispanic architecture. Yanhuitlán is in the Sierra Mixteca, where Dominican friars began evangelizing in 1526. Two other important centres in the region were San Juan Bautista at **Coixtlahuaca** and the open chapel at Teposcolula. The scenery and the altars, the huge convents in such a remote area, are a worthwhile day trip from Oaxaca. The new highway from **Nochixtlán** to Oaxaca (103 km) has been recommended for cyclists: wide hard shoulders and easy gradients.

Sleeping **D** *Mixli*, outskirts at intersection with new highway. Large beds, TV, parking. Recommended but 20 minutes' walk from town. **E** *Hotel Sarita*, around corner is **E** *Elazcan*, clean, OK.

Oaxaca

Oaxaca, the capital and administrative centre of the State of Oaxaca, is a colourful, charming city; its historical centre was declared a UNESCO World Heritage Trust Site in 1987. The city was founded by the Spanish with the name of Antequera in 1521 on the site where a Zapotec and Mixtec settlement already existed. It gracefully combines its colonial and native roots; fine stone buildings, churches, arcades and airy patios speak for its importance during the colonial period, while its markets, crafts, dances and feast days point to a more indigenous past. There are numerous sights to visit, the highlights for those with very little time include the Santo Domingo church and museum, a market, the Zócalo and the Monte Albán archaeological site overlooking the town.

Phone code: 951
Colour map 3,
grid C5
Population: 256,848
Altitude: 1,546 m

Ins and outs

Aeropuerto Xoxocotlán (OAX) is about 9 km south of the city. Airport taxis (*colectivos*) will take you into the city centre. The 1st class bus terminal is northeast of the Zócalo on Calzada Niños Héroes (some 2nd class buses also leave from here). The 2nd class terminal is west of the Zócalo on Calzada Valerio Trujano, near the Central de Abastos market. *Autobuses Unidos* (*AU*) have their own terminal northwest of the Zócalo at Prolongación Madero.

Getting there

Guerrero, Oaxaca and the Isthmus

Getting around Local town minibuses mostly charge US$0.20. For the 1st class bus terminal, buses marked 'VW' leave from Avenida Juárez; for the 2nd class terminal, buses are marked 'Central'. Most of the important sites are in or near the city centre and can be reached on foot.

Tourist information *Sedetur*, Independencia 607, T516-0123, F516-0984, open 0800-2000 daily, has maps, posters, postcards, information, friendly and very helpful; ask here about the *Tourist Yú'ù* hostel programme in local communities (see Excursions below). *Instituto Nacional de Estadística, Geografía e Informática (INEGI)*, Independencia 805 for topographic maps and information about the state. The local tourism website is at **www.oaxaca.gob.mx** There are several tourist publications, which include travel information, calendars of events, city map, etc. *Oaxaca Times*, English monthly; *Oaxaca*, monthly in Spanish, English and French; *Comunicación*, in Spanish, with a few articles translated to

Oaxaca

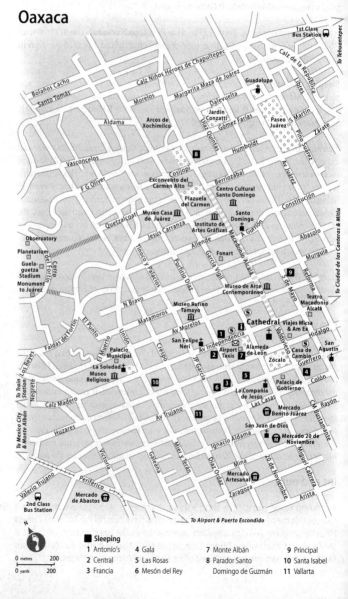

Guerrero, Oaxaca and the Isthmus

■ Sleeping			
1 Antonio's	4 Gala	7 Monte Albán	9 Principal
2 Central	5 Las Rosas	8 Parador Santo	10 Santa Isabel
3 Francia	6 Mesón del Rey	Domingo de Guzmán	11 Vallarta

0 metres 200
0 yards 200

nglish and French; *Guía Cultural*, published monthly by the Instituto Oaxaqueño de las
Culturas, has a complete listing of musical events, exhibitions, conferences, libraries, etc.

Sights

The Zócalo with its arcades is the heart of town, a pleasant park with a bandstand in the
centre and a few food stalls underneath. Because the streets surrounding the Zócalo
and the adjacent Alameda de León are closed to traffic, it is very pleasant to sit there or
stroll. It is always active, and the surrounding cafés and restaurants are always busy.
Free music and dance events are often held in the evenings. In the daytime vendors sell
food; in the evening they offer tourist wares and gardenias. It is especially colourful on
Saturday and Sunday nights when Indian women weave and sell their goods.

Avenida Independencia is the main street running east-west, the nicer part of the
old city is to the north of it; a simpler area, housing the cheaper hotels, lies to the
south. Independencia is also a dividing line for the north-south streets, which
change names here. Calle Macedonia Alcalá is a cobbled pedestrian walkway, which
joins the Zócalo with the church of Santo Domingo, many colonial buildings can be
seen along this mall; this street and Calle Bustamante, its continuation to the south,
are the dividing line for east-west streets, which change names here.

Worth visiting is the **Palacio de Gobierno**, on the south side of the Zócalo; it
has beautiful murals and entry is free. There are often political meetings or protests
outside. The **Teatro Macedonio Alcalá**, 5 de Mayo with Independencia, is an elegant theatre from Porfirio Díaz's times, it has a Louis XV-style entrance and white
marble staircase; regular performances are held here. Visit also the **Arcos de
Xochimilco** on García Vigil, starting at Cosijopi, some eight blocks north of the
Zócalo. In this picturesque area are the remains of an aqueduct, cobbled passageways under the arches, flowers and shops. The house of the Maza family, for whom
Benito Juárez worked and whose daughter he married, still stands at
Independencia 1306 (a plaque marks it). Similarly, a plaque marks the birthplace
of Porfirio Díaz at the other end of Independencia, in a building that is now a kindergarten, near La Soledad. DH Lawrence wrote parts of *Mornings in Mexico* in
Oaxaca, and revised *The Plumed Serpent*; the house he rented is on Pino Suárez.
The bar, *El Favorito*, on 20 de Noviembre, a couple of blocks south of the Zócalo, is
supposedly the original that inspired Malcolm Lowry's in his novel *Under the Volcano*. There is a grand view from **Cerro de Fortín**, the hill to the northwest of the
centre, here is the Guelaguetza amphitheatre; a monument to Juárez stands on a
hillside below. Atop the hill are an observatory and planetarium (shows Monday-Saturday 1230 and 1900, Sunday 1230, 1800 and 1900, US$1.10, students
US$0.55); best to take a taxi (about US$3.50) since the walk is dark and deserted. It
is a pleasant walk from town to the hill as far as the planetarium and antennas, but
muggings have been reported in the trails that go through the woods and the dirt
road that goes beyond.

Ciudad de las canteras, the quarries from where the stone for the city's monumental churches and public buildings was extracted, has been converted into a
beautifully landscaped park. It is located on Calzada Niños Héroes de Chapultepec,
at the east end of Calzada Eduardo Vasconcelos; several city bus lines go there. There
is a small stadium here and the site of the Expo Feria Oaxaca, a fair with rides, craft
exhibits, food and various live performances, held throughout the year (check in the
tourist information office for details).

Churches On the Zócalo is the 17th-century **cathedral** with a fine baroque façade (watch the
raising and lowering of the Mexican flag daily at 0800 and 1800 beside the cathedral), but the best sight by far, about four blocks from the square up the
pedestrianized Calle Macedonio Alcalá, is the church of **Santo Domingo** (closed
1300-1700, no flash photographs allowed) with its adjoining monastery, now the
Centro Cultural Santo Domingo (see below). The church is considered one of the

best examples of baroque style in Mexico. It first opened to worship in 1608 and was refurbished in the 1950s. Its gold leaf has to be seen to be believed. The ceilings and walls, sculptured and painted white and gold, are stunningly beautiful.

The massive 17th-century **Basílica de La Soledad** (between Morelos and Independencia, west of Unión) has fine colonial ironwork and sculpture (including an exquisite Virgen de la Soledad). Its interior is predominantly fawn and gold; the plaques on the walls are painted like cross-sections of polished stone. The fine façade is made up of stone of different colours, pinks and greens; it is considered the best example of carved stonework in the city. The church was built on the site of the hermitage to San Sebastián; begun in 1582, it was recommenced in 1682 because of earthquakes. It was consecrated in 1690 and the convent was finished in 1697. The **Museo Religioso de la Soledad**, Independencia 107, has a display of religious artefacts; it is at the back of the church. ■ *0900-1400 Mon-Sun, US$0.30 donation requested.* In the small plaza outside the encircling wall, refreshments and offerings are sold. There are elaborate altars at the church of **San Felipe Neri**, Avenida Independencia y García. At **San Juan de Dios**, 20 de Noviembre y Aldama, there is an Indian version in paint of the Conquistadores' arrival in Oaxaca and of an anti-Catholic uprising in 1700. This was the first church in Oaxaca, originally dedicated to Santa Catalina Mártir. The church of **San Agustín**, Armenta y López at Guerrero, has a fine façade, with bas relief of St Augustine holding the City of God above adoring monks (apparently modelled on that of San Agustín in Mexico City, now the National Library). The church of **La Compañía de Jesús**, Trujano, diagonal to the Zócalo, first built in 1579, has a wooden altarpiece; in the central niche is an image of the Virgin of the Immaculate Conception, hence it is also known as the **Iglesia de la Inmaculada**.

Museums   The **Centro Cultural Santo Domingo** is a cultural complex that includes a museum, exhibit halls, botanical garden, library, newspaper archives and bookstore; concerts are also performed here. It is housed in the former convent of Santo Domingo (Macedonio Alcalá y Gurrión), next to the Santo Domingo church. Construction of the convent started in 1575. It was occupied by the Dominican friars from 1608 to 1812. After the expulsion of the church it was occupied by the Mexican army between 1812 and 1972 later it housed the regional museum. Between 1994 and 1998, the convent was very beautifully restored, using only original materials and techniques. The **Museo de las Culturas de Oaxaca**, housed in the Centro Cultural Santo Domingo, and referred to as 'the Louvre of Oaxaca', is a superb museum that requires at least four hours to visit; exhibits are beautifully displayed and explained in Spanish (with plans to implement a system of recorded explanations in other languages); highly recommended. Fourteen galleries cover the history of Oaxaca from pre-Hispanic times to the contemporary period; the archaeology collection includes spectacular riches found in Tomb 7 of Monte Albán. There are also exhibits of different aspects of Oaxacan culture such as crafts, cooking, traditional medicine, etc, as well as temporary exhibits. ■ *1000-2000, closed Mon, US$2.70, free on Sun and holidays, use of video US$3.25.* The **Jardín Etnobotánico**, also in the Centro Cultural, offers free guided tours in Spanish at 1300 and 1800, one hour, sign up in advance, interesting. In high season English tours may be available. This garden aims to preserve different species of plants that are native to southern Mexico and have played and continue to play a role in the lives of different ethnic groups in Oaxaca; you can learn about the different species of *agaves* used to make mezcal, pulque and tequila; the trees used to make crafts; the *grana cochinilla*, an insect that lives in certain cacti and is used to dye cloth; the plants used in folk medicine; and many species more. Also part of the Santo Domingo complex, the **Biblioteca Francisco Burgoa** has a collection of 24,000 ancient volumes dating from 1484. There are temporary exhibits and the library is open to scholars for research. The **Hemeroteca**, corner Reforma and Gurrión, is a newspaper library. ■ *Mon-Fri, 0900-2000, Sat 0900-1700.*

The **Instituto de Artes Gráficas de Oaxaca** (IAGO), housed in an 18th-century building, is almost opposite the Centro Cultural at Alcalá 507; it has interesting exhibition rooms, a very good reference library and beautiful courtyards filled with flowers. ■ *Daily 0730-2200, closed Tue, free, but a donation is appreciated.*

At Alcalá 202 is **Museo de Arte Contemporáneo**, a good exhibition with library and café is housed in a late 17th-century house with a stone façade. ■ *Daily, 1030-2000, except Tue US$1.10.* The **Museo de Arte Prehispánico Rufino Tamayo**, Morelos 503, has an outstanding display of pre-Columbian artefacts dating from 1250 BC to AD 1100, donated by the Oaxacan painter Rufino Tamayo in 1974. Spanish only and not comprehensive. ■ *1000-1400, 1600-1900, Sun 1000-1500, closed Tue, entry US$1.50.* The **Museo Casa de Juárez**, at García Vigil 609, is where Juárez lived. It contains some of Juárez's possessions, historical documents and some bookbinding tools. ■ *1000-1800, Sun 1000-1700, closed Mon, US$1.40, free Sun and holidays.* The **Museo de Filatelia** Calle Reforma 504, has temporary exhibits, a philatelic library, and tours by appointment. ■ *0900-1900, closed Mon, free.* For photograph exhibits with Oaxacan motives, see Shopping below.

Markets

The colourful markets and varied crafts of Oaxaca are among the foremost attractions of the region. The city has four main markets, all of which are worth a visit; polite bargaining is the rule everywhere. The **Mercado de Abastos**, also known as the Central de Abastos, near the second class bus station, is the largest; a cacophony of sights, sounds and aromas, busiest on Saturdays and not to be missed. Prices here tend to be lower than in the smaller markets. Try the grasshopper-like critters called *chapulines* fried in huge vats on several of the stands. In the centre of town is the **Mercado 20 de Noviembre** (Aldama on the corner of 20 de Noviembre), with clean stalls selling prepared foods, cheese and baked goods. Next door, the larger **Mercado Benito Juárez** has a selection of household goods, fruits, vegetables, crafts, and regional products such as *quesillo* (string cheese), bread and chocolate. The **Mercado Artesanal** (Zaragoza and JP García) has a good selection of crafts intended for the tourist trade.

Safety Oaxaca is a generally safe city; however, sensible precautions are advised. Pickpockets are active in the markets, bus stations, and wherever there are crowds. Women should be aware of so-called 'Zócalo boys' or *gavacheros*, local young men who hang around the Zócalo picking up foreign women and seeking favours.

Essentials

Sleeping

There are over 160 hotels in Oaxaca in all price categories, and one can usually find some accommodation even at the busiest times of the year. If you wish to stay at a particular hotel however, reservations are recommended during peak holiday periods (Holy Week, Jul-Aug, Christmas and New Year).

L *Casa Cid de León*, Av Morelos 602, 2 blocks from the Zócalo, T514-1893, www.mexicoboutiquehotels.com/ciddeleon Intimate and charming with a fine terrace. **AL** *Casa Conzatti*, Gómez Farías 218, T513-8500, conzatti@oaxacalive.com 45 rooms in refurbished colonial house, a/c, safety deposit box, exchange, restaurant, new in 1999. **AL** *Marqués del Valle*, Portal de Clavería, right on the Zócalo by cathedral, T514-0688, F516-9961, hmarques@prodigy.net.mx Modern colonial-style, clean, friendly, good restaurant. Recommended. **AL** *San Pablo*, M Fiallo 102, T516-2553, F514-0860. In restored 16th-century convent of San Pablo, luxury suites, some with a/c, bathtubs, nice courtyard. **A** *Gala*, Bustamante 103 y Guerrero, southeast corner of Zócalo, T514-2251, F516-3660. Also suites, cable TV, with a/c, very nice (no elevator). **A** *Parador Santo Domingo de Guzmán*, Alcalá 804, T/F514-2171. An all-suite hotel with secure car parking, pool, cable TV. Suites have bedroom, sitting room and kitchen, daily maid included. Recommended. **A-B** *Casa María B&B*, Belisario Domínguez 205,

T515-1202, maria@oaxacalive.com Private house with large wooden garage doors, with same owners as *Casa Conzatti*, cater only to travellers. Bungalows and private rooms, friendly and helpful, breakfast included. **A-B** *Posada Catarina*, Aldama 325, T516-4270, F516-5338. Modern colonial, comfortable, nice, refurbished in 1999.

B-C *Antonio's*, Independencia 601, T516-7227, F516-3672, 1 block from Zócalo. Colonial patio, hot water, spotless, good restaurant, closed in evening. **B** *Ferri*, Las Casas 405, T514-5290, F514-5292. Modern, comfortable, clean, spacious, secure parking. Recommended. **B** *Francia*, 20 de Noviembre 212, T516-4811, F516-4251. Around enclosed courtyard, newly remodelled, popular, some rooms scruffy without windows, friendly and helpful. Recommended but noisy. **B** *La Casona del Llano*, Juárez 701, T514-7719, F516-2219. Nice location across from Paseo Juárez, pleasant, restaurant. **B** *Mesón del Rey*, Trujano 212, T516-0033, F516-1434, mesonrey@oax1.telmex.net.mx, 1 block from Zócalo. Clean, modern, fan, quiet except for street-facing rooms, good value, restaurant and travel agency, no credit cards. **B** *Monte Albán*, Alameda de León 1, T516-2777. Friendly, colonial-style, opposite cathedral, daily folk dance performances (see entertainment below). **B** *Parador San Andrés*, Hidalgo 405, 2 blocks from the Zócalo, T/F514-1011, sanders@prodigy.net.mx Comfortable, colonial-style, nice courtyard, new in 1999, very pleasant. **B-C** *Posada del Rosario*, 20 de Noviembre 508, T516-4112, F514-4911. Large courtyard (several others in same block). **C** *Las Rosas*, Trujano 112. Old charm, nice patio, clean, excellent, quiet, friendly, good view from roof. **C** *Posada del Centro*, Independencia 403, T/F516-1874, posadabb@prodigy.net.mx Modern colonial, nice, cheaper with shared bath, internet service. **C** *Principal*, 5 de Mayo 208, 2 blocks from the Zócalo, T/F516-2535. Colonial house, very clean, private shower with hot and cold water, morning coffee and cookies included. English spoken, rooms overlooking street are a bit noisy but still heavily booked. **C** *Vallarta*, Díaz Ordaz 309, T516-4967. Clean, good value, enclosed parking, street rooms noisy. **C** *Valle de Oaxaca*, Díaz Ordaz 208, T516-3707, F514-5203. Clean, comfortable, good restaurant. **C** *Yagul*, Mina 103, near Zócalo, T/F516-2750. Family atmosphere, use of kitchen on request.

D *Casa Arnel*, Aldama 404, Col Jalatlaco, T/F515-2856, www.casarnel.com.mx Homely, pleasant patio, good for meeting people, internet access, postal services, parking in next block, organize good tours. Reconfirm reservations. On the downside, not very central. **D** *Central*, 20 de Noviembre 104, 1 block from the Zócalo, T514-9425. With bath, hot water, good value but very noisy, fills up early. **D-E** *La Cabaña*, Mina 203, T516-5918. With bath, cheaper without, safe, clean but noisy, hot water 0700-1000, 1700-2100, good value. **D** *Nacional*, 20 de Noviembre 512, T516-2780. With hot water, clean, friendly. Recommended. **D** *Pasaje*, Mina 302. With bath, parakeets on the patio, hot water but you have to ask, clean, provides good town plan. **D** *Patria Querida*, Díaz Ordaz 307, 3 blocks from the Zócalo, New place with good reports, very clean and safe, small balcony (but no view). Parking. **D** *Posada del Rey*, Morelos 1001 y Reforma, T516-5555. Quiet with restaurant, parking and travel agency. A bit tatty, rooms on the street tatty and rather surly service, but otherwise OK. **D** *Posada El Palma*, JP García 504 y Mina, T516-4335. Cheaper without bath, convenient, friendly, family run, hot water in morning, only 1 shower upstairs, safe motorcycle parking. **D** *Posada Las Casas*, Las Casas 507 y Díaz Ordaz, T516-2325. Clean, with bath, cheaper without bath, normally friendly, good value. **D** *Posada Margarita*, Labastida 115, near Santo Domingo, T516-2802. With bath, hot water, clean, quiet, basic. **D** *Villa Alta*, Cabrera 303, T516-2444, 4 blocks from Zócalo. With bath, friendly service, stores luggage, and parking, bit run down but still OK.

E *Don Mario*, Cosijopi 219 and Rufino Tamayo, T514-2012. Clean, former house of famous painter Rufino Tamayo, internet service, close to ex-convent of Santo Domingo. Recommended. **E** *Lupita*, Díaz Ordaz 314, T516-5733. Large, pleasant rooms, upstairs rooms are bright with a brilliant views across the city and mountains from the flat rooftop. Recommended. **E-F** *Ninivé*, Periférico 108 and Las Casas, T514-4907, across from Mercado Mayorista, near 2nd class terminal. Basic, shared bath, noisy street. **E** *Posada Halcón*, Aldama 316, T516-1707. Without bath. Recommended. **E** *San José*, Trujano 412, T516-3948. Basic, dirty, cheap, lively, friendly. **E** *Yalalag*, Mina 108, T516-2892. Basic, noisy. A fairly new place receiving good reports is **F** *Don Diego*, on Callejón del Carmen, north of the centre. Clean, shared rooms with hot shower, use of kitchen and friendly staff. **F** *Hostal Santa Isabel*, Mier y Terán 103, T514-2865 (3 blocks from Zócalo). Friendly, kitchen, luggage store, bicycle rental. Recommended.

Hostels **F** per person *Guadalupe*, Juárez 409 and Abasolo, T516-6365. **F** per person in dorm, **D** for private room with shared bath, separate male and female dorms, hot water, kitchen, laundry, lockers. **F** per person in dorm at *Hostal Misión San Pedro*, Juárez y Morelos, T/F516-4626. **D** for private room, hot water, kitchen, laundry, TV room. **F** *Magic Hostel*, Fiallo 305, T516-7667, www.magichostel.com.mx Popular and full of tourists, friendly, kitchen and laundry facilities, bathrooms could be cleaner, stores luggage, internet access, purified water, good place to meet travellers. Good breakfast. **F** *Plata Gelatina*, Independencia 504, T514-9391, youthhostel_platagelatina@hotmail.com, 1 block from Zócalo. Funky atmosphere, clean, baggage storage, internet access, Mexican owned. **F** per person in dorms at *Paulina Youth Hostal*, Trujano 321, T516-2005, www.paulinahostel.com Brand new, friendly and clean with garden. Will store luggage, cheaper with Youth Hostal card. Recommended.

Many cheap hotels in the block formed by the streets Mina, Zaragoza, Díaz Ordaz and JP García; also on Trujano four blocks from the Zócalo (areas not safe at night)

Camping *Oaxaca Trailer Park*, Violeta 900, Colonia Reforma, north of town off the road to Mitla at a sign marked 'Infonavit' (corner of Pinos and Violetas). US$4.50 for a tent, US$6 for a camper van, secure; bus 'Carmen-Infonavit' from downtown.

Long stay *Villa María*, Arteaga 410A, T516-5056, F514-2562, 5 blocks from the Zócalo. Pleasant, modern, well-furnished apartments from US$300 per month with 24-hr security, maid service if required, daily rate **B**. Recommended.

Outside Oaxaca In 13 towns, throughout the Central Valleys around Oaxaca, there are tourist accomodations known as *Tourist Yú'ù* run by local communities (**F** per person, US$2.70 to camp). Each house has room with 6 beds, equipped kitchen, bathroom with hot water. For details contact T516-0123, F516-0984. See Excursions from Oaxaca, page 397.

Around the Zócalo Most restaurants on the main square cater for tourists, and are there-fore pricey (efficiency and standards depend a bit on how busy they are, but generally they are good). On the west side; *Bar Jardín*. A nice place to sit and watch all the activity (music, parades, aerobics, etc) in the Zócalo; upstairs is *Asador Vasco*. Live Mexican music in the evening, good food and service. *La Primavera*. Good value meals, international and traditional dishes, good expresso coffee, slow. On the north side, *Portal de la Soledad*, has fine dining on the plaza with exciting adaptions of regional food. *Pizza, Pasta y Más*. Popular. On the east side, *Café El Portal*, Portal Benito Juárez. Good food, quick service. *Café Amarantos* and *Mario's Terranova Restaurant*. Excellent food, friendly and efficient service, pricey. On Hidalgo at northeast corner. *El Mesón*. Buffets 0800-1830, good at US$2.50, breakfast, *comida corrida* poor value, good tacos, clean, quick service. Almost opposite is *La Piñata*. Good lunches. *La Casita*, Av Hidalgo 612 near main post office, 1st floor. Good food, sample platter of 7 Oaxacan *moles*, live music. On Bustamante, just south of Zócalo. *Gala*. Good breakfast, opens 0730, not cheap.

Eating

Along Macedonio Alcalá *Hostería de Alcalá*, at No 307. Excellent food and quiet atmo-sphere in colonial courtyard, good service, expensive. *María Bonita*, at No 706B. Typical Oaxaca food, small restaurant with pleasant atmosphere, closed Mon. *Pizza Nostrana Angelo*, opposite Santo Domingo. Very good, reasonable prices. Recommended. *Quing Long*, at Nos 407-32, upstairs. Beijing and Szechuan specialities. Mid-range.

North of Independencia Several good places for cheap *menú del día* on Porfirio Díaz, such as *Guidos*. Popular, with cheap pasta and coffee. *Arte y Tradición*, García Vigil 406. Craft cen-tre with courtyard café, excellent service and food, open Mon-Sat 1100-2200. *Bamby*, García Vigil 205. Cheaper beer than elsewhere, good breakfast, good value. *Catedral Restaurant*

Oaxacan cooking

The food of the state of Oaxaca is a fine representation of the complexity and variety of its cultures. The region's cuisine ranges from sublime to highly unusual.

A stroll through any of Oaxaca's markets will quickly bring you into contact with vendors selling chapulines. These small grasshopper-like creatures are fried, turning them bright red, and then served with lime. Another interesting ingredient in the diet is gusanito, a small red worm that is used to make a special sauce or ground with salt to accompany mezcal.

There are local curiosities for vegetarians as well. Flor de calabaza, squash flowers, are used in soup, empanadas, or as a garnish. Soup is also prepared from nopales, the young leaves of the prickly-pear cactus.

The most typical regional snacks are tlayudas, huge crispy tortillas, covered with a variety of toppings (beef, sausage, beans or cheese) and grilled over the coals. Oaxacan string cheese, known as quesillo, is also famous, as is the area's excellent chocolate,

best enjoyed as a hot beverage. A slightly fermented drink made from corn flour is known as atole.

Barbacoa is a pork, lamb or beef dish combining several different types of chillies and special condiments such as avocado leaves. The colour of the resulting sauce is a very deep red, reminiscent of another platter appropriately called mancha manteles (tablecloth stain).

The essence of Oaxacan cooking, however, and the recipes for which the state is most famous, are its many moles, which come in all colours of the rainbow. They are served as sauces accompanying beef, chicken, turkey or pork. The most complex by far is mole negro (black), combining at least 17 different ingredients including cocoa beans and sesame seeds. Mole colorado (red), or just coloradito, is also very typical and quite spicy. Almendrado (also red) is milder and slightly sweet. Mole verde (green) is a bit tangy, while mole amarillo (yellow) rounds out Oaxaca's culinary chromatic spectrum.

Bar, corner of García Vigil and Morelos, 1 block from cathedral. Good for international and local specialities, steaks, good *tamales*, classical music, excellent buffet for US$7. Recommended. *El Bicho Pobre II*, Calzada de la República. Lunch only, very popular and will serve platters of various dishes. Highly recommended. *El Decano*, 5 de Mayo and Murgia, open 0800-2400. Serves *comida corrida* from 1400-1500, Mexican dishes, good value. Also a good night spot. *El Infierno*, Crespo 210, T516-3921, good crêpes, international fare. *El Sol y la Luna*, Reforma 502. Good international food, not cheap, nice setting, live music Thu-Sun, open evenings only. *La Verde Antequera*, Matamoros 3 blocks north of Zócalo. Good daily lunch specials, best *comida corrida* in town for US$1. *Los Arcos*, García Vigil 306 under *Calesa Real* hotel. Good food in pretty setting and friendly service. *Los Chapulines*, Murguia 104. Upscale cooking, good desserts, pricey. *Marco Polo*, 5 de Mayo 103, open 0800-2300. Mexican and international dishes, good. Not cheap. *Pizza Rústica*, original location on Belisario Domínguez and Carranza, great pizza, popular and friendly. *Quince Letras*, Abasolo opposite *Hotel Santo Tomás*. Excellent food, friendly service. *Santa Clara*, Reforma and Independencia. Good breakfast, set meal. *Trece Cielos*, Matamoros 101. Good, cheap daily *menú*. *Tito's*, García Vigil No 116. Good food at very reasonable prices.

South of Independencia *Flor de Oaxaca*, Armenta y López 311. Pricey but excellent meals and delicious hot chocolate. *El Naranjo*, Trujano 203. In courtyard of 17th-century house, traditional Oaxaca fare, expensive but good, known for its *moles*. If you like the food, why not join one of the cooking classes. *Café Alex*, Díaz Ordaz 218 y Trujano. Good *comida corrida* and varied *à la carte*, coffee and breakfasts, delicious pancakes with fruit, good value. Recommended. *Coronita*, Díaz Ordaz 208 below *Hotel Valle de Oaxaca*. Tasty lunches, traditional Oaxacan dishes. *Hipocampo's*, Hidalgo 505. Good-value set meals, popular with locals, open late. *Flami*, on Trujano near Zócalo. Good food. *La Quebrada*, Armenta y López. Excellent fish, open only to 1800. *El Patio Grande*, Hidalgo 412, 2 blocks from Zócalo. Cheap *comida corrida*, Guelaguetza dancing (see below).*El Paisaje*, 20 de Noviembre. Good, cheap chicken dishes. *María Cristina's*, in Mercado 20 de Noviembre. Excellent *caldos* and *comidas*.

Fiesta, Las Casas 303. Good for breakfast or *comida corrida*. *El Shaddai*, Av Hidalgo 121 y Galeano. Family-run, good and cheap. The most authentic Oaxacan food is found in the *comedores familiares*, such as *Clemente*, *Los Almendros*, *La Juchita*, but they are way out of town and could be difficult to get to, or in *comedores populares* in the market. *Makedonia*, Trujano 122 y 20 de Noviembre. Greek food, *souvlaki*.

Vegetarian *Arco*, Niños Héroes de Chapultepec opposite *ADO* bus station. loud music. *Café Fuente y Señor de Salud*, Juárez just north of Morelos. Pleasant, reasonable food. *Flor de Loto*, Morelos 509, next to Museo Rufino Tamayo. Good value, clean, vegetarian and Mexican, *Supesteka* is delicious, also breakfast. *Girasoles*, 20 de Noviembre 102. Small, good food. Recommended. *La Abeja*, Porfirio Díaz 610 y Carranza. Breakfast and lunch, set meals, bakery, garden setting. *Los Olivos*, Carranza Madero, Good menu and buffet. *Manantial Vegetariano*, M. Alcalá 407, close to Santo Domingo cathedral. Excellent cheap meals, buffet US$4, pleasant patio. Live music at weekends. Recommended.

Pizza Nostrana, corner of Allende close to Santo Domingo church, 1300-2300. Delicious Italian cuisine, specializing in vegetarian dishes. Cheap-mid-range. *Gaia,* Labastida 115, organic meals, energizing juices and tarot card reading, open 0900-2100.

Snacks The most popular place to eat *tlayudas* (oversized tortillas) and other local snacks in the evening is from stalls and restaurants along Aldama, between Cabrera and 20 de Noviembre.

Cafés and bakeries *French Pastry Shop*, Trujano, 1 block west of Zócalo. Good coffee, pastries, desserts. *Café y Arte Geono*, Macedonio Alcalá 412. Nice garden, good coffee and cakes. *Café Plaza*, 5 de Mayo near Santo Domingo. Courtyard, good coffee. Recommended bakeries and pastry shops are: *Tartamiel*, Trujano, ½ block east of Zócalo; *La Vasconia*, Independencia 907; *La Luna*, Independencia 1105; *Pan Bamby*, García Vigil y Morelos. Good *dulcería* (sweet shop) in the 2nd class bus station. A local bread called *pan de yema*, made with egg yolk, at the Mercado de Abastos (the *Hermanas Jiménez* bakery is most recommended). *La Brew Coffee and Wafflehouse*, García Vigil 409B, 4 blocks from the Zócalo, T514-9673. Owner Susan McGlynn sincerely believes she has the best coffee in all of Oaxaca – test her out and get a refund if it isn't true! Great breakfast and delicious treats of brownies, muffins, cookies, breads and bagels. She is also on a quest to save the stray dogs of Oaxaca – big job, donations accepted.

Folk dancing Guelaguetza-style shows at the following hotels: *Casa de Cantera*, Murguia **Entertain-** 102, T514-9522, US$10, US$21 includes buffet dinner; *Camino Real*, Fri 1900, US$32 **ment** includes buffet dinner; *Monte Albán*, nightly at 2030, US$7, photography permitted; *El Patio Grande*, US$8 cover, 2030-2200, large, basic and cheaper option.

Nightclubs *Snob*, Niños Héroes Chapultepec, young crowd, free Wed; live salsa at *Rojo Caliente* on Porfirio Díaz; *Candela*, Murguía 413 y Pino Suárez, salsa, merengue, live music from 2200, also restaurant, popular with visitors and locals, cover US$5; *Bongos*, Nezahualcóyotl 218, Col Reforma, Thu-Sat 2100 onwards, salsa club, recommended. *La Tentación*, Murguía between Macedonio Alcalá and García Vigil, salsa, merengue, live music starting 2230, open late, friendly atmosphere, cover US$3.25. *Casa de Mezcal*, in front of the market, popular drinking hole. *Nitro*, H Escuela Naval Militar 103, the new in-place disco.

Cinemas *Ariel 2000*, Juárez y Berrizabal, subtitled films for US$2, ½ price Mon. *Cine Versalles*, Av Melchor Ocampo, north of Hidalgo (3 blocks east, ½ block north of Zócalo). *Cine Oaxaca*, Morelos near Alcalá; *Plaza Alameda*, Independencia y 20 de Noviembre; another cinema on Trujano, 1 block west of Zócalo. *Multimax*, Plaza del Valle; new multi-screen complex (with shopping mall), 2 for 1 Wed, normally US$3.

Adventure tourism Some of the leading organizations for 'adventure tourism' include **Sport & leisure** *Tierra Dentro*, Reforma 528B, Centro, T514-9284, www.tierradentro.com, and *Eco-x-plore*, M Bravo 210-D, Centro, T514-7204 with cycling, climbing, parapenting and rappelling.

Guerrero, Oaxaca and the Isthmus

Guelaguetza or Lunes del Cerro

This impressive annual celebration in July is where all the colour and variety of Oaxaca's many different cultural groups comes together in one place. For those with an interest in native costumes, music and dance, it must not be missed.

The word Guelaguetza originally means something like 'reciprocity' in Zapotec, the interchange of gifts or favours. Some elements of the celebration may well date from pre-Hispanic times, however the contemporary event is a well-organized large-scale folklore festival. Guelaguetza is heavily promoted by the state government to attract tourism, which it does in great numbers. Estimated revenues totalled US$10mn in 1999.

The main event is a grand folk dance show held at the Guelaguetza stadium on the slopes of Cerro del Fortín, on Monday morning. The performance is lively and very colourful, with the city below serving as a spectacular backdrop. Nine different groups are selected each year to represent the principal ethno-linguistic regions of the state.

Among the favourite presentations are always Flor de Piña, danced by women from the Tuxtepec area with a pineapple on their shoulder, and Danza de la Pluma, performed by men from the central valleys using enormous feather head-dresses. The most elaborate costumes are those of the women from the Isthmus of Tehuantepec, including stiffly starched lace resplandores (halos) on their heads. At the end of each performance, gifts are thrown from the stage to the audience – watch out for the pineapples!

Los Lunes del Cerro are usually the last two Mondays in July, but the exact dates can vary, so prospective visitors should enquire

beforehand. Tickets for seats in the lower galleries (A and B) are sold in advance through Sedetur and cost US$30 in 1999. The upper galleries (C and D) are free, line up before 0600, gates open around 0700, the performance begins at 1000 and finishes around 1400. Take a sweater as it is chilly in the morning, but the sun is very strong later on. A sun hat and sun-screen are essential, a pair of binoculars is also helpful in the upper galleries. Drinks and snacks are sold.

In addition to the main event, there are scores of other happenings in Oaxaca at this time of year, ranging from professional cycling races to classical music concerts, a Feria del Mezcal, and several smaller celebrations in nearby villages. Many events are free and a complete programme is available from Sedetur.

On the Saturday before Lunes del Cerro, at around 1800, participating groups parade down the pedestrian mall on Macedonio Alcalá, from Santo Domingo to the Zócalo. This is a good opportunity to see their splendid costumes close up and to meet the participants. On Sunday is the election of the Diosa Centeotl (goddess of the new corn), who presides over the following week's festivities. Candidates are chosen based on their knowledge of native traditions.

On Monday night, following the Guelaguetza, the Donají legend is presented in an elaborate torchlight performance at the same stadium starting around 2000. Donají was a Zapotec princess who fell in love with a Mixtec prince, Nucano, and eventually gave her life for her people. Some claim that the two lovers are buried in the same grave in Cuilapan de Guerrero.

Cycling *Bicicletas Bravo*, García Vigil 409C, T516-0953, roger@spersaoaxaca.com.mx New aluminium-frame bikes, front suspension, US$10 for 24-hour rental. Will also provide photocopied sections of topographic maps to guests upon request. Guided mountain biking trips available rated from 'easy' to 'technically challenging' all great itineraries. Wonderful way to see surrounding countryside. Minimum 2 people, US$28 each, make reservations at least one day before. Recommended. **Bird-watching** Almost 700 species of birds can be found in the State of Oaxaca. Its strategic location at the junction between North and Central America and its geographic diversity, spanning the Pacific and Atlantic watersheds, result in great diversity. There are birding opportunities in the Central Valleys, in the mountain range separating the Central Valleys from the Pacific coast, in the coastal lagoons, the thorn forests along Route 190, and in the cloud forests and lowlands of the Atlantic coast (see Valle Nacional). **Horse-riding** *La Golondrina*, Borde del Río Atoyac 800, San Jacinto Amilpas,

452-7570, thoroughbred Andalucían horses. **Public baths** *Baños Reforma*, Reforma 407, open 0700-1800, US$4 for steam bath US$2, sauna US$1, US$3. *Baños San Rafael*, Tinoco y Palacios 514, Mon-Sat 0600-1800, Sun 0600-1530, hot water. *Temazcal*, Reforma 402, 516-1165, www.mexonline.com/temazcal.htm Indigenous ancient ceremonial steam bath with herbs, also offer massages and aromatherapy. **Caving** Southwest of Oaxaca is San Sebastián de las Grutas, with a large system of caves (see page 404).

The most important festival is the *Guelaguetza*, also called *Los Lunes del Cerro*, when a fes- **Festivals** tive atmosphere permeates the city for over 2 weeks at the end of **Jul** (see page 392). *El Señor del Rayo*, a 9-day event in the 3rd week of **Oct**, including excellent fireworks. **2 Nov**, *Day of the Dead*, is a mixture of festivity and solemn commemoration, best appreciated at the Panteón General (main cemetery). Always ask before photographing. **8-18 Dec** with fine processions centred around the Basílica de la Soledad, patroness of Oaxaca, and throughout the city. On the night of **23 Dec**, *Noche de Rábanos*, outside the Palacio de Gobierno, there is a unique contest of figures carved out of radishes, many groups participate, stands made of flowers and corn stalks have been added in recent years to this old tradition. During the 9 days before Christmas, the *Novenas* are held, groups of people go asking for shelter, *posada*, as did Joseph and Mary, and are invited into different homes. This is done in the centre as well as other neighbourhoods like San Felipe (5 km north) and at Xoxo, to the south. The *posadas* culminate on the night of **24 Dec** with what is known as *Calendas*, a parade of floats representing allegories from the birth of Christ; every church in town prepares a float honouring their patron saint, the groups from all the parishes converge at the cathedral at 2300 (best seen from balcony of the restaurants around the Zócalo; go for supper and get a window table). *Buñuelos*, crispy fried dough rings, covered in syrup, are sold and eaten in the streets during a number of festivals, the clay dishes are ceremonially smashed after serving.

Crafts Many crafts are produced throughout the state of Oaxaca. Crafts are sold in nearby **Shopping** villages or they may be purchased in the city of Oaxaca, at the markets listed below. There are endless shopping temptations such as green and black pottery, baskets and bags made from cane and rushes, embroidered shirts, skirts, wooden painted animals called *alebrijes*, hammocks, tooled leather goods, woven wall hangings and rugs. The *Mercado Artesanal* at JP García y Zaragoza has a large selection of all kinds of crafts. The *Mercado Benito Juárez*, in the centre, has a sampling of different wares including a selection of leather bags and straw hats. At the *Mercado de Abastos* you are likely to find better prices; there is a selection of pottery and basketry used by locals and a section with other crafts. *Aripo*, on García Vigil 809, T516-9211. Government-run, cheaper and better than most, service good, with very good small market nearby on junction of García Vigil and Jesús Carranza, for beautiful coloured belts and clothes. *Arte y Tradición*, García Vigil 406. Superior craft shops, offer excellent selection of quality rugs at good prices. For the highest quality rug collection visit *La Mano Mágica*, Alcalá 203. *Sedetur* (see under Tourist offices, page 384) run a shop selling crafts and profits go to the artisans, good prices, recommended. *Casa Breno*, near Santo Domingo church, has unusual textiles and spindles for sale, happy to show visitors around the looms. *Lo Mexicano*, García Vigil, at end furthest from centre, excellent selection of high-quality crafts at reasonable prices, run by young Frenchman. *Pepe*, Av Hidalgo, for jewellery, cheap local crafts. *Yalalag*, 5 de Mayo y Murguía, has good selection of jewellery, rugs and pottery, somewhat overpriced. *Maro*, 5 de Mayo 204 between Morelos y Murguía. Good range of clothes from several regions and some crafts. *El Palacio de las Gemas*, Alcalá 100 block, is recommended for gemstones, good selection at reasonable prices. Cheapest and largest selection of pottery plus a variety of fabrics and sandals at *Productos Típicos de Oaxaca*, Belisario Domínguez 602; city bus near *ADO* depot goes there. Fine cream and purple-black pottery (Zapotec and Mixtec designs) available at *Alfarería Jiménez*, Zaragoza 402. *Mujeres Artesanas de las Regiones de Oaxaca* is a regional association of Oaxacan craftswomen with a sales and exhibition store at 5 de Mayo 204, T516067, open daily 0900 to 2000. *Corazón del Pueblo*, Alcalá 307, has fine crafts.

Bookshops *Librería Universitaria*, Guerrero 104, buys and sells books including English and a few German books. *Proveedora Escolar*, Independencia 1001 y Reforma, large, excellent selection on all subjects, cheaper. *Códice*, Alcalá 403. *Amate*, Alcalá 307, foreign-language books and magazines and a nice selection of books about Oaxaca and Mexico.

Photography *Foto Rivas*, Juárez 605 opposite Parque Juárez and 20 de Noviembre C-502, has an excellent collection of photographs of Oaxacan themes, new and old, also sell postcards and film. *Centro Fotográfico Alvarez Bravo*, Murguía 302, photo exhibits and sales. Likewise at *Galería Nunduá*, Nicolás Bravo 206.

Regional food and drink On Mina and 20 de Noviembre, opposite the 20 de Noviembre market, are several mills where they grind cacao beans, almond, sugar and cinnamon into a paste for making delicious hot chocolate, the cacao smell permeates the air in this area. Some of the brands sold are *Mayordomo* (very good), *Guelaguetza* and *La Soledad*. These same outlets sell Oaxacan *mole*, a thick paste used for preparing sauces. *Mole* and *quesillo*, the regional string cheese, are sold at the Benito Juárez market, where *La Oaxaqueña* stalls are recommended. Also at Mina y 20 de Noviembre is *La Casa del Dulce* sweet shop. Mezcal, the local hard drink (see page 404), is readily available throughout town. There are several mezcal factories on the Mitla road, which show the process of making Mezcal and sell it in black pottery bottles.

Transport **Local Bus**: buses, mostly US$0. 25. To the first-class bus station, buses marked 'VW' go from Avenida Juárez. Many lines marked 'Central' go by the second-class bus station. To airport US$1.70. **Car hire**: phone ahead to book, a week before if possible. *TTN*, 5 de Mayo 217-7 y Murguía, T516-2577; *Hertz*, La Bastida 115, T516-2434, F516-0009; *Arrendadora Express*, 20 de Noviembre 204A, T/F516-6776, cars motorcycles and bicyles. **Car park**: safe parking at *Estacionamiento La Brisa*, Av Zaragoza y Cabrera, US$3.50 per night, closed Sun.

Long distance **Air**: the Xoxocotlán (OAX) airport is about 9 km south, direction Ocotepec. The airport taxis (*colectivos*) cost US$1.85 per person. Book at Transportación Terrestre Aeropuerto on Alameda de León No 1-G, opposite the cathedral in the Zócalo (T514-4350) for collection at your hotel to be taken to airport, office open Mon-Sat 0900-1400, 1700-2000, must book at the office. To **Mexico City** with AeroMéxico, Mexicana, Aerocaribe and Aviacsa, several daily, US$155 1-way (US$128 advance booking), under 1 hr. To **Puerto Escondido** and **Huatulco**, with Aerocaribe, at 1030 and 1705, US$120 1-way (US$85 advance booking), same price both destinations. To **Puerto Escondido** with Aerotucán, daily US$120. To **Tuxtla Gutiérrez**, with Aerocaribe at 1210 and 1440, with Aviacsa at 1235, US$146 1-way. To **Tapachula**, with Taesa at 1005, US$100. To **Ciudad Ixtepec** (Tehuantepec Isthmus), with Aerocaribe, at 0840, US$85 1-way. For other destinations it is necessary to make a connection in Mexico City.

Shuttle vans: a new service running to Pochutla and Puerto Escondido. *Auto Expess de Turismo*, Atlantida. Reservations and tickets at Officina Matriz, La Noria 101, T514-7077 and Suc Maihuatlan, 3 de Octubre 114. T572-0380. Comfortable vans have hotel pick, available for other destinations also for groups. Pochutla: 0700, 1100, 1500, 1700, 2130 and 2330, US$18; Puerto Escondido: 0700, 1500 and 2330, US$14.

Buses: for 1st class buses, you may buy tickets in advanced at the Ticket Bus Office, 20 de Noviembre 103, T515-1214, Mon-Sat 0800-2200, Sun 0900-1600. 1st class terminal, also referred to as *ADO* terminal is northeast of Zócalo on Calzada Niños Héroes de Chapultepec (no luggage office, taxi from centre US$2.50). *ADO*, *Cristóbal Colón*, *Sur* and *Cuenca* operate from here. Note that many 2nd class buses leave from here too. 2nd class terminal is west of Zócalo on Calzada Valerio Trujano, just west of the Periférico, across from the Central de Abastos, it is referred to as the 'Central Camionera' (has left-luggage office, open until 2100). Some 2nd class companies also offer superior service on some runs. The *Autobuses Unidos* (AU) terminal (2nd class, 2 levels of service, 1 is very good, modern buses but without a/c) is at Santa Rosa, near the Teatro Alvaro Carillo. 1st class terminal is the only one for Villahermosa and the Yucatán. Tickets for *ADO*, *Cristóbal Colón*, *AU*, *Sur* and *Cuenca* can also be purchased at Periférico 152, T516-3222, by the pedestrian crosswalk across from the Mercado de Abastos. For long-distance travel, you must book in advance; beware of thieves at all bus terminals, but especially on arrival of *plus* services. To **Mexico City** most go to Tapo (Mexico City east bus terminal) but there are also services to the North and South terminals if that makes for a better connection, 6 hrs; some 2nd class buses go along the old Carretera Federal through the Cañada region, 8-9 hrs. Many buses throughout the day and night, prices from US$38 to US$21. To **Puebla**: 1st class and some 2nd class buses take the Autopista, 4 hrs, other 2nd class buses go on the old road, 5-6 hrs, good scenery in both cases, many buses throughout the day, US$19 to US$13. To **Veracruz**: it is 7½ hrs via the Autopista and Orizaba. Luxury service: *Cristóbal Colón Plus*, at 2330, US$26.40; 1st class: *ADO*, at 0830 and 2030, US$22.70; 2nd class: *Cuenca* (1st class terminal) at 2400, US$13.15; *AU* (*AU* terminal), at 2230, US$16.80; book early, alternatives are to change at Puebla or go via Tuxtepec. *Cristóbal Colón* to **Villahermosa**: daily at 1700 and 2100, US$22.70, 14 hrs, book well ahead. To **Mérida**: *Cristóbal Colón*, Sun at 0900, 16½ hrs.

The route to Chiapas from Oaxaca is via Tehuantepec, the 1st 2 hrs are on very windy roads. To **Tuxtla Gutiérrez** and **San Cristóbal de las Casas**, luxury service: *Cristóbal Colón Plus*, at 2000, US$26.40, 10½ hrs (Tuxtla); US$27, 12½ hrs (*San Cristóbal*); 1st class: *Cristóbal Colón*, at 1930 (both) and 2215 (Tuxtla only), US$20.30 (Tuxtla), US$23.50 (San Cristóbal). 2nd class to Tuxtla only: with Oaxaca-Istmo 4 daily, with *Fletes y Pasajes* 6 daily, several daytime departures, US$18, 10-11 hrs. To **Tapachula**, 1st class, *Cristóbal Colón*, US$24, 11 hrs; 2nd class, with *Fletes y Pasajes*. Book well in advance as buses often come almost full from Mexico City. To **Tehuantepec**, scenic, 1st class: *Cristóbal Colón*, 13 daily, US$9.60, 5½ hrs; 2nd class: with Oaxaca-Istmo and *Fletes y Pasajes*, every 30 mins 0600-2400, US$7.40, 5½ hrs. To **Ciudad Cuauhtémoc**: US$33, 12 hrs. To **Arriaga**: US$7, 6 hrs, 5 a day.

All 1st class services to the Pacific Coast go through Tehuantepec in the Isthmus, a long detour, making 2nd class service more convenient for all coastal destinations except Salina Cruz. To **Pochutla**, 1st class: *Cristóbal Colón*, via Isthmus, 4 daily, US$14.70, 11 hrs; 2nd class: direct route, very scenic, with Oaxaca-Pacífico and *Estrella del Valle*, direct service (comfortable buses but no a/c) at 0945, 1415 and 2230, US$6.75, 6 hrs; regular service, same companies, every 30 mins throughout the day. Night bus to Puerto Angel, 2315, arrives 0600. To **Puerto Escondido**, 1st class: *Cristóbal Colón*, via Isthmus, 0100, 0930 and 2400, US$14.80, 12 hrs (night bus via Pochutla 7 hrs); 2nd class: via Pochutla, with Oaxaca-Pacífico and *Estrella del Valle*, direct service (comfortable buses but no a/c) at 0945, 1415 and 2230, US$7.60, 7 hrs; with *Estrella Roja*, superior service at 2245, US$8.70, direct service 4 daily, US$7.60; with *Tran-Sol* via Sola de Vega, at 0600, 1300 and 2200, US$7.60, 7 hrs (Oaxaca-Sola de Vega US$2.70). To **Huatulco**, 1st class: *Cristóbal Colón*, via Isthmus, 4 daily, US$14.60, 9½ hrs; 2nd class: via Pochutla, with Oaxaca-Pacífico at 2200, 7 hrs, or take a day bus to Pochutla and transfer there.

Airline offices *Mexicana*, Fiallo 102 y Av Independencia, T516-8414, Mon-Fri 0900-1900, Sat-Sun 0900-1800. *Aerocaribe*, Fiallo 102 y Av Independencia, T516-0266. *AeroMéxico*, Av Hidalgo 513 Centro, T516-3229. *Aviacsa*, Pino Suárez 604, T518-4566. *Aerotaxi (Turoca)*, Calz Porfirio Díaz 104, Col Reforma, T515-7270. *AeroTucán*, Alcalá 201, T501-0532.

Banks Get to banks before they open, long queues form. *Bancomer*, on García Vigil, 1 block from Zócalo, exchanges TCs in own *casa de cambio*, 0900-1600, and has cash dispenser for Visa card. *Banco Santander Mexicano*, Independencia 605, cash and TCs, good rates, TCs changed Mon-Fri 0900-1330. *Amex* office *Viajes Micsa*, at Valdivieso 2, T516-2700, just off Zócalo, very helpful, but lots of paperwork (no travel reservations). *Escotiabank*, on Periférico near Mercado de Abastos, best rates. *Casa de Cambio*, Abasolo 105, 0800-2000 changes TCs. *Casa de Cambio* at Armenta y López, near corner with Hidalgo, 0800-2000 Mon-Sat, shorter hrs on Sun. No problem to change TCs at weekends, many *casas de cambio* around the Zócalo.

Communications Internet: many cyber cafés and in the post office, Mon-Fri 0800-1900, with fairly good set ups, charging US$1/hr. **Post office:** on Alameda de León, Independencia y 20 de Noviembre.

Directory
For airline websites, see page 34

Courier *DHL*, office at Amado Nervo 104D, esq Héroes de Chapultepec, open Mon-Fri 0900-1800, Sat 0900-1400, no credit card payments. **Telephone:** public card phones are the easiest way to make long-distance calls, otherwise shop around for rates at long-distance phone establishments.

Embassies and consulates *Canada* (Honorary Consulate), Pino Suárez 700 local 11B, T513-3777, F515-2147. *Italy*, Alcalá 400, T516-5058. *US* (Consular Agency), Alcalá 407-20, Plaza Santo Domingo, T514-3054, conagent@prodigy.net.mx

Language schools There are many in the city; the following have been recommended: *Amigos del Sol*, Libres 109, T514-3484 amisol@oaxacanews.com Small groups and low rates. *Becari*, M Bravo 210, Plaza San Cristóbal, CP 68000, T/F514-6076, www.becari.com.mx, 4 blocks north of Zócalo, US$75 per 15-hr week, fully qualified teachers, courses including culture, history, literature and politics, with workshops on dancing, cooking or art, flexible programmes, recommended. *Centro de Idiomas*, Universidad Autónoma Benito Juárez, Burgoa, 5 blocks south of Zócalo, weekly or monthly classes (US$200 per month), or private tuition, very professional and good value for money, recommended. In addition to Spanish classes, local crafts and culture (including dance, cooking, weaving and pottery) are taught at the *Instituto Cultural Oaxaca*, Av Juárez 909, T53404, www.instculturaloax.com.mx, daily, 4 hrs of formal Spanish teaching are complemented with 2 hrs spent in cultural workshops and 1 hr of informal conversation with a native speaker; US$105 per week, US$400 per month; accommodation can be arranged. *Instituto de Comunicación y Cultura*, M Alcalá 307-12, 2nd Floor, T/F516-3443, www.iccoax.com, cultural workshops and field trips included in the programme, US$100 per week, US$350 per month; accommodation can be arranged. *Instituto Johann Goethe*, JP García 502, T/F43516, wide variety of courses, eg 4 weeks, 2 hrs a day US$160. *Vinigulaza*, Abasolo 209, T/F514-6426, vinigulaza@prodigy.net.mx, small groups, good place to talk with Mexican students, also cooking and salsa classes. See also Learning Spanish in Essentials, page 27.

Cooking classes *Susan Trilling*, www.seasonsofmyheart.com Recommended (also see above as many language schools also have cooking classes).

Laundry *Lavandería Azteca*, Hidalgo 404 between Díaz Ordaz y J P García, Mon–Sat 0830-2000, quick service, delivers to nearby hotels, 3½ kg US$3.80. *Lavandería Hidalgo*, Hidalgo esq J P García, Mon–Sat 0800-2000, 3½ kg US$3.80. *ELA, Super Lavandería Automática*, Antonio Roldán 114, Colonia Olímpica, washes and irons.

Libraries *Biblioteca Circulante Benedict Crowel Memorial*, Macedonio Alcalá 305, looks like an apartment block, English lending library with very good English books, a few French and Spanish, also English newspapers (*The News* from Mexico City), used books and magazines for sale (open Mon-Fri 1000-1300, 1600-1900, Sat 1000-1300), US$13 per year plus US$13 returnable deposit. *The News* is also sold round the Zócalo by newsboys, from mid-morning, or from street vendor at Las Casas y 20 de Noviembre. The *Biblioteca Pública Central*, at Alcalá 200 (no sign) has a lovely courtyard and a reading room with Mexican newspapers and magazines. Next door is the library of the Museo de Arte Contemporáneo. For the libraries at the Centro Cultural Santo Domingo and the Instituto de Artes Gráficas, see Museums above.

Medical services Pharmacy: 20 de Noviembre y Ignacio Aldama, open till 2300. **Dentist**: *Dra Marta Fernández del Campo*, Armenta y López 215, English-speaking, very friendly, recommended. **Doctor**: *Dr Victor Tenorio*, Clínica del Carmen, Abasolo 215, T62612, close to centre (very good English). *Dr Marco Antonio Callejo* (English-speaking), Belisario Domínguez 115, T53492, surgery 0900-1300, 1700-2000.

Tour operators There are many in town, most running the same tours, eg daily to Monte Albán; El Tule, Mitla and, sometimes, another village on this route; city tour; Fri to Coyotepec, Jalietza and Ocotlán; Thu to Cuilapan and Zaachila; Sun to Tlacolula, Mitla and El Tule. Basically, the tours tie in with local markets. Regular day tours run US$11-13 per person; special tours on demand about US$22 per hr for 4 passengers. Judith Reyes at *Arte y Tradición*, García Vigil 406, runs good tours to outlying villages in her VW van, US$8 per hour. *Expediciones Sierra Norte*, García Vigil 406. T514-8271, F516-7745, www.sierranorte.org.mx, run hiking and mountain-bike tours in the Sierra Juárez, north of the town of Benito Juárez. Tours depart daily from office at 0930, call day before for reservations. *Tierraventura*, Boca del Monte 110, T/F514-3043, tierraventura@yahoo.com, run tours to the highlands (Sierra Juárez, Sierra Mixteca, Hierve el Agua) and coast, US$20-30 per day. *La Brujita Tours*, García Vigil 409B, T548-7334, labrujita_oax@yahoo.com Flamboyant and friendly Susan McGlynn organizes personalized tours that take you to the heart of Oaxacan markets, home-cooked meals with local families and to visit local artisans at work in their shops. She can be found at her coffee shop *La Brew Coffee and Wafflehouse* (see under Cafés and bakeries above).

Useful addresses Immigration: Pensamientos 104, Col Reforma, open Mon-Fri 0900-1400, 2nd floor. **Luggage storage**: Servicio Turístico de Guarda Equipaje y Paquetería, Av Tinoco y Palacios 312, Centro, T516-0432, open 24 hrs. **Tourist police**: on Zócalo near cathedral, friendly and helpful. *Centro de Protección al Turista*, T516-7280.

Excursions from Oaxaca

The Central Valleys of the State of Oaxaca, which surround the capital, make a fine destination for several interesting day-trips or overnight visits. The area features awe-inspiring archaeology (Monte Albán, Mitla and Yagul are but the best known of many different sites), authentic native towns and villages, their people, markets, crafts, and fiestas. There is good walking with impressive views throughout the region, as well as the interesting mineral deposits at Hierve El Agua. The area has good public transport and excursions can easily be organized.

Oaxaca is a growing hotbed of eco-tourism, with many options for tours (see Sport and leisure, page 391). For good hikes, take local bus to **San Felipe del Agua**, north of the city. To the left of where the buses stop at the end of line is a car parking area, just below it starts a dirt road; follow this road and in five minutes you will reach the San Felipe Park entrance and a booth where you register with the guard. Several trails fan out from here; one follows the river valley, it goes by some picnic areas and a swimming pool, continues upstream crossing the river several times before reaching a waterfall in about one hour. There are longer walks to the mountain to the north, crossing through several vegetation zones, from low dry shrub to pleasant pine forest; allow five or six hours to reach the summit.

Monte Albán

Colour map 3, grid C5
There are tri-lingual
(Spanish, English and
Zapotec) signs
throughout the site

From the ruins
at Monte Albán
there are paths
leading to the
valleys below

Monte Albán is situated about 10 km (20 minutes) west of Oaxaca, on a hilltop dominating the surrounding valley. The ruins were declared a UNESCO World Heritage Trust site in 1987, and additional restoration was carried out between 1992 and 1994, when a museum and visitors centre were built. Monte Albán features pyramids, walls, terraces, tombs, staircases and sculptures of the ancient capital of the Zapotec culture. The place is radiantly colourful during some sunsets, but permission is needed to stay that late (take a torch/flashlight).

Although the city of Monte Albán extended far beyond the confines of the Main Plaza, it is to the latter area that archaeologists, art historians, historians and tourists have looked to assess and interpret the raison d'être of this fascinating site. Constructed 400 m up a steep mountain, without immediate access to water or cultivable land, the Main Plaza has at times been considered the site of a regional marketplace or ceremonial centre. The marketplace theory becomes less convincing when access to the site is considered: not only would the visitor have had to haul merchandise up the back-breaking hill, but entrance to the plaza was severely restricted. The modern access roads did not exist in ancient times and the only way into the site was through three narrow passageways, which could easily have been guarded to restrict entry. The modern ramp cuts across what was the ball-court to the southeast of the North Platform. The space at the centre of the Main Plaza would seem ideal for religious ceremonies and rituals: the absence of religious iconography contradicts this interpretation. The imagery at Monte Albán is almost exclusively militaristic, with allusions to tortured captives and captured settlements.

To the right, before getting to the ruins, is Tomb 7, where a fabulous treasure trove was found in 1932; most items are in the Centro Cultural Santo Domingo and the entrance is closed off by a locked gate. Tomb 172 has been left exactly as it was found, with skeleton and urns still in place, but these are not visible. Tombs 7 and 172 are permanently closed.

The Main Plaza The Main Plaza at Monte Albán is delineated north and south by the two largest structures in the city, which have been interpreted as palace and/or public building (North Platform) and temple (South Platform). Apart from these two impressive structures, the ball court and the arrow-shaped building in front of the South Platform, the Main Plaza has 14 other structures, six along the west side of the Plaza, three in the middle and five along the east side. One structure, known as Edificio de los Danzantes (Dancers), has bas reliefs, glyphs and calendar signs (probably 5th century BC). During the period AD 450-600, Monte Albán had 14 districts beyond the confines of the Main Plaza: it has been proposed that each of the 14 structures located within the Main Plaza corresponded with one of the districts outside. Each pertained to a distinct ethnic group or polity, brought together to create a pan-regional confederacy or league. The arrow-shaped structure functioned as a military showcase; it also has astronomical connotations.

The Confederacy The presence of a number of structures in or bordering the Main Plaza that housed representatives of distinct ethnic groups supports the theory that Monte Albán came into being as the site of a confederacy or league. Its neutral position, unrelated to any single polity, lends credence to this suggestion. The absence of religious iconography, which might have favoured one group over the others, emphasizes the secular role of the area, while the presence of the Danzantes sculptures suggests a trophy-gathering group. However, although Monte Albán may have served defensive purposes, the presence of the Danzantes and the captured town glyphs argues for an offensive and expansionist role. In all, about 310 stone slabs depicting captives, some of whom are sexually mutilated with streams of blood (flowers) flowing from the mutilated parts, have been found. Some of these woeful captives are identified by name glyphs, which imply hostilities against some

Monte Albán

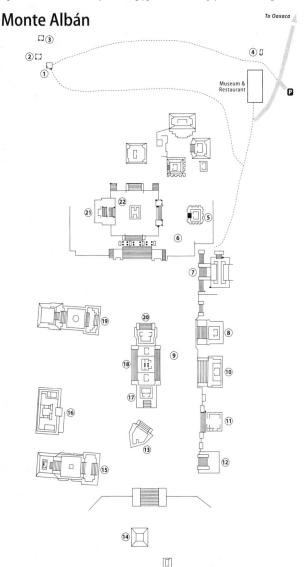

To Oaxaca

Museum & Restaurant

1 Tomb 104	**10** Building P	**17** Building I
2 Tomb 103	**11** Palace (Building S)	**18** Building H
3 Tomb 172	**12** Building Q	**19** Complex IV
4 Tomb 7	**13** Observatory (Building J)	**20** Building G
5 Mound A	**14** South Platform	**21** Building B
6 North Platform	**15** Complex M	**22** Sunken Patio
7 Ball Court	**16** Building of the Dancers	
8 Building U	(with Building L	
9 Chapel	superimposed)	

0 metres 50
0 yards 50

Guerrero, Oaxaca and the Isthmus

settlement and the capture of its warriors. The fact that most of them are nude denotes the disdain and contempt with which they were treated by their captors: nudity was considered shameful and undignified by the peoples of Mesoamerica. It is very likely that the rulers of Monte Albán were determined to bring into the confederacy as many polities as possible in order to extract tribute, which would permit the expansion of the capital. The growth of the confederacy at Monte Albán was a direct response to events in the Valley of Mexico, where Teotihuacán was exercising dominion over most of the polities in that area. Although Monte Albán had been developing a policy of offence and capture as early as 200 BC, the growth of the city really gained impetus with the growth of Teotihuacán, whose administrators must have cast an avaricious eye on the rich soil of the Valley of Oaxaca. From the ceramics and architecture analysed at Monte Albán, it is clear that Teotihuacán never realized its ambitions in that area. The confederacy clearly functioned well.

The Collapse Monte Albán reached its maximum size around AD 600, with a population estimated at between 15,000-30,000. Shortly after that date, the city changed dramatically in form and function. There was a decrease in population of nearly 82%, the Main Plaza was abandoned and the majority of the people moved nearer to the valley floor, but behind protective walls. They were much closer to major roads, implying that Monte Albán was now becoming more commercially minded and aspired to be self-sufficient, which it had never been in its long history.

The abandonment of the Main Plaza was a direct result of the collapse of the political institution centred there. This collapse has been seen as a consequence of the fact that, beginning early in the seventh century AD, Teotihuacán was already showing signs of decadence. Gaining momentum, the decadence led to the massive abandonment of that great centre. It is unlikely to have been coincidental that the Main Plaza at Monte Albán was abandoned around this time. The removal of the Teotihuacán threat made redundant the confederacy that was so costly to maintain: the collapse was complete.

Readers interested in the archaeology of Monte Albán are referred to: Richard E Blanton, *Monte Albán*, AP, New York, 1978.

The site **museum** is good, exhibiting stone glyphs and sculptures as well as smaller artiefacts; explanations are in Spanish only, and flash photography is prohibited. Informative literature and videos in several languages are sold in the bookstore in the visitors' centre, which also houses a small restaurant. (Recommended literature is the Bloomgarden *Easy Guide to Monte Albán* or *Easy Guide to Oaxaca*, covering the city and all the ruins in the valley, with maps. It is available in major hotels or the bookshop at Guerrero 108, and all the ruins.)

■ *The ruins are open 0800-1800. Entrance US$3.80, free on Sun and public holidays (and for Mexican students). A charge of US$3 is made to use video cameras; fees for the guides who hang around the site are variable, ask several of them and beware of overcharging. Monte Albán receives many visitors during high season. Most people go in the morning, so it may be easier to catch the afternoon bus.*

Transport
If you're in reasonable shape consider hiring a bike for the day, and enjoy the ride down at least

To Monte Albán: *Autobuses Turísticos* depart from *Hotel Rivera del Angel*, Mina 518 near Díaz Ordaz (bus tickets available from hotel lobby) every ½ hr from 0830 to 1600 (schedule may vary with season) fare US$1.50 return, last bus back at 1800; 1½ hrs at the site, allowing not nearly enough time to visit ruins before returning (you are permitted to come back on another tour on 1 ticket for an extra US$1 but you will not, of course, have a reserved seat for your return). Several buses from *Hotel Trébol*, 1 block south of Zócalo, US$1.30, 0930, 1030, returning 1330, 1400. Local city buses marked 'Colonia Monte Albán', US$0.20, pass along the street outside *Hotel Rivera del Angel*. You can also catch the same bus as it begins its route in front of the *Panadería México* next to the Mercado de Abastos. Either way you will be left at the end of the bus route in the Col Monte Albán neighborhood at the foot of the hill of the Monte Albán ruins. There are a few friendly kiosks where you will be dropped off. Ask them or the way and you should find yourself walking or hitching up a somewhat steep, black paved road for about 4 km to the ruins. The hike offers nice views but it's best not to go alone. Take the tourist bus to Monte Albán, see the ruins at your leisure, then walk 4 km downhill from the ruins to Colonia Monte Albán and get a city bus back from there. Some prefer to walk up and take the tourist bus back. Taxis charge about US$10 per hour for touring.

Route to Mitla

It is 42 km from Oaxaca to Mitla, on a poor paved road (Route 190), but with many potholes and occasional flooding. On the way you pass **El Tule** (12 km east of Oaxaca), which in the churchyard has what is reputed the world's largest tree, a savino (*Taxodium mucronatum*), estimated at 2,000 years old. It is 40 m high, 42 m round at base, weighs an estimated 550 tons, and is fed water by an elaborate pipe system. ■ *US$0.25*. Bus from Oaxaca, second class bus station, every 30 minutes, US$0.25, buy ticket on the bus, sit on the left to see the Tule tree; alternatively *colectivos* for surrounding villages leave from near the second class bus station, bus El Tule-Mitla US$0.40. El Tule has a market with good food on sale and *La Sonora* restaurant on eastern edge of town has quite tasty food, also *El Milenario* Restaurant at Guerrero 4-A.

Continuing east along Route 190, 5 km from El Tule is **Tlacochahuaya**, with a 16th-century church and vivid Indian murals; visit the cloisters at the back and see the decorated organ upstairs. ■ *US$0.45 to church*. Bus from Oaxaca second class terminal, US$0.30.

Another 5 km further, a paved road leads off Route 190 to **Teotitlán del Valle**, where wall hangings and *tapetes* (rugs) are woven, and which is now becoming rather touristy. There is an artesans' market near the church, and a **Museo Comunitario**. ■ *Mon-Sat 1000-1800, US$0.50*. Since 1999 a *Fiesta 'Antigua' Zapoteca* is celebrated in July, to coincide with the *Guelaguetza* in Oaxaca. The feast of *Virgen de la Natividad* is on 8 September, and on 3 May *Fiesta de las Cruces*, when people climb to a cross on a beautiful summit above town (across the river); good hiking at any time of the year. The best prices for weavings are to be had at the stores along the road as you come into town, but they may be even cheaper in Oaxaca where competition is stronger. Buses leave every hour from 0700-2100, from second class bus terminal (US$0.40); the second class bus may provide the contacts you need to buy all the weavings you want! From the town of Teotitlán del Valle you can walk up to the nearby hills across the river or hike north to the town of Benito Juárez.

Teotitlán del Valle
Make sure you know whether you are getting all wool or a mixture and check the quality. A well-made rug will not ripple when unfolded on the floor

Sleeping and eating There is a *Tourist Yú'ù* for those wishing to stay overnight, situated far from town, by the turn-off from Route 190. 1 simple *restaurant* in town.

Tlacolula has a most interesting Sunday market and the renowned Capilla del Santo Cristo in the church. The chapel is similar in style to Santo Domingo in Oaxaca, with intricate white and gold stucco, lots of mirrors, silver altar rails and sculptures of martyrs in gruesome detail. Two beheaded saints guard the door to the main nave (**Fiesta**: 9 October). There is a pleasant walled garden in front of the church. A band plays every evening in the plaza, take a sweater, cold wind most evenings, starts at 1930. On the main street by Parque Juárez is *Casa de Cambio Guelaguetza*, cash only, fair rates. The towns people are renowned for their mezcal preparation. The indoor market next to the church is very interesting. Between the church and the market you might see a local lady selling dried grasshoppers! Tlacolula can be reached by bus from Oaxaca, from the second class bus station every 10 minutes, 0600-1900, US$0.80. Taxis stop by the church, except on Sunday when they gather on a street behind the church; ask directions. Tlacolula's bus station is just off the main highway, several blocks from the centre; pickpockets are common here, be especially careful at the Sunday market and in the scrum to board the bus.

Tlacolula
Colour map 3, grid C5

Guerrero, Oaxaca and the Isthmus

Sleeping and eating *Hotel Fiesta*, across from gas station at entrance to town. Shared bath, cold water, basic; also a *Tourist Yú'ù*. There are several simple restaurants in town.

Santa Ana del Valle
Quality weavings can be found at Santa Ana del Valle (3 km from Tlacolula). The village is peaceful and friendly with a small museum showing ancient textile techniques; ask any villager for the keyholder. There are two fiestas, each lasting three days. One takes place the second week of August, the other at the end of January. There is an important rug market. Buses leave from Tlacolula every 30 minutes.

Yagul
Further east along Route 190 is the turn-off north for Yagul, an outstandingly picturesque archaeologic site where the ball courts and priests' quarters are set in a landscape punctuated by candelabra cactus and agave. Yagul was a large Zapotec and later Mixtec religious centre. The ball court is said to be the second largest discovered in Mesoamerica; it also one of the most perfect discovered to date. There are fine tombs (take the path from behind the ruins, the last part is steep) and temples, and a superb view from the hill behind the ruins. Recommended. ■ *Daily 0800-1730, US$1.40, free on Sun. Guided tours in English on Tue, US$10, from Oaxaca travel agencies.* Take a bus to Mitla from the Oaxaca second class terminal (see below) and ask to be put down at paved turn-off to Yagul (five minutes after Tlacolula terminal). You will have to walk 1 km uphill from the bus stop to the site (overpriced *Restaurant El Centeotl* half way, open 1100-1900, stock up on water, none at site) and you can return the same way or walk 3 km west to Tlacolula along Route 190 to catch a bus to Oaxaca.

Mitla
Phone code: 951
Colour map 3, grid C5
A further 5 km past the turn-off for Yagul along Route 190, a paved road branches left and leads 4 km to Mitla (meaning 'place of the dead') where there are ruins of four great palaces among minor ones. Some of the archaeology, outside the fenced-in site, can be seen within the present-day town.

Magnificent bas reliefs, the sculptured designs in the Hall of Mosaics, the Hall of

Around Oaxaca

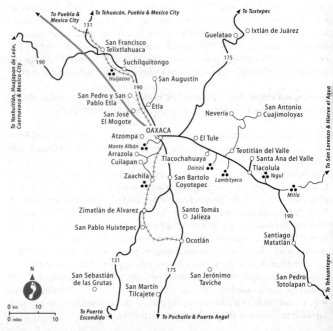

Zapotec Indians

The Zapotec language is used by over 300,000 people in the state as a first or second language (about 20% of Oaxaca State population speaks only an Indian language). The Zapotec Indians, who weave fantastic toys of grass, have a dance, the Jarabe Tlacolula Zandunga, performed by barefoot girls splendid in most becoming coifs, short, brightly coloured skirts, ribbons and long lace petticoats, while the men, all in white with colourful handkerchiefs, dance opposite them with their hands behind their backs. Only women, from Tehuantepec or Juchitán, dance the slow and stately Zandunga, costumes gorgeously embroidered on velvet blouse, full skirts with white pleated and starched lace ruffles and huipil.

the Columns and, in the depths of a palace, *La Columna de la Muerte* (Column of Death), which people embrace and then measure what they can't reach with their fingers to know how many years they have left to live (rather hard on long-armed people). We have been informed that the column can no longer be embraced but do not know if this is a temporary or permanent arrangement. ■ *Daily 0800-1730, entry US$2 (Sun free, use of video US$3.00), literature sold at entrance.*

By the site, there is a soberly decorated colonial church with four cupolas, built on top of a pre-existing native structure (no access from church to ruins, or vice versa). A small museum (included in entry fee) displays a few artefacts. Crafts and souvenirs are sold at the entrance to the site (bargaining recommended). Away from the ruins the town is very relaxed, and has a pleasant plaza adorned with bright bougainvillea.

Sleeping and eating D *Hotel y Restaurante Mitla*, on town square, T80112. Private bath, simple, clean, friendly, local food. D *Hotel y Restaurante La Zapoteca*, before bridge on road to ruins, T958-0026. Private bath, hot water, parking, friendly, good food. *María Teresa* restaurant 100 m from site towards village. Good *comida corrida*.

Transport Taxi costs US$10 each to Mitla for 4 sharing, with time to take photographs at Tule and Mitla and to buy souvenirs at ruins, or approximately US$10 per hour for touring as you please. Tours (1000 till 1300, rather rushed) to Tule, Mitla and Tlacolula from Oaxaca agencies, cost US$7.50, not including entry fees. Buses from Oaxaca 2nd class station every 10 mins, 0600-1900, US$0.90, 40 mins; the ruins are 10 mins' walk across the village (from the bus stop on the main road, 2 blocks from the square).

Hierve el Agua From Mitla take a bus to San Lorenzo Albarradas (one hour, US$1). Three kilometres from there (57 km from Oaxaca) is the village of Hierve el Agua. Due to the concentration of minerals, a pre-Hispanic irrigation system and various waterfalls are now petrified over a cliff, forming an enormous stalactite. You can swim in the mineral pools in the dry season. There is a village-run hotel, **E** *Tourist-Yú'ù*, Oaxaca T516-0123. Rooms for six people with kitchen, hot water, discounts for students, good restaurant. There are two second class buses a day from Oaxaca, which pass through Hierve El Agua, departing 0810 and 1400, returning around noon and early the following day. Most visitors recommend staying overnight to have enough time to enjoy the surroundings.

Excursions south of Oaxaca

Along Route 175 to Pochutla are several towns that specialize in the production of different crafts. **San Bartolo Coyotepec**, 12 km southeast of Oaxaca, is known for its black pottery. Doña Rosa de Nieto accidentally discovered the technique for the black glazed ceramics in the 1930s, and her family continues the tradition, as do many other potters in town. **San Martín Tilcajete**, 21 km from Oaxaca, 1 km west of

Guerrero, Oaxaca and the Isthmus

Mezcal

Produced throughout the dry central valleys of Oaxaca, mezcal has become one of the best-known symbols of the state. This liquor is prepared from the heart of the agave espadín (Agave angustifolia). Mature plants (12 years old) are selected and first stripped of their swordlike leaves by machete. The hearts are baked in dry ovens – a large pit filled with red-hot coals covered by stones, the agave, and finally a layer of earth. This part of the process gives the drink its characteristic smoky flavour. The baked agave hearts are traditionally ground by teams of oxen and the mash fermented for 10 days in wooden vats. It is then double-distilled with various essences depending on the variety of mezcal. Most famous among these is pechuga, for which raw chicken breasts are hung in the still, a touch apparently much appreciated by the connoisseur. Today some mezcals are flavoured with sweetened fruits, but the original is still drunk straight, accompanied only by lime wedges dipped in sal de gusano – salt into which a special bright red worm has been ground. The squeamish may find some reassurance in the drink's high alcohol content, which is sure to neutralize all the other unusual ingredients!

the main road, is the centre for the *alebrije* production, animals carved from *copal* wood, painted in bright colours, often having a supernatural look to them. **Santo Tomás Jalieza** is the centre for cotton and wool textiles produced with backstrap looms and natural dyes, in the surrounding villages. Market day Friday.

Cuilapan In **Cuilapan de Guerrero**, 12 km southwest of Oaxaca, there is a vast unfinished 16th-century convent, now in ruins, with a famous nave and columns, and an 'open chapel', whose roof collapsed in an earthquake. The last Zapotec princess, Donaji, daughter of the last ruler Cosijoeza, married a Mixtec prince at Tilantengo and was buried at Cuilapan. On the grave is an inscription with their Christian names, Mariana Cortez and Diego Aguilar. Reached by bus from Oaxaca from second class bus station, on Calle Bustamante, near Arista (US$0.50).

North of Cuilapan and 6 km west of the main road is **San Antonio Arrazola**, another town where *alebrijes*, mythical animals made of *copal* wood are sold by the artisans. **Zaachila**, 5 km beyond Cuilapan, was the last capital of the Zapotec empire. Today this town still mantains some of its ancestral traditions in the local cooking (several local restaurants). There is black pottery production, and market day is Thursday. Here are the partially excavated ruins of Zaachila, with two Mixtec tombs; the outer chamber has owls in stucco work and there are carved human figures with skulls for heads inside. ■ *US$1.50*. Take bus to Zaachila (US$0.60), which leaves every 30 minutes, then walk to unexcavated ruins in valley.

Eighty kilometres south on Route 131 is **San Sebastián de las Grutas** (about 10 km northwest of El Vado, off the main road) where there is a system of caves. One 400-m long cave, with five chambers up to 70 m high, has been explored and is open to visitors. Ask for a guide at the Agencia Municipal next to the church. ■ *Guide obligatory, US$1.50*. Take bus 175 from Oaxaca, terminal at Calle Bustamante, US$0.25 or Solteca buses bound for Sola de Vega from the second class terminal.

Excursions north of Oaxaca

At **Santa María Atzompa**, 8 km northwest of Oaxaca, at the foot of Monte Albán, green glazed and terracota ceramics are produced, you can see the artisans at work, their wares are sold at La Casa del Artesano; buses from the second-class terminal.

Etla Valley The Etla Valley, along which Route 190 runs, had a number of important settlements in pre-Hispanic times. Seventeen kilometres along this road and 2 km to the west is **San José el Mogote**, an important centre before the rise of Monte Albán; there is a small museum housing the artefacts found at this site. **San Pedro y San**

Pablo Etla, 19 km from Oaxaca, has an important Wednesday market specializing in Oaxacan foods such as *quesillo* string cheese, *tasajo* (dried meat) and different types of bread; the town has a 17th-century church and convent. At **Santiago Suchilquitongo**, 27 km from Oaxaca and atop a hill, are the ruins of **Huijazoo**, once an important centre that controlled the trade between the Central Valleys and the Cañada region; the local museum has a reproduction of a Huijazoo polychromatic mural, which has been compared to those at Bonampak (see page 458). The town of **San Agustín Etla** (turn-off east from Route 190 at Guadalupe Etla) was once an important industrial centre and in the 19th century it had two large cotton mills; with the introduction of synthetic fibres came a decline to this area. Since 1998, the town has found a new use for the cotton and other natural fibres available in the region, with the production of handmade paper for artists. Cotton, agave fibers, pineapple, nettle, ash, limestone and other raw materials are used in the workshop, which welcomes visitors. Further information from the Instituto de Artes Gráficas on Alcalá 507 in Oaxaca city.

The Sierra Norte or Sierra Juárez is a region of beautiful landscapes and great biolog- **Sierra Juárez** ical diversity; seven of the nine types of vegetation that exist in Mexico can be found in this area. The region is starting to develop ecotourism with community participation; permits are required to camp on community land. The mountains gradually drop to the Papaloapan valley to the north. There are two access roads, Route 175 from Oaxaca to Tuxtepec, and the small roads that go north from Route 190, past Teotitlán and Santa Ana del Valle (see page 401). *Viajes Rua-Via* in Ixtlán (T553-6075), and *Expediciones Sierra Norte* (T/F513-9518) and *Tierraventura* (T/F514-3043) in Oaxaca run hiking and mountain biking tours in this region. The Oaxaca-Tuxtepec road has been recommended as exhilarating for cyclists.

Along the road to Tuxtepec, 65 km from Oaxaca is the village of **San Pablo de Guelatao**, the birthplace of Benito Juárez. The town is located in the mountainous Sierra Juárez, and can be reached by bus (any service going to Tuxtepec, US$1.50, three hours) along a paved but tortuously winding road (for a more detailed description of this road and area see page 366). Guelatao means 'small lake' and by the shores of this small lake is a statue of Juárez as a shepherd with his lambs. There is also a memorial and a museum to Juárez on the hillside within the village. ■ *US$0.20*. The area is beautiful although the town is rather neglected. A few kilometres north of Guelatao is **Ixtlán de Juárez** (*Population: 2,095*), a larger town with a petrol station, hotel, shops and some simple eating establishments.

The Oaxaca Coast

The 510 km of Oaxaca's Pacific Coast, stretching from Guerrero to the west and Chiapas to the east, includes some truly spectacular shoreline and provides most varied opportunities for seaside recreation. Many beaches are still entirely virgin (accessible only on foot or by sea), while others are being developed for various tastes and to varying degrees; a very few have been burnt out by overcrowding, pollution, drugs or crime. Palapas, thatched roof shacks, are found all along the coast; these are dwellings or simple restaurants and places to stay. Huatulco is the best-known international resort on the Oaxaca Coast, but there are many other popular areas including Puerto Escondido, Puerto Angel, Salina Cruz, and their respective surroundings.

All of the above are linked by Highway 200, the Carretera Costera, fully paved and in generally good condition, with frequent bus service along its entire length, as well as transport to several nationwide destinations. Three main roads connect the coast with the city of Oaxaca and the central valleys of the highlands: Route 131 from Puerto Escondido, Route 175 from Pochutla and Route 190 (the Panamerican Highway) from Tehuantepec; daytime travel is safest along all of them. There are airports at Puerto Escondido, Huatulco and near Tehuantepec, with service to Mexico City, Oaxaca and Chiapas.

Santiago Pinotepa Nacional, the westernmost of Oaxaca's coastal towns, is known for its cheerful, witty people, dressed in bright colours, and the happy rhythm of their *chilena* dances. The local festival, rich in music and dance, is held on 24 February. From Pinotepa Nacional you can visit the Mixtec Indian village of **Pinotepa de Don Luis** by *camioneta* (US$1, 50 minutes). These leave from beside the Centro de Salud in Pinotepa Nacional, taking paved road, via Tlacamama, to Don Luis (last one back to Pinotepa Nacional at 1300, nowhere to stay). The women there weave beautiful and increasingly rare sarong-like skirts (*chay-ay*), some of which are dyed from the purple of sea snails. They also produce half-gourds incised with various designs. The *ferias* of Don Luis (20 January) and nearby San Juan Colorado (29-30 November) are worth attending for the dancing and availability of handicrafts. Another village, **Huazolotitlán**, is known for mask making; take *camioneta* from near *Hotel Las Palomas*, three blocks from plaza, 40 minutes. **Fiesta**, first Friday in February with masked dancers.

Sleeping **B** *Pepes*, Carretera a Acapulco, Km 1, T/F543-3602. A/c, restaurant, parking. **C** *Hotel Carmona*, Porfirio Díaz 127, T543-2222. Restaurant, good value but poor laundry service, helpful advice on visiting surrounding villages, parking. **C** *Marisa*, Avenida Juárez 134, near Zócalo, T543-2101, F543-2696. With bath, more expensive with a/c, **E** with fan. **C** *Gaviota*, 3 Oriente and 2a Sur, T/F543-2626. Hot water, TV, restaurant, parking. **E** *Tropical*, Fan, clean, large rooms, quiet, parking.

Transport Buses to Oaxaca, with *Cristóbal Colón*, 1 daily, 9½ hrs, US$15.90; with Oaxaca Pacífico, 2 daily via Pochutla, 9 hrs, US$12.00; with Trans-Sol, 2 daily via Sola de Vega, 8 hrs, US$10.90.

Puerto Escondido

The town and its surroundings offer some stunningly beautiful beaches with world-class surfing, many facilities for vacationers, and a good base for various interesting excursions. Sadly, however, Puerto Escondido is at risk of becoming a case study in unsustainable tourism development. It was a small and sleepy fishing village as recently as the 1980s, until the population rapidly increased, perhaps in response to grandiose plans for Acapulco-style development. These never panned out and tourism instead developed low-rise and haphazardly, creating considerable environmental and social impact. Drugs and crime followed, largely ignored by the authorities until an American celebrity (a member of the Kennedy clan) was murdered at the south end of Zicatela beach in 1998. Publicity of the slaying brought home the need to clean up the town. There has since been considerable improvement with much better security and more responsible environmental as well as general practices by the area's tourism industry. The newly formed state tourist police now patrol both the main beach and tourist areas on quad bikes. They are English speaking and helpful.

At present, Puerto Escondido is a bustling and very commercial seaside resort. El Adoquín, the city's pedestrian tourist mall along Avenida Pérez Gasga near the beach (also known as the *Andador Turístico*), teems with vacationing Mexican families in season, sunburnt foreigners and hard-core surfies throughout the year; December-January are the most crowded, May-June are the quietest (and hottest) months. A handful of luxury hotels and resorts are clustered above Playa Bacocho, while Playa Zicatela is ideal for surfers, and the majority of tourist facilities are found in the vicinity of El Adoquín. The real town, where prices are lower and there is less of a hard-sell atmosphere, is located up the hill on the other side of the highway. There is an ample selection of hotels and restaurants in all areas. Many fast-talking '*amigos*' are found at all the nearby beaches and other sites frequented by tourists offering an impressive array of goods and services for sale or hire; be polite and friendly (as are most of the vendors) but also wary, since there is no shortage of over-pricing and trickery. **Tourist offices** Sedetur information kiosk at the west end of El Adoquín, run by Gina Machorro, a very helpful, friendly person who is knowledgeable about the town and the region. She speaks English, Spanish and French. Sedetur office and information, Avenida Juárez, at the entrance to Playa Bacocho, T582-0175, open Mon-Sat.

Beaches

The **Playa Principal**, abutting El Adoquín pedestrian mall, has the calmest water but it is very close to the city and not clean. A few fishermen still bring in the catch of the day here and a small pier is being built for them and the tourist craft, which offer sport fishing and excursions to nearby bays and beaches. Immediately to the south is **Playa Marinero**, with slightly stronger surf (reportedly a good place for beginners), also very built up with hotels, bars and restaurants. Further south, past a rocky point called Rocas del Morro, lies the long expanse of **Playa Zicatela**, which claims to be the best surfing beach in Mexico, with the fastest-breaking waves anywhere in the world. It is suitable only for experienced surfers and very dangerous for swimming. To the west of the main bay, past a lovely headland (being built up with condominiums) and lighthouse, are a series of picturesque bays and beaches, all accessible by road or boat from town. **Playa Manzanillo** and **Puerto Angelito** share the Bahía Puerto Angelito and are the closest, an easy 15-minute walk; they are pretty with reasonably safe swimming but very commercial; every square millimetre of shade is proprietary here. Further west is **Playa Carrizalillo**, with swimming and more gentle surfing than Zicatela, accessible along a steep path, or by boat (US$3), or taxi (US$1.50). **Playa Bacocho** is next, a long beautiful stretch of less developed beach, where the ocean, alas, is too dangerous for swimming.

Excursions

Seventy-four kilometres west of Puerto Escondido is the 140,000-ha **Lagunas de Chacahua National Park**, a wildlife refuge of sand dunes, interconnected lagoons, mangroves and forest. La Pastoría is the largest lagoon, connected to the sea by an estuary; it has nine islets that harbour thousands of birds, both resident and migratory. On the shores of the lagoon is the village of Chacahua, home to some of the area's small Afro-Mexican population. There is a crocodile hatchery nearby, aimed at preserving this native species. A tour is the easiest way to see the park and learn about its wildlife (see Tour operators below). To go independently you need two days; take a bus to Río Grande (from Carretera Costera and 3a Norte), then another one to Zapotalito from where there are boats (US$4.50 per person if there are enough passengers) to the village of Chacahua, where you can find very basic accommodations in the **F** price range; take a mosquito net.

Closer and easier to access than Chacahua are the **Lagunas de Manialtepec**, 16 km west of Puerto Escondido, also a good place for bird-watching and watersports. Tours are available (see Tour operators in Directory below) or take a minibus towards Río Grande (from Carretera Costera and 3ra Norte, US$0.65) or a taxi (US$6). Get off at the village of Manialtepec; at restaurants *Isla de Gallo* and *Puesta del Sol* you can hire a boat for four persons (US$33.00 for two hours).

Santos Reyes Nopala is a mountain town 43 km northeast of Puerto Escondido. The original Chatino settlement here is believed to date from around 800 BC; stelae can be seen in the municipal palace and the Chatino language is still spoken. Colourful celebrations are held 6-8 January. Further north is **Santa Catarina Juquila** with the Santuario de la Virgen de Juquila, a very popular pilgrimage site; the local **fiesta** is 8 December; there are several hotels here.

Safety

Even with the vast improvements in security, safety is an especially important issue in and around Puerto Escondido. A safe and pleasant stay here is possible with the appropriate

Guerrero, Oaxaca and the Isthmus

precautions, but carelessness can have the most severe consequences. Never walk on any beach at night, alone or in groups. The ocean can also be dangerous.

Sleeping
■ *on map*

Puerto Escondido has more than 85 hotels in all categories, mostly along the beaches. There is little air-conditioning, many of the cheaper hotels have no hot water and cheap cabañas may be full of mosquitos, especially in the wet season (Jun-Oct). High season is during Easter week, the last 2 weeks of Jul, all of Aug, and Nov-Feb; discounts of 10-30% may be obtained at other times. Hotels right on El Adoquín may be noisy because of nearby discos.

L-AL *Aldea del Bazar*, Benito Juárez 7, T582-0508. A veritable Sultan's palace, complete with Middle Eastern dress for the staff, huge garden with palms, pool, large rooms, good restaurant. Recommended. **AL** *Santa Fe*, Calle del Moro, Playa Marinero, T582-0170, F582-0260. A/c, pool, very good food, including vegetarian. **A** *Paraíso Escondido*, Unión 10, Centro, T582-0444. Away from beach, a/c, pool, colonial style, restaurant open in high season.

B *Barlovento*, Camino al Faro 3, Centro, T582-0220, F582-0101. Pool, fridge, very comfortable, on the way to the lighthouse. Recommended. **B** *Kootznoowoo*, Calle Vista al Mar y Av del Morro, T582351, A/c, on Playa Zicatela. Recommended. **B** *Le P'tit*, Andador Soledad 379, T5823178. Nice colonial house, clean. **B-C** *Bungalows Casa del Mar*, Retorno A6, Fraccionamiento Bacocho, T/F582-2377. Equipped bungalows.

C *Bungalows Acuario*, Calle del Moro, Playa Marinero, T582-0357, F582-1027. Cheaper with shared bath, pool, gym, scuba diving centre, the 1st in the area to treat its waste water. Recommended. **C** *Bungalows Zicatela*, Calle del Moro, Playa Marinero, T/F582-0798. A/c, cheaper with fan, fridge, pool, small restaurant. **C** *Inés*, Calle del Moro, T582-0792. Fan, hot water, pool, restaurant. **C** *Ben Zaa*, 3a Sur 303, T582-0523, on hill climbing to the lighthouse. Fan, hot water, pool. **C** *Casa Blanca*, Av Pérez Gasga 905 (Adoquín), T582-0168. Fan, hot water, clean, well furnished, balconies, pool. **C** *Flor de María*, 1st entrance, Playa Marinero,

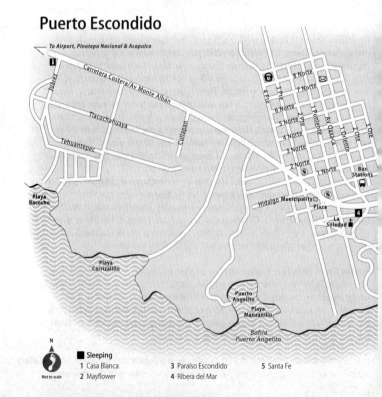

Puerto Escondido

Guerrero, Oaxaca and the Isthmus

Sleeping
1 Casa Blanca
2 Mayflower
3 Paraíso Escondido
4 Ribera del Mar
5 Santa Fe

Not to scale

T582-0536. Fan, hot water, pool, restaurant. **C** *Rincón del Pacífico*, Av Pérez Gasga 900 (Adoquín), T582-0193. Hot water, on beach, restaurant, very popular, always full.

D *Art and Harry's*, Playa Zicatela. On oceanfront, free use of surfboard. **D** *Bungalows Villa Marinero*, Carretera Costera, Playa Marinero, T582-0180, F582-0716. On seafront, kitchen/eating area, pool, friendly. **D** *Casa Loma*, Camino al Faro opposite Escuela Las Primeras Luces, on road to lighthouse. Cook prepares meals on request (including your catch). **D** *Castillo de Reyes*, Av Pérez Gasga 210, T582-0442. Clean, nice rooms, hot water, quiet, good beds, friendly, good value. Highly recommended. **D** *Central*, Av Oaxaca, Centro, T/F582-0116, in bus terminal area. Clean, friendly. **D** *Cocoa Beach*, Fundadores esquina Felipe Merklin, T582-0428, near the church. Small rooms, mosquito nets, family-run. **D** *El Alemán*, Av Las Brisas, Santa María, Zicatela, T/F582-1995. Fan, ocean views. **D** *Liza's Restaurant*, off Carretera Costera, Playa Marinero. Fan, very clean, safe deposit. Highly recommended. **D** *Mayflower*, Andador Libertad, T582-1755, on pedestrian walkway perpendicular to El Adoquín. With bath, fan, **F** per person in dormitory, friendly, good value. English and German spoken. Recommended. **D** *Papaya Surf*, Calle del Moro, Zicatela. Fan, mosquito net, hot water, pool. **D** *Roca Mar*, Av Pérez Gasga 601, T582-0330. Upper rooms with a/c and balcony, hot water, restaurant. Recommended.

E *Casa de Huéspedes Naxhiely*, Av Pérez Gasga 301. Simple, fairly clean. **E** *Casa de Huéspedes San Martín*, 1a Oriente 106, Centro, T5820883. Basic, private bath, fan, clean, close to bus stations. **E** *Girasol*, Av Oaxaca 403, T/F582-1168, in bus station area. With bath, fan, parking. Many other economic hotels in the Centro, near the bus station as well as bungalows and cabins on Playa Zicatela. **E** *Ribera del Mar*, Felipe Merklin 205, T/F582-0436, behind Iglesia de la Soledad. Fan, hot water, clean, quiet, laundry facilities, good value. **E** *San Rafael*, Av Hidalgo y 2a Oeste, T582-1052, near bus stations. Basic, with bath, fan. **F** *Rockaway*, Calle del Moro, Zicatela, far end of Zicatela strip. Popular hangout with hippie twist and a well-maintained pool.

Camping *Trailer Park Palmas de Cortés*, Av Pérez Gasga y Andador Azucena, T582-0774. Clean bathrooms, shade, US$10.00 per car, US$5.00 per tent. Recommended. *Trailer Park Neptuno*, Av Pérez Gasga, T582-0327, on waterfront. Space for vehicles, tents and hammocks, pool, cold showers, electricity, run down, US10.00 per car with 2 people.

Eating Many restaurants along the main street, Avenida Pérez Gasga, especially on the pedestrian mall: *Baguettería Vivaldi*, Good breakfast and sandwiches. *Banana's*, Italian and Mexican. *San Angel*. For fish, Italian and international dishes. *Hermann's Best*. Good value, popular. *Mario's Pizzaland*. Excellent pizzas, friendly. *La Galería*. Italian, good pizzas but pricey. *La Estancia*. Good, warm service. *La Sardina de Plata*. Popular. *Cappuccino*. Good coffee, fruit salads, some dishes pricey.

In Playa Marinero are: *Liza*, off Carretera Costera. Good food, nice location. *La Gota de Vida*, Calle del Moro. Good vegetarian. *Cipriano's Pizza*, Calle del Moro. Italian and regional. *Hotel Santa Fé*. Excellent vegetarian, but expensive. *El Tabachín*, behind Hotel Santa Fe. Also vegetarian and café. *El*

Cafecito, Calle del Moro, Zicatela. Excellent breakfasts, chocolate bread. Highly recommended. *Super Café Puro*, off top flight of stairs of walkway that starts at the tourist information kiosk. Good for breakfast, pleasant terrace. *Pepe's*, 8a Nte, near market. Great sandwiches. *Carmen's Bakery*, on a path to the beach from main road, Zicatela. Great pastries baked on the premises, also second-hand books and magazines. *Gelatería Giardino*, Av Pérez Gasga 609, just east of El Adoquín. Excellent Italian ice-cream and fruit ices, made on the premises, also cappuccino coffee. Highly recommended (closed May-Jun). *Un Tigre Azul*, Av Pérez Gasga on El Adoquín, upper floor. Bar, coffee and snacks, nice views.

Entertainment
It is not advisable to stay at bars and discos past 0300

Tequila Sunrise, Av Marina Nacional, just west of El Adoquín. Open-air disco, varied music, international crowd. *El Son y la Rumba*. Rooftop bar with live salsa and rumba at night. Restaurant serves *comida corrida* during the day. Opposite is *El Tubo*. Disco, popular with local surfers. *Barfly*. Good music, regular screening of films and videos. *Bar Banana's*, Av Pérez Gasga y Andador Azucena. Drinks and food. *Los 3 Diablos*. Av Pérez Gasga 604, www.los3diablos.com.mx, new lively bar with pool table, nice friendly staff. *Wipeout*. Rock and techno music.

Sports

Diving The region's coastline offers good opportunities for snorkelling and scuba diving; snorkelling from the beach is easiest at Puerto Angelito. Tours and diving lessons with Jorge Pérez Bravo, *Aventura Submarina*, Av Pérez Gasga at west end of El Adoquín, T/F582-2353. You are likely to see turtles and dolphins on the way to the snorkelling and diving sites. Snorkelling, 3 hrs, US$22 per person. Diving lessons, US$55 for 1 tank. If qualified, US$38 for 1 tank, US$55 for 2. **Fishing** Boats can be hired for fishing at Playa Principal or through travel agencies for approximately US$27 per hour for up to 4 passengers. **Kayaking** New to Puerto Escondido, US$7 per hr, enquire at *Las Hamacas* at Matialtepec Lagoon. Recommended. **Pelota Mixteca** A modern version of an ancient Mixtec ball game is played on Sat and Sun in Bajos de Chila, 15 mins from Puerto Escondido, on the road to Acapulco. In a 9 m by 35 m court, teams of 5-7 players propel a rubber ball weighing almost 1 kg, using elaborately decorated leather mits that weigh between 3½ kg and 6 kg. A game can take up to 4 hrs. **Surfing** Playa Zicatela is a surfer's haven, but dangerous for the novice. See beaches above.

Festivals The city's festivities are held throughout the month of **Nov**, along with a surfing tournament. In the middle of the month is the *Festival Costeño de la Danza*, with colourful, lively folk dances. The *Master World Surf Championship* is held in **Aug**.

Shopping Crafts and souvenirs from shops all along **El Adoquín**, stalls on the main street, east of El Adoquín and on **Andador Libertad**, a walkway going uphill from about the middle of El Adoquín. Shop around, vendors on the beach are likely to ask for higher prices and you may find better value in shops north of the highway. *Papi's* souvenir shop has a small selection of foreign books for sale or trade. Surfing gear and clothing from shops in Zicatela. *Ahorrara*, 3a Poniente y 5a Nte, large well-stocked supermarket.

Transport **Air** Airport (PXM) 10 mins' drive west of town, orange juice and coffee sold. With *Aerocaribe* (T582-2023), daily from **Mexico City** at 1140, to Mexico City at 1300, 1 hr, US$87; daily from Oaxaca at 0955 and 1640, to Oaxaca at 1045 and 1820, 30 mins, US$70.00. With *Aerovega* (T/F582-0151) daily from **Oaxaca** at 0700, to Oaxaca at 0900, US$100.00. Also with *Aerotucán* (T501-0532) daily from Oaxaca, US$110. *Colectivo* from airport, US$2.80 per person, T582-0030.

Roads The Sierra Madre del Sur lies between the coast and Oaxaca's central valleys, where the state capital is located. All routes must cross this steep mountain range and are subject to landslides and damage, especially during the rainy periods. Enquire locally as to current conditions. **Car hire** *Budget*, Av Juárez at the entrance to Bacocho, T582-0312.

Buses To **Pochutla**, from corner Carretera Costera and Av Oaxaca, every 20 mins, 0500-1900, 1½ hrs, US$1.30. For **Puerto Angel**, **Zipolite** and other beaches: transfer in Pochutla to pick-up or *colectivo* taxi .

To **Acapulco**: *Estrella Blanca*, a/c service every couple of hours, 9 hrs, US$23.00; regular service, hourly 0400-1500, US$29. To **Mexico City**: *Estrella Blanca*, 1st class at 1930 and 2000, US$39.00, 12 hrs via Acapulco, to travel during the day go to Acapulco and transfer there; Oaxaca-Pacífico/*Estrella del Valle*, 1st class, at 1745, US$31.00, 12 hrs via Oaxaca, arrives at *Fletes y Pasajes* terminal near TAPO (east terminal). To **Oaxaca**: for better safety, travel only during the daytime and take the direct services that run better vehicles and do not stop to pick up passengers along the way; *Oaxaca-Pacífico/Estrella del Valle*, Av Hidalgo 400 near Av Oaxaca, direct service at 0815, 1245, 2215, US$7.60, 7½ hrs, 1st class at 2230, US$9.50. *Cristóbal Colón*, 1a Nte 207, 3 daily via Tehuantepec, US$14.80, 12 hrs (this 1st class service takes the Isthmus route since it is not allowed to take passengers on the more direct routes where local companies operate). *Trans Sol/Solteca*, station near the market, via Sola de Vega, 3 daily, US$7.60, 7 hrs. To **Puebla**: *Oaxaca-Pacífico/Estrella del Valle*, 1st class, at 1745, US$25.00, 10 hrs via Oaxaca, leaves you by the highway, not CAPU. To **Salina Cruz**: *Estrella Blanca*, Av Oaxaca, 4 a day, 5 hrs, US$6.50. To **Tapachula**: *Cristóbal Colón*, 2000, 14-15 hrs, US$27.00. To **Tuxtla Gutiérrez** and **San Cristóbal de las Casas**: *Cristóbal Colón*, 0845 and 2130, Tuxtla US$4, 12 hrs, San Cristóbal, US$29.00, 14 hrs. To **Zihuatanejo**: *Estrella Blanca*, 1 direct bus daily.

Banks Some 11 banks have ATMs around town. *Bancomer*, 1a Nte y 2a Poniente, cash and TCs **Directory** 0800-1400. *Bital*, 1a Nte y 3a Pte, cash and TCs, cash advance on Visa and MasterCard, Mon-Sat 0800-1900. *Banamex*, Av Pérez Gasga east of El Adoquín, 0900-1300. *2 Casas de Cambio* on El Adoquín, open till 2000, poor rates. **Communications** Internet: *Cibercafé Un Tigre Azul*, on El Adoquín, US$5.40 per hour, coffee, snacks, gift shop, friendly service, open 1100. *Graficom*, Av Pérez Gasga 302, west of El Adoquín, US$5.40 per hour. Post office: 7a Nte by Av Oaxaca. **Laundry** Lavandería at east end of El Adoquín, US$1 per kg or US$3.25 per load, self-service, Mon-Sat, 0900-2100. Another one at Av Pérez Gasga by Hotel Nayar, US$1.5 per kg. **Medical services** Dr Francisco Serrano Severiano, 1a Nte y 2a Pte, opposite Bancomer, speaks English, 0900-1300, 1700-2000. *Clínica de Especialidades del Puerto*, Av Oaxaca, has been recommended. *Clínica Santa Fe*, Av 5a Poniente. *Farmacia La Moderna*, Av Pérez Gasga 203, T582-0214, has a physician in house, open 24 hrs. **Tour operators** *Gina Machorro* (speaks English and French), offers a 2-hr walking tour of Puerto Escondido's local culture and history, US$16 per person (Wed and Sat only during the winter). Contact through the tourist information kiosk. Ana Márquez of *Ana's Ecotours* (contact at *Tigre Azul*, Av Pérez Gasga) is a certified, recommended guide, speaks English and is very knowledgeable about the region and especially its birds. Tours to all the natural attractions in the area and cultural tours of her native Mixtec community, day trip, US$32 per person. *Michael Malone*, a Canadian ornithologist, is another recommended guide who is in Puerto Escondido Nov-Mar (ask at tourism information kiosk). *Margarito* takes visitors to the Manialtepec lagoon for US$16 per person. Hard to find but he normally walks the beach near *Cafecito*.

Pochutla

Sixty-six kilometres east of Puerto Escondido and 240 km south of Oaxaca is San Pedro Pochutla, a hot and busy supply town with an imposing church set on a small hill. Its pleasant **Plaza de las Golondrinas**, where folks stroll in the cool of the evening, is filled with many singing birds; countless swallows line up on the electric wires here every night. There is a prison in Pochutla, and the inmates carve crafts out of coconut husks for sale by their families and local shops. The *Fiesta de San Pedro* takes place on 29-30 June.

Phone code: 958
Colour map 3, grid C5
Population: 10,251

A road runs south of Pochutla 9 km to Puerto Angel, then turns west along the coast past the **beaches** of Zipolite, San Agustinillo and Mazunte (details below). Also along this route are El Mariposario, a private butterfly reserve that welcomes visitors, the Centro Mexicano de la Tortuga, where sea turtles can be observed, and La Ventanilla, on a lagoon with birds and crocodiles. Past Ventanilla, the road turns back north to meet Highway 200 at San Antonio.

C *Posada San José*, Constitución behind Oaxaca bus terminal, T584-0153. A/c, small pool, **D** **Sleeping** with fan. **D** *Loma Real*, Mina 17 by entrance from Oaxaca, T584-0645. A/c, cheaper with fan, pool, garden, parking. **D** *Izala*, Lázaro Cárdenas 59, T584-0115. A/c, cheaper with fan, clean,

Guerrero, Oaxaca and the Isthmus

comfortable. **E** *Pochutla*, Francisco Madero 102, at corner of Plaza, T584-0003. Bath, ceiling fan, good value. **E** *Santa Cruz*, Lázaro Cárdenas 88, across from Oaxaca terminal, T584-0116. Fan, basic. **E** *El Patio*, Lázaro Cárdenas, across from market. Fan, basic, parking. **E** *Gloria Estela*, Constitución 23, T584-0095. Bath, fan, hot water.

Eating *San Angel*, at Plaza. Nice atmosphere, terrace overlooking park. *Panadería Las 7 Regiones*, Lázaro Cárdenas at Oaxaca end. Recommended.

Transport **Roads** Highway 175 from Oaxaca to Pochutla is a very scenic but extremely winding paved road. In the central valleys it goes through the craft towns of **Ocotlán de Morelos** (*Posada San Salvador*) and **Ejutla de Crespo** (*Hotel 6* and several other places to stay), before climbing the Sierra Madre del Sur to its pine-clad ridges and the pass. Just south of the pass is San José del Pacífico, a hamlet with nice views and a restaurant where buses make a rest stop.

Local For Puerto Angel, Zipolite, and other beaches, pick-up trucks with benches in back and shared taxis (*colectivos*) do round trips on the coastal road in both directions, these taxis also offer private service (*carreras*); in Pochutla, wait at marked bus stops along the main road. To Puerto Angel, truck US$0.25, *colectivo* US$0.50 per person, taxi US$3-4. To Zipolite, truck US$0.40, *colectivo* US$1, taxi US$6. To Mazunte, truck US$0.50, *colectivo* US$1, taxi US$6. Beware of over-charging, which is especially common in this area. Taxi drivers have been known to wait for unwary visitors and charge US$7, Pochutla-Zipolite. To Puerto Escondido, *colectivo* US$3, taxi US$20. To Huatulco, *colectivo* US$1.50, taxi US$10.

Buses **Acapulco**: *Estrella Blanca*, 0600, 1000, 2200, 8½ hrs, US$19. **Huatulco** (La Crucecita): small buses from lane near Oaxaca-Pacífico terminal, every 15 mins 0500-2000, 1 hr, US$0.90. **Mexico City**: *Estrella Blanca*, 1st class, via Acapulco, 1900, US$36, 12-13 hrs; Oaxaca Pacífico, via Oaxaca, 1800 and 1900, 13hrs, US$24. **Oaxaca**: *Oaxaca-Pacífico/Estrella del Valle*, direct service 0945, 1415, 2300, 6 hrs, US$7.25. 2nd class service, 14 daily, 9hrs, US$6.20; with *Cristóbal Colón* via the Isthmus, at 1445 and 1930, US$14.70. **Puerto Escondido**: small buses from side street near church, every 20 mins 0500-1900, 1½ hrs, US$1.30; also with through buses coming from Oaxaca or Salina Cruz. **Salina Cruz**: with *Cristóbal Colón*, 5 daily; with *Estrella Blanca*, 3 daily, 3-4 hrs, US$7. **Tapachula**: *Cristóbal Colón*, 2100, 12 hrs, US$24. **Tuxtla Gutiérrez**: *Cristóbal Colón*, 0945 and 2230, 10 hrs, US$19.

Directory **Banks** All on main street: *Bancomer*, 0830-1400, cash and TCs. *Bancrecer*, 0830-1400, cash and TCs. *Bital*, 0830-1700, cash and TCs. **Communications** Email, in a shop on Lázaro Cárdenas, a whopping US$26 per hour! **Medical services** Public hospital just south of town.

Puerto Angel

Phone code: 958
Colour map 3, grid C5
Population: 2,433

Twenty minutes south of Pochutla along a pretty road that winds through hilly forest country before dropping to the sea is Puerto Angel. Until the 1960s it was a busy port from which coffee and timber were shipped to Asia; with the fall in coffee prices, the local population turned to selling turtle skins until 1990, when this activity was banned in Mexico. Tourism and fishing are currently the main economic activities here. The town lies above a beautiful flask-shaped bay; unfortunately the turquoise water is polluted, but there are hopes for improvement if a planned sewage system is installed. Because of its lovely setting it has been described as 'the ideal place to rest and do nothing'. The beach right in town is neither clean nor attractive. A short walk away, either along the road or on a concrete path built on the rocks (not safe at night), is **Playa del Panteón**, a small beach in a lovely setting, but crowded with restaurants (touts await visitors on arrival) and many bathers in season. There are cleaner and more tranquil nearby beaches east of town. **Estacahuite**, with simple cabañas, 1 km from town, about a 20-minute walk, has good snorkelling (gear rental from hut selling drinks and snacks) but beware of strong waves, currents and sharp coral that can cut you; La Boquilla, with comfortable Canadian-run bungalows, is 3 km away, off a signed track on the road to Pochutla. There is a **fiesta** on 1 June to celebrate the *Día de la Marina* and another on 1 October, the *Fiesta de San Angel*. For transport to and from Puerto Angel see Pochutla above. **Safety**: Take extra care in the sea as the currents are very dangerous. Also watch your belongings.

Sleeping **C** *Villa Florencia*, Av Principal Virgilio Uribe across from town beach, T/F584-3044. A/c, cheaper with fan, clean, comfortable, friendly, Italian-Mexican run, restaurant, bar, library. **C** *Cañón De Vata*, Playa del Panteón, T584-3048, lopezk@spin,com.mx Clean but dark, lovely setting, booked continuously, popular with Americans, restaurant. **D** *Casas Penélopes*, on road to Zipolite and Mazunte. Friendly, beautiful location. Highly recommended. **C** *El Rincón Sabroso*, T584-3095. Beautiful views, clean, quiet, friendly, no hot water. **D** *La Cabaña*, Playa del Panteón, T584-3105. Fan, clean, friendly, free coffee in the morning. Recommended. **D** *Puesta del Sol*, on road to Playa del Panteón, T584-3096. Fan, cheaper with shared bath, clean, restaurant, very friendly, English and German spoken. Recommended. **E** *Anahi*, on road to Playa del Panteón. Fan, basic. **E** *Capy's*, on road to Playa del Panteón, T584-3002. Fan, clean, nice restaurant. Recommended. **E** *Casa de Huéspedes Gladys*, above Soraya, T584-3050. Clean, fine views, balcony, owner can prepare food. Recommended. **E** *Casa de Huéspedes Gundi y Tomás*. Shared bath, clean, **F** in hammocks, good value, popular with travellers, stores luggage, breakfast and snacks served (cook prepares dinner every day for guests, but expensive), often recommended; Gundi also runs *Pensión El Almendro*, with café (good ice-cream) and library. **E** *Casa de Huéspedes Leal*, T584-3081. Shared bath, washing facilities, friendly. Recommended.

Camping There is a camp ground halfway between Puerto Angel and Pochutla, very friendly, driveway too steep for large vehicles, US$8.50 for 2 in campervan. Recommended.

Eating An excellent restaurant at *Villa Florencia* hotel. Good food, Italian and Mexican dishes, charming place. *Beto's* by turn-off for Playa del Panteón. Good fish (fresh tuna) and cheap beer, nice views. Nearby are *Capy's*. Good food. *Cañón de Vata*. Also good, mainly vegetarian. *Pensión Puesta del Sol*. Excellent restaurant. *Mar y Sol*. Cheap, good seafood. *Sirenita*. Popular for breakfast and bar, friendly. *Cangrejo*, by Naval Base gate. Popular bar, also good breakfasts and excellent tacos. Several fish restaurants along the main street; 2 restaurants by fishing harbour, cheap, popular with locals.

Sports Scuba diving with *Hotel La Cabaña*, T584-30116, experienced instructors, up-to-date equipment, PADI service available. English spoken.

Directory **Banks** Cash and TCs changed at *Hotel Soraya*. Banks in Pochutla. **Communications** Internet: *Caseta Puerto Angel*. C José Vasconcelos 3 (next to *Hotel Soraya*), T584-3038. **Post office:** next to Agencia Municipal near *Hotel Soraya*.

West of Puerto Angel

Zipolite Four kilometres west of Puerto Angel is Zipolite, one of the few nude beaches in Mexico and once an inspirationally beautiful spot that still attracts many foreign visitors. Sadly, a few years ago, it became a veritable Paradise Lost, notorious for drugs, crime and violence, including murder. Things seem to be cleaning up a little, and the interest is recovering. The beach here is very steeply shelved and there are dangerous undercurrents, especially near the rocks at the east end.

Sleeping and eating The shore is lined with *palapas* offering cheap meals and accommodation (beds from US$3.50 per night, hammocks from US$2.50, shared bath, basic facilities), with informal discos at night. **B-C** for up to 4 people at *Solstice*, www.solstice-mexco.com 4 cabañas around a palm-shaded courtyard. According to the many readers who have written in, it's a quiet spot, complemented perfectly by the yoga classes run by the hosts Brigette and Guy (US$5/hr). The *Livélula* bar is a quiet little bar, open 0800-0200, Wed, Sat. Ping

Guerrero, Oaxaca and the Isthmus

pong, table football, hammocks and plenty of time to relax. There are also a few more solid structures toward the west end of the beach and a number of establishments had been recommended by visitors in the past.

Another 3 km west lies **San Agustinillo**, a long, pretty beach, with an extraordinary cave in the cliffs. The western end is quite built up with private homes, simple cabañas in the **E** range, and restaurants; nude bathing is prohibited. Swimming is safest at the west end of the beach, surfing best near the centre. There is one larger hotel, **E** *Posada San Agustín*. With private bath, ceiling fan, mosquito net, nice views, friendly.

Mazunte One kilometre further west is Mazunte, perhaps the least-developed major beach in the area but rapidly changing, so responsible tourism is especially important here (see Responsible tourism, page 39). The beach is on federal land and drug laws are strictly enforced here; nude bathing is prohibited, the safest swimming is at either end of the bay. At the east end of Mazunte is the **Centro Mexicano de la Tortuga**, a government institute that studies sea turtles and works to conserve these frequently endangered species, as well as to educate visitors and the local population (interested researchers may contact the director at cmtvasco@angel.umar.mx). There are interesting viewing tanks to observe many species of turtles underwater. ■ *Guided tours in Spanish and English, open Tue-Sat 1000-1630, Sun 1000-1430, US$2, children under 12 US$1, crowded with tour buses from Huatulco 1100-1300 during high season.* A trail leads from the west end of the beach to **Punta Cometa**, a spit of land with lovely views of the thundering breakers below, a popular spot to view the sunset, well worth the 30-minute walk.

Sleeping B *Posada Alta Mira*, T/F(958)43104, www.labuenavista.com, on a wooded hillside overlooking the west end of the beach. 10 lovely cabañas, spacious, clean, comfortable, spectacular views, no electricity yet. Restaurant serves the best food in Mazunte. Immediately adjacent is *Balam Juyu*. Simpler but in the same splendid setting, breakfast and drinks served. **D-E** *Posada Brisa Marina*, Col Roca Blanca, F584-3070. New large rooms on the beach. Friendly. **E** *Ziga*, at the east end near the *Centro Mexicano de la Tortuga*. Semi-private bath, fan, mosquito net, clean, friendly, family run, nice views, good value. Recommended. Next door is **E** *Porfiria*, basic, friendly, kitchen facilities, small bar. Several *palapas* offer simple accommodation along the middle of the beach.

Eating There are many simple (but not necessarily cheap) restaurants including *Lupita*, at west end of beach. Large portions. *Pizzería Iris*, on track between the west end of the beach and the road. *La Dolce Vita*, on main road at west end. Good Italian pizza and home-made pasta, pricey. *El Paso*, on main road west of the bridge. Inexpensive and friendly. *Posada Alta Mira*, see above.

Shopping There are several shops with basic supplies, other items may be brought from Pochutla. At the west end of Mazunte is *Cosméticos Naturales de Mazunte*, where *Body Shop*-type cosmetics are made with natural ingredients. Especially recommended is their natural mosquito repellent.

Ventanilla Two kilometres west of Mazunte is a signed turn-off for Ventanilla. It is 1½ km from here to the village and visitors' information centre on the shores of a lagoon. Tours are run by local residents who are working on a mangrove reforestation project (in 1997 Hurricane Pauline wiped out part of the mangroves here) and have a crocodile farm to repopulate the area. The tour combines a rowing boat ride through the mangroves for up to 10 persons, a visit to the crocodile farm, and a walk on the beach, US$3.25 per person, many birds, crocodiles and iguanas may be seen, guides speak Spanish only. Recommended. Horse-riding tours along the beach are also available for US$5.40 per hour. Those wishing to spend the night can camp or stay with a family. Simple meals are available in the village.

Thirty kilometres west of Pochutla is the **Criadero de Iguanas Barra del Potrero de** Cozoaltepec **Cozoaltepec**, which raises iguanas to repopulate areas where they have become endangered. Take a bus towards Puerto Escondido and get off at the Río de Cozoaltepec, Km 178; the *iguanario* is just east of the river. Green and black iguanas may be seen. ■ *Daily, free admission but a donation is recommended.*

Huatulco

East of Pochutla (50 km, one hour), and 112 km west of Salina Cruz on the coast *Phone code: 958* road is Huatulco, a meticulously engineered resort complex surrounded by 34,000 *Colour map 3, grid C5* ha of forest reserve and nine splendid bays. It offers golf, swimming pools, international and Mexican cuisine, nightlife, beaches, watersports and excursions into the forest. The product is safe, clean, efficient, and claims to be environmentally friendly (see The Huatulco Experiment); an international vacation resort in a lovely setting with a mild Mexican flavour. Huatulco's high seasons include Holy Week, July-August, and November-March, with regular charter flights from the US and Canada during the latter months; prices can as much as double during these periods.

The Huatulco complex encompasses several interconnected towns and development areas; a regular city bus service connects them, and there are many taxis. **Tangolunda**, on the bay of the same name and also known as the Zona Hotelera, is set aside for large luxury hotels and resorts including a Club Mediterranée; it also has the golf course and the most expensive restaurants, souvenir shops and nightlife. **Chahué**, on the next bay west, where development only began in 1999, has a town park with nothing around it, a marina and a few hotels. Further west (6 km from Tangolunda) is **Santa Cruz Huatulco**, once an ancient Zapotec settlement and Mexico's most important Pacific port during the 16th century (later abandoned). It has the marina where tour boats leave for excursions, as well as facilities for visiting yachts, several upscale hotels, restaurants, shops and a few luxury homes. An open-air chapel by the beach here, the Capilla de la Santa Cruz, is attractive; nearby is a well-groomed park. **La Crucecita**, located 2 km inland, is the functional hub of the Huatulco complex, with housing for the area's employees, bus stations, banks, a small market, ordinary shops, plus the more economical hotels and restaurants. It also doubles as a Mexican town, which the tourists can visit, more cosmetic by the manicured Plaza Principal, less so towards the highway. The old-looking, but brand-new Templo de Guadalupe church stands on a small hill next to the plaza. **Santa María Huatulco**, in the mountains 25 km further inland, is a pre-existing

Bays of Huatulco

Guerrero, Oaxaca and the Isthmus

town where the municipal offices are located; there is said to be good walking in the area but little else of interest for the visitor.

Tourist office: Sedetur, Blvd Benito Juárez near the golf course, Tangolunda, T/F581-0176, sedetur6@oaxaca-travel.gob.mx, helpful, informative. Other websites are **oaxaca-travel.mx/sedetur** and **www.baysofhuatulco.com.mx**

Bays and beaches Huatulco's coastline extends for almost 30 km between the Río Copalita to the east and the Río Coyula to the west. Hills covered in deciduous forest, very green during the rainy season (June-September), yellow and parched in the dry, sweep down to the sea. Nine turquoise bays with 36 beaches line the shore, some bays have road access while others can only be reached by sea.

Excursions Full-day boat tours to see the different bays are offered by travel agencies for US$17-27 per person, with stops for swimming, snorkelling and a meal; there are catamarans, sail boats, yachts and small launches. Trips can also be arranged at the Santa Cruz marina directly with the boatsmen, they will probably speak Spanish only. Some of the bays can also be reached by land, and there are tours on all-terrain, quad bikes (*cuatrimotos*).

In the Huatulco area the Sierra Madre del Sur mountains drop from the highest point in the state of Oaxaca (3,750 m) right down to the sea. There are ample opportunities for day-hiking, see Sports on page 417. In the hills north of Huatulco are a number of coffee plantations that can be visited. Huatulco travel agencies arrange for full-day plantation tours, which include a meal with traditional dishes at the farm and bathing in fresh water springs or waterfalls; US$44 per person.

Day trips to the different coastal attractions to the west, including Puerto Angel, Mazunte and Puerto Escondido are offered by travel agencies for US$20. Much ground is covered so it is a long day.

Sleeping **Tangolunda** L *Gala Royal Maeva*, Blvd. Benito Juárez 4, T581-0000, F581-0220,
Discounts of up www.galaresorts.com.mx All-inclusive resort, on the beach, several pools, discotheque.
to 50% can be **L-AL** *Plaza Huatulco*, Blvd Benito Juárez 23, T581-0035, F581-0027. Small luxurious hotel
expected in the with personalized service.
low season **Chahué AL** *Posada Chahué*, Mixie y Mixteco, T587-0945, F587-1240, posadachaue@
huatulco.net.mx A/c, pool, terrace restaurant, **A** with fan.
Santa Cruz L *Marina Resort*, Tehuantepec 112, T587-0963, F587-0830,
hmarinaresort@huatulco.net.mx Pools, restaurants, disco. **AL** *Meigas Binniguenda*, Blvd
Sta Cruz 201, T587-0077, F587-0284, binniguenda@huatulco.netmx Colonial-style, gardens, pool.
La Crucecita AL *Gran Hotel Huatulco*, Carrizal 1406, at the entrance to town, T587-0077,
587-1346, toll free Mexico 01-800-712-7355. A/c, pool. **B** *Busanvi*, Carrizal 601, T587-0056.
A/c and fan, hot water, apartments with kitchenette, pool. **B** *Misión de los Arcos*, Gardenia
902 y Tamarindo, T/F587-0165, losarcos@huatulco.net.mx A/c, hot water, cheaper with fan,
nice rooms. **C** *Posada Michelle*, Gardenia 1301, 2nd floor, T/F587-0535. A/c, cheaper with
fan. **C** *Posada de Rambo*, Guarumbo 307, near main plaza, T587-0958. With bath, fan,
some with hot water. **C-D** *Posada del Carmen*, Palo Verde 307, T587-0593. Nice rooms, cold
water, cheaper with 1 double bed. **D** *Benimar*, Bugambilia esq Pochote, T587-0447. With
bath, fan, hot water, simple rooms. **D** *Casa de Huéspedes Koly*, Bugambilia near Plaza,
T587-1075. With bath, fan.

Camping *Trailer Park Los Mangos*, Blvd Santa Cruz, at Chahué and Santa Cruz.

Eating **Tangolunda** Luxury restaurants at Tangolunda hotels. *La Pampa Argentina*, Centro
Restaurants on Comercial Punta Tangolunda, Blvd Benito Juárez, across from the golf course. For
the beach, out Argentinian-style beef and pasta, pricey. *Don Porfirio*, Blvd Benito Juárez. Fish and seafood
of town, tend to specialities, also steak. *Jarro Café*, across from *Sheraton*. Oaxacan and international cuisine.
be the cheapest **Santa Cruz** *Mar y Luz*, Bahía Santa Cruz. Seafood specialities. *Jardín del Arte*, Paseo Mitla

at *Hotel Marlín*. French and international. *Tipsy's*, Bahía Santa Cruz, by the beach. Seafood, burgers, salads. *Café Huatulco*, near the marina, to sample regional coffee and snacks.
La Crucecita Cheaper prices, especially as you get away from the plaza, several restaurants along Gardenia including *Oasis Café*, Bugambilia esq Flamboyán and Flamboyán 211, by main plaza. Varied menu, grill, seafood, Oaxacan food. *María Sabina*, Flamboyán 306, by plaza. Grill and lobster. *La Crucecita*, Bugambilia esq Chacah. Breakfast, snacks, set meals. *Los Portales*, Bugambilia 603, Plaza Principal. Breakfast, tacos and other snacks, open late. *Don Wilo*, Plaza Principal. Oaxacan specialities and pizza. *El Pato Mojado*, Jazmín. Seafood and regional dishes cooked in wood oven. *Il Giardio del Papa*, Flamboyán 204. Italian, chef was the Pope's cook. *Origami*, Carrizal 504. Japanese food. *El Sabor de Oaxaca*, Guamuchil 206. Regional cooking, Oaxacan *mole*.

Entertainment Several luxury hotels have shows such as the *Sheraton*'s *Fiesta Mexicana with Mariachis*, folk dancing, Mexican buffet, reservations T581-0055. La Guelaguetza folklore show at *Noches Oaxaqueñas*, Blvd Benito Juárez, Tangolunda, reservations T581-0001. Latin dancing at *Magic Tropic*, Santa Cruz. *Magic Circus*, also in Santa Cruz. European-style disco.

Festivals The *Fiesta del Mar* takes place in the 1st week of Apr, the religious *Fiesta de la Santa Cruz* on **3 May**. There is an international sail-fishing tournament during the 1st week of May. The *Fiesta de la Virgen* is on **8 Dec**.

Shopping The *Mercado de Artesanías de Santa Cruz*, Blvd Santa Cruz, corner Mitla, has a variety of regional crafts. The *Museo de Artesanías Oaxaqueñas*, Flamboyán 216, Plaza Principal, La Crucecita, also exhibits and sells a variety of Mexican crafts.

Sports **Cycling** A mountain bike is a good way to get around this area and to reach the high points with the many views of the bays. Bike rentals in La Crucecita from restaurants *La Tropicana*, *Gardenia*, and *Guanacastle* near the plaza, US$1.65 per hr and *Origami*, Carrizal 504, US$2.25 per hour. Rentals and cycling tours from *Motor Tours*, *Eco Aventuras* and other agencies (see Tour operators).
    Diving and snorkelling There are good snorkelling opportunities on reefs by the beach at La Entrega (Bahía Santa Cruz), Riscalillo (Bahía Cachacual) and San Agustín (Bahía San Agustín). The islands of Cacaluta (Bahía Cacaluta) and La Montosa (Bahía Tangolunda) are also surrounded by reefs with several species of coral, many different organisms can be seen here in relatively shallow water. Snorkel and fins rented at Santa Cruz marina, US$4.35 or through agencies who organize tours. There are good scuba diving opportunities as well the cliffs that separate the different bays continue underwater an average of 30 m. Diving lessons and tours from **Action Sports Marina** (*Sheraton Hotel*), **Buceo Sotavento** (*Hotel Club Plaza Huatulco*) and other agencies. Lessons run at about US$82, diving tour if you have your certificate, US$65.
    Fishing Launches and yachts for deep-sea fishing charge US$100 per hr, minimal rental 3 hrs.
    Golf The Tangolunda golf course offers 18-hole, par-72 golf with nice views of the surroundings. Reservations T581-0037, F581-0059.
    Hiking There are opportunities for hiking in the forested hills to the north of Huatulco. Because part of the forest is deciduous, the experience is very different in the rainy season, when it is green, and in the dry season when the area is brown and even some cacti change from green to violet. The Río Copalita to the north and east of Huatulco is quite scenic. It has waterfalls and rapids, walking here can be combined with a visit to the Punta Celeste Zapotec archaeological site.
    Horse-riding Rancho Caballo de Mar, on the shores of the Río Copalita, east of Huatulco and south of Route 200, T587-0530, offers riding tours along the river, on forested trails and on the beaches of Bahía de Conejos, US$45 for 3 hrs.
    Rafting Several companies run tours down the Copalita and Zimatán rivers. These can be as basic as a float down the river or as challenging as class 4-5 rapids; ask enough questions to find the tour that best suits you. Half-day tours US$33-40, full day for US$65-76 per

The Huatulco Experiment

It has been argued with some justification that mass tourism by any other name is equally harmful to the local physical and social environments. Huatulco claims to be different however, and even the most fundamentalist opponents of industrial-scale resort development might want to consider its unique experiment.

Begun in 1987 and perhaps designed to avoid some of the mistakes of Acapulco or Cancún, it is certainly a contrast to the haphazard development of nearby Puerto Escondido. Huatulco was meticulously planned and executed; the land (34,000 ha comprised mostly of virgin forest) and its spectacular shoreline were all expropriated beforehand by the Mexican federal government. There could be no upward spiral of property values here, nor fragmentation of lots to impede orderly development. With the tiny local population relocated outside the area, there was no social impact to consider and the design concentrated on creating a comprehensive infrastructure in harmony with the natural environment.

A comprehensive infrastructure has certainly been achieved, with an international airport, four-lane divided access roads lined with landscaped greenery, marinas, parks, plazas, public transport, medical facilities, employee housing, commercial areas, sewage systems, huge concrete drainage canals, international courier services and cellular phones. Huatulco's harmony with its natural environment is a matter of debate, but at least the water looks reasonably clean in the nine bays, and fish swim alongside the bathers and jet-skis, while basket-shaped nests hang from the trees overhead.

Courses on working with tourists are provided for the area's residents, all of whom make their living directly or indirectly from the industry; the atmosphere is cordial and there is little crime. In fact the only thing Huatulco really lacks is authenticity, but while its detractors may focus on how artificial it all is, its promoters can point out that it works.

In the meantime, the project – which continues to be guided by the federal government agency Fonatur – has not grown as rapidly as expected.

person. Note that from Feb-May there may not be enough water. Providers include: *Aventuras Piraguas*, Plaza Oaxaca Local 19, on Flamboyán across from the plaza, La Crucecita, T/F587-1333, canoe trips and rafting in up to class 5 rapids. *Copalita River Tours*, Gardenia esquina Palo Verde (*Posada Michelle* lobby), La Crucecita, T/F587-0535, kayak and rafting tours. *Huatulco Outfitters*, Plaza Comercial, Punta Tangolunda, T581-0315.

Rock climbing There are rock climbing opportunities at Piedra de los Moros a few kilometres north of Route 200, on the road to Pueblo Viejo, the turn-off is west of the Bahías de Huatulco entrance road; by the Copalitilla waterfall, on the Copalita river canyon, 65 km from Huatulco; and in Punta Celeste, at the Botazoo Park, 8 km from Huatulco.

Watersports Those looking for wind surfing, sailing, wave running, and water skiing, can rent equipment at the major hotels and beach clubs.

Transport **Local** **Bus**: a city bus runs from corner of Carrizal and Av Oaxaca in La Crucecita to Chahué, Tangolunda and Santa Cruz. 2nd class buses to Pochutla from Blvd Chahué and Riscalillo, La Crucecita, every 15 mins 0500-2000, US$0.90, 1 hr. 2nd class buses to Salina Cruz from Blvd Chahué and Bugambilia, frequent departures, 3 hrs. **Car hire**: *Dollar*, at *Sheraton Hotel* and airport, T587-1528. *Advantage*, at *Hotel Castillo Huatulco*, Santa Cruz, T587-1379. *Pesos*, at *Los Portales* restaurant, main plaza, La Crucecita, T587-0070, beach buggies.

Long distance **Air**: Aeropuerto Bahías de Huatulco (HUX), is located 17 km northwest of Huatulco along Route 200, T581-9099; airport van service T581-9024, US$27. Taxi US$11, shared taxi (*colectivo*) US$6.50 per person, 20 mins. From **Mexico City**, *Mexicana*, daily at 1005 and 1335, returning from Huatulco 1150 and 1520; discounts for advanced purchase. From **Oaxaca**, *Aerocaribe* daily at 0700 and 1705, returning from Huatulco at 0750 and 1755. All international flights are charters and run in the boreal winter only.

Guerrero, Oaxaca and the Isthmus

Buses: **Acapulco**: with *Estrella Blanca*, 1st class, 4 daily, 9 hrs, US$21; 2nd class, 3 daily, 11 hrs, US$15.60. **Mexico City**: with *Cristóbal Colón*, 1st class, 4 daily (arriving at various terminals), 14 hrs, US$41, via Isthmus and Oaxaca: with *Estrella Blanca*, 1st class, at 1800, 13 hrs, US$40, via Acapulco. **Oaxaca**: 1st class with *Cristóbal Colón*, Gardenia corner Ocotillo, La Crucecita, 2 daily, US$15, via Isthmus 8 hrs, luxury *Plus* service at 2100, US$18.50. 2nd class with *Oaxaca-Pacífico*, Calle Jazmín, La Crucecita, 1 daily, 7 hrs, US$8.70, via Pochutla. **Puerto Escondido**: with *Cristóbal Colón*, 1st class, 4 daily, US$4.35, 2 hrs; with *Estrella Blanca*, Gardenia corner Palma Real, La Crucecita, 1st class, 4 daily, 2½ hrs, US$4.70, 2nd class, 3 daily, US$3.50. **Salina Cruz**: with *Cristóbal Colón*, 1st class, 4 daily continuing to Tehuantepec and Juchitán, 2½ hrs, US$5.60; *Plus* service, 2 daily, US$6.50; with *Estrella Blanca*, 3 daily, 2½ hrs, US$5.80. **Tapachula**: with *Cristóbal Colón*, 1st class, at 2200, 10 hrs, US$22.**Tuxtla Gutiérrez**: with *Cristóbal Colón*, 1st class, 1045 and 2330, 8 hrs, US$17.

Airline offices *Mexicana*, Hotel Castillo Huatulco, Santa Cruz, T587-0223, airport T581-9007. *Aerocaribe*, Hotel Castillo Huatulco, Santa Cruz, T587-1220, airport T581-0155. **Banks** *Bital*, Bugambilia corner Sabalí, La Crucecita, cash and TCs, cash advances through ATM only. *Bancomer*, Blvd Santa Cruz y Otitlán del Valle, Santa Cruz, cash and TCs. *Inverlat*, Blvd Santa Cruz, Santa Cruz, cash and TCs. *American Express*, Bahías Plus, Carrizal 704, La Crucecita, cash and TCs at good rates, Mon-Sat 0900-1400. *Casa de Cambio*, Guamuchil near the Plaza, La Crucecita, poor rates. **Communications** Internet: *Informática Mare*, Guanacastle 203, 2nd floor, near market, US$3 per hour. **Post office**: on Blvd Chahué, at south end of La Crucecita. **Laundry** *Lavandería Abril*, Gardenia 1403 y Pochote, La Crucecita, US$0.75 per kilo. *Lavandería Estrella*, Flamboyán y Carrizal, La Crucecita, US$0.75 per kilo, Mon-Sat 0800-2100. **Medical services** *Especialidades Médicas* Santa Cruz, Flamboyán at Plaza, La Crucecita, private, English spoken. *Central Médica Huatulco*, Flamboyán 205, La Crucecita, T587-0104, private. *IMSS* social security hospital, Blvd Chahué, just south of La Crucecita. **Tour operators** *Bahías Plus*, Carrizal 704, La Crucecita, T/F587-0811 and at *Hotel Binniguenda*, Santa Cruz, T/F587-0216, bahiasplus@huatulco.net.mex, airline reservations, tours, helpful, American Express representatives on 2nd floor of La Crucecita office. *Paraíso Huatulco*, at *Hotel Flamboyán*, La Crucecita, T587-0181, F587-0190 and at *Sheraton Resort*, Tangolunda, T581-0218 ext 788, Tangolunda, paraiso@ huatulco.net.mx, local and regional tours, diving, fishing, quad bikes. *Motor Tours*, at *Hotel Club Plaza Huatulco*, Tangolunda, T581-0024, *Hotel Castillo Huatulco*, Santa Cruz, T587-0050, local and regional tours, motorcycles and quad bikes. *Action Sports Marina*, at *Sheraton Resort*, Tangolunda, T581-0055, ext 842, F587-0537, diving lessons and tours, watersports. *Eco Aventuras*, La Crucecita, T587-0669, adventure tours, cycling, rock climbing, kayaking, bird-watching. *Jungle Tour*, at *Royal Maeva Hotel*, T581-0000 ext 729, quad tours.

Directory

Isthmus of Tehuantepec

From the city of Oaxaca, Route 190 heads southeast towards the Golfo de Tehuantepec and the Pacific. At Km 116, in **San José de Gracia**, is the hotel and restaurant *El Mirador*, **D**. Clean, very friendly, noisy from passing trucks, overlooking a beautiful valley, parking in front. At Km 134, in the village of **El Camarón** is **E** *Hotel Santa Elena*. Clean, friendly, fan and TV.

Only about 210 km separate the Atlantic and the Pacific at the hot, once heavily jungled Isthmus of Tehuantepec, where the land does not rise more than 250 m. This narrowest point of Mexico is also the geographic boundary between North and Central America. There is a railway (freight service only) and a Trans-Isthmian Highway between Salina Cruz and Coatzacoalcos, the terminal cities on the two oceans. The regional airport at Ixtepec has flights to Oaxaca and Mexico City.

The Isthmus has a strong cultural character all of its own. The people are *mestizo* and descendants of several different indigenous groups, but Zapotecs predominate. Once a matriarchal society, Zapotec women continue to play a very important role in local affairs. Their typical dress is most intricate and beautiful, and they are high-pressure saleswomen. The men for the most part work in the fields, or as potters or weavers, or at the Salina Cruz oil refinery.

The Isthmian region of Oaxaca is dominated by three neighbouring cities: **Tehuantepec** is the smallest and most authentic; **Juchitán** has the largest and most

Guerrero, Oaxaca and the Isthmus

interesting market; while **Salina Cruz** is a modern industrial city and port. The climate throughout the area can be oppressive, very hot and quite humid, hence the region's many cultural events usually take place late in the evening. Winds are very strong on and near the Isthmus, because of the intermingling of Pacific and Caribbean weather systems.

Salina Cruz

Phone code: 971
Colour map 3, grid C6
Population: 76,392

A modern and industrial city and port, with broad avenues and a large central plaza, Salina Cruz is surrounded by hills and many poor neighbourhoods. The centre is pleasant enough however and, although there is little of outstanding interest here, it offers a good selection of accommodations and services for those breaking a journey or visiting for work. Salina Cruz is located 17 km south of Tehuantepec and 174 km east of Huatulco, at the junction of the Carretera Transístmica (185) and the Carretera Costera (200). Some of the nearby beaches are quite scenic but oil pollution, high winds, dangerous surf and sharks all conspire against would-be bathers. Do not park close to the beach, as your vehicle may be sandblasted. The **tourist office**, Regiduría de Turismo, is at city hall opposite the plaza. The *Fiesta de la Santa Cruz* is held 3-6 May.

Excursions Ten kilometres to the southeast is a picturesque fishing village with **La Ventosa** beach, which, as the name says, is windy. In 1528 the Spanish conquerors established a shipyard here; the old lighthouse, **El Faro de Cortés**, can still be seen. Buses go to the beach every 30 minutes from a corner of the main square. **Sleeping D** *La Posada de Rustrian*. Overlooking the sea, with bath in new block, half in old block, poor value; several other *pensiones* in **D** and **E** ranges. Friendly family at the top of the dirt road coming from Salina Cruz (on the right) and 200 m after the first path that leads down to the beach, rents hammocks, US$1 a night, fried fish US$1. *Champas*, or hammocks under thatch shelters by the beach, US$1 a night. Many seafood restaurants and bars in town; at the end of the road which crosses the village is a good restaurant under a high palm roof, excellent fish.

The coast west of Salina Cruz is quite scenic, with several high sand dunes and lagoons; shrimp farms have been set up in this area. Just west of the city is the village of Salinas del Marquez; the beach of **Las Escolleras** in Salinas is popular with locals. Urban bus service from the park in Salina Cruz every 30 minutes.

Sleeping **B** *Altagracia*, 5 de Mayo 520, T714-0726. A/c, bar. **B** *Bugambilias*, 5 de Mayo 24, T714-4402, F714-1896. A/c, hot water, **E** with fan. **B** *Costa Real*, Progreso 22, near Avila Camacho, T714-0293, F714-5111. A/c, restaurant, parking. **B-C** *El Parador*, Carretera Transístmica Km 60, T716-2951. A/c, pool. Recommended. **C** *María del Carmen*, Manzanillo 17 and Tampico, T714-5625, F714-5421. A/c, modern, nice, **D** with fan. **C** *Las Palmas*, Mazatlán 46, T714-0362, F714-0357, 1 block from plaza. A/c, clean. **C** *Fuentes*, Avila Camacho 411, T714-3403. Bath, a/c, **E** with fan.

D *Pacífico*, Avila Camacho 709, T/F714-5552. A/c, cheaper with fan, restaurant. **D** *Posada del Jardín*, Avila Camacho 108, T714-0162. A/c, bath, **E** with fan. **E** *Ríos*, Wilfrido Cruz 405, T714-0337. Reasonable.

Eating *El Lugar*, corner of Acapulco and 5 de Mayo on 1st floor, opposite the plaza. Mexican food, good. *Aloha*, Wilfrido Cruz 13-A. Seafood and regional dishes. *Aguascalientes*, Avila Camacho 422. Fish. *Vittorios Pizza*, 5 de Mayo 404. Italian. *Olimpo Pizzas*, Tampico 73. Italian and fish. Several restaurants in outdoor settings along the Carretera Transístmica; many seafood restaurants at La Ventosa beach.

Transport **Air** Regional airport at Ciudad Ixtepec, transport to airport US$9 per person.

Buses Regional service to **Tehuantepec** (US$0.65) and **Juchitán** (US$1.40) every 10 mins with Istmeños, 0500-2400, from Progreso west of Tampico, by train tracks. Frequent 2nd class service to **Huatulco**, 3 hrs. There is a joint bus station for *Cristóbal Colón*, *ADO*, *AU* and *Sur* at the north end of town, by the Carretera Transístmica.

To **Coatzacoalcos**: 6 hrs, US$14.50. To **Oaxaca**: 1st class: *Cristóbal Colón*, 8 daily, 6 hrs, US$13; 2nd class: Oaxaca-Istmo, 3 daily, 6 hrs, US$10. To **Pochutla**: 1st class: *Cristóbal Colón*, 5 daily; 2nd class: *Estrella Blanca*, 3 daily, 3-4 hrs, US$9. To **Puerto Escondido**: 2nd class, *Estrella Blanca*, 4 daily, 5 hrs, US$6.50. To **Tapachula**: *Cristóbal Colón* 2nd class, along the coast, 9-10 hrs, 0740 and 2030, US$17, 1st class bus at 2000, US$21. To **Tuxtla Gutiérrez** and **San Cristóbal de las Casas**: 2 daily buses come from Oaxaca or Puerto Escondido and are very often full, book well in advance, US$15 (Tuxtla), US$18 (San Cristóbal); alternatively, take a 2nd class bus to **Juchitán**, then to Arriaga and from there to Tuxtla and San Cristóbal.

Banks *Bancomer*, Avila Camacho. *Bital*, Avila Camacho and Coatzacoalcos. Both change cash and TCs. **Communications** Internet: service from *Edtzin*, Tampico 40 and *Nautinet*, Tampico 15; both US$2.20 per hour. **Laundry** *Alborada*, Tampico and Guaymas, US$1.65 per kilo. **Medical services** Hospital Civil, Avila Camacho, Centre, T714-0110. **Tour operators** *Servicios Turísticos Gilsa*, Tampico 53, T/F714-4497, airline reservations, transport to airport, helpful. — **Directory**

Tehuantepec

Santo Domingo Tehuantepec, 257 km from Oaxaca, is a colourful town that conserves the region's indigenous flavour. Robust Zapotec matrons in bright dresses ride standing in the back of motorized tricycles known as *moto-carros*. Life moves slowly here, centered on the plaza, which has arcades on one side, and an adjacent market, the best place to admire the Zapotec dress. In the plaza is a statue of Máximo Ramón Ortiz (1816-55) composer of the *zandunga*, the legendary music of the Isthmus, which is still very popular. The meandering Río Tehuantepec is two blocks from the plaza, by the highway. Due to the importance of Tehuantepec during the early colonial period, many churches were built here; attractive white churches with coloured trim dot the landscape. Houses are low, in white or pastel shades.

Phone code: 971
Colour map 3, grid C6
Population: 36,888
Altitude: 150m

Tehuantepec

Sleeping
1 Casa de Huéspedes Istmo
2 Donají
3 Oasis
4 Posada Hasdar

Eating
1 Café Colonial
2 Scaru

Not to scale

Guerrero, Oaxaca and the Isthmus

The **Casa de la Cultura** is housed in the 16th-century Dominican ex-convent Rey Cosijopi. The building is quite run down, but original frescoes can still be seen on some walls. There is a library and some simple exhibits of regional archaeology, history and costumes. Ask the caretaker to open the exhibits for you. The **Museo Casa de la Señora Juana C Romero** is a chalet built entirely with materials brought from France; Sra Romero's great-granddaughter lives there today, ask for permission to visit the house.

Excursions To the northwest of town, off the road to Oaxaca, are the unrestored ruins of **Guiengola**, 'the Mexican Machu Picchu', so called because of its lonely location on a mountain. It has walls up to 3 m high, running, it is said, for 40 km; there are the remains of two pyramids and a ball court. This last fortress of the Zapotecs was never conquered (*guiengola* is the Zapotec word for fortress); Alvarado and his forces marched past it in 1522. Take the 0500 bus from Tehuantepec towards Oaxaca and get off at the Puente las Tejas bridge (8 km from Tehuantepec); this is the last place to buy water on the way to the ruins. Take the turning at the signpost 'Ruinas Guiengola 7 km'. Walk 5 km then turn left, uphill, to the car park. From here it is 1½ hours' walk to the ruins, there are no facilities or entry fees. Try to return before 0900 because it gets very hot; take plenty of water. Alternatively, take a taxi to the car park and ask the driver to return for you three hours later (US$5.50 each trip).

Nine kilometres from Tehuantepec, taking the turn-off at *Hotel Calli* and going past the Santa Teresa Trailer Park, is **Santa María La Mixtequilla**, on the shores of the Tehuantepec river, where many herons can be seen at dawn and dusk. Take the blue Mixtequilla city bus from the Monte de Piedad bus stop in the centre of town.

Sleeping
■ *on map*
B *Calli*, on the road to Juchitán, just north of town, T715-0085, F715-1113. A/c, pool, gardens, restaurant, parking. **C** *Guiexhoba*, on the road to Oaxaca, T715-0416, F51710. A/c, mini-fridge, pool, restaurant, parking. **D** *Donají del Istmo*, Juárez 10, T715-0064, F715-0448, in Centre. A/c, **E** with fan, clean, friendly. Recommended. **D** *Oasis*, Melchor Ocampo 8, T715-0008, F715-0835, 1 block from plaza. Good atmosphere, with bath and a/c, **E** with fan, simple, safe parking, owner Julín Contreras is helpful, good information on local history and traditions. **E** *Casa de Huéspedes Istmo*, Hidalgo 31, T715-0019, 1½ blocks from the main plaza. Quiet, basic, with lovely patio. **E** *Casa de Huéspedes La Tehuanita*, Aldama 62. Fan. **F** *Posada Hasdar*, next to *Oasis*. Fan, shared bath, very basic.

Camping *Santa Teresa Trailer Park*, east side of town, 8 km off Route 190 (take side road at *Hotel Calli* and follow signs or Mixtequilla city bus from the centre of town), by sugar cane plantation and mill. US$5.50 for car and 2 people, US$3.80 per tent, cold showers, public conveniences, drinking water, restaurant, lovely mango grove, very friendly owner.

Eating
● *on map*
Café Colonial, Juana C Romero 66. Good *comida corrida* and à la carte, a variety of Mexican dishes, clean, friendly. *Restaurant Scaru*, Leona Vicario 4. Good food, fish and seafood specialities, upscale, nice courtyard and mural. *Nanixe*, at *Hotel Calli*. Good regional and international food. *Guiexhoba*, at *Hotel Guiexhoba*. Also regional and international. *Mariscos Silvia*, Av Juárez by the park. Excellent shrimp, moderate. *Mariscos Angel*, 5 de Mayo No 1, by entrance from Salina Cruz. Seafood, moderately priced. Cheap food on top floor of market, here you can get the local speciality, pork or chicken, stuffed with potatoes, but beware of hygiene. The local *quesadillas* made of maize and cheese are delicious; sold at bus stops.

Festivals Festivals and traditions are very important in Tehuantepec. There are many colourful and ceremonious celebrations throughout the year, for which the women don their elaborate embroidered dresses and lace halos, known as *resplandores*. The town is divided into 15 wards; each one has a patron saint. *Fiestas Patronales* are held in each neighbourhood for several days in honour of the local patron, these culminate on the saint's day. In the centre of Tehuantepec the *Fiestas of Santo Domingo* are held during the 1st week of Aug, in the San José neighbourhood the fiestas in honour of St John the Baptist are held during the week leading up to **24 Jun**, and so forth. Another type of celebration are *velas*, very formal dances; the *Vela Zandunga* is held **19 May**, while the *Velas de Agosto* are held throughout the Isthmus in **mid-Aug**, and the *Vela Tehuantepec* is on **26 Dec**.

Local 3-wheeled motorized rickshaws (*moto-carros*) take locals around town; you have to stand and hold on to the railing.   **Transport**

Long distance **Air**: the regional airport is in Ciudad Ixtepec.

Road Tehuantepec is at the junction of the Carretera Transístmica (185) and Route 190, which connects it with Oaxaca, 257 km away.

    Buses: regional Istmeños buses leave from the highway (Carretera Cristóbal Colón), by the river, at the end of 5 de Mayo: to **Salina Cruz**, every 10 mins, 0500-2400, US$0.65, 45 mins; to *Juchitán*, every 10 mins, 0500 to midnight, US$0.80, 1 hr. There is a joint bus station for *Cristóbal Colón*, *ADO*, *AU* and *Sur* on the outskirts of town; taxi to Zócalo US$1, *moto-carro* US$0.50 or 15 mins' walk (walking not recommended at night).

    To **Arriaga**: 0600, 0800, 1800 to connect to Tonalá (not confirmed). It is not always possible to get a reservation with *Cristóbal Colón* in Tehuantepec, for Chiapas destinations; you have a better chance from Salina Cruz or Juchitán, where more buses stop. To **Cancún**: *ADO* at 1430, US$68. To **Coatzacoalcos**: *ADO* and *Sur*, 1st class 5 daily, 6 hrs, US$13; 2nd class every 30 mins, US$10. To **Oaxaca**, **Pochutla**, and **Puerto Escondido**: *Cristóbal Colón*, 1st class 4 daily, US$7.50 (Huatulco), US$10 (Pochutla), US$14 (Puerto Escondido); to Huatulco 2nd class, 0600, 1330, US$6. To **Mexico City**: *Cristóbal Colón*, *Plus* service, 2030, US$42.60; 1st class, 2000, 2145, US$48. To **San Cristóbal de la Casas**: *Cristóbal Colón*, 0030 and 1400, 6½ hrs, US$16. To **Tonalá** and **Tapachula**: *Cristóbal Colón*, 2 nightly, US$9 (Tonalá), US$19 (Tapachula). To **Tuxtepec** and **Veracruz**: *AU* via Sayula, 1040, 2140, US$14, 6 hrs (Tuxtepec), US$23 (Veracruz). To **Tuxtla Gutiérrez**: *Cristóbal Colón*, 0030, 1400, 2200, 4½ hrs, US$13. To **Villahermosa**: *Cristóbal Colón* 1st class, US$17, 8 hrs, 2nd class US$14.

Banks *Bital*, Juana C Romero, open 0800-1700. *Bancomer*, 5 de Mayo. *Bancrecer*, 5 de Mayo. All   **Directory** change cash and TCs. **Communications Internet:** service in Salina Cruz or Juchitán. **Tourist offices** SEDETUR regional delegation for the Isthmus, Carretera Transístmica 7, 2nd floor, opposite the petrol station, T51236, F50802. Regiduría de Turismo at Palacio de Gobierno.

Juchitán

Twenty-seven kilometres from Tehuantepec is the larger and more modern city of Juchitán de Zaragoza, an important commercial and cultural centre on the Isthmus. It has a nice plaza next to impressive colonial municipal buildings and many churches including that of **San Vicente Ferrer**, the city's patron saint. Many Zapotec women here still wear traditional costumes as everyday dress. The **tourist office** is at the Palacio de Gobierno.

Phone code: 971
Colour map 3, grid C6
Population: 78,493

The **Mercado Central 5 de Septiembre** is the largest market on the Isthmus; traditional barter still takes place here. The meat and produce section is dirty, but the crafts section on the second floor is well worth a visit; this is the best place to see the elaborate embroidered Zapotec dresses which sell for up to US$600.   **Sights**

South of Juchitán and stretching for some 100 km to the east are three very large, shallow lagoons. On the shores of Laguna Superior, the closest one, 10 km south of the city, is the fishing village of **Playa Vicente**; across from here are several scenic islands. In Laguna Mar Muerto, the furthest one to the east, there are salt pans.   **Excursions**

B *Santo Domingo*, Carretera Transístmica, T711-1959, F711-3642. A/c, restaurant, pool.   **Sleeping** **C** *Don Alex Lena Real*, 16 de Septiembre 48, T711-1064, F711-1063. Modern comfortable rooms, a/c, clean. **D** in older wing, cheaper with fan, restaurant. **C** *La Mansión*, 16 de

Guerrero, Oaxaca and the Isthmus

Septiembre 11, T711-2055, F711-1241. A/c, restaurant. **C** *Lidxi Biuxa*, 2 de Abril 79, T711-1299. A/c, pool. **D** *Alfa*, Carretera Panamericana Km 821, T711-0327. A/c, bath, cheaper with fan. **D** *Hotel Casa Río*, has an Indian name, *Coty*, not posted, next to *Casa Río* shop, near market. Clean. **E** *Modelo*, 2 de Abril 64, T711-1241, near market. With bath, fan, basic. The Casa de Cultura can help if you want to stay with local people and learn about their culture, eg with Florinda Luis Orozco, Callejón de los Leones 18, between Hidalgo and Aldama.

Eating   *Café Colón*, Carretera Panamericana, close to the bus station. Good. *Casa Grande*, Juárez 125, on the main square. In a beautifully restored colonial house, good food, live music. *Deyaurihe*, 5 de Septiembre esquina Aldama. Mexican food, *comida corrida* and à la carte. *La Tablita*, 5 de Septiembre 15. Regional and other Mexican dishes. *Los Chapulines*, 5 de Septiembre esq Morelos. Regional and international food, *comida corrida* and à la carte, a/c. *Mariscos Angel*, Aldama 100 and 5 de Septiembre. Seafood. *Pizzería La Vianda*, 5 de Septiembre 54-B. Pizza and seafood.

Festivals   Although every birth and wedding is reason for a colourful celebration, best known are the *velas*, formal dances in a decorated setting resembling a European palace, for which the attendees wear traditional dress. Some *velas* also include a *regada de frutas y convite de flores* in which the participants offer gifts of fruits and flowers. There are *velas* throughout the year, the most important ones are held during **May** in honour of *San Vicente Ferrer*.

Transport   **Air**   The regional airport is at Ciudad Ixtepec.

Road   Juchitán is 26 km northeast of Tehuantepec. At La Ventosa, 14 km northeast of Juchitán, the road splits: the Carretera Transístmica (Route 185) continues north towards Coatzacoalcos on the Gulf of Mexico, and the Carretera Costera (Route 200) goes east to San Pedro Tapanatepec, where it splits again, 1 road going to Tuxtla Gutiérrez and the other to Tapachula.

Buses   Regional bus service to **Tehuantepec** (US$0.80) and **Salina Cruz** (US$1.40): every 15 mins with Istmeños, 0500-2400, from Prolongación 16 de Septiembre, by the highway to Tehuantepec. Joint bus station for *Cristóbal Colón*, *ADO*, *Sur* and *AU* at Prolongación 16 de Septiembre, just south of the highway to Tehuantepec. To **Huatulco**: *ADO* 0600, US$8.60; *Cristóbal Colón*, 5 daily, US$9; *Sur*, 3 daily, US$5.55.

To **Coatzacoalcos**: *ADO* 13 daily, US$13; *Sur*, every 20 mins, US$8. To **Mexico City**: *ADO* luxury, at 2145, US$72, *ADO* 1st class, 1900 and 2100, US$52; *AU* 6 daily US$42. To **Oaxaca**: *ADO* luxury, 3 daily, US$16; 1st class: *ADO* 3 daily, *Cristóbal Colón* 7 daily, 6 hrs, US$13. To **Pochutla** and **Puerto Escondido**: *Cristóbal Colón*, 4 daily, US$14 (Puerto) US$12 (Pochutla); *Sur*, 2330, US$12 (Puerto), US$9 (Pochutla). To **San Cristóbal de las Casas**: *Cristóbal Colón*, 3 daily, US$16. To **Tapachula**: *ADO* at 0230, US$23; *Cristóbal Colón*, 2 nightly, US$19; *Sur* 0230 and 1600, US$16. To **Tuxtepec**: *AU* at 1115, US$13. To **Tuxtla Gutiérrez**: *Cristóbal Colón*, 5 daily, US$14. To **Veracruz**: *ADO* 0055 and 2130, US$215; *AU* 1115, US$24.

Directory   **Banks**   *Bancomer*, 16 de Septiembre by the main plaza, Mon-Fri 0830-1400, cash and TCs. *Bital*, 16 de Septiembre y Alvaro Obregón, Mon-Fri 0800-1900, Sat 0900-1400, cash and TCs. **Communications** Internet: *Servitel*, Efraín Gómez and 16 de Septiembre, US$4.35 per hr. *Istmored*, just north of town on the road to Ixtepec, US$3.25 per hr. **Tour operators**   *Viajes Zaymar*, 5 de Septiembre 100B, T/F711-0792.

Ciudad Ixtepec   A road runs 19 km northwest to Ciudad Ixtepec railway junction. South of Ixtepec is
Colour map 3, grid C6   a military base and the regional airport.

Sleeping and eating   All hotels in the vicinity of the train station: **D** *El Regente Turista*, Nicolás Bravo 10, T/F713-0237. A/c, restaurant. **E** *Casa de Huéspedes San Gerónimo*, close to train station and market. Clean, good. **E** *San Juan*, 16 de Septiembre 127. Bath, some with a/c, acceptable. *La Flor del Café*, Av Ferrocarril. Regional food. *La Tropicana*, 16 de Septiembre. Mexican cooking. *La Manzana*, Nicolás Bravo 10. Seafood and international cooking.

Transport Air: To **Mexico City**, with *Aeromar*, 2 daily flights weekdays, 1 daily flight weekends, US$168-US$257. To **Oaxaca**, with *Aerocaribe*, 1 daily flight at 0935, US$85.

Crossing the Isthmus

From Juchitán, Route 185 crosses the **Isthmus of Tehuantepec** to Sayula, passing through **Matías Romero**, a quiet town set in the hills, with a less oppressive climate than other parts of the Isthmus.

Sleeping and eating C *Real del Istmo*, Carretera Transístmica Km 136, T722-1300, F722-0088. A/c, safe parking, good restaurant. In the centre. **D** *Juan Luis*, Carretera Transístmica Km 195, T722-0611. Pool, restaurant. **E** *Gil Mary*, Hombres Ilustres 607b, T722-0624, F722-0224. As well as the restaurant in the Real del Istmo, there is *Piscis*, Guerrero 302. Seafood. *Chava*, 16 de Septiembre, 218. Regional food. *Las Flores*, Carretera Transístmica Km 197. Mexican dishes.

Petrol and food on sale at the halfway point, **Palomares**, where there is a paved road to Tuxtepec (see page 363), 2½ hours' drive. A few kilometres south of Palomares a gravelled road enters on the eastern side; this passes under an imposing gateway, **La Puerta de Uxpanapa**, where some 24,500 families are being settled on land reclaimed from the jungle.

Further north the Carretera Transístmica reaches the junction with the Veracruz-Villahermosa Gulf Coast road at **Acayucan**.

Sleeping: **D** *Hotel Joalicia*, Zaragoza 4. **D** *Hotel Ritz*, Av Hidalgo 7, T715-0024. Shower, fan, noisy, parking. **D** *Los Angeles*. Cheaper without TV, clean, fans, friendly, pool, owners speak some English, space for car inside. **E** *San Miguel*. With bath, hot water and fan, not very attractive, but OK. **E** *Iglesias*, 267 km from Veracruz on toll road (1st class buses 'de paso', very hard to get on, 4 hrs to Veracruz, 2nd class 5½ hrs).

From Acayucan, continue on Route 180 for Minatitlán, Coatzacoalcos (Veracruz) and Villahermosa (Tabasco).

Tabasco and Chiapas

Tabasco and Chiapas

The states of Tabasco and Chiapas merge to form a geographical block that separates Mexico from Guatemala, and from the Yucatán Peninsula. Until recently, low-lying, jungly Tabasco was considered an oil state that held little appeal for tourists, but oil wealth has brought Villahermosa, the state capital, a certain self-assurance and vibrancy, which invites exploration, and the parks, nature reserves and huge meandering rivers in the eastern and southern regions of the state are beginning to attract visitors. Its lands once gave rise to the first great civilization of Mesoamerica, the Olmec, whose influence was felt through vast zones of Mexico and further afield.

In Chiapas, the land of the Classic Maya (whose descendants still inhabit the highland villages today), the attractions are better known: San Cristóbal de las Casas is the end of the line for many travellers who base themselves in this unique Colonial-Indian town while they soak up the atmosphere and explore the jungle waterfalls, the dramatic canyon, the multicoloured lakes, and – highlight of any trip to Mexico – the ruins at Palenque, whose jungle setting is probably the most atmospheric and beautiful of all the Mayan sites. Chiapas is also a good entry point for Guatemala. You can head straight for northern Guatemala and the ruins of Tikal or a more genteel entry through the west of the country, the highlands and the idyllic Lake Atitlán. For details see Routes to Guatemala, page 460.

Villahermosa

Phone code: 993
Colour map 4, grid B1
Population: 275,000

Capital of Tabasco state, Villahermosa is on the Río Grijalva, navigable to the sea. It used to be a dirty town, but is improving, though it is very hot and rainy. The city is heaving under pressure from the oil boom, making it an expensive place.

The **cathedral**, ruined in 1973, has been rebuilt, its twin steeples beautifully lit at night; it is not in the centre. There is a warren of modern colonial-style pedestrian malls throughout the central area. The **Centro de Investigaciones de las Culturas Olmecas** (CICOM) is set in a new modern complex with a large public library, expensive restaurant, airline offices and souvenir shops, a few minutes' walk south, out of town along the river bank. The **Museo Regional de Antropología Carlos Pellicer**, on three floors, has well laid out displays of Maya and Olmec artefacts. ■ *0900-1900, closed Mon, US$1.* Two other museums worth visiting are the **Museo de Cultura Popular**, Zaragoza 810 (■ *Tue-Sun, 0900-2000, free*), and the **Museo de Historia de Tabasco**, Avenida 27 de Febrero esq Juárez, ■ *Tue-Sun 0900-2000, Sun 1000-1700, US$0.50.* **Mercado Pino Suárez**, on the corner of Pino Suárez and Bastar Zozaya, is sensory overload as every nook and cranny is taken up with a variety of goods; everything from barbecued *pejelagarto* to cowboy hats, colourful handmade fabrics, spices and dangling naked chickens en route to the kettle. The local drink, *pozol*, is believed to cure a hangover. You can watch it being made here as the *pozoleros* grind the hominy into a thick dough to then mix it with cacao and water; its grainy starchiness is somewhat of an acquired taste. Nonetheless it is popular, and the *pozoleros* will serve you the drink *al gusto*, that is, with as much or as little sugar as you want. At the northwest side of town (west of the downtown area) is **Tabasco 2000**, a futuristic mall/hotel/office area with an original statue of fishermen.

The new **Insitute of Tourism**, Av de los Ríos y C 13, T316-3633, T346-7246, intuit@tnet.net.mx, is good for maps, advice on excursions throughout Tabasco State. Open 0800-2000 every day, English spoken.

Parque Nacional La Venta

Be sure to take insect repellent for the visit

In 1925 an expedition of archaeologists discovered huge sculptured human and animal figures, urns and altars in almost impenetrable forest at La Venta, once the centre of the ancient Olmec culture, 120 km west of Villahermosa. In the 1950s the monuments were threatened with destruction by the discovery of oil nearby. The poet Carlos Pellicer got them hauled all the way to a woodland area near Villahermosa, now the Parque Nacional de La Venta, also called the Museo Nacional de la Venta, Boulevard Adolfo Ruiz Cortines, T314-1652. The park, with scattered lakes, next to a children's playground, is almost opposite the old airport entrance (west of downtown). There, the 33 exhibits are dispersed in various small clearings. The huge heads, one of them weighing 20 tons, are Olmec, a culture that flourished about 1150-150 BC; this is an experience that should not be missed. There is also an excellent zoo with creatures from the Tabasco jungle: monkeys, alligators, deer, wild pigs and birds. Recommended. ■ *0800-1600, closed Mon, US$2. It takes up to 2 hrs to do the park justice; excellent guides, speak Spanish and English (US$6.65 for 1 hr 10 mins).* . There is nothing to see at the original site of La Venta. Outside the park, on the lakeside is an observation tower, **Mirador de las Aguilas**, with excellent views. Entry free but only for the fit as there are lots of stairs.

Getting there Taxis charge US$1.50. It is possible to take a bus although the routes change often, if in doubt ask at the *ADO* terminal. To walk from *ADO*, left at front entrance, left again at the overpass and straight ahead. Bus Circuito No 1 from outside 2nd class bus terminal goes past Parque La Venta. From Parque Juárez in the city, take a 'Fraccionamiento Carrizal' bus and ask to be let off at Parque Tomás Garrido, of which La Venta is a part.

Excursions **Parque Yumká**, T356-0107, a safari park containing 108 ha of Tabasco's three major habitats – jungle, savannah and lagoon, is a 'zoo without cages' offering walking, trolley and boat tours of each habitat. While the ecological park partly promotes the diversity of the region's flora and fauna, there are also animals from Asia and Africa. It's an easy day trip. ■ *Open 0900-1600, US$2, take the colectivo to the airport and the park is next door. Most tour agencies offer round trips for about US$8.*

Northwest of Villahermosa are the Maya ruins of **Comalcalco**, reached by bus (two a day by *ADO*, 1230 and 1800, US$2.50, or local *Souvellera* bus, US$2, 1 hour over paved roads; *Souvellera* bus leaves from near the bridge where Avenida Universidad crosses Ruiz Cortines, 4-5 blocks north of Central Camionera in Villahermosa). Whichever bus you take, you will need to walk 3 km or take a *colectivo* to the ruins, US$0.50. Otherwise, take a taxi as far as the entrance to the park, US$1, and walk the rest of the way (1 km). The ruins are unique in Mexico because the palaces and pyramids are built of bricks, long and narrow like ancient Roman bricks, and not of stone. ■ *Daily 0900-1600, US$3.* From Comalcalco go to **Paraíso** near the coast; frequent buses run from town to the beach 8 km away. Interesting covered market with good cocoa. **D** *Centro Turístico* is a beach hotel, clean, no hot water, food and drink expensive. In the centre is **E** *Hotel Hidalgo*, clean.

L *Casa Inn*, Madero 418, T358-0102, www.casainn.zl.com.mx central, newly refurbished, some rooms with good views, clean, helpful, with good terrace restaurant overlooking Calle Madero. Nearby parking. **AL** *Cencali*, Juárez y Paseo Tabasco, T315-1999, F315-6600. Excellent breakfast. Highly recommended. **A** *Maya-Tabasco*, Blvd Ruiz Cortines 907, T312-1111, F312-1133. All services, ask for special offers – sometimes as cheap as **C**. **B** *Provincia Express*, Lerdo 303, T314-5376, F314-5442. Recently refurbished and upgraded. Clean, modern with DirecTV and a/c. Good. **C** *Chocos*, Lino Merino 100 and Constitución, T312-9444, F312-9649, near *ADO* terminal. Friendly, clean, a/c.

D *La Paz*, Madero 919, central with fan. **D** *Madero*, Madero 301, T312-0516. Clean, better than many on Madero, some rooms cheaper for 4. **D** *Oriente*, Madero 425, T312-0121. Clean, hot shower, fan, good restaurant. Recommended. **D** *San Miguel*, Lerdo 315, T312-1426. Quiet, clean, shower, fan, very friendly, no windows, run down. **D** *Sofía*, Zaragoza 408, T312-6055. Central, tolerable but overpriced, a/c. **D** *Tabasco*, Lerdo 317, T312-0077. Not too clean, cold water, mosquitoes. Several others on Lerdo. Cheap hotels,

Sleeping
■ *on map*
The price difference between a reasonable and a basic hotel can be negligible, so you might as well go for the former

Try to book hotel rooms in advance, especially during the holiday season (May onwards)

Villahermosa

Sleeping
1 Cencali
2 Madero
3 Provincial Express

0 metres 500
0 yards 500

N

from **E** per person, on Calle Constitución (come out of main entrance of bus terminal, turn right then 1st left and continue for 5 blocks, but it's the red-light district). **E** *Del Río*, Av Constitución 206 and Reforma, on plaza off Madero, T312-6055. Central, tolerable, with fan, noisy bar below.

Eating A good restaurant at *Hotel Madan*, Madero 408. Good breakfast, inexpensive fish dishes, a/c, newspapers, a good and quiet place to escape from the heat. *Aquarius*, Javier Mina 309, near Av Méndez. Vegetarian food, juice bar and health food store. *Blanca Mariposa*, near entrance to Parque La Venta. Recommended. *Bruno's*, Lerdo y 5 de Mayo. Cheap, good, noisy, good atmosphere. *Café El Portal*, Independencia 301, delicious typical food of the region with some exotic regional platter such as empanadas stuffed with *pejelargarto*, a strange-looking freshwater fish with an impressive set of alligator-type jaws and curiously leathery skin. Service is very friendly, artsy atmosphere. *Café La Cabana*, Juárez 303-A, across the way from the Museo de Historia de Tabasco. Has outdoor tables where town elders congregate to debate the day's issues over piping cups of cappuccino. Very entertaining to watch. No meals. *Cafetería La Terraza*, Reforma 304, in *Hotel Miraflores*. Good breakfast. Good coffee, quiet, pleasant. *El Café de la Calle Juárez*, Juárez 513, indoor/outdoor café. Great for breakfast, good coffee, a new menu every month. Outdoor tables are great for people watching. *El Matador*, Av. César Sandino No 101a, local meat dishes, good value. *El Torito Valenzuela*, next to *Hotel Madero*. Mexican specialities, excellent and inexpensive. Highly recommended. *Los Tulipanes*, Malecón, south of Paseao Tabasco, typical food. Recommended. *Rodizio do Brasil*, Parque la Choca, Stand Grandero, speciality *espadas*, good Brasilian food. *Zona Luz*, Aldama 615. Typical Mexican/Tabasqueña food. Cheap, quaint, airy with a charming colonial feel about it.

Bars & discos *Dasha*, Tabasco 2000 complex, Expensive nightclub. Suggested you leave the sandals behind and dress up to the nines. Good dancing. *Ku Hardrock*, corner of Malecón and Sandino. Varied music, less strict on clothing.

Festivals *Ash Wednesday* is celebrated from 1500 to dusk by the throwing of water in balloon bombs and buckets at anyone who happens to be on the street – get wet!

Transport **Local** Taxis run on a zone basis, most fares downtown cost from US$1.30 to US$1.80. **Car hire** *Hertz* car rental is available from the airport. *Agrisa*, M Ocampo esq Paseo Tabasco y Malecón, T312-9184, good prices, eg US$40 per day including taxes and insurance, but it is expensive to return the car to another city.

Air Airport Carlos R Pérez (VSA), 18 km from town. Flights to Cancún, Ciudad del Carmen, Havana (Cuba), Houston (Texas), Mérida, Mexico City, Monterrey, Oaxaca, San José (Costa Rica), Tampico, Tuxtla Gutiérrez and Veracruz. VW bus to town US$3 each, taxi US$9.50 for 2.

Road If arriving with a trailer you must contact the tourist offices before arrival to arrange facilities in Parque Tabasco.

Reserve your seat as soon as you can; buses to Mexico City are often booked up well in advance

Buses 1st class, *ADO* bus terminal is on Javier Mina between Méndez and Lino Merino, 12 blocks north of centre, computerized booking system. A taxi to the *ADO* terminal costs US$1.30. Left luggage at *ADO* terminal, 0700-2300, US$0.30 per piece per hr, often closed. Alternatively, go to Sra Ana in minute restaurant/shop at Pedro Fuentes 817, 100 m from *ADO*, reliable, open till 2000, small charge made, or upstairs at 203 Javier Mina, opposite *ADO*, US$0.10 per piece per hr. Other private luggage depositories by the bus station also make a small charge. The Central Camionera 2nd class bus station is on Avenida Ruiz Cortines, near roundabout with fisherman statue, 1 block east of Javier Mina, opposite Castillo, 4 blocks north of *ADO* (ie 16 from centre); usually in disarray and it is difficult to get a ticket.

Several 1st class buses to **Mexico City**, 12 hrs, US$30, direct bus leaves 1815 (*Cristóbal Colón*) or 1650 (*ADO*) then frequent through the night, expect to wait a few hours for Mexico City buses and at least 30 mins in the ticket queue.

Catazajá: 1½ hrs, US$4; **Chetumal**: 10 a day, 10 hrs, US$16, but the road is now in a very bad state and it can take much longer, 4 buses, erratic service; **Campeche**: 6 hrs, US$16.50, reservation required; **Mérida**: many daily, 8-10 hrs, US$19.50; if coming from Oaxaca to make a connection for Mérida, be prepared for long queues as most buses pass through en route from México City; **Oaxaca**: via Coatzacoalcos and Tehuantepec, with *Cristóbal Colón* from *ADO* terminal at 1930 and 2130, 1st class, stops at about 7 places, US$27.50; **Palenque**: 8 a day from the *ADO* terminal, 2½ hrs, US$2.50 to US$4.60; **Puebla**: *ADO* 'GL' *plus* service via autopista, US$30, 1st class US$25.50; **San Andrés Tuxtla**: 6 hrs, US$12.50; **San Cristóbal de las Casas**: every couple of rs, 6 hrs, US$9; also 2nd class bus with 1 change at Tuxtla, leaves 0800, arrives 2100, fine scenery but treacherous road; **Tapachula**: 14 hrs, US$20; **Veracruz**: many a day with *ADO*, 7 hrs, US$36 *Primera Plus*; **Xalapa**: with *ADO*, 3 a day, 10 hrs.

To **Emiliano Zapata** and **Tenosique** (for Río San Pedro crossing into Guatemala, see page 460): buses 0700, 0800, 1330, 3-4 hrs.

Airline offices *Aerocaribe*, Javier Mina 301-A, T314-3202. *AeroMéxico* office, Periférico Carlos Pellicer 511, T312-6991. *Aviacsa*, T316-5736. *Mexicana*, Av Madero 109, or Desarrollo Urbano Tabasco 2000, T316-3132. **Banks** *Banco Internacional*, Suárez and Lerdo, changes TCs at good rates. *Banamex*, Madero and Reforma, open from 0900-1700, closed at weekends. *American Express*, Turismo Nieves, Sarlat 202, T314-1818. **Communications** Internet: *C@fe internet*, Aldama 404-C, lobby of the *Hotel Howard Johnson*. US$1.50/hr. Many others scattered around town. **Post office**: on Ignacio in the centre. *DHL*, parcel courier service, Paseo Tabasco. **Cultural centres** *El Jaguar Despertado*, Saenz 117, T314-1244, forum for artists and local Villahermosino intellectuals. Hosts concerts, art exhibitions and book presentations. *Centro Cultural*, Corner of Madero and Zaragoza, T312-5473. Presentations of local artists and photographers. Live music, workshops in literature, local handicrafts and musical interpretation, among others. **Tour operators** *Turismo Nieves*, Sarlat 202, T314-1888, www.turismonieves.com.mx Offers guided trips to ruins of Comalcalco, Cocona, and transportation to Parque Yumká. English speaking, very friendly, recommended.

Directory

South of Villahermosa

The Maya ruins at Palenque (see page 450), southeast of Villahermosa, are reached by turning off the inland Route 186, at **Catazajá**, 117 km from Villahermosa. There are no petrol stations until Catazajá; if you need fuel there's a PEMEX in **Macuspana**. Municipal **fiesta** 15-16 August.

Sleeping: **D** *América*. Basic, clean, comfortable, safe parking, and **D** *Carisma*, Calle Hidalgo 209. T362-1263. Palenque is 26 km away on a good but winding paved road (minibus US$1.15, 30 mins, taxi US$10).

Twenty kilometres southwest of Villahermosa via Cárdenas is the hot and dirty town of **Huimanguillo** (basic hotel *El Carmen*). Continuing up into the Sierra de Huimanguillo the road reaches Malpasito (taxi US$33 from Huimanguillo) where there is a lodge, *El Pava* (reservations at *Hotel El Carmen*). Beyond are the Raudales de Malpaso (cataracts) on Presa Netzahualcóyotl (accommodation, **E**, at *ADO* bus station, bus service once a day from Huimanguillo). There is a regular launch across the dam (0600, 0700, 0900, 1100 1300, 1500) to Apic-Pac (see page 431) where you can take a pick-up (2½ hours, bumpy road) to Ocozocuautla and on to Tuxtla Gutiérrez (see page 430).

South of Villahermosa on Route 195 this is a nice, clean little town with several hotels and beautiful surroundings. The square is pleasant, and you can swim in the river or in the sulphur pool. Also in Teapa are the **Grutas de Cocona**, which house a stunning array of stalagmites and beautiful displays of colour. The caves are approximately ½ km deep and a fresh and inviting river runs through them. There is a restaurant and campsite in the area. Most tour companies offer trips to the area. **Tapijulapa**, on the Chiapas border, can be visited from Teapa for more beautiful views.

Teapa
Phone code: 932
Colour map 4, grid B1

Tabasco and Chiapas

Sleeping and eating C *Quintero*, Eduardo R Bastar 108, T322-0045, behind Zócalo. A/c, fan, clean, friendly, enthusiastic restaurant. **D** Simple hotel in grounds of *El Azufre*, entry to pool included, no restaurant. **D** *Jardín*, at the top of the square. Friendly. Recommended. Good restaurant on main square, *El Mirador*. *Familiar*, main street 125. Friendly, not cheap but filling. Recommended.

Transport Buses: there are buses between Teapa and Villahermosa, 50 km, 1 hr, US$2.20. Also to Chiapa de Corzo at 0730, through lovely, mountainous landscape (see page 434).

Pichucalco
Phone code: 932
Colour map 4, grid B1

Southwest of Teapa on Route 195 is Pichucalco, an affluent town with a lively and safe atmosphere. The Zócalo throngs in the evening with people on after-dinner *paseos*. Buses hourly to Villahermosa, US$4.

Sleeping and eating There are many good restaurants and bars. **D** *Hotel La Loma*, Francisco Contreras 51, T323-0052. With bath, a/c, or fan, ample parking, clean (opposite is a cheaper *posada* with resident monkey). **E** *Hotel México*, on left turn from bus station. With bath, fan, clean but musty. *Vila*, on Plaza. **D** *Jardín*, noisy.

South of Pichucalco on Highway 195 on the way to Tuxtla Gutiérrez, is **Bochil**, an idyllic stopover (**D** *Hotel/Restaurant María Isabel*, 1 Avenida Sur Pte 44, basic but nice, delicious simple food). Highway 195 is fully paved, but narrow and winding with landslides and washouts in the rainy season, high altitudes, beautiful scenery.

Chiapas Heartland

Although in some ways the Chiapas Heartland has fallen victim to the progress bug, it nevertheless seems impervious to the intrusion of outsiders, most of whom are eager to experience a step back in time, or perhaps a time warp. The Lost World feeling is created indigenous inhabitants and those from the outlying villages who make everything seem timeless. Many visitors will know something about the dreadful treatment they have suffered over centuries, the fundamental cause of the rebellion on 1 January 1994, which led to the occupation of San Cristóbal by the revolutionaries. What the visitor is unprepared for is the great dignity demonstrated by these people who resist the intrusions of outsiders. The result of clinging to ancient traditions in dress, crafts, food, religious practice, festivals and especially languages. Following the EZLN uprising in early 1994, it is advisable to check on political conditions in Chiapas state before travelling in the area.

Tuxtla Gutiérrez

Phone code: 961
Colour map 4, grid B1
Population: 467,000
Altitude: 522 m

The capital of Chiapas, Tuxtla Gutiérrez is a busy, shabby city with a couple of points of interest to the tourist. The main sights are a long way from the centre and too far to walk, the gem being the zoo. The feast of the Virgen de Guadalupe is celebrated on 12 December.

To find your way around the complicated street-naming system, see Transport page 432

The **tourist office** is at Boulevard Belisario Domínguez 950, Plaza Instituciones, T602-5127, F602-5345. ■ *Mon-Fri 0900-2100, Sat 0900-2000, Sun 0900-1500 (take a colectivo from the junction of Avenida Central and Calle 2 Oriente).* There is also an office in the *ADO* bus terminal on Calle 2 Poniente Norte and Avenida 2 Norte Poniente, which has more or less the same limited information as the main office. The local tourism website is at **www.turismochiapas.gob.mx**

Sights

In the Parque Madero at the east end of town (Calzada de los Hombres Ilustres) is the **Museo Regional de Chiapas** with a fine collection of Mayan artefacts, an auditorium and a library. ■ *Tue-Sun, 0900-1600, US$3.30.* Nearby is the **Jardín Botánico** (botanical garden). ■ *Tue-Sun, 0900-1600, free.* Also in this park is the **Teatro de la Ciudad**.

There is a superb **zoo** some 3 km south of town up a long hill. It was founded by Dr Miguel Alvarez del Toro, who died in 1996. His philosophy was to provide a free zoo for the children and indigenous people of the area. The zoo has always been free, but the new administration proposes a small charge for tourists. At the moment donations are welcome, and are recommended to help keep up the ecological work being carried out. All the animals are regional to Chiapas, except for a few species from other parts of Mexico. The zoo is very large and many of the animals are in open areas, with plenty of room to run about. Monkeys are not in cages, but in areas of trees pruned back so they cannot jump out of the enclosure. Some birds wander along the paths among the visitors. The zoo makes for a very pleasant and educational afternoon. Recommended. Take mosquito repellent. ■ *Tue-Sun 0830-1730; in Spanish only, the donations box is in front of the educational centre on the right as you enter the zoo. Getting there: colectivos to 'Zoológico' and 'Cerro Hueco' from Mercado, Calle 1a Ote Sur y 7 Sur Ote, pass the entrance every 20 mins; taxi US$2.50-3.00 from centre. Town buses charge US$0.20. When returning, catch the bus from the same side you were dropped off as it continues up the hill to the end of the line where it fills up for the return journey.*

Excursions

Two vast artificial lakes made by dams are worth visiting: **La Angostura**, southeast of Tuxtla; and the **Presa Netzahualcóyotl**, or **Malpaso**, 77 km northwest of the city. You can reach the latter by taking two buses from Tuxtla: the first is for Ozozocoautla; *colectivos* leave all day from Calle 4 Poniente between Avenida 3 y 2 Sur. The second bus goes to Apic-Pac near the lake. Information from the tourist office. Malpaso can also be visited from Huimanguillo (see page 429).

Route 190 continues beyond Ozozocoautla (airport for Tuxtla. **D** *Posada San Pedro*, noisy, not recommended) to Cintalapa (**D** *Hotel Leos*, recommended and restaurant. **E** hotel on main street, clean with bath and fan) whence there is a steep climb up an escarpment. Thirty kilometres before Cintalapa a gravel road leads north (last section very rough) to the beautiful waterfall in **El Aguacero National Park** (small sign), which falls several hundred feet down the side of the Río La Venta canyon. There is a small car park at the lip of the canyon; 798 steps lead down to the river and the base of the waterfall. Good camping but no facilities.

Tuxtla Gutiérrez

Sleeping
■ *on map*

There is plenty of budget accommodation a short walk from the 1st class ADO terminal. Exit from the main entrance, turn left, past the hotels *Santo Domingo* and *María Teresa* (neither recommended) and head east along Av 2 Nte Ote; go under the underpass (well-policed) beneath the plaza; as soon as you emerge, there are a number of cheap *posadas* along the continuation of the street.

AL *Bonampak*, Blvd Belisario Domínguez 180, T602-5916, F602-5914, west end of town, hotbonam@prodigy.net.mx Social centre of the city, clean, noisy at night, expensive restaurant. **AL** *Flamboyant*, Blvd Belisario Domínguez 1081, T615-0888, F615-0087. Comfortable with good swimming pool. **B-C** *Palace Inn*, Blvd Belisario Domínguez, 4 km from centre, T615-0574, F615-1042. Generally recommended, lovely garden, pool, noisy videobar. **C** *Regional San Marcos*, 1 Sur y 2 Ote Sur 176, T613-1940. Cheaper without TV, close to Zócalo, bath, fan or a/c, clean. **C** *Conquistador*, Libramiento

Sleeping
1 Casa Blanca
2 Catedral
3 Estrella
4 La Posada
5 María Dolores
6 María Teresa & Santo Domingo
7 Mar-Inn
8 Plaza Chiapas
9 Regional San Marcos

Tabasco and Chiapas

Sur Pte, Km 2 (towards the zoo), T613-0820. **C** *Casa Blanca*, Av 2 Nte Ote, near Plaza Chiapas, T611-0305. OK. **C** *Catedral*, 1 Nte Ote y 3 Ote Nte, T613-0824. Not very friendly, but has large indoor car park.

D *Plaza Chiapas*, Av 2 Nte Ote y 2 Ote Nte, T613-8365. Clean, with fan and hot shower, most rooms have balconies, good value, good restaurant, enclosed car park. Recommended. **D** *Mar-Inn*, Av 2 Nte Ote 347, T612-5783. Pleasant, clean. Opposite *Cristóbal Colón* bus station is **D** *María Teresa*, 2 Nte Pte 259-B, T613-0102. **D** *Estrella*, 2 Ote Nte 322, T612-3827. With bath, friendly, clean, quiet, comfy, a bit run down but safe, free drinking water. Recommended. **E** *La Posada*, Av 1 Sur Ote y 5 Ote Sur, T612-6827. With or without bath, laundry facilities, friendly. **E** *María Dolores*, 2 Ote Nte 304, between Av 2 y Av 3 Nte Ote, T612-3683. Hot water only between 0600 and 1000. **E** *Posada de Chiapas* , 2 Sur Pte 243, T612-3354. Small rooms with bath, TV, friendly. **E** *Santo Domingo*, opposite *ADO* bus terminal, with shower, good if you arrive late, but noisy and very basic.

F *Posada del Sol*, 3 Pte Nte, 1 block from *Cristóbal Colón* buses. With hot shower and fan, good service, good value and basic, mixed reports. **F** *Posada Maya*, 4 Pte Sur 322. Fan, clean. Recommended. *Posada Muñiz*, 2 Sur Ote 245, near 2nd class bus station. Not recommended but useful for early departures. **F** *Tuxtleca*, Av 2 Nte Ote, near *Casa Blanca*. One of the cheapest in town, OK if a bit scruffy.

Motels **C** *El Sumidero*, Panamericana Km 1,093, on left as you enter town from east. A/c, comfortable, but much passing trade. **C** *La Hacienda*, trailer-park-hotel, Belisario Domínguez 1197 (west end of town on Route 190), T615-0849.

Camping US$7-8 per tent, 4 spaces with hook-up, hot showers, restaurant, minipool, US$13.50 for car and 2 people, a bit noisy and not easily accessible for RVs over 6 m, owner speaks English.

Eating *Alameda*, Av 1 Nte 133, near plaza. Good breakfast. *Bing*, 1 Sur Pte 1480. Excellent ice-cream; many others. Coffee shop below *Hotel Avenida*, Av Central Pte 224. Serves excellent coffee. *Café Avenida*, on Av Central just past *Aerocaribe* office. There are several cheap taco places on Calle 2 Ote Nte between 2 Nte and Av Central. Good coffee shop, does cappuccino and espresso. Popular with locals. *Café Mesón Manolo*, Av Central Pte 238. Good value, reasonably priced. *Cantón*, 2 Nte Pte y 6 Pte Nte. Chinese, open 1300-2300. *El Chato*, opposite *Hotel San Marcos*. One of the few touristy places, *huaraches*, grilled meat, OK, moderate prices. *La Parcela*, 2 Ote Sur, near *Hotel Plaza Chiapas*. Good, cheap, good breakfasts. Recommended. *Las Delicias*, 2 Nte Pte between Central and 1 Nte Pte, close to *Cristóbal Colón* terminal. Good breakfasts and snacks. *Las Pichanchas*. Pretty courtyard, typical food, dancing from Chiapas with *marimba* music between 1400-1700 and 2000-2300, on Av Central Ote 857. Worth trying. *Los Arcos*, Real de Guadalupe 67. Good international food. *Los Gallos*, Av 2 Nte Pte, 20 m from *Cristóbal Colón* terminal. Open 0700-2400, good and cheap. *Maryen*, 2 Ote Nte between 1 Nte and Av Central. Good, cheap tacos. *Mina*, Av Central Ote 525, near bus station. Good cheap *comida*. *Parrilla La Cabaña*, 2 Ote Nte 250. Excellent tacos, very clean. *Pizzería San Marco*, behind cathedral. Good. Nah Yaxal, 6 Pte Nte, just off Av Central Pte. Vegetarian, modern design, popular with students. *Restaurant Imperial*, Av Central Nte. Recommended. *Tuxtla*, Av 2 Nte Pte y Central, near plaza. Good *comida corrida* and fruit salad. Recommended.

Transport **Local** The street system here is as follows: Avenidas run from east to west, Calles from north to south. The Avenidas are named according to whether they are north (Norte) or south (Sur) of the Avenida Central and change their names if they are east (Oriente) or west (Poniente) of the Calle Central. The number before Avenida or Calle means the distance from the Centre measured in blocks. You know whether it's an Avenida or a Calle by the order of the address: Avenidas have their number, then Sur or Norte followed by east or west; Calles have the east or west position first. For example, 1 Norte Oriente is the eastern part of the first avenue north of Avenida Central; 2 Oriente Norte is the north part of the second street west of Calle Central. It all sounds very complicated, but as long as you check map and road signs very carefully, it is not difficult to navigate your way around the city.

Taxis: mostly VW beetles, easy to flag down anywhere. US$2 within the centre, US$2.50-3 to the zoo, US$5 to Chiapa de Corzo (for Sumidero Canyon), frequent local buses, US$0.50.

Long distance   Air: Terán airport is the main one. It is a military airport converted for civilian use. It has no facilities for bad weather, so if there is fog, flights are re-routed to Llano San Juan, further out of town. Taxi to Terán US$3. Flights to **Hualtulco**, **Mérida**, **Mexico City**, **Oaxaca**, **Palenque**, **San Cristóbal de las Casas**, **Tapachula**, **Veracruz** and **Villahermosa**.

Buses: *Cristóbal Colón* 1st class bus terminal is at Av 2 Nte Pte 268 (opposite *UNO* and *Maya de Oro*), **Left luggage** at *Juguería* opposite bus station, will guard bag for US$0.50, a better service at *Maya de Oro* bus station, opposite the *ADO* (San Cristóbal) terminal, US$0.50 a bag and under lock and key.
    Cancún: 1230, US$42. **Córdoba**: *ADO*, 1725, 1900, *Cristóbal Colón* 2130, US$38. To **Chetumal**: 1430, US$44. **Ciudad Cuauhtémoc**: towards Guatemala, 7 a day, 0500-2230, including Altos, US$10. **Comitán**: 0500 then each hr to 1900 and 1 at 2300, Altos, US$5.80. **Mexico City**: 4 a day, 16 hrs, US$64, 1st class, US$42, 2nd class. **Villahermosa**: at 1500, 2300, 8½ hrs, US$10.30, *Altos de Chiapas* 6 a day between 0700 and 2345. **Mérida**: change at Villahermosa if no direct service at 1530 (*Altos*), US$26. The scenery between Tuxtla and Mérida is very fine, and the road provides the best route between Chiapas and the Yucatán. **Oaxaca**: 1130, 1915, 10 hrs, US$24 1st class, US$18 2nd class. **Palenque**: Altos, 6 a day, 0500-2300, 7 hrs, US$9.40, other buses pass through Palenque. **Pochutla**: at 0935 and 2015, 10 hrs, US$24. **Puebla**: *ADO* US$42, departs 1900, *Cristóbal Colón* 4/day pm, *UNO* US$65, 14 hrs. *Oaxaca Pacífico* buses to **Salina Cruz**: from 1st class bus terminal. Take travel sickness tablets for Tuxtla-Oaxaca road if you suffer from queasiness. Frequent buses 0500-2300 to **San Cristóbal de las Casas**: 2 hrs, US$3.50 (2nd class US$3 superb mountain journey; *colectivos* from near Av 2 Ote Sur y 2 Sur Ote do the journey for US$3. **Tapachula**: 16 a day; there are more 1st class than 2nd class to the Talismán bridge (1st class is less crowded), US$16. **Tonalá**: 1615, US$13. **Tulum**: 1230, US$51. **Veracruz**: 1930, US$34.

Airlines *Aviacsa*, Av Central Pte 1144, T612-6880, F612-7086, 40 mins. **Banks** *Bancomer* Av Central Pte y 2 Pte Nte, for Visa and TCs, open 0900-1500. *Banco Bital (Banco Internacional)*, opens Mon-Sat 0800, good rates and service. For cheques and cash at 1 Sur Pte 350, near Zócalo. There are ATMs in various branches of Farmacia del Ahorro, all over the city. **Communications Internet**: free at library of Universidad Autónoma de Chiapas, Route 190, 6 km from centre. *Compucentro*, 1 Nte Pte 675, upstairs. US$1 per hour. Various other internet cafés springing up, costing about US$1/hr. **Post office**: on main square. **Telephone**: international phone calls can be made from 1 Nte, 2 Ote, directly behind post office, 0800-1500, 1700-2100 (1700-2000 Sun). **Tour operators** *Viajes Miramar*, in *Posada del Rey*, 1 Ote Nte 310, T612-3983, F613-0465, viajesmiramar@ infosel.net.mx Good, efficient service for national flight bookings. *Viajes Kali*, Av Central Ote 507 esq 4 Ote, T/F611-3175, heugenia@chis1.telmex.net.mx Tours to Sumidero Canyon with English/French/ Italian-speaking guide, also books national flights. *Carolina Tours*, Sr José Narváez Valencia (manager), Av Central Pte 1138, T612-4281; reliable, recommended; also coffee shop at Av Central Pte 230. **Useful addresses** Immigration Office, 1 Ote Nte.

Directory

Sumidero Canyon

An excellent paved road through spectacular scenery leads to the rim of the 1,000-m deep Sumidero canyon, now a national park. Indian warriors, unable to endure the Spanish conquest, hurled themselves into the canyon rather than submit. ■ *0600-1800*. Camping is permitted outside the gate (bus US$3; *colectivo* from San Cristóbal de las Casas bus terminal, US$2.50; taxi fare US$25 return; try to get a group together and negotiate with a combi driver to visit the viewpoints on the road into the canyon, US$15 per vehicle, leave from 1 Nte Ote). To get to the first viewpoint only, take *colectivo* marked 'Km 4', get out at the end and walk about 3 km up the road. With your own car, you can drive up to the last *mirador* (restaurant), a 2-3 hour trip, 20 km east of the city. At Cahuaré, 10 km in the direction of Chiapa de Corzo, it is possible to park by the river. If going by bus, US$1.50 each way, get out just past the large bridge on the Chiapa de Corzo road. Boat tours

Especially recommended at sunset

Hardship for Chiapas Indians

For the visitor to Chiapas, the state's wonders are many: lush tropical jungle, quaint colonial villages, or the modern, prosperous capital, Tuxtla Gutiérrez. However, the peacefulness masks the troubles of the state's indigenous peoples. Their plight was splashed across the world's press with the Zapatista uprising of January 1994 and has remained a photogenic story ever since (see Recent Politics, page 545). Chiapas, the southernmost state and one of Mexico's poorest, appears much like its neighbour, Guatemala, and shares many of the same problems. Subsistence has been a way of life for centuries, illiteracy and infant mortality are high, particularly among those who have retained their languages and traditions, shunning the Spanish culture. The Chiapas government estimates that nearly one million Indians live in the state, descendants of the great Maya civilization of 250-900 AD. The Chiapas Indians of today are not a monolith; they are spread out across the state, they do not speak the same language, nor dress alike, have the same customs nor the same types of tribal government.

The Tzotziles and Tzeltales total about 626,000 and live mainly on the plateau and the slopes of the high altitude zones. The Choles number 110,000 and live in the towns of Tila, Tumbalá, Salto de Agua, Sabanilla and Yajalón. The 87,000 Zoques live near the volatile Chichonal volcano. The 66,000 Tojolabales live in Margaritas, Comitán, La Independencia, La

Trinitaria and part of Altamirano. On the high mountains and slopes of the Sierra Madre are the 23,000 Mames and the 12,000 Mochós and Kakchikeles. The Lacandones, named after the rainforest they occupy, number only 500 today. Along the border with Guatemala are 21,500 Chujes, Kanjobales and Jacaltecos, although that number includes some refugees still there from the Guatemalan conflict, which ended in a negotiated peace in late 1996.

A minority of the Indians speak Spanish, particularly in the Sierra Madre region and among the Zoques. Many have dropped their típica clothing. Customary positions of authority along with stewardships and standard bearers have been dropped from tribal governance, but medicine men continue to practise. They still celebrate their festivals in ways unique to them and they think about their ancestors as they have for centuries. Many now live in the large cities, some even working for the government, but those who remain in el campo are, for the most part, poor. They get by, eating tortillas with salt, some vegetables and occasionally beans. Many who leave for the city end up as domestic servants, labourers or street pedlars. The scarcity of land for the indigenous has been a political issue for many decades and limited land reform merely postponed the crisis that eventually erupted in the 1990s, and continues to cause President Fox considerable difficulties.

start from below this bridge, where there is also a car park and restaurant serving good seafood. Boat trip into the Sumidero Canyon costs US$6.50 per person for 2 hours; boats leave when full. US$65 to hire boat for private group. Take a sweater; the boats go very fast. From Tuxtla: Taxi to all *miradores* US$18, first *mirador* only US$10. Or taxi to Chiapa de Corzo, US$5, then a *colectivo* boat from there. A licensed taxi service from Tuxtla to the Canyon can be booked at Avenida 1 Sur Pte 1203, T613-7033.

Tours from San Cristóbal including boat trip costs US$22-25. It is easier to find people to make up numbers in Chiapa de Corzo than in Cahuaré, as the former is a livelier place with more restaurants, launches and other facilities.

Chiapa de Corzo
Phone code: 961
Colour map 4, grid B1
Population: 60,000
Altitude: 456 m

Fifteen kilometres on, a colonial town on a bluff overlooking the Grijalva River, is more interesting than Tuxtla: see a fine 16th-century crown-shaped fountain; the 16th-century church of Santo Domingo whose engraved altar is of solid silver; and famous craftsmen in gold, jewellery and lacquer work who travel the fairs. Chiapa de Corzo was a pre-classic and proto-classic Maya site and shares features with early Maya sites in Guatemala; the ruins are behind the Nestlé plant, and some unrestored mounds are on private property in a field near modern houses. There are 1½- and 2-hour boat trips along the river to spot crocodiles, turtles, monkeys and hummingbirds, cost US$50 or US$60 for 12 passengers; wait by water's edge, boats soon fill up.

Sleeping and eating B *La Ceiba*, T616-0773. With fan, a/c extra, bath, restaurant, pool. Recommended. **D** *Hotel Los Angeles*, on Plaza, T616-0048. Often full, warm shower, fan, beautiful rooms, indoor parking. Good value. **Shopping** Painted and lacquered vessels made of pumpkins are a local speciality.

Jardín Turístico on main plaza, open until 2000 (*plato jardín* is a selection of different regional dishes). Good seafood restaurants by the riverside. Along the pier there are many restaurants, including the *Verónica*. Good food, cheap, slow service. The adventurous might want to try the local non-alcoholic drink *pozole*, a corn drink with *cacao* and *pinole*. Best version is the *pozole negra*, with a distinctive chocolate flavour, choose carefully as sometimes purified water is not used. **Bars** Plaza filled with bars playing jukeboxes.

Festivals The fiestas here are outstanding; they reach their climax on **20-23 Jan** (in honour of San Sebastián) with a pageant on the river. But there are daylight fiestas, *Los Parachicos*, on **15**, **17** and **20 Jan**, and the *Chunta Fiestas*, at night, from **9-23 Jan**. The *musical parade* is on **19 Jan**. There is another fiesta in early Feb and *San Marcos* festival on **25 Apr**, with various *espectáculos*.

Transport Buses from Tuxtla Gutiérrez, Calle 3 Ote Sur, US$0.50, frequent; several buses a day (1 hr) to **San Cristóbal de las Casas**, 2nd class, US$3.50. *Cristóbal Colón* to **Mexico City**, 1815, US$36.50.

The waterfall at the **Cueva de El Chorreadero** is well worth a detour of 1 km (one restaurant here, but better to take your own food). The road to the cave is 10 km past Chiapa de Corzo, a few kilometres after you start the climb up into the mountains to get to San Cristóbal. Camping is possible but there are no facilities; take a torch to the cave.

Thirty-five kilometres east of Tuxtla, just past Chiapa de Corzo, a road runs north, 294 km, to Villahermosa via Pichucalco (see page 430), paved all the way. If driving to Villahermosa, allow at least 5 hours for the endless curves and hairpins down from the mountains, a very scenic route nevertheless.

San Cristóbal de las Casas

One of the most beautiful towns in Mexico, San Cristóbal de las Casas is stunningly located in the fertile Jovel Valley, with the mountains of Huitepec to the west and Tzontehuitz to the east. The city is a charming blend of colonial architecture and indigenous culture, laid out in the colonial period with 21 indigenous barrios on the city's perimeter, which were later integrated into the totally mestizo city that existed by the 18th century. The Indians now form an important part of San Cristóbal's atmosphere, many of them earning a living by selling handicrafts in the town's two markets. The centre is rich in architectural variety, with excellent examples of baroque, neo-classical and plateresque, a Mexican style characterized by the intricate moulding of façades, resembling the work of silversmiths, hence the name, which means 'like a silversmith's'.

Phone code: 967
Colour map 4, grid B1
Population: 116,729
Altitude: 2,110 m

For trips to the nearby villages, see page 445

Tabasco and Chiapas

Ins and outs

San Cristóbal's new airport is 15 km from town, mostly for local charter flights. There is a 1st class bus terminal that services destinations all over Mexico, and two 2nd class terminals for local buses to destinations within Chiapas and to the Guatemalan border (for details, see Transport page 443). Those travelling to Palenque by car can use the new 210 km paved road, which has fine views (avoid night-time journeys because of armed robberies). **Getting there**

Getting around   Most places are within walking distance of each other although taxis are available in the town and to the nearby villages; the cheaper *colectivos* run on fixed routes only.

Climate   Due to its altitude, San Cristóbal has a pleasantly mild climate compared to the hotter Chiapas towns such as Palenque and Tuxtla. During Jun, Jul and Aug, it is warm and sunny in the morning, while in the afternoon it tends to rain, with a sharp drop in temperature. Warm, waterproof clothes are needed, though the heavy rains conveniently stop in the evening, when you can enjoy San Cristóbal's many cheap restaurants and friendly bars and cafés.

Tourist office   Tourist offices at the government offices, Hidalgo 1, T678-6570. Very helpful with all types of information, good maps provided, usually someone there who speaks English. ■ *Mon-Sat 0800-2000, Sun 0900-1400*. There is a municipal office on the main plaza, in the Palacio Municipal, T678-0665. Ask here for accommodation in private houses. Information on eco-tours to Huitepec nature reserve. Good free map of town and surroundings. A new tourist trolley *El Coleta* at the Mercado de Dulces y Artesanías, Av Insurgentes 24, gives a 1-hr city tour visiting the main sights. Good for orientation. ■ *Hourly from 1000-1300 and 1600-1900*.

Sights

The main square is Plaza 31 de Marzo, with a gazebo built during the era of Porfirio Díaz

In front of the plaza is the neo-classical **Palacio Municipal**, built in 1885. A few steps away is the **Catedral de San Cristóbal**, built in the 16th century, painted in ochre, brown and white, with a baroque pulpit added in the 17th century. Adjacent to the cathedral is the church of **San Nicolás**, which houses the historical archives of the diocese. The building dates from 1613, and is believed to be the only church in Mexico to preserve its original design in the architectural style of indigenous people's churches. Just off the plaza, at the beginning of Insurgentes, is the former **Casa de la Sirena**, now the *Hotel Santa Clara*. Built at the end of the 16th century, this is a rare example of colonial residential architecture in the plateresque style. The interior has the four classic corridors of renaissance constructions. Heading off the plaza in the opposite direction, going north up 20 de Noviembre, you reach the **Church and Ex-Convento de Santo Domingo**. By far the most dramatic building in the city, it features an elaborate baroque façade in moulded mortar, especially beautiful when viewed in the late afternoon sun, which picks out the ornate mouldings with salmon pink hues. The church's altarpieces are covered in gold leaf, and the pulpit is intricately carved in a style peculiar to Mexico, known as churrigueresque, even more elaborate than the baroque style of Europe. Outside the market is the main handicraft market, with dozens of stalls selling traditional textiles, handmade dolls, wooden toys and jewellery. To the west of the centre, and up a strenuous flight of steps, is the **Templo del Cerrito**, a small church with fine views of the city and the surrounding mountains. The church is so-called (*cerrito* meaning 'small hill') because it is set on an isolated, tree-covered hill. At the other end of the city, to the east, is another little church on a hill, the **Templo de Guadalupe**. This church is used by the indigenous people of the barrio de Guadalupe, the nearest to the centre of the 21 such indigenous neighbourhoods. Each neighbourhood is characterised by the dress of the Indians, depending on which indigenous group they belong to, and by the handicrafts produced by them. Guadalupe is the barrio of candle makers, saddle makers, and wooden toy makers. The other barrios, such as Mexicanos, the oldest in the city, are further afield and not recommended for unguided visits. The cultural centre **Na Bolom** (see Museums) is very helpful for information on all aspects of indigenous culture.

Museums   The **Museo de Los Altos** (Anthropological Museum) contains a history of San Cristóbal, with an emphasis on the plight of the indigenous people, as well as a good selection of locally produced textiles. There is a small library with books on Chiapas at the back. Calzada Lázaro Cárdenas, next to Santo Domingo church. ■ *Tue-Sun 1000-1700. US$3, free on Sun and bank holidays.*

Na Bolom Museum and Cultural Centre, Vicente Guerrero 33, T678-1418, is situated in a neo-classical mansion dating from 1891. Na Bolom was founded in 1951 by the Danish archaeologist Frans Blom and his wife, the Swiss photographer Gertrudis Duby. After the death of Frans Blom in 1963, Na Bolom became a study centre for the universities of Harvard and Stanford, while Gertrudis Duby continued campaigning for the conservation of the Lacandón area. She died in 1993, aged 92, after which the centre has continued to function as a non-profit making organization dedicated to conserving the Chiapan environment and helping the Lacandón Indians. The photographic archives in the museum contain a detailed visual history of 50 years of daily life of the Maya people with beautifully displayed artefacts, pictures of Lacondón Indians, and information about their present way of life. There are five galleries with collections of pre-Columbian Maya art and colonial religious paintings. There is a good library. A shop sells products made by the indigenous people helped by the centre. ■ *Guided tours Tue-Sun, 1130 in Spanish, 1630 in English. US$2.50 including video, 1½ hrs. Recommended. You cannot see the museum on your own.   Library opens Mon-Fri 0930-1330, 1630-1900. www.ecosur.mx/nabolom/*

Na Bolom run various projects, entirely staffed by volunteers. Prospective volunteers spend a minimum of three months, maximum six, at the centre. They must have skills that can be useful to the projects, such as anthropology, organic gardening, or multi-linguists. Volunteers are given help with accommodation and a daily food allowance. Contact Allison Motto for further information. Na Bolom also has 12 rooms to rent in the **B** range (see Sleeping). They run tours (Tuesday-Sunday) to San Juan Chamula and San Lorenzo Zinacantán. US$10 per person, good guides, thorough explanations, respectful to indigenous locals. Contact details for Na Bolom, Avenida Vicente Guerrero 33, CP 29220, San Cristóbal de las Casas, Chiapas, T/F678-1418, www.ecosur.mx/nabolom/

The **Templo del Carmen**, Crescencio Rosas y Alvaro Obregón, with a unique archery tower in the Moorish style, is the home of the museum of fine art and the El Carmen Cultural Centre. ■ *Tue-Sun 0900-1700. Free.*

The **Centro de Desarrollo de la Medicina Maya**, Salomón González Blanco, has a herb garden with detailed displays on the use of medicinal plants by the Maya for various purposes, including child delivery. ■ *Mon-Fri 0900-1800, Sat-Sun 1000-1600. US$2.*

Essentials

A *Casa Mexicana*, 28 de Agosto 1, T678-0698, F678-2627. Cable TV, telephone, indoor patio with fountain, very plush and comfy, same owner as *La Galeria* restaurant. Highly recommended. **A** *Casa Vieja*, María A Flores 27, T678-2598, F678-6268. Elegant converted colonial house, relaxing, TV, good restaurant, hot water, will heat rooms on request if weather cold, parking, laundry service. **A** *Plaza Magnolias*, Insurgentes 14, T678-8600, magnolias@plazamagnolias.com.mx   New rustic Mexican motif, colourful and enchanting, good restaurant, parking available. Recommended. With the same owners is **A** *Mansión de Los Angeles*, Francisco I Madero 17, T678-1173. Beautiful 17th-century building, neo-classical style, lovely courtyard restaurant. **A** *Posada Diego de Mazariegos*, María A Flores 2, T678-0833, F678-0827, 1 block north of plaza. Comfortable, quiet, restaurant, live music regularly in the evening in bar *Tequila Zoo*. Recommended. **B** *Bonampak* (Best Western), Calzada México 5, T678-1621, F678-1622. Pool, restaurant, bar and excellent travel agency run by Pilar. **B** *Na Bolom*, Vicente Guerrero 33. Beautiful, 12-room guesthouse in cultural centre (see above), bath, fireplace, 3 meals available, lunch and dinner US$5 each with 3 hrs' notice. Recommended. **B** *Rincón del Arco*, Ejército Nacional 66, T678-1313, F678-1568, 8 blocks from centre. Friendly, bar, restaurant. Warmly recommended. **B** *D'Mónica*, Insurgentes 33, T678-0732, F678-2940. Nice patio, restaurant, bar, recommended, and smaller at 5 de Febrero 18, T678-1367. **B** *Posada de los Angeles*, Madero 17, T678-1173, F678-2581. Very good value, hot water, with bath and TV. **B** *Posada El Paraíso*, Av 5 de Febrero 19, T/F678-0085. Mexican-Swiss owned, impeccable rooms varying in size, many open onto pretty patio, excellent restaurant, nearby parking beneath cathedral. Highly recommended. **B** *Santa Clara*, Insurgentes 1, on

Sleeping
■ *on map page 440*
Price codes:
see inside front cover

Tabasco and Chiapas

Plaza, T678-1140, F678-1041. Colonial style, clean, some rooms noisy, good restaurant, swimming pool and pool bar. Highly recommended.

C *Don Quijote*, Av Cristóbal Colón 7, T678-0920, F678-0346. Bath, 24-hr hot water, garage, no credit cards. **C** *Palacio de Moctezuma*, Juárez 16, T678-0352, F678-1533. Colonial style, good Mexican food. Highly recommended. **C** *Posada San Cristóbal*, Insurgentes 3 near Plaza, T678-6881. With bath, colonial style, renovated, pleasant. **C** *Real del Valle*, Av Real de Guadalupe 14, T678-0680, F678-3955, next to plaza. With breakfast, very clean, friendly, hot water, laundry, credit cards accepted, parking. Avoid noisy room next to kitchen. **C** *Real del Valle*, Av Real de Guadalupe 14, T678-0680, F678-3955, next to plaza. With breakfast, very clean, friendly, avoid noisy room next to kitchen, hot water, laundry, credit cards accepted, parking. **D** *Barón de Las Casas*, Belisario Domínguez 2, T678-0881, www.travelbymexico.com Clean and comfortable, good value. **D** *Capri*, Insurgentes 54, T678-3018, F678-0015, near *Cristóbal Colón* bus terminal. Clean, helpful. Recommended. **D** *El Cerrillo*, Belisario Domínguez 27, T678-1283. Lovely rooftop patio, single rooms available or **F** per person dormitory. Recommended. **D** *Fray Bartolomé de las Casas*, Insurgentes and Niños Héroes, T678-0932, F678-3510. Attractive courtyard, with bath, nice rooms (some dark) and patio with *Café Kate*, can be noisy, extra blankets available, hot water 0700-1000 and 1900-2000, safe parking. **D** *Posada Los Morales*, Ignacio Allende 17, T678-1472. Cottages with open fires (wood US$0.80), kitchen (no pots or pans) and hot showers, beautiful gardens overlook city, parking possible (some cottages are very basic, with no water), beautiful bar/restaurant with live music. Owner is a collector and exporter of rustic-style Mexican furniture. **D** *Posada Vallarta*, Hermanos Pineda, near *Cristóbal Colón* bus terminal. Cheaper if you pay for several nights in advance, clean, quiet, hot water, car parking. Recommended. **D** *San Martín*, Real de Guadalupe 16, T678-0533, near plaza. Clean, hot water, left-luggage. Highly recommended. **D** *Villa Real*, Av Benito Juárez 8, T678-2930. Clean, hot water, luggage deposit, safe. Recommended. **D-E** *Posada Los Robles*, Francisco I Madero 30 y Colón, T678-0054. Hot water, own bath, all rooms have 2 beds, good value. **D-F** *Posada Media Luna*, María Adelina Flores 24, T678-8814, paint49@hotmail.com Free taxi from bus station, laundry service, hot water, internet, cable TV, pretty garden.

E *Casa di Gladys* (*Privates Gästelhäus Casa Degli Ospiti*), Cintalapa 6, between Av Diego Dugelay and Huixtla T673-9396, casagladys@hotmail.com, or **F** per person in dormitory, patio, hot showers, clean bathrooms, comfortable, breakfast available. 5- min walk from the Zócalo, internet access, will pay your taxi ride from the bus stop if you are a group of 2 or more. Gladys and her son are extremely friendly, helpful and attentive. Highly recommended. Laundry facilities, horse-riding arranged, luggage store. **E** *Posada Casa Blanca*, Insurgentes 6-B, 50 m south of Zócalo. With shower, hot water, friendly owner. **E** *Posada Doña Rosita*, Ejército Nacional 13, 3 blocks from main plaza (**F** Dormitory accommodation), fleas, kitchen and laundry facilities, breakfast included, Doña Rosita is very knowledgeable about local affairs and herbal medicine, but you may be moved around to fit in other guests. The herbal medicine course consists of at least 10 hrs of classes, an introduction to vegetarian cooking and 5 meals, costing about US$30. **E** *Posada Insurgente*, Av Insurgentes 73, T678-2435. Clean, refurbished, good bathrooms with hot water, cold rooms, 1 block from *Cristóbal Colón* station. **E** *Posada Isabel*, Francisco León 54, T678-2554, near Av JM Santiago. With hot shower, clean, quiet, good value, parking. Recommended. **E** *Posada Lucella*, Av Insurgentes 55, T678-0956, opposite Iglesia Santa Lucía (noisy bells!). Some rooms with bath, hot water, others shared, good value, clean, safe, quiet rooms around patio, large beds. Recommended. **E** *Posada Lupita*, near bus terminal on Insurgentes. Nice plant-filled courtyard, popular, often full. **E** *Posada Margarita*, Real de Guadalupe 34, T678-0957. Private room without bath, spotless, washing and toilets, friendly, hot water, popular with backpackers, attractive restaurant (not cheap), wholefood. Recommended. **E** *Posada Maya*, Av Crescencio Rosas 11. Hot water in shared showers, cheap café next door. Recommended. Look on the bulletin board outside the tourist office for guesthouses advertising cheap bed and breakfast. **E** *Posada San Agustín*, Ejército Nacional, T678-1816. Large rooms, shared bath, family-run, friendly. Recommended. **E** *Posada Santiago*, Real de Guadalupe 32, T678-0024. With private bath, clean, hot water, good *cafetería*. Recommended. **E** *Posada*

Virginia, Cristóbal Colón y Guadalupe. For 4 in room with bath, hot water, clean. Recommended. **E** *Santo Domingo*, 28 de Agosto 3, 3 blocks north of Zócalo. With bath, **F** without, hot showers, very friendly. **E-F** *Posada Jovel*, Flavio Paniagua 28, T678-1734. Villa style, roof terrace, clean, quiet, limited hot water, extra blankets available, will store luggage, restaurant, horses for hire, laundry facilities. Recommended. **E-F** *Posada Memetik*, on Dr José Flores 34. Clean, pretty patio, including breakfast. Recommended.

F *Baños Mercederos*, 1 de Marzo 55. Shared quarters, good cheap meals, steam baths (highly recommended, US$2 extra). **F** *Casa de Huéspedes Chamula*, Julio M Corzo 18. Clean, hot showers, washing facilities, friendly, parking, noisy, with shared bath, some rooms without windows. Recommended. **F** *Casa de Huéspedes Santa Lucía*, Clemente Robles 21, T678-0315. Shared bath, ask for hot water, refurbished, 1 of the cheapest. Recommended. **F** *Casa Nostra*, Real de Guadalupe 88B, near Av Vicente Guerrero. Shared bath, hot water, laundry, clean, quiet, friendly. Recommended. **F** *Hospedaje Bed and Breakfast*, Madero 83, 10 mins from Zócalo. Clean, small breakfast, popular with backpackers. **F** *Los Anafres*, Calle Flavio Paniagua 2b. Probably the cheapest place in town, restaurant, small rooms, without bath, famous 25-peso rooms, more with breakfast. **F** per person *Ma Adelina Flores 24*, address as name. Including lunch or dinner. **F** *Posada Casa Real*, Real de Guadalupe 51. Communal bath, clean, friendly. **F** *Posada Chilam Balam*, Niños Héroes 9. Family-run, hot water, very pleasant. **F** *Posada del Candil*, Real de Mexicanos 7, T678-2755. Hot shower, parking, clean, laundry facilities, good value. **F** *Posadita*, Flavio Paniagua 30. With bath, clean, laundry facilities. Recommended.

Youth Hostels F *Youth Hostel*, Juárez 2. 24-hr hot water, popular with backpackers. **F** *Los Camellos*, Guadalupe 101. Price includes breakfast, popular with backpackers, T678-0665. *Qhia*, Tonalá 5, T678-0594. Including breakfast, kitchen, laundry facilities, warm water, often full.

Camping *Rancho San Nicolás*, T678-0057, at end of Francisco León, 1½ km east of centre. Beautiful, quiet location, is a trailer park, but do take warm blankets or clothing as the temperature drops greatly at night, hot showers, US$7 for room in cabaña, US$5 to camp, US$12 for camper van with 2 people (electricity hook-up), children free, laundry facilities. Recommended. **Trailer park** *Bonampak* on Route 190 at west end of town. 22 spaces with full hook-up, hot shower, heated pool in season, restaurant, US$10 per vehicle, US$5 per person.

Expensive *El Teatro*, next to Teatro Municipal on 16 de Septiembre. Good quality French food. There is a good restaurant at *Hotel Ciudad Real*. Rustic setting, good crêpes. *La Parrilla*, Av Belisario Domínguez 32. Excellent grilled meats and cheese, open fire, cowboy décor with saddles as bar stools, closed Mon. *La Margarita*, Real de Guadalupe 34. Open for breakfast at 0700. Live music in the evenings, flamenco, rumba and salsa, good tacos. *Los Balcones*, Real de Guadalupe. Friendly, good atmosphere. *Pierre's*, Real de Guadalupe 73. Good-quality French cuisine, will prepare custom dishes given notice.

Eating
● *on map page 440*

Mid-range *Capri*, Insurgentes 16 (not associated with the hotel of the same name). Good food, set meals at reasonable prices. *Doña Lolita*, Insurgentes 7. Excellent, cheap, good for breakfast and lunch. *El Manantial*, 1 de Marzo 11. Good *licuados* and juices. *El Pavo Real*, Insurgentes 60, near *Cristóbal Colón* terminal. Regional food. *El Tapanco*, Guadalupe 24B. Good crêpes, friendly – not to be confused with *El Tapanco Cybercafé*. *Flamingo*, Madero 14. Nice décor, reasonable food (good *paella*). Next door is *El Mirador II*. Good local and international food, excellent *comida corrida* US$3. Recommended. *Kau Lom*, Madero, opposite *Maya Pakal*. Chinese. *Kukulcán*, Insurgentes Sur 3. Mexican food. *La Galería*, Hidalgo 3, a few doors from Zócalo. Popular with tourists, best coffee, good breakfast, good pasta, international (many German) newspapers, art gallery, videos at night, pool table, live music at weekends. *La Langosta*, Madero 9. Mexican and seafood. *París-México*, Madero 20. Smart, French cuisine, excellent breakfasts, reasonably priced *comida corrida*, classical music. Not cheap, apart from the 3 daily menus (very good). Highly recommended. *Shanghai*, 20 de Noviembre 7B, Chinese. *Tuluc*, Insurgentes 5, open 0630-2200. Good value especially

Tabasco and Chiapas

breakfasts, fresh *tamales* every morning, near plaza, popular, classical music, art for sale and toys on display (SODAM, see below). Recommended.

Cheap The cheapest places for lunch in San Cristóbal are the stalls in the craft market on Insurgentes. They do set meals for US$1.20, usually beef or chicken. Numerous stalls nearby sell punch, often made with *posh*, the alcoholic brew made by the people of Chamula.

Chamula's Grill, Real de Guadalupe 1a. Excellent breakfast, good coffee, internet only US$0.50 per hour. *El Gato Gordo*, Madero and Colón. Cheap set breakfast, crêpes, *tortas*, vegetarian. *El Huarache Real*, Juárez between Madero y J F Flores, no sign, next to *Todo*

San Cristóbal de las Casas

N

0 metres   100
0 yards   100

■ Sleeping
1 Capri *E2*
2 Casa de Huéspedes
  Chamula *D3*

3 Casa di Gladys *B4*
4 Casa Mexicana *B2*
5 Casa Vieja *B3*
6 Don Quijote *B3*
7 Fray Bartolomé de las
  Casas *D2*
8 Hospedaje Bed &
  Breakfast *C4*
9 Jovel *B3*
10 Palacio de Moctezuma *D3*
11 Posada Casa Blanca *C2*
12 Posada Casa Real *C3*

13 Posada del Candil *A1*
14 Posada Diego de
  Mazariegos *B2*
15 Posada El Paraíso *B1*
16 Posada Insurgente *E2*
17 Posada Los Morales *D1*
18 Posada Lucella *E2*
19 Posada Lupita *E2*
20 Posada Margarita *C3*
21 Posada San Cristóbal *C2*
22 Posada Santiago *C3*
23 Posada Vallarta *E2*

24 Posadita *C4*
25 Real del Valle *C2*
26 Rincón del Arco *B4*
27 San Martín *C2*
28 Santa Clara *D2*
29 Villa Real *C3*
30 Youth Hostel *D3*

● Eating
1 La Casa del Pan *B3*
2 La Galería *C2*
3 Madre Tierra *D2*

Tabasco and Chiapas

Especial. Excellent *huaraches*, a thick kind of taco served flat with topping, many varieties. *El Suadero*, Insurgentes 69. Very good 3-course *comida corrida*, US$2.50, open till 2300. *Fulano*, Madero 12, near Plaza. Excellent set meal. *Juguería Ana Banana*, Av Miguel Hidalgo 9, good cheap typical Mexican food and fresh juices. *La Alpujarra*, Diego Dugelay 11, is a bakery-cum-pizzeria, with the best European-style crusty white bread in town. Half a block away on the other side of the Real de Guadalupe, *Lacteos Maya*, Av J M Santiago, has excellent locally made yogurt. *Los Anafres*, Calle Flavio Paniagua 2b, speciality is *anafres*, table top BBQ, US$5.50 per person. *Maya Pakal*, Madero, 1st block east of plaza. Excellent 3-course set lunch and dinner, ex-chef of *Madre Tierra*, many vegetarian options, horses for rent to Chamula, book day before T678-5911, Francisco Ochoa. *Merendero*, JM Corzo y Insurgentes, OK. Several other cheap, local places on Madero east of Plaza 31 de Marzo. Very good *panadería*, **Pan Chico**, on Rosales next to *Hotel Casa Mexicana*, excellent bread and cakes. Unnamed restaurant at *Real de Guadalupe 85*, between Isabel la Católica and Díaz del Castillo. Chiapan specialities are *chalupas*, *tortillas* with beans, pork and vegetables in tomato sauce; also *pan compuesto*, bread with pork, carrots and sauce.

Taco restaurants *Emiliano's Moustache*, Av Crescencio Rosas 7. Popular with Mexicans (no facial hair required). Recommended. *La Salsa Verde*, 2 on 20 de Noviembre. *El Ambar*, Almolonga 43. Friendly, cheap. Recommended. *El Pastorcito de Los Altos*, esq Allende y Clemente Robles. Cheap. *El Pastor Coleto*, Panamericana and Hidalgo, near Pastorcito. Popular with locals.

Health food/vegetarian *Madre Tierra*, Insurgentes 19 (opposite Franciscan church). Anglo-Mexican owned, European dishes, vegetarian specialities, good breakfasts, wholemeal breads from bakery (also takeaway), pies, brownies, chocolate cheesecake, classical music, popular with travellers, not cheap. Much recommended. *Las Estrellas*, Dr Navarro 201. Good cheap food, including vegetarian, good brown bread, try the *caldo Tlalpeño*, nice atmosphere, Mexican/Dutch owned. Recommended. *Café San Cristóbal* on Cuauhtémoc. Good coffee sold in bulk too, chess hangout. *Naturalissimo*, 20 de Noviembre 4. Healthy, low-fat vegetarian food, fresh (delicious) yoghurt, fruit sherbet and juices, wholewheat bread and homebaked goodies, pleasant courtyard inside. *La Selva Café*, Crescencio Rosas and Cuauhtémoc. 30 types of really delicious organic coffees, owned by growers' collective, art gallery, lively in evenings. Good breakfast and cakes. Recommended. *Café Centro*, Real de Guadalupe. Popular for breakfast, good *comida*. *La Casa del Pan*, on B Domínguez and Dr Navarro 10. Excellent wholemeal bread, breakfasts, live music, closed Mon. Highly recommended but not cheap. *Tortas Tortugas*, Guadalupe Victoria, near corner of Av 20 de Noviembre. Excellent sandwiches.

Cafés *La Fe Café,* Diego Mazarriegos and 12 de Octobre. T678-9978. Cappuccinos and a sawdust floor (for that little extra fibre), express home delivery (for a coffee shop!) open 1600-2230. *La Llorona Kafe-Pub*, 1 de Marzo 14 Bis, la_llorona2001@hotmail.com Happy hour from 1800-2000. Open Wed-Mon 1600 until late. Comfortable atmosphere to read, hang out, down some beers, and then pass out in the hammocks by a cosy fireplace. Sandwiches and burgers are also available. *Namandi*, Diego Mazarriegos. Coffee and crêpes, also breakfast, sandwiches and deserts. *Todo Natural*, B Domínguez and Madero. Juice bar, huge variety, any combination of fruit, yoghurt and alfalfa, open 0800-2100.

Bars *A-Dove*, Hidalgo, just off plaza, above a shop. Open Fri and Sat from 2200 until very late. *Blue Bar*, Av Crescencio Rosas 2, live music after 2300, salsa, rock, reggae, pool table, good atmosphere. *Cocodrilo*, Insurgentes 1, cafebarcocodrilo@hotmail.com, T678-0871. Cappuccinos, cocktails, beer and live music every night: reggae, trova, flamenco and rumba. *Emiliano's Moustache* (see Eating) has a bar open until 0100. *Las Velas*, Madero, ½ block from plaza. Reggae, Honduran music, sometimes live, happy hour 2000-2200, open till dawn. *Los Latinos*, Madero and Benito Juárez. Caribbean music. *Revolución*, 20 de Noviembre and 1 De Marzo, Café, bar with internet upstairs, happy hour 1500-1700, live soul, blues and rock music at 2000, good atmosphere.

Tabasco and Chiapas

Entertainment *Cine Santa Clara*, Av 16 de Septiembre, Mexican and alternative films, international film festival 2nd half Feb. Video films are also shown at Centro Bilingüe in the **Centro Cultural** *El Puente* (see Cultural centres, page 444), Real de Guadalupe 55, usually about local issues. Every day except Sunday 3 good films in original version, US$1.25. Film schedules are posted around town. *Santa Clara*, Insurgentes 1, daily schedule posted outside. *Teatro Daniel Zebadúa*, 20 de Noviembre and 1 de Marzo, film festivals each month, films at 1800 and 2100 US$2 (US$1.50 students).

Festivals In early **Nov** you will catch the *Maya-Zoque Festival* which lasts 4 days, promoting the 12 different Maya and Zoque cultures in the Chiapas region, with dancing and celebrations in the main plaza. There is a popular *spring festival* on **Easter Sun** and the week after. *La Fiesta de Guadalupe* is celebrated on **12 Dec**.

Shopping Part of the ex-convent of Santo Domingo has been converted into a cooperative, *Sna Jolobil*, selling handicrafts from many Indian villages especially textiles (best quality and expensive); also concerts by local groups. *La Casa del Jade*, Av 16 de Septiembre 16. The shop, which sells top quality jade, also has a museum with replicas of jade relics and the Tomb of Pakal (Mayan King of Palenque), which is now more difficult to visit at Palenque. *Taller Lenateros*, Flavio A Paniagua 54, T678-5174, conjuros@sancristobal.com.mx A paper-making workshop run primarily by a Maya group. Their paper and prints are made from natural materials and their profits help support around 30 Maya families. Also offers demonstrations and workshops US$6.50 per day. *Weavers Co-op J'pas Joloviletic*, Utrilla 43. *SODAM* (Mutual Aid Society) with their shop at Casa Utrilla, Utrilla 33, is a cooperative of Indian craftspeople selling beautiful wooden dolls and toys. Sales go towards a training fund for Chamula Indians, with a workshop based at Yaalboc, a community near San Cristóbal. For local goods try *Miscelánea Betty*, Utrilla 45, good value. *Souvenir markets* on Utrilla between Real de Guadalupe and Dr A Navarro. *Amber museum* in Plaza Sivan shop, Utrilla 10, T678-3507. Many shops on Av Real de Guadalupe for amber and jade plus other artesanías. The **market** north of Santo Domingo is worth seeing as well. The craft market beside Santo Domingo church is soon to be moved to a new covered location on Insurgentes, at the current location of the smaller craft market in Parque Fray Bartolomé de las Casas. At this market you will find stands offering an assortment of local sweets such as *cocada*, balls of sweetened and caramelized shredded coconut, as well as small, perfectly shaped animal figurines made, strangely enough, of sweetened hard-boiled egg yolks. Different, yet tasty. *La Casona*, corner of 16 de Septiembre and 5 de Febrero. Cute little shop filled to the brim with quality Mexican crafts; hand-painted jewellery boxes and picture frames, beautiful water pitchers and matching glasses. *Pasaje Mazariegos* (in the block bounded by Real de Guadalupe, Av B Domínguez, Madero and Plaza 31 de Marzo) has luxury clothes and bookshops, restaurants and travel agents. *Casa de Artesanías*, Niños Héroes and Hidalgo. Top-quality handicrafts. The shop is also a museum. *Mujeres por la Dignidad*, on Belisario Domínguez 8, is a cooperative with a few hundred members from San Andrés, San Juan Chamula and Chenalho. They're happy to take special orders in addition to selling more regular items. *Jolom Mayaetik*, 28 de Agosto on the corner of Av 5 de Mayo, has worked some 'new' designs in to the traditional offerings.

Bookshops *La Pared*, Av Miguel Hidalgo 2, T678-6367, lapared@prodigy.net.mx, opposite the government tourist office. Books in English and a few in other European languages, many travel books including Footprint *South American Handbook*, book exchange, good quality amber jewellery, American owner Dana Gay is very helpful with local information, also offers cheapest phone service in town (see under **Communications**). *Soluna*, Real de Guadalupe 13B, has a few English guidebooks, a wide range of Spanish titles and postcards. *Librería Chilam Balam*, Casa Utrilla, Av Utrilla 33, good range of books, mostly in Spanish, also cassettes of regional music. *La Quimera*, Real de Guadalupe 24.

Sports **Horse hire** Carlos, T678-1873. Horses can be hired from *Casa de Huéspedes Margarita*, prices US$16-20 for horse and guide, to Chamula, 5 hrs, US$9, reserve the day before; or from

Sr José Hernández, Calle Elías and Calle 10 (1 block from Av Huixtla and Chiapa de Corzo, not far from Na Bolom), US$10 for half a day, plus guide US$11.50; Real de Guadalupe 51A, to Chamula US$6.50, also to Rancho Nuevo and San José; Francisco Ochón, T678-5911, goes to Chamula, US$6.50. *Viajes Chincultik* (see below in Directory under Tour operators) also offer horse-riding tours to San Juan Chamula, US$11. **Rafting** There are several rivers in the area surrounding San Cristóbal that offer great rafting opportunities. *Explora-Ecoturismo y Aventura*, T678-4295, www.prodigyweb.com.mx/explora Eco-sensitive company with good recommendations offer rafting, caving, sea kayaking, river trips and multi-day camping expeditions on a variety of rivers. Price for a 6-day river and camping trip US$520.

The active might want to try *Patty's Aerobics*, T678-6090, Pedro Moreno 14. US$2.50 a class. Or there is the *Physical Center Gym*, T678-1207, Av Allende, between Cuauhtémoc and Diego Mazariegos. Weights and sauna, US$4 a day, or US$10 a week. *Club Deportivo*, on the south side of town off the Pan-American, has a clean pool but not much else.

Local **Taxi**: US$1.60 anywhere in town, *colectivo* US$0.70. **Bike hire**: *Los Pingüinos* on Av Ecuador, T678-0202, open 0915-1430, 1600-1900, rents mountain bikes for US$3/hr or US$9/day, US$12 for 24 hrs. Guided biking tours half or full days, English, German spoken, guide Joel recommended, prices from US$8 to US$14, beautiful countryside and knowledge-able guides, highly recommended. *Rodada 28*, on María Adelina Flores, opposite *Hotel Casa Vieja*, open Mon-Sat 0900-1330, 1600-2000, US$2/hr, US$8/day. Bike shops: *Bicipartes*, on Alvaro Obregón and 2 shops on Utrilla between Navarro and Primero de Marzo have a good selection of bike parts. **Car hire**: *Budget*, Mazariegos 36, T678-1871, in *Mansión del Valle Hotel*.

Transport

Long distance **Air**: San Cristóbal has a new airport (SZT) about 15 km from town, Aerocaribe flies to Tuxtla Gutiérrez. There are also daily direct flights to **Mexico City**. There are also charter flights to see **Lacanjá**, **Bonampak** and **Yaxchilán** on the Río Usumacinta, 7 hrs in all (US$100 per person if plane is full, more if not). All with *Aerochiapas* at airport. *Aeromar* take small planes to Mexico City US$230 return. T5133-1111.

Buses: It is recommended you buy tickets in advance at the ticket office, corner of Real de Guadalupe and Belisario Domínguez, T678-8503, for the following bus lines: *ADO, UNO, Cristóbal Colón, Sur, Av, Altos, ETN, Primera Plus, Estrella de Oro* and *Maya De Oro*, The 1st class bus terminal serves all destinations in the country. There are 2 other 2nd class terminals across the road, only serving Chiapan destinations. Book tickets as far in advance as possible; during Christmas and Holy Week buses are sometimes fully booked for 10 days or more. Ticket prices may also increase at this time.

From the 1st class terminal, on Allende: **Campeche**: 0930, US$25. **Cancún**: 1430, 1635, 18 hrs, US$47. **Cárdenas**: *ADO* US$17. **Chetumal**: 1430, 11 hrs, US$29. **Arriaga**: at 1200 via Tuxtla Gutiérrez, US$6. **Ciudad Cuauhtémoc**: several daily, 3 hrs, US$5 – see below for buses to Guatemala. **Coatzacoalcos**: at 0630, US$14.80. Campeche, *servicio plus*, 2100. **Comitán**, 7 per day, 1½ hrs, US$3.60. **Mérida**: 0930, 1730, 13 hrs, US$34. **Mexico City**: 1350, 1530, 1800, 18 hrs, US$55. **Oaxaca**: 2 with *Cristóbal Colón* at 1700 and 2000, US$28, 1 with *Maya de Oro* at 2200, US$35. **Palenque**: 10 daily, 5½ hrs, US$9. **Playa del Carmen**: US$42. **Puebla**: 1530 and 1730, US$46. **Puerto Escondido**: with *Cristóbal Colón*, 1st class, 0745,1815, US$27. **Tapachula**: 5 a day, 9 hrs, US$14.30. **Tuxtla Gutiérrez**: 12 a day, US$3.60 (US$6 with *Uno* luxury 1st class – with seats that are practically beds, at 1800 and 1445). **Tulum**: US$40. **Veracruz**: 1840, US$35. **Villahermosa**: 1125, 1830, 7 hrs, US$13.

Lacandonia 2nd class bus to **Palenque** from 2nd class bus station, also on Allende, 7 a day between 0100 and 2015, 4-5 hrs, US$9 (via Agua Azul, US$6); *Cristóbal Colón*, 1st class ser-vice, up to 4 times daily (including at least 1 *servicio plus*) US$10, bookings 5 days in advance; *Maya de Oro*, from *Cristóbal Colón* terminal, 3 times daily, a/c, videos, non-stop; *Rodolfo Figueroa*, 5 times a day, US$4.50, a/c. (On reaching Ocosingo it is not uncommon to be told the bus is going no further; your onward fare to Palenque will be refunded but you will have to make your own way.) *Autotrans Tuxtla*, F Sarabia, between Carretera Panamericana and Alvaro Obregón, 2nd class to Palenque, reserved seats, US$5. Minibuses to **Tuxtla Gutiérrez** leave from in front of 1st class bus station, when full, US$2.

Buses to Guatemala: *Cristóbal Colón*, south end of Av Insurgentes (left-luggage facilities open 0600-2000 excluding Sun and holidays), clean station, direct 1st class buses to the Guatemalan border at **Ciudad Cuauhtémoc**, 170 km, several daily from 0700, 3 hrs, US$3.50 (leave bus at border, not its final destination). 1 *ADO* bus a day to the border at 1900, book in advance. *Altos* to Ciudad Cuautémoc/border, 3 a day, US$5. *Cristóbal Colón* to **Comitán** (if you can't get a bus to the border, take 1 to Comitán and get a pick-up there, US$0.50), hourly from 0700. 87 km (a beautiful, steep route). *Colectivos* also leave for Comitán from outside the *Cristóbal Colón* bus station, US$2. 2nd class to border with *Autotransportes Tuxtla*, US$2.75 (do not take 1430 *ACL* 2nd class, next to *Trans Lacandonia*, on Carretera Panamericana, as it arrives too late for onward transport). For details on crossing the border at La Mesilla see page 464.

Viajes Chincultik, see Tour operators in Directory below, run a shuttle to the Guatemalan border and beyond on Tue and Fri. **La Mesilla** (US$20), **Quetzaltenango** (US$40), **Panajachel** and **Lake Atitlán** (US$50) and **Antigua** (US$60).

Directory   **Airlines** *Aviacsa*, in *Xanav* agency, Pasaje Mazariegos, local 2, Real de Guadalupe, T678-4441, F678-4384 – although they do not fly from San Cristóbal.

Banks *Casa Margarita* will change dollars and TCs. Banks are usually open for exchange between 0900 and 1300 only, check times. *Bancomer*, Plaza 31 de Marzo 10, charges commission, cash advance on Visa, American Express or Citicorp TCs, good rates and service. *Banco Internacional (Bital)*, Diego de Mazariegos, good rates for cash and TCs (US$ only), fast, efficient, cash advance on MasterCard, open Sat afternoons. *Banamex*, Real de Guadalupe y Portal Oriental, changes cheques without commission, 0900-1300. *Banca Serfín* on the Zócalo, changes Euro, Amex, MasterCard, TCs. *Casa de Cambio Lacantún*, Real de Guadalupe 12, open daily 0900-1400, 1600-1900, Sat/Sun 0900-1300 (supposedly, may close early), no commission, at least US$50 must be changed. 24-hr ATM at Bancrecer, 5 de Febrero, adjacent to cathedral. Quetzales can be obtained for pesos or dollars in the *cambio* but better rates are paid at the border.

Communications **Internet**: many internet cafés all over town with rates as low as US$0.60/hr. Service is generally good. Free ½ hour on the internet at the Telmex office, very slow, poor service, must have identification. **Post office**: Cuauhtémoc 13, between Rosas and Hidalgo, Mon-Fri 0800-1900, Sat 0900-1300. **Telephone**: *Computel*, Insurgentes 64B, fax, guards luggage; *Telmex*, Niños Héroes and Hidalgo, also has 24-hr ATM. *La Pared*, Av. Miguel Hidalgo 2, owner Dana Gay offers long-distance calling service, cheap rates, and a bookshop to browse. Long-distance phone calls can be made from the *Boutique Santo Domingo* on Utrilla, on corner of Paniagua, takes credit cards, collect call possible; and at shops at Av 16 de Septiembre 22, Madero 75 and Av Insurgentes 60. Phone and fax services available at the tourist office in the Plaza. International calls from 2nd class bus station.

Cultural centres The *Casa de Cultura*, opposite El Carmen church on junction of Hermanos Domínguez and Hidalgo, has a range of activities on offer: concerts, films, lectures, art exhibitions and conferences. *El Puente*, Real de Guadalupe 55, T678-4157, 1 block from the plaza, has restaurant, internet centre and a small cinema. Check their notice board for forthcoming events. A good place to meet other travellers. *Taller de Artes y Oficios Kun Kun*, Real de Mexicanos 21, T678-1417. Exhibits hand-woven woollen textiles made on primitive looms held around the weaver's waist, also ceramics. Some items available to buy. *Casa/Museo de Sergio Castro*, Guadalupe Victoria 47 (6 blocks from plaza), T678-4289, excellent collection of indigenous garments, talks (in English, French or Spanish) and slide shows about customs and problems of the indigenous population, open from 1800-2000, best to make appointment, entry free but donations welcome.

Language schools *Centro Cultural El Puente*, Real de Guadalupe 55, Caja Postal 29230, T/F678-3723, spanish@mundomaya.com.mx (Spanish programme), rates range from US$6 per hour to US$8.50 per hour depending on number in class and length of course, home stay programmes available from US$180 per week, registration fee US$100. *Universidad Autónoma de Chiapas*, Av Hidalgo 1, Dpto de Lenguas, offers classes in English, French and Tzotzil. *Instituto Jovel*, María Adelina Flores 21, Apdo Postal 62, T/F678-4069, jovel@sancristobal.podernet.com.mx Group or 1-to-1 classes, homestays arranged, said to be the best school in San Cristóbal as their teachers undergo an obligatory 6-week training course.

Laundry *Superklin*, Crescencio Rosas 48, T678-3275, US$1.30 per kg, for collection after 5 hrs. *La Rapidita*, Insurgentes 9. New coin-operated machines for self-service or they will launder clothes for you 1-3 kilos US$3.50. *Lavorama* at Guadalupe Victoria 20A; *Lavasor*, Real de Guadalupe 26, US$1.30 per kg, Mon-Sat 0800-2030. *Tinto Clean*, Guadalupe Victoria 20A. Recommended. Clothes washed and mended by Isaiah and friendly staff, B Domínguez 8, near corner of Real de Guadalupe. *Orve*, Belisario Domínguez no 5, T678-1802. Open 0800-2000, US$1.20 per kilo, service wash available.

Medical Services *Dra Carmen Ramos*, Av Insurgentes 28, next to (south of) Templo de Santa Lucía, T678-1680, best to call ahead if possible or make an appointment through tourist office. **Red Cross:** Calle Prolongación Ignacio Allende, T678-0772. Recommended. *Regina Centro*, 24-hr pharmacy on Diego de Mazariegos and Crescencio Rosas; another on Hidalgo and Cuauhtémoc, open 0700-2300, with a homeopathic and natural remedy shop next door. *Farmacia Bios*, corner of Cuauhtémoc and Hidalgo. Well-stocked pharmacy. *Servicio Médico Bilingüe*, Av Benito Juárez 60, T678-0793, Dr Renato Zarate Castañeda speaks English, is highly recommended and if necessary can be reached at home, T678-2998.

Tour operators There are many agencies to choose from. As a rough guide to prices: to San Juan Chamula and Zinacantán, US$12. Horse-riding to San Juan Chamula, US$12. Sumidero Canyon, US$23, Montebello Lakes and Amatenango del Valle, US$26. Palenque Ruins, Aqua Azul and Misol Há, US$37. Toniná Ruins, US$26. There's also a 3-day jungle trip option taking in Agua Azul, Misol-Há, the ruins at Bonampak, Cedro River Falls, Yaxchilán and Palenque ruins. Camping in the jungle, US$175.

    Viajes Pakal, Cuauhtémoc 6A, T678-2818, F678-2819, pakal@mundomaya.com.mx Manager Mike Ramos is from the area and runs a reliable agency and culturally friendly tours, several branches in other cities. Good for flight bookings, though some require 4 days' notice. *Viajes Chincultik*, Real de Guadalupe 34, T/F678-7832, ag.chincultik@mundomaya.com.mx Runs group tours to the Lagunas de Montebello (US$25), to the Sumidero Canyon (US$22); also to Yaxchilán, Bonampak and Tikal in Guatemala. *Santa Ana Tours*, Madero, ½ block from plaza, T678-0422. Recommended for local and international flight bookings. *Mercedes Hernández Gómez*, tours of local villages, starting at 0900 from kiosk on the Plaza 31 de Mayo (arrive early), returns about 1500, about US$12 per person. Mercedes speaks English, is very informative, somewhat eccentric. Many others take tours for a similar price. *Raúl and Alejandro*, T678-3741, chamul@hotmail.com Offer tours to San Juan Chamula and Zinacantán. They depart from in front of the cathedral at 0930 and return at 1400, in blue VW minibus, US$11, in English, Spanish and Italian. Friendly, very good and highly recommended. *Viajes Navarra*, Real de Guadalupe 15D, T678-1143, guided tours to Tenam Puente ruins, Sumidero Canyon and more. *Héctor Mejía*, T678-0545, walking tour (Tue and Thu, 0900, from outside Santo Domingo, US$11, 4 hrs) around cottage industries, eg candymaker, dollmaker, toymaker. Longer tours such as to Bonampak and Yaxchilán can be booked by tour operators in San Cristóbal, eg *Yaxchilán Tours*, Guadalupe 26D, but they are much cheaper if booked in Palenque, take care to check what is included in cheaper packages. Tours also offered from the Na Balom museum (see above).

Useful addresses Immigration: on Carretera Panamericana and Diagonal Centenario, opposite *Hotel Bonampak*. From Zócalo take Diego de Mazariegos towards west, after crossing bridge take Diagonal on the left towards Highway, 30-min walk. Only 15-day extensions due to state controls.

Villages near San Cristóbal

Check on the situation before you visit the surrounding villages. Travellers are strongly warned not to wander around on their own, especially in the hills surrounding the town where churches are situated, as they could risk assault. Warnings can be seen in some places frequented by tourists. Remember that locals are particularly sensitive to proper dress (that is neither men nor women should wear shorts, or revealing clothes) and manners; persistent begging should be countered with courteous, firm replies.

    You are recommended to call at Na Bolom (see Museums, above) before visiting the villages, to get information on their cultures and seek advice on the reception you are likely to get. Photography is resisted by some Indians because they believe the camera steals their souls, and photographing their church is stealing the soul of God, but also it is seen as invasive and sometimes profiteering. Many Indians do not speak Spanish. You can visit the villages of San Juan Chamula, Zinacantán and Tenejapa. While this is a popular excursion, especially when led by a guide, several visitors

It is best not to take cameras to villages; there are good postcards and photographs on sale

Tabasco and Chiapas

have felt ashamed at going to look at the villagers as if they were in a zoo; there were many children begging and offering to look after private vehicles in return for not damaging them.

Getting there Get to outlying villages by bus or communal VW bus (both very packed); buses leave very early, and often don't return until next day, so you have to stay overnight; lorries are more frequent. To Zinacantán catch also VW bus from market. Buses and combis (US$1.50) from the market area to San Andrés Larrainzar (bus at 1000, 1100, 1400, with return same day, US$0.80 1-way) and Tenejapa. *Transportes Fray Bartolomé de las Casas* has buses to Chanal, Chenalhó (US$15 with taxi, return, 1 hr stay), Pantelhó, Yajalón and villages en route to Ocosingo. *Transportes Lacandonia* on Av Crescencio Rosas also go to the villages of Huixtán, Oxchuc and Yajalón, on the way to Palenque and to Pujiltic, La Mesilla and Venustiano Carranza. If you are in San Cristóbal for a limited period of time it is best to rent a car to see the villages.

Zinacantán
Tours from San Cristóbal, US$12

Zinacantán is reached by VW bus from the market, US$0.75, 30 minutes' journey, sometimes with frequent stops while the conductor lights rockets at roadside shrines; taxi US$4. The Zinacantán men wear pink/red jackets with embroidery and tassels, the women a vivid pale blue shawl and navy skirts. Annual festival days here are 6 January, 19-22 January, 8-10 August; visitors are welcome. At midday every day the women prepare a communal meal, which the men eat in shifts. The main gathering place is around the church; the roof was destroyed by fire (US$0.40 charged for entering church, official ticket from tourist office next door; photography inside is strictly prohibited). There are two museums but both have recently closed because the community felt that they only benefited those most involved in them. Check before planning a visit. **Ik'al Ojov**, off Calle 5 de Febrero, five blocks down Avenida Cristóbal Colón from San Lorenzo church, and one block to the left; the museum includes two traditional *palapas* or huts that people used to live in and there is a small collection of regional costumes. It occasionally holds shows and there is an annual festival on 17 February. Tiny gift shop. Donation requested. The second museum is the **Museo Comunitario Autzetik ta jteklum**, one block from San Lorenzo church, which is run by women from Zinacantán and also has exhibits on local culture.

San Juan Chamula
Colour map 4, grid B1

Signs in Chamula warn that it is dangerous to walk in the area; robberies have occurred between Chamula and both San Cristóbal and Zinacantán. Also seek full advice on any travel outside San Cristóbal de las Casas in the wake of events since early 1994

In this Tzotzil village 10 km northwest of San Cristóbal the men wear grey, black or light pink tunics, while the women wear bright blouses with colourful braid and navy or bright blue shawls. One popular excursion is to visit the brightly painted church. A permit (US$1) is needed from the village tourist office and photographing inside the church is absolutely forbidden. There are no pews but family groups sit or kneel on the floor, chanting, with rows of candles lit in front of them, each representing a member of the family and certain significance attached to the colours of the candles. The religion is centred on the 'talking stones' and three idols as well as certain Christian saints. Pagan rituals are held in small huts at the end of August. The pre-Lent festival ends with celebrants running through blazing harvest chaff. This happens just after Easter prayers are held, before the sowing season starts. Festivals in Chamula should *not* be photographed; if you wish to take other shots ask permission, people are not unpleasant, even if they refuse (although children may pester you to take their picture for a small fee). Take great care when visiting this village; some readers found an unreceptive attitude toward tourists, in particular to those drinking the local liquor *posh*.

There are many handicraft stalls on the way up the small hill southwest of the village. This has a good viewpoint of the village and valley. Take the road from the southwest corner of the square, turn left towards the ruined church then up a flight of steps on the left.

To get to Chamula, you can catch a VW bus from the market in San Cristóbal every 20 minutes, last at 1700, last one back at 1900, US$0.70 per person (or taxi, US$4). It is an interesting walk from San Cristóbal to Chamula along the main road to a point 1 km past the crossroads with the Periférico ring road (about 2½ km from own centre); turn right on to an old dirt road, not sign-posted but it is the first fork you come to between some farmhouses. Then head back via the road through the village of Milpoleta, some 8 km downhill; allow five hours for the round trip (one hour for Chamula). Best not done in hot weather. Also, you can hike from Chamula to Zinacantán in 1½ hours: when leaving Chamula, take the track straight ahead instead of turning left onto the San Cristóbal road; turn left on a small hill where the school is (after 30 minutes) and follow a smaller trail through light forest. After about an hour you reach the main road 200 m before Zinacantán.

Just past the 3 km sign from San Cristóbal, on the road to Chamula, is the **Huitepec** nature reserve. The 2½-km long trail is administered by Pronatura-Chiapas. The 135 ha reserve contains grassland, oakwood forest, rising to cloud forest at 2,400 m. As well as a wide diversity of plants, there are many birds, including some 50 migratory species and snakes. ■ *Tue-Sun 0900-1600, (take combi heading for Chamula from behind market). US$1.25. Guided tours restricted to Tue, Thu, Sat 0930-1100. Colectivos go there, US$0.50. Tours can be organized 2-3 days in advance at Pronatura office, María Adelina Flores 21, T678-4069.*

The Thursday market is traditionally fruit and vegetables, but there are a growing number of other stalls. Excellent woven items can be purchased from the weavers' cooperative near the church. They also have a fine collection of old textiles in their regional ethnographic museum adjoining the handicraft shop. The cooperative can also arrange weaving classes. The village is very friendly and many men wear local costume. Few tourists visit Tenejapa (**F** *Hotel Molina*, simple but clean; several *comedores* around the market). Buses leave from San Cristóbal market at 0700 and 1100 (1½ hours' journey), and *colectivos* every hour, US$1. Ask permission to take pictures and expect to pay. The market thins out by noon.

Tenejapa
Phone code: 967

Drunkenness is quite open and at times forms part of the rituals

Two other excursions can be made, by car or local bus, from San Cristóbal south on the Pan-American Highway (30 minutes by car) to **Amatenango del Valle**, a Tzeltal village where the women make and fire pottery in their yards, and then southeast (15 minutes by car) to **Aguacatenango**, a picturesque village at the foot of a mountain. Continue one hour along this road past Villa Las Rosas (hotel) to **Venustiano Carranza**, where the women wear fine costumes, and there is an extremely good view of the entire valley. There is a good road from Las Rosas to Comitán as an alternative to the Pan-American highway. Frequent buses.

Las Grutas de San Cristóbal (caves), 10 km southeast of the town, contain huge stalagmites and are 2,445 m deep but only lit for 750 m. ■ *US$0.30*. Refreshments are available. Horses can be hired at Las Grutas for US$13 for a five-hour ride (guide extra) on beautiful trails in the surrounding forest. Some of these are best followed

Other excursions
Parts of the forest are a military zone

Around San Cristóbal de las Casas

on foot. Yellow diamonds on trees and stones mark the way to beautiful meadows. Stay on the trail to minimize erosion. The land next to the caves is taken up by an army football pitch, but once past this, it is possible to walk most of the way back to San Cristóbal through woods and fields.

Transport Las Grutas are reached by *Autotransportes de Pasaje* '31 de Marzo' *colectivos* every 15 mins (0600-1900 US$0.60) from Av Benito Juárez 37B, across the Pan-American Highway just south of *Cristóbal Colón* bus terminal (or take *camioneta* from Pan-American opposite San Diego church 500 m east of *Cristóbal Colón*). *Colectivos* are marked 'San Cristóbal, Teopisca, Ciudad Militar, Villa Las Rosas', or ask for minibus to 'Rancho Nuevo'. To the bus stop take 'San Diego' *colectivo* 1 block east of Zócalo to the end of Benito Juárez. When you get to Las Grutas, ask the driver to drop you at Km 94; the caves are poorly signed.

Tours from San Cristóbal to the **Sumidero Canyon** (see page 433) including boat trip cost around US$15 with numerous travel agencies, 0900-1600. San Cristóbal can also serve as a base for exploring the Mayan ruins at **Palenque** (210 km away, see page 450), **Bonampak** and **Yaxchilán**, near the Guatelmalan border (see page 458).

The route to Palenque

Ocosingo
Phone code: 919
Colour map 4, grid B1
Population: 120,000

Palenque (see page 450) can be reached by paved road from San Cristóbal de las Casas, a beautiful ride via Ocosingo, which has a local airport, a colourful market and several hotels (**C** *Central* on Plaza, T673-0024, shower, clean, veranda. **E** *Bodas de Plata*, Av 1 Sur, clean, hot water. **E** *San Jacinto*, just off lower side of Plaza, with bath, hot water, clean, friendly. *Agua Azul*, simple rooms around courtyard, parking; *Posada Morales*) and clean restaurants, including *La Montura*, on the Plaza, good. It was one of the centres of fighting in the Ejército Zapatista de Liberación Nacional uprising in January 1994. Many buses and *colectivos* to Palenque, 2½ hours, US$3.30 and San Cristóbal de Las Casas.

Toniná
Colour map 4, grid B1

The perfect place to enjoy the countryside and Maya architecture in peace and quiet, with no crowds

The Maya ruins at Toniná are 12 km from Ocosingo, with bus links to San Cristóbal de las Casas. The road is unpaved but marked with signs once you leave Ocosingo. Beside the road is a marsh, frequented by thousands of swallows in January. A tour from San Cristóbal to Toniná costs US$15 it is possible to drive in an ordinary car, or take a taxi (US$6). There are also *colectivos* (15 mins, US$1) running from the market. To walk from Ocosingo, start in front of the church on the plaza and follow the signs, or take the 0900 bus from the market to the jungle and get off where the road forks (ask). There is a short cut through the fields: after walking for two hours you come to an official sign with a pyramid on it; don't follow the arrow but take the left fork for about 15 minutes and go through a wooden gate on your right; follow the path for 2-3 km (across a little stream and two more gates, ask farmers when in doubt). You end up in the middle of one of the last classic Maya sites, with the palace high on a hill to your left. It is well worth visiting the ruins, which were excavated by a French government team. The temples are in the Palenque style with internal sanctuaries in the back room, but influences from many different Maya styles of various periods have been found. The huge pyramid complex, seven stone platforms making a man-made hill, is 10 m higher than the Temple of the Sun at Teotihuacán and is the tallest pyramidal structure in the Mayan world. Stelae are in very diverse forms, as are wall panels, and some are in styles and of subjects unknown at any other Maya site. A beautiful stucco mural was discovered in December 1990. Ask the guardian to show you the second unrestored ball court and the sculpture kept at his house. He will show you round the whole site; there is also a small museum. ■ *0900-1600, US$1.30.* (Drinks are available at the site; also toilets and parking.)

Sleeping 10 mins' walk from Toniná is **C** *Rancho Esmeralda*. Owned by an American couple, cabañas, good meals, home-made bread, horse-riding, US$20 per person for a couple of hrs.

The series of jungle waterfalls and rapids at Agua Azul run for 7 km and are breathtakingly beautiful. They are easily visited on a day trip from Palenque. All the travel agencies, as well as many of the hotels, offer a tour there for about US$11, including a visit to the waterfall at Misol-Há (see below). Agua Azul's main swimming area has many restaurants and Indian children selling fruit. Swimming is good, in clear blue water during good weather, in muddy brown water during bad (but still refreshing if very hot, which it usually is). Swimmers should stick to the roped areas where everyone else can see them; the various graves on the steep path up the hill alongside the rapids are testament to the dangers of swimming in those areas. One of the falls is called 'The Liquidizer', an area of white water in which bathing is extremely dangerous. On no account should you enter this stretch of water; many drownings have occurred. Even in the designated areas, the currents are ferocious – the strongest swimmer will not make any progress trying to swim against them. Beware of hidden tree trunks in the water if it is murky. The path on the left of the rapids can be followed for 7 km, with superb views and secluded areas for picnics. There are also several *palapas* for hammocks, and plenty of space for free camping. ■ *Entry US$1, US$3 for cars.* Entry price is included in day trips from Palenque, which allow you to spend at least three hours at Agua Azul. *Posada Charito* in Palenque does the trip for US$7, marginally less than all the travel agencies. Kim Tours in Palenque town do a day trip taking in Agua Azul, Misol-Há *and* the Palenque ruins for US$8; a bargain, but a gruelling, hot day of excursions. Similar tour from San Cristóbal costs US$37.

To get off the tourist path, find Gerónimo, proprietor of *Casa Blanca* (see below under Sleeping and eating), who has a solid grasp of the area and its surrounding trails. He can take you either on foot or on horseback to an area beyond the falls through thick and lush forest to a series of five waterfalls that are known locally as Bolon Ahao or 'Waterfalls of the King Jaguar'. This is not a well-travelled path so it is advisable to wear long trousers, take plenty of water, some food and insect repellent. The hike takes approximately four hours round trip and costs US$5 per person; or US$3 per hour on horseback.

Agua Azul

Violent robberies have been reported; the river bridge is a particularly risky spot. Never go alone; groups of at least four are best

Sleeping and eating At Agua Azul there are many restaurants and food stalls (if on a tight budget, bring your own). There are 2 places with cabañas for hammocks (hammock rental US$1.50 and up; US$3.50 per person in beds in dormitory); if staying, be very careful of your belongings; thefts have been reported. *Camping Agua Azul* is popular and reliable, opposite the parking lot; camping costs US$1.75, US$3.30 for 2 in camper van, and US$0.15 for use of toilets (100 m further on are free public toilets). RVs can stay overnight at Agua Azul, using the facilities, without paying extra (as long as you do not leave the park). Plenty of food stalls, 2 restaurants. Follow the path up the falls to a 2nd site, cheaper, less crowded. There are more cabañas and nice places to sling a hammock further upstream, all cheaper and less touristy than lower down. *Camping Casa Blanca*, next to *Comedor El Bosque*, 2 km upstream, has 4 cabañas (**F** for a bed, US$2 for a hammock) with toilets and showers, and breakfast for a little more. *Restaurant Económico* will rent out a small hut with hammocks, friendly, helpful, excellent food, safe luggage store.

Eight kilometres from Agua Azul along the river is **Agua Clara**, a nature reserve with a small zoo, horse-riding and kayaking. Some travel agencies in Palenque include this as part of the day trip. One hotel and restaurant (ask for details at tourist office in Palenque). At Misol-Há there is a stunning waterfall usually visited first on day trips from Palenque. A narrow path winds around behind the falls, allowing you to stand behind the immense curtain of water without getting your camera wet. Swimming is possible in the large pool at the bottom of the tumbling cascade of water, but it is usually better to wait until you get to Agua Azul for a good swim. However, during the rainy season swimming is reported to be better at Misol-Há, so go by bus or check with your tour operator, as some only allow a brief stop at Misol-Há.

Misol-Há

Sleeping and eating D *cabañas* are for rent and there is a restaurant.

Tabasco and Chiapas

Warning: there are occasional military checks between Palenque and San Cristóbal de las Casas; buses and cars are stopped. If stopped at night in a private car, switch off engine and lights, and switch on the inside light. Always have your passport handy.

All the travel agencies in Palenque do a cheap tour to both Misol-Há and Agua Azul, about US$8 per person. Most tours allow about ½ hr at Misol-Há and 3-4 hrs at Agua Azul. Bring a swimsuit and plenty of drinking water. *Colectivos* from Hidalgo y Allende, Palenque, for Agua Azul and Misol-Há, 2 a day, US$9; *colectivos* can also be organized between Misol-Há and Agua Azul, in either direction. Taxi US$45 with 2 hrs at Agua Azul, or to both falls US$65. Several buses from Palenque daily (direction San Cristóbal de las Casas or Ocosingo), to crossroads leading to the waterfall, US$3.35, 2nd class, 1½ hrs. You can purchase bus tickets from *Transportes Figueroa*, about 100 m from the *ADO* bus station (in direction of the town centre) in Palenque. Bus time is approximately 1½ hrs from Palenque to the turn-off to the Agua Azul road. From the crossroads walk the 4 km downhill to the falls on a beautiful jungle-lined road (or hitch a ride on a minibus for US$1). If, after a long day at the falls, you have no desire to walk the 4 km back to the main road (steep) you can always catch a ride back to Palenque on tour buses that have extra space US$4. They leave from the Agua Azul parking lot from 1500-1800. Back from the junction 1400-1600 with *Transportes Maya* buses. There are buses between San Cristóbal de las Casas and Palenque (to 2nd class bus station, *Transportes Maya*), which will stop there, but on a number of others you must change at Temo, over 20 km away, north of Ocosingo.

Palenque

Colour map 4, grid B1

Built at the height of the Classic period on a series of artificial terraces surrounded by jungle, Palenque is one of the most beautiful of all the Maya ruins in Mexico. Palenque was clearly built for strategic purposes, with evidence of defensive apertures in some of the retaining walls. In the centre of the site is the Palace, a massive warren of buildings with an asymmetrical tower rising above them, and fine views to the north. The tower was probably used as an astronomical observatory and a watchtower. The outer buildings of the palace have an unusual series of galleries, offering shade from the jungle heat of the site.

It is extremely hot and humid at the ruins especially in the afternoon so it is best to visit as early in the day as possible

From about the fourth century AD, Palenque grew from a small agricultural village to one of the most important cities in the pre-Hispanic world, although it really achieved greatness between AD 600-800. During the long and illustrious reign of Lord Pacal, the city rapidly rose to the first rank of Maya states. The duration of Pacal's reign is still a bone of contention among Mayanists because the remains found in his sarcophagus do not appear to be those of an 81-year-old man, the age implied by the texts in the Temple of the Inscriptions.

Since its discovery, choked by the encroaching jungle that pushed against its walls and scaled the stairs of its temples once climbed by rulers, priests and acolytes, the architecture of Palenque has elicited praise and admiration and begged to be reconstructed. The corbelled vaults, the arrangement of its groupings of buildings, the impression of lightness created by walls broken by pillars and open spaces make Palenque-style architecture unique. It was only later that archaeologists and art historians realized that the architecture of Palenque was created mainly to accommodate the extraordinary sculptures and texts that referred not only to historical individuals and the important events in their lives, but also to mythological beings who endorsed the claims of dynastic continuity or 'divine right' of the rulers of this great city. The structures most illustrative of this function are the Palace, a group of buildings arranged around four patios to which a tower was later added, the Temple of the Inscriptions that rises above the tomb of Lord Pacal, and the temples of the Group of the Cross, used by Chan Bahlum, Pacal's successor, who made claims in the inscriptions carved on the tablets, pillars and balustrades of these exceptional buildings, claims which, in their audacity, are awe-inspiring.

The Palace

The Palace and Temple XI are located in the centre of the site. The Palace stands on an artificial platform over 100 m long and 9 m high. Chan Bahlum's younger brother, Kan Xul, was 57 when he became king. He devoted himself to enlarging the palace, and apparently built the four-storey tower in honour of his dead father. The top of the tower is almost at the level of Pacal's mortuary temple, and on the winter solstice the sun, viewed from here, sets directly above his crypt. Large windows where Maya astronomers could observe and chart the movement of the planets, ancestors of the royal lineage of Palenque, pierce the walls of the tower. Kan-Xul reigned for 18 years before being captured and probably sacrificed by the rulers of Toniná. During his reign Palenque reached its greatest degree of expansion, although recent excavations at the site may prove differently.

The Temple of the Inscriptions

The Temple of the Inscriptions, along with Temple XII and Temple XIII, lies to the south of the Palace group of buildings and is one of the rare Maya pyramids to have a burial chamber incorporated at the time of its construction. Access to the tomb has been restricted but may be possible around 1600, ask the local security officer. This building was erected to cover the crypt in which Lord Pacal, the founder of the first ruling dynasty of Palenque, was buried. Discovered in 1952 by Alberto Ruz-Lhuillier, the

Palenque archaeological site

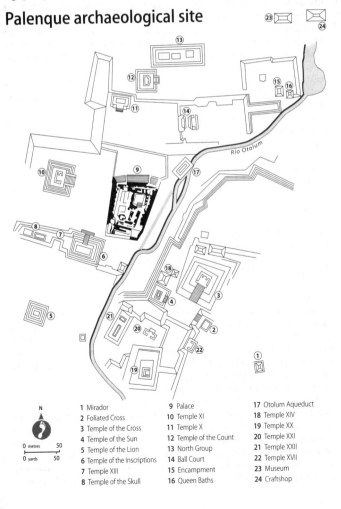

1 Mirador	9 Palace	17 Otolum Aqueduct
2 Foliated Cross	10 Temple XI	18 Temple XIV
3 Temple of the Cross	11 Temple X	19 Temple XX
4 Temple of the Sun	12 Temple of the Count	20 Temple XXI
5 Temple of the Lion	13 North Group	21 Temple XXII
6 Temple of the Inscriptions	14 Ball Court	22 Temple XVII
7 Temple XIII	15 Encampment	23 Museum
8 Temple of the Skull	16 Queen Baths	24 Craftshop

0 metres 50
0 yards 50

N

burial chamber measured 7 m long, 7 m high and 3.75 m across, an incredible achievement considering the weight of the huge pyramid pressing down upon it. According to the inscriptions, Lord Pacal was born in AD 603 and died in AD 684. Inside Ruz-Lhuillier discovered his bones adorned with jade jewellery. Around the burial chamber are various figures carved in stucco, depicting the Bolontikú, the nine lords of night of Maya mythology. There was a narrow tube alongside the stairs, presumably to give Pacal spiritual access to the outside world. Pacal also left a record of his forebears in the inscriptions. These three great tablets contain one of the longest texts of any Maya monument. There are 620 glyph blocks; they tell of Pacal's ancestors, astronomical events and an astonishing projection into the distant future (AD 4772). One of the last inscriptions reveals that, 132 days after Pacal's death, his son, Chan Bahlum, ascended to power as the new ruler of Palenque.

While finishing his father's funerary monument, Chan Bahlum had himself depicted as a child being presented as heir by his father. The portraits of Chan Bahlum, on the outer pillars of the Temple of the Inscriptions, display features that are both human and divine. He took and assumed attributes that rightly belong to the gods, thus ensuring that the heir to the throne was perceived as a divine human.

The sarcophagus lid

The sarcophagus, or coffin, is carved out of a solid piece of rock, with a carved slab covering it. Every element in the imagery of the sarcophagus lid is consistent with Maya iconography. It is exquisitely beautiful. The central image is that of Lord Pacal falling back into the fleshless jaws of the earth monster who will transport him to Xibalba, the realm of the dead. A cruciform world-tree rises above the underworld maw. The same world-tree appears on the tablets in the sanctuaries at the backs of the buildings known as the Group of the Cross. A long inscription runs around the edge of the lid, which includes a number of dates and personal names that records a dynastic sequence covering almost the whole of the seventh and eight centuries.

Four plugs in the corners of the lid filled the holes used with ropes to lower the lid into place; the plug in the southeast corner had a notch cut in it so that the channel, built into the stairway leading to the upper world, would allow spiritual communion between the dead king and his descendants above. Although the imagery of the sarcophagus lid refers to Pacal's fall into Xibalba, the location of the tower of the palace ensures that he will not remain there. The sun, setting over the crypt on the winter solstice, will have to do battle with the Nine Lords of the Night before re-emerging triumphantly in the east; the nine tiers of the pyramid represent the nine battles to be fought during his downward journey. Pacal, who awaits the sun at the point where the final battle had been fought, will accompany the sun as he re-emerges from Xibalba in the east. Palenque, the westernmost city of the Classic Maya, was in the 'dead zone', which placed it in the perfect position to accommodate the descent of the sun and Lord Pacal into the underworld.

The Group of the Temples of the Cross

To the extreme southeast of the centre of the site lie the temples of the Group of Cross and Temple XIV. The buildings known as the Grupo de la Cruz include the Temple of the Sun, with beautiful relief carvings, which would probably have been painted in their day. The three temples in this group all have dramatic roof-combs, originally believed to have a religious significance, although traces of roof-combs have been found on buildings now known to have been purely residential. In all of the temples there was discovered a huge stone tablet with bas-relief, now removed to the museum, from whose images the name of each temple was taken.

Human and mythological time come together in the inscriptions of these temples. In each tableau carved on the tablets at the back of the temples, Chan Bahlum, the new ruler, receives the regalia of office from his father, Pacal, now in the underworld and shown much smaller than his living son. The shrines in the three temples are dedicated to the Palenque Triad, a sacred trinity linked to the ruling dynasty of the city, whose genealogy is explained in the inscriptions. They were certainly long lived: the parents of the triad were born in 3122 or 3121 BC and the children arrived on 19 October, 23 October, and 6 November, 2360 BC. It has been shown that these were dates of extraordinary astronomical phenomena: the gods were intimately related to heavenly bodies and events. They also provided a mythological origin for the dynasty which is detailed on the three main tablets from the group of the Cross. Rulers died and gods were born in an impressive merging of historical and mythological events. At their completion, the three temples of the Group of the Cross housed the divine sanction for the dynasty as a whole and gave the rationale for its descent through females as well as males.

On each set of balustrades, Chan Bahlum began his text with the birth of the patron god of each temple. On the left side of the stairs, he recorded the time elapsed between the birth of the god and the dedication of the temple. Thus, mythological time and contemporary time were fused. Each temple was named for the central image on its inner tablet. When Chan Bahlum died in 702 after ruling 18 years, his younger brother and heir erected a fourth shrine to record the apotheosis of the departed king (Temple XIV). On these reliefs, Chan Bahlum emerges triumphantly from the underworld and dances towards his mother, Lady Ahpo-Hel.

The lengths to which the rulers of Palenque went to establish legitimacy for their claims of divine right could not guarantee the survival of Palenque after the collapse felt throughout the Classic Maya region, when the building of élite religious structures stopped and stelae where no longer engraved with the details of dynastic events. Toniná, the city that captured and probably sacrificed the Palenque ruler Kan-Xul, outlived the great centre made glorious by Pacal and Chan Bahlum. The last-known dated monument from the Maya region registers AD 909 at the lesser site; it is to be supposed that soon afterwards, Toniná went the way of the other centres of the Classic Maya world. ■ *0800-1700. US$4, free on Sun. There are lots of handicraft stalls at the main entrance. Colectivos back to the town leave from outside the main entrance, US$0.80, every 15 minutes. From Palenque town, take a colectivo from either of the two points (see Transport).*

The museum is on the way back to the town, with an expensive restaurant and gift shop – buy water in town. Many of the stucco carvings retrieved from the site are here, as well as jade pieces of jewellery, funerary urns and ceramics. ■ *Tue-Sun 1000-1600.* Readers wishing to learn more about the iconography and writing system of the Classic Maya are referred to: *A Forest of Kings*, L Schele and D Freidel, William Morrow and Company, NY 1990.

Warning: the ruins are surrounded by thick, mosquito-infested jungle so wear insect repellent and make sure you're up to date with your tablets (May-November is the worst time for mosquitoes). It is extremely hot and humid at the ruins, especially in the afternoon, so it is best to visit early. Unfortunately, as well as mosquitoes, there have also been reports of criminals hiding in the jungle. There are also occasional reports of muggings in out of the way places. As ever, try and leave valuables at home to minimize any loss.

Palenque town

A friendly, colourful little town whose sole reason to exist is to accommodate the tourists heading for the famous archaeological site nearby. There is plenty of accommodation for every budget, with dozens of cheap *posadas* around the centre, and a new tourist barrio, **La Cañada**, with more expensive hotels, restaurants and bars. Souvenirs are available at lower prices than elsewhere on the Ruta Maya, making Palenque a convenient place to stop off en route to the southerly Chiapan towns of San Cristóbal and Tuxtla Gutiérrez. Travellers coming to Palenque from Mérida, Campeche and other cities in the Yucatán Peninsula will find it much hotter than those places, particularly in June, July and August. The *Fiesta de Santo Domingo* takes place in the first week of August.

The **tourist office** is on Juárez, a block below the plaza and next to the *Artesanía* market. They are very helpful and provide good free map of Palenque and the ruins.

Phone code: 916
Colour map 4, grid B2
Population: 22,000

Visitors to Palenque and other communities in Chiapas should respect the local customs and dress so as not to offend – footwear and shirts should always be worn

Tabasco and Chiapas

■ *Open daily 0800-2000. There's another City Tourism Office in the Palacio Municipal on Independencia.* ■ *Daily 0800-1500 and 1600-2000.* A new **tourist polic**-office, on Av Reforma and Francisco Javier, T345-0788, works in conjunction with the tourist office. ■ *0900-1300 and 1800-2100.* Also check out the website a **www.palenque.com.mx**

Sleeping

■ *on map*
Price codes:
see inside front cover

It is convenient to stay at hotels near the Pemex service station, as they are also nearer the ruins and the bus stations.

Prices treble around fiesta time

AL *Maya Tucán*, on road into town, T345-0290. Swimming pool, a/c, bar, restaurant, lovely views from rooms. **B** *Chan Kah Centro*, corner of Juárez and Independencia, T345-0318, F345-0489. A/c, restaurant, street car parking, terrace bar with happy hour. **B** *Maya Tulipanes*, Cañada 6, T345-0201, F345-1004, www.mayatulipanes.com.mx A/c, cable TV, rooms vary in size, price and quality, garage, pool, bar/restaurant next door. Recommended **B-C** *Kashlan*, 5 de Mayo 105, T345-0297, F345-0309. With bath, fan or a/c, hot water, quiet, clean, will store luggage, mosquito nets, helpful owner Ada Luz Navarro, tours to Agua Azul and Misol-Há falls, US$13 per person, laundry opposite, restaurant with vegetarian food in same building, bus and boat tours to Flores in Guatemala offered, internet US$1.50/hr. Recommended. **B-C** *Los Leones*, Km 2.5, T345-1110, F345-0033. About 5 km before ruins on main road, hot water, a/c, TV, quiet, large restaurant, 'gringo' food.

C *La Cañada*, Merle Green 13, T345-0102, F345-0446. Very rustic but very clean, with fan, good value, lovely garden, expensive restaurant, the owner, Sr Morales, is an expert on the ruins. **C** *Nikte-Há*, Juárez between Allende and Aldama, T345-0934. New, modern building, friendly, a/c, TV.

D *Lacroix*, Hidalgo 30, T345-0014, next to church. With bath, fan, no hot water, some cheaper rooms, pleasant place. **D** *La Posada*, at La Cañada, T345-0437. Hot water, fans, basic, a little run down but OK, 'designed for young travellers, international ambience', peaceful, luggage store. **D** *Naj K'in*, Hidalgo 72. With bath and fan, hot water 24 hrs, purified water in reception and cooler in hallway, safe parking. **D** *Posada Mallorca*, on highway, T345-0838. Small rooms, comfortable. **D** *Posada Shalom*, Av Juárez 156, T345-0944. New, friendly, clean, noisy, stores luggage. Recommended. **D** *Xibalba*, Merle Green 9, T345-0411, F345-0392. Spacious rooms, clean, hot water, a/c, fan. Recommended.

D-E *Marantha*, 20 de Noviembre 19, T345-1007. New hotel. Same owners as *Posada Charito* (T345-0121). Family-run, friendly service, some rooms have TV at no extra charge.

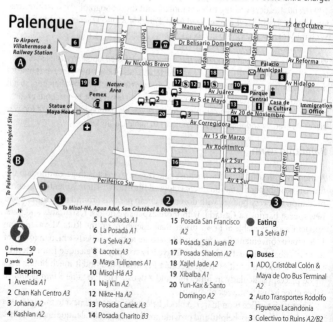

Palenque

Sleeping
1 Avenida *A1*
2 Chan Kah Centro *A3*
3 Johana *A2*
4 Kashlan *A2*
5 La Cañada *A1*
6 La Posada *A1*
7 La Selva *A2*
8 Lacroix *A3*
9 Maya Tulipanes *A1*
10 Misol-Há *A3*
11 Naj K'in *A2*
12 Nikte-Ha *A2*
13 Posada Canek *A3*
14 Posada Charito *B3*
15 Posada San Francisco *A2*
16 Posada San Juan *B2*
17 Posada Shalom *A2*
18 Xajlel Jade *A2*
19 Xibalba *A1*
20 Yun-Kax & Santo Domingo *A2*

● **Eating**
1 La Selva *B1*

🚌 **Buses**
1 ADO, Cristóbal Colón & Maya de Oro Bus Terminal *A2*
2 Auto Transportes Rodolfo Figueroa Lacandonia
3 Colectivo to Ruins *A2/B2*

Tabasco and Chiapas

-E *Xajlel Jade*, Hidalgo 61, T345-0463. Clean, comfortable rooms in quiet street, family-run, ot water. Recommended. **D-E** *Yun-Kax*, Av Corregidora 87 (behind *Santo Domingo*), 345-0146. Quiet, clean, large rooms, hot water. Recommended.

E *Avenida*, Juárez 216, T345-0116. With restaurant, clean, large rooms with fan, parking, ut does not display price in rooms so ask for government list to check, no hot showers, ome rooms with balcony. **E** *La Selva*, Av Reforma 69. Newly renovated, very good value, ame owners as *Posada Charito*, clean. **E** *Misol-Há*, at Juárez 12, T345-0092. Fan, with bath, ot water, clean, owner Susana Cuevas speaks English. **E** *Posada Kin*, Abasolo s/n, 20 de oviembre y 5 de Mayo T345-1714, very near Zócalo. Clean doubles with bathroom, fan, ours available, safe and luggage store. **E** *Posada San Francisco*, Hidalgo 113 and Allende. Vith bath, clean, quiet, no curtains, basic. **E** *San Miguel*, Hidalgo and Aldama, above Union Pharmacy. T345-0152, new, big clean rooms, balcony, hot water and fan, good value. Recommended. **E** *Vaca Vieja*, 5 de Mayo 42, T345-0388, 3 blocks from plaza. With bath, popular with gringos, good restaurant. **E-F** *Posada Canek*, 20 de Noviembre. More expensive rooms ave bath, all with fan and toilet, very clean, ground floor dormitory near reception noisy, helpful staff, prices are per person, fills up early in peak time, arrive before 1000 check-out ime. **E-F** *Posada Nacha'n Ka'an*, 20 de Noviembre 25 and Allende. Hot water, fans, cheaper rooms in the dormitory. Recommended. **E-F** *Posada San Juan*, T345-0616 (from *ADO* go up he hill and 1st right, it's on the 4th block on the left). With bath, cheaper without, cold water, and fan, clean, quiet, firm beds, secure locks, nice courtyard, very good for budget accommo-dation, safe parking available (also near buses, Santo Domingo, 20 de Noviembre 19, T345-0146, stores luggage).

F *Johana*, 20 de Noviembre and Allende. Large, clean, airless rooms with fan and bath. **F** *Posada Charito*, 20 de Noviembre 15B, T345-0121. Clean, friendly, family-run, very good value, basic, some rooms very airless, ground floor best, laundry service. Opposite is **F** *Posada Kushul-ha*, 20 de Noviembre 131. T345-0483. New, clean rooms with bath, fan, TV. Close to bus stations. Next door **F** *Santo Domingo*, 20 de Noviembre 119, T345-0146, cheap and cheerful, marginally clean, but one of cheapest in town close to bus, cold showers.

Camping *Trailer Park Mayabel*, on road to ruins, 2 km before entrance (bus from town US$0.30). For caravans and tents, US$8 per vehicle with 2 people. US$2.35 for tent or to sling hammock (an *ambulante* sells hammocks once a day, or you can hire them for an additional US$2.50), palmleaf huts, bathrooms, hot showers, good restaurant but not cheap, nice set-ting (double room with shower US$12.50). Cabins for US$30 and US$40 with a/c available, popular so can be noisy, the place is not to everyone's taste; many mosquitoes and many ticks in long grass. Watch your belongings; management sometimes stores luggage during the day (reluctant to store valuables). At night, around 0100, you can often hear the howler monkeys screaming in the jungle; quite eerie.

El Panchan Camping, on road to ruins, is host to a fascinating mix of very different phi-losophies, foods and intellectual interests. Don Moisés, founder of Panchan, first came to Palenque as an archaeologist and was one of the first guides to the ruins. He bought a plot of land, named it Panchan – Maya for 'heaven on earth' – and started to raise a family. Now he has divided lots among his children who run the following businesses: **D-E** *Chetos Cabins*, hot water, private bath, 2 apartments with kitchenettes for longer stays and *Don Mucho* restaurant, completely outdoors, excellent Italian-Mexican food, fantastic break-fast, people come from Palenque town to eat here, often with fire dancing at night, quite exotic given the forest backdrop, will host 'passing through,' travelling musicians. **D-E** *Ed and Margaritas*, edcabanas@yahoo.com, the plushest cabins at Panchan. Private thatched roof cabins, very comfortable, very clean, private bath, hot water, caretaker Pablo is friendly and helpful. **E-F** *Rakshita*, cabins, place to sling a hammock, Maya study area, meditation area, *Rakshita's Vegetarian Restaurant*, whimsical, doused in spirituality, housed by a throng of belly danceresque gals, good array of vegetarian platters. Deli-ciously original fruit shakes. There is also a steam bath at Panchan (US$3 for 1½ hrs) and perhaps refreshing to know that: it is about 10° cooler at Panchan than Palenque town due to the dense foliage cover. Although vastly different, all businesses at Panchan have inter-twined themselves into the natural jungle that surrounds them; an almost Robinson

Tabasco and Chiapas

Crusoe setting. Recommended. F *Jungle Palace*, quiet place to sling hammocks. **F** *Beto* sling a hammock, prepare for loud dance music at night, outside bar.

Good swimming at *Calinda Nututún* (entry US$1), 3½ km along Palenque-Ocosingo roa T345-0100, F345-0620. US$3.30 per person, vehicle free, US$2 per camping site per nigh rather run down, no tent rentals, rooms (**B**) are neglected, toilets and bath; beautiful lake an waterfall open to the public for a small fee. Misol-Há, 2 km off same road at Km 19, see abov **F** *Elementos Naturales*, on road to ruins, past Panchan, enpalenque@hotmail.com Yout hostel, can sling hammock US$3 or camp US$3. Includes breakfast. Pleasant outdoor feel.

Eating **Expensive** The classier restaurants are in the barrio La Cañada, behind the Maya head as yo enter the town, eg *El Tapanco Grill*, Av Juárez 65, 2 blocks below Plaza above *Bing* ice-cream shop. Good steak, balcony dining. *Las Tinajas*, 20 de Noviembre 41 y Abasolo. Good, fam ily-run, excellent food, huge portions, highly recommended. At Km 0.5 on Hidalgo (road t ruins) is La Selva. Excellent, smart dress preferred, live music at weekends, recommended.

Mid-range *El Herradero*, Av Juárez 120. Breakfast and reasonably priced meals, fast ser vice, open 24 hours. Recommended. *Don Mucho*, at *Panchan Camping*, road to ruins, excel lent Italian-Mexican food and great breakfast. *Rakshitas Vegetarian Restaurant*, a *Panchan Camping*, road to ruins, across the walkway from *Don Mucho*. Delicious vegetarian cuisine. See *Panchan* above. *Merolec*, down street from *La Posada*. Good atmosphere and service. *Lakan-Há*, Juárez 20. Good tacos, fast, efficient. *El Rodeo*, Juárez 116, near plaza Does good breakfasts and meat dishes, popular with travellers. Recommended *Pizzería Palenque*, Juárez 168 and Allende, T345-0332. Good pizzas and prices. *Mara's*, Juárez 1, by the Zócalo. Excellent food, very welcoming, colourful ambience, cheap set menus. *Artemio*, Av Hidalgo, near plaza. Reasonably priced food. Recommended. *Casa Grande*, upstairs on plaza. Good value, set menu and happy hour, good for people watching. *Chan Kah*, on plaza. Good value, accepts credit cards. *Yunuen*, at *Hotel Vaca Vieja*. Generous portions at reasonable prices, good steaks, popular with local ranchers. *Restaurante Maya*, Hidalgo and Independencia. Very popular, fills up by 1900, set-menu lunches and à-la-carte dinner, mainly Mexican.

Cheap *Los Portales*, Av 20 de Noviembre and Independencia. Cheap, good. Recom mended. Good *pollo rostizado* in restaurant inside *ADO* office. Good tacos at food stalls east of Parque Central. Try the ice-cream at *Holanda*, Av Juárez s/n, 4 doors west of *Banamex*, in the centre. *Mundo Maya*, Juárez 10, friendly, good and cheap Mexican fare. **Cafés** Opposite *Hotel Kashlan*, *Café de los Altos*. Good coffee. *Café de Yarra*, Hidalgo 66. New café, stylish setting, good for breakfast, Reasonable prices and relaxed atmosphere. *El Rinconcito*, Allende, across from *Kashlan*. Good, economical.

Bars *El Rocamar*, Plaza Independencia and Av 5 de Mayo. Restaurant/bar. Watch your change. *Discoteca Kichan*, 20 de Noviembre, varied music.

Shopping Av Juárez is lined with souvenir shops selling hammocks, blankets, Maya figurines and hats. Sales staff are much less pushy than in towns in the Yucatán Peninsula, but bargaining is still necessary to get good prices.

Sports **Horse-riding** tours can be booked at the *Clínica Dental Zepeda*, Juárez s/n – the dentist owns the horses – good way of checking their health! Also through *Cabañas de Safari* in Palenque archaeological zone Km 1 T345-0026, *Gaspar Alvaro* also rents horses. He can be located at his house on the road to the ruins, directly in front of *Mayabel*. Gaspar will take you on a 3-hr ride through rainforested trails in the surrounding area of the ruins. Good chance of seeing monkeys and toucans. US$15 for 3 hrs. Tell him specifically that you want to go through the rainforest and not on the road. **Microlight** for the upwardly mobile. *Fernando Maza*'s house is next door to Gaspar's (see above). He operates a powered hang glider; for US$35 and in 10 mins he will take you soaring over Palenque ruins.

Local Buses: micro buses run back and forth along the main street, passing the bus station area, to and from the ruins, every 10 mins, US$0.80 (taxi US$5). All bus companies have terminals close to each other at west end of Av Juárez with 20 de Noviembre. **Taxis**: charge a flat rate of US$1 within the town, US$4 to the *Panchan* and nearby *Mayabel* camping areas. **Colectivos** to the ruins run from 2 places, every 15 mins starting at 0600; last one passes by Panchan at 1830: Allende between Hidalgo and Juárez, and from Allende between 20 de Noviembre and Corregidora. US$0.70, but they pass along the main road and only drop you at the ticket office before the ruins; it is a further 1 km uphill from there, US$0.50. *Colectivos* to Playas de Catazajá (for Escárcega and Campeche) leave from Allende between 20 de Noviembre and Corregidora, US$0.80. There is also a collectivo service to Sant Elena/Flores – see Hotels for booking.

Transport

Long distance Air: *Aerocaribe* flies daily during the high season to Palenque from **Cancún** via Flores, Guatemala – check with travel agents. There are also flights from **Huatulco**, **Mérida**, **Oaxaca** and **Tuxtla Gutiérrez**. For flights to Bonampak and Yaxchilán, see below.

Bus: there are 3 bus terminals, 2 smaller 2nd class ones serving destinations in Chiapas state, and the *ADO/Cristóbal Colón* terminal, with buses to Chiapas destinations as well as longer journeys, all on 1st class buses. **Cancún**: 1st class terminal, 2000, 13 hrs, US$30. 2nd class buses, 2345, US$23. **Campeche**: 1st class terminal, 2345, US$30, 0800 and 2100, 5 hrs, US$13 (*ADO*); 2nd class buses, 2345, US$10. **Escárcega**: 1st class terminal, 1410, 1730, 3 hrs, US$10; 2nd class 2345, US$6. **Mérida**: 1st class terminal, 0800, 2100, 9 hrs, US$20; 2nd class buses, 2345, US$15. **Mexico City**: 1st class terminal, 1800, 2000, 16 hrs, US$41. **Oaxaca**: 1st class terminal, 1730, 15 hrs, US$30 (*ADO*). **San Cristóbal**: 1st class terminal, 0930, 1830, 5 hrs, US$6.50 (also 1st class service from *Lacandonia* terminal, 2 doors down, 8 a day, US$11); 2nd class buses, same times as Tuxtla, US$5.50; from the *Lacandonia* terminal, next door to *Express Plus*, 0530, 0645, 0845, US$5. **Tulum**: 1st class terminal, 2000, 11 hrs, US$26. **Tuxtla Gutiérrez**: 1st class terminal, 0930, 1200, 1830, 6 hrs, US$9.40; 2nd class buses, 3 a day from 0730, US$7. **Villahermosa**: 2nd class buses, 6 per day from 0500, US$4.

Banks Exchange rate only comes through at 1000, then banks open until 1200. *Bancomer*, changes TCs, good rates. *Yax-Há Cambio* on Juárez, open 0700-2000 daily, changes US$ cash and TCs. Next door at No 28, is *Banamex*, open Mon-Fri 0930-1400, slow. *Restaurante El Rodeo* also changes TCs at bank rate. At weekends TCs can be changed at many travel agencies and other shops on Av Juárez; also, the owner at *Farmacia Central* will change US$ at a reasonable rate. ATMs at *Bancomer* and *Banamex*, but with long queues.

Directory

Communications Internet: several internet café's along Juárez with good service and prices ranging from US$1-US$1.50/hr. **Post office**: Independencia, next to Palacio Municipal, helpful, open Mon-Fri 0900-1300. **Telephone**: long-distance telephones at *ADO* bus terminal, cheaper than many other telephone offices; at *Mercería* bookshop in Aldama near Juárez, and a shop by *Hotel Palenque* in Zócalo.

Laundry Opposite *Hotel Kashlan*, US$2 per 3 kg, open 0800-1930. At the end of Juárez is a laundry, US$3 per 3 kg.

Tour operators *Inter Travel*, Juárez 48, T345-1566, www.palenque.com.mx/intertravel, domestic and international flight arrangements, hotel reservations, a new tour to **Lagunas Catazajá** (27 km from Palenque). Includes a 3-hr motor boat ride and a visit to a bird sanctuary, US$45 per person, minimum 4 people. *Na Chan Kan*, corner of Hidalgo and Jiménez, T345-0263, www.palenquemx.com/viajesnachan Offer a wide selection of packages ranging from tours to Agua Azul to tours of the Yaxchilán and Bonampak ruins as well as transportation to Guatemala. *Toniná*, Juárez 105, T345-0384, or small office on Juárez ½ block from plaza, mixed reports, questionable reliability, clarify prices before tour, tours to Bonampak and Yaxchilán, 2 days, US$55 per person. *Yax-Há*, Av Juárez 123, T345-0798, F345-0767. English spoken. Recommended. *Shivalva* (Marco A Morales), Merle Green 1, La Cañada, T345-0411, F345-0392, tours of Palenque, Yaxchilán, Bonampak, Tikal, Guatemala City, Belize, Copán. *Viajes Mayasol*, Juárez 191, T345-1006, F345-0282, mayasol@hotmail.com Adventure tours to Chacamax River, all-day trek, rafting, lunch US$58. Many other rafting and adventure trips of between 1 and 6 days. *Kim Tours*, Juárez opposite *Banamex*. 2-day trip to Yaxchilán and Bonampak US$48, 4-hr jungle walk with swim and visit to ruins with guide, US$15, also adventure trips on the Usumacinta River. *Alonso Méndez* is a well-versed guide with extensive knowledge of flora, fauna, medicinal uses of plants and an intimate knowledge of the Palenque ruins. A respected authority on Chiapan ethnobotany, Alonso has a unique gift of academic and spiritual understanding of the rainforest. He speaks English, Spanish and Tzeltzal and can be found at his home in the *Panchan* camping site. Full-day hiking trips US$50 for a group of 6-8 people. Highly recommended.

Yaxchilán and Bonampak

Colour map 4, grid B2

Take suitable footwear and rain protection for jungle walking, drinking water, insect repellent and passport (military checkpoints). Beware of mosquitoes and sandflies, which can cause river blindness

Yaxchilán is a major Classic Maya centre built along a terrace and hills above the Río Usumacinta. The temples are ornately decorated with stucco and stone and the stone lintels are carved with scenes of ceremonies and conquests. There are more howler monkeys than people in Yaxchilán. Bonampak, originally under the political domination of Yaxchilán, was built in the late Classic period on the Río Lacanjá, a tributary of the Usumacinta. It is famous for its murals, dated at AD 800, which relate the story of a battle and the bloody aftermath with the sacrificial torture and execution of prisoners.

From around AD 200 to the early 10th century, the era known as the Classic Maya witnessed the growth of many small settlements into great centres noted for wonderful architecture, sculpture, painted ceramics, impressive advances in mathematics and hieroglyphic writings, and the growth of an elite who often created alliances with other polities through marriage. Wide causeways, *sacbés*, were built between centres enabling the inhabitants to maintain contact with those of other towns. All these great advances came to an end around AD 909, when the Classic Maya civilization collapsed. For many years Mayanists have postulated about the cause of the collapse: some have suggested land exhaustion, others have suggested invasion from the Central Highlands, while still others believe in a peasant revolt against the conspicuous consumption of an ever-expanding elite. The painted walls of Structure 1 at Bonampak illustrate well the extravagance indulged in by the elite of this centre on the margins of the Lacandón rainforest.

An article in National Geographic, February 1995, reproduces some of the murals with computer enhancement to show their original colours and most of the details

The murals at Bonampak are very realistic with an excellent use of colour and available space. Painted on the walls, vault rises and benches of three adjoining but not interconnecting rooms, they describe the rituals surrounding the presentation at court of the future ruler. Some of the rituals were separated by considerable intervals, which adds to the solemnity of the ceremony. It is very possible that the rituals illustrated were only a small selection of a far greater series of events. The people participating were mainly elite, including the royal family, and a strict hierarchy was observed in which eminent lords were attended by minor nobility.

In Room 1, the celebration opens with the presentation of the young prince, a simple act in which a porter introduces the child to an assembly of lords, dressed for the occasion in white robes. The king, dressed simply, watches from his throne. Also present are two representatives from Yaxchilán, one male and one female. It is probable that the female is the wife or consort of Chaan-Muan, the ruler of Bonampak. After this simple opening, the spectacle begins. Lords are represented dressing in sumptuous clothing and jewellery, musicians appear playing drums, turtle carapaces, rattles and trumpets and they all line up for a procession, which will bemuse the peasantry, labourers and artisans waiting outside. We never see the lower orders, but, open-mouthed, we can stand with them to observe the spectacle. The headdresses alone are enough to bedazzle us and the great diversity in the attire of the participants illustrates the wide spectrum of social functions fulfilled by those attending the ceremony.

The imagery and text of the sculptured lintels and stelae at nearby Yaxchilán proclaim the right of the heir to accede to the throne while emphasizing the need to take captives to be sacrificed in honour of the king-to-be. This need is echoed in the paintings of Room 2, Structure 1, at Bonampak. A ferocious battle is in progress in which the ruler, Chaan-Muan, proves his right to the throne. In the midst of battle, he shines out heroically. The local warriors pull the hair of those of the opposite side, whose identity is not known. Many captives were taken. In the ensuing scene, the full horror of the fate of those captured by the Maya is illustrated.

On a stepped structure, the ruler Chaan-Muan oversees the torture and mutilation of the captives taken in the recent battle. This event is clearly in the open air and surely witnessed by the inhabitants of Bonampak, whose loyalty is rewarded by admission to the bloody circus. The torture of the captives consisted of mutilation of the hands; some disconsolate individuals hold up their hands dripping blood, while one has clearly been decapitated, his head resting on a bed of leaves. It is to be supposed that the torture of the captives would be followed by death, probably by decapitation. The gods demanded sacrifice, which was provided by the rulers in an extravaganza of bloodletting. It must be understood that what appears to be outright bloodthirstiness was a necessary part of Maya ritual and probably accepted by all the polities throughout the Classic Maya region. It is very probable that the heir would not have been acceptable without this gory ritual.

The murals of the third room at Bonampak express the events that were meant to close the series of rituals designed to consolidate the claim to the throne by the son of the ruler. At first sight, the paintings that cover the walls of room three of Structure 1 appear to celebrate the sacrifices of the previous depictions in an exuberant public display of music, dance and perhaps song. The background is a pyramid, and ten elegantly dressed lords dance on different levels, colourful 'dance-wings' sprouting from their hips. The dominant dancer on the uppermost level is believed to be the ruler, Chaan-Muan. However, it has been noted that a very strong element of sacrifice accompanies the extrovert display. In a more private corner, the royal family is portrayed preparing to engage in blood sacrifice; a servant proffers them a container that the sacred bloodletting instruments. There are also indications that the male dancers had already drawn blood by means of penis perforation. As at Yaxchilán, blood endorsed the dynastic claims of the royal family.

The rituals portrayed on the walls of Structure 1 at Bonampak are thought to have been performed between 790 and 792, a time when the collapse of the Classic Maya was beginning to be felt. The extravagant use of enormous amounts of fine cloth, expensive jaguar pelts, jade beads and pectorals, elegant costumes, headdresses made from rare feathers, and spondylus shells was not enough to reverse the decadence of the civilization that had produced magnificent works in art, architecture, jewellery, mathematics, astronomy and glyphic writing: within a hundred years, the jungle was to claim it for its own. ■ *0800-1600 (both sites). US$3 entry to Yaxchilán. At Bonampak site entrance is officially free, but there appears to be a charge several kilometres from the gate of US$7, and then an additional entrance charge of US$2.50.*

Sleeping There is basic accommodation at the site, take hammock and mosquito net. Thieving has been reported.

Transport A new road has been built to **Bonampak**: 2 lanes, paved. *Autotransportes Comitán Lagos de Montebello* (Manuel Velasco 48, 2 blocks west of plaza, Palenque) buses at 0300, 0430, 0630, 0900 and 2000 all pass the turn-off to Bonampak, US$5.50, check details in advance. Last *colectivo* returning from Echeverría to Palenque passing crossroads for Bonampak at 1500. Buses from Palenque from Chancalá bus terminal every 3 hrs or so, from 0730 to **San Javier**, 3 hrs; *colectivos* US$4. From San Javier, a jungle trail leads to Bonampak, easy to follow but several hrs' walk with nowhere to stay en route. Take your own tent, hammock and sleeping bag as it gets cold at night, as well as food and drink. **Yaxchilán** is reached by 1-hr boat journey from Echeverría; you must register at the immigration office here if you are continuing on to Guatemala. US$67 for up to 4 people, US$92 for more than 5, to hire a motorboat for the round trip. There is no problem finding a boat (max 10 people, cost includes boatman staying overnight), but try to be there before 0900 to meet other travellers wanting to share launch, you may be able to share with tour parties who arrive from 0900 onwards. It is a beautiful ride, with rewarding ruins at the end of it. The custodian of the ruins is very helpful. Camping is restricted to the INAH site on the Usumacinta.

Air: flights from Palenque to **Bonampak** and **Yaxchilán**, in light plane for 5, about US$600 per plane, to both places, whole trip 6 hrs. Prices set, list available; *Viajes Misol-Há* Juárez 48 at Aldama, T345-0911, run charter flights to Bonampak and Yaxchilán for US$150 per person return, minimum 4 passengers. *ATC Travel Agency*, agents for *Aviacsa*, at Av Juárez and Allende, open 0800-1800 daily except Sun, to Bonampak; book at airport, may be cheaper from Tenosique, best to visit in May – the driest month. **Road**: Bonampak is over 30 km from Frontera Echeverría/Corozal and can be reached from the crossroads to Lacanjá on the road to Echeverría/Corozal.

Directory Tour operators: from Palenque, a 2-day road and river trip to Bonampak and Yaxchilán is sold by travel agencies, US$55 per person, all transport and food included; or 1-day trip to Yaxchilán, US$35; entrance to sites included in cost. Strenuous, but good value: the usual schedule is 4-hr bus ride to Echeverría/Corozal (mostly tarmac), 1 hr boat to Yaxchilán, next day boat to Echeverría, 1 hr bus to Bonampak turn-off, walk to Bonampak and back, 3-4 hrs bus to Palenque (arriving 2200). *Colectivos Chambala* at Hidalgo y Allende, Palenque, also run 2-day trips, slightly cheaper, again all-inclusive, minimum 6 passengers. Taxis charge US$20 per person for the return trip to Bonampak. Lacandón Indians running an ecotourism project take passengers in 3-wheelers to the ruins (or to Lacanjá Chansayab community), US$7.

Lacanjá At Lacanjá (9 km from Bonampak) there is a community of Lacandón Indians. They have curly hair, rare in Mexico, and wear white gowns. For more details ask at Na-Bolom in San Cristóbal de las Casas. There are four campsites here where you can sling a hammock: *Kin Bor, Vicente K'in, Carlos Chan Bor* and *Manuel Chan Bor* (best to bring food and mosquito net). Local guides can be hired for hikes in the jungle and to the ruins of Bonampak. Lucas Chambor at the *Casa de Cultura* is a good source of advice. There have been some reports of hostility towards tourists. Transport Lacanjá-Bonampak with locals US$6.50-9. The walk through the jungle is beautiful and crosses several streams. Another walk in the area is to the **Cascadas de Moctuniha** (one hour each way US$6.50 with guide).

Routes to Guatemala

There are two main border crossings into Guatemala: one at Ciudad Cuauhtémoc, reached via Route 190 from San Cristóbal de las Casas, and the other at Tapachula along the coastal Route 200 from the neighbouring state of Oaxaca. A third option is to cross the border by boat, east of Palenque, along the rivers San Pedro or Usumacinta. Note: if planning on returning to Mexico after an excursion to Guatemala, ensure you get an exit stamp, at the immigration office. When you re-enter you will then have to pay US$18 for a visa. Pick up your tourist card and a slip of paper, take this to any bank, pay US$18 and the slip is stamped. Not doing this can lead to problems when you try to leave Mexico again.

River travel to Guatemala

Tenosique & Río San Pedro route The Río San Pedro route starts at Tenosique, a friendly place east of Palenque (money exchange at clothing shop, Ortiz y Alvarez at Calle 28 No 404, good rates for dollars to quetzales, poor for dollars to pesos). From here the route takes you by road to La Palma, boat to El Naranjo, in Guatemala, and then road to Flores.

Sleeping and eating D *Rome*, Calle 28, 400, T342-2151. Clean, will change dollars for residents, bath, not bad. **E** *Azulejos*, Calle 26, 416. With bath, fan, clean, hot water, friendly, helpful owner speaks some English, opposite church. **E** *Casa de Huéspedes La Valle*, Calle 19. With bath, good, but a little grubby.

Transport You can get to Tenosique from **Villahermosa** by *ADO* bus (0430, 0700, 0800, 1330), 4 hrs, from **Emiliano Zapata** by frequent 1st or 2nd class bus, US$2. From Palenque minibuses Libertad leave from 20 de Noviembre y Allende from 0700 to Emiliano Zapata, 1 hr, US$2.50 (take 0700 to be sure of making the boat at La Palma); and from there to Tenosique at 0800 or 0900, 90 mins, US$2. *ADO* have a direct bus to Tenosique from **Palenque** at 0430, 2 hrs, US$3.25. Many travel agents in Palenque organize *colectivos* direct to **La Palma** at 1000, US$14 per person to connect with the boat to **El Naranjo** (4 passengers minimum). Alternatively, take a *colectivo* before 0645 to Playas de Catazajá from the stop just up from *ADO* (US$1.00, 30 mins); get off at the El Crucero de la Playa crossroads on the Villahermosa-Tenosique road and wait for the bus to pass at 0730 (2 hrs to Tenosique, US$2). Similarly, from Tenosique to Palenque, take the Villahermosa bus (every hour or so during the day) as far as El Crucero de la Playa, and then take one of the regular minibuses running to Palenque. Bus also from **Mexico City**: *ADO*, 16½ hrs, arrives 0700, US$45.50.

Tour operators For planes to Bonampak contact Sr Quintero, T342-0099. *Hotel Kashlan*, Palenque, offers 2-day and 3-day trips to Flores via Yaxchilán and Bonampak. Reliable and recommended. *Kim Tours*, Av Juárez 27, Palenque, T345-1499. Do similar trips, 'strenuous but great', US$100 per person. Recommended. Travel agencies in Palenque also do the trip to Flores via La Palma and El Naranjo, US$35-55 per person, 3 passengers minimum (agencies will make up the numbers), departs 0500, arrive Flores 1900; via Corozal/Bethel, US$35 per person, via Yaxchilán and Bonampak, see below, minimum 5 people. It may take several days before you can join an organized trip in low season. On Av Juárez several agencies offer tours to Flores by minibus and/or taxi, boat and public bus, via Tenosique, La Palma and El Naranjo. You probably won't meet any other travellers. Difficult to find enough people during the low season (otherwise you pay the whole trip yourself), about US$70 per person, 16-hrs trip.

From Tenosique to **La Palma** on the Río San Pedro, colectivos starting at 0600 from in front of the market, one hour, US$1, two hours by bus (from Tenosique bus station, which is outside town, take taxi, US$1.70 or colectivo to 'Centro', or walk 20 minutes). Taxi to La Palma US$7, shared by all passengers. From La Palma boats leave to El Naranjo (Guatemala) at 0800 (or when they have enough passengers), but timings are very irregular (they wait for a minimum of five passengers before leaving), at least 4½ hours, US$22 (to check boat times, T343-0811 Rural at the Río San Pedro). Be at the boat one hour early, it sometimes leaves ahead of schedule; if this happens ask around for someone to chase it, US$3-4 per person for three people. If there are fewer than five passengers, the boat may be cancelled, in which case you must either wait for the next one, or hire a *rápido* (US$125, maximum four people). You may be able to arrange a slower boat for up to six people for US$100. In La Palma, two restaurants are poor value; one restaurant will change money at weekends at a reasonable rate.

It is a beautiful boat trip, through mangroves with flocks of white herons and the occasional alligator, dropping people off at homesteads. There is a stop at the border post two hours into the journey to sign out of Mexico, a lovely spot with a lake and lilies. In the rain, your backpack will get wet; take waterproofs and a torch/flashlight. There are no officials on arrival at the jetty in El Naranjo; immigration is a short way uphill on the right (entry will cost US$5 in quetzales or dollars, beware extra unofficial charges at customs); bus tickets to Flores are sold here.

At **El Naranjo** there are hotels (basic) and restaurants (you can wait in a restaurant till the 0100 bus departs, but electricity is turned off at 2200). The grocery store opposite immigration will change dollars into quetzales at a poor rate. From El Naranjo there is a dirt road through the jungle to Flores; buses leave at 0200, 0400, 0600, 1100, 1400 for Flores (minimum 4-5 rough, crowded hours, US$3), or hitchhiking is apparently possible.

The Río Usumacinta route takes you by road to Benemérito (southeast of Uaxchilán and Bonampak), boat to Sayaxché, Guatemala and then road to Flores. Autotransportes Comitán Lagos de Montebello buses (Avenida Manuel Velasco Suárez, Palenque, three blocks from food market) run eight a day starting at 0400 until 1530 to **Benemérito**, on the Mexican side of the Usumacinta, 7-12 hours but will be quicker when the new paved road is completed; basic buses, dreadful road, crowded (it's about half the time in a *camioneta* if you can hitch a ride). You must visit

Río Usumacinta route
Latest reports suggest this post may be closed check in Palenque before leaving

Tabasco and Chiapas

immigration, about 3 km from Benemérito, to sign out of Mexico (the bus will wait)

Once in Benemérito where there is a 2100 curfew (two basic *pensiones*), hope for a boat to Guatemala; this may take a couple of days. The boat goes to Sayaxché and should stop at Pipiles for immigration. A trading boat takes two days, US$4-5; a motorized canoe eight hours, US$5-10. From Sayaxché, buses run to Flores.

Alternatively, take the bus Palenque-Frontera Echeverría, now more often known as Puerto Corozal, 1000, four hours by good road, US$5.50; or minibuses at 0730, 1100, 1400 from 5 de Mayo by *Restaurante El Caimito*, US$4.50 (many travel agencies in Palenque run minibuses on this route, leaving at 0600, to connect with the boat to Bethel, 35 minutes, and on to Flores as below). From Echeverría/Corozal there is a five-minute launch ride to La Técnica, then 20 minutes by bus to Bethel in Guatemala, from where a regular bus service goes to Flores at 1200, five hours, although some reports suggest this service has now stopped. Alternatively launches go directly to Bethel, US$40-45 per boat. At Echeverría/Corozal there is an immigration office; **F** *Posada XX*, nearby, and **F** *Posada Tumbala*, better of the two; near the *embarcadero* are **C** *cabañas* with two double beds, built by the river boat company (Cooperativa Escudo Jaguar de Corozal) and two cheap *comedores*. Coming from Guatemala you may well get stuck at the border as the 0500 Santa Elena-Bethel bus does not connect with buses to Palenque (you may be able to get a lift with a pick-up, or one of the tour buses, which start arriving around 1200; bargain hard). Passengers have to wait until 0400 next day. Bus from Frontera Echeverría to Palenque, 0500, US$3 and at 1230, US$5. Many military checkpoints.

San Cristóbal to the border

Comitán
Phone code: 963
Colour map 4, grid B1
Population: 87,000
Altitude: 1,580 m

South of San Cristóbal and heading for Guatemala, follow the 170 km paved road via **Teopisca** (*pensión*, **E**, comfortable; *La Amistad* trailer park, run down, one dirty shower and bathroom, no electricity, not recommended), to **Comitán de Domínguez**, a lively, attractive town with a large, shady plaza. **Tourist office** On main square, in Palacio Municipal, ground floor. ■ *Mon-Fri 1000-1400, 1700-2000.*

Sleeping Accommodation inferior in quality and almost twice the price of San Cristóbal. **B** *Internacional*, Av Domínguez 22, T632-0111, near plaza. Good, decent restaurant. **B** *Los Lagos de Montebello*, T632-0657. On Pan-American Highway, Km 1,257. Noisy but good. **B** *Real Balún Canán*, Av 1 Pte Sur 5, T632-1094. Restaurant. **D** *Delfín*, Av Domínguez 19-A, T632-0013, on plaza. Small rooms but hot water, helpful and clean. **E** *Posada Panamericana*, Av 1 Pte Nte 2, T672-0763. Dirty. 1 block away is **E** *Hospedaje Montebello*. Clean, sunny courtyard, laundry, fax service, friendly. Recommended. **F** *Hospedaje Primavera*, Calle Central Benito Juárez 42, ½ block off Plaza. Room without bath.

Eating *Helen's Enrique*, on plaza opposite church. Good food in pleasant surroundings. *Nevelandia*, Central Nte 1. Clean. Recommended. *Café Casa de la Cultura*, on the plaza. Sandwiches only. *Buffalo Café*, near plaza, Av Central y Calle Nte. Live music daily at 2030. Several small *comedores* on the plaza and at market (cheap).

Transport Buses from San Cristóbal de las Casas with *Cristóbal Colón*, frequent between 0730 and 2030, US$3.75, 2 hrs, last bus back at 1930. One *Cristóbal Colón* bus goes on to Tuxtla (via *San Cristóbal*), US$3.50, 4 hrs. Minibuses from Comitán to Tuxtla leave from the *Cristóbal Colón* bus station. Buses, combis and pick-up trucks from Comitán run to the border at Ciudad Cuauhtémoc. Petrol is available in Comitán, in centre of town on east side of Pan-American Highway, and another 2 km south of town, open 24 hrs.

Directory Airline offices: *Aviacsa*, Calle 3 Sur Pte, 12a, T672-3519, F672-0824, helpful, recommended. **Banks**: *Bancomer*, on plaza will exchange Amex TCs; 2 others on plaza, none change dollars after 1200; also a *casa de cambio*. **Embassies and consulates**: *Guatemala*, at Calle 1 Sur Pte 26

Av 2 Pte Sur, T672-0491. Mon-Fri 0800-1200, 1400-1700, Sat 0800-1400; tourist card US$10 (even for ose for whom it should be free), valid 1 year, multiple entry.

agunas de Montebello and Chinkultic

ix kilometres south of Comitán take a right turn for the Mayan ruins of **Tenán** uente (5 km), situated in a forest; there is a shortcut on foot. In 1996 the tomb of a Maya nobleman (AD 1000) was discovered here. The buildings at Tenán are more estored than those at Chinkultic (see below). A road branches off the Pan-American lighway, 16 km further on, to a very beautiful region of vari-coloured lakes and caves, ne **Lagunas de Montebello** (a national park). On no account visit the Lagunas alone or stay the night, because of rapes and robberies at gunpoint (see Sleeping below). Off he road to Montebello, 30 km from the Pan-American Highway, lie the ruins of Chinkultic, with temples, ball court, carved stone stelae and a *cenote* (deep round ake, good swimming) in beautiful surroundings; from the signpost the ruins are bout 3 km along a dirt road. ■ *Close at 1600, US$3.* Watch and ask for the very small ign and gate where the road to the ruins starts (about 1 km back along the main road, owards Comitán, from *Doña María's*, see below, don't attempt any short cuts); worth visiting when passing. Colectivo from Comitán US$1.

Some Mexican maps show a road running along the Guatemalan border from Montebello to Bonampak and on to Palenque; this road is not complete and no public transport or other traffic makes the trip

Combi vans or buses marked 'Tziscao' or 'Lagos' to the Lagunas de Montebello National Park (60 km from Comitán, US$1.30 about one hour), via the **Lagunas de Siete Colores** (so-called because the oxides in the water give varieties of colours), eave frequently from Avenida 2 Pte Sur y Calle 3 Sur Poniente, four blocks from the plaza in Comitán; buses go as far as Laguna Bosque Azul, a one-hour journey. For those with their own transport there are several dirt roads from Comitán to the Lagunas; a recommended route is the one via La Independencia, Buena Vista, La Patria and El Triunfo (beautiful views), eventually joining the road west of the Chinkultic ruins.

Tziscao is 9 km along the road leading right from the park entrance, which is 3 km before Bosque Azul; five buses a day Comitán-Tziscao; the last bus and colectivo back connecting with the 1900 bus to San Cristóbal is at 1600. The last combi to Comitán is at 1700. A trip to the Lagunas de Siete Colores from Comitán can be done in a day (note that the less accessible lakes are hard to get to even if staying in the vicinity). It is also possible to hire a combi, which takes 12 people, to go to the Lakes and Chinkultic for US$15 per hour. A day trip to Chinkultic and the lakes from San Cristóbal de las Casas is also possible, if exhausting (take passport and tourist card with you). The Bosque Azul area is now a reserve. The area is noted for its orchids and birdlife, including the famous *quetzal*; very crowded at weekends and holidays.

Tziscao

Sleeping Before planning to spend the night in the area check with the Tourist Office. In 1999 rapes and robberies at gunpoint brought official advice to travellers not to stay the night. There are, as well as picnic areas, an *Albergue Turístico* on the shores of Lake Tziscao (10 km, **F** per person, rooms for 4-6, toilet, blankets available, no hot water, reasonable kitchen facilities and bathrooms, excellent, reasonably priced meals, camping including use of hotel facilities; boats for hire, friendly owners, one of whom, Leo, speaks good English and has an intimate knowledge of the region); a small, family-run restaurant at Laguna Bosque Azul with a wooden hut for sleeping, **F**, bring sleeping bag; 2 very basic food shops in the village (best to bring your own food from Comitán market); and there are small caves. *Posada Las Orquídeas* (better known as 'Doña María'), Km 31, on the road to Montebello near Hidalgo and the ruins of Chinkultic, dormitory or cabin, **F** per person, family-run, very basic (no washing facilities, often no water, 2 toilets, urn in a shack) but friendly, small restaurant serving plentiful Mexican food. Next door are cabañas/restaurant *El Pino Feliz*. **Youth Hostel** *Las Margaritas*. *Hotel Bosque Bello*, 34 km, reservations in Tuxtla, T611-0966, or Comitán T672-1702.

Tabasco and Chiapas

Border with Guatemala

Ciudad Cuauhtémoc
Colour map 4, grid B2

Mexico is one hour ahead of Guatemala

From Comitán the road winds down to the Guatemalan border at Ciuda Cuauhtémoc via La Trinitaria (near the turn-off to Lagunas de Montebello, restau rant but no hotel). Ciudad Cuauhtémoc, despite its name, is not a city, but just a few buildings; the *Cristóbal Colón* bus station is opposite Immigration, with an over priced restaurant and an excellent **E-F** *Hotel Camino Real*. Extremely clean an quiet, changes dollars to pesos. Highly recommended. Be sure to surrender you tourist card and get your exit stamp at Mexican immigration in Ciudad Cuauhtémo before boarding a pick-up for Guatemalan immigration; you will only have to g back if you don't. A pick-up to the Guatemalan border, 4 km, costs US$0.65 per per son. Walk 100 m to immigration and customs, open until 2100. Beyond the Guate malan post at La Mesilla, a beautiful stretch of road leads 85 km to Huehuetenango This route is far more interesting than the one through Tapachula; the border cross ing at Ciudad Cuauhtémoc is also reported as easier than that at Talismán.

Entering Mexico from Guatemala

Tourist cards and visas are available at the border; recent reports say only 15 days are being given, but extensions are possible in Oaxaca or Mexico City. It is forbidden to bring in frui and vegetables.

Crossing by private vehicle

Drivers entering Mexico: at the border crossing your vehicle is fumigated, US$7.25, ge receipt (if re-entering Mexico, with documents from a previous entry, papers are checked here). Proceed 4 km to Migración to obtain tourist card or visa, or have existing visa checked Then go to *Banjército* to obtain the necessary papers and windscreen sticker or, if re-entering Mexico, to have existing papers checked. ■ *Mon-Fri 0800-1600, Sat-Sun 0900-1400.*

Transport

Buses are *de paso* from San Cristóbal so no advance booking is possible. The *Cristóbal Colón* bus leaves Comitán 0800, 1100 (coming from San Cristóbal) and in the afternoon-- for the border at Ciudad Cuauhtémoc, fare US$2.75. *Autotransportes Tuxtla* leave from Comitán (on the main highway at approximately Av 2 Sur) at regular intervals for the border, 1½ hrs. There are at least 8 buses to Comitán 0800-1930 from Ciudad Cuauhtémoc, with 2nd class buses during the evening. Pick-ups charge US$1.55 per person Comitán-border; beware short-changing. From here take a taxi, US$1.65, or colectivo, to the Guatemalan side (4 km uphill, minimum 3 people) and get your passport stamped. *Cristóbal Colón* (terminal near the Pan-American Highway, Comitán) has 1st class buses to **Mexico City** at 0900, 1100 and 1600 (which leave the border 2½ hrs earlier), fare US$40.75 (from Mexico City to Comitán at 1415 and 2040, fully booked 2 hrs in advance); to **Oaxaca** at 0700 and 1900, US$33; to **Tuxtla Gutiérrez** at 0600 and 1600, US$8, and to **Tapachula** (via Arriaga) at 1200 and 2000, US$20. Entering Mexico from Guatemala, to San Cristóbal, direct buses US$3.50, or take a minibus to Comitán, US$1.55; these connect with combis at the *Autotransportes Tuxtla* terminal for San Cristóbal de las Casas.

Director   Banks: Don't change money with the Guatemalan customs officials: the rates they offer are worse than those given by bus drivers or in banks (and these are below the rates inside the country). There is nowhere to change TCs at the border and bus companies will not accept cheques in payment for fares. 300 m after the border, however, you can get good rates for TCs at the *Banco de Café*. The briefcase and dark glasses brigade changes cash on the Guatemalan side only, but you must know in advance what quetzal rates are.

Route to Tapachula

Travelling from the neighbouring state of Oaxaca, Routes 190 and 200 merge to cross the Isthmus of Tehuantepec. Accommodation is available at **Zanatepec**, **C-D** *Posada San Rafael*. Motel. Very comfortable, safe parking. At **Tapanatepec**, **D** *Motel La Misión* on Highway 190 on northern outskirts, T(971) 717-0140. Fan, hot water, clean, TV, hammock outside each room, affiliated restaurant, very good.

This is where Highway 190 heads northeast to Tuxtla Gutiérrez and Highway 200 continues southeast along the coast of Chiapas to the Guatemalan border.

Arriaga

Phone code: 966
Colour map 3, grid C6
Population: 18,000

Arriaga is a good stopping place just across the state border that separates Oaxaca from Chiapas; many banks around Zócalo for exchange. The road from Arriaga to Tapachula is a four-lane divided freeway.

Sleeping and eating C *Ik-Lumaal*, near Zócalo, T662-0895. A/c, clean, quiet, good restaurant. *El Parador*, Km 47 on road to Tonalá, T662-0164. Clean with swimming pool. D *Colonial*, Callejón Ferrocarril, next to bus station, T662-0856. Clean, friendly, quiet, limited free parking. E *Arbolitos*. Fan, basic, clean, off main road. F *Hotel Iris*, Callejón Ferrocarril, near bus station. Bath, fan, basic. *Restaurant Xochimilco*, near bus stations.

Transport Buses: to many destinations, mostly 1st class, to **Mexico City**: US$26.50, 12-13 hrs, at 1645. **Tuxtla**: with *Fletes y Pasajes* at 1400 and 1600, 4 hrs, US$7. **Oaxaca**: 6 hrs, US$7.

Tonalá

Phone code: 966
Colour map 3, grid C6

From Arriaga, Route 200 continues to Tonalá, formerly a very quiet town but now noisy and dirty, with a small museum; good market (bus Tonalá-Tapachula, three hours, US$6.75; also buses to Tuxtla). This is by far the most direct road for travellers seeking the quickest way from Mexico City to Guatemala.

Sleeping and eating B *Galilea*, Av Hidalgo y Callejón Ote, T663-0239. With bath, a/c, good, basic cheap rooms on 1st floor, balconies on main square, with good restaurants. C *Tonalá*, Hidalgo 172, T663-0480, opposite museum. E *Casa de Huéspedes El Viajero*, Av Matamoros, near market. With bath, rough but OK. E *Farro*, 16 de Septiembre 24, near plaza, T663-0033.

For eating try *Santa Elena*, at the south end of town, near *Cristóbal Colón* bus station on outskirts. Good. On the plaza, *Nora*. Numerous Chinese-named restaurants; good breakfast at restaurants on Zócalo.

Puerto Arista

Phone code: 961
Colour map 3, grid C6

Along the coast from Tonalá to Tapachula there are several fine-looking and undeveloped beaches, although waves and currents are dangerous. Puerto Arista (17 km south of Tonalá) is now being built up, but it is still a relatively peaceful area with 32 km of clean beach to relax on with no sales people; bus/colectivo from Tonalá every hour, 45 minutes, US$0.60, taxi US$2; plenty of buses to Arriaga, US$0.75. Many hotels, motels and restaurants on the beach; hot and, in the wet season, sandflies. B *Arista Bougainvilla*, Blvd Zapotal, T600-9044. With private beach, a/c, swimming pools, restaurant. Some restaurants (closed by 2000) have rooms to rent, eg F *Turquesa*, small hotel/restaurant three blocks down on the right from where the road reaches the beach coming from Tonalá and turns right, next to bakery. No fan, basic. **Camping** E-F *José's Camping Cabañas* (ask colectivo from Tonalá to take you there, US$0.60 extra), at east edge of town, follow signs. Canadian-run, well organized, clean, laundry, restaurant (including vegetarian), library.

Buses also from Tonalá to **Boca del Cielo** further down the coast, which is good for bathing and has cabañas with hammocks, and similarly **Cabeza del Toro**. **Paredón**, on the huge Laguna del Mar Muerto, 14 km west of Tonalá, has excellent seafood and one very basic guest house. You can take a local fishing boat out into the lagoon to swim; the shore stinks because fishermen clean fish on the beach among dogs and pigs. Served by frequent buses.

On the way to Tapachula you pass through **Pijijiapan** where there is the *Hotel Pijijilton*(!) next to the *Cristóbal Colón* bus station; also C *Hotel El Estraneo* Av Central, T(918) 645-0264. Very nice, parking in courtyard. E *Sabrina*. Nice, clean and quiet, safe parking. Many on Route 200, eg E *El Navegante Los Reyes* per bed, doubles only. Also **Huixtla**, which has a good market, no tourists (E *Casa de Huéspedes Regis*, Independencia Norte 23). From Huixtla, a good, scenic road winds off into

Tabasco and Chiapas

the mountains parallel to the border, towards Ciudad Cuauhtémoc and Comitán (see above). En route is the small, modern town of **Motozintla de Mendoza** with an attractive zócalo and three hotels: one on the plaza, another, *Rendón*, at Central Norte 415, friendly, parking, limited hot water, noisy; also, cheaper, **D** *Alberto*, Central Norte 305, quiet.

Tapachula

Phone code: 962
Colour map 4, grid C1
Population: 271,000

Tapachula is a pleasant, neat, but expensive and hot commercial town (airport; cinemas in centre). *Avenidas* run north-south, *calles* east-west (Oriente-Poniente). Odd-numbered *calles* are north of Calle Central, odd *avenidas* are east of Avenida Central. It is the road and rail junction for Guatemala (road crossings at the Talismán bridge or at Ciudad Hidalgo).

Tourist offices 4 Nte 35, Edificio del Gobierno del Estado, 3rd floor, between 3 and 5 Poniente, T626-5470, F626-5522. ■ *Mon-Fri 0900-1500, 1800-2000, helpful.*

Excursions The coastal town of **Puerto Madero**, 18 km from Tapachula (bus US$1.80), is worse than Puerto Arista, because it is more built up and the beaches stink from rubbish being burned. Intense heat in summer. (**E** *Hotel Pegado*. Run down, not recommended. Better is unnamed *hospedaje*, also **E**. **F** *Hotel Puerto Madero*, accommodation in what are really remains of cement block room.) Water defences are being built, but the graveyard is under threat of being washed into the sea. There are many fish restaurants on the beach.

Visit the ruins of **Izapa** (proto-Classic stelae, small museum) just off the road to Talismán; the part of the site on the north is easily visible but a larger portion is on the south side of the highway, about 1 km away, ask caretaker for guidance. These buildings influenced Kaminal Juyú near Guatemala City and are considered archaeologically important as a proto-Mayan site. Some findings from the ruins are displayed in the **Museo Regional del Soconusco** on the west side of the Zócalo in Tapachula. To reach Izapa take combi from Unión Progreso bus station. 45 km northeast of Tapachula, beyond the turning to Talismán, is **Unión Juárez** (**E** *Hotel Alijoat*, hot shower, reasonable restaurant. **E** *Hotel Colonial*; *Restaurant Carmelita* on the square is modest with fair prices). In Unión Juárez you can have your papers stamped and proceed on foot via Talquián to the Guatemalan border at Sibinal.

A worthwhile hike can be made up the **Tacaná volcano** (4,150 m), which takes 2-3 days from Unión Juárez. Ask for the road to Chiquihuete; no cars. The Tapachula tourist office can help; in Unión Juárez ask for Sr Umberto Ríos at *Restaurante Montaña*, he will put you in touch with guide Moisés Hernández, who charges US$15 a day. It is possible to stay overnight in Don Emilio Velásquez's barn halfway up, US$2; he offers coffee and *tortillas*. At the top are some cabañas in which you sleep for free; sleeping bag essential.

Sleeping
■ *on map*

AL *Loma Real*, Carretera Costera 200, Km 244, T626-1440, 1 km north of city, www.travelodge.com.mx Operates as a 1st class hotel, use of swimming pool, cold showers. **C** *San Francisco*, Av Central Sur 94, T626-1454, F625-2114, 15 mins from centre. Good, a/c, large rooms, hot water, TV, restaurant, safe parking. **C** *Santa Julia*, next to *Cristóbal Colón* terminal, in centre within 1 block of Plaza Central, T626-2486. Bath, phone, TV, a/c, clean, good. **D** *Alfa*, Calle 11 Pte 53, T626-5442. Clean, fan, cold shower, similar. **D** *Posada de Calú*, Calle 11 Pte 34, T626-5659. **D** *Tabasco*. With shower, close to 1st class bus station, poor value but friendly. **E** *Atlántida*, Av 6 Nte between Calle 11 and 13 Pte, T626-2136. Helpful, clean, cheaper without window, fans, noisy, safe parking for 2. **E** *Cinco de Mayo*, Calle 5 Pte y Av 12 Nte. With bath (cheaper without), not very clean, convenient for Talismán *colectivos*, which leave ½ block away. **E** *Colonial*, Av 4 Nte 31. Attractive courtyard, about 1 block from central square, good value, clean, safe. **E** *El Retorno*, opposite, on Calle 5 Pte. Unhelpful and noisy. **E** *Hospedaje Madrid*, Av 8 Nte, 43, T626-3018. Shared bath. Many hotels along Avs 4, 6, 8 (near plaza). **E** *Pensión Mary*, Av 4 Nte 28, T626-3400. Has cheap *comidas*. **E** *Plaza Guizar*,

Av 2 Nte. Old, pleasant, clean, hot water, rooms differ so ask to see more than 1. **E** *Rex*, Av 8 Nte 43, T625-0376. Similar. **E** *San Román*, Calle 9 Pte between Av 10 y 12 Nte. Shower, fan, safe motorcycle parking, clean, quiet, friendly, drinks for sale.

Eating

Snoopy, Av 4 no 19. Friendly, excellent *tortas*, breakfasts. *Viva Pizza*, Av Central. Good pizza, reasonable price. Good, cheap chicken on Central Nte. *Heladas Irma*, Calle 13 Pte between Av 4 y 6. Good ice-cream.

Shopping

Rialfer, supermarket, Blvd Díaz, 2 doors from *Banamex*.

Transport

Air Flights from **Mérida**, **Mexico City**, **Tuxtla Gutiérrez**, **Veracruz** daily. Combis to airport from Calle 2 Sur No 40, T625-1287. From airport to border, minibuses charge US$26 for whole vehicle, so share with others, otherwise take *colectivo* to 2nd class bus terminal and then a bus to Ciudad Hidalgo.

Buses *Cristóbal Colón* bus Mexico City-Guatemala City takes 23 hrs, with a change at the border to *Rutas Lima*. *Transgalgos*, 7a Avenida, T230-5058, run a new direct service to Guatemala City and Antigua 0930 and 1330, US$45.

Mexico City-Tapachula, 20 hrs (*Cristóbal Colón*, 1st class, Av 3 Nte y 17 Ote, T626-2880; 2nd class, Prolongación 9 Pte s/n, T626-1161). To/from Tapachula to **Mexico City**, US$40, 5 a day, all in the afternoon (frequent stops for toilets and food, also frequent police checks, no toilet or a/c on bus) much better to take *plus* service, 1915, US$58. Buses from Mexico City all leave in the afternoon; the 1545 and 1945 go on to Talismán. The 2nd class bus station is at Av 3 Nte, Calle 9 Ote.

Tapachula

Sleeping
1 Colonial
2 Pensión Mary
3 Santa Julia

Tabasco and Chiapas

Bus to **Oaxaca**, *Cristóbal Colón* and *Fipsa* (Calle 9 Ote, T626-7603) has luggage store, 14 hrs, US$19,many passport checks (Fipsa has 4 a day, continuing to Puebla and Córdoba, take 1830 to see sunrise over the Sierra Madre; also has 2 a day to Mexico City). To **Puebla**: 16 hrs, plus US$47; UNO, US$53. To **San Cristóbal de las Casas** and **Tuxtla Gutiérrez** at 1100. To **Tehuantepec** and **Salina Cruz**: 0915, 8 hrs, US$14.80;

Directory **Airlines** *Aviacsa*, Calle Central Nte 52-B, T/F626-3159. *AeroMéxico*, Av 2 Nte 6, T626-3921. *Taesa*, T626-3702. **Banks** Avoid the crowds of streetwise little boys at the border; exchange is rather better in the town, bus station gives a good rate (cash only). *Banamex*, Blvd Díaz Ordaz, open 0830-1230, 1400-1600, disagreement over whether TCs are changed. *Bital* is the only bank open Sat, changes TCs. *Casa de Cambio Tapachula*, Av 4 Nte y Calle 3 Pte, changes dollars, TCs, pesos, quetzales, lempiras and colones (open late Mon-Sat), but not recommended, poor rates, very difficult to change money on Sun. Try the supermarket. **Communications** **Telephone:** several long-distance phone offices, eg *Esther*, Av 5 Nte 46; *La Central*, Av Central Sur 95; *Monaco*, Calle 1 Pte 18. **Embassies and consulates** *Guatemalan Consulate*, Calle 2 Ote 33 and Av 7 Sur, T626-1252, taxi from *Cristóbal Colón* terminal, US$1. Open Mon-Fri 0800-1600; visa US$10, friendly and quick, take photocopy of passport, photocopier 2 blocks away. **Laundry** There is a laundry, at Av Central Nte 99 between Calle 13 y 15 Ote, US$3 wash and dry, 1 hr service, about 2 blocks from *Cristóbal Colón* bus station, open Sun. Also on Central Nte between Central Ote y Calle 1, opens 0800, closed Sun. **Tour operators** *Viajes Tacaná*, operated by Sr Adolfo Guerrero Chávez, Av 4 Nte No 6, T626-3502; trips to Izapa ruins, to mountains, beaches and can gain entry to museum when closed. **Useful addresses** Migración/Gobernación: Av 14 Nte 57, T626-1263.

Border with Guatemala-Talismán

It is 8 km from Tapachula to the border at Talismán (open 24 hours a day).

Immigration The Mexican customs post is 200 m from the Guatemalan one. Exit tax US$0.45. Lots of pushy children offer to help you through border formalities; pay US$2-3 for one, which keeps the others away.The toilet at immigration at the crossing is dangerous, hold-ups have been reported day and night. **Guatemalan consulate** In Tapachula, above.

Crossing into Guatemala by car can take several hours. If you don't want your car sprayed inside it may cost you a couple of dollars. Do not park in the car park at the control post, as it is very expensive. **Driving into Mexico** See Essentials, Motoring, on the temporary importation of vehicles, page 79. Car papers are issued at the Garita de Aduana on Route 200 out of Tapachula. There is no other road, you can't miss it. Photocopies of documents must be made in town; no facilities at the Garita. Reported to be a frustrating procedure – be prepared and patient.

Sleeping There is a *hospedaje* at the border.

Exchange Exchange in town rather than with men standing around customs on the Guatemalan side (check rates before dealing with them, and haggle; there is no bank on the Guatemalan side).

Transport Combi vans run from near the Unión y Progreso bus station, about US$1; colectivo from outside *Posada de Calú* to Talismán, US$0.60, also from Calle 5 Pte between Avs 12 y 14 Nte. Taxi Tapachula-Talismán, negotiate fare to about US$2. There are few buses between the Talismán bridge and Oaxaca or Mexico City (though they do exist); advisable therefore to travel to Tapachula for connection, delays can occur there at peak times. A taxi from Guatemala to Mexican Immigration will cost US$2, but it may be worth it if you are in a hurry to catch an onward bus. Hitchhikers should note that there is little through international traffic at Talismán bridge.

Border with Guatemala-Ciudad Hidalgo

There is another crossing south of Tapachula, at **Ciudad Hidalgo**, opposite Tecún Umán (you cannot change travellers' cheques here); there are road connections to Coatepeque, Mazatenango and Retalhuleu.

mmigration A few blocks from the town plaza is Mexican Immigration, at the foot of the 1-km long bridge across the Río Suchiate; cycle taxis cross the bridge for about US$1, pedestrians pay US$0.15.

Transport From Calle 7 Pte between Av 2 Nte and Av Central Nte, Tapachula, buses go to Hidalgo', US$1.25.

Yucatán Peninsula

Mexico City

The Yucatán Peninsula, which includes the states of Campeche, Yucatán and Quintana Roo, is sold to tourists as the land of Maya archaeology and Caribbean beach resorts. And there's no denying it, the warm turquoise sea, fringed with fine white-sand beaches and palm groves of the 'Mayan Riviera' are second to none. And it would be a crime not to tread the beaten path to the sensational ruins at Chichén Itzá, Uxmal and Tulum. But it more than pays to explore beyond the main itineraries to visit some of the lesser-known Maya sites such as Cobá, Edzná or Dzibilchaltún, or the imposing Franciscan monastery and huge pyramid at Izamal. There are flamingo feeding grounds at Celestún and Río Lagartos and over 500 other species of bird, many of which are protected in Sian Ka'an Biosphere Reserve, which covers 4,500 sq km of tropical forest, savanna and coastline. Ever since Jacques Cousteau filmed the Palancar Reef in the 1960s, divers have swarmed to the clear waters of Cozumel, the 'Island of the Swallows', to wonder at the many species of coral, and other underwater plants and creatures at what has become one of the most popular diving centres in the world. Also popular and specialized, is diving in the many cenotes, or sink holes, including the famous Nohooch Nah Chich, part of the world's largest underground cave system.

History

After the Maya arrived in Yucatán about 1200 BC, they built monumental stone structures during the centuries leading up to the end of the pre-Classic period (AD 250). Later they rebuilt their cities, but along different lines, probably because of the arrival of Toltecs in the ninth and 10th centuries. Each city was autonomous, and in rivalry with other cities. Before the Spaniards arrived the Maya had developed a writing system in which the hieroglyphic was somewhere between the pictograph and the letter. Fray Diego de Landa collected their books, wrote a very poor summary, the *Relación de las Cosas de Yucatán*, and with Christian but unscholarly zeal burnt most of the codices, which he never really understood.

The Spaniards found little to please them when they first arrived in the Yucatán: no gold, no concentration of natives; nevertheless Mérida was founded in 1542 and the few natives were handed over to the conquerors in *encomiendas*. The Spaniards found them difficult to exploit: even as late as 1847 there was a major revolt, fuelled by the inhumane conditions in the *henequén* (sisal) plantations, and the discrimination against the Maya in the towns, but it was the expropriation of the Maya communal lands that was the main source of discontent. In July 1847 a conspiracy against the *Blancos*, or ruling classes from Mexico, was uncovered in Valladolid and one of its leaders, Manuel Antonio Ay, was shot. This precipitated a bloody war, known as the *Guerra de Castas* (Caste War) between the Maya and the *Blancos*. The first act was the massacre of all the non-Maya inhabitants of Tepich, south of Valladolid. The Maya took control of much of the Yucatán, laying siege to Mérida, only to abandon it to sow their crops in 1849. This allowed the governor of Yucatán to counter-attack, driving the Maya by ruthless means into southern Quintana Roo. In Chan Santa Cruz, now called Felipe Carrillo Puerto, one of the Maya leaders, José María Barrera, accompanied by Manuel Nahuat, a ventriloquist, invented the 'talking cross', a cult that attracted thousands of followers. The sect, called Cruzob,

Yucatán Peninsula

established itself and renewed the resistance against the government from Mexico City. It was not until 1901 that the Mexican army retook the Cruzob's domain.

People

The people are divided into two groups: the Maya Indians, the minority, and the *mestizos*. The Maya women wear *huipiles*, or white cotton tunics (silk for fiestas), which may reach the ankles and are embroidered round the square neck and bottom hem. Ornaments are mostly gold. A few of the men still wear straight white cotton (occasionally silk) jackets and pants, often with gold or silver buttons, and when working protect this dress with aprons. Carnival is the year's most joyous occasion, with concerts, dances and processions. Yucatán's folk dance is the *Jarana*, the man dancing with his hands behind his back, the woman raising her skirts a little, and with interludes when they pretend to be bullfighting. During pauses in the music the man, in a high falsetto voice, sings *bambas* (compliments) to the woman.

The Maya are a courteous, gentle people. They drink little, except on feast days, speak Mayan, and profess Christianity laced with a more ancient nature worship.

Access to sites and resorts

Many tourists come to the Yucatán, mostly to see the **ancient Maya sites** and to stay at the new coastal resorts. A good paved road runs from Coatzacoalcos through Villahermosa, Campeche and Mérida (Route 180). An inland road from Villahermosa to Campeche gives easy access to Palenque (see page 450). If time is limited, take a bus from Villahermosa to Chetumal via Escárcega, which can be done overnight as the journey is not very interesting (unless you want to see the Maya ruins off this road, see page 542). From Chetumal travel up the coast to Cancún, then across to Mérida. Route 307 from Chetumal to Cancún and Puerto Juárez and is all paved and in very good condition. Air services from the US and Mexico City are given under Mérida, Cancún and Cozumel.

The state of Quintana Roo is on the eastern side of the Yucatán Peninsula and has recently become the largest tourist area in Mexico with the development of the resort of Cancún, and the parallel growth of Isla Mujeres, Cozumel and the 100 km corridor south of Cancún to Tulum. Growth has been such, in both Yucatán and Quintana Roo, that there are insufficient buses at peak times; old second class buses may be provided for first class tickets and second class buses take far too many standing passengers. There is also a lack of information services. Where beaches are unspoilt they often lack all amenities. Many cheaper hotels are spartan. **Warning**: So many of the tourists coming to the coastal resorts know no Spanish so price hikes and short-changing have become very common, making those places very expensive if you are not careful. In the peak, winter season, prices are increased anyway, by about 50%.

Quintana Roo (and especially Cozumel) is the main area for **diving** and **watersports** in the Yucatán Peninsula, and the options are mentioned in the text. However, watersports in Quintana Roo are expensive and touristy, although operators are generally helpful; snorkelling is often in large groups. On the more accessible reefs the coral is dying and there are no small coral fish, as a necessary part of the coral life cycle. Further from the shore, though, there is still much reef life to enjoy.

The use of tripods for photography at sites is subject to an extra fee of US$3.50, but for using video cameras the fee is US$7.50. Since the major archaeological sites get very crowded, it is best to visit them just before closing time. Note also that in spring and summer temperatures can be very high; take plenty of drinking water and adequate protection against the sun. See page 551 for recommended reading.

State of Campeche

Take time out to explore the State of Campeche. Colonial architecture is plentiful, there are several fortified convents and Campeche City itself was fortified to protect its citizens from pirate attacks. There are many archaeological sites, most demonstrating influences of Chenes architecture. Relax at the resorts of Sihoplaya and Seybaplaya while watching pelicans dive and iguanas scurry. You can try the beaches at Ciudad del Carmen, eat delicious red snapper and buy a cheap, but sturdy, Panama hat. The exhibits at several museums reflect the seafaring nature of the area and the pre-Conquest civilization that occupied these lands.

There are two routes to Campeche from the neighbouring state of Tabasco: the inland Highway 186, via Escárcega, with two toll bridges (cost US$4.25), and the slightly longer coastal route through Ciudad del Carmen, Highway 180; both converge at Champotón, 66 km south of Campeche. Highway 186 passes Villahermosa's modern international airport and runs fast and smooth in a sweeping curve 115 km east to the Palenque turn-off at Playas del Catazajá; beyond, off the highway, is **Emiliano Zapata** (**Fiesta**: 26 October), a busy cattle centre, with Pemex station. There is a mediocre hotel here on a quiet plaza by the river, 200 m from the main road. On the main road is restaurant *La Selva*, good food.

Transport Bus: from Emiliano Zapata, all *ADO*: to **Tenosique**: almost hourly, 1½ hrs US$2.80 (plus 2, 2nd class companies); to **Villahermosa**: 17 departures between 0600 and 2000, US$8; to **Mérida**: 5 a day between 0800 and 2100, US$29; to **Escárcega**: 5 between 0630 and 2100, US$7.50; to **Chetumal**: 2130, US$20.

The river town of **Balancán** is a further 60 km northeast and has a small archaeological museum in its Casa de Cultura (**E** *Hotel Delicias*, T344-0033); **fiesta**: **14 December**. In 10 km the main highway has crossed the narrow waist of Tabasco state and entered Campeche, a popular destination for hunters and fishermen.

FranciscoEscárcega

Escárcega, a shortening of its full name Francisco Escárga, is a major hub for travellers on their way south to the states of Tabasco and Chiapas, north to Mérida in the state of Yucatán, east to Maya sites in Campeche and Quintana Roo states, and further east to the city of Chetumal. The town itself is not particularly enticing, set on a busy highway with a dusty Wild West atmosphere. If stuck here overnight, all you need to know is that there is a clean budget hotel around the corner from the bus terminal (*Escárcega*, see below), one bank nearby and several cheap restaurants.

Phone code: 982
Colour map 4, grid B2
Population: 50,541

Yucatán Peninsula

Sleeping

C *María Isabel*, Justo Sierra 127, T824-0045. A/c, restaurant, comfortable, back rooms noisy from highway. **C** *Motel Akim Pech*, on Villahermosa highway. A/c or fans and bath, reasonable rooms, restaurant in motel, another across the street, also Pemex station opposite. **D** *Casa de Huéspedes Lolita* on Chetumal highway at east end of town. Pleasant. **D-E** *Escárcega*, Justo Sierra 86, T824-0188, around the corner from the bus terminal (turn left twice). Clean, bath, parking, hot water, good restaurant, small garden. **D-E** *El Yucateco*, Calle 50 No 42-A, T824-0065. With or without a/c, central, tidy, fair value. **E** *Las Gemelas*, behind Pemex on Highway 186, west of intersection and *ADO*. Noisy, decrepit, overpriced. **E** *San Luis*, Calle 28 facing the Zócalo. Simple and lazily maintained.

Eating

Not many places used to serving tourists, but there is a good and cheap *lonchería* opposite the bus terminal. For a more expensive meal in a/c surroundings, try *Titanic*, on the corner of the main highway and the road to the train station (first turning on the right after turning right out of the bus terminal).

Transport Buses Most buses from Chetumal or Campeche drop you off at the 2nd class terminal c the main highway. To buy tickets, you have to wait until the outgoing bus has arrived; sit ne the ticket office and wait for them to call out your destination, then join the scrum at th ticket office. There is an *ADO* terminal west of the 2nd class terminal, a 20-min walk. Fro there, 1st class buses go to **Palenque**, several daily, 3 hrs, US$14. **Chetumal**: 4 a day, 4 hr US$13. **Campeche**: 5 a day, 2 hrs, US$8.

From the 2nd class terminal, there are buses to *Campeche*, 16 a day, 2½ hrs, US$5.6 *Chetumal*, 3 a day, 4 hrs, US$11; *Mérida*, 4 a day, 6 hrs, US$13.50; *Playas de Catazajá*, connec ing with colectivos to Palenque, at 0830, 0930 and 1030, US$5; *Villahermosa*, 12 a day, 4 hr US$12.50. *Colectivos* to *Palenque* leave from outside the 2nd class terminal at 1300, US$5.50.

The coast road

Although Highway 180 via Ciudad del Carmen is narrow, crumbling into the sea i places and usually ignored by tourists intent on visiting Palenque, this journey is beautiful one and more interesting than the fast toll road inland to Campeche. Th road threads its way from Villahermosa 78 km north through marshland and ric cacao, banana and coconut plantations, passing turn-offs to several tiny coastal vil lages with palm-lined but otherwise mediocre beaches. It eventually leads to th river port of **Frontera** (*Population*: 28,650), where Graham Greene began th research journey in 1938 that led to the publication of *The Lawless Roads* and later t *The Power and the Glory*. The *Feria Guadalupana* is held from 3-13 December, wit an agricultural show, bullfights, *charreadas* and regional dances.

Sleeping and eating in Frontera C *Chichén Itzá*, Aldama 671, T332-0097. Not very clean fan, shower, hot water. **D** *San Agustín*, Pino Suárez, T332-0037. Very basic, fan, no mosquitc net. *Restaurant Conquistador*, beside church. Very good.

The road briefly touches the coast at the Tabasco/Campeche state border. It then runs east beside a series of lakes (superb bird-watching) to the fishing village ol **Zacatal** (93 km), at the entrance to the tarpon-filled **Laguna de Términos** (named for the first Spanish expedition, which thought it had reached the end of the 'island' of Yucatán). Just before Zacatal is the lighthouse of **Xicalango**, an important pre-Columbian trading centre. Cortés landed near here in 1519 on his way to Veracruz and was given 20 female slaves, including 'La Malinche', the Indian prin cess baptized as Doña Marina who, as the Spaniards' interpreter, was to play an important role in the Conquest. A bridge crosses the lake's mouth to Ciudad del Carmen.

Ciudad del Carmen

Phone code: 938
Colour map 4, grid B1
Population: 171,367

This is the hot, bursting-at-the-seams principal oil port of the region and is being developed into one of the biggest and most modern on the Gulf. Its important shrimping and prawning fleets are also expanding and much ship building is under taken. The site was originally established in 1588 by a pirate named McGregor as a lair from which to raid Spanish shipping; it was infamous until the pirates were wiped out by Alfonso Felipe de Andrade in 1717, who then named the town after its patroness, the Virgen del Carmen.

Carmen is situated on a narrow, largely forested (coconut palm) island, little more than a sandpit, 38 km long and 51 sq km in all. It is joined to the mainland at either end by bridges, which are among the longest in the Americas. One, on the east end of the island at Puerto Real, called La Unidad, 3,222 m long and built in 1922 (US$1.85 toll), links with Isla Aguada; the other, 3,865 m, between Zacatal (main-land) and La Puntilla, was completed in 1994. The town is principally concentrated at the west end of the island and shows few signs of the ugliness often associated with oil-boom centres (the rigs are mainly way off-shore). It is not, as yet, visited by many ourists, but is well worth a detour en route to, or from, the Yucatán, and is a good lace for those curious to see something of the development of the Mexican fishing nd oil industries.

Most streets in the centre are numbered; even numbers generally run west-east, nd odd south-north. Calle 20 is the seafront *malecón* and the road to the airport and University is Calle 31. The **tourist office**, on Calle 20 near Calle 23, has little to pronote in this non-tourist town; the emphasis is on fishing excursions, a basic street nap is available. **Fishing excursions** can be arranged through the *Club de Pesca Velo Manjárrez*, T382-0073, at Calle 40 and Calle 61. Coastal lagoons are rich in tarpon *(sábalo)* and bonefish.

The attractive, cream-coloured **cathedral** (Parroquia de la Virgen del Carmen), begun 1856, is notable for its stained glass. The **Palacio Municipal** and library, stands on the **Plaza Principal**, or Plaza Zaragoza, a lush square laid out in 1854, near the waterfront, with wooden gazebo (free band concerts Thursday and Sunday evenings), Spanish lanterns, brick walkways and elegant wrought-iron railings from Belgium. There is a modest **Archaeological Museum** in the Liceo Carmelita showing locally excavated items. ■ *US$0.25.* **La Iglesia de Jesús** (1820) opposite Parque uárez is surrounded by elegant older houses. Nearby is the Barrio del Guanal, the oldest residential quarter, with the church of the **Virgen de la Asunción** (1815) and houses with spacious balconies and tiles brought from Marseilles. Close by is the **Casa de la Cultura** in a French-style building (1860s) with library and temporary exhibitions and concerts.

There are several good **beaches** with restaurants and watersports, the most scenic being Playa Caracol (southeast of the centre) and the Playa Norte, which has extensive white sand and safe bathing.

Living costs in Carmen tend to be higher than the norm, partly on account of the spending power of the oil workers but also because most commodities have to be brought in. However, there are hotels and restaurants in the budget range.

Sights

AL *EuroHotel*, Calle 22 No 208, T382-3044, reganem@prodigy.net.mx Large and modern, 2 restaurants, pool, a/c, disco, built to accommodate the flow of Pemex traffic. **B** *Lli-Re*, Calle 32 y 29, T382-6408. Commercial hotel with large, sparsely furnished a/c rooms, TV, oddly old-fashioned but comfortable, restaurant with good but not cheap fish dishes. **C** *Acuario*, Calle 51 No 60, T382-3947. A/c, comfortable. **C** *Lino's*, Calle 31 No 132, T382-1766. A/c, pool, restaurant, also has 10 RV spaces with electricity hook-ups.

D *Hotel Playa Dorna*, on Playa Norte. Clean, friendly, pool, TV, hot water, 2 strip bars loud and late at weekends. **D** *Zacarías*, Calle 24 No 58, T382-3506. Modern, some cheaper rooms with fans, brighter a/c rooms are better value. Recommended. **E** *Internacional*, Calle 20 No 21, T382-1344. Uninspiring outside but clean and friendly, 1 block from plaza, some a/c. **E** *Casa de Huéspedes Carmen*, Calle 20 No 142, *Villa del Mar*, Calle 20 y 33. There are several **E** range hotels near the *ADO* bus station on Av Periférica eg *El Ancla*. Simple rooms, TV, a/c, good restaurant in spectacular waterside setting.

Sleeping
Price codes:
see inside front cover

The better hotels have good restaurants; others recommended are *Pepe's*, Calle 27 No 15. A/c, attractive seafood dishes. *Vía Veneto*, in the *EuroHotel*. Reasonable prices, good breakfasts. *El Kiosco*, in *Hotel del Parque* with view of Zócalo. Modest prices, eggs, chicken, seafood and Mexican dishes, but not clean, poor service. *La Mesita*, outdoor stand across from ferry landing. Well-prepared shrimp, seafood cocktails, extremely popular all day. *La Fuente*, Calle 20. 24-hr snack bar with view of the Laguna.

For 'best coffee in town' try *Café Vadillo* or other tiny cafés along pedestrian walkway (Calle 33) near the Zócalo. Inexpensive snacks also available in the thriving Central Market (Calle 20 y 37, not far northwest of Zócalo).

Eating

The town's patroness is honoured with a cheerful fiesta each year between **15-30 Jun**.

Festivals

Yucatán Peninsula

Transport **Local Car hire** (not cheap): *Auto-Rentas del Carmen*, Calle 33 No 121, T382-2376; *Fas* T382-2306 and *Auto Panamericana*, Calle 22, T382-2326.

Air Carmen's efficient airport (CME, 5 km east of the plaza) has also benefited from the oil traffic with flights daily to **Mérida**, **Mexico City**, **Poza Rica**, **Tampico**, **Veracruz** and **Villahermosa**.

Buses *ADO* bus terminal some distance from centre. Take bus or colectivo marked 'Renovación' or 'ADO', they leave from around the Zócalo. At least 8 *ADO* services daily to **Campeche**, 3 hrs and **Mérida**, 9 hrs, US$19, includes 3 departures between 2100 and 2200 (worth considering if stuck for accommodation); hourly bus to **Villahermosa** via the coast, hrs. A connection can be made to **Palenque** at 2330 or 0400, a slow but worthwhile trip. Buses also travel via **Escárcega**, where connections can be made for Chetumal and Belize.

Directory **Directory Airlines**: *Mexicana*, Calle 22 y 37, T382-1171. **Banks** *Banco del Atlántico* or *Banamex* both at Calle 24 y 31. **Communications** Post office: at Calle 29 y 20, 1 block from the plaza.

Isla Aguada
Phone code: 982
Colour map 4, grid B2

Eleven kilometres beyond Carmen is the *Rancho El Fénix*, with an interesting iguana (*lagarto*) hatchery. Highway 180 runs northeast along the Isla del Carmen and crosses the bridge to Isla Aguada (**C** *Hotel Tarpon Tropical*. **D** *Motel La Cabaña* and Trailer Park at former boat landing just after the toll bridge. Full hook-up, hot showers, laundry facilities, quiet, US$12 for vehicle and two people), actually a narrow peninsula with more deserted shell-littered beaches on the Gulf shore. The road then undulates its way northeast through tiny fishing villages towards Campeche; there are many offshore oil rigs to be seen. At Sabancuy (85 km from Carmen) a paved road crosses to the Villahermosa-Escárcega highway, 57 km away. Sixty-three bumpy km later, Highway 180 reaches Champotón (see below).

Maya ruins in south Campeche

Calakmul Three hundred kilometres southeast from Campeche town, and a further 60 km off the main Escárcega-Chetumal road, the ruins of Calakmul are only accessible by car. The site has been the subject of much attention in recent years, due to the previously concealed scale of the place. It is now believed to be one of the largest archaeological sites in Mesoamerica, and certainly the biggest of all the Maya cities, with somewhere in the region of ten thousand buildings in total, many of them as yet unexplored. There is evidence that Calakmul was begun in 300 BC, and continually added to until AD 800. At the centre of the site is the Gran Plaza, overlooked by a pyramid whose base covers five acres of ground. One of the buildings grouped around the **Gran Plaza** is believed, due to its curious shape and location, to have been designed for astronomical observation. The **Gran Acrópolis**, the largest of all the structures, is divided into two sections: **Plaza Norte**, with the ball court, was used for ceremonies; **Plaza Sur** was used for public activities. The scale of the site is vast, and many of the buildings are still under excavation, which means that information on Calakmul's history is continually being updated. To reach Calakmul, take Route 186 until Km 95, then turn off at Conhuás, where a paved road leads to the site, 60 km. ■ *US$2.50, free on Sun.*

Xpujil
Phone code: 983

The name means a type of plant similar to a cattail. The architectural style is known as Río Bec, characterized by heavy masonry towers simulating pyramids and temples, usually found rising in pairs at the ends of elongated buildings. The main building at Xpujil features an unusual set of three towers, with rounded corners and steps that are so steep they are unscalable, suggesting they may have been purely decorative. The façade features the open jaws of an enormous reptile in profile on either side of the main entrance, possibly representing Itzamná, the Maya god of creation. Xpujil's main period of activity was AD 500-750; it began to go into decline around 1100. Major excavation on the third structure was done as recently as 1993, and there are still many unexcavated buildings dotted about the site. It can be very peaceful and quiet in the early mornings, compared with the throng of tourist activity at the more accessible sites such as Chichén Itzá and Uxmal. ■ *0800-1700. US$1.50, free on Sun. US$3 to use a video camera.*

The tiny village of Xpujil, on the Chetumal-Escárcega highway, is conveniently located for the three sets of ruins in this area, Xpujil, Becán and Chicanná. There are two hotels and a couple of shops. Guided tours to the more remote sites such as Calakmul and Río Bec can be organized through either of the two hotels listed below, costing about US$20-30 per person for the whole day.

Sleeping C *Calakmul*, 800 m from the bus stop, T/F832-9162. Recently renovated, modern fixtures, good restaurant, quiet, safe, clean. **D** *Mirador*, just past Calakmul. Cabaña accommodation. A bit run down, restaurant.

Transport 2nd class buses from Chetumal and Escárcega stop on the highway in the centre of Xpujil, some 800 m east of the 2 hotels. There are 4 buses a day to Escárcega, between 1030 and 1500, 3 hrs, US$6. 8 buses a day go to Chetumal, 2 hrs, US$5. Change at Escárcega for buses to Palenque or Campeche. 1st class buses will not stop at Xpujil.

Becán
Phone code: 996

Seven kilometres west of Xpujil, Becán is another important site in the Río Bec style, its most outstanding feature being a moat, now dry, surrounding the entire city, believed to be one of the oldest defence systems in Mesoamerica. Seven entrance gates cross the moat to the city. The large variety of buildings on the site are a strange combination of decorative towers and fake temples, as well as structures used as shrines and palaces. The twin towers, typical of the Río Bec style, feature on the main structure, set on a pyramid-shaped base supporting a cluster of buildings, which seem to have been used for many different functions. ■ *0800-1700. US$2, free on Sun.*

Chicanná
Phone code: 981

Located 12 km from Xpujil, Chicanná was named upon its discovery in 1966 in reference to Structure II: *chi* - mouth, *can* - serpent, and *ná* - house, 'House of the Serpent's Mouth'. Due to its dimensions and location, Chicanná is considered to have been a small residential centre for the rulers of the ancient regional capital of Becán. It was occupied during the late pre-Classic period (300 BC-AD 250); the final stages of activity at the site have been dated to the post-Classic era (AD 1100). Typical of the Río Bec style are numerous representations of the Maya god Itzamná, or Earth Mother. One of the temples has a dramatic entrance in the shape of a monster's mouth, with fangs jutting out over the lintel and more fangs lining the access stairway. ■ *0800-1700. US$1.50, free on Sun.* A taxi will take you from Xpujil bus stop to Becán and Chicanná for US$10, including waiting time.

Sleeping AL *Eco-Village Resort*. Km 144, T816-2233. Discount for members of Sanborn's Amigo Club.

Hormiguero

Twenty kilometres southwest of Xpujil, Hormiguero is the site of one of the most important buildings in the Río Bec region, whose elaborate carvings on the façade show an excellent example of the serpent's-mouth entrance, with huge fangs and a gigantic eye.

Río Bec

In the opposite direction to the other group of sites in this area, Río Bec is south off the main highway, some 10 km along the road to Chetumal. Although the site gave its name to the architectural style seen in this area, there are better examples of it at the ruins listed above. Río Bec is a cluster of several smaller sites, all of which are very difficult to reach without a guide. Guided tours to all the sites in this region can be arranged in Xpujil.

Champotón
Phone code: 982
Colour map 4, grid A2
Population: 18,000

Back near the west coast of Campeche State, Route 261 runs 86 km due north from Escárcega through dense forest to the Gulf of Mexico, where it joins the coastal route at Champotón, a relaxed but run-down fishing and shrimping port spread along the banks of Río Champotón. In pre-Hispanic times it was an important trading link

Yucatán Peninsula

between Guatemala and Central Mexico; Toltec and Maya mingled here, followed by the Spaniards; in fact blood was shed here when Francisco Hernández de Córboba was fatally wounded in a skirmish with the inhabitants in 1517. On the south side of town can be seen the remnants of a 1719 fort built as a defence against the pirates who frequently raided this coast. The *Feast of the Immaculate Conception* (8 December) is celebrated with a joyous festival lasting several days.

Sleeping and eating B *Snook Inn*, Calle 30 No 1, T828-0018. A/c, fan, pool, owner speaks English, favourite with fishing enthusiasts and bird hunters. **C** *Gemenis*, Calle 30 No 10, T828-0008. **E** *Imperial*, Calle 28 No 38. Simple, with fans, river views, regular food. **E** *Casa de Huéspedes*, Calle 30. Clean, basic, big rooms. Recommended. A few unpretentious restaurants, usually seafood menus but *venado* (venison) and *pato* (duck) plentiful in season: *La Palapa*, on the seafront. Covered terrace, speciality is fish stuffed with shrimp, very fresh. Recommended.

Directory Banks Try *Banco del Atlántico* for currency transactions, open Mon-Fri 0900-1230.

Sihoplaya &
Seybaplaya
Phone code: 982

Continuing north, Highways 180 and 261 are combined for 17 km until the latter darts off east on its way to Edzná and Hopelchen (bypassing Campeche, should this be desired). A 66-km toll *autopista*, paralleling Highway 180, just inland from the southern outskirts of Champotón to Campeche, is much quicker than the old highway. Champotón and Seybaplaya are bypassed. But from the old Highway 180, narrow and slow with speed bumps, you can reach the resort of **Sihoplaya**. Here is the widely known **C** *Hotel Siho Playa*, T826-2989. A former sugar hacienda with a beautiful setting and beach facilities, pool, disco/bar, breezy rooms, etc, but, despite remodelling in the past, it has seen better days; camping possible, US$5; restaurant is overpriced and poor but there is nowhere else to eat nearby. Regular buses from Campeche US$1. A short distance further north is the larger resort of **Seybaplaya**. This is an attractive place where fishermen mend nets and pelicans dry their wings on posts along the beach. On the highway is the open-air *Restaurant Veracruz*, serving delicious red snapper (fresh fish at the seafront public market is also good value), but in general there is little to explore. Only the *Balneario Payucán* at the north end of the bay makes a special trip worthwhile; this is probably the closest decent beach to Campeche (33 km), although a little isolated, since the water and sand get filthier as one nears the state capital. Nevertheless, there is still much reef life to enjoy.

Campeche

Phone code: 981
Colour map 4, grid A2
Population: 171,367

At the end of the 20th century, the town of Campeche was declared a Cultural Heritage Site by UNESCO. The clean streets of brightly painted houses give the town a relaxed Caribbean feel. A hurricane in 1996 destroyed the Malecón, which has since been rebuilt and is now a beautiful promenade where people stroll, cycle, walk and relax in the evening in the light of the setting sun.

Highway 180 enters the city as the Avenida Resurgimiento, passing either side of the huge **Monumento al Resurgimiento**, a stone torso holding aloft the Torch of Democracy. Originally the trading village of Ah Kim Pech, it was here that the Spaniards, under Francisco Hernández de Córdoba, first disembarked on Mexican soil (22 March 1517) to replenish their water supply. For fear of being attacked by the native population, they quickly left, only to be attacked later by the locals further south in Champotón, where they were forced to land by appalling weather conditions at sea. It was not until 1540 that Francisco de Montejo managed to conquer Ah Kim Pech, founding the city of Campeche on 4 October 1541, after failed attempts in 1537 and earlier in 1527. The export of local dyewoods, *chicle*, timber and other valuable cargoes soon attracted the attention of most of the famous buccaneers, who constantly raided the port from their bases on Isla del Carmen, then known as the Isla de Tris. Combining their fleets for one momentous swoop, they fell upon

Campeche on 9 February 1663, wiped out the city and slaughtered its inhabitants. Five years later the Crown began fortifying the site, the first Spanish colonial settlement to be completely walled. Formidable bulwarks, 3 m thick and 'a ship's height', and eight bastions (*baluartes*) were built in the next 36 years. All these fortifications soon put a stop to pirate attacks and Campeche prospered as one of only two Mexican ports (the other was Veracruz) to have had the privilege of conducting international trade. After Mexican Independence from Spain, the city declined into an obscure fishing and logging town. Only with the arrival of a road from the 'mainland' in the 1950s and the oil boom of the 1970s has Campeche begun to see visitors in any numbers, attracted by its historical monuments and relaxed atmosphere (*campechano* has come to mean an easy-going, pleasant person).

Like many of the Yucatán's towns, Campeche's streets in the Old Town are numbered rather than named. Even numbers run north/south beginning at Calle 8 (no one knows why) near the Malecón, east to Calle 18 inside the walls; odd numbers run east (inland) from Calle 51 in the north to Calle 65 in the south. Most of the points of interest are within this compact area. A full circuit of the walls is a long walk; buses marked 'Circuito Baluartes' provide a regular service around the perimeter.

The **state tourist office** is on the Malecón in front of the Palacio de Gobierno (walk down Calle 61 towards the sea), T816-7364. ■ *0800-2100*. There is a smaller office at Baluarte Santa Rosa, Calle 14. ■ *0800-2000*. The state tourism website is at **www.campeche.gob.mx** For a good orientation take the Centro Histórico tour, a regular tourist tram running from the main plaza. ■ *Daily 0900-1300 and 1700-2000, 45 mins, English and Spanish spoken.*

Campeche

■ Sleeping	4 Posada del Angel	● Eating	4 Lonchería
1 Baluartes	5 Regis	1 Del Parque	
2 Campeche	6 Roma	2 La Parroquia	
3 Del Mar	7 Teresita	3 La Perla	

Yucatán Peninsula

Sights Of the original walls, seven of the *baluartes* and an ancient fort (now rather dwarfed by two big white hotels on the seafront) remain. Some house museums (see below).

The heart of the city is the Zócalo, where the austere Franciscan **cathedral** (1540-1705) has an elaborately carved façade; inside is the Santo Entierro (Holy Burial), a sculpture of Christ on a mahogany sarcophagus with a silver trim. There is plenty of shade under the trees in the Zócalo, and a small pagoda with a snack bar.

Right in front of the Zócalo is the **Baluarte de la Soledad** (see **Museums**), the central bulwark of the city walls, from where you can do a walking tour of the *Circuito Baluartes*, the remains of the city walls. Heading south, you will come to the **Puerta del Mar**, formerly the entrance to those permitted to enter the city from the sea, which used to come up to this point. Next along the *Circuito* is a pair of modern buildings, the **Palacio de Gobierno** and the **Congreso**. The latter looks like a flying saucer, and makes for a bizarre sight when viewed with the 17th-century **Baluarte de San Carlos** in the background. Baluarte de San Carlos now houses a museum (see below). Heading west on the continuation of the *Circuito*, you will come to **Templo de San José**, on Calle 10, an impressive baroque church with a beautifully tiled façade. It has been de-consecrated, and is now an educational centre. Back on to the *Circuito*, you will next reach the **Baluarte de Santa Rosa**, now the home of the tourist information office. Next is **Baluarte de San Juan**, from which a large chunk of the old city wall still extends, protecting you from the noisy traffic on the busy road beyond it. The wall connects with **Puerta de la Tierra**, where a Luz y Sonido (Light and Sound) show takes place. ■ *Tue, Fri and Sat 2030, (for information, contact the tourist office).* The continuation of the *Circuito* will take you past the **Baluarte de San Francisco**, and then past the market, just outside the line of the city walls. **Baluarte de San Pedro** flanks the northeast corner of the city centre, and now houses a museum (see below). The *circuito* runs down to the northwest tip of the old city, where the **Baluarte de Santiago** houses the Botanical Gardens (see **Museums**).

Further from the city walls is the **Batería de San Luis**, 4 km south from the centre along the coast road. This was once a lookout post to catch pirates as they approached the city from a distance. The **Fuerte de San Miguel**, 600 m inland, is now a museum (see below). A 20-minute walk along Avenida Miguel Alemán from Baluarte de Santiago is the **San Francisco** church, 16th century with wooden altars painted in vermilion and white. Nearby are the **Portales de San Francisco**, a beautifully restored old entrance to the city, with several good restaurants in its shadow.

Museums **Museo Regional de Campeche**, in the Casa Teniente del Rey, Calle 59 between Calle 14 y Calle 16, charts a history of the state of Campeche since Maya times with interesting displays. ■ *Tue-Sat 0800-1400, 1700-2000, Sun 0900-1300, US$3.*

Museo de la Cultura Maya, in the Fuerte de San Miguel, contains the results of continual excavations at the ruins of Calakmul, including jade masks and a mummified body. ■ *Tue-Fri 0800-2000, US$1.* **Museo de la Escultura Maya**, Baluarte de la Soledad, has three well-laid out rooms of Maya stelae and sculpture. ■ *Tue-Sat 0900-1400, 1600-2000, Sun 0900-1300. US$1.* **Museo Gráfico de la Ciudad**, Baluarte de San Carlos, contains interesting scale models of the 18th-century defences and a collection of colonial arms and seafaring equipment, small library, a fine view from the cannon-studded roof, dungeons and a government-sponsored handicrafts market; for a few pesos, guides will conduct you through underground passageways, which once provided escape routes from many of the town's houses (most have now been bricked up). ■ *0900-1300, 1700-2000. Free.* **Exposición de Artesanías**, Baluarte de San Pedro, is a permanent collection of local handicrafts with a shop. ■ *Mon-Fri 0900-1300, 1700-2000. Free.*

Jardín Botánico Xmuch'Haltun, in Baluarte de Santiago, is a small, but perfectly formed collection of tropical plants and flowers in a peaceful setting. ■ *Mon-Sat 0900-1300, 1800-2000, Sun 0900-1300. Free.* **Centro Ecológico de Campeche**, Avenida Escénica s/n, T811-2528, has a good collection of local wildlife. ■ *Tue-Fri 0900-1300, Sat and Sun 1000-1630.*

The **Fuerte de San Miguel**, on the Malecón 4 km southwest, is the most atmospheric of the forts (complete with drawbridge and a moat said to have once contained either crocodiles or skin-burning lime, take your pick!); it houses the **Museo Arqueológico**, with a well-documented display of pre-Columbian exhibits including jade masks and black funeral pottery from Calakmul and recent finds from Jaina. ■ *Tue-Sat, 0900-2000, Sun 0900-1300, US$1. Recommended.*

Excursions

Lerma is virtually a small industrial suburb of Campeche, with large shipyards and fish-processing plants; the afternoon return of the shrimping fleet is a colourful sight. The *Fiesta de Polk Kekén* is held on 6 January, with traditional dances. The nearest beach is Playa Bonita, some 7 km south of Campeche. It gets very packed in the high season with locals, and the water is not very *'bonita'* at all, but dirty and polluted. The nearest decent beaches are at Seybaplaya (see page 476), 20 km south of Campeche. There, the beaches are clean and deserted; take your own food and drink as there are no facilities. Crowded, rickety buses marked 'Lerma' or 'Playa Bonita' run from Campeche, US$1, 8 km.

Sleeping
■ *on map*

In general, prices are high. Beware of overcharging and, if driving, find a secure car park

AL *Del Mar*, Av Ruiz Cortines 51, T816-2233, F811-1618, 5-star hotel on the waterfront with pool, gym, good bar and restaurant. **A** *Baluartes*, Av 16 de Septiembre 128, T816-3911. Recently remodelled, on the foreshore, very good restaurant, pool.

C *América*, Calle 10 No 252, T816-4588. Hot water, friendly, no safe deposit, clean, fans but hot, safe parking, with night watchman. **C** *Regis*, Calle 12 No 148, between 55 y 57, T816-3175. Nice setting among cool colonial columns in the centre, good service.

D *La Posada Del Angel*, Calle 10 No 307, T816-7718 (on the side entrance of the cathedral). A/c, attractive, some rooms without windows, clean. Recommended. **D** *Autel El Viajero*, López Mateos 177, T816-5133. Overcharges, but often the only one left with space in the afternoon. **D** *Central*, on Gobernadores opposite *ADO* bus station. Misleadingly named, a/c, hot water, clean, friendly, noisy. **D** *López*, Calle 12 No 189, T816-2488. Interesting art deco design, clean if a bit musty, with bath, uncomfortable beds, a/c. **D** *Roma*, Calle 10 No 54, T816-3897. Run-down, dirty, dark, difficult parking, not safe (but often full).

E *Campeche*, Calle 57 No 2, across from the cathedral on the Zócalo, T816-5183. Fan, cold water, grubby, run-down – has been a hotel since 1939 and is long overdue a paint job! **E** *Reforma*, Calle 8 No 257, T816-4464. Dirty, run down, upper-floor rooms best, basic. **E** *Teresita*, Calle 53 No 31, 3 blocks northeast of plaza. Very basic rooms with fans, no hot water. Cheapest in town, but good if you're on a tight budget.

Camping *Trailer Park Campeche*, on Agustín Melgar and Calle 19, 5 km south of centre, close to the bay in uninviting suburb of Samulá (signposted). 25 spaces and tent area, full hook-ups, good amenities, cold showers, pleasant site, owners speak some English, US$3.25 per person, US$6.50 for car with 2 people, 'Samulá' bus from market (US$0.15) or a 'Lerma' bus down coast road, get off at Melgar and walk.

Youth hostel *Villa Deportiva Univeritaria*, Av Agustín Melgar s/n, Col Buenavista, T816-1802, in the south suburbs, near University, take Samulá or *ISSSTE* bus from market US$0.25 (*ISSSTE* bus also from bus station). Get dropped at the intersection with Av Melgar, take the road toward the coast about 200 m and it is on the left. Call beforehand to check availability, as they can be full of students and sports groups. Segregated dormitories with 4 bunk beds in each room (US$1.50 per person), lovely grounds, pool, cafetería (breakfast 0730-0930, lunch 1400-1600, dinner 1930-2130, about US$1.50), clean and friendly, towels provided.

Eating
on map, page 477
Price codes:
see inside front cover

Campeche is widely known for its seafood, especially *camarones* (large shrimps), *esmedregal* (black snapper) and *pan de cazón* (baby hammerhead shark sandwiched between corn *tortillas* with black beans). Food stands in the market serve *tortas, tortillas, panuchos* and *tamales* but hygiene standards vary widely; barbecued venison is also a marketplace speciality. Fruit is cheap and in great variety; perhaps best to resist the bags of sliced mangoes and peel all

Yucatán Peninsula

fruit yourself. (The word 'cocktail' is said to have originated in Campeche, where 17th-century English pirates enjoyed drinks adorned with palm fronds resembling cocks' tails).

La Perla, Calle 10 between 57 and 59. Good fish, busy and popular, venison, squid, locals' haunt, sometimes erratic service, off plaza. *Mirador*, Calle 8 y 61. Good fish, moderate prices. *Marganza*, Calle 8. Upmarket, good breakfast and meals, excellent service. *Heladería Bing*, Calle 12 y 59. Good ice-cream. *Av Fénix*, on Juárez where the street bends towards the terminal. Generous breakfasts. Good food in the market, but don't drink the tap water. It is hard to find reasonably priced food before 1800; try the restaurant at the *ADO* terminal, or *La Parroquia*, Calle 55 No 8. Open 24 hours, good local atmosphere, friendly and clean. Recommended. *Los Portales*, Calle 10 No 86. Authentic local atmosphere, try the *sopa de lima*, open 1900-midnight. *Bar El Portón*, Calle 18 between 61 and 63, near walls. Courtyard, friendly. *Restaurant del Parque*, on the plaza opposite the cathedral. Good, cheap seafood. *La Pigua*, Av Miguel Alemán, opposite *Cine Estela*. Seafood in pleasant garden setting. *Lonchería Guayín*, Calle 53 between 16 and 14. Cheap *comida corrida*, good *licuados*, also houses Miguel Angel, spiritualist, fortune teller and feng shui consultant.

Festivals *Feria de San Román*, 2nd 2 weeks of Sep. *Fiesta de San Francisco*, **4-13 Oct**. Good *Carnival* in **Feb/Mar**. **7 Aug** is a *state holiday*.

Shopping Excellent cheap Panama hats *(jipis)*, finely and tightly woven so that they retain their shape even when crushed into your luggage (within reason); cheaper at the source in Becal. Handicrafts are generally cheaper than in Mérida. The market, from which most local buses depart, is beside Alameda Park at the south end of Calle 57. Plenty of bargains here. Try ice-cream, though preferably from a shop rather than a barrow. *Super 10* supermarket behind the post office has an excellent cheap bakery inside. There are souvenir shops along Calle 8, such as *Artesanía Típica Naval* (No 259) with exotic bottled fruit like *nance* and *marañón*, or *El Coral* (No 255) with a large variety of Maya figurines; many high-quality craft items are available from the *Exposición* in the Baluarte San Pedro. Camping and general supplies, and laundrette, at *Superdíaz* supermarket in Akim-Pech shopping area at Av Miguel Alemán y Av Madero, some distance north of the Zócalo. ■ *0800-2100*. *Casa de Artesanía*, Calle 10. Good-quality handicrafts displayed on bizarre Maya dummies, with a mock-up hammock-making cave.

Transport **Local Car hire**: next to *Hotel Del Mar*, Av Ruiz Cortines 51, T816-2233. *Hertz* and *Autorent* car rentals at airport. **Tourist buses** run to **Edzná** from Puerta de la Tierra, in front of the market, 0900 and 1400, US$20 return, also cheaper combis from the same stop. Buses to **Calakmul** depart from Baluarte de San Pedro, weekends only at 1700. Buses to **Seybaplaya** leave from the tiny Cristo Rey terminal opposite the market, 9 a day from 0615, 45 mins.

Long distance Air: modern, efficient airport (CPE) on Porfirio, 10 km northeast. *AeroMéxico* direct daily to **Mexico City**, T816-5678. If on a budget, walk 100 m down service road (Av Aviación) to Av Nacozari, turn right (west) and wait for 'China-Campeche' bus to Zócalo.

Buses: the main bus station is to the northeast on Av Gobernadores. The following times and prices are for 2nd class buses, the *ADO* terminal is next door. Prices are higher but greater comfort and speed. **Cancún**: 2200, 2330, US$23; **Chetumal**: 1200, US$18; **Ciudad del Carmen**: 9 a day from 0745, US$9; **Escárcega**: hourly from 0200, 2 hrs, US$7.50; *Cristóbal Colón*, 2210, US$7; **Mérida**: 11 a day from 0545-1930, 2½ hrs, US$9; *Maya de Oro*, 0400, US$11; *Cristóbal Colón*, 2030, US$7.50; **Mexico City**: 1600, US$78; **Oaxaca**: 2155, 2400, US$55; **Palenque**: 1st class with *ADO*, 3 a day from 0030, 5-7 hrs, US$17; **San Cristóbal de las Casas**: *Maya de Oro*, 2400, 14 hrs, US$33; *Cristóbal Colón*, 2210, US$26; **Veracruz**: 1st class, 1030, 1300 and 2100, 14 hrs, US$49; **Villahermosa**: 5 a day from 0900, 6½ hrs, US$18.

Directory **Banks** *Banamex*, Calle 10 No 15. *Bancomer*, opposite the Baluarte de la Soledad. *Banco del Atlántico*, Calle 50 No 406; open 0900-1300 Mon-Fri; all change TCs and give good service. *American Express*, T811-1010, Calle 59, Edificio Belmar, oficina 5, helpful for lost cheques, etc. Plenty of places to get cash on edit cards and ATMs. **Communications** Internet: *Cybercafé Campeche*, Calle 61 between Calle 10 and 12, open 0900-1300, US$1.50/hr, several others around but somewhat slower; *Telmex*, Calle 8 between Calle 51 y 53, free; Calle 51 No 45, between 12 and 14. *Intertel*, long-distance phones and fax, Calle 57 No 1 between 10 and 12. **Post office:** Av 16 de Septiembre (Malecón) y Calle 53 in Edificio Federal go to the right upon entry for telegraph service); open Mon-Fri 0800-2000, Sat 0900-1300 for *Lista de Correos*, registered mail, money orders and stamps. **Cultural centres** Casa del Teniente de Rey, on Calle 9 No 38 between 14 and 16, houses the Instituto Nacional de Antropología e Historia (INAH), dedicated to the restoration of Maya ruins in the state of Campeche, as well as supporting local museums. INAH can be visited for information regarding any of the sites in the state, T811-1314, inah@campeche.sureste.com *Centro Manik*, Calle 59 No 22 between 12 and 14, T/F62448, opened 1997 in restored house in centre, vegetarian restaurant, bookshop, handicrafts, art gallery, music lessons, conferences, concentrates on ecology, environmentalism and health, also developing ecotourism in southern Campeche. **Hospitals** Red Cross, T815-2378, emergency T815-2411. **Laundry** Calle 55 between 12 and 14, US$0.60 per kg. **Tour operators** *Viajes del Golfo*, Calle 10 No 250 D, T816-4044, F816-6154. Tours to Edzná, Calakmul. *Viajes Chicanná*, Av Augustín Melgar, Centro Comercial Triángulo del Sol, Local 12, T811-3503, F811-0735. Flight bookings to Cuba, Miami and Central America. *Intermar Campeche*, Miguel Alemán Av, T816-9006, intercam@prodigy.net.mx Useful addresses The *Oficina de Migración* at the Palacio Federal will extend Mexican visas. Take copies of your passport as well as the original.

Maya sites east of Campeche

A number of city remains (mostly in the unfussy Chenes architectural style) are scattered throughout the rainforest and scrub to the east of Campeche; little excavation work has been done and most receive few visitors. Getting to them by the occasional bus service is possible in many cases, but return trips can be tricky. The alternatives are one of the tours run by some luxury hotels and travel agencies in Campeche (see above) or renting a vehicle (preferably with high clearance) in Campeche or Mérida. Whichever way you travel, carrying plenty of drinking water is strongly advised.

The closest site to the state capital is Edzná ('House of Grimaces'), reached by the highway east to Cayal, then a right turn onto Highway 261 (the road to Uxmal, see page 483), a total distance of 61 km. A paved short cut southeast through China and Poxyaxum (good road) cuts off 11 km; follow Avenida Nacozari out along the railway track. Gracefully situated in a lovely, tranquil valley with thick vegetation on either side, Edzná was a huge ceremonial centre, occupied from about 600 BC to AD 200, built in the simple Chenes style mixed with Puuc, Classical and other influences. The centrepiece is the magnificent, 30-m tall, 60 sq m **Temple of the Five Storeys**, a stepped pyramid consisting of four levels of living quarters for the priests and a shrine and altar at the top; 65 steep steps lead up from the Central Plaza. Opposite is the recently restored **Paal U'na**, Temple of the Moon. Excavations are being carried out on the scores of lesser temples by Guatemalan refugees under the direction of Mexican archaeologists, but most of Edzná's original sprawl remains hidden away under thick vegetation. Imagination is still needed to picture the extensive network of irrigation canals and holding basins built by the Maya along the valley below sea level. Some of the site's stelae remain in position (two large stone faces with grotesquely squinting eyes are covered by a thatched shelter); others can be seen in various Campeche museums. There is also a good example of a *sacbé* (white road). Edzná is well worth a visit especially in July (exact date varies), when a Maya ceremony to Chac is held, either to encourage or to celebrate the arrival of the rains. ■ *Tue-Sun 0800-1700, US$2, free on Sun; small comedor at the entrance. Local guides available.* There is a tourist bus that leaves from Chetumal town wall at 0900, US$10 per person. At weekends take a bus towards Pich from Campeche market place at 0700, 1000 and 1030 (one hour trip) but it may leave hours late; return buses pass the site (five minutes' walk from the Highway) at 0930, 1230 and 1300. In the week, the Pich bus leaves Campeche at 1400, which is only of any use if you are prepared to sleep rough as there is nowhere to stay in the vicinity; hitching back is difficult, but you may get a ride to El Cayal on the road to Uxmal.

Edzná
Colour map 4, grid A2

Yucatán Peninsula

Directory Tour operators: *Viajes Programados*, Calle 59, Edificio Belmar, in Campeche offer daily 2-hr tours at 1000, US$20; tours from the *Hotel Baluartes*. *Picazh Servicios Turísticos*, Calle 1 No 348 between 357 and 359, T816-4426, run transport to ruins, with or without guide, US$20 Recommended.

Hochob   Of the more remote and even less-visited sites beyond Edzná, Hochob and Dzibilnocac are the best choices for the non-specialist. **Hochob** is reached by turning right at **Hopelchén** on Highway 261, 85 km east of Campeche. This quiet town has an impressive fortified 16th-century church but only one hotel, **D** *Los Arcos*. A traditional Honey and Corn Festival is held on 13-17 April; another fiesta takes place each 3 May on the Día de la Santa Cruz. From here a narrow paved road leads 41 km south to the village of **Dzibalchén**; no hotels but hammock hooks and toilet facilities upon request at the Palacio Municipal, there are some small eating places around the Zócalo. Don Willem Chan will guide tourists to Hochob (he also rents bikes for US$3.50 per day), helpful, speaks English. Directions can be obtained from the church here (run by Americans); essentially you need to travel 18 km southwest on a good dirt road (no public transport, hopeless quagmire in the rainy season) to the village of Chenko, where locals will show the way (4 km through the jungle). Remember to bear left when the road forks; it ends at a small *palapa* and, from here, the ruins are 1 km uphill with a magnificent view over the surrounding forest. Hochob once covered a large area but, as at Edzná, only the hilltop ceremonial centre (the usual Plaza surrounded by elaborately decorated temple buildings) has been properly excavated; although many of these are mounds of rubble, the site is perfect for contemplating deserted, yet accessible Maya ruins in solitude and silence. The one-room temple to the right (north) of the plaza is the most famous structure, deep-relief patterns of stylized snakes moulded in stucco across its façade were designed to resemble a mask of the ferocious rain god Chac. A door serves as the mouth. Some concentration is needed to see this due to erosion of the carvings. A fine reconstruction of the building is on display at the Museo de Antropología in Mexico City. ■ *Daily 0800-1700, US$4.35.* Early morning second class buses serve Dzibalchén, but, returning to Campeche later in the day is often a matter of luck.

Dzibilnocac   Twenty kilometres northeast of Dzibalchén at Iturbide, this site is one of the largest in Chenes territory. Only three temples have been excavated here (many pyramidal mounds in the forest and roadside *milpas*); the first two are in a bad state of preservation, but the third is worth the visit: a unique narrow edifice with rounded corners and remains of a stucco façade, primitive reliefs and another grim mask of Chac on the top level. Much of the stonework from the extensive site is used by local farmers for huts and fences, keep an eye out in the vegetation for thorns and snakes. ■ *Daily 0800-1700, US$4.35.* A bus leaves Campeche at 0800, 3 hours, return 1245, 1345 and 1600, US$3.35. If driving your own vehicle, well-marked 'km' signs parallel the rocky road to Iturbide (no accommodation); bear right around the tiny Zócalo and its attendant yellow church and continue (better to walk in the wet season) for 50 m, where the right branch of a fork leads to the ruins. Other sites in the region require four-wheel-drive transport and to appeal only to professional archaeologists.

Jaina   The small limestone island of Jaina lies just off the coast, 40 km north of Campeche. Discovered by Morley in 1943, excavations on Jaina have revealed the most extensive Maya burial grounds ever found, over 1,000 interments dating back to AD 652. The bodies of religious and political leaders were carried long distances from all over the Yucatán and Guatemala to be buried beneath the extremely steep **Pyramids of Zacpol** and **Sayasol** on Jaina. The corpses were interred in jars in crouching positions, clutching statues in their folded arms, some with jade stones in their mouths; food, weapons, tools and jewellery accompanied the owner into the afterlife. Terracotta burial offerings (including figurines with movable arms and legs) have provided a revealing picture of Maya customs, dress and living habits. Many of these are now on display in Campeche or in the museum at Hecelchakán (see below). The island is Federal property, well guarded and currently closed to visitors. Major restoration and excavation is in progress and the island will reopen in a few years as an accessible tourist attraction.

Campeche to Mérida

There are two routes north from Campeche to Mérida, capital of the state of Yucatán: the so-called *Camino Real*, *vía corta* or short route (173 km via the shortcut along the railway line to Tenabó), using Highway 180 through Calkiní, Becal and Umán (taken by all first class and *directo* buses), and the *Ruta Maya* or long route (254 km), Highway 261 through Hopelchén and Muná, which gives access to many of the peninsula's best-known archaeological sites, especially Uxmal (see page 498).

On the direct route, State Highway 24 provides a convenient link from Campeche to Highway 180 at **Tenabó** (36 km against 58 km), from where the well-paved road runs on through rising ground and sleepy villages, each with its traditional Zócalo, solid church and stone houses often made from the materials of nearby Maya ruins, to **Hecelchakán** (18 km, large service station on the bypass), with a 1620 Franciscan church and the rustic Museo Arqueológico del Camino Real on the Zócalo. Although dusty, the museum's five rooms give an informative overview of Mayan cultural development with the help of maps, stelae, a diorama and many Jaina burial artefacts. ■ *Tue-Sat 0900-1400, US$1.85.*

The highway bypasses **Calkiní** (E *Posada del Viajero*, not recommended, in a state of decay; service station) and after 33 km arrives at **Becal** (*Population*: 4,000), the centre for weaving Panama hats, here called *jipis* (pronounced 'hippies') and ubiquitous throughout the Yucatán. Many of the town's families have workshops in cool, moist backyard underground caves, necessary for keeping moist and pliable the shredded leaves of the *jipijapa* palm from which the hats are made. Most vendors are happy to give the visitor a tour of their workshop, but are quite zealous in their sales pitches. Prices are better for *jipis* and other locally-woven items (cigarette cases, shoes, belts, etc) in the *Centro Artesanal, Artesanías de Becaleña* (Calle 30 No 210), than in the shops near the plaza, where the hat is honoured by a hefty sculpture of three concrete *sombreros*! More celebrations of homage take place each 20 May during the *Feria del Jipi*.

State of Yucatán

The archaeological sites of Chichen Itzá, Oxkintoc, Uxmal, Kabah and Labná are just a few of the many strewn throughout the State of Yucatán. Try not to miss Dzibilchaltún; the intrusion of European architecture is nowhere more startling than here. The region's many cenotes (deep pools created by the disintegration of the dry land above an underground river) were sacred to the Maya who threw precious jewels, silverware and even humans into their depths; many are perfect for swimming. On the coast, boat trips are organized to observe pelicans, egrets and flamingos in their natural habitat. It is possible to visit some of the impressive henequén (sisal) haciendas in the more rural areas and admire the showy mansions that line the Paseo de Montejo in Mérida.

Just beyond Becal, en route from Campeche, Highway 180 passes under a 19th-century stone arch, which is supposed to mark the Campeche/Yucatán border (although nobody seems totally sure of where the line is) and runs 26 km to **Maxcanú**. Here the road to Muná and Ticul branches east (see page 499); a short way down it is the recently restored Maya site of **Oxkintoc**. The Pyramid of the Labyrinth can be entered (take a torch) and there are other ruins, some with figures. ■ *US$3.* Ask for a guide at the village of Calcehtoc, which is 4 km from the ruins and from the Grutas de Oxkintoc (no bus service). These, however, cannot compare

Yucatán Peninsula

with the caves at Loltún or Balancanché (see pages 497 and 504). Highway 180 continues north towards Mérida through a region of numerous *cenotes*, soon passing a turn-off to the turn-of-the-century Moorish-style *henequén* (sisal) hacienda at **San Bernardo**, one of a number in the state that can be visited; an interesting colonial museum chronicling the old Yucatán Peninsula tramway system is located in its lush and spacious grounds. Running beside the railway, the highway continues 47 km to its junction with the inland route at **Umán**, a *henequén* processing town (*Population: 7,000*) with another large 17th-century church and convent dedicated to St Francis of Assisi; there are many *cenotes* in the flat surrounding limestone plain. Highway 180/261 is a divided four-lane motorway for the final 18 km stretch into Mérida. There is a ring road around the city.

Mérida

Phone code: 999
Colour map 4, grid A2
Population: 703,324

The capital of Yucatán state and its colonial heart, Mérida is a bustling, tightly packed city full of colonial buildings in varying states of repair, from the grandiose to the dilapidated. There is continual activity in the centre, with a huge influx of tourists during the high season mingling with busy Meridanos going about their daily business. Although the city has been developed over many years for tourism, there is plenty of local flavour for the traveller to seek out off the beaten track. Attempts to create a sophisticated 'Champs-Elysées' style boulevard in the north of the city at Paseo Montejo have not quite cracked it; the plan almost seems to go against the grain of Mérida's status as an ancient city, which has gradually evolved into a place with its own distinct identity. Mérida is a safe city, with its own tourist police force, recognizable by their brown and white uniforms. It is worth noting that during July and August, although very hot, Mérida is subject to heavy rains during the afternoon.

Ins and outs

Getting there All buses from outside Yucatán State arrive at the CAME terminal on Calle 70 between Calle 69 y 71, a few blocks from the centre. There is another bus terminal around the corner on Calle 69, where buses from local destinations such as Uxmal arrive. The airport is 8 km from the city, bus 79 takes you to the centre. Taxi to the centre from the airport charge US$9.

Getting around You can see most of Mérida on foot. Although the city is big, there is not much to concern the tourist outside a few blocks radiating from the main plaza. The VW Beetle taxis are expensive, due to their scarcity; fares start at US$3 for a short journey. Colectivo buses are difficult to locate; they appear suddenly on the bigger roads in the city, you can flag them down anywhere. They terminate at the market; flat fare US$0.25.

The main **tourist office** is inside the Teatro Peón Contreras, Calle 60 y Calle 57 (just off Parque Hidalgo). ■ *0800-2000 daily.* Very helpful, often staffed by trainees who are very enthusiastic about giving help. There are other tourist offices at the airport and in the main plaza. The state tourism website is at **www.yucatan.gob.mx**

Background

Mérida was originally a large Mayan city called Tihoo. It was conquered on 6 January 1542, by Francisco de Montejo. He dismantled the pyramids of the Maya and used the stone as the foundations for the cathedral of San Ildefonso, built 1556-59. For the next 300 years, Mérida remained under Spanish control, unlike the rest of Mexico, which was governed from the capital. During the Caste Wars of 1847-55, Mérida held out against the marauding forces of indigenous armies, who had defeated the Mexican army in every other city in the Yucatán Peninsula except Campeche. Reinforcements from the centre allowed the Mexicans to regain control of their city, but the price was to relinquish control of the region to Mexico City.

Sights

The city revolves around the large, shady Zócalo, site of the **cathedral**, completed in 1559, the oldest cathedral in Latin America, which has an impressive baroque façade. It contains the Cristo de las Ampollas (Christ of the Blisters), a statue carved from a tree that burned for a whole night after being hit by lightning, without showing any

Mérida

N		
0 metres 300	3 Casa Becil *E2*	12 Margarita *D2*	2 Café Petropolis *E1*
0 yards 300	4 Casa Bowen *E2*	13 Mucuy *C3*	3 El Trapiche *D2*
	5 Del Gobernador *C2*	14 Pantera Negra *E1*	4 El Tucho *C3*
	6 Del Parque *C3*	15 Posada del Angel *E2*	5 Jugos California *D2*
	7 Dolores Alba *D4*	16 Posada Toledo *C3*	6 La Prosperidad *C3*
	8 Gran *D3*	17 San Juan *C3*	7 Los Almendros *C4*
■ **Sleeping**	9 La Paz *E2*		8 Pizza Bella *D2*
1 América *E3*	10 Las Monjas *D2*	● **Eating**	9 Pizza Chief *C2*
2 Caribe *C3*	11 Los Aluxes *C3*	1 Amaro *C2*	10 Tianos *C3*

damage at all. Placed in the church at Ichmul, it then suffered only a slight charring (hence the blistering name) when the church was burned to the ground. To the left of the cathedral on the adjacent side of the plaza is the **Palacio de Gobierno**, built 1892. It houses a collection of enormous murals by Fernando Castro Pacheco, depicting the struggle of the Maya to integrate with the Spanish. The murals can be viewed until 2000 every day. **Casa de Montejo** is on the south side of the Plaza, a 16th-century palace built by the city's founder, now a branch of Banamex. Away from the main Plaza along Calle 60 is Parque Hidalgo, a charming tree-filled square, which borders the 17th-century **Iglesia de Jesús**. A little further along Calle 60 is the **Teatro Peón Contreras**, built at the beginning of the 20th century by an Italian architect, with a neo-classical façade, marble staircase and Italian frescoes.

There are several 16th- and 17th-century churches dotted about the city: **La Mejorada**, behind the Museum of Peninsular Culture (Calle 59 between 48 and 50), **Tercera Orden**, **San Francisco** and **San Cristóbal** (beautiful, in the centre). The **Ermita**, an 18th-century chapel with beautiful grounds, is a lonely, deserted place 10-15 minutes from the centre.

Museums **Museo de Antropología e Historia**, Paseo de Montejo 485, housed in the beautiful neo-classical Palacio Cantón, has an excellent collection of original Maya artefacts from various sites in the Yucatán state. The displays are very well laid out, explanations all in Spanish. Many examples of jade jewellery dredged from *cenotes*, and examples of cosmetically deformed skulls with sharpened teeth. This is a good overview of the history of the Maya. ■ *Tue-Sun 0800-2000. US$2, free on Sun.*

Museo Macay, Calle 60, on the main plaza, has a permanent exhibition of Yucatecan artists, with temporary exhibits by contemporary local artists. ■ *Daily 1000-1730. US$2.* **Museo de Arte Popular**, Calle 59 esquina 50, Barrio de la Mejorada, has a permanent exhibition of Mayan art, handicrafts and clothing, with a good souvenir shop attached. ■ *Tue-Sat 0900-2000, Sun 0800-1400. Free.* **Museo de la Canción Yucateca**, Calle 63 between 64 and 66, in the Casa de la Cultura, has an exhibition of objects and instruments relating to the history of music in the region. ■ *Tue-Sat 0900-2000. Free.* **Pinacoteca Juan Gamboa Guzmán**, Calle 59 between Calle 58 and 60, is a gallery showing old and contemporary painting and sculpture. ■ *Tue-Sat 0800-2000, Sun 0800-1400. US$1, Sun free.*

Essentials

Sleeping The prices of hotels are not determined by their location. You can easily find a budget hotel
■ *on map page 485* right near the plaza, next door to a 5-star luxury establishment. If booking into a central hotel,
Price codes: see always try to get a room away from the street side, as noise on the narrow streets begins as
inside front cover early as 0500.

LL *Xcanatun*, Km 12, Carretera Mérida-Progreso, T/F941-0273. hacienda@xcanatun.com Carefully restored hacienda, 10 mins out of town, relaxed atmosphere with great attention to detail, full breakfast included, restaurant possibly the best in Mérida without an expensive price tag, located in a converted machine room with ceilings high enough to give you vertigo, live music every day. Highly recommended. **AL** *Calinda Panamericana*, Calle 59 No 455 esq 54, T923-9111, F924-8090. Good, expensive, with elaborate courtyard in the Porfirian style, very spacious and airy, ordinary rooms in new building behind, good buffet breakfast, with swimming pool, 5 blocks from centre. **AL** *Los Aluxes*, Calle 60 No 444, T924-2199. Delightful, pool, restaurants with live music, very convenient, 1st class, 2 large new wings away from traffic noise. **AL** *del Gobernador*, Calle 59 Nos 533 and 66, T923-7133, F928-1590. A/c, bar, restaurant, good pool. Highly recommended. **A** *Gran Hotel*, Parque Hidalgo, Calle 60 No 496, T923-6963, F924-7622. A/c, TV, hot water, phone, clean, helpful, owner speaks English. Popular with the stars of film and stage, and politicians including Fidel Castro. Pizza/pasta restaurant, free parking nearby. **B** *Aragón*, Calle 57 No 474 between 52 and 54, T924-0242. A/c, clean, good breakfast offering free coffee all day. Good value. **B** *Caribe*, Parque Hidalgo, Calle 59 No 500, T924-9022. A/c, cheaper with fan, modern, elegant, tasteful patio, tiny pool, helpful. **B** *Del Parque*, Calle 60 No 497 esq 59, T924-7844, F928-1429. With bath and a/c, clean, friendly. Recommended.

C *Casa San Juan*, Calle 62 No 545A between 69 and 71, T923-6823, F986-2937, c.sanjuan@sureste.com Restored 19th-century house with pleasant courtyard, large rooms with bath, a/c, includes breakfast. **C** *Dolores Alba*, Calle 63, No 464 between 52 and 54, T928-5650. Rooms with bath and fan, some with a/c, quiet, friendly, good breakfast for US$4.50, pool, safe parking in courtyard, will make reservations for sister establishment at Chichén Itzá. No credit cards. **C** *México*, Calle 60 No 525 esq 67, T924-7207, F923-2256. Good restaurant, attractive. **C** *Posada Toledo*, Calle 58 No 487 esq 57, T923-1690, F923-2256, hptoledo@pibil.finred.com.mx Good value, central, a/c extra, in charming old house with lots of plants, cheap breakfast, has paperback exchange. **C** *Trinidad*, Calle 62 No 464 esq 55, T923-3033. Old house, dorm rooms **E**, hot water, clean bathrooms, tranquil, courtyard, lovely garden, sun roof, can use pool at the other hotel, lots of rules and regulations. Recommended.

Near the airport There are 2 hotels near the airport: **C** *Alfonso García*, Av Aviación 587 y Calle 53, T984-2651. **C** *Posada Maya*, Calle 81A No 841 y Av Aviación.

D *Casa Becil*, Calle 67 No 550-C, between 66 and 68. Convenient for bus station, fan, bath, hot water, clean, safe, popular, owner speaks English, quiet, friendly, make you feel at home. Recommended. **D** *Casa Bowen*, restored colonial house (inside better than out), corner of Calle 66 No 521-B, esq 65, near *ADO* bus station, T928-6109. Often full at weekends, rooms on the main street noisy, bath, hot water but irregular supply, exchanges dollars, stores luggage, clean, mosquitoes, some rooms with kitchen (but no utensils). Good. **D** *Del Prado*, Calle 50 and 67; **E** with a/c, fan, safe parking, pool. Recommended. **D** *Hospedaje San Juan*, 1 block north of arch by Iglesia San Juan. Clean rooms with fan and bath. **D** *Meridano*, Calle 54 No 478 between 55 and 57, T923-2614. Nice courtyard, parking, fan, a/c, clean, hot water. **D** *Mirador del Centro*, Calle 57 No 519-A between 64 and 66, T928-0861. Good, a/c, fan, TV, basic, clean. Recommended. **D** *Mucuy*, Calle 57 No 481 between 56 and 58, T928-5193. Good, but 1st floor rooms very hot, with shower, use of fridge, washing facilities, efficient, nice gardens. Highly recommended (although owner can be irritable, his wife is very nice). **D** *Posada del Angel*, Calle 67 No 535 between 66 and 68, T923-2754. Clean, with shower and fan. **D** *San Jorge*, across from *ADO* bus terminal. With fan and bath, stores luggage, clean, but take interior room as the street is noisy. **D-E** *Nacional*, Calle 61 between 54 and 56 (3 blocks from Plaza Mayor), T924-9255. Large clean rooms with fan, a/c, café, friendly, pool.

E *América*, Calle 67 between 60 and 58, T928-5879. On busy street near market, cheaper rooms with cold water, OK, comfortable, bit run down. **E** *Centenario*, Calle 84 between 59 and 59A, T923-2532. With bath, friendly, clean, safe. **E** *Centenario II*, Calle 69 between 68 and 70, opposite *ADO* bus station. Fan, small rooms, friendly. **E** *del Mayab*, Calle 50 No 536A between 65 and 67, T928-5174. With bath, clean, friendly, tiny pool, car park. **E** *La Paz*, Calle 62 between Calle 65 and 67, T923-9446. Tall, eccentric rooms in old colonial house, some noise in the morning from nearby bus station, but otherwise quiet. **E** *Las Monjas*, Calle 66A and 63. Clean, quiet, luggage store, good value. Recommended. **E** per person *Latino*, Calle 66 No 505 esq 63, T923-5087. With fan and shower, friendly and clean, parking outside. **E** per person *Lol-be* Calle 69 between 66 and 68. With bath, hot water, fan, friendly. **E** *Margarita*, Calle 66 No 506 and 63, T923-7236. With shower, clean, good, rooms a bit dark, downstairs near desk noisy, cheaper rooms for 5 (3 beds), friendly. **E** *Pantera Negra*, Calle 67 No 547B and 68, T924-0251. Beautifully restored old colonial house, with cool, quiet patio, well-stocked bookshelves, clean, communal bath, very friendly English owner. Recommended. **E** *Rodríguez*, Calle 69, between Calle 54 and 56, T923-6299. Huge rooms, with bath, central, clean, safe. **E** *San Clemente*, Calle 58 No 586, T928-1795. Bath, hot water, basic, clean, good value. **E** *San José*, west of Plaza on Calle 63 No 503, T928-6657. Bath, hot water, basic, clean, friendly, rooms on top floor are baked by the sun, one of the cheapest, popular with locals, will store luggage, good cheap meals available, local speciality *poc chuc*. Recommended. **E-F** *Nómadas Youth Hostal*, Calle 62 No 433, at the end of Calle 51, 5 blocks north of the plaza, T924-5223, nomadas1@prodigynet.mx Private rooms, dorms and camping, hot water, full kitchen, drinking water, clean, friendly, owner Raúl speaks English and is very helpful, best value.

Camping *Trailer Park Rainbow*, Km 8, on the road to Progreso, is preferable, US$5 for 1 or 2, hot showers. *Oasis Campground*, 3 km from Mérida on Highway 180 to Cancún, F432160. With hook-ups, hot showers, laundry, run down, US manager, US$7 for car and 2 people.

Eating
● *on map page 485*
Price codes:
see inside front cover

Expensive *Casa de Piedra 'Xcantun'*, in *Hacienda Xcantun* (see above). Km 12 Carretera Mérida-Progreso. T941-0213. Fine dining, best restaurant in the area (although a bit out of town). Reservation recommended. Popular with locals. Highly recommended. *Pórtico del Peregrino*, Calle 57 between 60 and 62. Dining indoors or in an attractive leafy courtyard, excellent food. *El Mesón*, in *Hotel Caribe*. Pleasant, with tables on the square. *Tianos*, Calle 59 No 498 esq Calle 60 (outdoor seating). Friendly, touristy, good food, check your change, sometimes live music.

Mid-range *Los Almendros*, Calle 50A No 493 esq 59, in high-vaulted, whitewashed thatched barn. For Yucatán specialities, first rate. *El Tucho*, Calle 60 near University. Good local dishes and occasional live music. A good hotel restaurant for value and cooking is *El Rincón* in *Hotel Caribe. Alberto's Continental*, Calle 64 No 482 esq Calle 57. Local, Lebanese and international food, colonial mansion. Recommended. *La Prosperidad*, Calle 53 y 56. Good Yucatecan food, live entertainment at lunchtime. *El Escorpión*, just off plaza on Calle 61. Good cheap local food. *Bologna*, Calle 21 No 117a Col Itzimná, Italian, great pizza and hand-made pasta (pizza oven imported from Italy!), beautiful plaza with hanging pots, live music Fri and Sat at night. Recommended. The café at the *Gran Chopur* department store serves good food, large portions, a/c. *Amaro*, Calle 59 No 507 between 60 and 62. With open courtyard and covered patio, good food, especially vegetarian, try *chaya* drink from the leaf of the *chaya* tree, their curry, avocado pizza and home-made bread are also very good, open 1200-2200, closed on Sun.

There are a number of taco stands, *pizzerías* and sandwich places in Pasaje Picheta, a small plaza off the Palacio de Gobierno, on the plaza. *Pizza Chief*, Calle 62 between Calle 57 and 59. Many other branches, good pizzas. *Café Habana*, Calle 59 y Calle 62. International cuisine, a/c, nice atmosphere. *Lido*, Calle 62 y 61. Good-value meals and breakfast. *Pizza Bella* on the main plaza. Good meeting spot, pizzas US$4-7, excellent cappuccino. *Café Restaurante Express*, on Calle 60, at Parque Hidalgo. Breakfast, good *comida*, traditional coffee house where locals meet, nice atmosphere, good food, occasional absence of alcohol due to licence problems.

Cheap *Café Petropolis*, Calle 70 opposite CAME terminal. Existed long before the terminal was built, family-run, sometimes staffed entirely by children, who do a very good job, turkey a speciality, excellent quality, good *horchata* and herb teas. *La Alameda*, Calle 58 No 474 between Calle 57 and 55. Arabic and Mexican cuisine, lunch only, closes at 1800. *Eric's*, Calle 62 between Plaza and Calle 57. Huge sandwiches filled with roast chicken or pork, cheap set breakfast. *El Trapiche*, a few doors down on Calle 62. Excellent pizzas and freshly made juices. *Café Continental*, Calle 60 between 55 and 53. Open 0630-1400, buffet breakfast, nice setting, classical music. Recommended. *Marys*, Calle 63 No 486, between Calle 63 and 58. Mainly Mexican customers. Recommended. *Alameda*. Excellent-value Lebanese food, some vegetarian, can ask for half portions. Recommended. *Mily's*, Calle 59 between 64 and 66. *Comida corrida* for under US$3; *La Pérgola* (both drive-in and tables), at corner Calle 56 and 43. Good veal dishes. Warmly recommended. Also in Col Alemán at Calle 24 No 289A. *Los Cardenales*, Calle 69 No 550-A esq 68, close to bus station. Good value, open for breakfast, lunch and dinner. Both *El Ardillo* and *El Viajero*, near bus station, offer good local meals. Cold sliced cooked venison (*venado*) is served in the Municipal Market. *Mil Tortas*, Calle 62 between 65 and 67, good sandwiches. *Tortacos*, Calle 62 y 65. Good Mexican food. Many other *torta* places on Calle 62, but check them carefully for best value and quality. *Kuki's*, Calle 61 esq 62, opposite taxi stand. Very good coffee, snacks, expresso, cookies by the kilo.

ighly recommended. Good banana bread and wholemeal rolls at *Pronat* health shop on alle 59 No 506 esq Calle 62 (but don't have breakfast there). *Café Club*, Calle 55 No 446 etween 58 and 60, T923-1592. Caters for both vegetarian and non-vegetarian, will deliver. *ugos California*, good fruit salads, Calle 60, in Calle 65, at the main bus station and many ther branches all over city. *El Colón Sorbetes y Dulces Finos*, Calle 62 near Colón, Serving e-cream since 1907, great sorbets, *meringue*, good menu with explanation of fruits in Eng-sh. Highly recommended. 13 blocks from centre, about 30 different flavours of good e-cream. Good *panadería* at Calle 65 y 60, banana bread, orange cake. Another good bak-ry at Calle 62 y 61. Good cheap street fare at Parque Santa Ana, closed middle of day.

here are several good bars on the north side of the plaza, beer is moderate at US$1.20, **Bars &** hough food can be expensive. *Café Expresso*, on Parque Hidalgo, is good for an early eve- **nightclubs** ing beer (if they aren't having liquor licence problems). *Panchos*, Calle 59 between Calle 60 nd 62. Very touristy, staff in traditional gear, but lively and busy, live music, patio. There are a umber of live music venues around Parque Santa Lucía, a couple of blocks from the main laza. *El Trovador Bohemio*, on the park itself, has folk trios in a tiny 50's Las Vegas-style set-ng, cover charge US$1, beer US$2. Around the corner on Calle 60 are 2 more music venues. *l Tucho* is a restaurant (see above), open till 2100 only, with live music, often guest perform-rs from Cuba. Two doors down towards the Plaza is *El Establo*, upstairs from the street, pen 2100-0230. Live local bands, plus occasional Cuban cabaret entertainers. Free entry, rinks US$2 and over.

heatre *Teatro Peón Contreras*, Calle 60 with 57. Shows start at 2100, US$4, ballet, etc. The **Entertainment** niversity puts on many theatre and dance productions. **Cinema** There is a cinema show-ng subtitled films in English on Parque Hidalgo; also *Cine Plaza Internacional*, Calle 58 etween 59 and 57. There is a multiscreen cinema in the huge shopping complex Gran Plaza, orth of the city; colectivo 20 mins from Plaza Mayor. See the free listings magazine *Yucatán oday,* available at hotels and the tourist office, for other evening activities.

Carnival during the week before **Ash Wednesday** (best on Sat). Floats, dancers in regional **Festivals** costume, music and dancing around the Plaza and children dressed in animal suits. On **6 Jan** Mérida celebrates its birthday. Every **Sun** the central streets are closed off to traffic, live music and parades abound.

Many souvenir shops are dotted in the streets around the plaza. They all specialize in ham- **Shopping** mocks (see box, page 491), they also sell silver jewellery from Taxco, Panama hats, *guayabera* shirts, *huaraches* (sandals with car-tyre soles), baskets and Maya figurines. Always bargain hard, the salesmen are pushy, but they expect to receive about half their original asking price. The main handicraft market is on Calle 56 y 67. Bargaining and pushy sales staff as well. There is a smaller handicraft market on Calle 62, 1 block from the plaza. The *Mercado de Artesanías*, on Calle 67 between 56 and 58, has many nice things, but prices are high and the sales people are also pushy. Good postcards for sale, though. There are several frequently recommended shops for hammocks (there is little agreement about their respective merits, best to compare them all and let them know you are comparing, shops employing touts do not give very good service or prices): *El Hamaquero*, Calle 58 No 572, between 69 and 71. Popular, but beware the very hard sell. *El Campesino*, the market. Eustaquio Canul Cahum and family will let you watch the weaving. *El Mayab*, Calle 58 No 553 and 71, friendly, limited choice but good deals available; and *La Poblana*, Calle 65 between 58 and 60, will bargain, especially for sales of more than 1, huge stock, a bit curt if not buying there and then; also *Jorge Razu*, Calle 56 No 516B between 63A and 63, very convincing salesman, changes TCs at good rates. Recommended. *El Aguacate*, Calle 58 No 604, corner of Calle 73. Good ham-mocks, no hard sell. Recommended. Another branch on Calle 62 opposite *El Trapiche*. Help-ful, bargaining possible if buying several items. *Santiago*, Calle 70 No 505 between 61 and 63. Very good value. Good silver shops and several antique shops on Calle 60 between 51 and 53. *Bacho Arte Mexicano*, Calle 60 No 466 between 53 and 55. Also sells other jewellery and ornaments. *La Canasta*, No 500. Good range of handicrafts, reasonable prices.

Good Panama hats at *El Becaliño*, Calle 65 No 483, esq 56A, diagonally opposite post office. *Paty*, Calle 64 No 549 between Calle 67 and 69. Stocks reputable 'Kary' brand *guayabera*, also sells hammocks. *Tita*, Calle 59 between Calle 60 and 62. Enthusiastic hard sell, they onl. sell sisal hammocks, good selection, give demonstrations. *Miniaturas*, Calle 59 No 507A near plaza. Traditional folk art, Day of the Dead miniatures, wrestling masks. Calle 62 between Calle 57 y 61, is lined with *guayabera* shops, all of a similar price and quality. Embroidered *huipil* blouses cost about US$25. Good, cheap *guayabera* shop on northwest corner of Parque San Juan, prices half those of the souvenir shops in the centre. Clothe shopping is good along Calle 65 and in the *García Rejón Bazaar*, Calle 65 y 60. Good leathe *huaraches* sandals, robust and comfortable, from the market, US$10. Excellent cowboy boot for men and women, maximum size 10, can be bought around the market for US$46. There i a big supermarket, *San Francisco de Assisi*, on Calle 67 y 52, well stocked; also *San Fran cisco de Assisi* at Calle 65, between Av 50 and 52.

Bookshop *Librerías Dante*, Calle 59, No 498 between 58 and 60. Calle 61 between 62 and 64 (near *Lavandería La Fe*) used books. Also *Libros Usados*, Calle 57, between Calle 60 y 62 Used English books, will buy, swap or sell.

Cameras and film Repairs on Calle 53 y 62. *Mericolor*, Calle 67 y 58. Recommended for ser vice and printing; also *Kodak* on Parque Hidalgo. Many processors around crossing of Calle 59 y 60. Prices are high by international standards. **Camera repairs** *Fotolandia*, Calle 62 No 479G y 57, T924-8223.

Backpack repair *Industria de Petaquera del STE*, Calle 64 No 499, T928-3175. *Macay* Pasaje Revolución, beside cathedral, run by University.

Transport **Local** **Car hire**: car reservations should be booked well in advance wherever possible; there is a tendency to hand out cars that are in poor condition once the main stock has gone, so check locks, etc, on cheaper models before you leave town. All car hire firms charge around US$40-45 a day although bargains can be found in low season. Cheapest in 1999 was *World Rent a Car*, Calle 60 No 486A, between 55 and 57, T924-0587, US$40. *Hertz*, Calle 55 No 479, esq 54, T924-2834. Most car hire agencies have an office at the airport, and, as all share the same coun-ter, negotiating usually takes place. Many agencies also on Calle 60: *Executive*, down from Gran Hotel. Good value. *Tourist Car Rental*, Calle 60 No 421 between Calle 47 and 45, T924-6255. *Alamo*, T946-1623 (airport). *MeriCar*, Calle 41 No 504A between Calle 60 and 62, T924-0949. *Maya Car*, Paseo Montejo 486 between Calle 41 and 43, T924-0445. All agencies allow vehicles to be returned to Cancún at an extra charge. **Car service**: *Servicios de Mérida Goodyear*, very helpful and competent, owner speaks English, serves good coffee while you wait for your vehi-cle. Honest car servicing or quick oil change on Calle 59, near corner of Av 68. **Toll road**: tariffs from Mérida: Chichén Itzá, US$5.50; Valladolid, US$10; Cancún, US$30.

Taxis: there are 2 types: the Volkswagens, which you can flag down, prices range from US$3.50-7; cheaper are the 24-hr radio taxis, T928-5328, or catch one from their kiosk on Parque Hidalgo. In both types of taxi, establish fare before journey; there are set prices depending on the distance, the minimum is an expensive US$3.50 even for a few blocks.

Long distance **Air**: Aeropuerto Rejón (MID), 8 km from town. From Calle 67, 69 and 60, bus 79 goes to the airport, marked 'Aviación', US$0.35, roughly every 20 mins. Taxi US$8, voucher available from airport, you don't pay driver direct; colectivo US$2.50. There is a tourist office with a hotel list. No left-luggage facilities. Lots of flights to **Mexico City** daily, 1¾ hrs. Other internal flights to **Acapulco**, **Cancún**, **Chetumal**, **Ciudad del Carmen**, **Guadalajara**, **Huatulco**, **Monterrey**, **Oaxaca**, **Palenque**, **Tapachula**, **Tijuana**, **Tuxtla Gutiérrez**, **Veracruz** and **Villahermosa**. International flights from **Belize City**, **Houston**, **Miami** and **Havana**. Package tours Mérida-Havana-Mérida are available (be sure to have a confirmed return flight). For return to Mexico ask for details at Secretaría de Migración, Calle 60 No 285.

Know your hammock

*Different materials are available for hammocks. Some you might find are: **sisal**, very strong, light, hard-wearing but rather scratchy and uncomfortable, identified by its distinctive smell; **cotton**, soft, flexible, comfortable, not as hard-wearing but good for 4-5 years of everyday use with care. It is not possible to weave cotton and sisal together, although you may be told otherwise, so mixtures are unavailable. Cotton/silk mixtures are offered, but will probably be an artificial silk. **Nylon**, very strong, light but hot in hot weather and cold in cold weather. Never buy your first hammock from a street vendor and never accept a packaged hammock without checking the size and quality. The surest way to judge a good hammock is by weight: 1,500 g (3.3 lb) is a fine item, under 1 kg (2.2 lb) is junk (advises Alan Handleman, a US expert). Also, the finer and thinner the strands of material, the more strands there will be, and the more comfortable the hammock. The best hammocks are the so-called 3-ply, but they are difficult to find. There are three sizes: single (sometimes called doble), matrimonial and family (buy a matrimonial at least for comfort). If judging by end-strings, 50 would be sufficient for a child, 150 would suit a medium-sized adult, 250 a couple. Prices vary considerably so shop around and bargain hard.*

Buses: buses to destinations outside Yucatán state leave from the 1st class terminal at Calle 70 No 555, between Calle 69 and 71 (it is called CAME). The station has lockers; it is open 24 hrs a day. About 20 mins' walk to centre, taxi US$3.50. Most companies have computer booking. Schedules change frequently. The *ADO* terminal, around the corner, is for Yucatán destinations, with the single exception of buses to Chichén Itzá, which depart from the CAME terminal.

Mexico City: 24-28 hrs, about 6 rest stops, US$78 (*ADO*, 5 a day); direct *Pullman* bus Mexico City 1400 and 1700. Regular 2nd class buses to **Campeche**: with *ATS* (2½ hrs, US$5.50) also pass Uxmal, 6 a day between 0630 and 1900; 1st class fare (not via Uxmal), *ADO*, 8 daily, 2½ hrs, US$9. To **Celestún**: 2nd class, frequent departures, 2 hrs, US$3.50. **Chetumal**: see Road to Belize below. **Ciudad del Carmen**: 11 a day, 1st class, *ADO*, 9 hrs, US$20. **Coatzacoalcos**: 14 hrs, US$45. Buses to **Palenque**: 0830, 2200, US$30 and 2330, US$25 from *ADO* terminal, 8-9 hrs, *Cristóbal Colón* luxury service US$30; alternatively take Villahermosa bus to Playas de Catazajá (see page 429), US$18.50, 8½ hrs, then minibus to Palenque, or go to Emiliano Zapata, 5 buses a day US$23, and local bus (see page 471). Buses to **Progreso**: US$1.10 with *Auto Progreso*, leave from the bus station on Calle 62, between Calle 65 and 67 every 15 mins from 0500-2100. **Puerto Juárez** and **Cancún** (*Autobuses de Oriente*): every hour 0600 to 2400, 2nd class, US$12, 1st class, US$16, *plus*, 4½ hrs, US$20. Buses to and from Cancún stop at Calle 50, between Calle 65 and 67. If going to **Isla Mujeres**, make sure the driver knows you want Puerto Juárez, as the bus does not always go there, especially at night. Buses to **Tulum**: via Chichén Itzá, Valladolid, Cancún and Playa del Carmen, several daily, from main terminal, 6 hrs, US$12, 2nd class, drops you off about 1 km from the ruins. For buses to Uxmal and Chichén Itzá see under those places. To **Valladolid**: US$8, 1st Express, US$6, 2nd class (9 a day). **Veracruz**: *ADO*, 1030, and 2100, 16 hrs, US$55. Many buses daily to **Villahermosa**: US$30, 1st class (several from 1030 to 2330) 11 hrs, US$25; **Tuxtla Gutiérrez**: 1st class bus daily at 1330 via Villahermosa and Campeche, arrives 0630 next day, US$35 with *Autotransportes del Sureste de Yucatán*, also with *Cristóbal Colón*, US$30. **San Cristóbal de las Casas**: 1915, US$31 (arr 0900-1000), and another at 0700 (*Autotransportes del Sureste de Yucatán*); also 2 a day with *Cristóbal Colón*, 1915 and 2345. Buses to Celestún and Sisal from terminal on Calle 71, between Calle 64 and 66. **Tenosique**: 2100, US$28. To **Tizimín**: **Cenotillo** and **Izamal**: buses leave from Calle 50 between Calle 65 and 67. Route 261, Mérida-Escárcega, paved and in very good condition.

To **Guatemala** take a bus from Mérida to San Cristóbal and change there for Comitán, or to Tenosique for the route to Flores. A more expensive alternative would be to take the bus from Mérida direct to Tuxtla Gutiérrez (times given above), then direct either Tuxtla-Ciudad Cuauhtémoc or to Tapachula.

Yucatán Peninsula

Road to Belize paved all the way to Chetumal. Bus Mérida-Chetumal US$18.50, luxury, US$18, 1st class, takes 7 hrs (*Autotransportes del Caribe*, *Autotransporte Peninsular*), US$13, 2nd class.

Directory   **Airline offices** *Mexicana* office at Calle 58 No 500 esq 61, T924-6633, and Paseo Montejo 493 (airport T946-1332). *AeroMéxico*, Av Colon 451 and Montejo, T920-1260, airport T946-1400. *Aviacsa*, T926-9087. *AeroCaribe*, Paseo Montejo 500B, T928-6790, airport T946-1361. *Aviateca*, T926-9087. *Aerolineas Aztecas*, T01-800-229-8322.

Banks *Banamex*, at Calle 56 and 59 (Mon-Fri 0900-1300, 1600-1700), ATM cash machine, quick service, good rates. Many banks on Calle 65, off the plaza. Most have ATM cash machines, open 24 hours. Reliable ATM machine at *Inverlat Red Servicaja*, Calle 62 No 513, between 65 and 67. Cash advance on credit cards possible only between 1000 and 1300. *Centro Cambiario*, Calle 61 between Calle 54 and 52. *Casa de Cambio*, Calle 56 No 491 between 57 and 59, open 0900-1700 Mon-Sun. Exchange office on Calle 65 and 62, good rates for TCs, open Mon-Fri 0830-1700, Sat 0830-1400. 2nd branch on plaza, near Palacio de Gobierno, open daily 0800-2100.

Communications Internet: multitude of internet cafés, most charging US$1-1.50. **Post office**: Calle 65 and 56 will accept parcels for surface mail to US only, but don't seal parcels destined overseas; they have to be inspected. For surface mail to Europe try Belize, or mail package to US, *poste restante*, for collection later if you are heading that way. An airmail parcel to Europe costs US$15 for 5 kg. Also branches at airport (for quick delivery) or on Calle 58. *DHL* on Av Colón offers good service, prices comparable to post office prices for air mail packages over 1 kg. **Telephone**: international telephones possible from central bus station, airport, the shop on the corner of Calle 59 and 64, or public telephones, but not from the main telephone exchange. Many phone card and credit card phone booths on squares along Calle 60, but many are out of order. Collect calls can be made on Sat or Sun from the *caseta* opposite central bus station, but beware overcharging (max US$2). Telegrams and faxes from Calle 56, between 65 and 65A (same building as post office, entrance at the back), open 0700-1900, Sat 0900-1300. *Tel World* offer long-distance fax service from offices on Calle 60 No 486, between 55 and 57.

Cultural centres *Alliance Française*, Calle 56 No 476 between Calle 55 and 57. Has a busy programme of events, films (Thu 1900), a library and a cafetería open all day.

Embassies and consulates *British Vice Consul*, also *Belize*, Major A Dutton (retd), MBE, Calle 58-53 No 450, T928-6152, 0900-1600. *US*, Paseo Montejo 453 y Av Colón, T925-5011. *Canada*, Av Colón, 309-D, T925-6419. *Cuba*, Calle 1-D No 320, between 44 and 4D, T944-4215. *Germany*, T981-2676. *France*, T925-2886. *Switzerland*, T927-2905.

Medical services Hospitals: *Red Cross*, T924-9813. *Centro Médico de las Américas* (CMA), Calle 54 No 365 between 33A and Av Pérez Ponce. T926-2619, F926-4710, emergencies T927-3199. Affiliated with Mercy Hospital, Miami, Florida, US. **Hospital:** *IDEM*, Calle 66, between 67 and 65, open 24 hrs, specializes in dermatology. **Dermatologist:** *Dr José D Cerón Espinosa*, Calle 66 No 524 between 65 and 67, T923-9938. **Dentist:** *Dr Javier Cámara Patrón*, Calle 17 No 170 between Calle 8 and 10, Colonia García Gineres, T925-3399. US-trained, English spoken.

Language schools *Instituto Technológico de Hotelería* (ITECH), Calle 57 No 492 between Calle 56 and 58, T924-0387, dccmid@minter.cieamer.conacyt.mx, www.itech.edu.mx Courses in Spanish, also courses in local cooking (in Spanish) and Maya culture. Homestays arranged, advanced booking necessary. *Modern Spanish Institute*, Calle 29 No 128 between Calle 26 and 28, Col México, T927-1683, www.modernspanish.com Courses in Spanish, Maya culture, homestays. *Instituto de Español*, Calle 29, Col México, T927-1683.

Laundry *Lavandería* on Calle 69 No 541, 2 blocks from bus station, about US$3 a load, 3-hr service. *La Fe*, Calle 61 No 518, between Calle 62 and 64. US$3.30 for 3 kg. Highly recommended (shoe repair next door). Self-service hard to find.

Library English library at Calle 53 between Calle 66 and 68. Many books on Mexico, used book for sale, bulletin board, magazines, reading patio. ■ *Tue, Thu, Fri 0900-1300, 1400-1900; Mon, Wed, Sat 0900-1300.*

Yucatán Peninsula

Tour operators *Yucatán Trails*, Calle 62 No 482 between Calle 57 and 59, T928-2582, F924-1928, yucutantrails@hotmail.com Tours to all the popular local destinations such as Uxmal, Celestún and Progreso; they do a train trip to Izamal, Sun only, full day with lunch, tour of convent, folklore ballet, guide, trip in horse and cart, US$18. *Mayaland Tours*, in *Hotel Casa del Balam*, T926-3851, and *Fiesta Americana*, T925-0622, have their own hotel at Chichén Itzá. *Mayan Iniciatic Tours*, Paseo de Montejo 481, T920-2328, F920-1912, mayan@yuc1.telmex.net.mx *Carmen Travel Services*, *Hotel María del Carmen*, Calle 63 No 550 y Calle 68, T923-9133, 3 other branches.

Useful addresses Tourist police: T925-2555.

Around Mérida

A small, dusty fishing resort much frequented in summer by Mexicans, Celestún stands on the spit of land separating the Río Esperanza estuary from the ocean. The long beach is relatively clean except near the town proper (litter, the morning's fishing rejects, insects, weeds that stick to feet, etc), with clear water ideal for swimming, although rising afternoon winds usually churn up silt and there is little shade; along the beach are many fishing boats bristling with *jimbas* (cane poles), used for catching local octopus. There are beach restaurants with showers. A plain Zócalo watched over by a simple stucco church is the centre for what little happens in town. Cafés (some with hammock space for rent) spill onto the sand, from which parents watch offspring splash in the surf. Even the unmarked post office operating Monday-Friday, 0900-1300, is a private residence the rest of the week.

Celestún
Phone code: 998
Colour map 4, grid A2

The immediate region is a National Park, created to protect the thousands of migratory waterfowl (especially flamingos and pelicans) who inhabit the lagoons; fish, crabs and shrimp also spawn here, and manatees, toucans and crocodiles may sometimes be glimpsed in the quieter waterways. Boat trips to view the wildlife can be arranged with owners at the river bridge 1 km back along the Mérida road (US$35

Facilities

15 roomy and comfortably furnished cabins, all with a beautiful view of the emerald green Gulf of Mexico.
Surrounded by a coconut grove, at the border of one of the most fascinating Mexican biological reserves, in the middle of our 3 mile virgin beach,

the hotel is fully oriented towards environment protection.
Freshwater swimming pool, spectacular white sand beach covered with thousands of seashells and spacious gardens with exotic coastal dune flora.

Hotel Eco Paraíso Xixim,
Km 10 del viejo camino a Sisal,
Celestún,
Yucatán,
México.

ECO PARAISO
CELESTUN. YUCATAN. MEXICO

Tel: ++52 (988) 916 21 00/916 20 60
Fax: ++52 (988) 916 21 11
E-mail: info@ecoparaiso.com &
reservations@ecoparaiso.com
www.ecoparaiso.com

Yucatán Peninsula

for one large enough for six to eight people, 1½ hours, bargaining possible). Trips also arranged at *Restaurant Avila*, US$8 per person, seven to a boat, one to two hours, and from the beach in front of *Hotel María del Carmen*, US$42 per boat, three hours (but much time is spent on the open sea). It is often possible to see flamingos from the bridge early in the morning and the road to it may be alive with egrets, herons and pelicans. January-March is best time to see them. Important to wear a hat and use sunscreen. Hourly buses to Mérida 0530-2030, one hour, US$3.

Sleeping LL *Eco Paraíso*, Km 10 off the old Sisal Highway, T916-2100, F916-2111, www.ecoparaiso.com In coconut grove on edge of reserve, pool, tours to surrounding area including flamingos, turtle nesting, etc. **D** *Gutiérrez*, Calle 12 (the Malecón) No 22. Large beds, fans, views, clean. **D** *María del Carmen*. New, spacious and clean. Recommended. **E** *San Julio*, Calle 12 No 92. Large bright rooms and clean bathrooms, owner knowledgeable about the area.

Eating Many beachside restaurants along Calle 12, but be careful of food in the cheaper ones; recommended is *La Playita*, for fried fish, seafood cocktails; bigger menu and more expensive is *Chemas*, for shrimp, oysters and octopus; *Avila* also safe for fried fish. Food stalls along Calle 11 beside the bus station should be approached with caution.

Transport Buses leave every 2 hrs from Calle 71 between 66 and 64 in Mérida, 2-hr journey, 1st class, US$3.50, 2nd class, US$2.80.

Hunucmá Twenty-nine kilometres west of Mérida is Hunucmá, an oasis in the dry Yucatán, about 30 minutes from the Central Camionera bus station, US$0.50.

The road divides here, one branch continuing 63 km west to **Celestún**, the other running 24 km northwest to the coast at **Sisal**, a languid, faded resort that served as Mérida's port from its earliest days until it was replaced by Progreso last century; the old Customs House still retains some colonial flavour; snapper and bass fishing from the small wharf is rewarding; the windy beach is acceptable but not in the same league as Celestún's. Sisal's impressive lighthouse, painted in traditional red-and-white, is a private residence and permission must be sought to visit the tower, the expansive view is worth the corkscrew climb. Frequent buses from Mérida (0500-1700), Calle 50 between Calle 65 y 67, two hours, US$1.50.

Sleeping and eating AL *Sisal del Mar Hotel Resort*, in US T800-451-0891 or 305-341-9173. Luxury accommodation. More modest are **E** *Club Felicidades*, a 5-min walk east of the pier, bathrooms not too clean; **E** *Club de Patos*, similar but a slight improvement; **E** *Los Balnearios*, with shower (cold water) and fan, prickly mattresses; **E** *Yahaira* (**F** low season), large, clean rooms. *Restaurant Juanita*, reasonable.

Progreso
Phone code: 969
Colour map 4, grid A2
Population 48,692

Thirty-six kilometres north of Mérida, Progreso has the nearest beach to the city. It is a slow-growing resort town, with the facilities improving to service the increasing number of US cruise ships which arrive every Wednesday. Progreso is famous for its industrial pier, that at 6 km is the longest in the world. It has been closed to the public since someone fell off the end on a moped. The beach is long and clean and the water is shallow and good for swimming.

Sleeping B *Siesta Inn*, Calle 40 No 238 between Calle 23 and Calle 25, T935-1129. Away from the tourist zone, but near the beach, pool, restaurant, bar, TV, a/c. **B-C** *Tropical Suites*, Av Malecón and Calle 20, T935-1263, F935-3093. Suites and rooms with cable TV, a/c, sea views. **C** *Progreso*, Calle 29 No 142, T935-0039, F52019. Simple rooms in the centre. **D** *Real del Mar*, next door to Tropical Suites on the Malecón, T935-0798. Some rooms with sea views. **E** *Carismar*, Calle 21 No 151A, T935-2907. 1 block from the beach, sea views, family-run, pleasant. **E-F** *Xcaret*, in front of bus terminal. Basic, friendly, cheaper rooms have fan.

Eating The Malecón is lined with seafood restaurants, some with tables on the beach. *Casablanca*, *Capitan Marisco* and *Le Saint Bonnet* have been recommended. For cheaper restaurants, head for the centre of town, near the bus terminal.

Shopping Worth a visit is *Mundo Marino*, Calle 80 s/n, 1 block from the beach, T915-1380. A souvenir shop whose friendly owner Luis Cámara once caught a great white shark. Many shark-related as well as other marine souvenirs are on sale.

Transport Buses from Mérida leave from the small terminal on Calle 62 between 67 and 65, next to Hotel La Paz, every 10 mins. US$0.80 1-way/US$1.50 return. Return journey every 10 mins until 2200. **Boats** Can be hired to visit the reef of *Los Alacranes* where many ancient wrecks are visible in clear water.

A short bus journey (4 km) west from Progreso are Puerto Yucalpetén and **Chelem**, a dusty resort. Balneario Yucalpetén has a beach with lovely shells, but also a large naval base with further construction in progress.

Puerto Yucalpetén

Sleeping and eating AL *Fiesta Inn* on the beach and **AL** *Mayaland Club* (Mayaland Resorts, in US T305-341-9173). Villa complex. Yacht marina, changing cabins, beach with gardens and swimming pool. Between the Balneario and Chelem there is a nice hotel with some small bungalows, *Hotel Villanueva* (2 km from village, hot rooms), and also *Costa Maya*, on Calle 29 y Carretera Costera, with restaurant. In Chelem itself is a new hotel, **B** *Las Garzas*, Calle 17 No 742, T244735. A/c, cable TV, bar, good restaurant, private beach club, pool, pleasant. Fish restaurants in Chelem, *Las Palmas* and *El Cocalito*, reasonable, also other small restaurants.

Five kilometres east of Progreso is another resort, **Chicxulub**; it has a narrow beach, quiet and peaceful, on which are many boats and much seaweed. Small restaurants sell fried fish by the *ración*, or kilo, served with *tortillas*, mild chilli and *cebolla curtida* (pickled onion). Chicxulub is reputed to be the site of the crater made by a meteorite crash 65 million years ago, which caused the extinction of the dinosaurs. The beaches on this coast are often deserted and, between December and February, 'El Norte' wind blows in every 10 days or so, making the water turbid and bringing in cold, rainy weather.

Chicxulub

Forty-five kilometres east of Progreso is Telchac Puerto, a laid-back village on the coast with a luxury hotel and many private beach homes for rent. Not many tourists come here, due to its location. The village has a small plaza, with a lighthouse just off it; there is good swimming in the sea, and there are two large lagoons with interesting wildlife just beyond the village. The ruins of **Xtampu** are nearby, on the road to Progreso, a large site with an impressive pyramid, currently under reconstruction. For years, the locals have been using the stones from this site to build their homes. There is also a Catholic church built from the same stone right among the ruins.

Telchac Puerto
Phone code: 991

Sleeping and eating AL *Reef Club*, T917-4100. Exclusive resort set around a small bay just outside the village, rooms with private terrace, watersports, health spa, nightly entertainment, 2 restaurants, fishing trips, special deals for families. **B** *Casa del Mar*, Apdo 13, Cordemex 97310, Yucatán, T922-0039, Yuctoday@finred.com.mx Maya-style thatched bungalows with modern fittings, kitchen, pool, on the beach. To enquire about **renting private homes**, contact Miguel Solís Lara, PO Box 102, Progreso, Yucatán, T/F993-54080, www.multired.net.mx/misola *Bella Mar* is a seafood restaurant on the beach just outside the village. There are a few restaurants around the plaza serving seafood.

Halfway between Mérida and Progreso turn right for the Maya ruins of Dzibilchaltún. This unique city, according to carbon dating, was founded as early as 1000 BC. The site is in two halves, connected by a *sacbé* (white road). The most

Dzibilchaltún

Yucatán Peninsula

important building is the **Templo de Las Siete Muñecas** (Seven Dolls, partly restored and on display in the museum) at the east end. At the west end is the ceremonial centre with temples, houses and a large plaza in which the open chapel, simple and austere, sticks out like a sore thumb. The evangelizing friars had clearly hijacked a pre-Conquest sacred area in which to erect a symbol of the invading religion. At its edge is the **Cenote Xlaca** containing very clear water and 44 m deep (you can swim in it, take mask and snorkel as it is full of fascinating fish); there's a very interesting nature trail starting halfway between temple and *cenote*; the trail rejoins the *sacbé* halfway along. ■ *0800-1700, US$4.50, free with ISIC card.* The museum at entrance by ticket office (site map available). VW combis leave from Parque San Juan, corner of Calle 62 y 67A, every one or two hours between 0500 and 1900, stopping at the ruins en route to Chablekal, a small village further along the same road. There are also five direct buses a day on weekdays, from Parque San Juan, marked 'Tour/Ruta Polígono'; bus returns from site entrance on the hour, passing the junction 15 minutes later, taking 45 minutes from junction to Mérida (US$0.60).

The Convent Route

A popular day trip from Mérida, this tour unfortunately cannot be done on public transport, so a car is necessary. The route takes in Mayan villages and ruins, colonial churches, cathedrals, convents and *cenotes*. It is best to be on the road by 0800 with a full gas tank. Get on the *Periférico* to Ruta 18 (signs say Kanasín, not Ruta 18). At Kanasín *La Susana* is known especially for local delicacies like *sopa de lima*, *salbutes* and *panuchos*. Clean, excellent service and abundant helpings at reasonable prices. Follow the signs to **Acanceh**. Here you will see the unusual combination of the Grand Pyramid, a colonial church and a modern church, all on the same small plaza (see Tlatelolco in Mexico City; page 104). About four blocks away is the Temple of the Stuccoes, with hieroglyphs. Eight kilometres further south is **Tecoh**, with an ornate church and convent dedicated to the Virgin of the Assumption. There are some impressive carved stones around the altar. The church and convent both stand at the base of a large Maya pyramid. Nearby are the caverns of **Dzab-Náh**; you must take a guide as there are treacherous drops into *cenotes*. Next on the route is **Telchaquillo**, a small village with an austere chapel and a beautiful *cenote* in the plaza, with carved steps for easy access.

Mayapán A few kilometres off the main road to the right you will find the Maya ruins of Mayapán, a walled city with 4,000 mounds, six of which are in varying stages of restoration. Mayapán, along with Uxmal and Chichén Itzá, once formed a triple alliance, and the site is as big as Chichén Itzá, with some buildings being replicas of those at the latter site. The restoration process is ongoing; the archaeologists can be watched as they unearth more and more new buildings of this large, peaceful, late-Maya site. Mayapán is easily visited by bus from Mérida (every 30 minutes from terminal at Calle 50 y 67 behind the municipal market, one hour, US$1 to Telchaquillo). It can also be reached from Oxcutzcab. ■ *US$4.35.*

Thirty kilometres along the main road is **Tekit**, a large village containing the church of San Antonio de Padua, with many ornate statues of saints in each of its niches. The next village, 7 km further on, is called **Mama**, with the oldest church on the route, famous for its ornate altar and bell-domed roof. Another 9 km is **Chumayel**, where the legendary Mayan document *Chilam Balam* was found. Four kilometres ahead is **Teabo**, with an impressive 17th-century temple. Next comes **Tipikal**, a small village with an austere church.

Maní Twelve kilometres further on is Maní, the most important stop on this route. Here you will find a large church, convent and museum with explanations in English, Spanish and Mayan. It was here that Fray Diego de Landa ordered important Maya documents and artefacts to be burned, during an intense period of Franciscan conversion of the Maya people to Christianity. When Diego realized his great error, he set about trying to write down all he could remember of the 27 scrolls and hieroglyphs he had destroyed, along with 5,000 idols, 13 altars and 127 vases. The text, entitled *Relation of Things in Yucatán*, is still available today, unlike the artefacts. To return to Mérida, head for Ticul, to the west, then follow the main road via Muná.

Eighty kilometres south of Mérida, Ticul is a small, pleasant little village known for its *huipiles*, the embroidered white dresses worn by the older Maya women. You can buy them in the tourist shops in Mérida, but the prices and quality of the ones in Ticul will be much better. It is also a good base for visiting smaller sites in the south of Yucatán state such as Sayil, Kabah, Xlapak and Labná (see below).

Ticul
Phone code: 997
Colour map 4, grid A2
Population: 32,728

Sleeping and eating C *Plaza*, on the Zócalo, T972-0484. Clean, a/c. **D-E** *Sierra Sosa*, Calle 26, near Zócalo, T972-0008. Cheaper rooms dungeon-like, but friendly, clean and helpful. **E** *San Miguel*, Calle 28 near the market, T972-0382. Quiet, good value, parking. **E** *Motel Buganvillas*, on the edge of town on the road to Mérida, T972-0761. Clean, basic rooms. **E** *Cerro Motor Inn*, also on outskirts, near *Motel Buganvillas*. Run down. *Los Almendros*, Calle 23. Nice colonial building with patio, good Yucatecan cuisine, reasonable prices. *El Colorín*, near Hotel Sierra Sosa on Calle 26. Cheap local food. *Pizzería La Góndola*, Calle 23. Good, moderately priced pizzas.

Transport There are frequent VW colectivos from Parque San Juan, in Mérida, US$2.

Sixteen kilometres southeast of Ticul is Oxkutzcab, a good centre for catching buses to Chetumal, Muná, Mayapán and Mérida (US$2.20). It is a friendly place with a large market on the side of the plaza and a church with a 'two-dimensional' façade on the other side of the square.

Oxkutzcab
Phone code: 997

Sleeping and eating C *Tucanes*, Calle 64 No 99, T975-0378. With a/c, **D** with fan, not very clean, by Pemex station. **E** *Casa de Huéspedes*, near bus terminal. Large rooms with bath, TV, fan, friendly. Recommended. *Bermejo*, Calle 51 No 143. **D** *Trujeque*, just south of main Plaza. A/c, TV, clean, good value, discount for stays over a week. **E** *Hotel Rosario*, turn right out of bus station then right again. Double room, shower, cable TV. Hammocks provided in some private houses, usually full, fluent Spanish needed to find them. *Su Cabaña Suiza*, Calle 54 No 101. Good, cheap set lunch, family-run. Recommended.

Nearby, to the south, are the caverns and pre-Columbian vestiges at Loltún (supposedly extending for 8 km). ■ *Caves are open Tue-Sun 0930, 1100, 1230 and 1400. US$3 with obligatory guide, 1 hour 20 mins. Recommended. Caretaker may admit tours on Mon, but no lighting.* Take pick-up (US$0.30) or truck from the market going to Cooperativa (an agricultural town). For return, flag down a passing truck. Alternatively, take a taxi, US$10 (can be visited from Labná on a tour from Mérida). The area around Ticul and Oxcutzcab is intensively farmed with citrus fruits, papayas and mangoes. After Oxkutzcab on Route 184 is **Tekax** with restaurant *La Ermita* serving excellent Yucatecan dishes at reasonable prices. From Tekax a paved road leads to the ruins of **Chacmultún**. From the top you have a beautiful view. There is a caretaker. All the towns between Muná and Peto, 14 km northeast of Tzucacab off Route 184, have large old churches. Beyond the Peto turn-off the scenery is scrub and swamp as far as the Belizean border.

Grutas de Loltún

The Puuc Route

These four sites (Kabah, Sayil, Xlapak and Labná) can be visited in a day, as well as Uxmal, on the 'Ruta Puuc' bus, which departs from the 1st class bus station in Mérida every day except Sun at 0800, US$7, entry to sites not included. This is a good whistle-stop tour, but does not give you much time at each of the ruins; if you want to spend longer seeing these sites, it is recommended that you stay overnight in Ticul. ■ *The following sites all cost US$1.70, free on Sun.*

Yucatán Peninsula

Kabah On either side of the main road, 37 km south of Uxmal and often included in tours of the latter, are the ruins of Kabah. On one side there is a fascinating **Palace of Masks** (or *Codz-Poop*), whose façade bears the image of Chac, mesmerically repeated 260 times, the number of days in the Almanac Year. Each mask is made up of 30 units of mosaic stone. Even the central chamber is entered via a huge Chac mask whose curling snout forms the doorstep. On the other side of this wall, beneath the figure of the ruler, Kabal, are impressive carvings on the door arches, which depict a man about to be killed, pleading for mercy, and of two men duelling. This side of the road is mostly reconstructed; across the road the outstanding feature is a reconstructed arch marking the start of the *sacbé* (sacred road), which leads all the way to Uxmal, and several stabilized, but unclimbable mounds of collapsed buildings. The style is Classic Puuc. Watch out for snakes and spiders. ■ *US$2.40.*

Sayil, Xlapak Sayil means 'The Place of the Ants'. Dating from AD 800-1000, this site has an inter-
& Labná esting palace, which in its day included 90 bathrooms for some 350 people. The simple, elegant colonnade is reminiscent of the architecture of ancient Greece. The central motif on the upper part of the façade is a broad mask with huge fangs, flanked by two serpents surrounding the grotesque figure of a descending deity. From the upper level of the palace you can see a tiny ruin on the side of a mountain called the Nine Masks.

Thirteen kilometres from Sayil, the ruins of **Xlapak** have not been as extensively restored as the others in this region. There are 14 mounds and three partially restored pyramids.

Labná has a feature that ranks it among the most outstanding sites of the Puuc region: a monumental arch connecting two groups of buildings (now in ruins), which displays an architectural concept unique to this region. Most Maya arches are purely structural, but the one at Labná has been constructed for aesthetic purposes, running right through the façade and clearly meant to be seen from afar. The two façades on either side of the arch differ greatly in their decoration; the one at the entrance is beautifully decorated with delicate latticework and stone carving imitating the wood or palm-frond roofs of Maya huts. ■ *Entrance US$8.*

Uxmal

Phone code: 997 Built during the Classic Period, Uxmal is the most famous of the ruins in the Puuc
Colour map 4, grid A2 region. The characteristic features of Maya cities in this region are the quadrangular layout of the buildings, set on raised platforms, and an artificially created underground water-storage system. The **Pyramid of the Sorcerer** is an unusual oval-shaped pyramid set on a large rectangular base; there is evidence that five stages of building were used in its construction. The pyramid is 30 m tall, with two temples at the top. The **Nunnery** is set around a large courtyard, with some fine masks of Chaac, the rain god, on the corners of the buildings. The east building of the Nunnery is decorated with double-headed serpents on its cornices. There are some plumed serpents in relief, in excellent condition, on the façade of the west building. The **House of the Governor** is 100 m long, and is considered one of the most outstanding buildings in all of Mesoamerica. Two arched passages divide the building into three distinct sections that would probably have been covered over. Above the central entrance is an elaborate trapezoidal motif, with a string of Chaac masks interwoven into a flowing, undulating serpent-like shape extending to the façade's two corners. The stately two-headed jaguar throne in front of the structure suggests a royal or administrative function. The **House of the Turtles** is sober by comparison, its simple walls adorned with carved turtles on the upper cornice, above a short row of tightly-packed columns, which resemble the Maya *palapas*, made of sticks with a thatched roof, still used today. The **House of the Doves** is the oldest and most damaged of the buildings at Uxmal. What remains of it is still impressive: a long, low platform of wide columns topped by clusters of roof combs, whose similarity to dovecotes gave the building its name. ■ *0800-1800. US$10, free on Sunday. Son et*

Yucatán Peninsula

Lumière shows cost US$3, in Spanish; rental of translation equipment US$2.50. Shows are at 2000 in summer and 1900 in winter. There are six buses a day from Mérida, from the terminal on Calle 69 between 68 and 70, US$1.80. Return buses run every two hours, but if you've just missed one, go to the entrance to the site on the main road and wait for a colectivo, *which will take you to Muná for US$0.50. From there, many buses (US$1.70) and* colectivos *(US$1.40) go to Mérida. Parking at the site costs US$1 for the whole day. Uxmal is 74 km from Mérida, 177 km from Campeche, by a good paved road. If going by car from Mérida, there is a new circular road round the city: follow the signs to Campeche, then Campeche via* ruinas, *then to Muná via Yaxcopoil (long stretch of road with no signposting). Muná-Yaxcopoil is about 34 km. Parking US$1.*

AL *Misión Uxmal*, 1-2 km from ruins on Mérida road, T976-2022, F976-2023, Km 78, www.hotelesmision.com.mx Rooms a bit dark, pool. **L** *Hacienda Uxmal*, T976-2013, 300-400 m from ruins. Good, efficient and relaxing (3 restaurants open 0800-2200), a/c, gardens, swimming pool; also owns **L** *Lodge Uxmal*, T976-2102, at entrance. Comfortable, a/c, bath, TV, fair restaurant. **A** *Club Méditerranée Villa Arqueológica*, Mérida T928-0644. Beautiful, close to ruins, good and expensive restaurant, excellent service, swimming pool. Recommended. **C** *Rancho Uxmal*, about 4 km north of ruins, T923-1576. Comfortable rooms, hot and cold water, camping for US$5, pool, reasonable food but not cheap (no taxis to get there). **D-F** *Sacbe Bungalows*, at Km 127 on Highway 261, T858-1281, sacbebungalow@ hotmail.com A mix of bungalows, rooms and campsite, with space for hammocks, and solar-powered showers, and breakfast and dinner for a little more. For cheap accommodation, go to Ticul, 28 km away (see below). Restaurant at ruins, good but expensive.

Sleeping & eating
There is no village at Uxmal, just the hotels

Camping No camping allowed, but there is a campsite, *Sacbé*, at Santa Elena, about 15 km south, between Uxmal and Kabah, on Route 261, Km 127 at south exit of village. Postal address: Portillo, Apdo 5, CP 97860, Ticul, Yucatán. (2nd class buses Mérida-Campeche pass by, ask to be let out at the Campo de Baseball.) 9 electric hook-ups (US$7-10 for motor home according to size), big area for tents (US$2.75 per person with tent), *palapas* for hammocks (US$2.65 per person), for cars pay US$1, showers, toilets, clothes-washing facilities, also 3 bungalows with ceiling fan (**E**), breakfast, vegetarian lunch and dinner available (US$2.65 each); French and Mexican owners, a beautifully landscaped park, fastidiously clean and impeccably managed. Highly recommended.

On the road from Uxmal to Mérida is Muná (15 km from Uxmal, 62 km from Mérida); delightful square and old church, no hotel, but ask in *Restaurant Katty*, just on plaza, whose owner has two rooms with two double beds at his home, **E**, clean, friendly, hot showers. Recommended (restaurant has good, cheap *enchiladas en mole*). Also ask in shops by bus stop in town centre for accommodation in private homes. There is a new direct road (Highway 184 and 293) from Muná to Bacalar, Quintana Roo, just north of Chetumal.

Muná

Yucatán Peninsula

Izamal

Sixty-eight kilometres east of Mérida is the friendly little town of **Izamal** (reached by direct bus either from Mérida or Valladolid). Once a major Classic Maya religious site founded by the priest Itzamná, Izamal became one of the centres of the Spanish attempt to Christianize the Maya.

*Phone code: 988
Colour map 4, grid A3
Population: 22,998*

Fray Diego de Landa, the historian of the Spanish conquest of Mérida (of whom there is a statue in the town), founded the huge **convent** and **church**, which now face the main **Plaza de la Constitución**. This building, constructed on top of a Maya pyramid, was begun in 1549 and has the second largest atrium in the world. If you examine carefully the walls that surround the magnificent atrium, you will notice that some of the faced stones are embellished with carvings of Maya origin, confirming that, when they had toppled the pre-Columbian structures, the Spaniards re-used the material to create the imported architecture. There is also a throne built for the Pope's visit in 1993. The image of the Inmaculada Virgen de la Concepción in the magnificent church was made the Reina de Yucatán in 1949, and the patron saint of the state in 1970. Just 2½ blocks away, visible from the convent across a second square and signposted, are the ruins of a great mausoleum known as the **Kinich-Kakmo** pyramid. ■ *0800-1700, free. The entrance is next to the tortilla factory.* You climb the first set of stairs to a broad, tree-covered platform, at the end of which is a further pyramid (still under reconstruction). From the top there is an excellent view of the town and surrounding *henequén* and citrus plantations. Kinich-Kakmo is 195 m long, 173 m wide and 36 m high, the fifth highest in Mexico. In all, 20 Maya structures have been identified in Izamal, several on Calle 27. Another startling feature about the town is that the entire colonial centre, including the convent, the arcaded government offices on Plaza de la Constitución and the arcaded second square, is painted a rich yellow ochre, giving it the nickname of the 'golden city'.

Sleeping and eating C *Macan-Che*, Calle 22 and Calle 33, T954-0287. 4 blocks north of the plaza, pleasant bungalows, breakfast. Recommended. **D** *Kabul*, Plaza de la Constitución. Poor value, cell-like rooms. **E** *Canto*. Basic, Room 1 is best, friendly. *Tumben-Lol*, Calle 22 No 302 between 31 and 33. Yucatecan cuisine. *Kinich-Kakmó*, Calle 27 No 299 between 28 and 30. Near ruins of same name, local food. Several restaurants on Plaza de la Constitución. *Gaby*, just off the square on Calle 31. *El Norteño* at bus station. Good, cheap. *Wayane*, near statue of Diego de Landa. Friendly, clean.

Entertainment Activity in town in the evening gets going after 2030.

Shopping Market, Calle 31, on Plaza de la Constitución, opposite convent, closes soon after lunch. *Hecho a mano*, Calle 31 No 332 between 36 and 38. Folk art, postcards, textiles, jewellery, papier-mâché masks.

Transport Bus station is on Calle 32 behind government offices, can leave bags. 2nd class to **Mérida**, every 45 mins, 1½ hrs, US$1.50, lovely countryside. Bus station in Mérida, Calle 50 between Calle 65 and 67. 6 a day to/from **Valladolid** (96 km), about 2 hrs, US$2.30-3.

Directory Banks Bank on square with statue to Fray Diego de Landa, south side of convent. **Communications Post office**: on opposite side of square to convent.

From Izamal you can go by bus to **Cenotillo**, where there are several fine *cenotes* within easy walking distance from the town (avoid the one *in* town), especially **Ucil**, excellent for swimming, and **La Unión**. Take the same bus as for Izamal from Mérida. Past Cenotillo is Espita and then a road forks left to Tizimín (see page 506).

The cemetery of **Hoctún**, on the Mérida-Chichén road, is also worth visiting; indeed it is impossible to miss, there is an 'Empire State Building' on the site. Take a bus from Mérida (last bus back 1700) to see extensive ruins at **Aké**, an unusual structure. Public transport in Mérida is difficult: from an unsigned stop on the corner of Calle 53 y 50, some buses to Tixkokob and Ekmul continue to Aké; ask the driver.

An interesting detour off the Chichén-Mérida highway is to turn in the direction of Yaxcaba at Libre Unión, then after 3 km turn on to a dirt road, signposted to **Xtojil**, a beautiful *cenote* with a Maya platform, which has well-preserved carvings and paintings.

Chichén Itzá

Colour map 4, grid A3 Route 180 runs southeast from Mérida for 120 km to Chichén Itzá where the scrub forest has been cleared from over 5 sq km of ruins. Chichén Itzá means 'Mouth of the well of the water-sorcerer'. The city was built by the Maya in late Classic times (AD 600-900). By the end of the 10th century, the city was more or less abandoned. It was reestablished in the 11th-12th centuries, but much debate surrounds by whom.

Whoever the people were, a comparison of some of the architecture with that of Tula, north of Mexico City (see page 144), indicates that they were heavily influenced by the Toltecs of Central Mexico.

The major buildings in the north half display a Toltec influence. Dominating them is **El Castillo**, its top decorated by the symbol of Quetzalcoatl/Kukulcán. The balustrade of the 91 stairs up each of the four sides is also decorated at its base by the head of a plumed, open-mouthed serpent. There is also an interior ascent of 61 steep and narrow steps to a chamber lit by electricity; here the red-painted jaguar that probably served as the throne of the high priest burns bright, its eyes of jade, its fangs of flint (■ *1100-1500, and 1600-1700, closed if raining)*. To reach the chamber you have to clamber up very narrow, slippery steps as high as seven tiers of pyramid (count them from the outside) - definitely NOT for the claustrophobic.

There is a **ball court** with grandstand and towering walls, each set with a projecting ring of stone high up; at eye-level is a relief showing the decapitation of the winning captain (sacrifice was an honour; some theories, however, maintain that it was the losing captain who was killed). El Castillo stands at the centre of the northern half of the site, and almost at a right angle to its northern face runs the *sacbé*, sacred way, to the **Cenote Sagrado**, the Well of Sacrifice. Into the Cenote Sagrado were thrown valuable propitiatory objects of all kinds, animals and human sacrifices. The well was first dredged by Edward H Thompson, the US Consul in Mérida, between 1904 and 1907; he accumulated a vast quantity of objects in pottery, jade, copper and gold. In 1962 the well was explored again by an expedition sponsored by the National Geographic Society and some 4,000 further artefacts were recovered, including beads, polished jade, lumps of *copal* resin, small bells, a statuette of rubber latex, another of wood, and a quantity of animal and human bones. Another *cenote*, the Xtoloc Well, was probably used as a water supply. To the east of El Castillo is the **Temple of the Warriors** with its famous reclining Chacmool statue. This pyramidal platform has now been closed off to avoid erosion.

Old Chichén, where the Maya buildings of the earlier city are found, lies about 500 m by path from the main clearing. The famous **El Caracol**, or Observatory, is included in this group, as is the **Casa de las Monjas**, or Nunnery. A footpath to the right of Las Monjas leads to the **Templo de los Tres Dinteles** (the Three Lintels) after 30 minutes' walking. It requires at least one day to see the many pyramids, temples, ball courts and palaces, all of them adorned with astonishing sculptures. Excavation and renovation is still going on. Interesting birdlife and iguanas can also be seen around the ruins. ■ *0800-1700, US$10, free Sun and holidays, when it is incredibly crowded, you may leave and re-enter as often as you like on day of issue. Guides charge US$4-6 per person for a 1½-hour tour (they are persistent and go too fast). Recommended guide from Mérida: Miguel Angel Vergara, Centro de Estudios Maya Haltun-Ha, T927-1172, PO Box 97148. Guided tours US$37 per group of any size; it is best to try and join one, many languages available. Check at entrance for opening times of the various buildings. Best to arrive before 1030 when the mass of tourists arrives. Son et lumière (US$5 in English, US$1.35 in Spanish) at Chichén every evening, in Spanish at 1900, and then in English at 2000; nothing like as good as at Uxmal. A* tourist centre has been built at the entrance to the ruins with a restaurant, free cinema (short film in English at 1200 and 1600), a small **museum**, books and souvenir shops (if buying slides, check the quality), with exchange facilities at the latter; luggage deposit free. ■ *0800-1700. Car park US$1.50.* Drinks and snacks are available at the entrance (expensive) and at the *cenote*, also guidebooks (**Panarama** is the best) and clean toilets at the former. There are more toilets on the way to Old Chichén, and a drinks terrace with film supplies. The site is hot, take a hat, sun cream, sunglasses, shoes with good grip and drinking water.

Grutas de Balankanché Tours run daily to the Balankanché caves, 3 km east of **Excursions** Chichén Itzá just off the highway. There are archaeological objects, including offerings of pots and *metates* in an extraordinary setting, except for the unavoidable,

Yucatán Peninsula

'awful' *son et lumière* show (five a day in Spanish; 1100, 1300 and 1500 in English; 1000 in French; it is very damp and hot, so dress accordingly). ■ *0900-1700, US$3.45, free Sun (allow about 45 mins for the 300 m descent), closed Sat and Sun afternoons. The caretaker turns lights on and off, answers questions in Spanish, every hour on the hour, minimum six, maximum 20 persons. Getting there: Chichén Itzá or Pisté-Balankanché bus hourly at a quarter past, US$0.50, taxi US$15.*

Chichén Itzá

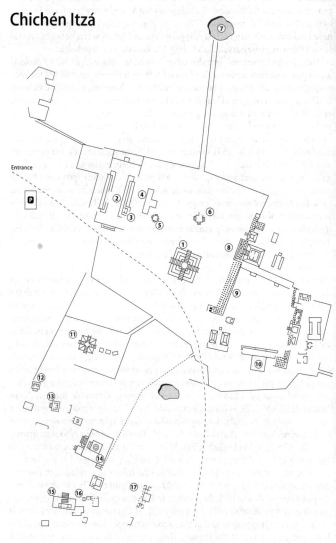

N

0 metres 100
0 yards 100

1 Castillo	**7** Well of Sacrifice	**12** House of the Deer
2 Ball Court	**8** Temple of the Warriors	**13** Red House
3 Temple of the Jaguar	& Chacmool Temple	**14** El Caracol (Observatory)
4 Platform of the Skulls	**9** Group of a Thousand	**15** Nunnery
(Tzompantli)	Columns	**16** 'Church'
5 Platform of Eagles	**10** Market	**17** Akabdzilo
6 Platform of Venus	**11** Tomb of the High Priest	

Close to the ruins: AL *Hacienda Chichén*, T851-0045. Once owned by Edward Thompson with charming bungalows. **AL** *Villas Arqueológicas*, T851-0034, Apdo Postal 495, Mérida. Pool, tennis, restaurant (expensive and poor). Both are on the other side of the fenced-off ruins from the bus stop; you cannot walk through ruins, either walk all the way round, or take taxi (US$1-1.50).

Not so close to the ruins: A *La Palapa Chichén*. With breakfast and dinner, a few kilometres from the ruins, excellent restaurant, modern, park with animals. **A** *Hotel Misión Chichén Itzá*, Pisté. A/c, pool, disappointing, gloomy, poor restaurant, not easily seen from the road; it has staircases with plumed serpents and a big statue facing north on top. **B** *Sunset Club*, 10 mins' walk from Pisté village, 30 mins from Chichén Itzá. Takes credit cards, room with bath, hot water, fan, TV, swimming pool. Recommended. **D** *Maya Inn*, on main road to Chichén Itzá. With bath, **E** without, also hammock space, clean. **D** *Posada Chac Mool*. Fan, bath, clean, laundry service, safe parking, a bit noisy. Recommended. **D** *Posada Olalde*, 100 m from main road at end of Calle 6. Quiet. **D** *Posada Novelo*, near *Pirámide Inn*. Run by José Novelo who speaks English, guest access to pool and restaurant at nearby *Stardust Inn*. **D** *Posada el Paso*, on main road into village from Chichén. With shower, good value, very friendly, safe parking, nice restaurant. A lot of traffic passes through at night, so try to get a room at the back.

A little out of town are: **C** *Pirámide Inn*, 1½ km from ruins, at the Chichén end of Pisté, T851-0115. Clean but run-down, with good food, swimming pool, hammocks and *palapas*, friendly English-speaking owner, Trailer Park and camping US$6.50 for 2 plus car in front of hotel, US$4.50 in campground (owned by *Stardust*, see below, but still check in at hotel reception, cold showers). **D** *Dolores Alba*, Km 123, T928-5650. Small hotel (same family as in Mérida, where you can make advance reservations, advisable in view of long walk from ruins), 2½ km on the road to Puerto Juárez (bus passes it), in need of renovation, with shower and fan, clean, has swimming pool and serves good, expensive meals, English spoken, RVs can park in front for US$5, with use of toilets, shower and pool, free transport to the ruins (be careful if walking along the road from the ruins after dark, there are many trucks speeding by, carry a flashlight/torch).

B-C *Stardust Posada Annex*, Pisté, about 2 km before the ruins if coming from Mérida (taxi to ruins US$2.50). Good value, especially if you don't want TV or a/c (fans available), swimming pool, popular with German tour groups, average restaurant.

There is a small pyramid in the village opposite *Hotel Misión Chichén Itzá*; close by is a huge plumed serpent, part coloured, almost forming a circle at least 20 m long. Unfortunately the serpent has been largely destroyed to make way for the *Posada Chac Mool*. There is no sign or public path, climb over gate into scrubland, the serpent will be to right, pyramid to left. The whole construction is an unabashedly modern folly made 25 years ago by a local stone mason who used to work on the archaeological expeditions.

Mostly poor and overpriced in Chichén itself (cafés inside the ruins are cheaper than the restaurant at the entrance to the ruins, but they are still expensive). *Hotel Restaurant Carrousel* (rooms **D**); *Las Redes*; *Nicte-Ha*, opposite, is cheaper and has chocolate milk shakes; fiesta in Pisté, Calle Principal. Yucatecan specialities, touristy but good. Next door is a place serving good *comida corrida* for US$5.35; *Poxil*, Mérida end of town, for breakfast; *El Paso* in Pisté. Good meals but doesn't open for breakfast as early as it claims. *Sayil* in Pisté. Has good *pollo pibil* for US$2.60. Restaurants in Pisté close 2100-2200.

Hammocks are sold by *Mario Díaz* (a most interesting character), excellent quality, huge, at his house 500 m up the road forking to the left at the centre of the village. 35 km from Chichén is Ebtún, on the road to Valladolid, a sign says 'Hammock sales and repairs'. It is actually a small prison, which turns out 1st class cotton or nylon hammocks; haggle with wardens and prisoners; there are no real bargains, but good quality. Silver is sold at orange-coloured shops opposite *Posada Novelo* in Pisté.

Road If driving from Mérida, follow Calle 63 (off the plaza) out as far as the dirt section, where you turn left, then right and right again at the main road, follow until hypermarket on left and make a left turn at the sign for Chichén Itzá. Hitchhiking to Mérida is usually no problem.

Sleeping

Eating

Shopping

Transport

Yucatán Peninsula

Buses Chichén Itzá is easily reached (less so during holiday periods) from Mérida by (*ADO*) 2nd class, 2½ hrs, US$4 from 0500, bus station on Calle 71 between 64 and 66. 1st class bus, US$5.80. Return tickets from the gift shop near entrance to site. Buses drop off and pick up passengers until 1700 at the top of the coach park opposite entrance to *artesanía* market (thereafter take a taxi to Pisté or colectivo to Valladolid for buses). Monday morning 2nd class buses may be full with workers from Mérida returning to Cancún. Many buses a day between 0430 and 2300 go to **Cancún** and **Puerto Juárez**, US$8. The 1st bus from Pisté to Puerto Juárez is at 0730, 3 hrs. *ADO* bus office in Pisté is between *Stardust* and *Pirámide Inn*. Budget travellers going on from Mérida to Isla Mujeres or Cozumel should visit Chichén from Valladolid (see below), although if you plan to go through in a day you can store luggage at the visitors' centre. Buses from **Valladolid** go every hour to the site, the 0715 bus reaches the ruins at 0800 when they open, and you can return by standing on the main road 1 km from the entrance to the ruins and flagging down any bus going straight through. Colectivo entrance-Valladolid, US$2.30. Bus **Pisté-Valladolid** US$1.50; **Pisté-Tulum**, 1 bus only at 1300, US$4. **Chichén Itzá-Tulum**, bus at 1330 and 1445, 4 hrs, very crowded.

Directory   **Banks** Bank in Pisté, *Banamex*, open 0900-1300. **Communications** Telephone: international calls may be placed from *Teléfonos de México*, opposite *Hotel Xaybe*.

Valladolid

Phone code: 985
Colour map 4, grid A3
Population: 19,300

Situated roughly halfway between Mérida and Cancún, Valladolid is a pleasant little town, until now untouched by tourism. Its proximity to the famous ruins of Chichén Itzá, however, means that Valladolid has been earmarked for extensive development by the Mexican government. Construction is under way of a new international airport at Kaná, in the deserted land near Chichén Itzá, which will open Valladolid's doors to a much larger influx of travellers than the trickle it receives at the moment, and two new luxury hotels are being built on the outskirts of the town. This doesn't mean that the area will receive a Cancún-like transformation, because the airport will be for those travellers in search of the historic-cultural aspects of this area, as opposed to the golden beaches and nightclubs of Quintana Roo.

Valladolid is set around a large plaza, flanked by the imposing Franciscan cathedral. Most of the hotels are clustered around the centre, as well as numerous restaurants catering for all budgets, favouring the lower end. There is a slightly medieval feel to the city, with some of the streets tapering off into mud tracks. The Vallisoletanos, as they are known, are friendlier than their Meridano neighbours, and Valladolid's location makes it an ideal place to settle for a few days, while exploring the ruins of Chichén Itzá, the fishing village of Río Lagartos on the north coast, and the three beautiful *cenotes* in the area, one of which is right in the town itself, on Calle 36 y 39.

The **tourist office**, on the southeast corner of the plaza, is not very helpful but they give a useful map. Much more helpful information from **Antonio 'Negro' Aguilar**, on Calle 44 No 195. Something of a local celebrity, he was a baseball champion in the 1950s and 60s, playing for the Leones de Yucatán and the Washington Senators. He was also the Chief of Police in Valladolid for three years. Now semi-retired, he runs a shop selling sports equipment, rents bicycles and rents very cheap accommodation (see below). He is glad to offer information on any of the tourist attractions in the area; if cycling around, he will personally draw you a map of the best route you should take. Antonio can also help organize tours in a minivan to the ruins at Ek-Balam, minimum four people, US$3 per person.

Sights   **Cenote Zací** is an artificially lit *cenote* where you can swim, except when it is occasionally prohibited due to algae in the water. There is a thatched-roof restaurant and lighted promenades. The *cenote* is right in town, on Calle 36 between Calle 37 and 39. ■ *0800-1800, US$2, half price for children.* There is a small town **museum** on Calle 41, housed in Santa Ana church, showing the history of rural Yucatán and some exhibits from recent excavations at the ruins of *Ek-Balam*. ■ *Free.*

Seven kilometres from Valladolid is the beautiful **Cenote X-Kekén** at Dzitnup, the name by which it is more commonly known. It is stunningly lit with electric lights, the only natural light source being a tiny hole in the cavernous ceiling dripping with stalagtites. Swimming is excellent, the water is cool, clean and refreshing, and harmless bats zip around overhead. Exploratory walks can also be made through the many tunnels leading off the *cenote*, for which you will need a torch. ■ *0800-1800, entry US$1.20.* Colectivos leave hourly from in front of Hotel María Guadalupe, US$1, they return until 1800, after which you will have to get a taxi back to Valladolid, US$4. Alternatively, hire a bicycle from Antonio Aguilar (see above) and cycle there, 25 minutes. Antonio will explain the best route before you set off.

There is also a newly discovered, easily reached *cenote* close by, called **Samulá**.

B *Mesón del Marqués*, north side of Plaza Principal, T859-1985, F856-2280. A/c, with bath, pool, on square, with good but pricey restaurant, cable TV, excellent value. Recommended. **B-C** *Zací*, Calle 44 No 191, T856-2167. A/c, cheaper with fan, TV, good pool, clean, quiet. **C** *María de la Luz*, Calle 42 No 193-C, Plaza Principal, T856-1181. Good, a/c, swimming pool (non-residents, US$0.50), excellent restaurant, buffet breakfast US$3.50, *comida corrida* US$5, closes at 2230. Takes Visa. **C** *San Clemente*, Calle 42 No 206, T856-2208. With a/c, spacious, quiet, clean, has car park, TV, small swimming pool, restaurant, opposite cathedral, in centre of town. Recommended.

D *María Guadalupe*, Calle 44 No 198, T856-2068. Quiet, fan, clean, good value, hot water, washing facilities. Recommended. **D-E** *Maya*, Calle 41 No 231, between 48 and 50, T856-2069. Fan or a/c, clean, quiet, good value. **D** *Mendoza*, Calle 39 No 294 between Calle 44 and 46. Recommended.

E *Albergue La Candelaria*, Calle 35 No 201-F, T856-2267, fidery@valladolid.com.mx New and good cheap option, especially for solo travellers. Single-sex dorms with fan, clean, hot water, kitchen, washing facilities, hammocks out the back in the garden, TV room. Recommended. **E** *Antonio 'Negro' Aguilar* rents rooms for 2, 3 or 4 people. The best budget deal in the town for 2 or more, clean, spacious rooms on a quiet street, garden, volley-ball/basketball court. The rooms are on Calle 41 No 225, before the *Maya Hotel*, but you need to book them at Aguilar's shop on Calle 44 No 195, T856-2125. If the shop is closed, knock on the door of the house next door on the right of the shop. **E** *Lily*, Calle 44 No 192. Hot shower, cheaper with shared bath, fan, basic, not too clean, good location, laundry facilities, friendly. **E** per person *Sr Silva* (see Transport: bike hire), rents large, airy rooms with fan and bathroom. Recommended.

Sleeping
■ *on map*
Price codes:
see inside front cover

Los Portales, on southeast corner of main square. Very good and cheap. *La Sirenita*, Calle 41 No 168-A, a few blocks east of main square. Highly recommended for seafood, popular, only open to 1800, closed Sun. *Plaza Maya*, Calle 41 No 235, a few blocks east of main square.

Eating

Yucatán Peninsula

Valladolid

To Albergue La Candelaria
To Bus Station
To Mérida
Telmex
Antonio Bike Rental
Sr Silva Bike Rental
To Albergue Deportivo — Bar El Zaguán
Banco del Atlántico
To Ex-convent of San Bernardino & Cenote Dzitnup
N
Cenote Zací
Palacio Municipal
Plaza
Bancomer
Cathedral
To Cancún

0 metres 100
0 yards 100

■ **Sleeping**
1 Lily
2 María de la Luz
3 María Guadalupe
4 Mendoza
5 Mesón del Marqués
6 San Clemente
7 Zací

● **Eating**
1 Cocinas Familiares
2 Los Portales

Good *comida corrida*, step up from the rest below. Next to *Hotel Lily* are **Panadería La Central** and **Taquería La Principal**. Marginally cheaper food at the **Cocinas Familiares**, Yucatecan food, pizzas, burgers, etc, northeast corner of Plaza Principal, next to *Mesón del Marqués*. Cheap meals in the market, Calle 37, 2 blocks east of the Cenote Zací. There is a well-stocked supermarket on the road between the centre and bus station. **Cafés** Nice café on the corner of Calle 40 and 39, off the plaza. Open till late but doesn't serve alcohol. **Bars** El Zaguán, Calle 41 and 41A, 2 blocks west of the plaza. One of the few places serving alcohol without a meal, nice setting in plant-filled courtyard, music, open until about 0300.

Shopping Quality cheap leather goods from **Mercado de Artesanías**, Calle 39 between 42 and 44.

Transport **Bike hire** Antonio Aguilar (see page 504) rents bicycles.

Buses The main bus terminal is on Calle 37 and Calle 54. **Cancún** *Express Oriente*, 9 a day, 2 hrs, US$8, *Avante* 3 a day, US$8. **Chichén Itzá**, 10 a day, 45 mins, US$2. **Izamal** 2 a day, 2 hrs, US$3.80. **Mérida**, 9 buses a day with various companies, 2½ hrs, US$7-8 goes via Chichén Itzá. **Playa del Carmen** 9 a day, 4 hrs, US$8. **Tizimín** (for Río Lagartos), 10 a day, 2 hrs, US$2 (for some strange reason it costs the same for a return ticket to Tizimín, make sure you ask for it if planning to return to Valladolid).

Directory **Banks** *Bancomer* on east side of square, changes TCs between 0900 and 1330. *Banco del Atlántico*, corner of Calle 41 and 42, quick service for TCs, from 1000. *Banco del Sureste* has a branch in the shopping centre on Calle 39, 5 blocks west from the Plaza. Open Mon-Fri 0900-2100, Sat and Sun 0900-1400, 1700-1930. **Communications** Internet: *Internet café* on corner of Calle 46 and 37, open Mon-Sat 1000-2100. *Modutel Communication* on Calle 42 No 197, on the plaza, Mon-Sun, 0700-2200, US$1.50/hr. There are many others for a small town as this becomes the main form of communication for many local people. **Post office:** on east side of Plaza, 0800-1500 (does not accept parcels for abroad). **Telephones:** Telmex phone office on Calle 42, just north of square; expensive Computel offices at bus station and next to *Hotel San Clemente*; Ladatel phonecards can be bought from *farmacias* for use in phone booths. **Laundry** *Teresita*, Calle 33 between 40 and 42, US$6 for 5½ kg.

North of Valladolid

Ek-Balam Twenty-five kilometres north of Valladolid are the recently opened Maya ruins of Ek-Balam meaning 'Black Jaguar'. The ruins contain an impressive series of temples, sacrificial altars and residential buildings grouped around a large central plaza. The main temple, known as 'The Tower', is an immaculate seven-tiered staircase leading up to a flattened area with the remains of a temple. The views are stunning, and because they are not on the tourist trail, these ruins can be viewed at leisure, without the presence of hordes of tour groups from Cancún. ■ *0800-1700, US$2, free on Sun.* To get there by car, take Route 295 north out of Valladolid. Just after the village of Temozón, take the turning on the right for Santa Rita. The ruins are some 5 km further on. A recommended way for those without a car is to hire a bike, take it on the roof of a colectivo leaving for Temozón from outside the Hotel María Guadalupe, and ask to be dropped off at the turning for Ek-Balam. From there, cycle the remaining 12 km to the ruins. There are also minivans to Ek-Balam run by Antonio Aguilar (see page 504).

Tizimín Tizimín is a dirty, scruffy little town en route for Río Lagartos, where you will have to change buses. If stuck, there are several cheap *posadas* and restaurants, but with frequent buses to Río Lagartos, there should be no need to stay the night here.

Sleeping and eating There are several hotels, eg **D** *San Jorge*, on main plaza. A/c, good value. **D** *San Carlos*, 2 blocks from main square. With bath, fan, clean, good. **D** *Tizimín*, on main square. **D** *Posada* next to church. There is a good but expensive restaurant, *Tres Reyes*, also *Los Portales* , on main square, and others, including many serving cheap *menú del día* around the plaza.

Entertainment On the edge of town is a vast pink disco, popular with Meridanos.

Transport There are 2 terminals side by side. If coming from Valladolid en route to Río Lagartos, you will need to walk to the other terminal. Río Lagartos, 7 per day, 1½ hrs, US$2. Valladolid, 10 per day, 1 hr, US$1.50. Mérida, several daily, 4 hrs, US$4. There are also buses to Cancún, Felipe Carrillo Puerto and Chetumal.

Communications Telephone: long-distance phone at Calle 50 No 410, just off plaza.

Río Lagartos

Colour map 4, grid A3
Population: 3,000

An attractive little fishing village on the north coast of Yucatán state, whose main attraction is the massive biosphere reserve containing thousands of pink flamingos, as well as 25 other species of bird. The people of Río Lagartos are extremely friendly and very welcoming to tourists, who are few and far between, due to the distances involved in getting there. The only route is on the paved road from Valladolid; access from Cancún is by boat only, a journey mainly made by tradesmen ferrying fish to the resort. Development in Río Lagartos, however, is on the horizon. The former *posada* is being refurbished as an expensive hotel, and the so-far unspoilt Malecón could easily be the home to luxury yachts in the not-too-distant future.

Excursions

Boat trips to see the flamingo reserve can be easily arranged by walking down to the harbour and taking your pick from the many offers you'll receive from boatmen. You will get a longer trip with fewer people, due to the decreased weight in the boat. As well as flamingos, there are 25 other species of bird, some very rare, in the 68 km reserve. Make sure your boatman takes you to the larger colony of flamingos near **Las Coloradas** (15 km), recognizable by a large salt mound on the horizon, rather than the smaller groups of birds along the river. Early morning boat trips can be arranged in Río Lagartos to see the flamingos (■ *US$35, in 8-9 seater, 2½-4 hours, cheaper in five-seater, fix the price before embarking; in mid-week few people go so there is no chance of negotiating, but boat owners are more flexible on where they go; at weekends it is very busy, so it may be easier to get a party together and reduce costs).* Check before going whether the flamingos are there; they usually nest here during May-June and stay through July-August (although salt mining is disturbing their habitat).

Fifteen minutes' walk east from the Río Lagartos harbour is an *ojo de agua*, a pool of sulphurous water for bathing, supplied by an underground *cenote*. The waters are supposed to have curative properties - locals say it is better than Viagra.

Buses run from Río Lagartos to **San Felipe** (13 km), where you can bathe in the sea; access to the beach is by boat only; there is basic accommodation in the old cinema, **F**, ask in the shop *Floresita*; also houses for rent; Miguel arranges boat trips to the beach (US$3), he lives next door to the old cinema; good cheap seafood at *El Payaso* restaurant; on the waterfront is *La Playa* restaurant, recommended; on a small island with ruins of a Maya pyramid, beware of rattlesnakes.

Sleeping and eating The *Hotel Nefertiti* will soon be renamed and upgraded to the **B-C** range. There are 3 **E** rooms for rent at the house of Tere and Miguel, near the harbour (ask at the bus terminal). Very nicely furnished, double and triple rooms, 1 with an extra hammock, sea views. Recommended. For a fishing village, seafood is not spectacular, as most of the good fish is sold to restaurants in Mérida and Cancún. *Isla Contoy*, Calle 19 No 134, average seafood, not cheap for the quality. *Los Negritos*, off the plaza, moderately priced seafood. There are a couple of smaller restaurants around the plaza, and a grocery shop, useful for stocking up on supplies for the boat trip to see the flamingos, which usually departs around 0600 in the morning.

Festivals 12 Dec, *Virgen de Guadalupe*. The whole village converges on the chapel built in 1976 on the site of a vision of the Virgin Mary by a local non-believer, who suddenly died, along with his dog, shortly after receiving the vision. On **17 Jul** there is a big local *fiesta*, with music, food and dancing in the plaza.

Yucatán Peninsula

Transport There are frequent buses from **Tizimín** (see above), and it is possible to get to **Río Lagartos** and back in a day from Valladolid, if you leave on the 0630 or 0730 bus (taxi Tizimín-Río Lagartos US$25, driver may negotiate). Last bus back from Río Lagartos at 1730.

El Cuyo
Colour map 4, grid A3

The road goes east along the coast on to El Cuyo, rough and sandy, but passable. El Cuyo has a shark-fishing harbour. Fishermen cannot sell (co-op) but can barter fish. Fry your shark steak with garlic, onions and lime juice. El Cuyo is a very quiet, friendly place with a beach where swimming is safe (there is less seaweed in the water the further from town you go towards the Caribbean). *La Conchita* restaurant (good value meals) has cabañas with bath, double bed and hammock (**D**). Opposite *La Conchita* bread is sold after 1700. From Tizimín there are combis (US$2.70, 1½ hours) and buses (slower, four times a day) to El Cuyo, or take a combi to Colonia and hitch from there.

State of Quintana Roo

Holbox Island
Phone code: 984
Colour map 4, grid A3

The beach is at the opposite end of the island to the ferry, 10 minutes' walk

Also north of Valladolid, but in the neighbouring state of Quintana Roo, turn off the road to Puerto Juárez after Nuevo Xcan (see page 536), to Holbox Island. Buses to **Chiquilá** for boats, three times a day, also direct from Tizimín at 1130, connecting with the ferry, US$2.20. The ferry leaves for Holbox 0600 and 1430, one hour, US$1, returning to Chiquilá at 0500 and 1300. A bus to Mérida connects with the 0500 ferry. If you miss the ferry a fisherman will probably take you (for about US$14). You can leave your car in the care of the harbour master for a small charge; his house is east of the dock. Take water with you if possible. During 'El Norte' season, the water is turbid and the beach is littered with seaweed.

Sleeping *Delfín Palapas*, on the beach. Expensive but nice. *Cabañas*, **D**, usually occupied; take blankets and hammock (ask at fishermen's houses where you can put up), and lots of mosquito repellent. **E** *Hotel Holbox* at dock. Clean, quiet, cold water, friendly. House with 3 doors, ½ block from plaza, rooms, some beds, mostly for hammocks, very basic, very cheap, outdoor toilet, no shower, noisy, meals available, which are recommended; rooms at pink house off plaza, **D**, clean, with bath. **Camping** Best camping on beach east of village (north side of island).

Eating *Lonchería*, on plaza. Restaurant on main road open for dinner. All bars close 1900. Bakery with fresh bread daily, good. Fish is generally expensive.

There are five more uninhabited islands beyond Holbox. Beware of sharks and barracuda, though very few nasty occurrences have been reported. Off the rough and mostly unpopulated bulge of the Yucatán coastline are several islands, once notorious for contraband. Beware of mosquitoes in the area.

Cancún

Phone code: 998
Colour map 4, grid A3
Population: 500,000

In 1970, when Cancún was discovered by the Mexican tourist board, it was an inaccessible strip of barren land with beautiful beaches; the only road went straight past Cancún to Puerto Juárez for the ferry to Isla Mujeres, which had been a national tourist destination since the 1950s. Massive international investment and government sponsorship saw the luxury resort of Cancún completed within 25 years. The 25-km hotel zone, set on a narrow strip of land in the shape of a number seven alongside the coast, is an ultra-modern American-style boulevard, with five-star hotels, high-tech nightclubs, high-class shopping malls, and branches of McDonald's, Burger King and Planet Hollywood - enjoy or avoid.

Mexico's most famous resort is not the only attraction the State of Quintana Roo has to offer. There are several other luxury resorts and, in contrast to Cancún, Isla Mujeres provides a much more laid-back atmosphere for the weary traveller. Diving and other watersports can be enjoyed at almost any point along the coastlines of Quintana Roo,

*which also has its fair share of fascinating archaeological sites. Those interested in wild-
life will enjoy the sanctuary on Isla Contoy or the Sian Ka'an Biosphere Reserve.*

Ins and outs

Cancún airport is 16 km south of the city. There are 2 terminals, but only the main one is used
for international departures and arrivals. Colectivo taxi to the Hotel Zone or the centre costs
US$9; pay at the kiosk outside airport. Drivers go via the Hotel Zone, but must take you to
whichever part of the city centre you want. If going to the centre, make sure you know the
name and address of your hotel before you get in the taxi, or the driver will offer to take you
to a budget hotel of his own choice. Buses go to the centre via Av Tulum every ½ hr from the
airport. Taxi to the airport from the centre, US$10. Buses go from several stops, marked
'Aeropuerto', along Av Tulum, catch the bus from the centre road, every ½ hour, US$0.50.
There is a tourist information kiosk in the airport, and a *casa de cambio* with poor rates.

Getting there

Ruta 1 and Ruta 2 buses go from the centre to the Hotel Zone, US$0.55; Ruta 1 runs 24 hrs
and goes via Av Tulum; Ruta 2 runs 0500-0330 and goes via Av Cobá to the bus terminal.

Getting around

Around Cancún

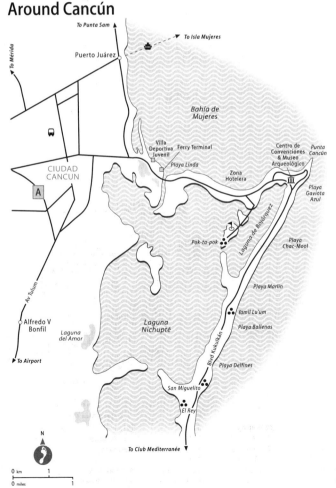

Related map
A Cancún centre,
page 510

Yucatán Peninsula

Buses to the hotel zone can be caught from many stops along Av Tulum. Buses to Puerto Juárez leave from outside *Cinema Royal*, across Av Tulum from the bus terminal, US$0.55. To get around in the centre, get on a bus at Plaza 2000 and ask the driver if he's going to Mercado 28; those buses go along Av Yaxchilán; all others go to the hotel zone. Taxis are cheap and abundant in Cancún. Flat rate for anywhere within the centre is US$1-1.50; hotel zone from centre US$3; Puerto Juárez US$3. Many taxis stop at El Crucero, the junction of Av Tulum and Av López Portillo outside Plaza 2000, but there are often queues.

During July and August the rains can be very heavy during the afternoon. This is true for the whole of the Yucatán Peninsula

Two-and-a-half million visitors arrive in Cancún every year, staying in a total of 24,000 rooms in the **hotel zone** alone, a figure expected to rise to 37,000 in the next few years. The prices are geared towards the wealthy US package tourist, and the atmosphere at night is not unlike Las Vegas, but without the casinos or the glamour. Every hotel has its own strip of beach; the beaches are supposedly public, but locals complain of being refused entry to some of them if not lodged in the hotel.

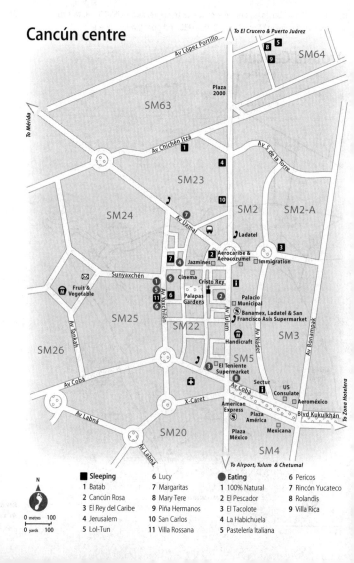

Cancún centre

■ Sleeping	6 Lucy	● Eating	6 Pericos
1 Batab	7 Margaritas	1 100% Natural	7 Rincón Yucateco
2 Cancún Rosa	8 Mary Tere	2 El Pescador	8 Rolandis
3 El Rey del Caribe	9 Piña Hermanos	3 El Tacolote	9 Villa Rica
4 Jerusalem	10 San Carlos	4 La Habichuela	
5 Lol-Tun	11 Villa Rossana	5 Pastelería Italiana	

Cancún City is a world apart from the hotel zone. It evolved from temporary shacks housing the thousands of builders working on the hotel zone, and is now a massive city with very little character. Architecture has not had a role to play in its geography; there is no definite centre, unlike most Mexican cities, in fact visitors may feel as if they are always on the outskirts, groping their way towards a non-existent *zócalo*. Hastily cobbled together over the last 25 years, the extent of town planning has merely been to name the broad avenues and narrow streets as they have appeared over the years. The main avenue is Tulum, formerly the highway running through the city when it was first conceived. It is now the location of the handicraft market, the main shops, banks and the municipal tourist office. There are also restaurants, but the better ones are along Av Yaxchilán, which is also the main centre for nightlife.

The cheaper end of the city, and a good area for budget travellers to base themselves, is around the junction of Av Tulum and Av López Portillo, known locally as El Crucero. The rest of the city is fairly expensive, but not as much as the hotel zone. The city is laid out in *supermanzanas* (SM), the blocks of streets between avenues, with smaller *manzanas* (M), or blocks, within them. Often the address you are given is, for example, SM24, M6, L3. L stands for *lote*, and is the precise number of the building within its *manzana*. This can lead to confusion when walking about, as the streets also have names, often not mentioned in the addresses. Look closely at street signs and you will see the SM and the M numbers. Taxi drivers generally respond better to addresses based on the *manzana* system. More confusion arises from the fact that most side streets are named in pairs; they rejoin the main avenue after forming a U shape. If you can't find what you're looking for, walk to the end of the street and find the continuation (right or left) leading back to the main avenue.

The **tourist office** is at Av Tulum 26, in a building that also houses local government offices. Typically for Quintana Roo state, it is not very helpful; most tourists seem to get palmed off with a glossy pocket guide to Cancún full of adverts for expensive restaurants. There is a new and well-equipped office at the conventions and visitor bureau, on the corner of Av Cobá and Av Bonampak, T884-6531. Here the staff are helpful and friendly with information on new attractions, hotels and excursions. The official government website for Quintana Roo is at **www.qr.gob.mx**

Essentials

Accommodation in the hotel zone costs upwards of US$50, mostly much more, and is best arranged as part of a package holiday. The centre (or Downtown, as it is known locally) has many cheaper options, but prices are still higher than other parts of the Yucatán Peninsula.

Hotel zone There is no shortage of all-inclusive hotels with prices ranging from affordable to dreamy. On the up side many have all-inclusive activities, but in reality do not generally target the independent traveller. If circumstances find you in the market head along the strip and find one that takes your fancy – discounts can be considerable in the quiet season (Apr-Nov) and outside the northern hemisphere's summer holidays. The best of the bunch are the sumptuous **LL** *Le Meridien*, Retorno del Rey Km 14, T881-2200, F881-2201, and **L** *Presidente Inter-Continental*, Av Kukulcán Km 7.5, T883-0200, F883-2602.

Town centre Many hotels, especially the budget ones, tend to be full during Jul. It is best to get to them as early as possible in the morning, or try to make a reservation if planning to return to Cancún after a trip to the interior or Isla Mujeres.

AL *Margaritas*, Yaxchilán y Jasmines, T/F884-9333. Modern, efficient service, outside restaurant, bar, pool, travel agent and care hire. **AL** *Xbalamqué*, Av Yaxchilán 31, SM22, T/F884-9690, 24-hr room service, a/c, pool, gym, internet, elegant décor. **A** *Batab*, Chichén Itzá 52, SM23, T884-3822, F884-3821. A/c, cable TV, beach club, restaurant, bar. **A** *El Rey del Caribe*, Av Uxmal esq Náder, SM2A, T884-2028, F884-9857, reycarib@ cancun.com.mx A/c, gardens, parking, pool, jacuzzi.

Sleeping
■ *on maps, opposite and page 510*
Price codes: see inside front cover

Some of these hotels have special offers during July and August, listed in Riviera Maya Hotels Guide, available free at the airport

Yucatán Peninsula

B *Cancún Rosa*, Margaritas 2, local 10, T884-2873, F884-0623. Close to bus terminal. A/c, TV, phone, comfortable rooms. **B** *Colonial*, Tulipanes 22 y Av Tulum, T884-1535. A/c, with bath, cheaper with fan, quiet, TV, phone, poor service, not too clean. **C** *El Alux*, Av Uxmal 21, T884-0662, turn left and first right from bus station. A/c with bath, clean, TV, some rooms cheaper, good value. Recommended. **C** *Lucy*, Gladiolas 25, between Tulum and Yaxchilán, T884-4165. A/c, kitchenettes, takes credit cards. **C** *María Isabel*, Palmera 59, T884-9015, near bus station and Av Tulum. Fan and a/c, hot water, TV, small and clean, friendly, helpful, will store luggage, avoid rooms backing onto noisy air shaft. **C** *Villa Rossana*, Av Yaxchilán opposite *Mexhotel*, Lotes 67, 68, 69, T884-1943. Popular, central and spacious, good location. **C** *Las Palmas*, Palmeras 43, T884-2513. Huge rooms, clean with TV, a/c, fan, kitchen. **E** in dormitory, good value. Recommended.

El Crucero, location of some of the budget hotels, is said by locals to be safe during the day, but unsafe at night

D *Guadalupe*, Av López Portillo, SM65, M2, L6 (NE corner of Crucero), T884-5740. Quiet, small, clean. **D** *Jardín*, SM64, M14, Lote 20, No 37, T884-8704. Clean, friendly, a bit noisy. **D** *Jerusalem*, Av Tulum 64, T884-0506. Cheaper with fan, on busy avenue near bus terminal. **D** *San Carlos*, Cedro 10 (2nd turning on to Cedro from bus terminal), T884-0786, near and handy for the bus terminal. Mixed bag of rooms, some cramped and shabby, the upper floor is OK and slightly more expensive. **D** *Soberanis Hostal*, Av Cobá 5, next to *El Teniente* supermarket, T884-4564. New hostel, includes breakfast, safe boxes, lockers in room, clean, good location, **B** for private rooms. Recommended. **D** *Tankah*, Av Tankah 69, T884-4844. Slightly more with a/c, TV and parking. Recommended. **D** per person *De Valle*, Av Uxmal (near Av Chichén Itzá), T884-5123. Noisy club next door but clean, OK.

The following 4 hotels are all in a barrio near the Crucero. Walk to Plaza 2000, 500 m north of the bus terminal on Av Tulum; directly opposite is Calle 10, which leads into Supermanzana 64, where there are also cheap restaurants (if going by taxi, ask for 'Supermanzana 64'). **D** *Alda*, next door to *Piña Hermanos*. OK as last resort. **D** *Lol-Tun*, SM64, M6, L21, T884-3205. Noisy, OK, good service. *Mary Tere*, SM64, M6, L1, 2, 3, T884-0496. Large, chaotic service, busy, OK. **D** *Piña Hermanos*, Calle 7 No 35, SM64, M6, L14, T884-2150. Very clean, nice decor, restaurant, friendly staff. Highly recommended.

E *Mexico Hostel*, Palmera 30, T887-0191, www.mexicohostels.com The best budget deal in Cancún, very clean, dormitories, breakfast included, TV, lockers, kitchen. Recommended and a good place to stop when just arriving.

Camping Not permitted in Cancún town except at the Villa Deportiva youth hostel. There is a trailer park, *Rainbow*, just south of the airport. *El Meco Loco*, campground, 2 km north of passenger ferry to Isla Mujeres. Full hook-ups for RVs, good showers, small store, access to small beach, buses into town. **Youth hostel E** *Villa Deportiva Juvenil*, is at Km 3.2 Blvd Kukulkán, T883-1337, on the beach, 5 mins' walk from the bridge towards Cancún town, next to *Club Verano Beat*. Dormitory-style, price per person, US$10 deposit, 10% discount with membership card, 8 people per room, friendly, basic, dirty, plumbing unreliable, sketchy locker facilities, camping US$5.

Yucatán Peninsula

The hotel zone is lined with expensive restaurants, with every type of international cuisine imaginable, but with a predominance of Tex-Mex and Italian. Restaurants in the centre are cheaper, and the accent is on local food. Av Yaxchilán has many restaurants in the mid-price range, as well as a few budget *loncherías*; Av Uxmal is slightly cheaper, with more street stalls.

Eating
● *on map*
*Price codes:
see inside front cover*

Restaurants in the centre   Expensive: *Rolandis*, Av Cobá 12. Italian, also branch on hotel zone at Km 9. Recommended. *Matilda*, Plaza Las Américas, Av Tulum 260. French bistro style, freshly baked bread. *La Habichuela*, Margaritas 25. Caribbean seafood, tropical garden setting, jazz music. *Pericos*, Av Yaxchilán 71. Themed *Mexican*, staff in fancy dress, lively atmosphere. *El Pescador*, Tulipanes 28. Good seafood, well established with excellent reputation but expensive. **Mid-price**: *Yamamoto*, Av Uxmal and Nader. Japanese food, popular, good quality. *Villa Rica*, Yaxchilán 35. Veracruz seafood specialities, live band, good service. *Ciao*, Yaxchilán 37, SM22. Tacos, pizzas, touristy, live music, garden, happy hour. *100% Natural*, Yaxchilán y Sunyaxchén. Some vegetarian dishes, seafood, healthy breakfasts. *Los Almendros*, Bonampak 60. Good Yucatecan food. *El Tacolote*, Cobá 19. Tacos, good variety. *La Placita*, Yaxchilán 12. Good local food, good service. *La Doña*, on Av Yaxchilán between Av Uxmal and Av Sunyaxchén. Good, cheap breakfast, and lunch, clean, a/c, friendly. *Rincón Yucateco*, Av Uxmal 24, opposite *Hotel Cotty*. Good Mexican breakfasts, popular. *Pop*, next to *Hotel Parador*. For quicker-type food, good value. *Torta y Torta*, Av Tulum (opposite *McDonald's*). Good juices, cheap. *Bing*, Av Tulum y Uxmal, close to Banpais bank. Best ice-cream. *Piemonte Pizzería*, Av Yaxchilán 52. Good food and value, appetizing aperitifs on the house. Recommended. *Las Tejas*, Av Uxmal, just before Calle Laurel. Good food at reasonable prices. On Av Tulum, *Olé Olé*. Good meat, friendly. *Comida Casera*, Av Uxmal opposite bus terminal. Good coffee. *La Chiquita del Caribe*, Av Xel-Há at Mercado 28. Great seafood, good value. Recommended. **Cheap**: the cheapest area for dinner is SM64, opposite Plaza 2000. Popular with locals, especially on Sun when it is hard to get a table, there are 4 or 5 small family-run restaurants serving local specialities. *Comida corrida* for as little as US$2. Mercado 28 (see map) is the best budget option for breakfast or lunch, with many cheap outdoor and indoor *loncherías* serving *comida corrida*, very popular with locals, quick service. *Mr Greek*, Uxmal 40 between Yaxchilán and Tulum. Outdoor stand with authentic Greek food and tacos. *Los Huaraches*, on Uxmal opposite Yaxchilán. Fast food, cheap *empanada* specials after 1300. *Pastelería Italiana*, Yaxchilán, just before turning of Sunyaxchén. Excellent coffee and pastries, friendly. A few other cheap eateries along Yaxchilán, tucked away between the pricey themed restaurants, some open during the day only. *Jaguari*, in the Zona Hotelera. Brazilian, opens 1700, set price, has been recommended.

A night out in the hotel zone will set you back anywhere between US$20 and US$50. There are many nightclubs, most of them branches of US-run chains, throughout Mexico. Attendance tends towards 16-21 year-old Americans, who can drink under age here. The clubs all try to outdo each other by offering wild and wacky entertainment; this usually involves drinking and dancing competitions, all having very little connection with Mexico. *Señor Frogs* is one of the most popular, while *La Boom* is said to be the craziest. The only place for a cheap beer is right opposite *Señor Frogs*, where there is a grocery store selling beer, which you can drink at the tables outside. They also sell pizzas, and there is a burger stall open from 2300.

**Bars &
nightclubs**

   In Cancún City, there are cheaper and more down-to-earth nightclubs, where you might even hear a bit of local music. Av Yaxchilán has several nightclubs and bars, the most popular with locals being *Bum-Bum*, which has a dress code, and is open till late. *Blue Bar*, next to *Restaurant Villa Rica*, fills up about 11pm, open till very late. Many of the restaurants along Av Yaxchilán will serve a beer without ordering any food.

Cinemas: the main one is *Cine Royal*, on Av Tulum near the bus terminal. *Multiplex*, showing mostly Hollywood blockbusters with Spanish subtitles, entry US$2.30. There are a couple of smaller cinemas near the Crucero, one of them, on Calle 10, SM64, shows vintage Mexican gangster films in Spanish. Also a multiplex cinema in the Zona Hotelera at Plaza Kukulcán.

Entertainment

Yucatán Peninsula

Shopping There are several US-style shopping malls in the Zona Hotelera, the main one being *Plaza Kukulcán*, with over 200 shops, restaurants, a bowling alley and video games. It is open from 1000-2200, and the prices are high for most things, including souvenirs. The main 'handi-craft' market in the centre is on Av Tulum near Plaza Las Américas; it is a huge network of stalls, all selling exactly the same merchandise: silver jewellery from Taxco, ceramic Maya figurines, hammocks, jade chess sets. Prices are hiked up to the limit, so bargain hard: most vendors expect to get half what they originally ask for. The market called *Mercado 23* (at the end of Calle Cedro, off Av Tulum) has cheaper souvenirs and less aggressive salesmen, but the quality is shoddy; *guayabera* shirts are available on one of the stalls. The only bookshop in the city is the modestly stocked *Fama*, on Av Tulum, which mostly sells glossy books on the Maya and American thrillers. Several new smoking shops have appeared, cashing in on the craze for Cuban cigars; these are all located on or just off Av Tulum. Cheaper clothes shops than the hotel zone can be found at the north end of Av Tulum, near Plaza 2000. Pricey leather goods, clothes and jewellery can be bought in *Plaza 2000* shopping mall.

Sport A variety of watersports can be organized on the beaches along the hotel zone, including parasailing, water-skiing, windsurfing and jet-skiing. There is also a **Bullfighting** ring, which has shows every Wednesday at 15.30. Admision US$33.00, tickets available at travel agents and the ring (Plaza del Toros) on Av Bonompak south.

Transport **Car hire**: *Budget Rent-a-Car* in Cancún has been recommended for good service. A 4-door Nissan Sentra, a/c, can be hired for US$24 per day from *Budget* at the airport, insurance US$15. *Avis*, Plaza Caracol, cheapest but still expensive. There are many car hire agencies, with offices on Av Tulum, in the Zona Hotelera and at the airport; look out for special deals, but check vehicles carefully. Beware of overcharging and read any documents carefully before you sign. Rates vary enormously, from US$40 to US$80 a day for a VW Golf (VW Beetles are cheaper), larger cars and jeeps available. Car parking: do not leave cars parked in side streets; there is a high risk of theft. Use the parking lot on Av Uxmal.

International departure tax is US$22 **Air** Cancún airport (CUN) is 16 km south of the town (very expensive shops and restaurant, exchange facilities, double check your money, especially at busy times, poor rates too, 2 hotel reservation agencies, no rooms under US$45). 2 terminals, Main and South (or 'FBO' building), white shuttle minibuses between them. From Cancún there are domestic flights and connections throughout the country.

For international connections see Getting there on pages 35 and 74.

Buses Cancún bus terminal, at the junction of Av Tulum and Uxmal, is small but very well organized. It is divided into two halves: the west section is for 2nd class bus services, while the east section handles the 1st class traffic. Left luggage is found in the 2nd class section. The bus station is the hub for routes west to Mérida and south to Tulum and Chetumal, open 24 hrs, left luggage US$0.55 per hr. Many services to **Mérida**, 4 hrs, ranging from *Plus* with TV, a/c, etc, US$28, to 1st class US$19, to 2nd class US$11; all services call at **Valladolid**, US$8 1st class, US$7.20 2nd class; to **Chichén Itzá**, many buses, starting at 0630, *Expreso de Oriente* 1st class to Mérida, US$8.50, 2½ hrs. *Expreso de Oriente* also has services to **Tizimín** (3 hrs, US$8), Izamal, Cenotillo and Chiquilá. To Palenque, US$44, and **San Cristóbal**, 3 a day, US$52, 18 hrs. To **Villahermosa**, US$60. *Autotransportes del Oriente* to **Playa del Carmen** have been recommended, 2nd class, US$2.25. *Inter Playa Express* every 30 mins to **Puerto Morelos**, US$1, **Playa del Carmen**, US$2.25 and **Xcaret**, US$2.25; 3 times daily to **Puerto Aventuras**, US$2.50, **Xel-Há**, US$3.30 and **Tulum**, US$4.25. Other services to Playa del Carmen and Tulum are more expensive, eg 1st class *Caribe Inter* to Playa del Carmen US$3, 2nd class US$2.35, and US$4.75 to Tulum. Last bus to Playa del Carmen 2000, first bus to Tulum 0430. These services are en route to **Chetumal** (US$19 luxury, US$25 1st class, US$15 2nd, 5 hrs). The 0800 departure for Chetumal arrives for connection to Flores and will get you to Belize City by around 2000. Several other services to Chetumal include Caribe Express, deluxe service with a/c.

Yucatán Peninsula

Ferries and cruises The ferry to Isla Mujeres is much cheaper from Puerto Juárez (see below). The one from Cancún departs from Playa Linda Pier, at the mainland side of the bridge across Canal Nichupté, about 4 km from centre, opposite the *Calinda Quality Cancún Beach*. Playa Linda has shops, agencies for boat trips, a snack bar and Computel. The ferry leaves 9 times a day between 0900 and 1645, US$12.50 return, 20 mins' journey. Returns 7 times a day between 0900 and 1700. Trips to Isla Mujeres, with snorkelling, bar, shopping, start at US$27.50, or US$35 with meal. *M/V Aqua II* has all-inclusive day cruises to Isla Mujeres starting from US$44 (sometimes discounts for user of the *Handbook*), T887-1909.
Boat trips: *Nautibus*, a vessel with seats below the waterline, makes trips to the reefs, 1½ hrs, a good way to see fish, Playa Linda dock, T883-3552. There are a number of other cruises on offer. *Atlantis* submarines offer trips in a 48-passenger vessel to explore natural and man-made reefs off Cancún. For more information contact Robert Theofel on T883-4963.

Airline offices *Aerocaribe* and *Aerocozumel*, Av Cobá 5, Plaza América SM4, T884-2000. *AeroMéxico*, Av Cobá 80, SM3, T884-3571. *American Airlines*, Aeropuerto, T883-4460. *Aviacsa*, Av Cobá 37, SM4, T887-4211. *Aviateca*, Av Cobá 5, Plaza América SM4, T887-4110. *Continental*, Aeropuerto, T886-0006. *Cubana de Aviación*, Av Yaxchilán 23, T887-7373. *Iberia*, Aeropuerto, T886-0243. *Lacsa*, Av Cobá 5, Plaza América SM4, T887-3101. *Mexicana*, Av Tulum, T887-4444.

Directory

See page 34, for Airline websites

    Banks There are 11 Mexican banks along Av Tulum, all in SMs 4 and 5. American Express, for changing their own TCs at better rates than anywhere else, is on Av Tulum, just south of Av Cobá. Many *casas de cambio* in the centre, mainly around the bus terminal and along Av Tulum. *Casas de cambio* in the hotel zone give slightly lower rates for TCs than those in the centre.

    Communications Internet: numerous cafés charging US$1-1.50/hr. Generally good servers, open until around 2300. Post office: at the end of Av Sunyaxchén, near Mercado 28, open Mon-Fri 0800-1900, Sat 0900-1300. **Telephones:** many public phones everywhere, phone cards available from general stores and pharmacies, for US$2, $3 and $5. Collect calls can be made without a card. Also many public phones designed for international calls, which take coins and credit cards. **Fax:** at post office, Mon-Sat, and at San Francisco de Asís shopping mall, Mon-Sat until 2200.

    Cultural centres *Casa Tabasco*, Av Tulum 230, displays and handicrafts for sale from the state of Tabasco, a good place to go if bored of the same old souvenirs in Cancún.

    Embassies and consulates The following consulates are in the hotel zone: *Canada*, Plaza Caracol, 3rd floor, T883-3360. *France*, Hotel Casa Turquesa, T885-2924. *Netherlands*, Hotel Presidente, T883-0200. *Spain*, Oasis Corporativo, T883-2466. *Sweden*, Switzerland, Hotel Caesar Park, T881-8013. *UK*, Hotel Royal Caribbean, T881-0100. *US*, Plaza Caracol, 3rd floor, T883-0272. The following consulates are in the centre: *Austria*, Cantera 4, SM15, T884-7505; *Germany*, Punta Conoco 36, SM24, T884-1898; *Finland*, Nader 28, SM2, T884-1557; *Italy*, Alcatraces 39, SM22, T884-1261.

    Language schools *El Bosque del Caribe*, Náder and Uxmal, T/F884-1065, bcaribe@ mail.cancun-language.com.mx

    Laundry *Alborada*, Nader 5, behind Tourist Information building on Av Tulum. *Cox-boh*, Av Tankah 26, SM24.

    Medical services *American Hospital* (24-hr) Viento 15, Centre, T884-6133. *Total Assist* (24-hr) Claveles 5, Centre, T884-1058. *American Medical Centre*, Plaza Quetzal, Zona Hotelera Km 8, T883-0113.

    Tour operators *Colors Travel*, Av Yaxchilán 7C, SM24, T887-7929, colors@correoweb.com Very friendly and helpful owner Martha Reyes Sangri; all-inclusive package deals to Río Lagartos and Ek-Balam with guides in various languages; overnight trip by plane to Tikal ruins in Guatemala; flights to Cuba, many other trips, reliable service. *Mayan Destinations*, Cobá 31, Edificio Monaco, SM22, T884-4308. All the usual destinations, such as Chichén Itzá, Xcaret, Tulum, as well as flights to Cuba. Many others in the centre and at larger hotels. Most hotels on the hotel zone have their own travel agency. *American Express*, Av Tulum 208, esq Agua, SM 4, T884-5441, F884-6942.

    Useful addresses Immigration office is on the corner of Av Náder and Av Uxmal. There is also an office in the airport, T886-0492, where the staff are better trained and speak English.

Cancún to Isla Mujeres

A strip of coastline north of Punta Sam is officially part of Isla Mujeres. It is being developed as a luxury resort, but without the high-rise buildings of Cancún's hotel zone. Accommodation will be in luxury bungalows and cabañas. The first of these, now completed, is **AL** *Villas Chalet Maya* , Km 9 Punta Sam Highway (for

Punta Sam

Yucatán Peninsula

reservations, contact COMITSA, Km 12.5, Zona Hotelera, Cancún, T885-1418, F885-1498). Ocean views, elaborate ethnic interiors, pool, beach, restaurant.

Puerto Juárez
Colour map 4, grid A3

About 3 km north of Cancún, Puerto Juárez is the dock for the cheaper ferry services to Isla Mujeres; there is also a bus terminal, but services are more frequent from Cancún. There are many buses between Cancún and Puerto Juárez, for example No 8 opposite the bus terminal (US$0.70), but when the ferries arrive from Isla Mujeres there are many more taxis than buses (taxi fare should be no more than US$2, beware overcharging).

Sleeping and eating A *Hotel Caribel*. Resort complex, with bath and fan; in the same price range is *San Marcos*. Other hotels include **D** *Kan Che*, 1st hotel on right coming from Cancún. Fan, clean, swimming pool on beach, good value. *Posada Hermanos Sánchez*, 100 m from bus terminal, on road to Cancún. **D** *Fuente Azul*, opposite the dock. **E** *Pina Hermanos*, SM 68, M 6, Lote 14, Puerto Juárez, T884-2150, 10 mins from Cancún by bus depot. Excellent value, friendly, clean, secure. *Cabañas Punta Sam*, on the beach. Clean, comfortable, **D** with bath (**C** in high season). Possible to camp, with permission, on the beach near the restaurant next door. A big trailer park has been built opposite *Punta Sam*, 150 spaces, camping **F** per person, shop selling basic commodities. Irregular bus service there, or hitchhike from Puerto Juárez. Check to see if restaurant is open evenings. Take mosquito repellent. **Restaurants** *Natz Ti Ha* and *Mandinga* by the ferry dock in Puerto Juárez, serve breakfast.

Transport Buses: regular buses to Cancún from outside the ferry dock, US$0.50. On the whole it is better to catch outgoing buses to more distant destinations in Cancún rather than in Puerto Juárez as there are more of them.

Ferry to Isla Mujeres There are 2 types of ferry: the more expensive costs US$3.80 and leaves Puerto Juárez every 45 mins between 0500 and 1830. Passengers are packed inside; badly functioning a/c makes for a hot and airless journey of 30 mins. The cheaper ferry is in an open-decked boat with cool breezes, much nicer but slightly slower journey, 45 mins, cost US$1.80, departures every 2 hours. Car ferries leave from Punta Sam 5 times a day from 0800, US$7-8 per car, US$1.50 passengers, 45 mins. There is a luggage store, 0800-1800, and a tourist information desk at the jetty.

Isla Mujeres

Phone code: 998
Colour map 4, grid A3

A refreshing antidote to the urban sprawl of Cancún, Isla Mujeres is a good place to relax for a few days away from the hurly-burly of package tourism. The island is especially nice in the evening, when all the Cancún day-trippers have gone. The town is strictly low-rise, with brightly coloured buildings giving it the feel of a Caribbean island such as Trinidad. The island's laws prohibit the construction of any building higher than three floors, and US franchises such as *McDonald's* and *Walmart* are not allowed to open branches here.

There are several good beaches on Isla Mujeres, the best being **Playa Cocos** on the northwest coast, five minutes' walk from the town. Further south, there are several places to swim, snorkel and observe marine life. Restaurants and nightspots are plentiful, good quality and cheaper than those on the mainland, and the people are friendlier. There are several ways to explore the island: you can rent a golf cart, many of which chug around the streets all day, good for families; mopeds and bicycles are cheap and plentiful to rent, and a public bus runs all the way from the town to El Paraíso, almost at the southern tip of the island.

The name Isla Mujeres refers to the large number of clay female idols found by the Spaniards here in 1518. The island contains the only known Maya shrine to a female deity: Ixchel, goddess of the moon and fertility. Sadly, the ruins of the shrine at the southern tip of the island have recently been bought by developers. They will be made into part of a new tourist complex like Xcaret, and locals are furious at having to pay a fee to view them. The tourist office, Rueda Medina, opposite the ferry dock, is very helpful. ■ *Mon-Fri 0900-2100, Sat 0900-1400.* Immigration office is next door.

Most of the sights south of the town can be seen in a day. The first of these, 5 km from the town, is the **Turtle Farm**, T877-0595, with hundreds of sea turtles weighing from 170 g to 270kg in a humane setting. ■ *Daily 0900-1700, US$1.* To get there, take the bus to the final stop, Playa Paraíso, double back and walk five minutes along the main road. **Sights**

At the centre of the island are the curious remains of a pirate's domain, called **Casa de Mundaca**. A big, new arch gate marks its entrance. Paths have been laid out among the large trees, but all that remains of the estate (called Vista Alegre) are one small building and a circular garden with raised beds, a well and a gateway. Fermín Mundaca, more of a slave-trader than a buccaneer, built Vista Alegre for the teenage girl he loved. She rejected him and he died, broken-hearted, in Mérida. His epitaph there reads *Como eres, yo fui; como soy, tu serás* ('What you are I was; what I am you shall be'). See the poignant little carving on the garden side of the gate, *La entrada de La Trigueña* (the girl's nickname). To get there, get off the bus at the final stop, and turn the opposite way to the beach; the house is a short walk away. ■ *Daily 0900-1700, US$1.*

El Garrafón, T877-1100, is a snorkelling centre 7 km from the town, being developed into a luxury resort in the style of Xcaret, on the mainland. Snorkelling is still possible, US$15, lockers US$2, plus deposit, equipment rental available. There is a 12-m bronze cross submerged offshore, trips to snorkel around it cost US$13, 1½ hours, no lunch. There is an expensive restaurant and bar at El Garrafón, and a small beach. The snorkelling is good past the pier, along a reef with some dead coral. Large numbers of different coloured fish can be seen at very close range. If you want to walk to El Garrafón from the bus stop at Playa Paraíso, take the second path on the right to the beach from the main road. The first path leads through Restaurant Playa Paraíso, which charges US$1 for the privilege of walking through their premises to the beach. Playa Paraíso is an expensive mini-resort for Cancún day-trippers; there is a swimming-with-sharks option, during which harmless nurse sharks are treated cruelly so that tourists can have their picture taken with them. Once on the beach, you can walk all the way to El Garrafón along the coast, though it gets very rocky for the final part. It is easier to go as far as the cluster of beach villas, then cut through one of them (ask for permission) to the main road. The whole walk takes about half an hour. When you arrive at El Garrafón, turn right at the building site, go down the hill to *Hotel Garrafón* del Castillo, which is the entrance to the snorkelling centre.

A further 15 minutes' walk from El Garrafón, at the tip of the island, are the ruins of the Maya shrine **Santuario Maya a la Diosa Ixchel,** to Ixchel, goddess of fertility. Unfortunately, these are no longer free to visit. They have been bought and developed as part of the El Garrafón 'National Park', and it now costs US$5.50. A cultural centre has been built here with large sculptures by several international artists.

A small island north of Isla Mujeres, **Isla Contoy** has been designated as a bird and wildlife sanctuary, with good bird-watching. Trips can be arranged through agencies; the specialist is Ricardo Gaitán, at Av Madero 16, T877-0434. His trips include snorkelling, fishing and a fish lunch. Many touts around the main dock will offer trips to Isla Contoy for around US$50 for a full day. **Excursions**

AL *María del Mar*, Av Carlos Larzo 1, on the road down to the north beach. T/F8770179. Close to the best beach, restaurant, pool, cabañas and rooms, overlooks Coco beach. Lovely beach bar with hammocks and rocking chairs for 2. **A** *Condominio Nautibeach*, on Playa Los Cocos, T877-0606. 2-bed apartments, a/c, pool, right on beach facing the sunset. **A** *Francis Arlene*, Guerrero 7, T/F877-0310. Modern, pleasant, efficient service. **B** *Rocamar*, Nicolás Bravo y Zona Marítima, T/F877-0101. On the eastern side, quiet, nice views. **Sleeping**

Yucatán Peninsula

C *Casa Maya*, Zazil-Ha (near Playa Los Cocos) T/F877-0045. Bungalows right next to beach, palm trees, garden, kitchen. **C-D** *El Caracol*, Matamoros 5, T877-0150, F877-0547. Cheaper with fan, hot water, terrace, stoves for guests' use, bar, coffee shop, laundry, central, clean, good value. Recommended. **C** *El Paso*, Morelos 13. With bath, clean, facing the pier. **C** *Isleño*, Madero and Guerrero, T877-0302. Very clean, with bath, cheaper without, helpful. **C** *Isla Mujeres*, next to church. With bath, renovated, run by pleasant Englishman. **C** *Rocas del Caribe*, Madero 2, 100 m from ocean. Cool rooms, big balcony, clean, good service. **C** *Vistalmar*, on promenade about 300 m left from ferry dock, T877-0209 (**D** for longer stays). Ask for rooms on top floor, bath, balcony, a/c, fan, TV, insect screens, good value.

D *Caribe Maya*, Madero 9. Central, modern, a/c, cheaper with fan, very clean and comfy. **D** *Las Palmas*, Guerrero 20. Central, 2 blocks from north beach, good, clean. **D** *María José*, Madero 25, T872-0130. Clean, fans, friendly, scooter hire. **D** *Osorio*, Madero, 1 block from waterfront. Clean, fan, with bath and hot water, friendly, reception closes at 2100. Recommended. **D** *Posada Suemi*, Matamoros 12, T877-0122. Nice, recently opened, family-run, clean, well-furnished rooms, 4 to a room for US$5 extra. Recommended. **D** *San Jorge*, Juárez between López Mateos and Matamoros. Small, quiet, friendly. Recommended.

F (per person) *Poc-Na Hostel*, top end of Matamoros on the northeast coast, T877-0090. Mixed-sex dormitories, 6-14 to a room, also 2 double rooms (**E**), sheets US$10 deposit, restaurant, bar, big screen TV with movies. **F** camping or in hammock. Busy, often booked up in summer and Dec. Recommended but sometimes dirty.

Eating **Expensive** *Rolandis*, Hidalgo, T877-0700. Italian, terrace overlooking street, busy. Recommended. *Meson del Bucanero*, Hidalgo, opposite *Rolandis*. Steak, seafood, terrace, classy. *Miramar*, Rueda Medina opposite ferry dock. Seafood, Mexican. *Lo Lo Lorena*, Guerrero 7, esq Matamoros. Authentic French bistro, lobster, shrimp, also has international dishes.

Mid-range *El Balcón de Arriba*, Hidalgo 12, above souvenir shop. Varied menu, excellent fish and seafood, some vegetarian and tempura dishes, very friendly staff, large portions. Highly recommended. *Velázquez*, on the beach next to the ferry dock. Excellent fresh seafood (except the shrimp), tables on the sand. *Manolos*, Juárez. Small, nice décor, seafood, barbecue, baked potatoes. *Isla Tequila*, Hidalgo 19a. Popular, steak, seafood, good bar, live music, helpful, friendly owners, who also have a bookstore next door. *Pizzería Los Amigos*, Hidalgo. Small, with 2 tables outside, excellent pizzas and pasta. *All Natural*, Plaza Karlita on Hidalgo. Speciality grilled fish, many varieties, some vegetarian dishes.

Cheap *Poc-Chuc*, Juárez y Madero. Very good local food, big portions, good *tortas*. Next door is *La Susanita*. Excellent home cooking, friendly locals' place; when closed it is the family's living room. There are 4 *loncherías* at the northwest end of Guerrero, open till 1800. Good for breakfast, snacks and lunch. All serve the same local fare at similar prices. Opposite is *Lonchería Chely*, similar food and prices. *La Mexicana*, Guerrero 4, T877-0006. Chicken joint, daily 1300-1700.

Cafés *Aluxes Café*, Av Matamoros, next to *Al Forno Pizza*. Good café, with cappuccinos, lattes, tea, muffins, bagels and juices. Recommended. *Cafecito*, Matamoros 42. Nice breakfast place, waffles, juice, sandwiches, 0800-1400. *Red Eye*, Av Hidalgo Centro, north end. Open early, breakfast, coffee.

Bars Most of the bars have a permanent happy hour, with 2 drinks for the price of 1. Not particularly good value, since the prices are double the usual. It works out if 2 people are having the same drink: simply order one! *Daniel's*, Hidalgo between Madero and Morelos. Very popular (and loudest) in the early evening, live music every night. *Kokonuts*, Hidalgo 65, towards beach from centre. Most popular in town, fills up after 2200, dance floor, happy hour, young crowd. Further along towards the beach is *Chile Locos*, more sedate than *Kokonuts*, with live marimba music. *La Palapa*, on Playa Los Cocos. Cocktails and snacks, busy during the day until everyone leaves the beach, then fills up again after midnight. There is sometimes live music at *La Taverna*, on the harbour near the ferry dock. Nice location on wooden stilts in the sea, but the venue is having difficulty competing with the popularity of places in the centre like *Daniel's* and *Kokonuts*. *Mr Papas*, Hildago below Matamoros. Lively bar and nightclub with good variety of DJ music.

Festivals

Between **1-12 Dec** there is a fiesta for the *Virgin of Guadalupe*, fireworks, dances until 0400 in the Plaza. In Oct there is a festival of music, with groups from Mexico and the US performing in the main square.

Shopping

Souvenirs: Av Hidalgo is lined with souvenir shops, most of them selling the same things: ceramic Maya figurines and masks; hammocks; blankets; and silver jewellery from Taxco. Bargaining is obligatory - try and get the desired item for half the original asking price, which is what the vendors expect to receive. There are more souvenir shops along the harbour front, where the salesmen are more pushy, and more shops along Av Morelos. **Books**: *Cosmic Cosas*, Matamoros 82, T876-3495. New and used books bought, sold and exchanged, CDs, internet café, US-run, good place to meet fellow travellers. **Cigars**: *Tobacco & Co*, Hidalgo 14. Cuban cigars and smoking paraphernalia. There are several other shops in the centre selling Cuban cigars. **Supermarkets**: the largest supermarket is on the Zócalo; there is a smaller one on Juárez between Morelos and Bravo.

Sport

Scuba diving and snorkelling: there are various reefs for diving and snorkelling, as well as a sunken cross specifically placed in deep water for divers to explore (see above). **Dive centres**: *Sea Hawk*, Zazil-Ha (behind *Hotel Na-Balam*) T/F877-0296. Certified PADI instructors, 2-tank dive US$50, introductory course including shallow dive US$75. Also snorkelling trips and fishing trips. *Coral*, Av Matamoros 13A, T877-0763, F877-0371, coral@coralscubadivecenter.com The only dive centre on the island affiliated with PADI, over 20 years' experience, bilingual staff, over 50 local dive sites, including reef, adventure or Ultrafreeze options. *Bahía*, Av Rueda Medina 166, opposite the ferry dock, T877-0340. Snorkelling trips depart from the ferry dock daily between 1000 and 1100. They include 2 hrs' snorkelling in various spots and lunch, returning at 1430. US$150 per person. Lots of touts along the seafront, who will tell you that the snorkelling centre at El Garrafón is closed. It is not.

Transport

There is a public **bus**, which runs from the ferry dock to Playa Paraíso every ½ hr, US$0.25. A **taxi** doing the same journey will cost US$1-2, taxi from town to El Garrafón US$3.40. For the return journey, sharing a taxi will work out marginally more expensive than the bus for 4 people. A taxi from El Garrafón to the bus stop at Playa Paraíso is US$1. Taxis charge an additional US$1 at night.

There are several places renting **golf carts**, eg *Ciros*, on Matamoros near Playa Cocos. Rates are generally US$40-50 per day. A credit card is usually required as a deposit. **Mopeds**: many touts along Hidalgo offer similar rates: US$8 per hour, US$20 full day. *Sport Bike*, Av Juárez y Morelos, has good bikes. *Cárdenas*, Av Guerrero 105, T/F877-0079, for mopeds and golf carts. **Bicycles** are usually offered by the same places as mopeds for about US$8 per day.

Air The small airstrip in the middle of the island is mainly used for private planes. Flights can be booked to Cancún and Chichén Itzá through *Mundaca Travel*, on Hidalgo, T877-0025, F877-0076. Charters with *Island Airtours*, contact T877-0331, Helena or Adriana. Also directly with Capt Joaquín Ricalde T9845-3038 (mob) for sightseeing trips to Isla Mujeres, Holbox, Cozumel, Tulum, Chichén Itzá.

Ferry For information on ferries to and from the island, see page 516.

Directory

Banks *Banco del Atlántico*, Av Juárez 5. *Banca Serfín*, Av Juárez 3. Both can get very busy. Good rates, varying daily, are offered by several *casas de cambio* on Av Hidalgo. The one opposite *Rolandis* is open daily 0900-2100. **Communications** **Internet**: several new internet cafés operate on the island. Rates

Yucatán Peninsula

between US$2-2.50/hr, but speeds can be a little slow. **Post office**: at the end of Guerrero towards the beach. Phone cards can be bought at some of the souvenir shops along Hidalgo. International calls and faxes at *Gold & Silver*, Av Hidalgo 58. **Laundry** Tim Pho, Juárez y Abasolo. **Language school** *Ixchel Language Institute*, Matamoros 82, 1-wk survival courses, US$10/hr, individual, US$5.50 group lessons. **Medical services** *Dr Antonio Salas*, Hidalgo, next to *Farmacia*, T877-0477. 24-hrs, house calls, English spoken, air ambulance. *Dr Antonio Torres*, Av Matamoros esq Guerrero, T877-0050. 24 hrs, English and German spoken. **Tour operators** *Prisma Tours*, Av Juárez 22, T/F877-0938. Tours to Tulum, Cobá, Chichén Itzá, Uxmal, Sian Ka'an in a/c vans. Also cheap and reliable airport transfer from Cancún Airport-Puerto Juárez. *Tercer Milenio*, Abasolo 46, between Juárez and Hidalgo, T877-0795, F877-0794. Tours to archaeological sites in Quintana Roo, airport transfer, high-class van rental, reservations for cruises, golf cart, moped and car rental, scuba diving, flights to Cuba, Belize, Guatemala.

South of Cancún

Puerto Morelos
Phone code: 998
Colour map 4, grid A3

A quiet little village 34 km south of Cancún, Puerto Morelos is one of the few places that still retains some of the charm of an unspoilt fishing village (but not for much longer!), making it a good place to stop over en route to larger towns further south, such as Playa del Carmen. The village is really just a large plaza right on the seafront with a couple of streets going off it. If on arrival at Cancún airport you don't wish to spend the night in the city, get a taxi directly to Puerto Morelos. This is also the place to catch the car ferry to the island of Cozumel. The *Sinaltur* office on the plaza offers good snorkelling, kayak and fishing trips. *Goyos*, just north of the plaza, offers jungle adventures and rooms for rent, erratic hours maintained.

Sleeping & eating

L-AL *Caribbean Reef Club*, just past the car ferry dock on the beach, T871-0162. Luxury resort hotel with organized watersports and a pool. Next door is **A** *Rancho Libertad*, T871-0181. Thatched cabañas, price includes breakfast, scuba diving and snorkelling gear for rent. **A** *Hacienda Morelos*, on the seafront, T871-0015. Nice rooms with sea views. **D** *Posada Amor*, opposite the beach, T871-0033, F871-0178. Very pleasant, well-built cabañas with good mosquito nets, the cheaper ones have outdoor communal showers, good restaurant, prices are reduced considerably out of season, ie Feb-Jun/Sep-Nov. Recommended. There are several restaurants on the plaza, eg *Johnny Cairo*, with good typical food. *Pelicano*. Has very good seafood.

Transport

There are buses to Cancún and Playa del Carmen every ½ hr. Buses depart from the main road, taxi to bus stop US$3. Car ferries to Cozumel depart twice a day at 0600 and 1500, the dock is 500 m south of the plaza. Taxi from Cancún airport to Puerto Morelos, US$25-35.

Directory

Communications There is an internet café on the corner of the plaza opposite *Posada Amor*, US$2.50/hr, open Mon-Sat 1000-1400, 1600-2100.

Playa del Carmen

Phone code: 984
Colour map 4, grid A3
Population: 45,000

What use to be a pleasant little town on the beach has lost the charms of its former existence as a fishing village. Recent development for tourism has been rapid, but Playa, as it is known locally, has not had the high-rise treatment of Cancún. The beach is dazzling white, with crystal-clear shallow water, ideal for swimming, and further out there is good scuba diving. There is accommodation for every budget, and plenty of good restaurants and bars of every description. Many travellers choose Playa as their base for trips to the ruins of Tulum in the south, and archaeological sites such as Cobá in the interior.

The town is laid out in a grid system, with the main centre of tourist activity based on Avenida 5 (pedestrianized in the central section at night between 1800 and 0200) one block from and parallel with the beach. This is where the more expensive hotels and restaurants are, as well as being the centre for nightlife. Cheaper accommodation can be found up Avenida Juárez and further north of the beach.

Tourist information is scant, although there is a new tourism office on the corner of Av Juárez and Avenida 15, T873-0263, which has useful information and maps, and the kiosk on the main plaza will provide a copy of *Destination Playa del Carmen*, a useful guide with maps produced by US residents.

Most luxurious is **L** *Continental Plaza Playacar*, T873-0100, F873-0105. A huge new development just south of the ferry terminal, excellent in every respect, non-residents can use swimming pool. **AL** *Alhambra*, Calle 8 Nte, on corner with the beach, T873-0735, F873-0699, www.alhambra-hotel.net All rooms with balcony or sea view, family-run, French and English spoken. Recommended. **AL** *Las Molcas*, T873-0070, near ferry pier. Pool, a bit shabby, friendly staff, interesting architecture, its open-air restaurant across street is good and reasonable. At the north end of town, on a popular stretch of beach between Calle 12 y 14, is **AL-B** *Blue Parrot*, T873-0083, F874-4564 (toll free in the US on 800-634-3547). Price depends on type of room and facilities, has bungalows, no a/c, with excellent bar (Happy Hour 2200) and café, volleyball court, deep-sea fishing expeditions. Highly recommended.

B *Costa del Mar*, T873-0058, on little road by beach between Calle 10 and 12. Clean, restaurant (disappointing) and bar, pool. **B** *Maya Bric*, Av 5, between Calle 8 and 10, T873-0011. Hot water, clean, friendly, pool, *Tank-Ha* dive shop (see below). **B** *Mom's*, Av 30 y Calle 4, T873-0315, about 5 blocks from bus station or beach. Clean, comfortable, small pool, good restaurant with Chinese home cooking and plenty of vegetables. **B-F** *Cabañas Alejari*, Calle 6 going down to beach, T873-0374. Very nice, shop has long-distance phones. **B-C** *Casa de Gopala*, Calle 2 Nte and Av 10 Nte (PO Box 154), T/F873-0054. Bath and fan, 150 m from beach, quiet and central, American/Mexican owned, large rooms, quiet and comfortable. Recommended.

C *Cabañas Tuxatah*, 2 mins from sea, 2 blocks south from Av Juárez, T873-0025). German owner, Maria Weltin, speaks English and French. Bath, clean, comfortable, hot water, laundry service, beautiful gardens, breakfast US$4. Recommended. **C** *Nuevo Amanecer*, Calle 4, west of Av 5. Very attractive, fans, hot water, hammocks, mosquito nets, clean, laundry area, poolroom, helpful. Recommended. **C** *Posada Las Flores*, Av 5 between Calle 4 and Calle 6. Popular, friendly, courtyard, near beach. **C** *Playa del Carmen*, Av Juárez, between Calle 10 y 15, T873-0293, opposite bank. **C** *Siesta Fiesta*, Av 5 between 8 and 10, T873-0203, Nice rooms, relaxed feel. Recommended. **C-D** *Castillo Verde*, Calle 26 between Av 5 and 10, T/F873-0990, 10 mins from centre at north end of town. With bath, hot water, garden, free coffee, Swiss-German owned. **C-D** *Posada Marinelly*, Av Juárez between Calle 10 and Calle 15. T873-0140. Near the centre, some rooms noisy, very clean, nice staff, family-run, good cheap café downstairs. **C-D** *Posada Papagayo*, Av 15 between Calle 4 and 6. Fan and bath, mosquito net, very nicely furnished rooms, friendly. Highly recommended.

D *Casa Tucán*, Calle 4 Nte, between 10 and 15 Av Nte, T/F873-0283. Nice patio, small but clean rooms. **D** *Colorado*, Calle 4 Nte between 20 and 25. Remodelling, Swedish owned and run, balony, fridge, TV, hot water, good value. Recommended. **D** *El Bucanero*, Av 25 and Calle 4, T873-1454. Comfortable rooms away from the noisy centre. **D** *Las Brisas*, at the beach end of Calle 4 ask at shop *Nall Ha*, T873-2644. Newly renovated, near beach, courtyard and lagoon, cold water, big rooms, family run. Recommended. **D** *Posada Lily*, Av Juárez opposite the bus stop. With shower, fan, safe, clean, but noisy in the morning and cell-like rooms. **D** *Posada Marixchel*, Calle 30 and 1 Sur, T872-0823. Shower, safe, fan, clean. Recommended. **D** *Posada Mar Caribe*, Av 15. Small, friendly. Recommended.

E *Posada Fernández*, Av 10 opposite Calle 1. Bath, hot water and fan, friendly. Recommended. **E** *Urban Hostel*, Av 10 between 4th and 6th, T879-9342, urbanhostel@yahoo.com Dormitories, hot water and fan, mosquito nets, kitchen facilities, lockers under the beds, curtains separate the rooms so watch out for wandering hands in the night.

Lots of new places are going up, but none under US$10 a night. Small apartments on Av 5, esq Calle 6. Approximately US$200 per month, with kitchen; also rooms near basketball court, US$100 per month.

Youth Hostel F *Villa Deportiva*, 5 blocks up from Av 5, on Calle 24 Nte, T875-2548, camping, in dormitory (hot with only 2 fans and a lot of beds), for up to 4 in cabin with fan and private shower, comfortable, with basketball court, clean, difficult to find, especially after dark, but it is signposted. Recommended.

Sleeping

■ *on map*
Price codes:
see inside front cover

Prices quoted are for the high season - July/August and December; during the low season prices will drop by about 25%

Yucatán Peninsula

Camping See above under *La Ruina* and *Villa Deportiva Juvenil*; also **Punta Bete**, 10 km north, the right-hand one of 3 campsites at the end of a 5 km road, on beach. US$3 for tent, also 2 restaurants and cabañas. **Outback**, small trailer park on beach at end of Calle 6. US$10 for car and 2 people.

Eating

● *on map, page 522*
Price codes: see inside front cover

Expensive *Idea Pasta*, Av 5 between Calle 12 and Calle 14. Good Italian, seafood. *Panchos*, Av 5 between Calle 10 and Calle 12. Traditional Mexican food, speciality international flambées and flaming Spanish coffee. *La Galleria*, Calle 8 between 5th and the beach

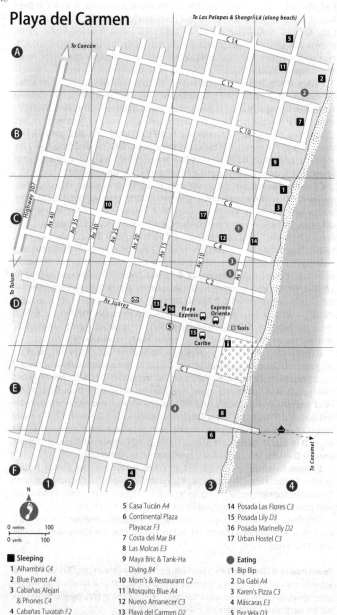

Playa del Carmen

To Las Palapas & Shangri-Lá (along beach)

Sleeping
1 Alhambra *C4*
2 Blue Parrot *A4*
3 Cabañas Alejari & Phones *C4*
4 Cabañas Tuxatah *F2*
5 Casa Tucán *A4*
6 Continental Plaza Playacar *F3*
7 Costa del Mar *B4*
8 Las Molcas *E3*
9 Maya Bric & Tank-Ha Diving *B4*
10 Mom's & Restaurant *C2*
11 Mosquito Blue *A4*
12 Nuevo Amanecer *C3*
13 Playa del Carmen *D2*
14 Posada Las Flores *C3*
15 Posada Lily *D3*
16 Posada Marinelly *D2*
17 Urban Hostel *C3*

Eating
1 Bip Bip
2 Da Gabi *A4*
3 Karen's Pizza *C3*
4 Máscaras *E3*
5 Pez Vela *D3*

by *Tree Tops* hotel. Good international food. *Jazzy Cat*, Calle 6 between Av 5 and Av 10. Rib roasts, oven-baked lasagne, home-made pasta. *Limones*, Av 5 and Calle 6. Good seafood, sunken garden, popular.

Mid-range *Argentino Bar Restaurant*, Calle 12, between 5th and the *Blue Parrot*. Great BBQs, good breakfast cheap, good sports bar. Recommended. *Máscaras*, on square. Highly recommended. Also on the square, *El Tacolote*. Tacos, etc, and *Las Piñatas*. *California Buffet*, corner of Av Uxmal and Nader. Clean with good prices, all you can eat option for US$9. *Da Gabi*, just up Calle 12 from *Blue Parrot*, good pastas, Mexican dishes, breakfast buffet, also has rooms in **C** range. *Tarraya*, on seafront. Seafood, closes 2100. Recommended. On or near Avenida 5: *Pez Vela*, Av 5 y Calle 2. Good atmosphere, food, drinks and music (closed 1500-1700). *Pollo Caribe*, near bus station between Calle 2 and Juárez. Set chicken menu for US$2, good, closes early when chicken runs out. Recommended. *La Parrilla*, Av 5 y Calle 8. Large portions, good service, live music every night, popular. *Buenos Aires*, Calle 6 Nte between Av 5 and Av 10, on Plaza Playa. Speciality Argentine meats, run by Argentines, nice for a change from Mexican food. *La Choza*, Av 5 between Av Juárez and Calle 2. Good breakfasts, Tex-Mex dinners. *Bip Bip*, Av Constituyentes between Av 5 and the beach. Good pizzas. *Media Luna*, Av 5 between Calle 8 and Calle 10. Excellent vegetarian and seafood. *Sabor*, Calle 4 and Av 5. Vegetarian and health food, bakery. *The Lazy Lizard*, Av 5 between Calle 2 and Calle 4. Canadian-run, US-style food, burgers. *Yaxche*, Calle 8 between Av 5 and Av 10. Traditional Maya cuisine. *Karen's Pizza*, Av 5 between Calle 2 and 4. Pizzas, Mexican dishes, cable TV, popular. *Le Bistro*, Calle 2. Good French cheese/Caribbean chicken and wine. Recommended. *Los Almendros*, Calle 6 and Av 10. Excellent Mexican food, friendly. Recommended. *La Choza*, 5 Av between Juárez and Calle 2. Great food, set menus. *El Chino*, Calle 4 Nte between Calle 10 and 15. Popular with Mexicans.

Cheap *Lonchería Maquech*, Calle 1 between Av 5 and 10. Set lunch daily, cheap, friendly. Recommended. *El Correo*, just beyond *Posada Fernández*. Mexican, cheap, excellent *menú del día* and *pollo pibil*. Recommended. *Tacos Senjansen*, Av Juárez between Calle 10 and Calle 15. Nice open-air café under *Posada Marinelly*, for good breakfast and snacks. *Cielito Lindo*, Av 20 s/n y Av Juárez. Good filling meals, varied menu, popular with locals, surly staff. Nice *palapa* (no name) for snacks, on Av 20 Nte and Calle 2 Nte. Popular with locals. *Taquería El Poblano*, Av. Juárez between Calle 15 and 20. Mexican food. Reccomended. *Pizza y Pasta de Fofo*, Calle 4 between Av 5 and 10. Recommended.

Cafés and bakeries *Coffee Press*, Calle 2 between Av 5 and the beach. Espresso, cappucino, latte, breakfast. *Java Joe's*, Av 5 between Calle 10 and Calle 12. Italian and gourmet coffees, sandwiches, pastries. *El Molino*, Av 30 and Calle 4. Sandwiches, pastries. *Chedraue*, Juáraz and highway. Excellent bakery in supermarket.

Bars *The Blue Parrot Inn*, Calle 12 y Av 1, next to beach. Live music every night, happy hour 1700-2000 and 2200-2400. *Bouron Street*, Av 5 between Calle 6 and 8. Live Louisiana blues and jazz, Cajun food, great, relaxed atmosphere earlier, draught beer. Owner Paul Anderson is friendly and helpful. *Tequila Barrel*, 5th between 10th and 12th. Live blues music 2000-2400 daily, Tex Mex Bar and grill, friendly owner (Greco) and staff.

Bars & nightclubs

Nightclubs *Señor Frogs*, by the pier. Part of large chain throughout Mexico, live reggae and karaoke, open from 2200 till late. *Fiesta Latina*, Calle 8 y Av 25. Live Latin music and ballet show. *Buena Onda*, Av 5 between Calle 26 and Calle 28. Live music, salsa, funk, reggae. *Crocodillos*, Juárez, disco, small cover, popular with the locals, good at weekends. *Espiral*, Av 5 off the main plaza. House and techno.

Lots of souvenir shops clustered around the plaza, pricey. Cheaper shops, for day-to-day items, can be found on Av Juárez. There is a cheap *panadería* at the beginning of Av Juárez. For developing photos and buying film, there are several places along Av 5. Recommended jewellers is *Joyería Cobá*, Av 5.

Shopping

Yucatán Peninsula

Sport **Scuba diving** The best is said to be *Abyss*, Calle 12 and the beach, near the *Blue Parrot*, T873-2164, abyss@playadelcarmen.com Run by fully certified American instructor David Tomlinson, PADI courses cost US$324; 1-tank dive costs US$40, 1-day introductory course US$69, also cave dives and night dives. *Adventures Underwater*, on plaza, T873-2647. Diving courses in English, French or Spanish, 3 certified instructors, 1-day beginner course US$60, open water PADI US$350, advanced refresher course US$250, cave diving in 2 *cenotes* US$100. Other recommended centres are *Tank-Ha*, in *Maya Bric Hotel*, T873-0011, www.tankha.com and *Phocea Caribe*, Av 5 between Calle 12 and Calle 14, T873-1024.

Transport **Local Taxis**: Cancún airport US$25. Beware of those who charge only US$5 as they are likely to charge an extra US$20 for luggage. Tours to Tulum and Xel-Há from kiosk by boat dock US$30; tours to Tulum, Xel-Há and Xcaret, 5-6 hrs, US$60; taxi to Xcaret US$6.65. Taxis congregate on the Av Juárez side of the square (Sindicato Lázaro Cárdenas del Río, T873-0032).

Car hire *Caribetur*, Av 10 No 128 between Calle 2 and 4 Nte, T873-2292. *Freedom*, Av 5, T873-1459. *Happy*, Plaza Tucán, Local 6, T873-1739. *Hertz*, T873-0703. *Budget*, T873-0100.

Long distance Buses: The *ADO* bus terminal is on Av Juárez between Av 5 and 10. All buses depart from here. The following prices and times are for *ADO* buses (1st class, a/c, usually showing a video on longer journeys); *Premier*, also 1st class; *Maya de Oro*, supposed to be 1st class but quality of buses can be poor; *Cristóbal Colón*, good 1st class service. **Cancún:** 8 per day, 1 hr 15 mins, *ADO* US$2.40, *Playa Express* US$2. **Mérida:** 4 per day, 7 hrs, US$10. **Valladolid:** 0730 and 1115, 3½ hrs, US$8 (most buses going to Mérida stop at Valladolid. 2nd class buses to Valladolid go via Tulum, US$6.50). **Chichén Itzá:** 6 per day, 4 hrs, US$7. **Tulum:** 5 per day, 1 hr, US$2. **Xcaret:** frequent service, 10 mins, US$1. **Xel Há:** 2 per day, 1 hr, US$2. **Chetumal:** 8 per day, 5 hrs, US$10. **Mexico City:** 3 per day, 24 hrs, US$54. **San Cristóbal de las Casas:** 3 per day, 16 hrs, US$37.

Transport to Cozumel Ferries depart from the main dock, just off the plaza, every hr on the hr, 0400-2200, ½ hour, US$8 1-way, buy ticket 1 hr before journey. There are also flights from the nearby airstrip; touts will mingle with the queues for the ferry to get passengers. Flights cost US12.50 1-way, 10 mins.

Directory **Banks** *Bancomer*, Av Juárez between Calle 25 and Calle 30. *Banamex*, Av Juárez between Calle 20 and Calle 25. A few doors down is *Santander*. *Bancrecer*, Av 5 between Av Juárez and the beach. *Inverlat*, Av 5 between Av Juárez and Calle 2. *Bital*, Av Juárez between Calle 10 and 15, also at Av 30 between Calle 4 and 6. There are several *casas de cambio* along Av 5, which change TCs with no commission. Count your money carefully as short changing is not uncommon. **Communications** Internet: all the cybercafés in town charge between US$1.50-2/hr. Post office: Av Juárez y Av 15, open Mon-Fri 0800-1700, Sat 0900-1300. Telegraph office is around the corner on Av 15. **Language schools**, *Academia de Español*, 'El Estudiante', Av 15 between Calle 2 and 4, T/F873-0050. US$7.00/hr. Recommended. Also offer courses in English and German. *Playalingua*, Calle 20 between 5 and 10, T873-3876, cidi@playalingua.com, weekend excursions, a/c, library, family stays, US$75 enrolment fee, US$150 per wk (20 hrs). **Laundry** Av Juárez, 2 blocks from bus station; another on Av 5. *Maya Laundry*, Av 5 between Calle 2 and Calle 4, Mon-Sat 0800-2100. Laundry in by 1000, ready in the afternoon. **Medical services** *International Medical Services*, Dr Victor Macías Orosco, Av 35 between Calle 2 and 4, T873-0493. 24-hr emergency service, land and air ambulance, ultrasound, most major insurance accepted. *Tourist Divers Medical Centre*, Dr Mario Abarca, Av 10 between Av Juárez and Calle 2, T873-0512. Air and land ambulance service, hyperbaric and diving medicine, affiliated with South Miami Hospital, all insurance accepted. **Dentist:** *Perla de Rocha Torres*, Av 20 Nte s/n between 4 and 6, T873-0021, speaks English. Recommended. **Tour operators** *Classique Travel*, Calle 6 between Av 5 and Av 10, T/F 873-0142, boletaje@ mail.classique.com.mx Long-standing and reliable agency with a branch in Cancún, tours to Chichén Itzá US$72, including transport from hotel, guide, entrance, food, also bookings for national and international flights, helpful staff. *Euro Latino*, Av 5 no 165B, between Calle 6 and 8, T873-0549, F873-0550, eurolatino@grupasesores.net.mx An efficiently run agency with young European staff, 2 of their tours are: dawn in Tikal (Guatemala) US$278, including flight, overnight stay in hotel, all meals, all transfers; weekend on Cozumel, including dive (all levels) plus 2 nights and the ferry, US$72. **Useful addresses** *Police station*, Av Juárez, next to the post office, T873-0291. *Immigration office*, Centro Comercial, Plaza Antigua, Av 10 Sur, T873-1884.

Yucatán Peninsula

Cozumel

The town, San Miguel de Cozumel, is a seedy, overpriced version of Playa del Carmen.
Daily tour groups arrive on cruises from Miami and Cancún, and the town's services
seem geared towards this type of tourist. But Cozumel is a mecca for scuba divers, with
many beautiful offshore reefs to explore, as well as much interesting wildlife and
birdlife. Travellers looking for a beach holiday with some nightlife will find the island
disappointing compared to Playa del Carmen. There is only one nice beach on the west
side, and the eastern, Atlantic coast is far too rugged and choppy for swimming.

Phone code: 987
Colour map 4, grid A3
Population: 175,000

Ins and outs

The airport is just north of San Miguel with a minibus shuttle service to the hotels. There are **Getting there**
10-min flights to and from the airstrip near Playa del Carmen, as well as flights linking to Mexico City, Cancún, Chichén Itzá and Houston (Texas). The passenger ferry from Playa del Carmen runs every 2 hrs (see above), and the car ferry leaves twice daily from Puerto Morelos (see page 520).

There are no local buses, but Cozumel town is small enough to visit on foot. To get around **Getting around**
the island, there are organized tours or taxis; otherwise, hire a jeep, moped or bicycle.

Sights

The island's only town has very little character, mainly due to the construction of a **San Miguel**
US air base during the Second World War, whose airfield has now been converted **de Cozumel**
for civilian use. The buildings are mostly modern and functional, with many restaurants and bars cluttering the centre. The outskirts are reserved for large banks and airline offices. There is a variety of accommodation, with a few budget hotels, but mainly focusing on the luxury end of the market.

On the waterfront between Calle 4 and 6, the **Museo de la Isla** provides a well laid-out history of the island. ■ *US$3.30.* There is a bookshop, art gallery and rooftop restaurant, which has excellent food and views of sunset, good for breakfast, from 0700 (*The Quick* is excellent value). Recommended.

In the north of the island the beaches are sandy and wide, although those at the Zona **Beaches**
Hotelera Norte were damaged in 1989 and are smaller than they used to be. At the *The best public*
end of the paved road, walk up the unmade road until it becomes 'dual carriageway'; *beaches are some way*
turn left for the narrow beach, which is a bit dirty. Cleaner beaches are accessible *from San Miguel town*
only through the hotels. South of San Miguel, **San Francisco** is good if narrow
(clean, very popular, lockers at *Pancho's*, expensive restaurants), but others are generally narrower still and rockier. All the main hotels are on the sheltered west coast.
The east, Caribbean coast is rockier, but very picturesque; swimming and diving on the unprotected side is very dangerous owing to ocean underflows. The only safe place is at a sheltered bay at **Chen Río**. Another bay with possibilities is **Punta Morena**, which is a good surf beach, there is good accommodation and seafood (try the ceviche). D *Cabañas Punta Morena*, contact Matt at *Deep Blue*, on Salas 200, for more information and transport. Three good (and free) places for snorkelling are: the beach in front of *Hotel Las Glorias*, 15 minutes' walk south from ferry; you can walk through the hotel's reception. **Playa Corona**, further south, is too far to walk, so hitch or take a taxi. There is a small restaurant and pier; **Xul-Ha**, further south still, has a bar and comfortable beach chairs.

There are some 32 archaeological sites on Cozumel; those on the east coast are **Archaeological**
mostly single buildings (thought to have been lookouts, navigational aids). The easi- **sites**
est to see are the restored ruins of the Maya-Toltec period at **San Gervasio** in the

Yucatán Peninsula

north (7 km from Cozumel town, then 6 km to the left up a paved road, toll US$1). ■ *0700-1700, US$3.50. Guides are on hand, or you can buy a self-guiding booklet at the librería on the square in San Miguel, or at the Flea Market, for US$1.* It is an interesting site, quite spread out, with *sacbés* (sacred roads) between the groups of buildings. There are no large structures, but a nice plaza, an arch, and pigment can be seen in places. It is also a pleasant place to listen to birdsong, see butterflies, animals (if lucky), lizards, landcrabs and insects. **Castillo Real** is one of many sites on the northeastern coast, but the road to this part of the island is in very bad condition and the ruins themselves are very small. **El Cedral** in the southwest (3 km from the main island road) is a two-room temple, overgrown with trees, in the centre of the village of the same name. Behind the temple is a ruin, and next to it a modern church with a green and white façade (an incongruous pairing). In the village are large, permanent shelters for agricultural shows, rug sellers and locals who pose with *iguanas doradas* (golden iguanas). **El Caracol**, where the sun, in the form of a shell, was worshipped, is 1 km from the southernmost Punta Celarain. At Punta Celarain is an old lighthouse.

Excursions A circuit of the island on paved roads can easily be done in a day (see Local transport below). Head due east out of San Miguel (take the continuation of Avenida Juárez).

Cozumel

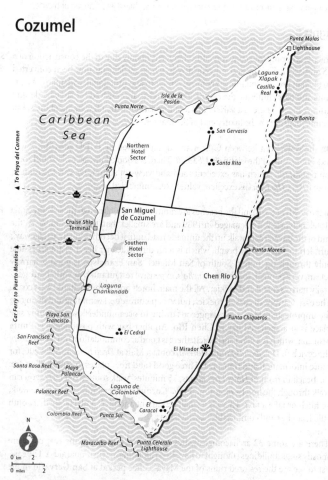

Make the detour to San Gervasio before continuing to the Caribbean coast at *Mescalito's* restaurant. Here, turn left for the northern tip (road unsuitable for ordinary vehicles), or right for the south, passing Punta Morena, Chen Río, Punta Chiqueros (restaurant, bathing), El Mirador (a low viewpoint with sea-worn rocks, look out for holes) and Paradise Cove. At this point, the paved road heads west within an unpaved road continues south to Punta Celarain. Here there is the **Punta Sur Ecological Reserve**, T872-2940, funpaymu@cozumel.com.mx, an eco-tourism development, with a variety of natural landscapes with lagoons and mangrove jungles. A snorkel centre has opened here as well as viewing platform. On the road west, opposite the turn-off to El Cedral, is a sign to *Restaurante Mac y Cía*, an excellent fish restaurant on a lovely beach, popular with dive groups for lunch. Next is Playa San Francisco (see above). A few more kilometres lead to the former *Holiday Inn*, the last big hotel south of San Miguel. Just after this is Parque Chankanab, which used to be an idyllic lagoon behind the beach (9 km from San Miguel). After it became totally spoilt, it was restored as a National Park, with the lagoon, crystal clear again, a botanical garden with local and imported plants, a 'Maya Area' (rather artificial), swimming (ideal for families with young children), snorkelling, dive shops, souvenirs, expensive but good restaurants and lockers (US$2). ■ *0800-1600, US$4, snorkelling mask and fins US$5, use of underwater camera US$25.* Soon the road enters the southern hotel zone at the *Stouffer Presidente*, coming to the cruise ship dock and car ferry port on the outskirts of town.

Essentials

Out of town Several luxury hotels including **A** *Tontan*, 3 km north of town (taxi US$1) on waterfront. Pool, clean, safe, snorkelling, cheap restaurant. Recommended.

In town In **AL-A** range: *Bahía*, Av Rafael Melgar y Calle 3 Sur, T872-1791, F872-7651. A/c, phone, cable TV, fridge, breakfast included, free internet, even-numbered rooms have balcony. Recommended. *Barracuda*, Av Rafael Melgar 628, T872-0002, F872-0884. Popular with divers. *Mesón San Miguel*, on the plaza, T872-0233, F872-1820. *Plaza Cozumel*, Calle 2 Nte 3, T872-2711, F872-0066. A/c, TV, phone, pool, restaurant, car hire, laundry.

A-B *Amaranto*, Calle 5 sur, between 15 and 20, T872-3219, amaranto@cozumel.com.mx Bungalows, fridge, microwave, new, run by Eliane and Jorge, Spanish, English and French spoken, child care on request. Recommended. **B** *Maya Cozumel*, Calle 5 Sur 4, T872-0011, F872-0781. A/c, pool, good value. **B** *Tamarindo*, Calle 4 Nte 421, between 20 and 25, T/F872-3614. Bed and breakfast, 3 rooms, shared kitchen, hammocks, dive gear storage and rinse tank, purified drinking water, laundry, safe deposit box, TV, also run by Eliane and Jorge, Spanish, English and French spoken, child care on request.
    C *Al Marestal*, Calle 10 y 25 Av Nte, T872-0822. Spacious, clean rooms, fan or a/c, cool showers, swimming pool, very good. **C** *Pepita*, Av 15 Sur y Calle 1 Sur, T/F872-0098. Very pleasant rooms around a plant-filled courtyard, modern fittings, a/c, fridge in all rooms, free coffee and cookies in the morning. Recommended. **C** *Posada Cozumel*, Calle 4 Nte 3, T872-0314. Pool, showers, a/c, cheaper with fan, clean. **C** *Posada Marruang*, A R Salas 440, between Av 20 Sur and Av 25 Sur, T872-1678. Very spick and span, large comfortable rooms set back from road; barking dog ensures occasional noise and total security. **C** *Posada Zuanayoli*, Calle 6 Nte between Av 10 and Av 15 Nte, T872-0690. Tall, old building in quiet street, TV, modern facilities, fridge, fan, free coffee, drinking water.
    D *Blanquita*, 10 Nte, T872-1190. Comfortable, clean, friendly, owner speaks English, rents snorkelling gear and motor-scooters. Recommended. **D** *Flamingo*, Calle 6 Nte 81, T872-1264. Showers, fan, clean, family-run, good value. Recommended. **D** *Flores*, A R Salas 72, off plaza, T872-1429. 50 m from the sea, very cheap for central location. A/c, cheaper with fan. **D** *José de León*, Av Pedro J Coldwell y Calle 17 Sur. Fairly clean, showers. **D** *Paraíso Caribe*, 15 Av Nte y Calle 10. Fan, showers, clean. **D** *Posada del Charro*, 1 block east of *José de León*. Same owner, same facilities. **D** *Posada Edem*, Calle 2 Nte 124, T872-1166. Kitchen, a/c, fan, also apartments

Sleeping
■ *on map, page 528*
Price codes: see inside front cover

Prices may rise by up to 50% around Christmas

Yucatán Peninsula

in **B** range, clean, very good value. Recommended. **D** *Posada Letty*, Calle 1 Sur y Av 15 Sur, T872-0257. Hot water, clean, good value. Recommended. **E** *Saolima*, A R Salas 260, T872-0886. Clean, fan, showers, hot water. Recommended.

Camping Not permitted although there are 2 suitable sites on the south shore.

Eating

● *on map, page 528*
Price codes: see
inside front cover

Expensive *Morgans*, main square. Elegant, good. *Café del Puerto*, 2nd floor by pier. South-Seas style. *El Capi Navegante*, 2 locations: by market for lunch, and Calle 3 y Av 10 Sur. More upmarket. Seafood at each. *Pepe's Grill*, waterfront, 2 blocks south of pier. Excellent. *Pancho's Backyard*, Rafael Melgar 27, in *Los Cinco Soles* shopping complex in big courtyard out the back. Mexican food and wine elegantly served, good food. *La Choza*, A R Salas 198. Expensive, Mexico City food. Recommended. *Lobster's Cove*, Av Rafael Melgar 790. Seafood, live music, happy hour 1200-1400. *Prima*, A R Salas, 109. Northern Italian seafood, hand-made pasta, brick oven pizzas, non-smoking area.

Mid-range *Las Palmeras*, at the pier (people-watching spot). Very popular for breakfast, opens 0700, always busy. Recommended. *Plaza Leza*, main square. Excellent and reasonable. *Miss Dollar*, A R Salas y Av 20. Good Mexican food, US$2 *comidas*, very friendly. *El Moro*, 75 Bis Nte 124, between 4 and 2. Good, closed Thu. *Santiago's Grill*, Av 15 Sur y A R Salas. Excellent, popular with divers. *La Yucatequita*, Calle 9 Sur y Av 10 Sur. Genuine Mayan food,

San Miguel de Cozumel

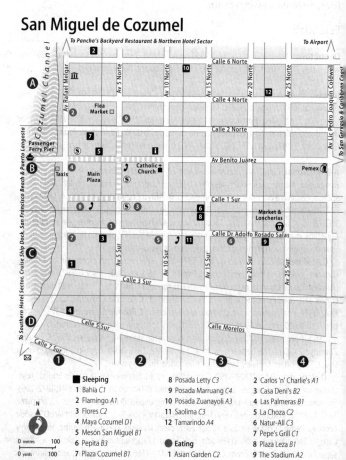

■ Sleeping
1 Bahía *C1*
2 Flamingo *A1*
3 Flores *C2*
4 Maya Cozumel *D1*
5 Mesón San Miguel *B1*
6 Pepita *B3*
7 Plaza Cozumel *B1*

8 Posada Letty *C3*
9 Posada Marruang *C4*
10 Posada Zuanayoli *A3*
11 Saolima *C3*
12 Tamarindo *A4*

● Eating
1 Asian Garden *C2*

2 Carlos 'n' Charlie's *A1*
3 Casa Deni's *B2*
4 Las Palmeras *B1*
5 La Choza *C2*
6 Natur-All *C3*
7 Pepe's Grill *C1*
8 Plaza Leza *B1*
9 The Stadium *A2*

closes at 2130, best to go day before and discuss menu. *La Misión*, Av Juárez y Av 5 Nte. Good food, friendly atmosphere. *Acuario*, on beach 6 blocks south of pier. Famous for seafood, aquarium in restaurant (ask to see the tanks at the back). *Carlos 'n' Charlie's*, restaurant/bar. Popular, in the new Plaza Pointe Langostina, south of the *Mi Chabalita*, Av 10 Sur between Calle 1 Sur and A R Salas. Friendly, cheap and good Mexican food. *Asian Garden*, 5 Ave 148, between 1a Sur and Salas. Good Chinese food. *Guido's*, Av. Rafael Melgar 23. Swiss restaurant, dining inside plaza with exuberant plants, great lasagne and sangría. *Pepe Pelícano*, 2 houses left of *Hotel Saolima*. Cheap and clean. *Casa Deni's*, Calle 1 Sur 164, close to plaza. Open-air restaurant, very good, moderate prices. *The Stadium*, Calle 2 Nte y Av 5. US-style, breakfasts, burgers, steaks, lobster, satellite TV, money exchange, phones for USA; US-style breakfasts also at *Los Cocos*, next to ProDive on A R Salas. *Sonora Grill*, Av 15 Nte No 2 between Av Juárez and Calle 2 Nte. Tex-Mex, steaks, seafood. *Los Moros del Morrito*, Av 35 Sur between Calle 3 and Morelos. Typical Yucatecan cuisine and seafood.

Cheap There are few eating options for the budget traveller. The cheapest places for breakfast, lunch or an early dinner are the *loncherías* next to the market on A R Salas, between Av 20 and Av 25. There are several of them, all serving fairly good local *comida corrida*, open from 0800-1930.

Cafés and bakeries *Coffee Bean*, Calle 3 Sur 9 near waterfront. Good coffee, great pies, cakes and brownies.

Bars & nightclubs
The Stadium, see above. *Havana Club*, Av Rafael Melgar, north of the ferry. Cigar Jazz Bar, with live Jazz, 1330-1800, Wed and Fri. *Café Salsa*, 10 Av Between Juárez and 2 Nte. Salsa Bar, popular alternative and slightly more authentic. *Scaramouche*, Av Rafael Melgar y A R Salas. The best. *Neptuno*, Av Rafael Melgar y Calle 11, south of centre. The last 2 are state-of-the-art discos, as well as hotel nightclubs.

Shopping
Lots of very expensive diamond and gold shops along the seafront, aimed at the US cruises arriving daily from Miami. Souvenirs are more expensive than Playa del Carmen, with pushy sales staff.

Sport
See Cenote diving, page 533

Scuba diving The island is famous for the beauty of its underwater environment. The best reef for scuba diving is **Palancar**, reached only by boat. Also highly recommended are **Santa Rosa** and **Colombia**. For more experienced divers the reefs at **Punta Sur**, **Maracaibo** and **Baracuda** should not to be missed. There are at least 20 major dive sites. Almost all Cozumel diving is drift diving, so if you are not used to a current, choose an operator you feel comfortable with. There are 2 different types of dive centre: the larger ones, where the divers are taken out to sea in big boats with many passengers; the smaller, more personalised dive shops, with a maximum of 8 people per small boat. The best of the smaller centres is said to be *Deep Blue*, A R Salas 200, esq Av 10 Sur, T/F872-5653, www.deepbluecozumel.com Matt and Deborah, an English/Colombian couple, run the centre. All PADI and NAUI certifications, eg Open Water Diver US$360; 3-5-day dive packages US$165-250; cavern and *cenote* diving, including 2 dives, transport and lunch US$130. Other small dive centres are: *Black Shark*, Av 5 between A R Salas and Calle 3 Sur, T/F872-5657. *Diving Adventures*, Calle 5 No 2, T872-3009. *Blue Bubble Divers*, Av 5 Sur, esq Calle 3, T872-1865. Cozumel has 3 **decompression centres**: *Buceo Médico Mexicano*, Calle 5 Sur No 21B, T872-2387, immediate localization (24-hr) VHF 16 and 21. It is suported by US$1 per day donations from divers with affiliated operators. *Cozumel Hyperbarics* in Clínica San Miguel, Calle 6 Nte No 135 between Av 5 and Av 10, T872-3070, VHF channel 65. *Nachicocom*, T872-1430. A new one on the seafront and Calle 5 Sur.

Transport
There is no bus service, but taxis are plentiful. The best way to get around the island is by hired moped or bicycle. Mopeds cost US$25-30 per day, credit card needed as deposit; bicycles are around US$8 per day, US$20 cash or TC deposit. *Rentadora Cozumel*, Av 10 Sur No 172 between A R Salas y Calle 1 Sur, T872-1120. *Splash*, Calle 6 Nte, T872-3977. **Car rental** There are many agencies, including *Less Pay*, in Hotel Barracuda (see under Sleeping) T872-4744. *Budget Jeep and Auto*, Av 5 y Calle 2, T872-0903. *Aguila jeep and Moto*, Calle 11 No 101, T872-0729.

Yucatán Peninsula

Air Cozumel-Mexico City direct with Mexicana, or via Cancún; Continental to Houston; Aerocaribe to Cancún and Chichén Itzá. Aerocaribe and Aerocozumel have almost hourly flights to Cancún.

Directory **Airline offices** Most are based at the airport, 2 km north of the town. Aerocozumel T872-3456. Continental T872-0847. Mexicana, P Joaquin between A R Salas and Calle 3 Sur, next to Pemex, T872-0263. **Banks** 4 banks on the main square, all exchange money in morning only, but not at same hours: *Bital*, on Juárez (all with ATM machines), *Bancomer*, *Banamex*, *Atlántico*. *Casas de cambio* on Av 5 Nte and around square, 3.5% commission, open longer hours. **Communications** Internet: several internet cafés set up recently charging around US$1.50/hr. **Laundry** *Express*, A R Salas between Av 5 and Av 10, T872-3655. Coin-op and service washes, US$9 medium load, collection service and dry cleaning. **Post office:** Av Rafael Melgar y Calle 7 Sur, Mon-Fri 0900-1800, Sat 0900-1200. **Telephone:** Ladatel phones on main square at corner of Av Juárez and Av 5, or on A R Salas, just up from Av 5 Sur, opposite *Roberto's Black Coral Studio* (if working). For calls to the US, go to *The Stadium*. Telmex phone offices on the main square next to *Restaurant Plaza Leza*, 0800-2300, and on A R Salas between Av 10 and 15. There are also expensive Computel offices in town, eg at the cruise ship dock. Telephone centre for long distance on corner of Rafael Melgar and Calle 3 Sur. Also public telephone *caseta* at Av 5 esq Calle 2, 0800-1300, 1600-2100. **Medical services** Hospitals: *Red Cross*, A R Salas between Calle 20 and Calle 25 Sur, T872-1058. *Centro Médico de Cozumel*, Calle 1 Sur No 101, esq Av 50, T872-3545. English spoken, international air ambulance, 24-hr emergency service. *Pharmacy*, A R Salas between Av 12 and Av 20. Open 0700-2400. **Dentists:** Dr Hernández, T872-0656. **Tour operators** *Ferinco Travel Tours*, T872-1781. Own airline with flights to all major Maya sites.

Playa del Carmen to Tulum

Xcaret Back on the mainland, there are some Maya ruins at Xcaret, a turn-off left on Route 307 to Tulum, after Playa del Carmen. The Maya site, an ancient port called Polé, was the departure point for voyages to Cozumel. It has now been turned into an overpriced and very tacky theme park catering exclusively for day-trippers. ■ *US$37, children under 5 free.* This entry fee entitles you to visit the small ruins, the aviary, the beach, lagoon and inlet, to take an underground river trip (life vest included) and to use all chairs, hammocks and *palapas*. Everything else is extra: food and drink (none may be brought in), snorkel rental (US$7), snorkel lessons, reef trips (US$10), diving, horse-riding (US$30) and lockers (for which you have to pay US$1 each time you lock the door). There are also dolphins in pens; you don't actually swim with them, rather they jump or pass over you (US$50). No suntan lotion may be worn in the sea, but there is a film of oils in the sea nonetheless. Buses from Playa del Carmen leave you at the turn-off (US$0.65), by a roadside restaurant that is very clean. There is a 1 km walk from the entrance to Xcaret. The alternative is to take a taxi, or a tour from Playa del Carmen or Cancún (in a multicoloured bus). You can also walk along the beach from Playa del Carmen, three hours.

Paamul, just south of Playa del Carmen and about 92 km south of Cancún, is a fine beach on a bay, planned for development, with chalets (**C** with bath, fan, terrace for hammocks, comfortable, pretty, clean, recommended) and campsites (recommended). There is snorkelling and diving and a reef a few metres off shore. Second class buses from Cancún and Playa del Carmen pass.

Akumal
Colour map 4, grid A3

A luxury resort, 102 km south of Cancún, 20 km north of Tulum, Akumal is reached easily by bus from there or from Playa del Carmen (30 minutes). There is a small lagoon 3 km north of Akumal, good snorkelling. The coastline from Playa del Carmen down to just short of Tulum to the south is known as the 'Riviera Maya' – a strip of upmarket, generally all-inclusive hotels.

Sleeping and eating **L** *Hotel Club Akumal Caribe.* One of many luxury hotels, villas and condos, which can be booked in the US through *Caribbean Fantasy*, PO Box 7606, Loveland, Colorado 80537-0606, caribbfan@aol.com, accommodation is all **LL-AL** *Playa Aventuras* is a huge beach resort south of Akumal. **LL** *Club Puerto Aventuras*, sandwiched between the sea and marina, all-inclusive with 309 rooms. Two ferries run daily to Cozumel.

Also just south of Akumal are **Chemuyil** (*palapas*, thatched shelters for hammocks, US$4, free shower, expensive restaurant, laundry facilities) and **Xcacel** (campground has water, bathrooms, cold showers and restaurant, very clean, US$2 per person, vehicles free, snorkel hire US$5 a day, beautiful swimming in the bay). Ask guards if you can go on turtle protection patrol at night (May-July).

Laguna Xel-Há

Thirteen kilometres north of Tulum, 122 km from Cancún (bus from Playa del Carmen, 45 minutes), this beautiful clear lagoon is full of fish, but fishing is not allowed as it is a National Park. ■ *0800-1630, US$10*. Snorkelling gear can be rented at US$7 for a day, but it is often in poor repair; better to rent from your hotel. Lockers cost US$1. Arrive as early as possible to see fish as the lagoon is full of tourists throughout most of the day. Snorkelling areas are limited by fencing.Bungalows, first-class hotels and fast-food restaurants are being built. The food and drink is very expensive. There is a marvellous jungle path to one of the lagoon bays. Xel-Há ruins (known also as **Los Basadres**) are located across the road from the beach of the same name. ■ *US$3.35*. Few tourists but not much to see. You may have to jump the fence to visit; there is a beautiful *cenote* at the end of the ruins where you can have a lovely swim. Small ruins of **Ak** are near Xel-Há. Closer to Tulum, at **Tancáh**, are newly discovered bright post-Classical Maya murals, but they are sometimes closed to the public.

Tulum

Colour map 4, grid A3

The Tulum ruins, Maya-Toltec, are 131 km south of Cancún, 1 km off the main road. They are 12th century, with city walls of white stone atop coastal cliffs. The temples were dedicated to the worship of the Falling God, or the Setting Sun, represented as a falling character over nearly all the west-facing doors (Cozumel was the home of the Rising Sun). The same idea is reflected in the buildings, which are wider at the top than at the bottom.

The main structure is the **Castillo**, which commands a view of both the sea and the forested Quintana Roo lowlands stretching westwards. All the Castillo's openings face west, as do most, but not all, of the doorways at Tulum. Look for the alignment of the **Falling God** on the temple of that name (to the left of the Castillo) with the pillar and the back door in the **House of the Chultún** (the nearest building in the centre group to the entrance). The majority of the main structures are roped off so that you cannot climb the Castillo, nor get close to the surviving frescoes, especially on the **Temple of the Frescoes**.

Tulum is crowded with tourists (best time to visit is between 0800 and 0900). Take towel and swimsuit if you wish to scramble down from the ruins to one of the two beaches for a swim (the larger of the two is less easy to get to). The reef is from 600 m to 1,000 m from the shore, so if you wish to snorkel you must either be a strong swimmer, or take a boat trip. ■ *The site is open 0800-1700, entry US$3, parking US$1.50, students with Mexican ID free, Sun free*. There is a tourist complex at the entrance to the ruins. Guide books can be bought in the shops; the *Panorama* guide book is interesting; others are available. Local guides can also be hired. About two hours are needed to view at leisure. The parking area is near Highway 307, and there's a handicraft market. A small train takes you from the parking area to the ruins for US$1, or it is an easy 500 m walk. The paved road continues down the coast to **Boca Paila** and beyond, access by car to this road from the car park is now forbidden. To reach the road south of the ruins, access is possible 1 km from Tulum village.

Public buses drop passengers at El Crucero, a crossroads 500 m north of the car park for Tulum Ruinas (an easy walk) where there is an *ADO* bus terminal that opens for a few hours at 0800; at the crossroads are some hotels, a shop (will exchange travellers' cheques), on the opposite side of the road a naval base and airstrip, and a little way down Highway 307 a Pemex station. The village of **Tulum** is 4 km south of El Crucero. A taxi from the village to the ruins costs US$2.50. It is not very large but is growing rapidly and has a bus station, post office, bank (Bital); there are five to six grocery shops, two *panaderías*, a hotel and restaurants.

There is a **tourist information office** in the village, next to the police station, two blocks north of the bus terminal. The information centre set up by the *Weary Traveller* backpacker centre has taken over as the primary source of information for this area. Located at the southern end of town a block away from the *ADO* bus terminal. Friendly and knowledgeable staff give fairly impartial information on hotels, excursions and restaurants.

Also try the **Sian Ka'an Information Centre** in Tulum (Av Tulum between Satélite and Géminis), T/F871-2363, siankaan_tours@hotmail.com, which has information about visiting the reserve and several other areas of interest.

Sleeping & eating
When arriving by bus, get off at El Crucero for the ruins and nearby accommodation

At El Crucero **C** *Riviera Maya*. TV, a/c, OK, restaurant serving pizzas, Mexican dishes and very expensive drinks. Almost opposite bus stop is a new hotel, **C**, large, clean, a/c, parking, with restaurant (24 hours), good food and service.

At Tulum village Many new hotels and restaurants have sprung up turning Tulum Av into a lively spot, and worth a visit on any stay, and new budget accommodation makes it a good choice for backpackers. The only limitation is the mafia-like control of public transport by the strong taxi union. This means there are no public buses to the beach, a taxi will cost you US$3.50 or more. Along Tulum Av.

B-C *Chilam-Balam*, central, T871-2042. Restaurant serves good food. **C** *L'Hotel*, 1 block north of bus stop. A/c or fan, hot showers, new and clean.

D-E *Hotel Maya*, near bus stop, T871-1234. Fan, shower, reasonable, restaurant with slow service, small shop, parking in front. **D-E** *Rancho Tranquilo*, far south end of town. Cabañas, nice setting, quiet as the name suggests.

Good budget options are opening up including **E-F** *Papaya Playa*, has a few bungalows next to the beach. No hot water but good food and a lively bar in the evenings. **F** *Cabañas Diana*, has small bungalows and showers. **F** *Weary Traveller Hostel*, 1 block south of *ADO*. Bus terminal, backpackers' hostel, good meeting place, price includes basic breakfast and dinner, bunk rooms with comfy beds, book exchange, information centre, internet (US$2.5/hr).

Several chicken restaurants along Tulum Av, working from south to north. *Doña Tinas*, good basic and cheap, in a grass hut at southern end of town. *El Mariachi*, taco bar with good fajitas, cheap. *Bistro Nocturne*, Tex-Mex food, very good value dining, nice décor (check out the bones on the ceiling above the bar). Recommended. *El Tacontento*, 2 blocks north of *ADO* station. Good basic Mexican, cheap tacos. *París de Noche*, French-Mexican food, lobster, outside garden setting, mid-range good value.

Cabañas To reach the following accommodation it is better to get off the bus in town and take a taxi (US$3-5 depending on season), otherwise ½-hr walk from the bus stop. In high season cabañas are difficult to get. Establishments are listed according to proximity to the ruins (see map); **E-F** *Cabañas El Mirador*. Small, quiet, cabins (won't rent to singles), hammocks available, camping, 2 showers, use of restaurant toilets (clean), bar and restaurant with excellent views, 10 mins' walk from ruins; next is **E** *Santa Fe*. Basic cabañas, T880-5854, new toilets and showers but only 4 and 2 of each, US$1 extra for mosquito net, hammocks or tents, water problems, reported insecure, watch your belongings, has a restaurant, good breakfasts and fish dinners, reggae music, English, French and Italian spoken, basic toilets, laid-back atmosphere, but cheaper cabins are badly constructed and lack privacy, free camping possible further up the beach. **C-D** *Cabañas Don Armando*, T871-2743. Cabañas for up to 4, prices variable, the best, very popular, staff are friendly and helpful, cheap but limited restaurant with long queues, bar with noisy disco till 0200, certain bus tickets available. **E** *Cabañas Mar Caribe*. Smaller complex than its neighbour *Don Armando*, but a friendly atmosphere, and much more peaceful. **A** *El Paraíso*, beach club and cabañas, beautiful beach with bar, good restaurant, dive and snorkel shop. Recommended. Small beachside restaurant. **B** *Cabañas Diamante K*, on the beach, T871-2283. Rustic with nice bar and restaurant, with hints of the Crystal Maze.

Cenote diving

There are over 50 cenotes in this area, accessible from Ruta 307 and often well signposted, and cave diving has become very popular. However, it is a specialized sport and, unless you have a cave diving qualification, you must be accompanied by a qualified dive master. A cave diving course involves over 12 hours of lectures and a minimum of 14 cave dives using double tanks, costing around US$600. Specialist dive centres offering courses are: **Mike Madden's CEDAM Dive Centres**, *PO Box 1, Puerto Aventuras, T/F873-5129, mmadden@cancun.rce.com.mx;* **Aquatech**, *Villas de Rosa, PO Box 25, Aventuras Akumal No 35, Tulum, T875-9020, www.cenotes.com;*

Akumal Dive Centre, PO Box 1, Akumal, Playa del Carmen. The above have a 100% safety record. Other operators include **Yax-Há Dive Centre**, **Akumal Explorers**, *and* **Dos Ojos (Divers of the Hidden World)**. *Some of the best cenotes are 'Carwash', on the Cobá road, good even for beginners, with excellent visibility; 'Dos Ojos', just off Ruta 307 south of Aventuras, the second largest underground cave system in the world; it has a possible link to the Nohoch Nah Chich, the most famous cenote and part of a subterranean system recorded as the world's largest, with over 50 km of surveyed passageways connected to the sea.*

Recommended. **AL** *La Conchita*, colourful and tasteful décor, with sea-shell floors in a long-house design. Beautiful, recommended restaurant. **AL** *Posada del Sol*. On other side of the road. Four rooms with terrace, hot water. **B-D** *Nohoch Tunich*, 1-hr walk from ruins. Clean cabañas, good food; near the cabaña resort are exchange facilities, dive shop and 2 bike rental shops. **AL-A** *Piedra Escondida*. Modern, 2-storey thatched cabañas.

D-E *La Perla*, 5 km south of Tulum. Cabañas, camping and restaurant, comfortable, good food, family atmosphere, near beach. Recommended. **D** *Hemingways*, various types of cabañas, good value. **L** *Posada Margherita*, T876-3072, www.posadamargherita.com Well-designed hotel with complete wheelchair access, runs scuba courses for handicapped. Good Italian restaurant. Recommended. **A** *Los Arrecifes*, T879-7307, cabañas, live music and shows, restaurant. **A** *Anna y José*, restaurant, 6 km south of ruins, T887-5470. Also has cabañas and rooms, some are right on the beach, with pool, very clean, comfortable and hospitable. Trips can be arranged to the Sian Ka'an Biosphere Reserve (see page 536). Recommended. **B** *Cabañas Tulum*. Solid stone cabañas near the beach, bar and restaurant, electricity till 2200.

E *Tita Tulum*. Eco hotel, with bath; taxi to Tulum, US$3-5. **F** *Playa Selva*. Camping, can rent tents US$5, kitchen facilities, good value. **AL** *Dos Ceibas*, 9 km from the ruins. Luxury cabins on the edge of the Sian Ka'an Biosphere Reserve. **A** *Tierra del Sol*. Rustic cabañas, with bath, quiet, double beds with mosquito nets, good French restaurant, last place before Sian Ka'an Bioshere Reserve.

For places to stay in Sian Ka'an Biosphere Reserve, see page 536

Diving Several dive shops all along the Tulum corridor. See page 533 for cave diving opera- **Sports** tors and specialist courses. Many untrained snorkelling and diving outfits, take care. *Aktun*, next to *Hotel El Mesón*, 1 km out of Tulum on main road, T871-2311, www.aktundive.com, German/Mexican-run, experienced NACD and IANTD instructor, very friendly, speaks English, French and Dutch. *Hidden World's Cenotes*, at Dos Ojos caverns (largest in the world), T877-8535, www.hiddenworlds.com.mx Only technical fill station in Tulum, snorkel (US$40) diving trips (from US$50), several trips a day.

Buses 2nd class buses on the Cancún-Playa del Carmen-Felipe Carrillo Puerto-Chetumal **Transport** route stop at Tulum. Some buses may be full when they reach Tulum; very few buses begin their journeys here. **Felipe Carrillo Puerto**: several between 0600-1200 and 1600-2200, 1 hr, US$4.70, continuing to **Chetumal**: 4 hrs, 2nd class, US$10, 1st class US$12. For **Cobá**: take the Playa del Carmen-Tulum- Cobá-Valladolid bus which passes El Crucero at 0600, 1100 and 1800 (in the other direction buses pass Tulum at 0715 and 1545, all times approximate, may leave 15 mins early). **Tulum-Cobá**: US$1.35, 45 mins. **Mérida**: several daily, 6 hrs, US$10, 2nd class.

Yucatán Peninsula

Tizimín: daily at 1400, via Cancún and Valladolid. **Escárcega** and **Córdoba:** 0800, **Palenque** US$34. **San Cristóbal:** 1845, often late, US$45. **Villahermosa**: 1630, 2100, US$35. **Mexico City:** 0815, 1315, 2100, US$85. Autobuses del Caribe offices are next door to *Hotel Maya*. Buy tickets here rather than wait for buses at the crossroads, but this still does not ensure getting a seat. It may be better to go to Playa del Carmen (US$1.40) for more connections to nearby destinations. If travelling far, take a bus to Felipe Carrillo Puerto and transfer to *ADO* there.

Taxis Tulum town to ruins US$3.50; to the cabañas US$3.50; to Cobá about US$25.

Bicycles can be hired in the village at US$1 per hr, a good way to visit local centres (*Cristal* and *Escondido* are recommended as much cheaper, US$2, and less commercialized than *Xcaret*).

Directory **Banks** 4 money exchange booths near bus station in Tulum village. TCs can be changed at the offices of the GOPI Construction Company, though not at a very good rate. **Communications** **Telephone:** long-distance phones in *ADO* terminal in town; also fax office, F9871-2009 and bike rental.

Cobá
Colour map 4, grid A3

An important Maya city in the eighth and ninth centuries AD, whose population is estimated to have been between 40,000 and 50,000, Cobá was abandoned for unknown reasons. The present-day village of Cobá lies on either side of Lago Cobá, surrounded by dense jungle, 47 km inland from Tulum. It is a quiet friendly village, with few tourists staying overnight.

The entrance to the ruins of this large but little-excavated city is at the end of the lake between the two parts of the village. A second lake, **Lago Macanxoc**, is within the site. There are turtles and many fish in the lakes. It is a good bird-watching area. Both lakes and their surrounding forest can be seen from the summit of the **Iglesia**, the tallest structure in the **Cobá Group**. There are three other groups of buildings to visit: the **Macanxoc Group**, mainly stelae, about 1½ km from the Cobá Group; **Las Pinturas**, 1 km northeast of Macanxoc, with a temple and the remains of other buildings that had columns in their construction; the **Nohoch Mul Group**, at least another kilometre from Las Pinturas. Nohoch Mul has the tallest pyramid in the northern Yucatán, a magnificent structure, from which the views of the jungle on all sides are superb. You will not find at Cobá the great array of buildings that can be seen at Chichén Itzá or Uxmal, nor the compactness of Tulum. Instead, the delight of the place is the architecture in the jungle, with birds, butterflies, spiders and lizards, and the many uncovered structures that hint at the vastness of the city in its heyday (the urban extension of Cobá is put at some 70 sq km). An unusual feature is the network of ancient roads, known as *sacbés* (white roads), which connect the groups in the site and are known to have extended across the entire Maya Yucatán. Over 40 *sacbés* pass through Cobá, some local, some of great length, such as the 100 km road to Yaxuná in Yucatán state.

At the lake, toucans may be seen very early; also look out for greenish-blue and brown mot-mots in the early morning. The guards at the site are very strict about opening and closing time so it is difficult to gain entry to see the dawn or sunset from a temple.

The paved road into Cobá ends at **Lago Cobá**; to the left are the ruins, to the right *Villas Arqueológicas*. The roads around Cobá are badly potholed. Cobá is becoming more popular as a destination for tourist buses, which come in at 1030; arrive before that to avoid the crowds and the heat (ie on the 0430 bus from Valladolid, if not staying in Cobá). Take insect repellent. ■ *0800-1700, US$2.50, free on Sunday*. Guide books: Bloomgarten's *Tulum and Cobá*, and *Descriptive Guide Book to Cobá* by Prof Gualberto Zapata Alonzo, which is a little unclear about dates and details, but is still useful and has maps. Free map from *Hotel Restaurant Bocadito*.

Sleeping **B** *Villas Arqueológicas* (Club Méditerranée), about 2 km from site on lake shore. Open to non-members, excellent, clean and quiet, a/c, swimming pool, good restaurant with moderate prices, but expensive beer. Do not arrive without a reservation, especially at weekends; on the other hand, making a reservation by phone seems to be practically impossible. In the village, on the street leading to the main road, is **E** *Hotel Restaurant El Bocadito*. Run-down, spartan rooms with fan, intermittent water supply, poor security, good but expensive restaurant (which is popular with tour groups), books and handicrafts for sale. Recommended.

There are plenty of restaurants in the village, on the road to *Villas Arqueológicas* and on the road to the ruins, they are all quite pricey; also a grocery store by *El Bocadito* and souvenir

Eating

Tulum to Chetumal

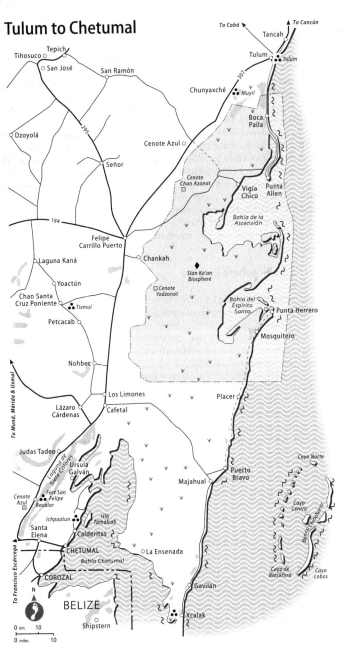

To Cobá
To Cancún
Tancah
Tihosuco
Tepich
San José
San Ramón
Tulum
Tulum
307
Chunyaxché
Muyil
Boca Paila
Dzoyolá
Cenote Azul
Cenote Chan Azonot
Vigía Chico
Punta Allen
Señor
Bahía de la Ascensión
184
Felipe Carrillo Puerto
Chankah
Sian Ka'an Biosphere
Laguna Kaná
Yoactún
Cenote Yodzonot
Chan Santa Cruz Poniente
Tixmul
Bahía del Espíritu Santo
Punta Herrero
Petcacab
Mosquitero
Nohbec
Los Limones
Placer
Lázaro Cárdenas
Cafetal
Judas Tadeo
Laguna de Siete Colores
Úrsula Galván
Cayo Norte
Cenote Azul
Fort San Felipe
Bacalar
Majahual
Puerto Bravo
Ichpaatun
Isla Tamalcab
Cayo Centro
Banco Chinchorro
Santa Elena
Calderitas
CHETUMAL
Bahía Chetumal
La Ensenada
COROZAL
Gavilán
Cayo de Blackford
Cayo Lobos
BELIZE
N
Xcalak
0 km   10
Shipstern
0 miles   10

To Muná, Mérida & Uxmal

To Francisco Escárcega

Yucatán Peninsula

shops. *Nicte-Ha*, good and friendly. *Pirámides*, on corner of track leading to *Villas Arqueológicas*. Highly recommended.

Transport **Local** Buses into the village turn round at the road end. There are 3 a day to Valladolid, coming from Playa del Carmen and Tulum, passing through at 0630, 1130 and 1830, 2 hrs to Valladolid, US$2.50; 2 buses a day to Tulum and Playa at 0630 and 1500, US$1 to Tulum. A taxi to Tulum costs around US$25. If you miss the bus there is a taxi to be found at *El Bocadito*.

Directory **Banks** *Sterling Store*, opposite entrance to ruins.

Cobá via Nuevo Xcan The road linking Tulum with Cobá turns off the main Highway 307 just before Tulum town. This road joins the *vía libre* Valladolid-Cancún road at **Nuevo Xcan**, thus greatly shortening the distance between Chichén Itzá and Tulum (do not take the *cuota* road, which no longer exits at Nuevo Xcan). The Cobá-Valladolid bus passes Nuevo Xcan (no hotel but the owner of the shop where the road branches off to Cobá may offer you a room). There is an *aduana* post in Nuevo Xcan, which is at the border between Yucatán and Quintana Roo states; police searches are made for on leaving Quintana Roo for items that may transmit plant and other diseases. If going from Valladolid or Cancún to Cobá, follow the *Villas Arqueológicas* sign at Nuevo Xcan. **NB** Many maps show a road from Cobá to Chemax, west of Xcan. This road does not exist; the only road from the north to Cobá is from Nuevo Xcan. For drivers, there is no Pemex station between Cancún and Valladolid, or Cancún-Cobá-Tulum, or Valladolid-Cobá-Tulum; all are journeys of 150 km without a fill-up.

Between Nuevo Xcan and Cobá is the tiny village of **Punta Laguna**, which has a lake and forest, preserved through the efforts of ecotourists. Ask for Serapio to show you round.

Sian Ka'an Biosphere Reserve

Colour map 4, grid A3 The Reserve covers 4,500 sq km of the Quintana Roo coast. About one-third is covered in tropical forest, one-third is savannah and mangrove and one-third coastal and marine habitats, including 110 km of barrier reef. Mammals include jaguar, puma, ocelot and other cats, monkeys, tapir, peccaries, manatee and deer; turtles nest on the beaches; there are crocodiles and a wide variety of land and aquatic birds. For all information, go to the office of Los Amigos de Sian Ka'an, Plaza América, Avenida Cobá 5, 3rd floor, suites 48-50, Cancún (Apdo Postal 770, 77500 Cancún, T884-9583, sian@cancun.rce.com.mx); very heplul. ■ *0900-1500, 1800-2000.* Do not try to get there independently without a car. *Ecocolors*, Cancún, T/F884-9580, in collaboration with Los Amigos, run tours to the Reserve, US$115 for a full day, starting at 0700, pick up at hotel, everything included: in winter the tour goes through a canal, in summer it goes bird-watching, in both cases a visit to a Maya ruin, a *cenote*, snorkelling, all equipment, breakfast and evening meal are included. Two-day camping trips can be arranged. Two-hour boat trips through the Biosphere can be taken for US$50. Trips can also be arranged through *Cabañas Ana y José*, near Tulum, US$50, daily except Sunday (see page 533). It is possible to drive into the Reserve from Tulum village as far as Punta Allen (58 km; the road is opposite the turning to Cobá; it is not clearly marked, and the final section is badly potholed); beyond that you need a launch. From the south it is possible to drive to Punta Herrero (unmade road, see **Majahual**, below). No explanations are available for those going independently.

Sleeping At **Punta Allen** is a small fishing village with houses for rent (cooking facilities), and a good, non-touristy restaurant, *La Cantina* (US$3-4 for fish). There are also 2 comfortable cabañas at a place called **A** *Rancho Sol Caribe*. With bath, restaurant. Recommended. Reservations to: Diane and Michael Sovereign, Apdo Postal 67, Tulum, CP 77780, T871-2091, F871-2092. **Punta Herrero** is 6 hrs from Chetumal, 10 hrs from Cancún; *rancheros* are very hospitable, camping is possible but take all food and plenty of insect repellent.

Yucatán Peninsula

In the Reserve, 8 km south of Tulum, are the quiet, pleasant **AL** *Cabañas Los Arrecifes*, with smart chalets on the beach and others behind, cheaper, with good fish restaurant shaped like a ship (no electricity), limited menu. 100 m away are **D** *Cabañas de Tulum*, also with good restaurant, clean cabins with shower, electricity 1730-2100; interesting fish in the *cenote* opposite, take taxi there (US$5-6 from ruins car park), empty white beaches. *Pez Maya* and *Boca Paila* are expensive fishing lodges. *Casa Blanca* is an exclusive hotel reached only by small plane. *Rancho Retiro*, camping US$2, food and beer served, very relaxed atmosphere.

The ruins of Muyil at **Chunyaxché**, three pyramids (partly overgrown), are on the left-hand side of the road to Felipe Carrillo Puerto, 18 km south of Tulum. One of the pyramids is undergoing reconstruction; the other two are relatively untouched. They are very quiet, with interesting birdlife although they are mosquito-infested. ■ *US$4*. Beyond the last pyramid is Laguna Azul, which is good for swimming and snorkelling in blue, clean water (you do not have to pay to visit the pool if you do not visit the pyramids).

Muyil

The cult of the 'talking cross' was founded here. The Santuario de la Cruz Parlante is five blocks west of the Pemex station on Highway 307. The beautiful main square, which has playground equipment for children, is dominated by the Catholic church, built by the Cruzob in the 19th century (see page 469). Legend has it that the unfinished bell tower will only be completed when the descendants of those who heard the talking cross reassert control of the region.

Felipe Carrillo Puerto
Colour map 4, grid A3

Sleeping and eating *Hotel Carrillo Puerto* has been recommended. **C** *El Faisán y El Venado*, 2 blocks northeast of main square. Mixed reports on cleanliness, but hot water and good-value restaurant, popular with locals. **D** *San Ignacio*, near Pemex. Good value, a/c, bath, towels, TV, secure car park; next door is restaurant *Danburger Maya*. Good food, reasonable prices, helpful. **D** *Tulum*, with better restaurant. **E** *Chan Santa Cruz*, just off the plaza. Good, basic, clean and friendly (*Restaurante 24 Horas* is open 24 hrs, OK). **E** *Hotel Esquivel*, just off plaza. Fair, noisy. **F** *María Isabel*, on same road. Clean, friendly, laundry service, quiet, safe parking. *Restaurant Addy*, on main road, south of town. Good, simple. There are a few food shops in the village selling sweet breads, and mineral water.

Transport Bus station opposite Pemex. *Autotransportes del Caribe* (*Playa Express*) to **Cancún** daily from 0600, 1st and 2nd class to **Tulum**, US$2, and **Playa del Carmen** *en route*. Bus Felipe Carrillo **Puerto-Mérida**, via Muná, US$10, 4½ hrs; to **Valladolid**, 2nd class, 2 hrs, US$3.75; to **Chetumal**, 1st class, 2 hrs, US$3.35.

Further south on Route 307, at Cafetal, is an unpaved road east to Majahual on the coast (56 km from Cafetal), a peaceful, unspoilt place with clear water and beautiful beaches. A combi from the bus terminal next to *Hotel Ucum* in Chetumal at 0600, returns 1300. Accommodation at *Restaurant Los Piratas del Caribe*. It is owned by a French family, simple rooms without bath, excellent restaurant, inexpensive. Excursion possible to **Banco Chinchorro** offshore, where there is a coral bank and a white sandy beach.

Majahual

About 2 km before Majahual a paved road to the left goes to **Puerto Bravo** and on to Placer and **Punta Herrero** (in the Sian Ka'an Biosphere Reserve, see above). Just over 3 km along this road a right turn goes to the *Sol y Mar* restaurant, with rooms to rent, bathrooms and spaces for RVs, also coconut palms and beach. Another 10½ km along the Punta Herrero road, again on the right, is *Camidas Trailer Park*, with palm trees, *palapas*, restaurant and restrooms, space for four RVs, US$5 per person, car free.

Across the bay from Chetumal, at the very tip of Quintana Roo, is Xcalak, which may be reached from Chetumal by private launch (two hours), or by the unpaved road from Cafetal to Majahual, then turning south for 55 km (186 km by road from

Xcalak
Colour map 4, grid B3
Population: 250

Yucatán Peninsula

Chetumal, suitable for passenger cars but needs skilled driver). Daily colectivos from Chetumal, 0700-1900, 16 de Septiembre 183 y Mahatma Ghandi, check return times. Bus runs Friday 1600 and Sunday 0600, returning Saturday morning and Sunday afternoon (details from Chetumal tourist office). Xcalak is a fishing village with a few shops selling beer and basic supplies and one small restaurant serving Mexican food. A few kilometres north of Xcalak are two hotels, *Costa de Cocos* and *Villa Caracol*, both American-run; the latter is good, with comfortable cabañas, though expensive. From here trips can be arranged to the unspoiled islands of Banco Chinchorro or to San Pedro, Belize. *Villa Caracol* has sport fishing and diving facilities. In the village you may be able to rent a boat to explore Chetumal Bay and Banco Chinchorro. Do *not* try to walk from Xcalak along the coast to San Pedro, Belize; the route is virtually impassable.

Chetumal

Phone code: 983
Colour map 4, grid B3
Population: 120,000

State capital of Quintana Roo, Chetumal is a necessary stopover for travellers en route to Maya sites in the south of the peninsula, and across the frontier to Belize and Guatemala. Though tourist attractions are thin on the ground, Chetumal does have the advantage of being a small Mexican city not devoted to tourism, and therefore has a more authentic feel than most other towns on the Riviera Maya. It is 240 km south of Tulum. The Chetumal Bay has been designated a Natural Protected Area for manatees, and includes a manatee sanctuary.

The avenues are broad, busy and in the centre lined with huge shops selling cheap imported goods. The main local activity is window-shopping, and the atmosphere is more like a North American city, with an impression of affluence that can be a culture shock to the visitor arriving from the much poorer country of Guatemala. The **tourist offices** at Avenida Miguel Hidalgo 22, 1st floor, esq Carmen Ochoa de Merino, is mainly for trade enquiries. There is very little tourist information in Chetumal; it is usually best to go to a travel agent such as *Tu-Maya* (see below).

Sights

The *paseo* near the waterfront on Sunday night is worth seeing. The State Congress building has a mural showing the history of Quintana Roo. The **Museo de la Cultura Maya**, on Avenida Héroes de Chapultepec by the market, has good models of sites and touchscreen computers explaining the Mayan calendar and glyphs. Although there are few original Maya pieces, it gives an excellent overview; some explanations are in English, guided tours available, and there's a good bookshop with English magazines. ■ *Tue-Thu 0900-1900, Fri and Sat 0900-2000, Sun 0900-1400, US$1.50. Cold a/c. Highly recommended.*

Sleeping
■ *on map*

A *El Marqués*, Av Lázaro Cárdenas 121, T832-2998, 5 blocks from centre. Fan, a/c, hot water, restaurant. Recommended. **AL** *Los Cocos*, Héroes de Chapultepec 138, T832-0544, F832-0920. Reductions for AAA members, a/c, pool, restaurant. Recommended. **C** *Real Azteca*, Belice 186, T832-0720. Cheerful, friendly, but no hot shower. 2nd floor rooms best, but still not too good. **B** *Príncipe*, Av Héroes 326, T832-4799. Clean, a/c, TV, pool and parking. A bit run down, but good for the price. **C** *Caribe Princess*, Av Obregón 168, T832-0520. A/c, TV, good, very clean, no restaurant. Recommended. **C** *Ucum*, Gandhi 4, T832-0711. A/c, fan, bath, pleasant, quiet (rooms away from street), expensive laundry, parking in enclosed car park included in price, good value, restaurant next door recommended for *ceviche*. **C-D** *Jacaranda*, Av Obregón 201, T832-1455. Clean, good, bath, safe parking. **C-D** *El Dorado*, Av 5 de Mayo 42, T832-0315. Hot water, a/c, very friendly, quiet. Recommended. **E** *Big Ben*, Héroes 48-A, T832-0965. Clean, shabby, safe, cheaper rooms for 4, with bath. Arabic restaurant downstairs. **E** *Motel Casablanca*, Alvaro Obregón 312. Clean, quiet, very good value. Recommended. **E** *Crystal*, Colón y Av Belice. Fan, bath, parking. **E** *María Dolores*, Alvaro Obregón 206, T832-0508. Bath, hot water, fan, clean, windows don't open, noisy, restaurant *Solsimar* downstairs good and popular. Recommended. **E** *Tulum*, Héroes 2, T832-0518, above market. The noise starts 0530, but clean, with bath and fan, friendly, large rooms. **E-F** *Cuartos Margot*, 5 de Mayo 30. Some with bath, clean, charming. **F** *Ejidal*, Av Independencia between Obregón and Othón P Blanco. With bath, clean. Recommended. Plenty more.

Camping *Sunrise of the Caribbean*, Trailer Park on the road to Calderitas. US$15 for car and 2 people, cold showers, electricity, laundry facilities, *palapas*, boat ramp.

Youth hostel Calzada Veracruz y Alvaro Obregón, referred to as CREA, T832-3465, CP 77050. Hot water, clean, run down, friendly, good breakfast, camping US$2. Recommended.

Chicho's Lobster House, Blvd Bahía esq Vicente Guerrero, T832-7249. Expensive but good **Eating** seafood, friendly. *Bambino Pizzas*, Othón P Blanco 215. Good. *Hotel Los Cocos*, Good breakfasts, US$5. *Lonchería Ivette* on Mahatma Gandhi 154. Cheap snacks. *Mar Caribe*, 22 de Enero between Madero and Independencia, snacks only. *Pandoja*, Gandhi y 16 de Septiembre. Good food. *Sergio Pizza*, Obregón 182. Pizzas, fish, and expensive steak meals, a/c, good drinks, excellent service. Several places a block west of intersection of Héroes and Obregón, eg *Bienvenidos*, good. *Arcada*, Héroes y Zaragoza, open 24 hrs, with mini-market at the back. *El Vaticano*. Popular with locals, good atmosphere, cheap. *Solsimar*, Obregón 206 (closed Sun). Popular, reasonable prices. Another area with many restaurants is about 4 blocks north of market, then 3 blocks west, eg *Barracuda*, good seafood. Good juices at *Jugos Xamach*, corner of Salvador y Quintana Roo, friendly local spot. *Pacho Tec*, small lunch room next to electricity plant, try the chicken broth. Delicious yoghurt ice in shop opposite market. Cheap meals in the market at the top of Av Héroes, but the service is not too good and tourists will be stared at a lot.

Chetumal

■ Sleeping
1 Big Ben
2 Caribe Princess
3 Crystal
4 El Dorado
5 Jacaranda
6 Los Cocos
7 María Dolores
8 Real Azteca
9 Tulum
10 Ucum

Entertainment Try *Safari* roadhouse in Calderitas suburb for enterprising nightlife.

Shopping Shops are open from 0800-1300 and 1800-2000. Avenida Héroes is the main shopping street. Good for foreign foodstuffs - cheaper at the covered market in the outskirts than in the centre. A new commercial centre is being built at the site of the old bus station. *Super San Francisco* supermarket, near bus station, is better than the one behind *Arcada* restaurant.

Transport **Taxis** No city buses; taxis operate on fixed price routes, US$0.50 on average. Cars with light-green licence plates are a form of taxi. **Fuel** Petrol station just outside Chetumal on the road north at the beginning of the road to Escárcega, and another at Xpujil. **Garage** *Talleres Barrera*, helpful, on Primo de Verdad; turn east off Héroes, then past the electrical plant.

Air Airport (CTM) 2½ km from town. Flights to Cancún, Mérida, Belize City (*Aerocaribe*), Mexico City, Monterrey and Tijuana (*Aviacsa*, T872-7765).

Buses The main bus terminal is 3 km out of town at the instersection of Insurgentes y Belice. Modern. Taxi into town US$1.20. There is a bus into the centre from Av Belice. Left luggage lockers cost US$0.20 per hr. If buying tickets in advance, go to the *ADO* office on Av Belice esq Ghandi, 0800-1600. There are often more buses than those marked on the display in the bus station. Always ask at the information desk. Many buses going to the border, US$0.30; taxi from Chetumal to border, 20 mins, US$6 for 2. Long-distance buses are often all booked a day ahead, so avoid unbooked connections. Expect passport checks on buses leaving for Mexican destinations. **Mexico City**: *Autobuses del Caribe*, 1630 and 2100, 22 hrs, US$62. **Villahermosa**: 0800, 8 hrs, US$22, the road is bad and it can take longer; *ADO*, 3 per day. **Puebla**: US$58; **Escárcega**: 6 departures, 1300-2100, 4 hrs, US$12 1st class, US$11 2nd class. **Palenque**: *ADO*, 1st class at 2215, *Maya de Oro*, 1st class at 2200, 9 hrs, US$28, 2nd class at 2130, US$19, otherwise a change is necessary at Emiliano Zapata (bus at 0900, 1300, US$15), then change again at Catazajá, or to Catazajá itself (then take a colectivo), or Escárcega. **San Cristóbal**: *Maya de Oro* 1st class, 2300, US$39. *Lacandonia* has 2nd class bus to San Cristóbal via Palenque at 2130, US$27. **Tuxtla Gutiérrez**: *Maya de Oro*, 2300, US$42; *Cristóbal Colón*, 2115, US$36. **Mérida**: 4 per day, luxury US$18.30, US$21 1st class (*Caribe Express* and *Autobuses del Caribe*), about 7 hrs, 2nd class US$16. **Felipe Carrillo Puerto**, US$4, 1½ hrs, many daily, on excellent road. **Cancún**: 5½ hrs, boring road, 10 per day, 0630-0100, luxury US$31, 1st class US$27, 2nd class US$25. **Tulum**: several 2nd class from 0630, US$9, 1st class from 0700, 4 hrs, US$11. **Playa del Carmen**: 1st class US$13, 2nd class US$9. **Minatitlán**: 12 hrs, US$28. There are also buses to **Veracruz**, **Campeche**, **Villahermosa**, **Córdoba**, **Xpujil** and **Puerto Juárez**.

Colectivos to Bacalar and Francisco Villa (for Kohunlich and Xpujil) depart from the junction of Av Miguel Hidalgo and Francisco Primo de Verdad. Bacalar buses are very frequent (several per hr). To Francisco Villa (US$1.30) and Xpujil (US$4) at 1300 and 1600.

To **Belize**, *Batty Bus* from *ADO* to **Belize City**, 5 per day, schedules change frequently, taking 3½-5 hrs on paved road, US$7. Money-changers in the bus terminal offer marginally poorer rates than those at the border. Venus Bus to Belize City leaves from the square by Mercado Nuevo on Calzada Veracruz y 2° Circuito Periférico, 3 blocks from main terminal (US$1 taxi ride), morning departures, again frequent schedule changes, first bus leaves at 0600. Be there in good time; they sometimes leave early if full. If intending to stay in Belize City, do not take a bus that arrives at night as it is not recommended to look for a hotel in the dark. Bus **Orange Walk**, 2½ hrs, US$4.50. It is difficult to hitch to the Belizean border. To hitch once inside Belize, it is best to take the colectivo from in front of the hospital (1 block from the bus station, ask) marked 'Chetumal-Santa Elena', US$1. *San Juan Travel* at the main bus station has a direct daily service to **Flores** (US$30) and **Tikal** (US$33) in Guatemala, at 1430 from *ADO* terminal, 8 hrs to Flores, 6 hrs to Tikal.

Directory **Airline offices** Aerocaribe, Plaza Varudi, Av Héroes 125. **Banks** The banks all close at 1430. There are several ATMs. For exchange, *Banamex*, Obregón y Juárez, changes TCs. *Banco Mexicano*, Juárez and

Cárdenas, TCs or US$ cash, quick and courteous service. Several on, or near, Av Héroes with ATMs. Banks do not change quetzales into pesos. Good rates at *Bodegas Blanco* supermarket beside bus terminal; will change US dollars and Belize dollars (only if you spend at least 15 of the total on their groceries!). *Batty Bus* ticket counter will change pesos into Belizean dollars. Try also *Casa Medina*, L Cárdenas. Pemex stations will accept US and Belizean dollars, but at poor rates for the latter. *San Francisco de Assisi* supermarket changes TCs, next to bus station. **Communications** Internet: *Eclipse*, 5 de Mayo 83 between PE Calles and Zaragoza. Open 0930-1500, 1800-2100. Not very friendly but cheap at US$3 per hour. *Los Cebollones*, Calzada Veracruz 452, T872-9145. Also restaurant and cocktail bar. **Post office** at 16 de Septiembre y PE Calles. Open Mon-Fri 0800-1730, Sat 0900-1300. Packets to be sent abroad must be taken unwrapped to the bus terminal to have them checked by customs before taking them to the post office. Better to wait till another town. Parcel service not available Sat. Western Union office attached to Post office, same hours. **Embassies and consulates** *Guatemala* Av Héroes de Chapultepec 354, T872-6565. Open for visas, Mon-Fri 0900-1700. Visas to Guatemala not required by nationals of EU, US and Canada or Mexico and Central America. For other nationals, it is far better to organize your visa, if required, in your home country before travel. *Belize* Hon Consul, Lic Francisco Lechón Rosas, Rotondo Carranza 562 (behind Super San Francisco) , T878-7728; visas can take up to 3 weeks to get, and many are only issued in Mexico City. **Laundry** *Lavandería Automática* 'Lava facil', corner of Héroes and Confederación Nacional Campesina. **Medical services** Malaria prophylaxis available from Centro de Salud, opposite hospital (request tablets for *paludismo*). **Tour operators** *Tu-Maya*, Av Héroes de Chapultepec 165A, next to *Holiday Inn*, T872-0555, F872-9711. One-day tours to Guatemala, Belize and Calakmul. *Premier*, Av Juárez 83, esq Zaragoza, T872-3096, F872-1247, otocarybe@mpsnet.com.mx Eco and adventure tours, car rental. *San Juan Travel Agency*, based at Chetumal bus station, T872-5110. Leaves 1500 for Flores, arriving 2100, returns 0500 connecting to 1400 bus to Cancún. US$35 one way plus US$3 at the Belize-Guatemala border.

Customs and immigration procedure can be slow, particularly at peak holiday times when Belizeans come on charter buses for cheap shopping; over the bridge is Belizean passport control. For people entering Mexico, tourist cards are available at the border. It has been reported that only 15 days are given but you can get an additional 30 days at the Servicios Migratorios in Chetumal. Note that fresh fruit cannot be imported into Belize.

Border with Belize

Leaving Mexico by car, go to the Mexican immigration office to register your exit and surrender your vehicle permit and tourist card; very straightforward, no charges. Go to the office to obtain compulsory Belizean insurance (also money changing facilities here). Entering Belize, your car will be registered in your passport.

Money is checked on entering Belize. Excess Mexican pesos are easily changed into Belizean dollars with men waiting just beyond customs on the Belize side, but they are not there to meet the early bus. You can change US for Belizean dollar bills in the shops at the border, but this is not necessary as US$ are accepted in Belize. If you can get a good rate (dollars to pesos) in the bank, it is sometimes better to buy Belizean dollars with pesos in *casas de cambio* than to wait until you enter Belize where the US dollar/Belize dollar rate is fixed at 1:2.

Excursions north of Chetumal

Six kilometres north are the stony beaches of **Calderitas**, bus every 30 minutes from Colón, between Belice and Héroes, US$1.80 or taxi, US$5, many fish restaurants. Camping at Calderitas, signposted, OK, US$2.75. Beyond are the unexcavated archaeological sites of **Ichpaatun** (13 km), **Oxtancah** (14 km) and **Nohochmul** (20 km). Sixteen kilometres north on Route 307 to Tulum is the **Laguna de los Milagros**, a beautiful lagoon for swimming. Further on, 34 km north of Chetumal, is **Cenote Azul**, over 70 m deep, with a waterside restaurant serving inexpensive and good seafood and regional food (but awful coffee) until 1800. There is also a trailer park (Apartado 88, Chetumal), a relaxing place to camp; other *cenotes* in area. Both the *laguna* and the *cenote* are deserted in the week.

About 3 km north of Cenote Azul is the village of **Bacalar** (nice, but not special) on the **Laguna de Siete Colores**, which has swimming and skin-diving; colectivos from terminal (Suchaa) in Chetumal, corner of Miguel Hidalgo and Primo de Verdad, from 0700-1900 every 30 minutes, US$1.60, return from plaza when full;

Bacalar

also buses from Chetumal bus station every two hours or so, US$1.60. There is a Spanish fort there overlooking a beautiful shallow, clear, fresh-water lagoon, and abundant birdlife on the lake shore. This is the fort of **San Felipe**, said to have been built around 1729 by the Spanish to defend the area from the English pirates and smugglers of logwood (there is a plaque praying for protection from the British). ■ *US$0.70, small museum.* The British ships roamed the islands and reefs, looting Spanish galleons laden with gold, on their way from Peru to Cuba. There are many old shipwrecks on the reef and around the Banco Chinchorro, 50 km out in the Caribbean (information kindly provided by Coral Pitkin of the *Rancho Encantado*, see below). There is a dock for swimming from north of the plaza, with a restaurant and disco next to it. North of Bacalar a direct road (Route 293) runs to Muná, on the road between Mérida and Uxmal.

Sleeping and eating 3 km north of Bacalar is the resort hotel **AL** *Rancho Encantado*, on the west shore of the lagoon. Half-board also available, Apdo 233, Chetumal, T/F872-0427, www.encantado.com, with private dock, tour boat, canoes and windsurf boards for rent, private cabins with fridge and hammock, very good. At Bacalar is **D** *Hotel América*, 700 m north of the bus stop on the plaza (walk in the opposite direction to Chetumal). Recommended. **D** *Hotel Las Lagunas*, about 2 km south of Bacalar (on left-hand side of the road going towards the village). It is very good, wonderful views, helpful, clean, comfortable, hot water, swimming pool and opposite a fresh-water lake; restaurant is poor and overpriced. Several houses rent rooms (**E**) 500 m north of the plaza, look for signs on fence. *Restaurant La Esperanza*, 1 block north from plaza. Thatched barn, good seafood, not expensive. 1 cheap place on the plaza, *Punta y Coma*. *Orizaba*, 3 blocks from Zócalo. Inexpensive, large menu including vegetarian. Recommended. Several lakeside bars also serve meals, mostly fish. Camping possible at the end of the road 100 m from the lagoon, toilets and shower, US$0.10, but lagoon perfect for washing and swimming. *Balneario Ejidal*, with changing facilities and restaurant (good fried fish). Recommended; gasoline is sold in a side-street.

West of Chetumal

From Chetumal you can visit the fascinating Mayan ruins that lie on the way (Route 186) to Escárcega, if you have a car. There are few tourists in this area and few facilities. Take plenty of drinking water. About 25 km from Chetumal at **Ucum** (fuel), you can turn off 5 km south to visit **Palmara**, located along the Río Hondo, which borders Belize; there are swimming holes and restaurant.

Kohunlich
Colour map 4, grid B3

Just before Francisco Villa (61 km from Chetumal) lie the ruins of **Kohunlich**, 8½ km south of the main road, 1½ hours' walk along a sweltering, unshaded road; take plenty of water. Descriptions in Spanish and English. Every hour or so the van passes for staff working at **AL** *Explorer Kohunlich*, a luxury resort hotel halfway to the ruins, which may give you a lift, but you'll still have 4 km to walk. There are fabulous masks (early Classic, AD 250-500) set on the side of the main pyramid, still bearing red colouring; they are unique of their kind (allow an hour for the site). ■ *US$2.* About 200 m west of the turning for Kohunlich is a Migración office and a stall selling beer; wait here for buses to Chetumal or Xpujil, which have to stop, but first class will not pick up passengers. Colectivos 'Nicolás Bravo' from Chetumal, or bus marked 'Zoh Laguna' from bus station pass the turning.

Dzibanché

Other ruins in this area are Dzibanché and **Knichná**. Both are recent excavations and both are accessible down a dirt road off the Chetumal-Morocoy road. The remains of a Maya king have recently been disinterred (June 1999) at Dzibanché, which is thought to have been the largest Maya city in southern Quintana Roo, peaking between AD 300 and 1200. Its discoverer, Thomas Gann, named it in 1927 after the Maya glyphs he found engraved on the sapodilla wood lintels in Temple VI - *Dzibanché* means 'writing on the wood' in Maya. Later excavations revealed a tomb in Temple I, believed to have belonged to a king because of the number of offerings it contained. This temple is also known as the **Temple of the Owl** because one of the artefacts unearthed was a vase and lid carved with an owl figure. Other important structures are the **Temple of the Cormorants** and **Structure XIII**, known as 'The Captives', due to its friezes depicting prisoners. ■ *Free*. Knichná means 'House of the Sun' in Maya, christened by Thomas Gann in reference to a glyph he found there. The **Acropolis** is the largest structure. ■ *Free*. To reach these sights follow the Chetumal-Escárcega road, turn off at Km 58 towards Morocoy, 9 km further on. The road to Dzibanché is 2 km down this road, crossing the turning for Knichná.

Background

History

Of the many Indian nations in the vast territory of Mexico, the two most important before the Conquest were the Aztecs of Tenochtitlán (now Mexico City) and the Maya of Yucatán. The Aztecs, a militarist, theocratic culture, had obtained absolute control over the whole Valley of México and a loose control of some other regions. The Maya were already in decline by the time the Spaniards arrived. A brief history of these and other pre-Conquest, Mexican people is given in pre-Columbian civilizations, page 59.

Pre-conquest

The remarkable conquest of Mexico began when 34-year-old **Hernán Cortés** disembarked near the present Veracruz with about 500 men, some horses and cannon, on 21 April 1519. They marched into the interior; their passage was not contested; they arrived at Tenochtitlán in November and were admitted into the city as guests of the reigning monarch, Moctezuma. There they remained until June of the next year, when Pedro de Alvarado, in the absence of Cortés, murdered hundreds of Indians to quell his own fear of a rising. At this treacherous act the Indians did in fact rise, and it was only by good luck that the Spanish troops, with heavy losses, were able to fight their way out of the city on the Noche Triste (the Night of Sorrows) of 30 June. Next year Cortés came back with reinforcements and besieged the city. It fell on 30 August 1521, and was utterly razed. Cortés then turned to the conquest of the rest of the country. One of the main factors in his success was his alliance with the Tlaxcalans, old rivals of the Aztecs. The fight was ruthless, and the Aztecs were soon overcome.

Spanish rule

There followed 300 years of Spanish rule. In the early years all the main sources of gold and silver were discovered. Spanish grandees stepped into the shoes of dead Aztec lords and inherited their great estates and their wealth of savable souls with little disturbance, for Aztec and Spanish ways of holding land were not unlike: the *ejido* (or agrarian community holding lands in common), the *rancho*, or small private property worked by the owner; and that usually huge area that paid tribute to its master, the Spanish *encomienda*, soon to be converted into the hacienda, with its absolute title to the land and its almost feudal way of life. Within the first 50 years all the Indians in the populous southern valleys of the plateau had been Christianized and harnessed to Spanish wealth-getting from mine and soil. The more scattered and less profitable Indians of the north and south had to await the coming of the missionizing Jesuits in 1571, a year behind the Inquisition. Too often, alas, the crowded Jesuit missions proved as fruitful a source of smallpox or measles as of salvation, with the unhappy result that large numbers of Indians died; their deserted communal lands were promptly filched by some neighbouring *encomendero*: a thieving of public lands by private interests, which continued for 400 years.

By the end of the 16th century the Spaniards had founded most of the towns that are still important, tapped great wealth in mining, stock raising and sugar-growing, and firmly imposed their way of life and belief. Government was by a Spanish-born upper class, based on the subordination of the Indian and *mestizo* populations and a strict dependence on Spain for all things. As throughout all Hispanic America, Spain built up resistance to itself by excluding from government both Spaniards born in Mexico and the small body of educated *mestizos*.

Background

Revolution & civil war The standard of revolt was raised in 1810 by the curate of Dolores, **Miguel Hidalgo**. The Grito de Dolores: 'Mueran los gachupines' (Perish the Spaniards), collected 80,000 armed supporters, and had it not been for Hidalgo's loss of nerve and failure to engage the Spaniards, the capital might have been captured in the first month and a government created not differing much from the royal Spanish government. But 11 years of fighting created bitter differences.

A loyalist general, **Agustín de Iturbide**, joined the rebels and proclaimed an independent Mexico in 1821. His Plan of Iguala proposed an independent monarchy with a ruler from the Spanish royal family, but on second thoughts Iturbide proclaimed himself Emperor in 1822: a fantasy that lasted a year. A federal republic was created on 4 October 1824, with General Guadalupe Victoria as President. Conservatives stood for a highly centralized government; Liberals favoured federated sovereign states. The tussle of interests expressed itself in endemic civil war. In 1836, Texas, whose cotton-growers and cattle-ranchers had been infuriated by the abolition of slavery in 1829, rebelled against the dictator, Santa Ana, and declared its independence. It was annexed by the United States in 1845. War broke out and US troops occupied Mexico City in 1847. Next year, under the terms of the treaty of Guadalupe Hidalgo, the US acquired half Mexico's territory: all the land from Texas to California and from the Río Grande to Oregon.

Benito Juárez A period of reform dominated by independent Mexico's great hero, the Zapotec Indian, Benito Juárez, began in 1857. The church, in alliance with the conservatives, hotly contested by civil war his liberal programme of popular education, freedom of the press and of speech, civil marriage and the separation of church and state. Juárez won, but the constant civil strife wrecked the economy, and Juárez was forced to suspend payment on the national debt. Promptly, Spain, France and Britain landed a joint force at Veracruz to protect their financial rights. The British and the Spanish soon withdrew, but the French force pushed inland and occupied Mexico City in 1863. Juárez took to guerrilla warfare against the invaders.

The **Archduke Maximilian of Austria** became Emperor of Mexico with Napoleon III's help, but US insistence and the gathering strength of Prussia led to the withdrawal of the French troops in 1867. Maximilian, betrayed and deserted, was captured by the Juaristas at Querétaro, tried, and shot on 19 June. Juárez resumed control and died in July 1872. He was the first Mexican leader of any note who had died naturally since 1810.

General Porfirio Díaz Sebastián Lerdo de Tejada, the distinguished scholar who followed Juárez, was soon tricked out of office by Gen Porfirio Díaz, who ruled Mexico from 1876 to 1910. Díaz's paternal, though often ruthless, central authority did introduce a period of 35 years of peace. A superficial prosperity followed upon peace; a civil service was created, finances put on a sound basis, banditry put down, industries started, railways built, international relations improved, and foreign capital protected. But the main mass of peasants had never been so wretched; their lands were stolen from them, their personal liberties curtailed, and many were sold into forced labour on tobacco and *henequen* plantations from which death was the only release. It was this open contradiction between dazzling prosperity and hideous distress that led to the upheaval of November 1910 and to Porfirio Díaz's self-exile in Paris.

Mexican Revolution A new leader, **Francisco Madero**, who came from a landowning family in Coahuila, championed a programme of political and social reform, including the restoration of stolen lands.

Madero was initially supported by revolutionary leaders such as **Emiliano Zapata** in Morelos, **Pascual Orozco** in Chihuahua and **Pancho Villa** in the north. During his presidency (1911-13), Madero neither satisfied his revolutionary supporters, nor pacified his reactionary enemies. After a coup in February 1913, led by Gen Victoriano Huerta, Madero was brutally murdered, but the great new cry, 'Tierra y Libertad' (Land and Liberty) was not to be quieted until the revolution was made safe by the election of Alvaro Obregón to the Presidency in 1920. Before then, Mexico was in a state of civil war, leading first to the exile of Huerta in 1914, then the dominance of Venustiano Carranza's revolutionary faction over that of Zapata (assassinated in 1919) and Villa.

Later, **President Lázaro Cárdenas** fulfilled some of the more important economic objectives of the revolution; it was his regime (1934-40) that brought about the division of the great estates into *ejidos* (or communal lands), irrigation, the raising of wages, the spread of education, the beginnings of industrialization, the nationalization of the oil wells and the railways. Later presidents nationalized electric power, the main airlines and parts of industry, but at the same time encouraged both Mexican and foreign (mainly US) entrepreneurs to develop the private sector. All presidents have pursued an independent and non-aligned foreign policy.

Modern Mexico

In 1946, the official party assumed the name **Partido Revolucionario Institucional (PRI)**, since when it held a virtual monopoly over all political activity. Having comfortably won all elections against small opposition parties, in the 1980s electoral majorities were cut as opposition to dictatorship by the party grew. Corruption and fraud were claimed to be keeping the PRI in power. The PRI candidate in 1988, **Carlos Salinas de Gortari**, saw his majority dramatically reduced when **Cuauhtémoc Cárdenas** (son of the former president), at the head of a breakaway PRI faction, stood in opposition to him. The disaffected PRI members and others subsequently formed the **Partido de la Revolución Democrática (PRD)**, which rapidly gained support as liberalization of many of the PRI's long-held political and economic traditions became inevitable. In 1989, for the first time, a state governorship was conceded by the PRI, to the right wing party, **Partido de Acción Nacional (PAN)**.

Recent politics

On New Year's Day of the election year, 1994, at the moment when the North American Free Trade Agreement (NAFTA - Mexico, the US and Canada) came into force, a guerrilla group briefly took control of several towns in Chiapas. The **Ejército Zapatista de Liberación Nacional (EZLN)** demanded social justice, indigenous people's rights, democracy at all levels of Mexican politics, an end to government corruption, and land reform for the peasantry. Peace talks were overshadowed by the assassination in Tijuana on 23 March of the PRI's appointed presidential candidate, Luis Donaldo Colosio. Further disquiet was caused by the murder of the Tijuana police chief and the kidnapping of several prominent businessmen and other linked killings in subsequent months. To replace Colosio, President Salinas nominated **Ernesto Zedillo Ponce de León**, a US-trained economist and former education minister. Despite continued unrest in Chiapas, Zedillo won a comfortable majority in the August elections, as did the PRI in Congress. Zedillo's opponents, Cuauhtémoc Cárdenas of PRD and Diego Fernández Cevallos of PAN claimed fraud, to no effect.

On 20 December, just after his inauguration, Zedillo devalued the peso, claiming that political unrest was causing capital outflows and putting pressure on the currency. In fact, devaluation was necessary for a variety of economic reasons, but Zedillo linked the economic necessity with the political situation in the south. On 22 December, however, a precipitate decision to allow the peso to float against the dollar caused an immediate crisis of confidence and investors in Mexico lost billions of dollars as the peso's value plummeted.

The 1994 devaluation

Economic problems mounted in the first half of 1995 and Mexicans were hard hit by the recession. The PRI was heavily defeated by the PAN in state elections in Jalisco (February) and in Guanajuato (May). In the same month, a narrow PRI victory in Yucatán was hotly disputed. In August the PAN retained the state governorship of Baja California Norte, first won in 1989. In Chiapas, Zedillo suspended the controversial PRI governor, but the tension between EZLN and the army continued. A 72-hour campaign to apprehend the EZLN leader, Subcomandante Marcos, was a failure. Talks recommenced in April, with the EZLN calling a ceasefire but the first peace accord was not signed until February 1996.

Zedillo appointed as attorney-general Antonio Lozano of PAN, who uncovered PRI involvement in Colosio's murder and ordered the arrest of Raúl Salinas, brother of ex-president Carlos Salinas, for masterminding the murder of PRI general secretary José Ruiz Massieu in 1994. This broke the convention granting former presidents and their families immunity from criticism or prosecution. Carlos Salinas left Mexico under a cloud. Meanwhile, scandal within the PRI continued: Mario Ruiz Massieu, brother of José Luis, was arrested in the US on suspicion of

Intrigue & corruption

Background

covering up Raúl Salinas' involvement in the Ruiz Massieu murder and of receiving money from drugs cartels when he was in charge of anti-narcotics operations. Raúl Salinas was also investigated for alleged money laundering and illicit enrichment after his wife was arrested in Switzerland trying to withdraw US$84 mn from an account opened in a false name. Stories of his massive fortune in land and investment filled the Mexican newspapers.

Political reform
Political reform advanced in 1996. Despite a boycott of talks by the PAN, the other major parties agreed: to introduce direct elections for the mayoralty of Mexico City; abolish government control of the Federal Electoral Institute, which will become independent; introduce constitutional reforms to allow referendums and guarantee fairer access to the media for party broadcasts during elections. The President's campaign to clean up government was strengthened when he sacked the governor of Guerrero for his alleged involvement in a peasant massacre.

Mid-term congressional elections were held in July 1997 for six state governorships, the entire 500-seat Congress and one third of the Senate, as well as the mayoralty of Mexico City. The PRI suffered a huge blow at the polls, and for the first time ever it lost control of Congress, winning only 239 seats. The PRD surged to become the second largest party in the lower house, with 125 deputies, while the PAN won 122. The PRD also gained the mayoralty of Mexico City (Cuauhtémoc Cárdenas, son of the popular 1930's president, took office in December having won almost twice as many votes as his PRI rival) and the Speaker of the Legislature (Porfirio Muñoz Ledo, unanimously elected by the new, four-party opposition bloc).

The Chiapas massacre
In 1997 the EZLN renewed its protests at the slow pace of change after a year of no negotiations, accusing the government of trying to change the terms of the agreed legal framework for indigenous rights. The low-intensity war continued in Chiapas, where 60,000 troops heavily outnumbered the EZLN fighters hiding in the Lacandón forest. In December 1997, 45 people were massacred in Acteal, Chenalhó, near San Cristóbal de las Casas, by paramilitaries linked to the PRI. The victims, refugees from communities previously attacked by paramilitaries, were mostly women and children. Human rights groups and church leaders blamed the government for failing to disarm paramilitary groups and not negotiating a solution to the Chiapas conflict. The local mayor was implicated and arrested with 39 others, charged with taking part in the massacre. There were calls for more senior government officials to be removed. Early in 1998 the Interior Minister resigned, followed by the State Governor. The army increased its pressure on the EZLN and its civilian supporters in its search for weapons in defiance of the 1995 Law of Dialogue, which forbade persecution of Zapatistas unless peace talks were abandoned. Meanwhile, foreign observers were deported for violating their tourist visas and engaging in 'political activity' in Chiapas.

Background

Presidential elections 2000
During 1999 the political parties manoeuvred and schemed prior to choosing their presidential candidates. President Zedillo relinquished his traditional role in nominating his successor and the PRI had a US-style primary election to select a candidate. **PAN**, meanwhile, chose former Coca-Cola executive **Vicente Fox** to lead their campaign. On 2 July 1999, Mexicans turned out to vote in what proved to be an historic election, which gave power to Fox, former governor of Guanajuato, and the PAN, prising it from the PRI for the first time in 71 years.

Fox promotes himself as a down-to-earth man of the people and he spent much time in the lead-up to elections, touring the country on horseback. An admirer of 'third way' politics and of US President Bill Clinton and UK Prime Minister Tony Blair, Fox, who took office on 1 December 2000, announced czar-led initiatives that would tackle government corruption, drug-trafficking, crime and poverty, and the economic conditions that drive migration to the US. One critic dismissively said Fox was "90% image and 10% ideas."

Soon after election Fox adopted the role of president, visiting many of the Latin nations early in his presidency and quickly met up with US President George W Bush. His early popularity has only waned by about 10% since election, and his policies are still a little too early to assess in the light of global changes. In his first State of the Union address, or *Informe*, Fox lamented the recession in the US, Mexico's leading trade partner and the recipient of most of her exports, as the cause of economic woes. He also suggested that government had been cleaned up and drug cartels destroyed in the battle against organized crime.

The Zapatista movement, however, was not prepared to tread water until the new president had found his feet. A two-week long nationwide march round the country to highlight the ongoing demands for the indigenous people ended with a 100,000-strong crowd gathering in the heart of Mexico City, the Zócalo, to hear the rousing cries for greater autonomy. Although Congress passed a bill in late April 2001 supporting the claims, the Zapatista movement rejected the proposal, claiming the bill did nothing to improve their rights - if anything it simply clarified the rights of the landowners. Fox claimed he could sort out the Chiapas problem in '15 minutes' – a year into his presidency he has found that getting the balance between indigenous rights and the opportunities is a difficult task, even more so when you need approval from Congress.

Fox's early international posturing reached its highest peak in March 2002 with the United Nations Development Summit held in Monterrey, which saw almost 60 heads of states converge on the northern city to set the 'goal' of reducing the wealth gap between rich and poor nations. Fox appeared to be using the posturing to good effect when he threatened to stop US trucks entering Mexico because the US denied access to Mexican trucks in contravention of the North American Free Trade Agreement (NAFTA).

The vulnerability of pushing the statesman card became clear when the economy slipped into recession in the last half of 2001, the knock-on effect of the economic downturn in the US. The international stance took a further knock when Congress, which collectively has to authorize presidential trips, vetoed travel plans to Canada and the US.

For Fox, the honeymoon is almost over. Mexicans will be expecting signs of real change in 2003.

Economy

Mexico has been an oil producer since the 1880s and was the world's leading producer in 1921. By 1971 the country had become a net importer, a position reversed in 1972 with the discovery of major new reserves. Today Mexico benefits greatly from the reserves and is the world's sixth largest producer with 65% of production coming from offshore wells in the Gulf of Campeche. Mexico's mineral resources are legendary and it is the world's leading producer of silver, fluorite and arsenic, and a major producer of many other minerals. Agriculture has been losing importance since the beginning of the 1970s and now contributes only 5.8% of GDP.

Manufacturing, including oil refining and petrochemicals, contributes 17.6% of GDP. While the capital used to be a focal point for manufacturing the government now offers incentives to companies relocating away from major industrial centres. The boom has been with the creation of 3,600 *maquiladoras* along the US border which employ some 1.3 million people, earning US$1.5 bn for the economy. Tourism is a large source of foreign exchange and the largest employer, with about a third of the workforce. About 6.7 million tourists visit Mexico every year, with about 85% come from the US.

Recent trends

In 1982 Mexico, like many countries, was unable to service its debts forcing the economy to restructure under the guidance of the International Monetary Fund. Improving economic conditions stimulated negotiations with the US and Canada on the creation of the North America Free Trade Agreement (NAFTA) to open markets, encourage investment and pave the way for migration of many state-owned industries.

Growth in the early 1990s wobbled with domestic political unrest, which saw the peso devalued and allowed to float freely against the dollar. The loss of US$4 bn in just two days created the 'Tequila effect' which rippled through Latin markets. While economic figures began to recover the pain of austerity measures hit hard and laid the foundations of dissent within the middle and lower classes.

Background

Towards the end of the 1990s devaluation in Brazil caused the stock market to tumble, weakening the peso just months before presidential elections. The increasingly international nature of business in Mexico was reinforced with the purchase of *Banamex* by *Citigroup* in 2001 – the largest deal of its kind in Latin America.

The 2000 Census confirmed the importance of the *maquila* industry to the Mexican economy, as well as over US$9 bn sent home from family living abroad. But in 2002, the Mexican economy will simply be trying to ride out the impact of recession in the US, which has created a domino effect in Mexico, and recover from the recession that hit the country in late 2001 due to reduced exports to the US.

Government

Under the 1917 Constitution Mexico is a federal republic of 31 states and a Federal District containing the capital, Mexico City. The President, who appoints the Ministers, is elected for six years and can never be re-elected. Congress consists of the 128-seat Senate, half elected every three years on a rotational basis, and the 500-seat Chamber of Deputies, elected every three years. There is universal suffrage.

Local administration The states enjoy local autonomy and can levy their own taxes, and each state has its Governor, legislature and judicature. The President has traditionally appointed the Chief of the Federal District but direct elections were held in 1997 for the first time.

Culture

People The Census of 2000 gave Mexico a total population of 97.4 million people, an increase of 16.2 mn in 10 years. About 9% are considered white and about 30% Indian; about 60% are *mestizos*, a mixture in varying proportions of Spanish and Indian; a small percentage (mostly in the coastal zones of Veracruz, Guerrero and Chiapas) are a mixture of black and white or black and Indian or *mestizo*. Mexico also has infusions of other European peoples, Arab and Chinese. There is a national cultural prejudice in favour of the Indian rather than the Spanish element, though this does not prevent Indians from being looked down on by the more Hispanic elements. There is hardly a single statue of Cortés in the whole of Mexico, although he does figure, pejoratively, in the frescoes of Diego Rivera and his contemporaries. On the other hand the two last Aztec emperors, Moctezuma and Cuauhtémoc, are national heroes.

Indians Among the estimated 24 million Indians there are 54 groups or sub-divisions, each with its own language. The Indians are far from evenly distributed; 36% live on the Central Plateau (mostly Hidalgo, and México); 35% are along the southern Pacific Coast (Oaxaca, Chiapas, Guerrero), and 23% along the Gulf Coast (mostly Yucatán and Veracruz): 94% of them, that is, live in these three regions. There are also sizeable concentrations in Nayarit and Durango, Michoacán, and Chihuahua, Sinoloa and Sonora. The main groups are: Pápago (Sonora); Yaqui (Sonora); Mayo (Sonora and Sinaloa); Tarahumara (Chihuahua); Huastec and Otomí in San Luis Potosí; Cora and Huichol (Nayarit); Purépecha/Tarasco (Michoacán); scattered groups of Nahua in Michoacán, Guerrero, Jalisco, Veracruz and other central states; Totonac (Veracruz); Tiapaneco (Guerrero); in Oaxaca state, Mixtec, Mixe and Zapotec; in Chiapas, Lacandón, Tzoltzil, Tzeltal, Chol and others; Maya in Campeche, Yucatán and Quintano Roo.

Land ownership The issue of access to the land has always been the country's fundamental problem, and it was a despairing landless peasantry that rose in the Revolution of 1910 and swept away Porfirio Díaz and the old system of huge estates. The accomplishments of successive PRI governments have been mixed. Life for the peasant is still hard. The minimum wage barely allows a simple diet of beans, rice and *tortillas*. The home is still, possibly, a shack with no windows, no water, no sanitation, and the peasant may still not be able to read or write, but something was done to redistribute the land in the so-called *ejido* system, which gave either communal or personal control of the land. The peasant was freed from the landowner, and his family received some basic health and educational facilities from the state. In 1992 new legislation was approved that radically overhauled the outdated agricultural sector with far-reaching political and economic consequences. Farmers now have the right to become private property owners, if two-thirds of the *ejido* votes in favour; to form joint ventures with private businessmen; and to use their land as collateral for loans. Private property owners may form joint stock companies, thereby avoiding the constitutional limits on the size of farms and helping them to raise capital. The failure of any agricultural reforms to benefit the peasants of Chiapas was one of the roots of the EZLN uprising in early 1994.

Mexican music is particularly attractive and vibrant and a vigorous radio, film and recording industry has helped make it highly popular throughout Latin America. There can be no more representative an image of Mexico than the *mariachi* musician and his *charro* costume. The Spanish conquistadores and the churchmen that followed them imposed European musical culture on the defeated natives with a heavy hand and it is this influence that remains predominant. Nobody knows exactly what pre-Columbian music sounded like and even the music played today in the Indian communities is basically Spanish in origin although African slaves introduced a third ingredient. The music brought from Europe has over the centuries acquired a highly distinctive sound and style of which every Mexican is justly proud, even if many of the young now prefer to listen to Anglo-American rock and pop, like their counterparts the world over.

Music & dance

There is a basic distinction between Indian and Mestizo music. The former is largely limited to the Indians' own festive rituals and dances, religious in nature and solemn in expression. The commonest instruments are flute and drum, with harp and violin also widely used. Some of the most spectacular dances are those of the Concheros (mainly urban), the Quetzales (from the Sierra de Puebla), the Voladores (flying pole – also Sierra de Puebla and Veracruz), the Tarascan dances from around Lake Pátzcuaro and the Yaqui deer dance (Sonora).

Mestizo music clearly has more mass appeal in what is an overwhelmingly mixed population. The basic form is the *son* (also called *huapango* in eastern areas), featuring a driving rhythm overlaid with dazzling instrumentals. Each region has its own style of *son*, such as the *son huasteco* (Northeast), *son calentano* (Michoacán/ Guerrero), *chilena* (Guerrero coast), *son mariachi* (Jalisco), *jarana* (Yucatán) and *son jarocho* (Veracruz). One *son jarocho* that has achieved world status is *La Bamba*. Instrumental backing is provided in almost all these areas by a combination of large and small guitars, with the violin as virtuoso lead in the *huasteca* and the harp in Veracruz. The *chilena* of Guerrero was inspired by Chilean sailors performing their national dance, the *cueca*, during a naval visit to Acapulco in 1822, while Yucatán features a version of the Colombian *bambuco*. The *son* is a dance form for flirtation between couples and often involves spectacular heel-and-toe stamping by the man. Another widespread dance rhythm is the *jarabe*, including the patriotic 'Jarabe Tapatío', better known to the English-speaking world as the 'Mexican Hat Dance'. Certain regions are known for more sedate rhythms and a quite different choice of instruments. In the north, the Conjunto Norteño leads with an accordion and favours the polka as a rhythm. In Yucatán they prefer wind and brass instruments, while the Isthmus of Tehuantepec is the home of the *marimba* (xylophone), which it shares with neighbouring Guatemala.

For singing, as opposed to dancing, there are three extremely popular genres. First is the *corrido*, a narrative form derived from old Spanish ballads, which swept across the country with the armies of the Revolution and has remained a potent vehicle for popular expression ever since. A second is the *canción* (literally 'song'), which gives full rein to the romantic, sentimental aspect of the Mexican character, and is naturally slow and languid. *Las Mañanitas* is a celebrated song for serenading people on their birthdays. The third form is the *ranchera*, a sort of Mexican Country and Western, associated originally with the cattle-men of the Bajío region. Featured in a whole series of Mexican films of the 1930s and 1940s, *rancheras* became known all over the Spanish-speaking world as the typical Mexican music. The film and recording industry turned a number of Mexican artists into household names throughout

Background

Latin America. The 'immortals' are Pedro Infante, Jorge Negrete, Pedro Vargas, Miguel Aceves Mejía and the Trio Los Panchos, with Agustín Lara as an equally celebrated and prolific songwriter and composer, particularly of romantic *boleros*. To all outsiders and many Mexicans however there is nothing more musically Mexican than *mariachi*, a word said to be derived from the French *mariage*, introduced at the time of Maximilian and Carlota.

Originating in the State of Jalisco, *mariachi* bands arrived in Mexico City in the 1920s and have never looked back. Trumpets now take the lead, backed by violins and guitars and the players all wear *charro* (cowboy) costume, including the characteristic wide-brimmed hat. They play all the major musical forms and can be found almost every evening in Mexico City's Plaza Garibaldi, where they congregate to be seen, heard and, they hope, hired. This is the very soul of Mexico.

Finally, there are a number of distinguished 20th-century composers who have produced symphonies and other orchestral works based on indigenous and folk themes. Carlos Chávez is the giant and his *Sinfonía India* a particularly fine example. Other notable names are Silvestre Revueltas *(Sensemayá)*, Pablo Moncayo (*Huapango*), Blas Galindo (*Sones de Mariachi*) and Luis Sandi (*Yaqui Music*).

Religion   Roman Catholicism is the principal religion, but the state is determinedly secular. Because of its identification firstly with Spain, then with the Emperor Maximilian and finally with Porfirio Díaz, the Church has been severely persecuted in the past by reform-minded administrations, and priests are still not supposed to wear ecclesiastical dress (see *The Lawless Roads* and *The Power and the Glory*, by Graham Greene). Rapprochement between State and Church was sought in the early 1990s.

Land and environment

Geography   Mexico has an area equal to about a quarter of the US, with which it has a frontier of 2,400 km. The southern frontier of 885 km is with Guatemala and Belize. It has a coast line of 2,780 km on the Gulf of Mexico and the Caribbean, and of 7,360 km on the Pacific and the Gulf of California.

The structure of the land mass is extremely complicated, but may be simplified (with large reservations) as a plateau flanked by ranges of mountains roughly paralleling the coasts. The northern part of the plateau is low, arid and thinly populated; it takes up 40% of the total area of Mexico but holds only 19% of its people. From the Bolsón de Mayrán as far south as the Balsas valley, the level rises considerably; this southern section of the central plateau is crossed by a volcanic range of mountains in which the intermont basins are high and separated. The basin of Guadalajara is at 1,500 m, the basin of México at 2,300 m, and the basin of Toluca, west of Mexico City, is at 2,600 m. Above the lakes and valley bottoms of this contorted middle-land rise the magnificent volcano cones of Orizaba (5,700 m), Popocatépetl (5,452 m), Ixtaccíhuatl (5,286 m), Nevado de Toluca (4,583 m), Matlalcueyetl or La Malinche (4,461 m), and Cofre de Perote (4,282 m). This mountainous southern end of the plateau, the heart of Mexico, has ample rainfall. Though only 14% of the area of Mexico, it holds nearly half of the country's people. Its centre, in a small high intermont basin measuring only 50 sq km, is Mexico City, with 20 or so million inhabitants.

The two high ranges of mountains which rise east and west of the plateau, between it and the sea, are great barriers against communications: there are far easier routes north along the floor of the plateau to the US than there are to either the east coast or the west. In the west there are transport links across the Sierra Madre Occidental from Guadalajara to the Pacific at the port of Mazatlán, continuing northward through a coastal desert to Nogales. The Sierra Madre Oriental is more kindly; in its mountain ramparts a pass inland from Tampico gives access to Monterrey, a great industrial centre, and the highland basins; and another from Veracruz leads by a fair gradient to the Valley of México.

South of the seven intermont basins in the south-central region the mountainland is still rugged but a little lower (between 1,800 and 2,400 m), with much less rainfall. After some 560 km it falls away into the low-lying Isthmus of Tehuantepec. Population is sparse in these southern mountains and is settled on the few flat places where commercial crops an be grown. Subsistence crops are sown on incredibly steep slopes. The Pacific Coast ere is forbidding and its few ports of little use, though there is massive development of ourism in such places as Acapulco, Zihuatanejo, Puerto Escondido and Huatulco. Very ifferent are the Gulf Coast and Yucatán; half this area is classed as flat, and much of it gets nough rain the year round, leading to its becoming one of the most important gricultural and cattle raising areas in the country. The Gulf Coast also provides most of Mexico's oil and sulphur. Geographically, North America may be said to come to an end in he Isthmus of Tehuantepec. South of the Isthmus the land rises again into the thinly populated highlands of Chiapas.

The complex land mass that is Mexico is the result of millions of years of geological moulding, a process that still continues today. The country was ignited literally by the spectacular eruptions of Popocatépetl, 60 km to the east of the capital, in 2001, which has been slowly wakening from a 65-year slumber for several years. Likewise to the west of the capital, Colima Volcano is closed to climbers, as activity that has been growing steadily in the last few years looks certain to result in an eruption.

Climate

Climate and vegetation depend upon altitude. The *tierra caliente* takes in the coastlands and plateau lands below 750 m. The *tierra templada*, or temperate zone, is at 750 to 2,000 m. The *tierra fría*, or cold zone, is from 2,000 m upwards. Above the tree line at 4,000 m are high moorlands (*páramos*).

The climate of the inland highlands is mostly mild, but with sharp changes of temperature between day and night, sunshine and shade. Generally, winter is the dry season and summer the wet season. There are only two areas where rain falls the year round: south of Tampico along the lower slopes of the Sierra Madre Oriental and across the Isthmus of Tehuantepec into Tabasco state; and along the Pacific coast of the State of Chiapas. Both areas together cover only 12% of Mexico. These wetter parts get most of their rain between June and September, when the skies are so full of clouds that the temperature is lowered: May is a hotter month than July. Apart from these favoured regions, the rest of the country suffers from a climate in which the rainy season hardly lives up to its name and the dry season almost always does.

But extremes of weather do happen, however. In 2001 both the Caribbean and Pacific coastlines were battered by severe storms or hurricanes.

Books and films

Travellers wanting more information than we have space to provide, on archaeological sites for instance, would do well to use the widely available *Panorama Guides* and the *Easy Guides* written by Richard Bloomgarden, with plans and good illustrations. Also available are Miniguides to archaeological and historical sites, published in various languages by INAH, US$0.75 each. Do not expect to find leaflets or books at the sites, so stock up before you visit. For ornithologists: *A Field Guide to Mexican Birds*, Peterson and Chalif, Houghton Mifflin, 1973, has been recommended; *Finding Birds in Mexico*, by Ernest P Edwards, Box AQ, Sweet Briar, Virginia 24595, US, is recommended as detailed and thorough. Two books by Rudi Robins are: *One-day Car Trips from Mexico City*, and *Weekend Trips to Cities near Mexico City*. Highly recommended, practical and entertaining is *The People's Guide to Mexico* by Carl Franz (John Muir Publications, Santa Fe, NM), now in its 11th edition, 1998; there is also a *People's Guide Travel Letter*. Another publication *Back Country Mexico, A Traveller's Guide and Phrase Book*, by Bob Burlison and David H Riskind (University of Texas Press, Box 7819, Austin, Texas, 78713-7819), has also been recommended. *Mexico From the Driver's Seat*, by Mike Nelson, is published by Sanborn's (see Motoring, above).

The essential recommended reading for the Maya archaeological area: *The Maya*, by MD Coe (Pelican Books, or large format edition, Thames and Hudson).

On the international big screen Mexico has probably suffered more than most from stereotypical images painting the whole nation as a bunch of lazy, good-for-nothing

Background

scoundrels, crooks and corrupt officials. The Western genre relied heavily on the scenic locations around Durango producing classics from the 1950s through the works of Sam Peckinpah up to the more recent all-star *Mask of Zorro*. Many other US productions have used Mexico's tropical locations for films such as *Night of the Iguana*, *Romancing the Stone* and *Medicine Man*, and the blockbuster *Titanic*, which was shot at Rosarito, Baja California, close to Tijuana.

But the national film industry has grown in prominence in recent years with international successes including *Como agua para chocolate* (*Like Water for Chocolate*), *Danzón*, *Amores Perros* (nomiated for an Oscar and winner of the 2002 Bafta for best foreig film), and the latest domestic hit released *Y tu mamá también*, a road movie about love, sex friendship, politics and the blind haste to grow up.

Guatemala

4

Guatemala

Essentials

Guatemala is the most popular Central American republic for independent travellers and for good reasons. The Maya live on in culture and language in the western regions, where the highest volcanoes in Central America cast long shadows over hundreds of small communities that till the soil. Impressive ruins stand as monuments to the skills of the ancient civilization, with discoveries still revealing new secrets. Landscapes encompass Pacific and Caribbean coastline, and densely forested areas throughout the country provide a panacea of possibilities for getting close to nature. In short, Guatemala offers a great opportunity to get lost in mind, body, soul, or all three.

Planning your trip

Guatemala City is a modern, commercial and polluted capital. It is the main entry point for travellers by air and long-distance bus. While there are one or two sites of interest in the city centre, few stay long, preferring to head west to the clean air and relaxed atmosphere of **Antigua**. Once the capital, **Antigua** was built by the Spanish Conquistadores. Later destroyed by several huge earthquakes, the grand ruins of colonial architecture remain and the dramatic location, at the foot of three volcanoes, as well as its prominence as a centre for Spanish studies, make Antigua a justifiably popular destination.

Where to go

Heading northeast from Guatemala City towards the Caribbean, lie the highlands of the Verapaz region. **Cobán** is the main focus, with access to nearby traditional villages, the caves at Lanquín, the natural bridge of Semuc Champey and, at Purulhá, the Mario Dary Rivera Reserve which protects the habitat of the quetzal, the national bird. Skirting the northern shores of Lago de Izabal, is the newly formed Bocas del Polochic Wildlife Reserve which is plentiful with monkeys, avifauna and other wildlife. The beautiful scenery and rivers close to El Estor are slowly being discovered as perfect for hiking and swimming.

South of the lake, the highway runs close to one of the country's main Maya archaeological sites, **Quiriguá**, which once competed with Tikal and nearby Copán, in Honduras, for dominance of the Maya heartlands. On Guatemala's short **Caribbean** shore is Lívingston, popular with young travellers and close to the dramatic landscapes of El Golfete Biotopo Chocón-Machacas, a manatee and wildlife reserve. From Lívingston boats go to Puerto Barrios for the trip north to Belize or south to Honduras.

The forested northern lowlands of **El Petén** hide most of Guatemala's archaeological sites. The majestic **Tikal** is the most developed for tourism, but many others can be reached including Uaxactún and El Ceibal. For the truly adventurous, a number of exciting trips can be made to outlying Maya cities. **Flores**, sitting on an island in Lago Petén Itzá, is the centre for exploring El Petén. There are routes from here to Belize and Mexico.

West of Guatemala City, beyond Antigua, the mountainous highlands overflow with the influence of the Maya. Market days filled with colour, fiestas crammed with celebrations, each community is characterized by unique costumes and crafts. Several villages are dotted around the shores and hills of **Lago Atitlán**, a spectacular and sacred lake protected on all sides by silent volcanic peaks. From the popular town of **Panajachel**, ferries and trails link to the small communities each offering different levels of seclusion and fun. **San Pedro La Laguna** is currently the chief chill out and hang loose spot on the lake's shores.

An hour north of Atitlán is the famous market of **Chichicastenango**, a town where Maya and visitors converge in a twice-weekly frenzy of buying goods and produce, alongside textiles and tapestry. The market is alive with colour and a must for any visitor. While Chichi stands out, there are many other markets and districts with their own customs in the Quiché region or the Ixil Triangle to the north.

Towards the Mexican border, the towns of Quetzaltenango, Retalhuleu and Huehuetenango provide good opportunities for discovering the charms of western Guatemala. To the north, in the heart of the Cuchumatanes mountains, **Todos Santos Cuchumatán** stands firm as a town that has restricted Western influences and is increasingly

Guatemala

Guatemala

popular as a place to learn about the Mam way of life, including language and weaving classes. As in much of southern Guatemala, volcanoes dominate the landscape, with hot springs, hiking possibilities and magnificent scenery lining the roads which descend from the highlands to the Pacific lowlands. Along the western coastline, the turtle nesting sites of **Monterrico** are attracting visitors to this forgotten district of Guatemala.

When to go　Climate is dependent upon altitude and varies greatly. Most of the population lives at between 900 and 2,500 m, where the climate is healthy and of an even springlike warmth – warm days and cool nights. The majority of visitors spend most of their time in the highlands, where the dry season lasts from November to April. Some places enjoy a respite from the rains (the *canícula*) in July and August. Days are warm and nights are cool, so you will need to take some warm clothing, especially for the higher altitudes. On the Pacific and Caribbean coasts you can expect rain all year round, heaviest on the Pacific in June and September with a dry spell in between, but with no dry season on the Caribbean. In the lowlands of El Petén, the wet season is roughly the same as the highlands, May to October, and this is also the time when the mosquitoes are most active. December to February are cooler months, while March and April are hot and dry.

Finding out　**Instituto Guatemalteco de Turismo (INGUAT)**, 7 Avenue 1-17, Zona 4, Centro Cívico, **more**　Guatemala City, T3311333347, www.travel-guatemala.org.gt, free information T1-801-INGUAT-1 (local). Inguat provides bus timetables, hotel lists and road maps. Tourist information is provided at the Mexican border for those entering Guatemala. Maps include Belize as Guatemalan territory. Roads marked in El Petén are often inaccurate.

Tourist offices overseas　INGUAT (If an address is not given, see the Embassies box, page 557): *Canada*, T001-613-2332349. *Germany*, Joachim Karntaz-Alle 45-47, 10557, Berline Tiergarten; *Italy*, Viale Prassilla 152, 00124, Rome, T390-6-50916626. *Mexico*, T0052-52021457, turismoembagua@prodigy.net.mx *Spain*, Calle Rafael Salgado 9, 4th Izquierda, 28036 Madrid, T/F34-91-4573424, guatemala@retemail.es. *USA*, T001-202 5185514, embaguat@sysnet.net In the UK, information on Guatemala and the Maya of Guatemala, Mexico, Belize and Honduras can be found at *The Guatemalan Indian Centre*, 94A Wandsworth Bridge Rd, London SW6 2TF, T/F020-7371-5291, www.maya.org.co.uk Library, video archive and textile collection. Admission free. Closed January and August, and two weeks at Easter.

Guatemala on the web　Guatemala is rapidly connecting to the internet. The Guatemalan Tourist Board (INGUAT) has good general information at **www.travel-guatemala.org.gt** Regional sites covering some of the more popular areas include **www.atitlan.com**, **www.mayaparadise.com** (Río Dulce/Livingston), and **www.xelapages.com** (Quetzaltenango). Of the several publications with websites (see below), the *Revue*, www.revuemag.com is probably the most useful to the visitor. If you're thinking of staying around, **www.terra.com.gt** has an incredible amount of information, whille **www.spanishconnection.com** has a Guatemala-based search engine.

Working in　If you would like to **volunteer** it is best to try and make contact before arriving, if only by a **Guatemala**　few days. Such is the demand for positions that unskilled volunteers very often have to pay for board and lodgings. Work needs to be planned and, although there is always work to do, your time will be used most efficiently if your arrival is expected and planned for. In Antigua there is **El Arco Volunteer Work Center**, 5 Avenida Norte 25 B, T/F832-0162, www.rudderfn.org, places people in short or long term positions. Helpful with plenty of contacts across the country. Also in Antigua is *Project Mosaic Guatemala*, 1 Avenida Sur 21, T813-5758, F832-7337, www.pmg.dk/, an information centre and clearing house for volunteers, with access to opportunities all over the country. To help in local children's homes, contact *Casa Guatemala*, 14 Calle, 10-63, Zona 1, Guatemala City, T232-5517, www.casa-guatemala.com which runs a project for abandoned and malnourished children at Río Dulce. See page 659. *Casa Alianza* is a project that helps street kids. It is based at

Guatemala embassies and consulates

Austria, Salesianergasse 25/5, A-1030, Vienna, T1-7143570, F7143569 (also covers *Hungary* and *Romania*).

Australia and *New Zealand*, see Japan.

Belgium, Av Winston Churchill 185, 1180, Brussels, T2-3459058, F3446499, embbelgica@minex.gob.gt (also covers Holland and Luxembourg).

Belize, No 8 'A' St, Belize City, T2-33314, F35140, embbelice1@minex.gob.gt

Canada, 130 Albert St, Suite 1010, Ottawa, Ontario, KIP 5G4, T613-2337237, F2330135, embcanada@minex.gob.gt

Chile, Casilla No 36, Correo 10, Las Condes, Santiago, T2-3414012, F2253630.

Colombia, Transversal 29 A, No 139A-41, Bogotá, T1-2580746, F2745365.

Costa Rica, De la Pops de Curridabat, 500 sur, 30 este, 2da casa izquierda, San José, T283-2555, F283-2556, embcostarica@minex.gob.gt

El Salvador, 15 Av Norte, No 135, San Salvador, T271-2225, F221-3019, embelsalvador@minex.gob.gt

France, 73 Rue de Courcelles, 75008, Paris, T1-42277863, F47540206 (also covers *Portugal* and *Switzerland*).

Germany, Joachim-Karnatz-Alle3 47 D-10557, Berlin, T302064363, F20643659, embalemania@minex.gob.gt

Honduras, Calle Arturo López Redezno 2421, Colonia Las Minitas, Tegucigalpa, T231-1543, F232-8469, embhonduras@minex.gob.gt

Israel, Junction Haifa-Tel Aviv, rehov Medinat Hayedulm 103 Belt Ackerstein entry B, floor 2, Herzliya Pituach, T099577335, F9518506, embisrael@minex.gob.gt (covers *Greece*).

Italy, Via Dei Colli della Farnesina 128, 00194, Rome, T6-36303750, F3291639, embitalia@minex.gob.gt

Japan, No 38 Kowa Bldg, Room 905, Nishi-Azabu, Minato-Ku, Tokyo 106, T3-38001830, F34001820, embjapon@minex.gob.gt (also covers *Australia*, *Bangladesh*, *India*, *Iraq*, *Philippines* and *Thailand*).

Mexico, Av Explanada No 1025, Lomas de Chapultepec, 11000 México DF, T5540 7520, F5202 1142, www.ourworld.compuserve.com/homepages /embaguate

Nicaragua, Km 11½ on road to Masaya, Managua, T2-799609, F799610, embanic@minex.gob.gt

Norway, Oscars Gate 59, 0258, Oslo, T22-556004, F556047 (also covers *Denmark*).

Panama, Calle Abel Bravo y Calle 57, Bella Vista, Edif Torre Cancún, Apt 14-A, Panama City, T2693475, F2231922.

Peru, Inca Ricap No 309, Lima 11, T/F14-635885 (also covers *Bolivia*).

Spain, Calle Rafael Salgado No 3, 4th Izquierda, 28036, Madrid, T1-3441417, F4587894, www.arrakis.es/-~embaguat (also covers *Morocco*).

Sweden, Wittstockgaten 30, S 115, 27 Stockholm, T8-6805229, F6604229 (also covers *Finland*).

United Kingdom, 13 Fawcett Street, London SW10 9HN, T020-7351 3042, F7376 5708.

USA, 2220 R St NW, Washington DC, 20008, T202-7454952, F7451908, www.guatemala-embassy.org

Venezuela, Avenida Francisco Miranda, Torre Dozsa, Primer Nivel, Urb El Rosal, Caracas, T2-952-1166, F952-1992.

Avenida Simeón Cañas 7-06, Zona 2, Guatemala City, T254-1259, F201-6170, guatemala@casa-alianza.org For more information see page 577. There are also opportunites to work in children's homes in Quetzaltenango (Xela). Two organizations are *Casa Hogar de Niños* and the *Asociación Hogar Nuevos Horizontes*. See page 634 for more information. Also check out Xela-based volunteering information organization www.entremundos.org **Proyecto Ak 'Tenamit** is based at Clínica Lámpara, 15 minutes up river from Lívingston. It was set up to help 7,000 civil-war displaced Q'eqchi' Maya who now live in the region in 30 communities. For further information ring Steve Dudenhoefer on T9083392, www.aktenamit.org In Guatemala City, 11 Avenida 'A', 9-39, Zona 2, T254-1560.

Volunteers are welcomed by the **Fundación Mario Dary** which operates conservation, health and education projects on the Punta de Manabique. For more information contact Erwin Herdocia, 17 Calle between 5 and 6 Avenida, Puerto Barrios. T9480944, fundarymanabique@intelnet.net.gt or in the capital at Diagonal 6, 17-19, Zona 10,

Guatemala

T333-4957, www.fundarymanabique.guate.net   Other projects involving working with nature and wildlife include the **Asociación de Rescate y Conservación de Vida Silvestre (ARCAS)**, T/F2535329, T9262022 or arcaspeten@intelnet.net.gt, which returns wild animals to their natural habitat. They take volunteers at their site, accessible by boat, near Flores.

Several language schools in Quetzaltenango (Xela) fund community development projects and seek volunteers. Make enquiries in the town or via www.xelapages.com At *Quezaltrekkers*, www.quetzaltrekkers.com, volunteer hiking guides might be required. Also the *Guatemala Solidarity Network*, 46 The Street, Old Basing, Hampshire, RG24 7BX, UK, gsn_mail@yahoo.com, can assist with finding projects that look at human rights issues.

Before you travel

Visas & immigration
Identification must always be carried in Guatemala in case of police checks

Only a valid **passport** is required for citizens of: all Western European countries; USA, Canada, Mexico and all Central American countries; Brazil, Chile, Paraguay, Uruguay and Venezuela; Australia, Israel, Japan and New Zealand. The majority of visitors will get 90 days on arrival. **Tourist cards** (US$10) which can be bought at the border or visas (US$25) are required by citizens of Bahrain, Kuwait, Saudi Arabia, Czech Republic, Slovakia, Poland, Philippines, Iceland and South Africa. All other nationalities, including UK colonies, must have a visa, which may require reference to immigration authorities in Guatemala which takes three to four weeks.

Visa renewal   This must be done in Guatemala City **after 90 days**, or on expiry. Passport stamp renewal on expiry for those citizens only requiring a valid passport to enter Guatemala must also be done at the immigration office at **Dirección General de Migración**, 7 Avenida, 1-17, Zona 4, Guatemala City, 2nd floor of the blue and white INGUAT building, T361-8476/78/79. Open Monday-Friday 0800-1600, but until 1230 for payments. This office extends visas and passport stamps only once for a further period of time, depending on the original time awarded. These rules have been introduced to stop people leaving the country for 72 hours (which is the legal requirement) every six months and returning, effectively making them permanent residents. The new rules deliberately cause the 'resident tourist' hassle every 90 days, unless they leave every 90 days for 72 hours. The process is meant to take two full working days, but up to a week is possible. To flout these rules will incur a US$1.30 fine per day of each day of overstaying.

Customs

You are allowed to take in, free of duty, personal effects and articles for your own use, two bottles of spirits and 80 cigarettes or 100 g of tobacco. Temporary visitors can take in any amount in quetzales or foreign currencies; they may not, however, take out more than they brought in. The local equivalent of US$100 per person may be reconverted into US dollars on departure at the airport, provided a ticket for immediate departure is shown.

What to take

Most of the areas you are likely to visit in Guatemala are over 1,500 m and, while temperatures may well be comfortably warm in the day, it will be cold in the evening and at night. Bad weather may bring noticeable drops in temperature. In many tropical areas where mosquitoes and other biting insects are common, take long trousers and long-sleeved shirts for after dusk. The sun is strong everywhere at midday, so you will probably need a hat.

Money

Currency
Torn notes are not always accepted

The unit is the quetzal, divided into 100 centavos. There are coins of one quetzal, 50 centavos, 25 centavos, 10 centavos, five centavos and one centavo. The paper currency is for 50 centavos and one, five, 10, 20, 50 and 100 quetzales.

Banks

There are numerous banks in Guatemala and a large majority in cities and towns have ATMs (*cajeros automáticos*). All will change US dollars cash into quetzales, the majority will change TCs, see below, and a large majority will accept Visa to obtain cash, but only a few will accept MasterCard.

isa is the most widely recognized and accepted bank card, whereas MasterCard is only generally accepted at *G&T Continental* (where there is a daily withdrawal limit of US$65) and at *Credomatic/Banco de América Central*, which are few and far between.

Similarly Visa ATMs are much more common than MasterCard ATMs. ATMs for the withdrawal of cash are available for Visa most commonly at *Banco Industrial* and *Bancafé*, and MasterCard/Cirrus sometimes at *Banco G&T Continental*. Others such as *Credomatic* are only found in the capital, Antigua and Quetzaltenango. Banks usually charge up to 2% per transaction to advance quetzales on a credit card and you will probably get a less favourable rate of exchange. It is common for the majority of establishments to make a charge for use of credit cards – regrettably it's about US$3. Check before you sign. All top class hotels and restaurants accept cards but very few hostels do. Amex cards are not very widely accepted. Visa assistance, T1-800-9990115; MasterCard T1-800-9991480. American Express T1-800-9990245. Amex cheques are less easy to change outside the main cities than Citicorp and Visa. Your passport is needed to change them and in some cases a purchase receipt is required, especially in the capital. **Thomas Cook** travellers' cheques are not accepted.

Credit cards & TCs
There is often a shortage of small change, but when you arrive in Guatemala and change money, insist on being given some small notes to pay hotel bills, transport, etc

Getting there

From the USA *American* (Atlanta; Chicago; Miami), *Continental* (Houston), *Delta* (Atlanta), *United* (Los Angeles), *Grupo Taca* (Miami). **From Canada** Connections are made through San Salvador, Los Angeles or Miami.

From Europe *Iberia* flies from Madrid via Miami, with connecting flights from other European cities. Long haul operators from Europe will share between airlines, taking passengers across the Atlantic normally to Miami, and using *Taca*, for example, to link to Guatemala City. *Air France* daily from Paris.

From Central America From San Salvador: *Taca* and *Copa*. From Tegucigalpa: *Taca*. From San Pedro Sula: *Taca* and *Copa*. From Mexico City: *Mexicana*. From Cancún: Taca. From Belize: *Taca* (see under Flores for flights from Belize and Mexico to El Petén). From Managua: *Copa*. From San José: *Lacsa*. From Panama: *Copa*, *Taca* (via San Salvador), *Lacsa* (via San José). See page 45, for regional airpasses.

From the Caribbean Copa from Santo Domingo and San Juan; Copa from Kingston and Montego Bay, Jamaica, and from Port au Prince via Panama. Copa from Havana.

From South America Lacsa from Bogotá via San José, Copa via Panama. **NB** If flying to Colombia you will have to have an outward ticket to be allowed a visa (though worth checking with Colombian embassy first); round-trip tickets Guatemala-Colombia are stamped 'Refundable only in Guatemala', but it is possible either to sell the return part on San Andrés island – at a discount – or to change it to an alternative destination. Lacsa flies from Santiago (Chile) and Lima with a stopover in San José, otherwise Copa flies via Panama.

Air
For international flights to Flores see Flores Transport

There are good road crossings with all of Guatemala's neighbouring countries. Several crossing points to Western Guatemala from southern **Mexico**, with additional routes through the jungle from Palenque. From **Belize** it is possible to cross from Benque Viejo del Carmen. Links with **Honduras** are possible on the Caribbean near Corinto, and for the ruins at Copán the best crossing is El Florida. There are three road routes in to **El Salvador**.

Overland

Touching down

There is a 17% ticket tax on all international tickets sold in Guatemala. A US$5 tourism tax is levied on all tickets sold in Guatemala to Guatemalan residents for travel abroad. There is no official entry tax, except for those nationalities needing a tourist card. There is also a US$30 or quetzal equivalent, airport and international departure tax, and a Q7.50/US$1 domestic departure tax. There is usually an unofficial tourist tax charge (10Q) at all borders, charged on leaving overland (borders may not be open 24 hours). These taxes vary from one border crossing to another, and from one official to another, and may be charged on entry as well as departure. Bribery is rife at border crossings, whether you are entering with a car or on foot.

Airport tax, entry & exit information

Guatemala

Touching down

Official time 6 hours behind GMT.
IDD 502.
Hours of business Business offices are open from 0800-1200, and 1400-1800 except Saturday. **Shops**: 0900-1300, 1500-1900, often mornings only on Saturday. **Banks** in Guatemala City: 0900-1500. In the main cities some banks are introducing later hours, up to 2000, while in the main tourist towns, some banks are open 7 days a week.
Voltage Generally 110 volts AC, 60 cycles. Electricity is generally reliable in the towns but can be a problem in the remoter areas, like

Petén. Take a torch to be on the safe side.
Weights and measures The metric system is obligatory on all Customs documents: specific duties are levied of weight, usually gross kilograms. United States measures are widely used in commerce; most foodstuffs are sold by the pound. The metric tonne of 1,000 kilograms is generally used; so is the US gallon. Old Spanish measures are often used; eg vara (33 inches/13 cm), caballería (111.5 acres/45 ha), manzana (1.7 acres/.7 ha), arroba (25 pounds/11 kg), and quintal (101 pounds/46 kg).

Always ask for a receipt and, if you have time and the language ability, do not give in to corrupt officials. Report any complaint to an INGUAT representative.

Local customs & laws **Begging** Guatemalan children can be persistent in asking for money in some tourist areas, a practice usually brought on by visitors offering money in the first place. If you give in to one another dozen will immediately appear.

Tipping Hotel staff: bell boys, US$0.25 for light luggage, US$0.50 for heavy. Restaurants 10% in the better places (see if a service charge has already been added to the bill). Airport porters: US$0.25 per piece of luggage. Taxi drivers: none.

Prohibitions Caught with drugs and you'll wind up in prison where the minimum penalty is five years. In the traditional laid-back travellers' drug haven of San Pedro on Lake Atitlán a number of police have been installed. Take care with gambling in public places and do not take photos of military installations.

Safety
National police T110; Tourist police in Antigua, T8327290

Since the 1996 ceasefire between government and URNG forces, travellers should not encounter difficulties, but if going to very isolated areas it may be wise to check conditions prior to travelling. In some parts of the country you may be subject to military or police checks. Local people are reluctant to discuss politics with strangers; it is best not to raise the subject. Do not necessarily be alarmed by 'gunfire' which is much more likely to be fireworks, etc, a national pastime, especially early in the morning.

Robberies and assaults on tourists are becoming more common. While you can do nothing to counter the bad luck of being in the wrong place at the wrong time, sensible precautions can minimize risks. Single women should be especially careful, but tourist groups are not immune and some excursion companies take necessary precautions. Bus hijacks are becoming more frequent; if possible travel by day, especially on the road between the Flores and Tikal in El Petén, and Flores and the Belizean border. Show sensitivity at all times when meeting people and children, especially with your camera. Specific warnings are given in the text, but visitors are advised to seek up-to-date local advice on places to avoid at the earliest opportunity.

Where to stay

Hotels
Rooms in the more expensive hotels are subject to 12% IVA (VAT) and 10% tourism tax

The tourist institute INGUAT publishes a list of maximum prices for single, double and triple occupancy of hundreds of hotels throughout the country in all price ranges, though the list is thin on the budget hotels. They will deal with complaints about overcharging if you can produce bills or other proof. Room rates should be posted in all registered hotels. Ask if taxes (*impuestos*) are included when you are given the room rate. Busiest seasons: Easter, December and the European summer holiday (July-August). Most budget hotels do not supply toilet paper, soap or towels. There are no official campsites in Guatemala.

Getting around

Air *Inter*, part of Grupo Taca, links Guatemala City with Flores/Santa Elena, T361-2144 (Guatemala City), www.flyinter.com   See under Flores/Santa Elena for services to Tikal.

Bus There is an extensive network of bus routes throughout the country. The chicken buses are mostly in a poor state of repair and overloaded. Faster and more reliable Pullman services operate on some routes. Correct fares should be posted up. We receive regular complaints that bus drivers charge tourists more than locals, a practice that is becoming more widespread. One way to avoid being overcharged is to ask the locals, then tender the exact fare on the bus. Many long-distance buses leave very early in the morning. Make sure you can get out of your hotel/*pensión*. For long trips, take snacks and water. For international bus journeys make sure you have small denomination local currency or US dollar bills for border taxes. At Easter there are few buses on Good Friday or the Saturday but they run again on Easter Sunday. On several popular tourist routes, for example Antigua-Panajachel, there are minibuses, comfortable and convenient, but a little overpriced and not as much fun as regular buses. They can be booked through hotels and travel agencies and will usually pick you up from your hotel. **NB** Many long names on bus destination boards are abbreviated: Guate = Guatemala City, Chichi = Chichicastenango, Xela = Xelajú = Quetzaltenango, etc. Buses in the west and north are called *camionetas*. Regarding pronunciation in Guatemala, 'X' is pronounced 'sh', as in Xela (shay-la).

Road There are 13,100 km of roads, 27% of which are paved

Car and motorcycle The paved roads have vastly improved in the past two years and are now of a high standard, making road travel faster and safer. Even cycle tracks (*ciclovías*) are beginning to appear on new roads, eg near San José. However, a new driving hazard in the highlands is the deep gully (for rainwater or falling stones) alongside the road. High clearance is essential on many roads in remoter areas and a four-wheel drive vehicle is useful.

Bringing a vehicle into Guatemala requires the following procedure: presentation of a valid International Driving Licence; a check by *cuarantena agropecuaria* (Ministry of Agriculture quarantine) to check you are not importing fruit or veg; at *Aduana* (Customs) you must pay Q35 for all forms and a tourist vehicle permit for your vehicle. A motorcycle entry permit costs the same as a car. The description of your vehicle on the registration document must match your vehicle's appearance exactly. You must own the car/motorcycle and your name must be on the title papers. When entering the country, ask the officials to add any important accessories you have to the paper. Car insurance can be bought at the borders.

On leaving the country by car or motorcycle, two stamps on a strip of paper are required: surrender of the vehicle permit at customs and the *cuarantena agropecuaria* (quarantine) inspection, which is not always carried out. It is better not to import and sell foreign cars in Guatemala as import taxes are very high.

Gasoline costs US$2.07 'normal', US$2.12 'premium' for the US gallon. Unleaded (*sin plomo*) is available in major cities, at Melchor de Mencos and along the Pan-American Highway, but not in the countryside, although it is gradually being introduced across the country. Diesel costs US$1.30 a gallon. All gas is cheaper in the capital than anywhere else.

Security   Spare no ingenuity in making your car or motorbike secure. Try never to leave the car unattended except in a locked garage or guarded parking space. Lock the clutch or accelerator to the steering wheel with a heavy, obvious chain or lock. Street children will generally protect your car fiercely in exchange for a tip. Don't wash your car: smart cars attract thieves. Be sure to note down key numbers and carry spares of the most important ones. Try not to leave your fully laden motorbike on its own. An Abus D or chain will keep the bike secure. A cheap alarm gives you peace of mind if you leave the bike outside a hotel at night. Most hotels will allow you to bring the bike inside. Look for hotels that have a courtyard or more secure parking and never leave luggage on the bike overnight or whilst unattended. Also take a cover for the bike. Just about all motorbike parts and accessories are available at decent prices in Guatemala City at *FPK*, 5 Calle, 6-75, Zona 9.

Border crossings From Mexico to Western Guatemala: *Tecún Umán/Ciudad Hidalgo* is the main truckers' crossing. It is very busy and should be avoided at all costs by car. *Talismán*,

Guatemala

the next border crossing north, is more geared to private cars; there are the usual hordes of helpers to guide you through the procedures, for a fee. *La Mesilla* is the simplest for private cars and you can do your own paperwork with ease. All necessary documents can be obtained here. Any of the crossings from Guatemala into Mexico are straightforward.

Car hire cars may not always be taken into neighbouring countries (none is allowed into Mexico or Belize); rental companies that do not allow their vehicles to cross borders charge US$15 for the permits and paperwork. Credit cards or cash are accepted for rental.

Cycling

Reports of harassment by police asking for protection fees have been received

The scenery is gorgeous, the people friendly and colourful, but the hills are steep and sometimes long. The Pan-American Highway is OK from Guatemala City west; it has a shoulder and traffic is not very heavy. Cycling is hard, but enjoyable. Buses are frequent and it is easy to load a bicycle on the roof; many buses do so, charging about two-thirds of the passenger fare. On the road, buses are a hazard for cyclists, Guatemala City is particularly dangerous. Look out for the cycle tracks (*ciclovías*) on a few main roads.

Hitchhiking

Hitching is comparatively easy, but risky, especially for single women. Also beware of theft of luggage, especially in trucks. The best place to try for a lift is at a bridge or on a road out of town; be there no later than 0600, but 0500 is better as that is when truck drivers start their journey. Trucks usually charge US$1-1.50 upwards for a lift/day. Recently, travellers suggest it can be cheaper by bus. In remote areas lifts in the back of a pick-up are usually available; very crowded, but convenient when bus services are few and far between, or stop early in the day.

Train

The railways were closed down in 1995 though the track mostly remains.

Maps

The *Instituto Geográfico Nacional* (IGN - www.ign.gob.gt) produces detailed maps, see Guatemala City. The best internationally available map of the country is from ITMB (No 642, Third Edition 1998, 1:500,000).

Keeping in touch

Internet

Internet cafés are found in all the popular tourist destinations, ask around in the cities for the best rates. Rates vary depending on supply and demand from US$1 to US$5 an hour.

Post

Airmail to Europe takes 10-14 days. Letters cost US$0.52 for the first 20 g and between US$5.85 for 100 g to US$48 for a maximum weight of 2 kg. Airmail letters to the US and Canada cost US$0.39 for the first 20 g. Airmail parcel service to the US is reliable (four to 14 days) and costs US$3.76 for 100 g up to US$31.90 for 2 kg. Note, that parcels over 2 kg may only be sent abroad from Guatemala City, Correos y Telégrafos, 7 Avenida y 12 Calle, Zona 1. See in the text under Panajachel and Chichicastenango for alternative services.

Telephone

All phone numbers in the country are on a 7-figure basis. No prefixes (eg 0 for numbers outside Guatemala City) are necessary. For directory enquiries, dial 1524

There are two main service providers for the traveller – *Telgua* and *Telefónica*. *Telefónica* sell cards with access codes for up to Q45, which can be used from any private or public *Telefónica* phone. *Telgua* phone booths are ubiquitous. They use cards sold in values of Q20, Q30 and Q50. The price of a local call is US$0.05 per minute; a national call costs US$0.77 per minute. Most businesses offering a phone call service charge a minimum of US$0.13 for a local call, therefore it's a cheaper option to buy a phone card. International calls can be made from these booths, however unlike the local calls it is cheaper to find an internet café or shop who tend to offer better rates (eg in Antigua some companies offer calls through the internet at US$0.26 per minute to Europe). Operator calls are more expensive. For calling card and credit card call options you need a fixed line in a hotel or private house. First you dial 9999 plus the following three-digit number: For Sprint USA, dial 195; MCI USA: 189; AT&T USA: 190; Germany: 049; Canada: 198; UK (BT): 044; Switzerland: 041; Spain: 034, Italy: 039. Collect calls may be made from public *Telgua* phones by dialling T147 120.

Newspapers The main newspaper is *Prensa Libre* (www.prensalibre.com). *The Guatemala* **Media**
Post is published in English. *Siglo Veintiuno* is a good newspaper, started in 1989
(www.sigloxxi.com). Mega popular is *Nuestro Diario*, a tabloid with more pics than copy. *The*
Revue, produced monthly in Antigua, carries articles, advertisements, lodgings, tours and
excursions, covering Antigua, Pana, Xela, Río Dulce and Guatemala City.

Food and drink

Traditional Central American/Mexican food such as tortillas, tamales, tostadas, etc are found **Food**
everywhere. Tacos are less spicy than in Mexico. *Chiles rellenos*, chillies stuffed with meat and
vegetables, are a speciality in Guatemala and may be *picante* (spicy) or *no picante*. *Churrasco*,
charcoal-grilled steak, is often accompanied by *chirmol*, a sauce of tomato, onion and mint.
Guacamole is also excellent. Local dishes include *pepián* (thick meat stew with vegetables) in
Antigua, *patín* (tomato-based sauce served with *pescaditos*, small fish from Lake Atitlán
wrapped in leaves), *cecina* (beef marinated in lemon and bitter orange) from the same region.
Fiambre is widely prepared for families and friends who gather on All Saints' Day (1
November). It consists of all kinds of meat, fish, chicken, vegetables, eggs or cheese served as a
salad with rice, beans and other side dishes.

   Desserts include *mole* (plantain and chocolate), *torrejas* (sweet bread soaked in egg and
panela or honey) and *buñuelos* (similar to profiteroles) served with hot cinnamon syrup.

   For breakfast try *mosh* (oats cooked with milk and cinnamon), fried plantain with cream,
black beans in various forms. *Pan dulce* (sweet bread), in fact bread in general, and local
cheese are recommended. Try *borracho* (cake soaked in rum).

Local beers are good (Monte Carlo, Cabra, Gallo and Moza, a dark beer); bottled, carbonated **Drink**
soft drinks (*gaseosas*) are safest. Milk should be pasteurized. Freshly made *refrescos* and
ice-creams are delicious made of many varieties of local fruits; *licuados* are fruit juices with
milk or water, but hygiene varies, so take care. Water should be filtered or bottled.

Shopping

Visiting a **market** in Guatemala can be one of the most enjoyable and memorable experiences
of any trip. Bartering in the markets is the norm and is almost expected and unbelievable
discounts can be obtained. But getting the discount is less important than paying a fair price.
Woven goods are normally cheapest bought in the town of origin. Try to avoid middlemen and
buy direct from the weaver. You won't do better anywhere else in Central America.

   Guatemalan **coffee** is highly recommended, although the best is exported; coffee sold
locally is not vacuum-packed. **Kerosene** is called *gas corriente*, and is good quality, US$1 per
US gallon; sold only in gas stations. **Film for transparencies** is hard to find but it is normally
available in Guatemala City at 9 C, 6-88, Zona 1, and in other large cities.

Holidays and festivals

1 January; Holy Week (four days – very good in Antigua); **1 May**: Labour Day; **30 June**; **15**
August: (Guatemala City only); **15 September**: Independence Day; **12 October**: Discovery of
America; **20 October**: Revolution Day; **1 November**: All Saints; **24 December**: Christmas Eve:
from noon; **25 December**: Christmas Day; **31 December** (from noon). 12 October and
Christmas Eve are not business holidays. During Holy Week, bus fares may be doubled.
Although specific dates are given for fiestas there is often a week of jollification beforehand.

Sport and special interest travel

Archaeology is the big attraction. Consequently there are a huge number of organizations **Archaeology**
offering tours. There are also a number of tour operators that operate out of Flores and Santa
Elena in the Petén using local villagers to help with expeditions, so that there is some
economic benefit to those places that many travellers pass through. Others include *Maya*

Guatemala

Expeditions, 15 Calle "A", 14-07, Zona 10, Guatemala City, T363-4955, F3634965, www.maya expeditions.com They offer trips to Piedras Negras with archaeologists, who worked on the 1990s excavation of the site, Río Azul, the Petexbatún area, El Mirador, led by Doctor Richard Hansen, the chief archaeologist of the site, and a brand new trip to the recently discovered Cancuen site, led by its chief archaeologist, Doctor Arthur Demarest. *Explorations*, 27655 Kent Road, Bonita Springs, Florida, FL 34135, T1-941-9929660, Toll free T1–800-446-9660, has tours led by an archaeologist and Maya specialist Travis Doering. Use first class services.

Bird-watching Contact the **Guatemalan Birding Resource Center**, 7 Calle, 15-18, Zona 1, Quetzaltenango, T7677339, www.xelapages/gbrc or Anne Berry, 7361 Hawthorne Lane, Indianapois, IN46250, T317-8421494, an American ornithologist who has spent some time on the ground seeking out the best spots. *Footprint Adventures*, 5 Malham Drive, Lincoln, UK, LN6 OXD, T01522-804929, F804928, www.birding-tours.co.uk in the UK offer country-wide birding tours led by ornithologists. *Aventuras Naturales*, Avenida La Reforma, 1-50, Zona 9, Edif El Reformador, Guatemala City, T/F3345222, aventuras@centramerica.com specializes in guided birding tours.

Fishing Sailfish, bill fish, marlin, tuna, dorado, roosterfish, yellowfin, and snapper can all be found in large
The Pacific coast is numbers, especially bill fish. **Tour operators:** *Artmarina*, www.artmarina.com, one of the biggest
world renowned for concerns at Iztapa running a fishing lodge, *Fish 'n' Feathers Inn* also.
deep sea fishing www.fishinginternational.com/location/guatemala, www.tropicalfishing.com/guatemala See also under Iztapa and Monterrico.

Mountain Mountain biking is an increasingly popular activity in Guatemala. There are numerous tracks
biking and paths that weave there way across the country, passing hamlets as you go. There are two recommended operators in Antigua, which also deal in the gear, should you be biking around independently: *Mayan Bike Tours*, 3 Calle Poniente y 7 Avenida Norte, T8323743, www.mayanbike.com, offer guided tours from US$15 per person. *Old Town Outfitters*, 6 Calle Poniente 7, T8324243, www.bikeguatemala.com offer mountain bike tours starting at US$25 for a half-day tour.

Mountain & Guatemala represents a wealth of opportunity for climbers – with more than 30 volcanoes
volcano on offer. There are also the heights of the Cuchumatanes Mountains in the Highlands, which
climbing claims the highest non-volcanic peak in the country at 3,837 m, and those of the relatively
For volcano climbing unexplored Sierra de Las Minas in eastern Guatemala close to the Río Motagua Valley. For
around Guatemala climbing in the Sierra de las Minas, a biosphere reserve, contact *La Fundación de la*
City and Antigua see *Naturaleza*, 19 Av "B", 0-83, Zona 15, Vista Hermosa II, T369-5151, www.defensores.org.gt, to
page 579 and 591 obtain a *permiso*.

Nature The majority of tour operators listed in this guide will offer nature-oriented tours. There are
tourism several national parks, *biotopos* and protected areas in Guatemala, each with their highlights. **CECON** (*Centro de Estudios Conservacionistas*) and INGUAT have set up conservation areas (*biotopos*) for the protection of Guatemalan wildlife (the quetzal, the manatee, the jaguar, etc) and their habitats. Several other national parks (some including Maya archaeological sites) and forest reserves have been set up or are planned. Many of these are administered by the national parks and protected areas authority **CONAP** (*Consejo Nacional de Areas Protegidas*), 5 Avenida, 6-06, Zona 1, Guatemala City, T238-0000, http://conap.online.fr Another useful organization is the non-profit making ecological project, **Proyecto Ecológico Quetzal**, 2 Calle, 14-36, Zona 1, Cobán, T/F9521047, bidaspeq@guate.net, run by David Unger.

Spiritual There is a spiritual centre on the shores of Lake Atitlán that offers courses in accordance with the
interest cycle of the moon: *Las Pirámides* is in San Marcos La Laguna and offers yoga, meditation as well as spiritual instruction year round (see also page 609). At the *Takilibén Maya Misión* in Momostenango, day keeper Rigoberto Itzep offers courses in Maya culture. You can leave a message for him on T7365051 from Mon-Fri between 0800-1200, 1400-1700, www.geocities.com/rainforest/jungle/989 See also page 620.

Guatemala

It is possible to get weaving lessons in many towns and villages across the Highlands. See the text for details. Weaving lessons can also be organized through Spanish schools.

Textiles & weaving

Diving You can dive in Lake Atitlán with *ATI Divers* at *La Iguana Perdida* in Santa Cruz, T7622646, santacruz@guate.net Also run dive trips off the Caribbean Coast.

Water sports

Kayaking Kayak tours (five days for US$350) are run by *Old Town Outfitters*, 6 Calle Poniente 7 Antigua, T8324243, www.bikeguatemala.com

Waterskiing Possible at Río Dulce from *Hacienda Tijax*, www.tijax.com, see page 658, and from *La Iguana Perdida* in Santa Cruz La Laguna, see under diving for the address.

Whitewater rafting This water sport can be done on a number of rivers in Guatemala of different grades. However, none of the trips are turn up and go – they have to be arranged in advance, and, as with most things, the larger the group, the cheaper the cost. The country's best outfitter is *Maya Expeditions*, see address under Archaeology. They raft the Río Cahabón in Alta Verapaz, (Class III-V), the Río Naranjo close to Coatepeque (Class III), the Río Motagua close to Guatemala City (Class III-IV), the Río Esclavos, near Barbarena (Class III-IV), the Río Coyolate close to Santa Lucía Cotzumalguapa (Class II-III) and the Río Chiquibul in the Petén (Class II-III). They also run a rafting and caving tour in the Petén and a combined archaeology and rafting tour where you would raft through a canyon on the Río Usumacinta (Class II). *Maya Expeditions* also arrange bungee jumping at Río Dulce.

Guatemala

Health

Guatemala is healthy enough if precautions are taken about drinking-water, milk, uncooked vegetables and peeled fruits; carelessness on this point is likely to lead to amoebic dysentery, which is endemic. In Guatemala City three good hospitals are: *Bella Aurora*, 10 Calle A Zona 14, *Centro Médico*, 6 Av 3-47, Zona 10, T332-3555, and *Herrera Llerandi*, 6 Av/9 C, Zona 10, T334-5959, but you must have full medical insurance or sufficient funds to pay for treatment. English and other languages are spoken. Most small towns have clinics. At the public hospitals, which are seriously underfunded and where care for major problems is not good, you may have an examination for a nominal fee, but drugs are expensive. There is an immunization centre at *Centro de Salud* No 1, 9 C, 2-64, Zona 1, Guatemala City (no yellow fever vaccinations). In the highlands avoid excessive exertion. If going to the Maya sites, jungle areas and coastal regions, prophylaxis against malaria is strongly advised; there may also be a yellow fever risk. Cholera has been reported since 1991 and you should be particularly careful buying uncooked food in market *comedores* where good hygiene may be doubtful. You may pick up parasites if you swim in lakes.

Guatemala City

Smog-bound and crowded, Guatemala City is the commercial and administrative centre of the country. A sprawl of industrial activity lightly sprinkled with architectural treasures and out-of-place tributes to urban sculpture. Rarely rated by visitors, this is the beating heart of Guatemala and worth a couple of days if you have time and can bear the noise. Guatemala City is surrounded by active and dormant volcanoes easily visited on day trips.

Guatemala City □

Colour map 5, grid C2
Population: 1,150,452
Altitude: 1,500m

Ins and outs

The airport is in the south part of the city at La Aurora, 4 km from the Plaza Central. The Zona 4 chicken bus terminal between 1-4 Av and 7-9 C serves the Occidente (west), the Costa Sur (Pacific coastal plain) and El Salvador. The area of 19 C, 8-9 Av, Zona 1, next to the Plaza Barrios market, contains many bus offices and is the departure point for the Oriente (east), the Caribbean zone, Pacific coast area towards the Mexican border and the north, to Flores and Tikal. First-class buses often depart from company offices in Zona 1 (see map).

Getting there

Guatemala

Getting around
All addresses in the text are Zona 1 unless stated otherwise

Any address not in Zona 1 – and it is absolutely essential to quote zone numbers in addresses – is probably some way from the centre. Addresses themselves, being purely numerical, are usually easy to find. For example, 19 C, 4-83 is on 19 C between 4 Av and 5 Av at number 83.

Tourist office Inguat, 7 Av, 1-17, Zona 4 (Centro Cívico), 24 hrs 1801-INGUAT-1, T331-1333, F331-8893, www.travel-guatemala.org.gt English is spoken They are very friendly and provide a hotel list, a map of the city, and general information on buses, market days, museums, etc. They also have other maps and information on major tourist attractions. Open Mon-Fri 0800-1600. For information on the Biotopos (nature reserves) contact **CECON**, Av La Reforma 0-63 Zona 10, T361-5450, cecon@usac.edu.gt

Background

Guatemala City was founded by decree of Charles III of Spain in 1776 to serve as capital after earthquake damage to the earlier capital, Antigua, in 1773. Almost completely destroyed by earthquakes in 1917-18, it was rebuilt in modern fashion, or in copied colonial, only to be further damaged by earthquake in 1976. Most of the affected buildings have been restored.

Sights

For sights close to Guatemala City, see Excursions from Guatemala City and Antigua on page 592

The old centre of the city is Zona 1. It is still a busy shopping and commercial area, with several good hotels and restaurants, and many of the cheaper places to stay. However, the main activity of the city has been moving south for some years, first to Zona 4, now to Zonas 9, 10 and 14. With the move have gone companies, commerce, banks, embassies, museums and the best hotels and restaurants. Industry is mostly to the north and southwest. The best residential areas are in the hills to the east, southeast and west. The different centres add to the dispersed feel of the capital.

Around Zona 1

At the city's heart lies the **Parque Central**. It is intersected by the north-south running 6 Avenida, the main shopping street. The eastern half has a floodlit fountain; on the west side is **Parque Centenario**, with an acoustic shell in cement used for open-air concerts and public meetings. The Parque Central is popular on Sunday with many *indígenas* selling textiles. To the east of the plaza is the **Catedral**. It was begun in 1782 and finished in 1815 in classical style with notable blue cupolas and dome. Inside are paintings and statues from ruined Antigua. Solid silver and sacramental

Related maps
A Guatemala Zone 1 page 568
B Guatemala City, Zona 9, 19 & 13, page 571

Guatemala City orientation

N

0 km 1
0 miles

To Mapa en Relieve
C 5
C 2
A
Av 6A
Plaza Mayor
C 8
Av 10
ZONA 1
C 18
Buses to Antigua
To Hyatt Regency Hotel (Tikal Futura), Kaminal Juyu, Antigua & the West
Av Bolívar
Teatro Nacional
Centro Cívico
ZONA 4
B
Av 6
Av Reforma
Muse Popo Vuh
Museo Ixchel
ZONA 9
ZONA 10
Diagonal 12
Museo Nacional de Arqueología y Etnología
Av 11
La Aurora International Airport
ZONA 13

eliquary are in the east side chapel of the Sagrario. Next to the cathedral is the colo-
ial mansion of the Archbishop. Aside from the cathedral, the most notable public
buildings constructed between 1920 and 1944, after the 1917 earthquake, are the
Palacio Nacional, built of light green stone (the guards have keys and may show you
round the state rooms), the Police Headquarters, the Chamber of Deputies and the
Post Office. To the west of the cathedral are the **Biblioteca Nacional** and the *Banco
del Ejército*. Behind the **Palacio Nacional** is the Presidential Mansion.

Most of the churches worth visiting are in Zona 1. **Cerro del Carmen**, 11 Av y 1 Calle **Churches**
A, Zona 1, was built as a copy of a hermitage destroyed in 1917-18, containing a
famous image of the Virgen del Carmen. Situated on a hill with good views of the
city, it was severely damaged in the earthquake of 1976 and remains in poor shape.
La Merced, 11 Av y 5 C, dedicated in 1813, has beautiful altars, organ and pulpit
from Antigua as well as jewellery, art treasures and fine statues. **Santo Domingo**, 12
Av y 10 C, 1782-1807, is a striking yellow colour, reconstructed after 1917, image of
Nuestra Señora del Rosario and sculptures. **Santuario Expiatorio**, 26 C y 2 Av,
holds 3,000 people; the colourful, exciting modern architecture was by a young
Salvadorean architect who had not qualified when he built it. Part of the complex
(church, school and auditorium) is in the shape of a fish. **Las Capuchinas**, 10 Av y
10 C, has a very fine St Anthony altarpiece, and other pieces from Antigua. **Santa
Rosa**, 10 Av y 8 C, was used for 26 years as the cathedral until the present building
was ready. The altarpieces are again from Antigua (except above the main altar). **San
Francisco**, 6 Av y 13 C, a large yellow and white church which shows earthquake
damage outside (1976), has a sculpture of the Sacred Head, originally from
Extremadura, in Spain. **Carmen El Bajo**, 8 Av y 10 C, was built in the late 18th century; again the façade was severely damaged in 1976.

Museo Nacional de Historia, 9 C, 9-70, T253-6149, has historical documents and **Museums**
objects from Independence onward. ■ *Mon-Fri 0800-1700, free.*

   Museo de la Universidad de San Carlos de Guatemala (MUSAC) charts the
history of the university. The Salon Mayor, opposite the entrance, is where Guatemala signed its independence from Mexico in 1823, and in 1826, the Central American Federation, with Guatemala as the seat of power, abolished slavery in the union.
Also, the country's president from 1831-38, Doctor Mariano Gálvez, is buried
behind part of the salon wall and a marble bust of him sits outside the salon door.
The Universidad de San Carlos was the first university in Guatemala City.
■ *Mon-Fri 0930-1730, except Tue. Sat 0930-1300, 1400-1730, US$1.05. Guided
tours are available at 1100 and 1500. Large groups need to reserve. T232-0721,
musac@intelnet.net.gt, 9 Av, 9-79.*

   Casa MIMA is the only authentic turn-of-the-19th-century family home open to
the public, once owned by the family Ricardo Escobar Vega and Mercedes
Fernandez Padilla y Abella. It is furnished throughout in European-influenced style
with 15th- to mid 20th-century furniture and ornaments. ■ *Mon-Sat, 0900-1230,
1400-1700, US$2 adults, US$1.30 students, US$0.65 children, no photography,
T253-6657, CasaMima@hotmail.com, 8 Av, 14-12.*

To the north, in Zona 2, is the fine **Parque Minerva**, where there is a huge relief map **Zona 2**
of the country made in 1905 to a horizontal scale of 1:10,000 and a vertical scale of
1:2,000. The park has basketball and baseball courts, swimming pool, bar and restaurant and a children's playground (it is unsafe at night). ■ *0900-1700, US$2.
Buses V21 from 7 Av, Zona 4.*

Guatemala

South of the centre: Avenida La Reforma

Each museum has a sign to the effect that Guatemala prohibits the exportation from the country of any antique object, either pre-Columbian or colonial

The modern **Centro Cívico**, which links Zona 1 with Zona 4, includes th Municipalidad, the Palacio de Justicia, the Ministerio de Finanzas Públicas, th Banco de Guatemala, the mortgage bank, the social-security commission and th tourist board. The **Teatro Nacional** dominates the hilltop of the west side of th Centro Cívico. There is an excellent view of the city and surrounding mountain from the roof. An old Spanish fortress provides a backdrop to the Open Air Theatr

djoining the blue and white mosaic-covered Teatro Nacional. ■ *Open Mon-Fri 0800-1630 for tours, free, but tips appreciated.*

To see the finest residential district go south down 7 Av to Ruta 6, which runs diagonally in front of Edificio El Triángulo, past the **Capilla de Yurrita** (Ruta 6 y Vía 8). Built as a private chapel in 1928 on the lines of a Russian Orthodox church, it has been described as an example of "opulent 19th-century bizarreness and over-ripe extravagance". There are many woodcarvings, slender white pillars, brown/gold ornamentation and an unusual blue sky window over the altar. Ruta 6 runs into the wide tree-lined **Avenida La Reforma**.

To the east, in Zona 10, are some good museums. **Museo Ixchel del Traje Indígena**, in the Campus of Universidad Francisco Marroquín, 6 C Final, has a collection of Indian costumes. In addition to costumes there are photos from the early 20th century, paintings and very interesting videos. A shop sells textiles that aren't usually available on the tourist market, prices are fixed. ■ *Mon-Fri 0900-1700, Sat 0900-1300, US$2.60, students US$1.05, T331-3622.* **Museo Popol Vuh de Arqueología**, also at 6 C Final. Extensive collection of pre-Columbian and colonial artefacts, as well as a replica of the Dresden Codex, one of the only Maya parchment manuscripts in existence. ■ *Mon-Fri 0900-1700, Sat 0900-1300, US$2.60, students US$1.05, US$2 charge to take photographs, T361-2301.* **Museo de Historia Natural de la USAC y Jardín Botánico**. Gardens, stuffed animals and live serpents. ■ *Mon-Fri 0800-1600, US$1.30, C Mcal Cruz 1-56, T334-6065.*

In **Parque Aurora**, Zona 13, in the southern part of the city, are La Aurora International Airport, the Observatory, racetrack and **Parque Zoológico La Aurora**. ■ *Tue-Sun 0900-1700, US$1.05.* The newer areas show greater concern for the animals' well-being. There are also several museums. **Museo Nacional de Antropolgía y Etnología**, Salón 5, Parque Aurora, Zona 13, T472-0489, contains outstanding Maya pieces including stelae from Piedras Negras and typical Guatemalan costumes, as well as good models of Tikal, Quiriguá and Zaculeu, and other Maya items. There are sculptures, murals, ceramics, textiles, a collection of masks

N
litres 200
rds 200

Sleeping
Belén *D3*
Capri *E3*
CentroAmérica *E3*
Chalet Suizo *D2*
Colonial *E3*
Continental *D2*
Monteleone *E2*
Pan American *C2*
Pensión Meza *C3*
Ritz Continental *C2*
Spring *D3*

Eating
Altuna *D2*
Arrin Cuan *A2*
Café de Imeri *B2*
Europa *D2*
Helados Marylena *B1*
Rey Sol *C2*
Rey Sol 2 *C2*

Bars
Bodeguita del Centro *D2*
El Encuentro *D2*
El Portal *C2*
Ephebus *B2*
Las Cien Puertas
& El Tiempo *C2*
Tzijolaj *C2*

Transport
Escobar-Monja
Blanca to Cobán *E3*
Fuente del Norte to
Río Dulce & Santa
Elena/Flores *E3*

3 Línea Dorada to Río
Dulce & Flores *E3*
4 Líneas Américas to
Quetzaltenango *E1*
5 Los Halcones to
Huehuetenango *E3*
6 Marquensita to
Quetzaltenango *F1*
7 Rutas Orientales to
Chiquimula & Esquipulas
& Transportes Fortaleza
to Tecún Umán *F3*
8 Tacana to
Quetzaltenango *F1*
9 Terminal for
buses to Chimaltenango,
Panajachel & Santa Cruz
del Quiché *F1*
10 Transportes Alamo to
Quetzaltenango *F1*
11 Transportes Centro
América to San
Salvador *E3*
12 Transportes Galgos
to Mexico *F2*
13 Transportes Litegua to
Puerto Barrios &
Río Dulce *E3*
14 Transportes Poaquileña
to Tecpán *F2*
15 Transportes Rebuli to
Panajachel *F1*
16 Transportes Rosita to
Santa Elena/Flores &
Melchor de Mencos *E3*
17 Transportes Unidos to
Antigua *E2*
18 Transportes Velásquez to
Huehuetenango
& La Mesilla (Mexican
border) *F1*

Guatemala

and an excellent jade collection. ■ *Tue-Fri 0900-1600, Sat-Sun 0900-1200 1330-1600, US$3.90, no photos.* Around the corner is the **Museo Nacional de Historia Natural**, which houses a collection of national fauna, including stuffed birds, animals, butterflies, geological specimens, etc. ■ *Mon-Fri 0900-1600, Sat-Sun 0900-1200, 1400-1800, US$1.30, T4720468.* Opposite the archaeology museum, the **Museo de Arte Moderno**, Salón 6, Parque Aurora, Zona 13, T4720467, has a modest but enjoyable collection, but was closed at the time of writing. Next door is the **Museo de los Niños**, an interactive museum with a gallery of Mayan history and the Gallery of Peace which houses the world's largest single standing artificial tree - a *ceiba.* ■ *Tue-Fri 0800-1200, 1300-1700. Sat-Sun 1000-1330, 1430-1800, US$4.50, T4755076.*

Kaminal Juyú On the western outskirts in Zona 7 are the Maya ruins of Kaminal Juyú (Valley of Death). About 200 mounds have been examined by the Archaeological Museum and the Carnegie Institute. The area is mainly unexcavated, but there are three excavated areas open to the public, and a sculpture shed. ■ *0900-1600, free. Bus T2000 goes to the site and can be picked up at the 2 Av and 17 C, Zona 1.*

Essentials

Sleeping

Hotel prices are subject to a 10% tourist tax and 12% VAT (IVA). Make sure the price you have been quoted includes the tax. Thefts from hotel rooms and baggage stores occur and not just from the budget places. You can get better prices in the more expensive hotels by booking corporate rates through a travel agent or simply asking at the desk if any lower prices are available. Hotels are often full at holiday times, eg Easter and Christmas. At the cheaper hotels single rooms are not always available. There are many cheap *pensiones* near bus and railway stations and markets; those between C 14 and C 18 are not very salubrious.

Zona 1
■ *on map, page 568*
Price codes:
see inside front cover

Hotels are listed by zone and price category. All hotels have hot water unless otherwise stated

AL-A *Pan American*, 9 C, 5-63, T232-6807, F232-6402, www.hotelpanamerican.com Quiet and comfortable rooms with TV, but try to avoid rooms on the main road side. Parking, and breakfast included. Restaurant with good food in the mid-range price bracket. Meals are served by staff in typical costumes, which look a tad ridiculous, especially in contrast to the maelstrom of Zona 1 just outside. **A** *Ritz Continental*, 6 Av "A", 10-13, T238-1871, F238-1684. Standard rooms with TV, a pool and a pleasant mid-range priced restaurant.

B *Colonial*, 7 Av, 14-19, T232-6722, F232-8671. Reasonable restaurant for breakfast. Rooms are quiet with TV and nice dark cedar wood beds and furniture. It's pleasant and friendly too. Recommended. **B** *Posada Belén*, 13 C "A", 10-30, T232-9226, F251-3478, www.posadabelen.com A colonial-style house run by the friendly Francesca and René Sanchinelli, who speak English. Laundry, email service, luggage store and good dining-room. Recommended. They also run tours and a well-researched website: www.guatemala web.com

C-D *Chalet Suizo*, 14 C, 6-82, T251-3786, F232-0429. In a good central position with constant hot-water showers (cheaper with shared bathroom). It is popular, so often crowded. There is a locked luggage store, safety box, and the rooms are secure. However, those rooms facing the main street are noisy. Also, avoid rooms 9 to 12 as a noisy pump will disturb sleep and 19 to 21 have very thin walls.

D *Capri*, 9 Av, 15-63, T232-8191. Private showers (cheaper without). Some rooms are noisy and dark, others bright, but all are clean, with TV. It's a good deal for single travellers and the management is friendly. Just check out the available rooms before putting your bags down. **D-E** *CentroAmérica*, 9 Av, 16-38, T220-6371. 58 rooms with or without bathroom, TV costs extra. There's a safe deposit, cheap restaurant next door, iced drinking water and internet

(US$4/hr). Peaceful, with helpful staff and an excellent deal for single travellers. **D** *Continental*, 12 C, 6-10, T230-5814, F251-8265. Two floors up in a central building with a very secure street entrance. It has absolutely vast, comfortable rooms, but they're spartan; some quadruples available. All are very clean with private bath, TV costs extra. **D** *Spring*, 8 Av, 12-65, T2302858, F232-0107. Bright rooms with TV (costs a little extra) in this quiet haven of tranquillity and flowers amid the pollution of Zona 1. Rooms without private shower are cheaper. There is a patio garden, good breakfasts, and parking near by; popular. Free coffee, email service at US$1.30/hr, phone calls, luggage store at US$1 daily. Probably the nicest place to stay in this zone for this price. Recommended.

E *Monteleone*, 18 C, 4-63, T238-2600, F238-9205, monteleone@intelnet.net.gt In front of Antigua bus terminal. This hotel wins no prizes either for its façade, which looks seriously run down from the outside, but inside there are clean rooms, some with private bathroom. It's secure and safe, and staff are helpful. **F** *Pensión Meza*, 10 C, 10-17, T232-3177. A large ramshackle place with beds in dormitories **F** per person. It is popular, staff are helpful and English is spoken. It is reported as noisy and some rooms are damp. Other rooms are darker than a prison cell, but cheered by graffiti, poetry and paintings. There is a ping pong table and book exchange. Beware of petty theft.

Guatemala

Zona 9, 10 & 13

■ Sleeping		7 Westin Camino Real *C2*	7 Los Ranchos *C2*
1 Aguilar *A2*			8 Sophos *C2*
2 Holiday Inn & Las		● Eating	
Mañanitas Restaurant *C2*		1 Hacienda de los	● Bars
3 Istmo *A1*		Sánchez *B3*	9 Cheers *B2*
4 Posada de Los		2 Hacienda Real *C2*	10 El Establo *C3*
Próceres *C2*		3 Jimmy John's *B2*	11 Shakespeare's
5 Princess Reforma *C2*		4 Kacao *C2*	Pub *C2*
6 San Carlos & Residencial		5 Lai-Lai *C2*	
Reforma La Casa Grande *B2*		6 Los Alpes *B2*	

Zona 9
■ *on map, page 571*

AL *Hotel Princess Reforma*, 13 C, 7-65, T334-4545, F334-4546, princgua@guate.net Attractive and comfortable rooms with a/c and all mod cons, including cable TV, and phone. There's also a pool and excellent service. **B** *Carillón*, 5 Av, 11-25, T/F3324036. 16 rooms all with private bath, a/c and TV, handy for the airport so can be noisy, but friendly. **C-D** *Hotel del Istmo*, 3 Av, 1-38, Zona 9, T332-4389. A stone's throw from the Zona 4 terminal, and right above the El Salvador bus terminal. Its 27 rooms are nicer than the *Aguilar's* (see below) with private bath and TV (cheaper without TV), and there's 24-hr security, and free coffee, but it's a bit more expensive, and probably a lot noisier. **E** *Aguilar*, 4 Av, 1-51, close to the Zona 4 terminal, T334-7164. Modern, with 34 clean rooms, private bath and TV and good cheap food in the restaurant. Can be a bit noisy, but handy if you are going to El Salvador by bus.

Zona 10
■ *on map, page 571*

L *Westin Camino Real*, Av La Reforma and 14 C, T333-4633, F337-4313, www.westin.com An excellent value hotel in this range for a long time, good restaurants open 0600-2330, gym, pool, spa, airport shuttle, and live Cuban music Fri and Sat at 2100. **AL** *Hotel San Carlos*, Av La Reforma, 7-89, T362-9076, F331-6411, hscarlos@gua.net A small, charming hotel, with pool and plant-filled patio. More expensive than the *Residencial Reforma* (see below). Recommended. **AL** *Residencial Reforma La Casa Grande*, Av La Reforma, 7-67, T/F3320914. Near the US Embassy, with nicer rooms than the next door *San Carlos*. All rooms come with TV. There's a good small restaurant, open 0630-2100, a bar and internet service. Good value in this price range. **A** *Posada de Los Próceres*, 16 C, 2-40, T363-0744, F3681405, posadazv@gua.net Includes breakfast in the room price. Some rooms are quite musty, which is off-putting. Staff are friendly and there's internet and TV. It's secure and 5 mins from the airport. **B** *Holiday Inn*, 1 Av, 13-22, T332-2555, F332-2567, holidayinn@guate.net This is an excellent value hotel in this range with a pool, gym, restaurant, email centre, and free airport shuttle available. There's an atmospheric little restaurant – *Las Mañanitas* – next door (see eating).

Zona 11

LL *Hyatt Regency*, Calzada Roosevelt, 22-43, T4401234, F4404050. A large convention hotel and centrepiece of the 'Tikal Futura' commercial zone. It has all the top-class services, but is isolated from the city. It offers live Cuban music from Mon-Sat at 2100.

Zona 13 & airport area

AL *Meliá Guatemala*, Av Las Américas, 9-08, T339-0666, www.lasamericas.hotel.com Top-class hotel with a new pool and spa club, suites are available. **C** *Hotel Aeropuerto Guest House*, is 5 mins' walk from the airport at 15 C "A", 7-32, T332-3086, F362-1264, hotairpt@guate.net Free transport to and from the airport. It has shared baths, and is clean and safe. Staff will order takeaway food for you from near by. **B** *Hincapié Guest House*, Av Hincapié, 18-77, T332-7771, ruedapinillos@yahoo.com On the far side of the airport runway. Continental breakfast included and free airport transport. Cable TV in the rooms. **E** *Dos Lunas Guest House*, 21 C, 10-92, Aurora II, T334-5264, lorena@intelnet.net.gt A comfy B&B, with prices per person. There are 4 rooms with shared bath and one with private bath that costs a little more. Very close to the airport with free transport to or from the airport. There's internet at US$3 per hr, storage service, free coffee and water and tourist information. Lorena, the landlady, also organizes shuttles and taxis and tours. English spoken. Reservations are highly advisable as it's usually full to the brim. **C-D** *Economy Dorms Guest House*, 8 Av, 17-74, T331-8029. Rooms with bath, cheaper without, and continental breakfast included, as well as a free airport transfer.

Eating

There are all kinds of food available in the capital, from the simple national cuisine to French, Chinese and Italian food. There is a plethora of fast food restaurants and traditional *comedores* in all commercial zones of the city, where you will get good value for money; a reasonable set meal will cost no more than US$2.50. The cheapest places to eat are in street stalls and the various markets, but some of these may not be the most hygienic of places – take the normal precautions.

Mid-range *Altuna*, 5 Av, 12-31, serves huge tasty portions of Spanish food, in huge portions. Lobster is available but expensive. Delicious coffee is served. This hotel has a beautiful traditional Spanish bar interior, reminiscent of some of the older Barcelona restaurants, with great ambience. Recommended. If you can't afford to eat here, step off the street for a drink. There is also a branch in Zona 10 at 10 C, 0-45. The best lunchtime menu is at the **Hotel Pan American**, 9 C, 5-63 (see Sleeping).

Zona 1
● *on map page 568*
*There are many
modest but
good places to
eat in the area*

Cheap *Cafe de Imeri*, 6 C, 3-34, serves sandwiches, salads, soups and pastries in a patio garden. It's popular with young professional Guatemalans. Try the *pay de queso de elote* (maize cheesecake). Closed Sun. More expensive, but a famous local institution is **Arrin Cuan**, 5 Av, 3-27, which specializes in traditional food from Cobán (*subanik*, *gallo en chicha*, and *kak ik*). Unfortunately turtle soup is on the menu as well. The restaurant is centred around a small courtyard with a little fountain. There is also live lunchtime music. There is a second restaurant on the 16 C, 4-32, Zona 10.

Seriously cheap *La Bodeguita del Centro*, see Bars below. **Restaurante Vegetariano Rey Sol**, 8 C, 5-36, is a prize vegetarian find – a wholesome food and ambience oasis amid the fumes of Zona 1, and popular with the locals. Delicious veggie concoctions at excellent prices served canteen style by friendly staff. Breakfasts and *licuados* are also served. And, if you're not full up on leaving, buy some freshly baked breads and pastries at the entrance. Closed Sun. There is also a newer, larger and brighter branch with upstairs seating as well, at 11 C, 5-51. **Helados Marylena**, 6 C, 2-49, not quite a meal but almost. This establishment has been serving up the weirdest concoctions for 90 years. From the probably vile – fish, chile, yucca and cauliflower ice-cream – to the heavenly – beer and sputnik (coconut, raisins and pineapple). The *elote* (maize) is good too. Other palatable or not so palatable flavours include beetroot, sweet potato, cereal and beans. This city institution is credited with making children eat their vegetables! Anyone travelling with fussy eaters should stop by here. Cones start from US$1.30. It's open daily from 1000-2200 and run by a friendly *señora*!

Most of the best restaurants are in the 'Zona Viva', within 10 blocks of the Av La Reforma on the west side, between 6 C and 16 C in Zona 10. Zona 9 is just across the other side of Av La Reforma. Drinks, particularly wines, are expensive in the majority of these places.

Zona 9 & 10
● *on map page 571*

Expensive *Hacienda Real*, 13 C, 1-10, Zona 10, is opposite the *Holiday Inn*, with an excellent steak selection and meaty smells always wafting out of the doors. Recommended. **Los Ranchos**, 14 C, 1-42, Zona 10, has a Nicaraguan owner with staff serving up fine steaks in pleasant surroundings. However, the service at reception leaves a lot to be desired.

Mid-range *Altuna*, 10 C, 0-45, Zona 10, see under Zona 1. **Hacienda de Los Sánchez**, 12 C, 2-25, Zona 10, good steaks and local dishes, but seriously crowded at weekends, and so not the most pleasant of settings compared with other steakhouses in the vicinity. **Kacao**, 2 Av, 13-44, Zona 10, has a large variety of ample portions of delicious local and national dishes, which are attractively prepared. The setting is fantastic – a giant thatched room, with beautiful candle decorations, some options are expensive. Highly recommended.

Cheap *Arrin-Cuan*, 16 C, 4-32, Zona 10, see under Zona 1. **Café Vienes**, is in the *Camino Real*, Zona 10, one of the best places for coffee and cakes. **Cafesa**, 6 Av, 11-64, Zona 9, is a 24-hr diner serving a range of Western and Guatemalan food with some seriously cheap options on offer too. **Lai Lai 2**, 7 Av, 13-27, Zona 9. Chinese, popular, good value, especially the set menus. Takeaway, T332-4628. Recommended. **Los Alpes**, 10 C, 1-09, Zona 10, is a Swiss/Austrian place with light meals, which also offers a smorgasbord of excellent cakes with piles of cream and flavours, and chocolates if you've still got room. It's popular with Guatemalan families. Closed Mon.

Seriously cheap *Las Mañanitas*, next to the *Holiday Inn*, 1 Av, 13-22. Excellent value tacos with good spicy relish and wonderful smells. **Sophos**, Av La Reforma, 13-89, El Portal 1, Zona

Guatemala

10, is an attractive indoor and outdoor café with a bookshop. On Thu nights there are literary events until 2300, T332-3242, sophos@gold.guate.net *Jimmy John's*, is on the corner of 8 C and 7 Av, Zona 9. Huge, very filling sub sandwiches to eat in or take away.

Entertainment

Bars & nightclubs

Bars *Cheers*, 12 C, 0-60, Zona 10, is a basement sports bar with pool tables, darts, and large cable TV. Open Mon-Sat 0900 0100, Sun 1300-2400ish. Happy hour until 1800. One of Guate's hotspots, and worth a visit, is the totally funky *Colloquia*, inside La Cúpula building at 7 Av 13-01, Zona 9. On Tue nights there are poetry meetings and on Thu nights there's techno, trance and house music. Open 0900-2400, Tue-Sat. *El Establo*, 14 C, 5-08, Zona 10, is a highly popular drinking hole with an English pub atmosphere in a huge barn with pounding Western sounds and a large circular bar. It's open until 0100 and the crowd is a mixture of Guatemalans, travellers and ex-pats. *El Portal*, Portal del Comercio, 8 C, 6-30, Zona 1. This was a favourite spot of Che Guevara and you can imagine him sitting here holding court at the long wooden bar. A massive stuffed bull's head now keeps watch over drinkers. To get there, enter the labyrinths of passageways facing the main plaza at number 6-30 where there is a Coke stand. At the first junction bear round to the left and up on the left you will see its sign. Open Mon-Sat 1000-2200. *Europa*, 11 C, 5-16, Zona 1, popular peace-corps/travellers' hangout, sports bar, shows videos, books for sale. Open Mon-Sat 0800-0100. *La Bodeguita del Centro*, 12 C, 3-55, Zona 1, T239-2976. The walls of this hip place in an old stockhouse are adorned with posters of Che Guevara, Bob Marley, and murdered Salvadorean Archbishop Romero. There's live music Thu-Sat at 2100, talks, plays, films, exhibitions upstairs. Wooden tables are spread over 2 floors, free popcorn is offered with drinks and seriously cheap nachos and soup are on the menu. The *menú del día* is US$2. It's an atmospheric place to spend an evening. Call in to get their Calendario Cultural leaflet. Open daily 0900-0100. *La Casa Comal*, 1 Av, 10-41, Zona 10, T332-6274, casacomal@internetdetelgua.com.gt, is another hot capital nightspot with jazz, rave, reggae, 80s and techno nights (Fri-Sat), along with cinema nights on Wed and art displays on Mon-Tue. The club is open Fri and Sat 2000-0100 and the displays are available to see 0800-1700. *Las Cien Puertas*, Pasaje Aycinea, 7 Av, 8-44, just south of Plaza Mayor, Zona 1, has a wonderful atmosphere with political, satirical and love missives covering its walls. There's excellent food and outdoor seating and it's friendly. Open daily 1600-2400. Opposite is *El Tiempo*, which has the same bohemian atmosphere but better political satire on its walls and busier. *Shakespeare's Pub*, 13 C, 1-51, Zona 10, English-style basement bar with a good atmosphere, American owner, a favourite with ex-pats and locals, safe for women to go and drink. Open Mon-Fri 1100-0100, Sat-Sun 1400-0100. *Tzijolaj*, 11 C, 4-53, Zona 1, T220-3262. This place often has live singing and music, eg jazz. It also sells music.

Cinema & theatre

Cinemas There are numerous and they often show films in English with Spanish subtitles. *Cine Lux*, opposite *Piccadilly Restaurant*, corner of 6 Av and 11 C, Zona 1. *Cine Capitol*, 6 Av between 12 and 13 C, Zona 1. **Theatres** **Teatro Nacional**, Centro Cívico. Most programmes are Thu-Sun. *La Cúpula*, 7 Av, 13-01, Zona 9, T334-2606, lacupula2001@hotmail.com Contemporary plays, concerts, dance and alternative cinema; details in the press. There is a restaurant, bar, bookshop and shops in the same complex.

Shopping

Bargain hard at all markets in Guatemala. It is expected. Better in Antigua

The **Central Market** operates underground behind the cathedral, from 7 to 9 Av, 8 C, Zona 1. One floor is dedicated to native textiles and crafts, and there is a large, cheap basketware section on the lower floor. Silverware is cheaper at the market than elsewhere in Guatemala City. The market is, however, recommended for all local products. Other markets include the **Mercado Terminal** in Zona 4, and the **Mercado de Artesanía** in the Parque Aurora, near the airport, which is for tourists. Large shopping centres have been opened in the last few years, which are good for a wide selection of local crafts, artworks, funky shoes, clothes and the local scene. Don't miss the *dulces*, candied fruits and confectionery. The best centres are

Guatemala

Centro Comercial Los Próceres, 18 C and 3 Av, Zona 10, the *Centro Comercial La Pradera*, Carretera Roosevelt and Av 26, Zona 10. There is a large *Paiz* supermarket on 18 C and 8 Av and a vast shopping mall *Tikal Futura* at Calzada Roosevelt and 22 Av.

For more upmarket things visit **Rodas Antiques**, 5 Av, 8-42, Zona 1 and **Barrientos Antigüedades**, 10 C, 4-64, Zona 1, which sell highly priced silver and antiques. At Av La Reforma and C 14, Zona 9, there are some long-established shops and a market area that is good for handicrafts, furniture and antiques, in varying price ranges. **Pasaje Rubio**, inside the Portal del Comercio, 8 C on the Plaza Mayor, a labyrinth of passages and good for antique silver charms and coins.

Bookshops *Museo Popol Vuh* bookshop has a good selection of books on pre-Columbian art, crafts and natural history. The *Museo Ixchel* also has a bookshop. **Librería del Pensativo**, La Cúpola, 7 Av, 13-01, Zona 9, has a large selection of books with helpful staff on hand. **Luna y Sol**, 12 C, 3-55, Zona 1, next to *Bodeguita del Centro*, good selection of books, cassettes, etc.

Maps Maps can be bought from the **Instituto Geográfico Nacional** (IGN), Av Las Américas, 5-76, Zona 13, T332-2611, F331-3548. Open Mon-Fri 0900-1730. The whole country is covered by about 200 1:50,000 maps available in colour or photocopies of out of print sections. None is more recent than 1991. There is, however, an excellent 1996, 1:15,000 map of Guatemala City in 4 sheets. A general *Mapa Turístico* of the country is available here, also at INGUAT and elsewhere. All map sheets cost US$5.70.

Transport

Bus In town, US$0.10 per journey on regular buses, US$0.14 on the larger red buses known as *gusanos* ('worms') and other standard red city buses. (Except on Sun and public holidays when they charge US$0.11 and US$0.16 respectively.) One of the most useful bus services is the *101*, which travels down 10 Av, Zona 1, and then cuts across to the 6 Av, Zona 4, and then across Vía 8 and all the way down the Av La Reforma, Zona 10. You can pick it up at 6 Av and 20 C near the Antigua bus terminal. Bus no *V21* also goes to the Zona Viva (Zona 10) travelling down from the Plaza Mayor on the 6 Av, Zona 1. The *82* also travels from Zona 1 to 10 and can be picked up on the 10 Av, Zona 1 and the 6 Av, Zona 4. Bus *85*, with the same pick-up points, goes to the cluster of museums in Zona 13. Any bus saying 'Terminal' is heading for the Zona 4 bus terminal. Buses *37, 35, 32* all head for the general immigration office and INGUAT building which is the large blue and white building in the Centro Cívico complex. *40B* goes from the 6 Av, Zona 4, to the Tikal Futura shopping complex – a good spot to catch the Antigua bus, which pulls up by the bridge to the complex. Buses leaving the 7 Av, Zona 4, just 4 blocks from the Zona 4 bus terminal, for the Plaza Mayor, Zona 1, are *gusano V21, 35, 36, 82,* and *101*. The *T64* goes to the Botanical Gardens, Natural History Museum and the office of CECON, which are all next to each other.

Local
Buses operate between 0600-2000 after which you will have to rely on taxis

Car Car hire companies include: *Hertz*, 7 Av, 14-76, Zona 9, T334-2540, and at *Camino Real*, and the airport, www.hertz.com *Budget*, at the airport T331-0273, also at Av Hincapíe, 11-01, Zona 13, www.drivebudget.com *Tabarini*, 2 C "A", 7-30, Zona 10, T331-2643, airport T331-4755, www.tabarini.com *Rental*, 5 Av 16-62, Zona 10, T337-2600, good rates. *Tally*, 7 Av, 14-60, Zona 1, T232-0421, tally@infovia.com.gt (have pick-ups), very competitive. Recommended. *Ahorrent*, Blvd Liberación, 4-83, Zona 9, T361-5661, and at airport T362-8922, good service, hotel delivery. Check carefully the state of the car when you hire to avoid being charged for damage already done. Average rates are US$50-80 per day. Local cars are usually cheaper than those at international companies; if you book ahead from abroad with the latter, take care that they do not offer you a vehicle that is not available. If you wish to drive to Copán, you must check that this is permissible and you need a letter authorizing you to take the vehicle in to Honduras; *Tabarini* and *Hertz* do allow their cars to cross the border. Insurance rates (extra) vary from US$4-6 a day; check carefully what excess will be charged (it could be as high as US$500 but travel insurance should cover this in the event of an accident). **Car and motorcycle repairs** Honda, *Frank Autos*, 10 C, 7-20, Zona 9, T331-9287.

Avenidas have priority over Calles (except in Zona 10, where this rule varies)

Good car service. *Mike and Andy Young*, 27 C, 13-73, Zona 5, T331-9263, open Mon-Fri 0700-1600. Excellent mechanics for all vehicles, extremely helpful. Honda motorcycle parts from *FA Honda*, Av Bolívar, 31-00, Zona 3, T4715232. Some staff speak English. Car and motorcycle parts from *FPK*, 5 C, 6-75, Zona 9, T331-9777.

Always bargain for a better fare

Taxi There are 3 types of taxis and all are safe – *Rotativos, Estacionarios* and the ones that are metered, called *Taxis Amarillos*. *Rotativos* are everywhere in the city cruising the length and breadth of all zones. You will not wait more than a few minutes for one to come along. They are numbered on their sides and on their back windscreen will be written TR (*Taxi Rotativo*) followed by 4 numbers. Most of them have a company logo stamped on the side as well. *Estacionarios* also have numbers on the sides but are without logo. On their back windscreen they have, the letters TE (*Taxi Estacionario*) followed by 4 numbers. They are to be found at bus terminals and outside hotels or in other important places. They will always return to these same waiting points (good to know if you leave something in a taxi). Do not get in a taxi that does not have either of these labels on its back windscreen. *Rotativos* and *Estacionarios* are unmetered, but *Estacionarios* will always charge less than *Rotativos*. The fact that both are unmetered will nearly always work to your advantage because of traffic delays. You will be quoted an inflated price by *Rotativos* by virtue of being a foreigner. *Estacionarios* are fairer. It is about US$5.25 from the airport to Zona 1. From Zona 1 to 4 is about US$3. The metered *Taxi Amarillo* also moves around but less so than the *Rotatvos*, as they are more on call by phone. They only take a couple of minutes to come. Within zones or from one zone to the next a metered fare should be between US$3.25-4.50 and from Zona 1 to the airport should be about US$6.50, but it does depend on the traffic. Taxis of the *Amarillo Express*, T332-1515, are 24-hr, and charge Q3.85 per km, but if there is a waiting period of 40 seconds it charges up at Q0.75 for each period. There is a minimum fare of nearly US$2 between 0900-1700 and between 1700-0700 it's US$2.60.

Long-distance

Air Flights to Flores and Petén, with *Tikal Jets* and *Grupo Taca*, leave daily. See under Flores for more information, page 675, and under directory for contact details.

See the city maps for bus station locations and individual places for more detailed transport information

Bus There are numerous bus terminals in Guatemala City. The majority of first-class buses have their own offices and departure points around Zona 1 (see map). Antigua has its own chicken bus (second-class bus) terminal in Zona 1. (See below and on map.) Hundreds of chicken buses for the south and west of Guatemala leave from the Zona 4 terminal, as well as local city buses. International buses have their offices scattered about the city. (The cheaper Salvador buses leave from near the Zona 4 terminal.) The Zona 4 bus terminal has to be the dirtiest and grimmest public area in the whole of the city and the Zona 1/18 C bus area seems like it's perfumed with flowers in comparison. Watch your bags everywhere, but like a hawk in the Zona 4 terminal and don't spend a second more than you need to in this part of town.

The main destinations with companies operating from Guatemala City are: to **Antigua**, 1 hr, US$0.60, until 2000 with *Transportes Unidos*, 18 C, 4-5 Av, Zona 1. To **Biotopo del Quetzal** and **Cobán**, 3½ hrs and 4½ hrs respectively, hourly from 0400-1700, US$3.90, with *Escobar-Monja Blanca*, 8 Av, 15-16, Zona 1, T238-1409. To **Zacapa**, **Chiquimula** (for El Florido, Honduras border) and **Esquipulas** with *Rutas Orientales*, 19 C, 8-18, Zona 1, T253-7282, every 30 mins from 0430-1830. To Zacapa 3¼ hrs, US$2.40. To Chiquimula, 3½ hrs, US$2.60, and to Esquipulas, 4½ hrs, US$3.65. To **Huehuetenango**, with *Los Halcones*, 7 Av, 15-27, Zona 1, T238-1929, 0700, 1400, 1700, US$3.80, 5½ hrs, and *Transportes Velásquez*, 20 C, 1-37, Zona 1, T221-1084, 0800-1700, *hourly*, 5 hrs, US$2.60. To **Panajachel**, with *Transportes Rebuli*, 21 C, 1-34, Zona 1, T2513521, hourly from 0530-1530, 3 hrs, US$1.50. To **Puerto Barrios**, with *Transportes Litegua*, 15 C, 10-40, Zona 1, T253-8169, www.litegua.com, 0445-1700, hourly, 5 hrs, US$5.20, and **Río Dulce**, 0530, 1130, 5 hrs, US$5.20. To **El Petén** with *Fuente del Norte* (same company as *Líneas Máxima de Petén*), 17 C, 8-46, Zona 1, T251-3817, going to **Río Dulce** and **Santa Elena**. There are numerous departures from midnight to 2130; 5 hrs to Río Dulce, US$5.20; to Santa Elena, 9-10 hrs, US$10.40. *Línea Dorada*, 16 C, 10-03, Zona 1, T232-9658, www.lineadorada.com, at 1400 and 2100, normal service,

S$14; 1000, 2000, 2200, luxury service to **Flores**, US$28, 8 hrs and on to **Melchor de Mencos**, 10 hrs, US$28. *Transportes Rosita*, 15 C, 9-58, Zona 1, T253-0609, to **Santa Elena** nd **Melchor de Mencos**, 1500, 1700, 2000 *especial* US$10, 1900 normal, US$6.50, 10 hrs.)n to Melchor, 12 hrs, *normal* US$8.45, *especial* US$10. To **Quetzaltenango** (Xela) and **San Marcos**, with *Tacana*, 2 Av, 20-42, every 30 mins from 0400-1630, 4hrs, US$2. To San Marcos, hrs, US$2.50. Pullman at 0900, 1400, 1500, US$3.25. First-class bus to Xela with *Transportes lamo*, 21 C, 0-14, Zona 1, T251-4838, from 0800-1730, 5 daily Mon-Sat, 4 hrs, US$3.90. *Líneas méricas*, 2 Av, 18-47, Zona 1, T232-1432, 0500-1930, 7 daily to Xela, US$3.65. *Galgos*, 7 Av, 9-44, Zona 1, T253-4868, between 0530-1700, 5 daily to Xela, 4 hrs, US$4.15. *Marquensita*, 1 \v, 21-31, Zona 1, T253-5871. Hourly from 0600-1700, US$4.30, to Xela. To **Tecpán**, with *ransportes Poaquileña*, 20 C, Av Bolívar, Zona 1, 0530-1900, every 15 mins, 2 hrs, US$0.90.

At 20 C and Av Bolívar, Zona 1, opposite *Transportes Poaquileña*, there is a small bus sta- ion, with chicken buses leaving for **Chimaltenango**, **Panajachel** and **Santa Cruz del Quiché**. Walk under the underpass (safe for all) and bear to the right, where you will emerge n 6 Av opposite the Centro Cívico. To reach the 18 C and the Antigua bus terminal, take a eft. Chicken buses for the following destinations leave from the Zona 4 bus terminal. To Chichicastenango, and **Santa Cruz del Quiché**, hourly from 0500-1800, Zona 4 terminal vith *Veloz Quichelense*. *Delta y Tropical*, to **Escuintla** and **Taxisco**, every 30 mins, 0600-1830, ½ hrs. *Chantla Gomerana* to **La Democracia**, every 30 mins from 0600-1630 via Escuintla, 2 rs. *Transportes Cubanita* to **Reserva Natural de Monterrico** (La Avellana) at 1040, 1230, 430, 3 hrs, US$2. Numerous buses to **Santa Lucía Cotzumalguapa**, **Puerto San José** and ztapa, **Jalapa** and **San Pedro Pinula** between 0500-1800.

Shuttles Shuttle services are possible between Guatemala City and all other destinations, but t's a case of reserving them first. Contact shuttle operators in Antigua, see Transport, Antigua.

nternational buses To **San Salvador**: *King Quality*, 18 Av, 1-96, Zona 15, T369-0404,)uses leave daily at 0630, 0800, 1400, 1530, US$24 one way, US$42 return, booking advisable hough space usually available on early buses. Tickets from all travel agencies in Guatemala City and Antigua. *Confort Lines*, leaves from the same address, US$20 one way, US$33 return to San Salvador, 0630, 0800, 1400, 1530. *Melva Internacional* and *Pezzarossi*, 3 Av, 1-38, Zona 9, are half a block from the Zona 4 terminal, T331-0874, 0515-1615, every hour, US$8, but JS$10 at 0700 and 1515. Both these companies have onboard toilets and TV. *Pullmantour*, from the *Holiday Inn*, 1 Av, 13-22, Zona 10, T332-9785, daily departures at 0700, 1300, and 1500, US$37 one way, US$51 return. *Ticabus*, 11 C, 2-72, Zona 9, T331-4279 at 1300 daily, to **San Salvador** (US$9, 5 hrs) with connections to **Managua** (US$38), **San José** (US$49) and **Panama** (US$77). This company no longer calls in at Tegucigalpa, Honduras. *Transportes Centro América*, 16 C, 7-75, Zona 1, T232-0235, to Puerto bus terminal, San Salvador, Tue-Sun 0600 from this office, 5hrs, US$7.80. Door to door, US$16. One of the cheapest ways to get to San Salvador is with *Mermes*, 1 C, 4-59, Zona 9, T334-3151, at 0900 and 1300, US$6.50. To **Honduras**: avoiding El Salvador, take a bus to Esquipulas, then a minibus to the border. To **Mexico**: *Trans Galgos Inter*, 7 Av, 19-44, Zona 1, T253-9131, www.transgalgosinter.com, has 2 daily buses to **Tapachula** via **El Carmen**, 0730, 1330, 7 hrs, US$20. *Línea Dorada* to **Tapachula** at 0700 and 1600, US$32.50. *Transportes Velásquez*, 20 C, 1-37, Zona 1, 0800-1600, hourly to **La Mesilla**, 7 hrs, US$3.90. *Transportes Fortaleza*, 19 C, 8-70, Zona 1, T232-3643 to **Tecún Umán**, 0130, 0300, 0330, 0530 via **Retalhuleu**, 5 hrs, US$5.20.

Reserve the day before if you can. Taking a bus from Guatemala City as far as, say, San José is tiring and tiresome (the bus company's bureaucracy and the hassle from border officials all take their toll). Break up the journey

Directory

Local airlines: *Grupo Taca* at the airport and *Hotel Intercontinental*, Zona 10, T331-8222, for reservations, T334-7722, www.taca.com *Tikaljets*, Hangar 8 at the airport, Av Hincapié, Zona 13, T3346855, reservations T3610042, good rates. *Tapsa*, T3319180, private flights only at US$350/hr. Offices at the airport. **International airlines**: *Air France*, Av La Reforma, 9-00, Zona 9, Plaza Panamericana, T334-0043. *American Airlines*, Hotel Marriott, 7 Av, 15-45, Zona 9, T337-1177, www.aa.com *British Airways*, 1 Av, 10-81, Zona 10, Edificio Inexsa, 6th floor, T3327402/4. *Continental Airlines*, 18 C, 5-56, Zona 10, Edif Unicentro, T366-9985, www.continental.com *Copa*, 1 Av, 10-17,

Airline offices

Guatemala

Guatemala

Zona 10, T385-5555. *Delta Air Lines*, 15 C, 3-20, Zona 10, Edif Centro Ejecutivo, T337-0642 www.delta.com *Grupo Taca* (includes Aviateca, Lacsa, Nica and Inter), see above. *Iberia*, Av La Reforma, 8-60, Zona 9, Edif Galerías Reforma, T3320911. *JAL* (Japanese Airlines), 26 Av, 2-14, Zona 14 T367-0854, jal~cu@guate.net *KLM*, 6 Av, 20-25, Zona 10, T367-6179, nc.@netherlands.com *Lufthansa*, Diagonal 6, 10-01, Zona 10, T336-5526, www.lufthansa.com *Mexicana*,13 C, 8-44, Zona 10, Edif Plaza Edjma, T333-6001/5, www.mexicana.com *United*, Av La Reforma, 1-50, Zona 9, Edif La Reformador, 2nd floor, T332-1994.

Banks

The legal street exchange for cash may be found on 7 Av, between 12 and 14 C, near the post office (Zona1), but be careful; don't go alone

Banks change US dollars into quetzales at the free rate, but actual rates and commission charges vary; if you have time, shop around. *Banco Industrial*, Av 7, opposite the central post office, Visa cards only Mon-Fri 0900-1530. *Bancafé*, 18 C, 8-75, near the Zona 1 bus terminals, has 24-hr Visa ATM. *Lloyd Bank plc*, 6 Av, 9-51, Zona 9, Edif Gran Vía, also at 14 C and 4 Av, Zona 10, with 24-hr ATM. Open Mon-Fri, 0900-1500. *Banco Uno*, 10 C, 5-40, Visa and 24-hr ATM. Open Mon-Fri 0930-1730, Sat 1000-1300. *Bancafé*, Av La Reforma, 9-30, Zona 9, T331-1311, open Mon-Fri until 2000. Quetzales may be bought with MasterCard at *Credomatic*, beneath the *Bar Europa*, at 11 C, 5-6 Av, Zona 1. Open Mon-Sat 0800-1900. MasterCard ATM also at: *Banco Internacional*, Av La Reforma and 16 C, Zona 10 *Western Union*, T360-1737, collect 1-800-360-1737.

Communications

Internet: *Mesón Don Quijote*, 11 C, 5-27, opposite *Bar Europa*, Zona 1, US$1.45 per hr. *Café Internet* opposite *Telgua* office, US$1.30 per hr. *Café Net*, US$1.80 per hr in *Centro Comercial Real del Parque* on the corner of the Plaza Mayor where *Wendy's* is. **Post**: the main post office is at 7 Av and 12 C, Zona 1 Open Mon-Fri 0830-1700. This is the only post office in the country from which parcels over 2 kg can be sent abroad. See Essentials for postage rates. Poste restante keeps mail for 2 months. **Telephone** *Telgua*, 7 Av, 12-39, Zona 1.

Embassies & consulates

Addresses change frequently. Office hours are Monday-Friday unless otherwise stated

Austria, 6 Av, 20-25, Zona 10, T368-2324. Open 0900-1200. *Belgium*, Av Las Américas, 7-20, Zona 13, Local 17, Centro Comercial Real America, T361-1998. Open 0900-1400. *Belize*, Av La Reforma 1-50, Zona 9, Edif El Reformador, Of 803, T3345531. Open 0900-1200, 1400-1600. *Canada*, 13 C, 8-44, Zona 10, T333-6104. Open Mon, Thu, Fri 0800-1630. *Costa Rican Consulate*, Av La Reforma, 8-60, Zona 9, Edif Galerías Reforma, T3320531. Open 0900-1400. *Cuba*, Av Las Américas, 20-72, Zona 13, T3612860. Open 0900-1300. *Danish Consulate*, Carretera Villa Canales Km 14.8, Boca del Monte, Interior Industrias Unidades, T238-1091. Open 0900-1200. *El Salvador*, 5 Av, 8-15, Zona 9, T3607670. Open 0800-1400. *Finland*, 2 C, 18-37, Zona 15, Vista Hermosa I, T3659270. Open 0830-1200. *France*, 16 C, 4-53, Zona 10, Edif Marbella, 11th floor, T3370647. Open 0900-1200. *Germany*, 20 C, 6-20, Zona 10, T337-0028. Open 0900-1200. *Honduras*, 12 C, 1-25, Zona 10, T3353281. Open 0900-1300 (takes 24 hrs to get a visa, quicker in Esquipulas, T9431143, open 0900-1800). *Israel*, 13 Av, 14-07, Zona 10, T333-6951. Open 0900-1400. *Italy*, 5 Av, 8-59, Zona 14, T337-4558. Open 0830-1230. *Japan*, Av La Reforma, 16-85, Zona 10, Edif Torre Internacional, T367-2244. Open 0930-1200. *Mexico*, 15 C, 3-20, Zona 10, T333-7254/8. Open 0900-1300, 1500-1800; *Mexican Consulate*, Av La Reforma, 6-64, Zona 9, T339-1007. Open 0800-1200, for tourist card applications. *Netherlands Consulate General*, 16 C, 0-55, Edif Torre Internacional, 13th floor, Zona 10, T3674761. Open 0800-1630. *Nicaragua*, 10 Av, 14-72, Zona 10, T368-0785. Open 0900-1300, English spoken. *Norway*, 14 C, 3-51, Zona 10, T366-5908. Open 0900-1200. *Panama*, 10 Av, 18-53, Zona 14, T368-2805. Open 0830-1430. *South Africa*, 10 Av, 30-57, Zona 5, Of Cidea, T334-1531. Open 0900-1200, 1400-1700. *Spain*, 6 C, 6-48, Zona 9, T334-3757. Open 0900-1400. *Sweden*, 8 Av, 15-07, Zona 10, T333-6536. Open 1030-1230, 1430-1600. *Switzerland*, 16 C, 0-55, Zona 10, Edif Torre Internacional, 14th floor, T3675520. Open 0900-1130. *UK*, Av La Reforma, 16-00, Zona 10, Edif Torre Internacional, 11th floor, T367-5425. Embassy open Mon-Thu 0800-1230, Fri 0800-1200. Consulate open Mon-Thu 0830-1200, Fri 0830-1100. Passports normally replaced within 5 working days or less, helpful, report all attacks/thefts. (Australian/New Zealand citizens should report loss or theft of passports here.) *USA*, Av La Reforma, 7-01, Zona 10, T331-1541, www.usembassy.state.gov/guatemala Open 0800-1700.

Laundry

Una Hora El Siglo, 12 C, 3-42, Zona 1, wash and dry US$2.60. Open 0800-1800.

Medical services

See page 565 for hospitals

Dentists: *Centro Médico*, 6 Av, 3-69, Zona 10, T332-3555, English spoken by some staff. **Doctors**: *Dr Boris Castillo Camino*, 6 Av, 7-55, Zona 10, Of 17, T3345932. Open 0900-1230, 1430-1800. Recommended. **Opticians**: *Optico Popular*, 11 Av, 13-75, Zona 1, T238-3143, excellent service for repairs. **Emergency**: T128 for ambulance, T122/123 for the *bomberos*, the fire brigade who also get called to accidents.

Aire, Mar y Tierra, Plaza Marítima, 6 Av, 20-25, Zona 10, T337-0149, Airemar@terra.com.gt **Tour operators**
Recommended. *Anfañona*,11 Av, 5-59, Zona 1, T238-1751, walkinguate@hotmail.com Offers walking
tours of the historical centre. Tours are Mon-Fri, 2 hrs, US$10 per person, including hotel pick-up,
minimum 2 people. Reserve in advance. *Aventuras Naturales*, Av La Reforma, 1-50, Zona 9, Edif El
Reformador, T/F334-5222, aventuras@centramerica.com Specialized trips in Guatemala including
guided birding tours. *Clark Tours*, Centro Gerencial Las Margaritas, Torre II, 7th floor, Of 702, Diagonal
6, 10-01, Zona 10, T339-2888, www.clarktours.com.gt and several other locations in Zonas 9 and 10,
long established, very helpful, tours to Copán, Quiriguá, etc. *Gufo Tours*, Av Las Américas 19-30, Zona
13, T360-0842, www.gufo.com Arranges hotels, flights, shuttles as well as tailored tours. *Interconti
Travel*, Princess Plaza, 13 C, 7-74, Zona 9, T331-5800, F331-5776, interconti@guate.net English and
German spoken. *Marsans*, 43 Av, 0-44, Zona 11, Col Alvarado, T/F591-0789, www.marsans.amigo.net
Good for bus excursions, German spoken. *Maya Expeditions*, 15 C "A", 14-07, Zona 10, T363-4955,
F363-4965, www.mayaexpeditions.com Very experienced, and helpful with varied selection of short
and longer river/hiking tours, white-water rafting, bungee jumping, cultural tours, tours to Piedras
Negras. *Nancy's*, 11 C, 5-16, Zona 1, T253-3271, Marisa@nancystravel.com Very helpful. *Salga Travel*,
14 C, 0-61, Zona 10, T/F333-7445, is also very helpful. *Setsa Travel*, 8 Av, 14-11, Zona 1, T230-4726, very
helpful, tours arranged to Tikal, Copán, car hire. *Tourama*, Av La Reforma, 15-25, Zona 10, T368-1820,
tourama@guate.net German and English spoken. Recommended. *Viajes de Guatemala*, 15 C, 7-75,
Zona 10, Local 6, Villa Begonia, T/F368-2252, arranges helicopter flights from Flores to Uaxactún, Río
Azul and Mirador, and helicopter rental. *Viajes Internacionales*, Edif Torre Café, Of 204, 7 Av, 1-20, Zona
1, T331-9392, interquetzal@gold.guate.net Helpful, English spoken.

Fire service: T122/123. **Immigration office**: 7a Av 1-17, Zona 4, 2nd floor of INGUAT building. For **Useful
extensions of visas. If you need new entry stamps in a replacement passport (ie if one was stolen), a **addresses**
police report is required, plus a photocopy and a photocopy of your passport. They also need to know
your date and port of entry to check their records. **Police**: T120/110.

Antigua

Antigua is rightly one of Guatemala's most popular destinations, overflowing as it is   Colour map 5, grid C2
with colonial architecture and fine churches on streets that are linked by squat houses,   Population: 43,000
painted in ochre shades and topped with terracotta tiles, that bask in the fractured light   Altitude: 1,520m
of the setting sun.
    *Apart from the ruins, Antigua is a very attractive place. It is the cultural centre of
Guatemala, arts flourish here and indigenous music can be heard everywhere. Maya
women sit in their colourful costumes amid the ruins and in the Parque Central. In the
late-afternoon light buildings such as Las Capuchinas are very attractive, and in the
evening the cathedral is beautifully illuminated as if by candlelight.*

Ins and outs

Avenidas are numbered upwards running from east (Oriente, Ote) to west (Poniente, Pte), **Getting around**
and Calles upwards from Norte to Sur and are in relation to where 5 C and 4 Av cross on the
corner of the Parque Central; however, unlike Guatemala City, house numbers do not give
one any clue about how far from the Parque Central a particular place is.

INGUAT office, corner of 5 C Ote and 4 Av Sur, is very helpful, with lots of maps and informa- **Tourist office**
tion. English, Italian and a little German spoken. Open 0800-1700, normally daily, T8320763.
The monthly magazine *The Revue* is a useful source of information with articles and advertisements in English, free. There is also the Guatemala Post in English.

Unfortunately, despite its air of tranquillity, Antigua is not without unpleasant incidents. Take **Security**
care and advice from the tourist office on where to go or not to go. The situation has
improved with the arrival of the tourist police (green uniforms) who are helpful and conspicuous; their office is at 4 Av Norte at the side of the Municipal Palace. If you wish to go to Cerro

de la Cruz (see Sights), check with them. Antigua is generally safe at night, but it's best to keep to the well-lit area near the centre. Report incidents to police and the tourist office.

Background

Until it was heavily damaged by an earthquake in 1773, Antigua was the capital city. Founded in 1543, after the destruction of an even earlier capital, Ciudad Vieja, it grew to be the finest city in Central America, with numerous great churches, a University (1676), a printing press (founded 1660), and a population of around 50,000, including many famous sculptors, painters, writers and craftsmen.

Antigua has consistently been damaged by earthquakes. Even when it was the capital, buildings were frequently destroyed and rebuilt, usually in a grander style, until the final cataclysm in 1773. For many years it was abandoned, with most of the accumulated treasures moved to Guatemala City. Although it slowly repopulated in the 19th century, little was done to prevent further collapse of the main buildings until late in the 20th century when the inestimable value of the remaining monuments was finally appreciated. Since 1972 efforts to preserve what was left have gained momentum. The major earthquake of 1976 was a further setback, but now you will see many sites that are busy with restoration, preservation or simple clearing. If the city was not treasure enough, the setting is truly memorable. Agua volcano (3,766 m) is due south and the market is to the west, behind which hang the imposing peaks of Volcán Acatenango (3,976 m) and Volcán Fuego (3,763 m) which still emits the occasional column of ash as a warning of the latent power within.

Sights

Most of the sites offer student and child discounts

In the centre of the city is the **Parque Central**, the old Plaza Real, where bullfights and markets were held in the early days. The present park was constructed in the 20th century though the fountain dates back to the 18th century. The **Catedral**, to the east, dates from 1680 (the first cathedral was demolished in 1669). Much has been destroyed since then and only two of the many original chapels are now in use. The remainder can be visited. ■ *US$0.40*. **The Palacio de los Capitanes Generales** is to the south. The original building, dates from 1558, was virtually destroyed in 1773 but was partly restored in the 20th century and now houses police and government offices. The **Cabildo**, or Municipal Palace, is to the north and an arcade of shops to the west. The **Museo de Santiago** is in the municipal offices to the north of the Plaza, as is the **Museo del Libro Antiguo**, which contains a replica of a 1660 printing press (the original is in Guatemala City), old documents and a collection of 16th-18th century books (1,500 volumes in library). The **Museo de Arte Colonial** is half a block from Parque Central at Calle 5 Oriente, in the building where the San Carlos University was first housed. It now has mostly 17th-18th century religious art, well laid out in large airy rooms around a colonial patio. ■ *All open Tue-Fri 0900-1600, Sat-Sun 0900-1200, 1400-1600, US$1.30 and US$3.25 respectively.*

The **Casa Popenoe** (1632), 1 Av Sur, on the corner of 5a Calle, is a restored colonial house containing many old objects from Spain and Guatemala. ■ *Mon-Sat 1400-1600, US$1.30.*

Hotel Casa Santo Domingo

The Casa Santo Domingo is one of Antigua's most beautiful sites - a converted old Dominican church and monastery property. Recent archaeological excavations have turned up some unexpected finds at the site. During the cleaning out of a burial vault in September 1996, one of the greatest finds in Antigua's history was unearthed. The vault had been filled with rubble, but care had been taken in placing stones a few feet away from the painted walls. The scene is in the pristine colours of natural red and blue, and depicts Christ, the Virgin Mary, Mary Magdalene and John the Apostle. It was painted in 1683, and only discovered by placing an ultraviolet light over it. A Guatemalan specialist was called in to prevent climate changes and

Semana Santa

This week-long event is a spectacular display of religious ritual and floral design. Through billowing clouds of incense, accompanied by music, processions of floats carried by purple-robed men make their way through the town.

The cobbled stones are covered in carpets of flowers known as alfombras, made up of coloured sawdust and flowers.

The day before the processions leave from each church, Holy Vigils (velaciones) are held, and the sculpture to be carried is placed before the altar (retablo), with a backdrop covering the altar. Floats (andas) are topped by colonial sculptures of the cross-carrying Christ. He wears velvet robes of deep blue or green, embroidered with gold and silver threads, and the float is carried on the shoulders by a team of 80 men (cucuruchos), who heave and sway their way through the streets for as long as 12 hours through the town. The processions, arranged by a religious brotherhood (cofradía), are accompanied by banner and incense carriers, centurions, and a loud brass band.

*The largest processions with some of the finest carpets are on **Palm Sunday** and **Good Friday**. Not to be missed are: the procession leaving from La Merced on Palm Sunday at 12-1300; the procession leaving the church of San Francisco on Maundy Thursday; the 0200 sentencing of Jesus and 0600 processions from La Merced on Good Friday; the crucifixion of Christ in front of the cathedral at noon on Good Friday; and the beautiful candlelit procession of the crucified Christ which passes the central park between 2300 and midnight on Good Friday.*

This is the biggest Easter attraction in Latin America so accommodation is booked way ahead. If you plan to be here and haven't reserved a room, arrive a few days before Palm Sunday. If unsuccessful, commuting from Guatemala City is an option.

■ *Don't rush: each procession lasts up to 12 hours.*

■ *The whole week is a fantastic opportunity for photographs – and if you want a decent picture remember the Christ figure always faces right, so make sure you're on the right side of the street.*

■ *Arm yourself with a map (available in kiosks in the central park) and follow the processional route before the procession to see all the carpets while they are still intact.*

Guatemala

---

preserve the Calvary scene under the Chapel of Nuestra Señora del Socorro. Also, while opening a vent to resolve a humidity problem in 1997, human remains were found. These were found to be 'feeding' the lichens on the mural. Within the monastery grounds are the **Colonial Art Museum**, with displays of Guatemalan baroque imagery and silverware and the **Archaeological Museum** is situated in the original meeting room of the monastery and includes some Maya ceramics and pots. There are also human remains in the crypt on display. ■ *0900-1600, US$1.60. Entry for hotel guests is free. 3 C Ote 28.*

There are many fine colonial religious buildings. Top of the list are the cloisters of the convent of **Las Capuchinas** (1736), with immensely thick round pillars adorned with bougainvillea. ■ *0900-1700, US$3.90, 2 Av Nte y 2 C Ote.* The church and monastery of **San Francisco**, with the tomb of Hermano Pedro, is much revered by all the local communities who hope for his canonization in due course. The church has been restored and is in use, and there is a small museum in the south transept. ■ *1 Av Sur y 7 C Ote.* The convent of **Santa Clara**, was founded in about 1700 and became one of the biggest in Antigua, until the nuns were forced to move to Guatemala City. The adjoining garden is an oasis of peace. ■ *US$3.90, 6 C Ote y 2 Av Sur.* **El Carmen** has a beautiful façade with strikingly ornate columns, tastefully illuminated at night, but the rest of the complex is in ruins. ■ *3 C Ote y 3 Av Nte.* Likewise **San Agustín**, was once a fine building, but only survived intact from 1761 to 1773; earthquake destruction continued until the final portion of the vault collapsed in 1976, leaving an impressive ruin. ■ *5 C Pte y 7 Av Nte.* **La Compañía de Jesús** at one time covered the whole block. The church is closed for restoration but you can

Churches, convents & monasteries

access the rest of the ruins from 6 Av Norte. (There is a craft market in front of the church.) ■ *3 C Pte y 6 Av Nte*.

The church and cloisters of **Escuela de Cristo** (1720-30) a small independent monastery, have survived and were restored between 1940 and 1960. The church is refreshingly simple and has some interesting original artwork. ■ *C de los Pasos y de la Cruz*. **La Recolección**, despite being a late starter (1700), became one of the biggest and finest of Antigua's religious institutions. It is now the most awe-inspiring ruin in the city. ■ *0900-1700, US$3.90, C de la Recolección*. **San Jerónimo** (early 1600s) was at first a school for La Merced, three blocks away, but later became the local customs house. There is an impressive fountain in the courtyard. ■ *0900-1700, US$3.90, C de la Recolección*. **La Merced** (1767) with its white and yellow façade dominates the surrounding plaza. The church and cloisters were built with earthquakes in mind and survived better than most. The church remains in use and the cloisters (US$0.26) are being further restored. Antigua's finest fountain is in the courtyard. ■ *1 C Pte y 6 Av Nte*. **Santa Teresa**, 4 Avenida Norte, was a modest convent, but the church walls and the lovely west front have survived. It is now the city's men's prison.

Other ruins including **Santa Isabel**, **Santa Cruz**, **La Candelaria**, **San José El Viejo** and **San Sebastián** are to be found round the edges of the city, and there is an interesting set of the Stations of the Cross, each a small chapel, from San Francisco to **El Calvario** church, which was where Pedro de Betancourt (Hermano Pedro) worked as a gardener and planted an esquisuchil tree. He was also the founder of the **Belén Hospital** in 1661, which was destroyed in 1773. However, some years later, his name was given to the **San Pedro Hospital** which is one block south of the Parque Central.

There is a fabulous panorama from the **Cerro de la Cruz**, which is 15 minutes' walk from the northern end of town along 1 Avenida Norte.

Essentials

Sleeping

All hotels listed have hot water unless otherwise stated
■ *on maps*
Price codes: see inside front cover

In the better hotels, advance reservations are advised for weekends and Dec to Apr. During Holy Week hotel prices are significantly higher, sometimes double for the more expensive hotels. In the Jul-Aug period, find your accommodation early in the day.

L *Casa Santo Domingo*, 3 C Ote 28, T832-0140, F832-0102, www.casasanto domingo.com.gt This is a beautifully designed hotel in the ruins of a 17th-century convent with pre-Hispanic archaeological finds, with good service, beautiful gardens, a pool, good restaurant with breakfast included. It is worth seeing just to dream. Even if you can't stay here at least you can have a drink! (See also Sights.) **L** *Hotel Antigua*, 8 C Pte 1, T832-2801, F832-0807, www.hotelantigua.com.gt Has all the benefits associated with a hotel in this range as well as beautiful gardens and a pool. It is some 4 blocks from the plaza on a quiet street. **L-AL** *La Casa de los Sueños*, 1 Av Nte 1, T/F832-0802, www.lacasadelossuenos.com A richly furnished, beautiful, colonial building, with friendly and helpful owners. Some rooms are grander than others so make sure you know what you're taking. Breakfast is included and served at a vast table, medieval-style. The gardens have a swimming pool and patio. An airport shuttle is offered. Recommended. **L** *Posada del Angel*, 4 Av Sur 24A, T/F832-0260, www.posadadelangel.com A stay here includes breakfast. It is a colonial-style hotel with wood fires in beautifully furnished rooms.

AL-B *Casa Capuchinas*, 2 Av Nte 7, T/F832-0121, www.casacapuchinas.com Has fine, large, colonially furnished rooms, with fireplaces and massive beds, with adjoining beautiful tiled bathrooms with special touches. A continental breakfast is included. Airport shuttle available. Highly recommended. **A** *Aurora*, 4 C Ote 16, T/F832-0217, www.hotel-aurora-antigua-guatemala.com The oldest hotel in the city with old plumbing (but it works) and 1970s features. Quieter rooms face a patio, which is overflowing with beautiful flowers.

Breakfast is available, and English is spoken. **A** *La Sin Ventura*, 5 Av Sur 8, T832-0581, F832-4888, www.lasinventura.com Has very comfortable rooms, but some may suffer noise at weekends due to the re-location of the *Mono Loco Restaurant and Bar,* which is next door. Periodically slashes its prices so you may want to check out its billboard. **B** *San Jorge*, 4 Av Sur 13, T/F832-3132, sanjorge@terra.com.gt Behind gates with a stunning red bougainvillea. Rooms with fireplaces, room service and continental breakfast is served.

C *El Descanso*, 5 Av Nte 9, T832-0142. Rents 4 clean rooms on the 2nd floor, with private bath. There's a family atmosphere here and the place is extremely friendly and welcoming. It is run by Pedro and Graciela González, who run a small bar service as well. **C** *La Tatuana*, 7 Av Sur 3, T832-1223, latatuana@micro.com.gt Colourful with a beautiful leafy courtyard. It's friendly, clean and safe; discounts are available off-season. Some rooms are a little dark. Choose carefully. (Allegedly Tatuana was a witch condemned to death by the Spanish Inquisition and burnt in the central plaza in the capital.) **C** *Posada del Sol,* C de los Nazareno 17, T/F832-6838, posadsol@hotmail.com 6 large, attractively decorated rooms with private bath in a colonial building. The owners are friendly and helpful and create a family atmosphere. A laundry service is available. There is a 20% discount following a 3-night stay. Recommended. **C-D** *Bugambilia*, 3 C Ote 19, T/F832-5780. 24 rooms, some with bath. Rooms have extra furnishings such as table, bedside lamp and candles and there's a small patio and balconies to hang out on. There is parking for US$3.25 a night and a small restaurant/pizzería attached to the hotel. There's also an apartment with 4 beds and a small kitchen for rent at US$55 per night.

D *Casa de Sta Lucía No 2*, Alameda Sta Lucía Nte 21. All 12 rooms with private bathroom, hot water twice a day only, free drinking water. **D** *Casa de Santa Lucía No 3*, 6 Av Nte 43A, T8321386. There are 20 standard clean rooms here all with private bathrooms, towels, soap, hot water and free drinking water. Although pleasant it has a bit of a corridor atmosphere. However, the **D** *Casa de Sta Lucía No 4*, Alameda Sta Lucía Sur 4, is way more attractive than numbers 2 and 3, with 30 rooms for the same price. Only 5 yrs old, it has been built in a colonial style, with dark wood columns and is decorated with large clay bowls in the patio. **D** *Las Rosas*, 6 Av Sur 8, T832-0644. 13 clean, quiet rooms, family atmosphere, friendly. **D** *Posada Doña Luisa*, T832-3414, 7 Av Nte 4. Near the San Agustín church, a clean and very friendly place with a family atmosphere. It has 8 rooms with private bath and a small cafeteria. **D-E** *Hotel Backpacker's Place*, 4 C Pte 27, above *La Bodegona* supermarket, T832-7743. Offers a warm welcome and 10 rooms, some with bath. Shared bathrooms are ultra clean with good showers. Free coffee, cable TV in reception. It is sometimes a little noisy from the street *bulla*, but recommended. You can store luggage safely here. **D-E** *Posada Juma Ocag,* Alameda Santa Lucía Nte 13, T832-3109. A small, but clean and nicely decorated hotel, using local textiles as bedspreads. It has an enclosed roof terrace, is quiet and friendly.

E *Posada Landivar*, 5 C Pte 23, T832-2962, is also close to the bus station. There are no single rooms here but the beds are good and it's cheaper without bath. It's safe and there are clothes-washing facilities. Recommended. Close by is **E** *Posada La Quinta*, 5 C Pte 19, which is basic. Some single rooms are cell-like but they have their own shower and are a good deal for single travellers who want their own bathroom. It's all clean and has the added advantage of being opposite the supermarket. Luggage can be stored here. **E** *Posada Refugio Hotel*, 4 C Pte 30. Popular, rooms with or without shower, but not always clean. There are some cooking facilities and, with lots of comings and goings, it has been reported as not being very secure. There is a curfew at 0100 and gates locked until 0400. Parking for US$1.30 in the adjacent courtyard.

F *Hospedaje El Pasaje*, Alameda Sta Lucía 3, T832-3145. A clean and friendly place, but noisy. Avoid damp ground-floor rooms. A good view of the volcanoes can be had from the roof. The *hospedaje* has washing facilities, use of kitchen, and will store luggage for US$0.50. Doors shut at 0100. **F** *Hostelling Internacional*, 2 Av Sur 6. Dormitories with clean shared bathroom and hot water, 5% discount with IYHA card. You might want to try this place if you arrive at Easter without a reservation. **F** *Posada Ruiz*, Alameda Sta Lucía 17. Noisy and popular. There's a washing

Guatemala

Guatemala

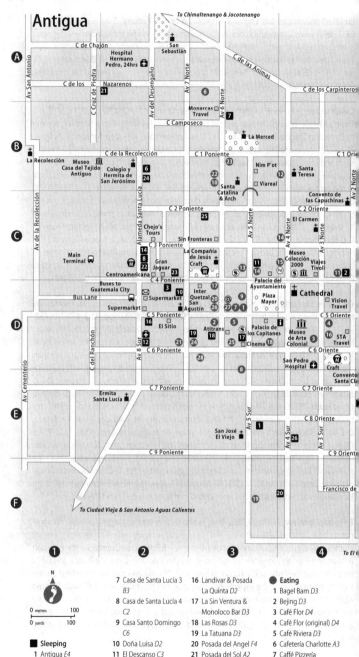

Antigua

N
0 metres 100
0 yards 100

■ **Sleeping**
1 Antigua *E4*
2 Aurora & La Fuente
    Restaurant *C4*
3 Backpacker's Place *D2*
4 Bugambilia *C5*
5 Casa Capuchinas *B4*
6 Casa de Santa Lucía 2 *B2*

7 Casa de Santa Lucía 3
    B3
8 Casa de Santa Lucía 4
    C2
9 Casa Santo Domingo
    C6
10 Doña Luisa *D2*
11 El Descanso *C3*
12 El Pasaje *D2*
13 Hostelling
    International *E4*
14 Juma Ocag *C2*
15 La Casa de los Sueños
    D5

16 Landivar & Posada
    La Quinta *D2*
17 La Sin Ventura &
    Monoloco Bar *D3*
18 Las Rosas *D3*
19 La Tatuana *D3*
20 Posada del Angel *F4*
21 Posada del Sol *A2*
22 Primavera & Comedor
    Antigueño *C2*
23 Refugio *C2*
24 Ruiz *B2*
25 Ruiz 2 *C3*
26 San Jorge *E4*

● **Eating**
1 Bagel Barn *D3*
2 Bejing *D3*
3 Café Flor *D4*
4 Café Flor (original) *D4*
5 Café Riviera *D3*
6 Cafetería Charlotte *A3*
7 Caffé Pizzería
    Asjemenou *D3*
8 Cinema Bistro *D3*
9 Condesa *D3*
10 Da Vinci *B3*
11 Doña Luisa's *C4*
12 El Sereno *B4*

machine available and it's close to the bus station. **F** *Posada Ruiz No 2*, 2 C Pte 25. Safe and even more popular, and can be very busy. Have a look at the room before taking it – some are not much bigger than the bed itself. Sometimes the shared bathrooms are not cleaned frequently enough and with loads of people passing through these can get pretty **grim**. **F** *Primavera*, 3 Cjón, off 3 C Pte near Alameda Sta Lucía. 15 rooms with shared bathrooms that are clean, but which could do with a serious lick of paint. Good for the price though and in a quiet location. Two rooms have private bathroom (**E**).

Look on the notice boards in town. Rooms and apartments are available from about US$25 a week up to US$500 per month. You don't have to be on a language course to stay with local families and it's cheap and convenient, about US$40-60 a week including meals, and a good way of meeting local people. One recommended family is *Estella López*, 1 C Pte 41A, T8321324, who offers board and lodging on a weekly basis. The house is clean, and the family friendly. **For longer stays**

Eating

El Sereno, 4 Av Nte 16, has a grand entrance with massive imposing plants in the courtyard; it's popular at weekends. *La Casserole*, Cjón de Concepción 7, close to *Casa Santo Domingo*. Sophisticated cooking with great seafood options served at tables set in a beautiful courtyard. Closed Mon. *Mesón Panza Verde*, 5 Av Sur 19, one of the best restaurants in town with a great staircase in the courtyard. Closed Mon. **Expensive**
● *on maps*

Caffé Mediterraneo, 6 C Pte 6A, 1 block south of the plaza. Absolutely mouth-watering Italian cuisine with great candlelit ambience. Highly recommended. Closed Tue. *Da Vinci*, 7 Av Nte 18B, serving such tempting delights as smoked pork chop in Amaretto, and pork with pears and blue cheese, plus lots of delicious pastas, including many vegetarian options, in a richly coloured interior. Pizza is also on the menu. Closed Mon. *Fonda de la Calle Real*, 5 Av Nte 5 and No 12, also at 3 C Pte 7. Its speciality is *queso fundido*. They also serve local dishes including *Pepían* (and a vegetarian version) and *Kak-ik*, a Verapaz speciality. **Mid-range**

Guatemala

Guatemala

Cheap *Café Flor*, 4 Av Sur 1, has full-on delicious Thai and Tandoori food, delivered up between 1000-2400. The stir-fries are delicious, but a little overpriced. Discount offers sometime available. Staff are friendly. Now also at 3 Av Sur 4. *Café Masala*, 6 Av Nte 14A, wicked curries tofu stir-fries and salads in peanut sauce, in small candlelit restaurant. Great vegetarian options. Highly recommended. Closed Wed. *Caffé Pizzería Asjemenou*, 5 C Pte 4. Serve Italian dishes, good food, excellent espresso and cappuccino, always full, good breakfast excellent bread, slow service at times, but recommended. *Café Riviera*, 5 C Pte 7A, is an Italian restaurant with courtyard and interior seating. Prices are good value, but portions don' err on the generous side. Try the Greek-style chicken in orange sauce. Closed Mon. *Café Rocío*, 6 Av Nte 34. This is a palace of Asian food delight. Virtually everything on the menu i mouthwateringly delicious, which will leave you no choice but to return. Don't leave withou indulging in the *mora crisp*, hot blackberry sauce sandwiched between slices of vanilla ice-cream! This restaurant comes more than highly recommended. *Cinema Bistro Café Restaurante*, 5 Av Sur 14, burritos and pastas and budget *menú del día* at US$2.30, happy hour 1800-2100, also shows videos (see Cinemas) and has a movie meal deal, with a film and a meal with a drink for US$3.90. Recommended. *Personajes de La Antigua*, on 6 Av Nte 7 with great ambience, classical music and black and white photos on the wall, and outdoor stone seating as well. Large breakfast range and delicious salad selection. *Rainbow Café*, 7 Av Sur, on the corner of 6 C Pte, vegetarian food served in a pleasant courtyard surrounded by hanging plants, top filling breakfasts, indulgent crepes, popular, recommended for word-of-mouth information, also poetry evenings, book exchange and *Bar Pacific* at nigh with happy hour and ladies' nights. Recommended. *Restaurante Beijing*, corner of 6 Av Su and 5 C Pte, excellent Chinese restaurant with large portions, oyster and crab dishes available, as well as chow mein and vegetarian options. Highly recommended. Closed Tue.

Seriously cheap *Café Sol*, 1 C Pte 9, delicious shish kebabs and vegetarian burritos, excellent value. Shame about the not too attractive courtyard. Cheap internet available. English spoken, friendly Recommended. *Comedor Antigüeño*, Alameda Sta Lucía 4, near the PO. This locally run place offers an absolute bargain of a *menú del día* (fish, chicken), which includes a soup, all for only US$1.70; sometimes a drink is included for that price. This place is extremely popular and can get ridiculously busy, so best to turn up before 1300 for lunch. Recommended *Helas Taberna Griega*, 4 Av Nte 4, inside *La Escudilla*, see below. Delicious food including pitta bread stuffed with goodies, Greek olives, tzatsiki, all surrounded by a Greek ruin and sea mural, fishing net and shells. Closed Wed. *La Escudilla*, 4 Av Nte 4, in the same building as the popular *Rikki's Bar* (see under bars). The food here is always delicious and extremely good value. The plant-filled courtyard is a good place to meet and mingle. Recommended. *Travel Menu*, 6 C Pte 14, big fat juicy sandwiches and tofu stir-fry, in candlelit place with great montage on the wall, friendly. Closed Mon until 1730. For the cheapest of the cheap go to the stalls on the corner of 4 C Pte and 7 Av Nte, and those at the corner of 5 C Pte and 4 Av Sur. During the Easter period, the plaza in front of La Merced is transformed into a food market. At all these places you can pick up *elote, tortillas, tostadas* and *enchiladas*.

Cafés *Bagel Barn*, 5 C Pte 2, near the southwest corner of the plaza, popular, snack deals with bagels. *Cafetería Charlotte*, Cjón de los Nazarenos 9, between 6 and 7 Av Nte, good breakfasts, light meals, cakes, good coffee, German books and newspapers, and German films. *Café Condesa*, 5 Av Nte 4, west side of the main plaza in a pretty courtyard, popular, a little pricey for the portions given, breakfast with free coffee fill-ups, desserts, top quiches, popular Sun brunches, friendly. *Doña Luisa Xicotencatl*, 4 C Ote 12, 1½ blocks east of the plaza, a popular meeting place with an excellent bulletin board, serving pies and bread, breakfasts, tasty ice-cream (especially the cherry), good coffee, good burgers, extensive menu, large portions. Steer clear of the baked potatoes – way too dry. It's worth eating in the upstairs dining-room for the views to Volcán Agua. *Fernando's Kaffee*, 7 Av Nte 43D esq with C Camposeco, tasty quiche, muffins, home-made ice-cream and coffee-grinding workshops for US$13! Recommended and very cheap. *La Cenicienta*, 5 Av Nte 7, cakes and cookies until you can eat no more. Try the cinnamon roll. *La Fuente*, next to *Doña Luisa*, delicious falafel dishes with pitta bread, good pasta, light meals and cakes at tables set around fountain, colourful and popular. A *huipil* market is held in the courtyard on Sat 0900-1400. Recommended. *Peroleto*, Alameda Sta Lucía 36, next to San Jerónimo church, stop by here for the wickedest *licuados* in town and you probably won't be able to bypass the cake cabinet either. It has a *ceviche* restaurant next door open until 1800. *Tostaduría Antigua*, 7 Av Sur No 12A, roasts and brews good coffee, many say the best in town. You can smell the coffee half a block away in each direction.

Café 2000, 6 Av Nte, between 4 and 5 C Pte, kicking most nights with indie music, and hard, cool lines in décor, but the free films shown on a giant screen can alter the balance in the bar between those on a bender and those glued to the screen. Daily hours are 0800-0100. *Casbah*, 5 Av Nte 30, just past the arch, has a medium-sized dance floor with a podium. It plays a mixture of mostly good dance sounds plus some Latin music. It's probably the closest place to a nightclub atmosphere in Antigua. Open Thu-Sat 1800-0100, Sun 2000-0100. Gay night is Thu. *La Canoa*, 5 C Pte, near the plaza, good mix, salsa, crowded. Doors open at 1930 until 0100. *MonoLoco*, 5 Av Sur 6, rooftop veranda, heaving at weekends big time, happy hour 1700-2000, open 1100-2400. See under eating. Guatemalans love the *Peña Cubana*, on 6 C Pte 31, a huge bar with podium in a large courtyard, giving the impression that it's open air, but it's actually covered by a rather graceful big top tent roof. Gringoless and the place to come to mix with the locals, dance to Western and Latin sounds, and sometimes win a free bottle of rum. Open until 0100. *Rikki's Bar*, 4 Av Nte 4, inside *La Escudilla*, usually packed full of gringos, but attracts a young Guatemalan crowd as well, popular with students and visitors and the gay fraternity. Good place to meet people. A good mix of music, including jazz.

Bars & nightclubs
Most bars have a happy hour between 1800-2100

Entertainment

Cinemas Antigua must be the home of the lounge cinema. All show films or videos in English, or with subtitles. Look out for flyers for showings. *Café 2000*, 6 Av Sur, shows free films daily. *Cinema Bistro*, 5 Av Sur 14, food and film deal, US$3.90, 12 films daily. *Ciné Sin Ventura*, 5 Av Sur 8, US$1.30. The only real screen in town, auditorium can get cold, and they could do with hitting the brightness button. *Tecún Umán*, 6 C Pte 34A, near *Rainbow Café*, 2 films a day at 1700 and 2000, US$1.30. **Dance lessons** *Menéalo Dance School*, Casa de los Nahuales, 3 Av Sur 6, T832-7137, beginners and intermediates.

Festivals

Semana Santa: see box, page 581. **21-26 Jul** for the feast of *San Santiago* (St James). **31 Oct-2 Nov** (All Saints and All Souls, in and around Antigua). On **7 Dec**, the citizens celebrate the *Quema del Diablo* (burning of the Devil) by lighting fires in front of their houses and burning an effigy of the Devil in the Plazuela de La Concepción at night, thereby starting the Christmas festivities. **15 Dec** sees the start of what's known as the *Posadas*, where a group of people leave from each church, dressed as Mary and Joseph, and seek refuge in hotels. They are symbolically refused lodging several times, but eventually allowed in.

Shopping

Antigua is a shopper's paradise, with textiles, furniture, candles, fabrics, clothes, sculpture, candies, glass, jade and ceramics on sale everywhere. The main municipal market is on Alameda Santa Lucía next to the bus station, where you can buy fruit, clothes and shoes. There are *artesanía* stalls inside. There are also plenty of photo developing shops in town.

There are numerous **bookshops** selling books in English and Spanish, postcards, posters, maps and guides including *Footprint Handbooks*. For example: *Casa Andinista*, 4 C Ote 5A; *Culture Shack*, 6 C Pte 7 and 5a Av Sur, inside *Cinemaya*; *Un Poco de Todo*, near *Casa del Conde* on 5 Av Nte on the Plaza; *Casa del Conde*, 5 Av Nte 4; *Librería El Pensativo*, inside *Nim P'ot*, 5 Av Nte 29; *Rainbow Café*, 7 Av Sur 18, second-hand books; *Hamlin y White*, 4 C Ote 12A. Books on Guatemala are cheaper here than at *Casa del Conde*. **Crafts, clothes and jewellery** The **Mercado de Artesanías** is next to the main market at the end of 4 C Pte.

Guatemala

Craft market also on 4 C Pte between 7 and 6 Av Nte next to La Compañía de Jesús; but bargain very hard here. There are also stalls in the plaza on 3 C Pte between 2 and 3 Av Sur in front of the Santa Clara Convent. *Casa de Artes*, 4 Av Sur 11, for traditional textiles and handicrafts, jewellery, etc. *Casa de los Gigantes*, 7 C Ote 18, for textiles and handicrafts. *El Telar*, Loom Tree, 5 Av Sur 7, all sorts of coloured tablecloths, napkins, cushion covers, and bedspreads are sold here. *Milagroso*, 5 C Pte 13, sells cotton clothes, some of them embroidered with flowers. For Western-style clothes and jewellery try *Diva*, at 5 Av Nte 16 and inside *La Fuente*, and *Shooga*, 5 Av Nte 9, which has clothes and cards. There is a traditional *hulpil* market held in the courtyard of *La Fuente* every Sat 0900-1400. The display is very colourful and if the sun is out this is an excellent place for photos. There are many other stores selling textiles, handicrafts, antiques, silver and jade on 5 Av Nte between 1 and 4 C Pte and 4 C Ote. *Nim P'ot*, 5 Av Nte 29, a mega-warehouse of traditional textiles and crafts brought from around the country, www.nimpot.com A number of jade-carving factories may be visited, including *Jades, SA*, 4 C Ote 34 (branches on same street Nos 1 and 12), and *La Casa del Jade*, 4 C Ote 10. *Colibrí*, 4 C Ote 3B, sells quality weavings. *Calzado Fase*, 6 Av Nte 61A, makes made-to-measure leather boots. *Tabaquería*, 4 C Pte 38B, sells all sorts of Cuban and Central American cigars; if you can't get to Cuba, best buy here. For items that will make your eyes pop, visit *Angelina*, at 4 C Ote 22, for some wild pieces of furniture carved from gigantic slabs of wood. *Antigua Tattoo*, Paseo de los Corregidores, 5 Av Sur 6, ta2mike@hotmail.com

Food *Doña María Gordillo*, 4 C Ote 11, is famous throughout the country. It is impossible to get in the door most days but, if you can, take a peek, to see the *dulces*, as well as the row upon row of yellow wooden owls keeping their beady eyes on the customers. The *Tienda de Doña Gavi*, 3 Av Nte 2, behind the cathedral, sells all sorts of lovely potions and herbs, candles, and home-made biscuits. Doña Gaviota also sells Guatemala City's most famous ice-creams in all sorts of weird and wonderful flavours (see *Helados Marylena*, page 573, for the story). *La Bodegona*, 5 C Pte 32, opposite *Posada La Quinta* on 5 C Pte and below *Hotel Backpacker's* on 4 C Pte, large supermarket.

Sport

Pampering parlours *Antigua Spa Resort*, San Pedro El Panorama, lote 9 and 10 G, T832-3960, www.antiguaspa.centroamerica.com Swimming pool, steam baths, sauna, gymnasium, jacuzzi, beauty salon. Open daily 0900-2100. Reservations advised. *Fraternidad Naturista Antigua*, C Real 30, Jocotenango, T831-0379, Sun-Thu 0700-1800, Fri 0700-1300, massage US$5.20 and saunas. *Mayan Spa*, Alameda Sta Lucía Nte 20, T832-0381. Massages are US$12 per hr and pampering packages, including sauna, steam baths and jacuzzi, are available. Open Mon-Sat 0900-1900. **Riding** *Club Ecuestre La Ronda*, based at the Establos La Ronda, *Centro Cultural La Azotea*, Jocotenango, rents horses and does guided tours, T832-0907, T508-2535 (mob). You can also hire horses in Santa María de Jesús. **Swimming** Non-residents may use the pool at the *Hotel Antigua* for a charge of US$6.50 from Mon-Fri, US$7.80 on Sat-Sun; also at the *Radisson Antigua* (Ciudad Vieja exit), T832-0011-15, for US$6.50 per day. Both hotels have special Sun prices for buffet lunch, swimming and marimba band. There is a public pool on the outskirts of the city on the way to Santa María de Jesus. Take any bus heading this way and ask to be dropped at the Escuela INVAL, 10 mins. Just before the school on the left is a short path to the *Paraíso Azul*, a small leisure area, US$2.60 for use.

Transport

Local **Bike hire** See Tour operators. **Car hire** *Tabarini*, 6 Av Sur 22, T832-8107, also at the *Radisson*, T832-7640, www.tabarini.com **Horse-drawn carriage** Available at weekends and during fiestas around the plaza. US$1.30 for a trip around 12 blocks of the town centre. **Motorcycle hire** *La Ceiba*, 6 C Pte 15, T832-0077, www.laceiba.centroamerica.com

Long distance **Bus** To **Guatemala City**. Buses leave when full between 0530 and 1900, US$0.60, 1-1½ hrs, depending on the time of day, from the Alameda Santa Lucía near the market, from an exit

Learning the lingo

Antigua is overrun with language students and so some say it is not the most ideal environment in which to learn Spanish. There are about 70-plus schools, open year round. At any one time there may be 300-600 overseas students in Antigua. Not all schools are officially authorized by INGUAT and the Ministry of Education. INGUAT has a list of authorized schools in its office. Rates depend on the number of hours of tuition per week, and vary from school to school. As a rough guide, the average fee for 4 hrs a day, 5 days a week is US$85 (US$125 for 8 hrs a day), at a reputable school, though many are less and some schools offer cheaper classes in the afternoon. You will benefit more from the classes if you have done a bit of study of the basics before you arrive. There are guides who take students around the schools and charge a high commission (make sure this is not added to your account). They may approach tourists arriving on the bus from the capital.

All schools offer one-to-one tuition; if you can meet the teachers in advance, so much the better, but don't let the director's waffle distract you from asking pertinent questions. Paying more does not mean you get better teaching and the standard of teacher varies within schools as well as between schools. Beware of 'hidden extras' and be clear on arrangements for study books. Some schools have an inscription fee. Several schools use a portion of their income to fund social projects and some offer a programme of activities for students such as dance classes, Latin American film, tours, traditional clothing and weaving and football. Before making any commitment, find somewhere to stay for a couple of nights and shop around at your leisure. Schools also offer accommodation with local families, but check the place out if possible before you pay a week in advance. Average accommodation rates with a family with three meals a day are US$40-60 per week. In some cases lodging is group accommodation, run by the schools; if you prefer single accommodation, ask for it.

Guatemala

next to *Pollo Campero,* not from behind the market. All other buses leave from behind the market. To **Chimaltenango**, on the Pan-American Highway, from 0700-1800, every 30 mins, US$0.32, for connections to **Los Encuentros** (for Lake Atitlán and Chichicastenango), **Cuatro Caminos** (for **Quetzaltenango**) and **Huehuetenango** (for the Mexican border). It is possible to get to Chichicastenango and back by bus in a day, especially on Thu and Sun, for the market. Get the bus to Chimaltenango and then change. It's best to leave early. See Chimaltenango for connections. The only direct bus to **Panajachel** leaves at 0700, from 4 C Pte, in front of *La Bodegona* supermarket, US$4, 2½ hrs. Returning 1100. To **Escuintla**, at 0645, 0730, 0745, 0800, 1000, and 1600, 1½-2 hrs, US$0.65. For local transport to the following towns and villages, see Excursions from Guatemala City and Antigua. **Ciudad Vieja, San Antonio Aguas Calientes, Santa María de Jesús, San Miguel Dueñas,** and **San Juan Alotenango. Shuttles** Hotels and travel agents run frequent shuttle services to and from Guatemala City and the airport (1 hr) from 0400 to about 2000 daily, US$7-10 depending on the time of day: details from any agency in town. There are also shuttles to Chichicastenango, US$12, Panajachel, US$10-12, Quetzaltenango, US$25, and other destinations, but check for prices and days of travel. Private shuttle to or from Guatemala City US$10-30, depending on the number of people.

Directory

Most banks are open 0900-1800 and 0900-1300 on Sat. *Bancafé,* on 4 C Pte between 5 Av and 6 Av Nte, near the plaza, with a 24 hr ATM for Visa, Plus. Fairly quick service. *Banco de América Central*, on the plaza, Visa and MasterCard ATM (Cirrus and Plus), but bank hours only. *Banco Industrial*, 5 Av Sur 4, near the plaza, gives cash on Visa ATM (24 hr) and Visa credit card at normal rates, no commission. Extremely quick service. *Banquetzal* on the plaza, good rates, no commission, MasterCard (Cirrus) ATM. *Lloyds TSB*, 4 C Ote 2 on the northeast corner of plaza, changes TCs and deals with MasterCard. There are a number of other banks dotted around town and on the Alameda Sta Lucía.

Banks
No banks change money in the week between Christmas and New Year. Banks also close from Wed-Sun of Holy Week

Guatemala

Communications Internet Some internet cafés offer discount cards, which are worth buying if you are in town for any length of time. The following are recommended: *Conexión*, inside *La Fuente*, 4 C Ote 14, open daily 0830-1900. *Enlaces*, 6 Av Nte 1, discount cards available. Open Mon-Sat 0800-2000, Sun 0800-1300. *FunkyMonkeyNet*, Paseo de los Corregidores, 5 Av Sur 6, half a block from the plaza. Open daily 0800-2230. **Post office**: at Alameda Sta Lucía and 4 C Pte, near the market. Open Mon-Fri 0800-1830, Sat 0830-1400; *Lista de correos* keeps letters for a month. There is also a post box in the *Hotel Cortés y Lazarro*, 6 Av Sur, between 5 and 6 C. **Courier services**: There are several couriers in town, including *DHL*, 6 C Pte and 6 Av Sur. **Telephones**: *Telgua*, 5 Av Sur on the corner of the plaza for international and local calls, but not as helpful as they could be. There are cheaper rates in the internet cafes eg *FunkyMonkeyNet* (see above). There is a line of public phone boxes inside the building, which are quieter to use than the couple under the arches on the west side of the square. Open Mon-Fri 0800-1800, Sat 0800-1200.

Cultural centres *El Sitio*, 5 C Pte 15, T832-3037, elsitio@guate.net has concerts and other cultural activities, and a very good library including books in English, and a quiet coffee shop. Open Tue-Sun 1100-1900.

Language schools *Footprint* has received favourable reports from students for the following language schools: *Academía de Español Guatemala*, 7 C Ote 15, T832-5060, aegnow@guate.net, *Alianza Lingüística 'Cano'*, Av El Desengaño 21A, T832-0370, F832-3580. Private classes are also available. *Amerispan*, 6 Av Nte 40 and 7 C Ote, T832-0164, F832-1896, amerispan@guate.net, www.amerispan.com *Centro Lingüístico Maya*, 5 C Pte 20, T/F832-0656, www.clmmaya.com *CSA* (Christian Spanish Academy), 6 Av Nte 15, Aptdo Postal 320, T832-3922, F832-3760, www.learncsa.com *Don Pedro de Alvarado*, 6 Av Nte 39, T8326645, F832-4180, www.guacalling.com/donpedroschool 20 years' experience. *Latinoamérica Spanish Academy*, 3 C Pte 19A, Lotificación Cofiño, T832-1484. *Proyecto Bibliotecas Guatemala (PROBIGUA)*, 6 Av Nte 41B, T/F832-0860, www.probigua.conexion.com, gives a percentage of profits towards founding and maintaining 14 public libraries in rural towns; frequently recommended. *Proyecto Lingüístico Francisco Marroquín*, 7 C Pte 31, T832-3777, www.plfm-antigua.org *Quiché*, 3 Av Sur 15A, T8320780. *Sevilla Academia de Español*, 1 Av Sur 8, T/F832-5101, www.sevillaantigua.com *Spanish School Antigüeño*, 1 Pte 10, T/F832-7241, www.granjaguar.com/antiguena *Tecún Umán*, 6

C Pte 34A, T/F832-2792, www.tecunuman.centramerica.com Also check ads in Doña Luisa's and others around town and the tourist office for private lessons. Recommended private teachers: *Julia Solís*, 5 C Pte 36, T8325497, julisar@hotmail.com She lives behind the tailor's shop. *Armalia Jarquín*, Av El Desengaño 11, T8322377. There are, unbelievably, numerous number 11s on this road. Armalia's has a sign up and is opposite number 75, which has a tiled plaque.

Laundry All charge about US$0.75 per kg and close Sun and half-day Sat. *Lavandería Gilda*, 5 C Pte between 6 and 7 Av, very good and can do a wash and dry in 2 hrs. *Central*, 5 C Pte 7B. There are many others scattered around the centre of town.

Left luggage Jungle Party Smoothie Bar, Paseo de los Corregidores, 5 Av Sur 6, T832-7181, jungleparty2001@ yahoo.com Long-term rates negotiable. *Luna Maya*, 6 Av Nte 4, T832-0489, short and long term rates available.

Medical services Casa de Salud Santa Lucía, Alameda Sta Lucía Sur 7, T832-3122. Open 24 hrs, good and efficient service. Consultation prices vary. **Hospital Privado Hermano Pedro**, Av El Desengaño 12A, T832-6419. **Doctor**: *Dr Julio Castillo Vivar*, Alameda Sta Lucía 52 esq 6 C Pte, next to *Farmacia El Pilar*. Helpful, speaks English, recommended, open late. **Hospital emergency**: *Hospital San Pedro*, T8320301. **Opticians**: *Optica Santa Lucía*, 5 C Pte 28, T832-0384. Sells contact lens solution and accessories.

Tour operators Adventure Travel Center Viareal, 5 Av Nte 25B, T/F832-0162, viareal@guate.net, daily trips to Guatemalan destinations (including Río Dulce sailing, river and volcano trips), Monterrico, Quiriguá, El Salvador and Honduras. *Antigua Tours*, Casa Santo Domingo, 3 C Ote 22, T832-5821, www.antiguatours.net Run by Elizabeth Bell, author of 4 books on Antigua. She offers walking tours of the city (US$18 per person), book in advance, Mon 1400-1630, Tue-Wed, Fri-Sat 0930-1230. Also, slide show every Tue 1800-1900 at 6 Av Nte 15, US$3. During Lent and Holy Week there are extra tours, giving insight into the processions and carpet making. Highly recommended. *Archaeology EcoTours*, 5a Av Norte 24 "A", T/F832-1851, http://archaeology-ecotours.com, specialize in archaeology and ecological Maya tours. *Atitrans*, 6 Av Sur 8, T832-0644, atitrans@quick.guate.com Good, reliable shuttle service (they will also drive to private addresses in the remoter zones of Guatemala City), and tours to surrounding villages and Guatemala City. *Aventuras Vacacionales*, 1 Av Sur 11B, T/F832-3352, www.sailing.conexion.com Highly recommended sailing trips on *Las Sirenas* with Capt John Clark (see also under Río Dulce, page 659). *Centroamericana Tourist Service*, 4 C Pte 38F, T/F832-5032, centroamericana@yahoo.com Operates a reliable shuttle service. *Eco-Tour Chejo's*, 3 C Pte 24, T832-5464, ecotourchejos@hotmail.com Offers well-guarded walks up volcanoes. Agua US$20 for two, Pacaya US$10. Interesting tours are also available to coffee *fincas*, flower plantations and a macadamia nut plantation etc, shuttle service, horse-riding, very helpful. *Gran Jaguar*, 4 C Pte 30, T832-2712, www.guacalling.com/jaguar/ Well-organized volcano tours with official security, great fun, shuttles and trips to Tikal. Very highly recommended for the Pacaya trip. *Mayan Bike Tours* offer guided tours around Antigua, Lake Atitlán and other areas, at the former *Villa San Francisco*, 1 Av Sur 15, T/F8325836. Spanish, English, German, French, Italian spoken. Also at 3 C Pte and 7 Av Nte, T8323743, www.mayanbike.com From US$15 per person. Recommended. *Monarcas Travel*, 6a Av Nte 60A, T8324305, F832208, monarcas@conexion.com.gt Reliable airport shuttle service and trips to

Guatemala

Guatemala

Copán (US$25, 0400), Semuc Champey and the kite festival at Santiago Sacatepéquez on 1 Nov. Also medicinal plant tours. *Old Town Outfitters*, 6 C Pte 7, T832-4243, www.bikeguatemala.com Mountain bike tours (US$25 half-day tour), kayak tours (5 days US$350), outdoor equipment on sale, maps, information, very helpful. *Rainbow Travel Center*, 7 Av Sur 8, T832-4202, F832-4206, rainbowtravel@gua.gbm.net Full local travel service, specialists in student flights and bargain international flights, they will attempt to match any quote. They also sell ISIC, Go25 and teachers' cards. Recommended. Manager Phillipa Myers is also the warden for the British Embassy in the area. English, French, German and Japanese spoken as well as Spanish. *Servicios Turísticos Atitlán*, 2 Av Sur 4A, T832-1493, at night T762-2421, www.atitlan.com Comprehensive and good shuttle service, air tickets, hotel reservations and organized tours. *Sin Fronteras*, 3a C Pte 12, T832-1226, F832-2674, www.sinfront.com Local tours, horse-riding, bicycle tours, national and international air tickets including discounts with ISIC and Go25 cards. They also sell travel insurance. They are agents for rafting experts *Maya Expeditions*. *Space*, 5 C Pte 3A, T/F832-7143, spacegua@terra.com.gt Shuttles, tours, flights, deep-sea fishing (between US$200-1,200 a day), bungee jumping (US$25 1 jump), helicopter tours (US$500 per hr), golf and bird-watching. Closed Sun. *Tivoli Travel*, 4 C Ote 10, T832-4274, F832-5690, antigua@tivoli.com.gt Helpful with any travel problem, English, French, Spanish, German, Italian spoken, reconfirm tickets, shuttles, hotel bookings, good-value tours. Useful for organizing independent travel as well as tours. Recommended. Closed Sun. *Turansa*, in *Hotel Radisson Antigua*, Ciudad Vieja exit, T832-2928, www.turansa.com Good for flights, eg to Tikal, extensive travel service. *Viajes Inter Quetzal*, 5 C Pte 13B, T/F832-5938, interquetzal@guate.net.com Helpful, reconfirms flights, can also arrange travel insurance. Closed Sun. *Vision Travel*, 3 Av Nte 3, T832-3293, F832-1955, www.GUATEMALAinfo.com, offer a wide range of tours, run by Nancy Hoffman and Luis Ramirez, English spoken. Frequently recommended. *Vision* also has guidebooks for reference or to buy, along with a water bottle filling service to encourage recycling. Cheap phone call service. Shuttles and tours. Closed Sun.

Useful addresses   **Tourism police**, 4 Av Nte, between 3 and 4 C Ote down the side of City Hall, T832-7290. The office is open from 0700-2200 daily and there is night cover for emergencies or flooding/rain problems, 2200-0700, Jun-Oct. Just knock on the door or ring their number. **National Police** are based in Antigua, in the *Palacio de los Capitanes General*, on the south side of the plaza, T832266. For **Volunteer work**, see Essentials.

Excursions from Guatemala City and Antigua

Ciudad Vieja, San Miguel de las Dueñas and San Juan del Obispo
Whether you're staying in Guatemala City or Antigua, the places in this section can be conveniently visited as a day or overnight trip

Ciudad Vieja – the former capital – is 5½ km southwest of Antigua at the foot of Agua volcano. In 1527, Alvarado moved his capital, known then as Santiago de Los Caballeros, from Iximché to San Miguel Escobar, now a suburb of Ciudad Vieja. On 11 September 1541, after days of torrential rain, an immense mudslide came down the mountain and swallowed up the city. Alvarado's widow, Doña Beatriz de la Cueva, newly elected Governor after his death, was among those drowned. There are few ruins to be seen, those in the north of the village are believed to be part of a small monastery. Today Ciudad Vieja is itself a suburb of Antigua, but with a handsome church, founded 1534, one of the oldest in Central America. There's a **fiesta** on December 8. Bus from Antigua, US$0.10, every 30 mins, 15 mins. Between Ciudad Vieja and San Miguel de las Dueñas is the **Valhalla macadamia nut farm**. ■ *Visits and nut tasting are free, T831-5799. Getting there: take a bus marked 'Dueñas'*. At **San Juan del Obispo**, 5 km south of Antigua, is the restored palace of Francisco Marroquín, first bishop of Guatemala, which is now a convent. The parish church has some fine 16th-century images.

Jocotenango   The music museum, **Casa K'ojom**, is now in the Centro Cultural La Azotea. Recommended, with displays of traditional Maya and colonial-era instruments. ■ *Mon-Fri 0830-1600, Sat 0900-1400, US$3.25*. Jocotenango also has a butterfly enclosure, **Mariposario Antigua**, 800 m from La Azotea and public saunas at the **Fraternidad Naturista Antigua**, C Real 30. ■ *Closed Sat. T831-0379*.

Santa María de Jesús   Beyond San Juan del Obispo, beside Agua volcano, is the charming village of Santa María de Jesús, with its beautiful view of Antigua. In the early morning there are good views of all three volcanoes from 2 km back down the road towards Antigua. Colourful *huipiles* are worn, made and sold from a couple of stalls, or ask at the shops on the plaza. **Fiesta** on 10 January. *Frequent buses to and from Antigua every 30 mins, 35 mins, US$0.20.* **Sleeping** at **E** *Restaurante Posada El Oasis*, T832-0130. The owner hires horses and offers a guide service for the volcano.

About 3 km northwest of Ciudad Vieja is San Antonio Aguas Calientes. The hot springs unfortunately disappeared with recent earthquakes, but the village has many small shops selling locally made textiles. *Carolina's Textiles* is recommended for a fine selection, while on the exit road *Alida* has a shop almost as large. You can watch the weavers in their homes by the roadside. Some women offer weaving lessons, ask in town. You will need some time (say several afternoons) to make progress. There is a market most days in the centre. **Fiestas**: 16-21 January; Corpus Christi, 1 November. ■ *Buses from Antigua, every 30 mins, 15 mins, US$0.13.*

San Antonio Aguas Calientes

About 7 km from Antigua is *Finca Los Nietos*, a coffee farm at San Lorenzo El Cubo which conducts tours of the crop and its processing, toasting and packaging. ■ *0800-1100, US$6, T831-5438.* Take bus heading to San Antonio Aguas Calientes.

At the village of San Felipe (US$0.05 by bus, or 15 minutes walk from Antigua) is a figure of Christ which people from all over Latin America come to see. *Restaurant El Prado* is recommended. There is a small silver workshop which is worth visiting.

Five kms beyond San Lucas Sacatepéquez, at Km 29½, Carretera Roosevelt (usually known as the Pan-American Highway), is **Santiago Sacatepéquez**, whose **fiesta** on 1 November, Día de los Muertos (All Souls Day), is characterized by colourful kite-flying (*barriletas*); also 25 July. Market days are Wednesday and Friday.

North of Guatemala City is **Mixco Viejo**, the excavated site of a post-classic Mayan fortress, which spans 14 hilltops, including 12 groups of pyramids. Despite earthquake damage it is worth a visit and is recommended. It was the 16th-century capital of the Pokomam Maya. There are a few buses a day from the Zona 4 bus terminal, Guatemala City. The bus goes to Pachalum; ask to be dropped at the entrance. A bridge now allows you to drive to the site, refreshments available.

Volcanoes

With Agua and Pacaya you get a considerable head start by starting from villages that are on their flanks. The three volcanoes surrounding Antigua give incomparable views of the surrounding countryside and are best climbed on a clear night with a full moon, or after a very early morning start. Altitude takes its toll and plenty of time should be allowed for ascending. Take lots of water and fleeces, as the summits are cold. Climbing boots are recommended, especially on Fuego and Pacaya, to cope with the cinder. The descents take from a third to a half of the ascent time. The tourist office in Antigua is helpful; enquire there about conditions before setting out. They also have a list of authorized independent guides if you would rather use one of them. Robberies and rapes have occurred even where large parties are climbing these volcanoes. None of these have been on Pacaya, since the security set-up was introduced a few years ago, however there have been a few incidents on Agua in the last year, including climbers being robbed of all their clothes and having to descend starkers.

The most exciting to climb is Pacaya because it's active and you can moon wander near the crater on rubble that is black, sharp and lifeless

At 2,552 m, the still-active Volcán Pacaya can't be missed. The cone is covered in black basaltic rock shed from the crater. The rocks get warm and are lethally sharp. At the lip of the crater the sulphurous gases that are being belched out are chokingly disgusting, but the yellow, green and red colours blotched on the crater lip are striking. The roaring magma-filled mouth can be seen on the far side of the crater once the gaseous winds disperse. As the sun sets on the horizon, Agua is silhouetted in the distance, a weak orange line streaked behind it.

Volcán Pacaya

One of the highlights of this trip is surfing down the scree at high speed as the sun sets

Guatemala

Should you be in Antigua when Pacaya erupts you may see some spectacular lava flows

Pacaya has erupted about 20 times since 1565, but since the mid-1960s it has been erupting continuously. In the late 1980s it produced lava flows and in 1998 several villages were evacuated following eruptions and the airport was shut as the runway was carpeted in ash. Always check its alert status before signing up for a tour. Tours are available for US$5 upwards per person, depending on the number in the party, with *Gran Jaguar, Eco-Tour Chejo's* and *Tivoli*, and other Antigua tour agencies. In addition there is a US$3.25 fee to be paid at the official entrance in San Francisco de Sales (where there are toilets). Every climber must pay the entrance fee to the Volcán Pacaya National Park. Do not try to avoid this and do not go with a guide who tries to avoid it, not least because such guides have faced potentially dangerous situations with locals. It is about 1½ hours to the base of the crater, then a further 30-45 minutes scrambling up the scree and volcanic throw up – depending on how good you are at tackling the 'one step forward, two steps back' syndrome. The trick is to walk on your toes and not your heels. The popular time for organized trips is to leave Antigua at 1300 and return at 2100. Try to avoid going on a mid-morning departure, which usually results in an arrival at the summit just as it is covered in cloud. Take torch/flashlight, refreshments and water and – it may sound obvious – but wear boots or trainers, not sandals. Security officers go with the trips and police escorts ensure everyone leaves the area after dark.

Check the situation in advance for **camping** (which is well below the crater lip); the guides will point out the area – ignore their advice at your own peril. If it's safe, take a torch and warm clothing and a handkerchief to filter dust and fumes. Tour agencies can arrange camping with a guide and guard, at around US$70, negotiable, including transport. Sunrise comes with awesome views over the desolate black lava field to the distant Pacific (airborne dust permitting) and the peaks of Fuego, Acatenango and Agua.

Volcán Agua The easiest of the three Antigua volcanoes, at 3,760 m, is climbed from Santa María de Jesús. Ask for directions in the village or speak to Aurelio Cuy Chávez at the *Posada El Oasis,* who offers a guide service. For Agua's history, see under Ciudad Vieja, page 592. The crater has a small shelter (none too clean), which has a shrine, and about 10 antennae. There are great views (though not guaranteed) of Volcán de Fuego. It's a three- to five-hour climb if you are fit, and at least two hours down. Make sure you get good directions if you do it alone (although this is not recommended by INGUAT); there are several old avalanches you have to cross before regaining the trail. If you do not, you may get lost. To get the best views before the clouds cover the summit, it is best to stay at the radio station at the top. Climbing at night is recommended, either by torchlight or by the light of the moon; Saturday-Sunday is recommended for the ascent. Take an early bus from Antigua to Santa María de Jesús, which allows you to climb the volcano and return to Antigua in one day. Most organized tours with Antigua tour operators are during the day and cost about US$20 per person with guide and security, but less if there is a larger party. Trips normally leave Antigua about 0500, returning in the evening.

Agua can also be climbed from **Alotenango**, a village between Agua and Fuego volcanoes, south of Ciudad Vieja. It's 9 km from Antigua and its name means 'place surrounded by corn'. It has a **fiesta** from 18-20 January. Buses go from Antigua to Alotenango from 0700-1800, 40 mins. Looking at the market building in Alotenango, take the left route up; turn left at the T-junction, then first right and up. There are only two decision points: take the right fork, then the left. It is not advisable to descend Agua towards Palín in the southeast, as there is precipitous forest, steep bluffs, and dry watercourses, which tend to drop away vertically and a route is hard to plot.

Volcán Acatenango Acatenango is classified as a dormant volcano and is the third-tallest in the country (3,975 m) with two peaks to its name. Its first recorded eruption was in 1924. Two other eruptions were reported in 1924-27 and 1972. The best trail (west of the one shown on the 1:50,000 topographic map) heads south at the village of La Soledad, 2,300 m (15 km west of Ciudad Vieja), which is 300 m before the road (Route 5) turns right to Acatenango (good *pensión*, **F**, with good cheap meals). A small plateau, La Meseta on maps, known locally as El Conejón, provides a good camping site two-thirds of the way up (three to four hours). From here it is a further three to four hours' harder going to the top. There is a shelter, holding up to 15 people, on the lower of the two summits. Though dirty and in poor condition, this is the best place to sleep. The climb to the higher peak takes about 45 minutes. The views of the near by (lower) active crater of Fuego are excellent and you can watch the activity of Pacaya at night. To reach La Soledad, take a bus heading for Yepocapa or Acatenango village and get off at La Soledad. Be sure to take the correct track going down (no water on the way). If you do this climb independently of a tour agency, ask for a guide in La Soledad.

This volcano (3,763 m) can be climbed via Volcán de Acatenango, sleeping on the col between the two volcanoes where there is a primitive shelter, then climbing for a further four hours over tiring loose ash to the crater. Harder is the long climb from Alotenango. For the first hour or so, until the trees, take a guide. Or go down from Alotenango market place, over the river and, at the concrete gateway, turn right up the main track. Ignoring the initial left fork, plantation/orchard entrances and all 90° turn-offs, take the next three left forks and then the next two right forks. Do not underestimate the amount of water needed for the climb. It is a seven-hour ascent with an elevation gain of 2,400 m – it's a very hard walk, both up and down, and easy to lose the trail. There are steep, loose cinder slopes, which are very tedious, in many places. It is possible to camp about three-quarters of the way up in a clearing. Fuego has had frequent dangerous eruptions in recent years though generally not without warning. Its last major eruption was in 1974. Check in Antigua before attempting to climb. It is recommended by INGUAT that you take a guide, as for all the volcanoes in Guatemala. If driving down towards the south coast you can see the red volcanic rock it has thrown up.

Volcán Fuego
This one is for experienced hikers only

Guatemala

Lake Atitlán and the Highlands

□Guatemala City

Beautiful scenery stretches west of the capital, through the Central Highlands amongst volcano landscapes dotted with colourful markets and Indians wearing traditional costumes in the towns and villages. Decide for yourself whether Aldous Huxley was right to call Lake Atitlán "the most beautiful lake in the world". Further north you can explore the streets and alleys of Chichicastenango as the town fills with hawkers and vendors at the weekly markets serving tourists and locals alike. North of Chichicastenango, the Quiché and Ixil Triangle regions have small, very traditional hamlets set in beautiful countryside that is easily explored by bus.

Guatemala City to Lago de Atitlán

The Pan-American Highway heads west out of the capital passing through Chimaltenango and on to Los Encuentros where it turns north for Chichicastenango, Santa Cruz del Quiché, Nebaj and the Ixil Triangle, and south for Sololá and the Lake Atitlán region. It continues to the western highland region of Quetzaltenango, Totonicapán, Huehuetenango and the Cuchumatanes Mountains.

Guatemala

**Chimalte-
nango**
Chimaltenango is busy with traffic, moving people and produce in the noisy, clumsily efficient style unique to the local Guatemalan buses. Here, another road runs left, 20 km, to Antigua. This tree-lined road leads to Parramos where it turns sharp left. Straight on through the village, in 1½ km, is **B** *Posada de Mi Abuelo*, Carretera a Yepocapa, T839-1842, a delightful inn formerly a coffee farm, good restaurant. This road continues through mountains to Pastores, Jocotenango and finally to Antigua.

Transport Buses to **Antigua** leave from the corner of the main road and the road south to Antigua where there is a lime green and blue shop – *Auto Repuestos y Frenos Nachma*, 45 mins, US$0.32. To **Chichicastenango**, every 30 mins, 0600-1700, 2 hrs, US$1.70. To **Cuatro Caminos**, 2½ hrs, US$2. To **Quetzaltenango**, every 45 mins, 0700-1800, 2½ hrs, US$2.20. To **Tecpán** every 30 mins, 0700-1800, 1 hr. Any bus heading west from Guatemala City stops at Chimaltenango, so you can always make a head start on your journey if you don't want to wait for a direct bus. Taxi to Antigua, US$8-9.

At **San Andrés Itzapa** (6 km south of Chimaltenango) there is a very interesting chapel to Maximón (San Simón) which is well worth a visit. Open till 1800 daily. Shops by the chapel sell prayer pamphlets and pre-packaged offerings.

Beyond Chimaltenango is Zaragoza, a former Spanish penal settlement, and beyond that a road leads 13 km north to the interesting village of **Comalapa**: This is the best place to see *naíf* painting and there are plenty of galleries. **D** *Pixcayá*, 0 Avenida 1-82, T8498260, hot water, parking. Colourful market Monday-Tuesday.

**The routes
west**
Returning to the Pan-American Highway the road divides 6 km past Zaragoza. The southern branch, the **old Pan-American Highway**, goes through Patzicía (see next page) and Patzún (see next page) to Lake Atitlán, then north to Los Encuentros. The northern branch, the **new Pan-American Highway** which is used by all public

Lake Atitlán

Distances
Sololá - Panajachel 8 km
Panajachel - Santa Catarina 4 km
Santa Catarina - San Antonio 6 km

San Andrés Sem - Godínez 10 km
San Lucas - Santiago 16 km
San Marcos - Tzununá 3 km
Tzununá - Santa Cruz 5 km

------ Small
boat service

N
Not to scale

transport, goes past Tecpán and over the Chichoy Pass, and then to Los Encuentros. From Los Encuentros there is only the one road west to San Cristóbal Totonicapán, where it swings northwest to Ciudad Cuauhtémoc, at the Mexican border. The old route goes west through Quetzaltenango to Tapachula, in Mexico.

From Zaragoza the Pan-American Highway runs 19 km to near **Tecpán**, which is slightly off the road at 2,287 m. It has a particularly fine church with silver altars, carved wooden pillars, odd images and a wonderful ceiling which was severely damaged by the 1976 earthquake. The church is slowly being restored. There is accommodation (**B-E**), restaurants and banks. Near Tecpán are the important Mayan ruins of **Iximché**, once capital and court of the Cakchiqueles, 5 km of paved road south of Tecpán. The first capital of Guatemala after its conquest was founded near Iximché; followed in turn by Ciudad Vieja, Antigua and Guatemala City. The ruins are well presented with three plazas, a palace, and two ball courts on a promontory surrounded on three sides by steep slopes. ◼ *0800-1700, US$3.25.*

Tecpán
The women wear most striking huipiles, best displayed at market on Thursday and Sunday

Transport Buses From Guatemala City (Zona 4 terminal), 2¼ hrs, every hr, US$1.05; easy day trip from Panajachel or Antigua.

The old and new Pan-American Highways rejoin 11 km from Sololá at the El Cuchillo junction. 2 km east is Los Encuentros, the junction of the Pan-American Highway and the paved road 18 km northeast to Chichicastenango.

Los Encuentros
Altitude: 2,579 m

Rewarded by amazing views of Lake Atitlán and the surrounding volcanoes, travellers of the southern road from Zaragoza to Lake Atitlán encounter a much more difficult route than the northern option, with several steep hills and many hairpin bends. Nevertheless, if you have the time and a sturdy vehicle, it is a rewarding trip.

To Lake Atitlán along the old Pan-American Highway

The route goes through **Patzicía**, a small Indian village founded in 1545 (no accommodation). Market on Wednesday and Saturday. **Fiesta**: 22-27 July. The famous church, which had a fine altar and beautiful silver, was destroyed by the 1976 earthquake. Beyond is the small town of **Patzún**; its famous church, dating from 1570, is severely damaged and, while it is still standing, is not open to the public. Sunday market, which is famous for the silk (and wool) embroidered napkins and for woven *fajas* and striped red cotton cloth; other markets Tuesday and Friday. **Fiesta**: 17-21 May. Accommodation, ask at the *tiendas* in town.

The road leaves Patzún and goes south to Xepatán and on to **Godínez**, the highest community overlooking the lake. There are several buses to Panajachel, US$0.35 and one bus daily Patzún-Godínez. From Godínez, a good paved road turns off south to the village of San Lucas Tolimán and continues to Santiago Atitlán.

The main (steep, paved) road continues straight on for Panajachel. The high plateau, with vast wheat and maize fields, now breaks off suddenly as though pared by a knife. From a viewpoint here, there is an incomparable view of Lake Atitlán, 600 m below. The very picturesque village of **San Antonio Palopó** is right underneath you, on slopes leading to the water. It is about 12 km from the viewpoint to Panajachel. For the first 6 km you are close to the rim of the old crater and, at the point where the road plunges down to the lakeside, is **San Andrés Semetabaj** which has a beautiful ruined early 17th-century church. Market on Tuesday. Bus to Panajachel, US$0.30.

Sololá

On the road down to Panajachel is Sololá, 11 km from the junction, which has superb views across Lake Atitlán. A fine modern white church, with brightly coloured stained-glass windows and an attractive clocktower dated 1914, dominates the west side of the plaza. Sololá is even more special for the bustling market that

Colour map 5, grid C1
Population: 40,785
Altitude: 2,113m

brings the town to life every Tuesday and Friday, when Indians gather from surrounding commuties to buy and sell local produce. Women and particularly men wear traditional dress. While it is primarily a produce market, there is also a good selection of used *huipiles*. Even if you're not in the market to buy, it is a colourful sight. Markets are mornings only, go early, Friday market gets underway on Thursday. Great **fiesta** 11-17 August.

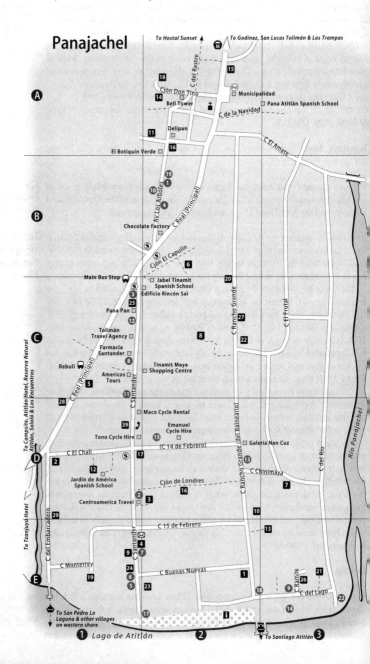

Panajachel

Del Viajero, 7 Av, 10-45, T762-3683, on Parque Central, also annexe around the corner on C 11, rooms with bath, cheaper without, spacious, clean and friendly, good food in restaurant on plaza (El Cafetín). **E** *Belén*, 10 C, 4-36, T762-3105, hot water, restaurant, parking, pleasant, clean. **E** *El Paisaje*, 9 C, 5-41, 2 blocks from Parque Central, T762-3820, pleasant colonial courtyard, shared baths and toilets, clean, hot water, restaurant, good breakfast, family run, laundry facilities. There are many simple places to eat near the Parque Central.

Sleeping & eating
Little accommodation here. Any F-grade accommodation is very basic

Buses To **Chichicastenango** US$0.39, 1½ hrs. Bus to **Panajachel**, US$0.20, every 30 mins, 20 mins, or 1½-2 hrs' walk; to **Chimaltenango**, US$1.05; to **Quetzaltenango**, US$1.50. *Colectivo* to **Los Encuentros**, US$0.15; to **Guatemala City** (*Rebuli*) direct US$1.50, 3 hrs.

Transport

From Sololá the old Pan-American Highway weaves and twists through a 550 m drop in 8 km to Panajachel. The views are impressive at all times of day, but particularly in the morning. Time allowing, it is quite easy to walk down direct by the road (two hours), you also miss the unnerving bus ride down.

Guatemala

Panajachel

The old town of Panajachel is charming and quiet but the newer development, strung along a main road, is a tucker and trinket emporium. It's mainly brash, loud and busy, and will probably swallow a lot of your cash as you make your way down the main road, which is crammed with stalls to tempt. It is a gringo magnet, and if you want to fill up on international cuisine and drink then it's a good place to stay for a few days.

Colour map 5, grid C1

Called 'Pana' by the Guatemalans and pronounced Pana ha' chel

The town centre is the junction of C Principal and C (or Av) Santander. The main bus stop is here, stretching south back down C Real, and it marks the junction between the old and the modern towns. There is no local transport, but everywhere is within walking distance. It takes about 10 mins to walk from the junction to the lake shore. C Rancho Grande is sometimes called C del Balneario and other streets have variants. **INGUAT** is on the lake shore (see map), open daily 0900-1700, T762-1392.

Ins & outs
See page 599 for more detailed transport information

The original settlement was tucked up against the steep cliffs to the north of the present town, about 1 km from the lake. Virtually all traces of the original Kaqchikel village have disappeared, but the early Spanish impact is evident with the narrow streets, public buildings,

Background

Sleeping

1 Barceló *E2*
2 Cacique Inn *D1*
3 Dos Mundos *D2*
4 El Chaparral *E2*
5 Fonda del Sol *C1*
6 Hospedaje Casa Linda *B2*
7 Hospedaje Eddy *D3*
8 Hospedaje El Príncipe *C2*
9 Hospedaje El Viajero *E1*
10 Hospedaje Jere *D2*
11 Hospedaje Pana *A2*
12 Hospedaje Sánchez *D1*
13 Hospedaje Tzutujil *E3*
14 Hospedaje Villa Lupita *A2*
15 Las Casitas *A2*
16 Londres *D2*
17 Mario's Rooms *D1*
18 Montana *A2*
19 Monterrey *E1*
20 Müllers Guest House *C2*
21 Playa Linda *E3*
22 Posada de Doña Carmen *C2*
23 Posada de Don Rodrigo *E2*
24 Posada de los Volcanes *E1*
25 Primavera *C1*
26 Ramos I & II *E3*
27 Rancho Grande *C2*
28 Riva Bella *D1*
29 Santa Isabel *D1*

Eating

1 Al Chisme *B2*
2 Bombay *D1*
3 Chez Alex *C1*
4 Circus Bar *B2*
5 Deli 2 *E1*
6 El Bistro *E1*
7 El Pájaro Azul *E2*
8 El Patio, Chinitas *C1*
9 Los Pumpos *E3*
10 Flyin' Mayan Yacht Club *B2*
11 Guajimbos *C1*
12 Hamburgesa Gigante *C1*
13 Jhanny's *D2*
14 Lakeside Comedores *E3*
15 Last Resort *D*
16 La Zanahoria Chic *A2*
17 Sunset Café *E2*
18 Toyocal *E2*

Bars

19 El Aleph *B2*

0 metres 100
0 yards 100

plaza and church. The original Franciscan church was founded in 1567 and used a the base for the Christianization of the lake area. Later, the fertile area of the rive delta was used for coffee production, orchards and many other crops, some of which are still grown today, and can be seen round the back of the tourist streets or incor porated into the gardens of the hotels. Tourism began here in the early 20th century with several hotels on the waterfront, notably the *Tzanjuyú* and the *Monterrey*, the latter originally a wooden building dating from about 1910, rebuilt in 1975. In the 1970s came an influx of young travellers, quite a few of whom stayed on to enjoy the climate and the easy life. Drugs and the hippy element eventually gave Panajachel a bad name, but rising prices and other pressures have encouraged this group to move on – some to San Pedro across the lake. Others joined the commercial scene and stil run services today.

Sights

Fiesta: 1-7 Oct, the main days are at the weekend and on 4 Oct

The old town is 1 km from the lake and dominated by the **church**, originally built ir 1567, but now restored. It has a fine decorated wooden roof and a mixture of Catholic statues and Maya paintings in the nave. A block up the hill is the daily **market** worth a visit on Sunday mornings especially for embroideries.

In contrast, the modern town, almost entirely devoted to tourism, spreads out towards the lake. Calle Santander is the principal street, leading directly to the short but attractive **promenade** and boat docks. The section between Calle Santander and Calle Rancho Grande has been turned into a park, which delightfully frames the traditional view across the lake to the volcanoes. Near the promenade, at the *Hotel Posada de Don Rodrigo*, is the **Museo Lacustre Atitlán** created by Roberto Samayoa, a prominent local diver and archaeologist, to house some of the many items found in the lake. The geological history is explained and there is a fine display of Maya classical pottery and ceremonial artefacts classified by period. A submerged village has been found at a depth of 20 m, which is at present being investigated. It has been named Samabaj in honour of Don Roberto. ■ *Daily 0900-1700, US$4.60.*

For those interested in local art, visit **La Galería** (near *Rancho Grande Hotel*), where Nan Cuz, an Indian painter, sells her pictures evoking the spirit of village life. She has been painting since 1958 with international recognition. Her painting of a children's procession was adopted by UNICEF for their Christmas cards in 1971.

Excursions

On the road past the entrance to *Hotel Atitlán* is the **Reserva Natural Atitlán**, T762-2565, natres@atitlan.com, a reserve with a bird refuge, butterfly collection, monkeys and native mammals in natural surroundings. A guide (free) is available. Picnic area, herb garden, waterfall, visitor centre, café, access to the lakeside beach. Ask about camping. ■ *Daily 0800-1800, US$4, children under 12, US$2.*

Sleeping

Accommodation and restaurants have been grouped into: Lakeside, Old Town and Centre

■ *on maps*
Price codes: see inside front cover

Lakeside LL *Barceló Del Lago*, C Rancho Grande, T762-1560/1555, F762-1562, www.barcelo.com Includes full board, many services, all rooms have lake view, pool. Recommended. **L** *Atitlán*, 1 km west of centre on lake, 2nd turning off the road to Sololá, T762-1441/1416 (T360-8405, F334-0640, for reservations), www.hotelatitlan.com Full board available, colonial style, excellent rooms and service, beautiful gardens, pool, private beach, top class restaurant. **AL** *Posada de Don Rodrigo*, C Santander, overlooks the lake, T762-2326, pool, terrace, gardens, good restaurant, comfortable, houses museum. **A** *Playa Linda*, on main promenade, T762-1159, F762-0096, www.hotelplayalinda.com Cheaper without lake view, run by US couple, friendly, comfortable,TV, fireplaces, good. **A** *Visión Azul*, on the road to *Hotel Atitlán*, T/F762-1426, restaurant, pool, picturesque, attractive gardens, campground on lakeside US$2 per person, vehicle US$3, tent hire US$6. **B** *Monterrey*, C Monterrey, T762-1126, only hotel in the centre with its own shoreline, run down, great garden, fine for sunsets. **B** *Tzanjuyú*, first left on road to Sololá, T762-1317/18, superb position on bluff overlooking lake, in need of renovation but good value, well-kept flower gardens, restaurant, pool, romantic spot, camping possible. **E** *Hospedaje Ramos*, close to public beach, run by Maya family, friendly, safe, loud music from nearby cafés, with bath, hot water, clean, good value.

Guatemala

Old Town C *Montana*, Callejón Don Tino, near the bell tower in the Old Town, T762-0326, F762-2180, comfortable, TV, hot water, parking. D *Las Casitas*, C Real, T762-1224/1069, neat bungalows, breakfast available, with bath, hot shower, attractive gardens, friendly, next to police station and market, buses stop outside but it's quiet at night. E *Hospedaje Casa Linda*, Callejón El Capulín, T762-0836, hot shower, garden, friendly, clean and quiet. Good value. Recommended. E *Hostal Sunset*, follow C del Rastro from the bell tower, 10 mins' walk to gate, dozens of steps up to hostel, reward is the view, dormitories, very clean and friendly, hot water with private showers, comfortable. F *Hospedaje Pana*, opposite *Hospedaje Eli*, clean, friendly, hot water, coffee, fruit juice and beer available, luggage store. F *Hospedaje Villa Lupita*, Callejón Don Tino, T762-1201, hot showers, clean, friendly, parking, good value, recommended.

Centre B *Cacique Inn*, C del Embarcadero, T/F762-1205, large, comfortable rooms, no credit cards, swimming pool, magnificent house and garden, English spoken, good food. Recommended. B *Dos Mundos*, C Santander, T762-2078, F762-0127, dosmundos@atitlan.com Pool, cable TV, fireplaces, good mid-level place to stay, good Italian restaurant (*La Lanterna*). B *Müllers Guest House*, C Rancho Grande, 1-81, T762-2442. Comfortable, quiet, good breakfast. Recommended. B *Posada de los Volcanes*, C Santander, 5-51, T762-0244, F762-2367, posadavolcanoes@atitlan.com With bath, hot water, clean, comfortable, quiet, friendly owners, Julio and Janet Parajón. B *Primavera*, C Santander, T762-2052, F762-0171. Clean, expensive restaurant serves German food, washing machine, friendly. Recommended. B *Rancho Grande*, on C Rancho Grande, T762-1554, F762-2247, cottages in charming setting, 4 blocks from beach, popular for long stay, good, including breakfast with pancakes. Recommended. C *Riva Bella*, C Real, T762-1348/1177. Bungalows with parking, with bath, good, clean, nice garden. Recommended. D *El Chaparral*, C Santander, T762- 0540, F762- 2204, next to post office, attractive building, with excellent restaurant *Pajaro Azul*, hot water, TV, parking, good value. D *Fonda del Sol*, C Real, T762-1162, with bath, cheaper without, parking, occasional hot water, comfortable, garden, good restaurant, credit cards. D *Santa Isabel*, C del Embarcadero, T762-1462, two rooms in large house, hot water, with bath, pleasant, nice gardens, also bungalow available for longer rent. D *Utz-Jay*, C 15 de Febrero, T762-0217, T/F762-1358, 2 blocks from the lake, nice large garden, very clean and quiet, friendly owners, owner arranges tours, often full. Recommended. E *Hospedaje Casa Loma*, C Rancho Grande, T762-1447, with bath, cheaper without, attractive garden, good. E *Hospedaje El Viajero*, final C Santander, T762-9128, with bath, comfortable large rooms, hot water, friendly, laundry facilities, nice flower garden, OK. E *Hospedaje Jere*, C Rancho Grande, T762-2781, with bath and TV, cheaper without, clean, expanding, good. E *Hospedaje Tzutujil*, off C Rancho Grande, cheaper without bath, nice small garden, clean, good. E *Mario's Rooms*, C Santander, T762-1313, cheaper without bath, with garden, clean, laundry, hot showers US$0.35, good breakfast, popular. E *Villa Martita*, C Santander, T762-0244, close to lake, friendly. Recommended. F *Hospedaje Eddy*, C Chinimaya, off C Rancho Grande, T762-2466, hot water, basic, friendly, quiet. F *Hospedaje Sánchez*, C El Chali, T762-2224, clean, friendly, hot shower, get up early to enjoy it, family run, quiet, comfortable, 2nd floor with hammocks. Recommended. F *Posada de Doña Carmen*, C del Balneario, hot water, attractive garden, quiet, very friendly, good value, motorcycle parking. G *Hospedaje El Príncipe*, Cjón Los Yach, off C Rancho Grande – follow signs, T762-0228, hot water shower, simple, good value. G *Londres*, Callejón Londres, off C Santander, good atmosphere, friendly, very basic.

For **long stay**, ask around for houses to rent; available at all prices from US$125 a month for a basic place, to US$200, but almost impossible to find in Nov and Dec. *Apartamentos Boheme* at Cjón Chinimaya rent furnished bungalows. Break-ins and robberies of tourist houses are not uncommon. The water supply is variable.

Camping Possible in the grounds of *Hotel Visión Azul* and *Tzanjuyú* – see Hotel entries. G *Campana*, on the road to Santa Catarina, F762-2223/2479, kitchen, shower, laundry, books, free pick-up. There is free camping in Jucanyá on the lakeshore beyond the river south of the public beach, but it's not recommended.

Guatemala

Guatemala

Eating
● on map, page 598

The quality of restaurant food in Panajachel is not high. This reflects the many years when the demand was for quantity not quality, junk food rather than gourmet, and cheap not expensive. Good service was not expected. There has been a noticeable improvement recently, with a few upmarket restaurants opening and more competition driving out the worst establishments. This does not apply to the better hotels where then, as now, the food and service can be excellent. Almost all of these open their restaurants to the public: in some a reservation may be advisable.

Lakeside Mid-range *Los Pumpos*, varied menu, bar, good fish and seafood dishes. *Tocoyal*, on beach near *Hotel del Lago*, good for breakfast, good value. All these are on C del Lago. Overlooking the lake at the end of C Santander: *Sunset Café*, superb location, excellent for drinks, light meals and main dishes, but you pay for the view. **Cheap** Down by the dock *Restaurante Las Olas* serves the absolute best nachos, great for just before catching the boat. There are many *comedores* and kiosks round the promenade area.

Old Town Mid-range *Circus Bar*, Av Los Arboles, has Italian dishes including good pizzas, good coffee, German/French owners, popular. *Al Chisme*, Av Los Arboles, good food, try eggs 'McChisme' for breakfast, good fresh pasta, excellent banana cake, good atmosphere, popular, a bit pricey, open 0700-2200 daily except Wed. **Cheap** *La Zanahoria*, or *The Carrot*, also known as *Casa de Pays*, Av Los Arboles, pie shop, good food, good value, clean, also has rooms (shows English language videos in the evening, US$1). *Flyin' Mayan Yacht Club*, Av Los Arboles, excellent pizzas and banana pie, coffee, newspapers to read.

Centre Expensive *Chez Alex*, C Santander, T762-0172, French menu, good quality, credit cards accepted. *El Patio*, C Santander, good food, very good breakfast, quiet atmosphere. **Mid-range** *El Bistro*, at end of C Santander, dinner only, homemade Italian dishes, great salads and chocolate mousse, good value. Recommended. *El Pájaro Azul*, C Santander, café, bar, creperie with gorgeous stuffed sweet or savoury crepes. Vegetarian options available. Reasonable prices, good for breakfasts, occasional slow service. Recommended. *Guajimbo's*, C Santander, good atmosphere, excellent steaks, fast service, live music some evenings. Recommended. **Cheap** *Bombay*, C Santander, vegetarian recipes from several countries, German beer, good food, set lunch popular, good service. *Deli 2* at end of C Santander, for light meals, delightful garden, classical music, go for the *pastel del día*. Recommended. *Hamburguesa Gigante*, C Santander, good honest burgers. *Jhanny's*, C Rancho Grande, local menu, don't be put off by the premises, the food is good. *Las Chinitas*, C Santander, Chinese, cooked in front of you, inexpensive, friendly, good. *The Last Resort*, C El Chali, 'gringo bar', classic spot, all-you-can-eat breakfasts, friendly, huge portions and reasonable prices, open all day, bar, table tennis, good information. Has open fire going in the colder months. **Seriously cheap** In and around the market. If you want to eat with the view, go to the stalls on the lakefront. However, be warned that the locals are accustomed to the local water, which may be used in the preparation of food.

For good bread and cakes *Delipan*, Av Arboles and *Pana Pan*, C Santander, which has excellent wholemeal breads and pastries, banana bread comes out of the oven at 0930, wonderful, cinnamon rolls also recommended. Also, look out for *Margarita* who sells freshly made bread and cookies from her bicycle in C Santander daily 1630-1830.

Entertainment

Bars and clubs *Chapiteau Disco*, Av Los Arboles, nightclub open 2000 to early morning Tue-Sat, US$1-1.50 cover charge. *Circus Bar*, good live music at weekends, open 1700-0100 daily. *El Aleph*, Av Los Arboles, is one of a number of video bars. **Cinema** *Turquoise Buffalo*, Av Los Arboles, choice of two major films each evening.

Shopping
Bartering is the norm

Sometimes there are better bargains than in Chichicastenango

The main tourist shops are on C Santander, the upmarket places near the centre, eg *El Güipil*, with a selection of the best quality items available. Part way down is *Tinamit Maya Shopping Centre*, C Santander, with many stalls for typical items, bargain for good prices. Maya sell their wares cheaply on the lakeside; varied selection, bargaining easy/expected. *Chalo's Tienda*, on C Real, is the town's 'mini-supermarket'.

Diving *ATI Divers*, Edif Rincón Sai, C Santander, T762-2646, santacruz@guate.net Open Mon-Sat 0930-1300, PADI Advanced Course (4 days) US$140, beginners US$175, fun dive US$25, two for US$45. PADI Rescue and Dive Master also available. Dives are made off Santa Cruz La Laguna and are of special interest to those looking for altitude diving. Here there are spectacular walls that drop off, rock formations you can swim through, trees underwater, and because of its volcanic nature, hot spots, which leaves the lake bottom sediment boiling to touch. Take advice on visibility before you opt for a dive. **Fishing** Lake fishing can be arranged, black bass (*mojarra*) up to 4 kg can be caught. Boats for up to 5 people can be hired for about US$15. Check with INGUAT for the latest information. **Hang-gliding** (*Vuelo Libre*). Rogelio at *Americos Tours*, C Santander will make arrangements, at least 24 hrs' notice is required. Jumps, costing about US$50, are made from San Jorge La Laguna or from above Santa Catarina, depending on weather conditions. **Horse-riding** Enquire locally round the lake for possibilities. In Panajachel, *Americos Tours* has good information. The best, though expensive, option is 10 km south of Santiago (see page 606). **Kayak hire** US$2 per hr. Ask at the hotels, INGUAT and at the lakeshore. **Paragliding** Call Roger, T7104630, about US$50. **Sail boat trips** The friendly Kiwi-US couple who run *Johnny's Place* at Monterrico have a 36-ft catamaran, *Shin Tzu*, that does trips around the lake. It is based out of Panajachel and is the only sail boat on the lake. 3-hr trips for US$19 take in the hot springs and San Antonio. Call the Atitlán Nature Reserve to reserve, T762-2565. **Waterskiing** Arrangements can be made in Panajachel, or with ATI Divers at the *Iguana Perdida* in Santa Cruz.

Sport
A bad storm the previous night may not make ideal diving conditions in the lake the following day

Local Bicycle hire Several rental agencies on C Santander, eg *Maco Cycle Rental* and *Tono Cycle Rental* and also *Alquiler de Bicicletas Emanuel/Gaby*, on C 14 de Febrero. The cost is US$0.65 up per hr or about US$5 for 8 hrs.

Transport

Boat There are two types of transport – the scheduled ferry service to Santiago Atitlán and the *lanchas* to all the other villages. The boat service from Panajachel to Santiago Atitlán runs from the dock at the end of C Rancho Grande from 0600 to 1630, at least 6 sailings a day, US$1.30 each way, 1¼ hrs in the large ferry or 20-35 mins in the fast *lanchas*. Some *lanchas* to all the other villages leave from here, but most from the dock at the end of C Embarcadero. If you set off from the main dock the *lancha* will pull in at the C Embarcadero dock as well. These *lanchas* leave when full, but there is normally one every hour or so. If there is a demand, there will almost always be a boatman willing to run a service but non-official boats can charge what they like. Virtually all the dozen or so communities round the lake have docks, and you can take a regular boat to any of those round the western side; the price for a trip is between US$1.30 and US$2. (To San Pedro La Laguna from the dock at the end of C Embarcadero, US$2, 45 mins, or longer, if they call at docks along the western shore.) You may well be asked for more but unless there are special circumstances, just offer the standard fare. Note that, officially, locals pay less. The only reliable services back to Panajachel are from Santiago or San Pedro up to about 1600. If you wait on the smaller docks round the western side up to this time, you can get a ride back to Panajachel, flag them down in case they don't see you, but they usually pull in if it's the last service of the day. Only buy tickets on the boat – if you buy them from the numerous ticket touts on the dockside you will be overcharged. There are no regular boats to Santa Catarina, San Antonio or San Lucas: pick-ups and buses serve these communities. Bad weather can, of course, affect the boat services. Crossings are generally rougher in the afternoons, which is worth bearing in mind if you suffer from sea-sickness.

The tourist office has the latest information on boats

Private boat hire Boats (*lanchas*) can be hired to take you anywhere round the lake, about US$26 one way, US$30 round trip, maximum passengers about 10 (negotiable). For round trips to San Pedro and Santiago and possibly San Antonio Palopó, with stopovers, go early to the lakefront and bargain. Trip takes a full day, eg 0930-1500, with stops of 1 hr or so at each, around US$6-7, if the boat can be filled. If on a tour, be careful not to miss the boat at each stage – if you do, you will have to pay again. Alternatively, you can take the regular boats (see below). You can hire canoes, kayaks, etc, check at INGUAT for the best deals or negotiate at

Guatemala

the beach, most about US$2 per hr. At almost any time of year, but especially in Jan-Mar, strong winds occasionally blow up quickly across the lake (*El Xocomíl*). This can be dangerous in small boats.

Motorcycle hire About US$6 per hr, plus fuel and US$100 deposit. Try *Maco Cycle* near the junction of C Santander and 14 de Febrero, and 2 places near *Circus Bar*. Bikes generally poor, no locks or helmets provided. Motorcycle parts from *David's Store*, opposite *Hotel Maya Kanek*, good prices, also does repairs.

Bus *Rebuli* to **Guatemala City**, 3½ hrs, US$2.50, crowded, 9 a day between 0500 and 1430. From Guatemala City either *Transportes Rebuli* or alternatively take any bus heading for Quetzaltenango and the west as far as Los Encuentros, and a local bus (up to 1830) to Panajachel. Direct bus to **Quetzaltenango**, 8 a day between 0530 and 1415, US$1.40, 2½ hrs. There are direct buses to **Los Encuentros** on the Pan-Amercan Highway (US$0.50 but at busy times the buses at Los Encuentros may be already full). To **Chichicastenango** direct, 11 a day between 0645 and 1700, US$1.40, 1½ hrs. There are direct buses to **Cuatro Caminos**, US$1.30 (see page 619) from 0530, for connections to Totonicapán, Quetzaltenango, Huehuetenango, etc. To **Chimaltenango** US$1.40, change there for **Antigua**. There is also a direct bus (*Transpopeye*) to Antigua leaving 1030-1100, Mon-Sat US$4, which leaves from opposite the bank (leaves Antigua 0700 daily). To **Sololá**, US$0.20, 20 mins, every 30 mins. You can wait for through buses by the market on C Real. *Rebuli* buses leave from opposite *Hotel Fonda del Sol* on C Real, otherwise, the main stop is where C Santander meets C Real. The fastest way to **Mexico** is probably by bus south to Cocales, 2½ hrs, 5 buses between 0600 and 1400, then many buses along the Pacific highway to Tapachula on the border.

Shuttles Services are now available, run jointly by travel agencies, from Guatemala City-Antigua-Panajachel, 4 a day, ask if they will collect/deliver at hotels. Cost US$10 per section, call *Atitrans* T332-8877 (Guatemala), T832-0648 (Antigua), T7622336 (Panajachel). There are also shuttle services connecting Panajachel with Chichicastenango US$10, Quetzaltenango US$15 and the Mexican border US$35.

Car *Dalton Rent-a-Car*, Av Los Arboles, T7621275, not necessarily open off season. Best to hire in Guatemala City or Antigua if you wish to explore this area by car.

Directory **Banks** *Banco Industrial*, C Santander (TCs and Visa ATM), *Banco de Comercio*, C Real, US$TCs and cash, Visa ATM opposite. There is a *cambio* on the street near *Mayan Palace* for US$ cash and TCs, good rate. **Communications** Internet: many in centre, shop around for best prices: standard price is US$2 per hr. **Post office**: on C Santander. Difficult but not impossible to send parcels of up to 1 kg abroad as long as packing requirements are met. *Get Guated Out*, Centro Comercial, Av Los Arboles, T/F762-2015, good but more expensive service, they use the postal system but pack and deal with formalities for you. *DHL*, Edif Rincón Sai, C Santander. **Telephone**: *Telgua*, on C Santander. **Language schools** *Jardín de America*, Callejón off C El Chalí, T762-2637,www.atitlan.com/jardin.htm US$65 for 20 hrs per week tuition, US$85 for 30 hrs per week, lodging with family, US$50 per week. *Jabel Tinamit*, behind Edif Rincón Sai, T762-0238, span1school@starnet.net.gt Similar tariff. *Pana Atitlán Language School*, C de la Navidad, 0-40, T762-1196. **Medical services** *Centro de Salud* on C Real, just downhill from the road to San Antonio Palopó. *Dr Hernández Soto*, office near the *Texaco* station, US$5 for a short consultation. *Dra Zulma Zenin Buttrago*, C Real near junction with Av de los Arboles. *Farmacia Santander*, top end of C Santander, very good and helpful. Outbreaks of cholera have been reported in the lake area since 1991. Enquire locally about the safety of water, lake fish, etc. Fleas are endemic. Take care to treat bites in case of infection. **Tour operators** *Tolimán Travel*, C Santander, T762-2455. *Americos Tours*, C Santander, T762-2641. *Atitrans*, Edif Rincón Sai, T7622336. *Centroamericana Tourist Service*, C Santander, T762-0324, T/F762-2496. Several others on C Santander. All offer shuttle services to Chichicastenango, Antigua, etc, see under Transport, and can arrange most activities on and around the lake.

Around the lake

Travelling round the lake is the best way to enjoy the stunning scenery and the effect of changing light and wind on the mood of the area. The slower you travel the better, and walking round the lake gives some fantastic views. With accommodation at towns and villages on the way, there is no problem finding somewhere to bed down for the night if you want to make a complete circuit. The lake is 50 km in circumference and you can walk on or near the shore for most of it. Here and there the cliffs are too steep to allow for easy walking and private properties elsewhere force you to move up 'inland'. For boat information see Transport, Panajachel. At almost any time of year, but especially between January-March, strong winds (*El Xocomil*) occasionally blow up quickly across the lake. This can be dangerous for small boats.

The town has an attractive adobe church. Reed mats are made here, and you can buy *huipiles* (beautiful, green, blue and yellow) and men's shirts. Watch weaving at *Artesanías Carolina* on way out towards San Antonio. Bargaining is normal. There are hot springs close to the town and an art gallery. Houses can be rented. **Fiesta** 25 November. There are frequent pick-ups from Pana and boat services.

Santa Catarina Palopó
Within easy walking distance (4 km) of Panajachel

Guatemala

Sleeping and eating A *Villa Santa Catarina*, T762-1291/2827, F762-2013, villasdeguatemala@intelnet.net.gt Comfortable rooms with balconies round pool, most with view of lake, good restaurant. Less than 1 km beyond Santa Catarina, on the left up a steep hill is **LL** *Casa Palopó*, T762-2270, F762-2721, www.casapalopo.com One of the finest hotels in the country, opened 2001, 6 beautiful rooms, flowers on arrival, excellent service, heated pool, top class restaurant – reservations necessary. A further 3 km to **B** *San Tomas Bella Vista*, T762-1566, F485-7474, below the road to San Antonio, overlooking lake, bungalows for 5 people, set down the hill, 2 private beaches, children's playground, pool, ecological gardens, trails for bird watching, bar, restaurant, camping possible.

Six kilometres beyond Santa Catarina, San Antonio Palopó has another fine 16th-century church. Climbing the hill from the dock, it lies in an amphitheatre created by the mountains behind. Up above there are hot springs and a cave in the rocks used for local ceremonies. The village is noted for the costumes and headdresses of the men, and *huipiles* and shirts are cheaper than in Santa Catarina. A good hike is to take the bus from Panajachel to Godínez, take the path toward the lake 500 m south along the road to Cocales, walk on down from there to San Antonio Palopó (one hour) and then along the road back to Panajachel via Santa Catarina Palopó (three hours). You can walk on round the lake from San Antonio, but you must eventually climb steeply up to the road at Agua Escondida. Frequent pick-ups from Pana. Enquire about boats.

San Antonio Palopó
Fiesta: 12-14 June

Sleeping B *Hotel Terrazas del Lago*, T762-0157, F762-0037, on the lake with view, bath, clean, restaurant, a unique hotel built up over the past 28 years. You can stay in private houses (ask around) or rent rooms (take sleeping bag).

San Lucas is at the southeastern tip of the lake. It is known for its fiestas and markets especially Holy Week with processions, arches and carpets on the Thursday and Friday, and 15-20 October. Market days are Tuesday, Friday and Sunday (the best). Enquire about boats. There are buses to Santiago Atitlán, hourly and to Guatemala City via Panajachel. There are two banks and an internet centre.

San Lucas Tolimán

B *Pak'ok*, Av 6, one block from the lake, T722-0033, rooms and suites, colonial style, good but expensive restaurant (reservations), gardens, good. **D** *Brisas del Lago*, Av 6, on lakeside, T722-0028, unattractive building – a sort of clumsy rustic, 10 rooms, restaurant, bar. **D** *La Cascada de María*, C 6, 6-80, T722-0136, F722-0161, with bath, TV, parking, garden, restaurant, good. **D** *Villa Real*, Av 7 (Pavarotti), T722-0102, with bath, hot water, restaurant, parking, friendly, good value. *Comedor Victoria*, Av 6 near plaza, Guatemalan food, also rooms to

Sleeping & eating

Guatemala

let. *Café Tolimán*, Av 5 on lakeside, home-made yoghurt and local dishes. *Fonda La LLave*, Av 6/C 3, 1 block north of plaza, clean, good local food. *Oaklans*, Av 6/C 3, local and Chinese food. Bar *Casa Vieja*, Av 5, opposite *Texaco*, popular bar.

Climbing Atitlán & Tolimán
Cloud on the tops is common, least likely November-March

There have been reports of robbery so consider taking a guide, or at least local advice, when climbing the volcanoes

From San Lucas the cones of **Atitlán**, 3,535 m, and **Tolimán**, 3,158 m, can be climbed. The route leaves from the south end of town and makes for the saddle (known as Los Planes, or Chanán) between the two volcanoes. From there it is south to Atitlán and north to the double cone (they are 1 km apart) and crater of Tolimán. Though straightforward, each climb is complicated by many working paths and thick cover above 2,600 m. If you are fit, either can be climbed in seven hours, five hours down. Ask Father Gregorio at the Parroquia church, two blocks from the Central Plaza, or at the Municipalidad for information and for available guides. Father Greg has worked in the area for 37 years so has a vested interest in recommending safe and good guides. One such recommendation is Carlos Huberto Alinan Chicoj who charges US$28 for the day trip, leaving at midnight with torches to arrive at the summit by 0630 to avoid early cloud cover.

Santiago Atitlán

Santiago is a fascinating town, as much for the stunningly beautiful embroidered clothing of the locals, as for the history and character of the place with its mix of Roman Catholic, evangelical and Maximón worship. There are 35 evenagelical temples in town as well as the house of the revered idol Maximón.

You will be taken to the house of Maximón for a small fee. The fine church, with a wide nave decorated with colourful statues, was founded in 1547. The original roof was lost to earthquakes. At certain times of the year, the square is decked with streamers gently flapping in the breeze. The women wear fine costumes and the men wear striped, half-length embroidered trousers. There is a daily market, best on Friday and all sorts of art work and crafts can be bought. **Fiesta**: 5 June and 23-27 July. The celebrations of Holy Week are worth seeing, but it may be hard to find a room, and include the display of Maximón.

Near town is the hill, **Cerro de Oro**, with a small village of that name on the lake. The summit (1,892 m) can be reached from the village in 45 minutes. Seven kilometres south of Santiago Atitlán is the **Quetzal Reserve**, a mirador and *refugio* where a path winds through rainforest. Follow the path past the *Posada de Santiago*, then go left at the fork and stay on the road until you come to the reserve and viewpoint, both on the left.

Sleeping

B *Bambú*, on the lakeside, 500 m by road towards San Lucas, T721-7179, cabins in attractive setting, restaurant, a few minutes by *lancha* from the dock (US$3). **B** *Posada de Santiago*, 1½ km south of town, T/F721-7167, posdesantiago@guate.net Comfortable stone cottages, some cheaper accommodation, good restaurant with home-grown produce, canoeing, mountain biking, horse-riding arranged. Recommended. **E** *Hotel Chi-Nim-Ya*, walk up from the dock, take the first left and walk 50 m and it's there on the left, T721-7131, good, clean, comfortable and friendly, cheaper without bath, good value, good café opposite, cheap, large helpings. **E** *Tzutuhil*, on left up the road from the dock to centre, T721-7174, above *Ferretería La Esquina*, with bath, restaurant, great views, good. **F** *Pensión Rosita*, to the right of the church, friendly, safe, basic, restaurant. Camping possible near *Hotel Bambú*.

Eating
Many cheap comedores near the centre

The best restaurants are at the hotels. *El Pescador*, on corner 1 block before *Tzutuhil*, full menu good but expensive. Close by is *Brisas del Lago*. The chicken is a better option than the bony *mojarra* fish. The attitude of the staff here is so bad it has to be experienced! *Santa Rita* to the left of the church, brightly decorated, good food and cheap.

Sports

Aventura en Atitlán, Jim and Nancy Matison, *Finca San Santiago*, T811-5516 (Guatemala City), wildwest@amigo.net.gt 10 km outside Santiago. Offer riding and hiking tours.

Bus To **Guatemala City**, US$2.15 (5 a day, first at 0300).Two *Pullmans* a day, US$2.80. To **Panajachel**, 0600, 2 hrs, or take any bus and change on the main road just south of San Lucas. **Boat** 6 sailings a day to and from Pana, 1¼ hrs, US$1.30, or by *lancha* when full, 20-35 mins, US$1.30-2. Santiago to **San Pedro** by *lancha* at 0800, 0900, 1030, 45 mins, US$1.30.

San Pedro La Laguna

San Pedro is a small town set on a tiny promontory with coffee bushes threaded around tracks lined with hostels and restaurants on the lakeside fringes, and with the Tz'utujil Maya dominating the main part of the town up a very steep hill behind. San Pedro is now the favourite spot to hang out in for a couple of days or longer. It's a place to relax, to soak

Guatemala

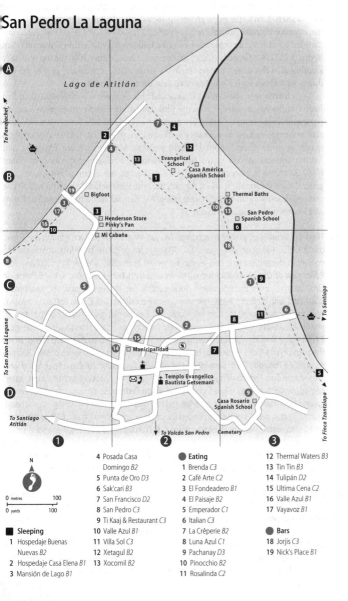

San Pedro La Laguna

Sleeping
1 Hospedaje Buenas
   Nuevas *B2*
2 Hospedaje Casa Elena *B1*
3 Mansión de Lago *B1*
4 Posada Casa
   Domingo *B2*
5 Punta de Oro *D3*
6 Sak'cari *B3*
7 San Francisco *D2*
8 San Pedro *C3*
9 Ti Kaaj & Restaurant *C3*
10 Valle Azul *B1*
11 Villa Sol *C3*
12 Xetagul *B2*
13 Xocomil *B2*

Eating
1 Brenda *C3*
2 Café Arte *C2*
3 El Fondeadero *B1*
4 El Paisaje *B2*
5 Emperador *C1*
6 Italian *C3*
7 La Crêperie *B2*
8 Luna Azul *C1*
9 Pachanay *D3*
10 Pinocchio *B2*
11 Rosalinda *C2*
12 Thermal Waters *B3*
13 Tin Tin *B3*
14 Tulipán *D2*
15 Valle Azul *B1*
16 Valle Azul *B1*
17 Vayavoz *B1*

Bars
18 Jorjis *C3*
19 Nick's Place *B1*

in hot baths, learn a bit of Spanish and horse-ride. Some of the semi-permanent gringo inhabitants now run bars and cafés or sell home-made jewellery and the like. Grass is easily available and harder drugs can be found, however police have been drafted in for greater law enforcement. **Fiesta**: 27-30 Jun with traditional dances. The cobbled road from the dock facing Panajachel (known as the *muelle)* climbs up to the centre and another goes down, more or less at right angles, to the other dock (known as the *playa –* beach) facing Santiago with the village arranged around.

The town lies at the foot of the **Volcán San Pedro** (3,020 m), which can be climbed in four to five hours, three hours down. It's not difficult except for route-finding through the coffee plantations and heavy cover. A guide is therefore advisable unless you walk part of the way the day before to make sure you know where you are going. The route starts 1½ km along the road to Santiago, and where the road takes a sharp turn to the right, go left through coffee plantations to the west flank of the volcano; after one hour there is only one path and you cannot get lost. A recommended guide is Ventura Matzar González, Calle Principal, Cantón Chuacante, San Pedro, T7621140. Go early (0530) for the view, because after 1000 the top is usually smothered in cloud; also you will be in the shade all the way up and part of the way down. Also check with *Bigfoot* in town or at the tourist booth.

The **church** is in the centre. Evangelical churches are well represented in San Pedro, and you can hardly miss the pink and white *Templo Evangelico Bautista Getsemaní* in the centre. Canoes are made here (US$3.20 hire for two hours) and a visit to the rug-making co-operative on the beach is of interest. Backstrap weaving is taught at some places, about US$0.50 per day. Market days are Thursday and Sunday (better). A visit to the **thermal baths** is a relaxing experience at about US$2.50 a session. Note that the water is solar heated, not chemical hot springs. For general local information ask at *Bigfoot*, near the Panajachel dock, who will advise you on horse-riding to neighbouring villages, guides for climbing Volcán San Pedro and whatever else you have in mind.

Sleeping

Accommodation is mostly cheap and laid-back, your own sleeping bag, etc will be useful. Take care of your belongings

There are virtually no private telephones. You can try to make contact through the *Telgua* office, T762-2486, or general email 703110@amigo.net.gt Put the place/person you want to contact in the subject line. Houses can be rented from US$5 a week to US$50 a month **E** *Mansión de Oro*, up a hill with good views, with bath, hot water, good value. **E** *Punta de Oro*, 10-mins' walk from Santiago dock, suitable for families, beach site, overpriced. **E** *Sak'cari*, with bath, hot water, lake view, clean. Recommended. **E** *Villa Sol* (also known as *Pensión Chuazanahi* and the *Colonel's Place*), up from the *playa*, with bath, cheaper shared, reasonable meals, good banana pancakes, friendly staff, nice rooms. Recommended. **F** *Hospedaje Buenas Nuevas*, small, friendly, hot shower. **F** *Hospedaje Casa Elena*, along the path behind *Nick's Place*, with bath or shared bath, clean, good views of lake. Recommended. **F** *Posada Casa Domingo*, hot showers, opposite *La Crêperie*. **F** *Hotel* and *Hospedaje San Francisco*, rooms with lake view, garden, cooking facilities, cold water, helpful owner, washing facilities, good value. **F** *San Pedro*, near *Chuazanahi*, police on the ground floor, bargain for a decent price, laundry and hot shower if you stay more than 1 night, balcony, noisy, not recommended for single women, clean, basic. **F** *Xocomil*, clean, basic, cold water, washing facilities, helpful. **G** *Ti Kaaj*, simple rooms, hammock space, wooden cabins a few metres from *playa*, popular with backpackers, lovely garden, but basic. **G** *Valle Azul*, 100 m to the right of the Panajachel dock, good value, nice view, good restaurant, but very run down. **G** *Xetagul*, primitive, but hot shower and kitchen use.

Eating & bars

Be careful of drinking water in San Pedro; both cholera and dysentery exist here

Brenda, good, cheap *comedor*. *Café Arte*, uphill from *Hotel San Pedro*, all meals, vegetarian dishes, good value. *Comedor Sta Elena*, near *Nick's Italian*. Seriously cheap and filling breakfasts. *El Fondeadero*, good food, lovely terraced gardens, reasonable prices. *El Pasaje*, thatched house opposite *Hotel Santa Elena*, local food, OK. *Emperador*, up the hill, *comedor*, good local dishes. *La Crêperie*, light meals, good crêpes. *Luna Azul*, along shore beyond *Valle Azul*, popular for breakfast and lunch, good omelettes. *Mata Hari*, another good *comedor*. *Nick's Place*, on the left up from the *muelle*, cheap, popular, comfy sofas, free films every night. *Nick's Italian*, by the *playa* (Santiago dock), good Italian menu, open 0800-2200. *Pachanay*, along the road opposite *Hotel San Pedro*, lunch and dinner, cheap rice dishes, reggae music, chilled, gallery. *Pinocchio*, Italian, popular for breakfast, reasonable prices, closed Sun. *Rosalinda*, near centre of village, friendly, breakfasts (eg *mosh*), local fish and good for banana and chocolate cakes.*Thermal Baths* along the shore from the *playa*, good vegetarian food and coffee, expensive. *Ti Kaaj*, good Italian and local dishes, bar. *Tin Tin*, good value. Recommended. *Tulipán*, in town, has wide variety and vegetarian dishes. *La Ultima Cena*, opposite the *Municipalidad*, good pizzas, pancakes, very popular, service for food can be very slow but beer comes quickly. *Valle Azul*, opposite hotel, popular restaurant overlooking lake. *Vayavos*, run by Israelis, Italian dishes. **Bars** *Nick's Place* is popular, and well frequented in the evening. *Bar Jorji's* is another popular spot. Others include *Ti Kaaj* and *Tony's Bar*, next to *Hotel Bella Vista*.

Up to 10 *lanchas* a day leave from **Panajachel** for San Pedro. The boat fare is about US$2 (US$5 to take motorcycle in boat). There are launches from **Santiago** to **San Pedro** that leave when full (45 mins, US$1.30). To **Santiago** at 1100, 1200, 1300, 1400, 45 mins, US$1.30. There are daily buses to **Guatemala City**, several leave in the early morning and early afternoon, 4 hrs, US$2.50 and to **Quetzaltenango**, in the morning, 3½ hrs, US$2.

Transport *Frequent pick-ups to other villages along the western shore*

Banks There are no banks in San Pedro. **Language schools** This is a popular place for learning Spanish. *Casa América*, *Casa Rosario* and *San Pedro* Spanish schools. Tuition for 1 week/20 hrs about US$50. Here most students make their own accommodation arrangements. *Casa Rosario*, www.artemaya.com/pro5.html, offers classes for US$50, homestay plus tuition is US$90/week. *San Pedro*, T703-1100, is US$90/ for tuition and a week's homestay and has a great location with gardens close to the lakeshore. **Medical services** *Centro Médico* opposite Educación Básica school has a good doctor who does not speak English.

Directory

The road north from San Pedro passes around a headland to San Juan La Laguna (2 km), which also has a *Nick's Place* and a bank. Look for *Los Artesanos de San Juan* and another image of Maximón displayed in the house opposite the Municipalidad.

San Juan La Laguna *There are simple places to eat*

On the road towards San Pablo there is a good viewpoint from the hilltop with the cross; a popular walk. A more substantial walk, about three hours, is up behind the village to Santa Clara La Laguna, 2,100 m, passing the village of **Cerro Cristalino** with its attractive, large white church with images of saints around the walls.

Santa Clara La Laguna

A short distance (500 m) to the west, separated by a gully, is another smaller place, Santa María Visitación. As with Santa Clara La Laguna, this is a typical highland village, friendly, full of colourful textiles and unspoilt by tourism. San Juan is connected to San Pablo by the lakeshore road, an attractive 4 km stretch mainly through coffee plantations. San Pablo, a busy village set 80 m above the lake, is known for rope making from *cantala* (maguey) fibres, which are also used for bags and fabric weaving.

Santa María Visitación & San Pablo La Laguna

San Marcos La Laguna

San Marcos is deceptive with the main part of the community 'hidden' up the hill. The quiet village centre is set at the upper end of a gentle slope that runs 300 m through coffee and fruit trees down to the lake, reached by two paved walkways. Beyond the centre, 300 m to the east is the main dock of the village down a cobbled road. Down the pathways are the hotels, some with waterfront sites have their own docks. There is a slanting **trail** leaving the village up through dramatic scenery over to Santa Lucía Utatlán, passing close to Cerro San Marcos 2,918 m, the highest point in the region apart from the volcanoes.

If arriving by boat and staying in San Marcos, ask to be dropped at the Schumann or the Pirámides dock

Down the first walkway (beside fruit stall), 200 m on the left, is **Las Pirámides**, a meditation centre. The month course costs US$10 per person per day, accommodation included. Shorter courses can be arranged. In the grounds are a sauna, a

Guatemala

vegetarian restaurant with freshly baked bread and a library. This is a relaxing, peaceful place. For information T205-7151 or www.laspiramides.com.gt **Reiki Shiatsu massage** available down second pathway with Beatrice, full treatment US$20.

Sleeping & eating

All the hotels are in the sector (Zona 3) below the centre and towards the lake. They are all simple and traditional, converted small *fincas* or purpose built to blend into the local environment. **Down the first pathway** (beside the fruit stall), in order: **E** *Paco Real*, T801-2297. Cabins, shared bath, cheaper in dormitory, clean, good restaurant. **F** *La Paz*, T702-9168. 3 bungalows, vegetarian restaurant, quiet, but popular. **F** *San Marcos*, 4 rooms with 2 beds, shared bath, basic. **D** *Posada Schumann*, T202-2216. With waterfront and dock, bungalows in attractive gardens, some with kitchenettes, sauna, restaurant, comfortable. *Il Giardino*, attractive garden, Italian owners, good breakfasts. **Down the second pathway**: **F** per person, *Quetzal*, 4 bunk rooms, shared bath, restaurant. **F** *Unicornio*, with self-catering, bungalows, shared kitchen, may be closed in low season.

Transport

Road Frequent **pick-ups** from the village centre and anywhere along the main road. To **San Pedro** US$0.40, less to intervening villages. Occasional pick-up to **Tzununá**. **Buses** to **San Pedro** to Pan-American Highway can be boarded at San Pablo. **Boat** Service roughly every ½ hr to **Panajachel** and to **San Pedro**. Wait on any dock. Fare US$1.30 to either.

San Marcos to Santa Cruz

Arguably the best walk in the Atitlán area is from Jaibalito to Santa Cruz

From the end of San Marcos where the stone track goes down to the dock, a rough track leads to **Tzununá**, passable for small trucks and four-wheel drive vehicles, with views across the lake all the way. The village of Tzununá is along the treelined road through coffee plantations with a few houses up the valley behind. There is a dock on the lakeside but no facilities. The bridge over the intermittent stream is the end of the road and the path passes through stretches of forest too steep to cultivate, though higher up there are the usual maize fields. From here to Panajachel there are no roads or vehicular tracks and the villages can only be reached by boat, on horse or on foot. Also from here are some of the most spectacular views of the lake and the southern volcanoes. **Jaibalito** is smaller still than Tzununá, hemmed in by the mountains. Here **D** *La Casa del Mundo*, T204-5558, F762-2333, casamundo@yahoo.com, enjoys one of the most spectacular positions on the entire lake. Various cheaper alternatives, many facilities, good food, standard family-style dinner US$6.50, lakeside hot tub, a memorable place. Highly recommended.

Santa Cruz La Laguna

Behind the village are steep, rocky forested peaks, many too steep even for the locals to cultivate

Santa Cruz village is set in the most dramatic scenery of the lake. Three deep ravines come down to the bay separating two spurs. A stone roadway climbs up the left-hand spur, picks up the main walking route from Jaibalito and crosses over a deep ravine (unfortunately used as a garbage tip) to the plaza, on the only flat section of the right spur, about 120 m above the lake. The communal life of the village centres on the plaza. The hotels, one of them over flowing with flowers, are on the lake shore. The **fiesta** takes place 7-11 May.

There is good **walking** here. Apart from the lake route, strenuous hikes inland eventually lead to the Santa Lucía Utatlán-Sololá road. From the left-hand (west) ravine reached from the path that runs behind the lake shore section, a trail goes through fields to an impossible looking gorge, eventually climbing up to Chaquijchoy, Finca María Linda and a trail to San José Chacayá (about four hours). In the reverse direction, the path southwest from San José leads to the Finca María Linda, which is close to the crater rim from where due south is a track to Jaibalito, to the left (east) round to the trail to Santa Cruz. Others follow the ridges towards San José and the road. These are for experienced hikers, and a compass (you are travelling due north) is essential if the cloud descends and there is no one to ask.

Guatemala

D *Arca de Noé*, to the left from dock, T306-4352, thearca@yahoo.com Bungalows, cheaper in dormitory with shared bath, good restaurant, BBQ, lake activities arranged, nice atmosphere, veranda overlooking really beautiful flower-filled gardens and the lake, low voltage solar power. **E** *La Casa Rosa*, to the right from dock, T416-1251, la_casa_rosa@hotmail.com Bungalows and rooms, with bath, cheaper without, home-made meals, attractive garden, sauna. **E-G** *La Iguana Perdida*, opposite dock, T762-2646, with bath, **F** without, **G** dormitory, lively, especially weekends, delicious vegetarian food, BBQ, popular, friendly, good atmosphere, *ATI Divers* centre (see page 603), waterskiing; kayaks US$0.65 per hr. There's no electricity so bring a torch. **G** *Hospedaje Hernández*, up the hill just across bridge before plaza (remember, no transport), basic, cold water only. Beyond the beach, about 15 mins' walking is **Paxanax**, with **A** *Villa Sumaya*, T810-7199, T/F76-20488, www.virtualguatemala.com/villasumaya/index.html Including breakfast, with its own dock, sauna, massage and healing therapies, comfortable, peaceful.

Sleeping & eating
Near the dock are the three main hotels

From Santa Cruz to Panajachel along the coast is difficult, steep and unconsolidated, with few definitive paths. If you do get to the delta of the Río Quiscab, you may find private land is barred. The alternatives are either to go up to Sololá, about 6 km and 800 m up, or get a boat.

Guatemala

Chichicastenango

Often called 'Chichi' but also known as Santo Tomás, Chichicastenango is the hub of the Maya-K'iche' highlands. The name derives from the *chichicaste*, a prickly purple plant like a nettle, which grows profusely, and *tenango*, meaning 'place of'. Today the locals call the town 'Siguan Tinamit' meaning 'place surrounded by ravines'. The townsfolk are also known as *Masheños*, which comes from the word *Max*, also meaning Tomás. About 1,000 *ladinos* live in the town, but 20,000 Indians live in the hills nearby and flood the town for the Thursday and Sunday markets.

Colour map 5, grid B1
Altitude: 2,071 m
Nights are cold

The town itself has winding streets of white houses roofed with bright red tiles, which wander over a little knoll in the centre of a cup-shaped valley surrounded by high mountains. The men's traditional outfit is a short-waisted embroidered jacket and knee breeches of black cloth, a woven sash and an embroidered kerchief round the head. The cost of this outfit, now over US$200, means that fewer and fewer men are wearing it. Women wear *huipiles* with red embroidery against black or brown and their *cortes* have dark blue stripes.

Chichicastenango is a curious blend of mysticism and commercialism. It is famous for its market where hundreds come for a bargain buy. On market mornings the steps of the church are blanketed in flowers as the women, in traditional dress, fluff up their skirts, amid baskets of lilies, roses and blackberries. But, with its mixture of Catholic and indigenous religion readily visible, it is more than just a shopping trolley stop. On a hilltop peppered with pine, villagers worship at a Maya shrine; in town, a time-honoured tradition of brotherhoods focuses on saint worship. Coupled with the mist that encircles the valley late afternoon, you can sense an air of intrigue.

A large plaza is the focus of the town, with two white churches facing one another: **Santo Tomás** the parish church and **Calvario**. Santo Tomás, founded in 1540, is open to visitors, although photography is not allowed, and visitors are asked to be discreet and enter by a side door (through an arch to the right). Next to Santo Tomás are the cloisters of the Dominican monastery (1542). Here the famous Popol Vuh manuscript of the Maya creation story was found. A human skull wedged behind a carved stone face, found in Sacapulas, can be seen at the **Museo Arqueológico Regional**, on the main plaza. Also a jade collection once owned by 1926-1944 parish priest Father Rossbach. ■ *Tue, Wed, Fri, Sat 0800-1200, 1400-1600, Thu and Sun 0800-1400, closed Mon, US$1.30, photographs and video camera not permitted.*

Sights
There is a tourist office, 7 C, half a block east from the main square. Open daily from 0800-2000 Thursday, Saturday and Sunday, Wednesday until 1900, Monday and Friday until 1800

There are the Sunday and Thursday **markets**. Both are very touristy, and bargains are harder to come by once shuttle loads of people arrive mid-morning. Articles from all over the Highlands are available: rugs, carpets and bedspreads.

Pascual Abaj

If you wish to undergo a ceremony to plead for a partner, or to secure safety from robbery or misfortune, you may ask the curandero (US$7 including photographs)

This idol, Pascual Abaj, a god of fertility, is a large black stone with human features, which can just about be made out. Crosses in the ground surrounding the shrine are prayed in front of for the health of men, women and children, and for the dead. Fires burn and the wax of a thousand candles, flowers and sugar cover the shrine. One ceremony you may see is that of a girl from the town requesting a good and sober husband. To reach the deity, walk along 5 Avenida, turn right on 9 Calle, down the hill, cross the stream and take the second track from the left going steepest uphill, which passes directly through a farmhouse and buildings. The farm now belongs to a mask-maker whom you can visit and buy masks from. (There is also another mask shop next to this plot to the left.) Follow the path to the top of the pine-topped hill where you may well see an Indian ceremony in progress. It's about half an hour's walk. ■ *The site can be easily visited by yourself, or an INGUAT-approved guide can take you there and explain the history and significance. US$6.50, 1-2 hrs.*

Sleeping

You won't find accommodation easily on Sat evening, when prices are increased

As soon as you get off the bus, boys will swamp you and insist on taking you to certain hotels. Even if you say 'no' they will accompany you. Two hotels that pay them commission are the *Posada Belén* and *Salvador* – between 3-10 *quetzales* that will be added to your room charge. Insist that you have walked there yourself and refuse to pay extra.

AL *Mayan Inn*, corner of 8 C and 3 Av, T756-1176, F756-1212, is a classic, colonial style courtyard hotel with antique furniture and fireplaces. The staff are very friendly. **AL** *Santo Tomás*, 7 Av, 5-32, T7561-061, F756-1306, is a very attractive building with beautiful

Chichicastenango

	Sleeping				Eating
■	1 Belén		7 Pensión Girón &	●	1 Buenaventura, La Villa
	2 Chalet House		Restaurante Las		de los Cofrades &
	3 Chugüilá		Brasas		La Fonda de Tzijolaj
	4 El Arco		8 San Jerónimo		2 Caffé Tuttos
	5 El Salvador		9 Santo Tomás		3 La Villa de los Cofrades
	6 Mayan Inn		10 Villa Grande		4 Tziguan Tinamit

0 metres 100
0 yards 100

colonial furnishings. It is often full at weekends, pool, sauna, good restaurant and bar. The attendants are in traditional costume. **AL** *Villa Grande*, just outside town, T756-1053, F756-1140, stpvillas@intelnet.net.gt **C** *Chugüilá*, 5 Av, 5-24, T/F756-1134, some rooms with fireplaces. Avoid the front rooms, which are noisy. **D** *Chalet House*, 3 C, 7-44, T/F756-1360, is a clean, guest house with family atmosphere. Don't be put off by the dingy street. **D** *Pensión Girón*, Edif Girón on 6 C, 4-52, T756-1156. Clean rooms with bath, cheaper without, with hot water. **D** *Posada El Arco*, 4 C, 4-36, T756-1255, clean, very pretty, small, friendly, garden, washing facilities, negotiate lower rates for stays longer than a night, some large rooms, good view, English spoken. **E** *Hospedaje San Jerónimo*, at the end of 5 Av near *El Salvador*, T756-1204, with private bath. **E** *El Salvador*, 10 C, 4-47, 50 large rooms with bath and fireplace (wood available in market), good views, **F** in small rooms without bath. **E** *Posada Belén*, 12 C, 5-55, T756-1244, with bath, cheaper without, hot water, clean, will do laundry, fine views from balconies and hummingbirds in the garden. **Camping** Free overnight vehicle parking at Shell station next to the *Hotel Santo Tomás*. There is also secure parking at *Mayan Inn*.

There are several good restaurants in the Centro Comercial Santo Tomás on the north side of the plaza (market). *Restaurant Las Brasas Steak House*, in same building as *Hotel Girón*, nice atmosphere, good steak menu, accepts credit cards. Also upstairs *La Fonda de Tzijolaj*, great view of the market below, good meals, prompt service, reasonable prices. *Restaurante Buenaventura*, good value, inside market building, but slow service. *La Villa de los Cofrades*, café downstairs, good for breakfasts, good value. Up the street and upstairs is another *La Villa de los Cofrades*, great people-watching location and an escape during market days. *Tziguan Tinamit*, on the corner of 5 Av, 5-67, some local dishes, steaks, tasty pizzas, breakfasts, but a little more expensive than most places, good. *Caffé Tuttos*, near *Posada Belén*, good breakfast deals, pizzas, and *menú del día*, reasonable prices.

Eating

The best food is in the top hotels, but is expensive

On market days there are plenty of good food stalls in the centre of the plaza

1 Jan: *Padre Eterno*; Jan: *San Sebastián*; 19 Mar: *San José*; Fridays in Lent: *Jesús Nazareno* and *María de Dolores*; 29 Apr and 29 Jun: *San Pedro Mártir*; *Corpus Christi*; *El Sacramento*; 3 May and 14 Sep: *Santa Cruz*; 18 Aug: *Virgen de la Coronación*; 29 Sep and 1 Nov: *San Miguel*; 30 Sep: *San Jerónimo Doctor*; 1st Sun of Oct: *Virgen del Rosario*; 2nd Sun in Oct: *Virgen de Concepción*; 13-22 Dec: *Santo Tomás*, with 21 Dec being the main day. There are processions, traditional dances, the *Palo Volador*, marimba music, well worth a visit – very crowded. Other fiesta dates are **20 Jan**; *Holy Week*; the end of **May**; **24 Jun** (shepherds) and *New Year's Eve*.

Festivals

The 14 Cofradías/ Brotherhoods

Buses run through Chichi to and from Santa Cruz del Quiché. Buses passing through all stop at 5 Av/5 C by the *Hotel Chugüilá*, where there are always police and bus personnel to give information. To **Guatemala City**, every 15 mins from 0200 to 1730, 3 hrs, US$2. To **Santa Cruz del Quiché**, at least every ½ hr between 0600-2000, US$0.40, 30 mins or 20 mins, depending on whether the bus driver is aiming for honours in the graduation from the School of Kamikaze Bus Tactics. To **Panajachel**, 1 hr, US$1.50, 0700, 0900, 1200, 1400, or take any bus heading south and change at Los Encuentros (US$0.40). Same goes for **Antigua**, where you need to change at Chimaltenango. To **Quetzaltenango**, 5 between 0430-0830, 2½ hrs. To **Mexico**, and all points west, take any bus to Los Encuentros and change. To **Escuintla** via Santa Lucía Cotzumalguapa, between 0300-1700, 3 hrs, US$2. There are additional buses to local villages especially on market days. **Shuttles** There are 2 tour operators in town: *Chichi Turkaj Tours*, 5 Av, 4-42, T756-2111, 0800-2000 daily. Shuttles to the capital, Xela, Panajachel, Huehuetenango and Mexican border. *Maya Chichi Van*, 6 Av, 6-45, T756-2187, M713-6870. Shuttles and tours ranging from US$10-650.

Transport

Banks There are a number of banks in town (see map) taking Visa and MasterCard. *Bancafé*, corner 5 Av/6 C, also has 24 hr Visa ATM. *Mayan Inn* will exchange cash. **Communications** Internet: There is occasional connection at *Aces*, inside *Hotel Girón*, 6 C, 4-52, expensive. **Post office**: 7 Av, 8-47. **Telephone**: *Telgua*, 6 C between 5 y 6. **Shipping service**: *Cropa Panalpina*, 7 Av opposite post office, T7561028, cropachi@amigo.net.gt Will pack and ship your purchases back home by air cargo.

Directory

Guatemala

Santa Cruz del Quiché

Population: 7,750
Altitude: 2,000 m

Santa Cruz del Quiché, often simply called Quiché, is a quaint, friendly town, with a colourful daily market covering several blocks. There are few tourists here and prices are consequently reasonable. Its main attraction is Utatlán, the remains of the Maya K'iche' capital. **Fiesta**: 14-20 Aug (but varies around Assumption).

Sights   The large Parque Central has a military garrison on the east side with a jail on the lower floor and a sinister military museum with reminders of recent conflicts above.

Three kilometres away are the remains of temples and other structures of the former Quiché capital, **Gumarcaj**, sometimes spelt **K'umarkaaj**, and now generally called **Utatlán**. The city was largely destroyed by the Spaniards, but the stonework of the original buildings can be seen in the ruins, which can be reached on foot, and the setting is very attractive and well maintained. From the bus station, walk west along 10 Calle for 40 minutes, until you reach a small junction, with a blue sign (SECP). Take the right lane up through gates to the site. There are two subterranean burial chambers (take a torch, as there are unexpected drops) still used by the Maya for worship and chicken sacrifices. There's a small but interesting museum at the entrance with a scale model of Utatlán, which should be visited before the site. Ask at the site for a good guide. Utatlán is a huge site and only a small part is open to the public, although much of it belongs to the local municipality. The seven plazas, many temples, ball court, gladiator's archway and other features are marked. ■ *0800-1700, US$1.30.*

Sleeping   **C** *Rey K'iché*, 8 C, 0-9, 2 blocks from bus terminal, clean, comfortable, hot water, parking, restaurant, TV. **D** *Maya Quiché*, 3 Av 4-19, T755-1667, with bath, hot water, restaurant. **E** *San Pascual*, 7 C, 0-43, T555-1107, with bath, **F** without, occasional hot water in morning only, dirty shared bathroom, quiet, locked parking. **F** *La Cascada*, 10 Av, 10 C, friendly, clean.

Eating   *El Torito Steak House*, 4 C, ½ block west directly opposite church, good meat and chicken dishes, a little dingy around the edges. *La Casona*, 6 Av, 2-66, Zona 1, old colonial house, very reasonable prices, nice atmosphere, also vegetarian, good quality. Recommended. *Musicafé*, 1 Av, 1-16, good food, reasonable, with pleasant ambience. *La Cabañita Café*, 1 Av, 1-17, charming small café with pinewood furniture, home-made pies and cakes , excellent breakfasts (pancakes, cereals, etc), eggs any way you want 'em, great snacks, for example *sincronizadas*. Recommended. Looks a little jaded from the outside, a favourite for tea with the military! *Comedor Los Viajeros*, 1 Av, 8 C, near bus terminal, clean, good. *La Toscan*, a little pizza and pastelería with checked cloth covered tables. Lasagne lunch a bargain at just under US$2 with garlic bread, pizza by the slice also. It's on 1 Av just north of the church, same road as *Musicafé* and *La Cabañita*.

Try sincronizadas, hot tortillas baked with cubed ham, spiced chicken and cheese

Transport   Bus terminal at 10 C y 1 Av, Zona 5. To **Guatemala City**, at 0300 until 1700, 3 hrs, US$2. To **Nebaj** and **Cotzal**, 8 a day, US$1.30, 3 hrs; a rough but breathtaking trip, arrive in good time to get a window seat (may leave early if full. See Nebaj for route description). Buses leave, passing through Sacapulas (1 hr, US$0.90), at 0800, 0900, 1000, 1030, 1400, 1500, 1600, 1700. To **Uspantán**, via **Sacapulas**, for **Cobán** and **San Pedro Carchá** (see below) at 0930, 1300, 1500, 1530, 3 hrs, US$1.30. To **Joyabaj**, several daily, via Chiché and Zacualpa, US$0.50, 1½ hrs. First at 0800 with buses going on to the capital. Last bus back to Quiché at 1600. It is possible to get to **Huehuetenango** in a day via Sacapulas, then pick-up from bridge to **Aguacatán** and bus from there to Huehuetenango. Last bus to Huehue from Aguacatán, 1600. Daily buses also to **Quetzaltenango**, **San Marcos**, and to **Panajachel**.

Directory   **Banks** *Banco Industrial*, 3 C y 2 Av, top corner of Parque Central, cash on Visa cards and TCs; *G&T Continental*, 6 C y 3 Av, Visa and MasterCard TCs. **Communications** Internet: *Megatel*, 1 Av and 3 C, Zona 5. **Post office:** 3 C between 1 Av and 0 Av, Zona 5. *Telgua*: 1 Av/2 C, Zona 5.

There is a paved road east from Quiché to (8 km) **Santo Tomás Chiché**, a pictur- **Chiché**
esque village with a fine rarely visited Indian Saturday market (**fiesta**, 25-28 December). There is also a road to this village from Chichicastenango. Although it is a
short-cut, it is rough and virtually impassable in any vehicle. It makes a good three to
four-hour walk, however. Further east (45 km) from Chiché is **Zacualpa**, where
beautiful woollen bags are woven. The church has a remarkably fine façade and
there is an unnamed *pensión* near the plaza. Market days are Sunday and Thursday.

Here women weave fascinating *huipiles* and there is a colourful Sunday market, fol- **Joyabaj**
lowed by a procession at about noon from the church led by the elders with drums
and pipes. This was a stopping place on the old route from Mexico to Antigua. There
is good walking in the wooded hills around, for example north to Chorraxaj (two
hours), or across the Río Cocol south to Piedras Blancas to see blankets being
woven. Ask at the Conalfa office in Joyabaj for information or a guide. The *Centro
Xoy* arranges tours (for the benefit of community development) and offers Spanish
and K'iche' lessons. During **fiesta** week (9-15 August) Joyabaj has a *Palo Volador*
and other traditional dances. There is a restaurant next to the *Esso* station on the
Santa Cruz end of the plaza with a bank opposite (will change US$ cash). ■ *Getting
there: Joyita bus from Guatemala City between 3 and 4 Av, and 7 and 9 C, Zona 4, 10 a
day between 0200 and 1600, 5 hrs, US$1.50.*

Off the main road, 35 km northeast of Quiché is **San Andrés Sajcabaja**, an Indian **San Andrés**
village on the Río Xoljá situated in a terraced landscape, wooded above, semi-arid **Sajcabaja**
lower down. **D** *Posada San Rafael*, T755-1834, including full board, traditional
adobe rooms, ecotourism project run by Guatemalan/French family, horse-riding,
hiking, visits to local Maya sites. There are buses from Quiché.

A paved road goes north from Quiché, 48 km, to Sacapulas, a quiet, friendly town at **Sacapulas**
the foot of the Cuchumatanes Mountains, where there are the remains of a bridge *Colour map 5, grid B1*
over the Río Negro, built by Fray Bartolomé de Las Casas. There's a market under *Altitude: 1,220 m*
two large ceiba trees on Thursday and Sunday (larger, selling local wares, baskets,
some traditional clothing). There is a *Banrural* bank on the plaza.

Sleeping and eating **F** *Restaurante Río Negro*, 20 rooms, basic, friendly, cold communal
showers, but hot springs opposite, clean, good meals well prepared, excellent milkshakes.
Small *tiendas* near the plaza.

Transport The ride from Quiché to Sacapulas is on a paved road and takes 1 hr, 10 mins.
Thereafter going north it is unpaved. All buses from Quiché to Uspantán and Aguacatán go
through Sacapulas. Bus to **Huehuetenango** via **Aguacatán** (see also page 623), at 0300,
0430 and 0530, (2¼ hrs, US$1.20); this road is beautiful, but can be closed in the rainy season
(it's a tough road at any time). There are 8 buses a day to **Nebaj** between 0900-1745, 2 hrs,
US$0.80, coming from Quiché. There is a bus around midday to **Uspantán** and one also to
Nebaj, which both appear to wait for the morning arrival from Aguacatán. These buses leave
from the north side of the river over the bridge.

The road east to Cobán

The road east from Sacapulas is one of the most beautiful, and roughest, mountain *There have been*
roads in all Guatemala, with magnificent scenery in the narrow valleys. Several trucks *occasional reports*
to Cobán, daily in the morning; US$1.25, seven hours if you're lucky, usually much *of robberies on*
longer. Start very early if you wish to make it to Cobán the same day. There is no direct *the road between*
bus to Cobán; instead, take one of the three Quiché-Uspantán buses (0930, 1300, *Uspantán and Cobán*
1500), passing Sacapulas at about 1030, 1400, 1600, there is also a departure from
Sacapulas around midday or a truck to **Uspantán**. Coming from Huehuetenango via
Aguacatán to Sacapulas, see page 623. Stay the night at the **F** *Galindo*, four blocks east

Guatemala

of the Parque Central, clean, friendly, recommended. There are also a couple of other *hospedajes* in town. There are several places to eat, including *Cafetería Kevin*, which is good and serves up decent food and vegetables. Then take the early morning bus at 0300 to Cobán. Truck to Cobán 0800-0900. Hitchhiking to Cobán is also possible. (Truck Uspantán-San Cristóbal Verapaz, US$1.25.) Buses to Quiché at 0300, 2200, but other early morning departures are reported.

It is a five-hour walk from Uspantán south to **Chimul**, the birthplace of Rigoberta Menchú, the Nobel Peace Prize winner in 1992. The village was virtually wiped out during the 1980s, but settlement is coming to life again. Only pick-ups head towards the village.

The Ixil Triangle

The Ixil Triangle is made of up of the highland communities of Nebaj, Chajul and Cotzal. The forested mountainous scenery provides great walking opportunities, although sadly, out of local necessity, many of the slopes have been badly deforested and the wood burnt for fires. The traditional costume of the Nebaj women – an explosion of primary colours – is spectacular. Much of this area was decimated during the Civil War and then repopulated with the introduction of 'model villages' established by the government. Evidence of wartime activities can still be seen and more remote Maya Ixil-speaking villages are gradually opening up to visitors with the introduction of hostel and trekking facilities.

Nebaj

Colour map 5, grid B1

There is an excellent website for Nebaj by Solidaridad Internacional: www.Nebaj.org

The town of Nebaj is high in the Cuchumatanes Mountains, and its green slopes are often layered with mist. It is coloured by the beautiful costume worn by the local women, in an extravaganza of predominantly green, with red, yellow, orange, white and purple. The *corte* is mainly maroon with vertical stripes of black and yellow; some are bright red, and the *huipil* is of a geometric design. The women also wear a headdress with colourful bushy pom-poms on them. The men hardly ever wear the traditional costume. Their jacket is red and embroidered in black designs. The main plaza is dominated by a large, simple white church. At the edge of the plaza there are weaving co-operatives selling *cortes, huipiles* and handicrafts from the town and the surrounding area – bargaining is possible.

When you arrive, boys will meet you from incoming buses and will guide you to a *hospedaje* – they expect a tip. Nebaj has Sunday and Thursday markets and a **fiesta** on 12-15 August with traditional dancing.

Excursions

See also Tour operators for details

There is good walking west of Nebaj, and the roads are better in this direction than to Chajul and Cotzal since there are a number of 'model villages' resettled by the government following the widespread destruction in this region. These include **Acul**, founded on 22 December 1983. Follow 5 Calle out of town (the road to the right if you are facing the church at the bottom of the plaza), downhill, then over the bridge. Another 50 m further on the main path veers left, but go straight on; from here the route is self-evident, any forks come back together, approximately two hours. By road leave town on Avenida 4, the *Shell* station road; at the first fork after the 'tower', follow the main road left and at the next fork take the small, unsigned track to the left. **Finca San Antonio** is a good cheese farm 1 km west of the village, whose late Italian owner made Swiss cheese for 50 years (the cheese is for sale, US$9.10 lb).

La tumba de la Indígena Maya is a shrine just outside Nebaj (15 minutes) where some of those massacred during the war were buried. Take the same route as to Ak'Tzumbal, but at the bottom of the very steep hill, immediately after the bridge over the river, take a left, walk straight on over a paved road, then you come to a small junction – carry straight on until you see a minor crossroads on a path with an orange house gate to your left. Look up and you will see a small building. This is the shrine. Walk to your right where you will see a steep set of stairs leading to the shrine.

There is a walk to **Ak'Tzumbal**, through fields and meadows, where rabbits can be seen, and through long, thin earth tunnels used by the military and guerrillas during the war. You need a guide to walk this cross-country route. Alternatively you can take the road to Ak'Tzumbal, where the new houses still display signs warning of the danger of land mines. Walk down 15 Avenida de Septiembre away from the church, and take a left just before *El Triangulo* gas station past *El Viajero Hospedaje*, then left and then right down a very steep hill and keep walking (1½ hours). When you reach a small yellow tower just before a fork – take the right (the left goes to Salquil Grande) to reach the 'model village'. Above the village of Ak'Tzumbal is **La Pista**, an airstrip used during the war. Next to it bomb craters scar the landscape. Only a few avocado trees, between the bomb holes, survive, and the *gasolinera* to refuel planes, is still there, although covered in corrugated iron. There are plans to erect a memorial here. Ask for directions.

E-F *Ilebal Tenau*, bottom of Av 15 de Septiembre, *salida a* Chajul, hot water, shared and private bath, very clean, friendly, parking inside. **F** *Ixil*, 5 Av, 10 C, on the road in from Sacapulas, in a colonial house, clean, pleasant and comfortable, big rooms, hot water. **G** per person. **E** *Ixil*, 2 Av, 9 C, 1 block back up the slope from the bus terminal and one block to the left, cream building with maroon base, no sign, T755-1091, private bath, TV, cheaper without TV, quiet. **E** *Hotel Turanza*, 1 block from plaza down 5 C, T779-7850, formerly *Posada Don Pablo*, but has changed hands, tiny rooms, but very clean, soap, towels, second floor rooms are nicer, TV and parking, little shop in entrance, phone call service. **F** *Hospedaje Esperanza*, 6 Av, 2-36, **G** per person, very friendly, clean, hot showers in shared bathroom, noisy when evangelical churches nearby have activities, hotel is cleaner than it looks from the outside. **F** *Hostal Don Juan*, T755-4014, part of *Programa Quiché*, run with the support of the EU, there are 6 beds in 2 rooms, **G** per person, each bed with a locked strongbox, and hot showers. The colonial building has a traditional sauna, *chuj*, US$2, plus a *boxbol*. The hostel is at 0 Av A, 1 C B, Canton Simocol. Take Av 15 de Septiembre and take a left at *Comedor Sarita*, which is opposite the grey office of PRODONT-IXIL, then it's 100 m to the right, on the right.

Sleeping

El Boxbolito, a *comedor* on the main square, open at 0630 for breakfast. Good value *menú del día* of chicken, rice, salad and fried potatoes, friendly and recommended. Closes at 2200. *Maya Inca*, on the plaza, substantial food, but more expensive than *El Boxbolito*, run by Peruvians hence the name. *Pizza del César*, opposite *Bancafé*, has mouth-watering strawberry cake every day, open 0730-2100. *Restaurant Campestre*, serves up chicken dishes, *licuados* and the only place serving some Western fare – cornflakes and hash browns for breakfast. One block from the plaza and open from 0730-2100. Just after the gas station *El Triangulo* on Av 15 de Septiembre there is an excellent bakery – *El Trigal*.

Eating

Boxboles are squash leaves with masa and chopped meat or chicken spread on them, rolled tightly, boiled and served with salsa and fresh orange juice

The bus ride to Quiché is full of fabulous views, hair-raising bends, and bus drivers who seem hell-bent on leaving the unpaved road for the tarmac from Sacapulas south, at which point they up the speed even more. There is at least 1 rusting bus roof down a chasm to be viewed. Buses to **Quiché** (US$1.30, 3 hrs) passing through **Sacapulas** (1¾ hr from Nebaj, US$0.78) leave 2400, 0100, 0200, 0300, 0400, 0530, 0630-0700, 0800, 1100. You can travel to Cobán in a day by getting a truck or pick-up from outside the village or earliest bus to Sacapulas, get off at the junction to Cunén (1 hr from Nebaj) and hitch or catch a bus from there. There is a lone bus shelter on the mountain road at this junction and you may not wish to wait there if you are on your own, in which case continue to Sacapulas to pick the bus up there (another 40 mins from the junction.)

Transport

Directory **Banks** *Bancafé* and *Banrural*, TCs only. **Communications** Internet: There are 2 email services in town. The **post office** is behind *Bancafé*. **Tour operators** *Solidaridad Internacional*, Av 15 de Septiembre. The PRODONT-IXIL (Proyecto de Promoción de Infraestructuras y Ecoturismo) office is in a grey building on the right 1 block after the *gasolinera El Triangulo* on the road to Chajul.

Directory

Guatemala

www.nebaj.org They have supported 6 hostels in the villages of Xexocom, Chortiz, Xeo, Cocop, Cotzc and Parramos Grande where there is room for 5 people. **G** per person. For further information call in t see the director Pascual, who is very helpful. *Gaspar Terraza Ramos* guides tourists to all the loca places. He usually waits near the bus station or in the plaza and will probably find you. He lost both hi parents during the war and fled to Chiapas for 5 years. He can arrange horse hire.

Chajul This, the second largest village in the Ixil Triangle, is known for its part in the Civi War, where Rigoberta Menchu's brother was killed in the plaza, as relayed in he book *I, Rigoberta Menchu*. According to the Nobel Peace Prize winner on 9 Septem ber 1979, her 16-year-old brother Petrocinio was kidnapped after being turned ir for 15 *quetzales*. He was tortured in the plaza by the army along with numerous oth ers. Villagers were forced to watch the torture under threat of being branded com munists. People were set on fire, but the onlookers had weapons and looked ready tc fight. This caused the army to withdraw. Chajul's main festival is the second Friday in Lent. There is also a pilgrimage to Christ of Golgotha on the second Friday in Lent beginning the Wednesday before (the image is escorted by 'Romans' in blue police uniforms). Market day is Tuesday and Friday. It is possible to walk from Chajul tc Cotzal. It is a six-hour walk from Nebaj to Chajul.

Cotzal Cotzal is spread over a large area on a number of steep hills. *Hostal Doña Teresa* (**G** per person) has a sauna, patio and honey for the face for sale. Ask Teresa about trips from the village or ask for Sebastian Xel Rivera who leads one-day camping trips. The vil lage's **fiesta** is 21-24 June, culminating in the day of St John the Baptist on 24 June. In Cotzal the market is on Wednesday and Saturday. You can hire bikes for US$0.52 an hour from *Maya Tour* on the plaza next to the church. There is also *Cafeteria and Hospedaje Christian,* **G** per person, alongside the church, and *Comedor and Hospedaje El Maguey,* **G** per person where a bland meal, but decent size, plus drink, are served up for for US$1.70. Don't stay here though, unless you're desperate. Nebaj to Cotzal is a pleasant four-hour walk. There's no accommodation or restaurants in other small vil lages and it is difficult to specify what transport is available in this area as trucks and the occasional pick-up or commercial van are affected by road and weather conditions. For this reason, be prepared to have to spend the night in villages. Buses to Chajul, and Cotzal, do not run on a set schedule. It is best to ask the day before you want to travel, at the bus station. There are buses and numerous pick-ups on Sundays when villagers come to Nebaj for its market, which would be a good day to visit the villages. There is a definite 0500 bus to Chajul on Tuesday returning 1200. Alternatively, bargain with a local pick-up driver to take you on a trip.

To Huehuetenango and the Cordillera de los Cuchumatanes

Just before the volcanic highlands reach their highest peaks, this part of the western highlands divides into scores of small market towns and villages, each with its own character and features – the loud animal market at San Francisco El Alto, the extra-planetary landscape at Momostenango, and its Maya cosmovision centre, and the dancing extravaganzas at Totonicapán. The modern *ladino* town of Huehuetenango sits at the gateway to the Cordillera de los Cuchumatanes, among which hides, in a cold gash in a sky-hugging valley, the Indian village and weaving centre of Todos Santos Cuchumatán.

Nahualá- Before the major four-way junction of Cuatro Caminos (see page 619), the
Cuatro Pan-American Highway runs past Nahualá, an Indian village at 2,470 m. The tradi-
Caminos tional *traje* is distinctive and best seen on market days on Thursday and Sunday,
31 km when finely embroidered cuffs and collars are sold, as well as very popular *huipiles*.
Fiesta (Santa Catalina) on 23-26 November (main day 25).

There is an unpaved all-weather road a little to the north and 16 km longer, from Los Encuentros (on the Pan-American Highway) through Totonicapán (40 km) to

San Cristóbal Totonicapán. The route from Chichicastenango to Quiché, Xecajá and Totonicapán takes a day by car or motorcycle, but is well worth taking and recommended by cyclists. There are no buses.

Cuatro Caminos is a busy junction with roads, east to Totonicapán, west to Los Encuentros, north to Huehuetenango and south to Quetzaltenango. Buses stop here every few seconds so you will never have to wait long for a connection. There are lots of stalls and food vendors to keep you fed and watered. Just north of Cuatro Caminos is San Cristóbal Totonicapán, noted for its *huiples*.

Totonicapán

Colour map 5, grid B!
Population: 52,000
Altitude: 2,500 m

The annual fair is on 24-30 September in celebration of the Archangel San Miguel, with the main fiesta on 29 September

The route to San Miguel Totonicapán, the capital of its Department, passes through pine-forested hillsides, pretty red-tiled roofs and *milpas* of maize on the road side. The 18th-century beige church stands on one of the main squares, unfortunately now a parking lot, at 6 y 7 Avenida between 3 and 4 Calle. The market is considered by Guatemalans to be one of the cheapest, and it is certainly very colourful. Saturday is the main market noted for ceramics and cloth, with a small gathering on Tuesdays. There is a traditional dance **fiesta** on 12-13 August, music concerts and a chance to see *cofradía* rituals. The **Casa de Cultura,** 8 Avenida, 2-17, T7661575, www.larutamayaon line.com/aventura, displays an excellent collection of fiesta masks, made on site at the mask factory, and for sale. It has a cultural programme with a number of tour options. You need to reserve in advance. ■ *Mon-Fri 0800-1200, 1400-1630, run by Carlos Humberto Molina.*

Sleeping and eating D *Hospedaje San Miguel*, 3 C, 7-49, Zona 1, T766-1452, rooms with or without (**E**) bath, hot water, communal TV. **F** *Pensión Blanquita*, 13 Av and 4 C, 20 rooms, **G** per person, hot showers, good. Opposite this *pensión* is a Shell Station. **Eateries include** *Centro Siam*, 2 blocks from the church, Thai and Chinese dishes. *Comedor Letty*, 3 C, 8-18, with typical Guatemalan fare. *Comedor Brenda 2*, 9 Av, 3-31, also good, serving local food.

Transport Buses every 15 mins from **Quetzaltenango**, US$0.32, 45 mins. Last bus returns 2000. Bus to **Los Encuentros**, US$1.50. From Cuatro Caminos, 30 mins, US$0.20.

San Francisco stands high on a great big mound in the cold mountains at 2,640 m above the great valley in which lie Totonicapán, San Cristóbal and Quetzaltenango. It is famous for its market, which is stuffed to capacity, and for the animal market held above town, where creatures from piglets to kittens to budgies are for sale.

San Francisco El Alto

The town's fiesta is on 1-6 October in honour of St Francis of Assisi

The market is packed to bursting point on Fridays with locals buying all sorts, including woollen blankets for resale throughout the country. It's an excellent place for buying woven and embroidered textiles of good quality, but beware of pickpockets. Go early to see as much action as possible. Climb up through the town for 10 minutes to see the animal market (ask for directions all the time as it's hard to see 5 m ahead the place is so chocka). Here, on a small dusty plain, stand locals with their piglets, puppies, calves, budgies, ducks, turkeys and kittens. They stand in separate groups as if waiting judgement in an animal show. The sun sizzles up here and the unsold piglets are virtually hot dogs by closing time. Potential buyers can be seen inspecting the eyes, teeth and tongues of pigs, which screech as if about to succumb to the slaughter here and then.

The church on the main square is magnificent; notice the double-headed Hapsburg eagle. It is often full on market days with locals lighting candles, and their live purchases ignoring the 'Silencio' posters. The white west front of the church complements the bright colours of the rest of the plaza, especially the vivid green and pink of the Municipalidad. You can get a good view of the stall-covered plaza on market day by climbing the bandstand in the centre above a small fountain.

Sleeping and eating D *Vista Hermosa*, 2 C, 2-23, T738-4010, 36 rooms, cheaper without bathroom (**E**), hot water, TV. **F** *Hotel Vásquez*, 4 Av, 11-53, T738-4003, rooms all with private bathroom, but the owner is unwelcoming. Parking available. There are a number of *comedores*, including a line of them on C 3, just below the plaza.

Guatemala

Transport 2 km along the Pan-American Highway heading north from Cuatro Caminos is a newly paved road, which runs to San Francisco El Alto (3 km) and then to Momostenango (19 km). Bus from Quetzaltenango takes 50 minutes on Fri, US$0.33. The last bus back is at 1800.

Directory Banks *G&T Continental*, 2 Av, 1-95, takes MasterCard and changes TCs; *Banco de Comercio*, 2 C, 2-64, cashes TCs, takes Visa cards. *Bancafé*, 2 C, 3-23. Takes Visa and TCs.

Momostenango

Colour map 5, grid B1

The town's very popular fiesta is between 21 July and 4 August, with the town's patron saint of Santiago Apóstol celebrated on 25 July. The Baile de Convites is held in December with other dances on 8, 12 and 31 December and 1 January

Momostenango is set in a valley with ribbons of houses climbing higgledy-piggledy out of the valley floor. Some 300 medicine men are said to practise in the town. Their insignia of office is a little bag containing beans and quartz crystals. Momostenango is the chief blanket-weaving centre in the country, and locals can be seen beating the blankets (*chamarras*) on stones, to shrink them. There are also weird stone peaks known as the *riscos* nearby – eroded fluted columns and draperies formed of volcanic ash strange stone formations on the outskirts of town. Momostenango, at 2,220 m, represents *Shol Mumus* in K'iche', meaning 'among the hills', and on its outlying hills are numerous altars and a hilltop image of a Maya god.

The town is quiet except on Wednesday and Sunday **market days**, the latter being larger and good for weaving, especially the blankets that sell for around US$16 for a single size. On non-market days try *Tienda Manuel de Jesús Agancel*, 1 Avenida, 1-50, Zona 4, near *Bancafé*, for good bargains, especially blankets and carpets. There is also *Artesanía Paclom* at the corner of 1 Calle and 3 Avenida, Zona 2, just five minutes along the road to Xela. This family have the weaving looms in their back yard and will show you how it's all done if you ask.

The Feast of Wajshakib Batz' Oj (8 Thread (first day), pronounced 'washakip', is celebrated by hundreds of *Aj Kij* (Maya priests) who come for ceremonies. New priests are initiated on this first day of the ritual new year; the initiation lasting the year. At **Takilibén Maya Misión**, Chuch Kajaw (Day keeper) Rigoberto Itzep welcomes all interested in learning more about Maya culture and cosmology. He offers courses in culture and does Maya horoscope readings (US$2.60). He also has a Maya sauna (*Tuj*) open Tuesdays and Thursdays 1400-1700, US$6.50. You can leave a message for him on T736-5051 from Mondays-Fridays between 0800-1200, 1400-1700. www.geocities.com/rainforest/jungle/9089 He can be found just after the Texaco garage on the right on the way in from Xela at 3 Avenida, 6-85, Zona 3.

Excursions Just outside town are three sets of *riscos* (eroded columns of sandstone with embedded quartz particles) creating a strange eerie landscape of pinnacles that look like rocket lollipop ice-creams (if you know what I mean). They also resemble parts of the cave dwelling region of Cappadocia in Turkey. ■ *Getting there: take the 2 Calle, Zona 2, which is the one to the right of the church, for 5 mins until you see a sign on a building pointing to the left. Follow the signs until you reach the earth structures (5-10 mins), which are close to some homes.*

Sleeping & eating **E** *Ixcel*, also known as *Estiver*, downhill away from plaza at 1 C, 4-15, Zona 4, T736-5036, 12 rooms, hot water, cheaper without bath, clean. **E-F** *Hotel La Villa*, 1 Av, 1-13, Zona 1, below *Bancafé*, T736-5108, 6 rooms, warm water only, communal TV, clean and nicely presented. **F** *Hospedaje y Comedor Paclom*, close to central plaza, at 1 C, 1-71, Zona 4, pretty inner courtyard with caged birds and plants, hot water in shared bathrooms; the attached *comedor* has cheap meals, including snacks. *Comedor Santa Isabel*, next door, friendly, cheap and good breakfasts. *Flipper*, 1 C y 2 Av A, good *licuados* and a range of fruit juices.

Transport Bus service from Cuatro Caminos (US$0.40) and Quetzaltenango, US$0.52, 1-1½ hrs. Buses to **Xela** every 30 mins from 0430-1600, US$0.52, 1½ hrs.

Directory Banks *Banrural*, on plaza, TCs only. *Bancafé*, esq 1 Av y 1 C, Zona 2, takes Visa. **Language schools** *Patzite*, 1 C, 4-33, Zona 2, T736-5159, www.patzite.20 m.com

Huehuetenango

Huehuetenango is a quiet, pleasant, large town with little to detain the visitor, and is colloquially known as Huehue. However, it is a busy transport hub serving the Cuchumatanes Mountains and the Mexican border. Its bus terminal 2km from town, is one of the busiest in the country. There are Maya ruins near the town, which were badly restored by the infamous United Fruit Company, and new adventure tourism opportunities opening up nearby. Trips to more remote spots in the Huehuetenango region to see forests, haciendas and lakes are being organized by a new tour agency, *Unicornio Azul*, call T205-9328 for more information. There is a useful local website at www.interhuehue.com/

Population: 39,000
Colour map 5, grid B1
Altitude: 1,905 m

The town is pronounced 'way-way'

The neo-classical **cathedral** has had more than its fair share of knocks in its relatively short life. Built between 1867-1874, it was destroyed by earthquake in 1902, and took 10 years to repair. In 1956 the image of the patron saint la Virgen de la Concepción was burnt in an altar fire. Then, during the 1976 earthquake, 80% of it was damaged, save the bells, façade and cupola. The skyline to the north of the city is dominated by the Cuchumatanes Mountains, La Cordillera de los Cuchumatanes, the largest area over 3,000 m in Central America.

The ruins of **Zaculeu**, the old capital of the Mam Maya, are 5 km west of Huehuetenango on top of a rise with steep drops on three sides – a site chosen because of these natural defence measures. Its original name in Mam was *Xinabajul*, meaning 'between ravines'. In K'iche' it means 'white earth'. It was first settled in the Early Classic period (AD 250-600), but it flourished during the Late Post-Classic (AD 1200-1530). In July 1525, Gonzalo de Alvarado, the brother of Guatemala's conqueror, Pedro de Alvarado, set out for Zaculeu with 80 Spaniards, 40 horses and

Guatemala

Huehuetenango

■ Sleeping	4 Mary	● Eating	4 La Fonda de
1 Casa Blanca	5 Maya	1 Café Bougambilias	Don Juan
2 Central	6 Todos Santos	2 El Jardín	5 Mi Tierra Café
3 La Sexta	7 Vásquez	3 La Cabaña del Café	Internet

0 metres 100
0 yards 100

N

2,000 indigenous fighters, passing Mazatenango and Totonicapán on the way. The battle lasted four months, during which time the soldiers and residents of Zaculeu were dying of hunger, and eating their dead neighbours. The weakened Kaibil Balam, the Zaculeu *cacique* (chief), called for a meeting with Gonzalo. Gonzalo told the Mam chief that peace was not on the cards. Negotiations followed with the outcome being that Kaibil Balam be instructed in Christianity, obey the Spanish king and leave the city, whereupon Gonzalo de Alvarado would take possession of the Mam kingdom settlement in the name of the Spanish crown. Half a dozen structures were restored by the United Fruit Company in the 1940s by covering the surfaces in white concrete. The museum has many exhibits from the site. ■ *0800-1800, free. Getting there: bus leaves Salvador Osorio School, final C 2, every 30 mins, US$0.13, 15 mins, last return 1830. Taxi, US$7, including waiting time. To walk takes about 1 hr – either take 6 Av north, cross the river and follow the road round to the left, through Zaculeu modern village to the ruins, or go past the school and turn right beyond the river. There are signs, but they are barely visible.*

Chiantla, just 5 km north of Huehuetenango, has a great pilgrimage to the silver Virgen de La Candelaria on 28 January to 2 February. The church has a wonderful roof and an impressive see-through altar with an ambulatory to the vestry, where the Virgin and child, virtually encased in silver, can be visited; ask the priest's permission to take photos. During the pilgrimage period, however, a replica is processed through the town as the original weighs too much. The town is also famous for its leather workshops, which are open during the day. Many of the workshops are on 7 Calle. ■ *Getting there: buses leave from corner of 5 Av and 4 C and from 1 Av and 1 C, Huehuetenango, 25 mins, US$.013. In Chiantla they pass the Parque Central with the last bus returning at 1900.*

Fifteen kilometres north of Chiantla is **El Mirador**. At about 3,300 m, a short distance to the left of the road, there are incredible views to the south. In good visibility, you can see most of the volcanoes from Tacaná on the Mexican border to those overlooking Antigua. There are nine small pyramids inscribed with verses of the poet Juan Diéguez Olaverri with a garden and monument to peace in the centre. This commemorates the end of the Civil War in December 1996.

Sleeping
■ *on map, see previous page*

Bus station area **C** *Cascata*, opposite terminal, T764-1188, hot water, TV, although restaurant disappointing. **D** *Trinitaria*, T764-3922, rooms with bath, **E** without, hot water.

In town **C** *Casa Blanca*, 7 Av, 3-41, T769-0777, F769-0777. Comfortable, good restaurant in a pleasant garden, very popular and good value. **D** *Maya*, 3 Av, 3-55, T764-0369, F764-1622, this former basic hotel has been remodelled with spa facilities, offering free coffee in reception, hot water and cable TV in rooms. It is ultra-clean, but some rooms are a little small. **E** *La Sexta*, 6 Av, 4-29, T764-6612, with bath, cheaper without, cable TV, restaurant, good for breakfast, clean, good value, phone call facility. **E** *Mary*, 2 C, 3-52, T764-1618, with bath, cheaper without, good beds, hot water for 3 hrs in the morning and at night only, cable TV, parking, clean, quiet, safe, good value. Recommended. **E** *Todos Santos Inn*, 2 C, 6-74, T764-1241, shared bath and private bath available, hot water, TV, helpful, clean, luggage stored. Recommended. Better value for single travellers than *Mary*. **E-F** *Vásquez*, 2 C, 6-67, T764-1338, with bath, cheaper without, TV lounge, parking, clean. **F** *Central*, 5 Av, 1-33, communal baths, hot water, basic, parking, restaurant, looking a little poky.

Eating
● *on map, see previous page*

Casa Blanca, 7 Av, 3-41, try the breakfast pancake with strawberries and cream. The plate of the house is a meat extravaganza, fish and good salads served, open 0600-2200. *Café Bougambilias*, 5 Av near 4 C, on the plaza, large, unusual 4-storey building, most of which is a popular, cheap, restaurant, very good breakfasts, *almuerzos*, sandwiches. Recommended. *La Fonda de Don Juan*, 2 C, 5-35, Italian (try the *cavatini*), sandwiches, big choice of desserts, *licuados*, good pizzas, also *comida típica*, with reasonable prices all served in a bright environment with red-and-white checked table cloths. Open daily 0600-2200. *La*

Cabaña del Café, 2 C, 6-50, log cabin café with to-die-for cappuccino, snack food and good breakfasts, but service is lamentably slow. Live music on Sat. Open Mon-Sat 0800-2100. Recommended. *Mi Tierra Café Internet* , 4 C, 6-46, good drinks and light meals, Mexican offerings – try the *fajitas*, nice setting, popular with locals and travellers, recommended. Open 0700-2200. *El Jardín*, 6 Av y 3 C, Zona 1, meat dishes, good pancakes and milk shakes, local dishes, *menú del día* US$2.20. It's worth eating here just to check out the toilets, which are right out of the 3rd-and-a-half floor of the office in the movie *Being John Malkovich*! Open daily 0600-2200. *Le Kaf*, 6 C, 6-40, Western-style, varied menu, live music between Thu-Sun 0700-2200, good travel information. Recommended. Open 1100-2300. *Numerous cheap comedores* near the market.

Local From the terminal to town, take 'Centro' bus , which pull up at cathedral, US$0.08, 5 mins. Taxis from behind the covered market building for US$2.60. To walk takes 20-25 mins. **Bus** To **Guatemala City**, 5 hrs, US$3.75, *Los Halcones*, 7 Av, 3-62, Zona 1 (they do not leave from the terminal) at 0430, 0700, 1400, reliable. From the bus terminal there are 12 a day to the capital from 0215-1600 via Chimaltenango, 5 hrs, US$3.70. Via Mazatenango there are 5 daily. Heading north: to **Todos Santos Cuchumatán** 0300, 0500, 1200, 1400, 1500, 1600, 2-3 hrs, US$1.25. To **Barillas**, via San Juan Ixcoy (2½ hrs), Soloma (3 hrs), and San Mateo Ixtatan (7 hrs), 10 daily from 0200-2330, US$3.25. There are also buses to **San Rafael la Independencia** passing through Soloma and Sta Eulalia, US$3.25. **Heading northwest:** to **La Mesilla** for Mexico: frequent buses between 0330-1700, US$1.05, 2½ hrs, last bus returning to Huehue, 1800. To **Nentón**, via La Mesilla at 0530, 0930. To **Gracias a Dios**, 0500, 1230. **Heading south**: to **Quetzaltenango**, 13 a day from 0600-1600, US$1.05, 2-2¼ hrs. To **Cuatro Caminos**, US$1, 2 hrs; to **Los Encuentros**, for Lake Atitlán and Chichicastenango, 3 hrs, US$2.60. **Heading east**: To **Aguacatán**, 12 daily, 0600-1900, 1 hr 10 mins, US$0.52. To **Nebaj** you have to get to Sacapulas via Aguacatán as the 1130 direct bus no longer runs as far as Nebaj, although it is still advertised; to **Sacapulas**, 1130, 1245; to **Cobán**, take the earliest bus to Aguacatán and then Sacapulas and continue to Uspantán.

Transport

Guatemala

Banks Many local bank taking Visa and MC, some open Sat morning. The bigger banks change Tcs. Mexican *pesos* can be got from *Camicard*, 5 Av, 6-00. **Communications** Internet: The cheapest is just outside the centre opposite El Triangulo shopping mall: *Los Angeles 2*, US$2.30 per hr, phone calls also. Several places around the centre, eg *Mi Tierra Internet Café*. Post office: 2 C, 3-54. Telephone: *Telgua*, Edif El Triángulo, 9 Av, 6-142, on main road out of town. **Embassies and consulates** The Honorary *Mexican Consul*, Lic Tomás Del Cid Fernández, T764-1366, at the *Farmacia del Cid* (5 Av y 4 C) will provide you with a Mexican visa. Open Mon-Fri 0900-1200, 1500-1700. **Language schools** Some operate in the summer months only (see box, Learning the lingo, page 589). *Señora de Mendoza*, 1 C, 1-64, Zona 3, T764-1987. *Rodrigo Morales* (at *Sastrería La Elegancia*), 9 Av, 6-55, Zona 1. Recommended. *Spanish Academy Xinabajul*, 6 Av, 0-69, Zona 1, T764-1518, www.worldwide.edu/guatemala/xinabaj/ *Abesaida Guevara de López*, 10 C 'A', 10-20, Zona 1, T7642917. Recommended. Information on schools and other tourist information is posted in *Mi Tierra Café Internet*. **Laundry** *Lavandería Cintya*, 7 Av, 3-00, Mon-Sat 0800-1900. **Useful addresses** Car insurance: for Mexico and Guatemala, arranged at *Banco G&T Continental's* agent, Edif Villa Rosa opposite *Mi Tierra Café Internet*.

Directory

Huehuetenango would be a good spot to learn Spanish, as there are fewer chances of meeting gringos and conversing in your own tongue

The women of Aguacatán wear the most stunning headdresses in the country. They are a long, slim textile belt of woven threads using all the colours of the rainbow. On sale in *tiendas* in town. The women also wear beautiful costumes – the *cortes* are dark with horizontal stripes of yellow, pink, blue and green. The town **fiesta** is 40 days after Holy Week, Virgen de la Encarnación. ■ *Getting there: bus from Huehue, 1 hr 10 mins, US$0.52. Returning between 0445 and 1600. Buses and pick-ups for Sacapulas and for onward connections to Nebaj and Cobán leave from the main street going out of town. Wait anywhere along there to catch your ride. A bus leaves between 1030-1100 to Sacapulas and there are meant to be more buses until 1400, after which you will have to rely on pick-ups. It is 1½ hrs, US$0.65 from Aguacatán to Sacapulas. To Guatemala City at 0300, 1100. See also Sacapulas, page 615.*

Aguacatán

Colour map 5, grid B1
Altitude: 1,670 m

26 km east of Huehuetenango on a semi-paved route (good views); 36 km from Sacapulas

Guatemala

 Todos Santos Festival

The horse festival of Todos Santos is one of the most celebrated and spectacular in Central America – it is also a frenzied day that usually degenerates into a drunken mass. Quite simply the riders race between two points, having a drink at each turn until they fall off.

According to Professor Margarito Calmo Cruz, the origins of the fiesta lie in the 15th or 16th century with the advent of the conquistadores to Todos Santos. They arrived on horseback wearing large colourful clothes with bright scarves flowing down their backs and feathers in their hats. The locals experimented, imitating them. They enjoyed it and the tradition was born.

When the day begins, the men are pretty tipsy, but sprightly and clean. The race is frantic and colourful with the scarves flying out from the backs of the men. As the day wears on, they get completely smashed, riding with arms outstretched - whip in one hand and beer bottle in the other. Their faces are mudspattered, they look dishevelled and filthy, and they are moaning and groaning from the enjoyment and the alcohol which must easily have reached a poisonous level.

At times the riders fall, and look pretty lifeless on the track. They are dragged by the scruff of the neck, regardless of serious injury or death, to the edge of the fence as quickly as possible, to avoid trampling.

The men guzzle gallons of beer and the aim is to continue racing all day. A fall means instant dismissal from the race. There are wardens on the side lines with batons, whose primary job is the welfare of the horses, changing them when they see necessary. But they also deal with protesting fallen riders, who try and clamber back onto their horses.

By the end of the day the spectacle is pretty grotesque. The horses are drenched with sweat and wild-eyed with fear. The men look hideous and are completely paralytic. The edge of the course and the town is littered with semi-comatose bodies. A large proportion of these are lying in the streets with people stepping over them as if they were rocks.

The race takes place on the road that winds its way out of town, not the incoming road from Huehue. It starts between 0800 and 0830. There are about 15 riders on the course at any one time. It continues until noon, stops for lunch and cerveza guzzling begins again at 1400 and ends at 1700.

Todos Santos Cuchumatán

*Colour map 5, grid B1
Altitude: 2,470 m
Strong sun
during the day,
cold at night*

High in the Cuchumatanes, the Mam-speaking Todos Santeros maintain a traditional way of life with their striking, bright, traditional costume and their adherence to the 260-day Tzolkin calendar. The town is hemmed in by 3,800-m high mountains either side that squeeze the town into one long, 2-km street down the valley. The town is famous for its weaving, and even more famous for the horse-race held on 1 November – a riot of colour, energy, festival dancing and drunkenness.

To get to Todos Santos, you have to climb the front range of the Cuchumatanes Mountains above Chiantla by a steep road from Huehuetenango. Looking down on a clear day the cathedral at Huehuetenango looks like a blob of orange blancmange on the plain. At the summit, at about 3,300 m, there is *El Mirador* (see page 622). The new paved road continues over bleak moorland to Paquix where the road divides. The unpaved road to the north continues to Soloma. The other to the west goes through Aldea Chiabel, noted for its outhouses, more obvious than the small dwellings they serve. Here, giant agave plants appear to have large pom poms attached – reminiscent of the baubles on Gaudi's cathedral in Barcelona. On this journey you often pass through cloud layer eventually surfacing above it. On cloudier days you will be completely submerged until descending again to Huehuetenango. The road crosses a pass at 3,394 m before a difficult long descent to Todos Santos, about 50 km from Huehuetenango. Walking northwest from Chiantla to Todos Santos Cuchumatanes, can be done in around 12-14 hrs, or better, 2 days, staying overnight at El Potrillo in the barn owned by Rigoberto Alva. This route crosses one of the highest parts of the Cordillera at over 3,500 m. Alternatively, cycle the 40-km part-gravel road, which is steep in places, but very rewarding.

Some of Guatemala's best weaving is done in Todo Santos. Fine *huipiles* may be bought in the co-operative on the main street and direct from the makers. The men wear the famous red-and-white striped trousers. Some wear a black wool over-trouser piece. Their jackets are white, pink, purple and red-striped with beautifully coloured, and intricately embroidered, collars and cuffs. Their straw hat is wrapped with a blue band. You can buy the embroidered cuffs and collars for men's shirts, the red trousers, and gorgeous colourful crocheted bags made by the men. The women wear navy blue *cortes* with thin, light blue, vertical stripes.

There is a colourful Saturday **market** and a smaller one on Wednesday. A big reforestation project is under way around Todos Santos where cypress, pine, alder and eucalyptus are being planted. The **church** near the park was built in 1580. There is a spectacular annual **fiesta** on 1 November – see below under festivals, and box, previous page. The local men make a promise one year beforehand that they will ride in the *corrida* (horse-race). If they don't fulfil this promise, they believe they will die.

Excursions

Horses can be hired from Casa Mendoza for US$2.60 an hour

The closest walk is to **Las Letras**; where the words 'Todos Santos' are spelt out in white stone on a hillside above the town. The walk takes an hour. To get there take the path down the side of *Restaurant Cuchumatlan*. The highest point of the Cuchumatanes, and the highest non-volcanic peak in the country, **La Torre** at 3,837 m, is to the northeast of Todos Santos and can be reached from the village of Tzichem on the road to Concepción Huista. When clear, it's possible to see the top of Volcán Santa María, one of the highest volcanoes in Guatemala. The hike takes about five hours (for a shorter version see below). The best way to do it is to start in the afternoon and spend the night near the top. It is convenient for camping, with wood but no water. There are also two guards at the top minding antennae and solar panels who have two beds in a cabin (**G**, including supper) and offer a cuppa for US$0.13! A compass is essential in case of mist. A shorter version is to take the 0630 bus to Laventosa, US$0.40, and from there, it's a 1½-hour climb. From Todos Santos, you can also hike south to **San Juan Atitán**, four to five hours, where the locals wear an interesting *traje típica*. Market days are on Mondays and Thursdays. From there you can hike to the Pan-American Highway - one day walk. **G** *Hospedaje San Diego*, only three beds, basic, friendly, clean, food. **Fiesta**: 22-26 June. Walking southwest from Todos Santos it is possible to reach **Santiago Chimaltenango** in seven hours (you can stay in the school, ask at the Municipalidad), then on to San Pedro Necta, and on to the Pan-American Highway for bus back to Huehuetenango. Walking to Nebaj in the Ixil Triangle can also be done in three days. Ask in Todos Santos if you want a guide. If you camp, secure your belongings.

Sleeping

Reservations would only really be necessary in the week before the November horse-race, but even if you turn up and the town is full, locals offer their homes

F *Casa Familiar*, myearth@c.net.gt, up the hill, close to central park. Run by the friendly family of Santiaga Mendoza Pablo. Hot shower, sauna, breakfast, dinner US$2.50, but slow service (chase them up), delicious banana bread, spectacular view, popular. The Mendoza family make and sell *típicas* and give weaving lessons, US$1 per hr. **F** *Hospedaje El Viajero*, around the corner and then right from *Hotelito Todos Santos*, 5 rooms, 2 shared baths with hot water. **F** *Hotelito Todos Santos*, above the central park, hot water, clean, small café, but beware of boys taking you to the hotel quoting one price, and then on arrival, finding the price has mysteriously gone up! **G** *Casa Mendoza*, basic, hot shower is some way from the rooms, free sauna. **G** *Hotel La Paz*. Friendly, great view of the main street from balconies, excellent spot for the 1 Nov fiesta, shared showers have seen better days, enclosed parking. **G** *Hotel Mam*, next to *Hotelito Todos Santos*. Friendly, clean, hot water, but needs 1 hr to warm up, not too cold in the rooms as an open fire warms the building, good value.

Eating

Comedor Katy, will prepare vegetarian meals on request, good value *menú del día*, US$2. *Cuchumatlan*, has sandwiches, pizza and pancakes, and is popular at night. *Patz Xaq*, signposted 100 m down a track opposite and just before *Hotel La Paz* on the right, serving *comida típica* from 0700-2100, great view. *Tzolkin*, good food, the most popular gringo hangout, can also arrange local tours. Next door *Café Ixcanac* was due to open. There are *comedores* on the 2nd floor of the market selling very cheap meals.

Guatemala

Festivals **1 Nov**, horse-race. The festival begins on 21 Oct. See box. You need to arrive a few day before the race to secure a room in the town. If all rooms are full, and you walk around look ing lost, you may be taken in by a family for the remainder of the time. On **2 Nov** is *Day of the Dead* when locals visit the cemetery and leave flowers and food.

Shopping The following shops all sell bags, trousers, shirts, *huipiles*, jackets and clothes. Prices have more or less stabilized at the expensive end, but the best bargains can be had at the *Tienda Maribel*, further up the hill from *Casa Familiar* and the **Cooperativa Estrella de Occidente** on the main street. *Casa Mendoza*, just beyond *Tienda Maribel*, is where Telésforo Mendoza makes clothes to measure. A pair of trousers including material costs US$19.50. His young daughter, Isabela, is a keen businesswoman, and will offer you items in exchange for your watch or some jewellery, her parents unaware! *Domingo Calmo* also makes clothes to measure. A pair of trousers will cost US$3.90 plus material. Takes 4-5 hrs. His large, brown house with tin roof is on main road to the Ruinas (5 mins) – follow the road up from *Casa Familiar*. Ask for the Casa de Domingo.

Transport Bus to **Huehuetenango**, 2-3 hrs, crowded Mon and Fri, 0400, 0500, 0600, 0615-30, 1145, 1230, 1300. Possble changes on Sat so ask beforehand. For petrol, ask at *El Molino*.

Directory
Only travellers' cheques and cash can be changed here

Bank *Banrural* TCs and dollars cash only. **Communication** Post office: central park. **Language schools** All the local co-ordinators are on friendly terms with each other but all are competing for your business. Take your time and visit all 3 schools. *Hispano Maya*, opposite *Hotelito Todos Santos*, http://www-persona.umich.edu/~kakenned/, US$15 with homestay. *Nuevo Amanecer*, T308-7416, mitierra@c.net.gt; US$115 with homestay: *Proyecto Lingüístico de Español*, US$115 with homestay, food reported as basic. There is also a volunteer project to teach English in a nearby village where food and board is provided. Weaving can be taught at US$0.65 per hr.

Jacaltenango
Much pride is taken in marimba playing, eg at football matches

The road from Todos Santos continues northwest through Concepción Huista. Here the women wear towels as shawls and Jacalteco is spoken. **Fiesta:** 29 January- 3 February with fireworks and dancing. The hat maker in Canton Pilar supplies the hats for Todos Santos, he welcomes viewers and will make a hat to your specifications (but if you want a typical Todos Santos leather *cincho*, buy it there). ■ *Getting there: from Huehuetenango at 0330, 0500, returning at 1130 and 1400, also pick-ups.*

Beyond Jacaltenango, is **Nentón**, and **Gracias a Dios** at the Mexican border. When the road north out of Huehue splits at Paquix, the right fork goes to **San Mateo Ixtatán**, with ruins nearby. The road crosses the roof of the Cuchumatanes, before descending to San Juan Ixcoy, Soloma and Santa Eulalia, where the people speak O'anjob'al as they do in Soloma. East along a scenic route is Barillas. There are several *pensiones* in these places and regular buses from Huehue.

Border with
Mexico

La Mesilla/Ciudad Cuauhtémoc The Pan-American Highway runs west from the junction to Huehuetenango to La Mesilla. Guatemalan immigration: open 0700-1900. You may be able to pass through out of hours for a surcharge. The Mexican border post is in Ciudad Cuauhtémoc (just a few buildings, not a town), about 4 km from the Guatemalan border. There are pick-ups during the day. Crossing by private vehicle is reported to be fairly simple. **Sleeping**: There are a couple of *pensiones* at the border inside Guatemala should you get stuck, including **F** *Hotel Mily's*, 10 rooms, hot water. **Transport**: Buses from La Mesilla to **Huehuetenango** run from 0330 to 1800, 2 hrs, US$1.05. Express buses run by *Transportes Velásquez* go to Guatemala City (US$5, 7 hrs). **Banks**: Rates are not usually favourable at the border in either currency. *Banrural* in La Mesilla, or haggle in the street.

Entering Guatemala A tourist card for Guatemala can be obtained at the border. See Essentials, Guatemala. For visas, also see this section and for border 'charges'.

Crossing by private vehicle Full details under Getting around by car, page 561.

Mexican consulates Mexican visas are available at the border, but better at *Farmacia El Cid*, Huehuetenango, see page 623. See also Quetzaltenango, Embassies and consulates.

Heading south to Quetzaltenango (Xela) you pass the small *ladino* town of Salcajá, where jaspé skirt material has been woven since 1861. If you fancy a taste or a whiff of some potent liquor before bracing yourself for an entry into Quetzaltenango then this is the place to halt. It is worth a visit not only for the booze but its famous church – the oldest in Central America – and for its textiles, often seen being produced in the streets. In 1524 the first church in Central America was founded by the conquering Spaniards. **San Jacinto** is a small church on 6 Avenida y 2 Calle, the church is being restored and may not always be open. *Caldo de frutas*, a highly alcoholic drink with quite a kick, is not openly sold but is made in the town and drunk on festive occasions. It is illegal to drink it in public places. It is a concoction of *nances*, cherries, peaches, apples and *membrillos* and is left to ferment in rum. There is also *Rompope*, a drink made with eggs. Sold in various shops around town, the smallest bottle of bright yellow liquid sold at the *Fábrica de Pénjamo*, 2 Avenida, 4-03, Zona 1, is US$1.55 and it slips down the throat very nicely!

Salcajá is a town that also revolves around textiles with shops on every street. Yarn is tied and dyed, untied, and wraps are then stretched around telephone poles along the road or along the riverside. One of these can be seen outside San Jacinto church. There is a textile workshop that can be visited near the church.

Salcajá
Market day is Tuesday

All buses heading to Quetzaltenango from Cuatro Caminos pass through Salcajá, 10 minutes

Guatemala

Quetzaltenango

Quetzaltenango (commonly known as Xela – pronounced 'shayla') is the most important city in western Guatemala. The country's second city is set among a group of high mountains and volcanoes, one of which, Santa María, caused much death and destruction in 1902. The bulk of the city is modern, but its 19th-century downtown revamp and its narrow streets gives the centre more of an historical feel. There are breathtaking views and a pleasant park with its beautifully restored façade of the colonial church. It is an excellent base from which to visit nearby hot springs, religious idols, volcanoes and market towns.

Colour map 5, grid C1
Population: 118,000
Altitude: 2,335 m

General information can be found at www.xelapages.com

Most visitors arrive by bus. It is 30 mins (14.5 km) southwest of Cuatro Caminos , US$0.18. Buses pull into the Zona 3 Minerva Terminal. To get a bus into the city centre, take a path through the market at its far left or its far right, which brings you out in front of the Minerva Temple. Buses for the town centre face away (left) from the temple. All *Santa Fe* services go to Parque Centro América, US$0.6-0.10. Alternatively take a taxi, US$2.60.

The town centre is compact and all sites and most services are within walking distance. The *Santa Fe* city bus goes between the terminal, the *rotonda* and the town centre. Out of town destination buses stop at the *rotonda* and it is quicker to get here from the town centre than to the terminal. City buses for the terminal leave from 4 C and 13 Av, Zona 1, and those straight for the *rotonda* leave from 11 Av and 10 C, Zona 1, US$0.6-0.10. A taxi within Zona 1, or from Zona 1 to a closer part of Zona 3, is between US$1.30-2. *INGUAT*, 7 C, 11-35, on the park, T761-4931. Open Mon-Fri, 0900-1300, 1400-1700, Sat 0900-1300.

Ins & outs
See page 633 for further details

Watch out for very clever pickpockets walking through this market

The most important battle of the Spanish conquest took place near Quetzaltenango (see page 629) when the great K'iche' warrior Tecún Umán was slain. In October 1902 the Volcán Santa María erupted showering the city with half a metre of dust. An ash cloud soared 8.6 km into the air and some 1,500 people were killed by volcanic fallout and gas. A further 3,000 people died a short while later from malaria due to plagues of mosquitoes which had not been wiped out by the blast. Some 20 years on a new volcano, which was born after the 1902 eruption, began to erupt. This smaller volcano, Santiaguito, spews clouds of dust and ash on a daily basis and is considered one of the most dangerous volcanoes in the world. The city's prosperity, as seen by

History
9-17 September and Holy Week, October fiesta of La Virgen del Rosario

the grand neoclassical architecture in the centre, was built on the back of the success of the coffee *fincas* on the nearby coastal plain. This led to the country's first bank being established here.

Sights

Museo de Historia Natural must rate as having one of the most bizarre collections in the world

The central park, **Parque Centro América**, is the focus of the city. It is surrounded by the cathedral, with its beautifully restored original colonial façade, and a number of elegant neoclassical buildings, constructed during the late 19th and early 20th century. The modern cathedral, **Catedral de la Diócesis de los Altos**, was constructed in 1899 and is set back behind the original. The surviving façade of the 1535 **Catedral del Espíritu Santo** is now visible after being under wraps for restoration since 1996. It is beautiful, intricately carved and with restored portions of murals on its right side. On the south side of the park is the **Casa de la Cultura**. Inside are the **Museo de la Marimba** with exhibits and documents relating to the 1871 Liberal Revolution. On the right hand side of the building is the totally curious **Museo de Historia Natural**. Deformed stuffed animals are cheek by jowl with Pre-Columbian pottery, sports memorabilia, fizzy drink bottles, a lightning-damaged mirror and dinosaur remains. It satisfies the most morbid of curiosities with its displays of a two-headed calf, Siamese twin pigs, an eight-legged goat, and a strange sea creature

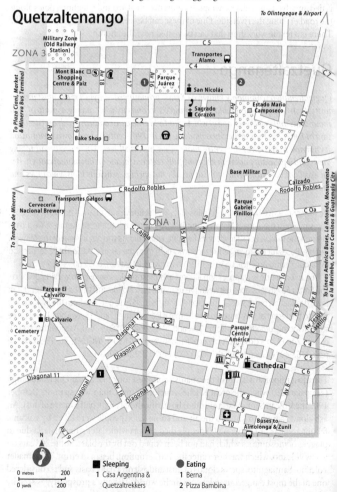

Quetzaltenango

To Olintepeque & Airport

ZONA 3

Military Zone (Old Railway Station)

Mont Blanc Shopping Centre & Paiz

To Plaza Cioni, Market & Minerva Bus Terminal

C 3

Parque Juárez

Transportes Alamo

C 5

C 4

San Nicolás

Sagrado Corazón

Estado Mario Camposeco

C 2

C 1

Bake Shop

Base Militar

C 6

To Templo de Minerva

Transportes Galgos

Cervecería Nacional Brewery

Rodolfo Robles

ZONA 1

C Cajola

Calzado Rodolfo Robles

Parque Gabriel Pinillos

C Oa

C 0

C 1

Parque El Calvario

C 4

El Calvario

Cemetery

Diagonal 12

Diagonal 11

C 5

Parque Centro América

C 6

Cathedral

C 8

C 9

C 10

Buses to Almolonga & Zunil

Diagonal 11

A

To Lineas América Buses, La Rotonda, Monumento a la Marimba, Cuatro Caminos & Guatemala City

N

Related map
A Quetzaltenango centre, page 630

0 metres 200
0 yards 200

■ **Sleeping**
1 Casa Argentina & Quetzaltrekkers

● **Eating**
1 Berna
2 Pizza Bambina

Guatemala

that looks like an alien, known as *Diabillo del Mar*. ■ *Mon-Fri, 0800-1200, 1400-1800, US$0.90*. On the park's southwest side is the **Museo de Arte**, with a collection of contemporary Guatemalan art, and the unique **Museo del Ferrocarril Nacional de los Altos**, recounting the story of an electric railway between Xela and the Pacific slope. ■ *Mon-Fri 0800-1200, 1400-1800. US$0.90. 7 C/12 Av*. The **Banco de Occidente**, founded in 1881, and the first bank to opened in Guatemala, dominates the northern edge of the park. The overly wired up **Municipalidad** straddles the eastern edge of the park with its neoclassical columns. Its first building blocks were laid in 1881, but it wasn't completed until 1897.

The stately **Teatro Municipal** (1892-96) is on 14 Avenida y 1 Calle and can be visited outside of performance hours. Restored at a cost of four million quetzales it has an imposing presence. To its left, on Avenida 14 "A", is the Teatro Roma. Building began in 1898, but was not completed until 1931, when it became the first cinema to open in Guatemala. It was restored in 2000 as a theatre with a capacity for 1,400 and is open for performances. See page 633.

There is a sickly-green modern church, the **Sagrado Corazón**, on the Parque Benito Juárez near the market. Inside is a gigantic, free-standing, Chagall-influenced painting with swooping angels, and Christ in a glass box, built into the picture. The church of **La Transfiguración**, near the corner of 11 Calle and 5 Avenida, Zona 1, houses he largest crucified Christ figure (San Salvador del Mundo) to be found in Central America – it is almost 3 m in height and now housed behind glass. At 20 Avenida and 4 Calle is the city's Cementerio. Inside are the remains of the Quetzalteco President, Estrada Cabrera (1898-1920) in a small cream neoclassical temple. Behind his tomb are the unmarked graves of a large number of cholera victims wiped out in a 19th-century epidemic. Manuel Lisandra Barillas, (Guatemalan President 1885-1892) is also entombed here. There is a small patio area known as Colonia Alemana lined with graves of German residents; a large area where those that died as martyrs in the civil war lie; and a memorial to those that perished in the September Revolution of 1897. This was prompted by the extravagant spending on buildings by the then president in the face of plummetting coffee prices affecting those in the western part of the country. ■ *0700-1900*.

Churches & cemetery
There is a great view of the city from the plaza in front of the church of La Transfiguración and Cerro del Baúl behind

According to folklore, on the Llanos de Urbina near **Olintepeque**, 6 km north of Quetzaltenango (on a road parallel to the main road), Pedro de Alvarado slew Tecún Umán in single combat, on 18 February 1524. Tecún Umán had been contacted by the chief of Xelajú (Quetzaltenango). He was forewarned that the Spaniards were coming, and was sent by the K'iche' Kingdom to do combat. He lined up 8,000 warriors for the battle. Legend says that Tecún Umán struck Alvarado three times and killed his horse. Alvarado quickly secured another horse and thrust his spear into his enemy's chest. When Tecún Umán was struck, a quetzal is said to have landed on his chest, and so the story goes as to why the bird has a scarlet-red chest. The river here is still known as *Xequizel*, the river of blood. Market day is Tuesday and there is an emphasis on animals. The local idol, San Pascual Baillón, has its own little church. **Fiesta**: June 20-25. ■ *Buses from Xela, US$0.13*.

Excursions
For trips further afield see page 635

San Andrés Xecul is a small village in stunning surroundings with an extraordinarily lurid coloured church, 8 km north of Xela. Painted a deep-mustard yellow in 1900, its figurines, including angels, have been given blue wings and pastel-pink skirts. At its peak are jaguars clutching a white pole. Its columns are entwined in evergreen vines, and oodles of plant material sprouts out of red vases. The apostles sport blue crowns and blue musical instruments. Climb the hill a bit above the town and catch a glimpse of the fantastic dome – mulitcoloured like a beach ball.

With your back to the church climb the cobbled street leading up the right hand side of the plaza to a yellow and maroon chapel peering out across the valley. The view from here is spectacular. There is a small but attractive market on Thursdays opposite the church. **Fiesta**: 21 November, 30 November and 1 December. ■*Getting there: bus*

Guatemala

from Xela, US$0.22, 30 mins. Or take any bus heading to Cuatro Caminos and getting off at the Esso station on the left-hand side, and then almost doubling back on yourself to take the San Andrés road. There are pick-ups from here, S$0.65.

Some 6 km southeast is **Almolonga**, noted for its fine 16th-century church and beautiful costumes. Strung along the main road, are a number of thermal baths. *El Manantial* is the cleanest (US$2 or 3.90 for a luxury bath). Bus from Xela, US$0.13. Near Almolonga is the dormant **Volcán Cerro Quemado** at 3,197 m, which provides the hot springs of Almolonga. It is a three-hour climb to the top.

Quetzaltenango centre

N

0 metres 100
0 yards 100

Sleeping
1 Altense *D3*
2 Andina *C3*
3 Anexo Modelo *B1*
4 Bonifaz *B2*
5 Casa Iximulew & El
  Rincón de los
  Antojitos *B1*
6 Casa Mañen *C3*
7 Casa Suiza *B1*
8 Enríquez *C2*
9 Horiani *B2*
10 Kaehler *B2*
11 Kiktem-Ja *C2*
12 Los Olivos *B2*
13 Modelo *B1*
14 Occidental *C2*
15 Villa Real Plaza *B2*

● **Eating**
1 Baviera *C2*
2 Blue Angel *C1*
3 Cardinali *B2*
4 Delí Crepe *B2*
5 El Kopetin *B2*
6 Enanos *C2*
7 La Luna *C3*
8 La Salida *D2*
9 Las Calas *B1*
10 Mana *C2*
11 Royal Paris &
  Guatemaya
  Intercultural Travel
  Agency *B1*
12 Ut'z Hua *B2*

● **Bars**
13 Casa Verde *B2*
14 El Zaguan &
  Bukana's *A1*
15 La Duende *A1*
16 Las Tacas *A1*
17 La Taberna de
  Don Rodrigo *A2*
18 Salón Tecún *C2*

L-A *Casa Mañen*, 9 Av, 4-11, Zona 1, T765-0786, F765-0678, www.comeseeit.com Reports are consistently good, serve great breakfasts, friendly staff offer a very warm welcome. Room 2 is a great option with a bed on a mezzanine. Some rooms have microwave, all are comfortable, and furnished with attractive wooden accessories. There is a small, pretty courtyard area. **A** *Pensión Bonifaz*, 4 C, 10-50, T765-1111, F763-0671, www.quetzalnet.com/QuetzalNET/bonifaz/default.html Not a *pensión* but a hotel. Has 75 clean, comfortable rooms with TV. Pool (noisy at times) which is occasionally heated. Good restaurant and bar. Parking. **B** *Modelo*, 14 Av "A", 2-31, T761-2529, F763-0216, www.xelapages.com/ Friendly hotel with 20 rooms with TV, some set around a garden patio. Hot showers, restaurant and bargain breakfasts from 0715. Safe parking. Part of the same management is: **C** *Anexo Hotel Modelo*, 14 Av "A", 3-22, T761-2606. 9 rooms with private bath and TV, good value. **B** *Villa Real Plaza*, 4 C, 12-22, T761-4045, F761-6780. Dignified colonial building, 58 carpeted rooms with TV. Restaurant has good vegetarian food, and is good value. No parking.

D *Casa Suiza*, 14 Av "A", 2-36, T763-0242, all rooms with bath. **D** *Hotel Los Olivos*, 13 Av, 3-22, T761-0215, F761-0216. 12 pleasant rooms above a parking area with private bathroom, TV, and a restaurant with cheap breakfasts and meals for around US$4. **D** *Kiktem-Ja*, 13 Av, 7-18, T761-4304, F761-2667. A central location with 16 colonial-style rooms, nicely furnished, locally-made blankets on the beds, wooden floors, all with bath, hot water, open fires, car parking inside gates. Recommended. **D** *Pensión Enríquez*, next to Pasaje Enríquez, T765-2296. 12 rooms with shared bathroom and hot water. It has a local information office and offers shuttles, open daily 0800-2200.

E *Altense*, 9 C, 8-48, T765-4648. 16 rooms with bath, hot water, parking, secure and friendly. However, if your room is on the 9 Av side, you will be woken by rush hour traffic. This is a good town centre deal for single travellers. Recommended. **E-G** *Casa Argentina*, Diagonal 12, 8-37, T761-2470, lemovi@yahoo.com 25 clean rooms, hot water, 10 shared bathrooms, cheaper in18-bed dorm, cooking facilities with purified water, friendly, laundry service. Monthly room rates, US$78. **E** *Casa Iximulew*, 15 Av, 4-59, 1 twin room, and 1 single room (**G**) with or without breakfast (a little extra), hot water at low pressure. Also, 2 fully furnished apartments (**E**) with 2 bedrooms, TV and kitchen facilities, minimum 1 week, US$235 a month, US$70 a week, restaurant next door *El Rincón de los Antojitos* is under the same ownership. **E** *Casa Kaehler*, 13 Av, 3-33, T761-2091. 6 very nice old rooms, clean, hot water all day in private bathrooms, 1 room without bath, some rooms are very cold though. **E** *Hotel Occidental*, 7 C, 12-23, T765-4069. 10 rooms, 1 of the cheapest budget rooms right in the town centre. Lack natural light, but there's hot water and the town's on your doorstep. **E** *Pensión Andina*, 8 Av, 6-07, T761-4012. Private bathrooms, hot water 0630-0900 only, friendly, clean, sunny patio, restaurant, good value, parking. **F** *Pensión Horiani*, 12 Av and corner of 2 C. 6 rooms in this family-run place with shared bathroom and hot water. Unfortunately the friendliest being around here is the the caged parrot.

For apartments see *Casa Iximulew* above and notice boards around town. There is also a house for volunteers in Xela: *Guesthouse Tecún*, 4 C "A", 10-55 A, Zona 4, 3 rooms and 10

Sleeping
All addresses are Zona 1 unless stated

At Easter, 12-18 September and Christmas, rooms need to be booked well in advance

Guatemala

beds and is a very good deal if you're staying to volunteer for a while. For more information contact *Adrenalina Tours*, see Tour operators below.

Eating

All restaurants and cafés are in Zona 1 unless otherwise stated

Mid-range *Restaurante Royal París*, 14 Av "A", 3-06, delicious food (try the fish in a creamy mushroom sauce), excellent choices, including vegetarian. Also cheap options. Run by Stéphane and Emmanuelle. Recommended. Live music from 2000 on Fri. **Cheap** *El Kopetín*, 14 Av, 3-51, friendly, good, meat and seafood dishes, try the fish cooked in garlic. Some mid-range options. *El Rincón de los Antojitos*, 15 Av y 5 C, (French/Guatemalan owned, Thierry y María Roquet), vegetarian and local cuisine, good food, closed Sat and Sun. *Las Calas*, 14 Av "A", 3-21. Breakfasts, salads, soups, paella and pastas served around a court-yard with changing art works hanging from the walls. The food is tasty with delicious bread to accompany, but small portions are served. The breakfast service is far too slow. Adjoining bar. Open Mon-Sat. *Pizza Bambina*, 14 Av, 3-60, Zona 3, good prices, popular with gringos, excellent vegetarian pizza. *Restaurant Cardinali*, 14 Av, 3-25, owned by Benito, a NY Italian, great Italian food, including large pizzas with 31 varieties: two for one on Tue and Thu; tasty pastas of 20 varieties, extensive wine list. Recommended. Also does home delivery in 30 mins, T7610924. *Salón Tecún*, Pasaje Enríquez, off the park at 12 Av y 4 C, bar, local food, breakfasts also, US$2.60-4, TV, always popular with gringos and locals. They are often looking for bar workers. *Ut'z Hua*, Av 12, 3-02, on the corner. This prettily decorated restaurant with purple tablecloths does typical food, which is always very good and filling. Don't miss the *pollo con mole* or fish. Recommended. **Seriously cheap** *El Deli Crepe*, 14 Av, 3-15, good tacos, *almuerzo* US$1.50 with soup, great milkshakes, savoury and sweet crêpes, juicy fajitas that arrive steaming, but the restaurant is a little dirty around the edges though. *Café Taberna Enanos*, 5 C near Av 12 and Parque Central, good cheap breakfast, also has *menú del día*, US$1.75. Open daily, except Sun, 0715-2000. *La Salida*, corner of 10 C and 9 Av. Heavenly vegetarian options including tofu and tempeh concoctions, closed Wed.

Cafés

Blue Angel Café, 7 C, 15-22, great salads, light meals, service a little slow though, movies shown on a monthly rotation, useful noticeboard. *Café Baviera*, 5 C, 13-14, good cheap meals and excellent pies, huge cake portions (try the carrot cake) and coffee in large pre-mises, with walls lined from ceiling to floor with old photos and posters. Good for breakfasts, but these are a little on the expensive side. Popular, but lacks warmth. *Café Berna*, 16 Av, 3-35, Zona 3, good breakfasts, great cappuccino, excellent sandwiches. Cheesecake and other *pasteles* are a little expensive though. *Café El Mana*, 13 Av y 5 C. Delicious coffee, cheap breakfasts, including Western fare, and snacks, in this small locally run corner café. *Café y Chocolate La Luna*, 8 Av, 4-11, delicious hot chocolates with or without added luxu-ries, good cheap snacks, also top chocolates and *pasteles* (the strawberry and cream pie is recommended), pleasant atmosphere in a colonial house decorated with moon symbols, fairy lights, and old photos (and a bed pan in the women's toilet!), good meeting place.

Not a café exactly but deserves a huge mention: *Bakeshop* at 18 Av, 1-40, Zona 3, is a Mennonite bakery that is Xela's answer to *dulce* heaven. They bake a whole range of cookies, muffins, breads, and cakes and sell fresh yoghurt and cheeses. Note, so as not to be disap-pointed, it is only open on Tue and Fri, 0900-1800 and get there early if you can as all the goodies go really fast. Another popular Xela bakery is *Xelapán*, at several locations.

Bars & nightlife

Casa Verde, 12 Av, 1-40, T763-0271, is the place to be on a Thu night when the townsfolk and the gringos flock to shake a bit of salsa leg. There are plenty of partners to go around and the women may even have to turn some of the men down (where and when does this ever happen girls?) just to have a breather. Music, drinking and dancing from 2000 until half past midnight. *Salón Tecún*, Pasaje Enríquez, off the park, 12 Av y 4 C. See eating for more details. *El Zaguan*, 14 Av "A", A-70, across the road from the Teatro Principal, is a disco-bar open 1900-2430, on Wed, Thu, Fri, Sat. US$3.25 on Fri and Sat from 2100, drink included; plays salsa music. *Bukana's*, 14 Av "A", A-80, next to *El Zaguán*, is a *discoteca* playing a mixture of music and a favourite among more wealthy young Guatemalans. Open Thu, Fri, Sat from 2000-2445. US$3.25 on Fri and Sat. *La Duende*, 14 Av "A", 1-40, popular café-bar, open 1800-2330. A favourite among Guatemalans and gringos. Opposite is *Las Tacas*, 14 Av "A",

Guatemala

-49, which plays a mixture of salsa, rock and indie music. Good ambience with nooks and crannies to sit in. Open Mon-Sun 1800-2400. *La Taberna de Don Rodrigo*, 14 Av, C C-47, cosy bar, reasonable food served in dark wood atmosphere, draught beer.

Cinemas *Cadore*, 13 Av and 7 C, next to *Despensa Familiar*. *Alpino*, Plaza Ciani, 24 Av y 4 C, Zona 3. *Cinema Paraíso Café*, 14 Av "A", 1-04, art house, and some in Spanish only, 2 showings daily, 3 at weekends, US$1.30, students US$1.05, café inside. **Dance** *Latin Dance School*, in the *Casa Verde*, (address under Theatre), Mon-Fri 1700-1800 merengue, 1800-1900, salsa, US$3.25 per hr. **Theatre** *Roma*, 14 Av "A", C A-24. *Teatro Municipal*, 14 Av y 1 C, main season May-Nov, theatre, opera etc, tickets about US$7.

Entertainment

It's two for the price of one at the pictures on Wednesday

The main **market** is at Templo de Minerva at the western edge of town (take the local bus, US$0.10); at the southeast corner of **Parque Centro América** is the Centro Comercial Municipal, a shopping centre with craft and textile shops on the upper levels, food, clothes, etc below. There is another market at 2 C y 16 Av, Zona 3, south of Parque Benito Juárez. Every first Sun of the month, there is an *artesanía* market in the central park, with a marimba band. **Bookshops** *Bellas Letras*, 3 C, 12-31 and *Vrisa*, 15 Av, 3-64, T761-3237, has a good range of English language second-hand books. **Supermarkets**: *Mont Blanc* commercial centre, *Paiz*, 4 C between 18-19 Av, Zona 3. *Despensa Familiar*, 13 Av, 6-94.

Shopping

Local Bicycle hire: *Adrenalina Tours*, see above, also from *Vrisa* bookstore. **Bus**: City buses run between 0630 and 1900. Between the town centre and Minerva terminal, bus No 6, *Santa Fe*, US$0.10, 15-30 mins, depending on traffic. Catch the bus at the corner of 4 C and 13 Av by Pasaje Enríquez. Buses to the *Rotonda* leave from the corner of 11 Av and 10 C, US$0.10, or catch bus No 6, 10 or 13, from Av 12 y 3 C as they come down to the park, 15 mins. To catch buses to San Francisco El Alto, Momostenango, the **south coast** and Zunil, get off the local bus at the *Rotonda*, then walk a couple of steps away from the road to step into a feeder road where they all line up. **Car**: *Tabarini Renta Autos*, 9 C, 9-21, Zona 1, T763-0418. **Taxi**: These can be found all over town, notably lined up along Parque Centro América. A journey within town is US$2.60. *Taxis Xelaju*, T761-4456.

Transport

Long distance Buses: To **Guatemala City**, *Galgos*, C Rodolfo Robles, 17-43, Zona 1, T761-2248, 1st class buses, 15 a day from 0300-2015, US$3.90, 4 hrs, will carry bicycles (mixed reports on services to the city); *Marquensita* several a day (office in the capital 21 C, 1-56, Zona 1), leaves from the Minerva Terminal, US$3.90, comfortable, 4 hrs. *Líneas América*, from 7 Av, 3-33, Zona 2, T761-2063, US$3.60, 4 hrs, between 0515-1930, 7 daily. *Transportes Alamo* from 4 C, 14-04, Zona 3, T767-7117, between 0430 and 1430 Mon-Sat, 5 daily, Sun from 0800-1500, 5 buses, US$3.90, 4 hrs. For **Antigua**, change at Chimaltenango (*Galgos*, US$2 to Chimaltenango, *Marquensita*, US$2.90). The following destinations are served by buses leaving from the Minerva Terminal, Zona 3 and the *Rotonda*. To **Almolonga**, via **Cantel**, every 30 mins, US$0.20, 10 mins. (Buses to **Almolonga** and **Zunil** not via Cantel, leave from the corner of 10 Av and 10 C, Zona 1.) To **Chichicastenango** with *Transportes Veloz Quichelense de Hilda Esperanza*, at 0500, 0600, 0930, 1045, 1100, 1300, 1400, 1530, US$1.05, 2½ hrs. To **Cuatro Caminos** US$0.18, 30 mins. To **Huehuetenango** 0545-1515, 12 daily, US$1.05, 2 hrs, and *Transportes Velásquez* to **Huehuetenango**, every 30 mins 0500-1730, US$1.05, 2½ hrs. To **La Mesilla** at 0500, 0600, 0700, 0800, 1300, 1400 with *Transportes Unión Fronteriza*, US$1.60, 4 hrs. To **Los Encuentros**, US$1.30. To **Malacatán**, US$2, 5 hrs. To **Momostenango**, every 30 mins, US$0.52, 1½ hrs. To **Panajachel**, with *Transportes Morales*, at 0500, 0600, 0800, 1100, 1200, 1500, US$1.40, 2½-3 hrs. To **Retalhuleu**, US$0.78, 1½ hrs. To **Salcajá**, every 30 mins, US$0.20, 15 mins. To **San Andrés Xecul** every 2 hrs, US$0.26, 1 hr. To **San Cristóbal Totonicapán**, every 30 mins, US$0.26, 20 mins. To **San Francisco El Alto** every 30 mins, US$0.33. To **San Marcos**, every 30 mins, US$0.78, 1 hr. To **San Martín Sacatepéquez/San Martín Chile Verde**, US$0.40, 1 hr. To **Santiago Atitlán**, with *Ninfa de Atitlán* at 0800, 1100, 1230, 1430, 4½ hrs. To **Tecún Umán** every 30 mins, 0500-1400, US$1.60, 4 hrs. To **Totonicapán**, every 20 mins, US$0.33, 1 hr. To **Zunil**, every 30 mins, US$0.26, 20-30 mins.

Guatemala

Guatemala

Directory

Banks Many banks on Parque Centro América. There is a *Bancared*, 24 hr Visa ATM on the park next t *Banrural*. *Banco Industrial*, corner of 5 C y 11 Av, 24 hr Visa ATM, Visa accepted. *G&T Continental*, 14 A 3-17. You can take out up to US$65 on MasterCard here. For more of an advance against MasterCard go t *Credomatic*, 2nd floor of the Montblanc commercial building, 4 C, between 18-19 Av, Zona 3 (also Visa).

Communications Internet: *Alfa International*, 15 Av, 3-51, international phone calls also. *May Communications*, inside *Bar Salón Tecún*, phone call service. *Comunicaciónes y Más*, 12 Av between and 4 C. **Post office**: 15 Av y 4 C. **Telephone**: *Telgua* 15 Av across from the post office,1st floor. *Ka Shop*, 8 Av, 4-24, Zona 1.

Embassies and consulates *Mexico*, 21 Av, 8-64, Zona 3, T7675542, open Mon-Fri 0800-1100, take photocopies of your passport.

See also the box on page 589

Language schools There are many schools, which offer individual tuition, accommodation with families, extra-curricular activities and excursions. Some also offer Mayan languages. Several schools fund community development projects, and students are invited to participate with voluntary work. Some schools are non-profit making, but some advertise that they are, but are not. Enquire carefully. Extra-curricular activities are generally better organized at the larger schools (despite the factory atmosphere). Prices start from US$100 per week including accommodation, but rise in Jun-Aug to US$120-150. Some schools offer volunteer opportunities but may require a fee to sort out a position for you or may receive monies from the organization in question. If you want to steer clear of these rules it is suggested you contact organizations direct. These are listed below under voluntary work. Many of Xela's schools can be found at www.xelapages. com/schools.htm The following schools have been recommended: *Centro de Estudios de Español Pop Wuj*, 1 C, 17-72, T/F761-8286, www.pop-wuj.org *Desarrollo del Pueblo*, 11 C, Diagonal 2, 2-46, Zona 5, near the Marimba monument, T7650701, desapu@hotmail.com *Guatemalensis*, 19 Av, 2-14, Zona 1, 7651-384, www.infovia.com.gt/gssxela/ *Instituto Central América (ICA)*, 1 C, 16-93, Zona 1, T/F763-1871, www.xelapages.com/ica *INEPAS (Instituto de Estudios Español y Participación en Ayuda Social*, 15 Av, 4-59, T765-1308, F765-2584, www.xelapages.com/iximulew Keen on social projects and has already received a primary school in a Maya village, extremely welcoming. *International Language School English Club*, Diagonal 4, 9-71, Zona 9, T767-3506, www.angelfire.com/country/englishclub/index Harry Danvers is an expert on indigenous culture, worth a visit. You can also learn K'iche' and Mam. *Juan Sisay Spanish School*, 15 Av, 8-38, Zona 1, T/F7651318, juansisay@yahoo.com *Kie-Balam*, Diagonal 12, 4-46, Zona 1, 7761-1636, F761-0391, kie_balam@hotmail.com Offers conversation classes in the afternoon in addition to regular hours. *La Paz*, Diagonal 11, 7-38, T/F761-2159, escuela_lapaz@hotmail.com *Latin Arts*, 10 Av, C-09, T/F761-0424, www.quetzal.net/latin *Minerva Spanish School*, 24 Av, 4-39, Zona 3, F767-4427, www.xelapages.com/minerva *Proyecto Lingüístico Quetzalteco de Español*, 5 C, 2-40, Zona 1, T/F763-1061, plq@c.net.gt *Proyecto Lingüístico 'Santa María'*, 14 Av "A", 1-26, T/F765-1262, www.spanishgua@c.net.gt Volunteer opportunities and free internet access. *Ulew Tinimit*, 7 Av, 3-18, T/F761-6242, www.spanishguatemala.org *Sakribal*, 6 C, 7-08, Zona 1, 7761-2057, www.kcyb.com/sakribal Community projects are available. There is a female director. *Utatlán*, 12 Av, 4-32, Pasaje Enríquez, Zona 1, T763-0446, www.xelapages.com/utatlan Voluntary work opportunities, one of the cheaper schools. Private lessons from Mike Pinot, a Cuban-American, mickeypiekey@hotmail.com

Laundry *Minimax*, 14 Av, C-47, US$2.60. *Lavandería Pronto*, 7 C, 13-25, good service at US$1.56. *Lavandería El Centro*, 15 Av, 3-51, Zona 1, US$2.10, very good service.

Medical services *San Rafael Hospital*, 9 C, 10-41, T761-2956. *Hospital Rodolfo Robles*, a private hospital on Diagonal 11, Zona 1, T761-4229. *Hospital Privado Quetzaltenango*, C Rodolfo Robles, 23-51, Zona 1, T761-4381.

When taking a tour up any of the volcanoes make sure your guides stay with you all the time: it can get dangerous when the cloud rolls down

Tour operators *Adrenalina Tours*, inside Pasaje Enríquez, T308-9139, M503-3095, www.adrenalinatours.xelalinea.com Numerous tours are on offer including bike and volcano tours. *Guatemaya Intercultural Travel Agency*, 14 Av "A", 3-06, T/F765-0040, www.xelapages.com/ guatemaya, very helpful. *Agencia de Viajes SAB*, 1 C, 12-35, T761-6402, F761-8878, good for cheap flights. *Guatemalan Birding Resource Center*, 7 C, 15-18, T767-7339, www.xelapages.com/gbrc open 1430-1800. Bird- watching and eco-tours. Jason Berry and his wife Anrea Pinto will also take trips further afield to Tikal and Cerro San Gil, near the Río Dulce. Recommended. *Mountain Tours*, Diagonal 13, 15-53, T761-5993, www.xelapages.com/mountaintours/mountain.htm and ask about volunteering. Numerous tours are on offer. There is also a shuttle service. *Quetzaltrekkers*, based inside *Casa Argentina* at Diagonal

2, 8-37, T761-5865. This recommended, established, non-profit agency is known for its 3-day hike Sat am-Mon pm) from Xela across to Lake Atitlán, US$60. Proceeds go to the *Escuela de la Calle School* or kids at risk, and a dorm for homeless children. See www.beef.brownrice.com/ streetschool/hikers.htm Hiking volunteers are also needed for a 3-month minimum period: hiking experience and reasonable Spanish required. *Thierry Roquet* at *INEPAS*, 15 Av, 4-59, www.mayaexplor.com Arranges all sorts of trips. He can also arrange longer tours with advance notice and arrange treks in various parts of the country, eg, from Nebaj to Todos Santos. Recommended. *Xela Sin Limites*, 12 Av, C C-35, T/F761-6043, www.trafficman.com/xelapages/ xelasinlimites/

Useful addresses Insurance: *G&T Continental* offers motoring insurance. **Mechanic**: *José Ramiro Muñoz R*, 1 C, 19-11, Zona 1, T761-8204. Also *Goodyear Taller* at the *Rotonda* and for motorbikes *Moto Servicio Rudy*, 2 Av, 3-48, Zona 1, T765-5433.

Police: T761-5805
Fire: T761-2002
Red Cross: T761-2746

Voluntary work *Associación Hogar Nuevos Horizontes*, nhcoordinadoras@ hotmail.com or Aida T761-6122. *Entre mundos*, www.entremundos.org puts people in touch with opportunities. *Hogar de Ninos*, Llanos de Urbina, Cantel, T761-1526, hogardeninos@altavista.com

Around Quetzaltenango

Sout east of Xela is Cantel which has the largest and oldest textile factory in the country. Sunday is market day and the town's **fiesta** is 12-18 August (main day 15). At Easter a passion play is performed. A little further on, on the outskirts of town, on the right hand side (one minute on the bus), is the white **Copavic glass factory** where you can watch and photograph the workers blow the recycled glass. ■ *Mon-Fri 0500-1300, Sat 0500-1200, 15 mins by bus (11 km), and US$0.13 from Xela on the way to Zunil, but you need to take the bus marked for Cantel Fábrica and Zunil, not Almolonga and Zunil.*

Cantel
In the surrounding fields, apples and pears are grown

Pinned in by a very steep sided valley is the town of Zunil, 9 km from Quetzaltenango. It is visited for the nearby hot thermal baths that many come to wallow in, and for its worship of its well-dressed idol San Simón (Maximón). The **market** is held on Mondays. The town's **fiesta** is 22-26 November (main day 25) and there is a very colourful Holy Week. The **church** is striking both inside and out. It has a large decorated altarpiece and a small shrine to murdered Bishop Gerardi at the altar. The façade is white with serpentine columns wrapped in carved ivy and decorated with dangling large coloured bulbs.

Zunil

San Simón (Maximón) is worshipped in the town and is often dressed in different clothes at different times. For example he might be wearing ski wear: hat, scarf, gloves and sunglasses or a black suit and wide-brimmed hat, complete with cigar. He is moved from time to time to different houses. Here, at Zunil, he has firewater poured down his throat causing him to 'pee' into a basin below! Enquire locally for the present location. A small charge is usually made for the upkeep. To the left of the church is the *Santa Ana Co-operative* which sells beautiful *huipiles*, shirt and skirt materials, as well as bags and bookmarks. ■ *Getting there: bus to Xela via Almolonga leaves from the bridge. Walk down the left-hand side of the church to the bottom of the hill, take a left and you'll see the buses the other side of the bridge, US$0.20.*

The nearby extinct Volcán Pico Zunil, rises to 3,542 m to the southeast of the town. On its slopes are the **thermal baths of Fuentes Georginas**, which you'll know you're approaching by the wafts of sulphurous fumes that come your way. There are several different-sized pools set into the mountainside surrounded by thick luscious vegetation and enveloped in the steam that continuously rises up in wafts from the hot pools. There are spectacular views on the way to the baths. ■ *Mon-Sat 0800-1700, Sun 0800-1600, US$1.30, children US$0.65. Reached either by walking the 8 km uphill just to the south of Zunil, 2 hrs (300 m ascent; take the right fork after 4 km, but be careful as robbery has occurred here), by pick-up truck in 15 mins (US$9.10 return with a 1 hr wait), or hitch a ride. If you come by bus to Zunil and are walking to*

Guatemala

the Fuentes, don't go down into town with the bus, but get off on the main road at the Pepsi stand and walk to the entrance road, which is visible 100 m away on the left.

Sleeping and eating: **D** *Turicentro Fuentes Georginas*, 6 cold bungalows with 2 double beds and 2 bungalows with 3 single beds. They have cold showers, fireplaces with wood, electricity from 1700-2200 and barbecue grills for guests' use near the baths. Guests can use the baths after public closing times. Reasonably priced restaurant with breakfasts at US$1.60, snacks and drinks (open 0800-1800).

Just beyond Zunil on the left-hand side of the road heading to the coast (Km 210) is *Las Cumbres Eco Saunas y Gastronomía*. This is just the place for some R&R with saunas emitting natural steam from the geothermal activity nearby. There are 12 rooms, with sauna, **C**, without sauna, **D**. There are separate saunas (US$3.25) and jacuzzis for day visitors, and a restaurant serving wholesome regional food and natural juices. Highly recommended. Open 0700-1800. T210-3062.

The thermal baths of **Aguas Amargas** are on Zunil Mountain below Fuentes Georginas. They are reached by following the road south and heading east (left) by Estancia de La Cruz. This road passes fields of flowers and would make a great trip on a bike. ■ *0715-1700, US$1.30, children, US$0.26.*

The road descends through Santa María de Jesús to bypass **San Felipe**, at 760 m, 35 km from Zunil, where you can buy tropical jungle fruits. The pass from the Highlands to the tropical lowlands is amazing. You'll immediately notice the change in temperature and the appearance of fruits like bananas, coconuts and pineapples. Some 3 km beyond is **San Martín**, with a branch road to Mazatenango.

El Viejo Palmar This is Guatemala's Pompeii. The river that cuts through here flows directly down from the active Santiaguito volcanic cone following a series of serious lahars (mudflows of water and volcanic material) that took place in the 1990s. The small town of 10,000 was evacuated leaving an extraordinary legacy. In August 1998, the whole south end of the ghost town was destroyed by a massive lahar which crushed the church. This also shifted the course of the Río Nimá I which began to flow directly through the centre of the church remains. Very heavy erosion since leaves the west front and the altar separated by a 30-m deep ravine – an unbelievable site.

You can still see the school building in one of the streets of El Palmar Viejo. Everywhere is now overgrown, with homes looking more like greenhouses. The town is some 4 km from the road; follow the paved road to its natural end. The beginning of the urban zone is marked by a pale green building on the right. Walk further in as far as you can and then bear to the right and you will see the **ravine**. Be very careful when at the edge of the ravine, as some areas have been undercut by the river. To cross the ravine on an Indiana Jones-type wooden bridge, with a scary view of the gorge below, return to the green abandoned building and turn right until you reach the gorge. ■ *Just before San Felipe, and just before the Puente Samalá III, if you're heading south, is the turn to the right for El Viejo Palmar. Getting there: take any bus heading to the south coast, and asked to be dropped off at the entrance and walk. Or, take a pick up from San Felipe park. Ask for Beto or Brígido. A taxi from Xela round trip is US$20.*

Volcán Santa María & Santiaguito
Do not attempt to climb Santiaguito – it is considered one of the most dangerous volcanoes in the world

Santiaguito's mother is Santa María (3,772 m). To reach the volcano take the bus to Llano del Pinal, 7 km away, from the Minerva Terminal (every 30 minutes, last bus back 1800). Get off at the crossroads and follow the dirt road towards the right side of the volcano until it sweeps up the right (about 40 minutes) where you should take the footpath to the left (where it is marked for some distance); bear right at the saddle where another path comes in from the left, but look carefully as it is easily missed. A rough 5½-hour climb (1,500 m). You can see Santiaguito (2,488 m) below, erupting mostly with ash blasts and sometimes lava flows – an incredible sight. It is possible to camp at the summit, or on the saddle west of the summit, but it is cold and windy, but worth it because dawn provides views of the entire country's volcanic chain and an almighty shadow is cast across the area by Santa Maria's form. **Santiaguito** is a fairly new volcano that formed after the eruption of Santa María out of its crater. It erupts continuously on a daily basis throwing up ash. To see it erupting you need to climb Santa María where you will look down on this smaller volcano.

It takes half an hour to reach **San Juan Ostuncalco** (15 km away). It's a pleasant, prosperous town with a big white church noted for its good weekly market on Sunday and beautiful sashes worn by men. Its **fiesta**, *Virgen de la Candelaria*, is held on 29 January-2 February. The road, which is paved, switchbacks 37 km down valleys and over pine-clad mountains to a plateau looking over the valley in which are San Pedro and San Marcos. San Marcos has a few places to stay and eat. It is a transport hub with little to see. **San Pedro Sacatepéquez** has a huge market on Thursday. The Maya women wear golden-purple skirts.

To Mexico

This extinct volcano, at 4,220 m, is the highest in Central America. The volcano can be reached by getting to the village of San Sebastián from San Marcos. There are buses from San Marcos that take about two hours. It's about a five-hour climb and a three-hour descent. Once you have reached the ridge on Tajumulco, turn right along the top of it; there are two peaks, the higher is on the right. The peak on the left (4,100 m) is used for **shamanistic rituals**.

Volcán Tajumulco
Start very early in the day if you plan to return to San Marcos by nightfall

Dormant Tacaná (4,093 m) on the Mexican border may be climbed from the village of Sibinal. It is the second highest volcano in Guatemala with a 400-m wide crater and fumaroles on its flanks. Take a bus to Sibinal from San Marcos. It is a six-hour difficult climb to the summit and it's recommended that you ask for a guide in the village.

About 15 km west of San Marcos the road begins its descent from 2,500 m to the lowlands. In 53 km to **Malacatán** it drops to 366 m. It is a winding ride with continuous bends, but the scenery is attractive. There is accommodation.

Volcán Tacaná
Its last eruption was 1949, but there was activity in 2001, so check before climbing

El Carmen – Talismán The international bridge over the Río Suchiate at Talismán into Mexico is 18 km west of Malacatán. The last staging post in Guatemala is El Carmen. Beyond the bridge the road goes on to Tapachula. Guatemalan immigration, open 24 hrs. It is a 200-m walk between the 2 border posts. If entering by car, especially a rented car, be prepared for red tape, miscellaneous charges, vehicle fumigation and frustration.
Sleeping B-C *Hospedaje El Paso*, T776-9474, 13 rooms with bath, TV, a/c, cheaper without. There is a *hospedaje* at the border, but better accommodation nearby (see above) or in Mexico. **Transport** For long distance travel see Transport, Guatemala City. Travelling by bus to Mexico is quicker from Quetzaltenango (Xela) than from San Marcos. Most traffic seems to go via Coatepeque and not via San Marcos. However, from Quetzaltenango, there are frequent buses to **Talismán** via San Marcos or Coatepeque; buses from Xela marked 'Talismán' usually involve a change in Malacatán, 40 mins from the border. From **San Pedro Sacatepéquez**, there are frequent local buses from 0430 to 1630 to Malacatán, from where *colectivos*, often crowded, will get you to the border. Or, take a bus from Quetzaltenango to **Retalhuleu**, 1½ hrs, US$0.78, and then another to the border, 2 hrs, US$1.85. This border is not used much by heavy transport. Hitchhikers will find Tecún Umán better.

Border with Mexico

The road to the coastal plain from San Juan Ostuncalco (see page 637) is the most attractive of all the routes down from the highlands, bypassing most of the small towns through quickly changing scenery as you lose height. After San Juan, go south for 1½ km to **Concepción Chiquirichapa**, with a bright blue and yellow church, which is one of the wealthiest villages in the country. It has a small market early every Thursday morning and a **fiesta** 5-9 December. About 6 km beyond is **San Martín Sacatepéquez**, which used to be known as San Martín Chile Verde, and is famous for its hot chillies. This village appears in Miguel Angel Asturias' *Mulata de Tal*. It stands in a windy, cold gash in the mountains. The slopes are superbly steep and farmed, giving fantastic vistas on the climb up and down from Laguna Chicabal (see

Guatemala

below). The men wear very striking clothing of a long red and white striped tunic, beautifully embroidered around its hem. Market day is Sunday. **Fiesta:** 7-12 November (main day November 11).

Laguna Chicabal

The Maya believe the waters are sacred and it is thought that if you swim in the lake you will become ill

San Martín is where the two-hour climb to Laguna Chicabal, at 2,712 m, starts. This is a jelly-green lake in the crater of the extinct volcano (2,900 m) of the same name, with wild white lilies, known as *cartucho*, growing at the edges. The highlight of a trip here is the sight of the clouds tumbling down over the circle of trees that surround the lake, that then appear to bounce on the surface before dispersing. Ceremonies of Maya initiation are held at the lake in early May, known as *Jueves de la Ascensión*, on rotating annual dates. The walk from San Martín takes about two hours. Take the path that is signposted from the main road, on the left-hand side, if approaching from Xela. You climb before descending to a second closer entrance before climbing again and descending to the lake. It's possible to camp at the lake and walk around it. Start early as soon after, the mist rolls down, and the whole area is covered in cloud and views are lost. ■ *0700-1800, US$1.30. Getting there: the last bus to Quetzaltenango leaves at 1900, 1 hr. Parking at the entrance, US$1.30. It is a 40 -min walk from the car park (and you'll need a sturdy vehicle if you attempt the steep first ascent in a car).*

Guatemala City

Southern Guatemala

The southern coastal plain of Guatemala supports many plantations, of coffee, sugar and tropical fruit trees and its climate is unbearably hot and humid. Amid the fincas some of the most curious archaeological finds have been unearthed, a mixture of monument styles such as Maya and Olmec, including Abaj Takalik, the cane field stones at Santa Lucía Cotzumalguapa and the big 'Buddhas' of Monte Alto. On the coast are the black-sand beaches and nature reserves of the popular and laid-back Monterrico and Sipacate resorts, where nesting turtles burrow in the sand and masses of birds take to the skies around. Casting a shadow over the coast, the Central Highland volcanoes of Lake Atitlán, and the Antigua trio of Fuego, Acatenango and Agua, look spectacular, looming on the horizon above the lowlands.

Guatemala City to the Pacific Coast

The main road from the capital heads to Escuintla, which connects Guatemala City with all the Pacific ports. There is also a direct route to Escuintla from Antigua. South of Guatemala City is **Amatitlán** on the banks of the lake of the same name. The lake is seriously polluted. The main reason for coming here would be for the *Day of the Cross* on 3 May when the Christ figure is removed from the church and floated out of a boat amid candles and decorations. ■ *Getting there: buses from Guatemala City (every 30 mins, US$0.26) from 0700-1900 from 20 C and 2 Av, Zona 1.*

Palín has a Sunday market in a plaza under an enormous ceiba tree. The textiles are exceptional, but are increasingly difficult to find. Palín has great views of Pacaya to the east as you head down to the coast, Agua Volcano to the northwest, and the Pacific lowlands to the west. An unpaved road runs northwest from here to Antigua via **Santa María de Jesús** (see page 592). **Fiesta:** 24-30 July. There are *hospedajes* (**F**).

Escuintla

Colour map 5, grid C2

Escuintla is a large, unattractive provincial centre in a rich tropical valley. Already Grottsville, in June 2001 it gained notoriety for being the place from which 78 dangerous prisoners escaped from its high-security prison known as *El Infierno* ('Hell').

The bus terminal is the most interesting thing for travellers. Buses leave from the Zona 4 terminal in **Guatemala City** for Escuintla (1½ hrs), and return to the capital from the 8 C and 2

Av, Zona 1, near the corner of the plaza in Escuintla. (See below for getting to this spot.) However, buses that have come along the Pacific Highway and are going on to the capital pull up at the main bus terminal on 4 Av. From the busy terminal there are buses direct to **Antigua** at 0700, 1200, 1300, 1500, 1630, 1800 1½ hrs, US$0.65. See page 589. To **Taxisco** every 30 mins, 0700-1700, 40 mins, US$1.05 for **La Avellana**, for boats to **Monterrico**. There are frequent buses to **Iztapa** with the last bus departing at 2030. If you are changing in Escuintla for **Santa Lucía Cotzumalguapa** to the west, you need to take a left out of the bus terminal along the 4th Av up a slight incline towards the police fortress and take a left here on its corner, the 9 C, through the market. Head for 3 blocks straight, passing *the Cinammon Pastelería y Panadería* on the right at 9 C and 2 Av. At the end here are buses heading to Santa Lucía and further west along the Pacific Highway. It is a 5-10-min walk. Buses leave here every 5 mins. To Santa Lucía Cotzumalguapa (the bus *ayudantes* shout 'Santa'), 35 mins, US$0.45. On the return, buses pull up at the corner of the 8 C and 2 Av, where the Guatemala City buses also pass. If heading for Antigua you can wait here for the buses that pass by or walk to the bus terminal, which you will need to do for other southern destinations. To get to the bus terminal from here, take a right down the 8 C, passing the waiting capital-bound buses. When you hit the church take a right, then take a first left down 9 C at the edge of the plaza and through the market. At the corner of the police station on 9 C and 4 Av, take a right down the hill for a couple of mins until you see a sea of buses emerging from the terminal.

To the Mexican borders

The Pacific Highway goes west from Escuintla to the Mexican border at **Ciudad Tecún Umán**, see page 645, some 200 km away, passing Siquinalá, where there is a brand new bypass that emerges the other side of Santa Lucía Cotzumalguapa (buses run through the centre of these places), and on to Mazatenango (see page 644) and Retalhuleu (see page 644). To the east the highway heads to Taxisco for the El Salvador border at **Cuidad Pedro de Alvarado**, see page 646.

Puerto San José
52 km beyond Escuintla

South of Escuintla the fast tarmacked highway heads to Puerto San José. Puerto San José used to be the country's second-largest port and first opened for business (especially the coffee trade) in 1853. The climate is hot, the streets and most of the beaches dirty, and at weekends the town fills up with people from the capital. Fishing is available (see under Iztapa below), and there are swimming beaches near by, but beware of the strong undercurrent. A newer harbour, **Puerto Quetzal**, taking all shipping alongside is 3 km to the east.

Sleeping   **AL-A** *Hotel y Turicentro Eden Pacific*, Barrio El Laberinto, T881-1605, with 17 a/c rooms with TV, private beach and pools. **B** *Club Vacacional Agua Azul*, Km 106.5, T/F881-3445, 32 rooms, with TV, a/c and a choice pools, reasonable food. **D** *Hospedaje María Piedad*, Cjón 6, Barrio Miramar, T881-2965, 10 rooms. **D** *Papillon*, Barrio Miramar, T881-1064, on the beach, bar, restaurant and pool. ■ *Regular buses from the capital passing through Escuintla, 2 hrs, US$1.30. From Puerto San José to Iztapa US$0.13.*

Some 5 km to the west of Puerto San José is **Chulamar**, a popular beach at weekends with good bathing. It is lifeless during the week with nowhere but expensive resorts to stay. **Sleeping LL-L** *Villas del Pacífico*, T362-6030, www.omegaresorts.com The usual luxuries available. A day pass costs US$40 per person, but the food is reported to be extremely bad value. **B** *Santa María del Mar*, T881-1287, pools, restaurant, and a private beach with changing facilities.

Iztapa is world renowned for deep-sea fishing, so much so that Guatemala's sailfish sport fishing was ranked as the best in the world in 1995. Sail fish, bill fish, marlin, tuna, dorado, roosterfish, yellowfin, and snapper are to be found in large numbers. See Tour operators for further details. The Chiquimulilla Canal runs either side of Puerto San José parallel to the coast, for close to 100 km. From here a trip can be taken through the canal by *lancha* to the old Spanish port of Iztapa, now a bathing resort a short distance to the east. If you are heading further east by road along the coast to Monterrico, you need to cross the canal to Pueblo Viejo by ferry,

Guatemala

five minutes (US$2.20 per car and US$0.40 per foot passenger from 0600 to 2045 daily). There are regular buses between Iztapa and Escuintla.

Sleeping and eating C *Hotel Club Sol y Playa Tropical*, 1 C, 5-48, T881-4365, is on the canal, with pool, friendly staff, and standard rooms with fans. Good food at restaurant. There are a number of *comedores* in town. **Tour operators** *Artmarina*, www.artmarina.com One of the biggest fishing tour concerns at Iztapa also runs the *Fins 'n Feathers Inn* fishing lodge. Also check out www.sailfish.guatemala.com www.fishinginternational.com/location/guatemala.htm, and www.tropicalfishing.com/guatemala.html Most organizations have HQ in the US.

Monterrico

Colour map 5, grid C2

Monterrico is a small black-sand resort where the sunsets are a rich orange and the waves crash spectacularly on to the shore. If you are in the area between September and January you can sponsor a baby turtle's waddle to freedom by taking part in a competition. The baby turtles are lined up just before sunset for a race to the sea.

Getting around

Female travellers should take care even in front of all the hotels on the beach after dark

The landing stage is 10 mins' walk from the ocean front, where you'll find the main restaurants and places to stay. When you step off the dock take the first left, and keep left, which heads directly to the main cluster of beach hotels. This road is known as Calle del Proyecto or Calle del Muelle. Walking straight on from the dock takes you to the main drag in town. When you get to the main drag and want to walk to the main group of hotels, take a left along the beach or take the sandy path to the left one block back from the beach where the sand is a tiny bit easier to walk on.

Monterrico's popularity is growing fast but mainly as a weekend and holiday resort with views that are undisturbed by high-rise blocks. All the hotels, mostly rustic and laid-back, are lined up along the beach, and there are a few shops and *comedores*, not linked to hotels, in the village of just 1,500 people. Do not underestimate the ocean – people have died here. The sand is blisteringly hot and there is no shade on the beach. Take insect repellent for dusk. The village is surrounded by canals carpeted in aquatic plants and mangrove swamps with bird and turtle reserves in their midst. These areas make up the **Monterrico Nature Reserve**. Anteater, armadillo, racoon and weasel live in the area. It is well worth taking a boat trip at sunrise or sunset, to see migratory North and South American birds, including flamingo. However, the real stars in this patch are the olive ridelys – Parlama Blanca and Parlama Negra turtles, which lay eggs between July and October, and the Baule turtle, which lays between between October to February. There is a **turtle hatchery**. Just behind the hatchery, there are 300 breeding crocodiles, 150 turtles and iguanas. ■ *Daily 0800-1230, 1400-1700, free.* The turtle liberation event takes place every Saturday during the aforementioned period at 1700. **Fishing** along the coast will also provide rich pickings including tuna, dolphin fish, roosterfish and mackerel. Those preferring to stay on land can rent horses for a jaunt on the beach. Lancha and turtle-searching tours are operated by a couple of agencies in town. See below under Tour operators.

Sleeping

There are no land line telephones, so all numbers shown are mobiles or are in Guatemala City

Most hotels are fully booked by Sat midday. If you know you are arriving at a weekend it is worth booking beforehand. There is little pleasure in walking with your rucksack from hotel to hotel in the boiling sand and blistering heat looking for a place to sleep! **B** *San Gregorio*, behind *El Kaiman* on Calle del Proyecto, T/F238-4690, has 22 modern rooms with bath, fan and mosquito nets. There is a large part-shaded pool, a restaurant set around the pool. Non-guests can use the pool for US$3.90 per person. **B-C** *Hotel Pez de Oro*, T204-5249, T368-3684, at the end of the main strip to the east with 11 spacious bungalows attractively set around a swimming pool. All rooms have private bathroom, mosquito lamps, pretty bedside lights and fan. Rooms are **B** at weekends. The hotel has the popular and consistently good *Restaurant Italiano*, where the delicious fish is a better option than shrimps. **C** *Eco Beach Place*, 250 m west of the main drag, T611-6637. Facing the ocean, take a right off Calle principal down the path opposite *Las Margaritas*, 1 street back from the beach. This cosy place has clean and spacious rooms with bath, mosquito nets and fans. There is a pool, and restaurant. Breakfast included in the room price. There is a discount on stays of 3 nights or more. **D** *El Delfín*, T202-0267 (Guatemala City T591-1970), ELDELFIN99@yahoo.com Bungalows, with mosquito nets, fans and private bathroom and rooms. Surfboards for hire at US$2 per hr. Although the hotel is on the beach, most people hang out in the courtyard and by the pool at the back. Non-guests can use the pool for US$3.25. **D** *El Mangle*, T611-5547 (Guatemala City T369-7631) rooms with fans and mosquito nets (some are a little dark), centred around a nice clean pool, set a little back from the beach front. It's quieter than some of the others and recommended. **D** *Hotel El Baule Beach*, T478-3088, with 20 rooms that are nearly clean, with bath, and mosquito nets, but no fans. There are 2 pools and restaurant. **D** *Hotel Restaurante Dulce y Salado*, T817-9046, is some way away from the main cluster of hotels and a 500 m hard walk east through sand if you are on foot. The compensations are the sea view and the fantastic uninterrupted view of the Highland volcanoes behind. Run by a friendly Italian couple, Fulvio and Graziella, the hotel has 8 clean and nice rooms, with bath, fans and mosquito nets, set around a pool. Breakfast included. **D** *Hotel y Restaurant Kaiman*, T703-4284, (Guatemala City T334-6214), big bar on the beach side (1000 'til you're done at the weekends, and from 1500 in the week) with a pool table, restaurant, serving such delights as squid in its own ink. The rooms are very clean, with bath, fan, and mosquito nets. There are 2 pools for adults and children, but they are not in top shape. Prices rise at weekends. Discounts are available for longer stays. Shuttle tickets to Antigua are sold here – US$10-15 per person. **D-E** *Johnny's Place*, T206-4702, johnnys@backpackamericas.com is run by a super-friendly US and Kiwi couple, Sid Eschenbach and Jan Clarke. There are 7 equipped bungalows, rooms with bath, cheaper without, and a dorm, **F** per person. All windows have mosquito netting. Prices rise at weekends and discounts are possible during the week. Internet, table tennis; swimming pools and a restaurant with free coffee fill-ups, and barbecues at weekends. Fishing can be arranged for US$64 for 2. Recommended. **D-F** *La Sirena*, T307-5531, is very popular with Guatemalans. Its rooms vary in price: some have private bathroom, others are very basic, with shared bathroom. All have fans. Also equipped bungalows for a bargain price (**F** per person); 3 pools, restaurant and bar, cheap breakfasts.

Eating

Be careful especially with ceviche: bad stomachs are not unknown.

Neptuno, alongside the *San Gregorio* hotel, has very good food and service. Closed Tue. If you find the *Neptune* closed, food is served in *La Jaula*, next door. *La Jaula*, as its name would suggest, is a funky giant cage-cum-bar open from 1800 onwards. Apart from the drinks there's a food and a book exchange and it's mosquito-free. Closed Mon. *El Animal Desconocido* is another newish bar in town. It's right on the beach next to *El Delfín* and open until the early hours. It's possible that by the time you read this there will be a branch of Antigua's *Mono Loco* bar and restaurant on the beach. There are lots of local *comedores* along Calle Principal, which leads to the beach.

Transport

The **first route** to Monterrico involves heading direct to the Pacific coast by taking a bus from the capital to Puerto San José, 1 hr, and changing for a bus to Iztapa. Or take a direct bus from Escuintla to Iztapa. Then cross the inlet by ferry to Pueblo Viejo for US$2.20 per car, and US$0.40 per foot passenger, from 0600 to 2045 daily, 5 mins. Then take a bus to Monterrico, about 25 km east, 1 hr, US$0.65. Buses run to and from Pueblo Viejo between 0600-1500, from the corner of main street and the road to Pueblo Viejo to the left, 3 blocks north of the beach, just past the Catholic church on the right. The **second route** involves getting to Taxisco first and then La Avellana. Antigua to Escuintla by bus is 1-1½ hrs, US$0.65. From there, there are regular departures to Taxisco, 40 mins, US$1.05. From Taxisco to La Avellana, buses leave hourly until 1800, US$0.40, 45 mins. Direct *Cubanita* buses from Guatemala City, Zona 4 terminal, to La Avellana via Taxisco at 1030, 1230 and 1420, 3 hrs, US$3. At La Avellana take the motor boats through mangrove swamps, 20 mins, US$0.26 for foot passengers, cars US$6.50, from 0630 and then hourly until 1800. The journey via this route from Antigua to Monterrico uses 3 public buses and the boat, and takes about 3¼ hrs if your connections are good. Return boats to La Avellana leave at 0330, 0530, 0700, 0800, 0900, 1030, 1200, 1300, 1430, 1600. Buses leave La Avellana for Taxisco hourly until 1800, US$0.40. Buses pull up near the *Banco Nor-Oriente* where numerous buses heading to Guatemala and Escuintla pass.

Guatemala

Alternatively, numerous travel agencies in Antigua run **shuttles**, US$10-12 one way. You can book just a return shuttle journey for about US$12 in Monterrico by going to the *Don Quijote* office at the *ALM School* (see below) on the road that leads to the dock, Calle de Proyecto, in Antigua T832-7513, donquijotetravel@yahoo.com Also see *El Kaimán* above which sells shuttle tickets. The shuttles mainly go via Iztapa and it takes 2 hrs from Antigua

Directory **Communications** Post office: near *Hotel Las Margaritas* on the Calle Principal. **Language school** *ALM, Academia Lingüística Mayense*, 7days homestay with classes is US$85, T815-0999, www.inch.com/~quake/alm **Tour operators** *El Arco de Noé* is run by the friendly Noé Orantes, an INGUAT-registered guide, T703-3781. His blue-painted house is just a couple of mins up from the dock on the way to the beach on Calle del Proyecto. He runs tours along the canals at 0600 and 1800 daily for US$5 per person. *Iguana Tours*, 1 block from the dock on Calle Principal, T/F885-0688, and with a rep at the sanctuary, runs a number of trips. Office hours are 0800-1900 daily.

West of Escuintla at Siquinalá (see below) is a turn-off south to **La Democracia** (10 km), where big fat sculptures found on the nearby Monte Alto and Costa Brava *fincas*, are displayed in the main plaza. These stones, carved from basaltic boulders, are believed to date from 400 BC or earlier and show clear Olmec influence. Many of them are vast, their figures like Buddhas, revealing oriental eyes or fat eyelids, flattened noses and flat foreheads. There is an associated museum on the plaza. ■ *Mon-Sun 0800-1200, 1400-1600, US$1.30. It takes 20 mins to reach the town from Santa Lucía Cotzumalguapa. From Escuintla takes 25 mins, US$0.52.*

From La Democracia the road heads to the coast for 40 km to **Sipacate** where the Chiquimulilla Canal runs along much of this coast separating the mainland from the narrow black-sand beach. To get to the beach here, take a canoe across the canal. You can enjoy good swimming in the ocean, provided there are calm conditions (the dangers of bathing along this coast must not be underestimated). There is a good beach east towards Puerto San José as far as Buena Vista in the bird and turtle sanctuary of Sipacate-Naranjo National Park. There are a couple of cheap and basic *hospedajes* in Sipacate. ■ *Getting there: there is a half-hourly bus service through La Democracia from the Zona 4 bus terminal, Guatemala City. Buses also serve this route between the coast and Siquinalá.* The main Pacific Highway continues 8 km west from Siquinalá to Santa Lucía Cotzumalguapa, where you will pass strange stelae-shaped hills in to your right-hand side, used for Maya ceremonies.

Santa Lucía Cotzumalguapa Amid the sugar-cane fields and fincas of this Pacific town lie an extraordinary range of carved stones and images with influences from pre-Maya civilizations, believed mostly to be ancient Mexican cultures, including the Izapa civilization from the Pacific coast area of Mexico near the Guatemalan border. The town is just north of the Pacific Highway where some of the hotels and banks are.

Population: 60,000

See the next page for further details

Ins and outs You can visit all the sites on foot. However, you are advised not to go wandering in and out of the cane fields at the Bilbao site as there have been numerous assaults in recent months. You can walk along the tarmacked road north to the El Baúl sites (6 km and 8 km respectively from town), but there is no shade, so take lots of water. Ask for directions. There is an occasional bus saying *Río Santiago*, which goes as far as Colonia Maya, close to where the El Baúl hilltop is. Only workers' buses go to *Finca El Baúl* in the morning, returning at night. To get to the museum, head west along the Pacific Highway and take a left turn into the *finca* site. Alternatively, take a taxi from town (next to the plaza) and negotiate a trip to all four areas. They will charge around US$16-19. Do not believe any taxi driver who tells you that *Las Piedras* (the stones) have been moved from the cane fields to the museum because of the increasing number of assaults. This is not true.

There is considerable confusion about who carved the range of monuments and stelae scattered around the town. However, it is safe to say that the style of the monuments found in the last 150 years is a blend of a number of pre-Columbian styles. Some say, that the prominent influence is Toltec, the ancestors of the Maya K'iche', Kaqchikel, Tz'utujil and Pipiles. It is thought the Tolteca-Pipil had been influenced in turn by the Classic culture from Teotihuacán, a massive urban state northeast of the present Mexico City, which had its zenith in the seventh century AD. However, some experts say that there is no concrete evidence to suggest that the Pipiles migrated as early as AD 400 or that they were influenced by Teotihuacán. All in all, the cultural make-up of this corner of Guatemala may never be known.

Four main points of interest entice visitors to the area. **Bilbao**: first re-discovered in 1860, with a couple of monumental carved stone boulders hidden deep in the sugar cane. **El Baúl**, a ceremonial centre, with two carved stone pieces. **Finca El Baúl** with a collection of sculptures and stelae gathered from the large area of the *finca* grounds. The **Museo Cultura Cotzumalguapa** at *Finca Las Ilusiones* displays numerous artefacts collected from the *finca* and a copy of the famous Bilbao Monument 21 from the cane fields. It is less than 1 km east of town.

The remnants of **Bilbao** are mainly buried beneath the sugar cane but monuments found above ground show pre-Maya influences. It is thought that the city was inhabited between 1200 BC-AD 800. There are four large boulders – known locally as 'Las Piedras' – in sugar-cane fields, which can be reached on foot from the tracks leading from the end of 4th Avenida in town. **El Baúl** is a Late Classic site 6 km north of Santa Lucía. Most of its monuments were built between AD 600-900. To reach the site, go along 3 Avenida to the end and into the countryside north of the town where you will cross the Río Santiago by bridge. Shortly after this, the road forks. Bear to the right (marked to Los Tarros sugar refinery), along another tarmacked road with the village of Colonia Maya on your right. After 1 km, beyond the extent of the village, you will come to a small crossroads where to your left and right there are well-defined cane-field tracks. Take the track to the right. This is marked on the main tarmacked road by a half-metre white stone block with orange metal tubing poking out of the top. The left fork on the main road heading out of town leads to the **Finca El Baúl** refinery. Here numerous stones have been found and collected together. The centrepiece of the stone collection is a well-preserved jaguar sitting up on its haunches. **Museo Cultura Cotzumalguapa** on the *Finca Las Ilusiones* estate displays stelae, a replica of the large onument from the Bilbao site, carved stone human limbs, figurines, mushroom stones, a waist yoke worn for ball games, numerous obsidian pieces and flowerpots. There are also a few stone carvings in front of the museum. Those further beyond the museum next to the driveway are copies. ■ *Mon-Fri 0800-1600, Sat 0800-1200, US$1.30. The museum will be closed when you arrive. You will have to ask and search for the person who is in charge, who will have the key.*

Sleeping and eating B *Santiaguito*, on the Pacific Highway at Km 90.4, T882-5435, F882-2585, with air-conditioned rooms, TV and hot and cold water, pool and restaurant. Non-guests can use the pool for US$2.60. **C-D** *Hotel El Camino*, diagonally opposite *Santiaguito* across the highway at Km 90.5, T882-5316. Rooms with bath, tepid water, fan, some rooms with a/c (more expensive). All have TV. Good restaurant. A stone's throw from the park on 4 Av, 4-71, is the **E** *Hospedaje La Reforma*. Large number of dark box rooms and dark shared showers. Clean though. *Pastelería Italiana*, Calzada 15 de Septiembre, 4-58, open early for bakery business.

These are all in town unless stated

Transport Bus Regular departures from the Zona 4 terminal in the capital. Buses plying the Pacific Highway also pass through, so if you are coming from Reu in the west or Escuintla in the east you can get off here. If you are driving, there are a glut of 24-hr *Esso* and *Texaco* gas stations here.

Directory Banks *Banco G&T Continental*, on the highway, accepts MasterCard. *Banco Industrial*, accepts Visa, 3 Av between 2 and 3 Calle. There's a *Bancared* Visa ATM on the plaza. **Communications** Telephone: *Telgua*, Cda 15 de Septiembre near the highway.

Guatemala

Beyond Santa Lucía Cotzumalguapa is **Cocales**, where a good road north leads to Patulul and after 30 km, to Lake Atitlán at San Lucas Tolimán. ■ *Getting there: buses a day Cocales-Panajachel, between 0600 and 1400, 2½ hrs, US$1.05.*

The Pacific Highway continues through San Antonio Suchitepéquez to **Mazatenango** (where just beyond are the crossroads for Retalhuleu and Champerico) and on to Coatepeque and Ciudad Tecún Umán for the border with Mexico. Mazatenango is the chief town of the Costa Grande zone. While it is not especially attractive, the Parque Central is very pleasant with many fine trees providing shade. There is a huge festival in the last week of February, when hotels are very full and double their prices. At that time, beware of children carrying (and throwing) bags of flour. There are a number of mid-range to cheap places to stay. ■ *Frequent buses to and from Guatemala City, US$1.56; to the border at Tecún Umán US$1.56.*

<table>
<tr><td>

Retalhuleu

Colour map 5, grid C1

Retalhuleu is normally referred to as 'Reu', pronounced 'Ray-oo'

</td><td>

Retalhuleu is the capital of the department. The entrance to the town is grand with a string of royal palms lining the route, known as Calzada Las Palmas. It serves a large number of coffee and sugar estates and much of its population is wealthy. The original colonial church of **San Antonio de Padua** is in the central plaza. Bordering the plaza to the east is the neo classical *Palacio del Gobierno*, now housing the Municipalidad, with a giant quetzal sculpture on top. The **Museo de Arqueología y Etnología**, next to the *palacio*, is small. Downstairs are exhibits of Maya ceramics. ■ *Tue-Sat 0830-1300, 1400-1800, Sun 0900-1230, US$1.30.*

</td></tr>
</table>

The site was discovered in 1888 by botanist Doctor Gustav Brühl

Take water and snacks.

One of the best ancient sites to visit outside El Petén is **Abaj Takalik**, a ruined city that lies in sweltering conditions on the southern plain. Its name means 'standing stone' in K'iche'. It is believed to have flourished in the Late Preclassic period of 300 BC to AD 250 strategically placed to control commerce between the Highlands and the Pacific coast. However, it was first occupied much earlier than this, evidenced by the presence of Olmec-style monuments. It is thought that the site was abandoned and then reoccupied. There are some 239 monuments, which include 68 stelae, 32 altars and some 71 buildings, all set in peaceful surroundings. The environment is loved by birds and butterflies, including blue morphos, and by orchids, which flower magnificently between January and March. In the very well-presented part that you can see, the main temple buildings are mostly up to 12 m high, suggesting an early date before techniques were available to build Tikal-sized structures. Human and animal Olmec-style figures abound – frogs facing east for fertility and birth, jaguar and crocodile facing west towards darkness and the afterlife. A collection of threatened indigenous animals also lives at the site. ■ *Daily 0700-1700, US$3.25, guides are volunteers so tips are welcomed. Getting there: take a bus to El Asintal from Retalhuleu and walk the hot 4 km to the site entrance. Or, take any bus heading along the Pacific Highway and get off at the El Asintal crossroads. A pick-up from here to El Asintal is US$0.52. Then, take a pick-up from the town square to Abaj Takalik. If the pick-up is almost full, which would be rare, it should cost you only US$0.40. However, since there are only fincas along this road, you will probably be on your own, in which case it is US$3.90 to the site or US$6.50-7.50 round trip, including waiting time. Bargain hard though. A taxi from the central plaza in Reu to the site and back including waiting time is US$13.*

Sleeping In town B *Posada de Don José*, 5 C, 3-67, T771-4176, F771-1179, donjose@infovia.com.gt Rooms with a/c and fan, TV. There is a very good restaurant serving such mouthwatering temptations as lobster sautéed in Cognac. Restaurant and café are set beside the pool. Non-guests can use the pool for US$1.30. **C** *Astor*, 5 C, 4-60, T771-0475, F771-2562, hotelastor@terra.com.gt A colonial-style place with a small feel with 27 rooms with a/c, hot water, TV, set around a pretty courtyard where there's a pool and jacuzzi. Parking and restauarant. *Bar La Carreta* is inside the hotel with MTV on the go all the time. Non-guests can use the pool and jacuzzi here (nicer than the one at *Posada de Don José*) for US$2. **D** *Modelo*, 5 C, 4-53, T771-0256, opposite the *Astor*, is run by a friendly old couple, with rooms like barns set around a basic patio, with bath and fan. Those with windows on the main street will suffer from noise. **F** *Hilman*, 7 Av, 7-99. Rooms have fans and it's clean. Basic but acceptable. **Out of town B** *La Colonia*, 1½ km to the north at Km 178, T771-0054. Rooms with a/c and TV, pool, and good food. **B** *Siboney*, 5 km northwest of Reu in San Sebastián, Km 179, T771-0149. Rooms are with bath, a/c and TV, set around pool. Try the *caldo de mariscos* or *paella* in the excellent restaurant. Non-guests can use the pool for a fee.

Eating *Restaurante La Luna*, 5 C, 4-97, on the corner of the plaza. Good *típico* meals served: *menú del día* at US$2.50, cheap breakfasts. *El Volován*, on the plaza, delicious cakes and pies. *El Patio*, corner of 5 C/4 Av, with *menú del día* US$1.60, cheap breakfasts. Limited.

Transport Bus Services along the Pacific Highway to Mexico leave from the main bus terminal, which is beyond the city limits at 5 Av 'A' on the right-hand side, just before a *tienda* sign saying 'Caseta Sonia'. To **Coatepeque** (0600-1800), **Malacatán**, **Mazatenango** and **Champerico** (0500-1800). Buses also leave from here to **El Asintal**, 30 mins, US$0.13, every 30 mins from 0600-1830, last bus back to Reu 1800). Or catch them before that from the corner of 5 Av 'A' and the Esso gas station as they turn to head for the village. Leaving from a smaller terminal at 7 Av/10 C, there are regular buses to **Tecún Umán**, **Talismán** and **Guatemala City** via the Pacific route, and to Xela (1¾ hrs, US$0.80, every hr 0500-1800).

Directory Banks: There are plenty of banks in town taking Visa and MC. ATMs also. **Communications** Internet: *La Casona*, 4 C, 4-58, open daily 0830-1230, 1500-1800. **Post office**: on the plaza. **Telephone**: 5 C, 4-18. **Embassies and consulates** Mexican inside the *Posada de Don José*. Open Mon-Fri 0700-1230, 1400-1800. **Useful addresses** Hospital Nacional de Retalhuleu, Blvd Centenario, 3 Av, Zona 2, 10 mins along the road to El Asintal, T771-0116.

Colomba, an attractive typical village, is east of Coatepeque in the lowlands, with a basic *hospedaje*. The main road runs 21 km east off the Pacific Highway to **Coatepeque**, one of the richest coffee zones in the country. There is a bright, modern church in the leafy Plaza Central. **Fiesta**: 11-19 March. There are several hotels, *hospedajes* and restaurants. ■ *Getting there: bus from Quetzaltenango, US$0.40, or catch any bus heading to Ciudad Tecún Umán from Reu.*

Border with Mexico

The Pacific Highway goes to **Ciudad Tecún Umán**, 37 km west, on the Mexican border, separated by the Río Suchiate from the Mexican town of Ciudad Hidalgo. Guatemalan immigration: the 1 km bridge over the river separates the 2 border posts. For a fee, boys will help you with your luggage. Normally open 24 hrs. For Mexican consulates, see Quetzaltenango and Reu.

Essentials Sleeping: **D** *Hotel Don José*, C Real del Comercio, T776-8164, rooms with bath. **D** *Hotel Villazul* , 3 Av, 5-28, T776-8827. Rooms with bath and a/c. **Transport**: Buses run from the Mexican side of the border to Tapachula, 30 mins. To Guatemala City, US$5.20, run by *Fortaleza*, 4 direct daily, 5 hrs. Frequent slower buses via Reu and Mazatenango. *Colectivo* from Coatepeque, US$0.52. See also Talismán page 637 for crossing into Mexico. **Directory**: There are numerous banks and plenty of money changers.

Routes to El Salvador

Three routes pass through Southern Guatemala to El Salvador. The main towns are busy but scruffy with little to attract the visitor.

Pan-American Highway The first route heads directly south along the paved Pan-American Highway from Guatemala City (CA1) to the border at San Cristóbal Frontera. **Cuilapa**, the capital of Santa Rosa Department, is 65 km along the Highway. There is a busy market at the top end of the town, and **D** *Hospedaje K-Luy*, 4 Calle, 1-166, T886-5372, which has clean, comfortable rooms with private bath and

Route 1
If travelling by international bus to El Salvador, see page 575

hot water and cable TV. About 9 km beyond Los Esclavos is the El Molino Junction. An unpaved road goes north from the El Molino junction to Ayarza, where nearby is **Lake Ayarza**, which is slightly sulphurous, formed by a twin peaked volcano. Around the lake grow orchids and bromeliads. Fishing for *tilapias* and *mojarras* is permitted. Take the left fork at the El Molino Junction for San Cristóbal Frontera crossing. **Jutiapa**, some 50 km on, is a pleasant, lively town with a big food market in Zona 3. Jutiapa has at least six hotels/*hospedajes* nearby.

Beyond, just off the Pan-American Highway, is the village of **El Progreso**, dominated by the imposing Volcán Suchitán, at 2,042 m. There is **E** *Hotel Najarro*, 2 C and 7 Av, Zona 2, opposite *Banco Banoro*, T843-4321. The town **fiesta** with horse-racing is between 10-16 November. From El Progreso, a good paved road goes north 43 km to Jalapa (see page 650) through open, mostly dry country, with volcanoes always in view. There are several crater lakes including **Laguna del Hoyo** near **Monjas** that are worth visiting. The higher ground is forested. Beyond Jutiapa and El Progreso the Pan-American Highway heads east and then south to Asunción Mita. Here there is a turning left to Lago de Güija. Before reaching the border at San Cristóbal Frontera the Pan-American Highway dips and skirts the shores (right) of **Lago Atescatempa**, with several islands set in heavy forest.

Border crossing El Salvador – San Cristóbal Frontera This is the principal crossing. Heavy transport and international buses favour this route. Guatemalan immigration is open 0600-2000 but it is usually possible to cross outside these hours with additional charges.

Route 2 Via Jalpatagua The second, quicker way of getting to San Salvador is to take a highway which cuts off right from the first route at El Molino Junction, about 7 km beyond the Esclavos bridge. This cut-off goes through El Oratorio and Jalpatagua to the border at Valle Nuevo, continuing then to Ahuachapán and San Salvador.

Border crossing Valle Nuevo/Las Chinamas Since the construction of the Santa Ana bypass, this has become a popular route for lighter traffic between the two countries. Guatemalan immigrationr is officially open 0800-1800.

Route 3 El Salvador (La Hachadura) via the border at Ciudad Pedro de Alvarado This coastal route goes from Escuintla to the border bridge over the Río Paz at La Hachadura (El Salvador). It takes two hours from Escuintla to the border. You pass **Auto Safari Chapín**, east of Escuintla, an improbable wildlife park, but busy at weekends and holidays. It is at km 87.5, T363-1105, open daily 0900-1700, except Monday, US$3.25. **Taxisco** is 18 km beyond and just off the road. It's a busy place, which has a white church with a curious hearts and holly design on the façade. To the east is Guazacapán which merges into **Chiquimulilla**, 3 km to the north, the most important town of the area, with good quality leather goods available. **Sleeping** If you need to stay there is **E-F** *San Carlos*, Barrio Santiago, T885-0187. A side excursion can be made from Chiquimulilla up the winding CA 16 through coffee *fincas* and farmland. About 20 km along there is a turning to the left down a 2-3 km steep, narrow, dirt road which goes to **Laguna de Ixpaco**, an impressive, greenish-yellow lake that is 350 m in diameter. It is boiling in some places, emitting sulphurous fumes and set in dense forest. This trip can also be made by heading south off the Pan-American Highway after Cuilapa (just before Los Esclavos) towards Chiquimulilla on the CA 16, with old trees on either side, some with orchids in them, where you will reach the sign to Ixpaco, after 20 km. Thirty kilometres beyond on the Pacific Highway at **Ciudad Pedro de Alvarado** on the border there are several *hospedajes* (all **G**, basic) but it is not recommended that you plan to stay here.

Ciudad Pedro de Alvarado/La Hachadura This is becoming a busier crossing as roads on both sides have improved. The last bus for Sonsonate in El Salvador leaves at 1800.

Guatemala City to the Caribbean

Guatemala City

The Atlantic Highway to the Caribbean

The Carretera al Atlántico or Atlantic Highway, stretches from Guatemala City all the way to Puerto Barrios on the Caribbean Coast in the department of Izabal. Most of the worthwhile places to visit are off this fast main road, along the Río Motagua valley, where cactus, bramble, willow and acacia grow.

Teculután

Before Teculután is **El Rancho** at Km 85, the jumping-off point for a trip north to Cobán (see page 664). There are a few places here to stay. Geologists will be interested in the Motagua fault near Santa Cruz, between Teculután and Río Hondo. Just before Río Hondo (Km 138), a paved road runs south towards Estanzuela. Shortly before this town you pass a monument on the right commemorating the 1976 earthquake, which activated a fault line that cut across the road. It can still be seen in the fields on either side of the road. The epicentre of this massive earthquake, which measured 7.5 on the Richter scale, and killed 23,000 people, was at Los Amates, 65 km further down the valley towards Puerto Barrios.

Estanzuela

Estanzuela is a small town fronting the Highway. Its **Museo de Palaeontología, Arqueología y Geología** displays the incredible reconstructed skeletal remains of a 4 m prehistoric giant sloth found in Zone 6, Guatemala City and a giant armadillo among others. ■ *Daily 0800-1700, free. Getting there: take a minibus heading south from Río Hondo and ask to be dropped at the first entrance to the town on the right, where there is an Orange Crush Caseta Ana No 2. Then walk right, into the town, and continue for 600 m to the museum, 10 mins. When you reach the school, walk to the right and you will see the museum.*

Zacapa
Colour map 5, grid B3
Population: 15,000
Fiesta: 4-9 December
and 30 April-1 May
Zacapa is 8 km further
on from Estanzuela

Zacapa is known for its sharp cheese, *quesadilla*, a Madeira-type cheesecake sold throughout the country, cigars, and palm hat manufacture. There are banks around the central plaza that will change travellers' cheques. **Sleeping and eating D** *Miramundo*, 17 Av, 5-41, T941-2674, 40 rooms, a/c, TV. Some rooms are not too clean, with restaurant. **F** *Hotel de León*, T941-0125, cheaper without bath, clean, a little run down, friendly, with restaurant. Eateries include: *Magic*, diagonally opposite *Hotel Miramundo*, with burgers and snacks. *La Unica*, a pizzería and pastelería.

Transport Bus: From Guatemala City to **Zacapa**, US$2.25 with *Rutas Orientales*, 0500-1830, every 30 mins, 2¾-3 hrs. To **Esquipulas** with same service that continues from Zacapa, US$1, 1½ hrs. To **Puerto Barrios**, US$2, 3¼ hrs. With *Vargas* 0430-1730, 3½ hrs, US$2.35, every 30 mins. Minibus leaving from next to church, 0700-0730 and 1200-1230, for the turn-off to the Quiriguá ruins, 1 hr 50 mins, US$1.05. To **Estanzuela**, 10 mins, US$0.26.

Chiquimula
Colour map 5, grid B3
Population: 42,000
21 km from Zacapa

Chiquimula is a stop-off point for travellers who stay here on their way to or from Copán Ruinas, Honduras, if they can't make the connection in one day (see page 648 for border crossing details). **Fiesta:** 11-18 August, including bullfighting.

Sleeping C *Hotel Posada Don Adán*, 8 Av, 4-30, T942-0549. All rooms with private bathroom, a/c, telephone, TV. Run by a friendly, older, couple. **D** *Posada Perla del Oriente*, 2 C between 11 and 12 Av, T942-0014, F942-0534. All rooms with TV, some with a/c, parking, pool, quiet. Restaurant. Recommended. **D-E** *Victoria*, 2 C, 9-99, T942-2732, F942-2179, next to the bus station, so ask for rooms away from street. All rooms have bath, cold water, fan, cable TV, towels, soap, shampoo, some rooms (more expensive), have a/c, drinking water provided, good restaurant, good value, will store luggage. Recommended. **E** *Chiquimulja*, 3 C, 6-51, on the central plaza, T942-0387. With bath, a/c, fan, TV, clean, inside parking, good value. With restaurant *El Patio* behind, see Eating. **E** *Hotel Hernandez*, 3 C, 7-41, T942-0708, hotel@guate.net Cheaper without bathroom, fans. TVs in rooms and a pool add to its attractions. It's family run, quiet and friendly, but not such a good deal for single travellers (although you usually can't get the use of a pool at this price). **E** *Hotel Palmeras*, 10 Av, 2-00, T942467, F942-0763. Clean rooms with private bathroom, fan, a/c and TV, close to bus terminal. **F** *Hospedaje Martínez*, close to bus station. Clean, safe, cold showers, but noisy in the mornings. **F** *Hotel Dario*, 8 Av, 4-40, T942-0192. Some rooms with shared bath, clean, but the private bathrooms are a cement block in the room, and could do with some serious redecoration, TV, fans, friendly, English spoken.

Eating *El Patio*, behind *Hotel Chiquimulja*, is a great thatch-roofed, open-air wooden restaurant with wicker furniture. Good breakfasts and *fajitas* on the main menu. It's popular and recommended. *Magic*, corner of 8 Av and 3 C, is a good place from which to watch the world go by, and most of what's on offer is seriously cheap. Sandwiches, *licuados* and burgers all available. *Pastelería Las Violetas*, 7 Av, 4-80, and another near *Hotel Victoria*, is an excellent cake shop with a fine spread, good-value sandwiches too, plus great cappuccino, and all while enjoying the air conditioning. Next door is its bakery *Superpanadería Las Violetas*. There are also many small *comedores* between 3 C and 4 C with good *licuados* and *batidos* and a huge *Paiz* supermarket on the main square.

There are 3 small terminals in Chiquimula, all within 50 m of each other

Transport Bus To **Guatemala City**, *Transportes Guerra* and *Rutas Orientales*, hourly, US$3, 3¼-3½ hrs, leave from 11 Av between 1 and 2 C, as do buses for **Puerto Barrios**, several companies, every 30 mins, between 0300-1500, 4 hrs, US$2.60. To **Quiriguá**, US$1.55, 1 hr 50 mins. Take any Puerto Barrios-bound bus. On to **Río Dulce** take the Barrios bus and get off at La Ruidosa junction and change, or change at Bananera/Morales. Buses to **Ipala** and **Jalapa** also leave from here; 4 buses daily to Jalapa between 0500-1230, 4½ hrs, US$1.80; to Ipala, US$0.65. Supplemented by minibuses 0600-1715 to Ipala, US$0.65. To **Zacapa** US$0.52, 25 mins, from the terminal inside the market at 10 Av between 1 and 2 C. Same for those to **Esquipulas**, every 10 mins, US$1.05, until 1900. To and from **Cobán** via El Rancho (where a change must be made), US$1.65. Buses to **El Florido** (Honduras border) leave from inside the market at 1 C, between 10 and 11 Av. See page 648, Border with Honduras.

Directory There are several **banks** accepting MasterCard and Visa, and ATMs, two **internet** centres, a **post office** (close to the bus terminal inside the market) and a **telephone** office on the plaza.

Volcán de Ipala
The crater lake is cool and good for swimming

Southwest of Chiquimula, the extinct Volcán de Ipala (1,650 m) can be visited. Take an early bus to Ipala (two basic *hospedajes*), stay on the bus and ask the driver to let you off at Aldea El Chaparroncito (10 minutes after Ipala). From here it's a 1½-hour ascent, following red arrows every now and then. Another ascent goes via Municipio Agua Blanca. Take a minibus to Agua Blanca from Ipala and get out at the small village of El Sauce, where the trail starts. ■ *Last bus from Ipala to Chiquimula is 1700.*

To Copán Ruinas – Honduras

At **Vado Hondo**, 10 km south of Chiquimula, on the road to Esquipulas, a smooth dirt road branches east to the Honduran border (48 km) and a further 11 km beyond to the great Maya ruins of Copán.

The border is 1 km after the village

Border with Honduras – El Florido Open 0700-1900. If you are going to Copán for a short visit, the Guatemalan official will give you a 72-hr pass, stapled into your passport. You must return through this border within this period, but you will not require a new visa. Exit fees of US$1.30 are being charged. **Honduran consulate** If you need a visa to enter Honduras, go to the lobby of the *Hotel Payaquí*, Esquipulas, where there is a consulate office, manned by very helpful staff. It's reportedly quicker to get your Honduran visa here than in the capital.

Transport There are buses from Chiquimula to the border at El Florido with *Transportes Vilma*, 1 C, between 10 and 11 Av, T942-2253, between 0530-1230 on the hour, and then 1320, 1345, 1430, 1500, 1530, 1630, US$1.05, 2 hrs. Buses return from the border at 0530, 0630 and then hourly 0700-1700. Taxi Chiquimula-border US$16. Chiquimula-Copán and back the same day in a taxi costs US$32. It is impossible to visit Copán from Guatemala City by bus and return the same day. However travel agents do a 1-day trip in minibuses for about US$35 per person to US$125 including an overnight stop. **Crossing by private vehicle** If crossing by car make sure you have all the right paperwork. If you are in a Guatemalan hire car you will need a letter of authorization from the hire company allowing you to take the car across the border to Honduras. You can leave your car at the border and go on to Copán by public transport, thus saving the costs of crossing with a vehicle.

For a better road to Honduras from Chiquimula, see Agua Caliente, page 650

The Honduran immigration office is at El Florido on the border. They charge an entry fee of US$1.50 and an exit fee of US$0.75. Ask for a receipt for any 'extra' charges. Pick-up trucks run all day every day when full until 1700 between Copán Ruinas and the border, 30 mins, connecting with buses to Guatemalan destinations. The cost is around US$2.50. Bargain for a fair price. They leave from one block west of the park, near the police station. See Chiquimula, Transport, page 648. There is a direct minibus service Copán-Antigua – Guatemala, run by *Monarcas Travel*, next to *Posada del Annie*, Copán, US$29 one way, 1500 daily, pick-up from hotels. If leaving with a vehicle, you need 3 stamps on your strip from Migración, Tránsito (where they take your *Proviso Provisional*), and Aduana (where they take your *Pase Fronterizo* document and cancel the stamp in your passport).

Border with Guatemala
There are many money changers but for US$ or TCs, change in Copán, better rates

Guatemala

Esquipulas is dominated by a large white basilica, which attracts millions of pilgrims from across Central America to view the image of a Black Christ. The town has pulled out the stops for visitors, who, as well as a religious fill, will lack nothing in the way of food, drink and some of the best kitsch souvenirs on the market. If it's possible, stop at the mirador, 1 km from the town, for a spectacular view on the way in of the basilica, which sits at the end of a 1½ km main avenue.

Esquipulas
Population: 7,500

The history of the famous *Cristo Negro* records that in 1735 Father Pedro Pardo de Figueroa, suffering from an incurable chronic illness, stood in front of the image to pray, and was cured. A few years later, after becoming Archbishop of Guatemala he ordered a new church to be built to house the sculpture. The **basilica** was completed in 1758 and the *Cristo Negro* was transferred from the parish church shortly after that. Inside the basilica, the Black Christ is on a gold cross, elaborately engraved with vines and grapes. It was carved by Quirio Cataño in dark balsam wood in 1595. The image attracts over 1,000,000 visitors per year, with some crawling on their hands and knees to pay homage. The main pilgrimage times are 1-15 January, with 15 January being the busiest day, during Lent, Holy Week and 21-27 July. Surrounding the church are hundreds of sellers of candles, relics, mementoes, and some top kitsch stuff – if you want something to swing from your car rear mirror. ■ *The basilica closes at 2000.*

Near town is the **Cueva de Las Minas**, a cave 50 m deep, used for Maya rituals. There is a little café by the river, picnic tables, and a small zoo with tropical animals, including a margay. They are kept in clean conditions, but the enclosures are, sadly, way too small. ■ *Daily 0700-1700, US$0.65, US$0.26 for kids. Take a lamp for the cave. Getting there: walk behind Pollo Campero (to the right of the basilica), and look for the signposted entrance gates.*

Sleeping Plenty of hotels, *hospedajes* and *comedores* all over town, especially in and around 11 C, also known as Doble Via Quirio Cataño. Prices tend to double before the Jan feast day. They also rise at Easter and at weekends. When quiet, midweek, bargain for lower room prices. **A** *Hotel Chortí*, on the outskirts of town at Km 222, T943-1148, F943-1551. All 20 rooms have a/c, TV, phone and *frigobar*. There are 2 pools, a restaurant and bar. **B** *Legendario*, 3 Av and 9 C, T943-1824, F943-1022, built around a garden, 2 pools, restaurant, TV, parking. **C** *Hotel Villa Zonia*, looking a little Alpine, at 10 C, 1-84, T943-1133. **C-D** *Hotel El Peregrino*, just up from the *Hotel Esquipulao*, T943-1054, F943-1589, has clean

Some hotels in the E-G range charge per person

rooms in a newer part. **C-D** *Hotel y Restaurante Esquipulao*, 2 Av, 11-68, T943-2023, marojas@yahoo.com Rooms with TV and hot water. A few unpleasant insects in the room though and some staff aren't too friendly. **D** *Los Angeles*, 2 Av, 11-94, T943-1254, F943-1343 spotless rooms with bath, TV and fans, parking, friendly service. Recommended. **D** *Payaquí* 2 Av, 11-26, T943-1143, F943-1371, www.payaqui.com The 40 rooms are extremely nice, with *frigobars*, full of beers for the pilgrims to guzzle, hot-water showers and free drinking water, swimming pool, parking, restaurant, bar; credit cards, Honduran *lempiras* and US dollars accepted. **E** *Hotel Calle Real*, 3 Av, 10-00, T794-32405, rooms all with private bathroom with TV, hot water, clean. **E** *Hotelito*, 2 Av, 10-30, T943-2636, 40 rooms, cold water only. **E** *Pensión Casa Norman*, 3 Av, 9-20, T943-1503, rooms with bath and hot water. **F** *San Carlos 2*, used to be known as *París*, 2 Av, 10-48, T943-1276, 28 very clean rooms and a much better option than its neighbour, *Santa Rosa*. Cheaper without bath, hot-water showers.

Eating *Café Pistachos*, clean cheap snack bar with burgers, hotdogs, etc. *Jimmy's*, a pizzería alongside the park. *La Hacienda*, 2 Av, 10-20, has delicious barbecued chicken and steaks. Kids' menu available, breakfasts available, probably one of smartest restaurants in town. *Restaurante Payaquí*, 2 Av, 11-26, inside the hotel of the same name, with specialties including turkey in *Pepian*, also lunches and breakfasts. A poolside restaurant makes a pleasant change. There are a couple of *comedores* on 3 Av near the park, including *La Favorita*, which does good cheap breakfasts with fast service, as well as *La Beato Hermano Pedro*, *Restaurante Calle Real* and *Comedor San Carlos*.

Plenty of restaurants, but prices are high for Guatemala

Transport Buses from the capital every 30 mins, 0400-1800 (see also page 575), US$3.60, 4-4½ hrs, with *Rutas Orientales*. Leaving Esquipulas, 1 Av "A" and 11 C, T943-1366, for **Guatemala City** every 30 mins from 0200-1700, 4½ hrs, US$3.60. To **Chiquimula** by minibus, every 30 mins, 0430-1830, US$1.05. To **Agua Caliente** (Honduran border) and **Anguiatú** for El Salvador, see below. *Transportes María Elena*, 12 C, between 5 and 6 Av, to **Santa Elena, Petén** at 0400, 0900, 1300, 11 hrs, US$7.80.

Directory Banks There are a number of banks and ATMs in town close to the park, Visa and MasterCard accepted. There are money changers in the centre if you need *lempiras*. Better rates than at the borders. **Communications Post office:** end of 6 Av, 2-43.

Border with Honduras

Agua Caliente Immigration open 0600-1900. The Honduran consulate is in *Hotel Payaquí*, Esquipulas, very helpful. Open 0930-1800, T943-1143. Minibuses run from Esquipulas, US$0.65, 15 mins. By taxi US$6.50. From Chiquimula, US$1.80, every 10 mins.

Border with El Salvador

Anguiatú This border is 19 km from the Padre Miguel Junction on the main road and 33 km from Esquipulas. Immigration open 0600-1900. There are *colectivos* to/from Padre Miguel junction connecting with buses to Chiquimula and Esquipulas. From Esquipulas, minibuses run every 30 mins, 0600-1720, US$1.05, 40 mins. By taxi, US$26. From Chiquimula there are minibuses every 30 mins from 0515-1700, 1½ hrs, US$1.20.

Alternative route to Chiquimula & Esquipulas

From the southeast corner of Guatemala City (Zona 10), the Pan-American Highway heads towards the Salvadorean border. After a few kilometres there is a turning to **San José Pinula; fiesta:** 16-20 March. After San José, an unpaved branch road continues for 203 km through fine scenery to Mataquescuintla, Jalapa (several *hospedajes*, good bus connections; **fiesta:** 2-5 May), San Pedro Pinula, San Luis Jilotepeque, and Ipala to Chiquimula (see page 647).

Quiriguá

The remarkable Late Classic ruins of Quiriguá include the tallest stelae found in the Maya world. The UNESCO World Heritage Site is small, with an excavated acropolis to see, but the highlight of a visit is the sight of the ornately carved tall stelae and the zoomorphic altars. The Maya here were very industrious, producing monuments every five years between AD 751-806, coinciding with the height of their prosperity and confident rule. The earliest recorded monument dates from AD 480.

It is believed that Quiriguá was an important trading post between Tikal and Copán, inhabited since the second century, but principally it was a ceremonial centre. The Kings of Quiriguá were involved in the rivalries, wars and changing alliances between Tikal, Copán and Calakmul. It rose to prominence in its own right in the middle of the eighth century, around the time of Cauac Sky who ascended to the throne in AD 724. Cauac Sky was appointed to the position by 18 Rabbit, powerful ruler of Copán (now in Honduras), and its surrounding settlements. It seems that he was fed up with being a subordinate under the domination of Copán, and during his reign, Quiriguá attacked Copán and captured, 18 Rabbit. One of the stelae tells of the beheading of the Copán King in the plaza at Quiriguá as a sacrifice after the AD 738 battle. After this event 18 Rabbit disappears from the official chronicle and a 20-year hiatus follows in the historical record of Copán. Following this victory, Quiriguá became an independent kingdom and gained control of the Motagua Valley, enriching itself in the process. And, from AD 751, a monument was carved and erected every five years for the next 55 years.

The tallest stelae at Quiriguá is Stelae E, which is 10.66 m high with another 2.5 m or so buried beneath. It is 1.52 m wide and weighs 65 tonnes. One of its dates corresponds with the enthronement of Cauac Sky, in AD 724, but it's thought to date from AD 771. All of the stelae, in parkland surrounded by ceiba trees and palms, have shelters, which makes photography difficult. Some monuments have been carved in the shape of animals, some mythical, all of symbolic importance to the Maya. ■ *Daily 0730-1630, US$3.25. Take insect repellent. There are toilets, a café and you can store your luggage with the guards. There is no accommodation at the site, but you can camp (see below). The site is reached by a dirt road from the Atlantic Highway. The village of Quiriguá is about half way between Zacapa and Puerto Barrios on the highway, and about 3 km from the entrance road to the ruins.*

Sleeping Quiriguá D-E *Hotel y Cafetería Edén*, T947-3281, helpful, cheaper with shared bath, basement rooms are very dark, clean. The bus comes as far as here, which is where the back route walk to the ruins starts. **E** *Hotel y Restaurante Royal*, T947-3639, with bath, cheaper without, clean, mosquito netting on all windows, good place to meet other travellers in town to see the ruins, restaurant. You can **camp** in the car park of the ruins for free, but facilities are limited to toilets and very little running water. In **Los Amates**, 2 km south of Quiriguá village on the highway, there is **E** *Hotel Restaurante Santa Mónica*, T946-3602, 8 rooms all with private bath, TV and fan, restaurant. It is next to a 24-hr *Texaco* gas station. Convenient if you don't want to walk the 10-15 mins into Quiriguá village for the 2 hotels there. There are a couple of shops, banks, and *comedores* here.

Emphasize to the bus driver you want Quiriguá pueblo, not the ruinas. Countless travellers have found themselves left at the ruins and having to make a return journey to the village

Transport To get to the ruins **directly**, take any bus heading along the highway towards Puerto Barrios and ask to be let off at the *ruinas*. At this ruins crossroads, take a pick-up (very regular), 10 mins, US$0.40, or bus (much slower and less regular) to the ruins 4 km away. Last bus back to highway, 1700. You can walk, but take lots of water, as it's hot and dusty with little shade. To get to the **village** of Quiriguá, 3 km south from the ruins entrance road, it is only a 10-min walk to the *Hotel Royal*. Keep to the paved road, round a left-hand bend, and it's 100 m up on the left. Or take a local bus heading from the highway into the village (US$0.13). The *Hotel Eden* is a further 5 mins on down the hill. There is a frequent daily bus service that runs a circular route between Los Amates, Quiriguá village and then on to the entrance road to the ruins, US$0.13. You can also walk through the banana plantations from Quiriguá village to the ruins as well. From *Hotel Royal* walk past the church towards the old train station and the *Hotel Eden*, and follow the tracks branching to the right, through the plantation to the ruins.

Thirteen kilometres from Quiriguá is the turn-off for Mariscos and Lago de Izabal (see page 661). A further 28 km on are the very hot twin towns of Bananera/Morales. ■ *From Bananera there are buses to Río Dulce, Puerto Barrios and the Petén.*

Bananera/Morales
Fiesta: 15-21 March

Puerto Barrios

Colour map 5, grid B3
Population: 37,800

The town is 297 km from the capital and 5 hours by bus

Puerto Barrios, on the Caribbean coast, is a hot and dusty port town, still a central banana point, but now largely superseded as a port by Santo Tomás (see next page). The launch to the Garífuna town of Lívingston leaves from the municipal dock here. While not an unpleasant town, it is not a destination in itself, but rather a launch pad to more beautiful and happening spots. The *Fundación Mario Dary*, 17 C between 5 and 6 Av, Puerto Barrios. T948-0944, www.fundarymanabique.guate.net, has information about visiting Punta de Manabique, see page 657. The **fiesta** is 16-22 July. On the way into town, note the cemetery on the right-hand side, where you will pass a small, Indian mausoleum with elephant carvings. During the 19th century, *culi* (coolies) of Hindu origin migrated from Jamaica to Guatemala to work on the plantations.

Sleeping   **A-D** *Hotel del Norte*, at the end of the 7 C, T/F948-0087, a rickety, old wooden structure with sloping landings on the seafront side. All rooms have bath, some with a/c. There is a pool and expensive restaurant, but worth it for the English colonial tearoom atmosphere, no credit cards, but will change US$ cash. **B** *Hotel Valle Tropical* is a new, bright green hotel with 59 rooms on 12 C between 5 and 6 Av, T948-7084, F948-1156, vtropical@guate.net All rooms with a/c and private bathroom, inviting pool, gym and restaurant, parking. Non-guests can use the pool for US$5.20. **C** *El Reformador*, 16 C and 7 Av 159, T948-5489, F948-1531, reformador@intelnet.net.gt 51 rooms with bathroom and TV, some with a/c, some with fan, restaurant, laundry service, clean, quiet, accepts credit cards. Recommended. **D** *Español*, 13 C between 5 and 6 Av, T/F948-0738, with bath, clean, comfortable, good value, cheaper without a/c, friendly and helpful management. **D** *Hotel Europa 2*, 3 Av between 11 and 12 C, T/F948-1292, has rooms with private bathrooms, fan, 24 hr parking. **D-E** *Hotel y Restaurante La Caribeña*, 4 Av, between 10 and 11 C, T948-0384, F948-2216. 43 rooms, some with a/c and TV, parking, close to boat and bus terminals, popular restaurant serving fish dishes. **E** *Hotel Europa*, 8 Av, between 8 and 9 C, T948-0127, 23 clean rooms, with bath, fan, 2 rooms with a/c, more expensive (**C**) good restaurant, parking, friendly Cuban management. Next door is *Restaurant La Habana Vieja*. **E** *Hotel Lee*, 5 Av, between 9 and 10 C, T948-0830, convenient for the bus station and dock, 24 rooms with fan and TV, with private bath, cheaper without. Noisy restaurant opposite. Friendly service. **E-F** *Hotel Xelajú*, 8 Av, between 9 and 10 C, T948-1117, 15 rooms, with bath, cheaper without, fans, quiet, and ultra-clean shared bathrooms. This hotel is up along near *Hotel Europa*, and not facing the market, where there is a hotel of the same name.

Eating   *La Fonda de Quique*, an orange and white wooden building at 5 Av and corner of 12 C,

Most hotels have restaurants

nicely air conditioned with hand-made wooden furniture, serving lobster, fish and meats, plus snacks. *La Habana Vieja*, run by a Cubano serving Cuban food, among other things, plus a café serving bagels and fast food. The bar serves mojitos too. Recommended. *Restaurante Safari*, at the north end of 5 Av and 1 C, overlooking the bay with views all around. Basically serving up oceans of fish, including the whole fish (US$6.50-10) plus ceviche and fishburgers. Just past the Hotel del Norte, overlooking the sea is *The Container*, an unusual bar constructed from the front half of an old ship equipped with portholes, and a number of banana containers from the massive banana businesses just up the road. It's open from 0700-2300. One of the most popular spots in Puerto Barrios is the thatched bar Mariscos de Izabal. Mostly a drinking den but with tacos, tortillas and burgers served amid beating Latin rhythms. You can hang out until here 0100.

Transport   **Bus** To **Guatemala City**, with *Litegua*, 6 Av between 9 and 10 C, T948-1002,

The airport is 5 mins in a taxi from the centre

www.litegua.com 20 a day, 5 hrs, US$5.20. Bus to **El Rancho** (turn-off for Biotopo del Quetzal and Cobán), 4 hrs, take any bus to Guatemala City. To **Quiriguá**, 2 hrs, US$2, take any capital-bound bus. To **Chiquimula**, operated by *Carmencita*, 4 hrs, US$3. Alternatively, catch a bus to Guatemala City, getting off at Río Hondo, and catch a *colectivo* or any bus heading to Chiquimula. For **Río Dulce**, take any bus heading for Guatemala City and get off and change at **La Ruidosa** (15 mins). For minibuses to **Entre Ríos**, for the El Cinchado border crossing to **Honduras (Corinto)**, with connections to Omoa, Puerto Cortés and La Ceiba, see page 653.

Sea It's a 10-min walk to the municipal dock at the end of C 12, from the *Litegua* bus station. Taxi, US$0.65 per person. Ferries *(barca)* leave for Lívingston at 0500 and 1030 (1½ hrs, US$1.30). *Lanchas* also leave when a minimum of 16 people are ready to go, 35 mins, US$3.25. The first and only scheduled *lancha* leaves at 0630, and the last will leave, if there are enough people, at 1800. *Transportes El Chato*, 1 Av, between 10 and 11 C, T948-5525, pichilingo2000@ yahoo.com, also does trips from here to Punta de Manabique, and other places near and far, from US$32 up to US$195 from between 1-10 people. **To Belize** *Lanchas* leave for Punta Gorda at 1000 with *Transportes El Chato*, address above, returning at 1600, 1 hr, US$13. There is also one at 1400. To the southern Belize Cayes, US$325 for 1-10 people. To Placencia, US$390. **To Puerto Cortés, Honduras** Min 6 people in *lancha*, US$300.

Banks *Lloyds*, 15 C and 7 Av, handles MasterCard only *Bancafé*, 13 C and 7 Av, with Visa ATM. *Banco G&T Continental*, 7 C and 6 Av, it's possible to withdraw up to US$65 on MasterCard and Visa. TCs. *Banco Industrial*, 7 Av, 7-30, 24hr Visa ATM and cash on Visa cards. **Communications** Post office: Corner of 6 C and 6 Av. **Telephone:** *Telgua*, corner of 10 C and 8 Av. **Internet:** *Café Internet*, opposite gas station, corner of 6 Av and 13 C, US$3.25/hr. **Useful addresses** *Immigration*, corner of 12 C and 3 Av, open 24 hrs. — **Directory**

Puerto Barrios and Lívingston/Punta Gorda Guatemalan immigration offices are in Puerto Barrios and Lívingston , both open 24 hrs. There are exit fees to leave Guatemala by boat, but the official fee varies according to the time of day you leave. You must have your exit stamp from immigration before you can buy a ticket. If you come to Guatemala by boat you must go straight to the Puerto Barrios or Lívingston immigration offices. — **Border with Belize**

You can get your exit stamp at the Guatemalan immigration offices in Puerto Barrios or Lívingston if you are leaving by boat to Honduras. If you come into Guatemala by boat you must go straight to either of these offices. **Honduran consulate** If you need a visa, you must obtain it in Guatemala City, or at Esquipulas. Minibuses leave the market on 8 C in Puerto Barrios for Entre Ríos every 15 mins between 0630-1800, US$0.40. They pull up at the immigration post beyond Entre Ríos at El Cinchado and wait for you to complete formalities. The minibus continues the journey (15 mins) over a new bridge over the Río Motagua. There is nothing here except a handful of moneychangers and a pick-up or two to take you the 30 mins, over track, to Honduran immigration in Corinto. There is no entry tax here. pICK-UP to Tegucigalpita (1½ hrs). The trip from the border to Tegucigalpita costs US$3. This road from Corinto to Tegucigalpita, via Cuyamelito, is now also covered by an hourly bus service with *Línea Costeños*. If you take a pick-up, it leaves you at the bus stop heading for Omoa (US$0.40, 1¼ hrs) and on to Puerto Cortes (US$0.80, 2 hrs). With swift connections the journey is just under 4 hrs from Puerto Barrios to Omoa. It would not be wise to leave Puerto Barrios later than 0800 for this crossing due to pick-up connections. In the rainy season, start even earlier. — **Border with Honduras**

A few kilometres south of Puerto Barrios on Santo Tomás bay is **Santo Tomás de Castilla**. This port is now the country's largest and the most efficient on the Caribbean. There are a couple of hotels and some banks. Above Santo Tomás, to the southwest, is the **Cerro San Gil**, which rises to 1,300 m and is classified as 'super humid rainforest'. This is being conserved as a wildlife refuge.

Lívingston

Lívingston, or La Buga, is populated mostly by Garífuna blacks, who bring a colourful flavour to this corner of Guatemala. It is a funky town, with its tropical sounds and smells, and a good place to hang out for a few days, sitting on the dock of the bay, or larging it up with the locals, punta-style. Coco pan and cocado (a coconut, sugar and ginger *dulce*) and locally made jewellery are sold in the streets . The town is the centre of fishing and shrimping in the Bay of Amatique and only accessible by boat.

Lívingston can only be reached by boat. It is nearly 23 km by sea from Puerto Barrios and there are regular daily boat runs which take 35 mins in a fast *lancha*. The bulk of the town is up a small steep slope leading straight from the dock, which is at

Colour map 5, grid B3
Population: 5,000

Festivals : 24-31 December, in honour of the Virgen del Rosario, with traditional dancing including the Punta. Garífuna Day, 26 November

Guatemala

the mouth of the Río Dulce estuary. The other part of town is a linear spread along the river estuary, just north of the dock and then first left. The town is small and everything is within walking distance. The Caribbean beach is pretty dirty nearer the river estuary end, but a little further up the coast, it is cleaner, with palm trees and accommodation. Closer to the town are a couple of bars and weekend beach discos.

The town's **Centro Cultural Garífuna** is perched on a hillock, and has the best views in the whole of Lívingston. At the other side of town, near the hotel *African Place*, is the **Asociación Garífuna Guatemalteca Büdürü-Ogagua**, T947-0105, which focuses on dance, music, *artesanía*, food and ecotourism. There is also the *Büdürü bar*, see below. ■ *0800-1200, 1400-2000.*

Excursions

Don't stroll on the beach after dark and be careful at the Siete Altares end: there's a serious risk of robbery. Women should not go alone or even in pairs

Northwest along the coastline towards the Río Sarstún, on the border with Belize (where manatee can be seen), is the Río Blanco beach (45 minutes by *lancha* from Lívingston), followed by **Playa Quehueche** (also spelt Keueche). Beyond Quehueche, about 6 km (1½ hrs) from Lívingston, is **Los Siete Altares**, a set of small waterfalls and pools hidden in the greenery. They are at their best during the rainy season when the water cascades down to the sea. In the drier seasons much of the water is channelled down small, eroded grooves on large slabs of grey rock, where you can stretch out and enjoy the sun. Early *Tarzan* movies were filmed here.

Sleeping and eating On the beach, on the way to Siete Altares, there is a hotel and restaurant, **E** *Hotel Ecológico Siete Altares*, T501-4039, altares@hotmail.com Also along the coast, towards Siete Altares, is the fantastically located **E** *Salvador Gaviota Ecological Resort*, T404-7380. Rooms are with shared bath, but the bungalows for 2 or 4 people (**D**) have private bath. There is a bar and restaurant, and free *lancha* service – just ring beforehand.

For one of the best trips in Guatemala take a boat up the **Río Dulce** through the sheer-sided canyon towards El Golfete, where the river broadens out. Trees and vegetation cling to the canyon walls, their roots plunging into the waters for a long drink below. The scenery here is gorgeous, especially in the mornings, when the waters are unshaken. Tours can be arranged from Lívingston for US$9, see under Tour operators below. You can also paddle up the Río Dulce gorge on *cayucos*, which can be hired from some of the hotels in Lívingston.

The **Biotopo Chocón Machacas** is one place where the elusive **manatee** (sea cow) hangs out, but you are unlikely to see him munching his way across the lake bottom, as he is very shy and retreats at the sound of a boat motor. (The manatee is an aquatic herbivore, which can be up to 4 m long when adult, and weigh more than 1,000 lb. They eat for six to eight hours daily and can consume more than 10% of their body weight in a 24-hour period.) Administered by CECON (*Centro de Estudios Conservaciónistas*), the reserve is a mangrove zone, half way between Río Dulce town and Lívingston, on the northern shore of El Golfete – an area where the Río Dulce broadens into a lake that is 5 km across. Four Q'eqchi' communities of 400 people live on land within the 6,245 ha reserve. Within the reserve are carpets of water lilies, dragonflies, blue morpho butterflies, pelicans and cormorants. On land spot army ants, crabs, mahogany trees and the *labios rojos* ('hot lips') flower. ■ *0700-1600, US$2.60. Campsite in the reserve, 400 m from the entrance, next to a pond, with grills for cooking on, and toilets, but no food or drink for sale.*

Proyecto Ak' Tenamit (meaning 'new village' in Q'eqchi'), www.aktenamit.org, T254-1560is 15 minutes upriver from Lívingston. It was set up to help 7,000 Q'eqchi' Maya displaced by the civil war. Volunteers are needed for a minimum of a month's work. Board and transport, and weekends off. A working knowledge of Spanish is required. Near here is the Río Tatin tributary and the wonderfully sited **E-F** *Finca Tatin*, with great dock space to hang out on, T902-0831, www.fincatatin.centroamerica.com It's B&B, whether you opt for a room with private bath, or a dorm bed. Spanish classes (20 hours), and 7 days lodging is US$120 a week. Take a *lancha* from Lívingston (US$5.20) to get there.

Guatemala

Reserva Ecológica Cerro San Gil with its natural pools, karstic caves and biostation, can be visited from here, or from Río Dulce. Contact FUNDAECO, T948-5487, T504-1070 (mob), Guatemala City T440-4609, fundaeco@quetzal.net , or call in to see them at their offices next to the *Hotel Henry Berrisford*.

Boats can be hired in Lívingston to visit beaches along the coast towards San Juan and the Río Sarstún, or to cross Amatique Bay to the north to the tip of the long finger of land beyond Puerto Barrios, known as Punta de Manabique.

Sleeping
■ *on map*
Price codes:
see inside
front cover

AL *Tucán Dugú*, T947-0078, F947-0614, or Guatemala City T334-7813, tukansa@guate.net Cheaper in low season. All rooms have sea view, and have baths. There is a swimming pool (available to non-guests when the hotel is not busy for US$3.25), and a large restaurant overlooking the sea. **C** *Hospedaje Doña Alida,* 150 m to the right beyond *Tucán Dugú*, in a quiet location, T947-0027, hotelalida@hotmail.com This place has direct access to the beach and some rooms with great sea views and balconies, with restaurant. **D-E** *Casa Rosada*, a pastel pink house set on the waterfront, 600 m from the dock,

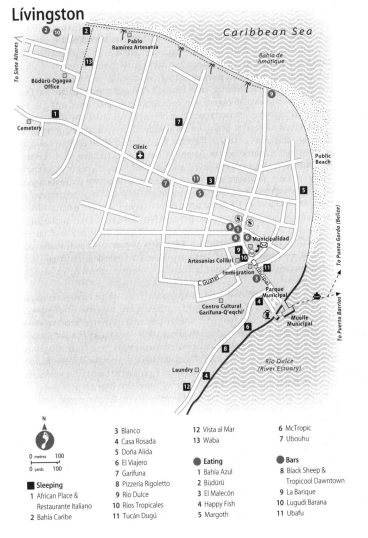

Guatemala

Lívingston

T947-0303, F947-0304, info@hotelcasarosada.com 10 bungalows furnished with attractively decorated hand-painted furniture. But, even better for budget travellers is a large, but uncrowded dorm upstairs, overlooking the bay. Meals are set for the day, ranging from pasta to delicious shrimps bathed in garlic, for the evening meal. Often full, so reservations are advisable. On the beach is the rather incongruous-looking **D-E** *Hotel Bahía Caribe*, at the time of writing, was the only hotel right on the beach, at Barrio París, T947-0399. Rooms are clean, and cool, and vary in price according to whether they have private bath and a/c. All have TV. Its restaurant *Pelican* is open 24 hrs a day. A communial jacuzzi costs an extra US$6.50 for guests and non-guests for unlimited time, 24 hrs. **D-E** *Hotel Ríos Tropicales*, T957-0158. This place has some nice touches to distinguish it from the majority of other places in town, like funkily designed mirror frames and terracotta-tiled floors. There are 8 rooms, with fans, 2 with private bath, a laundry and an 8% discount on meals at the *McTropic* restaurant up the road. **D-E** *Hotel Vista al Mar*. This is a peculiar place with some adventurous mural work, and a friendly owner. Basic and clean bungalows are set in a small yard, restaurant, laundry service, kayaks and bicycles ror rent, US$1.30 per hr. **E** *African Place*, T947-0218, built in Moorish style with beautiful tile work, and a garden, but it looks very out of place in Lívingston. It is right at the end of the main street, so quite a walk from the dock. There are 24 clean rooms with bath, cheaper without, but some are a little musty. The owners are Spanish. **E** *Garífuna*, T947-0183, has 10 comfortable, ultra-clean rooms with private bath, laundry. Recommended. **E** *Hotel Blanco*, T947-0267, labocadelabuga@yahoo.com All rooms with 3 or 4 beds with private bathrooms, upstairs with balcony and hammocks. It's clean, but the rooms could do with a general spruce up. Laundry service, book exchange, small *Side Walk Café*, and internet. **E** *Hotel Río Dulce*, T947-0059, is an early 19th-century wooden building on the main street, with a seriously sloping landing on the first floor, a good place from which to watch life pass by. Try and get a room upstairs rather than behind the old building. There is a restaurant on the ground floor with some tables directly on the street. The restaurant serves delicious Italian food prepared with panache by the hospitable Italian chef. Recommended. **E** *Pizzería Rigoletto*, T947-0772, run by Alix, a Brit, who has 1 twin room to rent out with a fan, and shared bathroom. If you want something that resembles a bit of home ambience, a garden on the river with an almond tree, and 5 star hospitality, then this is the place. See also Eating and Tour operators. **E** *Waba*, barrio Pueblo Nuevo, T947-0193, is run by a friendly family offering upstairs rooms with a balcony and sea views. Rooms with private bath are clean and cool, with fan. *Comida típica* is served at a little wooden restaurant (0700-2130) on site. Good value and recommended. **F** *El Viajero*, popular, clean and friendly, rooms with fans. Some have private bath, cheaper without. If the front desk is unmanned take a walk down the garden, where you'll probably find those in charge having a nap!

Eating

● *on map,*
see previous page
Fresh fish is available
everywhere, ask for
tapado in restaurants
– a rich soup with
various types of
seafood, banana and
coconut

Bahía Azul, excellent breakfasts, but dreadful coffee. Tables on the street as well as a dining-room inside.There is a tourist information service and the *Exotic Travel Agency*. *El Malecón*, *50 m from the dock on the left*, serves *Chapín* and Western-style breakfasts, seafood and chicken fajítas, all served in a large airy wooden dining area. *Happy Fish*, just along from the *Hotel Río Dulce*, is a popular restaurant with internet café. Serves a truckload of fish (not quite so happy now) with good coffee. Occasional live music at weekends. At the *Margoth*, don't be put off by the building, the food is good, especially the baked fish, and reasonably priced. *McTropic*, opposite the *Hotel Río Dulce*, with street tables, great breakfasts, and cocktails. Good service and popular. *Pizzería Rigoletto*, serving delicious pizzas, 18 flavours, made with real mozzarella cheese. Also sandwiches, salads, cocobread and teas (including Earl Grey all the way from England!). You can sit in the garden on the riverfront and enjoy a beer. There's a book exchange, laundry service, packed lunch service and tours are offered. *Restaurante Italiano*, new Italian-run restaurant in *Hotel African Place*. The *melanzane* eggplant/aubergine dish is divine. *Ubouhu*, with street tables outside, near the *Ubafu*. This Garífuna-run place, meaning world, has *pollo*, *bisteck* and shrimps on the menu, as well as drinks. It's one of the popular local gossip exchanges. Women sell *pan de coco* on the streets. You can buy cold, whole coconuts, split for you with a machete, US$0.20, from the orange crush stand on the main street, or from a *tienda* next to *Bancafé*.

The *Black Sheep Cinema and Bar* is a popular Bob Marley shrine with happy hour as well as a cinema showing afternoon movies. Open 1400 until dawn. On the beach is the *Büdürü Bar y Restaurante*, at Barrio París, 15 mins along the beach from town (see also under Tour operators). Next to the *Hotel Bahía Caribe* on the beach is the popular *Happy Fisherman's Place*, open all day. *La Barique,* on the beach, is open 0900-0100, Fri and Sat. Also on the beach is *Lugudi Barana disco,* open Sun only, 1500-0100. *Tropicool Dawntown Disco-Bar*, around the corner from *Bahía Azul*, is one of the most popular hang-outs from 0800-0100, with happy hour until 2100. The unmissable *Ubafu* , on the road down to *African Place*, is heaving most nights as locals and travellers dance the *punta*. A live band plays nightly from about 2100 with drums, a conch shell and turtle shells, the *punta*'s instrument ensemble. This large wooden bar, decked out in Bob Marley posters and Rastafarian symbols, is definitely worth a visit. Try the *Coco Loco*, rum and coco milk served up in a coconut. At the weekends the place is a little less packed as it vies for attention with the beach bars and discos.

Bars & nightclubs
Garífuna music CDs are sold at the Hotel Blanco – ask for Greg Lucas

Ferries Ferry from **Puerto Barrios to Lívingston** (22½ km), daily at 1000 and 1700, 1½ hrs, US$1.30. Returning to Puerto Barrios, 0500 and 1400 daily (to theoretically connect with the last bus to Guatemala City). Private launches taking 16-25 people also sail this route, 35 mins, US$3.25. They leave at 0630 and 0700 from Lívingston to Puerto Barrios and then when full. Note that the sea can get rough in the afternoons. **Lívingston to Río Dulce**, with short stops at Aguas Calientes and the Biotopo Chacón Machacas, US$9.10 one way, US$15.60 round trip. *Lanchas* definitely leave at 0900 and 1300 for Río Dulce, but these make no stops. **To Honduras (Omoa, Puerto Cortés, La Ceiba)**, *lanchas* can be organized at the dock: to Omoa, US$32.50 per person, min 7 people. With *Bahía Azul*, for US$35 per person including exit tax (see immigration below), 6 people min. With the same company to **Utila**, US$90, 2 days. **To Belize** (Punta Gorda, Placencia, Cayos Zapotillos), there is no regular ferry service from Lívingston. Anyone who takes you must have a manifest with passengers' names, stamped and signed at the immigration office. Most days fast *lanchas* make the trip to Punta Gorda. Enquire at the dock and negotiate a fare with the *lanchero* association, US$13 per person, min 8 people. To the cayes, US$39 per person round trip, max 8 people. Boats to Placencia, with *Bahía Azul*, for US$50 per person, 4 people min. Boats to Zapotilla cayes, US$35 per person, 6 people min with the same company.

Transport
The ferry from Puerto Barrios to Lívingston has been referred to as the 'barfy barque', as there is much pitching and heaving

Banks *Bancafé*. Cash advance on Visa and MasterCard, TCs and cash changed. Has a 24-hr Visa-only ATM. *Banco de Comercio* will change Amex and MasterCard TCs and cash. Some hotels will change cash, including *Casa Rosada*. **Communications** Internet: *Happy Fish*, US$4.70/hr. The *Black Sheep Cinema and Bar* has internet. **Post office**: Next to *Telgua*, behind the Municipalidad, take the small road to the right. **Telephone**:*Telgua*, open 0800-1800. **Laundry** *Lavandería Doña Chila*, opposite the *Casa Rosada*, does laundry for US$0.65 per lb. *Pizzería Rigoletto* also does laundry, at US$0.20 per piece. **Tour operators** *Büdürü Bar y Restaurante* offers guided tours in English and Spanish on Garífuna culture, US$7-10, T9470603. It's on the beach at Barrio París 15 mins from the town centre. *Exotic Travel Agency*, in the *Bahía Azul* restaurant, T947-0049, F947-0136, exotictravelagency@ hotmail.com Both the *Casa Rosada* and *Pizzería Rigoletto* make more stops on their Río Dulce trip including the Project Ak' Tenamit, and the Río Tatin and the *lagunetas*. You can also contract any of the *lancheros* at the dock to take you to any destination. They charge US$9.10, US$15.60 round trip to Río Dulce; to Playa Blanca, US$9.75; to Siete Altares, US$26, 4 people maximum. **Useful addresses** *Immigration*, on C Principal, opposite *Hotel Tucán Dugú*, is open 24 hrs daily, T947-0240. Just knock if the door is shut. *Port Captain*, T947-0029.

Directory

Punta de Manabique is a fine, finger-shaped peninsula coated in a beach of white sand on its eastern side, and by mangrove on the other. Travelling north to the point of the peninsula, you pass the Bahía de Graciosa, where dolphins frolic. Manatees are also to be found munching under the surface. In its virgin tropical forest live howler monkeys, parrots, snakes, pizote, tapirs and peccary and on its beaches, turtles. There is a visitor centre and a scientific station near the tip and the **E** *Saraguate Hotel*. Meals are extra and cost between US$2-4. Advance reservations need to be made either via the person in charge, Luis Alonso, T948-2331, or by ringing the *Fundación Mario Dary*. It costs US$78 to get to the tip of Punta de Manabique from

Punta de Manabique

Guatemala

Puerto Barrios. See details on pages 653 and 657. Volunteers are welcomed by the *Fundación Mario Dary*, which operates conservation, health, education and ecotourism projects. Volunteers receive free lodging. For more information contact the helpful Erwin Herdocia who is in charge of ecotourism at the *Fundación* T948-0944, www.fundarymanabique.guate.net

Lago de Izabal

This area can be wet in the rainy season, but it experiences a lull in July, known as the canícula

The vast Lago de Izabal narrows to form a neck at the town of Fronteras, better known as Río Dulce. Río Dulce is best known for its riverside setting and there are some beautiful places around the lake and river in which to stay. Just south of Río Dulce on the lake is the Castillo de San Felipe. On the northern shore of the lake is the town of El Estor, and on its southern shore the smaller town of Mariscos. Further east, beyond Río Dulce, the river broadens out to El Golfete, where there is the Biotopo Chacón Machacas. It then narrows into one of the finest gorges in the world, and opens out at its estuary, with Lívingston at its head (see page 654).

Fronteras/Río Dulce

Río Dulce is a good place to stop and kick back for a couple of days. Allow yourself to be tempted to laze on a boat for the afternoon, walk in the nearby jungle, or eat and drink at one of several dockside restaurants. Río Dulce is 23 km upstream from Lívingston at the entrance to Lago de Izabal, is easily accessible from Puerto Barrios by road, and is the last major stop before the Petén. It's also a good place to collect information about the area stretching from El Estor to Lívingston. Río Dulce website is at www.mayaparadise.com See also under Tour operators, below. For a trip to the Castillo de San Felipe, see page 660.

El Paraíso waterfall Between Río Dulce and El Estor is *Finca El Paraíso*, a hot waterfall with waters that plunge into a cool-water pool below. It is a delightful place to swim, and the hot water has eroded the rock behind it to form a piece of cool rock art. ■ *Getting there: from Río Dulce, take a bus from the corner of the main street and a road turning left at Pollandia north of the bridge, 45 mins , US$0.90. Ask to be dropped at the entrance: US$0.65. Buses to Río Dulce pass the finca between 40 and 50 mins past the hour.*

Essentials

Sleeping & eating **A** *Catamaran*, T930-5109, www.mayaparadise.com Finely decorated cabañas, 40 rooms set around the lake edge, an inviting pool, large restaurant with good food, *lancha* (US$6.50 from Río Dulce, 10 mins downstream, or call for a pick-up). **A-E** *Bruno's* is on the lake, and a stone's throw from the where the buses stop, T930-5174, www.mayaparadise.com/brunoe.htm Rooms overlook the lake, there's a dormitory, camping, campervan parking, pool, restaurant. Non-guests can pay US$1.60 to use pool. The marina has 28 berths. Popular. **A-F** *Hacienda Tijax*, T902-0858, www.tijax.com 2 mins by *lancha* from the dock, jungle lodges, and other simpler accommodation; camping facilities. There is a beautiful jungle trail, a rubber plantation, bird sanctuary, natural pools to swim in, horse-riding, rowboat hire and a medicine trail. Excellent food in the riverside bar and restaurant, tranquil and beautiful. Also afternoon sails until sunset, US$25, min 2 people, including snacks and drinks, and water skiing. To get there, ask at the *Tijax Express* office near the dockside. The Lívingston *lancha* will pass by here if you pre-arrange at reception. Highly recommended. **A-F** *Hotel La Ensenada*, Km 275, 500 m to the right at the Shell station, T930-5240, F930-5299, riverside location, breakfast included, restaurant, pool, nice gardens, camping and campervan facilities. **B-E** *Turicentro Las Brisas*, T930-5124, a stone's throw from the dock, near where the buses pull up. Rooms with private bath and a/c, some without a/c, and dorms with fans and private bath, and dorms with shared bath. **C-D** *Tortugal Marina*, T306-6432, T902-0174 (mob), tortugalmarina@hotmail.com If you can afford it, stay here in the 5 beautifully presented bungalows with gorgeous soft rugs on the floor. Bathrooms are shared. There is a riverside restaurant and bar, pool table in a cool upstairs attic room with books, internet, phone and fax service. Highly recommended. **D** *Posada del Río*, a new hotel under the bridge with river views, across the road and behind *Bruno's*, T930-5167, 5 standard rooms with private bath and fan, some with TV. **D-F** *Hospedaje Riverside*, about 200 m on the left heading north after the bridge, T930-5188. Very basic downstairs rooms, with fan, cold water and shared bath, are much cheaper than the upstairs rooms with private bath, a/c, and TV. Friendly landlady. **D-F** *Hotel Backpacker's*, by the bridge on the south bank of the river, T208-1779, www.mayaparadise.com/backpe.htm Restaurant and bar, dorms with lockers, internet and telephone service, profits go to Casa Guatemala (see below). Recommended. **E** *Café Sol*, 500 m north of the bridge on the road to Tikal, T930-5143, friendly, clean, fans, good-value rooms, cheaper without bath, TV costs a bit extra. Useful if you have to catch an early bus. *Restaurante y Pizzería Río Bravo*, friendly management, dockside location serving breakfasts, seafood, chicken, pastas and pizzas up to US$8. Open 0700-2300 daily.

Sailing Captain John Clark's sailing trips on his 46-ft Polynesian catamaran, *Las Sirenas*, are highly recommended. Trips include the Río Dulce canyon, to El Paraíso falls, Castillo de San Felipe, and Belize Cayes. Food, taxes, snorkelling and fishing gear, and windsurf boards are included. Contact *Aventuras Vacacionales SA*, 1 Av Sur, 11B, Antigua, T/F832-3352, www.sailing.conexion.com *Discover Paradise*, runs 7-day trips on *That*, a 62' trimaran, to the Belize Cayes. Contact *ATI Divers*, at the *Iguana Perdida*, Santa Cruz, Lake Atitlán, T762-2646, santacruz@guate.net

Sports

Local Boat *Colectivo lanchas* leave for Lívingston at 0900 and 1300, US$10. Private *lanchas* can be arranged at the dock to any of the river or lakeside hotels. **Bus** To **Finca El Paraíso**, US$0.90, 45 mins; to **El Estor**, US$1.30, 1½ hrs on a partially paved road, 0500-1600, hourly, returning 0500-1600. These buses leave north of the bridge, from the corner of the first road to the left, where there is a *Pollandia* restaurant. To get to the Castillo de San Felipe, see page 660. To **Puerto Barrios**, take any bus to **La Ruidosa** and change.

Transport

Buy bus tickets at Tijax Express or Information Río Dulce near the dock

Long-distance Bus To **Guatemala City** and **Flores**: through buses stop at Río Dulce. To **Guatemala City** with *Litegua*, T930-5251, www.litegua.com, 0300, 0545, 0745 and 1200, US$3.90, 6 hrs. **Fuente del Norte**, T930-5111, 20 services daily, first at 0700, then virtually every hour on the half-hour from 1030 until 0230. *Línea Dorada*, Lineadorada@intelnet.net.gt at 2400 and 1300, luxury service, 5 hrs, US$30. To **Flores** from 0630-0300, 20 buses daily, 4½ hrs with *Fuente del Norte*. This bus also stops at **Finca Ixobel** and **Poptún**, US$3.90. *Línea Dorada*, to Flores, 2400, 1430, 3½ hrs, luxury service with a/c, TV and snacks, US$30, and on to **Melchor de Mencos** for Belize and returning. Fuente del Norte, also to **Melchor de Mencos**, US$11, at 1230, 2030, 2230-0300, **Sayaxché** at 2200 and one to **Naranjo** at 2100. **Shuttles** *Atitrans* runs a shuttle service at 1600 to **Antigua**, minimum 2 people, US$37, 6½ hrs. To Río Dulce from **Antigua**, at 0400. Contact *Atitlán* in Río Dulce for tickets, see above, or *Atitrans* itself.

Banks There are 2 banks: Visa, Tcs and cash only. **Communications** Internet and telephone: *Captain Nemo's Communications* behind *Bruno's*, US$6.50/ hr and phone call service. *Tijax Express*, US$7.80/hr. *Hotel Backpacker's* has internet as does *Information Río Dulce*, near the dock (also telephone service). **Post office:** Near the banks. **Tour operators** On the little road heading to the dockside is *Atitlán*, also known as *Information Río Dulce*, T930-5111, 24 hrs, riodulceinfo@itelgua.com Offers good independent advice on hotels. They also run a shuttle service to many mainstream places, but also to Quiriguá. Opposite is *Tijax Express*, T930-5196/7, tijax@guate.net, which also has an internet service. Next to them is *Otiturs*, T930-5402, otiturs@hotmail.com Offers a minibus service as well as tours to local sites, internal flights and boat trips. There are many **lancheros** offering trips on the river and on Lago de Izabal. **Volunteer work** On the shore of Lago de Izabal is *Casa Guatemala*, a children's orphanage, where you can work in exchange for basic accommodation and food. Contact 14 C, 10-63, Zona 1, Guatemala City, T232-5517, www.casa-guatemala.com, or the *Hotel Backpacker's*.

Directory

Guatemala

Castillo de San Felipe At the entrance to Lago de Izabal, 2 km upstream, is the old Spanish fort of Castillo de San Felipe. The fortification was first built in 1643 to defend the coast against attacks from pirates. ■ *0800-1700, US$1.30.*

Sleeping and eating **AL-A** *Banana Palms*, T930-5022, F930-5041, hotels@amigo.net.gt A luxury full service resort, with cheaper family rooms available, marina, 2 pools, kayak rental, ping pong, fishing rods available, basketball, restaurant. **B** *Mansión del Río Resort and Marina*, T930-5005, F930-5003, www.mercadeo.com.gt A new, all-inclusive resort, with a small supermarket on site, kid-friendly with dinosaur characters in and around the pool, which also has a waterslide. There are cheaper apartments to rent for 4 people. **B** *Viñas del Lago*, T930-5053, www.infovia.com.gt/hotelvinasdellago 300 m from the castle on the lakeside. Unfortunately the hotel has let its lakeside area go, and it's dirty and unkempt. All rooms have a/c. Pool and garden, but sadly, pet wild animals are kept. **D-E** *La Cabaña del Viajero*, 500 m from the castle, T930-5062. Small place with pool, traditional cabañas as well as larger family-style cabañas with private bathroom and some cute little attic rooms as well.
Transport Take a boat from Río Dulce, or *camioneta* from the corner of the main road to Tikal, and the first turning left after the bridge by *Pollandia*, US$0.26, 5 mins, or a 5-km walk.

El Estor

Colour map 5, grid B3
Population: 30,000

El Estor enjoys one of the most beautiful vistas in Guatemala. It is strung along the northwest shore of Lago de Izabal, backed by the Santa Cruz mountain range, and facing the Sierra de las Minas. The lake is the largest in Guatemala at 717 sq km. It is a great place to relax, swim (down a nearby canyon), go fishing and spot manatee. It is so laid back that young guys bicycle right through the doors of some restaurants screeching to a halt at the bar, and local men come round with buckets stuffed full of freshly plucked strawberries for sale. The town dates back to the days when the Europeans living in the Atlantic area got their provisions from a store situated at this spot, now the *Hotel Vista al Lago*. Briton Skinner and Dutchman Klee used to supply the region from *el store* from 1815 to 1850. Nickel-mining began just outside town in 1978, but was suspended at the **Exmibal plant** after the oil crisis of 1982, because the process depended on cheap sources of energy. The mine is still closed, but its huge hulks of motionless machinery remain, and the small town, built nearby for the plant's 1,000 or so workers, is now a ghost town. El Estor can be reached from Río Dulce, 43 km (dusty), 1¼ hrs by bus. (15 km of the road is paved from Río Dulce and the rest is all-weather unpaved.) The ferry from Mariscos no longer runs, but a private *lancha* can be contracted. For routes from El Estor to Cobán, via either Panzós and Tactic, or Cahabón and Lanquín, see page 668.

Excursions You can hire a boat from Río Dulce to El Estor for about US$60, passing near the hot waterfall, inland at *Finca El Paraíso* (see page 658), which can be reached by a good trail in about 40 minutes. The Sauce River cuts through the impressive **Cañon El Boquerón**, where you can swim with the current all the way down the canyon, which is brilliant fun. It's a deep canyon with lots of *barba de viejo* hanging down, strange rock formations, and otters and troops of howler monkeys whooping about. One of the locals will paddle you upstream for about 800 m, US$0.65. ■ *Take the Río Dulce bus and ask to be dropped at the entrance. Or, hire a bike from town (8 km) or a taxi, US$6.50, including waiting time.* Exploring the Río Zarco, closer to town, also makes for a good trip, with cold swimming. Sport fishing can be arranged on Lago Izabal with *robalo, mojarra,* and *tilapia* aplenty. The **Refugio de Vida Silvestre Bocas del Polochic (Bocas del Polochic Wildlife Reserve)** is a 23,000-ha protected area on the western shores of the lake. Howler monkeys are commonly seen. In addition to over 350 bird species, there are iguanas, turtles and the chance of sighting crocodiles and manatees. The NGO *Defensores de la Naturaleza* has a research station at Selempim with bunk beds (**F** per person), food, showers and kitchen. Contact them at the corner of 2 Calle and 5 Avenida, T/F949-7237, rbocas@defensores.org.gt ■ *2-3 hr boat ride from El Estor to Ensenada Los Lagartos.*

Sleeping

C *Marisabella*, 8 Av and 1 C on the waterfront, T949-7215, urlich@internet.detelgua.com.gt Large rooms with tiled private bathrooms, some with TV, internet service, US$11.70/hr. **C-D** *Hotel Ecológico Cabañas del Lago*, on the lake shore, with 200 m of private beach, T949-7245, or contact *Restaurante Hugo's*, taxi there, US$1.30 per person. **D** *Hotel Vista al Lago*, 6 Av, 1-13, T949-7205, has 21 clean rooms with private bath and fan. Ask for the lakeview rooms, where there is a pleasant wooden balcony on which to sit. Friendly owner Oscar Paz will take you fishing, and runs ecological and cultural tours. The new, family-run **E** *Hotel Central*, T949-7244, faces the park with lake views from the 2nd floor. It's extremely good value with 12 rooms with private bath and fan, and there's a communal TV. **E** *Villela*, 6 Av, 2-06, T949-7214. 9 big rooms with bath, clean, some rooms and showers quite dark though. Flower-filled garden with chairs to sit out in. Recommended.

Eating

Dorita, a *comedor* serving seafood, very good meals, excellent value (US$3 for 2) and popular with the locals. *Marisabella*, 8 Av and 1 C, good and cheap spaghetti, as well as fish and chicken, with lake views. *Restaurant Elsita*, 2 blocks north of the market on 8 Av. This is a great people-watching place. There's a large menu and the food is good. *Restaurante Hugo's*, with *mariscos*, *comida rápida*, vegetarian food and ice-cream. *Restaurante Típico Chaabil*, is a thatched restaurant right on the lakeside, with plenty of fish to eat. Prices range from US$2-7. Cheap breakfasts. *Super Joyita*, minisupermarket, near bus terminal on 8 Av.

Transport

Bus El Estor-Río Dulce, 0500-1600, hourly, 1¼ hrs, US$1.30. To **Cobán**, with *Transportes Valenciana*, 1200, 0200, 0400 and 0800, 8 long and dusty hrs, with no proper stop, US$2.60. The 0800 leaves its terminal and does a massive tour of the town before finally leaving from the park at 0900, but it's best to be there for 0800, because you will be swinging from the side wing mirror by the time it leaves, it's so packed. To **Guatemala City**, 0100 direct, via Río Dulce, 7½ hrs, or go to Río Dulce and catch one there. At 2400 and 0300 via Río Polochic Valley. Bus to **Santa Elena, Petén** at 0500.

Directory

Banks *Corpobanco* and *Banrural* accept TCs and cash. **Communications** **Internet**: *Café Internet Planeta Tierra*, US$5.45/hr. The post office is on the park. **Tour operators** *Aventuras Ecoturísticas y Café Internet Planeta Tierra*, 5 Av, 2-65, T913-5598, www.ecoturismoelestor.com Run by the helpful Eloyda Mejía, who offers tours to El Boquerón, the source of the Río Sauce, the nickel plant, *Finca El Paraíso* and to the Bocas del Polochic. Bicycle rent, horse rental, *lancha* tours and sport fishing can be arranged.

Mariscos is on the southern shore of Lago de Izabal. The best reason to come here is the nearby **D-F** *Denny's Beach*, with its gorgeous lakeside location, accessible by *lancha* from Río Dulce, or from Mariscos (US$2), or call in at *Shop-N-Go* in Mariscos to arrange for a pick-up, T7094990.

The Verapaces

□Guatemala City

Propped up on a massive limestone table eroded over thousands of years, the plateau of the Verapaz region is riddled with caves, underground tunnels, stalagtites and stalag-mites. Cavernous labyrinths used by the Maya for worship, in their belief that caves are the entrances to the underworld, are also now visited by travellers who marvel at the natural interior design of these subterranean spaces. Nature has performed its work above ground too. At Semuc Champey, pools of tranquil turquoise-green water span a monumental limestone bridge, and beneath the bridge a river thunders violently through. The quetzal reserve also provides the opportunity to witness a feather flash of red or green of the elusive bird, the quetzal, and dead insects provide curious interest in Rabinal, where their body parts end up on ornamental gourds. The centre of this region – the imperial city of Cobán – provides respite for the traveller with a clutch of muse-ums, honouring the Maya, coffee and orchid, and a fantastic entertainment spectacle at the end of July with a whirlwind of traditional dances and a Maya beauty contest.

History

Before the Spanish conquest of the region, Las Verapaces had a notorious reputation – it was known as Tezulutlán (land of war) for its aggressive warlike residents, who fought repeated battles for years with their neighbours and rivals, the K'iche' Maya. These warring locals were not going to be a pushover for the Spanish conquerors and they strongly resisted when their land was invaded. The Spanish eventually retreated in despair and the weapon was replaced with the cross. Thus, Carlos V of Spain gave the area the title of Verdadera Paz (true peace) in 1548. The region's modern history saw it converted into a massive coffee and cardamom growing region. German coffee *fincas* were established from the 1830s until the Second World War, when the Germans were invited over to plough the earth by the Guatemalan government. Many of the *fincas* were expropriated during the war, but some were saved from this fate, by naming a Guatemalan as the owner of the property. The area still produces some of Guatemala's finest coffee – served up with some of the country's finest cakes! The Germans also introduced cardamom to the Verapaces, when a *finquero* requested some seeds for use in biscuits.

Baja Verapaz

The small region of Baja Verapaz is made up of a couple of Achi'-Maya speaking towns, namely Salamá, Rabinal, San Jerónimo and Cubulco. The department is known for the quetzal reserve, the large Dominican finca and aqueduct, and the weird decorative technique of the crafts in Rabinal.

Sierra de las Minas Biosphere Reserve

Colour map 5, grid A2

Just north of El Rancho, in the department of El Progreso, is **San Agustín Acasaguastlán**, an entrance for the Sierra de las Minas Biosphere Reserve, one of Guatemala's largest conservation areas with peaks topping 3,000 m and home to the quetzal, harpy eagle and peregrine falcon fly here and puma, jaguar, spider monkey, howler monkey, tapir and pizote roam its mountains. To visit, get a *permiso* in San Augusín from the office of *La Fundació Defensores de la Naturaleza*, Barrio San Sebastián, one block before the Municipalidad, T945-1477. The contact is Claudia Paíz. Or from its offices in Santa Elena, Péten, at 5 C, 3 Av "A", Zona 2, T926-3095, or the capital at 19 Av B, 0-83, Zona 15, Vista Hermosa II, T369-5151. Inside the Sierra de las Minas is an ecotourism project, **D** *La Cabaña de Los Albores*. Chilascó, a 130 m-high waterfall, is nearby.

Biotopo del Quetzal

The Biotopo del Quetzal, or **Biosphere Mario Dary Rivera**, is between Cobán and Guatemala City at Km 160.5, 4 km south of Purulhá and 53 km from Cobán. There are two trails. Increasing numbers of quetzals have been reported in the Biotopo, but they are still very elusive. Ask for advice from the rangers. ■ *0700-1600 daily, US$2.60. Parking available, disabled entrance. Run by CECON (Centro de Estudios Conservacionistas), Av Reforma, 0-63, Zona 10, Guatemala City, T331-0904.*

Sleeping and eating B *Posada Montaña del Quetzal*, at Km 156, T331-0929, bungalows or rooms with private bathrooms, hot water, café, bar, swimming pool and gardens. **E-F** *Hospedaje Los Ranchitos,* clean rooms, hot water, and dorms, which are fairly basic, *comedor*. This is an excellent spot from where to see the quetzal in the early morning (0600) but especially between Jul-Nov. Opposite the reserve is *Biotopin Restaurante*. **Transport Bus** From Guatemala City, take a Cobán bus with *Escobar-Monja Blanca* and ask to be let out at the *Biotopo*, hourly from 0400-1700, 3½ hrs, US$3.90; Cobán-*Biotopo*, 1 hr, US$1.05, take any capital-bound bus; bus El Rancho-*Biotopo*, US$1.30, 1¼ hr. Cobán-Purulhá, local buses ply this route between 0645-2000 returning until 1730, US$0.52, 1 hr, 20 mins.

Salamá

Shortly before Salamá is **San Jerónimo**, where there is a Dominican church and convent, from where the friars tended vineyards, exported wine and cultivated sugar. There is an old sugar mill (*trapiche*) on display at the *finca* and a huge aqueduct of some 124 arches to transport water to the sugar cane fields and the town.

Salamá sits in a valley with a colonial cathedral, containing carved gilt altarpieces as its centrepiece. The town also has one of a few remaining Templos de Minerva in the country, which was built in 1916. Behind the Calvario church is a hill – Cerro de la Santa Cruz – from where a view of the valley can be seen. Market day is Monday and is worth a visit.

Sleeping and eating D *Tezulutlán*, Ruta 4, 4-99, Zona 1, T940-1643, just off the plaza – 1 of the best in town with bath, cheaper without, restaurant, some rooms have hot water. It's clean and quiet. E *San Ignacio*, 4 C "A", 7-09, T940-0186, behind the *Telgua* building, with bath and TV, clean and friendly. *Restaurante Las Tejas*, on the carretera a San Jerónimo, good, speciality is *caldo de chunto* (turkey soup). To get there take the Salamá-Guatemala bus, US$1.60; Rabinal-Salamá US$0.50, 1-1½ hrs.

The village of Rabinal was founded in 1537 by Fray Bartolomé de Las Casas. It has a handsome 16th-century church, and a busy Sunday market, where brightly lacquered gourds, beautiful *huipiles* and embroidered napkins are sold. The glossy lacquer is made from the body oil of a farmed scaly insect called the *Niij* (*Llaveia axin*). The male *Niij* is boiled in water to release its oil, which is then mixed with soot powder, to create the lacquer used to decorate the gourds. The **Museo Rabinal Achí** displays historical exhibits. ■ *2 C y 4 Av, Zona 3, T979-7820, musachi@intelnet.net.gt*

Rabinal

Sleeping and eating E-F *Posada San Pablo*, clean and friendly, will do the laundry, but there are hard beds and the *posada* has no hot water. F-G *Hospedaje Caballeros*, 1 C, 4-02, with bath, cheaper without. Getting theres: Rabinal is reached by travelling west from Salamá on a paved road. From Guatemala City, 5½ hrs, a beautiful, occasionally heart-stopping ride, or via El Progreso, and then Salamá by bus.

West of Rabinal, set amid maize fields and peach trees, **Cubulco** is known for its tradition of performing the pole dance, *Palo Volador*, which takes place every 20-25 July. Men, attached to rope, have to leap out from the top of the pole and spiral down, accompanied by marimba music. Buses leave 0330-1600 to Guatemala City via Salamá. There is a bus between Rabinal and Cubulco, supplemented by pick-up rides. There are three basic *hospedajes* (**F-G**) in town.

Cubulco

Alta Verapaz

The region of Alta Verapaz is based on a gigantic mountain, Sierra de Chamá. Dinosaurs roamed the area more than 65 million years ago before it was engulfed by sea. It later emerged, covered with limestone rock, which over millions of years has left the area riddled with caves, and dotted with small hills. In the far northwest of the department are the mystical emerald green waters of Laguna Lachuá.

On the main Guatemala City-Cobán road, Tactic is famous for beautiful *huipiles*, silverwork, and for its 'living well', in which the water becomes agitated as people approach. From here there is a route heading east through good hiking country to El Estor on the shores of Lago de Izabal (see page 658).

Tactic

Sleeping and eating D *Chi' Ixim*, Km 182.5, just beyond Tactic, T953-9198. Rooms with private bath, hot water and fireplaces, restaurant. D-E *Villa Linda*, 4 C, 6-25, Zona 1, T953-9216, near the plaza, with bath, cheaper without. F *Hotel Sulmy*, 4 Av, 1-02, Zona 2, nice and clean. All capital-bound buses from Cobán run through Tactic, or take a local bus between 0645-2000, returning between 0500-1730, 40 mins, US$0.32.

Santa Cruz Verapaz has a fine, white, 16th-century church and a **festival** between 1-4 May when you can see the wonderful Dance of the *Guacamayos* (scarlet macaws). **Poqomchi' Maya** village is 15 km northwest of Tactic at the junction with

Guatemala

the road to Uspantán. **Sleeping**: **B-C** *Hotel Park*, on the main road south of the junction to the village, T/F950-4539, rooms of varying prices with TV, restaurant, bar, gym, excellent gardens and a small zoo. To get there, take the San Cristóbal Verapaz bus, 25 minutes (see below), or take any bus heading to the capital, get off at the junction and walk the couple of hundred metres into the town.

Six kilometres west towards Uspantán is **San Cristóbal Verapaz**, which has a large, white, colonial church. From the church, a 1-km long, straight, road (Calle del Calvario) slopes down and then curves upwards to a hilltop **Calvario Church**. At Easter, the entire road is carpeted in flowers that rival those on display in Antigua at this time of year. There is **Museo Katinamit**, run by the Centro Communitario Educativo Poqomchi', dedicated to the preservation and learning of the Poqomchi' culture. ■ *Mon-Fri 0900-1200, 1500-1700, T950-4039, cecep@intelnet.net.gt*

Sleeping and eating **E-F** *Hotel El Portón Real*, 4 Av, 1-44, Zona 1, T950-4604. This hotel looks dreary from the outside, but inside it is lovely with lots of wood furnishings, and is run by a very friendly *señora*. Rooms, with bath, cheaper without, hot water, and free drinking water. The hotel closes its doors at 2130. **Fiesta 15, 20 Jan** and on **8 Dec** when the Devil-burning dance can be seen. **21-26 Jul** with the *Palo Volador*. **Transport** buses run from Cobán between 0600-1915 every 15 mins, US$0.26, 40 mins.

Cobán

Colour map 5, grid B2
Population: 70,000
Altitude: 1,320 m
Climate: semi-tropical

The cathedral and centre of the Imperial City of Cobán is perched on a long, thin plateau with exceptionally steep roads climbing down from the plaza. To the south the roads are filled with the odd well-preserved colonial building and a coffee finca. There is year-round soft rainfall, known as *chipi-chipi*, which is a godsend to the coffee and cardamom plants growing nearby. Most visitors use the city as a base from which to visit the sights around. Tourist information There's an unofficial **tourist office** on the Parque Central run by the helpful people at *Access Computación*, in the same building as *Café Tirol* (see Cafés and bars). English is spoken, they have lots of information and can help organize tours. Cobán has its own website: www.cobanav.com

Sights   The **cathedral** is on the east side of the Parque Central and dates from the middle of the 16th century. The church of **El Calvario**, in the northwest, now completely renovated, has its original façade still intact. On the way up to the church are altars used by worshippers. The **Museo El Príncipe Maya** is definitely worth a visit. It's a private museum of pre-Columbian artefacts. ■ *Mon-Sat 0900-1300, 1400-1800, US$1.30, 6 Av, 4-26, Zona 3*. The **Parque Nacional Las Victorias** is just west of El Calvario. It has two little lagoons in its 84 ha. There are paths and you can take a picnic and camp, but check with the tourist office first about safety before going. ■ *0700-1800 daily, US$0.80*. The daily market is near the bus terminal.

Starbucks coffee fans can check out where their mug of the old bean comes from – direct from **Finca Santa Margarita** on the edge of town. Tours in English and Spanish will tell you everything you need to know about our daily cuppa. ■ *Mon-Fri 0800-1230, 1330-1700, Sat 0800-1200, 45-min tour, US$2, 3 C, 4-12, Zona 2*.

Don't miss a visit to the flower-filled world of Vivero Verapaz, an orchid farm with more than 23,000 specimens, mostly flowering from December-February – the best time to go – with the majority flowering in January. ■ *Mon-Sat 0700-1800, US$1.30, 2½ km southwest of town, 40-min walk, or taxi ride, US$1.30*.

Southeast of Cobán (8 km) is **San Juan Chamelco** with an old colonial church. A one-hour walk from here is **Aldea Chajaneb** (see Sleeping below). Along this road are the caves of **Grutas Rey Marcos** (■ *US$1.30*) and **Balneario Cecilinda** (■ *Open weekends 0800-1700*). Buses run every 15 minutes from Cobán to San Juan Chamelco between 0530-1900, US$0.13 and leave from 5 Av and 3 C.

San Pedro Carchá is 5 km east of Cobán on the main road and used to be famous for its pottery, textiles, wooden masks and silver, but only the pottery and silver are available now. The local food speciality here is *kaq Ik*, a turkey broth. Buses leave Cobán every 10 minutes, US$0.13, 15 minutes, between 0600-1820.

B *La Posada*, 1 C, 4-12, Zone 2, T952-1495, F951-0646, laposada@c.net.gt 14 attractively decorated rooms all with private tiled bathrooms in a colonial hotel with well-kept flourishing gardens, credit cards accepted, restaurant. **C** *Hostal de Doña Victoria*, 3 C, 2-38, Zona 3, T951-4213, F951-4214, is in a 400-year-old former Dominican convent with colonnaded gallery, attractive gardens, and with a good restaurant (see below). Dorm room, **F** per person. Excursions arranged, recommended. **C-D** *Hotel Posada de Don Juan Matalbatz*, 3 C, 1-46, Zona 1, T/F951-0811, www.medianet.com.gt/discoverynat This is a colonial-style hotel with rooms set around a courtyard. Despite its proximity to the bus terminal it is very quiet and safe. All rooms have TV and there's a restaurant and pool table. Tours offered. **D-F** per person *Casa D'Acuña*, 4 C, 3-11, Zona 2, T951-0484, F952-1547, www.alfatravelguide.com Clean double rooms and dorm beds, ultra clean bathrooms with hot water, laundry service, excellent meals and coffee in *El Bistro* restaurant in a pretty courtyard (see Eating). The owners run a tourist office and tours. Recommended. **D** *Central*, 1 C, 1-79, T952-1442, has no sign, but is next to *Café San Jorge*, a stone's throw from the cathedral. There are 15 very clean large rooms, around a patio, with hot shower. Rooms with TV cost a little extra. **D** *Monja Blanca*, 2 C, 6-30, T951-190, F951-1899, all rooms are set around a pretty courtyard. The place is run by a couple of elderly *señoras* who are a bit mean when it comes to single travellers, for fear of losing the chance of earning on the other bed in the rooms. Local ecotours are also run from here. **D-E** *Hotel Posada de Don José*, 6 Av, 1-18 C, Zona 4, T951-4763, 14 rooms with private bathroom, TV, cheaper without, clean general bathrooms, friendly owner. **D-E** *Monterrey*, 6 Av, 1-12, T952-1131, 22 clean, big rooms, with bathroom, cheaper without, good value. Recommended. **E** *La Paz*, 6 Av, 2-19, T952-1358, hot water, safe

Sleeping
■ on map below
Price codes:
see inside front cover

Accommodation is extremely hard to find on the Friday and Saturday of Rabin Ajau and in August. For Rabin Ajau you need to be in town a few days beforehand to secure a room, or ring and reserve

Guatemala

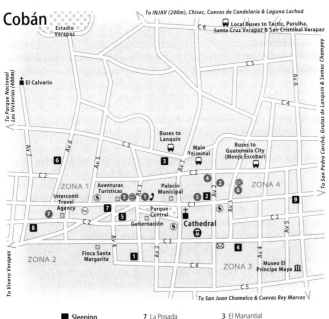

0 metres   100
0 yards   100
N

■ **Sleeping**
1 Casa D'Acuña
  & El Bistro Restaurant
2 Central
3 Don Juan Matalbatz
4 Doña Victoria
5 Familiar
6 La Paz
7 La Posada
8 Monja Blanca
9 Posada de Don José

● **Eating**
1 Argentine Empanada
2 Café y Fuente de Soda
  "Classe"
3 El Manantial
4 El Refugio
5 Tirol

● **Bars**
6 Milenio
7 Tofubu Café-Bar

parking, pleasant, comfortable beds in 28 rooms, cheaper without private bathroom, laundry facilities, café, garden, popular. **F-G** *Pensión Familiar*, Diagonal 4, 3-36, Zona 2, T952-1750, 1 block north of Parque Central, hot water, clean, but not too clean shared toilets, basic, two beautiful, but caged, pet toucans in the courtyard.

In Aldea Chajaneb B *Don Jerónimo's*, Km 5.3, *carretera* a Chamil, T/F308-2255, www.dearbrutus.com/donjeronimo Bungalows to rent, with full board including 3 vegetarian meals a day. All inclusive, hiking, swimming and tubing, massage, great for relaxation. From Cobán in a taxi, 30 mins, about US$6. Or, take a bus from Cobán to Chamelco, then a bus or pick-up to Chamil (no schedule) and ask to be let off at *Don Jerónimo's*.

Eating
● on map, see previous page

El Bistro, in Casa D'Acuña, excellent menu with massive portions served. Try the blueberry pancakes, and do not walk through the restaurant without putting your nose into the green cake cabinet! Breakfast is cheap. Recommended. *El Manantial*, this restaurant is tucked in at the back of the *El Gallo* shopping centre on 1 C, near the cathedral. It serves up good value breakfasts as well as Guatemalan fare and good cappuccino. It also does a child's menu. *El Refugio*, 2 Av, 2 C, Zona 3, next to the terminal has excellent waiter service and serves up substantial portions at good value prices – steaks but also fish, chicken and snacks. The restaurant inside *Hostal de Doña Victoria*, 3 C, 2-38, Zona 3, serves up breakfast, lunch and supper in a semi-open area with a pleasant, quiet ambience. Pasta, including vegetarian options, is the speciality of the house. The *menú del día* is US$2. *Argentine Empanadas*, is a stand on the Parque Central next to the *Telgua* office, delicious chicken or cheese-filled options at bargain prices. *Café y Fuente de Soda 'Classe'*, this is a bargain find. It probably has some of the cheapest brekkies in town and is close to the bus terminal.

Cafés & bars

Café El Tirol, 1 C, 3-13, on the main park, good meals. There are 52 coffee concoctions, 17 teas and 9 hot chocolate options, also homemade wholemeal bread, good cakes. Recommended for the coffees. *Café La Posada*, part of the hotel, *La Posada*, has divine brownies and ice-cream, with a view of the central park and, unfortunately, some very ugly satellite dishes. **Bars** *Tofubu Café-Bar*, 2 C, 6-09, Zona 2, is a popular continental European-type bar. *Milenio*, 3 Av between 1-11 C, Zona 4, with pool tables, is a more popular place with an older crowd.

Festivals

Holy Week. *Rabin Ajau* is the election of the *reina indígena*, the Maya Beauty Queen. Around this time the *Paa banc* is also performed, which is when the chiefs of brotherhoods are elected for the year during ceremonies. **1-6 Aug** is the town's own fiesta in honour of its patron, Santo Domingo, with various activities.

Transport
It is four hours direct from Guatemala City by bus

Local   Car hire: *Ochoch Pec*, at the entrance to town, T951-3474. **Long distance Bus**: To Guatemala City with *Transportes Escobar-Monja Blanca*, hourly from 0200-1600, 4 hrs, US$3.90, from its own offices near the terminal. From the main Cobán terminal: to **El Estor**, 10 daily, first at 0400, and mostly morning departures, but check in the terminal beforehand, 8 hrs, US$2. To **Fray Bartolomé de Las Casas**, between 0600-1600 by bus, pick-up and trucks, every 30 mins. To **Raxrujá** at 0500, 0630 (Sayaxché bus) and 1300. The bus to **Sayaxché** leaves at 0630, 6-6½ hrs, US$3.25. To **Uspantán**, 1000 and 1200, 5 hrs, US$1.40. Cobán can be reached from **Santa Cruz del Quiché** via Sacapulas and Uspantán, and from **Huehuetenango** via Aguacatán, Sacapulas and Uspantán. There are also buses to and from **Flores** via Sayaxché and Sebol (also see page 686). To **Salamá**, minibus, US$1.75, 2¼ hrs.

Directory

Banks Most banks around the Parque Central will change money. MasterCard accepted at *G&T Continental*, corner of 1 C and 2 Av. Visa ATM at *Bancafé*, just down from the cathedral on 1 Av. **Communications** Internet: *Access Computación*, in the same building as *Café Tirol*, US$3.90 per hr. Offers a fax and collect call phone service only. *Infocel*, 3 Av, between 1-2 C, Zona 4. US$2.60/hr. **Post office**: corner of 2 Av and 3 C. **Telephone**: you can make international calls from *Telgua*. **Language schools** *Active Spanish School*, 3 C, 6-12, Zona 1, T952-1432 (Nirma Macz). *La Escuela de Español Muq'bil' B'e*, 6 Av, 5-39, Zona 3, T951-2459 (Oscar Macz), muqbilbe@intelnet.net.gt Offers Spanish and Q'eqchi'. *School of Arts and Languages*, at Telepate, outside Cobán, T953-9276, www.lagomio.com/Spanish/index.htm Offers

Spanish, Q'eqchi' and Poqomchi', weaving, silverwork and marimba lessons. **Laundry** *Lavandería Providencia*, opposite *Café Tirol*. **Medical services** Hospital: *Policlínica y Hospital Galen*, a private institution on 3 Av, 1-47, Zona 3, T951-2913. **Tour operators** *Interconti*, 2 C, 6-01, Zona 2, T951-3191, amazing@intelnet.net Offers travel agency services and local tours. Very helpful. *Aventuras Turísticas*, 1 C, 3-25, Zona 1, T9511358, also offers tourist information. *Proyecto Ecológico Quetzal*, 2 C, 14-36, Zona 1, Cobán, T/F952-1047, Bidaspeq@guate.net Contact David Unger. Trips are organized to the multicoloured Río Ikbolay, northwest of Cobán, see page 667, and the mountain community of Chicacnab.

Near **Playa Grande**, to the far northwest of Cobán, is Parque Nacional Laguna Lachuá. The deep velvet-green lake, formed by a meteor impact at 170 m high, is 5 sq km and 220 m deep in places. It is surrounded by dense jungle, which is virtually unspoilt, and the chances of seeing wildlife at dawn and dusk are high. There is a guided nature trail and camping. **Sleeping E** per person in bunk beds with mosquito netting, **F per person** for camping. Bring your own food and rubbish bags. There are fireplaces, showers and toilets. ■ *US$5.20. Heading for Playa Grande from Cobán, also known as Ixcan Grande, ask the bus driver to let you off before Playa Grande at 'La entrada del parque', from where it's a 4.2-km (1-hr) walk to the park entrance. Buses leave Cobán at 0500, 1000 and 1230, the first 2 via Chisec, 4½ hrs, US$3.90. There are also minibuses that leave when full for US$5.20.*

Parque Nacional Laguna Lachuá

In this area is the **Río Ikbolay**, a green river that runs underground through caves. When it emerges out the other side it is blue. The river has changed its course over time leaving some of its run-through caves empty, making it possible to walk through them. The *Proyecto*, see page 667, runs jungle hikes in this area. On the borders of the national park on the bank of the **Río Chixoy** is **E-G** *Finca Chipantun*, T951-3423, chipantun@hotmail.com With rooms, hammocks or camping space. Three meals a day are provided at extra cost but at excellent value – the most expensive is dinner at US$3. Lots of great things to do around here.

Lanquín and Semuc Champey

Lanquín is surrounded by mountainous scenery reminiscent of an Alpine landscape. It nestles in the bottom of a valley, where a river runs through it. With a hammock bar at the village entrance, caves, and the clear water pools at Semuc Champey, it is worth kicking back for a few days and inhaling the high altitude air.

Colour map 5, grid B2
56 km east of Cobán, 10 km from the Pajal junction

Just before the town are the **Grutas de Lanquín**, in which the Río Lanquín rises. The caves are lit for 200 m and strange stalactite shapes are given names such as the eagle and the tower, but it's worth taking a torch as well. The cave, whose ceiling hangs with thousands of stalactites, is dangerously slippery, although handrails will help you out. The sight of the bats flying out at dusk is impressive. Outside the cave you can swim in the deep, wide river, and camp for free. ■ *0800-1600, US$2.60, 30-min walk from town.*

At weekends the place can be converted into a noisy adventure playground; if you can, visit on weekdays

From Lanquín you can visit the natural bridge of **Semuc Champey**, a liquid paradise stretching 60 m across the Cahabón Gorge. The limestone bridge is covered in stepped, clear blue and green water pools, that span the length and breadth of it. Upstream you can see the water being channelled under the bridge. As it thunders through, it is a spectacular sight. At its voluminous exit you can climb down from the bridge and see it cascading down. All the pools can be swum in with little hot flows pouring into some of them – great therapy after days or weeks on the road. ■ *0600-1800, US$2.60, parking (US$0.65). It is possible to camp for as long as you want, once you've paid the entrance fee. There are toilets and cooking areas. Take insect repellent, a mosquito net, and all food and water. Semuc Champey is a 10-km walk to the south from Lanquín, 3 hrs' walking along the road, which is quite tough for the first hour as the road climbs very steeply out of Lanquín. If planning to return to Lanquín the same day, start very early to avoid the midday heat. To get there in a pick-up start early (0630), US$0.65, or ask around for a private lift (US$13 return). Transport is very irregular so it's best to start walking and keep your fingers crossed. By*

Guatemala

1200-1300 there are usually people returning to town to hitch a lift with. However, if you are on your own and out of season, it would be wise to arrange a lift back.

Hikes

Unless you speak Q'eqchi', conversation is difficult with local people, few of whom speak Spanish

You can hike from Cobán or San Pedro Carchá to Lanquín via Semuc Champey in five or six days, camping beside rivers. For information and guide possibilities, enquire at *Casa D'Acuña* in Cobán. From Cahabón village, 24 km east of Lanquín, it is possible to cross the mountains to Senahú (see below). There is accommodation, **F**, in Cahabón and tourist information in the town hall. The hike takes a full day (if setting out from Senahú, it may be possible to hitch a lift to Finca Volcán, then it's only six hours; either way it is quicker than by road).

Sleeping & eating

C *El Recreo*, T952-2160, at the village entrance, clean, good meals, friendly, pool, but this isn't always filled with water. **F-G** *El Retiro*, campsite, cabañas, dorm beds and restaurant, in a gorgeous riverside location. There's an open fire for cooking, hammocks to chill out in, and tubes for inner tubing the river. To get there don't get off in town, continue on the road to Cahabón for 5 mins and ask to be dropped off. Highly recommended. **G** *Hospedaje El Centro*, close to the church, friendly, good simple dinner, basic. **F** *Hospedaje La Divina Providencia*, hot water and a cheap restaurant (*menú del día* US$1.70 including drink), small, dark rooms, friendly. *Comedor Shalom*, in town, which has excellent value, if basic, meals US$1.35 including drink. There are *tiendas* selling good fruit and veg, and there are a couple of bakeries, all open early, for stocking up for a trip to Semuc Champey. For a chilled beer check out the hammock bar, *Rancho Alegre,* at the entrance to the village.

Transport

There is a gas station in Lanquín near the church

Bus From **Cobán** with *Rutas Belenju*, 0600, 1200, 1500, 3 hrs, US$1.30 – continuing to **Cahabón**, 1 hr more. Return from Cahabón at 0300, 0500 and 1300 passing Lanquín at 0400, 0600 and 1400. With *Nicte Ameli*, near *Rutas Belenju* in Cobán, leaving 1230 daily, returning 1200 daily. From Cahabón to **El Estor** at 0400, 3-3½ hrs. From Lanquín to **Flores**: take the 0400 or 0600 Cobán bus to **Pajal**, 1 hr, US$0.30, then any passing bus or vehicle to **Sebol**, 2-2½ hrs, (there are Las Casas-Cobán buses passing hourly in the morning only, see below for times) and then pick-up, hitch or bus to Sayaxché and then Flores.

North of Cobán & the southern Petén crossroads

About 100 km northeast of Cobán is **Sebol**, from where roads go north to Sayaxché, east to Modesto Méndez, and south to Río Dulce. Just south of Sebol are the **Grutas de Candelaria**. An extensive cavern system with stalagmites, it is said to be the fifth longest in the world. ■ *US$3.25 including a guided tour.* Take the road to Raxrujá and look for a sign saying '*Escuela de Autogestión Muqbilbe*' and enter here to get to the caves and eco-camp. Nearby on the main road is a farmhouse, *Rancho Ríos Escondidos*. Ask for Doña América and you can camp here for **G** per person. ■ *Getting there: see under Las Casas. Local transport in the form of minibuses and pick-ups connects most of these towns before nightfall.*

Fray Bartolomé de las Casas

Ten kilometres east of Sebol, and 15 minutes by bus, is Fray Bartolomé de las Casas, a town that is just a stop-off for travellers on the long run between Poptún and Cobán or Sayaxché.

Sleeping and eating **E** *Hotel and Restaurante Las Diamelas*, just off the central park, T8101785, cleanest rooms in town. Restaurant food is OK and cheap. **F** *Hospedaje Lorena*, main street, dark rooms, shared bath. **G** *Hospedaje Ralíos*, shared bath, OK. There are a couple of *comedores* and a *Banrural*. **Transport** Bus to Poptún leaves at 0300 from the central park, 5¾ hrs, US$3.25. This road is extremely rough and the journey is a bone-bashing, coccyx-crushing one. Buses to Cobán at 0400 until 1100 on the hour. However do not be surprised if one does not turn up and you have to wait for the next one. To Flores via Sebol, Raxrujá and Sayaxché at 0700 (3½ hrs, US$3.90 to Sayaxché) a further ½-1 hr to Flores.

Raxrujá

A rough dirt road links Fray Bartolomé de Las Casas, Sebol and Sayaxché via unappealing Raxrujá, but tarmacking this route has begun and may be complete by the

Guatemala

ime you read this. The scenery is beautiful with luscious palms, solitary sheer-sided
rolinas and thatched-roofed homes.

Transport The road from Raxrujá via Chisec to Cobán is very steep and rocky. Chisec to
Cobán, 1½ hrs. The Sayaxché-Cobán bus arrives here for breakfast and continues between
0800-0900. This road is tarmacked now. You can also go from here to Sebol to Modesto
Méndez to join the highway to Flores, but it is a very slow, killer of a journey. Buses leave from
Cobán for Chisec from the market terminal at 0500, 0800, 0900. The 1000 Cobán-Playa
Grande bus also passes through Chisec.

South of Cobán, at Tactic, a very dusty, reasonable road runs east down the Polochic **Tactic to El**
valley to El Estor (see page 660). This road is served by the Cobán-El Estor buses and is **Estor**
also quite easy to hitch. Some 47 km beyond Tucurú on this road is a turn-off to
Senahú, where there is magnificent walking in the area. **Fiesta** in Senahú 9-13 June.
There are several *hospedajes* and *comedores*. ■ *Bus from Cobán, 6 hrs, from opposite*
INJAV building, from 0600-1400, 4 daily, US$2.35. If you are coming from El Estor, get
off at the Senahú turn-off, hitch or wait for the buses from Cobán. Trucks take this road,
but there is little traffic, so you will have to be at the junction very early to be in luck.

Guatemala

El Petén: the Maya
Centres and the Jungle

□ Guatemala
City

Deep in the lush lowland jungles of the Petén lie the lost worlds of Maya cities, pyramids
and ceremonial centres, where layers of ancient dust speak of ancient tales. Tikal,
whose temples push through the tree canopy, is wrapped in a mystical shroud, where
battles and burials are recorded in intricately carved stone. Although all human life has
vanished from these once powerful centres, the forest is humming with the latter day
lords of the jungle: the howler monkeys – that roar day and night. There are also tou-
cans, hummingbirds, spider monkeys, wild pig and coatimundi. Jaguar, god of the
underworld in Maya religion, stalks the jungle but remains elusive, as does the puma
and the tapir. Penetrating further into the undergrowth away from Tikal, the adven-
turous traveller can visit El Mirador, the largest Maya stronghold, El Zotz, El Perú, El
Ceibal and Uaxactún all by river, by foot and on horseback.

Predominatly covered in jungle, the Petén is the largest department of Guatemala **Background**
although it has the smallest number of inhabitants. The northern area was so impenetrable that its Maya settlers, the Itza's, were not conquered by the Spaniards until 1697.

In 1990 21,487 sq km of the north of the Petén was declared a **Reserva de la**
Biosfera Maya (Maya Biosphere Reserve), by CONAP, the National Council for
Protected Areas. It became the largest protected tropical forest area in Central
America. Inside the boundaries of the biosphere are the Parque Nacional Tikal,
Parque Nacional Mirador-Río Azul and Parque Nacional Laguna del Tigre.

The dry summer months and wet winter months offer different advantages and dis- **Climate**
advantages. In the summer months of Nov through to early May, access to all sites is
possible as all tracks are bone-dry. There are also less mosquitoes and if you are a
bird lover, the mating season falls in this period. In the rainy winter months, from
May-Nov, but sometimes into Dec, tracks become muddy quagmires making many
of them impassable, and with the rain comes greater humidity and pesky mosquitoes. However, this period's saving grace is that there is a far better chance of hearing
frog choruses and seeing wild animals, both large and small. There are, however,

Guatemala

some variations within the Petén – check under each area/site, and ask before visiting. Take plenty of repellent, and reapply frequently. It's also fiercely hot and humid at all times in these parts so lots of sun screen and drinking water are essential.

Poptún
Colour map 5, grid B3
107 km south of Flores

Poptún is best known for its association with **Finca Ixobel**. Otherwise, it is just a staging-post between Río Dulce and Flores, or where to switch buses for the ride west to Cobán. There are a couple of hotels and *pensiones*, a market and supermarket. *Finca Ixobel* is a working farm owned by Carole De Vine, widowed after the assassination of her husband in 1990. This highly acclaimed 'paradise' has become the victim of its own reputation and is frequently crowded especially at weekends. However, you can still camp peacefully and there are great treehouses, dorm beds and private rooms. Private rooms *(C)*, tree-houses **(E)**, dorm beds **(F)**, camping **(G)**. One of the highlights has to be the food. The *finca* offers a range of trips that could keep you there for days – swimming in a nearby lake, riding, inner tubing, many short and longer treks in the jungle, and the unmissable **River Cave Trip** (US$8).The *finca* runs transport to **Tikal** at 0800 returning at 1000. ■ *T410-4307, fincaixobel@conexion.com.gt It is 3 km south of Poptún and buses will drop you there in daylight, then it's a 15-20 min walk. A taxi costs US$2.60.*

Transport

Bus Take any *Fuente del Norte* bus or any bus heading to the capital from **Flores**, US$2.60, 2 hrs. To **Flores** 0830, 0930, 1030, or Flores-bound buses from the capital at 1130, 1230, 1500, 1730, 1900, 2230. Bus **Poptún-Río Dulce**, 2 hrs, US$3.90. Buses will drop you at the driveway to *Finca Ixobel* if that's your destination, just ask. To **Guatemala City** at 0930, 1030, 1130 (deluxe), 1230, 1330, 1730, 1830, 2130, 2230 (deluxe), 2330, 7-8 hrs, US$7.80-9.50, US$22.50 for the deluxe service. To the capital with *Transportes Rosita* at 0500, 2100, 2130, 2200, 8 hrs, US$6.50. There is a local bus to **San Luis** at 0930. The only bus that continues to **Fray Bartolomé de las Casas** (Las Casas on the bus sign) leaves at 1030, 5¾ hrs, US$3.25.

Flores/Santa Elena

Population of the Flores area: 320,000
Flores: 5,000
Colour map 5, grid A2

Flores is perched on a tiny island in Lake Petén Itzá'. Red rooves and palm trees jostle for position as they spread up the small hill, which is topped by the white twin-towered cathedral. Some of the streets of the town are lined with houses and restaurants that have been given lashings of colourful paint, giving Flores a Caribbean flavour. Lanchas, drifting among the lilies and dragonflies, are pinned to the lake edges. Santa Elena is the dustier, less elegant and noisier twin town on the mainland where the cheapest hotels, banking services and buses can be found.

Getting there
Sadly theft is common and watch out for rip-offs

Flores is 2 km from the international airport on the outskirts of Santa Elena. The airport departures hall has a *Banquetzal*, cash or TCs only. Tour operator and hotel representatives are based in the arrival halls. A causeway links Flores with Santa Elena. A taxi from the airport into Santa Elena or Flores, US$1.30, 5 mins, but bargain hard. Or take a local yellow school bus from the airport, US$0.13. If you arrive by long distance bus from Guatemala City, Mexico or Belize you will be dropped in the heart of Santa Elena. There are hotels within walking distance or you can walk to Flores across the causeway (10-15 mins) or take a taxi.

Tourist offices
If you wish to make trips independently to remote Maya sites, check with ProPetén to see if they have vehicles making the journey

INGUAT is open in the airport daily from 0700-1200, 1500-1800. There is also an office on the plaza. **ProPetén**, C Central, T/F926-0495, associated with *Conservation International*, is linked with *EcoMaya* (a tour operator) as part of an effort to involve local communities in tourism projects. **CINCAP** (Centro de Información sobre la Naturaleza, Cultura y Artesanía de Petén) on the plaza, T926-0718, alianzaverde@guate.net has free maps of Tikal, other local information and publishes a free magazine *Destination Petén*. Closed Mon and housed in the same building is the *Alianza Verde*, an organization promoting sustainable eco-tourism.

Security

Since Dec 2000 there has been a sharp rise in violence against tourists with rapes, a shooting, armed robberies and minibus hold ups. Most of these have occurred within certain areas of Parque Nacional Tikal, 2 incidents at the Biotopo Cerro Cahuí at El Remate and 1 incident in

he parking lot at Nakum. The hold ups have been between Flores and Tikal on the public
highway. The violators always seem to get away. Get independent up-to-date advice before
visiting these places and leave all valuables at your hotel.

History

This jungle region was settled by the Maya Itza' Kanek in about AD 600, with their
seat then known as La Isla de Tah Itza' (Tayasal in Spanish), now the modern-day
Flores. The Itza's were untouched by Spanish inroads into Guatemala until the Mexican conquistador Hernán Cortés and Spanish chronicler Bernal Díaz del Castillo
dropped by in 1525 on their way from Mexico to Honduras. In 1697 Martín Urzua y
Arismendi, the governor of the Yucatán fought the first battle of the Itza's, crossing
the lake in a galley killing 100 indigenous people in the ensuing battle, and capturing
King Canek. He and his men destroyed the temples and palaces of Tayasal and so
finished off the last independent Maya state. **Fiestas**: 12-15 Jan is the Petén *feria*.
11-12 Dec in honour of the *Virgen de Guadalupe*.

Sights

*There isn't much
in the way of sights
in the town*

The **cathedral**, Nuestra Señora de los Remedios y San Pablo del Itzá, is plain inside.
The cathedral houses a Black Christ (*Cristo Negro*), part of a chain of Black Christs
that stretches across Central America, with the focus of worship at Esquipulas.

Dugouts or fibreglass one or two-seaters can be hired for about US$2 per hour to
paddle yourself around Lake Petén Itza (ask at hotels). Swimming in the lake is not
advised. Do check the dugouts for lake-worthiness. **Paraíso Escondido** is home to
the zoo. ■ *US$0.25. Getting there: a dugout to island costs US$6-8 round trip.* Near
the zoo is **ARCAS** (Asociación de Rescate y Conservación de Vida Silvestre). They
care for rescued wild animals with the purpose of releasing them back into the wild.
Volunteers are welcome. Contact arcaspeten@intel net.net.gt Boat tours of the
whole lake cost about US$10 per boat, calling at the zoo and the **El Mirador** on the
Maya ruin of **Tayasal**. ■ *US$0.65.*

Guatemala

Santa Elena

Sleeping
1 Alonzo
2 Casa Elena
3 Jade
4 Maya International
5 Patio Tikal
6 Petén Esplendido
7 Sac Nicte
8 San Juan
9 Santander

Eating
1 Comedor Jennifer's
2 Doña Aminita's Pie
3 El Peténchel
4 El Rodeo
5 Mijaro

Excursions

San Andrés is 16 km by road from Santa Elena

San Andrés enjoys sweeping views of Lake Petén Itzá, and its houses climb steeply down to the lake shore. *Eco-Escuela de Español*, (supported by Eco Maya, see page 675), offers classes and homestay. Adonis, a villager, takes good value tours to El Zotz and El Mirador and has been recommended. His house is close to the shoreline. Ask around for him. **Sleeping** 2 km from the village on the Santa Elena road is **AL** *Hotel Ni'tun*, martsam@guate.net/Attention:Ni'tun/Monkey Luxury cabañas on a wooded hillside above the lake, run by friendly couple Bernie and Lore, who cook fantastic vegetarian meals and organize expeditions to remote sites. In town there are also a couple of *comedores* – *Angelita* and *La Troja* and one or two shops.

Transport Buses from Santa Elena with *Transportes Pinita*, leave at 1200, 30 mins and go on to San José, returning at 1300. Most people go by *lancha*, which is far better, leaving from San Benito from 0500 to 1100 and on demand (20 people) until late, US$0.40, 45 mins. If there are less people they will charge about US$0.80. You can take a *lancha* from *Hotel Santana* dock to San Benito to make the connection to the other side of the lake for US$1.30 in a *lancha privada*, or US$0.40 in a *colectivo*. Alternatively take a local bus to the San Benito *lancha* departure point from the Flores end of the causeway, or catch one from opposite *Fuente del Norte* in Santa Elena. Get off at the junction where it is signposted to Sayaxché. *Hotel Cali* is on the corner. Walk

Flores

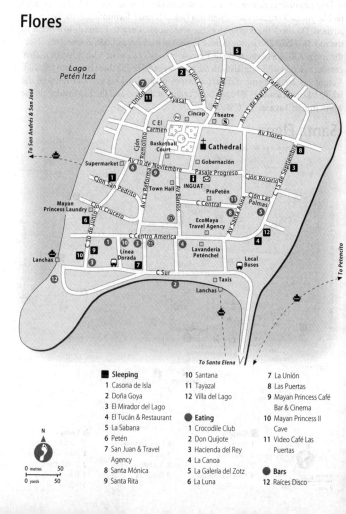

■ Sleeping
1 Casona de Isla
2 Doña Goya
3 El Mirador del Lago
4 El Tucán & Restaurant
5 La Sabana
6 Petén
7 San Juan & Travel Agency
8 Santa Mónica
9 Santa Rita
10 Santana
11 Tayazal
12 Villa del Lago

● Eating
1 Crocodile Club
2 Don Quijote
3 Hacienda del Rey
4 La Canoa
5 La Galería del Zotz
6 La Luna
7 La Unión
8 Las Puertas
9 Mayan Princess Café Bar & Cinema
10 Mayan Princess II Cave
11 Video Café Las Puertas

● Bars
12 Raíces Disco

Guatemala

right for 100 m until you see a sign saying 'Lanchas a San Andrés'. *Lanchas* also leave from *Hotel Casona de la Isla*, Flores, to San Andrés/San José at 1700 Mon-Fri, 1600 on Sat. From San Andrés/San José to Santa Elena/Flores daily at 0600, 0700, 1000, 1200, 1500, 1600, except Sun when there is no fixed schedule. From San José to San Benito/Santa Elena/Flores at 0730 and 1230 on weekdays, with no fixed schedule at weekends.

San José The attractive village of San José, a traditional Maya Itzá village, where efforts are being made to preserve the Itza' language and revive old traditions, is 2 km further northeast on the lake from San Andrés. Its painted and thatched homes huddling steeply on the lake shore make it a much better day trip than San Andrés. Some 4 km beyond the village a signed track leads to the Classic period site of **Motul**, with several plazas, tall pyramids and some stelae depicting Maya kings. The *Escuela Bio Itzá*, bioitzá@guate.net offers classes, homestay and camping. There is no **sleeping** in the village other than for students who stay at the school. However, should you wish to stay, and the student accommodation is not packed out, it may be possible to stay. It takes 20 minutes to walk between the two villages.

On 1 November San José hosts the Holy Skull Procession

Actún Kan caves These caves are a fascinating labyrinth of tunnels, where legend has it, a large serpent lived. They are 3 km south of Santa Elena and a 30-45 minute walk. ■ *0800-1700. US$1.30. Getting there: take the 6 Av out of Santa Elena to its end, turn left at a small hill, then take the first road to the right where it is well marked.*

Flores **B** *La Sabana*, T/F926-1248, including meals, with huge, spartan rooms, good service, clean, pleasant, good view, caters for European package tours, lakeside pool. **B** *Hotel Casona de Isla*, T926-0593, F926-0523, reservaciones@corpetur.com On the lake with elegant rooms, fans, clean, friendly, good restaurant, nice breakfasts, bar, garden, pool. **B** *Hotel Santana*, T/F926-0662, hotelsantana@guate.net Lakeside restaurant, pool, clean rooms, all with their own terrace and TV. **C** *Petén*, T926-0692, F926-0662. Lake view, clean, pool inside the foyer area, luggage stored, ask for new rooms at the front. **D** *Villa del Lago*, next to *El Tucán*, T926-0629, F926-0508. Very clean, cheaper with shared bath. There's a terrace with lake view where breakfast is served, but the service is excruciatingly slow. The breakfast menu is open to non-guests, but avoid it if it's the high season unless you don't mind a very long wait. **E** *Doña Goya*, C Unión, T926-3538. Clean, friendly family which run the place, breakfast available. **E** *Mirador del Lago*, C 15 de Septiembre, T926-4363. Beautiful view of the lake and a jetty to swim from. All with private bathrooms and hot water, but this is irregular. One of the better budget hotels and it has lake access. **E** *El Tucán*, T926-0677, on the lakeside. 4 internal rooms only, fan, 1 shared bathroom, comfortable. It's OK here, but can be very noisy because of the restaurant, and the shared bathroom means walking by some of the punters and cooks. **E** *Santa Rita*, C 30 de Junio, T926-3216. Bath, clean, excellent service. 2nd floor rooms have view of the lake, but rooms can get quite stuffy, despite the fans. **E** *Tayazal*, T926-0568. Rooms with 2 double beds, can sleep 4, fan, showers downstairs, roof terrace, drinking water available, very accommodating, can arrange a Tikal trip. **F** *Posada Santa Mónica*, near *Mirador del Lago*, basic rooms with private bath and fan, clean, quiet, bargain for single travellers, nice lounge area.

Santa Elena **AL** *Maya Internacional*, T926-2083, F926-0087, www.villasdeguatemala.com Beautifully situated on the lakefront with all services. **L** *Petén Esplendido*, 1 C, T360-8140, www.petenesplendido.com Has a great lake front restaurant setting (open 0600-2200), with beautiful pool on the lake. The pool can be used by non-guests for US$4. A full range of business services are available. **A** *Casa Elena*, Av 6, just before the causeway, T926-2238, F926-0097. With a beautiful tiled staircase, rooms with cable TV, pool (open to non-guests for US$3.50), restaurant. **C** *Del Patio Tikal*, T/F926-0104. Clean, modern rooms with a/c, TV, expensive restaurant, beautiful pool and gym. It's best booked as part of package for cheaper rates. **D-E** *Sac Nicte*, 1 C "A", T926-0092. Upstairs rooms have a balcony, electric showers, fan, occasional trouble with water and electricity. Rooms aren't always clean, but it's friendly and there's a minibus service to Tikal. There are lovely and clean thatched bungalows (**E**) in the garden here, which might be a better option. **D-F** *San Juan Hotel*, close to the Catholic

Sleeping
■ *on map, see previous page*
Price codes: see inside front cover

All hotels have hot water unless otherwise stated

Notices in cafés and around town advertise rooms and houses for rent if you are looking to stay for a while

■ *on map, see previous page*

Guatemala

church, T926-0562, F926-0041. Full of budget travellers in the older rooms, **F** with shared bath, not always spotless. There are also luxurious remodelled rooms (**C**) with a/c and TV. Credit cards are accepted, also cash advances on credit cards and TCs, exchanges US and Belizean dollars and Mexican pesos. It's safe, there's a public phone inside and parking available. There's a bus stop outside and you will probably be woken at 0400 whether you are travelling or not. **E-F** *Alonzo*, 6 Av, 4-99, T926-0105, with bath, **F** without, with bright yellow rooms, fan, popular, good deal for single travellers, minibus to Tikal. They also sell *Tikal Jets* tickets. It's quiet except on Fri when the evangelical church next door has an all night vigil. **E** *Posada Santander*, opposite *Banco Industrial*, T926-0574. Standard rooms, friendly owners who are expanding the hotel, free airport transfer. **F** *Jade*. Very simple, intermittent electricity, helpful, will store luggage, laundry facilities, try to choose your room.

Eating
● on map,
page 672

*Imported goods,
especially soft
drinks, are
expensive in Flores.
Do not order
tepezcuintle, a
rabbit-sized jungle
rodent that is
endangered*

Flores *Hacienda del Rey*, C Sur. Expensive Argentinian steaks are on the menu, but the breakfasts are seriously cheap. *La Luna*, refreshing natural lemonade, range of fish, meat and vegetarian dishes, some are in the cheap price range though. The restaurant has a beautiful courtyard with blue paintwork set under lush pink bouganvillaea, recommended. Colsed Mon. *The Crocodile Club*, European and Mexican food, and a good range of seriously cheap snacks, book exchange. Closed Tue. *Restaurante Don Quijote* , has a small number of tables on a barge on the lake in front of C Sur. A little rocky at times, but there's a cool breeze and it's a pleasant alternative to the other restaurants in town. The service is excellent but the menu is limited. *La Galería del Zotz*, with a wide range of food on offer, delicious pizzas, good service and presentation, and popular with the locals. *Restaurante La Unión*, deceptive from the outside, it has a gorgeous little thatched wooden terrace on the lake with great views. Try the fish. Recommended more for the setting than the food. *The Mayan Princess II Cave*, café, bar and dance club. Small menu but serving delicious pastas including shrimp in white wine and mushroom sauce. Cheap chef specials also. *Las Puertas Café Bar*, with seriously cheap breakfasts. Huge menu, good large pasta portions. It's popular with travellers here with Jackson Pollock splash paint effect on the walls, in an airy building, chilled atmosphere, games available. Popular at night. There is also *Las Puertas Video Café* opposite, which opens at 1530 with videos at 1900. *El Tucán*, see Sleeping, with cheap to mid range options. Its terrace is not particularly attractive and the service could be better. Closed Sun. *La Canoa*, good breakfasts (try the pancakes), dinners start at US$1.50, with good *comida típica*, very friendly owners. *The Mayan Princess Café and Cinema*, has the most adventurous menu on the island including daily specials, many with an Asian flavour, relaxed atmosphere, with bright coloured textile cloths on the tables. Internet and free films. Closed Sun.

● on map, page 672

Santa Elena If you want to splash out eat at the *Petén Esplendido*, which has a great terrace overlooking the lake towards Flores. *El Rodeo*, 2 C y 5 Av, excellent, reasonable prices but occasional slow service, classical music and sometimes impromptu singing performance from the locals! *Caffé Spaghettería Doña Aminita's Pie*, good value café/restaurant, fresh homemade pasta, friendly. Take lunch in the tree-filled patio along with the two resident parrots. Beware of falling fruit. Closed Mon. *Restaurante Mijaro*, great filling breakfasts and a bargain *menú del día* at US$1.70, all under a thatched roofed roadside location. *El Petenchel*, close to *El Rodeo*, vegetarian meals served here as well as conventional meats and meals. Excellent breakfasts. Good value *menú del día*. Music played and prompt service.

Transport
*Petrol is sold in Santa
Elena at the Texaco
Garage on the way to
airport. Open 24 hrs*

Local Bus: Local buses, US$0.13, Flores to Santa Elena, Flores to the airport, and Flores to San Benito. They leave from the end of the causeway in Flores. **Boat**: *Lanchas* leave from four points in the area: the corner of the *Hotel Petén Esplendido*, Santa Elena; from C Sur, Flores; from behind the *Hotel Santana*; and from the dock behind *Hotel Casona de Isla*. **Car hire**: there are plenty of agencies at the airport, mostly Suzuki jeeps, which cost about US$65-80 per day; *Hertz*, at the airport, T926-0332; *Jade* agency is recommended. Also ask at *Hotel San Juan*, T926-0041. *Garrido* at *Sac-Nicte Hotel*, Santa Elena, T926-1732, US$65 per day for a jeep.

Long distance **Air**: Several companies fly from Guatemala City to Santa Elena International Airport. The cost of a one-way flight is between US$50-77, shop around in Guatemala City and Antigua. *Grupo Taca*, T926-1238, leaves Guatemala City daily at 0640, 50 mins, returns 1620. *Tikal Jets*, T926-0386, tikalair@guate.net to Flores 0630 daily, returning 1630; 0900 on Mon, Fri, Sat and 1730 on Sun, 30 mins, returning Mon, Fri, Sat at 0730 and 1030 on Sun. To Cancún: *Grupo Taca* (0740). To **Belize City** with *Tropic Air*, T926-0348, at 0930 and 1530.

Be early for flights, as overbooking is common. Tikal Jets closes its check-in 45 minutes before departure from Santa Elena

Bus: Services from **Guatemala City**, see page 576. To **Guatemala City**, *Línea Dorada*, C Sur, Flores, daily between 0500-2200, T926-0528. In Santa Elena on the main drag, T9260070, www.lineadorada.com, leaves 1000, and 2100, 1st class, US$28; 2000, 2200, 2nd class, US$13, 8 hrs. Buses also to **Tikal**. *Fuente del Norte*, 18 buses between 0630-1930, US$8-10, 12 hrs. At 2000, 2015, 2030, US$10.40, 8 hrs; 2100, US$17, 8 hrs. With *Transportes Rosita* 1900, US$6.50, 2000, US$9.75. With *Rápido del Sur*, 2300, US$13, abi@correo.terra.com.gt If you are going only to **Poptún**, 2 hrs, US$2.60, or **Río Dulce** make sure you do not pay the full fare to Guatemala City: in practice, this means you will probably have to take a 2nd class bus, such as *Fuente del Norte*. To **Sayaxché** from the market area with *Pinita*, and *Rosío* 0500, 0700, 0800, 1000, 1300, 1500, US$1.95, 2 hrs. Buses run around the lake to **San Andrés**, with one at 1200 with *Pinita* continuing to **Cruce dos Aguadas** and **Carmelita** for access to El Mirador. To **Río Dulce**, US$8, with *Fuente del Norte*, 6 hrs. To **Belize City**, see page 685. To **Copán**, take *Transportes María Elena* to Chiquimula at 1400, US$6.50 then from Chiquimula to El Florido (see page 648) and finally on to Copán. Or, take any bus to the capital and change at Río Hondo. The *María Elena* bus continues onto Esquipulas, 8 hrs, US$7.80. To **Mexico**, see to Mexico through El Petén, and fast transport to Palenque on page 685. For local buses within the Petén with *Transportes Pinita, Hotel San Juan*, Santa Elena, 0800-1700, T926-0726.

All long distance buses leave from Santa Elena unless otherwise stated

Pinita operates daily, except Good Friday

Taxi: Taxis will take you anywhere for a price. For example to **El Remate** is US$20, to **Tikal**, approximately US$30 one way. *Taxi Mayrely*, T926-1600, T810-0445 (mob).

Banks Airport: *Banquetzal*, cash or TCs only. Open until 1700. **Flores**: *Banrural*, next to the church. TCs only. **Santa Elena**: *Banco del Café*, best rates for Amex TCs. *Banco de los Trabajadores*, MasterCard accepted. *Banco Industrial*, Visa ATM 24 hrs. *Banquetzal*, MasterCard only. The major hotels and travel agents change cash and TCs. There are other banks near the bus terminal. **Communications** Internet: *Tikal Net*, Santa Elena, US$3/hr, phone calls also. *Flores Net*, Flores, US$3/hr. *Tikal Net*, Flores. **Post office**: In Flores and in Santa Elena. **Telephone**: *Telgua* in Santa Elena. **Laundry** *Lavandería Petenchel*, US$3 for one load, wash and dry. *Mayan Princess Laundry*, US$3. **Medical services** *Hospital Nacional*, in San Benito, T926-1333, open 24 hrs. *Centro Médico Maya*, Santa Elena, Dra Sonia de Baldizón, T926-0714, speaks some English. Recommended. **Tour operators** Flores **EcoMaya**, C Centro América, T926-3202, www.ecomaya.com This agency was created by *ProPetén* and its tours involve and benefit the local community also. They also run shuttles and sell bus and air tickets. Santa Elena **Explore**, 1 C, close to the lakeshore, T926-2375, expeten@guate.net Offering tours to El Ceibal, Tikal, Aguateca and Sayaxché. This company has been recommended. *San Juan Travel Agency*, T/F926-2011/13, sanjuan@internetdetelgua.com.gt offers reliable transport to **Tikal**, US$30 including tour. Also runs excursions to **Ceibal**, US$30, and **Uaxactún**, US$20, with non-bilingual guide. Excellent service to **Belize**, US$20, 0500, arrives 1100, wake up call if you stay at *San Juan Hotel*, otherwise they will collect from your hotel. Also to Chetumal, Mexico, at 0500, US$30, arrives 1300. Also see local guide under San Andrés town, page 672. **Useful addresses** Immigration at the airport, T475-1390. For **volunteer** work, see ARCAS, page 558.

Directory

El Remate and Biotopo Cerro Cahuí

At the eastern side of Lake Petén Itzá is El Remate. The sunsets are superb and the lake is flecked with turquoise blue in the mornings. You can swim in the lake in certain places away from the local women washing their clothes and the horses taking a bath. West of El Remate is the **Biotopo Cerro Cahuí**, 700 ha, which opened in 1989 but closed in January 2001 because of incidents of rape and shooting by bandits inside its boundaries. It reopened with extra security on hand in April 2001. It is a lowland jungle area where three species of monkeys, deer, jaguar, peccary, ocellated wild turkey and some 450 species of birds can be seen. If you do not wish to walk alone, you can hire a guide. Ask at your *posada*. ■ *Daily 0700-1600, US$2.60, administered by CECON.* **Ixlú** is an unrestored ruin 100 m from the main road down a track, just before El Cruce (30 km from Santa Elena on the way to El Remate).

Sleeping   To reach the lodgings along the north shore of the lake can be up to a 2-km walk from El Remate centre depending on where you stay (turn left, west on the Flores-Tikal main road). There is light from the main road up to the *Posada del Cerro* until 2200 each night.

These places are listed with the furthest away from the main road first   About 1.8 km from the western entrance of the Biotopo Cerro Cahuí is **L** *Camino Real*, T926-0204, F926-0222, www.quetzalnet.com/caminoreal/CR-Tikal.html All rooms have views, good restaurant, a/c, cable TV etc. 1 km closer to the park on this side is **D-G** *El Gringo Perdido* (Guatemala City T232-5811, F253-8761, *Viajes Mundial*, 5 Av, 12-44, Zona 1, www.guate.net/gringo), with a restaurant, cabins (**D** without food), camping (US$3 a night), good meals. Just before the Biotopo entrance on its eastern, El Remate, side is **D-G** *Posada del Cerro*, T9260662, cahui@latinmail.com with beautiful thatched bright rooms – the top floor room is the best with a brilliant view. **G** Camping and hammock space. There is food and a laundry. **F** *Hotel and Restaurante La Casa Doña Tonita* , one of the most chilled out places along the shore and popular, with a friendly, warm, family running the place. Enormous portions of good food. Highly recommended. **E-G** *La Casa Roja*, a red house with a tranquil, oriental feel. Rooms are under thatched roofs, with separate bathrooms in attractive stone and wood design. The rooms don't have doors but there are locked trunks. Hammock space (**G**). Recommended. **D** *La Casa de Don David*, 20 m from the main road, T306-2190, www.lacasadedondavid.com Clean and comfortable, but a little overpriced, great view from the terrace restaurant with cheap food, bike hire free. Transport to Tikal.

These places are on the main road – Tikal road in El Remate Village   **AL** *La Mansión del Pájaro Serpiente*, overlooks the lake, suites set in the secluded hillside with an attractive garden. **E-G** *The Mayan Princess*. **G** for hammock comfort. Horse tours available, and two free video showings daily, restaurant. **F** *La Casa de Don Juan*. Rooms here have no doors, but it seems safe enough as the owner and his staff are always around. Restaurant, owner Don Juan offers tours. **F-G** *El Mirador del Duende*, T926-0269, F926-0397, miraduende@hotmail.com Overlooks lake, camping, cabins, vegetarian food, jungle trips, canoes, boat trips, mountain bikes, horses and guides are available. **G** *Posada Felin*, behind *La Casa de Don Juan*, all rooms have doors, but some are very dark. Friendly owners.

Eating   Between *Posada del Cerro* and *La Casa Doña Tonita* is **Restaurant Mon Ami**, with wines and seriously cheap chicken and pastas served. Camping available (**G**). *El Establo*, on the main road homemade veggie food with lashings of garlic and herbs, delicious. Served under shady wooden cabaña with seats and tables made of logs. Recommended.

Shopping   Strung along the lakeshore on the public highway are handicraft shacks selling carvings, trinkets, and salad servers in tropical hardwood, 15 mins walk from the cruce and El Remate.

Transport   Any bus or minibus heading for **Tikal** can stop at El Remate. To and from **Flores** it is about US$2-2.50. Or, get on a bus heading for the Belize border and get off at the turn off at El Cruce. Returning to Flores, pick up any minibus heading south (this is a lot easier after 1300 when tourists are returning). There is a bus service heading to **Flores** from El Remate at 0700, 0800, 0930, 1300 and 1400, US$0.80. But double check with your hotel as times shift.

Parque Nacional Tikal

With its Maya skyscrapers pushing up through the jungle canopy, Tikal will have you transfixed. Steep-sided temples for the mighty dead, stelae commemorating the powerful rulers, inscriptions recording the noble deeds and the passing of time, and burials that were stuffed with jade and bone funerary offerings, make up the greatest Maya city in this tropical pocket of Guatemala.

Colour map 5, grid A2
The park is 222 km sq

Getting there From Flores, it's possible to visit Tikal in a day. *San Juan Travel Agency* minibuses leave hourly between 0500 and 1000, and return between 1100 and 1800, 1 hr, US$7 return, US$4.50 one way. Several other companies also run minibuses. If you have not bought a return ticket you can often get a discounted seat on a returning bus if it's not full. Minibuses also meet Guatemala City-Flores flights. A taxi to Tikal costs US$30 one way. You can also visit Tikal with a package tour from Guatemala City or Antigua. Prices for 1-day excursions start at about US$135 return (including flights and transfers), 2 days US$160.

Ins & outs

Getting around It is best to visit the ruins after 1400, or before 0900, as there are fewer visitors. An overall impression of the ruins may be gained in 4-5 hrs, but you need at least 2 days to see it properly. Some of the pyramids cannot be climbed, including Temple I, Temple III and Temple V. Temple IV, the highest Tikal Temple, is climbed by hordes of tourists hoping to catch the sunrise. However, most mornings the temple is surrounded by mist and those rays will be just a figment of your imagination. Unbeatable is the Mundo Perdido complex at sunrise, where the ocellated turkeys meet for their morning gossip and toucans and parrots squawk for attention in the trees nearby.

If you enter after 1500 your ticket is valid the following day

Parque Nacional Tikal is open daily 0600-1800, US$7 (Q50) per day, payable at the national park entrance, 18 km from the ruins. It is no longer possible to get extended passes to see the ruins at sunrise/sunset following several security incidents including the rape of a tourist near Temple VI in Mar 2001. However, if you stay the night in the park hotels, you can enter at 0500 once the police have scoured the grounds. This gives you at least a 2-hr head start on visitors coming in from Flores. At the visitor centre there is a post office, which stores luggage. There is also a tourist guide service here (see below), exchange facilities, toilets, a restaurant and a few shops that sell relevant guidebooks. Take a hat, mosi repellent, water and snacks with you, as it's extremely hot, and drinks at the site aren't cheap, and there's a lot of legwork involved. There are locals selling cold drinks at various spots around the ruins and there are extra toilets close to Temple IV and picnic tables.

Essentials
From April to December it rains everyday for a while; it is busiest November to January, during the Easter and Northern Hemisphere summer holidays and most weekends

If you normally shy away from guides, Tikal is probably the one place where you should break the habit. The official *Tourist Guide Association* offers tours of varying natures and in different languages. For a minimum of US$10 per person (minimum 4) tours of 3-4 hrs are available. These are in Spanish, English or Italian. German and French tours are done for a minimum of US$50 (US$5 for 10 people or more) but an advance reservation is requested for these languages. All other tours start from 0800 onwards. Call T926-3133 in Santa Elena to reserve (Spanish only spoken), or come to the office in the visitor centre the day before. The guidebook *Tikal*, by W R Coe, in several languages has an excellent map (updated 1988), price US$6.50.

Guides & guidebooks
A guide is highly recommended as outlying structures can otherwise easily be missed

Tikal is a fantastic place for seeing animal and bird life of the jungle. Take binoculars. *The Birds of Tikal*, by Frank B Smithe, is available at the visitor centre, but for the serious bird-watcher, Peterson's *Field Guide to Mexican Birds: Mexico, Guatemala, Belize, El Salvador*, is recommended, and a quality guide to North American birds is helpful if visiting Tikal in the early months of the year. Wildlife includes spider monkeys, howler monkeys (re-established after being hit by disease), three species of toucan (most prominent being the keel-billed toucan - 'Banana Bill'), deer, foxes and many other birds and insects. Pumas have been seen on quieter paths and coatimundis (*pizotes*) in large family groups, are sometimes seen rummaging through the bins. The ocellated turkeys with their sky-blue heads with orange baubles attached are seen in abundance at the entrance, and at El Mundo Perdido.

Wildlife
December to April is the best time for bird tours with November to February being the mating season

Mosquitoes can be a real problem even during the day if straying away from open spaces

Guatemala

Guatemala

History The low lying hill site of Tikal was first occupied around 600 BC during the Preclassic era, but its buildings date from 300 BC. It became an important Maya centre from AD 300 onwards, which coincided with the decline of the mega power to the north, El Mirador. It was governed by a powerful dynasty of 30-plus rulers between about the first century AD until about AD 869, with the last known named ruler being Hasaw Chan K'awill II. At its height, the total 'urban' area of Tikal was over 100 sq km, with the population somewhere between 50,000-100,000.

Tikal's main structures, which cover 2½ sq km, were constructed from AD 550 to AD 900 during the Late Classic period. These include the towering mega structures of temples – shrines to the glorious dead – whose roof combs were once decorated with coloured stucco figures of Tikal lords. And, doorways on the temple rooms were intricately carved with figures and symbols, known as lintels – carved using the termite-resistant wood of the sapodilla tree. Tikal's stelae tell of kings and accessions and war and death. Its oldest stela dates from AD 292. Many Central Mexican influences have been found on the stelae imagery, in burial sites at Tikal, and in decorative architectural technique, which led archaeologists to conclude that the city was heavily influenced from the west by forces from the great enclave of Teotihuacán, now just outside Mexico City. This war-like state bred a cult of war and sacrifice and

Tikal

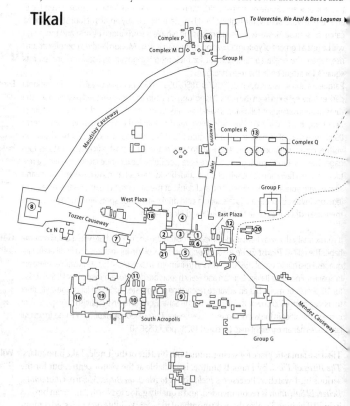

To Uaxactún, Río Azul & Dos Lagunas

Complex P
Complex M
Group H
Maudslay Causeway
Maler Causeway
Complex R — 13
Complex Q
Group F
Tozzer Causeway
West Plaza
East Plaza
Cx N
South Acropolis
Group G
Mendez Causeway

N

0 metres 100
0 yards 100

◯ **Sights**
1 Temple I (Temple of the Great Jaguar)
2 Temple II (Temple of the Masks)
3 The Great Plaza
4 North Acropolis
5 Palace Complex (Central Acropolis)
6 Ball Court
7 Temple III (Temple of the Jaguar Priest)
8 Temple IV (Temple of the Headed Serpent)
9 Temple V
10 Plaza of the Seven Temples Group
11 Triple Ball Court
12 Market
13 Twin Pyramid Plazas
14 North Group
15 Temple VI (Temple of Inscriptions)
16 El Mundo Perdido

seemed intent on spreading its culture far and wide. After the collapse of Teotihuacán in AD 600, a renaissance at Tikal was achieved by the ruler Ah Cacao (Lord Cocoa, Ruler A, Moon Double Comb, Hasaw Chan K'awil I, Sky Rain) who succeeded to the throne in AD 682 and died sometime in the 720s. However, in the latter part of the eighth century the fortunes of Tikal declined. The last date recorded on a stela is AD 889. The site was finally abandoned in the 10th century. Most archaeologists now agree the collapse was due to warfare with neighbouring states, over population, which resulted in environmental degradation and destruction, and drought. Tikal's existence was first reported by Spanish monk Andrés de Avendaño, but its official discovery is attributed to Modesto Méndez, Commissioner of the Petén, and Ambrosio Tut, Governor of the Petén, in 1848. They were both accompanied by an artist – Eusebio Lara.

The Great Plaza (3) is a four-layered plaza with its earliest foundations laid around **The ruins**
150 BC and its latest around AD 700. It is dwarfed by its two principal temples – Temples I and II. On the north side of the plaza between these two temples are two rows of monuments. It includes Stela 29, erected in AD 292, which depicts Tikal's emblem glyph – the symbol of a Maya city – and the third century AD ruler Scroll Ahau Jaguar, who is bearing a two-headed ceremonial bar.

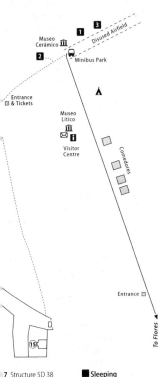

Temple I (Temple of the Great Jaguar) **(1)** on the east side of the Great Plaza rises to 44 m in height with nine stepped terraces. It was ordered to be built by the ruler Ah Cacao, who ruled between AD 682 to around AD 720-24, who probably planned it for use as his shrine. His tomb, the magnificent Burial 116, was discovered beneath Temple I in 1962 with a wealth of burial goods on and around his skeleton. The display is reconstructed in the *Museo Cerámico/Tikal*.

Temple II (Temple of the Masks) **(2)** faces Temple I on the Great Plaza and rises to 38 m, although with its roof comb it would have been higher. It's thought Ah Cacao ordered its construction as well. The lintel on the doorway here depicted a woman wearing a cape, and experts have suggested that this could be his wife.

The **North Acropolis (4)** contains some 100 buildings piled on top of earlier structures in a 2½ acres area and is the burial ground of all of Tikal's rulers until the break with royal practice made by Ah Cacao. In 1960, the prized Stelae 31, now in the *Museo Cerámico/Tikal*, see below, was found under the Acropolis. It was dedicated in AD 445. Its base was deliberately burnt by the Maya, and buried under Acropolis buildings in the eighth century. This burning was thought to be like a 'killing', where the burning ritual would 'kill' the power of

Guatemala

Museo Cerámico

Disused Airfield

Minibus Park

Entrance & Tickets

Museo Lítico

Visitor Centre

Comedores

Entrance

To Flores

7 Structure 5D 38
8 Structure 5D II
9 Great Pyramid 5C 54
20 Sweat House
21 Structure 5D 73

Sleeping
1 Jaguar Inn
2 Jungle Lodge
3 Tikal Inn

the ruler depicted on the monument, say, after death. It's thought to depict the ruler Stormy Sky (Siyah Chan K'awil), who died sometime around AD 457 having succeeded to the throne in AD 411. Yax Moch Xok (Great Scaffold Shark) is thought to be entombed in the first century AD grave, Burial 85. Surrounding the headless male body were burial objects and a mask bearing the royal head band. Under a building directly in the centre of this acropolis Burial 22 – that of ruler Great Jaguar Paw, who reigned in the fourth century, and died around AD 379 – was discovered. Also found here was Burial 10, thought to be the tomb of Curl Nose (Nun Yax Ayin I), who succeeded to the throne in AD 379 after Great Jaguar Paw. Inside were the remains of nine sacrificed servants as well as turtles and crocodile remains and a plethora of pottery pieces. The pottery laid out in this tomb had Teotihuacán artistic influences, demonstrating Tikal's links to the powers of Teotihuacán and Teotihuacán-influenced Kaminal Juyú. Burial 48 is thought to be the tomb of Curl Nose's son, Stormy Sky (Siyah Chan K'awil).

Central Acropolis (5) is made up of a complex of courts connected by passages and stairways, which have expanded over the centuries to cover four acres. Most of the building work carried out here took place between AD 550-900 in the Late Classic era. The **East Plaza** behind Temple I is the centre of the highway junctions of the Maler Causeway in the north, and the Méndez causeway heading southeast.

On the western side of the **West Plaza** is structure 5D II under which Burial 77 was brought to light. The skeleton was adorned with a jade pendant, which was stolen from the site museum in the 1980s.

Temple III (Temple of the Jaguar Priest) **(7)** is so called because of the scene of a figure in a glamorous jaguar pelt on a lintel found on the temple. Some experts believe this figure is Ah Chitam (Nun Yax Ayin II, Ruler C), son of Yax Kin, and grandson of the great Ah Cacao, and so propose that this is his shrine, although there has been no confirmation of this.Temple III was constructed around AD 810 and is 55 m tall.

Temple IV (Temple of the Double-Headed Serpent) **(8)** is the highest building in Tikal at 70 m. It was built in the Late Classic period around AD 741, as proven by hieroglyphic inscriptions and carbon dating. It's thought it was built to honour Yax Kin, the son of Ah Cacao, who became ruler in AD 734. A date on the lintel is AD 741, the same year that Temple I was dedicated.

Temple V (9) constructed between AD 700-750 during the reign of Yax Kin, is 58 m high. It is the mortuary temple of an unknown ruler.

El Mundo Perdido (The Lost World) **(16)** The Great Pyramid is at the centre of this lost world. At 30 m high, it is the largest pyramid at Tikal. It's flat topped and its stairways are flanked by masks. From the top a great view over the canopy to the tops of other temples can be enjoyed. Together with other buildings to the west, it forms part of an astronomical complex. The Lost World pyramid is a Preclassic structure, but was improved upon in the Early Classic. East of el Mundo Perdido is the **Plaza of the Seven Temples (10)**, constructed during the Late Classic period (AD 600-800). There is a triple court ball court lying at its northern edge.

Temple VI (Temple of the Inscriptions) **(15)** was discovered in 1951. The 12 m-high roof comb is covered on both sides in hieroglyphic text and is the longest hieroglyphic recording to date. It was carved in AD 766, but the temple was built under the rule of Yax Kin some years before. Altar 9 is at the base of the temple as is Stela 21, said to depict the sculptured foot of the ruler Yax Kin to mark his accession as ruler in AD 734. Unfortunately because of the location of this temple away from the rest of the main structures it has become a hideout for robbers and worse. Some guides no longer take people there. Take advice before going, if at all.

The North Group There are several twin pyramid complexes at the site, including Complexes Q and R, marking the passing of the *katun* – a Maya 20-year period.

Museums The **Museo Cerámico** (Museo Tikal) near the *Jungle Lodge* has a collection of Maya ceramics, but its prize exhibits are Stela 31 with its still clear carvings, and the reconstruction of the tomb of Tikal's great ruler, Ah Cacao. ■ *Mon-Fri 0900-1700, Sat*

Decline and fall of the Tikal Empire

Dr Patrick Culbert, of the University of Arizona, found two different kinds of skeletons in Tikal: those who died well nourished and others who suffered from malnutrition and lack of iron. He concluded that the normal dead must have been priests who fed on the sacrifices of food and drinks given by the peasants to the gods to ward off a poor harvest. The farmers must have died from starvation when the harvest failed. This theory has been confirmed by the findings in Belize of Dr David Pendergast, University of Toronto, which suggest that peasants looted the tombs of dead priests, but dared not threaten the living. The Tikal astronomer priests who prophesied good harvests erred in 790, after which there was drought, failed harvests and soil erosion, accompanied by malnourishment, starvation and death among the peasants. There was rebellion

among the peasants, while frustration and disillusionment followed within the priesthood. Their subsequent lack of interest in astronomy is reflected in the decline in the number of calendar stelae: 20 were dated AD 790, 12 of them 810, only 3 dated 830 and the last one AD 889. Competition between the Maya cities and the decline of the peasantry, leaving them outnumbered by the priesthood, led to the abandonment of Tikal around this time. Further research by scholars from the University of Florida, who conducted chemical analyses of lime and burned grass and roots of the Lake Chichancanab in the Yucatán, has shown that the lake was at its driest between AD 800-900. Similar effects on other lakes in Costa Rica, Mexico and wood fires in Costa Rica, all point to a massive drought in the area at that time, leading to the collapse of the Maya Empire.

Guatemala

and Sun, 0900-1600, US$2.60. The **Museo Lítico** is in the visitor centre. There are stelae and great photographs of the temples as they were originally found, and of their reconstruction, including the 1968 rebuild of the Temple II steps. ■ *Free. Photography is no longer allowed in either of these museums, T361-1399.*

Sleeping

It is advisable to book hotel rooms or camping space as soon as you arrive. In high season, book in advance. The telephone numbers given are in Flores; Tikal has no phones. If staying the night, take a torch: 24-hr electricity is not normally available.

AL-C *Jungle Lodge*, T361-4098, junglelodge@junglelodge.guate.com Spacious, comfortable bungalows, with bath, 24-hr hot water and fan (electricity 0700-2100), pool, **C** without bath. They will cash TCs, full board available (food fair, but service slow and portions small), *Jungle Lodge's* Tikal tours (US$5) have been recommended. **A-B** *Tikal Inn*, T926-0065, hoteltikalinn@internetdetelgua.com.gt, bungalows, **B** for hotel rooms, hot water between 1800-1900, electricity between 0900-1600, 1800-2200, beautiful pool for guests' use only. Natural history tours at 0930 for US$10, min 2 people, helpful. **A-E** *Jaguar Inn*, T926-0002, F926-2413, solis@quetzal.net full board, less without food. They will provide a picnic lunch for US$1.30, electricity (1800-2200), hot water in the morning or on request between Mar-Oct and between Nov-Feb 0600-2100. Will store luggage. There is a dormitory with six beds for US$10 per person. Hammocks with mosi nets and lockers, US$2.60.

Camping *Camping Tikal*, run by the *Restaurante del Parque*, reservations at hpesplen@guate.net or T360-8140, T926-0880. If you have your own tent or hammock it is US$3.25. If you need to rent the gear it is US$6.50. There are also cabañas with mattresses and mosquito nets for US$6.50 per person. They also do deals which include breakfast, lunch and dinner ranging from US$13-US$27 for a double. Communal showers available. Take your own water as the supply is very variable, sometimes rationed, sometimes unlimited, depending on the season. Same charge for vehicle overnight parking.

Eating

There are a couple of *comedores* inside the park: *Comedor Tikal*, *Imperio Maya* (opens 0530), *La Jungla*, good value food, but the chicken dish is not as good as at *Imperio Maya*. *Corazón de Jesús*. *Restaurant del Parque*, in an annexe of the visitor centre, more expensive than the *comedores*. Budget travellers are advised to bring their own food (you can pay US$2 for a candy bar) and especially drinks. Soft drinks, in the ruins, US$0.75.

Other Maya ruins

There are plenty of ticks eager for your blood in this region. If you're out walking take a pair of tweezers for the revenge attack

There are literally hundreds of Maya sites scattered around the Petén – the vast majority are just marks on a map – their existence is known, but it will be decades, if ever, before the tools of the archaeologist start revealing their history and their treasures. Some may never be excavated. Below are a handful of sites, whose ruins have been explored, and whose histories something is known.

Uaxactún

Colour map 5, grid A3 It is 24 km north of Tikal on an unpaved road. It is in fairly good condition taking less than one hour in any vehicle. See under transport

In the village of Uaxactún (pronounced Waash-ak-tún) are ruins, famous for the oldest complete Maya astronomical complex found, and a stuccoed temple with serpent and jaguar head decoration. The village itself is little more than a row of houses either side of a disused airstrip. At the *Hotel El Chiclero* there is a museum of the life and work of the *chicleros*, which also includes objects, especially vases, discovered in the excavations here and nearby. Uaxactún is one of the longest-occupied Maya sites. Its origins lie in the Middle Preclassic (1000 BC – 300 BC) and its decline came by the Early Post-Classic (AD 925 -1200) like many of its neighbouring powers. Its final stelae, dated AD 889, is one of the last to be found in the region. The site is named after a stela, which corresponds to Baktun 8 (8 x 400 Maya years), carved in AD 889 - Uaxac means 8, tun means stone. South of the remains of a ball court, in **Group B,** a turtle carving can be seen, and Stela 5, which marks the takeover of the city, launched from Tikal. Next door to this stela under Temple B-VIII were found the remains of two adults, including a pregnant woman, a girl of about 15 and a baby. It is believed this may have been the governor and his family who were sacrificed in AD 378. From Group B, take the causeway to **Group A**. In Group A, Structure A-V had 90 rooms and there were many tombs to be seen. The highest structure in the complex is Palace A-XVIII, where red paint can still be seen on the walls. In **Group E** the oldest observatory (E-VII-sub) ever found faces structures in which the equinoxes and solstices were observed. When the pyramid (E-VII) covering this sub-structure was removed, fairly well preserved stucco masks of jaguar and serpent heads were found flanking the stairways of the sub-structure. ■ *The ruins lie either side of the village, the main groups (**Groups A and B**) are to the northwest (take a left just before* Hotel El Chiclero *and follow the road round on a continuous left to reach this group). A smaller group (**Group E**) with the observatory is to the southwest (take any track, right off the airstrip, and ask. This group is 400 m away.*

Sleeping and eating **E** *El Chiclero*, T926-1095, chiclero@ecotourism-adventure.com is neat and clean, hammocks and rooms in a garden, also good food by arrangement (dinner US$5, breakfast US$3). **F-G** per person *Posada Aldana*, T801-2588, edeniaa@yahoo.com Little white casitas, tent and hammock space behind *El Chiclero*. Just before *El Chiclero* take a left on the road to the ruins and then first right until you see one of the whitewashed casitas on the right (2-min walk). Clean and run by a friendly family. *Comedor Imperial*, at the village entrance, which does a bargain *comida típica*, for US$1.30.

Transport To Uaxactún passing Tikal and El Remate at 1300 from Santa Elena arriving between 1600-1700, US$2.60, returning 0600 with *Transportes Pinita*. Unfortunately this does not give you much time to see the ruins if you plan to return the following day. Foreigners have to pay US$2 to pass through Parque Nacional Tikal on their way to Uaxactún. However, this appears to be enforced at random.

Directory Tour operators For guided walks around the ruins ask for any of the 13 trained experienced guides, US$9. Recommended is *Angela Fajardo*. For expeditions further afield, contact **Elfido Aldana** at *Posada Aldana*. All tours include food, transport and guide. Neria Baldizón at *El Chiclero*, has high clearance pick-ups and plenty of experience in organizing both vehicle and mule trips to any site. She charges US$195 per person to go to Río Azul.

El Zotz, meaning bat in Q'eqchi', is so called because of the nightly flight from a nearby cave of thousands of bats. The site is in a *biotopo* of 49,500 ha and, as always, there is some basic infrastructure for the guards, and you can camp. There is an alternative hiking route as well (see below). The temple ruins are 3 km from the camp and the majority of buildings are unrestored, but tragically slashed by looters. The tallest group, El Diablo, is a little further on. Incredibly, from Temple IV, the highest in the complex at 75 m, it is possible to see in the distance, some 30 km away, Temple IV at Tikal. The wooden lintel from Temple I (dated AD 500-550) is to be found in the *Museo Nacional de Arqueología y Etnología* in the capital.

El Zotz
Also accessible via Uaxactún

Each evening at about 1850 the sky is darkened for 10 minutes by the fantastic spectacle of tens of thousands of **bats** flying out of a cave near the camp. The 200 m-high cave pock marked with holes is a half-hour walk from the camp. If you have the luxury of spending two nights at the camp, walk to the cave the first night, where you can see the flight above you and get doused in a few bits of falling shit. On the second night, stay at the campsite and watch them streaking the dark blue sky with black in straight columns, like a Red Arrow performance above you.

One of the best trips you can do in the Petén is a **three-day hike** to El Zotz and on through the jungle to Tikal (known as the back door route). It's a one-hour truck ride to the village of Cruce dos Aguadas. From here it is a five-hour trek (24 km), with horses, if you have hired them, to the camp site at El Zotz. The terrain is not difficult, but is quite trying if you are biking it in the dry season because of the dried mud track grooves. The campsite is excellently made and there are rooved buildings for hammocks and tents. It is also possible to camp by a nearby *aguada*. On the third day, leaving at the crack of dawn, it is possible to walk through deep rainforest for eight hours (30 km) to Temple IV at Tikal. This route should not be attempted without a local guide as sometimes the path splits and sometimes it is not visible, except to the trained eye. Tours are offered by *EcoMaya*.

The journey, although long, is not arduous, and is accompanied by birds, blue morpho butterflies and spider monkeys chucking branches at you all the way

A visit to El Perú is included in the *Scarlet Macaw Trail*, a two to five day trip into the **Parque Nacional Laguna del Tigre** (see page 685), through the main breeding area of the scarlet macaw. There is little to see at the Maya site, but the journey to it is worthwhile. A more direct trip involves getting to the Q'eqchi'-speaking isolated community of Paso Caballos (1¾ hours). Here, the *Comité de Turismo* can organize transport by *lancha* along the Río San Pedro. From Paso Caballos it is one hour by *lancha* to the El Perú campsite and path. It's possible to stop off at the **Estación Biológica Guacamayo**, where there is an ongoing programme to study the wild scarlet macaws (*ara macao*). ■ *US$1.30*. The chances of seeing endangered scarlet macaws during March, April and May in this area is high, because they are reproducing. A couple of minutes upriver is the landing stage, where it's a 30 minutes' walk to the campsite of El Perú, where howler monkeys, hummingbirds, oropendola birds and fireflies abound. From the campsite, it is a two-hour walk to the El Perú ruins, while also taking time to look at the wildlife and plants. Small coral snakes slither about, howler monkeys roar, spider monkeys threaten you by chucking branches down on the path and charging white-lipped peccaries, nesting white turtles, eagles, fox and kingfishers have also been seen. Tapir and white-tailed deer are a little harder to come across. ■ *The trip may be impossible during Jun, Jul and Aug because of the rising of the rivers during the rainy season, and the fact that the unpaved road to Paso Caballos may not be passable. Doing it on your own is possible, though you may have to wait for connections and you will need a guide, about US$20 per day.*

El Perú and the Estación Biológica Guacamayo

El Mirador is the largest Maya site in the country. It dates from the Late Preclassic period (300 BC-AD 250) and is thought to have sustained a population of tens of thousands. It is just short of the northern border with Mexico. There are paintings and treasures; guards will show you around if no one else is on hand.

El Mirador
Colour map 5, grid A2

It takes five days to get to El Mirador. From Flores it is 2½-3 hrs to the village of Carmelita by bus or truck, from where it is seven hours walking, or part horse-riding to

Guatemala

Guatemala

El Mirador. It can be done in four days – two days to get there and two days to return. The route is difficult and the mosis and ticks and lack of respite from heat can make this a trying trip. Organized tours are arranged by *EcoMaya* in Flores, see page 675. If you opt to go to El Mirador independently, ask in Carmelita for the *Comité de Turismo* , which will arrange mules and guides. Take water, food, tents and torches. It is about 25 km to El Tintal, a camp where you can sling a hammock, or another 10 km to El Arroyo, where there is a little river for a swim near a *chiclero* camp. It takes another day to El Mirador, or longer, if you detour via Nakbé. You will pass *chiclero* camps on the way, which are very hospitable, but very poor. In May, June and July there is no mud, but there is little chance of seeing wildlife or flora. In July-December, when the rains come, the chances of catching a glimpse of wildlife is much greater and there are lots of flowers. It is a lot fresher, but there can be tonnes of mud, sometimes making the route impassable. The mosquitos are also in a frenzy during the rainy season.

The **site**, which is part of the Parque Nacional Mirador-Río Azul, is divided into two parts with the El Tigre Pyramid and complex in the western part, and the La Danta complex, the largest in the Maya world, in the east, 2 km away. The larger of two huge pyramids – La Danta – is 70 m high, where stucco masks of jaguars and birds flank the stairways of the temple complex. The other, El Tigre, is 55 m in height and is a wonderful place to be on top of at night, with a view of endless jungle and other sites, including Calakmul, in Mexico. In **Carmelita** ask around for space to sling your hammock or camp. There is a basic comedor, 1 bus daily with *Transportes Pinita* to Carmelita at 1200, US$2.60, 3 hrs. It returns daily at 0500, or hitchhike to Carmelita.

Around El Mirador

El Tintal, a day's hike from El Mirador, is said to be the second largest site in Petén connected by a causeway to El Mirador, with great views from the top of the pyramids. **Nakbé**, 10 km southeast of El Mirador, is the earliest known lowland Maya site (1000 BC- 400 BC), with the earliest examples of carved monuments.

Río Azul & Kinal

Hire a truck and driver from Uaxactún, see page 682, or organize a tour from Flores, see Tour operators, Flores

From Uaxactún a dirt road leads north to the *campamento* of Dos Lagunas, where the guards of the 45,900 ha *Biotopo Naachtún Dos Lagunas* live by the side of a small, tranquil lake. It is a lovely place to camp, with few mosquitoes, but swimming will certainly attract crocodiles. The guards' camp at **Ixcán Río**, on the far bank of the Río Azul, can be reached in one long day's walk, crossing by canoe if the water is high. If low enough to cross by vehicle you can drive to the **Río Azul** archaeological site, a further 6 km on a wide, shady, track. It is also possible to continue into Mexico if your paperwork is OK. A barely passable side track to the east from the camp leads to the ruins of **Kinal**. The big attraction at Río Azul are the famous black and red painted tombs, technically off limits to visitors without special permission, but visits have been known.

Yaxhá, Topoxte & Nakum

The road from Flores to the Belize border, passes through **El Cruce/Puente Ixlú**, and then north on to Tikal. There is a *campamento*, information and the ruins of Ixlú, see page 676. About 65 km from Flores, on this Belize road, is a turning left, a dry weather road, which brings you in 8½ km to Laguna Yaxhá. On the northern shore is the site of Yaxhá (meaning Green Water), the third-largest known Classic Maya site in the country, accessible by causeway. In the lake is the Late Post-Classic site (AD 1200-1530) of **Topoxte**. (The island is accessible by boat from Yaxhá, 15 minutes.) The site is unique **B** *El Sombrero*, T926-5229, F926-5198, sombrero@guate.net With comfortable cabins, restaurant. The owner organizes riding trips to Yaxhá and Nakum, and has a boat to take you to Topoxté. You can also camp for US$10 a person. About 20 km further north of Yaxhá lies Nakum, which it's thought was both a trading and ceremonial centre. You will need a guide and your own transport if you have not come on a tour.

Melchor de Mencos

You can get a bed for the night at the border at the **E** *Hotel Palace*, T926-5196, on the banks of the Río Mopan, with restaurant, private bathroom, no hot water, or at **F** *Zacaleu*, T926-5163, which is clean, fans, shared toilets/showers with cold water.

Melchor de Mencos/Benque Viejo Officials are charging the illegal US$1.30 fee to leave and US$4.50 to enter Guatemala – ask for receipts. There is also a 27.50 BZ dollar fee to leave Belize. If you need a visa for either Belize or Mexico obtain it at their consulates in Guatemala City. As a back-up there are 72-hr transit visas available at the border, which will cover you to the Mexican border at Chetumal, but not into Mexico. If you intend to stay in Belize, you may be able to get a visa at the border but there could be extra charges when you leave the country.

Transport There are several buses from **Santa Elena** to Melchor de Mencos, starting at 0500, 2-3 hrs. *Transportes Pinita* to Melchor de Mencos 0500, 0800, 1000, US$2, 2 hrs, returning 1100, 1300, 1400. Return bus to **Flores** also includes *Transportes Rosita*, US$1.30. Connecting buses for **San Ignacio**, **Belmopan** and **Belize City** wait at Melchor de Mencos (if you catch the 0500 bus from Santa Elena you can be in Belize City by 1200). In addition, there is a non-stop minibus service at 0500 from Santa Elena to Belize City, US$20, 5 hrs, returning at 1000 with *San Juan Travel Agency*. This service terminates at the A&R Station in Belize, from where boats to the Cayes leave. Also *Línea Dorada* at 0500, US$8, 4 hrs, returning 1800 to the capital, 8 hrs, US$29. Note that all buses stop and start at the border. Between Melchor de Mencos and Benque Viejo, there are taxis to take you the couple of kilometres, but rip offs are common – so bargain hard. **To Mexico through Belize**: there is a bus at 0500 direct to Chetumal, Mexico, arriving 1300 (Mexican time), US$30, plus US$3.50 to leave Belize with *San Juan Travel Agency*. Also *Línea Dorada* to Chetumal, 0500, US$15, 7 hrs.

Exchange There are good rates for quetzales, Belizean dollars and Mexican pesos on the street, but you might try the banks: *Bancafé* and *Banrural* in town.

Border with Belize
Open 0600-2130

Northwest Petén and the Mexican border

An unpaved road runs 151 km west from Flores to **El Naranjo** on the Río San Pedro, near the Mexican border. Just north of El Naranjo is the Laguna del Tigre National Park and Biotopo Laguna del Tigre Río Escondido. At *Posada San Pedro* (see below) there are guides and arrangements for travel as far as Palenque.

El Naranjo/La Palma C *Posada San Pedro* has simple cabañas with mosi nets, restaurant. Reservations T926-2083. F *Quetzal*, by the dock, basic, poor service, overpriced restaurant. Several even more basic *hospedajes* in town, but across the river, upstream from the ferry. The restaurant by the dugouts is expensive, others in town are better value.

Transport *Transportes Pinita* buses leave Santa Elena from *Hotel San Juan* for El Naranjo daily at 0500, 0800, 0900, 1100, 1200, 1500, 1600, 5 hrs, US$3.25, returning at 0300, 0400, 0600, 1100, 1400 and 1500. *Rosío* buses to El Naranjo at 0500, 0700, 0900. From El Naranjo, daily boats leave at 0600 and around 1300-1400, for La Palma in Mexico, US$22, cheaper to pay in quetzales, 4-5 hrs, including Mexican border crossing, from where buses go to Tenosique and on to Palenque. The 1300 boat will often get you to La Palma just in time to miss the last bus to Tenosique, so be prepared to stay the night. If there are fewer than 5 passengers for the boat, it may be cancelled and your alternatives are to wait for the next boat, or hire a *rápido*, maximum 6 people, US$125. Return from La Palma to El Naranjo at 0800. Bus La Palma-Tenosique at 1700, and 1 other, also *colectivos*; it is not possible to get to Palenque the same day unless you hire a taxi in La Palma. Mexican tourist cards can be obtained at the border. **Exchange** You can change money at the grocery store opposite immigration, which will give you a better US$/Q rate than the Mexican side of the border. Even so, rates here are poor.

Border with Mexico
Immigration is near the landing stage

The park and biotopo is a vast area of jungle and wetlands north of El Naranjo. The best place to stay is the CECON camp, the headquarters of the biotopo, across the river below the ferry; a boy will paddle you over in a canoe. This is where the guards live and they will let you stay in the bunk house and use their kitchen. Getting into the reserve is not easy and you will need to be equipped for a week or more, but a few people go up the Río Escondido. The lagoons abound in wildlife, including enormous crocodiles and spectacular bird life. Contact CECON, Av La Reforma, 0-63, Zona 10, Guatemala City, T361-5450, cecon@usac.edu.gt for more information.

Parque Nacional Laguna del Tigre & Biotopo Laguna del Tigre Río Escondido

Guatemala

Border with Mexico
You are advised to get your visa or Mexican tourist card in advance

Further south, another route leads into the Mexican state of Chiapas. There are 2 points on the Río Usumacinta, which you can reach by *lancha* and continue by bus into Mexico. They are **Frontera Echeverría**, also known as **Corozal** (immigration office near wharf) and **Benemérito** (frontier post upstream at **Pipiles**).

Frontera Echeverría Corozal For the first option, take a bus from Santa Elena via La Libertad to Bethel. *Transportes Pinita* bus, 0500, 0800, 1000, 1200, 1500, 3½ - 4 hrs, US$3.25. The bus leaves Bethel for Flores at 1200. The bus then continues to the *lancha* point for the boat ride, US$0.65. However, if the bus does not wait you will have to take a *lancha* from the immigration point, 20-min ferry ride, US$6.50 to Frontera Echeverría/Corozal on the Río Usumacinta. In Bethel there is accommodation at the **E** *Posada Maya Bethel*, T801-1799 (community phone), just over 1 km outside village. Only place to stay, open-sided thatched shelters with tents or hammocks and mosquito nets, all with clean sheets, built in plaza of a Maya site overlooking the river, cabañas, mainly used by passing tour groups. They run tours to Bonampak, Mexico, and Piedras Negras. You get your Mexican immigration stamp at Corozal. A dirt road leads up 18 km to the Frontier Highway (35 km to the San Javier junction for Lacanjá and Bonampak). From Frontera Echeverría/Corozal it is 4 hrs by bus to Palenque, US$5.50. To ensure getting to Palenque in 1 day, take the 0500 bus from Santa Elena and catch a pick-up, bus or tour buses. There is a daily shuttle service to Palenque, Mexico, 0500, US$30. Contact *San Juan Travel Agency* (see Tour operators, Flores). *Línea Dorada* also ply this route for US$30, 0600, 7 hrs, returning 1100 and 1400.

Benemérito/Pipiles Alternatively, go from Santa Elena to Sayaxché (see below), 60 km, and then take a boat down the Río de la Pasión to the military post at Pipiles (exit stamps must be given here – if you need a Mexican tourist card it's advisable to get it in advance to avoid paying bribes at the border) and on to the town of Benemérito. There are trading boats which take 8 hrs, US$5; motorized cargo canoe US$5-10, 8 hrs; private launch US$100, 4 hrs. At Benemérito, there are a couple of basic *hospedajes*. From Benemérito, buses at 0600, 0700, 0800 and 1300 to immigration just past the Río Lacantún (or hitch in a truck); buses wait here before continuing to Palenque on an unpaved road; 7-12 hrs by bus Benemérito-Palenque (more in the wet). Take a hammock, mosquito net, food and insect repellent; the only accommodation between Sayaxché and Palenque are a few rooms in Benemérito, and dollars cannot be exchanged. Yaxchilán and Bonampak in Mexico can be visited from the road Benemérito-Palenque, which is being improved.

Sayaxché
Colour map 5, grid B2

Sayaxché has a frontier town feel to it as its focus is on a bend on the Río de la Pasión. It is a good point from where to visit the southern Petén including a number of archaeological sites, namely El Ceibal. You can change US$ bills and TCs at *Banoro*. Mon-Fri 0900-1600, Sat 0900-1300.

Sleeping and eating C-D *Guayacán*, T928-6111, close to ferry, owner Julio Godoy is a good source of information. **E-F** *Hotel Posada Segura*, turn right from the dock area and then first left, T928-6162, some rooms with bath, TV, clean, one of the best options in town. **E-F** *Mayapán*, friendly, clean and very basic airless downstairs rooms with much nicer rooms upstairs. *El Botanero Café Restaurante and Bar*, straight up from the dock and second left. A funky wooden bar with logs and seats carved from tree trunks. Expensive food. *Restaurant La Montaña*, cheap food, local information given. *Yakín*, cheap, good food, try the *licuados*.

Transport Bus: there are buses to **Flores**, 0600, 0700, 1-2 hrs, US$2, then microbuses every 30 mins. To **Raxrujá** and on to Cobán via Chisec at 0400, US$3.25, 6½ hrs direct to Cobán. There are pick-ups after that. For Lanquín take the bus to Raxrujá, then a pick-up to Sebol, and then a pick-up to Lanquín, or the Lanquín *cruce* at Pajal, and wait for onward transport. If you are heading to Guatemala City from here it could be quicker to head north to Flores rather than take the long and rough road down to Cobán. However, this road is being tarmacked in stages, but the process is slow.

Directory Tour operators *Viajes Don Pedro*, on the river front near the dock, T928-6109, runs launches to **El Ceibal** (US$32 for up to 3), **Petexbatún** and **Aguateca** (US$52 for up to 5), **Dos Pilas**

US$45 for small group). Trip possible by jeep in the dry season, **Altar de los Sacrificios** (US$97 min 2) and round trips to **Yaxchilán** for 3 days (US$390). Open 0700-1800, 0700-1200 on Sun.

This major ceremonial site is reached by a 45-minute *lancha* ride up the Río de la Pasión from Sayaxché. It is about 1½ km from the left bank of Río de la Pasión hidden in vegetation and extending for 1½ sq km. The height of activity at the site was from 800 BC to the first century AD. Archaeologists agree that it appears to have been abandoned in between about AD 500 and AD 690 and then repopulated at a later stage when there was an era of stelae production between AD 771 to AD 889. It later declined during the early decades of the 10th century and was abandoned. There is now a difficult road linking Sayaxché with El Ceibal – impassable in the wet season. You can sling a hammock at El Ceibal and use the guard's fire for making coffee if you ask politely – a mosquito net is advisable, and take repellent for walking in the jungle surroundings. Tours can be arranged in Flores for a day trip to Sayaxché and El Ceibal (around US$35) but there is limited time to see the site. From Sayaxché the ruins of the **Altar de los Sacrificios** at the confluence of the Ríos de la Pasión and Usumacinta can also be reached. It was one of the earliest sites in the Péten, with a founding date earlier than that of Tikal. Most of its monuments are not in good condition. Also within reach of Sayaxché is **Itzán**, discovered in 1968. Further down the Río Usumacinta is Yaxchilán (see page 458), just over the border in Mexico with temples still standing, sculptures and carved lintels. **El Ceibal**

Still further down the Río Usumacinta in the west of Petén is Piedras Negras, a huge Classic period site. In the 1930s Tatiana Proskouriakoff first recognized the periods of time inscribed on stelae here coincided with human life spans or reigns, and so began the task of deciphering the meaning of Maya glyphs. Advance arrangements are necessary with a rafting company to reach Piedras Negras. *Maya Expeditions* (address on page 564), is the official tour operator for the project; they run expeditions, taking in Piedras Negras, Bonampak, Yaxchilán and Palenque. This trip is a real adventure. The riverbanks are covered in the best remaining tropical forest in Guatemala, inhabited by elusive wildlife and hiding more ruins. Once you've rafted down to Piedras Negras, you have to raft out. Though most of the river is fairly placid, there are the 30 m Busilhá Falls, where a crystal clear tributary cascades over limestone terraces, and two deep canyons, with impressive rapids to negotiate, before reaching the take-out two days later. **Piedras Negras**

From Sayaxché, the Río de la Pasión is a good route to visit other Maya ruins. From **Laguna Petexbatún** (16 km), a fisherman's paradise can be reached by outboard canoe from Sayaxché. Excursions can be made from here to unexcavated ruins which are generally grouped together under the title Petexbatún. These include **Arroyo de la Piedra**, Dos Pilas and Aguateca. **Dos Pilas** has many well-preserved stelae, and an important tomb of a king was found here in 1991 – that of its Ruler 2, who died in AD 726. Dos Pilas flourished in the Classic period when as many as 10,000 lived in the city. There are many carved monuments and hieroglyphic stairways at the site, which record the important events of city life. **Aguateca**, where the ruins are so far little excavated, gives a feeling of authenticity. The city was abandoned in the early ninth century for unknown reasons. Again, a tour is advisable. It's a boat trip and a short walk away. The site was found with numerous walls (it's known the city was attacked in AD 790) and a chasm actually splits the site in two. The natural limestone bridge connects a large plaza with platforms and buildings in the west with an area of a series of smaller plazas in the east. **Petexbatún**

Sleeping **B** *Posada Caribe*, T/F928-6114, including 3 meals, comfortable cabañas with bathroom and shower, excursion to Aguateca by launch and a guide for excursions. **AL** *Chiminos Island Lodge*, T335-3506, www.chiminosisland.com Includes all food. Jungle guides can be hired for US$1.50-2.50 per day. Camping is possible at Escobado, on the lakeside, occasional public *lanchas* from Sayaxché.

Guatemala

Background
History

For early history see page 59. On the eve of the Spanish conquest of Guatemala there were a number of dominant Maya groups, but dissent within some of these groups was exploited by the invading Spanish, who conquered the country bit by bit from 1524 through to 1697. Under Pedro de Alvarado the *encomienda* system was introduced whereby the Maya were forced to work land that was previously theirs and pay tribute to the colonialists in the form of crops. In return they received Christian instruction. They were treated like slaves and gradually died in their thousands from western diseases. At the end of the 18th century, Spanish power began to wane and Central American Independence was signed in 1821, followed by the creation of the Central American Federation. Full independence came in 1839. Liberals and Conservatives see-sawed in and out of power until 1944. Between 1839 and 1842 the Conservatives restored Spanish institutions. This hark back to the colonial era was continued by the fiercely pro-church Rafael Carrera who became president in 1844. He set about restoring church power and reinviting the Jesuits back into the country (they had been expelled in 1767). He went into exile in 1848 before returning to power in 1851 where he remained until 1865.

The 1871 Liberal Revolution On Carrera's death, General Vicente Cerna ruled Guatemala, where he repeatedly suffered liberal opposition, continuing the Conservative bent until 1871. In 1867, a Liberal revolt was launched in Guatemala, headed by Mariscal Cruz, an ally of the Liberal general Justo Rufino Barrios. Then, a small group of men, led by Barrios' troops invaded from Mexico. Initially they were forced back, but eventually Barrios' troops overthrew the Cerna regime, introducing a wave of liberal leadership. During his short term, Barrios supporter Miguel García Granados (1871-73) expelled leading clerics and overturned the invitation to the Jesuits.

Justo Rufino Barrios (1873-85) was elected president. He too was vehemently anti-clerical and church power was reined in. He expropriated church property, using the proceeds to found a national bank, secularised education and marriage, and aimed to restore the federation. This idea floundered and he resorted to dictatorial methods. When El Salvador refused to accept the notion of the federation he invaded and died in a battle at Chalachuapa. His term of office was characterized by huge infrastructure projects – including the construction of ports and railways. Coffee production was reformed, which transformed Guatemala into a major producer, but had detrimental effects on the lives of the *indígena*, who saw their plots of lands seized for coffee plantations, and who were forced to work the plantations. Until 1857, cochineal and indigo were the great exports, but both were wiped out by competition from synthetic dyes. The export vacuum left by indigo and cochineal was filled by *cacao*, followed by coffee and bananas, and essential oils.

Manuel Lisandra Barillas (1885-92) followed in the presidency and again tried to re-establish Central American union. He was in the same mould as Barrios and continued supporting the expanison of the coffee economy. In his Liberal footsteps followed General José María Reina Barrios (1892-98) who confiscated his enemies' property and spent much time quashing internal rebellion. During his term the price of coffee crashed on the world market, but public works using public money continued to be built, causing widespread outrage and revolts. He was assassinated.

Long-term dictatorship & the rise of the United Fruit Company In his place Manuel Estrada Cabrera (1898-1920) came to power. His was the longest one-man rule in Central American history. Cabrera encouraged foreign investment, expansion of the railways and encouraged the United Fruit Company's foray into Guatemala with the planting of bananas. The company acquired privileges, a monopoly on transport and free rein on their affairs without too much state intervention. The United Fruit Company's first plantations were at the mouth of the Río Motagua, near Puerto Barrios, then little more than a village. The company managed the electricity plant, ran supply shops, and was handed the contract to finish the railway line to the Atlantic and granted a 99-year right to use the existing railway line and the port. Land rights saw the company granted some 800,000 ha. Exports soared and American interests in Guatemala grew to the point where about 40% of all exports were US controlled – with the US consequently reaping much of the reward from Guatemala's natural resources. The nail in the coffin of the Cabrera government was its response to the 1917 earthquake. Stall holders were trying to earn money, but met with competition as the government set up its own stalls selling daily goods at cheaper prices. This provoked widespread demonstrations and Cabrera was eventually toppled.

Carlos Herrera followed as president and started on a fairly liberal path, but the old style military did not like his approach, and he was overthrown in a bloodless military coup, bringing José Maria Orellana to power. During Herrera's short presidency (1920-21) there were strikes against the United Fruit Company and the International Railways of Central America, which the fruit company also ran. Out of this anti-American sentiment again rose the idea of Central American unity, but Orellana knocked this idea on the head and negotiated more concessions for United Fruit and the railway company. However, workers' demands for rights were not to be suffocated, and organized protest grew, which was periodically met with government crackdowns. He, unlike some of his predecessors, died a natural death in 1926.

Jorge Ubico was an efficient but brutal dictator who came to power in 1931. He tightened political control, introduced a secret police, clamped down on workers' discontent and Communist movements, persecuted writers and intellectuals, and restricted books coming into the country because of his fear of Communism. He promoted forced labour, fixed low wage rates, and introduced an anti-vagrancy law, whereby the Maya had to work for free on a landlords's farm for 150 days a year. Ubico supported the US government during the Second World War, and during this period sent Germans living in Guatemala back to their homeland, or to camps in the US. He followed this up with expropriating German-owned land. He also extended privileges to the United Fruit Company. These, and other issues, and the fact that he sought constant re-election, led to demonstrations and a demand for his resignation. The demonstrations led to the suspension of constitutional rights. One teacher was shot dead during a demonstration demanding university autonomy. The demonstrators called for Ubico's resignation. He resigned in June 1944 and a triumvirate of generals assumed power.

Social reform

On 20 October 1944 there was an armed uprising of La Guardia de Honor, backed by popular support. This military trio drew up a democratic constitution, abolished forced labour, and upheld the autonomy of the university. Teacher Juan José Arévalo of the *Frente Popular Libertador* party was elected president following elections and drew up a plan of social reform. He separated the powers of state, introduced *comedores* for children of poor workers, set up the Department for Social Security, and accepted the existence of the communist party. He survived more than 20 military coups and finished his term of five years (1945-50).

October Revolution

Jacobo Arbenz Guzmán, a member of the 1945 military triumvirate, became the elected president in 1950. His biggest reforms focussed on land reform and the breaking up of American business monopolies in Guatemala. This set him on a collision course with the United Fruit Company. His 1952 Agrarian Reform Law saw the expropriation of large, under-utilised estates without adequate compensation awarded to their owners. The land was then distributed among the numerous landless peasantry, which aroused huge opposition from landowners. The value of the land was based on its declared taxable worth. Altogether, about 1.5 million acres of land was redistributed to around 100,000 families, at a cost of nearly US$8.5 million in government bonds. The biggest voice of discontent came from United Fruit, which for years had been under-declaring the value of its land for tax reasons. According to the company, of its 550,000 acres around the Caribbean, 85% of it was not farmed. It was offered a measly US$2.99 an acre for land (440,000 acres) which it said was worth US$75 – the seeds of the coup had begun to be sown.

Arbenz also attempted to dismantle the monopolies created by the likes of United Fruit. He made moves to build a government-funded port on the Caribbean coast, and started the

1954 American-backed military coup

construction of the Atlantic Highway to transport goods to compete with the fruit company-run railway line. He also ordered the construction of a hydroelectricity plant to compete with the existing plant run by an American company.

At the same time reports suggested there was increased Communist infiltration of the government. The reforms threatened American commercial interests in Guatemala, especially that of the United Fruit Company. The company's connections with the high-powered within the US Government and the CIA, and its constant complaint that Communism was percolating through the Guatemalan corridors of power, eventually persuaded the US to sponsor an overthrow of the Arbenz government.

According to the excellent investigative report *Bitter Fruit: The Story of the American Coup in Guatemala*, the US waited for tangible proof of the Guatemalan government's 'communist identity' before sponsoring the overthrow of the Arbenz regime. When a boat stockpiled with Czech weapons docked at Puerto Barrios there was no longer any need to delay action. According to the book's authors Stephen Schlesinger and Stephen Kinzer, President Eisenhower said weapons were one step away from establishing a Communist dictatorship.

A well-orchestrated propaganda war was also put in motion by United Fruit to persuade international opinion of the Communist threat. Military strikes were launched on the country in June 1954. At the end of the month Arbenz, under pressure from Guatemalan military and the US ambassador John Peurifoy, resigned. Arbenz went into exile. According to *Bitter Fruit*, the Eisenhower administration tried to distance itself from growing international criticism and it launched an anti-trust suit against United Fruit after investigating its land holdings in Guatemala. This, the book alleges, it did in an attempt to distance itself from the debacle and the opinion that it was defending United Fruit. The company was sued in a court case lasting four years. The company, in attempt to appease the government and extricate itself, offered 100,000 acres of its land (although it was mostly useless jungle) to landless *campesinos*. However, the government pursued the case and its effect caused the gradual break up and ending of United Fruit's long and highly controversial involvement in Guatemala.

Military rule   In June 1954, Colonel Carlos Castillo Armas, took over the presidencey. He persecuted and outlawed Communists. He was assassinated in 1957. His assasination provoked a wave of violence and instability in Guatemala and for the next three decades the army and its right-wing supporters suppressed left-wing efforts, both constitutional and violent, to restore the gains made under Arévalo and Arbenz; many thousands of people, mostly leftists but also many Maya without political orientation, were killed during this period.

**The rise of   On 13 November 1960, a military group, inspired by the Cuban Revolution, carried out an
the guerrilla   uprising against the government. It was suppressed but spawned the *Movimiento 13 de
movement**   *Noviembre*, which then joined forces with the Guatemalan Worker's Party. In 1962, student demonstrations ended in bloodshed, which resulted in the creation of the *Movimiento 12 de Abril*. These movements then merged to form *Fuerzas Armadas Rebeldes* (FAR) in 1962.

During this period, Arévalo made a move to re-enter the political fold. A coup d'état followed. Guerilla and right-wing violence began to increase in the late 1960s. In the early 1970s the guerrillas re-focussed. The FAR divided into FAR and the EGP – *Ejército Guerrillero de los Pobres* (Guerilla Army of the Poor) which operated in the north of the country. In 1972 the *Organización Revolucionaria del Pueblo en Armas* (ORPA) was formed. The EGP was led by Rolando Morán, a supporter of the Cuban Revolution. The group's first action took place in the Ixil Triangle in 1975. The ORPA was led by Commandante Gaspar Ilom, also known as Rodrigo Asturias, son of Nobel Prize Literature winner Miguel Angel Asturias.

**The worst of   Throughout the 1970s and early 1980s the worst atrocities of the war were committed.
the conflict**   General Kjell Eugenio Laugerud García's presidency was characterized by escalating violence, which led the US to withdraw its support for the Guatemalan government in 1974 and demand that human rights be respected.

A devastating earthquake struck Guatemala in 1976 killing 23,000 people. This prompted widespread social movements in the country to improve the lives of the poor. At the same time guerrilla activity surged. In 1978-82, during the term of General Romeo Lucas García and the presidency of Efraín Ríos Montt, the violence reached its peak.

The US, believing the human rights situation had improved, resumed military sales to Guatemala. But in 1981 the military unleashed a huge offensive against the guerrillas who united to confront it with the formation of the *Unidad Revolucionaria Nacional Guatemalteca* (URNG) in 1982. The government also set up the civil defence patrols, which were like neighbourhood watch movements, but with a sinister edge. They would set brother against brother and father against son, and were aimed at assisting the army in stopping the infiltration of guerrilla forces into Guatemalan society. Ríos Montt came to power in 1982 following a coup d'etat. He and his predecessor presided over the worst period of violence in the civil war with the introduction of the scorched-earth policy, which saw massacres of whole villages, literally wiping them off the face of the earth, in an attempt to root out bands of guerrillas in a massive counter-insurgency campaign. Ríos Montt was ousted by his defence minister, General Oscar Mejías Victores, in a coup in August 1983.

Mejía Victores permitted a Constituent Assembly to be elected in 1984, which drew up a new constitution and worked out a timetable for a return to democracy. He also created numerous 'model villages' to rehouse the displaced and persecuted Maya, who if they had survived massacre, had fled in their thousands to the forests, capital, Mexico and the US. Presidential elections, held in December 1985, were won by civilian Vinicio Cerezo Arévalo of the Christian Democrat party (DC), who took office in January 1986. He was the first democratically elected President of Guatemala since 1966. He opened the door to the first political dialogue between the government and the URNG, which took place in 1987. This was preceded by the establishment of the Commission for National Reconciliation formed in attempt to resolve the violent conflicts that had enveloped the entire region. In the 1990 elections the DC fared badly, their candidate failing to qualify for run-off elections between the eventual winner, Jorge Serrano Elías of the Solidarity Action Movement and Jorge Carpio of the National Centrist Union. Serrano Elías made Guatemalan history by being the first civilian to succeed a previous civilian president in a change of government.

Return of democracy

By 1993, the country was in disarray. Political, social and economic policies pursued by the government had alienated nearly everybody and violence erupted on the streets led by a wave of student riots. Amid growing civil unrest, President Serrano suspended the constitution, dissolved Congress and the Supreme Court, and imposed press censorship, with what appeared to be military support for his auto-coup. International and domestic condemnation of his actions was immediate and most foreign aid was frozen. After only a few days, Serrano was ousted by a combination of military, business and opposition leaders and a return to constitutional rule was promised. Congress approved a successor to Serrano, electing Ramiro de León Carpio, who had previously been the human rights ombudsman. This spectacular choice led to much optimism, which proved short-lived. Although progress was made in talks between the government and the URNG, human rights violations continued. Some communities, displaying no faith in the security and justice systems, took the law into their own hands in dealing with criminals. Land invasions also continued and strikes in the public and private sectors continued in 1994 and early 1995. In this climate, the public's distaste of corrupt congressional deputies and ineffectual government was not diminished. The president seemed powerless to restore any confidence because Congress deliberately failed to approve bills on constitutional, police, or tax reform, and other laws. The reform of election procedures and political parties had been called for by a referendum in 1994, which obliged Congressional elections to be called. The result gave a majority of seats to the Guatemalan Republican Front (FRG), led by ex-president Ríos Montt. Despite an alliance of four parties against the FRG's control of Congress, Ríos Montt was elected to the presidency of Congress for 1994-96. Ríos Montt's candidate in the 1995 presidential election, Alfonso Portillo, lost by a slim margin to Alvaro Arzú of the National Advancement Party. Arzú proposed to increase social spending, curtail tax evasion, combat crime and bring a speedy conclusion to peace negotiations with the URNG guerrillas.

Civil unrest

Towards peace
One of the earliest moves made by President Serrano was to speed up the process of talks between the government and the URNG, which began in March 1990. The sides met in Mexico City in April 1991 to discuss such topics as democratization and human rights, a reduced role for the military, the rights of indigenous people, the resettlement of refugees and agrarian reform. Progress, however, was slow. In August 1995 an accord was drawn up with the aid of the UN's Guatemala mission (MINUGUA) and the Norwegian government. The timetable proved over-ambitious, but, on taking office in January 1996, President Arzú committed himself to signing a peace accord. In February 1996 he met the URNG leadership, who called a ceasefire in March. On 29 December 1996 a peace treaty was signed ending 36 years of armed conflict. An amnesty was agreed which would limit the scope of the Commission for Historical Clarification and prevent it naming names in its investigations of human rights abuses. Although a demobilization of the guerilla was completed successfully, difficulties remained over human rights in the peace process. Nothing emphasized this more than the bludgeoning to death of Bishop Juan Gerardi, the ecclesiastical co-ordinator for the Project for the Recuperation of Historical Memory, in April 1998. Two days before his murder, the Project released *Guatemala Nunca Más* (*Guatemala Never Again*), a report detailing the deaths and disappearances in the conflict. Some 80% of the human rights violations, the report said, were caused by the military.

Peacetime elections & the Portillo Government
The 1999 elections went to a second round with self-confessed murderer Alfonso Portillo of the FRG winning 62% of the vote against his rival Oscar Berger, the candidate of President Arzú's ruling PAN. Portillo, while on the campaign trail, used to say that as someone that had defended his own life he could defend his countrymen's. (After he had gunned down two Mexican students in 1982, he fled the country saying he would not get a fair trial. The case against him was officially closed in 1995.) On coming to office in January 2000, Portillo committed his government to uphold the Peace Accord of 1996 adding that "all the political, economic and social changes this country needs are mandated under the peace accord". Portillo subsequently promised to reform the armed forces, solve the killing of Bishop Gerardi and disband the élite presidential guard, implicated in human rights abuses. Many fear that Portillo's government may come under the influence of his political mentor, the country's former military dictator Ríos Montt, who presided over some of the worst atrocities of the civil war. Ríos Montt is currently head of Congress. Portillo's presidency so far has been riddled with accusations of corruption and a lack of transparency. In April 2001, the country experienced 'Guategate' – Ríos Montt was accused of illegally changing the law regarding a tax on liquor sales. He claimed he was not in the room when the legislation was altered and escaped charges. In May the government was accused of a lack of priority in public expenditure and US$61.5 million went to prop up the *Promotor and Metropolitano* banks, owned by Portillo's friend and electoral campaign funder Francisco Alvarado MacDonald, who filed for bankruptcy. In addition, the *Banco de Guatemala* had to put up US$197 million to deal with the financial collapse of these banks, although it was promised the debt would be repaid. Although the banks, known as *los gemelos* (the twins), had US$120 million in financial holdings, US$108 million was lent with trustee backing to companies linked to Alvarado and, so it's thought, is virtually impossible to recover. In the same month Portillo was criticized for the cost of an official trip to Japan which cost about US$72,000. In June, 78 dangerous prisoners escaped from the country's high-security prison known as *El Infierno* (Hell). It was revealed the police knew about the planned escape the day before and sent staff to investigate but did not tighten security. Fantastic conspiracy stories ciculated for days, including the rumour that the escape was ordered to divert attention away from the government's proposed VAT (IVA) tax hike. Despite thousands of protests and a national strike on 1 August 2001, the 2% rise was introduced anyway, taking IVA to 12%. Common crime, as well as those more sinister crimes such as lynchings, have plagued Portillo's term and seem to be on the increase. Since the signing of the Peace Accords in 1996, MINUGUA has verified 347 lynchings throughout the country. As if things could not get worse, food shortages struck Guatemala in September 2001 due to the summer drought.

In 2002, human rights activists and forensic teams excavating burial sites of civil war victims continued to be threatened; the UN World Food Programme stepped in to aid 60,000 malnourished children; and Ríos Montt planned a legal challenge against a rule which prohibits former coup leaders running for president. Ex-paramilitaries blockaded Tikal trapping tourists in the grounds of the ruins after they demanded compensation for their roles in the civil war. The government said it would try and levy a tax to pay them compensation. In June, ex-president Jorge Serrano was ordered to be arrested on charges which included embezzlement of state funds. In July interior minister Eduardo Arevalo resigned his cabinet position citing personal reasons for his resignation. He was reported as saying his resignation had nothing to do with recent allegations of police brutality. The former interior minister Byron Barrientos resigned in December and now faces charges of misappropriating US$6million in state funds.

Economy

In 2000-01 tourism became the biggest earner for the country. The agricultural sector accounts for one-quarter of GDP, two-thirds of exports, and half of the labour force. Coffee, sugar, and bananas are the main produce, followed by vegetables, sesame and cardamom. There has been an attempt to diversify agricultural exports with tobacco, fruit and ornamental plants. Beef exports are increasing. The equitable distribution of occupied land is still a pressing problem. US Aid statistics show 68% of cultivable land is in the hands of just 2% of landowners, while medium and small landowners account for 20% and 10% of cultivable land, respectively. The industrial sector has been growing steadily; the main activities, apart from food and drink production, include rubber manufacture, textiles, paper and pharmaceuticals. Chemicals, furniture, petroleum products, electrical components and building materials are also produced. The encouragement of *maquila* (sweatshop) industries in the mid-1980s attracted foreign investment, much of it from the Far East, and created low-paid jobs for about 80,000 Guatemalans, mostly in garment manufacturing.

Culture

The indigenous people of Guatemala are mainly of Maya descent. The largest of the 22 indigenous Maya groups are K'iche', Q'eqchi' and Mam. When the Spaniards arrived from Mexico in 1524 those who stayed settled in the southern highlands around Antigua and Guatemala City and intermarried with the groups of native subsistence farmers living there. This was the basis of the present *mestizo* population living in the cities and towns as well as in all parts of the southern highlands and in the flatlands along the Pacific coast; the indigenous population is still at its most dense in the western highlands and Alta Verapaz. They form two distinct cultures: the almost self-supporting indigenous system in the highlands, and the *ladino* commercial economy in the lowlands. *Mestizo* are mixed Amerindian-Spanish or assimilated Amerindian – more commonly known as *ladino*. About half the total population are classed as Amerindian (Maya) – estimates of the Amerindian population vary from 40-65%. The remaining populaton comprises: *ladinos*, over 40%; whites, 5%; black, 2%; and other mixed race or Chinese, 3.9%. A 2001 study revealed that there are 5,944,222 Maya; 3,800,405 *ladinos*; 6,539 Garífuna; and 297 Xinca who are physically similar to the *ladinos* (little is known of this small population – some say they are descendants of the Inca).

Indian dress is unique and attractive, little changed from the time the Spaniards arrived: the colourful head-dresses, *huipiles* (tunics) and skirts of the women, the often richly patterned sashes and kerchiefs, the hatbands and tassels of the men vary greatly, often from village to village. Unfortunately a new outfit is costly, the Indians are poor, and denims are cheap. While men are adopting Western dress in many villages, women are slower to change.

People
The word ladino applies to any person with a 'Latin' culture, speaking Spanish and wearing Western clothes, though they may be pure Amerindian by descent. The opposite of ladino is indigena; the definition is cultural, not racial. Guatemala's population is 12,639,939

Costume & dress

Guatemala

Religion There is no official religion but about 70% consider themselves Roman Catholic. The other 30% are Protestant, mostly affiliated to evangelical churches, which have been very active in the country over the past 25 years.

Land and environment

A lowland ribbon, nowhere more than 50 km wide, runs the whole length of the Pacific shore. Cotton, sugar, bananas and maize are the chief crops of this strip. There is some stock raising as well. Summer rain is heavy and the lowland carries scrub forest. From this plain the highlands rise sharply to heights of between 2,500 and 4,000 m and stretch some 240 km to the north before sinking into the northern lowlands. A string of volcanoes juts boldly above the southern highlands along the Pacific. There are intermont basins at from 1,500 to 2,500 m in this volcanic area. Most of the people of Guatemala live in these basins, which are drained by short rivers into the Pacific and by longer ones into the Atlantic. One basin west of the capital, ringed by volcanoes and with no apparent outlet, is Lago de Atitlán. The southern highlands are covered with lush vegetation over a volcanic subsoil. This clears away in the central highlands, exposing the crystalline rock of the east-west running ranges. This area is lower but more rugged, with sharp-faced ridges and deep ravines modifying into gentle slopes and occasional valley lowlands as it loses height and approaches the Caribbean coastal levels and the flatlands of El Petén. The lower slopes of these highlands, from about 600 to 1,500 m, are planted with coffee. Above 1,500 m is given over to wheat and the main subsistence crops of maize and beans. Deforestation is becoming a serious problem. Where rainfall is low there are savannas; water for irrigation is now drawn from wells and these areas are being reclaimed for pasture and fruit growing. Two large rivers flow down to the Caribbean Gulf of Honduras from the highlands: one is the Río Motagua, 400 km long, rising among the southern volcanoes; the other, further north, is the Río Polochic, 298 km long, which drains into Lago de Izabal and the Bahía de Amatique. There are large areas of lowland in the lower reaches of both rivers, which are navigable for considerable distances; this was the great banana zone. To the northwest, bordering on Belize and Mexico's Yucatán Peninsula, lies the low, undulating tableland of El Petén almost one-third of the nation's territory. In some parts there is natural grassland, with woods and streams, suitable for cattle, but large areas are covered with dense hardwood forest. Since the 1970s large-scale tree-felling has reduced this tropical rainforest by some 40%, especially in the south and east. However, in the north, which now forms Guatemala's share of the Maya Biosphere Reserve, the forest is protected, but illegal logging still takes place.

Books and films

Guatemala for You by Barbara Balchin de Koose (Piedra Santa, Guatemala City); *I, Rigoberta Menchú*, by Rigoberta Menchú; *Sweet Waist of America: Journeys around Guatemala*, by Anthony Daniels (London: Hutchinson, 1990). The novels of Miguel Angel Asturias, notably *Hombres de maíz, Mulata de tal* and *El señor presidente*. Mario Payeras' *Los días de la selva* is a first-hand account of the guerrilla movement in the 1970s. On screen, *El Norte* (Gregory Nava, 1983) follows the plight of a Guatemalan brother and sister who seek a new life after experiencing the trials of their village massacre. *When the Mountains Tremble* (Yates & Sigel, 1983) is a hard-hitting film demonstrating the desperation of national governments, guerillas and meddling international military forces.

Guatemala

Belize

5

Belize

Essentials

Belize, formerly known as British Honduras, nestles on the coast between Mexico and Guatemala, and has a land area of about 8,860 sq miles, that includes numerous small islands known as *cayes*. Its greatest length (north-south) is 174 miles and greatest width 80 miles. Within this small territory the landscape varies incredibly, from mountainous, tropical rainforests with abundant wildlife, to fertile subtropical foothills where sugar, rice, cattle and fruit trees are cultivated, and to bird-filled coastal wetlands and cayes with beautiful beaches. The reefs and cayes form a 184-mile barrier reef with crystal clear water, and are a major tourist attraction for world-class diving, snorkelling and sport fishing. Inland rivers and rainforest invite you to head out on land or water, trekking, paddling, caving and biking through the above ground ruins and spiritual underworld of the Maya. Warm tropical breezes encourage the laid-back attitude of the small (just 240,000) but ethnically diverse population, who are 'as warm and friendly as the climate'.

Planning your trip

Belize

Where to go

While many travellers are dismayed by the reputation of **Belize City**, the authorities are working hard to clean it up and present a better face to tourists. Special tourist police have been introduced and crime is much less widespread than it was in the mid-1990s. That said, however, you may still be offered drugs on the streets. It is possible to avoid Belize City altogether, but it is worth spending a day or two having a look around and getting a feel for the old town – it's not possible to really know Belize if you haven't spent some time in the city. Generally, the longer people stay the better they like it and resident Belizeans are friendly and generally welcoming. The short journey to visit **Belize Zoo** is worthwhile. A little further on is the tiny capital of **Belmopan**, an hour's excursion from Belize City. Having recently earned its new status as a town with its own council, its finally on its way to becoming a cultural centre as well as being the seat of Government.

The **northern cayes**, a series of paradise islands with crystal clear waters, palm-fringed beaches and mangroves, are the main recipients of tourism to Belize. **Ambergris Caye**, more upmarket, and **Caye Caulker**, popular with budget travellers, are the two most developed cayes, from where you can take excursions to the smaller cayes and marine parks. Pleasant resorts and budget places attract a wide range of travellers wishing to sample the delights of a Caribbean island. The atmosphere is very laid back and there are lots of watersports for the active, with some spectacular diving, snorkelling on the barrier reef, and trips to outlying cayes and the world-famous **Blue Hole**.

On the mainland, the Northern Highway leads from Belize City to the Mexican border through some of the most productive farm land in the country. There is still plenty of room for wildlife, however, and several sanctuaries protect it, including the **Community Baboon Sanctuary**, for black howler monkeys; the **Crooked Tree Lagoons and Wildlife Sanctuary**, for birds; and the 22,000-acre **Shipstern Nature Reserve** incorporating hardwood forests, lagoons and savannah. The archaeological remains of **Lamanai**, one of Belize's largest archaeological sites with a 112-ft temple (the tallest known pre-classic Maya structure) is easily visited from Orange Walk, and **Altún Ha**, once a major Maya ceremonial site and trading post between the Caribbean and the interior, are essential visits for 'Maya-philes'. The largest town in the north, **Orange Walk**, is a multi-racial city of Mennonites, Creoles, Maya and other Central Americans who make their living from agriculture.

The Western Highway leads from Belize City, skirting the capital Belmopan, to **San Ignacio** and the Guatemalan border. San Ignacio and its twin town Santa Elena have a pleasant climate and are in a beautiful setting of wooded hills straddling the Macal River. Most people spend some time here before moving on to Guatemala and it is noted as one of the friendliest areas in the country. In the hills surrounding the town there are a number of eco-resorts, basic lodges and working farms offering accommodation in idyllic forest and riverside settings. A side trip to the **Mountain Pine Ridge** area offers great hiking, amid spectacular broadleaf forests, rivers, rapids, waterfalls and caves, making a worthwhile excursion with much to be enjoyed along the entire route to Caracol. There are several Maya sites, notably **Cahal Pech**, right at the edge of town overlooking the area; **El Pilar**, north through Bullet Tree Falls; **Xunantunich**, across the Mopan River by hand-cranked ferry at San José Succotz with its plazas, temples,

Belize

Belize

○ **Archaeological Sites**	4 Caracol	8 Cerros
1 Chan Chich	5 Las Milpas	9 Cuello
2 Altun Ha	6 Lubaantum	10 Nim Li Punit
3 Xunantunich	7 Lamanai	11 Mayflower

0 km 20

0 miles 20

ball court and *castillo*; and **Caracol** the country's largest site to date rivalling Tikal in size, if not splendour, where the Sky Palace pyramid reaches a height of 138 ft.

The Southern Highway runs along the eastern edge of the Maya Mountains, through sparsely populated countryside dotted with Indian settlements, to Dangriga and Hopkins Village and then past the world-famous **Cockscomb Basin Wildlife (Jaguar) Sanctuary**. The coastal area around **Placencia** offers idyllic palm-fringed beaches and some spectacular diving and sport fishing. Although the peninsula is developing rapidly, there are still plenty of accommodation choices for all budgets. Offshore cayes are reached by boat from **Dangriga** or Mango Creek, several of which are private or have very small settlements that offer seclusion, relaxation, lovely beaches and fabulous water. In the far south is **Punta Gorda** with the ruins of **Lubaantun**, a late-Maya ceremonial site where the infamous Crystal Skull was discovered. Nearby, you can stay at guesthouses in Maya villages as part of a community tourism projects.

When to go

Shade temperature is not often over 32°C on the coast, even in the hotter months of January to May (the 'dry season', but see below). The high season tends to run from mid-December to March, or even into May. Inland, in the west, day temperatures can exceed 38°C, but the nights are cooler and usually pleasant. Between November and January there are cold spells during which the temperature at Belize City may fall to 13°C. Humidity is normally high, making it 'sticky' most of the time in the lowlands.

There are sharp annual variations in rainfall, there is even an occasional drought, but the average at Belize City is 1,650 mm, with an average of 1,270 mm in the north and a huge increase up to 4,310 mm down in the south. Generally, the driest months are April and May; in June and July there are heavy showers followed by blue skies. Around August the *mauger* occurs, a mini-dry season of about six weeks. September, October and November tend to be overcast and there are more insects during these months. Hurricanes threaten the country from June to November, but these are rare. An efficient warning system has been updated post-Hurricane Mitch and most towns and large villages have their own hurricane shelters. 'Hurricane Preparedness' instructions are issued annually.

Finding out more

The Belize Tourist Board, in Belize City at New Central Bank Building, Level 2, Gabourel Lane, PO Box 325, T223-1913, F223-1943, www.travelbelize.org, provides information on hotels and a variety of handouts on parks and reserves. Also a freephone telephone service is provided from the USA and Canada on 1-800-624-0686. In Europe there are offices in **Germany** at Belize Tourist Board, Bopserwaldstr 40-G, D-71084, Stuttgart, T49-711-233947, F49-711-233954, btb-germany@t-online.de, and **UK**, c/o Belize High Commission (see Embassies and consulates below).

Belize on the web Given its size, the amount of information about Belize on the internet is phenomenal. **www.belizenet.com**, is a good search engine with general information as are **www.belize.net** and **www.belize.com** The government site on the country, **www.belize.gov.bz**, is packed with information on the official angle. Belize's strong focus on protected areas is supported on the net by **www.belizeaudubon.org**, and **www.pfbelize.org**, which cover most of the areas of interest. Regional websites also exist but are not fully inclusive of all services. One of the better ones is **www.placencia.com**, which comprehensively eliminates the need to go to the place! **www.ambergriscaye.com**, covers Ambergris Caye and **www.gocayecaulker.com** speaks for itself. **Belizex.com** covers much of the Cayo area, **BelizeEcotourism.org** has a member list to help choose environmentally sensitive lodging. Also recommended for online information is *Belize Report* at **www.belizereport.com**

Language

English is the official language, but Spanish is also used, especially in the border areas. Creole is widely spoken throughout the country, and some would consider it the second national language. A Low German dialect is spoken by Mennonite settlers in the north. Several Maya dialects and Garífuna are spoken by ethnic groups.

Belize

Belize

 Belize embassies and consulates

Belgium, Boulevard Brand Whitlock 136, 1200 Brussels, T/F2-732-6246

Canada (changes frequently), 1080 Cote Beaver Hill, Suite 1720, Montréal, Québec, H2Z 1S8, T514-871-4741, F514-397-0816.

Germany, Lindenstrasse 46-48 7120, Beitigheim, Bissingen, T7142-3924, F7142-33225

Guatemala, Edificio El Reformador 8th Floor, Suite 803, Avenida Reforma 1-50 Zone 9, Guatemala City, T334-5531, F334-5536

Honduras, Hotel Honduras Maya, Tegucigalpa, Postal address: Apto Postal 1586 Tegucigalpa. T220-5070, F220-5071

Israel, Asia house, 4 Weizman Street, Tele Aviv 4329, T3-695-4142, F3-255-816

Italy, Via Emilio de Cavalieri, 1200198 Rome, Italy, T06-841-7907, F06-841-5496

Mexico (Cancún), Nader 34, Cancun,

Quintana Roo, T998-887-8631

Netherlands, Henegouwselaan 51, 1181 CV Amsteleveen, T20-456-0206, F20-441-7656

Norway, Brunholmgt 1B, N6004 Alesund, T701-3600, F701-36630

Spain, Avdu Diagonal 469, 4th Floor 2 A, 08036 Barcelona, T93-430-3044, F93 405-3883

Switzerland, 1 Rue Pedro-Meylan, 1211 Geneva 17, T22-786-3883, F22-736-9939

UK, High Commission, 22 Harcourt House, 19 Cavendish Square, London, W1M 9AD, T020-7499-9728, F020-7491-4139.

USA, 2535 Massachusetts Ave, NW Washington DC 20008, T/F202-332-6888.

For more details check at www.belize.gov.bz/diplomats.html

Before you travel

Visas & immigration

All nationalities need passports, as well as sufficient funds and, officially, an onward ticket, although this is rarely requested for stays of 30 days or less. Visas are not usually required by nationals from countries within the EU, some Commonwealth countries, for example Australia and New Zealand, most Caribbean states, USA, Canada, Liechtenstein, Mexico, Norway, Finland, Panama, Sweden, Turkey, Uruguay and Venezuela. Citizens of India, Israel, Austria and Switzerland do need a visa. There is a Belizean Consulate in Chetumal, Mexico, at Avenida Alvaro Obregón 226A, T832-4908, US$25. If you do require a visa it is best to obtain one in Mexico City before arriving at the border . While visas cannot generally be purchased at the border, reports suggest it is possible if you have a visa for the US. Free transit visas (for 24 hours) are available at borders. It is possible that a visa may not be required if you have an onward ticket, but check all details at a consulate before arriving at the border. Those going to other countries after leaving Belize should get any necessary visas in their home country. Visitors are initially granted 30 days' stay in Belize; this may be extended every 30 days for US$12.50 for up to six months at the Immigration Office, Government Complex, Mahogany Street, Belize City, T222-4620 (to the west of the city. At the end of six months, visitors must leave the country for at least 24 hours. Visitors must not engage in any type of employment, paid or unpaid, without first securing a work permit from the Department of Labour; if caught, the penalty for both the employer and the employee is severe.

Border guards seem to have complete power to refuse entry to people whose looks they do not like. There have also been reports that tourists carrying less than US$30 for each day of intended stay have been refused entry. **Cyclists** should get a passport stamp to indicate an 'imported' bicycle.

What to take

Clothing The business dress for men is a short-sleeved shirt or *guayabera*, and trousers of some tropical weight material. Formal wear may include ties and jackets, but long-sleeved embroidered *guayaberas* are more common. Women generally wear dresses or lightweight suits. Casual attire such as shorts and T-shirts are suitable nearly everywhere for vacationers, however swimsuits are acceptable only on the beaches, cayes and at resorts.

Customs

Clothing and articles for personal use are allowed in without payment of duty, though laptop computers, video cameras, cellular phones, and CD players and radios that you bring may be

Touching down

Official time Six hours behind GMT.
Telephone IDD 501. Information T113.
International operator T115.
Hours of business Retail shops are open
0800-1200, 1300-1600 and Friday 1900-2100,
with a half day from 1200 on Wednesday.
Small shops open additionally most late
afternoons and evenings, and some on
Sunday 0800-1000. Government and
commercial office hours are 0800-1200 and
1300-1600 Monday to Friday.
Voltage 110/220 volts single phase, 60
cycles for domestic supply. Some hotels use 12
volt generators.
Weights and measures Imperial and US
standard weights and measures. The US
gallon is used for gasoline and motor oil.

stamped on your passport to ensure they leave with you. Other import allowances are: 200
cigarettes or ½ lb of tobacco; one litre of alcohol; one bottle of perfume. Visitors can take in an
unspecified amount of other currencies. No fruit or vegetables may be brought into Belize;
searches are infrequent, but can be thorough. Pets must have proof of rabies inoculations and
a vet's certificate of good health.

Money

The monetary unit is the **Belizean dollar**, stabilized at Bz$2=US$1. Currency notes issued by
the *Central Bank* are in denominations of 100, 50, 20, 10, 5, 2 and 1 dollar, and coinage of 2 and
1 dollar, 50, 25, 10, 5 and 1 cent is in use. The American expressions **quarter** (25c), **dime** (10c)
and **nickel** (5c) are used, although 25c is sometimes referred to as a shilling. US dollars are
accepted everywhere. A common cause for complaint or misunderstanding is uncertainty
about which currency you are paying in. The price tends to be given in US$ when the
hundred Belize dollar mark is breached; make sure it is clear from the start whether you are
being charged in US or Belizean dollars.

Currency
US$1=Bz$2

    Exchange See under Banks, Belize City. For Western Union, T227-5924. The government
has recently restricted the exchange of foreign currency to government-licensed *Casas de
Cambio*, but these only operate in major towns. You can still find some money changers at
the borders, but the exchange rate is not as high as it has been, and there is a risk of both you
and the money changer being arrested and fined.

The cost of living is high, compared to neighbouring countries, because of the heavy reliance
on imports and extra duties. But budget travellers will still be able to get by on about US$30
per person per day if travelling in twos. In addition, the licences that are required to provide
many services involve payment. Budget travellers also find exploring the interior difficult
because public transport is limited and car hire is beyond the means of many. VAT has been
replaced by an 8% sales tax which is charged on all services, but should **not** be charged on
top of the 7% hotel tax charged on your room. A 1% 'Environmental Tax' is levied on all goods
brought into the country. A recent enactment of 'Hotel Minimum Standards', developed to
allow Belize to compete in the international tourism arena, resulted in the elimination of
much of the cheaper, sub-standard accommodation.

**Cost of living
& travelling**

Getting there

With the exception of neighbouring countries, international services to Belize go through the
USA. Regular flights connect to Baltimore, Charlotte (North Carolina), Dallas/Fort Worth,
Hartford, Houston, Miami, Minneapolis, New Orleans, New York and Washington DC, with
American Airlines, **Continental**, **Grupo Taca** and **US Airways**. There are no direct flights
from Europe and the times of flights miss Miami connections necessitating an overnight stop
in Miami or Houston.

Air

    From Central America there are daily connections to San Salvador with **Grupo Taca**, and
Flores (Guatemala) and San Pedro Sula (Honduras) with **Maya Island Air** and **Tropic Air**.

Belize

Overland The most commonly used routes are with the Petén Department of Guatemala at Benque Viejo del Carmen and, to the north, at the border with Chetumal on Mexico's Yucután Peninsula, both scheduled for a remodelling in late 2002. A less widely used crossing, for non-vehicular travellers, is at La Unión, where there are immigration facilities but officials are only used to dealing with Mexicans and Belizeans so you may experience delays.

Boat Boat services link the south of the country with Honduras and Guatemala – for details see under Dangriga, Placencia, Mango Creek and Punta Gorda. From Puerto Barrios, Guatemala, there is a boat service to Punta Gorda; from Puerto Cortés, Honduras, a boat goes to Dangriga, and Placencia. Obtain all necessary exit stamps and visas before sailing – see under each town for details.

Touching down

Airline ticket & departure tax The main international airport and point of arrival is at Ladyville, 10 miles northwest of Belize City. For airport details, see page 708. Expect a departure tax of US$13.75 on leaving from the international airport, but not for transit passengers who have spent less than 24 hours in the country. There is also a security screening charge of US$1.25 and all visitors must pay the Bz$7.50 PACT tax on departure; see page 707, all in all totalling US$18.75.

There is now also a whopping US$10 departure fee levied by the newly established 'Border Management Authority' when crossing either the Northern border into Mexico or Western border into Guatemala.

Rules, customs and etiquette **Tipping** In restaurants, 10% of the bill; porters in hotels US$2; chambermaids US$1 per day. Taxi drivers are tipped depending on the length of the transfer, whether 'touring' took place or for extra stops, from US$1-10.

Safety Crimes against travellers are harshly punished, but precautions are still advised, particularly if travelling alone or at night or in deserted areas. Beware of becoming intoxicated, or risk being a victim of theft or 'date rape'. Despite the apparent availability of illegal drugs, the authorities are keen to prevent their use. The penalties for possession of marijuana are six months in prison or a US$3,000 fine, minimum.

Where to stay

Accommodation throughout the country varies greatly. For the budget traveller there are options in most towns of interest, although prices are higher than in neighbouring countries. While standard hotel options exist, the area around San Ignacio offers several secluded hideaways of varying price and to the south there are options for staying in Maya communities which helps to maintain the cultural identity of the region.

All **hotels** are subject to 7% government tax (on room rate only). **Camping** sites are gaining in popularity, and there are private camping facilities to be found in most tourist areas, with a variety of amenities offered. Camping on the beaches, in forest reserves, or in any other public place is not allowed. Butane gas in trailer/Coleman stove size storage bottles is available in Belize, and white gas for camp stoves is available at *Brodies* in Belmopan.

Getting around

Road **Bus** Public transport between most towns is by bus and, with the short distances involved, there are few long journeys to encounter. Trucks carry passengers to many isolated destinations, although they are no longer allowed to when travelling to places served by buses. Most buses are ex-US school buses with small seats and limited legroom. There are a few ex-*Greyhounds*, mostly used for 'express' services and charters. Several bus companies were recently acquired by *Novelos*, so services are expected to improve. It is recommended to buy tickets for seats in advance at the depot before boarding the bus.

Most buses have no luggage compartments so bags that do not fit on the luggage rack are stacked at the back. Get a seat at the back to keep an eye on your gear, but rough handling is more of a threat than theft.

Car Motorists should carry their own driving licence and certificate of vehicle ownership. Third party insurance is mandatory and can be purchased at any border (Bz$25 a week, Bz$50 a month, cars and motorbikes are the same, cover up to Bz$20,000 from the *Insurance Corporation of Belize*). Border offices are open Monday-Friday 0500-1700, Saturday 0600-1600, closed Sunday. There are also offices in every district. Valid International Driving Licences are accepted in place of Belize driving permits. Fuel costs Bz$6.58 (regular) or Bz$6.87 (super) for a US gallon but can be more in remote areas. Unleaded gasoline is now available in Belize.

Traffic drives on the right. When making a left turn, it is the driver's responsibility to ensure clearance of both oncoming traffic and vehicles behind; generally, drivers pull over to the far right, allow traffic from behind to pass, then make the left turn. Many accidents are caused by failure to observe this procedure. All major roads have been improved, but they are still poor in sections, particularly when it rains.

Car hire Only one car rental company (*Crystal* – see page 712) will release registration papers to enable cars to enter Guatemala or Mexico. Without obtaining them at the time of hire it is impossible to take hire cars across national borders. Car hire cost is high in Belize owing to the heavy wear and tear on the vehicles. You can expect to pay between US$65 for a Suzuki Samuri and US$125 for an Isuzu Trooper per day. Cautious driving is advised in Belize as road conditions, though improving steadily, are constantly changing and totally unpredictable, with speed bumps, cyclists and pedestrians appearing around every bend. When driving in the Mountain Pine Ridge area it is prudent to check carefully on road conditions at the entry gate; good maps are essential. Emory King's annually updated *Drivers' Guide to Belize* is helpful when driving to the more remote areas.

Selling cars Sellers of cars must pay duty (if the buyer pays it, he may be able to bargain with the customs official). The easiest type of vehicle to sell is either a pick-up or a four-door sedan. Smaller more economical cars are becoming more popular. Prices are quite good, particularly in Orange Walk (ask taxi drivers in Belize City). Also, *O Pérez & Sons*, at their grocery store, 59 West Canal Street, Belize City, T227-3439, may be able to help or refer you on to Norm, who sells cars for people at 10% commission (recommended for fast sale). The Belcan Bridge over Haulover Creek on the west side of town is a prime site for buying and selling cars. At the parking lot here you pay a small fee only if you sell your car. *Freetown Auto World and Club*, 150 Freetown Road, T223-0405, also buys and sells.

Hitchhiking Hitchhiking, while practised freely by locals, is risky and not recommended for travellers. If, however, this is your preferred mode of travel be prepared for long waits and break the journey down into smaller legs.

Sea **Boats** Several boats ferry passengers to the most popular cayes of Caye Caulker and Ambergris Caye, with regular daily services from the Marine Terminal by the swing bridge in Belize City. Further south boat transport is available at Dangriga to nearby cayes, with a service to Puerto Cortés, Honduras, also stopping at Placencia.

Air *Maya Island Air* and *Tropic Air* (see page 713) both provide in-country flights to the cayes, Dangriga, Placencia and Punta Gorda; both have good safety records and regular schedules. It costs less to fly from the Municipal Airport in Belize City than from the International Airport to the same destination. There is one exception: if making a connection for an international flight, it is cheaper to arrive at the International than taking a taxi from Municipal. Both airlines, plus *Javier's Flying Service* (T224-5332) and *Caribe Air Service* at the Municipal Airport, provide charters to airstrips that do not have regularly scheduled flights, such as Gallon Jug or Central Farm near San Ignacio.

Belize

Keeping in touch

Internet   The internet is a dream for countries like Belize which have much to sell but a limited infrastructure. Consequently a large number of hotels and resorts have websites and internet access, making for easy viewing and booking of services. The relatively high cost of telephone calls, however, makes surfing and internet cafés prohibitive. With the exception of San Ignacio, Ambergris Caye and Caye Caulker, internet cafés are less common than in neighbouring countries. When you do find one, the cost is upwards of US$5 per hour. *BTL* has been working more competitively as the telecommunications sector has been liberalized, and prices have reduced slightly in recent years. BTL loses its monopoly in early 2003 so the situation could change still further.

Post   Airmail postage to the UK takes 8 days. US$0.38 for a letter, US$0.20 for a postcard; US$0.50 for letter to European continent; US$0.30 for a letter to USA, US$0.15 for a postcard; US$0.30 postcard, US$0.50 letter to Australia, takes 2-3 weeks. **Parcels**: US$3.50 per ½ kg to Europe, US$0.38 per ½ kg to USA. The service to Europe and USA has been praised, but surface mail is not reliable. Belize postage stamps are very attractive, much in demand, and a trip to the **Philatelic Bureau** in Belize City may provide you with your most treasured souvenir. Mail may be sent to travellers at any local post office, c/o General Delivery.

Telephone
For information T113
For the international operator, dial 115

The much maligned Belizean telephone system is steadily modernizing and the first real impact began to take effect in May 2002 when telephone numbers were changed. All numbers are now seven-digit and there are no regional codes. The changes were planned to be a straight switch subject to a somewhat complicated forumla. However, there are some suggestions that the formula has been tinkered with and not all numbers conform to the conversion and many wrong numbers are listed in the phone book. While problems are being ironed out, contact **information** (T113) for assistance.

All towns have a telephone office and in most villages visitors can use the community phone. Payphones and cardphones are fairly commonplace in Belize City and elsewhere. If you have many calls to make a cardphone works out much cheaper although tapping in the multi-digit number does get frustrating. There is a direct-dialling system between the major towns and to Mexico and USA. Local calls cost US$0.25 for three minutes, US$0.12 for each extra minute within the city, US$0.15-0.55 depending on zone. *Belize Telecommunications Ltd* (known as *BTL*), Church Street, Belize City, open 0800-1800 Monday-Saturday, 0800-1200 Sunday and holidays, has an international telephone, telegraph and telex service. International calls from Belize cost far less than from neighbouring countries: US$3 per minute to UK and Europe (a deposit of US$15 required on all international calls); US$1.60 to North, Central and South America and the Caribbean; US$4 to all other countries. Collect calls to USA, Canada, Australia and UK only. International telex US$1.60 per minute to USA, US$3 to Europe, US$4 elsewhere.

Nearly all establishments throughout the country, with the exception of the poorest remote areas, are easily reached by cellular phone service. One drawback is that they aren't always listed under the business name, so it helps to know the name of the contact person.

Media   **Newspapers and magazines**   There are no daily newspapers in Belize. News is available in the weeklies, which generally come out on Friday morning, with the forthcoming Sunday's date. *The Belize Times* (PUP supported), *The Guardian* (UDP supported), *The Reporter and Amandala*. Good coverage of Ambergris Caye is provided by *The San Pedro Sun*. Small district newspapers are published sporadically. *Belize First!*, a quarterly magazine published in the USA (*Equator Travel Publications Inc*, 287 Beaverdam Road, Candler, NC 28715, USA, F828-667-1717), has articles on travel, life, news and history in Belize (US$29 a year in Belize, USA, Canada, Mexico, US$49 elsewhere) www.belizefirst.com

Food and drink

Food   Dishes suffer a wonderful preponderance on rice'n'beans – a cheap staple to which you add chicken, fish, beef and so on. For the cheapest meals, order rice which will come with beans

Belize

and (as often as not) banana or plantain, or chicken, vegetables or even a blending of beef with coconut milk. Belize has some of the best *burritos* in Central America but you have to seek them out, normally in hidden away stalls in the markets. Along the coastal region and on the cayes seafood is abundant, fresh and reasonably cheap, but try not to buy lobster out of season as stocks are worryingly low. Presentation varies and vegetables are not always served with a meat course. Better restaurants offer a greater variety and a break from the standards, often including a selection of Mexican dishes; there are also many Chinese restaurants, not always good and sometimes overpriced.

Drink Belikin beer is the local brew, average cost US$1.75 a bottle. Many brands of local rum are available. Several local wines and liqueurs are made from available fruit. One favourite is called *nanche*, made from *crabou* fruit and very sweet, as is the cashew wine, made from the cashew fruit rather than the nut. All imported food and drink is expensive.

Shopping

Indigenous arts and crafts are noticeable primarily for their absence. Carved hardwood objects are widely available. Jewellery made of black coral is occasionally offered but should not be bought. There are some fine Belikin/diving T-shirts. If you want to buy music, Andy Palacio is one of the best punta rock artists.

Belize

Holidays and festivals

1 January: New Year's Day. **February**: Carnival (Belize City and San Pedro, Ambergris Caye). **9 March**: Baron Bliss Day. **14-18 March**: San José Succotz Fiesta. **Good Friday and Saturday**. **Easter Monday. 21 April**: Queen's birthday. **Late April or May**: National Agricultural and Trade Show (Belmopan). **1 May**: Labour Day. **May (variable)**: Cashew Festival (Crooked Tree), Cayo Expo (San Ignacio), Coconut Festival (Caye Caulker). **24 May**: Commonwealth Day. **29 June**: San Pedro Day. **18-19 July**: Benque Viejo Fiesta. **August**: International Sea and Air Festival (San Pedro, Ambergris Caye) **10 September**: St George's Caye Day. **21 September**: Belize Independence Day. **12 October**: Pan-American Day (Corozal and Orange Walk). **19 November**: Garífuna Settlement Day. **25 December**: Christmas Day. **26 December**: Boxing Day.

Most services throughout the country close down Good Friday to Easter Monday: banks close at 1300 on the Thursday, buses run limited services Holy Saturday to Easter Monday, though local flights and boats to the Cayes are available. Christmas and Boxing Day are also limited in terms of services. Plan in advance, or you may find yourself without an open restaurant in which to eat on holidays. Many shops will open for a few hours on holiday mornings, but still may have limited choices for food. Independence Celebrations begin on St George's Caye Day, September 10, and there are events occurring daily through to Independence Day, September 21. The 'September Celebrations', as they are locally called, often start two or three days in advance and require a lot of energy.

Sport and special interest travel

Archaeology The protection of the Mayan heritage of Belize is high on the agenda. Excavation continues on several sites, supported by overseas countries and universities. In 1997 the European Union agreed to provide funding for the *Maya Archaeological Site Development Programme* (MASDP), specifically directed towards the protection, promotion and exhibition of various sites in Belize including Lubaantun, Nim Li Punit, Lamanai and Caracol. For information, contact MASDP at the Archaeology Department, T822-2106, in Belmopan, where there are plans underway for a new Museum of Archaeology.

Caving Belize has some of the longest caving systems in the world. While government permission is required to enter unexplored systems, simple cave exploration is easy. The best one-stop shop for all levels is the *Caves Branch Jungle Lodge* on the Hummingbird Highway close to the entrance to the Blue Hole National Park.

Diving The shores are protected by the longest barrier reef in the Western Hemisphere. The beautiful coral formations are a great attraction for scuba diving, with canyons, coves, overhangs, ledges, walls and endless possibilities for underwater photography.

Lighthouse Reef, the outermost of the three north-south reef systems, offers pristine dive sites in addition to the incredible Blue Hole. Massive stalagmites and stalactites are found along overhangs down the sheer vertical walls of the Blue Hole. This outer reef lies beyond the access of most land-based diving resorts and even beyond most fishermen, so the marine life is undisturbed. An ideal way to visit this reef is on a live-aboard dive boat. An exciting marine phenomenon takes place during the full moon each January in the waters around Belize when thousands of the Nassau groupers gather to spawn at Glory Caye on Turneffe Reef.

Note There are decreasing numbers of small fish – an essential part of the coral lifecycle – in the more easily accessible reefs, including the underwater parks. The coral reefs around the northerly, most touristy cayes are dying, probably as a result of tourism pressures, so do your bit to avoid causing further damage. Boats can only be hired for diving, fishing or sightseeing if they are licensed for the specific purpose by the government. This is intended to ensure that tourists travel on safe, reliable vessels and also to prevent the proliferation of self-appointed guides. Try to see that the boat which is taking you to the reef does not damage the coral in any way (ie by dropping its anchor on it). Old wrecks and other underwater treasures are protected by law and cannot be removed.

Fishing Belize is a very popular destination for sport fishing, normally quite pricey but definitely worth it if you want to splash out. The rivers offer fewer and fewer opportunities for good fishing, and *tilapia* escaped from regional fish farms now competes with the catfish, tarpon and snook for the food supply. The sea still provides game fish such as sailfish, marlin, wahoo, barracuda and tuna. On the flats, the most exciting fish for light tackle – the bonefish – are found in great abundance. Seasons are given below.

In addition to the restrictions on turtle and coral extraction noted above, the following regulations apply: no person may take, buy or sell crawfish (lobster) between 15 February and 14 July, shrimp from 15 April to 14 August, or conch between 1 July and 30 September.

Fishing seasons **Billfish**: blue marlin, all year (best November-March); white marlin, November-May; sailfish, March-May. **Oceanic**: yellowfin tuna, all year; blackfin tuna, all year; bonito, all year; wahoo, November-February; sharks, all year. **Reef**: kingfish, March-June; barracuda, all year; jackfish, all year; mackerel, all year; grouper, all year; snapper, all year; bonefish, November-April; tarpon, June-August. **River**: tarpon, February-August; snook, February-August; snapper, all year.

Operators In Belize City: *Belize River Lodge*, PO Box 459, T225-2002, F225-2298, www.belizeriverlodge.com Excellent reputation. *Seasports Belize*, 83 N Front Street, T223-5505.

Nature tourism Conservation is a high priority in Belize, with tourism vying for top spot as foreign currency earner in the national economy, and being the fastest growing industry. Nature reserves are supported by a combination of private and public organizations including the Belize Audubon Society, the government and international agencies.

The *Belize Audubon Society* (PO Box 1001, 12 Fort Street, Belize City, T223-5004, F223-4985, www.belizeaudubon.org) manages seven protected areas including **Half Moon Caye Natural Monument** (3929 ha), **Cockscomb Basin Wildlife Sanctuary** (41,310 ha – the world's only jaguar reserve), **Crooked Tree Wildlife Sanctuary** (6,480 ha – swamp forests and lagoons with wildfowl), **Blue Hole National Park** (233 ha), **Guanacaste National Park** (20.25 ha), **Tapir Mountain Nature Reserve** (formerly known as Society Hall Nature Reserve (2,730 ha – a research area with Maya presence) and the **Shipstern Nature Reserve** (8,910 ha – butterfly breeding, forest, lagoons, mammals and birds, contact BAS or the *International Tropical Conservation Foundation*, www.papiliorama.ch/ITCF/, Box 31, CH-2074 Marin-Neuchatel, Switzerland).

The **Río Bravo Management and Conservation Area** (105,300ha) bordering Guatemala to the northwest of the country, covers some 4% of the country and is managed by the *Programme for Belize*, T227-5616, F227-5635, www.pfbelize.org, PO Box 749, 1 Eyre Street, Belize City).

Other parks include the **Community Baboon Sanctuary** at Bermudian Landing, **Bladen Nature Reserve** (watershed and primary forest), **Hol Chan Marine Reserve** (reef eco-system). Recently designated national parks and reserves include: **Five Blue Lakes National Park**, based on an unusually deep karst lagoon, and a maze of exotic caves and sinkholes near St Margaret Village on the Hummingbird Highway; **Kaax Meen Elijio Panti National Park**, at San Antonio Village near the Mountain Pine Ridge Reserve; **Vaca Forest Reserve** (21,060 ha); and **Chiquibul National Park** (107,687 ha – containing the Maya ruins of Caracol). There's also **Laughing Bird Caye National Park** (off Placencia), **Glovers Reef Marine Reserve**, and **Caye Caulker** now has a marine reserve at its north end.

Belize Enterprise for Sustained Technology (BEST) is a non-profit organization committed to the sustainable development of Belize's disadvantaged communities and community-based ecotourism, for example Gales Point and Hopkins Village; PO Box 35, Forest Drive, Belmopan, T802-3043, F802-2563.

A Wildlife Protection Act was introduced in 1982 which forbids the sale, exchange or dealings in wildlife, or parts thereof, for profit. The import, export, hunting or collection of wildlife is not allowed without a permit; only those doing scientific research or for educational purposes are eligible for exporting or collecting permits. Also prohibited is the removal or export of black coral, picking orchids, exporting turtle or turtle products, and spear fishing while wearing scuba gear.

On 1 June 1996 a *National Protected Areas Trust Fund* (PACT) was established to provide finance for the "protection, conservation and enhancement of the natural and cultural treasures of Belize". Funds for PACT come from a Bz$7.50 Conservation Fee paid by all foreign visitors on departure by air, land and sea, and from 20% of revenues derived from protected areas entrance fees, cruise ship passenger fees, etc. For more information look at the site at www.pactbelize.org   Visitors pay only one PACT tax every 30 days, so if you go to Tikal for a short trip from Belize, for example, then leave from Belize airport, show your receipt in order not to pay twice.

Health

Those taking standard precautions find the climate pleasant and healthy. There are no mandatory inoculations required to enter the country unless coming from a country where yellow fever is a problem. Malaria prophylaxis is necessary only if staying in rural areas with poor medical care. Dengue fever is also rare but possible for travellers, and using insect repellent for mosquitoes is the best prevention for both diseases. Insect bites should be carefully scrutinized if not healing or if odd symptoms occur, as the possibilities of Chagas, leishmaniasis, or botfly larvae are all present. AIDS has increased substantially over the past few years, and has been transmitted both by sexual contact and blood transfusions, though no reports involve travellers as yet.

Medical services have improved dramatically in recent years with the completion of the Karl Heusner Memorial Hospital in Belize City, though many Belizeans still seek medical care for serious ailments in Mérida or Guatemala City. Myo'On Clinic Ltd, 40 Eve Street, Belize City, T224-5616, has been recommended, it charges reasonably for its services. Nearby is the Pathology Lab, 17 Eve Street, recommended. Also recommended are Belize Medical Associates, next to the new city hospital, and Dr Lizama, Handyside Street, consultation US$17.50. The British High Commission in Belmopan (T822-2146, brithicom@btl.net) has a list of recommended doctors and dentists.

Belize City ◻
◻ Belmopan

Belize City and Belmopan

Hardly large enough to warrant the title 'city', in any other country Belize City would be a dusty backwater, but in Belize it is the centre of the country, a blend of Latin American and Caribbean influences. Clapboard houses line garbage-strewn streets while people huddle in groups as the world drifts idly by. Born of the Belize River when the logs used to float downstream, it is still the main hub for maritime communications with boat services to the Cayes. Nearby Belize Zoo is a model for zoos throughout the world. The capital, Belmopan, enjoys the cursed pleasure of being a planned city. Founded after a devastating hurricane struck Belize, it has survived as the country's political centre, and has recently experienced a gentle rash of growth after several hurricanes have hit the country.

Belize City

Colour map 6, grid A1
Population: 59,050

Belize City is the old capital and the largest town in Belize. Most of the houses are wooden, often of charming design, with galvanized iron roofs. Most stand on seven-foot-high piles – signs of a bygone age when the city used to experience regular flooding. The city has improved greatly in recent years with the cleaning of the canal. Reclaimed land and a spate of building around the Eyre Street area, suggest plans to develop the city are well underway. The introduction of tourist police has had a marked effect on crime levels, and the situation now requires sensible caution rather than paranoia. Just under a quarter of the total population live here, with the African strain predominant. Humidity is high, but the summer heat is tempered by the northeast trades.

Hurricane Hattie swept a 10-ft tidal wave into the town on 31 October 1961, causing much damage and loss of life and, in 1978, Hurricane Greta caused further extensive damage. Belize City and the country escaped Hurricane Mitch in 1998 as it literally 'walked round Belize' turning south offshore hitting Honduras and the Bay Islands, before working its way through Guatemala. Hurricane Keith again threatened creeping round the western side of Ambergris Caye in October 2000 and caused localized damage.

Ins and outs

Getting there
International flights arrive at **Phillip Goldson International Airport**, 10 miles from Belize City along the northern highway. Facilities in the check-in area include toilets, a restaurant, bank (open daily 0830-1100 and 1330-1630), viewing deck and duty-free shop. No facilities on arrivals side but you can just walk round to the check-in area. Taxi fare to town is US$17, 20-30 mins, taxi drivers strongly discourage sharing so team up, if need be, before getting outside. Make sure your taxi is legitimate by checking for the green licence plates. Taxis all operate on a fixed rate, so you should get the same price quoted by every driver. Ask to see a rate sheet if you have doubts about the price. Any bus going up the Northern Highway passes the airport junction (US$0.75), then 1½ mile walk. Taxi from junction to airport US$2.50. For details of internal flights, see page 713.

The various **bus** stations are to the west of town, an area that requires caution. If taking an early morning bus, arrange for a taxi as walking through this part of town in darkness with luggage can be dangerous. If arriving in the late evening, you should be able to find a taxi; eg *Batty* bus station to the centre, US$3. For full bus details, see page 713.

From the **sea**, after passing the barrier reef, Belize City is approached by a narrow channel. This gives shelter to what would otherwise be a very choppy harbour. Belize is the nearest adequate port to Mexico's State of Quintana Roo, and re-exports mahogany from that area. It also handles substantial container traffic for Yucatán.

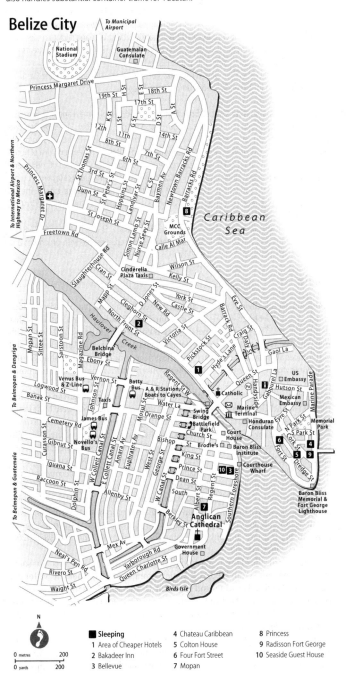

Belize City

Sleeping ■
1 Area of Cheaper Hotels
2 Bakadeer Inn
3 Bellevue
4 Chateau Caribbean
5 Colton House
6 Four Fort Street
7 Mopan
8 Princess
9 Radisson Fort George
10 Seaside Guest House

Belize

Security **Tourist police** wearing dark green uniforms patrol the city centre in an attempt to control crime and to give advice. The effect of their introduction has been encouraging and crime has greatly reduced in the city.

Nevertheless, a common-sense approach is needed and a careful watch on your possessions is recommended. Watch out for conmen who would like to disappear with your money. Guides have to be licensed and should carry a photo ID. Street money changers are not to be trusted either. It is wise to avoid small, narrow side streets and stick to major thoroughfares, although even on main streets you can be the victim of unprovoked threats and racial abuse. Travel by taxi is advisable particularly at night and in the rain.

Cars should only be left in guarded car parks. For a tip, the security officer at the *Fiesta Inn* will look after cars for a few days while you go to the Cayes.

Tourist offices *Belize Tourist Board*, New Central Bank Building, Level 2, Gabourel Lane, PO Box 325, T223-1913, F223-1943, freephone from USA and Canada T1-800-624-0686, www.travelbelize.org, open 0800-1200, 1300-1700 Mon-Thu, 1630 Fri), provides complete bus schedule (although it may be out of date) with a map of Belize City, as well as list of hotels and their prices. Also has *Central America and Mexico Handbook* for sale, a list of tour operators, recommended taxi guides and free publications on the country and its Maya ruins, practical and informative. Excellent maps of the country for US$3 (postage extra). The jail building right in front of the Central Bank is being developed into a Museum of Belize City, where the BTB will have an information office.

Belize Tourism Industry Association, 10 North Park St, T227-5717, F227-8710, www.btia.org is a private sector body for hotels, tour companies, etc with brochures and information on members throughout Belize.

Sights

Haulover Creek divides the city and is crossed by the antiquated **swing-bridge** which opens to let large vessels pass, if required, at 1700 daily. Three canals further divide the city. The main commercial area is either side of the swing-bridge, with most shops on the south side, many being located on Regent and Albert streets, and with offices and embassies generally on the northern side. The area around **Battlefield Park** (formerly Central Park) is always busy, with the former colonial administration and court buildings bordering the overgrown park adding to the sense of mischief in the area. At the southern end of Regent Street, the **Anglican Cathedral** (St John's) and **Government House** nearby are interesting. Both were built in the early 19th century and draw on the romantic and grand memories of colonialism. In the days before the foundation of the Crown Colony, the kings of the Mosquito Coast were crowned in the cathedral which was built with bricks brought from England as ships' ballast. In the cathedral (not always open, but with regular services), note the 19th-century memorial plaques which give a harrowing account of early deaths from 'country fever' (yellow fever) and other tropical diseases.

The museum in Government House contains some interesting pictures of colonial times, displays of furniture and silver and glassware, as well as a display showing fishing techniques and model boats. There are pleasant gardens surrounding the museum if you are looking for somewhere quiet. ■ *Mon-Fri, 0830-1200, 1300-1630, entry US$2.50.*

On the north side of the swing-bridge, turn left up North Front Street for some of the cheaper hotels and the A & R Station, from which some boats leave for the Cayes. The **Marine Terminal** and **Museum** are the sea side of the swing-bridge, with the post office right in front of you. Housed in a colonial building (the former fire station), the museum features a mangrove exhibition, reef exhibition and aquarium. ■ *Entry US$3.*

Further up Front Street is the new **Tourism Village** consisting of souvenir and gift shops and snack bars, along with several handicraft shops. This new development caters to tourists arriving from cruise ships. A little further on, at the tip of the peninsula, is **Memorial Park** on Marine Parade with a small obelisk, two cannon and concrete benches peppered with the holes of landcrabs. The views across the bay can be quite spectacular in the early morning. The small park by the **Fort George Lighthouse** has a children's play area and is a popular meeting place.

Belize Zoo (see page 733) is definitely worth a visit and not far from Belize City. The trip is short and very easy with buses passing the entrance hourly.

Essentials

Sleeping
■ on map page 709
Price codes: see
inside front cover

Belize

LL-A *Princess*, Kings Park, T223-2670, F223-2660, www.princessbelize.com On sea front (but not central), marina facilities, a/c, good food and service in restaurant and bar (a/c with sea views, expensive), good business facilities, informal calypso bar near the dock is lively at night, nice pool and children's play area. **LL-A** *Bellevue*, 5 Southern Foreshore, T227-7051, F227-3253, fins@btl.net Recently re-opened under new management. A/c, private bath, good laundry service, restaurant (nice atmosphere, good lunches with live music, steaks), leafy courtyard pool, nice bar with live music Fri and Sat nights, good entertainment. Recommended. **LL** *Radisson Fort George*, PO Box 321, 2 Marine Parade, T223-3333, F227-3820, www.radissonbelize.com In 3 wings (Club Wing, Colonial Section and former *Holiday Inn Villa*), each with excellent rooms, a/c, helpful staff, reservations should be made, safe parking, good restaurant, good pool (non-residents may use pool for US$10). Recommended. **L-A** *Chateau Caribbean*, 6 Marine Parade, by Fort George, T223-0800, F223-0900, www.chateaucaribbean.com Main building is beautiful, colonial, well-maintained with a/c, good bar, restaurant (excellent Chinese and seafood), sea view, good service, disco, parking.

A *Bakadeer Inn*, 74 Cleghorn St, T223-1286, F223-6506, mcfield@btl.net Private bath, breakfast US$4, a/c, TV, fridge, friendly. Recommended. **A** *Colton House*, 9 Cork St, T224-4666, F223-0451, www.coltonhouse.com Named after the owners, a delightful 1928 colonial-style home, private bath, some a/c, overhead fans, large rooms, friendly, helpful, quiet, recommended. **A** *Four Fort Street* (address as name), T223-0116, F227-8808, fortst@btl.net Full breakfast included, 6 rooms, all with 4-poster beds and shared bath, charming, excellent restaurant. Recommended.

B *Glenthorne Manor*, 27 Barrack Rd, T224-4212. With or without bath, colonial-style, safe, getting run-down, meals available, overpriced. **B** *Mopan*, 55 Regent St, T227-7351, www.hotelmopan.com Sixteen rooms with bath, breakfast, a/c, in historic house, has restaurant and bar, nice but pricey, new management very keen to help.

C *Freddie's*, 86 Eve St, T223-3851. With shower and toilet, fan, hot water, clean, very nice, secure, very small. **C** *Isabel Guest House*, 3 Albert St, above Matus Store, PO Box 362, T227-3139. 3 double rooms, 1 huge triple room, quiet except when nearby disco operating at weekends, private shower, clean, friendly, safe, Spanish spoken. Highly recommended. **C** *Seaside Guest House*, 3 Prince St, T227-8339, seasidebelize@btl.net **E** per person in bunk room, lots of rules but popular, very clean, pleasant veranda, a great place to stay. Credit cards accepted, internet access on site. Recommended.

D *Bon Aventure*, 122 North Front St, T224-4248. **E** in dormitory, purified water available, a bit run-down, not very clean, but one of the best cheap options in Belize City, Malaysian Chinese owners helpful and friendly, secure, Spanish spoken, laundry service, good meals at reasonable prices. Opposite is **D** *Mira Río*, 59 North Front St, T224-4790. Service criticized, rooms OK but small, shared hot shower, fan, toilet, clean, covered veranda overlooking Haulover Creek, Spanish spoken, good food, noisy bar opposite. **D** *Downtown Guest House*, 5 Eve St, T223-0951. Small rooms, hot shower in shared bath, secure, clean and friendly, if a little run down. **E** *North Front Street Guest House*, 124 North Front St, T227-7595. 1 block north of post office, no hot water, fan, book exchange, TV, friendly, laundry, good information, keep windows closed at night and be sure to lock your door, on street and a bit noisy.

Out of town is **B** *Belize River Lodge*, Ladyville, PO Box 459 Belize City, T225-2002, F225-2298, www.belizeriverlodge.com 10 mins from airport on Belize River, excellent accommodation and food popular for fishing (from lodge or cruises), also scuba facilities, numerous packages, call in advance.

Eating

It can be difficult to find places to eat between 1500 & 1800

Babb's, Queen and Eve Sts. Good pastries, meat pies, juices, friendly. **Blue Bird Cafe**, Albert St. Cheap fruit juices, specialities, basic, clean, reasonable. **DIT's**, 50 King St. Good, cheap. **Four Fort Street**, near Memorial Park. Nice atmosphere, sit out on the veranda in a beautiful setting, desserts a speciality. Recommended (see **Sleeping**). **Judith's Pastries**, south end of Queen St. Good cakes, pastries. **Macy's**, 18 Bishop St, T73419. Recommended for well-prepared local game, Creole cooking, different fixed menu daily, charming host. **Mar's**, 118 North Front St. Clean, pleasant, family cooking, reasonable prices, good. **Marlin**, 11 Regent St West, overlooking Belize River, T227-3913. Varied menu, good seafood.

   Memories of India, 35 Queen Street. Good Indian food. **New Chon Saan**, 55 Euphrates Av, T72709. Best Chinese in town, pleasant atmosphere (taxi ride), takeaway. **Pizza Pronto**, Barrack Rd. Very good cheap pizzas. **Pop 'n' Taco**, Regent St. Good sweet and sour chicken, cheap, friendly service. **Playboy**, 11 King St. Good sandwiches. **Tropicana**, Queen St, green building on corner next to *Hong Kong*. Good set-menu lunch. Other Chinese restaurants include: **Canton**, New Rd, large portions, good; **China Garden**, 46 Regent St. lunch specials; **Shek Kei**, 80 Freetown Rd, good; and **Ding Ho**, North Front St, good, try their 'special' dishes.

Nightlife

Bars Best and safest bars are found at major hotels, *Fort George, Biltmore Plaza, Bellevue* and *Four Fort Street*. If you want a little local charm **Lindbergh's Landing**, 164A Newtown Rd (next to *Mango*) is fun, open-air with sea view, big Latin dance evening on Sun. Lots of bars some with jukeboxes and poolrooms. **Privateer**, Mile 4½ on Northern Highway, on seafront, expensive drinks but you can sit outside. Try the local drink, anise and peppermint, known as 'A and P'; also the powerful 'Old Belizeno' rum. The local beer, Belikin, is good, as is the 'stout', strong and free of gas. Guinness is also served, but is expensive.

Clubs and discos **Hard Rock**, corner of Queen/Handyside Sts, good dance floor, a/c. **Club Calypso**, at the *Princess Hotel* has top bands at weekends. **Lumba Yaard**, 1 mile out of town along Northern Highway, recommended.

Shopping

The whole city closes down on Sunday except for a few shops open in the morning, eg Brodies in the centre of town. Banks and many shops are also closed on Wednesday afternoons

Handicrafts, woodcarvings and straw items are all good buys. The Belize Chamber of Commerce has opened a Belize crafts salesroom on Fort Street, opposite *Four Fort Street* restaurant, to be a showcase and promote craftspeople from all over Belize; come here first. **Nile**, 49 Eve St. Middle Eastern. **Go Tees**, 23 Regent St, T227-4082. Excellent selection of T-shirts (printed on premises), arts and crafts from Belize, Guatemala and Mexico: jewellery, silver, wood carvings, clothes, paintings, etc; also has a branch at Belize Zoo, good zoo T-shirts and cuddly animals. Zericote (or Xericote) wood carvings can be bought in Belize City, for example at **Brodies Department Store** (Central Park end of Regent St), which also sells postcards, the *Fort George Hotel*, the small gift shop at *Four Fort Street*, or from **Egbert Peyrefitte**, 11a Cemetery Rd. Such wood carvings are the best buy, but to find a carver rather than buy the tourist fare in shops, ask a taxi driver. (At the Art Centre, near Government House, the wood sculpture of Charles Gabb, who introduced carving into Belize, can be seen). Wood carvers sell their work in front of the main hotels. The market is by the junction of North Front St and Fort St. **Ro-Macs**, 27 Albert St. Excellent supermarket includes wide selection of imported foods and wines. **Thrift Center**, 2 Church St. Good food store.

Bookshops **Angelus Press**, 10 Queen St. Excellent selection of stationery supplies, books, cards, etc. **Book Centre**, 2 Church St, above *Thrift Center*. Very good, has second-hand books and back issues of US magazines. **The Book Shop**, 126 Freetown Rd. New and second-hand books, also exchange books.

Transport

Local Car hire: Most rental firms have offices opposite the international airport terminal building. **Avis**, at *Fort George Hotel*, T227-8637, airport T225-2385, largest fleet, well-maintained, Daihatsus and Isuzu Troopers. **Budget** PO Box 863, 771 Bella Vista (near International Airport, can pick up and drop off car at airport, office almost opposite *Biltmore Plaza Hotel*), T223-2435, good service, well-maintained vehicles, good deals (Suzukis and Isuzu Troopers); **Crystal**, Mile 1½ Northern Highway, T223-1600, Jay Crofton, helpful, cheapest deals in town, but not always most reliable, wide selection of vehicles including 30-seater bus, will release insurance papers for car entry to Guatemala and Mexico, he also buys second-hand cars but at a poor price; *National*, International Airport, T223-1586 (Cherokee Chiefs); *Pancho's*, 5747 Lizarraga Av, T224-5554; *Safari*, 11a Cork St, beside *Radisson Fort George Hotel*, T223-0268, F223-5395, Isuzu Troopers, also *Hertz* agents.

Taxis: have green licence plates (drivers must also have identification card); within Belize, US$2.50 for 1 person; for 2 or more passengers, US$1.75 per person. There is a taxi stand on Central Park, opposite *Barclays*, another on the corner of Collet Canal St and Cemetery Rd. Outside Belize City, US$1.75 per mile, regardless of number of passengers. Belize City to the resorts in Cayo District approximately US$100-125, 1-4 people (ask for Edgar August or Martin at *Radisson Fort George* desk, they are reliable and can do guided tours around Belize). Best to ask price of the ride before setting off. No meters, so beware of overcharging and make sure fare is quoted in Bz$. If you have a complaint, take the licence plate and report to the Taxi Union.

Air The International Airport is 10 miles from Belize City (see Ins and outs, page 708). There is also a municipal airstrip for local flights 15 mins drive from the centre on the northern side of town, taxi, US$7.50, no bus service. Services to San Pedro, Caye Chapel, Caye Caulker with *Tropic Air* and *Maya Island Air*, flights every 30 mins, 0700 to 1630. Flights to and from the islands can be taken from the International Airport and companies link their flights to international arrivals and departures; flights from the international airport cost about US$12 more each way. Services also to Corozal (*Tropic Air*). Big Creek, San Ignacio, Placencia, Dangriga, Punta Gorda, with *Maya Island Air* (T226-2435, www.mayaairways.com) and *Tropic Air* (T226-2012, www.tropicair.com)

Buses Within the city the fare is US$0.50. There are bus services to all the main towns. Heading north to **Chetumal** (see Mexico, Yucatán Peninsula), about 15 daily each way, several express *Batty* buses from 0600 stopping at **Orange Walk** and **Corozal** only, US$8.50, 3 hrs. Slower buses taking up to 4 hrs including crossing, US$7.50, service provided by two companies: *Batty* bus, 54 East Collet Canal St, T227-4924, F227-8991, and *Venus*, Magazine Rd, T227-3354, which has a midday service. If taking a bus from Chetumal which will arrive in Belize City after dark, decide on a hotel and go there by taxi.

Novelo's buses have recently purchased some bus companies. Ask locally for changes in service

Heading west towards **Guatemala** *Batty* bus to **Belmopan** and **San Ignacio**, express bus 0900, US$3, with refreshments and video, ordinary bus, Mon-Sat frequent 0600 to 1900, Sun 0630 to 1700. Novelo's run until 2000. The 0600, 0630 and 1015 buses connect at the border with services to Flores, Guatemala. To **San Ignacio**, Benque Viejo and the Guatemalan border via Belmopan, Novelo's, West Collet Canal, T228-2025 (can store luggage US$0.50), US$1.25 to Belmopan, US$3 to Benque, US$2.50 to San Ignacio, hourly Mon-Sat, 1100 to 1900. The last possible bus connection to Flores leaves the border at 1600, but it is better to get an earlier bus to arrive in daylight. Several *Batty* buses leave for **Melchor de Mencos**, from 0600 to 1030. To **Flores**, Guatemala, minibuses leave the A & R Station on Front Street at 0500, make reservation the previous day.

Heading south to **Dangriga**, via Belmopan and the Hummingbird Highway. *Southern Transport* (T227-3937), from *Venus* bus station, several daily 0800-1600, plus Mon 0600, US$5; to Dangriga via Coastal Highway (unsurfaced), *Richies Busline*, East Collet Canal Street, 1430, on to **Placencia**, 4½ hrs, US$7.50. *James Bus Line*, Pound Yard Bridge (Collet Canal), 9-12 hrs, to **Punta Gorda** via Dangriga, Cockscomb Basin Wildlife Sanctuary and Mango Creek, daily 0800 and 1500, US$11.

Boats For boats to the cayes and other places in Belize, see under each destination. There is also a peak-season boat service to Dangriga and Plancencia from the Marine Terminal. Enquire for details.

Airline offices Local: *Tropic Air*, Belize City T224-5671, San Pedro T026-2012, F026-2338, www.tropicair.com *Maya Island Air*, 6 Fort St, PO Box 458, Belize City T233-1794, San Pedro 226-2435, F226-2192, www.mayaairways.com **International:** *Aerovías*, in *Mopan Hotel*, 55 Regent St, T227-5383, F227-5383, for Flores/Guatemala. *American Airlines*, New Road and Queen St, T223-2168. *British Airways*, T227-7363, airport 225-2060. *Continental Airlines*, 32 Albert St, T227-8223, airport T225-2263. *Grupo Taca* (*Belize Global Travel*), 41 Albert St, T227-7363, F227-5213, airport T225-2454, F225-2453.

Directory

Belize

Belize

Banks It is easy to have money wired to Belize City. Guatemalan quetzales are very easy to obtain at the borders, less easy in Belize City. Money changers at *Batty* bus terminal just before departure of bus to Chetumal (the only place to change Mexican pesos except at the border). There are several ATMs in Belize City – few are found elsewhere at present. *Atlantic Bank*, 6 Albert St, or 16 New Rd (the latter in a safe area), quick efficient service, small charge for Visa/MasterCard, smaller queues than *Belize Bank* or Barclays. *Bank of Nova Scotia*. Banking hours: Mon-Thu 0800-1300, Fri 0800-1200 and 1300-1630. *Belize Bank* is particularly efficient and modern, US$0.50 commission on Amex cheques but a big charge for cash against Visa and MasterCard. *Barclays Bank International*, with some country branches, slightly better rates, 2% commission, no charge for Visa/MasterCard. *American Express*, good exchange rates at *Belize Global Travel Services*, 41 Albert St, T227-7185. *Khan's*, inside the Marine Terminal, will change currency, TCs and give cash advances.

All banks have facilities to arrange cash advance on Visa

Communications Internet: Service at *BTL* (see below), US$3 1½ hrs, 2 computers. Some hotels provide an email service. *Khan's*, inside the Marine terminal, has an email service. **Post office**: letters, Queen St and North Front St, 0800-1700 (1630 Fri); parcels, beside main post office, these must be wrapped in brown paper, sold by the yard in large stationery shop around the corner in Queen St. Letters held for a month. Beautiful stamps sold. **Telephone**: *Belizean Telecommunications Ltd* (BTL), 1 Church St, just off Central Park, 0800-1800, 0800-1200 on Sun. Also public fax service and booths for credit card and charge calls to USA, UK.

Cultural centres *Audubon Society*, see page 706. *Baron Bliss Institute*, public library, temporary exhibitions; has 1 Stela and 2 large discs from Caracol on display. *The Image Factory*, 91 Front St, has exhibitions of contemporary art, open Mon-Fri 0900-1800. The Belize crafts sales room on Fort St, opposite *Four Fort Street* has a good supply of books about Belize culture.

Embassies and consulates See also under Belmopan. *Belgium*, 126 Freetown Rd, T223-0748. *Canada*, 83 North Front St, T223-1060. *Costa Rica*, 8-18th St, Belmopan, T822-3801, F822-805. *Denmark*, 13 Southern Foreshore, T227-2172. *France*, 109 New Rd, T223-2708, F223-2416. *German Honorary Consul*, 57 Southern Foreshore, T227-7282, F222-4375. *Guatemala Consulate*, 6A Saint Matthew St, near municipal airstrip, T223-3150, open 0900-1300, will not issue visas or tourist cards here and will tell you to leave it till you reach San José Succotz (see page 742). *Guatemala Embassy*, 8 A St, Belize City, T223-3314, F223-5140. *Honduras*, 91 North Front St, T224-5889, F223-0562. *Israel*, 4 Albert and Bishop St, T227-3991, F223-0463. *Italy*, 18 Albert St, T227-8449. *Netherlands*, 14 Central American Blvd, T227-5663. *Norway*, 1 King St, T227-7031, F227-7062. *Panama Consulate*, 5481 Princess Margaret Drive, T223-4282. *Sweden*, 2 Daly St, T224-5176. *UK High Commission* (see Belmopan Directory below). *US Embassy*, 29 Gabourel Lane, T227-7161, F223-0802, consulate is on Hutson St, round corner from embassy's entrance on Gabourel Lane, consulate open 0800-1000 for visitor visas, library 0830-1200, 1330-1630 Mon-Fri, but mornings only on Wed.

Laundry *Belize Dry Cleaners and Laundermat*, 3 Dolphin St, or *Central American Coin-Op Laundry*, junction Barrack Rd and Freetown Rd, wash US$3.50, dryer US$1.50, powder US$0.50, self-service.

Tour operators *Quasar Náutica*, T(593-2)2463-660, F2436-625 (Ecuador), T(01962)779-317, F779-458 (UK), www.quasarnautica.com *Native Guide Systems*, 2 Water Lane, T227-5819, F227-4007, PO Box 1045. Individual and group tours. *S & L Guided Tours*, 91 North Front St, T227-7593, F227-7594, www.sltravelbelize.com Recommended group travel (minimum 4 persons for most tours, 2 persons to Tikal). A great many others both inside and outside Belize. Tourist Bureau has a full list. If booking tours in Belize from abroad it is advisable to check prices and services offered with a reputable tour operator in Belize first.

Belmopan

As capital of Belize, Belmopan has been the seat of government since August 1970. Its location, while curious, is easily explained. Following the devastation caused in Belize City by Hurricane Hattie in 1961, it was decided to plan a town which could be a centre for government, business and study away from the coast – Belmopan is the result. It is 50 miles inland to the west of Belize City, near the junction of the Western Highway and the Hummingbird Highway to Dangriga (Stann Creek Town). It has the National Assembly building (open to the public), two blocks of government

Colour map 6, grid A1
Population: 8,130

Belmopan has been described as 'a disaster for the budget traveller'

offices (with broadly Maya-style architecture), police headquarters, a public works department, a hospital, over 700 houses for civil servants, a non-governmental residential district to encourage expansion, and a market. It was projected to have a population of 40,000 but so far only a fraction of that have materialized – many government workers still commute from Belize City.

The near direct hit of Hurricane Mitch in 1998, and hurricanes in recent years have prompted a renewed interest in plans to develop the capital, and several government organizations are in the process of relocating to the city injecting a desperately needed 'heart' to this most eerie of capitals. One possible site of interest would be the **Department of Archaeology**, in the government plaza, which has a vault containing specimens of the country's artefacts. Unfortunately the vault is currently closed and there are no plans to open it in the near future, but there are plans to build a museum. The city can be seen in less than an hour – almost between bus journeys. The Western Highway from Belize City is now good (a one-hour drive), continuing to San Ignacio, and there is an airfield (for charter services only).

Excursions One very good reason for stopping nearby is **Guanacaste National Park**, just outside Belmopan, which is well worth a visit (see page 734). As Belmopan's accommodation is so expensive it may be better to take an early bus to the park from Belize City or San Ignacio rather than go from the capital.

Sleeping **L-AL** *Belmopan Convention*, 2 Bliss Parade, opposite bus stop and market, T822-2130, F822-3066. A/c, hot water, swimming pool, restaurant, bars. A 15-min walk east of the market through the Parliament complex, or a short taxi ride will take you to **A** *Bull Frog*, 23/25 Half Moon Av, T822-2111, F822-3155, bullfrog@btl.net A/c, good, reasonably priced, laundry **C** *El Rey Inn*, 23 Moho St, T822-3438. Big room with fan, hot and cold water, basic, clean, friendly, restaurant, laundry on request, central.

Eating
No cafés open on Sundays
Caladium, next to market, limited fare, moderately priced, small portions, and *El Rey*, see above; there are several *comedores* at the back of the market, and *International Café* near the market, recommended. Also a couple of bakeries nearby. Local food is sold by vendors, 2 stands in front sell ice-cream (closed Sat and Sun), fruit and vegetable market open daily, limited produce available Sun. Shops close 1200-1400.

Transport **Buses** To **San Ignacio**, 1 hr, US$1, frequent service by *Batty* and *Novelo* from 0730-2100. To **Belize City**, 1 hr, US$1.50 frequent service by *Batty*, *Z line* and others. To **Dangriga**, **Mango Creek** and **Punta Gorda**, several daily, see under those towns. To **Orange Walk** and **Corozal** take an early bus to Belize City and change.

Directory **Banks** *Barclays Bank International* (0800-1300, Mon-Fri, and 1500-1800 Fri). ATM, Visa transactions, no commission (but see Belize City). **Embassies & consulates** *Costa Rica*, 2 Sapodilla St, T822-2725, F822-2731. *El Salvador*, 2 Av Río Grande, visa on the spot valid 1 month for 90-day stay, 1 photo, US$38 cash, better to get it in Guatemala, maps available (PO Box 215, T/F822-3404). *Panama*, 79 Unity Blvd, T822-2714 (for Consulate see Belize City). *UK* (British High Commission), North Ring Rd, next to the Governor's residence (PO Box 91, T822-2146/7, F822-2761. brithicom@btl.net), has a list of recommended doctors and dentists.

The Northern Cayes

The cayes off the coast are attractive, relaxing, slow and very 'Caribbean' – an excellent place for all forms of diving, sea fishing or just lazing about. Palm trees fringe the coastline, providing day-long shade for resting in your hammock. They are popular destinations, especially in August and between December and May.

There are 212 square miles of cayes. St George's Caye, 9 miles northeast of Belize, *For southern cayes, see under Southern Belize page 742* *was once the capital and the scene of the battle in 1798 which established British possession. Before then the cayes and atolls were home to fishermen and resting points to clean the catch or grow coconuts. The Maya valued the cayes, building the site of Marco Gonzales on the southwestern tip of Ambergris Caye, the largest of the islands. Along with Caye Caulker they are popular destinations for visitors, while serious divers head for the Turneffe Islands. Other, smaller cayes are home to exclusive resorts or remain uninhabited, many being little more than mangrove swamps.*

Travel by boat to and between the islands is increasingly regulated and licensing requirements will probably drive the cheaper boats out of business. In general, it is easier to arrange travel between the islands once there, than from Belize City. Most boats to Caye Caulker (and some to Ambergris Caye) now leave from the new Marine Terminal opposite the post office. To **Caye Caulker** every 1½ hrs between 0900 and 1700, US$7.50. To **San Pedro-Ambergris Caye** at 0900, 1200 and 1500, US$7.50. *Triple J* leaves at 0900 from the North Front St gas station, *Seascape* departs from outside *Bellevue Hotel* at 1600. Timetables do change so check before travelling – your hotel will know. **Ins & outs**

Ambergris Caye

This island (pronounced Am-*ber*-gris), along with the town of **San Pedro**, has *Colour map 6, grid A2* grown rapidly over the last couple of years, with over 50 hotels and guesthouses now *Population: 4,499* registered on the island. Buildings are still restricted to no more than three storeys in height, and the many wooden structures retain an authentic village atmosphere. Hurricane Keith battered the western shore in late 2000, but repairs are now complete and new hotels are opening all the time. **Tourist information** office in the **Ambergris Museum**, T226-2298, opposite *Fido's*. The museum is new and has excellent displays on the history of the town and the caye.

It should be noted that, although sand is in abundance, there are few beach areas around San Pedro town. The emphasis is on snorkelling on the nearby barrier reef and Hol Chan Marine Park, and the fine scuba diving, sailing, fishing and board sailing. The main boat jetties are on the east (Caribbean Sea) side of San Pedro. It can be dangerous to swim near San Pedro as there have been serious accidents with boats. Boats are restricted to about 5 miles per hour within the line of red buoys about 25 yd offshore, but this is not always adhered to. There is a 'safe' beach in front of the park, just to the south of the Government dock. A short distance to the north and south of San Pedro lie miles of deserted beach front, where picnic barbecues are popular for day-tripping snorkellers and birders who have visited the nearby small cayes hoping to glimpse Rosets, spoonbills or white ibis. If you go north you have to cross a small inlet with hand-pulled ferry, US$0.50 for foreigners.

Just south of Ambergris Caye, and not far from Caye Caulker, is the **Hol Chan** **Excursions** **Marine Park**, an underwater natural park divided into three zones: Zone A is the *Only very experienced* reef, where fishing is prohibited; Zone B is the seagrass beds, where fishing can only *snorkellers should* be done with a special licence (the **Boca Ciega** blue hole is here); Zone C is man- *attempt to swim in* groves where fishing also requires a licence. Only certified scuba divers may dive in *the cutting between* the reserve. Several boatmen in San Pedro offer snorkelling trips to the park, US$25 *the reef and the open* (not including entry fee), two hours. Fish feeding, though prohibited, takes place at *sea; seek advice on* Shark-Ray Alley, where about 15 sharks and rays are fed for the entertainment of *the tides* tourists. Not the most natural of experiences but fascinating to see these creatures close up. ■ *Entry to the park is US$5. The park office (with reef displays and information on Bacalar Chico National Park to the north) is on Caribeña St, T226-2247. Contact the Reserve Manager in San Pedro for further information.*

San Pedro is well known for its diving. Long canyons containing plenty of soft and hard coral formations start at around 50-60 ft going down to 120 ft. Often these have grown into hollow tubes which make for interesting diving. **Tackle Box**, **Esmeralda**,

Belize

Cypress, **M & Ms** and **Tres Cocos** are only some of the dive sites which abound in the area. Visibility is usually over 100 ft. There is a recompression chamber in San Pedro and a US$1 tax on each tank fill insures treatment throughout the island.

You cannot, in practice, walk north along the beach from San Pedro to Xcalak, Mexico

Although offshore, Ambergris Caye airport makes arranging tours to visit places on the mainland very easy (for example Altún Ha US$60 per person; Lamanai US$125 per person) while still be able to enjoy other water experiences (catamaran sailing US$40 per person, deep-sea fishing US$150-400, manatee and Coco Solo US$75). Among the many operators, *Hustler Tours*, T226-2538 (Billy and his

The Cayes

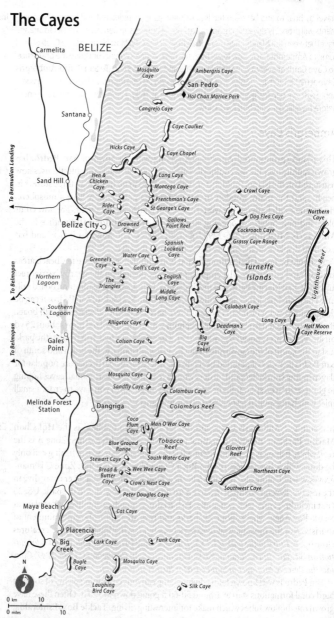

prothers are experienced and very helpful) are recommended. Day cruises to Caye Caulker and the barrier reef on the island trader *MV Winnie Estelle* is good value at US$45 per person, including snacks and soft drinks. Other day snorkelling trips from US$25 to Caye Caulker with stops at Sting Ray Alley and coral gardens. Snorkel rental US$5, discount through tour group.

In San Pedro LL *Belize Yacht Club*, PO Box 1, T226-2777, F226-2768, www.belizeyachtclub.com All rooms are suites with fully furnished kitchens, bar and restaurant, pool, docking facilities. **LL-AL** *Ramon's Village*, T226-2071, F2214, or USA T601-649-1990, (PO Drawer 4407, Laurel, MS 39441), info@ramons.com 61 rooms, a diving and beach resort, all meals and all diving, highly recommended even for non-divers (fishing, swimming, boating, snorkelling), very efficient, comfortable rooms, pool with beach club atmosphere. **L** *Mayan Princess*, T226-2778, F226-2784, mayanprin@btl.net Centre of village on seafront, clean, comfortable. **L-AL** *Paradise Resort Hotel*, T226-2083, F226-2232, www.ambergriscaye.com/paradiseresort Wide selection of rooms and villas, good location, villas better value, cheaper summer rates, all watersports.

AL *Rock's Inn Apartments*, T226-2326, F226-2358, rocks@btl.net Good value and service. **AL** *San Pedro Holiday Hotel*, T226-2014, F226-2295, holiday@btl.net 16 rooms in good central location, fun atmosphere with good facilities, reasonable value. **AL** *Sun Breeze*, T226-2191, F226-2346, www.sunbreeze.net Near airport, Mexican-style building, a/c, comfortable, all facilities, good dive shop. Recommended. **AL-B** *Coral Beach*, T226-2013, F226-2864 www.coralbeachhotel.com Central location, slightly run-down but good local feel and excellent watersports facilities including dive boat charter, tours for fishing and scuba available. **AL-A** *Spindrift*, T226-2018, F226-2251, spinhotel@btl.net 24 rooms, 4 apartments, unattractive block but central location, good bar and restaurant, popular meeting place, trips up the Belize River, a/c, comfortable. **AL-B** *Barrier Reef*, T226-2075, F226-2719, barrierreef@btl.net Handsome wooden house in centre, a/c, pool. **A** *Lily's*, T226-2059. Rooms with sea view, some with a/c, others with fan, clean.

B *Hideaway Lodge*, PO Box 43, Belize City, T226-2141, hideaway@btl.net Good value but a bit run-down. **B** *San Pedrano*, San Pedro, T226-2054. Clean and good value.

C *Thomas*, airy rooms, fan, bath (tub, not shower), drinking water, clean, friendly. **D** *Milo's Hotel*, T226-2033, F226-2198. 9 rooms, one of the cheapest hotels, bit run-down but still popular with backpackers. **D** *Rubie's*, San Pedro Town on the beach, T226-2063, fan, private bath, good views, beach cabaña, central, recommended as best value in town.

Just outside San Pedro there are several resort-style complexes offering seclusion and an ambience a little closer to paradise. **LL** *Mata Chica Resort*, 4 miles north, T/F226-3012, matachica@btl.net European-owned and managed, beautiful and stylish stucco and thatched cabañas on a lovely beach, fantastic restaurant, *Mambo*. **LL-L** *Captain Morgan's Retreat*, 3 miles north of town, T226-2567, F226-2616, captmorgan@btl.net Access by boat, thatched roofed cabañas with private facilities, pool, dock, secluded. Recommended. **LL-L** *El Pescador*, on Punta Arena beach 3 miles north, PO Box 793, Belize City, T/F226-2398, pescador@btl.net Access by boat, specialist fishing lodge with good reputation, a/c, good food and service. **LL-AL** *Victoria House*, PO Box 22, San Pedro, T226-2067, F226-2429 (USA T1-800-247-5159), www.victoria-house.com Including meals, 1 mile from town, 3 different types of room, excellent facilities, good dive shop and watersports, windsurfing US$15 per hour. Highly recommended. **AL** *Capricorn Resort*, 3 miles north of town, T226-2809, F220-5091, capricorn@ btl.net Wooden cabins on beach with great restaurant.

For those staying in villas, contact Denny 'The Bun Man' for fresh coffee, orange juice, and excellent cinnamon buns. He will deliver in time for breakfast, T226-3490. *Alijua*, in San Pedro, Croatian owned, good food, also rents suites with kitchen, US$100 for 4 persons. *Ambergris Delight*, pleasant, inexpensive, clean. *Celi's*, behind *Holiday Hotel*, good seafood. Recommended. *El Patio*, south of town, beyond Belize Yacht Club. Good, inexpensive Mexican-style food, live music in evenings. *Elvi's Kitchen*, popular, upmarket, live music and roof built around flamboyant tree, can be very busy, won international award 1996. *Estel's* on the

Sleeping
Price codes:
see inside front cover

Belize

Eating

beach, good food and 1940s-50s music. *Fido's Courtyard*, towards north end of Front St. Lively bar-restaurant often with live music, good lunch and dinner. *Jade Garden Restaurant*, Chinese, sweet and sour everything, drinks expensive. *Lily's Restaurant*, best seafood in town, friendly, good breakfast, excellent value but quite basic. *Little Italy*, at *Spindrift Hotel*, popular but expensive. *Rasta Pasta*, at *Sunbreeze Hotel*, south end of Front St. Great spicy food and barbecues.

Bars *Big Daddy's Disco*, open evenings but cranks up at midnight. For entertainment, try 'Chicken Drop' in Pier Lounge at *Spindthrift Hotel* on a Wed night, you bet US$1 on which square the chicken will leave its droppings. *Tarzan Disco*, nearby on Front St. Good atmosphere.

Sports **Diving**: instruction to PADI open water level widely available, from US$350-400 at: *Amigos del Mar*, T226-2706, F226-2648, www.amigosdive.com instructor Grant Crimmins, opposite *Lily's*; *Ramon's Village*, instructor Elbert Greer, www.scubalessonsbelize.com, and *Blue Hole* (Chris Allnatt, in centre of town, good for advice, information and trips), T/F226-2982, bluehole@btl.net *Amigos del Mar* and *Blue Hole* have been repeatedly recommended. Check diving shop's recent safety record before diving. **Sea kayaking** with expert guide, Elito Arceo, T226-3221 or T614-6043 (mob), office just north of airport. **Snorkelling** trips on the *Winnie Estelle*, a 40-ft motor cruiser with large deck area, US$55 day trip, open bar, snacks. Daniel Núñez, T226-3214, does trips to the Maya sites on the north of the caye in the new Bacalar Chico National Park.

Shopping *Island Supermarket*, across from *Ramon's*, has good range of supplies. There are many gift shops in the centre of town. Try *Fidos* which has *Sunsation Gift Shop*, *Belizean Arts* (paintings and prints by local artists), *Amber Jewelry* and *Realty Café*. Wave runners (US$50 per hr) and hobie cats (US$25 per hr) can also be hired here.

Transport **Air** *Tropic Air* (T226-2012) and *Maya Island Air* (T226-2345) have flights to/from both Belize City airports, many hourly. *Maya Island Air* also flies to Caye Caulker, while both airlines fly to Corozal, several daily flights.

Sea More interesting than going by air are the boats. To Belize City US$15 depending on boat. *Andrea* from San Pedro at 0700, returning from Courthouse Wharf at 1500. *Seascape* at 0800, returning from *Bellevue Hotel* at 1600. *Triple J*, the fastest and bumpiest, at 1500, returning from North Front St gas station at 0900; several other regular departures. All these call at Caye Caulker (and Caye Chapel and St George's Caye on request). Many regular boats between Caye Caulker and Ambergris Caye, US$7.50. Shuttle boats to hotels north of town, many from Fido's Dock.

Vehicle hire: golf carts US$10/hr, make sure battery is fully charged before hiring; gives quick access to southern, quieter end. Bicycles US$5 per hr, try negotiating for long-term rates, good way to get around.

Directory **Banks** *Atlantic Bank* and *Bank of Belize*, open Mon-Thu 0800-1300, Fri 0800-1630. Small denominations of US currency in regular use. **Tour operators** *Travel and Tour Belize* in town helpful, T226-2031. They can arrange charter flights to Corozal, with a request stop at Sarteneja (for the Shipstern Butterfly Farm see page 731).

Smaller cayes

St George's **Sleeping AL** *Cottage Colony*, PO Box 428, Belize City, T227-7051, F227-3253, fins@btl.net Colo-
Caye nial-style cabañas with dive facilities, price varies according to season, easy access from Belize City. **L** *St George's Island Lodge and Cabañas*, T220-9121, sgl.belize@btl.net, PO Box 625, Belize City, in USA, T1-800-678-6871, 8 rooms and 6 thatched cottages over the water, prices include 2 dives, all meals, transfer from international airport. Specialist diving resort including advanced and Nitrox certification. Boat fare is US$15, day trips are possible.

Caye Chapel was once a small, quiet caye dotted with palms and devoid of sandflies, close to its busier neighbour, where you could escape to a bit of quiet and solitude. That has all changed, as it is exclusive now as well as secluded.
Sleeping LL *Caye Chapel Golf Course and Marina*, PO Box 192, Belize City, T226-8250, F226-8201, golf@btl.net 12 deluxe villas with tennis courts, basketball and private airstrip.

Caye Chapel

Sleeping Middle Long Caye: *Moonlight Shadows Lodge*,T08-22587, still being developed. *Ricardo's Beach Huts*, Blue Field Range (59 North Front St, PO Box 55, Belize City, T224-4970), recommended, charming and knowledgeable host, rustic, authentic fish camp feel, overnight camps to Rendez-vous Caye, English Caye and Sargeants Caye can be arranged with Ricardo, excellent food, snorkelling. *Spanish Bay Resort*, PO Box 35, Belize City, T227-7288. Also under development, dive facilities. **Gallows Point Caye**: *The Wave* (9 Regent St, Belize City, T227-3054), 6 rooms, watersports facilities and diving.

Small caye resorts within easy reach of Belize City

Twelve miles off Belize City, English Caye is beautiful, but has no facilities; take a day trip only. It is part of the reef so you can snorkel right off the beach. *Sunrise Travel*, Belize City, T227-2051 or T223-2670, can help arrange a trip, book in advance.

English Caye

The islands form one of Belize's three atolls. On **Big Caye Bokel** is *Turneffe Islands Lodge*, PO Box 480, Belize City, info@turneffelodge.com, which can accommodate 16 guests for week-long fishing and scuba packages. *Turneffe Flats*, 56 Eve Street, Belize City, T224-5634, www.tflats.com, in a lovely location, also offers week-long packages for fishing and scuba; it can take 12 guests, but is to be expanded. *Blackbird Caye Resort*, c/o Blackbird Caye Co, 11a Cork Street, Belize, T223-2772, F223-4449, manager, Kent Leslie, weekly packages arranged, is an ecologically oriented resort on this 4,000-acre island used by the *Oceanic Society* and is a potential site for a biosphere reserve underwater project. Reservations in the USA, T713-658-1142, F713-658-0379. Diving or fishing packages available, no bar, take your own alcohol.

Turneffe Islands

Belize

Caye Caulker

A quiet lobster-fishing island (closed season 15 February-14 July) until quite recently, its extremely relaxing and laid-back atmosphere, gentle climate and the myriad small restaurants and bars have drawn gently increasing numbers of tourists to Caye Caulker. Small white sandy beaches fall to a sea of blue and green, while the reef can be seen a mile and a half from the shore. By day it's diving and snorkelling, sea and sand, by night it's eating, drinking and dancing.

Hurricane Keith gave the island quite a battering in late 2000, but repairs to the wooden houses, the majority on stilts, are now virtually complete. The caye is actually two islands separated by a small channel known as the 'cut', with all the services on the southern island and a marine reserve in the north. A **reef museum** has opened at the southern end of the south island with a small library, photos of reef fish. ■ *Free for school parties, tourists are asked for a US$2 donation to help expansion and to increase the work in ecology education.*

If swimming in the 'cut', beware of fishing and powerboats using it as a route from the ocean to the west side; several serious accidents have occurred

Tour operators and hotels on the island have worked hard to improve services for visitors. The atmosphere is friendly and easy-going, but the usual common sense rules apply with regards to personal safety. Drugs are readily available, but they are illegal and you shouldn't expect any sympathy should you get in to difficulties. Some think the atmosphere is more relaxed out of high season. Sandflies are ferocious in season (December-February); take long trousers and a good repellent. Make sure you fix prices before going on trips or hiring equipment, and, if you pay the night before, get a receipt. Golf buggies, available for hire, are the means of transportation on the island.

A walk south along the shore takes you to the new airstrip and to mangroves where the rare black catbird can be seen and its sweet song heard. A campaign is underway to make the black catbird's habitat and the associated reef a nature reserve

In this area there are lots of mosquitoes

(called Siwa-Ban, after the catbird's Maya name). Details from *Galería Hicaco* (Ellen McCrea, near *Tropical Paradise*), or 143 Anderson, San Francisco, California.

Excursions
Slightly cheaper from Caye Caulker than Ambergris Caye

See Tour operators, below; try to go with a small group of around six people; it's less enjoyable with larger numbers

Reef trips are the same as those found on Ambergris Caye, for more details see under San Pedro (page 717): Manatees US$27.50; San Pedro, Hol Chan and Shark Alley US$17.50. Both are full-day trips.

Generally trips offered at the same price by an agreement between tour operators, eliminating the need to shop around for a good price. By walking around you'll find somebody you like and trust. Tour operators share clients if numbers are not sufficient. This means you can be certain there is always a trip, but make sure that the boat operator is reliable. Anyone organizing trips must be approved by the *Tour Guide Association* and should have a licence to prove it. To encourage high standards, and for your own safety, insist on seeing evidence that your guide is licenced.

Protect against sunburn on reef trips, even while snorkelling. In the past, we have received reports of theft of valuables left on board while snorkelling, and even of swimmers being left in the water while the boatman went off to pick up another group, although these practices seem to have ceased.

Sleeping
In all accommodation take precautions against theft

The arrival pier is just about in the centre of town, with all the accommodation on or within a 15-min walk of the main street. The southern end of town is slightly quieter, but it is a long way from the 'Cut' for swimming or snorkelling. A map, which can be bought on arrival, lists virtually everything on the island. Camping on the beach is forbidden.

B *Tropical Paradise*, PO Box 1206 Belize City, T226-0124, F226-0225. Cabins, rooms from **D**, hot showers, clean, not very comfortable, restaurant (see below), good excursions. **B** *CB's*, further south than *Tropical Paradise*, T226-0176. With bath, clean, 12 beds, no advance bookings, good, small beds, restaurant. **B** *Rainbow*, on the beach heading north, T226-0123. 10 small bungalows, with shower, rooms also, **C**, hot water, good. Beach houses can also be rented for US$50-150 a month. **B** *Anchorage*, to the south, near *Ignacio's*, T226-0391, F226-0304, anchorage@btl.net New 2-storey building, comfortable, tiled rooms with private bathrooms, pleasant atmosphere, friendly family, breakfast and drinks served under shade on the beach.

C *Edith's*, T226-0161. Rooms with bath or private chalet, recommended, hot water, fan. **C** *Shirley's Guest House*, T226-0145, ccbtia@btl.net, south end of village. Very relaxing, recommended. **C** *Tree Tops*, T226-0008, F226-0115. Clean, spacious rooms, comfortable beds, beach views, German spoken, powerful fan, cable TV, friendly, good value, recommended. **C** *Vega's Far Inn*, T226-0142. Rents 7 rooms, all doubles, with ceiling fan and fresh linen, flush toilets and showers (limited hot water) shared with camping ground, which is guarded, has drinking water, hot water, clean toilets, barbecue, can rent out camping gear (camping costs US$6 per person, overpriced).

D *Tropical Star*, on the main street, T226-0196. OK rooms, with private bath and hot water. Cheaper for longer stays. **D** *Daisy's*, T226-0150. With shower, toilet and fan, reductions for longer stays, will store valuables, clean, friendly, safe, cheaper rooms downstairs, cash travellers' cheques, rooms with communal bathroom not good value, hot water. **D** *Ignacio Beach Cabins*, T226-0212 (PO Box 1169, Belize City). Small huts or hammocks just outside town, for double room, **C** for a hut for 3-4, quiet, clean, recommended, toilet and shower facilities in private cabins only, cheap lobster tails and free coconuts (Ignacio runs reef trips and he has equipment, he is principally a lobster fisherman). **D** *Marin*. With bath, clean, helpful, recommended (the proprietor, John Marin, will take you out for a snorkelling trip on the reef). **D** *Barbara's Guest House*, near north end, T226-0025. Canadian-run, good budget rooms, also safe hammock spaces, **E**, in thatched cabin with foot-lockers. **D-E** *Mira Mar*, T226-0307. 2nd-floor rooms best, clean showers, recommended, bargain if staying longer, helpful owner Melvin Badillo. **D-E** *Tom's*, T226-0102. With shared bath and fan, up to **C** in cabin with 3 beds, basic, clean, cold water, long walk from beach, laundry service US$5, safe deposit, barbecue. Tom's boat trips go to various destinations, including Hol Chan, coral gardens and Belize City. **E** *Sandy Lane*, T226-0217, 1 block back from main street. Bungalow-type accommodation, clean, shared toilet and hot showers, run by Rico and Elma Novelo, recommended. *Tina's Backpacker Hostel*, on the beach at the split, cheapest on the caye. Very popular and noisy – great for meeting people, but not the place if you want peace and quiet.

Menus don't vary much from restaurant to restaurant – fish, chicken, beans, burgers and burritos are the staple diet. Some places do not open for lunch. Many private houses serve food. Cakes and pastries can be bought at houses displaying the sign; recommended are *Daisy's*, *Jessie's* (open 0830-1300, 1500-1700), and a very good one near the telephone exchange office. Buy lobster or fish from the cooperative and cook it at the barbecue on the beach; beer is sold by the crate at the wholesaler on the dock by the generator; ice for sale at *Tropical Paradise*. *Chans Garden*, Chinese, try the chop suey, not cheap. *Glenda's*, near *Hotel Marin*, has delicious lobster, or chicken burritos – chicken, vegetables, chilli and sauce wrapped in a tortilla for US$0.50 – also good breakfast with cinnamon rolls, closed evenings. *Happy Lobster* on main street. Good food, recommended. *Hurricane Bar*, faces the beach on main street. Food OK, service can be a little slow. *I & I Bar*, take a right when you hit Tropical Paradise on main street. Excellent reggae bar, with Bob Marley paraphernalia everywhere. Mellow, laid-back, good views from upper deck. Highly recommended, open after 1700. *Lighthouse*, cantina on the main street. Serving coffee, cake and hot dogs, chairs on the street, always popular. *Little Kitchen*, fish and chips US$4, occasionally lobster, good *burritos* and top milk shakes. *Marin's*, good seafood in evening, cable TV, expensive but worth it. *Martínez*, good seafood, cheap prices. *Oceanside*, most popular bar on the island. Food is reasonable, dance floor and darts, open until midnight. *Paradise Burgers*, near the Split, also fish sandwiches. *Popeye's*, on the beach, live music some nights, opens at 0600 for breakfast. Also good for burritos is *Rainbow Bar and Restaurant*, with the restaurant on its own jetty, good value, beautiful view. *Sandbox Beach Bar and Restaurant*, T226-0200, sandbox@btl.net One of the Caye's social centres with a good atmosphere. Good chocolate cake, ice-cream, recommended. Very popular. *Sid's*, good fish, large portions, good fresh juices. *Sobre Las Olas*, cool restaurant right on the beach with coloured lights, on main street near *Chocolate's*. Excellent food. *Tropical Paradise* for excellent seafood, varied menu, slightly more expensive than others (also one of the few places selling ice-cream). *Wishwilly Bar and Grill*, up a side street, virtually opposite the *Hurricane Bar*. The fish is fantastic and barbecued in front of you. Highly recommended and frequented by Hollywood stars. *Yoo Hoo Deli*, next to the police station. Erratic opening hours, but great coffee, sub sandwiches and service always with a smile. Some chairs out on main street where you can watch the world go by. Book exchange.

Eating
All the island's ground-floor restaurants are carpeted in sand which makes it even easier to wander around bare-footed for days on end

Belize

Windsurfing: equipment hire from Orlando, US$10 per hr, poor quality, bring your own or go to San Pedro. **Canoes**: for hire from Salvador, at painted house behind *Marin's* restaurant, US$10 a day. **Sea kayaks**: from Ellen at *Galería Hicaco*, US$12.50 for ½ day, also next to *Ignacio Beach Cabins* at US$15 per ½ day, better kayaks. Go **fishing** with Rolly Rosardo, 4 hrs, US$45, up to 5 people, equipment, fresh bait and instruction provided. **Diving**: *Frenchie's Diving Service*, T226-0234, frenchies@btl.net charges US$330 for a 4-day PADI course, friendly and effective, 2-tank dive US$60, also advanced PADI instruction. Day-excursion diving Blue Hole, etc, US$65, snorkellers welcome. *Belize Diving Services*, PO Box 20, Caye Caulker, T226-0143, F226-0217, bzdiveserv@btl.net, is another dive shop on the island. Ask Chocolate for all-day trips to the manatee reserve in the south of Belize. It may be possible to hire a boat for 6-8 people to Chetumal.

Sports

There are at least 4 small 'markets' on the island where a variety of food can be bought; prices are 20-50% higher than the mainland. *Chan's Supermarket*, one street back from main street, open daily including Christmas and New Year's Day. Diagonally opposite is the bakery which sells delicious cinnamon rolls. Bookstore on opposite side of island to ferries sells many different magazines, including *Time* and *Newsweek*.

Shopping

On the island You can rent golf carts, US$5 per hr.

Air *Maya Island Air* flies to/from Belize City, Corozal and San Pedro, several daily. Flying is recommended if you have a connection to make.

Transport

Sea Boats leave from the Marine Terminal on North Front St (see above) for Caye Caulker between 0900-1700, returning 0630-1600, daily, US$12.50, buy tickets in advance from desk inside Marine Terminal, 45 mins one way (can be 'exciting' if it's rough). The Caye Caulker *Water Taxi Association* regulates schedules and fares; the office on Caye Caulker is opposite BTL. Recommended boats: Emilio Novelo's *Ocean Star* (good, cheaper than others); Chocolate's *Soledad* ('Chocolate' is white, over 70 years old and has a white moustache). Boats from San Pedro en route to Belize City 0700-0800, US$12.50. *Triple J* (see above, San Pedro) boat, recommended, daily service, from Ambergris Caye 0700, 45 mins, US$12.50. To get to Flores or Chetumal buy onward tickets at any travel agency on the caye and take the boat at 0800.

Directory **Banks** Rates for cash and TCs are reasonable. *Atlantic Bank* (Visa advances; US$5 commission) and many other places for exchange. Gift shops will charge a commission.

Communications Internet: *Caye Caulker Cyber Café*. open 0700-2200, US$6/hr. **Telephone**: international telephone and fax connections available on Caye Caulker (telephone exchange is open 0900-1230, 1400-1630; cardphone outside the BTL office can be used for international calls. Collect calls possible at least to North America at no charge. Fax number at telephone exchange is 501-226-0239). **Post office** on west side of the island.

Laundry Several locals will take washing in – look out for the signs. *Marie's Laundry*, 1 block back from main street, operates self service or you can leave your stuff. US$5 for 4 kg.

If trying to arrange a trip to a smaller island, you may have to try a few operators, or ask around for a boatman

Tour operators *Dolphin Bay Dive Travel*, PO Box 374, Belize City, T/F226-0214, is very helpful and can arrange domestic and international flights as well as local excursions. Highly recommended. **Reef trip operators** *Neno Rosado* (T226-0302) has been approved by the association and is reliable and knowledgeable. *Mervin*, a local man, is reliable for snorkelling trips, he will also take you to Belize City. *Driftwood Snorkelling*, T226-0011, on the front by the *Miramar Hotel*, good snorkelling and diving trips and information. Lobster fishing and diving for conch is also possible. *Chocolate's*, a few tours, but mainly a shop with beautiful sarongs and dresses imported from Guatemala. *E-Z Boy Tours*, opposite Driftwood on main street, tours taken by Carlos. T226-0349. Snorkelling, manatee, river and Mayan site tours. Manatees and Goff Caye (a paradise perfect circular island with good snorkelling around), US$30, Hol Chan Shark-Ray alley, US$23. Equipment included. *Island Sun*, near the Cut, local husband and American wife, very conscientious. They offer day tours to reef, plus snorkel hire (1000-1400), and a day tour to San Pedro and Hol Chan, plus snorkel hire, plus entry fee for reserve, recommended. *Stone Crab* Captain Leroy and Sons. Reef trips, sunset sails, and tours by arrangement. Ask for them at the *lancha* ticket office near the Sand Box. Mixed reports. *Capt Jim Novelo*, of *Sunrise* boat, does trips to Hol Chan and San Pedro, 1000-1600, and snorkelling excursions to the Turneffe Islands, Half Moon Caye, Bird Sanctuary and Blue Hole, 0630-1700, every Tue, Dec-Apr, Jul-Aug, or on request, US$67.50 including lunch and drinks, T226-0195, F226-0239. A sailing boat also goes to Hol Chan, but the trip takes a long time, leaving only a short while for snorkelling, departs 1000, US$12 for a day. Mask, snorkel and fins for US$2.50 cheapest (for instance at the post office). *Benji*, owner of a small sailboat and Joe Joe, his Rasta captain, will take you on a fun trip to Placencia or the Cayes. Recommended **guides** include *Ras Creek*, 'a big man with a big heart', in his boat, US$12.50 including lunch; *Alfonso Rosardo*, reef trips for up to 6 people, 5-6 hrs, sometimes offers meals at his house afterwards; *Obdulio Lulu* at *Tom's Hotel* goes to Hol Chan and San Pedro for a full day (if he catches a barracuda on the return, he will barbecue it at the hotel for US$0.75); *Raoul and Charles*, also from *Tom's Hotel*, US$12.50; also *Harrison* (ask around for him, he goes to see manatees, then to a small island to see the coral reef, US$25, recommended).

Lighthouse Reef

There are no facilities, so take all food, drink and fuel

Lighthouse Reef is the outermost of the three north-south reef systems off Belize and is some 45 miles to the east of Belize City. Trips out here are not cheap, but if you like diving and have the money, this is one of the best dive sites in the world. There are two cayes of interest: Half Moon Caye (on which the lighthouse stands) and, 12 miles to the north, the atoll in which the diving shrine of the **Blue Hole** (see below) is found. **Half Moon Caye** is the site of the **Red-Footed Booby Sanctuary**, a national reserve. Besides the booby, magnificent frigate birds also nest on the island. The sea-birds nest on the western side, which has denser vegetation (the eastern side is

Belize (side margin)

covered mainly in coconut palms). Of the 98 other bird species recorded on Half Moon Caye, 77 are migrants. The iguana, the wish willy (smaller than the iguana) and the *anolis allisoni* lizard inhabit the caye, and hawksbill and loggerhead turtles lay their eggs on the beaches. The Belize Audubon Society in Belize City maintains the sanctuary, providing a lookout tower and a trail. The lighthouse on the caye gives fine views of the reef. It was first built in 1820: the present steel tower was added to the brick base in 1931 and nowadays the light is solar powered. Around sunset you can watch the boobies from the lookout as they return from fishing. They land beside their waiting mates at the rate of about 50 a minute, seemingly totally unperturbed by humans. ■ *On arrival you must register near the lighthouse with the warden who will provide maps and tell you where you can camp (US$5 per person).*

In Lighthouse Reef is the **Blue Hole**, recently declared a National Monument, which is a circular sinkhole, 1,000 ft across and with depths exceeding 400 ft. The crater was probably formed by the collapsed roof of a subterranean cave, and was studied by Jacques Cousteau in 1984. Stalagmites and stalactites can be found in the underwater cave and it is rated as one of the best dives in the world. Entry to the Blue Hole is US$4. Scuba diving is outstanding at Lighthouse Reef, and includes two walls which descend almost vertically from 30-40 ft to a depth of almost 400 ft.

Excursions Frenchie, of *Frenchie's Diving*, runs regular trips from Caye Caulker to **Half Moon Caye** and the **Blue Hole**, US$65 for snorkellers, more for divers. To charter a motor boat in Belize City costs about US$50 per person if 10 people are going (six hours' journey). Organized trips can be booked through any dive shop in San Pedro. Bill Hinkis, in San Pedro Town, Ambergris Caye, offers three-day sailing cruises to Lighthouse Reef for US$150 (you provide food, ice and fuel). Bill and his boat *Yanira* can be found beside the lagoon off Back Street, just north of the football field. *Out Island Divers,* San Pedro, do various two to three-day trips. Other sailing vessels charge US$150-250 per day. Speedboats charge US$150 per person for a day-trip including lunch and three dives, recommended. A two-day overnight trip including five dives, costs US$250. The main dive in the Blue Hole is very deep, at least 130 ft (almost 50 m); the hole itself is 480 ft deep. Check your own qualifications as the dive operator probably will not. It is well worth doing if you are qualified. Keep an eye on your computer or dive charts if doing subsequent dives.

Sleeping It's possible to stay on one of the reef's private islands, 12 km from the Blue Hole, all-inclusive 1-week stays; contact PO Box 1435, Dundee, Fla, US, T1-800-423-3114, F1-813-439-2118 (US).

Northern Belize

North Belize is notable for the agricultural production of sugar, fruit and vegetables and for providing much of the country's food. But amongst the fields of produce are some well-hidden gems. The Maya ruins of Lamanai are just about visible in the dense jungle, and Chan Chich is truly remote. Wildlife can easily be seen at the Community Baboon Sanctuary, the wildlife reserves of Shipstern, the vast Río Bravo Conservation Area and the Crooked Tree Wildlife Sanctuary which is home to thousands of beautiful birds. If you have time, Northern Belize is definitely worth exploring.

Belize City to the Mexican border Heading north out of Belize City, the Northern Highway leads to the Mexican border. You can do the journey in a day, but you won't see a thing. However, if you have time, this route passes some impressive wildlife sanctuaries, the spectacular ruins of Lamanai, and the largely untouched wilderness of the Shipstern Peninsula. More difficult to reach is the Río Bravo Conservation Area – at over 260,000 acres Belize's largest, privately owned protected area.

Bermudian Landing and the Community Baboon Sanctuary

About 15 miles out of Belize City a road heading west leads to the small settlement of **Bermudian Landing** (12 miles on a rough road from the turn-off) that has been thrust into the global conservation spotlight. The small Creole village was once a transfer point for the timber that floated down the Belize River, but now there's a local wildlife museum – sponsored by the Worldwild Fund For Nature (WWF) – and the **Community Baboon Sanctuary** nearby, with over 1,000 black howler monkeys, locally called baboons. Local farmers have agreed to protect the riverside habitat of the howlers, realizing that by doing so they not only protect their land from annual floodwaters, but that this also retains a natural balance to the area. Aims have been made to ensure that the benefits of this 'community' project are returned to the community and not to individuals. Trails have been made in and around the reserve, which encompasses eight villages. Check with the Sanctuary warden if you wish to visit, PO Box 1428, Belize City, T220-9181, baboon@btl.net Boats can be hired from the warden for river trips to see monkeys and birds. An excellent booklet (US\$3) is available from the *Audubon Society*, 12 Fort Street, Belize City. A guided walk costs US\$6 per person. The warden will also arrange accommodation locally and may allow overnight parking at the site for a small donation. Many freelance guides seek business from arriving vehicles, but it is better to get a licensed guide from the visitors' centre.

Sleeping **At Bermudian Landing** L-B *Howler Monkey Lodge*, 400 m from museum, T220-2158, www.belizemall.com/jungled PO Box 694, Belize City, screened windows, fans, cheaper with shared bath, discounts for students, TCs, Visa, MasterCard accepted, camping US\$5 per person, bring tent, river tours US\$20 per person recommended, transport from Belize City in pick-up, US\$40, 1-4 people, on request, breakfast, lunch and dinner, US\$2.50-7.50. Many good tours available including night-time crocodile adventures and river trips from US\$25 per person. Canoe rentals in Burrell Boom for trips on Belize River to see birds, howler monkeys, manatee, hicatee. **C** *Cabañas* are available alongside the visitors' centre, bath, hot water. Basic lodging is also available with families in the village.

Transport Bus from **Belize City:** *Mcfadzean Bus* from corner of Amara Av and Cemetery Rd at 1215 and 1715 Mon-Fri; 1200 and 1400 Sat. *Rancho Bus* (*Pook's Bus*) from *Batty* bus terminal on Mosul Street, 1700 Mon-Fri, 1300 Sat, check details, US\$1.50-2, 1 hr. Alternatively, any bus travelling the Northern Highway can drop you off at the turn-off to Bermudian Landing where you can wait for a bus, or hitch a ride. A day trip giving any meaningful time in the sanctuary is difficult by public transport, so it is best to stay the night.

Crooked Tree Wildlife Sanctuary

The Northern Highway continues to **Sand Hill**, and a further 12 miles to the turn-off for the Crooked Tree Wildlife Sanctuary which was set up in 1984 and is an exceptionally rich area for birds. The network of lagoons and swamps attracts many migrating birds and the dry season, October-May, is a good time to visit. You may see the red collar of the jabiru stork, the largest flying bird in the Western Hemisphere at a height of 5 ft and a wingspan of 11-12 ft, which nests here as well as herons, ducks, vultures, kites, ospreys, hawks, sand pipers, kingfishers, gulls, terns, egrets and swallows. In the forest you can also see and hear howler monkeys. Other animals include coatimundi, crocodiles, iguanas and turtles. Glenn Crawford is a very good guide as is Sam Tillet (see Sleeping below). The turn-off to the sanctuary is signposted but keep an eye out for the intersection which is 22 miles from Orange Walk and 32 miles from Belize City. There is another sign further south indicating the sanctuary but this just leads to the park boundary, not to the Wildlife Sanctuary. The mango and cashew trees in the village of Crooked Tree are said to be 100 years old. Bird-watching is best in the early morning but, as buses do not leave Belize City early, for a day trip take an early Corozal bus, get off at the main road (about 1¼ hours from Belize City) and hitch to the sanctuary. The village is tiny and quaint, occupied mostly by Creoles. Boats and guides can be hired for approximately US$70 per boat (maximum four people). It may be worth bargaining as competition is fierce. Trips include a visit to an unexcavated Mayan site. It is easy to get a lift, and someone is usually willing to take visitors back to the main road for a small charge. Entry is US$4 (Belizeans US$1); you must register at the visitors' centre, drinks are on sale, but take food. There is a helpful, friendly warden, Steve, who will let you sleep on the porch of the visitors' centre.

A *Bird's Eye View Lodge*, T223-2040, F222-4869, www.belizenet.com/birdseye.html, **Sleeping** (owned by the Gillett family; in USA New York T/F718-845-0749). Single and double rooms, shower, fan, also bunk accommodation, US$10, camping US$5, meals available, boat trips, horse-riding, canoe rental, nature tours with licensed guide, ask for information at the *Belize Audubon Society* (address above). **A** *Paradise Inn*, T02-44333. Run by the Crawfords, cabins with hot showers, restaurant, is well maintained and friendly, boat trips, fishing, horse-riding and tours available.

B-C *Sam Tillet's Hotel*, T225-7044, www.adventurecamera.com, in centre of village. Wood and thatch cabin, tiny restaurant, great trips. Cabins may be rented at US$33 for a night, up to 4 people. Camping and cheap rooms (house of Rev Rhayburn, **E**, recommended, meals available) can also be arranged if you ask.

Buses from Belize City with *JEX* (1035) and *Batty* (1600); return from Crooked Tree at **Transport** 0600-0700, sometimes later. *Batty* bus also on Sun, leaves Belize City 0900, returns 1600.

Altún Ha

The Maya remains of Altún Ha, 31 miles north of Belize City and 2 miles off the Old *Colour map 6, grid A1* Northern Highway, are worth a visit. Altún Ha was a major ceremonial centre in the Classic Period (250-900 AD) and also a trading station linking the Caribbean coast with Maya centres in the interior. The site consists of two central plazas surrounded by 13 partially excavated pyramids and temples. What the visitor sees now is composite, not how the site would have been at any one time in the past. The largest piece of worked Maya jade ever found, a head of the Sun God Kinich Ahau weighing 9 ½ lb (4.3 kg), was found here in the main temple (B-4) in 1968. It is now in a bank vault in Belize City. Nearby is a large reservoir, now called **Rockstone Road** ('Altún Ha' is a rough translation of the modern name). ■ *0900-1700, US$1.50 (insect repellent necessary).*

Just north of Maskall is **LL** *Maruba Resort*, T322-2199 also USA 713-799-2031, **Sleeping** www.maruba-spa.com A hotel, restaurant and spa, all rooms different, some a/c, German spoken, good bird-watching, including storks in the nearby swamp; has caged animals and birds. There is no accommodation in nearby villages.

Since there is so little transport on this road, hitching is not recommended, best to go in a pri- **Transport** vate vehicle or a tour group. Vehicles leave Belize City for the village of **Maskall**, 8 miles north of Altún Ha, several days a week, but same-day return is not possible. With warden's permission, vehicle overnight parking is permitted free.

Orange Walk

The Northern Highway runs to Orange Walk (66 miles), the centre of a district *Colour map 6, grid A1* where about 17,000 Creoles, Mennonites and Maya Indians earn their living from *Population: 13,483* timber, sugar planting and general agriculture. Nearby are the impressive ruins of Lamanai. This is also the departure point for the Shipstern Peninsula and for the long overland trip to Río Bravo Conservation Area, Chan Chich and Gallon Jug.

Belize

There is little to draw the visitor for an extended stay in Orange Walk, but it is the best base for planning a trip to the impressive ruins of Lamanai – see below. An agricultural centre and the country's second city, it is busy with the comings and goings of a small town. Orange Walk is a truly multi-cultural centre with inhabitants coming from all over Central America which makes Spanish the predominant language. Originally from Canada, Mennonnites live in nearby colonies using the town as their marketing and supply centre. The only battle fought on Belizean soil took place here, during the Yucatecan Caste Wars (1840-70s); the Maya leader, Marcus Canul was shot in the fighting in 1872.

Buses plying the route from Belize City to the Mexican border stop on Queen Victoria Avenue, the main street, by the town hall in front of the park. While a few pleasant wooden buildings remain on quiet side streets, most are worn out and in bad need of repair. Many have been pulled down and replaced by the standard concrete box affairs, which lack either inspiration or style.

A toll bridge (Bz$0.25 for motorbikes, Bz$0.80 for cars) now spans the New River a few miles south of the town at Tower Hill. A market overlooks New River, and is well organized, with good food stalls and interesting architecture.

Sleeping   **B-D** *Mi Amor*, 19 Belize-Corozal Rd, T322-2031. With shared bath, with bath and fan, or with a/c, nice, clean, restaurant. **C** *d'Victoria*, 40 Belize Rd (Main St), T322-2518. A/c, shower, hot water, parking, quite comfortable, pool, but somewhat run-down. **C** *Chula Vista*, Trial Farm, T322-2227, at gas station (closed) just north of town. Safe, clean, helpful owner, but over-priced. **C** *St Christopher's*, 10 Main St, T/F322-1064. Beautiful clean rooms and bathrooms, highly recommended and the best in town. **E** *Jane's*, 2 Baker's St, T322-2473 (Jane's II on Market Lane). Large house in pleasant location but smelly. **E** *La Nueva Ola*, 73 Otro Benque Rd, T322-2104. Large car park, run down, probably the cheapest. Neither of these is recommended but there are not many 'budget' options in Orange Walk to choose from. Parking for vehicles is very limited at hotels.

Eating   The majority of restaurants in town are Chinese, eg *Golden Gate*, Baker's St. Cheap. *Hong Kong II*, next to *Mi Amor*. *King Fu*, Baker's St. Excellent, filling, US$5 per person. *Juanita's*, 8 Santa Ana St (take road beside Shell station), open 0600 for breakfast and all meals. Good, inexpensive creole cooking. Similarly at *Julie's*, near police station. Many good bars eg *San Martín*. On Clarke St, behind the hospital, is *The Diner*, good meals for US$3, very friendly, taxi US$4 or walk.

Transport   Bus station is on street beside the fire station, on the main road. All Chetumal buses pass Orange Walk Town (hourly); **Belize**-Orange Walk, US$3. **Corozal**-Orange Walk, US$1.50, 50 mins. For **Lamanai** take bus to Indian Church (Mon, Wed, Fri 1600). Buses to **Sarteneja** outside *Zeta's Store* on Main St, 1530.

Directory   **Banks** *Belize Bank* on Main St (down Park St from Park, turn left); same hours as Belize City (see page 715). *Scotia Bank* on Park, Bz$1 commission. Shell Station will change TCs. **Tour operators** *Jungle River Tours*, PO Box 95, 20 Lovers' Lane, T322-2293, F322-3749, in *Lovers' Café* on the southeastern corner of the park. Organize and run trips to Lamanai (US$55) and New River area, regular trips, *the* specialists on the region and highly recommended.

West & south of Orange Walk   From Orange Walk a road heads west, before turning south, running parallel to the Mexican and then Guatemalan border, where it becomes unpaved. Along this road are several archaeological sites: First is **Cuello**, 4 miles west on San Antonio road, behind Cuello Distillery (ask there for permission to visit); taxi about US$3.50. The site dates back to 1000 BC, but, though it has yielded important discoveries in the study of Maya and pre-Maya cultures, there is little for the layman to appreciate and no facilities for visitors. At **Yo Creek** the road divides, north to San Antonio, and south through miles of cane fields and tiny farming settlements as far as **San Felipe** (20 miles via San Lázaro, Trinidad and August Pine Ridge). At August Pine Ridge here is a daily bus to Orange Walk at 1000. You can camp at the house of Narciso Novelo (T323-3019), a relaxing place to stay. At San Felipe, a branch leads southeast to Indian Church/Lamanai, 35 miles from Orange Walk (one hour driving, four-wheel drive needed when wet). Another road heads west to Blue Creek Village on the Mexican border (see below).

Lamanai

Near **Indian Church**, one of Belize's largest archaeological sites, **Lamanai** is on the west side of New River Lagoon, 22 miles by river south of Orange Walk. Difficult to get to and hidden in the jungle, it is a perfect setting to hide the mysteries of the Maya and definitely worth a visit. While the earliest buildings were erected about 700 BC, culminating in the completion of the 112-ft major temple, N10-43, about 100 BC (the tallest known preclassic, Maya structure), there is evidence the site was occupied as long ago as 1500 BC. As a Maya site, it is believed to have the longest history of continuous occupation and, with the Spanish and British sites mentioned below and the present-day refugee village nearby, Lamanai's history is impressive. The Maya site has been partially cleared, but covers a large area so a guide is recommended. The views from temple N10-43, dedicated to Chac, are superb; look for the Yin-Yang-like symbol below the throne on one of the other main temples, which also has a 12-ft tall mask overlooking its plaza. Visitors can wander freely along narrow trails and climb the stairways.

Colour map 6, grid A1

At nearby Indian Church a Spanish mission was built over one of the Maya temples in 1580, and the British established a sugar mill here last century. Remains of both buildings can still be seen. Note the huge flywheel engulfed by a strangler fig. The archaeological reserve is jungle again and howler monkeys are visible in the trees. There are many birds and the best way to see them is to reach Lamanai by boat, easily arranged in Orange Walk. The earlier you go the better, but the trips from Orange Walk all leave at pretty standard times. The mosquitoes are vicious in the wet season (wear trousers, take repellent). The community phone for information on Indian Church, including buses, is T320-4015.

At Indian Church AL *Lamanai Outpost Lodge*, T/F223-3578, www.lamanai.com Run by the incredibly friendly Colin and Ellen Howells, this beautiful lodge is a short walk from Lamanai ruins, overlooking New River Lagoon, package deals available, day tours, thatched wooden cabins with bath and fan, hot water, electricity, restaurant, still expanding. A resident archaeologist and a naturalist run field study courses here. Nazario Ku, the site caretaker, permits camping or hammocks at his house, opposite path to Lamanai ruins, good value for backpackers.

Sleeping

Boats Herminio and Antonio Novelo of *Jungle River Tours* run boat trips from Orange Walk, T322-2293, F322-2201, PO Box 95, 20 Lovers Lane, 5 passengers per boat, US$55 per person including lunch, 1½-2 hrs to Lamanai. The brothers are excellent and knowledgeable tour guides, constantly recommended. For transport to Lamanai, see Orange Walk, Buses.

Transport

West of San Felipe is Blue Creek (10 miles), largest of the Mennonite settlements. Many of the inhabitants of these close-knit villages arrived in 1959, members of a Canadian colony which had migrated to Chihuahua, Mexico, to escape encroaching modernity. They preserve their Low German dialect, are exempt from military service, and their industry now supplies the country with most of its poultry, eggs, vegetables and furniture. Some settlements, such as Neustadt in the west, have been abandoned because of threats by drug smugglers in the early 1990s. In 1998 Belize and Mexico signed an agreement to build an international bridge from Blue Creek across the river to La Unión, together with a river port close to the bridge. It is not known when work will start; at present there is a canoe-service for foot passengers across the Blue Creek.

Blue Creek
Colour map 6, grid A1

A vast area to the south along the **Río Bravo** has been set aside as a conservation area (see page 706). Within this, there is a study and accommodation centre near the Maya site of **Las Milpas**: **AL** *La Milpa Field Station*, four double cabañas, spacious, comfortable, with a thatched roof overhanging a large wooden deck, or a dormitory sleeping up to 30. There is also the *Hill Bank Field Station*, on the banks of the New River Lagoon, with a dormitory also sleeping up to 30. Both places make a good base for exploring trails in the region and bird-watching. For more information call T323-0011, or contact the Programme for Belize in Belize City (T227-5616, www.pfbelize.org). To reach La Milpa, go six miles west from Blue Creek to Tres Leguas, then follow the signs south towards the Río Bravo Escarpment. The reserve is privately owned and you will need proof of booking to pass the various checkpoints. The site of Las Milpas is at present being excavated by a team from the University of Texas and Boston University, USA.

A good road can be followed 35 miles south to **Gallon Jug**, where a jungle tourism lodge has been built in the **Chan Chich** Maya ruin: **LL** *Chan Chich*, PO Box 37, Belize City, T/F223-4419 or in the USA and Canada 1-800-343-8009, www.chanchich.com With or without meals, recommended. The journey to Chan Chich passes through the Río Bravo Conservation Area, is rarely travelled and offers some of the best chances to see wildlife. Chan Chich is believed to have the highest number of jaguar sightings in Belize, and is also a bird-watchers' paradise. Another road has recently been cut south through Tambos to the main road between Belmopan and San Ignacio, but travel in this region is strictly a dry-weather affair. Phone before setting out for Chan Chich for reservations and information on the roads. Flights to Chan Chich from Belize City, 0900 Mon, Wed and Fri, US$98 return, can also be chartered from elsewhere.

Northeast of Orange Walk

From Orange Walk a complex network of roads and tracks converge on **San Estevan** and Progresso to the north. The Maya ruins near San Estevan have reportedly been 'flattened' to a large extent and are not very impressive. Ten miles from San Estevan is a road junction: straight on is **Progresso**, a village picturesquely located on the lagoon of the same name. The right turn, signposted, runs off to the Mennonite village of Little Belize and continues (in poor condition) to **Chunox**, a village with many Maya houses of pole construction. In the dry season it is possible to drive from Chunox to the Maya site of Cerros (see below).

Sarteneja Leaving the Northern Highway a road heads east to Sarteneja, a small fishing and former boat-building settlement founded by Yucatán refugees in 19th century. The main catch is lobster and conch. On Easter Sunday there is a popular regatta, with all types of boat racing, dancing and music. There are remains of an extensive Maya city scattered throughout the village, and recent discoveries have been made and are currently being explored to the south around the area of Shipstern Lagoon.

Sleeping Recommended accommodation at *Fernando's Guest House*, on seafront near centre, T423-2085; *Sayab Cabañas*, by water tower, with thatched cabins and private bath; **D** *Diani's*, on the seashore, restaurant, seems to be undergoing eternal refurbishment. Houses can be rented for longer stays.

Transport Sarteneja is 40 miles from Orange Walk; 1-hr drive, only impassable in the very wet. It can be reached by **boat** from Corozal in 30 mins, but only private charters, so very expensive (compared with 3 hrs by road). Boats will soon be available to northern Ambergris Caye and the **Bacalar Chico Nature Reserve**. Enquire at your hotel for details. **Bus** from Belize City with *Venus*, 1200, and *Pérez*, 1300 (from the gas station on North Front St). Buses also leave from Corozal (1400), passing through Orange Walk (1530). No buses Sun.

Three miles before Sarteneja is the visitors' centre for the reserve, which covers 22,000 acres of this northeastern tip of Belize. Hardwood forests, saline lagoon systems and wide belts of savannah shelter a wide range of mammals (most likely coatis and foxes, but all the fauna found elsewhere in Belize, except monkeys), reptiles and 200 species of bird. Also, there are mounds of Maya houses and fields everywhere. The remotest forest, south of the lagoon, is not accessible to short-term visitors. There is a botanical trail leading into the forest with trees labelled with Latin and local Yucatec Maya names; a booklet is available. At the visitors' centre is the **Butterfly Breeding Centre**. ■ *0900-1200, 1300-1600 except Christmas and Easter, US$5 including excellent guided tour*. Mosquito repellent is essential. There is dormitory accommodation at the visitors' centre, rather poor, US$10 per person. A day trip by private car is possible from Sarteneja or Orange Walk.

Shipstern Nature Reserve

Choose a sunny day for a visit if possible; on dull days the butterflies hide themselves in the foliage

Corozal

The Northern Highway continues to Corozal (96 miles from Belize City), formerly the centre of the sugar industry, now with a special zone for the clothing industry and garment exports. Much of the old town was destroyed by Hurricane Janet in 1955 and it is now a mixture of modern concrete commercial buildings and Caribbean clapboard seafront houses on stilts. Like Orange Walk it is economically depressed, and while both towns once shared an economic dependence on marijuana, Corozal is much the safer place. It is open to the sea with a pleasant waterfront where the market is held. There is no beach but you can swim in the sea and lie on the grass. You can check out the local website at www.corozal.com

Colour map 5, grid B3
Population: 7,888

Belize

Between Orange Walk and Corozal, in San José and San Pablo, is the archaeological site of **Nohmul**, a ceremonial centre whose main acropolis dominates the surrounding cane fields (the name means 'Great Mound'). Permission to visit the site must be obtained from Sr Estevan Itzab, whose house is opposite the water tower.

Excursions

From Corozal, a road leads 7 miles northeast to **Consejo**, a quiet, seaside fishing village on Chetumal Bay. No public transport, taxi about US$10.

A-C *Tony's*, South End, T422-2055, F422-2829, www.tonysinn.com With a/c, clean, comfortable units in landscaped grounds, recommended, but restaurant overpriced. **B** *Hok'Ol K'in Guest House*, 4th Av and 4th St South, T422-3329, F422-3569, www.corozal.net Immaculate rooms. Runs tours to Cerros. **C** *Maya*, South End, T422-2082, F422-2827 www.corozal.com/tourism/hotelmaya Hot water, quieter than *Nestor's*, food good, meal US$5, the owners are very helpful and know everything about the area, *Tropic Air* agents for flights to San Pedro, Ambergris Caye. Ask the bus driver to drop you off. **C** *Nestor's*, 123, 5th Av South, T422-2354, nestors@btl.net With bath and fan, OK, *refrescos* available, good food, lively bar downstairs. **D** *Caribbean Village Resort*, South End, PO Box 55, T422-2045, F422-3414. Hot water, US$5 camping, US$12 trailer park, recommended, restaurant. **D** *Central Guest House*, 22 6th Av, T422-2358, F422-3335, www.corozal.com/tourism/cgh Basic, clean rooms, shared area with TV, lots of information about Belize and the area. Close to the bus terminal. Next door to *Nestor's*, **E** *Papa's Guest House*, basic but cheap. **E** *Capri*, 14 4th Av, on the seafront, T422-2042. A bit run down but OK for a night or 2, with or without private bath, towels and soap provided but no mirror, bar and dance hall downstairs. Pleasant, clean guesthouse, **E**, to the north of town, on east side of main street, no name but look for sign which reads: 'Rrooms/comfortable and clean', next to used car dealer, very friendly, fan, good value.

Sleeping

Camping *Caribbean Motel and Trailer Park*, see above, camping possible but not very safe (US$4 per person), shaded sites, restaurant.

Nestors, *Tony's* and *Maya* all have hotel restaurants. The best restaurant is *Café Kela*, in a beach-front palapa on the shore. Intimate setting, fine food, mid-price and good value for money, just sit back and enjoy. *Club Campesino*, decent bar, good fried chicken after 1800.

Eating

Corozal Garden on 4th Av, one block south, has good, quick local food. *Gongora's Pastry* southwest corner of main square, hot pizza pieces US$1-1.50, cakes and drinks. *Skytop*, 5th Av South, friendly, good food, excellent breakfast, recommended, good view from roof. Many Chinese restaurants in town including Border, 6th Av South, friendly Chinese, good food, cheap. *Newtown Chinese*, 7th Av, just north of the gas station on the other side of the main road, large portions, good quality, from US$3, slow service. *Rexo*, North 5th St.

Transport **Air** *Maya Island Air*, 3 flights daily from Belize City via Caye Caulker and San Pedro (Ambergris Caye); *Tropic Air* daily from San Pedro. Airstrip 3m south, taxi US$1.50. **Buses** There are 15 buses a day from Belize City by *Venus*, Magazine Rd, and *Batty* bus, 54 East Collet Canal, normal buses 3 hrs, US$4, express buses 2½-3 hrs, US$5. Both continue to Chetumal where they terminate at the market, 1 km from the Mexican bus terminal, but they pass the terminal; ask the driver to let you off there; because of the frequency, there is no need to take a *colectivo* to the Mexican border unless travelling at unusual hours (US$2.50). The increased frequency of buses to Chetumal and the number of money changers cater for Belizeans shopping cheaply in Mexico, very popular, book early. For those coming from Mexico who are more interested in Tikal than Belize, it is possible to make the journey border to border in a day, with a change of bus, to *Novelo's*, in Belize City (but you will be missing out a lot of interesting places). Timetables change frequently, so check at the time of travel. There are also tourist minibuses which avoid Belize City.

Directory **Banks** *Atlantic Bank* (charges US$2.50 for Visa cash advances), *Bank of Nova Scotia*, and *Belize Bank* (does not accept Mexican pesos, charges US$7.50 for Visa cash advances), open same hrs as Belize City. For exchange also ask at the bus station (see page 715).

Six miles northeast of Corozal, to the right of the road to Chetumal, is **Four Mile Lagoon**, about quarter of a mile off the road (buses will drop you there). Clean swimming, better than Corozal bay, some food and drinks available; it is often crowded at weekends.

Cerros & Santa Rita Across the bay to the south of Corozal stand the mounds of **Cerros**, once an active Maya trading port whose central area was reached by canal. Some of the site is flooded but one pyramid, 69-ft high with stucco masks on its walls, has been partially excavated. Boat from Corozal, walk around bay (boat needed to cross mouth of the New River) or dry-season vehicular trail from Progresso and Chunox (see above). Ask in *Hotel Maya* for information about local guides and visits. More easily accessible are the ruins of **Santa Rita**, only a mile out on the Northern Highway, opposite the Coca Cola plant; once a powerful and cosmopolitan city, and still occupied when the Spaniards arrived in Belize, the site's post-classic murals and buildings have long been destroyed; only 50-ft tall Structure Seven remains standing. ■ US$1.

Border with Mexico Eight miles north beyond Corozal is the Mexican border at **Santa Elena**, where a bridge across the Río Hondo connects with Chetumal, 7 miles into Mexico. The border can be very busy, and therefore slow, especially at holiday times when chartered coaches bring shoppers to Mexico.

Immigration **Belizean immigration** Border crossing formalities are relatively relaxed. The border is open 24 hours a day. Exit tax including PACT (see page 707) US$10.
Crossing by private vehicle If driving to Belize, third party insurance is obligatory. It can be purchased from the building opposite the immigration post.
Mexican Immigration Mexican tourist cards for 30 days are available at the border. To extend the tourist card beyond 30 days, go to immigration in Cancún. The Mexican Embassy is in Belize City if you need a visa.

Transport The Northern Highway is in good condition. Driving time to the capital 3 hrs. There are frequent buses from the border and Corozal to Belize City, see under Corozal. All northbound buses from Belize City go to Chetumal: *Batty* in morning, *Venus* in the afternoon up to 1900. Contact Henry Menzies in Corozal, T422-3415, who runs taxis into Chetumal for about US$25, quick and efficient way to get through to the border. If leaving Mexico, he will collect you in Chetumal.

Directory Exchange: Money changers are on the Belize side of the border. You can buy pesos at good rates with US and Belizean currency. Rates for Belizean dollars in Mexico will be lower. Coming from Mexico, it is best to get rid of pesos at the border. Compare rates at the small bank near the frontier with the street changers on the Belizean side. The shops by the border will also change money.

Western Belize

Impressive sights – man-made and natural – line the route from Belize City to the Guatemalan border, starting with Belize Zoo – a pleasant break from the norm. Monkey Bay Wildlife Sanctuary and Guanacaste National Park are both worth a visit. From the bustling town of San Ignacio, there are canoe trips down the Macal River and dramatic cave systems, journeys into the impressive limestone scenery of Mountain Pine Ridge, and the spectacular Maya ruins of Caracol, Xunantunich and Cahal Pech to explore. Day-trippers can also cross the border for a quick visit to Tikal in Guatemala.

Belize City to San Ignacio

The Western Highway leaves Belize City past the cemetery, where burial vaults stand elevated above the boggy ground, running through palmetto scrub and savannah landscapes created by 19th-century timber cutting. At Mile 16 is **Hattieville**, originally a temporary settlement for the homeless after Hurricane Hattie in 1961. It has become a permanent town of some 2,500 people and the new Belize prison with its many juvenile offenders is just a few miles out of town on an all-weather road that runs north to **Burrell Boom** with access to the Community Baboon Sanctuary (see page 726) and the Northern Highway, a convenient bypass for motorists wishing to avoid Belize City. The highway roughly parallels the Sibun River, once a major trading artery where mahogany logs were floated down to the coast in the rainy season; the placename 'Boom' recalls spots where chains were stretched across rivers to catch logs being floated downstream.

The small but excellent **Belize Zoo** is at Mile 28½ , watch out for the sign, or tell the **Belize Zoo** driver where you're going. It is a wonderful collection of local species (originally gathered for a wildlife film), lovingly cared for and displayed in wire-mesh enclosures amid native trees and shady vegetation, including jaguar and smaller cats, pacas (called 'gibnuts' in Belize), snakes, monkeys, parrots, crocodile, tapir ('mountain cow'), peccary ('wari') and much more. Highly recommended, even for those who hate zoos. Get there early to miss the coach party arrivals. Tours by enthusiastic guides, t-shirts and postcards sold for fundraising. ■ *Open daily, 0900-1700, US$7.50, www.belizezoo.org Getting there: take any bus from Belize City along the Western Highway (1 hr).*

Sleeping and eating L *Jaguar Paw Jungle Lodge*, on curve of Caves Branch River on road south at Mile 31, enquiries T223-5395, with 3 meals. Possible basic dorm-style lodging at the *Tropical Education Centre* at Belize Zoo, ask at the reception, take a torch. *Cheers*, 'with a tropical twist', serves good burgers and local dishes, has a nice orchid collection.

At Mile 31½, the Wildlife Sanctuary protects 1,070 acres of tropical forest and savannah between the highway and the Sibun River (great swimming and canoeing). Birds are abundant and there is a good chance of seeing mammals. Guided tours of the trails are available. Dormitory accommodation US$7.50 per person, or you can camp on **Monkey Bay Wildlife Sanctuary**

Belize

wooden platform with thatched roof for US$5, swim in the river, showers available, take meals with family for US$4 (it is planned to provide cooking facilites in the future). Write to the manager, PO Box 187, Mile 31 Western Highway, Belmopan, T820-3032, F822-3661, www.watershedbelize.org Nearby at Mile 33 is *JB's* bar and restaurant, a popular stopping place with good food and reasonable prices.

Guanacaste National Park

Forty-seven miles from Belize City, a minor road runs 2 miles north to **AL** *Banana Bank Ranch*, T/F820-2020, PO Box 48, Belmopan, bbl@pobox.com Resort accommodation, with meals, horse-riding, birding, river trips, etc. A mile further on is the highway junction for Belmopan and Dangriga. At the confluence of the Belize River and Roaring Creek is the 50-acre **Guanacaste National Park**, protecting a parcel of 'neotropical rainforest' and a huge 100-year-old *guanacaste* (tubroos) tree, which shelters a wide collection of epiphytes including orchids. Many mammals (jaguarundi, kinkajou, agouti, etc) and up to 100 species of bird may be seen from the 3 miles of nature trails cut along the river. This is a particularly attractive swimming and picnicking spot at which to stop or break the journey if travelling on to Guatemala. It has a visitors' centre, where luggage can be left. ■ *US$2.50. Take an early morning bus from Belize City, see the park in a couple of hours, then pick up a bus going to San Ignacio or Dangriga.*

Roaring Creek
Population: 952

Soon after the junction to Belmopan is Roaring Creek, once a thriving town but now rather overshadowed by the barely illuminated capital nearby. At Teakettle, turn south along a dirt road for 5 miles to Pook's Hill Reserve and **AL** *Pook's Hill Lodge*, PO Box 14, Belmopan, T820-2017, F822-3361, a 300-acre private nature reserve on Roaring Creek, run by Ray and Vicki Snaddon, six cabañas, horses, rafting and bird-watching. Further along the highway at mile 56 is **AL** *Warrie Head Lodge*, PO Box 244, Belize City, T227-7185, F227-5213, www.warriehead.com A working farm offering accommodation, they cater mainly for groups but it is well kept, homey and a lovely spot for river swimming.

Baking Pot, Georgeville & Spanish lookout
Ask in San Ignacio if you are interested in visiting this area

At Mile 60 is **A** *Caesar's Place*, PO Box 48, San Ignacio, T824-2341, under same ownership as *Black Rock* – see page 738 – four rooms with bath, clean riverside campground with security, four full hookups for RVs, with showers and bathroom facilities, restaurant and bar, gift shop, swimming, musicians welcome to play with 'in-house' group. The important but unimpressive **Floral Park** archaeological site is just beyond the bridge over Barton Creek (Mile 64). Two miles further is **Georgeville**, from where a gravel road runs south into the **Mountain Pine Ridge Forest Reserve** (see below). The highway passes the turn-off at Norland for Spanish Lookout, a Mennonite settlement area 6 miles north (*B & F Restaurant*, Centre Road, by Farmers' Trading Centre, clean, excellent value). The Central Farm Agricultural College, the village of Esperanza and other small settlements along the way keep the road interesting until it reaches Santa Elena. Formerly only linked by the substantial Hawkesworth suspension bridge to its twin town of San Ignacio, it now has a small, one-lane 'temporary bridge' you must take to cross the river to San Ignacio. Watch for the 'diversion' sign, turn right in front of the Social Security building, then left at the end of the block. The next right turn leads you to the bridge. The Hawkesworth Bridge is now only used to route traffic back across from San Ignacio.

San Ignacio

Colour map: 6, grid A1
Population: approx 13,260 including Santa Elena

All shops and businesses close 1700-1900

Sixty-eight miles from Belize City and 10 miles from the border, San Ignacio (locally called **Cayo**) is the capital of Cayo District and western Belize's largest town, an agricultural centre serving the citrus, cattle and peanut farms of the area, and a good base for excursions into the Mountain Pine Ridge and Western Belize. It stands amid attractive wooded hills at 200-500 ft, with a good climate, and is a nice town to rest in if coming from Guatemala. The town is on the eastern branch of the Old, or Belize River, known as the Macal. The 185-mile river journey down to Belize City has become internationally famous as the route for the annual 'Ruta Maya Belize River Challenge' a gruelling three-day canoe race held the weekend of Baron Bliss Day, March 9.

There are several options for accommodation around San Ignacio. In the centre of town, a selection of hotels spans all levels. Out of town, resorts and lodges offer relaxing hideaways often in the midst of the jungle. Although these tend to be for the higher price bracket, there are a few good exceptions.

In centre of town A *Martha's Guest House*, 10 West St, T804-2276. Comfortable rooms with balcony, lounge area, good restaurant, friendly, clean, kitchen facilities, the family also runs *August Laundromat*. **B** *Plaza*, 4a Burns Av, T824-3332. A/c, cheaper without, with bath, parking. **C-D** *Venus*, 29 Burns Av, T824-3203, daniels@btl.net With or without bath, fan, clean, hot water, free coffee and fruit, thin walls, noisy, Sat market and bus station behind hotel. **D** *New Belmoral*, 17 Burns Av, T824-2024, belmoral@btl.net With shower, cable TV, hot water, fan or a/c, a bit noisy (clean and friendly). **D** *Tropicool*, Burns Av, T824-3052. Shared bath, fan, clean. **D** *Princesa*, Burns Av and King St. With bath, clean, helpful, secure, manager Matthew Galvez. **E** *Central*, 24 Burns Av, T824-2253. Clean, secure, fans, shared hot showers, book exchange, friendly, veranda with hammocks, uncomfortable beds but recommended, no restaurant but eat at *Eva's Bar* next door. **E** *Hi-Et*, 12 West St, T824-2828. Noisy, fans, low partition walls, nice balcony, friendly, helpful, family-run, clothes washing permitted, no meals, use of kitchen possible. **F** *Mrs Espat's*, up the hill from *Hi-Et*, rooms next door to small shop and house.

At the southern end of town, up the hill, as you turn left on the San Ignacio side of the suspension bridge, is **AL-B** *San Ignacio*, 18 Buena Vista Rd, T824-2034, F824-2134, www.sanignaciobelize.com On road to Benque Viejo, with bath, a/c or fan, hot water, clean, helpful staff, swimming pool, excellent restaurant. Highly recommended. **D** *Piache*, 18 Buena Vista Rd, around the bend in the road from the *San Ignacio*, PO Box 54, T824-2032 With or without bath, cold water, basic, overpriced, bar, also tour agent.

Sleeping
■ *on map*
Price codes: see inside front cover

Some hotels in town and on Cahal Pech Hill may be noisy at weekends from loud music, and during the day from traffic and buses

Belize

San Ignacio

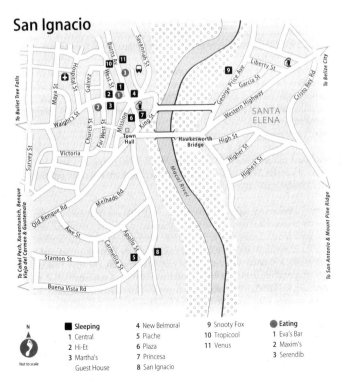

	Sleeping ■	4 New Belmoral	9 Snooty Fox	● Eating
	1 Central	5 Piache	10 Tropicool	1 Eva's Bar
	2 Hi-Et	6 Plaza	11 Venus	2 Maxim's
	3 Martha's Guest House	7 Princesa		3 Serendib
		8 San Ignacio		

N — Not to scale

Close to Cahal Pech are **B** *Cahal Pech Village*, T824-3740, daniels@btl.net Thatched cabins or a/c rooms, restaurant, bar, meeting facilities. **B** *Chiclero Camp*, T824-4119. Small rustic cabins in lush jungle setting, good restaurant, inconsistent management, call first. **B** *Rose's Guesthouse*, T824-2282, rosesguesthouse@btl.net 5 rooms in a private house, Rose is a charming hostess, lovely garden restaurant, closest to entrance Cahal Pech ruins.

In Santa Elena C *Aguada Hotel*, T824-3609, aguada@btl.net Full-service hotel, 12 rooms, private baths, a/c US$5 more, fresh water pond and heart-shaped swimming pool, quiet part of town, excellent restaurant and bar. **D** *Snooty Fox*, 64 George Price Av, overlooking Macal River. Rooms and apartments, some with bath, others shared bath, good-value canoe rental.

Camping *Mida's*, ½ mile from town on Branchmouth Rd near river, go down Burns Av, turn right down unpaved road after wooden church, after 200 yd turn left, campground is 300 yd on right, US$15 per car and 2 people including electricity, cabins available at US$20, hot showers, electricity, water, restaurant, very helpful, good value, also organize trips to Tikal. ½ mile further is *Cosmos* camping, US$2.50 per person for tents, washing and cooking facilities, cabins **E**, run by friendly Belizean family, good breakfasts, canoe and bikes for hire, good. West of San Ignacio at Mile 68¼, *Inglewood Camping Grounds*, T824-3555. *Palapas*, tent camping, RV hookups, hot and cold showers, maintained grounds, some highway noise.

Eating
● *on map*

The *Blue Angel* on Burns Av is good fun and popular with the younger crowd, live bands, dancing, small admission charge. *Erva's*, 6 Far West St, T824-2556, vegetarian available, reasonable prices. *Eva's Bar*, 22 Burns Av, T804-2267. Good diner-style restaurant, local dishes, helpful with good local information, bike rental, internet facilities, tours. *Martha's Kitchen*, below *Martha's Guest House*. Very good breakfasts and Belizean dishes, good information. *Maxim's*, Bullet Tree Rd and Far West St. Chinese, good service, cheap, very good food, popular with locals, noisy TV at the bar. *Running W*, in the *San Ignacio Hotel*, is one of the best restaurants in town. *Serendib*, 27 Burns Av. Good food and good value, Sri Lankan owners, good, tasty Indian-style food, open 1030-1500, 1830-1100, closed Sun. *The Sand Castle*, take a right turn off King St to river. The open-air restaurant is at the back of the building, music, good food and prices. *Cafe Sol*, between Burns Av and West St, serves delicious coffee and pastries, with vegetarian, chicken and seafood dishes for lunch and dinner. Also has bookstore and giftshop.

On a hill, with TV station, beside the road to Benque Viejo before the edge of town is *Cahal Pech* tavern, serving cheap drinks and meals, with music and dancing at weekends, *the* place to be, live bands are broadcast on TV and radio all over Belize, good views. On a hill across the track from the tavern is Cahal Pech archaeological site (see above). *Sanny's Grill*, several blocks down the hill off the Western Highway past the Texaco station, serves the 'world's best conch ceviche', full dinner menu, charming setting.

Shopping

Black Rock Gift Shop, near *Eva's*, linked to *Black Rock Lodge*, luggage can be left here if canoeing from Black Rock to San Ignacio, large selection of arts and crafts, workshop. Fruit and vegetable market every Sat morning.

Transport

Buses To **Belize City**: *Batty* bus departs 1300, 1400, 1500 and 1600; early-morning buses from the border stop at the bridge in front of the police station and from the bus terminal at 0500, 0600 and 0700. Later morning trips go from Benque Viejo at parking area behind Burns Av, US$2.50, 3½ hrs. A 1000 or 1100 bus will connect with the 1500 bus to Chetumal. Novelo, starts at 0400 and runs on the hr until about 1200. To **Belmopan**, 1 hr, US$1. **Taxi**: to Guatemalan border, about US$5 (*colectivo* US$2.50, bus US$0.75), to Xunantunich US$20, to Belize City US$75, to Tikal US$100. **Minibuses**: also run to Tikal, US$20 per person return, making a day trip possible. Organized tours cost about US$70.

Directory

Banks *Belize Bank* offers full service, TCs, Visa and MasterCard cash advances. *Atlantic Bank*, Burns Av, also does cash advances. Both charge US$5 commission for cash advances. *Eva's Bar* changes TCs at a very good rates. Changers in the town square give better rates of exchange for dollars cash and TCs than you can get at the border with Guatemala. The best place to change dollars into quetzales is in

Guatemala. **Communications** Internet: *Eva's Bar*, US$2.50 for 30 mins. **Post office**: above the police station, reliable parcel service. **Telephone**: *BTL* office at further end of Burns Av, opposite *Venus Hotel*, long-distance calls and fax service. **Tour operators** A recommended guide is *Ramón Silva* from *International Archaeological Tours* (*IAT*), West St, next to *Martha's Guest House*, T804-3991, F804-3991, iatours@btl.net, who arrange tours throughout Belize and in Petén. *IAT* are very helpful with advice about the area and, not surprisingly, also know absolutely everything about travel in the area and throughout Belize and northern Guatemala. Also recommended is *David's Adventure Tours*, near main bus stop, T804-3674, for visits to Barton's Creek Cave or guided canoe trips along the Macal River. For **horse-riding** try *Easy Rider*, Bullet Tree Rd, T804-3310. Full-day tours for US$40 including lunch. *Eva's Bar*, T804-2267, run by Bob from the UK, is the best starting point for information on any of the trips although your hotel will also have details and suggestions. Canoe trips with bird and wildlife watching (US$12.50 per person, 2-3 people), visiting medicinal plant research farm (US$5 extra), small rapids, etc, 0830-1600, good value; or jungle river trips, US$30 for 2 in a canoe, all-day tour. Highly recommended. Bob is very helpful and will organize tours for you but you may end up with an indifferent guide, make sure you tell him exactly what you want. Trips to Caracol start at around US$40 per person including Río Frío Cave, Río On pools and García sisters' gift shop, 12 hrs; cheaper to hire a car if with a group, difficult to get lost.

A short walk from San Ignacio (800 m from *Hotel San Ignacio*) is **Cahal Pech**, an impressive Maya site and nature reserve on a wooded hill overlooking the town, with a visitor centre and museum. ■ *Open daily, US$2.50.* The man who sells tickets will lend you a guidebook written by some of the archaeologists who worked on the site, but it must be returned.

Excursions from San Ignacio

Four miles west of San Ignacio on a good road is **Bullet Tree Falls**, a pleasant cascade amid relaxing surroundings on the western branch of the Belize River, here in its upper course known as the Mopan River.

Twelve miles north of San Ignacio, near Bullet Tree Falls, is **El Pilar Archaeological Reserve for Maya Flora and Fauna**, an archaeological site which straddles the border with Guatemala. Although it is a large site (about 94 acres), much of it has been left intentionally uncleared so that selected architectural features are exposed within the rainforest. The preserved rainforest here is home to hundreds of species of birds and animals. There are five trails – three archaeological, two nature – the longest of which is a mile and a half long. There are more than a dozen pyramids and 25 identified plazas. Unusually for Maya cities in this region, there is an abundance of water (streams and falls). Take the Bullet Tree Road north of San Ignacio, cross the Mopan River Bridge and follow the signs to El Pilar. The reserve is 7 miles from Bullet Tree on an all-weather limestone road. It can be reached by vehicle, horse or mountain bike (hiking is only recommended for the experienced; carry lots of water). The caretakers, who live at the south end of the site in a modern green-roofed house, are happy to show visitors around. The Cayo Tour Guides Association works in association with the Belize River Archaeological Settlement Survey (BRASS) and can take visitors. See also *Trails of El Pilar: A Guide to the El Pilar Archaeological Reserve for Maya Flora and Fauna* (published 1996).

The renowned Rainforest Medicine Trail in Ix Chel closed recently but Dr Arvigo sells selections of herbs (the jungle salve, US$5, has been found effective against mosquito bites) and a book on medicinal plants used by the Maya (US$8, US$2 postage and packing, from General Delivery, San Ignacio, Cayo District). The herbs are also sold in most local gift shops.

Local tour operators (see below) generally offer similar tours at similar prices. Canoe trips up the **Macal River** are well worthwhile. They take about three hours upstream, 1½ hrs on return, guides point out iguanas in the trees and bats asleep on the rock walls. Hiring a canoe to go upstream without a guide is not recommended unless you are highly proficient as there are Class II rapids one hour from San Ignacio. Another trip is to **Barton Creek Cave**, a 1½-hour drive followed by a 3½-hour canoe trip in the cave. The cave vault system is vast, the rock formations are beautiful, the silence is eerily comforting and all can be explored for a considerable distance by canoe (US$20 per person minimum three people).

Belize

Trips to the nearby ruins of **Xunantunich** (see below) are very easy by bus, with regular traffic going to the Guatemalan border. Tours of **Mountain Pine Ridge** are available (see below), but shop around carefully – if you decide to go with a taxi you probably won't get far in the wet season. Trips to **Caracol** are best arranged from San Ignacio, and if you only want to visit Tikal in Guatemala, you can arrange a day trip which will maximize your time spent at the ruins.

Sleeping outside San Ignacio In the area surrounding San Ignacio there are many jungle hideaways. Ranging from secluded and exclusive cottages to full activity resorts, and covering a wide range of budgets, these places are normally an adventure on their own. But before going, make sure you know what costs are included; food is often extra.

West of San Ignacio: at Mile 68, **AL** *Windy Hill Cottages*, on Graceland Ranch 2 miles west off highway, T804-2017, F804-3080, www.windyhillresort.com 14 cottage units, all with bath, dining room, small pool, nature trails, horse-riding and river trips can be arranged, expensive. Also try *Richie's Place* restaurant across the street. Also across the street, **A** *Log Cab-Inns*, T804-3367, logcabins@btl.net Mahogany log cabins with private bath and fans, pool, restaurant. Down a signed track on the Benque road, around Mile 70 is **C-D** *Clarissa's Falls*, on Mopan River. Owned by Chena Galvez, thatched cottages on riverbank by a set of rapids, also bunkhouse with hammocks or beds, US$7.50 per person, camping space and hookups for RVs, rafting, kayaking and tubing available, wonderful food in the restaurants. **AL-A** *Nabitunich Cottages* (Rudi and Margaret Juan), turn off the Benque road 1½ miles beyond Chial, T803-2309, F803-2096, rudyjuan@btl.net, or c/o Benque Viejo post office. Offers spectacular views of Xunantunich and another, unexcavated Maya ruin, jungle trails, excellent bird-watching, with fields going down to beautiful Mopan River, working farm, own transport recommended, very homely if slightly basic, restaurant. You can camp here, US$6 per person.

South of San Ignacio Halfway between Clarissa Falls turn-off and Nabitunich is Chial Rd, gateway to adventure. A half-mile down the road is a sharp right turn that takes you through **Negroman**, the modern site of the ancient Maya city of **Tipu** which has the remains of a Spanish Mission from the 1500s. Across the river from here is *Guacamallo Camp* (home of David Simpson of *David's Adventure Tours*, see page 737), rustic jungle camping and starting point for his canoe trips on the Macal River. 2 miles further up, also across the river, is **L** *Ek Tun*, T809-3002, in USA 303-442-6150, www.ektunbelize.com, 500-acre private jungle retreat on the Macal River with access by boat only, with 2 very private deluxe thatched guest cottages, excellent food, spectacular garden setting, secluded sandy river beaches, bird-watching, caving, mineral pool for swimming, miles of hiking trails, canoeing and tubing down the river. Highlights cave tours, adventure and a special Tikal Extension. Advance reservations only, no drop-ins. Further along at the end of the road, find **AL-B** *Black Rock Lodge*, T804-2341, www.blackrocklodge.com Road sometimes requires 4-WD depending on weather, own transportation recommended. Another spectacular setting, though clearing and barbed wire fences detract, 6 cabañas, solar-powered electricity and hot water, hiking, riding, canoeing, bird-watching, excursions, breakfast US$7, lunch US$8, dinner US$15. Just past the Negroman turn on the Chial Rd, **AL** *Green Heaven Lodge*, T820-4034, www.ghlodgebelize.com 4 cabins, excellent swimming pool, French restaurant and bar, close alternative to dining at the area resorts. Several miles further on, after the turn to Ix Chel Farm, is the fork to **LL** *The Lodge at Chaa Creek*, on the Macal River, T824-2037, F824-2501, www.chaacreek.com, or hotel office at 56 Burns Av, San Ignacio. In 20 years of operation it has evolved from jungle cottages at the riverside on a working farm, to upscale accommodation, amenities and tours, with a spa, conference centre, morpho butterfly breeding centre, natural history movement and an adventure centre. Strong supporters of environmental groups and projects, and sponsors of the La Ruta Maya River Challenge. *Chaa Creek Inland Expeditions* offers tours and excursions to all local attractions. The Macal River Camp, recently upgraded from tents on platforms to a more solid construction, offers less expensive accommodations in more rustic surroundings at US$100 double, including meals. To reach **L** *duPlooys'*, continue past by the Chaa Creek road, then follow (including one steep hill) to its end above the Macal River, T804-3101, F804-3301, www.duplooys.com Several choices of accommodation and packages are available, enjoy their 'Hangover Bar' with cool drinks on the deck overlooking trees and river. New **Belize Botanic Gardens**, on 50 acres of rolling hills, is next to lodge with hundreds of orchids, dozens of named tree species, ponds and lots of birds. Run by the du Plooy family, good food. Recommended.

North of San Ignacio is C *Parrot Nest*, T820-4058, www.parrot-nest.com Near village of Bullet Tree Falls, 3 miles from San Ignacio (taxi US$5), small but comfortable tree houses in beautiful grounds by the river, breakfast and dinner included, canoeing, bird-watching, horse-riding available. Also near Bullet Tree Falls is a restaurant, *Terry's*, limited menu but good food.

East of San Ignacio **AL-B** *Maya Mountain Lodge* (Bart and Suzi Mickler), ¾ mile from San Ignacio at 9 Cristo Rey Rd, Santa Elena, PO Box 46, San Ignacio, T804-2164, F804-2029, www.mayamountain.com Welcoming, special weekly and monthly rates and for families, restaurant, excursions are more expensive than arranging one in town, 10% service charge, laundry, postal service, self-guided nature trail, swimming, hiking, riding, canoeing, fishing can be arranged. *Mountain Equestrian Trails*, Mile 8, Mountain Pine Ridge Rd (from Georgeville), Central Farm PO, Cayo District, T824-3310, F822-3361, reservations in USA T1-800-838-3913, www.metbelize.com Accommodation in 4 double cabañas with bath, no electricity, hot water, mosquito nets, good food in *cantina*, offers ½-day, full-day and 4-day adventure tours on horseback in Western Belize, 'Turf' and 'Turf 'n' Surf' packages, and other expeditions, excellent guides and staff, bird-watching tours in and around the reserve. *Chiclero Nature Trails*, tents under rainforest canopy, US$499 for 4 nights, including meals, trip to Caracol, bird-watching, caving, etc. Highly recommended. Owners Jim and Marguerite Bevis, in conjunction with neighbouring landowners, have set up a biosphere reserve, incorporating nearby Salvadorean refugees. **LL-AL** *Blancaneaux Lodge*, Mountain Pine Ridge Rd, Central Farm, PO Box B, Cayo District, T/F824-3878, www.blancaneauxlodge.com Once the mountain retreat of Francis Ford Coppola and his family, now villas and cabañas, full amenities, overlooking a stream, private air strip. **AL** *Five Sisters Lodge*, 2½ miles beyond *Blancaneaux Lodge*, T/F804-1005. Rustic cottages lit by oil lamps, great views, good-value restaurant, recommended. **AL** *Pine Ridge Lodge*, on road to Augustine, just past turning to Hidden Valley Falls, T606-4557, www.PineRidgeLodge.com Cabañas in the pinewoods, including breakfast.

Xunantunich

At Xunantunich ('Maiden of the Rock'), now freed from heavy bush, there are Classic Maya remains in beautiful surroundings. The heart of the city was three plazas aligned on a north-south axis, lined with many temples, the remains of a ball court, and surmounted by the Castillo. At 130 ft this was thought to be the highest man-made structure in Belize until recent measurement of the Sky Palace at Caracol. The impressive view takes in the jungle, the lowlands of Petén and the blue flanks of the Maya Mountains. Maya graffiti can still be seen on the wall of Structure A-16 – friezes on the Castillo, some restored in modern plaster, represent astronomical symbols. Extensive excavations took place in 1959-60 but only limited restoration work has been undertaken. ■ *0800-1700, US$2.50. A leaflet on the area is available from the Archaeological Dept for US$0.15. Helpful guides at the site.* Apart from a small refreshment stand, there are no facilities for visitors, but a new museum has been built, and a couple of stelae have been put on display in a covered area. Beware of robbery on the road up to the ruins, government employees accompany visitors up the hill (try hitching back to the ferry with tourists travelling by car). It is in any case an extremely hot walk up the hill, with little or no shade, so start early. Just east of the ferry, Magaña's Art Centre and the Xunantunich Women's Group sell locally made crafts and clothing in a shop on a street off the highway. About 1½ miles further north are the ruins of **Actuncan**, probably a satellite of Xunantunich. Both sites show evidence of earthquake damage.

Colour map 6, grid A1

You can swim in the river after visiting the ruins

F per person *Trek Stop*, near the Xunantunich ferry on the way to Benque Viejo, has small wooden cabins, or you can camp for a few dollars. Also home to Tropical Wings Nature Center.

Sleeping

Belize

Transport **Bus** from San Ignacio towards the border as far as San José Succotz (7 miles), where a hand-operated ferry takes visitors and cars across the Mopan River (0800-1600, free); it is then a 20-min walk
uphill on an all-weather road. Return buses to San Ignacio pass throughout the afternoon.

San José Below Xunantunich is a large Yucatec Maya village where Spanish is the first lan-
Succotz guage and a few inhabitants preserve the old Maya customs of their ancestral village
(San José in the Petén). The colourful fiestas of St Joseph and the Holy Cross are cel-
ebrated on 19 March and on a variable date in early May each year. There is a Guate-
malan Consulate on the Western Highway, opposite the Xununtunich ferry (see
Border with Guatemala, on page 742).

Mountain Pine Ridge

Colour map 6, grid A1 Mountain Pine Ridge is a Forest Reserve (146,000 acres) which covers the northwest
section of the Maya Mountains, an undulating landscape of largely undisturbed pine
Note the frequent and gallery forest, and valleys of lush hardwood forests filled with orchids, bromeliads
changes of colour of and butterflies. There's river scenery to enjoy, high waterfalls, numerous limestone
the soil and look out caves and shady picnic sites; it's a popular excursion despite the rough roads. Hitching
for the fascinating is difficult but not impossible. Try contacting the Forestry Conservation Officer,
insect life. If lucky T824-3280, who may be able to help. Two reasonable roads lead into the reserve: from
you may see deer Georgeville to the north and up from Santa Elena via Cristo Rey. These meet near **San
Antonio**, a Mopan Maya village with many thatched-roof houses and the nearby
Pacbitun archaeological site (where stelae and musical instruments have been
unearthed). At San Antonio, the García sisters have their workshop, museum and
shop where they sell carvings in local slate, and guesthouse (**D**). You can sample Maya
food and learn about the use of medicinal plants. This is a regular stop on tours to the
Mountain Pine Ridge. A donation of US$0.50 is requested; US$12.50 is charged to
take photos of the sisters at work. Two buses a day from San Ignacio, 1000 and 1430,
from market area, but check times of return buses before leaving San Ignacio.

On the Mountain Pine Ridge Road from Georgeville, one mile from the junction
near San Antonio, is *Green Hills* and the **Belize Butterfly House**, opened by Jan
Meerman and Tineke Boomsma, and its fine collection of butterflies in a natural
environment. There is an associated botanical collection which provides foodplants
for the butterflies. A fascinating place for the enthusiast. ■ *0900-1600, from Christmas to Easter, US$2.50, outside this period and for further information contact: Belize
Tropical Forest Studies, PO Box 208, Belmopan, T822-3310, F822-3361.*

The main forest road meanders along rocky spurs, from which unexpected and
often breathtaking views emerge of jungle far below and streams plunging hundreds of
feet over red-rock canyons. A lookout point has been provided to view the impressive
Hidden Valley Falls, said to be over 1,000 ft high (often shrouded in fog October-Jan-
uary). On a clear day it is said you can see Belmopan from this viewpoint. There is a
picnic area and small shops here. It is quite a long way from the main road and is probably not worth the detour if time is short, particularly in the dry season when the flow is
restricted. Eighteen miles into the reserve the road crosses the **Río On**. Here, where the
river tumbles into inviting pools over huge granite boulders, is one of Belize's most
beautiful picnic and swimming spots. The rocks form little water slides and are good
for children. However, bathing is not possible in the wet season.

Five miles further on is the tiny village of **Augustine** (also called Douglas D'Silva,
or **Douglas Forest Station**), the main forest station where there is a shop, accommodation in two houses (bookable through the Forestry Dept in Belmopan, the area
Forestry Office is in San Antonio) and a camping ground, US$1, no mattresses (see
rangers for all information on the area). Keep your receipt, a guard checks it on the
way out of Mountain Pine Ridge. A mile beyond Augustine is a cluster of caves in
rich rainforest. The entrance to the **Río Frío Cave** (in fact a tunnel) is over 65 ft high,
and there are many spectacular rock formations and sandy beaches where the river
flows out. Trees in the parking area and along the Cuevas Gemelas nature trail,

which starts one hour from the Río Frío cave, are labelled. It's a beautiful excursion and highly recommended.

Forestry roads continue south further into the mountains, reaching **San Luis** (6 miles), the only other inhabited camp in the area, with post office, sawmill and forest station, and continuing on over the granite uplands of the Vaca Plateau into the **Chiquibul Forest Reserve** (460,000 acres).

At the driest time of year, February to May, there is an ever-present danger of fire. Open fires are strictly prohibited and you are asked to be as careful as possible.

The four forest reserves which cover the Maya Mountains are the responsibility of the Forestry Department, who have only about 20 rangers to patrol over a million acres of heavily forested land. A hunting ban prohibits the carrying of firearms. Legislation, however, allows for controlled logging; all attempts to have some areas declared national parks or biosphere reserves have so far been unsuccessful.

Caracol

About 24 miles south-southwest of Augustine, Caracol (about one hour by four-wheel drive) is a rediscovered Maya city. The area is now a National Monument Reservation. Caracol was established about 300 BC and continued well into the Late Classic period (glyphs record a victorious war against Tikal). Why Caracol was built in such a poorly watered region is not known, but Maya engineers showed great ingenuity in constructing reservoirs and terracing the fields. The **Sky Palace** (*Caana*) pyramid, which climbs 138 ft above the site, is being excavated by members of the University of Central Florida. Excavations take place February-May but there are year-round caretakers who will show you around. Currently very knowledgeable guides escort groups around the site twice daily and a new information centre has been built. ■ *US$10*. The road has been improved and is passable for much of the year with two-wheel drive and year-round with four-wheel drive. It is an interesting journey as you pass through the Mountain Pine Ridge, then cross the Macal River and immediately enter a broadleaf tropical forest. Several tour companies in the San Ignacio area offer trips to Caracol for $50-$60 per person in a group, or $200 for a private tour (1-4 people). Take your own food as there is none at the site. Otherwise *Pine Ridge Lodge*, *Five Sister's Lodge* or *Blancaneaux Lodge* are open for lunch (see page 739).

See map, page 698

Transport Mountain Pine Ridge has no public transport. Apart from tours, the only alternatives are to take a taxi or hire a vehicle or a mountain bike (from *Eva's Bar* or somewhere in San Ignacio). Everything is well signposted. The private pick-ups which go into San Ignacio from Augustine are usually packed, so hitching is impossible. Taxis charge US$88 for 5 people. Roads are passable but rough Jan-May, but after Jun they are marginal and are impossible in the wet (Sep-Nov); essential to seek local advice at this time.

Benque Viejo On a good road 9 miles west of San Ignacio is the tranquil town of Benque Viejo, near the Guatemalan border. Many of the inhabitants are Maya Mopan Indians.

Sleeping AL-A *Mopan River Resort*, T823-2047, F823-3272, www.MopanRiverResort.com Belize's first all-inclusive, luxury resort on the Mopan River, opposite Benque Viejo, accessible only by boat, 12 thatched cabañas with verandas nestled in a lush coconut grove, swimming pool, water garden, minimum stay 7 nights, includes airport transfers, meals, drinks, daily tours plus Tikal and Caracol, tax and service, rates from US$680 per person per week, open Nov-Jun, contact Pamella S Picon, Manager, for advance booking.

The hotels on the Guatemalan side are much cheaper than those in Belize.

Eating Meals at *Oki's* and *El Sitio*, on main street, and *Hawaii*, down past the town hall, all recommended. *Long Luck Chinese* restaurant has the best Chinese in town, on George Price Blvd, up the hill on the left, just after the Hydro road.

Transport Road *Novelo's* run many daily buses from Belize City to **Benque Viejo**, and frequent buses from San Ignacio to Benque Viejo, taxi US$10, or *colectivo* from central square, US$2 (or US$2 to Melchor de Mencos in Guatemala, 10 mins). Not all buses go through the

From Benque to the border is a 20-minute walk

Belize

border to Melchor de Mencos. Get off the bus and walk the short distance to the border post or take a taxi. All buses that do cross stop at the border (contrary to what the taxi drivers might tell you).

Border with Guatemala

Belizean immigration Border hours are 0800-1200 and 1400-1700. Everyone leaving Belize has to pay the PACT exit tax (see page 707). Additional exit taxes of approximately US$10 are often charged but not required by law. Asking for a receipt can remove the need for payment.

Guatemalan consulate Opposite the ferry in San José Succotz, open Mon-Fri 0900-1300; visas for those who need them easily arranged. Most nationalities can obtain a tourist card (sometimes a visa) at the border.

Transport From Benque Viejo to Melchor de Mencos, by taxi US$1.50, by *colectivo* US$0.50. For bus services, see under Benque Viejo.

On the Guatemalan side someone will carry the luggage to **Melchor de Mencos** (see Guatemala, page 684 where there is a landing strip (flights to Flores). There is also a very rough road to Santa Elena, for Flores (a bus leaves the border for Flores at 1330, US$2.65, or several daily buses from Melchor de Mencos, 3½ hrs, US$2.65, leave Belize City at 0600, 0630 or 1015 to make a connection to Flores); unless you take a tourist minibus, it is only possible to get to Tikal by bus by asking the driver of the border-Flores bus to let you off at the road junction (El Cruce), where you can get a connecting bus to Tikal (see page 684). For direct minibus services between Flores/Santa Elena and Belize City, see page 685.

Directory Exchange: You will get better rates purchasing quetzales at the border than anywhere before Puerto Barrios or Guatemala City. Compare rates at the *Banco de Guatemala* with the money changers. Check what you receive and do not accept damaged notes. Belizean dollars are difficult to change beyond Santa Elena.

Southern Belize and the Southern Cayes

Southern Belize is the remotest part of the country and has poor roads, but it is worth exploring. Dangriga is the largest of several Garífuna settlements that burst into life every year on Settlement Day. The paradise beaches of Hopkins and Placencia are perfect for watersports and relaxing. Cockscomb Basin Wildlife (Jaguar) Sanctuary offers one of the best chances of seeing one of Central America's big cats in the wild, while the sparsely populated far south around Punta Gorda has many Maya settlements to visit, and the region is dotted with impressive Maya ruins.

Gales Point

Boat tours of the lagoon are recommended

About 2 miles beyond the Belize Zoo on the Western Highway, the **Coastal Highway** (a good dirt road) runs southeast to Gales Point, a charming fishing village on a peninsula at the south end of Manatee Lagoon, 15 miles north of Dangriga. The villagers are keen to preserve their natural resources and there are still significant numbers of the endangered manatee and hawksbill turtles. Gales Point can be reached by inland waterways from Belize City, but buses have largely superseded boat services. At least two daily *Southern Transport* buses between Belize City and Dangriga use the coastal road.

Sleeping LL *Manatee Lodge*, resort fishing camp, 7-day all-inclusive package; T/F220-8040, in the US T1-877-462-6283, www.manateelodge.com The *Gales Point Bed and Breakfast Association* arranges basic accommodation, **E**, no indoor plumbing, meals available, contact Hortence Welch on arrival or call T220-9031 in advance.

Directory Tour operators: There's a wide variety of day and overnight excursions, from US$30 per boat holding 6-8 people. Contact Kevin Andrewin of *Manatee Tour Guides Association* on arrival. Community phone, T02-12031, minimum 48 hrs notice is advisable, ask for Alice or Josephine.

Along the Hummingbird Highway

The narrow Hummingbird Highway branches off the Western Highway 48 miles west of Belize City, passes Belmopan and heads south. Skirting the eastern edge of Mountain Pine Ridge, the newly surfaced highway meanders through lush scenery of cohune palms, across vast flood plains filled with citrus trees which provide a spectacular backdrop for the 52-mile journey southeast to Dangriga.

The Hummingbird Highway climbs through rich tropical hardwood forest until reaching Mile 13, where a visitor centre marks a track leading off to St Herman's Cave. Two paths, with good bird-watching, lead through shady ferns before descending in steps to the cave entrance with its unique microclimate. You can walk for more than a mile underground but it can be slippery if wet: torch and spare batteries essential. There is a three-mile trail to a campsite from the visitor centre.

St Herman's Cave

Two miles further on is the Blue Hole National Park, an azure blue swimming hole fringed with vines and ferns, fed by a stream which comes from St Herman's Cave. This is typical karst limestone country with sinkholes, caves and underground streams. After its long journey underground, the water here is deliciously cool until it disappears again into the top of a large underwater cavern. Eventually this joins the Sibun River which enters the sea just south of Belize City. There is a rough 2½ mile trail, through low secondary forest, between St Herman's Cave and the Blue Hole; good hiking boots are required. A sign on the roadway warns visitors against thieves; lock your car and leave someone on guard if possible when swimming. An armed guard and more wardens have been hired to prevent further theft and assaults. ■ *0800-1600 daily. US$4 entry to the park. There is a visitor centre at the entrance.*

Blue Hole National Park

Sleeping AL-A *Caves Branch Jungle Lodge*, PO Box 356, Belmopan, ½ mile past St Herman's Cave, T/F822-2800, www.cavesbranch.com Reached along ½-mile track, signed on the left, any bus between Belmopan and Dangriga will stop, secluded spot on banks of Caves Branch River, comfortable cabañas with private baths or **E** per person in the bunkhouse, camping US$5 per person, good, clean, shared bathrooms, delicious meals served buffet-style. More than just accommodation, this is very much an activity centre. Great trips through caves, 7-mile underground floats, guided jungle trips, pricey for some budgets starting at around US$60 but highly recommended.

The peaks of the mountains continue to dominate the south side of the highway until about Mile 30, when the valley of Stann Creek begins to widen out into Belize's most productive agricultural area, where large citrus groves stretch along the highway. The drive to Dangriga from Belmopan can take from 2- 2½ hours, depending on road conditions.

Canoeing or tubing trips can be organized down Indian Creek, visiting the imaginatively named Caves Five, Four and Three and then Daylight Cave and Darknight Cave, from *Over-the-Top Camp* on the Hummingbird Highway, or *Kingfisher/Belize Adventures* in Placencia. Vehicle support is brought round to meet you on the Coastal Highway near Democracia.

Turn east at Mile 32 for 4 miles along a gravel road to **Tamandua**, a wildlife sanctuary in **Five Blue Lakes National Park**. Follow the track opposite *Over-the-Top Camp*, turning right and crossing the stream for Tamandua, then for another 2 miles or so straight on following the signs for the National Park, 1½ miles, where there is camping. ■ *For further information on Five Blue Lakes,*

Belize

Friends of 5 Blues, PO Box 111, Belmopan, T809-2005, or the warden, Lee Wengrzyn, a local dairy farmer, or else Augustus Palacio (see below).

Sleeping **On the Hummingbird Highway** At Mile 31, **E** *Palacios Mountain Retreat*, Augustus Palacio, St Martha, Hummingbird Highway, Cayo District. Good for relaxing, cabañas, friendly, helpful, family atmosphere, safe, good local food, swimming in river, tours to waterfall in forest, caves and lagoon, Five Blue Lakes National Park, beware sandflies.

Dangriga

Colour map 6, grid A1
Population: 8,814

The chief town of the Stann Creek District is on the seashore, which has the usual Belizean aspect of wooden clap-board houses elevated on piles, and is a cheerful and busily commercial place with a population largely of Black Caribs (Garífunas). North Stann Creek meets the sea at Dangriga, coming alive with flotillas of boats and fishermen. There are several gas stations, a good hospital and an airfield with regular flights. The beach has been considerably cleaned up and extended, being particularly nice at the far north of town at the *Pelican Beach Hotel*, where it is raked and cleaned daily. Palm trees have been planted by *Pal's Guest House* where the beach has been enlarged. Dangriga (until recently called Stann Creek) means 'standing waters' or 'sweet water' in Garífuna.

Sleeping **AL** *Pelican Beach*, outside town (PO Box 14), on the beach north of town, T522-2044, F522-2570, www.pelicanbeachbelize.com With private bath, hot water and a/c, veranda, pier with hammocks, 20 rooms, restaurant, bar, games lounge, gift shop, tours arranged, helpful (taxi from town US$2.50, or 15-min walk from North Stann Creek). **AL** *Bonefish*, Mahogany St, on seafront near post office, T522-2165, bonefish@btl.net A/c, colour TV with US cable, hot water, takes Visa, good restaurant.
　C-D *Chaleanor*, 35 Magoon St, T522-2587, dssusher@btl.net Fairly large rooms, some with TV and fan, some with sea views, rooftop restaurant. **C-E** *Pal's Guest House*, 868A Magoon St, Dangriga, T522-2095, palBze@btl.net 10 units on beach, all with balconies, sea views, bath, fan, cable TV, cheaper rooms in main building, shared bath downstairs, private upstairs; *Dangriga Dive Centre*, T522-3262, runs from next door, Derek Jones arranges fabulous trips to the cayes (see also Hangman's Caye below). **D** *Bluefield Lodge*, 6 Bluefield Rd, T522-2742. Bright hotel, owner Louise Belisle very nice, spotless, comfortable beds, very helpful, secure. Highly recommended. **F** *Catalina*, 37 Cedar St, T522-2390. Very small, not that clean, but family-run and friendly, store luggage.

Eating *Comedor Elizabeth*, good local food. *Pola's Kitchen*, 25a Tubroose St, near *Pal's Guest House*, excellent breakfasts, cheap, clean, good atmosphere. *Ricky's*, good reasonable local food. *Ritchie's Dinette*, on main street north of police station. Creole and Spanish food, cheap, simple, large portions, popular for breakfast. *Riverside Café*, south bank of river, just east of main road, nicer inside than it looks, good breakfast, good service and food, best place to get information on boats to Tobacco Caye. *Starlight* near *Cameleon*, towards bridge. Chinese, quite cheap, good.

Entertainment Listen for local music 'Punta Rock', a unique Garífuna/African-based Carib sound, now popular throughout Belize. **Local Motion Disco**, next to *Cameleon*, open weekends, punta rock, reggae, live music. *Riviera Club*, between bridge and *Bank of Nova Scotia*, popular nightclub at weekends (see Eating above). Homemade instruments are a Garífuna speciality, especially drums. Studios can be visited.

Festivals **18-19 Nov**, *Garífuna*, or **Settlement Day**, re-enacting the landing of the Black Caribs in 1823, having fled a failed rebellion in Honduras. Dancing all night and next day; very popular. Booking is advisable for accommodation. At this time, Private homes rent rooms, though. At this time, boats from Puerto Barrios to Punta Gorda (see below) tend to be full, but launches take passengers for US$10 per person.

Air *Maya Island Air* and *Tropic Air* from Belize City several daily, also from Punta Gorda via Placencia. Tickets from the airstrip (T522-2294), or *Pelican Beach Hotel*.

Buses From **Belize City**, *Southern Transport*, Magazine St, several daily from 0800, plus 0600 Mon, returning daily from 0530, US$5, 4½ hrs (buy ticket in advance to reserve numbered seat, the bus stops at the Blue Hole National Park); also via Coastal Highway, 2 hrs. Bus to **Placencia** daily at 1200 direct, 1630 (*Southern Transport*) via Hopkins and Sittee River, US$4.50 (prices and schedules change often, as do bus companies); to **Belmopan**, 2½ hrs, US$4.50. The *Southern Transport* bus terminal is at the junction at the south end of town.

Sea A fast skiff leaves 0900 (be there at 0800) on Sat for Puerto Cortés, Honduras, US$50, stopping en route at Placencia if there are passengers; departs from north bank of river by bridge, T522-3227, ask for Carlos. Crossing takes 3 hrs and can be dangerous in rough weather. Check in advance procedures for exit formalities, if PACT exit tax has to be paid and you will have to pay to enter Honduras. You can hire a boat for around US$25 per person in a party to Belize City, enquire locally.

Banks *Bank of Nova Scotia, Barclays Bank International*, MasterCard and Visa, and ATM. *Belize Bank* (Visa cash advances). Same hours as Belize City (see page 707). **Communications** Internet: at *Val's laundry* and *Pelican Beach Hotel*. Post office: on Mahogany Rd. **Telephone**: BTL office is on the main street. **Laundry** *Val's* on Mahogany Rd, near *Bonefish* – also has internet access. **Tour operators** *Treasured Travels*, 64 Commerce St, T522-2578, is very helpful, run by Diane; *Pelican Beach Hotel* runs tours to Cockscomb Basin, Gales Point and citrus factories. *Rosado's Tours*, T522-2119, 35 Lemon St. Government Services. **Useful addresses** *Immigration Office* at south end of Commerce St. *New Southern Regional Hospital*, T522-2078, F522-2805, dannhis@btl.net

Cayes near Dangriga

This tiny island, 35 minutes by speedboat from Dangriga (US$15), is quite heavily populated, but has lots of local flavour and charm and, though becoming a little commercialized, still has an authentic feel. It sits right on the reef and you can snorkel from the sandfly-free beach although there are no large schools of fish; snorkelling equipment for rent. Boats go daily, enquire at *Riverside Café*. US$12-15 per person.

Sleeping AL *Ocean's Edge Fishing Lodge*, T520-7004, USA T713-894-0548, beltex@ symet.net Full board, 6 cabins on stilts joined by elevated walkways, run by Raymond and Brenda Lee, excellent food, diving and fishing can be arranged. **C** *Reefs End Lodge*, PO Box 10, Dangriga, T522-2419. Basic, small rooms, excellent host and food, boat transfer on request from Dangriga. **C** *Hotel Larnas*, T522-2571/2, USA T909-943-4556. Has its own fishing pier, snorkelling equipment hire $10 per day, good Caribbean-style food, mosquito net, shared shower. Recommended. **C** *Island Camps*, PO Box 174 (51 Regent St, Belize City, T227-2109). Owner Mark Bradley will pick up guests in Dangriga, A-frame huts and campground US$5 per person a night, meals on request, reef excursions, friendly, good value. Recommended. **D** *La Gaviota*, next to *Ocean's Edge*, rather basic, communal facilities. There is no electricity on the island.

There is a new dive resort on this tiny private island, consisting of six attractive cabañas with balcony over the sea, private bath, restaurant and bar.

South Water Caye, the focus of a new marine reserve, is a lovely palm-fringed tropical island with beautiful beaches, particularly at the south end.

Sleeping Part of the caye is taken up by **AL** *Blue Marlin Lodge*, PO Box 21, Dangriga, T522-2243, F522-2296, marlin@btl.net An excellent dive lodge offering various packages, small sandy island with snorkelling off the beach, good accommodation and food, runs tours. **AL** *Frangipani House* and *Osprey's Nest* are 2 comfortable cottages owned by the *Pelican Beach Hotel* in Dangriga, available for rent; the hotel also has *Pelican University*, which is ideal for groups as it houses 10-22 at US$60 per person per day including 3 meals. **B** *Leslie Cottages*, 5 units, T522-2119, F522-3152, izebelize@aol.com

Belize

South of Dangriga

The Southern Highway, now completely paved except for a stretch of a mile or so, connects Dangriga with Punta Gorda in the far south. Six miles inland from Dangriga the road branches off the Hummingbird Highway and heads south through mixed tropical forests, palmettos and pines along the fringes of the Maya Mountains. West of the road, about 5 miles from the junction with the Hummingbird Highway, a track leads to **Mayflower**, a Mayan ruin. Some minimal work has begun on opening it up and some say it will eventually be the biggest archaeological site in southern Belize.

Hopkins Fifteen miles from Dangriga a minor road forks off 4 miles east to the Garífuna fishing village of Hopkins. Watch out for sandflies when the weather is calm. The villagers throw household slops into the sea and garbage on to the beach.

Sleeping **LL** Hamanasi, Sittee Point, T/F520-7073, www.hamanasi.com 17-acre resort, 20 rooms and suites with a/c. Swimming pool, full dive operation. South of Hopkins, just north of Sittee River, is **LL-L** *Jaguar Reef Lodge*, T520-7040, F520-7091, www.jaguarreef.com 14 a/c rooms with refrigerators. Central lodge on sandy beach, swimming pool, diving, snorkelling, kayaking, mountain bikes, bird-watching and wildlife excursions. **LL** *Pleasure Cove Lodge*, Sittee Point, T/F520-7005. Small new beachside resort. **L-AL** *Beaches and Dreams*, Sittee Point, T/F523-7078, dreams@btl.net 4 extremely well-furnished beach-front rooms. Room rate includes full breakfasts, Dangriga transfers, use of bikes and kayaks. **A** *Hopkins Inn*, T523-7013, hopkinsinn@btl.net White cabins with private bathroom on beach south of centre, very clean and friendly, German spoken. Room rates include breakfast, owners are knowledgeable about the area.

C-D *Tipple Tree Beya Inn*, tipple@ btl.net English/American-run, 3 rooms in a wooden house and small cabin apartment just before *Sandy Beach Lodge*, camping US$4.50 per person **C** *Sandy Beach Lodge*, T522-2023. A women's cooperative, run by 14 women who work in shifts, arrive before 1900 or they will have home gone, 6 thatched beachside cabañas, 20-min walk south of village, quiet, safe, friendly, clean. **E** *Swinging Armadillos*, T522-2016. On the pier, 5 rooms, outdoor shower, seafood restaurant, bar, usually the best in the village.

Eating *Over The Waves* has good food. *Ronnie's Kitchen*, turquoise house on stilts north of the police station (follow the road left from the bus stop). Excellent food, friendly service, open 0630-2100, lunch includes burritos and chicken US$4-8, Ronnie also runs a library and gives good local advice.

Diving: *Second Nature Divers*, T/F523-7038, divers@btl.net, or enquire at *Hamanasi*. English-owned, good guides and equipment, recommended spot to visit is Sharks' Cave.

Transport **Buses** From Dangriga or Placencia, *Southern Transport* around 0700, 1500, 1530 and 1800, which travel on to Placencia or Dangriga depending on which way you are going. From Placencia, *Southern Transport* around 0530, 0600 and 1330, which travel on to Dangriga.

Cockscomb Basin Wildlife Sanctuary

The rainy season here extends from June-January

Four miles further on, the Southern Highway crosses the Sittee River at the small village of **Kendal** (ruins nearby). One mile beyond (20 miles from Dangriga) is the village of **Maya Centre** (or Center) from where a poor seven-mile track winds west through Cabbage Haul Gap to the Cockscomb Basin Wildlife Sanctuary (102,000 acres), the world's first jaguar sanctuary and definitely worth an extended visit if you have two or three days. This was created out of the Cockscomb Basin Forest Reserve in 1986 to protect the country's highest recorded density of jaguars (*Panthera onca*), and their smaller cousins the puma ('red tiger'), the endangered ocelot, the diurnal jaguarundi, and that feline cutey, the margay. Many other mammals share the heavily forested reserve, including coatis, collared peccaries, agoutis, anteaters, Baird's tapirs, and tayras (a small weasel-like animal). There are red-eyed tree frogs, boas, iguanas and fer-de-lances, as well as over 290 species of bird, including king vultures and great curassows. The sanctuary is a good place for relaxing, showering under waterfalls, tubing down the river, or listening to birds – hundreds of bird species have been spotted and there are several types of toucans, hummingbirds and scarlet macaws to be seen by early risers. This unique reserve is sponsored by the government, the *Audubon Society*, the *Worldwide Fund For Nature* and various private firms. Donations are very welcome. ■ *Entry US$5, Belizeans US$1.25.*

Around the sanctuary

Park HQ is at the former settlement of Quam Bank (whose milpa-farming inhabitants founded Maya Centre outside the reserve); here there is an informative visitors' centre. Eighteen miles of jungle trails spread out from the centre in a network of trails ranging in distance from a few hundred yards to 2½ miles. Walkers are unlikely to see any of the big cats as they are nocturnal, but if you fancy a walk in the dark you may be lucky. Note that the guards leave for the day at 1600. You will see birds, frogs, lizards, snakes and spiders. Longer hikes can be planned with the staff. Nearby is one of Belize's highest summits, Victoria Peak (3,675 ft) which is an arduous 4-5 day return climb and should not be undertaken lightly. There is virtually no path, a guide is essential; February-May are the best months for the climb. The most knowledgeable guides to the reserve live in Maya Centre; contact Julio Saqui, of *Julio's Cultural Tours*, T05-12020, who runs the village shop and can look after any extra luggage. At *Greg's Bar*, on the main road in the middle of the village, you can contact Greg Sho, a very experienced river and mountain guide who can also arrange kayak trips.

Sleeping

There is usually space on arrival, but to guarantee accommodation, travellers can contact the Belize Audubon Society, 12 Fort St, Belize City, T02-35004, F02-34985, base@btl.net **D** *Nu'uk Che'il Cottages*, Maya Centre, T05-12021. Simple thatched rooms in a garden next to the forest, take the botanical trail and learn about Maya medicine from Aurora Saqui; Ernesto, her husband, can arrange transport to the Park HQ. **C** *Mejen Tz'il's Lodge*, T520-2020; lsaqui@btl.net Owned by Liberato and Araceli Saqui, screened rooms with double beds or bunk beds, veranda, private hot water showers and toilets in a separate building, restaurant on premises. **E** per night per person in bunk beds. At the Park HQ there is a picnic area, camping area (US$1.50) and new purpose-built cabins, **B**, and dormitories, **D** per person. Drinking water is available, also earth toilets, but you must bring all your own food, other drinks, matches, torch, sheet sleeping bag, eating utensils and mosquito repellent. The nearest shop is at Maya Centre.

Other lodging in the area includes **AL** *Mama Noots Backabush Resort*, T520-7050, mamanoots@btl.net Electricity from solar, wind and hydro system, most fruits and vegetables grown organically on the grounds of the resort. 6 double rooms and 1 duplex thatched cabaña that sleeps up to 6. Private baths.

Tours

Full-day Mopan Mayan cultural tours of Maya Centre Village are available including visits to workshops on traditional Mayan cooking, crafts, language and natural tropical medicines. Contact *Destinations Belize*, info@destinationsbelize.com, to book in advance (at least 1 day is recommended, minimum 2 persons), or see Liberato or Araceli Saqui at Maya Centre Village.

Transport

Can be booked at time of reservation, or locals will drive you from Maya Centre, otherwise it is a 6-mile, uphill walk from Maya Centre to the reserve – allow 2 hrs for the walk to Maya Centre, if you leave early in the morning going either way you are likely to see quite a lot of wildlife. All buses going south from Dangriga go through Maya Centre, 40 mins, US$4; and north from Placencia, return buses from 0700 onwards to Dangriga. If walking, leave all unwanted gear in Dangriga in view of the uphill stretch from Maya Centre, or you can leave luggage at Julio's little store in Maya Centre for a daily fee. A taxi from Dangriga will cost about US$50, it is not difficult to hitch back.

Belize

Sittee River Village & Possum Point

Colour map 6, grid A1

Turning east towards the Caribbean just before Kendal a road leads down the Sittee River to Sittee River Village and Possum Point Biological Station.

Sleeping **L** *Lillpat Sittee River Resort*, PO Box 136, Dangriga, T/F520-2019, lillpat@btl.net 4 a/c rooms on the Sittee River, pool, restaurant, bar, very convenient for Cockscomb, bird-watching and fishing. Specializes in river and sea fishing. The Biological Station has a **D**, 16-room hotel, restaurant, specializes in student package tours from the US and discourages casual guests. **B-F** *Toucan Sittee*, 400 yd down river from *Glovers*, T523-7039. Run by Neville Collins, lovely setting, rooms with screens and fans, hot water, or fully equipped riverside apartments, great meals around US$6, grow most of their own fruit and veg, also over 50 medicinal plants. **E-F** per person *Glover's Guest House*, T802-2505. 5 rooms, on river bank, restaurant, camping, jungle river trips, run by Lomont-Cabral family and starting point for boat to their *North East Caye* (see below). **F** *Isolene's*, family house, Isolene cooks good meals in restaurant opposite.

Glover's Reef

Glover's Reef, about 45 miles offshore, is an atoll with beautiful diving and has been a Marine Reserve since 1993. The reef here is pristine, and the cayes are generally unspoilt, but yellow blight has hit the area killing most of the existing palm trees – especially on Long Caye. The combination of Mitch and high water temperatures in recent years has damaged the coral, and the snorkelling is not as good as it once was.

Sleeping and eating *Manta Reef Resort*, Glover's Reef Atoll, PO Box 215, 3 Eyre St, Belize City, T223-1895, F223-2764. 9 individual cabins with full facilities, in perfect desert island setting, 1 week packages available only, reservations essential, excellent diving and fishing, good food, highly recommended (E6 photo lab available). On 9-acre **North East Caye** is *Glover's Atoll Resort* (Gilbert and Marsha-Jo Lomont and Becky and Breeze Cabral), PO Box 563, Belize City, T614-7177 or T520-5016, F227-0156, www.belizemall.com/gloversatoll No reservations needed, 8 cabins with wood-burning stoves, US$99-149 per person per week, camping US$80 per person a week (add 7% room tax to rates). Weekly rates include round-trip transportation from Sittee River. Occasional rice and seafood meals, bring food, some groceries and drinking water (US$1.50 a gallon) available. A new beach has been created by Hurricane Mitch, and the resort also includes the 1-acre Lomont Caye and Cabral Caye which both have beaches and are within swimming distance. Boats for hire, with or without guide, also canoes, rowboats, windsurfer; full PADI/NAUI dive centre, snorkel and scuba rental, tank of air for shore dive US$14; boat dive includes air and gear US$36; no diving alone, certified divers must do tune-up dive, US$20, 4-day NAUI certification course US$295. Fly fishing with Breeze as guide, US$75 per ½ day. Families welcome. Contact the Lomonts in advance to obtain a full breakdown of all services and costs. Best to bring everything you will need including food, torch, soap, candles, sun screen, toilet paper, alcoholic and/or soft drinks, allowing for possible supply shortages or bad weather when boats stop running. Facilities are simple, don't expect luxury and guests are invited to help out occasionally.

Transport To North East Caye, 4 daily *Southern Transport* buses (T522-2160) from **Dangriga** to Sittee River and *Glover's Guest House* at Sittee River Village (see above). Also 3 daily buses from **Placencia**. Alternatively, take any bus going south to the Sittee junction and take a ride to the guesthouse. If you get lost, phone ahead for help. At 0800 Sun a sailing boat leaves for the reef, 5 hrs, US$20 per person one way (price included in accommodation package), returns Sat. At other times, charter a boat (skiff or sailing boat, US$200 one way, up to 8 people, diesel sloop US$350, up to 30 people).

Maya Beach & Seine Bight

Continuing down the Southern Highway watch out for signs to hotels (nothing official, look carefully). The road that heads east to Riversdale (after 9 miles) eventually turns south and follows a spit of land to **Maya Beach**, **Seine Bight** and, eventually, **Placencia**. The peninsula road is very rough from Riversdale to Seine Bight, with sand mixed with mud; a four-wheel drive vehicle is advisable.

Sleeping **L** *Green Parrot Beach Houses*, T/F523-2488, greenparot@btl.net Beach houses on stilts, all with sea view, sleep up to 5, kitchenettes, open-air restaurant and bar. **L** *Singing Sands Inn*, T/F523-2243. 6 thatched cabins with bathrooms, hot water, fans, ocean view, snorkelling in front of the resort at False Caye, restaurant and bar on the beach. **L-AL** *Maya Breeze Inn*, T523-8012, btolson@btl.net, 4 cottages on the beach, 2 with a/c, restaurant across the road. **AL-A** *Barnacle Bill's*, T523-8010, taylors@btl.net 2 cabañas, complete with queen-sized bed, sleeper/sofa in the living/dining area, full kitchen, private bath and fans. **A** *Inn at Maya Beach*, T523-8004, dafoolbewe@btl.net B&B with 1 room for nightly rentals. Private bath and use of family room and pier.

The road continues south to **Seine Bight**, becoming rougher, with sand mixing into mud, four-wheel drive advisable, huge holes appear and fill up with water in wet season. **LL** *Rum Point Inn*, T523-3239, F523-3240 (in US T504-465-0769, F464-0325), www.rumpoint.com Owned by an American entomologist, well-respected dive shop, very spacious units (some with a/c), swimming pool. **LL** *Luba Hati*, T523-3402, F523-3403, www.lubahati.com A little bit of Tuscany flavoured with Belizean spices, in a positively peaceful setting, each room uniquely decorated and with a/c. *Francos's Restaurant*, serving Mediterranean cuisine, is excellent. **A** *Kulcha Shak*, T523-4006, kulchashak@btl.net Clean, well-maintained rooms furnished with lots of local Garífuna art and local crafts, restaurant, gift shop and bar on the premises. Their entire operation promotes Garífuna culture and traditions. Several other new, higher and lower priced places to stay.

For an entertaining evening with dinner contact local artist Lola Delgado, who runs *Lola's Café and Art Gallery*, sign at south end of village.

Placencia

Placencia is a small, former Creole fishing village 30 miles south of Dangriga, at the end of a long spit of land. It was hard hit by Hurricane Iris in October 2001, but nevertheless is still becoming more and more popular among people looking for an 'end of the road' adventure, but it does have some modern amenities such as electricity, good water, telephones and internet services. There are no streets, just a network of concrete footpaths connecting the wooden houses that are set amongst the palms – the main sidewalk through the centre of the village is reported to be in the *Guinness Book of Records* as the world's narrowest street. Electricity and lighting have been installed on the main path and road. The atmosphere has been described as laid-back, with lots of Jamaican music, although litter can be a problem, particularly after Easter and Christmas celebrations. Rebuilding after the damage caused by Hurricane Iris is continuing but replacement of sections of the main sidewalk is expected to be finished by the end of 2002. Most hotels, restaurants, bars, dive shops and guide services re-opened once basic infrastructure was repaired after the hurricane.

Colour map 6, grid A1

The local **tourist office** (T523-4045, placencia@btl.net) is next to the petrol station. Services are maintained by the Placencia chapter of the Belize Tourism Industry Association which also produces the local monthly news sheet *Placencia Breeze* (online at www.placenciabreeze.com). You can also check out the local website at www.placencia.com

Big Creek, on the mainland opposite Placencia, is 3 miles from Mango Creek (see below). Fresh water is now piped from Mango Creek into Placencia and is of good quality.

LL *Turtle Inn*, on beach close to airstrip, T523-3244, F523-3245, www.turtleinn.com Completely destroyed by Hurricane Iris, the owner, Francis Ford Coppola, is rebuilding this resort with an opening date scheduled for mid-Dec 2002. **L** *Kitty's Place*, T523-3227, F523-3226, kittys@btl.net Barefoot casual beach cabañas, apartments and rooms. Good beach, restaurant and bar. **AL** *Serenity Resort*, just north of *Rum Point Inn*, itself just north of the airstrip, T523-3232, F523-3231, www.serenityresort.com 10 a/c hotel rooms, 12 beachside cottages, good beach, 2 bars – 1 on the Placencia Lagoon – and restaurant. **AL** *Rsanguana Lodge*, T/F522-3112, ranguana@btl.net Wooden cabins on the ocean, very clean. **A** *Trade*

Sleeping
Rooms may be hard to find in the afternoon, ie after arrival of the bus from Dangriga

Belize

Winds Cottages, South Point, T523-3122, F523-3201, trdewndpla@btl.net Mrs Janice Leslie, cabins and rooms in a spacious private plot on the south beach, completely rebuilt after Hurricane Iris. **A-D** *Seaspray*, T/F523-3148, seaspray@btl.net Cheaper in low season, very nice, good value, rooms range from beachside cabaña to small doubles in original building, the first hotel in Placencia Village.

C *Deb and Dave's Last Resort*, on the road, T523-3207, F523-3117, debanddave@btl.net 4 very good budget rooms with shared bathroom, hot water, kayak and bike rental. Walk-ins only, no advance reservations. **C-E** *Paradise Vacation Resort*, down by the piers, T523-3179, F523-3256, unbelizeable@btl.net 12 rooms with private baths and 4 rooms with shared. **D** *Lydia's Rooms*, T/F523-3117. 8 double rooms with shared toilet and shower, situated across the sidewalk on a quiet part of the beach, recommended. **E** *Lucille's Rooms*, run by Lucille and her family, private bath, fans, meals by arrangement.

Camping on the beach or under the coconut palms. The bus stop outside *Kingfisher* office is a good place to start looking for rooms, lots of budget accommodation nearby. Usually several houses to rent, US$200-550 per week, for less expensive houses try **Ted's Houses**, T523-3172, just past the market near where the buses stop.

Eating *Bella Beach*, directly on the beach just north of *Tipsy Tuna Bar* (the only 2-storey structure in the village), is the only Italian restaurant in the village. *BJ's Restaurant*, across from *Jake's*, good fried chicken and traditional Creole food. *Cozy Corner*, very nice beachside bar and restaurant with good barbecue and grilled seafood. *Daisy's*, good, reasonably priced meals. *Jake's Purple Space Monkey Internet Café*, on main road just west of the Placencia docks, very good US-style breakfasts and burgers for lunch, excellent espresso, cappuccino and lattes, dinner menu features local seafood, 5 computers for internet. *J-Byrd's Bar*, owned by Janice Leslie, owner and operator of *Tradewinds Hotel*. **John the Bakerman**, freshly baked bread and cinnamon buns each afternoon (takeaway only). *Merlene's*, in the Bakeder area south of the Placencia Village dock, one of the best, opens early for good breakfast, also has apartment for rent. *Miss Lilly's*, lunch only, authentic Creole food cooked by Miss Lilly, a village elder and local comedienne.

Omar's Fast Food, on the sidewalk, fish, meat, burgers, burritos, good cheap breakfasts – ask if they have fresh fish which Omar usually catches himself. *Pickled Parrot*, located next to *Wallen's Hardware*, good pizza, chicken and seafood. *The Galley*, good fish and shellfish (depending on the day's catch), try the seaweed punch, slow service. Recommended. *Tuna*, popular sports and karaoke beachside bar adjacent to *Bella Beach*.

Transport **Air** Placencia has its own airstrip. *Maya Island Air* and *Tropic Air* fly several times a day to Belize City (international and municipal), also Dangriga, Punta Gorda.

Buses From **Dangriga** at 1215 and 1530 direct, or 1630 via Hopkins and Sittee River, US$4.50, 3½ hrs, return at 0530, 0600 and 1330, connecting with 0900 buses to Belize City. From **Belize City** via Coastal Highway and Dangriga, 4 hrs, US$10, *Southern Transport*. Times, fares and operators change constantly, ask at the Placencia tourist centre at the dock next to the Shell gas station.

Visa extensions obtainable in Mango Creek (Thursday only) **Boats** Regular service across Placencia Lagoon from Mango Creek-Placencia, *Hokey Pokey*, 1000; return 1430, US$10 return; meets Dangriga and Punta Gorda buses. *Gulf Cruza*, leaves the Placencia dock on Fri for Punta Gorda and Puerto Cortés, Honduras, returning on Mon.

Directory **Banks** *Atlantic Bank* near the gas station at the south point is open Mon-Fri. **Communications** **Internet:** On the main road is *Jake's Purple Space Monkey Internet Café*, 5 computers for internet, and refreshments. Some hotels (*Kitty's Place*) also offer access. **Post office:** open Mon-Fri 0800-1200, 1330-1600. **Telephone:** *BTL* office in the centre where you can make international calls and receive and send fax messages. Payphones here, at the gas station and the ballfield. **Medical services** Basic medical care available at the clinic behind St John's Memorial School on the sidewalk. **Tour operators** Full PADI scuba diving courses are most local dive shops. Prices are from about US$75, plus 8% sales tax, for 2-tank dives to **Laughing Bird Caye**, US$105 to outer reef (gear extra). At *Seahorse Dive Shop*, T523-3166, www.belizescuba.com, ask for Brian Young. Also *Aquatic Adventures*, T523-3182, glenmar@btl.net *Rum Point Dive Shop*, T523-3239, rupel@btl.net, *Naudi Dive Shop*, T523-3595, nautical@btl.net, and *Robert's*

Grove Dive Shop, T523-3565, www.robertsgrove.com *Ocean Motion Guide Services* and *Nite Winds Guide Services*, T06-23487, renidrag_99@yahoo.com, located at or near the Placencia Village dock are reputable snorkelling tour operators. *Toadal Adventures*, T06-23207, F06-23334, debanddave@btl.net, is a very reputable tour operator for kayaking trips to local cayes and Monkey River. Doyle Gardiner (of *Nite Winds Guide Services* – see above), offers tours to Cockscomb Basin Wildlife Sanctuary. Benito Bol, a local Maya guide, conducts tours to Nim Li Punit and Lubaantun Ruins plus Blue Creek Cave. Contact *Fun Day Adventures*, T606-3870, bensadventures@yahoo.com **Fishing**, especially saltwater flyfishing, is excellent in the Placencia area, with recognized world-class permit fishing. Flats are hard-bottomed and good for wade fishing. Reputable licensed guides and tour operators include *Daniel*, *Wyatt* and *Egbert Cabral*, T523-3132, info@destinationsbelize.com, *Kurt*, T523-3277, and *Earl Godfrey*, T523-3433, lgodfrey@btl.net *Destinations Belize*, formerly known as *Kevin Modera Guide Services* offers combination cayes camping and fishing/snorkelling trips, plus whale shark interaction tours, T523-4018, info@destinationsbelize.com *Bruce Leslie*, T523-3370. Rates for a full day of light tackle and fly fishing, including lunch, average US$275 per day, plus 8% sales tax, maximum 2 anglers per boat for flyfishing.

Excursions from Placencia

Trips can be made to local cayes and the **Barrier Reef**, approximately 18 miles offshore. Day trips include snorkelling, with a beach BBQ lunch of lobster and conch, from US$45 per person, plus 8% sales tax.

Several hotels and guide services have kayaks that can be rented to explore some of the nearer islands or the quieter waters of the **Placencia Lagoon**. Those who want to keep their feet dry can go mountain biking on the peninsula or use it as a base for trips to **Cockscomb** and Maya ruins.

Day tours by boat south along the coast from Placencia to **Monkey River** and **Monkey River Village** are available. Monkey River tours feature howler monkeys, toucans, manatees and iguanas; cost approximately US$40 per person, plus 8% sales tax. Monkey River Village can be reached by a rough road, which is not recommended in wet weather. The road ends on the north side of the river and the town is on the south side, so call over for transport. Trips up river can also be arranged here with locals but kayaking is best organized in Placencia.

Sleeping Accommodations at or near Monkey River are under renovation after the destruction in the village caused by Hurricane Iris. Contact Placencia tourist centre (T523-4045, placencia@btl.net) for information on current accommodations.

Ranguana Caye

Ranguana Caye is private, and reached from Placencia. Reservations through *Destinations Belize*, T523-3132, info@destinationsbelize.com, or *Kitty's Place* (T523-3227). Getting there costs US$150 for up to four people. Three cabañas, each with a double and single bed and gas stove. Private hot showers and toilet in separate building. BBQ pits provided so bring food, but meal services is also available at US$25 per person. Divers must bring their own scuba equipment.

Sapodilla Cayes

At the southernmost end of the Mesoamerican Barrier Reef are the Sapodilla Cayes. Tours are arranged from Guatemala (for example see under Río Dulce-El Tortugal Resort) or can be made from Placencia. There are settlements on a few of the Cayes including **Hunting Caye**. A *Frank's Caye*, three cabañas with private baths, restaurant and bar. Contact Serenade Guesthouse (see above) for more information, and Lime Caye (tent camping – crowded). Very good fishing at certain times of the year (contact local guides for information).

Mango Creek
Colour map 6, grid A1

Mango Creek is a banana-exporting port on the mainland, 30 miles south of Dangriga as the quetzal flies. A boat service connects Mango Creek and Placencia. An all-weather road connecting Mango Creek to the rest of the country is currently being built, despite opposition on ecological grounds from several community groups.

Sleeping and eating C *Hello I Hotel* (at Independence) run by Antonio Zabaneh at the shop where the *Southern Transport* bus stops, clean, comfortable, helpful. D *Ursella's Guest*

Belize

House, 6 rooms. **F** Hotel above *People's Restaurant*, very basic, ask to borrow a fan and lamp, shower is a bucket of water in a cabin, basic restaurant. Food better at the white house with green shutters behind it (book 2 hrs in advance if possible). *Goyo's Inn/Restaurant Independence* (no accommodation), family-owned, good food.

Transport Air There is an airport at Independence, nearby. **Buses** Belize City-Mango Creek, *Southern Transport*, or the less regular *James Bus Service*, from Pound Yard Bridge, US$8.50. Mango Creek-Belmopan, US$10.50. **Sea** Motorized canoe from Mango Creek to **Puerto Cortés**, Honduras, irregular; ask Antonio Zabaneh at his store, T06-22011, who knows when boats will arrive, US$50 one way, 7-9 hrs (rubber protective sheeting is provided, hang on to it, usually not enough to go round, nor lifejackets, but you will still get wet unless wearing waterproofs, or just a swimming costume on hot days; it can be dangerous in rough weather). Remember to get an exit stamp, preferably in Belize City, but normally obtainable at the police station in Mango Creek, not Placencia (the US$10 departure tax demanded here is not official). See Placencia Transport for Mango Creek-Placencia boats.

Directory Banks *Belize Bank* is open Fri only 0900-1200.

The turn-off from the Southern Highway for Mango Creek, Independence and Big Creek comes 15 miles after the Riversdale turn-off, and the road runs 4 miles east through the **Savannah Forest Reserve** to the mangrove coast opposite Placencia. About 35 miles beyond the junction, 10½ miles north of the T-junction for Punta Gorda, half a mile west of the road, is the **Nim Li Punit** archaeological site which has a new visitors' centre and clean spacious housing for the stelae. Nim Li Punit ('The Big Hat') was only discovered in 1974. A score of stelae, 15-20 ft tall, were unearthed, dated 700-800 AD, as well as a ball court and several groups of buildings and plazas. The site is worth visiting – look for the sign on the highway. Day trips also offered from Placencia.

A short distance beyond, the highway passes **Big Falls Village**, almost completely destroyed by Hurricane Iris but rebuilding is ongoing. Take a short hike back to the hot springs for a swim, camp or sling a hammock, but first seek permission from the landowner, Mr Peter Aleman. Four miles from Big Falls, the Highway reaches a T-junction, know locally as the 'Dump', marked by a Shell station; the road to San Antonio branches right (west), the main road turns sharp left and runs down through another forest reserve for 13 miles to Punta Gorda. The road is paved all the way from Big Falls to Punta Gorda.

Punta Gorda

Colour map 6, grid B2
Population: 4,329

Rainfall in this region is exceptionally heavy, over 170 inches annually, and the vegetation suitably luxuriant

The capital of Toledo District, Punta Gorda is the southernmost town of any size in Belize, a marketing centre and fishing port with a varied ethnic makeup of Creoles, Kekchi, Mopan, Chinese, East Indians and descendants of the many races brought here over the years as labourers in ill-fated settlement attempts. Three miles north of **Toledo** are the remains of the sugar cane settlement founded by Confederate refugees after the American Civil War. The coast, about 10 ft above sea level, is fringed with coconut palms. Punta Gorda is a pleasant, breezy, quiet place. The seafront is clean and enjoyable – once you get away from Front Street, where the lively and colourful market on Wednesday, Friday and Saturday comes with the associated smells of fish and rotting vegetables. The *Voice of America* has an incongruous antenna complex to the south of town. On Main Street there is a pretty park with a clock tower, around which buses to local villages arrive and depart, while on the parallel Front Street are the civic centre, a new market hall and post office/government office. Most of the activity there takes place around the pier.

Toledo Visitors' Information Center, also called 'Dem Dats Doin', in booth by pier, PO Box 73, T22470, Alfredo and Yvonne Villoria, provide information on travel, tours, guiding, accommodation with Indian families (Homestay Program), message service and book exchange, for the whole of Toledo district, free. **Tourist Information Centre**, Front Street, T722-2834, F722-2835, can organize reservations for flights worldwide and for hotels, tours and boat trips to Honduras. ■ *Mon-Fri, 0830-1200, 1300-1800, Sat 0800-1200.*

Excursions

There are many tours that can be enjoyed on the numerous rivers in the Toledo District. Countless species of birds make their homes along the rivers, as do troops of howler monkeys and other wildlife. Kayaking is a good way to view wildlife on the rivers, while silently floating down the river. There are many white-sand beaches on the cayes off Punta Gorda for the beach comber, or camper. Fly fishing is becoming a popular sport and sport fishing, snorkelling and even scuba diving is available. **Toledo** is off the beaten path and has some of the most spectacular views, waterfalls, rivers, rainforest, cayes and friendly people – for some it is 'Last Frontier'.

Sleeping

Price codes:
see inside front cover

AL *Traveller's Inn*, near *Southern Transport* bus terminal, T722-2568. Including breakfast, bath, a/c, restaurant, bar, clinical atmosphere, information on tours and services. **A-D** *Tidal Waves Retreat*, south of the cemetery, T722-2111, bills_tidalwaves@yahoo.com Quiet, secluded, well-appointed cabins and camping, food available, nice spot. **A-B** *Sea Front Inn* PO Box 20, Front St, T722-9917, F722-2684, seafront@btl.net 14 rooms with private bath, hot water, a/c and TV, restaurant with great views and international menu. Agents for *Maya Island Air* and *Tropic Air*. **C** *Punta Caliente*, 108 José María Nuñez St, T722-2561. Double or king-size beds, excellent value, very good restaurant. **C** *Tate's Guest House*, 34 José María Nuñez St, T722-2196. A/c, cheaper without, clean, hot water, bathroom, TV, parking, friendly, breakfast before 0730, laundry service. **D** *Circle C*, 1 block from bus terminal. OK. **D** *Nature's Way Guest House*, PO Box 75, 65 Front St, T722-2119, thfec@btl.net Clean, good breakfast, ecologically-aware tours, fishing, sailing, has van, camping gear and trimaran for rent. Recommended. **D** *Pallavi*, 19 Main St, T722-2414. Recently enlarged, tidy, balcony, clean, friendly. **D** *St Charles Inn*, 23 King St, T722-2149. With or without bath, spacious rooms, fan, cable TV, good. **E** *Mahung's Hotel*, corner North and Main St, T722-2044. Reasonable, also rents mountain bikes, US$10 per day. **E** *Wahima*, T722-2542, on waterfront. Clean and safe, owner Max is local school teacher, friendly and informative. **F** per person *Airport Hotel*, quiet, OK, communal bathrooms, clean, spartan. You can flag down the 0500 bus to Belize in front of *Wahima* or *Pallavi*, buy a ticket the night before to get a reserved seat.

Eating

Several cafés around the market area with good views over the bay. *Bobby's* on Main St serves excellent fish dishes, Bobby is a local fishing guide and arranges trips. *Earth Runnings Café and Bukut Bar*, Main Middle St, also with tourist info. *El Café*, North St. *Gomier's* (vegan meals and soya products) located behind the *Sea Front Inn*. *Honeycomb* bar on Front St, especially good around Garífuna Day when spontaneous music, singing and dancing bursts forth. *Mangrove Inn* on Front St serves a wide selection of local and international dishes. Good Garífuna restaurant at the *Punta Caliente Hotel* at south end of town (see above).

Transport

Air Airstrip 5 mins' walk east of town. Daily flights with *Maya Island Air* and *Tropic Air* from Dangriga, Placencia, Belize City (both airports). Tickets at *Alistair King's* (at Texaco station), *Bob Pennell's* hardware store on Main St, the Sea Front Inn on Front St or the offices alongside the airstrip. Advance reservations recommended.

Buses From Belize, 8 hrs (longer in heavy rain), US$11, *Southern Transport*, Mon-Sat 0500, 0800, 1200 and 1500, Sun 0500, 1000 and 1500, ticket can be bought day before, beautiful but rough ride; *Southern Transport* bus to Belize City 0500, 0900, 1200 stopping at Mango Creek, Dangriga and Belmopan (schedules change on holidays). *Southern Transport* terminal is at very south end of José María Núñez St; lobby of *Traveller's Inn* serves as ticket office. *James* bus line to Belize City daily, 1100, after boat from Puerto Barrios arrives, also 0600 Sun; departs from government buildings near ferry dock. To San Antonio from square, see below for schedules; buses to San Pedro Columbia and San José, Wed and Sat 1200, return Wed and Sat morning. Buses can be delayed in the wet season. For the latest information on schedules contact Dem Dat's Doin at the pier by the Customs House.

Belize

Belize

 The Crystal Skull of Lubaantun

In 1927, a young woman by the name of Anna Mitchell-Hedges woke for her seventeenth birthday. For her it proved more eventful than most as she explored the recently excavated Maya site of Lubaantun to discover a finely crafted crystal skull made of pure quartz – setting off a tale of intrigue that remains to this day.

The size of a small water melon, the translucent skull of reflected light weighs just over 5 kg. The skull is one of only two ever found in Central America. Its date of manufacture is unknown – but some put it at over 3,600 years old – and its purpose is

equally curious. Local Maya people gave the Skull of Doom to Anna's father, the British explorer F A Mitchell-Hedges as a gift, saying it was used for healing and more sinisterly for willing death.

Dating the skull precisely is difficult because of the purity of the crystal, but the details of the finding are equally mysterious, with speculation that the skull was 'placed' to make that birthday so special.

Today the skull is reported to be an ornament in the house of the ageing Anna who has promised, one day, to reveal the truth about the skull's discovery.

Directory **Banks** *Belize Bank*, at one end of the park, will change excess Bz$ for US$ on production of passport and ticket out of the country. They do not change quetzales and charge US$7.50 for advancing cash against Visa. You can change Bz$ for quetzales at Customs in Punta Gorda and Puerto Barrios, but don't expect a good rate. **Communication** Internet: *Punta Graphics*, T722-2852, acapps@btl.net, round the back of the Texaco station. *Internet café* on Front St next door to the *Sea Front Inn. Carisha's*, located by the clock tower, *Earth Runnings* internet café and lunch. **Telephone**: calls from the *BTL* office on Main St and King St. **Laundry** *Sony's Laundry* Service near airstrip. **Tour operators** *Green Iguana Eco Adventures*, T722-2475, provide a wide range of tours and services including kayaking, diving, boat trips and rainforest treks.

Mango creek **Belizean immigration** Exit stamps for people and vehicles can be obtained at the Customs House next to the pier on Front St. Be there at least 1 hr before departure, or 2 hrs if loading a motorcycle. PACT exit tax payable, see page 707.

Guatemalan consulate If you need a visa it must be obtained in Belize City. Tourist cards are available in Puerto Barrios.

The weather can be bad, and you and your luggage may get wet **Transport** **Boats** *Requena Water Taxi*, 12 Front St, T722-2070, has fast skiffs leaving from the main dock in front of the immigration office every day at 0900, returning from Puerto Barrios at 0300. *Pichilingo* leaves daily at 1600, returning from Puerto Barrios or Lívingston at 1100. Both companies provide services to Puerto Barrios daily and to Lívingston by request. **Puerto Barrios** US$12.50, **Lívingston** US$10. There are also services to Izabal and Río Dulce (Guatemala) and Honduras. No need to book in advance though it's preferable so as to ensure space. Bike and motorbike transportation has been reported as difficult. Officials in Lívingston do not have the authority to issue vehicle permits to anything other than water craft.

Directory There are money changers at both ends of the crossing but it is better to buy quetzales in Guatemala. Neither side changes travellers' cheques. Try to get rid of any Bz$ in Belize.

San Pedro Columbia Inland from Punta Gorda there are several interesting villages in the foothills of the Maya Mountains. Take the main road as far as the 'Dump', the road junction (so named because soil was dumped here when clearing land for rice paddies) with the Southern Highway. Take the road west to San Antonio. After nearly 2 miles, there is a branch to **San Pedro Columbia**, a Kekchi village. The Kekchi are a sub-tribe of Maya who speak a distinct language. The Maya and Kekchi women wear colourful costumes, including Guatemalan-style *huipiles*. There are many religious celebrations, at their most intense on San Luis Rey day (5 August).

Sleeping and eating **C-D**, with Alfredo and Yvonne Villaria, *Dem Dats Doin'* (see Punta Gorda, Tourist offices). **E** *Guesthouse*, dormitory. You can buy drinks and get breakfast at the large yellow stone house.

Three miles beyond the village, up some very steep, rocky hills, is **L** *Fallen Stones Butter-fly Ranch*, leave messages at Texaco gas station in Punta Gorda, T722-2167. Excellent site and ideal for visiting the nearby ruins of Lubaantun. Owned by an Englishman, working butterfly farm exporting pupae. Price includes tax, service and breakfast, jungle tours, laundry, airport transfers.

Lubaantun

This whole region is a network of hilltop sites, mostly unexcavated and unrecognizable to the layman

Beyond San Pedro, continuing left around the church, then right and downhill to the concrete bridge, then left for a mile, is the road to the Maya remains of Lubaantun ('Fallen Stones'), the major ceremonial site of southern Belize. The site has a new visitor and information centre, and has undergone extensive work to clean and restore a large part of the ruins. It was last excavated by a Cambridge University team in 1970 and was found to date from 800-900 AD, late in the Maya culture and therefore unique. A series of terraced plazas surrounded by temples and palaces ascend along a ridge from south to north. The buildings were constructed with unusual precision and some of the original lime-mortar facings can still be discerned. Excavation revealed some interesting material: whistle figurines, iron pyrite mirrors, obsidian knives, conch shells from Wild Cane Caye, etc. One of the great controversies of the site was the discovery in 1927 of the Crystal Skull by the daughter of the explorer FA Mitchell-Hedges (see box). The site is seldom visited but is well maintained and a new visitor centre with interesting displays make it a worthwhile trip. ■ *0800-1600 daily, a caretaker will point out things of interest. Take refreshments.*

Blue Creek is another attractive Indian village which has a marked trail to Blue Creek caves and their Maya drawings. The trail leads through forest and along rock-strewn creeks. ■ *US$12.50 per person. The caretaker is the guide.* Good swimming nearby but choose a spot away from the strong current. Turn off 3 miles before San Antonio at *Roy's Cool Spot* (good restaurant; daily truck and all buses pass here). Halfway to Blue Creek is **E** per person *Roots and Herbs*, a couple of simple cabins with mosquito nets, Pablo is an excellent guide, good food. Turn left at *Jim's Pool Room* in Manfredi Village, then continue about 5 miles. Very basic accommodation at the house at the beginning of the trail to the caves.

Blue Creek

Close to the Guatemalan border, Pusilhá is one of the most interesting Maya cities and is only accessible by boat. Many stelae have been found here dating from AD 573-731, and carvings are similar to those at Quiriguá, Guatemala. Rare features are a walled-in ball court and the abutments remaining from a bridge which once spanned the Moho River. Swimming in the rivers is safe. There are plenty of logging trails and hunters' tracks penetrating the southern faces of the Maya Mountains, but, if hiking in the forest, do not go alone.

Pusilhá

San Antonio (21 miles from Punta Gorda) was founded by refugees from San Luis in Guatemala in the late 19th century. Nearby there are Maya ruins of mainly scientific interest. Community phone for checking buses and other information, T722-2144. *Dem Dat's Doin* in Punta Gorda will be able to give information (see above). There's medical centre in the village.

San Antonio

Colour map 6, grid B1

Sleeping and eating D *Bol's Hilltop Hotel*, showers, toilets, meals extra, clean; meals also from *Theodora or Clara*, next to hotel, and both with advance notice: local specialities are *jippy jappa/kula*, from a local plant, and chicken *caldo*.

Shopping *Lucio Cho* sells cold beer and soda and has the local post office; *Matildo Salam* is building a hotel above his shop. **Crafts** such as basketry made from *jippy jappa* and embroidery can also be found in this area.

Transport Bus from Punta Gorda, 1-1½ hrs, US$1.50, Mon, Wed, Fri, Sat 1230, from west side of Central Park, also 1200 on Wed and Sat, continuing to Santa Cruz, Santa Elena and Pueblo

Belize

Viejo (1 hr from San Antonio). Alternatively, hire a pick-up van in Dangriga, or get a ride in a truck from the market or rice co-operative's mill in Punta Gorda (one leaves early pm); or go to the road junction at Dump, where the northern branch goes to Independence/Mango Creek, the other to San Antonio; 6 miles, either hitch or walk. Bus from San Antonio to **Punta Gorda** Mon, Wed, Fri and Sat 0530 also 0500 Wed and Sat (having left Pueblo Viejo at 0400). If going to **Dangriga**, take the 0500, get out at Dump to catch 0530 *Southern Transport* bus going north. This area is full of places to explore and it is well worth hiring a vehicle.

Crossing into Guatemala

Although locals cross to shop in Guatemala, it is strictly illegal to cross this border

Transport can sometimes be arranged from Pueblo Viejo along a rough road to Jalacté (also reached by trail from Blue Creek and Aguacate), from where it is a 30-min hike to Santa Cruz del Petén (often muddy trail). From here trucks can be caught to San Luis on the highway near Poptún. There is no Guatemalan government presence at this border; entry stamps cannot be obtained. The area has been the focal point for several border disputes locally and visitors to the area should take local advice before travelling. Guatemalan maps are inaccurate.

Guesthouse Programme

An interesting alternative to Punta Gorda is to stay in Indian villages. Two schemes exist. The Guesthouse Programme is run by villagers as a non-competitive co-operative. **San Miguel**, **San José** (Hawaii), **Laguna**, and **Santa Cruz** are isolated villages beyond Dump towards San Ignacio. **Barranco** is a Garífuna village south of Punta Gorda, accessible by boat or poor road. These have joined together and have developed a visitor scheme which benefits all the villages. Each has built a well-appointed guesthouse, simple, but clean, with sheets, towels, mosquito nets, oil lamps, ablutions block, and a total of eight bunks in two four-bunk rooms. Visitors stay here, but eat in the villagers' houses on strict rotation, so each household gains equal income and only has to put up with intrusive foreigners for short periods.

Many village men and children speak English. They have expressed fears for what the arrival of power (and television) will do to their culture, and are keen to protect their heritage. The Indians have been relearning old dances from elderly villagers and are trying to rescue the art of making and playing the harp, violin and guitar to put on evening entertainments. Homemade excursions are arranged; these vary from a four-hour trek through local rainforest looking at medicinal plants and explaining agriculture, to seeing very out-of-the-way sights like caves and creeks (take boots, even in dry season). The village tour could be skipped, as it is easy to walk around and chat to people, although, by doing this on your own, you deprive the 'guide' of income.

One night for two people, with a forest tour and two meals, costs nearly US$50 but all profits go direct to the villages, with no outsiders as middlemen. Dormitory accommodation costs US$9 per person. All villagers share equally in the venture, so there is no resentment or pressure from competing households, and gross profits from the guesthouse are ploughed back into the villages' infrastructure, schools and other community projects. The scheme is co-ordinated by Chet Smith at *Nature's Way Guest House*, Punta Gorda, who offers free assistance and booking facilities for the scheme. You may have to arrange your own transport, or a vehicle can be hired. Hitching is not recommended as some villages are remote and may have onlyone car a day visiting. Enquire also at the *Toledo Information Centre* in Punta Gorda. Local attractions include: San Antonio waterfall, a two-minute walk from the roadside just outside the town; caves at San José (Hawaii); Uxbenka ruins and caves 2 ½-hour walk from San Antonio (turn off right just before Santa Cruz), with commanding view from ruins; and Río Blanco waterfalls, 10 minutes beyond the village. For Uxbenka and Santa Cruz, take Chun's bus on Wednesday and Saturday at 1300 from San Antonio and arrange return time. Do not take Cho's bus, it does not return.

The Homestay Programme is a similar scheme that involves actually staying with the family in their house. Several villages in the area have joined the programme. As you are living with the family, privacy is generally less and the experience more intense. Details can be discussed with *Dem Dat's Doin* in Punta Gorda, who will also help you arrange transport if required.

Both programmes are highly commended for their efforts to place control of visitors to the region with the Maya villages, and for the emphasis placed on environmental preservation. The experience is a unique way to explore the Maya villages, you are unlikely to find such an experience elsewhere.

There are no roads to the southern border with Guatemala along the Sarstoon (Sarstún) River. The newly created Sarstoon-Temash National Park is a wilderness of red mangroves and unspoilt rainforest. There are no visitor facilities at present. At **Barranco**, the only coastal hamlet south of Punta Gorda, there is a village guesthouse. A dirt road goes to Barranco through the village of Santa Ana, or you can go by boat.

Background

History

Throughout the country, especially in the forests of the centre and south, there are many ruins of the Classic Maya Period, which flourished here and in neighbouring Guatemala from the fourth to the ninth century and then, somewhat mysteriously (most probably because of drought), emigrated to Yucatán. It has been estimated that the population was then 10 times what it is now.

The first settlers were English, with their black slaves from Jamaica, who came in about 1640 to cut logwood, then the source of textile dyes. The British Government made no claim to the territory but tried to secure the protection of the wood-cutters by treaties with Spain. Even after 1798, when a strong Spanish force was decisively beaten off at St George's Caye, the British Government still failed to claim the territory, though the settlers maintained that it had now become British by conquest.

When they achieved independence from Spain in 1821, both Guatemala and Mexico laid claim to sovereignty over Belize as successors to Spain, but these claims were rejected by Britain. Long before 1821, in defiance of Spain, the British settlers had established themselves as far south as the River Sarstoon, the present southern boundary. Independent Guatemala claimed that these settlers were trespassing and that Belize was a province of the new republic. By the middle of the 19th century Guatemalan fears of an attack by the United States led to a *rapprochement* with Britain. In 1859, a Convention was signed by which Guatemala recognized the boundaries of Belize while, by Article 7, the United Kingdom undertook to contribute to the cost of a road from Guatemala City to the sea 'near the settlement of Belize'; an undertaking which was never carried out.

Heartened by what it considered a final solution of the dispute, in 1862 Great Britain declared Belize, still officially a settlement, a Colony, and a Crown Colony nine years later. Mexico, by treaty, renounced any claims it had on Belize in 1893, but Guatemala, which never ratified the 1859 agreement, renewed its claims periodically.

Independence & after

Belize became independent on 21 September 1981, following a United Nations declaration to that effect. Guatemala refused to recognize the independent state, but in 1986 President Cerezo of Guatemala announced an intention to drop his country's claim to Belize. A British military force was maintained in Belize from independence until 1993, when the British government announced that the defence of Belize would be handed over to the government on 1 January 1994, and that it would reduce the 1,200-strong garrison to about 100 soldiers who would organize jungle warfare training facilities. The last British troops were withdrawn in 1994 and finance was sought for the expansion of the Belize Defence Force. Belize was admitted into the OAS in 1991 following negotiations with Guatemala and Britain. As part of Guatemala's recognition of Belize as an independent nation (ratified by Congress in 1992), Britain will recompense Guatemala by providing financial and technical assistance to construct road, pipeline and port facilities that will guarantee Guatemala access to the Atlantic.

Belize

Belize

Border friction is an ongoing issue between Belize and Guatemala, and in early 2000 tensions overflowed when Guatemalans took some members of the Belizean Defence Force hostage for several days, eventually resulting in some Guatemalans being shot. Tensions were stretched to the limit, and periodically continue to rise and fall but now seem to have cooled and Guatemala has agreed to pursue its claim to half of Belizean territory through the international courts. On-going low-key negotiations continue between the two countries as they search for a mutually acceptable solution.

Hurricane Mitch brought flooding and wind damage in 1998, but Belize escaped the full force of the storm. A large-scale evacuation of coastal areas moved about 60,000 people to the interior. High tides and heavy rain flooded the cayes, but tourist facilities were back to normal by the winter season. One long-term impact of Hurricane Mitch could be the renewed interest in developing Belmopan. The vulnerability of Belize City became apparent as Mitch headed straight for the City, paused, pondered a few hours off the coast before heading south to strike Honduras and then north again to the west of Belize through Guatemala. Several government departments, embassies and NGOs are committed to move to the capital in the next couple of years.

As if to act as a word of warning, Belize was not so lucky with Hurricane Keith which hit Ambergris Caye in at the end of 2000. While there was no loss of life in Belize – ten people were killed in Nicaragua while trying to cross flooded rivers – Keith did cause widespread damage to the caye. In 2001 increased hurricane landfall gained greater support with the arrival of Hurricane Iris which hit the south of the country on the coastline around Monkey Town, Maya Beach and Placencia, where some 95% of buildings were flattened. In winds of 140 mph miraculously the only fatalities were offshore, when a tourist dive boat was capsized.

Government

Belize is a constitutional monarchy. The British monarch is the chief of state, represented by a Governor-General, who is a Belizean. The head of government is the Prime Minister. There is a National Assembly, with a House of Representatives of 29 members (not including the Speaker) elected by universal adult suffrage, and a Senate of eight: five appointed by the advice of the Prime Minister, two on the advice of the Leader of the Opposition and one by the Governor-General after consultation. General elections are held at intervals of no more than five years. The next election will be in August 2003 at the latest, with commentators predicting elections for spring of that year.

Mr George Price, of the People's United Party (PUP), who had been re-elected continuously as Prime Minister since internal self-government was instituted in 1964, was defeated by Mr Manuel Esquivel, of the United Democratic Party (UDP), in general elections held in December 1984 (the first since independence), but was returned as Prime Minister in 1989. The National Alliance for Belizean Rights (NABR) was created in 1992 by a defector from the UDP. General elections were held early in 1993 and, contrary to forecasts, the PUP was defeated. The UDP, in alliance with the NABR, won 16 of the 29 seats, many by a very narrow margin, and Mr Esquivel took office as Prime Minister with the additional portfolios of Finance and Defence. In the months following the elections, a corruption scandal rocked Belizean politics. Several PUP members, including the former Foreign Minister, were arrested on charges of offering bribes to two UDP members of the House of Representatives to persuade them to cross the floor. They were later acquitted.

Mr Price retired from the PUP party leadership in 1996, aged 77 after 40 years in the post. He was succeeded by Mr Said Musa, a lawyer. In 1997 the PUP had a spectacular success in the municipal elections, winning all seven Town Boards for the first time ever, reversing the 1994 position when the UDP had won them all. It continued its electoral success in 1998 in the August general election, when it won an unprecedented 26 of the 29 seats in the House of Representatives. The UDP won the other three, but Mr Esquivel lost his seat. The new government moved quickly to carry out its election promises. A review of the tax system was announced, the loss-making Broadcasting Corporation of Belize was privatized, logging licences to Malaysian companies were to be reviewed and allegations of corruption in state institutions under the former government were to be investigated. A 14-member Political Reform Commission was set up at the beginning of 1999 to look at Belize's system of governance and to make recommendations on how to achieve greater democracy. The Belizean electorate will assess the government's performance with a general election in 2003.

Economy

Belize's central economic problem is how to become self-sufficient in food: imports of food are still some 20% of the total. Conversely food exports – sugar, citrus fruits and bananas - are the most important sector of the Belizean economy, directly or indirectly employing more than half the population and bringing in 65% of the country's total foreign exchange earnings. Traditional exports include timber and marine products (for example shrimp and conch) both of which have been hit by conservation based protests and over extraction in some areas. Light industry and manufacturing (dominated by sugar refining and citrus processing), contribute about 14% of GDP. The value of clothing exports has risen to 10% of domestic exports.

With the emergence of ecotourism and natural history-based travel as a major expansion market within the travel industry, the Belize government is encouraging the development of tourism facilities and services. Tourism in Belize is the second largest foreign revenue earner, behind agriculture.

Culture

The 2000 National Census put the population of Belize at 240,204, given an annual population growth of 2.7% from the 1991 census figure of 189,392. The urban/rural distribution continues to be roughly 50:50 as it was in 1991. The fastest growing district over the 10-year period is Cayo which has gained at the expense of Orange Walk District and, to a far lesser extent, Belize District. The town of Orange Walk is now only a couple of hundred people more than San Ignacio/Santa Elena which has grown significantly – by Belizean standards – in the last 10 years.

People

About 30% of the population are predominantly black and of mixed ancestry, the so-called Creoles, a term widely used in the Caribbean. They predominate in Belize City, along the coast and on the navigable rivers. About 44% of the population are mestizo; 11% are Maya Indians, who predominate in the north between the Hondo and New rivers and in the extreme south and west. About 7% of the population are Garífuna (Black Caribs), descendants of those deported from St Vincent in 1797; they have a distinct language, and can be found in the villages and towns along the southern coast. They are good linguists, many speaking Mayan languages as well as Spanish and 'Creole' English. They also brought their culture and customs from the West Indies, including religious practices and ceremonies, for example *Yankanu* (John Canoe) dancing at Christmas time. The remainder are of unmixed European ancestry (the majority Mennonites, who speak a German dialect, and are friendly and helpful) and a rapidly growing group of North Americans. The Mennonites fall into two groups, generally speaking: the most rigorous, in the Shipyard area on The New River, and the more 'integrated' in the west, Cayo district, who produce much of Belize's poultry, dairy goods and corn. The newest Mennonite settlements are east of Progresso Lagoon in the northeast. There are also East Indian and Chinese immigrants and their descendants.

Language & education

English is the official language, although for some 180,000 the *lingua franca* is 'Creole' English. Spanish is the *lingua franca* for about 130,000 people. Spanish is widely spoken in the northern and western areas. In addition, it is estimated that 22,000 people speak Mayan languages, 15,000 Garífuna and 3,000 German. Free elementary education is available to everyone, and all the towns have secondary schools.

Land and environment

The coastlands are low and swampy with much mangrove, many salt and fresh water lagoons and some sandy beaches. In the north the land is low and flat, while in the southwest there is a heavily forested mountain massif with a general elevation of between 2,000 and 3,000 ft. In the east are the Maya Mountains, not yet wholly explored, and the Cockscomb Range which rises to a height of 3,675 ft at Victoria Peak. To the west are some 250 square miles of the Mountain Pine Ridge, with large open spaces and some of the best scenery in the country.

Cayes, meaning islands, are pronounced 'keys' From 10 to 40 miles off the coast an almost continuous, 184-mile line of reefs and cayes (or cays) provides shelter from the Caribbean, and forms the longest coral reef in the Western Hemisphere (the fifth-longest barrier reef in the world). Most of the cayes are quite tiny, but some have been developed into tourist resorts. Many have beautiful sandy beaches with clear, clean water, where swimming and diving are excellent. However, on the windward side of inhabited islands, domestic sewage is washed back on to the beaches, some of which are also affected by tar.

The most fertile areas of the country are in the foothills of the northern section of the Maya Mountains: citrus fruit is grown in the Stann Creek valley, while in the valley of the Mopan, or upper Belize River, cattle raising and mixed farming are successful. The northern area of the country has long proved suitable for sugar cane production. In the south bananas and mangoes are cultivated. The lower valley of the Belize River is a rice-growing area as well as being used for mixed farming and citrus cultivation.

Transport *There are no railways in Belize* Formerly the only means of inland communication were the rivers, with sea links between the coastal towns and settlements. The Belize River can be navigated to near the Guatemalan border for most of the year, but this route is no longer used commercially because of the many rapids. The Hondo River and the New River are both navigable for small boats for 100 miles or so. Although boats continue to serve the sugar industry in the north, the use of waterborne transport is much diminished.

Some 1,721 miles of roads connect the eight towns and many villages in the country. Many of the dirt roads are of high quality, smooth and well-maintained but, in outlying areas, others are impassable in the wet season. There are road links with Chetumal, the Mexican border town, and the Guatemalan border town of Melchor de Mencos. The main roads are the Northern Highway (from the Mexican border at Santa Elena to Belize City via Orange Walk), the Western Highway (from Belize City to the Guatemalan border at Benque Viejo del Carmen via San Ignacio), the Hummingbird Highway (from the Western Highway at Belmopan to Dangriga on the coast), the new Coastal Highway (from La Democracia on the Western Highway also to Dangriga) and the Southern Highway (from the Hummingbird Highway 6 miles west of Dangriga to Punta Gorda further down the coast). The road system has been upgraded in the interests of tourism and further improvements are planned.

Books

Suggested reading is *Hey Dad, this is Belize*, a collection of anecdotes by Emory King, a local celebrity who found himself in Belize after surviving a shipwreck out on the cayes. He had a cameo role in *The Mosquito Coast* starring Harrison Ford. More seriously, *Warlords and Maize Men*, a guide to the Mayan Sites of Belize, Association for Belize Archaeology, is available in bookshops. Maps and books on a wide range of topics including Belizean fauna are available at Angelus Press, Queen St, and at branches throughout Belize.

Belize

El Salvador

6

El Salvador

Essentials

Salvadoreans have for a long time been admired for their ability to weather hardship and suffering. Rightly or wrongly, the attractions of neighbouring countries – and the lack of anything truly comparable in El Salvador – stops a lot of travellers visiting or passing through El Salvador, but visitors always leave with memories of a friendly people, warm and helpful.

The devastating earthquakes of early 2001 literally brought the country to its knees. A huge earthquake measuring 7.6 on the Richter scale hit the country. A month later to the day, a second earthquake measuring 6.1 struck. In the three months following the first earthquake over 7,000 tremors shook El Salvador. The return to normal life was impressively quick. The rebuilding projects are replacing destroyed homes. For the visitor, the most visible sign of damage is the destruction and damage caused to hundreds of the nation's churches.

Planning your trip

El Salvador focuses strongly on San Salvador. All roads lead towards the capital like the spokes on a wheel with just a few exceptions. Consequently planning your trip will involve either a visit to San Salvador, or travelling along one of the main roads, cutting across, and then continuing a journey.

San Salvador is a cosmopolitan city with a variety of architectural styles that have been created by the multitude of rebuilding projects in a history dogged by earthquakes. The city centre is always busy and widely thought of as unsafe at night, so newcomers are best advised to head for the western areas around Boulevard de los Héroes, with its shopping malls and restaurants, and the residential districts of Escalón and the Zona Rosa.

Where to go

Throughout El Salvador volcanoes dominate the landscape, and the scenery is one of its main attractions. Close to the capital, **Parque Balboa** affords fine views through the dramatic Puerta del Diablo (Devil's Door). Below the park is **Panchimalco**, an old village with a growing handicraft industry. **Parque Nacional Cerro Verde**, just west of San Salvador, is a popular excursion for its prospect over Izalco and Santa Ana volcanoes and the deep-blue waters of the beautiful Lago de Coatepeque. Also a short distance west of the capital are the country's main archaeological sites of **San Andrés**, and the unique **Joya de Cerén**, where a Maya settlement has been preserved under volcanic ash. There are no grand temples and sculptures, just dwellings and everyday objects. The main city of the west is **Santa Ana**, which is an equally good base for visiting these sites and **Tazumal** to the west.

A little further south, **Sonsonate** is an interesting town leading to the *Ruta de las Flores* a handful of villages climbing the volcanic chains with good scenary and waterfalls, pleasant hiking and a smattering of crafts.

There are very few pockets of undisturbed land, mainly because El Salvador is farmed intensively. On the border with Guatemala and Honduras is **Montecristo**, a remnant of cloud forest administered jointly by the three countries, while another such survivor is **El Imposible** which, as its name suggests, is far from easy to reach.

North of San Salvador, near the Honduran border, is the town of **La Palma**, where handicrafts of brightly painted wood and other styles are made. Also north, but heading more to the east, is **Suchitoto**, one of the best-preserved colonial towns currently enjoying a revival that takes advantage of the beautiful scenery around Cerrón Grande resevoir. In eastern El Salvador are the cities of **San Vicente** and **San Miguel**, the port of La Unión/Cutuco and many small traditional towns. Those interested in the recent civil war can visit **Ciudad Segundo Montes**, north of San Miguel, where refugees have been repatriated close to the guerrillas' former headquarters of **Perquín**.

The Pacific coast at **La Libertad** is only a short trip from the capital and is a good place to start exploring the Balsam coast to the west, the surfing beaches and to get a feel for the country as a whole. The beaches of the **Costa del Sol** are definitely worth a stop for their long stretches of sand and estuaries. The **Gulf of Fonseca** has islands with secluded beaches

El Salvador

which you can explore. In some parts of the country the infrastructure for tourism is quite rudimentary, but in others (such as the capital and nearby places of interest and some of the beach resorts) it is well developed.

As it is a small country many facilities are designed for people driving from San Salvador for the day or weekend, but the independent traveller should not be put off as there is an efficient bus network as well as one of the few remaining passenger trains in Central America (San Salvador to Metapán, via Aguilares and Texistepeque).

When to go The most pleasant months are from November to January. El Salvador is fortunate in that temperatures are rarely excessively high. The average for San Salvador is 28°C with a variation of only about 3°C. March, April and May are the hottest months; December, January and February the coolest. There is one rainy season, from May to October, with April and November being transitional periods; there are only light rains for the rest of the year: the average annual rainfall is about 1,830 mm. Highest temperatures and humidity will be found on the coast and in the lowlands, with the heat at its greatest from March to May. Occasionally, in September or October, there is a spell of continuously rainy weather, the *temporal*, which can last from two or three days to as many weeks.

Finding out more Local information is available from the **Corporación Salvadoreña de Turismo** (**Corsatur**), Boulevard del Hipódromo 508, Col San Benito, San Salvador, T243-7835, F243-0427, www.elsalvadorturismo.gob.sv The *Revue* English-language magazine published in Guatemala, has a section on El Salvador.

El Salvador on the web The website www.buscaniguas.com.sv, gives access to lots of useful information, as does *El Diario de Hoy* at www.elsalvador.com, (look in 'Otros Sitios' for tourist information). Leftist newspaper *Co Latino* is at www.colatino.com, and *La Prensa Gráfica* newspaper at www.laprensa.com.sv For information on El Salvadorean political and social issues, see Centre for Investigation of El Salvadorean Public Opinion (CIOPS) at www.utec.edu.sv, (in Spanish). For advice on the next hurricane season go to www.huracan.com, while for political updates you can visit www.latinnews.com/newsroom.html

El Salvador

Spanish is spoken, but English is also widely understood in business circles. See directories of **Language**
individual towns for language schools.

Before you travel

Every visitor must have a valid passport. No visas or tourist cards are required for nationals of the following countries staying 30 days or less: Argentina, Austria, Belgium, Chile, Colombia, Costa Rica, Denmark, Finland, France, Germany, Guatemala, Honduras, Iceland, Ireland, Israel, Italy, Japan, Liechtenstein, Luxembourg, Netherlands, Nicaragua, Norway, Panama, Paraguay, South Korea, Spain, Sweden, Switzerland, United Kingdom and USA. All other nationalities require a visa, which costs US$30 in advance for a 30-day stay, or a tourist card which can be obtained at the frontier for US$10. Overstaying the limit on a tourist card can result in fines of US$3-7 a month. A visa application form should be requested from your nearest Salvadorean embassy/ consulate that will detail the requirements and cost. Evidence of your travel plans may be requested. Allow two weeks for processing. Immigration officials can authorize up to 90 days stay in the country; extensions may be permitted on application to Migración, Centro de Gobierno (see under San Salvador). Multiple-entry visas are only permitted to US citizens.

Visas & immigration
Always check at a Salvadorean consulate for any changes to the rules

Special arrangements should be made for business visitors, journalists, those wishing to study in El Salvador, residency/work permits, etc, that require authenticated documents to support the application, for example photographs, police good-conduct reports, certificates of good health, with varying charges up to US$100. Business visas can be arranged in 2 days.

Working journalists should register on arrival with the Secretaría Nacional de Comunicaciones (SENCO), T271-0058, office near the Casa Presidencial.

All personal luggage is allowed in free. Also permitted are: 50 cigars or 200 cigarettes, and 2 litres of liquor, two used cameras or a video recorder, one tape machine, one portable computer or typewriter and new goods up to US$500 in value (best to have receipts). There are no restrictions on the import of foreign currency; up to the amount imported and declared may also be exported.

Customs
You can't carry more than three bags through the 'Nothing to Declare' channel at the airport

Money

El Salvador adopted the dollar on 1 January 2001 and the national currency is being phased out. The exchange rate was set at US$1 to 8.75 colones. All US coinage and notes are widely used. You may find colones used in out of the way places so be prepared by learning your 8.75 times table. The colón (¢) is divided into 100 centavos. Banknotes of 5, 10, 25, 50 and 100 colones are used, with nickel coins for one colón, and for smaller amounts.

Currency
US$1=8.75 colones

Do not find yourself in the countryside without cash; travellers' cheques and credit cards are of no use outside cities. See under San Salvador, Banks, regarding exchange of travellers' cheques. Be aware that some banks will want to see your original purchase receipt. Credit cards are accepted in most upscale establishments. Transactions are subject to 5% commission and are charged at the official rate. There are international Visa and MasterCard ATMs in El Salvador and

Credit cards, TCs & banks

El Salvador

El Salvador

El Salvador embassies and consulates

Belgium, Av de Tervuren 171, 2nd Flr, 1150 Brussels, T733-0485.

Canada, 151 Bloor St, West Suite 320, Toronto, M5S 1S4, Ontario, T416-975-0812, also 209 Kent St, Ottawa, K2P 1Z8, 1613-238-2939; 1080 Beaver Hall, Bureau 1064, Montréal, Quebec, T514-861-6515.

France, 12 rue Galilée, 75116 Paris, T331-472-39803.

Germany, Adenaueralle 238, D-53113 Bonn 1, T228-49549913.

Italy, Via Gualtiero Castellini 13, scala B int, 3, 00197 Roma, T396-806-6605.

Japan, Kowa 38, Building 803, Nishi Azabu, Ch, Japan 106, T403-349-94461.

Spain, Calle Serrano 114, 2°Edif Izquierda, 28006 Madrid, T311-565-8002.

UK, Tennyson House, 159 Great Portland St, London W1N 5FD, T020-743-6 8282, visa information line T0891-444580.

US Embassy: 2308 Calif St NW, Washington DC, 20008, T202-387-6511; with consulates in several other large cities

---

larger cities throughout the country. For cash advances on Visa or MasterCard, go to **Aval-Visa** or **Credomatic de El Salvador**, see page 783.

Getting there

Air   **From Europe**   To Miami with any transatlantic carrier, thence to San Salvador with *American* or *Taca*. *Iberia* flies from Barcelona and Madrid via Miami, where you change planes.

   From USA and Canada   The main connection is with Miami. Other cities with flights to San Salvador are Atlanta, Dallas/Fort Worth, Houston, Los Angeles, Montreal, New Orleans, New York, Orlando, Phoenix, San Diego, San Francisco, Washington and Toronto (*Lacsa*).

   From Central America and Mexico   From Belize City, Guadalajara, Guatemala City, Managua, Mexico City, Monterrey, Panama City, Roatán, San José, San Pedro Sula and Tegucigalpa.

   From South America   Good connections to Colombian cities, with a few flights to South American capitals including Barranquilla, Bogotá, Buenos Aires, Cali, Caracas, Cartagena, Cucutá, Guayaquil, Quito, Lima, Medellín, Santa Marta and Santiago (Chile) with *Lacsa* via San José or *Copa* via Panama City.

   From the Caribbean   From Havana. Several other islands are connected through Panama City, for example Kingston, Port-au-Prince, San Juan, Santo Domingo or through Miami.

   From Asia there are flights connecting to Hong Kong via Los Angeles.

Touching down

Airport information   The international airport is at Comalapa, 62 km southeast of San Salvador off the Coastal Highway, reached by a 4-lane toll highway. There is a tourist information desk at the airport which is opens sporadically. If closed, you can still pick up some useful leaflets. Taxis and buses provide regular links to the capital. For transport details see page 770.

Airport & other taxes   There is a 13% tax on international air tickets bought in El Salvador and an airport tax of US$27 for anyone staying more than six hours. The airport has offices for all the main car rental companies and there are two banks, a tourist office and *Grupo Taca* and *American Airline* offices.

   Border formalities tend to be relatively brief although searches maybe carried out. There is an entry and an exit tax of about US$0.65. However, these taxes do not apply to every border crossing; they are payable only at the *Colecturía* office at borders; do not pay any other official.

Local customs & laws   Travellers can expect curiosity towards tourists of an unkempt appearance. Some rudeness has been reported, as has unwarranted attention towards women, but most Salvadoreans are friendly and eager to practise English. San Salvador has few places where foreigners gather (so far). Better for this are La Libertad, Zunzal and other recognized tourist areas.

Touching down

Official time *Time in El Salvador is six hours behind GMT.*
IDD *503.*
Hours of business *0800-1200 and 1400-1730 Monday to Friday; 0800-1200 Saturday. Banks in San Salvador 0900-1700 Monday to Friday, 0900-1200 Saturday; different hours for other towns given in text. Government offices: 0800-1600 Monday to Friday.*
Voltage *110 volts, 60 cycles, AC (plugs are American, two flat pin style). Supply is far from stable; mains supply alarm clocks will not work and important electrical equipment should have surge protectors.*
Weights and measures *The metric system is used alongside certain local units such as the vara (836 mm/32.9 in), manzana (7,000 sq m/1.67 acres) and the quintal (100 lbs/45 kg). Some US weights and measures are also used. US gallons are used for gasoline and quarts for oil.*

Tipping In upmarket restaurants: 10%, in others, give small change. Nothing for taxi-drivers except when hired for the day; airport porters, *boinas rojas*, US$1 per bag.

Safety

The legacy of many years of civil war has left its mark in certain areas, to the west and north of the country in particular. In addition, poverty abounds. Peace has left many ex-combatants armed but unemployed, which, together with the enforced return from the USA of Salvadorean gang members (*maras*), has led to El Salvador's unenviable distinction of having the worst levels of violent crime on the continent. Robbery at gunpoint is common, especially in the countryside and people in cars. Locals will talk incessantly about the country's problems and dangers but few actual examples materialize. Be cautious until you find your own level of comfort.

Since March 1996, the army and the civil police (PNC) have been patrolling the highways in an effort to reduce crime. Do not stop for lone gunmen dressed in military-looking uniforms. Vehicle theft is very common. If renting a car, buy a steering lock. Visitors to San Salvador should seek advice on where is not safe both inside and outside the city.

Foreigners are prohibited from participating in politics by Salvadorean law. Stay clear of any student rallies. Be prepared for police checks and possible body searches on buses (the officers are polite, if respected).

You are strongly advised to register with your embassy if staying for more than just a few days; carry their phone number with you. The British consulate, for example, advises on local legal procedures, lawyers, English-speaking doctors, help with money transfers and with contacting banks or relatives, and will make local hospital visits. The consulate cannot give free legal advice, supply money or obtain employment or accommodation. The services it does provide are only for those who have registered. Other consulates may provide the same services, but you should find out in advance about your country's diplomatic procedures.

Where to stay

Hotels As the most industrialized of the Central American states El Salvador has an impressive selection of international-standard business hotels in San Salvador. The country also has a good selection of higher-price hotels for those taking weekend breaks from the capital. At the lower end there is no shortage of cheap accommodation, but there is a shortage of *good*, cheap accommodation. If you have the time, shop around, don't check into the first hotel you come to. There are new places opening all the time.

Getting around

Bus services are good and cover most areas every 15-30 minutes, although the buses themselves are usually crowded. The best time to travel by bus is 0900-1500; avoid Friday and Sunday afternoons. All bus routes have a number, some also have a letter. Strange as it may seem, the system works and the route numbers don't change. Although it makes little difference to your journey, the buses are always brightly painted, particularly around San Miguel.

Bus

The cry of the Salvadorean bus boy is 'A Dios' – but the journeys are normally safe!

El Salvador

Transport is not difficult for the budget traveller as nearly all buses have luggage racks. For bigger bags there is space at the back where a couple of seats have been removed so sit there if you want to stay close to your bag. However, when problems on buses do occur they are usually at the back of the bus. The cheaper alternatives to the Pullman buses, that cross to Guatemala and Tegucigalpa from Puerto Bus Terminal in San Salvador, have luggage compartments beneath them and the luggage is tagged.

Car

Hitchhiking is comparatively easy

At the border, after producing a driving licence and proof of ownership, you are given a *comprobante de ingreso* (which has to be stamped by immigration, customs and quarantine) costing US$12 to stay for 60 days. You receive a receipt, vehicle permit and vehicle check document. Under no circumstances may the 60 days be extended, even though the driver may have been granted 90 days in the country. Other fees for bringing a car in amount to US$6. A few kilometres from the border the *comprobante* will be checked. When you leave the country a *comprobante de ingreso* must be stamped again and, if you don't intend to return, your permit must be surrendered; total cost US$2. Do not overstay your permitted time unless you wish to be fined. Leaving the country for a few days in order to return for a new permit is not recommended as customs officials are wise to this and may demand bribes. To bring a vehicle in permanently involves a complex procedure costing thousands of dollars.

Maps A good map, both of the republic and the capital, can be obtained from Texaco or Esso, or from the Tourist Institute. **Petrol** costs per US gallon US$2.25 (*sin plomo*, unleaded), US$2.25 (super), US$2 (regular), US$1.30 (diesel). **Roads** are generally good throughout the country, but look out for crops being dried at the roadside or in central reservations. Take care of buses which travel very fast, and of generally bad driving.

Insurance, third-party, is compulsory in El Salvador and can be arranged at the border (enquire first at consulates). Under the 1996 law, **seat-belts** must be worn; the fine for not doing so is US$34. The fine for **drink-driving** is US$55. Do not attempt to bribe officials.

Train

Passenger rail services exist in some rural areas, timetables don't. While it is a cheap way of travelling, it is more for the train lover than a genuinely useful way of moving around. There are 562 km of railway; rural passenger services run in the northwest of the country: San Salvador to Metapán and Aguilares to Texistepeque.

Keeping in touch

Internet

Internet cafés are beginning to pop up in places outside the capital. A few hotels will offer on-line access where internet cafés are not available.

Post

Air mail to and from Europe can take up to a month, but is normally about 15 days, US$0.35; from the USA, one week. Certified packets to Europe cost US$9.40, good service; swifter, but more expensive, is *EMS* (US$23 to Europe). Courier services are much quicker, but cost more. The correct address for any letter to the capital is 'San Salvador, El Salvador, Central America'. The main post office is at the Centro de Gobierno.

Telephone

There are no local area codes within El Salvador

Emergency numbers:
Police: 121
(In San Salvador)
Fire Service: T271-2227
Red Cross: T222-5155
Hospital: T225-4481
Maternity: T271-2555
Car accidents: 123

ANTEL, the state telecommunications company, was privatized in 1998 and was split into *CTE* (*Corporación de Telecomunicaciones de El Salvador*) for the terrestrial phone network, and Intelsa for cellular services. The market has been opened up to competition, a number of companies now operate and for the visitor passing through, confusion prevails.

Some hotels will provide direct dialling – by far the easiest option. If forced to use public services, most towns have a telephone office from where you can make national and international calls. Alternatively buy a *publitel* smart card (US$3) from a phone office and look for the little yellow telephone booths. National calls are charged at US$0.12 for the first three minutes. International calls carry a US$1.70 connection fee, after which charges per minute are as follows. Central America US$0.41, North America US$0.64, Europe and South America US$1.30 and Australasia US$1.69.

T114 for **information** (English spoken) and details of new phone numbers in San Salvador.

El Salvador

Newspapers In San Salvador: *Diario de Hoy* (right wing), www.elsalvador.com, and *La Prensa Gráfica* (centre) every morning including Sunday; both have the most complete listings of cultural events in San Salvador. *Co Latino* is a left-wing newspaper. *El Mundo* in the afternoons except Sunday. A popular, relatively new weekly is *La Noticia*. There are provincial newspapers in Santa Ana, San Miguel (for example *Periódico de Oriente*, weekly) and elsewhere. *Tendencias* is a leftish monthly magazine. US newspapers and magazines available at leading hotels. International newspapers can be read at the *British Club*.

Media

Radio Of the 80 radio stations: one is government owned and several are owned by churches.

Television There are four commercial television stations, all with national coverage, and one government-run station with two channels. There are three cable channels, all with CNN news, etc. Luxury and first-class hotels and some guesthouses in San Salvador have cable.

Food and drink

Pupusas, stuffed tortillas made of corn or ricemeal, are the quintessential Salvadorean dish. They come in several varieties including *chicharrón* (pork crackling), *queso* (cheese) and *revueltas* (mixed), typical, tasty and cheap. They are sold at many street stalls, and are better there than at restaurants, but beware stomach infection from the accompanying *corticlo* (pickled cabbage). On Saturday and Sunday nights people congregate in *pupuserías*. *Pavo* (turkey) is common and good, as are *frijoles* (red beans). A *boca* is an appetizer, a small dish of yucca, avocado or chorizo, served with a drink before a meal. Do not eat in restaurants whose menus do not give prices as you will very likely be overcharged.

Local cuisines
Apart from in San Salvador, restaurants tend to close early, around 2000.

Coffee makes an excellent souvenir and is good value. **Beers**: *Suprema* is stronger than *Pilsener*, while *Golden Light* is a reduced-alcohol beer. *Chaparro* is El Salvador's *chicha* or *agua dulce*. Although it is illegal to sell it, everyone has their source. *Chaparro curado* contains fruit or honey. It is a favourite at election times when alcohol sales are banned. Water bottles are emptied and filled with the clear *chaparro* for illegal swigging on the streets.

Drink

Shopping

Many of the villages in the northern regions, La Palma in particlar, are famous for brightly painted wood carvings and hand-embroidered tapestries.

Holidays and festivals

The usual ones are **1 January**, Holy Week (three days, government 10 days), **1 May**, **10 May**, Corpus Christi (half day), first week of **August**, **15 September**, **2 and 5 November** (half day), **24 December** (half day) and **Christmas Day**. Government offices are also closed on religious holidays. Little business in Easter Week, the first week of August, and the Christmas-New Year period. Banks are closed **29-30 June** and **30-31 December**.

If travelling at holiday times book accommodation in advance

Look in the newspapers for details of regional fiestas, rodeos and other fairs. There are many artesan fairs, for example at San Sebastián and San Vicente, which are worth a visit but which go largely unnoticed in the capital.

Health

Gastroenteritic diseases are most common. Visitors should take care over what they eat during the first few weeks, and should drink *agua cristal* (bottled water) or bags of water sold in the street. Precautions against malaria should be taken if a night is spent on the coast, especially in the east of the country. Cases of dengue are on the increase. The San Salvador milk supply is good, and piped water is relatively pure. For diarrhoea, mild dysentry and parasitic infections get *Intestinomicina* tablets from any chemist or large supermarket. For amoebic dysentry take *Nor-Ameb Forte* tablets.

El Salvador

Seven thousand tremors in three months

The devastation caused by the earthquakes that struck El Salvador in January and February 2001 makes for shocking reading. To be hit by one earthquake measuring 7.6 is devastating, the second quake served to compound the situation. The number of dead quickly rose to over 800, and almost one million people – one sixth of the country's population – were made homeless. The landslide in Santa Tecla, barely 10 km from the capital, caused the greatest loss of life, but the quake claimed lives in all but three provinces. Damage to property was massive. In San Miguel Tepezontes, 95% of the buildings were razed to the ground. In San Vicente, the town's two churches were reduced to rubble – nationwide over 330 churches were damaged in some way – and problems were exacerbated when the town's hospital was temporarily knocked out of operation. The second quake affected the provinces of Cuscatlán, La Paz and San Vicente but, with the epicentre closer to the centre, its destructive power was greater. The immediate concern of the authorities was to provide water and shelter. International aid organizations mobilized resources to set up water tanks, and provide shelter, medical assistance and much-needed emergency food supplies while the country was being continually battered by more than 7,000 tremors in the three months following January.

The cost of rebuilding the nation will run into millions of dollars, the cost to individuals who thought themselves fortunate to survive the first quake only to be hit by the second, is incalculable.

It goes without saying that, while visiting the country, you will experience places that have been thoroughly gutted – indeed it is likely that many of the places mentioned in this chapter have been affected. Charitable donations have greatly helped in reducing the financial burden for what has been a traumatic experience both for individuals and the nation. Salvadorean embassies around the world have set up bank accounts for donations. To find the one closest to you, look on the internet at www.rree.gob.sv

San Salvador

Colour map 6, grid C1
Population: 800,000
(estimated at
2.3 m if including
outlying suburbs)
Altitude: 680 m

Surrounded by a ring of mountains in a valley known as 'Valle de las Hamacas', San Salvador has suffered from both natural and man-made disasters. El Salvador's capital is a bustling cosmopolitan city with a rich blend of architectural styles; modern, yet retaining the charm of the Spanish era with the privilege of being one of the first European cities in the New World. Crumbling buildings await renovation and restoration, or the arrival of the next earthquake to deliver the final death knell. As always, some areas speed to recovery, and the shopping malls and wealthy suburbs to the west stand out in the pollution-filled valley.

There is little by way of natural attractions in the capital, but it is worth a visit. While you probably will not stay long, there are several day trips to nearby volcanoes, crater lakes and relaxing bathing pools to refresh your mind and body.

Ins and outs

Getting there The **international airport** (SAL) is at Comalapa, 62 km southeast of San Salvador towards Costa del Sol beach, reached by a 4-lane, toll highway. Taxis Acaya, 45 mins, US$18, T339-9182 (airport), 19 Av Nte y 3a Pte 1107, T271-4937 in San Salvador. *Colectivo* bus, US$2.85, from the airport at 0900, 1300 and 1730. From town at above address at 0600, 0700, 1000 and 1400. Some domestic flights use the old airport at Ilopango, 13 km east of the capital. Most **international buses** arrive at the Puerto Bus terminal, Alameda Juan Pablo II y 19 Av Nte, although luxury services and *Ticabus* have

El Salvador

their own terminals. Domestic bus lines use terminals at the east, south and west ends of the city. Details are given on page 713.

Getting around

The main focal points of the city are the historical centre, the commercial district some 3 km to the west around Boulevard de los Héroes and the residential and commercial districts of Escalón and Zona Rosa another 2 km further west. City buses and taxis are needed to get between the three (see page 781).

Four broad streets meet at the centre: Av Cuscatlán and its continuation Av España run south to north, C Delgado and its continuation C Arce, with a slight blip, from east to west. This principle is retained throughout: the *avenidas* run north to south and the *calles* east to west. The even-numbered *avenidas* are east of the central *avenidas*, odd numbers west; north of the central *calles*, they are dubbed Norte, south of the central *calles* Sur. The even-numbered *calles* are south of the two central *calles*, the odd numbers north. East of the central *avenidas* they are dubbed Oriente (Ote), west of the central *avenidas* Poniente (Pte). Sounding more complicated than it is, the system is straightforward and quickly grasped.

Security The city centre is widely considered to be dangerous after dark, but Blvd de los Héroes, the Zona Rosa and Escalón are relatively safe. At night, though, take taxis even for short distances, including on Blvd de los Héroes, especially the stretch east of the Esso gas station (known as 'Little America' – lots of crime). Armed security personnel are commonplace. Tourist police on bicycles now patrol Zona Rosa and Puerto de la Libertad day and night; there are plans to extend this to other areas. Consult them if in trouble, only use the emergency number 121 in very serious cases. Broadly speaking robberies, particularly on crowded city buses, have increased: pickpocketing and bag-slashing are both common. In downtown markets, don't carry cameras, don't wear watches or jewellery and don't flash money around. Women are advised not to wear expensive jewellery anywhere; they are also advised to carry a whistle at night, to attract attention in case of assault. Drivers, especially women, should take care at night at traffic junctions where windows should be kept closed (if the glass is tinted, so much the better).

Climate

The climate is semi-tropical and healthy, the water-supply relatively pure. Days are often hot, especially in the dry season, but the temperature drops in the late afternoon and nights are usually pleasantly mild. Since it is in a hollow, the city has a very bad smog problem, caused mainly by traffic pollution.

Tourist office

Corporación Salvadoreña de Turismo (*Corsatur*), Blvd del Hipódromo 508, Col San Benito, T243-7835, F243-0427, www.elsalvadorturismo.gob.sv, open 0800-1230 and 1330-1730 Mon-Fri: take bus 34 from centre, or 30B from Mundo Feliz or Salvador del Mundo; walk 4 blocks south and uphill from roundabout. Good information on buses, archaeological sites, beaches, national parks, etc. Both Texaco and Esso also sell good **maps** at some of their service stations. The best maps of the city and country (US$3 and $2 respectively) are available from the *Instituto Geográfico Nacional*, Av Juan Bertis 79, Ciudad Delgado. See also Finding out more, page 764.

Background

San Salvador was first established by Gonzalo, brother of the conquistador Pedro de Alvarado, in 1525. The settlement was named in honour of Christ the Saviour who, Pedro believed, had saved him from death in his first attempt to conquer the peoples of **Cuscutlán**, as the region was then known. In 1528 the town was moved to a site near present-day Suchitoto, only to be relocated 20 years later to its present location. Over the next three centuries it developed into the capital of the province of San Salvador. The city has been destroyed by earthquakes 14 times since 1575, the last being in 1986. Nowadays the buildings are designed to withstand seismic shocks, and most stood up well to the earthquake of 2001.

El Salvador

Sights

A number of important buildings are near the intersection of the main roads in the historic centre. On the east side of Avenida Cuscatlán is the **Plaza Barrios**, the heart of the city. A fine equestrian statue looks west towards the renaissance-style **Palacio Nacional** (1904-11). To the north is the **new cathedral**, which was left unfinished for several years after Archbishop Romero suspended its construction to use the money to reduce poverty. Work was resumed in 1990 and completed in 1999, the last consecration of a cathedral of the millennium. It now stands as a beacon of tranquility amid the dirt and noise of the downtown capital. It commands a striking presence, gleaming white and modern, its façade flanked by two giant murals vividly splashed with the colourful work of the country's most famous artist, Fernando Llort. Inside it is quite bare, but for the fabulous circular stained-glass window of a dove surrounded by a hundred shards of brilliant yellow glass, which in turn is framed by yellow stars set in deep lapis lazuli blue glass. Beneath the cathedral, a new chapel has been created to

San Salvador

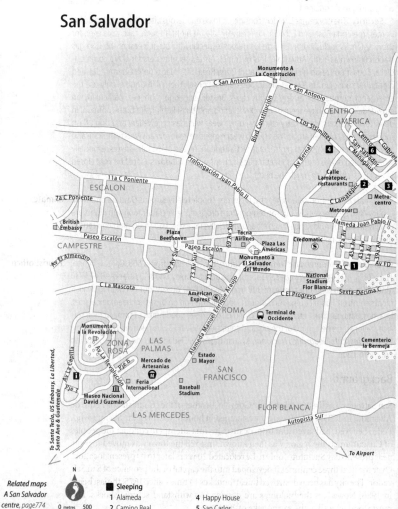

Related maps
A San Salvador
centre, page774

0 metres 500
0 yards 500

N

■ **Sleeping**
1 Alameda
2 Camino Real
3 Florida
4 Happy House
5 San Carlos
6 Ximena's Guest House

house the tomb of assassinated Archbishop Oscar Romero.

East of Plaza Barrios, on Calle Delgado, is the **Teatro Nacional** (the interior has been magnificently restored). If you walk along 2 Calle Oriente you pass, on the right, **Parque Libertad** with the rebuilt church of **El Rosario** on the eastern side where José Matías Delgado, father of the Independence movement, lies buried. The interior, decked out in modern sculpture, is fascinating, although knocked slightly by the earthquake. The **Palacio Arquiepiscopal** is next door. Not far away to the southeast (on 10 Avenida Sur) is another rebuilt church, **La Merced**, whose bell-tower rang out Father Delgado's tocsin call to Independence in 1811.

The church of El Rosario is San Salvador's best kept secret

One block north, across Calle Delgado, is the **Teatro Nacional** on **Plaza Morazán**, with a monument to General Morazán. Heading east along Delgado is the **Mercado Cuartel**, the expected confusion of sounds and smells that besiege the senses. Nearby are some of the cheapest hotels in the city. Running west from the Teatro Nacional Calle Arce leads to **Hospital Rosales** and its own gardens. On the way to the Hospital is the great church of **El Sagrado Corazón de Jesús**, which is

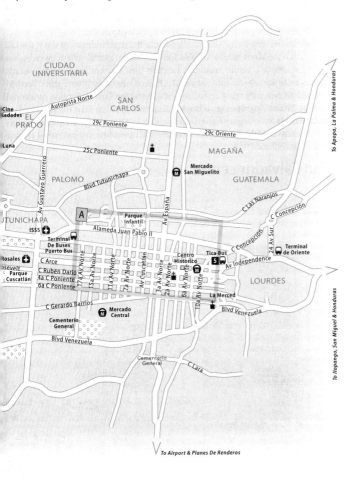

well worth a visit, don't miss the stained-glass windows. Turn left (south) here and you come after one block to the **Parque Bolívar**, with the national printing office to the south and the Department of Health to the north.

Four streets north of Calle Arce is the Alameda Juan Pablo II, an important road for bus transport, on which stands **Parque Infantil**, in which is the Palacio de los Deportes. One block west is the **Centro de Gobierno**, with many official buildings.

The north side of Parque Bolívar is Calle Rubén Darío (2 Calle Poniente), which becomes Alameda Roosevelt, then Paseo General Escalón as it runs through the commercial and residential districts west of the centre. Heading west this boulevard first passes **Parque Cuscutlán**. A major junction is with 49 Avenida: to the south this avenue soon passes the national stadium, **Estadio Olímpico Flor Blanca**, before becoming the main highway to the international airport. To the north, 49 Avenida crosses Alameda Juan Pablo II beyond which it changes name to **Boulevard de los Héroes**, home to the fashionable shopping centres, Metrocentro and the newer Metrosur, the *Camino Real* hotel, some of the city's better restaurants and a glut of fast-food places, a busy area at all times, especially at night. At the Shell station by Metrocentro, mariachis and other musicians gather each evening, waiting to be hired; others wander around the restaurants, playing to diners.

Continuing west along Alameda Roosevelt, the next landmark at the Plaza Las Américas is the **Monumento Al Salvador del Mundo**, a statue of Jesus standing on the Earth atop a column. From this junction the Carretera Panamericana heads southwest to Santa Tecla. Straight ahead is **Paseo General Escalón**, Parque Beethoven and an area with many restaurants, shops and the Colonia Escalón residential district. **Museo Antropólogico David J Guzmán**, opposite Feria Internacional on Avenida de la Revolución y Carretera a Santa Tecla. The only operating archaeological museums until the new museum has been built are at Joya de Cerén and Tazumal (see pages 790 and 794).

San Salvador centre

Sleeping ■

1 American Guest House
2 Custodio
3 León
4 Nuevo Panamericano

Another important residential and entertainment region is the **Zona Rosa** and **Colonia San Benito**, reached either from the Carretera Panamericana or from Escalón. In this leafy suburb, some of the most elegant restaurants and the *Hotel Presidente* are found. Also in Colonia San Benito is **Museo de Ciencias Físicas Stephen Hawking**, Avenida Reforma 179, T223-3027, with sections on astronomy, ecology, electronics and biochemistry. ■ *Mon-Fri by appointment only, Sat open to the public 1000-1600.*

Worth visiting is the **María Auxiliadora Church**, situated in Barrio San Miguelito. This multi-coloured marble temple is one of the city's landmarks, displaying a Venetian clock tower and with a spectacular view of the city from the belltower.

Museo Militar de las Fuerzas Armadas behind the presidential palace of San Jacinto at the former Cuartel El Zapote, hads a collection of exhibits of weapons, uniforms and decorations of the armed forces, also weapons captured from FMLN guerrillas.

Excursions

A good **sightseeing tour** of the surrounding area heads south to a couple of local places of interest. Lasting most of the day by bus (No 12) or two to three hours by car it starts a few blocks southwest of the main square on the eastern side of the Mercado Central. It includes the **Zoo**, which though small, is quiet and attractive. ■ *Tue-Sun 0900-1600, US$0.60. Getting there: Bus No 2 – Zoo, and No 12 from centre.* You then pass the Casa Presidencial and go on up to the new residential district in the mountain range of **Planes de Renderos**. This place is crowned by the beautiful **Parque Balboa** (good view of city from El Mirador at the foot of the park). Parque Balboa is a *Turicentro*, with cycle paths, playground and gardens. From the park a scenic road runs to the summit of **Cerro Chulo**, from which the view, seen through the Puerta del Diablo (Devil's Door), is even better. The Puerta consists of two enormous, nearly vertical rocks which frame a magnif-

The Zoo & Parque Balboa

icent view of the Volcán San Vicente. The rocks are very steep but the sides can be climbed on reasonable paths for an even better view. A little beyond the car park and drinks stands at the Puerta is a path climbing up a further summit, from which there are 360° views: to the coast, Lago Ilopango, the capital and volcanoes, including San Salvador, Izalco and Cerro Verde and San Vicente. ■ *Daily 0800-1800. Getting there: There are local buses to Parque Balboa (No 12, US$0.35 from eastern side of Mercado Central, and No 17, from same location to the Mirador), and to Puerta del Diablo (No 12-MC marked 'Mil Cumbres') almost hourly.* There are reports that mugging is increasingly common at Cerro Chulo; it is unsafe to make the trip alone, and do not stay after dark. At the foot of Cerro Chulo is Panchimalco (see page 786). The route to **Panchimalco** and the coast branches off the road to Parque Balboa at the village of Los Planes, a few kilometres before the park.

The Teleférico on Cerro San Jacinto overlooking the city and Lago de Ilopango has been closed due to earthquake damage.

El Salvador

Essentials

Sleeping

■ *on maps,*
pages 774 , and 772
Price codes: see
inside front cover

13% VAT (IVA) is
added to bills at
major hotels

Check Guía Activa
Yellow Pages for
local telephone
numbers, their office
is at Hotel Camino
Real, T243-8500

A useful landmark in front of the Metrocentro is **LL** *Camino Real*, Blvd de los Héroes, T211-3333, F211-4444, www.gruporeal.com, completely renovated, smart, formal atmosphere (popular with business visitors), *Avis* car hire, *Taca* desk, shop selling souvenirs, postcards, US papers and magazines. **AL** *Novo Apart Hotel*, 61 Av Norte 4617 (in cul-de-sac), T260-2288, F260-5053, www.novoaparthotel.com, rooms with bath and kitchen, mini swimming pool, garden, pleasant. **AL-A** *Mediterráneo Plaza*, 15 C Pte 4319, Escalón, T263-4592, F263-4612, www.hotelmedplaz.com.sv, a/c, cable TV, pool, garden, good. **AL-A** *Austria (Escalón)*, 1a C Pte 3843 (between 73 and 75 Av), T264-5869, www.casa-austria.com, small, quiet, family atmosphere, English and German-speaking owner, price includes coffee and toast, convenient. Also **A** *Casa Austria (Santa Elena)*, C Jucuaran, pl G No 1, Santa Elena, 400 m from US Embassy, hard to find (turn left Blvd Knights of Malta), buses 34, 44, T278-3401, F278-3105, www.casa-austria.com, renovated, clean, popular with business travellers, includes breakfast, good service, parking. **A** *Casa Blanca*, 89 Av Norte 719, T263-2545, F278-4466, jeafane@yahoo.com, with continental breakfast, new, cable TV, with bath, clean, good. **A** *Escalón Plaza*, 89 Av Norte 141-B, Col Escalón, T263-7480, F263-7464, www.escalonplazahotel.com, elegant, a/c, cable TV, good value, limited parking. **B** *Alameda*, 43 Av Sur and Alameda Roosevelt, T260-0299, F260-3011, www.hotelalameda.com, good service, tour information, parking, TV.

B *Good Luck*, Av Los Sisimiles 2943, Col Miramonte (turn left at *Camino Real* and go uphill 200 m), T260-1666, F260-1677, TV, shower, **C** without a/c, hot water, bright but simple, restaurant, secure parking. **B** *Myer's House*, Av Masferrer and 7a C Pte Bis 5350, T/F263-4176, hotmyers@quik.elsv.com, bus 52 from terminal, good service plus internet service, recommended. **B** *Posada Los Abetos*, C Los Abetos 15, Col San Francisco, near the Zona Rosa and the Carretera Panamericana, T224-3260, includes breakfast, quiet, TV, cafetería, discount with this *Handbook*, English, French and German spoken by owner Jill Lacaya. **B** *Townhouse* Bed & Breakfast, 3 C Pte 4409, Col Escalón, between Av 85-87 Norte, T223-0247, discount for groups and long stay, very nice, parking, English-speaking owner. **B** *Villa Antigua*, C Garbriela Mistral 571, Col Centroamérica, T/F226-5039, small, colonial-style, includes continental breakfast, reservations required, limited parking. **B-C** *Grecia Real* Av Sisimiles 2922, Col Miramontes, T/F261-0555, T/F260-1820. hotelgr@telemovil.net, with good Greek restaurant, recommended.

C *American Guest House*, 17 Av Norte 119 between C Arce y 1 C Pte, 3 blocks from Puerto Bus, T271-0224, F271-3667, with bath (cheaper without), hot water, fan, helpful, will store luggage, accepts credit cards, discounts for groups, weekly rates, *Cafetería La Amistad*, parking nearby, good. **C** *Family Guest Home,* T221-2349, 1 C Pte Bis 925, safe inside (don't walk alone outside late at night), clean, friendly, helpful, expensive meals available, convenient for Puerto Bus (advise owner if you have an early start), but overpriced and they may overcharge you if you arrive late. **C** *Hotel Florida*, Pasaje Los Almendros 115, off Blvd de los Héroes, T260-2540, F260-2654, all rooms with bath, fan, laundry service, secure, proprietor speaks English, good value, recommended. **C** *Happy House*, Av Sisimiles 2951, Col Miramonte, T260-1568,F260-8633, hotelgr@quik.elsv.com, good, friendly, often full, parking, restaurant, good breakfast. **C-E** *Ximena's Guest House*, C San Salvador 202-A, Col Centroamérica (René and Lisa Carmona), T260-2481, F260-2427, www.ximenasguesthouse.com, **C** with cable TV, a variety of rooms, **E** per person in 4-bed dormitory, discounts for long stay, clean, pleasant, cable TV in lobby, kitchen, fresh banana bread and carrot cake daily, breakfast US$1.75, other meals if ordered in advance, conveniently located, but not easy to find (it's roughly behind the Esso station on Blvd de los Héroes, take C Gabriela Mistral from Blvd de los Héroes.

D *Casa Clementina*, Av Morazán y Av Washington 34, Col Libertad, T225-5962, very friendly, clean, pleasant, garden. **D** *Centro*, 9 Av Sur 410, T271-5045, a bit box-like, checkout 0900, TV, phone, friendly, washing facilities, clean, safe, recommended. **D** *Occidental*, 49 Av Norte 171, T223-7715, renovated building, parking, popular with local business visitors, good.

B *Internacional Puerto Bus*, Alameda Juan Pablo II y 19 Av Norte, at Puerto Bus terminal, T/F221-1000, a/c, TV, wake-up service, etc. **D** *Nuevo Panamericano*, 8 Av Sur 112, T221-1199, F222-2959, with cold shower, safe, closes early (but knock on the door), will do laundry, meals from US$2 and parking space, recommended. **D** *San Carlos*, C Concepción 121, T222-8975, with bath, early morning call (extra charge), doors locked 2400, cold drinks available, good, resident cockroaches but otherwise clean, *Ticabus* leaves from outside (ticket reservations in lobby office hours), owner arranges evening tours of the city US$6 per person.

Close to the Historic Centre *In the downtown area, some hotels lock their doors very early*

E-F *Custodio*, 10 Av Sur 109, T222-5503, basic, clean, safe, and friendly, more expensive with private bath. **E** *Imperial*, C Concepción 659, T222-4920, serves reasonable meals and has car park, more expensive with toilet and shower. **E** *Hospedaje Izalco*, C Concepción 666, T222-2613, parking, most rooms with bath, TV lobby, dangerous area after dark. **E** *Pensión Rex*, 10 Av Norte 213, with bath, quiet, safe, run by Sra Rosalinda, recommended. **E** *Yucatán*, C Concepción, shared bath, safe, with parking. **E-F** *León*, C Delgado 621, T222-0951, friendly, safe with parking – OK for a budget spot. **F** *Hospedaje El Turista*, 1C y 12 Av Norte 210, fan, clean, quiet, dingy, little privacy, does laundry. **F** *Hospedaje España*, 12 Av Norte 123, fan, clean, bright, good value.

Many cheap *hospedajes* near **Terminal de Oriente**, dubious safety, not recommended for single women, avoid *La Avenida*. 3 doors along C Concepción is **F** *Emperador*, with bath, friendly, good value, clean, laundry facilities on roof, recommended.

Eating

Diligencia, 83 Av Sur, for good steaks, and *El Bodegón*, 77 Av Norte, proprietor Spanish, both excellent. *La Mar*, 75 Av Sur, seafoods, and *Siete Mares*, T224-3031, good seafood. *Asia* moderately priced Chinese. *La Fonda del Sol*, No 4920, opposite *Villas Españolas* shopping centre, Italian, popular with business set, good value, highly recommended. *La Pampa Argentina*, highly recommended for steaks, popular. *Quecos*, opposite Plaza Alegre, Mexican, good variety. *Las Carnitas*, Parque Beethoven, good beef, reasonable prices, less pretentious and costly than similar places. *La Fuente*, Leonel Fuentes, 83 Av Norte y 9 C Pte, Escalón, T263-3188, local food, family-oriented with play park for children, open noon-2100. *Pizzería Capri*, 85 Sur y J J Cañas, 1 block south of Paseo Escalón. *Beto's Escalón*, Pasaje Dordelly 4352 between 85 and 87 Av Norte (above Paseo Escalón), best seafood in the city, also Italian, great service, parking, recommended. *Sports Bar and Grill*, lower level Plaza Villavicencio, Paseo Escalón y 99 Av Norte, 1 block below Redondel Masferrer, 1100-2400 Mon-Thu, 1100-0200 Fri-Sat, 1100-2200 Sun, good varied menu, popular, English-speaking owner, friendly staff, trendy, TV screens, American-football theme. Tacos and *pupusas* at **Redondel Masferrer**, good view over the city, lively atmosphere, mariachis. In Col Escalón, *Rosal*, 93 Av Norte y C El Mirador, near *Hotel El Salvador*, Italian, good. *Kamakura*, 93 Av Norte 617, T223-1274, Japanese, expensive, good.

On the Paseo General Escalón *If staying in the older downtown area, note that there are few places open to eat after 1830. Restaurants are open later in the western sections of the city*

On Blvd de los Héroes there are many restaurants, including US and US-style fast-food places. *Neskazarra*, C Sierra Verde 3008, Col Miramonte, T226-8936, Basque, moderately priced, good. *Pueblo Viejo*, in Metrosur, T298-5318, open 1100-2000, popular for lunch, local and steak dishes, including *parrillada*, and seafood. *La Casa del Gran Buffet*, between *Camino Real* and Esso, T225-8401, all you can eat, lunch and dinner US$9. *Felipe's*, 27 C Pte off Blvd de los Héroes, popular Mexican, good value. Behind *Camino Real* is a row of restaurants on C Lamatepec: *Hola Beto's*, No 22, T226-8621, seafood; *Caminito Real*, No 19, local food, popular, good value, tasty; *Comida Lo Nuestro/Taco Taco*, local food, simple; *Hang Ly*, good Chinese, cheap; *Asia*, also Chinese, good portions, reasonable prices. Restaurant at *Hotel Good Luck* (see above) does good lunch specials, Chinese. *Tabasco*, Gabriela Mistral y Centroamérica, just up from Esso station on Blvd de los Héroes, Mexican, open 1200-2200. *Que Taco*, Av Pasco, Col Miramonte, good Mexican. *La Taberna del Viejo*, C Gabriela Mistral/Av 4 de Mayo 104, *pupusas* a speciality, good service. *Ipanema Grill*, Antigua C San Antonio Abad 1, T274-4887, Brazilian chef, good. *La Ventana-El Café*, C San Antonio Abad 2335, T226-5129, opposite Centro Comercial San Luis, about 500 m up from Cine Variedades,

In the Metrocentro area

El Salvador

European-style, international food, popular with foreigners, open 0800-2400, 0900-2300 Sun, US and European newspapers, recommended. *El Trapiche*, Av Bernal 587, Col Yumuri, T260-4663, Colombian and other South American dishes, recommended.

In the Zona Rosa Along Blvd Hipódromo, San Benito, restaurants are generally very good, but expensive. They include: *La Ola*, very good meals and moderately priced; *Ostería dei Cualtro Galti*, C La Reforma 232, T223-1625, Italian, good but expensive; *München*, German; *Paradise*, corner of Reforma, T224-4201 for steak and lobster, excellent food and service (*Pizza Hut* next door), another branch on Blvd de los Héroes (all popular); *Basilea/Schaffer's*, nice garden atmosphere and small shopping centre, restaurant and excellent cakes (from *Shaw's Bakery* next door; see also Coffee shops below). *Dynasty*, No 738-B, known for best Chinese food in city, but not cheap. Next door is *Madeira*, No 738, T298-3451, pleasant atmosphere, international, expensive. Also in San Benito, *Dallas*, 79 Av Sur 48, T279-3551, for steaks and seafood, very good, flamboyant service, prices from moderate to expensive, another branch on Autopista Sur (bus 44). Nearby, in Col La Mascota, *El Cortijo Español*, 79 Av Sur y Pasaje A, Spanish. *Texas Meats*, C La Mascota, good for steaks. *Tre Fratelli*, Blvd Hipódromo 307, moderate and popular.

Others include *China Palace*, Alameda Roosevelt 2731, excellent value (oldest Chinese restaurant in San Salvador); *Pupusería Margot*, opposite Estado Mayor on the road to Santa Tecla, good.

Vegetarian restaurants *Govinda's*, 51 Av Norte 147, Col Flor Blanca, T232468, take bus 44 (a bit hard to find, but worth it). *Kalpataru*, Av Masferrer 127, 100 m north of Redondel Masferrer, T279-2306, open 2230, full restaurant service and lunch buffet, nice atmosphere. *El Tao*, 21 Av Norte, C 27 y C 29 Pte, and Centro de Gobierno, 19 C Pte, and 19 Av Norte, Col Layco. *Todo Natural*, 39 Av Norte 934, T225-9918, near *Cine Variedades*, good, meals US$2-4, also has rooms **D** per person. *Koradi*, 9 Av Sur y 4 C Pte.

Comedores
Branches of the usual fast-food restaurants can be found in many parts of town
Good, cheap *comedores* in Occidente bus terminal. Food markets in various parts of the city have stalls selling cheap food. Gourmet and delicatessen fare at *Señor Tenedor*, Plaza Jardín, Av Olímpica 3544, opposite *Cine Deluxe*, 0900-2200, nearest thing to an American deli, good value, breakfast buffet, good choice of salads and sandwiches. *Pronto Gourmet*, lunch counter service, good value. *Kreef Deli*, in Metrosur near Pueblo Viejo, German style, and in Paseo Escalón 77 Av Sur 3945, T223-8063. *Comida a la Vista*, buffet *comedores* around centre, clean, cheap.

Cafés There are numerous *cafeterías* serving cheap traditional meals such as *tamales, pupusas, frijoles*, rice with vegetables, etc. Often these places can be found around the major hotels, catering for guests who find the hotel meals overpriced. *Café Don Alberto*, C Arce and 15 Av Sur, good and cheap. *Actoteatro*, 1 C Pte (between 15 and 13 Av north, near *American Guest House*), good atmosphere, patio, music, clown shows and theatre at weekends 1900, good buffet lunch, cheap, central, recommended. *Café de Don Pedro*, Roosevelt y Alameda, next to Esso filling station, good range of food, mariachi groups, open all night, another branch in Chiltiapan, near Plaza Merliot Mall, also 24 hrs. *Bandidos*, Blvd Hipódromo 131, snacks, drinks, live music Thu-Sat, cover US$3, opens 1900. *Café Teatro*, attached to the Teatro Nacional, serves very good lunches, good value (see also *La Ventana* above and Nightclubs below). *Shaw's* (good coffee and chocolates), Paseo Escalón 1 block west of Plaza Beethoven, Zona Rosa (see above) and at Metrocentro, also sell US magazines and greetings cards. *Victoria*, bakery, good for pastries.

Bars
Check for gigs in La Prensa Gráfica and El Diario de Hoy
Las Antorchitas, Blvd de los Héroes, good local orchestra with a dance floor, French and English spoken, cover charge US$1.20. *La Luna*, C Berlín 228, off Blvd de los Héroes, Urb Buenos Aires 3, T260-2921, www.lalunacasaysrte.com, great food and atmosphere, live musics some nights, décor and furniture designed by local artists. Popular and fashionable place to hang out. Reasonably priced drinks and snacks, cover charge US$2.30, closed Sun and Mon, but open for lunch Mon-Fri, 1200-1500, set menu about US$2.50, no cover except Fri Salsa nights, US$6, take taxi late at night. *Club 'M'*, C José Martí 7, San Benito,

T223-9321, trendy. *Sinatra's Bar*, Centro Comercial Loma Linda, T224-5736, piano-bar, expensive. *Villa Fiesta*, Blvd de los Héroes opposite Hospital Bloom, live music, popular, US$6 cover, good. On Calle San Antonio Abad, good places for **live music** are El Atrio, 3 Diablos and Las Celtas, all opposite Centro Comercial San Luis on the same stretch of road as *Las Ventanas*. Alongside Centro Comercial San Luis is *El Arpa* (run by Gerry from Ireland) and *Déjà Vu* which also have live music. See also *British Club* (see Cultural centres in Directory below) and Nightclubs.

All leading hotels have their own nightclub. All discos have ladies' night on Wed and Thu **Nightclubs** when women enter free and get a discount on drinks; go in a group. Zona Rosa, Colonia San Benito, has many bars/discos/open-air cafés in a 5-block area, well-lit, crowded Fri-Sat night (discos' cover charge is US$7), take bus 306 from near Esso/Texaco/Mundo Feliz on Boulevard de los Héroes before 2000, taxi thereafter. *Mario's* on Blvd Hipódromo, Zona Rosa, with good live music; *Café Teatro*, by National Theatre, Tue-Sat, jazz on Tue, various music other nights. *La Luna*, C Berlín 228, Urb Buenos Aires 3, 2 blocks from Blvd de los Héroes, see under Bars, above. *Villa Fiesta*, Blvd de los Héroes Norte, T226-2143 for reservation Fri-Sat, restaurant/bar, Mon-Wed Latin music (Grupo Fiesta), Thu 'Rumba Seis', Fri-Sat Latin music with guest bands (cover US$11). Marimba concerts Sat and Sun 1700-2100 at *La Tortuga Feliz*, 4a C Pte 1-5 Santa Tecla, not so happy turtle served in the speciality soup. *Zone Disco* and *Jungle* on Blvd del Hipódromo, popular with good dance music.

Entertainment

A few older-style cinemas in the centre are being overshadowed by the Multiplexes along **Cinema** the Blvd de los Héroes. Look in local press for listings. 'Arthouse' films are shown at *La Luna* (see Bars) on Tue 1800, free, *Cine Presidente* and *Cine Caribe*, Plaza Las Américas, see press for details. *Alliance Française* arranges film seasons, T223-8084.

Club Salvadoreño admits foreigners, owns a fine Country Club on Lago Ilopango called **Clubs** *Corinto* (with a golf course, green fee US$23), cabins for rent US$30 per day (not holidays), and has a seaside branch at Km 43 on the coast road, near La Libertad, much frequented during the dry season, Nov-Apr; T/F225-1634, Lic Oscar Paloma, Mon-Fri 0800-1200, 1330-1600. The *Automobile Club of El Salvador* has a chalet for bathing at La Libertad. See also *Atami Beach Club* under La Libertad, page 814. *Club Náutico*, at the Estero de Jaltepeque, famous for its boat races across the mud flats at low tide. *Lips*, Paseo General Escalón 5146, men's club with dancing girls, billiards, casino under construction.

Ballet and **theatre** at the *Teatro Nacional de Bellas Artes*, and music or plays at the Teatro **Music, dance** Cámera. **Folk music** in *Café Teatro*, in the Teatro Nacional, 2 Av Sur, C Delgado, T222-8760. **& theatre**

Baseball: on the field opposite Mercado Nacional de Artesanías, Tue-Fri 1700, Cuban and US **Spectator** coaches, local teams, admission US$1.25. **Bowling**: at Bolerama Jardín and Club **sports** Salvadoreño. **Motor racing**: at new El Jabalí autodrome on lava fields near Quetzaltepeque. *For all sporting* **Football**: is played on Sun and Thu according to programme at the Cuscatlán and Flor *events, check La* Blanca Stadiums. *Prensa Gráfica and El Diario de Hoy*

Festivals

During Holy Week, and the fortnight preceding **6 Aug**, the celebrations of *El Salvador del Mundo* are held. As a climax, colourful floats wend their way up the Campo de Marte (the park encompasssing the Parque Infantil and Palacio de Deportes; 9 C Pte and Av España). On **5 Aug**, an ancient image of the Saviour is borne before the large procession, before church services the next day, celebrating the *Feast of the Transfiguration*. On **12 Dec**, *Day of the Indian*, there are processions honouring the Virgin of Guadalupe in El Salvador (take bus No 101 to the Basílica de Guadalupe, on the edge of the city on the Carretera a Santa Tecla, to see colourful processions).

El Salvador

Shopping

For a one-stop shop crafts may be bought at the *Mercado Nacional de Artesanías*, opposite the Estado Mayor on the road to Santa Tecla (buses 101A, B or C, 42B, 79, 34, 30B), at prices similar to the Mercado Cuartel. Good cross section of items even if not that well presented. Some of the cheapest prices, open 0800-1800 daily.

Acogipiri, handicapped and women's project, ceramics retail and wholesale, Gabriela Mistral 4, Pasaje 11, No 563, Col Centroamérica, T226-7854, F226-5269, Eileen Girón Batres (speaks English), eilgiro@es.com.sv *Ava*, inside the *Ultima Alucinación Restaurant* (which serves great savoury pancakes), 7 C Pte No 5153 y Av Masferrer Nte, Col Escalón, T264 3848. Metal works of art by local artist Ana Evelyn using a technique known as *repujado*. Mon-Fri 1000-1800, Fri and Sat 2000-2200 and Sat 1000-1400. *El Arbol de Dios*, La Mascota y Av Masferrer, T224-6200, arts and crafts store, restaurant, museum and garden, operated by famed national artist Fernando Llort from La Palma, open Mon-Sat 1000-2200. (Llort designed the façade of the Metropolitan Cathedral). *La Cosecha*, Centro Cultural La Mazoroca, San Antonio Abad 1447, T226-5219, exhibitions and workshop producing T-shirts, posters, etc relating to Civil War, also wholesale prices. *Mercado Cuartel*, 8 Av Norte, 1 C Ote, crafts market, a few blocks east of the Teatro Nacional, rebuilt after a disastrous fire in 1995. **Towels** (Hilasal brand) may be bought here with various Maya designs. Good market in the centre on C Arce between 2 Av Sur and 7 Av Sur. Custom-made handicrafts (pottery, wood, jewellery, jade), antiques at *Pedro Portillo*, Antigua C San Antonio Abad, Urb Lisboa, Casa 3, 2nd floor, T284-4753 in advance. *Tienda de Artesanías La Cosecha*, in Casa Cultural La Mazorca, C San Antonio Abad 1447, T/F226-5219, 100m north of entrance to university, on left, good prices, large selection (bus 30B, 26, 44).

Metrocentro, the large shopping precinct with adequate parking on the Blvd de los Héroes, northwest of the city centre, contains 2 of best-known department stores, *Siman* and *Schwartz*, together with boutiques, gift shops and a small supermarket. An extension has some 35 further shops, including *El Rosal*, 8a Etapa, Local 278, wide variety of local handicrafts. It is accompanied by another shopping complex to the south, *Metrosur*, which has fewer shops (0900-2000 Mon-Sat, 0900-1900 Sun). Another shopping centre, *Villas Españolas*, is on the Paseo Escalón, 1 block south of the Redondel Masferrer; it is rather more exclusive, with expensive boutiques, several impressive furniture stores, and a minimarket specializing in tinned food from around the world. *Galerías Escalón*, Col Escalón, has department stores and cybercafés. The supermarket *Super Selectos* is on Redondel Masferrer itself. There is another called *Feria Rosa* opposite the Foreign Ministry on the road to Santa Tecla (Pan-American Highway), which is by no means fully occupied; similarly the *Plaza Merliot* in Merliot suburb. Also *Plaza San Benito*, San Benito, with *La Despensa de Don Juan*, best supermarket in the city. Paseo Escalón has a wide variety of boutiques and gift shops in all price ranges. Prices in shopping centres are much higher than in the centre of town. There are also some exclusive shops in the Zona Rosa. *El Sol* and *Europa* are 2 major supermarkets in Plaza Beethoven, Paseo Gen Escalón and Av 75 Norte.

For modern art and antiques try *Galería Rosenthal*, Centro Comercial El Manantial, C Reforma 232, San Benito, run by Pietro Yanelli, T224-0158, speaks Italian, some English, helpful. *Viejos Tiempos*, 3 C Pte entre 9 y 11 Av Norte, Centro, T222-6203, Jorge Antonio Sibrian, antiques, frames, odd articles, recommended. Several small galleries and antique shops around Escalón (side streets north of Paseo Escalón); nice gallery/antique store *Sol y Luna*, 7a C Pte, Polish/Salvadorean-owned. For those interested in cigars, *Timber Box* in *Hotel El Salvador*, T298-5444, sells fine cigars and other tobaccos and accessories, open Mon-Fri 0930-1230, 1330-1900, Sat 0930-1230, Lic Edward Neuwald Meza.

Bookshops At the Universidad de El Salvador (UES) and the Universidad Centroamericana (UCA). *Cervantes*, 9 Av Sur 114 in the Centre and Edif El Paseo 3, Paseo Escalón. *Bautista* (T222-2457), 10 C Pte 124, religious bookshop. *Cultura Católica*, opposite Teatro Nacional. *El Arabe* (T222-3922) 4 Av Norte. *Clásicos Roxsil* (T228-1212), 6 Av Sur 1-6, Santa Tecla. *Editorial Piedra Santa*, Av Olímpica 3428, Av 65-67 Sur, T223-5502. *Etc Ediciones* in Basilea Shopping Centre, San Benito. *Eutopia*, Av La Capilla 258, San Benito, new and used books, good prices. Some English books at *Librería Cultural Salvadoreña* in Metrosur. Others at *Librería Quixaje*, C Arce, and a few at *Shaw's* chocolate shops. American magazines and secondhand books at *La Revista*, Hipódroma 235, Zona Rosa, large selection. Magazines and newspapers in English can be bought at leading hotels and many shops sell US magazines.

Sports

Mountain biking: at *Bike Doctor Racing*, Centro Comercial Juan Pablo II 313A, Blvd San Antonio Abad, T260-0914. **Rollerskating**: Av La Reforma, 100 m from international school and Spanish Embassy, open daily, large, ample parking, skate rental, bus 308. **Tennis/squash**: *Raquet Club Complex*, opposite *Hotel El Salvador*, has 6 tennis courts and 6 squash courts. **Watersport**: *Amphibious*, Centro Comercial Plaza San Benito, C La Reforma 114, local 1-16, T279-4148, owner Robert Rotherham (and 2 sons), surfboard rental US$15 per day, kayak rental, windsurfing lessons, excursions arranged, also deep-sea fishing US$180 up to 6 people, English spoken, equipment for sale; also has mountain bike rental.s

Transport

Bus: city buses are either blue and white for normal services, or red and white for special services, *preferenciales*. Most routes have both normal and special buses. Fares are US$0.18 for normal services, more expensive after 1800; US$0.23 for special services. Most run 0500-2000, after which use taxis.

Local
Most buses stop running at 2100

    Some useful routes: 29 from Terminal de Oriente to Metrocentro via downtown; 30 Mercado Central to Metrocentro; 30B from Mundo Feliz (100 m up from Esso station on Blvd de los Héroes) to Escalón, 79 Av Norte, Zona Rosa (San Benito), Alameda Roosevelt and back to Metrocentro along 49 Av; 34 San Benito-Mercado de Artesanías-Terminal de Occidente-Mercado Central-Terminal Oriente; 52 'Paseo' Parque Infantil-Metrocentro-Plaza Las Américas-Paseo Escalón-Plaza Masferrer; 52 'Hotel' Parque Infantil-Metrocentro-*Hotel El Salvador*-Plaza Masferrer. Route 101 buses to/from Santa Tecla are blue and white for either class of service.

    Taxis: plenty (all yellow), don't have meters, ask fare before getting in. **Fares**: local journeys 3-4 km US$6 by day, US$6-US$7 at night. On longer trips, negotiate, about US$12 per hr or US$75 for a 6-7 hr day. Few drivers speak English. They will charge more in the rain. More expensive taxis may be hired from: *Acontaxis* (T270-1176/8), *Cobra* (T264-0327), *Dos Pinos* (T245-4743), *Acomet* (T276-5136). *Taxis Acacya* specializes in services to the airport (see below). For airport/beach trips call *Transportes Rapalo*, T225-1079, quick service.

Air: The international airport (SAL), T339-9455 and 339-9182, at Comalapa is 62 km southeast from San Salvador towards Costa del Sol beach, reached by a 4-lane toll highway. Acacya minibus to airport, from 3 C Pte y 19 Av Norte (San Salvador T271-4937, airport T339-9182, 0600, 0700, 1000, 1400 (be there 15 mins before), US$3 one-way. (Leave from airports when full, on right as you go out, but unreliable.) *Acacya*, T271-4937 also has a taxi service, US$20, the same as other radio taxi companies; ordinary taxis charge US$18, US$25 at night. A luxury bus service runs to 2 hotels for US$8.50, known as *Aerobuses*, T223-9206, and leaves the airport 4 times a day. Taxi to La Libertad beach US$20-30; to Costa del Sol US$20. There is a post office, a tourist office, two exchange desks, including Banco Hipotecario (open daily 0700-1900) and duty-free shopping for both departures and arrivals.

Long distance

    The old airport is at Ilopango, 13 km east of the city and is primarily used by the air force. However, small planes fly from Ilopango to San Miguel (30 mins), Usulután, Santa Rosa de Lima, San Francisco Gotera and La Unión; tickets from the civilian traffic offices (*TAES*, Taxis Aéreos El Salvador, T295-0363 or T/F295-0330, in San Miguel Sra de Domínguez T661-3954, or Gutiérrez Flying Service). *Línea Aérea Salvadoreña*, *LASA* (T243-1015, F243-2540) runs a daily service to San Miguel at 0630 and 1630, returning at 0715 and 1715, for US$35 return plus tax. Charter flights are easily arranged. For private aviation, tours, lessons, air taxis, *Club Salvador de Aviación Civil y Reserva*, T295-0391.

Car hire: local insurance (about US$10-15 per day plus a deductible US$1,000 deposit) is mandatory and 13% IVA applies: rentals from *Avis*, 43 Av Sur 137, T261-1212, F, also at leading hotels (ie *Camino Real*) can rent in advance from abroad. *Uno*, member of *Affinity*

El Salvador

International, Edificio Sunset Plaza, Av Masferrer Sur y C Mascota, Col Maquilishuat (bus 101D), T263-9371, 24-hr emergency service, cellular T298-1122, www.unorent.com, English and French spoken, good prices and service, free transfer from airport, excursions arranged. *Budget*, Cond Fuentes, Beethoven Loc 1, Escalón, T263-5583, airport T339-9186; www.budget.com   *Hertz*, Av Olímpica y 73 Av Sur Local 21, T279-0634, F279-0363, www.hertz.com *Superior Renta de Carros*, 3 C Poniente y 15 Av Norte 828, Centro, T222-9111, F221-2697, Superior@salnet.net   *Tropic Car Rental*, Av Olímpica 3597, Escalón, T279-3236, tropic@es.com.sv, (runs tours, has 4WD vehicle, good service). *Colón Renta Autos*, T/F274-1410, will collect at hotel, no English spoken. *Sandoval & Co*, T235-4405, sub compact late model cars from US$10 per day, English spoken; *Euro Rent-Cars*, T235-5232, near university area, daily rates from US$10; *Universal de Viajes*, 73 Av Norte 239, Colonia Escalón, T279-4767, F279-4434, English spoken.

Car repairs: Carlos Granicio, San Jacinto, Col Harrison T270-6830 for general car repairs. Julio Henríquez, *Auto-Inter*, 10 Av Sur 1-7, Santa Tecla, T228-8433, 0800-1600 Mon-Fri, speaks English, or contact through René Carmona at *Ximena's Guest House*. *Taller Mundar*, owned by English-speaking José Mungia, Pasaje Carolina Lote 15, Col Paraíso de la Escalón. Be aware that spare parts are hard to come by in El Salvador.

Insurance: Francisco Ernesto Paz, Asesor (for El Salvador and Central American companies), Blvd de los Héroes, Pasaje Los Angeles 151 (turn right at *Toto's Pizza*), T260-2985.

Car papers: Ministerio de Hacienda, 'Tres Torres', turn left on Boulevard de los Héroes 300 m past Texaco station. T226-1900.

Buses Domestic services go from **Terminal de Occidente**, off Blvd Venezuela, T223-3784 (take city buses 4, 7C, 27, 44 or 34); **Terminal de Oriente**, end of Av Peralta in Centro Urb Lourdes (take city buses No 29 from Metrocentro, 42 from Alameda, or No 4, from 7 Calle), T221-5379, very crowded with buses and passengers, keep your eyes open for the bus you want; and **Terminal Sur**, San Marcos, Zona Franca, about 9 km from the city (take city bus No 26 from Universidad Nacional area or Av España downtown, take taxi to city after 1830). Routes and fares are given under destinations.

International Buses Standard service to Guatemala: a confederation of buses (*Pezzarossi, Taca, Transesmer, Melva, Vencedora, Daniel Express* and *Centro América*) operate to Guatemala City more or less hourly (5½ hrs, US$8) from the Puerto Bus terminal at Alameda Juan Pablo II y 19 Av Norte; T222-3224, T222-2138; you can walk there from city centre, but not advisable with luggage; take bus 101D from Metrocentro, or bus 29, 52 to 21 Av Norte, 2 blocks south of terminal (city buses don't permit heavy luggage). The terminal has a *casa de cambio*, good rates, open daily, a restaurant (overpriced) and a hotel; alternatively stay at *American Guest House*, 5 mins' walk or US$3 by taxi with luggage (see above). There are 16 departures daily 0330-1600 Mon-Sat, 12 on Sun, and the fare is US$8, 5 hrs.

Luxury service to Guatemala: *King Quality*, Puerto Bus T271-3330 (or *Pullmantur* T243-1300), runs a daily service at 0630 and 1530 from *Hotel Presidente* to Guatemala City for US$27.50 (US$49.50 return), luxury service, with a/c, film, drinks and meals; also to Tegucigalpa 0700, US$45 return. *Confort Lines*, Al J Pablo II y Av Norte, T271-1361, US$18 one way, US$30 return. *Hotel Princess* has a luxury shuttle on microbus to Guatemala City US$30 one way. *Ticabus* (from address below, but calls at Puerto Bus) runs to Guatemala at 0530, US$9 one way. Reserve all *Ticabus* services in advance. Also from Terminal de Occidente, *El Cóndor* goes to **Talismán**, Mexico via Sonsonate, La Hachadura and Escuintla, US$12, 0330, 9½ hrs, also 0700-0800 to Guatemala City, compared with *Galgos* on the same route from Puerto Terminal, 1030 and 0300, 9 hrs, better service, US$10.30. If you want to go **direct to Mexico** with no stopover in Guatemala, call T260-5864, F262-5200, they will arrange 1st-class a/c bus to Tapachula with one change in Guatemala City, passport formalities done on bus.

To Tegucigalpa: through Pullman services: *Cruceros del Golfo* from Puerto Bus, T222-2158, 0600 and 1600 daily, US$18, 7 hrs, arrive early; *Ticabus* from *Hotel San Carlos*, C Concepción 121, T222-4808, US$15, leaves 0500, ticket office opens 0430, change buses in Honduras, direct to Managua. *King Quality* departs at 0600, US$25. Alternatively, take local services from Terminal de Oriente Ruta 306 to Santa Rosa de Lima, 4 hrs, US$2.20, less time by

El Salvador

express US$2.50, then Ruta 346 to the border at **El Amatillo**, 30 mins, US$0.40, last bus to border 1730; see Honduras chapter for onward transport.

To countries further south: *Ticabus* to **Managua** US$35, **San José** US$50, **Panama City** US$75. *King Quality* to Managua, departs from Puerto Terminal daily at 0530, US$40, a/c, 1st-class service.

Trains Services are very unreliable to the extent that there is no schedule. Trains do run and are used by locals. San Salvador-Sonsonate-Metapán, through coffee plantations. T221-1417.

Directory

Aerolíneas Argentinas, Alameda Roosevelt 3006, T/F260-5450. *Air France*, Blvd El Hipódromo 645, **Airline** T263-8192. *Alitalia*, 55 Av Sur entre Avs Olímpica y Roosevelt, T298-9553. *American*, Edif La **offices** Centroamericana, Alameda Roosevelt 3107, basement and 3rd floor, T298-0777. *British Airways*, 43 Av Norte 216, T260-9933. *Continental*, Edif Torre Roble, ground floor, Blvd de los Héroes, T260-3263. *Grupo Taca*, (Taca, Aviateca, Lacsa, Copa and Nica), main office 1st floor, Centro Comercial, Galerías Escalón, between 71 y 73 Av Norte (buses 52, 30B, 16) T298-5055 and T298-5077 *Iberia*, Centro Comercial Plaza Jardín, local C, Carretera a Santa Tecla, T223-2711, airport T339-9149. *Japan Airlines*, Edif Edim-Lama, Blvd Del Hipódromo 645, T263-8192, F264-3416. *KLM*, Av Los Angeles, Col Miramonte, T264-0604. *Lufthansa*, 87 Av Norte, FountainBlue Plaza, Col Escalón, T263-2850. *Mexicana*, Centro Profesional Presidente, Edif B, T243-3633. *United*, Galerías Escalón, Local 14, 71 Av Norte y Paseo Gen Escalón, Col Escalón, T298-5462, F298-5536.

Most banks (except *Cuscatlán*, see below) open 0900-1700 Mon-Fri, 0900-1200 Sat; *casas de cambio* **Banks** keep the same hours but most close 1300-1400 for lunch. The banks have branches in all the shopping malls and in large hotels such as *Princess*, *Radisson* (open daily till 1900). ATMs only give US dollars. *Banco Agrícola Comercial de El Salvador*, Paseo Escalón 3635, T279-1033, F263-3690, good for remittances from abroad, English spoken. International department of *Banco Cuscatlán* is in Santa Tecla (bus 101D), international currencies may be cashed here, 0900-1300, 1345-1600 Mon-Fri, 0900-1200 Sat. The branch at *Hotel El Salvador* is open 0900-2000 Mon-Fri, 0900-1200 Sat. There are *casas de cambio* throughout the city. Where TCs may be changed (several opposite Parque Infantil on Alameda Juan Pablo Segundo between 9 and 10 Avs Norte) with passport and one other form of photographic ID. *Banco Salvadoreño*, C Rubén Darío 1236, good rates for TCs and Visa card advances. Never change money with the street changers in Parque Infantil, in front of the *casas de cambio*. Quetzales, Mexican pesos and lempiras may be changed at *Casa de Cambio El Quetzal*, Alameda Juan Pablo Segundo y 19 Av Norte (Puerto Bus terminal), 0800-1700 Mon-Fri, 0800-1200 Sat. Accounts in dollars may be opened at *Citibank*, Edif Palic, CL Nueva 1, Alam Dr M E Araujo, Col Escalón, T245-1850.

Aval-Visa, Av Olímpica y 55 Av Norte (in Centro Comercial, behind Credomatic), does cash advances on Visa, T279-3077. In emergency, for Visa International or MasterCard, T224-5100; Visa TCs can only be changed by Visa cardholders. Visa ATMs can be found at Aval card 24-hr machines, the majority at Esso and Shell service stations (eg Esso Blvd los Héroes), but also at Metrocentro, 8th floor food court, and Centro de Servicio, Av Olímpica. See also pages 78-79 in the yellow pages. *American Express* is at *El Salvador Travel Service*, Carretera Panamericana y C Mascota, Km 4 on the road to Santa Tecla (by Shell Station, bus 42 and 101), T279-3844, F223-0035, www.elsaltravel.com.sv, to change TCs, get them stamped at the Amex desk then go upstairs round the back to *Banco del Comercio*, open 0900-1700, to get the cash; must take passport. Amex loss or theft, T223-0177. *Western Union* for money transfers, c/o *Banco Salvadoreño* branches, T225-2503 (48 other branches throughout the country, look out for the black and yellow sign), head office Alameda Roosevelt 2419 between 45 y 47 Av Sur, T298-1888, Mon-Fri 0800-1700, Sat 0800-1200, take passport and photographic ID (30 mins if from USA/Canada, 2-3 hrs from Europe).

Internet: Internet cafés all around the Universidad Nacional, especially on C San Antonio Abad. *Cyber* **Communi-** *Dreams*, Blvd Universitario 1951, cheap, US$1.20/hr, open 7 days a week. In the centre on C Arce there is a **cations** shopping mall, halfway betwen Hospital Rosales and the cathedral with half a dozen cafés all around US$1.20/hr. *Cafe Internet Ejje.com*, in Metrocentro 2nd level, also at Galerías Escalón, Paseo Escalón between 71 and 73 Avs, both open Mon-Sat 0900-2000, Sun 1000-1800. *Cyber Café Enlínea*, Av Río Lempa y C Marmara 18, Col Jardines de Guadalupe, about 6 km from downtown behind Universidad José S Cañas, a little below *Hotel Siesta*, buses 5, 27, 42, 44, 101-C, T243-0673, www.cybercafe.com.sv, and www.enlinea.com.sv, US$3.45 per hr, good food. *Cybercentro*, 25 Av Norte 583, T225-0588. *Cybermannia*,

El Salvador

Paseo Colón, Mon-Sat 0900-2100, Sun 1000-1900 US$3.50/hr. *Genesis, Hotel El Salvador*, T264-5437. *Quik Internet*, Av Masferrer Norte, C El Mirador y Av Rep Fed de Alemania, Block 162B, Col Escalón, T264-7001.

Post office: *Central Post Office* at the Centro de Gobierno with EMS, T271-4036, super-fast service: branches at *Almacenes Siman* (Centro), *Librería Hispanoamérica*, Centro Comercial Gigante (Col Escalón), Metrocentro, with EMS, Mercado Local 3, Mercado Modelo, 1st floor above *PHL* stationer on Plaza Morazán, Av Olímpica y 57 Av Norte, next to *Super Selectos* (behind *Casa de Regalos*, owned by Canadian Moe Heft, who repairs watches and is helpful, T223-5944, open 0830-1700 Mon-Fri and Sat am). Good service to Europe. Open Mon-Fri 0730-1700, Sat 0730-1200. *Lista de Correos*, Mon-Fri 0800-1200, 1430-1700, good service for mail collection.

Fax service: C Rubén Darío y 3 Av Norte, charge by the min, Guatemala US$0.92, USA US$2.35. **Courier services** many throughout the city. *DHL*, 43 Av Norte 228, T260-4466, F260-6084, www.dhl.com.sv *Gigante Express*, C 11 pte 3971, T264-2121, F263-3875. *León Express*, Alameda Roosevelt entre 49 y 51 Av Sur 2613, T224-3005, F224-3660, has *casa de cambio*. *International Bonded Couriers*, 1 C Poniente y 63 Av Norte, Escalón, Edif Comercial A&M 15, T279-0347, F279-1814. *UPS*, C El Progreso 3139, Col Roma, T/F245-3845.

Telephones: At the Centro de Gobierno, Metrocentro (open 0700-1930, 1830 for fax), and other locations. See Telephone services, page 768. **Phone boxes** throughout the city, card only, available at fast-food stores such as *Pollo Campero*, direct dialling to anywhere in the world, also collect calls.

Cultural centres *Alianza Francesa*, 5 Av Norte 152, Col Escalón. *American Society*, T224-1330, Chester Stemp, 0800-1600 Mon-Fri, at International School, or Pastor Don Dawson, T223-5505 (Union Church), cultural activities, open only to US citizens and their spouses and children, emergency assistance for US citizens. Family membership US$20 per year, single US$14. *British Club*, Paseo Escalón 4714, p2, Apdo postal (06) 3078, opposite *Farmacia Paseo*, T223-6765, F224-0420, open Mon-Sat 1700-midnight, Sun 1300-2100, has bar (with imported British beer), restaurant open to non-resident visitors (great fish and chips, US$4.50), British newspapers, an English-language library, darts, pool and snooker. *Club Arabe*, C Mirador, 3 blocks above *Hotel El Salvador*, open to members' guests, swimming pool, sauna, tennis, bar. *EL Centro Cultural*, Pasaje Senda Florida Sur, behind Edif Sisa, Carretera Santa Tecla, near Salvador del Mundo, T279-1868, Mon-Fri 0800-1800, Sat 0800-1200, art exhibitions, monthly shows. *El Centro Español*, off the Paseo Escalón, is open to non-members, has 2 pools (one for children), tennis courts, weight training room and aerobics salon.

Embassies & consulates *Belize*, Condominio Médico, local 5, p2, Blvd Tutunichapa, Urb la Esperanza, T/F226-3682. *Costa Rica*, Av Albert Einstein 11, Col Lomas de San Francisco, T273-3111. *Canada*, Av Las Palmas III, Col San Benito, T279-4659, F279-0765. *France*, 1 C Pte 3718, Col Escalón, T279-4260. *Germany*, 77 Av Norte y 7 C Pte 3972, T263-2099, F298-3580. *Guatemala*, 15 Av Norte 135 y C Arce, T271-2225, F221-3019, visas issued within 24 hrs. *Honduras*, 3A C Pte y 71 Av Norte, Col Escalón, T223-4975, F223-2221, *Mon-Fri 0900-1200, 1300-1500*. *Israel*, 85 Av Norte 619, Col Escalón, T263-3183, F263-3245. *Italy*, La Reforma 158, Col San Benito, T298-3050. *Mexico*, Pasaje 12 y C Circunvalación, San Benito, behind *Hotel Presidente*, T243-2037. *Nicaragua*, 71 Av Norte y 1 C Pte 164, Col Escalón, T223-1223, F223-7201. *Norway*, 73 Av Norte, Escalón, 100 m north of Paseo Escalón, near Galerías. *Panama*, Alameda Roosevelt y 55 Av Norte 2838, T260-5453. *Switzerland*, Pastelería Lucerna, 85 Av Sur y Paseo Escalón 4363, T279-3047. *UK*, Edif Inter Inversiones, 4828 Paseo Escalón y Calle La Ceiba, T263-6527, F263-6516. *US*, Blvd Santa Elena, Antiguo Cuscutlán, T278-4444, F278-6011, outside the city, reached by bus 101A.

Language schools *Academia Europea*, 99 Av Norte 639, Col Escalón, San Salvador, T263-4355, www.euroacad.edu.sv *Centro de Intercambio y Solidaridad*, Blv Universitario 4, T226-2623, www.cis-elsalvador.org Spanish school in the mornings 0800-1200, English school in the afternoons from 1700-1900 - volunteer English teachers needed for 10 week sessions. *Cihuatan Spanish Language Institute* (Ximena's), C San Salvador 202-B, San Salvador, Col Centro América (near *Hotel Camino Real*), T260-2481, F260-2427, ximenas@navegante.com.sv; rates are US$125 per week including board at *Ximena's Guesthouse* in the city or nearby farm, *Lisa's Inn*, 17 km from the capital between Apopa and Guazapa (buses San Salvador-Aguilares stop at the farm). *Escuela de Idiomas Salvador Miranda*, PO Box 3274, Correo Centro de Gobierno, T222-1352, F222-2849, US$125-150 per week including board. *Superior de Idiomas Cambridge*, Av La Capilla 226 Col San Benito, T/F264-1253, esi@ejje.com, good teachers, also sometimes require native speakers of English and other languages to teach.

Libraries The library of the *UCA* (Universidad Centroamericana), José S Cañas, Autopista Sur, the road to the airport, is said to be the most complete collection in the capital. US information library at *American*

Chamber of Commerce, 87 Av Norte 720, apto A, Col Escalón, Apdo Postal (05) 9, Sr Carlos Chacón, speaks English, helpful. *Centro Cultural Salvadoreño*, Av Los Sisimiles, Metrocentro Norte, T226-9103, 0800-1100, 1400-1700, English library, excellent. *Intercambios Culturales de El Salvador*, 67 Av Sur 228, Col Roma, T245-1488, F224-3084, extensive Spanish and English reference library, local artistic exhibitions, computer school.

Medical services

Dentist: *USAM Dental Clinic*, 19 Av Norte between 1 C Pte and Juan Pablo II, near Puerto Bus Terminal, bus 101D and 30A from Metrocentro, opens 0800, go early for emergency treatment. **Doctors:** *Medicentro*, 27 Av Norte is a good place to find doctors in most specialist fields, afternoon mostly after 1500. *Dr Jorge Panameno*, T225-9928, 24-hr beeper 298-1122, English-speaking, makes house calls at night for about US$35. **Hospitals:** *Hospital de la Mujer*, entre 81 y 83 Av Sur y C Juan José Cañas, Col Escalón (south of Paseo), bus 52 Paseo, T223-8955, F279-1441. *Hospital Pro-Familia*, 25 Av Norte 483, 11 blocks east of Metrocentro, T225-6100/4771, clinics and 24-hr emergency, reasonable prices. *Hospital Baldwin*, 37 Av Norte 297 y Prolongación C Arce, near Metro Sur, T298-5131, emergency, excellent; if short of cash or in emergency, public *Hospital Rosales*, 25 Av Norte y 3 C Pte, long waits. *Clínicas Médicas*, 25 Av Norte 640 (bus 3, 9, 44 centro from Universidad Nacional), T/F225-5233. If you contract a serious stomach problem, the doctor will send you for tests, which will cost US$5-6. **Opticians:** *Optica Ianuzzelli*, C Arce, Centro, between 11 and 13 Av Sur, T271-0182, free eye test.

Tour operators

Numerous tourist agents, including: *Amor Tours*, 73 Av Sur, Col Escalón, local 21 Edif Olimpic Plaza, T223-5130, F279-0363, www.amortours.com.sv 20 years' experience, expensive. *Dive Pacific*, 79 Av Sur 135, Col Escalón, T223-8304, F223-2774, Rodolfo González, PADI instructor, excellent but expensive, English spoken, for diving off the Pacific coast at Playa Los Cóbanos, fishing tours, and dives in lakes Coatepeque and Ilopango. *El Salvador Divers*, 3 C Pte 5020A, Col Escalón, T223-0961, F264-1842, www.elsalvadordivers.com, PADI dive centre offering crater diving, owner speaks English and German. *El Salvador Travel Service*, Carretera Panamericana y C Mascota, Km 4 on the road to Santa Tecla (by Shell Station, bus 42 and 101), T279-3844, F223-0035, www.elsaltravel.com.sv American Express agents and full services. *Jaguar Tours*, *Hotel Siesta*, near Col San Benito, T289-6031, F289-6030, for express transport options to Guatemala. *Oceánica*, 5-star PADI diving school also offering crater lake dives, C Circunvalación 17B, Col Escalón, T/F263-6931, oceanica@salnet.net 2-tank divies at Ilopango or Coatepeque, US$50, at Acajutla US$60.00. English, German, French and Portuguese spoken. *Network Travel*, Ciudad Merliot, in front of plaza Merliot, T243-8716, F243-5771, turavnet@sal.gbm.net, Guatemalan package tour specialists. *Pullmantur*, Av La Revolución, T243-1300, F243-1299, pullmantur@salnet.net, besides luxury bus service to Guatemala (see above), offers excellent package tours to Antigua. *Salva Natura*, 33 Av Sur 640, Col Flor Blanca, T279-1515, F279-0220, www.salvanatura.org for permission to enter and trips to Parque Nacional El Imposible. Day trips US$18 including transport, entrance, lunch and guide. *Salvador Tours*, Villas Españolas, local 3-b, Paseo General Escalón, T264-34110, F263-6687, www.puntamango.com.sv Recommended for for Punta Mango surf tours.

Useful addresses

Ambulance/rescue: (Comandos de Salvamento), T222-0817/221-1310. **Red Cross:** Av Henry Dunat y 17 Av Norte, T224-1330, emergency 24-hr T222-5155. **Immigration department:** in the Ministry of Interior Building, Centro de Gobierno, T221-2111, open Mon-Fri 0800-1600. They will consider sympathetically extending tourist visas, but be prepared with photos and plenty of patience. *Migración y Extranjería* in Plaza Merliot saves the trip to Centro de Gobierno. **Complaints:** Director General of Police, 6 C Ote, T271-4422. Also at Unidad Metropolitana Nacional Civil, I C Pte and 13 Av Norte. **Police:** emergency T121, 123, or 228-1156, no coin needed from new coin phones. In San Salvador, metropolitan police respond to tourist complaints. **For women visitors:** *Instituto de Estudios de la Mujer*, Cemujer, Blvd María Cristina 144, T/F226-5466, Spanish only (Raquel Cano, T/F221-5486, works with Cemujer; her husband is helpful with information). *American Women's Association*, Patricia Arias, T273-3204, for information, cultural and social events for English-speaking women, US$4.60 per year. *La Luna*, see above, is owned by women and has access to many women's organizations; ask for Beatriz, who speaks English and French; it is a safe place for women to go alone or in a group; office at C Berlín y 4 de Mayo, look for 'Ropero' sign, open daytime, T225-5054 (tell them Pato sent you). *Conamus Women's Center*, Florida Pasaje las Palmeras 130, T260-2671, open business hrs Mon-Sat, Marina Navarro is very helpful. **Others:** *Centro de Intercambio y Solidaridad (CIS)*, Blvd Universitario 4, next to Cine Reforma, T226-2623, www.cis-elsalvador.org, for language classes, brigade work, FMLN programmes and schools. *Instituto para el Rescate Ancestral Indígena Salvadoreño (RAIS)*, Av Santiago 20, Col San Mateo, has programmes for local aid to Indian communities and the Nahual language and customs. **Development and export of arts and crafts:** contact Salvador Monterrosa at Europe Union NGO Prodesar, Pasaje Los Pinos 241, Col Escalón

El Salvador

T263-2400, F263-5350, prodesar@gbm.net. **Work**: UCA University Simeon Cañas, T273-3503, English-language programme, always need certified English teachers, pay US$9 per hr. Also qualified teachers at university level often needed at The American University, T243-3527, speak to Dr Gavidia.

Around San Salvador

Many places can be visited in a day from San Salvador either on the frequent bus services or by car. Closest to the city is south to the indigenous village of **Panchimalco**, heading east are the beautiful setting and views around **Lago de Ilopango**; and to the southwest the crater of **Volcán San Salvador** (see Santa Tecla, below).

Heading west towards Santa Ana, but still manageable in a day, are the archaeological sites of **Joyo de Cerén**, El Salvador's Pompeii, and **San Andrés** and the peaks of **Volcán Izalco**, **Cerro Verde** (see page 791) with the deep blue waters of **Lago de Coatepeque** in the crater below.

The limits of a comfortable weekend trip will take you to the garden park of **Ichanmichen** is restful (see Zacatecoluca, page 816)and the pyramid of **Tazumal** (west of Santa Ana) is also worth a visit (page 794). At weekends the coast around La Libertad (see below) is very popular. Bus 495 from the Terminal del Occidente goes to the seaside resort of Costa del Sol (see page 816). The Mountaineering Club of the University of San Salvador sponsors day hikes every Sunday morning (recommended). Transport is provided from downtown San Salvador. See local papers on Saturday for details.

El Salvador

Panchimalco
14½ km south
by a paved road

This small town and the surrounding area is home to the Pancho Indians, descendants of the Pipil tribes, one of the region's dominant Indian groups prior to conquest; a few have more or less retained their old traditions and dress. Streets of large cobbles, with low adobe houses, thread their way between huge boulders at the foot of Cerro Chulo (see also page 775). A very fine baroque colonial church, Santa Cruz, has a white façade with statues of eight saints. Inside are splendid woodcarvings and wooden columns, altars, ceilings and benches. Note especially the octagonal ceiling above the main altar which is painted a silvery blue. There is a bell inscribed with the cypher and titles of the Holy Roman Emperor Charles V, and a colourful cemetery. An ancient ceiba tree shades the marketplace (disappointing market). The **Centro de Arte y Cultura Tonatiuh**, Calle Principal 14 bis, T280-8836/27, with gallery, museum and shop, has a good atmosphere, fair prices and supports local youth projects; ask for the painter, Eddie Alberto Orantes. The **fiesta** of Santa Cruz de Roma is held on 12-14 September, with music and traditional dances; on 3 May (or the second Sunday of the month) there is the procession of Las Palmas. Bus 17 from Mercado Central at 12 Calle Poniente, San Salvador, every 45 minutes, 45 minutes, or minibus from near Mercado Central, very crowded but quicker (30 minutess), and cheaper (US$0.35).

Lago de Ilopango
The eastern shore
is less polluted
and is reached
from Cojutepeque

Beyond the four-lane highway to Ilopango airport (14½ km east) lie the deep waters of Lago de Ilopango. Surrounded by mountains, the views around El Salvador's largest and deepest crater lake are impressive. Pre-Conquest Indians used to appease the harvest gods by drowning four virgins here every year. Private chalets make access to the lake difficult, except at clubs and the *Turicentro Apulo*, but it is well worth a visit.

There are a number of lakeside cafés and bathing clubs, some of which hire dug-outs by the hour. The cafés are busy in the dry season (try *Teresa's* for fish dishes), but often closed in the middle of the year. *Hotel Vista del Lago*, T227-0208, 3 km from Apulo turn-off on the highway, is on a hill top. Bus 15, marked Apulo, runs from the bus stop on Parque Hula Hula to the lake (via the airport), 1¼ hours, US$0.30. Entrance to the *Turicentro* camping site costs US$0.60; bungalow US$3.45; parking US$0.60; plenty of hammock-hanging opportunities; showers and swimming facilities, all rather dirty. The water is reported to be polluted in parts near the shore and it is busy at weekends.

Also known as Nuevo San Salvador, 13 km west of the capital by the Pan-American **Santa Tecla**
Highway, the town is 240 m higher in a coffee-growing district and much cooler. *Population: 63,400*
Although useful as a stopping point for visits to the nearby tourist centre of *Los*
Chorros (6 km – see below) and the route to Volcán San Salvador (see below), there is
little reason to stop here. It is here that the earthquake led to the greatest loss of life, not
due to structural collapse of buildings but from a landslide triggered by the tremors.

Sleeping D *Hotel Monte Verde*, on the main road towards Los Chorros, T228-1263.
F *Hospedaje San Antonio*, 4 Av Pte, 2 blocks south of Plaza, and an unnamed **F** *Hospedaje*,
C Daniel Hernández y 6 Av, 3 blocks from Parque San Martín, green door, good, safe, will store
luggage. **F** *Posada La Libertad*, Av Melvin Jones 4-1, 3 blocks south of Parque, T228-4071,
with bath, will store lugggage.

Eating *Restaurant La Tortuga Feliz*, 4 C Pte 1-5, marimba music, garden, pleasant setting, good local food. **Comedor y Pupusería Tikal**, 2 C, half block west of 1 Av Sur, pleasant, clean, cheap.

Transport Buses101 and 101-A, B and D, leave 3 Av Norte, near the junction with C Rubén
Darío, San Salvador, every 10 mins for Santa Tecla.

This large massif has an impressive crater, over 1½ km wide and 543 m deep, known **Volcán San**
as **El Boquerón**. About 2 km to the east is the equally dramatic peak of **El Picacho** **Salvador**
(1,960 m) which dominates the capital. A rough road goes north from one block east *La Laguna botanical*
of Plaza Central in Santa Tecla, through agricultural land, climbing up and passing *garden is near*
between the two features. A walk clockwise round the crater takes about two hours; *the summit*
the first half is easy, the second half rough. The views are magnificent, if somewhat
spoilt by TV and radio towers and litter. The inner slopes of the crater are covered
with trees, and at the bottom is a smaller cone left by the eruption of 1917. The path
down into the crater starts at the westernmost of a row of antennae studding the rim,
45 minutes down (don't miss the turn straight down after 10 minutes at an incon-
spicuous junction with a big, upright slab of rock 20 m below), one hour up.

   You can follow the road north and then turn right through extensive coffee plantations and forest to reach the summit of **El Picacho**. This also makes an excellent
climb from the Escalón suburb of San Salvador, in the early morning preferably,
which takes about three to four hours return trip (take a guide).

Transport Ruta 103 buses at 0800, 1100 and 1400, returning at 0930, 1230 and 1530, leave from
4 Av Norte y C Hernando for El Boquerón (US$0.30), or pick-ups from the Parque Central; from the
end of the bus line you must walk 45 mins to the crater, but you can drive to within 50 m.

Western El Salvador

Compact and with good transport links, western El Salvador combines the dramatic
volcanic landscapes of Cerro Verde, Volcán Izalco and Lago de Coatepeque – essential
for any visitor to the country – with the serene beauty and majesty of countless water-
falls and the colourful Ruta de las Flores. Little Indian villages and pre-Colombian
ruins contrast with the vibrancy of Santa Ana, El Salvador's second largest city. Three
routes lead to Guatemala, the northernmost passing close to the impressive cloud for-
ests of Parque Nacional Montecristo on the border with Honduras.

The 4 roads which cross into Guatemala are La Hachadura (see under Sonsonate, page 815), **Routes to**
San Cristóbal (via the Pan-American Highway, page 793), Las Chinamas (see under Santa **Guatemala**
Ana, page 796) and Anguiatú (beyond Metapán, page 798).

Izalco
Population: 43,000

From the junction with the Pan-American Highway, just west of Colón, route CA 8 heads west, past Armenia, to the town of Izalco at the foot of Izalco volcano (8 km from Sonsonate, bus 53C, US$0.10). The town has evolved from the gradual merging of the *ladino* village of Dolores Izalco and the Indian village of Asunción Izalco. **Sleeping F** *Hospedaje San Rafael*, next to the church on the Central Park, very basic, no shower, dirty, noisy, motorcycle workshop, but safe and friendly, no alternative. **Festivals** 8-15 August and during the Feast of St John the Baptist from 17-24 June.

Near Izalco, at the edge of town, is the spacious swimming pool of **Atecozol**, which is in the middle of a beautiful park with a restaurant. ■ *US$0.60, parking US$0.60, bungalow US$3.45.* The park is shaded by huge mahogany trees, palms, aromatic balsam trees and *amates*. There is a battlemented tower; a monument to Tlaloc, god of rain; another to Atlacatl, the Indian who, on this spot, shot the arrow which wounded the conquistador Pedro de Alvarado; and a statue to the toad found jumping on the spot where water was discovered.

The town of Izalco and Izalco volcano are not directly connected by road. A paved road branches off the highway 14 km before the turning for Izalco town (about 22 km from Sonsonate) and goes up towards Cerro Verde, Volcán Izalco and Lago de Coatepeque (see page 790).

Caluco

South of Izalco, a few kilometres off the main road, is **Caluco** with its colonial church and a ruined Dominican church (bus 432 from Sonsonate). Two kilometres from Caluco are **Las Victorias Falls** on the Río Chiquihuat, with a couple of caves above the falls. On the same road out of Caluco is the meeting of hot and cold streams at **Los Encuentros** which form the Río Shuteca/Aguas Calientes. Five kilometres southeast of the town is **La Chapina** pool and springs on the farm of the same name.

Sonsonate

Colour map 5, grid C6
Population: 120,000.
Altitude: 225 m

Sixty-four kilometres from the capital, Sonsonate is the chief cattle-raising region. It also produces sugar, tobacco, rice, tropical fruits, hides and balsam. The city was founded in 1552 and is now hot, dirty and crowded. The beautiful El Pilar church (1723) is strongly reminiscent of the church of El Pilar in San Vicente. The **Catedral** has many cupolas (the largest covered with white porcelain) and was badly damaged in the 2001 earthquake. The old church of **San Antonio del Monte** (completed 1861), 1 km from the city, draws pilgrims from afar (**fiesta** 22-26 August). There is a small **railway museum**, look for the locomotive at the entrance to the city on the highway from San Salvador (Km 65). An important market is held each Sunday. The market outside the church is quite well-organized. In the northern outskirts of the city there is a waterfall on the Río Sensunapán. Legend has it that an Indian princess drowned there, and on the anniversary of her death a gold casket appears below the falls. The main annual event is *Feria de Candelaria* in February.

Sleeping
Price codes: see inside front cover

B-C *Agape*, at Km 63 on outskirts of the town, take old road through Sonsonate, the hotel is on the exit street to San Salvador, just before the main roundabout on the right side, T451-2667, F452-4074, converted convent, gardens, suites and rooms, a/c or fan, safe parking, good restaurant, cable TV, pool and laundry service, recommended. **B** *Plaza*, C 9a Oriente, Barrio del Angel, T/F451-3610, a/c rooms, good restaurant, pool, recommended. **E** *Castro*, on main street 3 blocks from Parque, with bath, fan, good, safe, friendly, some rooms with bed and hammock. **E** *Orbe*, 4 C Ote y 2 Av Flavián Mucci, T451-1517, parking, good restaurant. **F** *El Brasil*, 4 Av Norte, basic, clean and friendly. **F** *Hospedaje Blue River*, near bus station, with bath, large, clean rooms.

Eating

Caften Teto, nearby, clean, friendly, good servings. *Restaurant Agape* at *Agape*, highly recommended. *Nuevo Hilary*, Av Rafael Campos 1-3, local and Chinese food, generous servings, moderate prices.

Buses Bus 248 to Santa Ana, US$1 along CA 12 north, 39 km, a beautiful journey through **Transport** high, cool coffee country, with volcanoes in view; to Ahuachapán, 2 hrs, slow, best to go early in the day; San Salvador to Sonsonate by bus 530, US$0.80, 1½ hrs, very frequent. There is also a bus from San Salvador along the coast at 0600 and 1300, a beautiful ride. Take care at the bus terminal and on rural routes (eg in Nahuizalco area). **Trains** The train up to the mountains and Metapán passes here about 1030-1100; see railway museum page 788.

Route CA 8 northwest to Ahuachapán (see page 794) has spectacular scenery climb- **Excursions** ing through impressive scenary along the Ruta de las Flores, with frequent buses **from** from Sonsonate (bus 249 and 285, US$0.50, two hours) covering the 40-km paved **Sonsonate** route. The road goes through the Indian village of **Nahuizalco**. Some of the older women here still wear the *refajo* (a doubled length of cloth made of tie-dyed threads worn over a wrap-round skirt), and various crafts are still carried on, including wood and rattan furniture, although use of the Indian language is dying out. The night market has ancient traditional food on sale. **Fiestas**: 19-25 June, religious festival, music, *Danza de los Historiantes* (see page 821) and art exhibitions; 24-25 December, music and *Danza de los Pastores*. (Bus 53 D from Sonsonate, US$0.10.)

A little further up the mountainside is **Juayúa** (just off the main road), with Los Chorros de la Calera 2 km further north (bus 249 from Sonsonate). The pretty town decorated with flowers – the name means 'River of Purple Orchids' in the local Nahuat dialect – sits nestling in a valley dominated by volcanoes. It's a peaceful spot where you can watch people at work through open doors, and kids playing in the semi-cobbled street. The surrounding region is blanketed in coffee groves; the bean was introduced to the area in 1838 and today the town produces about 10% of the coffee exported from El Salvador. Its church houses an image of the Black Christ carved by Quirio Cataño at the end of the 16th century. **Tourist information** is available from *Juayuatur*, T452-2002, juystur@navegante.com.sv City tours of the colonial architecture and churches, US$6.

There are several excursions you can do in the area to see wildlife including river otters, toucans, butterflies and many other animals. In the dry season **Laguna de las Ranas** (Laguna Seca) dries up attracting numerous reptiles as it shrinks. There are also trips to the 30-m high waterfall at Salto el Talquezal, the 50-m high Salto de la Lagunilla Azul and several other waterfalls in the region – seven in one day if you take a tour, with swimming and picnics on the way (see below). The La Feria Gastrónomica Internacional is in January and celebrates with dishes from all over the world; other festivals include Día de los Canchules (October 31), when people ask for candies and Día de los Mercedes (September 17), when the houses are decorated with branches and candles leading up to the procession of the Virgen de la Mercedes. Also gastronomic festival every Sunday with music and drinking.

Sleeping and eating C *Doña Mercedes*, 2 Avenida Sur, 6 Calle Oriente 3-6, one block south of *Farmacia Don Bosco*, T452-2287. D *Las Azaleas*, C Merceditas Caseres 2-3, T452-2421. No hot water, but private bath. *Café and Restaurante La Calera*, on the main square, T452-2002, serves sandwiches in a good spot to watch the world go by. *Lauras* is 'the best in town' according to one reader. *Sanita Helados* is a café on the corner of Parque Unión, with a tourist kiosk nearby.

Directory Banks: *Banco de Comercio*, 2 blocks behind the church on the road in to town, 0830-1630. **Internet**: *Mini Librería*, 4a C Oriente, ½ block from main square, 0730-1900 (slow) US$2.75/hr.

At Km 82 on the Carretera Salcoatitán to Juayua is *Parque y Restaurante La Colina*, T452-2916, with hammocks, arts and crafts, and horse-riding available. The town has a tiny colonial church and an orchid greenhouse. **Apaneca** (see under Ahuachapán page 794) is a short distance from Sonsonate.

Several **waterfalls** and other sites of natural beauty can be found in the Sonsonate district. To the west, near the village of **Santo Domingo de Guzmán** (bus 246 from

El Salvador

Sonsonate), are the falls of **El Escuco** (2 km north), **Tepechapa** (1½ km further) and **La Quebrada** (further still up the Río Tepechapa), all within walking distance of both Santo Domingo and each other. Walk through the town, then follow the river. Several spots to swim. **Festival** in Santo Domingo, 24-25 December, with music and dancing. A short distance north is **San Pedro Puxtla** (bus 246), with a modern church built on the remains of an 18th-century edifice. From here you can visit the **Tequendama Falls** on the Río Sihuapán. Bus 219 goes east to **Cuisnahuat** (18th-century baroque church; **fiesta**, 23-29 November, San Judas), from where it is 2 km south to the Río Apancoyo, or 4 km north to **Peñón El Escalón** (covered in balsam trees) and **El Istucal Cave**, at the foot of the Escalón hill, where Indian rites are celebrated in November.

Santa Tecla to Santa Ana

The new Pan-American Highway parallels the old one, bypassing Santa Ana and continuing northwest to the border with Guatemala at San Cristóbal. Santa Ana, acting as a transport hub, has routes out to Ahuachapán to the west and the border at Las Chiminas, and heading north to Metapán and beyond to the border crossing of Anguiatú.

Joya de Cerén   Fifteen kilometres from Santa Tecla, 7 km beyond the junction with the Sonsonate road, there is a junction to the right. This road forks immediately, right to **Quezaltepeque**, left (at *Joya de Cerén* café) to **San Juan Opico**. After a few kilometres on the San Juan road, you cross the railway by the Kimberley-Clark factory. At the railway is *Restaurante Estación Sitio del Niño* (seafood, steak, local dishes, in an old station, open from 0730 Tuesday-Sunday, horse-riding tours to San Andrés, see below, contact *Jaguar Tours* in San Salvador, US$60-70 per day per person including lunch and a/c transport). After the girder bridge crossing the Río Sucio there is a grain store beside which is **Joya de Cerén** (32 km from the capital). This is a major archaeological site, not for spectacular temples, but because this is the only known site where ordinary Mayan houses have been preserved having been buried by the ash from the nearby Laguna Caldera volcano in about AD 600. Buildings and construction methods can be clearly seen; a painted book and household objects have been found. All the structures are covered with protective roofing. The site has a small but good museum, café, toilets and car park. ■ *US$3, El Salvador and Central American nationals US$0.80, parking US$0.60. Children offer replicas for sale. Bus No 108 from San Salvador Terminal de Occidente to San Juan; US$0.45, 1 hr. Bus 201 from Santa Ana, US$0.60, 1 hr, ask the bus driver to drop you at Desvío Opico from where you can catch another bus to Joya de Cerén*

San Andrés   Back on the main road, heading west is the excavated archaeological site of San Andrés, halfway between Santa Tecla and Coatepeque on the estate of the same name (its full name is **La Campana de San Andrés**). It is located at Km 32.5 on the Pan-American Highway, just after the Hilasal towel factory. A group of low structures stands in the valley (Structure 5, the furthest from the entrance, is closed because of erosion). There are good views of the nearby hills. ■ *0900-1700, Tue-Sun, US$3, popular for weekend picnics, otherwise it is quiet, café. Getting there: Bus 201 from Terminal de Occidente, US$0.80, same bus from Santa Ana.*

Lago de Coatepeque

At El Congo, some 13 km before Santa Ana, a branch road leads south to the northern shore of the beautiful Lago de Coatepeque, a favourite weekend resort, with good sailing and fishing, near the foot of Santa Ana volcano. Many weekend homes line the north and east shores, making access to the water difficult, but there are public *balnearios*: *Casa Blanca* and *Recreativa El Jordán* ■ *US$0.05 per person, parking US$0.25*. There are two islands in the lake – **Anteojo** which is close to the hotels, and **Teopán** on the far side (**AL** *Teopán Resort*, T224-4658, F245-1751, teopanisland@mail.com, with nature reserve, archaeological excavations, hiking, biking, swimming and boating. Transport and ferries arranged with booking). Launches charge US$5.75-8.60 per person for lake trips, depending on the size of the group, or about US$15 for two hours (negotiate with the owners). **Fiesta**, Santo Niño de Atocha, 25-29 June.

B *Del Lago*, T446-9511, old (cheaper) and new rooms, good beds, nice setting, beautiful lakeside view, good restaurant (try the crab soup), very busy on Sun, recommended, mid-week specials. **B** *Torremolinos*, T441-6037, in Santa Ana on T447-2956, F447-3020, pool, good rooms (a couple with hot showers), restaurant and bar on pier out above the lagoon, boating excursions, popular at weekends with music, lively. **C/D** *Amaucuilco*, 300 m from CTE/Antel, very helpful manager (Sandra), 6 rooms (but avoid those which overlook the kitchen), reductions for weekly and monthly stays, art gallery, offers marimba classes and Spanish and Nahuat lessons, all meals available, live music Fri and Sat night, pool, great view with jetty over the lake, secure, recommended, boat excursions on lake, tours arranged from US$30-40 per day (US$100 per week includes breakfast and dinner). **F** *Ecoturismo Lajamaya*, final Calle los Planes, T871-5687, very nice and quiet park with pool, basic but safe. **F** basic, dirty rooms next to *Torremolinos*, towards the CTE/Antel office, unfriendly; also **F**, in white house across the street from *Amaucuilco*, friendly. Plenty of *comedores*.

Sleeping & eating

Buses From Santa Ana, bus 220 'El Lago' to the lake every 30 mins, US$0.35; from San Salvador, bus 201 to El Congo (bridge at Km 50) on Pan-American Highway, US$1, then pick up the No 220 bus to the lake, US$0.45. Other buses to Guatemala may also stop at El Congo, check. Taxi from Santa Ana US$10.

Transport

El Salvador

Cerro Verde and Volcán Izalco

From El Congo another road runs south, around the east shore of Lago Coatepeque. After reaching the summit, the paved road branches right, climbing above the south end of the lake to **Parque Nacional Cerro Verde** (2,030 m) with its fine and surprising views of the Izalco volcano (1,910 m). The road up to Cerro Verde is lined with beautiful flowers. A 30-minute walk, including a nature trail around the park, leads to a series of miradores with views of Lago Coatepeque and Santa Ana volcano, with Finca San Blas at its foot. There is an orchid garden. For the best view of Izalco go in the morning, although the afternoon clouds around the cone can be enchanting. ■ *Park entrance US$0.60, car park US$0.60.*

Cerro Verde and Volcán Izalco have been closed for most of 2002. There are plans to reopen in 2003. While climbing may not be possible, the views are spectacular and the place is almost deserted

Izalco, as can be seen from lack of vegetation, is a geologically young volcano. Historical records show that activity began in the 17th century as a sulphurous smoke vent but, in February 1770, violent eruptions formed a cone which was more or less in constant activity until 1957. There was a small eruption in 1966 through a blow-hole on the southeast slope testified by two 1,000 m lava flows. Since that time it has been quiescent.

Climbing Izalco
Izalco was known as the 'Lighthouse of the Pacific' because of the regularity of its fiery explosions

A path leads off the road (signposted) just below the car park on Cerro Verde. In 20-30 minutes descend to the saddle between Cerro Verde and Izalco, then it's 1-1½ hours up (steep, but manageable). The climb is three hours from base. Go in a group as thieves congregate at the base. Beware of falling rocks when climbing. There's a spectacular view from the top. For a quick descent, find a rivulet of soft volcanic sand and half-slide, half-walk down in 15 minutes, then it's about one hour back up the saddle. This 'cinder running' requires care, strong shoes and consideration for those below. Try to ensure that low cloud is not expected before planning to go.

Ask park guards for advice on climbing Izalco

NB Well-dressed bilingual thieves operate around Cerro Verde and Izalco. Don't give personal details (for example itinerary, room number) to smart English-speaking strangers and refuse offers of assistance or services. If driving to Cerro Verde, take care late afternoon/evening as assaults have been reported. Do not go alone.

Transport The junction 8 km from the top of Cerro Verde can be reached by the Santa Ana-Sonsonate bus, No 248 (US$0.80), first leaving Santa Ana at 0730, last at 1530 with several others in between, 1½ hrs (returning at 1000, 1100, 1300 and 1500 – with a couple of later buses at 1600 and 1730 going as far as El Congo). It can also be caught at El Congo (ask around for accommodation if you are stuck here), or, in the other direction, from the highway outside Izalco town; from the junction, hitch up to the national park and hotel (no problem, especially at weekends). 3 buses daily go up to Cerro Verde: 2 buses from El Congo arrive at the park at 0630 and 1700-1730, one from Santa Ana arrives at 1230 (departs Santa Ana 1030). Check carefully the times of the buses leaving Cerro Verde in the afternoon.

Volcán Santa Ana Three quarters of the way to Cerro Verde, a track branches off to the right to *Finca San Blas* (also can be reached on foot from Cerro Verde car park, 20 minutes). From there it is 30 minutes down to the saddle and a 1½ hours' walk straight up the very impressive Volcán Santa Ana, 2,365 m, the highest point in El Salvador apart from two places on the Honduran frontier. There are four craters inside one another; the newest has a lake and fuming columns of sulphur clouds. You can walk around the edge and down on to the ledge formed by the third crater (beware of the fumes). Spectacular views, but it can be hazy in the dry season. A rough map is available at reception in *Hotel Montaña*.

Santa Ana

Colour map 5, grid C6
Population: 400,000
Altitude: 776m

Santa Ana, 55 km from San Salvador and capital of its Department, is the second largest city in the country. On the foothills of Santa Ana volcano, the basin in which it lies is exceptionally fertile, producing large amounts of coffee, with sugar-cane coming a good second. The city, named Santa Ana La Grande by Fray Bernardino Villapando in 1567, is the business centre of western El Salvador. There are some fine buildings: the neo-Gothic **cathedral**, and several other churches, especially El Calvario, in neoclassical style. Of special interest is the classical **Teatro Nacional** on the north side of the plaza, originally completed in 1910, now in the latter stages of interior restoration and one of the finest theatres in Central America. A guide (small charge) will show you round on weekdays. A donation from the Organization of American States is being used to replace the seating. ■ *Watch local press for performances.* **Fiesta** 1-26 July, *Fiestas Julias.*

Sleeping **A-B** *Sahara*, 3 C Pte y 10 Av Sur, T447-8832, F447-8865, hotel_sahara@yahoo.com, good service, but a little overpriced. **B-D** *Internacional*, 25 C Pte y 10 Av Sur, T440-0810, with bath, restaurant in same building, safe parking for motorcycles, TV, not the most conventional of hotels.
      D *La Libertad*, near cathedral, 4 C Ote 2, T441-2358, with bath, good value budget choice, friendly, clean, helpful, safe car park across the street US$2 for 24 hrs. **E** *Livingston*, 10 Av Sur between C 7 and 9, T441-1801, with bath, cheaper without, cheap and clean. **E** *Pensión Lux*, on Parque Colón, Av JM Delgado 57, T440-3383, large rooms. **E** *Monterrey*, 10 Av Sur, T441-4842, without bathroom, but OK. *Venecia*, 11 C Pte between 14 and 16 Av Sur, T441-1534. **F** *Hospedaje San Miguel*, Av J Matías Delgado 26, T441-3465, cheaper without bath, basic, clean, car park. **F** *Hospedaje Tikal*, 10 Av Sur y C 9, clean, quiet, large rooms, free chilled drinking water, popular with the 1-hr crowd.

Eating *Expresión*, 11 Calle Pte 20, between Av 6 and 8, T/F440-1410, expresioncultural@yahoo.com A great little coffee bar, restaurant, bookshop and internet café, with occasional
Restaurants close quite early, between 2000 and 2100 art exhibitions. Cheap. *Kikos*, Av Independencia Sur, near 5 C, good chicken and pizza. *Kiyomi*, 4 Av Sur between 3 and 5C, good food and service, clean, reasonable prices. *Kyjau*, C Libertad near park, Chinese, large portions. *Los Horcones*, on main plaza next to the cathedral, like a jungle lodge inside, with pleasant balcony dining, good cheap meals. *Parrillada Texana*, Av Independencia Sur, good grilled chicken, garlic bread and salads, good value. *Pollo Campero*, Av Independencia Sur. *Pupusería Memita*, 25 C Pte, recommended for fresh *pupusas* made to order. *Talitunal*, 5 Av Sur 6, vegetarian, open 0900-1900, closed Sun, attractive, good lunch, owner is a doctor and expert on medicinal plants. *Veras Pizza*, Av

Independencia Sur, good salad bar. It is cheaper and usually good value to eat in *comedores*, or at the market in front of the cathedral. There are also food stalls on the side of the plaza. Look for excellent pineapples in season.

Entertainment

2 dance clubs on 15 C Pte near 4 Av Sur, good music Wed-Sat, dinner served. *El Gato*, Av Independencia Sur 24, theatrical co-operative, T447-6264 for programme, coffee-house atmosphere.

Transport

Buses No 201 from Terminal del Occidente, San Salvador, US$1, 1 hr, every 10-15 mins, 0400-1830. To La Libertad, take 'autopista' route bus to **San Salvador** and change buses in Nueva San Salvador. Buses (*Melva, Pezzarossi* and others) leave frequently from 25 C Pte y 8 Av Sur (T440-3606) for **Guatemala City**, full fare as from San Salvador, 4-4½ hrs including border stops. Alternatively there are local buses to the border for US$0.45; they leave from the market. Frequent buses to **Metapán** and border at **Anguiatú**. No 238 follows a beautiful route to **Juayúa**.

Directory

Banks Banks will change TCs. *Banco Salvadoreño*, and several other banks Av Independencia Sur, between Calle 3 and 7. **Communications** Internet: *Expresión*, has a couple of computers on the go in a very comfortable setting. **Post office**: 7 C Pte, between 2 Av and Av Independencia Sur. **Laundry** *Lavandería Solución*, 7C Pte 29, wash and dry US$2.50 per load, ironing service, recommended. **Tour operators** At 4 Av Nte y 2 C Pte, T447-7269, for flight reservations. **Useful addresses** Police: emergency T121.

Border with Guatemala – San Cristóbal

The border with Guatemala is 30 km northwest from Santa Ana along the paved Pan-American Highway at San Cristóbal (**F** *Hotel El Paso*, basic, friendly).This is the Carretera Panamericana crossing to Guatemala taken by the international buses and much heavy traffic. There is an *Inguat* office on the Guatemalan side.

Salvadorean immigration The border is open from 0600-2000. Some inconsistency has been reported about fees charged but, in general, expect standard procedures.

Santa Ana

To Metapán

Sleeping
1 Hospedaje San Miguel
2 La Libertad
3 Livingston
4 Monterrey
5 Sahara
6 Tikal
7 Venetia

Eating
1 Expresión
2 Kiyomi
3 Los Horcones

El Salvador

Transport To **Santa Ana**, bus 236, US$0.80, 1½ hrs, 0400-1800.

West of Santa Ana

Chalchuapa
Population: 34,865
Altitude: 640m

About 16 km from Santa Ana, on the road to Ahuachapán, lies Chalchuapa. President Barrios of Guatemala was killed in battle here in 1885, while trying to reunite Central America by force. There are some good colonial-style domestic buildings. The church of Santiago Apóstol is particularly striking, almost the only one in El Salvador which shows strong indigenous influences (restored 1997-98). **Fiestas** 18-21 July, Santiago Apóstol, and 12-16 August, San Roque. **Tazumal** ruins next to the cemetery in Chalchuapa, are probably the most impressive in El Salvador. Built about AD 980 by the Pipil Indians, with its 14-step pyramid now, alas, restored in concrete. The site has been occupied since 5000 BC and in the **Museo Regional de Chalchuapa** are the artefacts that were found in the mud under the lake. There are some very interesting bowls used for burning incense, intricately decorated with animal designs. Some of the exhibits from the Museo de Arqueología in San Salvador, damaged in the 1996 earthquake, are temporarily on show here. The ruin is only five minutes' walk from the main road. ■ *0900-1200 and 1300-1700, closed on Mon, US$3. Bus 218 from Santa Ana, 30 mins, US$0.20.* Near the ruins is a souvenir shop, *Tienda Tazumal* (selling good reproductions and jewellery), 11 Avenida Sur 31, T444-0803, on the main road. It is run by Elida Vides de Jaime, whose husband can act as a guide to Tazumal and other nearby ruins. He is helpful and speaks some English.

Sleeping and eating E *Gloria*, Av 2 de Abril, T444-0131. Opposite the entrance to the ruins is *Manhattan Bar and Grill*, 7 Av Sur y 5 C Ote 32, T444-0074, has disco 7 days a week, good service, clean, helpful. Also *5 Calles* by entrance to ruins. *Acajutla*, 7 C Ote 9, T444-0511, high-quality seafood, popular, not cheap, accepts credit cards.

Directory Embassies and consulates: Guatemalan consul in Chalchuapa, Av Club de Leones Norte, between Primero and C Ramón Flores, unmarked blue house, knock for attention.

Atiquizaya The road continues 12 km west to Atiquizaya, a small, quiet town with one *hospedaje* (**F**), several good *pupuserías* (1600-2100) and *Restaurante Atiquizaya*, 1 km at intersection with main highway to Ahuachapán, good. Also at the intersection there is a sculptor in metal who exhibits and sells his work (Km 89). There is a *Turicentro* 6 km west at hot springs (park, camping, turn off road to Ahuachapán at Finca La Labor, Km 94, 7 km on dirt road). At Cataratas del Río Malacachupán there is a beautiful 50-m high waterfall cascading into a lagoon; it's a 1-km hike to get there. Nearby is Volcán Chingo on the Guatemalan border. For a local guide, contact José Luis Estrada, who speaks English, T444-1672 (not Sunday) and who arranges long-term accommodation (**E-F**) in the area, English teachers welcome (will trade lessons Spanish-English). Camping is possible.

Transport There are frequent buses to the river from the central park in Atiquizaya; buses 202 and 456 from Terminal Occidente in **San Salvador**, 2 hrs, US$0.90. From **Santa Ana**, 45 mins, US$0.40. All Ahuachapán buses stop in the parque central.

Ahuachapán

Colour map 5, grid C6
Population: 80,000
Altitude: 785 m

A quiet town with low and simple houses, the department capital of Ahuachapán is an important distribution centre 35 km from Santa Ana. Coffee is the main product. Like many places in the area, it draws the mineral water for its bath-house from some hot springs close to the nearby falls of Malacatiupán. You can bathe in the river above the falls, and camp in the vicinity. The falls are over 70 m high and steam impressively, especially in the early morning. Downstream, where the hot water merges with the cold of the Río Frío, steam rises everywhere. This can be reached by

El Salvador (side margin text)

bus (hourly most of the day) or four-wheel drive along a 5-km dirt road from Atiquizaya (see above), or the same distance north of Ahuachapán. Pick-ups can be hired with driver for US$9 per day. Power is generated from the falls of Atehuezián on the Río Molino, which cascade prettily down the mountainside. See also the geo-thermal field of *los ausoles*, geysers of boiling mud with plumes of steam and strong whiffs of sulphur. The *ausoles* are used for generating electricity and only the small-est remains uncovered by drums and pipes. A yellow school bus leaves from the market, or there are *ATLA* private pick-ups/taxis, or you can walk. It is 3 km and marked on the road out of town to Apaneca as 'Planta Geotérmica'. You can't go into the plant, but when you arrive take the road to the right where, just a little way up the hill on the left, you hit a little *casita*. For US$0.50 the house owner will take you into his back garden to see the fumaroles and boiling pools.

Sleeping **B** *Casa Blanca*, 2 Av Norte y Gerardo Barrios, T/F443-1505, 2 rooms a/c, clean, good, recom-mended (owner's husband is a doctor, Dr Escapini). **B-C** *El Parador*, Km 103, 1½ km west of town, hotel and restaurant, a/c, good service, motel-style, relaxing, helpful owner, Sr Nasser, recommended. Buses to border stop outside, T/F443-0331, T443-1637. **E** *San José*, 6 C Poniente, opposite the park, T443-1820, with bath, clean, friendly, parking. **F** *Hospedaje Granada*, 3 blocks down from plaza by market, shared bath, clean. **F** *Hospedaje Milagro*, clean, basic, near bus station.

Eating Good meals at *Restaurant El Paseo*, *Restaurant Tanya* and *El Parador*. Good and inexpen-sive meals at *Mixta's Restaurante*. *Pastelería María*, good cakes and biscuits. *Super Selectos* supermarket in Centro Comercial at entrance to town.

Transport **Buses** Ahuachapán is 100 km from the capital by bus 202 (US$0.90), every 20 mins 0430-1830 to the capital, 2 hrs via Santa Ana. Microbuses to border in front of Almacén northwest corner of parque, US$0.45, 25 mins, slower buses same price. Frequent buses and minivans to the border at Km 117, Las Chinamas.

Tacuba This is an indigenous town, 15 km west of Ahuachapán. Head south out of town before going west. There are large, interesting colonial ruins at the entrance to town. ■*0900-1600, look for guard.* You can also visit the Casa de la Cultura office, *Concultura*, 3 km on main street north, to see an interesting display of photos. ■ *Same hours, closed 1230-1330*. The town is near the northern entrance of Parque Nacional El Imposible which is accessed by hiking or four-wheel drive in the dry sea-son, with permit only. There's nowhere to stay in town. *Café Tacuba*, 500 m above Casa de la Cultura, serves excellent food, fresh vegetables, inexpensive (Lydia de González, daughter Mónica and US husband speak English), open 0800-1600. The town is worth a visit, especially for the scenic ride through coffee plantations en route. **Transport**: buses leave the terminal in Ahuachapán every 30 minutes, 0500-1530, return 1630-1700, via Ataco; US$0.60, 45 minutes, rough road,

Apaneca
Population: 12,000
Altitude: 1,450m, the highest town in the country
Average temperature: 18°C

Between Ahuachapán and Sonsonate, heading south, is Apaneca (91 km from San Salvador, 29 km from Las Chinamas on the border) an extremely peaceful town with small cobbled streets, marking the northern end of the Ruta de las Flores. Founded by Pedro de Alvarado in 1543, the town has a colonial centre, one of the oldest parochial churches in the country, a traditional parque and a municipal market selling fruit, flowers and handicrafts. Other local industries include coffee, flowers for export and furniture. Have a look at the topiary creations outside the police station. There are two small lakes nearby to the north, **Laguna Verde** and **Laguna Las Ninfas**, whose crater-like walls are clothed in tropical forest, and where a swim, according to local leg-end, is meant to be very beneficial to your health. This is the Cordillera de Apaneca, part of the narrow highland belt running southeast of Ahuachapán. The lakes are pop-ular with tourists. It is possible to swim in the former, but the latter is too shallow and reedy. There is also a beautiful natural pool called the **Balneario de Azumpa**.

El Salvador

Sleeping and eating B *Las Cabañas de Apaneca*, T433-0500, F433-0400, cabanasapaneca@navegante.com.sv A dozen cabins many with good views, in pleasant gardens, **A** with full board. **C** *El Paraíso*, Av 15 de Abril, T433-0025, tidy rooms, southwest of the main plaza, close to Las Orquideas. Popular with locals. **C-D** *Las Orquideas*, Av Central 4, T433-0061, clean rooms, although the top ones a little overpriced. Also offer accommodation in a family home.

South of Apaneca is **AL** *Santa Leticia*, Careterra Sonsonate Km 86.5, T433-0351, 11 comfortable double rooms, decorated in locally carved wood, pool, gardens, live music on Sundays, restaurant, close to Santa Leticia archaeological site.

El Viejo Pescador, is a couple of blocks southeast of the plaza, good food, pleasant garden patio dining. Reasonably priced. *La Casona* and *La Cocina de Mi Abuela* are 2 popular locals spots that attract people from long distances, mid-priced. Several cafés beside the plaza offering cheap snacks.

Transport Local buses stop by the plaza, others pass on the main highway, a few blocks to the north, leaving you with a fairly long walk. Laguna Verde can be reached by walking from Apaneca to Cantón Palo Verde and Hoyo de Cuajuste, then a further 1 km from where the road ends.

Santa Leticia Close by, and 10 minutes by bus No 249 from Juaya, is the Santa Leticia archaeological site. The site is believed to be 2,600 years old and was rediscovered in 1968 by the farm owner. Three huge monuments are buried among the coffee groves and you feel like a first-time discoverer, especially as it is a winding route to get there. There are three stone spheres with human characteristics weighing between 14,000 and 24,000 pounds/6,000 and 11,000 kg. ■ *To visit the archaeological site is US$2. A coffee tour of two hours is US$20 and both combined is US$35.*

East of Apaneca is the **Cascada del Río Cauta** (take bus 216 from Ahuachapán towards Jujutla, alight 3 km after the turn-off to Apaneca, then walk along trail for 300 m).

Taking the northern road from Ahuachapán, 9 km west of town near the village of **Los Toles** are the Tehuasilla Falls, where the Río El Molino falls 60 m (take bus 293 from Ahuachapán to Los Toles, then walk 1 km). The road continues northwest through the treeless Llano del Espino, with its small lake, and across the Río Paz into Guatemala.

Border with Guatemala – Las Chinamas- Valle Nuevo This is a busy crossing as it is the fastest road link from San Salvador (117 km from Las Chinamas) to Guatemala City (121 km via the Santa Ana bypass, then to Ahuachapán and on to the border). The road to the border is being widened and repaved for its entire length, except where it passes through Chalchuapa at Km 78 and Ahuachapán at Km 100.

Salvadorean immigration A straightforward crossing: quick service if your papers are ready. **Crossing by private vehicle** If driving with non-Central American licence plates, expect about 45 mins for formalities; you can hire a *trámite* (young boy) to hustle your papers through, US$2-3. Your vehicle will probably be searched by anti-narcotics officers (DOAN); do not refuse as your papers will be checked again 300 m into El Salvador. PNC (police) are courteous and efficient.

Transport 300 m above immigration, frequent buses to Ahuachapán, No 265, US$0.45, 25 mins. Change there to a No 202 to San Salvador. Between 0800 and 1400 you may try for a space on one of the international Pullmans, negotiate with drivers' aide, about US$3.50 to the capital.

Directory Exchange: Coming from Guatemala, cash your quetzales at the border, check what you are given. Change money with the women in front of the ex-ISTU office next to Aduana, they are honest. Good quetzal-dollar rate, cash only.

North of Santa Ana

Texistepeque, 17 km north of Santa Ana on the road to Metapán, has an 18th-century baroque church, with **fiestas** on 23-27 December and 15 January. The town is on the San Salvador-Sonsonate-Metapán railway, which has erratic passenger services. A railway runs eastwards along the south bank of the Río Lempa to Aguilares. About 7 km east is the starting point for river trips on the Río Lempa (contact Carolina Nixon at *Corsatur*; her company, *Ríos Tropicales* has equipment rental, T/F223-2351 San Salvador).

Texistepeque

Metapán is about 10 km northeast of Lago de Güija. Its colonial baroque **Catedral de San Pedro** is one of the very few to have survived in the country (it was completed by 1743). The altarpieces have some very good silver work, using silver from local mines, and the façade is splendid. **Fiesta**: San Pedro Apóstol, 25-29 June. There are lots of easy walks with good views towards **Lago de Metapán** and, further on, **Lago de Güija**. There are many lime kilns and a huge cement plant.

Metapán
Population: 51,800
32 km north of
Santa Ana

Sleeping and eating B-C *San José*, Carretera Internacional Km 113, near bus station, T442-0556, a/c, quiet, cable TV, safe parking, good, restaurant on ground floor (Sra García, the manager, will help with transport to Montecristo). **F** *Ferrocarril*, west end of town. **F** *Hospedaje Central*, 2 Av Norte y C 15 de Septiembre, with bath, clean friendly, popular. *Rincón del Pelón*, best restaurant in town, helpful, friendly. *Comedor Carmencita*, 2 Av Norte, clean, popular, basic meals but cheap.

Transport From Santa Ana bus No 235, US$0.80, 1 hr. If driving San Salvador-Metapán, a bypass skirts Santa Ana**.**

Montecristo National Nature Reserve

A mountain track from Metapán gives access to El Salvador's last remaining cloud forest. Here there is an abundance of protected wildlife and it now forms part of El Trifinio, or the International Biosphere 'La Fraternidad', administered jointly by Guatemala, Honduras and El Salvador. Near the top of **Cerro Montecristo** (2,418 m), which is the point where the three borders meet, there is an orchid garden with over 100 species (best time to see them in flower is early spring), an orchard and a camping ground in the forest. The views are stunning as is the change in flora and fauna with the altitude.

If planning to walk in the hills near Metapán, seek local advice and do not walk alone

It is 20 km from Metapán to the park. It takes 1½-2 hours to go up, less to return. The trails to the summit take 1½ hours. ■ *Park employees escort visitors, best Mon-Fri. Admission is paid 5 km before the park, US$1.25 per person, plus US$3 for vehicle. 4WD is necessary in the wet season (mid-May to mid-Oct). Camping is permitted. To hire 4WD and driver costs US$45 return, 7 hrs; eg Sr Francisco Xavier Monterosa, Calle 15 de Septiembre Casa 40, T442-0373, c/o Isaac Monterosa. In San Salvador ask at* Salva Natura *for details on visiting the park.*

On the Guatemalan border is Lago de Güija, which is very beautiful and dotted with small islands, but not easy to reach. A new dam at the lake's outlet generates electricity for the western part of the country. It is possible to walk round parts of the lake, but there is no proper track and fences reach down to the water's edge. Ask permission to enter the hiking trails; vehicle access is difficult. Boat trip to **Isla Tipa**, once a sacred Maya site, can be arranged through *Amaucuilco Guest House* at Lago de Coatepeque (see page 790). Ask directions to the Cerro de Figuras where there are interesting rock drawings. Special excursions may be available through *Jaguar Tours* in San Salvador. The border with Guatemala passes through the lake so there is a chance that you may have to account for your presence there. Carry a copy of your passport and entry stamp in case you are questioned. Bus 235 from Santa Ana, US$0.55, one hour.

Lago de Güija

El Salvador

A good paved road runs from Metapán to the Guatemalan frontier at **Anguiatú**. 3½ km out of Metapán on this road is **E** *Montecristo*, with seven rooms.

Border with Guatemala – Anguiatú

This is normally a quiet border crossing except when there are special events at Esquipulas in Guatemala.

Salvadorean immigration   The usual requirements apply; relaxed crossing.

Transport   To Santa Ana, bus 235A, US$0.80, 1¾ hrs. To Metapán 40 mins, US$0.25. This is the best route from San Salvador to northwest Guatemala, Tikal and Belize but there is an alternative through Honduras (see under El Poy, page 802). There is a road of sorts from Metapán to El Poy and 2 buses a day, 4 hrs, US$1.80, but the poor state of the road is more than compensated for by spectacular scenery.

Directory   Good exchange rates reported.

Northern El Salvador

The route from San Salvador to Western Honduras heads north, skirting the vast arm of the Cerrón Grande reservoir with volcanoes in the distance. Small villages are interspersed with brand new settlements tucked amongst the fields and hills as the road winds through mountainous landscape – a snapshot of the old way of life, and the emergence of the new.Currently enjoying a cultural revival the charming colonial town of Sucitoto on the southern shore of the resevoir is definitely worth a visit.

To Western Honduras

There used to be much guerrilla and counter-insurgency activity in the northern areas, but there is now freedom of movement. The Troncal del Norte (Ruta CA 4) is paved throughout; the first 12 km, due north to Apopa, are autopista, thereafter it is being reconstructed. It is 2½ hours by car from San Salvador to La Palma, then 11 km to the border at El Poy. **NB** Most if not all the mines laid during the civil war have been cleared. However, if you are visiting the remoter areas, especially on foot, seek local advice.

Apopa & Tonacatepeque

Apopa is a friendly town with a good market and a new shopping centre. It is the junction with a good road to Quezaltepeque (12 km). Bus 38B from San Salvador to Apopa, US$0.15.

A paved road runs east from Apopa to Tonacatepeque, an attractive small town on a high plateau. It has a small textile industry and is in an agricultural setting. There has been some archaeological exploration of the town's original site, 5 km away. A paved road from Tonacatepeque runs 13 km south to the Pan-American Highway, some 5 km from the capital. In the other direction, a dry-weather road runs north to Suchitoto (see page 799).

Three kilometres beyond Apopa, on CA 4 Km 17, is **F** *Lisa's Guest House*, a *finca* belonging to the owners of *Ximena's Guest House* in San Salvador. It is being developed as an ecological centre with accommodation, restaurant and language school. *Restaurante Coma y Punto* serves local meals (it is planning to serve mostly natural foods, vegetarian meals with own-grown produce). *Lisa's Inn* will accommodate students in the Spanish-language school, and a hotel is to be built higher up the hill. It is planned to run tours to Suchitoto, the Cerrón Grande lake for watersports and to Guazapa volcano, which played a prominent part in the civil war. ■ *For information, contact René Carmona at Ximena's (address under San Salvador Sleeping) or T214-5281. Getting there: any bus from Terminal de Oriente to Aguilares passes the entrance, US$0.25.*

Aguilares

From Apopa, it's 21 km to Aguilares, 4 km beyond which are the ruins of **Cihuatán**. The name means 'place of women' and it was presided over by female royalty.

■ *Entry only with permission from the watchman*. A road from Aguilares heads west to Suchitoto, see page 799. If heading north, see page 801.

Suchitoto and Cerrón Grande

Suchitoto, meaning 'the place of birds and flowers', was founded by either the Pipíl or Yaqui Indians, and today is a small, very attractive colonial town with cobbled streets, balconied houses and an interesting church. Several hotels and restaurants in the town offer fantastic views towards Lake Suchitlán and Volcán Guazapa. Over 200 species of bird have been identified in the area, and white-tailed deer inhabit the local woods.

Population: 30,000

Suchitoto has its own website, at www.suchitoto elsalvador.com

The town was almost completely deserted in the early 1990s after 12 years of civil war which severely affected the region – 90% of the population left, leaving Suchitoto virtually a ghost town. It is now undergoing a population and cultural revival with a range of activities and events. Life centres on the main plaza which every evening becomes a bustle of people just wondering the streets. A street fair every Sunday includes live music, stalls and *comida típica*. **Casa de Los Mestizos**, a cultural centre and bar, is involving the town's young people in artistic and tourist projects. Suchitoto's telegraph poles have been decorated by artist Paulo Rusconi, and Parque San Martín, to the west end of town, is dotted with modern sculptures, some made using ex-war materials. Arts and cultural **festivals** take place every February, including the Palo Encebado, a competition involving attempts to clamber to the top of long greasy poles.

The **Teatro de Las Ruinas** is being restored, as is the **Iglesia de Santa Lucía**. Here there is a lot of stencil work inside and the church's columns are wooden and hollow. ■ *0800-1200, 1400-1600 Mon-Sat, all day Sun.* There is a splendid view from the church tower. **Casa Museo de Alejandro Cotto** is one of a couple of small museums. ■ *0830-1600 daily, US$3, guided tour in Spanish. For more information call Sr Cotto (T284-0040).* The other is **Museo de La Moneda**, which has a collection of stuffed animals and a large poster of a snake wrapped around a naked woman but also coins and notes from mostly Latin American countries including an 1832 coin from the short-lived American Federation of States (1823-1842), and the sought-after 3-peso Cuban note showing Che Guevara. ■ *0800-1700 Mon-Sun, $1.30. 4 Avenida Norte, 4 Calle Poniente, next to Restaurante La Casona.*

El Salvador

Suchitoto

To Buses to San Salvador, La Fonda El Mirador Hostal & Restaurant, Pupusería Vista al Lago, Casa Museo de Alejandro Cotto & Lago Suchitlán

BARRIO CONCEPCION

Parque San Martín

To Barrio San José & La Posada de Suchitlán

Museo de la Moneda

Theatre

BARRIO CENTRO

Banco de Fomento Agropecuario

ANTEL

Calle Francisco Morazán

Parque Centenario

San Sal

Casa de la Cultura

Santa Lucía

Galería Shanay

To Barrio San José & La Posada de Suchitlán

Av 15 de Septiembre
6 C Oriente
4 C Oriente
2 C Oriente
C San Martín
Pasaje de Sta Lucía
3 Av Norte
2 Av Norte
4 Av Norte
2 Av Sur
Av 6 de Noviembre
4 C Poniente
2 C Poniente
Av 15 de Septiembre

N
Not to scale

■ Sleeping
1 Casa de los Mestizos

● Eating
1 Café El Obraje
2 La Casona
3 Villa Balanza

El Salvador

Excursions A 30-minute walk north of town leads to **Lago Suchitlán**, with a few small restaurants and plans for some cheap accommodation in the pipeline. Boat excursions across to remote areas in neighbouring Chalatenango are available, ask around and negotiate prices. Los Tercios, a waterfall with striking, gigantic, black, hexagonal-shaped basaltic columns, can be reached by car, foot and by *lancha*. It is at its most impressive in the wet season when the full force of nature is on show. Walk 10-15 minutes from town down the very steep road towards the lake known as Calle al Lago Suchitlán. Lifts can be had for about $2-3 if you can't face the steep climb back to town afterwards. Ask around. At the lake shore, where there are *comedores*, ask for a *lanchero*. A *lancha* to the base of the trail to Los Tercios is US$5-6 (negotiable) and takes 10 minutes (ask the *lanchero* to point out the trail). There are thousands of flies on the lake shore, but they don't bite. Walk upwards for 10-15 minutes in a straight line till you reach the road. You will see *flor de fuego* trees, vultures, fish eagles, blue morpho butterflies and lizards. Turn right and walk for two minutes to the first basic house on the right; take a right just before the house, through their property (if the family is there, say *'con permiso'*, payment is not required). Follow the path down and up over the river to a mirador looking out over the lake. Veering to the right on the path descends steeply down black boulders where arching to the right, you will see these impressive hexagonal structures.

La Ciudad Vieja, one-time site of the capital, is 10 km from Suchitoto. An original Pipil town, it was taken over by the Spanish who made it their central base for 17 years before electrical storms, lack of water, and cholera forced them to flee. It is a private site but can be visited. There are plans for a museum and a café.

Boat trips go to lakeside villages associated with the FMLN in the recent civil war. 12 km away, on the road to Aguilares, a **Parque de la Reconciliación** is being developed at the foot of Cerro de Guazapa (contact Cedro in San Salvador, T228-0812, cedro@euromaya.com). Also, 3 km along this road is Aguacayo and a large church, heavily damaged in the war.

Sleeping & eating **B-C** *Posada de Suchitlán*, Final 4C Pte, at the eastern end of town, T335-1064, F335-1277, www.suchitlan.com, Swedish-run (Arne and Elinor Dahl) reservation required, colonial-style, beautifully tiled and decorated, excellent hotel and restaurant, stunning view. **D** *Fonda El Mirador*, C 15 de Septiembre, Barrio Concepción, on the road that leads to the lake, T335-1126, quintanilladavid@hotmail.com, next to restaurant of same name, with superb views of lake and good food too. **D-E** *Casa de Los Mestizos,* 3 Av N 48, Barrio Concepción, T848-3438, casamestizos@terra.com 5 rooms surrounding a gorgeous cobbled courtyard dominated by a flourishing mango tree, this haven is run by a group of artists who have added their artistic flair to the place, inside is the *Juan Palancapa Barricafé* and bar where you can enjoy a wide range of international beers. Great ambience, live music at weekends, videos, highly recommended. Offers guides to places of interest including Los Tercios (see above). **F** *Hostal El Viajero*, at entrance to town, very basic.

Local specialities include *salporitas* (made of corn meal) and *chachamachas*. Try the *pupusas* in the market and at the corner near CTE/Antel. Several eating options around the main plaza. In addition to the *La Posada* and *La Fonda El Mirador*, *Villa Balanza* services great food in a stylish setting. *Café El Barrio*, near El Mirador. Good service, nice courtyard. *Café El Obraje*, next to church, clean, reasonably priced, good breakfast variety. *Pupusería Vista al Lago*, Av 15 de Septiembre 89, good food. *Restaurant La Casona*, 4 Av N, 4 C Pte. Fresh water shrimp is served. Also sells artesanía. *Los Portales*, on the Parque Centenario, open until midnight.

Transport **Buses** to Aguilares, 8 a day, No 163 between 0500 and 1630, 2 hrs, poor road. There are regular buses (No 129) from Terminal Oriente, San Salvador, beginning at 0330. The bus stops at the market and leaves town for the capital from 3 Av N, near the *Casa de los Mestizos*.

Ferries cross the Embalse Cerrón Grande for San Luis del Carmen (25 minutes to San Luis 0800, 1010, 1300, 1700, returning at 0600, 0930, 1100, 1500), where there is *Comedor Carmen*, and buses linking to Chalatenango.

Bar and Disco Los Sánchez, 3 Av Norte which leads from the bottom left-hand corner of the church down towards the lake. Has terrace overlooking the town, open 1800-0100, US$1.30 which includes a drink.

Banks *Banco de Fomento Agropecuario. Western Union* available. Open 0800-1600 Mon-Fri, 0830-1200 Sat. Will cash TCs. No credit card facilities. **Internet**, is available on the main square.

A road runs east from Suchitoto to Ilobasco (see below) passing Cinquera, whose villagers returned home in February 1991 after six years displacement, and Tejutepeque.

Highway 4 continues north from Aguilares passing the western extremity of the Cerrón Grande reservoir. A branch to the east skirts the northern side of the reservoir to Chalatenango, capital of the department of the same name. Rural Chalatenango is mainly agricultural, with many remote villages and many non-governmental organizations working in the area. Chalatenango is a delightful little town with annual fairs and **fiesta** on 24 June and 1-2 November. It is the centre of an important region of traditional livestock farms. Good market and several craft shops, for example *Artesanías Chalateca*, for bags, hammocks, etc.

Take special care here if you walk in the countryside: areas off the main road may be mined. Local residents usually (but not always) know which places are safe.

Sleeping and eating E *California*, behind the market, and **E** *La Ceiba*, behind the military fort, with shower and bath, nice new 2-storey house. **F** *El Nuevo Amanecer*, basic, good views of the cathedral from the 2nd floor. *La Peña*, steaks and seafood, live music at night. *La Vieja Havana* serves good snacks and food, with photographs and occasional cultural events.

Transport Bus 125 from Oriente terminal, San Salvador, US$1.10, 2½ hrs.

The quiet village of La Montañona is located 20 km north along the road past Concepción Quezaltepeque in the department of Chalatenango. Situated at almost 1,400 m in a forest dominated by pines and oaks, the area also played an important role throughout the war. Various trails lead hikers to former guerrilla *tatús* (underground hideouts), offering sweeping vistas of the *embalse* and El Salvador volcano chain. Formed after the signing of the peace accords, the community of La Montañona is currently expanding its tourist infrastructure. *Hospedaje* or cabaña accommodation, food, guide service, horse-riding, and transportation can be arranged through locals Marcos Tulio (T735-5910), and/or Cesar (T723-6283).

La Palma

The main road continues north through Tejutla, with beautiful views, to La Palma (84 km from San Salvador), a charming village set in pine-clad mountains, and well worth a visit. It is famous for its local crafts, particularly brightly painted wood carvings and hand-embroidered tapestries. Also produced are handicrafts in clay, metal, cane and seeds. There are a number of workshops in La Palma where the craftsmen can be seen at work and purchases made. **Fiesta** mid- or late February, Dulce Nombre de María.

C-D *Hotel La Palma*, T/F335-9202, book ahead for weekends and holidays, 6 large rooms, clean, with bath, friendly, restaurant limited menu but good, beautiful gardens, nice pool, ceramics workshop, ample parking, recommended. *La Terraza Cafetería*, 2 blocks from church on road to El Poy, upstairs, open daily 0800-1900, good typical food, cheap, T335-9015. *El Poyeton*, 1 block down hill from *La Terraza*, 50 m on left, local food, also has basic rooms. *La Estancia*, next to *Gallery Alfredo Linares* (see below), on C Principal, open 0800-2000, good menu, bulletin board, T/F335-9049. *Del Pueblo*, C Principal 70, owner María Adela friendly, good basic and cheap menu, also incorporates *Artesanías El Yute*.

In San Ignacio, 6 km north of La Palma is *AL Entre Pinos*, T335-9370, F335-9322, reservations (San Salvador) T270-1151/7, 1st-class resort complex, a/c, pool, cable TV, sauna and small shop. Best budget accommodation in the region is at *E Posada San Ignacio*, on the main plaza. Cold rooms, clean and friendly.

Shopping

If unable to go to La Palma, visit El Arbol de Dios in the capital.

Handicrafts *Artesanías El Tecomate*, Carlos Alfredo Mancía, T335-9068, F335-9208, also good work in wood. Many of these products are also sold in San Salvador, but are much more expensive. *Artesanías El Típico*, Blanca Sola de Pineda, C Principal, T335-9210, good. *Cerámica San Silvestre*, T335-9202, opposite *Hotel La Palma*, wholesale/retail, good. *Cooperativa La Semilla de Dios*, Plaza San Antonio, T335-9098, F335-9010, the original cooperative founded by Fernando Llort in 1971, huge selection of crafts and paintings, helpful. *Gallery Alfredo Linares*, T335-9049 (Sr Linares' house), well-known artist whose paintings sell for US$18-75, open daily 0900-1700, friendly, recommended. (Ask in pharmacy if gallery is unattended). *Palma City*, C Principal behind church, T335-9135, Sra Alicia Mata, very helpful with finding objects, whether she stocks them or not, wood, ceramics, *telas*, etc. *Taller La Campina*, Marta Morena Solís, T335-9029, good handicrafts, good prices (phone in advance).

Transport **Buses** From San Salvador, Terminal de Oriente, to La Palma, bus 119, US$1.25, 3 hrs, last return leaves at 1630.

Six kilometres north of La Palma is the picturesque village of **San Ignacio**, which has two or three small *talleres* producing handicrafts; 20 minutes by bus, US$0.10 each way. Also near La Palma there is a river reached by rough road (14 km), beautiful, and the summit of **Miramundo**, about 2,000 m, with trails and wilderness. Be prepared to hike. Ask locally for a guide (recommended). Most areas are accessible by four-wheel drive.

Border with Western Honduras

The road continues north to the border at **El Poy**, for Western Honduras. From Citalá, an unexciting town 1 km west off the highway just before El Poy, an adventurous road goes to Metapán (see page 797). Two daily take three hours for the 40 km, rough but beautiful journey. If driving, use four-wheel drive. There is much reforestation under way in the area.

Border with Honduras – El Poy

The crossing is straightforward in both directions but it is best to arrive early in the day. At holiday times it can be busy. The border posts are 100 m apart.

Sleeping **D** *Hotel Cayahuanca*, Km 93.5, T335-9464, friendly, good but expensive restaurant. At Citalá is a small, basic hotel, *El Trifinio.*

Transport To San Salvador, Terminal de Oriente, bus 119, US$1.35, 3-4 hrs, often crowded, hourly, last bus from the capital 1600. The same bus to La Palma US$0.15, 30 mins.

Directory **Exchang**: bargain with money changers at the border for the best rate for lempiras. TCs can be changed in banks in Nuevo Ocotepeque.

This route is used from El Salvador to northwest Guatemala, crossing this border then into Guatemala at Agua Caliente, 45 minutes by car. However, roads are better through Anguiatú and there is only one border to cross. This is a good route for Copán and San Pedro Sula (7 hrs by car San Salvador-Copán, including 45 mins at border).

Eastern El Salvador

A primarily agricultural zone, the central region is lined with dramatic volcanoes, impressive scenery and the small towns of the Lempa Valley. Along the coast, quiet beaches and islands can be found on the way to the stunning Gulf of Fonseca to the east. In the north, an area of fierce disputes between the army and guerrillas in the civil war, small communities are slowly rebuilding, and opening up to visitors. There are two border crossings to Honduras to the north at Perquín, and the east at El Amatillo.

There are two roads to the port of La Unión/Cutuco on the Gulf of Fonseca: the Pan-American Highway, 185 km through Cojutepeque and San Miguel (see below); and the **Coastal Highway**, also paved, running through Santo Tomás, Olocuilta, Zacatecoluca, and Usulután (see page 812). Two crossings to Honduras exist, to the west at El Amatillo and to the northwest at Perquín.

To La Unión/ Cutuco

The **Pan-American Highway** is dual carriageway out of the city, but becomes single carriageway for several kilometres either side of Cojutepeque, sections that are twisty, rough and seem to induce some very bad driving. There is also a great deal of litter along the roadside; look beyond it for the fine views. A short branch road (about 2 km beyond Ilopango airport) leads off right to the west shores of Lago de Ilopango. A little further on another road branches off to the lake's north shore.

At San Martín, 18 km from the capital, a paved road heads north to Suchitoto (see page 799), 25 km on the southern shore of the Embalse Cerrón Grande, also known as Lago de Suchitlán. At Km 34.8 is *Guancora La Bermuda*, T226-1839, *estancia* and colonial-style restaurant with pool and B&B.

The capital of Cuscatlán Department, 34 km from San Salvador, is the first town on the Pan-American Highway encountered heading east. Lago de Ilopango is a short trip to the southwest and there is a good weekly market. The town is famous for cigars, smoked sausages and tongue, and its annual fair on 29 August has fruits and sweets, saddlery, leather goods, pottery and headwear on sale from neighbouring villages, and sisal hammocks, ropes, bags and hats from the small factories of Cacaopera (Department of Morazán). There is also a sugar cane **festival** on 12-20 January. That part of town on the Pan-American Highway is full of foodstalls and people selling goods to passengers on the many passing buses.

Cojutepeque
Colour map 6, grid C1
Population: 31,300

Cerro de las Pavas, a conical hill near Cojutepeque, dominates **Lago de Ilopango** and gives splendid views of wide valleys and tall mountains. Its shrine of Our Lady of Fátima draws many pilgrims. There are religious ceremonies on May 13.

Sleeping and eating E *Motel Edén*, with shower. E *Hospedaje Viajero*, 1 block east of *Turista* (also hourly rentals). E *Turista*, 5 C Ote 130, beware of extra charges. *Comedor Toyita*, good value. *Comedor Familiar*, good.

Transport Buses No 113 from Oriente terminal in San Salvador, US$0.55; buses leave from here on the corner of the plaza 2 blocks from the main plaza.

From **San Rafael Cedros**, 6 km east of Cojutepeque, a 16 km paved road north to Ilobasco has a branch road east to Sensuntepeque at about Km 13. The surrounding area, devoted to cattle, coffee, sugar and indigo, is exceptionally beautiful. Many of Ilobasco's population are workers in clay; its decorated pottery is now mass-produced and has lost much of its charm, but it is worth shopping around. Try *Hermanos López* at the entrance to town, or José y Víctor Antino Herrera, Avenida Carlos Bonilla 61, T332-2324, look for *Kiko* sign, fine miniatures for sale. Annual **fair** on 29 September.

Ilobasco
Population 48,100

El Salvador

An all-weather road leads from Ilobasco to the great dam and hydroelectric station of Cinco de Noviembre at the Chorrera del Guayabo, on the Río Lempa. Bus 111 from Terminal de Oriente US$0.80, 1½ hours. Another road with fine views leads to the Cerrón Grande dam and hydroelectric plant; good excursion by bus or truck. You can climb the hill with the CTE/Antel repeater on top for a view of the whole lake created by the dam.

Sleeping D *La Casona*, C Bernardo Perdomo y 3 Av Sur, 1332-2388, F284-1982, recommended. **E** *Hotel Ilobasco*, 4 Calle Pte, T332-2563, has the town's only real restaurant.

Sensunte-peque
Colour map 6, grid C1
Population: 45,000
Altitude: 900 m

Sensuntepeque, 35 km east of Ilobasco, is a pleasant town in the hills south of the Lempa valley. Once a great source of indigo, it is the capital of Cabañas Department. There are some interesting ceremonies during its **fair** on 4 December, the day of its patroness, Santa Bárbara. It can be reached from the Pan-American Highway from near San Vicente. **Sleeping E** *Hospedaje Jandy*. **E** *Hospedaje Oriental*.

From Sensuntepeque, the conventional way east is to head back to the Pan-American Highway by bus and continue to San Miguel. It is possible, however, to get off at Dolores (no accommodation), take a truck at dawn to the Río Lempa, cross in a small boat to San Juan, then walk three hours to **San Gerardo**, from where one bus goes daily at 1100 to Ciudad Barrios (see below). This area was badly damaged during the war. Most roads are appalling and water and electricity are often cut.

San Sebastián

Four kilometres from the turning to Ilobasco, further south along the Pan-American Highway at **Santo Domingo** (Km 44 from San Salvador), a paved road leads for 5 km to San Sebastián, where colourfully patterned cloth hammocks and bedspreads are made. You can watch them being woven on complex looms of wood and string. Behind *Funeraria Durán* there is a weaving workshop. Sr Durán will take you past the caskets to see the weavers. The Casa de Cultura, about 50 m from the plaza, will direct you to weaving centres and give information on handicrafts. Before buying, check prices and beware overcharging. Market on Monday. The 110 bus from the Oriente terminal runs from San Salvador to San Sebastián (one and a half hours, US$0.80). There are also buses from Cojutepeque.

San Vicente

Colour map 6, grid C1
Population: 56,800

Although all street signs have names, it seems that numbers are preferred

Founded in 1635, San Vicente is 61 km from the capital, and lies a little southeast of the Highway on the Río Alcahuapa, at the foot of the double-peaked **Volcán San Vicente** (or **Chinchontepec**), with very fine views of the Jiboa valley to the west. The town enjoys a lovely setting and is a peaceful place to spend a night or two. Its pride and joy is **El Pilar** (1762-69), the most original church in the country. It was here that the Indian chief, **Anastasio Aquino**, took the crown from the statue of San José and crowned himself King of the Nonualcos during the rebellion of 1832.

El Pilar stands on a small square 1½ blocks south of the Parque Central. On the latter is the cathedral, whose nave is draped with golden curtains. In the middle of the main plaza is a tall, open-work clock tower, quite a landmark when descending the hill into the city. Three blocks east of the main plaza is the *tempisque* tree under which the city's foundation charter was drawn up. The tree was decreed a National Monument on 26 April 1984. There is an extensive market area a few blocks west of the centre and hammock sellers can be found on nearby streets. An army barracks takes up an entire block in the centre. A small war museum opened in 1996-97; ask the FMLN office here or in San Salvador. Carnival day: 1 November.

Excursions

Three kilometres southeast of the town is the Balneario **Amapulapa**, a Turicentro. There are three pools at different levels in a wooded setting. ■ *US$0.60 entry and US$0.60 parking charges*. Unfortunately the site has a bad litter problem and a reputation for petty crime. Women should not walk there alone. Reached by buses 158,

El Salvador

177 and 193 from San Vicente bus station, US$0.10. **Laguna de Apastepeque**, near San Vicente off the Pan-American Highway, is small but picturesque. Take bus 156 from San Vicente, or 499 from San Salvador. Ask in San Vicente for guides for climbing the volcano.

Sleeping

D-E *Central Park*, on Parque Central, T/F333-0383, with bath, TV, a/c, phone, good, clean, cheaper with fan, cheaper still without TV, café downstairs. **D** *Villas Españolas*, ½ block from main square, T393-0322, smart, good value, parking. **E** *Casa Romero*, after the bridge, 1st turning on the left, no sign, clean, good meals. **F** *Casa de Huéspedes Germán y Marlon*, 1 block from plaza, T333-0140, shared bath, 1 bed and 1 hammock in each room, very clean and friendly. **F** *Casa de Huéspedes El Turista*, Indalecio Miranda y Av María de los Angeles, well kept, fan, good.

Eating

Taiwan, Parque Central. *La Casona*, on same plaza as El Pilar church. *Comedor Rivoli*, Av María de los Angeles Miranda, clean, good breakfast and lunches. *Comedor La Cabaña*, just off main plaza. *Casablanca*, good shrimps, steaks, and you can swim in their pool for US$1.15. *Chentino's Pizza*, good fruit juices. *Salón de Té María*, opposite barracks, café, cakes and snacks. *Pops*, next to *Banco Hipotecario* on main plaza, ice-cream. *La Nevería*, close to bus station, good ice-cream.

Transport

Bus 116 from Oriente terminal, San Salvador, every 10 mins or so, 1½ hrs, US$0.90. Returning to the capital, catch bus at bus station (Av Victoriano Rodríguez y Juan Crisóstomo Segovia), or outside the cathedral, or on the road out of town. To **Zacatecoluca**, bus 177, US$0.40 from bus station. Buses to some local destinations leave from the street that goes west-east through the market (eg 156 to **Apasteque**). You have to take 2 buses to get to **San Miguel** (see below), 1st to the Pan-American Highway (a few km), where there is a bus and food stop, then another on to San Miguel, US$1.30 total.

Directory

Banks *Banco Hipotecario* on main plaza, exchange counter at side, 'leave guns and mobile phones with the guard, please'. *Casa de Cambio León*, C Dr Antonio J Cañas, off northeast corner of main plaza.

El Salvador

San Vicente

To Pan American Highway & San Salvador

5 C Pte
5 C Ote/Domingo Santos
1 Av Norte
Av Canónigo R Lazo
2 Av Nte
Centro Judicial
Cambio León
Dr A J Cañas
Tempisque Tree
F A Figueroa/3 C Pte
Clock Tower
Cathedral
Lic Hernán Miranda
Daniel Díaz
Alcaldía
Zorra Tree
Bus to Apasteque
Army Barracks
Procuraduría para la Defensa de los Derechos Humanos
Ahorromet
Gobernación
1 de Julio 1823
Av Inocente Marín
Av F C Cañadas
Av Max Ramírez
Av María de los Angeles
Av María de los Angeles Miranda
Av José María Cornejo
Av José María
Av Pres M A Molina y Cañas
Av Ana Guerra de Jesús
Av Cayetano Molino Quiroz
European Commission
Lic Basilio Meriño
Alberto de Merino
El Pilar
Indalecio Miranda
Juan C Segovia

N

0 metres 100
0 yards 100

■ Sleeping	**● Eating**	
1 Casa de Huéspedes Germán y Marlon	1 Comedor La Cabaña	5 Salón de Té María
2 Central Park	2 Comedor Rivolí	6 Taiwan
3 Villas Españolas	3 La Casona	
	4 Pops	

Communications Post office: in Gobernación, which is 2 Av Norte y C 1 de Julio 1823. **Telephones:** CTE/Antel, 2 Av Norte/Av Canónigo Raimundo Lazo, southeast of plaza.

Berlín
Take care if driving in this area, especially after 1300

The Highway (in reasonable condition after San Vicente) used to cross the Río Lempa by the 411 m-long Cuscatlán suspension bridge (destroyed by guerrillas in 1983). Ten kilometres south of the Pan-American Highway is **Berlín**, known for its quality coffee plantations. *Hotel Berlines* and *Villa Hermosa*, both **E**.

From Berlín there is a road round the north of Volcán de Tecapa to **Santiago de María**, which itself is on a road between the Pan-American and coastal highways (**E** *Villa Hermosa*, 3 Avenida Norte 4, T663-0146; bus 309 from Terminal del Oriente, 2½ hours, US$1.15). Halfway along is Alegría from which you can visit the **Laguna de Alegría** in the crater of the volcano, fed by both hot and cold springs. (The volcano last erupted in 1878.) The lake level is low during the day but rises at 1600 each afternoon. Local guides charge US$12 per day.

San Miguel

Population: 380,000 approximately
Colour map 6, grid C2

Set at the foot of the volcano **San Miguel (Chaparrastique)**, which erupted in 1976, and **Chinameca**, San Miguel is the third largest city in El Salvador, 136 km from San Salvador. The capital of its Department, the town was founded in 1530 as a military fortress by Don Luis de Moscoso. It now has one of the fastest growing economies in Central America and some very pleasant plazas and a bare 18th-century cathedral. The city's theatre dates from 1909, but since the 1960s it has been used for various purposes other than the arts. The arid climate all year round makes the region ideal for growing maize, beans, cotton and sisal. Some silver and gold are mined and it is an important distribution centre. **Fiesta** of the Virgen de la Paz is on the third Saturday in November.

A new Metrocentro shopping centre has opened southeast of the centre. The Turicentro of Altos de la Cueva is 1 km north (take town bus 60, car parking US$0.60, swimming pools, gardens, restaurants, sports facilities, bungalows for rent US$3.45, busy at weekends).

Excursions

There is a charming church with statues and fountains in its gardens about 16 km away at Chinameca. **Aqua Park** is on the Pan-American Highway at Km 156 towards La Unión, T661-1864. It has 35-m high chutes, unique in Central America, playground, good restaurant, recommended. **El Capulín** natural pools are at the village of **Moncagua**, where the waters run from pumice stone caves and are said to be medicinal. Take bus towards Ciudad Barrios.

West of San Miguel a road goes south through hills and coffee plantations and has superb views of Volcán San Miguel. The volcano can be climbed from **Placita** on the road to San Jorge, about four hours up. Ask at Placita for information, a guide costs about US$5. To the northwest are the Indian ruins of **Quelapa** (bus 99, US$0.50), but there is not much to see. From Quelapa a road continues north to **Ciudad Barrios**.

Sleeping
Very few hotels in the centre, most on the entrance roads

A *Trópico Inn*, Av Roosevelt Sur 303, T661-1800, F661-1288, tropicoinn@yahoo.com, clean, comfortable, reasonable restaurant, swimming pool, garden, safe parking for motorbikes, recommended. **B** *El Mandarín*, Av Roosevelt N, T669-6969, a/c, pool, good Chinese restaurant. **C** *Motel Millián*, Panamericana Km 136, T669-5052, F669-7217, pool, good value, recommended, good restaurant. **D** *China House*, Panamericana Km 137, T669-5029, clean, friendly. **D** *Greco*, 10 C Pte 305, T661-1411, fan, good food and service, often full weekdays. **D** *Hispanoamericano*, 6 Av Norte y 8 C Ote, T661-1202, with toilet and shower, parking. **E** *Santa Rosa*, 8 Av Norte y 6 C, good. **E-F** *Caleta*, 3 Av Sur 601, T661-3233, basic, inexpensive, ample parking, fan, popular with local business travellers.

Plenty of cheap places near the bus station, eg **E** *Hospedaje Argueta*, 4 C Ote y 6-8 Av. **E** *San Rafael*, 6 C Ote y 10 Av Norte, T661-4113, with bath, clean, fan, parking. **E** *Hotel La Terminal*, opposite bus station, good breakfast. **F** *Migueleña*, 4 C Ote 610, very basic but good value, clean, large rooms, towels, bath, fan. **F** *Pension Lux*, 4 C Ote, 6 Av, reasonable.

Try *bocadillos de totopostes*, maize balls with either chilli or cheese; also *tustacos*, which are **Eating** like small tortillas with sugar or honey. Both are delicious and traditional in San Miguel. *La Puerta del Sol*, 3 Av Sur, 4 C Pte, good variety. *El Gran Tejano*, 4 C Pte, near cathedral, great steaks. *Chetino's Pizzería*, 5 C Pte, near Centro Médico. *Bati Club Carlitos*, 12 Av Norte. There are branches of *Pollo Campero*, and a *Burger King* and a *Wendy's* for fast-food lovers, and a good *Pizza Hut* 2 blocks north of the cathedral. South towards El Cuco at Km 142.5 is the *La Pema* restaurant, an interesting octagonal structure with the Chaparrastique volcano framed in one of the rear sections, popular, seafood specialities, moderate prices, open 1100-1700, closed Mon, T667-6055.

Local Car rental: Uno, Av Roosevelt Sur y C Chaparrastique 701, T661-7618.   **Transport**

Long distance Air Airport 5 km south of the centre, taxi US$4. Regular daily flights to the capital, see under San Salvador.

   Buses 301 from Oriente terminal, San Salvador (US$2.50, every 30 mins from 0500 to 1630, 2½ hrs). There are also 3 comfortable, express buses daily, US$5, 2 hrs. There are frequent buses to the Honduran border at El Amatillo, US$1. Four buses (No 332a) daily to Perquín, from 0600-1240, US$1.35, 2¾ hrs.

Airline offices *Taca*, Condominio San Benito, opposite *Hotel Trópico Inn*, Av Roosevelt, T661-1477.   **Directory** **Banks** Open: 0830-1200, 1430-1800. *Banco Cuscatlán* will change TCs, but you must produce receipt of purchase otherwise TCs are difficult to change. *Casa de Cambio Lego*, 2 C Poniente, overlooking market. **Useful addresses** Police: emergency T121.

El Salvador

San Miguel

| 0 metres | 200 |
| 0 yards | 200 |

■ **Sleeping**	3 Hispanoamericano	6 Pensión Lux
1 Caleta	4 Hospedaje Argueta	7 Santa Rosa
2 China House	5 Millián	8 Trópico Inn

Routes from San Miguel

Several routes radiate outwards from the city. From San Miguel a good paved road runs south to the Pacific Highway. Go south along it for 12 km, where a dirt road leads to Playa El Cuco (see page 817). Bus 320 from San Miguel, US$1. The climate in this area is good. A mainly paved, reasonable road goes to west to San Jorge and Usulután: leave the Pan-American Highway 5 km west of San Miguel, where the road passes hills and coffee plantations with good views of San Miguel volcano.

Another route heads northeast to the small town of Jocorro, where the road splits with options to Honduras. Heading north, San Francisco Gotera leads to the Perquín crossing. East of Jocorro the road leads to the border crossing at El Amatillo. Directly east from San Miguel lies La Unión, with connections north to El Amatillo .

San Francisco Gotera The capital of Morazán Department can be reached directly from the Oriente terminal in San Salvador, or from San Miguel (bus 328). Travel by foreigners used to be restricted beyond here, but reports suggest that travel to the Honduran border is now possible. Check for the latest details. Two places to stay: **C-E** *Hospedaje San Francisco*, Av Morazán 29, T654-0066, nice garden and hammocks; **E** *Motel Arco Iris*, next door, T664-0492. Beyond San Francisco, the road runs to **Jocaitique** (there is a bus) from where an unpaved road climbs into the mountains through pine forests to **Sabanetas**, near the Honduran border. Accommodation is available at Jocaitique and Sabanetas.

Corinto Northeast of San Francisco is Corinto which has two rock overhangs which show faint evidence of pre-Columbian wall paintings. They are 20 minutes north of the village on foot, just east of the path to the Cantón Coretito. The caves are open seven days a week; take an early bus, 327 from San Miguel, US$1.

Ciudad Segundo Montes Eight kilometres north of San Francisco Gotera is Ciudad Segundo Montes, a group of villages housing 8,500 repatriated Salvadorean refugees (the community is named after one of the six Jesuit priests murdered in November 1989). If you would like to visit this welcoming, energetic place, ask for the Ciudad Segundo Montes (CSM) office in San Salvador at the UCA university, or in San Francisco Gotera (T664-0033). When you get to CSM, ask to be let off at San Luis and go to the Oficina de Recepción. You will be put up in a communal dormitory; meals in *comedores* cost US$1; there is a bath house (spring-fed showers). Free tours of the community are given and there is beautiful hiking.

Fourteen kilometres north of San Francisco is **Delicias de la Concepción**, where fine decorated hammocks and ceramics are made; good prices, helpful, worth a visit. Buses every 20 minutes from San Francisco.

Perquín
Population: 5,000
Altitude: 1,200 m
Colour map 6, grid C2

Perquín – meaning 'Road of the Hot Coals', is 205 km from San Salvador and was the guerrilla's 'Capital', and the scene of much military activity. War damage is still visible around the town, but all is now peaceful and the scenery is very beautiful, surrounded by pine-topped mountains. Thousands who fled the fighting in the 1980s are now returning and rebuilding. There is a small central square with a Casa de la Cultura, post office and a **tourist information office**, T680-4086. Opposite is the plain Iglesia Católica Universal Progresista.

The **Museo de la Revolución**, clearly signposted from the plaza, has temporary exhibits as well as one on Romero and all the gory details of his murder – nothing is spared. The museum, run by ex-guerrillas, is poorly lit, but fascinating with plenty of photographs, propaganda posters, explanations, objects, pictures of the missing, and military paraphernalia. In the garden is the wreckage of an American-made helicopter, shot down by guerrillas in 1984. Sprawled like a piece of modern art, it wouldn't look out of place in a contemporary art gallery. ■ *Tue-Sun 0830-1630, US$1.20, T680-4053. No photos or filming allowed, guided tours in Spanish.*

El Salvador

Behind the town is the **Cerro de Perquín**. The views are fantastic with the town below nestling in the tropical scenery, green parrots flying through the pine trees, and the mountains stretching towards the border with Honduras. ■ *US$0.10 to climb*. **Fiesta**: The *Festival de Invierno* is a mixture of music, exhibitions and film running from 1-6 August. The festival honouring San Sebastión is on the 21-22 January, and for the Virgen del Tránsito, the patron saint of the church, on 14-15 August.

Nearby villages such as Arambala and El Mozote can be visited, or you can take a walking tour with the priest. At El Mozote is a memorial to a massacre in 1981. Five kilometres west of Perquín is **Arambala** which is slowly reconstructing. Locals will give you a tour of the town and church, destroyed by fire in the 1980s and now being rebuilt. Massacres took place here in the 1980s. Near Perquín, turn-off 2 km south, are the park and trails of **Cerro Pelón**. Nearby is El Llano del Muerto, a tourist area of naturally heated pools and wells. North of Perquín, straddling the new border with Honduras, is one of the few unpolluted rivers in the country. Contraband activity here means frequent military patrols; always carry a copy of your passport. The people of Morazán are more reserved with strangers than in the rest of El Salvador. It is best not to travel alone, or else arrange an escorted tour from FMLN in San Salvador. If travelling on your own, four-wheel drive or pick-up rental is advised.

Ruta de la Paz run by PRODETUR, T680-4086, provides walks, culture and adventure tourism and can organize accommodation. ■ *Open 0730-1630 daily, 0800-2100 during the winter festival. Tours are anything between 25 mins and 5 hrs, 1-10 people, US$1.30 an hr. 1½-hr tours walking to Llanos, 3 hrs to El Mozote.*

Sleeping **B** *Hotel Perkin Lenca*, Km 205.5 carretera a Perquín, T/F680-4080, www.perkinlenca.com Swiss cabins with restaurant *La Cocina de Ma'Anita*, open daily 0700-1900. **E** (per person) *Casa de huéspedes Gigante*, 5 mins from Perquín at the bottom of the hill, CTE Perquín T680-4037, countless partitioned rooms which would probably be noisy if full, but rarely is, clean, cold showers, friendly, meals served, power turned off at 2100. During the festival **G** *La Kinda*, ½ block to the right of the Casa de la Cultura, T680-4017, has mats you can bed down on with your sleeping bag in the town's kindergarten. Bathroom and outside shower (with curtain) available.

Camping is possible in the grounds of the Museo de la Revolución, near a crater formed by a 500-lb/227-kg bomb dropped in August 1981. Ask in the nearby *tiendas*.

Eating *Artesanía y Comedor 'La Muralla'*, on the corner of the park and main road out of town, is cosy, very friendly and popular. *Comedor El Comal*, 1 block from the town hall in the centre, 0600-2100. *Las Colinas*, at the top of the hill behind the Casa de la Cultura, near the entrance to the museum has good *comidas típicas*. *Comida Palmeras*, 1 block from Casa de la Cultura. Spacious, open late, but not much variety. **Bar** *Cueva de Torogoz* open 1100-2000 at weekends.

Transport **Bus** San Miguel-Perquín, 332A, 2¾ hrs, US$1.50. Bus from Terminal Oriente in San Salvador takes 6 hrs, very crowded, luggage a hindrance. Bus or truck from Ciudad Segundo Montes. Transport back to CSM or San Miguel may be difficult in the afternoons. If you're driving fill your tank before getting to Perquín because the last petrol station is 20 mins from the city and closes at 1700.

Border with Honduras – Perquín

The Honduran border has been moved, by treaty, to less than 3 km north of Perquín; this area has been the subject of disputes and definition problems for many decades. It was one of the basic causes of the 'football war' of 1969 (see page 64) and there were military confrontations between El Salvador and Honduras, in early 1997. There is a border crossing 5 km past the frontier here and the route to Marcala and La Esperanza Honduras, is open. There is a bus service from Marcala to San Miguel, 5 hrs, US$3.50, using this route, but the road may be impassable after heavy rains.

El Salvador

El Salvador

San Miguel to El Amatillo The shortest route from San Miguel to the Honduran border takes the Ruta Militar northeast through Santa Rosa de Lima to the Goascarán bridge at El Amatillo, a total of 58 km on newly paved road.

Santa Rosa de Lima
Population: 27,300

Santa Rosa is a charming little place with a wonderful colonial church set in the hillside. There are gold and silver mines, a market on Wednesday, and a curiously large number of pharmacies and shoe shops. The FMLN office here has details about the very interesting *Codelum Project*, a refugee camp in Monte Barrios. **Fiesta**: 22-31 August.

Sleeping and eating F *Florida*, Ruta Militar, helpful, fairly clean, basic, 3 parking spaces (arrive early). **F** *Hospedaje Gómez*, basic, hammocks, fan, clean. **F** *Hospedaje Mundial*, near market, rooms OK, with fan, basic, friendly, lots of parking space. **F** *Recreo*, 2 blocks from town centre, friendly, fan, noisy, basic. *El Tejano*, behind main church, friendly. Many *comedores*, most popular is *Chayito*, 'buffet', on Ruta Militar, and *Comedor Leyla*, next to bus stop, is good. *Martina*, near the bridge, good food including *sopa de apretadores* at US$7. Unnamed *comedor* on the Pan-American Highway, good and cheap.

Transport Buses to the Honduran border every 15 mins, US$0.50. Direct buses also to **San Salvador**, No 306, US$3 from 0400 until 1400, 3½ hrs.

Directory Banks *Banco de Comercio* will change TCs, also *Servicambio* near the church.

Border with Honduras – El Amatillo
The bridge over the Río Goascarán is the border, with El Amatillo on both sides

Salvadorean immigration The border closes at 1700 and may close for 2 hrs at lunchtime. This is a very busy crossing, but is easy for those going on foot. **Crossing by private vehicle** You will be hounded by *tramitadores* offering to help. There is no need to use their services as this is a fairly relaxed crossing. Procedures are detailed in Essentials, Motoring. Car searches are thorough at this crossing.

Sleeping Near the border are 2 *hospedajes*, both basic, **F** *Anita* with *comedor* and *Dos Hermanos*.

Transport To San Miguel, bus 330, 1 hr 40 mins, US$1.50. See also Santa Rosa de Lima.

Directory Exchange: There are money changers accepting all Central American currencies and TCs, but beware of short-changing on Nicaraguan and Costa Rican currencies. Good rates for lempiras.

La Unión/Cutuco

Colour map 6, grid C2
Population: 43,000

It is another 42 km from San Miguel to the port of La Unión/Cutuco, on the Gulf of Fonseca. The spectacular setting on the west shore of the Gulf does little to offset the heat and the faded glory of this port town which handles half the country's trade. Shortly before entering the town, the Pan-American Highway turns north for 33 km to the Goascarán bridge at **El Amatillo** on the border with Honduras (see above).

Excursions **Conchagua** is worth visiting to see one of the few old colonial churches in the country. The church was begun in 1693, after the original Conchagua had been moved to its present site following repeated attacks on the island settlements by the English. **Fiestas**: 18-21 January and 24 July. (Good bus service from La Unión, No 382, US$0.10.) **Volcán Conchagua** (1,243 m) can also be climbed and is a hard walk, particularly near the top where protective clothing is useful against the vegetation. It's about four hours up and two hours down. You will be rewarded by superb views over Volcán San Miguel to the west and the Gulf of Fonseca, which is bordered by El Salvador, Honduras and Nicaragua (where the Cosigüina volcano is prominent) to the east.

You can take an early morning boat to the Salvadorean islands in the Gulf of Fonseca. These include **Isla Zacatillo** (about one hour), **Isla Conchagüita** and the largest **Isla Meanguera** (about 4 km by 7 km) which takes about 2 hours. English and Spanish pirates occupied the island in the late 1600s, and international claims remained until the International Tribunal of the Hague awarded the island to El Salvador in preference to claims from Honduras and Nicaragua. Meanguera has attractive small secluded beaches with good bathing, for example Marahual, fringed with palm trees. About 5,000 people live on the carless island where painted boats float in the cove surrounded by small *tiendas* and *comedores* that serve fish, shark and prawns. The highest point on the island is **Cerro de Evaristo** at 512 m. The local **fiesta**, Patronales de San José Mar, lasts a fortnight from 15-29 March. There is just one hotel, **E** *Mirador*, T648-0072, with good views of the sea and neighbouring islands. The owner can take you back to La Unión in his launch, or even to Honduras or Nicaragua if you have visited immigration in La Unión first to get the necessary paperwork. Locals will allow you to camp and may offer a room (better to arrange in La Unión before you arrive). Launches leave La Unión at 1000, back very early, 0500 Monday and Friday from Marahual beach, cost US$1.50. For information of excursions to the islands, contact Carolina Nixon through Corsatur in San Salvador, otherwise go to *Hotel El Pelícano* and enquire. Local boatmen offer trips; negotiate a price.

You can reach El Tamarindo on the mainland coast (see below) from La Unión, bus 383, US$0.50. Also from La Unión, the ruins of **Los Llanitos** can be visited.

Sleeping **C** *Centroamérica*, 4C Ote, 1-3 Av, T664-4029, with fan, more with a/c, noisy. **D** *Portobello*, 4a Av Norte, 1a C Pte 1-3, T604-4113. A/c and fan, good. **E** *El Pelícano*, Final C Principal El Hüisquil, T664-4648, 20 rooms. **E** *San Carlos*, opposite railway station, good meals available. Opposite *Hospedaje Annex Santa Marta*, a bit further away from plaza is **E** *San Francisco*, T664-4159, clean, friendly, some rooms with hammocks and fan, safe parking, noisy, but OK. **F** *Hospedaje Annex Santa Marta*, with shower and fan, not bad, but rents by the hour!

Eating *Amanecer Marino*, beautiful view of the bay. *Capitan John's*, 3a Av Sur y 4a Calle Ote, T604-3013, best seafood in town, big portions, cheap, nice place on the terrace – try *tazón de sopa de pescado*.*Comedores Gallego* and *Rosita*, recommended. *Comedor Tere*, Av Gen Menéndez 2.2, fairly good. *La Patia*, for fish. Bottled water is impossible to find, but *agua helada* from clean sources is sold (US$0.05 a bag).

Transport **Bus** Terminal is at 3 C Pte (block 3); to San Salvador, bus 304, US$2, 4 hrs, many daily, direct or via San Miguel, one passes the harbour at 0300. (Bus 320 to San Miguel US$0.45). Bus to Honduran border at El Amatillo, No 353, US$1.65.

Boats *Lanchas* leave for Potosí in Nicaragua daily, weather permitting, at 0400, 3hrs, US$12. Ask at *Comedor Montecristo* by the docks. Outboards cross most days from La Unión-Potosí (Nicaragua), weather permitting. You must get your exit permission in La Unión. Make arrangements 1 day ahead, and check at customs office. There is reportedly a boat to Honduras, but it is easier to go by land.

Directory **Banks** Exchange at *Cafetín Brisas del Mar*, 3 Av Norte y 3 C Ote. *Banco Agrícola Comercial* for US$ cash and TCs. Black market sometimes in centre. **Useful addresses** Customs: 3 Av Norte 3.9. **Immigration**: at 3 C Ote 2.8.

El Salvador

The Pacific Coast

Running the length of the country to the south, the Pacific Coastline is a blend of stunning views, quiet beaches and private resorts. If basking in the sun isn't enough, the coast is a big hit with the surf crowd. For a little more activity, you can go west and visit the impressive El Imposible National Park. Heading east, towards Nicaragua, the islands of the Gulf of Fonseca are equally cut off. Travel along the coastline is easy with regular bus services, although access to some of the beaches may require a little more initiative.

La Libertad

Colour map 6, grid C1
Population: 22,800

La Libertad is very crowded at weekends and holidays. Service can be off-hand. Do not stay out alone late at night

Just before Santa Tecla, a branch road turns south for 24 km to the small fishing port of La Libertad. 34 km from San Salvador and just 25 minutes from the Comalpa International Airport, this is a popular seaside resort in the dry season. The pier is worth seeing for the fish market awnings and, when the fleet is in, for the boats hauled up out of the water along its length. The cemetery by the beach has tombstones curiously painted in the national colours, blue and white. On the seafront (Calle 4 Poniente) are several hotels, lodgings and restaurants. At a small plaza, by the *Punta Roca* restaurant, the road curves left down to the point, for fine views of La Libertad bay and along the coast. The market street is two blocks inland from the seafront.

The coast to the east and west has good fishing and surf bathing (El Zunzal beach is the surfers' favourite, see below). If the waves don't get you, watch out for the undercurrents and sharks. Don't worry too much though, as there have only been two shark attacks in 25 years. The beaches are black volcanic sand (which can get very hot). Surf season is November-April. La Libertad is laid-back and not very clean, but the surf is magnificent. Watch your belongings on the beach. The town holds an annual **Gastronomic Festival** in early December and has resurrected the tradition of *lunadas* – full-moon parties that take place in the dry season. Bonfires are lit on the beach, restaurants stay open late offering *comida típica* and some places provide live music and themed nights.

The Costa del Bálsamo (Balsam Coast), running west from La Libertad and Acajutla (see below), gave its name to the pain-relieving balsam, once a major export of the region, but which has almost disappeared. However, on the steep slopes of the departments of Sonsonate and La Libertad, scattered balsam trees are still tapped for their aromatic juices. Buses travel along the coast to Sonsonate at 0600 and 1300, about four hours.

Sleeping La Libertad is at Km 34 from San Salvador. Continuing west from the port, Playa Conchalío is at Km 36 and, while quieter than La Libertad, some would advise against going to the area even in groups.

In La Libertad Turning right from 4 C Pte at the *Punta Roca* restaurant which has 2 rooms (**A**) with terraces overlooking the sea, the following are on the road to the point: **A** *La Posada de Don Lito*, T335-3166, and beside it **B** *La Hacienda de Don Rodrigo*, older hotel with character, OK. Next to *Don Lito* is **C** *Rick*, T335-3235, with bath, clean, friendly, restaurant, good value. **C-D** *Puerto Bello*, 2 C Pte, on the main avenue, with bath, run-down, small rooms. **D** *La Posada Familiar* on 5 Av Sur, just up from beach front, **F** without bath, popular with surfers and backpackers, basic, meals, clean, good value, hammocks, parking. Next door is *La Paz*, budget accommodation. Nearby is **E** *Pensión Amor y Paz*, very basic, small rooms, no ventilation, dirty, friendly owner. **E** *Nuevo Amanecer*, 1 C Pte 24-1, safe, clean. *Miramar* lets price negotiable rooms, restaurant. **F** *Rancho La Amistad*, on front, some rooms are tiny, balcony. **F** *Comedor Margoth,* next to *La Posada Familiar*, run-down but clean.

At Playa Conchalío **B-C** *Conchalío*, T335-3194, large, nice, but no a/c, good restaurant, pool, and **C** *Los Arcos*, T335-3490, better value, a/c, TV, 300 m from beach, safe, quiet, with pool, garden and restaurant.

Seafood is good in the town, especially at *Punta Roca* (American-owned, Robert **Eating** Rotherham), try the shrimp soup, T/F335-3261, open 0800-2000, or 2300 weekends, safe, English spoken, son Lonnie offers advice for travellers. Also offers fishing tours for *dorado*, sailfish and marlin. Opposite *La Posada de Don Lito* is *Rancho Mar El Delfín*. By 4 C Pte: *El Nuevo Altamar* for good seafood. *Sagrado Corazón de Jesús*, 1 Av Norte, good value, large helpings, try their *pupusas de queso*. *Pupusería*, specializes in snacks, recommended. *Los Mariscos*, good, reasonable prices, popular, closed Mon. *Rancho Wilmer,* thatched *comedor* on front serving seafood. Cheap restaurants near the pier and in the market. *La Fonda Española*, *Los Amigos*, *Sandra* and others around Playa La Paz are cheap.

Surfing A surfing guide to El Salvador can be found at www.puntamango. com.sv *Hospi-* **Sport** *tal de Tablas*, next to *Comedor Margoth*, 5 Av Sur, for surfboard hire and repair.

Local Bus: 102 from San Salvador leaves from 4 C Pte, between 13 and 15 Av Sur, 1 hr via **Transport** Santa Tecla, US$0.45. To **Zacatecoluca** at 0500, 1230 and 1530. La Libertad bus terminal is on 2 C Ote, east of the pier. **Minibuses** to La Flores and Conchalío leave from 4 Av Norte, C Gerardo Barrios, every 10 mins. **Taxi**: US$15-20 one-way, US$30 return, negotiate. There is also a mini-van service that will take groups on tour anywhere in the country, contact Robert Rotherham at Punta Rock T335-3261 (see above). **Car repairs**: good workshop on 7 Av Sur, Francisco is helpful, good-quality work, you can sleep in vehicle while the job is being done.

Banks There are no credit card bank facilities or ATMs in La Libertad. *Banco de Fomento Agropecuario*. **Directory** Open 0800-1600 Mon-Fri, 0800-1200, Sat. Also has *Western Union*. *Banco Desarollo* takes TCs. Open 0830-1630 Mon-Fri, 0830-1200 Sat. **Communications Post office**: Up the side of the Telecom office. Open 0800-1200, 1400-1700. *Telepunto*, next to *Hotel Puerto Bello*, 2 C Pte (open 0630-0830) Cheap rates. *Telecom* on same road. **Language School** 5 Av Norte, close to Punta Roca restaurant, T449-0331, or in the USA T413-549-5924, salvaspanischool@mailcity.com, sites.netscape.net/salvaspanischool **Useful addresses Police**: C Gerardo Barrios and 1 Av Sur. **Tourism police**, based here, patrol the town and beach areas at weekends. A tourist kiosk is planned for the entrance to town.

The eastern end of La Libertad is **Playa La Paz**, 2 km beyond which is **Playa Obispo** . **Around La** **Sleeping** **A** *El Malecón de Don Lito*, T335-3201; **D** *Rancho Blanco*, T335-3584. On the **Libertad** beach are several good-value seafood restaurants, for example *Mariscos Freddy* and *La Marea*. Opposite the motel there is a trail up the Río San Antonio which leads after 1 km to the 50-m waterfall Salto San Antonio (50 m) and after 2 km to the 60-m Salto y Cueva Los Mangos. Bus 287 from La Libertad to the San Antonio quarry will get you there. About 1 km further east is **Playa Las Flores** with excellent seafood restaurant *La Dolce Vita*, 200 m east of the Shell gas station, T335-3592, also *La Curva de Don José*, T335-3436, recommended. About 1 km east of La Curva, on the right towards San Diego is the *Fisherman's Club* (T335-3272), with pool, tennis courts and a good restaurant. Entry US$6. Good beach but beware of rip tide, only advisable for surfers.

Eight kilometres from La Libertad, on a turn-off from the Carretera Litoral, is **Playa San Diego**, nice but deserted: *Río Mar Club*, T222-7879; *Mad Mike's Bed & Breakfast*, run by surfer Miguel Johnson, private property facing the beach, with short and long-term accommodation available. Bus for San Diego beach, from Calle 2 Oriente in La Libertad, US$1, 30 minutes.

West of La Libertad

Continuing west from Playa Conchalío at **Km 38** you reach **Playa El Majahual** with *If heading east,* **D** *Cabañas Don Chepe* at the start, and **D** *Hospedaje El Pacífico*, a surfers' hotel, at *see page 815* the other end. This beach does not have a safe reputation, nor is it clean. Other

El Salvador

cheaper hotels include **F** *Hospedaje Surfers-Inn*, very basic but friendly, run by Marta, who serves meals. All reached on bus No 80 from La Libertad.

A little further on to **Km 42**, **Playa Zunzal** is the best surfing beach in this area and is where the *Club Salvadoreño* and the *Automobile Club* have their beach premises. *El Bosque Club*, T335-3011, day cabins only, closes 1800. Many local houses for rent. At **Km 49.5** is the *Atami Beach Club*, T223-9000, with large pool, private beach, expensive restaurant, two bars, gardens, a beautiful place. In the grounds of *Atami* is a private *rancho* (kitchen, two bedrooms, small pool, hammocks, 150 m from private beach, cooking, safe, US$100 for maximum four). Access to *Club Atami* for US and other non-Central American passport-holders US$8, including cabaña for changing.

At **Km 51** just before El Zonte on the main road, is *Rosa's*, east of the river, three basic rooms with fan, separate toilet, cold showers, **F** for room, US$1 for hammock space, very helpful, excellent meals (US$2-3), very quiet during the week, beautiful beach with fine sunsets.

A short distance beyond, **Km 53**, is **El Zonte** and the *Turicentro Bocana*. **F** *Doña Rosa*, friendly place with basic rooms in a family atmosphere. Good food in the restaurant and will rent, sell or repair surfboards. **F** *La Casa de Frida*, T257-1496, miriamulloa:yahoo.com, rooms and a restaurant right on the beach. Very popular with foreign visitors. **F** *Horizonte Surf Camp*, saburosurfcamp@hotmail.com, simple bungalow and a camping area, nice garden, kitchen available for use.

At **Km 64**, turn inland to the large village of **Jicalapa**, which is on high rockland overlooking the ocean. There is a magnificent **festival** here on St Ursula's day (21 October). The Carretera Litoral continues for a further 40 km or so to Acajutla past rocky bays, remote black-sand beaches and through tunnels. Take great care with the sea if you bathe along this coast.

Acajutla
Colour map 5, grid C6
Population: 36,000

At the junction of San Julian, a short journey south from Sonsonate, the coastal road heads south to the lowlands city of Acajutla, El Salvador's main port serving the western and central areas, 85 km from San Salvador (the port is 8 km south of the Coastal Highway). It handles about 40% of coffee exports and is a popular seaside resort during the summer, with good surfing, though beaches are dirty and suffer from occasional oil spills. The beaches around Los Cóbanos, near Remedios Point, are popular at weekends.

Sleeping and eating **C** *Miramar*, with bath and fan, clean, reasonable restaurant/bar. *Lara*, by beach, with bath and fan, clean, car parking. **E** *Pensión Gato Negro*, opposite Belinda store, run by Japanese couple, with good restaurant, varied food, generous portions, meals US$1 to US$1.50. There are 2 motels, **D**, on the outskirts of town. *Pizza y Restaurante Perla del Mar* serves good shakes and food at reasonable prices. There are good seafood restaurants in Barrio La Peña.

Buses No 207 from Occidente terminal, San Salvador, US$2.80, or No 252 from Sonsonate US$0.30. 58 km from Santa Ana.

South of Acajutla

The rocky beach of **Los Cóbanos** (14 km south of Acajutla via San Julian, bus from Sonsonate) is very popular with weekending Salvadoreans and has some coral reef making it a popular dive spot. **Sleeping D** *Sol y Mar*, T451-0137, weekends only; **E** *Mar de Plata*, at Punta Remedios, 24 cabins, T451-3914. *Dive Pacific* (see page 785) has a guesthouse for clients. Abraham Ríos runs deep-sea fishing charters, US$180 per day, four people, English spoken, enquire locally. Fishermen arrange boat trips, negotiate a price.

West of Acajutla

The newly paved coastal road heads west running along the coast for 43 km before reaching the Guatemalan frontier at **La Hachadura**.

The black-sand beaches northwest of Acajutla at **Metalío** (safe for camping, but no formal place to stay) and **Barra de Santiago** are recommended, although there are few public facilities. At Barra de Santiago, 30 km west of Acajutla, the beach is reached across a beautiful lagoon. A bird sanctuary is being developed on the estuary and nearby is a turtle farm and museum. D *El Capricho Beach House*, same owners as *Ximena's* in San Salvador (see page 776) rent rooms here (clean, safe, including gas stove, guardian has motor launch for excursions, closed May-June, transport can be provided from the capital with advance notice). There are government plans to develop the nearby **Isla del Cajete** into a tourist complex to attract Guatemalans. Also recommended is **Salinitas**, scenic and peaceful, but too many rocks for safe bathing; a modern tourist complex here contains cabins, restaurants, gardens, pool and a zoo.

So called because of the difficulty of getting into it, this 'impossibility' has also helped to preserve some of the last vestiges of El Salvador's flora and fauna on the rocky slopes and forests of the coastal **Cordillera de Apaneca**. Among the mammals are puma, ocelot, agouti and ant bear, and birds include black-crested eagle, white hawk and other birds of prey, black and white owl, and woodpeckers. There is also a great variety of reptiles, amphibians and insects, the greatest diversity in the country. There are eight different strata of forest, with over 300 species of tree that have been identified. The 3,130-ha park is managed by the *Centro de Recursos Naturales* (CEREN) and the *Servicio de Parques Nacionales y Vida Silvestre* (SPNVS), under the auspices of the Ministerio de Agricultura y Ganadería. It is maintained by Salva Natura and US Peace Corps volunteers: contact Salva Natura at 33 Av Sur 640, Col Flor Blanca, San Salvador, T279-1515, F279-0220, www.salvanatura.org for permission to enter and trips to Parque Nacional El Imposible. Access (suitable only for four-wheel drive or hiking) is from the road to La Hachadura, either from the turn-off by the Olmec site of **Cara Sucia** (currently being excavated), 12 km before La Hachadura, or by two routes leading to San Francisco Menéndez. If travelling independently you need to get a permit from San Salvador (although you may be lucky if you just turn up). There are two buses a day from the junction at 0900 and 1400, and a few pickups make the journey.

Reserva Nacional Bosque El Imposible

El Salvador

The border is at the bridge over the Río Paz, with a filling station and a few shops nearby.

Border with Guatemala – La Hachadura-Pedro de Alvarado

Salvadorean immigration The immigration facilities are on either side of the bridge; a relaxed crossing. **Crossing by private vehicle** The border crossing is quite straightforward but a private vehicle requires a lot of paperwork (about 2 hrs). Several boys will offer their services with the administration process. You don't need to use them – go straight to Aduana.

Sleeping In La Hachadura F *El Viajero*, safe, clean, good value, with fans.

Transport To **San Salvador**, Terminal de Occidente, bus No 498, 3 hrs; to **Ahuachapán**, by market, bus No 503, US$0.75, 50 mins.

East of La Libertad

This is the second route to La Unión/Cutuco, running east through the southern cotton lands. It begins on a four-lane motorway to the international airport at Comalapa. The first place of any importance after leaving the capital is (13 km) **Santo Tomás** where there are Indian ruins at **Cushululitán**, a short distance north. A new road to the east, rising to 1,000 m, runs south of Lago de Ilopango to join the Pan-American Highway beyond Cojutepeque.

Ten kilometres on from Santo Tomás is **Olocuilta**, an old town with a colourful market on Sunday under a great tree, famed for its rice dough *pupusas*. Good church. Both Santo Tomás and Olocuilta can be reached by bus 133 from San Salvador.

The highway to the airport crosses the Carretera Litoral (CA 2) near the towns of San Luis Talpa and Comalapa. The coastal highway goes east, through Rosario de la Paz, across the Río Jiboa and on to Zacatecoluca.

El Salvador

Costa del Sol Just after Rosario, a branch road to the south leads to **La Herradura** (Bus 153 from Terminal del Sur to La Herradura, US$0.90, 1½ hours) and the Playa Costa del Sol on the Pacific, which is being developed as a tourist resort. Before La Herradura is a small supermarket on the left. The beach is on a narrow peninsula, the length of which are private houses which prevent access to the sand until you reach the *Turicentro* (0800-1800). Here cabañas can be rented for the day, or for 24 hours (not suitable for sleeping), admission and car parking US$0.80 each, US$1.60 overnight (camping and cabaña rental may be refused). It is crowded at weekends and on holidays. Vehicle camping possible on the beach. There are extensive sandy beaches, but the sea has a mild undertow; go carefully until you are sure.

Sleeping LL *Bahía del Sol Marina and Yacht Club*, T278-5222/6661, F278-5252, bahia@salnet.net, 104 villas with luxury fittings, docking for boats. A *Izalco Cabaña Club*, T264-1170, F338-2127, izalcocabanaclub@saltel.net, good value, 30 rooms, pool, seafood a speciality. D *Miny Hotel y Restaurant Mila*, Km 66 opposite police station, very friendly, owner Marcos speaks English, clean, simple, fan, pool, good food, beach access. Take bus 495 from Terminal Sur, San Salvador; buses are very crowded at weekends, but the resort is quiet during the week. Cheaper accommodation can be found 1 km east on the next beach, Los Blancos, and also in La Herradura, eg E *La Sirena*, by the bus terminal, 10 rooms, fan, restaurant.

Tasajera island At the southeast end of the Costa del Sol road, near the *Pacific Paradise* hotel, a ferry (US$1.75) leaves for Tasajera island in the Estero de Jaltepeque (tidal lagoon). For boat excursions, take Costa del Sol bus to the last stop and negotiate with local boatmen. To hire a boat for the day costs US$75 (per boat), including pilot, great trip into the lagoon, the mangroves, dolphin watching and up the Río Lempa. There is interesting wildlife on the island.

Back on the coastal highway Between Rosario de la Paz and Zacatecoluca, a road branches north to the small towns of **San Pedro Nonualco** and **Santa María Ostuma** (with an interesting colonial church and a famous **fiesta** on 2 February). Both are worth visiting, but not easy to get to. Bus 135 from Terminal del Sur goes to San Pedro. If you get off this bus at the turn off to San Sebastián Arriba, you can walk to the **Peñón del Tacuazín** (or del Indio Aquino), 480 m above sea level, which is 4½ km north of Santiago Nonualco. A cave at its summit was used as a refuge by Anastasio Aquino (see page 804), before his execution in April 1833.

Zacatecoluca
Colour map 6, grid C1
Population: 81,000
Altitude: 201 m

The capital of La Paz Department is 56 km from San Salvador by road and 19 km south of San Vicente. Good place to buy hammocks, eg nylon 'doubles', US$13. José Simeón Cañas, who abolished slavery in Central America, was born here. There is a cathedral in the Moorish style, and an excellent art gallery.

Sleeping D *El Litoral*, on the main road Km 56. F *Hospedajes América* and *Popular* clean. F *Hospedaje Primavera*, clean, friendly, fan. *Comedor Margoth* (beware overcharging).

Buses Bus 133 from Sur terminal, San Salvador. Direct bus to La Libertad 1540, US$0.65, or take San Salvador bus and change at Comalapa, 2 hrs.

Ichanmichen Near the town is the garden park and *Turicentro* of Ichanmichen ('the place of the little fish'). It is crossed by canals and decorated with natural spring pools where you can swim. It is very hot but there is plenty of shade. Admission and car parking each US$0.75, bungalow rental US$4. Take bus 90 from Zacatecoluca.

Between Km 69 and 70, turn south for **Centro Recreativo Las Ruedas**, T393-0865, or take Usulután bus from Terminal Sur, San Salvador, 1½ hours. ■ *Entry US$0.90*.

Both the road and a railway cross the wide Río Lempa by the Puente de Oro (Golden Bridge) at **San Marcos**. (The road bridge has been destroyed; cars use the railway bridge.) Off the main road near here is **La Nueva Esperanza** where there is a community that has returned from Nicaragua, dormitories to sleep and a good place to go and help if you have a few days to spare. Beyond the bridge (20 km), a branch road (right) leads to tiny **Puerto El Triunfo** on the Bahía de Jiquilisco, with a large shrimp-freezing plant (**E** *Hotel/Restaurant Jardín*). Boats can be hired to take you to the islands in the **Bahía de Jiquilisco**, which are being developed with holiday homes, but are still very beautiful.

About 110 km from the capital is Usulután, capital of its Department. It's large, dirty and unsafe, and only useful as a transit point. Bus 302 from San Salvador, US$1.40. The Coastal Highway goes direct from Usulután to La Unión/Cutuco. **Sleeping E** *España*, on main plaza, T662-0378, recommended. Nice patio, restaurant, bar and discotheque. Several other hotels in same price range.

Usulután
Colour map 6, grid C2
Population: 69,000

Playa El Espino can be reached from Usulután, by car (four-wheel drive) pick-up or slow bus from Usulután; it is very remote but lovely. A luxury resort complex is under construction, but there is no other lodging.

Playa El Espino

Beyond Usulután, the impressive silhouette of Volcán Chaparrasque rises out of the flat coastal plain. Two roads go northeast to San Miguel, the first from 10 km along at El Tránsito, the second further 5 km east, which keeps to the low ground south and east of Volcán San Miguel. Two kilometres beyond this turning on the Carretera Litoral is a short road to the right leading to Laguna El Jocotal, a national nature reserve supported by the World Wildlife Fund which has an abundance of birds and snakes. ■ *The reserve can be visited; enquire at the entrance.*

Laguna El Jocotal
You will see more if you hire a boat

About 12 km from the junction for San Miguel there is a turn to the right leading in 7 km to Playa El Cuco, a popular beach with several places to stay (**F**), near the bus station (bus 320 to San Miguel, US$0.45, one hour last bus 1600). The main beach is liable to get crowded and dirty at weekends and holidays, but is deserted mid-week. Single women should take care here; locals warn against walking along the beach after sunset.

Another popular beach, **El Tamarindo**, is reached by following the coastal road a little further before taking a right turn.

Playa El Cuco
Cases of malaria have been reported from El Cuco

Sleeping Near the centre is **F** *El Rancho*, hammocks only, in cane shacks, basic, friendly, shower from bucket drawn from well. **D** *Hotel La Tortuga*, cheap, good for backpackers. **D** *Los Leones Marinos*, T619-9015, with bath, clean and tidy. **D** *Cucolindo*, 1 km along the coast, cabin for 4, basic, cold water, mosquitos. Another 1½ km gets you to **B** *Trópico Club*, T823-3520, with several cabins, pool and open air dining. Leads directly to the beach. Run by the *Trópico Inn* in San Miguel which can provide information.

At El Tamarindo Cabañas for rent at: **AL** *Playa Negra*, T661-1726, F661-2513; **A** *Torola Cabaña Club*, run by *Izalco Club* at Costa del Sol, T612-0251, F224-0363. Pool looking out to sea with a great open air bar/restaurant, friendly and welcoming owner, recommended; and basic *pensión*. In Tamarindo you can stay at the *Workers' Recreational Centre*, but first obtain a permit from the Ministry of Labour, 2 Av Sur 516, San Salvador. Entry is usually only granted to those related to members and smartly dressed ones at that.

Transport Boat from El Tamarindo across the bay leads to a short cut to La Unión; bus from La Unión 20 mins.

El Salvador

Background

History

When Spanish expeditions arrived in El Salvador from Guatemala and Nicaragua, they found it quite densely populated by several Indian groups, of whom the most populous were the Pipiles. By 1550, the Spaniards had occupied the country, many living in existing Indian villages and towns. The settlers cultivated cocoa in the volcanic highlands and balsam along the coast, and introduced cattle to roam the grasslands freely. Towards the end of the 16th century, indigo became the big export crop: production was controlled by the Spaniards, and Indians provided the workforce, many suffering illness as a result. A period of regional turmoil accompanied El Salvador's declaration of independence from the newly-autonomous political body of Central America in 1839: Indian attempts to regain their traditional land rights were put down by force.

Coffee emerged as an important cash crop in the second half of the 19th century, bringing with it improvements in transport facilities and the final abolition of Indian communal lands.

The land question was a fundamental cause of the peasant uprising of 1932, which was brutally crushed by the dictator General Maximiliano Hernández Martínez. Following his overthrow in 1944, the military did not relinquish power: a series of military coups kept them in control, while they protected the interests of the landowning oligarchy.

1980s Civil War The most recent military coup, in October 1979, led to the formation of a civilian-military junta which promised far-reaching reforms. When these were not carried out, the opposition unified forming a broad coalition, the Frente Democrático Revolucionario, which adopted a military wing, the Farabundo Martí National Liberation Front (FMLN) in 1980. Later the same year, the Christian Democrat Ing José Napoleón Duarte was named as President of the Junta. At about the same time, political tension reached the proportions of civil war.

Duarte was elected to the post of President in 1984, following a short administration headed by Dr Alvaro Magaña. Duarte's periods of power were characterized by a partly-successful attempt at land reform, the nationalization of foreign trade and the banking system, and violence. In addition to deaths in combat, 40,000 civilians were killed between 1979 and 1984, mostly by right-wing death squads. Among the casualties was Archbishop Oscar Romero, who was shot while saying mass in March 1980. Nothing came of meetings between Duarte's government and the FMLN, which were aimed at seeking a peace agreement.

The war continued in stalemate until 1989, by which time an estimated 70,000 had been killed. The Christian Democrats' inability to end the war, reverse the economic decline or rebuild after the 1986 earthquake, combined with their reputation for corruption, brought about a resurgence of support for the right-wing National Republican Alliance (ARENA). An FMLN offer to participate in presidential elections, dependent on certain conditions, was not accepted and the ARENA candidate, Lic Alfredo Cristiani, won the presidency comfortably in March 1989, taking office in June.

Peace talks again failed to produce results and, in November 1989, the FMLN guerrillas staged their most ambitious offensive ever, which paralysed the capital and caused a violent backlash from government forces. FMLN-government negotiations resumed with UN mediation following the offensive, but the two sides could not reach agreement about the purging of the armed forces, which had become the most wealthy institution in the country following 10 years of US support.

Peace negotiations Although El Salvador's most left-wing political party, the Unión Democrática Nacionalista, agreed to participate in municipal elections in 1991, the FMLN remained outside the electoral process, and the civil war continued unresolved. Talks were held in Venezuela and Mexico after initial agreement was reached in April on reforms to the electoral and judicial systems, but further progress was stalled over the restructuring of the armed forces and disarming the guerrillas. There were hopes that human rights would improve after the establishment in June 1991 of a UN Security Council human rights observer commission (ONUSAL), which was charged with verifying compliance with the human rights agreement signed by the Government and the FMLN in Geneva in April 1990. Finally, after considerable UN assistance, the FMLN and the Government signed a peace accord in New York in January 1992 and a formal ceasefire began the following month. A detailed schedule throughout 1992 was established to demobilize the FMLN, dismantle five armed forces elite battalions and to initiate land requests by ex-combatants from both sides. The demobilization process was reported as completed in December 1992, formally concluding the civil war. The US agreed at this point to 'forgive' a substantial portion of the US$2bn international debt of El Salvador. In March 1993, the United Nations Truth Commission published its investigation of human rights abuses during the civil war. Five days later, the legislature approved a general amnesty for all those involved in criminal activities in the war. This included those named in the Truth Commission report. The Cristiani government was slow to implement not only the constitutional reforms proposed by the Truth Commission, but also the process of land reform and the establishment of the National Civilian Police (PNC). By 1995, when Cristiani's successor had taken office, the old national police force was demobilized, but the PNC suffered from a lack of resources for its proper establishment. In fact, the budget for the implementation of the final peace accords was inadequate and El Salvador had to ask the UN for financial assistance.

Presidential and congressional elections on 20 March 1994 failed to give an outright majority to any presidential candidate. The two main contenders, Armando Calderón Sol of Arena and Rubén Zamora, of a coalition of the FMLN, Democratic Convergence and the National Revolutionary Movement, faced a run-off election on 24 April, which Calderón Sol won. Besides his government's difficulties with the final stages of the peace accord, his first months in office were marked by rises in the cost of living, increases in crime, strikes and protests, and occupations of the Legislature by ex-combatants. The government's failure to solve these problems continued into 1996, with the United Nations adding its weight to the criticisms especially of the lack of progress on implementing the social projects designed to reintegrate civil war combatants into civilian life. This contributed to the electorate's sense of disillusion, exacerbated by a considerable realignment of the country's political parties. The congressional and mayoral elections of March 1997 highlighted these issues further. Only 41% of the electorate bothered to vote. In the National Assembly, Arena won 29 seats, FMLN increased its tally to 28 seats, the National Conciliation Party (PCN) won 11, the Christian Democrats (PDC) nine and minority parties seven seats. FMLN managed to run neck-and-neck with Arena until within a year of the March 1999 presidential elections. The party's inability to select a presidential candidate, however, caused it to lose ground rapidly, so much so that in the poll Arena's candidate, Fransisco Flores, won with sufficient votes to avoid a second ballot. Since less than 40% of the electorate voted, Flores could not claim a clear mandate in the face of such a huge rejection of the political system. Most interpreted the abstention as a lack of faith in any party's ability to solve the twin problems of poverty and crime.

1994 elections & after

If the devastating earthquakes of early 2001 were not enough for the country to deal with, droughts through the summer months led to a food crisis that required United Nations intervention. Old rivalries flared briefly as Honduras expelled two Salvadorian diplomats on spying charges, something hotly denied by El Salvador, displaying the fragility of the cordial relations with the northern neighbour. In a year that demonstrated the ease with which instability can become the status quo, El Salvador also hosted the meeting of Mexican and Central America presidents to develop the *Plan Puebla* regional integration project which would link the Mexican city of Puebla with Panama City along an economic

The new Millennium

El Salvador

investment corridor designed to create jobs. Promising signs of progress, and support for the future led President Bush to drop in on the country in his whirlwind trip to Latin America in early 2002.

El Salvador

Government

Legislative power is vested in a unicameral Legislative Assembly, which has 84 seats and is elected for a three-year term. The head of state and government is the president, who holds office for five years. The country is divided into 14 departments.

Economy

Agriculture is the dominant sector of the economy, accounting for three quarters of export earnings. Coffee and sugar are the most important crops, but attempts have been made at diversification and now soya, shrimp, sesame, vegetables, tropical flowers and ornamental plants are promoted as important foreign exchange earners. The sector has been badly effected in recent years by drought, the El Niño phenomenon and Hurricane Mitch. Land ownership had been unevenly distributed with a few wealthy families owning most of the land, while the majority of agricultural workers merely lived at subsistence level. In 1992 the Government and the FMLN agreed to distribute 166,000 ha of land to about 48,000 Salvadoreans at a cost of US$143 mn, a process that was beset by problems.

The most important industries are food processing and petroleum products: others include textiles, pharmaceuticals, shoes, furniture, chemicals and fertilizers, cosmetics, construction materials, drink processing and rubber goods. *Maquila* factories have grown rapidly in recent years, providing an estimated 20,000 jobs. Exports of manufactured goods, mostly to other Central American countries, account for some 33% of foreign exchange earnings.

In 1975 a geothermal power plant came into operation at Ahuachapán, with a capacity of 30 MW, and was expanded by 60 MW in 1978. Hydraulic resources are also being exploited as a means of generating power and saving oil import costs.

Attempts in the late 1990s to stablize El Salvador's economic problems were voiced by President Flores in the first month of his term in June 1999 when he outlined his economic priorities as reducing the fiscal deficit through reorganization of the tax system and controls on government spending. Help for the agricultural sector would be complemented by road-building and by efforts to stem violence in rural areas and to cut smuggling.

Economically, the main shift has been to adopt the dollar as national currency. A ground swell of rumbling opposition to dollarization was apparent before the earthquake placed the focus on other events. The long-term impact of the earthquakes has been compounded by droughts in the east of the country resulting in the need for United Nations' emergency food relief.

Culture

People The population is far more homogeneous than that of Guatemala. The reason for this is that El Salvador lay comparatively isolated from the main stream of conquest, and had no precious metals to act as magnets for the Spaniards. The small number of Spanish settlers intermarried with those Indians who survived the plagues brought from Europe to form a group of mestizos. There were only about half a million people as late as 1879. With the introduction of coffee, the population grew quickly and the new prosperity fertilized the whole economy, but the internal pressure of population has led to the occupation of all the available land. Several hundred thousand Salvadoreans have emigrated to neighbouring republics because of the shortage of land and the concentration of land ownership, and, more recently, because of the civil war.

Handicrafts of El Salvador

The artists' village of La Palma, in a pine-covered valley under Miramundo mountain, is 84 km north of the capital, 10 km south of the Honduran frontier. Here, in 1971, the artist Fernando Llort "planted a seed" known as the copinol (a species of the locust tree) from which sprang the first artists' cooperative, now called La Semilla de Dios (Seed of God). The copinol seed is firm and round; on it the artisans base a spiritual motif that emanates from their land and soul. The town and its craftspeople are now famous for their work in wood, including exotically carved cofres (adorned wooden chests), and traditional Christmas muñecas de barro (clay dolls) and ornamental angels. Wood carvings, other crafts and the designs of the original paintings by Llort, are all produced and exported from La Palma to the rest of El Salvador and thence worldwide. In 1971 the area was almost exclusively agricultural; today 75% of the population of La Palma and neighbouring San Ignacio are engaged directly or indirectly in producing handicrafts. The painter Alfredo Linares (born 1957 in Santa Ana, arrived in La Palma 1981 after studying in Guatemala and Florence) has a gallery in La Palma, employing and assisting local artists. His paintings and miniatures are marketed abroad, yet you will often find him working in the family pharmacy next to the gallery. Many of La Palma's images are displayed on the famous Hilasal towels. If you cannot get to La Palma, visit the shop/gallery/workshop of Fernando Llort in San Salvador, Arbol de Dios.

Twenty kilometres from the capital is the indigenous town of Panchimalco, where weaving on the loom and other traditional crafts are being revived. Many nahuat traditions, customs, dances and the language survived here as the original Indians hid from the Spanish conquistadores in the valley beneath the Puerta del Diablo (now in Parque Balboa). In 1996 the painter Eddie Alberto Orantes and his family opened the Centro de Arte y Cultura Tunatiuh, named after a nahuat deity who is depicted as a human face rising as a sun over a pyramid. The project employs local youths (from broken homes, or former addicts) in the production of weavings, paintings and ceramics.

In the mountains of western El Salvador, villages in the coffee zone, such as Nahuizalco, specialize in weaving henequen, bamboo and reed into table mats and wicker furniture. There are also local artists like Maya sculptor Ahtzic Selis, who works with clay and jade. East of the capital, at Ilobasco (60 km), many ceramic workshops produce items including the famous sorpresas, miniature figures enclosed in an egg shell. In the capital there are crafts markets in which to bargain for pieces, while throughout the country, outlets range from the elegant to the rustic. But everywhere artists and artisans welcome visitors into their workshops.

El Salvador

Of the total population, some 10% are regarded as ethnic Indians, although the traditional Indian culture has almost completely vanished. Other estimates put the percentage of pure Indians as low as 5%. The Lenca and the Pipil, the two surviving indigenous groups, are predominantly peasant farmers. Only 1% are of unmixed white ancestry, the rest are mestizos.

With a population of 280 to the sq km, El Salvador is the most densely populated country on the American mainland. Health and sanitation outside the capital and some of the main towns leave much to be desired, and progress in this area was very limited in the 1980s and early 1990s because of the violence.

Music & dance

The Mexican music industry seems to exert an overwhelming cultural influence, while the virtual absence of an Indian population may also be partly responsible, since it is so often they who maintain traditions and hold to the past. Whatever the reason, the visitor who is seeking specifically Salvadorean native music will find little to satisfy him or her. El Salvador is an extension of 'marimba country', but songs and dances are often accompanied by the guitar and seem to lack a rhythm or style that can be pinpointed as specifically local. An exception is the music played on the pito de caña and tambor which accompanies the traditional dances called Danza de los Historiantes, La Historia or Los Moros y Cristianos. Over 30 types of dance have been identified, mostly in the west and centre of the country, although there are a few in the east. The main theme is the conflict between christianized *indígenas* and 'heretic' *indígenas* and the dances are performed as a ritual on the local saint's day.

Education & religion Education is free if given by the government, and nominally obligatory. There are 43 universities, three national and the others private or church-affiliated. There is also a National School of Agriculture. The most famous are the government-financed Universidad Nacional and the Jesuit-run Universidad Centroamericana (UCA). Roman Catholicism is the prevailing religion.

Land and environment

El Salvador is the smallest, most densely populated and most integrated of the Central American republics. Its intermont basins are a good deal lower than those of Guatemala, rising to little more than 600 m at the capital, San Salvador. Across this upland and surmounting it run two more or less parallel rows of volcanoes, 14% of which are over 900 m high. The highest are Santa Ana (2,365 m), San Vicente (2,182 m), San Miguel (2,130 m), and San Salvador (1,893 m). One important result of this volcanic activity is that the highlands are covered with a deep layer of ash and lava which forms a porous soil ideal for coffee planting.

The total area of El Salvador is 21,041 sq km. Guatemala is to the west, Honduras to the north and east, and the Pacific coastline to the south is approximately 321 km long. Lowlands lie to the north and south of the high backbone. In the south, on the Pacific coast, the lowlands of Guatemala are confined to just east of Acajutla; beyond are lava promontories before another 30-km belt of lowlands where the 325-km long Río Lempa flows into the sea. The northern lowlands are in the wide depression along the course of the Río Lempa, buttressed to the south by the highlands of El Salvador and to the north by the basalt cliffs edging the highlands of Honduras. The highest point in El Salvador, Cerro El Pital (2,730 m) is part of the mountain range bordering on Honduras. After 160 km the Lempa cuts through the southern uplands to reach the Pacific; the depression is prolonged southeast till it reaches the Gulf of Fonseca.

El Salvador is located on the southwest coast of the Central American Isthmus on the Pacific Ocean. As the only country in the region lacking access to the Caribbean Sea, it does not posses the flora associated with that particular coastal zone. El Salvador nevertheless has a wide variety of colourful, tropical vegetation; for example over 200 species of orchid grow all over the country. As a result of excessive forest cutting, and hence the destruction of their habitats, many of the animals (such as jaguars and crested eagles) once found in the highlands of the country, have diminished at an alarming rate. In response to this problem several nature reserves have been set up in areas where flora and fauna can be found in their most unspoilt state. Among these nature reserves are the Cerro Verde, Deininger Park, El Imposible Woods, El Jocatal Lagoon and the Montecristo Cloud Forest.

Books and films

The novels of Manlio Argueta, *One day of Life* (1980) and *Cuzcatlán* (1986), look at peasant rebellion during El Salvador's 20th-century history. *Rincón Mágico de El Salvador* and *El Salvador Prehistórico*, both available at *Banco Agrícola Comercial*, Paseo Escalón 3635, San Salvador (US$72). *Amor de Jade*, by Walter Raudales, to be published in English too, is a novel based on the life of El Salvador's Mata Hari (now ex-comandante Joaquín Villalobos' wife).

On the big screen Raúl Julia takes the lead in *Romero* (1989), which covers the story surrounding the archbishop's assassination. Oliver Stone's *Salvador* takes the journalist's view of events in the country's civil war circa 1980.

El Salvador

823

Honduras

7

824

Honduras

Essentials

Honduras is larger than the other Central American republics except Nicaragua, but its population is smaller – less than a fifth the size – than that of neighbouring El Salvador. Bordered by Nicaragua, Guatemala and El Salvador, and a narrow coastal Pacific strip, the northern Caribbean coast and beautiful Bay Islands are a natural focus and a prime destination for visitors.

Inland, the mountainous terrain creates natural obstacles to easy, direct travel round the country, but it also means that, for trekking and hiking, there are great swathes of beautiful hillside, many of which are dotted with small communities largely disinterested in the comings and goings of the few travellers who venture so far off the beaten track.

In October 1998 Hurricane Mitch deluged Honduras with torrential rain causing great loss of life and major damage to almost all parts of the country. News reports at the time painted a bleak picture, but recovery in many places was swift. By 2000 over half a million foreigners had visited to enjoy the delights of this often overlooked country.

Planning your trip

Where to go

With the popularity of the Bay Islands as a diving destination, mainland Honduras is often missed in the frenzied rush to hit the water. And, while the beauty of the the islands cannot be overstated, picking a route that takes in some of the smaller towns of Honduras gives a far better understanding of the country as a whole.

The capital and administrative centre is **Tegucigalpa**, which has an older, colonial sector and a newer section with modern hotels, shops and businesses. Across the Río Choluteca is Tegucigalpa's twin city, **Comayagüela**, the working heart of the city with the markets and bus terminals. Around the capital, colonial villages, old mining towns, handicraft centres and good hiking areas, including **Parque Nacional La Tigra**, make ideal trips for a day or two.

West of Tegucigalpa, near the border with Guatemala, is Honduras' premier Maya archaeological site **Copán**, where new discoveries are still being made, and some fine Maya art can be seen. A short distance from the site, the well-restored town of **Copán Ruinas** is a colonial gem and, nearby, the recently opened site of **El Puente** is beginning to reveal treasures hidden for centuries. Closer to the capital, quiet colonial towns such as **Gracias** and graceful **Santa Bárbara** are the site of opal mines, Lenca Indian communities and **national parks** such as **Mount Celaque**. There is lots of good hiking in the vicinity of the increasingly popular colonial city of **Santa Rosa de Copán**. A good way to explore this more traditional part of the country is to pick a route, travel in short distances and soak up the calm and tranquillity.

From Tegucigalpa a paved highway runs north to San Pedro Sula, the second city of the republic and the country's main business centre. The road passes the old colonial capital of Comayagua and beautiful Lago Yojoa. North of San Pedro Sula, the **North Coast** has a number of centres of interest to the visitor. The main port is **Puerto Cortés** to the west of which is Omoa, an increasingly popular beach and fishing village with an old fort, from which an overland route enters Guatemala. East of Puerto Cortés are **Tela**, a more established resort, and **La Ceiba**, a good place for visiting the nearby national parks of Pico Bonito and Cuero y Salado, a base for whitewater rafting trips on the Río Cangrejal and departure point for the Bay Islands. Further west Trujillo, sitting at the southern end of a palm-fringed bay, was once the capital of the country. Dotted along the Caribbean several areas are set aside as wildlife refuges and national parks.

The **Bay Islands**, Utila, Roatán and Guanaja, plus the smaller Hog Islands, are one of Honduras' main tourist destinations. Travellers visiting just one part of Honduras often pick the islands which curve northeast from the coast. The diving in the area is excellent and Utila and Roatán are currently the cheapest dive centres in the Caribbean. The islands also have good beaches.

Northeast of Tegucigalpa is the province of Olancho, an agricultural and cattle-raising area which leads eventually to the Caribbean coast at Trujillo. Juticalpa and Catacamas are the main towns, and the mountains of the district have cloudforest, hiking trails and beautiful conservation areas. Beyond Olancho is **Mosquitia** which is forested, swampy and almost uninhabited. Efforts

Honduras

are being made to preserve this relatively untouched area and to promote sustainable development among the Miskito and Pech Indians. Ecotourism initiatives have been set up in some of the communities on the coast and inland, making for adventurous and rewarding travel where the main ways of getting around are by boat, small plane or on foot.

Honduras' short **Pacific** coast on the Gulf of Fonseca is little visited, other than en route to Nicaragua and El Salvador. The main towns in the region are Choluteca and, in the gulf, Amapala, on the extinct volcanic Isla del Tigre. Another route to Nicaragua is that **east of the capital** through the town of Danlí, which passes the Panamerican Agricultural School at Zamorano and the old mining town of Yuscarán.

When to go The Caribbean coast is wet all year round, but the heaviest rain falls from September to February. The dry season inland is November to April, December and January being the coolest months, April and May the hottest. Some of the central highland areas enjoy a delightful climate, with a freshness that makes a pleasant contrast to the humidity and heat of the lowland zones. In Tegucigalpa lowest average temperatures are 14°C in January and February, and the highest 30°C in April and May. The cooler season in San Pedro Sula is November to February, but the rest of the year is very hot.

Finding out more The **Ministerio Hondureño de Turismo**, T800-222-8687 (toll free number in Honduras). The main office at Edificio Europa, Avenida Ramón E Cruz y Calle República de México, Colonia San Carlos, Tegucigalpa, T238-3974, F238-2102. There is also an office at Toncontín Airport and several regional tourist offices (see also under Tegucigalpa, page 833). *HONDURAS tips*, edited by John Dupuis in San Pedro Sula, Apartado Postal 2699, Edificio Rivera y Cía, piso 7, oficina 705, 3 Calle 6 Avenida 50, T/F552-9557, **www.hondurastips.honduras.com**, is a biannual publication full of interesting and useful tourist information, in English and Spanish, free (available in Tegucigalpa from Ministerio Hondureño de Turismo).

Honduras on the web **www.honduras.com**, has lots of information about Honduras with links to national newspapers. The official homepage of Honduras is at **www.hondurasinfo.com** whilst **www.hondurastips.honduras.com**, is the official guide to tourism in Honduras on the net and comes with a selection of photographs. Try **www.netsys.hn**, for business links. Several regional guides are being developed and these are mentioned within the text, including, for example, **www.copanruinas.com**, for the town and ruins.

Language Spanish is the main language, but English is often spoken in the north, in the Bay Islands, by West Indian settlers on the Caribbean coast, and is understood by large businesses.

Before you travel

Visas & immigration
For embassies and consulates in Honduras see page 841

Neither a visa nor tourist card is required for nationals of Western European countries, USA, Canada, Australia, New Zealand, Japan, Argentina, Chile, Guatemala, Costa Rica, Nicaragua, El Salvador, Panama and Uruguay. Citizens of other countries, including Israelis, need either a tourist card, which can be bought from Honduran consulates for US$2-3, occasionally less, or a visa, and they should enquire at a Honduran consulate in advance to see which they need. The price of a visa seems to vary depending on nationality, and according to where it is bought. It is imperative to check entry requirements in advance at a consulate. Two-day transit visas costing US$5, for any travellers it seems, are given at the El Florido border for visiting Copán, but you must leave at the same point and your right of return to Guatemala is not guaranteed, especially if your Guatemalan visa is valid for one journey only.

Visitors from all countries who do not need a visa may stay for 30 days. Visitors from Germany, Japan and Chile are allowed 90 days; some travellers, regardless of nationality, have reported 90-day permits given at airport immigration. Make sure border officials fill in your entry papers correctly and in accordance with your wishes. Extensions of 30 days are easy to obtain (up to a maximum of six months' stay, cost US$5). There are immigration offices for extensions at Tela, La Ceiba, San Pedro Sula, Santa Rosa de Copán, Siguatepeque, La Paz and Comayagua, and all are more helpful than the Tegucigalpa office. A ticket out of the country is

Honduran embassies and consulates

Belgium (also the Netherlands and Luxembourg), Avenue des Gaulois 8, 1040 Brussels, T322-734-0000, F322-735-2626.
Canada, 151 Slater Street, Suite 805-A, Ottawa, Ontario K1P 5H3, T613-233-8900, F613-232-0193.
France, 8 rue Crevaux, 75116 Paris, T4755-8645, F4755-8648.
Germany, Ubierstrasse-1, D-53173 Bonn, T228-356394, F228-351981.
Israel, Calle Zohar Tal No 1, Herzlya Pituach, CP46741, T99577686, F99577457.
Italy, Gian Battista de Vico 40, Interno 8, Roma, T06-320-7236, F06-320-7973.
Japan, 38 Kowa Bldg, 8F No 802, 12-24 Nishi Azabu 4, Chome Minato Ku, Tokyo 106,

T03-3409-1150, F03-3409-0305.
Mexico, Alfonso Reyes 220, Colonia Condesa, México DF, T211-5747, F211-5425.
Spain, Calle Rosario Pino 6, Cuarto Piso A, Madrid 28020, T341-579-0251, F341-572-1319.
Sweden, Sturegatan 12, 114, 36 Stockholm, T665-3231, F665-0917.
UK, 115 Gloucester Place, London W1H 3PJ, T020-7486-4880, F020-7486-4550.
USA, 3007 Tilden Street NW, Pod 4M, Washington, DC 20008, T202-966-7702, F202-966-9751.
For information on visa requirements and embassies look on the web at www.sre.hn

necessary for air travellers – if coming from USA, you won't be allowed on the plane without one – and onward tickets must be bought outside the country. It is not impossible to cash in the return half of the ticket in Honduras, but there is no guarantee and plenty of time is needed. Proof of adequate funds is sometimes asked for at land borders.

Customs

There are no customs duties on personal effects. You are allowed to bring in 200 cigarettes or 100 cigars, or ½ kg of tobacco, and two quarts of spirit.

Money

Currency

The unit of currency is the **lempira** (written La and referred to as *lemps* within a few days of arrival) named after a famous Indian chief that lost his life while fighting the invasion of the Spaniards. In general, it is reasonably stable against the dollar. Divided into 100 centavos, there are nickel coins of 5, 10, 20 and 50 centavos. Bank notes are for 1, 2, 5, 10, 20, 50, 100 and 500 lempiras. No one has change for larger notes, especially the 500. Any amount of any currency can be taken in or out of the country.

US$1=17.14 lempiras

Money may be changed at the free rate in banks, but a street market offers rates which are usually slightly higher than the official rate. Not all banks accept travellers' cheques. Good exchange rates are available at the borders if you speak Spanish.

Credit cards & TCs

MasterCard and *Visa* are accepted in major hotels and most restaurants in cities and larger towns. *American Express* is accepted in more expensive establishments. Cash advances from *Credomatic*, Boulevard Morazán, Tegucigalpa, and branches of *Banco Atlántida*, *Aval Card* and *Honducard* throughout the country. *Credomatic* represents *American Express* and issues and services Amex credit cards. Cash advances using *MasterCard* cost US$10 in banks. Acceptance of credit cards in Honduras is patchy and commissions can be as high as 6%. Most businesses will try to tack on a service charge to credit card purchases which is illegal. If a hotel or restaurant tries to add an additional charge, dispute it with the manager. Asking the manager to call Credomatic will yield the answer that the added charge is in fact illlegal. It is advisable to have travellers' cheques available and US$ in cash as well.

Cost of living & travelling

Honduras is not expensive for the visitor (two people can travel together in reasonable comfort for US$25 per person per day – less if on a tight budget), but prices for services offered to tourists fluctuate greatly. Transportation including domestic flights is still the cheapest in Central America. Diving will set you back a bit, but at US$150 or so for a PADI course, it is still the cheapest in Central America.

Honduras

Honduras

Getting there

Air Tegucigalpa, La Ceiba, San Pedro Sula and Roatán all have international airports. There are no direct flights to **Tegucigalpa** from Europe, but connecting flights can be made via Miami, then with *American Airlines* or *Taca*. There are flights to Tegucigalpa from Houston with *Continental*. *Taca* flies daily from Guadalajara, Guatemala City, Mexico City, Monterrey (Mexico), San Salvador, and San José (Costa Rica).

Iberia flies to **San Pedro Sula** via Miami from Madrid and Barcelona five days a week. *American Airlines* fly daily from Miami, as do *Taca* and *Iberia*. *Taca* also fly once a week from New Orleans. *Continental* flies from Houston, New York and West Palm Beach once a week, and have a daily service from Los Angeles. *Taca* flies from San José to San Pedro Sula direct, with flights from Belize City, Guatemala City, Panama City, San José and San Salvador. *Sol Air* have recently introduced daily flights from Miami to San Pedro Sula and Tegucigalpa.

There are twice-weekly flights from Grand Cayman Island to La Ceiba. For flights to Roatán, see page 912. *Atlantic Air* serves La Ceiba, San Pedro Sula, Teguc, Roatán, Utila, Guanaja, Puerto Lempira, Caquira and Ahuas. *SOSA* is the largest domestic carrier, serving Roatán, Utila, Guanaja, Palacios, San Pedro Sula, Tegucigalpa and other destinations in Honduras.

Overland There are numerous border crossings with Guatemala to the east near Copán Ruinas at El Florida, or on the Caibbean coast at Corinto. To the south, the crossings at El Poy and Perquín lead to Suchitoto and San Miguel respectively. The border post of Guasale leads 116 km on a very bad road to the Nicaraguan town of León, while the inland routes at Las Manos and El Espino guide you to Estelí and Matagalpa, in the northern hills. Most bridges that lead to the border with Nicaragua were washed away by Hurricane Mitch so be prepared for badly marked detours. Crossing through the Mosquitia Coast is not possible – officially at least.

Sea There are weekly boats from Lívingston in Guatemala in high season. Contact *Gunter's Dive Shop*, Utila, for details see page 903.

Touching down

Taxes **Airport** There is an airport departure tax of US$25 (not charged if in transit less than nine hours), and a 10% tax on all tickets sold for domestic and international journeys.

The border offices close at 1700 (not 1800 as in most other countries); an extra fee is charged after that time

Land borders Taxes are charged on entry and exit at land borders, but the amount charged varies from border to border, despite notices asking you to denounce corruption. Entry is 20 lempiras (or US$1.50) and exit is 10 lempiras. Double is charged on Sunday. If officials make an excess charge for entry or exit, ask for a receipt. Do not attempt to enter Honduras at an unstaffed border crossing. When it is discovered that you have no entry stamp you will either be fined US$60 or escorted to the border, and you will have to pay the guard's food and lodging (you may be able to defray some of this cost by spending a night in jail).

Local customs & laws **Clothing** On the north coast, where the climate is much hotter and damper, dress is less formal. **Tipping** Normally 10% of the bill but more expensive places add a service charge to the bill. **Identification** It is advisable to carry some form of identification at all times, because spot checks have increased, especially when entering or leaving major towns. **Safety** Unfortunately we are forced to report greater concerns over general security in Honduras. At the time of Hurricane Mitch predictions suggested social problems would be prevalent in a few years. Reports of muggings and theft have increased but verifying the reports is difficult. Take local advice and be cautious when travelling alone or off the beaten track. But remember, the vast majority of Hondurans are honest, friendly, warm and welcoming.

Touching down

IDD 504; Local operator 192; General
information 193; International operator 197.
Hours of business 0900-1200, 1400-1800
Monday to Friday; 0800-1200 Saturday, and
some open in the afternoon. In San Pedro Sula
and along the north coast most places open
and close half an hour earlier in the morning
and afternoon than in Tegucigalpa. **Banks** in
Tegucigalpa 0900-1500 Monday-Friday;
0800-1100 only along the north coast on

Saturday. **Post offices**: 0700-2000
Monday-Friday; 0800-1200 Saturday.
Voltage Generally 110 volts but, increasingly,
220 volts is being installed. US-type flat-pin
plugs.
Weights and measures The metric system
of weights is official and should be used, but
the libra (pound) is still often used for meat,
fish, etc. Land is measured in varas (84 cm)
and manzanas (0.7 ha).

Accommodation in Honduras varies greatly. In Tegucigalpa and San Pedro Sula you will find
a mix of business-style hotels ranging from international standards down to the base for the
bus travelling salesman. In popular tourist spots the focus is more on comfort and costs rise
accordingly. Get off the beaten track and you'll find some of the most basic and cheapest
accommodation in Central America – complete with accompanying insect life it can be
unbearable or a mind-broadening experience depending on your mood.

Getting around

There are airstrips in all large towns and many of the cut-off smaller ones. Airlines which make **Air**
internal flights are: *Isleña*, *Sosa*, *Rollins Air* and *Atlantic Air*. Details are given in the text. It is
worth checking the price for longer flights as they are occasionally discounted to levels that
compete with bus travel. La Ceiba is the main hub for domestic flights, especially for *Sosa* and
Atlantic, and most flights to and from the islands stop there. The cheapest way to the islands is
to get a bus to La Ceiba and then catch a flight.

The road system throughout the country – apart from **La Mosquitia** which is only reached **Road**
by light aeroplane – has improved rapidly in recent years and Honduras probably has the *If hiring a car,*
best roads in Central America. However many roads were built and maintained with US *make sure it has*
money when Honduras was supporting the contras in Nicaragua and many are now *the correct papers,*
showing signs of lack of maintenance. Traffic tends to travel fast on these apparently good *and emergency*
roads, and road accidents are second only to Costa Rica in Latin America. If driving take care *triangles which*
and avoid driving at night. Total road length is now 15,100 km, of which 3,020 km are paved, *are required by law*
almost 10,000 km are all-weather roads and the remainder are passable in the dry season.

Buses There are essentially three types of service: local (*servicio a escala*), direct (*servicio directo*) and luxury (*servicio de lujo*). *A escala* is very slow, with frequent stops and detours,
using school buses and is uncomfortable for long periods. *Servicio directo* is faster, slightly
more expensive and more comfortable. *Servicio de lujo* has air-conditioned European and
Brazilian buses with videos.

Buses tend to set out early in the day, with a few night buses running between major
urban centres. Try to avoid bus journeys after dark as there are many more accidents and
even occasional robberies. If you suffer from motion sickness, the twisty roads can become
unbearable. Avoid sitting at the back of the bus, take some water and sit by a window that will
open. Minibuses normally travel faster than buses, so the journey can be quite hair-raising.
Pick-ups which serve out-of-the-way communities will leave you covered in dust (or soaked)
– sit near the cab if possible.

Honduras

There are frequent police searches on entry to or exit from towns and villages. Only stop if signalled to do so. Be alert if there are police around, they will try to spot the tiniest infraction of the laws to collect a fine. Your licence will be taken until the fine is paid; on-the-spot fines are not legal, but are common. Try to go to a police station

Driving Regular **gasoline/petrol** costs US$2.45 per US gallon. Unleaded petrol is available everywhere, US$2.40, diesel US$1.66. On entering with a car (from El Salvador at least), customs and the transit police give a 30-day permit for the vehicle. This must be renewed in Tegucigalpa (anywhere else authorization is valid for only one department). Charges for motorists appear to be: on entry, US$30 in total for a vehicle with two passengers, including provisional permission from the police to drive in Honduras, US$1 (official minimum) for car papers, fumigation and baggage inspection; on exit, US$2.30 in total. Motorcyclists face similar charges. These charges are changing all the time and differ significantly from one border post to another (up to US$40 sometimes). They are also substantially higher on Saturday, Sunday and holidays and by bribery. You will have to pass through Migración, Registro, Tránsito, Cuarentena, Administración, Secretaría and then a police vehicle check. At each stage you will be asked for money, for which you will not always get a receipt. On arriving or leaving with a vehicle there are so many checks that it pays to hire a *tramitador* to steer you to the correct officials in the correct order (US$1-2 for the guide). No fresh food is allowed to cross the border. The easiest border crossing is at Las Manos.

The Pan-American in Honduras is in bad condition in parts. One reader warns to "beware of potholes that can take a car. They suddenly appear after 20 km of good road without warning."

Cycling Bicycles are regarded as vehicles but are not officially subject to entrance taxes. Bicycle repair shops are difficult to find, and parts for anything other than mountain bikes may be very hard to come by. Some buses and most local flights will take bicycles. Most main roads have hard shoulders and most drivers respect cyclists. It is common for cars to blow their horn to signal their approach.

Hitchhiking is relatively easy. Travel is still by foot and mule in many rural areas.

Train The railways are in the north. In 1993 the *Tela Railroad Company* closed its entire operation along the Atlantic coast, while the *Ferrocarril Nacional de Honduras* has since downgraded its one remaining passenger service between Tela and Puerto Cortés to a twice-weekly ferrobus.

Maps The *Instituto Geográfico Nacional* produces two 1:1,000,000 maps (1995) of the country, one a tourist map which includes city maps of Tegucigalpa, San Pedro Sula and La Ceiba, and the other a good road map although it does not show all the roads. Both maps are widely available in bookshops in major cities and some hotels. *International Travel Maps* (*ITM*) have a 1:750,000 map of Honduras.

Keeping in touch

Internet Internet cafés are widely available in the capital and in popular locations. Connections tends to be on the slow side, but inexpensive. Details of cafés and places offering email and internet services to travellers are given in the text.

Post Air mail takes four to seven days to Europe and the same for the US. Letters up to 20 g cost US$0.40 to all parts of the world. Small packages – 500 g to 1 kg – US$3 to USA or Europe. Sea mail to Europe US$3 up to 5 kg, US$4.50 up to 10 kg, takes several months. Note that this service is not available in Guatemala, so it might be convenient to send things from Tegucigalpa or San Pedro Sula main post offices.

Telephone *Hondutel* provides international telephone and fax services from stations throughout the country. The system is the most basic and most expensive in Central America Telephone service between Honduras and Europe costs about US$4.81 per minute; calls to USA US$2.70 per minute. Collect calls to North America, Central America and some European countries (not possible to Netherlands, Australia, Switzerland or Israel) can be made from *Hondutel* office in Tegucigalpa. Fax charges are per page, plus 12% tax, to North America US$1.80, to Europe US$1.80, to South America and the Caribbean US$2, to the rest of the world US$3. To receive a fax at *Hondutel* costs one lempira per page.

Honduras

Newspapers The principal newspapers in Tegucigalpa are *El Heraldo* and *La Tribuna*. In **Media**
San Pedro Sula are *El Tiempo* and *La Prensa* (circulation about 54,000). Links on the net at
www.honduras.com The English weekly paper *Honduras This Week*, Centro Commercial
Villa Mare, Boulevard Morazán, T232-8818, F232-8818, www.marrder.com/htw/, available at
limited locations throughout the country, comes out on Saturday, costs US$0.35, also online
edition on website.

Television There are six television channels and 167 broadcasting stations. Cable TV is
available in large towns and cities.

Food and drink

Cheapest meals are the *comida corriente*, or the sometimes better prepared and more expensive **Cuisine**
comida típica, which usually contain some of the following: beans, rice, meat, avocado, egg,
cabbage salad, cheese, *plátanos*, potatoes or yucca, and always tortillas. *Carne asada* is charcoal
roasted meat and served with grated cabbage between tortillas, good, though rarely prepared
hygienically. Make sure that pork is properly cooked. *Tajadas* are crisp, fried *plátano* chips topped
with grated cabbage and sometimes meat; *nacatamales* are ground, dry maize mixed with meat
and seasoning, boiled in banana leaves. *Baleadas* are soft flour tortillas filled with beans and
various combinations of butter, egg, cheese and cabbage. *Pupusas* are thick corn tortillas filled
with *chicharrón* (pork scratchings), or cheese, served as snacks with beer. *Tapado* is a stew with
meat or fish (especially on the north coast), plantain, yucca and coconut milk. *Pinchos* are meat,
poultry, or shrimp kebabs. *Sopa de mondongo* (tripe soup) is very common.
   Cheap fish is best found on the beaches at Trujillo and Cedeño. While on the north coast,
look out for *pan de coco* (coconut bread) made by Garífuna (Black Carib) women, and *sopa de
camarones* which are prepared with coconut milk and lemon juice.

Soft drinks are called *refrescos*, or *frescos* (the name also given to fresh fruit blended with **Drink**
water, check that bottled water is used as tap water is unsafe); *licuados* are fruit blended
with milk. Bottled drinking water is readily available in most places. Orange juice, usually
sweetened, is available in cartons everywhere. *Horchata* is *morro* seeds, rice water and
cinnamon. Coffee is thick and sweet. The main brands of beer are Port Royal Export,
Imperial, Nacional and Salva Vida (more malty than the others). Local rum is cheap, try
Flor de Caña white, or seven-year-old amber. Twelve-year-old *Flor de Caña Centenario* is
the best.

Shopping

The best articles are those in wood. Straw items are also highly recommended. Leather is
cheaper than in El Salvador and Nicaragua. As a single stopping point, the region around
Santa Bárbara is one of the best places, with outlets selling handicrafts from nearby villages.
Alternatively you can explore the villages yourself and see the goods being made.
   The coffee is good. Note that film can be expensive, but *Konica* film can be bought for
US$4-5 for 36 exposures, for example at *Laboratorio Villatoro*, stores in major towns. For bulk
purchases (say 50 rolls) try their head office on Calle Peatonal, Jardín de Italia, Tegucigalpa. Be
aware that film is rarely of good quality.
   Sales tax is 12%, often only charged if you ask for a receipt; 15% on alcohol and tobacco.
There is also a 4% extra tax on hotel rooms.

Holidays and festivals

Most of the feast days of the Roman Catholic religion. Also 1 January: New Year's Day; 14 April:
Day of the Americas; Holy Week: Thursday, Friday, and Saturday before Easter Sunday; 1 May:
Labour Day; 15 September: Independence Day; 3 October: Francisco Morazán; 12 October:
Columbus' arrival in America; 21 October: Army Day.

Honduras

Sport and special interest travel

*Honduras is
slowly developing
its special interest
travel opportunities*

Diving off the Bay Islands has for a long time been the number one attraction, whether seeking some of the best and most varied diving in Central America, or looking to kick start your scuba skills with some of the cheapest PADI courses on the planet. Snorkelling is also excellent off the Bay Islands if you've reached your dive limits or simply find the whole thing just a little too unnatural.

Whitewater rafting is growing steadily in Honduras with the hotspot being the River Cangrejal, close to La Ceiba, where Class II, III and IV rapids test both the novice and experienced paddler. The sport is relatively new to the country and sites are certain to be found in the coming years.

Adventure tourism is beginning to take off with the usual array of activities. Mountain biking is increasingly popular as is horse-riding around Copán. Hard-core adventure can be found in the swamp wetlands of Mosquitia, usually by taking an organized tour.

Nature trips take advantage of the wide variety of national parks in Honduras (see below). Birders have for years known about the treasures of the country, but hikers and trekkers are beginning to venture out through the valleys and across the hills that are often shrouded in cloud forest.

**National
parks**
*For location, see
colour map 6 at
the back of the book*

The extensive system of national parks and protected areas provides the chance to enjoy some of the best scenery Honduras has to offer, much of it unspoilt and rarely visited. The National Parks' Office, **Conama**, is next to the Instituto Nacional Agrario in Tegucigalpa; chaotic but friendly and a good source of information. **Cohdefor**, the national forestry agency, is also much involved with the parks, they have an office at 10 Avenida 4 Calle NO, San Pedro Sula, T253-4959. The parks system has been in existence legally since a congressional decree was passed in 1987. Parks have different levels of services – see individual parks for details. Natural Reserves continue to be established and all support and interest is most welcome. Parks in existence are **La Tigra**, outside Tegucigalpa (page 843), and the **Biosphere of the Río Plátano** (page 921). Under development since 1987 are **Monte Celaque** (page 859), **Cusuco** (page 876), **Punta Sal** (page 885), **Capiro y Calentura** (page 895), **Cerro Azul-Meámbar** (page 868), **Montaña de Yoro** (page 896) and **Pico Bonito** (page 890) (these parks have visitors' centres, hiking trails and primitive camping). The following have been designated national parks by the government: **Montecristo-Trifinio** (page 863), **Santa Bárbara** (page 870), **Pico Pijol** (Yoro, page 896), **Agalta** (Olancho, page 917) and **Montaña de Comayagua** (page 867). Wildlife Refuges covered in the text are **Punto Izopo** (page 884), **Cuero y Salado** (page 891), **Las Trancas** (page 862) and **La Muralla-Los Higuerales** (page 915). For information on protected areas in the **Bay Islands**, see page 897.

Health

Dysentery and stomach parasites are common and malaria is endemic in coastal regions, where a prophylactic regime should be undertaken and mosquito nets carried. Inoculate against typhoid and tetanus. There is cholera, so eating on the street or at market stalls is not recommended. Drinking water is definitely not safe; drink bottled water which is available almost everywhere. Ice and juices are usually made with purified water. Otherwise boil or sterilize water. Salads and raw vegetables are risky. There are hospitals and private clinics in Tegucigalpa, San Pedro Sula and all the larger towns.

Tegucigalpa

Genuinely chaotic, Tegucigalpa – or Tegus as it is called by locals – is cramped and crowded, but still somehow retains a degree of charm in what remains of the colonial centre. If you can bear to stay away from the Caribbean for a few days, it has much more history and charisma than its business-orientated rival San Pedro Sula, to the north. Surrounded by sharp, high peaks on three sides, the city is built on the lower slopes of El Picacho. The commercial centre is around Boulevard Morazán, an area known as 'zona viva' full of cafés, restaurants and shops. For contrast to the modern functional city, you can visit some of the centuries-old mining settlements set in forested valleys amongst the nearby mountains that are ideal for hiking.

Colour map 6, grid C2
Population: 900,000
Altitude: 1,000 m

Ins and outs

Getting there The international airport, Toncontín, is 6½ km south of the centre. The airport is in a narrow valley creating difficult landing conditions: early morning fog or bad weather can cause it to close. There is no central bus station and bus companies have their offices scattered throughout Comayagüela. On arrival it is advisable to take a taxi to your hotel until you get to know the city. The Carretera del Sur (Southern Highway), which brings in travellers from the south and from Toncontín Airport, runs through Comayagüela into Tegucigalpa. It goes past the obelisk set up to commemorate 100 years of Central American Independence, and the Escuela Nacional de Bellas Artes, with its decorated Mayan corridor and temporary exhibitions of contemporary paintings and crafts.

Getting around The Tegucigalpa section of the city uses both names and numbers for streets, but names are used more commonly. In Comayagüela, streets designated by number are the norm. Addresses tend not to be very precise, especially in the *colonias* around Boulevard Morazán east and south of the centre of Tegucigalpa. There are buses and taxis for city transport.

Tourist information *Ministerio Hondureño de Turismo*, Edif Europa, Av Ramón E Cruz y C Rep de México, 3rd floor, above Lloyds Bank (see Banks), Col San Carlos, T238-3974, F238-2102, also at Toncontín Airport. Open 0830-1530, provides lists of hotels and sells posters, postcards (cheaper than elsewhere) and slides. Information on cultural events around the country from *Teatro Manuel Bonilla* is better than at regional tourist offices. *El Mundo Maya*, a private tourist information centre, is behind the cathedral next to the Parque Central, T222-2946.

Climate The city's altitude gives it a reliable climate: temperate during the rainy season from May to November; warm, with cool nights in March and April; and cool and dry with very cool nights from December to February. The annual mean temperature is about 74°F (23°C).

Safety Generally speaking, Tegucigalpa is cleaner and safer (especially at night) than Comayagüela. If you have anything stolen, report it to Dirección de Investigación Criminal (DIC), 5 Av 7-8 C (next to Edif Palermo), T237-4799.

Background

Founded as a mining camp in 1578, Tegucigalpa means silver hill in the original Indian tongue, and miners first discovered gold at the north end of the current Soberanía bridge. The present-day city comprises the two former towns of Comayagüela and Tegucigalpa which, divided by the steeply banked Río Choluteca, became the capital in 1880 and are now united administratively as the Distrito Central.

Being off the main earthquake fault line, Tegucigalpa has not been subjected to disasters by fire or earthquake, unlike many of its Central American neighbours, so it has retained many traditional features. The stuccoed houses, with a single, heavily barred entrance leading to a central patio, are often attractively coloured. However, the old low skyline of the city has been punctuated by several modern tall buildings, and much of the old landscape changed with the arrival of Hurricane Mitch.

The rains of **Hurricane Mitch** in October 1998 had a devastating effect on the Distrito Central. But the damage caused by the Choluteca bursting its banks is hard to see these days, with the exception of the first avenue of Comayagüela, where abandoned homes and buildings remain empty. Bridges washed away by the floodwaters have now been replaced, power supplies are back and, in some respects, traffic is actually better now, since many routes were diverted from the heart of downtown. While Hurricane Mitch lives on as painful memory, the physical impact has now been completely removed from the capital.

Sights

Crossing the river from Comayagüela by the colonial Mallol bridge, on the left is the old Casa Presidencial (1919), now the **Museo de la República de Honduras** (formerly the Museo Histórico), which is better on the 19th than the 20th century. Visitors can see the President's office and the Salón Azul state room. ■ *Mon-Sat 0830-1630, US$1.20, reduced for Central Americans, children and students. (The*

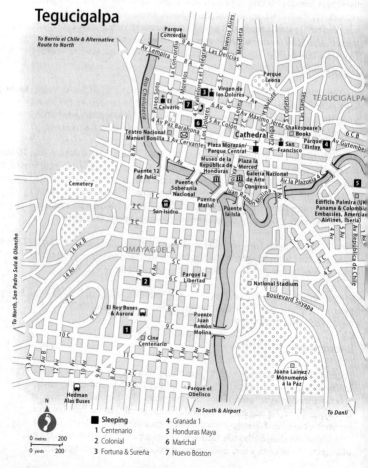

Tegucigalpa

Honduras *(side tab)*

Sleeping		
1 Centenario	**4** Granada 1	
2 Colonial	**5** Honduras Maya	
3 Fortuna & Sureña	**6** Marichal	
	7 Nuevo Boston	

new Presidential Palace is a modern building on Boulevard Juan Pablo II in Colonia Lomas del Mayab.)

Calle Bolívar runs through the area and contains the Congress building and the former site of the University, founded in 1847. The site adjoining the church in Plaza La Merced is now the **Galería Nacional de Arte**, a beautifully restored 17th-century building, housing a very fine collection of Honduran modern and colonial art, prehistoric rock carvings and some remarkable pre-Colombian ceramic pieces. There are useful descriptions of exhibits, and explanations of the mythology embodied in the prehistoric and pre-Colombian art (in Spanish only, but a brochure in English and Spanish is in preparation). ■ *Tue-Sat 1000-1700, Sun 1000-1400, US$5, bookshop and cafetería with a permanent art exhibition.*

Calle Bolívar leads to the main square, Plaza Morazán (commonly known as Parque Central). On the eastern side of the square are the **Palacio del Distrito Central**, and the domed and double-towered **Catedral**, built in the late 18th century. See the beautiful gilt colonial altarpiece, the fine examples of Spanish colonial art, the cloisters and, in Holy Week, the ceremony of the Descent from the Cross.

Avenida Miguel Paz Barahona, running through the northern side of the square, is a key avenue. On it to the east is the church of **San Francisco**, with its clangorous bells, and (on 3 Calle, called Avenida Cervantes) the old **Spanish Mint** (1770), now the national printing works.

To El Picacho & Parque las Naciones Unidas

San Pablo Ⓜ

COLONIA VIERA

COLONIA REFORMA

COLONIA MATAMOROS

Spanish Embassy

Av La Paz

US Embassy

To Valle de Angeles

COLONIA PALMIRA

Lloyds Ⓢ

Centro Comercial Los Castaños

Boulevard Morazán

ⓘ

From Plaza Morazán, heading west towards the river to Avenida Miguel Paz Barahona and then right along 5 Calle (Calle Los Dolores), is the 18th-century church of **Iglesia de Nuestra Señora de los Dolores**. Two blocks north and three blocks west of the church is the beautiful Parque Concordia with good copies of Maya sculpture and temples. On a hilltop one block above Parque Concordia, on Calle Morelos 3A, is **Museo de la Historia Republicana Villa Roy**, the former site of the Museo Nacional and, in 1936, home of former President Julio Lozano. The building was restored, reconstructed and reopened in 1997. There are seven main rooms presenting Honduras' history from Independence in 1821 right up to 1963, as well as cultural presentations and temporary exhibits. ■ *0900-1630, closed Sun, US$1.50.*

Back on Avenida Miguel Paz Barahona, and further west, are the **Teatro Nacional Manuel Bonilla**, with a rather grand interior (1915) inspired by the Athenée Theatre in Paris and, across the square, the beautiful old church of **El Calvario**. Built in elegant colonial style, El Calvario's roof is supported by 14 pillars. It contains images of the Virgen de la Soledad, San Juan, and the archangels San Miguel and San Rafael. On Easter Friday processions start and end here.

Honduras

Crossing the bridge of 12 de Julio (quite near the theatre) you can visit Comayagüela's market of San Isidro. In the Edificio del Banco Central, 12 Calle entre 5 y 6 Avenida, Comayagüela, is the **Pinacoteca Arturo H Medrano**, which houses a collection of approximately 500 works by five Honduran artists and, in the same building, the **Museo Numismático**, which has a collection of coins and bank-notes from Honduras and around the world. ■ *Mon-Fri, 0900-1200, 1300-1600.* Funds have been set aside to restore the older parts of Comayagüela which should make the place more enjoyable to explore.

In Colonia Palmira, to the southeast of the city, is Boulevard Morazán, with shop-ping and business complexes, embassies, banks, restaurants, cafeterías and bars. You can get a fine view of the city from the **Monumento a La Paz** on Juana Laínez hill, near the Estadio Nacional (National Stadium). ■ *Open till 1700.*

The backdrop to Tegucigalpa is the summit of **El Picacho**, with the Cristo del Picacho statue looming up to the north (see Excursions, below), although this can be hard to see during spring because of smog. From Plaza Morazán go up 7 Calle and the Calle de la Leona to **Parque La Leona**, a small handsome park with a railed walk overlooking the city. Higher still is the reservoir in El Picacho, also known as the **United Nations Park**, which can be reached by a special bus from the No 9 bus stop, behind Los Dolores church (in front of Farmacia Santa Bárbara), Sunday only, US$0.15; alternatively, take a bus to El Piligüin or Corralitos (daily) at 0600 from the north side of Parque Herrera in front of the Teatro Nacional Manuel Bonilla.

Essentials

Sleeping

There is a 4% tax on hotel bills, plus 12% sales tax; check if it is included in the price

■ *on map Price codes: see inside front cover*

In Tegucigalpa: Several 5-star choices including **LL** *Real Intercontinental*, T231-1300, www.interconti.com, right in front for the Mall Multiplaza. All services, excellent, and **LL** *Honduras Maya*, Av República de Chile, Colonia Palmira, T220-5000, F220-6000, www.hondurasmaya.hn Rooms and apartments, casino, swimming pool US$3.50, bars (the main bar is relaxed and has US TV channels), cafeterías (*Black Jack's Snack Bar*, *Cafetería 2000*), restaurant (*El Candelero*), conference hall and convention facilities for 1,000, view over the city from uppermost rooms. Excellent travel agency in the basement that can book your flights to Roatán for no extra charge. **L** *Plaza San Martín*, on Plaza San Martín (near *Honduras Maya*), Colonia Palmira, T232-8267, F231-1366, hpsmresv@ns.gbm.hn Good cafetería, nice bar, great views of the city from the top terrace. **AL** *Alameda*, Blvd Suyapa (some dis-tance from centre), T232-6902, F232-6932. Comfortable, pool, restaurant *Le Chalet* (T232-6920). **AL** *Humuya Inn Guest House*, Colonia Humuya 1150, 5 mins from airport, T239-2206, F239-5099, www.humuyainn.com, rooms and service apartments, US owner. Recommended. **A** *Plaza*, on Av Paz Barahona, in front of post office, T237-2111, F237-2119. Good, *Papagayo* restaurant good for breakfast and set lunch. **A-B** *Rosemarie Bed & Break-fast*, Col Elvel, 5 C, behind Tiendas Carrión, T232-5766, F239-1134. A/c, bath, cable TV, phone, free local calls, comfortable, continental breakfast, safe. **A** *Suites La Aurora*, Apart-Hotel, Av Luis Bográn 1519, Colonia Tepeyac, T232-9891, F232-0188. Rooms with kitchenette, cable TV, excellent restaurant, swimming pool, helpful staff.

C *MacArthur*, Av Lempira betweem Telégrafo and Los Dolores, T237-5906, F238-0294. A/c, TV, private bath, cheaper without a/c. Recommended. **C-D** *Krystal*, Máximo Jérez y S Mendieta, T237-8804, F237-8976. TV, a/c, good rooms, not very welcoming, parking, restau-rant for 1,000 (special events only), rooftop bar with good view.

D *Granada 1*, Av Gutemberg 1401, Barrio Guanacaste, T222-2654. Hot water on 2nd floor only, good, clean, safe, TV lounge, table tennis. **D** *Granada 2 and 3*, on the street leading uphill (to Barrio Casamate) from northeast corner of Parque Finlay, T237-7079, F238-4438. Good beds, hot water in all rooms, safe parking, both can be noisy from passing traffic so try to get a room away from the street. Recommended. **D** *Nuevo Boston*, Av Jérez No 321, T237-9411. Good beds, spotless, cable TV, hot water, central. Good value, no credit cards, rooms on street side noisy, friendly, free coffee, mineral water and cookies in lounge, stores luggage, well run. Repeatedly recommended.

D-F *Nan Kin*, Av Gutemberg, Barrio Guanacaste, opposite San Miguel gas station, T238-0291, F238-0299. Clean, friendly, safe, hot water, huge Chinese meals, laundry service, good value, recommended. **E** *Marichal*, Los Dolores y Colón, T237-0069. Ask for a back room, noisy but clean, centrally located.

F *Hospedaje Sureño*, next door but one to *Fortuna*. Friendly, safe, shared bath, room to dry laundry. **F** *Fortuna*, Av P Valledores, beside Virgin de Los Dolores church. Without bath, blanket, towel, soap or toilet paper (more expensive with bath), good, clean, friendly, basic, stores luggage; there are several other cheap hotels in this area. **F** *Iberia*, Peatonal Los Dolores, T237-9267. Hot showers, clean, friendly, refurbished, stores luggage, cheaper without fan. **F** *Tegucigalpa*, Av Gutemberg 1645. Basic but OK.

Comayagüela: Convenient for buses to the north and west and there are many cheap **pensiones** and rooms. It is noisier and dirtier than Tegucigalpa, and many establishments are unsuitable for travellers. If you are carrying luggage, take a taxi. **C-D** *Centenario*, 6 Av, 9-10 C, T222-1050. Safe parking. Recommended. **D-E** *Real de Oro*, Av Cabañas, 11 and 12 C. Clean, friendly. **E** *Condesa Inn*, 7 Av, 12 C. Clean, hot shower, a/c, TV, cafetería, very friendly, a bargain. Recommended. **E** *San Pedro*, 9 C, 6 Av, with bath, **F** without or with private cold shower, popular, restaurant. **F** *California*, 6 Av, 22-23 C. Private bath, friendly, close to Mi Esperanza bus station for Nicaragua. **F** *Colonial*, 6 y 7 Av, 6 C, No 617, T237-5785. With bath, hot water, clean, secure (but unsafe area), front desk unhelpful, otherwise good service and value, restaurant next door (serves breakfast). **F** *Hotelito West*, 10 C, 6-7 Av. Towels and soap, hot water all day, very friendly, changes TCs. Recommended. **F** *Ticamaya*, 6 Av, 8 C. Soap, towels and clean sheets daily, quiet, friendly, restaurant. **F** *Hotelito Latino*, 6 Av, 8 C. Very basic, friendly, safe, cafetería.

Eating

Alondra, Av República de Chile on east side of Honduras Maya. Good but expensive. *Casa María*, Av Ramón E Cruz, Col Los Castaños, 1 block off Blvd Morazán. Good food and atmosphere. *Duncan Maya*, Av C Colón 618 opposite central *Pizza Hut*. Good and reasonably priced. *El Arriero*, Av República de Chile, near *Honduras Maya*. Very good steaks, also seafood, expensive. *El Gachupín*, off Blvd Morazán, Col El Castaño Sur. Superb, Mediterranean-style, garden setting. *El Ganadero*, C La Isla, behind the Congress building. Steaks, chicken, seafood, good. *El Padrino*, 1 block off Blvd Morazán, Col Montecarlo behind *Popeye's*. Very good pizzas and other dishes. *El Patio 2*, easternmost end of Blvd Morazán. Excellent traditional food and kebabs, good service and atmosphere, good value for the hungry. Recommended. *El Pórtico*, near Blvd Morazán, T236-7099. Good food but don't be in a hurry. *El Trapiche*, Blvd Suyapa, opposite National University. Colonial ranch atmosphere, good steaks, expensive. Recommended. *José y Pepe's*, Av República de Panamá. Excellent steaks, good service, good value. Warmly recommended. *La Gran Muralla*, opposite *Hotel Nan Kin* (see above). Good cheap food, very friendly. Recommended. *Rojo, Verde y Ajo*, 1 Av B, Col Pamira. Good food, reasonable price, closed Sun. *Roma*, Av Santa Sede, C Las Acacias 1601, 1 block off Av Rep de Chile, Col Palmira. The oldest Italian restaurant in the city, good pizzas and other food. *Taco Loco*, Paseo Rep Argentina behind Blvd Morazán. Mexican fast food. *Tito*, ½ block off Blvd Morazán on Av Juan Lindo. Good pizzas. *Tony's Mar*, Blvd Juan Pablo II y Av Uruguay, Col Tepeyac, T239-9379. Seafood, good, simple, New Orleans style, US$8 per person. *Veracruz*, C del Telégrafo between M Jérez and Colón, near hotels *Boston* and *Fortuna*. Good breakfast, closed Sun. For Garífuna food, try *Yurumey*, Av JM Gálvez.

China Food, 2 blocks before the easternmost bridges on Blvd Morazán, ½ block to the right. Good-value Chinese. *Mei-Mei*, Pasaje Midence Soto, central. Chinese. Recommended. There are several good Chinese restaurants on C del Telégrafo in centre, enormous helpings at reasonable prices. *Taiwan*, round corner from *Hotels Granada 2* and *3*, on Av Máximo Jérez. Huge portions, good value. There are several Japanese restaurants, including *Daymio*, on Plaza Benito Juárez, Col Palmira. *Suchi Bar* in the Bakery Center, 1 Av B, Col Palmira.

A meal in a good restaurant costs between US$6-11; for hotel restaurants, see above. Most places are closed on Sunday

Honduras

Basilio's Repostería y Panadería, C Peatonal between Los Dolores and S Mendieta. Good cakes, breads and pastries. *Pastelería Francesa*, opposite French embassy. Recommended *Salman's* bakeries, several outlets in the centre, good bread and pastries. *Sirias*, next door to *Hotel Granada 3*. Best place to eat in the immediate neighbourhood. *Super Donuts*, Peatonal, Blvd Morazón. Good for filling buffet breakfasts (not just doughnuts!), popular with locals.

Centro Comercial Multiplaza in Colonia Lomas del Mayab has a large food court with many different outlets. There are several *Burger Kings*, *McDonalds*, *Pizza Huts*, one near Parque Central (with good salad bar), *Pollos Camperos* all over the city as well as *Popeye's* and *Wendy's*.

Cafeterías *Al Natural*, C Hipólito Matute y Av Miguel Cervantes. Some vegetarian, some meat dishes, huge fresh fruit juices, antiques, caged birds, nice garden atmosphere. *Bar Mediterráneo*, C S Mendieta entre Máximo Jérez y Colón. Delicious goat meat, and cheap set meals. *Brik Brak*, C Peatonal just off the Parque Central. Open 24 hrs. Recommended. *Cafetería Típica Cubana*, Parque Finlay. Open 0700-1800 (1200 Sun), good breakfast, good service. *Café y Librería Paradiso*, Av Paz Barahona 1351. Excellent coffee and snacks, good library, paintings, prints and photos to enjoy, newspapers and magazines on sale, good meeting place. *Chomy's Café*, Centro Comercial Asfura, Av Cervantes and two branches in Col San Carlos (C Ramón Rosa and C San Carlos). Good quiches, desserts, coffee, tea. *Don Pepe's Terraza*, Av Colón 530, upstairs, T222-1084. Central, cheap, live music, but typical Honduran atmosphere. Recommended. *Stacolosal*, Paseo de Panamá y Paseo Argentina off Av Rep de Chile, Col Palmira. Good cheap eating place, classical music and friendly owner, open 0700-1900.

In Comayagüela *Bienvenidos a Golosinas*, 6 Av, round corner from *Hotel Colonial*. Friendly, basic meals, beer. *Cafetería Nueva Macao*, 4 Av No 437. Large portions, Chinese. *Comedor Tulin*, 4 Av between 4 and 5 C. Good breakfasts.

Entertainment

Bars and clubs In front of the Universidad Nacional on Blvd Suyapa is *La Peña*, where every Fri at 2100 there is live music, singing and dancing, entrance US$1.40. Blvd Morazán has plenty of choice in nightlife including *Taco Taco*, a good bar, sometimes with live mariachi music; next door *Tequila*, a popular drinking place only open at weekends. *Iguana Rana Bar* is very popular with locals and visitors, similarly *Confettis* disco. Blvd Juan Pablo II has discos with various types of music. *La Puerta del Alcalá*, 3½ blocks down from *Taca* office on Blvd Morazán, Col Castaño Sur. Pleasant open setting.

Cinemas Plazas 1 to 5 in Centro Comercial Plaza Miraflores on Blvd Miraflores. *Regis*, *Real* and *Opera* at Centro Comercial Centroamérica, Blvd Miraflores (all have good US films). *Multiplaza*, Col Lomas del Mayab, has 6-screen cinema. In city centre, 2-screen cinemas *Lido Palace*, and *Variedades*. *Tauro* and *Aries*, 200 m up Av Gutemberg leading from Parque Finlay to Col Reforma (same street as *Hotel Granada* 2 and 3), tickets US$1.65.

Shopping

Bookshops *Metromedia*, Edif Casa Real, Av San Carlos, behind Centro Comercial Los Castaños, Blvd Morazán, English books, both new and second-hand, for sale or exchange (small fee for exchange), wide selection of US magazines. *Shakespeare's Books*, Centro Commercial La Ronda, half a block away from *Hotel La Ronda* on Av Máximo Jérez. Mon-Fri 0900-1930, Sat 0900-1200, has a large selection of second-hand English-language books. US owner also runs *Tobacco Road Tavern* and *Au Natural* on C Matute with email and internet available. *Librería Paradiso* (see under Cafetería listing above). For books in Spanish on Honduras and Central America, *Editorial Guaymuras*, Av Miguel Cervantes 1055. Good book and news-stand, and maps in *Hotel Honduras Maya*. Second-hand bookstalls in Mercado San Isidro (6 Av y 2 C, Comayagüela), good value.

Mercado San Isidro, 6 Av at 1 C, Comayagüela. Many fascinating things, but filthy, do not **Markets**
buy food here. Sat is busiest day. *Mercado de Artesanías*, 3 Av, 15 C next to Parque El
Soldado. Good value (the market was swept away by the Mitch floods). Good supermarkets:
Sucasa, in Blvd Morazán, Más y Menos, in Av de la Paz. Chinese supermarket on C Salvador, 1
block south of Peatonal, near the post office in the centre, open till 2000.

Kodak on Parque Central and Blvd Morazán for excellent, professional standard develop- **Photography**
ment of slides. *Fuji* in front of the Catedral and on Blvd Morazán.

Candú, opposite *Hotel Maya*, and in Av Rep de Chile. Also in Valle de Angeles, see Excursions. **Souvenirs**
The big, swanky hotels all have souvenir shops.

Transport

Buses Cost US$0.08-US$0.12; stops are official but unmarked. **Local**

Car hire *Avis*, Edif Palmira and airport, T232-0088; *Budget*, Blvd Suyapa and airport,
T/F235-9531. *Hertz*, Centro Comercial Villa Real, Col Palmira, T239-0772, F232-0870. *Maya*,
Av Rep de Chile 202, Col Palmira, T232-0992. *Molinari*, 1 Av 2 C Comayagüela and airport,
T237-5335. *Toyota*, T235-6694. *Thrifty*, Col Prados Universitarios, T235-6077.

Car repairs *Metal Mecánica*, 1 block south of Av de los Próceres, Col Lara. Volkswagen
dealer near Parque Concordia, good for repairs.

Taxis About US$1.40-US$2 per person (no reduction for sharing), but you can often bargain down to around US$1 a trip in the city. More after 2200, but cheaper (US$0.25) on designated routes, eg Miraflores to centre.

Air Toncontín Airport opens at 0530. Check-in at least 2 hrs before departure; snacks, sou- **Long distance**
venir shops, several duty free stores. Buses to airport from Comayagüela, on 4 Av between 6
and 7 C, or from Av Máximo Jérez in downtown Tegucigalpa; into town US$0.06-0.19, 20
mins from left-hand side outside the airport; yellow cabs, US$4, smaller *colectivo* taxis, US$2
or more. Agree taxi fare at the airport.

Buses To **San Pedro Sula**: on Northern Highway, 4 hrs. several companies, including: *Sáenz*,
Centro Comercial Perisur, Blvd Unión Europea, T233-4229; *El Rey*, 6 Av, 9 C, Comayagüela,
T237-6609; *Hedmán Alas*, 11 Av, 13-14 C, Comayagüela, T237-7143; *Viajes Nacionales* (*Viana*),
Servicio Ejecutivo Clase Oro, terminal on Blvd de Las Fuerzas Armadas, T235-8185. *Sáenz* and
Hedman Alas both have a highly recommended luxury service (book in advance), with a/c, film,
snacks and refreshments, 3¼ hrs. To **Tela** and **La Ceiba**: *Viana Clase Oro*, and Etrusca, 8 Av, 12 y
13C, T222-6881. To **Choluteca**: Mi Esperanza, 6 Av, 23-24 C, Comayagüela, T225-1502. To
Trujillo: Cotraibal, 7 Av 10-11 C, Comayagüela, T237-1666. To **La Esperanza**: Empresa Joelito,
4 C, No 834, Comayagüela. To **Comayagua**: most going to San Pedro Sula and *Transportes*
Catrachos, Col Torocagua, Blvd del Norte, Comayagüela. To **Valle de Angeles** and **Santa**
Lucía: from stop on Av La Paz (near filling station opposite hospital). To **Juticalpa** and
Catacamas: Empresa Aurora, 8 C, 6-7 Av, Comayagüela, T237-3647. For **Danlí** and **El Paraíso**,
for the Nicaraguan border at Las Manos, see under those towns in 'East of Tegucigalpa'.
    For travellers leaving Tegucigalpa, take the Tiloarque bus on Av Máximo Jérez, by C Pal-
ace, and get off in Comayagüela at Cine Centenario (Av 6) for nearby *Empresa Aurora* buses
(for **Olancho**) and *El Rey* buses (for **San Pedro Sula**). 3 blocks northwest is *Cine Lux*, near
which are *Empresas Unidas* and *Maribel* (8 Av, 11-12 C, T237-3032) for **Siguatepeque**.
Tiloarque bus continues to Mi Esperanza bus terminal (for **Choluteca** and **Nicaraguan**
border). Take a 'Carrizal' or 'Santa Fe' bus ascending Belén (9 C) for *Hedmán Alas* buses to
San Pedro Sula and for Comayagua buses. The *Norteño* bus line to San Pedro Sula is alongside Mamachepa market, from where there are also buses for **Nacaome** and **El Amatillo**
border with El Salvador.

Honduras

International buses *Ticabus*, 16 C, 5-6 Av, Comayagüela, T222-0590, office opens 0730, t Managua 0900 (US$20, 9 hrs), **San José** (US$35), **San Salvador** (US$15), **Guatemala Cit** (US$25) and **Panama** (US$60) daily. Make sure you reserve several days ahead, you have to go t the office to reserve (taxi from centre US$2). Visa ATM near to offices. Alternatively to **Nicaragua** take *Mi Esperanza* bus to San Marcos de Colón, then taxi or local bus to El Espino on border. To San Marcos, 4 a day from 0730, and direct to border at 0400, US$2.50, 5 hrs (0730 is the latest one that will get you into Nicaragua the same day). Or *Mi Esperanza* bus to Río Guasaule border, several daily, 4 hrs, US$2. To **San Salvador**, *Cruceros del Golfo*, Barrio Guacerique, Blvd Comunidad Económica Europea, Comayagüela, T233-7415, US$18, at 0600 and 1300, 6 hrs travelling, 1 hr o more at border, connections to Guatemala and Mexico; direct bus to border at El Amatillo US$2.50, 3 hrs, several daily; alternatively from San Pedro Sula via Nueva Ocotepeque and El Poy To **San Salvador** and **Guatemala**, with *King Quality* from Tegucigalpa (T225-5415) from Cruceros del Golfo terminal, 0600 and 1300 and San Pedro Sula (T553-4547) at 0630. Alternatively, to Guatemala go to San Pedro Sula and take Escobar, Impala or Congolón to Nueva Ocotepeque and the Border at Agua Caliente, or take the route via Copán (see page 649).

Directory

Airline offices For national flights: *Atlantic Airline*, T234-9702. *Isleña Airlines*, Galerías La Paz, Av de la Paz, at Toncontín Airport, T237-3410, *Sosa Airline*, at the airport, T233-7351.

International carriers: *Air France*, Centro Comercial Galería, Av de la Paz, T237-0229; *Alitalia*, Col Alameda, 5 Av, 9 C No 821, T239-4246; *American*, Ed Palmira, opposite Honduras Maya, 1st floor, T232-1414 (airport T233-9685); *British Airways*, Edif Sempe, Blvd Comunidad Económica Europea, T225-5101; *Continental*, Av República de Chile, Col Palmira, T220-0999; *Grupo Taca*, Blvd Morazán y Av Ramón E Cruz, T239-0148 or airport T233-5756; *Iberia*, Ed Palmira, opposite *Honduras Maya*, T232-7760; *Japan Airlines*, Edif Galería La Paz, 3rd floor, Local 312, 116 Av La Paz, T237-0229; *KLM*, Ed Ciicsa, Av Rep de Chile y Av Rep de Panamá, Col Palmira, T232-6410; *Lufthansa*, Edif Plaza del Sol, No 2326, Av de la Paz, T236-7560.

Banks All banks have several branches throughout the city; we list the main offices. Branch offices are unlikely
There are lots of to change TCs, only US dollars cash. *Bancahsa*, 5 C (Av Colón) in the centre. *Bancahorro*, 5 C in front of
ATMs in the Plaza Morazán. *Banco Atlántida*, 5 C in front of Plaza Morazán (may agree to change money on Sat up
centre of the city to 1200). *Banco de Honduras (Citibank)*, Blvd Suyapa. *Banco del País*, C Peotonal in the centre, changes TCs. *Banco de Occidente*, 3 C (Cervantes) y 6 Av (S Mendieta) in the centre. *Banexpo*, Av Rep de Chile, Col Palmira. *Lloyds Bank*, Av Ramón E Cruz, off Blvd Morazán and Av de la Paz, take any San Felipe bus (Rivera y Cía), get out above US Embassy, walk back, turn left and bank is 300 m on right. Open 0900-1500, closed Sat, Sterling and Canadian dollars changed.

Visa, MasterCard and American Express cash advances (no commission) and TCs at *Credomatic de Honduras*, Blvd Morazán, and at *Honducard*, Av de la Paz y Ramón E Cruz and at *Aval Card*, Blvd Morazán. Anywhere with the *Credomatic* symbol should be able to arrange cash advances, but it may be simpler to go straight to *Credomatic*. Banks are allowed to trade at the current market rate (see Currency in Essentials), but there is a street market along the C Peatonal off the Parque Central, opposite the post office and elsewhere. Exchange can be difficult on Sat, try *Coin*, a *casa de cambio* on Av de la Paz, inside *Supermercado Más y Menos*, same rates as banks, no commission, Mon-Fri 0830-1730, Sat 0900-1200, changes TCs but will photocopy cheques and passport; another branch of *Coin* on C Peatonal, good rates. Recommended.

Communications Internet: *Café Don Harry*, Av Rep de Chile 525, Edif Galerías TCB, T220-6174, pipo1@sigmanet.hn *@ccess Cyber Coffee*, Centro Commercial La Ronda, Av M Jérez next to *Super Donuts*, Mon-Sat 0800-1900, US$1.50 for 30 mins. *Café Cyberplace*, Barrio La Plazuela, Av Cervantes 1215, opposite *Souvenirs Maya*, T220-5200, open 0900-1830, US$2 for 30 mins. *Cyberiada Internet Café*, Plaza Brezani, Av Jérez, C H Matute, open 24 hrs, US$1.80 per hr with free coffee. *Multinet*, 1 Av B, Galerías Maya, Col Palmira, T232-3181, 0800-2100, US$4.45 per hr, also at Mall Multiplaza, local 114, Blvd Juan Pablo II, Col Lomas del Mayab, adae@usa.net *PC Cyber*, Edif Paz Barahona, Calle Peatonal, Mon-Fri 0830-1700, Sat 0830-1400. *Shakespeare's Books* (see under Bookshops). **Post office:** Av Paz Barahona/C del Telégrafo, Lista de Correos (Poste Restante) mail held for 1 month, US$0.20 per letter. Mail boxes in main supermarkets. Books should be packed separately from clothes, etc when sending packages. The post office will send and receive faxes. **Telephone:** *Hondutel*, C del Telégrafo y Av Colón, has several direct AT&T lines to USA, no waiting. Phone, fax and telegrams; open 24 hrs for phone services only. Also at 6 Av, 7-8C, Comayagüela, with post office.

Alianza Francesa, Colonia Lomas del Guijarro, T239-1529, cultural events Fri afternoon, French films **Cultural** Tue 1930. *Centro Cultural Alemán*, 8 Av, C La Fuente, T237-1555, German newspapers to read, cultural **centres** events. *Instituto Hondureño de Cultura Interamericana* (IHCI), C Real de Comayagüela,T237-7539, has an English library and cultural events.

Argentina, Col Rubén Darío 417, T232-3376. *Belize Consulate*, T220-5000, Ext 7770. *Brazil*, Colonia **Embassies &** La Reforma, Casa 1309, T236-5223. *Canada*, Ed Financiero Banexpo, Local 3, Col Payaqui, Boulevar **consulates** Juan Bosco II, T232-4551, F232-8767. *Chile*, Av Las Minitas, Casa 501, T232-2114. *Colombia*, Edificio Palmira No 200, opposite *Honduras Maya*, 4th floor, T232-1709, F232-8133. *Costa Rica*, Colonia El Triángulo, 1a C, opposite No 3451, T232-1768, F232-1876, bus to Lomas del Guijarro to last stop, then walk up on your left for 300 m. *Ecuador*, Av Juan Lindo 122, Col Palmira, T236-5980. *El Salvador*, Colonia San Carlos 2 Av Calzada Rep de Uruguay, Casa 219, T236-8045, F236-9403. *France*, Colonia Palmira, 3 C, Av Juan Lindo, T236-6432, F236-8051. *Germany*, Ed Paysen, 3rd floor, Blvd Morazán, T232-3161, F232-9518. *Guatemala*, Col Las Minitas 4 C, Casa 2421, T232-9704, F232-8469, Mon-Fri, 0900-1300, take photo, visa given on the spot, US$10. *Italy*, Av Principal 2602, Col Reforma, T236-6391, F236-5659. *Japan*, Colonia San Carlos, entre 4 y 5 C, 2 blocks off Blvd Morazán and Av de la Paz, T236-6828, F236-6100, behind Los Castaños Shopping Mall. *Mexico*, Av República de México, Paseo República de Brasil 2402, Col Palmira, T232-6471, T231-4719, opens 0900, visa takes 24 hrs. *Netherlands* (Consulate), Edif Barahona, Col Alameda, next to INA, T231-5007, F231-5009. *Nicaragua*, Colonia Lomas del Tepeyac, Av Choluteca 1130, bloque M-1, T232-9025, F231-1412, 0800-1200, US$25, visa usually issued same day, but can take up to 2 days, has to be used within 4 weeks of issue; for Nicaraguan embassy, take Alameda bus from street behind Congress building (from Parque Merced descend towards river, but don't cross bridge, instead turn left behind Congress and ask for bus stop on right-hand side), alight before Planificación de Familia and climb street on left beside Planificación. *Norway*, consular services in front of Residencial el Limonar, T557-0856. *Panama*, Edificio Palmira No 200, opposite *Honduras Maya*, 2nd floor, T239-5508, F232-8147. *Peru*, C La Reforma 2618, Col La Reforma, T221-0596. *Spain*, Col Matamoros 801, T236-6589, near Av de la Paz and US Embassy. *Sweden* (Consulate), Av Altiplano, Retorno Borneo 2758, Colonia Miramontes, T/F232-4935. *UK*, Edif Palmira, 3rd floor, opposite *Hotel Honduras Maya* (Apdo Postal 290, T232-0612, F232-5480). *USA*, Av La Paz, 0800-1700, Mon-Fri, take any bus from north side of Parque Central in direction 'San Felipe', T236-9320, F236-9037. *Venezuela*, Col Rubén Darío 2116, T232-1879.

La Cisne, 1602 C La Fuente/Av Las Delicias, US$2.50 up to 5 kg, same-day service. Recommended. **Laundry** *Lavandería Italiana*, Barrio Guadalupe, 4 blocks west of Av Rep de Chile 300 block. *Lavandería Super Jet*, Av Gutemberg, about 300 m east of *Hotel Granada*, US$0.20 per kg. Recommended. *Mi Lavandería*, opposite Repostería C Real, 3 C, 2 Av, Comayagüela, T237-6573, Mon-Sat 0700-1800, Sun and holidays 0800-1700. Recommended.

Dentist: *Dra Rosa María Cardillo de Boquín*, Ed Los Jarros, Sala 206, Blvd Morazán, T231-0583. **Medical** Recommended. *Dr Roberto Ayala*, DDS, C Alfonso XIII 3644, Col Lomas de Guijarro, T232-2407. **services** **Pharmacy**: *Farmacia Rosna*, in pedestrial mall off Parque Central, T237-0605, English spoken. Recommended. *Regis Palmira*, Ed Ciicsa, Av República de Panamá, Col Palmira. *El Castaño*, Blvd Morazán. **Private hospitals:** Hospital y Clínica Viera, 5 C, 11 y 12 Av, Tegucigalpa, T237-7136. Hospital la Policlínica SA 3 Av, 7 y 8 C, Comayagüela, T237-3503. Centro Médico Hondureño, 3 Av, 3 C, Barrio La Granja, Comayagüela, T233-6028.

Columbia, C Principal between Av 11 y 12, Blvd Morazán, T232-3532, columbiatours@sigmanet.hn **Tour operators** Excellent for national parks, including Cusuco, Pico Bonito and Cuero y Salado, as well as Punta Sal and Bay Islands. Air and ground transportation. *Explore Honduras Tour Service*, Ed Medcast, 2nd level, Blvd Morazán, T236-7694, F236-9800, www.explorehonduras.com, Copán and Bay Islands. *Gloria Tours* across from north side of Parque Central in Casa Colonial, T/F238-2232, information centre and tour operator. *Mundirama*, Edif Ciicsa, Av Rep de Panamá, Col Palmira, T553-0192, F557-9092. *Trek Honduras*, Av Julio Lozano 1311, T239-9827, F237-5776, downtown, tours of the city, Bay Islands, Copán, San Pedro Sula, Valle de Angeles and Santa Lucía.

Immigration: Dirección Gen de Migración, Av Máximo Jérez, next to *Hotel Ronda*, Tegucigalpa. **Peace** **Useful** **Corps**: opposite Edif Ciicsa, on Av República de Chile, uphill past *Hotel Honduras Maya*. The volunteers **addresses** are a good source of information.

Honduras

Around Tegucigalpa

Suyapa Southeast of Tegucigalpa, the village of Suyapa attracts pilgrims to its big church, home to a tiny wooden image of the Virgin, about 8 cm high, set into the altar. A **fiesta** is held 1-4 February, during which they hold a televised *alborada* with singers, music and fireworks, from 2000-2400 on the second evening. Take a bus to the University or to Suyapa from 'La Isla', one block northwest of the city stadium.

Santa Lucía
Population: 4,230
Altitude: 1,400-
1,600 m

Northeast of Tegucigalpa, on the way to Valle de Angeles, a right turn goes to the quaint old mining village of Santa Lucía which is perched precariously on a steep mountainside overlooking the wide valley with Tegucigalpa below. The town has a beautiful colonial church with a Christ given by King Philip II of Spain in 1592. There is a charming legend of the Black Christ which the authorities ordered to be taken down to Tegucigalpa when Santa Lucía lost its former importance as a mining centre. Every step it was carried away from Santa Lucía it became heavier. When it was impossible to carry it any further they turned round, and by the time they were back in Santa Lucía, it was as light as a feather. The town is lively with parties on Saturday night, and there is a festival in the second and third weeks of January. There are souvenir shops in the town, including *Cerámicas Ucles* just past the lagoon, second street on left, and another ceramics shop at the entrance on your right. There are good walks up the mountain on various trails, with fine views of Tegucigalpa.

A good circuit is to descend east from the mountain towards San Juan del Rancho through lovely landscapes on a good dirt road, then connect with the paved road to El Zamorano. From there continue either to El Zamorano, or return to Tegucigalpa (see below for opposite direction).

Around Tegucigalpa

Eating One small *comedor* next to the plaza/terrace of the municipality, but on Sun food is available on the streets. Also a Czech restaurant *Miluka* serving Czech and Honduran food. Recommended.

Transport Bus to Santa Lucía from Mercado San Pablo, hourly service, US$0.30, past the statue of Simón Bolívar by the Esso station, Av de los Próceres, Tegucigalpa.

About a 30-minute drive from Tegucigalpa, **Valle de Angeles** is on a plain below **Monte San Juan**, with **Cerro El Picacho**, (2,270m) and **Cerro La Tigra** nearby. The 22-km road between the capital and Valle de Angeles was damaged in many places by Hurricane Mitch. With the road repaired, it is once more a popular spot for trips from the city, with a cool climate year round and surrounded by pine forests. There are tracks going through the forests, old mines to explore, a picnic area and a swimming pool; consequently it is crowded on Sundays. At the top of Cerro El Picacho there is a stunning view of the city, and if so inclined you can visit the zoo of mostly indigenous animals including jaguar, spider monkeys and other animals and birds. ■ *Daily, 0800-1500, US$0.20.* Hospital de los Adventistas, in the valley, is a modern clinic selling vegetables and handicrafts. There are handicraft shops throughout the town and in the Parque Central, good for leather goods, wooden items, hats, musical instruments and so on. A visit to the pavilion of arts and crafts organized by the national Asociación de Artesanías is recommended.

Valle de Angeles
Population: 6,635
Altitude: 1,310 m

Sleeping and eating *Centro Turístico La Florida* is a large development at Km 20, T766-2121, with hotel, restaurant and sports facilities, horse-riding, swimming pool, zoo (day entry US$2.30, open all year). Opposite is the Dutch-owned restaurant *Las Tejas*. **C** *Hotel y Restaurante Posada del Angel*, swimming pool, indifferent service, moderate prices. **D** per person *Los Tres Pinos*, Bed & Breakfast Inn, Casa 907, Barrio El Edén, Carretera a San Juancito, T766-2879. English spoken, with bath, hot water, laundry facilities, horse rental, airport pick-up, excursions. Recommended. On Parque Central is *El Anafre*, good for pasta, with *Restaurante Epocas* next door. *Rudy's Café and Grill*, 1 block north of Parque Central, T766-2628, rudys@hondutel.hn, and next door *La Casa de las Abuelas*, T766-2626, corporealminas@hotmail.com, has a pleasant courtyard with wine bar, café, library, satellite TV, video, email, fax and phone service, tourist information and art gallery. *Restaurant Papagayo* for typical dishes. *Restaurante Turístico de Valle de Angeles*, on top of hill over-looking town, also good. Several others.

Transport Buses to Valle de Angeles every 45 mins, US$0.40, 1 hr, leaves from San Felipe, near the hospital. To San Juan de Flores 1000, 1230, 1530.

Continue to San Juan de Flores (also called Cantarranas) and San Juancito, an old mining town. From here you can climb the La Tigra cloud forest and even walk along the top before descending to El Hatillo and then to Tegucigalpa.

There are good climbs to the heights of Picacho and excellent hikes in the **Parque Nacional La Tigra** cloud forest. Only 11 km from Tegucigalpa, this cloud forest covers 238 sq kms and is considered one of the richest habitats in the world with great diversity of flora and fauna – bromeliads, orchids, arborescent ferns and over 200 species of birds. Single hikers must have a guide. There are two approach routes: go to **El Piligüin** (see below) for the Jutiapa entrance, from where you can start hiking, or to *Gloriales Inn*, in El Hatillo. You can also walk 24 km from Tegucigalpa to the Jutiapa entrance. Then hike to the visitors' centre of La Tigra at El Rosario (10 km, three hours, easy hiking, superb). Alternatively, go to **San Juancito** (**F** *Hotelito San Juan*, six rooms with shared bathroom, grocery store next door also sells fuel, drinks and can prepare *comida corriente*, same owners, T766-2237), above which is the national park (well worth a visit, a stiff, one-hour uphill walk to El Rosario visitor centre, park offices and six trails ranging from 30 minutes to eight hours, bring

Parque Nacional La Tigra
Early Sunday morning is a good time but weekdays are quieter

Honduras

insect repellent. A recommended hike is the **Sendero La Esperanza**, which leads to the road; turn right then take the **Sendero Bosque Nublado** on your left. The whole circuit takes about one hour 20 minutes. A few quetzal birds survive here, but you will need a good eye. In the rainy season (June, July, October-November) there is a spectacular 100-m waterfall (Cascada de la Gloria) which falls on a vast igneous rock. Do not leave paths when walking as there are steep drops. Also get advice about personal safety, as robberies have occurred. ■ *US$10 entry. Go first to the Amitigra office, Edificio Italia, 6th floor, about 3 blocks southwest of Amex office in Av República de Panamá, T232-6771, F237-5503; helpful. Book a visit here in advance.*

Sleeping **E** per person *Eco Albergue La Tigra*, in the old hospital of the mining company, rooms named after local birds, capacity for 50. Meals are available at the house of Señora Amalia Elvir, before El Rosario.

Transport Buses leave from San Pablo market, Tegucigalpa, for San Juancito from 1000, 1½ hrs, on Sat and Sun bus at 0800 packed with people visiting their families, US$0.75; passes turn-off to Santa Lucía and goes through Valle de Angeles. Return bus from San Juancito at 1500 from across the river and up the hill, opposite the park. On Sat, buses return at 0600 and 1200 from church, board early. Note that the return Sun bus at 1300 is even fuller, board early, leaves from near edge of town not at terminal point where it dropped you, double check local information. Alternatively, from behind Los Dolores church in Tegucigalpa you can take a bus to El Piligüin/Jutiapa at 0600; it passes through beautiful scenery by El Hatillo and other communities. From El Piligüin, it is a long hot walk up to the park entrance.

From Parque Herrera buses throughout the day go to the village of **El Piligüin**, north of Santa Lucía. A delightful 40-minute walk down the pine-clad mountainside leads to El Chimbo (meals at *pulpería* or shop, ask anyone the way), then take bus either to Valle de Angeles or Tegucigalpa.

At Km 24 on the road to Danlí, there are climbs to the highest peak through the Uyuca rainforest, information from Escuela Agrícola Panamericana in the breath-taking **Valle del Zamorano**, or from their office near the Edificio Italia, Colonia Palmira (see *Amitigra*, above) T233-2717, in Tegucigalpa. The school has rooms for visitors. Visits to the school are organized by some tour operators. On the northwest flank of Uyuca is the picturesque village of **Tatumbla**.

Ojojona

Population: 6,670
Altitude: 1,400 m

Ojojona is another quaint, completely unspoiled, old village about 30 minutes (24 km) south of Tegucigalpa; turn right off the Southern Highway. The village pot-tery is interesting but make your selection carefully as some of it is reported to be poor. *La Casona del Pueblo* offers the best handicrafts in town, including fine rus-tic ceramics. **Fiesta** 18-20 January. There are two well-preserved colonial churches in Ojojona, with fine paintings, plus two more in nearby Santa Ana which is passed on the way from Tegucigalpa. **Sleeping and eating** **F** *Posada Joxone*, comfortable and *Comedor*.

Transport **Bus** every 15-30 mins from C 4, Av 6, Comayagüela, near San Isidro market, US$0.40, 1 hr. From same location, buses go west to **Lepaterique** ('place of the jaguar'), another colonial village, over 1-hr drive through rugged, forested terrain. Distant view of Pacific on fine days from heights above village.

Sabanagrande

Further south (40 km) is Sabanagrande, just off the main highway. This typical colo-nial town, complete with cobbled streets, is a good day trip from Tegucigalpa. There is an interesting colonial church (1809), Nuestra Señora del Rosario 'Apa Kun Ka' (the place of water for washing), with the **fiesta** of La Virgen de Candelaria from 1-11 February. At 1,000 m it has a mild climate, beautiful scenery with pleasant walks, including views to the Pacific and the Gulf of Fonseca. The town is famous for its *rosquillas* (a type of biscuit).

North of Tegucigalpa

Taking the Olancho road, you come to **Talanga**, with post office and Hondutel near the market on the main road. From Talanga it is a short trip to the historic and beautiful settlements of **Cedros** and **Minas de Oro**. From the Parque Central an unpaved road leads south to the Tegucigalpa-Danlí road making a triangular route possible back to the capital.

Talan

This is one of Honduras' earliest settlements, dating from Pedro de Alvarado's mining operations of 1536. It is an outstanding colonial mining town with cobbled streets, perched high on an eminence amid forests. The festival of El Señor del Buen Fin takes place in the first two weeks of January. Buses to Talanga, Cedros and San Ignacio: Reynita de San Ignacio in Mercado Zonal Belén, Comayagüela, T224-0066.

Cedros

On a forested tableland, Minas de Oro is a centre for walking in attractive hill country and is a picturesque old mining town. There is a fine view from Cerro Grande which overlooks the town, and a more interesting hike up Cerro El Piñón about 3 km north towards Victoria. From Minas de Oro to Victoria (18 km) the road is poor but heads to Sulaco (bus service) with connections to Yorito, Yoro and San Pedro Sula and to Cedros. Several buses daily Sulaco-Yoro.

Minas de Oro
Population: 6,000
Altitude: 1,060m

Sleeping and eating Several *pensiones*, including **F** *Hotelito Girón* and *Los Pinares* (meals US$1). *Comedor El Rodeo*, or eat at *Doña Gloria's* house, good, large helpings, US$0.80.

Transport 4-hr bus ride with *Transportes Victoria*, 10 Av 11 C Barrio Belén, Comayagüela at 1300, returning from Minas de Oro at 0400 daily (US$1.90). Just beyond Talanga, an unpaved road turns north to Cedros. After 41 km take the small road to your left. Further on is the turn off to Equías (8 km). Straight on for Minas de Oro (66 km). The last part of the road to Minas de Oro is in poor condition, high clearance recommended.

North of Tegucigalpa

To the west of Minas de Oro it is 3 km to Malcotal and a further 4 km to Minas de San Antonio, both surrounded by hills which are mostly stripped of trees. Four-wheel drive recommended if driving. There is a good two-hour forested walk over to **Esquías** (good comedor, *Tita's*, accommodation available in private houses, ask at *Tita's*), which has a fine church with one of the most fascinating colonial façades in Honduras with extravagant palm motifs, floating angels and, at the apex, a bishop with hands outstretched in blessing. There is a monument in the plaza to a local hero, the American Harold Brosious, 1881-1950, who arrived in Malcotal in 1908 to prospect for gold. He founded a school here (closed since his death) for the children of local *campesinos*. As Brosious' fame as a

Honduras

read, pupils arrived from throughout Honduras and neighbouring coun-
us services Esquías- Tegucigalpa and Esquías-Comayagua.
res east of Minas de Oro is San José del Potrero, beyond which is **Sulaco**
a de la Flor region, with settlements of Xicaque Indians. These are also
the lowlands around Victoria where they sell their handicrafts.

Copán and Western Honduras

Close to the Guatemalan border, the serene ruins of Copán are Honduras' major Maya attraction. Treasured for its exceptional artistry when compared to other Maya sites, Copán enjoys a calm and pleasant setting. The quiet town of Copán Ruinas nestles among hills nearby. In fact, the whole area is sprinkled with interesting towns and villages, mostly in delightful hilly surroundings, some with an interesting colonial history, others with their foundations in Lenca Indian communities, and many producing handicrafts. The ruins of Copán aside, one of the enjoyable aspects of Western Honduras is that there are no 'must-sees' – just pick a route, take your time and enjoy the scenery and whatever else you find.

West to Copán

The Western Highway runs parallel to the border from San Pedro Sula southwest along the Río Chamelecón to Canoa (58 km, from where there is a paved road south to Santa Bárbara, a further 53 km). Continuing along the Western Highway, the road from San Pedro Sula towards Guatemala runs southwest to La Entrada (115 km from San Pedro), where it forks again left for Santa Rosa (see below) and right for an attractive 60-km road through deep green scenery to Copán. The regular bus is recommended rather than the dangerous minibus service, which can be a bit hair-raising. The road is paved throughout and in good condition. **La Entrada** is a hot, dusty town and the place to change buses. Going south takes you to Santa Rosa and towards El Salvador, west to Copán and Guatemala. *Banco Sogerín* will cash travellers' cheques.

Sleeping in La Entrada C-E *San Carlos*, at junction to Copán Ruinas, T898-5228, a/c, modern, cable TV, bar, swimming pool, restaurant (T/F661-2187), excellent value. **E** *Central*, by Shell station, with 2 beds, **F** with 1, either with bath, fans, cold water, OK. **F** *Hospedaje Copaneco*, 1 Av No 228, T898-5181, Barrio El Progreso, on road to San Pedro Sula. Opposite is **F** *Hotel Gran Bazar*, basic, **E** with bath. **F** *Hospedaje Golosino Yessi*, parking, small rooms, OK. **F** *Hospedaje María*, good, limited food. Eat in the market or at the bus station (to west, on Santa Rosa road), or at *Comedor Isis*, excellent. Plenty of other good restaurants.

El Puente El Puente is a National Archaeological Park reached by taking a turn-off, 4½ km west from La Entrada on the Copán road, then turning right on a well signposted, paved road 6 km to the Visitors' Centre. It is near the confluence of the Chamelecón and Chinamito rivers and is thought to have been a regional centre between AD 600 and 900 . There are over 200 structures, many of which have been excavated and mapped since 1984 by the Instituto Hondureño de Antropología e Historia (Honduran Institute of Anthropology and History) together with the Japanese Overseas Cooperation Volunteers, and have only opened to visitors since 1994. Several of the structures have been cleared and partially restored, including a 12-m high pyramid; there are also stelae. The visitors' centre has a cafetería and a souvenir shop. There is a small museum of anthropology, well worth a visit and an introduction to Copán. ■ *0800-1600, US$5, US$1.50 for Central Americans. You are not allowed to camp at the site, but ask the locals nearby.*

Transport From **La Entrada** the cheapest transport is by truck. From **Copán** ask about a truck by *Hotel Paty* and negotiate for the 60 km, 1-hr ride, about US$25 for 2 includes 1½ hrs at the site and a stop at **Las Lagunas** to see the roosting cattle egrets (recommended).

A few kilometres beyond La Entrada is the small town of **La Florida**, with primitive accommodation. The owner of the gas station here will advise archaeologists about the many Maya ruins and hilltop stelae between La Florida, Copán and the border.

Copán Ruins

A charming town set in the hills just to the east of the border with Guatemala, Copán *Colour map 6, grid B1* Ruins – to give the town its full name – thrives and survives on visitors passing through to visit the nearby ruins. Nevertheless, it is arguably the best-preserved and most pleasant colonial town in Honduras. Close to the border with Guatemala, most people stop briefly before heading straight to San Pedro Sula (172 km) and the Bay Islands or Tegucigalpa (395 km), but if time allows, in addition to the impressive ruins of Copán, there are a few waterfalls, horse-riding and unspoilt hiking trails to

Honduras

Western Honduras

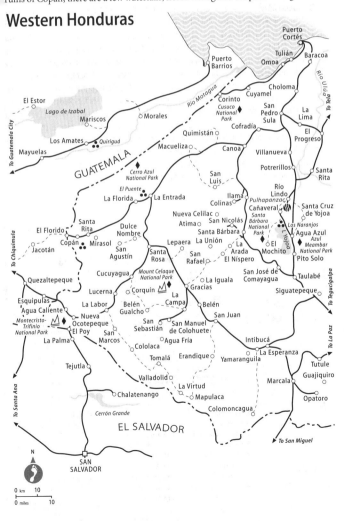

be enjoyed. Ask locally for the very latest updates. You'll find more information a[...] www.copanruinas.com

The **Copán Museum** on the town square has good explanations in Spanish of th[...] Maya Empire and stelae. There is a good selection of artefacts, a burial site and recently unearthed tomb that was uncovered during a roadbuilding project. It is [...] good idea to visit the museum before the ruins. ■ *Mon-Sat, 0800-1600, US$2[...]* **Enchanted Wings Butterfly House**, two blocks west of the cemetary on the road t[...] Guatemala, is run by Bob 'The Butterfly Guy' Gallardo, specialist in Honduran But[...] terflies. The garden is beautiful and there are exhibits of rare butterflies with a new orchid garden. Recommended. ■ *0800-1700. US$5. T651-4133.*

Sleeping
■ *on map*

Hotels are generally expensive here compared with other places in Honduras

AL *Posada Real de Copán*, on hill overlooking Copán, T651-4480, F651-4497 www.mayanet.hn/posadareal, full service major hotel, restaurant, too far from town to walk. **AL-C** *Marina Copán*, on the Plaza occupying almost an entire block, T651-4070, F651-4477, www.hotelmarinacopan.com, swimming pool, sauna, restaurant, bar, live marimba music at weekends, also caters for tour groups, large rooms with TV, suites, very tasteful and spacious, friendly, nice atmosphere. Recommended.

B *Camino Maya*, corner of main plaza, T651-4646, F651-4517, hcmaya@david.intertel. hn, with bath, good restaurant, rooms bright and airy, cable TV, fans, rooms on courtyard quieter than street, English spoken, nice patio garden with parrot, balcony on some upstairs rooms. **B** *La Casa de Café*, 4½ blocks west of Plaza, T651-4620, F651-4623, www.todomundo.com/casadecafe, renovated colonial home, with breakfast, coffee all day, library, good information, beautifully designed garden, lovely views, friendly and interesting hosts, English spoken, very popular so best to reserve in advance, protected parking. Recommended. **B** *Los Jaguares* on Plaza opposite *Marina*, T651-4451, 10 rooms, with bath, TV, a/c, hot water, friendly staff, locked parking, no restaurant. **B** *Madrugada*, T651-4092, F557-8830, take street from southeast corner of Parque, go down steps and turn right, by the river, unprepossessing exterior but nice colonial-style interior, 15 rooms (upstairs best). **B-C** *Bella Vista*, on hill by former police barracks, T445-1036, clean, safe but poorly situated, good value. **C** *Hotelito Brisas de Copán*, T651-4118, terrace, modern rooms with bath, hot water, quiet, limited parking. Recommended. **C-D** *Yaragua*, ½ block east of the Plaza, T651-4050, with bath, hot water, safe, clean, friendly.

Copán Ruinas

Honduras

D *Café ViaVia Copán*, next to *Tunkul*, T651-4652, part of a worldwide Belgian network of cafés (*Joken Tours*), breakfast US$2.75, special price for students with card and discounts for more than one night, hot water, good beds, bar. **D** *Paty*, T651-4021, F651-4109, fan, bath, no meals, good value, lots of parking. Recommended. **D** *Popul Nah*, on street off southeast corner of Plaza, T651-4095, fan, hot shower, safe parking, very clean, hospitable. **E** *California*, opposite *Los Gemelos*, T651-4314, fan, laundry, book exchange, nice lawn. **E** *Hotelito Yaxpac*, 1 block north of Parque Central, T651-4025, 4 rooms with bath, cold water, nice view of countryside from balcony. **E** *La Siesta*, 2 blocks west of main plaza on street that is plaza's northern edge, with bath, cheaper without, fan, laundry facilities on roof. **E-F** *Hostel Iguana Azul*, next to *La Casa de Café* and under same ownership, dormitory-style bunk beds in 2 rooms, shared bath, also 3 more private double rooms, hot water, laundry facilities, garden patio, colonial décor, clean, comfortable, common area, books, magazines, travel guides (including the Handbook), maps, garden, fans, safe box, English spoken. Good for backpackers and women travelling alone. Recommended.

F *Hospedaje Los Gemelos*, 1 block down from *Banco de Occidente*, T651-4077, F651-4315, maricela@hondutel.hn, without bath, clean, fans, good value, best place for backpackers, friendly, pleasant patio, good for single women, also laundry facilities, email, phone and fax service. Recommended. **F** *Posada del Viajero*, on road into town from the border, T651-4638, some rooms with bath, cheaper without, cold shower, meals, relaxing.

Out of town is the **B** *Hacienda San Lucas*, guest centre in town 2 blocks north of the Parque Central, T651-4106, www.geocities.com/sanlucascopan much cheaper in groups of 4, 2 rooms with private hot water bath, restaurant, renovated hacienda home, lovely views of Copán River Valley, hiking trails.

Camping Good place to camp is *Hacienda San Lucas*, with a restaurant and lovely views. Also some houses will accommodate cheaply, enquire. Also good camping at the Agua Caliente hot springs (see Excursions above).

Eating
● *on map, opposite*

Café Vamos a Ver, 1 block from Plaza, Dutch-owned, lots of vegetables, good sandwiches and snacks, complete dinner US$5, pleasant, good value, open 0700-2200. Recommended. *Café ViaVia Copán* (see above), food, bar, lodging. *Café Welchez* in *Hotel Marina Copán*, good cakes but expensive and coffee 'unpredictable'. *Carnitas Nía Lola*, 2 blocks south of Parque Central, at end of road, nice view over river valley, popular meeting place, open 0700-2200, see 'la fragua' bellows and brazier, *comida típica*, inexpensive, busy bar, relaxed atmosphere and book exchange. *Comedor El Jacal*, opposite *El Sesteo*, typical food, recommended for decent budget meal, breakfast, lunch and dinner, cable TV, can arrange rented rooms. *Comedor Isabel*, next to *Llama del Bosque*, typical comedor atmosphere, slow service, relatively clean, average food, dinner US$2.50. *Elisa's* at *Camino Maya*, excellent food at reasonable prices, pleasant, good service. Recommended. *El Sesteo*, next to *Hotel Paty*, typical lunch US$3, dinner US$3-4.50, friendly but rather nondescript atmosphere. *Llama del Bosque*, 2 blocks west of Plaza, open for breakfast, lunch and dinner, bar, pleasant, recommended, large portions of reasonable food, try their *carnitas típicas*, meals about US$5.50, soup US$2.25. *Tunkul*, opposite *Llama del Bosque*, good food includes vegetarian meals, large portions, not cheap, happy hour 2000-2100, large outdoor patio, nice for relaxing breakfast, helpful. Recommended.

Shopping

Selling all sorts of local crafts are *Galería de Arte Mahchi*, 0800-1200 and 1400-1900, Mon-Sun. *La Casa de Todo*, just down the street from *Banco de Occidente*, is Copán's best crafts shop, run by Carin Steen who also runs *Copán Pinta* which sponsors art projects for kids in local villages. *Pabellón Maya*, in the old *colegio* on the Parque Central, also home to a new interactive kids museum about the Maya. 0900-1200 and 1300-1800, Tue-Sun. The *El Jaral* shopping centre and cinema is 6 km from town on the road to San Pedro Sula.

Transport

Air 1- to 3-day trip from Guatemala City to Copán can be arranged by air (40 mins' flight to a *finca* airstrip, then bus, 25 mins), US$180 includes guide for 1 day, hotel accommodation

Honduras

extra. Try *Jungle Flying* (also charter flights between Tikal and Copán), T651-4023, in Copán or T360-4920, F331-4995 in Guatemala City, or many other agencies.

Buses New first-class direct service to San Pedro Sula with connections to **Tegucigalpa** and **La Ceiba** with *Hedman Alas*, leaving at 0530 and 1430 daily, 1030 service on Sat and Sun, 2½ hrs to San Pedro (US$6.50), connecting with buses to Tegulcigalpa and La Ceiba Direct buses from San Pedro Sula in parking lot next to *Hotel Palmira*, to Copán Ruinas, *Gama Express*, T661-4421, 0600, returns from Copán 1500 (tickets from *Maya Connections* or *Café ViaVia*), Casasola-*Cheny Express*, 0700, returns 1400, tickets in Copán from *Souvenirs Mundo Maya* next to *Los Gemelos*, both comfortable, reclining seats, efficient, good value, highly recommended. Express minibus service to San Pedro Sula, airport and Tela from *Hotel Paty*, US$11, and to La Ceiba US$18.50. Numerous small boys greet you on arrival to carry bags or offer directions for a small fee. There are regular slow buses (*Copanecos* or *Torito* lines) from San Pedro Sula to La Entrada, US$1.50 (2½ hrs), 0345-1700; from La Entrada to Copán, US$1.85 by bus (2½ hrs), from 0500 every 45 mins (or when full) till 1630, stops at entrance to ruins. If going by bus from San Pedro Sula, and returning, it is impossible to see Copán in 1 day. Buses from Copán to La Entrada for connecting buses going north or south, 0400-1700. Children meet arriving buses so use them as guides only if you want. Direct **Copán Ruinas-Antigua**, leaves 1430, US$25, *Monarcas Travel*.

Motoring There is a Texaco filling station by the ruins. The main bridge into town was badly damaged by Hurricane Mitch. A huge landslide also wrecked a part of the road between Santa Rita and Copán. The bridge and road have now been fully repaired.

Directory **Banks** *Banco Atlántida* and *Banco de Occidente* both on the plaza both changes TCs and take Visa. *Banco Credimatic*, has similar services and an ATM for MasterCard and AmEx. Guatemalan currency can be changed at Copán; it is possible to change quetzales near where buses leave for the border or with money changers in front of *Hotel Paty*. **Communications** Internet: *Copán Net*, 1 block southwest of Parque Central, copannet@hondutel. hn, open 0800-2100 (but Sat morning is for local children), 2 La per min. *Maya Connections*, next to *Los Gemelos*, US$6 per hr, 0730-1800, Mon-Sun. **Post office**: next to the market, open Mon-Fri 0800-1200, 1300-1700, Sat 0800-1200, beautiful stamps available. **Telephone**: phone calls can be made from the office of Hondutel 0800-2100. **Language schools** *Academia de Español Guacamaya*, T/F651-4360, www.guacamaya.com, classes US$175 a week, with homestay US$175, recommended. *Ixbalanque*, T/F651-4432, www.copanruinas.com/ixbalanque.htm, one-to-one teaching plus board and lodging with local family, US$125 for 1 week, 4 hrs teaching a day. **Tour operators** *Go Native Tours*, T651-4432, ixbalan.gbm.hn Information at Paris Copán. *MC Tours*, in *Hotel Marina*, T651-4453, www.mctours-honduras.com local and countrywide tours. *Monarcas Travel*, for shuttle service to Guatemala City and Antigua, next to *Posada del Annie*, T651-4361, monarcas@honduras.com, 0800-1800, Mon-Sun. Horses for hire (but look around and bargain). You will probably be approached with offers of horse hire which is a good way of getting to nearby attractions. **Horse-riding** to Los Sapos and Las Sepulturas, US$10 for 3 hrs. **Birding** guide and naturalist Robert Gallardo (T651-4133, rgallardo32@hotmail.com) is the owner of the Butterfly Garden and an expert on Honduran flora and fauna. He leads birding trips, **natural history** tours, orchid and serpent tours around Copán and other parts of Honduras, including La Mosquitia. Recommended. *Yaragua Tours*, next to hotel of same name, T651-4050, yaraguatour@yahoo.com, horse-riding and coffee *fincas*. 0700-2100, Mon-Sun. Recommended. **Useful addresses Immigration:** in old Colegio building on the Parque Central.

Copán archaeological site

The magnificent ruins of Copán are one of Central America's major Maya sites, certainly the most significant in Honduras, and they mark the southern most limit of Mayan dominance. Just 1 km from the village, there is a signposted path beside the road from Copán to the ruins which passes two stelae en route. Get to the ruins as early as possible, or stay late in the day so you have a chance to be there without hordes of people.

Museo de Escultura Maya The Museum of Mayan Sculpture, opened in 1996 next to the Visitors' Centre, is an impressive and huge two-storey museum and sculpture park which houses the newly excavated carvings. In the middle of the museum is an open-air courtyard with a full-size reproduction of the Rosalila temple, found intact buried under Temple 16 with its original paint and carvings (see below). A reproduction of the doorway to Temple 16 is on the upper floor. The new museum houses the original stelae to prevent weather damage, while copies will be placed on site. Over 2,000 other objects found at Copán are also in the museum. It is essential to visit the museum before the ruins. Good explanations in Spanish and English. The exit leads to the ruins via the nature trail. ■ *US$10, ticket from main ticket office, not at the museum.*

Copán archaeological site

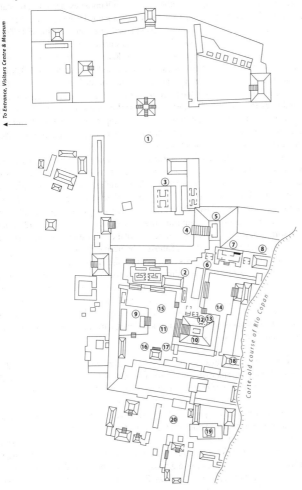

N

0 metres   50
0 yards   50

1 Main Plaza with Stelae	9 Structure 13	14 East Court/Plaza de los
2 Acropolis	10 Structure 16	Jaguares
3 Ball Court	11 Altar Q	15 Plaza Occidental
4 Hieroglyphic Stairway	12 Rosalila Building	16 Altar I
5 Structure 26	(within Structure 16)	17 Altar H
6 Council House, Temple 22A	13 Hunal Building	18 Temple 18
7 Temple of Meditation/	(beneath Rosalila)	19 Structure 32
Temple 22	& Tomb of Founder	20 Zona Residencial
8 House of Knives		

The ruins

Some of the finest examples of sculpture from Copán are now in the British Museum or at Boston

When Stephens and Catherwood examined the ruins in 1839, they were engulfed in jungle. In the 1930s the Carnegie Institute cleared the ground and rebuilt the Hieroglyphic Stairway, and since then they have been maintained by the Government. Some of the most complex carvings are found on the 21 **stelae**, or 3-m columns of stones on which the passage of time was originally believed to have been recorded. Under many of the stelae was a vault; some have been excavated. The stelae are deeply incised and carved with faces, figures and animals. There are royal portraits with inscriptions recording deeds and the lineage of those portrayed as well as dates of birth, marriage and death. Ball courts were revealed during excavation, and one of them has been fully restored. The **Hieroglyphic Stairway** leads up a pyramid; its upper level supported a temple. Its other sides are still under excavation. The Stairway is covered for protection, but a good view can be gained from the foot and there is access to the top via the adjacent plaza. After Hurricane Mitch, the **Rosalila Temple**, in Temple 16, was opened to the public, as were other previously restricted excavations, in an effort to attract more visitors. Recently the Rosalila and Jaguar tunnels below the site have been opened to visitors at additional cost (US$12). Much fascinating excavation work is now in progress, stacks of labelled carved stones have been placed under shelters, and the site looks like becoming even more interesting as new buildings are revealed. The most atmospheric buildings are those still half-buried under roots and soil. The last stela was set up in Copán between AD 800 and 820, after less than five centuries of civilized existence. The nearby river has been diverted to prevent it encroaching on the site when in flood.

Also near the ruins is a **Sendero Natural** (nature trail) through the jungle to the minor ball court; take mosquito repellent if you intend to stand still. The trail takes 30 minutes. After 1600 is the best time to see animals on the Sendero Natural, which is open until 1700. About 4 km from the main centre is the ceremonial site known as **Los Sapos** (The Toads), a pre-classic site with early stone carvings. The sapo was a Mayan symbol of fertility. East of the main ruins near Los Sapos is a stone, Estela 12, which lines up with another, Estela 10, on the other side of the valley at sunrise and sunset on 12 April every year. Horse rides to Los Sapos can be arranged with guides at main Visitors' Centre at Copán for US$25, 3-4 hours, or through *Yaragua Tours*, US$15.

One kilometre beyond the main ruins, along the road to San Pedro Sula, is an area called **Las Sepulturas**, a residential area where ceramics dating back to 1000 BC have been found; entry to this site is included in the main Copán ticket. Exhibits from the site are on display in the Copán Museum. It is a delightful site, beautifully excavated and well maintained, peaceful and in lovely surroundings. ■ *The entrance is almost 2 km from the main site.*

Essentials

Entry to ruins and Las Sepulturas US$10 (US$2.50 for Central Americans), open 0800-1600, admission valid for 1 day. Entrance to the tunnels is an extra US$12. Guided tours available all year (recommended, US$20 for 2 hrs); recommended is Antonio Ríos, T898-3414, owner of restaurant/shop opposite the ruins. The Copán Guide Association has a table set up in the visitor centre where qualified bilingual guides can be hired at a fixed rate. Photographs of the excavation work and a maquette of the site are located in a small exhibition room at the ruins' visitors' centre. There is a cafetería by the entrance to the ruins, and also a handicrafts shop. There is a tourist office in the Parque Arqueológico, next to the bookshop, with local and country maps, and a Spanish/English guide book for the ruins, which is rather generalized. Useful recent books are: *Scribes, Warriors and Kings: City of Copán*, by William and Barbara Fash (1991), and *History Carved in Stone*, a guide to Copán by William Fash and Ricardo Argucía (3rd edition, 1998, US$3), published locally and available at the site. Luggage can be left for no charge.

Around Copán

There are many caves around Copán to visit – some of which have unearthed Mayan artefacts. Ask locally or check with *Yaragua Tours*. Also here, and in the neighbouring part of Guatemala, are a few remaining Chorti Indian villages, interesting to visit, particularly on 1 November, Día de Los Muertos, when there are family and communal ceremonies for the Dead.

After all the trekking has ruined your body a trip to the **Agua Caliente**, 20 km north from Copán, thermal springs will be just what you need. Reached by a road through villages and beautiful scenery, it's a 45 minute journey by vehicle, pick-ups go sometimes for about US$17, shared between passengers. Cross the river and follow the trail up to the springs, but only swim in the river where the very hot water has mixed with the cold. There are changing facilities and toilets in the park which gets busy at weekends. Take all food and water. ■ *0800-2000, US$1.50.*

Also on the road to Guatemala is the **Enchanted Wings Butterfly House**. ■ *0800-1700. US$5.*

Nine kilometres east of Copán is **Santa Rita**, a small colonial town on the Copán River with cobblestones and red rooves (*Hospedaje Santa Rita* and unnamed outdoor restaurant recommended, off main road next to Esso, speciality *tajadas*, huge portions, cheap). A lovely one-hour walk goes upstream (expect to get wet feet, take swimsuit) to **El Rubí**, a boulder and waterfall, and beyond to a small rock canyon, more waterfalls, and return through the countryside with lovely views of the valley and town. There have been several robberies of people visiting the area. The advice is not to go at present, but ask for local advice, and if you really want to go, take nothing and then there's nothing to steal! Nearby **Balneario Mitch** is a newly opened swimming complex that is positively heaving at weekends. **Sleeping** Outside Santa Rita, 11 km from Copán Ruinas, is **A** *Hacienda El Jaral*, T/F552-4891, formerly a working farm, now a hotel with a cluster of duplex cottages on a broad, tropical flower-lined lawn, with a pool, good horses to hire or for guided tours, mountain hiking nearby and a lake where egrets return in the evening theroughout most of the year; October-May up to 3,000 have been seen here. The hacienda, owned by the Bueso family, is included on several tour programmes. Recommended. Also has a petrol/gas station, shopping mall and a cinema.

Honduran immigration The Honduran immigration office is at **El Florido** on the border and you get stamps there. They charge entry and exit fees (see Touching down, page 828) ask for a receipt for any 'extra' charges.

Leaving Honduras by private vehicle If leaving with a vehicle, you need 3 stamps on your strip from Migración, Tránsito (where they take your Proviso Provisional), and Aduana (where they take your Pase Fronterizo document) and cancel the stamp in your passport.

Guatemalan consulate For visas, either San Pedro Sula or Tegucigalpa. Guatemalan tourist cards are available at the border.

Transport Minibuses run all day every day until 1700 between Copán Ruinas and the border at El Florida, 30 mins, connecting with buses to Guatemalan destinations. Catch the buses behind the Municipal market. The cost should be about US$2.50. Bargain for a fair price. If heading for Antigua, there is a direct minibus service Copán-Antigua, Guatemala, run by *Monarcas Travel*, next to Posada del Annie, Copán, US$25 one way, 1430 daily, pick up from hotels (in Antigua 7 Av Nte No 15A, T/F783-24779, geotours@gua.net, leaves 0400).

Just to visit Copán, those needing visas can get a 72-hr exit pass at the border but you must re-cross at the same border post before expiry.

To enter (or return to) Guatemala an alternative route is via Santa Rosa de Copán and Nueva Ocotepeque (see below and Guatemala chapter).

Border with Guatemala
There are many money changers, but for US$ or TCs, change in Copán for better rates

Santa Rosa de Copán

Santa Rosa is an important regional town with a colonial atmosphere of cobbled streets and some of the best colonial architecture in Honduras. Originally known as Los Llanos, it was made a municipality in 1812 and became capital of the

Colour map 6, grid B1
Population: 35,000
Altitude: 1,160 m

Honduras

department of Copán when it was split from Gracias (now Lempira). The town is set in some of the best scenery in Honduras and the fine weather makes it ideal for hiking, horses and mountain bike riding.

Santa Rosa owes its wealth to the fact it's an agricultural and cattle-raising area. Maize and tobacco are grown here, and visitors can see traditional hand-rolling at the Flor de Copán **cigar factory** three blocks east of the bus terminal. They do give tours – ask for the production manager. ■ *Open until 1700, Mon-Fri, closed 1130-1300 for lunch.* The central plaza and church are perched on a hilltop. There is a quieter plaza at Calle Real Centenario y 6 Av SO, which is fenced, a nice place to relax. The main market is at 1 C and 3 Av NE, which has good leather items. Farmers' markets are held daily in Barrio Santa Teresa, take 4 Calle SE past 5 Avenida SE, and at 4 Calle SE and 5 Avenida SE on Sunday 0500 to 1000. The town holds a festival to Santa Rosa de Lima from 21 to 31 August with the 'Tobacco Queen' crowned at the end of the week. There is also a smaller fair around May 15. A visitor information centre has opened in the Casa de la Cultura. ■ *Mon-Fri, 0800-1200, 1300-1700, T662-0800.*

Sleeping
■ *on map below*
Price codes: see
inside front cover

B *Elvir*, C Real Centenario SO, 3 Av SO, T/F662-0805, hotelelvir@hondudata.com, overpriced, safe, clean, quiet, all rooms have own bath, TV, hot water, drinking water, good but pricey meals in cafetería or restaurant. Recommended. **C-D** *Continental*, 2 C NO y 2-3 Av, T662-0801, F662-0802, on 2nd floor, musty, with bath, hot water, fan, cable TV, friendly management. **D** *Copán*, 1 C 3 Av, T662-0265, with bath, hot water at times and TV, cheaper without, cell-like rooms but clean, safe, hot water in morning. **E** *Castillo*, next door to *Maya Central*, T662-0368, clean. **E** *Hospedaje Santa Eduviges*, 2 Av NO y 1 C NO, good beds, clean, pleasant, good value but some rooms damp. **E** *Maya Central* (not to be confused with *Hospedaje Maya*), 1 C NO y 3 Av NO, T662-0073, with bath, cold shower, pleasant. **E** *Rosario*, 3 Av NE No 139, T662-0211, cold water, with bath, **F** without.

Santa Rosa de Copán

With thanks to Michael J Grey

Not to scale

■ Sleeping
1 Blanca Nieves *B2*
2 Castillo *B1*
3 Continental *B1*
4 Copán *B2*
5 Elvir *B1*
6 Hospedaje Calle Real *B3*
7 Hospedaje San Pedro *B2*
8 Hospedaje Santa Eduviges *B1*
9 Hospedaje Santa Rosa *B2*
10 Hospedaje Suyapa *B2*
11 Maya Central *B1*
12 Rosario *B2*

● Eating
1 Chiky's *B1*
2 El Rodeo *C2*

3 Flamingo *B2*
4 Las Haciendas *C2*
5 Las Haciendas II *C1*
6 On Fu *B1*
7 París *B1*
8 Pizza Pizza *B3*
9 Rincón Colonial *C2*
10 Well *C2*

F *Blanca Nieves*, 3 Av NE, Barrio Mercedes, T662-1312, safe, shared bath with cold water, good value, laundry facilities. **G** *Hospedaje Calle Real*, Real Centenario y 6 Av NE, clean, quiet, friendly, best of the cheaper places but sometimes water failures. **G** *Hospedaje San Pedro*, 2 C NE, basic, dirty, OK at night, noisy by day. **G** *Hospedaje Santa Rosa*, 3 Av NE No 42, Barrio Mercedes, T662-1421, basic, clean, safe, cold water, laundry facilities, welcoming. **G** *Hospedaje Suyapa*, 2 C NE, basic, noisy in the day, OK at night.

Chikys, 1 C SO y 1 Av SO, Mexican, good food, atmosphere, music and beer. Recommended. **Eating**
El Rodeo, 1 Av SE, good menu, specializes in steaks, nice atmosphere, plenty of dead animals ● *on map opposite*
on the walls, pricey. *Flamingo*, 1 Av SE, off main plaza, T662-0654, relatively expensive but good pasta and chop suey, popular with locals. *On Fu*, 1 Av SO, near *Chikys*, 2nd floor, Chinese and local dishes, large servings, good vegetables, attentive service. *Las Haciendas*, 1 Av SE, varied menu, filling *comida corriente*. Recommended. *Las Haciendas II*, 1 C SO, smaller, more intimate, same menu. *Paris*, C Real Centanario, ½ block from Parque Central, expensive but very good food, nice garden, cigars for sale. *Pizza Pizza*, Real Centenario 5 Av NE, 4½ blocks from main plaza, one of the best in town, good pizza and pasta, pleasant surroundings in old colonial house, great coffee, best meeting place, internet access, US owned, good source of information, book exchange. Recommended. *Rincón Colonial*, 1 Av SE, typical local cuisine, good, less expensive than its neighbours. *Well*, 3 C SE, Chinese, a/c, huge portions, good value and service.

There is a good *comedor* at the bus terminal, *Merendera El Campesino*. On the carretera *La Gran Villa*, some of the tastiest meats and meals in Santa Rosa, run by Garífuna family. Recommended.

Nightclubs *Glamour*, shows videos Mon-Thu night. **Cultural Centre** ½ block south of **Entertainment**
Parque Central with live music and singing, sculpture and picture galley.

Buses from Santa Rosa to **Tegucigalpa** (lovely scenery, lush pine forests, colonial villages), **Transport**
Toritos, leaves at 0400 from terminal, Mon-Sat, 0400 and 1000 Sun, US$6, 7-8 hrs. To **Gracias**
Transportes Lempira, several 0745-1800, 2 hrs, US$1.3 (road paved). To **San Pedro Sula**,
US$2.50, 4 hrs, every 45 mins from 0400-1730, express service daily 2½ hrs, US$3.50 (*Empresa Torito*), bus to **La Entrada**, 1 hr, US$0.90. To **Copán Ruinas**, 4 hrs on good road, US$2.90, several direct daily (eg *Etumi* at 1130, 1215, 1345), but you may have to change at La Entrada. South on paved road to **Nueva Ocotepeque** 6 daily, US$1.80, 2 hrs. There you change buses for El Salvador and Guatemala (1 hr to border, US$1, bus leaves hourly until 1700). Local 'El Urbano' bus to centre from bus station (on Carretera Internacional, 2 km below town, opposite *Hotel Mayaland*), US$0.35; taxi US$0.50. If coming from the Guatemalan border at Nueva Ocotepeque, the bus will stop at the end of town near Av Centenario (main street).

Banks *Atlántida*, has Visa ATM, maximum withdrawal US$30, and *Banco de Occidente* (best **Directory**
exchange rates) both on main plaza. *Banadesa*, and 2 branches of *Bancahsa* (fast service) on C Real Centenario (*Occidente* and *Bancahsa* change TCs). **Communication** Internet: *Pizza Pizza* has email at US$4 per hr, good machines. **Post office and Hondutel** are on the park, opposite side to the cathedral. **Laundry** *Lavandaría Florencia*, C Centenario. **Medical services** *Clínica Médica Las Gemas*, 2 Av NO, near Hotel Elvir, T666-1428, run by Dr Soheil Rajabian (speaks English among other languages), first class attention. Hospital Medico Quirurgico, Barrio Miraflores, Carretera Internacional, T/F662-1283, fast and efficient, but not cheap. **Dentist**: *Dr Ricardo Reyes*, 3 Av 349, Barrio Santa Teresa, T662-0007. **Shopping** *Supermercado Martín* is three blocks south of *Pizza Pizza*. **Tour operators** *Lenca Land Trails*, at *Hotel Elvir*, T/F662-1375, lenca@hondutel.hn, run by Max Elvir, organizes cultural tours of the Lenca mountain villages in western Honduras, hiking, mountain biking, the lot, excellent source of information about the region. **Guide**: Ask at *Flor de Copán* cigar factory for *José Pineda* who runs tours to tobacco plantations at weekends, informative, only 30 mins from town, lovely countryside. **Useful addresses** *Immigration*, Av Alvaro Contreras y 2 C NO, helpful, extensions available. **Voluntary work** *Hogar San Antonio*, run by nuns across the street from the City Playground, welcome volunteers.

Entertainment

Honduras

Around Santa Rosa de Copán

Taking time to explore some of the forested hills around Santa Rosa will lead yo' through some spectacular scenery and give an insight into the life of agricultura Honduras.

There are buses from Santa Rosa west to the small town of **Dulce Nombre d** **Copán** (US$0.55). There are rooms available next to the *Hondutel* office. Hiker heading for Copán and the border can continue west through themountains to sta at the primitive village of **San Agustín** (buses and pick-ups from Santa Rosa), take hammock or sleeping bag, continuing next day through Mirasol you reach the Ruinas road at El Jaral, 11 km east of Copán ruins (see Copán Excursions above).

Numerous buses head south daily to **Corquín** (US$0.75, two hours), which ha: two good *pensiones*, one **F** with a charming garden, recommended. They pas: through **Cucuyagua** (40 minutes, US$0.60, restaurant *Brisas de Copán*, on side street, ask directions, good, clean), with a scenic river, good swimming and camping on its banks, and **San Pedro de Copán**, an attractive village and an entry point into the Parque Nacional Celaque.

Belén
Gualcho
From here take a bus, six a day (also one bus a day from Santa Rosa de Copán) or a rough, dusty, 1½-hour ride in a pick-up truck (US$0.75) to Belén Gualcho, a Lenca village 1,500 m up in mountains and a good base to explore the surround- ing mountains and valleys, especially north towards Monte Celaque. Belén Gualcho is perched on the mountainside with two colonial churches, one archi- tecturally fine with three domes and a fine colonnaded façade with twin bell tow- ers, the other more rustic. There is an interesting Sunday market from 0500, over by 1000. There are numerous short walks from town in most directions, all affording wonderful views. You can walk two hours to waterfalls (90-m drop). Head for El Paraíso then ask for directions. Everyone knows where they are. There is a **fiesta** on 24 June.

Sleeping
& eating
Hotels fill up quickly on Sat as traders arrive for the Sun market. **G** *Hotelito El Carmen* (2 blocks east down from the church in the plaza), friendly, clean, good views, recommended.. **G** *Hospedaje Doña Carolina*, electricity goes off at 2130 so take a torch and candle. Films are shown every evening at 1930, ask anyone, US$0.10. *Comedor Mery*, 1 block northwest of plaza, good food in a welcoming family atmosphere. *Las Haciendas*, also good. Two more *comedores* on south side of plaza and east side on corner with store.

Transport
To Santa Rosa daily at 0430 (Sun at 0930). To Gracias from main plaza at 0400, 0500, 1330.

A mule trail connects Belén Gualcho with **San Manuel de Colohuete** (1,500 m), which has a magnificent colonial church whose façade is sculpted with figures of saints. Buses to San Manuel from Gracias at 1300, four hours, and usually a pick-up returning in the evening. There are no hotels so you must ask villagers about places to stay. There is an equally fine colonial church 30 minutes by four-wheel drive vehicle to the southwest at **San Sebastián Colosuca** (1,550m). The village has a mild climate (two hospedajes; or try Don Rubilio; food at Doña Clementina García or Doña Alicia Molina). The *Feria de San Sebastián* is on 20 January. No alcohol may be sold in the village and there are no soldiers here. An hour's walk away is the Cueva del Diablo and 6 km away is Cerro El Alta with a lagoon at the top. From San Sebastián, a mule trail goes via the heights of **Agua Fría** to reach the route near the border at **Tomalá**.

Alternatively, you can walk five hours east from San Manuel to **La Campa** with its nice colonial church, or take a daily bus San Manuel-La Campa-Gracias. Irregular transport on the 18-km dirt road to Gracias. There is a *hospedaje* in La Campa, ask at Hondutel. Red pottery is made there. San Matías, the patron saint's **fiesta** is 23-24 February, well worth visiting, thousands celebrate the mostly indigenous traditions.

Walking from San Manuel Colohuete to Belén Gualcho

There is a well-defined, well-used and easy to follow mule trail linking these two villages, which makes a good one or two day hike. Maps are not essential as there are communities at many points along the way where advice can be sought. If required, a map of the area is available from the Lenca Cultural Centre in Gracias.

The path leading away from the village leaves from opposite the pulpería and comedor where the bus drops you, heading west and downhill into a valley. The path is used by four-wheel drive vehicles and continues to San Sebastián. Just after the community of San José, after passing the last house, the path to Belén branches off. A smaller path leaves the four-wheel drive track and climbs steeply up to your right and more northwest.

One hour: just after Peña Blanca, the path direction becomes unclear after it crosses an area of white chalky rocks. There are several other paths here. The main path heads north and steeply downhill at this point.

Two hours: there is water all the year round in the Quebrada de Rogán.

Three hours: all year round water in Río Gualmite, a short descent. After this there is a longish, steep ascent.

Four hours: just after this point the path branches on a large flat grassy area. Both paths lead to Belén Gualcho. The one to the left drops and crosses the river and then you are faced with a long, arduous and very steep ascent. We would recommend taking the path to the right, which exits to the far right of a grassy area by three small houses.

Five hours: the path climbs as it skirts around the Cerro Capitán. Just after passing the steepest part, a small landslide forces the path into a descent almost to the river. From here, only 2 m above the river, you can walk steeply down off the path to the river bank where there is the most perfect camp site. Flat sandy soil in some shade on the edge of a coffee plantation and 2 m from the river.

Six hours: from the camping site there is a long, continuous climb before dropping down sharply to cross the river. It is possible, but difficult, to cross the river at the point the path meets it. Take a small path off to the right just before the river, which leads to a suspension bridge. From the river it is a long climb, not especially steep, but continuous, to Belén Gualcho. It is situated between two small peaks that can be seen clearly after crossing the river. There are increasing numbers of houses after crossing the river and the odd pulpería where you can buy refrescos or food.

A paved road runs east from Santa Rosa to San Juan de Opoa, where it turns southeast towards Gracias. At Km 25 from Santa Risa to Gracias is *Las Tres Jotas* (the 3 'J's) run by the Alvarenga family (T662-0530), a tobacco plantation with swimming pools, hot water tubs and a man-made lake in a beautiful setting. There is live marimba music, a nice restaurant and drinks. ■ *Entry at weekends about US$1 to use all facilities.* Good walking and views of the Río Higuito; ask about camping. From Santa Rosa there are buses at 0630 and 0730 (US$1, 2 hours) to tiny **Lepaera** (very basic *hospedaje*, **G**, opposite market, and *comedores*, the best one is next to the market) perched on a lovely mountainside east of San Juan de Opoa (also reached from Gracias). You can climb **Cerro Puca** (2,234 m, stiff climb, start early morning for day trip) or descend on foot by an old mule trail heading back to Santa Rosa (4½ hours), crossing the river on a swingbridge (*hamaca*), then hitchhiking.

Also on the road between Santa Rosa and Gracias is **La Montanita**, 15 minutes by bus (US$0.50, or US$0.40 in a pick-up truck), a small park run by the Honduran Forestry Service with a lagoon, picnic area and camping. It's popular with the locals. Just around the corner is a private recreation centre called **Doricentro**. It has pools, water slides, picnic area, snack bar, and music. ■ *Only open weekends.*

Gracias

Background
Colour map 6, grid B1
Population: 19,380
Altitude: 765m

One of the oldest and most historic settlements in Honduras, dominated by Montañas de Celaque, Puca and Opulaca – the country's highest peaks – Gracias is a charming, friendly town. Just 50 km from Santa Rosa, both the town and the surrounding countryside are worth a visit. Gracias was the centre from which Francisco de Montejo, thrice Governor of Honduras, put down the great Indian revolt of 1537-38. Alonso de Cáceres, his lieutenant, besieged Lempira the Indian leader in his impregnable mountain-top fortress at Cerquín, finally luring him out under a flag of truce, ambushed him and treacherously killed him. When the Audiencia de los Confines was formed in 1544, Gracias became for a time the administrative centre of Central America.

Sights There are three colonial churches, San Sebastián, Las Mercedes and San Marcos (a fourth, Santa Lucía, is southwest of Gracias), and a restored fort, with two fine Spanish cannon, on a hill five minutes' walk west of the centre. The fort, **El Castillo San Cristóbal**, has been well restored, and at the foot of the northern ramparts is the tomb of Juan Lindo, President of Honduras 1847-1852, who introduced free education through a system of state schools.

Sleeping
■ on map

C-E *Posada de Don Juan*, C Principal opposite *Banco de Occidente*, T/F656-1020, Dutch-owned, good beds, great hot showers, nice big towels, laundry, some rooms have TV, parking. Recommended. **D** *Guanacascos* at the west end of Hondutel road, T656-1219, F656-1273, fronica@datum.hn, bath, hot water, TV, also rents 2-room cabin at *Villa Verde* adjacent to Monte Celaque Visitors' Centre. **D** *Hotel Rosario*,T656-1447, hot water, private bath, clean and friendly. **E** *Colonial*, 1 block south of *Erick*, T656-1258, with bath, fan, bar, restaurant, very good. **F** *Iris*, 3 blocks south of Plaza, 1 block west, opposite San Sebastián church, T656-1086, clean, cold water, closes at 2200, disco Saturday. **F** *Erick*, same street as bus office, T656-1066, with bath, cheaper without (cold shower), TV, comfortable beds, fresh, bright, clean, good value, laundry facilities, stores luggage, and shop open daily with trekker food, very convenient. Recommended. **F** *Herrera*, shared bath, noisy, basic. **F** *Hospedaje Corazón de Jesús*, on main street by market, clean, OK. **F** *Hospedaje El Milagro*, north side of market, basic. **F** *San Antonio*, no sign, main street, 2 blocks from Texaco station, T656-1071, clean, pleasant, friendly, good.

Gracias To Santa Rosa de Copán

Río Arcagual

To Castillo San Cristóbal

To Santa Lucía & Celaque

Cohdefor

Las Mercedes

Palacio Municipal

Parque Central

San Marcos

San Sebastián

To La Campa

To La Esperanza & Aguas Termales

N

Not to scale

4 Iris
5 Posada de Don Juan
6 Rosario
7 San Antonio

■ **Sleeping**
1 Colonial
2 Erick
3 Guanacascos

● **Eating**
1 Alameda
2 El Señorial
3 La Fonda

Alameda, 3 blocks west of *La Fonda*, white house, no sign, open 1100-2200 for lunch and dinner, excellent cooking, meat, fish, some vegetarian dishes, salads, main courses US$3-4, *comida corriente* US$2, elegant setting, dining room faces wild garden with fruit trees, not to be missed, under same management is **Comedor Graciano** and **Pollo Gracianito** on main street, good value. **El Señorial**, main street, simple meals and snacks, once house of Dr Juan Lindo. **La Fonda**, on Parque Central, good food, good value, attractively decorated, but no written menu – good practice for your Spanish. Recommended. **Rancho de Lily**, 3 blocks west of Hondutel, good value, rustic cabin, bar service, good snacks. For breakfast, *comedores* near the market, or, better, the restaurant at *Hotel Iris* (good *comida corriente* too) or *Guancascos*.

Eating
● *on map opposite*

A mail car goes to **La Esperanza** Tue, Thu, Sat, 0400, or take bus to Erandique, 1315, get off at San Juan from where bus goes to La Esperanza the next day, or hitch, or rides can be taken on very dusty and bumpy pick-up trucks for US$3 – beware overcharging (dep 0700 or earlier from south end of main street on highway). The road is much improved as far as San Juan. You can easily find a pick-up this far, 1½ hrs, US$1.50. Thereafter it is all-weather and can be rough. There is a bus service from Gracias to **Santa Rosa de Copán**, US$1.80, from 0530, 5 times a day, 2 hrs, last one at 1630; beautiful journey through majestic scenery, the road is paved. Daily bus service to **Lepaera** 1400, 1½ hrs, US$1.50; daily bus to **San Manuel de Colohuete** at 1300. Cotral bus ticket office is 1 block north of Parque Central. Torito bus, a few metres from the main terminal, has buses to the Guatemalan frontier at Agua Caliente, one at 1000, change buses at Nueva Ocotepeque.

Transport

Banks *Bancafé*, *Bancrecer* and *Banco de Occidente*, but none take Visa yet. **Communications** Hondutel and Post office: 1 block south of Parque Central, closes 1100 on Sat. **Cultural centres** Music lessons including marimba and flute, available from Ramón Alvarenga, 2 blocks west of the parque central on the same side as Iglesia San Marcos. **Tour operators** *Guancascos Tourist Centre* at the *Guancascos Hotel* arranges tours and expeditions to Monte Celaque Parque Nacional, local villages and other attractions. *Celaque Aventuras Tours*, run by Christophe Condor is based in Guancascos, T656-1219, F656-1219, has walking tours, visits to La Campa, the national park, thermal baths, horse hire, US$8, includes horse-riding, visit to thermal pools day or night, visiting natural caves. Just hot springs, including entry, is US$4.

Directory

Honduras

Around Gracias

Some 6 km from Gracias along the road to Esperanza (side road signposted), are Balneario Aguas Termales – hot, communal thermal pools in the forest for swimming (one hour by a path, one hour 20 minutes by road). To find the path, walk 2 km beyond the bridge over Río Arcagual to a second bridge before which turn right by a white house. Climb the hill and walk about 50 m along the top where a left-hand path leads to the pools. ■ *Daily 0600-2000, US$1.50, rental of towels, hammock, inner tube, restaurant/bar, recommended. Good place to barbecue.*

La Campa (see page 856) is 18 km away. From Gracias buses go through coffee plantations to San Rafael (makeshift accommodation), from there you can hitch to El Níspero (*pensión*) and catch a bus to Santa Bárbara. Also on the road to San Rafael, a short detour leads to **La Iguala**, a tiny village attractively set between two rivers, magnificent colonial church. Irregular transport from/to Gracias.

It takes at least a day to climb from Gracias to the summit of Monte Celaque (2,849 m, the highest point in Honduras). Most people allow two days to enjoy the trip. The trail begins from behind the visitors' centre of the **Parque Nacional Celaque** (1,400 m) which is 8 km from Gracias, two hours' walk. There are several intersections, best to ask at each. ■ *Entry fee US$3 plus US$3 per night camping in the mountain.* Not much of the 8-km road from Gracias to the park is passable without a high-clearance or four-wheel drive vehicle when wet. Transport can be arranged through the Lenca Centre. Armando Mondragon, at Texaco station, T898-4002, does trips, including lunch. At the centre there are seven beds, shower and cooking facilities, US$1, drinks

Monte Celaque
Visiting the other peaks around Gracias is more complicated but interesting. Information, maps which you can photocopy, camping gear and guided tours can be found at the Lenca Cultural Centre

available, well maintained. There is another cabin nearby with 10 beds. Take a torch and sleeping bag. Behind the centre is a trail going down to the river where a crystal clear pool and waterfall make for wonderful bathing. Ask the guide the exact way or pay US$6 for the guide. There is a warden, Miguel, living nearby who can supply food and beer but safer to take supplies from Gracias. Contact Cohdefor in Gracias before leaving for full information. There is a trail all the way to the summit (trees are marked with ribbons) which takes at least six hours: the first three are easy to a campsite at 2,000 m (Campamento Don Tomás) where there is small hut, the rest of the way is steep. A better campsite if you can make it is *Campamento Naranjo*, with water, at about 2,500 m – but you'll need a tent. Between these two sites, the climb is particularly steep and in cloud forest. Look out for spider monkeys. Above 2,600 m quetzals have been seen. Many hikers don't bother with the summit as it is forested and enclosed; it's four hours down to the visitors' centre. Don't forget good hiking boots, warm clothing, insect repellent and, given the dense forest and possibility of heavy cloud, a compass is recommended for safety. Also, beware of snakes. There are plans to extend the trail westward from the summit to Belén Gualcho (see above) and to create a nature trail near the visitors' centre.

Gracias to Erandique

After Gracias, the road runs 52 km to **San Juan del Caite** (two *hospedajes*, *Lempira* and *Sánchez*, two restaurants nearby, helpful people and Peace Corps workers). From here a dirt road runs 26 km south to the small town of **Erandique**. Founded in 1560 and and set high in pine-clad mountains not far from the border with El Salvador, it is a friendly town, and very beautiful. Lempira was born nearby, and was killed a few kilometres away. The third weekend in January is the local **Fiesta de San Sebastián**. Best time to visit is at the weekend. Market days are Friday and Sunday. Each of the three *barrios* has a nice colonial church. There is one basic *hospedaje*, **G**, run by the elderly Doña Bárbara in the main street and the simple *Comedor Inestroza* can serve you eggs, beans and tortillas; there is no electricity and a torch is essential. Ask around as there are lakes, rivers, waterfalls, springs and bathing ponds in the vicinity. Camping is allowed outside town by the small lagoon. Nearby is **San Antonio** where fine opals (not cut gems, but stones encased in rock) are mined and may be purchased. The many hamlets in the surrounding mountains are reached by roads that have been either resurfaced or recently built and the landscapes are magnificent.

Transport There are minibuses to Erandique from bridge on road to La Esperanza 1100 daily, although most people go by truck from Gracias (there is sometimes a van service as far as San Juan) or La Esperanza (change trucks at San Juan intersection, very dusty). Return minibus to Gracias at 0500 daily, which connects with the bus to La Esperanza in San Juan. Trucks leave Erandique 0700 daily, but sometimes earlier, and occasionally a second one leaves around 0800 for Gracias, otherwise be prepared for a long wait for a pick-up.

There are several roads radiating from Erandique, including one to **Mapulaca** and the frontier with El Salvador (no *migración* or *aduana* or bridge here, at the Río Lempa), a road to San Andrés and another to Piraera (all passable in a car).

La Esperanza
Colour map 6, grid C2
Altitude: 1,485 m

Beyond San Juan del Caite the main, but still rough and stony, road winds through beautiful mountain pine forests to La Esperanza. It is 43 km from San Juan del Caite and another 98 km on a good road to Siguatepeque. Capital of Intibucá Department, La Esperanza is an old colonial town in a pleasant valley. It has an attractive church in front of the park. There is a grotto carved out of the mountainside west of the town centre, a site of religious festivals. Good views. Market on Thursdays and Sundays when Lenca Indians from nearby villages sell wares and food but no handicrafts. Nearby is the Indian village of **Yaramanguila**. It's an excellent area for walking in forested hills, with lakes and waterfalls, although very cold in December-January. You can hike to **Cerro de Ojos**, a hill to the northwest and visible from La Esperanza.

It is forested with a clearing on top littered with many cylindrical holes; no one knows how they were formed, and they are a strange phenomenon. The turning to this hill is on the La Esperanza to San Juan road. Ask for directions.

Sleeping There are simple but pleasant *pensiones*, eg **E** *Hotel Solis*, T898-2080, 1 block east of market, bath and hot water, restaurant. Recommended. **E** *La Esperanza*, T898-2068, with bath, cheaper without, warm water, clean, TV, friendly, good meals. **F** *El Rey*, in Barrio La Morera, T898-2078, clean, friendly. **F** *Hotel Mina*, T898-2071, good beds, clean, very friendly, 1 block south of east side of market, food available. **F** *Hotel y Comedor San Antonio*. **F** *Mejía Batres*, ½ block from Parque Central, with bath, clean, friendly, excellent value. **F** *Rosario*, basic, on road to Siguatepeque.

Eating *Café El Ecológico*, corner of Parque Central, home-made cakes and pastries, fruit drinks, delicious home-made jams. *Lucky's*, excellent meat dishes as well as hamburgers. *Pizza Venezia*, on edge of town towards Marcala, good Italian dishes. *Restaurant Magus*, 1 block east of Plaza, 'good food in a formica video bar atmosphere'. Unnamed restaurant in front of Iglesia de la Esperanza, very good *comida corriente*, worth it.

Festivals The third week in **July** is the *Festival de la Papa*. **8 December** is the fiesta of the *Virgen de la Concepción*.

Transport Buses from La Esperanza to **Tegucigalpa** several daily, 1½ hrs (Cobramil, also to San Pedro Sula, and Joelito, 4 hrs, US$2.60), to **Siguatepeque** 0700, 0900, last at 1000, US$1.20, 2 hrs; bus, La Esperanza, Siguatepeque, Comayagua at 0600; buses also go from La Esperanza to the Salvadorean border; bus stops by market. Hourly minibuses to Yaramanguila, 30 mins. Daily bus to **Marcala** 2 hrs at 1230 (but check), US$0.80 (truck, US$1.20, 2¼ hrs). Minibus service at 1130, US$1.50. Daily minibus service to San Juan, dep between 1030-1200 from a parking space midway between the two bus stops, 2½ hrs, pick-ups also do this journey, very crowded; for Erandique, alight at Erandique turn off, 1 km before San Juan and wait for truck to pass (*comedor* plus basic *hospedaje* at intersection). If going to Gracias, stay on the La Eseranza-San Juan bus until the end of the line where a pick-up collects passengers 15 mins or so later, 1 hr San Juan-Gracias. Buses to Lake Yojoa, 2 hrs, US$2.50.

Directory Banks *Banco de Occidente*, *Banco Atlántida* and *Banadesa*.

Marcala

Colour map 6, grid C2
Population: 10,770
Altitude: 1,300m

From La Esperanza, an unpaved road runs southeast to Marcala in the Department of La Paz (a paved road goes to La Paz). During the hotter months from March to May, a cooler climate can be found in the highlands of La Paz, with pleasant temperatures during the day and cold (depending on altitude) at night. Ideal for hiking and with beautiful scenery and dramatic waterfalls in the surrounding area, Marcala is a good base from which to visit Yarula, Santa Elena, Opatoro, San José and Guajiquiro (see page 865). The Marcala region is one of the finest coffee-producing areas of Honduras and a visit to 'Comarca', at the entrance to town, gives a good idea of how coffee is processed. *Semana Santa* is celebrated with a large procession through the main street and there is a **fiesta** in honour of San Miguel Arcángel in the last week of September.

Sleeping **D-E** *Medina*, on main road through town, T898-1866, the most comfortable, clean, modern with bath, cafetería, free purified water. Highly recommended. **F** *Hospedaje Edgar*, main street, beginning of town, clean, basic, no sheets (under US$3). **F** *Hospedaje Jairo*, with bath, 2 blocks east of main square.

Eating *Café Express*, beside Esso, good breakfast and *comida corrida*. Recommended. *Darwin*, on main street in centre, cheap breakfasts from 0700. Recommended. *El Mirador*, on entering town by petrol station, nice views from veranda, good food. Recommended. *Jarito*, opposite market entrance, good. *Riviera Linda*, opposite *Hotel Medina*, pleasant atmosphere, spacious, a little pricey but good food.

Honduras

Entertainment Discotheque *Geminis*.

Transport Buses to **Tegucigalpa** 0500, 0915 and 1000 daily via La Paz, 4 hrs, US$2.40 (bus from Tegucigalpa at 0800 and 1400, Empresa Lila, 4-5 Av, 7 C, No 418 Comayagüela, opposite *Hispano* cinema); bus to **La Paz** only, 0700, 2 hrs, US$1; several minibuses a day, 1½ hrs, US$1.50. Bus also from Comayagua. Pick-up truck to **San José** at around 1000 from market, ask for drivers, Don Santos, Torencio, or Gustavo. Bus to **La Esperanza** at about 0830, unreliable, check with driver, Don Pincho, at the supermarket next to where the bus is parked (same street as *Hotel Medina*), 1½-2 hrs, otherwise hitching possible, going rate US$1.20. Bus to **San Miguel**, El Salvador, *Transportes Wendy Patricia*, 0500, 1200, 7 hrs, US$3.50, office ½ block southeast of market.

Directory **Banks** *Banco de Occidente*, *Banhcafé*, and *Banco Sogerín*.

Around Marcala

Near Marcala is Balneario **El Manzanal**, 3 km on the road to La Esperanza; it has a restaurant, two swimming pools and a boating lake, open weekends only. For panoramic views high above Marcala, follow this hike (one hour): head north past *Hotel Medina*, turn right (east) after the hotel and follow the road up into hills. After 2 km the road branches. Take the left branch and immediately on the left is a football field. A small path leaves from this field on the west side taking you through a small area of pine trees then out onto a ridge for excellent views. The track continues down from the ridge back to town, passing an unusual cemetery on a hill.

Estanzuela is an area next to a small village of the same name. A favourite spot to visit at weekends, it is a large grassy area next to a river where a dam has been built to provide an area for bathing, excellent camping (no food or drinks sold here). Best visited in the rainy season as the river is higher and the area greener. Take the road to La Esperanza from the Marcala to La Paz road. After 20 minutes (by car) take a right hand turning to Estanzuela. It is a one-hour walk from the turn-off passing the village of Estanzuela to the area.

There are caves nearby on **Musula** mountain, the Cueva de las Animas in Guamizales and Cueva de El Gigante and El León near La Estanzuela with a high waterfall close by. Other waterfalls are El Chiflador, 67 m high, Las Golondrinas, La Chorrera and Santa Rosita. Transport goes to La Florida where there is good walking to the village of **Opatoro** and climbing **Cerro Guajiquiro**. Between Opatoro and Guajiquiro is the **Reserva las Trancas**, a heavily forested mountain where quetzales have been seen.

Yarula and **Santa Elena** are two tiny municipalities, the latter about 40 km from Marcala, with beautiful views (bus Marcala-Santa Elena 1230 returns 0500 next day, two hours 45 minutes, enquire at Gámez bus office opposite market; truck daily 0830 returns from Santa Elena at 1300). Sometimes meals are available at *comedores* in Yarula and Santa Elena. The dirt road from Marcala gradually deteriorates, the last 20 km being terrible, high clearance essential, four-wheel drive recommended. In **La Cueva Pintada**, south of Santa Elena, there are pre-Columbian cave paintings (*pinturas rupestres*) of snakes, men and dogs; ask for a guide in Santa Elena. Ask also in this village about the *Danza de los Negritos*, performed at the annual **fiesta** of Santiago, 24-25 March, in front of the church. A special performance may be organized, the dancers wearing their old wooden masks, if suitable payment is offered.

Altitude: 1,700 m

The village of **San José** is a Lenca Indian community where the climate can be cool and windy even in the hottest months. The scenery is superb. Good hill walking (see box for two examples; there are many others; also rivers for swimming). Frequent pick-ups from Marcala, and two daily minibuses at about 0815 and 0900; from San José to Marcala minibuses depart at 0615 and 0645, one hour, US$1. There is a good *comedor* 500 m before plaza on main road, clean and cheap, and an unnamed hotel, **F**, run by British man, Nayo, or Nigel Potter, basic but comfortable and clean, with meals. He also takes groups to stay in Lenca villages, US$5 per person plus US$10 per person for accommodation in a village; ask for the house of Doña Gloria, Profe Vinda, Nayo or Ruth. At least one of these will be present to meet visitors. Nayo knows most

Hiking around San José

Hike 1 From San José (see page 862), head northwest down through Limón. Take a small path to the left towards some high ground, a large area covered with pine above some rocky escarpments, about one hour from the centre of San José. A 30-minute trail runs along the outer edge of the high ground with many vantage points overlooking the forest, canyons and mountains. There are many paths which lead down into valleys and canyons below, and a couple of small communities.

Hike 2 Five kilometres from San José is a turn-off called Cerro Bueno (ask locally for directions), with a few houses and a comedor. Explore the terrain to the south, where there are valleys, canyons and waterfalls. Ask for the path to Portillo Norte and Sapotal. Sapotal is a small community in an attractive valley from where you can continue via Aguacatal and Grandeo back to the main La Paz-Marcala road. There are many small villages in this fertile area and almost no tourists.

of the local pathways. There is good camping 10 minutes' walk away. (Write to Nigel J Potter at San José, Marcala, Depto La Paz, CP15201, Honduras.)

South of Marcala the road crosses into El Salvador, 3 km before Perquín (see page 808). There have been several confrontations with the Honduran military in the area but the border dispute has been settled by treaty. Ask locally for security conditions but more travellers are reporting no problems in crossing. There are buses from Marcala to San Miguel, El Salvador, and from Perquín to the frontier in the early morning. The rustic border crossing office is about 5 km inside Honduras. The road is not shown on some Honduran maps. **Border with El Salvador**

Nueva Ocotepeque

Heading south from Santa Rosa, Nueva Ocotepeque gives access to good hiking and leads to the borders with Guatemala and El Salvador. The old colonial church of La Vieja (or La Antigua) between Nueva Ocotepeque and the border, is in the village of Antigua Ocotepeque, founded in the 1540s, but destroyed by a flood from Cerro El Pital in 1934. *Colour map 6, grid B1*

The **Guisayote Biological Reserve** protects 35 sq km of cloud forest, about 50% virgin and is reached from the Western Highway, where there are trails and good hiking. Access is from El Portillo, the name of the pass on the main road north. El Portillo to El Sillón, the park's southern entrance, three to five hours. Twice daily *buseta* from El Sillón to Ocotepque. **El Pital**, 3 km east of Nueva Ocotepeque, but 2 km vertically above the town, 2,730 m; the third highest point in Honduras with several square kilometres of cloud forest. The park has not been developed for tourism.

The **Parque Nacional Montecristo** forms part of the Trifinio/La Fraternidad project, administered jointly by Honduras, Guatemala and El Salvador. The park is quite remote from the Honduran side, two to three days to the summit, but there are easy-to-follow trails. Access is best from Metapán in El Salvador. From the lookout point at the peak you can see about 90 of El Salvador and 20 of Honduras on a clear day. The natural resources office, for information, is opposite Texaco, two blocks from *Hotel y Comedor Congolón* at the south end of town. Raymond J Sabella of the US Peace Corps has written a very thorough description of the natural and historical attractions of the Department, including hikes, waterfalls and caves.

In Nueva Ocotepeque C *Sandoval*, opposite *Hondutel*, T653-3098, F653-3408, rooms and suites, breakfast included, private bath, hot water, cable TV, mini-bar, phone, room service, restaurant attached, good value. **D** *Maya Chortis*, Barrio San José, 4 C 3 Av NE, T653-3377, nice rooms with bath, double beds, hot water, fan, TV, mini-bar, phone, room service, quieter rooms at back, including breakfast, good restaurant, good value. **D** *Santander*, clean, good **Sleeping**

Honduras

restaurant. **E-F** *San Antonio*, 1 C, 3 Av, T653-3072, small rooms but OK. **F** *Gran*, with bath, cold water, pleasant, clean, single beds only, about 250 m from town at the junction of the roads for El Salvador and Guatemala, just north of town, at Sinuapa. **F** *Hotel y Comedor Congolón*, also bus agency, shared bath, very noisy in morning. **F** *Hotelito San Juan*, pleasant and cheap. **F** *Ocotepeque*, by *Transportes Toritos*, clean but noisy.

Eating Best at **Sandoval** and **Don Chepe** at *Maya Chortis*, excellent food, main courses US$4-6, small wine lists, good value. Recommended. **Comedor Nora**, Parque Central, and **Merendera Ruth**, 2 C NE, just off Parque Central, both offer cheap *comida corriente*, preferable to *comedores* around bus terminal.

Transport *Transportes Escobar* daily service Tegucigalpa-Nueva Ocotepeque/Agua Caliente, via La Entrada and Santa Rosa de Copán (12 Av entre 8 y 9 C, Barrio Concepción, Comayagüela, T237-4897; *Hotel Sandoval*, T653-3098, Nueva Ocotepeque). From Nueva Ocotepeque, buses to San Pedro Sula stop at La Entrada (US$1.70), 1st at 0030, for connections to Copán. There are splendid mountain views. From San Pedro Sula there are regular buses via Santa Rosa south (6 hrs, US$4.50); road is well paved.

Directory **Banks** *Banco de Occidente* will change TCs. *Banco Atlántida* has Visa facilities.

Border with Guatemala You can cross into Guatemala at Agua Caliente, 16 km from Nueva Ocotepeque. There are three banks (open 0800-1700, Saturday 0800-1500), a tourist office on the Honduran side, the *Comedor Hermanos Ramírez* for food, and one *hospedaje* (bargain).

This can be a busy crossing but is quicker, cheaper (less graft) and more efficient than the crossing at El Florido

Honduran immigration All formalities completed at the border, open 0700-1800. There is an army of money changers outside the Honduran Migración building, keep lempiras for exit stamp and minibus ride Agua Caliente-Atulapa.

Guatemalan consulate The nearest Guatemalan consulate is in San Pedro Sula.

Transport There are several buses a day from San Pedro Sula to Agua Caliente, 1st at 0300 (eg Congolón, Toritos) US$4.45, 6-7 hrs. Buses from Nueva Ocotepeque to Agua Caliente every 30 mins from 0630, US$0.60. Money changers get on the bus between Nueva Ocotepeque and the border, good rates for US$ cash. Minibuses go to Esquipulas, US$0.25, with connections to destinations in Guatemala.

Border with El Salvador Take bus from Nueva Ocotepeque to El Poy on the border, 15-20 mins, US$0.30. The exit tax is US$5.50. Buses leave El Poy to San Salvador regularly, 3-4 hrs.

Tegucigalpa to San Pedro Sula

Connecting the capital and the country's second largest city, San Pedro Sula, the main road heads north through beautiful scenery along the shore of Lago Yojoa, skirting villages of Lenca Indian communities. Though the tendency is to head north for the warmth and beauty of the beaches, a slow gentle journey along the road can be very rewarding.

Támara The Northern Highway between Tegucigalpa and San Pedro Sula leaves the capital and enters the vast valley of Támara, with the village of the same name. A turning leads to the San Matías waterfall, in a delightful area for walking in cool forested mountains.

Sleeping 500 m southwest of the toll station near the Balneario San Francisco is **F** *Hotel Posada Don Willy*, with bath (electric shower), clean, quiet, fan, excellent value.

The road climbs to the forested heights of **Parque Aventuras** at Km 33, open at weekends, good food, swimming pools, horses, bikes, then to **Zambrano** at Km 34 and **Parque Aurora** at Km 36, midway between Tegucigalpa and Comayagua. It has a small zoo, nice swimming pools and a picnic area among pine-covered hills, a lake with rowing boats (hire US$1 per hour), a snack bar and lovely scenery. Good bird-watching. This spot is perfect for camping and for large vehicles, which need to avoid the narrow streets and congestion of Tegucigalpa (camping US$0.50 per person, admission US$0.70, food supplies nearby). Zambrano village is west of the highway; there is not a lot there but, once off the main road, it is very peaceful with a good year-round climate, and good walking among the pine trees with several 100-m high waterfalls nearby.

Zambrano
Altitude: 1,450 m

Sleeping **A-C** *Casitas Primavera*, Barrio La Primavera (Zambrano), 1½ km west of main road, cosy, rustic houses, lovely setting, sleep 6 (arrangements can be made for 1 or 2 people, **E**), T898-6625 weekends, T239-2328 weekdays. **L-A** *Caserío Valuz*, T898-6755 (Zambrano), T996-4294 (mob), 15 rooms with bath, most with balconies, 1, 2 and 3-night packages including all meals, also rooms for backpackers, **E**, with use of kitchen, volunteer work in exchange for room and board possible, a great place to relax, hike, read, paint; it is 1½ km from the highway, 20 mins' walk on the road to Catarata Escondida. The Dippsa fuel station has a restaurant.

Transport From the capital take any bus going north to Comayagua, Siguatepeque or La Paz and tell the driver where you want to get off.

Before descending to the Comayagua valley, the Northern Highway reaches another forested mountainous escarpment. A track leads off to the right (ask for directions), with about 30 minutes' climb on foot to a tableland and the natural fortress of **Tenampua**, where Indians put up their last resistance to the conquistadores, even after the death of Lempira. It has an interesting wall and entrance portal.

Soon after the Tenampua turning, a short road runs west, through Villa San Antonio, to La Paz, capital of its Department in the western part of the Comayagua valley. From the new church of the Virgen del Perpetuo Socorro on the hill, there is a fine view of the town, the Palmerola airfield and the Comayagua Valley. The town's roads are all paved and it has a soccer stadium and many public services, thanks to ex-president Córdoba who lives there. The Casa de la Cultura in the centre has an attractive exhibit of Lenca handicrafts. ■ *Open daily*.

La Paz
Colour map 6, grid B2
Population: 19,900
Altitude: 690 m

A paved road runs southwest from La Paz to Marcala (see page 861, frequent minibuses two hours, US$1). 2 km off this road, at 1,400 m, lies **San Pedro de Tutule**, the marketplace for the Indians of **Guajiquiro** (one of the few pure Indian communities in Honduras), several kilometres south of Tutule. Markets are held Sunday morning and Thursday. Accommodation at **F** *Hospedaje Valestia*, good, basic, *comedor* opposite. **Ajuterique**, with a fine colonial church, is 5 km north of La Paz, on the paved road to Comayagua, and is worth a visit.

Sleeping and eating in Ajuterique All **F** *Pensión San Francisco* (quite nice). *Ali*, friendly, 5 rooms, bath, hot water, eat at *Ali's Restaurant*, food and lodging excellent. *Rico Lunch*, near church, good and friendly.

Transport Buses from Comayagua, Cotrapal (opposite Iglesia La Merced), every hour from 0600, US$0.40, passing Ajuterique and Lejamaní; frequent minibus Comayagua-La Paz, 35 mins, US$0.50. Lila bus from the capital, from opposite *Hispano* cinema in Comayagüela.

Honduras

Colectivo taxi from main north-south highway to La Paz, US$2. In La Paz all buses leave from boulevard crossroads, look for the statue of the soldier. Minibus to Marcala, 3 daily, 0530 0630, 0800, 1½ hrs, US$1.50.

Directory Banks *Bancahsa, Banco Atlántida* and *Banadesa.*

Comayagua

Colour map 6, grid B2
Population: 59,535
Altitude: 550 m

Founded on 7 December 1537 as Villa Santa María de Comayagua on the site of an Indian village, by Alonzo de Cáceres, Comayagua is a colonial town in the rich Comayagua plain, 1½ hours' drive (93 km) north from the capital. On 3 September 1543, it was designated the Seat of the Audiencia de los Confines by King Philip II of Spain. President Marco Aurelio Soto transferred the capital to Tegucigalpa in 1880.

There are many old colonial buildings in Comayagua, reflecting the importance of Honduras' first capital after Independence in 1821. The city is looking a little jaded these days, but is still worth a visit for the impressive architecture.

Comayagua was declared a city in 1557, 20 years after its founding. Within a couple of centuries a rash of civic and religious buildings were constructed. The former University, the first in Central America, was founded in 1632 and closed in 1842 (it was located in the Casa Cural, Bishop's Palace, where the bishops have lived since 1558). Others include the churches of La Merced (1550-58) and La Caridad (1730), San Francisco (1574) and San Sebastián (1575). San Juan de Dios (1590 but destroyed by earthquake in 1750), the church where the Inquisition sat, is now the site of the Santa Teresa Hospital. El Carmen was built in 1785. The wealth of colonial heritage has attracted funds for renovation which have produced a slow transformation in the town. The most interesting building is the **cathedral** in the Parque Central, inaugurated in 1711, with its plain square tower and façade decorated with sculpted figures of the saints, which contains some of the finest examples of colonial art in Honduras (closed 1300-1500). Of the 16 original hand-carved and golded altars, just four survive today. The clock in the tower was originally made over 800 years ago in Spain and is the oldest working clock in the Americas. It was given to Comayagua by Felipe II in 1582. At first it was in La Merced when that was the cathedral, but it was moved to the new cathedral in 1715. Half a block north of the cathedral is the ecclesiastical museum. ■ *Daily 0930-1200, 1400-1700, US$0.60.* One block south of the cathedral, at the corner of 6 Calle and 1 Avenida NO, is the **Museo de Arqueología** (housed in the former Palacio de Gobernación), small scale but fascinating, with six rooms each devoted to a different period. Much of the collection came from digs in the El Cajón region, 47 km north of Comayagua, before the area was flooded for the hydroelectricity project. ■ *Wed-Fri 0800-1600, Sat, Sun 0900-1200, 1300-1600, US$1.70.*

There are two colonial plazas shaded by trees and shrubs. A stone portal and a portion of the façade of Casa Real (the viceroy's residence) still survives. Built in 1739-41, it was damaged by an earthquake in 1750 and destroyed by tremors in 1856. The army still uses a quaint old fortress built when Comayagua was the capital. There is a lively market area.

In Easter Week festivities build to a crescendo, starting on Palm Sunday with a symbolic journey on a donkey, and continuing throughout the week following the religious elements of Holy Week, with processions through the streets.

Excursions The friendly coffee town of **La Libertad** (hourly bus, two hours, US$0.75) has several *hospedajes* and *comedores*. Before La Libertad is **Jamalteca** (1½ hrs by bus, US$0.50), from where it is a 40-minute walk to a large deep pool into which drops a 10-m waterfall surrounded by lush vegetation. Great place for a swim, picnic or camping, it is on private property and a pass must be obtained from the owner before visiting (ask at *Supermercado Carol* in Comayagua). Best to avoid weekends, when the owners' friends may be there.

Parque Nacional Montaña de Comayagua is only 13 km from Comayagua, reached from the villages of San José de la Mora (four-wheel drive necessary) or San Jerónimo and Río Negro (usually passable). Contact Fundación Ecosimco at 0 Calle y 1 Avenida NO in Comayagua, T772-4681, for further information about the trails which lead through the cloudforest to waterfalls. The mountain (2,407 m) has about 6,000 ha of cloud forest and is a major watershed for the area.

A-B *Santa María*, Km 82 on the Tegucigalpa Highway, T772-7872. Private bath, a/c, cable TV. Best hotel in town, although not in the centre. **C** *Quan*, 8 C NO, 3 y 4 Av, T772-0070, hquan@hondutel.hn Excellent, with private bath, popular.

Sleeping
Price codes:
see inside front cover

D *América Inc*, 2 Av y 1 C NO, T772-0360, a/c, hot water, private bath, TV, cheaper with fan. **D** *Imperial*, 3 Av SO, Barrio Torondón, opposite *Norymax*, T772-0215. With bath, fan, TV, clean, friendly, good value, parking. **D** *Norymax*, C Central y 3 Av SO, Barrio Torondón, T772-1210, a/c, all with bath, hot water, cheaper rooms available and car park. **D-E** *Emperador*, C Central y 4 Av SO, Barrio Torondón, T772-0332. Good, a/c, cable TV, cheaper with fan. **E** *Honduras*, 2 Av NO, 1 C, clean, friendly, some rooms with bath. **E** *Libertad*, south side of Parque Central. Nice courtyard, much choice of room size, clean apart from the toilets, cold water shower outside, helpful, good restaurant 2 doors away. **E** *Motel Puma*, off the same Blvd. Garage parking, hot water, with bath, caters for short-stay clientele.

F *Luxemburgo*, 4 Av NO y 2 C. Laundry facilities, good value, rooms at front are noisy. For **F**-grade *hospedajes* – basic, not very clean but cheap – try, *Galaxia*, *Miramar*, *Primavera*, *Terminal* and *Tío Luis*, all within a couple of blocks of the bus stop on the Panamericana.

Fruty Tacos, 4 C NO, just off southwest corner of Parque Central. Good snacks and *licuados*. *Hein Wong* on Parque Central. Chinese and international food, good, a/c, reasonable prices. *Juanis Burger Shop*, 1 Av NO, 5 C, near southwest corner of Parque Central. Friendly, good food, OK. *Las Palmeras*, south side of Parque Central, T772-0352, good breakfasts, open for dinner and lunch as well, good portions, reasonable prices. *Venecia*, in front of Supermercado Carol, T772-1734, popular café-style restaurant. *Villa Real*, behind the cathedral, T772-0101, mixes colonial atmosphere with good international and Honduran cuisine. Probably the best in town.

Eating
Parque Central is
surrounded by
restaurants and
fast-food
establishments

Cinema Valladolid, at north end of 2 Av.

Entertainment

Air The US military base at Palmerola, 8 km from Comayagua, was designated to be a commercial national and international airport in 1993, initially for cargo and later to take passenger traffic.

Transport

Buses To **Tegucigalpa**, US$1.10, every 45 mins, 2 hrs (Hmnos Cruz, Comayagua, T772-0850). To **Siguatepeque**, US$0.55 with Transpinares. To **San Pedro Sula**, US$1.50, 3 hrs, either catch a bus on the highway (very crowded) or go to Siguatepeque and change buses there. Incoming buses to Comayagua drop you on the main road outside town. From here you can walk or taxi into town. Buses depart from Torocagua: *colectivo* from C Salvador y Cervantes in town, **Car rental**: Amigo, on the road to Tegucigalpa and San Pedro Sula, T772-0371.

Banks Only *Bancahsa* near Parque Central changes TCs, but others for cash: *Banco Atlántida, Banco de Occidente, Bancahorro, Banco Sogerín, Banhcafé, Ficensa, Banadesa, Bamer* and *Banffaa*. **Medical services** Dentist: *Dr José de Jesús Berlioz*, next to Colegio León Alvarado, T772-0054. **Tour operators** *Cramer Tours* in Pasaje Arias. *Rolando Barahona*, Av Central. *Inversiones Karice's*, 4 Av NO, very friendly and helpful. **Useful addresses** Immigration: Migración is at 6 C NO, 1 Av, good place to get visas renewed, friendly.

Directory

The Northern Highway crosses the Comayagua plain, part of the gap in the mountains which stretches from the Gulf of Fonseca to the Ulúa lowlands. Set in forested highlands 32 km northwest of Comayagua is the town of Siguatepeque, which has a cool climate. It is the site of the Escuela Nacional de Ciencias Forestales (which is worth a visit) and, being exactly halfway between Tegucigalpa and San Pedro Sula (128 km), is a collection point for the produce of the Intibucá, Comayagua and

Siguatepeque
Colour map 6, grid B2
Population: 39,165
Altitude: 1,150 m

Honduras

Lempira departments. The Cerro and Bosque de Calanterique, behind the Evangelical Hospital, is a 45-minute walk from the town centre. The Parque Central is pleasant, shaded by tall trees with the church of San Pablo on the north side and the cinema, *Hotel Versalles* and *Boarding House Central* on the east; *Hondutel* and the post office are on the south side.

Sleeping **D** *Zari*, T773-2015. Hot water, cable TV, own generator, parking. **E** *Boarding House Central*, Parque Central, T773-2108. Simple, but very good value, beware of the dog which bites. **E** *Internacional Gómez*, 21 de Junio, T773-2868. With bath, **F** without, hot water, clean, use of kitchen on request, parking. **F** *Mi Hotel*, 1 km from highway on road into town. With bath, parking, restaurant. **F** *Versalles*, on Parque Central. Excellent, with restaurant.

Eating *Bicos*, southwest corner of Parque Central. Nice snack bar/patisserie. *Cafetería Colonial*, 4 Av SE (just behind the church). Good pastries and coffee, outside seating. *Juanci's*, also on main street. US-style hamburgers, good steaks and snacks, open until 2300. *Pollos Kike*, next door. Pleasant setting, fried chicken. *Supermercado Food* has a good snack bar inside. There are several restaurants on the Northern Highway, including *Granja d'Elia*, open all day, lots of vegetables, also meat, All-U-Can-Eat buffet US$2.50, French chef, veg from own market garden and bread on sale outside. Recommended. *Nuevo* and *Antiguo Bethania*, quite a long way out of town, good, cheap and huge meals.

Shopping A good leatherworker is Celestino Alberto Díaz, Barrio San Antonio, Casa 53, 2 C NE, 6 Av NE. 1 block north of Celestino's is a good shoemaker, leather shoes made for US$25.

Transport Bus to **San Pedro Sula**, from the west end of town every 35 mins, US$1.35. **Tegucigalpa** with *Empresas Unidas* or *Maribel*, from west plaza, south of market, US$1.50, 3 hrs. Alternatively take a taxi, US$0.50, 2 km to the highway intersection and catch a Tegucigalpa-San Pedro Sula bus which passes every ½ hr. To **Comayagua**, *Transpinares*, US$0.50, 45 mins; to **La Esperanza** buses leave from near *Boarding House Central*, 1st departure 0530, several daily, taxi from town centre US$0.50.

Directory **Banks** *Bancahsa*, *Banco Atlántida*, *Banco de Occidente* and *Banco Sogerín*.

Southwest from Siguatepeque, a beautiful paved road travels through lovely forested mountainous country, via **Jesús de Otoro** (two basic *hospedajes* and Balneario San Juan de Quelala, US$0.30 entry, cafetería and picnic sites), to La Esperanza (see page 860). North from Siguatepeque, the Highway goes over the forested escarpment of the continental divide, before descending towards Lago Yojoa. Just south of **Taulabé** on the highway are the caves of Taulabé (illuminated), with both stalactites and bats. ■ *Open daily, US$0.40. Guides available.* Just north of Taulabé, and 16 km south of the lake, and is the turn-off northwest of a paved road to Santa Bárbara (see page 870).

Lago Yojoa
Colour map 6, grid B2
Altitude: 635 m

Sitting pretty among the mountains is the stunningly impressive Lake Yojoa, 22½ km long and 10 km wide. To the west rise the Montañas de Santa Bárbara which include the country's second highest peak and the **Parque Nacional de Santa Bárbara** (see page 870). To the east is the **Parque Nacional Montaña Cerro Azul-Meámbar**. Pumas, jaguars and other animals live in the forests, pine-clad slopes and the cloud forest forming part of the reservoir of the Lago Yojoa basin. The national parks also have many waterfalls. The 50-sq km Azul-Meámbar park is 30 km north of Siguatepeque and its highest point is 2,047 m. To get to any of the entry points (Meámbar, the main one, Jardines, Bacadia, Monte Verde or San Isidro) a four-wheel drive is necessary. A local ecological group, *Ecolago*, has marked out the area and is to offer guided tours of the park. *Ecolago* has guides who are expert in spotting regional birds; at least 373 species have been identified around the lake. At one time the lake was full of bass, but overfishing and pollution have decimated the fish stocks. Efforts are being made to clean up the lake and limited fishing is again possible. ■ *For local information contact Enrique Campos or his son at Motel Agua Azul (see below). For more information, contact Proyecto Humuya, behind Iglesia Betel, 21 de Agosto, Siguatepeque (T773-2426), or Proyecto de Desarrollo Río Yure, San Isidro, Cortés, Apartado 1149, Tegucigalpa.*

The Northern Highway follows the eastern margin to the lake's southern tip at **Pito Solo**, where sailing and motor boats can be hired. On the northern shore of Lago Yojoa is a complex of pre-Columbian settlements called **Los Naranjos**, which are believed to have had a population of several thousand. It is considered to be the country's third most important archaeological site spanning the period from 1000 BC to AD 1000 , and including two ball courts. The site is slowly being developed for tourism by the Institute of Anthropology and History but it may take several years for the site to open to the public. For the timebeing there is a forest walking trail. Excavation work is currently in progress and you can visit the site, but be warned that all you will see is work in progress. The local office of the Institute (T557-8197) is at the *Hotel Brisas de Lago*. From the lake it is 37 km down to the hot Ulúa lowlands.

Sleeping and eating L *Gualiqueme*, luxurious cottage at edge of lake, for information contact Richard Joint at Honduyate, T882-3129, F882-3620. 4 bedrooms in main house, 2 in annex, daily, weekly, monthly rental, weekend packages include ferry and fishing boat. **A-C** *Brisas del Lago*, close to Peña Blanca at the northern end of the lake, T553-4884, F553-3341. Large hotel, good restaurant but overpriced, launches for hire.

B-C *Oasi Italiana*, on San Pedro Sula Highway in Yoya Cortés, some 20 km from the lake, T991-1195. Motel rooms with fans or a/c, swimming pool and great Italian food. **B** *Finca Las Glorias*, close to Peña Blanca, T566-0462, F566-0553, www.hotellasglorias.com Bath, a/c, hot water, TV, bar, good restaurant, pool, great views – currently being restored. **C-D** *Hotel Agua Azul* (at north end of lake, about 3 km west from junction at Km 166), T/F991-7244. Basic clean cabins for 2 or more persons, meals for non-residents, but food and service in restaurant is poor, beautiful gardens, manager speaks English, swimming pool, fishing, horse-riding and boating, launches for hire, mosquito coils. Good reduction in low season. Recommended (except when loud karaoke is in full swing). **C** *Los Remos*, T557-8054, has cabins and camping facilities (**F**) at Pito Solo, at the south end of the lake, and rooms in **E** range, clean, beautiful setting, good food, nice for breakfasts, no beach but swimming pool, boat trips, parking US$3.

Comedores on the roadside serving bass fish caught in the lake. *Restaurant Margoth*, 1 km north of *Los Remos*. Recommended. Roadside stalls near Peña Blanca sell fruit. Buses between Tegucigalpa and San Pedro stop to let passengers off at *Los Remos*, and at Peña Blanca, 5 km from the turning for *Agua Azul.*

Transport Bus to Lake from San Pedro Sula, US$1, 1½ hrs; bus from Lake to Tegucigalpa with Hedmán-Alas, US$3, 3-5 hrs, 185 km.

A paved road skirts the lake's northern shore for 12 km via Peña Blanca. One unpaved road heads southwest to **El Mochito**, Honduras' most important mining centre. A bus from 2 Avenida in San Pedro Sula goes to Las Vegas-El Mochito mine where there is a cheap *pensión* (**F**) for walks along the west side of Lago Yojoa. Buses will generally stop anywhere along east side of lake. Another unpaved road heads north from the northern shore, through Río Lindo, to **Caracol** on the Northern Highway. This road gives access to the Pulhapanzak waterfall, with some unexcavated ceremonial mounds adjacent, and to Ojo de Agua, a pretty bathing spot near Caracol.

Peña Blanca is, according to one reader, a 'very ugly town' on the north side of the lake. Almost makes you want to stay. **Sleeping** The options are **F** *Hotel Maranata*, clean, near bus stop, friendly, and *Comedor Vista Hermosa*, nearby has good, cheap food. *Brisas del Canal*, local food. Recommended, but small portions. *Panadería Yoja*, one block from *Hotel Maranata*, good juices and pastries.

The impressive 42-m waterfall at Pulhapanzak is on the Río Lindo. There is swimming in terrace-like pools about 20 minutes' walk from Pulhapanzak (for a small tip

Pulhapanzak waterfall

Honduras

boys will show off their diving skills). The waterfall is beautiful during, or just after the rainy season, and in sunshine there is a rainbow at the falls. There is a picnic area, a small cafetería and a good *comedor* 15 minutes' walk away down in the village, but the site does get crowded at weekends and holidays; there is a small admission charge (US$1). The caretaker allows camping for US$0.85. Recommended. There are two rooms available (under US$3) and a hotel is planned. Leave early for the trip.

Transport By car it's a 1½-hr drive from San Pedro, longer by bus. There is a bus from Peña Blanca every 2 hrs to the falls, or take a Mochito or Cañaveral bus from San Pedro Sula from the bus station near the railway (hourly 0500-1700) and get off at the sign to the falls, at the village of Santa Buena Ventura, US$0.95. Alternatively stay on the bus to Cañaveral (take identification because there is a power plant here), and walk back along the Río Lindo, 2 hrs past interesting rock formations and small falls. Last bus returns at 1630 during the week.

Santa Bárbara

Colour map 6, grid B2
Population: 23,000
Altitude: 290 m

Santa Bárbara, surrounded by high mountains, forested hills and rivers, lies in a hot lowland valley 32 km west of Lago Yojoa (see page 868). One of the nicest main towns in Honduras, it has little of architectural or historical interest compared with Gracias, Ojojona or Yuscarán, but it is here that you will find Panama hats and other goods made from *junco* palm. The majority of the population is fair-skinned (some redheads) and the people are vivacious. In addition to being a pleasant place to stay, Santa Bárbara is also a good base for visiting villages throughout the Santa Bárbara department. Nearby the ruined colonial city of **Tencoa** has recently been rediscovered. A short local trek behind the town climbs the hills to the ruined site of **Castillo Bogran**, with fine views across the valley and the town. Heading south out of Santa Bárbara, the paved road joins the Northern Highway south of Lago Yojoa.

Excursions
The Department of Santa Bárbara is called the *Cuna de los Artesanos* (cradle of artisans), with over 10,000 craftspeople involved in the manufacture of handicrafts. The main products come from the small *junco* palm, for example fine hats and baskets. The main towns for *junco* items are **La Arada**, 25 minutes from Santa Bárbara on the road to San Nicolás (see below) and then branching off south, and **Ceguaca**, on a side road off the road to Tegucigalpa. Flowers and dolls from corn husks are made in Nueva Celilac (see also below). *Mezcal* is used to make carpets, rugs and hammocks, which are easy to find in towns such as **Ilama**, on the road to San Pedro Sula, which has one of the best small colonial churches in Honduras (no accommodation). People here also make *petates* (rugs) and purses.

Between Santa Bárbara and Lago Yojoa is the **Parque Nacional de Santa Bárbara** which contains the country's second highest peak, Montaña de Santa Bárbara at 2,744 m. The rock is principally limestone with many subterranean caves. There is little tourist development as yet, with just one trail, and you can track down a guide in Los Andes, a village above Peña Blanca and Las Vegas. The best time to visit is the dry season, January-June. For more information contact Asociación Ecológica Corazón Verde, at the Palacio Municipal, Santa Bárbara. There is a Cohdefor office just below the market (look for the sign) but they are not helpful.

In the Department of Santa Bárbara is an area known as **El Resumidero**, home to the Quezapaya mountain, and six others over 1,400 m, as well as a number of caves (Pencaligüe, Los Platanares, El Quiscamote, and others). From Santa Bárbara, go southwest to El Níspero and then to El Quiscamote. Or go to San Vicente Centenario (thermal springs nearby), and on to San Nicolás, Atima, Berlín, and La Unión, all of which have thermal waters, fossils, petrified wood and evidence of volcanic activity.

San Nicolás, which is 20 km from Santa Bárbara on a paved road, was founded on 20 February 1840 after the disappearance of Viejo Celilac, near Cerro Capire. There is a nice Catholic church and, in the centre of town, is the big tree called *Anacahuite* – in Lenca 'place of reunion' – planted in 1927. Other points of interest are La Peña, Las Cuevas del Masical (you will probably not find them on your own, a local guide will take you to the caves for a fee), Quebrada Arriba and El Violín. You can drive to the ruined church of Viejo Celilac and on to Nueva Celilac, high on the mountain, a pleasant little town with a Vía Crucis procession on Good Friday.

North of Santa Bárbara is **Colinas**, also reached by bus from San Pedro Sula (from near Avenida Los Leones). The village is picturesque, with a basic *pensión* (**G**), near the church; excellent set meals from *Chinita* near the gas station. Climb the mountain with El Gringo Guillermo (Bill Walton) to Laguna Colorada, US$3 (a long drive through coffee *fincas*); he plans to build tourist cabins.

C-E *Boarding House Moderno*, Barrio Arriba, T643-2203, rooms with fan better value than with a/c, with hot shower, quiet, parking. Recommended. **C-E** *Gran Hotel Colonial*, 1½ blocks from Parque Central, T643-2665, fans in all rooms, some with a/c, cold water, sparsely furnished, friendly, clean, good view from roof. Recommended. **F** *Hospedaje Rodríguez*, with bath, dark, clean, friendly, helpful, walls don't meet the ceiling, noisy. **F** *Rosileí*, clean, pleasant, *comedor* attached. **F** *Ruth*, C La Libertad, T643-2632, rooms without windows, fan.

Sleeping

Comedor Everest, by bus stop on Parque Central, friendly, good *comida corriente*. *Comedor Norma*, family food, friendly. *Doña Ana*, 1 block above Parque Central, no sign but restaurant in Ana's dining room, crammed with bric-a-brac, only meat, rice, beans and bananas, plentiful and good food if a little boring. *El Brasero*, ½ block below Parque Central, extensive menu of meat, chicken, fish, Chinese dishes, good food, well prepared. Recommended. *Las Tejas*, near Rodríguez, friendly, good pizzeria. *Pizzería Don Juan*, Av Independencia, very good pizzas. *Repostería Charle's*, on Parque Central, excellent cakes, pastries, about the only place open for breakfast. On main street, *McPollo*, clean, smart, good, and *Comedor Remembranzas del Verde*, good, cheap *comida corriente*.

Eating

Buses to **Tegucigalpa**, 0700 and 1400 daily, weekends 0900, US$3, 4½ hrs with *Transportes Junqueños* (passing remote villages in beautiful mountain scenery); to **San Pedro Sula**, 2 hrs, US$1.90, 7 a day between 0500 and 1630. Bus to San Rafael at 1200, 4 hrs. Onward bus to **Gracias** leaves next day.

Transport

Banks *Banadesa*, *Bancafé*, *Banco Atlántida*, *Banco de Occidente* and *Banco Sogerín*.

Directory

Continuing towards the coast, 10 km north of Lake Yojoa on the Northern Highway, is the turn-off for the village of **Santa Cruz de Yojoa** (**F** *Hospedaje Paraíso*, with bath, clean, fan, friendly), and at 24 km is the **El Cajón** hydroelectric project (to visit the dam apply at least 10 days in advance: T222-2177, or in writing to Oficina de Relaciones Públicas de la ENEE, 1 Avenida, Edif Valle-Aguiluz, Comayagüela, DC). El Cajón hydroelectric dam (226 m high) has formed a 94-sq km lake, which lies between the departments of Cortés, Yoro and Comayagua. The dam is 22 km from Santa Cruz de Yojoa.

Santa Cruz de Yojoa
Colour map 6, grid B2

At Km 46, south of San Pedro Sula, a paved road runs east through banana plantations to Santa Rita, and from there either east to Yoro, or north to Progreso and Tela. This allows drivers heading between Tegucigalpa and the north coast to shorten their route by avoiding San Pedro Sula. Shortly before San Pedro Sula, the road divides and becomes a toll road.

San Pedro Sula

San Pedro Sula is the second largest and most industrialized city in the country and a centre for the banana, coffee, sugar and timber trades. It is a distribution hub for northern and western Honduras with good road links. Its business community is mainly of Arab origin, and it is considered the fastest growing city between Mexico and Panama.

Colour map 6, grid B2
Population: 500,000
Altitude: 60-150 m

Honduras

Honduras

By Central American standards, San Pedro Sula is a well-planned, modern city, but it's not a city you'll be inclined to stay in for long, although if you do have to stop, there is enough to keep you entertained.

Ins & outs

Getting there San Pedro Sula is a more important international gateway than Tegucigalpa. Its **airport**, Ramón Villeda Morales (SAP) is 15 km from the city centre along a good 4-lane highway. See also page 875. There is no bus station; companies have their own terminals, mostly in the southwest part of the city.

The higher and cooler suburb of Bella Vista, with its fine views over the city, affords relief from the intense heat of the town centre

Getting around The city is divided into 4 quadrants: Noreste (Northeast, NE), Noroeste (Northwest, NO), Sudeste (Southeast, SE) and Sudoeste (Southwest, SO), where most of the hotels are located, although newer hotels, shopping malls and restaurant chains are in the Noroeste. There are buses, minibuses and taxis for getting around town. Though pleasant in the cooler season from Nov-Feb, temperatures are very high for the rest of the year. It is, nevertheless, a green city, clean and the traffic is not too bad.

Background The city was founded by Pedro de Alvarado on 27 June 1536 in the lush and fertile valley of the Ulúa (Sula) River, beneath the forested slopes of the Merendón mountains. The flooding that accompanied Hurricane Mitch all but wiped out the banana plantations in the Ulúa valley, east and north of San Pedro Sula. Now it has been replanted and exports have recommenced.

Sights The large neocolonial-style **cathedral** was completed in the 1950s. **Museo de Antropología e Historia**, 3 Avenida, 4 Calle NO, has displays of the cultures that

San Pedro Sula

N		
0 metres (approx) 300		
0 yards (approx) 300		

Sleeping ■	6 Gran Hotel Sula	12 Suites Delvalle	4 Citul
1 Acrópolis	7 Montecristo		5 Toritos y
2 Bolívar	8 Palace Internacional	**Transport** 🚌	Copanecos
3 Brisas del Occidente	9 París	1 Hedmán Alas	6 Atlántico
4 Ejecutivo	10 San José	2 El Rey	7 Gama & Casasola
5 Gran Hotel San Pedro	11 San Juan	3 Impala	

nce inhabited the Ulúa valley up to Spanish colonization and, on the first floor, ocal history since colonization. ■ *Open Mon, Wed-Sat, 0900-1600, Sun 0900-1500, US$0.75. First Sun of the month is free.* There is a museum café in the adjacent garden with fine stela and a good set lunch. **Museo Jorge Milla Oviedo**, 3 Avenida 9 Calle NE, Barrio Las Acacias, T552-5060, run by the foundation which cares for the Cuero Salado Wildlife reserve (see page 891). **Expocentro**, Avenida Junior, off Boulevard to Puerto Cortés, has temporary exhibitions, conferences and fairs. For train enthusiasts there is an old steam engine on display next to the train station.

A taxi ride up the mountain behind the city has good views and costs US$2-2.50. Parque Nacional Cusuco, 20 km west of San Pedro Sula, offers some excellent hikes, trails and bird-watching in cloud forest – see below.

Excursions

LL *Camino Real Inter-Continental*, T553-0000, F550-6255, Blvd del Sur at Centro Comercial Multiplaza, full service, new and the best in town. **LL** *Copantl*, Col Los Arcos, Blvd del Sur, T556-8900, F556-8848, copantl2@copantl.hn   Corporate rates available, Olympic-sized pool, tennis courts, gym, sauna, disco, casino (the only one in town, foreigners only, take passport), car and travel agencies. **AL** *Holiday Inn*, Boulevard Morazán, 1ra calle between Av 10 y 11, T550-8080, ventas@holiday-inn.sps.com Gym, pool, 24-hr coffee shop. Best location in town, walking distance to the main square and restaurants. **AL** *Suites Delvalle*, Apart-hotel, 6 Av 11C NO, T552-0134, F552-0137, fcastro@globalnet.hn Big, comfortable rooms with cooker, fridge, cable TV, coffee machine in hall, buns provided for breakfast, good.

A-B *Palace Internacional*, 3 C 8 Av SO, Barrio El Benque, T550-3838, F550-0969. A/c, helpful staff, internet service, parking, pool, bar, restaurant OK. **B-C** *Ejecutivo*, 2 C 10 Av SO, T552-4289, F552-5868, a/c, cable TV, café/bar, phone, own generator. **C** *Acrópolis*, 3 C 2 y 3 Av SE, T/F557-2121. A/c, cable TV, parking, café, comfortable, friendly, good value. **C** *Bolívar*, 2 C 2 Av NO, T553-3224, F553-4823. Recently redecorated (but not all rooms), a/c, TV, own generator, pool, restaurant, OK but reception unhelpful. **C** *Gran Hotel San Pedro*, 3 C 2 Av SO, T550-1513, F553-2655. Private bath, a/c, **E** with fan, popular, clean, good value, rooms overlooking street are noisy, stores luggage, secure parking. **C** *Manhattan*, 7 Av 3-4 C SO, T550-2316. A/c, a bit run down. **D** *Palmira 1*, 6 C 6 y 7 Av SO, T553-6522. Clean, convenient, large parking area. **D** *Terraza*, 6 Av 4-5 C SO, T550-3108, F557-4798. Dining room dark, friendly staff, **E** without a/c.

E *El Nilo*, 3 C 2 Av SO, T553-4689. Nice rooms, friendly. **E** *La Siesta*, 7 C 2 Av SE, T552-2650, F558-0243. Private bath, a/c or fan, double or twin beds, clean, but noisy. **F** *Brisas del Occidente*, 5 Av 6-7 C SO, T552-2309. 5-storey building, fan, some rooms without window, laundry facilities, friendly, grubby. **F** *Montecristo*, 2 Av 7 C SE, T557-1370. Noisy, not very clean, fan, safe. **F** *París*, 3 Av 3 C SO, near *El Nilo* and bus station for Puerto Cortés. Shared bath, poor water supply, clean but noisy. **F** *San José*, 6 Av 5 y 6 C SO, just round corner from *Norteños* bus station, T557-1208. Friendly, clean, safe, cheap and cheerful. **F-G** *San Juan*, 6 C 6 Av SO, T553-1488. Modern building, very noisy, clean, helpful, good value. **F** *Parador*, 6 C 1 Av SE, safe, good value.

Sleeping
■ *on map*
Price codes: see inside front cover

International In all the top hotels and *Applebees*, Circunvalación, is highly recommended with good food, good service, good prices. *Bar El Hijo del Cuervo*, 13 C 7-8 Av NO, Barrio Los Andes. Authentic Mexican cuisine, informal setting of *champas* in tropical garden with fountain, à la carte menu, tacos, *quesadillas*. *Chef Mariano*, 16 Av 9-10 C SO, Barrio Suyapa, T552-5492. Garífuna management and specialities, especially seafood, Honduran and international cuisine, attentive service, a/c, not cheap but good value, open daily for lunch and dinner. *Copa de Oro*, 2 Av 2 y 3 C SO. Extensive Chinese and western menu, a/c, pleasant. Recommended. *Don Udo's*, Blvd Los Próceres, restaurant and café-bar, T553-3106. Dutch owner, big international menu, good wine list, Sun brunch 1000-1400. *Gamba Tropic*, 5 Av 4-5 C SO. Delicious seafood, good wine, medium prices, a/c. Recommended. *Italia y Más*, 1 C 8 Av NO. Genuine Italian food, pizza, homemade ice-cream, very good. *La Espuela*, Av Circunvalación, 16 Av 7 C. Good grilled meats. Recommended. *La Fortuna*, 2 C 7 Av NO. Chinese and international, very good, not expensive, smart, good service, a/c. *La Huerta de España*, 21 Av 2 C SO, Barrio Río de Piedras, 4 blocks west of Av Circunvalación. Supposedly

Eating

Honduras

best Spanish cuisine in town, open daily until 2300. *Las Tejas*, 9 C 16 y 17 Av, A Circunvalación. Good steaks and fine seafood, as also at nearby sister restaurant *La Tejana* 16 Av 19 C SO, Barrio Suyapa, T557-5276. *Pamplona*, on plaza, opposite *Gran Hotel Sula* Pleasant décor, good food, strong coffee, excellent service. *Pat's Steakhouse*, Av Circunvalación SO. Very good. *Shanghai*, 4 Av, C Peatonal. Good Chinese, popular on Sun a/c. *Sim Kon*, 17 Av 6 C NO, Av Circunvalación. Arguably the best Chinese in town. Enormous portions. Try *arroz con camarones* (prawns with rice). *TGI Friday's*, Blvd Los Próceres, 1 block from Av Circunvalación. 1st branch of US chain in Honduras, new, smart, a/c.

Cafés *Café del Campo*, 5 C 10 Av NO. Best coffee in town, 20 varieties, good à la carte breakfasts, big sandwiches, fish and prawn specialities US$6-8, bartender is cocktail specialist smart, a/c, good service, very nice. *Café Nani*, 6 Av 1-2 C SO. Very good *pastelería*. *Café Skandia*, ground floor, *Gran Hotel Sula*. Open 24 hrs, best place for late night dinners and early breakfasts, good club sandwiches, good service. *Café Suisse*, Blvd los Oroceres, across the street from *Frogs*, Swiss specialities. *Café Venecia*, 6 Av 4-5 C. Good juices, cheap. *Espresso Americano*, 2 branches, in C Peatonal, 4 Av, off southwest corner of Parque Central, and in Megaplaza shopping mall. Closed Sun, great coffee, cookies. *La Fuente de Salud y Juventud*, Av 8 SO y C 5 and 6. Vegetarian lunch counter, generous portions, nice outside patio, get there early (1130-1200), very popular and food goes fast.

Bars & nightclubs

Bars A thriving night life exists beyond the casinos. *Frogs Sports Bar*, Blvd Los Próceres, just above *Don Udo's*. 3 different bars, a/c, pool tables, 2nd-storey open deck overlooking their own beach volleyball court, giant TV screens showing US sports, snack bar, disco at weekends (karaoke), open 1700 until late, happy hour 1800-1900. *Mango's*, 16 Av 8-9 C SO, Barrio Suyapa. Open 1900 onwards, open terrace, pool tables, dance floor, rock music, snacks. Other nightclubs include *Henry's* and *Confetis*, both on Av Circunvalación NO; more exclusive is *El Quijote*, 11 C 3-4 Av SO, Barrio Lempira, cover charge.

Entertainment

Cinemas There are 8 a/c cinemas, all showing Hollywood movies, look in local press for details. **Theatre** *The Círculo Teatral Sampedrano* stages occasional amateur productions (see below, Cultural centres). The *Proyecto Teatral Futuro*, is a semi-professional company presenting contemporary theatre of Latin American countries and translations of European playwrights, as well as ballet, children's theatre, and workshops. Offices and studio-theatre at 4 C 3-4 Av NO, Edif INMOSA, 3rd Flr, T552-3074.

Festivals The city's main festival, *Feria Juniana*, is in the last days of **June**.

Shopping

Bookshops *La Casa del Libro*, 1 C 5-6 Av SO. Comprehensive selection of Spanish and English-language books, good for children's books and games, microfiche information, central, just off Parque Central. *Librería Atenea*, Edif Trejo Merlo, 1 C 7 Av SO. Wide choice of Latin American, US and British fiction, philosophy, economics and so on. *Librería Cultura*, 1 C 6-7 Av SO, cheap paperbacks, Latin American classics. *Librería Editorial Guaymuras*, 10 Av 7 C NO. Wide range of Hispanic authors, including their own publications.

Food *Gourmet Foods*, Blvd Los Próceres, between *Don Udo's* and *Frogs*. Delicatessen, lots of expensive goodies, eg French and Dutch cheeses, caviar, smoked salmon, Italian sausages, champagne, etc, T553-3106 (home delivery). *Supermercado Colonial*, good supermarket, strategically located at the intersection of C Oeste and Av Circunvalación.

Handicrafts Large artesan market, Mercado Guamilito Artesanía, 6 C 7-8 Av NO. Typical Honduran handicrafts at good prices (bargain), with a few imported goods from Guatemala and Ecuador, also good for fruit and vegetables. Open 0800-1700. *Danilo's Pura Piel*, factory and shop 18 Av B/9 C SO. *Honduras Souvenirs*, C Peatonal No 7, mahogany woodcraft. The *IMAPRO Handicraft School* in El Progreso has a retail outlet at 1 C 4-5 Av SE, well worth visiting, fixed prices, good value, good mahogany carvings. *La Maison du Cuir*, Av Circunvalación opposite *Los Andes* supermarket. *La Placita*, 6 C, 9 A, NE, great for souvenirs,

Honduras

cigars and coffee,which you can sample first! Open Mon-Sat. For fine leatherwork, *Latino's Leather*, 7 C 12-13 Av SO, superb bags, belts, briefcases, etc. *Lesanddra Leather* at Megaplaza Shopping Mall. The *Museum Gift Shop*, at the Museo de Antropología e Historia has lots of cheap *artesanía* gifts open during museum visiting hours.

Local Local buses cost US$0.10, smaller minibuses cost US$0.20. **Car rentals**: *Avis*, 1 C, 6 Av NE, T553-0888; **Blitz**, *Hotel Sula* and airport (T552-2405 or 668-3171); **Budget**, 1C 7Av NO, T552-2295, airport T668-3179; **Maya Eco Tours**, 3 Av NO, 7-8 C, and airport (T552-2670 or 668-3168); **Molinari**, *Hotel Sula* and airport (T553-2639 or 668-6178); **Toyota**, 3 Av 5 y 6 C NO, T557-2666 or airport T668-3174. Rental of a 4WD car costs US$85 per day includes tax and insurance after bargaining, good discounts for long rental. **Car repairs**: *Invanal*, 13 C, 5 y 6 Av Northeast, T552-7083, excellent service from Sr Víctor Mora. **Bike repairs**: there are few shops for parts. One with some imported parts is *Dibisa* on 3 Av y 11 C SO. **Taxi**: ask the price first and bargain if necessary. Parque Central to Av Circunvalación costs about US$1.50, to *Hotel Copantl* US$4.

Transport *If coming from the south, and wishing to avoid the city centre when heading for La Lima or El Progreso, follow signs to the airport*

Long distance Air A taxi to the airport costs US$8 per taxi, but bargain hard. No hotels near the airport. Yellow airport taxis cost US$13. Free airport shuttle from big hotels. Buses and *colectivos* do not go to the airport terminal itself; you have to walk the final kilometre from the La Lima road (bus to this point, US$0.10). Parking US$3.50 a day, but park close to the entrance as several cars stolen in 2001. Duty free, Global One phones, *Bancahsa* for Visa and Amex Tcs (two other banks don't change TCs – money changers give a good rate for dollars and will exchange lempiras into dollars), restaurant on 2nd floor. Flights to Tegucigalpa (35 mins), La Ceiba, Utila and to Roatán. See Essentials for international flights.

    Buses To **Tegucigalpa**, 4½ hrs, 250 km by paved road, main bus services with comfortable coaches and terminals in the town centre are: *Hedmán Alas*, 8-9 Av NO, 3 C, T553-1361, 0630 to 1730 (US$5), recommended, TV movies; *Transportes Sáenz*, 8 Av 5-6 C SO, T553-4969, better buses, meals, US$8; *El Rey*, Av 7, C 5 y 6, T553-4264, or *Express* 10 Av 8-9 C, Barrio Paz Barahona, T557-8355; *Transportes Norteños*, 6 C 6-7 Av, T552-2145, last bus at 1900; *Viana*, Av Circunvalación, T556-9261. The road to **Puerto Cortés** is paved; a pleasant 45-min journey down the lush river valley, buses to Puerto Cortés with *Empresa Impala*, 2 Av, 4-5 C SO No 23, T553-3111, several each hour, or Citul, 6 Av, 7-8 C. To **Omoa** (3 C East from 0600), east to **La Lima**, **El Progreso**, **Tela** and **La Ceiba** (Tupsa and Catisa, 2 Av SO, 5-6 C, hourly on the ½ hr between 0530 and 1830, US$2.50, 2½-3 hrs) some with a change in El Progreso, others direct. Also first class to La Ceiba with *Viana* at 10:30 am and 5:30 pm To **Trujillo**, 3 per day, a/c, US$5, 6 hrs, comfortable, Cotraibal departs from 1 Av, 7-8 C SE.

    Buses run south to **Lago Yojoa** and Tegucigalpa, and southwest to **Santa Rosa** and then through the Department of Ocotepeque, with its magnificent mountain scenery, to the **Guatemalan border** (US$3.40 to the border by bus). Congolón and Torito/Copanecos, 6-7 Av, 11C SO (1 block from the Citul bus arriving from Puerto Cortés), serve **Nueva Ocotepeque** (US$5) and **Agua Caliente** on the Guatemalan border with 7 buses a day; Congolón, 8 Av 10 C SO, T553-1174, Torito, 11 C 7 Av SO, T557-3691,1 block apart; to **Santa Rosa de Copán**, with connections at La Entrada for **Copán**, *Empresa Toritos y Copanecos* (T563-4930) leaving from 6-7 Av 11 C SO, every 20 mins, 0345-1715, 3 hrs, US$2.50, to Santa Rosa. Direct bus to Santa Rosa US$2.50, 4 daily. Take these buses to La Entrada, 2 hrs, US$1.30, or US$1.45 on the fast bus, for connection to Copán (3 hrs). Road paved all the way. Direct first-class bus to Copán with *Hedman Alas*, 0950 and 1430, also 0700 Fri-Sat, 2½ hrs, US$6.50 with a/c, movie and bathrooms. Also direct service with *Casasola-Cheny Express*, 1400, or *Gama Express* (T552-2861/6) at 1500, both from 6 C 6-7 Av, by *Hotel Palmira*, 3 hrs, see under Copán for details.

    Train Enquire to see if services on the Tela-Puerto Cortés line continue to San Pedro Sula.

Airline offices *American*, Ed Firenze, Barrio Los Andes, 16 Av, 2-3 C, T558-0524, airport T668-3241. *Atlantic*, airport, T668-7309. *Continental*, Plaza Versalles, Av Circunvalación, T557-4141, airport T668-3208. *Grupo Taca* 13 Av NO esq Nte de la Circunvalación, Barrio Los Andes, T557-0525, airport T668-3333. *Iberia*, Edif Quiroz, 2 C, Av 2, 1st floor, T550-1604, airport T668-3216/9. *Isleña*, Edif Trejo Merlo, 1 C 7 Av SO, T552-8322, airport T668-3181. *Sosa*, 8 Av 1-2 C SO, Edif Román, T550-6548, airport 668-3128.

Directory

Honduras

Banks *Bancahorro*, has a beautiful mural in its head office, 5 Av, 4 C SO. *Bancahsa*, 5 Av, 6-7 C SO, changes TCs. *Banco Atlántida*, on Parque Central, changes TCs at good rates. *Lloyds Bank* at 4 Av SO 26, between 3 y 4 C. *Banco de Honduras (Citibank). Banco Continental*, 3 Av, 3-5 C SO No 7. *Banco de Occidente*, 6 Av, 2-3 C SO. *Bancomer*, 4 C, 3-4 Av NO. *Banhcafé*, 1 C, 1 Av SE and all other local banks. *Credomatic* for Visa, MasterCard and Amex is at, 5 Av y 2 C NO. These 2 also at *Aval Card*, 14 Av NO y Circunvalación, and *Honducard*, 5 Av y 2 C NO. Also dealers buy dollars in Parque Central and the pedestrian mall.

Communications Internet: Internet cafés are easily found throughout town. Internet Café in Multiplaza centre, T550-6077, US$5 per hr. **Post office:** 3 Av SO between 9-10 C. **Telephone:** *Hondutel*, 4 C 4 Av SO. Collect calls can be made from lobby of *Gran Hotel Sula*.

Cultural centres *Alianza Francesa*, on 23 Av 3-4 C SO, T/F553-1178, b.espana@publinet.hn, 552-4359/553-1178, offers French and Spanish classes, has a library, French films on Wed, and cultural events on Fri. *Centro Cultural Sampedrano*, 3 C, 4 Av NO No 20, T553-3911, USIS-funded library, cultural events, occasional concerts, art exhibitions and theatrical productions.

Embassies and consulates *Belize*, Km 5 Blvd del Norte, Col los Castaños, T551-0124, 551-0707, F551-1740. *Costa Rica*, Hotel St Anthony, T558-0744, F558-1019. *El Salvador*, Edif Rivera y Cía, 7th floor, local 704, 5 y 6 Av 3 C, T/F553-4604. *France*, Col Zerón, 9 Av 10 C 927, T557-4187. *Germany*, 6 Av NO, Av Circunvalación, T553-1244, F553-1868. *Guatemala*, 8 C 5-6 Av NO, No 38, T/F553-3560. *Mexico*, 2 C 20 Av SO 201, Barrio Río de Piedras, T553-2604, F552-3293. *Nicaragua*, Col Trejo, 23 Av A entre 11 C B y 11 C C No 145, T/F550-3394. *Spain*, 2 Av 3-4 C NO 318, Edif Agencias Panamericanas, T558-0708, F557-1680. *Italy*, Edif La Constancia, 3rd floor, 5 Av 1-2 C NO, T552-3672, F552-3932. *Netherlands*, 15 Av 7-8 C NE, Plaza Venecia, Local 10, T557-1815, F552-9724. *UK*, 13 Av 10-12 C SO, Suyapa No 62, T557-2046, F552-9764.

Laundry *Excelsior*, 14-15 Av Blvd Morazán. *Lava Fácil*, 7 Av, 5 C NO, US$1.50 per load. *Lavandería Almich*, 9-10 Av, 5 C SO No 29, Barrio El Benque. *Rodgers*, 4a C, 15-16 Av SO, No 114.

Medical services Dentist: *Clínicas Dentales Especializadas*, Ed María Antonia, 3a C entre 8 y 9 Av NO, apartamento L-1, Barrio Guamilito, T558-0464.

Tour operators *Explore Honduras*, Edif Paseo del Sol, 1 C 2 Av NO, T552-6242, F552-6239, interesting short and multi-day tours and activities, with a/c bus, to Copán from US$60, Lake Yojoa and Pulhapanzak waterfall, to Lancetillo Botanical Park, Omoa, all around US$65 including guided tour, entrance fees, lunch. *Maya Tropic Tours* in lobby of *Gran Hotel Sula*, T/F557-8830, mayatt@netsy.hn, run by helpful Jorge Molamphy and his wife. *Mesoamerica Travel*, Colonia Juan Lindo, 8 C and 32 Av NO 710, T557-8447, F557-8410, www.mesoamerica-travel.com, individual and group tours arranged, recommended for quality of service and reliability. *Javier Pinel*, PO Box 2754, T/F557-4056, local and regional tours, also offers bed and breakfast.

Useful addresses Immigration: C Peatonal, just off Parque Central, or at the airport.

Parque Nacional Cusuco Twenty kilometres west of San Pedro Sula, the cloud forests of Cusuco National Park are managed by the Fundación Ecológica Héctor Rodrigo Pastor Fasquelle (HRPF). Exploited for lumber until the 1950s, is was declared a protected area in 1959 when the Venezuelan ecologist, Geraldo Budowski, reported the pine trees here were the highest in Central America. Cutting was stopped and the lumber company abandoned the site. It is a splendid location and well worth the effort to get there. The area includes tropical rainforest and cloud forest with all the associated flora and fauna. It includes both **Cerro Jilinco**, 2,242 m, and **Cerro San Ildefonso**, 2,228 m. There are four trails, ranging from 30 minutes to two days. They use old logging roads traversing forested ridges with good views. HRPF produces a bird checklist which naturally includes the quetzal.

Park essentials Entrance to the park is US$10 which includes a guided trip; you cannot go on your own. Contact the HRPF at 5 Av, 1 C NO, San Pedro Sula, T552-1014, F557-6620. Also contact Cohdefor, 10 Av, 5 C NO, Barrio Guamilito, San Pedro Sula, T553-4959, or Cambio CA, who run tours. Permission from HRPF is required to walk through the park to Tegucigalpita on the coast.

Hike from Buenos Aires to Tegucigalpita

This route to the coast follows a mule trail around the northeast side of the Parque Nacional Cusuco. The scenery is superb and you see a good range of wildlife.

From Buenos Aires walk east along an unpaved track to Bañaderos. A smaller track branches left just before you enter Bañaderos and immediately twists its way down, with frequent switchbacks, to a river in the valley below the road. It takes about an hour to reach the river, from where the path is fairly straightforward. Heading northeast, the trail climbs steeply away from the river before dropping again to another village (two hours) where there is a small shop selling drinks.

From the village the path climbs to the pass (four to five hours). Much of the ascent is steep

and water sources are scarce. There are some flat areas to camp as you approach the pass. After the pass head north to the village of Esperanza. Signs that you are nearing the village are clear as you begin to enter small coffee plantations among the heavily forested slopes. On this side of the pass water sources are plentiful. Esperanza has two shops and you can camp on the village football field.

It is about four hours, almost all downhill, from Esperanza to the coast road. There are no more water sources and temperatures can be very high. Where the path meets the road there is a well-stocked shop. From there it is a 30-minute walk on a tarmac road to Tegucigalpita (hospedaje); the bus terminal is just past the turning for the village.

There is a visitors' centre but bring your own food. You cannot stay or camp in the park, but camping is possible outside. Access by dirt road from Cofradía (*Cafetería Negro*, one block northwest of plaza, good food), on the road to Santa Rosa de Copán, then to **Buenos Aires**: 2 hrs by car from San Pedro Sula, 4WD recommended; bus San Pedro Sula-Cofradía, 1 hr, US$0.15, from 5 Av, 11 C SO (buses drop you at the turn-off 1 km from town); pick-up Cofradía-Buenos Aires 1½ hrs, US$1.75, best on Mon at 1400 (wait at the small shop on outskirts of town on Buenos Aires road); the park is 12 km from Buenos Aires. Ask in Buenos Aires for Carlos Alvaréngez-López who offers lodging and food halfway to the park, very friendly, camping possible US$3 per person. No hotels in the village but you can stay in the small, cockroach-infested house owned by the park authorities. 2 *comedores* in town; *Comedor Tucán*, good.

The North Coast

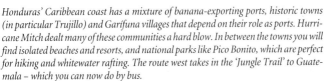

Honduras' Caribbean coast has a mixture of banana-exporting ports, historic towns (in particular Trujillo) and Garífuna villages that depend on their role as ports. Hurricane Mitch dealt many of these communities a hard blow. In between the towns you will find isolated beaches and resorts, and national parks like Pico Bonito, which are perfect for hiking and whitewater rafting. The route west takes in the 'Jungle Trail' to Guatemala – which you can now do by bus.

Running parallel to the coast, a route from El Progreso runs south of the coastal mountain chain Cordillera Nombre de Dios leading to rarely visited national parks, pristine cloud forest and an alternative route to La Ceiba.

Puerto Cortés

Stuck out on the northwestern coast of the country, Puerto Cortés is backed by the large bay of Laguna de Alvarado. The climate is hot, tempered by sea breezes, and there are many beautiful palm-fringed beaches nearby. The mosquitoes are ferocious, especially during the rainy season. The success of the place is its location and most Honduran trade passes through the port which is just 58 km from San Pedro Sula by road and rail, and 333 km from Tegucigalpa. It has a small oil refinery, a free zone and, being two days' voyage from New Orleans, is arguably now the most important port in Central America.

The Parque Central contains many fine trees but focuses on a huge Indian poplar in

Colour map 6, grid B2
Population: 65,000

Honduras

the centre that provides an extensive canopy. The tree was planted as a sapling in 1941. The park was remodelled in 1996/97 with new flowerbeds, fountain and bronze statues.

Sleeping
■ *on map*
Avoid 4 C between 1 and 2 Av (bars, drunks and beggars) and the area on 1 Av opposite the dockyards (prostitution and drunks), unpleasant by day, dangerous at night

AL *Playa*, 4 km west at Cienaguita, T665-1105, F665-2287. Hotel complex, directly on beach, cable TV, good fish dishes in restaurant. Mountain bikes for rent, available to non-guests. **B** *Costa Azul*, Playa El Faro, T665-2260, F665-2262. Restaurant, disco-bar, billiards, table tennis, pool, horse-riding, volley ball, good value. **C** *International Mr Ggeer*, 9 C, 2 Av E, T665-0444, F665-0750. No hot water, very clean, a/c, bar, video, satellite TV. Recommended. **C-E** *El Centro*, 3 Av 2-3 C, T665-1160. With bath, a/c, hot water, cable TV, parking, garden, café, pleasant, well furnished. **C** *Hotel-restaurante Costa Mar*, Playas de la Coca Cola, T665-1367. Pleasant. **E** *Frontera del Caribe*, Playas de Camaguey, calle a Travesía, T665-5001. Very friendly, quiet, safe, on beach, restaurant on 1st floor, open, airy, good food, 7 rooms on 2nd floor, private bath, cold water, linen changed daily, fan. Recommended. **F** *Formosa*, 3 Av 2 C E. With bath (some without), no towel, but soap and toilet paper provided, clean, fan, good value, friendly Chinese owner. **F** *Colón*, 3 Av 2 C O. Diagonally opposite *Hotel Puerto Limón* in clapboard building, clean, safe, basic.

Eating
● *on map*

Burger Boy's, 2 Av 8 C. Lively, popular with local teenagers. *Comedor Piloto*, 2 Av 1-2 C. Open 0700-1800, closed Sun, clean, satellite TV, fans, good value and service, popular. *El Zaguán*, 2 Av 5-6 C, closed Sun popular with locals, good for refreshments, cheap. *Kasike's Restaurant-Bar-Peña*, 3 Av y 9 C and *Carnitas Tapadera*, on same block. Recommended. Next door is *Candiles*, 2 Av, 7-8 C. Good grills, reasonable prices, open-air seating. *Kobs* ice-cream, 2-3 Av, 9 C Este. *La Cabaña*, 2 Av 6-7 C, bar and restaurant, on same block as *Matt's*, a/c, nice bar, good food, not expensive, and *Pekin*, Chinese, a/c, excellent, good service, a bit pricey but recommended. *Supermercado Pekin* next door. *Repostería y Pastelería Plata*, corner of 3 Av and 2 C E, near Parque Central. Good bread and pastries, excellent cheap *almuerzo*, buffet-style, kids' playroom. Recommended. *Repostería Ilusión*, 4 C E opposite Parque. Pastries, bread, coffee, nice for breakfast. *Wendy's* on the Parque with inside play centre for children.

Festivals In **August**, including *Noche Veneciana* on 3rd Sat.

Shopping There is a souvenir shop, Marthita's, in the Aduana administration building (opposite *Hondutel*). The market in the town centre is quite interesting, 3 C entre 2 y 3 Av. *Supertienda Paico* on the parque.

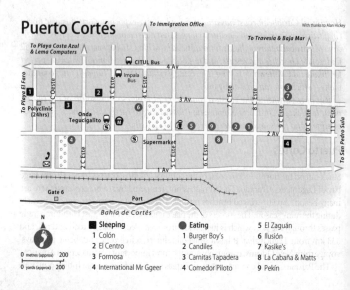

Puerto Cortés

With thanks to Alan Hickey

	Sleeping ■			
	1 Colón	2 El Centro	3 Formosa	4 International Mr Ggeer
	Eating ●			
	1 Burger Boy's	2 Candiles	3 Carnitas Tapadera	4 Comedor Piloto
	5 El Zaguán	6 Ilusión	7 Kasike's	8 La Cabaña & Matts
	9 Pekín			

Honduras

Buses Virtually all buses now arrive and leave from 4 Av 2-4 C. Bus service at least hourly to **San Pedro Sula**, US$0.75, 45 mins, Citul (4 Av entre 3 y 4 C) and **Impala** (4 Av y 3 C, T255-0606). *Expresos del Caribe, Expresos de Citul* and *Expresos del Atlantic* all have minibuses to **San Pedro Sula**. Bus to **Omoa** and **Tegucigalpita** from 4 Av, old school bus, loud music, very full, guard your belongings. *Citral Costeños* go to the Guatemalan border, 4-5 Av, 3C Este.

Transport

Sea If entering Puerto Cortés by boat, go to Immigration immediately (don't be persuaded by the boat captain to fill in your tourist card on the boat). Passports are sometimes collected at the dock and you must go later to Immigration to get them; US$1 entry fee, make sure that you have the stamp. This is the only official payment; if asked for more, demand a receipt. **To Guatemala** A boat leaves from Omoa for Lívingston, no fixed schedule, US$25 per person. Irregular boats also leave for Puerto Barrios. Ask at *Fisherman's Hut*, Omoa, for Sr Juan Ramón Menjivar (phone line pending). In Puerto Cortés information from Ocean Travel at 3 Av, 2 blocks west of plaza. **To Belize** Boats to Belize leave from beside the bridge over the lagoon (Barra La Laguna), buy tickets at blue wooden shack next to *joyería* near Los Coquitos bar just before bridge. Open 0800-1700. A launch leaves Puerto Cortés for Mango Creek, Belize, US$50, 7 hrs, no fixed schedule; can be dangerous in rough weather. Boats leave for Belize at 1000, Mon and Tue, US$40 per person. More boats at Easter. Remember to get your exit stamp. To be sure of getting an exit stamp go to Immigration in town (address below). The bridge linking the ticket office and the dockside was closed for hurricane damage repairs until Feb 2001. This means allowing more time to buy the tickets and then taking a taxi (5 mins) to the other side of the bridge on a diversion route to catch the boat.

There are occasionally boats to the **Bay Islands**, but none scheduled. It is possible to visit the harbour on Sun morning, ask at the gate. Most boats wait until they have sufficient cargo before they set sail. Price is around US$10.

Trains The railway station is near the harbour entrance to La Laguna de Alvarado. There are 2 trains a week (Fri and Sun) to **Tela**, 0700, 3½ hrs, US$0.70, returning for Puerto Cortés at 1300 arriving at 1800. Timetables change check locally.

Banks *Bancahsa*, 2 Av, 2 C. All banks open Mon-Fri 0800-1700, Sat 0830-1130. *Banco de Comercio* cashes TCs. *Banco de Occidente*, 3 Av 4 C E, cashes Amex TCs, accepts Visa/MasterCard. *Banco Ficensa* has ATM for MC and Amex only, 2 Av, 2C. Banks along 2 Av E, include *Atlántida* (2 Av, 3-4 C, has Visa ATM), *Bamer, Bancahsa, Bancomer, Sogerín*. **Communications** Internet: *Lema Computers*, 5-6Av, 2C, open Mon-Sat. **Post office**: next door to *Hondutel*. **Telephone**: *Hondutel*, at dock entrance, Gate 6, includes fax and AT&T. Direct to USA. **Medical services** *Policlínica*, 3 Av just past 1 C, open 24 hrs. **Tour operators** *Bahía Travel/Maya Rent-a-Car*, 3 Av, 3 C, T665-2102, F665-0218. *Irema*, 2 Av 3-4 C, T665-1506, F665-0978. *Ocean Travel*, Plaza Eng, 3 Av 2 C, T665-0913. **Useful addresses** Immigration: the Immigration Office is on 5 Av y 3-4 C next to Port Captain's office. Open daily 0800-1800.

Directory

Head west to **Tulián**, along the bay, for picnics and very good freshwater bathing. Minibuses leave from the Esso petrol station in the centre (US$0.35 each way) and travel along the coast past Tulián west to the laid-back village of Omoa (or three hours' walk, 15 km from Puerto Cortés) with its popular beach (see below).

Around Puerto Cortés

Tours from Puerto Cortés to Copán to visit the Maya ruins and tourist parties at the Ustaris Hacienda can be arranged with travel agents. Buses from Puerto Cortés go east to coconut palm beaches at **Travesía, Baja Mar**, and others, which are beautiful, unspoilt and with a small café at each. The best stretch of beach is between the two villages, but the width of sand is narrow even at low tide. The fishing communities are very friendly. Beware of sunburn, and mosquitoes at dusk.

Omoa

Omoa, 15 km from Puerto Cortés, is set in the beautiful Bahía de Omoa where the mountains, lusciously carpeted in jungle, tumble towards the sea. You can watch fine purple sunsets from the quiet laid-back bars on the beach. It has an 18th-century castle, Fortaleza de San Fernando, now renovated and worth a visit It was built

Colour map 6, grid B2
Population: 2,500

Honduras

by the Spaniards to protect the coast and shipments of silver from British pirates. According to Roli, one of the guides, it is the only one in the world that features curved walls – the result of a cost-cutting exercise. There is a Visitors' Centre and a small but interesting museum. ■ *Tue-Sun 0800-1700, US$1.40, tickets on sale at gate, guides available.*

During the week Omoa is a quiet, friendly fishing village, but at weekends it gets a little busier with Hondurans from San Pedro, and the place becomes littered, followed by a grand clean-up the following Monday morning. Roli (Swiss) runs tours of Honduras and Guatemala. Lancha hire to the cayos (a handful of small islands, 1½ hours away), good snorkelling – US$200-300. Near Omoa are two waterfalls (Los Chorros), with lovely walks to each, and good hiking in attractive scenery both along the coast and inland.

Sleeping At Omoa you can stay at **C-D** *Bahía de Omoa*, T658-9076, F658-9075, on beach, with bath, a/c, English, German and Dutch spoken, use of washing machine, comfortable and clean, owner Heinz has motor launch for fishing or scuba diving, sleeps 4. **C** *Gemini B*, on main access road to beach, T658-9137. Bath, fan, cafetería, parking, comfortable. **D** *Aquí Pancha*, T658-9172, basic. D-E *Tatiana*, on beach. With bath, clean and quiet. **F** *Hospedaje Champa Julita*, on beach, T658-9174, friendly, fan, basic, rundown. **F** *Hospedaje El Centro* is in the centre of the village. **F** *Pia's*, on the beach, T658-9076 (same owners as *Bahía de Omoa*). Popular backpacking stop, with living room, small porch with hammocks, and laundry facilities – seems to have encroached on *Roli's* market so watch the hotel rivalry develop! F *Roli's Place*, T/F658-9082, www.yaxpactours.com 100 m from beach, clean rooms with private bath and hot water, more planned, good information here of the region, email, fax and phone service, bikes and kayaks for guests' use, games, garden, campground, Roli will change TCs, quetzales and dollars. Recommended. The *tienda* (F) where the bus stops has cheap, basic rooms, shared bathroom, OK.

Eating Restaurants include *Cayuquitos*, on beachfront, good value meals all day, but service is very slow; next door is *Stanley*, on the beach is good value, with good shakes and juices. *La Macarela*, northwest end of beach, good food, owner Silvia speaks English, good view. *Fisherman's Hut*, 200 m to right of pier, new, clean, good food, seafood, recommended. Don't expect early Sun breakfasts after the partying the night before.

Transport A **bus** leaves Puerto Cortés at 0700 passing Omoa at 0730 to get to Corinto. Buses also leave Omoa for the border at 1000, 1400 and 1700. . **Boats** leave Omoa for Lívingston, Guatemala

Northwestern coast

on Tue and Fri around 1000. Ask around to confirm. Omoa to Puerto Cortés is 30 mins.

Directory

Banks In Omoa, *Banco de Occidente* does not take credit cards, but will cash TCs. Some shops will change dollars. Ask around. **Useful addresses** Immigration: *Migración* has an office on the main road opposite Texaco. If you come from Guatemala by car you have to get a police escort from Corinto to Puerto Cortés.

The coastal road heads southwest from Omoa towards the Honduras-Guatemalan border at Corinto. About 8 km from Omoa is a nice stretch of beach at the mouth of the Río Coto, with the very pleasant **D** *Río Coto Hotel-Restaurant*, a/c, pool, good, but has some caged animals. 15 km southwest of Omoa (Km 30½, Carretera de Puerto Cortés a Cuyamel) at **Pueblo Nuevo** on the banks of the Río Coco, is **A** *EcoRancho*, a dairy hacienda owned by César López. It is a beautiful ranch at the foot of the Omoa mountain range with luxury accommodation, fine family cooking, hiking, riding, bird and butterfly watching, swimming, fishing and even learning to milk a cow. Also **B** cabins in two mountain sites, one at Esmeralda (500 m), the other at Río Coco (1 km), both organic coffee and cardamom plantations, camping also available, equipment provided. Tour packages arranged to include Ranguana Caye (Belize), Río Dulce (Guatemala) and other lodges. Contact the manager, Rafael Aguilera at PO Box 130, San Pedro Sula, T/F556-6156. Continuing along the coast road you come to a Garífuna village, **Mazca** (or Masca), where Doña Lydia has built bamboo and palm-thatched cabins on stilts beside her house behind the beach, under US$3, warm family atmosphere, good Garífuna cooking. A few *champas* on the beach provide fish meals and cold drinks. There are also a couple of good hikes in the area.

Border with Guatemala

Honduran immigration Immigration is now available at Corinto if crossing to Guatemala on the former jungle trail. If taking a boat get your exit stamp from the Oficina de Migración in Puerto Cortés (see under Puerto Cortés Shipping), or Omoa.

    Entering Honduras There is now an immigration office just beyond Entre Ríos in Guatemala where the buses drop you. After crossing the border into Honduras, a pick-up will take you to Honduran immigration in Corinto. If you enter Honduras by boat you must go to immigration in Puerto Cortés as soon as possible. You may be asked for an entry tax, ask for a receipt (see Documents, page 826).

    Guatemalan Consulate See San Pedro Sula.

Transport Buses leave Puerto Cortés for Omoa and **Corinto** on the border every hour or so (Línea Costeños, Ruta 3 or 4).

The crossing to Guatemala, which used to be possible only on foot and by boat, has now been greatly simplified with more buses running and bridges spanning the Río Motagua. A road now connects Puerto Cortés and Puerto Barrios (Guatemala), with a new bridge over the river, although one section of the journey is track. Take a bus to Corinto (as above) or, from Omoa, take a bus to Tegucigalpita (30 km) and from there a bus or pick-up to Corinto (20 km). After completing immigration at Corinto, take a pick-up from Tegucigalpita to the border crossing. The road goes through **Cuyamelito** where there is **G** *Hospedaje Monte Cristo*, behind the bridge. From Corinto a pick-up goes 10 km to the suspension bridge at the frontier (a new concrete bridge is being built 800 m upriver). Across the bridge, in Guatemala, is Finca Arizona, from where there is an hourly bus to Puerto Barrios. From Cuyamelito it is still possible to go overland: it is a 2 km walk to the wharf from where a dug-out takes you through the swamps to the border, US$1.50, 1st at 0600, no controls. Another boat, US$2.50, on the Guatemalan side (Río Tinto) takes you to the Barra de Motagua and on to Finca la Inca banana plantation where you have to wait for a bus or hitch to Puerto Barrios. Take protection against the sun and mosquitoes, and be prepared for delays in wet season.

Honduras

Tela

Colour map 6, grid B2
Population: 67,890

*The local Fiesta
de San Antonio
takes place in June*

Tela, 88 km northeast of San Pedro Sula, used to be an important banana port before the pier was partly destroyed by fire. Easily reached from San Pedro Sula with a frequent bus service via El Progreso, it is pleasantly laid out with a sandy but dirty beach. Tela Viejo to the east is the original city joined by a bridge to Tela Nuevo, the residential area built for the executives of the American banana and farming company *Chiquita* which established itself in the city. There is a pleasant walk along the beach east to Ensenada, which has a café and not much else, and Triunfo, or west to San Juan (see Excursions; also see Security, below).

*See Security below,
regarding walking in
and around Tela*

A **Garífuna Museum** at the river end of Calle 8 (also known as J Calle del Valle, its original name), is an interesting and colourful introduction to Garífuna history and culture, with special emphasis on the contribution made by Honduran and Belizean Garífunas to contemporary music in the form of the frenetic rhythms of *punta*, a blend of rock, Afro-Caribbean and Spanish influences, originally a ritual dance. Also here is the art gallery of the Tela Artists Association, which exhibits many local artists. The museum shop sells *artesanía* and oil paintings. ■ *Open until 2100. US$0.40, T448-2244.* Check out the local website at www.tela-honduras.com

Sleeping

*During Easter week,
the town is packed;
room rates double
and advance
booking is essential*

AL-A *Telamar*, T448-2196, F448-2984, www.villastelamar.com A complex of wooden bungalows, set on a palm-fringed beach, price for rooms, villas from **AL**, restaurant, bar, golf club, swimming pool, conference centre. **B** *César Mariscos*, T448-2083. On beach, a/c, large rooms, restaurant. **B** *Gran Central*, in the centre of town, T/F448-1099. French-owned, beautifully restored historic banana port era hotel. 5 apartments, kitchen, hot water, color tv/cable, a/c, security, safe box in each room. Highly recommended. **B** *Sherwood*, T448-1065, F448-1063. On waterfront, some cheaper rooms, a/c, TV, hot water, upper rooms have balconies and are airy, new pool, English speaking owner, TCs or credit cards accepted, staff friendly and honest, restaurant busy at weekends. **B-C** *Maya Vista*, T/F448-1497, www.mayavista.com At top of hill, steep flight of steps starting opposite *Preluna*, Canadian-owned, French and English spoken, bath, a/c, hot water, bar, restaurant, delicious French-Canadian cuisine, fantastic views, very highly recommended.

C *Bahía Azul*, 11 C, 6 Av NE, T448-2381. With a/c or fan, on western end of beach, avoid rooms on road side, good restaurant overlooking the sea, fine location. **C** *Ejecutivos*, 8 C 3 Av NE, T448-1076. A/c, hot water, TV, 8 rooms with kitchenette. **C** *Nuevo Puerto Rico*, T448-2413. On the waterfront, lovely situation but exposed in Jun-Dec wet season, a/c or fan, small rooms, fridge, balcony, TV, poor service, run-down, large restaurant. **C** *Tía Carmen*, 8 C 5 Av, next to Bancahorro, T448-1476. A/c, hot water, TV, comfortable, well-furnished rooms, friendly, efficient, excellent restaurant. **C-D** *Tela*, 9 C, 3-4 Av NE, T448-2150. Clean, airy, fans, hot water, will do laundry, with restaurant, but meagre breakfast, otherwise very good. **D** *Bertha's*, 8 C, 9 Av NE, T448-1009. Near bus terminal, new brick building, with bath, a/c, cheaper with fan, clean. Recommended.

E *Mar Azul*, 11 C, 5 Av NE, T448-2313. With fan and bath, charming helpful owner. **E** *La Posada del Sol*, 8 C 3 Av NE, opposite *Ejecutivos*, T448-2111. With bath, **F** without, clean, laundry facilities, nice garden, bookshop on ground floor sells US magazines. **E** *Mundo Unido*, Col 4 de Enero, dirección San Juan. 5 mins out of town by bus or taxi (US$1), French-owned, helpful, cabins, mosquito nets, hammock space, cooking facilities, advanced horse-riding US$25-30 per day. Recommended. **E-F** *Mi Casa es Su Casa*, 6 Av 10-11 C. Bed and breakfast, private house, sign outside, friendly, family atmosphere. **F** *Preluna*, 9 C, 7-8 Av NE, opposite bus terminal. Delightful clapboard building, restaurant, quiet but reportedly deteriorating. **F** *Sara*, 11 C, 6 Av behind the restaurant *Tiburón Playa*, T448-1477. Basic, with bath, or without, poor sanitation, has 3 good cabins priced according to number of occupants, popular with backpackers, friendly, noisy especially at weekends from all night discos.

Out of town, 3 km on highway to La Ceiba, *El Retiro*, set back from the road by a small river, attractive setting, camping in vehicle allowed.

Prolansate

The Fundación Para la Protección de Lancetilla, Punta Sal y Texiguat (Prolansate) is a non-governmental, apolitical, non-profit organization based in Tela. Originally set up by Peace Corps volunteers, it is now operated by local personnel and is involved in environmental programmes to protect and educate in conjunction with comunity development and ecotourism. It is currently managing four protected areas: Parque Nacional 'Jeannette Kawas' (Punta Sal), Jardín Botánico Lancetilla, Refugio de Vida Silvestre Texiguat and Refugio de Vida Silvestre Punta

Izopo. There are plans to extend the area of the national park (see map), named after a former Treasurer and President of Prolansate who was assassinated in 1995, but there are complications with the location of several Garífuna villages. The Prolansate Visitors' Centre is at Calle 9 Avenida 2-3 Northeast, T448-2035. They organize trips to Punta Sal, Punta Izopo and Lancetilla, with expert guides, and provide information about other national parks, wildlife refuges and bird sanctuaries.

Eating

The best eating in Tela is in the hotel restaurants

Alexandro's, pedestrian mall. International menu, popular, often crowded, seafood specialities, open daily from 0800. *Casa Azul*, Barrio El Centro. Italian restaurant and bar, good food and nice atmosphere, French-Canadian owners, helpful. *César's* (also hotel, see above). Nice location on the beach, serves good seafood, open from 0700, very good breakfast menu. *Comedor Acuario*, near *Sara*. Local food, cheap. Recommended. *El Magnate*, 11 C 1 Av NE, close to old bridge. A la carte menu, pork chops speciality, open until midnight, good, disco Fri-Sun. *Garífuna*, at river end of 8 C. With *champas* at river's edge, typical Garífuna fare, conch soup, *tapado* (fish stew with coconut and yuca). *Iguana Sports Bar,* on road between two town bridges leading out of town. Open-air and music. *La Cascada*, on the pedestrian mall, modest *comedor* in clapboard shack, cheap, home cooking, good, open early until late. Next door is *La Cueva*, smart, big menu includes steak, chicken, seafood, pricey. *Los Angeles*, 9 C, 2 Av NE. Chinese, run by Hong Kong owners, large helpings, good. *Luces del Norte*, of Doña Mercedes, 11 C, 2 Av NE, towards beach from Parque Central, next to *Hotel Puerto Rico*. Delicious seafood and good typical breakfasts, very popular, also good information and book exchange. *Mango Café*, by the river at the Garífuna Tours dock with views of the river, mango@honduras.com, T448-2856. Italian, seafood and Garífuna specialities, run by owner of Garífuna Tours, Spanish school and internet on premises. Great place to eat before or after tours, Garífuna Museum on premises, and good place to meet travellers. *Maya Vista*, in hotel (see above). Run by Québécois Pierre, fine cuisine, one of the best in Tela, highly recommended. *Merendero Tía Carmen*, at the hotel. Good food, Honduran specialities, good *almuerzo*. *Pizzería El Bambino*, 11 C, 50 m from new bridge. Good pasta, pizza, open-air eating on terrace, nice children's playground. Also *Sherwood's*, see above. Good food, attractive, popular, enjoy the view from the terrace, also opens 0700 and serves excellent breakfast. *Tuty's Café*, 9 C NE near Parque Central. Excellent fruit drinks and good cheap lunch specials, but slow service.

In Tela Nueva, all along the boulevard, *Cafetería La Oso*, offshoot of *Hotel Tía Carmen's Merendero*. *Estancia Victoria*, elegant restaurant/bar, a/c, not cheap, good, international menu. *Los Pinchos*, shish-kebab speciality, meat and seafood, very good, nice patio, soothing music, closed Mon. *Marabú*, excellent, also rooms to rent (**C**). *Repostería y Baleadas Tía Carmen*, across the boulevard, same excellent Honduran specialities, very good.

Security

In the last few years, Tela has suffered a law and order crisis, made worse by Hurricane Mitch-related problems. As of March 2002, Tela was the first place in Honduras to receive a contingent of the new specially trained Tourist Police. With luck the recent problems and reputation will be replaced in time. Nevertheless, for the time being, express caution when walking alone and after dark.

Transport

Local Bicycle: hire from *Garífuna Tours*, 9 C y Parque Central (see below).

Honduras

Long distance Buses: *Catisa* or *Tupsa* lines from San Pedro Sula to **El Progreso** (US$0.50) where you must change to go on to **Tela** (3 hrs in total) and **La Ceiba** (last bus at 1900). On Catisa bus ask to be let off at the petrol station on the main road, then take a taxi to the beach, US$0.50. Bus from Tela to **El Progreso** every 30 mins, US$1; to **La Ceiba**, 2½ hrs, US$1. Direct to **Tegucigalpa**, Traliasa, 1 a day from *Hotel Los Arcos*, US$4.50, same bus to **La Ceiba** (this service avoids San Pedro Sula); to **Copán**, leave by 0700 via El Progreso and San Pedro Sula to arrive same day. *Garífuna Tours* (see below) also offer a shuttle service direct to Copán Ruinas, US$29.

Trains: The railway service to Puerto Cortés runs Fri and Sun at 1300, 4 hrs, US$1. Check locally for exact schedule, can be daily in high season.

Directory **Banks** *Banco Atlántida* (with ATM), *Bancahsa*, 9 C 3 Av, Visa and MasterCard, *Banadesa*, *Bancahorro*, 8 C 5 Av, changes TCs. *Casa de Cambio La Teleña*, 4 Av, 9 C NE for US$, TCs and cash. Exchange dealers on street outside post office. **Communications** Internet service at the *Mango Café*. **Telephone and post office:** both on 4 Av NE. Fax service and collect calls to Europe available and easy at *Hondutel*. **Laundry** *El Centro*, 4 Av 9 C, US$2 wash and dry. *Lavandería Banegas*, Pasaje Centenario, 3 C 1 Av. *Lavandería San José*, 1 block northeast of market. **Medical services** *Centro Médico CEMEC*, 8 Av 7 C NE, T/F448-2456. Open 24 hrs, X-rays, operating theatre, smart, well-equipped. **Tour operators** *Garífuna Tours*, southwest corner of Parque Central, T448-2904, www.garifuna-tours.com knowledgeable and helpful, day trips to Punta Sal (US$20) and Punta Izopo (US$16), good value, also mountain bike hire, US$4.60 per day, internet service. Highly recommended. *Barana Tours*, 30 m south of Parque Central, T448-1173, good personal service, English spoken, good-value trips. Also provide shuttle service to San Pedro Airport (US$11) and City (US$13), La Ceiba (US$14) and Copán US$30. *Galaxia Travel Agency*, 9 C 1 Av NE, near river, T448-2152, F448-2942, for reservations and confirmations of national and international flights. **Useful addresses** Immigration: *Migración* is at the corner of 3 Av and 8 C.

Around Tela

Local buses and trucks from the corner just east of the market go east to the Garífuna village of **Triunfo de la Cruz** which is set in a beautiful bay. Site of the first Spanish settlement on the mainland, a sea battle between Cristóbal de Olid and Francisco de Las Casas (two of Cortés' lieutenants) was fought here in 1524.

Sleeping **A** *Caribbean Coral Inn*, T448-2942, www.globalnet.hn/caribcoralinn, with bath, fan. **F** *Hotel El Triunfo*, with bath or **D** furnished apartments. Cheap houses and cabañas for rent in Triunfo de la Cruz. **Transport** **Bus** to Triunfo de la Cruz, US$0.40 (about 5 km, if no return bus, walk to main road where buses pass).

Beyond Triunfo de la Cruz is an interesting coastal area that includes the cape, **Punta Izopo** (1½-hour walk along the beach, take water – 12 km from Tela) and the mouth of the Río Leán. This, and its immediate hinterland, is now a National Park, and a good place to see parrots, toucans, turtles, alligators and monkeys as well as the first landing point of the Spanish conqueror Cristóbal de Olid. For information contact Prolansate. To get right into the forest and enjoy the wildlife, it is best to take an organized tour (see Tour operators in Directory above). A trip to Punta Izopo involves kayaking through mangrove swamps up the Río Plátano Indiana-Jones style. While it may be exciting, it is hard work as the kayaks get stuck on the roots. Trips also include a visit to Triunfo de la Cruz and a chance to taste the local Garífuna drink *gifiti*.

The area west of Tela is planned for tourism development with investment in infrastructure, hotels and resorts – but for the meantime it is still virgin beach. The Carib villages of **Tornabé** and **San Juan** (4 km west of *Villas Telamar*) are worth a visit, and the food's beautiful (fish cooked in coconut oil). In Tornabé (taxi US$3) there are eight bungalows for rent, some a/c, some fan, hot water, at **A-B** *The Last Resort*, T/F984-3964, with breakfast, run by the Pacheco family, several cabins for different size groups, a great place to relax, full board available, good restaurant.

Further northwest, along palm-fringed beaches and blue lagoons, is P... lovely place now protected within the boundaries of the 80,000-ha P... **Nacional Jeannette Kawas** (Punta Sal), contact Prolansate for informatio... ■ *Entrance US$2* It is one of the most important parks in Honduras and has two distinctive parts, the peninsula and the lagoon. During the dry season some 350 species of birds living within the lagoon, surrounded by forest, mangroves and wetlands. Once inhabited only by Garífuna, the area has recently suffered from the immigration of cattle farmers who have cleared the forest, causing erosion, and from a palm oil extraction plant on the Río San Alejo, which has dumped waste in the river and contaminated the lagoons. Conservation and environmental protection programmes are now under way.

Sleeping and eating There is a small hotel in Río Tinto, two *comedores* and accommodation is also available in private houses.

Transport To get there you need a motor boat, or take a bus (3 a day) to Tornabé and hitch a ride 12 km, or take the crab truck at 1300 for US$0.40 (back at 1700), on to **Miami**, a small, all-thatched fishing village (2 hrs' walk along beach from Tornabé), beer on ice available, and walk the remaining 10 km along the beach. There are also pick-ups from Punta Sal to Miami, contact Prolansate for information. The direct route from Tela along the coast may be impassable (sand and water) to passenger cars, though you can leave your car in Tornabé safely in the hands of locals for a few lempiras and walk from there. *Garífuna Tours* (address above) in Tela, run recommended tours for US$15, food extra. Alternatively, take a motorized *cayuco* from Tela to **Río Tinto** beyond Punta Sal, and explore from there.

From Río Tinto it is possible to walk west along the beach to Puerto Cortés; it is about 20 km from Río Tinto to Baja Mar (4-5 hrs' walk), from where buses run to Puerto Cortés. This would be quicker than taking buses Tela-Progreso-San Pedro Sula-Puerto Cortés, but not quicker than the train. *Cayucos* arrive in Tela early morning for shopping, returning to Río Tinto between 1000 and 1200, very good value.

Jardín Botánico at **Lancetilla** (established 1926), is 5 km inland, and was originally founded as a plant research station by United Fruit Co. Managed by Prolansate, over 1,000 varieties of plants and over 200 bird species have been identified. It has fruit trees from every continent, the most extensive collection of Asiatic fruit trees in the Western Hemisphere, orchid garden, plantations of mahogany and teak alongside a 1,200-ha virgin tropical rainforest. ■ *Mon-Fri, 0730-1530, Sat, Sun and holidays 0830-1600, US$5.50. Not well signposted – a guide is recommended, ask at the Cohdefor office.*

Jardín Botánico
Good maps available in English or Spanish US$0.30

Be warned, there are many mosquitoes

Sleeping E *Turicentro Lancetilla*, T448-2007, a/c and *comedor*, full at weekends. No camping allowed. **Transport** Either take employees' bus from town centre at 0700, or take a taxi from Tela, US$1.55, but there are few in the park for the return journey in the afternoon, so organize collection in advance.

La Ceiba

La Ceiba, the capital of Atlántida Department and the third largest city in Honduras, stands on the narrow coastal plain between the Caribbean and the rugged Nombre de Dios mountain range crowned by the spectacular Pico Bonito (2,435 m) – see page 890. The climate is hot, but tempered by sea winds. Once the country's busiest port, trade has now passed to Puerto Cortés and Puerto Castilla, but there is still some activity, mainly serving the Bay Islands. The close proximity to Pico Bonito National park, Cuero y Salado Wildlife Refuge and the Cayos Cochinos Marine Reserve gives the city the ambitious target of becoming an important ecotourism centre. Watch out for developments.

The main plaza is worth walking around to see statues of various famous Hondurans including Lempira, a couple of ponds with basking alligators and turtles; there

Colour map 6, grid B3
Population: 80,160

La Ceiba is the usual departure point for trips to the Bay Islands

...on kiosk. Not far from town are some white sand beaches ...(for example Venado, 3 km up the Río Cangrejal); but the ...are not recommended (for details see under Excursions ...ífuna community by the beach at the end of Calle 1E.

...nsect museum has a collection of 5,000 butterflies, roughly ...nd snakes at Colonia El Sauce, Segunda Etapa Casa G-12. Inter- ...ou get a 25-minute video in both Spanish and English and Robert ...nan guide visitors expertly through the lives and loves of the but- ...ted butterfly T-shirts for sale. ■ *Mon-Sat 0800-1200, 1400-1700,* ...*rnoon, US$1.30, student reductions, T442-2874, rlehman@gbm.hn* ...a **Butterfly Farm** on the grounds of *The Lodge* at Pico Bonito. ■ ...*daily, entry US$6.*

Excursions

Many bridges on the roads leading to La Ceiba were washed away by Hurricane Mitch, mainly over the Bonito and Aguán rivers. A Bailey bridge was erected over Río Bonito in early 1999 and all services in the city were back to normal by the middle of the same year

Fig Tree Medical Centre, 25 km east of La Ceiba on the highway to Jutiapa, is a famous centre for alternative medicine. Operated by Dr Sebi, this facility is treating cancer and diabetes utilizing vegetarian diet, medications and the local hot springs. For more information or to visit call in advance T440-0041 (in La Ceiba). **Jutiapa** is a small dusty town with a pretty little colonial church. Contact United Brands office in La Ceiba (off main plaza) to visit a local pineapple plantation. **Corozal** is an interesting Garífuna village near La Ceiba, at Km 209½, with a beach – Playas de Sambrano – and **B** *Villa Rhina*, T443-1222, F443-3558, www.honduras.com/villarhina, with pool and restaurant near the turn-off from the main road. **Sambo Creek**, another Garífuna village, has nice beaches and a simple hotel-restaurant **E** *Hermanos Avila*, clean, food OK, and *La Champa* restaurant, seafood Garífuna style, bar, delightful location. Recommended. Near the towns of **Esparta** and **El Porvenir** thousands of crabs come out of the sea in July and August and travel long distances inland. The **Catarata El Bejuco** waterfall is 7 km along the old dirt road to Olanchito (11 km from La Ceiba). Follow a path signposted to Balneario Los Lobos to the waterfall about 1 km upriver through the jungle. There is good swimming from a pebbly beach where the river broadens. Along this road is El Naranjo near *Omega Adventure Lodge*, T440-0334, omegatours@laceiba.com with rooms (**E**), cabañas and good food. Rafting and kayaking are available on the Río Cangrejal, and varied holidays can be arranged (see page 890).

Yaruca, 20 km down the old road to Olanchito, is easily reached by bus and offers good views of Pico Bonita. **Eco-Zona Río María**, 5 km along the Trujillo highway (signposted path up to the foothills of the Cordillera Nombre de Dios), is a beautiful walk through the lush countryside of a protected area. Just beyond Río María is **Balneario Los Chorros** (signposted), a series of small waterfalls through giant boulders into a deep rock pool that is great for swimming (refreshments nearby).

La Ceiba and the coast

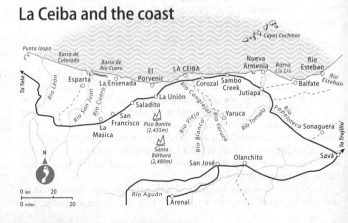

Upstream there is some beautiful scenery and you can continue walking through the forest and in the river, where there are more pools. Another bathing place, Agua Azul, with restaurant is a short distance away. The active will want to get on the **Río Cangrejal** for the exhilarating rush of Class II, III and IV **whitewater rapids**, which can be combined with treks in to the lush wilderness of **Parque Nacional Pico Bonito** (see below).

Beaches

Beaches in and near La Ceiba include Playa Miramar (dirty, not recommended), La Barra (better), Perú (across the Río Cangrejal at Km 205½, better still, quiet except at weekends, deserted tourist complex, restaurant, access by road to Tocoa, 10 km, then signposted side road 1½ km, or along the beach 6 km from La Ceiba) and La Encenada (close to Corozal).

The beaches near the fishing villages of Río Esteban and Balfate are very special and are near Cayos Cochinos (Hog Islands) where the snorkelling and diving is spectacular. The Hog Islands (see page 898) can be reached by *cayuco* from **Nuevo Armenia**, a nondescript Garífuna village connected by road to Jutiapa. E *Chichi*, three small rooms, fan, mosquito net, clean, friendly, good food available. Bus from La Ceiba at 1100 US$0.75, 2½ hours. At the bus stop is the office of the man who arranges boat trips to Hog Islands, US$10, trips start at 0700, you may see dolphins. Take whatever you need with you as there is almost nothing on the smaller cayes. However, the Garífuna are going to and fro all the time.

Sleeping
■ *on map*
Price codes: see inside front cover

Electricity is irregular, have candles/torches at the ready

Honduras

A *La Quinta*, exit carretera La Ceiba-Tela, opposite Club de Golf, T443-0223, F443-0226. Restaurant, laundry, cable TV, swimming pool, immaculate, good value. B *Partenon Beach*, T443-1176, F443-0434. Greek-owned, family apartments, new annex with very nice rooms, cable TV, English speaking desk staff, swimming pool, expensive but excellent restaurant, home made pasta, lovely salad bar. Highly recommended. B *Gran Hotel París*, Parque Central, T/F443-2391. Newly renovated, new management, a/c, own generator, swimming pool, parking, good value. B *Tesla's Guest House*, C Montecristo 212, Col El Naranjal, opposite Hospital La Fe, T/F443-3893. 5 rooms, private bathrooms, hot water, a/c, pool, phone, minibar, BBQ, laundry, friendly family owners speak English, German, French and Spanish, airport collection.

C *Ceiba*, Av San Isidro, 5 C, T443-2737. With fan or a/c and bath, restaurant and bar, uncomfortable, but good breakfast. Next door to *Ceiba* is C *Iberia*, T443-0401, a/c, windows without screen. Recommended. C *Italia*, 4 doors from the *Colonial*, on Av 14 de Julio, T443 0150. Clean, a/c, good restaurant with reasonable prices, parking in interior courtyard. C *Paraíso*, C 4 E, Barrio La Isla, T443-3535. Bath, a/c, hot water, TV, restaurant, 4 blocks from beach, bar, restaurant.C *Posada Don Giuseppe*, Av San Isidro at 13 C, T/F442-2812. Bath, a/c, hot water, E with fan, TV, bar, restaurant, comfortable.

D *Colonial*, Av 14 de Julio, between 6a and 7a C, T443-1953, F443-1955, a/c, sauna, jacuzzi, cable TV, rooftop bar, restaurant with varied menu, nice atmosphere, tourist office, tours available. D *Gran Hotel Líbano*, at bus terminal, T443-2102. Good, restaurant, a/c or fan, bath. D *Granada*, Av Atlántida, 5-6 C, T443-2451. Bath, a/c, clean, safe, cheaper with fan. D *Príncipe*, 7 C between Av 14 de Julio and Av San Isidro, T443-0516. Cheaper with fan and shared bath, bar/restaurant, TV. D *El Conquistador*, Av La República, T443-3670. Cheaper with fan, shared bath, safe, clean, TV. E *Amsterdam 2001*, 1 C, Barrio La Isla, T442-2292. Run by Dutchman Jan (Don Juan), good for backpackers, dormitory beds or rooms, with laundry, bit run down, *Dutch Corner Café* for great breakfasts. E *Tropical*, Av Atlántida between 4 y 5 C, T442-2565. With bathroom, fan, basic, small rooms, noisy, cold drinks and water sold in foyer. E *Florencia*, Av 14 de Julio. Some a/c, TV, clean, bath, friendly, dark rooms but recommended. E *Rotterdam Beach*, 1 C, Barrio La Isla, T440-0321. On the beach, with bath, fan, clean, friendly, pleasant garden, good value. Recommended. E *San Carlos*, Av San Isidro, 5 y 6 C. Bit grotty, colourful cafetería, and its own bakery, good breakfasts, where Bay Islanders assemble Tue mornings for boat trip to Utila. Hotel at airport entrance F *El Cique*, basic but convenient. F *Las 5 Rosas*, C 8 near Av Le Bastilla, opposite Esso. Clean, simple rooms, bath, fan, laundry, good value.

Many cheap hotels on Av La República, beside railway line leading from central plaza to pier, eg *Arias*, *Los Angeles*, but most of them are dirty, noisy, short-stay places.

Out of town L *The Lodge* at Pico Bonito is Honduras' first world-class ecolodge at the base of Parque Nacional Pico Bonito, T954-472-3881 (in the USA), www.picobonito.com 22 rooms, full-service nature lodge, swimming pool, gourmet restaurant, tours, guides, butterfly farm. 5 mins out of town on the road to Tela is **E** *Cabañas del Caribe* in Dantillo. T441-1421 (997-8746 cell). 6 big cabins, some with jacuzzi, and 7 rooms on the beach, restaurant serving breakfast. Video screen in restaurant. Great place to relax. Call one day ahead to collect from town. Buses from La Ceiba for Dantillo every 30 mins.

Eating *Café El Pastel*, Av San Isidro with 6 C. Good cheap breakfasts, set lunches, snacks, open 0700-2100. *Café le Jardin*, Av La Bastilla, 7-8 C, Barrio La Isla. Owners Michel (chef) and Lisette (la patronne), outstanding French cuisine, good value wine, open lunch and dinner Mon-Sat. Highly recommended. *Cafetería Mi Delicia*, Av San Isidro, 11 C. Good and cheap, big breakfasts, family atmosphere. *Cobel*, 7 C, opposite *Príncipe*. Good breakfasts, excellent set lunches, very popular with locals, closes 1730. Recommended. *Cric Cric Burger*, Av 14 de Julio, 3 C, facing attractive Parque Bonilla. Good fast food, several branches in town. Recommended. *Deutsch-Australian Club*, beach end of Av 14 de Julio. Run by German retired to Honduras after living in Australia, German food and seafood, busy bar, open 1200 until very late. *El Canadiense*, Parque Manuel Bonilla, north end of Av 14 de Julio. Steaks etc, busy bar, open 1300-2300, Sun 1600-2300, book exchange, operates Harry's Horseback Riding trips to Pico Bonito, 6 hrs, US$25, expat guide, food provided. *Expatriates Bar and Grill and Cigar Emporium*, at Final de C 12, above Refricón, 3 blocks south, 3 blocks east of Parque Central. Open 1600-2400, closed Wed, Canadian owned, very expat atmosphere, US TV and newspapers, sports shown, barbecue and Mexican food, US$2-5 a meal. Recommended. *La Carreta*, 4 C, 2 Av E, Barrio Potrerito (near Parque Manuel Bonilla). Good value, BBQ about US$17 for 2, try *anafre*, a bean and cheese dish. Recommended. *La Chavelita*, end of 4 C E, overlooking Río Cangrejal. Open daily, lunch and dinner, seafood, popular.

Las Dos Fronteras, Av San Isidro, 13 C. Good Mexican and American food, open 0700-2200, good food, limited choice. *Masapán*, 7 C Av San Isidro-Av República. Self-service, varied, well-prepared choice of dishes, fruit juices, good coffee, open 0630-2200. Recommended. *Palace*, 9 C, Av 14 de Julio. Large Chinese menu, surf 'n' turf. Recommended. *Paty's*, Av 14 de Julio between 6 and 7 C. Milkshakes, wheatgerm, cereals, donuts, etc, purified water, clean. Opposite is an excellent pastry shop. There are two more *Paty's* at 8 C E and at the bus terminal. *Pizza Hut*, on main plaza. Good salad bar, large restaurant, US$2.25 lunchtime special, pizza, salad, drink, playground. *Ricardo's*, Av 14 de Julio, 10 C. Very good seafood and steaks, garden setting and a/c. Recommended. *Toñita*, opposite *Hotel Partenon*. Good seafood, pleasant atmosphere. *Toto's*, Av San Isidro, 17 C. Good pizzería. There are several good fish restaurants at end of C 1 E, *El*

La Ceiba

Caribbean Sea

Sleeping ■
1 Ceiba & Iberia
2 Colonial
3 Gran Hotel París
4 Italia
5 Príncipe

Eating ●
1 Cobel
2 Expatriates
3 Ricardo's

Not to scale

Honduras

Pescado and *Brisas de la Naturaleza* and *La Barra*, overlooking the river, good prawn s̪
music and dancing in bar from 2100, very pleasant garden setting.

Cinema *Cinema Tropical*, 8 C y Av San Isidro in Plaza Tropical commercial centre, new, **E**
comfortable, digital Dolby stereo. **Nightclubs** *Buho's*, 1 C, Thu-Sat 2000-0400, free with
dinner on Thu. Several others along 1 C.

San Isidro, La Ceiba's patron saint, is on **15 May**. The celebrations continue for 2 weeks, end- **Festivals**
ing 28 May, the highlight being the international carnival on the third Sat in May, when La
Ceiba parties long and hard to the Afro-Caribbean beat of *punta* rock.

Carrion Department Store, Av San Isidro with 7A C. *Deli Mart* late-night corner store on 14 **Shopping**
de Julio, round corner from Internet Café, shuts at 2300. *El Regalito*, good quality souvenirs
at reasonable prices in small passage by large Carrión store. *T Boot*, store for hiking boots, C
1, east of Av San Isidro, T443-2499. Supermarket *Super Ceibena* 2 on Av 14 de Julio and 6A C.

Air Golosón (LCE), 10 km out of town. See Getting there, in Essentials, for international ser- **Transport**
vices. For full details of flights to Bay Islands, see next section. *Isleña* (T443-0179 airport), flies
to San Pedro Sula, Trujillo, Puerto Lempira, Roatán and Guanaja; *Taca* and *Lacsa* fly to Tegucigalpa and San Pedro Sula. *Sosa*, the most reliable domestic airline flies to Utila and to Roatán,
office on Parque Central, T443-1399, F443-2519. *Atlantic Air*, T/F440-2347, atlan-
tic@caribe.hn, the cheapest, and *Rollins Air* also have services. Standard fare to Roatán on
Sosa or Atlantic one-way US$20. Slightly more on *Isleña*. At weekends there are some charter
flights which may be better than the scheduled flights. Taxi to town US$4 per person or walk
200 m to the main road and share for US$1 with other passengers, also buses from bus sta-
tion near *Cric Cric Burger* at end 3 Av, US$0.15. Intercity buses pass by the entrance.
　　Car rental: Molinari in *Hotel París* on Parque Central, T/F443-0055. **Maya Rent-a-Car**,
Hotel La Quinta, T443-3071, F443-0226; **Dino's Rent-a-Car**, *Hotel Partenon Beach*,
T443-0404, F443-0434.
　　Buses Taxi from centre to bus terminal, which is a little way west of town (follow Blvd 15
de Septiembre), costs US$0.75 per person, or there are buses from Parque Central. Most
buses leave from here. *Traliasa*, *Etrusca* and *Cristina* bus service to **Tegucigalpa** via Tela sev-
eral daily, US$6, avoiding San Pedro Sula (US$1 to Tela, 2 hrs); also hourly service to **San
Pedro Sula**, US$2 (3-4 hrs). *Empresa Tupsa* direct to San Pedro Sula almost hourly from 0530
until 1800. Also 1st class with *Hedman Alas* – take taxi to separate terminal. To **Trujillo**, 3 hrs
directo, 4½ hrs *local* (very slow), every 1½ hrs or so, US$3; daily bus La Ceiba-Trujillo-Santa
Rosa de Aguán; to **Olanchito**, US$1, 3 hrs; also regular buses to Sonaguera, Tocoa, Balfate,
Isletas, San Esteban and other regional locations.
　　Sea *Safeway Maritime* operates the passenger vessel *Galaxy II*, T445-1795, F445-5056.
The timetable is La Ceiba-Utila 0930, Utila-La Ceiba 1030, La Ceiba-Roatán, 1500, Roatán-La
Ceiba 0700. Boats from the new dock (Muelle de Cabotaje) about 15 mins taxi ride from
town, US$2-3 per person if sharing with 4 people.

Banks *Bancahsa*, 9 C, Av San Isidro and *Bancomer*, Parque Central, both cash TCs. Open 0830-1130, **Directory**
1330-1600; Sat 0800-1200. *Banco Atlántida*, Av San Isidro and 6 – 7 C, has ATM that accepts Visa and
they will cash TCs at good rates. Cash advances on Visa and MasterCard from *Credomatic* on Av San
Isidro opposite *Hotel Iberia* between 5 – 6 C; also American Express. *Honducard*, Av San Isidro for Visa,
next to *Farmacia Aurora*. Better rates for US$ cash from *cambistas* in the lounges of the bigger hotels
(and at travel agency next door to *Hotel Príncipe*). *Money Exchange*, at back of *Supermercado Los
Almendros*, 7 C Av San Isidro with Av 14 de Julio, open daily 0800-1200, 1400-1800, T443-2720, good
rates for US$ cash and TCs.
　　Communications Internet: *Hondusoft*, in Centro Panayotti, 7A C between San Isidro and Av 14
de Julio, Mon-Fri 0800-2000, Sat 0800-1800, discount between 1800-2000 US$3 instead of US$6 an hr.
In *La Ceiba Internet Café*, Barrio El Iman, 9 C, T440-1505, Mon-Sat 0900-2000, US$3 per hr. *Intercon
Internet Café*, upstairs in Plaza del Sol Shopping Centre, Av San Isidro, opposite *Atlántida* ATM.
Mon-Thu 0800-2000, Fri 0800-1700, Sun 0900-1600. US$5 an hr. Post office: Av Morazán, 13 C O.
Telephone: *Hondutel* for international telephone calls is at 2 Av, 5 y 6 C E.

ol *Centro Internacional de Idiomas*, T/F440-1557, cii@leceiba.com, provide a homestay options. Also *Central America Spanish School*, Av San Isidro No 110, C ndio, T/F440-1707, www.ca-spanish.com.

Doctor: *Dr Gerardo Meradiaga*, Edif Rodríguez García, Ap No 4, Blvd 15 de ctitioner, speaks English. *Dr Siegfried Seibt*, Centro Médico, 1 C and Av San ospital: *Vincente D'Antoni*, Av Morazán, T443-2264, private, competent, well nd doctor's fees about US$40 per day for in-patients.

several agencies to choose from, ask around to find a tour that suits your ntials. *Caribbean Travel Agency*, run by Ann Crichton, Av San Isidro, Edif awas, Apdo Postal 66, T/F443-1360, ctravel@caribe.hn, helpful, shares office with *Ríos Honduras* (affiliate of Rocky Mountain Outdoor Center, Howard, Colorado, USA), T443-0780, rios@hondurashn.com, offering whitewater rafting, trips on the Río Cangrejal, spectacular, reservations 1 day in advance. *Junglas River Rafting*, T440-1268, jungle@laceiba.com Zona Viva, ½ block south of *Hotel Rotterdam*. Whitewater rafting on the Cangrejal (Class II, III and IV rapids) 4 hrs down the rapids with expert guides, US$35. Highly recommended. *La Ceiba Ecotours*, Av San Isidro, 1st block, 50 m from beach, T/F443-4207, hiking and riding in Parque Nacional Pico Bonito, visits to other nearby reserves, whitewater rafting, trips to La Mosquitia. *Laffite*, Av San Isidro between 5 y 6 C, T443-0115, F443-0354, helpful and informative. *La Moskitia Eco Aventuras*, Av 14 de Julio at Parque Manuel Bonilla, T/F442-0104, www.honduras.com/moskitia Jorge Satavero, very knowledgeable, enthusiastic and flexible. Specializes in trips to Mosquitia. Recommended. *Omega Tours*, T440-0334, omegatours@laceiba.com, runs rafting and kayaking trips on the Río Cangrejal and jungle hikes, and own hotel 30 mins upstream (see page 886). *Pedal and Paddle*, Av 14 de Julio, T443-2762, rafting possible all year. *Tourist Options*, *Hotel Caribbean King*, Av 14 de Julio, T/F443-0859, touristoptions@caribe.hn, good value tours.

Parque Nacional Pico Bonito

Pico Bonito (674 sq km) is the largest national park in Honduras and home to the country's highest point, Pico Bonito, at 2,435 m. The Río Cangrejal, a mecca for whitewater rafting, marks the eastern border of the park. After visiting the area, US-published *Outside Magazine* said the experience offered "adventure and unparalleled natural beauty" – commendation indeed. It has deep tropical hardwood forests which shelter, among other animals, jaguars and three species of monkey, deep canyons and tumbling streams and waterfalls (including Las Gemelas which fall vertically some 200 m).

Development of the park by Curla (Centro Universitario Regional del Litoral Atlántico) continues under the supervision of Cohdefor, the forestry office, and the Fundación Parque Nacional Pico Bonito (FUPNAPIB), office on C 15, half a block east of Av 14 de Julio, La Ceiba. Curla has a *campamento* with accommodation under construction for visiting scientists, but you can camp. The camp is 5 km (1½ hours' walk) on a good path from **Armenia Bonito** to the west of La Ceiba, frequent buses from Parque Manuel Bonilla by the Ruta 1 de Mayo urban bus (one hour). Visitors can take the path to the Río Bonito which has some spectacular river scenery. Swimming is possible in deep rock pools. A route is being created around the foothills and there are a few interesting trails in the forest. Pico Bonito itself (2,435 m) has seldom been climbed as it takes at least nine days. The preferred route is along the Río Bonito, starting from near the *campamento*, and from there up a ridge which climbs all the way to the summit. Expertise in rock climbing is not necessary, but several steep pitches do require a rope for safety; good physical condition is also a necessity. Poisonous snakes, including the fer-de-lance will probably be encountered en route.

Park information and tours For further information on the Park contact Cohdefor at their local office 6 km out of town along the Carretera La Ceiba-Tela, T443-1033, where the project director is Sr Allan Herrera. FUPNAPIB can be contacted at Av San Isidro, El Centro Edificio Reyes 3, La Ceiba, T443-3824, fupnapib@laceiba.com Maps are being prepared by Curla but are not yet available. Take care if you enter the forest: tracks are not yet developed, a compass is advisable. Tour companies in La Ceiba arrange trips to the park. A day trip, horse-riding through the park, can be arranged through Harry's at *Bar El Canadiense*, 14 de Julio, near Parque Manuel Bonilla. Trip includes food and guide, US$25. Recommended.

Cuero y Salado Wildlife Reserve

Near the coast, between the Cuero and Salado rivers, 37 km west of La Ceiba , is the Cuero y Salado Wildlife Reserve, which has a great variety of flora and fauna, including manatee, jaguar, monkeys and a large population of local and migratory birds. It extends for 13,225 ha of swamp and forest. The reserve is managed by the Fundación Cuero y Salado (Fucsa) – Refugio de Vida Silvestre, one block north and three blocks west of Parque Central (see map) to the left of the Standard Fruit Company, La Ceiba, T/F443-0329, Apartado Postal 674. The foundation is open to volunteers, preferably those who speak English and Spanish. Part of the programme is to teach environmental education at two rural schools.

Early morning is the best time for views of the Parque Nacional Pico Bonito, for its birdlife and howler monkeys

Nilmo, a knowledgeable biologist who acts as a guide, takes morning and evening boat trips for those staying overnight, either through the canal dug by Standard Fruit, parallel to the beach between the palms and the mangroves, or down to the Salado lagoon. Five kayaks are available for visitors' use. In the reserve are spider and capuchin monkeys, iguanas, jaguar, tapirs, crocodiles, manatee, hummingbirds, toucans, ospreys, eagles and vultures. A five-hour trip will take you to Barra de Colorado to see the manatees. Ask to see the garden where local people are taught to grow food without burning the forest. The beach along the edge of the reserve is 28 km long, with a strip of sea also protected by Fucsa. Fishing is possible, and camping at Salado Barra, but you need a permit for both. There are extensive coconut groves along the coast owned by Standard Fruit Company.

Fucsa's administration centre, on the banks of the Río Salado, has photos, charts, maps, radio and a two-room visitors' house, sleeping 4 in basic bunks, electricity from 1800-2100. No mosquito nets, so avoid Sep and Oct if you can. Don't wear open footwear as snakes and yellow scorpions can be found here. The refuge is becoming increasingly popular, so book lodging in advance. There is space for tents. Meals cost extra and are served by Doña Estela Cáceres (refried beans, egg, tortillas, etc) in her main family room, with pigs, chickens and children wandering in and out. Give her prior notice. It is worth bringing your own provisions too, especially drinking water.

Sleeping & eating

Although it is possible to go to the Salado and hire a villager and his boat, a qualified guide will show you much more. It is essential to bring a hat and sun lotion with you. Travel agencies in La Ceiba run tours there, but **Fucsa** arranges visits and owns the only accommodation in the reserve. Before going, check with Fucsa in La Ceiba. Although the office only has basic information, they are helpful and there are displays and books about the flora and fauna to be found in the park. A charge of about US$10 is made to enter the reserve, which you can pay at Fucsa, keep the receipt, plus US$5 per person for accommodation. A guide and kayak for a 1-hr trip costs about US$10. Boatmen charge about US$20 for a 2-hr trip or US$40 for 5 hrs (6-7 persons maximum) US$6-7 for the guide.

Tours

To get there independently, take a bus to **La Unión** (every hour, 0600 until 1500 from La Ceiba terminus, US$0.30, 1½ hrs, ask to get off at the railway line, *ferrocarril*, or Km 17), an interesting journey through pineapple fields. There are several ways of getting into the park from La Unión. Walking takes 1½ hrs (avoid midday sun), take water. Groups usually take a *motocarro*, a dilapidated train which also transports the coconut crop – there is no fixed timetable – but if you're lucky enough to catch it, it costs US$12, payable at the Park Office, 15 mins' journey. From near Doña Tina's house (meals available), take a *burra*, a flat-bed rail-car propelled by two men with poles (a great way to see the countryside) to the community on the banks of the Río Salado (9 km, 1 hr, US$8 each way).

Transport

To return to La Unión, it is another *burra* ride or a 2-hr walk along the railway, little shade; then, either wait for a La Ceiba bus, last one at 1500, or ask for the short cut through

Honduras

grapefruit groves, 20 mins, which leads to the main La Ceiba-Tela road on which there are many more buses back to town, 20 mins, US$0.40.

La Ceiba to Trujillo A paved road runs from La Ceiba to Trujillo (see below) and Puerto Castilla. At Savá, the bridge over the Río Aguán was washed away by Mitch, but traffic is now passing through here without problems. Like the Ulúa, the Aguán valley was flooded extensively by Mitch. The La Ceiba-Trujillo road meets the road heading southwest to Olanchito and Yoro, newly paved to Olanchito and a good gravel surface thereafter, which involves a river crossing.

Between Savá and Trujillo is the rapidly growing town of **Tocoa**, also in the Aguán valley. The town has several banks and the Catholic church is the modern design of a Peace Corps volunteer.

Sleeping and eating **E** *San Patricio*, Barrio El Centro, T444-3401. With bath, a/c, cheaper without, TV. **F** *Hotelito Rosgil*, near bus station. With bath but water problems. *Rigo*, Barrio El Centro. Good Italian food and pizzas. *Gran Vía*, on east side of park. Good *comedor* opposite the bus station. **Transport** Several buses daily to La Ceiba US$2.50, and to Trujillo, US$1.

Trujillo

Colour map 6, grid B3
Population: 45,000

Once a major port and the former capital, Trujillo sits on the southern shore of the palm-fringed Bay of Trujillo. It is a quiet, pleasant town with clean beaches nearby and calm water that is ideal for swimming. Founded in 1525 by Juan de Medina, it is the oldest town in Honduras. Hernán Cortés arrived here after his famous march overland from Yucatán in pursuit of his usurping lieutenant, Olid. Filibuster William Walker (see under Nicaragua) was shot near here in 1860; a commemorative stone marks the spot in the rear garden of the hospital, one block east of the Parque Central, and the old cemetery (near *Hotel Trujillo*) is his final resting place.

Fortaleza Santa Bárbara, a ruined Spanish fortress overlooking the bay, is worth a visit. Most of the relics found there have been moved to the museum of Rufino Galán, but there are still a few rusty muskets and cannon balls. ■ *US$1.* Twenty minutes' walk from Trujillo plaza (follow on road beyond *Hotel Trujillo*) is the **Museo y Piscina Rufino Galán Cáceres** which has a swimming pool filled from the Río Cristales with changing rooms and picnic facilities. Close by, the wreckage of a US C-80 aircraft which crashed in 1985 forms part of Sr Galán's museum. Inside the museum is more information and memorabilia about the accident. The rest of the collection is a mass of curios, some very interesting. ■ *US$1, US$0.50 for swim.* The cemetery is rather overgrown, with collapsed and open tombs, but it does give a feel for the origins of early residents. **Fiesta**: San Juan Bautista in June, with participation from surrounding Garífuna settlements.

West of Trujillo, just past the football field on the Santa Fe road, is the **Río Grande**, which has lovely pools and waterfalls for river bathing, best during rainy season. Take the path on far side of river, after about 10 minutes cut down to the rocks and follow the river upstream along the boulders. **C** *Campamento*, 2 km along the road, T434-4244, has a round thatched bar, good food, and 10 rooms, lovely setting, mountain backdrop, on unspoilt beach, showers, palm trees, shade, basic but clean, ask about camping.

Beaches
Before setting out ask which beaches are safe

Good beaches are found both on the peninsula and around Trujillo Bay. Take a bus from near the Parque Central towards Puerto Castilla and ask the driver to let you off at the path about 1 km beyond the bridge over the lagoon. Other beaches around Puerto Castilla are separated by mangroves, are littered and have sandflies. Other sandy beaches can be reached by taking any bus from the Parque Central 1½ km, to the side road leading to the landing strip and *Bahía Bar-Restaurant*; the white sand stretches for many kilometres northwards. The beaches in town tend to be less clean. If you're tempted to walk westwards towards Santa Fe to find a cleaner stretch of sand don't walk alone; it is not safe; tourists here have been assaulted and robbed.

Honduras

A-B *Christopher Columbus Beach Resort*, outside town along the beach, drive across airstrip, T434-4966, F434-4972. 72 rooms and suites (**L-AL**), a/c, cable TV, swimming pool, restaurant, watersports, tennis, painted bright turquoise. **B-C** *Villa Brinkley* (known locally as Miss Peggy's), T434-4444, F434-4045. On the mountain overlooking the bay, swimming pool, good view, large rooms, wooden furniture in Maya style, big bathrooms, sunken baths, fan, cheaper rooms in annex, full of character and friendly, motorbike rental, restaurant good for evening meal. **C** *Colonial*, T434-4011, F434-4878. With bath, on plaza, hacienda style, restaurant (*El Bucanero*, see below), a/c, safe and clean, recently refurbished. **C** *O'Glynn*, T434-4592. Smart, clean, good rooms and bathrooms, a/c, TV, fridge in some rooms.

Sleeping
Price codes:
see inside front cover

D *Trujillo*, T434-4202, up the hill from the market. Fan, clean sheets daily, rooms with shower and toilet, TV, good value. Recommended, but ask for a corner room, cockroaches in ground floor rooms, nice breeze. **E** *Albert's Place*, T434-4431, 2 blocks south of Parque Central. Red brick house, beautifully restored, nice garden, good value, English spoken. **E** *Mar de Plata*, up street west, T434-4458. Upstairs rooms best, with bath, fan, friendly and helpful, beautiful view from roof. **E-F** *Catracho*, 3 blocks south of church, then a block east, T434-4438. Basic, clean, noisy, no water at night, wooden cabins facing a garden, camping space US$1.50, parking. **F** *Buenos Aires* opposite *Catracho*, T434-4431. Monthly rates available, pleasant, clean, peaceful, but cabins damp and many mosquitos, organizes tours to national park. **F** *Coco Pando*, Barrio Cristales, behind beach, T434-4748. Garífuna-owned, clean, bright airy rooms, restaurant serving typical Garífuna dishes, runs popular weekend disco nearby.

In the village of Silin, on main road southeast of Trujillo, is **B** *Resort y Spa Agua Caliente Silin*, T434-4249, F434-4248. Cabañas with cable TV, pool, thermal waters, restaurant, massage given by Pech Indian, Lastenia Hernández, very relaxing.

El Bucanero, on main plaza, a/c, video, good breakfast, *desayuno típico*, for US$2. *Don Perignon*, uphill from *Pantry*, some Spanish dishes, good local food, cheap. *Galaxia*, 1 block west of plaza. Good seafood at reasonable prices, popular with locals. *Granada*, in the centre. Good Garífuna dishes, seafood and standard meals, great *sopa de camarones*. Recommended. Breakfasts and snacks, also bar, friendly service, good value. *Oasis*, opposite Bancahsa. Outdoor seating, Canadian owned, good meeting place, information board, good food, bar, English books for sale, book exchange, local tours. *Nice and Ease*, sells ice-cream and cakes. Nearby is *Pantry*, Garífuna cooking and standard menu, cheap pizzas, a/c.

Eating
Don't miss the coconut bread, a speciality of the Garífuna

Bahía Bar-Restaurant, T434-4770, on the beach by the landing strip next to Christopher Columbus. Popular with ex-pats, also Hondurans at weekends, good vegetarian food, showers, toilets.

Nightlife In Barrio Cristales at weekends there's Punta music and a lively atmosphere. Recommended. The **cinema** shows current US releases.

Entertainment

Garí-Arte Souvenir, T434-4207, in the centre of Barrio Cristales, is highly recommended for authentic Garífuna souvenirs. Owned by Ricardo Lacayo and open daily. *Tienda Souvenir Artesanía* next to *Hotel Emperador*, handicrafts, hand-painted toys. 3 supermarkets in the town centre.

Shopping

Air Trujillo has an airstrip east of town near the beach hotels. *Isleña* flies daily to La Ceiba to connect with flights to San Pedro Sula and Tegucigalpa. Booking office at *Christopher Columbus Resort*, T434-4966.

Transport

Buses Trujillo can be reached by bus from San Pedro Sula, Tela and La Ceiba by a paved road through Savá, Tocoa and Corocito. From La Ceiba it is 3 hrs by direct bus, 4 hrs by *local*. 3 direct *Cotraibal* buses in early morning from Trujillo, buses every 1½ hrs, 6 hrs, US$5. Bus from **Tegucigalpa** (Comayagüela) with *Cotraibal*, 7 Av between 10 and 11 C, US$6, 9 hrs; some buses to the capital go via La Unión, which is not as safe a route as via San Pedro Sula. To **San Pedro Sula**, 5 daily 0200-0800, US$5. Public transport also to San Esteban and Juticalpa (leave from in front of church at 0400, but check locally, arriving 1130, US$5.20 – see page 915). Bus to **Santa Fe** at 0930, US$0.40, leaves from outside *Glenny's Super Tienda*; to **Santa Rosa de Aguán** and **Limón** daily.

Sea Cargo boats leave for ports in Mosquitia (ask all captains at the dock, wait up to 3 days, see page 917), the Bay Islands (very difficult) and Honduran ports to the west. Enquire at the jetty.

Directory **Banks** *Banco Atlántida* on Parque Central and *Bancahsa*, both cash US$, TCs and handles Visa. *Banco de Occidente* also handles MasterCard and Western Union. **Communications** Post office and *Hondutel*: (F434-4200) 1 block up from church. **Laundry** Next to *Disco Orfaz*, wash and dry US$2.50. **Libraries** Library in middle of square. **Medical services** Hospital on main road east off square towards La Ceiba. **Tour operators** *Hacienda Tumbador Crocodile Reserve*, privately owned, accessible only by 4WD and with guide, US$5 entry, eg **Turtle Tours** at *Hotel Villa Brinkley* (address above – agency at *Oasis Café*), run trips to Río Plátano, 6 days, 5 nights US$400, also to beaches, jungle hikes, etc. Guided tours by motorbike, 7-17 days with back-up vehicle. Bike rental US$35 per day. Very helpful even if you want to travel independently to Mosquitia, German, English, Spanish spoken, T/F434-4431. Several other enterprises organize tours to Capiro y Calentura, Guaimoreto and the *Oasis*, *Gringo's Bar*. *Gringo's* also advertises trips to Tumbador followed by a visit to the beach near Puerto Castilla and lunch. **Useful addresses** *Migración* is opposite *Mar de Plata*.

Around Trujillo

West of Trujillo There are interesting Garífuna villages west of Trujillo. The road is rough, often impassable in wet weather, and jeeps are needed even in the dry season. **Santa Fe**, 10 km west of Trujillo (US$0.30 by bus, leaves when full, get there by 0800 for a seat), is a friendly place with several good Garífuna restaurants, for example *Comedor Caballero* (also known as *Pete's Place*, good for lunch, huge portions, lobster, vegetarian food, highly recommended) and *Las Brisas de Santa Fe*, on the endless white sandy beach. The bus service continues to **San Antonio** (good restaurant behind the beach) and **Guadalupe**. Walk in the morning along the beach to Santa Fe and then get a bus back to Trujillo, taking plenty of water and sun block. This stretch of beach is outstanding, but watch out for *marea roja*, a sea organism which colours the water pink and can give irritating skin rashes to bathers. Also, be warned, there have been attacks on the beach and local people consider this walk unsafe. It's best to go in a large group.

Trujillo & the coast

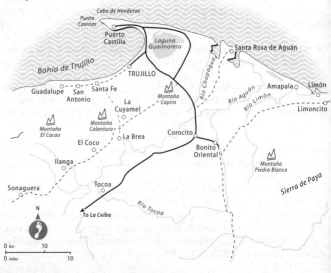

Puerto Castilla is one of the two containerized ports of the Honduran Caribbean coast, mainly exports including bananas, grapefruit and palm oil. In addition to a meat-packing station and active shrimping centre, there is a naval base and helicopter station. The restaurant *Brisas de Caribe* is good. Near the village, a large crucifix marks the spot where Columbus reputedly conducted the first mass on American soil in 1502.

Puerto Castilla

One of the largest Garífuna communities, Santa Rosa de Aguán is an interesting coastal town of 7,000 hospitable English and Spanish-speaking inhabitants some 40 km from Trujillo. The spreading settlement lies at the mouth of the Río Aguán, the greater part on the east of the bay. It suffered great loss of life and property in Hurricane Mitch. Check on conditions before going there. Bus from Trujillo's Parque Central Monday-Saturday. Also bus service from La Ceiba. If driving from Trujillo, turn left at Km 343, 20 km along the highway, where a good gravel road runs another 20 km to Santa Rosa. From where the road ends at the west bank, take a canoe ferry across to the east side. A white sand beach stretches all the way to Limón (see page 920), and the thundering surf is an impressive sight. Take drinking water, insect repellent, mosquito coils and high factor sun screen.

Santa Rosa de Aguán

The **Parque Nacional Capiro y Calentura** encompasses these two mountains overlooking Trujillo. The four- to six-hour walk to the summit gives spectacular views and on a clear day Isla Roatán can be seen in the distance. The walk is best done early in the morning when the forest is alive with the sounds of birds, monkeys and other wildlife. The path can be reached by walking (or taking a taxi) up the hill past the *Villa Brinkley Hotel*. The road to the summit is in poor condition from the entrance of the park and can be driven only in a four-wheel drive. There used to be a secret military tracking station at the top but this is now a Hondutel relay installation and there are no longer any restrictions on access. Insect repellent is needed if you pause. The park is run by the **Fundación Capiro Calentura Guaimoreto (Fucagua)**, which has a temporary office first left after *Hotel Mar de Plata*, a couple of doors before the cinema, open Monday-Friday. They have information on all the reserves in the area and also on hiking and tours. Until a new office is built in the park, entry tickets must be bought here before going to Capiro y Calentura. They are opening up new trails, improving old ones and organizing guided tours through parts of the forest. The hike along the Sendero de la Culebrina uses the remnants of a colonial stone road used to transport gold from the mines in the Valle de Aguán. It runs along the Río Mojagua and leads to **La Cuyamel**, 37 km from Trujillo, just off the road to Sonaguera. Halfway up the **Cerro de las Cuevas**, 7 km beyond Cuyamel, are impressive caves showing traces of occupation by pre-Columbian Pech Indians.

National parks
As with all walking in this area, it is best to go in a group to avoid attacks

Fucagua also administers the **Refugio de Vida Silvestre, Laguna de Guaimoreto (RVSLG)**, northeast of Trujillo, where there is a bird island (Isla de los Pájaros), monkeys and good fishing. To visit, either arrange a trip with Fucagua, a tour agency such as *Turtle Tours*, or take a bus from Trujillo towards Puerto Castilla, get off just after the bridge which crosses the lagoon, then walk away from the lagoon for about 200 m to a dirt track on the left. Follow this and cross a low bridge and on the left is the house of a man who rents dugout canoes. The Isla de los Pájaros is about 3 km up the lagoon, a bit too far for a dugout. Another alternative is to go down to the wharf in Trujillo and ask for Reinardo, who runs the local fishermen's co-op. He hires out motorized canoes and launches (price depends on the number of passengers and length of trip). There are no roads, paths or facilities in the area.

East from El Progreso

While most people make straight for the coast at Tela, heading east from El Progreso leads through mountain scenery up to the small town of Yoro, beyond to Olanchito and a link to La Ceiba. With everyone else rushing to the Bay Islands, you could well have the place to yourself.

Honduras

El Progreso
Colour map 6, grid B2
Population: 106,550

This important but unattractive agricultural and commercial centre (no longer just a banana town) on the Río Ulúa, is 30 minutes' drive on the paved highway southeast of San Pedro Sula en route to Tela.

Sleeping **D** *Gran Hotel Las Vegas*, 2 Av, 11 C N, T666-4667. Smart, a/c, good restaurant called *La Copa Dorada*. **D** *Municipal*, 1 Av, 7-8 C N, T666-4061. With a/c and bath, clean. **E** *Plaza Victoria*, 2 Av, 5-6 C S, T666-2150. Opposite Migración, with bath, cheap laundry, pool, good. **E** *Honduras*, 2 Av 3 C, T666-4264, in front of Banco Atlántida. With bath, run-down, meals US$1.25. **F** *Emperador*, 2 Av, 4-5 C S, 8 blocks west of bus terminal. Attractive, with bath, cheaper without. **F** *La Casa Blanca*, 4 C, 2 Av N. Traditional white and yellow clap-board house with covered balcony, quiet, cockroaches.

Eating *Comida Buffet América*, 2 Av N, ½ block east of market. Open 0700 to 1500, good vege-tarian food. *Mr Kike*, on the ground floor of the *Hotel Municipal* building, a/c, good. *Red Dragon Pub*, 4 C, 1-2 Av N. Owned by an Englishman, Steve, good source of local information, good bar and restaurant. *Los Tarros*, on San Pedro Sula road just before bridge. Good but not cheap. *La Parrilla*, next to *gasolinera* on road to Santa Rita. Good steaks and international food, a/c.

Festivals *La Virgen de Las Mercedes*, 3rd week of **Sep**. Visit the Santa Isabel handicraft centre, where women are taught wood carving.

Shopping Good artesanía, *Imapro*, T266-4700, on the road to Tela.

Transport *Transportes Ulúa*, (18 C y 6 Av, Barrio Villa Adela, Comayagüela, T238-1827) 4 daily, a/c; in El Progreso, 5 Av y Blvd, T666-3270.

Directory Banks About a dozen different banks in town. **Tour operators** *Agencia de Viajes El Progreso*, 2 Av 3-4 C N, T666-4101.

The Santuario Señor de Esquipulas is 5 km south of El Progreso in the village of **Arena Blanca**, where there is a festival on 13 January in honour of the Black Christ of Esquipulas. The temple has baroque and modern architecture, with trees and gardens.

The highway is paved 25 km south of El Progreso to Santa Rita; if you continue towards the San Pedro Sula-Tegucigalpa highway, you avoid San Pedro Sula when travelling from the north coast to the capital. About 10 km south of El Progreso on the paved highway to Santa Rita, at the village of Las Minas, is **El Chorro** (1 km off the highway), a charming waterfall and natural swimming pool. A rugged hike can be made into the mountains and on to **El Negrito** from here.

Parque Nacional Pico Pijol
Colour map 6, grid B2

This park protects the 2,282 m summit of primary cloud forest that is home to many quetzales. It is 32 km from the town of **Morazán** in the Yoro Department, which is 41 km from Progreso (bus from Progreso or Santa Rita). In Morazán are *Hospedaje El Corazón Sagrado*, several restaurants and a disco. The lower slopes of Pico Pijol have been heavily farmed. Access by vehicle is possible as far as Subirana. A guide is needed from there to a large cave nearby and access is difficult, with no infrastruc-ture. Another trail to the summit (2,282 m) starts at **Nueva Esperanza** village (bus from Morazán, Parque Central); ask for the correct trail. The first day is tough, all uphill with no shade; the second is tougher and requires a lot of clearing with a machete. Take a compass and a topographical map. Also in the park is the waterfall at **Las Piratas**; take a bus from Morazán to Los Murillos and then walk to El Ocotillo (ask for Las Piratas). Further up the river are some beautiful deep pools.

Yoro
Colour map 6, grid B2

The paved highway to the prosperous little town of Yoro passes through pleasant countryside surrounded by mountains and dotted with ranches and farms. The **Parque Nacional Montaña de Yoro** is 8 km to the southeast (access from Marale), comprising 257 sq km of cloud forest, home to the Tolupanes indigenous people, also known as Xicaques. The Asociación Ecológica Amigos de la Montaña de Yoro has an office in the Parque Central in Yoro.

Sleeping and eating E *Nelson*, comfortable rooms with bath, fan, modern, good restaurant/bar and nice outdoor swimming pool on 3rd floor, bar/disco on roof with marvellous views. Warmly recommended. **E-F** *Palacio*, on main street, restaurant, nice, all rooms with bath and fan. **F** *Aníbal*, corner of Parque Central, restaurant, excellent value, private or shared bath, clean, pleasant, wide balcony. Best restaurants in hotels, several *comedores* along main street. **Transport** Hourly bus service to **El Progreso**, several daily to **Sulaco**.

Directory Banks *Banco Atlántida* on Parque Central. **Communications** Post office and *Hondutel* 1 block from Parque Central.

From Yoro a dirt road continues to Olanchito via **Jocón**, through attractive country as the road snakes along the pine-forested slopes of Montaña Piedra Blanca and Montaña de la Bellota, with fine views of the surrounding valleys and distant mountain ranges. **F** *Hospedaje*, clean, basic and other accommodation, ask around. Buses from Yoro to Olanchito go as far as Río Aguán (US$1.50) which is a bit too deep to ford. Cross the river in an ox cart or giant inner tube with waterproof floor pushed across by wading drivers, US$0.35, then get on a waiting bus to Olanchito, US$1.

A prosperous but hot town (also called La Ciudad Cívica) in the Agúan valley in the hills southeast of La Ceiba. The town was founded, according to tradition, by a few stragglers who escaped from the destruction of Olancho el Viejo, between Juticalpa and Catacamas, then a wealthy town. They brought with them the crown made of hides which the image of the Virgin still wears in the church of Olanchito. There is a natural bathing spot, **Balneario El Higueral**.

Olanchito
Colour map 6, grid B3
Population: 12,200

Sleeping D *Hotel Olanchito*, Barrio Arriba, C La Palma, T446-6385, a/c, under same management is **E** *Valle Aguán y Chabelito*, 1 block north of Parque Central, T446-6718, single rooms, with a/c, double rooms with fan, all rooms with cable TV, best in town, with best restaurant. **F** *Colonial*, C del Presidio, good value, bath, fan, cheaper with shared bath, restaurant, parking. Opposite is **E** *Olimpic*, bath, a/c, TV. **Eating** *Comedor Doña Luisa* in front of Radio Station and 3 blocks south of Park. *La Ronda*, best in town, Chinese and international, main dishes US$4. Recommended.

Entertainment Cinema *Cine Gardel*. **Festivals** 2nd week of **Sep**, *Semana Cívica*.

Transport Buses from **La Ceiba**, 2½ hrs, US$1 via Jutiapa and Savá (Cotol 7 times a day; Cotrail); to **Trujillo**, 3 hrs, US$3.75 via Savá and Tocoa (Cotol); to Yoro 0545 and 1000 daily, US$2.80.

Directory Banks *Bancahsa* changes TCs. *Importadora Rosita* has better exchange rates.

The Bay Islands

A string of islands off the northern coast of Honduras, the Bay Islands are the country's most popular tourist attraction. Warm, clear Caribbean waters provide excellent diving – some of the cheapest in the Caribbean – on the coral reef. Equally enjoyable are the white sand beaches, tropical sunsets and the relaxed atmosphere which positively encourage you to take to your hammock, lay back and relax. The culture is far less latino *than on the mainland. English is spoken by many and there are still Black Carib descendants of those deported from St Vincent in 1797.*

Getting there Transport to the Bay Islands is easy with regular and flights with *Isleña, Sosa, Atlantic Airlines* and *Rollins Air* from La Ceiba and San Pedro Sula to Utila and Roatán. *Taca* has an international service from Miami to Roatán. There is also a daily boat service from La Ceiba to Roatán and Utila.

Population: 60,000

The beautiful Bay Islands, or **Islas de la Bahía**, of white sandy beaches, coconut palms and gentle sea breezes form an arc in the Caribbean, some 32 km north of La Ceiba. The three main islands are **Utila**, **Guanaja** and, the largest and most developed, **Roatán**. At the eastern end of Roatán are three smaller islands: **Morat**, **Santa Elena**, and **Barbareta**; with many islets and cayes to explore. Closest to the mainland are the small, palm-fringed **Hog Islands**, more attractively known as **Cayos Cochinos**. The Bay Islands have their own websites at www.caribbeancoast.com/bayislands/index.cfm and www.bayislandsdirectory.com

The underwater environment is one of the main attractions and is rich and extensive; reefs surround the islands, often within swimming distance of the shore. Caves and caverns are a common feature, with a wide variety of sponges and the best collection of pillar coral in the Caribbean. There are many protected areas including the Marine Parks of Turtle Harbour on Utila, and Sandy Bay/West End on Roatán, which has permanent mooring buoys at the popular dive sites to avoid damage from anchors. Several other areas have been proposed as marine reserves by the Asociación Hondureña de Ecología: the Santuario Marino de Utila, Parque Nacional Marino Barbareta and Parque Nacional Marino Guanaja. The Bay Islands have their own conservation association (see under Roatán, below).

The traditional industry is fishing, mostly shellfish, with fleets based at French Harbour; but the supporting boat-building is a dying industry. Tourism is now a major source of income, particularly because of the scuba diving attractions. English-speaking blacks constitute the majority of the population, particularly on Roatán. Utila has a population which is about half black and half white, the latter of British stock descended mainly from the settlers from Grand Cayman who arrived in 1830. Columbus anchored here in 1502, during his fourth voyage. In the 18th century the islands were the base for English, French and Dutch buccaneers. They were in British hands for over a century, but were finally ceded to Honduras in 1859. Latin Hondurans have been moving to the islands from the mainland in recent years. The government schools teach in Spanish, and the population is bilingual.

The islands are very beautiful, but beware of the strong sun (the locals bathe in T-shirts), sandflies and other insects. Basic etiquette for snorkelling and diving applies. Snorkellers and divers should not stand on or even touch the coral reefs; any contact, even the turbulence from a fin, will kill the delicate organisms. Unfortunately, security has become a cause for concern. Take care when walking at night.

Cayos Cochinos

The **Hog Islands** (Cayos Cochinos), 17 km northeast of La Ceiba, constitute two small islands and 13 palm-fringed cayes. **Cochino Grande** is the larger island, rising to an altitude of just 143 m, and **Cochino Pequeño** is the smaller. Both have lush tropical vegetation with primeval hardwood forests and there are fewer biting insects than in the Bay Islands. There are Garífuna fishing villages of palm-thatched huts at Chachauate on Lower Monitor Cay, and East End Village on Cochino Grande. Transport to the Hog Islands can be sought on the supply *cayuco* from

Cayos Cochinos/ Hog Islands

Honduras (side margin)

Nuevo Armenia (see page 887), or by chartering a boat from Utila. There is a small dirt airstrip. Dugout canoes are the local form of transport. The islands are privately owned and access to most of the cayes is limited, being occupied only by caretakers. The Cayos Cochinos and surrounding waters are now a National Marine Reserve and rangers are currently being trained. Spear fishing, nets and traps are not allowed, although line fishing is permitted.

Plantation Beach Resort, T/F442-0974, VHF 12, www.plantationbeachresort.com, on Cochino Grande, rustic cabins on hillside, hot water, fans, diving offshore, yacht moorings, good steep walk up to lighthouse for view over cayes to mainland, music festival end-Jul, local bands and dancers, they charge US$30 for the trip from La Ceiba. At Chachauate, stay with fishing family or rent thatched hut (US$6) and a Garífuna woman will cook for you. Small restaurant but bring your own drinking water. A few small *tiendas* sell beer and sodas. Short wade to *Pelican Bar*, run by Al, opens on demand. This island is free of mosquitoes and sandflies. Bring snorkelling equipment, kayaks can be hired. **Cayo Timón** (also known as North Sand Cay) can be visited from Utila, 1¼ hrs by boat; you can rent the caye, **E** per person, minimum 6, 8 is comfortable, A-frame, Polynesian style, do overnight diving trips, very basic, quiet, peaceful, or phone Roy and Brenda at *Thompson's Bakery*, Utila, T425-3112, for information.

Sleeping & eating

Utila

Utila is the cheapest and least developed of the islands. Only 32 km from La Ceiba, it is low lying, with just two hills, Pumpkin and the smaller Stewarts, either side of the town known locally as **East Harbour**. The first inhabitants were Paya Indians and there is scant archaeological evidence of their culture. Later the island was used by pirates; Henry Morgan is reputed to have hidden booty in the caves. The population now is descended from Black Caribs and white Cayman Islanders with a recent influx from mainland Honduras. Independence Day (15 September) festivities, including boxing and climbing greased poles, are reported to be worth staying for.

Colour map 6, grid B3
Area: 41 sq km
Population: 2,400

Honduras

There are no big resorts on the island, although a couple of small, lodge-style, upmarket places have opened, otherwise the accommodation is rather basic. Sunbathing and swimming is not particularly good and has changed a bit post-Mitch. There is a swimming hole near the airport. At the left-hand end of the airstrip (from the town) is one of the best places for coral and quantity of fish. **Jack Neal Beach** has white sand with good snorkelling and swimming. **Chepee's White Hole** at the end of Blue Bayou peninsula has a beach for swimming. Snorkelling is also good offshore by the *Blue Bayou* restaurant, a 20-minute walk from town, but you will be charged

Around the island

Utila

US$1 for use of the facilities. There are hammocks and a jetty which is great for fishing at sunset, and the only place to get away from the terrible sandflies. There is also sandfly relief at **Big Bight**, **Redcliff** and **Rocky Point**. Look out for the American, Dick (with a beard and a parrot on his shoulder), who takes four-hour snorkelling trips for US$10. *Laguna Beach Resort* is on the other side of the lagoon.

You can hike to **Pumpkin Hill** (about 4 km down the lane by *Bancahsa*, bikes recommended) where there are some freshwater caves with a beach nearby (watch out for sharp coral). It is also possible to walk on a trail from the airfield to Big Bight and the iron shore on the east coast, about 2 km, exploring tidal pools; nice views and beach but it is rocky so wear sandals. Trails to the north coast through the swamp and past the dead forest are only passable in the dry months (April-September), it is best to hire a local to show you the way. An interesting way of visiting the north coast is to hire a canoe (or kayak from *Gunter's*) and paddle from the lagoon past the *Blue Bayou* through the mangroves and the canal (about three hours). But look out for crocodiles – a huge one was killed in 1995. Take snorkelling gear and explore the reef offshore if the sea is not too rough. Canoe hire US$10 per day. On dry days and when there is no breeze sandflies are most active. Coconut oil, baby oil or Avon *Skin-so-Soft* helps to ward them off. Take insect repellent; *Off*, sold at *Henderson's* supermarket, is effective.

The Cayes A 20-minute motorboat ride from East Harbour are the cayes, a chain of small islands populated by fisherfolk off the southwest coast of Utila which is known as the Cayitos de Utila. **Jewel Caye** and **Pigeon Caye** are connected by a bridge and are inhabited by a fishing community which reportedly settled there to get away from the sandflies on Utila. E *Hotel Kayla* is a European-style hotel run by Donald Cooper. There is also the basic hotel, *Vicky's*, a few restaurants, a Saturday night disco and little else. **Diamond Caye** is privately owned and is looking for a new owner – in the meantime, the snorkelling offshore is excellent. **Water Caye** is a coconut island with 'white hole' sandy areas and with wonderful bathing in the afternoons. It is the only place where you can camp, sling a hammock or, in an emergency, sleep in or under the house of the caretaker; take food and fresh water, or rent the caretaker's canoe and get supplies from Jewel Cay. The caretaker collects a US$1.25 per person fee for landing and the same for a hammock. There are no facilities, but you can get supplies delivered by the boatman who brings you over. The best snorkelling is off the south shore, a short walk from the beach. To hire a motorized canoe or dory costs US$15 per person; many boatmen go and will collect you in the evening, recommended. You may also be able to go out with a diving party and be picked up in the afternoon, or persuade a boatman to take you to one of the remoter cayes. *Gunter's Dive Shop* in Utila runs water taxis to the cayes for US$10, as does the *Bundu Café*.

Sleeping **L-AL** *Laguna Beach Resort*, on point opposite *Blue Bayou*, T/F425-3239, www.utila.comlodge, with bungalows each with own jetty, 6-day package includes meals and diving US$750-800,

Honduras

non-diver US$600-650, fishing offered, can accommodate maximum 40. **B** *Sharky's Reef Cabins*, the Point, T425-3212, hjackson@hondutel.hn, a/c, cable TV, porch over lagoon, fans. **B** *Utila Lodge*, T425-3143, F425-3209, bicdive@hondutel.hn, an all-wooden building with decks and balconies, harbour view, a/c, 8 rooms, clean and modern, meals only when they have guests, dive shop (*Bay Islands College of Diving*) on site. **B** *Utila*, on water next to *Lodge*, T425-3340, cheaper rooms downstairs, very clean, 24-hr water and power, fan, nice view, secure.

Cheaper hotels are along main street or just off it. **D** *Bay View*, T425-3114, 100 m from *Utila Lodge*, with or without bath, private pier, family run. **D** *Mango Inn*, T425-3335, with bath, cheaper without, fan, spotless, helpful, roof terrace, reduction for students with *Utila Dive Centre*, good restaurant and coffee bar. Recommended. **D-E** *Margaritaville*, at very end of the village, T425-3366, very clean, big rooms with 2 double beds, private bathroom, friendly, but no water or electricity at night.

E *Countryside*, T425-3216, 10 mins' walk out of town, shared bath, rooms and apartments, quiet, clean, friendly, fan, porch, ask in town for Woody and Annie. **E** *Cross Creek* (see also *Diving* below), T425-3134, clean basic rooms, bathrooms, for divers on courses, cheaper than for non-divers. **E** *Harbour View*, T425-3159, F425-3359, right on water, *Parrot's Dive* on site, cheaper rooms with shared bathrooms upstairs, rooms with private bath downstairs, hot water, own generator, cleaning done only on arrival, TV, fans, run by Roger and Maimee. **E** *Laguna del Mar*, opposite and owned by *Trudy's*, T425-3103, terrace, very clean, fans, mosquito nets, diving offered with *Underwater Vision*. **E** *Seaside*, T425-3150, including private bathroom, very popular with budget travellers, laundry service, noisy in the mornings from cockerels and locals' music. **E** *Trudy's*, T/F425-3103, 5 mins from airport, with and without bath, very clean, comfortable. Recommended. *Underwater Vision* dive shop on site.

F *Blue Bayou*, 25 mins out of town, 1 hr walk from airfield, very basic, insanitary, bad sandflies, good place to hire a bike, snacks and drinks available, restaurant only in high season, hammocks on the beach US$1, free to guests, take torch for night-time. Cheap and very basic rooms at **F** *Blueberry Hill*, T425-3141, and houses for rent, lots of signs along the road. **F** *Celena*, main street, T425-3228, with bath, clean, fan, Visa and MasterCard accepted. Recommended. **F** *Coopers Inn*, T425-3184, cheaper if you dive with Captain Morgan's, very clean and friendly, Danish cook. Recommended. **F** *Delaney's*, good value, good small restaurant. **F** *Lizzie*, clean, comfortable, fan, shared facilities, friendly, no power from 0000-0600. **F** *Loma Vista*, beyond *Bucket of Blood Bar*, T425-3243, clean, fan, shared bath, very friendly, washes clothes cheaply. **F** *Tropical*, Mammie Lane, 15 double rooms, kitchen, fans, has own water supply and generator, safe.

Honduras

Eating

Menus are often ruled by the supply boat: on Tuesday restaurants have everything, by the weekend some drinks run out

Bundu Café, excellent food, quiche, salads, sandwiches, juices and other drinks, run by friendly couple Steve and Fran, good book exchange, also has a **video cinema**, with movies nightly at 1930, US$1.50, also run trips to Water Cay, popular hangout. Recommended. *Capt Jack's*, next to Gunter's Dive Shop, good, 0630-2100. *Delaney's Island Kitchen*, open 1730-2200 for pizza, lasagne and veg dishes, Danish cook, good specials nightly. *Frosty Sea Frog*, near the Golden Rose, with *fajitas* and pizza, 0700-2300. *Golden Rose*, opposite Utila Lodge, superb food, reasonable prices, highly recommended, Mon-Sat 1000-2200, Sun 1400-2200. *Jade Seahorse*, open 1100-2200, opposite *Bucket of Blood*, good seafood, excellent vegetarian food and *licuados*, coolest décor in town, includes the *Treetanic* bar, high up in the trees 1700-2400. Closed Thu. *Las Delicias*, open 0800-2400, local food, lively bar with music each night, live music Tue and Fri. *Looney Lagoon* is a new bar and restaurant in town. *Mermaid's Corner*, breakfast from 0700, huge pizza (US$6) and pasta, about US$2.50-3 main course, good value and popular but nothing special. *Myrtle's*, open 1000-2330, by far the quickest lunch in town, delicious *comida corriente* served by Terricina, opposite casino, locals' hangout. *Ormas*, simple but good food, excellent coconut bread, also serves beer. *RJ's BBQ and Grill House*, "absolutely the best top notch food in town", barbequed meat and fish, with generous portions. Very highly recommended. Wed, Fri and Sat from 1730. *Selly's*, very good food, closed to regular custom but Selly will cook if you get a group of 6 minimum, great kingfish, also rooms available. *Sharky's Reef*, near airport, open Wed-Sun 1800-2100, good portions, well prepared, try their vodka sours. *The Galley*, below the Seaside Inn, set evening meal only, very good. *Thompsons Bakery*, open 0600-1200, best place for breakfast, very informal, friendly, good cakes, lots of information. Good yogurt, cakes, bottled water at *Henderson's* store.

Bars *Bahía del Mar*, bar with pier, swimming. *Bar in the Bush,* is the place to go, 100 m beyond the *Mango Inn*, very popular, lots of dancing and always packed, Wed 1800-2330, Fri and Sun 1800-0300. *Bucket of Blood*, run by Evita and Milkie, make mine a double. *Club 07*, opens Sat, free rum 2200-2300, good dancing. *Coco Loco*, on jetty at harbour front near Scuba Libre sign, very popular, 1600-0000, closed Sun. *Las Delicias*, and *Casino* are busy on Sat nights. *Sea Breaker*, thatched bar, on waterfront behind *Orma's*, open Tue, Fri and Sat, 1730-2300, happy hour 1730-1900, jugs of cocktails, popular.

Sports

www.roatanet.com, has plenty of information about Utila and its dive sites

Diving There are currently around 50 dive sites around Utila, where permanent moorings have been established to minimize damage to the coral reef. Although the reef is colourful and varied, there are not a lot of fish, and lobster have almost disappeared. The dive sites are close to shore at about 20 m depth but they are all boat dives. Diving off the north coast is more spectacular, with drop-offs, canyons and caves. Fish are more numerous, helped by the establishment of the *Turtle Harbour Marine Reserve and Wildlife Refuge*.

Recently there have been improvements in conservation with the arrival of Coral Caye Conservation to investigate Utila. Project Utila started with a dive shop survey in October 1999 using 10 weeks of diving records to assess diving intensity on Utila´s reefs. The project is mapping the reefs to check their health and plans to establish a programme of coral reef monitoring which can eventually be maintained by Honduran scientists. The project's aims are broad, including providing information for the management of Turtle Harbor Marine Reserve and the proposed Raggedy Caye Marine Reserve, and assessing the status of some of the marine species which are exploited for commercial and subsistence use. The long-term aim is to promote conservation of the marine ecosystems of Utila through education, training and the dissemination of information. Work on studying the migratory patterns of the whale shark, which passes through Honduran waters, has also begun on Utila.

Dive with care for yourself and the reef at all times

Utila is essentially a very popular dive training centre. You can learn to dive here cheaper than anywhere else in the Caribbean, especially if you include the low living expenses. It is best to do a course of some sort; students come first for places on boats and recreational divers have to fit in. In recent years Utila has developed a reputation for poor safety and there have been some accidents requiring emergency treatment in the recompression chamber on Roatán. Serious attempts have been made to change this by the diving community of Utila. Michel Bessette, manager and owner of *Paradise Divers* and a committee member of the Utila Clinic, says that the 3 or 4 accidents that happen annually are a result of cowboy divers and drug or alcohol abuse.

Choose an **instructor** who you get on with, and one who has small classes and cares about safety; follow the rules on alcohol/drug abuse and pay attention to the dive tables. There is a rapid turnover of instructors; many stay only a season to earn money to continue their travels, and some have a lax attitude towards diving regulations. Check that equipment looks new and well maintained. Boats vary, you may find it difficult to climb into a dory if there are waves. Not all boats have oxygen on board.

There is **price agreement** across dive shops in Utila. Out of the revenues the Utila Dive Supporters' Association can budget for spending, facilities and eventually conservation. Whatever you may think of the idea, one benefit, according to Bessette, is greater safety and better organized protection of the reef. Whether this works remains to be seen, but the price of saving a few dollars could end up costing lives. Dive insurance at US$3 per day for fun divers, US$9 for students (advanced, or open water), US$30 for divemasters is compulsory and is available from the BICA office. It covers air ambulance to Roatán and the recompression chamber. Treat any cuts from the coral seriously, they do not heal easily.

A **PADI Open Water** course costs US$159 (including certificate) with 4 dives, an Advanced course costs US$159 with 5 dives. Credit cards, if accepted, are 8 extra. Competition is fierce with over 15 dive shops looking for business, so you can pick and choose. Once qualified, fun dives are US$25 for 2 tanks, US$125 for 10 tanks. Most schools offer instruction

in English or German; French and Spanish are usually available somewhere, while tuiti
handbooks are provided in numerous languages including Japanese. A variety of courses is
available up to instructor level. If planning to do a diving course, it is helpful but not essential
to take passport-sized photographs with you for the PADI certificate. *Cross Creek*, run by
Ronald Janssen, T425-3134, F425-3234, www.ccreek.com, 2 boats, maximum 8 people per
instructor, 2-3 instructors, new equipment, 8 kayaks for hire (US$10 per day), accommoda-
tion on site for students, 18 rooms. *Gunter's* dive school based at Sea Side Inn, T/F425-3350,
www.riconet.com/ecomarine run by Roland from Austria and Miri, an Israeli. The instructor,
Pascal Floss, is experienced, has been on the island a long time and is recommended as the
best person for finding fish and other aquatic life on the reef. Gunter's also offer trips to Water
Caye and are the contact for trips to Lívingston, Guatemala. *Utila Watersports*, T/F425-3239,
run by Troy Bodden; quality of instructors varies. Troy also hires out snorkelling gear, photographic and video equipment and takes boat trips. Chris Phillips from the *Utila Dive Centre*,
T425-3326, F425-3327, www.utiladivecentre.com, very professional courses, well-maintained equipment, sometimes takes divers to north coast in fast dory, recommended but no
shade, surface interval on cayes. *Bay Islands College of Diving*, on main street close to
Hondutel tower, T425-3143, www.dive-utila.com, 5-star PADI facility, experienced and well
qualified staff, good boats ranging from 50 ft, for large parties to skiff for smaller ones, environmentally sound. *Paradise Divers*, on the seafront behind Hendersons supermarket,
relaxed and friendly, T425-3148, F425-3348, www.todomundo.com/paradisedivers/ *Captain Morgan's*. T/F425-3161, captm@hondutel.hn, has been recommended for small
classes, good equipment, friendly staff.

Salty Dog Productions specialize in underwater videos, underwater photography
courses, camera rental and photo processing. T/F425-3363, saltydog@hondutel.hn

Shopping

Arts and crafts: *Bay Islands Original Shop* sells T-shirts, sarongs, coffee, hats, etc. Mon-Fri
0900-1200 and 1300-1800, Sat and Sun 0900-1200. Also *Annie Maude Gift Shop* and *Utila
Lodge Gift Shop*. Gunter Kordovsky is a painter and sculptor with a gallery at his house, good
map of Utila, paintings, cards, wood carving.

Entertainment

Reef Cinema, opposite *Bay Islands Originals* shop, shows films at US$2 per person, they also
do cash advances on Visa, MC and American Express. Also see the *Bundu Café*.

Festivals

The *Sun Jam* is on Water Cay at a weekend at the beginning of *Aug* – watch out for details
locally. 50 La entrance to the island, bring your own tent/hammock, food and water.

Transport

Local   Bike hire about US$5 per day. *Delco Bike* or *Utila Bike Rental* below *Howell's Internet*.

Long distance   Air   *Sosa* has scheduled flights to La Ceiba, US$16.50, 3 times a day Mon-Sat.
Also *Rollins Air* (T443-3206) to Utila. Always reserve flights and make onward reservations in
advance. Get there 15 mins before flight. Local transport between airport and hotels.

Sea   The *Galaxy II* is the only passenger boat going to Utila, operated by *Safeway Maritime*,
T445-1795. Fare is 185 La single, with a 10 La dock fee charged when leaving Utila. Daily services at La Ceiba-Roatán 1500, Roatán-La Ceiba 0700, La Ceiba-Utila 0930, Utila-La Ceiba
1030, weather permitting. There are irregular boats to **Puerto Cortés**, times posted in main
street, 7 hrs, US$7.50, ask at public dock. Boats from Utila to Roatán can be chartered for
about US$70. Occasional freight boats, eg *Utila Tom*, take passengers from Utila to Roatán.
It's a 3-hr journey and you and your possessions are liable to get soaked.

A boat service from Utila to **Lívingston**, Guatemala runs weekly in high season, and fort-
nightly in low season. US$98 for the overnight trip stopping at Puerto Cortés, 10 people max,
food provided. See Gisela and Tom at *Gunter's Dive Shop*.

Directory

Banks   Dollars are accepted on the island, and you can pay for diving courses with dollars, TCs and credit
cards, although the latter carry an 8-10% charge. Have some dollars with you for diving courses. Banks
(*Bancahsa* and *Banco Atlántida*) open 0800-1130, 1330-1600 Mon-Fri, 0800-1130 Sat. *Bancahsa* changes

...sh against a Visa, but not MasterCard. *Thompson's Bakery* will change dollars and TCs. ...*Cross Creek Divers* does Amex, Visa and MasterCard advances plus 8%, so will Michel ...of *Paradise Divers*. Other establishments do the same. **Communications** Internet: ..., near the dock, 0800-1730, closed Sat, extortionate at US$0.15 a min. *Seaside Internet*, next ...0900-1400 and 1600-1800 Mon-Fri. Also internet café on road to *Mango Inn*, 0900-1700, ...re is a **post office** at the pier opposite *Captain Morgan's Dive Centre* (0800-1200, 1400-1600 ...)0-1100 Sat) and a *Hondutel* office (0700-1100 and 1400-1700 Mon-Fri, 0700-1100 Sat) near ...e. The main service is reported as unreliable. *Hondutel* sends (and receives) faxes, F425-3106, ...erica US$1.80, Europe US$2.25, South America and Caribbean US$2, rest of world US$3 per page ...tax. Ronald Janssen also runs *Intertel*, an international phone service: North America US$4 per min, Europe US$7.50 (2 mins minimum), Mexico and Central America US$2, South America US$7, elsewhere US$8.50; incoming fax US$1.

Medical services *Utila Community Clinic* (0800-1200, Mon-Fri), has a resident doctor. There was a case of malaria in early 1999, and a spate of dengue fever cases in late 1999. Sandflies are not infected.

Tour operators Shelby McNab runs *Robinson Crusoe Tours* and takes visitors on half-day tours around the island (US$10 per person) explaining his theory that Daniel Defoe based his famous book on Utila (not Alexander Selkirk off Chile), fascinating. *Tropical Travel Agency*, for flights and clothes, 0800-1100 and 1400-1700, Mon-Fri.

Useful information Electricity: goes off between 2400 and 0600. The **BICA Visitor Centre** in front of *Mermaid's Restaurant* has information on Honduran national reserves and sells Utila T-shirts. Marion Howell is the current President of BICA. Donations welcomed for conservation efforts.

Roatán

Colour map 6, grid B3
127 sq km
Population: 10,245

Roatán is the largest of the islands and has been developed quite extensively. But its idyllic charm is still apparent and quiet beaches are often just a short walk away. There is a paved road running from West End through to French Harbour, almost to Oak Ridge, continuing unpaved to Punta Gorda and Wilkes Point, and other unmade roads.

Tourist offices *Bay Islands Conservation Association*, Edif Cooper, C Principal, Coxen Hole, T/F445-1424, Farley Smith, an American volunteer, is extremely helpful. BICA manages the Sandy Bay/West End Marine Reserve and has lots of information about the reef and its conservation. Excellent map of the island at about 1:50,000 supplied by Antonio E Rosales, T445-1559. Local information maps also from *Librería Casi Todo*, West End. Two websites providing local information are **www.roatanet.com** and **www.roatan.com**

Coxen Hole The capital of the department Coxen Hole, or Roatán City, is on the southwest shore. Planes land and boats dock here and you can get transport to other parts of the island. It is a scruffy little town with not much of tourist interest but some souvenir shops are opening. Besides being the seat of the local government, it has immigration, customs and the law courts. There is a post office, supermarket, several

Roatán

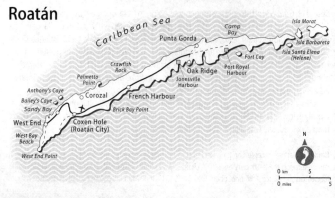

Related maps
Roatán - West End &
West Bay page 906

handicraft shops, photo shops, banks, travel agents, a bookshop and various other stores making it an ideal spot to stock up on supplies. Buses leave from outside the supermarket. You can find cheap accommodation and all public transport starts or ends here. If taxis are shared, they are *colectivos* and charge the same as buses.

Sandy Bay A short journey from Coxen Hole, en route to West End, is Sandy Bay, one of the quieter towns on the island. The **Carambola Botanical Gardens**, created in 1985, contain many flowering plants, ferns and varieties of trees which can be explored on a network of trails. A 20-minute walk from the garden takes you to the top of **Monte Carambola** past the **Iguana Wall**, a breeding ground for iguanas and parrots. There is a visitor centre and gift shop and plans to locate a tourist campground above the gardens. For details contact Bill or Irma Brady, T445-1117. ■ *Daily 0700-1700, US$3, guided tours or nature trails, well worth a visit.* The **Roatán Museum** has displays covering the history of the island, with plenty of information about the pirates who called Roatán home, and a collection of artefacts (■ *US$4*), and the **Institute of Marine Sciences** with a dolphin pool and performance twice a day is at *Anthony's Key Resort*, Sandy Bay. ■ *Mon-Fri, 1000 and 1500, Sat and Sun 1000, 1300 and 1600. US$4, free for guests. Swimming with dolphins arranged for extra cost.* The **Tropical Treasures Bird Sanctuary** at Sandy Bay has macaws, toucans and parrots native to Honduras, as well as many others from throughout Latin America. ■ *US$5 includes guided tour.*

Transport From Coxen Hole to Sandy Bay is a 2-hr walk, or a US$1 bus ride, hourly 0600-1700; taxi drivers will try to charge much more. The per person fare from Coxen Hole is US$1. If you take a private taxi, *privado*, negotiate the price in advance. The official rate from the airport to Sandy Bay/West End is US$8 per taxi regardless of the number of passengers.

West End Five minutes by road beyond Sandy Bay, the popular community of West End is at the western tip of the island and is the most popular place to stay. It's a narrow beach on a palm-fringed bay with a distinctly relaxed and laid-back atmosphere. The **Sandy Bay/West End Marine Park** protects marine life in the area and large numbers of fish have flourished along the coast creating spectacular images for snorkellers. There are numerous good foreign and local restaurants with lots of pizza/pasta places, as well as hotels, cabañas and rooms to rent for all budgets. It is a stiff walk from Coxen Hole over the hills (three hours) to West End, or take the bus on the paved road for US$1, 20 mins. From West End you can take a small motor boat from *Foster and Vivian's Restaurant* for a short ride to West Bay (0900-2100, US$1.10 each way, more at night), or walk along the beach, 45 minutes. You can also take a boat from West End to West Bay. *Colectivos* charge US$1.50 per person.

West Bay is a beautiful clean beach with excellent snorkelling on the reef, particularly at the west end, where the reef is only 10-20 m off shore and the water is shallow right up to where the wall drops off 50-75 m out and scuba diving begins. Paradise comes at a price and the sandflies here are a nightmare, but there are a couple of jetties where you can escape the sandflies which lurk in the powdery white sand. Take your own food and drinks, and insect repellent. Developers have recently discovered the delights of West Bay and the atmosphere is changing fast. Apartments, hotels, bars and restaurants are springing up. A variety of luxury cabins and homes are available for daily, weekly and monthly rental. Watch out for jellyfish in the shallow water at certain times of the year. A taxi from the airport to West Bay costs US$15, to West End, US$10.

French Harbour, on the south coast, with its shrimping and lobster fleet, is the main fishing port of Roatán. There is no beach and there are two seafood packing plants. The road passes *Coleman's (Midway) Bakery*, where you can buy freshly baked products. The bay is protected by the reef and small cayes which provide safe

East of Coxen Hole

Honduras

anchorage. *Roatan Dive and Yacht Club* and *Romeos Marina* (at Brick Bay) offer services for visiting yachts. Several charter yachts are based here. There are a few cheap, clean places to stay, as well as expensive hotels and dive resorts. *Eldon's Supermarket* is open daily and has a range of imported US food. *Gios Restaurant* and *Casa Romeos* serve top quality seafood.

Across the island The main road goes across the mountain ridge along the island with side roads to Jonesville, Punta Gorda and Oak Ridge. You can take a bus on this

Roatán - West End & West Bay

Sleeping
1 Anderson's *B1*
2 Bananarama *D1*
3 Belvedere's
  & Glass Bottom Boat *B1*
4 Burke's *A1*
5 Cabaña Roatana *D1*
6 Casa Calico *A1*
7 Coconut Tree 2 *D1*
8 Coconut Tree Cabins
  & Supermarket *A2*
9 Georphi's Tropical Hideaway *B2*
10 Half Moon Bay Cabins
  & Restaurant *A1*
11 Jimmy's Lodge *C1*
12 Keifitos Plantation Resort *C1*
13 Las Rocas *C1*
14 Mermaid Beach &
  Native Sons Water Sports *C2*
15 Robert's-Hill *C1*
16 Sam's *C2*
17 Sea Breeze *B2*
18 Seagrape Plantation *A1*
19 Sunset Inn (above Ocean Divers) *B2*
20 Valerie's *B2*
21 West Bay Lodge *D1*

Eating
1 Bite on the Beach *C1*
2 Cindy's Place *B2*
3 Neptuno Seafood Grill *C1*
4 Papagayos *B1*
5 Pinocchio's *B2*
6 Pura Vida *B2*
7 Sea View *B2*
8 Stanley's *B2*

route to see the island's hilly interior, with beautiful views from coast to coast. Alternatively, hire a small four-wheel drive, which is almost as cheap if shared between four people and allows you to explore the dirt roads and empty bays along the island's northern tip. **Jonesville** is known for its mangrove canal, which is best reached by hiring a taxi boat in Oak Ridge. **Oak Ridge**, situated on a caye (US$0.40 crossing in a dory from the bus stop), is built around a deep inlet on the south coast. It is a charming little fishing port, with rows of dwellings on stilts built on the water's edge (bus Coxen Hole-Oak Ridge, one hour depending on passengers, US$1.10). Numerous boatmen will meet you at the dock offering mangrove tours. Make sure they take you to the Jonesville mangroves: turn right out of the harbour. The mangrove tunnel is a 40-minute dory tour of the mangroves. There is a clear canal at the end of the tunnel which is recommended for snorkelling, US$10-12 per boat. As well as the hotels, there is a grocery store and a couple of good restaurants.

Punta Gorda to Camp Bay In Punta Gorda on the north coast, the oldest established community on Roatán, Black Caribs retain their own language, music, dance, food, crafts and religion. **Carib Week**, 8-12 April, is a good time to experience their customs. Bus from Coxen Hole US$1. There are also boat tours which include Punta Gorda (and the mangrove tunnel, US$25 per person with Averyll at *Librería Casi Todo* in West End, T445-1255). There is a bar/restaurant serving local food. The paved road ends at the turning for Punta Gorda and from here the road is rough and sometimes too muddy for vehicles to get through. **Marble Hill Farms** is down a small track to the left on the north coast, where you can buy a variety of tropical jams, jellies and spices. The gardens have been landscaped over many years by Lisa and Brian Blancher and their produce is all home grown. Lisa also creates batik and tie dye clothing not on sale anywhere else (0900-1700 Monday-Saturday). Beyond here the road deteriorates but leads to Diamond Rock, Camp Bay (5 km from the paved road) and Paya Beach. Camp Bay has a nice beach but parts of it have been closed off. It is a long swim to the reef. New resorts and timeshare developments are being built along this stretch of coast.

You can hire a boat to **Port Royal**, famous in the annals of buccaneering but now just a community of private houses; old British gun emplacements on Fort Cay, 1 km off-shore. No bus from Port Royal to Oak Ridge, and it's a tough three-hour walk. The **Port Royal Park and Wildlife Refuge** is the largest highland reserve on Roatán, protecting pines and endemic species of flora and fauna which are threatened by hunting, the pet trade and habitat destruction. At present it lacks facilities or management and is relatively inaccessible (contact Bay Islands Conservation Association – see above – for information). There are also several archaeological sites of the Payan inhabitants.

At Coxen Hole C *Caye View*, C Principal, T445-1222, F445-1179, a/c, bath, TV, phone, **Sleeping**
laundry, restaurant, bar, overlooks water, overpriced. **C-E** *Mom*, on main road into Coxen Hole, above pharmacy, next to hospital, private or shared bath, modern, clean, a/c, TV. **E** *El Paso*, T445-1367, next door to *Caye View*, shared bath, restaurant. **F** *Naomi Allen*, near the bus depot, fan, clean, good. Many of the cheaper hotels in the **F** range have water shortages.

At Sandy Bay LL *Anthony's Key Resort*, T445-1003, F445-1140, www.anthonys-key.com, glorious location, accommodation in small wooden cabins, launch and diving facilities (only open to resident guests), the owner, Julio Galindo, is very serious about helping the environment and local community. Dolphin pool at the resort looked after by the Institute of Marine Sciences. **A** *Ocean Side Inn*, T445-1552, F445-1532, www.roatanet.com/oceanside_f.htm, full board, clean, comfortable, friendly owners Joseph and Jenny, nice deck with view of bay, superb restaurant, diving packages offered, but no beach nearby, otherwise recommended. **B-C** *Caribbean Seashore Bed and Breakfast*, on the beach at West Sandy Bay, T445-1123, hot water, private bath, cooking facilities, friendly management.

Honduras

At West End and Half Moon Bay **AL** *Half Moon Bay Cabins*, T445-1075, F445-1213, bungalows and cabins with bath, restaurant with excellent seafood. **AL-B** *Coconut Tree* (owner Vincent Bush), across the road from Half Moon Bay, T445-1648, private cabins (3 double beds), a/c, kitchen, balcony, hot water, fan, fridge, clean, friendly, discounts in low season. **A** *Hillside Garden Cabins*, on the hill above *Lost Paradise* cabins, T445-0505, with hot water, fan, quiet, friendly and helpful owner. **A** *Seagrape Plantation*, T445-1428, cabins with 2 beds, bathroom, hot water, family atmosphere, friendly, Visa accepted, nice location on rocky promontory but no beach, snorkelling, full service restaurant and bar, inclusive packages available. Shoredives for US$15 with equipment. **A-B** *Casa Calico*, T445-1946, F445-1171, comfortable, cable TV, videos, rooms and apartments, fan, 2 rooms with a/c, garden, huge balconies, apartments sleep 4 or more with kitchen, hot water, noisy in morning, owned by Frances Collins, friendly, helpful. **A-B** *Georphi's Tropical Hideaway*, T445-1794, F445-1205, individual cabins, 2 bedrooms, kitchens, coffee shop under trees with excellent cookies and pancakes, open all day. **A-B** *Mermaid Beach*, T445-1335, clean, quiet, with bath, fan or a/c, dive shop next door. **A-B** *Posada Arco Iris*, T445-1264, apartments in Halfmoon Bay, kitchen, hot water, fan, large balcony, friendly owners. New restaurant on premises specialising in grilled meats. Highly recommended. **A-B** *Pura Vida*, T/F445-1141, www.puravidaresort.com, a/c, cheaper with fan, hot water, restaurant/bar/pizzeria open all day. **A-D** *Sunset Inn*, T445-1925, oceandivers@globalnet.hn, **A-C** in main hotel, private bath, some with kitchen and up to 5 beds, some with a/c, hot water, friendly, **D** rooms above *Ocean Divers* dive shop, shared bathroom, recommended, good discounts with diving in low season, Italian seafood restaurant.

B-D *Roberts-Hill*, T445-1176, basic rooms with bath and fan, 2-storey cabaña and new cabins on the beach next to *Keifitos*. **C** *Belvedere's* cabins on beach behind *Chris's Tienda*, T445-1171, private bath, restaurant serving steaks, seafood, pasta and salad. **C** *Burke's* cottages, east end of village past Half Moon Bay, T445-1252, private bath and kitchen, laundry, **D** without, cold water. **C** *Dolphin Resort*, T445-1280, centre of Half Moon Bay, private bathroom, a/c and fan. Recommended. **C** *Sea Breeze*, T445-0020, nice rooms, hot water, baths, a/c optional at US$5 per night, suites and studios available with kitchens, windsurfers and kayaks for rent. **C-D** *Anderson's*, T455-5365, basic rooms, shared bath, clean, fan, lower rates for longer stays, behind *Chris' Tienda*. **D** *Chillies*, in Half Moon Bay, double rooms and dormitory, clean, fully equipped kitchen, lounge, big balcony, camping and hammocks available, excellent value. **D** *Bamboo Hut*, T455-5365, cabins, shared bathroom, central, next door to *Ocean Divers*, also laundry US$4 per load. **D** *Pinocchio's*, owner Patricia, 4 double rooms behind *Sea View Restaurant*, follow *Stanley's* signs, good restaurant. **D-E** *Sam's*, end of Miller Av, double rooms and dormitory, some fans, island-style dinners. Other **D-F** places to stay include *Hotel Suárez*, *Kenny's* (also camping, under US$3), all basic but friendly, water and electricity not guaranteed, take insect repellent.

E *Dora Miller* (no sign), 2 houses behind *Jimmy's*, washing facilities, no fan, no mosquito nets, basic, noisy, friendly. **E** *Jimmy's Lodge*, hammocks or communal rooms, popular with backpackers, extremely basic, smelly, ground floor room has crabs at night, very friendly, cheap meals, snorkelling gear and horse-riding available, it is very cheap to string a hammock here, but very exposed and tin roof, you'll be bitten by sandflies, hosepipe as a shower. **E-F** *Valerie's*, dormitory accommodation, communal central area with cooker and fridge, private rooms **D**, hospitable, but watch your belongings, reports of theft, basic but friendly.

At West Bay **AL** *Island Pearl*, F445-1205, double storey apartments on the beach, a/c, hot water, tiled kitchen, handmade furniture, nicely decorated. **AL-B** *Las Rocas*, T/F445-1841, www.lasrocasresort.com, duplex cabañas next to *Bite on the Beach*, very close together, hot water, balcony, smaller cabins sleep 3, larger ones sleep 6, free boat transport to West End and back, new dive shop opened. **AL** *Cabaña Roatana*, T991-5659, comfortable beachfront rooms with half kitchen, a/c, hot water, beach towels, some snorkelling gear, café open 1100-1600 for sandwiches, beer, snacks. Recommended. **AL-A** *Coconut Tree 2*, T445-1648, luxury cabins with hot water, a/c, balcony on the beach. **A-B** *Bananarama*, just behind *Cabaña Roatana*, T992-9679, F445-1271, with bath, hot water, fan, PADI dive courses available, breakfast included for guests, good value, recommended. **B** *West Bay Lodge*, F445-1471, westbaylodge@globalnet.hn, cabins with hot water and fan, good breakfast included. **B-C** *Keifitos Plantation Resort*, bungalows on hillside above beach, beautiful setting, short walk from village, mosquitoes, bar, good breakfasts to 1300, champagne breakfasts Sun, horses for rent with guide, friendly owners, very quiet, very clean. Recommended.

At Brick Bay C *Palm Tree Resort*, T445-1986, cabins with bath, homecooking island style, quiet, diveshop, wall diving with boat available.

At Mount Pleasant A-B *Executivo Inn*, on road to French Harbour opposite electricity plant, T455-5658, nice rooms, a/c, hot water, TV, pool, no beach.

At French Harbour L *Coco View Resort*, T455-5011, F445-1416, www.cocoviewresort.com, good shore diving, on lagoon. **A-B** *Casa Romeo's* , T455-5518, comfortable rooms with views over the bay, transport to beach, ask about scuba diving packages, excellent restaurant good for seafood. **AL-A** *Roatan Dive and Yacht Club*, T445-5233, F445-5407, cable TV in every room, suites available, nice location, view over yacht harbour, small pool, dive packages, expensive but good food (especially lunch). **A-B** *The Faro Inn*, T455-5214, above *Gios* seafood restaurant, TV, phone, a/c, large rooms, including continental breakfast. **E** *Britos*, with fan, very good value. **E** *Dixon's Plaza*, past the *Buccaneer*, good. **E** *Hotelito*, sometimes no water, in the village. **E** *Hotelito Joe*, rooms with fan and private bath, clean restaurant downstairs serving local dishes. **E** *Isabel*, comfortable, restaurant, free transport to airport.

At Oak Ridge L *Reef House Resort*, T435-2297, F435-2142, including meals, various packages, includes diving, wooden cabins with seaview balconies, seaside bar, private natural pool, dock facilities, good snorkelling from the shore. **E** *San José Hotel*, with bath (2 rooms), cheaper without (3 rooms), clean, pleasant, good value, water shortages, good food, English-speaking owner, Louise Solórzano.

At Punta Gorda L-A *Henry's Cove*, T435-2180, secluded retreat on hill, a/c, pool, cabins sleep 6, or rooms, seafood restaurant; rooms to rent with local families. *Ben's Restaurant*, on coast road south out of village, has nice cabins to rent, **B**, T445-1916, dive shop (US$35 per dive), limited equipment, disorganized, wooden deck over sea, local food, bar, friendly, safe parking.

At Paya Bay L *Paya Bay Dive Resort*, T/F435-2139, www.payabay.com cabins, private bath, hot water, wonderful ocean and beach views, owned by Mervin and Lurlene McNab, beautiful restaurant, seafood US$5-10, beach bar and showers, open breakfast, lunch, dinner, homemade soursop juice, remote, long rough drive but worth it.

Coxen Hole *Comedor Ray Monty*, very cheap, set meal US$1.50 but avoid the meat, fish good. *El Paso*, next to the *Caye View*, good seafood soup. *El Punto*, bar with one basic dish, very cheap. *Gloria's*, good local food, reasonable prices, TV, popular with locals. *HB Warren*, large well-stocked supermarket (best place on island for fresh fruit) with cafetería, mainly lunch and snacks, open 0700-1800. Pizza stand opposite *Warren's*, slices US$1.50. *Hibiscus Sweet Shop*, homemade fruit pies, cakes and biscuits. *Pizza Rey*, opposite Warren's, pizza slices. *Qué Tal Café*, good, export quality coffee, herbal teas, sandwiches and pastries, shares space with bookstore, on road to West End. There is a good seafood restaurant on Osgood Caye a few minutes by free water taxi from wharf.

Eating
Evening meals cost US$4-10

West End *Belvedere's*, on water, nice setting, tasty Italian food, open 1900-2100. Recommended. *Big Blue*, above *West End Divers*, serving good Thai food. *Cannibal Café*, in the *Seabreeze*, excellent Mexican food, large helpings, good value. *Cindy's Place*, next to *Sunset Inn*, local family breakfast, lunches and dinner in garden, fish caught same morning, also lobster and king crab. Recommended. *Coral Reef*, Mexican and seafood, good tacos, good prices. *Deja Blue*, Asian and Middle East specialities, good location, salad buffet, expensive but worth it. *Papagayos* is on a jetty, good atmosphere for pre-prandial tipple, reggae music, basic meals, no sandflies, great sundeck, Thu is band/dance/party night, also rooms to rent, **B**, T445-1008. *Half Moon Bay* restaurant, nice location to sit on terrace overlooking sea, more expensive than most, dishes

Honduras

between US$6-US$15, but excellent food, service can be very slow. *Keifito's Hangout*, good breakfasts, champagne on Sun, reasonable prices. *Lighthouse*, on the point after *Belvedere's*, local dishes, good coffee and breakfasts, fried chicken and seafood. *Online Café*, *Starbucks* coffee, bagels, light meals and refreshments etc, email service. *Pinocchio's*, along same path, excellent pasta, great stir fry and delicious salads, run by Patricia and Howard. *Punta del Ovest* music village, exotic, clay oven pizzas, 200 m along path behind *Bamboo Hut*, one of the best in town. Shows a film every night. *Pura Vida*, Italian, restaurant and pizzeria next to *West End Divers*, good atmosphere. *Rick's American Café*, Sandy Bay, tree top bar, shows all sports events, best steaks on Roatán, US$10. Open from 1700, except Wed. Recommended. *Rudy's*, has good pancakes and cookies for breakfast, sandwich combos, good atmosphere but pricey, open all day. *Salt and Pepper Club*, entrance to West End, supermarket, BBQ and live music. *Sea View Restaurant*, Italian chef/manager, extensive menu, pasta, fish, chicken, pizza, good salads. *Stanley's*, up north about 50 m north of *Sunset Inn*, small sign up path, island cooking, menu changes daily, evening meal only, at 1900, cheap, good food, try their coconut dinner, friendly. *The Cool Lizard*, Mermaid Beach, seafood, vegetarian and chicken, homemade bread, salads, nice atmosphere, good. *Tony's Pizzeria*, in the *Sunset Inn*, fresh fish, good food, big portions. *Twisted Toucan*, bar serving curries on Tue nights. *Tyll's Kitchen*, in Tyll's Dive Shop, now open for breakfast, happy hour for rum and beer goes on all day. *Woodys Supermarket*, cheap hot dogs and *baleadas* at lunch between 1100 and 1300, good. *Velva's Place*, at the far end of Halfmoon Bay, island style seafood and chicken dishes, try the conch soup, good prices. *Tartines and Chocolate*, French bakery/patisserie in Half Moon Bay, good bread and pastries.

West Bay *Neptuno Seafood Grill*, between *Fosters* and *Coconut Tree 2*, seafood, paella, barbecued crab, extensive bar, open daily for lunch and dinner. *The Bite on the Beach*, open Wed-Sat and Sun brunch, huge deck in gorgeous position on the point over West Bay, excellent, fresh food and great fruit punch. Recommended and very much what Roatín is about – get down there. *West Bay Lodge* serves a good breakfast on a nice balcony with sea view.

French Harbour *Roatan Dive and Yacht Club*, daily specials, pizza, salads, sandwiches, usually very good. *Gios*, seafood, king crab a speciality. *Iguana Grill*, international cuisine, suckling pig. *Romeo's*, (Romeo is Honduran-Italian), good seafood, and continental cuisine. *Tres Flores*, on the hill, good views, Mexican specialities, they will pick up groups from West End T245-0007. There is a *taquería* close to Bancahsa on the main road, good tacos, burritos and hamburgers.

At Oak Ridge *BJ's Backyard Restaurant*, at the harbour, island cooking, fishburgers, smoked foods, reasonable prices. There is a pizzeria and, next door, a supermarket. *Pirate's Hideaway*, at Calabash Bay, east of Oak Ridge, seafood, friendly owner.

Entertainment **Nightclubs** Mostly come alive about midnight, play reggae, salsa, *punta* and some rock. In **West End** is *Bahía Azul*, Fri is party night, DJ, dancing. *Foster's*, the late night hotspot in West End, dance music Thu night as well as band nights. *Lone's Bar*, Mermaid Beach, nightly BBQ, reggae music. On the south side of the island is *Harbour View*, Coxen Hole, Thu-Sun nights, late, US$0.50 entrance, very local, usually no problem with visitors but avoid local disputes, hot and atmospheric. *Al's*, Barrio Las Fuertes, before French Harbour, closed Sat night, salsa and plenty of *punta*. *Bolongas*, French Harbour, weekends, late, US$1 entrance, more upmarket, modern building, sometimes live Honduran bands and classy stripshow.

Shopping **Supermarkets** Best to buy supplies in Coxen Hole. *Coconut Tree* at West End expensive. *Woods* is cheaper. *Eldon* in French Harbour is also expensive. *Ezekiel*, West End, opposite church, fruit and vegetables, selection varies.

Sports **Diving** The creation of the *Sandy Bay/West End Marine Park* along 4 km of coast from Lawson Rock around the southwest tip to Key Hole has encouraged the return of large numbers of fish in that area and there are several interesting dive sites. Lobsters are still rare, but large grouper are now common and curious about divers. Mooring buoys must be used,

If you don't want to dive, the snorkelling is normally excellent

anchoring and spear fishing are not allowed. If the sea is rough off West End try diving around French Harbour (or vice versa) where the cayes provide some protection. There are more mangroves on this side, which attract the fish. Flowers Bay on the south side has some spectacular wall dives, but not many fish, and it is calm during the 'Northers' which blow in Dec-Feb. Few people dive the east end except the liveaboards (Bay Islands Aggressor, The Aggressor Fleet, Romeo Tower, French Harbour, T445-1518, F445-1645 (T800-348-2628 in USA or Canada) and people on camping trips to Pigeon Cay, so it is relatively unspoilt. Because fishing is allowed to the east, tropical fish are scarce and the reef is damaged in places. In addition to a few stormy days from Dec to Feb, you can also expect stinging hydroids in the top few feet of water around Mar and Apr which bother people who are sensitive to stings (with friends like these, who needs anemones?). Vinegar is the local remedy. Divers are usually unaffected as they go below the hydroids.

As on Utila, the dive operators concentrate on instruction but prices vary (since Dec 1994 the municipal government has set minimum prices). If you are planning to learn, you can normally find a course starting within a day or two. There is more on offer than in Utila; not everyone teaches only PADI courses. Prices for courses and diving vary with the season. In low season good deals abound. Open Water US$225, Advanced US$160, fun dives US$25. Despite the huge number of dive students, Roatán has a good safety record but it still pays to shop around and find an instructor you feel confident with at a dive shop which is well organized with well-maintained equipment. As in other 'adventure' sports, the cheapest is not always the best. Dive insurance is US$2 per day, and is sometimes included in the course price. If you do not have dive insurance and need their services, the hyperbaric chamber charges a minimum of US$800. They also treat other diving related problems for a minimum fee.

West End *Aquarius Divers*, PADI courses, fun dives, excursions to the south walls in conjunction with Scuba Romance dive shop, Brick Bay. *Native Son's Water Sports*, next to *Mermaid* cabins, run by Alvin, local instructor, PADI and PDSI courses and fun dives. *Ocean Divers* at *Sunset Inn*. Recommended, T/F445-1925, oceandivers@ globalnet.hn, run by Carol and Phil Stevens with emphasis on safety and fun, good equipment, multilingual instructors, PADI courses, BSAC, the only shop with nitrox instruction, fast boats, also rooms and restaurant, dive/accommodation packages available. *Sueño del Mar Divers*, good, inexpensive, American-style operation, they tend to dive the sites closest to home, T445-1717. *Tyll's Dive*, multilingual instructors, PADI, SSI courses, good boats, accommodation also available. *West End Divers*, Italian owned, competent bilingual instructors, PADI Dive Centre. **West Bay** *Bananarama*, in centre of beach, small, friendly, run by young German family, boat and shore diving. **Gibson Bight** *The Last Resort*, T445-1838, F445-1848, (in USA T305-893-2436), mostly packages from the USA. **Sandy Bay** *Anthony's Key Resort*, mostly hotel package diving, also swim and dive with dolphins, see above. **Dixon Cove** *Scuba Romance*, new shop and equipment, large diesel boat and compressor, diving the south wall and the reef at Mary's Place, overnight trips to Barbareta, 6 dives, US$80, sleeping on the boat, work with *Palm Cove Resort*, cabin-style accommodation, home cooking.

Tours At *Belvedere's Lodge* on the headland at Half Moon Bay, Dennis runs snorkelling trips to secluded bays beyond Antony's Key in a glass-bottomed yacht. He also takes charters and sunset cruises all along the coast. Horse-riding available from *Keifitos* or *Jimmy's* in West End. Alex does day trips to Punta Gorda and 2/3 day trips in his sailboat *Adventure Girl*. His boat is moored at Ocean Divers dock, contact here or at *Tyll's*. *Far Tortugas* charters, trimaran *Genesis*, does sailing trips with snorkelling and reef drag (snorkellers towed behind slow moving boat), US$45 per day, US$25 per ½ day, contact *Casi Todo*, West End, T445-1347. *Coconut Tree* have a rainforest tour to Pico Bonito, US$112 including guide, transport, lunch and snorkelling.

Fishing arranged through Eddie, contact at *Cindy's* next to *Ocean Divers*, West End, small dory, local expert, good results, US$30 per hr, but prices can vary. Alternatively, go fishing in style from French Harbour, *Hot Rods* sports fisher, US$500 per day charter, T445-1862. See *Casi Todo* for the *Jimni* fishing tours, half and full day. Fishing trips also available on *Flame*, contact Darson or Bernadette, T445-1616, US$20 per hr. They also do trips to Cayos Cochinos (diving available), Utila and island tours, US$250 per boat. Kayak

Honduras

rentals and tours from Seablades, contact Alex at *Casi Todo,* 3-7 day kayak tours, US$150-250. Full and half-day rental US$20 and US$12 (with instruction), kayaks available at *Tyll's. Genesis* used as support boat for 2-7-day trips around Roatán (US$175 and US$1,250, respectively), ask for Sally or T443-0780 in La Ceiba. From **Rick's American Café**, Casablanca charters on yacht *Defiance III*, sunset cruises, party trips, full-day snorkelling, also can be arranged through *Casi Todo*. At West Bay beach is a glass-bottomed boat, *Caribbean Reef Explorer*, US$20 per 1½ hrs, unfortunately includes fish feeding, which upsets the reef's ecological balance. Glass-bottomed boat and 3-person submarine tours from the dock at Half Moon Bay, US$25 per person. Day trips to the mainland, whitewater rafting on the Río Cangrejal with **Ríos Honduras** is US$125 per day round trip with lunch, T443-0780, or contact *Casi Todo*. Mopeds, bikes, island tours: **Captain Van's Rentals**, West End; also from **Ole Rentavan**, T445-1819.

Transport **Local Car rental**: *Captain Van*, West End, vans, also mopeds and bicycles, good information about the islands, **Roatan Rentals**, West End, range of vehicles, pickups and vans for rent; **Sandy Bay Rent-A-Car**, US$42 per day all inclusive, jeep rental, T445-1710, F445-1711, agency also in West End outside *Sunset Inn*; **Toyota**, opposite airport, have pickups, US$46, four-wheel drive, US$65, Starlets US$35 per day, also 12-seater bus, US$56 per day, T445-1166;

Long distance Air If travelling to or from the mainland, check fares available on the day of travel, it may be cheaper to fly than to go by sea. The airport is 20 mins' walk from Coxen Hole, or you can catch a taxi from outside the airport for US$1.50. There is a hotel reservation desk in the airport, T445-1930. Change in Coxen Hole for taxis to West End. US$1 per person for *colectivos* to West End, US$2 to Oak Ridge. If you take a taxi from the airport they charge US$10 per taxi; if you pick one up on the main road you may be able to bargain down to US$5. *Isleña*, *Sosa*, *Atlantic Air* and *Rollins* fly from **La Ceiba**, US$20 one way (fewer Sun); flights also to and from **Tegucigalpa**, US$60, via **San Pedro Sula** (*Isleña*), US$50, frequency varies according to season. No other direct flights to other islands, you have to go via La Ceiba (to Utila US$38.50, to Guanaja US$51). Always buy your ticket in advance (none on sale at airport), reservations are not always honoured.

From the USA, *Taca* flies on Sat from **Houston**, on Sun from Miami. From Central America, daily flights from **Belize City** (*Isleña*), Sat from **San Salvador** (*Taca*). Airlines: *Taca*, at airport T445-1387; *Isleña*, airport T445-1550; *Sosa*, airport T445-1154. *Casi Todo* sells all inter-Honduras at same price as airlines.

Sea *Galaxy II* sails from La Ceiba to Coxen Hole. Roatán-La Ceiba 0700, La Ceiba-Roatán 0930, T445-1795. No sailings in bad weather. At times the crossing can be rough, sea-sick pills available at ticket counter. Irregular boats from Puerto Cortés and Utila. Cruise ships visit from time to time, mostly visiting Tabayana Resort on West Bay.

Directory **Banks** *Banco Atlántida*, *Bancahsa*, *Banco Sogerín* and *Banffaa* in Coxen Hole, there is also a **Credomatic** office where you can get a cash advance on your Visa/MasterCard, upstairs, before *Caye View Hotel* on the main street; 5 banks in French Harbour; **Bancahsa** in Oak Ridge, T245-2210, MasterCard for cash advances. No banks in West End. No exchange facilities at the airport. Dollars and lempiras can be used interchangeably for most services.

Communications Internet: send or receive email at **Online Café** and the **Sunset Inn**. **The Lucky Lemp**, opposite *Qué Tal* coffee shop, main street Coxen Hole, phone, fax and email services. **Paradise Computer**, Coxen Hole, 10 mins' walk down road to West End. **Post office**: in Coxen Hole, stamps not always available, bring them with you or try *Librería Casi Todo* in West End. **Telephone**: very expensive, you will be charged as soon as a call connects with the satellite, whether or not the call goes through. *Hondutel* in Coxen Hole, fax is often broken. *Supertienda Chris*, West End, T/F445-1171, 1 min to Europe US$10, USA, Canada $5. Both *Librería Casi Todo* and *Rudy's Cabins* in West End have a fax, US$10 per page to Europe, US$5 to USA. *Rudy's* charge US$2 a min to receive phone calls.

Medical services Ambulance and Hyperbaric Chamber: Anthony's Key with full medical service. Local hospital, Ticket Mouth Rd, Coxen Hole, T445-1499. **Dentist**: upstairs in the Cooper building for emergency treatment, but better to go to La Ceiba or San Pedro Sula. **Doctor**: Dr Jackie Bush has a clinic in Coxen Hole, no appointment necessary, for blood or stool tests, etc.

Tour operators Airport travel agency at the airport, has information on hotels, will make bookings, no commission. *Bay Islands Tour and Travel Center*, in Coxen Hole (Suite 208, Cooper Building, T445-1585, F445-1146) and French Harbour. *Casi Todo 1* in West End or *Casi Todo 2* in Coxen Hole can arrange tours, locally and on the mainland, including fishing, kayaking, island tours, trips to Barbareta and Copán. Local and international air tickets also sold here as well as new and second-hand books, open Mon-Sat, 0900-1630 (see above Excursions). *Columbia Tours*, Barrio El Centro, T445-1160, good prices for international travel, very helpful. *Tropical Travel*, in *Hotel Caye View*, T445-1146. Carlos Hinds, T445-1446, has a van for trips, reasonable and dependable.

East of Roatán, Barbareta Island is a private nature reserve with beaches, good diving and sport fishing, and a network of hiking trails. The adjacent Pigeon Cayes are ideal for snorkelling, shallow scuba diving and picnics. There are stone artefacts on the island, and you can hike in the hills to caves which may have once been inhabited by Paya Indians. Isla Barbareta, plus its neighbours Santa Elena and Morat, are all part of the proposed Barbareta National Marine Park.

Isla Barbareta
The island was once owned by the descendants of Henry Morgan

Sleeping Comfortable accommodation, services and sports at **LL** *Barbareta Beach Club*, PO Box 63, La Ceiba, T445-1255, www.wildernessriver.com/barbareta/, VHF 88A. Book in advance. One-day walking tours with guide, lunch, snorkelling, US$35.

Guanaja

Columbus called Guanaja the Island of Pines, but Hurricane Mitch swept most of them away. Since then, a great replanting effort has started and, until the new pines have grown, there are many flowering and fruiting plants thriving on the island. The island was declared a forest reserve in 1961, and is now designated a national marine park.

Colour maps 6, grid A3
Area: 56 sq km
Population: 5,000

Honduras

Guanaja

Good (but sweaty) clambering on the island gives splendid views of the jungle and the sea and there are several attractive waterfalls, which can be visited on the hills rising to the summit of 415 m. The first English settler was Robert Haylock, who arrived in 1856 with a land title to part of the island, the two cayes which now form the main settlement of Bonacca and some of the Mosquito coast. He was followed in 1866 by John Kirkconnell who purchased Hog Caye, where the Haylocks raised pigs away from the sandflies. These two families became sailors, boat builders and landowners, and formed the basis of the present population.

Much of Guanaja town, locally known as **Bonacca** and covering a small caye off the coast, is built on stilts above sea water, with boardwalks and concrete pathways, hence its nick-name: the 'Venice of Honduras'. There are three other small villages: **Mangrove Bight**, **Savannah Bight** and **North East Bight** on the main island. Much of the accommodation is all-inclusive resorts, but it is possible to visit independently as well. Swimming is made somewhat unpleasant by the many sandflies. These and mosquitoes cannot be escaped on the island, and none of the beaches offer respite (coconut oil, baby oil or any oily sun-tan lotion will help to ward off sandflies). The cayes are better, including Guanaja town. South West Caye is especially recommended.

Sleeping **LL** *Bayman Bay Club*, beautiful location, see the sunset from the tree house deck, T453-4191, F453-4179 (USA T1-800-524- 1823, F954-572-1907), and **LL** *Posada del Sol*, on an outlying caye, T/F668-3347, www.posadadelsol.com Both include meals, launch trips, diving, fitness studio, 1st class, the latter has a good underwater photographic and video facility for divers. **B-C** *Alexander*, T453-4326, 20 rooms, or US$100 in 3-bed, 3-bathroom apartment, diving and fishing resort, packages: US$98 per person includes 3 dives a day, US$110 per person includes bone fishing and trawling, US$85 per person includes snorkelling and hiking, all with 3 meals a day and lodging. **B-C** *El Rosario*, T453-4240, with bath and a/c, nice. **C-D** *Harry Carter*, T455-4303, ask for a fan, clean. **E** *Miss Melba*, 3 rooms in boarding house, run by friendly old lady with lots of interesting stories and island information, shared bathroom, cold water, great porch and gardens just before *Hotel Alexander* sign on left, house with flowers.

Eating *Harbour Light*, through *Mountain View* nightclub, good food reasonably priced for the island. *The Nest*, T453-4290, good eating in the evening. *Glenda's*, good standard meals for under US$1, small sandwiches. *Fifi Café*, named after the hurricane which wiped out most of the houses in 1974, popular local hangout.

Sports **Diving and sailing** The most famous dive site off Guanaja is the wreck of the *Jado Trader*, sunk in 1987 in about 30 m on a flat bottom surrounded by some large coral pinnacles which rise to about 15 m. Big black groupers and moray eels live here, as does a large shy jewfish and many other fish and crustaceans. *End of The World*, next to Bayman Bay Club, T/F991-1257, www.guanaja.com, diving instruction, beach front bar, restaurant, cabins, kayaks, canoes, hobbie cats, white sand beach, fishing. Highly recommended resort. *Jado Divers*, beside *Melba's*, US$26 for 2 dives, run by Matthew from US. Preston Borden will take snorkellers out for US$25 per boat load (4-6 people), larger parties can be accommodated with larger boat, or for customized excursions, very flexible, T453-4326. *SV Railovy*, T453-4135, F453-4274, is a 40-ft yacht running local cruises and excursion packages; also sailing, diving and snorkelling services, and PADI courses. Ask for Hans on VHF radio channel 70.

Transport **Air** The airport is on Guanaja but you have to get a water taxi from there to wherever you are staying; there are no roads or cars; *Sosa* and *Isleña* (T453-4208) fly daily from La Ceiba, 30 mins. Other non-scheduled flights available.

Sea The *Suyapa* sails between Guanaja, La Ceiba and Puerto Cortés. The *Miss Sheila* also does this run and goes on to George Town (Grand Cayman). *Cable Doly Zapata*, Guanaja, for monthly sailing dates to Grand Cayman (US$75 one way). Irregular sailings from Guanaja to Trujillo, 5 hrs.

Directory **Banks** *Bancahsa* and *Banco Atlántida*.

Northeast of Tegucigalpa

Through the agricultural and cattle lands of Olancho State, a road runs near to the Parque Nacional Sierra de Agalta and beyond to Trujillo on the Caribbean coast. To the west, reachable only by air or sea, is the Mosquitia Coast – a vast expanse of rivers and swamps, coastal lagoons and tropical forests filled with wildlife but very few people.

The Carretera de Olancho runs from the capital northeast to the Caribbean coast. Passing through **Guaimaca** (hotel, **F**, on plaza above restaurant *Las Cascadas*, good value, clean, friendly) and **San Diego** (restaurant *El Arriero*), **Campamento**, 127 km, a small, friendly village surrounded by pine forests (*Hotelito Granada* and *Hospedaje Santos*), and on to the Río Guayape, 143 km.

By the river crossing at **Los Limones** is an unpaved road north to **La Unión** (56 km), deep in the northern moutains passing through beautiful forests and lush green countryside. There are several *comedores* in La Unión and **F** *Hospedaje San Carlos* serves good vegetarian food. To the north is the **Refugio de Vida Silvestre La Muralla-Los Higuerales**, wh ere quetzales and emerald toucanettes can be seen between March and May in the cloud forest. For those that have made the effort to get to this spot, if you're camping you may experience the frissonic pleasure of jag-uars 'screaming' during the night. The Park comprises the three peaks of La Muralla, 1,981m, Las Parras, 2,064 m and Los Higuerales, 1,985 m. Cohdefor has an office on the main plaza for information, closed weekends. You are now required to take a guide with you on the trail. Cost is US$4, arrange in La Unión. Four trails range from 1-10 km and are recommended. There are two campsites in the forest (contact Cohdefor on T/F222-1027 for prior arrangements), or there is accommodation for one or two at the visitors' centre. ■ *Park entrance fee US$1.* Buses from Comayagüela to La Unión, daily, take four hours. To get to the park, hire a truck from La Unión for about US$18. There's little traffic so it's difficult to hitchhike. If driving from San Pedro Sula, take the road east through Yoro and Mangulile; from La Ceiba, take the Savá-Olanchito road and turn south 13 km before Olanchito.

The main road continues another 50 km from Los Limones to Juticalpa, the capital of Olancho department, in a rich agricultural area for herding cattle and growing cereals and sugar-cane. There is a paved road northeast through the cattle land of Catacamas, continuing to just beyond Dulce Nombre de Culmí.

Juticalpa
Colour map 6, grid B3
Population: 74,000
Altitude: 420 m

Sleeping **D** *Antúñez*, 1 C NO y 1 Av NO, a block west of Parque Central, T885-2250, with bath, **F** without, friendly, clean, also annex in same street. **D** *Las Vegas*, 1 Av NE, T885-2700, central, ½ block north of Parque, cafetería, clean, friendly. **D** *El Paso*, 1 Av NE y 6 C NO, 6 blocks south of Parque (on way to highway), T885-2311, quiet, clean, bath, fan, laundry facili-ties. Highly recommended. **F** *Familiar*, 1 C NO between Parque and Antúñez, with bath, clean. Basic but recommended. **F** *Fuente*, 5 minutes from bus station on left side of main road to town centre, basic but large and clean rooms. **F** *Regis*, 1 C NO, balcony, good value.

Eating *Casa Blanca*, 1 C SE, quite smart with a good cheap menu, good paella. *Comedor Any*, 1 Av NO, good value, friendly. *El Rancho*, 2 Av NE specializes in meat dishes, wide menu, pleasant. *El Tablado*, 1 Av NE entre 3 y 4 C NO, good fish, bar. *Helados Frosty*, near Parque Central, with ice-creams. *La Galera*, 2 Av NE, specializes in *pinchos*. *Tropical Juices*, Blvd de los Poetas, good fruit juices. From 0600 Saturday the market in Parque Central has good selection of food, fruit, vegetables and souvenirs, said to be best outdoor market in Olancho.

Transport Bus station is on 1 Av NE, 1 km southeast of Parque Central, taxis US$0.50. Hourly to **Tegucigalpa** from 0330 to 1800; bus to **San Esteban** from opposite Aurora bus terminal

Honduras

Honduras

Kicking Ass

From February to May you can taste the vino de coyol which is extracted from a palm (a hole is made at the top of the trunk and the sap which flows out is drunk neat). With sugar added it ferments and becomes alcoholic (chicha), so strong it is called patada de burro (mule kick).

at 0800, 6 hrs, US$2.25. Bus to **Trujillo** dep 0400, 9 hrs, US$5.20. Bus to **Tocoa** at 0500.

Directory Banks Local banks: *Bancahsa* (the only one that will change TCs, with insistence), *Banco Atlántida*, *Bancahorro*, *Banco de los Trabajadores*, *Banco de Occidente*, *Banco Sogerín* and *Banhcafé*. **Communications Post office:** 2 blocks north from Parque Central, opposite Shell station. **Telephone:** *Hondutel* on main street, 1 block from Parque Central.

Catacamas

Colour map 6, grid B4
Altitude: 400 m

Catacamas lies at the foot of Agalta Moutain in the Río Guayape valley in the Department of Olancho, 210 km from Tegucigalpa. The Río Guayape (named after an Indian dress, *guayapis*) is famous for its gold nuggets.

The town was established by the Spaniards and the colonial church dates from the early 18th century. It is an agricultural and cattle-raising district. The National School of Agriculture (ENA) is based here, ask if you wish to visit their agricultural demonstration plots in the Guayape valley, 5 km south of the town. El Sembrador school, which offers room and board, is also south of the town towards San Pedro and is run by North Americans. It is more or less self contained with its own farms and electricity generators. Catacamas received a boost in the 1980s when the US built a military base in El Aguacate, 20 km to the northeast, which was later used by the Nicaraguan 'Contras'. **Fiesta**: St Francis of Assisi, 4 October.

Excursions   Hiking in the mountains behind Catacamas is beautiful. From Murmullo there are trails to coffee farms. **Río Talgua**, 4 km east of Catacamas, is interesting with caves in which significant pre-Columbian remains have been found. The area and caves are worth a visit. Hiking to **El Boquerón**, stop off at the main road near Punuare, 17 km west of Catacamas, and walk up **Río Olancho**, which has nice limestone cliffs and a pretty river canyon. Through much of the canyon the stream flows underground.

Sleeping   **E** *Central*, in Barrio El Centro, T899-4276, with bath, cheaper without, big mango tree in
& eating   front. **E** *Juan Carlos*, Barrio José Trinidad Reyes, T899-4212, good restaurant. Recommended. **E** *La Colina*, T899-4488, with bath, hot water, fan, TV, parking. *Continental*, chicken dishes, pizza, US beer. *Asia*, Chinese. *Comedor Ejecutivo*, buffet-style meals US$2, local craft decorations. *As de Oro*, good beef dishes, Wild West décor.

Entertainment   **Cinema** *Cine Maya*, Barrio El Centro. **Nightclubs** *Fernandos*. *Extasis*. *Montefresco*, outside town towards Tegucigalpa, pool (US$1.20), live music 2 evenings a week.

Transport   **Buses** **Tegucigalpa** to Juticalpa/Catacamas, *Empresa Aurora*, 8 C 6-7 Av, Comayagüela, T237-3647, hourly 0400-1700, 3¼ hrs US$2 to Juticalpa, 4 hrs US$2.75 to Catacamas. Juticalpa-Catacamas, 40 mins, US$0.60. Bus Catacamas-**Dulce Nombre de Culmí** (see below), 3 hrs, US$1.35, several daily.

Directory   **Banks** *Banco Atlántida*, *Banco de Occidente*, *Banco El Ahorro Hondureño*, *Banco Sogerín*, all in Barrio El Centro. **Medical services** Dentist: *Elvia Ayala Lobo*, T899-4129.

Beyond Catacamas, a rough road continues northeast up the Río Tinto valley to **Dulce Nombre de Culmí**, **F** *Hospedaje Tania*, very basic, on the main street, several *comedores* on the main plaza. Further on is **Paya** where the road becomes a mule track but, in three to four days in the dry season, a route can be made over the divide (Cerro de Will) and down the Río Paulaya to Mosquitia (see next section). Local police say that there is a path in the dry season from Dulce Nombre to San Esteban (about 30 km).

Juticalpa to Trujillo

There is a fine scenic road from Juticalpa to Trujillo. From Juticalpa head northeast and turn left where the paved road ends, to **San Francisco de la Paz** (several *hospedajes*, **F**). Beyond San Francisco is **Gualaco**, which has an interesting colonial church. There are several plac es to stay including **G** *Calle Real*, near Parque Central, basic, friendly, will store luggage, and **G** *Hotelito Central*, which is similar. *Comedor Sharon* is one of several places to eat. Buses to Juticalpa and to the north coast (Tocoa and Trujillo) are fairly frequent.

San Esteban is 23 km from Gualaco. On the way you pass Agalta mountain, and **San Esteban** some of the highest points in Honduras, and several waterfalls on the Río Babilonia. San Esteban has a lurid recent history. For 10 years after 1987 there was a violent family dispute between the Nájeras and the Turcios which engulfed the whole community. Eighty people were killed before a truce was agreed in 1997 which has so far held. There is a military detachment here primarily to supervise the ceasefire. If it sounds like the 'Wild West', remember that electricity arrived here in 1994 and the telephone only in 1997 – there are no internet cafés!

Sleeping   F *Centro*, very clean, nice family, best. **F** *Hotel Hernández*, cheapest. **F** *Hotel San Esteban*, very friendly, clean. 3 nice *comedores* nearby.

After San Esteban the road continues to **Bonito Oriental** (via El Carbón, a mahogany collection point with Paya Indian communities in the vicinity). There are four hotels here. The final 38 km from Bonito Oriental to Trujillo are paved, through Corocito. There are many dirt roads between San Francisco and Trujillo. If driving, ask directions if in any doubt. Fuel is available in the larger villages but there is none between San Esteban and Bonito Oriental.

Between the roads Juticalpa-Gualaco-San Esteban and Juticalpa-Catacamas- Dulce **Parque** Nombre de Culmí lies the cloud forest of the Parque Nacional Sierra de Agalta, extend- **Nacional Sierra** ing over 1,200 ha and reaching a height of 2,590 m at Monte de Babilonia, a massif with a **de Agalta** number of interesting mountains. Several different ecosystems have been found with a wide variety of fauna and flora: 200 species of bird have been identified so far. There are several points of entry. Contact Cohdefor in Juticalpa, Culmí, Gualaco, San Esteban or Catacamas for information on access, maps, guides, mules and lodging. There is no infrastructure in the park, but a base camp is being built. A good trail leads to **La Picucha** mountain (2,354 m). Access is from El Pacayal, 750 m, a short distance towards San Esteban from Gualaco (bus at 0700 which goes on to Tocoa). There are two campsites on the trail, the first at 1,060m is just short of **La Chorrera** waterfall which has a colony of white-collared swifts that nest in the cave behind the falls. Four to six hours above is the second campsite at 1,900 m. The final section is mainly dwarf forest with low undergrowth on the summit. There is much wildlife to be seen and a good viewpoint 1 km beyond at the site of two abandoned radio towers. Hiking time two days.

From Gualaco there are other trails into Mount Babilonia with spectacular views over Olancho and Mosquitia; from La Venta you can visit the double waterfall of the Río Babilonia, another track from the east side skirts the flank of Montaña de Malacate. To the west of Gualaco, there is an area of limestone with some fine caving possibilities; enquire in Gualaco.

Mosquitia

Forested, swampy and almost uninhabited, Mosquitia is still well worth visiting. The western boundary is Cabo Camarón near Palacios and the mouth of the Río Sico. Apart from the one road that stretches 100 km from Puerto Lempira to Leimus and a further

100 km to Ahuasbila, both on the Río Coco, there are no roads in the Honduran Mosquitia. Many places can only be reached by plane, boat or on foot.

Malaria is endemic in this area; take anti-malaria precautions

MOPAWI (Mosquitia Pawisa) is the best source of information and provides the main means of access for travellers to communities in Mosquitia. It is a non-profit-making, non-sectarian organization dedicated to the development of the region and the conservation of the biodiversity of its flora and fauna. The head office is in Puerto Lempira, T898-7460, and there are offices in Tegucigalpa (Residencias Tres Caminos 4b, lote 67, Aptdo 2175, T235-8659, mopawi@optinet.hn), and in La Ceiba (Av La República, half a block from the old dock, Apdo 776, T/F443-0553). It also has offices in several other villages.

MOPAWI is concerned with the protection of natural and human resources throughout Mosquitia and the Department of Gracias a Dios. Among its many programmes is the conservation of marine turtles and the green iguana. In Mosquitia the **Reserva Biósfera Río Plátano** (525,100 ha – see below) is destined to be joined with the Reserva Antropólogica Tawakha and the Reserva Nacional Patuca which, together with Mosquitia Nicaragüense, will constitute one of the largest forest reserves north of the Amazon. This will not happen until Tawakha and Patuca receive congressional decree.

Eastern Honduras

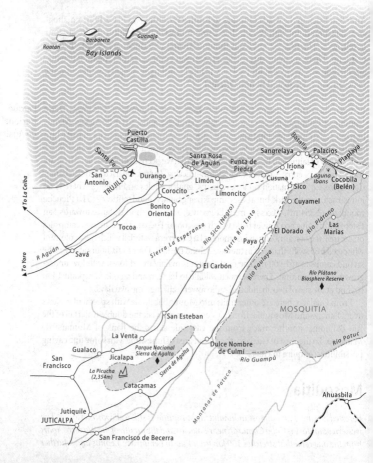

Mosquitia was very badly affected by Hurricane Mitch, but by mid-1999 it was perfectly possible to visit the region. Although previously discouraged, the Río Patuca increasingly welcomes visitors to the region, with locals being friendly and helpful to visitors passing through. If you wish to visit this area go with an organized tour. In fact, it is best to go with a guide anywhere in the region, especially if you do not speak Spanish. Having said that, few Pech speak Spanish.

Air   From **Tegucigalpa:** *Setco* flies Tue and Thu to Mocorón and Puerto Lempira, US$64 one way, US$120 return, T233-1711; agent in Mocorón is Charly (who also has a restaurant), and in Puerto Lempira the wife of Federico, the local mechanic. *Alas de Socorro* fly to **Ahuas**, T233-7025. This company charters planes for US$565, but per person it is US$60 one way to Ahuas (see Medical services, below). From **La Ceiba:** *Isleña* flies daily except Sun to **Palacios**. *Isleña* and *Sosa* fly daily except Sun to **Puerto Lempira** and *Sosa* flies Mon, Wed, Fri to **Brus Laguna** and **Ahuas**. *SAMi* flies to various villages from Puerto Lempira, eg Ahuas, Brus Laguna, Belén. There are expensive express flights to places like **Auka**, **Raya**, **Kaukira**.

Transport

Sea   Coastal vessels leave irregularly from La Ceiba to Brus Laguna and Puerto Lempira and back (2-3 day journey), carrying passengers and cargo. Information is available from the Mopawi office in **La Ceiba**, or at the pier itself. Essential equipment: torch. From **Trujillo**, ask

at the dock on the east part of the beach, wait 1½-3 days, take sleeping bag (not recommended for women, especially single women: all-male crews). **Trujillo-Palacios** US$4.50, **Brus Laguna** US$6.80; sometimes boats go to **Puerto Lempira**.

Directory **Tour operators** *La Moskitia Eco Aventuras* with Jorge Satavero, office in La Ceiba, T442-0104, www.honduras.com/moskitia who specializes in trips to La Mosquitia. *Mesoamerica Travel* and Fundación Patuca (Hauke Hoops), see page 876, also specialize in travel in this region. *Mesoamerica* is the only company to run tours to the Zona Arriba of the Río Patuca (5 or 10 days). Bob 'The Butterfly, Bird and Bug Guy' Gallardo leads highly regarded birding and other specialized nature trips to La Mosquitia, rgallardo32@hotmail.com, based in Copán Ruinas. Also see under San Pedro Sula, La Ceiba and Trujillo. **Medical services** *Alas de Socorro* operates from Ahuas to collect sick people from villages to take them to Ahuas hospital, contact the Moravian church (in Puerto Lempira Reverend Stanley Goff, otherwise local pastors will help).

Palacios Palacios, situated on a lagoon near Cabo Camarón, was once an old English fort. It is now the main access point for travellers to Mosquitia. You can cross the lagoon by cayuco from Palacios to the Black Carib village of **Batalla** (US$0.50), from where it is 112 km west along the beach to Limón (see below). It is easy to get boats from Palacios to Plaplaya (on Lago Ibans, the next lagoon east), Raísta (US$15) and Cocobila/Belén. Trips down the Río Plátano are possible, boats have to be arranged through Felix Marmol. Trips can go as far as Las Marías (see below).

Sleeping There is a hotel at the airport (**E**), good, but meals at the airport are poor value. Room for US$3 with Félix Marmol, everyone calls him Don Félix, who has information on boats to lagoons and meals for US$2. **D** *Río Tinto Lodge*, T/F237-4793, Don Félix has recently opened this ecotourist hotel, 10 rooms, bath, purified water, all woodwork locally made, beautiful view of Laguna Bacalar, guided tours of Río Plátano Biosphere Reserve, nearby is the World Wildlife Fund's Turtle Conservation Project, also a butterfly farm and a botanical garden. A 7-room *hospedaje* has been built by *Trek de Honduras*, accommodation for 14 guests, electricity, filtered water, restaurant, 5-day tours (including fishing expeditions) arranged out of La Ceiba; T238-1944, *Trek de Honduras*, or USA T1-800-654-9915, *Trek International*. Alternatively, you can go independently at considerably less cost, and ask around for somewhere to stay, eg the local teacher may let you sleep at the school.

Transport **Air** There are flights direct to Palacios from **La Ceiba** 6 days a week (see above), US$25 one way. A US$10 fee for entering Mosquitia was introduced at Palacios airport in 1995. **Boat** 2 boats, the *Margarita* and the *Sheena Dee* sail irregularly from **La Ceiba** to Palacios; also fishing boats from **Trujillo**.

Sico *Colour map 6, grid B4* You can take a picturesque cayuco trip from Palacios or Plaplaya up the Río Sico for US$50 for a hired trip, or about US$6 if you can get a lift on a cargo cayuco to Sico village. Contact Carlos Mejía who speaks perfect English and has basic rooms to rent, **F**, his wife Ofelia sells meals for US$2, also possible food and meals with David Jones, who runs the store. At Sico the remains of a railway built in the late 1920s by a banana company can be seen, including the pillars of a bridge over the river. This was abandoned after disastrous floods in the 1930s. There is no public electricity or piped water in Sico but there are two schools, a health centre and alligators in the river.

There is a gruelling beach route out of Mosquitia from Palacios/Batalla, but this is not recommended in the wake of Hurricane Mitch as it is not advisable to walk alone on empty beaches. If you wish to leave Mosquitia overland, the best possibility would be to try to get a boat to **Icoteya** on the Río Sico. From Icoteya the Río Sico is navigable downstream to Sico village past the farms of Los Fales, Los Naranjos and Los Andes. Cayucos can be hired, though they are expensive.

From Icoteya there are two buses daily to Tocoa through Limoncito (for Limón on the coast) and Francia. There are buses from La Ceiba and Trujillo to Limoncito and Limón. At **Limón** there is a fine, clean beach, with lovely swimming;

accommodation is available at *Hospedaje Martínez* (also serves meals) and there is a friendly *comedor, Bar-Restaurant Kerolyn*. This is a Spanish-speaking Garífuna community. Transport: two buses a day run from Trujillo to Limón, first at 0830; from Limón, there are several buses daily to Tocoa and La Ceiba.

Mosquito-free **Cocobila** (Belén), picturesquely situated on a sandspit between the ocean and the huge freshwater Ibans Lagoon. Excellent meals (US$2) with Miss Erlinda, but be sure to order in advance; ask at the MOPAWI office about accommodation. Boats go to **Plaplaya** at the mouth of the Río Sico (bad mosquitoes and *niguas* which burrow into the soles of your feet), or walk the distance in over two hours along the beach. Room and meals with Doña Evritt de Woods at Plaplaya. Accommodation here is very basic (US$3, no toilet facility). After Plaplaya is the village of **Raísta**, where there is a butterfly farm which breeds species for export. For US$3, Ed will give explanations. Accommodation (US$3) is in rooms in a large house in a fenced-off compound; river water for washing, toilet hut, laundry area. There is a restaurant near the landing stage.

Transport Boats to **La Ceiba**, or up the Río Sico to **Sico**. A boat leaves Plaplaya at 0600 for the 0730 plane out of Palacios. For the same plane a boat leaves **Raísta** at 0400 (boatman Umberto Marmol). **Plátano** village, at the mouth of the Río Plátano, can be reached by lobster boat from **Guanaja** or by the supply ships from La Ceiba to **Brus Laguna** (in all cases cayucos take passengers from ship to shore); Plátano-Brus Laguna, 1½ hours, US$2.50 (plus 45 mins-1 hr on foot between the westernmost edge of the lagoon, **Barra**, and Plátano), Plátano-La Ceiba, US$25.

The Reserve was established by the Honduran government in 1980 to protect the outstanding natural and cultural resources of the Río Plátano valley and its environs. In 1982 the UN declared the Reserve a World Patrimony site. The tropical jungles that still cloak the landscape here shelter a number of endangered birds, mammals, and fish, among them scarlet macaws and harpy eagles, jaguars and tapirs, and the cuyamel, a prized food fish fast becoming extinct throughout Honduras. In addition, there are a number of archaeological sites about which little is known, and the fabled lost White City of the Maya is said to be hidden somewhere in the thick jungles of the Plátano headwaters.

Reserva de la Biósfera Río Plátano

Miskito and Pech Indians living along the lower Plátano cultivate yuca, bananas, rice, corn and beans, and also feed themselves by hunting and fishing. The upper (southern) portion of the Plátano watershed was virgin jungle until quite recently, but is being quickly populated by mestizo immigrants from the poverty-stricken south of Honduras. These new residents are cutting down the forest to plant crops, hunting wildlife mercilessly, and using home-made dynamite in a very destructive form of fishing. The government's intention in 1995 officially to allow settlers into the Sico and Paulaya valleys, on the western edge of the reserve, was roundly criticized. It was feared that the agrarian reform programme would lead to the desertification of Río Plátano. Given the pressure the Reserve is under, it is recommended to visit it sooner rather than later.

Transport To get there you can fly or take one of the boats that periodically leave from **La Ceiba** and **Trujillo** to either Palacios, Cocobila/Belén or Barra Río Plátano, the main villages in the vicinity of the river mouth. Expect to pay perhaps US$25 for passage from La Ceiba or US$5 from Trujillo. A boat from **Palacios** to Cocobila/Belén cost US$3 per person, US$20 for the whole boat, 45 mins. From Belén to the Biosphere headquarters in **Kuri** is a 45-min walk or 10-min ride (US$2). The staff and locals are friendly and the staff or the teacher (of the few who can speak Spanish) can probably put you up for the night. They can also help you contract with a *tuk-tuk* (motorized dugout canoe) to carry you upriver as far as **Las Marías**, the cost is about US$80 per person return and it takes 6-8 hrs (3-4 downstream). Daily boat rental costs about US$20.

Las Marías
It is harder to advance upriver during the rainy season, from June-December

A Miskito-Pech village that is the furthest limit of upstream settlement. There is a hospital in Las Marías where you may be able to stay (chocolate and hand woven bags for sale to make money for the community), but usually you are assigned accommodation in the village: 3-4 *hospedajes* (family houses, US$3), also serving meals, US$2. Each *hospedaje* has a map in several languages explaining local routes and attractions. No drinks for sale, purify your water. The journey upstream to Las Marías, although beautiful, can become very tedious and uncomfortable. On arrival in Las Marías, arrange return at once. Bird-watching can provide a diversion; there are three species of toucan as well as tanagers, herons, kingfishers, vultures, hawk eagles and oropendolas. If lucky you might see crocodiles or iguanas.

An alternative route to Las Marías is by boat across Ibans Lagoon, 45 minutes by *tuk-tuk*, then 6 ½ hours' walk through jungle (rough path, hot, mosquitoes, take lots of water and insect repellent, and wear good hiking boots). In Belén, ask for Rosendo Mejía or Sergio to act as a guide. Bargain hard for a rate (about US$12.50 per person) and pay separately for the one-way boat trip.

Once in Las Marías, it is possible to arrange at El Comité de Ecoturismo for guides (US$5) or trips upstream in a *pipante*. This is a shallow dugout canoe manoeuvered with poles (*palancas*) and paddles (*canaletes*). Each *pipante* can carry up to two passengers and their gear, plus three villagers who pole it upstream. The cost per day to rent pipante and crew is about US$12.50 per person (negotiable, you must provide all food, for crew as well). Among the sights are pre-Columbian rock carvings, some involve a two-day trip. It is also possible to take an excursion into the forest for four, or eight hours. The very pacy walk is an interesting way to see tropical jungle, but do not expect to see much wildlife. High prices are charged for everything in Las Marías, but remember that it is their only source of income. On your return, if not on an organized tour, use the radio in Kuri to call Palacios for a boat to fetch you in Belén, and don't forget to reserve a flight out of Palacios if you need one. On any trip take drinking water, or water purifiers, food, insect repellent, sun protection for boat journeys, candles and camping gear.

Brus Laguna
Colour map 6, grid B5

It is a 15-minute scenic flight from Puerto Lempira (see below) above Caratasca Lagoon and grassy, pine-covered savannas to **Ahuas**, one-hour walk from the Patuca River (fabled for gold). There is a hospital here, as well as four missions, but poor accommodation and not much else besides. **F** *Hospedaje y Comedor Suyapa*, basic, no electricity, meals, US$1.25; mosquito repellent and coils absolutely essential here. Irregular cayucos sail down to **Brus Laguna** for US$2.50, at the mouth of the Patuca River, or US$12.50 (15 minutes) scenic flight in the mission plane. The airstrip is 4 km from village, take a lift for US$1. There is a disco at the riverside to the left of the bridge. Plague of mosquitoes for all but five months of the year (winter and spring).

Sleeping and eating *George Goff* rents rooms (good but basic, limited electricity, **F**) and his wife Elga cooks tasty meals for US$2, he speaks English and will also help with mission-plane flights. Behind his house is a *hospedaje* being built by the 'Medio-Francés', *Colindre* (who speaks English, German, French, 'Scandinavian' and Spanish); he operates tours on the Brus Laguna and Río Plátano (can pick up people in La Ceiba if requested). Food and lodging only to those on tour with him. Meals generally to be ordered in advance, try *Hospedaje Cruz* or *Doña Norma*, *Doña Aurora* or *Doña Gladys*.

Puerto Lempira
Colour map 6, grid B5

Puerto Lempira is on the large Caratasca Lagoon. In Puerto Lempira is the main office of MOPAWI (see above). The airstrip is only five minutes' walk from town. Regular *tuk-tuks* (motorized canoes) cross the lagoon to **Kaukira**, US$1.20 (a nice place, but nothing there), **Yagurabila** and **Palkaka**. The *tuk-tuks* leave Kaukira daily, except Sunday, at 0500, returning during the morning. In the afternoon the lagoon is usually too rough to cross.

Sleeping **D** *Gran Hotel Flores*, some rooms with bath. Recommended. *Villas Caratascas*, huts with bath, restaurant, disco. **F** *Pensión Moderno* (good, friendly, electricity 1800-2230), and inferior **F** *Pensión Santa Teresita*, Barrio El Centro, T898-7434.

Eating *La Mosquitia*, Centro Comercial Segovia in main street, breakfasts and cheap fish. *Glorieta*, left of landing bridge, fish, lagoon breezes. *Delmy*, 3 blocks north of main street, chicken and other dishes, noisy. *Doña Aida*, north side of main road to landing bridge, fresh orange juice. *Quinto Patio*, good breakfasts.

Discotheque *Hampu*, by landing bridge.

Entertainment

Airline offices *SAM*, T898-7491. *Sosa*, T898-7467. **Banks** *Banco Nacional de Desarrollo Agrícola* changes dollars at poor rates, bad reputation.

Directory

Inland by road from Puerto Lempira are **Mocorón** (*Charly's* restaurant, see above, rooms available **F** per person) and **Rus Rus** which may be visited with difficulty (there is no public transport but any vehicle will give a lift); a beautiful, quiet village (accommodation at Friends of America hospital's house; meals from Capi's next door, ask Friends about transport out). A branch off this road leads southeast to **Leimus** on the Río Coco and the frontier with Nicaragua. Ask for Evaristo López (at whose house you can get breakfast) who can arrange transport to Leimus, most days, 3-4 hours for about US$3.50. He is also knowledgeable about area safety.

Honduran immigration If you wish to cross here, obtain your exit stamp in Puerto Lempira. The Office of *Migración* is open until 1100, Mon-Fri. This office is reported as very helpful and a good source of information.

Border with Nicaragua

For further details see the section on the Nicaraguan Mosquitia under **The Caribbean Coast** (page 918). The road continues south to the small town of **Ahuashbila** on the upper river of the Río Coco which marks the border with Nicaragua.

Tegucigalpa to the Pacific and Nicaragua

From the capital to the Golfo de Fonseca the route twists through mountain valleys down to the volcanic islands and Honduras' Pacific ports San Lorenzo and Amapala. Near the coast the Pan-American Highway leads west to El Salvador and east though the hot plains of Choluteca, the quiet but popular beaches of Cedeña and Ratón and ultimately to Nicaragua. An alternative route to Nicaragua heads east, through the agricultural town of Danlí, to the border at Las Manos. Short detours from the highway lead to picturesque colonial villages and old mining centres in the hills.

From the capital a paved road runs south through fine scenery. Beyond Sabanagrande (see page 844) is **Pespire**, a picturesque colonial village with the beautiful church of San Francisco, which has triple domes. Pespire produces small, delicious mangoes. At **Jícaro Galán** (92 km; *Population*: 3,000) the road joins the Pan-American Highway, which heads west through **Nacaome** (*Population*: 4,475), where there is a colonial church, to the border with El Salvador at **Goascarán** (*Population*: 2,190). At Jícaro Galán, *Ticabus* and other international buses from San Salvador, Tegucigalpa and Managua meet and exchange passengers.

Tegucigalpa to Goascarán

Sleeping **Jícaro Galán**: **C** *Oasis Colonial*, T881-2220, hotel, nice rooms, good restaurant and pool, in hot sticky area, and an unnamed basic guesthouse. **Nacaome**: **D** *Perpetuo Socorro*, Barrio el Centro, T895-4453, a/c, TV. **F** *Intercontinental* in centre, basic, tap and bucket shower, friendly. **F** *Suyapa*, basic, cheap. **Goascarán**: There are very basic hotels at the border. Restaurants at all these places.

Border with El Salvador The Santa Clara bridge over the Río Goascarán is the border with El Salvador. **El Amatillo** straddles the border.

Honduran immigration The border closes at 1700. Try to avoid lunchtime when there may be a 2-hr break. This border is very relaxed.

Crossing by private vehicle Expect to be besieged by young *tramitadores* touting for your business. They wear a black and white uniform of sorts with name badges, carry an identity card issued by the border station, and will take the strain out of the 3-4 hr border crossing. Expect to pay about US$25 to the various officials on both sides.

Salvadorean consulate See Choluteca below.

Sleeping 2 cheap *hospedajes*, *San Andrés* and *Los Arcos* on the Honduran side.

Transport Bus Tegucigalpa-El Amatillo, hourly, US$1.50, 4 hrs. El Amatillo-Choluteca, US$1, 3 hrs, every 30 mins, microbuses.

A temporary pass can be purchased on the Honduran side for US$1.50 for a visit to the Salvadorean town of **El Amatillo**, for an hour or so. Many Hondurans cross to purchase household goods and clothes.

Directory **Exchange** Moderate rates of exchange from money changers.

San Lorenzo
Colour map 6, grid C2
Population: 21,025

The Pan-American Highway continues south from Jícaro Galán, to the Pacific coast (46 km) at San Lorenzo, a dirty town on the shores of the Gulf of Fonseca. The climate on the Pacific litoral is very hot. The shrimp farms on this part of the coast, an essential part of the local economy, were largely washed away in the 1998 storm.

Sleeping and eating **D** *Miramar*, Barrio Plaza Marina, T881-2038, 26 rooms, 4 a/c, good restaurant, overpriced, in rough dockside area, best not to walk there. **E-F** *Perla del Pacífico*, fan, bath, comfortable, clean, friendly, central, charming. Recommended. *Restaurant-Bar Henecán*, on Parque Central, a/c, good food and service, not cheap but worth it.

Transport Frequent *busitos* from Tegucigalpa to San Lorenzo (US$1) and Choluteca (US$1.50).

Directory **Banks** *Bancahorro* (changes US$ cash and TCs), *Banco Atlántida*, and *Banco de Occidente* (no exchange); Chinese grocery gives good rates for US$ cash.

Amapala
Colour map 6, grid C2
Population: 7,925

The Pacific port of **Amapala**, on Isla del Tigre, has been replaced by Puerto de Henecán in San Lorenzo, and is reached by a road which leaves the Pan-American Highway at the eastern edge of San Lorenzo. The **Isla del Tigre** is yet another place reputed to be the site of hidden pirate treasure. In the 16th century it was visited by a number of pirates, inlcuding Sir Francis Drake. Amapala was capital of Honduras for a brief period in 1876 when Marco Aurelio Soto was president. Today, in addition to a naval base, Amapala is 'a charming, decaying backwater'. The 783-m extinct Amapala volcano has a road to the summit where there is a US army unit and a DEA contingent. You can walk round the island in half a day. There is a ferry service from Coyolito, but fishermen will take you to San Lorenzo for a small fee, not by motor launch, and the trip takes half a day. The deep-sea fishing in the gulf is good. It is possible to charter boats to La Unión in El Salvador.

Sleeping and eating B *Hotel Villas Playa Negra*, Aldea Playa Negra, T898-8534, F898-8580, 7 rooms with a/c, 7 with fan, pool, beach, restaurant poor value, very isolated, lovely setting. Ask for Doña Marianita, who rents the 1st floor of her house, **F** *Al Mar*, above Playa Grande, fan, scorpions (if you're lucky), lovely view of mountains and sunset. **F** *Pensión Internacional* on the harbour, very basic, otherwise only local accommodation of low standard. *Restaurant-Bar Miramar* by the harbour, overlooking the sea, pleasant, very friendly, good meals, hamburgers and boquitas, and you can hang your hammock. Several clean *comedores* in the new Mercado Municipal.

Transport A 31-km road leaves the Pan-American Highway 2 km west of San Lorenzo, signed to Coyolito. It passes through scrub and mangrove swamps before crossing a causeway to a hilly island, around which it winds to the jetty at **Coyolito** (no *hospedajes* but a *comedor* and *refrescarías*). Motorized launches run between Coyolito and Amapala, US$0.35 per person when launch is full (about 10 passengers), about US$4 to hire a launch (but you will probably have to pay for the return trip as well). First boat leaves Amapala at 0700 to connect with first Coyolito-San Lorenzo bus at 0800; next bus from Coyolito at 0900.

Directory Banks *Banco El Ahorro Hondureño*.

Choluteca

Choluteca is expanding rapidly on the back of the local industries of coffee, cotton and cattle which flourish despite the hot climate. The town was one of the earliest settlements in Honduras (1535) and still has a colonial centre. The church of **La Merced** (1643) is being renovated and is due to be reconsecrated. The **Casa de la Cultura** and **Biblioteca Municipal** are in the colonial house of José Cecilio del Valle on the corner of the Parque Central. A fine steel suspension bridge crosses the broad river at the entrance into Choluteca from the north (it was built in 1937). The social centre of San José Obrero is at 3 Calle SO, where handicrafts, in particular carved wood and chairs, can be bought.

Colour map 6, grid C3
Population: 87,889

Honduras

The city was heavily damaged by floods during Hurricane Mitch. The suspension bridge still stands, but both banks of the Río Choluteca suffered badly.

Excursions

Cedeño beach, on the eastern side of the Gulf of Fonseca 40 km from Choluteca, is a lovely though primitive spot, with clean sand stretching for miles and often thundering surf (the beach shelves sharply). Avoid public holidays, weekend crowds and take a good insect repellent. Spectacular views and sunsets over the Gulf of Fonseca south to Nicaragua and west to El Salvador, and of the volcanic islands in the bay. Hourly bus from Choluteca (US$0.60, 1½ hours). A turn-off leads from the Choluteca-Cedeño road to Ratón beach, much more pleasant than Cedeño. Bus from Choluteca at 1130; returns next morning.

Sleeping

B *La Fuente*, Carretera Panamericana, past the bridge, T882-0253, F882-0273, with bath, swimming pool, a/c, meals. Will let motorbikes in if you insist. Recommended. D *Camino Real*, road to Guasaule, T882-0610, F282-2860, swimming pool, good steaks in restaurant. Recommended. D *Centroamérica*, near *La Fuente*, T882-3525, F882-2900, a/c, good restaurant, bar, pool, good value. D-E *Pierre*, Av Valle y C Williams, T882-0676, with bath (ants in the taps), a/c or fan, TV, free protected parking, cafetería has good breakfasts, very central, credit cards accepted. Recommended. E *Brabazola*, Barrio Cabañas, T882-5535, a/c, comfy beds, TV, good. E *Pacífico*, near Mi Esperanza terminal, outside the city, clean, cool rooms, fan, hammocks, quiet, safe parking, fresh drinking water, breakfast US$1.50. F *Hibueras*, Av Bojórquez, Barrio El Centro, T882-0512, with bath and fan, clean, purified water, *comedor* attached, good value. F *San Carlos*, Paz Barahona 757, Barrio El Centro, with shower, fan, very clean, pleasant. F *Santa Rosa*, 3 C NO, in the centre, just west of market, T882-0355, some with bath, pleasant patio, laundry facilities, clean, friendly. Recommended.

East of Choluteca is D per person *Escuela de Español Mina Clavo Rico*, El Corpus, Choluteca 51103, T/F887-3501, US$90 per week, full board, living with local families, language classes (US$4 per hour), riding, craft lessons, work on farms, excursions.

Eating *Alondra*, Parque Central, old colonial house, open Fri-Sun only. *Comedor Central*, opposite side of Parque, *comida corriente* daily specials, *licuados*, sandwiches, good for breakfast. Local specialities are the drinks *posole* and *horchata de morro*. *El Conquistador*, on Pan-American, opposite *La Fuente*, steaks etc, outdoor seating but you have to eat inside, good but slow service. Will change money for customers. Recommended. *Frosty*, on main street, owned by *Hotel Pierre*, good food and juices. Recommended. The *Tico Rico* on C Vincente Williams has been highly recommended.

Festivals The local feast day of the **Virgen de la Concepción** on **8 Dec** begins a week of festivities, followed by the **Festival del Sur**, 'Ferisur', which attracts many visitors from Tegucigalpa.

Shopping *Mercado Municipal*, 7 Av SO, 3 C SO, on outskirts.

Transport Buses to El Espino (Nicaraguan border) from Choluteca, US$1.15, 1 hr, 1st at 0700, last at 1400. Also frequent minibuses to El Amatillo (El Salvador border) via San Lorenzo, US$1, from bus stop at bridge. Buses to Choluteca from Tegucigalpa with Mi Esperanza, Bonanza and El Dandy; Bonanza continue to San Marcos and depart Tegucigalpa hourly from 0530, 4 hrs to Choluteca, US$1.90. The municipal bus terminal is about 10 blocks from the new municipal market, about 8 blocks from cathedral/Parque Central; Mi Esperanza has its own terminal 1 block from municipal terminal.

Directory **Banks** Of the many banks in town *Banco Atlántida* has a Visa ATM, and only *Banco de Comercio* changes TCs. Can be difficult to exchange money in Choluteca. **Communications** Post office: 0800-1700, 0800-1200 on Sat, US$0.15 per letter for Poste Restante. **Telephone**: collect calls to Spain, Italy, USA only. **Embassies and consulates** The *El Salvadorean Consulate* is to south of town, fast and friendly, open 0800-1500 daily. **Tour operators** *Agencia de Viajes Tropical*, Edif Rivera y Compañía, T882-2831.

San Marcos de Colón
Population: 9,570
Altitude: 915 m

Beyond Choluteca is the long climb to San Marcos de Colón, a clean, tidy, peaceful and beautifully cool town in the hills.

Sleeping **E** *Colonial*, friendly, clean, erratic water supply. **F** *Hospedaje Flores*, friendly, clean, cell-like rooms, washing facilities, breakfast and typical dinner, good, exchange. **F** *Hotelito Mi Esperanza*, 1 block west of *Banco Atlántida*, near the bus terminal, T281-3062, 17 rooms, nice, clean, friendly, cold showers.

Eating *Parrillada Candilejas*, good food, children's play area. *Restaurante Bonanza*, near main plaza, clean, good food, friendly service, Also *Taquería Bonanza*, 2 blocks from Pan-American highway on road to centre, Mexican specialities, clean, inexpensive.

Transport Bus from Choluteca throughout the day, US$0.75, 1½ hrs; buses from Tegucigalpa, Mi Esperanza, 6 Av 23 or 26 C, Comayagüela and Bonanza, 5 a day from 0530, US$2, 4 hrs.

Border with Nicaragua – El Espino
Border formalities can be particularly tedious at El Espino

Honduran immigration Immigration is 100 m from the border, open 0800-1600 (till 1630 on Nicaraguan side). Beware of taxis offering to take you to the border after 1600. **Nicaraguan consulate** In Tegucigalpa.

Transport Taxis/minibuses run from Choluteca and San Marcos (10 km) to the border. From San Marcos they only leave when full, US$1, US$0.50 for locals. To Tegucigalpa, there is a direct bus through Choluteca with Empresa Esperanza, 4 hrs.

Directory **Exchange** is easy at this crossing for dollars and córdobas, but the rate for córdobas is better on the Nicaraguan side.

Border with Nicaragua at Río Guasaule

There is another route from Choluteca to Nicaragua through **El Triunfo** to the border at the bridge over the Río Guasaule. This route is preferred by the international buses as the road is better. It may be worth choosing one of the many 'helpers' to steer you to the correct officials. Fix price beforehand.

Honduran immigration Open 0800-1600. On *Ticabus*, passengers' passports are collected by an official as the bus enters Honduras. Entry tax is paid to the official, who returns passports after sniffer dogs have checked the bus for drugs. No other customs checks.

Exchange There is a bank, but lots of money changers offer rates slightly worse than in the capital. Watch out for children who try to distract you while changing money.

Transport Bus Choluteca-Guasaule, US$1, 45mins.

East of Tegucigalpa

A good paved road runs east from Tegucigalpa through the hills to Danlí, 92 km away in the Department of El Paraíso. There are no signs when leaving Tegucigalpa so ask the way. Some 40 km along, in the Zamorano valley (see page 844), is the Escuela Agrícola Panamericana which is run for all students of the Americas with US help: it has a fine collection of tropical flowers (visits should be booked in advance at the office in Tegucigalpa – see page 844).

At **Zamorano** (Km 29) a narrow winding road leads, after about 6 km, to the picturesque old mining village of **San Antonio del Oriente** and its beautiful church, much favoured by Honduran painters such as Velásquez. At Zamorano the bus will drop you off a few hundred metres before the road junction to San Antonio, from where a small path on the left goes through some trees for 10 minutes before joining the main dirt road. From here on up it is a winding, rocky route through tall thin pine woods, rising quickly for an impressive view of the broad flat valley. After about 40 minutes the main road turns sharply to the right, while a smaller track continues in roughly the same direction along the left-hand slope of a mountain. If you go to the right this leads to San Antonio del Oriente after climbing for an hour. If it is sunny, the path is dusty and glaring and there is little shade in the middle of the day. But reaching the village is well worth it: red-tiled rooves and white plastered walls cling to the hillside, and a very quaint little church overlooks the valley. There is one *pulpería*. From here, a steep 15-minute climb over the ridge leads to **San Antonio del Occidente**, an even smaller village (also with one tiny *pulpería*). A much shorter (about 30 minutes) walk from San Antonio del Occidente, down the other side of the mountain, comes back to the junction mentioned above. The hike can be done in reverse, which is probably easier. It is little problem to hitch back to Tegucigalpa.

Hike to San Antonio de Oriente

Transport Direct bus to San Antonio del Oriente from Tegucigalpa at 0630, return trip 0400, US$1.75.

From Zamorano, a road goes south to Güinope, a pretty, white and dusty town with a church (1820) blessed with a charming façade. The town is famed for its oranges and jam; try the orange wine 'La Trilla', matured in oak barrels, US$2.50 per bottle. Good walking in the area. **Fiesta**: Festival de la Naranja, at the end of March.

Güinope

Sleeping F *Merlin*, with bath, clean, good value. *Comedor Lilian*, down side street. Snack bar next to bus office on Parque Central.

Transport Bus from Tegucigalpa, Mercado Jacaleapa, 1st at 0730, 1st from Güinope at 0515, frequent service. Some buses to Güinope continue south to San Lucas and San Antonio de Flores.

At Km 47½, a paved road branches south to Yuscarán, in rolling pineland country preserved by the **Reserva Biológica de Yuscarán** which protects much of the land around Montserrat mountain. The climate here is semi-tropical. Yuscarán was an important mining centre in colonial days and is a typically picturesque colonial village, with cobbled streets and houses on a steep hillside. Ask to see the museum near

Yuscarán
Colour map 6, grid C3
Population 9,270
Altitude: 1,070 m

Honduras

the town plaza, you have to ask around to find the person who has the key, antiques and photographs are displayed in a restored mansion which belonged to a mining family. There is a Caa de Cultura in the former Casa Fortín, open Monday-Saturday. The Yuscarán distilleries, one in the centre, the other on the outskirts, are considered by many to produce the best *aguardiente* in Honduras (tours possible). The Montserrat mountain which looms over Yuscarán is riddled with mines. The old Guavias mine is close to Yuscarán, some 4 km along the road to Agua Fría. About 10 km further along, a narrow, winding road climbs steeply through pine woods to the summit of **Pico Montserrat** (1,891 m), with fine views all around.

Sleeping and eating D-E hotel, owned by Dutchman Freek de Haan and his Honduran wife and daughter, T892-7213; private or dormitory rooms, beautiful views of Nicaraguan mountains in the distance. **F** *Hotel Carol*, 6 modern rooms with bath and hot water, annex to owner's fine colonial house, safe, family atmosphere, good value. *Cafetería Colonial*, opposite *Banco de Occidente*, serves excellent *desayuno típico* and *comida corriente*.

Transport Frequent buses to **Zamorano** and **Tegucigalpa**; from the capital buses leave from Mercado Jacaleapa. For information, ask anyone in the Parque Central in Yuscarán.

Danlí
Colour map 6, grid C3
Population: 30,000
Altitude: 760 m

Danlí, 102 km from Tegucigalpa, is noted for sugar and coffee production, a large meat-packing company (Orinsa), and is a centre of the tobacco industry. There are four cigar factories. The Honduras-América SA factory (right-hand side of *Cine Aladino*) produces export quality cigars at good prices. ■ *Mon-Fri, 0800-1200, 1300-1700, Sat 0800-1200*. Also *Placencia Tabacos*, on the road to Tegucigalpa, where you can also watch cigar-making. Better prices than at Santa Rosa. From Danlí to the north is Cerro San Cristóbal and the beautiful Lago San Julián.

Sleeping C-D *Gran Hotel Granada*, T883-2499, F883-2774, bar, cable TV, accepts Visa, restaurant and swimming pool, locals pay half price. Recommended. **E** *La Esperanza*, Gabriela Mistral, T883-2106, next to Esso station, bath, hot water, fan (**D** with a/c), TV, drinking water, friendly, good car parking. **F** *Apolo*, El Canal, T883-2177, next to Shell station, with bath, clean, basic. **F** *Danlí*, C El Canal, opposite *Apolo*, without bath, good. **F** *Eben Ezer*, 3½ blocks north of Shell station, T883-2655, basic, hot showers. **F** *Las Vegas*, next to bus terminal, noisy, restaurant, washing facilities, parking. **F** *Regis*, 3 blocks north of Plaza Central, with bath, car park, basic.

Eating *Comedor Claudio*, good *comida corriente*, good information from locals. *El Gaucho* and *España*, in the centre of town, are good. *El Paraíso de las Hamburguesas*, cheap, good, owner very friendly. *McBeth's*, snackbar, good ice-cream. *Pizzería Picolino*, 2 blocks southwest of Parque Central, good pizzas, pleasant atmosphere. *Rancho Típico* near *Hotel Danlí*, excellent.

Festivals The *Fiesta del Maíz* lasts all of the 3rd week of **Aug**, with cultural and sporting events, all-night street party on the Sat; it gets very crowded with people from Tegucigalpa.

Transport Buses From **Tegucigalpa**, US$2, from Blvd Miraflores near Mercado Jacaleapa (from left-hand side of market as you face it), Colonia Kennedy, Tegucigalpa, hourly, 2 hrs, arrive 1½ hrs before you intend to leave, long slow queues for tickets (take 'Kennedy' bus from C La Isla near the football stadium in central Tegucigalpa, or taxi, US$1.20, to Mercado Jacaleapa). Express bus from Colonia Kennedy, 0830, 1230 and 1700, US$2. One road continues east from Danlí to Santa María (several buses daily), crossing a mountain range with panoramic views.

Directory Banks *Banco Atlántida* changes TCs without problems. Cash on Visa card, maximum US$50. Other banks as well. **Medical services** Dentist: *Dr Juan Castillo*, Barrio El Centro, T883-2083.

El Paraíso
Colour map 6, grid C3
Population: 27,291

Another paved road goes south 18 km to El Paraíso, and beyond to the Nicaraguan border at Las Manos/Ocotal. El Paraíso is a picturesque town in an area producing coffee, bananas and rice.

Sleeping E-F *5a Av Hotel y Restaurant*, 5 Av y 10 C, T893-4298, with bath, hot water, parking, restaurant specializes in Mexican-American food. **F** *Lendy's*, Barrio Nuevo Carmelo, by ~~b~~us station, T893-4461, clean, friendly, prepares food.

Eating *Comedor Edith*, on a small square on main road, after Parque Central towards border, US$0.85 for a meal.

Transport Minibuses run from Danlí terminal to El Paraíso, frequent (0600 to 1740), US$0.40, 30 mins, don't believe taxi drivers who say there are no minibuses. *Emtra Oriente*, Av 6, C 6-7, runs 4 times a day from Tegucigalpa to **El Paraíso**, 2½ hrs, US$1.50. Buses from El Paraíso to **Las Manos**, about every 1 ½ hrs, US$0.35, 30 mins, or taxi US$4, many people willing to share, 15 mins bumpy ride.

Directory Banks Several branches in town including *Bancahsa*, *Banco Atlántida*, *Banadesa*, *Banhcafé* and *Banco Sogerín*.

Honduran immigration Border at **Las Manos** open 0800-1600.

Crossing by private vehicle Whether entering or leaving Honduras, you will find *tramitadores* will help you through the paperwork, and are recommended. Total costs are about US$25 and the receipts may not quite tally with what you have paid.

Exchange Buy and sell your córdobas in Nicaragua.

Transport Direct bus Las Manos to Tegucigalpa, 0930, US$2.

Border with Nicaragua
This is recommended as the best of the 3 routes from Tegucigalpa to Nicaragua

Honduras

Background

History

Honduras was largely neglected by Spain and its colonists, who concentrated on their trading partners further north or south. The resulting disparity in levels of development between Honduras and its regional neighbours caused problems after Independence in 1821. Harsh partisan battles among provincial leaders resulted in the collapse of the Central American Federation in 1838. The national hero, General Francisco Morazán was a leader in unsuccessful attempts to maintain the Federation and the restoration of Central American unity was the main aim of foreign policy until 1922.

For Honduras' early history, see page 59

Honduras has had a succession of military and civilian rulers and there have been 300 internal rebellions, civil wars and changes of government since Independence, most of them in the 20th century. Political instability in the past led to a lack of investment in economic infrastructure and socio-political integration, making Honduras one of the poorest countries in the Western Hemisphere. It earned its nickname of the 'Banana Republic' in the first part of the 20th century following the founding of a company in 1899, by the Vaccaro brothers of New Orleans, which eventually became the Standard Fruit Company and which was to make bananas the major export crop of Honduras. The United Fruit Company of Boston was also founded in 1899 and, 30 years later, was merged with the Cuyamel Fruit Company of Samuel Zemurray, who controlled the largest fruit interests in Honduras. United Fruit (UFCo), known as El Pulpo (the octopus), emerged as a major political influence in the region with strong links with several dictatorships.

Banana Republic

The 1929 Great Depression caused great hardship in the export-oriented economies of the region, and in Honduras it brought the rise of another authoritarian régime. Tiburcio

The Great Depression

Cariás Andino was elected in 1932 and, through his ties with foreign companies and other neighbouring dictators, he was able to hold on to power until renewed turbulence began in 1948, and he voluntarily withdrew from power a year later. The two political parties, the Liberals and the Nationals, came under the control of provincial military leaders and, after two more authoritarian Nationalist governments and a general strike in 1954 by radical labour unions on the north coast, young military reformists staged a palace coup in 1955. They installed a provisional junta and allowed elections for a constituent assembly in 1957. The assembly was led by the Liberal Party, which appointed Dr Ramón Villeda Morales as President, and transformed itself into a national legislature for six years. A newly created military academy graduated its first class in 1960, and the armed forces began to professionalize their leadership in conjunction with the civilian economic establishment. Conservative officers, nervous of a Cuban-style revolution, pre-empted elections in 1963 in a bloody coup which deposed Dr Villeda, exiled Liberal Party members and took control of the national police, which they organized into special security forces.

Football War In 1969, Honduras and El Salvador were drawn into a bizarre episode known as the 'Football War', which took its name from its origin in a disputed decision in the third qualifying round of the World Cup. Its root cause, however, was the social tension aroused by migrating workers from overcrowded El Salvador to Honduras. In 13 days, 2,000 people were killed before a ceasefire was arranged by the Organization of American States. A peace treaty was not signed until 1980, and the dispute provoked Honduras to withdraw from the Central American Common Market (CACM), which helped to hasten its demise.

Tensions between the two countries can still easily rise. Disputes over the border and fishing rights in the Gulf of Fonseca are a cause of friction, and in August 2001, Honduras expelled two Salvadoreans on spying charges. Honduras also has disputed land claims with Nicaragua to the east. However, regional cooperation is sufficiently well developed for regional conferences to tackle the problems with commitments to non-aggressive solutions.

Transition to The armed forces, led chiefly by General López Arellano and his protégés in the National
democracy Party, dominated government until 1982. López initiated land reform but, despite liberal policies, his régime was brought down in the mid-1970s by corruption scandals involving misuse of hurricane aid funds and bribes from the United Brands Company. His successors increased the size and power of the security forces and created the largest air force in Central America, while slowly preparing for a return to civilian rule. A constituent assembly was elected in 1980 and general elections held in 1981. A constitution was promulgated in 1982 and President Roberto Suazo Córdoba of the Liberal Party assumed power. During this period, Honduras cooperated closely with the USA on political and military issues, particularly in covert moves to destabilize Nicaragua's Sandinista government, and became host to some 12,000 right wing Nicaraguan contra rebels. It was less willing to take a similar stand against the FMLN left wing guerrillas in El Salvador for fear of renewing border tensions. In 1986 the first peaceful transfer of power between civilian presidents for 30 years took place when José Azcona del Hoyo (Liberal) won the elections. Close relations with the USA were maintained in the 1980s, Honduras had the largest Peace Corps Mission in the world, non-governmental and international voluntary agencies proliferated and the government became increasingly dependent upon US aid to finance its budget.

In 1989, the general elections were won by the right wing Rafael Leonardo Callejas Romero of the National Party, which won a 14-seat majority in the National Assembly. Under the terms of the Central American Peace Plan, the contra forces were demobilized and disarmed by June 1990. The Honduran armed forces have come under greater pressure for reform as a result of US and domestic criticism of human rights abuses. A report published in April 1993 recommended a series of institutional reforms in the judiciary and security services, including the resolution by the Supreme Court of all

:ases of jurisdictional conflict between civilian and military courts. This and other measures led to some, but by no means all, improvements in respect of human rights.

Liberal
government
since 1993

In the campaign leading up to the 1993 general elections, the Liberal candidate, Carlos Roberto Reina Idiáquez, pledged to provide every citizen 'techo, trabajo, tierra y tortilla' (roof, work, land and food), arguing for a more socially-conscious face to the economic adjustment programme inaugurated by President Callejas. Reina duly won the elections with a 53.4 majority over his National Party rival, Oswaldo Ramos Soto. Although many of his economic policies were unpopular, and he was unable to alleviate widespread poverty in the short term, President Reina received approval for his handling of the military and investigations of human rights' abuses.

The 1997 presidential elections were again won by the Liberal candidate, Carlos Flores Facusse, with 53 of the vote over the National Party candidate, Nora Gúnera de Melgar, who received 42. Carlos Flores had the support of the business community, who believed he would control public spending and reduce the government deficit in line with IMF targets, but he also campaigned against economic austerity and in favour of bridging the gap between rich and poor. The passage of Hurricane Mitch over Honduras in October 1998 forced the Flores administration to refocus all its attention on rebuilding the country at all levels, social, economic and infrastructural. The president set up a 'reconstruction cabinet' to oversee this mammoth task.

Elections on 26 November 2001 saw Ricardo Maduro of the National Party beat his counterpart Rafael Pineda Ponce of the Liberal Party, to assume the presidency in January of 2002 in a ceremony attended by many Central American leaders. Maduro, born in Panama in 1946 and an economics graduate from Stanford University in the US, is a successful businessman from Tegucigalpa. One of his main commitments, to fight violent crime with a 'zero tolerance' policy, is based on the dramatic rise in crime in recent years and the death of his son who was kidnapped four years ago.

Other policies include reducing government spending and waste, fighting corruption and promoting tourism. Several of these goals have proved to be the Achille's heel of Latin goverments. One real concern is that the policy of zero tolerance could lead to an increase in human rights violations – something which the military of Honduras is only slowly learning to avoid.

Economy

Honduras has the unfortunate honour of being the poorest economy in Central America with one of the lowest income rates per head in all Latin America. The distribution of land continues to be a pressing problem, with an estimated 170,000 farming families lacking sufficient land for subsistence agriculture. Unemployment (and under-employment) is about 40% of the working population with estimates that 80% of the population live in poverty and the minimum wage has not kept pace with inflation.

Over half of the population lives by the land: coffee, bananas and shrimp are traditionally the main export crops. Cotton, once important, is now far less so. Tobacco, maize, beans, rice and sugar are grown mostly for domestic use, but small quantities are sometimes exported. Cigars have a good international reputation. Cattle raising is important and exports of both meat and livestock are growing, as are exports of timber. Honduras has considerable reserves of silver, gold, lead, zinc, tin, iron, copper, coal and antimony, but only lead, zinc and small quantities of gold and silver are mined and exported. Considerable offshore exploration for petroleum is in progress. There is an oil refinery at Puerto Cortés and another at San Lorenzo on the Pacific. The US$600 mn hydroelectric scheme at El Cajón was constructed to reduce the country's oil bill.

Local industries are small, turning out a wide range of consumer goods. *Maquila* industries, accounting for 20% of total exports, in the northern cities of San Pedro Sula, Choloma and Villanueva, in Comayagua and elsewhere grew rapidly in the 1980s but stagnated in the mid-1990s.

Honduras

Recent trends

Honduras' total external debt amounted to some US$4.5 bn in 2000 – roughly one third of foreign exchange receipts are spent on debt servicing. The entire economic framework was shattered by Hurricane Mitch. According to estimates 70% of economic output was lost, with the main export crops (bananas, shrimps) largely destroyed or prevented from reaching ports by road damage. Joblessness, especially in the agricultural sector, increased greatly. By mid-2000 the estimated economic damage caused by Mitch was put beyond US$4 bn. The difficult years following Mitch changed little in 2001 when drought hit the southern region of Choluteca in June causing most crops to fail in an area that had already suffered greatly from the effects of El Niño and Mitch. The north Atlantic coast also took a battering with the arrival of Hurricane Michelle in November, which killed 10 people.

Outgoing President Flores left with one final flurry, choosing to recognize Cuba. The decision leaves El Salvador and, of course, the US as the only two American nations not to recognize the Caribbean country.

Incoming President Maduro's government proposes a broad sweep of crime-tackling measures, including greater resources for the police and a beefed-up judicial system. Commitments to improving the national economy are matched by prudence and cut backs on wasteful spending, with government employees, including the President, no longer entitled to first-class air travel.

Economically, the country has been hit by low coffee prices on world markets, the almost terminal decline in the banana industry and low yields from over fishing. Growth that does exist is present in the *maquila* industries and tourism. But in real terms, the greatest single source of foreign income is from money being sent to Honduras from abroad.

Government

Honduras is a multi-party republic. The Legislature consists of a single 128-seat Chamber. Deputies are elected by a proportional vote. Executive authority rests with a President, directly elected for four years. No President may serve two terms in succession. The National Assembly elects members of the Supreme Court which, together with the Court of Appeal, Justices of the Peace and lesser tribunals, constitutes the judiciary. The Constitution was revised by a Constituent Assembly elected in April 1980. The country is divided into 18 departments, each with its own administrative centre, and further subdivided into 297 municipalities.

Culture

People There are few pure Indians (an estimated 7% of the total population), and even fewer of pure Spanish or other European ancestry. The two largest concentrations of Indians are the Chortis from Santa Rosa de Copán westwards to the border with Guatemala, and the Lencas in the departments of Lempira, Intibucá and, above all, in the highlands of La Paz. There are also about 45,000 Miskito Indians who live on the Caribbean coast, alongside several communities of Garífunas (black Caribs). The population is 90% *mestizo*. Some 53% are peasant farmers or agricultural labourers, with a low standard of living.

Religion & education Education is compulsory, but not all the rural children go to school – 33% of the population over the age of 10 have had no formal schooling. According to UNESCO 27.1% of people over 15% are illiterate. The National University is based in Tegucigalpa though it also has departments in Comayagua, San Pedro Sula and La Ceiba. Also in Tegucigalpa are the Universidad José Cecilio del Valle, the Universidad Católica (with campuses in San Pedro Sula and Choluteca), the Universidad Tecnológica Centro Americana and the Universidad Pedagógica Nacional; there is also the Universidad de San Pedro Sula, the

Universidad Pedagógica Francisco Morazán and the Universidad Tecnológica Centroamericana. The majority of the population is Catholic, but there is complete freedom of religion.

The visitor seeking specifically Honduran native music will find little to satisfy him or her. **Music** Honduras shares with Belize and Guatemala the presence of Garífuna or Black Caribs on the Caribbean coast. These descendants of Carib Indians and escaped black slaves were deported to the area from St Vincent in the late 18th century and continue to maintain a very separate identity, including their own religious observances, music and dances, profoundly African in spirit and style.

Land and environment

With a territory of 112,492 sq km, Honduras is larger than all the other Central American republics except Nicaragua. Bordered by Nicaragua, Guatemala and El Salvador, it has a narrow Pacific coastal strip, 124 km long on the Gulf of Fonseca, and a northern coast on the Caribbean of 640 km.

Inland, much of the country is mountainous: a rough plateau covered with volcanic ash and lava in the south, rising to peaks such as Cerro de las Minas in the Celaque range (2,849 m), but with some intermont basins at between 900 and 1,800 m. The volcanic detritus disappears to the north, revealing saw-toothed ranges which approach the coast at an angle; the one in the extreme northwest, along the border with Guatemala, disappears under the sea and shows itself again in the Bay Islands. At most places in the north there is only a narrow shelf of lowland between the sea and the sharp upthrust of the mountains, but along two rivers (the Aguán in the northeast, and the Ulúa in the northwest) long fingers of marshy lowland stretch inland between the ranges. The Ulúa lowland is particularly important; it is about 40 km wide and stretches southwards for 100 km where the city of San Pedro Sula is located. From its southern limit a deep gash continues across the highland to the Gulf of Fonseca on the Pacific. The distance between the Caribbean and the Pacific along this trough is 280 km; the altitude at the divide between the Río Comayagua, running into the Ulúa and the Caribbean, and the streams flowing into the Pacific, is only 950 m. In this trough lies Comayagua, the old colonial capital. The lowlands along the Gulf of Fonseca are narrower than they are along the Caribbean; there is no major thrust inland as there is along the Ulúa.

The prevailing winds are from the east, consequently the Caribbean coast has a high rainfall and is covered with deep tropical forest. The intermont basins, the valleys and the slopes sheltered from the prevailing winds bear oak and pine down to as low as 600 m. Timber is almost the only fuel available. In the drier areas, north and south of Tegucigalpa, there are extensive treeless savannas.

The Spaniards, arriving in the early 16th century, found groups of Indians of the Maya and other cultures. Pushing east from Guatemala City they came upon silver in the southeast, and in 1578 founded Tegucigalpa near the mines. The yield was comparatively poor, but enough to attract a thin stream of immigrants. Settlement during the ensuing century was mostly along the trail from Guatemala City: at Gracias, La Esperanza, Comayagua and the department of Santa Bárbara, where the largest white population is located. Gradually these settlements spread over the south and west and this, with the north coast, is where the bulk of the population lives today. The Spaniards and their descendants ignored the northern littoral and the Ulúa lowlands, but during the 19th century US companies, depending largely on black workers from the British West Indies and Belize, developed the northern lowlands as a great banana-growing area. Today the largest concentration of population per sq km is in the Department of Cortés, which extends northwards from Lago Yojoa towards the Caribbean; it includes the major portion of the river basins of Ulúa and Chamelecón, also known as the Sula valley: the most important agricultural area in the country, with San Pedro Sula as its commercial centre and Puerto Cortés as its seaport. The Atlantic littoral consumes two-thirds of the country's imports, and ships the bananas which are the country's major export.

Even today, land under some form of cultivation is only 18 of the total, while meadows and pastures make up 14 of total land use. Rugged terrain makes large areas unsuitable for any kind of agriculture. Nevertheless, there is undeveloped agricultural potential in the flat and almost unpopulated lands of the coastal plain east of Tela to Trujillo and Puerto Castilla, in the Aguán valley southward and in the region northeast of Juticalpa. The area further to the northeast, known as the Mosquitia plain, is largely unexploited and little is known of its potential.

Climate   Rain is frequent on the Caribbean coast during the whole year; the heaviest occurs from September to February inclusive. In Tegucigalpa the dry season is normally from November to April inclusive. The coolest months are December and January, but this is when heavy rains fall on the north coast, which could impede travel. The driest months for this area are April and May, though they are very hot. However, weather predictions in this area have become more difficult in recent years, whether because of the *El Niño* phenomenon or for other reasons. Rain, when it comes, is usually heavy, but of short duration. You will get plenty of sunshine everywhere.

Books and films

Recommended are Paul Theroux's *The Mosquito Coast* (Penguin, 1996) which was also turned into a film starring Harrison Ford, and Norman Lewis' *The Volcanoes Above* (1954). Keen film enthusiasts could hunt down *Latino* (Haskell Wexler, 1985), which follows the twists, turns, loves and contradictions of a latino US soldier drafted to Honduras to provide military training in the mid-1980s.`

Nicaragua

Nicaragua

Essentials

With a history of dictators and revolutions spanning the political divide, it is a strong sense of national pride running through the heart of all Nicaraguans that keeps this once turbulent country together. The largest of the Central American republics, Nicaragua is located at the junction of three continental plates which regularly cause earthquakes and volcanic eruptions to shake the country – at times to its foundations.

The political upheavals have been equally dramatic, with democracy replacing the Revolution of 1979, which had in turn replaced an earlier dictatorship. The people and most of the economic activity are concentrated in the western highlands, around the two great lakes (Managua and Nicaragua), and to the west of the volcanic chain which runs parallel to the Pacific shore. Stretching inland from the Caribbean coast, the largely unpopulated lowlands are challenging country for travelling and a nature paradise for those with the energy and time to spare.

Planning your trip

Where to go

Dramatic evidence of tectonic power can be seen in the capital, **Managua**, where the centre was destroyed by an earthquake in 1972. The old cathedral stands open to the skies, preserved as a museum. Other sites in the old colonial centre, close to the shores of **Lago de Managua**, reflect Nicaragua's recent civil war. The idealism of revolution no longer leads the country's development and the capital is now a rapidly changing place, with new construction, symbolized by the startling new cathedral to the south. Within easy reach are the Pacific beaches of **Pochomil** and **Masachapa**, busy at weekends and holidays, but quiet otherwise.

Southeast of Managua is the colonial city of **Masaya**, a major centre for handicrafts in the region and a base to visit the smoking crater of **Santiago** volcano. The road continues to **Granada**, one of Nicaragua's major colonial cities, passing close to the crystal clear waters of the beautiful Apoyo crater lake. Founded on the shores of **Lago de Nicaragua** in 1524, Granada is the oldest continually inhabited city on the mainland of the Americas, with fine Spanish buildings and impressive churches carefully and faithfully restored. Lake Nicaragua has the added attraction of an archipelago of 354 islands which are interesting for boat trips and nature watching. Accessible from Granada is **Isla Zapatera**, an extinct volcano and pre-Columbian site.

Ometepe, more easily reached from the lakeside town of **San Jorge**, near **Rivas**, is the largest island in the lake with two forest-covered volcanoes ideal for climbing, indigenous petroglyphs and welcoming residents. **San Carlos** marks the southeast corner of Lake Nicaragua at the outlet of the **Río San Juan**, which flows along the Costa Rican border to **San Juan del Norte**. Passing through some of Central America's most unspoilt forest; the potential for nature tourism is enormous. A short trip from San Carlos is the **Solentiname archipelago**, a group of forested islands and home to a community of artists. On the south Pacific coast, heading towards Costa Rica, the town of **San Juan del Sur** provides beachlife and fabulous sunsets, with deserted beaches nearby best reached by boat. Close by is the country's most important turtle nesting ground at **La Flor**.

Two routes head round Lago de Managua from the capital, heading north to **Honduras**. The main route runs south of the lake shore arriving at the former capital of **León**, a city of colonial houses, beautiful churches and captivating festivals. As the birthplace of Rubén Darío, one of Latin America's greatest poets, the city is rightly proud of its cultural heritage. Nearby are the Pacific beaches of **Poneloya**. Heading north is **Chinandega** and the national park of **Cosigüina** volcano, overlooking the Gulf of Fonseca. Further inland is the frontier post at El Guasale. A second route goes east of Lake Managua through the highland agricultural towns of **Matagalpa**, **Jinotega** and **Estelí** where a gentle climate and beautiful scenery make ideal country for walking and hiking.

On the Caribbean coast Bluefields and **Puerto Cabeza** are sleepy port towns. Bluefields is a bumpy bus and boat journey from Managua, Puerto Cabeza makes for a long journey on a

Nicaragua

Nicaraguan embassies and consulates

Belgium, 55 Avenue de Wolvendael, 1180 Brussels, T02-375-6500, F02-375-7188.

Canada, 130 Albert Street, suite 407, Ottawa, Ontario KIP 5G4, T613-234-9361/2, F613-238-7666.

France, 34 Avenue Buaeaud, 75116 Paris, T1-4405-9042, F1-4405-9242.

Germany, Konstantinstrasse 41, D-53179 Bonn, T228-352787, F354001.

Israel, Touro 17, Jerusalem, Israel 94102, T2-256997.

Italy, Via Brescia 16, sala 1, int 7, 00198 Roma, T6-841-3471, F841-1695.

Japan, Kowa Bldg 38, RM 903, 4-1-24, Nishi-Azabu, Minato-Ku, Tokyo 106, T3-499-0400, F499-3800.

Mexico, Payo de Rivera 120, Lomas de Chapultepec, CP 11000, T540-56256, F520-6960.

Spain, Paseo de la Castellana 127, 1 B, 28046 Madrid, T1-555-5510, F555-5737.

Sweden, Sandhamnsgatan 40, 6TR, 11528 Stockholm, T8-667-1857, F8-662-4160.

UK, Vicarage House, 58-60 Kensington Church Street, London W8 4DB, T020-7938 2373, F020-7937 0952.

USA, 820, 2nd Avenue, 8th floor, suite 802, New York, NY 10017, T212-983-1981, F212-989-5528; 8370 West Flagler Street, suite 220, Miami, FL33144, T305-220-0214, F220-8794; 870 Market Street, suite 1050.

couple of buses. Out to sea, the **Corn Islands**, fringed with coral, are popular for bathing, snorkelling and diving. All can be reached by plane from Managua.

When to go The dry season runs from December to May, when temperatures can be unbearable, the wettest months are usually June and October. The most popular time to visit is just after the rainy season in November.

Finding out more **Tourist information** The Institute of Tourism, PO Box 5088, Managua, information line T222-6652 or the office at T222-2962, F222-6610, www.intur.gob.ni, has a wide range of brochures and information packs. The first-floor office is one block west of Inter Plaza (see Managua map page 943). In the **USA**, PO Box 140357, Miami, FL 33114-0357, T305-860-0747, F860-0746. Local information service, T112.

Nicaragua on the web The tourist board site is at **www.intur.gob.ni** Another useful government site, **directory.centramerica.com/** (no www), has a Yahoo-style search engine with news links and general information. **www.toursnicaragua.com**, has a good selection of photographs and images if you want to have a look before you go. If you're staying in the country for a while **www.nicaragua.com**, provides an e-community for getting to know what is going on.

Language A basic knowledge of Spanish is essential for independent travel in Nicaragua. On the Caribbean coast English is widely spoken, but in the rest of the country it is Spanish only, except at expensive hotels, tour companies and airline offices.

Before you travel

Visas & immigration Visitors must have a **passport** with a minimum validity of six months, and may have to show an onward ticket and proof of funds in cash or cheques for a stay of more than a week in the country. In reality this has not been requested for many years. No visa is required by nationals of most Western countries. Nationals of the following countries do not need a visa for a stay of 90 days or less: Guatemala, El Salvador, Honduras, Chile, Bolivia, Argentina, Uruguay, USA, Belgium, Denmark, Finland, Greece, Hungary, Ireland, Liechtenstein, Luxembourg, Netherlands, Norway, Poland, Spain, Sweden, Switzerland or the United Kingdom. **Visas** are only required by citizens of Cuba, Afghanistan, Libya, Iraq and China.

Visa rules are changing frequently, check before you travel (www.cancilleria.gob.ni/consular). If you need a visa it can be bought before arriving at the border, is valid for arrival within 30 days, and for a stay of up to 30 days, it costs US$25; two passport photographs are required. A full 30-day visa can be bought at the border, but it is best to get it in advance. Visas take less than two hours to process in the embassies in Guatemala City and Tegucigalpa, but have been known to take 48 hours elsewhere. When consultation with Managua is required it takes longer. **Extensions** can be obtained at the Dirección de Migración y Extranjería in Managua, Semáforo Tenderí, 1½ c al norte, T244-3989 ext 3, dgm@migracion.gob.bi (Spanish only). Arrive at the office before 0830. From the small office on the right-hand side you must obtain the *formulario* (three córdobas). Then queue at the *caja* in the large hall to pay US$18 for your 30 or 60-day extension. This can take hours. In the meantime you can complete the forms. With the receipt of payment you queue at the window on the right. With luck you will receive the extension stamp by midday; at any event you should get it the same day. Another possibility is to leave the country for at least 72 hours and re-enter on a new visa.

Customs Duty-free import of ½ kg of tobacco products, 3 litres of alcoholic drinks and one large bottle (or three small bottles) of perfume is permitted.

Money

Currency
US$1=13.40 córdobas

The unit of currency is the **córdoba** (C), divided into 100 centavos. It was introduced in July 1990, at a par with the US dollar. Notes in circulation are for 1, 5, 10 and 25 centavos, 1, 5, 10, 20, 50 and 100 córdobas. Coins in circulation are 20 and 50 centavos and 1 and 5 córdobas (replacing notes of these values). Try to avoid obtaining the larger notes, as no-one ever has enough change. The import and export of foreign and local currencies is unrestricted. US dollars are accepted almost everywhere but change is given in córdobas.

Bank queues can be very long and you should allow plenty of time, especially on Monday mornings and the 15th and 31st of every month. It is not possible to change currencies other than US dollars and Euros (*BanCentro* only) in Nicaragua. Money changers on the street (*coyotes*) during business hours are legitimate and their rates differ little from banks.

Credit cards & TCs
Credit cards are more widely used than they used to be, but ATMs are hard to find outside the capital

Visa and MasterCard are accepted in nearly all restaurants and hotels, and in many shops. This applies to a lesser extent to Amex, Credomatic and Diners Club. But don't rely exclusively on credit cards. In Managua ATM machines are found in the airport, at the Metrocentro and Plaza Inter shopping malls and in many gas station convenience stores. Outside the capital ATM's are quite rare.

Travellers' cheques can only be changed in Managua at *Multicambios* in Plaza España and other limited locations. Changing travellers' cheques outside Managua is difficult; but the situation is improving, it is best to carry US dollar notes and sufficient local currency away from the bigger towns. All branches of *Bancentro* can change travellers' cheques and arrange cash advances although some branches appear not to know this. Similarly banks showing Credomatic signs and all *Banco de America Central* (BAC) branches should be able to help. *Banco de Finanza* only changes American Express TCs.

Cost of living & travelling

Nicaragua is not an expensive country as far as hotel accommodation is concerned, and public transport is also fairly cheap. For food, as a rough guide, a *comida corriente* costs about US$1.40 (meals in restaurants US$6-13, breakfasts US$2.50-3.50). However, on the islands or in out of the way places where supplies have to be brought in by boat or air, you should expect to pay more.

Getting there

Air
See Essentials page 34 for contact details

From Europe Take any transatlantic flight to Miami or Houston and connect to *American*, *Continental*, *Grupo Taca* or *Iberia*, flights from Madrid via Miami with connections to other European cities.

From USA Regular daily flights from Miami and Houston with either *American*, *Contintental*, *Iberia* or *Taca*. Also regular flights from Atlanta, Los Angeles and Orlando.

Nicaragua

Touching down

Official time 6 hours behind GMT.
IDD 505. Equal tones with long pauses indicate it is ringing. Equal tones with equal pauses means engaged.
Hours of business 0800-1200, 1430-1730 or 1800. Banks: 0830-1200, 1400-1600, but 0830-1130 on Saturday. Government offices are not normally open on Saturday in Managua, or in the afternoon anywhere.

Voltage 110 volts AC, 60 cycles.
Weights and measures The metric system is official, but local terms are frequently used; The principal local weights are the arroba=25 lb/11.3 kg and the quintal=101.4 lb/46 kg. Other measures in use include US gallon for petrol, US quart and pint for liquids and the vara (33 in/84 cm) for short distances.

From Latin America Good connections with connections to Barranquilla (Colombia), Bogotá, Bucuramanga (Col), Buenos Aires, Cali (Col), Cancún, Caracas, Cartagena (Col), Guatemala City, Guayaquil (Ecuador), Havana, Kingston (Jamaica), La Paz (Bolivia), Lima, Medellín (Col), Mexico City, Panama City, Port au Prince (Haiti), Quito, San José (Costa Rica), San Juan (Puerto Rico), San Salvador, Santiago, Santo Domingo (Dominican Republic) and Sao Paulo.

Road The main road links to the north are at El Guasaule and further inland on the Pan-American Highway at El Espino with a third option at the border north of Ocotal at Las Manos in Honduras. In the south the most commonly used crossing is at Peñas Blancas.

Boat From San Carlos there is a less frequently used immigration post which links with a boat journey on the Río Frío to Los Chiles in Costa Rica. There is no official border crossing between San Juan del Norte and Costa Rica.

Touching down

Airport tax, entry & exit information All passengers arriving by air pay an entry tax of US$5, while departing passengers must pay an airport tax of US$25, payable in US dollars. All passengers have to pay a sales tax of US$5 on tickets issued in and paid for in Nicaragua; a transport tax of 1% is levied on all tickets issued in Nicaragua to any destination. For information on Managua airport, see page 943.

The cost of entry overland is US$8, although this may be less on weekdays. Exit tax for foreigners is US$2 in cash, US$5 at weekends. If in the slightest doubt about charges, insist on being given a receipt and go to the Immigration Department in Managua to verify the charge. Officials in Las Manos are reported to try and overcharge – be firm. Motorists see Driving below.

Local customs & laws **Clothing** Dress is informal although shorts are never worn by men except at the beach.
Tipping US$0.50 per bag for porters; no tip for taxi drivers. Most restaurants add 10% to bills, it is not mandatory, but is almost always paid.

Safety Visitors to Nicaragua must carry their passports (or a photocopy) with them at all times. There are police checkpoints on roads and in outlying districts; the police search for firearms. They may inspect luggage on entering and leaving Nicaragua. Do not photograph military personnel or installations.

Pickpocketing and bagslashing occur in Managua in crowded places, and on buses throughout the country. Apart from Managua at night, most places are generally safe. Reports of robberies and assaults in northern Nicaragua indicate that care should be taken in this area, enquire about conditions before going, especially if proposing to leave the beaten track.

Working in Nicaragua Volunteer work in Nicaragua is not as common as it was during the Sandinista years. Foreigners now work in environmental brigades supporting the FSLN, construction projects, agricultural co-operatives and environmental organizations. Certain skills are in demand, as elsewhere in the developing world; to discover the current situation, contact non-governmental organizations in your home country (for example **Nicaraguan Network**, 1247

Nicaragua

East St, SE, Washington, DC 20003, T202-544-9355, F544-9360, or PO Box 4496, Fresno, CA 93744, T209-226-0477, in the USA), twin town/sister-city organizations and *Nicaraguan Solidarity Campaigns* (NSC/ENN Brigades, 129 Seven Sisters Rd, London N7 7QG, T020-727-29619, www.gn.apc.org/nsc *Dutch Nicaragua Komitee*, Aptdo Postal 1922, Managua). *Casa Danesa*, T267-8126, F278-6684 (Managua), may be able to help find volunteer work, usually for three months, but shorter times are sometimes acceptable.

Where to stay

Most hotel accommodation is run by independent operators with a few international chains beginning to enter the top end of the market. Standards vary greatly but there is plenty of competition in mid to low-budget range in most towns. In smaller towns you will have to put up with whatever is available.

Getting around

Domestic flights should always be reconfirmed immediately on arrival for return. There is a 9 **Air** kg hand luggage limit. Stowed luggage 13.5 kg free, maximum 45 kg. Domestic departure tax is 15 córdobas.

La Costeña, T263-1228, F263-1281, www.flylacostena.com, operates internal air services to Bluefields, Corn Island, Minas (Bonanza/Siuna/Rosita), Puerto Cabeza, San Carlos and Waspám (see text for details). *Atlantic Airlines* provide similar coverage.

The **road** has been greatly extended and improved in recent years. The Pan-American Highway **Road** from Honduras to Costa Rica is paved the whole way (384 km) as is the shorter international road to the Honduran frontier via Chinandega. The road between Managua and Rama (for Bluefields) is paved, but not in good condition. There are 17,146 km of road, of which just 15% are paved.

Bus Local buses are the cheapest in Central America, and often the most crowded. Baggage loaded on to the roof or in the luggage compartment may be charged for, usually at half the passenger rate or a flat fee of US$0.50.

Driving Motorists and motorcyclists must pay US$20 in cash on arrival at the border (cyclists pay US$2, and up to US$9 at weekends, though this tends to vary from one customs post to the next). There are no exit fees. For **motorcyclists**, the wearing of crash helmets is compulsory. Several cyclists have said that you should take a 'proof of purchase' of your cycle or suggest typing out a phoney 'cycle ownership' document to help at border crossings. Motorists also pay the same entry tax as other overland arrivals (see above). Make sure you get all the correct stamps on arrival, or you will encounter all sorts of problems once inside the country. Do not lose the receipts, they have to be produced when you leave; without them you will have to pay again. Vehicles not cleared by 1630 are held at customs overnight. Up to four hours of formalities are possible when entering Nicaragua with a vehicle. On leaving, motorists pay five córdobas, as well as the usual exit tax. For procedures at each border, see the relevant sections of text. Low octane gasoline costs US$1.60 per litre; diesel, US$1.35. Unleaded petrol is widely available, US$1.70 super, US$1.55 regular. Service stations close at 1700-1800. In general, major roads are not in very good condition. Be careful when driving at night, many cars have no lights, most roads are not lit and there are many people, animals and holes in the road. Your car may be broken into if unattended and not in a secure place. Someone will normally offer to watch your car for a tip; good insurance for one or two córdobas.

Car hire Renting a vehicle costs around US$30 a day for a basic car, rising to US$85 for a jeep. Weekly discount rates are significant and if you want to cover a lot of sites quickly it can work out to be worthwhile. A minimum deposit of US$500 is required along with an international drivers' licence or a licence from your country of origin. Insurance is US$10-23 depending on cover. Before signing up check insurance and what it covers and also ask about mileage allowance. Most agents have an office at the international airport and a few have offices in other parts of Managua. Check to see if you can drop the vehicle off in a different location.

Hitchhiking is widely accepted, but not easy because so many people do it and there is little traffic – offer to pay a small contribution.

Sea The main **Pacific ports** are Corinto, San Juan del Sur and Puerto Sandino. The two main **Atlantic ports** are Puerto Cabezas and Bluefields.

Keeping in touch

Internet Internet cafés are widley available in Managua, Masaya and Granada with services becoming more common in León, Estelí and other regional cities. Prices are somewhere between US$3-5 per hour. Beyond these places the technology revolution is occurring behind the scenes.

Post Airmail to Europe takes two to four weeks (letter rate 10 córdobas); from Europe seven to 10 days; to USA six córdobas (five to Miami); to Australia six córdobas.

Telephone Phone lines are owned by the *Empresa Nicaragüense de Telecomunicaciones* (*Enitel*),
The international code parented by *Telcor*. Automatic national and international telephone calls are possible from any
for Nicaragua is T505 private or public phone.

Phone numbers in Nicaragua have seven digits. Outside Managua each town has a three-figure prefix, followed by four digits. If you are phoning from inside the prefix zone you dial the seven digits, but if you are dialling a different zone you put 0 in front, for example to dial a Managua number from Masaya would be 0266-8689. Card phones were introduced in 1994.

International or national calls can be made at any Enitel office, 0700-2200. All phone calls can be paid for in córdobas. Rates: US$10 for three minutes to USA, US$11.50 to Europe. You may have to wait a long time for a line, except for early in the morning on weekdays. You have to say in advance how long you want to talk for. Person-to-person calls are charged extra. Collect calls to the USA are easy (*por cobrar* or *a pagarse allá*), also possible to Europe. For SPRINT, dial 171; AT&T 174 and MCI 166. To connect to phone services in Germany dial 169, Belgium 172, Canada 168, Spain 162, Netherlands 177, UK 175. International Fax services are available in all major cities, US$4.50 per page to Europe.

Media **Newspapers** All published in Managua, but many are widely available in the country: **Dailies**: *La Prensa*, centre, the country's best, especially for coverage of happenings outside Managua; *El Nuevo Diario*, centre-left and sensationalist; *La Noticia*, right, government paper, only afternoon daily. **Weeklies**: *El Seminario*, left-leaning, well written with in-depth analysis; *7 Días*, pro-Government; *Tiempo del Mundo*, owned by Rev Moon, good coverage of South America, not much on Nicaragua. **Monthlies**: *El País*, pro-Government, good features.

Food and drink

Restaurant bills attract Try *nacatamales*, cornflower dumplings stuffed with meat and vegetables, and boiled in
a 15% tax and 10% banana leaves, an excellent value meal; or *gallo pinto*, a tasty dish of rice and beans. Fizzy
service is added or drinks are known as *gaseosas* in Nicaragua as in neighbouring countries. Fresh fruit-based
expected as a tip drinks and juices are *frescos*. Coffee can be terrible as most good Nicaraguan beans go for export and locals drink instant – ask for *café perculado*.

Shopping

What to buy Masaya is the centre for *artesanía* selling excellent crafts, leather goods and colourful woven rugs often used as wall hangings and wicker furniture. Ceramics are produced in many parts of the country.

Holidays and festivals

1 January: New Year's Day; **March or April**: Maundy Thursday and Good Friday; **1 May**: Labour Day; **19 July**: Revolution of 1979; **14 September**: Battle of San Jacinto; **15 September**:

Independence Day; **2 November**: All Souls' Day (Día de los Muertos); **7 and 8 December**: Immaculate Conception (*La Purísima*); **25 December**: Christmas Day.

Businesses, shops and restaurants all close for most of Holy Week; many companies also close down during the Christmas-New Year period. Holidays which fall on a Sunday are taken the following Monday. Local holidays are given under the towns.

Sport and special interest travel

The national game is baseball, which is even more important than soccer. The season runs from November to the end of February.

Opportunities for **nature tourism** are growing rapidly with the lowlands of the Caribbean coast and the highlands around Matagalpa attracting keen nature watchers. The islands of Lake Managua are a popular destination for trekking. Granada is experiencing a steady rise in interest and activities like mountain biking are growing rapidly. The Pacific coast has a few good swimming beaches, and excellent surfing opportunities to the south. Out on the Corn Islands, snorkelling and diving is possible on nearby coral reefs.

Health

Take the usual tropical precautions about food and drink. Tap water is not recommended for drinking outside of Managua, León and Granada, generally and avoid uncooked vegetables and peeled fruit. Intestinal parasites abound; if requiring treatment, take a stool sample to a government laboratory before going to a doctor.

Malaria risk exists especially in the wet season, with the high risk areas being east of the great lakes; take regular prophylaxis. **Dengue fever** is also present, including in Managua; as always, avoid being bitten by mosquitoes.

Managua

Managua, the nation's capital and commercial centre since 1852, was destroyed by an earthquake in March 1931 and then partially swept away by fire five years later. Rebuilt as a modern, commercial city, the centre was again destroyed by an earthquake in December 1972 when just a few modern buildings we re left standing. Severe damage from the Revolution of 1978-79 and flooding of the lakeside areas as a result of Hurricane Mitch in October 1998 both added to the problems. It's a tribute to the city's resilience that Managua still has the energy to carry on.

Colour map 7, grid A1
Population: 1,028,695
Altitude: 40-200 m

Ins and outs

The airport is 12 km east of the city, near the lake. Buses and taxis (US$15 to Barrio Martha Quezada) run from the airport to the city. International bus services arrive at several terminals throughout the city. Conveniently *Ticabus, Cruceros del Golfo, Panaline* and *Nicabus*, are in Barrio Martha Quezada, where most of the cheap hotels are to be found. Provincial bus services have 3 main arrival/departure points (see also page 952). City buses and taxis serve the provincial terminals.

Getting there

Managua is on the southern shores of Lake Managua (Lago Xolotlán), 45 km from the Pacific. Since 1997, the old centre has become a garden monument consisting mainly of open spaces, ageing buildings and lakeside cafés and restaurants. Despite lying over 14 seismic faults and the warnings of seismologists, some important new buildings have now been built in the old centre, including a new presidential palace between the ruins of the old cathedral and the lake front – the epicentre of the 1972 earthquake.

Two areas now lay claim to being the heart of Managua and both have multilevel shopping centres. The older of the two is based around the *Hotel Intercontinental*, with a shopping and

Getting around

cinema complex, complete with US-style 'food court' and to the west **Barrio Martha Quezada** with many mid- and budget-range hotels, and international bus services. To the south, nearby **Plaza España** has the country's best supermarket and numerous shops, banks, travel agents, tour companies and nearly every airline office in the country. The other heart of the city is to the south based on the **Carretera a Masaya**, running from the new cathedral to Camino de Oriente. This stretch of four-lane highway includes the **Rotonda Rubén Darío**, the **Metrocentro** shopping complex, numerous restaurants, the new Pellas family business centre with the new *BAC* and *Credomatic* headquarters, and the cinema, disco and offices of Camino de Oriente. To get there, or to the provincial bus terminals, some form of city transport will have to be taken. **Buses** are cheap, crowded and infamous for their pickpockets. Their routes can be hard to fathom; some of the main ones are given on page 952. **Taxis** have either red number plates (licensed so in theory safer) or blue (pirates and illegal). Taxi-sharing in Managua is standard for non-radio taxi, so don't be surprised if the driver stops to pick someone up on roughly the same route. For more details, see page 952.

Directions are given according to landmarks; in place of cardinal points, the following are used: *al lago* (north), *arriba* (east), *al sur* (south), *abajo* (west). This applies to the whole country (although *al norte* is used outside of Managua). Even where there are street names or numbers Nicaraguans give direction by landmarks.

Tourist office *Instituto Nicaragüense de Turismo* (Intur), 1 block west of *Hotel Intercontinental*, enter by side door, Apdo Postal 122, T222-2962, F228-1187, **www.intur.gob.ni** Information service T112 or information line T222-6652. Airport T233-1539. Closed Sat. Standard information available, including on all types of transport in the country. Maps of Managua with whole country on reverse, US$2. Information on national parks and conservation should be obtained from *Sistema Nacional de Areas Protegidas* (Sinap), at Ministerio de Medio Ambiente y Recursos Naturales (Marena), Km 12.5 Carretera Norte, T263-2617. *Guía Fácil*, the Managua listings magazine, is at **www.guiafacil.com.ni**

Security Nicaraguans are incredibly friendly and, although Managua is one of the safest cities in Latin America, a few simple guidelines may be useful. Never walk at night unless you are in a good

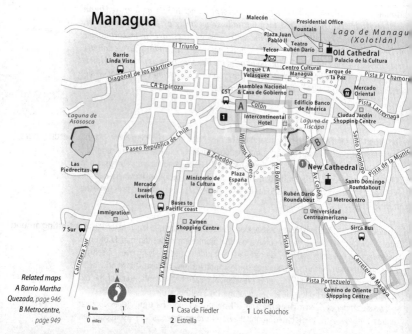

Managua

Related maps
A Barrio Martha
Quezada, page 946
B Metrocentre,
page 949

0 km 1
0 miles 1

■ Sleeping
1 Casa de Fiedler
2 Estrella

● Eating
1 Los Gauchos

area or shopping centre zone. If you are worried about taking a city bus, avoid them altogether. If you find yourself in a very poor neighbourhood simply take the next taxi, they are cheap and friendly, use them (for added security, take a radio taxi.. Arriving in Managua at night is not a problem, but choose your hotel in advance and take a taxi straight there. Long-distance buses are fine, but be careful in the market when you arrive to take the bus, try for a window seat and then relax. Barrio Martha Quezada is much safer than it used to be, but youth gangs are present and walking alone at night is best avoided. The Mercado Oriental (not to be confused with the Camino de Oriente which is safe and fun), is said to be the largest informal market in Latin America and its barrio, Ciudad Jardín, should be avoided at all costs (60% of all crime in the entire country occurs here with assaults both day and night). Roberto Huembes (Mercado Central) has the best crafts section outside of the Masaya market and is safe.

Sights

In the old centre of Managua near the lake shore, the Palacio Nacional de la Cultura, previously the Palacio de los Héroes de la Revolución, is one example of colonial architecture still standing. Beautifully restored, it has permanent and temporary exhibits in the Nicaraguan National Gallery, the **Museo Nacional** and the National Library. ■ *Daily 0800-1700, US$1, includes 20-min introductory guided tour in English and French.*

Damaged by earthquake the old cathedral now has a roof of narrow steel girders and side-window support bars to keep it standing, the atmosphere is of an old and sad building past its prime, left in ruins, but still worth a look. ■ *Closed and likely to fall down soon.* The **Centro Cultural Managua**, behind the Palacio Nacional de Cultura, has a good selection of before and after photos of quake-struck Managua in 1972. The centre is also home to the National Art School and the National Music School. There are some antique and craft shops and art exhibits in galleries downstairs. Upstairs, to the right and to the far end, is the office of *Guía Fácil*, the most comprehensive guide to what's happening in Managua (see above).

The garishly painted **Presidential Palace** is in front of the Palacio de la Cultura on the opposite corner to the old cathedral. These buildings are situated on the **Parque Central** and provide a striking contrast with the modern **Teatro Rubén Darío** on the lake shore which hosts good plays, folkloric dances and musical events. ■ *US$1.50 to US$20 depending on show.* There are usually temporary exhibitions in the theatre so, in the day, ask at the window to view the exhibit and you can probably look at the auditorium as well. The **Parque de la Paz**, just southeast of the Parque Central, is part of the rebuilding programme for the old centre. The park is a graveyard for weapons and a few dozen truckloads of AK-47s are buried there, some of which can be seen sticking out of the cement.

Three blocks south of the Parque Central are the offices of the Nicaraguan parliament, which include the city's only high-rise building, once the *Bank of America*, now the offices of the *diputados* (congressmen and women).

A significant landmark is the *Hotel Intercontinental*, similar in design to a Maya pyramid, about a dozen blocks south of the old cathedral (not too far to

Nuevo Diario

To Airport & Hotel Las Mercedes

Carretera Norte

Ciudad Xolotlán

Bello Horizonte Shopping Centre

Pista Portezuelo

Blvd Buenos Aires

2

Mercado Iván Montenegro

Pista Sábana Grande

Roberto Huembes/ Mercado Central

To Plaza El Mayoreo Bus Station

Managua Shopping Centre

Nicaragua

walk). Its entrance is on Avenida Bolívar and just in front is the new Plaza Inter shopping centre with cinemas, restaurants and shops. The Bolívar-Buitrago junction, at the northwest corner of Plaza Inter, is on a number of important bus routes.

From the hilltop behind the *Intercontinental* the **Parque Nacional de la Loma de Tiscapa** provides the best views of the capital and of the **Laguna de Tiscapa** on the south side of the hill. From the top a giant black silhouette of Sandino stands looking out over the city. Since the 1996 change in government it has not been well maintained, but the spot has much historical significance. It is the site of the former presidential palace, Sandino signed a peace treaty here with Somoza and was abducted (and later killed) at the entrance to the access road. Underneath the park facing the *laguna* (now blocked by a fence) are the prison cells of the Somoza regime where inmates were said to have been tortured before being tossed into the lake. ■ *0800-1630 daily.* Take the road behind the *Intercontinental* to top of hill using an access road for the Nicaraguan military headquarters. Guards at the park are nervous about photography. Ask permission and photograph only downtown and towards the stadium – do not take photos on the access road up to the park

To the west of the *Intercontinental* is **Barrio Martha Quezada**. This district (see Ins and outs above) is a mixture of well-to-do housing alongside poorer dwellings. South again, through the Bolonia district, is **Plaza España** by the Rotondo El Güengüense roundabout. Plaza España is reached either by continuing over the hill above the *Intercontinental* and branching right at the major junction, or by going south on Williams Romero, the avenida at the western edge of Barrio Martha Quezada (bus 118).

Avoid flash photography when people are praying and don't enter via the side doors during Mass

From Tiscapa hill, the **new cathedral**, inaugurated in 1993, can be seen 500 m to the south of the lake. Designed by the Mexican architect Ricardo Legoreto, comments on the exterior range from 'strikingly beautiful' to 'sacreligious'. The interior, which is mostly unadorned concrete, has been described as 'post-nuclear, with an altar resembling a futuristic UN Security Council meeting room'. Many visitors are fascinated by the Sangre de Cristo room, where a lifesize bleeding Christ is encased

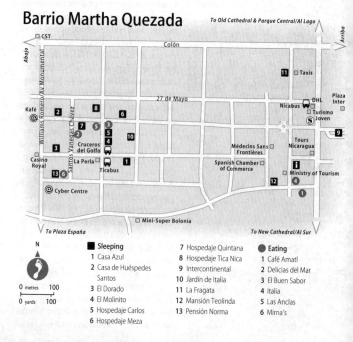

Barrio Martha Quezada

To Old Cathedral & Parque Central/Al Lago

N

0 metres 100
0 yards 100

■ **Sleeping**
1 Casa Azul
2 Casa de Huéspedes Santos
3 El Dorado
4 El Molinito
5 Hospedaje Carlos
6 Hospedaje Meza
7 Hospedaje Quintana
8 Hospedaje Tica Nica
9 Intercontinental
10 Jardín de Italia
11 La Fragata
12 Mansión Teolinda
13 Pensión Norma

● **Eating**
1 Café Amatl
2 Delicias del Mar
3 El Buen Sabor
4 Italia
5 Las Anclas
6 Mirna's

Nicaragua

in a glass and steel dome, illuminated by a domed roof with hundreds of holes for the sun to filter through. At night, the dome sparkles with the glow of lightbulbs in the holes. Pedestrian access is possible from the Metrocentro junction. Vehicles need to approach from the east.

From the Metrocentro, around which much new construction is taking place, the Carretera a Masaya passes through the district of Altamira (restaurants, a few hotels, internet cafés, Sirca bus) to the financial centre, the Semáforos de Centroamérica and Camino de Oriente.

The **Iglesia Santa María de los Angeles**, Barrio Riguero (east of Metrocentro, south of Pista de la Municipalidad), was the initial setting for the *Misa Revolucionaria*, a Catholic/secular mass, now celebrated only on special occasions and not necessarily at this church.

Essentials

Sleeping

Try to choose a central hotel (ie near *Intercontinental* or Plaza España) since transport to the outskirts is so difficult. Close to the airport is **L-AL** *Las Mercedes*, Km 11 Carretera Norte, T263-1011, F263-1083, www.lasmercedes.com.ni, excellent food, but expensive, charming open-air restaurant, pool, tennis court, barber shop, all rooms have cable TV, a/c, bath, fridge, phone, 3 levels of room Standard, Premiere and Executive (avoid Standard), local phone calls can be made here when airport office is shut, the outdoor café is the best place to kill time near the airport.

Other luxury hotels include: **LL** *Intercontinental Metrocentro*, next to Metrocentro shopping centre, T271-9483, F278-4545, www.interconti.com Managua's finest hotel, excellent service, very good restaurant, excellent location, 157 rooms with all amenities of a new (opened 2000) 5-star hotel. Weekend and multi-day discount rates with some tour operators. **L** *Intercontinental*, 'El Inter', PO Box 3278, 101 Octava C SO, in front of the Plaza Inter shopping centre, T228-3530, F228-3087, some rooms with lake view, rooms small for the price, slow service, sauna, use of swimming pool for non-residents on Sun for US$18, bookshop, handicraft shop, buffet, breakfast and lunch (see below), Visa cards accepted; **L-AL** *Mansión Teodolinda*, Bolonia, T228-1050, F222-4908, www.teodolinda.com.ni, a/c, private bath with hot water, kitchenette with refrigerator, cable TV, telephone, pool, bar, restaurant, laundry service, very clean, often full with business people, good location; and **L-AL** *Las Colinas*, Las Colinas, Embajada de España 3 c al lago, T276-0035, a/c, with bath, hot water, cable TV, bar, restaurant, pool, secure parking, far from centre (no taxis or buses).

AL *Casa Real*, de la Rotonda Rubén Darío 2 c al sur 1½ c Este. T278-3838, F267-8240, casareal@ibw.com.ni, private bath, hot water, A/C, telephone, cable TV. Recommended. **AL-A** *Hostal Real*, Bolonia, opposite German Embassy, T266-8133, private bath with hot water, breakfast included, internet, cable TV, interesting and unique airy rooms decorated with antiques and art, 'the most beautiful hotel interior in Nicaragua', central, very clean and very booked up, so reserve in advance. Highly recommended. At Km 8.5 on Carretera Sur is **A** *César*, T265-2760, cesar@ibw.com.ni, great value, often fully booked, call ahead, Swiss-run, garden, safe, very good food, garage, swimming pool for children. **A** *El Conquistador*, 1 c al sur, 1 c abajo, T222-4789, F222-3657, elconquistador@ideay.net.ni, 11 rooms, a/c, private bath, cable TV, refrigerador, lake view terrraza, good value and location. **A** *Estrella*, Semáforos de Rubenia 2CN, T289-7213, F289-7104, hestrella@ibw.com.ni, a/c, swimming pool, with breakfast, long way from centre, book in advance as it's very popular. **A** *La Posada del Angel*, opposite San Francisco church, Bolonia, T/F266-1347, pdelangel@interlink.com.ni, private bath with hot water, cable TV, a/c, mini-bar, telephone, laundry service. Recommended. **A-B** *Europeo*, Bolonia, Canal 2, 75 m abajo, T/F268-5999, europeo@ibw.com.ni, a/c, private bath, hot water, cable TV, includes continental breakfast, restaurant, bar, fax, secure parking, laundry service, internet, very clean, interesting furnishings, each room unique, very friendly and helpful staff, hotel proceeds go to a drug rehabilitation programme, quiet but central location. Highly recommended.

■ *on maps, pages 944, 946 and 949 Price codes: see inside front cover*

15% tax is added to hotel bills. The Government stipulates a small additional charge for rooms with a telephone (whether used or not)

Nicaragua

B *Colón*, Km 4½ Carretera a Masaya, del Lacmiel 2 c arriba, near Sirca bus terminal, T278-2490, hcolon@ibw.com.ni, with bath and a/c, **C** with fan, cable TV, secure, clean, good restaurant. **B** *La Fragata*, Estatua Simón Bolívar 1 c al oeste, 50 m al sur, a block west of the *Intercontinental*, T222-4179, F222-4133, remodelled, good value, includes full breakfast, good restaurant, new beds, hot showers (not electric), cable TV, a/c, central, disabled acess. Recommended. **B** *Las Cabañitas*, near Plaza 19 de Julio, T278-3235, F277-2740, hoteleco@interlink.com.ni, good, helpful, with pool and decent restaurant next door. **B** *María La Gorda*, Iglesia El Carmen, 1 c al sur, ½ c arriba, ½ c al sur, T268-2455, F268-2456, 8 rooms, a/c, private bath with hot water, e-mail access, cable TV, telephone, just west of Martha Quezada, nice. **B-C** *Posadita de Bolonia*, Canal 2, 3 c abajo, 75 m al sur, casa 12, T266-2081, 7 rooms private bath, cable TV, internet, quiet area, homey and friendly, owner Sandra speaks English.

Most budget travellers stay in Barrio Martha Quezada, or else in Granada or Masaya, visiting Managua on regular minibuses

C *Ay Caramba*, Montoya 2 c al lago, T266-6284, F266-2194, 10 rooms, a/c, private bath, cable TV, telephone, not ideal location but good service and value, often recommended. **C** *Casa de Fiedler*, 8 c suroeste 1320 (western limit of Barrio Martha Quezada – from CST 2 blocks south and 1½ blocks west), T266-6622, with bath and a/c or fan, comfortable, soft mattresses, clean, friendly, popular, accepts TCs, cold Victoria beer sold, good breakfasts, coffee all day, has interesting collection of pre-Columbian ceramics. **C** *Casa San Juan*, C Esperanza 560, T278-3220, F267-0419, sanjuan@nicanet.com.ni, shared bath and private bath, clean, owner's family sleeps in, safe, excellent breakfasts for US$3, friendly, good value. Highly recommended.

D *Casa de Huéspedes Castillo*, Casa del Obrero 1 c arriba, 1½ al Sur, 2 blocks from *Ticabus*, also known as *Casa Ramiro*, with bath, fan, some with a/c, clean, quiet, safe. **D** *Casa Gabrina Los Españoles*, Ticabus 1 c al sur, ½ c arriba, frente a radio La Primerísima, T222-6650, 4 rooms with fan, cable TV, cheap food, group discounts. **D** *Los Felipes*, Ticabus 1½ c abajo, T222-6501, 26 rooms with private bath and hot water, cable TV, nice garden, parking.

Most hotels in this price range have very thin walls and can be noisy!

There are many hotels west of the Hotel *Intercontinental* in the Barrio Martha Quezada and near the Cine Dorado (now called *Casino Royale*, but still ask for 'Cine Dorado'). To get from *Intercontinental* to the Cine Dorado, walk west for 10 mins to a main north-south road, Av Williams Romero, Cine Dorado is just south.

E *Casablanca*, Ticabus ½ c al lago, T222-3178, 5 rooms, some with private bath)). **E** per person *Jardín de Italia*, Ticabus 1 c arriba, ½ al lago, T222-7967, some rooms with a/c (**C**), with bath, basic but friendly. Mixed reports. Take care of your belongings. **E** *El Pueblo*, 3 blocks north, 2 blocks east from *Intercontinental*, simple, old house, big rooms, private bath, friendly. **E** *Hospedaje Carlos*, ½ block north of *Ticabus*, T222-2554, rooms on left at the back better than on right, cold shower, fan, a/c extra, good value, clean.

Children tout for hotels in Barrio Martha Quezada, especially at Ticabus; don't always believe them if they say a place is full

F *Hospedaje Meza*, from *Ticabus* 1c al lago, ½ c arriba, T222-2046, 10 rooms with shared bath and fan. TV. **F** *El Dorado*, turn left out of *Ticabus* station, clean, small rooms of varying standard, key deposit charged. **F** *Hospedaje Quintana*, from *Ticabus*, 1 block north, then ½ block west, rooms with fan, shared shower (cold), laundry, clean, good value, family-run. Recommended for longer stays. **F** *Hospedaje Tica Nica*, 1½ blocks north of *Ticabus*, with or without bath, noisy, use of kitchen. **F** per person *Sultana*, at the *Ticabus* terminal, dormitory accommodation, friendly, clean, fan, handy if you have an early bus, otherwise noisy from 0500 and overpriced. The owners of **F** *Hospedaje Mangaia* often wait at *Ticabus*, free transfer to and from terminal, 1 block south then about 5 towards Plaza España, turn left in C Gabriel Cardinal Cabrera, 2nd house on right, No 930, T268-0480 (*Optica Nicaragüense*). In the same block as *Ticabus* is **F** *Casa Azul*, 70 m arriba, T222-3713. 10 rooms with private bath and ceiling fan, popular, brusque service. **F** *El Molinito*, ½ block from *Ticabus*, T222-5100. 14 rooms with private bath and fan, good value, basic, clean and hot during day. Also **F** *El Molinito 2*, Ticabus 1 c arriba, T222-5100, 4 rooms, private bath with, **D** with a/c and cable TV. **F** *Casa de Huéspedes Santos*, from *Ticabus*, 1 block north, 1½ west, with bath but washbasins outside, no soap, towel or toilet paper, bright, basic, good value, spacious courtyard with hammocks, friendly, serves meals, including breakfasts and snacks. Very popular, good place to meet travellers. **F** *Pensión Norma*, Antiguo Cine Dorado 1c al sur, 75 m abajo, T222.3498. Shared rooms, basic, popular but poor beds (*Comedor Mirna's* nearby). **F** *El Viajero*, Ticabus 80 m abajo, T228-1280. 9 rooms with fan, shared bath, laundry service.

Metrocentro

Laguna de Tiscapa

✝ New Cathedral

La UNI (University)

Av Colón

Rubén Darío (Metrocentro) Roundabout

Metrocentro Shopping Centre

2

To Bar Charman

To Legendis Hotel & Hard Rock Café

Lacmiel

3 **6** **1**

Alianza Francesa

@ Mi Oficina

Optica Matamoros

Mexican Embassy

5

@ Kafé

Distribuidora Vicky @

Coconut Grove Plaza & Cyber Café

1

@ Sirca Bus

☒ Kodak

Banic □ ⑤ Forex

To Rostipollo Restaurant

Carretera a Masaya

To Mercado Roberto Huembes

BAC ⑤

Ⓜ La Colonia

Centroamérica Roundabout

Pista Portezuelo

Camino de Oriente Shopping Centre

4

To Masaya & Granada

N

Not to scale

● **Eating**
1 Bongo
2 La Cocina de Doña Haydée
3 La Fonda
4 Las Brasas
5 María Bonita
6 Pizza Valenti

■ **Sleeping**
1 Colón
2 Intercontinental Metrocentro

Eating

The *Hotel Intercontinental* serves enormous buffet breakfasts (0600-1100) for US$10 (plus 15% tax and service charge), and an excellent lunch between 1200 and 1500, US$12 for as much as you want, open to non-residents (best dress smartly); major credit cards accepted. *Hotel Las Mercedes* also serves a good US$12 buffet lunch on weekdays. New restaurants in Managua are opening all the time, other established ones are moving to new areas.

● *on maps, pages 943, 946 and 949*

Expensive *Hotel César*, Km 8½ Carretera Sur, T265-2760, good, try duck in orange sauce, best place for those craving real Euro-food, cheeses, wines, etc *Las Delicias del Bosque*, Colegio Centroamericana 5 Km al sur, T08830071, restaurant for the Nicaraguan power brokers, lovely setting in hills, good food, Wed-Sat only. *El Mesón Español*, *Mansión Teodolinda* 3 c al sur, Spanish very good, either totally empty or completely full with high level of government employees. *La Marseillaise*, C Principal Los Robles, T277-0224, closed Sun, daily specials, good wine list, very expensive and tasty. *La Casa del Pomodoro*, de Lacmiel 100 m al sur, Km 4½ Carretera a Masaya, good Italian, try the *calzone*. *Rincón Español*, Iglesia El Carmen, 2 c al lago, 1 c abajo, good Spanish. *El Churrasco*, Rotonda El Güegüense (Plaza España), expensive and very good beef dishes. *Harry's Grill Argentino*, Km 8 Carretera a Masaya, contiguo a Texaco Las Colinas, T276-2858, Argetine beef grill in 7 different cuts, daily 1130-2330, very good. *Los Gauchos*, Carretera a Masaya Km 3.5, very famous, very overpriced, locals eat elsewhere. *El Cartel*, across Carretera a Masaya from Metrocentro, T277-2619, traditional fare, dance floor, nice setting, popular with Miami crowd. *Jalapeño's*, Rotonda Metrocentro, 1 c abajo, ½ al sur, T278-6341, overpriced trendy California-style Mexican restaurant, good *tacos*, *tortilla* soup. *Las Lugo*, Colonial Los Robles, antiguo restaurante *Lacmiel* 4 c al este, T277-3090, Mon-Sat 1100-2300. Best seafood, expensive but worth it. *La Estrella de Oriente*, across from *Mansión Teodolinda*, maki sushi, crab, salmon, nice cosy décor, embassy crowd.

Mid-range *Italia*, Bolonia next to Institute of Tourism, Managua's best Italian food, try Spaghetti Mariscos, seafood pizza or octopus in tomato and garlic sauce, also

Nicaragua

excellent soups and pastas. Highly recommended. *Pasta Fresca*, del Sandy Carretera a Masaya 2 c arriba, great bread, recommended by some. *Kameleón*, Colonial Los Robles, T277-2700, interesting varied menu, Swiss owners. Recommended. *El Mesón Express*, at the Plaza Inter and the Metrocentro food courts, budget Spanish food, good paella for US$4, cup of wine US$1, good value, but noisy, overlit location. *María Bonita*, Altamira, de la Vicky 1½ c abajo, T270-4326, Mexican, closed Mon, wildly popular on weekend nights with live music and a noisy, happy crowd, good food and service, fun. Recommended. *La Hora del Taco*, Sandy's Carretera a Masaya 1 c arriba, T277-0949, traditional Mexican fair, good, nice setting outside at back.

La Plancha, various locations, T278-2999 for nearest one, good value, very generous portions, good beef, very popular, 1 can often feed 2. Recommended. For the best value, *Las Brasas*, behind *Cinema 1 and 2*, Camino Oriente, good cheap Nicaraguan fare, traditional, outdoors, great atmosphere, sea bass US$5.50, churrasco steak US$5, best deal to drink rum with friends, ½ bottle comes with bowl of ice, limes, a coke and 2 plates of food, US$9.50. *La Cocina de Doña Haydée*, opposite *Pastelería Aurami*, Planes de Altamira, T270-6100, once a popular family kitchen eatery that has gone upscale, traditional Nicaraguan food at higher prices than elsewhere, very popular with foreign residents, good, try the *surtido* plate for 2, US$6.50, and the carrot/orange *fresco*. *Bongo*, Carretera a Masaya across from Colegio Teresiano, Cuban, food not special but good cocktails, upper class crowd, good live music at weekends. *China de Asia*, de Lacmiel 1 c arriba, ½ al sur, Taiwanese specialties, good. *La Ballena que Cayó del Cielo*, next to Camino de Oriente, T277-3055, Nicaragua's best hamburgers, good grilled chicken, salsa and merengue videos.

Cheap *Hollywood Diner*, Carretera a Masaya, frente a Lacmiel, T270-2822, American-style food, big omelet's, hamburgers, salads, popular with gringos, daily 0600-2000, Sun 0800-1200 only. *Pizza Valenti*, Colonial Los Robles, best cheap pizza, US$4.50, home delivery, very popular. *Rincón Salvadoreño*, Enel Central 2 c al lago, T0886-7584 *pupusas, tamales* and *quesadillas*, very cheap, simple and good. *Topkapi*, Camino de Oriente, across from Alhambra cinema, pizza (US$2.50), tacos, Nicaraguan food, good people-watching, outdoor seating. Recommended. *La Fonda*, de Lacmiel 1 c al este, next to *Pizza Valenti*, good, try *quesadilla suprema*, also has vegetarian. *Tacos al Pastor*, Carretera a Masaya across from Camino de Oriente, T278-2650, budget Mexican, burritos and *enchiladas*, popular with young crowd. *Tacos Charros*, de la Plaza el Café, 1 c abajo, cheap, generous servings. Highly recommended. *Rincón Chino*, Km 4½ Carretera Norte, T244-0155, popular, traditional fare. *La Crema Batida*, Camino de Oriente, T277-2517, North American-style foods with many ice-cream combinations, family crowd. *La Sazón*, Cine Cabrera, 3 c al sur, 1½ abajo, T222-2243, Mon-Fri 1200-1500 only, buffet US$2, great value, often very crowded.

Vegetarian Most Nicaraguan restaurants will make a big salad or a rice, *plátano* and bean dish, but there are a few places just for veggie lovers. *Anada*, Estatua de Montoya 10 m arriba T228-4140, Nicaragua's first non-meat eatery and still the best, also good fruit juices, daily 700-2100. *Healthy Food*, Plaza El Sol 4 c al sur, Casa 211, T270-4091, 278-2453, low calorie breakfast and lunch buffets, vegetarian dishes, whole grain and soy galore, fruit juices, Mon-Fri 700-1900 and Sat 0700-1500. *Nutrem Food*, Portón principal de la UCA, 150 m abajo, soy-based foods, vegetarian menu, Mon-Sat 0700-1800).

The **Metrocentro** shopping centre has several good restaurants in its food court, the best being *El Guapinol*, next to *Pizza Hut*, with grilled beef, chicken and fish. Try Copinol dish with grilled beef, avocado, fried cheese, salad, tortilla and *gallo pinto* US$4. *Oriental King*, T271-9333, big Chinese combo dishes for US$4 with drink, from 1000 daily. *Rostipollo*, next to *McDonalds*, has chicken cooked over wood fire, tasty combo dishes with breast, beans, tortilla, salad and onions for US$4. Across the street from shopping centre behind *BDF* bank is *Emiliano's*, T278-5689, Azteca soup, great *chimichangas*, daily 1300-2300.

In the **Plaza España/Barrio Martha Quezada area**: *Comedor Sara*, next to *Ticabus*, cheap, popular with gringos, serves breakfast, has noticeboard. *Eskimo* ice-cream, on C 27 de Mayo efore ex-Cine Cabrera. Near *Santos*, **China Bien Bien**, on 27 de Mayo, 1 block south and 1 block down from CST, excellent fast food, Chinese. *Delicias del Mar*, ½ block from *Santos* on Santos Vargas Chávez, reported good. *El Buen Sabor*, *Ticabus* 1 c al lago, T222-3021, cheap lunch buffet, Mon-Fri 1100-1500. *Las Anclas*, 1 block from *Casa Santos*, good food and huge portions but watch your bill. *Mirna's*, near *Pensión Norma*, open 0700-1500, good economic breakfasts and *comidas*, popular with travellers and Nicaraguans, friendly service. 1 block north of the roundabout at Plaza España is *Rincon Cuscalteco*, T266-4209, good cheap *pupusas Salvadoreñas*, also *vigorón* and *quesillos*, daily 1200-2200.

Bars

Look in newspapers for listings of what's on in Managua and throughout the country; also check Guía Fácil at www.guiafacil.com.ni

Bar Chaman, Colonial Los Robles, US$2 entrance, young, wild crowd, salsa, rock and disco on tape, lots of dancing and sweating, great fun. *El Quelite*, Entel Villa Fontana 5C al oeste, T267-0126, open air, typical Nicaraguan dance bar with good food (try the Corvina a la plancha (sea bass) US$5, lots of dancing, live acts Thu-Sun. **Island Taste** *H*, Km 6 Carretera Norte, T240-0010, Garífuna, Socca and reggae music from Nicaragua's Caribbean, only authentic bar of its kind in Managua, Wed-Sun 1800-0400, not a nice area, use caution and a taxi. *La Casa de Los Mejía Godoy*, Plaza El Sol 2 c al sur, T278-4913, 270-4928, Thu-Sat from 2130, reservations recommended, live music in small setting of the legendary folk/revolutionary singers Carlos and Luis Enrique Mejía Godoy, US$10 entrance, well worth it, unique experience. *La Curva*, on main road behind old *Intercontinental*, T222-6876, traditional Nicaraguan dishes, cheap pitchers of beer, keep track of bill, daily 1700-0200. *La Ruta Maya*, de Montoya 150 m east, entrance US$5, good live Nicaraguan bands Thu-Sat. *El Parnaso*, UCA 1 c arriba, 1 c al lago, bohemian crowd, live music Thu-Sat. *El Quetzal Colonia Centro América*, opposite Shell, fun crowd who fill big dance floor and dance non-stop, no entrance fee, live music, ranchera, salsa, merengue. *Café Amatl*, Bolonia, terminally hip crowd, bookshop open during the day, set lunch US$2, nice outdoor setting, good crêpes at night, good live music at weekends, Brazilian, reggae, folk. Recommended. *Shannon Bar Irlandés*, 1 block east and 1 block south of *Ticabus*. Recommended with excellent food, whisky and Guinness – which runs dry due to popularity.

Entertainment

Cinemas

Cinemateca Nacional, Parque Central south corner, US$2, best movies in Managua, Mon-Fri 1830, 2000, Sat, Sun 1600, 1800, 2000. *Alianza Francesa*, Altamira, 1 block north of Mexican embassy, Fri 1900, free, French films, art exhibits during the day. *Cinema 1 & 2*, Camino de Oriente, US films, Spanish subtitles, US$3. *Alhambra 1, 2 & 3*, Camino de Oriente, US films, Spanish subtitles, US$3, bring sweater for polar a/c. *Plaza Inter*, 4 screens, American films, subtitles in Spanish, buy tickets in advance for weekend nights. *Metrocentro*, 4 screens, small theatres with steep seating, arrive early, US$3.

Dance

Ballet Tepenahuatl, folkloric dances in the ruins of the *Gran Hotel* and at the Teatro Rubén Darío. Folkloric and Latin dance classes at the Escuela de Danza, across from UNI.

Nightclubs

Zima, Camino de Oriente, T267-0123, the largest disco in Central America. *La Cabaña* in the *Intercontinental* and the *Piano Bar* across the street, the latter is a cultural experience. *Cat's Club*, at the edge of the Martha Quezada district, good dance music.

Spectator sports

The national sport and passion is **baseball**, with games on Sun mornings at the Estadio Denis Martínez. The season runs from Nov-Feb and tickets cost US$1-4. Other popular sports include **basketball** and **football** although none have a regular venue and season. Nicaragua has had four lightweight world champion **boxers** but the big fights are staged outside the country. There is also **cockfighting** and **bullfighting** (but no kill).

Festivals

Santo Domingo is the patron saint of Managua. His festival is held at El Malecón from **1-10 Aug**: church ceremonies, horse-racing, bull-fights, cock-fights, a lively carnival; proceeds to the General Hospital. **1 Aug** (half day) and **10 Aug** are local holidays.

Nicaragua

Shopping

Mercado Oriental is not recommended, see Security page 944

The best place to buy handicrafts, and just about anything else, is the **Mercado Ricardo Huembes** (also called **Mercado Central**). *Artesanía* from all parts of the country at the northeast end of the parking lot. Some handicrafts (goldwork, embroidery, etc) are available in the refurbished **Metrocentro**, in the new **Plaza Inter** and in **Centro Comercial Managua** (good general shopping here). For Mercado Huembes, on Pista Portezuelo, buses 110 or 119. A smart shop selling Nicaraguan arts and crafts is *Takesa*, del *Intercontinental* 2 c al sur, ½ abajo, Edif Bolívar 203, T268-3301, high quality and high prices. *Mi Pueblo* at Km 9.5 on Carretera Sur, T882-5650, sells handicrafts, plants and also has a good restaurant. Post cards for sale at Tourist Office, Ministry of Culture, Mercado Huembes and *Hotel Intercontinental* (several times more expensive); also at *Tarjetas Gordión*. Most ordinary shops are in private houses without signs. **Almacenes Internacionales** (formerly *Dollartienda*, and *Diplotienda*), opposite *Los Gauchos* restaurant on Carretera a Masaya, offers Western-style goods, take your passport, accepts dollars and travellers' cheques if to value of purchase. There is an a/c supermarket on Plaza España. For chocolate, *Chocolatería Gorbea*, Calle Principal Los Robles, Pizza House 50 m al sur, T278-4091.

Bookshops *Amatl Libro Café* above. **Hispamer**, UCA, 1 c arriba, 1 c al sur, 1 c arriba, best Spanish-language bookstore in country. Many bookshops sell maps, postcards, badges, stickers and other tourist items. Small selection at the **Centro Sandinista de Trabajadores**, Ho Chi Minh Way.

Transport

Beware of pickpockets on the crowded urban buses, particularly those on tourist routes

Local Bus: service in Managua costs US$0.13 approximately. City buses run every 10 mins 0530-1800, every 15 mins 1800-2200, when last services begin their routes; buses are frequent but it is difficult to fathom their routes. The principal bus routes are: 101 from Las Brisas, passing CST, *Hotel Intercontinental*, Mercado Oriental, then on to Mercados San Miguel and Mayoreo; 103 from 7 Sur to Mercado Lewites, Plaza 19 de Julio, Metrocentro, Mercado San Miguel and Villa Libertad; 109 from Teatro Darío to the Bolívar/Buitrago junction just before *Intercontinental*, turns east, then southeast to Mercado Huembes/bus station; 110 runs from 7 Sur to Villa San Jacinto passing en route Mercado Lewites, Plaza 19 de Julio, Metrocentro, Mercado Huembes/bus station and Mercado San Miguel; 113 from Ciudad Sandino, Las Piedrecitas, CST, *Intercontinental*, to Mercado Oriental; 116 runs east-west below *Intercontinental*, on Buitrago, also passing CST; 118 takes a similar route but turns south on Williams Romero to Plaza España, thence to Israel Lewites bus station; 119 runs from Plaza España to Mercado Huembes/bus station via Plaza 19 de Julio; 123 runs from Mercado Lewites via 7 Sur and Linda Vista to near Palacio Nacional de Cultura, and Nuevo Diario.

Car hire: *Avis*, by Centro Comercial Nejapa, T265-0112. *Budget*, Barrio Altagracia, Estatua Montoya 1 c al sur 1 c al oeste, T266-6226, F222-5567, budget@budget.com.ni *Hertz* at the airport, *Hotel Intercontinental* (T222-2320, F266-8400, hertzni@interlink.com.ni), or Edif Caribe Motors, Km 4 Carretera Sur, T266-8399, F266-8400. *Leo's* southwest side of Rotonda Güegüense, T266-3719. *Toyota* T222-2275, F222-2269. Rates are US$30 per day Group A to US$65 per day Group G (all a/c), unlimited mileage, US$10-23 per day accident protection, tax not included, discounts for 2 weeks or more. Given the poor public transport and the decentralized layout of Managua, you may find that renting a car is the best way to get around. Alternatively, hire a taxi for journeys out of Managua, about US$10 per hour from an office opposite *Hotel Intercontinental*, T222-3469 (opens 0930). *Renault garage*: Km 6 Carretera Norte, in front of Coca Cola; efficient spare parts service.

Taxis: can be flagged down along the street. They also cruise the bus stations looking for arriving passengers, but it is cheaper to get a taxi on the street nearby. There is a taxi stand just below *Hotel Morgut*, west of *Intercontinental*. Taxis are the best method of transport for foreigners in Managua; bargain the fare before entering (fares range from US$0.80-US$1 for a short trip, US$1.50-US$2.50 across town, US$8 to airport). Fares are always per person, not per car. After telling the driver your desination, if travelling far or in a different direction to other passengers he may decide not to take you. If he says yes, ask how much (*¿por cuánto* *he lleva?*) then get in. If travelling alone and the front seat is empty take it as back seat will be lled *en route*. It may be handy to have the telephone number of your hotel with you. Street ames and numbers are not universal in the city and the taxi driver may not know your destination, make sure you know the co-ordinates of your destination if it is a private residence. If eading for Barrio Martha Quezada, ask for the *Ticabus* if you do not know your exact destination. Recommended radio taxis which do not stop for other passengers (for early flights or ate night transport) are **Coop 25 de Febrero**, T222-5218, or **Coop 2 de Agosto**, T263-1512, et price quote on the phone, normally 80-100% more expensive.

ong distance Air César Augusto Sandino (MGA), modernized 1998-99. Take any bus narked 'Tipitapa' from Mercado Huembes, Mercado San Miguel or Mercado Oriental (near Victoria brewery), US$0.16. Alternatively, take a taxi for no more than US$8. Be early for international flights since formalities are slow and thorough and can take 2 hrs. Artesan stalls and cheap food upstairs above the bank. X-ray machines reported safe for film. 2 duty free shops, café, toilets through immigration. You are not allowed to stay overnight in the airport. The bank at the airport closes at 1600, does not always change travellers cheques but does have an ATM machine accepting Visa and Mastercard.

Inter-city buses Buses for destinations south of Managua leave from **Mercado Roberto Huembes** (also called **Mercado Central**). **Masaya**, every 30 mins, 0415-2200, 1 hr, US$0.40; *Express*, every 30 mins, 0500-2100, 40 mins, US$0.80. **Granada**, every 20 mins, 0500-2100, 1½ hrs, US$0.70; *Express* from *La UCA*, every 30 mins, 0500-2200, 1 hr, US$1. **Rivas**, every 20 mins, 0400-1830, 2¾ hrs, US$1.50. **San Jorge** (dock), 0830 and 1500, 2½ hrs, US$2. **San Juan del Sur**, every hr, 0400-1600, 3½ hrs, US$2.25. **Peñas Blancas**, 0400, 3½ hrs, US$3.50. **San Carlos**, daily at 0500, 0600, 0700 and 1300, 9½ hrs, US$7.

For return times see individual destinations

For destinations east and then north or south, the buses leave from **Mercado Mayoreo**. **Boaco**, every 30 mins, 0430-1800, 2½ hrs, US$1.50. **Juigalpa**, every hr, 0500-1700, 3 hrs, US$2.25. **El Rama**, every hr, 0400-1100, 8-10 hrs, US$5.25. **San Carlos**, every hr, 0505-1310, 9 hrs, US$5.25. **Matagalpa**, every hr, 0500-1800, 2½ hrs, US$2.25. **Jinotega**, every hr, 0500-1730, 3½ hrs, US$3. **Estelí**, every hr, 0545-1745, 2¾ hrs, US$3.25. *Express luxury*,1315 and 1515, 2¾ hrs, US$3. **Ocotal**, every hr, 0510-1700, 3½ hrs, US$3.25. **Managua-Somoto**, 1330, 1530 and 1645, 3½ hrs, US$3.

For destinations west and northwest, buses leave from the **Mercado Israel Lewites** (also called **Mercado Boer**). **Pochomil**, every 30 mins, 0600-1830, 2½ hrs, US$0.75. **Diriamba**, every 20 mins, 0530-2130, 1¼ hr, US$0.80. **Jinotepe**, every 15 mins, 0500-2100, 1 hr 20 mins, US$1. **León**, every 30 mins, 0500-1900, 2½ hrs, US$1. **El Sauce**, 1400, 3½ hrs, US$4. **Chinandega**, every 30 mins, 0500-1800, 2½ hrs, US$2.25. **Corinto**, every hr, 0500-1715, 3 hrs, US$3. **Guasaule**, 0300, 4 hrs, US$3.

International buses International buses are a cheap and efficient way to travel between Nicaragua and other Central American countries. Buses are available to and from Honduras, El Salvador and Guatemala in the north, Costa Rica and Panama to the south. When leaving Managua you will need to check in 1 hr in advance with passport and ticket. The buses all have a/c, toilet, reclining seats; most have television screens and offer some sort of snacks. The most famous is *Ticabus*, which parks in Barrio Martha Quezada, from Cine Dorado, 2 c arriba, T222-3031. Leaving next door are the buses of *Cruceros del Golfo*, T228-1454. Just across from the Plaza Inter shopping plaza, behind the DHL office, is *Nicabus*, T228-1383, while *Transnica* is a long-haul bus option, 150 m east of the Santo Domingo roundabout (the one with the big Jesus Christ) in Centro Comercial Lucila, No 8, T278-2090.

For **Costa Rica** *Ticabus* leaves Managua twice daily at 0545 and 0700, 9 hrs, US$10. *Transnica* at 0530 and 0700, US$12.50. *Nicabus* at 0600, US$10. To **El Salvador** *Transnica* leaves Managua at 0500, 11½ hrs, US$25. *Ticabus* leaves Managua at 0500, US$20. *Cruceros del Golfo* leaves at 0430, US$30. To **Guatemala City** *Ticabus* leaves Managua at 0500, 15½ hrs US$30 (plus overnight costs in El Salvador). *Cruceros de Golfo* leaves Managua at 0430, US$53 (plus overnight costs in El Salvador). To **Honduras** *Ticabus* leaves Managua at 0800, 9 hrs, US$20. *Cruceros de Golfo* leaves at 0430. For **Panamá** *Ticabus* leaves Managua at 0545 to connect with 1600 bus in San José to Panamá, 22 hrs, US$35.

Nicaragua

A cheaper way of travelling to San José is to take a bus Managua-Rivas, then *colectivo* t‹ border and another between the border posts, then take local bus to San José; takes 15 hr altogether, cost about US$8. Similarly, taking local buses to Tegucigalpa will cost you abou‹ US$5. International buses are always booked-up many days in advance and tickets will no‹ be sold until all passport/visa documentation is complete. Look in *El Nuevo Diario* Sección 2‹ 'Servicios', for buses running to San Salvador, Tegucigalpa, Guatemala City and Mexico.

Directory

Airline offices Around Plaza España: *Air France*,T266-2612, *American Airlines*, T266-3900, *British Airways*, in the Grupo Taca office,T266-3136, *Grupo Taca*, T266-3136, *Iberia*, T266-4440, *Japan Airlines* T266-3588, *LanChile*, T266-6997. *Alitalia*, de Los Pipitos 1½ c abajo, T266-6997. *Continenta‹* (T270-3403), Carretera a Masaya Km 4. *Copa*, 1 c abajo de *Sorbet Inn*, Carretera a Masaya, T267-5438. *La Costeña* (for the Atlantic coast), at the airport, T263-1228, F263-1281. *LTU*, Rotonda Güegüense, 2½ c arriba, T266-7734.

Banks The best 2 banks for foreigners are *Banco de América Central (BAC)* and *Banco de Finanzas (BDF)*
Any bank in Nicaragua their acronyms are used regularly. *BAC* offers credit card advances, uses the Cirrus debit system and
will change US$ to changes all travellers' cheques with a 3% commission. *BDF* changes American Express travellers'
córdobas and cheques only, also with a 3% commission. See page 32 for more details on street changing and ATMs.
vice-versa. TC receipts *BDF* central office across Av Bolívar from the old *Intercontinental*. Other locations include: across the
may be required Carretera a Masaya from Metrocentro, T277-0343, at the Mayoreo market, T233-4350, in Martha
in banks when Quezada next to *Cine Dorado*, T268-5662, and at immigration, T248-6272. *BAC*'s slick new office
changing money headquarters is at Casa Pellas, Km 4 Carretera a Masaya, T277-3624. There is a *BAC* in Plaza España, T266-7062, and at Metrocentro, with long hours including Sun afternoon, T278-5510.

Several money changers hang out at the road junction in Altamira by the restaurants *La Fonda* and *Casa del Pomodoro* and outside *La Colonia* shopping centre in Plaza España. After 1800 and on Sun they are usually tricksters. On Sun you can change money at the *Intercontinental*, major hotels or banks inside *Metrocentro*.

Communi- **Internet**: *Cyber-Café*, de la Distribuidora Vicky 1 c al oeste y 2 c al sur, Plaza Coconut Grove, T278-8526,
cations servicio@cybercafe. com.ni, Mon-Sat 0900-2200, US$3 per hr, serves coffee. *Kafe@Internet*, No 1, Martha Quezada, de la CST 120 m al sur, T0864-2700, US$3 hr, Mon-Sat 0800-2000. Sun 0900-1800. *Kafe@Internet*, Edif Fontaine Blue, carretera a Masaya across from *Friday's*, T270-5670, US$3 hr, Mon-Sat 0900-2100, Sun 0900-1800. **K@LU Internet**, Martha Quezada, Cine Cabrera, 2 c arriba, contiguo a Plaza Jiménez, T222-2602, internet and international calls, Mon-Sat 0830-2000, Sun 0900-1800. **Post office**: of 21 locations around Managua, the main office for the country is 1 block west of Parque Central. Wide selection of beautiful stamps. Poste Restante (*Lista de Correos*) keeps mail for 45 days, US$0.20 per letter. There is another post office in the Centro Comercial Managua and at the airport. **Telephone**: *Enitel*, same building as post office, open 0700-2230. There is a small office in the international airport. Telephone offices are spreading around Managua; most are next to or near the *correos*.

Cultural **Library** *Casa Ben Linder*, 3 blocks south 1½ blocks east of Estatua Monseñor Lezcano, also good book
centres exchange, T266-4373. *Alianza Francesa*, in Altamira near Mexican Embassy, films on Fri evenings, friendly.

Embassies & *Canada*, costado este de Casa Nazaret, 1 c arriba, C El Nogal No 25, T268-0433, F268-1985, open
consulates Mon-Thu 0900-1200. *Costa Rica*, Montoya 1½ c east, C 27 de Mayo, T266-3986, F266-3955, open 0900-1500. *Denmark*, Rotonda El Güegüense 1 c abajo, 2 c al lago, ½ c abajo, T268-0250, F266-8095, open 0800-1400. *Netherlands*, del Canal 2, 1 c al norte, 1 c al oeste, Apdo 3534, T266-6175, F266-0364, open 0800-1600. *Finland,* Hospital Militar 1 St North, 1½ c west, T266-7947, open 0800-1200, 1300-1500. *France*, Iglesia El Carmen 1½ c abajo, T222-6210, F228-1057, open 0800-1600. *Germany*, 200 m north of Plaza España (towards lake), T266-3917, F266-7667, open Mon-Fri 0900-1200. *Guatemala*, Km 11 Carretera a Masaya, T279-9609, F279-9610, fast service, 0900-1200 only. *Honduras*, Reparto San Juan del Gimnasio Hercules, 1 c al sur, 1 arriba, Calle San Juan 312, 15 mins' walk from the *Hotel Intercontinental*, T278-3043, open Mon-Fri, 0900-1200. Visas in a couple of hours, US$10. *Italy*, Rotonda El Güegüense 1 c al lago, T266-6486, F266-3987, open 0900-1200. *Mexico*, from Km 4.5 on Carreta a Masaya, take the 2nd st on the left and it's at the 1st crossroads on your right, in Altamira, T277-5886, F178-2886. *Panama*, Col Mantica, el Cuartel General de Bomberos, 1 c abajo, casa 93, T/F266-8633, open 0830-1300, visa on the spot, valid 3 months for a 30-day stay, US$10, maps and

nformation on the Canal. *Sweden*, from Plaza España, 1 c west (abajo), 2 c al lago, ½ c abajo, Apdo Postal 2307, T266-0085, F266-6778, open 0800-1200. *Switzerland*, *Restaurante Marseillaise* 2 c al lago, Apdo Postal 166, T277-3235, F278-5263. *UK*, El Reparto, 'Los Robles', Primera Etapa, Entrada Principal de la Carretera a Masaya, Cuarta Casa a la mano derecha, T278-0014, F278-4083, Apdo Aéreo 169, open 0900-1200. *US*, Km 4½ Carretera del Sur (T266-6010, F266-3865), open 0730-0900. *Venezuela*, Km 10.5 Carretera a Masaya, T276-0267, F267-8327.

Language schools

Spanish classes and a thorough introduction to Nicaragua: *Casa Nicaragüense de Español*, Km 11.5 Carretera Sur; accommodation with families. *Huellas*, Col Centroamérica, Callejón El Ceibo G-414, T277-2079, intensive classes, private classes and regular classes (0880-1200). *Nicaragua Spanish School*, Rotonda Bello Horizonte, 2 c al sur, 2 c arriba, T244-4512, nssmga@ibw.com.ni, regular and private classes. *Universidad Americana*, Centro de Idiomas Extranjeros, T278-3800 ext 301, open course with flexible hrs and regular class of 5 months, crgila@uam.edu.ni *Universidad Centroamericana* (*UCA*), Centro de Idiomas Extranjeros, T278-3923, 267-0352 ext 242-351, 5 week regular classes of all levels and open classes with flexible hrs.

Medical services

Hospitals: are generally crowded and queues very long. The best are *Hospital Bautista*, near Mercado Oriental, T249-7070, F249-7327; *Hospital Militar*, T222-2172, F222-2391 (go south from *Intercontinental* and take 2nd turn on left); and *Hospital Alemán-Nicaragüense* Km 6 Carretera Norte Siemens, 3 blocks south, 249-3368, operated with German aid, mostly Nicaraguan staff. Phone for appointment first if possible. Private clinics are an alternative. *Policlínica Nicaragüense*, consultation US$30. *Med-Lab*, 300 m south of Plaza España, is recommended for tests on stool samples, the director speaks English. **Doctors**: **Internal medicine**, Dr Enrique Sánchez Salgado, T278-1031, Dr Mauricio Barrios, T266-7284. **Paediatricians**, Dr Alejandro Ayón, T268-3103, Dr César Gutiérrez Quant, T278-6622, T278-5465 (home). **Gynaecologists**, Dr Walter Mendieta, T278-5186, T265-8543 (home), Dr Edwin Mendieta, T266-6591. **Ophthalmologist**, Dr Milton Eugarrios, T278-6306. **Dentists**: Dr Claudia Bendaña, T277-1842 and Dr Mario Sánchez Ramos, T278-1409, T278-5588 (home).

Tour operators

Aeromundo, east corner of Plaza España, T266-8725, F266-8784, aeromundo@ibw.com.ni, contact Esmeralda. *Atlántida*, Plaza España, 1 block east, ½ block north, T266-4050, F266-4160, contact Francis or Lisette. *Careli Tours*, calle Principal Colonial Los Robles, Apdo C-134, T278-2572, F278-2574, www.carelitours.com, offer guided tours through western Nicaragua and down the Río San Juan. *Momotombo Tours*, Ciudad Jardín, casa F-35, T249-8224, contact Enrique. *Otec*, Hospital Militar 1 c al lago, ½ c abajo, T268-1583, F268-1698, otec@munditel.com *Schuvar Tours*, Plaza España Edif Bamer No 4, T266-3588, F266-3586, schuvar@ibw.com.ni, contact Mercedes. *Tours Nicaragua*, Plaza Barcelona, next to the *Galería Internacional*, T270-8417, T088-41712 (mob), F270-7851, www.toursnicaragua.com A wide variety of tours to all parts of the country in vans, boats, small plane and 4WD, English-, German- and French-speaking guides. Contact Mike Newton, helpful. *Turismo Joven*, Calle 27 de Mayo, del Cine Cabrera 3 c al este, T222-2619, F222-2143, turjoven@munditel.com.ni (same block as *Nicabus* and *Panaline*), travel agency and representative for international student identity cards, affiliated to Youth Hostel Association. *Viajes Globo*, Bolonia, Edif Policlínica, T266-4515, contact María José.

Useful addresses

Customs: Km 5 Carretera del Norte, bus No 108. **Immigration**: near Ciudad Jardín, Antiguo Edif del Seguro Social, bus 101, 108, open 0800-1600, T244-3989. **Police**: T118 in an emergency. The local police station number will depend on what *distrito* you are in. Start with the Metrocentro area number, T265-0651. **Fire**, dial T115 in an emergency; the central number is T265-0162. **Red Cross**, dial T128 in an emergency, to give blood T265-1517.

Around Managua

Laguna de Xiloá

There are several volcanic-crater lakes close to Managua, some of which have become centres of residential development, with swimming, boating, fishing and picnicking facilities for the public. Among the more attractive of these lakes is Laguna de Xiloá, 16 km from Managua just off the new road to Léon. At Xiloá there is a private aquatic club (El Náutico), with small restaurants and hotels, boats for rent, bathing possible on the narrow beach, with caves. On Saturday and Sunday, the only days when buses run, Xiloá gets very crowded. It is quiet during the week and you can camp there, but without public transport you will have to walk or take a taxi. ■ *Getting there: take bus 113 to*

Nicaragua

Las Piedrecitas for Xiloá, Sat and Sun only (US$0.35); admission US$1.60 for cars, US$0.30 for pedestrians. Other lakes within a 45-min drive of Managua are the Laguna de Masaya and Laguna de Apoyo (see pages 978 and 979).

Huellas de Acahualinca

The Huellas de Acahualinca are Managua's only site of archaeological interest. These are prehistoric animal and human footprints (6,000 years old), which have been preserved in the sedimentary tufa, located close to the old centre of town, near the lakeshore at the end of the south Highway. There is still some debate as to the origin and purpose of the footprints – the theory that they were left by people fleeing a volcanic eruption has now been discarded due to the distance between the footsteps. What is known is that there were several different groups of nomadic people who left their tracks. There is also a small, interesting museum which exhibits a variety of prehistoric artefacts. ■ *Entry US$1, US$2.50 extra for photographs, all explanations in Spanish.* Getting there: taxi or car recommended, not a nice neighbourhood. From the Portón de Gadala María, 1½ blocks towards the lake. Buses 102, 12 or 6 pass the site, look out for a concrete tower and a huge stone slab by a small red footbridge. Off the main road there are no signs. By road, take the street that leads west (*abajo*) from the old centre and continue to the big building of López Richardson International Inc. Turn right (*al lago*) immediately before López Richardson; the pavement becomes a dirt road and, just after it does, the museum is on the right.

Laguna de Asososca

It's a 10-km drive down Carretera Sur – the Pan-American Highway – to Laguna de Asososca (the city's reservoir) and another small lake, Laguna de Nejapa (meaning medicinal waters) in the wooded crater of an old volcano. Piedrecitas Park is to one side of the lake: with playgrounds for children, a café, and splendid view of Lake Managua, Laguna de Asososca and of Momotombo volcano. The Pan-American Highway continues to **Casa Colorada** (hotel), 26 km from Managua, at 900 m, with commanding views of both the Pacific and of Lake Managua, and a delightful climate (but no trees due to poisonous gases from Santiago volcano, see page 976).

Mateare & Momotombito

Beware of snakes when hiking around the island – there are lots

Thirty kilometres northwest of Managua is Mateare, a pleasant fishing and agricultural town with some of the finest lake fish in Lake Managua (eat at your own risk). Distanced from the capital by a large peninsula, the lake is much cleaner here than on the Managua side. The fishermen can take you to the small volcanic island of Momotombito. The best time of year to visit is during the rainy season, when the island is green and the swell on the lake small. The boat ride in the dry season can be alarming and you may get very wet. Price about US$60 for the day. There are other small islands in the shadow of the smoking Momotombo volcano, which appears to loom over the lake from the mainland shore. Momotombito is a nature reserve, and has much bird and reptile life and a legendary family of albino crocodiles. There is a small military outpost on the calm side of the island. Stop there to check in if you wish to hike on the islands. Bring drinks or food as gifts for the (non-uniformed) guards, who are very friendly and usually quite bored. They might take you hiking for a small fee to see what is left of many pre-Columbian idols, most of which have been robbed, though one can be seen in the Museo Nacional. The guards know of others still on the island.

Pacific beaches

Don't sleep on the beach, mosquitoes will eat you alive

There are several beaches on the Pacific coast, about an hour's drive from Managua. Because of their proximity to the capital, these get very crowded during the high season (January-April). The nearest are **Pochomil** and **Masachapa** (54 km from Managua, side by side, bus service from terminal in Israel Lewites market every 35 minutes, US$1 to Pochomil).

Out of season, except at weekends, Pochomil is deserted; it is cleaner the further south you go, but there are rock and strong waves here, so swim with care. It is a tourist centre with a few hotels and many small family owned restaurants, most of which serve freshly caught snapper (*pargo*).

Nicaragua

At the entrance to Masachapa is the access road to the **Montelimar Resort**. Just before the gates of the resort, at the entrance to a new housing development is the dirt access road to the area's nicest public beach, *Montelimar Gratis* or *El Muelle de Somoza*, which is a long deserted stretch of clean sand that runs from the crumbling, old Somoza family pier to the rocky point that separates the resort from the rest of Masachapa. Take bus to Masachapa and walk from main highway on entrance road or in car to the pier, then walk north.

Sleeping Near Pochomil and Masachapa is the **LL** *Montelimar Resort*, T269-6769, F269-7669, montelimar@ns.tmx.com.ni, built by the Sandinistas, now owned by Spain's *Barceló* group. It is expensive, becoming popular with package tours, has full services and is often booked solid from Nov to Apr. It has a broad, unspoilt sandy beach ideal for bathing and surfing. The nearest public transport is 3 km away at Masachapa, taxi from Managua US$30 (70 km), or hire a car.

There are few hotels in **Pochomil** at present, **A** *Ticomo Mar*, just south of the presidential beach house on the nicest part of Pochomil beach, T265-0210, a/c and bath, best hotel in the region apart from Montelimar (see below), but still poor value. **B** *Villas del Mar*, just north of Pochimal centre, T266-6661, crowded, overpriced food, party atmosphere, use of swimming pool $5 per person. **Masachapa** is cheaper but dirtier and rocky. There are hotels on beach, **D** *Hotel Summer* on the main street to the beach, restaurant, OK. **F** *Hotel Rex*, very basic. Very slow bus journey from Managua.

La Boquita, is the nearest beach to the villages south of Managua and is visited by turtles from August to November. **B** *Hotel Palmas del Mar*, centre of beach, T552-8715, pglo@tmx.com.ni, beach front, private bath, a/c or fan, bit noisy, but best on the beach. **D** *Suleyka*, Centro Turístico La Boquita, T552-8717. Six rooms with shared baths and fan, good restaurant with fresh fish dishes. Muggings have been reported at La Boquita in the past but no problems for several years.

Casares (69 km from Managua), is the next beach south of La Boquita. The town itself is a rough little fishing villages, but empty beaches are just south of the village, access is a long hike or journey by four-wheel drive; lodging is available at **A** *Lupita*, Centro Turístico Casares, Laminic 500 m abajo, T552-8708, 18 rooms with private bath, TV, a/c, swimming pool and restaurant.

Heading north from Managua, a visit to the broad, sandy **El Velero** beach (turn off at Km 60 on the old road to León and then follow signs) is recommended, despite the entrance charge and poor road. All facilities are controlled by the INSSBI for the benefit of state employees. Weekends are fully booked for weeks in advance. ■ *Entry US$3.50.* **AL-B** *Centro Vacacional El Velero*, 8 km from Puerto Sandino, T222-6994, 32 rooms with private bath, refrigirators, a/c or fan, or you may be able to rent a cabin (**E** for two) in the week, pay extra for sheet and pillows. You can eat in the expensive restaurant, *Pirata Cojot*, at the INSSBI cafetería (bring your own cutlery and buy meal ticket in advance) or take your own food. However, the beach itself is beautiful, and the sea is ideal for surfing and swimming. **El Tránsito** is another lovely, undeveloped Pacific beach. Bus from Managua at 1200, 1315, 1500 (from Terminal Lewites), return at 0600 or 0700, US$0.70. Good cheap meals from Señora Pérez on the beach (possible accommodation); *Restaurant Yolanda*, beach flats for four to six people normally available midweek at north end (*Centro Vacacional de Trabajadores*, good value).

Nicaragua

Managua to the Northern Highlands

Managua

A couple of routes to the Honduran border use the Pan-American Highway heading north of Lake Managua. The road rises and winds through hilly country, with fields set aside for agriculture and coffee growing, giving way to mining and pine forests. Damage from the Revolution is evident in the small town of Estelí, as it is throughout the region. A short detour south of Estelí takes a paved road to good walking and wildlife country in Matagalpa and Jinotega. North of Estelí the road splits, leading to Somoto and Ocotal, and completing the 214-km paved road from the capital to Honduras.

Tipitapa
Colour map 7, grid A1

Heading east out of Managua along the southern shore of the lake is Tipitapa (21 km). Once a tourist resort with hot sulphur baths and a casino, some of the buildings are in ruins, but the resort has been reopened and you can swim in clean water in the baths. There is a colourful market, and the **Fiesta del Señor de Esquipulasis** on 13-16 January. You can swim in El Trapice park. ■ *US$0.50.*

Sleeping and eating *Hospedaje (Lazo)* is at the main road junction. *Entre Ríos*, main street opposite Texaco, T295-3245, very good lake perch, sweet and sour shrimp in nut sauce, daily, 1000-2100. *Salón Silvia*, no frills. Slightly cheaper, but good, is the a/c restaurant attached to the thermal baths.

Buses from **Managua**, Plaza Mayoreo, via La Fanisa, Waspan, La Subasta, Aeropuerto and Zona Franca, every 10 mins, 0530-2100, 45 mins, US$0.25. Bus to **Estelí**, US$1.40, pick-up on the road coming from Managua, every 30 mins, 0455-1755. Bus to **Masaya**, US$0.35, every 20 mins, 0500-1900, 1 hr, change there for Granada.

Ciudad Darío

The Pan-American Highway goes north through Tipitapa to **Sébaco**, passing through Ciudad Darío, where the poet Rubén Darío was born. You can see the house, which is maintained as a museum. There is an arts festival for the week of his birthday, 18 January. Sébaco and the surrounding area was badly affected by Hurricane Mitch, and Sébaco itself was damaged almost beyond repair

Sleeping and eating **Ciudad Darío** **F** *Hospedaje* El, 1½ blocks before the bridge on left, basic, friendly. Cheap good food from *Comedor Crismar* on Plaza Central. **Sébaco** is **D** *El Valle*, on the highway 1 km towards Ciudad Darío, with restaurant, clean, fan, shower, quiet, patio with pool, English and Italian spoken. *Los Gemelos*, next to *ENEL*, T622-2004, moderate price, seafood and good steaks, try the Churrasco steak with garlic and parsley sauce. *El Sesteo*, *Banco del Café*, 2c al oeste, T622-2242, mid-range, chicken, shrimp, onion steak, clam cocktail, fried fish. East of the highway is **Esquipula**, 2½ hrs by bus, a good place for hiking, fishing and riding. **F** *Hotel Oscar Morales*, clean, shower, friendly.

Matagalpa

Colour map 6, grid C4
Population: 62,000
Altitude: 672 m

From Sébaco a road leads to Matagalpa, and some of the best walking country in Nicaragua. Matagalpa has an old church, and while it is about the only colonial-style building left, the town retains a simple agrarian charm. Badly damaged in the Revolution, the coffee boom of the last five years has benefitted the region greatly creating a very strong local economy, and all war damage has now been repaired. Matagalpa is the birthplace of **Carlos Fonseca**, one of the founder members of the FSLN. The house he was born in, one block east of Parque San José, is a museum that looks certain to remain closed for the foreseeable future, but the local FSLN office reportedly has the keys. The cathedral is in the main square to the north, as is the **Galería de los Héroes y Mártires**. The gallery is closed but the monument is quite impressive. The Centro Popular de la Cultura is 2½ blocks north, four blocks east from the northeast corner of the cathedral plaza. The **tourist office** next to the Iglesia Adventista, Monday-Friday 0800-1700, has useful information, English spoken. Coffee, the region's main source of employment, is harvested in November and December and can be seen drying in the sun at the southern edge of town. There is also some cattle ranching in the area, and the chief industry is the Nestlé powdered-milk plant. A 32-km road runs from Matagalpa east to the Tuma valley.

A *Lomas de Guadalupe*, 500 m east of INAA, T612-7505, F612-6408, 26 rooms, private bath with hot water, cable TV, telephone, minibar, internet access, new and pretty view, not central. **B-C** *Ideal*, Tienda Rosalinda ½ c al oeste, T612-2483, with bath and TV, **E** without, better rooms are upstairs, beware overcharging, good but expensive restaurant, disco on Sat.   **D** *Fountain Blue*, Colegio Santa Teresita, ½ c al este, T612-2733, private bath with hot water, fan, cable TV. **D** *Wanpani*, Shell La Virgen, ½ c al sur, 20 m al este, T612-4761, F612-2893, 12 rooms, cafetería, private bath and fan. **E** *Caoba*, Colegio Santa Teresita, 1½ c al norte, T612-3515, private bath and fan. **E** *Soza del Río*, with bath, nice patio, good value, opposite river, basic, meals

Sleeping

Many places shut their doors by 2200-2300

The town has an erratic water supply

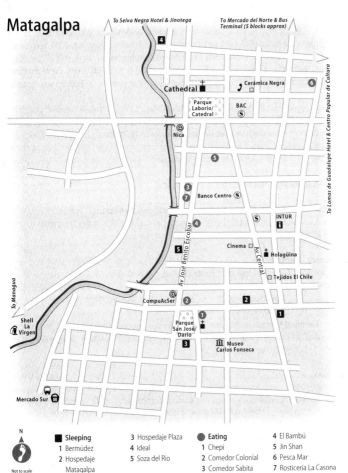

Matagalpa

To Selva Negra Hotel & Jinotega

To Mercado del Norte & Bus Terminal (5 blocks approx)

Cathedral

Cerámica Negra

Parque
Laborio/
Catedral

BAC

Nica

Banco Centro

INTUR

Av José Benito Escobar

Cinema

Holagüina

Av Central

Tejidos El Chile

To Managua

CompuAcSer

Shell
La
Virgen

Parque
San José/
Darío

Museo
Carlos Fonseca

Mercado Sur

To Lomas de Guadalupe Hotel & Centro Popular de Cultura

N

Not to scale

■ **Sleeping**
1 Bermúdez
2 Hospedaje
  Matagalpa
3 Hospedaje Plaza
4 Ideal
5 Soza del Rio

● **Eating**
1 Chepi
2 Comedor Colonial
3 Comedor Sabita
4 El Bambú
5 Jin Shan
6 Pesca Mar
7 Rostería La Casona

Nicaragua

available. **E** *Hospedaje Matagalpa*, 1 block east of Parque San José, T612-3834, with bath, **F** without, clean, light and airy. **F** *Bermúdez*, 2 blocks east of Parque San José, some with bath, poor, rundown, but popular, good car parking, helpful, meals. **F** *Hospedaje Plaza*, on south side of Parque San José, small rooms with thin walls and peepholes, poor beds, mosquitoes, basic.

Out of town 10 km on road to Jinotega at Km 139½ is **L-C** *Selva Negra*, at 1,200 m, T612-5713, F612-3883, www.selvanegra.com, cabins in a private cloud forest reserve with howler monkeys and quetzals. Good, expensive restaurant (reserve in advance at weekends), good starting point for walks, private rainforest reserve, with 14 different paths (visitors US$2.50 for which credit is given in the restaurant), ask hotel for free map. Horses available for rent and they offer coffee plantation tours. **B** *Campestre San Ramón y Finca Esperanza Verde*, San Ramón east of Matagalpa, T612-5003, new place built for ecotourism and specifically for observation of butterflies, 2 rooms with private bath, fan, telephone, internet access. There are also guesthouses in the area. Call the same number.

Eating At the north end of town is *White House Pizza*, 1½ c al norte, T612-7575, open daily, will deliver in local area. *Jinshan*, 1 block south of Parque San José, Chinese, good. *Sabita*, 2 blocks south of Laborio on Av José Benito Escobar, family-run, good breakfasts and lunch. Nearby is *La Casona*, Av José Benito Escobar, cheap chicken and on the same street *El Bambú*, is popular with locals. *La Vita e Bella*, an Italian run restaurant at the north end town, has received strong praise from a couple of readers. It's up some alleyway, but well worth the effort and very reasonable. *Pesca Mar*, Cancha del Brigadista 3 c al este, T612-3548, shrimp in garlic butter, red snapper in onions, open daily until 2200. *Zinica*, frente a Casa Pellas, T612-5921, tacos, sandwiches and chicken, daily 0900-2100. Very cheap.

Close to Parque San José is *Bay Pay*, smoked pork, hot pepper steak, mid-priced, good, daily 0900-2000. *Chepi*, large portions, excellent value, popular. Close by is *Comedor Colonial*, good in the evening. *La Posada*, Parque Darío ½ c al norte, T612-2330, fish a la Tipitapa

Bars & clubs Several good bars in town. At the south end of town is *La Posada* and a couple of blocks further south is *Rancho Escondido* which is better and has live music on weekends. Neaby is *La Licor* another popular hang-out. On Parque San José is *Vi Pay* bar and a couple of blocks east, near *Hotel Bermúdez* is a new sports bar. But the most popular spot by far is *Disco Luz de la Luna*, 4 km out of town on the road to Managua.

Festivals 24 Sep, *Virgín de las Mercedes*, is a local holiday.

Shopping *Mercado del Norte*, close to northern highway (filthy). *Mercado del Oeste*, is 2 blocks west of *Royal Bar*, busy and not the healthiest market around, but look for fine black pottery made in local co-operatives.

Transport **Buses** **Terminal Sur**, by Mercado del Sur is used for destinations north, south and west including Managua, Estelí and Jinotega. **Estelí**, every 30 mins, 0515-1800, 1½ hrs, US$1. **Jinotega**, every 30 mins, 0500-1800, 1½ hrs, US$1. **León**, 0600 and 1500, 3 hrs, US$2.25 (luggage US$1), **Managua**: every 30 mins, 2½ hrs, US$2.50. **Masaya**, 0700, 1400 and 1530, 4 hrs, US$2. **Tipitapa**, every 30 mins, 2 hrs, US$2.

Terminal Norte, by Mercado del Norte, is for destinations within Matagalpa department, ie **San Ramón** and **El Tuma**. **Taxi** between terminals US$0.75. **Car hire** *Budget Rent a Car*, Km 131 at exit to Managua, T612-3041.

Directory **Banks** *Bancentro* on Av Central changes cash and TCs. *Credomatic,* hidden behind the Toyota dealer off the main plaza, cash advances on Visa and MC. Several other banks close to *Bancentro*, and money changers near the cathedral (varying rates). **Communications** Internet *CompuacSer Internet* on Av José Benito Escobar, 1 block north of Parque San José.

Jinotega
Colour map 6, grid C4
Population: 33,000
Altitude: 641 m

A rough road spirals north from Matagalpa rising out of the valley and into one of the most scenic paved highways in the north. The highway to **Jinotega** is lined by highland farms, virgin cloud forest and affords breathtaking views of the

urrounding valleys and mountains. At Km 143 in the of the coolest and freshest
places in the region is *Diparate de Potter*, T612-6228, with beef and chicken dishes
and worth a stop to enjoy the scenery, daily 0900-2100.

Jinotega, a pleasant, friendly town which has famous images in the church; if
closed, ask around. The Somoza jail has been converted into a youth centre. There
is a beautiful hike from behind the cemetery to the cross above the city, 1½ hours'
round trip. As with Matagalpa, excellent coffee grown in the region. Several banks
near the main plaza. Road (18 km) to El Tuma power station; another to Estelí,
through La Concordia, unpaved, picturesque, but there's very little transport from
La Concordia to Estelí. The INTUR **tourist office** is at *Banco Caley Dagnal*, 25 m al
este, T632-4552.

Sleeping and eating **B** *Sollentuna Hem*, del Batazo 5 c al norte, T632-2334, 23 rooms, private bath with hot water, fan, restaurant, garage, best in town. **C** *La Colema*, Banco Mercantil
½ c al este, T632-2017, private bath, TV. **D** *Bolper*, south side of Shell El Carmen, T632-2966,
10 rooms, private bath with hot water, cable TV, simple and friendly. **E** *Cubulcan*, barrio
Centroamérica, frente a taller Luna, T632-2727, 5 rooms with private bath, cheap food, parking. **F** *Hotel y Soda La Tica*, next to bus station, motel-type, beware of overcharging in the
restaurant. **F** *Hotel Tito*, Banco Caley Dagnal 1½ c al este, T632-2607. 7 rooms, some with
shared bath, clean, friendly and helpful owners, very good value, cheap fast food and fresh
fruit drinks. *Jinocuba No 1*, Alcaldía 5 c al norte, T632-2607, *mojito cubano, pollo habanero*,
daily 1200-1200. *El Rincón de Don Pancho*, next to Esso, T632-3413, cheap and good local
food, mariachi music Sat and Sun nights, open Tue-Sun, 1030-2230.

Transport Most destinations will require a change of bus in Matagalpa. **Matagalpa**, every
½ hr, 0500-1800, 1½ hrs, US$0.90. **Managua**, every 1½ hrs, 0400-1700, 3 hrs, US$3. **San
Rafael de Norte**, every 15 mins, 0600-1700, 1 hr, US$0.70.

From Jinotega an 80 km unpaved road goes to the main highway at Condega, 51 km
from the Honduran border (see below). There are still some bridges down as a result
of Hurricane Mitch and a wide river must be crossed just outside Condega, so passage is only possible in good four-wheel drive or for crazed bus drivers. Crime has
been reported in the region and travelling between Estelí passing through Yali and to
Jinotega is not safe at night. If aiming for Condega, the best route is via the highway
from Estelí. This road passes through **San Rafael del Norte** (**F** *Hospedaje Rocío*, just
south of the petrol station, T652-2313, private and shared bath, 3 good set meals at
US$1.50 each, small, homey and very clean, good value.). There are some good
murals in the local church, and a chapel on the hill behind, at Tepeyak, built as a spiritual retreat; very interesting recent history, involved in Sandinista struggle. There's
a bus to Jinotega every 15 minutes, 0600-1800 1 hour, US$0.70. Trucks from
Jinotega market to San Rafael del Norte at 0700, 0800 and 0900, thereafter regular
buses; trucks to Estelí at 0700, US$1, 3 hours.

From Sébaco (see above) a 134-km section to the border at El Espino is through **North of**
sharp hills with steep climbs and descents, but quite well banked and smooth. A rea- **Sébaco**
sonable road leads off the Pan-American Highway 10 km northwest of Sébaco, near
San Isidro (**F** *Camposinos*), to join the Pacific Highway near **León** (110 km). This is
an attractive alternative route to Managua through the Chinandega cotton growing
area, past the spectacular chain of volcanoes running west from Lake Managua, and
through León. (Bus Estelí-San Isidro, every 30 mins, two hours, US$0.50, San
Isidro-León, every 30 mins, three to four hours, US$1.50.)

After San Isidro, the Pan-American Highway goes through **La Trinidad**, an
attractive mountain village set in a canyon (*Cafetería Los Coquitos*, good-value
meals, and *Antojitos del Desierto*, Comunidad Santa Cruz, grilled rabbit, chicken
soup, before reaching Estelí.

Nicaragua

Estelí

Colour map 6, grid C3
Population: 73,000
Altitude: 844 m

This is a rapidly developing departmental capital, heavily damaged during the Revolution of 1978-79. Worth visiting is the **Casa de Cultura**, which has a small exhibition of petroglyphs found in the area and military memorabilia, and the **Galería de los Héroes y Mártires** next door, with mementoes and photographs of those killed defending the Revolution and wonderful, moving paintings on the outside walls. Leave a donation as they are desperate for funds to maintain the museum. Many co-operative and support organizations were developed in the aftermath of the Revolution. The Salvadorean co-operative on Calle Principal south of the Cathedral Plaza is good and has some crafts and a café with posters all over the walls. The Ministry of Health Information Centre, also on the Calle Principal, four blocks from Plaza, is involved with projects to revive traditional medicine and healing and offers advice on a wide range of herbal remedies. Ask at the Reforma Agraria Office (above *Banco de América*) if you wish to see any local farming co-operatives. The Amnlae women's centre has social and educational projects which are interesting to visit and may welcome volunteers.

The INTUR **tourist office** at antiguo Hospital Alejandro Dávila Bolaños, T713-6799, F713-6798, has information on the city and surrounding attractions, all in Spanish.

Sleeping
■ on map opposite
Price codes:
see inside front cover

B *Alameda*, Shell Esquipulas 1 c al este, 1½ c al sur, T713-6292, F713-5219, a/c, private bath with hot water, cable TV, pool, restaurant. **B** *Alpino*, Texaco ½ al este, T713-2828, F713-2368, 18 rooms and 4 apartments, private bath, a/c or fan, cable TV. **B** *Moderno*, T713-2378, F713-4315, east corner of cathedral, 2½ blocks south, hot water, clean, friendly. On the Pan-American Highway is **B** *Panorama No 1*, T713-3147, private bath, hot water, a/c, cable TV, noisy but convenient for buses. **B** *Panorama No 2,* in city centre close to Casa de Cultura, T713-5023, same features as No 1, better rooms upstairs, but much quieter at night with good acess to town centre and restaurants, secure parking. **D** *El Mesón*, Av Bolívar, 1 block north of cathedral and plaza, T713-2655, F713-4029, barlan@ibw.com.ni, with shower, fan, restaurant, TV, changes TCs. Very thin walls but friendly service.

D *Mariela*, behind bus station, clean, safe, washing facilities, very small rooms, parking inside gates, basic **E** *Nicarao*, 1½ blocks south of main plaza, Av Bolívar/C Principal, T713-2490, with shower (cheaper without), restaurant in leafy courtyard with good breakfasts, ideal for sitting around and relaxing, closes at 2200. Recommended. **E** *Barlop*, 5 blocks north of main square, T713-2486, 12 rooms, 6 of which are good, 6 basic, former have showers, good, friendly. **E** *Sacuanjoche*, Enitel 2½ c al sur, T713-2482, 13 rooms private bath, breakfasts, good location. **F** *San Francisco*, on Calle Principal, clean and simple. **F** *Miraflores*, 1 block north of the plaza, restaurant, private bathroom, hot water, TV in restaurant, basic, but OK if others are full. **F** *Rizo*, Ferretería Briones 75 m al sur, T713-2862, 7 rooms with shared bath and fan.

Eating
● on map

China Garden, on main plaza, good food, friendly waiters, but a bit like a hangar. On the same street *El Caporal*, offers simple meat and fish dishes at good prices. *El Mesero*, Cine Estelí 2 c al este, T713-6539, attentive service, giant chicken soup US$3, with salad, rice, tortilla and cheese, best deal in town, daily 1100-2200. *Estanzuela*, Supermercado Las Segovias 75 m al norte, T713-4522, good cheap tacos, *enchiladas, nacatamales,* sandwiches, daily 0730-1830. About 3 blocks north of park on Av Bolívar is *Panadería España*, good but pricey. *Las Brasas*, just off northwest corner of central park, T713-4985, very good Nicaraguan food, try *cerdo asado* (grilled pork), very popular, liveliest place during the week. Open Tue-Sun, 1130-2400. Recommended. *Rincon Pinareño*, across from *Panorama No 2*, T713-4369, smoked chicken, *vaca frita, sandwich cubano*, cheap, good, excellent deserts, daily 1100-2200. *Soda La Confianza*, 1 block south of Parque Central, cheap, good food. *Sopas El Carao*, Almacén Sony 1 c al sur, 1 c al oeste, T713-3678, chicken, crab and iguana soups, grilled meats, very *Nica*, daily 0900-2000.

To Las Praderas Bar & Restaurant, Somoto & Honduras

To Cigar Factory (Segovia Cigars)

Taksi Disco

Río Estelí

Gran Vía Bolívar

1

@ berplace **4**

5 Crafts **2**

Soluciones @ Computarizados

3

China Garden · Parque Central · **Cathedral** · Galería de los Héroes y Mártires · Estelí Cigar SA

BDF

8 Casa de Cultura C Perú

ANIC

Amnlae Women's Centre

7

6

Carretera Panamericana

Salvador Cooperative

Ministry of Health Information Centre

C Principal

Cenac Language School

INTUR Craft

orizontes Spanish School

Parque Infantil

Bus Station North

Gran Vía Bolívar

Buses South

To Managua

N

Not to scale

■ **Sleeping**
1 Barlop
2 El Mesón
3 Hospedaje San Francisco
4 Mariela
5 Miraflor
6 Moderno
7 Nicarao
8 Panorama 2

● **Eating**
1 El Caporal
2 El Mesero
3 Las Brasas
4 Panadería España

Bars

Villa Vieja, ½ block north of Parque Central on Av Bolívar, good atmosphere, live music at weekends. North of town on highway at Km 154 is *Las Praderas*. Decent food, great atmosphere, open-air dance floor, good fun Thu-Sat nights.

Shopping

La Esquina, is a craft shop opposite *Hotel Mesón*. 2 small markets, 1 north, 1 south of Parque Central. Big *Supermercado Económico*, on C Principal.

Transport

Buses There are two terminals in town. The **south terminal**, next to the southern market, serves all routes to the south including destinations that are accessed via Sébaco: **León**, 0625 and 1500, 2 hrs, US$1.50. Alternatively, take any bus going south on the Panamericana and change at **San Isidro**, ½ hr, US$0.50; from here wait by the roadside for buses south to León. **Managua**, every hr, 0445-1515, 2¾ hrs, US$2.25; Express 0545 and 0645, US$3, 2¼ hrs.

North terminal (which has small shops and cheap places to eat) serves northern destinations: **El Sauce**, 0900, 3 hrs, US$1.25. **Jinotega**, every hr, 0730-1530, 2 hrs, US$1.50. **Ocotal**, for border crossing at **Las Manos**, every hr, 0600-1730, 2 hrs, US$1. **Matagalpa**, every hr, 0620-1730, 1½ hrs, US$1.50. **San Juan de Limay**, 0915 and 1215, 4 hrs, US$2.25. **Somoto**, for border crossing at **El Espino**, every ½ hr, 0530-1800, 1½ hrs, US$1.

Directory

Banks Bancentro, 1 street west of C Principal and *Banpro*, Parque Central, Visa cash advance, US$3 commission, efficient. *Agencia de Viajes Tisey* in *Hotel El Mesón* changes TCs at the official rate; many street changers, for cash only, on Av Bolívar. **Communications** Internet: *Computer Soluciones*, on northwest corner of plaza, US$5 per hr. **Language schools** *Cenac* (Centro Nicaragüense de Aprendizaje y Cultura), Apdo 10, Estelí, T/F713-2025, cenac@ibw.com.ni, 500 m north of the north bus terminal, 20 hrs of Spanish classes, living with a family, full board, travelling to countryside, meetings and seminars, opportunities to work on community projects, cost US$120 per week. Also teaches English to Nicaraguans and others and welcomes volunteer tutors. *Cenac* is run by women, but is separate from the *Movimiento de Mujeres*, **Casa Nora Astorga**, Apdo 72, Estelí, which also occupies one of the *Cenac* buildings and offers classes. Also *Casa de Familias*, Costado Noreste del Hospital, 1 block from Carretera, US$100 per week.

Nicaragua

Los Pipitos-Sacuanjoche Escuela de Español, ½ block south of Teatro Nancy, Apdo 80, T713-5511, sacuanjoche@ibw.com.ni, all profits go to disabled children and their families, excursions to local co-operatives, social projects and nature reserve (see below) are part of the course, staying with families, US$120-170 per week, flexible, co-ordinator is German Katharina Pförtner. *Horizonte Nica*, Estelí, INISER 2 c al este, ½ c al norte, T713-4117, 4-week intensive course, Mon-Fri 800-1200 1400-1700, horizont@ibw.com.ni **Tour operators** *Tisey*, next to *Hotel El Mesón* and run by same management. Apdo Postal No 63, T713-2655, F713-4029.

Around Estelí

Miraflor
Altitude: 800-1,500 m
Area: 5,675 ha

Miraflor is a nature reserve 28 km northeast of Estelí in the Department of Jinotega. It has a wide range of flora and fauna (including the quetzal) and the **Laguna de Miraflor**. The Unión de Cooperativas Agropecuarias Héroes y Mártires de Miraflor operates in the reserve, has a tourism project and is in charge of environmental protection. This has been stepped up after the damage caused by Hurricane Mitch, with wooden huts, basic facilities and accomodation at **C-F**, meals, horse hire (US$2 for 2 hours), guided walks, US$20 per person. Contact Porfirio Zepeda (speaks English), T/F713-2971, miraflor@ibw.com.ni, (address: contiguo a Talleres del Mingob, Estelí), or Katharina Pförtner (see *Los Pipitos-Sacuanjoche*, above) and Gene Hinz, T713-4041. Recommended for a visit to see rural life, beautiful area for riding. Travelling to the region at night is not recommended due to reported crimes. Police have been installed at the entrance to the Miraflor reserve.

Puente La Sirena

Near Estelí at Puente La Sirena, 200 m off the road to Condega, or Salto Estanzuela, 5 km south of Estelí, is a 25-m waterfall, with a deep pool at the bottom and, surrounded by trees and flowers (including orchids – only worth it in the rainy season). It is at least 5 km off the Managua road, and a four-wheel drive is recommended. Take the dirt road, starting 500 m south of Estelí on Pan-American Highway, through San Nicolás. Since there are no signs, it is worth hiring a guide.

El Sauce

A very poor but spectacular gravel road just north of Estelí runs to El Sauce where there is a large 16th-century church (burnt down in 1997 and refurbished in 2002), and a place of pilgrimage from all over Central America for the black Christ of Esquipulas who is celebrated in a giant **festival** culminating 15-18 January. (**F** *Hospedaje Diana*, clean, basic. *Viajero*, noisy, fan, friendly, good food. *Restaurant Mi Rancho* and others). After 20 km, an equally rough road branches north to Achuapa. North of **Achuapa**, an unmade road continues through the artesanía town of **San Juan de Limay** (one *hospedaje*) which is famous thoughout Nicaragua for its great soap-stone carvings. The artists are happy to invite you into their house to watch them carve (average sculpture costs $8 or less). Further on, **Pueblo Nuevo** (two basic *hospedajes*) is near an archaeological site. From here the road goes on to join the Pan-American Highway a few kilometres east of Somoto.

Condega
Population: 8,000
Altitude: 561 m

From Estelí, the Pan-American goes north to **Condega**, a quiet town producing agricultural goods, mostly beans and corn. Its name means 'pottery makers' and the Indian village was once known for its ceramics. A lot of pottery is still made here and is some of the most beautiful in the country. *Ducuale Grande Ceramic Cooperative*, opposite the Colegio Ana Velia de Guillén, T752-2374, is an all women co-op that makes a very rustic and attractive red-clay earthenware. Visitors are welcome and there's a small store inside the workshop. *Condega* has a small and well-kept **archaeological museum** on its central plaza, Julio C Salgado, Casa de Cultura de Condega, opposite the Policía Nacional, T752-2221, permanent expositions of discoveries from the region. ■ *Tue-Sun 0800-1200 and 1400-1800.*

Sleeping and eating **E-F** *Pensión Baldovinos*, frente al Parque, T752-2222, 6 rooms, cheaper with shared bath, fan, group discounts. **G** *Hospedaje Framar*, on main plaza next to

Casa de Cultura, T752-2393, 14 very clean and pleasant, cold showers, shared facilities, nice garden, safe, friendly, owner speaks English, excellent value. Safe parking for motorcycles. Recommended. About 6 very cheap eating places including *Comedor Rosa Amelia Peralta*, 1 block north off main plaza, *Linda Vista*, 6 blocks southwest of main plaza.

The road junction at **Yalagüina** (F *Hospedaje*, with restaurant, at intersection), splits leading west to Somoto and El Espino and north to Octoal.

Continuing along the highway you reach Somoto, a pleasant town in a lovely setting. Recent excavations have uncovered unusual pre-Columbian remains which are on display at the **Museo Arqueológico de Somoto**, located inside the mayors office, opposite the old *Banco del Café*. ■ *Mon-Fri 800-1200*. The town is also famous for the best *rosquillas* in Nicaragua – a traditional toasted food, dry but tasty, made of egg, cheese, cornmeal and butter. Try the *viejita* which also has pure cane sugar in the centre. There are many road-side stands en route from Estelí to Somoto.

Somoto
Population: 14,000
Altitude: 700 m

Sleeping and eating D *Hotel Colonial,* just north of main plaza, very smart rooms in family-run hotel. Restaurant. **D-E** *Panamericano*, on main plaza, T722-2355. Quiet, landlord helpful, speaks English. 20 rooms, TV and private bath in newer ones, which are much nicer, great value, unparalleled artisan store with rare crafts of the entire northern region, highly recommended. **E** *El Bambu*, Profamilia 1 c al este, T722-2330. 24 rooms, a/c, private bath, **F** with fan, simple and nice, good restaurant. **F** *Baghal*, Centro de Salud 1½ c al sur, T722-2358, 7 rooms, shared bath, fans, TV, breakfast. Helpful and recommended. **F** *Internacional,* 1 block from central plaza, clean and basic.

El Almendro, parque central ½ c al sur, T722-2152, beef dishes, popular, mid-priced, daily 1100-2200. *La Llanta*, Petronic 100 m al oeste, T722-2291, good pork and chicken dishes, jalapeño steak, daily 1000-2200. *Tepecxomoth*, Farmacia El Pueblo 25 m al este, T722-2667, grilled rabbit and deer, beef ribs, daily 1000-2200.

Nicaraguan immigration 20 km beyond Somoto is El Espino, 5 km from the Honduran border at **La Playa**. The Nicaraguan passport control and customs are in the ruined customs house, 100 m from the Honduran border. The Nicaraguan side is open 0900-1300 and 1400-1700. **Crossing by private vehicle** Motorists leaving Nicaragua should enquire in Somoto if an exit permit has to be obtained there or at El Espino. This also applies to cyclists.

Border with Honduras – El Espino
There's nowhere to stay in El Espino

There's a duty-free shop and a food bar on the Nicaraguan side and several cafés on the Honduran side

Transport Minibuses run between Somoto and the border US$0.40 plus US$0.40 per bag, and at least 2 buses daily Somoto-Estelí 0610 and 1410 which continue to Managua, US$2.15, 5 hrs; Managua-Somoto 0700 and 1400, 3¾ hrs, US$3. On the Honduran side, taxis go between the border and the *Mi Esperanza* bus stops, when totally full, ie 9-10 people, US$1 for foreigners, less for locals. On the Nicaraguan side taxis wait to take you to Somoto, they will probably try to overcharge, pay no more than US$8.

Directory Banks: no money changers on Nicaraguan side but locals will oblige, even with lempiras.

A road turns off right to **Ocotal** (18 km), a clean, cool, whitewashed town on a sandy plain and well worth a visit. It is near the Honduran border, to which a road runs north (bus marked Las Manos), wonderful scenery. From Ciudad Sandino – formerly Jícaro – 50 km east from Ocotal, you can get to **San Albino**, where there are many gold mines and the nearby Río Coco is used to wash the gold.

Ocotal
Colour map 6, grid C3
Population: 27,000
Altitude: 606 m

Sleeping At Ocotal D *Bel Rive*, across from Shell Ramos on Pan-american Highway, T732-2146, cable TV, fan, private bath with hot water, restaurant, good value noisy locale. **D** *Benmoral*, opposite *Enel* at entrance to city off highway, T732-2824, private bath with hot water, fan, cable TV, good restaurant, best value in town, recommended. **E** *Hotel Restaurant Mirador*, opposite bus station, clean, friendly, with bath. **F** *El Portal*, no sign, some new rooms, shared bath, clean, reasonable. Recommended. **F** *Pensión Wilson*, good, friendly.

Nicaragua

F *Hospedaje El Castillo*, basic, quiet, close to bus, candles provided for blackouts. **F** *El Viajero*, Esso 3½ c al oeste, T732-2040, with shared bath and fan, **D** with private bath, cheap set meals.

Eating *La Cabaña*, frente a Enel, T732-2415, soups, seafood and grilled meats, mid-range daily 1000-2300. *La Llamarada del Bosque*, on central park, T732-2643, good-priced buffet for breakfast, lunch and dinner, delivery, Mon-Sat 0630-2000. *La Quinta*, Petronic 200 m Abajo, T732-3420, shrimp, sea bass, filete mignon, late hours until 0400 with live music on Fri.

Transport The bus station is on the highway, 1 km south of town centre, 15-20 mins' walk from Parque Central. **Ciudad Antigua**, 1 daily, 1200, 1 hr, US$1. **Estelí**, leaves the city market every hr, 0600-1700, 2 hrs, US$1. **Las Manos/Honduras Border**, every 30 mins, 0545-1730, 45 mins, US$0.50. **Managua**, every hr, 0510-1515, 4 hrs, US$3.25. **Somoto**, every 45 mins, 0600-1600, 2½ hrs, US$1.50.

Directory Banks: *Banco Banic* (near the plaza) will change TCs. Shell petrol station changes dollars.

Border with Honduras – Las Manos/Ocotal
This is recommended as the best route from Tegucigalpa to Managua

Nicaraguan immigration Open 0800-1200, 1300-1600. All those arriving must fill in an immigration card, present their luggage to the customs authorities and obtain a receipt, and then present these to the immigration authorities with passport and entry fees. Leaving the country, fill out a card, pay the tax and get your passport stamped.

Crossing by private vehicle After completing immigration procedures, go to Tránsito to pay for the vehicle permit, obtain clearance from Revisión, and get your vehicle permit from Customs (*Aduana*). Travellers advise that if it is busy, go first to Customs and get your number in the queue – if necessary shout at the clerks until they give you one. On leaving the country, complete the immigration requirements, then go to Tránsito to have the vehicle checked, and to Customs to have the vehicle stamp in the passport cancelled. Surrender the vehicle permit at Customs and take another form back to Tránsito; this will be stamped, signed and finally handed over at the exit gate.

Transport Bus from 4 blocks north of main plaza in Ocotal, US$0.40, otherwise take a truck or hitch. Beware of taxis: agree the fare before getting in. See above for onward buses.

Directory Money changers operate on both sides offering córdobas at a little better than the street market rate in Nicaragua – if they have them. Rates for cash and TCs are better in Estelí.

León and the West

A third route to Honduras leaves the capital heading through the Pacific lowlands to the Gulf of Fonseca in the shadow of a chain of volcanoes from Momotombo on Lake Managua to Cosigüina overlooking the gulf. This route takes in León, a city deeply involved in Nicaraguan history since colonial times. On the Pacific coast are the beaches at Poneloya and the major port of Corinto. From León, 88 km from Managua, the Pacific Highway continues north to the industrial town of Chinandega. From here, routes lead west to the port of Corinto, north to the Gulf of Fonseca and east to Guasaule and the Honduran border.

The old paved road to León crosses the Sierra de Managua, offering fine views of the lake. It is no longer than the Pacific Highway and is in good condition.

About 60 km down the new road to León lies the village of **La Paz Centro**, with several truck-stop restaurants and accommodation at **F** *Hospedaje El Caminante*, close to the highway, basic, friendly, cheap, and **F** *Hospedaje El Buen Gusto*, friendly, fairly clean, basic. There is a good range of cheap, handmade pottery here, and you can ask to see the potters' ovens and production of bricks. Try the local speciality *quesillo*, mozzarella cheese, onions and cream wrapped in tortilla, served ready-to-eat in plastic bags, available all along the highway. Frequent bus service from Managua, Terminal Lewites, every 30 minutes. From here you can reach **Volcán Momotombo**, which dominates the Managua skyline from the west. It is possible to camp on the lakeside with great views of the volcano.

You need a permit from *Empresa Nacional de Luz y Fuerza* in Managua to climb Momotombo from the south as they have built a geothermal power station on the volcano's slopes. Alternatively, ask police in Puerto Mombotombo for a permit (very difficult to get). We understand no permit is required to climb the volcano from the north but one reader has urged us to remove that information after a gruelling 11-hour climb which, at times got 'extremely dangerous'.

At the foot of the volcano lies León Viejo, destroyed by earthquake and volcanic eruption on 31 December 1609 and now being excavated. It was here that the brutal first Spanish governor of Nicaragua Pedrarias and his wife were buried in La Merced church next to Francisco Hernández de Córdoba, the country's founder who had been beheaded under order of Pedrarias. Archaeological excavations have revealed the **cathedral**, the **Convento de la Merced**, the **Casa del Gobernador**, as well as the bodies of Cordoba and Pedrarias, which have been placed in a special tomb in the the Plaza Mayor. The ruins themselves are little more than low walls and probably only of serious interest to archaeologists, but you can see the ground plan of the old Spanish town. ■ *US$2 entrance fee includes Spanish-speaking guide. Getting there: bus (0830) from Managua to La Paz Centro, then another to León Viejo. Walk 1 km to the ruins. Return bus at 1400.*

León Viejo

León

León has a colonial charm unmatched elsewhere in Nicaragua, except perhaps by Granada. It has narrow streets, red-tile roofs, low adobe houses and time-worn buildings everywhere. Founded by Hernández de Córdoba in 1524 at León Viejo, 32 km from its present site (see above), it was moved here after the devastating earthquake of 1609. The existing city was founded in 1610. In recent years, economic factors have taken precedence over the cleaning up of old buildings, but the work is going ahead slowly.

Colour map 6, grid C3 Population: 184,792 Altitude: 50 m

Nicaragua

Ins and outs

Regular buses to León run from Managua and Chinandega, with frequent routes from Estelí and Matagalpa. International buses will drop you off, if asked, at the entrance to town. The bus terminal is at the northeastern end of town, a-20 minute walk, or short taxi journey from the centre.

Getting there

Most attractions are within a few blocks of the centre so choosing a fairly central hotel makes it an easy city to explore on foot. Local buses will take you to the terminal and a network of pick-up trucks work as cheap taxis. If you're getting a little tired just ask a passing driver or in a shop and the local knowledge will get you there.

Getting around

The tourist office on Parque Central, next to restaurant *El Sesteo*, is the most central. It has brochures in Spanish and helpful staff. Guides can be arranged but there's little information available. *INTUR*, Parque Rubén Darío 2½ c al norte, T311-3682, maps for sale, reference books, friendly staff.

Tourist office

Background

As the capital, León was the dominant force in Nicaragua until Managua took control in 1852. Today, it is still thought of as the 'intellectual' capital, with a university (Universidades Nacionales Autónomas de Nicaragua, known as UNAN), founded 1804, religious colleges, the largest cathedral in Central America, and several colonial churches. It is said that Managua became the capital, although at the time it was only an Indian settlement, because it was half-way between violently Liberal León and equally violently Conservative Granada.

Sights

Cathedral The Basílica de la Asunción, begun in 1746 and not completed for 100 years, is an enormous building. Legend has it that the plans for the cathedrals of Lima (Peru) and León were switched by mistake. It has a famous shrine, 145 cm high, covered by white topazes from India given by Philip II of Spain – too bad it is kept in a safe in the vestry, to which the bishop holds the key. The cathedral also houses a very fine ivory Christ, the consecrated Altar of Sacrifices and the Choir of Córdoba, the great Christ of

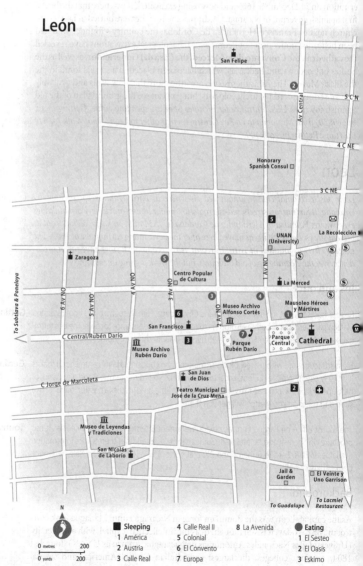

León

Sleeping ■
1 América
2 Austria
3 Calle Real

4 Calle Real II
5 Colonial
6 El Convento
7 Europa

8 La Avenida

Eating ●
1 El Sesteo
2 El Oasis
3 Eskimo

squipulas – a colonial work in bronze with a cross of very fine silver – and statues of he 12 Apostles. At the foot of one of these statues is the tomb of Rubén Darío, the 9th-century Nicaraguan poet, and one of the greatest in Latin America, guarded by a orrowful lion. All the entrances to the cathedral are guarded by lions. The old Plaza de armas, in front of the cathedral, is now **Parque Jérez**, but is usually referred to as Parque Central; it contains a statue of General Jérez, a mid-19th century Liberal leader.

.eón has the finest colonial churches in Nicaragua, more than 12 in all, and they are the ity's most significant attraction. **La Recolección**, with a beautiful baroque Mexican açade, built in 1786, has a neoclassical interior with mahogany woodwork. **La Merced**, which was built in 1615 and burned by pirates in 1685, is notable for its seven different altars. It is one of the oldest churches in León and has fine woodwork inside and a newly restored exterior (1999). **San Felipe** was built at the end of the 16th century for the religious services of the black and mulatto population of the city. It was rebuilt in the 18th century in a manner true to its original form, a mixture of baroque and neoclassical. During the same period **El Calvario** was constructed, and is notable for its neoclassical façade attributed to the growing French influence in Spain at the time. The Convent and Church of **San Francisco**, founded in 1639, is the oldest convent with a church in León. It still has two plateresque altars from Spain and its original pillars. In 1830, after the expulsion of the Franciscans from Nicaragua, it was used by various civic organizations and is now a gallery. ■ *US$1.50*. **Iglesia de San Nicolás de Laborío**, founded in 1618 for the local Indian population, is the most modest of the León churches, constructed of wood and tiles over adobe walls with an unostentatious façade and a simple altar, 10 m high. The celebration for San Nicolás is 10 September. **Iglesia de Nuestra Señora Pilar de Zaragoza** was built from 1884-1934 and has two unusual octagonal turrets and arched doorway with tower above. There is a pleasant walk south across the bridge, past the church of Guadalupe, to the cemetery.

Other churches

To see inside or attend Mass, plan to visit in the morning usually from 0700-0900, or in the afternoon from 1600-1800

The house of poet Rubén Darío, the famous 'Four Corners' in Calle Rubén Darío, is now the Museo-Archivo Rubén Darío. It has an interesting collection of personal possessions, photographs, portraits and a library with a wide range of books of poetry in Spanish, English and French. Darío died in 1916 in another house in the northwest sector (marked with a plaque). Alfonso Cortés – another of Nicaragua's finest poets who wrote a famous poem while

Museo-Archivo Rubén Darío

Nicaragua

4 Hong Kong
5 La Casa Vieja
6 Rinconcito Flor de Sacuanjoche

● **Bars & clubs**
7 Ruinas

chained to the bars in front of Rubén's old bed – lived in Darío's house until hi death in 1969, leaving behind the museum-archive. ■ *Tue-Sat 0900-1200 1400-1700, Sun 0900-1200, entry and guided tour free but donations accepted.*

Two blocks west of La Merced church is the **Centro Popular de la Cultura** which has frequent exhibitions and events, and is the only place in León to see live folk concerts (schedule on the front door).

Subtiava The western end of the city is the oldest, and here is the oldest of all the churches, the parish church of **San Juan Bautista** in Subtiava (1530). Local literature dates the current district at 1681 and the church at 1700. Las Casas, the Apostle of the Indies, preached here on several occasions. It has a fine façade, the best colonial altar in the country and an interesting representation of *El Sol* (the sun), carved in wood in mid-nave on the ceiling. The church has been beautifully reconstructed. The roo was rebuilt under the supervision of the 'Comisión 500 Años'. Near the church is a small **Comunidad Indígena Subtiava**, with an anthropological and historical museum. ■ *US$1.* The ruins of the nearby parish churches of Vera Cruz and Santiago are both crumbling and unapproachable. Also in the suburb of Subtiava is the **Casa de Cultura** with several interesting murals adorning the walls. Inside there are a couple of cafés, information about prominent Nicaraguan cultural figures and the offer of a free history and cultural lesson on Thursdays (1500) in basic Spanish.

Descriptions of León's fight against the Somoza régime can be found in 'Fire from the Mountain: The Making of a Sandinista', by Omar Cabezas

During the **1978-79 Revolution**, León was the centre of heavy fighting. There are many monuments from that time in the city. A plaque marks the spot in the centre of the city where the first President Somoza was assassinated in 1956 by poet Rigoberto López Pérez.

Visitors can see **El Fortín**, the ruined last stronghold of Somoza's national guard. A commemorative march goes there each July. From the cathedral, go west about 10 blocks, then south; it's best in early morning for the great views of town and several volcanoes. It is also home to the León city garbage dump, ask the men in hammocks for permission to enter the old fort. **El Veinte Uno**, the national guard's 21st garrison, was also ruined, and the scene of an important battle in April 1979; the jail around the corner (three blocks south of cathedral) has been converted into a garden with a statue to *El Combatiente Desconocido* (the unknown warrior) . A statue of **Luisa Amanda Espinoza**, in Barrio San Felipe, seven to eight blocks north of the market behind the cathedral, remembers the first woman member of the FSLN to die (in 1970). The women's organization AMNLAE is named after Espinoza.

Across the street from the north side of the cathedral is an interesting mural covering the history from pre-Columbian times to the Sandinista Revolution, completed in 1990. (Sadly it seems many of the murals are being painted over as the images of the Revolution are gradually removed and replaced.) It surrounds a commemorative park, the **Mausoleo Héroes y Mártires**. There is also the **Galería Héroes y Mártires** at Calle 1 NO, between Avenidas 1 and 2, which sells handicrafts and houses the twinning office with New Haven (US).

Essentials

Sleeping
■ *on map, page 968*
Price codes: see inside front cover

AL *Hotel El Convento*, connected to San Francisco church, T311-7053, F311-7222, new, a/c, hot water in private bath, cable TV, beautiful colonial design decorated by antiques with a lovely interior garden, moderate priced restaurant, Nicaragua's most charming colonial hotel and Leon's best. **B** *Austria*, Costado Oeste de la Catedral 1 c al sur, ½ abajo, T311-1206, central, best and often fully booked, hot water, a/c, cable TV, clean, secure parking, often full, breakfast US$3. Recommended. **B** *Colonial*, 50 m north of UNAN, 2½ blocks north of Parque Central, T311-2279, F311-3125, pleasant, fine old building and patio but small rooms and in need of refurbishment, a/c, **C** with fan, bath (**D** without), good views from upstairs, front rooms with balcony can be noisy from disco opposite at weekends, restaurant (breakfast US$3, other meals US$4). **B** *Europa*, 3 C NE, 4 Av, 2 blocks south of railway station, T311-6040, F311-2577, with

(sidebar, rotated) Nicaragua

bath and a/c, **D** with fan, cold water, brusque service, comfortable patios with bar and shade, coffee available, restaurant expensive, limited parking inside, guard will watch vehicles parked on street. **B** *Grand Hotel*, from bus terminal ½ block south, T311-1327, with bath, a/c, clean, safe parking, breakfast US$4, other meals US$ 5, book ahead.

D *América*, Av Santiago Argüello, 2 blocks east of cathedral, with bath and fan, clean, good value, a bit run down, friendly, nice garden, breakfast US$2, other meals US$3, cold drinks, convenient location, secure garage nearby. **D** *Avenida*, near Mercado San Juan, T311-2068, **F** without bath, family run, fan, cable TV, good food US$1-2, friendly, laundry facilities, popular. **D** *La Casona Colonial*, Parque San Juan ½ c abajo, T311-3178, private bath, fan, internet access. **D** *Primavera*, on exit road to Chinandega, T311-4216, with bath and a/c, **E** with fan, helpful and friendly, secure parking, breakfast US$1.50, other meals US$3. **E** *California*, with bath, across from the bus station and new market, friendly family run, with nice patio, purified water and TV. Recommended. **E** *La Cabaña*, Ermita de Dolores 1 c al sur, ½ c al este, T311-0467, clean simple rooms with shared bath and fan. **E** *Vía Vía*, del Servicio Agrícola Gurdián 75 m al sur, T311-6142, cheap food, dance and Spanish classes. **F** per person *Hotelito Calle Real*, C Rubén Darío opposite San Francisco, T311-1120, with bath and fan, has *comedor*. **F** per person *Hotelito Calle Real II*, Av 2 SE, ½ block north of C Rubén Darío, T311-2510, is a response to the shortage of beds, basic rooms without fan and shared bathroom. **F** per person *La Posada del Doctor*, 20 m from Parque San Juan, T311-4343, F311-5986, shared bath, fan, clean, some rooms with bunks, good value, very nice. **F** *Yenín*, Av Cdte Pedro Aráuz, pleasant, garden, good value. **F** *Telica*, Proquinsa 2 ½ c al norte, T311-5853 , shared bath, basic, cheap food.

Casa Popular de Cultura, 1 block north of plaza central, 2½ blocks west, sandwiches and hamburgers, nice atmosphere, find out what's going on. *Central*, C 4 Norte, good *comida corriente*. *El Barcito*, northwest of Parque Central, popular, soft drinks, milk shakes, slow service. *El Oasis*, C 5 and Av Central, good value, limited menu, popular. *El Rincón Azul*, C Central Rubén Darío, about 1½ blocks west of Parque Jérez, an excellent bar, very cheap, also a local art gallery, open 1500-2400. Recommended. *El Sesteo*, next to cathedral, on Parque Central, renovated, mid-priced, excellent food and *the* place for watching the world go by. Across the street from the beautifully restored Teatro Municipal is *El Taquezal*, T311-7282, pleasant atmosphere, classic León decor, mid-priced dishes of shrimp, calamari, pastas, very good, Mon -Sat 1200-2300. *Eskimo* good ice-cream parlour, C Rubén Darío at the back of San Francisco. *Hong Kong* Chinese restaurant, 1 C NO, ½ block north of Parque, T311-6572, popular with locals, mixed reports. *La Casa Vieja*, 1½ blocks north of San Francisco church, pleasant bar, good quality snacks, good value. Highly recommended. *Lacmiel*, 5 blocks south of cathedral, good food, live music, open air. Recommended. *Metrosoda*, UNAN León 75 m al sur, T311-5112, cheap hamburgers, sandwiches, salads, daily 0800-2100. *Payitas*, across from parque La Merced, T311-5857, jalapeño steak, hamburgers, sandwiches, daily 1000-1400. *Rinconcito Flor de Sacuanjoche*, northeast corner of University UNAN-León, 75 m abajo, T311-1121, best vegetarian meals, meat dishes, lunch and breakfast, good, daily 0900-2300. *Ruinas*, 1 block west of *Enitel* (*Telcor*) on Rubén Darío, friendly, live music at weekends. *White House Pizza* has a couple of branches close to the centre.

  In Subtiava is *Caperas*, good Nicaraguan food, inexpensive. *Los Pescaditos*, Iglesia de Subtiava 1 c al sur, 1 c al oeste, near Subtiava church, excellent fish at reasonable prices, daily 1200-2230. Recommended. On the Carretera Circunvalación, *Caña Brava*, the best food in town, try their *pollo deshuesado* (boneless chicken). *Montezerino*, Km 91 on the bypass, T311-2638, outdoor, good meat and fish, pleasant.

Eating
● *on map, page 968*

Few restaurants have signs so you'll have to be standing outside the door before you realize you're there. Many restaurants are closed all day Sunday

Bars *Bar El Alamo*, 1 block north of Plaza, good atmosphere, cheap draught beer. *Don Señor*, across from parque La Merced, T311-1212, karaoke on Wed and Fri good place to see Nicaraguans cut loose, open Wed-Sun after 2000. Just north of the Teatro Municipal is *Rincón Azul*, T311-4779, very trendy and crowded, beautiful spot and people, appetizers, beer and rum, Mon-Fri 1500-2400, Sat and Sun until 0200. **Cinema** Next to *La Unión* supermarket, 1 block north and 1 block east of *El Sesteo* in Plaza Siglo Nuevo, T311-7080/ 83. Films in English with Spanish subtitles. **Nightclubs** Like all Nicaraguans, the Leoneses love to

Entertainment

Nicaragua

dance; all dancing is to taped music played at full volume. *Discoteca Dilectus*, at south entrance to city, upmarket crowd, a/c, parking, US$5 entrance, drinks and food expensive, Wed-Sun. *Discoteca Nueva Túnel*, at exit to Carretera a Chinandega, US$2 cover. *Video Luna*, across the street from *Hotel Colonial*, entrance US$1, Sat and Sun only. *Las Ruinas*, next to Parque Rubén Darío, T311-4767, dancing in the bombed-out ruins of the 1979 Revolution, Thu-Sun from 1900. Also next to La Merced park is a small disco upstairs, in a brown wooden house, unsigned and unnamed, but very popular.

Festivals   The *Holy Week* ceremonies are outstanding, as are the festivities *Día de la Concepción* on **7 Dec**; much singing, dancing, fireworks and festive crowds. Throughout **Dec**, *Santa Lucía* is celebrated in Subtiava; there are processions, religious and cultural events, sports and *Pepe Cabezón* (a giant head on legs) accompanies *La Gigantona* (an impossibly tall princess) through the city. **20 Jun**, *Liberation by Sandinistas*, 24 Sep; 1 Nov, *All Saints' Day*.

Shopping   The old market (dirty) is near the centre, behind the cathedral, and the new market is at the bus terminal, 5-6 blocks east of the old railway station, which itself is now Mercado San Juan, not touristy, good local atmosphere. Good supermarket, *La Unión*, on C 1 Norte, 1 block north of central market. **Bookshops**   *Libro Centro Don Quijote*, next to *Hotelito Calle Real*, has secondhand books, a few in English.

Transport   **Local**   Small trucks ferry people between the bus terminal and town on circuitous routes for US$0.25. Taxis around town charge US$0.40 in the day and US$0.80 at night.
    Bus The bus terminal is in the far eastern part of town, a long walk or short taxi ride from the centre. **El Guasaule**, 0500, 2½ hrs, US$2. **El Sauce**, every hour, 0800-1600, 2½ hrs, US$1.50. **Chichigalpa**, every 11 mins, 0400-1800, 1 hr, US$0.75. **Chinandega**, every 11 mins, 0500-1800, 1 hr 45 mins, US$1. **Corinto**, every 30 mins, 0500-1800, 2 hrs, US$1. **Estelí**, 0500 and 1500, 3 hrs, US$2.25. **Matagalpa**, 0500 and 1500, 3 hrs, US$2.25. **Managua**, every 30 mins, 0425-2000, 1½ hrs, US$1.50. **Salinas Grandes**, 0600 and 1200, 1½ hr, US$0.40. **San Isidro**, every 30 mins, 0420-1730, 2½ hrs, US$1.50.

Directory   **Banks** Most of the country's banks are represented in the blocks north of the cathedral. *Bancentro*, C 1 NE between Central y 1 E will change dollars and all TCs, 3% commission. *Banpro* changes dollars cash. Cash advances from *Credomatic* ½ block to the west on C Central. *Interbank* is behind *El Sesteo*.

León & Los Maribios volcanic chain

Communications Internet: *León Net*, Iglesia La Recolección 75 m arriba, T311-5515, internet rental, international calls, typing service, daily 800-2000. *Puerto Café*, corner opposite UNAN, T311-0548, internet, typing service, 0900-2300, Mon-Sat, 0800-1200, Sun. **Post office:** opposite the Recolección church. **Telephone:** *Enitel* (*Telcor*), Parque Central, opposite cathedral. International calls possible. Small *Enitel* office on Darío, on road to Subtiava, about 10 blocks from main plaza, open till 2200, and another in the bus terminal. **Language classes** *Nicaragua Spanish School León*, Iglesia La Merced, 1½ c abajo, T311-2116, escleon@ibw.com.ni, regular classes and private tutors, with cultural interaction and trips to beach, theatre, etc. *Hotel Vía Vía*, Servicio Agrícola Gurdián 75 m al sur, T311-6142, tutored study with flexible hours. US$5 per hr, US$400 per month.

Poneloya & Las Peñitas

A bumpy road from León heads west to Poneloya and Las Peñitas, a couple of relaxed and very friendly beach communities 19 km from León. Both contain long stretches of beautiful sandy beaches and a mixture of humble houses and rich vacation homes. Most of the coast has big waves and strong currents (swim here with great caution – there are drownings every year). The south end of Las Peñitas and Puerto Mántica, at the north end of Poneloya, are the best for swimming, with good surfing in between, but no boards available to rent. The sun is very strong here and there's not much shade. During the week you will have the beaches to yourself, but at weekends young people and families come from León and in Semana Santa it's sardine time. It is possible to rent quadbikes from the *pulpería* at the intersection of the road to Las Peñitas and Poneloya, called *Licorería Estela de los Mares* (US$10 per hour, you must also show driving licence, sign a release form and pay a US$10 deposit).

Sleeping and eating C *Suyapa Beach Hotel*, in Las Peñitas, T088-5834, F311-6257 (León), best in region, a/c, **D** with fan, ask for rooms with ocean view and nice breeze upstairs, all with private bath, very clean, swimming pool in season and outdoor beach shower, group discounts, restaurant is good, try *pescado a la suyapa*, fresh snapper in a very nice tomato, pepper and onion sauce, excellent, mid-range with great view. Recommended. C *La Montaña*, Playa Las Peñitas, T317-372, 4 rooms with a/c and private bath or **D** with fan and shared bath, restaurant. **D** *Posada de Poneloya*, opposite Lacayo, T311-4612, cabinas with bath, a/c or fan, car park. **E** *Lacayo*, great location, dusty rooms, restaurant has good *repochetas*, basic, meals, bats in the roof and beware of insects at night, bring coils. *Restaurante Cáceres*, good *comida corriente*. *La Peña del Tigre*, good restaurant down the road, huge portions (great *repochetas*), friendly, open air, nice views – it is near a tall rock on the beach where bathing is dangerous and prohibited.

Transport Take **bus** 101 from León's Terminal Interurbana, or the central market west to the bus stop near Subtiava church on C Rubén Darío, then walk 3 mins to Terminal Poneloya outside the market, from where a small bus leaves every hr or so for Las Peñitas (US$0.5) at the south end of Poneloya beach. **Taxi** from León costs around US$6.

San Jacinto

A fast camera shutter will catch mud flying through the air

On the road to Estelí, 12 km north of the intersection with the Chinandega-León road, is **San Jacinto**. About 200 m to the west of the road is a field of steaming, bubbling mud holes, which is worth visiting. These *hervideros* are, in fact, an exposed vein of the active Volcán Telica seen in the distance, not of the closer San Jacinto Volcano – also called Santa Clara. You should approach carefully, the ground may give and scald your legs; follow other footmarks for safety, avoiding walking on the crystallized white sulphur and listen for hissing. Or, safer still, hire one of the local children as a guide (US$2-3 tip) to show you where it is safe to walk. It is normal to be surrounded by children who will ask for money; buying a small clay pre-Columbian imitation from their mothers may be a better option for supporting the children.

Chinandega
Colour map 6, grid C3
Population: 137,940
Altitude: 70 m

About 40 km beyond León, Chinandega is one of the hottest and driest towns in Nicaragua. Agriculturally, this is one of the richest areas in Central America producing bananas, peanuts, sugar cane and shrimps. There's a good market by the bus terminal and you can hire horse-drawn cabs. Local **fiesta**: 26 July.

The **tourist office**, main entrance Reparto Los Angeles, T341-2040, has a very helpful representative who speaks English and Italian.

Sleeping A *Los Volcanes*, Km 129 Carretera a Chinandega, at entrance to city, T341-1000, F341-1010, hotelosvolcanes@tec.com.ni, hot water, a/c, cable TV, telephone, bar, restaurant, clean, good service. Recommended. **C-D** *Glomar*, Mercado Central 1 c al sur, T341-2562, **C** with private bath, bar and restaurant, may be closed Sun evening, owner will change dollars, but mistrusts foreigners, his son is friendly, good food, cold beer.

E *Aniram*, Shell 1½ c al este, T341-4519, private bath, cable TV, fan or a/c, cheap meals, parking, good value. **E** *California*, Esso El Calvario 1 c al este, 1½ c al sur, T341-0936, private bath, a/c or fan, cable TV, homey and friendly. **E** *Casa Granada*, antiguo *Interbank* ½ c al oeste, T341-0325, private bath with fan and cable TV, **C** with a/c, fax and laundery service, restaurant, excursions to San Cristóbal volcano. **F** *Chinandega*, basic, fan, shared bath, decent. **F** *Pensión Cortés*, south of Parque Central, basic.

Eating *Caprax Pizza*, 1 block east of Parque Central. *Central Palace*, 1½ blocks east of Parque Central. *Chiles Café*, Shell Central 1½ c al norte, T341-0520, good tortilla soup, Mexican fare, daily 1200-2300. *Corona de Oro*, Iglesia San Antonio 1½ c al este, T341-2539, curry chicken, shrimp skewers. *El Mondongazo*, south side of Colegio San Luis, T341-4255, traditional Nicaraguan foods, sopa mondongo (tripe soup), beef, chicken and meatball soup. *El Refugio*, Esso El Calvario ½ c al sur, T341-0834, beef specialities, try the breaded tongue. *Hungaro*, COPEPACH ½ c arriba, T341-3824, far from centre, Hungarian-style sweetbreads, beef fillet in paprika sauce, friendly staff, daily 1100-2300. *Italian Pizza*, Iglesia San Antonio 175 m al este, good. *Parador*, Texaco Los Encuentros 300 m al norte, T341-0885, cheap sandwiches, hamburgers and fruit drinks, daily 1100-2300.

Entertainment Try *Monserrat*, main entrance Reparto Monserrat 2 c al este, T341-3465, has a big dance floor, appetizers, rum and cold beer, dance music, Thu-Sun after 2000.

Transport Bus: Most buses leave from the new market at southeast edge of town. **Corinto**, every 20 mins, 0600-2100, 30 mins, US$0.30. **Guasaule**, every 2 hrs, 0600-1600, 2 hrs, US$2. **León**, every 11 mins, 0600-1700, 1¾ hr, US$1. **Managua**, every 30 mins, 0600-1600, 3 hrs, US$2.25. **Somotillo**, every 3 hrs, 0900-1500, 2 hrs, US$2.

Buses for **Potosí**, **El Viejo** and **Puerto Morazán** leave from the Mercadito at northwest of town. A local bus connects Terminal, Mercado and Mercadito.

Directory Communications Post office and **telephone**: in *Enitel* building opposite *Caprax Pizza*. **Consular offices** *Costa Rica*, Chinandega, *Banpro* 20 m al norte, T341-1584, 0800-1200 and 1300-1530, Mon-Fri. *Honduras*, Chinandega, frente a *Enitel*, T341-0949, 0830-1630, Mon-Fri. *El Salvador*, Chinandega, corner opposite La Curacao, Tel: 341-2049, 0800-1400, Mon-Fri.

Chichigalpa

Not far away, near Chichigalpa, is Ingenio San Antonio, the largest sugar mill in Nicaragua, with a railway between the town and the mill (five trains a day each way May-November, passengers taken, US$0.10; also bus US$0.30). While there are no official tours of the installations, you can apply at Gate (*Portón*) 14 to be shown around. On the edge of Chichigalpa itself is the **Flor de Caña** distillery, maker of what many believe to be the finest rum in the world, aged up to 21 years and made in over 15 flavours. On leaving you will recognize the picture on the bottle labels, a palm-shaded railway leading towards Chichigalpa with volcanoes in the background.

Corinto
Colour map 6, grid C3
Population: 17,414
Altitude: 3 m

Twenty-one kilometres from Chinandega, Corinto is the main port and the only one at which vessels of any considerable size can berth. About 60% of the country's commerce passes through here. The town itself is on a sandy island, Punto Icaco, connected with the mainland by long railway and road bridges. There are beautiful old wooden buildings with verandas, especially by the port. (Entry to the port is barred to all except those with a permit.)

On the Corinto-Chinandega road is Paseo Cavallo beach (*Restaurante Buen Vecino*). The sea is treacherous here and people drown every year. There are no facilities in Corinto's barrier islands, but they are beautiful with crashing surf on one side, calm and warm swimming water on the other. The journey can be negotiated with any fisherman, but there are two who are particularly trustworthy and reliable, named Isidro and Lester. They can be contacted in advance through their aunt, Guadalupe Hernández, who lives next to the *Alcoholics Anonymous* building in Corinto, T342-2490. Tell her you want to visit Castañones, US$10 each way, pre-arrange departure and pick-up times. Bring anything you might need with you to the island. A *panga* can be rented for the whole day for US$40 so you can explore the numerous islands and mangroves. Lots of birdlife but also lots of sandflies, bring repellent (see Bay Islands section, Honduras, for suggestions).

Sleeping and eating D *Central*, in front of Port Buildings, clean, a/c. **F** *Hospedaje Luvy*, fan, dirty bathrooms, 2 blocks from plaza. *El Imperial*, evenings only, *Meléndez*, on main plaza, good but pricey; cheapest meals in *market*, but not recommended.

North of Chinandega

The road north to Puerto Morazán passes through the village of **El Viejo** (US$0.20 by bus from Chinandega, 5 km) where there is an old church, La Basílica del Viejo, famous throughout the country for its celebration called *La Lavada de la Plata*, which consists of devotees washing all silver parts of the altar. The Basílica has la Virgen del Hato, which leaves the altar every December in a major pilgrimage to visit Corinto, Chinandega, León and Managua. **Eating**: *Tezoatega*, Basílica 1½ c al norte, T344-2436, chicken and beef dishes, very good, cheap, daily 1200-2300.

Puerto Morazán, 26 km from Chinandega (eight buses a day, 1½ hours, US$0.40, one hotel) is a poor, muddy village with reed huts on a navigable river running into the Gulf of Fonseca. From Chinandega there are four buses a day to **Potosí** (at least three hours, US$1.20); *Comedor Adela*, 24-hour service, cheap. You can sling your hammock at the *comedor* 150 m past immigration for US$0.50. Ask Héctor for permission to stay in the fishing co-operative. The fishermen are very friendly. In the centre of the village there are warm thermal springs in which people relax each afternoon. There are also pleasant black-sand beaches; the sea, although the colour of coffee, is clean. The passenger ferry from Potosí to La Unión (El Salvador) has been suspended, but there is an ad hoc open boat from La Unión. Ask around.

It is a four-hour hike to the cone of **Volcán Cosigüina**. The path is overgrown and very difficult to follow, so you may need a guide. There is plenty of wildlife in the area, including poisonous snakes, so take a machete. On 23 January 1835, one of the biggest eruptions in history blew off most of the cone, reducing it from 3,000 m to its present height of 800 m, throwing ash as far as Colombia. From the cone there are beautiful views of the Golfo de Fonseca shared by Nicaragua, Honduras and El Salvador. The volcano and the surrounding dry tropical forest are a Reserva Natural, administered by the Ministry of the Environment and Natural Resources in Managua.

Nicaragua

Jiquilillo beach, 42 km from Chinandega, is reached by a mostly paved road branching off the El Viejo-Potosí road. Lying on a long peninsula, there are a few lodgings and small restaurants.

From Chinandega a rough paved road goes to the Honduran border on the **Río Guasaule** near **Somotillo** (E *Las Vegas*, small rooms, fan, not too clean, restaurant; *Hospedaje/Bar El Panamericano*), where the road improves heading to Choluteca, Honduras. Bus from Chinandega, 1¾ hours, US$1.25.

Most of the bridges on the Highway in León and Chinandega departments and all between Chinandega and the border, and the border bridge itself, were washed away by Hurricane Mitch. All roads are now repaired in this region from the hurricane.

Border with Honduras – Guasaule

Nicaraguan immigration The distance between the border posts is 500 m. There are no *colectivos*, so you must walk, take one of the tricycles with parasol or hitch a lift. Vehicles drive through the water. Foot passengers are ferried across the river in small boats if the bridge is down. International buses use this crossing. The procedure when leaving Nicaragua (on *Ticabus*, at least) is that an official takes all passports from passengers as soon as the bus leaves Chinandega and he fills out all the immigration forms and collects the exit tax. At the border, the official with the passports and documents disappears and passengers alight from the bus to await his return and be called by name to re-embark. This takes about 1 hr. Once back on the bus, a Honduran official takes your passport and you go through Honduran immigration procedures.

Transport **Buses** run every 30 mins from the border to Chinandega, US$0.80. Express bus to Managua, Mercado Lewites terminal at 0500 and 1545, 3½ hrs, US$2.85 via Somotillo and León. From Managua to Río Guasaule at 1810.

Directory Money changers offer the same rates for córdobas to lempiras as on the Honduran side. *Banco de Crédito Centroamericano*, beside immigration, is recommendee, good rates, no commission, and will accept photocopy of passport if yours is being checked by immigration.

Managua to Granada and Lake Nicaragua

The journey from Lago de Managua to Lago de Nicaragua passes several volcanoes including Volcán Santiago whose crater constantly spews out tonnes of sulphurous gases over Parque Nacional Volcán Masaya. Nearby Masaya town is a centre for handicrafts in a tobacco-growing zone. The blasted remains of Mombacho are near the historical city of Granada. The perfect cone of Concepción, on Isla de Ometepe, rises out of the waters of Lago de Nicaragua which has a number of other islands that can be visited by boat.

Parque Nacional Volcán Masaya
Take drink, a hat and hiking boots if planning much walking. If walking to the summit, leave early as there is little shade along the road

The dramatic Santiago crater of Masaya Volcano is a spectacular sight and definitely worth visiting. The entrance to Parque Nacional Volcán Masaya is at Km 23 on the road from Managua. Two volcanoes are within the perimeter of the park. Volcán Nindirí last erupted in 1670. The more active Volcán Masaya burst forth in 1772 and again in 1852, forming the Santiago crater between the two peaks; this in turn erupted in 1932, 1946, 1959 and 1965 before collapsing in 1985, and the resulting pall of sulphurous smoke made the soil uncultivable in a broad belt to the Pacific. Although research into the activity of Volcán Masaya is limited, gaseous emissions range from 500 to 3,000 tonnes a day, making the volcano one of the largest natural polluters in the world. Ninety years ago German engineers Schomberg and

Scharfenberg, attempting to produce sulphuric acid from the volcano's emissions, drilled into an unexpected 400 m-wide lava tube, resulting in explosions and landslides. Remains of these old installations can still be seen; consult the *guardabosques* (park rangers) for information.

Masaya Volcano was called **Popogatepe** or 'mountain that burns' by the indigenous Chorotega people who believed that eruptions were a sign of anger from the goddess of fire, Chacitutique. To appease her they made sacrifices to the lava pit, which often included children and young women. In the 16th century Father Francisco de Bobadilla planted a cross on the summit of Masaya to exorcize the 'Boca del Infierno' (Mouth of Hell); the cross visible today commemorates the event. Many Spanish chroniclers visited the crater, including Oviedo in 1529 and Blas de Castillo in 1538, who actually descended into the crater in search of gold!

Created in 1979, Volcán Masaya is the country's oldest national park. It covers an area of 54 sq km, contains 20 km of trails leading to and around two volcanoes rising to around 400 m, five craters and one lake. The *Centro de Interpretación Ambiental* (visitors' centre) is 1½ km in from the entrance. Shortly after is a beautiful area with toilets, picnic facilities and barbecues (*asadores*) for the use of visitors. Camping is possible here but no facilities after the visitors' centre closes. From here a short path leads up to Cerro El Comalito, with good views of Mombacho, the lakes and the extraordinary volcanic landscapes of the park; longer trails continue to Lake Masaya and the San Fernando crater. Because of the potential danger involved, visits to the fumaroles at Comalito require special authorization from rangers, who warn that they may have to place this area off-limits if visitors are injured touching or throwing the surrounding rocks. The paved road (20-25 kph speed limit) continues south across the 1670 lava flow to the twin crests of Masaya and Nindirí, which actually consist of five craters (Santiago – still emitting sulphurous gases, San Fernando, San Juan, Nindirí and San Pedro). There is parking and a recreation area here. Park guides and rangers are very knowledgeable about the area's history and early indigenous inhabitants. ■ *0900-1700, Tue-Fri, and until 1900 on Sat and Sun. Entrance US$4 per person. Soft drinks, bottled water and sometimes fresh coconut water are available at the summit of Santiago crater. Getting there: ask bus driver to drop you off at Km 23 on the Managua-Masaya route. It's easy to hitchhike from either city, especially on Sun.*

Sleeping and eating close to the park entrance, **C** *Hotel Volcán Masaya*, Km 23 Carretera a Masaya, T522-7114, F522-7115, bath, a/c, fridge, and lobby area for relaxing, very comfortable. Great view of the volcano and park. *Restaurants* on main road.

Ciudad de Masaya

Masaya lies 29 km southeast of Managua, and is the folkloric and crafts centre of Nicaragua, home to more artesans than any other place in the country. The town is in almost constant celebration with religious festivals, including Central America's longest party, the **San Jerónimo festival**. Running for three months from September 30, the festival includes many traditional dances, countless processions and music. Smaller festivals happen every Thursday with the *Jueves de Verbena* which has local dancing, music, food and drinking late into the night. The late-baroque **church**, constructed from 1833-93 in the centre of the plaza, is currently being restored.

Indian handicrafts are sold in the market near the bus station and in the new **Centro de Artesanías** (closed Sundays) in the old market. The newly restored 19th-century market was ruined during the Revolution. The 'new' market is very popular with Nicaraguans and sells excellent hammocks, nice leather work, colourful woven rugs used as wall hangings and wicker furniture. The 'old' market, close to the bus park, is marginally cheaper but crowded, dirty, claustrophobic and not particularly recommended. Masaya is also the centre for Nicaraguan rocking chairs, which can be purchased in kit form, packed for taking by air. The *Co-operativa Teófilo Alemán* has a good selection at around US$35.

Colour map 7, grid A1
Population: 140,000
Altitude: 234 m

There are some very pretty horse-drawn carriages for hire in Masaya

Nicaragua

The best place for Indian craft work is the barrio of **Monimbo** and 15 minutes from Masaya is **Nindirí**, named after its former Indian chief represented by a statue in the central park. Known as the city of myths and legends, it is one of the oldest settlements in Nicaragua with evidence of over 3,000 consecutive years of habitation. It is so rich in ceramic history that its small museum, the privately owned **Museo Nindirí,** one block north of the Rubén Darío library, has one of the country's most impressive pre-Columbian collections and Spanish colonial relics. It is run by the aging wife of the founder who will show you around. ■ *Tue-Sat, donation of US$1-2 requested.* The town suffered severely in the Revolution of 1978-79 and you can visit the **Museo de Héroes y Mártires**. ■ *Mon-Fri.* Another museum is that of **Camilo Ortega**, which has interesting exhibits on recent history. ■ *45 mins' walk from Plaza Central, ask directions.*

The small **Laguna de Masaya** is at the foot of Masaya volcano, the water too polluted for swimming, but it's an attractive view from the town. Santiago volcano is also near the town.

Sleeping
Price codes: see inside front cover

D ***La Ceiba Inn***, Plaza 2000 2½ c arriba, Calle El Calvario, T522-7632, 4 rooms with private bath and fans, friendly secure parking. **D** ***Montecarlo***, 1½ blocks north of *Regis* on same side, small rooms, clean, friendly, bar, restaurant serves good burgers. **E** ***Maderas' Inn***, Cuerpo de Bomberos 1½ c al sur, private bath with fan, **C** with a/c, breakfast, T522-2528, F522-5825, clean comfortable rooms although a little small. Very friendly owners. **E** ***Regis***, Sergio Delgadillo (main street), T522-2300, shared bath, fan, clean, very good breakfast (other meals if ordered), fruit juices, very helpful owner who is very knowledgeable about the town and surrounding area. Highly recommended. **F** ***Masayita***, 2 blocks west of central park, clean, basic and cheapest place in town, but reports of theft.

On the outskirts of town is **C** ***Motel Cailagua*** (Km 29.5, Carretera a Granada, T/F522-4435), about 2 km from Masaya, with bath and a/c, **D** with bath and fan, large rooms, clean, good, very friendly, meals available (but breakfast only by arrangement), reasonably priced, parking inside gates. Recommended.

Eating

There are 2 *Fuentes de Soda* near the northeast corner of the Parque Central. A host of places have congregated on the southwest corner of the main plaza. 5 blocks north of the Parque Central is a small park with a Pepsi stand that sells excellent fresh *tutti-frutti* fruit juice. Others include ***Alegría***, C Real San Gerónimo, ½ block north of Parque Central, good, clean, comfortable, not expensive, good pizzas. ***Coconut Sports Bar*** is a trendy bar, good for a beer, hamburger and cable TV. ***La Jarochita***, near park, Mexican, excellent, mid-range, try chicken *enchilada* in *mole* sauce. ***Panadería Corazón de Oro***, 2-3 blocks towards highway from the

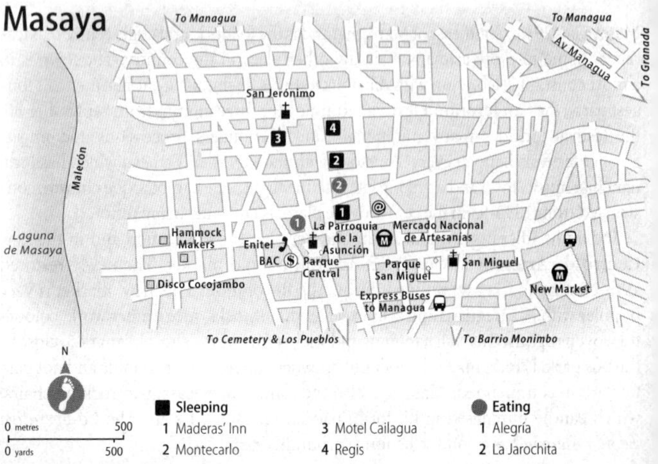

church, excellent cheese bread (*pan de queso*), US$0.50 a loaf. *Pochil*, near park, good food, ask for vegetarian dishes. *Restaurante Che Gris*, ½ block south around corner from *Regis*, very good food in huge portions, excellent *comida corriente* for US$2.50, nice garden. Recommended. *Xochild,* 50 m north of *Hotel Regis*, has good *comida corriente*. Inside artesan's market, between the bus terminal and town, are several small places to eat, best during day is *Sacuanjoche* with chicken tacos US$2.

Buses Buses leave from the new market or you can also catch a non-express bus from the Carretera a Masaya towards Granada or Managua. Express buses leave from Parque San Miguel to La UCA in Managua when full or after 20 mins.   **Granada**, every 30 mins, 0600-1800, 45 mins, US$0.40. **Jinotepe**, every 30 mins, 0500-1800, 1½ hrs, US$0.40. **Managua**, every 30 mins, 0400-1800, 1 hr, US$0.40. Express to **Managua**, every 30 mins, 0400-2100, 40 mins, US$0.80. **Matagalpa**, 0600 and 0700, 4 hrs, US$2.25.

 Taxi Fares around town are US$0.30-0.80. **Granada**, US$15; **Managua** US$20; **airport** US$25. Horse-drawn carriages (*coches*) US$0.30.

Transport

Banks *Bancentro* and *Banco Americano* on Parque Central change TCs and cash at good rates. Street changers around market and plaza. **Communications** Internet: *Intecomp*, is south of the main plaza. *Mi PC a colores*, on Sergio Delgadillo. **Post office**: on Sergio Delgadillo. **Telephone**: *Enitel* office on Parque Central. **Medical services** Doctors: *Dr Freddy Cárdenas Ortega*, near bus terminal, recommended gynaecologist. *Dr Gerardo Sánchez*, next to town hall, speaks some English. **Tourist office** On main highway in the block between the 2 main roads into Masaya; helpful, mostly Spanish spoken.

Directory

Just outside Masaya to the north, on the road from Managua, is an old hilltop fortress, **Coyotepe**, also called La Fortaleza, built in the 19th century to protect Masaya. ■ *US$0.50*. Once a torture centre used first by the Somozistas, later by the Sandinistas, it is now a clubhouse for the Boy Scouts. It is deserted and eerie (take a torch, or offer a boy scout US$1-2 to show you around). Even if you don't want to see the fort, the view from the top of the hill is spectacular.

Around Masaya

Near Masaya Lake, to the south of the town, there are caves with prehistoric figures on the walls; ask around for a guide.

The nearby village of **Niquinohomo** is Sandino's birthplace (see Background), and the house where he lived from the age of 12 with his father is opposite the church in the main plaza. There used to be a museum here but the exhibits have now been transferred to Managua.

San Juan de Oriente is a charming colonial village with an interesting school of pottery (products are for sale). Nearly 80% of the inhabitants are engaged in the ceramic arts. Ask at the artists' co-operative at the entrance to the village to visit an artesan's house. Buses from Granada cost US$0.30. It is a short walk to neighbouring **Catarina** (famous for ornamental plants), and a 1 km walk or drive uphill to **El Mirador**, with a wonderful view of **Laguna de Apoyo** (Granada and Volcán Mombacho in the distance on a clear day) which is very clean, beautiful for swimming and well worth a visit. Quiet during the week but busy at weekends. ■ *Entrance fee US$0.20, US$1 in a car*.

Sleeping **E** *Jaaris*, Iglesia Santa Catalina 1 c abajo, 30 m al sur, T558-0020, 5 rooms, private bath with fan. **On lake shore**: **A-B** *Norome*, T0883-9093, noromeresort@yahoo.com, accessed by the shore road to the east, this charming lakefront lodge has 8 rooms, a/c, bar, restaurant, very clean, smartly decorated rooms, great views and setting, jacuzzi, and a small dock. **C-E** *Monkey Hut*, bottom of the lake access road, 100 m west, T552-4028. Can be booked with transfer from Granada, dormitory and private rooms, breakfast and dinner included, canoe, kayak and sailboat rentals. It's also possible to stay at the *Proyecto Ecológico Espacio Verde* (see *Apoyo Intensive Spanish School* in Directory, below).

Transport **Buses** to Valle de Apoyo from Masaya once a day for US$0.70, then walk down the road that drops into the crater. Buses also run between Masaya and **Granada** every 15 mins. You will have to get off at Km 37.5 and walk down the 5-km access road (it's very dusty

Nicaragua

in the dry season, so bring a bandanna). Hitchhiking is possible though traffic is sparse during the weekdays. *Monkey Hut* offers transfers from their Granada hotel, *The Bearded Monkey* (see Granada Sleeping) for US$1.25 twice weekly (Granada-Laguna de Apoyo: Tue 1200, Fri 1000; Laguna de Apoyo-Granada: Wed 1100, Fri 1400). The other alternative is a taxi from Granada, US$15-20, or from Managua, US$35-40.

Directory Language schools *Apoyo Intensive Spanish School*, T0882-3992, econic@guegue.com.ni, groups of 4, 5 hrs' tuition per day. 5-day programme, US$195, US$230 for a week including accommodation and food or US$750 per month, family stays available. It is also possible to stay in the lodge without enrolling in the school, prices start at US$16 plus meals, contact the *Proyecto* for information.

Granada

Colour map 7, grid A1
Population: 111,506
Altitude: 60 m

Situated on the northwest shore of vast Lake Nicaragua, and at the foot of Volcán Mombacho, Granada is currently the best place to hang out in the country. Founded in 1524 by Hernández de Córdoba on the site of the Indian village of Xalteva, it is the oldest city on continental Latin America. The prosperous city was attacked on at least three occasions by British and French pirates coming up the San Juan and Escalante rivers, and much of old Granada was burnt by filibuster William Walker in 1856; but Granada, the third largest city of the republic, still retains many beautiful buildings and has faithfully preserved its Castilian traditions.

Ins and outs

Getting there Very regular and quick bus and minibus service to the capital makes this a good base even if your interest is the capital. International buses pass the western side of town, adding to the convenience.

Getting around Small and manageable on foot, the focal point of the town if the Parque Central. Heading east takes you to Lake Nicaragua and the Complejo Turístcio (tourist centre). South of the Parque is the working heart of the city with the market and many bus departure points. East, west and north of the park, the streets are a bit quieter. If you feel you've walked far enough, you can hire one of the horse-drawn carriages and rest your feet.

Tourist office The local INTUR office on Parque Central next to the cathedral has good maps of Nicaragua and general information on the country.

Sights

To view the interiors of Granada's churches you must time your visit from 0600-0800, or from 1500-1700

The centre of the city, about 10 blocks from the lake, is the **Parque Central**, with many trees and food stalls selling Granada's famous *vigorón*, a popular dish of fried pork skins, yucca, and cabbage salad served on a big banana leaf. Bordering the park are many civic buildings, the landmark *Hotel Alhambra*, the cathedral and the local branch of the Nicaraguan Tourist Office (southeast corner). In between the red house of the Bishop and the cathedral is the century cross with a time capsule of belongings from 1899 buried underneath in the hope of a peaceful 20th century. This practice was repeated in 1999 with another cross and time capsule in front of the La Merced church in the hope of a peaceful 21st century (let's hope they have better luck!). The **cathedral**, rebuilt in neoclassical style, is simpler in design and ornamentation than the church of **La Merced** to the west, which was built in 1781-83, half-destroyed in the civil wars of 1854 and restored in 1862. Its interior is painted in pastel shades, predominantly green and blue. It has some unusual features and interesting lighting. Continuing away from the centre, beyond La Merced, is the church of **Jalteva** (or Xalteva – the indigenous name of Granada), which faces a pleasant park with formal ponds. Not far from Jalteva is **La Pólvora**, an old fortress that has been partially restored and opened to the public. Donations accepted by the caretaker, nice rooftop with church and volcano view east from the turrets. Also nearby is **Museo de las Arenas**, in a restored fortress. Heading towards the Managua bus terminal from Jalteva, you pass the now-dilapidated **Hospital** which was built in 1886 and is a beautiful building. The chapel of **María Auxiliadora**, where Las Casas, Apostle of the Indies, often preached, is hung with Indian lace and needlework. ■ *Church open to public at 1600. Heading southwest from Jalteva, the cemetary is well worth a visit as the resting place of key figures from recent Nicaraguan history.*

Directly north of Parque Central is the restored **La Casa de Los Leones**, restored and run by the international foundation **Casa de los Tres Mundos**. It is a beautiful colonial house, with art exhibits and concerts. Free admission during the day, check bulletin board for events. Heading west is the fortress-church of **San Francisco**, Nicaragua's oldest, though burned many times and now only the front steps are from 1524; inside there are wonderful sculptures. Next door is the **Museo del Convento de San Francisco**. Originally a convent (1524), then a Spanish garrison, William Walker's garrison, a university and more recently an institute, the cloister surrounds about three dozen tall palms. Restoration is now complete and it is the country's most interesting pre-Columbian museum, housing 28 sculptures from Isla Zapatera in the lake. They date from AD 800-1200, note especially the double sculptures of standing or seated figures bearing huge animal masks, or doubles, on their heads and shoulders (lizard, tortoise, jaguar, etc). The museum also contains several galleries with changing exhibits of Nicaraguan art and a snack bar. ■ *0800-1800, US$1 entrance, US$2.50 extra for photography.*

A road runs from the Parque Central to Plaza España by the dock on the lake; the church of **Guadalupe** is on this road. From Plaza España it is a 30-minute walk along the lakeshore to the **Complejo Turístico**, a large area with restaurants and bars (see below), paths and benches. ■ *US$0.12.* The lake beach is popular, having been cleaned up and built into a nice, if often windy park; marimba bands stroll the beach and play a song for you for a small fee. If you're wondering why Granada is empty at night it's because everyone decants to the club and bars of the Complejo in the evenings!

Horse-drawn carriages are for hire and are used here, as in Masaya, as taxis by the locals. The drivers are happy to take foreigners around the city, US$4.50 for half an hour, US$9 for one hour. You can see most of the city's sites in a half-hour rental. A nice walk, or carriage ride, starts from La Pólvora and continues down Calle Real, past La Capilla María Auxiliadora, La Jalteva, La Merced to Parque Central. From the cathedral you can then continue to La Virgen de Guadalupe and to the lake front along the Calle la Calzada.

The latest additon to things to do is the **Canopy Tour** provided by *Mombotour*. See Tour operators below.

L *Colonial*, 25 m north of central park, T552-7299, F552-6029, 27 rooms, private bath with hot water, a/c, cable TV, telephone, pool, very nice, French owned and operated. **AL** *La Casona de los Estrada,* 50 m west of the Convento San Francisco, T552-7393, F552-7395, www.casonalosestrada.com.ni, pleasant well-lit rooms, most luxurious in Granada, decorated with antiques and charm, expensive restaurant, English spoken. **A-B** *Alhambra*, Parque Central, T552-4486, F552-2035, pleasant, comfortable rooms although some are a bit run down, with bath, large restaurant, good fruit breakfasts, high prices, terrace is nice place for a beer overlooking Plaza Central, parked cars guarded by nightwatchman.

B *Granada*, C La Calzada, opposite Guadalupe church, T552-2178, F552-4128, a/c, cable TV, electric showers, poor beds, restaurant for all meals (overpriced), café, disco, bar, lovely view from front balcony but rather faded. **B** *Posada Don Alfredo*, from La Merced 1 block to the north, T/F552-4455, charlyst@tmx.com.ni, with bath and hot water, **C** without, beautifully maintained 165-year-old house with much of the original flavour (slatted doors and windows which allow sounds through), high ceilings, dark rooms, English and German spoken by friendly, very helpful owner Alfred, clean, good location, buffet German breakfast for US$7. **B** *Italiano*, La Calzada, T/F552-7047, next to Iglesia Guadalupe, Italian-owned, with bath and a/c, **C** without, nice patio, restaurant and bar, good value. **C** *Hospedaje El Maltese*, Plaza España 50 m al sur, opposite *malecón* in the **Complejo Turístico**, T552-7641, new

Sleeping
■ *on map*
Price codes: see inside front cover

There is a shortage of hotels and restaurants in Granada. Try not to arrive too late at night

Nicaragua

hotel with 8 very clean rooms with private bath, nice furnishings, Italian spoken, also restaurant *La Corte Del Maltese*, 1600-2200, Mon-Fri.

D *Another Night in Paradise*, next to *Granada*, T552-7113, donnatabor@hotmail.com, bath, fan, Spanish, English, Danish and German spoken, no sign, look for the mural, very helpful. **E** *Hospedaje Cocibolca*, C La Cazada, T552-7223, good and friendly, clean, bath, use of kitchen, family-run, friendly, internet access. **E-G** *Hospedaje Esfinge Don Alfredo*, opposite market, T552-4826, rooms with character, 50 years old, patio with washing facilities, friendly, clean, motorcycle parking in lobby, safe, laundry frowned upon. Recommended. **E** *Hospedaje Familiar*, malecón ½ c al oeste, calle San Juan del Sur, T552-4906. 8 rooms with private bath, cable TV and fan, **D** with a/c, good restaurant. **E** *La Calzada*, C La Calzada near Guadalupe church, big rooms some with bath, fan, friendly, great breakfasts.

F *Central*, C la Calzada, friendly, clean, laundry facilities, popular with backpackers, mosquito nets, good restaurant. **F** *Hospedaje Granada*, cathedral 3½ c al lago, T552-3716 with bath and fan, cheaper in shared bath, nice location. **F** *The Bearded Monkey*, C 14 de Septiembre, near the fire station, T552-4028, dormitory accommodation with footlockers, shared bath, relaxed common areas, food and excellent breakfasts, bar, cable TV, internet access, films in the evening, great atmosphere, comfortable and very friendly.

Eating
● *on map*

Most restaurants close on Monday. Hotel restaurants (ie Central and The Bearded Monkey) are popular meeting places

Café Converso, next to La Casa de Los Leones, T552-5626, coffee, sodas, beer, fast food, internet (US$2.70/hr), very good, great outdoor and indoor setting, open 1000-2000. *Gran Café*, Convento San Francisco 75 m al oeste, T552-7257, Miami Cuban café, sandwiches, hamburgers, fruit salads, salsa music played loud from 0900. On C Caimito *Doña Conchi's*, beautiful restaurant with Spanish, Mediterranean and seafood, homemade bread, small artesanía shop. Recommended but a bit pricey, and you should wear something tidy. *Don Luca's*, Calle La Calzada, near *Hospedaje Cocibolca*, excellent pizza, pasta, cheap, nice setting. *El Ancla*, across from *Hotel Granada*, fresh outdoor setting, decent food and service, Nicaraguan dishes. *El Zaguán*, on road behind cathedral, T552-2522, great grilled meats cooked on wood fire, best beef dishes in Granada, friendly service, nice setting in colonial home on quiet

Granada

To Managua

Parque Sandino (Sin Nombre)
Minibuses to Managua

San Francisco & Museo Antiguo Convento

Av Arellano

Nicabus

Casa de los Leones

Guadalupe

La Calzada

Plaza de Independencia

To Managua

Cathedral

Parque Central

C Caimito

To Managua

Palacio de Cultura

Ticabus

Alcaldía

Minibuses to Managua

La Merced

La Jalteva

C Real

Doña Elba (Cigar Factory)

Ticabus & Nueva Sirca

C Atravesada

Av Vega

Fortaleza de la Pólvora

Capilla María Auxiliadora

To Masaya

To Rivas

To Cemetery (300m) & Nandaime

To Mombacho & Rivas

N

0 metres 100
0 yards 100

■ **Sleeping**
1 Alhambra
2 Another Night in Paradise
3 Central
4 Colonial

5 Hospedaje Cocibolca
6 Hospedaje Esfinge
7 La Barba del Mono (Bearded Monkey)
8 Posada Don Alfredo

● **Eating**
1 Café Converso
2 Doña Conchi's
3 Las Bocaditas
4 Mediterráneo

Nicaragua

street, mid-range, excellent, 1100-1500 and 1800-2300, Mon-Fri, 1100-2200, Sat – Sun. *Eskimo's*, C La Calzada, good ice-cream; between *El Ancla* and *Eskimo's* is a cheap, good grilled meats place. *La Gran Francia*, corner of park, historic house, classic setting, expensive French cuisine, bar, new 2002. *Los Portales*, Plaza Central, opposite *Enitel*, simple, good. *Mediterráneo*, C Caimito, T552-6764, open daily 0800-2300, lovely colonial house, quiet garden setting, expensive but worth it and popular with foreigners, Spanish owners and menu, very good seafood. *TelePizza*, C Caimito, great pizzas and quick service.

Several cheap places near the market including **Tasa Blanca**, friendly, good coffee. Nearby is *Restaurant Querube's*, popular with locals, set menu for lunch (US$1.50). Good breakfasts at the market.

The best place to find a good *vigorón* – a large banana leaf filled with fried pork skin, yucca and tomato, covered in cabbage salad, a mixture of chilli peppers and lime juice – is on central park, try *Kiosko La Gata*, which also offers traditional *Nica* drinks like *chicha* and *cacao con leche*. Next to the mayor's office on Parque Central, in the corner house, is the seriously cheap lunch buffet of *Don Daffa*, with very fresh food, served in a clean setting, great value.

Granada's most famous dish is the cheap, filling and messy vigorón, well worth trying

On C Atravezada behind the *Hotel Alhambra*, are: *Bullpen*, from Los Cocos, 1 block east, very cheap drinks and good soups. *Dragón Dorado*, mid-range Cantonese fare, attentive service, mediocre food. *El Volcán*, Calle Estrada, iglesia La Merced 1C al sur, T552-2878, shish kebabs, *quesillos* and sandwiches, daily from 1000. *La Colina del Sur*, excellent lake fish and avocado salad, expensive but worth it, recommended. *Number One*, Calle Real Xalteva, *Supermercado Lacayo* ½ c al lago, T552-7679, Italian and Nicaraguan food in a posh setting, nice patio and wood decor, cannelloni, *churrasco*, 1100-2200 daily except Thu. Near the Shell station, *Tito Bar*, good local place, with inexpensive typical Nicaraguan food.

In the **Complejo Turístico** on the lakeshore there are many places for dancing and eating (flying insects can make it a miserable place at the beginning of the rainy season). *La Terrazza La Playa*, mid-range, great *cerdo asado* and *filete de guapote*. *César*, open Fri and Sat only, recommended for dancing and drinking very popular, inexpensive bar, merengue and salsa music.

Entertainment

Cinema 1 block behind *Hotel Alhambra*, good, modern, 2 screens. **Nightlife** The street that runs behind the *Hotel Alhambra*, C Atravezada, has, or is close to, most of Granada's nightlife and restaurants. On this street, next to the cinema, is the very popular *Flamingo* canteen with cheap beer and a very diverse clientele, particularly at night. Upstairs is *Leidy's Bar*, with dancing and karaoke. Near Iglesia La Merced is *La Fábrica*, an old colonial-style house with modern bar, nice patio, young crowd, cheap beer rock music, full of foreigners.

Circuit Breaker, 1 c north of *Hospedaje Cocibolca*, young hip crowd, rock music, corner colonial house, tattoo salon, piercing and drinking until early hours. *Matchico*, Calle La Calzada 3 c al lago, across from *Hospedaje Cocibolca*, T0888-7992, crêpes and salads, bar and cocktails, French and Spanish cuisine. Live music. Open Mon–Sun 1200-2400.

Festivals

La Serenata dancing and foodstalls every Fri. *Folklore, Artesanía and Food Festival* for 3 days in **Mar** (check locally for precise dates). *Holy Week. Assumption of the Virgin*, 14-30 Aug; and *Christmas* (masked and costumed performers).

Nicaragua

Lago de Nicaragua

To San Carlos

Dock

Plaza España

Complejo Turístico

To Las Isletas

To Puerto Asese

5 Osteria Pane e Vino
6 Pizza Hot

Shopping

Market (large green building south of Parque Central) is dark, dirty and packed; lots of stalls on the streets outside, also horse cab rank and taxis. Main shopping street runs north-south, west of plaza. *Supermercado Lacayo*, C Real. Next to the outdoor market is *Supermercado Pali*. *Almacén Internacional* is near *Hotel Alhambra*.

Transport

For boat travel see Lago de Nicaragua below

Local Bike rental available from several places in town. (US$12) and **kayak** (US$10) rental from *Posada Don Adolfo*, Av Atravasado. **Taxis** Granada taxi drivers are useful for finding places away from the centre, average fare US$0.75-1.50. **Managua** US$16, but make sure the taxi looks strong enough to make the journey.

There is no central bus station – check locally for bus terminal information

Long distance Ferry: The Granada-San Carlos ferry leaves the main dock on Mon and Thu at 1400, 15 hrs, US$4. It stops in Altagracia, Ometepe after 14 hrs.

Bus Express mini-buses to **Managua** leave from Parque Sandino and from a small lot just south of BAC on Parque Central, US$1.25.

Leaving from the Shell station, 1 c south of the Mercado: **Masaya**, every 30 mins, 0500-1800, 40 mins, US$0.40; **Rivas**, every 45 mins, 0540-1510, 2 hrs, US$1; **Niquinohomo**, every 45 mins, 0430-1610, 45 mins, US$1, use this bus for visits to Diriá, Diriomo, San Juan de Oriente, Catarina; or **Jinotepe**, 0630 and 1200, 1½ hrs, US$0.80, for visits to Los Pueblos, including Masatepe and San Marcos.

From the bus terminal next to the old hospital to the west of town: **Managua**, every 20 mins, 0400-1900, 1½ hrs, US$0.75. **Nandaime**, every 20 mins, 0500-1800, 1 hr, US$0.70.

International *Tica*, *Trica* and *Nica* buses heading to San José and Costa Rica all pass through Granada and have offices on Av Arellano. *Nicabus*, T228-1373, 0700, Tue-Sun, US$10. *Ticabus*, T552-4301, has several buses a day. *Tricabus*, T522-6619, 0615, 0800, 1100, daily, US$10.

Directory

Banks *Banco de Centro América* on Parque Central and *Banco Centro* (1 block west of plaza) will change TCs and you can buy US$ using Visa. Can also change TCs and cash dollars on the street. **Communications**: Internet: *Computer Internet Service*, from Casa Pellas 75 m west of *Enitel* (see below), T552-2544, F552-3061, US$5 per hr. Other places include **Compunet** beside cathedral, US$5.50 per hr; one behind *Hotel Alhambra*, also in several *hospedajes* (see above). *Internet Don Bosco*, calle Real Xalteva, opposite Colegio Salesiano, T552-3359, internet service, with scanners, and general e-services. **Post office** and **telephone**: (*Enitel*) on corner northeast of Parque Central, by Casa de los Leones, open until 2200. **Language schools** *Casa Xalteva*, C Real Xalteva 103, T/F552-2436, www.ibw.com.ni/~casaxal, small Spanish classes, 1 week to several months, US$125 a week, home stays arranged, US$60 a week, voluntary work with children, recommended. *GLSN*, C Real Xalteva, 6½ blocks west of Parque Central, 1 block from Jalteva church, US$55 per week, or US$85 with accommodation, 4 hrs tuition per day. Recommended. *Nicaragua Spanish School*, Palacio de la Cultura, frente al Parque Central, T552-7114, classes daily 0800-1200. *One on One*, calle La Calzada 450, T552-6771, flexible classes, on an hourly basis. Also see *Apoyo Intensive Spanish School*, on Laguna de Apoyo, page 979. **Tour operators** *Auxiliadora Travel Agent*, Iglesia La Merced 1 c al oeste, C Real Xalteva, Apdo 180, T298-3304, F298-5638, most helpful and efficient. *Mombotour*, Cutirre Canopy Tour, west side of Iglesia La Merced, T552-4548, 17 platforms located between 3 m and 20 m above the ground on the lake side of Volcán Mombacho, coffee tours, birding walks, 2 departures per day to the ranch from their office, canopy US$35 and includes transfers to the site. In the same office is *Island Kayaks*, offering 'sea kayaking' in Lake Nicaragua, classes given in Las Isletas. *Oro Travel*, Convento San Francisco ½ c al norte, T552-4568, F552-6512, www.orotravel.com, owner Pascal speaks French, English and German, friendly, helpful, good tours of Mombacho volcano reserve, recommended. *Viajes Griffith*, C Real No 414, T552-4358, F552-6262, English spoken.

Lago de Nicaragua

Colour map 7, grid A2

The 'Gran Lago de Nicaragua' or **Lago Cocibolca**, 148 km long by 55 km at its widest (8,264 sq km), is a freshwater lake full of saltwater fish which have swum up the Río San Juan from the sea and adapted to the fresh water. These fish exist in no other lake in the world, like the sawtooth fish and the shark recently bought to fame by the author Edward Marriott in *Savage Shore*. Seen regularly on the east side of Isla Ometepe, is a

Lake Nicaragua – El Mar Dulce

A lake so vast the Spanish conquistadors dubbed it the 'Freshwater sea' (Mar Dulce), Lago de Nicaragua or Cocibolca covers 8,264 sq km. In a little country like Nicaragua, this is massive. The lake is fed by numerous rivers in Nicaragua and northern Costa Rica and its waters drain into the Caribbean Sea, via the Río San Juan. Lago de Nicaragua is home to more than 430 volcanic islands. This is the earth as it was being formed millions of years ago, for Cocibolca is actually a 160 x 65 km floodplain with the earth rising up around it and inside it. Its average depth is 20 m with some deep sections near Ometepe at 60 m. The two continents were finally connected on the lake's west coast, some four or five million years ago, blocking off the Caribbean from the Pacific and forming a land bridge that allowed the flora and fauna of the two great continents to mix.

For an estimated 30,000 years, the bridge has been used by humans too. Some of the

lake's islands were, without a doubt, very important religious sites, places of organized worship, human sacrifice and ritual cannibalism. Indeed, getting to the islands in canoes must have been a religious experience in itself. Thanks to its shallow floor, Cocibolca's waves change by the hour. The lake can go from calm to swells, and from swells to rough in no time at all.

Lake Nicaragua is also unique in its freshwater sawtooth fish, sharks, sardines and the prehistoric gaspar fish. A visit to Nicaragua without a visit to its freshwater sea is like touring Egypt without visiting the pyramids or Peru without visiting the Andes. Still free of resorts, pleasure yachts, jet skis and commercial fishing boats, Cocibolca, the world's second biggest lake in the tropics, remains as it has been for thousands of years: a place of volcanoes, mysteries and murmurs from the past;

a huge body of clean, fresh water, teeming with fish, asleep under an endless sky.

rare freshwater member of the bull shark family (*Carcharhinus nicaragüensis*). Terrapins can be seen sunning themselves on the rocks and there are many interesting birds. The lake has three major archipelagos (over 400 islands) as well as the largest lake island in the world, Ometepe. Created by a massive eruption of Volcán Mombacho 3,000 years ago, **Las Isletas Archipelago**, just southeast of Granada, consists of 354 islands, most of which are uninhabited, covered with lush vegetation. The **Zapatera Archipelago** is the most significant pre-Columbian site in Nicaragua and a national reserve. Guided tours are available from tour operators in Managua. In the southeastern part of the lake is the Solentiname Archipelago (see below).

Sleeping & eating **A** *Nicarao Lake Resort* on the island of La Ceiba, T266-1316, F266-0704, nlr@nicaraolake.com.ni, includes all meals, a/c, good beds, part-time generator, delightful setting, lake perch in restaurant. *Restaurante Asese*, T459-2269, on the lake, good value, fish specialities.

Transport **Boats** The islands can be visited either by hired boats or motor launches, from the restaurant at the end of the road beyond the Complejo Turístico (see above), at US$10 per hr for the whole boat, US$50 per hr for 6 in a motor launch, or US$10 per hr for 2 in a rowing boat. Another option is to take the morning bus (or taxi US$3.50) from Granada to **Puerto Asese**, 3 km further south, a tranquil town at the base of the Asese peninsula at the head of the Ensenada de Asese. Boats can be hired for US$10-12 per hr for 2 people. Trips to various lake destinations (Zapatera, El Muerto, the Solentiname Islands, Río San Juan) can be arranged in the yacht *Pacífico*, up to 15 people on day trips, 8 for overnight voyages, lunch included, recommended for a group (information and reservations in Granada, T459-4305). See San Jorge, below, for the most frequently used service.

San Jorge
Colour map 7, grid A2

San Jorge is the main departure point for Ometepe Island, but on Sundays in summer the town itself is very lively with music, baseball, swimming and lots of excursion buses. **D** *Mar Dulce*, 300 m south of dock, bath, TV, parking. **F** *Nicarao*, left off the Rivas-San Jorge road, a short distance from the dock, basic meals, friendly. From

Nicaragua

San Jorge a road runs away from the shore through Rivas (see page 990) to the port of San Juan del Sur (see page 991). Taxi to Rivas, US$1.50, *colectivos* US$0.40. From Rivas, the Pan-American Highway runs along the west coast of the lake to Sapoá and the Costa Rican border.

Ometepe

Colour map 7, grid A2
Population: 32,000
Altitude: 60-1610 m

The largest freshwater island in the world, Ometepe is a highlight of any trip to Nicaragua and is definitely worth a visit. It has two volcanoes, one of them, Concepción, a perfect cone rising to 1,610 m; the other, Volcán Maderas, rises to 1,394 m. There are two main villages on the island on either side of Volcán Concepción: **Moyogalpa** and **Altagracia**, which are connected by bus. Moyogalpa has the atmosphere of a tourist port; Altagracia, like other small villages on the island, is more charming. Ometepe has the kindest people in Nicaragua, partly because the Revolution and Civil War were never waged here. There are many indigenous petroglyphs in several locations on the island, the best being near Finca Magdalena.

There is not much to hold you in Moyogalpa, unless you're catching an early boat the following day. If you have time to kill you can hire a bicycle and ride to Punta Jesús María, 4-5 km and well signposted from the road just before Esquipulas, where there is a nice beach for swimming, a small café and a good panoramic view of the island. You can change money in the two biggest grocery stores (one opposite *Hotel Colonial*), or in some of the hotels.

Pick-ups meet boats arriving at Altagracia to provide transport for the 2-km ride into town. In the main plaza there is a sculpture park of pre-Columbian-style ceramics with some large basalt statues, similar to those housed in the San Francisco museum in Granada. The **Museo de Omotepe** has displays of archaeology covering local ethnographic and environmental themes, half a block from the central park. ■ *US$1, guide in Spanish.* Ask for the bird-watching site about 3 km from Altagracia; birds fly in the late afternoon to nest on offshore islands. You can stroll to the base of **Volcán Concepción** (which had its last major eruption in 1954 but was still throwing ash in December 1999), for good views of the lake in the company of many birds and howler monkeys (*congos*).

To climb the volcano, leave from **Cuatro Cuadros**, 2 km from Altagracia, and make for a cinder gully between forested slopes and a lava flow. There are several

Isla de Ometepe

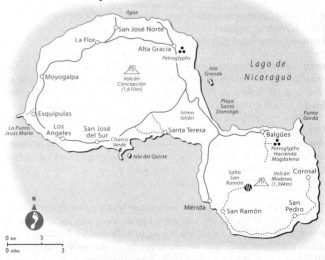

fincas on the lower part of the volcano. The ascent takes about five hours (take water), with Alpine vegetation, heat from the crater and howler monkeys as attractions. It gets very steep near the summit. It's worthwhile getting a guide as visibility is often restricted by clouds and it is easy to get lost, especially in the final stages (US$25 per group). You can get a guide by asking near the pier; otherwise Eduardo Ortiz and his son José, of Cuatro Cuadros, will guide; or Borman Gómez, who meets boats from San Jorge; his house is two blocks east, half a block south of the dock (ask for Casa Familia Gilberto Arcia), US$3.60 per person, speaks English. There is an alternative route up Volcán Concepción from behind the church in Moyogalpa. Again, a guide is recommended for route-finding in jungle sections (machete useful) and cloud, eight hours up. Camping is possible near the top. South of Volcán Concepción is Charco Verde lagoon and a waterfall worth visiting.

Between Altagracia and **Balgües** (small basic *hospedaje*) is Santo Domingo, with a wide grey-sand beach. There is a small place to eat at the north end of the beach. **Around the island**

For **Volcán Maderas**, take an early bus (0430 or 0530) from Altagracia to Balgües (or stay overnight there), ask for Finca Magdalena (20 minutes' walk), go up through banana plantations and forest to the top, beautiful lagoon in the crater, two to three hours up (can be very muddy, strong boots recommended). This is one of the country's two finest Pacific basin cloud forests with howler monkeys accompanying your journey to the top. On the southwest flank of Volcán Maderas is Salto San Ramón, a 110-m waterfall. You'll need a rope if you want to enter the crater and you're not with a guide – you may be able to borrow one from *Finca Magdalena*. The climb to the summit of Volcán Maderas is not technical, but a guide may be helpful. Guides can be found at the coffee co-operative in Balgües, *Finca Magdalena*, or at *Hotel Ometepetl* in Moyogalpa, ask for Antonio. Take water on all hikes and climbs.
■ *There is an entrance fee of US$1.75 to climb Maderas.*

Altagracia D-E *Central*, on main street to Moyogalpa, attractive courtyard and dining room, good friendly service, with bath, nice patio, cabañas in garden. Recommended. **F** *Castillo*, on same road, friendly, good food, slow service, water problems, trips can be organized to rock carvings on the volcano, US$4 per person or US$12 for a group guide. *Las Cabañas*, close to Playa Santa Domingo, new. In **Moyogalpa B** *La Isla*, del Puerto 1 c arriba, T459-4258, shared baths, a/c, row boat, bicycle rental. **C** *Ometepetl*, on main street from dock, T459-4276, F459-4132, bath, a/c, rooms dirty, friendly, poor food, best rental cars on the island. **C-E** *Cari*, ½ block from pier, T459-4263, F459-4283, best location, poor service, some a/c, restaurant. **D** *El Pirata*, rotonda del puerto 3 c al este, T459-4262, 9 rooms with private bath and a/c, run down, very attentive friendly service. **F** *Casa Familiar*, del puerto 2 c al este, 20 m al sur, T459-4240, private bath with fan and good restaurant with vegetarian, fried fish, fish casserole, daily 0630-2100. **F** *El Colonial*, on main street from dock, with bath, clean, balcony, good food. Recommended. **F** *El Puerto*, next to La Portuaria, T459-4194, shared bath with fan. **F** *Pensión Aly*, opposite Shell, clean, uncomfortable beds, helpful, poor value and service in restaurant. **G** *Pensión Jade*, good atmosphere, friendly, water problems, meals available good value. **E** *Los Ranchitos*, on same street as telephone company, excellent food, reasonable prices, 2 branches, both good. Highly recommended. In **Santo Domingo C-F** *Villa Paraíso*, vparaiso@ibw.com.ni, in cabañas with bath and fan or in lodge without bath, Austrian owner, German spoken, clean, lake view, friendly, peaceful, lovely setting, best food on the island (but won't permit you to bring own food to hotel), good bird-watching. Highly recommended. **C** *Finca Santo Domingo*, Playa Santo Domingo, T265-7831, 16 rooms with private bath and a/c, bar restaurant, nice, relaxed, day trips by boat and horse. **D** *Istián*, south of *Villa Paraíso*, across the beach, reservations through *Ometepetl*, basic, fan, bath, views of both volcanoes, friendly. In **San Ramón C** with full board *Ometepe Biological Station*, T453-0875, Managua office 277-1130, www.studyabroad.com/lasuerte Mainly for biology students, the station manages about 325 ha of conservation land in the San Ramón area. Includes mountain bikes, kayaks, buffet-style meals. Rooms are simple with shared bath outside. At **Sleeping**

Nicaragua

trail head for good path to San Ramón 35-m waterfall, 2-3-hr hike. Don't bathe in waterfall as it is drinking water for the community of San Ramón.

Near San Ramón is the beautiful and breezy area of **Mérida**, **F** *Hacienda Mérida*, is a former ranch of Somoza García that was confiscated by the Sandinistas and then given to the Institute of Tourism by Violeta Chamorro. Simple hostel beds or camping, seriously cheap food well prepared with fresh ingredients from the island. Mountain bike and kayak rentals. The 2-km-long Istian River flows through swamps that has a large diversity of shore birds including 9 species of egret. There is a trail that leads from the hostel to the highest part of Maderas, hiking time 8-10 hrs. A local guide US$8. The *Hacienda* has gear to enter the crater which holds a misty lake.

In **Balgües F** *Finca Magdalena,* a working co-operative farm, hammock space US$1, good meals around US$2, friendly, basic, very popular with travellers. You can work in exchange for lodging, 1 month minimum. Camping possible.

In **San José de Sur** near the legendary Charco Verde lagoon, **C** *Finca Playa Venecia*, 250 m from the road, T887-0191, 1 cabin for 2 and another for 4 people, **E** for 3 double rooms with outside toilet, meals available, horse rental, trips to Charco Verde.

Transport

Anyone prone to seasickness can buy Nausil from the farmacia before travelling; the lake can have very big wind swells

Boat The best access route to the island is from **San Jorge** on the lake's southwest shore (see above) to **Moyogalpa**. Cars are transported. 5 boats per day Mon-Sat, 2 boats on Sun; the best boat, *La Señora del Lago*, leaves 1100 from San Jorge and returns 1300 from Moyogalpa, US$1.50 each way, 1 hr. Early-morning boats are cheaper at US$1 (they have no bar). **Express buses** from Mercado Huembes bus terminal in **Managua** to San Jorge at 0830 and 1500 (2 hrs, US$1.60) meet ferries to Moyogalpa. Return from San Jorge to Managua 0745 and 1445, connecting with 0600/0630 and 1230/1330 ferries from Moyogalpa.

Launches sail from **Granada-Altagracia** Mon, Thu and Sat, 1200 and 1600, ticket office open 0900. 5 hrs to Altagracia, US$1.60. Boats leave Altagracia for Granada on Wed, Fri and Sun. Everything left on deck will get wet. As it can be very crowded, a good spot for sleeping is on the cabin roof. Snacks and soft drinks sold on board. A cargo boat at 1100 from Altagracia takes passengers, 4 hrs. Ticket office in Granada is at the dock; ENAP T552-2745.

Bus on the island, several daily from Moyogalpa to Altagracia (1 hr, US$0.50), Balgües (1 hr, US$0.75), and San Ramón (3 hrs, US$1) and return; reduced service on Sun.

Directory

Banks In Moyogalpa, change money in the 2 biggest grocery stores (1 opposite *Hotel Colonial*), or in hotels. **Communication** Internet, *Tienda Fashion*, 1 block from *Hotel Central* towards the plaza (US$2.90/hr) and will change TCs (at a poor rate). **Tour operator** Local guides can be found at *Ecotur Ometepe*, T/F459-4118. *Ometepe Tours*, in Moyogalpa, ½ block north of BND, T459-4105, sells a useful booklet with maps and information, next to the dock, T453-4779.

Solentiname Islands

Colour map 7, grid A2

One hour by fast boat (two or more hours by public boat) from San Carlos (see below), is the 36-island Archipelago of Solentiname. These sparsely populated islands are covered with humid tropical forest and are home to many birds and a unique school of painting and balsa wood sculptures.

Apart from the hotel (see below), there is no electricity on the island, so take a torch

On **San Fernando Island**, many locals carve and paint balsa wood figures. The diet on the island is somewhat limited but there is lots of fresh fruit. Ask for Julio Pineda or his sister Rosa, one of the local artists. The island has a new **museum** with a variety of natural and cultural history exhibits as well as a spectacular view of the archipelago, especially at sunset, if closed ask in village if it can be opened. ■ *US$1.*

Isla La Venada, named for its plentiful population of deer (*venado*), is also home to artists, in particular the house of Rodolpho Arellano who lives on the south side of the island. He is one of the region's best painters and his wife, daughters and grandson all paint tropical scenes and welcome visitors to see and purchase their works. On the north side of the island is a series of semi-submerged caves with some of the best examples of petroglyphs from the pre-Columbian Guatuso tribe. **Isla El Padre** is privately owned and the only island inhabited by howler monkeys. If you circle the island in a boat they can usually be spotted in the trees.

Isla Mancarrón is the largest in the chain, with the highest hill at 250 m. This is where the famous revolutionary/poet/sculptor/Catholic priest/Minister of Culture, Ernesto Cardenal, made his name by founding a primitivist school of painting, poetry and sculpture, and even decorating the local parish church in naïve art. There is no Mass said in the church but it is currently being restored and should be open soon. There is a monument to the Sandinista flag outside the church. Hiking is possible on the island where many parrots and Moctezuma oropendolas make their home. The island's hotel of the same name is part of the local folklore as its founder Alejandro Guevara was a hero of the Sandinista Revolution, and his widow Nubia and her brother Peter now look after the place.

On **Mancarrón L** *Refugio Mancarrón*, up the hill from the dock and church, T265-2716 (Managua), T552-2059 (Solentiname), szerger@ibw.com.ni, includes 3 meals per day, clean airy rooms with screened windows, generated power at night, rocky beach, great bird-watching, meals are traditional Nicaraguan fare with fruit juices, bar, purified water, hiking on the island led by the always fun Peter (in Spanish only, US$10 for 4), also to other islands and Los Guatusos in boat. Water supply can be problematic, and ask to see your room first as some are becoming run down. Even so, it's recommended. **D** *El Refugio*, T283-0083, low-ceiling cabins in need of care, big grassy grounds, food available, library. Turn right before church and yell at gate (¡*Buenas!*), rustic cabins with full board included, some with private bath, some with shared, owned by the famed priest Ernesto Cardenal (can be booked through his *Galeria de Los Tres Mundos*, in Managua, T278-5781). On **San Fernando C** *Albergue Solentiname,* with meals, safe, pretty grounds. Shared baths, tiny rooms with weak beds and no windows. New cabins due to open with private bath and lake views. Alternatively, you can stay in basic but generally very clean private homes. **Sleeping**

Private transfers from San Carlos to Solentiname 1-1½ hr, US$55-85 per boat. The public boat goes Tue and Fri only at 1100 from San Carlos, 0300 from Mancarrón, 3½ hrs, US$2.15. **Transport**

Managua to Costa Rica

Travelling towards Costa Rica, the Pan-American Highway passes through agricultural land, with branches heading east to Granada and west to the Pacific coast. Rivas makes a good stopping place for trips to Lago de Nicaragua and Isla de Ometepe, or you can head for the coast and the spectacular sunsets and surf beaches of San Juan del Sur, or the turtle nesting sites of Astillero and La Flor.

The Pan-American Highway has bus services running all the way to the border with Costa Rica (148 km). The road runs into the Sierra de Managua, reaching 900 m at Casa Colorada, 26 km from Managua. Further on, at El Crucero (a cool and pleasant place), a paved branch road goes through the Sierra south to the Pacific beaches of Pochomil and Masachapa (see page 956).

The highway continues through the beautiful scenery of the Sierras to **Diriamba**, 42 km from Managua in a coffee-growing district. In the centre of the town is the **Museo Ecológico de Trópico Seco**, with displays of local flora and fauna, including coffee and turtles, and a section on volcanoes. ■ *Tue-Sat 0800-1200, 1400-1700, Sun 0800-1200, US$1.* **Fiesta** on 20 January. There is a 32-km dirt road direct to the beach at **Masachapa** (no buses).

Diriamba
Colour map 7, grid A1
Population: 57,682
Altitude: 580 m

  Five kilometres north of Diriamba a paved road branches off the main highway and runs east through San Marcos, Masatepe (famous for wooden and rattan furniture) and Niquinohomo to Catarina and Masaya. A road also leads to **La Concepción**, a small, industrious village in the highlands, very typical of this part of Nicaragua, where almost no travellers go. The area is rich in pineapple,   *pitaya,* coffee, mandarins and oranges and the people are welcoming. Access is by bus from Jinotepe, every 20 minutes, US$0.50, or from Managua's Roberto Huembes terminal, every half an hour, US$0.75.

Sleeping and eating **B** ***Naranjal***, La Concepción, a 1½ km from Instituto Guillermo Ampié, T0883-4060. 20 rooms, with a/c, jacuzzi, restaurant and pool. **E** ***Diriangén***, Shell 1 c al este, ½ c al sur, T422-2428, private bath with fan, parking. Good fish at restaurant ***2 de Junio***. Before Diriamba on the Carretera Sur, just after the turning to Masatepe at Las Esquinas, is ***El Patio de Don Pedro***, mostly Mexican food, mid-range, nice décor, sleepy service.

Jinotepe
Population: 42,566
Altitude: 569 m

Five kilometres beyond Diriamba is Jinotepe, capital of the coffee-growing district of Carazo. It has a fine neoclassical church with modern stained-glass windows from Irún, in Spain. **Fiesta**: July 5 is celebrated as 'Liberation Day' here. The fiesta in honour of St James the Greater runs from 24-26 July.

Sleeping and eating **B** *Hotel Casa Grande*, T412-3284, F412-3512, private bath, hot water, cable, some rooms with a/c, nice building, central location, very clean. Recommended. **C** ***Montreal***, Esso 3 c al sur, T412-2847, 8 rooms with private bath and hot water, fans **F** ***Hospedaje San Carlos***, no sign, ask around for it. ***Pizza Danny's*** is very good, 50 m north of municipal building (try their *especial*, small but delicious, US$7).

Transport **Buses** for **Managua** leave from the terminal in the northeast corner of town, every 20 mins, US$0.55; to **Nandaime** every 30 mins, US$0.35; to ***Diriamba-Masaya*** every 20 mins. **Banks** Black market for dollars in Parque Central.

Nandaime

From Nandaime, 21 km south of Jinotepe, a paved road runs north to Granada (bus US$0.50). Nandaime has two interesting churches, El Calvario and La Parroquia (1859-72). The annual **fiesta** is 24-27 July, with masked dancers.

Sleeping and eating **C** *Brisas del Mombacho*, Km 66.5 Carretera a Rivas, T452-2312, private bath with a/c and TV, **D** with fan. Unnamed ***hospedaje***, **E**, and restaurant ***La Cabaña***, good local dishes, a favourite with truck drivers.

Rivas

Colour map 7, grid A2
Population: 41,764,
Altitude: 139 m

About 45 km beyond Nandaime (US$0.40 by bus) is Rivas. The Costa Rican national hero, the drummer Juan Santamaría, sacrificed his life here in 1856 when setting fire to a building captured by the infamous William Walker (see Background) and his men. On the town's Parque Central is a lovely old church (in need of repair). In the dome of the Basilica, see the fresco of the sea battle against the ships of Protestantism and Communism. The Parque has some old, arcaded buildings on one side, but also some new buildings. Rivas is a good stopping place if in transit by land through Nicaragua. The bus station, adjacent to the market, is on the northwest edge of town about eight blocks from the main highway. The road from the lake port of San Jorge joins this road at Rivas; 11 km beyond Rivas, at La Virgen on the shore of Lake Nicaragua, it branches south to San Juan del Sur. **Tourist information** (INTUR) is located 3½ c west of the Texaco station, T453-4914; ask for Sr Francisco Cárdenas. They have good maps of Nicaragua and general information.

Sleeping

C ***Cacique Nicarao***, 2 blocks west of Parque Central, next to the cinema (3 blocks south and 2 east from bus terminal), T453-3234, F453-3120, with a/c, cheaper with fan, comfortable, slow service, shower, cold water, best in town, clean, well-equipped, good restaurant, Visa accepted, secure parking. Recommended. **E** ***Hospedaje Lidia***, near Texaco, clean, noisy, family-run. (At the Texaco station, Lenín, who speaks English, is very helpful.) **E** ***Pensión Primavera***, small rooms but clean, shared bath, friendly, basic. **F** ***El Coco***, on Pan-American Highway near where bus from border stops, noisy, basic, small rooms, shower, interesting bar, *comedor* with vegetarian food, nice garden. **F** ***Hospedaje Delicia***, on main

Managua-border road, basic and dirty, but friendly. **F** *Hospedaje Internacional*, where the *Sirca* bus stops, near the Texaco station, good breakfast.

Comedor Lucy, on street leaving Parque Central at corner opposite *Banco de Nicaragua*, **Eating** *comidas corrientes y vegetarianos*. *Restaurant Chop Suey*, in the arcade in Parque Central. *Restaurant El Ranchito*, near *Hotel El Coco*, friendly, serves delicious chicken and *churrasco*. *Rinconcito Salvadoreño*, in the middle of the Parque Central, open air, charming.

Bus Managua, every ½ hr, 0330-1800, 2¾ hrs, US$1.50. Granada, every 45 mins, **Transport** 0530-1625, 1¾ hr, US$1. **Rivas-Jinotepe**, every ½ hr, 0540-1710, 1¾ hr, US$1. **Rivas-San Juan del Sur**, every ½ hr, 0600-1830, 45 mins, US$0.70. **Peñas Blancas/Sapoá – Costa Rica**, every ½ hr, 0500-1600, 1 hr, US$.60. Taxi to **San Jorge**, the best way to get to the dock, US$1.50, *colectivos* US$0.40.

Banks *Banco de Finanzas* for changing cash and American Express travellers' cheques, from the fire **Directory** station, 1 c south, 75 m east, T453-0743. **Communications** *Enitel* is 3 blocks south of Parque Central, or 7 blocks south and 3 blocks east from bus terminal. **Tour operators** *Tour Nicarao*, 1 block south from Plaza, T453-4157, F453-3371, arranges local tours, good place to send faxes.

Between Nandaime and Rivas are various turnings south which lead eventually to **Refugio de** the **Pacific coast** (all are rough, high clearance better than four-wheel drive). One of **Vida Silvestre** these turnings, 89 km from Managua if going via Diriamba and Jinotepe (61 km **Río Escalante** from Peñas Blancas), just south of the Río Ochomogo bridge, is signposted Refugio **Chacocente** de Vida Silvestre Río Escalante Chacocente. This 4,800-ha reserve of forest and beach is the second most important turtle nesting site in the country and one of the biggest tracts of tropical dry forest in the Pacific basin. The forest is full of mammal, reptile and birdlife and the beach is long and empty. Bring your own hammock and shade. The rough dirt road to the coast (45 km) goes to Las Salinas. Turn right here to **Astillero**, which has a fishing co-operative, and continue to the reserve. You will probably have to ask directions to the reserve several times and cross a number of rivers, the last of which is very wide (it can't be crossed after rain without a very strong four-wheel drive, lots of speed and bravado). Camping is safe and you can buy fish from the co-op. At **Chacocente**, there is a Marena office, a govern-ment-sponsored turtle sanctuary (the only signs after Astillero say 'authorized per-sonnel only'; don't be put off, they welcome visitors, but ask for directions). The Marena wardens protect newly hatched turtles and help them make it to the sea (a magnificent sight during November and December). Unfortunately, newly laid tur-tle eggs are considered to have aphrodisiac properties and are used as a dietary sup-plement by the locals. Marena is virtually powerless to prevent egg theft, although for two months a year the place is protected by armed military personnel. The Marena personnel are friendly and helpful – ask about similar projects around the country. ■ *US$0.70 entry to the refugio.*

San Juan del Sur

San Juan del Sur on the Pacific coast has a beautiful bay, and the sunsets have to be *Colour map 7, grid A2* seen to be believed. A sandy beach and some rocky caves can be reached easily by *Population: 14,521* walking round the point opposite the harbour. The town is 28 km from Rivas south *Altitude 4 m* along the Pan-American Highway and then right to the coast along a road which is in good condition. There is also a direct dirt road from Rivas going through beautiful countryside, but it is only good when dry.

The town beach is cleaned daily, but at weekends and on holidays, especially at *Semana Santa*, San Juan is busy; otherwise the beaches are quiet during the week.

Nicaragua

Sleeping

Note that hotel prices in San Juan del Sur double for Semana Santa, Christmas and New Year

A *Casablanca*, opposite *Bar Timón*, T/F458-2135, F458-2307, casablanca@ibw.com.ni, a/c, cable TV, private bath, restored house, clean, friendly, small swimming pool, laundry service, secure parking, transfers to San Jorge or Peñas Blancas US$25 per person, in front of beach. Recommended. **B** *Aramara Lodge*, from la Cabañita 1 block north, T458-2259, aguzman@uam.edu.ni **A** at weekends, includes breakfast, a/c, cable TV, pool, traditional house, very cute with balconies and living room, friendly, 1 block from beach. Recommended. **B** *Villa Renata*, behind the church to the left, T458-2568, marked by small wooden sign, 5 rooms, includes breakfast, a/c, fan, private bath, very clean, prices are negotiable at low season, lovely wooden house with hardwood floors, well decorated with ample windows and light, English spoken, 4 blocks from beach. **C** *Joxi*, T458-2348, friendly, clean, a/c, bath, bunk beds, Norwegian-run, restaurant, bar, sailing trips on the boat *Pelican Eyes* can be arranged here.

E *Buengusto*, very basic but very friendly, helpful, good fish restaurant, on seafront. **E** *Hospedaje Casa No 28*, 40 m from beach, near minibus stop for Rivas, big airy rooms, shared showers, laundry facilities, clean, friendly owners, good. On same street as *Joxi* is **E** *Estrella*, on Pacific, with meals, balconies overlooking the sea, partitioned walls, shower, take mosquito net and towel, clean, popular. **E** *Guest House Elizabeth*, opposite bus terminal, T458-2270, clean, fan, friendly and helpful owner, with tied-up monkey – please give it some food and water. **F** *Gallo de Oro*, 500 m north of town, very basic but friendly, nice setting at end of beach. **F** *Hospedaje Juliet*, from the church 1 block north, T458-2333, dark clean rooms, ask for fan, some with bath, others without, basic, soft beds, breakfast US$1.50, family-run, 4 blocks from beach. **F** *Hospedaje La Fogata*, clean, friendly, family-run, good food, keep an eye on your things. **F** *Youth Hostel Casa Oro*, 1 block from beach on church street (corner house), T0777-2453. 2 dormitories, 4 double rooms and plenty of hammocks, free use of fully equipped kitchen, beautiful garden. There are a couple of cheap, very basic places near the market, **F** *Eleonora*, Mercado ½ c al este, T458-2191, 4 rooms with shared bath and fan. **F** *Las Flores*, Mercado 1½ c al norte, T458-2284, 5 rooms, shared bath with fan, **E** with private bath.

Camping Customs Office may give permission for camping and to park motor-caravans and trailers on the wharves if you ask them nicely. Motor-caravans and trailers may also be parked on Marsella beach: coming south, turn right on entering San Juan, by shrimp-packing plant.

Eating *Las Lugo*, from post office 1 block east, expensive seafood, fresh fish, despite being by the sea, this is nothing like as good as its sister restaurant in Managua. Nearby is *Rinconcito Mexicano*, de *Las Lugos* 1 c al norte, T458-2594, tacos, quesadillas and nachos, daily 1000-2200. *O Sole Mio*, from *Hotel Casablanca* 500 m north, best Italian, mid-range, pizza and pasta. Recommended. *Salón Siria*, good. *Soya*, vegetarian and meat dishes, fruit, *refrescos, chorizo de soya*, good, cheap and friendly, also has a room to rent (**F**). The beach-front restaurants all serve good fish (about US$4 a meal), eg *Bar Timón* , lobster (US$9) and prawns are specialities, most popular place in town, good fish, slow service, very laid back and Nicaraguan. Next door is *Iguana Beach*, T458-2481 with European dishes. *Marie Bar*, OK food, English and German spoken, the owner George arranges evening trips to the reserve to see the turtles. *Ricardo's Bar*, north of *Bar Timón* on beach, popular with foreigners, good chicken salad, cybercafé.

The restaurants popular with the locals are along the beach front near the *Hotel Estrella*. *Brisas Marinas*, *Hotel Estrella* 20 m al oeste, T458-2176, seafood soup, *ceviche*, from 0700 daily. *Eskimo*, *Hotel Estrella* 75 m al sur, sundaes, banana splits, and malts, daily 0930-2300. In the same space is *El Globo*, chicken and beef burgers, cold beer from 0900 until dawn, inexpensive. Also *Lago Azul*, *Hotel Estrella* ½ c al sur, T458-2325, garlic shrimp, sandwiches, daily 0800-2300.

Breakfast and lunch in market, eg *Comedor Zapata*. *Comedor Angelita* serves very good fish dishes. *La Fogata*, south side of market, T458-2271, fried fish, sandwiches, daily from 0700 and *Las Flores*, Mercado 1½ c al norte, T458-2284, Greek stew, chicken *cacciatore*, daily 1100-0100 (except Thu). Good *panadería* 1 block from beach. Good *cafés* along the beach for breakfast and drinks.

Nicaragua

Surfing: The coast north and south of San Juan del Sur is among the best in Central America **Sports** for surfing, all access is by boat or long treks in 4WD. Ask around for information about the best spots and how to get there.

Bus Managua, every hr, 0500-1600, 3½ hrs, US$2.25. **Rivas**, every ½ hr, 0630-1700, **Transport** 40 mins, US$0.70.

Banks There is no bank. Hotels *Casablanca* and *Joxi* and some shops, like *Pulpería Sánchez*, will **Directory** change money. **Communications** Internet: *Capitan Erick*, *Hotel Estrella* 1 c al sur, T458-2180, with scanning and printing services. *Casa Joxi* and at *Ricardo's Bar*. Post office: 150 m left (south) along the seafront from the main junction. **Laundry** Most of the mid to upper-range hotels will do laundry for their guests on request. Near *Soya Restaurant* (ask there), hand wash, line dry. **Language schools** *Spanish Doña Rosa*, *Hotel Villa Isabella* 1 c al este, 1 c al norte, 1 c al este, spanish_rosa@latinmail.com, private lessons, 'dynamic' classes. *Spanish Nicaraguita*, del Mercado ½ c al oeste, T458-2388, individual tutoring, flexible hours. *Spanish School San Juan del Sur*, escuela Integral de San Juan del Sur, frente a la Bahía, T458-2115, escsjds@ibw.com.ni, regular morning classes, tutoring with flexible hours. **Medical services** The dispensary, where you have to pay for medicines, has good service.

You can take a boat to more pristine beaches such as **Playa del Coco** on the poor **South of San** road to Ostional. **Sleeping L-E** *Parque Marítimo El Coco*, 18 km south of San Juan **Juan del Sur** del Sur, T458-2512, apartments, bungalows and houses for 4-10 people, some on beach, others ocean view, very nice and closest lodging to La Flor Wildlife Refuge. **Eating** *Puesta de Sol*, broiled lobster, baked chicken, ceviche, with great fruit drinks on sand (Monday-Friday 1000-1600; Saturday-Sunday 1000-2000). The surfing on nearby beaches is good. **Refugio de Vida Silvestre La Flor** covers 800 ha of tropical dry forest, mangroves, estuary and beach. A beautiful, sweeping cove with light tan sand and many trees, it is the most important and heavily visited beach by nesting sea turtles from August to November. Armed guards protect the turtle arrivals during high season and the rangers are very happy to explain, in Spanish, the creature's reproductive habits. Arrivals are at times in the thousands and usually for a period of three days. Many birds live in the protected mangroves at the south end of the beach. ■ *Entrance costs US$5, US$2.50 student discount, and can be made by 4WD or on foot.* Exit for the dirt path south is 200 m before the entrance to San Juan del Sur, 21 km from the highway. Several rivers must be crossed, most with solid bottoms. Camping is provided (one tent only) during the turtle arrivals, US$10 per night, first come, first served. Bring hammock and mosquito netting, insects are vicious at dusk. Ranger station sells soft drinks and will let you use their outhouse.

Eating This is the only road crossing between the 2 countries. There are 2 duty-free shops **Border with** (not worth bothering with), *Hospedaje El Mesón* with *Cafetín Sapoá*, frente a *Bancentro*, **Costa Rica –** T454-0021, jalapeño steak, garlic shrimp, lobster in tartar sauce, Wed-Mon, 0800-1900, and **Peñas Blancas** several *comedores* on the Nicaraguan side.

Nicaraguan immigration Open 0800-1200 and 1300-1745. When entering the country, *There is no fuel going* you show your passport at the border completing Costa Rican exit formalities and then walk *into Nicaragua until* the 500 m to the new Nicaraguan border controls. International bus passengers have to dis- *Rivas (37 km)* embark and queue for immigration to stamp passport. Then you must unload your baggage and wait in a line for the customs official to arrive. You will then be asked to open your bags, the official will give them a cursory glance and you reload. Passports and tickets will be checked again back on the bus. For travellers not on a bus, there are plenty of small helpers on hand. Allow 45 mins to complete the formalities.

Leaving the country you pay US$1 to enter the customs area at the border and then com- plete formalities in the new customs building where you pay US$2 to have your passport checked. Then walk the 500 m to the Costa Rican border and get your passport stamped. You then need to buy a Cruz Roja stamp (US$3) from the window by the restaurant – if you don't get the Cruz Roja stamp you may have problems later in the country. Buses and taxis are available from the border – hitching is difficult.

Nicaragua

Crossing by private vehicle Entering: After you have been through Migración, find an inspector who will fill out the preliminary form to be taken to Aduana. At the Vehículo Entrando window, the vehicle permit is typed up and the vehicle stamp is put in your passport. Next, go to Tránsito to pay for the car permit. Finally, ask the inspector again to give the final check.

Leaving: First pay your exit tax at an office at the end of the control station, receipt given. Then come back for your exit stamp, and complete the *Tarjeta de Control Migratorio*. Motorists must then go to Aduana to cancel vehicle papers: exit details are typed on to the vehicle permit and the stamp in your passport is cancelled. Find the inspector in Aduana who has to check the details and stamp your permit. If you fail to do this you will not be allowed to leave the country – you will be sent back to Sapoá by the officials at the final Nicaraguan checkpoint.

Transport There is an hourly bus service from Sapoá to Rivas from 0730-1630, US$0.70, 1 hr. The last bus Rivas-Managua is at 1630, US$1.40, 2½ hrs. There can be long waits when the international buses are passing through. A good time to cross, if you are going independently, is around 0900, before the buses arrive.

Directory Exchange: same rates on either side, so try to find out the rate before arriving at the border to avoid being stung.

□Managua

Río San Juan

Nicaragua

The Río San Juan, running through deep jungles, drains Lake Nicaragua from its eastern end into the Caribbean at San Juan del Norte. Over 190 km long and with more than 17 tributaries, it runs the length of the southern border of the Indio Maíz Biological Reserve (see below) and makes the most natural connection between the Atlantic and Pacific Oceans. This great river has played an integral part in Nicaragua's colonial and post-colonial history and is one of the most accessible of the country's many pristine nature-viewing areas. First sailed by the Spanish in 1525, the complete length of the river was not navigated until 24 June 1539, the day of San Juan Bautista, hence its name. In colonial times it was a vital link between the Spanish Caribbean and the port of Granada. After three attacks by Caribbean pirates on Granada, the Spanish built a fortress at El Castillo in 1675. The English tried to take the fort twice in the 18th century, failing the first time thanks to the teenage Nicaraguan national heroine Rafaela Herrera, and then succeeding with Lord (then Captain) Nelson, who later had to withdraw owing to tropical diseases. Later it became the site of many aborted canal projects, one of which was abandoned after just 1 km had been dredged. Today it is a most rewarding boat journey.

San Carlos

Colour map 7, grid A2
Population: 39-536
Altitude: 39 m

San Carlos is the capital of Río San Juan Department and the jumping-off point for excursions to Solentiname (see above), Río Frío to Los Chiles in Costa Rica and the Río San Juan itself, with irregular launches to the river from the lakeside. Nearby are the two great nature reserves of Los Guatusos (see above) and Indio Maíz (see below). Much of the town was destroyed by fire in 1984, but rebuilding is almost complete. In the wet it is a very muddy place. At San Carlos there are the ruins of a fortress built for defence against pirates.

Sleeping & eating
All hotels are basic. If yours has no running water, there is a bathhouse by the pier

One possibility is **B** *Cabinas Leyka*, Policía Nacional 2 c al oeste, T283-0354, with bath, a/c, **D** with fan, balcony with view of the lake, serves breakfast, best in town; another is **F** *Costa Sur*, Consejo Supremo Electoral 50 m al sur, T283-0224. 10 rooms with shared or private bath and fan, meals available. **F** *Hospedaje Peña*, near central plaza, T283-0265, share bath, unhelpful. **F** *Casa de Protocolo*, top of town on park opposite church, clean, nets, private bath. *Restaurante Río San Juan*, good meals, room for rent, **F**, dirty, noisy. Also **F** *Hotelito San*

Carlos, by jetty, with fan, basic, breakfast US$1.25, and *Yuri*, nice room, cheap, friendly. Several *comedores* including *El Mirador*, west end of town in ruins of fort, lovely view of lake, Río Frío and Río San Juan, decent food with dishes starting at US$3. *Félix Dining Room*, 2 plastic tables on the main street but good meals for US$1.50. *Bar-restaurant Kaoma*, Río San Carlos, fresh fish caught by the owner, good food with occasional live music. Recommended. *Oasis*, by the lake. *Bar Miralago*, by the lake, painted pink and purple, good grilled meat and salad, but fearsome mosquitoes in the evening. Several good, cheap *comedores* including *Comedor Londras* on the jetty next to *BDF* and also in the covered market.

Air *La Costeña* has daily flights from Managua Mon-Sat, US$76 return, sit on right side on way to San Carlos for breathtaking views over Ometepe's 2 volcanoes. Flights depart at 1000, except Sun and Fri when they depart at 1300. You will be asked your body weight as there is a maximum weight accepted for flight. Flight lands and takes off within 5 mins, so early arrival is recommended. Taxi from airstrip to dock US$1.

Transport

Ferry San Carlos-Granada ferry leaves from main dock Tue and Fri, 1400, 15 hrs, US$4.

Small motor boats are called 'pangas'; long, narrow ones are 'botes', and big broad ones are 'planos'

Boat **Solentiname Archipelago**, stopping at islands La Venada, San Fernando and Mancarrón from San Carlos, and in reverse en route to San Carlos: **San Carlos- Solentiname**, Tue and Fri 1300, 2½ hrs, US$4. **Solentiname-San Carlos**, Tue, Fri 0400.

Los Guatuzos Wildlife Refuge, stopping at village of Papaturro, **San Carlos-Río Papaturro**, Tue and Fri 0800, 5½ hrs, US$5. **Río Papaturro-San Carlos**, Mon, Thu 0500.

San Carlos-El Castillo, 0800 (daily except Sun) and 1400 (daily), 3-4 hrs, US$5. **El Castillo-San Carlos**, daily 0430, 0500, 0600.

San Carlos-San Juan del Norte, Thu 0800, 12-14 hrs, US$15. **San Juan del Norte-San Carlos**, Sun 0330, 13-15 hrs.

Crossing to **Costa Rica** from **San Carlos-Los Chiles**, 1000 (daily), 2 hrs, US$4. **Los Chiles-San Carlos**, 1600 (daily).

Private boats are expensive but are faster and provide freedom to stop and view wildlife. Ask at docks, restaurants, taxi drivers or at tourism office. Average round-trip rates: **El Castillo** US$190-250, **Solentiname** US$75-100. Group tours are available from tour operators in Managua.

Bus **Managua-San Carlos** is a brutal ride, but the locals prefer it to the Granada ferry boat trip. There are some lovely mountain ranges and formations during the early part and pure pain in the kidneys at the end. **San Carlos- Managua**, daily at 0200, 0600, 0800 and 1100, 9½ hrs, US$7. Returning from Mercado El Mayoreo at 0500, 0600, 0700 and 1300.

Banks *BDF*, next to dock for Solentiname. No exchange for TCs, only cash with street changers.

Directory

San Carlos

To Airport, Police, Acoyapa & Managua

Enitel

To El Castillo & San Juan del Norte

Public Baths
La Costeña Office
Main Dock (ENAP)

Taxis
Immigration & Customs

Fort San Carlos

Taxis

Dock (Muelle Flotante)

Río San Juan

New Dock

New Dock

Lago de Nicaragua

Río Frío

To Costa Rica

N

0 metres 200
0 yards 200

■ **Sleeping**
1 Cabinas Leyka
2 Hospedaje Peña
3 Hospedaje Yuri

● **Eating**
1 El Mirador
2 Kaoma

Known as the cradle of wildlife for Lake Nicaragua, Los Guatuzos Wildlife Reserve is home to many exotic and varied species of bird and reptile. It is also heavily populated by monkeys, especially howlers. The reserve is crossed by

Los Guatusos Wildlife Reserve
500 sq km area of wetland, rainforest and gallery forest

Nicaragua

three rivers, Guacalito, Zapote and (most popular for boat touring) Papaturro. It is essential to be at the park for sunrise to see the best of the wildlife. After 1030 the river often becomes busier with the immigration traffic of labourers heading to Costa Rica. A new **research centre** built by Friends of the Earth and the Government of Spain has a collection of over 90 orchids native to the region and a butterfly farm. Visitors are welcome. Explanations in Spanish only, ask for Armando who is a native and an enthusiastic expert on orchids. ■ *US$4*. Lodging is also possible in the research station (**E** per person, bunk beds with mosquito netting and shared bath). There is a public boat San Carlos-Papaturro daily except Sunday at 1100 and 1400, US$1, 1½ hours; check return schedule locally. It is only 30 minutes to one hour from Mancarrón into the reserve. Your name and passport number may have to be given to the police post at Papaturro. Tours can be booked with Managua tour operators, or at the *Hotel Mancarrón* in Solentiname (see above). Cost US$85-125 per boat for 5-6 hours.

Lake Nicaragua's eastern shore Heading south down the eastern shore of Lake Nicaragua, a good road passes through **Juigalpa** before leaving by a track at **Lovago** on a road that runs parallel to the shoreline through **Acoyapa**, San Bartolo and down to the shore where, about 45 km north of San Carlos, is **San Miguelito**. This small fishing village is where the boats call between San Carlos and Granada; vendors with drinks and food board the boats. **D** *Cocibolca*, at the end of the jetty, T552-8803, F552-6104, colonial style, ask for a room with balcony, hard beds, riding arranged by the owner, Franklin, as well as day trips to El Boquete and El Morro Islands.

Border with Costa Rica – San Carlos to Los Chiles This has now become a frequented crossing point between Nicaragua and Costa Rica and is normally quick and hassle free. There is a track of sorts from the south side of the Río San Juan, but most travellers go by boat up the Río Frío.

Sleeping The Nicaraguan side of the Río Frío is part of the *Los Guatuzos Wildlife Refuge* and there is a research station and lodge on the river, **E** *Reserva La Esperanza Verde*, 15 mins by boat from San Carlos, T283-0354, F283-0080, 5 rooms with shared baths, meals available, hiking and birding.

Nicaraguan immigration Border is now open 7 days a week 0800-1600. Exit stamp, costing US$2, must be obtained in San Carlos Mon-Fri only. If travelling into Costa Rica the exit stamp must be obtained in San Carlos. Entrance stamps into Costa Rica (US$8) are only available via Limón or Los Chiles. Check with the police in advance for the latest position.

Transport There several launches a day from San Carlos to Los Chiles, US$3.50, 1½ hrs, from 1000. If you get on last at San Carlos, you will be first off at Los Chiles for the Costa Rican *Migración* which closes at 1200 for lunch.

The entire Nicaragua-Costa Rica border along the Río San Juan is ill-defined and the subject of inter-government debate and tension. The Costa Rican border reaches the south banks of the Río San Juan 2 km down river from El Castillo but the river in its length is Nicaraguan territory. It is best to travel in Nicaraguan boats on the river, as Costa Rican ones could be detained or turned back.

El Castillo Some 60 km down river is El Castillo, built around the restored ruins of the 18th-century Spanish fort called La Fortaleza de la Inmaculada Concepción. The old fort has a good history museum inside. ■ *Closes at 1200 for lunch, US$1. The tourist office on the quay has a leaflet about the fort and town.* It was here that Nelson did battle with the Spanish forces (see above). There are great views of the river in both directions from the fortress. The town is on a wide bend in the river where some shallow but tricky rapids run the whole width. Horse-riding is possible (about US$6 per hour).

Nicaragua

Sleeping and eating **C** *Albergue El Castillo*, next to fortress above city dock, T892-0174, *El Castillo is a* new but oddly designed, comfortable rooms with shared balcony overlooking river, shared *good place to pick* bath and good restaurant downstairs. The restaurant serves very good food, mid-range/cheap *up food on the river* with great view of river from outdoor deck, good *camarones del río* (river shrimp) in garlic butter. **F** *Hospedaje Manantial*, on left of main street as you leave the boat, not too clean, no view, basic, breakfast US$1.50, lunch US$2. **F** *Hospedaje Aurora*, basic, but kindly owners, veranda with rocking chair overlooking river, serves food. *Bar Cofalito*, on the jetty, crayfish on menu, good view but poor quality. Better value is the *soda* facing the quay. *Doña Amelia*, good meals also on the wharf, very clean, cheap. *Naranjano*, good food.

Transport There are about 4 daily boats from San Carlos to El Castillo (2½ hrs, US$1.50), schedules seem to change frequently. Other boats do the trip but without fixed schedules. If you plan to continue beyond El Castillo, it can only be done by prior arrangement in San Carlos or Managua, or with lots of patience – and cash.

A few kilometres downstream is the Río Bartola and the beginning of the Indio Maíz **Reserva** Biological Reserve, 3,000 sq km of mostly primary rainforest and home to over 600 **Biológica Indio** species of bird, 300 species of reptile and 200 species of mammal including many big **Maíz** cats and howler, white-faced and spider monkeys.

Sleeping **B** per person *Refugio Bartola*, T289-7924, including 3 meals (**C** without food), fruit juices, simple rooms with solid beds, ask for mosquito netting, excellent meals great *camarones del río, cerdo a la plancha*, purified water, very clean. Pet spider monkey at lodge, Daniela, loves men and bites women. *Refugio Bartola* is also a research station and training ground for young Nicaraguan biologists; it has a labyrinth of well-mapped trails behind the lodge in the reserve. The hotel guides are very knowledgeable, but one speaks only Spanish. They will also take you down the Río Bartola in canoe, great wildlife viewing and birding. Fantastic. Make all transport arrangements with care. **Camping** is possible: ask the lone park ranger where you may camp, his guard house is across the Río Bartola from the *Refugio Bartola* lodge.

The river past Bartola becomes more beautiful and unpopulated. Here the Costa **Bartola to the** Rican border reaches to the south bank of the river, and while the Costa Rican side is **Caribbean** partially deforested and populated, the Nicaraguan side containing the Indio Maíz Reserve is almost entirely intact. Many turtles, birds and crocodiles can be seen in this section of the river. Two hours minimum down river is the Río Sarapiquí and immigration check-points for both Costa Rica and Nicaragua – no stamps available though.

There is a simple, friendly, Nicaraguan-owned lodge on the Sarapiquí called *Paraíso de la Frontera* or Doña Adilia's place, **D** per person, private bath, not terribly clean, shared bath, fan, restaurant with set meals, US$3. She also has a small store for supplies and a pool table next door, popular for games between Nicaraguan and Costa Rican military. If coming from the Río San Juan to Río Sarapiquí you will need to check in with the Costa Rican guard station if you want to spend the night, or even if you just want to pick up something at the store. If continuing down the river without stopping you only need to check in at the Nicaraguan station on the Río San Juan. The guards there will let you use their toilet for a smile and a thank you.

Past the Sarapiquí, the San Juan branches north, and both sides of the river (heavily forested) become part of Nicaragua again as the Río Colorado heads into Costa Rica. Two hours or so later, the San Juan reaches the Caribbean via a series of magnificent forest-wrapped lagoons. The Río Indio must be taken to reach the isolated but surprisingly wealthy village of San Juan del Norte.

San Juan del Norte

One of the wettest places on the American continent at over 5,000 mm of rain per year, *Colour map 7, grid A3* San Juan del Norte is also one of the most beautiful, with primary rainforest, lagoons, rivers and the Caribbean Sea. It is settled by a small, gregarious population (estimated

Nicaragua

at 275), though it was once a boom town in the 19th century, when the American industrialist Cornelius Vanderbilt was running his steamship line between New York and San Francisco. Then called **Greytown**, San Juan del Norte was the pick-up point for the steamship journey to the Pacific via the Río San Juan, Lake Nicaragua to La Virgen and then by mule overland to San Juan del Sur. This service was quite popular during the 'gold rush' of San Francisco and Mark Twain made the crossing as a young man from San Francisco to New York. He recounted the journey in his book *Travels with Mr Brown*. This town remained in its location on the Bahía San Juan del Norte (actually a coastal lagoon) until the 1980s, when fighting caused its population to flee. Re-established in its current location on the Río Indio, the village is separated from the Caribbean Sea by a dense wedge of rainforest, 400 m wide, on the east bank of the Río Indio. The population is a mix of Miskito, Creole, Rama and Hispanic. There is no land route from here to Bluefields – the boat takes about 3 hours, US$600.

Due to its proximity to Limón, in Costa Rica, colones are the standard currency here as all the food and supplies are more easily bought there than in San Carlos. In Sarapiquí and San Juan del Norte córdobas, colones and dollars are all accepted, with change normally given in colones.

Sleeping Turn left out of the ferry and follow the river about 500 m down for **D** per person *Hotel Lost Paradise* (or *Melvin's Place*), on the river, ceiling fan, private bath, clean, bring coils or mosquito netting, owner Melvin speaks some English and is very helpful, bar, restaurant, night-time generated power, hammocks on the gazebo by the river, sometimes have bottled water for sale, highly recommended. Tell the kitchen in advance if you want meals. Nearby is **F** *Greytown Lodge*, no sign, basic and friendly with cooking facilities.

Eating The food in San Juan del Norte is simple, fresh lobster if in season, if not the fried snook is rec-
Advance notice ommended. Other seafood is fresh too. *Doña Ester's Place*, just down the river from *Melvin's*
needed for meals *Place*, is the town's restaurant, though others are to open soon, average dish of fantastic food costs US$3. Drinks in town consist of Costa Rican beer, Nicaraguan rum and Coca-Cola. There is a pleasant bar just up river from *Doña Ester's Place* with a big palm ranch and somewhat cold beer, card-playing locals and friendly Rama Indians. At times it can be difficult to find someone in San Juan to cook a meal, so bring snack supplies and arrange meals at *Doña Ester's* or *Melvin's Place* in advance, they will buy supplies and cook.

Entertainment **Discos** There is 1 disco which is full of festive locals on weekend nights. Dancing to reggae as well as salsa, rap and merengue. If staying at *Melvin's Place* (and Melvin is in town) he will take you to the disco at night to make sure you have a good time and make it back home. It is a short walk but a ride in his *super-panga*, if offered, is not to be missed; hold on tight. There are no police in San Juan and while the locals are very honest, this is frontier country and care should be taken at night.

Excursions If coming in your own boat (chartered), a trip further down the **Río Indio** is recommended, with lots of wildlife, virgin forest and Rama Indians (please respect their culture and privacy). A visit to the ruins of old **Greytown** is also interesting, with a well-marked trail that leads through various cemeteries buried in the forest and to the town centre where only foundations and the church bell remain. It has been described as 'incredibly atmospheric' with amazing wildlife ('spider monkeys and a puma skulking amongst gravetones'). Swimming is best in the **Blue Lagoon**, though the Caribbean is also accessible, but with many sharks. If coming on the public boat from San Carlos, Melvin can arrange tours with one of his *pangas*. Reckon on US$15-20 for a boat.

Border with This area of the Caribbean coast is a narcotics zone, with drugs being landed from
Costa Rica – San Andrés (Colombia). Before attempting to cross, seek information on safety.
Greytown

Nicaraguan immigration There is no official immigration in San Juan del Norte. Although travellers have reported being able to get stamps from the authorities here that were accepted when checked elsewhere, this is not recommended. Alternatively you must go to Bluefields or to one of the posts up the Río San Juan. Equally take advice on what to do on arrival in Costa Rica, where the official entrance is Limón.

Transport You can go by boat from San Juan del Norte to Barra del Colorado in Costa Rica, ask about fishing boats and canoes.

Eastern lowlands and the Caribbean

Managua

Nicaragua's eastern tropical lowlands make for a striking change from the rest of the country. Gone are the volcanoes, hills and valleys, and in their place is lush, tropical rainforest that is drenched between May and December with heavy rainfall. Most of the population are the African-influenced Miskito Indians who live in the northern lowlands, mainly around Puerto Cabezas. Their economy is based on timber, fishing and mining. To reach the Caribbean port of Bluefields and the idyllic and peaceful Corn Islands, you can fly or take the famous 'Bluefields Express' down river. English is widely but not universally spoken.

This area, together with roughly half the coastal area of Honduras, was never colonized by Spain. From 1687 to 1894 it was a British Protectorate known as the Miskito Kingdom. It was populated then, as now, by Miskito Indians, whose numbers are estimated at 75,000. There are two other Indian groups, the Sumu (5,000) and the Rama, of whom only a few hundred remain, near Bluefields. Also near Bluefields are a number of Garífuna communities. Today's strong African influence has its roots in the black labourers brought in by the British to work the plantations and in Jamaican immigration. The Afro-Nicaraguan people call themselves *criollos* (creoles). The largest number of inhabitants of this region are Spanish-speaking *mestizos*. The Sandinista Revolution, like most other political developments in the Spanish-speaking part of Nicaragua, was met with mistrust. Although the first Sandinista junta recognized the indigenous peoples' rights to organize themselves and choose their own leaders, many of the programmes initiated in the region failed to encompass the social, agricultural and cultural traditions of eastern Nicaragua. Relations deteriorated and many Indians engaged in fighting for self-determination. A low point was reached when the Sandinista Government ordered forced resettlement of many Miskito villages, burning to the ground what was left behind. About half the Miskito population fled as refugees to Honduras, but most returned after 1985 when a greater understanding grew between the Sandinista Government and the people of the east coast. The Autonomous Atlantic Region was given the status of a self-governing region in 1987; it is divided into **Región Autonomista Atlántico Norte** (RAAN) and **Región Autonomista Atlántico Sur** (RAAS).

Background
In Nicaragua, the Caribbean coast is almost always referred to as the Atlantic coast

Nicaragua

Managua to Rama

At **San Benito**, 35 km from Managua on the Pan-American Highway going north, the Atlantic Highway branches east, paved all the way to Rama on the Río Escondido. Shortly after Teustepe, a paved road goes northeast to Boaco. A turn-off, unpaved, goes to **Santa Lucía**, a village inside a crater, with a women's handicraft shop. There is also a co-operative here with an organic farming programme (information from *Unag* in Matagalpa). **F** *Casa de Soya*, good food, friendly owners, single room for rent, basic. Good views from nearby mountains. Two trucks a day from Boaco, US$1, one bus a day to/from Managua. **Boaco** (84 km from Managua), is called the city of two floors because it is split-level nature. The upper floor has a nice square with good views of the surrounding countryside. On the square is **F** *Hotel Sobalvarro*, simple and clean. On the first level is **E** *Hotel Boaco*, opposite Cooperativa San Carlos, T842-2434, small beds, private and shared baths, friendly owners who include one of the country's finest archaeologists, Edgar Espinoza, the current director of the Museo Nacional de Nicaragua. It may be possible on the weekend to convince Edgar to guide to some hidden petroglyph sites in the surrounding hills, call ahead. Boaco is cattle country and there a many good places to enjoy a local steak. *La Casona*, next to Texaco, T842-2421, try their *lomo de costilla* or *plato típico*, daily 0800-2300, or *La Cueva*, south side of the Parroquia Santiago church, T842-2438, very good steaks, with chicken and fish.

From Boaco, unpaved roads go north to **Muy Muy** and **Matagalpa**, and south to **Comoapa**. Bus Managua-Boaco every 40 minutes from Plaza Mayoreo (two hours 10 minutes, US$1.50).

Juigalpa
Colour map 7, grid A2
Population: 41,000

The Atlantic Highway continues through Juigalpa. A pleasant town with one of the best museums in Nicaragua, housing a collection of idols resembling those at San Agustín, Colombia. The bus terminal is in the town centre near the market, up the hill. Banks on main plaza accept dollars cash only.

139 km from Managua
Buses every 30 minutes, US$1.85, 2½ hours

Sleeping D *Hotel La Quinta*, on main road at the east end of town, a/c or fan, bath, clean, friendly, restaurant has good food and a fine view of surrounding mountains. **E** *Hospedaje Rubio*, on main road going north, clean, friendly, with bath (**F** without), TV, laundry. **F** *Hospedaje Central*, basic and noisy, just about OK. *Hospedaje Angelita* next door, a bit more expensive, better. The *hospedaje* in *Comedor San Martín* is unfriendly; better is *Presillas* (Km 269), unnamed, beside *Comedor González*; all **F** per person.

Around Juigalpa

A gravel road goes north to La Libertad, a goldmining town at 600 m, and on to Santo Domingo. Heading south a road goes direct to the shore of Lake Nicaragua at Puerto Díaz. From here pick-ups will go to the monastery of **San Juan de las Aguas**, founded in 1689. The guide will show you the path through swamps to the monastery for about US$1.20 per person, minimum four people (Pedro Córtez is recommended). It's a little neglected, but has several wooden statues. The monks are very friendly and will let you stay the night if you ask. Take your own food and leave a donation. Ask to see the cave/tunnel complex that was used when the monks hid from besieging Indians. Twenty-five kilometres south of Juigalpa an unpaved road turns off to **Acoyapa**, El Morrito, San Miguelito and San Carlos on Lake Nicaragua (see page 994).

Rama

The main road continues east to **Santo Tomás** and smaller villages (including La Gateada, turn-off to **Nuevo Guinea**, centre of cacao production, connected by air from Managua via San Carlos on Friday with La Costeña, T285-0160), to **Cara de Mono**, on the Río Mico, and finally to Rama, 290 km from Managua. The town was badly hit by Hurricane Joan in October 1988 when the river rose 16 m above normal height. It is now poor, dirty with what can best be called 'a frontier charm'.

Sleeping and eating *Hospedaje Ramada Inn* seems to be the best. *Hotel Las Cabinas*, T817-0021, F817-0013 has a/c and garage parking. *El Viajero* is quite good. Hotels *Amy* and *Johanna* both **E**, neither has showers, *Amy* cleaner and quieter, near main jetty. Good cheap food at *Comedor Torres*.

Transport Buses. From Managua buses leave from the Mercado Mayoreo. **Managua**-Rama, every hr, 0400-1130, 8-10 hrs, US$5.50. To Managua, hourly from 0400-1130. To **Juigalpa**, every hr, 0800-1500, 6 hrs, US$3.75. Juigalpa-El Rama, hourly from 0800-1500.

Rama to Bluefields

The ferry from Rama to Bluefields – the **Bluefields Express** – is packed with hundreds of people, assorted animals and goods. The journey passes through the sparsely populated eastern half of Nicaragua. The river is wide and fast flowing, passing land that is mostly cultivated, with the occasional subsistence farmer's dwelling.

Transport The schedule appears to be express boat **Rama-Bluefields**, Tue, Thu, Sat, Sun at 1700, **Bluefields-Rama** at 0500; ordinary boat Rama-Bluefields, Mon, Wed and Fri in the early morning, from Bluefields-Rama between 1100 and 1300, 5 hrs, US$3.50. Food and soft drinks are sold on the ferry. Fast boats, *pangas*, can be hired for US$12-15 per person Rama-Bluefields, taking 1½ hrs, or hitch on a fishing boat. There is usually one waiting when the bus arrives.

Bluefields

Dirty, chaotic yet curiously inviting, Bluefields, the most important of Nicaragua's three Caribbean ports, gets its name from the Dutch pirate Abraham Blaauwveld. It stands on a lagoon behind the bluff at the mouth of the Bluefields River (Río Escondido), which is navigable as far as Rama (96 km). In May there is a week-long local festival, *Mayo-Ya!* with elements of the British Maypole tradition, local music, poetry and dancing. **Fiesta**: 30 September for San Jerónimo. Bananas, cabinet woods, frozen fish, shrimps and lobsters were the main exports until the hurricane in 1988. The **tourist office**, INTUR, next door to the old Migración building, T822-1111.

Colour map 7, grid A3
Population: 42,665

Tragically, in October 1988, Hurricane Joan destroyed virtually all of Bluefields, but the rebirth is now complete. There are several bars, a couple of reggae clubs, *comedores* and restaurants (two with a/c), and an *Almacén Internacional*. Prices are about the same as in Managua. Be prepared for frequent power and water cuts.

B *Bluefields Bay Hotel*, Barrio Pointeen, T/F822-2838, a/c, with bath, clean, owned by the autonomous regions university URACAN. Rooms upstairs are better. Excursions offered to surrounding areas. Highly recommended. **B** *La Casona*, Barrio Central, frente a discoteca Bacchus, T822-2436, with breakfast, private bath, cable TV, a/c. **C** *Caribbean Dreams*, opposite *Hollywood*, T822-0107, with bath, water erratic, basic but clean, owners helpful. **C** *South Atlantic*, near central square, next to *Enitel*, run by Fanny Chambers (native language English), with bath, safe, a/c, cable TV, fridge, clean, friendly, excellent food, *South Atlantic II*, T822-2265, F822-1219, new annex in the main street, with *Sports Bar* looking across the bay and main street. **D** *Marda Maus*, T822-2429, 1 of the nicer places in its price range with bath and fan, dark, not too clean, no restaurant, soft drinks available, near market. **E** *El Dorado*, quiet spot away from main street, may offer floor space to late arrivals. **E** *Hollywood*, Barrio Punta Fría, Mercado Teodoro Martínez ½ c arriba, T822-2282, 12 rooms, some with fan others more expensive with a/c and cable TV. Has its own well and generator, friendly, restaurant, clean. **F** *Airport*, above *Costeña* office at airport, clean, friendly. **F** *Claudia*, clean, comfortable, room on street side best. **F** *Las Brisas*, Barrio Central, Muelle de las Pangas, T822-1471, 12 basic rooms with fan and shared baths. **F** *Pearl Lagoon*, Barrio Central, frente a UNAG, T822-2411, private bath, laundry service, restaurant, good value.

Out of town A-D *The Groovy Ant Farm*, T/F822-2838, tiairene@ibw.com.ni, is the locally well-known Carol Bidon's new venture. Formerly an agroforestry demonstration farm, it is now ideal for nature lover's, fishing and bird-watching, cabaña accommodation, with running water, 15 mins by *panga* from town. Call in advance to book and for group rates.

Sleeping
Hotels may be full if you arrive late, or are last off the ferry

Café Central, good-value meals, provides accommodation, has colour TV. *Restaurant Flotante*, built over the water at the end of the main street, average prices, slow service, great view. *Cocktails*, international menu, but good seafood, reasonably priced, recommended. *Bay View Restaurant*, next to Tía Irene, beautiful spot on the water to watch the world go by with a drink, popular.

Eating

Air The airport is 3 km from the city centre; either walk (30 mins) or take a taxi jeep (US$0.80) that waits by the runway. *La Costeña* (Managua T263-1228, Bluefields T822-2500) and *Atlantic Airlines* (Managua T233-2791, Bluefields T822-1299) share the service to Bluefield, US$45 1-way, US$78 return. *Costeña* has 3 flights a day (0700, 0830, 1600, Mon-Sun). *Atlantic*

Transport

Nicaragua

also has 3 daily flights (0645, 1030, 1410, Mon-Sun). Flights also connect to daily flights to Puerto Cabezas and the Corn Islands (see below). Managua offices of the airlines are in the domestic terminal at the airport. Bring passport, it is sometimes asked for in the departure lounge. There is a customs check on return to Managua. Flights rarely leave on time, and sometimes leave early.

Sea Several wharfs near the market provide access to the port. *Pangas* can be rented for trips within the area. From the main wharf small boats leave irregularly for villages on the coast and Laguna de Perlas, such as Tasbapounie (*hospedaje*); food may be scarce in all settlements. A boat leaves daily 0800 to **Laguna de Perlas** (Pearl Lagoon), 80 km north of Bluefields 3-6 hrs, US$4.35.

Directory **Banks** Branches of *Caley Dagnall* and *Banco de Nicaragua* in town.

Laguna de Perlas The lagoon itself is some 50 km long with mostly Creole villages round its shores, eg Pearl Lagoon, Haulover, Brown Bank, Marshall Point and San Vicente. La Fe and Orinoco are Garífuna villages and Raitipura and Kakabila are Indian villages. In Raitipura there is a Danish housing project, run by Mogens Vibe who takes on volunteers (minimum 1 week), recommended. At the village of Pearl Lagoon there is a hostel, *Miss Ingrid's*, very friendly, stay with the entertaining family. Within walking distance of the village the swimming beach of Awas has basic accommodation. Larger vessels may be available for transport to Puerto Cabezas, but there is no transport south of Bluefields.

El Bluff is a small island with a village harbour, some oil tanks and a small, dirty beach. It is accessible by *panga* from the wharf at the Bluefields market. When the *panga* is full, pay your fare (no more than US$1.70). **Sleeping and eating** **E** *El Bluff*, with bath, cheaper without, fan, limited water, friendly, restaurant, pleasant. *El Buen Gusto*, next to Pescasa, sector No 1, T827-0121, good cheap food, sandwiches, hamburgers, *vigorón*, fruit drinks (Monday-Saturday 1000-2200).

Nicaragua

Outlying areas of the Región Autonomista Atlántico Sur The **Río Kurinwás** area north of Bluefields is a fascinating, largely uninhabited jungle area, where it is possible to see monkeys and much other wildlife. It might occasionally be possible to get a boat to **Tortuguero** (also called Nuevo Amanecer) a *mestizo* town which will really give you a taste of the frontier. Tortuguero is about a six-hour speedboat ride from Bluefields up the Kurinwás River; several days by regular boat.

The **Río Grande** is the next river north of the Kurinwás, connected to the Pearl Lagoon by the Top-Lock Canal. At its mouth are five interesting villages: the four Miskito communities of Kara, Karawala, Sandy Bay Sirpi, and Walpa, and the Creole village of La Barra. **Sandy Bay Sirpi** is situated on both the river and the Caribbean, and has a nice beach. Travelling upriver, the Río Grande is a noticeable contrast to the Río Kurinwás; it is much more settled, dotted with farms and cattle grazing. Quite a bit upriver (also about a six-hour speedboat ride from Bluefields, several days by regular boat), you reach the *mestizo* town of **La Cruz de Río Grande**. It was founded in about 1922 by Chinese traders to serve workers from a banana plantation (now defunct) further upriver. La Cruz has a very pretty church, and there are resident expatriate (US) priests of the Capuchin order in the town. The adventurous can walk between La Cruz and Tortuguero; each way takes about 10 hours in the dry season, 12 in the rainy. There is partial damage from Hurricane Mitch on the Río Grande, eg at Karawala and La Cruz de Río Grande.

Corn Islands

Colour map 5, grid A2

Everything is more expensive than on the mainland

The Corn Islands, opposite Bluefields, are two small islands fringed with white coral and slender coconut trees, perfect for relaxation. **Little Corn**, the smaller of the two and far more idyllic, escaped serious damage in the 1988 hurricane and can be visited by boat from the larger island, **Big Corn**, a one-hour ride by *panga*. On Little

Corn Island there is no electricity and no phones, just pristine white-sand beaches and some of the Caribbean's finest undisturbed coral reefs. Big Corn is a popular Nicaraguan holiday resort; its bathing facilities make it ideal for tourists (best months March and April). The nicest beaches are Long Bay and Brik Bay.

If you climb the mountain, wear long trousers as there are many ticks. On Little Corn you can climb the lighthouse for fantastic views of the whole island (not recommended if you are uncomfortable with heights).

The language of the islands is English. The islanders are very friendly but petty thievery has been reported, even clothes stolen off a washing line. Be wary of touts who greet you at the airport, posing as impartial guides, who may charge you for their services. The local coconut oil industry has been devastated by Hurricane Joan, but lobsters provide much prosperity. An Italian resort is planned, so visit now.

Dollars are widely used. Since the price of everything is generally high and there is only one bank (*Caley Dagnall*), take the cash you need with you. In an emergency there is a *Western Union*, opposite the *Bayside Hotel*. There is a post office about 100 m south of the airport shack.

On **Big Corn B** *El Paraíso Club Cabinas*, Briggs Bay, T285-5111, F285-5125, with bath, porch with hammock, clean, bar, restaurant, slow service, horses, bicycles and snorkelling gear for rent, noisy part of the island but popular, recommended. Some misunderstandings with restaurant bills have been reported, keep track of your tab. **B** *Bayside Hotel*, T285-5001, F249-0451, all rooms with a/c and cable TV, oceanfront on the best snorkelling reef on the island, suffered hurricane damage in 1996, a bit run-down. **B-C** *Panorama*, close to beach, clean, simple, private bath. **D** *Beachview*, next to *Panorama*, some rooms with bath, run-down. **D** *Hospedaje Miramar* is recommended, serves meals. **D** *Hospedaje Playa Coco*, also serves meals. **E** *Brisas del Mar*, Playa Coco, good but simple, friendly and good breakfast, restaurant. **E** *Casa Blanca* (actually blue), at Playa Coco, Miss Florence's house, running water, noisy. The chief problem in all the hotels is rats, which may not be dangerous, but neither are they pleasant. Electric power 1400-2400 only, failures are not uncommon. **E** *Estrella*, *Enitel* 80 m este, 73 m sur, T822-0523, shared bath with fan. **E** *Sweet Pearly*, Barrio Central del Muelle 8 m al sur, T822-0512, 24 rooms, with private and cheaper shared baths, fan, laundry.

On **Little Corn B** *Casa Iguana*, www.casaiguana.net, on a 3-ha bluff overlooking the sea, US-owned, friendly, helpful, 4 smart cabins with bath, 2 cabins with shared bath. Can hire out snorkelling equipment and arrange fishing trips. TCs accepted. **E** *Derek's*, on beach in beautiful remote setting, per person in 4-bed cabins. Can also camp for a small fee. **F** *Bridget's*, in village, very basic (stifling heat at night) but good food.

Sleeping
A map by the airline offices shows all the accommodation

On **Big Corn** *Sevva's Place*, 500 m past *Bayside Hotel*, T285-5058, great seafood, chicken, fine location, good food, mid-range, try breakfast on rooftop seating overlooking Caribbean. Beach in front of *Sevva's* good for swimming. Highly recommended. *Fisherman's Cave*, next to dock, popular, mid-range, average food, terrible service. *Comedor Lissie*, good hearty meal US$2. *Comedor Blackstone*. *Mini Café*. Ice-cream parlour. Several bars and reggae clubs. *Dugout de la Tonia* has the cheapest beer and good *punta* music. Ask around for where meals are available; the restaurants serve mainly chicken and chop suey, but in private houses you can find much better fare. Try fresh coconut bread (from family stores, a must), banana porridge and sorrel drink (red, and ginger-flavoured). Main market area is near Will Bowers Wharf and is a cheap place to eat.

On **Little Corn** All the hotels have restaurants, though you should book. *Comedor Isleta/Miss Rosie's* in village, next to *Bridget's* has simple good food.

Eating

Swimming: the best beach for swimming is Long Beach on Long Bay; walk across the island from Playa Coco. For **fishing** (barracuda, etc), contact *Ernie Jenkie* (about US$5 per hr). It is possible to **dive** off the Corn Islands. There are reports that the equipment is rather old, but the reef is good, however, and dives are very cheap through the couple of diver operators on the islands (US$25 a dive).

Sports

Nicaragua

Transport **Land** Buses and *colectivos* travel clockwise and anti-clockwise round the island. US$0.70 per person regardless of distance travel or time of day.

Air *La Costeña* flies from Managua and Bluefields to the Corn Islands, daily at 0630 and 1400 from Managua, 0700 and 1535 from Corn Islands (0845 and 1535 on Sun), US$105 return. The same advice on passport and customs applies as under Bluefields. Air services are suspended from time to time because of the poor state of the runway on Big Corn. Book well in advance and book return immediately on arrival.

Sea A boat leaves Big Corn for Little Corn, if the weather's ok, twice a day, 0900 and 1600 – it runs to coincide with the plane timetable. Starts in Little Corn first, leaving for Big Corn 0630 and 1400. Not for the faint-hearted if it's choppy. US$5 each way.

Passenger-carrying cargo boats leave Bluefields for the Corn Islands from the docks of Copesnica, north of town, around a small bay and past the ruined church: Wed, Fri, Sun 0700-1000, return Thu, Sun, Tue, US$4.35 one way. The water around Bluefields is dirty, muddy brown, soon becoming a clear, sparkling blue. There is usually a boat from Bluefields (the *Lynx Express*), via El Bluff on Wed at 0830, 4 hrs, but there is no guarantee. Boats back to Bluefields leave from Will Bowers Wharf; tickets available in advance from nearby office. You may be able to find a lobster, or other fishing boat that will take you but make sure the boat is properly equipped and seaworthy. Check with the *Capitanía* in Bluefields, or in El Bluff and with anyone else you can find who has information. Trips take 5-8 hrs. To hire a boat, go to the dock and ask around, normal charge US$40 one way, US$80 for the *panga* for a full day.

Puerto Cabezas

Colour map 6, grid B6
Population: 50,941
Altitude: 10 m

Puerto Cabezas, capital of the RAAN (Región Autonomista Atlántico Norte), has a distinctly different atmosphere from Bluefields. It is principally a large Miskito village, and it offers an excellent introduction to the Miskito part of the country. You can arrange to stay in small Miskito villages, for example near Haulover, a few hours by boat south of Puerto Cabezas. There are significant minorities of *mestizos* (referred to on the coast as *españoles* or the Spanish) and Creoles, many of whom came to 'Port' by way of Las Minas (see below). Spanish is a second language for the majority of residents, although most speak it well (at least those who live in Puerto itself); many speak at least some English, and for some, English is their native language. The local name for Puerto Cabezas is **Bilwi**, although the name is of Sumo origin. The Miskitos conquered the Sumos to obtain the town sometime in the last century.

There are two main roads, the only paved streets, which run parallel to each other and to the sea. At the southern end of the town is the port area; a walk along the pier at sunset is highly recommended. The airport is at the northern end. The main market occupies the central part of town. Travellers' cheques can be changed by Augusto Chow, ask for 'El Chino'.

Beaches There is a beach within the town limits, but it is reputed to be dirty. A clean, and lovely, beach, **Poza Verde**, can be found several kilometres north of town: it has white sand, calm water and sandflies. Take the road out of town for about 15 minutes and turn right on the track marked *SW Tuapi*; follow it for a few kilometres to the sea. You can also walk 6 km along the beach from Puerto Cabezas, or take a taxi (US$30, 3 hrs; it's a very bad track).

Sleeping **C** *El Cortijio*, Barrio San Pedro, calle Comercio, T282-2223, 6 rooms with bath, a/c, cable TV, parking, fax, laundry. **D** *Cayos Miskitos*, 2 blocks east of the plaza, good, comfortable rooms with bath, clean, friendly, breakfast by arrangement in advance only. **D** *El Viajante*, also clean, central, very friendly, basic wooden rooms with fan, singles only, shared baths, *comedor* serves good breakfast to its guests. **D** *Ricardo Pérez*, T/F282-2362, friendly, clean, all rooms have windows, meals available.

Eating The 3 best restaurants are the *Atlántico*, *Jumbo*, which serves Chinese food and is close to the sea, and *Pizzería Mercedita*, near the harbour, very good, expensive. Recommended.

Nicaragua

Wide liquor selection, good service. *El Zaire*, popular, with TV, food and service disappointing. There are also numerous **comedores**. Prices are much higher than elsewhere in Nicaragua because almost everything has to be brought in by air.

Air The airstrip is 3 km from the town. From the airport, it is possible to get a taxi that will charge US$1 to any point in Puerto (it is also possible to walk). *La Costeña* (T263-1281) flies daily from Managua in small 20-seater planes. There are also daily flights via Bonanza, Siuna and Rosita. Cancellations are not infrequent so it's best to make reservation and pay just before plane leaves. Bring your passport: there are 'immigration' checks by the police in Puerto, and sometimes in the waiting lounge in Managua; also, there is a customs check when returning from the coast by air to Managua.

Transport

Road It is not possible to rent a vehicle or bicycle in Puerto, but arrangements for a car and driver can be made with a taxi driver or others (ask a taxi or at your *hospedaje*). Public bus service is available between Puerto and **Waspám** (see below) and from **Matagalpa** (14 hrs). Furthermore, Puerto is connected by road to **Managua**; however, this 559-km trip should only be attempted in the dry season (early Jan to mid-May) in a 4WD vehicle. With luck, it will take only 2-3 days (the road, almost all of it unpaved, is not bad from Managua to Siuna, but becomes very difficult after that); do not drive at night. If you drive back from Puerto to Managua, take the road out of town and turn left at the sign, *SW Wawa*. Check on the road conditions; Hurricane Mitch caused damage in the highlands around Matagalpa on this route.

Medical services Hospital: located on the outskirts of Puerto, on the road leading out of town.

Directory

Waspám and the Coco River

The Coco River (called *Waspán* in Spanish and *Wanghi* in Miskito) is the heart of Miskito country and the town of Waspám is often referred to as 'the capital of the Río Coco'. There is a road from Puerto to Waspám; during the dry season the 130-km trip should take about three hours by four-wheel drive vehicle, several hours longer by public bus (leaves Puerto 0700, Monday-Saturday, with luck returns from Waspám 1200). The bus can be boarded at several points in Puerto along the road leading out of town, cost is US$5 to go to Waspám. This trip will take you through the pine forests, red earth, and plains north of Puerto towards the Coco River (the border with Honduras), and you will pass through two Miskito villages, Sisin and Santa Marta. Hitching rides is possible; if you cannot get all the way to Waspám, make sure you are left at Sisin, Santa Marta or La Tranquera. You can take lifts from the military; never travel at night.

Population: 38,701
Altitude: 14 m

This area of Nicaragua was the worst hit by Hurricane Mitch. Many Miskito communities along the Coco River have vanished. Make thorough enquiries in advance before travelling to the region

Las Minas

This area comprises the gold-mining towns of Siuna, La Rosita and Bonanza, and is part of the RAAN (Northern Atlantic Coast Autonomous Region), but is significantly inland from the coast almost directly west of Puerto Cabezas. Las Minas is a somewhat depressed region since the demise of the mines, but the atmosphere is still very much frontierish. A Canadian company has bought the mines in Siuna and Bonanza, which are now the only working mines.

Colour map 6, grid B5/C5

Siuna is the largest of the three towns, and, while all are predominantly *mestizo*, there is a Creole minority and the surrounding rural areas have a significant Sumo population as well as some Miskitos. There is a bank in Siuna.

Siuna
Colour map 6, grid C5

Sleeping and eating In Siuna E *Chino*, the best and most expensive. **F** *Troysa*, clean. **F** *Costeño*, 100 m east of airstrip, basic. In Barrio La Luz there is a hotel above a billiard hall. A recommended place to eat is either of the 2 *comedores* called **Desnuque**, 1 in the market, and the other on a hill near the baseball stadium and airstrip, the latter has good pizza as well as typical Nicaraguan food. **Comedor Siuna**, opposite *Hotel Costeño*, has good *comida corriente*.

Nicaragua

In Rosita, a recommended place to eat is *Comedor Jassy*, near the entrance of town on the Siuna side; there is an *hospedaje*, **E**, no name, near the market (noisy, but basically clean).

Transport Air *La Costeña* flies from daily to Siuna, reservations in Siuna, T263-2142.

Do not drive after dark **Road** There are two road links from Managua: one is through Matagalpa and Waslala; the other goes through Boaco, Muy Muy, Matiguás and Río Blanco, a very scenic 330-km drive, about 7 hrs by four-wheel drive vehicle in the dry season; check on the security situation before starting out. There are also bus links. **La Rosita** is 70 km east of Siuna, and it is also possible to drive on through to Puerto Cabezas, although the road is in very poor shape.

Parque Nacional Saslaya

Colour map 6, grid B4 Created in 1971, Saslaya was the first national park in Nicaragua, located within the **Bosawás Biosphere Reserve** which contains the largest tropical cloud forest in Central America. Development is now underway to encourage local communities to get involved in ecotourism as an incentive to preserve the area's rich natural and cultural heritage. One of these projects is the *Proyecto Ecoturístico Rosa Grande*, supported by Nature Conservancy and the Peace Corps. The community of **Rosa Grande**, 25 km from Siuna, is near an area of virgin forest with a trail, waterfall on the river Labú and lots of wildlife including monkeys and large cats. One path leads to a lookout with a view over the **Cerro Saslaya**; another circular path to the northwest goes to the **Rancho Alegre falls**. Guides can be hired for US$7 a day plus food. Excursions for two or more days cost only US$13 per person for guide, food and camping equipment. You may have to pay for a camp guard while hiking. Tourism is in its infancy here and you may find little things 'added on' to your bill. Be certain you have enough supplies for your stay. ■ *For information contact Don Trinidad at the comedor on arrival in Santa Rosa. In Siuna you can contact the office of the Proyecto Bosawás, 200 m east of the airstrip; open Mon-Fri, 0800-1700. Groups of 5 or more must reserve in advance; contact the Amigos de Saslaya, c/o Proyecto Bosawás, Siuna, RAAN, by post or telegram. Large groups are not encouraged.*

Sleeping **G** *Bosawás Field Station*, on the river Labú, has hammocks but not many, clean but simple,
& eating locally produced and cooked food about US$1.25. In Rosa Grande a meal at *Comedor Melania* costs about US$1.

Transport **Bus** Daily from Siuna market at 0500 and 0730, sometimes another at 1100, US$2.25.

Background

History

For more on Nicaragua was at the crossroads between northern and southern pre-Hispanic cultures. In
Nicaragua's early Managua, near the crater lake of Acahualinca, there are some well-preserved human and
history, see page 59. animal footprints of what appears to be a mass flight from a volcanic eruption 6,000 years ago. The best understood cultures are the Chorotegas, who came from Mexico around AD 800, and the Nicaraos, from the same region who partially displaced the Chorotegas in the Pacific basin around AD 1200. The Nicaraos set up a very successful society which traded with people from Mexico to Peru. The more primitive Chorotegas (Nahua speakers) remained in the areas not occupied by the Nicarao (Nahuat speakers), though some were pushed down into Guanacaste and the complete relationship between the two has yet to be fully explained. The most interesting pre-Columbian remains are the many petroglyphs left by unnamed pre-Chorotega cultures, and the Chorotegas' own large basalt figures

found in and around Lake Nicaragua, in particular on the islands of Zapatera and Ometepe. Nicaragua is rich in ceramic history, with traces of 3,000 years of continuous occupation being found in some areas. The Ramas and Sumos, of South American lowland origin, populated the eastern seaboard regions, but are almost extinct today. Other pre-Columbian cultures of note were the mountain Matagalpa people, thought to be related to the Lenca, the strangely primitive, understudied Chontales, who inhabited the eastern side of the two lakes and, in the area that is now León, the Subtiava people who are perhaps from Baja California in Mexico.

Christopher Columbus arrived on the Caribbean shores of Nicaragua in 1502 on his fourth and final voyage. The Spanish explorer Gil González Dávila arrived in 1522 overland from Panama and, searching for the wealthiest chief of all, arrived on the western shores of Lake Nicaragua to meet the famous Nicaraguas chief, Niqueragua. The 16th-century Spanish chroniclers described the Nicaraguas' land as the most fertile and productive they had ever seen in the Americas. The chief Nicaragua and Dávila engaged in long philosophical conversations conducted through a translator and eventually the great chief agreed to accept Christianity. After the conversion to Christianity of more than 900 people, Dávila was chased out of Nicaragua by the fierce Chorotega chieftain Diriangen, whose troops decimated Dávila's small force. In 1524 a stronger army was sent and the populace was overcome by Francisco Hernández de Córdoba. Granada and León were founded on the shores of Lake Nicaragua and Lake Managua respectively. In 1570 both colonies were placed under the jurisdiction of Guatemala.

The local administrative centre was not rich Granada, with its profitable crops of sugar, cocoa, and indigo, but impoverished León, then barely able to subsist on its crops of maize, beans and rice. This reversal of the Spanish policy of choosing the most successful settlement as capital was due to the ease with which León could be reached from the Pacific. In 1852 Managua was chosen as a new capital as a compromise, following violent rivalry between Granada and León.

The infamous filibustering expedition of William Walker is often referred to in the text. William Walker (1824-60) was born in Nashville, Tennessee, graduated at the University, and studied medicine at Edinburgh and Heidelberg, being granted his MD in 1843. He then studied law and was called to the bar. On 5 October 1853, he sailed with a filibustering force to conquer Mexican territory, declared Lower California and Sonora an independent republic and was then driven out. In May 1855, with 56 followers armed with a new type of rifle, he sailed for Nicaragua, where Liberal Party leaders had invited him to help them in their struggle against the Conservatives. In October he seized a steamer on Lake Nicaragua belonging to the Accessory Transit Company, an American corporation controlled by Cornelius Vanderbilt. He was then able to surprise and capture Granada and make himself master of Nicaragua as Commander of the Forces. Two officials decided to use him to get control of the Transit Company; it was seized and handed over to his friends. A new government was formed, and in June 1856 Walker was elected President. On 22 September, to gain support from the southern states in America, he suspended the Nicaraguan laws against slavery. His Government was formally recognized by the USA that year. A coalition of Central American states, backed by Cornelius Vanderbilt, fought against him, but he was able to hold his own until May 1857, when he surrendered to the US Navy to avoid capture. In November 1857, he sailed from Mobile with another expedition, but soon after landing near Greytown, Nicaragua, he was arrested and returned to the USA. In 1860 he sailed again from Mobile and landed in Honduras. There he was taken prisoner by Captain Salmon, of the British Navy, and handed over to the Honduran authorities who tried and executed him on 12 September 1860. Walker's own book, *The War in Nicaragua*, is a fascinating document.

In 1909, US Marines assisted Nicaraguan Conservative leaders in an uprising to overthrow the Liberal president, José Santos Zelaya. In 1911 the USA pledged help in securing a loan to be guaranteed through the control of Nicaraguan customs by an American board. In 1912 the United States sent marines into Nicaragua to enforce control. Apart from short

Walker's expedition
Nicaragua became an independent state in 1838

US involvement

Nicaragua

intervals, they stayed there until 1933. During the last five years of occupation, nationalists under General Augusto César Sandino waged a relentless guerrilla war against the US Marines. American forces were finally withdrawn in 1933, when President Franklin Roosevelt announced the 'Good Neighbour' policy, pledging non-intervention. An American-trained force, the Nicaraguan National Guard, was left behind, commanded by Anastasio Somoza García. Somoza's men assassinated General Sandino in February 1934 and Somoza himself took over the presidency in 1936. From 1932, with brief intervals, Nicaraguan affairs were dominated by this tyrant until he was assassinated in 1956. His two sons both served a presidential term and the younger, General Anastasio Somoza Debayle, dominated the country from 1963 until his deposition in 1979; he was later assassinated in Paraguay.

1978-79 Revolution The 1978-79 Revolution against the Somoza Government by the Sandinista guerrilla organization (loosely allied to a broad opposition movement) resulted in extensive damage and many casualties (estimated at over 30,000) in certain parts of the country, especially in Managua, Estelí, León, Masaya, Chinandega and Corinto. After heavy fighting General Somoza resigned on 17 July 1979, and the Government was taken over by a Junta representing the Sandinista guerrillas and their civilian allies. Real power was exercised by nine Sandinista *comandantes* whose chief short-term aim was reconstruction. A 47-member Council of State formally came into being in May 1980; supporters of the Frente Sandinista de Liberación Nacional had a majority. Elections were held on 4 November 1984 for an augmented National Constituent Assembly with 96 seats; the Sandinista Liberation Front won 61 seats, and Daniel Ortega Saavedra, who had headed the Junta, was elected president. The Democratic Conservatives won 14 seats, the Independent Liberals nine seats and the Popular Social Christians six (the Socialists, Communists and Marxists/Leninists won two seats each). The failure of the Sandinista Government to meet the demands of a right-wing group, the Democratic Co-ordinating Board (CDN), led to this coalition boycotting the elections and to the US administration failing to recognize the democratically elected government.

The Sandinistas Despite substantial official and private US support, anti-Sandinista guerrillas (the 'Contras') could boast no significant success in their war against the Government. In 1988, the Sandinistas and the contras met for the first time to discuss the implementation of the Central American Peace Plan, drawn up by President Oscar Arias Sánchez of Costa Rica and signed in August 1987. To comply with the Plan, the Nicaraguan Government made a number of political concessions. By 1989 the contras, lacking funds and with diminished numbers, following a stream of desertions, appeared to be a spent force; some participated in general elections held on 25 February 1990. The Sandinista Government brought major improvements in health and education, but the demands of the war against the contras and a complete US trade embargo did great damage to the economy as a whole. The electorate's desire for a higher standard of living was reflected in the outcome of the elections, when the US-supported candidate of the free market National Opposition Union (UNO), Sra Violeta Chamorro, won 55.2% of the vote, compared with 40.8% for President Ortega. The 14-party alliance, UNO, won 52 seats in the National Assembly, the FSLN 38 and the Social Christian Party one seat. Sra Chamorro, widow of the proprietor of *La Prensa*, who was murdered by General Somoza's forces in 1978, took office on 25 April 1990. The USA was under considerable pressure to provide substantial aid for the alliance it created and promoted, but of the US$300 mn promised for 1990 by the US Congress, only half had been distributed by May 1991. President Chamorro's refusal to dismiss the Sandinista General Humberto Ortega from his post as head of the armed forces (EPS), and to drop the Nicaraguan case against the USA at the International Court of Justice, were said to be hindrances to more rapid disbursement. The Court in The Hague found the USA guilty in 1986 of crimes against Nicaragua in mining its harbours.

The lack of foreign financial assistance prevented any quick rebuilding of the economy. The Government's scant resources did not permit it to give the disarmed contra forces the land and services that had been promised to them. Demilitarized Sandinistas and landless peasants also pressed for land in 1991, with a consequent rise in tension. Factions of the two groups rearmed, to be known as recontras and recompas; there were many bloody conflicts. Divisions within the UNO coalition, particularly between supporters of President Chamorro and those of vice-president Virgilio Godoy, added to the country's difficulties. Austerity measures introduced in early 1991, including a devaluation of the new córdoba, strained the relationship between the administration, Sandinista politicians and the National Workers' Front (FNT), the so-called 'concertación', a pact which the private sector refused to sign. Pacts signed in January 1992 between Government, recontras and recompas failed to stop occasional heavy fighting over the next two years. In 1994, however, a series of bilateral meetings between previously entrenched parties and ceasefires announced by the EPS and the main recontra group, FN 3-80 (Northern Front 3-80) contributed to a disarmament accord, proposed by archbishop Miguel Obando y Bravo, between the Government and FN 3-80.

The achievement of a more peaceful state of affairs, if not reconciliation, did not remove other political tensions. After the UNO coalition realigned itself into new political groupings and returned to the National Assembly following a boycott in 1993, the FSLN began to fall apart in 1994. By early 1995, the Sandinistas had become irrevocably split between the orthodox wing, led by Daniel Ortega, and the Sandinista Renewal Movement (MRS), under Sergio Ramírez. The MRS accused the orthodox wing of betraying Sandinista principles by forming pacts with the technocrats and neo-liberals of the Government. The MRS was itself accused of opportunism. Linked to this was considerable manoeuvring over UNO-inspired constitutional reform. The National Assembly approved 67 amendments of the constitution, among which were the strengthening of the legislative branch of government at the expense of the executive, and the prohibition of relatives of the president from seeking that office. President Chamorro denied the validity of the reforms, but the National Assembly unilaterally adopted them in February 1995.

Movement towards a real & lasting peace

In 1995 the National Assembly approved legislation governing the 20 October 1996 presidential elections. The frontrunner was Arnoldo Alemán, former mayor of Managua, of the Liberal alliance. His main opponent was Daniel Ortega of the FSLN, who regarded Alemán's policies as a return to Somoza-style government. After reviewing the vote count because of allegations of fraud, the Supreme Electoral Council (CSE) announced on 8 November that Arnoldo Alemán had won 51% of the vote compared with 37.7% for Daniel Ortega with the rest divided among the other 21 candidates. The FSLN appealed and called for new elections in Managua and Matagalpa but this was rejected. The OAS declared the elections fair but flawed. Ortega announced he would respect the legality but not the legitimacy of the Government of Alemán, whose position was weakened by his Liberal Alliance failing to win an outright majority in the National Assembly.

The 1996 elections

The Sandinistas have maintained pressure on the Alemán government, with strikes, protests and intermittent negotiations. A deal was reached in 1997 on compensation for properties expropriated under the Sandinista government, involving 1,293 claims by foreigners. The agreement avoided a suspension of US aid and the USA gave Nicaragua a year to sort out property rights involving US citizens.

In 1998 two meteorological events caused even greater hardship for parts of the country: the drought (and related fires) from the El Niño phenomenon and, much more costly in terms of lives lost and property destroyed, the floods and storm damage from Hurricane Mitch. In July of 2000 an earthquake measuring almost six points on the Richter scale hit western Nicaragua killing four people and causing damage near the epicentre at Laguna de Apoyo, near Masaya.

Nature plays her hand

Political machinations continue to create uncertainty, not just between parties, but within parties themselves. The Sandinistas' divisions were sharpened in 1998 by accusations against Daniel Ortega by his stepdaughter, Zoilamérica Narváez Murillo, that he had sexually abused her in her youth. Narváez and a colleague, Henry Petrie, belonged to a dissident faction of the

Political & economic uncertainty

Nicaragua

FSLN which was expelled from the party at the time of the accusations. Both Ortega's wife and Narváez' brother said the charges were false. The inability to make economic advances also remains a major problem and international and domestic observers point out that over 70% of Nicaraguan families live below the poverty line.

A new opportunity In November of 2001, with Daniel Ortega of the FSLN leading in the polls over ex-vice president for outgoing president Arnoldo Alemán, Enrique Bolaños, Nicaraguans turned out in record numbers to vote. In a country where voting is not mandatory, the astonishing 96% voter turnout was taken as a sign that democracy is stronger than ever in Nicaragua. The voters chose Enrique Bolaños of the Liberal Party (PLC) by more than a 15-point margin in what many believed to be a vote against Ortega rather than approval of the Liberal Party, one that had been accused of rampant corruption. In Enrique Bolaños' first 3 months of office in 2002 he shocked many by taking a very aggressive stance against corruption and his administration has exposed several cases of embezzlement under the Alemán adminstration, whom by mid-2002 are fleeing the country or being imprisoned. New hope abounds in Nicaragua that a half-millennium of corruption may finally be minimized or at least de-institutionalised. Bolaños faces heavy opposition from his own majority party in the parliament, but the minority seats of the Sandinistas and some defectors from Alemán's loyalists to the Bolaños 'clean house' policy mean that the tide could turn in the fight against government corruption. An internal victory the world's poorest Spanish speaking country so desperately needs.

While Bolaños is presented with the positively uncomfortable prospect of sorting out the country's desolate prospects, many predicted Ortega's third attempt and subsequent failure to secure the presidency would mark the end of his political career. But suprisingly in March of 2002 he was reelected as leader of the FSLN continuing the legacy of the Sandanista Revolution.

Economy

The World Bank classes Nicaragua among the world's poorest countries and its per capita income is the lowest in Latin America. The economy is based on agriculture, which contributes almost 35% of GDP. The principal export items are coffee, sugar, beef, seafood and bananas. Main industries are food processing (sugar, meat, shrimps), textiles, wood, chemical and mineral products. Mineral resources are scarce but there are gold, copper and silver deposits.

Since the late 1970s GDP has fallen, starting with a decline of 29% in 1979. In 1981-90 it fell by an annual average of 2.4%, with only one year of positive growth. In the same period per capita income fell by an average of 5.6% a year, a collapse caused by guerrilla insurgency, the US trade embargo, fluctuations in Central American Common Market trade, floods, drought and changing commodity prices.

In 1990 the US-supported Government of President Violeta Chamorro took office amid great optimism that the economy could be revived on the back of renewed trade with the USA. Trade sanctions were lifted and the US Congress was asked to provide US$300 mn in aid immediately, to be followed by a further US$200 mn. Other countries were also asked for US$100 mn. By mid-1991 disbursements had been insufficient to help the administration out of its circumstances as attempts to rebuild the economy floundered.

President Alemán promised to continue the structural adjustment programme of the Chamorro government and to create 100,000 jobs a year by reactivating agriculture, tourism and attracting foreign investment. The reduction of poverty and the promotion of growth were to be given high priority.

Nicaragua's entire economic outlook was radically altered, however, by Hurricane Mitch. With reconstruction forced to the top of the agenda and a new focus given to debt relief, there were signs that financial resources were being targeted at areas of greatest need, and that a political unity not seen for many years was now emerging.

Annual inflation dropped from just over 11% to 9% between 1999 and 2000. Export earnings have risen slowly since 1990 with a total of US$625.3 mn in 2000 compared to the 1990 earnings total of US$330.5 mn, but the earnings are certain to be hit hard by the fall in world coffee prices that is dramatically effecting producing communities in the north of the country. The economic latitude afforded President Bolaños is so narrow that fighting corruption is seen by some commentators as a valid contribution to the economic strategy. But with few promising economic signs on the horizon, the best prospect for the country must be cancellation of debt.

Government

A new Constitution was approved by the 92-member National Constituent Assembly in 1986 and signed into effect on 9 January 1987. Legislative power is vested in a unicameral, directly elected National Assembly of 92 representatives, each with an alternate representative, with a six-year term. In addition, unelected presidential and vice presidential candidates become representatives and alternates respectively if they receive a certain percentage of the votes. Executive power is vested in the President, assisted by a Vice President and an appointed Cabinet. The Presidential term is five years.

Constitution

Culture

Population density is low: 38.1 persons to the sq km, compared with El Salvador's 269. Nine out of 10 Nicaraguans live and work in the lowlands between the Pacific and the western shores of Lake Nicaragua, the southwestern shore of Lake Managua, and the southwestern sides of the row of volcanoes. It is only in latter years that settlers have taken to coffee-growing and cattle-rearing in the highlands at Matagalpa and Jinotega. Elsewhere, the highlands, save for an occasional mining camp, are very thinly settled.

People

The densely forested eastern lowlands fronting the Caribbean were neglected, because of the heavy rainfall and their consequent unhealthiness, until the British settled several colonies of Jamaicans in the 18th century at Bluefields and San Juan del Norte (Greytown). But early this century the United Fruit Company of America (now United Brands) opened banana plantations inland from Puerto Cabezas, worked by blacks from Jamaica. Other companies followed suit along the coast, but the bananas were later attacked by Panama disease and exports today are small. Along the Mosquito coast there are still English-speaking communities of African, or mixed African and indigenous, descent. Besides the *mestizo* intermixtures of Spanish and Indian (69%), there are pure blacks (9%), pure Indians (5%) and mixtures of the two (mostly along the Atlantic coast). A small proportion is of unmixed Spanish and European descent. For a brief survey of the people of eastern Nicaragua, see the introductory paragraphs of The Caribbean Coast.

Nicaragua is 'marimba country' and the basic musical genre is the *son*, this time called the *Son Nica*. There are a number of popular dances for couples with the names of animals, like *La Vaca* (cow), *La Yeguita* (mare) and *El Toro* (bull). The folklore capital of Nicaragua is the city of Masaya and the musical heart of Masaya is the Indian quarter of Monimbó. Here the marimba is king, but on increasingly rare occasions may be supported by the *chirimía* (oboe), *quijada de asno* (donkey's jaw) and *quijongo*, a single-string bow with gourd resonator. Some of the most traditional *sones* are *El Zañate*, *Los Novios* and *La Perra Renca*, while the more popular dances still to be found are *Las Inditas*, *Las Negras*, *Los Diablitos* and *El Torovenado*, all involving masked characters. Diriamba is another centre of tradition, notable for the folk play known as *El Güeguense*, accompanied by violin, flute and drum and the dance called *Toro Guaco*. The Caribbean coast is a totally different cultural region, home to the Miskito Indians and English-speaking black people of Jamaican origin concentrated around Bluefields. The latter have a maypole dance and their music is typically Afro-Caribbean, with banjos, accordions, guitars and of course drums as the preferred instruments.

Music & dance

Nicaragua

Religion & education Roman Catholicism is the prevailing religion, but there are Episcopal, Baptist, Methodist and other Protestant churches. Illiteracy was reduced by a determined campaign by the Sandinista government in the 1980s. Higher education at the Universidad Nacional Autónoma de Nicaragua at León, with three faculties at Managua, and the private Jesuit Universidad Centroamericana (UCA) at Managua is good. There are two separate Universidades Nacionales Autónomas de Nicaragua (UNAN).

Land and environment

There are three well-marked regions: (1) A large triangular-shaped central mountain land beginning almost on the southern border with Costa Rica and broadening northwards; the prevailing moisture-laden northeast winds drench its eastern slopes, which are deeply forested with oak and pine on the drier, cooler heights. (2) A belt of lowland plains which run from the Gulf of Fonseca, on the Pacific, to the Costa Rican border south of Lake Nicaragua. Out of it, to the east, rise the lava cliffs of the mountains to a height of 1,500-2,100 m. Peninsulas of high land jut out here and there into the lowland, which is generally from 65 to 80 km wide along the Pacific, but is at its narrowest 20 km between La Virgen on Lake Nicaragua and San Juan del Sur. (3) A wide belt of eastern lowland through which a number of rivers flow from the mountains into the Atlantic.

Lakes In the plains are the two largest sheets of water in Central America and 10 crater lakes. The capital, Managua, is on the shores of Lake Managua (Xolotlán), 52 km long, 15-25 km wide, and 39 m above sea-level. Its maximum depth is only 30 m. The Río Tipitapa drains it into Lake Nicaragua, 148 km long, about 55 km at its widest, and 32 m above the sea; Granada is on its shores. The 190-km Río San Juan drains both lakes into the Caribbean and is one of 96 principal rivers in the country. The longest at 680 km is the Río Coco, on the border with Honduras.

Volcanoes Lying at the intersection of three continental plates, Nicaragua has a very unstable, changing landscape. Through the Pacific basin runs a row of 28 major volcanoes, six of which have been active within the 20th century. The northernmost is Cosigüina, overlooking the Gulf of Fonseca, at 800 m with a lake in its crater. Its final eruption was in 1835. Northeast of Chinandega begins the Maribios volcanic chain, with Chonco (1,105 m) and the country's highest, the cone of San Cristóbal (1,745 m), which recommenced erupting in 1971 after a long period of inactivity. This volcano's lava discharge was used as a lighthouse by Pacific pirates in a very destructive raid on the colonial capital of León in 1685. Just south rises Volcán Casita which is notable for its pine forest, the southernmost of its kind in the American continent's northern hemisphere. A side of Casita collapsed during the torrential rains of Hurricane Mitch (1998), burying numerous villages in Posoltega and killing hundreds of people. Further south, just before León, is the very active Telica (1,061m) with eruptions occurring every five years, and the extinct cones of little Santa Clara and Orata (836 m), which is believed to be the oldest in the chain. Just south of León is one of the youngest volcanoes on the planet, Cerro Negro, which was born in 1850 and has risen from sea level to 450 m in this short period. Its most recent eruptions occurred in 1992 and 1995 and it frequently coats León in a thick black soup. Volcán Pilas is formed of various craters, the highest of which rises to 1,001 m and contains one active crater known as El Hoyo, which last erupted in 1954. Other extinct cones lie between Pilas and the majestic Momotombo (1,300 m), which overlooks the shores of Lake Managua and last erupted in 1905, though a geothermal plant utilizes its energy daily. The chain ends with little Momotombito, which forms an island in Lake Managua. Managua's volcanoes are all extinct and six contain crater lakes. The Dirianes volcanic chain begins just north of Masaya with the complex of the same name, including the smoking, lava-filled Santiago crater and four extinct craters and a lagoon. Masaya is the only volcano on the American continent with a consistent lava pool. The last eruptions occurred in 1965 and 1979 and, after a nine year period of calm, it began to smoke heavily again in 1995 with an eruption expected soon. South between Masaya and Granada is the extinct Apoyo, which died very violently 2,000 years ago, leaving the deep blue Laguna de Apoyo, 6 km in diameter. Along the shores of Lake Nicaragua, and shadowing Granada, is Volcán Mombacho (1,345 m), wrapped in cloud forest. Mobacho had a major structural collapse in 1570 and the resultant explosion not only wiped out an indigenous village at its base, but also fathered hundreds of Las Isletas in nearby Lake Nicaragua. The volcanoes of Lake Nicaragua include the Isla de Zapatera (600 m), a national park and pre-Columbian site, and the final two in the Nicaraguan chain which make up the stunning Isla de Ometepe: the symmetrical and active cone of Concepción (1,610 m), which last erupted in 1956, and the cloud forest covered Maderas (1,394 m), which holds a lake at its summit.

Climate

The wet, warm winds of the Caribbean pour heavy rain on the Atlantic coastal zone, especially in the southern basin of the Río San Juan, with more than 6 m annually. While the dry season on the Atlantic coast is only short and not wholly dry, the Pacific dry season, or summer (November to April), becomes very dusty, especially when the winds begin to blow in February. There is a wide range of climates. According to altitude, average annual temperatures vary between 15° and 35°C. Midday temperatures at Managua range from 30° to 36°C, but readings of 38° are not uncommon between March and May, or of 40° in January and February in the west. It can get quite cold, especially after rain, in the Caribbean lowlands. Maximum daily humidity ranges from 90% to 100%.

Books and films

Rubén Darío stands as the quintessential Latin American author, expressing the emotions of many with words that are difficult to silence. *Cuentos Completos* is the collected stories of this great Nicaraguan poet. Descriptions of León's fight against the Somoza régime can be found in *Fire from the Mountain: The Making of a Sandinista* by Omar Cabezas. Salman Rushdie's *The Jaguar Smile* romanticizes the Revolution but maybe that's only with the benefit of hindsight. *Savage Shore: Life and Death with Nicaragua's Last Shark Hunters* by Edward Marriott looks at the life of the shark hunters of Lake Nicaragua.

Fans of the big screen can see an insightful, if feverishly pro-Sandinista portrayal of Nicaragua post-Revolution in the Ken Loach film *Carla's Song*. Set during the Revolution and starring Nick Nolte and Gene Hackman, *Under Fire* mixes a lot of fact with some fiction. While the setting may be Nicaragua, it was filmed entirely in Mexico.

Nicaragua

Books and films

Costa Rica

Costa Rica

Essentials

Geographically Costa Rica is the smallest but two of the Central American republics (after El Salvador and Belize) and only Panama and Belize have fewer inhabitants. Despite these diminutive tendencies, the Rich Coast has carved out a niche market as *the* nature destination in Central America with a network of well-developed national parks and biological reserves protecting large tracts of unspoilt tropical wilderness. Adventure activities are an option to sap untapped adrenaline and there are plenty of glorious beaches for lazing around and soaking up the perfect climate.

Known throughout Latin America as the continent's purest democracy, Costa Rica celebrated a centenary of democracy in 1989. The country has the highest standard of living in Central America, the second lowest birth rate (after Panama) and the greatest degree of economic and social advancement.

Planning your trip

Costa Rica's main attractions are its countryside, nature and wildlife – although the country has a colourful history, most of the colonial heritage has been lost in earthquakes over the centuries. San José, the capital, is a lively city, and well enjoying for a couple of days visiting museums and sights while organizing visits to other parts of the country.

Where to go

Surrounding San José is the **Meseta Central** draped in the quirky charms and graceful aire of **Zarcero** and **Sarchí, Heredia** and **Alajuela** in the heart of this agricultural and coffee producing region. Just 57 km from the capital, the impressive crater and easily reached summit of **Volcán Poás** steams and puffs in a national park with a sprinkling of wildlife and a few trails. To the east the former capital **Cartago** is overshadowed by **Volcán Irazú**, with spectacular views from the summit. Nearby the **Orosí Valley** leads to the hidden beauty of **Parque Nacional Tapantí**. Further east on the Caribbean slope, **Turrialba** is a prime site for world-class **whitewater rafting** on the scenic Reventazón and Pacuare rivers, staying in secluded lodges offering comfortable nature tourism and guided tours.

Heading north the Pan-American Highway leads towards the Nicaraguan border. **Lake Arenal** is the backdrop to the most spectacular of Costa Rica's volcanoes – the highly active **Arenal**. A perfect cone, it is best watched at night when the red hot lava can be seen spewing out of the top before rolling and crashing down the mountainside. Nearby **Fortuna** at the foot of Arenal, is a good base for a number of trips including visits to the wetlands of **Caño Negro Wildlife Refuge** near **Los Chiles** which makes an interesting boat trip, is a bird-watcher's paradise and a route between Costa Rica and Nicaragua.

South of Lake Arenal is Monteverde Forest Reserve, a private reserve and a guiding light in the world of conservation. Difficult to reach, the epiphyte-laden cloud forest spans the continental divide, protecting the habitat of the resplendent quetzal and many other beautiful tropical birds. Nearby **Santa Elena** and several other private reserves offer nature visits and dramatic canopy tours for visitors.

Guanacaste, in the northwest, is drier with open plains once used for cattle ranching inspiring a distinctive regional music, dance and culture. From the town of **Liberia**, trips to **Parque Nacional Rincón de la Vieja** reveal an array of geothermal curiosities including mudpots and hot springs. Close to the Nicaraguan border, **Parque Nacional Santa Rosa** protects rare dry tropical forest and Pacific beaches used by nesting turtles. Beach lovers should head for the **Nicoya Peninsula** with miles of white sand beaches. Resorts are springing up if you want parties, dancing and services, but smaller towns exist for solitude, sun-loving and surf.

Puerto Limón is the main town on the Caribbean with a vibrancy and rhythm that shines through at carnival each October. While much of the region is given over to banana cultivation, on the coast towards the Nicaraguan border is **Parque Nacional Tortuguero**, reached through a network of inland canals and waterways full to bursting with tropical avifauna, basking crocodiles, noisy monkeys and beaches used by turtles to nest.

Costa Rica

South of Puerto Limón the road leads to Panama through the towns of **Cahuita**, **Puerto Viejo** and **Manzanillo**. Strong local cultures, a proud expatriate community and protected tropical rainforest attract backpackers and the discerning traveller to this forgotten corner of Costa Rica. It's also a great route to Bocas del Toro in Panama.

Back on the Pacific side, beautiful beaches fringe the coast south from the transport hub of **Puntarenas** through the surf hangout of **Jacó**, the justifiably popular **Quepos** with nearby **Parque Nacional Manuel Antonio**, and the quieter spots around **Dominical** and **Playa Hermosa**. In the far south, the **Osa Peninsula** draws naturalists to the beauty of **Parque Nacional Corcovado**'s protected primary rainforest. It's tough, hot, sweaty, not for the faint hearted and you won't regret the effort.

The Pan-American Highway takes the high road down the southern spine of the country from San José to Panama through the spectacular mountain scenery of the Cordillera Talamanca. The country's highest mountain **Chirripó Grande**, at 3,820 m is climbed from **San Gerardo** near **San Isidro de El General**. Throughout the area lodges catering for all budgets offer bird-watching and guided tours in the mountains, where the **Parque Nacional Chirripó** and neighbouring **Parque Internacional La Amistad** protect the largest area of virgin forest in the country with the greatest biological diversity.

When to go
In general, December to February is the best time to visit, within the dry season, running from December to April, but before the temperatures really rises in March and April. Two main factors contribute to the local climatic conditions – altitude and location – whether on the Pacific or Caribbean side. The climate varies from the heat and humidity of the Caribbean and Atlantic lowlands, usually around the mid-20s, falling to warm temperate on the Meseta Central and chilly temperate at greater heights – in the Cordillera Talamanca, the average temperature is below 16°C.

Altitude, as elsewhere in Central America, determines the climate, though the major temperature changes start at about 300 m lower on the Pacific than on the Atlantic side.

There are dry and wet seasons: on the Pacific side there is a well-defined wet season from May to November with a little decrease during July-August. The Atlantic side, which is wetter, has no specific dry season but there is less rainfall between March and September.

Finding out more
The information office of the **Instituto Costarricense de Turismo** (**ICT**) is underneath the Plaza de la Cultura, C 5, A Central-2 (T223-1733, F223-5452, toll free 800-012-3456, **www.tourism-costarica.com**), open 0800-1600 Mon-Fri. All tourist information is given here along with a good free map of San José and the country. For more details, see page 1027.

Costa Rica on the web There are a number of useful websites. Recommended is Costa Rica's Travelnet at **www.centralamerica.com**, which contains general information on tourist-related suvbjects. At **www.infocostarica.net** you'll find a Yahoo-style search engine for all things Costa Rican. A good general site for the country is found at **www.yellowweb.co.cr**

Language
Spanish is the first language, but you will always find someone who can speak some English – ranging from perfect to just a few words – in almost every place you visit. In the Caribbean, particularly around Limón, the Afro-Caribbean population speak a regional creole dialect with elements of English. With a good ear you can just about work out what's going on.

Before you travel

Visas & immigration
Those arriving by air from Colombia will be searched thoroughly because of drug trafficking. Do not get involved with drugs in Costa Rica; many dealers are undercover police agents

For visits of up to 90 days the following do not need visas: nationals of most Western European countries, Argentina, Canada, Hungary, Israel, Japan, Panama, Paraguay, Poland, Romania, South Korea, Uruguay and the USA. The following also do not need a visa, but visits are limited to 30 days: citizens of Australia, Iceland, Monaco, New Zealand, Singapore, South Africa, Taiwan, most East European countries, most Middle Eastern countries, most Caribbean countries and most Central and South America countries, including Brazil, El Salvador Guatemala, Guyana, Honduras and Mexico. For the latest information check www.costarica-embassy.org To find your nearest embassy look at www.rree.co.cr In spite of this, some travellers report that 90 days may be allowed for nationals of some of these countries. All other nationalities need a visa, costing US$20, valid for only 30 days. Make absolutely sure that you get an entry stamp in your passport and insist even if border officials tell you otherwise. Failure to have a stamp can lead to numerous problems on departure. Some nationalities have to have a tourist card, US$2 on entry.

After requesting an **extension**, when departing Costa Rica you will have to pay a US$38 departure tax (the same as Costa Ricans or residents). If you overstay the 30- or 90-day permitted period, you must report to Immigration before leaving the country. A fine of US$2 per month will be charged, you will be given five days to leave the country and will have to pay the departure tax. For longer stays ask for a Prórroga de Turismo at Migración in San José. For this you need three passport photos, an airline or bus ticket out of the country and proof of funds (for example travellers' cheques); you can apply for an extension of one or two months, 300 colones per month. The paperwork takes three days. If you leave the country, you must wait 72 hours before returning, but it may be cheaper and easier to do this and get a new 30-day entry. Travel agents can arrange all extension and exit formalities for a small fee.

An onward ticket (a bus ticket, which can be bought at the border immigration office or sometimes from the driver on *Tica* international buses or a transatlantic ticket will sometimes do) is asked for, but can be refunded in San José with a loss of about US$3 on a US$20 ticket. Cashing in an air ticket is difficult because you may be asked to produce another ticket out of the country. Also, tourists may have to show at least US$300 in cash or travellers' cheques before being granted entry (especially if you have no onward ticket).

What to take

Climate is generally very comfortable in Costa Rica limiting the necessity for specialist clothing. If choosing to go to the higher altitudes, Chirripó for example, be sure to take warm clothing and rain gear. At lower altitudes, umbrellas are preferred to raincoats in the rain. If considering jungle treks take gear that will protect you from insect bites.

Customs

Half a kilo of manufactured tobacco and 3 litres of liquor are allowed in duty-free. Any amount of foreign or local currency may be taken in or out.

Money

Costa Rica

Currency
US$1=372.85 colones

The unit is the colón. Small, golden-coloured coins are also minted for 5, 10, 25, 50 and 100 colones. Notes in use are for 50, 100, 500, 1,000, 2,000, 5,000 and 10,000 colones. US dollars are widely accepted but don't depend on them.

Banks, credit cards & TCs
For card loss or theft: MasterCard/Visa T0800-011-1084; Amex T0800-011-0216

US dollars can be exchanged in most banks, for bank drafts and transfers commission may be charged. Banks may charge whatever commission they please on TCs (no commission on US$ cash) and other services: shop around for the best deal. General opening times: Mon-Fri, 0900-1500, although more banks are starting to stay open later.

Most tourist and first-class hotels will change dollars and TCs for guests only, the same applies in restaurants and shops if you buy something. Hardly anyone will change damaged US dollar notes. It is almost impossible to exchange any other major currency in Costa Rica. Most banks will process cash advances on Visa/MasterCard. ATMs which accept international Visa and/or MasterCard are widely available at most banks, and in shopping malls and at San José airport. However, travellers report that Visa is more acceptable than MasterCard. Credomatic handles all credit card billings; they will not accept a credit card charge that does not have the imprint of the borrower's card plus an original signature. This is the result of fraud, but it makes it difficult to book tours or accommodation over the phone.

Cost of living and travelling

Costa Rica is more expensive than countries to the north. While transport is reasonably cheap, you get less for you money in the hotels. You will be able to survive on US$30 a day, but that does not allow for much in the way of activities.

Getting there

Air **From Europe** Direct scheduled flights from Amsterdam (*Martinair*). From most European cities flights connect in the US – Miami, Houston, Dallas and many others – with *American Airlines*, *Continental* and *Grupo Taca*. There are charter flights in season from several European cities including London (*British Airways*) and Frankfurt (*Condor*).

From North America Flights from the US are many and varied, again some stop in Miami so check if a direct flight is important. Here is a selection: Atlanta *(Delta)*, Boston (*American Airlines*), Chicago (*Continental*), Dallas (*American Airlines, Grupo Taca*), Houston (*Continental*), Los Angeles (*America, Grupo Taca, United*), Miami (*American, Grupo Taca, Martinair, Iberia*), New York (*American, Continental, Grupo Taca*), Orlando (*Martinair*), San Francisco (*United, Grupo Taca*), Toronto (*AeroMéxico, Grupo Taca, Mexicana*), Washington DC (*American*).

Daniel Oduber International Airport, on the Nicoya Peninsula near Liberia, receives charter flights throughout the year. Specials available from time to time include New York – Costa Rica US$99. Enquire at travel agents for details. Also weekly flights from Detroit and Minneapolis with *North West*.

From South America Flights from most South American capitals including Bogotá (*Copa, Grupo Taca*), Cali (*SAM, Grupo Taca*), Caracas (*Grupo Taca*), Cartagena (*SAM*), Guayaquil (*Grupo Taca*), Lima (*Grupo Taca*), Quito (*Grupo Taca*), Santiago (*Grupo Taca*).

GRUPO TACA is the alliance of the main Central American airlines (AVIATECA, LACSA, NICA and TACA)

From Central America The *Grupo Taca* alliance provides connections with all capitals and several of the more popular tourist destinations including Cancún (*Grupo Taca*), Guatemala City (*United, Grupo Taca, Aviateca, Copa*), Managua (*Copa, Grupo Taca*), Mexico City (*Grupo Taca, Mexicana, United*), Panama City (*Grupo Taca*), San Pedro Sula (*Grupo Taca*), San Salvador (*Copa, Grupo Taca*), Tegucigalpa (*Grupo Taca*).

From the Caribbean There are a couple of flights a week to Havana (*Cubana, Grupo Taca*) and San Andrés (*SAM*). Also flights to Santo Domingo (*Copa*).

Overland Road links to the north are on the Pan-American Highway at Peñas Blancas with immigration services and buses connecting to and from Nicaragua. It is possible to cross the northern border close to Los Chiles making the journey by land or boat to San Carlos. Crossing the border on the North Pacific is possible but immigration services are non-existent and transportation is irregular.

The main crossing to Panama at Paso Canoas is straightforward and problem free. On the Caribbean coast Sixaolo links with the Panamian town of Guabito over the old banana bridge. Immigration services on both sides but only in normal office hours.

Sea The main port for international cargo vessels is Puerto Limón which has regular sailings to and from Europe. Contact shipping agents, of which there are many, in Puerto Limón for details. Cruise vessels arrive at Puntarenas and Puerto Limón normally stopping for little more than 24 hours.

Touching down

Airport information and exit tax

250 colones (US$0.90) has to be paid on arrival and departure at land frontiers

The main international airport is at San José, see page 1027. There is an airport departure tax for tourists of US$20, payable in colones or dollars (travellers' cheques not accepted). There is a 5% tax on airline tickets purchased in the country.

If leaving overland, you will have to purchase a 'cruz roja' which is pasted in your passport. These can be obtained in San José from the major banks for 250 colones or at the border normally for around 300 colones.

Exit taxes, by air or land, and legislation regarding visa extensions, are subject to frequent change and travellers should check these details as near to the time of travelling as possible.

Touching down

Official time *Standard time is six hours behind Greenwich Mean Time.*
Hours of business *0800 or 0830 to 1100 or 1130 and 1300 to 1700 or 1730 (1600, government offices), Monday to Friday, and 0800 to 1100 on Saturday. Shops: 0800 to 1200, 1300 to 1800 Monday to Saturday.*
IDD *506. Operator 113, international operator 116.*

Voltage *110, 60 cycles, AC (US flat-pin plugs).*
Weights and measures *For Customs the metric system of weights and measures is compulsory. Traders use a variety of weights and measures, including Imperial and old Spanish ones.*

Safety Generally speaking, Costa Rica is very safe, but as ever there are some problem areas. Look after your belongings in hotels – use the safe. If hiring a car do not leave valuables within sight and leave nothing unattended on beaches or buses. Theft (pickpockets, grab-and-run thieves and muggings) is on the increase in San José, especially in the centre, in the market, at the *Coca Cola* bus station, in the barrios of Cuba, Cristo Rey, México, 15 de Septiembre and León XIII. Keep away from these areas at night and on Sunday, when few people are around as we have received reports of violent robberies. Street gangs, known as *chapulines*, are mostly made up of kids. A couple of US students were murdered close to Cahuita in 2000, and a tourist bus was held up near San José in March 2001. The police do seem to be attempting to tackle the problem but you can help yourself by avoiding potentially dangerous situations.
Useful phone numbers Police: T117. **Fire**: T118. **Medical**: T128. (**Police, Fire, Red Cross** bilingual operators: T911).

Local customs & laws *You must carry your passport (or a photocopy) with you at all times and make sure your papers are in order*

Tipping A 10% service charge is automatically added to restaurant and hotel bills, as well as 15% sales tax. Tip porters, hairdressers and cloakroom attendants.

Where to stay

Accommodation in Costa Rica strongly favours couples and groups – the price of a single room is often the same as a double, and the price of a room for four is often only twice that of the price for one. If you can get in a group, the cost per person falls considerably.

A 13% sales tax plus 3.39% tourism tax (total 16.39%) are added to the basic price of hotel rooms. A deposit is recommended at the more expensive hotels in San José, especially in the high season, December-April, to guarantee reservations. If you arrive late at night, even a guaranteed reservation may not be honoured.

The Costa Rica Bed & Breakfast Group has 200 **AL-D** Bed & Breakfast inns and small hotels around the country in its membership. See page 1036.

Getting around

Airports There are domestic airports, with scheduled services provided by *Sansa* or *Travelair* at Barra Colorado, Carrillo, Coto 47, Fortuna, Golfito, Liberia, Nosara Beach, Palmar, Puerto Jiménez, Punta Islita, Quepos, Tamarindo, Tambor and Tortuguero. For details see page 1041.

Air

Costa Rica has a total of 35,600 km of roads of which 17% are paved. The Pan-American Highway runs the length of the country, from the Nicaraguan to the Panamanian borders. A highway has been built from Orotina to Caldera, a new port on the Gulf of Nicoya which has replaced Puntarenas as the principal Pacific port, and a highway is being built from Orotina to Ciudad Colón. Another road has been completed from San José via Guápiles and Siquirres to Puerto Limón. Also a road was completed in 1993 from Orotina to Playas de Jacó to improve access to the Pacific beaches. This has still to be extended to Parrita and Quepos, but the road is generally good between Dominical and Ciudad Cortés. All four-lane roads into San José are toll roads, varying in price from US$0.30-US$1.

Road *It is illegal to ride in a car or taxi without wearing seatbelts. Motorcyclists must wear crash helmets*

Costa Rica

Cycling Cycling is easier in Costa Rica than elsewhere in Central America; there is less heavy traffic and it is generally 'cyclist friendly'. However, paving is thin and soon deteriorates; look out for cracks and potholes, which bring traffic to a crawl. The prevailing wind is from the northeast, so if making an extensive tour travelling in the direction of Panama-Nicaragua is slightly more favourable. Be prepared for a lot of rain. Particularly bad for cyclists is the Nicoya Peninsula; a mountain bike is recommended for the terrain and the poor road state.

Recommended reading for all users: Baker's *The Essential Road Guide to Costa Rica*, with detailed strip maps, kilometre by kilometre road logs, motoring information plus *San José map and Bus Guide* (Bill Baker, Apdo 1185-1011, San José, T/F220-1415). Cycle shop: *Bicicletas Cannondale*, La Uruca, T222-4222, F223-0986, good stock of newest bicycle parts.

Driving With a few precautions, driving in Costa Rica allows for greater flexibility when travelling. Many of the nature parks are in remote areas and four-wheel drive and high-clearance is recommended and sometimes essential; in the wet season some roads will be impassable. Always ask locals or bus drivers what the state of the road is before embarking on a journey, but do not assume that if the buses are running, a car can get through too.

Tourists who come by car or motorcycle pay US$10 road tax and can keep their cars for an initial period of 90 days. This can be extended for a total period of six months, for about US$10 per extra month, at the Instituto Costarricense de Turismo, or at the Customs office, Avenida 3, Calle 14, if you take your passport, car entry permit, and a piece of stamped paper (*papel sellado*) obtainable at any bookshop. If you intend to drive in the country for more than three months, you are required to apply for a Costa Rican Driver's Licence at Avenida 18, Calle 5, San José. Cars are fumigated on entry: exterior US$8. It is now mandatory for foreign drivers to buy insurance stamps on entry; US$17.75 for one month (US$8 for motorcycles), US$27.70 for two months, US$37.65 for three months. If you have an accident, contact Policía de Tránsito, San José T226-8436 or 227-2189.

Discounts are available during the 'green season', May-November

Car hire If hiring a car, be very careful to make sure you have all the costs and details explained – in the past we have received many complaints. As with all rentals, check your vehicle carefully as the company will try to claim for the smallest of 'damages'. Most leases do not allow the use of a normal car off paved roads. Always make sure the spare tyre is in good order, as holes are frequent. You can have tyres fixed at any garage for about US$3 in 30 mins. Tyres without rims are confiscated and burnt by the Customs. Guideline prices: smallest car US$47 per day includes unlimited mileage or US$282 per week; jeep costs US$54 per day, US$390 per week, includes unlimited mileage. Driver's licence from home and credit card generally required. Insurance costs US$10-17 per day extra; excess is between US$750 and US$1,500. Four-wheel drives are very popular and in limited supply, you may have to reserve a week in advance, but if staying on the main roads a sedan is normally OK. Cash deposits or credit card charges range from US$600 to US$1,000, so check you have sufficient credit. You can often obtain lower rentals by making reservations before arrival with the major companies. If you plan to drop off a hired car, check with several firms for their charges: Elegante, Ada and National appear to have the lowest drop-off fees. Insurance will not cover broken windscreens, driving on unsurfaced roads or damaged tyres.

If you have an accident always call the traffic police and rental car company. Licence plates will automatically be removed. Do not move your car until the police arrive. Never bribe traffic police, ask them to issue a ticket. Some traffic police will tell you to return to San José, or another place, trying to get you to bribe them to avoid interrupting your trip. Always report any demands for money to the tourism authorities. Beware of policemen trying to charge on-the-spot fines for speeding. Fines in Costa Rica are paid in the Banco Central in San José and major towns and carry 30% in addition to the actual fine. If you pay a fine immediately, you still run the risk of getting reported and having to pay when you leave the country.

Security Never leave anything in a hired car and never leave your car on the street, even in daylight. Secure parking lots are available in San José, roughly US$1.25 per hour. Regular reports of break-ins at national parks.

Car parts are very expensive because of high import tax. If the parts are needed for leaving the country you can order them from abroad yourself and avoid the tax but it takes

Costa Rica

time. It is best not to try and sell your car here as the import tax is 70%. Spares are available for Japanese makes in San José. San José is also the best place to get Land Rover spares. Try Oswaldo von Breymann, Avenida 7, Casa 27, Calle 5-7, San José, for motorcycle spares; he is a good mechanic. Yamaha dealer, Lutz Hermanos y Cía Ltda, La Uruca, T222-2130.

Fuel Main fuel stations have regular (unleaded) US$0.48 (148 colones) and diesel US$0.34 (105 colones) per litre; super gasoline (unleaded) is available throughout the country, US$0.51 (158 colones).

Road tolls vary between US$0.30 and US$1. The following are 60 colones: San José-San José airport; San José-Santa Ana; San José-Cartago. 120 colones: San José airport-San Ramón. 200 colones: San José-Guápiles. San José-Cartago, San José-Santa Ana and San Ramón-airport have automatic machines accepting 5, 10, 20 colón coins.

Hitchhiking is easy and generally safe by day in the week, but take the usual precautions.

Sea Ferries serve the southern section of the Nicoya Peninsula from Puntarenas. There is also a vehicle and passenger ferry service crossing the Gulf of Nicoya close to the mouth of the Río Tempisque. The Osa Peninsula has a regular service from Golfito. Irregular boats travel to Tortuguero from Moín close to Puerto Limón and from Cariari, north of Guápiles.

Train There used to be 1,286 km of railways. The spectacular line from San José to Puerto Limón suffered major damage from landslides in 1991 and all the lines are now closed. For the truly devoted there is talk of reintroducing a tourist 'banana' from Siquirres to Matina on the Caribbean side. Ask locally for details. A couple of tourist trains runs at weekends on the Pacific side. One leaves Santa Ana at 0800, travelling to Orotina (US$59), the other leaves from San José at 0600, travelling to Caldera for US$25. The tours are in refurbished 1940s German wagons. ■ *Contact America Travel, T233-3300, americatravel@msn.com*

Maps The *Instituto Geográfico*, Av 20, C 9-11, at the Ministry of Public Works and Transport in San José, supplies very good topographical maps for walkers, 0730-1200. *ITM* have a 1:500,000 travel map of Costa Rica, available at bookstores throughout the country. Maps are also available in San José at *7th Avenue Books* and *Lehmann* on Av Central, C 1-3.

Keeping in touch

Internet Internet cafés are increasingly popular and connections in the towns tend to be good. Prices vary greatly but a rough guide is US$1.50 for 30 minutes.

Post Mail by sea from the UK takes from two to three months and 10 to 14 days by airmail. Airmail letters to Europe cost 90 colones, postcards 70 colones; to North/South America, letters 70 colones, 55 colones for postcards; to Australia, Africa and Asia, letters 70 colones, postcards 65 colones. 'Expreso' letters, 55 colones extra, several days quicker to USA and North Europe. Registered mail, 150 colones. All parcels sent out of the country by foreigners must be taken open to the post office for clearance. *Lista de Correos*, charges 50 colones per letter and will keep letters for four weeks. The contents of incoming parcels will be the subject of plenty of paperwork, and probably high duties. You normally have to come back the next day.

Telephone

Call 911 for emergencies

Public phones use 5, 10 and 20 colón coins

Long-distance telephone services are run by the Instituto Costarricense de Electricidad (ICE) and by Radiográfica Costarricense S.A. (RACSA). Rates at RACSA Telecommunications Centre, A 5, C 1, San José, to US, Canada, Mexico and South America are US$0.45 a minute, Central America and Belize are US$0.28, Panama is US$0.40 and the rest of the world US$60. Standard rates are charged between 0700 and 1900, reduced between 1900 and 2200 and reduced again between 2200 and 0700 and throughout the weekend. Add 13% sales tax, open 0800-1900, Sat 0800-1200, closed Sun. Phone cards with 'Personal Identification Numbers' are available for between US$0.80 and US$10. These can be used for national and international direct dialling from a private phone which is cheaper than rates from a public phone or RACSA office. Calls abroad can be made from phone booths; collect calls abroad may be made from special booths

Costa Rica

in the RACSA office, or from any booth nationwide if you dial 116 for connection with the international operator. Phone cards can be used. Country Direct dialling codes are (all prefix 0800): MCI 012-2222, AT&T 0114-114, Sprint 013-0123, Italy 039-1039, Germany 049-1049, Switzerland 041-1184, Belgium 032-1032, Britain 044-1044, Canada 015-1161, France 033-1033, Worldcom 014-4444, Denmark 045-1045, Spain 034-1034, Finland 358-1358, Holland 031-1111, Japan 081-1081, New Zealand 064-1064.

Media   **Newspapers** The best San José morning papers are *La Nación* (www.nacion.co.cr) and *La República* (www.larepublica.net); there is also *Al Día*. A good evening paper is *La Prensa Libre* (www.prensalibre.co.cr); *Libertad*, is a weekly newspaper (socialist); *El Debate* is another good weekly. Three weekly news magazines are: *Rumbo* (political), *Triunfo* and *Perfil* (popular). *La Gazette* is the official government weekly paper. *Tico Times* (www.ticotimes.co.cr) is out on Fridays, San José, T258-1558, F233-6378, and *Costa Rica Today* (free in better hotels and restaurants, subscriptions Ediciones 2000 SA, Acc No 117, PO Box 025216, Miami FL 33102) in English (look in the classifieds for Spanish classes). The former is better for news and classifieds and publishes *Exploring Costa Rica* annually (US$12); the latter has weekly features of interest to travellers.

Television Six local TV stations, many MW/FM radio stations throughout the country (new radio station 'Welcome Radio' is in English, Spanish and German, 800 Khz AM). Local Voz de América (VOA) station. Many hotels and private homes receive one of the four TV stations offering direct, live, 24-hour TV from the USA (Canal 19, Supercanal, Cable Color and Master TV-channels 56, 58, 60. All US cable TV can be received in San José on the two cable stations).

Food and drink

Local cuisine   *Sodas* (small restaurants) serve local food, which is worth trying. Very common is *casado*, a
Sales tax of 13%   cheap lunch which includes rice, beans, stewed beef or fish, fried plantain and cabbage. *Olla*
plus 10% service   *de carne* is a soup of beef, plantain, corn, yuca, *ñampi* and *chayote* (local vegetables). *Sopa*
charge added to   *negra* is made with black beans, and comes with a poached egg in it; *picadillo* is another meat
restaurant bills   and vegetable stew. Snacks are popular: *gallos* (filled tortillas), *tortas* (containing meat and vegetables), *arreglados* (bread filled with the same) and *empanadas*. *Pan de yuca* is a speciality, available from stalls in San José centre. For breakfast, try *gallo pinto* (rice and beans) with *natilla* (a slightly sour cream). Best ice-cream can be found in *Pops* shops. *Schmidt* bakeries are highly recommended; they also serve coffee. Also *La Selecta* bakeries. In general, eating out in Costa Rica is more expensive than elsewhere in Central America.

Drink   There are many types of cold drink, made either from fresh fruit, or milk drinks with fruit (*batidos*) or cereal flour whisked with ice cubes. Drinks are often sugared well beyond North American tastes. The fruits range from the familiar to the exotic; others include *cebada* (barley flour), *pinolillo* (roasted corn), *horchata* (rice flour with cinnamon), *chan*, 'perhaps the most unusual, looking like mouldy frogspawn and tasting of penicillin' (Michael J Brisco). All these drinks cost the same as, or less than, bottled fizzy products. Excellent coffee. Local beers are Bavaria, Bremen, Pilsen, Imperial and Tropical (which is low alcohol).

Shopping

What to buy   Best buys are wooden items, ceramics and leather handicrafts. Many wooden handicrafts are made of rainforest hardwoods and deforestation is a critical problem. Coffee should have 'puro' on the packet or it may have additives.

Holidays and festivals

1 January: New Year's Day; **19 March**: St Joseph; **Easter**: three days; **11 April**: Battle of Rivas; **1 May**: Labour Day; **June**: Corpus Christi; **29 June**: St Peter and St Paul; **25 July**: Guanacaste Day; **2 August**: Virgin of Los Angeles; **15 August**: Mothers' Day; **15 September**: Independence

Day; **12 October**: *Día de la Raza* (Columbus Day); **8 December**: Conception Immaculate; **25 December**: Christmas Day; **28-31 December**: San José only.

During Holy Week, nearly everyone is on holiday. Everything is shut on Thursday, Friday and Sunday, and many shops close on Saturday and most of the previous week as well.

The main **festival** is Carnival in Puerto Limón on 12 October when the focus of the country for once dwells on the country's largest Caribbean town. Music, dance, street processions and general festivities. Hotels book up, but it's definitely worth making the effort.

Sport and special interest travel

Tourists particularly enjoy the many well-kept and well-guarded national parks and nature reserves which protect some samples of the extraordinarily varied Costa Rican ecosystems. The variety is daunting including some of the last patches of dry tropical forest in the Parque Nacional Santa Rosa, the cloud forest of Monteverde and the Talamanca Mountains, and several active volcanoes including Rincon de la Viejo, Poás, Irazú and of course Arenal.

Nature tourism

There is a standard entrance fee of US$6 for all national parks. Manuel Antonio, Guayabo, Cabo Blanco and Braulio Carrillo (Quebrada González ranger station) are closed Monday. Cabo Blanco is also closed Tuesday.

Bird-watchers and butterfly lovers have long flocked to Costa Rica to see some of the 850 or so species of bird (the whole of the US counts about 800) and untold varieties of butterflies. All of these can best be seen in the parks, together with monkeys, deer, coyotes, armadillos, anteaters, turtles, coatis, raccoons, snakes, wild pigs, and, more rarely, wild cats and tapirs.

Although the national parks and other privately owned reserves are a main tourist attraction, many are in remote areas and not easy to get to on public transport; buses or coaches that do go tend to stay for a short time only. There is a growing tendency for tour companies to dominate the National Park 'market' to the exclusion of other public transport. For those on tight budgets, try making up a party with others and sharing taxis or hiring a car. Descriptions of the individual parks, and how to get there, will be found in the text.

The **Sistema Nacional de Areas de Conservación** (SINAC, T234-0973, F283-7343, PO Box 10104-1000, write in advance or call) in San José administers the National Park System. For information and permits to visit and/or camp in the Parks apply to **Fundación de Parques Nacionales** (FPN), 300 m north and 150 m east of Santa Teresita Church, Barrio Escalante, Calle 23, Avenida 15, San José, T257-2239, F222-4732, open Mon-Fri 0800-1200, 1300-1700. Most permits can be obtained at park entrances, but check in advance if your trip depends on gaining entrance. To contact park personnel by radio link or make accommodation reservations, T233-4160, but good Spanish is a help (bilingual operators at National Parks can be reached by dialing 192). If you make reservations at their San José office, make sure they have made them direct with the park and that you have clear references on the confirmation to avoid difficulties on arrival. If you want to work as a volunteer in the parks, contact SINAC. An alternative is to contact ASVO, Avenida 8, Calle 25, San José, T222-5085, F233-4989, asvo89@racsa.co.cr

The rivers of Costa Rica have proved to be highly popular for **whitewater rafting**, **kayaking** and **canoeing**, both for the thrill of the rapids and the wildlife interest of the quieter sections. The five most commonly run rivers are the Reventazón (and the Pascua section of it), Pacuare, Corobicí, Sarapiquí and El General. You can do a day trip but to reach the Class IV and V rapids you usually have to take two to three days. The Reventazón is perhaps the most accessible but the Pacuare has been recommended as a more beautiful experience. The Corobicí is slow and popular with bird-watchers. Ríos Tropicales (see San José Travel Agencies, page 1045) has been recommended for its guides and its equipment.

Watersports
Heavy rain may cause cancellations for reasons of safety, so you need flexibility in your plans

Offshore, **sea kayaking** is increasingly popular. **Snorkelling** and **scuba diving** are offered by several hotels, but you have to pick your spot carefully. Anywhere near a river will suffer from poor visibility and the coral reef has died in many places because of agricultural pollutants washed downstream. Generally, on the Caribbean side you can see wrecks and coral reefs, particularly in the southeast towards the Panamanian border, while on the Pacific side you see large pelagics and sportfish. Liveaboard dive boats head for the islands of Caño

Costa Rica

and Isla del Coco. Divers are not permitted in national parks or reserves, nor within 500 m of the protected sea turtle zone north of Parque Nacional Tortuguero. **Windsurfing** is good along the Pacific coast, particularly in the bay close to La Cruz and world-class on Lake Arenal, particularly the west end. Lots of hotels have equipment for hire and operators in San José will know where the best conditions prevail at any time. Be careful of obstacles in the water along rocky coastlines and near river mouths. **Surfing** is very popular on the Pacific and southern Caribbean beaches, attracting professionals who follow storm surges along the coast. Beginners can get classes in some resorts like Tamarindo, Jacó and Dominical, and proficient surfers can get the local advice on waves from surf shops in these areas.

Sport fishing is done off either coast and at different times of the year. Snook and tarpon are caught in the Caribbean, the largest snook being found in September and October, mostly north of Limón (where there are several fishing lodges), but also towards Panama. Exciting it may be, cheap it is not.

Other sports **Football** (soccer) is the national sport (played every Sunday at 1100, September to May, at the Saprissa Stadium). The national side's single greatest achievement came in the 1990 World Cup when they defeated Scotland. Qualification for the 2002 World Cup in Japan and South Korea led to a temporary halt in activities while Costa Rica remained in the running.

Mountain biking is popular throughout most parts of the country with options to simply rent the bike and push out on your own, or join a guided trip.

There are several **golf courses** close to the capital, and a few on the Nicoya Peninsula and at *Los Sueños Marriott*, near Jacó. For the capital see under San José. There is **swimming** on both Atlantic and Pacific coasts (see text). The Meseta is good country for **horse-riding**; horses can be hired by arrangement directly with owners. Most fiestas end with **bullfighting** in the squares, an innocuous but amusing set-to with no horses used. Bullfights are held in San José during the Christmas period. There is no kill and spectators are permitted to enter the ring to chase, and be chased by, the bull. If you're looking for a last big spending celebration **Hot-air balloon** rides can be organized throughout Costa Rica from Turrialba. And the final suggestion is to go and jump off a bridge… try **bungee jumping** off the Colorado bridge, close to Grecia in the Meseta Central (see page 1039).

Health

Drinking water is safe in all major towns; elsewhere it should be boiled, but bottled water is widely available. Intestinal disorders are prevalent in the lowlands although Chagas disease is now rare. Malaria is on the increase; malaria prophylaxis is advised for visitors to the lowlands, especially near the Nicaraguan border; in Costa Rica it is available only from the Ministerio de Salud (T223-0333) in San José (free), or at the Nicaraguan border. If visiting jungle areas be prepared for insects bites with repellent and appropriate clothing. Dengue fever has been recorded in Liberia and Puntarenas. Uncooked foods should not be eaten. The standards of health and hygiene are among the best in Latin America.

Costa Rica

San José

□San José

Nestled in a broad, fertile valley producing coffee and sugar-cane, San José was founded in 1737 and became capital in 1823 after struggles for regional ascendency between competing towns of the Central Valley. Frequent earthquakes have destroyed most of the colonial buildings and the modern replacements do little to inspire the arriving visitor. But, like any city, if you can get under the skin, the mix of museums and general attractions make it worth staying a couple of days. The climate is comfortable, with temperatures between 15° and 26°C, though the evenings can be chilly. The rainy season lasts roughly May to November; the rest of the year it's mainly dry.

Ins and outs

Getting there The international airport is 16 km from the centre along a good *autopista*. A taxi costs US$10-12 and there are efficient buses running every 10 mins from outside the terminal building to the city centre. Long-distance buses have their terminals scattered round town (see map) but the majority are closed to the Coca Cola Terminal. Bus connections in Costa Rica and with other Central American countries are very good.

Getting around
Few buildings have numbers, so find out the nearest cross-street when getting directions; 200 m means two blocks

For pedestrians navigating the streets of San José is easy. Streets cross one another at right-angles. *Avenidas* run east-west; *Calles* north-south. *Avenidas* to the north of Av Central are given odd numbers; those to the south even numbers. *Calles* to the west of C Central are even-numbered; those to the east odd-numbered. The 3 main streets, Av Central, Av 2 and the intersecting C Central, encompass the business centre. The main shops are along Av Central. The **Instituto Costarricense de Turismo** (**ICT**) provides an excellent free map of the city, marking all the important sights and business houses.

Some people find the narrow streets are too heavily polluted with exhaust fumes and prefer to stay in the suburbs of Escazu, Alajuela or Heredia. It's probably a good choice if you've already visited San José, but if it's your first time in the capital you should give it a try for a couple of days at least. That said, regular buses run in and out of the city centre to outlying districts, so it is easy to come in to town if you choose a hotel in the suburbs. A circular bus route travels along Av 3 out to Sabana Grande and back making a useful circuit and an impromptu city tour. Taxis can be ordered by phone or hailed in the street; they are red and should have meters.

Traffic is congested especially between 0700 and 2000, so you are not recommended to drive in the city centre. If you do drive, watch out for no-parking zones. Seven blocks of the Av Central, from *Banco Central* running east to Plaza de la Cultura, are closed to traffic and there are several poorly signposted one-way streets.

Tourist offices *Instituto Costarricense de Turismo*, information office: under the Plaza de la Cultura, Calle 5, A Central-2, T223-1733, F223-5452, toll free T800-012-3456, open Mon-Fri 0800-1600. Also at Juan Santamaría airport (very helpful, will check hotels for you) and at borders. Free road maps of Costa Rica, San José and the metropolitan area and public transport timetables available. *Otec, youth and student travel office*, extremely helpful, Calle 3, Av 1-3, Edif Ferenz, T256-0633, F233-2321, Apdo 323-1002 San José, good special discounts, for ISTC and FIYTO members, has discount booklet for shops, hotels, restaurants, museums, cinemas, theatres, tourist attractions and more, excellent for travel arrangements, special student airfares to Latin America, US, Europe, bus and car rental arrangements, good tours of Costa Rica.

Costa Rica

Sights

Colour map 7, grid B3
Population: 968,367
Altitude: 1,150 m

Student cards
give reductions in
most museums

Many of the most interesting public buildings are near the intersection of Av Central and C Central. The **Teatro Nacional** (1897), with marble staircases, statues, frescoes and foyer decorated in gold with Venetian plate mirrors, is just off Avenida Central, on Calle 3. It has a good coffee bar run by Café Britt and guided tours. ■ *Mon-Sat 0900-1700, US$3, T221-5341.* Nearby is **Plaza de la Cultura**, Av Central, Calle 3-5, which, in addition to being a great place for people-watching, hosts occasional public concerts. The **Museo de Oro**'s booty of golden treasure is buried beneath the Plaza de la Cultura complex with art museums adjoining the Teatro Nacional. Fine golden figures of frogs, spiders, raptors and other creatures glisten in the spectacular museum sponsored by the *Banco Nacional.* ■ *Tue-Sun, 1000-1600, US$5, US$1 with student card,* In the same complex is the **Museo Numismático** with a small exhibition displaying the history of Costa Rican money.

The **Museo Nacional** is east from the Plaza de la Cultura, at C 17, Av Central-2. It has very interesting archaeology, anthropology and national history displays and some gold, ex-President Arias' Nobel Peace Prize, information in Spanish and English, replicas of pre-Columbian jewellery may be bought at reasonable prices. ■ *Tue-Sun, 0900-1630, US$3.20, children free, T257-1433.* Facing it is the **Plaza de la Democracia**, a concrete cascade constructed to mark the November 1989 centenary of Costa Rican democracy. The **Palacio Nacional** (Av Central, C 15) is where the Legislative Assembly meets; any visitor can attend debates, sessions start at 1600.

South of the Museo Nacional is **Museo de Criminología**, Av 8, C 17-19, display of forensic medicine and various grisly exhibits, ■ *Mon-Fri 0700-1630, free.*

Two blocks north of the Museo Nacional is the **Parque Nacional**, with a grandiloquent bronze monument representing the five Central American republics ousting the filibuster William Walker (see Nicaragua, History section) and the abolition of

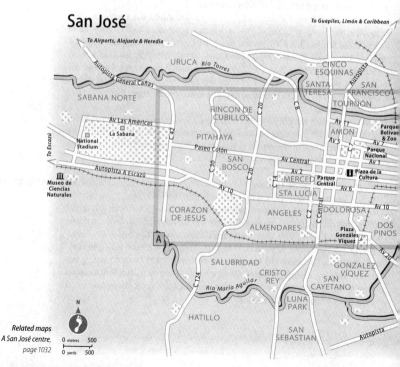

San José

To Guapiles, Limón & Caribbean

Related maps
A San José centre,
page 1032

0 metres 500
0 yards 500

slavery in Central America. There is also a statue donated by the Sandinista Government of Nicaragua to the people of Costa Rica. To the north of the park is the **Biblioteca Nacional**. In the old liquor factory next to the Biblioteca Nacional, now the Centro Nacional de la Cultura, is the **Museo de Arte Contemporáneo y Diseño**, Avenida 3, Calle 15-17, ■ *Tue-Fri 1000-1700, Sat 1000-1600, free.*

Along Calle Central, west of the Teatro Nacional, is **Parque Central**, with a bandstand in the middle among trees, again with occasional performances. East of the park is the monumental architecture of the **Catedral Metropolitana**; to the north is the **Teatro Melico Salazar** with a good mix of performances throughout the year and regular folklore performances every Tuesday evening. ■ See press for details or call T221-4952.

In **Braulio Carillo Park** opposite the eclectic neo-gothic design of **La Merced** church is a huge carved granite ball brought from the Diquis archaeological site near Palmar Norte. There are others at the entrance to the Museo de Ciencias Naturales.

At the end of Paseo Colón, at Calle 42, is **Parque Sabana** which was converted from the former city airport in the 1950s; the old airport building is now the **Museo de Arte Costarricense**, with a small but interesting display of paintings and sculptures. ■ *Tue-Sun, 1000-1600, Sun free, US$2, US$1 for students.* T222-7155. Further west in the park is the **Estadio Nacional**, with seating for 20,000 spectators at (mainly) football matches, basketball, volleyball and tennis courts, a running track, lake and swimming pool.

At the southwest corner of Parque Sabana are the impressive natural displays of the **Museo de Ciencias Naturales**, Colegio La Salle. ■ *Mon-Sat 0800-1600, Sun 0900-1700, US$2, (in the grounds of the Ministry of Agriculture; take 'Estadio Sabana' bus from Av 2, C 1 to the gate).*

North of Avenida Central, on Calle 2, is the **Unión Club**, the principal social centre of the country. Opposite is the **General Post and Telegraph Office** which also houses the **Museo Filatélico**, on the second floor. ■ *Mon-Fri 0800-1700, free.*

A couple of blocks to the west is the hustle and bustle of the **Mercado Central**, rich with the shouts, cries, smells and chaos of a fresh produce market. Good cheap meals for sale as well as some interesting nic-nacs for the passing tourist.

The Disneyesque building on the horizon to the north of the city is the **Centro Costarricense de Ciencias y Cultura** (Scientific and Cultural Centre) in the old city penitentiary with the **Galería Nacional**, **Biblioteca Carlos Luis Saénz**, the **Auditorio Nacional** and **Museo del Niño**. Interesting as much for the well-restored building as for the exhibits using former prison cells and spaces to good effect. C 4, Av 9. ■ *Tue-Fri 0800-1500, Sat-Sun 1000-1700, US$2, children US$1.30.*

Along Avenida 3, north of the Plaza de la Cultura, are the four gardens of the remodelled **Parque Morazán**, with another bandstand at the centre. A little to the northeast, **Parque España**, cool, quiet, and intimate, has for neighbours

Costa Rica

the **Casa Amarilla** (Yellow House), seat of the Ministry of Foreign Affairs, and the **Edificio Metálico**, which houses several of the main schools.

One of the best museums in the city is the **Museo del Jade Fidel Tristan** in the INS building, at Av 7, C 9-13, on the 11th floor, with jade carvings, pottery and sculpture, interesting, explained in Spanish and English, a 'must', and a beautiful view over the city. Renovated late 2000. ■ *Mon-Fri, 0830-1630, US$3.*

To the south of Parque Morazán the **Serpentarium** is worth a visit especially if you are going to the National Parks or the jungle. Good variety of snakes and other reptiles. Staff helpful if you speak Spanish. ■ *Mon-Sun 0900-1800, US$4,* Av 1, C 9-11, on the second floor of an office block.

To the north of Parque Morazán is **Parque Simón Bolívar**, now turned into a recreation area, with **Simón Bolívar National Zoo and Botanical Gardens**. It's been remodelled and much improved, with all native plants numbered and listed in a brochure; animals' cages are small. ■ *Mon-Fri, 0800-1600, Sat-Sun, 0800-1600, US$2, also restaurant and souvenir shop. Av 11, just east of C 7 (go down C 7 about three blocks from Av 7)*

To the north of town, a reasonable walk or a short taxi ride, is **Spirogyra**, 100 m east, 150 m south of Centro Comercial El Pueblo (near *Hotel Villa Tournón*). Fascinating little butterfly farm close to the city but filled with life. ■ *Daily, 0800-1500, printed guide in English, last guided tour 1430, US$6, U$$3 students, take 'Calle Blancos' bus from Calle 3 and Avenida 5 to El Pueblo.*

Out to the east of San José in San Pedro is the **Museo de Entomología**, in basement of School of Music building of the University of Costa Rica in San Pedro, west of the capital, many beautiful insects, only museum of its kind in Central America. ■ *Mon-Fri 1300-1700, US$3.*

Excursions

San José is a good base for excursions into the beautiful Meseta Central. Excursions to the spectacular Orosí Valley and Irazú Volcano are given under Cartago (see page 1055). Volcán Poás gently simmers and steams from its elevated position at the northern limit of the Central Highlands and can be visited from Alajuela (described on page 1048). To reach Volcán Barva in Parque Nacional Braulio Carillo, take a bus to San José de la Montaña (see page 1054). Enquire first about the likely weather when planning a visit to Poás, Irazú or Barva as cloud will limit the views.

A road runs northeast of San José (11 km) to **San Isidro de Coronado**, a popular summer resort (bus from Terminal Coronado, Avenida 7, Calle Central and 1). Those interested in medical research can visit the **Instituto Clodomiro Picado** snake farm. ■ *Mon-Fri 0800-1600, snake feeding Fri only 1400, T229-0335, Spanish speaking only*. Take Dulce Nombre de Coronado bus from Avenida 3, Calle 3-5, 30 mins, or San Antonio Coronado bus to end of line and walk 200 m downhill.

San Antonio de Escazú, a western suburb of San José popular with the expatriate community, hosts the Día del Boyero (National Oxcart Drivers' Day) on the second weekend in March. Festivities culminate on the Sunday in a colourful oxcart parade from the school to the centre, accompanied by typical *payasos*. Open-air dancing in the evening to music played on a marimba.

Water Land, formerly Acua Mania, is a water park just off airport highway at traffic lights, 600 m south of *Hotel Herradura*, on the San Antonio de Belén road. ■ *Tue-Fri 0900-1700, Sat and Sun members only. US$6.50 per person. T293-2891.* Further west is **Ojo de Agua**, T441-2808, a spring-fed water park about 6 km south of Alajuela. ■ *Open until 1700 daily, US$1.20.* Direct bus from Av 1, C 20-22 in San José or take bus to Alajuela and then on to San Antonio de Belén. **Parque de Diversiones**, 2 km west of Hospital México, has the **Pueblo Antiguo** theme park next to it depicting Costa Rica through the ages from 1880-1930 with thematic regions of representative of different

:owns, and different parts of the country and coast. ■ *US$7*. Held at the theme park
.s a *Vivencias Costarricenses* show (■ *Wed-Sun 1000-1400, US$35 includes show,*
'unch, transport, guide and taxes) and *Noches Costarricences* show (■ *Sat-Sun,*
1800-2100, US$35 includes show, dinner, transport, guide and taxes).

In **La Guácima**, 35 minutes west of San José, 20 minutes south of Alajuela, is a **Butterfly Farm**, dedicated to rearing and exporting over 120 species of butterflies. The
first such farm in Latin America, now with over 100 associated farmers throughout
Costa Rica, it is believed to be one of the second largest exporters of farm-bred butterflies in the world (the largest is in Taiwan). Created by Joris Brinckerhoff, a former
Peace Corp volunteer and his wife in 1984, the farm opened to the public in 1990. All
visitors receive a two-hour guided tour. Visit in the morning as butterflies require heat
from the sun for the energy to fly so when it is cool or cloudy, there may be less activity.
■ *Daily, 0830-1700, US$15 adults, US$9 students, US$7 children under 12, includes*
guided tour every 2 hrs T438-0400. Getting there: bus for La Guácima Mon-Sat from Av
1, C 20-22, 1100 and 1400, return 1515, 1 hr, US$0.40, at last stop walk 300 m from
school south to the butterfly sign (also minibuses, US$5). From Alajuela take bus marked
'La Guácima abajo' from Av 2 between C 8-10, Pali Pacifico 75 m east, 40 mins, at 0830,
1030, 1230 and 1430, returning at 1110, 1310 1510, 1710.

From San José you can take a tour of **Café Britt's coffee farm** near Barva de
Heredia where you can see the processing factory, tasting room and a multi-media
presentation using professional actors of the story of coffee. You can arrange to be
picked up at various points and hotels in San José. ■ *Tours 0900, 1100 and 1500 in*
high season, 2 hrs, US$20, T260-2748, T238-1848 for details.

Essentials

Sleeping

L *Aurola Holiday Inn*, C 5, Av 5, pool, T233-7233, F222-0090, aurola@racsa.co.cr, mainly **Central**
business clientèle, casino (smallest wager US$4, free drinks if you play), good view of city ■ *on map*
from the top floor bar/casino. **L-AL** *Del Rey*, Av 1, C 9, Apdo 6241-1000, T257-7800,
F221-0096, www.hoteldelrey.com, nice single, double, triple rooms, standard or deluxe,
suites, children under 12 free, free city tour on a/c bus, walls a bit thin, restaurant, casino.
AL *Europa*, C Central, Av 5, T222-1222, F221-3976, europa@racsa.co.cr, pleasant, comfortable rooms, cable TV, pool, central, good for business visitors, suites available, prior reservation recommended, rooms on street side can be noisy, good restaurant. **AL** *Fleur de Lys*,
C13, Av 2-6, T223-1206, F257-3637, www.hotelfleurdelys.com, restored Victorian mansion
house, good restaurant, bar. Recommended and stylishly elegant. **A** *Best Western San José*
Downtown, Av 7, C 6-8, T234-8055, F234-8033, www.bestwestern.co.cr, bath, TV, a/c,
includes breakfast, rustic rooms, free coffee and bananas all day, pool, sauna, parking. Recommended. **A** *Doña Inés*, C 11, Av 2-6, PO Box 1754-1002, T222-7443, F223-5426,
www.amerisol.com/costarica/lodging/ines.html, clean, quiet, safe, Italian-run.

B *Diana's Inn*, C 5, Av 3, Parque Morazán, near *Holiday Inn*, T223-6542, F233-0495, an old
building formerly used by the president, now restored, includes breakfast and taxes, discounts available, a/c, TV, hot water, noisy, luggage storage, safe box. **C** *Centroamericano*,
Av 2, C 6-8, T221-3362, F221-3714, private bath, clean small rooms, very helpful, will arrange
accommodation in other towns, free shuttle (Mon-Fri) to airport, laundry facilities. Recommended. **C** *Diplomat*, C6, Av Central, T221-8133, F233-7474. 29 rooms, very central and reasonably priced. Private bath and hot water. **C** *Fortuna*, Av 6, C 2 y 4, T223-5344, F221-2466,
hfortuna@infoweb.co.cr, quiet, helpful. Recommended. **C** *Pensión de la Cuesta*, Av 1, C
11-15, T256-7946, F255-2896, www.suntoursandfun.com A little off the wall in style with
artwork all over the walls of this old colonial home. Shared bath and use of the kitchen.
C *Ritz*, Av 8-10, C Central, T222-4103, F222-8849, ritzcr@racsa.co.cr Private bath, cheaper
without, TV lounge, storage boxes, credit cards accepted. Ritz Eco-Tourismo travel agency

Costa Rica

downstairs. Smallish rooms but popular with friendly service and congenial atmostphere. Discounts available in the green season. Recommended.

D *Bienvenido*, C 10, Av 1-3, T233-2161, F221-1872, very clean, hot shower, good restaurant, near centre and airport bus, best hotel near Coca-Cola bus station. **D** *Boston*, C Central, Av 8, T221-0563, F257-5063, with or without bath, good, very friendly, but noisy, will store luggage. A couple of other cheap options in the area including the *Berlin* almost next door. **D** *Compostela,* C 6, Av 3-5, T257-1514, bath, friendly, small rooms, family-run, quiet, door locked at 2300. Recommended. **D** *Johnson*, C 8, Av Central, T223-7633, F222-3683, very friendly and helpful staff, clean, restaurant and bar, good value, although some rooms a little dark. Recommended. **D-E** *Pensión Continental*, C Central, Av 8, T222-4103, avoid small rooms downstairs, hot water, clean, friendly, laundry, helpful, coffee available, no meals

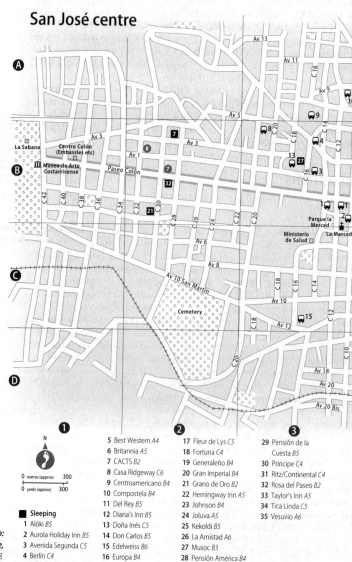

San José centre

Sleeping		
1 Alóki *B5*	13 Doña Inés *C5*	25 Kekoldi *B5*
2 Aurola Holiday Inn *B5*	14 Don Carlos *B5*	26 La Amistad *A6*
3 Avenida Segunda *C5*	15 Edelweiss *B6*	27 Musoc *B3*
4 Berlín *C4*	16 Europa *B4*	28 Pensión América *B4*
5 Best Western *A4*	17 Fleur de Lys *C5*	29 Pensión de la Cuesta *B5*
6 Britannia *A5*	18 Fortuna *C4*	30 Príncipe *C4*
7 CACTS *B2*	19 Generaleño *B4*	31 Ritz/Continental *C4*
8 Casa Ridgeway *C6*	20 Gran Imperial *B4*	32 Rosa del Paseo *B2*
9 Centroamericano *B4*	21 Grano de Oro *B2*	33 Taylor's Inn *A5*
10 Compostela *B4*	22 Hemingway Inn *A5*	34 Tica Linda *C5*
11 Del Rey *B5*	23 Johnson *B4*	35 Vesuvio *A6*
12 Diana's Inn *B5*	24 Joluva *A5*	

0 metres (approx) 300
0 yards (approx) 300

Related Map:
San José centre,
page 1028

Costa Rica

except for breakfast. Recommended. **D** *Pensión Musoc*, C 16, Av 3-5, T222-9437, with or without private bath, very clean, hot water, luggage stored, will do laundry, friendly, near bus stations so somewhat noisy, but recommended. **D** *Príncipe*, Av 6, C Central-2, T222-7983, with bath, top rooms best, quiet, friendly.

E *Casa Ridgeway*, Centro de Amigos para la Paz, C 15, Av 6-8, T/F233-6168, friends@racsa.co.cr, 1-4 beds in room, shared bath, use of kitchen, very friendly, laundry possible. **E** *Generaleño*, Av 2, C 8-10, T233-7877, with bath, cold water, good value. **E-F** *Gran Imperial*, on the western side of the Central Market, C 8, Av 1-Central, T222-8463, F256-9650, granhimp@racsa.co.cr Current backpacker hang-out, mixed reports, small rooms, thin walls, clean, sometimes noisy, limited hot showers, restaurant with good prices, best to reserve, good for meeting other travellers with

Costa Rica

● Eating
1 Café Parisienne *B5*
2 Choza del Sabor *B4*
3 Gran Diamente *B4*
4 La Esmeralda *C5*
5 La Hacienda *B5*
6 La Perla *B4*
7 Le Croissant *B2*
8 Machu Picchu *B2*
9 Morazán *B5*
10 Polla a la Leña *B4*
11 Soda El Parque *C4*
12 Tin Jo *C5*
13 Vishnu *B5*

🚍 Buses
1 Alajuela & Airport Buses *B3*
2 Heredia Buses *B3/B4*
3 Liberia Buses *B3*
4 Panaline Bus *B3*
5 San Isidro Buses *D4*
6 Sirca Bus *C5*
7 Ticabus *C5*
8 Transnica Bus *B3*
9 Terminal Alfaro *A3*
10 Terminal Atlántico Norte *A3*
11 Terminal Caribe (Sixaola) *A4*
12 Terminal Cartago *D5*
13 Terminal Coca Cola *B3*
14 Terminal Los Santos *D6*
15 Terminal Puntarenas *C3*
16 Terminal Turrialba *C5*

balcony overlooking Central Market a great spot for relaxing, locked luggage store, TV. **E** *Marlyn*, Av 7-9, C 4, T233-3212, more with bath, hot showers, good security, will store luggage, parking for motorcycles (just). On the other side of the road is **F** *Pensión América*, Av 7, C 4, T221-4116, clean, large rooms, good value. **E-F** *Rialto*, Av 5, C 2, 1 block from Correos, shared bath, hot water, safe, friendly but can be very noisy. **E** *Roma*, C 14, Av Central-1, T223-2179, uphill from Alajuela bus station, clean, safe, good value but windowless rooms, stores luggage. **E-F** *Otoya*, C 1, Av 3-5, T221-3925. Close to the centre, cleanish, friendly and quite popular, you're allowed to use the telephone which can be a bonus. Hot water throughout and some rooms with private bath. Luggage store, internet access and English spoken. Recommended.

F *Americana*, C 2, Av 2, T221-9799. Rooms are large, basic and with shared bath and mixed reports. On the good side the place is friendly, there is luggage store and laundry facilities. **F** *Pensión Boruca*, C 14, Av 1-3, Coca-Cola market, T223-0016, without bath, hot water, laundry service, rooms a bit dark but friendly owner.

Ticabus
terminal
Southeast of centre

E *Avenida Segunda*, Av 2 No 913, C 9-11, T222-0260, acebrisa@racsa.co.cr, price varies, friendly, stores luggage. **F** *Tica Linda*, Av 2, C 9-11, T221-9332. Dormitory accommodation, use of kitchen, hot water and laundry, TV in communal area. Will store luggage, popular with travellers. No sign, just a notice on the front, currently yellow door. Not the *Hilton*, but perfectly OK for the price and in an OK part of town – moves often, ask locally. There are several hotels in **F** and **G** range between the Mercado Central, Mercado Borbon and the Coca Cola terminal. Cheaper hotels usually have only wooden partitions for walls, so they are noisy. Hotels in the red light district, C 6, Av 1-5, near Mercado Central, charge on average US$10 with toilet and shower for a night.

Barrio Amón
Northeast of centre

L-AL *Britannia*, C 3, Av 11, T223-6667, F223-6411, britania@racsa.co.cr, 1910 Spanish-style beautifully restored mansion, high standard, antique furniture, very good service, excellent restaurant, worth the money. **AL** *Alóki*, C 13, Av 9, T380-7159, www.traveltocostarica.com, US-owned, elegant 19th-century restored mansion, antique furnishings, only 7 rooms, restaurant recommended, book in advance, bar, patio, very pleasant, no credit cards, front doors locked at 2300. **AL-A** *Don Carlos*, C 9, Av 7-9, T221-6707, F255-0828, www.doncarlos.co.cr, 36 rooms, interesting traditional building, much artwork and statuary, sundeck, free coffee, Annemarie's giftshop good selection, credit cards accepted, airport shuttle, tours arranged. **AL** *La Casa Verde Inn*, C 7, Av 9, Barrio Amón, T/F223-0969, small, renovated old house, deluxe, good breakfast, helpful.

A *Hemingway Inn*, Av 9, C 9, T/F221-1804, www.geocities.com/hemingwayinn, central, quirky old Spanish home with wood-panelling and circuitous corridors, includes breakfast, patio and tropical garden. **A** *Taylor's Inn*, Av 13, C 3-3b, T257-4333, F221-1475, www.catours.co.cr, with breakfast, old house nicely restored. **A-B** *Kekoldi*, Av 9, C 3b, T248-0804, F248-0767, www.kekoldi.com, old house imaginatively refurbished with delightfully colourful, breezy pastel designs, 14 big rooms with bath, includes breakfast, helpful, snacks and bar service, some traffic noise. **B** *Cinco Hormigas Rojas*, C15, Av 9-11, T/F257-8581, cincohormigasrojas@ertimes.com, nice décor, small house. Recommended. **B-C** *Joluva*, C 3b, Av 9-11, T223-7961, F257-7668, www.joluva.com, with breakfast, old house, friendly, safe, good laundry service, good value. A relaxing and gay-friendly hotel.

Barrio Otoya
Northeast of centre

A *Vesuvio*, Av 11, C 13-15, T/F256-1616, www.hotelvesuvio.com, includes breakfast, 20 rooms, private bath, secure parking, very quiet, comfortable, email, good restaurant, show your *Handbook* for 20% discount. **A** *La Amistad*, Av 11, C 15, T221-1597, F221-1409, wolfgang@racsa.co.cr, with breakfast, very popular, good value, with bath, TV, fan, net café, German owned. 20% discount with this guide. **B** *Edelweiss*, Av 9, C 13-15, 100 m east of Condovac offices, T221-9702, F222-1241, www.edelweisshotel.com, English, German and Spanish spoken, clean, comfortable, native hardwood furniture and carved doors, pleasant courtyard bar, helpful, friendly. Recommended.

Paseo Colón
West of centre

A *Rosa del Paseo*, Paseo Colón, C 28-30, T257-3225, F223-2776, www.online.co.cr/rosa/, beautifully restored mansion, breakfast included. Good location for access to the city centre but not in the heart of town. **LL-AL** *Grano de Oro*, C 30, Av 2, T255-3322, F221-2782, www.hotelgranodeoro.com, exquisite converted 19th-century mansion, 35 rooms and suites,

Costa Rica

beautiful terrace gardens, friendly, tasteful, good value. **B** *CACTS*, Av 3 bis, C 28-30, near *Pizza Hut* Paseo Colón, T221-2928, F221-8616, www.tourism.co.cr/hotels/cacts/cacts.htm, safe, good service, breakfast included, TV, friendly. Recommended. **B-C** *Ritmo del Caribe*, Paseo Colón y C 32, T221-2928, F221-8616, www.ritmo-del-caribe.com, simple, good rooms and friendly atmosphere, free airport shuttle, good value. German owner Tomas also runs *Wild Rider Motorcycles* (see Transport, Motorcycle rental page 1040).

LL-L *Costa Rica Marriott*, 10 minutes from Juan Santamaría airport, San Antonio de Belén, T298-0000, F298-0011, www.marriotthotels.com/SJOCR More an experience than a hotel. Full service, luxury hotel with conference facilities. Built in the style of a coffee plantation. **LL-L** *Meliá Cariari*, 10 minutes from the airport, T239-0022, F239-2803, www.solmelia.com Full service business hotel with 3 pools, tennis, 18-hole golf course.

San José-Airport highway (Autopista General Cañas)

In the area of **Los Yoses, San Pedro,** University of Costa Rica are: **AL** *Milvia*, 4 km west of downtown in San Pedro, 250 m northwest of De Muñoz y Nane shopping centre, T225-4543, F225-7801, www.hotel-milvia.co.cr, attractive boutique hotel, converted wooden mansion once the home of a 1930s revolutionary, personal service.

Eastern suburbs

Apartotels (with kitchen, etc) can be cheaper for longer stays, weekly or monthly rates. **C** *Apartamentos Scotland*, C 29, Av 1, T223-0033, F257-5317, www.goin2travel.com/a525.htm, weekly (from US$275) or monthly (from US$650) for furnished apartments **B-E** Studio apartments from US$100 to US$300 a week, one week minimum, through *Cabet Travel*, Av 2, C5 – 7, T257-8920, F256-1554, cabet1@racsa.co.cr Apartments are in Barrio Yoses, 1 wk minimum, ideal for language students, business trips and others seeking a secure spot with a sense of home. Apartments range from a basic and simple room, to comfortable studio flats with TV, telephone, kitchen and dining-room.

AL *Tennis Club*, Sábana Sur, Apdo 4964, T232-1266, F232-3867, crtennis@racsa.co.cr On the southern side of Parque Sabana, the 11 tennis courts will obviously attract the tennis player. There are also 3 pools, a gym and a spa. Each of the 27 rooms have AC, cable TV and private bathroom. Recommended.

La Sabana

Around **Escazú** and **Santa Ana** are **LL-L** *Tara Resort Hotel*, San Antonio de Escazú, T228-6992, F228-9651, www.tararesort.com, beautiful mansion, includes breakfast and transport, suites, conference facilities, recommended restaurant, pool, beautiful views, climb nearby Pico Blanco mountain. **LL-L** *Camino Real Intercontinental* Próspero Fernández Highway, Multiplaza Mall, Escazú, T289-7000, F289-8998, www.interconti.com, 260 rooms, in a full service, top-quality international business hotel. Every comfort imagineable with some nice touches to remind you of Costa Rica's natural heritage.

Western suburbs

A *Pico Blanco Inn*, San Antonio de Escazú, T228-1908, F289-5189, all rooms with balconies and views of Central Valley, several cottages, English owner, restaurant with English pub, Costa Rican flavour, pool, airport pickup can be requested. Recommended. **A-B** *Costa Verde Inn*, 300m south of the cemetery, T228-4080, F289-8591, www.hotelcostaverde.com A secluded and charming country home with 12 imaginatively decorated rooms – a popular choice away from the centre of town. **C** *Linda Vista Lodge Bed and Breakfast*, Escazú, cosy rooms, spectacular views.

AL *Hampton Inn*, T443-0043, F442-9523 (toll free within Costa Rica 800-HAMPTON), www.hampton.hotel.co.cr Closeset hotel to airport, handy for early and late flights (see Alajuela, Sleeping).

At the airport

Toruma Youth Hostel, Av Central, C 29-31, T234-8186, F224-4085, www.hostelling-costarica.com, 95 beds, clean, hot water, crowded but safe, lockable compartments in each room, restaurant on site, **E** per person including breakfast, **D** for those who do not hold ISIC or YHA membership; music, free for guests, on Fri and Sat nights; a good place for meeting other travellers to arrange group travel, and for booking other hostels in the country. You can leave bags for US$0.50 per day. There are 11 affiliated Youth Hostels throughout Costa Rica.

Youth hostel

Costa Rica

Bed & breakfast B&B accommodation in San José and Costa Rica is very popular and covers a wide range of price brackets. *Costa Rica Bed and Breakfast Group*, c/o Pat Bliss, Interlink 978, PO Box 025635, Miami, Florida 33152, T/F 228-8726, www.catch22.com/~vudu/bliss2.html They offer a reservation and itinerary planning service. They have over 200 inns and hotels covering the **AL-D** range in their directory.

Trailer park *Belén*, in San Antonio de Belén, 2 km west of intersection at Cariari and San Antonio, 5 km from airport, turn off Highway 1 on to Route 111, turn right at soccer field then 1st left for 1 km, T239-0421, F239-1316, US$10 per day, American-owned, shade, hot showers, laundry, friendly, recommended, good bus service to San José.

Eating

● *on map, page 1032* Dining in San José takes its inspiration from across the world. Traditional dishes, feasting on a steady supply of rice and beans, tend to be a little on the heavy side but definitely worth trying. Beyond *Tico* food, inspiration comes from as wide a source as the capital's citizens. Italian, French and Chinese restaurants are many but more diverse dishes can also be found.

Expensive
Smarter restaurants add sales and service tax totalling 23%

Apart from the hotels, the best restaurants include: *Ana Italiana*, T222-6153, C 24 y 26, good Italian and friendly. Recommended. *La Bastille*, Paseo Colón, C 22, T255-4994. Stylish French food in elegant surrounds. Closed Sun. *Lobster Inn*, Paseo Colón, C 24, T223-8594, seafood, large choice, expensive. *Masia de Triquell*, Edif Casa España, Sabana Norte, T296-3528, Catalan, warmly recommended, closed Sun. *La Cocina de Leña*, T255-1560, north of the centre in El Pueblo, Barrio Tournón, excellent menu of the very best in *Tico* cuisine, upmarket, pricey, but warm, friendly ambience.

In **Los Yoses** is *Buenos Aires Tango*, Paseo Rubén Darío, C 29, Barrio la California, T233-9729, F233-9954. Argentine *parrillada* with a wide range of international dishes à la carte, a vaguely Mediterranean atmosphere in a Bavarian house. *Euro Café (Rómulo & Remo)*, Paseo Rubén Darío and C 41, T289-5206. Chic, crisp décor, with service to match. You can choose to eat on the garden patio or dine in the pure white dining-room. *Jurgen's*, C 41 and Paseo Rubén Darío, Los Yoses, T224-2455, F224-2166. First-class service, excellent international menu in a sophisticated atmosphere. Recommended. *Le Chandelier*, T225-3980, 100 m south and 100 m west of the ICE building in Los Yoses, one of the best French restaurants in town.

Mid-range
At lunchtime cheaper restaurants offer a set meal called a casado, US$1.50-2.50, which is good value

Al Andalus, Av 7 y 9 C, T257-6556, Spanish, Costa Rican and international, nice atmosphere, reasonable. *Café Mundo*, Av 9, C 13-15, opposite *Hotel Edelweiss*, old mansion tastefully restored, good salads, great pasta, wonderful bread, a stylish joint. *El Balcón de Europa*, C 9, Av Central-1, Italian, great atmosphere, popular, but some dishes rather small and tasteless. *La Esmeralda*, Av 2, C 7, reasonably priced with good local dishes, but it's the live *mariachi* music in the evenings that draws the crowd. A great institution, occasion and a must at least once. *La Esquina del Café*, Av 9, C 3b, speciality coffee roasters with good restaurant, souvenir shop, live music twice a month, daily 0900-2200. *La Estancia*, in El Pueblo, typical Costa Rican steakhouse, be sure to use the garlic sauce, recommended. *La Hacienda Steak House*, C 7, Av Central-2, good value when it's eat all you can on Sun, upstairs is a good Mexican *taquería* with an all-you-can-eat buffet at weekends between 1200 and 1500 for US$4. North of the Coca Cola district in Paso de la Vaca is *Mexico Bar* which although dead by day comes out at night with a flurry of music and good Mexican food. *Pizza Metro*, Av 2, C 5-7, good Italian, small and cosy, recommended. *Tin Jo*, C 11, Av 6-8, probably the best Asian cuisine in town taking inspiration from several different countries. *Tony's Ribs*, Av 6, C 11-13, good barbecued beef and pork.

Parque Sabana On the north side of Parque Sabana on Av 3 and about C 50 are 2 good restaurants, *El Chicote* (country-style, good grills) and *El Molino*. Also nearby is *La Flecha*, Centro Colón Building, Paseo Colón, superb. *Los Ranchos* Steak House, Sabana Norte near *Hotel Corobicí*, reliable, good food; *Marbella*, Centro Comercial de la C Real, San Pedro de Montes de Oca, T224-9452, fish, packed on Sun, very good.

A couple of recommended Peruvian restaurants are *Machu Picchu*, C 32, Av 1-3, and *Peruveana*, C 32, Av 1-3, reasonable prices.

If you're looking for something to fill you up, a stroll down Avenida 5 will take you passed several cheap Chinese restaurants, including *Gran Diamente*, Av 5, C 4 – 6, with a 'lively kitchen' where you can watch the food being prepared. Another cheap Chinese worth trying is *Lung Mun,* Av 1, C 5-7, and for Korean food go to *Fu Lu Su* at C 7, Av 2.

Specific recommendations include *Antojitos*, on Paseo Colón, on Pavas Highway west of Sabana and in Centro Comercial Cocorí (road to suburb of San Pedro), serves excellent Mexican food at moderate prices. *El Cuartel de la Boca del Monte*, Av 1, C 21-23, live music at night but a good and popular restaurant by day. Recommended. *Morazán*, C 9, Av 3, facing Parque Morazán, not touristy, popular with locals, friendly, excellent breakfast, delicious blackberry juice. *Pasta Factory*, Av 1, C 7, excellent Italian, recommended.

The fewer numbers of seriously cheap places do not indicate the absence of cheap eateries – more the lack of need to list them all. Reliable favourites are in the *Mercado Central*, around the Coca Cola bus terminal and the area to the southwest of Parque Central.

Places worth recommending are *Comedor* beneath 'Dorado' sign, C 8, Av 4-6, very cheap. *Pollo a la Leña*, C 1, Av 3-5, which has seriously cheap chicken, popular with the locals. *Choza del Sabor*, on the corner of Calle Central and Av 5, is a good, local *comedor* with a couple of gestures to décor but the *menú del día* a good and tasty bargain. On a Chinese theme one of the cheapest is *China Bonita* at Av 5, C 2 – 4.

Bagelman, Paseo Rubén Darío (Av Central), C 33, just east of Hostal Toruma. Smart and tasty fast food bagel heaven. *Café del Teatro*, Av 2, C 3, in foyer of National Theatre. Pricey but worth it for the sheer style and sophistication of the *belle époque* interior. Open Mon-Sat. *Café Parisienne* on the Plaza de la Cultura , the street café of the *Gran Hotel Costa Rica*. Food a little overpriced, but have a coffee and watch the world go by. Tucked away up in Barrio Amón is *La Esquina del Café*, Av 9, C 3b, a specialty coffee roasters with beans from 6 different regions to taste, also a good restaurant with a souvenir shop. Live music twice a month. Daily 0900-2200. *Le Croissant*, Av Central, C 30, divine croissants in this chique French bakery. *Musmanni*, has several outlets throughout the city but should be tried for crimes against flour, bread and pastry. *Ruiseñor*, Paseo Rubén Darío and C 41-43, Los Yoses. The smart place to take coffee and snacks out east. *Spoon* has a central bakery at Av Central, C 5-7, where you can have good coffee and pastries to take-out or eat in.

Don Sol, Av 7b No 1347, excellent 3 course lunch US$1.60, run by integral yoga society (only open for lunch). *El Edén*, Av 5, C Central. *La Mazorca*, in San Pedro, near University of Costa Rica (Rodrigo Facio site), vegetarian and health foods. *La Nutrisoda*, Edif Las Arcadas, open 1100 to 1800, homemade natural ice-cream. *Macrobiótica*, C 11, Av 6-8, health shop selling good bread. *Naturama Uno*, Av 1, opposite Omni building, cheap. *Shakti*, Av 8, C 13, excellent. *Soda Vegetariana*, next to *Librería Italiana*.

The best known is *Vishnu*, Av 1, C 1-3, good quality, cheap and good *plato del día*, try their soya cheese sandwiches and ice-cream, sells good wholemeal bread, also on C 14, Av 2, open daily, 0800-2000. Several branches throughout the city.

There are plenty of fast food outlets dotted throughout the city. *KFC*, can be found on Av 3, C 3-5, out by Hostal Toruma. *Pizza Hut*, C Central, Av 4-6, also several other branches. Several outlets of *Burger King* and *McDonald's* dotted throughout the city.

Food bars in the Mercado Central (C 6-8) are good for a quick breakfast and lunch, but none of them is open in the evening, but generally very clean. Also try *Corona de Oro*, Av 3, C 2-4 (next to *Nini*) is excellent. *Chicharronera Nacional*, Av 1, C 10-12, is very popular. *El Merendero*, Av 6, C Central-2, cheap local food, popular with *Ticos*. Try the snack bars in the *Galería* complex, Av Central-2, C 5-7. *Popular*, Av 3, C 6-8, good *casado*. Try *Soda Flor de Costa Rica*, entrada Noroeste, *pabellón de las flores*, very good and cheap meals, very clean, open 0700-1800.

Costa Rica

Ice-cream parlours & cafés	Several good ice-cream outlets to choose from. *Helados Boni*, C Central, Av 6-8, home-made ice-cream. *Helados Rena*, C 8, Av Central, excellent. *Pops* has excellent ice-cream too.

Several good ice-cream outlets to choose from. *Helados Boni*, C Central, Av 6-8, home-made ice-cream. *Helados Rena*, C 8, Av Central, excellent. *Pops* has excellent ice-cream too.

Churrería Manolo, Av Central, C Central-2 (new restaurant upstairs), and another branch on Av Central. Simple, quick food with takeaway options on the street, good sandwiches and hot chocolate. One of several sodas around Parque Central is *La Perla*. The food is OK, the service is poor, the waiters will stitch you up with a flurry of fingers over a calculator but it is open 24 hours. *La Vasconia*, Av 2, C 5, restaurant and soda bar has a good breakfast and is popular with locals. *Soda El Parque*, C 2, Av 4-6, is open 24-hours and a popular spot for business people by day and relaxing entertainers by night. Just north of the centre is the cheap and cheerful *Soda Nini* at Av 3, C 2-4. East out towards Los Yoses is *Soda La Luz*, Av Central, C 33, good filling meals, cheap.

Entertainment and nightlife

Bars

The Tico Times has a good listings section

North of town in Barrio Tournón is *Centro Comercial El Pueblo* where *Ticos* party in their finest, with restaurants, bars and discos. The ideal place to party the night away literally until dawn.

Other bars throughout the city include *Beatles*, C 9, Av Central, good music, popular with ex-pats. *Brew Pub Micro Brewery,* Av 0, C 26-8, serves various home-made beers in a pub atmosphere. *Chelle's*, Av Central, C 9, excellent 24-hour bar and round the corner is the slightly more upmarket *Chelle's Taberna*, Av Central-2 and C 9. A little east of the centre of town is *El Cuartel de la Boca del Monte*, Av 1, C 21-23, live music at weekends, popular with students, hip young things but without the flashy dress, recommended. There are several strip joints in the city, the best known is *Josephine's*, Av 9, C 2-4, T256-4396, 257-2269. Similar style entertainment in the *Blue Marlin Bar* at the *Hotel del Rey*. At some point while in San José you should visit the *mariachi* mecca of *La Esmeralda*, Av 2 , C5-7, T221-0530. *Las Risas*, C 1, Av Central, bars on 3 floors, good, popular with locals. *Nashville South*, C 5, Av 1-3, is a popular Country-and-Western-style gringo bar.

Nightclubs

Many restaurants and bars with varying styles of music at El Pueblo centre on road to San Francisco (take 'Calle Blancos' bus from C 1, Av 5-7, get off 500 m after river); also 3 discos here, *Cocoloco* is the liveliest, *Infinito* gets a slightly older crowd and *La Plaza* outside the centre, so often not as busy.

Several other less expensive places downtown: *El Túnel del Tiempo*, is close to the centre on Av Central and C 9-11. *Disco Salsa 54* on C 3, Av 1-3 is *the* place to go for salsa. *La Avispa*, C 1, Av 8-10, gay-friendly disco, but not exclusively so.

Cinemas

There are many excellent modern cinemas showing latest releases in the centre of town including *Cine Omni*, Av 1, C 3-5, T221-7903. *Sala Garbo*, Av 2, C 28, shows art house movies. *Cinemateca* at the UCR's Abelardo Bonilla auditorium (university), San Pedro, shows good films at 1700 and 1900 daily. Prices, US$2.50-US$3. See *La Nación* for films and times.

Theatre

All are closed on Mon. *Teatro Nacional*, Av 2, C 3-5 T221-1329 (recommended for the productions, the architecture and the bar/café), US$1.15 for guided tour, behind it is La Plaza de la Cultura, a large complex. *Teatro Arlequín* C 13, Av 2-Central, T221-4585. *Teatro Melico Salazar* on Parque Central for popular, folkloric shows every Tue, T221-4952. *Teatro del Angel*, Av Central, C 13-15, T222-8258, teaangel@racsa.co.cr, 3 modern dance companies.

Spectator sports

If you want to watch football, there are usually Saprissa games on Sun. The stadium is north of Downtown San José and you can just follow the gentle movement of people wearing purple shirts. International games are held in the national stadium in Parque Sabana – turn up and try your luck for a ticket.

Festivals

Christmas/New Year: festivities last from **18 Dec-5 Jan**, with dances, horse shows and much confetti-throwing in the crowded streets. The annual *El Tope* horse parade starts at noon on 26 Dec and travels along the principal avenues of San José. A carnival starts next day at about 1700 in the same area. Fairs, firework displays and bull running at El Zapote, frequent buses from the centre. The *International Festival of Culture* assembles musicians from throughout Central America in a week of performances in the Plaza de Cultura around the second week of **Mar**. Also parades during Easter week in the streets. Also the *Día del Boyero* celebrates Day of the Oxcart Driver on the second Sun of the month in San Antonio de Escazú. Parades of ox-drawn carts, with music, dancing and blessings from the priesthood. *Independence Day* on **15th Sep**, bands and dance troupes move through the streets, although things start to kick-off the night before.

Shopping

Market on Av Central, C 6-8, open 0630-1800 (Sun 0630-1200), good leather suitcases and wood. *Mercado Borbón*, Av 3-5, 8-10, fruit and vegetables. More and more *artesanía* shops are opening, *Canapi*, C 11, Av 1 (a co-operative, cheaper than most), *Mercado Nacional de Artesanía*, C 11, Av 4, T221-5012, Mon-Fri 0900-1800, Sat 0900-1700, and others on Av Central, C 1-3. *La Casona* (C Central, Av Central-1, daily 0900-1900), a market of small *artesanía* shops, is full of interesting little stalls.

Galería Namu, opposite the Alianza Francesa building on Av 7 and C 5-7, T256-3412, www.galerianamu.com, is the best one-stop shop for homegrown and indigenous art, with the distinctly bright coloured ceramics of Cecilia Figueres. Items can be shipped if required.

El Pueblo, near the *Villa Tournón Hotel*, is an area of shops, bars, restaurants and discos, built in a traditional 'pueblo' style. Another big new shopping centre is at San Pedro, on the eastern ring road. Also *Multiplaza Mall*, near *Camino Real*, Escazú, has excellent shops and lots of cinemas.

In **Moravia** (8 km from centre with stops often included on city tours) *El Caballo Blanco*, T235-6797, workshops alongside, and *HHH* are good for leatherwork.

Bookshops *Casa de la Revista*, C5, Av 1-3, T256-5092. Mon-Fri 0900-1800, Sat 0800-1700. Good selection of maps and some books. *Librería Francesa*, C 3, Av Central-1, T233-7979, Mon-Sat 0900-1700. Good selection of international magazines, newspapers and books. *Librería Lehmann*, Av Central, C 3, T223-1212, F233-0713, has a large and varied selection of Spanish and English books and magazines. They also stock several maps including the 1:50,000 topographical maps produced by the *Instituto Geográfico Nacional de Costa Rica* (IGN). *Librería Vlate*, Av 6, C 3-5, book exchange with a large choice of Spanish books and a few in English. *Mora Books*, Av 1, C 3-5, T/F255-4136, in Omni building above *Pizza Hut*, Mon-Sat 1200-1800. Large selection of used books, reasonable prices. *Papiros*, in the Yaohan Shopping Centre, Sabana Norte, T221-4664, Mon-Sat 0800-2145, Sun 0800-2045. Best selection of magazines and some books. *7th Street Books*, C 7, Av Central-Av 1, T256-8251, marroca@racsa.co.cr A wide range of new and used books covering all topics of interest to visitors to Costa Rica, including Footprint Handbooks and the *South American Handbook*. Open 0900-1800 daily. *Staufer*, Plaza del Sol shopping mall in Curridabat, English and German books. *Universal*, Av Central, C Central-1, T222-2222, F222-2992, for Spanish books and maps.

Photography 1-hr colour processing available at all *IFSA* (Kodak) branches. Fuji processing in 1 hr at *Universal* stores. *Taller de Equipos Fotográficos*, 120 m east of kiosk Parque Morazán, Av 3, C 3-5, 2nd floor, T223-1146 (Canon repairs – authorized workshop). *Tecfot*, Av 7, C Central, T221-1438, repairs all types of cameras, good service, reasonable rates.

Sport

If you're planning on staying in or around San José for a while, look in the *Calendar* pages of the *Tico Times* for clubs and associations.

Bungee jumping After Rafael Iglesias Bridge (Río Colorado), continue on Pan-American Highway 1½ km, turn right at *Salón Los Alfaro*, down track to Puente Colorado. *Tropical Bungee* operate 0900-1500 daily in the high season, US$45 1st jump, US$25 for the second, T232-3956, F232-3916, www.bungee.co.cr Exhilarating.

Costa Rica

Cycling *Geoventuras Bike Tours* run tours from San José, Tue, Thu, and Sat, 0800, return about 1700, US$85 including lunch, T221-2053. *Coast to Coast Adventures* also runs trips in the local area, T280-8054, F225-7806, www.ctocadventures.com For Cycle repairs, see below.

Golf *Costa Rica Country Club*, San Rafael de Escazú, T228-9333 9 holes. *Hotel Meliá Cariari Country Club* (near San José), 18 holes. *Los Reyes Country Club* (near Alajuela), 9 holes.

Swimming The best pool is at **Ojo de Agua**, 5 mins from the airport, 15 mins from San José. It is open until 1700; direct bus from Av 1, C 20-22, US$1.20 or take bus to Alajuela and then another to San Antonio de Belén. There is also a pool in **Parque Sabana** (at west end of Paseo Colón), entrance US$3, about 2 km from the city centre. Open-air pool at **Plaza González Víquez**, in the southeast section of the city.

Transport

Local **Buses**: in San José large buses cost US$0.10, small buses cost US$0.15 from the centre outwards. Hand baggage in reasonable quantities is not charged. A cheap tour of San José can be made on the bus marked 'periférico' from Paseo Colón in front of the Cine Colón, a 45-min circuit of the city. A smaller circuit is made by the 'Sabana/Cementerio' bus, pick it up at the Parque Morazán or on Av 3.

Car hire: www.rentacar.co.cr gives details of most of the companies, allowing for advance bookings. Most local agencies are to the north of Paseo Colón, and many also have a branch at the airport. **Adobe**, T221-5425, F221-9286, adobecar@racsa.co.cr, drop-off at the beach if you fly Travelair, flexible insurance, drivers aged 18-21 accepted with US$1,500 on credit card; *Avis*, Sabana Norte, T293-2222, F293-1111, airport T442-1321, www.avis.com *Budget*, C 30, Paseo Colón, T223-3284, F255-4966, www.budgetco.cr, open Mon-Sat, 0800-1900, Sun, 0800-1800, also at international airport, T442-2495, open Mon-Sun, 0600-2100, and at *Hotel Cariari*; *Dollar*, Paseo Colón and C 32, T257-1587, F222-1765, www.dollarcostarica.com, good rates; *Elegante*, C 10 Av 13-15, T221-0066, F221-5761, www.eleganterentacar.com, PO Box 30-1005, San José, cars, jeeps, vans. *Hertz*, C 38, Paseo Colón, T221-1818, F221-1949, airport T441-0097, hertzcr@racsa.co.cr; *National*, C 36, Av 7, T290-8787, F290-0431, www.natcar.com, easy to get on to autopista for Alajuela; *Santos*, T441-3044, F223-4030, www.casantos.co.cr; *Toyota*, Paseo Colón, T223-2250, F222-7875, info@toyotarent.com, good cars, helpful staff.

Motorcycle rental: from *Wild Rider Motorcycles*, Paseo Colón, C 32 diagonal Kentucky, in *Ritmo del Caribe Hotel*, T/F 258-4604, www.ritmo-del-caribe.com Suzuki DR 250s and DR 350s available for rent from US$30 a day. Very enjoyable, but experience essential not only to rent the bike, but also for your survival on the roads. *Harley Davidson Tours*, a service provided by *Apartotel* María Alexandera, T289-5552, F289-5551, www.mariaalexandra.com

Motorcycle repairs: *Taller Daytona 500*, in Pavas, 200 m east of US Embassy, T/F220-1726, run by Roberto Dachner, who speaks Spanish, English and Hebrew.

Cycle repairs: *Cyclo Quiros*, Apartado 1366, Pavas, 300 m west of US Embassy, the brothers Quiros have been repairing bikes for 20 years, good place for general info and repairs, highly recommended.

Taxis: minimum fare US$0.63 for 1st km, US$0.32 additional km, US$0.20 extra 2200-0500. Waiting time US$3.15 per hr. To order a taxi, T254-5847. Taxis are red and should have electronic meters (called 'marías'), if not, get out and take another cab or agree price before. For journeys over 12 km price should be negotiated between driver and passenger. Radio cabs can be booked in advance. *Coopeirazu*, T254-3211, *Taxi San Jorge*, T221-3434, *Taxis Unidos SA*, T446-6555, or look in the classified adverts of the *Tico Times* for car and driver hire.

Air The redeveloped and expanded Juan Santamaría International Airport (SJO) is at El Coco, 16 **Long distance**
km from San José along the Autopista General Cañas (5 km from Alajuela). Airport information,
T443-2622 (24 hrs). The Sansa terminal for domestic flights is next to the main terminal. Sansa
runs a free bus service to the airport for its passengers. There is another terminal about 1 km west
of the main terminal used by charter flights and private planes. Buses to city centre from main
street outside ground floor terminal. Buses to airport, continuing on to Alajuela from Av Central-2,
C 10, every 10 mins from 0500-2100; 45 mins, US$0.50 (good service, plenty of luggage space).
Taxi to and from airport, US$10-12, US$15 at night. Taxis run all night from the main square. For
early flights you can reserve a taxi from any San José hotel the night before. All taxi companies run
a 24-hr service. During the holiday period (Dec-Jan), Juan Santamaría airport allows only ticketed
passengers into the main terminal at peak times of 0600-0830, 1100-1400. Bank at the airport
open 0800-1600. ATMs at the airport accepts Visa and MasterCard. ICT has a helpful tourist office
in the main terminal for maps, information and hotel reservations.

Internal flights *Sansa* (next to the main terminal at Juan Santamaría airport) and *Travelair and light*
Travelair (from Tobias Bolaños) operate internal flights throughout the country. Sansa *aircraft use Tobias*
check-in is at office on Av Las Americas and C 42, 2 hrs before departure (free bus to and from *Bolaños Airport about*
airport). Check schedules on T221-9414, F255-2176, www.flysansa.com For Travelair reser- *8 km west of San José*
vations, T220-3054, F220-0413, www.travelair-costarica.com If you made reservations
before arriving in Costa Rica, confirm and collect tickets as soon as possible after arrival. Book
ahead, especially for the beaches. In Feb and Mar, planes can be fully booked 3 weeks ahead.
On all internal scheduled and charter flights there is a baggage allowance of 12 kg. Oversized
items such as surfboards, bicycles, etc are charged at US$15 if there is room in the cargo hold.
   From San José you can fly to Barra del Colorado, Coto 47, Golfito, Jacó, Liberia, Nosara, Palmar Sur, Puerto Jiménez, Punta Islita, Quepos, Sámara, Tamarindo, Tambor, Tortuguero.
   Charter flights: *Veasa*, T232-1010, F232-7934, long-established, at Pavas; *Alfa Romeo
Aéreo Taxi*, at Pavas, T/F296-4344, and Puerto Jiménez, T/F735-5112, Capitán Alvaro Ramírez.
Helisa (*Helicópteros Internacionales*) operate helicopter sightseeing flights to Monteverde,
etc, T231-6867, F222-3875. *Pitts Aviation*, T296-3600, F296-1429, www.pitts-aviation.com

Buses In the majority of cases, buses start or finish their journey at San José so there are services to most towns; see under relevant destination for details of times and prices. Check
where the bus stops at your destination, some routes do not go to the centre of towns, leaving passengers some distance away. Up to date timetables can be obtained from the ICT
office under the Plaza de la Cultura. Alternatively a free leaflet *Hop on the Bus*, giving times
but no prices, is distributed by Ecole Travel and KitCom and published on the internet,
updated every 2 months. Bus stations are scattered around town (see map): **Alajuela**
(including airport) from Av Central-2, C 10 during the day, from Av 2, C 10-12 after 2400;
Cahuita, Limón, Manzanillo, Puerto Viejo de Talamanca, Sixaola all served from Gran
Terminal del Caribe (*Guapileños, Caribeños, Sixaola*); **Jacó, Carará, Quepos, Manuel Antonio, Uvita** all depart from from Terminal Coca-Cola; **Santa Cruz** (½ block west), **Peñas
Blancas** (100 m north) from outside Terminal Coca-Cola; **Cartago** from Terminal Cartago
during the day, after 2030 from *Gran Hotel Costa Rica*, Av 2, C 3-5; **Ciudad Quesada (San
Carlos), Fortuna, Guápiles** (Braulio Carrillo), **Los Chiles, Caño Negro, Monteverde** (out-
side terminal), **Puerto Jiménez** (outside terminal), **Puerto Viejo Sarapiquí, Tilarán** (½
block north) from Terminal Atlántico Norte at Av 9 C 12; **Playa del Coco, Liberia** from C 14,
Av 1-3; **Golfito, Nicoya, Nosara, Palmar Norte, Paso Canoas, Sámara, San Vito,
Tamarindo** from Terminal Alfaro; **San Isidro de El General** (2 companies, *Musoc* and
Tuasur), new terminal down on Av 22-24, C Central, **Heredia** from Terminal Heredia or a
minibus from Av 2, C 10-12; **Volcán** *Irazú* from Av 2, C 1-3, opposite *Gran Hotel Costa Rica*;
Volcán Poás from Av 2, C 12-14; **Puntarenas** from Terminal Puntarenas, C 16, Av 10-12;
Santa María de Dota from Terminal Los Santos; **Turrialba** from Terminal Turrialba.

International buses If the timing of your journey is important book tickets; in Dec-Jan,
buses are often booked 2 weeks ahead, while at other times of the year outside holiday seasons there are plenty of spaces.

Costa Rica

Sirca (Av 3, C 16, T256-9072, open Sun-Fri 0800-1700, Sat 0800-1200) has a new service with video and a/c to Managua leaving at 0430, 8hrs, US$12. *Ticabus* terminal is at C 9-11, Av 4 (T221-8954, www.ticabus.com), office open Mon-Sun 0600-2200, book before Sat for Mon buses. It is here that all refund claims have to be made (have to be collected in person). *Ticabus* to **Guatemala City**, 0600, 0730, 60 hrs, US$35, with overnight stay in **Managua** and **San Salvador**. To **Tegucigalpa**, 0730, 1200, 48 hrs, US$42, overnight stay in Managua. To Managua, US$12, 11 hrs including 1 hr at Costa Rican side of border and another 2 hrs on Nic-araguan side while they search bags. The *Ticabus* journey from San José to **Panama City** leaves at 2200 daily, US$23 one-way, 18 hrs (book at least 3 days in advance). To get a Pana-manian tourist card you must buy a return ticket – you can get a refund in Panama but with a discount of 15%. The *Ticabus* from Panama City tends to arrive early between 0400 and 0500, and you are left on the street. There is a 24-hr café nearby if you wish to avoid the expense of a hotel. *Transnica*, C22, Av 3-5, T221-0953, runs new buses with TV, video, a/c, snacks, toilet, to **Managua** daily at 0530 and 0900, US$12 one way. Before departure have your ticket con-firmed on arrival at the terminal; when buying and confirming your ticket, you must show your passport. When boarding the bus you are given an immigration form. *Nicabus* at C 16 Av 3, T258-0022, to Managua 0600 and 0830, US$12.50 one way, US$20 return.

Panaline goes to Panama City daily at 1400 from C 16, Av 3, T258-0022, US$22 one way, US$41 return, reduction for students, arrives 0700; a/c, payment by Visa/MasterCard accepted. To **David**, from Terminal Alfaro, US$18 (buses daily at 0730 and 1200, 9 hrs); book in advance. They are modern, comfortable buses, although there is not much room for long legs, but they have the advantage of covering a scenic journey in daylight. A bus to **Changuinola** via the Sixaola-Guabito border post leaves San José at 1000 daily, 8 hrs, US$8, from opposite Terminal Alfaro, T556-1432 for information, best to arrive 1 hr before depar-ture; the bus goes via Siquirres and is the quickest route to **Limón**.

Directory

Airline offices *Aeroperlas*, 150 m east of *Hampton Inn*, Juan Santamaría airport, T440-0093. *Air France*, Condominio Vista Real, p 1, 100 m east of POP's, Curridabat, T280-0069. *Alitalia*, C 38, Av 3, Centro Comercial Los Alcazares,T222-6138. *American*, opposite *Hotel Corobicí*, Sabana Este, T257-1266, F222-5213. *Avianca*, Edif Centro, p 2, Colón, Paseo Colón, C 38-40, T233-3066. *British Airways*, C 13, Av 13, T223-5648. *Condor Airlines* (German charter airline), C 5, Av 7-9, T256-6161. *Continental*, Oficentro La Virgen No 2, 200 m south, 300 m east and 50 m north of American Embassy, Pavas, T296-4911. *Copa*, Av 5, C 1, T222-6640. *Delta*, 500 m east of Hampton Inn, T441-2487. *Grupo Taca*, see *Sansa* below. *Iberia*, Paseo Colón, C 40, T257-8266. *KLM*, Sabana Sur, behind Contoralía General Building, T220-4111. *Lloyd Aéreo Boliviano*, Av 2, C 2-4, upstairs, T255-1530. *LTU International Airways* (German charter airline), Condominio da Vinci, Oficina No 6, Barrio Dent. T234-9292. *Lufthansa*, C 5, Av 7-9, T256-6161. *Martinair*, Dutch charter airline – subsidiary of KLM, see above. *Mexicana*, C 5, Av 7-9, T257-6334, Mexican Tourist Card available here. *Saeta*, C 13, Av 11, T223-5648. *SAM*, Paseo Colón, C 38-40, Edif Centro Colón, p 2, T233-3066. *Sansa*, Casa Blanca, Calle 42 and Av Las Americas, La Sabana, T221-9414, see Internal flights above). *Singapore Airlines*, Av 1, C 3-5. T255-3555. *Servivensa*, Edif Centro Colón, p 2, Paseo Colón, C 38-40, T257-1441. *Swissair*, C Central, Av 1-3, T221-6613. *Travelair* (see Internal Flights above). *United Airlines*, Sabana Sur, behind Contoralía General Building, T220-2027. *Varig*, Av 5, C 3-5 T290-5222.

Banks Queues in banks in San José tend to be long, and using hotels is recommended if possible. The 15th and end of the month are especially bad as this is pay day for government employees and everyone wants their money. Visa and MasterCard ATMs are widespread and the best option in the capital. Queues tend to be shorter outside San José. *Banco Crédito Agrícola de Cartago*, 9 branches, also makes advances on Visa, no commission, no limits. *Banco de Costa Rica*, Av 2, C 4, changes TCs, open 0830-1500, long queues, 1% commission. *Banco de San José*, C Central, Av 3-5, commission 2.5%. Money can be sent through *Banco de San José* or *Banco de Costa Rica* at 4%. Credit card holders can obtain cash advances from *Banco de San José* (Visa, MasterCard) and *Credomatic Los Yoses* in colones (MasterCard ATM) and *Banco Popular y Desarrollo* (Visa ATM) minimum cash advance: US$50 equivalent. ATMs which will accept international Visa/MasterCard are available at most banks, shopping malls and San José airport. *Banco Mercantil*, Av 1, C Central-2, has safe deposit lockers for US$15 per month. *Banco Nacional*, head office, Av 1-3, C 2-4, will change TCs into dollars but you pay a commission, accepts Visa credit cards as do most of the bigger banks in San José and other major towns.

An alternative to the banks is *OFINTERSA*, Edificio Schyfter, behind *Banco Central*, 2nd floor, C 2, Av 1-Central. *Western Union*, Av 4, C 9-11, next to the *Ticabus* office. Money transfer services, quicker than banks but you pay a price premium.

Internet *Cybercafé*, in the basement of Edificio Las Arcadas, next to the *Gran Hotel Costa Rica*. Open 7 days a week, 0700-2300, very helpful and friendly staff, c250 10 mins, c600 1 hr. Terrace café outside serving excellent coffee and pizzas, newspapers, good atmosphere. If that's not enough, also self-service laundry. A genuine and complete internet cafe. *Internet Café*, 4th floor, Av C, C4, open 0800-2400. A better way to spend less money as it is just c500 for full or part hr, but not a café. Several branches around town including 2nd floor, Av Central, Calle Los Estudiantes, open 0900-2100, at the western end of Paseo Colón in Edifico Colón, C 38 – 40, and if you want to tap all night there is a 24-hr café in San Pedro, close to *Banco Popular*. The post office is supporting internet with *Punta.com* which shares the central post office buidling at Av 1, C 2. Open 0900-2100 Mon-Fri, 1000-2100 Sat and 1000-1800 Sun. 30 mins c300, 1 hr c500. *RACSA* provide internet access at their offices at Av 1, C 5 charging US$3 for 1 hr. **Post office** C 2, Av 1-3, open for sale of stamps Mon-Fri, 0700-1700, Sat-Sun 0700-1800 (outside these hours stamps may be bought from the lottery seller who sits under the big tree opposite the post office entrance). Stamp vending machine in main post office. Post office charges c50 for receiving letters (*Lista de Correos*, open Mon-Fri 0800-1700, quick service). **Couriers** *DHL*, Edificio Isabel, Paseo Colón, C 34, T290-3020, www.dhl.net *Jet Ex* (Federal Express agent), several offices near San José, T293-0505, F293-5839, www.jetex.co.cr, *UPS*, 50 m east of Edicificio La Virgen No 2, Pavas, San José, T290-2828, F232-8800, www.ups.com **Telephone** Faxes and internal telegrams from main post office. Fax abroad from RACSA, Av 5, C 1, 0730-2200, charges per page, also receives for US$1, unlimited pages, internet access and email, US$3 per hr (also see Essentials). *ICE, Instituto Costarricense de Electricidad*, Av 2, C 1, has a fax service, also phone calls here (phone card only), open 0700-2200, 3 min call to UK US$10, friendly service (cheaper than *Radiográfica*, but check). Some shops offer fax service. Collect/reverse charge telephone calls can be made from any public telephone. English-speaking operators are available. See also under Essentials.

Communications

Centro Cultural Costarricense Norteamericano, C 37, Av 1-5, Los Yoses, T207-7500, F290-2550, www.cccncr.com, good films, plays, art exhibitions and English-language library, open to 1930, free. *Alianza Francesa*, Av 7, C 5, French newspapers, French films every Wed evening, friendly.

Cultural centres

Argentina, 400 m south of *McDonalds*, Curridabat, T234-6270, 0800-1530, Mon-Fri. *Belgium*, Av 3, C 35-37, T225-6633, 0800-1330. *Brazil*, C 20-22, Av 2, T233-1544. *Canada*, Building 5 (3rd floor) of Oficentro Ejecutivo La Sabana, Sabana Sur, T296-4149, F296-4270, 0800-1630, Fri until 1330. *Chile*, Los Yoses, 50 m east, 225 m Oriente del Automercado, T224-4243, 0800-1200. *Colombia*, Barrio Dent, de Taco Bell San Pedro 150 m Oeste (on right), T283-6861. *Ecuador*, Sabana Sur, Colegio Médicos 100 m east, 125 m southwest, T232-1503, 0800-1400. *El Salvador*, C 30, Paseo Colón-Av 1, Casa 53, T224-9034, receives documents 0900-1300, returns them 1430-1500. *France*, Curridabat, 200 m south, 25 m west of Indoor Club, T225-0733, 0830-1200. *Germany*, Rohrmoser, 200 m north and 75 m east of la casa de Oscar Arias, T232-5533, 0900-1200. *Guatemala*, De la *Pizza Hut* en Plaza del Sol, Curridabat, 50 m east, 100 m north, 50 m east, Casa No 3, T283-2557, 0900-1300, visa given on the spot, US$10 in some cases (dollars only, see Guatemala Essentials). *Honduras*, del antiguo Ital 250 m east, 150 m north, 100 m east Yoses Sur, T234-9504, 0900-1230. *Israel* Edificio Colón, 11th floor, Paseo Colón, C 38-40, T221-6444, 0900-1200. *Italy*, Los Yoses, Av 10, C 33-35, T234-2326, 0900-1200. *Japan*, Rohrmoser, de la Nunciatura 400 m east and 100 m north, T296-1650, 0900-1200. *Mexico*, Consulate, Av 7, C 13-15, T225-7284, 0830-1230. *Netherlands*, Oficentro Ejecutivo La Sabana, Sabana Sur, T296-1490, Mon-Fri 0900-1200. *Nicaragua*, Av Central, C 25-27, opposite *Pizza Hut*, T233-8747, 0830-1130 and 1330-1500, US$25, dollars only, passport photo, 24-hr wait for visa or sometimes less. *Norway*, Centro Colón, p 10, T283-8222. Mon-Thu 1400-1700. *Panama*, C 38, Av 7 (275 m north of Centro Colón building, Paseo Colón area), T257-3241, strict about onward ticket, open 0900-1400, you need a photograph and photocopy of your passport, visa costs US$10 cash and takes up to 24 hrs, if they tell you to come back after 1300 to collect your visa, be there at 1245. *Paraguay*, T283-3504, 0830-1300. *Peru*, Los Yoses, 200 m Sur, 50 m Oriente del Automercado, T225-9145, 0900-1400. *Spain*, Paseo Colón, C 32, T222-1933. *Sweden*, honorary consul at Almacén Font, 100 m east of La Pozuelo, La Uruca, San José, T232-8549, F220-1854. *Switzerland*, Paseo Colón, Centro Colón, p 10, C 34/36, T221-4829, 0900-1200. *UK*, Centro Colón, p 11, end of Paseo Colón with C 38 (Apdo 815-1007), T258-2025, F283-6818. *USA*, in the western suburb of Pavas, opposite Centro Comercial, catch a ruta 14 bus to Pavas Zona 1 from Av 1 and C 16-18, T220-3050, 0800-1630. *Venezuela*, Los Yoses, de la 5a entrada, 100 m south, 50 m west, T225-8810, 0830-1230, visa issued same day, US$30, helpful.

Embassies & consulates

Costa Rica

Medical services   **Dentists** *Clínica Dental Dr Francisco Cordero Guilarte*, c26-28, Paseo Colón, T223-8890. *Dra Fresia Hidalgo*, Uned Building, San Pedro, 1400-1800, English spoken, reasonable prices, recommended, T234-2840. *Fernando Baldioceda* and *Silvia Oreamuno*, 225 m north of Paseo Colón on the street which intersects at the Toyota dealership: both speak English. *Alfonso Villalobos Aguilar*, Edif Herdocía, p 2, Av 3, C 2-4, T222-5709. **Doctor** *Dr Jorge Quesada Vargas*, *Clínica Internacional*, Av 14, C 3-5, speaks German. **Hospitals** *Social Security* hospitals have a good reputation (free to social security members, few members of staff speak English), free ambulance service run by volunteers: Dr Calderón Guardia, T222-4133, San Juan de Dios, T222-0166, México, T232-6122. *Clínica Bíblica* C 1, Av 14, 24-hr pharmacy, T257-5252, is frequently recommended and the one most used by the local expatriate community and offers 24-hr emergency service at reasonable charges with staff who speak English, better than the large hospitals, where queues are long. **Inoculations** *Bíblica* will arrange TB vaccinations, prepares Spanish summaries of treatment, medication, etc, accepts credit cards, and has addresses for emergencies it cannot handle. Yellow fever inoculation, *Ministerio de Salud* (Av 4, C 16), Dpto de Enfermedades Epidémicos, Dr Rodrígo Jiménez Monge, or at his private clinic, C 5, Av 4, T221-6658. Free malaria pills also from Ministerio de Salud, from information desk in office to left of ministry. Although the Ministerio de Salud does not have a stock of gamma globulin (Hepatitis A), they will inject it free if you buy it in a pharmacy.

Language schools   The number of schools has increased rapidly. Listed below are just a selection recommended by our readers. Generally, schools offer tuition in groups of 2-5 for 2-4 weeks. Lectures, films, outings and social occasions are usually included and accommodation with families is encouraged. Many schools are linked to the university and can offer credits towards a US course. Rates, including lodging, are around US$1,200 a month.
Academia Latinoamericana de Español, Aptdo 1280, 2050 San Pedro de Montes de Oca, Av 8, C 31-33, Barrio Francisco Peralta, T224-9917, F225-8125. Varied programme of homestays, latin dance, food and cultural events. US$155 for classes, add US$135 for homestay, recommended. *AmeriSpan*, PO Box 40007, Philadelphia, PA 19106-0007, T800-879-6640 (USA and Canada), T215-751 1100 (elsewhere), F215-751 1986, www.amerispan.com, has affiliated schools in Alajuela, Heredia, Monteverde and Manuel Antonio. At Playa Flamingo, on the Nicoya Peninsula, is *Casa de Lenguas*, www.casadelenguas.com, also affiliated to Amerispan. The *Instituto Británico* in Los Yoses, Apdo 8184, 1000 San José, T225-0256, F253-1894, www.institutobritanico.co.cr, teaches English and Spanish. *Comunicare*, Apdo 1383-2050, San José, T/F224-4473, www.comunicare.co.cr, offers language study (staying with families), volunteer work, and cultural activities. *Costa Rican Language Academy and Latin American Dance School*, Av Central, C 25-27, Apdo 336-2070 Sabanilla, Montes de Oca, T233-8914, F233-8670, www.learn-spanish.com, run by Aída Chávez, offers Latin American music and dancing as well as language study and accommodation with local families. *Costa Rica Spanish Institute*, in San Pedro district, T234-1001, www.cosi.co.cr US$280 per week with a homestay in San José or US$450 for the beach programme based in Playa Ballena. *Instituto de Español Costa Rica*, A 1, C Central – C 1, Apartado 1405-2100 Guadalupe, T/F283-4733, www.intensivespanish.com Close to the centre of San José, and complete with its own (**C**) B&B. English, French and German spoken. Many special offers including 2 for 1, where the 2nd person receives the course for free – if the offers ends, don't be pushed into taking the classes. *Instituto Universal de Idiomas*, in Moravia, T223-9662, F223-9917, www.universal-edu.com, stresses conversational Spanish. *Intercultura*, Apdo 1952-3000, Heredia, T260-8480, F260-9243, www.interculturacostarica.com, intensive courses with excursions to beaches, volcanoes, homestays available.

Costa Rica

Washing and dry cleaning at Centro Comercial San José 2000, 0730-2000, US$3.75 for large load. **Laundry** *Lavandería Costa Rica*, Av 3, C 19-21, US$5 for a large load. Below *Hotel Gran Imperial* is *Lavandería Lavamex*, US$3 to wash, US$3 to dry, quick and very friendly. Book swap, very popular with travellers, much more than a laundry thanks to the owners Karl and Patricia. *Martinizing*, US franchise, at Curridabat, Sabana Oriente (by new ring road) and Escazú, recommended. *Sixaola*, branches throughout San José, US$3.50 a load, 2 hrs dry cleaning available, expensive.

Biblioteca Nacional, opposite Parque Nacional, open Mon-Fri 0830-1630. Has art and photography **Libraries** exhibitions. *Centro Cultural Costarricense Norteamericano*, C 37, Av 1-5, has a good English-language library. *Universidad de Costa Rica*, in San Pedro suburb.

Aventuras Naturales, Av Central, C 33-35, T225-3939, F253-6934, www.toenjoynature.com Specialists in **Tour operators** whitewater rafting with their own lodge on the Pacuare which has a canopy adventure tour. Also several *It is much cheaper* other trips. *Aviatica*, C 1, Av 1, T222-5930, F222-7461, helpful for changing and buying airline tickets. *to take tours aimed* *COOPRENA*, Apdo 6939-1000, San José, T/F286-4203, www.agroecoturismo.net, (National Eco-Agricultural *at the local rather* Cooperative Network of Costa Rica), is a group supporting small farmers, it offers tours of mangroves, *than the foreign* rainforests, farms, beaches, etc, US$35 per day (accommodation and food included). *LADATCO*, *tourist market* T800-327-6162 (in USA), www.ladatco.com, specialists in tours (fixed and tailor-made) to Central and South America. *LA Tours*, PO Box 492-1007, Centro Colón, T221-4501, F224-5828, Kathia Vargas extremely helpful in rearranging flights and reservations. *Swiss Travel Service*, is one of the biggest tour operators with branches in many of the smarter hotels, T282-4898, F282-4890, www.swisstravelcr.com Can provide any standard tour, plus several specialist tours for bird-watchers. Good guides and warmly recommended. *Super Viajes*, *American Express* representative, Oficentro Ejecutivo La Sabana, Edif 1 Sabana, PO Box 3985, T220-0400, F220-0800. *Tam Travel Corporation*, 4 branches, 1 in *San José Palacio Hotel*, open 7 days a week, PO Box 1864, 24-hr answering service T256-0203, F222-1828, www.tamtravel.com *Viajes Alrededor del Mundo*, at the *Holiday Inn*, T223-6011, F222-0928, viamundo@racsa.co.cr, Eduardo Ureña is recommended for finding cheap flights to South America.

Those specializing in naturalist tours include: *Aguas Bravas*, T292-2072, F229-4837, *For independent* www.aguas-bravas.co.cr, whitewater rafting on various rivers including the Sarapaquí. *Arakari Tours*, *travel to Tortuguero,* C San Dimas y Av Castro Madriz, Barrio Cordoba, Apdo 1112-1011, San José, T227-1115, F226-3424, *see pages 1129* www.arakaritours.com A small *Tico*-owned operator started up in 1995 offering several tours and *and 1131* some interesting trekking options. *Braun Eco Tourism*, Av 8-10, C Central (in *Hotel Ritz*), T233-1731, F222-8849, basic but beautiful tours to out of the way places, recommended, but tour guides need to improve their biology. *Costa Rica Expeditions*, Av 3, C Central/2, T257-0766, F257-1665, www.costaricaexpeditions.com Upmarket wildlife adventures include whitewater rafting (US$89 for 1-day trip on Río Pacuare, includes lunch and transport, good, other rivers from US$69-85) etc, they own *Tortuga Lodge, Corcovado Lodge Tent Camp, Monteverde Lodge* and *Costa Rica White Water*. Open daily 0530-2100, highly recommended, good range of postcards in their souvenir shop next door. *Ecole Travel*, C 7, Av Central-Av 1, T223-2240, F223-4128, ecolecr@racsa.co.cr, Chilean-Dutch, highly recommended for budget tours to Tortuguero, Corcovado and tailor-made excursions off the beaten track. Shares office with 7th Avenue Books. *Green Tropical Tours*, C 1, Av 5-7, T/F255-2859, with options outside the norm including tours to Guayabo National Monument, Los Juncos and Cloud Forest. *Horizontes*, C 28, Av 1-3, T222-2022, F255-4513, www.horizontes.com One of the big operators in Costa Rica, high standards, educational and special interest, advice given and arrangements made for groups and individuals. *Mitur*, T255-2262, F255-1946, www.mitour.com A range of tours throughout the country, including Ilan Ilan to Tortuguero US$215, 3-days, 2 nights. *Ríos Tropicales*, C 38, between Paseo Colón and Av 2, 50 m south of Subway, T233-6455, F255-4354, www.riostropicales.com Specialists in whitewater rafting and kayaking, good selection and careful to assess your abilities, good food, excellent guides, US$250 for 2-day trip on Río Pacuare, waterfalls, rapids, including camping and food. Many other options throughout the country. *Typical Tours*, p 2-3, Las Arcadas, next to the *Gran Hotel Costa Rica*, PO Box 623-1007, T233-8486 24 hrs, F233-8474, city tours, volcano tours, nature reserves, rafting, cruising.

Several companies focus on trips to Tortuga Island off the southern tip of Nicoya Peninsula. Can be arranged direct or through operators above, try *Bay Island Cruises*, T258-3536, F258-1189, bayislan@racsa.co.cr, to Tortuga Island, or *Calypso Island Cruise* Wed, Fri, Sun, US$69 including lunch, T257-8787.

Useful addresses Immigration: is on the airport highway, opposite *Hospital México*. You need to go here for exit visas, extensions, etc. If they are busy, you could queue all day. To get there, take bus 10 or 10A Uruca, marked 'México', then cross over highway at the bridge and walk 200 m along highway – just look for the queue or ask the driver. Better to find a travel agent who can obtain what you need for a fee, say US$5. Make sure you get a receipt if you give up your passport. **Judiciary**: thefts should be reported in San José to Recepción de Denuncias, Organismo de Investigación Judicial (OIJ), C19, Av 6-8, T222-1365.

Meseta Central

Hilly and fertile with a temperate climate, the Central Highlands is a major coffee-growing area. Fairly heavily populated, picturesque and prosperous towns sit in the shadows of actives volcanoes. Exploring the towns and villages of the region – each with its own unique character and style – gives good insight into the very heart of Costa Rica.

Meseta Central West

From San José, the Pan-American Highway heads east through the Meseta Central for 332 km along good roads to the Nicaraguan border. While CA1 will take you north, by sticking to it you'll miss visiting the remnants of colonial architecture found in Alajuela, Heredia and the countless smaller towns that enjoy the spring-like temperatures of the highlands.

Whether taking a few days to explore the area, or just dipping into a couple of places, visiting the myriad of towns and communities in the region is certainly easier in a private vehicle. But frequent public buses and short journeys make hopping between towns fairly easy – if stepping out from San José it's probably worth dumping most of your luggage in the city and travelling as light as you can.

Alajuela

Population: 53,430
Altitude: 952 m
Colour map 5, grid B2

The provincial capital of Alajuela has a very slightly milder climate than San José making it a popular weekend excursion for *Josefinos*. Famous for its flowers and market days (Saturday market is good value for food), regular buses from San José make it an easy day trip. Alternatively stay in Alajuela and use the regular buses to visit the capital.

Alajuela, 5 km from the international airport, is handy for early flights and late arrivals

The town centres on the Parque Central with the 19th-century domed church on the eastern side. The unusual church of La Agonía five blocks further east is an interesting mix of styles. One block to the south Juan Santamaría, the national hero who torched the building in Rivas (Nicaragua) in which William Walker's filibusters were entrenched in 1856, is commemorated by a monument. One block north of the Parque Central the **Museo Histórico Juan Santamaría** tells, somewhat confusingly, the story of this war. ■ *Tue-Sun 1000-1800, Av 3, C 2.*

Six kilometres west of town is the **Ojo de Agua** swimming pool and sauna in beautiful surroundings, a popular bathing and boating resort. ■ *0800-1530 daily, US$1.20 per person, plus US$0.80 per vehicle.* The gushing spring which feeds the pool also supplies water for Puntarenas on the Pacific coast. At Río Segunda de Alajuela, southeast of town, is **Amigo de las Aves**, an experimental bird breeding farm hoping to reintroduce native macaws back into the wild. Contact owners, Richard and Margo Frisius (T441-2658), to arrange a visit.

Sleeping

In the town centre: **A-C** *Hotel 1915*, C 2, Av 5-7, 300 m north of park central, T/F441-0495. Old family home smartly refurbished with stylish garden patio café. Very good service. Rooms have cable TV, mini fridge, telephone and price includes breakfast. Best in town for the price. **B** *Charly's Place*, a couple of blocks north of the central park on Av 5, C Central-1, T/F441-0115, lilyhotel@latinmail.com Popular place, with 14 rooms most with private bathrooms, **C** without, some with TV. Good source of information. Credit cards accepted. **B** *Hotel Alajuela*, on corner across from Central Park at Av Central and C 2, T441-1241, F441-7912, alajuela@racsa.co.cr 50 generally good rooms and apartments all with private bathrooms. Exceptionally helpful staff and a garden patio and large restaurant for relaxing. Recommended for women travellers. **B** *Islands B&B*, Av 1, C 7-9, 50 m west of La Agonía church, T442-0573, F442-2909, islandbb@racsa.co.cr A small family-run *Tico*-owned B&B with 8 comfortable rooms. Some rooms have cable TV, free local calls. Airport pick-up available, very secure and 24-hour parking.

C *Mango Verde Hostel*, Av 3, C 2-4, T441-6630, mangover@racsa.co.cr 6 clean rooms with private bath and hot water, close to the centre of town. Courtyard and communal area create a relaxing atmosphere. Use of kitchen for guests and parking space. **C-D** *Pensión Alajuela*, Av 9, C Central-2, opposite the court house, T/F441-6251. Mixed bag of 10 simple rooms, some with private bath, some without. Small bar downstairs, laundry and fax service. 24-hour parking next door. **C-E** *Cortez Azul*, Av 3, C 2-4, 100 m west of Museo Juan Santamaría, T443-6145, corteazul@latinmail.com New place just opening up and already recommended, cheaper rooms in dormitories. **D-E** *Central Alajuela*, Av Central, C 8, close to the bus terminal, T443-8437. Under new administration the rooms are pretty basic, the shared bathrooms have cold water but it is reasonably clean. Popular with *Ticos* arriving from out of town. **E-F** *Villa Real*, Av 3, C 1, T441-4022. Claims of cleanliness largely unjustified, but it is popular with travellers and you can use the kitchen and wash clothes. Probably the cheapest place in town.

Out of town and nearby: **AL-A** *Hampton Inn*, T443-0043, F442-9532, www.hampton. hotel.co.cr, closest hotel to airport, 2 km east of Juan Santamaría, 100 rooms, double glazing, a/c, free form outdoor pool, bar, casino, fast food places nearby, children free and discounts for 3 or 4 adults sharing.

B *Tuetal Lodge*, 3 km north of Alajuela, T442-1804, tuetal@racsa.co.cr, www.islandnet. com/~tuetal/, cabins surrounded by 2 ha of gardens, some with kitchenette, pool, restaurant, also treehouses, camping area, plans to open a hostal.

5 km north of Alajuela is **LL** *Xandari*, T443-2020, F442-4847, toll free on 1-800-686-7879, www.xandari.com Once an old coffee finca overlooking the Central Valley, now it is a unique architectural treasure with 16 private villas, health restaurant, organic gardens, and many facilities. One of the best hotels in Costa Rica. 7 km north is

Meseta Central - west

Costa Rica

A *Buena Vista*, T442-8605, F442-8701, www.arweb.com/buenavista/, above the city with an all-round view, 25 rooms with bath, TV, pool, restaurant. Excellent service, beautiful restaurant with good wine list and very relaxing.

Eating Finding something to eat in Alajuela is not difficult, most restaurants and cafes are within 1 or 2 blocks of the Central Park. *El Cencerro*, actually on Parque Central, T441-2414, has good grills, especially steaks, good service, nice view over the park from the terrace. *Pizza Cayo*, C 1, Av 1-3, has a simple rustic charm, with good pizzas. *Restaurant da Lucia*, near Alajuela hotel on the corner of C 2 and Av 2, has good cheap meals overlooking Parque Juan Santamaría. *Señor Gazpacho* on Av Central, C Central-1, is a popular dining spot serving Mexican dishes.

Trigo Miel, Av 2, C Central-2 is one of a couple of patisserie cafés in Alajuela serving divine snacks and good coffee. *Café Almibar*, Av Central, C 1-3, is another snacking stop popular with locals. There are a number of sodas dotted round the square and down Calle Central.

Festivals *Juan Santamaría Day*, 11 Apr, sees the town celebrate the life of the town's most famous son with a week of general celebration, bands, concerts and dancing. **Mid-Jul** the fruitful heritage comes to the fore with a *Mango Festival* of parades, concerts and an arts and crafts fair.

Transport **Buses** Regular service between Alajuela and **San José**. Depart Alajuela from main bus terminal C 8, Av Central-1, or Av 4, C2-4 with both services arriving on Av 2 in the capital. Buses to **Heredia** from 0400 until 2300. Buses to the Butterfly Farm at **La Guácima** marked 'La Guácima abajo' leave from Av 2 between C 8-10. 1 block south of the terminal buses depart from a muddy block to several small villages in the area including **Laguna de Fraijanes** and **Volcán Poás**.

Directory **Banks** No shortage of banks, and all within 3 blocks of each other. *Banco Nacional*, C 2, Av Central-1, is facing Central Park. *Banco Interfin* next door has Visa and MasterCard ATMs. 1 block south of Central Park is *Banco Crédito Agrícola de Cartago*, C 2, Av Central-2, and 2 blocks north is *Banco de Santa Cruz*, C 2, Av 3, which is also the offices of *Credomatic*. **Communications** Internet: Several internet places around town but none firmly established. *Interplanet*, across from La Agonía church on Av Central and C 9, stands out largely due to the fluorescent lighting. Open every day 0830 until 2200. **Post office**: on the corner of Av 5 and C 1, Mon-Fri, 0730-1700. **Medical services** In emergency dial 911. **Hospital**: *Hospital San Rafael*, Av 9, C Central-1, north end of town, T440-1333, can help in a crisis.

Volcán Poás

Colour map 7, grid B3

Arrive early – clouds often hang low over the crater after 1000 obstructing the view. The volcano is very crowded on Sun go in the week if possible

Poás volcano (2,708 m) sits in the centre of the **Parque Nacional Volcán Poás** (6,506 ha), where the still-smoking volcano and bubbling turquoise sulphur pool are set within a beautiful forest. The crater is almost 1½ km across – the second largest in the world. The park is rich with abundant birdlife given the altitude and barren nature of the terrain and home to the only true dwarf cloud forest in Costa Rica.

From Alajuela two paved roads head north for 37 km to the volcano. The first through San Pedro de Poás and Fraijanes, the second follows the road to San Miguel branching left just before the town of Vara Blanca. In the park trails are well marked to help guide you from the Visitors' Centre to the geysers, lake and other places of interest. The main crater is 1 km along a road from the car park. There is a visitors' centre by the car park with explanations of the recent changes in the structure. There is also a good café run by Café Britt, alternatively bring your own food and water. ■ *0800-1530 daily, 1 hr later Fri-Sun, Dec-Apr, US$6, good café next door, and toilets further along the road to the crater. If you wish to get in earlier you can leave your car/taxi at the gates, walk the 3km up the hill and pay on your way out.*

Sleeping & eating You cannot camp in the park but there are several places advertising cabins on the road up to Poás and nearby. West of Poasito look for **L-A** *Poás Volcano Lodge*, PO Box 5723-1000, San José, 200 m from Vara Blanca junction on road to Poasito, at *El Cortijo* farm, sign on gate, 1 km to house, T482-2194, www.arweb.com/poas, English-owned, includes breakfast, dinner, good wholesome food, rooms in converted buildings with bath, or in farmhouse with shared bath, jungle trail, good walking, 25 mins to volcano by car, 1½ hrs from San José. *C Alberge Ecológica La Providencia*, near Poás NP (2 km from green entrance gate to volcano), private reserve, beautiful horse-riding tour US$25-30 including lunch, T232-2498, F231-2204.

The volcano can be reached by car from **San José**. A taxi for 6 hrs with a side trip will cost about US$50-60. There is a daily excursion bus from the main square of Alajuela right up to the crater, leaving at 0900 (or before if full), connecting with 0830 bus from San José (from Av 2, C 12-14); be there early for a seat; although extra buses run if necessary, the area gets very crowded, US$4 return, T237-2449. The bus waits at the top with ample time to see everything (clouds permitting), returning at 1400-1430. Daily bus **Alajuela-Poasito** 1200 (US$1) will take you part way to the summit. From **Poasito** hitch a lift as it is a 10-km walk. Other options include taking the 0600 or 1600 bus from Alajuela to **San Pedro de Poás**, hitch/taxi to Poasito and stay overnight, hiking or hitching up the mountain next morning. Taking a 0500 bus from Alajuela to Poasito arrives 2 hrs before the park gates open. **Transport**

From **Vara Blanca** the road continues north to the popular **La Paz waterfall**, round the east side of the volcano through Cinchona and Cariblanco. The road is twisty, winding through lush forest, with several waterfalls down to the lowlands at **San Miguel**. Here the road splits, leading either northeast heading to **La Virgen** and eventually **Puerto Viejo de Sarapiquí** (see page 1124), or northwest to **Venecia** (see below). **Heading north**

Ten kilometres northeast of San Miguel is La Virgen, near the Río Sarapiquí, a good spot for Class I, II and III rafting which is organized by the hotel *Rancho Leona*. From San José take the Río Frío bus which passes through San Miguel, or a bus from San Carlos, and ask to get off at *Rancho Leona*. Juan Carlos in La Virgen has been recommended as a guide for rafting, T761-1148, from US$25 per person. **La Virgen**

Sleeping In order as you reach them from San Miguel are **E** *Rancho Leona*, T/F761-1019, www.rancholeona.com, basic dormitories, free for kayak renters, original stained-glass windows for sale and the only 5-computer LAN with *Starcraft*, *Unreal Tournament* and *Ages of Empire* in the country! **A** *La Quinta de Sarapiquí Lodge*, Bajos de Chilamate on the Sardinal River, T/F761-1052, www.laquintasarapiqui.com, Costa Rica owned, family-run lodge, 23 rooms with bath and fan, bar and restaurant overlooking the rainforest, very popular with bird-watchers with bird list available. Also a frog and butterfly garden. At Chilamate is the **B** per person *Albergue Ecológico Islas del Río*, T292-2072, www.aguas-bravas.co.cr The operational centre of Aguas Bravas close to Puerto Viejo de Sarapiquí, includes meals, rooms with private and shared bathroom, ideal for groups. Río Sarapiquí trips arranged (affiliated to the Youth Hostel network). If continuing to Puerto Viejo de Sarapiquí, see page 1124.

Heading west from San Miguel, **Venecia** (three buses daily from San José, 4½ hours, US$4) has an interesting church with one hotel in the town to choose from, **F**, clean, friendly; *Restaurant El Parque*, near church, good local food. A strong recommendation is the **F** *Recreo Verde*, T472-1020, a recreational and ecological conservation park at Marsella, a short distance from Venecia. There are hot springs, primary forest, a few trails going to nearby caves and helpful, friendly staff. Also near Venecia are the pre-Columbian tumuli of **Ciudad Cutris**. A good road goes to within 2 km of Cutris, from where you can walk or take a four-wheel drive vehicle; get a permit to visit from the local *finca* owner.

West of Venecia is **Aguas Zarcas** where the road splits. Heading west on the road to San Carlos (also known as Ciudad Quesada), is the luxury health spa **LL-AL** *Melia Occidental El Tucano Resort and Thermal Spa*, T460-6000, F460-1692, occhcr@racsa.co.cr From here it is 8 km to San Carlos (see page 1060).

Heading directly north, the roads descends into the jungle lowlands, following the Río San Carlos towards the Nicaraguan border, passing through several small towns. After about 40 km, in **Boca Tapada**, is **A-B** *La Laguna del Lagarto Lodge*,

Costa Rica

T289-8163, F289-5295, www.adventure-costarica.com/laguna-del-lagarto, 12 rooms with bath, six with shared bath, friendly, 500 ha of forest, good for watching animals, boat trips down Río San Carlos to Río San Juan.

Grecia The road from Alajuela to San Carlos (see page 1060) passes through Grecia and several towns of the Meseta Central, with good paved roads leading to others. With coffee as the mainstay of the region, the hills are covered with green coffee bushes, interspersed with other plants for shade. Grecia is also a major pineapple producer, and has an interesting church made entirely of metal. The **Museo Regional de Grecia** is in the Casa de la Cultura. ■ *Mon-Fri, 0900-1700, free.* A short distance along the road to Alajuela is *El Mundo de los Serpientes*, a snake farm with over 50 species. ■ *0800-1600, US$11, reductions for biology students, information T/F494-3700, snakes@racsa.co.cr*

Sleeping **A-B** *Posada Mimosa*, Apdo 135-4100, Costa Rica, T/F494-5868, www.mimosa.co.cr A selection of rooms, suites and a couple of cabins set in beautiful tropical gardens. Cheaper options are **D** *Cabaña Los Cipreses*, and **G** *Pensión Quirós*, with bath.

Sarchí Heading west is the town of Sarchí, the country's artisan centre, where you can visit the *fábricas* that produce the intricately geometric and floral designs painted on ox-carts, which are almost a national emblem. In reality the town is divided between Sarchí Norte and Sarchí Sur, separated by some 4 km. The green church (until they paint it again) in Sarchí is especially attractive at sunset. Also **Valle de Mariposas** (next to Mercado de Artesanías), 40 species of butterflies, including morphos. ■ *0900-1700 daily, US$6.* Travel agents in San José charge around US$55 for a day trip to Sarchí usually combined with a trip to Volcán Poás.

Sleeping Just 800 m north of town is **B** *Hotel Villa Sarchí Lodge*, T454-3029, 11 rooms with private bath, hot water, cable TV and pool. **D** *Cabinas Daniel Zamora*, T454-4596, with bath, fan, hot water, very clean and extra blankets if cold at night. **E** *Cabinas Sarchí*, T454-4425, with bath, opposite *Banco Nacional*, you may have to call owner if unattended.

Shopping One of the largest *artesanías* is *Fábrica de Chaverri* in Sarchí Sur. *Taller Lalo Alfaro*, the oldest workshop, is in Sarchí Norte and worth a visit to see more traditional production methods. Both sell hand-made furniture, cowhide rocking chairs and wooden products as well as the ox-carts, which come in all sizes.

Transport Express bus from San José, C 16, Av 1-3, 1215, 1730 and 1755, Mon-Fri, returning 0530, 0615, 1345, Sat 1200, 1½ hrs, US$0.60. *Tuasa* buses every 30 mins, 0500-2200 from Alajuela bus station, 1½ hrs, US$0.50.

Directory *Banks: Banco Nacional* has branches in Sarchí Sur and Sarchí Norte. **Communications:** **Post office** services are also found in both villages.

Naranjo
Colour map 9, Grid B3
The road continues north to Naranjo, a quiet agricultural town with an exquisite bright white church undergoing restoration, and a shocking post-modern pyramidal structure in the main square.

Sleeping and eating **F** *La Bambo*, down the hill by the football pitch may muster up enough energy to let you stay in one of their simple rooms. On the Panamericana, 1 km west of the turn-off for Naranjo is **A** *Rancho Mirador*, T451-1302, F451-1301, good value cabañas, good restaurant with local food, a spectacular view of coffee *fincas* and San José in the distance, owner Rick Vargas was formerly a stunt pilot in the US. **Transport** *Transportes Naranjo*, T451-3655, have buses to and from San José's Coca Cola terminal every 20 mins. Buses connecting to other towns and villages in the area.

Directory *Banks: Banco Nacional*, on north side of plaza, has ATMs for Visa and MasterCard.

Frequent bus services from San José/Alajuela pass through Zarcero, on the lip of the **Zarcero** continental divide, en route to San Carlos (Ciudad Quesada). The town is famous for vegetable farming, dairy products and is notable for the topiary creations of Evangelista Blanco Breves that fill the main plaza. Bushes are clipped into arches leading up to the white church with twin towers, with shapes of animals, dancing couples, a helicopter, many designs of Henry Moore-like sculptures and a small grotto. The interior of the quaint church, overshadowed somewhat by the plaza, is made entirely of wood, even the pillars, painted cream and pale grey with patterns in blue, brown, green and pink; cartouches, emblems and paintings.

Sleeping and eating **B-C** *Don Beto*, by the church, T/F463-3137, with bath, very friendly, clean. *Soda/Restaurant El Jardín*, on 1st floor, overlooks the plaza with good view of topiary, local lunches and breakfasts. The town is also known for cheese and fruit preserves.

West of Naranjo along the Pan-American Highway is the town of **San Ramón**, **San Ramón** 76 km from San José. A clean town, known locally as the City of Poets, with an attractive Parque Central, and a street market on Saturday mornings. The **Museo de San Ramón**, Frente de Parque, records the history and culture of the local community. ■ *Tue-Fri, 1300-1700*. Good walking in the surrounding area. You can visit the coffee processing plant (in season) at the Cooperativa de Café in San Ramón. Twenty kilometres north of San Ramón is the private 800-ha **Los Angeles Cloud Forest Reserve**, (see *Hotel Villablanca* below) which offers hiking, guided tours, horse-riding and canopy ascents. ■ *US$15-39*. **Fiesta**: On the day of **San Ramón**, around 30 August, local saints are carried on litters to the town's church.

Sleeping and eating **B-D** *La Posada*, T/F445-7359, hoteles@racsa.co.cr, 400 m north of the cathedral, parking, 13 good rooms, with private bath, hot water. Use of kitchen, laundry, parking and small patio for relaxing. A new hotel is **C** *San Ramón*, 100 m east of *Banco de Costa Rica*, T44-2042. 30 spotless rooms (but pretty garish décor), with private bathroom, hot water and cable TV. Parking. **E** *Gran Hotel*, 150 m west of central park, T445-6363. Big rooms, private bathrooms, hot water, OK. Friendly, communal TV area. **F** *Hotel Nuevo Jardín*, 5 blocks north of the Central Park, T445-5620, simple, clean and friendly. *Restaurant Tropical*. Excellent ice-cream parlour near the northwest corner of the Parque. Several restaurants and sodas dotted around town.
   On the San Ramón to La Tigra/Fortuna road Heading north, is **L** *Hotel Villablanca*, set in the 800 ha Los Angeles Cloud Forest Reserve, T228-4603, F228-4004, www.villablanca-costarica.com Naturalist hikes, some up to 8 hrs, canopy tour and horse-riding – you don't have to stay to visit. Also **AL** *Valle Escondido Lodge*, at San Lorenzo much lower in altitude on the same road, T231-0906, F232-9591, www.valleescondido.com, comfortable rooms with private bath, set in 100 ha of primary forest, riding, bird-watching.

Transport Heading north the road forks, left to Zarcero (20 km) and finally Ciudad Quesada. The right fork heads north to La Tigra and Fortuna passing the Los Angeles Cloud Forest Reserve (see below). Many **buses** going to San Ramón continue to Puntarenas. They originate at the *Empresarios Unidos* stop in San José at C 16, Av 10-12, 10 a day, every 45 mins or so. There is also a service via Alajuela. Buses run to surrounding villages and towns.

Palmares (one hotel), 7 km southeast of San Ramón, has a pretty central park with **Palmares** lovely tall trees, where sloths are occasionally spotted. The quiet town comes alive in January for the annual **Fiestas de Palmares** with food, carnival rides and parades.

After Palmares you can pick up the Pan-American Highway and head to the coast or **Atenas** return to San José, or continue south to Atenas. The church and main plaza in *Colour map 7, grid B3* Atenas lie on an earthquake fault. The local speciality, *toronja rellena*, is a sweet-filled grapefruit. Atenas is reputed to have the best climate in the world, with stable temperatures of between 17 and 32°C the year round (plus rain of course).

Costa Rica

Sleeping AL *El Cafetal Inn*, T446-5785, F446-7028, www.cafetal.com, out of town in St Eulalia, 4.7 km towards Grecia, private house, nice setting, large pool, 10 rooms, recommended. **B** *Ana's Place*, T446-5019, includes breakfast, private bathroom, special weekly/monthly rates. **C** *Villa Tranquilidad*, T446-5460, 6 rooms, Canadian owned, quiet, welcoming, hard to find, phone for reservations/directions. **Transport** The library on the plaza also serves as the office for the bus company, *Cooptransatenas*, T446-5767. Many daily buses to **San José**, either direct or via **Alajuela**, US$0.60.

Atenas to Alajuela

La Garita de Alajuela — Completing the loop heading from Atenas towards Alajuela, you pass *Fiesta del Maíz* soda/restaurant, where they sell products made only from maize, you can try spoonfuls before you buy. Open weekends only, it's very busy and a stopping place for weekenders on their way to Jacó Beach. Nearby is the Enchanted Forest, popular with children. Also **Zooave**, between Atenas and Alajuela in La Garita de Alajuela, Canadian owner, over 100 species of native birds and 25 exotic species, toucans, parrots, black swans, eagles, also four types of monkey as well as other mammals and reptiles. Now recognized as a Wildlife Rescue Centre, Zooave has been successful in breeding endangered birds. ■ *0900-1700 daily, US$9. T433-8989, F433-9140, www.zooave.org Getting there: from Alajuela take a bus to La Garita.*

Sleeping AL *Chatelle Country Resort*, T487-7781, F487-7095, www.hotelchatelle.com 15 rooms with bath, some with kitchenette, TV, spacious, comfortable beds, beautiful gardens, good restaurant, pool, weekly/monthly rates, airport pick-up available at no extra charge. Opposite the is an orchid nursery with a marvellous variety of blooms, run as a hobby by an enthusiastic English-speaking optometrist, who will give you a guided tour for US$3.50. **A** *Río Real*, T/F487-7022, includes breakfast, pool, restaurant, bar. **Eating** In addition to *Fiesta del Maíz* try *Mi Quinta*, good food, swimming pools, sports facilities also available for a small charge.

Aserrí to San Pablo de Turrubares

Ten kilometres south of San José is **Aserrí**, a village with a beautiful white church. On Friday and Saturday evenings, street bands begin the fiesta with music from 2000, followed by marimbas. Extremely popular among locals, the dancing is fabulous, with *chicharrones*, *tortillas* and plenty of other things to eat and drink. Further along the same road is *Mirador Ram Luna*, a restaurant with a fine panoramic view. At the end of the road is **San Ignacio de Acosta**, again with a good church containing life-size Nativity figures. Buses from San José (Calle 8, Avenida 12-14 in front of the Baptist church) via Aserrí hourly from 0500-2230, return 0430-2100, one hour. The unpaved road continues to **Santiago de Puriscal**, which was the epicentre for many earthquakes in 1990. Although the church is now closed as a result, there are excellent views from the town and the road. From here it is possible to take a dirt road to the Pacific coast, joining the coastal road near Parrita (see page 1100). Alternatively, take the road to **San Pablo de Turrubares**, from where you can either head west for Orotina, via an unpaved road through San Pedro and San Juan de Mata, or for Atenas via Quebradas, then east to Escobal, next stop on railway, then four-wheel drive necessary to Atenas.

A road has been built from San José west to Ciudad Colón by-passing Escazú and Santa Ana (**AL** *Hotel Posada Canal Grande*, T282-4089, F282-5733, www.novanet.co.cr/canal) The road will eventually pass San Pedro de Turrubares going to Orotina, with the aim of replacing the Pan-American Highway to the coast.

Heredia

Population: 30,968
Altitude: 1,200 m

Ten kilometres from San José, Heredia is capital of the province of the same name and an important coffee centre. It is a convenient and pleasant place to stay, away

Costa Rica

from the pollution of San José but close to the capital and the airport, and with good public transport. The town is mostly new with only the main square maintaining a colonial atmosphere in its architecture. The short squat **Basílica de la Inmaculada Concepción** built in 1797 has survived countless earthquakes. To the north of the central plaza, with a statue to the poet Aquileo Echeverría (1866-1909), is the solitary defensive structure of El Fortín. Across the street the Casa de la Cultura is a fine colonial home that now hosts concerts and exhbitions. The School of Marine Biology at the Universidad Nacional campus has a **Museo Zoológico Marino** (check locally for opening times).

Excursions One of the largest coffee *beneficios* is **La Meseta**.The bus from Heredia to Santa Bárbara will drop you at the gate and you can ask for a guided tour. A more popular tour is of **Café Britt's coffee farm**near Barva de Heredia where you can see the processing factory, tasting room and multimedia presentation of the story of coffee. You can arrange to be picked up from Heredia or at various points in San José. ■ *US$20, tours at 0900 and 1100, also 1500 in high season, 2 hrs, in low season at 0900 and 1100, T260-2748, F238-1848 for details, www.cafebritt.com*

North of Heredia is the historic town of **Barva**, on the slopes of Barva Volcano; frequent buses to/from Heredia. *Los Jardines Bed and Breakfast*, T260-1904. At Barva the Huetar Gallery is recommended for arts, crafts and delicious food. There is also a **Museo de Cultura Popular**, 500 m east of the Salón Comunal de Santa Lucía de Barva. Beyond Barva is **Santa Bárbara**, good seafood at the *Banco de los Mariscos* on the north side of the central plaza. Five kilometres west of Heredia is **San Joaquín de Flores**, a small town in a rural setting with views of Barva and Poás volcanoes.

A short distance south of Heredia on the road to Santo Domingo is **INBio Parque**, an educational and recreational centre which explains and gives insight into Costa Rica's incredible biological diversity. In a remarkably small area you can visit the ecosystems of Central Highland Forest, Dry Forest and Humid Forest, with trails set out for bromelias and guarumo. ■ *Open daily 0730-1600. US$18, under-12s free, T244-4730, F244-4790, www.inbio.ac.cr/inbioparque*

Sleeping **AL** *Valadolid*, C 7, Av 7, PO Box 1973-3000, T260-2905, F260-2912, valladol@racsa.co.cr 11 spacious rooms and suites, all with a/c, private bath, telephone and cable TV. 5th floor has sauna, jacuzzi and *Bonavista Bar* with fine views overlooking the Central Valley. The best option in town. **A-B** *Apartotel Vargas*, Apdo 510-3000, Heredia, 800 m north of Colegio Santa Cecilia and San Francisco Church, T237-8526, F260-4698, lmasis@ hotmail.com, 8 large, well-furnished apartments with cooking facilities, hot water, laundry facilities, TV, enclosed patio with garage and nightwatchman, English speaking staff, Sr Vargas will collect you from airport. Excellent choice if taking language classes and in a group. Recommended.

D *Hotel Heredia*, C 6, Av 3-5, T238-0880. 10 rooms, some quite dark, but all have private bath and hot water. **D** *Las Flores*, Av 10, C 12-14, T382-3418, with bath, clean, quiet and recommended. **F** *Colonial*, C 4-6, Av 4, clean, friendly and family run, will park motorcycles in restaurant. **F** *El Parqueo*, C 4, Av 6-8, T237-5258, next to central market, rooms on street side are slightly better, close to bus terminal. **F** *Pension Herediano*, C6, 2 blocks south of the cathedral, T237-3217, US$11, private bath, safe parking, OK and friendly owner.

Out of town LL *Finca Rosa Blanca*, 1.6 km from Santa Bárbara de Heredia, T269-9392, F269-9555, www.finca-rblanca.co.cr Deluxe suites in an architectural orgasm of style and eloquence, romance and exclusivity at the extremes of imagination and fantasy, restaurant and bar for guests only. **AL** *Bougainvillea de Santo Domingo*, just west of Santo Domingo, T244-1414, F244-1313, www.bouganvillea.co.cr, includes breakfast, excellent service, pool, spectacular mountain setting, free shuttle bus to San José. Highly recommended.

Eating & drinking *Bulevar Bar*, Av Central, C 5-7, is one of the happening places with a lively balcony bar upstairs and fast food and bocas available. *Café Azzura*, on the southwest corner of the main plaza, great ice-cream, cakes, shakes, cappuccino, great people-watching. From around

Costa Rica

US$5. Good noticeboard outside with apartments and local information for anyone thinking of hanging around for a while. *Cowboy Restaurant*, C 9, Av 5, is a mid-price grill option where the Mid-West meets Costa Rica. Lively bar in the evenings. Credit cards accepted. *El Gran Papa*, C 9, Av 3, gets the majority of lunchtime business trade, with a good range of *bocas*, pastas and cocktails. From US$10. *Fresas*, C 7, Av 1, T237-3915, diner-style restaurant serving everything you could possible want including snacks, sandwiches, breakfast, full meals, fresh fruit juices and strawberries. *La Nueva Floresta*, south side of main square, Chinese, balcony, large portions, good value from US$4. Recommended. *La Rambla*, C 7, Av 7, services a good mix of *comida típica* and international dishes. From US$8.

Le Petit Paris on C 5 and Av Central-2, is a little piece of France simply oozing style in the heart of Heredia. The ambience shifts between the bar, restaurant and patio café, the food is French, divine and there is live music on Wed. US$4 upwards. *Pollo Frito*, cook it quick and sell it cheap *comedor* specializing in *pollo frito*. *Vishnu*, C 7, Av Central-1, good wholesome vegetarian served fast food style out front or a little more leisurely out back.

Shopping **Bookshop** *Book Swappers*, diagonal to *McDonalds*, run by Jill Chalfont and Frank García, new and used books, newspapers, CDs, postcards, open Mon-Sat 0930-1900.

Transport **Buses** From **San José** from Av 2, C 12-14, buses every 10 mins daily, 0500-0015, then every 30 mins to 0400, 25-min journey, US$0.30, or minibus from Av 2, C 10-12, every 15 mins 0600-2000. Return buses from Av 4, C Central. Local buses leave from Av 8, C 2-4, by market.

Directory **Language schools** *Centro Panamericana de Idiomas*, in San Joaquín de Flores, PO Box 151-3007, T265-6866, F265-6213, www.cpi-edu.com, accommodation with local families. Also have schools in Monteverde and Playa Flamingo. *Intercultura Costa Rica*, in Heredia, T/F260-9243, www.spanish-intercultura.com, small intensive classes.

Volcán Barva Parque Nacional Braulio Carrillo (see page 1122) to the north of Heredia includes Barva Volcano, 2,906 m. This section of the park is ideal for hiking with a good trail leading up to the summit with three lagoons nearby, and excellent views and wildlife encounters for the few that make the effort. The really enthusiastic can hike all the way down to the lowlands arriving close to La Selva Biological Station near Puerto Viejo de Sarapaqui but careful planning is required. Ranger station and camp site near the entrance 4 km north of Sacremento, from where it's a 3 km easy climb to the top. ■ *Park entry US$6, no permit needed.*

Transport Accessible from Heredia, there is no route from the San José-Limón Highway. Buses leave from market at 0630, 1230 and 1600, returning at 0730, 1300, 1700. Arriving at Porrosati. Some buses continue as far as Sacramento otherwise walk 6 km to park entrance then 4 km to lagoon. Be careful if leaving a car, regular reports of theft from rental cars.

From **San José de la Montaña** it is four hours' walk to Sacramento but some buses continue towards Sacramento halving the walk time (otherwise walk, hitchhike, or arrange a ride with the park director). Taxi Heredia-Sacramento, US$7.

Sleeping On the western slopes of Volcán Barva between Birri and Sacramento, all with beautiful views across the Meseta Central: **A** *El Pórtico*, T260-6000, F260-6002, cosy, clean, pool, sauna, good food. Recommended.

On the main highway heading east is **B** *Hotel Villa Zurqui*, just off Limón highway at **San Luis de Santo Domingo**, 5 mins from entrance to Parque Nacional Braulio Carrillo, T/F268-8856, www.online.co.cr/zurqui/ 6 rooms with private or shared bathroom, including breakfast. Just south of the main highway, in the village of **San Jerónimo** is **B** *San Jerónimo Lodge*, T292-3612, F292-3243, 20-ha reserve, 20 mins from San José on Guápiles road, 800 m east of church at San Jerónimo de Moravia, horse-riding, hiking, biking.

Meseta Central East

Cartago

Cartago, at the foot of the Irazú Volcano, is encircled by mountains. Founded in 1563, it was the capital of Costa Rica for almost 300 years until San José assumed the role in 1823. Since then the town has failed to grow significantly and remains small, though densely populated. Earthquakes in 1841 and 1910 destroyed many of the buildings, and ash from the Irazú engulfed the town in 1963. While colonial-style remnants exist in one or two buildings, the town feels as if it is still reeling from the impact of so much natural devastation and is keeping quiet waiting for the next event.

Population: 33,539
Altitude: 1,439 m

22½ km from San José on a toll road (US$0.75)

The most important attraction in town and the focal point for pilgrims from throughout Central America is the **Basílica de Nuestra Señora de Los Angeles**, the patroness of Costa Rica, on the eastern side of town. Rebuilt in 1926 in Byzantine style, it houses the diminutive **La Negrita**, an Indian image of the Virgin under 15 cm high, worshipped for her miraculous healing powers. The high point of the pilgrimages is on 2 August (see Festivals below). The Basilica houses an extraordinary collection of finely made silver and gold images, no larger than 3 cm high, of various parts of the human anatomy, presumably offered in the hope of being healed. Also worth seeing is **La Parroquia** (the old parish church), roughly 1 km west of the the the Basílica, ruined by the 1910 earthquake and now converted into a delightful garden retreat with flowers, fish and hummingbirds.

Excursions

Aguas Calientes is 4 km southeast of Cartago and 90 m lower, with a warm-water *balneario* ideal for picnics. 8 km from Cartago on the road to Paraíso is the **Jardín Lankester orchid garden** (run by the University of Costa Rica, T551-9877), 10 minutes' walk from the main road. The best displays are between February and April. Although off the beaten track, the gardens are definitely worth a visit. ■ *0800-1500 daily except Christmas, Easter and New Year, US$3.10.* Cartago-Paraíso bus departs every 30 minutes from south side of central park in Cartago (15 minutes); ask the driver to let you out at Campo Ayala. Taxi from Cartago, US$3. 1 km further on is Parque Doña Ana (La Expresión), a lake with picnic area, basketball courts, exercise track and bird-watching. ■ *0900-1700, US$0.50. Get off bus at Cementerio in Paraíso and walk 1 km south.* At Paraíso, *Restaurant Continental* is recommended.

Sleeping B *Los Angeles Lodge B&B*, close to the Basílica at Av 4, C14-16, T551-0957, clean, nice rooms. At the Las Ruinas end of town is **D** *Dinastia*, C 3, Av 6-8, close to the old railway station, T551-7057, F551-0626, slightly more with private bath. The rooms are small although better with a window. Safe hotel but in lively area north of the central market. Credit cards accepted. **F** *Familiar Las Arcadas*, rents rooms hourly late into the night. Nearby is **F** *Venecia*, basic, with cold water. **Eating** *Salón París*, very good food. *City Garden*, Av 4, C 2-4. *Puerta del Sol*, in front of the Basilica. *Pizza Hut*, opposite La Parroquia ruins. *Auto 88*, east of public market, meal US$2-3, cafetería style, beer drinking room adjoining dining-room. Restaurants, among other places, are closed on the Thu and Fri of Holy Week, so take your own food.

Festivals **2 Aug** is the most important date in the pilgrims' calendar when the image of *La Negrita* is carried in procession to churches in Cartago with celebrations throughout Costa Rica.

Shopping The noisy and sometimes colourful Thu-Sun **market** is at Av 4, C 1-3. *Fuji* has a store selling slide and print film at Av 2, C 4-6.

Transport A good bus service supplies the surrounding area. To San José every 10 mins from Av 4, C 2-4. Arrives and departs **San José** from C 5, Av 18-20 for the 45-min journey. After 2030 buses leave from *Gran Hotel Costa Rica*, Av 2, C 3-5. **Orosí/Río Macho**, for Parque Nacional Tapanti

Costa Rica

every 30 mins from C 6, Av 1-3, journey time of 35/55 mins. **Turrialba**, every hr from Av 3, C 8-10, 1 hr direct, 1 hr 20 mins *colectivo*. **Cachí**, via Ujarrá and Paraíso from C 6, Av 1-3, every 1½ hrs, 1 hr 20 mins. **Paraíso**, every 5 mins from Av 5, C 4-6. **Aguacalientes**, every 15 mins from C 1, Av 3-5. **Tierra Blancas** for Irazú, every 30 mins from C 4, Av 6-8.

Closest bus for Irazú rides to San Juan de Chichua, still some 12 km from the summit. The bus leaves Cartago from north of the central market, Av 6, C 1-3, at 1730, returning at 0500 the next day, so you have to spend at least two nights on the volcano or in a hotel if you can't get a ride. To visit **Turrialba** take a bus from C 4 y Av 6 to the village of San Gerardo.

Directory **Banks** No shortage of banks if funds are running low, most with ATMs. *Banco de Costa Rica*, Av 4, C 5-7. *Banco Interfin*, Park Central at Av 2, C 2. *Banco Nacional*, Av 2, C 1-3. **Communications** Staying in touch in Cartago is challenging. Internet:*Café Línea*, Av 4, C 6-8, the only internet place in town, looks decidedly temporary. **Post office** Formerly on C 1, Av 2-4, the post office has moved and nobody appears to know to where! Try '800 m west of Parque Central'. Better still, post letters elsewhere. **Medical services** Hospital Dr Max Peralta, entrance on C 3, Av 7. Pharmacies can be found along Av 4 between C 1-6. Useful addresses in emergencies call 911. **Tour operators** *Mercatur*, next to Fuji at Av 2, C 4-6, provides local tourist information.

Volcán Irazú

Colour map 7, grid B3
Altitude: 3,432 m

Irazú volcano crater is an impressive half-mile cube dug out of the earth, surrounded by desolate grey sand, which looks like the surface of the moon – or what you might imagine it to look like. President Kennedy's visit in 1963 coincided with a major eruption, and in 1994 the north wall of the volcano was destroyed by another eruption that sent detritus down as far as the Río Sucio, within sight of the the San José-Limón Highway.

Wear good shoes and a hat, the sun is strong. Those with sensitive skins should consider face cream if the sulphur fumes are heavy

The views are stupendous on a clear day and the main reason for the trip. But the clouds normally move in enveloping the lower peaks and slopes by 1300 (sometimes even by 0900 or 1000 between July and November), so get there as early as you can to have a greater chance of a clear view of the mountains and the sun shining on the clouds in the valley below. There's little wildlife other than the ubiquitous Volcano Junco bird and the few plants which survive in this desert, but ongoing colonization is attracting more birds.

It's definitely worth the trip and an early start. As one traveller writes: "In the afternoon the mountain top is buried in fog and mist or drizzle, but the ride up in the mist can be magical, for the mountainside is half displaced in time. There are new jeeps and tractors, but the herds of cattle are small, the fields are quilt-work, hand-carts and oxcarts are to be seen under the fretworked porches of well-kept frame houses. The land is fertile, the pace is slow, the air is clean. It is a very attractive mixture of old and new. Irazú is a strange mountain, well worth the ride up."

In addition to a short trail, there is a small exhibition centre and souvenir shop. National Park rules forbid visitors to walk around the crater: on the north side the '*Prohibido pasar*' sign should not be passed. ■ *US$6, 0800-1530 most of the year.*

Sleeping & eating If you want to stay on the slopes of Irazú on the way up in **San Juan de Chicúa** is **D** *Hotel Gestoria Irazú*, T253-0827. Simple rooms with private bath, hot water and extra blankets to get you through the cold winter nights. A little further uphill is *Restaurantes Linda Vista* with spectacular views, as you'd expect from Costa Rica's highest restaurant, and apparently good food and drinks. But most people stop to post, stick, pin or glue a business card, or some other personal item, to the wall.

Getting there It is possible to get a **bus** from Cartago to Tierra Blanca (US$0.33) or San Juan de Chicúa (which has one hotel) and hitch a ride in a pick-up truck. Alternatively you can take a bus from Cartago to Sanatorio. Ask the driver to drop you at the crossroads just outside Tierra Blanca. From there you walk 16 km to the summit. If you're looking for a **day trip** from San

José a yellow 'school' express bus run by *Buses Metropoli SA*, T272-0651, runs from San José, Sat, Sun and holidays, 0800 from *Gran Hotel Costa Rica*, stops at Cartago ruins 0830 to pick up more passengers, returns 1215 with lunch stop at *Restaurant Linda Vista*, US$6.

A **taxi** from Cartago is US$32 re turn. A taxi tour from Orosí costs US$10 per person, minimum 3 people, and stops at various places on the return journey, eg Cachí dam and Ujarrás ruins. Since it can be difficult to find a decent hotel in Cartago, it may be easier to take one of the guided tours leaving from San José, about US$35, 5½ hrs includes lunch, transport from San José. If **driving** from San José, take the turn-off at the *Ferretería San Nicolás* in Taras, which goes directly to Irazú, avoiding Cartago.

The Orosí Valley

Heading further east from Cartago a trip round the Orosí Valley makes a beautiful circular trip, or a fine place to hang out for a while in a valley that is often overlooked as the crowds rush to the more popular spots on the coast. The centrepiece of the valley is the artificial Lake Cachí used for hydro-electric generation. Heading round the lake counter-clockwise the road passes through Orosí, clips the edge of Parque Nacional Tapantí, continuing to the Cachí Dam and completes the circuit passing through Ujarrás. Along the way there are several miradores which offer excellent views of the Reventazón Valley. For transport see each destination. Day trips can be easily arranged from San José.

In Orosí there is an 18th-century mission with colonial treasures (closed on Mon), **Orosí** and just outside two *balnearios* (US$1.60) with restaurants serving good meals at fair prices. It's a good place to hang out, take some low-key language classes, mixed with mountain biking and trips to the national park and other sites of interest nearby.

Sleeping B *Orosí Lodge*, T/F533-3578, sites.netscape.net/timeveit/orosilodge, 7 rooms with balcony overlooking the valley towards Volcán Irazú each with private bath, hot water and kitchenette. Just about everything you could want; divine home-baked cookies, mountain bikes, kayaks and horses for rent and an internet service. Credit cards accepted. Excellent value. **B-C** *Cabinas Media Libra*, T533-3838, F533-3737. Rather stark and characterless rooms, with telephone, TV, fridge. But clean and friendly service, and good local knowledge. Credit cards accepted.

F-G *Montaña Linda*, T/F533-2153 (international calls), T533-3640 (if dialing locally), www.montanalinda.com A classic backpackers' place, with a range of options. Dormitory rooms, options for camping (**G**), and a bed and breakfast service (**B-C**) if you just can't get out of bed! Toine and Sara are friendly and know their patch very well organizing trips to local sights. In **Palomo**, just south of Orosí, **D** *Río Palomo*, cabins, pool, laundry facilities, good restaurant.

Directory Language schools: *Montaña Linda Language School* uses local teachers to get you *hablando español* with a homestay option if you want total submersion. Recommended.

Buses from Cartago to Orosí/Río Macho from C 6, Av 1-3 every 30 mins, journey time of 35/55 mins. US$0.50. **Transport**

Twelve kilometres beyond Orosí is the **Parque Nacional Tapantí-Macizo de la Muerte**, the country's newest national park and one of the wettest parts of the country, some parts reportedly receiving as much as 8 m of rain a year. Approached from Orosí and just 30 km from Cartago the national park is suprisingly easy to reach and packs in the interest.

Parque Nacional Tapantí-Macizo de la Muerte
From June to November/December it rains every afternoon

Covering 58,000 ha, Tapantí Macizo includes the former Tapantí National Park and much of the Río Macho Forest Reserve. The park protects the Río Orosí basin which feeds the Cachí Dam hydro power plant. Strategically the southern boundary of the park joins with Chirripó National Park extending the continuous protected area that makes up La Amistad Biosphere Reserve. The park incorporates a wide range of life zones with

Costa Rica

altitudes rising from 1,220 m to over 3,000 m at the border with Chirripó. The diverse altitudes and relative seclusion of the park has created an impressive variety of species – 260 bird species, 45 mammals, lizards, snakes – list which is currently incomplete due to the recent creation of the park. There are picnic areas, a nature centre with slide shows (ask to see them) and good swimming in the dry season (November-June), and trout fishing (1 April-31 October). ■ *Daily 0700-1700, US$6.*

Sleeping B *Kiri Lodge*, 1½ km from the park entrance (T284-2024, beeper T225-2500, San José T257-8064, F257-8065), excellent lodging and food, peaceful, very friendly, good trails. **Camping** The guards may let you camp on or near the parking lot at the entrance.

Transport 0600 **bus** from Cartago to Orosí gets to Puricil by 0700, then walk (5 km), or take any other Cartago-Orosí bus to Río Macho and walk 9 km to the refuge. Alternatively take a **taxi** from Orosí (US$7 round trip, up to 6 passengers), or San José, US$50.

Cachí Continue round the lake to **Cachí** and the nearby *Casa del Soñador* (Dreamer's House) which sells wood carvings from the sculpture school of the late Macedonio Quesada. The road crosses the dam wall and follows the north shore to Ujarrás, then back to Cartago. The Charrarra tourist complex, 30-mins' walk from Ujarrás, has a good campsite, restaurant, swimming pool, boat rides on the lake and walks. Can be reached by direct bus on Sun. Buses leave from Cartago 1 block north of the Cartago ruins.

Ujarrás Ujarrás (ruins of a colonial church and village) is 6½ km east of Paraíso, on the shores of the artificial Lago Cachí. There is a bus every 1½ hours from Paraíso that continues to Cachí. Legend has it that in 1666 English pirates, including the youthful Henry Morgan, were seen off by the citizens of Ujarrás aided by the Virgin. The event is now celebrated annually in mid-March when the saint is carried in procession from Paraíso to the ruined church.

Turrialba

Colour map 7, grid B3
Population: 20,000
Altitude: 646m

Turrialba (62 km from San José) bridges the Central Valley highlands and the Caribbean lowlands, and was once a stopping point on the old Atlantic railway between Cartago and Puerto Limón. The railway ran down to Limón on a narrow ledge poised between mountains on the left and the river to the right but no longer operates. The **Centro Agronómico Tropical de Investigación y Enseñanza** (CATIE – T558-2000 ext 2275, F556-1533, www.catie.ac.cr) about 4 km southeast of Turrialba covers more than 2,000 acres of this ecologically diverse zone (with many fine coffee farms), has one of the largest tropical fruit collections in the world and houses an important library on tropical agriculture; visitors and students are welcome for research or bird-watching. Past CATIE on the south side of the river, a large sugar mill makes for a conspicuous landmark in Atirro, the centre for macadamia nuts. Nearby, the 256-ha Lake Angostura has now flooded some of the white waters of the Río Reventazón. What has been lost as world-class whitewater is believed, by some, to be a Lake Arenal in the making.

Excursions Many **whitewater rafting** companies operate out of Turrialba, with trips to the Reventazón and Pacuare rivers. The rafting is excellent; the Pascua section of the Reventazón can be Class V at rainy times. The Pacuare is absolutely perfect with divine scenary and more expensive. By contacting the guides in Turrialba you can save about 30% on a trip booked in San José, provided they are not already contracted. Added to companies in San José (ie *Ríos Tropicales*), local guides include Tico, at *Tico's River Adventures*, (T556-1231, www.ticoriver.com), the team at Jungla (on the road to CATIE, T556-2639, F556-6225, www.junglaexpeditions. com). *Serendipity Adventures*, T558-1000, F558-1010, or in USA T800-635-2325, www.serendipityadventures.com, have been recommended. A small locally owned

Costa Rica

operor is *Loco's Tropical Tours* (T556-6035, F556-6071, www.whiteh2o.com) with custom rafting trips on the Reventazón and Pacuare Rivers.

Turrialba volcano (3,329 m) may be visited from Cartago by a bus from C 4 y Av 6 to the village of San Gerardo. From Turrialba take a bus to Santa Cruz. From both an unpaved road meets at *Finca La Central*, on the saddle between Irazú and Turrialba.

AL *Wagelia*, Av 4, Entrada de Turrialba, T556-1566, F556-1596, 18 rooms with bath, some **Sleeping** a/c, restaurant. **C** *Alcázar*,C 3, Av 2-4, 25 m north of *Banco Norte*, T393-0767, F556-7397. Small terrace upstairs, each rooms has cable TV, telephone, fan and a private bath with hot water. Small, cheap bar/restaurant downstairs with frightening colour schemes.

D *Hotel Turrialba*, Av 2, C 2-4, T556-6396. Clean simple rooms with private bath, hot water and TV. There are also a couple of pool tables and drinks for sale. **E** *Laroche*, north of Parque Central on C 1, T556-6915. Simple and basic rooms but friendly with comfortable beds. Small bar downstairs. **F** *Whittingham*, C 4, Av 0-2, T550-8927. 7 fairly dark but OK rooms, some with private bath – an option if other places are full.

In a row facing the old railway station are: from **F** per person *Interamericano*, Av 1, T556-0142, www.hotelinteramericano.com Very friendly place run by mother-daughter team, popular with kayakers. Clean private or share bath. Safe for motorbikes. Internet service, bar and communal area with TV and books. **F** *Chemanga*, the last resort, some rooms OK, some definitely not. **F** per person *Central*, T556-0170, with bath, restaurant, basic.

Out of town 14 km southeast of Turrialba, 2 km before La Suiza, 1 km from main road at Hacienda Atirro, is **LL** *Casa Turire*, T531-1111, F531-1075, www.hotelcasaturire.com, 12 luxury rooms with bath, 4 suites, cable TV, phone, restaurant, pool, library, games room, in the middle of a 1,620-ha sugar, coffee and macadamia nut plantation. Now lakeside with the arrival of Lake Angostura. Virgin rainforest nearby, trails, horses, bike rental, lots of excursions.

On road to Siquirres - Limón **C** *Turrialtico*, T556-1111, F556-1575, www.turrialtico.com, on top of hill with extensive views, clean, private bath, comfortable, friendly. Going northeast from Turrialba, the main road follows the Río Reventazón down to Siquirres (see page 1126). On this road is the town of Pavones with **D** *Albergue Mirador Pochotel*, T556-0111.

Restaurant Nuevo Hong Kong, good, reasonable prices. *Pizzería Julián*, on the square. **Eating** *Soda Burbuja*, one block south of square on C Central, local dishes, excellent portions, very good value. *La Garza*, on main square, cheap, local good food.

Out of town heading south, *Kingston*, T556-1613, is the locally celebrated restaurant.

Buses run from San José every hr 0530-2200 from Terminal Turrialba, C 13, Av 6-8, 1½ hrs, **Transport** US$1.20; from Cartago, 1 hr, US$0.60, runs until about 2200.

About 19 km north of Turrialba, near Guayabo, an Indian ceremonial centre has **Monumento** been excavated and there are clear signs of its paved streets and stone-lined water **Nacional** channels. The archaeological site, 232 ha and 4 km from the town of Guayabo, is **Guayabo** now a National Monument, and dates from the period 1000 BC-AD 1400. There are excellent walks in the park, plenty of birds and wildlife to be seen. ■ *Tue-Sun 0800-1500, US$6, local guide available, water, toilets, no food.*

Sleeping D *Albergue y Restaurant La Calzada*, T556-0465, best to make a reservation. **Transport** From Turrialba, there are buses at 1100 (returning 1250) and 1710 (returning 1750), and on Sun at 0900, return 1700 (check times, if you miss it is quite difficult to hitch as there is little traffic), US$0.45 to Guayabo. If you can't get a bus all the way to Guayabo, several buses each day pass the turn-off to Guayabo, the town is a 2-hr walk uphill (taxi US$10, easy to hitch back). **Tour operators** in San José offer day trips to Guayabo for about US$65 per person (minimum 4 people), cheaper from Turrialba.

Further north along this road (1½ hours' drive) is Santa Cruz, from which the Turrialba volcano can be reached (see above). Following the old railway down the

Costa Rica

valley, in 10 km you come to **Peralta**, formerly a station and now more of a ghost village with a couple of sleepy bars. The old station is derelict but is the start of an interesting walk east down the track, through two tunnels full of large bats and past one of the landslides that closed the line in 1991. You can eventually reach Laguna Bonilla where there are boats for hire. The walk and return takes four to five hours, requires good footwear and you may see tiny red and blue poison dart frogs. You may be able to buy cheese from one of the local farmers.

Central Northwest

The Cordillera de Tilarán and the Cordillera de Guanacaste stretch to the Nicaragua border. Tucked in the eastern foothills is the vast man-made Lago Arenal, resting calmly beneath the highly active Volcán Arenal. A number of quieter spots can be found in the area with fine opportunities for fishing and seeing the wildlife, while the more active can go rafting, windsurfing, horse-riding and trekking.

San Carlos
Colour map 7, grid B3

Also known as **Ciudad Quesada**, San Carlos is served by frequent bus and can be reached by a road which branches for 44 km off the highway near Naranjo. Situated on the northern slopes of the central highlands mountain region, the temperatures rises and the speed of life slows down. San Carlos is the main town of the northern lowland cattle and farming region and is a hub of communications. True to form, the town has a frontier feel with an air of bravado and a pinch of indifference.

In a town without major sights, the huge church overlooking the main plaza stands out. The cavernous interior is matched for style by modern stained-glass windows and an equally massive sculpture of Christ above the altar.

Sleeping and eating **C-D** *Don Goyo*, T460-1780. A baker's dozen of clean, well-lit rooms, with private bathrooms – the best value in town. **C-D** *La Central*, T460-0301, F460-0391, with private bath, hot water, TV and casino. **D** *El Retiro*, on the western side of the plaza, T460-0463, with bath, hot water, clean and comfortable, popular with local business people. Several basic *pensiones* around corner from *Banco Popular* on Av 1 C 2-4, all **F**, eg *Diana*, T460-3319, and *Fernando*, T460-3314, which is probably the best of the bunch if you can get one of the new rooms. Next to the new bus terminal, roughly 1 km north of town, is **F** *Cabinas Balneario San Carlos*, T460-6857, F460-2145. Part of a sports complex, cabinas with cooking facilities, overlooking an athletics track, and with good swimming pool. Good value, good for buses, but long way from town.

Restaurant Crystal, on the western side of the plaza, sells fast food, snacks, ice-cream and good fruit dishes. *Los Geridianos* is a hip bar and restaurant serving up mean *bocas* and other dishes. Next to *Hotel Central* is *Coco Loco Steak House*, complete with wild west swing door.

The new bus terminal is about 1 km north of town

Transport Direct bus from Terminal Atlántico Norte, San José, 2¼ hrs, hourly, from 0645-1815, US$2.20, return 0645-1815. From San Carlos buses go northwest to Tilarán via Fortuna and Arenal (0630 and 1400), other buses go to Fortuna through El Tanque (6 daily, 1½ hrs), San Rafael de Guatuso and Upala, north to Los Chiles (hourly, 3 hrs), northeast to towns on the Río San Carlos and Río Sarapiquí, including Puerto Viejo de Sarapiquí (5 a day, 3 hrs), and east to the Río Frío district.

Directory **Banks**: *Banco Nacional*, on Av Central west of the church. *Banco de Costa Rica*, on east side of plaza has ATMs. Others nearby. **Communication** **Internet**: Ask around or try *Café Internet*, Av 1, C Central-1, c350/hr, but irregular hours. **Post office**: on Av 5, C 2-4 with internet service.

Costa Rica

San Carlos to Los Chiles

From San Carlos a paved road runs northwest to **Florencia** (service station). At *Many visit Los Chiles* Platanar de San Carlos, at Hacienda Platanar, is **AL** *Hotel La Garza* (8 km from *on a day trip from* Florencia, T475-5222, F475-5015, www.hotel-lagarza-arenal.com), 12 charming *Fortuna – prices work* bungalows with bath and fan, overlooking river. Idyllic spot with good views of *out about the same* Arenal. Guided tours, boat trips, fishing, 230 ha of forest and cattle ranch. Con- *allowing for transport* tinuing north for 13 km to **Muelle San Carlos** is **L-AL** *Tilajari Resort Hotel*, T469-09091, F469-9095, www.tilajari.com, luxury rooms, and suites, a/c, private bath, tennis courts, two pools, sauna, bar and restaurant, horses. Excursions organized. Justifiably popular with luxury groups.

Heading through the northern lowlands, a good road carves through rich red laterite **Los Chiles** soils in an almost straight line for 74 km through flat land where the shiny leaves of *Colour map 7, grid B3* orange and citrus fruit plantations have replaced forest. Just short of the Nicaraguan border is Los Chiles, where boat trips head through dense, tropical vegetation into the 10,171 ha **Caño Negro Wildlife Refuge** and Caño Negro Lake. Bird-watchers flock to the northern wetlands to see the amazing variety of birdlife which feasts at the seasonal lake created by the floodwaters of the Río Frío. The lake slowly shrinks in the dry season (Jan-Apr). The variety of habitats in the refuge makes a rewarding trip for anyone interested in seeing alligators, turtles and monkeys. Fishing trips for snook and tarpon are easily arranged.

Los Chiles is a small town on the banks of the Río Frío, a few hundred metres west of Highway 35. The central plaza is also a football pitch, and most places of interest are within a block or two. The days pass slowly as children chuck themselves off the dockside in the heat of the afternoon sun.

Tours and excursions Ask about guides at *Restaurant Los Petates, Restaurant El Parque* or Rancho Eco-Directa. A 4-hr tour with Esteban, Oscar Rojas (T471-1414) and Enrique, who have all been recommended, costs about US$50.

Alternatively, *Aventuras Arenal* in Fortuna run trips to Caño Negro (see below) approximately US$35/40. It is cheaper to get a boat from Los Chiles to the Park (US$60 for a boat, up to 4 people) rather than taking a tour from elsewhere (ie Fortuna) and convenient if you are going on to Nicaragua, but there are not always boats available nor sufficient numbers to fill one economically. Call the park administration, T661-8464, F460-0644, or FPN in San José on T257-2239 (see page 1025), for reservations for food and lodging.

Fishing trips are likely to be beyond the budgets of many with a full day's fishing on the Río Frío and the Río San Juan for 2 (rods, drinks and boat included), working out at around US$350 – but then you could catch a 2-m-long tarpon.

Sleeping C *Rancho Eco-directa*, one block west of the central park opposite the immigration offices, T471-1197, new, good restaurant, 8 clean well-appointed rooms with bath and hot water. Can arrange a wide variety of tours in the area including river safaris, fishing trips and the manager Oscar Rojas is useful for information on travelling to Nicaragua.

A good choice is **E** *Cabinas Jaribú*, (**F** for Youth Hostel members), 100 m from the bus stop, a few blocks from the central park, T/F471-1055. Good but simple rooms with private bathrooms, fan, some with TV and parking. Postal service, internet, fax and laundry and a range of interesting tours. Cheapest to Caño Negro (US$20 per person, min 3) and to El Castillo de la Concepción in Nicaragua.

G *Carolina*, close to the main highway, T471-1151, small, fairly dark rooms but very clean and well-maintained – the best of the budgets. Of the strip facing the football pitch your best bet is **G** *Onassis*, T471-1001, southwest corner of main plaza, basic rooms, clean, fan if requested, shared bath.

Costa Rica

Eating *Restaurant El Parque* on the main plaza, with good home cooking. *Los Petates*, on road running south of the central park, has good food, cheap with large portions but check the bill. Supermarket *El Chileno* is unfriendly and overcharges.

Transport Bus Going into Costa Rica, there are direct buses to **San José** daily, 0500, 1500, 5 hrs, from San José Terminal Atlántico Norte to Los Chiles at 0530, 1530, alternatively take one of the hourly buses to **San Carlos** (Ciudad Quesada) from where there are good services. From **Fortuna**, take the bus to San Carlos, get off at Muelle and wait for a connection.

Directory Bank *Banco Nacional*, with ATM, on central park. **Communication** Postal and internet services provided by *Cabiñas Jabirú*.

Frontier with Nicaragua - Los Chiles
This crossing point is now open to foreigners but the road link is a dirt track, and San Carlos on the Nicaraguan side is remote from the rest of that country.

Costa Rican immigration All formalities are in Los Chiles which is a few kilometres short of the border. The office is close to the river and leaving procedures are normally straightforward. Open 0800-1600, usually closed for lunch. If entering Costa Rica, officials can be more difficult, mainly because they are sensitive about the many Nicaraguan immigrants wishing to enter the country. Crossing purely overland is possible. It is some 4 km to the border post, and a total of 14 km to San Carlos with no regular transport.

Transport Boat A regular launch goes down the Río Frío across the Río San Juan to San Carlos, 0800 or when full, 45 mins, US$5. There are other launches if demand is sufficient. You can follow the track north to the San Juan River and then find a ferry to cross, but enquire before trying this route.

See under **Nicaragua – San Carlos** and **San Juan del Norte/Greytown** for details on the Río San Juan border.

Fortuna

Colour map 7, grid B3
Population: 7,658
Altitude: 254 m

The small town of Fortuna, is an ideal base for exploring the Arenal region with the ominous silhouette of the highly active Volcán Arenal looming above the town. Reached on a paved road running west from Florencia or along the northern shore of Lake Arenal it's worth a few days of your travels.

Once a quiet town that shuddered in the shadow of the volcano's power, Fortuna has grown to accommodate the regular influx of visitors keen to see the active volcano. While the numbers have grown, the quiet feel has not quite disappeared. The place is busy with visitors and coach parties in the day but, with so many activities in the area, most get tired by the day's events and the streets are often pretty empty by around 2100.

Sleeping
Generous discounts in the green/low season are common

Town centre: **A** *Luigi's Lodge*, a couple of blocks west of the church, T479-9636, F479-9898, www.luigislodge.com 20 comfortable rooms with private bath, tub, hot water and coffee machine, small balconies overlooking a pool and with good views of the volcano; email service for guests. **A-B** *San Bosco*, T479-9050, F479-9109, www.arenal-volcano.com, all rooms with private bath, quiet, signs on main road, clean, friendly, nice gardens with terrace, pool and view of the volcano, excellent service and attention to detail, slighty less without a/c. **B** *Cabinas Guacamaya*, T479-9393, F479-9087, www.cabinasguacamaya.com 10 good-sized rooms sleeping 3 or 4, all with private bath and hot water, fridge and a/c. Clean and tidy, with plenty of parking.

C *Cabinas Monte Real*, 1 block west and south of the main plaza, T/F479-9243. Close to the centre, quiet and friendly, big rooms with private bath and hot water, next to the river and also close to centre. Parking. **C** *Las Colinas*, at the southeastern corner of the central park, T/F479-9305, hcolinas@racsa.co.cr 20 tidy rooms, with private bathroom, some with excellent views. Friendly management, good discounts in the low season. Recommended. **D** *Cabinas*

Costa Rica

Herri, south of church on road to the river, T479-9430, bright rooms, private bath with hot water, a/c or fan. Balcony with view of the church, good discounts in the green season. **D** *Cabinas La Amistad*, T479-9364, clean, friendly, hot water, hard beds. **D** *Fortuna*, one block southeast of the central park, T479-9197, simple rooms, but very clean. Price includes breakfast **E** *Cabinas Carmela*, on the south side of the church, T/F479-9010, www.hostelling-costarica.com 12 rooms with private bath, floor and ceiling fans, some with fridge. Very central, hot showers, can arrange tours, discount for youth hostel members. Apartment sleeping 5 available **E** per person. **F** *Cabinas Manuel*, south of the church on road to the river, T479-9079, basic wall-panelled rather dark rooms in a family home. **F** *Burio B&B*, down small driveway next to *Canopy Tours*, T479-9454. Shoddy rooms, but clean, with hot water in shared bathrooms. **F-G** per person *Sissy*, office is 100 m south and 100 m west of church, T479-9256. Quiet spot beside the river, basic rooms with private bathroom; others have shared bath, and there's access to a kitchen and camping spaces (US$2 per person); simple but friendly.

G per person *La Posada Inn*, a couple of blocks east of the parque central, T479-9793. 4 simple, but spotless rooms, shared bath with hot water, fan but mosquitoes reported. Small communal area out front, and the friendly owner Thadeo is very helpful.

West of town towards the volcano In the order you meet them heading out of town: **C** *Hotel Arenal Rossi*, T479-9023, F477-9414, cabrossi@racsa.co.cr, 1 km towards the volcano, with breakfast, friendly owner, hot water, fan, watch the volcano from the garden, horses rented, good value. 2 km on road towards the volcano is **C** *Cabinas Las Flores*, T479-9307, F479-8042. Clean, basic but a little overpriced. **A** *Albergue Ecoturístico La Catarata*, 2 km from town, rough road, T479-9522, F479-9168, www.agroecoturismo.net Reservations essential for these 8 cabins in co-operative with organic garden, homemade soaps and shampoos, good fresh food, butterfly farm, taxi US$2, hot water, laundry, all meals. Run by community association and supported by WWF Canada and CIDA Canada.

East of town In order are **B** *Cabinas Villa Fortuna*, 500 m south of the bridge, 1 km from the central plaza, T/F479-9139. 10 bright and tidy cabins, with neat bathrooms, fans or a/c, nice pool and simple gardens. 500 m beyond is **A** *Las Cabañitas*, T479-9400, F479-9408, www.cabanita.com 30 cabins with private baths, a couple of pools, observatory for viewing Arenal volcano, restaurant. Recommended.

Costa Rica

Fortuna

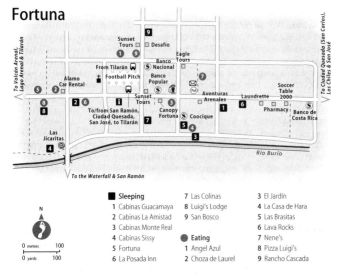

Sleeping	7 Las Colinas	3 El Jardín
1 Cabinas Guacamaya	8 Luigi's Lodge	4 La Casa de Hara
2 Cabinas La Amistad	9 San Bosco	5 Las Brasitas
3 Cabinas Monte Real	**Eating**	6 Lava Rocks
4 Cabinas Sissy	1 Angel Azul	7 Nene's
5 Fortuna	2 Choza de Laurel	8 Pizza Luigi's
6 La Posada Inn		9 Rancho Cascada

South of town **AL** *Arenal Country Inn*, T479-9670, F479-9433, www.costaricainn.com A former working hacienda with 20 large, fully equipped cabinas set in pleasant tropical gardens. After eating in the dining-room – once a holding pen – you can rest by the pool before heading out to explore.

Eating *Angel Azul*, north side of central park, good, cheap vegetarian food. Open all day. *Choza de Laurel*, west of the church, T479-9231, typical food in a rustic setting, serving breakfast, lunch and dinner, US$2-US$4.50, ocassionally greeted by passing hummingbirds. *El Jardín*, on the main street opposite the gas station, good menu with a mix of local and fast food, *menú del día* US$2.25, good place to watch the world go by. *La Casa de Hara*, round the side of Hotel Fortuna, very good local food, fast service and normal prices – where the locals eat. *La Fortuna*, open-air restaurant serving good, simple food, quiet spot but nothing special. *Las Brasitas*, open air restaurant serving pizzas, pastas with a laid-back European-café style. *Las Jicaritas*, near bridge, nice setting, internet service. *Lava Rocks*, south side of the church, smooth open-air café restaurant serving excellent coffee, good food with chilled music. Travel agency on site for any questions. Definitely worth a visit. *Nene's*, good food, pleasant service, not expensive. Recommended. *Pizza Luigi's*, forma, mid-rangel open-air restaurant with distinctly Italian pretentions toward pizza and pasta. Good wine list for Fortuna. *Rancho Cascada*, on corner of Parque with high conical thatched roof, mid-range with good *bocas*, films shown in evenings.

West of town towards the volcano just 500 m or so are: *La Vaca Muca*, a bit out of the village on the way to Tabacón. Public phone with international access. *Nene*, good food, pleasant service, not expensive. *Steakhouse Arenal* next to *Hotel Las Flores*, mid-priced steak house with Texan tendencies. *Vagabondo* reasonably priced pizza and pasta.

Entertainment There are a couple of bars in town if you want a drink. Also seek out *Soccer Table 2000*, table soccer like you've never seen it. 0700-2100 daily.

Transport **Buses** There are daily buses at 0615, 0840, 1130, from Terminal Atlántico Norte, San José, 4½ hrs, via San Carlos, US$2.50, return at 1245, 1445; 6 buses a day from San Carlos, 1 hr, US$1, 4 different routes. 2 buses a day to Tilarán, 0800 (connecting to 1230 bus Tilarán-Santa Elena/Monteverde and 1300 bus Tilarán-Puntarenas) and 1700, US$2.90, 4 hrs. Subject to demand, there are direct minibuses to Monteverde and Tamarindo (US$25 per person, min 6). **Taxis** in the area overcharge. Agree on price before travelling. **Car hire** Alamo, T479-9722, have an office in town.

Directory **Banks** *Banco Nacional de Costa Rica* will change TCs, US$1 commission, ATM. *Banco Popular*, Visa ATM. *Coocique*, open Sat mornings 0800-1200, Visa ATM. **Communication** **Internet**: Prices in Fortuna are generally prohibitive and connections are poor. If desperate ask round town for the best current operator (*Los Jicaratas* US$3/hr), or ask at post office (punta.com). **Post office** down main street, shares building with the police so don't try a hold-up. **Laundry** *Lavandería La Fortuna*, 0800-2100, Mon-Sat, US$5 wash and dry 4 kg. **Medical services** *Farmacía Dr Max*, east down the main street, 0730-2030, Mon-Sat, 0800-1200 Sun. **Tour operators** *Aventuras Arenal*, on the main street, T479-9133, F479-9295, www.arenaladventures.com, provides all tours in the area, and has been around for many years. Can help with enquiries about other parts of Costa Rica. *Canopy Tour*, east down the main street, T/F479-9769, www.canopyfortuna.com, offer a short horseback journey from Fortuna, US$45, as well as quad tours, mountain bike rental and general tours. *Desafío*, just off main square by thatched restaurant, T/F479-9464, www.desafiocostarica.com Full range of tours, and with office in Monteverde. *Eagle Tours*, 1 block east of the park, T/F479-9091, aguilas@racsa.co.cr Helpful, with usual tours. *Sunset Tours*, behind Rancho Casado and on eastern corner of the central park, T479-9415, F479-9099, www.sunset-tours.com Reliable, long-standing company with a selection of tours. Recommended.

Excursions About 6 km south of Fortuna are the impressive **Río Fortuna Waterfalls,** plunging 70 m into the cloud of swirling mist and spray. It's a pleasant walk down the road for a couple of kilometres before heading uphill through yucca and papaya plantations. From the entrance a steep and slippery path leads to the falls so take shoes with a good tread. Admission US$3, drinks available at the entrance. Bathing is possible, so take swimming clothes, but safer 50 m downstream. If you don't want to walk there are several options. You can drive, but four-wheel drive is necessary. Bicycle hire (US$3 per hour, US$15 per day) is one option and hard work, or you can hire a horse for the day at around US$35. Two to three hours' climb above the falls is the crater lake of **Cerro Chato**. The top (1,100 m) is reached through mixed tropical/cloud forest, with a good view (if you're lucky) but beware of snakes on the path. A guide, if you need one, will charge US$9.

Safari river floats down the Río Peñas Blancas (US$40) and **whitewater rafting**, best in the wet season, (from US$69 for a one-day trip including all food and transport) is available through several tour operators.

Horse-riding through the forest to **Monteverde** costs around US$65 per person for the day trip. Luggage is taken on pack animals or by vehicles. Some operators seem to change the route once underway due to some 'unforeseen problem', so agree the route and try to arrange compensation if there are major changes. Due to competition for business, many horses are overworked on this route. Although difficult when on a budget, try not to bargain down the price, and ask to see the horses before beginning the journey. The journey is also possible by jeep-boat-jeep (US$30-35).

A small **snake farm** with 40 specimens, is a couple of kilometres west of Fortuna is a good opportunity to get up close and personal with these rather cool creatures. ■ *US$2*.

Thermal baths   Almost 5 km north of Fortuna is the **Baldi Thermae** complex, with four thermal pools ranging from 37° up to 63°C – the limits of endurance without departing poached. Poolside drinks, looks good, feels great. ■ *Open daily, 1000-2200. US$9. Taxi from town US$2, bus US$1.* 10 km northwest of Fortuna is **L** *Balneario Tabacón*, a kitcsh complex of thermal pools, waterfalls and (for residents) beauty treatments, with three bars and a restaurant. The water is hot and stimulating; there are a number of pools at descending heights and temperatures and there are waterslides and a waterfall to sit under. The food is good and the fruit drinks thirst quenching. ■ *1000-2200 daily. Day guests are welcome. Entry US$17, cheaper after 1800 (US$13). The resort is very popular with evening coach tours from San José. Taxi from Fortuna to Tabacón US$4.50.* There are cheaper hot springs across the road for US$6. Cheaper still are the hot waters about 4 km further along the road at Quebrada Cedeña, clean and safe, no sign but look for local parked cars.

Tour operators offer trips to view the volcano at night followed by a visit to the thermal baths; a typical four-hour tour, costing US$25 per person, leaves Fortuna at about 1815 and returns by 2200. Make sure the entry fee to the baths is included in the tour price.

Also near Fortuna are the limestone **Cavernas del Venado**. Tours from Fortuna with all necessary equipment, US$20. Buses from San Carlos en route to Tilarán daily, return transport to Fortuna at 2200.

Volcán Arenal

Skirting the slopes of the 1,633-m Volcán Arenal, the road travels north around the base to the man-made **Lago Arenal** and hydroelectric dam. The highly active volcano is beautiful, a classic Stromboli-type cone shape characterized by explosions sending out hot grey clouds of sulphurous gases which can descend the slopes at alarming speeds. The lava streams have moved from the west side to the northeast following activity in recent years. Although the side facing Fortuna is green, the side facing the lake is grey and barren, and the lava flows are clearly visible. There are three active craters and several fumaroles, with activity particularly impressive at night, as the red hot lava crashes, smashes and tumbles down the hillside accompanied by rumbles and intermittent roars (rather like someone moving furniture upstairs). The activity is fuelled by a magma chamber that vulcanologists believe is just 5 km below the surface.

Colour map 7, grid B3

Some say there is greater volcanic activity around full moon

Costa Rica

On no account walk up the volcano beyond the level of the vegetation – it's dangerous. However, there is good hiking on the lower slopes from Fortuna Take a flashlight if you plan to stay after dark

Arenal has been continuously active since July 1968, when an eruption killed 78 people and more or less destroyed three villages including Tabacón which is situated above the *balneario*. The most recent continuous major activity was in May 1998, but in August 2000 a small group travelled beyond the permitted area, were engulfed by a pyroclastic avalanche and the guide later died of third degree burns.

If you are visiting between May and December you may not see much as the volcano is usually obscured by clouds and rain and there can be bad weather for weeks on end. Clouds and rain are common in the afternoons all year round, but the clouds do break and you may be lucky. If you can hire a taxi for a trip at about 0400-0500 – and you can get up – the sky is often clearer.

To the east, the vast **Lago Arenal** reflects the moods of the volcano perfectly: smooth and calm from a distance, but whipped up to a waved frenzy by strong easterlies which are squeezed by the hills on either side. The surrounding area offers a multitude of opportunities for hiking, mountain biking, windsurfing and many other activities. There is also access to Santa Elena and Monteverde on foot or horseback.

Park information

Much of the area surrounding the volcano is a national park which most people visit as part of a tour. The most common entrance is through *Hotel Los Lagos* (see below), costing US$25 including a trip to *Baldi Thermae* baths. Following the eruption in 2000, the area was closed until considered safe again; if it has not reopened, tours will be developed to view lava flows from another point. Alternatively *Aventuras Arenal* will provide dependable advice.

You can also visit the park on your own. The entrance is on the western flank of the volcano, on the other side to Fortuna, 2 km down a bumpy road signposted to Arenal Observatory Lodge. 4 interesting trails, taking up to 1½ hrs each, lead through the national park going through a mixture of terrains, that flourish in the micro-climate of heavy rainfall bought on by the volcano.

Sleeping

Fortuna is the easiest place to stay if you don't have your own transport (see page 1062), but the whole area from Fortuna all along the shores of the lake is littered with hotels and eating options, each taking advantage of superb views and relative seclusion

C *Los Lagos*, T479-8000, F479-8009, 8 cabins with volcano view, 8 tents, sleep 4, **C**, camping areas, day visits US$2.75, excellent food and spectacular views of the volcano over the lake with a campsite US$2.75 per night, with good facilities and small café. There are 3 marked footpaths towards the lava fields and lakes through the forest. About 4 km from Fortuna on the road to Lake Arenal, turn at sign on left side of the road 'Bienvenidos a Junglas y Senderos Los Lagos'. Site is 2 km uphill, very steep, good facilities, **F** per person, tours to hot springs at night. This is one of the best places to watch the volcanic activity at night. There is a small campsite just before the park entrance with hook-ups for vehicles, US$2.50 per person. Great views of the volcano and a good spot for walking. Camping is also possible on edge of lake, no services but good view of volcano at night.

Heading west around the volcano several luxury hotels line the road including: **AL** *Volcano Lodge*, 6 km from Fortuna, T460-6080, F460-6020, volcanolodge@racsa.co.cr, with excellent open-air restaurant good for viewing the volcano, **A** *Cabañas Arenal Paraíso*, 7.5 km from Fortuna, T/F479-9006, 12 nice houses with bath, fridge and nice terrace views of the volcano. **L-AL** *Montaña de Fuego*, T460-7340, F460-7338, www.montanadefuego.com, 52 bungalows and rooms, with the stylish (and pricey) *Acuarelas* restaurant.

Hotels on the southern side of the lake are slightly cut off but have fantastic views

On the northwestern side of the volcano, 4 km after El Tabacón, a turn towards the lake follows a (signposted) gravel road which leads eventually to the **AL-B** *Arenal Observatory Lodge*, T695-5033, F257-4220, www.arenal-observatory.co.cr, 4-wheel drive recommended along this 9-km stretch (taxi-jeep from Fortuna, US$12). Set up in 1973, the observatory was purely a research station but it now has 42 rooms varying from cabins with bunk beds and bath, to newer rooms with queen-size beds. The service is excellent and there are stunning views of the volcano (which is frighteningly close), Lake Arenal, and across the valley of Río Agua Caliente. The lava flows on the other side of the volcano, but the trails are beautiful and the service excellent.

On the gravel road, taking the right fork *not* to the *Observatory* leads to **AL-A** *Linda Vista del Norte Lodge*, near *Arenal Vista Lodge*, T380-0847, F479-9443, www.lindavistadelnorte.

com, nice views, several good, unspoilt trails in the area, horse-riding tours, hot water. Recommended. **AL** *Arenal Vista Lodge*, T221-0965, F221-6230, 25 rooms with bath, arranges boat trips, riding and hiking.

North to Upala

A quiet route north leads from Fortuna to **San Rafael de Guatuso**. There is a 'voluntary' toll of US$1 between Jicarito and San Rafael for reconstruction work on this road. You can come back to the lake either by turning off before San Rafael through Venado (where there are caves), or from San Rafael itself, where there are a couple of basic hotels.

Three kilometres from Colonia Río Celeste near San Rafael de Guatuso is the **B** *Magil Forest Lodge*, set in 240 ha on the foothills of the 1,916-m **Volcán Tenorio** (now a national park of 12,871 ha with thermal waters, boiling mud and unspoilt forest). 10 rooms with private bath, price includes meals. If you continue along the road from San Rafael northwest towards the Nicaraguan border you come to **Upala** (airport, but no scheduled flights with *Sansa*) and a poor road east to Caño Negro. There is a direct bus from San José to Upala (from Av 3-5, C 10 at 1445, four hours), where there is **F** *Pensión Buena Vista*, basic, food available.

The San Rafael-Arenal road joins the lakeside road just north of Arenal town; no signs if driving from Arenal to San Rafael, it is just a track. If you turn left about 4 km out of San Rafael before the river, four-wheel drive necessary, you come to the Guatuso Indian villages of Tonjibe, Margarita and El Sol.

Fortuna to Tilarán (towards Monteverde)

A mostly paved road twists and winds round the northern shore of Lake Arenal, leading to Tilarán via Nuevo Arenal. Whether travelling by bus or car, you can get from Fortuna to Monteverde via Tilarán in a day, but set out early to make your connection with the 1230 bus in Tilarán or to avoid driving after dark. The lakeside road has improved greatly in recent years, but some sections are still unpaved. The main hazard is the winding road and some seriously pot-holed sections.

There is plenty of good accommodation around the lake shore, much of it in the higher price brackets. With only a couple of buses a day, and limited traffic, getting off the bus for a look will almost certainly delay you for a day.

If you do stop, an excellent café for a meal and drink with great views over the lake is *Toad Hall*, towards the northeastern end, which has an excellent souvenir shop with a good mix of Costa Rican crafts, some modern, some traditional, most desirable.

Around Lago Arenal

Arenal Botanical and Butterfly Gardens, 4 km east of Arenal town is a delightful place (still under development), with many flowers, birds and butterflies. ■ *0900-1600 (closed Oct), US$8. T694-4273.* **L-AL** *Villa Decary*, T383-3012 (mob), www.villadecary.com, has beautiful gardens and ethnic influences from all over Central America.

Sleeping Travelling round the lake from Fortuna. Just north of the dam wall up 2½ km steep road is **L-AL** *Arenal Lodge*, T/F383-3957, www.arenallodge.com Stunning views to the north and south. Rooms, suites, meal extra in excellent restaurant. Next is **A** *Hotel Los Héroes (Pequeña Helvecia)*, 10 km from Arenal towards Tilarán, T/F384-6315, heroes@racsa.co.cr Delightful Swiss owners with inspiring energy and a superb hotel, complete with Swiss train service. *Toad Hall*, café, restaurant and gift shop is followed shortly by **AL** *La Mansión Marina and Club*, T384-6573, www.lamansionarenal.com, on the lake, beautiful pool, very relaxing. A little further west is **C** *La Alondra*, T384-5575, with simple basic rooms sleeping up to 4. Nearby is the wonderfully underrated cheap, simple and tasty *Sabor Italiano* restaurant, serving pasta and pizza and fabulous Argentine-style *parrillada* grills. 6 km from Arenal is **A** *La Ceiba*, T385-1540, F694-4297, www.bbb.co.cr/ceiba, overlooking Lake Arenal, *Tico*-owned and run, good, helpful, great panoramic views, good breakfast.

Costa Rica

(Nuevo) Arenal With a head count of just over 2,500, Arenal is a small town with not much to see. The town is new, because it moved from its original location which now lies deep below the surface of the lake.

Sleeping and eating A little out of town is **AL** *Joya Sureña*, T694-4057, F694-4059, joysur@racsa.co.cr 28 big rooms on a former working cattle farm with a gym, sauna and pool. Options for horse-riding and fishing. **A-B** *Arenal Inn*, is a smarter option, with lake views from the rooms. Visa and MasterCard accepted. Overpriced but central. **A** *Aurora Inn B&B*, T694-4245, F694-4262, www.hotelaurorainn.com, with private bath, pool and jacuzzi overlooking Lake Arenal. Breakfast included. **E** per person *Cabinas Rodríiguez*, basic but clean, with private bath and hot water, cheapest in town.

Pizzería e Ristorante Tramonte, for Italian cuisine, excellent food and very friendly. *Típico Arenal*, T694-4159, good local dishes with seafood and vegetarian options. Large room upstairs (**C**) with private bath and hot water. The best cheap place in town.

Sport Fishing: several places rent fishing tackle, but if you want a boat, guide and full package try *Rainbow Bass Fishing Safaris*, run by Dave Myers, US$200 a day for 2 anglers, fishing licence US$30 for 2 months, PO Box 7758-1000, San José, T229-2550, F235-7662.

Directory *Banco Nacional* beside the football pitch.

Continuing west towards Tilarán, the western side of the lake is popular with windsurfers throughout the year, and between December and April the conditions are world class. A small pocket of hotels cater for windsurfers of all levels; there are many other options in the area so take your pick if you want to stop.

Sleeping **A** *Chalet Nicholas*, T/F694-4041, membersaol.com/ceiliam/chaletnicholas.html, bed and breakfast (a speciality), run by retired Americans, hot water, non-smokers only, friendly. Recommended. If passing through the area the best restaurant for miles is *Willy's Caballo Negro*, T694-4515, serving vegetarian, Swiss and seasonal fish dishes with organic salads. Warm family atmosphere, reasonably priced, but no credit cards.

A *Rock River Lodge*, on the road skirting the lake, T/F695-5644, www.rokriverlodge.com, 6 rooms and bungalows, with bathroom, good restaurant. Excellent activity spot with day options for surfing (US$35) and fishing (US$55) and good mountain biking. Just 8 km north of Tilarán is the **AL** *Hotel Tilawa*, T695-5050, F695-5766, www.tilawa-hotel.com, with great rooms, and excellent opportunities for wind surfing, bird-watching. Equipment for rent for US$55 a day. Guaranteed beginner lesson – if it's not fun it's free, try not to laugh and you've got a good deal. Good discounts off season.

Tilarán It is fair to say that few would visit Tilarán if it were not the transport hub for people
Colour map 7, grid B2 journeying between Fortuna, Santa Elena/Monteverde and Cañas on the Pan-American Highway.

Sleeping **B** *Naralit*, on the south side of the church, T695-5393, clean, new buildings. **C-D** *Hotel Guadalupe*, a block south and east of the church, T695-5943. 25 nice rooms with bath, hot water and cable TV. Recommended. **D** *Cabiñas El Sueño*, one block north of bus terminal/central park, T695-5347. Clean rooms around central patio, hot water, fan, TV, friendly and free coffee. Good deal. **D** *Hotel Restaurant Mary*, south side of church, T695-5479, with bath, small pleasant rooms upstairs recommended. **E** *Central*, round the back of the church, 1 block south, T695-5363, with shared bath (more with own bath), noisy.

Eating *Stefanie's* out of the bus station to the left on the corner of the main plaza is good and quick if you need a meal between buses. There is also *Restaurant Hotel Mary* which does a steady trade. *Restaurant La Carreta*, round the back of the church, is the place to go and relax if you have time to kill. Excellent pancakes, coffee and good local information.

Transport Buses Direct bus from **San José**, 4 daily, 4 hrs, from Terminal Atlántico Norte. 2 daily buses to **San Carlos** via Fortuna at 0700 and 1230. To Fortuna, 3 hrs, US$2.00. Daily bus to **Santa Elena** (for Monteverde), 1230, 2½ hrs, US$1.65, return 0700 daily. Tilarán-Puntarenas 0600, 1300, 3 hrs, US$3. 5 daily buses to/from Cañas (to at 0500, 0730, 1000, 1230 and 1530, 40 mins, US$1.25), where buses head north and south along the Pan-American. If you get the 1230 Tilarán-Liberia bus you can get from there to the Nicaraguan border before it closes.

If heading for Santa Elena and Monteverde see page 1071

Directory Banks *Banco Cootilaran*, a couple of blocks north of the Parque Central, has a Visa and MasterCard ATM, and there is also a *Banco de Costa Rica* in town.

Northwest

The route of the Pan-American Highway heads north passing near the world-renowned Monteverde Cloud Forest in the Cordillera de Tilarán, the marshes of the Parque Nacional Palo Verde, the active Volcán Rincón and the dry tropical forest of the Parque Nacional Santa Rosa on the Pacific coast, as it crosses the great cattle haciendas of Guanacaste before reaching the Nicaraguan border.

The Pan-American Highway from San José descends from the Meseta Central to **Esparza**, an attractive town with a turbulent early history, as it was repeatedly sacked by pirates in the 17th century, belying its peaceful nature today. **Sleeping E** *Hotel Castanuelas*, close to the highway, T635-5105, a/c, quiet, cooler alternative to Puntarenas. **F** per person *Pensión Córdoba*, clean and modern.

The stretch of the Highway between San Ramón and Esparza (31 km) includes the sharp fall of 800 m from the Meseta Central, often shrouded in mist and fog making conditions treacherous for road users. Beyond Esparza is the *Bar/Restaurant Mirador Enis*, a popular stopping place for tour buses breaking the journey at a service station with fruit stalls nearby, before a left turn at **Barranca** for Puntarenas, 15 km. In Barranca is the **D** *Hotel Río Mar*, with bath, restaurant, good. If going from San José to Monteverde it is possible to change buses in Barranca, rather than going all the way to Puntarenas, if you leave the capital before 1230.

Costa Rica

Puntarenas

Puntarenas fills a 5-km spit, thrusting out into the Gulf of Nicoya, east to west, but no wider than six *avenidas*. Although popular with locals, most visitors pass through, using it as a transport hub with links to the southern Nicoya Peninsula or to get a bus north or south to other parts of the country without returning to San José. If heading for Nicoya, see page 1094. If heading to Santa Elena/Monteverde see Transport below, and page 1074. It is also the Pacific destination, docking at Muelle de Cruceros on the Calle Central, for the bright white, cruise palaces that float through the Central American ports.

Colour map 7, grid B3
Population: 22,009
Mean temperature: 27°C

Watch your bags on the beach

Once the country's main Pacific port with rail links to the Central Highlands, it has since been superseded by Caldera a short distance to the south. The northern side of the peninsula, around Calle Central with the market, banks, a few hotels and the fishing docks, is run down and neglected, typical of small tropical ports. The southern side is made up of the **Paseo de los Turistas**, drawing crowds to the hot, sometimes dirty beach, especially at weekends. There are several hotels along the strip, as well as restaurants, bars and a general seafront beach atmostphere. There is a public swimming pool at the western end of the point (US$1 entrance), close to the ferries, and good surfing off the headland. There is a **Museo de la Historia Marina** in the Cultural Centre by the main church and tourist office. ■ *Mon-Fri 0830-1200, 1300-1630 daily, US$1.80.* Across the gulf are the hills of the Nicoya Peninsula. In the gulf are several islands including the Islas Negritas, a biological reserve reached by passenger launches.

There is talk of plans for a face-lift which would be a huge task, and long overdue. But the neglect may be to the town's eventual benefit. Overlooked and forgotten, a few charming architectural treasures and folly nightmares remain standing to the north of the peninsula.

Excursions

For crossing to Nicoya Peninsula see transport below and page 1085

Isla San Lucas, once a prison island with underground cells, is now a luxury resort. Launches leave Puntarenas on Sundays at 0900 and return at 1500, US$1.50, or can visit as part of an organized tour from San José. **Isla Jesuita**, in the Gulf of Nicoya, is home to the *Hotel Isla Jesuita*, lodge and cottages, reached by the hotel's boat or public launch from Puntarenas. Package rates are available from San José, or arrangements can be made in the USA, T800-327 9408.

Sleeping

Accommodation is difficult to find from December-April, especially at weekends

AL-A *Tioga*, on the beach front with C 17, T661-0271, F661-0127, www.hoteltioga.com 46 rooms, those with balconies are much better with good views. All with private bath, a/c, TV and telephone. Restaurant, swimming pool, casino, very good. **B-C** *Las Hamacas* on beach front between C 5-7, T661-0398. Rooms are OK, but noisy when the bar is in full flow. Small pool and gym. Could do with a lick of paint; for now overpriced.

C *Cayuga*, C 4, Av Central-1, T661-0344. 31 rooms with private bathroom, a/c, pretty dark rooms. There is a small garden patio but it's hardly paradise. **C** *Gran Imperial*, on the beach front, in front of the Muelle de Cruceros, T661-0579. Pleasant rooms, although a little dark, but clean with private bath and fan. Small garden patio, and a very chilled atmosphere. Good spot and handy for buses. **C** *La Punta*, Av 1, C 35, T661-0696, good spot 1 block from car ferry, with bath, friendly, clean, hot water, restaurant, secure parking, good pool, American-owned, big rooms. Recommended. **C** *Michael's Hotel*, on the waterfront on the corner with C 29, T661-4646. Half a dozen tidy rooms, with private bathroom, fan and TV. Small pool, with bar and snacks. Nothing special but friendly and nice quiet spot, parking. **C-D** *Gran Hotel Chorotega*, on the corner of C 1, Av 3 near the banks and market, T661-0998. Clean rooms with private bath, cheaper with shared. Efficient and friendly service. Popular with visiting business people. A good deal.

D *Cabezas*, Av 1, C 2-4, T661-1045, 23 rooms, some with private bath, cheaper without. Simple rooms with no frills but bright and clean. Good deal. **D** *Río*, Av 3, C Central-2 near market, T661-0331. Private bath, fans, good rooms. Friendly Chinese owners keen to help, lively, sometimes noisy but popular place. **G** *Monte Mar*, Av 3, C 1-3, T661-2731. Very basic, some rooms with fan, but bearable on a budget.

At **Roble**, 10 km east of Puntarenas, on the coast **B** *Villa del Roble*, by the sea, T663-0447, F255-3234, has 5 rooms, quiet, small pool, charming. **B** *Casa San Francisco*, T663-0148, near regional hospital, run by 2 Canadian women, with breakfast, pool, clean, laundry facilities, friendly and helpful. Recommended. *María Vargas*, bar and restaurant, friendly, good food, reasonable prices.

Eating

There are many bars and a couple of discos along the Paseo de los Turistas

Take a walk along the Paseo de los Turistas and take whatever your pick. Alternatively *Aloha*, on the seafront on C 17, is worth checking out. *Casa de Mariscos*, C 7-9 on the beach front, good seafood, reasonable prices. *Jardín Cervecero Bierstube*, on the seafront at C23-25, is good for sandwiches, hamburgers and a beer. *Kayte Negro*, north side of the peninsula on Av Badillo, C 17, good local food. *Mariscos Kahite Blanco*, next door, near launch, excellent and locally renowned seafood. *Soda Brisas del Mar*, on C Central, Av 2-4, is good for a snack. *Soda Macarena*, opposite the Muelle de Cruceros, is also handy while waiting for buses. *La Yunta*, on the beachfront at C 19, is a popular steak house. A number of Chinese restaurants on Av Central and C 1 (eg *Mandarín*, good value) and there is good, cheap food from market stalls, eg *sopa de carne*.

Festivals

On the Sat closest to the **16 Jul**, *Fiesta de la Virgen del Mar*, with a week of festivities leading to a carnival and regatta of decorated fishing boats and yachts.

Transport

Buses Bus terminal for San José is at C 2, Av 2-4, . Buses every 40 mins 0415-1900 to **San José**, 2 hrs, US$2.50. Buses from San José leave from Terminal Puntarenas C 16, Av 10-12, 0600-1900. Daily bus to **Santa Elena** for Monteverde, 1315 and occasionally at 1415, see page 1072. Buses south to **Quepos** from main bus station, 0500, 1100 and 1430 (high season) via Jacó, US$2.70, 4 hrs, return 0430, 1030, 1630. To Liberia with *Empresa Arata*, 5 a day, first at 0530, last 1500, 2½ hrs, US$1.50. To Tilarán via Cañas at 1130 and 1630. Good café at bus terminal where you can wait for your bus.

Ferries To southern Nicoya Peninsula from the dock at C 35. To Playa Naranjo at 0315, 0700, 1050, 1450 and 1900, returning at 0510, 0850, 1250, 1700 and 2100, 1½ hrs. T661-1069 for exact times. Pedestrians US$1.60, motorbikes US$3, cars US$12. The ferry dock is about 1 km from Puntarenas bus station, local buses run between the two, else walk or get a taxi. Buses meet the ferry for Nicoya (through Carmona, 40 km unpaved, 30 km paved road, crowded, noisy, frequently break down, US$1.25, 21/4 hrs), Sámara (US$1.30), Coyote, Bejuco and Jicaral. *Check which dock your ferry leaves from*

From the same dock a car ferry goes to Paquera at 0845, 1400, 2015, returning at 0600, 1115 and 1800, 1½ hrs. On arrival, get on the bus (which waits for the ferry) as quickly as possible (to Cóbano, 2-3 hrs, US$1.25, bad road, to Montezuma US$2.60, 1½ hrs at least), pay on the bus, or get a taxi. *Hotel Playa Tambor* (see page 1094) also runs a car ferry to **Paquera** at 0500, 1230, 1700, leaving Paquera 0800, 1430 and 2030. A bus to Tambor will be waiting at Paquera on your arrival.

Launch Paquera-Puntarenas leaves from behind the central market, directly north of the bus stop at 0600, 1100 and 1515, returning at 0730, 1230 and 1700. Pedestrians US$1.50, motorbikes US$1.80, T661-2830. Tickets are sold when the incoming boat has docked.

Banks *Banco Nacional* and *Banco de Costa Rica*, on Av 3, C 1-3 near the Central Market, changes TCs, and with ATM. . **Communications** Internet: *Millennium Cyber Café*, on the beach front with C 15, only one in town so popular, 1000-2200, c800 per hr. Free coffee if you're lucky. **Post office**: Av 3, C Central-1, close to Central Market. **Telephone**: ICE and Radiográfica, Av C, C 2-4. **Tour operators** *Turisol Travel Agency*, C 1, Av 3, T661-1212. See under San José Tour operators for Gulf of Nicoya cruises. **Directory**

Monteverde and Santa Elena

Monteverde Cloud Forest Reserve is one of the most precious natural jewels in Costa Rica's crown, an opportunity to see plants, insects, birds and mammals in grand profusion – well in theory at least. Protected by law, this private preserve is also protected by appalling access roads on all sides (the nearest decent road is at least two hours from the town). Santa Elena and Monteverde, although separate, are often referred to as the same place; in fact many of the sites of interest are between the town of Santa Elena at the bottom of the hillside and Monteverde Cloud Forest Reserve at the top.

Costa Rica

From the Pan-American Highway northwest to Km 149, turning right just before the Río Lagarto. Continue for about 40 km on mostly gravel road (allow 2½ hrs) to Santa Elena. Parts of the road are quite good, but in wet weather 4WD is recommended for the rough parts. If driving, check that your car rental agreement allows you to visit Monteverde. A 33 km shorter route is to take the Pipasa/Sardinal turn-off from the Pan-American Highway shortly after the Río Aranjuez. At the park in Sardinal turn left, then go via Guacimal to the Monteverde road. **Ins & outs**

Buses comes from Puntarenas via the Km 149 route. There are also buses from Tilarán to the north, linked with Fortuna by Volcán Arenal, and Cañas on the Pan-American Highway. 2 daily buses from San José.

Alternatively you can make the journey from Tilarán by bus or private transport. It's an equally poor road – a journey that takes a couple of hours, but if driving en route you can visit the quiet and dramatic **Cataratas de Viento Fresco**, some 11 km from Tilarán, 800 m down a very steep road, followed by a 400-m walk. Bit hairy if it's raining but worth the effort.

Santa Elena is a rugged and busy place, often packed with visitors exploring the options or just passing time. It is cheaper to stay in town than along the single, unpaved road that twists and turns for 5 km through the village of Monteverde, with hotels and places of interest situated along the road almost to the reserve itself. Santa Elena Reserve, Sky Trek and Sky Walk are to the north of Santa Elena, all other places of interest are east, heading up the hill. **Santa Elena**

■ *on map, page 1074* **Sleeping In the centre B** *Finca Valverde*, 300 m east of *Banco Nacional* up hill on road to the Reserve, T645-5157, F645-5216, www.monteverde.co.cr, with bath, nice gardens for bird-watching, bar, restaurant. **C** *Arco Iris*, 100 m north of *Banco Nacional*, T645-5067, F645-5022, arcoiris@racsa.co.cr, www.arcoirislodge.com, with bath, restaurant with good healthy breakfast, horses for rent, plenty of parking. **D** *Pensión Tucán*, T645-5017, bargain for lower price in low season, with bath in nice rooms, or **E** in basic cabins with shower (supposedly hot), friendly management, good breakfast and restaurant recommended but closed Sun lunch.

E *Pensión Santa Elena*, T645-5051, F645-6060, www.monteverdeinfo.com/pension.htm (**C** includes 3 meals), very popular, clean, good food, kitchen available, good source of information for the area, have a look at the excellent website, Jacques does the hard sell but he knows his stuff. **E** *El Colibrí*, clean, friendly, timber built, with balconies. **F** per person. *Hospedaje El Banco*, family-run, friendly, hot shower, clean, good information, English spoken. **F** *Pensión Cabinas Marín*, 500 m north of the centre past the Agricultural College, spacious rooms, room 8 has a nice view, good breakfasts, friendly. **E** *Pensión El Sueño*, very friendly, hot shower, small but nice rooms, clean, pricey meals, car park, run by Rafa Trejos who does horse-riding trips into the mountains to see quetzals, etc, US$35.

Leading into Santa Elena from the north is B *Miramontes*, T645-5152, F645-5297, www.multicr.com/miramontes, 6 comfortable rooms in a quiet spot, Swiss-run.

Eating There are a few places right in the centre of Santa Elena. *Chunches*, good expresso bar and snacks, used books, magazines, laundromat, opposite *Pensión Santa Elena*. *Daquiri* is another popular spot to hang out. *Morphos* has been recommended with a good atmosphere but not cheap.

Transport Buses Bus from **Puntarenas**, Terminal Empresarios Unidos, daily at 1415, occasionally at 1315 as well, 2½-4 hrs, returns 0600, US$2.20, this bus arrives in time to catch a bus to **Quepos** for Manuel Antonio. See Monteverde Transport, below, for buses from San José. For an alternative route to Santa Elena from Arenal, see page 1065.

To **Tilarán** the 0700 (US$1.80, 3 hrs) connects with the 1230 bus to Fortuna and others to Cañas for the Pan-American Highway, Liberia and Nicoya Peninsula. **Taxis** available between Santa Elena and Monteverde, US$6, and between Monteverde and the reserve, US$5.75 (hunt around for good prices). Not so easy to find a taxi for return trip, best to arrange beforehand. There is a service station, open Mon-Sat 0700-1800, Sun 0700-1200. **Horses** Several places rent horses; look for signs between Santa Elena and Monteverde or ask at your hotel. Try not to hire horses that look overworked – if you don't know, ask someone who does.

Directory Banks: *Banco Nacional*, open 0900-1500, to change TCs with commission and advance cash against Visa. ATM machine for Visa in the supermarket opposite the post office. **Communication Internet**: Several places are opening up, but with poor communication links are charging an exhorbitant US$6/hr.

Monteverde

Colour map 7, grid B3 Strung out along the road to the cloud forest, the settlement at Monteverde- between Santa Elena and the reserve – was founded by American Quakers in the 1950s. Without a centre as such, it started life as a group of dairy farms providing milk for a co-operative cheese factory. The cheese factory, now privately owned, still operates selling excellent cheeses of various types, fresh milk, ice-cream, milkshakes to die for and *cajeta* (a butterscotch spread) ■ *Shop closes 1600*.

Today, Monteverde maintains an air of pastoral charm, but tourism provides more revenue for the town than dairy produce ever could. It was the vision of the dairy farmers that led to the creation of the reserve to protect the community watershed. When George Powell and his wife spent time in the region studying birds they realized the importance of protecting the area. Working with local residents they created the reserve in 1972 – foresight that has spawned the creation of many other natural attractions locally and throughout the country.

Costa Rica

L *Monteverde Lodge*, T645-5057, F645-5126, T800-633 4734 toll free in USA, www.crexped.co.cr/monteverde.html or book through *Costa Rica Expeditions*, T222-0333, restaurant, jacuzzi, daily slide shows 1815. Recommended. **AL** *Cloud Forest Lodge*, 300 m north of *Sapo Dorado*, T645-5058, F645-5168, www.catours.co.cr, 18 rooms with bath, restaurant, beautiful views (*Canopy Tours*, T645-5243, offer tours of 5 platforms, connected by steel cables, to explore the forest canopy, US$45 per person, US$35 for students at *Cloud Forest Lodge*). **AL** *El Sapo Dorado*, 30 suites, 10 with fireplaces, T645-5010, F645-5180, www.cool.co.cr/usr/ apodorado, good but expensive restaurant open 0700-2100. **L-AL** *Heliconia*, T645-5109, F645-5007, www.centralamerica.com/cr/hotels/heliconia.htm, private bathroom, restaurant, very comfortable, excellent food. Highly recommended. A *El Establo*, next to *Heliconia*, T645-5110, F645-5041, www.establo.com, 22 carpeted rooms with private bathroom, restaurant, 50-ha farm with 50% cloud forest, own nature guide, good bird-watching, riding stables, 35 horses, family-run, very accommodating. Recommended.

E per person *Monteverde Inn*, T645-5156, down track opposite *Heliconia*, private bathroom, quiet, but run-down. Just beyond Establo, a short road on the right leads to **D** *Pensión Manakin*, T645-5080, F645-5517, manakin@racsa.co.cr 10 simple rooms, a few with private bath, or **E** with shared bath. Filling breakfast and evening meals are available, in a family atmosphere which is great for sharing stories with other guests. A small balcony at the back makes a calm place to sit and relax. The Villegas are very knowledgeable about the area, and will help arrange tours and transport up to the reserve if required.

AL *Hotel de Montaña Monteverde*, T645-5046, F645-5320, monteverde@ticonet.co.cr, comfortable, set meals, good, wholesome food, sauna, jacuzzi, horses for hire, good views of Nicoya, excellent bird-watching on 15-ha reserve, transport from San José available. Recommended. **AL-A** *Belmar*, T645-5201, F645-5135, www.hotelbelmar.com, 300 m behind service station, Swiss chalet-style, beautiful views of Nicoya, restaurant, good, transport from San José available. Just before the gas station is the **E** *Alberque Bellbird*, T/F645-5026. Half a dozen rooms in mainly dormitory-style accommodation, with shared bathrooms. **B-D** *El Bosque*, next to restaurant of same name, T645-5158, F645-5129, 26 rooms, hot showers, comfortable, clean, lovely rooms with fine views, beautiful gardens and short trail, safe parking.

B-C *Mariposa*, T645-5013, 3 rooms in a single block sleeping up to 3 people, with private bath. A family atmosphere with breakfast included in the price. **B** *La Colina Lodge*, T645-5009, F645-5588, between Monteverde and reserve, private bath, balconies with some rooms, or **D** per person in dormitory, helpful, luggage stored, small area for camping **F** per person, one of the original houses of Monteverde with some nice touches, Marvin Rockwell, the former owner and one of the original Quaker settlers, pops in to give talks when requested.

AL *Fonda Vela*, T257-1413, F257-1416, www.centralamerica.com/cr/hotel/fondavel.htm, private bathroom, hot water, 40 beautiful rooms and suites spread around 5 buildings, 25-min walk, 5-min drive to the reserve, on a 14-ha farm with forest and trail system, good birding, two excellent restaurants (open to public), bar, TV room, art gallery and conference room. **A** *Villa Verde*, T645-5025, F645-5115, 1½ km from reserve, rooms with hot showers, others with shared bath, some with kitchenette, includes breakfast, restaurant, clean, nice, excellent views.

Closest to the Reserve is the **AL** *Trapp Family Lodge*, T645-5858, F645-5990, www.trappfam.com, tidy, immaculate rooms, upstairs with balconies, downstairs with terraces, friendly and helpful hosts.

AL per person *San Luis Biological Station and Ecolodge*, 40-min drive from Monteverde, call ahead to book, T/F645-5277, on 65 ha of farmland and cloud forest in the San Luis Valley, adjoining Monteverde Cloud Forest, 5 cabins, horse-riding, swimming in river and other options.

In addition to the excellent hotel restaurants, *Johnny's Pizza*, on main road between Santa Elena and Monteverde, good wood oven-cooked pizzas in a relaxed atmosphere, café, souvenir shop, mid-priced. Tables outside give extra chance to see wildlife. *Restaurant Lucia's* down road opposite *Heliconia*, tasty lasagne, mid-priced. *Restaurant El Bosque*, next to *Casem* shop, good food, clean, open from 0630. *Stella's Bakery*, opposite *Casem*, has excellent wholemeal bread, cakes and good granola – there's a café if you want to eat in.

Sleeping
■ *on map page 1074*

Hotels in order as you head up the hill

Many hotels have slide shows – see below or ask locally for details

Eating

Costa Rica

Entertainment Apart from eating and drinking in Santa Elena and elsewhere, *Cinema Paradiso* is a long-awaited evening activity which is technically a bagel store which just happens to show a mix of good art and Hollywood blockbusters.

Festivals *Monteverde Music Festival*, classical and jazz concerts between **Dec** and **Mar** at sunset, local, national and international musicians. Programme from local hotels, US$9.

Shopping *Casem,* a co-operative gift shop, is located just outside Monteverde on the road to the reserve next to *El Bosque* restaurant. It sells embroidered shirts, t-shirts, wooden and woven articles and baskets. Shop selling Costa Rican coffee next door.

Transport **Buses** From San José a direct bus runs from Av 9, C 12, just outside Terminal Atlántico Norte, (4½ hrs, US$4) daily at 0630 and 1430. Leaves Monteverde from *Hotel Villa Verde* also at 0630 and 1430, picking up through town, stopping at Santa Elena bus stop (be early).

Monteverde & Santa Elena

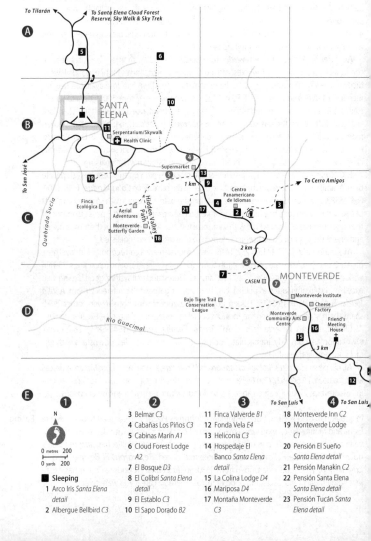

Costa Rica

Sleeping
1 Arco Iris *Santa Elena detail*
2 Albergue Bellbird *C3*
3 Belmar *C3*
4 Cabañas Los Piños *C3*
5 Cabinas Marín *A1*
6 Cloud Forest Lodge *A2*
7 El Bosque *D3*
8 El Colibrí *Santa Elena detail*
9 El Establo *C3*
10 El Sapo Dorado *B2*
11 Finca Valverde *B1*
12 Fonda Vela *E4*
13 Heliconia *C3*
14 Hospedaje El Banco *Santa Elena detail*
15 La Colina Lodge *D4*
16 Mariposa *D4*
17 Montaña Monteverde *C3*
18 Monteverde Inn *C2*
19 Monteverde Lodge *C1*
20 Pensión El Sueño *Santa Elena detail*
21 Pensión Manakin *C2*
22 Pensión Santa Elena *Santa Elena detail*
23 Pensión Tucán *Santa Elena detail*

To San Luis
To San Luis

0 metres 200
0 yards 200

Check times in advance, Sat bus does not always run in low season, T645-5032 in Santa Elena, T258-5674 in San José for information. This service is not 'express', it stops to pick up passengers all along the route, and is not a comfortable ride. Keep your day-bag with you at all times; several cases of theft reported. Alternatively, get a bus to Puntarenas and change there for Santa Elena, see above.

Directory

Cultural centres *Galería Extasis*, 250 m south of *La Cascada*, exhibits sculptures by the Costa Rican artist, Marco Tulio Brenes. **Language schools** A branch of the *Centro Panamericano de Idiomas*, in Heredia, has opened a school on the road up to the reserve, T645-5026, accommodation with local families. *Monteverde Studio of the Arts*, T645-5434, www.mvstudios.com, offers students the opportunity to study with local artists and craftsmen in a range of different materials. Classes are usually 20 hrs/wk-long, located in the artists studio, but shorter classes can be arranged.

Excursions from Santa Elena and Monteverde

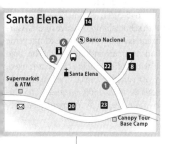

Five kilometres north of Santa Elena, off the road to Tilarán, **Sky Walk** uses six suspension bridges to take you through the cloud forest at canopy level, the highest being 42 m above the ground. ■ *Daily 0700-1600, US$12, student US$10, child US$4, for information T645-5238, www.skywalk.co.cr* **Sky Trek** is arguably even more popular and a breathtaking experience, as you fly through the air on a system of cables strung out from giant forest trees. On clear days the view from the highest tower is unbelievable. ■ *Daily 0700-1500, US$35, student US$28, T645-5238, www.skywalk.co.cr*

Very close to Santa Elena, at the start of the climb to Monteverde, is the **Serpentarium** with specimens of snakes and amphibeans found in the nearby cloud forest. ■ *Daily 0700-1700, US$3.*

A hundred metres beyond *Hotel Sapo Dorado* is the **Orchid Garden**, with about 400 species collected by Gabriel Barboza. ■ *Daily 0800-1700.*

A dirt road opposite the *Hotel Heliconia* leads to the **Monteverde Butterfly Garden**, a beautifully presented large garden planted for breeding and researching butterflies. ■ *Daily, 0930-1600, US$7 including guided tour, best time for a visit 1100-1300, wolfej@racsa.co.cr* Near the Butterfly Garden is **Finca Ecológica**, with three trails totalling around 5 km with bird lists for bird-watching and varied wildlife in this transitional zone between cloud and tropical dry forest, guides available. Good night tours.

24 Trapp Family Lodge *E5*
25 Villa Verde *E4*

● Eating
1 Chunches *Santa Elena detail*
2 Daiquiri *Santa Elena detail*
3 El Bosque *C2*
4 Johnny's Pizza *B2*
5 Lucia's *C2*
6 Morphos *Santa Elena detail*
7 Stella's Bakery *D3*

Costa Rica

■ *0700-1700 daily, US$5, free map.* Down the same path is **Aerial Adventures**, a ski-lift-style ride travelling slowly through the treetops. Ideal for bird-watching. ■ *Daily 0700-1800, US$12, T645-5960, wmvargas@racsa.co.cr*

From Monteverde to the reserve is a steep 45-minute walk uphill, about 4 km, but there are lovely views looking towards the sea and the Nicoya Peninsula, particularly in the evening (when you are coming down and can appreciate them).

Reserva Sendero Tranquilo is a private 200-ha reserve near the Monteverde cheese factory. Reservations and guides should be arranged through *El Sapo Dorado* hotel. ■ *Open daily, T645-5010. Entry restricted to 12 people at any one time.*

Just before the entrance to Monteverde Cloud Forest is the **Hummingbird Gallery**, where masses of different hummingbirds can be seen darting around a glade, visiting feeding dispensers filled with sugared water. ■ *0930-1700, slide shows daily at 1630 (3 times a week sometimes), US$4, T645-5030.* Outside the entrance is a small shop/photo gallery which sells pictures and gifts. There is also a slide show at *Hotel Belmar, The Hidden Rainforest*, by Bobby Maxson, 1930 daily except Friday.

Adjoining the Monteverde Cloud Forest is **El Bosque Eterno de los Niños** (the Children's Eternal Rainforest), T645-5003, F645-5104, acmmcl@racsa.co. Cr, established in 1988 after an initiative by Swedish schoolchildren to save forests. Currently at 22,000 ha, the land has been bought and is maintained by the Monteverde Conservation League with children's donations from around the world. The 'Bajo Tigre' trail takes 1½ hours, parking available with notice, a guide can be arranged, but no horses are allowed on the trail. Groups can arrange trips to the San Gerardo and Poco Sol Field stations, **B-C** including meals. ■ *0800-1600, entrance US$5, students US$2. Contact the Monteverde Conservation League for reservations at San Gerardo or Poco Sol. T645-5003, F645-5104, www.acmonteverde.com*

Monteverde Cloud Forest Reserve

Best months are January-May, especially February, March and April

Straddling the continental divide, the 10,500-ha Monteverde Cloud Forest Reserve is privately owned and administered by the Tropical Science Centre – a non-profit research and educational association. The reserve is mainly primary cloud forest and spends much of the year shrouded in mist, creating stunted trees and abundant epiphytic growth. It contains over 400 species of birds, including the resplendent quetzal, best seen in the dry months between January and May, especially near the start of the Nuboso trail, the three-wattled bellbird and the bare-necked umbrella bird. There are over 100 species of mammals, including monkeys, Baird's tapir and six endangered cats – jaguar, jaguarundi, margay, ocelot, tigrillo and puma – reptiles and amphibians. The reserve also includes an estimated 2,500 species of plant and more than 6,000 species of insect. The entrance is at 1,500 m, but the maximum altitude in the reserve is over 1,800 m. Mean temperature is between 16° and 18°C and average annual rainfall is 3,000 mm. The weather changes quickly and wind and humidity often make the air feel cooler.

The commonly used trails are in good condition and there are easy, short and interesting walks for those who do not want to hike all day. Trail walks take from two hours but you could easily spend all day just wandering around. Trails may be restricted from time to time if they need protection. There is a trail northwards to the Arenal volcano that is increasingly used, but it is not easy. There are three refuges for people wishing to spend the night within the reserve boundaries. Free maps of the Reserve at the entrance. Follow the rules, stay on the paths, leave nothing behind, take no fauna or flora out; no radios or tape recorders are allowed.

Essentials The reserve entrance is at the field station at the top of the road. Bus from Santa Elena head up the hill leaving at 0600 and 1100 returning at 1400 and 1700. The total number of visitors to the reserve at any one time is 150, but be there before 0700 to make sure of getting in during high season (hotels will book you a place for the following day). Tour buses come in from San José daily and be warned that travellers have told us there is little chance of seeing much

What is cloud forest?

Simply put, it's forest that spends much of the year blanketed in cloud, creating conditions of high humidity. In Monteverde, trade winds from the Atlantic force moist air up the Tilarán Mountains, cooling the air as it rises which condenses to create clouds.

The result is an abundance of plants and

epiphyte growth with tree trunks and branches covered in dense blankets of mosses and lichens, as well as twisting vines, fallen trees and giant tree ferns.

The cloud forest is an almost magical place, like the forests of fairy tales. Without the path imagine how quickly you could get lost.

wildlife. Entrance fee US$14 (students with ID half-price) valid for multiple entry during the day, cannot be purchased in advance. Office open 0700-1630 daily; the park opens at 0700 and closes at 1700. Shelter facilities throughout the reserve cost US$3.50 or US$5 a night, reserve entry fee for each night spent in the park, plus key deposit of US$5, bring sleeping bag and flashlight. You can make your own meals. Dormitory-style accommodation for up to 30 people at entrance, *Albergue Reserva Biológica de Monteverde*, T645-5122, F645-5034, montever@racsa.co.cr, US$23 full board only. Reservations required for all reserve accommodation (usually booked up by groups). A small shop at the office sells various checklists, postcards, print and APS film (up to 400ASA), slides, gifts and excellent t-shirts, the proceeds of which help towards the conservation project.

Guides Natural history walks with biologist guides, every morning and afternoon, 3-4 hrs, US$16 (children half price); advance reservations at the office or through your hotel are strongly recommended. If you use a private (non-reserve) guide you must pay his entrance fee too. An experienced and recommended guide is Gary Diller (Apdo 10165, 1000 San José, T645-5045). There are 25 others operating, of varying specialization and experience. Excellent night tours in the reserve are available normally with Ricardo Guindon, 1900 prompt, T661-1008, US$13. Day or night, a guide is recommended if you want to see wildlife, since the untrained eye misses a lot.

Donations for conservation are welcome. They can be made at the Monteverde Cloud Forest Reserve office or Tropical Science Centre (Apdo 8-3870-1000, San José, T225-2649, F253-4963, www.cct.or.cr) at El Higuerón, 100 m Sur y 125 m Este, Barrio La Granja, San Pedro, or the Monteverde Conservation League (Asociacion Conservacionista de Monteverde, Apdo Postal 10581-1000, San José, Costa Rica, T645-5003, F645-5104, www.acmonteverde.com). Donations are welcomed for purchasing additional land and maintaining and improving existing reserve areas. If you are interested in **volunteer work**, from non-skilled trail maintenance to skilled scientific assistance work, surveying, teaching or studying on a tropical biology programme, contact the reserve at the address above. US$14 per person, board and lodging, 2 weeks minimum. The Conservation League works with schools in the area on education regarding conservation.

Equipment Recommended equipment includes binoculars (750s-1040s), good camera with 400-1,000 ASA film, insect repellent, sweater and light rainwear. Rubber boots or good walking shoes are a must for the longer walks, at all times of year but especially in the rainy season, and can be rented at the park office for US$0.80 or at hotels.

Santa Elena Cloud Forest Reserve

One kilometre along the road from Santa Elena to Tilarán, a 5-km track is signposted to the reserve, managed by the **Centro Ecológico Bosque Nuboso de Monteverde**. It is 83% primary cloud forest and the rest is 17-year-old secondary forest at 1,700 m, bordered by the Monteverde Cloud Forest Reserve and the Arenal Forest Reserve. There is a 12-km path network and several lookouts where, on a clear day, you can see and hear Volcán Arenal. The 'canopy tour' is recommended: you climb inside a hollow strangler fig tree then cross between two platforms along

Costa Rica

aerial runways 30 m up, good views of orchids and bromeliads, then down a 30-m hanging rope at the end. There are generally fewer visitors here than at Monteverde. The Centro Ecológico Bosque Nuboso is administered by the local community and profits go to five local schools. It was set up by the Costa Rican government in 1989 with collaboration from Canada. The rangers are very friendly and enthusiastic. There is a small information centre where rubber boots can be hired and a small café open at weekends. Hand-painted t-shirts for sale. ■ *0700-1600, entrance US$8, students US$4, T/F645-5390, www.monteverdeinfo.com/reserve.htm, for information. It is a long, steep hike from the village, alternatively hire a taxi, carload US$6.50.*

North to Guanacaste Province

Rainfall is moderate: 1,000-2,000 mm a year, there is a long dry season which makes irrigation important, but the lowlands are deep in mud during the rainy season

North of Barranca, the Pan-American heads towards the province of Guanacaste – the cultural heartland of Costa Rica, home to the *sabinero* cowboy and the rolling plains of the northern ranches. The province also includes the Peninsula of Nicoya and the lowlands at the head of the gulf.

Guanacaste, with its capital Liberia, has a distinctive people, way of life, flora and fauna. The smallholdings of the highlands give way here to large haciendas and great cattle estates. The rivers teem with fish; there are all kinds of wildlife in the uplands.

The people are open, hospitable and fun-loving, and are famed for their music and dancing, in fact, the Punto Guanacasteco has been officially declared the typical national dance. There are many **fiestas** in January and February in the local towns and villages, which are well worth seeing.

Heading northwest on the Pan-American Highway, turn right just after the Río Aranjuez at Rancho Grande (or just south of the Río Lagarto at Km 149) to access a bumpy, dramatic and at times scenic route to Santa Elena-Monteverde (see page 1071).

Forty-three kilometres north of Barranca is the turn-off for **Las Juntas**, an alternative route to Monteverde for those using the Tempisque ferry or arriving from Guanacaste; a third of it is paved. After Las Juntas, there is a mining ecomuseum at **La Sierra de Abangares** with mining artefacts from a turn-of-the-(20th)century gold mine. ■ *0600-1800 daily, US$1.80.*

Four kilometres north, a left turn goes to the Tempisque car ferry and the north of the Peninsula. After about 6 km a road to the right at San Joaquín leads to the **A** per person *Hacienda Solimar Lodge*, a 1,300-ha cattle farm with over half dry tropical virgin forest bordering **Parque Nacional Palo Verde** (see below) near Porozal in the lower Tempisque River basin. The freshwater Madrigal estuary on the property is one of the most important areas for waterbirds in Costa Rica (only guests staying at the Hacienda can visit). Also surrounded by gallery forest, it is recommended for serious bird-watchers. Reservations essential, T669-0281 or contact *Birdwatch*, Apdo 6951, 1005 San José, T228-4768, F228-1573, eight rooms with private or shared bathroom, includes meals, minimum two nights, transport available on request, local guide, horse-riding.

Cañas Sixty-seven kilometres north of Barranca, Cañas has little to keep the visitor for long. There are a number of interesting sights nearby and, for the traveller arriving from the north, this is the cut-through to Tilarán and connecting buses to Arenal or Fortuna.

Sleeping and eating On the Pan-American is **C** *El Corral*, T669-1467, with bath. **D** *Cañas*, C 2, Av 3, T669-0039, with bath, clean, pleasant. **F** *Cabinas Corobicí*, T669-0241, 11 good rooms with bath and parking available.

Out of town 2½ km north of Cañas is **C** *Capazuri B&B*, T/F669-0580, www.hostelling-costarica.com, also good camping US$3 per person.

Restaurant Panchitos on main square is good and inexpensive. Good Chinese restaurants, eg *Central*, on main square. The restaurant *Rincón Corobicí*, next to *La Pacífica*, clean and pleasant, has a small zoo and offers rafting down Río Corobicí, T669-0544.

Transport Bus: the bus station is 500 m north of the centre, where all buses depart from except for those to **San José,** which leave from the terminal 300 m west of Parque Central on the Pan-American Highway. To and from **San José**: *Transportes La Cañera*, T669-0145, 8 daily from 0400, 3½ hrs, arriving and departing from C16, Av 1-3. To **Liberia** 10 daily from 0530. To **Puntarenas** 8 daily from 0600. To Upala for Bijagua and Volcán Tenorio, 7 daily from 0500, 1¾ hrs, US$1.50. To **Tilarán**, 7 daily from 0600. Buses to Tilarán for Nuevo Arenal, past the volcano and on to Fortuna, or for connections to Santa Elena and Monteverde. If going by road, the turn-off for Tilarán is at the filling station, no signs. For a description of this route in reverse see page 1060.

Directory Tour operators: *Safaris Corobicí* is 4 km past Cañas on the Pan-American Highway, 25 m before the entrance to Centro Ecológico La Pacífica (T669-2091, F669-1091, safaris@racsa.co.cr, www.nicoya.com). Float tours down the Río Corobicí, US$35 per person for 2 hrs rafting, US$60 ½-day. *Las Pumas*, behind Safaris Corobicí, a small, private, Swiss-run animal rescue centre specializes in looking after big cats, including jaguar – an unmissable if rather sad experience. Free but donations welcome and encouraged. *CATA Tours*, T296-2133, rafting tours and full-day tours to Parque Nacional Palo Verde.

If you turn north off the Pan-American Highway just after Corobicí, you will eventually come (58 km) to **Upala** (see page 1067). After 34 km you reach **Bijagua de Upala**, between the volcanoes Tenorio and Miravalles. The **B** *Bijagua Heliconias Ecotourist Lodge* had six cabins with private bathroom, a community project supported by WWF Canada and CIDA Canada. Book through *Tours of Exploration in Canada*, T(604)683-6511, F(604)886-7304, www.toursexplore.com

Further north at Bagaces, Route 164 heads north through **Guayabo** (**E** *Las Brisas*, bath, hot water, fans) and, at Km 30, you get to *Parador Las Nubes del Miravalles*, T671-1011 ext 280. Tent and mattress rental, horse rental, good hiking to **Volcán Miravalles** and waterfalls, very friendly and hospitable people on working *finca*. From here you can take a boat up the Río Pizote to Lake Nicaragua.

At the south of the neck of the Nicoya Peninsula is **Parque Nacional Palo Verde**, currently over 18,650 ha of marshes with many water birds. Indeed, in the Laguna over 50,000 birds are considered resident. Fantastic views from the limestone cliffs. Palo Verde Biological Station is a research station run by the Organization for Tropical Studies. They organize natural history walks and basic accommodation. T240-6696, www.ots.ac.cr/, ordinary visitors US$40 with three meals and a guided walk, student researchers, US$22, senior researchers, US$32. Day visits with lunch, US$35, minimum six persons. Make advance reservations. Turn off the Pan-American Highway at **Bagaces**, halfway between Cañas and Liberia, no public transport. The Palo Verde Administration offices are in Bagaces, next to service station, T671-1062. Camping and possible lodging in park. Two ranger stations, Palo Verde and Catalina. Check roads in wet season.

Parque Nacional Palo Verde

Costa Rica

Liberia

Known as the 'White City', Liberia is a neat, clean, cattle town with a triangular, rather unattractive modern church, and single-storey colonial houses meticulously laid out in the streets surrounding the central plaza. A well-paved branch road leads southwest to the Nicoya Peninsula.

Colour map 7, grid B2
Population: 40,000

There is a **tourist office** three blocks south of the plaza on Calle 1, Av 6, T666-1606, helpful, English spoken, leave donation as the centre is not formally funded (and information not always accurate). In the same building is the **Museo del Sabanero** (Cowboy Museum), a poorly presented display of artefacts. ■ *Museum and tourist office open 0800-1200, 1300-1600 Mon-Sat, US$0.45.* You can also get some tourist information across the plaza from the church.

Sleeping
● *on map*

AL *Las Espuelas*, 2 km south of Liberia, T666-0144, F666-2441, www.costasol.co.cr/espuelas/, good, a/c, satellite TV, swimming pool, round trip bus service from San José, day tour to San Antonio cattle ranch, US$60, Amex accepted. **AL** *Best Western El Sitio*, just off highway on road to Nicoya, T666-1211, F666-2059, htlsitio@racsa.co.cr, bath, a/c, good. **B** *Boyeros*, on Pan-American Highway with Av Central, T666-0722, F666-2529, pool, bath, restaurant. **B** *Hostal Ciudad Blanca*, Av 4, C 1-3, from Gobernación 200 m south, 150 m east, T666-3962, 12 nice but dirty rooms, a/c, hot water, phone, TV, restaurant/bar, parking, rooster wake up call. **B** *Hotel del Aserradero*, Interamerican y Av 3, T666-1939, F666-0475, 16 big rooms with bath, parking and fans.

C *Guanacaste*, C 12, Av 3, just round corner from bus stations, T666-0085, F666-2287, clean, bath, friendly, restaurant, safe parking, money exchange, *Ticabus* agency, transfers and tours, camping area, English spoken, group discount, 15 student discount, affiliated youth hostel. Recommended. **C** *Hotel Daysita*, Av 5, C11-13, T666-0197, F666-0927, restaurant, pool, quiet, not central. **D-E** to share 6-bedded room with own bath. **C** *La Siesta*, C 4, Av 4-6, T666-0678, with bath, restaurant, clean, swimming pool, helpful owner who speaks English. **D** *Liberia*, ½ block south of main square, T666-0161, F666-4091, with bath, **E** with shared bath, fans, clean, friendly, good information board and restaurant, laundry facilities. Recommended. **E** *La Casona*, Av 6, C Central, T/F666-2971, rooms for up to 4 people, shared bath, washing facilities, rooms facing street get very hot, **D** for new annex with private bath. **E** *Cabinas Sagitarios*, Av 11, C 2, T666-0950, with bath, run by Dutchman and Costa Rican, breakfast and dinner available on request, friendly. **F** *Anita*, C 4 y Av 8, T666-1285, F666-3364, bath, clean, family-run, friendly, café, shop, parking, best of the range. **F** per person *La Posada del Tope*, Rafael Iglesias, 1½ blocks south from cathedral, T666-3876, cold shower, laundry facilities, clean, friendly, helpful, parking, bike rentals, baggage storage, the owner Dennis has a telescope for star gazing.

Eating
■ *on map*

Chop Suey, C Central, Chinese, big helpings. *Hong Kong*, 1½ blocks east of church, Chinese, cheap and cheerful. *Copa de Oro*, next to *Hotel Liberia*, Chinese, huge dishes, good value. *Pronto Pizzeria*, C 1, Av 4, good food (not just pizzas) in a charming colonial house. *Buona Pizza*, La Immaculada, C 6, genuine clay oven. On the west side of the Plaza is

Liberia

■ Sleeping	6 El Sitio	12 Liberia	4 Jauja
1 Anita	7 Guanacaste		5 Las Tinajas
2 Aserradero	8 Hostal Ciudad Blanca	● Eating	6 Panymiel
3 Boyeros	9 La Casona	1 Buona Pizza	7 Pronto Pizzeria
4 Cabinas Sagitarios	10 La Posada del Tope	2 El Bramadero	
5 Daysita	11 La Siesta	3 Hong Kong	

0 metres 100
0 yards 100

Soda Las Tinajas, a great little open-air restaurant looking out on the plaza, which special-izes in *refrescos*. **Jardín de Azúcar**, just off plaza, self service, good variety and tasty; also in the bus station. **El Bramadero**, part of the *Hotel Bramadero* on the Pan-American, popular, mid-price range, breakfast from 0630, lively bar in the evenings. **Restaurante Jauja**, Av C, one street west of C 8, pizza and pasta. **Panymiel**, next to *Restaurante Jauja* and Av 1, C 2, bakery, snacks and drinks, good value.

Souvenirs *Tiffanys*, Av C-2, C 2, general gifts, cigars. *Mini Galería Fulvia*, on the main plaza, sells *Tico Times*, English papers and books, English spoken and helpful.

Shopping

Guanacaste Day on **25 Jul** sees dancing, parades and cattles related festivities.

Festivals

Air The Tomás Guardia International Airport, about 13 km from Liberia (LIR) on the road to the Nicoya Peninsula was reopened in 1992, revamped in 1995 and renamed Daniel Oduber Quirós Airport, after the former president who came from Guanacaste. The new runway can handle large jets and charter flights, and direct daily flights to Miami. *Lacsa*, T666-0306; *Sansa*, T221-9414; *Travelair*, T232-7883. There is a direct weekly flight to New York arriving Sat, through *Air-Tech*, www.airtech.com

Transport

    Buses Buses to San José leave from Av 5, C 10-12, with 14 a day, US$4.25, 4 hrs. Other buses leave from the local terminal at C 12, Av 7-9. Liberia to **Playa del Coco**, 6 a day, 0530-1815, **Playa Hermosa** and **Panama**, 1130 and 1900, **Puntarenas**, 7 a day, 0500-1530, **Bagaces/Cañas**, 4 a day, 0545-1710, **Cañas Dulces**, 3 a day, 0600-1730, **La Cruz/Peñas Blanca**, 8 a day 0530-1800. **Filedefia-Santa Cruz-Nicoya**, 0500-2020, 20 a day.

    Car rental *Sol* and *Toyota* car rental agencies (see map) offer same prices and allow you to leave the vehicle at San José airport for US$50.

Banks *Banco Popular* and *Bancrecer* both have Visa ATMs. *Banco de Costa Rica* is on the main plaza. *Credomatic*, Av Central, MasterCard ATM. For money exchange, try *Casa de Cambio* on C 2 or ask around, eg *Restaurant Chun San*, behind the cathedral. **Communications Internet**: *Ciberm@nia*, north side of main plaza, US$2 per hr. **Medical services** *Enrique Baltodano Hospital* T666-0011, pharmacies close to main plaza. **Tour operators** *Tiquicia Travel*, in *Hotel Guanacaste*, T666-4485. *Hotel Liberia* can organize tours, rent out bikes and assist with enquiries. A recommended guide for the nearby national parks is *Alejandro Vargas Rodríguez* who lives in front of the Cruz Roja, T666-1889.

Directory

Most easily visited from Liberia, Parque Nacional Rincón de la Vieja (14,161 ha) was created to preserve the area around the Volcán Rincón de la Vieja, to the northeast of the town, including dry tropical forest, mudpots, hot sulphur springs and several other geothermal curiosities. The volcanic massif reaches to 1,916 m, and can be seen from a wide area around Liberia when not shrouded in clouds. The area is cool at night and subject to strong, gusty winds and violent rains; in the day it can be very hot, although always windy. These fluctuations mark all of the continental divide, of which the ridge is a part. From time to time the volcano erupts, the last eruption being in November 1995, tossing rocks and lava down its slopes.

Parque Nacional Rincón de la Vieja
Entry US$6

    The park is home to over 350 recorded species of birds including toucans, parrots, the three-wattled bellbird and great currasows, along with howler monkeys, armadil-los and coatis, ticks and other biting insects. It also has the largest density of Costa Rica's national flower the *guaria morada* or purple orchid. Horses can be rented in the park from some of the lodges. If you want to climb the volcano you will need to camp near the top, or at the warden's station, in order to ascend early in the morning before the clouds come in. Trails through the park lead to most sights of interest, including beautiful waterfalls and swimming holes. There are several accommodation options in or near the park, and shorter trips easily arranged from Liberia.

Ins & outs There are 2 ways into the park: the southern route, which has less traffic, goes from Puente La Victoria on the western side of Liberia and leads, in about 25 km, to the Santa María sec-tor, closest to the hot springs. In this part, you can stay for US$2.50 per person in the old, spacious,

Costa Rica

and basic refurbished Santa María Hacienda 2 km inside the park. Bring your own food and bedding, or camp. From the old *hacienda* you can hike 8 km to the boiling mudpots (Las Pailas) and come back in the same day; the sulphur springs are on a different trail and only 1 hr away.

The northern route turns right off the Pan-American Highway 5 km northwest of Liberia, through Curubandé (no public transport on this route). Beyond Curubandé, you cross the private property of *Hacienda Lodge Guachipelin* (US$2 to cross), beyond which is *Albergue Rincón de la Vieja*.

To get there: a taxi costs US$30 1-way from Liberia. Most hotels will arrange transport for US$15 per person, minimum 6 passengers, depart 0700, 1 hr to entrance, return 1700, take food and drink. You can also hitch, most tourist vehicles will pick you up. If you take your own transport a 4WD is best, although during the dry season a vehicle with high clearance is adequate.

Sleeping All accessed through the northern route. **A-C** *Hacienda Lodge Guachipelin*, Lodge T384-2049, office 442-2818, F442-1910 , www.guachipelin.com, meals available, 18 rooms, camping US$1.70 but no fires, naturalist guides, riding, hot springs, sulphur springs, mud pools, waterfalls (transport from Liberia arranged, US$25 per person round trip). **C** *Albergue Rincón de la Vieja* down the road to Quebrada Grande (affiliated to the Youth Hostel network) T281-1117, F283-7148, www.hostelling-costarica.com/rvieja, includes food, pool, camping US$5, call the proprietor, Alvaro Wiessel, who will pick you up in Liberia. Also packages including transport from San José. The *Albergue* is on the edge of the park, there are horses for rent, guides, tours. From there it is 3¼ hrs to the volcano, 30 mins to Las Pailas, 45 mins to the thermal springs, Azufrales, 2¼ hrs to the Hidden Waterfalls.

Accessed through the Santa María sector. **F** *Miravieja Lodge*, T662-2004, Giovanni Murillo, rustic lodge in citrus groves, meals, transport and tours available.

Twenty kilometres north of Liberia is Costa Rica's first commercial ostrich farm, blueneck and black breeds; call T228-6646, Javnai Menahen for information on tours. A further 3 km north is the turn-off northeast to Quebrada Grande, 4 km from which is **B** *Santa Clara Lodge*, T/F224-4085, four rooms shared bath, one room with bath, cattle farm, riding, dry forest.

Guanacaste Conservation Area

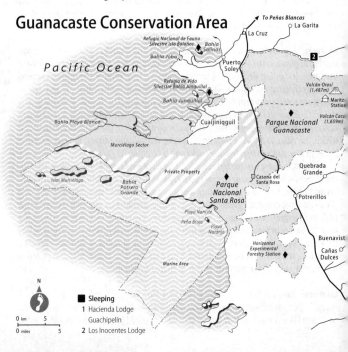

Costa Rica

Pacific Ocean

To Peñas Blancas
La Garita
La Cruz

Refugio Nacional de Fauna
Silvestre Isla Bolaños
Bahía Salinas
Bahía Jobo
Puerto Soley

Refugio de Vida
Silvestre Bahía Junquillal
Bahía Junquillal

Volcán Orosi (1,487m)
Maritz Station

Bahía Playa Blanca
Cuajiniqquil
Parque Nacional Guanacaste
Volcán Cace (1,659m)

Murciélago Sector

Private Property
Quebrada Grande

Islas Murciélaga
Bahía Potrero Grande
Parque Nacional Santa Rosa
Casona del Santa Rosa
Potrerillos

Playa Nancite
Peña Bruja
Playa Naranjo

Horizontal Experimental Forestry Station
Buenavist
Cañas Dulces

Marine Area

N

0 km 5
0 miles 5

■ Sleeping
1 Hacienda Lodge Guachipelin
2 Los Inocentes Lodge

About half-way to the Nicaraguan border from Liberia, is Parque Nacional Santa Rosa (38,673 ha). Together with the Murciélago Annex, the peninsula to the north of the developed park, it preserves some of the last dry tropical forests in Costa Rica, and shelters abundant and relatively easy-to-see wildlife. During the dry season, the animals depend on the water holes, and are thus easy to find until the holes dry up completely. Conservation work in the area is also attempting to reforest some of the cattle ranches of the area – helped by the fact that cattle have not been profitable in recent years.

Parque Nacional Santa Rosa

Close to the park headquarters and research buildings, the historically important La Casona was an essential visit for every *Tico* child as it is from here that the patriots repelled the invasion of the filibuster Walker in 1856, who had entrenched himself in the main building. Unfortunately the old hacienda building, once the **Museo Histórico de Santa Rosa**, was almost completely destroyed by fire in May 2001. ■ *Check with tourist offices or the park administrators for the latest information on rebuilding La Casona.* There are several good trails and lookouts in the park, the easiest of which is close to *La Casona*. Lasting a couple of hours, it leads through dry tropical forest with many Indio Desnudo (naked Indian) trees, which periodically shed their red flaky bark.

Deeper in the park, **Playa Naranjo** (12 km, three hours' walk or more, or use four-wheel drive, park authorities permitting) and **Playa Nancite** (about the same distance from the entrance) are major nesting sites of leatherback and Olive Ridley sea turtles. The main nesting season is between August and October (although stragglers are regularly seen up to January) when flotillas of up to 10,000 Ridley turtles arrive at night on the 7-km long Playa Nancite. Females clumsily lurch up the beach, scoop out a deep hole, deposit and bury an average of 100 ping-pong-ball sized eggs before returning exhausted to the sea (see also Ostional, page 1094). Playa Nancite is a restricted access beach; you need a written permit to stay plus US$2 per day to camp, or US$15 in dormitories. Permits from SPN in San José, and the Park Administration building at Santa Rosa. Make sure you have permission before going. Research has been done in the Playa Nancite area on howler monkeys, coatis and the complex interrelation between the fauna and the forest. Playa Naranjo is one of the most attractive beaches in the country. It is unspoilt, quiet and very good for surfing. There is good camping, drinking water (although occasionally the water is salty – checked before leaving park HQ) and BBQ facilities.

Costa Rica

Sleeping There is a pleasant campground at Park Administration, about 7 km from the entrance with giant strangler figs that shade your tent from the stupendously hot sun, and very adequate sanitary facilities, picnic tables, and so forth for US$2.15 per person per night. There is a small *comedor* for meals (breakfast 0600-0630, lunch 1100-1200, evening 1700-1800, good) and drinks near the camp ground but it is recommended you bring some of your own supplies; a tent is useful: essential in the wet season. You may be able to sleep on the veranda of one of the scientists' houses. Bring a mosquito net and insect repellent. If the water is not running, ask at Administration.

Transport Parque Nacional Santa Rosa is easy to reach as it lies west of the

Pan-American Highway, about 1 hr north of Liberia. Any bus going from Liberia to Peñas Blancas on the Nicaraguan border will drop you right at the entrance (US$0.70, 40 mins), from where it's a 7-km walk, but you may be able to hitch a ride. Last bus returns to Liberia about 1800. Coming from the border, any bus heading south will drop you off at the entrance.

La Cruz
Colour map 7, grid B2

The last town before the border, La Cruz has a bank (for cash, TCs or credit card transactions), a handful of hotels and absolutely incredible sunsets from the hilltop overlooking the Bahía de Salinas. Down in the bay the **Islas Bolaños Wildlife Refuge** and some of the best conditions for windsurfing in Costa Rica.

Sleeping **B** *Amalia's Inn*, 100 m south of Parque Central, T/F679-9181, stunning views, small pool, very friendly and excellent local knowledge. Extra person US$5, and one room sleeps 6. Excellent value for groups and recommended. **B** *Hostal de Julia*, on road out to the Pan-American, T/ F679-9084, clean, tidy rooms, ample parking. **C-D** *Cabinas Santa Rita*, 150m south of Parque Central, T679-9062, nice, clean, secure with good parking. Cheaper with fan. Would be great in any other town not competing with Amalia's. **G** per person, *Cabinas Maryfel*, opposite bus terminal, T679-9534, but no obvious sign. Dark and basic, but OK for the price.

Down on **Bahía Salinas** are a couple of all-inclusive resorts **LL-AL** *Ecoplaya Beach Resort*, T/F679-9380, well maintained with nice restaurant, and **A** *Three Corners*, T679-9444, www.threecorners.com (price includes activities and facilities).

West of La Cruz, on Bahía Salinas looking over to Isla Bolaños, is *Playa Morro Trailer Park y Cabinas*, T382-2989, drinking water, showers, toilets, tennis, barbecue, fishing boats and horses to rent, 1 km beach.

Sixteen kilometres east of La Cruz is **A** per person *Los Inocentes Lodge*, on slopes of Volcán Orosí, T/F679-9190, www.arweb.com/orosi, meals extra, 11 rooms with bath in beautiful former working hacienda, pool, horse-riding on the lower slopes of the volcano, forest trails and guides. Day trips possible for US$30 – call ahead.

Eating *Soda Estadio*, good, cheap. *Restaurant Mirador*, at the end of the only paved street, has superb views, good fish and rice. At nearby **Ciruelas de Miramar**, there is a good restaurant. Try the fried yucca at *Palenque Garabito*.

Transport Regular buses to **San José** from 0545 until 1630, 5 hrs. To **Liberia**, 5 daily from 0700 to 1730, 1½ hrs. To **Peñas Blancas**, 5 daily from 0730 to 1730, 1 hrs. To **Playa Jobo** in Bahía Solanos, at 0530, 1030 and 1500, from main plaza.

Isla Bolaños is a 25-ha National Wildlife Refuge protecting the nesting sites of the brown pelican, frigatebird and American oystercatcher. The island is covered with dry forest and you can only walk round the island at low tide. No camping allowed. The incoming tidal surge is very dangerous, be off the island before the tide comes in.

Border with Nicaragua – Peñas Blancas

Immigration Office hours 0800-1800 (Nicaragua 0800-1200 and 1300-1745). On leaving Costa Rica you have to go to Migración to surrender your passport to be stamped and to give in your immigration form. At another window you pay 75 colones for a 'Cruz Roja' stamp and to get your passport back. 'Helpers' may try and sell you the form before you arrive at the office – you do not have to buy it from them. Trolley pullers charge US$0.50 to carry bags between these posts, a short distance. Across the border, passports are inspected on the Nicaraguan side. Crossing to Nicaragua may be a slow process; if you arrive when a *Tica*, *Sirca* or other international bus is passing through this is especially true. When leaving Nicaragua you pay US$1 for the 'right to leave', another US$2 at customs and there are reports of a US$1 bus station tax on the Nicaraguan side. Visa stamps are given at the border. If you have no outward ticket for Costa Rica, and are challenged, you can buy a cheap bus ticket back to Nicaragua at the border (valid for 1 year).

Crossing by private vehicle Entering Costa Rica by car, first pay your entrance stamp, then go to Aduana Permiso de Vehículo for your vehicle permit (state how long you want);

purchase insurance at the 'Seguro Obligatorio' window. Your vehicle is then briefly inspected before you can depart. Fumigation cost US$3 for cars, US$4 for pick-ups. Leaving by car, just hand over the printed vehicle permit you were given on arrival. For documents and other requirements, see Essentials.

Transport There are several express or ordinary buses a day from/to San José, 100 m north of Coca-Cola terminal, 4 hrs or 6 hrs, US$5, only the earliest (at 0430 and 0500) from **San José** will get you to the border before it closes. Bus from the frontier to **Liberia**, US$1.25, 1½ hrs. Only a few buses from **La Cruz**, US$0.60, taxi costs US$4-5.

Directory Banks: there is a bank in *Aduana* (usually changes cash, does not change TCs, open 0800-1200, 1300-1600) and money changers to ease your passage. Good rates if you shop around, no great difference between rates on either side.

Nicoya Peninsula

San José

Fringed by idyllic white-sand beaches along most of the coastline, the Nicoya Peninsula is hilly and hot. There are few towns of any size and most of the roads not connecting the main communities are in poor condition. While a few large hotel resorts are increasingly taking over what were once isolated coves, they are generally grouped together and there are still many isolated beaches to explore. Several small areas of the peninsula are protected to preserve wildlife, marine ecosystems and the geological formations of Barra Honda.

Ins and outs

There are several ways of getting to the Nicoya Peninsula, the simplest being from the north by road via Liberia (bus Liberia-Nicoya, see page 1091). Further south on the mainland, leaving the Pan-American near Las Juntas, is the **Río Tempisque ferry**. After crossing on this ferry (hourly 0400-0000, car US$3, bicycle US$0.30, motorbike US$1, pedestrians free, queues of up to 1 hr on Sun) you can drive to Nicoya. Just across the river is **L** *Hotel Rancho Humo*, T255-2463, F255-3573, www.arweb.com/birds.html, boat trips on Tempisque and Bebedero rivers, visits to Palo Verde and Barra Honda national parks. (At La Mansión junction there is a good restaurant, *Tony Zecca Ristorante Il Nonno*, sandwiches and steaks, reasonable prices, menu in 6 languages, interesting international visitors' book to sign, open Sun).

    A 3rd route takes the **Salinero car ferry** from Puntarenas across the Gulf of Nicoya to *Playa Naranjo*. See page 1069. Buses meet the ferry for Nicoya, (US$1.25, 2¼ hrs), Sámara (US$1.30), Coyote, Bejuco and Jicaral. A 4th route also departs from Puntarenas to *Paquera* from the dock at C 35. See page 1069. On arrival, get on the bus (which waits for the ferry) as quickly as possible (to Cóbano, 2-3 hrs, US$1.25, bad road, to Montezuma US$2.60, 1½ hrs at least), pay on the bus, or get a taxi. *Hotel Playa Tambor* also runs a ferry service, Naviera-Tambor SA, between Puntarenas and Paquera, with a bus running between Paquera and the hotel in Tambor.

All the beaches on the Nicoya Peninsula are accessible by road in the dry season. Most places can be reached by bus from Nicoya. However, the stretch from Paquera to Montezuma and the Cabo Blanco Reserve is connected to Playa Naranjo and the north only by very poor roads. There is no bus connection between Playa Naranjo and Paquera and the road is appalling even in the dry season.

Getting there

Getting around

Costa Rica

Beaches on the Nicoya Peninsula

Even in high season, you will be able to find a beautiful beach which is uncrowded. There are so many of them, just walk until you find what you want. You will see plenty of wildlife along the way, monkeys, iguanas and squirrels as well as many birds. There can be dangerous undertows on exposed beaches; the safest bathing is from those beaches where there is a protective headland, such as at Playa Panamá in the north.

Santa Cruz Heading from Liberia by road, the first town you reach is Santa Cruz, known as Costa Rica's National Folklore City for its colourful fiestas, dancing and regional food. January is the month for the **fiesta** dedicated to Santo Cristo de Esquipulas, when it can be difficult to find accommodation. There is also a rodeo fiesta in January. But for the rest of the year, it's a quiet little town, with a charming modern church, providing supplies for the beach tourism industry. If you need to buy food, Santa Cruz is a good place to stock up.

Sleeping and eating B *Diria*, right on the main road, T680-0080, bath, restaurant and a couple of pools. **C-D** *La Pampa*, 25 m west of Plaza de los Mangos, T680-0586, a/c, cheaper without, close to parque, good and clean. **D** *Plaza*, on the plaza, T680-0169, next to bus station, friendly owner. **E** *Anatolia*, 200 m south, 100 m west of plaza, T680-0333, plywood partitions, dirty bathrooms. **G** per person *Pensión Isabel*, behind the church, T680-0173, simple box rooms. Several *sodas* around town. *Coopetortilla* is a local institution, a women's cooperative cooking local dishes on wooden fires. Very cheap and enjoyable.

Transport Bus Buses leave and arrive from terminals on Plaza de los Mangos. **San José**-Santa Cruz, 9 daily, 0700-1800, 4½ hrs, US$5, C 18-20, Av 3, ½ block west of Terminal Coca-Cola, return 0300-1700; bus Santa Cruz-**Tamarindo**, 2030, return 0645, US$1, also to **Playa Flamingo** and nearby beaches, 0630, 1500, return 0900, 1700, 64 km; Santa Cruz-**Liberia** every hr, US$1, 0530-1930; Santa Cruz-**Nicoya** hourly 0630-2130, US$0.35; taxi Santa Cruz-Nicoya, US$10.50 for 2 people.

Nicoya Peninsula

Directory Banks: *Banco Nacional*, with ATM, on main road. **Communication**: Post office 400 m west of Plaza de los Mangos.

In **Guaitíl**, 9 km east of Santa Cruz and 19 km north of Nicoya, local artisans specialize in reproductions of indigenous Chorotegan pottery. They work with the same methods used by Indians long ago, with minimal or no use of a wheel and no artificial paints. Ceramics are displayed at the local *pulpería*, or outside houses. At **San Vicente**, 2 km southeast of Guaitíl, local craftsmen work and sell their pottery.

In the community of Bolsón, 22 km east of Santa Cruz, you can stay in simple accommodation with local families at **B** *CoopeOrtega*, c/o *Simbiosis Tours* T/F286-4203, www.agroecoturismo.net which is part of the Cooprena network of community-based accommodation. Opportunities for exploring the Bolsón, Charco and Tempisque rivers to see crocodiles, birds and views of the Parque Nacional Palo Verde. Also horse-riding and to experience typical food, dances and music from the region.

West shore beaches

A number of beaches are reached by unpaved roads from the Santa Cruz-Liberia road. Many can be reached by bus from the Liberia bus station, others may require you to change buses at Santa Cruz.

After the town of **Comunidad** a road leads east to Playa del Coco and Playa Hermosa and the ever-pending resort development of Playa Panamá.

Playa del Coco is a popular resort some 8 km from the highway, set in an attractive islet-scattered bay hemmed in by rocky headlands. It's a good place to chill out, with a mix of good services without being too developed. The best beaches are to the south. All activities concentrate on the beach and fishing. Cocos is the starting point for surf trips to **Santa Rosa** spots by boat, such as **Witches Rock**. Snorkelling and diving are nothing special, but for a diving expedition to the Islas Murciélagos contact *Mario Vargas Expeditions* (see below).

There are bars, restaurants and one or two motels along the sandy beach. It is too small to get lost. To reach it, leave the road at Comunidad (road paved). Be wary of excursions to secluded Playa Verde, accessible by boat only, as some boatmen collaborate with thieves and reap the rewards later. A 2½-km road heads southwest from Playa del Coco to **Playa Ocotal**.

Playa del Coco & around

Costa Rica

Sleeping AL-A *La Puerta del Sol*, north of town, T670-0195, F670-0650, www.lapuertadelsol.com Great little family-run hotel. Great food in Italian restaurant, small pool and gym, friendly atmosphere and free scuba lesson in hotel pool. **A** *Villa del Sol*, at northern end of beach, T/F670-0085, www.villadelsol.com, Canadian owned (Quebec), pool, clean, friendly, safe, big garden with parrots. Recommended.

Good discounts (up to 40%) in green season

Esparza

To San Ramón & San José

Barranca

San Gerardo

Caldera

Puntarenas

Reserva Biológica
Isla Pájaros

*Golfo de
Nicoya*

Isla
San
Lucas

Playa
Naranjo

Reserva
Biológica
Islas
Negritos

Jicaral

Paquera

Curú

Refugio de Fauna
Silvestre Curú

Tambor

Playa Cocal

San Francisco
de Coyote

Cóbano

Montezuma

Playa
Coyote

Playa
Caletas

Cabuya

Malpaís

Reserva Natural
Absoluta
Cabo Blanco

Playa
Manzanillo

Playa
Balsitas

Ocean

B-D *Cabinas Chale*, north of town, T670-0036, Double rooms and villas, with private bath. Pretty quiet, small resort style spot, small pool, 50 m from beach. Good deal, especially villas which sleep up to 6. **B** *Coco Palms*, T670-0367, F670-0117, cocopalms@hotmail.com, beside football pitch, German-run, large pool, gringo bar and parking. **C** *Cabinas El Coco*, just north of the pier right on the beach, T670-0110, F670-0167, cocomar@racsa.co.cr, with bath and good reasonable restaurant. **C-D** *Luna Tica*, south of the plaza, T670-0127, F670-0459, also with an annex over the road (friendly, clean), both usually full at weekends. **At Playa Ocotal**: only top end accommodation but good diving services, **LL-AL** *El Ocotal Resort Hotel*, T670-0321, F670-0083, elocotal@racsa.co.cr, rooms, suites and bungalows, PADI dive shop on beach, sport fishing, surfing, tennis, 3 pools, car hire, excursions. **A** *Villa Casa Blanca*, T/F670-0448, 15 idylic rooms, with breakfast, friendly and informative, family atmosphere, small pool. Pricey but very good.

Eating *Cocos*, on the plaza, bit flashy and pricey for the area, good seafood. *El Roble*, beside the main plaza, is a popular bar/disco. *Mariscos la Guajira*, on southern beach, popular and beautiful beach-front location. *Papagayo*, good seafood, recommended. *Playa del Coco*, on beach is popular, open 0600. *Bananas* , on the road out of town, is the place to go drinking and dancing until the early hours. *Jungle Bar*, a little further out of town, is another lively, slightly rougher option.

Transport Bus from **San José** from C 14, Av 1-3, 0800, 1400, 5 hrs, return 0800, 1400 US$4.50. 6 buses daily from **Liberia** 0530-1815, return 0530-1800.

Directory Banks: *Banco Nacional*, closed Sat. *Café Internet 2000*, on road out of town. First and only internet café in town. **Tour operators**: *Deep Blue Diving*, beside *Hotel Coco Verde*, T670-1004, www.deepblue-diving.com, has diving trips to Islas Catalinas and Islas Murcielago, where sightings of manta rays and bull sharks are common. 2-tank dive, US$65 high season, US$50 low. Will also just rent gear. Other companies include *Rich Coast Diving*, TT/F670-0176, www.divecostarica.com and *Mario Vargas Expeditions*, PO Box 6398-1000, Playa del Coco, T/F670-0351, www.divexpeditions.com *Agua Rica Charters*, T670-0805, www.aguaricacharters.com or contact them through the internet café, can arrange transport to Witches Rock for surfers, approx US$400 for up to 10.

Playa Hermosa A spur road breaks from the main road to Playa del Coco heading north to Playa Hermosa. This is one of the nicest resorts and served by a paved road. Accommodation is mixed, but it's a good quiet alternative to other beaches in the region. Walking either to the left or the right you can find isolated beaches with crystal-clear water.

Sleeping At the southern end of the beach is **AL** *Villa del Sueño*, T/F672-0026, www.villadelsueno.com Canadian-owned, with big rooms, good restaurant, pool and live music. Apartments for longer stays. **B** *Hotel Playa Hermosa*, at the southern end of the beach, T/F672-0046. Italian run, 22 clean rooms, better prices for groups, very good Italian restaurant overlooking pleasant shaded gardens. Recommended. **E** *El Cenizaro*, T672-0186, 7 rooms on beach with bath, cold water. Hard beds. *Mini-Super* store next door. Further north is **AL** *El Velero*, T672-0036, F672-0016, elvelero@racsa.co.cr, or www.costaricahotel.net, right on the beach with an airy villa feel, nice rooms with a/c and private bathrooms, pool, clean, good reasonably priced restaurant. **B** *Iguana Inn*, T672-0065, 100 m from the beach, small place with 9 rooms, some with kitchen. Relaxed, laid-back spot, with use of kitchen, and laundry.

Transport Bus from Liberia, *Empresa Esquivel*, 0730, 1130, 1530, 1730, 1900, return 0500, 0600, 1000, 1600, 1700, US$0.80.

Diving *Bill Beard's Diving Safari*, based at the *Sol Playa Hermosa Resort* on Playa Hermosa, T672-0012, F672-0231, www.billbeardcostarica.com, one of the longest-running diving operations in the country, offering a wide range of diving options in the region.

Playa de Panamá The big Papagayo tourist complex near Playa Panamá, which once planned to provide as many as 60,000 hotel rooms, started in 1993. Objections from many quarters have delayed construction, but the project continues at a slower pace. **Sleeping** The area has several all-inclusive resort-style hotels (**LL**) including *El Natcuti, Hotel Costa Blanca* and *Hotel Esmeralda*.

South of Filadefia, close to Belén, a mostly paved but poor road heads east to the beach and popular surf spot Playa Tamarindo and other beaches nearby. Looking directly out to the west, the sunsets are incredible and while most make their way to the beach for that magic moment, the strong beach culture makes this a popular place to hang out.

Playa Tamarindo & around
Good surfing at north end of Playa Tamarindo

The beach is attractive – although not stunning – with strong tides in places so take care if swimming. The main reason to visit is that happy balance between good services without complete isolation or over development.

Either side of the magic moment, Tamarindo is a flurry of activity. Three good breaks provide a variety of options for the surf crowd that flock to town. Beyond surf and sun, the most popular excursion is an evening trip to **Playa Grande** and the leatherback nesting sights from October to March. While the town is driven by surfing, there's a good blend of hotels and bars to make it a good beach stop – not too busy, but not so quiet it's dead. The local website is at **www.tamarindo.com**

Sleeping **L-AL** *Tamarindo Diria*, near centre of town, T/F653-0031, tnodiria@racsa.co.cr, full range of services, good restaurants, beautiful pool, expensive tours offered with good guide. **L** *Capitán Suizo*, a long way south of the centre towards Playa Langosta, T653-0075, F653-0292, www.hotelcapitansuizo.com, 8 bungalows, 22 rooms with patio or balcony, a/c pool, restaurant, kayaking, scuba diving, surfing, sport fishing available, riding on hotel's own horses, Swiss management. One of Costa Rica's distinctive hotels.

Book well in advance at Christmas and New Year

A-B *Cabinas Hotel Zullymar*, T653-0140, F653-0028, www.tr506.com/zullymar, rooms with a/c and cheaper cabins, good beach bar. Recommended. **B** *Pozo Azul*, at the entrance to town, T653-0280, cabins, a/c, cheaper in low season, cooking facilities, clean, good, swimming pool. **B** *Cabinas Marielos*, T/F653-0141, www.asstcar.co.cr/marielos.htm, clean basic rooms, with bath, use of kitchen, popular, book ahead. **C** *Frutas Tropicales*, just south of *Tamarindo Vista Best Western*, T/F653-0041, 3 simple, spotless and quiet rooms.

E *Rodamar*, 50 m from *Tamarindo Vista*, T653-0109, no a/c or fan, no mosquito nets, but clean, helpful, use of kitchen, shared bath. Family atmosphere and cheapest good deal. **F** per person *Doly's*, basic, some rooms with bath, bars on balcony, unfriendly, key deposit only returned after room inspection, lots of rules and regulations, **camping** nearby, a cheap place to sling a hammock or rent a tent but thefts reported. **F** *Tsunami*, basic, tidy rooms, private bath and use of the kitchen. Turn up and see if there's free space – probably full of surfers more interested in water than comfort – great value.

Eating *Arco Iris*, on road heading inland, cheap vegetarian, great atmosphere. *Coconut Café*, pizzas, pastries and best fish on beach near *Tamarindo Vista*. Check the *sodas* for good breakfasts and cheap evening meals. *El Arrecife*, popular spot to hang out, good chicken and pizzas. *El Cocodrilo*, nice garden serving seafood and drinks. There's a new *Thai* restaurant at the northern end of town. *El Milagro*, buffet breakfast from 0700, surf and turf to the core. *Fiesta del Mar*, large thatched open barn on the loop at the end, good food, good value. *Frutas Tropicales*, near *Tamarindo Vista*, snacks and breakfast. *Iguana Surf* restaurant on road to Playa Langosta. Good atmosphere and food. *Portofino*, good ice-cream. *Stellas*, very good, try *dorado* with mango cream. Recommended.

Transport **Air** Several daily flights to Tamarindo (TNO) with *Sansa* (US$66 one way) and *Travelair* (US$73) from San José which connect with international arrivals. Daily flight from Fortuna with *Sansa*. **Buses** From **Santa Cruz**, 0410, 1330, 1500 daily. Tamarindo to Santa Cruz first bus at 0600, US$1. Express bus from **San José** daily from Terminal Alfaro, 1530, return 0600 Mon-Sat, 0600, 1230 Sun, 5½ hrs. Bus back to San José, can be booked through *Hotel Tamarindo Diria*, US$5.

Costa Rica

Directory Banks: *Banco Nacional* opposite *Hotel Diria*. **Internet**: *Interlink* continues to be the only internet service in town. Expensive. **Tour operators** Many provide tours to see the turtles nesting at night in Playa Grande. *Iguana Surf* rent out surf boards, they have one outlet near the beach, opposite the supermarket, the other in the restaurant of the same name. *Tamarindo Adventures*, T653-0108, F653-0640, tamaquad@racsa.co.cr, also offers a range of tours.

Playa Grande North of Playa Tamarindo is Playa Grande and the **Parque Nacional Marino Las Baulas de Guanacaste** (485 ha terrestrial, 22,000 ha marine), well known as a nesting site for leatherback turtles October-February. Organized trips to the beaches are possible from Tamarindo. The road from the main highway at Belén leads directly to Playa Grande, a sleepy town with almost no transport and no way of getting around.

Sleeping AL-A *Hotel Las Tortugas*, T653-0423, F653-0458, nela@cool.co.cr, www.cool.co.cr/usr/turtles, 11 rooms with bathroom, pool, restaurant, meals included, right on the beach in the centre of town, tours arranged. **B-C** *Lotus Surf Lodge*, T/F653-0490, www.lotussurflodge.com, formerly *Rancho Diablo*. 10 rooms with fan, good set up for surfers. **G** per person *Cabinas/Restaurante Playa Grande*, 500 m before beach at the entrance to town, T354-7661 (mob), 8 cabins with bath and kitchen, also camping.

Playa Flamingo & beaches to the north The bay around Playa Flamingo has white sand although the actual beach has some fairly intrusive developments with a grab-all approach to beachfront properties; in fact, the beach is now polluted and not as beautiful as it once was. But several other smaller beaches retain a relaxed atmosphere where life is governed by little more than the sunrise and beautiful sunsets. Of the following beaches, **Brasilito** is probably most suited to the budget traveller, but all make for interesting exploratory forrays.

Sleeping and eating At Playa Flamingo: **AL** *Mariner Inn*, T654-4081, F654-4024, mariner@costarica.net, 12 new rooms with bath, a/c, free camping on the beach. As well as several resorts.

   At Playa Conchal: is a beautiful 3-km beach full of shells which you can explore even if it is dominated by the **LL** *Meliá Playa Conchal*, T654-4123, F654-4181, mconchal@racsa.co.cr, 5-star resort with 18-hole golf course and supposedly the largest swimming pool in Central America.

   At Playa Brasilito: several hotels and cabinas along the road and near beach. **B-C** *Hotel Brasilito*, close to beach on plaza, T654-4237, F654-4247, www.brasilito.com Good rooms, also with horses (US$30 for 2 hrs), kayaks (US$10 for ½ day) and bikes (US$30 for ½ day) to rent. **C** *Ojos Azules*, T/F654-4343, run by Swiss couple, 18 cabins, good breakfasts with home-baked bread, nightmare décor. **F** per person at *Brasilito Lodge*, right on the beachT/F654-4890, www.brasilito-conchal.com Big rooms, good beds, bit of a bargain really. Internet service, several tours available. Also camping (**G**). *La Casita del Pescado* has some reasonably priced fish dishes which you have to eat quick because the stools are concrete. Restaurant *La Boca de la Iguana*, on beach, good value. *Pizzeria Il Forno*, serves a mean pizza.

   At Playa Potrero: a long, arching, black-sand beach: **A-B** *Cabinas Bahía Esmeralda*, T654-4480, F654-4479, Italian restaurant, garden, pool, hot water, roof ventilator. **A** *Bahía Potrero Beach Resort*, T654-4183, F654-4093, bar, pool, 10 rooms with bath. **A-B** *Cabinas Isolina* T654-4333, F654-4313, www.isolinabeach.com 250 m from beach, nice garden, roof ventilator. **E** per person *Cabinas Mayra*, T654-4213, on beach, friendly, with pretty, basically equipped cabins. Camping on the beach (**G**)

   Las Brisas, at the northern end of the beach, is a great spot for a beer and a snack, and surprisingly popular – well, 5 people – for its cut-off location. *Costa Azul*, by the football pitch, is popular with locals.

Transport Bus from **San José** to Flamingo, Brasilito and Potrero, daily from Av 3, C 18-20, 0800, 1000, 6 hrs, return 0900, 1400. From **Santa Cruz** daily 0630, 1500, return 0900, 1700, 64 km to Potrero.

Playa Junquillal is one of the cleanest beaches in Costa Rica and is still very empty. It is completely off the beaten track and has almost no tourist facilities. What it does have is a selection of stylish hotels, most of which are quite pricey. But there is camping if you have a tent.

Playa Junquillal, south of Tamarindo

Sleeping On the way in, just north of Junquillal, is **A-AL** *Iguanazul*, T653-0124, F653-0123, www.iguanazul.com, 24 different sizes of tiled-roof cabins on a cliff, great spot, hot water, fan or a/c, pool, restaurant, bar, great sunsets, sport fishing on 27-ft *Marlin Genie*, close to good surfing. **A** *Guacamaya Lodge*, T/F653-0431, www.guacamayalodge.com, immaculately maintained bungalows and one fully equipped house (sleeps 4, **C** per person) nice location with pool, ocean views, Swiss cuisine. **A** *El Lugarcito*, T/F653-0436, B&B, looks good. **B** *Tatanka*, T/F653-0426, 10 cabins with a pool, good restaurant with Italian, French and *Tico* dishes. **B-C** *Hibiscus*, T/F653-0437, big rooms with big windows and lots of natural light, seafood restaurant with German specialities, cared for garden, 50 m to beach, German-run. **B** *Playa Junquillal*, T653-0432, sleeping 2-4 so excellent value for a group. Right on the beach, great setting, ideal for surfers and beach lovers.

Hotels are listed in order encountered

    Camping, after *Iguanazul* at the northern entrance to town off main road down a dirt track at *Camping Los Malinches*, **G** per person, T653-0429, spectacular location, clean bathroom provided. Worth the effort, but bring all your own food.

Eating *La Puesta del Sol*, T653-0442. The only restaurant along the strip but then nothing could compete with the dishes from this little piece of Italy. US$10-15 for a dish, with a spectacular setting. Reservations required due to being so popular. **Transport** Daily bus from Santa Cruz departs 1030, returns to Santa Cruz at 1530.

Nicoya, at the heart of the Peninsula, is a pleasant little town distinguished by possessing the country's second oldest church, the 17th-century church of **San Blas**. Damaged by earthquake in 1822 it was restored in 1831, and is currently undergoing renovations. The Parque Central, on Calle and Avenida Central, is leafy and used for occasional concerts. Buses arrive at Av 1, C 3-5. Most hotels and banks are within a couple of blocks of the central park.

Nicoya
Colour map 7, grid B2

Sleeping **B** *Complejo Turístico Curime*, 500 m south of the centre on road to Sámara, T685-5238, F685-5530. Fully equipped bungalows, 3-m deep pool, private airstrip! The best in town, but needs touching up. **D** *Jenny*, or Yenny as the sign says, on the corner of C 1, Av 4, T685-5050, F686-6471, spotless, with bath, a/c, towels, soap and TV. Cavernous rooms – book in with a friend and play hide and seek. Recommended. **E** *Las Tinajas*, opposite Liberia bus stop on Av 1, T685-5081, F685-5777, with bath, modern, clean, good value. **E** *Pensión Venecia*, opposite old church on square, T685-5325, squidgy beds but good value for the price. Recommended. **F** *Chorotega*, C Central, Av 4-6, T685-5245, with bath (**F** without), very good value, clean, quiet. Rooms at back have windows. Clothes-washing facilities (good Chinese *soda* opposite).

Eating A good restaurant is *Chop Suey* (Chinese). *Daniela*, breakfast, lunches, coffee, *refrescos*, good. *Teyo*, near *Hotel Jenny*, good, quick service. Opposite *Chorotega* is *Soda El Triángulo*, good juices and snacks, friendly owners. *Café de Blita*, 2 km outside Nicoya towards Sámara, good.

Transport **Bus** from **San José**, 8 daily from Terminal Alfaro, 6 hr; from **Liberia** hourly 0430-1900; from **Santa Cruz** hourly 0630-2130. To **Playa Naranjo** at 0500 and 1300, US$1.45, 2¼ hrs. 2 buses to **Sámara**, 37 km by paved road, 1 to **Nosara**.

Directory **Banks** with ATMs on main square and C 3, with very welcome a/c. **Post office**: on corner of main square. **Useful addresses**: The area conservation offices (ACT) are on the northern side of central park. There is no general information for visitors, but they can assist with specific enquiries.

Costa Rica

Parque Nacional Barra Honda

A small park in the north of the Nicoya Peninsula (2,295 ha), Barra Honda National Park was created to protect a *mesa* with a few caves and the last remains of dry tropical forest in the region. The park office is near **Barra Honda** at Santa Ana (entry US$6, no permit required), at the foot of the *mesa*, and there are two different trails to the top; two hours' hiking. Also noteworthy are the *cascadas*, bizarre limestone fountains built by sedimentation on a seasonal riverbed. You'll need a guide to get here, as the trails are hopelessly muddled by cowpaths; arrange in advance for the visit to the cave. A full visit requires harnesses, ropes and guides, US$33 for three guides, US$11 per person for equipment. Avoid coming in the rainy season (May to November), but the dry season is very hot in the open fields. Bring your own food from Nicoya. *Turinsa* operates a Saturday tour from San José to the Barra Honda caves, T221-9185, US$90 includes breakfast and lunch. *Las Delicias Ecotourism Project*, owned and operated by local community at park entrance, T685-5580, three bungalows, comfortable accommodation, camping, **F**, Costa Rican meals at reasonable prices, guided tours available. ■ *Getting there: first go to Nicoya, from where there are several buses a day to* **Quebrada Honda** *(first bus 1030, last bus returns for Nicoya 1630, giving you only 2 hrs in the park), which is 1 hr's walk away from the park. Alternatively, get a lift.*

Sámara
Colour map 7, grid B2

Sámara is a smallish *Tico* village that has managed to maintain some of its regular way of life alongside steady tourist development. The beautiful beach at **Sámara**, 37 km from Nicoya on a paved road, is probably the safest and one of the best bathing beaches in Costa Rica. **Playa Carrillo** is 5 km away at the south end of the beach. The litter problem is being tackled with litter bins, warning signs, refuse collections and bottle banks. Both places have airstrips served by scheduled services from San José.

Sleeping and eating **AL** *Mirador de Sámara Aparthotel*, T656-0044, F656-0046, www.miradordesámara.com Very friendly, German-owned, rising up the hill above the village. 6 large, cool and comfortable suites with bath and kitchen. Recommended. **A** *Hotel Fénix*, T656-0158, F656-0162, www.fenixhotel.com On beach about 2 km east of the village. 6 slightly cramped double units with fans, hot water, small pool, friendly.

A-D *Cabinas Cantamar*, T656-0284, café, art gallery, simple rooms on the beach. Great for a peaceful or longer stay. **B** *Belvedere*, T/F 656-0213, Very friendly German-owners, with a cosy hotel sloping up the hill. 10 small rooms, very clean. Recommended. **B** *Marbella*, T656-0121, F656-0122, German-run, beautiful grounds, pool, good service, about 300 m from beach. Recommended. **B-D** *Casa Valeria*, on the beach near the supermarket, T656-0511. Friendly and good value, especially for 3 sharing, breakfast included, various different rooms, some with sea view, all nicely decorated, most with bath, hot water, kitchen and laundry available, small bar, tours, tickets and car rental arranged. Recommended. **E** *Arenas*, T656-0320, comfortable, cheaper for longer stays, good restaurant opposite, pleasant bar next door.

On the eastern side of the village, on the beach, try *Camping Coco*, T656-0496, with toilets, electricity until 2200 or *Camping San Martín*, T656-0336, same family, same deal, **G** in highest season. Slightly further from the beach is *Camping Los Mangos*.

There are several cheap *sodas* around the football pitch in the centre of town. Up a notch, but still cheap, is *Soda Sol y Mar*, serving a mixture of Costa Rican and western food. Opposite is *Las Brasas*, a mid-range Spanish restaurant and bar. Other mid-range restaurants include *Gaucho*, a short walk along the Nicoya road – cheaper *Soda Ananas* is next door – or try *Casa Naranja* in the hotel of the name. On the beach next to *Cabinas El Ancla* is the very good-value French-owned *Restaurant Delfín*, they also have cabinas, **B**, and close by is the untried but newly reopened *Restaurant Acuario* serving *Tico* and other food.

Nightlife *Bar La Góndola* is popular and opposite is *Bar Colocho*. *Dos Lagartos* disco is on the beach near *Al Manglar* and the disco at **Isla Chora** is the place to be during the season if you like resort discos.

Shopping The supermarket, near Casa del Mar, is well stocked and you can get fresh bread and croissants from *Chez Joel* .

Transport Buses From Nicoya, 45 km, US$1.15, 1½ hrs, 0800, 1500, 1600, return 0530, 0630, 1130, 1330, 1630. Express bus from Terminal Alfaro, San José daily at 1230, return Mon-Sat 0430, Sun 1300, 5-6 hrs. School bus to **Nosara** around 1600 – ask locally for details. It is not possible to go from Sámara along the coast to Montezuma, except in 4WD vehicle; not enough traffic for hitching. **Taxis** (official and others) stop outside bus station (US$20 to Nosara, US$10 to Nicoya).

Directory There is no **bank** in Sámara, although hotels may change money. There is no **internet** at present, although hotels may offer access. The **post office** is almost on the beach. **Tour operators** Most hotels will arrange tours for you. You can rent bikes from near the *ferretería* on the road to Cangrejal. Recommended, though, is the newer *Tip Top Tours* (T656-0650), run by a very nice French couple, offering the dolphin tours (from US$45 per person), mangrove tours (US$43 per person) and waterfall tours (US$20 per person). Naturalist guided tours to Barra Honda and Isla Chora (US$70 per person), as well as slightly more unusual trips like *Journée Cowboy* where you spend a day on the ranch roping cattle and eat with a *Tico* family.

Nosara (www.nosara.com) is a small village about 26 km north of Sámara without much to see or do in it – which makes it ideal if you like lying around on beaches. Indeed most come for the three unspoiled beaches which are not particularly close to the village.

Nosara
Colour map 7, grid B2

    Playa Nosara, to the north of the village across the Río Nosara where you may see turtles (see Ostional below), **Peladas** the prettiest and smallest, south of the river, and **Guiones**, which is safe for swimming and good for surfing. A colony of expatriates has formed the Nosara Civic Association to protect the area's wildlife and forests and to prevent exploitation.

Sleeping L *Hotel Playa de Nosara*, T682-0122, F682-0123, www.nosarabeachhotel.com, with amazing views, undergoing complete renovation, excellent restaurant. *Olga's Bar* is on the beach nearby. **A-B** *Rancho Suizo Lodge,* on Playa Pelada, T682-0057, F682-0055, www.nosara.ch. Swiss-owned, bungalows, restaurant, credit cards accepted, whirlpool, hiking, riding, bird and turtle-watching. **B** *Casa Río Nosara*, T682-0117, F682-0182, www.tropical-holiday.com, rancho-style house with cabins and nice garden, clean, friendly, camping, canoe tours and horse-riding arranged, German owners.

    D-E *Alan's Surf Camp* , T682-0251, michaelg@racsa.co.cr Almost on the beach, very chill surfer hang-out, rooms with bunkbeds, shared bath, very relaxed. Friendly manager and discounts for longer stays. Good value. **E** *Cabinas Chorotega*, in the village near the supermarket, T682-0129, 8 simple, clean rooms, shared or own bath. Bar and restaurant downstairs so can be noisy. **F** *Cabinas Agnell*, in the village, T682-0142, with bath, good value.

    Close to Nosara,17 km north of Sámara, is **A** *Villaggio*, at Punta Guiones de Garza, T686-0784, vilaggio@racsa.co.cr, an upmarket yet simply furnished beach hotel with vacation ownership plan, 30 bungalows, international restaurant, club house, bars, pool, disco, good packages arranged in San José, T233-2476, F222-4073.

Eating At Playa Peladas, try *Olga's* for seafood on the beach, or *La Luna* slightly up the hill for good food and ambience. The restaurant at *Hotel Amost Paradise* serves good food with a great view. In the middle section, try *Giardino Tropicale* for pizza, the European restaurant at *Casa Romántica* or the *Gilded Iguana* for gringo food and good company. *Alan's Surf Camp* does surfers' breakfasts. Finally, south along the road out of town, is *La Dolce Vita* for good but pricey Italian food. There are plenty of *sodas* in the village, including *Soda Vanessa* which is good and very cheap. Some of the nightlife is in the village as well – *Bambú*, *Disco Tropicana* and various other hang-outs line the football pitch.

Transport Buses daily from Nicoya to Nosara, Garza, Guiones daily from main station, 1300, return 0600, US$2, 2 hrs, 65 km; from San José daily from Terminal Alfaro at 0600, 6 hrs, return 1245. **Air** *Sansa* has daily flights to San José.

Directory Communications: *Nosara Office Centre*, offering email, fax, photocopies and international calls. **Language schools**: *Rey de Nosara* language school is in the village, T682

Costa Rica

0215. They can often advise about other things to see and do in the area and arrange tours. **Tour operators**: *Casa Río Nosara* for horse or river tours, and *Gilded Iguana* for kayaking and fishing. For turtle tours, try *Rancho Suizo* or *Lagarta Lodge* who are both sensitive to the turtles and don't exploit or bother them.

North of Nosara is **Playa Ostional** where Olive Ridley turtles lay eggs in July-November along the protected coastal strip of the **Refugio Nacional de Vida Silvestre Ostional**. The turtles arrive for nesting at high tide. The villagers are allowed to harvest the eggs in a designated area of the beach, the rest are protected and monitored. Outside the egg-laying period it is exceptionally quiet. Call the MINAE ranger station for more details.

Sleeping and eating There is very basic accommodation in cabins next to the village shop, **F** per person *Cabinas Ostional,* with bath, clean, friendly; also *Cabinas Guacamaya*, with bath, clean, good food on request. You can camp on the beach. 1 km south of *Cabinas Guacamaya* is a good restaurant, *Mirador de los Tortugueros,* coffee and pancakes recommended, good atmosphere. **Transport** There is 1 **bus** a day at 0500 to **Santa Cruz** and **Liberia**, returns at 1230 from Santa Cruz, 3 hrs, US$1.75.

Southern Nicoya Peninsula

Playa Naranjo The Southern Nicoya Peninsula is almost completely cut off from the north. Roads are appalling and those that exist are frequently flooded in part. For this reason most access the region by ferry from Puntarenas. Arriving at Playa Naranjo there are several expensive eating places by the dock and a gas station.

Sleeping **A** *Oasis del Pacífico* (**C** in rainy season), T/F661-1555, a/c, old building on beach, clean, quiet, pool, good restaurant, free transport from ferry. Recommended. **B** *El Paso*, T/F661-2610, with bath, **C** without, cold water, clean, pool. **E** *Cabinas Maquinay*, 1.3 km towards Jicaral, T661-1763, simple rooms with a pool and the attached *Disco Maquinay*.

Paquera is a small village 22 km along the coast from Playa Naranjo towards the main tourist areas. There are a few shops and some simple lodgings, for example *Cabinas Rosita* on the inland side of the village. It is separated from the quay by 1 km or so where, apart from a good *soda*, a restaurant, a public telephone and a branch of *Banco de Costa Rica*, there are no facilities.

Tambor This small village, 19 km from Paquera, has a dark-sand beach, some shops and restaurants. The beach is beautiful, 6-km long with rolling surf; 1½ hours on a bone-shaking road from the ferry. However cruise ships from Puntarenas come here, and part of the beach has been absorbed by the large and controversial *Hotel Playa Tambor*. Built around a cattle farm by the *Barcelo* group of Spain, the resort is alleged to have encroached on the public beach and drained a swamp which was a wildfowl habitat. A second stage is planned at Punta Piedra Amarilla, with a 500-boat yacht marina, villas and a total of 1,100 rooms.

Sleeping **L** *Hotel Playa Tambor*, T683-0303, F683-0317, www.barcelo.com 5-star all inclusive, every amenity. **L** *Tango Mar*, T683-0001, F683-0003, www.tangomar.com, 3 km from Tambor, all services including golf course and its own spectacular waterfall. **D** *Dos Lagartos*, T/F683-0236, cheap, clean, good value. On the beach, **D** *Cabinas Cristina*, with bath, T683-0028, cheaper without, good food; **D** *Cabinas del Bosque*, T683-0039, clean; and **E** *Hotel Hermosa Playa*, basic but clean, shared bath, restaurant, follow signs on main road as you enter town. *Bahía Ballena Yacht Club*, 15 mins' walk from Tambor, open in the high season only, friendly, free English book exchange, weekly traditional dances, good restaurant/bar, excellent place if you are looking for a crew position on a yacht Jun-Aug, many US craft here at that time. In the village there is a shop with public phones, a supermarket, agency for bicycle hire, and a good American-owned restaurant on the jetty. Take a torch for returning to hotel at night.

North of Playa Tambor is the **Curú National Wildlife Refuge**. Only 84 ha, but five different habitats exist here with 110 species of birds. Access is through private land, T661-2392 in advance and ask for Doña Julieta.

Cóbano, near Montezuma, can be reached by bus from Paquera ferry terminal, and buses for Tambor, Cóbano and Montezuma meet the launches from Puntarenas (there is an airstrip with flights from San José). Roads north, west and south out of Cóbano, require four-wheel drive. Cóbano has a petrol/gas station.

Montezuma

No longer a quiet sleepy hamlet, Montezuma is a very popular small village on the sea. It is a well-liked backpacking destination and at busy periods hotels fill up every day, so check in early. Although it gets crowded, there are some wonderful beaches, many are rocky, with strong waves making it difficult to swim, but very scenic. There are beautiful walks along the beach, sometimes sandy, sometimes rocky, always lined with trees, that visit impressive waterfalls. There is a **tourist office** at Monte Aventuras, which is very helpful and often knows which hotel has space; ask here first before looking around. The once popular *Cabinas Karen* are now closed. Prior to her death in 1994, Doña Karen donated her land to the National Parks in memory of her late husband creating what was to become **Reserva Natural Absoluta Cabo Blanco**. *Cabinas Karen* now house park guards.

Colour map 7, grid B2

Montezuma can be reached in 4 hours from Puntarenas if you get the early launch

Close to the village, 20 minutes up the Montezuma River, is a beautiful, huge waterfall with a big, natural swimming hole, beyond a smaller waterfall. Intrepid walkers can carry on up to further waterfalls but it can be dangerous and accidents have been reported. 6 km north of Montezuma is another waterfall with a pool right by the beach – follow the road out to the beach at the north end of town and keep going past three coves for about half an hour until you reach the trail off to the left (you can't miss it).

You can use Montezuma as a base for exploring the nearby **Reserva Natural Absoluta Cabo Blanco** (closed Monday and Tuesday). A shuttle service (US$3) leaves Montezuma at 0800 and 0900 and picks you up outside the park at 1500 or 1600. You can also arrange tours to **Isla Tortuga**. Many businesses rent horses – you should check the horses are fit and properly cared for.

Excursions

For organized tours and expeditions, see Tour operators below

Costa Rica

A *Horizontes*, on road to Cóbano, T/F642-0534, www.horizontes-montezuma.com, language school, restaurant, pool, hot water. Highly recommended. **AL-B** *Los Mangos*, a short walk south of the village, T642-0076. Large site comprising 9 bungalows (**AL**), each for 3 people with bath, hot water and fan, and 10 rooms, some with shared bath, some for 4 people (**A** or **B**). Different and fun. **B** *Cabinas Mar y Cielo*, on the beach, T642-0261, 6 rooms, sleeping 2-5 people, all the bath, fan and sea view. Recommended. **B** *Pargo Feliz*, T388-1731, has cabins with bath, and serves good food in a peaceful atmosphere – something the owners are keen on. **C-D** *La Aurora*, on the corner opposite *El Jardín*, T/F642-0051, 8 simple rooms with bath, cheaper without, fan, garden, hammocks, also boat trips for fishing or snorkelling, overpriced.

C *Montezuma Pacific*, 50 m west of the church, T642-0402, with private bath, hot water and a/c. **D** *Moctezuma*, T/F642-0058, 20 rooms with bath and fan, plans for hot water, clean and helpful. Very central and can be noisy. Sea view from rooms at the back. Bar and restaurant below serving usual selection of *típica* food – popular with *Ticos*. **E-F** *El Tucán*, T642-0284, wooden hotel on stilts, clean, small wood-panelled rooms, shared shower and toilet, fan, mosquito net on window. Recommended. **E** *Lucy*, follow road south past *Los Mangos*, T642-0273. One of the oldest hotels in town, 10 rooms with fans, some with sea view. Shared bath, pleasant balcony. Ultra-friendly *Tica* owner. Recommended. **E** *Pensión Arenas*, on the beach, T642-0308, run by Doña Meca, rustic small rooms, with fan, shared bath, no frills but pleasant balcony and sea view. Free camping.

Sleeping

Montezuma is a very small place; even hotels furthest from the centre are within a 10-minute walk

Out of town is **A** *Los Caballos*, 3 km north on road to Cóbano from Montezuma, T/F642-0124, www.centralamerica.com/cr, 8 rooms with bath, pool, outdoor restaurant, ocean views, gardens, 5 mins from beach, horses a speciality. **C** *Linda Vista*, T642-0104, on the hill, units sleep 6, with bath (cold water) and fan, ocean views. **D** *Cabinas Las Rocas*, 20 mins south of Montezuma, good but quite expensive meals, small, seashore setting, isolated. Also the *Mochila Inn*, T642-0030, 300 m outside Montezuma, has houses and apartments to rent, for around $350 per month.

Camping *Rincón de los Mono*, 500 m along the beach from the centre of Montezuma, T643-0048, clean, well organized, lockers for rent, many monkeys.

Eating For breakfast, don't miss the *Bakery Café* at the north end of town, which serves bread and cakes and vegetarian food. *El Chico*, popular beach hang-out. The best restaurant in town is the *Cocina Mediterránea* (also called *Playa de las Artistas*), mid-range, about 5 mins south of town on the road to Cabuya. For seafood, go to *Cocolores* on the beach behind *El Pargo Feliz* (closed Mon). In town try *El Sano Banano*, a health food restaurant, good vegetarian food, large helpings, daily change of menu, milkshakes, fresh fruit and yoghurt, owned by Dutch/Americans, free movies with dinner. *Los Mangos*, Greek food. *Pizzería*, next to *Hotel Montezuma*, self-service, good.

Several *sodas* around town, including *Soda El Caracol*, serving good *Tico* food. *Soda Monte Sol*, recommended for good Mexican burritos, good value, big helpings. *Soda Las Gemelas*, simple local food.

Shopping *El Hamaquero* sells locally made crafts and puts some of the profits back into the community. *Tienda Ecologica* also provides a post office service, international calls and money exchange. *Librería Topsy* sells books and maps – Mon-Fri, 0800-1400, until 1200 Sat.

Transport **Buses** Montezuma-**Paquera** daily at 0530, 1000, 1400, connecting with the car ferry, and also 0815, 1215 and 1600, connecting with the *lancha* to Puntarenas central docks. Tickets available in advance from tourist information centre; be at bus stop outside *Hotel Moctezuma*, in good time as the bus fills up quickly, US$2.60, 2 hrs. **Taxi** Montezuma-**Cóbano** US$3.50; taxi Paquera-Montezuma US$12.

Directory **Banks** Change money at *Hotel Moctezuma*, *Tienda Ecológica* and sometimes in *Aventuras en Montezuma* if they have enough colones (otherwise go to the *Banco Nacional* in Cóbano). **Communications** There is an *internet café* in the pizzeria next to the *Hotel Moctezuma*. **Laundry** Laundrette in *Pensión Jenny*. **Medical services** If you need a pharmacy, you will have to go to Cóbano. **Tour operators** *Montezuma Expeditions*,T642-0467, www.montezumaexpeditions.com, on the corner opposite *Soda Monte Sol*, offer a wide range of tours, including shuttle to Cabo Blanco (US$3), kayaking/snorkelling at Isla Cabuya (US$25 per person), day trip to Isla Tortuga (US$35 per person), horse rental (US$25) and bike rental (US$5 per day). Also boat/road transfers to Jacó/Tamarindo for around US$150 for up to 6 people. *Aventuras en Montezuma*, T/F642-0050, avenzuma@racsa.co.cr, offers a similar range, including whitewater rafting, canopy, sunset and wildlife tours for similar prices. Ivan and his staff are also exceptionally helpful as a tourist office and can advise on hotels and other matters locally and nationally.

Cabo Blanco Reserve Cabo Blanco Reserve (1,172 ha) is 11 km from Montezuma. The many marine birds include frigate birds, pelicans and brown boobies, and there are also monkeys, anteaters, kinkajou and collared peccary. Bathing in the sea or under small waterfall. ■ *0800-1600, closed Mon and Tue, entry US$6, jeep/taxi from Montezuma US$7, first at 0700, returns 1600.* At beautiful **Playa Balsitas**, 6 km from the entrance, there are lots of pelicans and howler monkeys.

At **Cabuya**, 2 km from Cabo Blanco Reserve, the sea can be cloudy after rough weather. Cabuya Island can be visited on foot at low tide. On the road west out of Cabuya, *Cafetería El Coyote* specializes in local and Caribbean dishes. On the west coast of the peninsula is the little village of **Mal País**. The coast here is virtually unspoilt with long white beaches, creeks and natural pools, and few facilities stretching further to the beach of **Santa Teresa**.

Costa Rica

Sleeping and eating In **Cabuya village**: **A** *Celaje*, T/F642-0374, on beach, very good Italian restaurant, pool, with bath, hot water, good. **D** *Cabinas y Restaurante El Ancla de Oro* (also some at **E**), T642-0369, some cabins with bath, others shared bathroom, seafood restaurant, lobster dinners US$10, filling breakfasts, owned by Alex Villalobos, horses US$20 per day with local guide, mountain bike rental, transport from Paquera launch available. *El Delfín* restaurant at crossroads, friendly, good-value local food.

At the road junction to **Mal País** is **A-E** *Frank's Place*, T640-0096, F640-0071, www.frankplace.com, is set in tropical gardens. Wide variety of rooms with private or shared bath, and self-catering options available. Good range of services and local advice. Heading south is **AL-C** *Mal País Surf Camp*, T/F640-0061, www.malpaissurfcamp.com, restaurant, pool, also camping **F** per person. **C** *Cabinas Mar Azul*, T642-0298, run by Jeannette Stewart, camping possible, delicious fried fish, shrimp, lobster. **D** *Cabañas Bosque Mar*, T640-0074, clean, large rooms, hot water shower, attractive grounds, good restaurant on beach nearby, 3 km to Cabo Blanco Reserve.

Continuing north along the coast, the next beach is **Playa Santa Teresa** with **AL** *Milarepa*, on beach, T/F640-0023, www.ticonet.co.cr/milarepa, nice bamboo bungalows, open-air bathroom. **D** *Cabinas Playa Santa Teresa*, T640-0137, 150 m from beach, surfboard rental, horses, German-run.

Transport Bus Montezuma-Cabuya US$1. There is a daily bus service between Cóbano and Mal País.

Central Pacific Coast

West of the Central Highlands lies a slim lowland strip of African palm with just the occasional cattle ranch. But for the visitor, it is the miles of beaches stretching from Jacó almost continuously south to Uvita. Parque Nacional Manuel Antonio is a major attraction with developed services. Further south, the beaches are quieter leading south to the Parque Nacional Marino Ballena, harder to get to and barely developed but interesting to divers and whale-watchers.

Costa Rica

From Esparza on the Pan-American Highway a road runs 21 km southeast to **San Mateo** (from where a road runs northeast to Atenas and the Central Highlands – see Meseta Central section). Just before San Mateo, at Higuito de San Mateo, is *Las Candelillas*, a 26-ha farm and reforestation project with fruit trees and sugar-cane. There is a camping area with showers, pool and riding, T428-9157, 428-8434. **AL** *El Rancho Oropéndola*, T/F428-8600 is at San Mateo, cabins with private bath or rooms with shared bath, rustic and peaceful, pool, nature trails.

From San Mateo a road runs south to **Orotina**, which used to be an important road/rail junction on the San José-Puntarenas route (**C** *Cabinas Kalim*, near plaza, T428-8082). From Orotina Finca Los Angeles, T224-5828, offers one-day nature tour on horseback through the mountains to the beach; US$65. Near Orotina is the **Iguana Park**, where the reptile-related options include watching, buying (as pets) or eating them, also 5 km trails and gift shop. ■ *0800-1600, US$15 entry, US$10 for guided tour, T240-6712.*

West of Orotina the road forks, northwest to the port of **Caldera** via Cascajal, and southwest to the Pacific Coast at Tárcoles.

The Costanera

The *Costanera* or coastal road passes through Jacó, Manuel Antonio and Quepos and on to Dominical before heading inland to **San Isidro de El General** or continuing south to Palmar Norte. If you want a popular beach, pick somewhere before Manuel Antonio. Beyond, although not deserted, you'll find things a lot quieter. If driving yourself, check the state of the roads and bridges before setting out to San Isidro. Just because buses are getting through, it doesn't mean cars can. The road is paved as far as Parrita (after Jacó) and with few potholes. Thereafter it is a good, but dusty, gravel road, paved in villages until Paquita, just before Quepos. After Quepos the road is unpaved to Dominical. From Dominical the road inland through Barú to San Isidro is paved but landslides can make this section hazardous. High clearance is needed if a bridge is down. South from Dominical, the Costanera drifts through small expat communities which are only just being explored by visitors. They cover a range of budgets, but all are for people seeking a little solitude… while it lasts.

Carara Biological Reserve

If travelling by car, leave nothing of value in your vehicle; thefts, robberies and scams are regularly reported in the area

Between Orotina and Jacó the Carara Biological Reserve (5,242 ha) is rich in wildlife. Three trails lead through the park, one lasting a couple of hours leaves from close to Tarcoles bridge, the others lasting a little over one hour from the ranger station to the south. The reserve protects a transitional zone from the dry north coast of the country to the very humid region of the southeast. Spider-monkeys, scarlet macaws and coatis can all be seen in the reserve. ■ *0700-1600, US$6.*

One of the most popular free experiences in Costa Rica is to dangle over the side of the Río Tárcoles bridge to see the opaque sediment filled waters broken only by the bony backs of the somnolent crocodiles below. It's easy to find the spot to stop, as parked cars cram the roadside, especially at dawn and dusk when scarlet macaws can be seen returning to their roosts from Carara National Park on the southern banks of the river.

You can get a closer look by taking a boat tours with *Jungle Crocodile Safari*, T292-2316, F225-4852, or *Crocodile ECO Tour*, T/F637-0426. US$25 per person from the dock in Tárcoles, US$39 round trip from Jacó.

Next to Carara is La Catarata, a private reserve with an impressive waterfall with natural pools for bathing; take the gravel road up the hill beside *Hotel Villa Lapas*: 5 km to entrance, 2½-km hike to falls and pools. Worth the effort. ■ *0800-1500, 15 Dec-15 Apr, US$7.50, T236-4140. There are signs on the main road.*

Sleeping & eating

AL *Hotel Villa Lapas*, next to the reserve (from Río Tarcolitos, turn left and go 500 m), reservations T637-0232, F637-0227, hvlapas@racsa.co.cr, with bath, pool, good restaurant, good bird-watching, easy access to mouth of Río Tárcoles, riding, guided tours to Carara, animals come close to the hotel at night. Recommended.

Nearby at **Playa Tárcoles**: **C** *Cabinas Carara*, T/F637-0178, basic, 16 cabins with bath, small, simple restaurant, pool, superb bird-watching at mouth of Río Tárcoles about 5 km along this road. 3 km from Tárcoles is *El Tico*, a good seafood restaurant.

Further south is **Punta Leona** with **L** *Villa Caletas*, to the south, T257-3653, F222-2059, www.distinctivehotels.com One of the distinctive hotels of Costa Rica, French owned, 8 rooms, 20 bungalows, atop a mountain with amazing views, spectacular sunsets, lush gardens, pool, restaurant, boat and nature tours. At **Playa Herradura** golfing enthusiasts with enjoy the **L** *Los Sueños Hotel and Golf Club*, T290-3311, F231-6040, www.los-suenos.com, full comfort, marina, hotel, 18-hole golf course.

Jacó

Be careful of the rip tides all along this coast

A short distance from Carara is Jacó, a large stretch of sandy beach, with a lively, youthful energy. It is popular with surfers, weekenders from San José and comes with a rough'n'ready, earthy commercial appeal. If you want to learn to surf, this is as good a place as any, with several surf shops offering courses and boards for rent.

Accommodation in Jacó is over-priced. Look for discounts May-November

Sleeping AL *Cabinas Tangeri*, T643-3001, F643-3636, modern, attractive landscaping leading to the beach, pool, excellent value for groups. **A** *Cocal*, T643-3067, F643-3082, cocalcr@racsa.co.cr, on beach near the centre of town, 2 pools, hammocks, German-owned, restaurant. Highly recommended. **A** *Paraíso del Sol*, T643-3250, F643-3137, parsolcr@racsa.co.cr, east of main street close to centre, apartments sleeping 2, 4 or 6 with kitchenette, pool. Recommended. **A** *Mar Paraíso*, T/F643-1947, www.hotelmarparaiso.com, tidy, mid-range beach resort. **A-B** *Pochote Grande*, T643-3236, F220-4979, www.centralamerica.com/cr/hotel/pochote.htm, beautiful German-owned hotel at the northern end of town, with bar and restaurant. Good rooms, free-form pool and a superb 500-year-old *pochote* tree shading the grounds. Good value. **B-C** *Cabinas Las Palmas*, north end of town, T643-3005, F643-3512, neat rooms, some with kitchenette, all with bath and fan, clean. Pretty gardens. **B-C** *El Jardín*, T/F643-3050, at north end of town, close to the beach, 10 rooms in quiet spot, friendly with small pool. **B-C** *Los Ranchos*, T643-3070, F643-1810, cobjm16@racsa.co.cr, central and close to the beach, 4 bungalows and 8 rooms sleeping 4-8 people, lively spot.

C *Alice*, south of central, T/F643-3061, tidy rooms with private bath, small terrace and pool. **C** *Bohío*, central and near beach, private bath, cold water, fan. **C** *Cabinas La Cometa*, T/F643-3615, central, with fan, shared bath, hot water, very clean. **D** *Cabinas Emily*, T643-3513, behind the restaurant of the same name not far from buses. Simple rooms, with private bath and fan. Good value. **D** *Cabinas Gipsy Italiano*, T/F643-3448, near beach at northern end, with bath, hot water. **E** per person *Hotel Paraíso Escondido*, 150 m east of the Catholic church on calle Los Cholos, T643-2883, F643-2884, paraisoescondido@racsa.co.cr, all rooms with a private bath, patio and a/c, rooms cheaper with fan. Swimming pool and laundry service. The owner often meets arriving buses. Good spot and worth the price.

Camping El Hicaco slightly south of the centre, is **G** per person and *Restaurant Los Hicacos* are both down same access route to the beach. *Camping Madrigal*, at the southern end of the beach, is a quiet spot.

Eating   In addition to the many *sodas* throughout Jacó you will find *Chatty Cathy's*, on the main drag, a popular dining spot. *Emily's*, just within the centre to the north, good *Tico* food, mainly fish. *La Fragata*, pasta and fish. *La Hacienda*, northern end, good bar serving snacks, there's a breezy balcony and gentle rock standards in the background. *La Ostra*, good fish in this pleasant open-air restaurant open all day. *Sunrise Grill Breakfast Place*, breakfast from 0700, closed Wed. *Wishbone*, on the main street serving big plates of Mexican. From US$6.

Nightlife   Several discos in town including *Central*, close to the beach, and *Las Tucanes*.

Transport Buses   From Coca-Cola bus station, 3 daily, 3 ½ or 4 ½ hrs, US$3.80 or US$4.60, arrive at Plaza Jacó-Complex terminal at north end of town, next to *Pizza Hut*. Also several buses to Quepos.

Directory   Bank *Banco Nacional* in centre of town. **Communication   Internet**: service on main road, but not really established – look out for new ones. **Post office**: at southern end near *Municipalidad* offices. **Language schools**   *City Playa Language Institute* offers Spanish classes.

Jacó to Quepos

From Jacó the pot-holed road runs down the coastline with lovely views of the ocean. The beaches are far quieter and, if you have a car, you can take your pick. A few kilometres south is **Playa Hermosa**, which is right on the main road. If travelling by car, 20 km further and a few kilometres off the road is **Playa Bejuco**, **Esterillos Centro** and **Playa Palma**, near Parrita; definitely worth exploring.

At **Playa Hermosa** a popular surfing beach,   **L** *Hotel Terrazas del Pacífico*, T643-3222,   **Sleeping** F643-3424, www.terraza-del-pacifico.com, with bath, phone, cable TV, 2 pools, wet bar, good surfing. **B** *Vista Hermosa*, T643-3422, on beach, pool, simple rooms. **E** *Rancho Grande*, T643-3529, large wooden house with communal kitchen, popular with surfers, great atmosphere. Small store for supplies.

At **Esterillos Centro** and **Playa Bejuco AL** *Hotel El Delfín*, T/F770-3808, swimming pool, all rooms with breezy balcony, secluded, clean, good restaurant, considered by many to be one of the best beach hotels in Costa Rica. Recommended. **C** *La Felicidad Country Inn*, T770-8332, F779-9960, lafelicidad.com (no www).

At **Esterillos Este B** *Auberge du Pelican*, F779-9236, www.aubergedupelican.home-stead.com, safe, French-Canadian owners, restaurant. Great little spot, airstrip out the back, beach out front – what more could you want?

Costa Rica

Great little beach and community at **Playa Palma B-C** *Cabinas Maldonado*, T286-1116, rooms sleeping 4, with bath, cold water, kitchen. **E** *Rooms/Restaurant Alex*, 2.6 km south, with bath, fan. Recommended. **F** *Las Brisas*, T779-9238, simple rooms near beach. **D** *Finca Don Herbert*, T779-9204, with bath, clean, parking.

At **Playa Palo Seco AL** *La Isla*, T779-9016, bar, pool, horse and canoe trips, hot water, a/c. **A** *Beso del Viento*, Playa Palo Seco, 5 km, T779-9674, www.besodelviento.com, swimming pool, French owners, stylish rooms

Beyond Parrita (*Banco Nacional, Banco de Costa Rica*, a gas station and a few stores) the gravel road travels through a flat landscape of endless African palm plantations. Many of the plantation villages are of passing interest for their two-storey, balconied houses laid out around a central football pitch, a church of some denomination and the obligatory branch of *AA*. The carriageway narrows to single track on bridges along this road so take care if you're driving, especially at night.

Quepos

Colour map 7, grid B3
Population: 14,674

Developed as a banana exporting port by *United Brands*, Quepos was forced to recreate itself following the devastation of banana plantations in the region overwhelmed by Panama disease in the early 1950s. Endless rows of oil-producing African Palm have replaced the bananas and Quepos has long since shrugged off the port-side image, to the extent that few even bother to explore the dock at the southern end of town.

South of Quepos, a winding road, lined with hotels, bars, restaurants and stores rises and falls for 7 km before reaching the beautiful coastline of Parque Nacional Manuel Antonio (see below) and nearby beautiful beaches. The impact on what was

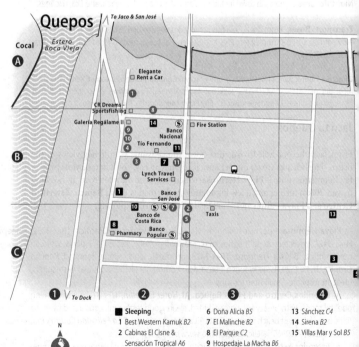

■ Sleeping	6 Doña Alicia *B5*	13 Sánchez *C4*
1 Best Western Kamuk *B2*	7 El Malinche *B2*	14 Sirena *B2*
2 Cabinas El Cisne &	8 El Parque *C2*	15 Villas Mar y Sol *B5*
Sensación Tropical *A6*	9 Hospedaje La Macha *B6*	
3 Cabinas Hellen *C4*	10 Majestic *C2*	**● Eating**
4 Cabinas Mary *C5*	11 Mar y Luna *B2*	1 Café Milagro *A2*
5 Ceciliano *C4*	12 Quepos *C5*	2 Dos Locos *C2*

once an attractive stretch of jungle-clad coastline is indisputable. For some it is an environmental catastrophe, for others it is a demonstration of the importance of planning to protect. Quepos plays an important role as a service town for local and foreign tourists. It is cheaper than the Manuel Antonio road, there is no shortage of restaurants, bars and shops, and regular buses make the journey to the national park.

Sleeping

Difficult to find accommodation on Saturday, December-April and when local schools are on holiday

Within a couple of blocks of the bus terminal are: **A** *Best Western Kamuk*, central, T777-0811, F777-0258, www.kamuk.co.cr, shower, TV, a/c, some ocean views, bar and restaurant at street level with large screen videos. **A** *Hotel Sirena*, T/F777-0528, new hotel with restaurant, pool, 14 quite good rooms with private bathroom, a/c. **B-D** *El Malinche*, T/F777-0093, 27 clean and good rooms, simply decorated, some with a/c much cheaper without. **E** *Cabinas Kali*, 200 m northeast of bus station, T777-1491, nice rooms, family-run, clean, friendly, safe but noisy. **E** *Majestic*, T777-0294, noisy, shared bath, on the same street as Banco de Costa Rica. **E** *Mar y Luna*, T777-0394, with or without bath, quiet, clean, friendly and popular. **F** per person *El Parque*, T777-0063, on waterfront road, friendly, clean, a bit rundown but good value, private bath, fan. **F** *Sánchez*, a couple of blocks east of the bus terminal, T777-0491, without bath, OK. Towards the eastern side of town, on the road leading to Manuel Antonio but still in town within walking distance are: **B-D** *Ceciliano*, T777-0192 with bath, family-run, quiet, small rooms, hot. **C** *Cabinas El Cisne and Sensación Tropical*, 75 m north of Catholic church and football pitch, T777-0719, safe, family-run, secure parking, bigger rooms on left, recommended. **C** *Hotel Quepos*, T777-0274, with bath, **D** without, simple, recommended. **C** *Villas Mar y Sol*, T777-0307, F777-0562, eight rooms with private bath and hot shower. Relaxed spot, parking. **D** *Cabinas Mary*, T777-0128, by football pitch close to *Iguana Tours*, clean, friendly, OK. **D** *Cabinas Hellen*, T777-0504, quite small rooms with private bath and fan, but clean and plenty of parking. **F** *Doña Alicia*, T777-0419, on walkway by football pitch, big cabin with bath, friendly, quiet, parking, can wash clothes. **F** *Hospedaje La Macha*, T777-0216, cheapest spot in town, next to post office on walkway by the football pitch, very basic but clean.

Eating

Café Milagro, on the waterfront, best expresso, cakes, pies, Cuban cigars, souvenirs, freshly roasted coffee for sale; another branch on the road to Manuel Antonio. *Dos Locos*, popular Mexican food, open to the street, occasional live music. *El Banco Sports Bar*, long bar with bright neon, and a good line on Tex Mex food. *Escalofrio*, pizza, pasta and ice-cream to die for from US$4. *El Gran Escape*, central, lively restaurant serving Tex Mex with a tropical twist. Good food, recommended. Dishes from US$10. *Isabel*, good breakfast choice, bulletin board, helpful staff, good food. *La Cueva del Marisco*, opposite *Hotel Sirena*. Pokey looking, small fish restaurant, cheap and very clean with much sought after chef who refuses to go and work for the bigger hotels. Recommended. *La Fuente*, upstairs close to *Hotel Sirena*, very popular new Chinese, with some good balcony tables. *La Marquesa*, very good, popular, cheap casados, lots of other dishes, good for breakfast. *L'Angolo*, opposite *Dos Locos*, excellent Italian delicatessen with pasta, cheeses, bread and meats. *Pizza Gabriels*,

Costa Rica

popular little spot with a lively undercurrent. Fine looking pizza and pasta from US$6. *Restaurant Pueblo*, lively bar with karaoke for the exhibitionists. *Rickshaws La Tropical*, a bustling, Chinese, popular with locals away from the bright neon. From US$4. Recommended. *Soda Nahomi*, good sandwiches divine ice-creams, next to *Lavanderías de Costa Rica*, on road out to Manuel Antonio. There are many good restaurants along the road towards Manuel Antonio.

In addition to some of the restaurants above, *Tío Fernando* is a tiny little joint, normally packed, playing jazzy little tunes and serving chilled beers.

Shopping The municipal market for fruit and bread is at the bus station. *L'angolo*, serves an absolutely divine mix of breads, olives, hams and everything you'd need for self-catering or picnicking in style. *La Buena Nota*, on road near the beach in Manuel Antonio, sells English language newspapers, a good place to seek local information, run by Anita Myketuk and Donald Milton, who has initiated a lifesaving programme and publicity on rip tides, T777-1002. *Galería Regálame II* has a good selection of gifts in Quepos and in their Manuel Antonio store next to the hotel *Sí como no*.

Transport **Air** There are several daily flights from San José, with *Sansa* and *Travelair* (US$45 one way). The *Sansa* office is under *Hotel Quepos*, T777-0683.

Buses Buses leave the capital from the Coca Cola Terminal. There are 2 express buses a day leaving **San José** at 0600, 1500, returning at 1230, 1900, 3½ hrs, US$4.50, book a day in advance, 6 regular buses, 4½ hrs, US$4. From **Quepos** there are buses northwest along the coast to **Puntarenas**, 3½ hrs, 0430, 1030, and 1500, return 0500, 1100, 1430, US$2.10. 2 daily buses via Dominical to **San Isidro de El General**, 0830 and 1700, 3½ hrs, US$2.50, connections can be made there to get to the Panamanian border, return 0700, 1330. **Taxis** congregate opposite the bus terminal, just up from *Dos Locos* restaurant. Minibuses meet flights at the airport.

Directory **Banks** Several branches in town including *Banco Nacional* which has a Visa ATM as does *Banco Popular* and *Banco San José*. The best place to exchange TCs or US$ cash is at *Distribuidora Puerto Quepos*, opposite *Banco de Costa Rica*, open 0900-1700, no paperwork, no commission, all done in 2 mins, same rate as banks. **Communications** Internet access available from above *Iguana Tours* on the road out of town. Fast machines. Also at *Jungle Net Cafe*, above restaurant *Dos Locos*. **Post office**, on the walkway by the football pitch, 0800-1700. **Language schools** *Escuela D'Amore*, in a great setting overlooking the ocean, halfway between Quepos and the national park, T777-1143, www.escueladamore.com, living with local families. *Escuela del Pacífico*, 2 km from town, T777-0805, www.escueladelpacifico.com, US$350 per week including lodging in owners' hotel, good classes. **Laundry** *Lavanderías de Costa Rica*, near the football pitch, good. **Medical services** The **hospital** is out of town, call T777-0922, or the **Red Cross**, T777-0118. **Tour operators** *Amigos del Río*, opposite the football pitch, T777-0082, F777-2248, amigorio@racsa.co.cr, tours, good guides. *Costa Rica Dreams*, sport fishing, office on the waterfront, T777-0593, www.crdreams.com *Iguana Tours*, close to the church on the football pitch, T777-1262, www.iguanatours.com Excellent local knowledge with many tours available. Friendly and helpful. *Lynch Travel Services*, right in the centre of town, T777-0161, www.lynchtravel.com **Useful addresses** Immigration: is on the same street as the *Banco de Costa Rica*. **Police**: T777-0196.

Parque Nacional Manuel Antonio

With 683 ha of mangrove swamps and beaches, home to a rich variety of fauna and flora, Manuel Antonio National Park can rightly claim to be one of Costa Rica's most popular protected areas – second only to Volcán Poás. Just 7 km south of Quepos on a paved road, three beautiful, forest-fringed beaches stretch along the coastline and around the headland of Punta Catedral: **Espadilla Sur**, **Manuel Antonio** and **Puerto Escondido**. Iguanas and white-faced monkeys often come down to the sand.

In addition to enjoying the beaches, hiking is also good in the park. A 45-minute trail, steep in places, runs round the Punta Catedral between Espadilla Sur and Manuel Antonio beaches. If you're early, and quiet, it is possible to see a surprising amount of wildlife. A second walk to Puerto Escondido, where there is a blow hole, takes about 50 minutes. The map sold at the entrance shows a walk up to a mirador, with good views of the coastline.

Manuel Antonio has been a victim of its own success with some of the animals becoming almost tame. But for all the criticism of recent years, it is still beautiful and highly enjoyable. Overdevelopment outside the park and overuse within has led to problems of how to manage the park with inadequate funds. In 1992 the National Park Service (SPN) threatened to close it and a number of tour operators removed it from their itineraries. You are not allowed to feed the monkeys but people do, which means that they can be a nuisance, congregating around picnic tables expecting to be fed and rummaging through bags given the chance. Leave no litter and take nothing out of the park, not even sea shells.

The range of activities in the area outside the park is slightly bewildering. Sea kayaking is possible, as is mountain biking, hiking, canopy tours, canyoning, deep-sea fishing and even quad biking. Most hotels can assist with booking trips, and there are agencies in Quepos (see above) that can also advise. The beaches in the park are safer than those outside, but rip tides are dangerous all along the coast. Beaches slope steeply and the force of the waves can be too strong for children.

Park essentials

Open 0700-1600, closed Mon, US$6. Guides available, but not essential, at entrance. The entrance to the park is reached by crossing a tidal river (plastic shoes recommended) or, when it is very high, a boat will take you across the river for US$0.55. Early and late are the best times to see the wildlife. Breakfast and other meals available from stalls just before the river, where cars can be parked and minded for US$1 by the stallholders. Basic toilets, picnic tables and drinks available by the beaches, cold water showers at Manuel Antonio and Espadilla Sur beaches.

Sleeping & eating

There are hotels all along the road from Quepos to Manuel Antonio, many of them the higher price bracket. From Quepos one of the first and cheapest hotels is **C** *Cabinas Pedro Miguel*, T/F777-0035, pmiguel@racsa.co.cr, with simple rooms, a small pool and very friendly *Tico* owners. Next door is the *Escuela del Pacífico*, see above. **AL-A** *Plinio*, T777-0055, F777-0558, www.hotelplinio.com, on hillside with 13 rooms, restaurant, bar, pool. Small nature trail with an observation tower. Recommended. **B** *Mono Azul*, T/F777-1954, monoazul@racsa.co.cr, friendly place with a couple of pools, and a good restaurant. *Escuela de Idiomas D'Amore*, T/F777-1143, www.esueladamore.com, Spanish school believes in the immersion technique. *Mot Mot* sells some great little souvenirs and next door is *Barba Roja* restaurant and bar, popular but not cheap, but good spot for sunsets.

A dirt road leads to Punta Quepos from opposite *Café Milagro*, where you find **LL** *Makanda by the Sea*, T777-0442, F777-1032, www.makanda.com, 6 villas and studios with superb open design, idyllic paradise spot for hopelessly romantic lovebirds. **LL** *El Parador*, 2 km from the main road, T777-1414, F777-1437, www.hotelparador.com (**AL** low season), 80 rooms, new all facility hotel, stunning views of the ocean, in style of Spanish *parador*, helicopter landing pad – just in case!

Back on the main road is **LL** *Byblos*, T777-0411, F777-0009, www.byblos.co.cr (**AL** low season), all in bungalows in a resort, sleep 1-4, French restaurant, pool. A little further on is the excellent gift shop *Regálame*, next door is the divine *Pickles Deli*, and then **LL-L** *Sí Como No*, T777-0777, F777-1093, www.sicomono.com, a superb hotel with beautiful touches of design using stunning stained-glass, all the comforts you would expect, and service *par excellence*. They even have a small cinema.

A-C *La Quinta*, T/F777-0434, 5 simple rooms, some with kitchenettes, overlooking the bay. Up above most of the activity, this is a charming spot away from the mêlée. Recommended. **AL** *Villa Nina*, unmistakable bubblegum pink, T777-1221, F777-1497, www.hotelnina.com, short walk to beach, 8 rooms, fully screened, bath, small pool, microwave ovens and fridges for hire, pleasant, friendly. The parked WWII plane – which is being decked out as a bar – marks the start of the downhill to the beach and the imminent arrival of **L** *Costa Verde*, at the train-carriage restaurant and reception, T777-0584, F777-0560, www.hotelcostaverde.com   Apartments for 2-4 people, with kitchenette and bath,

Many shut in the low season; in high season, it's best to book ahead. The area is full to bursting at weekends with many locals camping on the beach

Costa Rica

2-bedroom villas available, well-appointed, pool and a couple of restaurants. There are several nature trails out the back. Recommended. **B-D** *La Arboleda*, T777-1385, F777-0092, www.hotelarboleda.com, cabins on hillside leading down to beach sleep 2-3, bath, fan, Uruguayan restaurant, 8-ha wood, beware snakes, crabs and monkeys in the yard at night, recommended. Proceeding along the main road towards the beach, you come to **L** *Karahé*, on private road, T777-0170, F777-1075, www.karahe.com, includes breakfast, cabins on a steep hillside with lovely view, sleep 3-4, recommended, fridge, bath, a/c or fan, good restaurant, swimming pool across the road, access to beach, can walk to park along the beach. *La Buena Nota* is the stopping point for beachwear and everything cerebral you could want whether newspapers, books, postcards or just information. **D** *Cabinas Ramírez*, T777-0003, with bath, food and bar, hammocks and camping free, guests can help with cooking in exchange. Just off the road 25 m further on, in a small lay-by, is *Mar y Sombra*, T777-0003, good *casado especial* and jumbo shrimps with shady tables on the beach, sun-loungers for hire. Back on the main road towards Quepos is *Bar del Mar*, T777-0543, which rents surfboards, sells drinks and light meals and has a collection of English novels to read in the bar.

At the junction of a side road just before the park, there is a selection of *sodas*, surf board rental shops, and tour operators, information kiosks. Up the side road is **E** per person *Costa Linda*, T777-0304, double rooms or **F** per person in 6-bedded room, with cooking facilities, fan, water shortage, watch out for racoons raiding the outdoor kitchen in the night, good breakfasts, dinner rather pricey. **B-C** *Vela Bar*, T777-0413, large rooms with bath, fans, safes, very good restaurant, fishing and other trips, also has a fully equipped house to rent.

Back towards the park is *El Mono Loco*, serving up a full menu of international dishes, and lively in the evenings, and nearest is **D** *Hotel Manuel Antonio*, T777-1237, restaurant, good breakfast, camping possible nearby, ask in the restaurant. Handy, just minutes from the national park and the beach. If driving there is ample guarded parking in the area, US$6.

Transport There are 3 express buses a day (see Quepos, Transport), direct from **San José**, 4 hrs, US$5. At weekends buy ticket day before, bus fills to standing room only very quickly. Roads back to San José on Sun evening are packed. A regular bus service runs roughly ½-hourly from beside Quepos market, starting at 0545, to Manuel Antonio, last bus back at 1700, US$0.35. Taxi from Quepos, approximately US$10. Minibuses meet flights from San José to the airport at Quepos (see above), US$2.25.

Quepos to Dominical and Palmar Norte

Playa Matapalo Beaches, beaches, endless stretches of sandy beaches. Thirty kilometres southeast from the congestion of Quepos towards Dominical the unpaved coastal road drifts almost unnoticed through Playa Matapalo, where you'll find an expansive, beautiful sandy beach recommended for surfing, relaxing and playing with your ideas of paradise. Other activities, in an overwhelmingly Swiss community, include fishing, horse-riding and hiking to mountain waterfalls.

Sleeping and eating **A-C** *El Coquito del Pacífico*, T/F384-7220, www.elcoquito.com, comfortable cabins sleeping up to 4 with bath, palm gardens, good breakfast, Swiss-owned, fine restaurant, recommended. *Restaurant La Piedra Buena*, T/F771-3015, has basic accommodation, beach access, also Swiss-owned. Good restaurant, *Julio's*, also has rooms to rent.

Dominical
Colour map 7, grid B2
www.dominical.net
Twelve kilometres further on, at the mouth of the Río Barú, is Dominical, a small town with a population of a few hundred. No more than 500 m from one end to the other it's popular with surfers and often busy. If you want to surf (or learn) it's a great spot. Hotel prices soar in high season and most hotels are close to noisy bars. Treks and horse-riding trips to waterfalls are possible if the beach is just too much to bear. Just north of the town *Hacienda Barú* has a national wildlife preserve, with activities including abseiling, canopy tours and nature walks (see below). Booking hotels is slightly easier in the Dominical and Uvita area using regional specialists and central booking service of Selva Mar, T771-4582, F771-8841, www.exploringcostarica.com

Sleeping and eating **A-B** *Tortilla Flats*, formerly *Cabinas Nayarit* right on the sea front, T/F787-0033, tortflat@racsa.co.cr, or www.ecotourism.co.cr Rooms sleeping up to 3 people, with private bath and hot water. Bit overpriced if just for 2. **B-C** *Río Lindo*, T787-0028, F787-0078, www.dominical.net/hotelriolindo, at the entrance to town, clean, tidy rooms with a balcony or terrace. Private bath with fan or a/c. Pool and bar area. **C** *Diuwak*, T787-0087, F787-0089, www.diuwak.com Rooms and suites, sleeping up to 4 people, with private bath. Mini supermarket and (pricey) internet service. Book in advance.**C-D** *Albergue Willdale*, T787-0023. Fan and bath, bikes, boat trips, fishing and horses available. Reported to be winding down, taking only month longs bookings.**C-D** *Cabinas San Clemente*, on beach, T787-0026, F787-0055. Clean, with or without a/c, friendly, US owned, restaurant, **E** per person, rooms over bar, shared bath, fan; *San Clemente Bar & Grill*, bar/restaurant under same ownership, good, big portions. **D** *Posada del Sol*, 100 m from beach, T/F787-0085. Owned by local historian Mariela Badilla, 20-odd rooms, bath, fan, patio with hammocks, also 2-bedroom apartment with kitchen for US$150 per week. Rooms vary. **D-E** *Cabinas El Coco*, at end of main street, T787-0235, F787-0239. With or without bath, negotiate price, unfriendly, noisy, a last option. Camping possible.

Out of town **AL** *Villas Río Mar Jungle and Beach Resort*, T787-0052, F787-0054, riomar@racsa.co.cr, 500 m from beach, 40 bungalows with bath, fridge and fan, pool, jacuzzi, tennis court, trails, riding, all inclusive. **A** *Hotel/Restaurant Roca Verde*, on the beachfront about 1 km south of Dominical, T787-0036, F787-0013, www.hotelrocaverde.com, tropical rooms with a/c. Small balcony or terraces, with a pool. Big bar and restaurant. Recommended. **B** *Hacienda Barú*, about 2 km north of Dominical, T787-0003, F787-0004, www.haciendabaru.com, a 332-ha reserve that began life as a private reserve in 1972. Cabins sleeping 3 or more with private bath, hiking, riding. So much to see and do in such a small area. There is a canopy observation platform, tree climbing, night walks in the jungle and several self-guided trails.

Down the main (er, only) street there is *Soda Nanyoa* and a little further on *Restaurant Coco* serves good food. *Thrusters* is a hip spot for the surf crowd. *Capanna*, near the entrance to town, is universally acknowledged as the best restaurant in town. *Jazzy's River House*, is more an open-house cum cultural centre, with meals followed by musical contributions.

Punta Dominical is 4 km south (no transport). A poor dirt road follows a steep path inland up the *Escaleras* (stairs) to some secluded accomodation blending beach and rainforest **B** *Hotel Pacífico Edge*, T771-4582, www.exploringcostarica.com (*Selvamar* reservation service), 4 large cabins with great views of ocean and rainforest. **B** *Bella Vista Lodge,* T388-0155 or T771-4582 through the Selva Mar reservation service. Great view, good large meals, owned by local American 'Woody Dyer', organizes trips in the area. There are also houses to rent. **L** *Villas Escaleras*, T/F385-1526, www.villas-escaleras.com Beautiful fully equipped villas sleeping up to 10 people, spectacular views, a great spot to hideaway.

Transport Bus to Quepos 0545, 0815, 1350 (w/ends) and 1450. To San Isidro, 0645, 0705, 1450, 1530, 1 hr. To Uvita at 0950, 1010, 1130 (w/ends) 1710 and 2000. To Ciudad Cortés and Ciudad Neily 0420 and 1000. To San José, 0545, 1340 (w/ends), 7 hrs.

If you get the impression the southern Pacific coast is about beaches, you'd be right. **Uvita** Eighteen kilometres south of Dominical is the village of Uvita with beautiful beaches all along the coastline. You can take walks in the nearby forests, swim in nearby waterfalls or at the beach, take a boat trip and watch birds. **Ballena National Marine Park** (see below) protects over 5,000 ha of Pacific coral reef, and humpback whales can be sighted at nearby Ballena Island between December and April.

The road south from Uvita is being repaved as far as Ciudad Cortés, and access to the beaches of Playa Ballena and Playa Bahía is getting easier with consequent development of the area.

Costa Rica

Tell bus driver where you are going and he will drop you off at the closest point to your chosen hotel

Sleeping and eating In **Uvita**, which is not on the coast, there is **D** *Cabinas Los Laureles*, 200 m turn on the left, nice location, 3 *cabinas* with private bathroom, simple and quite good. A little further on is **C** *Coco Tico Ecolodge*, 250 m left, information c/o Pulpería, 6 clean *cabinas*, sleep 3, with private bathroom and trails outback. Up the hill you will find **E-G** *Cascada Verde*, a hostal, educational retreat and organic farm, German-run, vegetarian food, hilltop postition, workshops available. Take a bed, hammock, camp or work for your lodgings. Recommended and popular place to chill out.

In **Bahía Uvita**, **E** *Cabinas Punta Uvita*, T770-8066, opposite *Restaurant Los Almendros* close to the beach, simple, basic *cabinas* with private bathroom. Further away from the beach is **F** *Cabinas Betty*, with 3 simple cabins. **F** *María Jesús*, 4 simple cabins. **F** *Villa Hegalva*, T382-5780, Playa Bahía Uvita, simple rooms, with showers and bathrooms. Quiet spot with gardens for camping.

Colonia has a beautiful if very quiet beach. **B** *Cabinas El Chamán*, 2 km south on the beach, T771-2555, nice location, 8 simple *cabinas* with private bathroom, camping US$4 per person, and nearby is **D** *Villa Marie Luisa Lodge*, T236-6185, with simple cabins.

Transport Bus **San José** to Uvita from Terminal Coca-Cola, Mon-Fri 1500, Sat-Sun 0500, 1500, return Mon-Fri 0530, Sat-Sun 0530, 1300, 7 hrs. From **San Isidro** daily 0800, 1600, return 0600, 1400. Dominical-Uvita – last bus 1700 or 1800.

Parque Nacional Marino Ballena

The vast majority of Ballena (Whale) Marine National Park is coastal waters – 5,161 ha against 116 ha of protected land – which may go some way to explaining why there isn't a lot to see at this least-developed national park. The underwater world is home to coral reefs and abundant marine life that includes common and bottle-nosed dolphins as well as occasional visits from humpback whales at times seen with their calves.

Although there is a rarely staffed rangers station in Bahía (T/F786-7161), and signposts line the Costanera, the infrastructure in the park is non-existent. There is a nominal entrance fee of US$6 which is rarely collected. Along the beach at Bahía is a turtle nesting project administered by the local community. As with the park itself, the organization is very ad hoc – visitors and volunteers are welcome. Beachcombing is good, as is snorkelling when the tides are favourable. Boat trips to the island can be arranged from Bahía, and diving is starting up with the most recommended local being Máximo Vásquez, or Chumi as he is known.

The coastal road continues south to join the Pan-American Highway at Palmar Norte.

Sleeping **A** *Cabinas Ballena* and **C** *Rocaparadiso*, both 6 km south of Uvita in front of Parque Nacional Marino Ballena , T220-4263 for information.

New on **Playa Tortuga** is **AL** *Hotel Villas Gaia,* T/F788-8676, hvgaia@racsa.co.cr, 200 m to the beach, 12 spacious cabins with private bathrooms (hot water), fan and terrace. Swimming pool and restaurant serving Swiss, international and vegetarian dishes. Ocean view, diving school, horses. Several other quiet secluded options opening up. **B** *Posada Playa Tortuga*, T384-5489, ptortuga@racsa.co.cr, run by Gringo Mike, a great spot and place to stay, and Mike knows everything there is to know about the area.

San José to the Panama border

Heading through the Talamanca mountains, the Pan-American Highway reaches its highest point at Cerro de la Muerte (Peak of Death) and passes El Chirripó, Costa Rica's highest peak at 3,820 m as the scenic road drops down through the valley of the Río de El General to the tropical lowlands of the Pacific coast and the border with Panama. Private reserves along the route are ideal for bird-watching, the resplendent quetzal enjoys a quieter life than his Monteverde relations, and mountain streams are stocked with trout providing both sport and food. Lodges and hotels are usually isolated, dotted along the Pan-American.

Towards Costa Rica's most southerly point, the Osa Peninsula is a nature haven of beautiful pathways, palm-fringed beaches and protected rainforest – well worth the effort if you have the time.

From San José the Pan-American Highway runs for 352 km to the Panama border. It's a spectacular journey but challenging if you're driving, with potholes, frequent rockslides during rainy season, roadworks and generally difficult conditions.

From Cartago, the route heads south over the mountains, beginning with the ascent of **Cerro Buena Vista** (3,490 m), a climb of almost 2,050 m to the continental divide. A little lower than the peak, the highest point of the road is 3,335 m at Km 89 which travels through barren *páramo* scenery. Those unaccustomed to high altitude should beware of mountain sickness brought on by a too rapid ascent, see Health information, page 59. For 16 km the road follows the crest of the Talamanca ridge, with views of the Pacific 50 km away, and on clear days of the Atlantic, 80 km to the east.

At **Km 51** from San José, a side road leads off the Pan-American Highway to the peaceful and pleasant mountain village of Santa María (1,460 m) and several other small villages which collectively occupy the *Valle de los Santos* or **Valley of the Saints**. Quiet and beautifully situated, it is a good area for walking on short day trips of for the adventurous, it's a pleasant 10-hour hike from Santa María to the Pacific coast of the Puerto Quepos district. Whether travelling by car or bus you can explore the villages, each with a distinctive church.

Santa María
Colour map 7, grid B3

Sleeping At **Santa María** is D *Cecilia's Cabinas*, 15 mins' walk from the plaza on the outskirts of town, Apartado 805 1 (San José), T541-1233, run by Ana Cecilia Ureña, 7 cabins, rustic, clean, hot showers. Very friendly and recommended. F *Hotel and Restaurant Dota*, 25 m north of plaza, T541-1026, without bath. F *Hospedaje Fonda Marieuse*, T541-1176, shared bath, clean, very basic, friendly, run by an elderly lady, Doña Elsie, recommended. *Soda Gómez*, near the church, large portions, cheap.

At **San Marcos de Tarrazú**, 6 km west of Santa María, 15 mins by bus, US$0.25, the church, set on a west facing slope, is particularly impressive at sunset. D *Tarrazu*, T546-6022, close to main, simple rooms with private bath and hot water. E *Continental*, T546-6225, shared bath, cold water. F *Zacateca*, T546-6073, with bath and hot water. Several *sodas* around town and the fine *Pizzera Las Tejas*.

At **Km 58**, 6 km east of Santa María, or 7 km from Pan-American Highway, is **Copey de Dota** with A *El Toucanet Lodge*, T/F541-1435, www.ecotourism.co.cr/el_toucanet.htm, idyllic spot, breakfast included, 6 units, family run, with bath, hot water. Beautiful countryside with excellent bird-watching.

Costa Rica

Transport Bus from **San José** to Santa María via San Marcos, US$2.10, 1½ hrs, 13 daily from Av 16, C 19-21, Terminal Los Santos.

Directory *Banco Nacional* in Santa María and San Marcos de Tarrazú and *Banco de Costa Rica* in *San Marcos de Tarrazú*.

Genesis II   Four and a half kilometres east of Km 58 (Cañón church) is Genesis II, a privately owned 40-ha cloud forest National Wildlife Refuge, at 2,360 m, bordering the Tapantí-Macizo de la Merte National Park. Accommodation available at **A-B** *Genesis II Lodge*, T381-0739, F551-0070, www.genesis-two.com, in rooms with shared bath, for birders and naturalists. The trees are literally dripping with ephiphytes in this cloud forest and it is a worthwhile stopover. Camping (**G**) with bath and shower provided, tents available for rent. There is plenty to do including a **Treescape** canopy system, a suspension bridge, three platforms and a couple of zips. ■ *US$25 for guests, US$35 for day visitors.* There is also a volunteer programme minimum duration four weeks at US$150 per week. Contact Steve and Paula Friedman, Apartado 655, 7050 Cartago, or SJO 2031, Unit C-101, PO Box 025216, 1601 NW 97th Ave, Miami FL33102-5216, or volunteer@genesis-two.com

Sleeping along the Pan-American   At **Km 70** is **B** per person, *Finca Eddie Serano Mirador de Quetzales*, T/F381-8456, 43-ha forest property at 2,650 m, Eddie Serrano passed away recently, but one of his sons will show visitors quetzales (almost guaranteed but don't tell anyone at Monteverde Cloud Forest) and other endemic species of the highlands, 8 cabins, sleeping 2-5, with wonderful views, private bath, price includes breakfast, dinner and guided hike.

At **Km 78** is *Casa Refugio de Ojo de Agua*, a historic pioneer home totally overlooked but for a couple of picnic tables in front of the house.

At **Km 80** a steep, dramatic road leads down the spectacular valley of the Río Savegre to **San Gerardo de Dota**, a bird-watchers paradise: **A** *Trogón Lodge*, T223-2421, F222-5463, www.grupomawamba.com, 16 fine wooden cabins with private bathroom, set amongst beautiful gardens connected by paths used by dive-bombing hummingbirds. A little further down the slope is **AL** per person *Hotel de Montaña Savegre*, T771-1732, www.ecotourism.co.cr, and at the bottom of the hill is **F** *Los Ranchos*, T771-2376, camping in perfect surroundings. No transport down here, but pick-ups from the highway can be arranged.

The highest point is at **Km 89.5** (temperatures below zero at night). At **Km 95**: **E** *Hotel and Restaurant Georgina*, at almost 3,300 m Costa Rica's highest hotel, basic, clean, friendly, good food (used by southbound *Tracopa* buses), good bird-watching, ask owners for directions for a nice walk to see quetzales.

At **Km 107** at **División** turn-off and follow the signs for 4 km to **Avalón Nature Reserve**, where more than 60 species of bird have been recorded in the 151-ha private reserve. Several trails for walking through the cloud forest. **A-C** for private or shared rooms. Volunteers accepted, contact Glenn Richmond, T770-1341, or avalonreserve@yahoo.com

San Isidro de El General

Population: 45,145
Altitude: 702 m
Colour map 7, grid B3

The dramatic drop in altitude from the highlands to the fast-growing town of San Isidro passes through fertile valleys growing coffee and raising cattle. The huge cathedral on the main plaza is a bold architectural statement, with equally refreshing approaches to religious iconography inside. The **Museo Regional del Sur** is in the old marketplace, now the Complejo Cultural, Calle 2, Av 1-0. ■ *Mon-Fri, 0800-1200, 1330-1630, free.* 7 km north of San Isidro is the 750-ha **Centro Biológico Las Quebradas**, with trails, dormitory accommodation for researchers. ■ *0800-1400 Tue-Fri, 0800-1500 Sat-Sun, closed Oct, T771-4131.* San Isidro de El General is also the best place to stock up for a trip into Parque Nacional Chirripó and to climb Cerro Chirripó Grande (3,820 m).

Sleeping   **D** *Hotel/Restaurant Amaneli*, T771-0352, 41 quite good rooms with private bathroom, fan, some noisy. **D** *Hotel Iguazu*, Calle Central, Av 1, T771-2571, hot water, cable TV, clean, safe with parking. **E** *El Valle*, C 2, Av Central-2, T771-0246, F771-0220, clean and tidy, one of the better cheapies. **E-F** *Astoria*, on north side of square, T771-0914, expansive hallway, tiny but clean rooms.**E-F** *Hotel Chirripó*, south side of Parque Central, T771-0529, private or shared bath, clean, very good restaurant, free covered parking, recommended.

F *El Jardín*, Av Central, C Central-2, T771-0349, good value, small, rickety old building. Upstairs rooms have more light. Cheap restaurant downstairs. **F** *Hotel Balboa*, C 2, Av 1-3, T771-0606, close to centre, bath. **F** *Lala*, C Central, Av 1, T771-0291, basic and simple – just like the Telly Tubby. **F** *Pensión Jerusalem*, a dozen grubby rooms sharing a couple of baths.

Out of town the options include **A-B** *Del Sur*, 6 km south on the Pan-American, T771-3033, F771-0527, www.hoteldelsur.com, with bath, comfortable, swimming pool, tennis, good restaurant. On the road to San Gerardo is **A** *Rancho La Botija*, T382-3052, www.ecotourism.co.cr, restaurant, pool, hiking to nearby petroglyphs, open 0900 at weekends, great restaurant littered with fragments of *botijas*. Recommended. Nearby is **B** *Talari Mountain Lodge*, 10 mins from San Isidro, T771-0341, talari@racsa.co.cr, 8-ha farm, with bath, riverside cabins, rustic.

La Cascada, on Av 2 and C 2, is the balcony bar where the bright young things hang-out. *Las* **Eating** *Chapulines*, south of the main square opposite Pali, good tortillas snacks. *Restaurant Crestones*, south of the main plaza, serves a good mix of snacks, drinks and lively company. *Restaurant El Tenedor*, C Central, Av Central-1, good food, mid-range, friendly, big pizzas, recommended. *Soda Chirripó*, south side of the main plaza, gets the vote from the current gringo crowd in town. *Soda J&P*, the best of many in the indoor market south of the main plaza.

Bus terminal at Av 6, C Central-2 at the back of the new market and adjacent streets but most **Transport** buses arrive and depart from bus depots along the Pan-American Highway. To and from **San José** (just outside Terminal Coca-Cola), hourly service 0530-1700, US$3.30, 3 hrs (buses to the capital leave from the Interamericana, C 2-4). To **Quepos** via Dominical at 0700 and 1330, 3 hrs. However, *Tracopa* buses coming from San José, going south go from C 3/Pan-American Highway, behind church, to **Palmar Norte**, US$2.25; **Paso Canoas**, 0830-1545, 1930 (direct), 2100; **David** (Panama) direct, 1000 and 1500; **Golfito** direct at 1800; **Puerto Jiménez**, 0900 and 1500. Waiting room but no reservations or tickets sold. *Musoc* and *Tuasur* buses leave from the intersection of C 2-4 with the Pan-American.

Banks: *Banco Nacional*, on north side of plaza, Mon-Fri, 0830-1545. **Communications** Internet: **Directory** *Brucanet*, on north side of plaza. **Post** office: 3 blocks south of the church. **Telephone**: *ICE* office on C 4, Av 3-PAH. **Tour operators** *Ciprotur*, C 4, Av 1-3, T771-6096, www.ecotourism.co.cr with good information on services throughout the southern region. **Useful addresses** *Fuji* slide film from Av 1, C 2-4. *Selvamar*, C 1, Av 2-4, T771-4582, F771-8841, www.exploringcostarica.com, general tours and the main contact for out of the way destinations in the southern region.

Parque Nacional Chirripo

San Isidro de El General is west of Costa Rica's highest mountain **Cerro Chirripó Grande** (3,820 m) in the middle of **Parque Nacional Chirripó** (50,150 ha). Treks starts from San Gerardo de Rivas – see below. The views from the hilltops are splendid and the high plateau near the summit is an interesting alpine environment with lakes of glacial origin and diverse flora and fauna. The park includes a considerable portion of cloud forest and the walk is rewarding. ■ *US$6, crowded in season, make reservations in Oficina de los Parques Nacionales in San Isidro, T771-3155.*

Parque Nacional Chirripó neighbours **Parque Internacional La Amistad** (193,929 ha), established in 1982, and together they extend along the Cordillera de Talamanca to the Panamanian border, comprising the largest area of virgin forest in the country with the greatest biological diversity.

At San Isidro de El General (see below), get food and book accommodation at the MINAE office **Transport** (C 4, Av Central-2). Take the 0500 Pueblo Nuevo bus from northwest corner of Parque Central,

Costa Rica

Climbing the Chirripó peaks

The early morning climb to the summit of Cerro Chirripó, Costa Rica's highest mountain, is a refreshing slog after the relative comforts often encountered in Costa Rica. The hike takes you through magnificent cloud forest draped in mosses and ephiphytes before entering a scorched area of paramo grasslands with incredible views to the Pacific and Atlantic coastlines on clear days. The wildlife – birdlife in particularly – is incredible and, even if you don't see it, you will certain hear it. The trek itself is not difficult but it is tiring being almost consistently uphill on the way and a knee-crunching, blister bursting journey down.

From the refugio, you can also explore the nearby Crestones, a volcanic outcrop that has been etched on to the minds of every Costa Rican, and the creatively named Sabana de los Leones and the Valle de los Conejos.

If you wish to climb the Cerro Chirripó, Costa Rica's highest mountain, you must obtain information from the SPN office in San José (see National Parks) or San Isidro de El General. Start in the early morning for the 8-10 hours' hike to the refugio. The cost is US$6 entry for each day spent in the park, plus US$6 shelter fee per night, maximum 40 persons in park at any one time. The refugio

has simple but adequate accommodation, with space for about 80 people. The cold is a bit of a shock in contrast to the rest of Costa Rica, but you can rent sleeping bags from the refugio. Gas cookers are also available for hire. There are sufficient water supplies en route so you will need only to carry your food supplies. Book accommodation and equipment required in San José or San Isidro de El General if you can, especially in high season, otherwise pay and obtain permit at the Park office in San Gerardo. In addition to the high camp there is a shelter about half way up, Refugio Llano Bonito (2,500 m), simple and occasionally clean, wooden floor, two levels to sleep on, no door but wind protection, drinking water, toilet, about four hours' walk from San Gerardo, three hours' walk on to Refugios Base Crestones. Plan for two nights on the mountain – although you can do it with only one night if you want, although it's a long hard slog up and down for just a couple of days. While nights can be cold, daytime temperatures tend to be warm to hot, so go prepared. In the rainy season trails up the plateau are uncomfortably slippery and muddy, and fog obscures the views. Time your descent to catch the afternoon bus back to San Isidro.

or the 1400 from the new bus station to San Gerardo de Rivas (US$1.05, 1½ hrs, return at 0700 and 1600) which passes the entrance to the park. Interesting trip up the Río Chirripó valley.

San Gerardo de Rivas Situated in a cool, pleasant spot, San Gerardo de Rivas is at the confluence of the Río Blanco and the Río Pacifico Chirripó. Close to Parque Nacional Chirripó entrance, it is the starting point for the climb up Cerro Chirripó Grande (3,820 m). If you haven't booked accommodation at the refugio in San Isidro you can book it at the MINAE office. ■ *0600-1700 (see box).*

Handy for weary legs after the climb, there are hot springs in the area, entrance US$1. Before crossing the new concrete bridge turn left to 'Herradura' for 10 minutes then look for the sign after Parqueo Las Rosas; go down to the suspension bridge, cross the river and continue for 10 minutes to the house where you pay.

Most accommodation options share the same telephone. T771-1866

Sleeping At the very top, closest to the park entrance is **D** *El Uran*, with simple, clean rooms, lots of blankets and a restaurant that will feed you early before setting out. **D** *Pelícano*, T382-3000, 10 rooms with great views, a bar and restaurant. Beautiful setting with countless birds. **E** *Cabinas Bosque*, with a small bar and restaurant. Looks a bit scruffy from the outside, but spotless rooms, and great views over the valley from some rooms. Over the bridge you arrive at the home of Sr Francisco Elizondo Badilla (the local 'champion' speed climber and his family who have a small cabin **F** per person, *Cabinas El Descanso*, with 7 bunks, bathroom, hearty meals available, gas stove for hire, horses for rent and guide services offered, recommended. **E** *Cabinas/Restaurant Elimar*, swimming pool, simple restaurant, 4 quite good *cabinas* with private bathroom, hot water. **F** *Marín*, basic but friendly and good value. Next to

MINAE office. You can camp at or near the park office, in San Gerardo near the bus stop. Check in first and pay US$0.30.You can stay at the **F** *Roca Dura*, opposite the football pitch, built on a huge boulder, hot showers, good *comedor*, nice view, shop next door, ½ km out of village, friendly owners.

Continuing southeast, a good road sinks slowly through the Río General valley where the Talamanca Mountains dominate the skyline. At Km 197 (from San José), the change from coffee to fruit is complete, at the junction for Buenos Aires is the huge *Del Monte* cannery. The town, a few kilometres off the Pan-American, has some simple accommodation. **F** *Cabinas Violeta*, next to the fire station 200 m west of the plaza, T730-0104, is clean, simple, central and OK if you're stuck for the night. **F** *Cabinas Mary*, 800 m south of the centre close to the Aridikes office, T730-0187, quiet spot which tries to be clean. Several sodas around the main square, *Soda Kriss* on the east side is popular with locals.

Heading 17 km east towards the mountains is the Durika Biological Reserve, a privately owned reserve of roughly 800 ha, aiming to create a self-sustained community in the Talamanca mountains. Accommodation is available in rustic cabins (**B-C**), includes three vegetarian meals a day, with a wide range of activities including walks, hikes to the summit of Cerro Durika and cultural tours. Around US$10 per person on top of the daily rate. Contact T730-0657, www.gema.com/durika.

South along the Pan-American, the small towns of **Térraba** and **Boruca** are the most prominent remains of the nation's indigenous population. The community of Boruca, with a small hostal (**F**), has a small, poorly maintained museum, but every year the **Fiesta de los Diablitos** on the last day of December and first two days of January in Boruca and the last day of January and the first two days of February in Rey Curre see the culture come alive in a festival of music, dance and costume. Daily buses to Boruca from Buenos Aires, 0600 and 1300, 1½ hours.

At **Paso Real** the Pan-American heads west to Palmar Norte, with a turn heading towards San Vito (see below) and the Panamanian border.

Buenos Aires

Taking a sharp turn at Paso Real (straight on for San Vito – see below), the Pan-American heads west to Palmar Norte (Km 257 – with gas station) from where a paved road leads to Ciudad Cortés. A new road heads northwest to Dominical (see page 1104).

Palmar Norte

Sleeping **D** *Cabinas Tico-Alemán*, on the Interamericana near the gas station, T786-6232, 25 *cabinas* with private bathroom. Best in town. **D** cabin, **E** rooms *Hotel y Cabinas Casa Amarilla*, 300 m east of bus station on the plaza, T786-6251, with fan, rooms at back quieter, rooms over restaurant noisy but cheaper. **F** *Hotel Xinia*, 150 m east from bus station, T786-6129, 26 rooms, very basic but OK, shared bathroom.

Transport Express bus to Palmar Norte from Terminal Alfaro, with *Tracopa* from San José, 7 daily 0600-1800, 5 hrs, via San Isidro de El General, 5 buses return to the capital 0445-1300. 5 buses daily to Sierpe for Bahía Drake, 45 mins. Also buses north to Dominical, and south to the Golfito and the Panamanian frontier.

Crossing the Río Grande de Terraba leads to Palmar Sur, 90 km from the Panamanian border. There are several stone spheres in the area. A banana plantation close to town has stone spheres – 1½ m in diameter and accurate within 5 mm – of pre-Columbian Indian manufacture, though their use is a matter of conjecture. Recent theories are that they were made to represent the planets of the solar system, or that they were border markers. Daily flights with *Sansa* and *Travelair* San José-Palmar Sur (US$66 one way). From Palmar a bus goes to Sierpe, from where a boat sails to Bahía Drake (page 1120).

Palmar Sur

Through a matrix of cooperative banana and African plantations, a road leads to Sierpe on the Río Sierpe. **Sleeping** Several small hotels (**B** *Oleaje Sereno*,

Sierpe

Costa Rica

T/F786-7111, good rooms, with restaurant on river bank, **F** *Margarita*, T786-7574, 13 good rooms, friendly owners. Good value). **Transport** Five buses daily to Palmar Norte, 0530-1530, 45 minutes. Boats down Río Sierpe to Bahía Drake, 1½ hours, US$70 per boat. Many hotels in Drake have boats that pick up guests, you may be able to get a lift, US$15 per person.

To San Vito

Colour map 7, grid B4

The road from Paso Real to San Vito is now paved and has lovely views. La Amistad International Park has few facilities for visitors at present, but one lodge is found way up in the hills beyond Potrero Grande, just south of the Paso Real junction on the way to San Vito. **Sleeping AL** *Monte Amou Lodge*, T265-6149, a chalet lodge on a coffee plantation, with bath, guided walks with naturalists, electricity until 2200. Call ahead – impossible to reach without private transport.

Near the border is San Vito. Originally built by Italian immigrants among denuded hills, it is a prosperous but undistinguished town.

Excursions

On the road from San Vito to Ciudad Neily at **Las Cruces** are the world-renowned **Wilson Botanical Gardens**, T773-4004, F773-3665, www.ots.ac.cr, owned by the Organization for Tropical Studies, 6 km from San Vito. In 360 ha of forest reserve over 5,000 species of tropical plants, orchids, other epiphytes, and trees with 331 resident bird species. ■ *US$6, good self guide booklet for the principal trail US$2.20.* It is possible to spend the night here if you arrange first with the OTS in San José, T240-6696 (**AL** per person all inclusive, US$18 per person for day visits with lunch). On the same road is *Finca Cántaros*, T773-3760, specializing in local arts and crafts, owned by Gail Hewson Gómez. One of the best craft shops in Costa Rica – worth a look even if you don't buy anything.

Sleeping & eating

In **San Vito** Close to the centre of town is **C** *El Ceibo*, just down from main plaza, T/F773-3025, with bath, hot water and TV, good restaurant. **D-E** *Cabinas Rino*, right in the centre of town, T773-3071, clean and well maintained. Good deal. On the plaza area is **F** *Colono*, T773-4543, with new management trying to sweep out the old tired ways.

Close to the gas station, on the road from San Isidro is **F** *Cabinas Firenze*, T773-3741, 6 basic *cabinas*, sleep 5, with private bathroom. Nearby is **E** *Cabinas Las Huacas*, T773-3115, 13 OK *cabinas* with private bathroom, hot water, TV, which were looking very run down when visited.

On the road to Sabalito is **F** *Hotel Pitier*, ½ km out of town on road to Sabalito, clean, with bath. **F** *Las Mirlas*, T773-3714, in same location and price range but more attractive.

Lilianas is still showing homage to the Italian heritage of San Vito with good pasta dishes. *Jimar* on road out to Paso Real is OK. *Restaurant Nelly*, near *Cabinas Las Huacas*, serves good wholesome truck drivers fayre.

Transport

Bus Direct buses San José to San Vito, 4 daily, 0545-1445, from Terminal Alfaro, C 14, Av 5; direct bus San Vito-San José 0530, 6 hrs, *corriente* buses take 8 hrs. Alternative route, not all paved, via Ciudad Neily (see below); from San Vito to Las Cruces at 0530 and 0700; sit on the left coming up, right going down, to admire the wonderful scenery; return buses pass Las Cruces at 1510.

Directory

Bank There are branches of *Banco Nacional* and *Banco Popular* in San Vito. **Communications** The **post office** is at the northern end of town and should be getting **internet** connection soon.

Frontier with Panama - Sabalito

The road from San Vito to Ciudad Neily is paved, in good condition and offers some of the best coastal views in the country as the road rapidly falls through the hills. From San Vito a good gravel road, paved in places, runs via **Sabalito** (Banco Nacional) to the Panama border at Río Sereno. There are buses from Sabalito to San José. See Panama chapter, page 1216, for details of this frontier crossing.

Costa Rica

Palmar Norte to the border

From Palmar Sur the Pan-American Highway heads southeast to Chacarita (33 km) where a road turns off to the **Osa Peninsula**, to Río Claro (another 26 km) where a road leads to **Golfito**, another 15 km leads to **Ciudad Neily** which is 16 km from the border at Paso Canoas.

Golfito

Thirty-one kilometres north of the border a road branches south at Río Claro (several *pensiones* and a fuel station) to the former banana port of Golfito, a 6-km long linear settlement bordering the Golfo Dulce and steep forested hills. While elements of hard sweat and dock labour remain, Golfito's prominence today comes from being Costa Rica's only free port, set up in 1990, selling goods tax free at about 60% of normal prices. Popular with shoppers from throughout the country, it can be difficult to get a hotel room at weekends.

The **Refugio Nacional de Fauna Silvestre Golfito**, in the steep forested hills overlooking Golfito, was created to protect Golfito's watershed. Rich in rare and medicinal plants with abundant fauna, there are some excellent hikes in the refuge. Supervised by the University of Costa Rica, they have a field office in Golfito.

Thirty minutes by water taxi from Golfito, you can visit **Casa Orquídeas**, T775-1614, a family-owned botanical garden with a large collection of herbs, orchids and local flowers and trees, that you can see, smell, touch and taste. Tours last about 2½ hrs, closed Fridays.

To the north of Golfito is the **Parque Nacional Piedras Blancas** tropical wet forest.. The area was being exploited for wood products, but has been steadily purchased since 1991 with help from the Austrian government and private interests, notably the classical Austrian violinist Michael Schnitzler. All logging has now ceased and efforts are devoted to a research centre and ecotourism, concentrated in an area designated **Parque Nacional Esquinas**. Near the village of **La Gamba** a tourist lodge has been built: **AL** *Esquinas Rainforest Lodge*, T/F775-0901, www.esquinaslodge.com, full board, private baths, verandas overlooking the forest, tours, all profits to the local community. La Gamba is 6 km along a dirt road from Golfito, or 4 km from Briceño on the Pan-American Highway between Piedras Blancas and Río Claro.

Golfito also provides boat and ferry access to Puerto Jiménez and the Osa Peninsula, and popular fishing and surfing beaches to the south of the town

Entering the town from the south heading north there are a few hotels where the road meets the coast. In 2 km is the small town centre of painted buildings with saloon bars, open-fronted restaurants and cheap accommodation – probably the best stop for budget travellers. Nearby is the dilapidated *muellecito* used by the ferries to Puerto Jiménez and water taxis. A further kilometre north are the container port facilities and the Standard Fruit Company's local HQ though many of the banana plantations have been turned over to oil palm and other crops. Beyond the dock is the free port, airstrip and another set of hotels.

Sleeping

Listed in order from the south

4 km from Golfito **D** *La Purruja Lodge*, T/F775-1054, www.purruja.com, 5 duplex cabins with bath, plus camping US$2 per tent. As you arrive at the coastline from the south, the first place in town is **B-D** *El Gran Ceibo*, T/F775-0403, www.ecotourism.co.cr/elgranceibo/ Small pool, a/c, cheaper without. **B** *Las Gaviotas*, next to *El Gran Ceibo*, T775-0062, F775-0544, lasgaviotas@hotmail.com, 21 cabins and rooms, with bath, a/c and with excellent restaurant looking out over the waterfront. **D** *Mar y Luna*, T775-0192, F775-1049. Eight rooms sleeping 2-4, with bath, fan, restaurant on stilts above the sea, quiet spot, good deal.

A couple of km further down the road in the centre **E-F** *Delfina*, T/F775-0043. Shared bath, fan, friendly, basic. Some rooms with private bath much better. Rooms on street noisy, parking available. **F** *Melissa*, behind *Delfina*, T775-0443. 4 simple rooms, with private bath,

Costa Rica

clean and quiet, great spot overlooking bay. Parking and recommended. **F** *Golfito*, T775-0047. Quiet, central with a couple of rooms overlooking the bay. A little run down but OK. **F** *Costa Rica Surf*, T775-0034. 25 dark rooms, most with private bath. Big bar downstairs. Not the best in town but OK. **G** *El Uno*, above restaurant of same name, T775-0061. Very basic, mildy amusing if you fancy pretending to be a banana in a packing case, but friendly.

Close to the docks is **D-E** *Del Cerro*, T775-0006, 20 simple rooms sleeping 1-6, private bathroom, laundry services, fishing boat rentals. **F** *Cabinas Marlin*, a couple of streets back, T775-0191, small neat rooms, fan, hot water, *Tico*-run and very friendly.

At the northern most part of town, near the **airport** and **free zone** **B** *Sierra*, T775-0666, F775-0506, 72 double rooms, a/c, a couple of pools, restaurant. Rooms are better than the place looks from the outside. **C** *Golfo Azul*, T775-0871, F775-1849, golfazul@racsa. co.cr 20 comfortable large rooms, with bath and a/c, good restaurant.

Eating *Coconut Café*, in the centre opposite the gas station, good breakfasts, book swap and good local

Many seafood places along the seafront knowledge. *Cubana*, near post office, good food, try the *batidos*. *El Uno*, nearby, serves good, reasonably priced seafood. *La Dama del Delfín Restaurant*, new restaurant downtown, break-fast from 0700, snacks (hamburger, sandwiches, spaghetti), homemade bakery, closed for dinner and Sun. *Le Eurekita* in the centre serves a mean breakfast of *huevos rancheros*, cheap.

Transport **Air** Several daily flights San José-Golfito, with *Sansa* (US$66 one way) and *Travelair* (US$76), some via Coto 47 or Puerto Jiménez. Runway is all-weather, tight landing between trees; 2 km from town, taxi US$0.50. **Buses** From **San José** 0700 (8½ hrs), 1500 (6 hrs express) daily from Terminal Alfaro, return 0500 (express), 1300, US$6; from San Isidro de El General, take 0730 bus to Río Claro and wait for bus coming from Ciudad Neily. Bus Golfito to **Paso Canoas**, US$1.25, hourly from outside *Soda Pavo*, 1½ hrs. **Sea** ABOCAP (*Asociación de Boteros*), water taxis in and around Golfito, opposite ICE building, T775-0712, to Cacao Beach, Punta Zancudo, Punta Encanto or to order, US$20 per hr up to 5 persons. **Docks** *Land Sea Tours* (see below) and *Banana Bay Marina* (T775-0838, F775-0735, www.bananabaymarina.com) accommodates boats up to 150 ft – either of these places might be an option if heading south on a boat, but you'll need to ask nicely and be a bit lucky.

Directory **Banks** *Banco Nacional* near muelle, Mon-Fri 0830-1535. **Tour operators** *Land Sea Tours*, T/F775-1614, landsea@racsa.co.cr, know everything there is to know about the area. Can organize almost anything including national and international flights, and can advise on the minimal opportunities for crewing on yachts heading up and down the coast.

Beaches around Golfito

Playa de Cacao About 6 km (1½ hour walk) north round the bay from Golfito is the Playa de Cacao.

Beaches to the north A taxi boat from Golfito will take you there for US$2.50. Alternatively you can drive along an inland road, if it hasn't rained too heavily, starting left of the police station in Golfito and left again a few kilometres later.

B *Cabinas Playa Cacao*, T/F256-4850, www.cabinas-playa-cacao.co.cr, huts with small kitchen, private bathroom, hot water, thermal springs and kayak rental. Next to *Cabinas Palmas*, good, cheap restaurant, *Siete Mares*.

Playa San Josecito Beyond Playa de Cacao is Playa San Josecito and the **L** *Golfo Dulce Lodge*, T232-0400, F232-0363, the lodge is on T383-4839, www.golfodulcelodge.com, cabins with bath and hot water, guided hikes and trips, Swiss-owned. **AL-B** *Dolphin Quest*, T382-8630 (mob), F775-0373, www.dolphinquestcostarica.com, is a secluded jungle adventure centre and rainforest retreat, offering a wide range of land and sea-based activities.

Playa Cativo 30 mins by boat northwest of Golfito, at Playa Cativo **LL** *Rainbow Adventures*, *cabinas*, T690-7750, F690-7735, www.rainbowcostarica.com, includes all meals, snacks, beer and soft drinks, transport, private beach with no other hotels, jungle tours, tours of the gulf, fishing,

norkelling, bordered by national park, in US, 5875 northwest Kaiser Rd, Portland, Oregon
97229, T503-690-7750, F503-690-7735 for reservations.

At beautiful Playa Zancudo, about 15 km by sea south of Golfito (US$2 by *colectivo* ferry from the **Playa Zancudo**
small dock at 0600 and 1200, return 0500, 1300), you can stay at **AL-A** *Zancudo Beach Club*, *Beaches to the south*
T776-0087, www.zancudobeachclub.com, cabins and apartments with kitchenettes. Great spot
and atmosphere. **A-B** *Los Cocos*, Apdo 88, Golfito, T/F776-0012, www.loscocos.com, beach
front cabins at the ocean with private bathroom, hot water, mosquito net, fan, kitchenette, refrig-
erator, veranda. Discounts for longer stays. Heavenly. **B** *Casa Tranquilidad B&B*, T775-0449,
F775-0373, large house with terrace, 4 nice rooms with private bathroom, hot water, with breakfast. **B-C** *Coloso Del Mar*, T/F776-0050, www.coloso-del-mar.com Great little spot with 4 simple
cabins overlooking the beach. Meals extra. **B-C** *Sol y Mar*, T776-0014, F776-0015,
www.zancudo.com Run by Rick and Lori, 4 screened cabins, hot water, fan, 3-storey rental
house, US$450-550, 50 m from ocean, bar/restaurant, meals 0700-2000, home baked bread,
great fruit shakes, volleyball with lights for evening play, badminton, paddleball, boogie boards,
library. Highly recommended. **C** *Los Ultimos Paraísos*, T776-0050, with bath, fan, mosquito nets,
hammocks. **E** *Pensión Fin del Mundo*, over *Restaurant Tranquilo*, 6 simple rooms with fan, mosquito net, clean, shared bathroom. English book exchange at *Tienda Buen Precio*. *Bar y Restaurant Tranquilo*, a lively spot between *Zancudo Beach Club* and *Coloso Del Mar*. *Macondo* is a new
Italian restaurant which also has a couple of rooms.

South of Zancudo, is Pavones where a world-record left-hand wave has elevated the rocky **Pavones**
beach to the realm of legend. **Sleeping B** *Pavones Surf Lodge*, T222-2224, F222-2271 in
San José. Includes meals, 2 cabins with bath, 6 rooms with shared bath. Also at Pavones is
C *Cabinas La Ponderosa*, T384-7430, in USA on T407-783-7184. Owned by 2 surfers, large
cabins, fan, with bath, fishing, diving and surfing.

Transport A bus leaves **Golfito** for Pavones at 1400, and from Pavones to Golfito at 0500, 3 hrs,
US$2.50. A spit of land continues south to **Punta Burica** with no roads and only 1 or 2 villages.

South of Pavones, at the mouth of the Golfo Dulce, is Punta Banco with the **AL** *Tiskita Jun-* **Punta Banco**
gle Lodge, T233-6890, F255-2011, www.tiskita-lodge.co.cr, a 162-ha property including a
fruit farm, with excellent bird-watching, 14 cabins overlooking ocean, owned by Peter
Aspinall, c/o *Sun Tours*, Apdo 1195-1250 Escazú. Overlooks beach, cool breezes, waterfall,
jungle pools, trails through virgin forest – great spot..

Tour operators *Burica Adventures*, www.buricaadventures.com, provides land and water based
adventure tours in and around the Golfo Dulce area. They can also arrange transport to Pavones
from Golfito (US$60).

Ciudad Neily is about 16 km from the border. **C** *Cabinas Andrea*, T/F783-3784. 18 clean **Ciudad Neily,**
cabinas with private bathroom, a/c or fan, TV. Popular with *Ticos* coming through town, **Paso Canoas &**
handy for main bus terminal. **D** *Cabinas Helga*, a couple of blocks southwest of the bus termi- **Panama border**
nal, T783-3146. A dozen *cabinas*, sleep 4, with private bathroom, spotlessly clean and well
maintained. **D-E** *El Rancho*, just off the Pan-American T783-3060, F783-5435. 50 resort-style
cabins with bath, TV, much cheaper without. **E-F** *Cabinas Heileen*, north of plaza, T783-3080,
simple *cabinas* with private bathroom, fan. **F** *Cabinas Fontana*, 6 blocks north of the main
square, T783-3078, has simple but OK rooms. *Pizza Internet Los Colegios* for chips and bytes
next door. **F** *Hotel Musuco*, just off the Pan-American, T783-3048, with bath, cheaper without, fan, clean and quiet. Good deal. **F** *Hotel Villa*, north of *Hotel Musoc*, T783-5120, cheapest
and last option in town. There are plenty of *sodas* all over town, and also branches of *Banco
Nacional* and *Banco de Costa Rica*.

Transport Bus terminal in Ciudad Neily is at the northern end of town, beside the Mercado
Central. Daily bus to San José, with Tracopa, from main square (6 daily, US$6, 7 hrs, on Sun
buses from the border are full by the time they reach Ciudad Neily). Buses arrive at Av 5 and C

Costa Rica

Península de Osa – rain, snakes and mosquitoes

Avoid the rainy season. Bring umbrellas (not raincoats, too hot), because it will rain, unless you are hiking, in which case you may prefer to get wet. Shelters can be found here and there, so only mosquito netting is indispensable. Bring all your food if you haven't arranged otherwise; food can only be obtained at Puerto Jiménez and Agujitas in the whole peninsula, and lodging likewise. The cleared areas (mostly outside the park, or along the beach) can be devastatingly hot. Chiggers (coloradillas) and horseflies infest the horse pastures and can be a nuisance, similarly sandflies on the beaches; bring spray-on insect repellent. Another suggestion is vitamin B1 pills (called thiamine, or 'tiamina'). Mosquitoes are supposed to detest the smell and leave you alone but see Health, page 53. Get the Instituto Geográfico maps, scale 1:50,000. Remember finally that, as in any tropical forest, you may find some unfriendly wildlife like snakes (fer-de-lance and bushmaster snakes may attack without provocation), and herds of peccaries. You should find the most suitable method for keeping your feet dry and protecting your ankles; for some, rubber boots are the thing, for others light footwear which dries quickly.

14 in San José. Services to San Vito inland, and to Palmar, Cortés and Dominical (0600 and 1430, 3 hrs). Also to Puerto Jiménez at 0700 and 1400, 4 hrs. Bus for Golfito leave from the centre of town every 30 mins. The Pan-American goes south (plenty of buses, 20 mins, US$0.35) to **Paso Canoas** on the Panamanian border. *Colectivo* US$1.10, very quick.

Border with Panama - Paso Canoas

Shops sell luxury items brought from Panama at prices considerably lower than those of Costa Rica (for example sunglasses, stereo equipment, kitchen utensils, etc)

Immigration Border open 0600-2200 Costa Rica time. Remember Costa Rica is 1 hr behind Panama. For information on entering Panama, see Entry requirements on page 1149; for entry procedures see Panamanian immigration, page 1208. **Customs** No fruit or vegetables can be taken into Panama. **Crossing by private vehicle** Those motoring north can get insurance cover at the border for US$17 ensuring public liability and property damage.

Sleeping If you need to stay in town there is reasonable accommodation 1 block west from the border, south of the main road. **D-E** *Real Victoria*, T732-2586, simple rooms with a/c, cheaper with fan. Cable TV in all rooms. Swimming pool, open to non-guests. Credit cards accepted. **E** *Cabinas Jiménez*, T732-2258 quite good *cabinas* with private bathroom, fan. Very clean, good deal. **E** *Hilda*, south of town, T732-2873, good rooms, very clean, restaurant over the road. Recommended. **E-F** *Cabinas Interamericano*, T732-2041, with bath and fan, some with a/c, good value upstairs. **F** *Cabinas Jiménez Annexe*, T732-2258, OK if all else is full. **G** *Cabinas El Paso*, T732-2740, OK rooms with shower.

Transport Bus San José-Paso Canoas, US$9, 8 hrs from Terminal Alfaro at 0500, 1100 (direct), 1300, 1800, return 0400, 0730, 0900, 1500 (T223-7685). Not all buses go to the border. International buses that reach the border after closing time wait there till the following day. Hourly buses to **Ciudad Neily**, ½ hourly to Golfito.

Directory Banks either side of border close at 1600 local time. Slightly better dollar rate for colones on the Costa Rican side. No difficulty in getting rid of surplus colones with money changers.

Península de Osa

Across the Golfo Dulce is the hook-shaped appendage of the Osa Peninsula. Some distance from most other places of interest in the country, the journey is worth it as the peninsula is rightly world famous for the diversity of flora and fauna in Parque Nacional Corcovad which offers some of the best rainforest trekking and trails in the country.

Ins & outs Getting to the Peninsula is getting easier. There is a daily **ferry** service from Golfito arriving at the small dock in Puerto Jiménez. There are also **bus** services from San José, passing through

Costa Rica

San Isidro de El General and Palmar North, and from the south at Ciudad Neily. **Boats** ply the coastal route from Sierpe to Bahía Drake and you can **fly** from San José.

Puerto Jiménez

Once the gold-mining centre of the Osa Peninsula, Puerto Jiménez still has the feel of a frontier town even though most miners were cleared from the Parque Nacional Corcovado area in 1985.

Colour map 7, grid B4
Population: 2,500

Today, Puerto Jiménez is a popular destination with its laid-back, occasionally lively atmosphere, reasonable beaches nearby and, of course, the beautiful national park on the Pacific side of the peninsula. A particular charm of Puerto Jiménez, barely five blocks square, is its relative freedom from road traffic – Scarlet macaws can be seen roosting in the trees around the football pitch. There are good local walks to the jungle, where you will see monkeys and many birds, and to beaches and mangroves. Whale-watchers may be lucky between October and March with the seasonal migration of humpbacks.

Puerto Jiménez

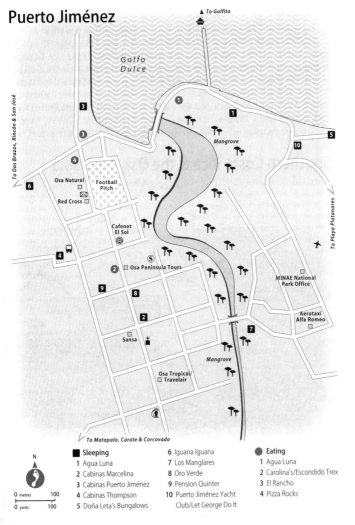

To Golfito

Golfo Dulce

To Dos Brazos, Rincón & San José

Mangrove

Osa Natural
Football Pitch
Red Cross

Cafenet El Sol

Osa Peninsula Tours

MINAE National Park Office

Aerotaxi Alfa Romeo

Sansa

Mangrove

Osa Tropical/ Travelair

To Playa Platanares

To Matapalo, Carate & Corcovado

N

0 metres   100
0 yards   100

■ **Sleeping**
1 Agua Luna
2 Cabinas Marcelina
3 Cabinas Puerto Jiménez
4 Cabinas Thompson
5 Doña Leta's Bungalows
6 Iguana Iguana
7 Los Manglares
8 Oro Verde
9 Pensión Quinter
10 Puerto Jiménez Yacht Club/Let George Do It

● **Eating**
1 Agua Luna
2 Carolina's/Escondido Trex
3 El Rancho
4 Pizza Rocks

Costa Rica

Geological treasures can be seen at the gold mine at **Dos Brazos** about 15 km west of town; ask for the road which goes uphill beyond the town, to see the local gold mines. Several buses a day to Dos Brazos, last bus back at 1530 (often late); taxi US$7.25. You can also take a long walk to **Carate** (see below) which has a gold mine. Branch to the right and in 4 km there are good views of the peninsula. A topographical map is a big help, obtainable from Instituto Geográfico in San José.

Sleeping   **In Puerto Jiménez** **AL-C** *Doña Leta's Bungalows*, left on the ferry near to *Let George Do It*, T735-5180, www.donaleta.com Fully equipped wooden cabins sleeping 1-5, beautiful spot, almost private beach. Cheaper in groups. **A-B** *Agua Luna*, facing pier, T/F735-3593, agualu@racsa.co.cr New rooms sleeping 2-4 with bath, good, although pricey, restaurant next door. **B-C** *Los Manglares*, T/F735-5002. Clean, well-maintained cabins with private bath, right beside the mangrove on the river. Small bar, regular visit from monkey, scarlet macaws and the occasional crocodile in the grounds by the river. Very friendly and recommended.

E *Hotel Oro Verde*, down main street, T735-5241, F735-5468, oroverde@racsa.co.cr Run by Silvia Duirós Rodríguez, 10 clean, comfortable rooms, with bath and fan, some overlooking the street. **F** *Cabinas Marcelina*, down main street, T735-5007, F735-5045. With bath, big clean, friendly, nice front yard, small discount for youth hostelling members. **F** *Iguana Iguana*, on road leading out of town, T735-5158. Simple rooms with private bath, small bar, pool in high season.

G *Cabinas Puerto Jiménez*, on the gulf shore with good views, T735-5090, F735-5215. Big rooms, friendly, spotless – arguably *the* best value cheap place in Costa Rica. **G** *Cabinas Thompson*, 50 m from the centre, T735-5910. With bath, fan, clean but a little dark. **G** per person *Pensión Quinter*, just off main street, T735-5078. Very simple wooden building, but clean and good value, will store luggage. Ask for Fernando Quintero, who rents horses and has a boat for up to 6 passengers, good value, he is also a guide, recommended. **G** *Puerto Jiménez Yacht Club*, more commonly known as *Let George Do It*, turn left off the ferry, T735-5313. Camping pushing up to the beach, with showers and bathrooms. Great spot and a wide range of tours

Southern Costa Rica & the Osa Peninsula

Outside Puerto Jiménez 5 km southeast of Puerto Jiménez behind the airstrip is **A** *Playa Preciosa Lodge*, T735-5062, F735-5043, 4 cabins, good swimming and surfing.

At **Dos Brazos**, **AL** *Bosque del Río Tigre*, T/F735-5440, www.osaadventures.com Small lodge set on the Río Tigre outside Dos Brazos, sleeps a maximum of 10, rustic and peaceful. **C** *Corcovado Ecology Lodge*, T775-1422, F735-5045. Friendly, rainforest tours US$25 per day, 5 simple, somewhat dark rooms, shared bathroom. **D** *Sr and Sra Talí*, T775-1422, have rooms, include breakfast, clean, shared bath, laundry facilities, jungle tours, riding, good food, recommended.

3 km from **Rincón**, on the road to Puerto Jiménez, a road heads west for 5 km to **B** per person *Centro Juvenil Tropical*, an environmental education naturalists' centre targetting Costa Rica kids with great access to the rainforest. Ideally for groups, but will accommodate guests. T735-5522, or contact Fundación Neotrópica, C 20, Av 3-5, T253-2130, in San José www.neotropica-tyc.org

At **Cabo Matapalo** on the tip of the peninsula, 18 km south of Puerto Jiménez are several expensive options. The cream of the crop is **LL** *Lapa Ríos Wilderness Resort*, T735-5130, F735-5179, www.laparios.com Includes meals, 14 luxury palm-thatched bungalows on private 400-ha reserve (80% virgin forest, US owners Karen and John Lewis but only locals employed), camping trips, boats can be arranged from Golfito. Idyllic, fantastic views, recommended.

In Puerto Jiménez *Carolina's*, down the main street, highly recommended for fish, everything actually, good prices. *Escondido Trex* office at back of restaurant. At the northern end of town is *El Rancho*, good pizzas and bar with music to 0100, and *Pizza Rock*, by the football pitch. *Restaurant Agua Luna*, stylish setting on the seashore, beautifully presented but pricey.

Eating

Air There are daily flights between Puerto Jiménez and Golfito with *Sansa* (US$66) and *Travelair* (US$76 one way) from San José. **Buses** arrive 1 block west of the main street. From **San José;** just outside Terminal Atlántico Norte (C 12, Av 9-11), there is one bus daily to Puerto Jiménez at 1200 via San Isidro, US$7, 8 hrs, return 0500, T735-5189. There are also buses from **San Isidro**, leaving from the Pan-American at 0930 and 1500 daily, US$4.50, returns at 0400 and 1300, 5 hrs. Puerto Jiménez to **Ciudad Neily** at 0500 and 1400, 3 hrs, US$3. A couple of *colectivos* to Carate depart from outside *Restaurant Carolina* daily 0530 and 0600, cost US$7. Service may be restricted in the wet season. **By road** To reach Puerto Jiménez from the Pan-American Highway (70 km), turn right about 30 km south of Palmar Sur; the road is newly paved to Rincón, thereafter a driveable road exists with many bridge crossings. There is a police checkpoint 47 km from the Pan-American Highway. **Sea** 2 boats leave from the Muelle in Golfito Muelle for Puerto Jiménez at 1100, US$2.50, 1½ hrs, return 0600, or you can charter a taxi boat for about US$60, up to 8 passengers.

Transport
A café by the bus terminal opens at 0430 when you can get a cheap but reasonable breakfast

Costa Rica

Banks Branch of *Banco Nacional*. **Communication** Internet *Café El Sol*, on main street, open 0700-1900, US$8 per hr – send a letter from the **Post office** opposite the football pitch. **Tour operators** *Escondido Trex*, in the

Directory

back of *Carolina's*. T/F735-5210, www.escondidotrex.com, running since 1992, excellent local information, treks, kayaking and jungle trips, from one-day upwards. *Osa Natural*, opposite the football pitch, T735-5007, can book accommodation and has a couple of internet machines. *Osa Peninsula Tours*, opposite *Carolina's*, T735-5135, good range of tours, with small book swap. Dormitory accommodation and camping facilities in Corcovado National Park should be booked through the *MINAE* office facing the airstrip, T735-5036.

Bahía Drake

Arriving by boat from Sierpe, Bahía Drake provides an entrance point to Osa Peninsula and Parque Nacional Corcovado. In March 1579, Sir Francis Drake careened his ship on Playa Colorada in Bahía Drake. A plaque commemorating the 400th anniversary of the famous pirate's nautical aberration was erected in Agujitas. Life in the bay is not cheap, and combined with transport costs quickly mount up. Drake Bay, which continues south merging seamlessly with Agujitas, is a popular destination for divers with Isla Caño nearby. Open water PADI courses (US$325) are available at *Cabinas Jinetes de Osa* or through *Caño Divers* at *Pirate Cove*.

Sleeping L *Aguila de Osa Inn*, the normal landing point, T296-2190, F232-7722, www.aguiladeosa.com, includes meals, fishing, hiking, canoeing and horse-riding available in comfortable cabins constructed with exotic hardwoods. Recommended. **L** per person *Drake Bay Wilderness Camp*, opposite *Aguila de Osa Inn*, T/F770-8012, www.drakebay.com, with meals, cabins, tents available, pleasant family atmosphere. Great views. Wide ranges of tours available. **L-AL** per person *La Paloma Jungle Lodge*, T/F239-0954, www.lapalomalodge.com, includes meals, 9 cabins with bath, guided tours with resident biologist. Packages available. **AL** *Cabinas Jinete de Osa*, T/F385-9541, www.costaricadiving.com Good hotel, run by 2 brothers from Colorado. Diving a speciality – PADI courses offered. Spacious and airy rooms, all with bath, hot water, fan. Recommended. **D** *Bella Vista Lodge*, on the beach at the southern end of town, T770-8051, the only budget option in town and disappointing. Basic rooms, 2 with bath, 3 shared (even more basic), meals (US$3-5) not included.

Towards the north of the bay **AL-A** *Pirate Cove*, northern end of the beach, T380-3670, www.piratecove.com Very pleasant tent-like cabins emulate an outdoor experience minus the mud. US$55 per person shared bath, US$70 with bath, 3 meals included. **A** *Rancho Corcovado Lodge*, in the middle of the beach, T786-7059. Simple, rustic rooms, many with view, all with bath. Friendly *Tico* owners nice open-air restaurant on beach serves *comida típica*. Camping permitted.

Camping (**F** per person) is allowed outside Rancho Corcovado (use of electricity and bathrooms included) or outside Pirate Cove (north end of beach – no fixed price but small charge for use of baths).

Parque Nacional Corcovado

Colour map 7, grid C4 Corcovado National Park, including **Isla del Caño Biological Reserve** (84 ha), comprises over 42,469 ha – just under half the Osa Peninsula. Consisting largely of tropical rainforests, swamps, miles of empty beaches, and some cleared areas now growing back, it is located on the Pacific Ocean at the western end of the peninsula. An ideal spot for just walking along endless beaches, the park is also filled with birds, mammals and six species of cat.

Ins & outs If short of time and/or money, the simplest way to the park is to take the pick-up truck from outside *Carolina's Restaurant* in Puerto Jiménez to **Playa Carate**, most days at 0600 and 1400, 2½ hrs, US$7 one way, returning at 0800 and 1600, ask in advance about departure. Alternatively call Cirilo Espinosa, T735-5075, or Ricardo González, T735-5068, for a 4WD jeep taxi. It is possible to book a flight from Puerto Jiménez to Carate or La Sirena in the park for US$99 per person, minimum 5. Ask at the airstrip or call T735-5178, F735-5112. The MINAE office in Puerto Jiménez is near the airport, open daily 0830-1200, 1300-1700, T735-5036; they will give permits for entering the park (US$6 for up to 4 days) and will book accommodation at **La Sirena** in dormitories, maximum 20 people, **F** for bed (reservation essential), take sheets/sleeping bag, camping **F**, no reservation needed, 3 meals available. Bring mosquito netting.

At **Carate** there is a dirt airstrip and a store, run by Gilberto Morales and his wife Roxana (they rent rooms, but often full of gold miners, they also have a tent for hire, but take sleeping bag). Thirty minutes' walk west along the beach is **AL** *Corcovado Lodge*, T257-0766, F257-1665, www.costaricaexpeditions.com, with 20 walk-in tents with two campbeds in each, in a beautiful coconut grove with hammocks overlooking the beach; walk-ins are possible but to be sure of space book through *Costa Rica Expeditions* in San José. Clean showers and toilets; good food, take a flashlight. Behind the camp is a trail into the jungle with a wonderful view of the bay from a clearing; many birds to be seen, plus monkeys and frogs.

> **Around the park**
> *You will find both hiking boots and sandals useful if you are walking any distance in the park*

Five minutes' walk further down the beach is **La Leona** park wardens' station and entrance to the park. To go beyond here costs US$6 per day, whether you are walking along the beach to La Sirena (18 km, six hours, take sun protection), or just visiting for the day. Lodging is available at La Leona, **F**, maximum 12 people in basic rooms or camping, meals available, book in high season through SINAC. Beyond here to the end of **Playa Madrigal** is another 2½-hours' walk, partly sandy, partly rocky, with some rock pools and rusty shipwrecks looking like modern art sculptures. The shore rises steeply into the jungle which grows thickly with mangroves, almonds and coconut palms. Check with wardens about high tide so you don't get stuck. There are a couple of rivers along the beach, the first, Río Madrigal, is only about 15 minutes beyond La Leona (lovely and cool, clear and deep enough for swimming about 200 m upstream, a good place for spotting wildlife). The best place for seeing wildlife, though, is La Sirena, where there are paths inland and the terrain is flatter and more isolated.

You can head inland from Sirena on a trail past three conveniently spaced shelters to **Los Patos** after passing several rivers full of reptiles (20 km, six to nine hours depending on conditions). The wooden house is the Ranger Station with electricity and TV, with four beds available at US$1.75 per night, meals possible if you do not bring your own food. Its balcony is a great observation point for birds, especially the redheaded woodpecker. From Los Patos you can carry on to the park border then, crisscrossing the Río Rincón to **La Palma** (small hostal), a settlement on the opposite side of the peninsula (13 km, six more hours) from which there are several 'taxis' making the one-hour trip to Puerto Jiménez (see above). An offshoot of this trail will lead you to a raffia swamp that rings the **Corcovado Lagoon**. The lagoon is only accessible by boat, but there are no regular trips. Caymans and alligators survive here, sheltered from the hunters.

From Sirena you can walk north along the coast to the shelter at **Llorona** (plenty of waterfalls), from which there is a trail to the interior with another shelter at the end. From Llorona you can proceed north through a forest trail and then along the beach to the station at **San Pedrillo** on the edge of the park. You can stay here, camping or under roof, and eat with the rangers, who love company. From San Pedrillo you can take the park boat (not cheap) to Isla del Caño, a lovely manned park outpost. See under Puerto Quepos for Taximar boat service from Quepos and Dominical to Isla del Caño or Bahía Drake.

Sleeping On round the coast is **LL** *Casa Corcovado Jungle Lodge*, T256-3181, F256-7409, www.casacorcovado.com, outside the park in the forest, but with 500 m of beach more or less opposite Isla del Caño, 7 bungalows, many facilities, packages from 2 nights full board with boat transport (2 hrs) from Sierpe.

Isla del Coco

This has to be one of the world's most distant island destinations, the steep-sided and thickly wooded island and national park of 24 sq km lies 320 km off the Osa Peninsula, on the Cocos Ridge which extends some 1,400 km southwest to the Galápagos Islands.

Costa Rica

There is virtually nothing on the island, apart from a few endemic species, but you can visit for some of the world's best diving. The BBC/Discovery Channel shot some dramatic sihouetted images of tiger sharks here for their *Blue Planet* series. Historically, though, it was a refuge for pirates who are supposed to have buried great treasure here, though none has been found by the 500 or so expeditions which have come in search of a spot marked by an 'x' or any other way. Finally the offshore waters are a fisherman's paradise. Arrangements for reaching it by chartered boat can be made in Puntarenas, after a government permit has been obtained, or you can take a scuba diving cruise on the *Okeanos Agressor*, 10 days, two sailings a month, T232-0572 ext 60 (in US: PO Drawer K, Morgan City, LA 70381, T504-385-2416, F504-384-0817). Understandably a trip would be expensive.

San José to the Atlantic Coast

San José

Heading east from San José the Central Highlands quickly fall away to the sparsely populated flat Caribbean lowlands. The tropical rainforest national parks of Tortuguero and Barra del Colorado, leading through coastal canals and waterways, are a nature lover's paradise with easily arranged trips, normally from San José, into the rainforest. South of the distinctly Caribbean city of Puerto Limón, coastal communities have developed to provide comfortable hang-outs and laid-back beach life for all budgets.

There are two routes from San José to Puerto Limón on the Atlantic coast. The newer main route goes over the Cordillera Central, through the Parque Nacional Braulio Carrillo down to Guápiles and Siquirres. This highland section is prone to fog and if driving yourself, requires extra care. The second, more scenic but considerably longer, route follows the old Atlantic railway to Cartago, south of Irazú volcano to Turrialba, joining the main highway at Siquirres.

Parque Nacional Braulio Carrillo

Colour map 7, grid B3   The third largest of Costa Rica's national parks Parque Nacional Braulio Carrillo was created to protect the high rainforest north of San José from the impact of the new San José-Guápiles-Puerto Limón highway. It extends for 47,583 ha, and encompasses five different types of forest with abundant wildlife including hundreds of species of bird, jaguar, ocelot and Baird's tapir. Various travel agencies offer naturalist tours, approximately US$65 from San José. San José to Guápiles and Puerto Limón buses go through the park.

The entrance to the **Quebrada González** centre on the highway is 23 km beyond the Zurquí tunnel, just over the Río Sucio at the Guápiles end. It has a new administration building. ■ *Open daily, 0800-1530. US$6.* Take any bus to the Atlantic coast and ask to be dropped off. There are three trails: Las Palmas, 1.6 km (need rubber boots); across the road are El Ceibo, 1 km, circular; and Botarrama, entry 2 km from Quebrada González (El Ceibo and Botarrama are to be joined). The trail has good bird-watching and the views down the Río Patria canyon are impressive. The **Zurquí** centre near the tunnel has been closed but may open again soon so ask at headquarters. It has services and the 250-m Los Jilqueros trail to the river.

Beyond Quebrada González (1½ km) is *Los Heliconios* butterfly garden with an insect museum and amphibians, entry US$6, 20-minute trail and others of 1-2 hours in Reserva Turística El Tapir which adjoins it (separate entry US$6).

An ingenious aerial tram (*teleférico*) lifts visitors high up into the rainforest, providing a fascinating up-close and personal view of the canopy life and vegetation. Best to go as early as possible for birds. It runs 0630-1600, except Monday 0900-1530 (tourist buses arrive 0800); 90 minutes' ride costs US$49.50 (including guided nature walk, students with ID and children half price, children under five not allowed). Office in San José: Rainforest Aerial Tram, Avenida 7, Calle 7, behind *Aurola Holiday Inn*, T257-5961, F257-6053. There's an all-inclusive package from San José leaving around 0800 daily, US$78.50, students and under 11s US$53.75, with pick-ups at most major hotels. Guarded car park for private vehicles. Restaurant for meals in the park. Can be difficult to get reservations during the high season.

Further on, at the *Soda Gallo Pinto* is the **Bosque Lluvioso** 170-ha private reserve, ■ *0700-1700, T224-0819*. It is at Km 56 on the Guápiles highway (Rancho Redondo), restaurant, trails in primary and secondary forest, entry US$15.

Parque Nacional Braulio Carrillo
& Puerto Viejo loop

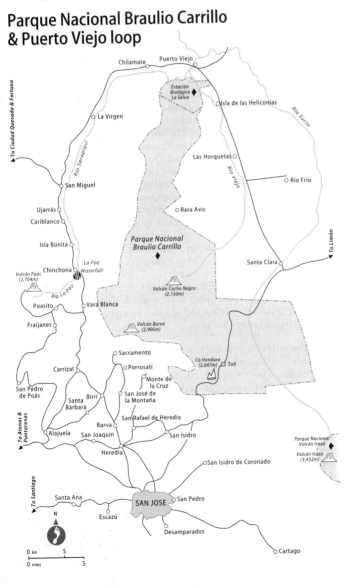

Thirteen kilometres before Guápiles is the turn off at Santa Clara to Puerto Viejo de Sarapiquí. At the junction is *Rancho Robertos*, a good, popular, reasonably priced roadside restaurant, T710-4609. For Guápile see below. Nearby is a new Tropical Frog Garden, T710-8347, an interesting short stop if your have the time.

There is a private reserve bordering the Parque Nacional Braulio Carrillo called *Río Danta*, 60 ha of primary rainforest, short limited treks (US$4) arranged with meals (US$6-9), for information contact Mawamba Group. T/F223-2421.

Puerto Viejo de Sarapiquí

Colour map 7, grid B3   Puerto Viejo de Sarapiquí (local website at www.sarapiquirainforest.com) is 40 km north of the San José-Limón highway, and 20 km from La Virgen to the southwest. Once an important port on the Río Sarapiquí, only occasionally do launches ply the Río Colorado to the Canales de Tortuguero. There is reported to be a cargo boat once a week to Barra del Colorado (no facilities, bring own food, hammock, sleeping bag; see pages 1129-1132), and on to Moín, about 10 km by road from Puerto Limón. But there is littletraffic, so you will need a bit of luck and a fair amount of cash. There is good fishing on the Río Sarapiquí.

In the neighbourhood is **La Selva Biological Station**, on the Río Puerto Viejo, run by the *Organization for Tropical Studies*. The floral and faunal diversity is unbelievable. Several guided and self-led walks are available. ■ *Guided natural history walk with bilingual naturalists from 0800-1130 or 1330-1600, US$20 per person. To visit it is essential to book in advance, T240-6696, reservas@ots.ac.cr*

Further south, hidden up a path from the hamlet of Montero close to the Río Isla Grande bridge, is **Los Heliconias Island**. Over 70 species of heliconia in 2 ha of beautifully landscaped gardens. Owned and run by the 'heliconiophile' Tim Ryan – as passionate about his subject as he is knowledgeable. If you doubt heliconias are interesting, a visit will certainly change your mind. ■ *US$7.50. T397-3948 (mob), helicon@sarapiquirainforest.com Camping E per day. Ask bus to drop you off at Las Chaves, 8 km south of Puerto Viejo, and follow signs.*

The Río San Juan is wholly in Nicaragua, so you technically have to cross the border and then return to Costa Rica. This will cost US$5 and you will need passport/visa   The river Sarapiquí flows into the San Juan, forming the northern border of Costa Rica. River trips on the Sarapiquí and on the Río Sucio are beautiful (US$15 for two hours); contact William Rojas in Puerto Viejo (T766-6108) for trips on the Río Sarapiquí or to Barra del Colorado and Tortuguero, or ask for the Lao brothers who will advise you. The cost of a launch to Tortuguero is about US$150 (US$350 for four people), but you may be able to find a place on a boat for US$40 or even less. The whole trip takes about five hours.

Sleeping & eating   **A** *El Bambú*, in centre north of park, T766-6005, F766-6132, www.elbambu.com, in centre, bath, fan, TV, including breakfast, very nice. **B** *Posada Andrea Cristina*, just out of town near the main road junction, T/F766-6265, comfortable small cabins, set amongst tropical gardens. Good local knowledge. **C** *Mi Lindo Sarapiquí*, overlooking park, T/F766-6074, lindo@sarapiquirainforest.com 6 spotless rooms with bath, fan, hot water and restaurant downstairs. Recommended. **F** *Cabinas Monteverde*, next to *El Bambú*, T766-6236, with bath, but pretty dirty. **F** *Hospedaje Gonar*, T766-6207, on road to the dock above hardware store (*ferretería*) without signpost, basic rooms, ones with windows slightly better. Shared bath, pretty dirty.

Out of town, in addition to *La Selva Biological Station* (see above), heading west a few kilometres towards La Virgen is **AL** *Selva Verde Lodge*, T766-6800, F766-6011, www.holbrooktravel.com, on over 200 ha of virgin rainforest reserve, 40 double rooms, 5 bungalows for 4, caters mainly for tour groups. Sensitively set in amongst the rainforest, evening lectures by biologists, excellent for bird-watchers and naturalists with extensive trail system, rafting, canoeing and riding through property; tours with biologists organized.

On the southern bank of the Río Sarapiquí, reached by taxi, is **AL-B** *El Gavilán Lodge*, T234-9507, F253-6556, www.gavilanlodge.com, includes breakfast, set in 100-ha private reserve by the river pier, good restaurant, good jungle paths, riding and river tours, 12 rooms private bath, special group and student/reseacher rates, day trips and overnight trips from San José. A dirt road just before the OTS station leads to **E** *Sarapiquí Ecolodge*, T766-6569 (daytime only), F236-8762, 4 rooms, shared bathroom, price per person, food extra. bird-watching, river trips, horse-riding. Great spot, but sometimes closed call ahead.

Mi Lindo Sarapaquí has good dishes. Good food on *el muelle* by the river with good views from the dockside.

Buses stop on north side of park. From **San José** 7 daily from Gran Terminal del Caribe, 1½ hrs through PN Braulio Carrillo, or through **Heredia**, 4 daily, 3½ hrs. From **Ciudad Quesada**, 5 daily, 2½ hrs.   **Transport**

Car To get there by car from San José, after passing through the PN Braulio Carrillo take Route 4, a paved road which turns off near Santa Clara to Puerto Viejo; it bypasses Río Frío and goes via Las Horquetas. A more scenic but longer route leaves from Heredia via San Miguel and La Virgen, and on to Puerto Viejo.

Banks *Banco de Costa Rica* and *Banco Nacional* both have branches in town.   **Directory**

Seventeen kilometres south of Puerto Viejo, near Las Horquetas de Sarapiquí, is *Rara Avis*, T253-0844, F764-4187, www.rara-avis.com, rustic lodges in a 600-ha forest reserve owned by ecologist Amos Bien. This admirable experiment in educating visitors about rainforest conservation takes small groups on guided tours (rubber boots provided), led by biologists. You must be prepared for rough and muddy trails, lots of insects but great bird-watching and a memorable experience.   **Las Horquetas de Sarapiquí**

Sleeping A range of accommodation options include **AL** *Waterfall Lodge*, a beautiful jungle lodge in an idyllic setting, includes meals, private bath. **L** *River-Edge Cabin*, even deeper in the rainforest. **A** *Albergue El Plástico*, 3 km before *Waterfall Lodge*, rustic with shared bath, minimum 2 nights, book well in advance. There is also treetop accommodation and rates for backpackers at the *Casita*. Call for details.

One hour from San José (bus US$1.45), Guápiles is the centre of the Río Frío banana region.   **Guápiles**
Colour map 7, grid B3

Sleeping and eating **C** *Centro Turístico Río Blanco*, on main road at entrance to town, T710-7857, with bath, fan. Recommended. **C** *Cabinas Car*, 50 m west of church, T710-0035, 10 clean and tidy rooms, with private bath, hot water, fan and TV. **E** *Cabinas de Oro*, north-east of bus terminal, T710-6663, clean rooms, private bath with hot water, cheaper without. Restaurant nearby. **F** *Hotel Cariari*, north of church on road out of town, T710-6048, bit untidy but essentially clean. Shared bath, restaurant and laundry downstairs. **G** *Hotel Alfaro (El Tunél)*, 50m west of bus terminal, T710-6293, simple rooms, no frills, but clean. Open 24 hrs, with a rather funky aluminium stairway. Good value.

Out of town, along the main highway is **A** *Casa Río Blanco*, about 6 km west of Guápiles, take first right before the Río Blanco bridge and follow signpost for 1 km, T/F382-0957, crblanco@racsa.co.cr, accommodates 12 guests in comfortable cabins, with breakfast, run by Dee and Steve, North Americans interested in biology and the environment, vegetarian food. Recommended. There are several *sodas* and snack bars around, but nothing stands out.

Transport Buses leave from a central terminal a block to the north of the church. Regular buses to **San José** and **Puerto Limón**. Buses to Puerto Viejo de Sarapiquí ever 2½ hrs, and to Río Frío every 1½ hrs.

The highway parallels the railway line to Guácimo. *Costa Flores* offer guided tours of the world's largest flower farm. ■ *US$15 per person, T220-1311.* **B** *Río Palmas*, T760-0330, F760-0296, 1 km past EARTH School, 30 rooms, private bathroom, pool, restaurant, the 200-ha property includes ornamental plant farm and rainforest.   **Guácimo**

Costa Rica

Siquirres
Colour map 7, grid B4

It is another 25 km from Guácimo to Siquirres, a clean, friendly town and junction for roads from Turrialba with the main highway and former railways.

Sleeping **D** *Centro Turístico Pacuare*, T768-6482, renovated, large pool. **D** *Don Quito*, 3½ km towards Siquirres, T768-8533, pleasant, good restaurant. **F** *Alcema*, 50 m east of market, T768-8157, some dark rooms, with fan, clean, shared bath.

Transport At least 1 bus per hr leaves Gran Terminal del Caribe in **San José**, 2½-hr journey.

Matina

Twenty-eight kilometres beyond Siquirres, heading north at the 'techo rojo' junction is Matina, a small, once busy town on the railway but off the highway. Today, it is an access point to Tortuguero (see page 1129) and the less well-known private **Pacuare Nature Reserve**, 30 km north of Puerto Limón, is accessible by canal from Matina. Run by Englishman John Denham, it has a 6 km stretch of leatherback turtle nesting beach, protected and guarded by the Reserve. Volunteers patrol the beach in May and June, measuring and tagging these magnificence marine turtles, US$50 per person per week, includes good meals and accommodation. For volunteer working, contact Carlos Fernández, Corporación de Abogados, Avenida 8-10, Calle 19, No 837, San José, T233-0508, F221-2820, fdezlaw@racsa.co.cr

Puerto Limón

Colour map 7, grid B4
Population: 61,494

On a rocky outcrops on an almost featureless coastline, Puerto Limón is the country's most important port. Built on the site of the ancient Indian village of Cariari, Columbus dropped anchor at Punta Uvita, the island off the coastline, on his fourth and final voyage. The climate is very humid and it rains almost every day. With a mainly black population, and a large Chinese contingent, the town has a distinctly Caribbean feel expressed particularly during carnival each October, but in most bars every weekend.

Parque Vargas and the seafront promenade at the rocky headland are popular places for social gatherings and killing time, making for ideal people watching territory, especially in the evening. Parque Vargas, sadly rather run down, is an impressive botanical display and has a colourful mural depicting the history of Limón and a bandstand. To complete the picture of neglect, the Hoffman's two-toed sloths which used to live in its trees seem to have disappeared. Long-running talk of refurbishment came to a head in late-2001 when the Ministry of Tourism announced a dramatic dockside redevlopment project. Keep an eye out for developments which should not only spruce up the city, but also make a visit to **Isla Uvita** a real possibility to commemorate the 500th anniversary of Columbus' arrival in 2002.

On the upside, the nightlife is good, particularly for Caribbean music and dancing, culimating in carnival every October, Costa Rica's largest festival. There is a small **Museo Etnohistórico de Limón**, Calle 2, Avenida 2, features material relating to Columbus' arrival in Limón. ■ *Mon-Fri, 0900-1200, 1300-1600.* The cargo docks are still active with international crews making regular journeys, as well as being the landing point for pristine floating palaces cruising the Caribbean.

Excursions

Playa Bonita and **Portete** have pleasant beaches about 5 km along the coastal road from Puerto Limón. **Moín**, a further 1½ km east along the road, is the sight of the new international docks which exports some 2.8 million bunches of bananas annually. The docks are also the departure point for barges to Tortuguero and Barra del Colorado (eight hours). Boats also run from Moín to Tortuguero (see below) and may be hired at the dockside. Buses run to Moín every 40 minutes from 0600-1740, 30 minutes, US$0.10. If shipping a vehicle check which dock.

A severe earthquake struck the Caribbean coast of Costa Rica and Panama in April 1991 raising much of the coastline, which is evident if you are travelling south, and causing the Tortuguero canals (see below) around Matina to dry up. Japdeva,

Costa Rica

the harbour authority, has carried out dredging work but boats for Tortuguero River now also depart from Hamburgo de Siquirres on the Río Reventazón.

Puerto Limón A-B *Park*, Av 3, C 1-2, T798-0555, F758-4364, neat little hotel with 34 rooms, sea facing rooms quiet and cool, recently renovated, restaurant good. **B-C** *Acón*, on corner of main square, C 3, Av 3, T758-1010, F758-2924, big rooms with private bath, a/c, clean, safe, good restaurant, a bit run down, popular daily disco *Aquarius* except Mon.

C-D *Miami*, next to *King* on Av 2, C 4-5, T/F758-0490, 35 rooms, all with private bath, some with a/c, others with fans. Secure and efficient. Credit cards accepted. **C** *Tete*, one block west of main square, Av 3, C 4-5, T758-1122, clean rooms, bright and good beds. Some sleeping up to 6 and some with balconies overlooking square.**C-D** *Caribe*, facing Parque Vargas, Av 2, C 1-2, T758-0138, big, immaculate rooms with private bath, hot water and swamp fan. Good deal.

D *Palace*, 1 block north of bus stops, C 2-3, Av 2, T758-0419, family-run hotel, with 33 mostly big rooms. Pretty clean, balcony overlooking street, popular with travellers and good place to make up groups for Tortuguero. **E** *Continental*, a little north of the centre, Av 5, C 2-3, T798-0532, 25 big, good and clean rooms with ceiling fans. **E** *International*, opposite the *Continental*, Av 5, C 2-3, T758-0434, with private bath, some with a/c other with fan, good deal. **E** *King*, next to post office near main square on Av 2, T758-1033, simple rooms, pretty dark, but clean and secure. **E** *Pensión Costa Rica*, 1½ blocks east of central park, Av 2, C 1-2, T758-0241, small, dark rooms, with a fan. **F** *Hotel Wilson*, on street west of main square, Av 3, C 4-5, T758-5028, clean, tidy and central, OK. **F** *Paraíso*, Av 2, C 4-5, plyboard partitions divide a once beautiful house in to tiny, dark, box rooms. Hard core roughing it and a little sad. **G** per person *Ng*, C 4, Av 5-6, T758-2134, 15 basic rooms some with bath, cheaper without. Basic and a bit untidy, but friendly. Good for the price.

Playa Bonita A *Matama*, T758-1133, F758-4499, matama@racsa.co.cr, tourist complex with palm-roofed huts aimed at local occasions, but with a couple of pools and smart

Sleeping
■ *on map*

Beware of theft at night, and remember it is a port; there are a lot of drunks roaming the streets

Costa Rica

Puerto Limón

To Springs Restaurant (400m), Portete & Moín (for Tortuguero)

To Swimming Pool (300m), Airport & Cahuita

■ **Sleeping**		
1 Acón	9 Paraíso	3 Doña Toda
2 Caribe	10 Park	4 Marisquería El
3 Continental	11 Pensión Costa Rica	Cevichito
4 International	12 Tete	5 Monte de Oro
5 King	13 Wilson	6 Palacio Encantador
6 Miami		7 Soda Mares
7 Ng	● **Eating**	8 Soda Yans
8 Palace	1 Antillita	
	2 Diplo's	

modern rooms. Boats for rent to Tortuguero. **B** *Cocorí*, T798-1670, F758-2930, restauran overlooking the beach and bay, 25 rooms with private bath and hot water, some with a/c boat trips to Tortuguero arranged. A little overpriced. **B-C** *Albergue Turístico Playa Bonita* T798-3090, F798-3612, relaxing little hotel, with small garden patio. 7 tidy rooms, with private bath, hot water and TV. 200 m from ocean.

Portete   AL *Maribú Caribe*, 3½ km out of Limón, T758-4543, F758-3541. 50 thatched bungalows on a rocky bluff overlooking the Caribbean – dreamy views from the restaurant balcony. **C-D** *Maeva del Caribe*, T758-2024, with a dozen cabins and a couple of pools. Looks good, but owners selling up.

Moín   B *Moín Caribe*, T758-1112, uphill from where the bus from Puerto Limón stops, reported to be friendly, nice, clean, good place to stay before Tortuguero.

Eating
● *on map*
It's not easy to find a good place to eat

Antillita, C 6, Av 4-5, Caribbean rice and beans, meat, open evenings only. *Brisas del Caribe*, facing Parque Vargas, Av 2, C 1, cheap noodles, meat, seafood, and good service. *Diplo's*, Av 6, C 5-6, the best, and cheapest, Caribbean food in town. *Doña Toda*, good, near market on main square. Cheap food available in the Central Market and around the outside. *Milk Bar La Negra Mendoza* at the central market has good milk shakes and snacks. *Casados* in market in the day, outside it at night, good, cheap food. Try *pan bon*, spicy bread from Creole recipe, sold near bus stop for San José. *Marisquería El Cevichito*, Av 2, C 3-4, good fish and *ceviche* and good spot for watching the world drift by. *Monte de Oro*, Av 4, C 3-4, serves good local dishes, in a rough and ready atmosphere. Handy for buses going south. *Palacio Encantador*, 50 m east of baseball park, good. *Park Hotel*, Av 3, C 1-2, does good meals, US$4. *Sabor Pizza*, corner of Av 3 and C 4, good pizza. *Soda Mares*, overlooking market square, open 0700-1400, good food. *Soda Yans* along Av 2, C 5-6, is a popular spot. *Springfield*, north of town opposite the hospital, stylish restaurant serving a mix of *Tico* and international dishes. Best restaurant in town. Several Chinese restaurants eg *Samkirson*, C 3, Av 3-4, good value.

Festivals   *Fiesta*: carnival lasts a few days leading up to **12 Oct**, Costa Rica's biggest; it's crowded, prices rise, but is definitely worth seeing if you can get a room.

Transport   **Buses** Town bus service is irregular and crowded. Service from **San José** with *CoopeLimón*, T233-3646 and *Caribeño*, T222-0610, at least every hr, 0500-2000, daily. Arrive and depart from C 2, Av 1-2, US$3, 2½ hrs. Also services to **Guápiles** and **Siquirres**. From same stop buses to Siquirres/Guápiles, 13 daily, 8 direct. Near *Radio Casino* on Av 4, C 3-4, buses leave for **Sixaola**, first 0500, last 1800, US$2.50, stopping at Cahuita, Puerto Viejo and Bri Brien route. To **Manzanillo**, at 0600, 1430, returning 1130, 1900, 1½ hrs, US$1.50. To **Moín** from C 5, Av 3-4, every 30 mins between 0600-2200.

Shopping   *La Casona del Parque* and *Mercado Artesanal Caribeño* on west side of Parque Vargas. *Fuji* film available at C 5, Av 4-5, and other film at *Rafael Barrantes* camera shop on Av 2, C 6.

Directory   **Banks** Usual banking hours and services, all with ATMs at *Banco de Costa Rica*, Av 2, C 1, open Mon-Fri 0900-1400. *Banco Nacional*, Av 2, C 3, with ATM. *Banco Popular*, C3, Av 1-2, with ATM. *Banco San José*, Av 3, C 3-4, with ATM. **Communications** Internet: *Edutec Internet*, on 2nd level above Plaza Caribe, US$2.30 per hr **Post office**: opposite central market. **Telephones**: *ICE* for international calls at Av 2, C 5-6 and at C 3, Av 4-5, open Mon-Thu, 0800-1700, Fri 0800-1600. **Laundry** Av 2, C 5-6, price per item, not that cheap, but 2-hr turnaround. **Medical services** *Red Cross*, C 3, Av 1-2, T758-0125. **Hospital** on the road to Moin, T758-2222.

The Atlantic Coast

Between Puerto Limón and the Río San Juan on the Nicaraguan border, the long stretch of Atlantic coastline and its handful of small settlements is linked by a canal system that follows the coastline. The region encompasses Tortuguero National Park, famed for its wildlife and turtle nesting beaches, and Barra del Colorado National Reserve. The Río San Juan forms the border between Costa Rica and Nicaragua, however the border is not mid-river, but on the Costa Rican bank. English is widely spoken along the coast.

Parque Nacional Tortuguero

Tortuguero is a 29,068-ha national park, with a marine extension of over 50,000 ha, protecting the Atlantic nesting sites of the green and leatherback turtle and the Caribbean lowland rainforest inland. As with much of Costa Rica, getting the timing right to see this natural phenomenon is essential. The green turtles lay their eggs at night on the scrappy, rather untidy beach from June to October, with the hatchlings emerging from the depths of their sandy nests until November at the latest. Leatherbacks can be seen from March to June. Hawksbill and loggerheads also nest at Tortuguero but numbers are minimal. Trips to look for nesting turtles are carefully monitored and you must be accompanied by a licensed guide at all times.

Colour map 7, grid B4

The beach is not attractive and the weather rarely inspires you to strip off but do not swim at Tortuguero – there are sharks

While your visit may not coincide with those of the turtles, the canals of jungle fringed waterways, teeming with bird and insect life, behind the beach are a pleasure throughout the year.

A **visitor centre**, close to the town of Tortuguero, has information on the park and the turtles. Round the back of the headquarters there is a well-marked 1.4 km nature trail, recommended. In the centre is a small gift shop. To the northern end of the village is the *Caribbean Conservation Corporation*, which has played a fundamental role in the creation and continued research of the turtle nesting grounds. There's an interesting and very informative **natural history museum**. ■ *1000-1200, 1400-1730, donation US$1. In San José T224-9215, www.cccturtle.org*

Where you stay in Tortuguero affects considerably your understanding of its layout

A guide is required for trips along the beach at night and recommended for trips through the waterways. If travelling with a lodge, tours will be arranged for you. If organizing independently, contact the information kiosk in the village for instructions and to link up with a registered guide. To visit the turtles at night you must pay US$7 park entrance fee, and US$5 each for a guide. A guide and tour in no way guarantees you will see a turtle or hatchlings. Unfortunately people still eat turtle eggs and meat, even though they are protected. It is depressing to see the nests robbed by morning.

Tours through the water channels are the best way to see the rainforest, ideally in a boat without a motor. The canal bordered with primary rainforest, gives way to smaller channels, and, drifting slowly through forest darkened streams, the rainforest slowly comes alive with wildlife including birds – over half of those found in Costa Rica – monkeys, sloths and, for the lucky, alligators, tapirs, jaguars, ocelots, peccaries, anteaters and even manatees. Take insect repellent against the ferocious mosquitoes, ticks and chiggers.

You can hire a canoe and guide for about US$6 per hour per person in a boat without a motor, excellent way to see wildlife including crocodiles, US$12 with a motor, minimum 4. Night tours, US$15 per person per hour. Fishing tours, with all equipment included are US$35 per person, minimum two. (See Directory, below, for tour operators and guides.)

Getting there Most people visit Tortuguero as part of a 2 or 3-day package tour from San José, flying in to the airport, or catching an agency bus and boat from Matina. However, it is possible to travel to Tortuguero independently. A regular vessel leaves from the Tortuguero dock in Moín at 1000, north of Limón. US$50 return, returning 1000 the next day. Book in advance if possible through the *Tortuguero Information Centre*, T392-3201, safari@racsa.co.cr The cheapest

Costa Rica

route to Tortuguero takes the 0900 direct bus to Cariari from the Terminal Gran Caribe. From here take the 1200 bus to GEEST Casa Verde and there will be a couple of boats waiting to take passengers, getting off the bus to Tortuguero. The journey is US$10 one way. Don't be talked into a package if you're not interested – there are plenty of services to choose from in Tortuguero (see below). The return services leaves at 0700 (and 1100 in the high season) giving you 1 or 2 nights in Tortuguero. There appears to be an attempt to monopolize this service but for the time being at least, there are a couple of boats in operation.

Sleeping

Top-end hotels normally target package deals, walk-in rates given where available

In town A *Casa Marbella*, in front of the the catholic church, T392-3201, casamarbella.tripod.com A new B&B with 4 small rooms, with private bath. Run by local guide Daryl Loth. A good source of information. **D** *Mary Scar*, basic stuff, foam mattresses, but friendly enough if things elsewhere are full. **D** *Miss Junie's*, T710-0523, 12 good cabins at the north end of town. **D** *Cabinas Sabina's*, winding down, the end of an era, with just 16 rooms remaining. Good views looking out over to the Caribbean. **D** *Cabinas Tortuguero*, 5 little cabins, each sleeping 3 with private bath, pleasant little garden with hammocks. Nice spot. **D** *Yoruki Lodge*, T233-3333 (pager), clean simple rooms looking over the river. There are many cheap cabañas in the **E-F** range, the boatmen or villagers will help you find them.

Places **out of town**, best visited as part of a package include: **AL** *Mawamba Lodge*, T710-7282, in San José T223-2421, F222-5463, www.grupomawamba.com Comfortable cabins with fans, pool, walking distance to town, turtle beaches behind property. **A** *Laguna Lodge*, T710-0355, F283-8031, www.lagunalodgetortuguero.com 50-odd cabins, with bath and fan, restaurant, bar, beautiful gardens.

Across the canal from the town is **AL** *Pachira Lodge*, T256-7080, F223-1119, www.pachiralodge.com, 3 day/2 night package includes transport, food, tours with bilingual guide, US$239. **A** *Jungle Lodge Hotel*, T233-0133, F233-0778, www.tortuguero.com 50 big, wooden panelled rooms, complete with pool, wet bar, games room and disco. **L** *Tortuga Lodge*, price per person includes meals, T257-0766 (San José), F257-1665, www.costaricaexpeditions.com, very comfortable accommodation, in big rooms each with veranda or balcony.

Cheaper walk-in and package options should be available at: **D** per person *El Manati*, T/F383-0330. *Tico* family run, simple rooms with a terrace. Relaxing spot, work with Ecole Travel in San José. Good value. **D** *Ilan Ilan*, through the Agencia Mitur in San José T255-2262, F255-1946, www.mitour.com, simple rooms in a line, with small terrace. Pool, jacuzzi and riverside bar. One channel back from Tortuguero is **B** *Caribbean Paradise*, T223-0238 and T223-2651 – difficult to reach, try going direct when you arrive – run by *Tico* Carlos and his wife Ana, includes 3 meals. 16 simple rooms, no set itinerary, no set activities, personal service, activities as you want them. A refreshing changes from the general offering, and very enjoyable. Recommended. Nearby is **B** with breakfast and dinner, **E** without at *Tortuguero Caribe Lodge*, T385-4676, 10 simple cabins, friendly *Tico* run and owned. Book direct or as package through Ecole Travel in San José.

Staying in town is better for the truly local economy

6 km north of Tortuguero is the *Caño Palma Biological Station*, administered by the *Canadian Organization for Tropical Education and Rainforest Conservation* (in Canada T905-683-2116), basic rooms for volunteer staff, **F** per person, includes meals, a good place for serious naturalists or just for unwinding, accommodation for up to 16 in wooden cabin, freshwater well for drinking and washing. Minimum stay 2 weeks. You can sometimes camp at the National Park office for US$2.50.

Eating

Good food is limited

El Dolar, simple restaurant, small menu, good *casado*. Almost legendary *Miss Junie's*, north end of town, has good local dishes, reservation necessary. *The Vine*, pizzas and sandwiches from US$3.

Shopping

The Jungle Shop specializes in handicrafts, and sells the odd T-shirt, postcard and nature book. Small tourist shop at the arrivals dock.

Transport

Air Daily flights from San José with *Sansa* and *Travelair* to Tortuguero, US$60 one way.

Costa Rica

Boat A regular boat leaves Moín at 0900, US$25, 4 hrs, returning about 1400, check the times which frequently change. Tickets sold once boat is under way. You can bargain at Moín for a boat to take you to Tortuguero and bring you back 3-4 days later, at around US$50-60 provided a party of 6 can be arranged. *Viajes Laura*, T758-2410, highly recommended, daily service, open return US$60 if phoned direct, more through travel agencies, pick up from hotel, will store luggage, lunch provided, excellent for pointing out wildlife on the way. It is also possible to take a bus from Siquirres to Freeman (unpaved road), a *Del Monte* banana plantation, from where unscheduled boats go to Tortuguero; ask around at the bank of the Río Pacuare, or call the public phone office in Tortuguero (T710-6716, open 0730-2000) and ask for Johnny Velázquez to come and pick you up, US$57, maximum 4 passengers, 4 hrs. Sometimes heavy rains block the canals, preventing passage there or back. Contact Willis Rankin (Apdo 1055, Limón, T798-1556) an excellent captain who will negotiate rampaging rivers. All river boats for the major lodges (see below) leave from **Hamburgo** or **Freeman**. If excursion boats have a spare seat you may be allowed on. Generally it is getting more difficult to 'do it yourself', but it is still possible, ask around the boat owners in Moín. Official tours and tourist guides with accommodation included are now normal, bargain for a good price. A 2-day, 1-night trip from Puerto Limón with basic accommodation, turtle-watching trip and transport (no food) costs from US$99 per person.

Road For independent travel to Tortuguero see Getting there above. A boat runs from Puerto Viejo de Sarapiquí to Barra del Colorado and from there to Tortuguero with the *Ilán Ilán Hotel* (US$135), but book in advance (see below). Caño Blanco Marina runs a daily bus-boat service San José-Tortuguero at 0700, US$50 return, T256-9444 (San José), T710-0523 (Tortuguero), from 2 Av, 1-3 C, San José. Book in advance – if you miss the boat, there is nothing else in Caño Blanco Marina.

Tour operators Tours from San José include transport, meals, 2 nights lodging, guide and boat trips for US$219-252 per person (double occupancy). The main tours are *Mawamba*, T223-2421, F223-7490, www.grupomawamba.com, minimum 2 people, 3 days/2 nights, daily, private launch so you can stop en route, with launch tour of national park included, accommodation at *Mawamba Lodge*, *Colorado Prince* boat, 3-day/2-night package, Tue, Fri, Sun US$200, using *Ilan Ilan Lodge*, T255-3031. *Tortuga Lodge* and *Laguna Lodge* also offer similar packages. OTEC (see page 1027) runs 3-day/2-night tours for US$180, with small student discount, a trip to see the turtles in Jul-Sep costs extra. Tours from Puerto Viejo de Sarapiquí, including boat trip to Tortuguero, meals, 2 nights' lodging, guide and transport to San José cost US$275-400 per person (double occupancy).

Several **local guides** have been recommended including Johnny Velázquez; Alberto who lives next to *Hotel Maryscar*; Rubén Bananero lives in the last house before you get to the National Park office, sign on pathway, recommended for 4-hr tour at dusk and in the dark; Chico lives behind *Sabina's Cabinas*, US$2 per hr, recommended local guide, will take you anywhere in his motor boat; Ernesto, born in Tortuguero, 15 years' experience as a guide, contact him at *Tropical Lodge* or through his mother, who owns *Sabina's Cabinas*; Rafael a biologist, recommended, speaks Spanish and English (his wife speaks French), lives ½ km behind Park Rangers' office, ask rangers for directions, he also rents canoes. There are several boats for rent from Tortuguero, ask at the *pulpería*.

Daryl Loth lives locally and runs *Tortuguero Safaris*, T392-3201, safari@racsa.co.cr Barbara Hartung of *Tinamon Tours*, pager 223-3030 ext 3761, www.tinamontours.de, is a biologist speaking English, German and Spanish who is recommended for boat, hiking and turtle tours in Tortuguero. US$5 per person per hr. All-inclusive trips from Limón 3-days, 2-nights, US$150. Both Daryl and Barbara are strong supporters of using paddle power, or at most electric motors. In 2001 the use of polluting 2-stroke motors was outlawed and the use of 4-stroke engines limited to 3 of the 4 main water channels. All in all moves that are better for visitors and, more importantly, the wildlife.

Directory (margin)

Costa Rica (margin)

Barra del Colorado

The canals pass many small settlements, and is often their only means of communication. The canals are part artificial, part natural; originally they were narrow lagoons running parallel to the sea separated from it by ¾ km of land. Now the lagoons are linked, and it is possible to sail as far as **Barra del Colorado**, in the extreme northeast of Costa Rica, 25 km beyond Tortuguero. The town is divided by the river, the main part being on the northern bank. Secluded and difficult to get to, The **Refugio Nacional de Fauna Silvestre Barra del Colorado** (81,213 ha) is a national wildlife refuge. The reserve and the Parque Nacional Tortuguero share some boundaries, making for a far more effective protected zone. The fame of the region's fauna extends to the waters which are world renowned for fishing.

Sleeping **AL** *Silver King Lodge*, T381-1403, F381 0849, toll free in US 1-800-847-3474, www.silverkinglodge.com, price per person, deluxe sport-fishing hotel, 5-night packages includes flights, meals, rooms with bath, fan, hot water. **C** *Tarponland Lodge*, T710-6917, cabins, run by Guillermo Cunningham, very knowledgeable and helpful. If you have a tent you may be able to camp at *Soda La Fiesta*, lots of mosquitoes.

Furthest south is **LL** *Samay Laguna*, T384-7047, F383-6370, www.samay.com, beautiful rooms, jungle tours and sport-fishing packages offered, transport by seaplane possible.

Transport **Air** Flight San José-Barra del Colorado daily with *Sansa* (US$55 one way). **Boat** From Barra to Tortuguero takes 1½ hr and costs US$50. A motorized canoe can take 8 people and costs up to US$80, 2 hrs. Try and arrive in a group as boats are infrequent.

Border with Nicaragua – Barra del Colorado

Once across the Río Colorado (which in fact is the south arm of the Río San Juan delta), you can walk to Nicaragua (see under Nicaragua, San Juan del Norte) along the coast, but it is a long 30-km beach walk, take food and lots of water. Most hikers overnight en route. Seek advice before setting out.

Costa Rican immigration This is not a regular border crossing and there are no formal facilities on the Costa Rican side. Do not leave for Nicaragua by boat or on foot without checking with the Guardia Civil in Barra del Colorado or Tortuguero, who are very helpful. Similarly, check with them if arriving from Nicaragua.

Transport Transport, mostly by boat, is costly, typically US$30 for a ½-day. There are several fishermen who will take you up the coast on their way to fish in Nicaraguan waters, US$20-30. You can go by irregular boat from Barra up the Río Colorado, Río San Juan and Río Sarapiquí to Puerto Viejo, about 5-6 hrs. A small boat for 4 without roof costs US$150 (or US$50 per person), a larger boat with roof (recommended) costs US$185 for 4; you see caimans, turtles and lots of birds. There are several border checkpoints. Non-Costa Rican nationals travelling along Río San Juan must pay US$5 entry and exit tax at Nicaraguan border checkpoint and receive stamp in passport.

An alternative if you have arrived from Nicaragua to going south along the coast to Puerto Limón, is by bus from the river bank opposite Isla Buena Vista 25 km up the Río Colorado, daily except Sun, leaves 0600, by dirt track to Cariari and then to Guápiles. Interesting trip through rainforest and then banana plantations.

South from Puerto Limón

Penshurst South of Limón, a paved road shadows the coastline normally separated by little more than a thin line of palms. At Penshurst a road (and the railway) branches to Valle de Estrella, a large Standard Fruit banana plantation. Beyond the town is the **Hitoy Cerere Biological Reserve.** If you have time, camping is easy in the hills and there are plenty of rivers for swimming. Further south the road leads to Cahuita, Puerto Viejo and on towards Manzanillo – all sleepy beach towns, with lively centres, comfortable hideaways, and coastal and nature opportunities to explore. If heading for Panama and the border, heading inland just north of Puerto Viejo takes you through Bri Bri and on to Sixaola.

Sleeping **AL** *Los Aviarios del Caribe*, T/F382-1335, aviarios@costarica.net, 30 km south of Limón just north of Penshurst, is a sloth rescue sanctuary with a small nature reserve. The friendly owners offer canoe trips in the Estrella River Delta and there's a volunteer programme if you have time to spare. They also have a number of comfortable room. Recommended.

AL *Selva Bananita Lodge*, T/F253-8118, www.selvabananito.com, 20 km from Puerto Limón at Cerro Mochila heading inland at Bananito, 7 cabins on secluded farm, solar heating, primary rainforest tours, tree climbing, horses and bikes to rent.

Transport Small buses leave Limón (C 4, Av 6) for Valle de Estrella/Pandora, 7 a day from 0500, at 2-hourly intervals, last at 1800, 1½ hrs (returning from Pandora at similar times). From Penshurst it is 11½ km to **Cahuita**; this stretch of the road is paved to the edge of Cahuita.

Cahuita and Parque Nacional Cahuita

The small town of Cahuita hides 1 km back from the main road, and enjoys a sleepy feel accordingly. A laid back community, it's a good spot to hide away in one of the secluded spots or to party in the centre of town. North of the town there is a beautiful black-sand beach ideal for swimming or just lazing about in a hammock, while to the south is the national park. Most people stay in Cahuita to explore the park.

Colour map 7, grid B4
Entry charge to the Park US$6

Cahuita National Park (1,068 ha) is a narrow strip of beach protecting a coral reef off shore and a marine area of 22,400 ha. The length of the beach can be walked in about three hours, and passes endless coconut palms and interesting tropical forest, through which there is also a path. It is hot and humid, so take drinking water, but a wide range of fauna can be seen, including howler monkeys, white face monkeys, coatis, snakes, butterflies and hermit crabs. Over 500 species of fish inhabit the surrounding waters and reef tours are available. An old Spanish shipwreck can be seen and reached without a boat. Snorkellers should take care to stay away from the coral which is already badly damaged by agricultural chemicals and other pollutants from nearby rivers.

The park extends from the southern limit of Cahuita town southeast to **Puerto Vargas**. The official entrance to the park is at Puerto Vargas, about 5 km south of Cahuita, where there are the park headquarters, a nature trail, camping facilities and toilets. Take the bus to Km 5, then turn left at the sign. There is a tourist complex in the area, and the restaurant *Marisquería*, at Puerto Vargas park entrance, Italian, jovial host, which also has rooms. You can enter the park for free from the southern side of Cahuita, which is ideal for relaxing on the beach, but leave a donation. If you have the option, visit during the week when it is quieter.

Note: Cahuita and Puerto Viejo have suffered from what locals believe is a lack of support and investment from central government. An under-current of problems, partially based on the perception that everyone on the Caribbean coast takes drugs, does mean that you may be hassled for drugs. If you are not interested, just say no. You should be aware there have been several violent attacks in the area and in March 2000 a couple of female students were murdered. In balance, the shock of this event after so many difficult years has produced some positive responses from the government and local community.

Sleeping
Hotels and lodges will give discounts for stays of over one week

Within a couple of blocks of the centre of town is **B** *Kelly Creek*, by entrance to national park, T755-0007, kellycr@racsa.co.cr, large rooms with veranda, ceiling fan to assist fresh sea breezes, good service and great spot. **C-D** *Hotel National Park*, T755-0244, F755-0065, opposite *Kelly Creek*, bright rooms, fan, just about friendly but the beach front restaurant makes it a good spot.

A little road from the bus stop goes straight to the seafront, passing **C** *Cabinas Palmar*, T755-0243, *Tico*-run, clean, good, friendly and very helpful. Internet café. Heading to the beach if **C** *Jenny's Cabinas* T755-0256, jenny@racsa.co.cr, clothes washing area, balconies with view, Canadian owned, bath, fan, breakfast available, running water, close to the sea with kayak tours available, but surrounding area a bit scruffy. **D** *Cabinas Seeside*, on beach close to *Jenny's Cabinas*, T755-0027, clean, English spoken, hammocks available.

Beware of theft on the beach, and drug pushers who may be undercover police. Exercise sensible caution

Costa Rica

Recommended. **D** *New Cabinas Arrecife*, T/F755-0081, right on the coastline close to Miss Ediths, OK rooms, but great spot and view from restaurant.

Facing the school is **E** *Cabinas Surf Side*, T755-0246, clean, good value and with parking. Towards the park entrance is **E** *Vaz Cabañas*, T755-0218, friendly, cold shower, some fans, quite clean, good restaurant, safe parking. Recommended. **F** per person *Cabinas Safari*, opposite *Cabinas Palmar*, T755-0078, F755-0020, simple rooms with fan and shared bath, friendly owner Wayne Palmer, clean, good value.

Heading north of Cahuita along **Playa Negra** in order. **D** *Cabinas Belo Horizonte*, T755-0206, a couple of good rooms, quite simple but on the beach. **C** *Cabinas Tito*, T755-0286, clean, quiet, little cabins sleeping 2-3, popular with families, good value. A path leads to 200 m away from beach to **D-E** *Cabinas Margarita*, T755-0205, simple rooms, quiet spot, nice atmosphere, clean. Back on the main road is **A** *Atlántida Lodge*, T788-0115, F755-0213, atlantis@racsa.co.cr, with private bath and ceiling fan. Pleasant gardens, pool, jacuzzi, health clinic, safe parking for cars and motorcycles.

A small track leads to **C-D** *Centro Turistico Brigitte's*, T/F755-0053, www.brigittecahuita.com Friendly, quiet, Swiss-run, good restaurant, good for wildlife, small cabin sleeping 2, excellent local information, knowledge, and many different tours. Recommended. **A** *Jardín Tropical & Cabinas Mambo*, T/F755-0033, jardintropical@racsa.co.cr 2 decent bungalows sleeping 2-4, or a house with kitchen for 5. Laid back, poison dart frogs in the gardens. **B-C** *Cabinas Iguana*, 800 m north of Cahuita, T755-0005, F755-0054, iguanas@racsa.co.cr Swiss-owned, cabins or houses to rent, with kitchen, fan, mosquito netting, balcony, clean, waterfall-fed pool, nice location. Big 2-for-1 book swap (English, German, French, Spanish and others). Very good value. Recommended.

Costa Rica

Cahuita

Playa Negra

Caribbean Sea

To La Piscina Natural Hotel (150m) & Playa Negra

Pub'n'Disco Nightlife

Plaza

Rainy Bay

Centro Turistico Brigitte

Laundrette

Cahuita Tours

Highway 36

To Highway 36

To Highway 36

N

0 metres 100
0 yards 100

■ **Sleeping**
1 Atlantida Lodge *A1*
2 Cabinas Belo Horizonte *A3*
3 Cabinas Iguana *B1*
4 Cabinas Margarita *C2*
5 Cabinas Palmar *B6*
6 Cabinas Safari *A2*
7 Cabinas Seeside *B6*
8 Cabinas Surf Side *B5*
9 Cabinas Tito *B3*
10 Camping Kontiki *A1*
11 Jardín Tropical *B1*
12 Jenny's Cabinas *B6*
13 Kelly Creek *C6*
14 National Park *C6*
15 New Cabinas Arrecife *A5*
16 Vaz's Cabinas *C6*

● **Eating**
1 Caribbean Roots *B5*
2 Cha Cha Cha *B5*
3 Ciao's Paradise *A1*

AL *Magellan Inn*, T/F755-0035, www.web-span.com/tropinet/magellan1.htm, includes breakfast, 2 km north of Cahuita, 6 beautifully decorated rooms with bath and fan, and 0,000-year-old pool (honestly) set in peaceful gardens.

Camping At *Kontiki* T755-0261, **G** per person, with laundry, showers and toilets, nd *Colibrís Paradise*, out of village close to Playa Negra. Also possible in Cahuita National Park (see below).

Eating
If the catch is good many restaurants have lobster at reasonable prices

n town *Cha Cha Cha*, international menu, great food and service, refreshing chic décor, very good pasta from US$4. *El Rancho* has the distinctly tropical feel with split-bamboo walls, sand floors and a good menu. Almost legendary *Miss Edith's*, delicious Caribbean and vegetarian menu, nice people, good value, no alcohol licence, take your own, many recommendations for breakfast and dinner, but don't expect quick service. *Pizza Cahuita*, right in centre, more than pizzas with good pasta, hamburgers and a fairly standard menu. *Sol y Mar*, good value, open 0730-1200, 1630-2000, need to arrive early and wait at least 45 mins for food, red snapper and volcano potato especially wicked, US$5, also good breakfasts, try cheese, egg and tomato sandwich, US$2. *Vista del Mar*, facing entrance to park, good fish and Chinese dishes.

Out along **Playa Negra** in order: *Pizzería El Cactus*, good food, service. *Sobre las Olas*, right on the beach serving *Tico* and Mexican, popular bar in the evening. *Ciao's Paradise*, good little reggae bar, with oropendula nests looking out to the beach. *La Casa Creole*, next to the *Magellan Inn*, 2 km north of Cahuita, T755-0104 for reservations, is a culinary feast of French and Creole creations. Dishes from US$8. Open 0600-0900, closed Sun. Recommended. *Restaurant Banana* at the top of Playa Negra, has a good restaurant and the bar is away from the crowds. Recommended. Worth the walk.

Casa de Locos Assylum and *Cocos Bar* are right in the centre of town. *Coffee Bar*, on the shore near *Cabinas Jenny*, is a good reggae spot. *Salón Vaz,* lively at weekends with reggae music, popular with travellers and locals, main gathering point, safe for lone women.

Nightlife

Snorkelling equipment and surf boards available for rent. Horses can be hired, but try to ensure they are in good shape. Bicycles can be hired for about US$7 per day and you can cycle to Puerto Viejo and the Panamanian border through some beautiful scenery.

Sports

Bus service direct from **San José** from Terminal del Caribe Sixaola, 0600, 1530, return 0730, 0930, 1100, 1630, US$4, T257-8129, *Transp Mepá*, 4 hrs, US$4.50, and from **Puerto Limón**, in front of *Radio Casino*, 0500-1800, return 0630-2000, 1 hr, US$0.80, T758-1572, both continuing to **Bribri**, and **Sixaola** (dirt road) on the Panamanian border (US$1, 2 hrs). The bus drops you at the crossing of the 2 main roads in Cahuita.

Transport

Banks There are none. Money exchange is difficult except occasionally for cash dollars (*Cahuita Tours* changes dollars and TCs). Take plenty of colones from Limón. Nearest bank is in Bribri (20 km) but several places accept credit cards. **Communications** Post office, next to

Directory

Costa Rica

4 El Rancho *B5*
5 La Sodas *C5*
6 Miss Edith's *A4*
7 Piccolo's *B2*
8 Pizza Cahuita *B5*
9 Pizzería El Cactus *B2*
10 Reggae *A1*

11 Robertos Restaurant & Tours *C6*
12 Sobre Las Olas *A2*
13 Sol y Mar *C6*
14 Vista del Mar *C6*

Raptor watch – an aerial freeway

If travelling through the southern Caribbean between September and November cast your eyes to the sky and look for a steady stream of raptors moving south along an imaginary aerial freeway. In the autumn of the northern hemisphere over one million raptors migrate from North America to over-winter in South America. A bird count in the fall of 2000 counted more than 1.3 million turkey vultures, broad-winged hawks, Swainson's hawks and Mississippi kites passing through the skies, one of only three sites in the world to record more than c million migrants in one season. The birds return from their winter break in the Amazon and throughout South America, reduced by as much as 30% due to mortality rates, between March and April.

police station at northern end of town. **Internet** *Cyberbet*, part of *Cabinas Palmar*, US$1.60 per hr. **Tour operators** Wide range of activities available including watersports and nature tours. *Cahuita Tours*, T758-0000, F758-0082, exotica@racsa.co.cr, excursions by jeep and glass-bottomed boat tours over the reefs, bike, diving and snorkelling equipment rental, international telephone service (ICE) and Western Union money transfer.

Puerto Viejo de Talamanca

Colour map 7, grid B4

Activities in the area are numerous and you could spend many days exploring the options

Where the paved road heads inland to Bri Bri, a road heads south to the popular beaches at Puerto Viejo de Talamanca, 19 km southeast of Cahuita. It's a good base and a quietly happening party town, with a number of good beaches stretching out to the south. There is reef diving nearby, or you can head south to Mandoca for lagoon diving from canoes. Surfers seek out the glorious **Salsa Brava** wave which peaks from December to February. Away from the beach nature trips range from tough treks in Gandoca-Manzanillo Wildlife Refuge through to gentle strolls around the self-guided **Botanical Gardens** to the north of town. There are also several cultural trips to KeKöLdi and BriBri indian reserves and the newest offering takes dug-outs to the inland town of **Yorkin**. The town has grown rapidly in recent years with a wide range of activites including diving, nature trails and cultural tours, as the local Afro-Caribbean population and resident expatriates blend ideas. The *Asociación Talamanqueña de Ecoturismo y Conservación* (ATEC, T/F750-0191, greencoast.com/atec.htm) provides **tourist information**, sells locally made crafts and T-shirts, guide services, rainforest hikes, snorkelling and fishing trips. The **South Caribbean Music Festival** takes place in the months leading up to Easter.

Sleeping

Discounts often available May to November

L *Samasati Lodge & Retreat Center*, T224-1870, F224-5032, www.samasati.com, near *Hotel Creek* on junction half way between Cahuita and Puerto Viejo, beautiful mountain location with 100-ha reserve, vegetarian restaurant, meditation courses, reservation recommended. **B** *Coco Loco Lodge*, south of town, T/F750-0281, www.clubs.privateweb.at/ karibikbungalows, quiet spot in expansive garden south of town, nice wooden cabins. Popular.

C *Cabinas Casa Verde*, T750-0015, F750-0047, www.greencoast.com/casaverd. htm Comfortable rooms with hammocks, private bath, cracked tile showers in beautiful gardens. Central. All very pleasant and far too relaxing. **C** *Cabinas Grant*, T758-0292, large clean rooms, with private bath and fan. Each with a small terrace. **C** *Cabinas Tropical*, T/F750-0283, rblancke@racsa.co.cr, 5 spotless rooms, with good mattresses, private bath and hot water. Pleasant gardens with shaded garden house for relaxing, small bar/café. Recommended. The German owner, Rolf Blancke, is a tropical biologist and runs tours. Recommended. **C** *Maritza*, central, T750-0003, F750-0313, in cabins, with bath, clean, clean, friendly. Affiliated to International Youth Hostel Association, English spoken, a map in the bar shows all the hotels and *cabinas* in the area. Highly recommended. **C-D** *Pura Vida*, T750-0002, F750-0296, Swiss-run, friendly, very clean, hammocks, although lacking in character. Recommended.

D *Jacaranda*, T750-0069, a very relaxed spot away from the beach set in beautiful gardens. Some rooms with bath, the highly respected *Garden Restaurant* is due to reopen soon. **D** *Los*

Costa Rica

Sueños, T750-0369, laid-back and very relaxing, just 4 rooms sleeping 2 or 3 people. Colourful and bright rooms. **E** *Cabañas Yoli*, 250 m from bus stop, clean, basic, fan, OK – one of the last *Tico* owned places. **E** *Cashew Hill*, classic backpacking hideaway. Quiet, very chilled, easy come easy go atmosphere with basic cabins. **E** *Puerto Viejo*, is in the centre of town and has rooms sleeping 1 to 5. Popular with surfers. **E** *Sol y Sombre*, at entrance to town, T750-0267, with the style of the French, 5 clean rooms, with fan and mosquito nets. Small restaurant downstairs. **F** *Cabinas Salsa Brava*, popular with surfers. **F** *Kiskadee*, T750-0075, small jungle lodge with 2 dormitories, kitchen available, American-run, about 200 m south of football field, from where it is signposted, take torch and rubber boots. Recommended.

South of town **D** *Cabinas Yucca*, T750-0285, nice beach garden, parking, German-run. **D** *Escape Caribeño*, 500 m along road to Punta Uva, T750-0103, German management, communal kitchen, free morning coffee, well-furnished cottages with TV, fully equipped.

Eating

Café Pizzería Coral, south of centre, good breakfasts from 0700, and good pizzas and meals for the rest of the day. Not cheap but recommended. *Bambú*, on the beach, good food. *Caramba* has excellent pizzas. *El Parquecito*, facing sea in the centre, nice breezy atmosphere, specializes in fish and seafood (evenings only). *Garden Restaurant*, in *Cabinas Jacaranda*, good Italian and Caribbean food, opens 1700. Highly recommended. *Johnny's Place*, on the beach front, serving sushi by day and a disco open Tue-Sun, by night. *Lidia's Place*, south of centre, good food and to-die-for chocolate cake that does not hang round for long. *Marcos Pizzería* does what it says on the tin. *Pan Pay*, good bakery on beach front. *Piranha* restaurant, in *Hotel Puerto Viejo*, popular, claims to serve the 'fattest plates in Costa Rica'. Hold them to that! *Salsa Brava*, Spanish food, closed Sun. Recommended. *Soda Miss Sam*, south of the centre, good local food piled high, good value. *Tamara*, on main street, open 0600-2100, local good fish dishes, popular throughout the day and packed at weekends.

Costa Rica

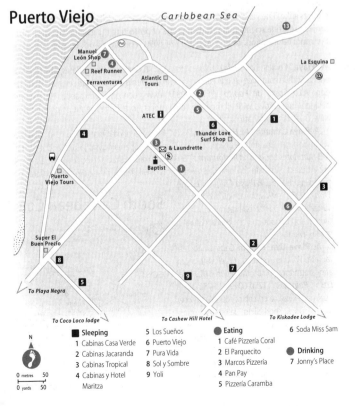

Sleeping		Eating	6 Soda Miss Sam
1 Cabinas Casa Verde	5 Los Sueños	1 Café Pizzería Coral	
2 Cabinas Jacaranda	6 Puerto Viejo	2 El Parquecito	**Drinking**
3 Cabinas Tropical	7 Pura Vida	3 Marcos Pizzería	7 Jonny's Place
4 Cabinas y Hotel	8 Sol y Sombre	4 Pan Pay	
Maritza	9 Yoli	5 Pizzería Caramba	

Nightlife *Stanford's Disco,* lively nightlife used in Coca Cola commercial. *Bar Sandborn*, recommended for an evening beer. *Taberna Popo*, lively bar-disco, live music some nights, Carib and rock.

Transport Daily **bus** from **San José** from Gran Terminal del Carine, 0600, return 0700, 0900, 1100, 1600, 4½ hrs, US$4.65; from **Limón** daily from Radio Casino, 0500-1800, return 0600-2000, 1½ hrs; 30 mins from **Cahuita**, US$0.45. To **Manzanillo** at 0700, 1530, 1900, returning 0500, 0830, 1700, ½ hr, US$0.80. To **Sixaola** 5 daily, 0545 until 1845, 2 hrs, US$1.80.

Directory **Bank** *Banco Nacional* is reported to be setting up a branch ½ a block south of ATEC. If not, change TCs and cash at *Manuel León's* general store on the beach. **Communications** Internet: from ATEC. Also *Cibercafé* just south of *Stanford's*. **Telephone**: there is a public telephone outside the ATEC office. **Post office**, ½ block south of ATEC. US$2 to send, US$1 to receive, atecmail@racsa.co.cr **Tour operators** ATEC are the easiest source of information but you can also try *Terraventuras* (T/F750-0426, terraventuras@hotmail.com) and *Atlántico Tours*, T/F750-0005, offer several trips. *Reef Runner Divers*, T/F570-0480, in Puerto Viejo, and *Aguamar Adventures*, who have been operating since 1993, offer diving courses and local trips. Prices from US$35. **Useful address** Police: on sea front.

Around Puerto Viejo

There are a number of popular beaches southeast along the road from Puerto Viejo. Traffic is limited, buses occasional, but you can walk if the weather is on your side. About 4 km away is **Playa Cocles** which has some of the best surfing on this coast, and 2 km further on is **Playa Chiquita** with many places to stay. Next is **Punta Uva**, beyond which after another 5 km you arrive in **Manzanillo**, followed by white sand beaches and rocky headlands to **Punta Mona** and the **Gandoca-Manzanillo Wildlife Refuge**, which is a celebration of Costa Rican diversity that has been largely left alone by prospectors and tourists alike. The variety of species is still growing as research continues. Among other projects, marine scientists are studying ways of protecting the giant leatherback turtle. For more information, contact ANAI, T224-6090. Volunteer work possible.

Sleeping
Most places aimed at mid-range and above

At **Playa Cocles** has a few places to stay. **A** *Cariblue Bungalows*, T/F750-0057, www.cariblue.com, nice natural complex complete with palm roofs and set in beautiful garden. **A** *La Costa de Papito*, T/F750-0080, www.greencoast.com/papito, 8 beautifully designed bungalows with all the style you'd expect from Eddie Ryan (*Carlton Arms Hotel*, New York), fan, with bath.

At **Playa Chiquita** **AL** *Hotel Kasha*, T/F750-0205, kashahotel@hotmail.com, 10 bungalows set in lush gardens on the beach, with bath and fan, open-air gym, jacuzzi and restaurant. **A-B** *Miraflores Lodge and Restaurant*, T750-0038, mirapam@racsa.co.cr, 10 rooms, a/c, breakfast included, with bath, fan, beautiful gardens, lots of wildlife, English and French spoken. Good spot, very relaxing. **B** *Playa Chiquita Lodge*, T/F750-0062, www.playachiquitalodge.com, 12 cabins with private bathroom, French restaurant and bar, 500 m from beach, naturalist guides available.

At **Playa Uva** **E** *Selvin Cabins* and restaurant, *Walaba Travellers Hostel*, with room and dormitory accommodation. **AL** *Hotel Las Palmas*, T750-0049, F750-0079, hpalmas@racsa.co.cr, cabins, 60 ocean-view rooms, pool, snorkelling, rainforest, tours, transport from San José on Wed, Fri, Sun, US$30 return, US$20 one way. **AL** *Almonds and Corals Tent Camp*, T272-2024, F272-2220, almonds@racsa.co.cr, geoexpediciones.com (without the www),

South Caribbean Coast

Moín
Puerto Limón

COSTA RICA

Penshurst
Valle de Estrella
Hitoy Cerere Research Centre
Cahuita
Playa Negra
Puerto Vargas
Puerto Viejo
Bribri
Reserva Biológica Hitoy Cerere
Parque Nacional Cahuita
Punta Pirikiki
Manzanillo
Refugio Nacional de Vida Silvestre Gandoca-Manzanillo
Gandoca
Sixaola
PANAMA

0 km 10
0 miles 10
N

luxury camping with bath and hot water in tents on platforms in the forest, pool, restaurant, trips arranged to Punta Mona, snorkelling (equipment rental), bike hire. Sleeping out in the wild, with a bit of comfort thrown in.

At **Manzanillo** **C** *Cabinas Pangea*, behind Aquamor, 2 nice rooms with bath, also house on beach with kitchen. **E** *Cabinas Las Veraneas*, rooms with shared bath. **E** *Cabinas/Restaurant Maxi*, T754-2266, basic, nice rooms, highly respected, and slightly pricey, seafood restaurant.

Transport Express **bus** to Manzanillo from Terminal Sixaola, **San José**, daily, 1600, return 0630. From Limón daily 0600, 1430, return 1130, 1900, 1½ hrs.

Bribri At Hotel Creek, north of Puerto Viejo, the paved road heads through the hills to the village of Bribri, at the foot of the **Talamanca Range Indian Reserve**. Halfway between Hotel Creek and Puerto Viejo is *Violeta's Pulpería*. From Limón, *Aerovías Talamaqueñas Indígenas* fly cheaply to **Amubri** in the reserve (there is a *Casa de Huéspedes* run by nuns in Amubri). Villages such as Bribri, Chase, Bratsi, Shiroles and San José Cabécar can be reached by bus from Cahuita. Several buses daily to Bribri from Limón. (For a good introduction to the Talamanca mountains, read *Mamita Yunai* by Fallas, or *What Happen: A Folk-History of Costa Rica's Talamanca Coast* by Paula Palmer.)

Continuing south from Bribri is **Sixaola**, on the border with Panama.

Border with Panama – Sixaola

Costa Rican immigration The border is open 0700-1700. The immigration office is just before the railway bridge, over the river Sixaola, which marks the frontier with Panama. A c300 exit *Cruz Roja* stamp has to be bought from the supermarket. Immigration do not sell them. Advance watches by 1 hr on entering Panama.

In both countries, the local greeting in this area is 'OK?'. This means, 'Good morning, how are you?', 'I'm not going to attack you', 'Can I help you?' If you don't want a chat, simply answer 'All right'

Sleeping At entrance to town is **E** *Imperio*, 8 basic cabins with ventilator, shared bath. **F** *Cabinas Sánchez*, T754-2105, clean and tidy, best option. **E** *El Siquirreño*, 200 m before railway, with bath, basic, restaurant downstairs. **F** *Doris*, T754-2207, basic rooms with fan and partitions, but friendly.

Transport A railway runs to Almirante (Panama) from Guabito, on the Panamanian side.

If crossing to Panama take the earliest bus possible to Sixaola (see Panama, The Northwestern Caribbean Coast, page 1217). Direct San José-Sixaola bus from Terminal del Caribe, *Autotransportes Mepe* (T221-0524), 5 hrs, US$6.30, 0600, 1000, 1330, 1530, plus 0800 on Sat, return 0700, 0830, 1300, 1530; also 6 daily from Puerto Limón (Radio Casino), 4 hrs.

Directory Banks There are no banks in Sixaola, but it is possible to change money in the supermarket, but rates, especially to the US dollar are very poor. Shops near the border in Panama will accept colones but shops in Changuinola and beyond do not.

Costa Rica

Background

History

Spanish settlement During his last voyage in September 1502, Columbus landed on the shores of what is now Costa Rica. Rumours of vast gold treasures (which never materialized) led to the name of Costa Rica (Rich Coast). The Spaniards settled in the Meseta Central, where the numbers of several thousand sedentary Indian farmers were soon greatly diminished by the diseases brought by the settlers. Cartago was founded in 1563 by Juan Vásquez de Coronado, but there was almost no expansion for 145 years, when a small number left Cartago for the valleys of Aserrí and Escazú. They founded Heredia in 1717, and San José in 1737. Alajuela, not far from San José, was founded in 1782. The settlers were growing in numbers but were still poor and raising only subsistence crops.

Independence & coffee Independence from Spain was declared in 1821 whereupon Costa Rica, with the rest of Central America, immediately became part of Mexico. This led to a civil war during which, two years later, the capital was moved from Cartago to San José. After independence, the government sought anxiously for some product which could be exported and taxed for revenue. Coffee was successfully introduced from Cuba in 1808, making Costa Rica the first of the Central American countries to grow what was to become known as the golden bean. The Government offered free land to coffee growers, thus building up a peasant landowning class. In 1825 there was a trickle of exports, carried by mule to the ports. By 1846 there were ox-cart roads to Puntarenas. By 1850 there was a large flow of coffee to overseas markets which was greatly increased by the opening of a railway in 1890 from San José and Cartago to Puerto Limón along the valley of the Reventazón.

From 1850, coffee prosperity began to affect the country profoundly: the birth rate grew, land for coffee was free, and the peasant settlements started spreading, first down the Río Reventazón as far as Turrialba, then up the slopes of the volcanoes, then down the new railway from San José to the old Pacific port of Puntarenas.

Banana industry Bananas were first introduced in 1878; Costa Rica was also the first Central American republic to grow them and is now the second largest exporter in the world. Labour was brought in from Jamaica to clear the forest and work the plantations. The industry grew and in 1913, the peak year, the Caribbean coastlands provided 11 mn bunches for export. Since then the spread of disease has lowered exports and encouraged crop diversification. The United Fruit Company then turned its attentions to the Pacific litoral, especially in the south around the port of Golfito. Although some of the Caribbean plantations were turned over to cacao, *abacá* (Manilla hemp) and African palm, the region has regained its ascendancy over the Pacific litoral as a banana producer. By the end of the century over 50,000 ha were planted to bananas, mostly in the Atlantic lowlands.

In the 1990s Chiquita, Dole and Del Monte, the multinational fruit producers, came under international pressure over labour rights on their plantations. Two European campaign groups targeted working conditions in Costa Rica where, despite constitutional guarantees of union freedom, there was a poor record of labour rights abuse. Only 10% of Costa Rica's 50,000 banana workers were represented by unions. The rest preferred to join the less political *solidarista* associations, which provide cheap loans and promote savings, and thus avoid being blacklisted or harassed. Del Monte agreed in 1998 to talk to the unions after a decade of silence, while Chiquita declared its workers were free to choose trade union representation.

Economic factors affecting the global banana trade are likely to seriously impact production in Costa Rica as producers – in particular independent and co-operatives – are caught in the cross-fire of US-European wrangling. The US supports full and free trade, Europe continues to offer preference to ex-colonies. While Ecuadorean producers dump produce on the global market, Costa Rica's production falls in the gap between, and the impact on the industry is having serious consequences for employment in the industry.

Costa Rica's long tradition of democracy began in 1889 and has continued to the present day, with only a few lapses. In 1917 the elected president Alfredo González was ousted by Federico Tinoco, who held power until 1919, when a counter revolution and subsequent elections brought Julio Acosta to the presidency. Democratic and orderly government followed until the campaign of 1948 when violent protests and a general strike surrounded disputed results. A month of fighting broke out after the Legislative Assembly annulled the elections, leading to the abolition of the constitution and a junta being installed, led by José Figueres Ferrer. In 1949 a constituent assembly drew up a new constitution and abolished the army. The junta stepped down and Otilio Ulate Blanco, one of the candidates of the previous year, was inaugurated. In 1952, Figueres, a socialist, founded the Partido de Liberación Nacional (PLN), and was elected President in 1953. He dominated politics for the next two decades, serving as President in 1953-58 and 1970-74. The PLN introduced social welfare programmes and nationalization policies, while intervening conservative governments encouraged private enterprise. The PLN was again in power from 1974-78 (Daniel Oduber Quirós), 1982-86 (Luis Alberto Monge), 1986-90 (Oscar Arias Sánchez) and 1994-98 (José María Figueres).

Democratic government

President Arias drew up proposals for a peace pact in Central America and concentrated greatly on foreign policy initiatives. Efforts were made to expel Nicaraguan contras resident in Costa Rica and the country's official proclamation of neutrality, made in 1983, was reinforced. The Central American Peace Plan, signed by the five Central American presidents in Guatemala in 1987, earned Arias the Nobel Peace Prize, although progress in implementing its recommendations was slow.

In the 1990 general elections, Rafael Angel Calderón Fournier, a conservative lawyer and candidate for the Social Christian Unity Party (PUSC), won a narrow victory, with 51% of the vote, over the candidate of the PLN. Calderón, the son of a former president who had been one of the candidates in the 1948 disputed elections, had previously stood for election in 1982 and 1986. The President's popularity slumped as the effects of his economic policies were felt on people's living standards, while his Government was brought into disrepute by allegations of corruption and links with 'narco' traffickers.

In the February 1994 elections another former president's son was elected by a narrow margin. **José María Figueres** of the PLN won 49.6% of the vote, 2.2% points ahead of his PUSC rival. In the Legislature, the PLN won 29 seats and the PUSC 25, while smaller parties won those that remained. The election was won on economic policies. Figueres argued against neo-liberal policies, claiming he would renegotiate agreements with the IMF and the World Bank, but in his first year of office a third Structural Adjustment Programme (backed by the international agencies and drawn up by the previous administration) was approved. A subsequent National Development Plan and a Plan to Fight Poverty contained a wide range of measures designed to promote economic stability and to improve the quality of life for many sectors of society. While the plans were partly responding to the protests that followed the approval of the Adjustment Programme, many of their proposals were at variance with the programme's policies.

PLN government, 1994-98

Labour strife increased in 1995-96 as tax increases and price rises cut into earnings. The granting of work permits to 50,000 Nicaraguan manual labourers was highly unpopular in the face of rising Costa Rican unemployment. Crime increased, particularly in San José, Limón and on the Caribbean coast, and the number of arriving tourists fell. The Government's popularity plummeted and the President was judged the least popular in recent history. There were allegations of corruption, links to 'narco' traffickers and money laundering, with involvement by legislators and the judiciary.

Elections were held in February 1998 and were won by the PUSC candidate, **Miguel Angel Rodríguez**, with 46.6% of the vote, 2% ahead of the PLN candidate. Thirty percent of voters abstained. The new president took office in May 1998, promising to make women, the young and the poor a priority for his government.

1998 elections

Costa Rica

2002 elections Typically for Costa Rica, the elections of early 2002 ran on a frenzy of neutrality with a head to head competition between Rolando Araya, of the PLN, and the victor Abel Pacheco, of the PUSC who received 58% of the vote. President Pacheco, 68 years old, stimulated just enough support to win after the election went to a run-off after none of the three candidates won outright victory in the first round. The general apathy in the electoral process which appeared in the elections of 1998 continued with an all-time low of 60% of voters turning out. The challenges to the candidates were to restimulate the economy, hit by the global downturn and the low coffee prices, and both claimed to be opposed to privatization of state-run industries.

Government

Costa Rica is a unitary multiparty republic with one legislative house, the Legislative Assembly of 57 deputies, elected by proportional representation for four years. Executive authority is in the hands of the President, elected for the same term by popular vote. Men and women over 18 have the right to vote. Voting is secret, direct and free. Judicial power is exercised by the Supreme Court of Justice. The re-election of former presidents is not permitted under the current constitution, but leading up to the elections of February 2002, there was growing pressure to review this policy, especially from Oscar Arias, former president and Nobel Peace prize winner.

Economy

The country's agricultural economy is based on the export of coffee, bananas, meat, sugar and cocoa. The Meseta Central with its volcanic soil is the coffee-growing area: here too are grown the staple crops: beans, maize, potatoes and sugar cane, and dairy farming is efficient and lucrative. More recently diversification of exports has been successful, with non-traditional crops now accounting for about 60% of revenues. Costa Rica remains the second largest banana exporter in the world, with production dominated by US multinational companies. The country's timber industry is very small although deforestation has occurred at an alarming rate.

High growth in the industrial sector has led to considerable economic diversification, and manufacturing accounts for about 19% of GDP, compared with 17% in the case of agriculture. The port of Caldera, near Puntarenas on the Pacific coast, has been improved and manufacturing for export is being encouraged. High education levels have successfully attracted a growing technology sector including the US microprocessor *Intel* whose assembly plant near San José is expected to earn more than bananas and coffee in exports.

Tourism is a major industry and one of the main sources of foreign exchange revenue, with over 1 mn visitors annually for the last four years. The construction of hotels and land prices have soared, driven up by foreign (mainly US) purchasers. Conservation groups have criticized larger developments due to environmental impact, the proximity of national parks and reserves and the destruction of ecosystems.

Recent trends

The Costa Rican economy suffers from large public sector deficits, partly because of a high level of government spending on social welfare. The country amassed a large foreign debt which, including accumulated arrears, amounted in 1989 to US$5 bn and was one of the highest per capita in the developing world. In the late 1980s, Costa Rica turned to the IMF and the World Bank for help in adjusting its economy, and was one of the first countries to take advantage of a US-sponsored debt reduction proposal.

In 1995 legislation was approved to liberalize the banking system, support privatization and end state monopolies. Labour unions opposed many of the economic measures ncluding the laying off of 8,000 public sector workers. There were many strikes, including an extended protest by teachers. Implementation was delayed until 1999, allowing another ound of elections in the interim.

Despite record growth of 8.3% in 1999, budgetary pressures led the government to announce a privatization programme that has met with more public demonstrations and oadblocks. Resistance to reforming ICE, the state-owned electricity and telecommunications monopoly, has hindered the economic restructuring that is considered essential for continued investment in the high-tech industry, and the continued move away from a reliance on coffee and banana exports.

While the economic downturn affected the economy overall, the shift towards technology based on high levels of education continue to reap rewards. In 2000 electrical manufacturing generated over US$2 bn for the economy – more than tourism.

Culture

In all provinces over 98% of the population are whites and *mestizos* excepts in Limón where 33.2% are blacks and 3.1% indigenous Indians, of whom only 5,000 survive in the whole country. There are three groups: the Bribri (3,500), Boruca (1,000) and Guatuso. Although officially protected, the living conditions of the indigenous Indians are very poor. In 1992 Costa Rica became the first Central American country to ratify the International Labour Organization treaty on indigenous populations and tribes. However, even in Limón, the percentage of blacks is falling: it was 57.1% in 1927. Many of them speak Jamaican English as their native tongue. Much of the Caribbean coastland, especially in the north, remains unoccupied. On the Pacific coastlands a white minority owns the land on the *hacienda* system which has been rejected in the uplands. About 46% of the people are *mestizos*. The population has risen sharply in the mountainous Peninsula of Nicoya, which is an important source of maize, rice and beans.

People
The national adjective, 'costarricense', is rather a mouthful: the universal short form is 'tica'

This is the southernmost in our string of 'marimba culture' countries. The guitar is also a popular instrument for accompanying folk dances, while the *chirimía* and *quijongo*, already encountered further north, have not yet totally died out in the Chorotega region of Guanacaste Province. This province is indeed the heartland of Costa Rican folklore and the *Punto Guanacasteco*, a heel-and-toe dance for couples, has been officially decreed to be the 'typical national dance', although it is not in fact traditional, but was composed at the turn of the last century by Leandro Cabalceta Brau during a brief sojourn in jail. There are other dances too, such as the *Botijuela Tamborito* and *Cambute*, but it must honestly be said that they will not be found in the countryside as a tradition, but are performed on stage when outsiders need to be shown some native culture. Among the country's most popular native performers are the duet Los Talolingas, authors of *La Guaria Morada*, regarded as the 'second national anthem' and Lorenzo 'Lencho' Salazar, whose humorous songs in the vernacular style are considered quintessentially *Tico*.

Music & dance

Some of the Republic's rapidly deculturizing Indian groups have dances of their own, like the *Danza de los Diablitos* of the Borucas, the *Danza del Sol* and *Danza de la Luna* of the Chorotegas and the *Danza de los Huesos* of the Talamancas. A curious ocarina made of beeswax, the *dru mugata* is still played by the Guaymí Indians and is said to be the only truly pre-Columbian instrument still to be found. The drum and flute are traditional among various groups, but the guitar and accordion are moving in to replace them. As in the case of Nicaragua, the Caribbean coast of Costa Rica, centred on Puerto Limón, is inhabited by black people who came originally from the English-speaking islands and whose music reflects this origin. The *sinkit* seems to be a strictly local rhythm, but the *calypso* is popular and the *cuadrille*, square dance and maypole dance are also found. There is too a kind of popular hymn called the *saki*. Brass, percussion and string instruments are played, as well as the accordion.

Costa Rica

Land and environment

Costa Rica lies between Nicaragua and Panama, with coastlines on the Caribbean (212 km) and the Pacific (1,016 km). The distance between sea and sea ranges from 119-282 km. A low, thin line of hills between Lake Nicaragua and the Pacific is prolonged into northern Costa Rica with several volcanoes (including the active Volcán Arenal), broadening and rising into high and rugged mountains and volcanoes in the centre and south. The highest peak, Chirripó Grande, southeast of the capital, reaches 3,820 m. Within these highlands are certain structural depressions; one of them, the Meseta Central, is of paramount importance. To the southwest this basin is rimmed by the comb of the Cordillera; at the foot of its slopes, inside the basin, are the present capital San José, and the old capital, Cartago. Northeast of these cities, about 30 km away, four volcano cones rise from a massive common pedestal. From northwest to southeast these are Poás (2,704 m), Barva (2,906 m), Irazú (3,432 m) and Turrialba (3,339 m). Irazú and Poás are intermittently active. Between the Cordillera and the volcanoes is the Meseta Central: an area of 5,200 sq km at an altitude of between 900 and 1,800 m, where two-thirds of the population live. The northeastern part of the basin is drained by the Reventazón through turbulent gorges into the Caribbean; the Río Grande de Tárcoles drains the western part of it into the Pacific.

There are lowlands on both coasts. On the Caribbean coast, the Nicaraguan lowland along the Río San Juan continues into Costa Rica, wide and sparsely inhabited as far as Puerto Limón. A great deal of this land, particularly near the coast, is swampy; southeast of Puerto Limón the swamps continue as far as Panama in a narrow belt of lowland between sea and mountain.

The Gulf of Nicoya, on the Pacific side, thrusts some 65 km inland; its waters separate the mountains of the mainland from the 900-m-high mountains of the narrow Nicoya Peninsula. From a little to the south of the mouth of the Río Grande de Tercels, a lowland savannah stretches northwest past the port of Puntarenas and along the whole northeastern shore of the Gulf towards Nicaragua. Below the Río Grande de Tercels the savanna is pinched out by mountains, but there are other banana-growing lowlands to the south. Small quantities of African palm and cacao are now being grown in these lowlands. In the far south there are swampy lowlands again at the base of the Península de Osa and between the Golfo Dulce and the borders of Panama. Here there are 12,000 ha planted to bananas. The Río General, which flows into the Río Grande de Térraba, runs through a southern structural depression almost as large as the Meseta Central.

Books

General   Several books are mentioned within the text but a few general texts will provide more background. *Costa Rica: A Guide to the People, Politics and Culture* (1998) from the In Focus series of the Latin America Bureau is a distilled analysis of the country.

Nature guides   The definitive field guide for bird-watchers is *Guide to the Birds of Costa Rica* by Gary Stiles and Alexander Skutch, Cornell University Press (1989). An excellent nature book is Les Beletsky's, *Costa Rica: The Ecotravellers' Wildlife Guide (1998)*.

Nature guides can be found at *7th Avenue Books* in San José, and there is also available an illustrated book, *The National Parks of Costa Rica*, by Mario A Boza (1986), which gives a good impression of the different parks. Also available is *Areas de conservación y sus parques nacionales* by the Asociación Ecologista de Vida Silvestre (1998), T/F223-0851. SINAC (see above) produce a couple of booklets with simple maps and background information.

Panama

10

Panama

Essentials

The S-shaped isthmus of Panama, just 80 km at its narrowest and 193 km at its widest, is one of the world's great crossroads, and its destiny has been entirely shaped by this junction. To the north, connections and links with the great civilizations of Central America and Mexico; to the south, the wilderness of the Darién leads to Colombia and the wealth of South America. For thousands of years people and animals have used the Panamanian corridor as a channel of communication. At the time of conquest, the Spaniards used it as a crossing point between the Atlantic and Pacific Oceans. In part Panama owes its creation to this positioning (it was, in fact, the outcome of a squabble between Colombia and the United States in 1903), and the make-up of its population and their distribution has been effected by this corridor ever since. Today, over 40% of Panamanians live in the two cities which control the entry and exit of the canal. International control continued until recently when, on 31 December 1999, the Canal Area, formerly the US Canal Zone, was returned to Panamanian jurisdiction. The hand-over was smooth as clockwork, despite the predictions and fears of international observers, and the next milestone in Panama's history is the centennial celebrations which will reach their peak on 3 November 2003.

Planning your trip

Panama City is a modern city, spread round the Bahía de Panamá. From the hilltop lookout of the unique Parque Natural Metropolitano, visitors enjoy spectacular views of the banks and high-rise buildings of the capital with the Canal in the distance. The rubble and ruins of Panamá Viejo lie to the east, the city's original location sacked by the pirate Henry Morgan. The fortified younger replacement of Casco Viejo dates from 1673 and is gradually being restored to its former glory.

Where to go

The city lies at the Pacific end of the **Panama Canal**, a feat of engineering which raises ocean-going liners 26 m to Lago Gatún on the 67½-km voyage between the Caribbean Sea and the Pacific Ocean. The financial cost of the canal was staggering; the price in human terms was over 22,000 lives. Owned and operated by the USA since its construction in 1914, the 16-km wide Canal Zone reverted to Panamanian ownership at the end of 1999. The Canal is surprisingly beautiful, consisting of the river-fed **Lago Gatún**, which is reached by a series of locks on the Pacific and Caribbean sides which raise and lower 30 ships a day. Within the lake is **Barro Colorado Island Biological Reserve**, to which animals fled when the basin flooded. **Parque Nacional Soberanía**, which forms part of the watershed of Lake Gatún, makes for an easier trip, just 30 minutes from the capital.

At the Caribbean end of the Canal is **Colón**, the country's major port for container traffic, shipping and, for the dedicated shopper, the second largest tax-free zone in the world. To the east is **Portobelo**, the site of flamboyant 16th- and 17th-century markets, where fortified warehouses filled with Peruvian gold and silver were guarded against pirate raids. Off the coast lies the marine burial site of the British buccaneering seaman Sir Francis Drake. Quiet, beautiful beaches await the visitor today. Further east, the 365-island **Archipiélago de San Blas** of crystalline waters and palms continues its autonomous existence under the guidance of the Kuna nation. The islands can be visited and hotels, lodges and simple cabinas are opening to cater for the growing tourist interest.

From Panama City to Costa Rica the Pan-American Highway runs almost parallel to the Pacific coastline, running through agricultural zones, Pacific beaches, colonial towns and mountain landscapes. The **Península Azuero** is dotted with old colonial towns, beaches perfect for surfing, and nature reserves of wetland birds, nesting turtles and quiet solitude. Open pastures and savannahs give way to sugar plantations on approach to **David**, the hot and humid third city of the Republic. It is an attractive hybrid city, both colonial and modern with good communications and an ideal base for the mountain resorts of **Boquete** and **Volcán**. Up in the cooler **Chiriquí Highlands** dominated by **Volcán Barú**, there is good hiking, horse-riding, river rafting and other adventure sports.

Panama

North of the **Talamanca Mountains**, the northern Caribbean lowlands that surround **Laguna de Chiriquí** are home to the banana, grown in vast quantities. The offshore islands of **Bocas del Toro** and the **Isla Bastimentos National Marine Park** are home to nesting turtles, birds and other wildlife. Once cut off and difficult to reach, the islands are growing in popularity. If lying around just relaxing on idyllic beaches isn't appealing enough, the snorkelling and diving on the unspoilt reefs is excellent.

Darién in the east is the most inhospitable part of Panama where all roads, including the Pan-American Highway, eventually just peter out. With no land links between Panama and Colombia, the fit and adventurous are tempted to cross one of the world's last great wildernesses by foot or boat to the border and Colombia beyond. While not impossible – what is? – armed insurgents from Colombia are currently active in the area, several high profile kidnappings have occurred and it is extremely dangerous.

When to go
Look out for centenary celebrations around November 2003

The most popular time to visit is between January and March. Temperatures vary little throughout the country. At lower altitudes, year-round daytime temperatures range between 30°-32°C (85°-90°F), dropping to 21°-22°C (70°-72°F) at night. Above 500 m temperatures fall, making the highland towns attractive spots to visit and cool off.

Rainfall, however, varies greatly. The Caribbean side of the central Cordillera is soaked with around 4,000 mm annually. On the Pacific slope, it is much lighter with an average of 1,700 mm, but both areas have marked pronounced seasonal variations. Rainfall begins to taper off sometime in December, and the months of January, February, March and sometimes April constitute the dry season or *verano* (summer). At this time rainfall on the Pacific side is scarce, or absent altogether, though on the Atlantic side you can expect a downpour 365 days a year. This is the period of school vacations and family holidays. In March or April the rains return throughout the country, and the season known in Panama as the *invierno* (winter) begins, although temperatures remain in the high 20°s and low 30°Cs (high 80°s and low 90°Fs). Even in the rainy season, however, the downpours, though very heavy, usually last only an hour or two, and almost always come in mid-afternoon.

The effect of this on the land is deep tropical forest along the Caribbean coast, on the northern slopes, in Darién and in the higher elevations of Chiriquí. On the Pacific coast the tropical forest gives way to semi-deciduous trees and, in the vast expanses cleared for grazing, to savannah between the sea and the mountains.

Finding out more

Before visiting, you can contact your nearest embassy for information or visit the *Instituto Panameño de Turismo* (IPAT) at **www.ipat.gob.pa** Information is currently only available in Spanish although they do offer an English information service by email. Once in country they have have an office in Panama City (see page 1159 for address).

Panama on the web An excellent overall site in English is **www.panamainfo.com**, with fast downloads, good general information on Panama and links to several other national sites including newspapers, government bodies and organizations and tourist services. A pure tourism site is **www.panamatours.com** with a good overview of the country. The Smithsonian Tropical Research Institute, with headquarters in Panama, can be viewed at **www.stri.org** Broader economic and political information is available at **www.businesspanama.com**

Language

Spanish is the national language, but English is widely understood. The older generation of West Indian immigrants speak Wari-Wari, a dialect of English incomprehensible to other English speakers, but the origin of much Panamanian Spanish slang. Indians in rural areas use their own languages, though many are bilingual.

Before you travel

Visas & immigration

Visitors must have a passport, and in most cases a tourist card (issued for 90 days and renewable for another 90 at the Immigration Office in Panama City, David or other provincial offices, eg Changuinola) or a visa (issued for 90 days, extendable for a further 90 days). Tourist

Panama embassies and consulates

Canada, 130 Albert St, Suite No 300 Ottawa, ON, Skip 5G4, T236-7177, F236-5775

France, 145 Avenue de Suffren, 75015 Paris, T4566-4244, F4567-9943

Germany, Lutzowstrasse 1, D 53173 Bonn, T228-361-036, F228-363-558

Israel, Hei Be 'iyar No.210 Tercer Piso, Aptdo 3, Kikar Hamedina, Apartado Postal 21260, Tel Aviv 62093, T696-0849, F691-0046.

Spain, Claudio Coello 86, Madrid 28006,

T576-5001, F576-7161

USA, 2862 McGill Terrace NW, Washington DC 20008, T202-483-1407, F202-483-8413

UK, 40 Hertford Street, London W1Y 7TG, T020-7493-4646, F020-7493-4333 8

There are embassies/consulates in most other European countries, many US cities, throughout the Americas, and selected countries elsewhere. These can be found on www.mire.gob.pa/embajadas.html

cards are available at borders, from Panamanian consulates, *Ticabus* or airlines. To enter Panama you must have an onward flight ticket, travel agent confirmation of same, or be able to demonstrate that you have sufficient funds to cover your stay and departure. 'Sufficient funds' do not have to be in cash; valid credit cards and travellers' cheques are accepted, or even notice of wire transfer awaiting you in Panama City. Recent travellers report these are asked for on the land frontier with Costa Rica and at Puerto Obaldía (Darién); generally officers are not very strict unless they fear you may be destitute. Once in Panama, you cannot get a refund for an onward flight ticket unless you have another exit ticket. *Copa* tickets can be refunded at any office in any country (in the currency of that country), but it can take up to five days to get your money back in Panama, compared with two days in San José, Costa Rica. If not entering Panama at the main entry points (Tocumen Airport, Paso Canoas), expect more complicated arrangements.

Citizens from Western Europe, the US, Canada, Australia, New Zealand and most Latin American countries can enter Panama with a visa or a tourist card.

Citizens of the following countries require a visa which incurs a nominal fee (local equivalent US$15): Czech Republic, Egypt, Peru, Singapore, Cyprus, Dominican Republic and Philippines. Before visiting Panama it is advisable to enquire at a Panamanian consulate whether you need a visa stamped in your passport, or whether a tourist card will suffice. You can check on the internet at www.panaconsul.com

Citizens of many African, Eastern European and Asian countries (including South Africa, Hong Kong, India, Poland, the former Soviet republics, and also Cuba) require authorization from Panama, which takes three to five days, before a visa will be issued.

Nationals not requiring visas can renew their 90-day tourist cards once for a total of 180 days, after which you must leave the country for three days. The necessary documents must all be obtained in advance: a photo-ID card (*carnét*), to be surrendered when you return for an exit visa, will be issued; allow one to two hours for this. Requirements are two passport photos, a ticket out of the country or proof of sufficient funds, a brief letter explaining why you wish to extend your stay, a letter from a permanent resident accepting legal and financial responsibility for you during your extra days in Panama, and two photocopies of the name page and the entry stamp page of your passport. All papers must be presented at *Prórrogas* in the immigration office and a fee of US$11 paid for each 90-day extension before the photo ID card is issued. Requirements for renewing a visa are similar, but include two photocopies of the original visa.

Exit visas Visitors from countries requiring visas and those who have been in Panama for more than 30 days must have an exit permit stamped in their passports before leaving. A *paz y salvo* slip must be obtained from the Ministerio de Hacienda y Tesoro by filling in a simple form, US$1. Present this with the ID card issued when you renewed your tourist card or visa to the *Permiso de Salida* window in the Inmigración y Naturalización for the exit stamp. Both have expiry dates, so plan accordingly as there are fines and time-wasting hassle if you miss the deadline. It is best to visit the government office early in the day. For where to go, see Useful addresses, under Panama City and David.

Panama

Customs Even if you only change planes in Panama, you must have the necessary papers for the airport officials. Panamanian Customs are strict; drugs without a doctor's prescription are confiscated.

Duty free and export restrictions Cameras, binoculars, etc, 500 cigarettes or 500 g of tobacco and three bottles of alcoholic drinks for personal use can be taken in free of duty. However, passengers leaving Panama by land are *not* entitled to any duty-free goods.

What to take Take clothes that are quick and easy to wash and dry. Loose-fitting clothes are more comfortable and can be layered at night in the highlands when it gets cooler. Also take good waterproofs.

Money

Currency
US$1=1 balboa

The unit of currency in Panama is the balboa (B/.), but Panama is one of the few countries in the world which issues no paper money; US banknotes are used exclusively, and US notes and coins are legal tender. There are 'silver' coins of 50c (called a *peso*), 25c (called *cinco reales* or *cuara*, from US 'quarter'), 10c, nickel of 5c (called a *real*) and copper of 1c. All coins are used interchangeably with US equivalents, which are the same in size and composition. There is great reluctance in Panama to accept US$50 and US$100 dollar notes because of counterfeiting. Do not be offended if asked to produce ID and sign a register when spending them. You can take in or out any amount of currency. If travelling north remember that US dollar notes, especially smaller denominations, are useful in all Central American countries and may be difficult to obtain in other republics. Stocking up on a supply of US$5 and US$1 notes greatly facilitates border crossings and traffic problems in Central America where 'fees' and 'instant fines' can become exorbitant if you only have a US$20 note.

Credit cards Visa ATMs are available at branches of *Telered* (T001-800-111-0016 if card is lost or stolen). MasterCard/Cirrus ATMs are available at *Caja de Ahorros* offices and others in the Pronto system (MasterCard emergency number, T001-800-307-7309). See under Banks, Panama City, for other ATMs and for credit card phone numbers. For *Western Union*, T269-1055.

Cost of living & travelling Prices are somewhat higher than in the rest of Central America, although food costs much the same as in Costa Rica. The annual average increase in consumer prices fluctuates in line with US trends. For business travellers, Panama was voted as one of the top three countries in Latin America to live, combining cost of living, safety and living standards.

Getting there

Air
For international airline websites see page 34

From Europe No direct services. Connecting flights go to Miami, then by *American* or *Copa* to Panama City. *Iberia* goes from Madrid via Miami. From Frankfurt, Paris, Madrid and London, there is a connection via Bogotá with *Avianca* and *SAM*.

From USA Direct flights from Atlanta, Dallas, Houston, Los Angeles, Miami, Copa, New York (some change planes in San José), Orlando, and Savannah. There are also flights from New Orleans, San Francisco and Washington. *Eva Airways* has a flight from Los Angeles which originates in Taipei. For other US cities, connections are made in Miami or Houston.

From Central America Flights from Guatemala City, Managua, San José and San Salvador. There are no direct flights to Tegucigalpa, only *Lacsa* with connection in San José or *Taca* in San Salvador, but *Copa* flies direct to San Pedro Sula. To Mexico City, Cancún, or connection via San José.

From South America Lots of flights from Colombia with *Copa* (Barranquilla, Bogotá, Cartagena, Cali, Medellín) and *SAM* (Bogotá). One-way tickets are not available from Colombia to Panama on *SAM* or *Copa*, but a refund on an unused return portion is possible, less 17% taxes, on *SAM*. *LAB* fly from Santa Cruz (Bolivia). From Guayaquil and Quito, *Continental*, *Ecuatoriana* and *Copa*. *Copa* from Santiago de Chile and Lima. From Caracas, *Mexicana*, *Copa* and *Aeropostal*.

From the Caribbean *Copa* has flights from Havana, Kingston, Montego Bay, Port-au-Prince, San Juan and Santo Domingo.

Panama

Touching down

Official time   *GMT minus five hours (Eastern Standard Time).*

IDD   *507. Operator and information 102; International operator 106.*

Hours of business   *Government departments, 0800-1200, 1230-1630 Monday to Friday.* **Banks:** *open and close at different times, but are usually open all morning, and often on Saturday.* **Shops and most private enterprises:** *0700 or 0800-1200 and 1400-1800 or 1900 every day, including Saturday.*

Voltage   *US-style 110 volt, 60 Hz AC throughout the country. 220 volt is occasionally available in homes and hotels.*

Weights and measures   *Both metric and imperial systems are used.*

Road

Overland passage to Panama from Costa Rica on the Pacific side is at **Paso Canoas**, where crossing is straightforward, simple and fast. International buses make the journey from Costa Rica to David and on to Panama City stopping briefly for paperwork at the border (see page 1208). A less popular and entertaining crossing point is **Sixaola/Guabito** on the Caribbean coast (see page 1223), made significantly more straightforward by new road between Almirante and Chiriquí Grande.

Passengers and vehicles (car or motorcycle) are given 30 days at the border. US$1 is payable for fumigation, US$3 for minibus. Rental vehicles are not allowed out of Panama.

Overland routes to Colombia are possible through the **Darién Gap**. The purist has a difficult, but not impossible challenge, alternatively it is possible to hop, skip and jump your way along the Caribbean coast taking canoes, but the cost can be considerable. For details see the Darién section, page 1224.

Sea

The Panama Canal is on the itineraries of some shipping services from Europe and the USA which take passengers. It is also possible to travel by sea to/from Colombia. See page 1196 for connections with San Blas.

There are several boats that make the journey from Isla Grande on the Caribbean across to Cartagena, charging US$150-200 for the journey.

There are about two boats a week from Colón to San Andrés Island, Colombia, from where there are connections to Cartagena; the *Johnny Walker* takes 30 hours, but the service is very irregular and travellers have sometimes had to wait over a week in vain. There are (contraband) boats from Coco Solo, Colón, to the Guajira Peninsula, Colombia. The uncomfortable three-day journey is undertaken entirely at your own risk and you may have to wait days for a sailing. You have to bargain for your fare on these boats and accommodation is a little primitive.

Staying closer to the coastline it is possible to cross the border to Colombia on the Caribbean side close to Puerto Obaldía, and on Pacific coast via Jaqué and possibly La Palma. These routes are not cheap and can take several days (see page 1229).

Touching down

Airport information & exit tax

Tocumen International Airport is 27 km east of the city centre. There are taxis (US$25) and buses for getting into Panama City as well as car hire. An airport exit tax of US$20 has to be paid by all passengers (cash only). There is a US$4 tax on air tickets over US$100 purchased in Panama.

Local customs & laws

Tipping In restaurants, 10% of the bill. Porters would expect US$1 for assistance at the airport. Taxi drivers don't expect tips, but see Taxis under Panama City.

Where to stay

Accommodation in Panama varies greatly. The very best in five-star luxury is available in Panama City, and several comfortable lodges are found in the larger towns and mountain

Panama

and jungle hideaways. If travelling further afield, accommodation in our **C** category and below is available in most towns of interest. Camping is generally tolerated – keeping a tidy campsite will certainly ease your path.

Getting around

Air There are local flights to most parts of Panama by several airlines. The most reliable is *Aeroperlas* (T315-7500), the *Grupo Taca* subsidiary, with destinations throughout the country. Other services include: *Ansa* (T226-7891) which flies to San Blas; *Parsa* (T226-3883, F226-3422) provides a charter service; *Transpasa* (T236-0842) has charter flights to San Blas; *Chitreana* (T226-4116) flies to Chitré, Los Santos, Las Tablas and Guararé, and *Aerotaxi* (T226-7891) operates a service to San Blas and charter flights.

On internal flights passengers must present their identity documents, declare their own weight in pounds (lbs) not kilos, and have their luggage weighed. As excess baggage charges are frequent, ask if it is cheaper to ship excess as air freight (*carga*) on the same flight.

Road There are now about 9,700 km of roads, of which 3,100 km are paved. Road building is complicated by the extraordinary number of bridges and the large amount of grading required. The highway running from Colón to Panama City, widened to four lanes in 1999, is the only fully paved road crossing the isthmus. A well-maintained and scenic road traverses the isthmus from Gualaca in Chiriquí to the town of Chiriquí Grande in Bocas del Toro, crossing the spectacular, Swedish-built Fortuna hydroelectric dam. In 1999 construction was completed to extend the road from Chiriquí Grande to Almirante and the regional centre of Changuinola, opening up a beautiful new route along the Caribbean. The Pan-American Highway, usually called the Interamericana in Panama, runs east from Panama City to Chepo and into the province of Darién, and west to the Costa Rican border. It is paved throughout (as far east as the Panama/Darién provincial border) and is being improved. There is a modern toll road between Panama City and La Chorrera, and the section between David and La Concepción is a modern, four-lane highway. Expressways were being built in 1999 to ease traffic congestion in and around Panama City.

Bus The bus network covers the entire country, generally with efficient, timely services. Some of the long-distance buses are small 'mini' buses, normally modern and comfortable, but large, modern air-conditioned buses are being introduced. They are more expensive than elsewhere in Central America, but nevertheless good value and recommended. Slower 'regular' buses run in country areas. 'Express' buses with air conditioning operate between Panama City and Colón and to David and the border with Costa Rica.

Companies listed under Panama City, Transport **Car hire** Rates vary from company to company and model to model. On average they range from US$24 per day for a small saloon to US$65 for four-wheel-drive jeep, free mileage, insurance US$8 per day, 5% tax, US$500 deposit (can be paid by credit card), minimum age 23, home driver's licence acceptable. If you require a four-wheel drive it is better to book a few days in advance. If planning to rent from an international company, consult them before leaving home. Sometimes very good deals are available that cannot be made at the Panama office. Rental cars are not allowed out of the country; they are marked by special licence plates.

Driving Super grade **gasoline** (called *super*) costs about US$1.90 per US gallon (3.78 litres); unleaded is available in larger towns. Low octane (*regular* or *normal*) costs about US$1.80; diesel is about US$1.30. For motorcyclists, note that a crash helmet must be worn.

Speed limit on the Pan-American Highway is 90 kph (but 60 kph is more realistic when planning a day's driving); the toll stretch (US$0.60) between Chame, La Chorrera and Panama City has a 100 kph limit. Observe 40 kph speed zones in villages. Most streets have no lighting, many hotel signs are unlit, so try to be at your destination before dusk (around 1800-1830). Driving in Panama City at night is inadvisable. Right turn against a red light is legal in cities if no vehicles are approaching from the left. If charged with a traffic violation, you should eceive a document stipulating the infraction; fines to be paid to Dirección Nacional de ⸀ránsito y Transporte Terrestre (Departamento de Infracciones Menores, Panama City, ⸀262-5687). In general, Panamanian highway police are helpful and approachable, but some ⸀panish is an advantage. If you *have* committed an infraction, accept the ticket and pay it later. ⸀ines are less than in Europe or the USA. However, if a traffic policeman is harassing you, speak ⸀nglish and insist firmly but courteously that you be given a ticket or be released. An example ⸀f harassment is to be asked to produce the driver's manual or the fire extinguisher, both ⸀mandatory, neither usually in the car.

Taking a car with Panamanian plates to Costa Rica requires a permit from the Traffic Police (*Tránsito*) obtainable on presentation of the ownership certificate and a document from the ⸀udicial Police (*PTJ*) indicating that the vehicle has not been reported stolen. A travel agency, ⸀or example *Chadwick's* in Balboa, will arrange this for you for US$30. Exit calls for four papers which cost US$4.20 (obtainable from Customs in Paitilla Airport).

It used to be virtually impossible for a tourist to sell a car in Panama unless it could be shown (with help from the Consulate) that the money was needed for a fare home. Recent reports suggest that the whole procedure is now a lot easier. A helpful office with ⸀nglish-speaking staff is in the same building as the Diablo Heights supermarket (in the street across the railway from the main entry of Marcos A Gelabert airport, the former Albrook air base), which deals with license plates, transfer of titles, etc. A great many US service personnel used this facility. Your embassy may be able to give you advice.

Sea

Boats and comfortable **yachts** provide tours all or part way through the canal. Contact tour operators in Panama City or Colón for details. It is also possible to travel through as a linehandling if you have sailing experience and turn up at the right time (see page 1185).

A regular ferry makes the journey to the island of Boca del Toro from Almirante and Chirquí Grande on the western Caribbean coast. To the east, canoes serves the archipelago of San Blas.

Access to and from Colombia is possible by sea, along the Caribbean or Pacific coasts, although the journey takes several days and can be costly. See page 1229.

Shipping a vehicle Taking a vehicle to Colombia, Venezuela or Ecuador is not easy or cheap. The best advice is to shop around the agencies in Panama City or Colón to see what is available when you want to go. Both local and international lines take vehicles, and sometimes passengers, but schedules and prices are very variable.

Theft is particularly prevalent on the Colombia route

To Panama, recommended agency is *Panalpina*, Los Andes 2, Ojo de Agua, Vía Transmística, Panama City, T273-7070, F273-7704, www.panalpina.com Jürgen Lahntaler speaks German, English and Spanish and cuts through the procedures with relative ease. *Panalpina* can also arrange shipment of vehicles to Ecuador, Venezuela and Chile.

To Colombia, agents include: *CSAV*, PO Box: 0832-2775, Edificio Frontenac, Local 2-B, C 50 y 54 Este, Ciudad de Panamá, T269-3344, F269-8003, www.csav.com, who also sail to many other countries in South America on both the Atlantic and Pacific side. To Barranquilla: Vicente Simones' Colón T195-1262, beeper 270-0000, code 700283, will arrange all paperwork for US$25: car passage US$800, motorcycle US$50, plus US$50 per passenger, no accommodation on ship other than hammock space, take food and drink for a week (even though voyage should be three days). To Cartagena, Captain Newball, Edificio Los Cristales, Piso 3, Calle 38 y Avenida Cuba, Panama City. On the same route *Central American Lines* sail once a week, agent in Panama, Colón T441-2880, Panama City T236-1036. Also, *Géminis Shipping Co SA*, Apdo Postal No 3016, Zona Libre de Colón, Rep de Panamá, T441-6269, F441-6571. Mr Ricardo Gil is helpful and reliable. Another agent, *Barwil*, PO Box 3002, Balboa, Panama, T263-7755, F223-0698, www.barwil-panama.com, will arrange shipments to Colombia (Cartagena) and elsewhere in Latin America from Balboa or Cristóbal. If sending luggage separately, make enquiries at Tocumen Airport, for example *Tampa*, T238-4439.

Some small freighters go only to intermediate ports such as San Andrés, and it is then necessary to get another freighter to Cartagena. *Navieras Mitchell* ship cars regularly to San Andrés and Barranquilla. Office at Coco Solo Wharf, T441-6942. You may have to wait up to a week in San Andrés to make the onward connection. From Colón to San Andrés takes two days and from San Andrés to Cartagena takes three days.

Panama

Customs formalities at the Colombian end will take up to three days to clear (customs offi cials do not work at weekends). Cartagena is the best port because it is privately run, more secure and more efficient. Go first to customs: DIAN, Manga CL27 A 24-83, Diagonal DIAN Jefe División de Servicio al Comercio Exterior. Here you will receive, free of charge, the neces sary documents to enter the port (takes about 24 hours).

To Ecuador, weekly (sometimes more often) sailings with combined services of *P&C Nedlloyd*, Edif Plaza Globus, 5th Floor, Av Samuel Lewis y C 55, Panama City, T206-5900 F206 5926, or visit www.ponl.com, to find your nearest office. *Hapaglloyd* agents are *AGENCO*, Edif Eurocentro, PB, Av Abel Bravo, Urb. Obarrio, Panama City, T269-1549 F263-8641, www.hapag-lloyd.com, about US$900 for a 6 m container. Shipping to Guayaquil from Panama's new container port of Manzanillo, next to Colón, is the best choice, preferable to Colombia or Venezuela. *TNE* (*Transportes Navieros Ecuatorianos*, T269-2022) ship vehicles to Guayaquil; agent in Cristóbal, Agencia Continental SA, T445-1818. Another agent recommended in Cristóbal is *Associated Steamships*, in Balboa, 232-5194, F232-5810, and in Cristobal, T445-0461, F441-2251, www.shipsagent.com Customs agents cost US$60 in Colón, US$120 in Guay aquil; 12 days from starting arrangements in Panama to leaving Guayaquil docks. Seek advice on paperwork from the Ecuadorean consul in Panama. *Barwil*, (see above for Colombia) will ship vehicles to Arica, Chile.

It is possible to ship a vehicle to Venezuela, from Cristóbal usually to La Guaira, but Puerto Cabello is also possible. In addition to those mentioned above, agents include: *Cia Transatlántica España*, T269-6300, to La Guaira. Also *Barwil Agencies* (see above) or *Vencaribe* (a Venezuelan line), agent in Cristóbal: *Associated Steamship* (*Wilford and McKay* – see above), T252-1258 (Panamá), T445-0461 (Cristóbal). There are several agencies in Colón/Cristóbal across the street from the *Chase Manhattan Bank* and next door to the *YMCA* building. Formalities before leaving can be completed through a travel agency – recom mended is *Continental Travel Agency*, at the *Hotel Continental*, T263-6162. In Venezuela there are customs complications (without carnet) and this route is not really recommended.

Air-freighting a vehicle Most people ship their vehicles from Panama to South America by sea but some find air-freighting much more convenient. Generally it is faster and avoids many of the unpleasant customs hassles, but it is more expensive; prices vary between carriers and from month to month so ask around if you have the time. The major carriers, if they permit it on a regular commercial flight, tend to charge more than the cargo lines and independents. You are generally not allowed to accompany the vehicle. For *Copa Cargo*, T227-5236, F227-1952, www.copaair.com, Tocumen Airport (T238-4290, F238-4391), talk to Jorge Arauz. Taking a motorcycle from Panama to Colombia can only be done on a cargo flight. Retrieving the bike in Colombia can take up to two days if there are any peculiarities in your documents.

Maps Topographic maps and aerial photos are sold by the ***Instituto Geográfico Nacional Tommy Guardia (IGNTG)***, on Vía Simón Bolívar, opposite the National University (footbridge nearby, fortunately), T236-2444, F236-1841, take Transístmica or Tumba Muerto bus, open 0800-1530, Mon-Fri: physical map of the country in 2 sheets, US$4 each. Other maps US$3.50 per map, eg 1:250,000 sheets covering Panama in sections, or 1:12,500 of Panama City; no survey maps sold of Canal Zone. *ITM* (www.itmb.com) have a 1:800,000 travel map of Pan ama. At the back of the Panama Canal Commission telephone books there are good maps of the Canal Area, Panama City and Colón.

Keeping in touch

Internet The web has spread extensively throughout the populated areas of the country. Charges average out at about US$1.50-2 an hour. Details of cyber cafés are given throughout the travelling text. For Panama City, see page 1176.

When sending mail, great care should be taken to address all mail as 'Panama' or 'RP' (Republic of Panama). Air mail takes up to 10 days, sea mail three to five weeks from Europe. Rates (examples) for air mail (up to 15 g) are as follows: Central, North and South America and Caribbean, 35c; Europe, 45c up to 10 g, 5c for every extra 5 g; Africa, Asia, Oceania, 60c. Parcels to Europe can only be sent from the post office in the El Dorado shopping centre in Panama City (bus from Calle 12 to Tumba Muerto).

Post
Post offices, marked with blue and yellow signs, are the only places permitted to sell stamps

International calls can be made from Panama at any time, day or night. Collect calls are permitted to Costa Rica, Italy, Spain, Sweden, UK, all of North America, Israel, Japan and some others, three minutes minimum, rates are higher than direct, especially to USA. Cable and Wireless now run the telephone system and have offices in most towns. Cost of direct dialled calls, per minute or fraction are as follows: Central America US$2.40, except Costa Rica US$1.04; USA US$1.12; Mexico and Canada US$2; Caribbean US$1.60-2.40 depending on country; South America, excluding Colombia, US$2; Colombia, US$1.60; West Europe, excluding Spain and United Kingdom, US$3.20, Spain and United Kingdom US$2.40 all day; Japan US$2.88 all day; elsewhere US$3.20, all plus US$1 tax per call. Calls are roughly 20-30% cheaper for most, but not all destinations from 1700-2200. Lowest rates apply Sunday all day.

Telephone
Local operator 102, international operator 106

Public payphones take 5, 10 and sometimes 25 cent coins. Phone cards are available in denominations of US$3, 5, 10, 20 and 50, for local, national and international calls. There are prepaid 'Aló Panamá' cards – dial 165 for connection (eg for use from hotel phones) in US$10, US$20, US$30 and US$50 denominations, but they are 50% more expensive than payphone cards. For *AT&T* dial T109. For *SPRINT* (collect calls only) T115 and for *MCI* T108. *BT Chargecard* calls to the UK can be made through the local operator.

Newspapers *La Prensa* (www.prensa.com) is the major local daily newspaper. Others are *La Estrella de Panamá*, *El Universal de Panamá* (www.eluniversal-pma.com), *El Panamá América* (www.epasa.com), and two tabloids, *Crítica Libre* (www. critica.com.pa) and *El Siglo*. *Colón News* (weekly – Spanish and English). In English is the bi-weekly *Panama News* (www.thepanamanews.com). The international edition of the *Miami Herald* is printed in Panama, and many other US newspapers are widely available in the capital.

Media

Food and drink

In Panama City the range of food available is very broad with a profusion of restaurants and well-stocked supermarkets. In the interior tastes are simpler and available ingredients less varied. Because country people do not traditionally use ovens, most food is boiled or fried in vegetable oil (usually soybean oil). Virtually every restaurant will have a *comida corriente* (meal of the day) which will include a serving of meat, chicken or fish, white rice and a salad, a dish of boiled beans garnished with a *tajada* (slice) of fried ripe plantain. It will cost about US$2 in towns, perhaps more in the city, less in villages. A bowl of *sopa de carne* (beef broth with vegetables) or *de pescado* (fish chowder) is usually available as a first course for US$0.50. Breakfast normally consists of eggs, a small beefsteak or a slice of liver fried with onions and tomatoes, bread and butter and some combination of *frituras* (see below).

Cuisine

The staple of Panamanian food is white rice, grown not in paddies but on dry land, and usually served at every meal, often with the addition of chicken, shrimp, vegetables, etc. Meat is usually fried (*frita*) or braised (*guisada*), rarely grilled except in the better restaurants. Beef is common; pork, chicken and the excellent fish are usually a better choice.

The national dish is *sancocho de gallina*, a stew of chicken, yuca, *ñame* (dasheen), plantain, cut-up pieces of corn on the cob, potatoes and onions and strongly flavoured with *culantro*, an aromatic leaf similar in flavour to coriander (*cilantro*). *Ropa vieja* ('old clothes') is beef boiled or steamed until it can be shredded, then sautéed with onions, garlic, tomatoes and green or red peppers, often served with yellow rice (coloured with *achiote*). Piquant *ceviche*, eaten as a first course or a snack with cold beer, is usually raw corvina or shellfish seasoned with tiny red and yellow peppers, thin slices of onion and marinated in lime juice; it is served very cold with crackers (beware of the bite). A speciality of the Caribbean coast is *sao*, pigs' feet pickled with lime and hot peppers. Also try *arroz con coco*, coconut rice, or the same with *tití*, tiny shrimp; also

Panama

fufú, a fish chowder with coconut milk. *Mondongo* is the stewed tripe dish called *menudo* in Mexico; the Panamanian version is less spicy, but very well seasoned.

For special occasions and whenever the young corn has been harvested (February and August), certain traditional corn dishes are prepared. Look for *serén*, a golden corn soup flavoured with *culantro* and mild peppers, or a sweeter version called *pesada* (or just *pesá*), with brown sugar and milk added. *Tamales* are thick cakes of corn-meal mush filled with spiced chicken or pork in *bijao* leaves and steamed, or the similar meatless version *bollo. Bollo de coco* is flavoured with coconut and either salt or sugar, steamed in coconut-palm or sugar-cane leaves.

Frituras are eaten at breakfast, as a snack or as a cheap, filling lunch: they include *carimañola*, a cigar-shaped cake of mashed yuca, filled with seasoned, chopped pork and fried golden brown; *tortillas* or *almojábanas* of corn-meal dough fried to a golden yellow; *patacones* (called *tostones* in Central America), slices of unripe green plantain fried till partially softened, flattened and refried until golden; *totorrones* or *turulitas*, fat, sweet cakes of corn batter with juicy kernels of young corn mixed in, fried dark brown; plus *bolitas de carne*, mildly spiced meatballs, *salchichas*, small sausages, *chicharrones*, pieces of pork rind with a thin strip of meat, deep fried; *tasajo*, smoked lean beef; *hojaldras* or *arepas*, thin cakes of wheat flour batter, leavened with baking powder and fried; *empanadas*, pastry-dough triangles filled with meat, chicken, cheese or sweetened fruit. Prices for these will normally be quoted by the *real* (multiples of US$0.05).

Sweets   Most *panaderías* sell good pastries: in Panama City most of the European standards are available; in the country, try *empanadas* (see above), *orejas, costillas* or *ma'mellena* ('fills me up more', a sweet bread-pudding with raisins; *dulces*, of coconut, pineapple, etc, are cakes or pastries, not sweets/candies as elsewhere (the latter are *confites*). In restaurants, as well as the ubiquitous *flan*, try *plátano a la tentación*, ripe plantain simmered with brown cane sugar, cinnamon and raisins, *sopa a la borracha*, a rich sponge cake macerated in rum, garnished with raisins and prunes marinated in sherry, *arroz con cacao*, chocolate rice pudding, *buñuelos de viento*, a puffy fritter served with syrup (called *sopaipillas* further north), and *sopa de gloria*, sponge cake soaked in cooked cream mixture with rum added. Local ice-creams are safe; try the fresh fruit flavours such as *guanábana* (soursop), mango, pineapple, etc. Among the items sold at the roadside you may see bottles stopped with a corncob, filled with *nance*, a strong-flavoured, yellow-green fruit packed with water and allowed to ripen and ferment slightly; *pifá/pixbae*, a bright orange fruit which, when boiled, tastes much like sweet potato (two or three will see you though to your next meal); *níspero*, the tasty, acidic yellow fruit of the chicle tree.

Drink   There are dozens of sweetened fruit drinks found everywhere in the country, making excellent use of the many delicious tropical and temperate fruits grown here: *naranja* (orange), *maracuyá* (passion fruit), *guayabo, zarzamora* (raspberry), *guanábana*, etc. The generic term is *chicha dulce* which also includes drinks made with rice or corn. Most common carbonated canned drinks are available. Panamanian beer tends to be low in alcohol, *Panamá* and *Soberana* the most popular locally. Foreign beers, some imported, others locally brewed, include *Löwenbrau* and *Guinness. Chicha fuerte* is the alcoholic form of corn or rice drink fermented with sugar, brewed mostly in the countryside. Sample with care. The local rum, for example *Carta Vieja*, is not bad. *Seco*, a harsh brand of 'white lightning' made from the juice of sugar cane, brand name *Herrerano*, deserves considerable respect.

Shopping

What to buy   More traditional Panamanian crafts include the colourful *molas* embroidered by the Kuna Indians of the San Blas islands. Masks, costumes, ceramics and woven hats can be found in several small villages dotted around the Azuero Peninsula. These are on sale in many places so keep looking for one you like rather than the first one you see. Straw, leather and ceramic items are also available, as are carvings of wildlife made from wood, nuts and other natural materials. And of course, don't forget the quintessential Panama Hat. Good ones are expensive. Duty-free imported goods including stereos, photographic equipment, perfume and clothes are cheap in the Colón Free Zone on the Caribbean coast. Most items are cheaper than at point of origin.

Holidays and festivals

1 January: New Year's Day; **9 January**: Martyrs' Day; **Shrove Tuesday**: Carnival. **Good Friday**; **1 May**: Labour Day (Republic); **15 August**: Panama City only (O); **1 November**: National Anthem Day (O); **2 November**: All Souls (O); **3 November**: Independence Day; **4 November**: Flag Day (O); **5 November**: Independence Day (Colón only); **10 November**: First Call of Independence; **28 November**: Independence from Spain; **8 December**: Mothers' Day; **25 December**: Christmas Day. School holidays are December-March when holiday areas are busy; make reservations in advance.

Holidays

O=Official holiday, when banks and government offices close. On the rest – national holidays – business offices close too

The fiestas in the towns are well worth seeing. Panama City at Carnival time, held on the four days before Shrove Tuesday, is the best (book hotels and car hire in advance at this time). During carnival women who can afford it wear the voluminous *pollera* dress, a shawl folded across the shoulders, velvet slippers, tinkling pearl and polished fish-scale hair ornaments (called *tembleques* from their quivering motion) in spirited shapes and colours. The men wear a *montuno* outfit: round straw hats, embroidered blouses and trousers sometimes to below the knee only, and carry the *chácara*, or small purse.

Festivals

At the Holy Week ceremonies at Villa de Los Santos the farces and acrobatics of the big devils – with their debates and trials in which the main devil accuses and an angel defends the soul – the dance of the 'dirty little devils' and the dancing drama of the Montezumas are all notable. The ceremonies at Pesé (near Chitré) are famous all over Panama. For other festivals in this region, see Exploring the Azuero Peninsula, page 1200. At Portobelo, near Colón, there is a procession of little boats in the canals of the city. See under Portobelo for the *Congos*, page 1192.

Bullfights, where the bull survives, are an important part of rural fairs, as are rodeo events.

The Ngöbe-Buglé (Guaymí) Indians of Chiriquí province meet around 12 February to transact tribal business, hold feasts and compete for brides by tossing balsa logs at one another; those unhurt in this contest, known as Las Balserías, are viewed as heroes and are regarded as promising suitors.

Sport and special interest travel

Panama's tourism potential for special interest travel is only just being truly appreciated. It is a paradise for fishermen and birders alike, there are fine beaches and beautiful islands along both Atlantic and Pacific coasts, several indigenous as well as colonist communities provide considerable cultural interest, ecotourists can find a variety of challenging activities, and there are few routes as appealing to the long-distance traveller as crossing the Darién Gap (should this become safe again, see page 1224). Although visitor facilities in Panama are well developed for those engaged in international commerce, off-shore banking and bargain-hunting shoppers, many other aspects of tourism are still in their infancy. However, they are all slowly evolving, as the country's tourist industry gradually becomes aware of its own broader potential.

Birdlife is particularly abundant and varied in Panama – they have been using it as a route for far longer than humans – and the country is an important destination for many bird-watchers. The Darién jungle, both coastlines, the forest fringe along the Canal, and the Chiriquí highlands (where quetzales, among many other species, may be seen) all provide their own special attractions for the birder. Those interested are referred to *A Guide to the Birds of Panama* by Robert S Ridgely and John A Gwynne Jr, Princeton University Press, 1992.

Bird-watching

With a relatively small population and much rugged terrain, Panama has a lot of remote and relatively unexploited areas. Some 43% of the country remains forested and a quarter of the land has protected status that includes 14 national parks, wildlife refuges and forest reserves that are home to over 900 recorded bird species – more than neighbouring Costa Rica – including the endangered great green macaw and the spectacular harpy eagle, the national

Nature tourism

Panama

bird. Most national parks can be visited without hindrance if you can get there – there is supposed to be a US$3 entry fee but it is rarely charged. Transport can be very difficult and facilities non-existent; the largest, Darién National Park, is a good example. But slowly the value of the National Park system to tourism is being realised and some parks now have accommodation in huts for US$5 a bed. Many of these protected places are mentioned in the text. For more information, contact Asociación Nacional de Conservación de la Naturaleza (ANCON – for address, see page 1178) or ANAM who have their headquarters near the domestic terminal at Albrook. (Note that they do not allow visitors wearing shorts.)

Hiking Volcán Barú, Panama's highest peak at 3,475 m, and nearby Cerro Punta are the two best climbs in the country but there are several excellent long walks. The hike from Cañita on the Darién road over the continental divide to Cartí is an alternative to flying to San Blas. The Caminos de Cruces and Real are tough jungle walks that follow in the footsteps of the Conquistadors crossing the continental divide and, if combined into an ocean-to-ocean hike, take eight days. A lesser known, but good range for hiking is the Serranía de Majé east of Panama City, visiting Embera villages and known for its howler monkey population. Closer is the Parque Nacional Chagres and a three-day walk from Cerro Azul to the coast.

Watersports With almost 2,000 km of coastline split between the Pacific and the Caribbean, and situated at the northern end of one of the wettest areas of the world, Panama has an awful lot of water in and around it. The potential for watersports is great, most of which remains unexploited.

Diving is the best locally developed sport and has great variety. The Caribbean coral reefs are similar to those of Belize and Honduras except that they extend southeast for 100 km along from the Costa Rica border and then from Colón 300 km to the border with Colombia. For information on these areas, see under Bocas del Toro, Portobelo and the San Blas Islands. The Pacific has quite different ecosystems owing to the much greater tidal ranges, differing water temperature and density. Because of easier accessibility, diving is better developed. Places to go include Taboga, the Pearl Islands, Iguana Island and Parque Nacional Coiba. A third, and perhaps unique experience, is diving in the lakes of the Panama Canal, mainly to visit wrecks, submerged villages and the odd train left behind by the filling of the canal. There's a good website at www.scubapanama.com

Snorkelling is popular in the less remote places mentioned under diving; equipment can be hired in most of the resorts.

Surfing is best along the Costa Arriba, east of Colón (namely Isla Grande, Playa Venado on the Azuero Peninsula, Santa Catalina on the Pacific coast of Veraguas and Bocas del Toro). Also in the capital, Jon Hanna, T227-7755, panamasurftours@hotmail.com offers tours to the more out of the way beaches.

Whitewater rafting and other forms of river running are best in the Chiriquí river system near David – Class III to IV on the Río Chiriquí (all year round) and the Chiriquí Viejo Palón section (December-April) when river is not in full speight. Also in the Parque Nacional Chagres area, north of Panama City, with Grades II and III which some consider better for the gentler activity of tubing – floating downriver on an inflated inner tube (generally best August-December).

Health

No particular precautions are necessary. Water in Panama City and Colón is safe to drink. In smaller towns, it is best to drink bottled or boiled water to avoid minor problems caused by indifferently maintained municipal distribution systems. Yellow fever vaccination is recommended before visiting Darién. Malaria prophylaxis for that area is highly recommended. It is currently very difficult to obtain chloroquine in Panama; stock up before arrival. In fact, stock up with all medicines, they are very costly in Panama. Hospital treatment is expensive; insurance underwritten by a US company would be of great help.

Panama City

Panama City is a curious blend of old Spain, US-style mall developments and the bazaar atmosphere of the east. Hardly surprising then that it has a polyglot population unrivalled in any other Latin American city.

Colour map 8, grid B1
Population: 484,261

Expanding rapidly since 1979, new developments have mushroomed along the southern end of the Canal and skyscrapers are springing up around the Bahía de Panamá. As new roads are constantly being built, Panama City is perhaps the only capital in the sub-continent which is developing to suit the automobile more than the pedestrian. Beyond the urban streets, palm-shaded beaches, the islands of the bay and encircling hills constitute a large part of Panama City's charm. And the cabarets and nightlife are an added attraction for any self-respecting hedonist.

Ins and outs

Tocumen International Airport is 27 km from the city centre. For flights see Essentials, page 1150. Set price taxis (US$25) and buses are available for getting into Panama City. The bus journey should take 1 hr but can take up to 3 hrs in the rush hour; see page 1174. Car rental companies also have offices at the airport. The city is well served by international buses from countries throughout Central America, with offices in the centre of town.

Getting there
For transport details, see page 1173

The old part of the city, Casco Viejo, can easily be toured on foot. There are old, usually crowded and very cheap buses for getting to other districts. The reasonably priced taxis charge on a zone system and can be shared if you wish to economize. Taxis can be hired by the hour for a city tour. At night, radio taxis are preferable. Many *avenidas* have both names and numbers, although locals are most likely to use the names, so asking for directions can be a bit complicated. Also, because there is no postal delivery to homes or businesses, few buildings display their numbers, so try to find out the nearest cross street.

Getting around
For maps of Panama, see page 1154

The wider metropolitan area has a population of approximately 720,000. Adjacent to the city, but constituting a separate administrative district, is the town of San Miguelito, a residential area for over 330,000 people. Once a squatter community, every available square inch of hillside has been built on and it is increasingly considered to be a part of greater Panama City.

Corredor Sur highway was built in 1999 to help combat the perpetual gridlock traffic jams along the main east-west avenues, but vehicular congestion and noise pollution are likely to be a part of life in Panama City for a long time to come.

Information office of the *Instituto Panameño de Turismo (IPAT)*, is in the Atlapa Convention Centre, Vía Israel opposite *Hotel Caesar Park*, Apdo 4421, Panamá 5, T226-7000 ext 112/113, F226-4002, www.panamainfo.com Office open 0900-1600; issues good list of hotels, *pensiones*, motels and restaurants, and a free *Focus on Panama* guide (also available at airport and all major hotels). There are IPAT kiosks at Tocumen Airport, in Panamá Viejo (Tue-Sun 0800-2200), on the pedestrian mall portion of Av Central (Mon-Fri 0900-1700) and a kiosk opposite *Hotel Continental* on España. Michèle Labrut's *Getting to Know Panama*, published by Focus Publications (Apdo 6-3287, El Dorado, Panamá 6A, RP, F225-0466, US$12), has been recommended as very informative.

Tourist information

Panamanians are generally very friendly and helpful. Accustomed to foreigners, they are casual about tourists. However, as in any large city with many poor people, certain areas can be dangerous after dark and reasonable precautions should be taken at all times. Attacks have been reported in the Casco Viejo (although this area is now well patrolled by police during the daytime) and Panamá Viejo. Marañón (around the market), San Miguelito (on the way in from Tocumen Airport) and Calidonia can all be dangerous; never walk there at night and take care in daylight, too. Poor districts like Chorillo, Curundú and Hollywood are best

Security
Tourist Police on mountain bikes are present in the downtown areas of the city, recognizable by their broad armbands

Panama

avoided altogether. Probably the safest area for budget travellers to stay is Bella Vista, although it is deserted after dark and street crime can take place here at any hour. Taxis are the safest way to travel around the city, and drivers will give you good advice on where not to go. If concerned, lock the doors of the taxi. See page 41.

El Chorrillo, the area west from Plaza Santa Ana to Ancón Hill, was largely destroyed in 'Operation Just Cause'; it was a dangerous area, so if you wish to visit it show a genuine interest in the district's recent history. We have received recent reports of muggings here.

Background

Modern Panama City was founded on its present site in 1673. The capital was moved from Old Panama (Panamá Viejo), 6½ km to the east, after Henry Morgan looted the South American treasure chest depot of Golden Panama in 1671. Today, it is a thoroughly modern city complete with congested streets and noisy traffic. Uncollected trash mouldering in the tropical heat and the liberal use of razor-wire are other eyesores but, despite its blemishes, the city does possess considerable charm. The old quarter, called Casco Viejo or San Felipe, massively fortified by Spain as the era of widespread piracy was coming to an end, lies at the tip of the peninsula at the eastern end of the Bay of Panama.

Sights

Casco Viejo   The principal districts of interest to vistors include El Cangrejo, Campo Alegre, Paitilla, and Coco del Mar, where the international banks, luxury hotels and restaurants are located. Calidonia, Bella Vista and Perejil are bustling with commerce, traffic, and mid-price hotels. Casco Viejo (the 'Old Compound' or San Felipe), which occupies the narrow peninsula east of Calle 11, is an unusual combination of beautifully restored public buildings, churches, plazas, monuments and museums alongside inner-city decay which, after decades of neglect, is now gradually being gentrified. Several budget hotels are found here, some very badly run-down but not without their faded glory. Created in 1673 after the sacking of old Panama, Casco Viejo is a treasure trove of architectural delights, some restored, others in a desperate state of repair, but most demanding a gentle meander through the shady streets.

Panama City orientation

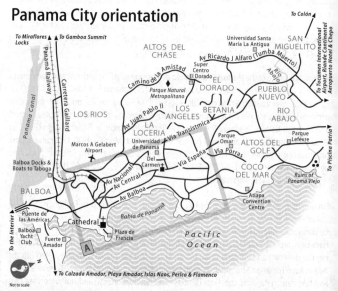

Related maps
A Main streets,
page 1162
A Central hotel
district, page 1168

Not to scale

n 1992 local authorities began reviving some of the area's past glory by painting the
post-colonial houses in soft pastels and their decorations and beautiful
wrought-iron railings in relief. New shops and restaurants are moving into restored
buildings in an attempt to make Casco Viejo a tourist attraction.

At the walled tip of the peninsula is the picturesque **Plaza de Francia**, with its
bright red poinciana trees and obelisk topped by a cockerel (symbol of the Gallic
nation), which has a document with 5,000 signatures buried beneath it. Twelve large
narrative plaques and many statues recall the French Canal's construction history
and personalities; the work of Cuban doctor Carlos Finlay in establishing the cause
of yellow fever is commemorated on one tablet. Facing the plaza is the French
Embassy, housed in a pleasant early 20th-century building; it stubbornly refused to
relocate during the years when the neighbourhood declined and is now one of the
main focus points in the area's renaissance. Built flush under the old seawalls around
the plaza are **Las Bóvedas** (The Vaults), the thick-walled colonial dungeons where
prisoners in tiny barred cells were immersed up to their necks during high tides.
Nine 'vaults' were restored by the Instituto Panameño de Turismo (IPAT) in 1982
and converted into an art gallery – **Galería Las Bóvedas**, (copies of *Focus on Panama* available) – and handicraft centre. ■ *Tue- Sun 1100-1900; students offer walking tours of the Casco Viejo from here during these hours.* The French restaurant *Las
Bóvedas* occupies another two 'vaults' next to the former Palacio de Justicia, partly
burned during 'Operation Just Cause' and now housing the **Instituto Nacional de
Cultura** (INC), with an interesting mural by Esteban Palomino on the ground floor.

Steps lead up from the Plaza Francia to the **Paseo de las Bóvedas** promenade which
runs along the top of the defensive walls surrounding the peninsula on three sides. This is
a popular place for an evening stroll; it is ablaze with bougainvillea and affords good
views of the Bahía de Panamá, the Serranía de Majé on the Panama/Darién provincial
border (on a clear day), Calzada Amador (known during the Canal Zone era as the
Causeway) and the islands beyond (see under Fuerte Amador, page 1181).

Two blocks northwest of the Plaza (Avenida A and Calle 3) are the restored ruins
of the impressive **Church and Convent of Santo Domingo** (1673, but later
destroyed by fires in 1737 and 1756), both with paired columns and brick inlaying
on their façades. The famous 15 m-long flat arch (*arco chato*) which formed the base
of the choir was built entirely of bricks and mortar with no internal support. When
the great debate as to where the Canal should be built was going on in the United
States Congress, a Nicaraguan postage stamp showing a volcano, with all its implications of earthquakes, and the stability of this arch – a supposed proof of no earthquakes – are said to have played a large part in determining the choice in Panama's
favour. A chapel on the site has been converted into the interesting **Museo de Arte
Colonial Religioso**, whose treasures include a precious golden altar, a delicate snail
staircase, silver relics and wooden sculptures from as far away as Lima and Mexico,
19th-century engravings of the city, and the skeleton of a woman found by archaeologists during excavation of the church. ■ *Tue-Sat 0830-1630, admission US$0.75,
students and seniors US$0.25. T228-2897.*

Not far from Santo Domingo, across Avenida Central, the neoclassical **Teatro
Nacional** (850-seat capacity) opened in 1908 with Verdi's *Aida* being performed in
what was then considered the state of the art in acoustics. French-influenced sculptures and friezes enliven the façade, while Roberto Lewis' paintings depicting the
birth of the nation adorn the theatre's dome. The ballerina Dame Margot Fonteyn,
who married a member of the prominent Arias family and was a long-time resident
of Panama until her death in 1991, danced at the theatre's re-inauguration in 1974.
■ *Open for visitors Mon-Fri 0800-1600, US$0.50.*

Diagonally opposite the Teatro Nacional (Avenida B and Calle 3) is the peaceful
Plaza Bolívar, with a statue of the Liberator Simón Bolívar, draped in robes, standing below a large condor surrounded by plaques of his deeds. Around the square are
the former *Hotel Colombia* (now restored and converted to condominiums), the
Church of San Felipe Neri (also undergoing restoration, interesting but only open

Panama

on 26 May), and many 19th-century houses still displaying roofs of red clay tile bearing the stamp 'Marseilles 1880'. On the east side stand **San Francisco Church** (colonial but 'modified' in 1917 and modernized in 1983 ■ *Mon-Sat 1430-1800, Sun all day*) and the **San Francisco Convent** (1678), largest of all the religious buildings, which was restored by Peruvian architect Leonardo Villanueva. The Bolivarian Congress of June 1826, at which Bolívar proposed a United States of South America, was also held in the Chapter Room of the Convent, now known as the **Salón Bolívar** and the 1904 Constitution was also drafted here. This northern wing was dedicated as the **Instituto Bolívar** in 1956; its wood panelling, embossed leather benches and paintings (restored in part by the government of Ecuador) may be viewed with an authorized guide from the Bolivarian Society, T262-2947. The adjacent Colegio Bolívar, built on a pier over the water, was closed in 1999 and is due to become the new Cancillería (Ministry of Foreign Affairs).

Another long block west of Plaza Bolívar, and one block north on the seafront (Avenida Eloy Alfaro) between Calles 5 y 6, is the **Palacio Presidencial**, the most impressive building in the city, built as an opulent residence in 1673 for successive colonial auditors and governors, enlarged and restored under President Belisario Porras in 1922. Graceful patios and mother-of-pearl decorated columns give a Moorish flavour, and murals by Lewis adorn the official reception salons. Visitors who ask permission at the guard office are allowed to approach the gate and view the courtyard from the outside. Exterior photography is allowed. Porras introduced two white Darién herons during one of his presidential terms and a number of their descendants are always to be seen strutting about the marble floor around the fountain of the Moorish patio, leading to the popular nickname of the residence: *Palacio de las Garzas* or 'Palace of the Herons'.

Panama City main streets

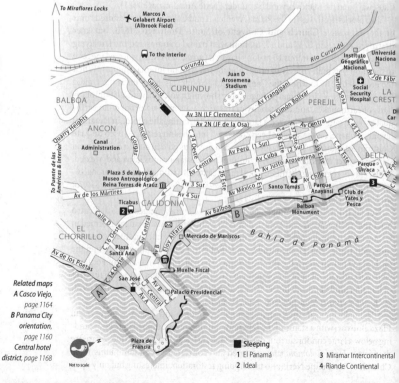

Related maps
A Casco Viejo,
page 1164
B Panama City
orientation,
page 1160
Central hotel
district, page 1168

Not to scale

Sleeping
1 El Panamá
2 Ideal
3 Miramar Intercontinental
4 Riande Continental

A few blocks west, Avenida Alfaro begins to curve north around the waterfront to the colourful **Central Market**, Mercado San Felipe (see Shopping, below) and the **Muelle Fiscal** wharf where coastal vessels anchor (a 15-m tidal range allows beaching for maintenance) and small cargo boats leave for Darién and sometimes Colombia. Two blocks further north, where Avenida Alfaro meets Avenida Balboa by the pier, is the modern **Mercado de Mariscos** (fish and seafood market), where fishermen land their catch.

Returning to Casco Viejo, two blocks south of the Palacio Presidencial is the heart of the old town, the **Plaza Catedral** or **Independencia**, with busts of the Republic's founders, and surrounding public buildings. On the west is the **cathedral** (1688-1794, refurbished in 1999), its twin towers, domes, classical façade encrusted with mother-of-pearl and three of the tower bells brought from the Old Panama Cathedral. To the right of the main altar is a subterranean passage which leads to other *conventos* and the sea. On the southwest corner with Calle 7 is the neoclassical **Palacio Municipal** (City Hall), on the first floor of which is the **Museo de Historia de Panamá**, which covers the nation's history since European landfall, and includes highlights of the treaty between Panama and the USA which led to the construction of the Canal. ■ *Mon-Fri 0800-1600, US$0.50.* The former post office next door, originally built in 1875 as the *Grand Hotel* ("the largest edifice of that kind between San Francisco and Cape Horn" according to a contemporary newspaper), is the city's best example of French architecture. It became de Lesseps' headquarters during Canal excavations in the 1880s and was sold back to Panama in 1912. It has been entirely gutted and converted into the **Museo del Canal Interoceánico** (Museum of the Panama Canal), on Plaza Catedral. It has a comprehensive and interesting history of Panama – covering mainly the central provinces – as shaped by its pass route, and is recommended.

■ *Tue-Sun 0930-1730, US$2.50, students and seniors US$0.75, free on Sun 0930-1730,* T/F262-0966, *www.sinfo.net/pcmuseum Photography not allowed. English- and French-speaking guides available, other languages if booked in advance. Hand-held English audio commentaries US$5.*

The east side of the Plaza is dominated by the former **Archbishop's Palace**, which was later occupied by a university, a shelter for runaway kids (now closed), and is now the run-down *Central Hotel* (1884), once the most luxurious in Central America. The interior featured a palm garden, restaurants, barber shop, 100 rooms with private baths and a wooden staircase imported from New York, and it was the centre of Panama's social life for decades. Today it is decrepit but still retains echoes of its former elegance.

There are a number of other interesting religious structures within two or three blocks of the cathedral, but the most-visited is the **Church of San José** (Avenida A and Calle 8, one block west and two south of the Plaza Catedral) with its famous Altar de Oro, a massive baroque altar carved from mahogany and, according to common belief, veneered with gold. This was one of the few treasures saved from Henry Morgan's attack on Old Panama in 1671 and legend records different versions of how it was concealed from the buccaneers: whitewashed by the priest, or even covered in mud by nuns; however, a remark attributed to Morgan hints that he was not deceived! A beautiful organ, an 18th-century original pulpit with a painting by an unknown artist on its tiny roof and several smaller carved wooden altars, can also be seen. Two blocks further west along Avenida Central is the church of **La Merced**, burnt down in 1963 and now completely restored. It was near here that the landward gate of the fortified city stood.

A block to the south down Calle 9 is the still run-down **Plaza Herrera**. The French influence is evident in the windows and flower-filled cast-iron balconies of the green and light pink houses and *pensiones*. Behind Plaza Herrera are the ruins of the **Tiger's Hand Bulwark**, where the defensive wall ended and the landward-side moat began. The strongpoint held a 50-man military post and 13 cannon; it was demolished in 1856 as the town expanded westwards but restored again in 1983. Portions of the moat can still be detected.

Avenida Central & Calidonia From Calle 10 heading north Avenida Central, Panama City's main commercial street, enters the 'mainland', curves northwest then sweeps northeast running almost parallel with the shore through the whole town. En route its name changes to Vía España – although signs reading 'Avenida Central España' exist in parts – on its course northeast to Tocumen Airport. At its crossing with Calle B, close to Casco Viejo, is the small **Plaza Santa Ana** with a colonial church (1764), a favourite place

Panama City: Casco Viejo

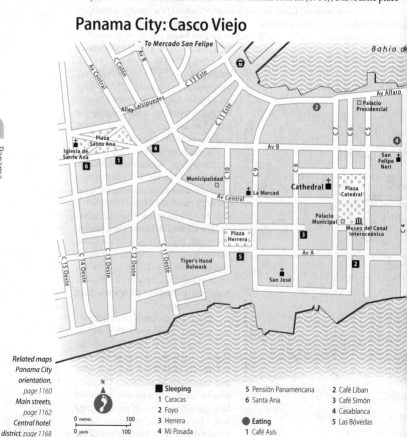

Related maps
Panama City
orientation,
page 1160
Main streets,
page 1162
Central hotel
district, *page 1168*

0 metres 100
0 yards 100

Sleeping
1 Caracas
2 Foyo
3 Herrera
4 Mi Posada

5 Pensión Panamericana
6 Santa Ana

Eating
1 Café Asís

2 Café Liban
3 Café Simón
4 Casablanca
5 Las Bóvedas

for political meetings; the plaza has many restaurants and is a good place to catch buses to all parts of the city. Nearby, running towards the Central Market between Avenida Central and Calle B (officially known as Carrera de Chiriquí), is an exotic, narrow alley called **Salsipuedes** – 'Get out if you can' – where crowded stalls sell everything from fruit to old books and medicinal plants. Over 75 of the street's residents in 1892 were Chinese merchants, but the city's Chinatown (**Barrio Chino**) is now largely confined to nearby Calle Juan Mendoza and adjacent Calle B with a typical Chinese archway at the entrance, good Chinese restaurants and general shops.

The next section of Avenida Central is a pedestrian precinct called **La Peatonal**, with trees and decorations, modern department stores and wandering street vendors. **Plaza 5 de Mayo** (at Calle 22 Este) is another busy bus stop from which buses leave for the Canal. In the centre of the Plaza is an obelisk honouring the firemen who died in a gunpowder magazine explosion on the site in May 1914. Housed in the old railway station (1913-46), almost opposite the Plaza de Lesseps, on Avenida Central south side of Plaza 5 de Mayo, is the **Museo Antropológico Reina Torres de Araúz**. It has five salons (partly looted during 'Operation Just Cause') exhibiting Panamanian history, anthropology and archaeology, rare collection of pre-Columbian gold objects and ceramics (Profesora Torres de Araúz, a renowned anthropologist and founder of the museum, died in 1982). It was closed for renovation in 1999, but has now re-opened hosting occasional performances. ■ *T262-4138*. One block east of Plaza 5 de Mayo is the **Museo Afro-Antillano**, which features an illustrated history of Panama's West Indian community and their work on the Canal. There's a small library. ■ *Tue-Sat 0900-1600, Sun 1500-1800, US$0.50. Justo Arosemena and Calle 24*. This area is the southern fringe of the **Calidonia** and **Curundí** districts, home to the descendants of British West Indian blacks brought in to build the railway and the Canal. Calidonia is a labyrinth of tightly packed wooden structures, exotic and unassimilated, where outsiders should exercise caution. The neighbourhood is safe enough during the day (watch for pickpockets in the crowd) but don't linger at night, best to leave before 1930.

La Exposición

East of Plaza 5 de Mayo, along the oceanside Avenida Balboa (a popular stretch for jogging), on a semi-circular promontory jutting out into the water by Calle 34, is a great monument to **Vasco Núñez de Balboa**, who stands sword aloft as he did when he strode into the Pacific on 15 September 1513. The 1924 statue stands on a white marble globe poised on the shoulders of a supporting group representing the four races of Man. To the east is Parque Anayansi, a pleasant shady park, popular with local couples and flocks of parrots in the late afternoon; this waterfront area was nicely refurbished in 1998. A short distance further east along Avenida Balboa are the British ambassador's residence and the fortified US Embassy. There are several hospitals in this area including the vast and run-down public Hospital

Panama

Santo Tomás.

Two more pleasant plazas, Porras and Arias, can be found west of Hospital Santo Tomás across Avenida 3 Sur (Justo Arosemena). This central part of the city is known as **La Exposición** because of the international exhibition held here in 1916 to celebrate the building of the Canal. Further east, as Avenida Balboa begins to curve around the other end of the Bay of Panama to Punta Paitilla, is **Bella Vista**, once a very pleasant residential district (many private homes now converted to business use) and site of many hotels in our **B** and **C** ranges. It includes the neighbourhood of Perejil ('parsley'), originally called Perry Hill. Bordering this on the north, where Vía España passes the Iglesia del Carmen, is **El Cangrejo** ('the crab') apartment and restaurant district, with many upmarket stores and boutiques. The University City is on the Transisthmian Highway making student demonstrations a frequent cause of traffic jams. Opposite the campus is the Social Security Hospital. All these areas are evidence of Panama City's sensational growth since the post-war economic boom and the spread of the centre eastwards; the attractive residential suburb of Punta Paitilla was an empty hill where hunting was practised as recently as the 1960s.

Claims to be the only natural forest within the limits of a Latin American metropolitan capital The 265-ha **Parque Natural Metropolitano** is located between Avenida Juan Pablo II and the Camino de la Amistad, west of El Cangrejo along the Río Curundú. ■ *Office open Tue-Sun 0900-1600. Park open 0730-1800.* As well as a *mirador* (150 m) with a great view over the city and a glimpse of the Canal, there are two interpretive walking trails from which tití monkeys, agoutis, coatis, white-tailed deer, sloths, turtles and up to 200 species of bird may be glimpsed (go early morning for best viewing); green iguanas sun themselves on every available branch. The Smithsonian Institute has installed a unique construction crane for studying the little-known fauna in the canopy of this remnant of tropical semi-deciduous lowland forest, which can be visited while walking the paths of the Metropolitan Park. Researchers and students wishing to use the crane need to apply through the Smithsonian Institute. The Visitors' Centre, on Avenida Juan Pablo II (T232-5516) runs guided one-hour tours and holds regular slide shows. No ANAM permit is required for this recommended, easy excursion. ■ *Getting there: bus, marked 'Tumba Muerto', from Avenida Central, and ask to be dropped at the Depósito. Park is signposted from here, otherwise make for the crane and the tree-covered hill.*

Other museums **Museo de Ciencias Naturales** has good sections on geology, palaeontology, entomology and marine biology. ■ *Tue-Sat 0900-1530, Sun 1300-1630, US$1, students and seniors US$0.25. Avenida Cuba y Calle 30, T225-0645.* **Museo Casa del Banco Nacional** contains a large numismatic and stamp collection and a history of banking from the 19th century, old postal and telephone items and historic photos, not widely known but worth a visit. ■ *Mon-Fri 0800-1230, 1330-1630, free. Calle 34 between Avs Cuba and Justo Arosemena.* **Museo Postal, Filatélico y Telegráfico**, Avenida Central, opposite Don Bosco church, has stamp collections, documents, equipment, maps, photos, etc. ■ *Mon-Fri 0830-1630, free.* **Mi Pueblitos**, north of Avenida de los Mártires, east of the Quarry Heights entrance, are nostalgic replicas of three different villages: one colonial from the Central Provinces, one Afro-Antillian, and one Indigenous; all very nicely portrayed. ■ *Open till 2200, small admission charge (on a busy road so best to take a taxi).*

Essentials

Sleeping

■ on map
Price codes: see inside front cover **LL-L** *Caesar Park* , Vía Israel y C 77, T270-0477, F226-4262, www.caesarpark.com, 4 restaurants , one with excellent vista over bay, another offering SE Asian cuisine, casino and sports bar, outdoor swimming pool. **LL** *Miramar Intercontinental*, Av Balboa y Av Federico Boyd, T214-1000, F223-4891, www.interconti.com Tallest building in the Republic, sea view, marina, pools, spa, restaurants. **L** *El Panamá*, Vía España, at Vía Venetto (C 55), T269-5000, F223-6080, www.elpanama.com Former *Hilton*, tropical Art Deco style, restaurant closed

Sun, vast rooms, good swimming pool, 'bags of charm'.

AL *Golden Tulip Costa del Sol*, Vía España y Federico Boyd, PO Box 8572, Zona 5, T206-3333, F206-3336, www.costadelsol-pma.com, 242 junior suites, kitchenettes, launderettes on all 7 floors, pool, 2 saunas, tennis, business centre, rooftop bar, restaurant and pizzería, shopping arcade with Indian restaurant, tour agency on site for excursions, airport transfer US$8. **AL** *Riande Continental Aeropuerto*, near Tocumen Airport (10 min), T220-3333, F290-3105, www.hotelesriande.com A/c, clean, free transport to airport, good breakfasts, pool (loud music all day), tennis, casino. Reductions for more than 1 night. **A** *R*, Av Justo Arosemena y C 33, T227-3844, F227-3711, www.hotelromaplaza.com Restaurant with Italian emphasis, rooftop pool. **B** *Veracruz*, Av Perú y C 30, T227-3022, F227-3789. With breakfast, very good restaurant, clean, good, but rooms at front noisy. **B** *Costa Inn*, Av Perú y C 39, T227-1522, F225-1281. A/c, hot water, TV, pool, use of fridge, safe parking, pool, restaurant noisy and smoky.

There is a 10% tax on all hotel prices. Most hotels are a/c, all others have fans

C *Acapulco*, C 30 Este y Av Perú, T225-3832, F227-2032. A/c, clean, comfortable, TV, private bath, excellent restaurant, safe parking, conveniently located. Recommended. **C** *Residencial Alameda*, C 30 Este, between Cuba and Justo Arosemena, T225-1758, F225-7806, clean, modern, a/c, hot water, cable TV, parking. **C** *Andino*, C 35 off Av Perú, beside Parque Parades, T225-1162, F227-7249, andino@sinfo.net Completely renovated with large rooms and all mod cons including TV and telephone. Family-run, friendly, free interent access, laundry (not cheap) quiet street. Highly recommended. **C** *Bella Vista*, Vía España y C 42. A/c, cable TV, private bath, safe deposit. Recommended. **C** *California*, Vía España y C 43, Bela Vista, T263-7736, F264-6144. With bath, a/c, modern, good value, TV, restaurant, friendly, safe. **C** *Caribe* Av Perú y C 28, T225-0404, F227-2525, caribehotel@hotmail.com, 153 rooms, one of the city's older hotels, rooftop pool, casino, restaurant open 0700-2300. **C** *Cobadonga*, C 29, between Cuba and Perú, T225-3998, F225-4011, marit@sinfo.net Small rooms but good rooftop terrace pool with views over the bay. **C** *Lisboa*, Av Cuba y C 31, T227-5916, F227-5919. Modern, a/c, TV, restaurant, good value. **C** *Montreal*, Vía España near *Restaurant Lesseps*, T263-4422, F263-7951. Shower, toilet, a/c, TV, phone, takes credit cards, rooms on street noisy, safe car park. **C** *Riazor*, C 16, T228-0777, F228-0986. A/c, cheaper with fan, with bath, hot water, good value, cheap restaurant downstairs next to the *Ticabus* office, therefore well placed as you arrive late from Costa Rica on the bus, but also noise from buses. **C-D** *Venecia*, Av Perú, between C 36 and 37, T227-7881, F227-5642, finitrivera@usa.net, new, modern, clean, smallish rooms, reasonable restaurant and bar.

Electricity and water cuts are frequent in Panama City, though usually very brief. Most better-class hotels have generators and large cisterns

D *Centroamericano*, Av Justo Arosemena y Av Ecuador, T227-4555, F225-2505. Very clean, hot water, good reading lights, TV, restaurant, good value. **D** *Arenteiro*, C 30 Este y Av Cuba, 227-5883, F225-2971. Hot water, TV, modern, clean, good value. **D** *Discovery*, Av Ecuador, T225-1140. Clean, fairly quiet, safe parking, good value. **D** *Caracas*, C 12 on Plaza Santa Ana, T228-7232. Large, clean rooms, friendly, a/c (**E** with a fan) , hot showers, be wary of rooms with outside windows. **D** *Dos Mares*, C 30 between Perú and Cuba, T227-6150, F227-3906. A/c, bath, hot water, pool on roof, good restaurant, TV, phone. Recommended. **D** *Ideal*, C 17 just off Av Central, between Plazas Santa Ana y 5 de Mayo, T262-2400. A/c (cold), shared hot shower, pool, cable TV, internet at US$1/hr, safe. **D** *Pensión Las Palmeras*, Av Cuba between C 38-39, T225-0811. With fan, shower (cheaper with shared toilet), clean, quiet in back rooms, short stay clientele. **D** *Pensión La Torre* Av Perú (S side), between C 36 y C37, T225-0172, a/c (**E** without), TV, clean, some rooms a bit dark. **D** *Residencial Volcán*, C 29, between Avs Perú and Cuba, T225-5263, opposite Migración, next to Museo de Ciencias Naturales. Fan, a/c extra, with shower, friendly, safe, clean.

Cheaper accommodation can be found in pensiones

  E *Foyo*, C 6, Santa Bárbara 8-25, T262-8023. Airy rooms, balcony, recommended, similar to **E** *Herrera*, Plaza Herrera y C 9, T228-8994. Basic, variety of prices, cheaper without bath, some dearer with a/c, TV, bars on main door, restaurant. **E** *Las Tablas*, Av Perú y C 29 Este. With bath, **E** without, cold water, fan, safe, quiet except for rooms overlooking street (opposite is *El Machetazo* supermarket, food for cheap meals, but crowded). **E** *Mi Posada*, C 12 y Av Central (Plaza Santa Ana). Basic, mixed reports. **E** *Rivera*, Av C 11 Ote, 8-14, off Av A. Pleasant and friendly, but noisy (monthly rates available). **E** *Pensión Panamericana*, C 10 y Av A, Casco

Panama

Viejo. Dark rooms, balcony rooms good value. **E** *Pensión Tropical*, C 8 (de San Blas) y Av A, T228-8894. With bath, fan, clean. **E** *Sevilla*, Av Justo Arosemena 46-40, T227-2436. With bath and a/c, cheaper without, good. **E** *Santa Ana*, overlooking Plaza Santa Ana, T228-7438. Helpful. **E** *Hostel Voyager*, C Ricardo Arias, Edif Comi Apto 1, above *Boutique de Diego*, T260-5913 Dormitory rooms, price includes breakfast, laundry service, TV, use of kitchen and free internet service for guests. Recommended. Many cheap places on Av México.

Apartments for rent, all have kitchenette, colour and cable TV, some with pool. Daily, weekly and monthly rates are available, at **AL** *Suites Ambassador*, in centre of El Cangrejo district, T263-7274, F264-7872. Well-furnished rooms, pool, gym, breakfast included. **AL** *Tower House Suites*, C 51 No 36, Bella Vista, T269-2244, F269-2869, www.towerhsuites.com Centre of commercial district, pool. **A** *Apartotel Las Vegas*, C 55 (Vía Veneto) y C Eusebio A Morales, T269-0722, F223-0047. Good restaurant on the patio. Recommended. **B** *Apartotel Plaza*, Av Batista opposite University campus, T264-5033, F264-2256.

Camping There are no official sites but it is possible to camp on some beaches or, if in great need in the Balboa Yacht Club car park. It is also possible to camp in the Hipódromo grounds (11 km east of the city, on Vía España) but there are no facilities; this is allowed if you are waiting to ship your vehicle out of the country. Also possible, by previous arrangement, at La Patria swimming pool nearby, and at the Chorrera (La Herradura) and La Siesta beaches on the Pan-American Highway. Camping Gaz is available at *Ferretería Tam SA*, Av B, No 54; at *Super 99* grocery stores, cheap.

Panamá City: central hotel district

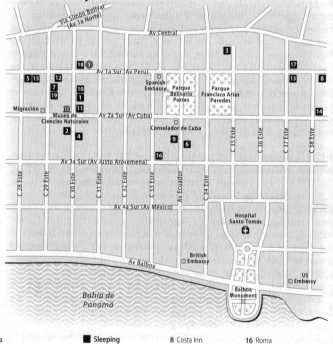

Panama

Eating

As a cosmopolitan city, there is a wide range of international restaurants, many of good quality in all styles and price ranges. There are good restaurants in most of the more expensive hotels, eg **Rendezvous**, at the *Riande Continental*, Vía España y C Ricardo Arias, T263-9999, is good value, open 24 hrs, superb Sun brunch from 1030-1500, US$9.50.

Bohío Turístico, Vía Cincuentenario, Panamá Viejo. On seafront, open air, palm thatched building (*bohío*). **El Trapiche**, Vía Argentina 10, T221-5241. Many dishes including *empanadas* (meat filled fritters), and *mondongo* (seasoned tripe), also in Panamá Viejo, Vía Cincuentenario, similar food with traditional music and dance programmes, call for information. **Jimmy's**, Paseo Cincuentenario just beyond Atlapa Centre, T226-1096. Good grills, seafood, fast food and fish, served under a thatched roof, very popular, also on Av Samuel Lewis opposite *Hotel Riande Continental*, a/c, self service, good for breakfast and lunch. **Las Tinajas**, on C 51, near *Ejecutivo Hotel*, T263-7890. Traditional entertainment most evenings at 2100, craft shop, closed Sun. Recommended. **Rincón Tableño**, Av Cuba No 5 y C 31. Several other locations, good *comida criolla*, lunchtimes only. Recommended. | **Panamanian**

Meat lovers should try **Gauchos Steak House**, C Uruguay y C 48. Choose your own steak, learn the names of the cuts, say you will salt your own, good. **La Tablita**, Transisthmian Highway, Los Angeles district, T260-1458. Good steaks, reasonable prices. **Los Años Locos**, opposite *Caesar Park Hotel*, T226-6966. Argentine *parrillada* steakhouse, good value. Also **Martín Fierro**, C Eusebio A Morales, T264-1927. Meat, seafood. | **Grills**

Gran China, Av Balboa, between C 26 y 27. Good value. **Kalua**, close to the *Hotel El Panamá*. Very good, reasonable prices. **Kwang Chow**, in the Salsipuedes area of Av Balboa, Chinese. Sells Tsingtao beer. Recommended. **Lung Fung**, Transistthmian Highway and Los Angeles. Very popular with Chinese residents for Sat and Sun, Cantonese-style brunch, very good food and value. **Madame Chang**, C 48 off Aquilino de la Guardia. Elegant, good food, but pricey and erratic service. **Palacio Imperial**, C 17 near *Ticabus* office. Good and cheap. **Tang**, C A y Cenbule, off Plaza Santa Ana. Cheap, friendly. Recommended. | **Chinese**

Benihana, C 60, Obarrio. Favoured by Japanese locals, closed Sat. **Ginza Teppenyaki**, C Eusebio A Morales, opposite *Hotel Granada*. Japanese, lobster, seafood, imported beef, diners surround the chef at his grill. **Korea House**, C 52, block north of Vía España opposite Cine Aries. Sushi bar, Japanese and Korean. **Club Fuji**, Vía Brazil, C 32, Obarrio. One of the best Japanese in town. **Matsuei**, Av Eusebio A Morales A-12. Japanese, excellent, pricey. | **Japanese & Korean**

Café du Liban Av Eloy Alfaro, Casco Viejo, on waterfront next to Presidential Palace, T212-1582, bit pricey, but good atmosphere and fine view of bay from balcony. | **Middle Eastern**

Calypso, Vía España y C 46, La Cresta, T223-0749. French restaurant and bar. **Casco Viejo**, C 50, Mansión Dante. Excellent French food, interesting décor, closed Sun. Expensive but recommended. **Dali**, Av Samuel Lewis y Santa Rita. Daliesque décor, French and Italian food. **La Cocotte**, C Uruguay 138, T213-8250. In former private house, excellent French cuisine, expensive, Hillary Clinton slipped out of the Embassy to eat here – but not on a Sun as it closes. **Las Bóvedas**, in converted dungeons at seaward end of Casco Viejo, T228-8068, best to take a taxi. Good French food, expensive, art galleries adjoining, live jazz Thu-Sat, closed Sun. **Le Bistrot**, Centro Comercial La Florida, C 53. French, good, expensive (under same ownership is **Siete Mares**, next to *El Cortijo*, see below). *1985*, next door to *Rincón Suizo* (see below) on Morales, same management. | **French**

El Rincón Suizo, C Eusebio A Morales, T263-8310. Charming mountain-hut atmosphere, good Swiss *rösti*, *raclette*, fondue, chef Willy Diggleman. | **Swiss**

Panama

Italian *Athen's*, C San Miguel, Obarrio (also C Ricardo Arias). Excellent pizza, also Greek and near-Eastern food, lively atmosphere, young people, very good. *Caffé Pomodoro*, Av Eusebio A Morales, north of C 55, in patio of *Apartotel Las Vegas*. Garden setting, also a/c, North Italian pasta and sauces, informal, moderately priced. *Il Rigoletto*, C Uruguay, Casa 1A-54, T214-9632. Italian, very good food and service, moderate-expensive prices. *Las Américas*, Av 1 Sur, C 57/58, 1 block south of Vía España, T223-4676. Elegant Italian, good cellar. *Nápoli*, C 57, Obarrio, 1½ blocks south of Vía España. Big, family-style, good Italian pizzas with real Italian dough, second location by Plaza 5 de Mayo.

Spanish *Angel*, Vía Argentina 68, T263-6411. Spanish, seafood, imported mussels, eel, *bacalao* (cod), closed Sun. *Café Balear*, C Colombia 17, north of Parque Urracá, T269-2415. Extensive Spanish menu, colonial-style town house. *Del Prado*, Vía Argentina, T264-2645. Spanish food, busy at lunchtime, full meals, sandwiches, open late. *El Cortijo*, between Eusebio A Morales and Vía Argentina on Calle D, T269-6386. *El Mesón del Prado*, Edif Alcalá, Tumba Muerto, T260-9466. Informal, Spanish, seafood, snacks, moderate prices. *Manolo*, Vía Argentina, sidewalk terrace. A favourite for politicians and young people in evenings and Sun morning, draught beer served with Spanish *tapas*, *churros* (doughnut-like fried cakes) a speciality, also on Vía Venetto y C Eusebio A Morales, tables or counter, same menu, prices and service. *Marbella*, Av Balboa y C 39. Seafood *cazuela de mariscos, paella*, good but not cheap.

Mexican *La Mejicanita*, Av Justo Arosemena y C 50, La Florida shopping centre. Good Mexican. *El Patio Mexicano*, Av 17, Galerías Miami, T236-4878, a bit pricey, closed Mon.

Vegetarian *Govinda's*, C 47, No 24, Marbella. Many specialities. *Mireya* C Ricardo Arango y C Ricardo Arias, near *Continental Hotel*, T269-1876. Health food bakery, good value, recommended, also at C 39 y Av Balboa, Bella Vista. *Mi Salud*, C 31 y Av México 3-30. Owned by dietary specialist Carlos Raúl Moreno, open Mon-Sat 0700-1900.

Seafood *Centolla's Place*, Vía España, Río Abajo, T221-7056. Caribbean seafood, catering to Antillean community, friendly, cheap, worth a taxi ride. Recommended. *La Fregata*, Av Samuel Lewis, Obarrio. Good seafood, reasonably priced. *Restaurante Mercado de Mariscos*, Av Balboa, above Mercado de Mariscos. Fresh catch of the day prepared for you, fish and other seafood.

Diners & pubs *La Cascada*, Av Balboa y C 25. Beef, pork, seafood, enormous helpings, open air, 'doggy bags' given, kitsch décor but good service, menus in charming English to takeaway. Highly recommended. Closed Sun, credit cards not accepted. The same management runs *Las Costillitas* on Vía Argentina. Same huge menu (which takes 30 mins to read), same reasonable prices, but closed on Sun. *La Victoria*, next to Minimercado Teresa on Av Central, open 1100-2300. Very cheap (US$1 a meal) with juke box and a/c. Recommended. Also recommended is unnamed restaurant opposite, very popular with locals. *Mango's Pub & Grill*, C Uruguay 1-24, T269-4856. US-style bar and food, many imported beers, best hamburger south of Houston, live music Tue and Sat, recommended for lunch and evening. *Niko's Café* with 4 locations at Vía España near *El Rey* supermarket, T264-0136, El Dorado Shopping Centre, T260-0022. Very good, cheap, self-service, Paitilla, past the old airport T270-2555, and behind the former Balboa High School in the Canal Zone T228-8888. *Ozone Café*, C Uruguay. Food from all over the world, upmarket, good and popular, many other restaurants in same area. *Pavo Real*, C 51, just west of C Ricardo Arias, Campo Alegre, T269-0504. Upmarket English pub with restaurant, darts, good food, ex-pat hangout, journalist's refuge during 'Just Cause', open 1200-2400 Mon-Tue, till 0330 Wed-Sat, live music from 2200, closed Sun. *Riazor*, C 16, 15-105, T228-2541. Just as it was 40-50 years ago, cheap local food served with style. Recommended. Take a taxi at night. *TGI Friday's*, C 49 y Av Aquilino de la Guardia, near Lloyds Bank, T269-4199. Huge US franchise operation, good food, hordes of young people, recommended to call ahead for waiting list.

Cafés & fast food *A & P* on Av Central opposite the National Museum. Good. *Café Coca Cola*, Av Central and Plaza Santa Ana. Pleasant, friendly, reasonably priced – US$3 for set lunch. *Café Central*, Av

Central, between C 28 and 29, Calidonia. Basic and cheap food, OK. *Café Jaime*, corner of C 12 and Av Central. Good *chichas* (natural drinks). *Dulcería Panadería La Gran Vida*, Av Central 11-64 (between C11 y 12). Good *chicha* juice, good cheap ice-cream, good *empanadas* and cakes. Recommended. Also *La Esquina*, Av A y C 12 Ote. *La Viña*, corner C 6 Ote and Av A, behind post office. Good, cheap. *La Conquista*, Calle J, up Av Central. *La Cresta* (good food from US$1), Vía España and C 45. *Markany*, Av Cuba y Av Ecuador. Good snacks. There are several good pavement cafés along Av Balboa.

Burger King, *Dairy Queen*, *Don Lee*, *Frutilandia*, *Kentucky Fried Chicken*, *Krispy*, and *McDonalds* all have branches throughout the capital.

Entertainment

La Chiva Parrandera is an open-sided bus that tours the hot-spots 2000-2330, T263-3144 for information, US$20 per person. Bacchus, Vía España y Elvira Méndez.

Capo's, Vía Cincuentenario. *Cubares*, C 50 diagonal a C Uruguay. *Fonda Antioqueña*, Panamá Viejo, T221-1268. Colombian restaurant, bar, disco, open 24 hrs. *La Parrillita*, Av 11 de Octubre in Hato Pintado district. Restaurant/disco in a railway carriage. *Las Molas*, entrance to *Chase Manhattan Bank*, Vía España, Los Angeles district. Small bands, rural décor, drinks US$1.50. *Unicornio*, C 50 y R Arias 23. Nightclub with discothèque and gambling; reasonable prices, will admit foreigners for US$3 a week.

In Casco Viejo, on Plaza Bolívar, the following all have tables on the square: *Café Asís*, reasonable set menu dishes, old style bar, runs art gallery (open late) next door; *Café Simón*, air conditioned, dark interior, bean bag seats, popular with young wealthy Panamanian crowd; *Café Bolívar*, small, snug bar; *Casablanca*, restaurant and bar, chrome filled interior, a/c.

Bars & nightclubs *Many late night haunts are now concentrated in the Marbella district such as Escape, La Cantina, Cocos, Mangos, Café Dalí*

The *Teatro Nacional* occasionally has shows and performances. There are regular folklore sessions every other Sun and monthly National Ballet performances when not on tour, check press for details. The *Anayansi Theatre* in the Atlapa Convention Centre, Vía Israel, San Francisco, has a 3,000-seat capacity, good acoustics, regular recitals and concerts. *Balboa Theatre* near Steven's Circle and post office in Balboa, with folkloric groups and jazz concerts sponsored by National Institute of Culture. *Guild Theatre* in the Canal Area at Ancón mounts amateur productions mainly in English. Cinemas cost US$2.50 except *Cine Balboa* near Steven's Circle, US$2; by law all foreign films must be subtitled in Spanish. *Cine Universitario* in the National University, T264-2737, US$1.50 for general public, shows international and classic movies, daily (not holidays) at 1700, 1900 and 2100.

Theatre & cinema *La Prensa and other newspapers publish daily programming (cartelera) of cultural events*

Café El Aleph, Vía Argentina north of Vía España, T264-2844. Coffee house atmosphere, snacks and full meals, Internet facilities, occasional art shows, live jazz at weekends, phone for programme. *Café Gardel*, Vía Argentina, T269-3710. Small restaurant, tiny bar, perfect atmosphere for jazz. *Giorgio's*, 1 block south of Vía Porras. Hotels *Granada* and *Soloy* (*Bar Maitai*, T227-1133) are recommended for live Latin music at weekends. *Nottingham*, Fernández de Córdoba, Vista Hermosa, T261-0314. Live salsa at weekends, no cover charge, restaurant. *Vino's Bar*, C 51 y Colombia, Bella Vista, T264-0520. Live salsa at weekends, cover charge, restaurant.

Live music

Hotel Riande Continental; *Josephine's*, C 50 y Av Uruguay, El Cangrejo. Cover charge US$20, continuous show 2100-0400 daily except Sun. *Le Palace*, C 52, opposite *Hotel El Ejecutivo*, T269-1844. No cover, shows from 2030 nightly. *Oasis*, Vía Brasil.

There are more than 20 state-managed casinos, some in the main hotels with profits intended for charitable public institutions. Most offer blackjack, baccarat, poker, roulette and slot machines (*traganikles*). Winnings are tax-free and paid without deductions. The *National Lottery* is solemnly drawn (televised) Wed and Sun at 1300 in Plaza de la Lotería between Av Perú y Cuba; 4-digit tickets, called *billetes* or *pedazos*, cost US$1, a win pays up to US$2,000; 'chance' tickets, with only 2 digits cost US$0.25, and pay up to US$14.

Cabarets, casinos & gambling

Cockfights At the *Club Gallístico*, Vía España near junction with Vía Cincuentenario, T221-5652, most Sun, same bus as for race track, but get out at crossing with C 150.

Spectator sports

Panama

Horse races Pari-mutuel betting. Held Sat, Sun and holidays at the Presidente Remón track (bus to Juan Díaz, entry from US$0.50-2.50).

Festivals

On *Independence Day*, **3 Nov**, practically the whole city – or so it seems – marches in a parade lasting over 3 hrs, through the old part of the city. Colourful, noisy and spectacular. Another parade takes place the following day. *Carnival* activities include a parade on Shrove Tuesday and have become more elaborate and interesting in recent years. The municipality has also instituted an annual *Christmas parade*, in which the growing displacement by US-style Christmas traditions of the Latin American emphasis on the *Nacimiento* and the Three Kings is much in evidence.

Shopping

Duty-free imported luxuries of all kinds are an attraction at the *Zona Libre* in Colón (purchases sealed and delivered to Tocumen Airport), but Panama City is a booming fashion and merchandise centre where bargains are not hard to find; anything from crystal to cashmere may be cheaper than at point of origin.

The smartest shops are along C 50 (Av 4 Sur) in Campo Alegre, and Vía España in Bella Vista and El Cangrejo, but Avenida Central is cheaper and the best and most popular place for clothing (not great quality), hi-fi and photographic equipment, perfumes, curios, souvenir t-shirts and Asian handicrafts. Colombian emeralds and pearls may also be purchased at reasonable prices from many establishments.

Traditional Panamanian *artesanía* includes *molas* (embroidered blouse fronts made by Kuna Indians, eg Emma Vence, T261-8009); straw, leather and ceramic items; *chunga nawala* (palm fibre) canasters; the *pollera* circular dress, the *montuno* shirts (embroidered), the *chácara* (a popular bag or purse), the *chaquira* necklace made by Ngöbe-Buglé (Guaymí) Indians, and jewellery. Indigenous Darién (Embera) carvings of jungle birds and animals from cocobolo wood or *tagua* nut (small, extremely intricate, also *tagua* necklaces) make interesting souvenirs (from US$10 up to US$250 for the best, museum-quality pieces). A good selection is at *Artesanías Nacionales* in Panamá Viejo, one of several Indian co-ops selling direct from open-air outlets, eg in the Canal Area at Balboa and along the road to Miraflores Locks at Corozal (daily if not raining). The YMCA has a good and varied shop. *Colecciones*, Vía Italia opposite *Hotel Plaza Paitilla Inn*, has a wide selection. Plenty of straw articles available, including baskets, bags, traditional masks and panama hats (US$150 for the best quality). Try *Flory Salzman* (not cheap) on Vía Venetto at the back of *El Panamá Hotel*, T223-6963, F264-4531, best place outside San Blas Islands for *molas*, huge selection, sorted by theme, ask for discounts, nearby *Inovación*, or *Indutípica*, Av A y C 8 Ote (opposite San José Church) for reproductions of pre-Columbian ceramics and jewellery, necklaces, Kuna *molas* (prices starting from US$2.50) from the Darién and Ngöbe-Buglé dresses from Bocas del Toro. The *Gran Morrison* department store chain (best-supplied is in Paitilla, also at *Hotel Continental* and on Vía España near C 51 Este) have good-quality handicraft sections, as well as postcards and books in English. The tourist office has a full list of *artesanía* shops available, including those in the main hotels. *Reprosa*, Av Samuel Lewis y C 54 (T269-0457) features a unique collection of pre-Columbian gold artefacts reproduced in sterling silver vermeil; David and Norma Dickson make excellent reproductions for sale (Panamá Guacas, T266-6176).

Of the various commercial centres, with banking, entertainment and parking facilities, the largest is *El Dorado Mall and Shopping Centre*, in the Tumba Muerto district at Av Ricardo Franco y C 71 (shops open Mon-Sat 0900-1900, Sun 1500-1900; cinema, plenty of restaurants and playgrounds).

Other centres include *Balboa Mall* on Av Balboa, the newest but closed on Sun. *Bal Harbour*, Vía Italia near Punta Paitilla (Mon-Sat 0900-1900, Sun 1100-1900); *Plaza California*, near *El Dorado*; *Plaza New York*, C 50, which has travel agencies and a well-known disco.

Supermercado El Rey has a branch on Vía España just east of *Hotel Continental*, at *El Dorado*, and at several other locations. *Super 99*, *Farmacias Arrocha*, *Casa de la Carne* (expensive) and *Machetazo*, also a department store (on Av Central, Calidonia) are said to be the best of the city's supermarkets.

Army-Navy store on Avenida Central near Plaza 5 de Mayo sells camping and hiking equipment. Similarly *Army Force*, east end pedestrianized section of Av Central, west of Plaza 5 de Mayo.

The central market *Mercado San Felipe*, close to the docks and Palacio Presidencial, is the place for fresh produce (pigs, ducks, poultry and geese) and pets. Most interesting part of the Market is the chaotic shopping area along C 13 and the waterfront (Terraplen). It's the best place to buy second-hand jungle and military supplies (eg powerful insect repellents, machetes, webbing and cooking equipment) for a trek into the forested interior. The nearby fish market is clean and prices are the best in town.

Bargain hard as prices are extremely competitive

Gran Morrison department stores around the city stock books, travel guides and magazines in English. A good bookstore is *Legends* T270-0097, C 50, San Francisco, diagonal to the Iglesia de Guadalupe de Panama, a cultural oasis – CD's, books, T-shirts and posters. *Librería Argosy*, Vía Argentina north of Vía España, El Cangrejo, T223-5344, very good selection in English, Spanish and French, also sells tickets for musical and cultural events. Recommended. *National University Bookshop*, on campus between Av Manuel Espinosa Batista and Vía Simón Bolívar, T223-3155, for excellent range of specialized books on Panama, national authors, social sciences and history, open Mon-Fri 0800-1600, closed weekends. Highly recommended. (The campus *Simón Bolívar Library* has extensive Panamanian material, only for matriculated students but visitors engaged in special research can obtain a temporary permit from the Director, Mon-Fri 0800-2000, Sat 0900-1300.) Near the University is *La Garza* bookshop, Av José de Fábrega y C 47, good supply of Latin American literature (Spanish only). The *Smithsonian Tropical Research Institute* (see under Ancon), Edif Topper, Av de los Mártires (opposite National Assembly), has a bookshop and the best English-language scientific library in Panama, open Mon-Fri 0800-1600. *Allegro* has a versatile selection of international music cds, literature as well as a coffee shop T226-6967.

Books & music

International edition of the *Miami Herald* printed locally on *La Prensa*'s presses, widely available at news-stands and hotels, as are leading US papers and magazines. Spanish and English magazines at branches of *Farmacias Arrocha, Super 99* and *Gago* supermarkets/drugstores.

Newspapers & magazines

Foto Decor and *Foto Enodi*, Vía Porras. Kodak slides developed in a day. Many other places for developing and equipment. In some places you will get a free film. Camera repairs at *Relojería*, watch shop, on C Medusin, off Av Central in Calidonia.

Photography

Panama

Sports

Golf   *Panama Golf Club*, T266-7777; *Coronado Beach Golf Club* (open to tourists who get guest cards at Coronado office on C 50). Similarly at *Fort Amador Golf Club* tourists can play, green fees and rented clubs US$20 for the day. A spectacular view of the canal and the city.

Swimming   *Piscina Patria* (the Olympic pool), take San Pedro or Juan Díaz bus, US$0.15. Piscina Adán Gordón, between Av Cuba and Av Justo Arosemena, near C 31, 0900-1200, 1300-1700 (except weekends to 1700 only). Admission US$0.50 (take identification), but beards and long hair frowned on (women must wear bathing caps); take a padlock for clothes locker. **Beaches**: many beaches within 1½ hrs' drive of the city. Fort Kobbe beach (US$7.50 admission, with vouchers given for drinks and hotdogs, bus from Canal Area bus station US$0.75, 30 mins) and Naos beach (US$1, Amador bus from same station, US$0.30, then 2 km walk along causeway) have been recommended. Veracruz beach is not recommended as it is both dirty and dangerous (all are dangerous at night).

Transport

Bus The traditional small buses known as *chivas*, consisting of locally made wooden bodies grafted onto truck chassis, have all but disappeared. Most buses in urban areas are

Local

second-hand US school buses brightly painted in fanciful designs, but poor condition. They are known as *diablos rojos* or red devils, and are notorious for roaring engines and aggressive drivers behind the wheel. During a downpour, windows are slammed shut and temperatures inside rise even further. Most out-bound (east) buses travel along Av Perú, through Bella Vista, before fanning out to their various destinations. In-bound (west) buses travel along Vía España and Av Central through the Calidonia shopping district. Basic fare US$0.15, usually paid to the driver upon descending; if there is a fare box, deposit upon entering. To stop at the next authorized stop, call out '*parada*' to the driver.

Taxis Service is generally good, but can be scarce during peak hours and many drivers have little clue where many streets are – it's good to have a rough idea of the address location; voluntary sharing is common but not recommended after dark. Most newer taxis have a/c, look for closed windows when hailing. If taxi already has a passenger, the driver will ask your destination to see if it coincides with the other passenger's. If you do not wish to share, waggle your index finger or say '*No, gracias*'. Similarly, if you are in a taxi and the driver stops for additional passengers, you may refuse politely. Zone system: US$1 for 1 passenger within 1 zone, US$0.25 for each additional zone (US$2 is a common overcharge in zone 1). Additional passengers US$0.25 each regardless of zones; sharing passengers each pay full fare. Panamanians rarely tip, but foreigners may add US$0.25 or US$0.50 to the fare. Hourly hire, recommended for touring dubious areas, US$7 per hr, US$8 with a/c. Radio taxis summoned by telephone highly recommended. Listed in yellow pages under 'Taxis'. Add US$0.40 to fare for pick-up. 'Tourist taxis' at major hotels (aged, large American cars with 'SET' number plates) have a separate rate structure: they are more expensive than those you can flag down on the street. Agree on fares in advance, or arrange through the hotel concierge.

Car rental At the airport *Avis*, T238-4056; *Budget*, T238-4068; *Dollar*, T238-4032; *Hertz*, T238-4081 and *National*, T238-4144.

Offices in El Cangrejo: *Avis*, Vía Venetto, T264-0722; *Barriga*, Edif Wonaga 1 B, Calle D, T269-0221; *Budget*, T263-9190; *Dollar*, T269-7542. *Gold*, C 55, T264-1711; *Hertz*, Hotel *Caesar Park*, T226-4077 ext 6202, C 50, T264-1111, El Cangrejo T263-6663; *International*, Vía Venetto, T264-4540.

Traffic system Several major downtown arteries become one-way during weekday rush hours, eg Av 4 Sur/C 50, one-way heading west 0600-0900, east 1600-1900. The Puente de las Américas can be used only to go into or out of town depending on time and day, mostly weekends; these directions are not always clearly signed.

Cycling *Almacén The Bike*, C 50 opposite Telemetro, good selection of cycle parts.

Long distance

Airport information T238-4160 or T238-4322

Air Tocumen International Airport (PTY), 27 km. Official taxi fare is US$25 to or from Panama City, maximum 2 passengers in same party, US$14 each sharing with one other, or US$10 per person if you share making it a *colectivo*. US$2 extra if you go by the toll road – much quicker. Bargaining is possible with regular cabs but not with the tourist taxis found at the airport. You might try leaving the terminal area and walk 300 m to the traffic circle where there is a bus shelter, safe but hot during the day. For about US$3 (should only be US$1.20) driver takes you by Panamá Viejo, just off the main airport road. Buses to airport are marked 'España-Tocumen', 1 hr, US$0.35, but if going at a busy time, eg in the morning rush hour, allow 1½-3 hrs. From airport to city, walk out of the terminal and across the main road to the bus shelter. There is a 24-hr left-luggage office near the *Budget* car rental desk for US$1 per article per day (worth it, since theft in the departure lounge is common). The official IPAT tourist office at the airport remains open to meet late flight arrivals. There are duty-free shops at the airport with a wide selection and good prices. Most facilities are found in upper level departure area (*Banco Nacional de Panamá*, *Cable & Wireless* office for international phone, fax and internet access); car rental is downstairs at Arrivals.

Airport information T226-1622

Domestic flights operate from Marcos A Gelabert airport at Albrook in the Canal Area. There is no convenient bus service, taxi US$1-2. Good self-service café especially for fried breakfast before early flight to San Blas. *Aeroperlas* (see Airline offices, below) operates daily flights to 17 destinations throughout the country (eg Colón US$36, David US$57, Bocas del

Toro US$50, Yaviza/El Real US$39, all fares one-way). *Mapiex Aéreo* and *Aviatur* also fly to several destinations throughout the country, and there are charter flights to many Darién outposts. Sample hourly rates for private hire: Twin Otter 20 passenger, US$630; Rodolfo Causadias of *Transpasa*, T226-0842 is an experienced pilot for photographic work.

Buses   Orange buses to all **Canal Area** destinations (Balboa, Miraflores, Paraíso, Kobbe, etc) leave from SACA terminal near Plaza 5 de Mayo; from the Plaza, walk past the National Assembly tower and turn left.

A new, air terminal-like bus terminal was built in 1999 in Albrook, near the domestic airport. All buses leave from here. Taxi US$2 to centre. Facilities at terminal include ATMs, internet access, clothes shops, luggage shops, bakeries and basic restaurants.

Unlike urban vehicles, most long-distance buses are fairly modern and in good condition, usually with a/c. Except for the longest routes, most are 24-seater 'Coaster'-type mini-buses. Check if a/c on next bus out is functioning.

Buses and routes, offices arranged in long line – from right to left in terminal: **Chitré (Los Santos)**, 20 per day, 0600-2300, 4½ hrs, US$6; **Tonosi (Los Santos)**, 0745 and 1300, 5½ hrs, US$8.50; **Macaracas (Los Santos)**, 0830, 1030, 1230, 1345, 1530 (Mon-Sat, no 1345 service on Sun), 5 hrs, US$7; **Las Tablas (Los Santos)**, 11 per day, 0600-1900, 5 hrs, US$6.50; **Calobre (Las Palmas)**, 0800, 0930, 1100, 1240, 1500, 1700, 4½ hrs, US$6; **Las Palmas**, 0830, 4½ hrs, US$8; **Cañaza (Las Palmas)**, 0845, 1045, 4½ hrs, US$7; **Santiago**, 21 per day, 0300-2400, 4 hrs, US$7, with *Expreso Veraguense* 16 per day, 0100-2300; **Ocú (via Las Minas)** 8 per day, 0700-1700, 5½ hrs, US$6; **Pesé (Las Minas)**, 4½ hrs US$6; **Yaviza**, 0415, 1400, 8-10 hrs, (delays possible during rainy season) US$14; **Agua Fría**, 7 per day, 0600-1530, US$7; **Colón**, many buses, less frequent at weekends, express buses leave every 20 mins, peak weekends book or be prepared to wait, 1½ hrs, US$2, pay on bus; **David** and on to **Frontera** (*Trans 5 Estrellas*) 1030, 1630, 1930, 1130, 6 hrs, US$10.60 (US$10 to David), and further down terminal – with Padafront – 11 per day, 0700-2400, US$12, express buses at 2300 and 2400 (US$17), also with Utranschiri US$10.60; **Cañita**, (*Utracasa*) 17 per day, 0640-1740, 2½ hrs, US$2.50; **San Carlos-Chamé**, 1½ hrs, US$2.50; **El Valle de Antón**, US$3.50; **Penonomé**, every 20 mins, 2½ hrs US$3.70; **El Copé** and **La Pintada**, (*Utracopa*) 0600-1800, 3½ hrs US$5; **Aguadulce**, (*Utasa*), many buses, 3 hrs, US$4.70; **Olá**, calling at Río Hato, daily at 1500, US$4.50.

International buses   Buses going north through Central America tend to get booked up so make sure you reserve a seat in advance and never later than the night before departure. *Ticabus*, with office on the first floor of the *Hotel Ideal*, C 17 Ote, T262-2084 or 262-6275, www.ticabus.com, run a/c buses to **San José**, daily at 1100, arriving at 0500, US$25 1-way (but check times and prices which change at regular intervals); continuing to **Managua**, US$40; **Tegucigalpa**, US$60, and on as far as **Tapachula** on the Mexico-Guatemala Pacific coast border, US$98, via **Guatemala City**, US$83 (4½ days, overnight in Managua and El Salvador, US$75), a/c rarely works. (Tickets are refundable; they pay on the same day, minus 15%.) *Panaline* to San José from *Hotel Internacional* in the Plaza 5 de Mayo leaves daily at 1300. The buses have a/c, TV/videos and drinks and are reported more comfortable than Ticabus, US$22. Whichever route you choose (international bus, Padafront Panama City-Paso Canaos then change to *Tracopa* for San José, or Panama City-David, David-frontier, then change to Costa Rican buses), it should be possible to go between the two capitals in under 24 hours. *Ticabus* and *Panaline* do not stop in David but take passengers at the border at 1800 and 1900 respectively.

Trains   Station on Carretera Gaillard. A luxury train now runs daily to Colón US$20 one way, US$35 return, 0700, returns 1730, 1¼ hrs. For information call *Aventuras 2000*, T227-2000, info@colon2000, who operate the service.

Directory

Aerolíneas Argentinas, Vía Brasil y Av Ramón Arias, T269-3815. *Aeroméxico*, Av 1B Nte, El Cangrejo, T263-3033. *Aeroperlas*, reservations T315-7500, airport T238-4767, F315-7580, www.aeroperlas.com *AeroPerú*, T269-6970. *Air France*, C Abel Bravo y 59 Obarrio T269-7381. *Alitalia*, T269-2161. *American Airlines*, C 50, Plaza New York, reservations T269-6022, airport T238-4615, F269-0830. *Avensa*, Calle MM

Airline offices
For airline international websites see page 34

Panama

Icaza, T264-9906, F263-9022, avensa@sinfo.net *Avianca*, T223-5225, F263-7797. *Aviatur*, airport T315-0311, F315-0316. *British Airways*, Centro Comercial Siglo XXI AV Ricardo J Alfaro, T236-8335, F236-8334. *Continental*, Av Balboa y Av 4, Ed No 17, T263-9177, F264-6778. *Copa*, Av Justo Arosemena y C 39, for reservations T227-6060, F227-1952, airport T238-4100. *Cubana*, Av Justo Arosamena, T227-2122, airport T238-4147. *El Al*, T264-8320. *Delta*, Edif World Trade Centre, C 53E, Marbella, T214-8118, at airport T238-4793. *Grupo Taca*, World Trade Center, T269-6066, gtaca@sinfo.net *Iberia*, Av Balboa y C 43, T227-2505, reservations T227-3966 F227-2070, ptyuu@iberia.es *KLM*, Av Balboa y C Uruguay, Edif Plaza Miramar, reservations T264-6395, F264-6358. *LAB*, C 50, Ed Bolivia, T263-6771, F263-6767. *LanChile*, Ed Aerogoldo, T226-0133, lanchile@sinfo.net *Lufthansa*, C Abel Bravo y 59 Obarrio, Ed Eurocentro, T269-1549, F263-8641, rlince@agenco.com *Mapiex Aéreo*, Hotel Riande Continental T223-0299, airport T315-0888, F315-0289. *Mexicana*, C Manuel María Icaza, T264-9855. *SAM*, C MM Icaza No 12, Edif Grobman, reservations T269-1222, airport T238-4096. *United Airlines*, World Trade Centre, T213-9824 F225-7525. *Varig*, C MM Icaza, T264-7666 for reservations, airport T238-4501, F263-8179.

Banks See also Money in Essentials. Panamanian banks' hours vary, but the core open hours are 0800-1500 Mon-Fri, 0800-1200 Sat. *Visa* T264-0988; *MasterCard* T263-5221; *Diners* T263-8195.

Try to avoid 15th and last working day of the month, paydays

   Algemene Bank Nederland changes *Thomas Cook* TCs. *American Express*, Agencia de Viajes Fidanque, C 50 y 59, T264-2444, Mon-Fri 0800-1715, does not exchange TCs, clients' mail only. International Service Center, T001800-111-0006. ATM for withdrawals at *Banco Continental* near hotel of same name. *Banistmo*, C 50, open Mon-Fri 0800-1530, Sat 0900-1200, changes TCs, no commission on AMEX, US$5 per transaction for other TCs. *Banco General* takes American Express, Bank of America and Thomas Cook TCs, 1 commission, min US£2 per transaction. Branch at Av Central y 4 Sur (Balboa) can be used for cash advances from ATMs on Visa. *Bank of America*, Av José de la Cruz Herrera, C 53 Este, no commission on own TCs, US$0.10 tax. You can buy AMEX TCs at *Banco Mercantil del Istmo* on Vía España (they also give cash advances on MasterCard). *Banco Sudameris* will also change Thomas Cook TCs. *Chase Manhattan Bank*, US$0.65 commission on each TC, Visa advances. *Citibank* has plenty of ATMs for cash withdrawals for its own debit or credit cardholders, also Visa cash advances. Deutschmarks exchanged at *Deutsch-Südamerikanische Bank*. *Lloyds Bank*, C Aquilino de la Guardia y C 48, Bella Vista, T263-6277, T263-8693 for foreign exchange, offers good rates for sterling (the only bank which will change sterling cash, and only if its sterling limit has not been exhausted).

   Possible to change South American currencies (poor rates) at *Panacambios*, ground floor, Plaza Regency, behind *Adam's Store*, Vía España, near the Banco Nacional de Panamá and opposite *Hotel Riande Continental* (it also has postage stamps for collectors).

Communi-cations **Internet** Plushest is *Internet Café*, C 76 y Av 5 B Sur, diagonally opposite *Hotel Caesar Park*, San Francisco, T270-1052, cruiser@inter-cafe.com, open Tue-Sat 1130-2300, Sun 1300-2300, 12 stations US$3/hr until 1700, then US$4 (US$10 monthly rate), food and bar. More central is *PC Mall*, C Eusebio A Morales, 2 doors west of Vía Venetto, El Cangrejo, T269-1919, pcmall@cwpanama.net, Mon-Fri 0730-1800, Sat 0900-1500, 15 stations US$1.50/hr, light food, no bar; in Los Tucanos Shopping Center, Blvd El Dorado. *Internet*, Av Perejil west of C 43, Edif Marlynsa, 1st floor, Oficina 6, opposite Antiguo Palacio del Millón, T214-6644, open Mon-Sat 0900-2100, US$1.75/hr.

Post There is no home postal delivery service in Panama. Recipients either have a post office box (*apartado*), or receive mail via General Delivery/Poste Restante (*Entrega General*). The new main post office is close to Casco Viejo at the west end of Av Balboa at Av B, opposite the Mercado de Mariscos, open Mon-Fri 0700-1745, Sat 0700-1645; 'Poste Restante' items are held for a month. Official name and zone must be included in the address: **Main Post office**: 'Zona 1, Central, Av Balboa opposite Mercado de Mariscos'; **C 30 East/Av Balboa**: 'Zona 5, La Exposición'; **El Dorado Shopping Centre**, Tumba Muerto: 'Zona 6A, El Dorado'; **Vía España, Bella Vista** (in front of Piex store): 'Zona 7, Bella Vista'. Parcels sent 'poste restante' are delivered either to **Encomiendas Postales Transístmicas** at the El Dorado Centro Comercial or the main post office if there is no duty to pay on the goods. The post office operates a courier system called *EMS* to most Central and South American countries, Europe, US and some Asian countries. Packages up to 20 kg: 2 to 3 days to USA (500 g documents to Miami US$13); 3 to 4 days Europe US$20; Asia US$25. Also private courier services, eg *UPS*, Edif Fina, C 49, El Cangrejo, ½ kg to London or Paris, 3-4 days, US$30; *Jet Express (Federal Express)*, Edif Helga, Vía España y Av 4 Sur/C 50, ½ kg to Miami, 2 days, US$19. Panama issues highly regarded stamps; foreigners may open a 'philatelic account' and order stamps, 1st-day covers, commemorative issues, etc, provided a minimum US$20 in account: Dirección de Filatelia, Dirección de Correos y Telégrafos, Apdo 3421, Panama 1 (Vía España, Calidonia, opposite Don Bosco Church).

Panama

Telephone *Cable & Wireless* has its main office in Vía España, on the ground floor of *Banco Nacional* building. It offers excellent but expensive international telephone, telex, fax and modem (use Bell 212A type) facilities. Collect calls to 21 countries, dial T106. For cost of phone cards and international calls, see Essentials, page 1155. Local calls in Panama City, US$0.10 for 3 mins, US$0.05 for each additional min; anywhere else in the country, US$0.15 per min.

Alianza Francesa, C 49, Bellavista, T264-2737, film each Wed at 2000. **Cultural centres**

Canada, World Trade Centre, Galeria comecial, piso 1, Marbella, T264-9731, open 0830-1300. *Chile*, Vía **Embassies &** España, Edif Banco de Boston, T223-9748, 0900-1200, 1400-1600. *Colombia*, MM Icaza 12, Edif **consulates** Grobman, 6th floor, T264-9266, 0800-1300. *Costa Rica*, Av Samuel Lewis, T264-2980, open 0830-1330. *Cuba*, consular services at Av Cuba y Ecuador, frente a Parque Porras, T227-5277 *Denmark*, Vía Cincuentario 28, T270-0944, open 0800-1200, 1330-1630. *Ecuador*, Edif Grobman, 3rd floor, T264-7820, open 0830-1300. *El Salvador*, Av Manuel Espinoza Batista, Edif Metropolis 4A, T223-3020, open 0900-1300. *Germany*, Edif Bank of America, C 50 y 53, T263-7733, 0900-1700. *Guatemala*, Edif Altamira, 9th floor, 9-25, Vía Argentina, T269-3406, F223-1922, 0800-1300. *Honduras*, Av Justo Arosemena y C 31, Edif Tapia, 2nd floor, T225-8200, 0900-1400. *Israel*, Edif Grobman, C MM Icaza, 5th floor, PO Box 6357, T264-8022. *Italy*, Av Bal boa Edif Banco Exterior, T225-8948, open 0900-1200. *Japan*, C 50 y 60, Edif Don Camilo, Urb Obarrio, T263-6155, open 0830-1200, 1400-1700. *Mexico*, Edif Credicorp, C 50, T210-1523, open 0800-1200. *Netherlands*, Altos de Algemene Bank, C MM Icaza, 4, T264-7257 open 0830-1300, 1400-1630. *Nicaragua*, Av Manuel E Batista, T269-6721, open 0900-1300, 1500-1800. *Norway*, Edif Comasa, 5th floor, Av Samuel Lewis, T263-1955, 0900-1230, 1430-1630. *Spain*, Plaza Porras, entre Av Cuba y Av Perú, C 33A, T227-5122, 0900-1300. *Sweden*, consulate at Av Balboa y C Uruguay, T264-3748, 0900-1200, 1400-1600. *Switzerland*, Av Samuel Lewis y C Gerardo Ortega, Edif Banco Central Cancellería, 4th floor, T264-9731, PO Box 499 (Zona 9A), open 0845-1145. *UK*, Torre Swiss Bank, C 53, Zona 1, T269-0866, F223-0730, Apdo 889, 0800-1300. *USA*, Av Balboa y 40, Edif Macondo, 3rd floor, T227-1777, F227-1964, 0800-1700. Consulate in new Miramar building, C 39, y Av Balboa, ground floor (hotel and restaurant in same building). *Venezuela*, Edif Hong Kong Bank, 5th floor, Av Samuel Lewis, T264-2524, 0830-1100.

Lavamático Lavarápido, C 7 Central No 7-45, ½ block from Plaza Catedral, Mon-Sat 0800-2000, Sun **Laundry** 0900-1400, US$0.75 with hot water, US$0.60 cold, soap and drying extra. Many around Plaza Catedral; wash and dry US$2.

ILERI, 42G Vía La Amistad, Altos del Chase, El Dorado T/F 260-4424, small school in suburban house. **Language** US$10/hr one-to-one tuition. **Schools**

Dentist: *Balboa Dental Clinic*, El Prado, Balboa, T228-0338, good, fair price. Dr Daniel Wong, *Clínica* **Medical** *Dental Marbella*, Edif Alfil (ground floor), near Centro Comercial Marbella, T263-8998. Dr D Lindo, **services** T223-8383, very good but fix price before treatment. Hospitals: the *US Gorgas Army Community Hospital* has closed and US medical facilities have moved to the Howard Air Force Base, across the Puente de Las Américas. Private clinics charge high prices; normally visitors are treated at either the *Clínica San Fernando*, T229-2004, or the *Clínica Paitilla*, T269-6060, which both have hospital annexes. For inoculations buy vaccine at a chemist, who will recommend a clinic; plenty in La Exposición around Parque Belisario Porras.

Services in English at *Baha'i Temple*, Mile 8 on Transístmica Highway (Ojo de Agua district), Baha'i HQ **Places of** for all of Latin America, modern, white domed, worth seeing for its architecture (open daily 1000-1800, **worship** Sun service 1000). *Baptist*, C Balboa 914, La Boca, Sun 1100 and 1900. *Kol Shearith Israel Synagogue*, Av Cuba y C 36, services Fri 2000, Sat 1100. *Methodist*, Av Central y C 16 Este, Sun 0900. *St John's Episcopalian*, Av 12 de Octubre y La Paz, Betania, Sun 0700.

Airemar, C 52 y Ricardo Arias 21, T223-5395, F264-2316, airemar@pty.com Highly recommended for **Tour** flights to South American destinations. *Ancon Expeditions*, Calle Elvira Méndez, next to *Marriott Hotel*, **operators** T269-9415, F264-3713, www.anconexpeditions.com, this is the tour operator for the environmental agency ANCON (see under Useful Addresses). *Arco Iris*, Av Justo Arosemena y C 45, Bella Vista, Edif Dollar, T227-3318, F227-3386, for full range of local tours. *Cinco Continentes*, Av Principal La Alameda, Edif Plaza San Marcos, T260-8447, F260-8414, helpful with shipping a car. Recommended. *Continental SA*, Av 7 y

Panama

Vía España, T263-5531, in *Riande Continental* building, friendly, good. *EcoCircuitos and Margo Tours*, next to *Las Tinajas* restaurant, T264-8888, F264-5355, www.ecocircuitos.com, specializes in ecotourism for small groups with emphasis on using local guides, can book various lodges and excursions. *Extreme Tours*, Altos del Bosque Calle del Laurel, No 47-E, T/F230-6835, http://adventurepanama.tripod.com Specialist in hiking, rock climbing, very knowledgeable about Darién and the old colonial roads, very active on looking for new opportunities. Good store of equipment with the unusual option of naturist hiking if the mood takes you and weather suits. *Marsal*, C Eusebio y Av Morales, Edif IBC, PB, T223-5321, F 263-5604, marsal@pan.gbm.net, helpful, efficient, English spoken. *Panama Jones*, C Ricardo Arias, Edif Zart, near *Hotel Continental* T265-4551, F265-4553, www.panamacanal.com English spoken, specialists in adventure tourism. *Panamá SA*, C 52 y Av Federico Boyd, Edif Costa del Sol, T223-0644, T223-0619, viajepma@sinfo.net English spoken. *Pesantez Tours*, Plaza Balboa, oficina 2, Punta Paitilla, T263-7577 F263-7860, www.pesantez-tours.com *Rapid Travel*, C 53, El Cangrejo, Edif Las Margaritas, T264-6638, F264-6371. *Riande*, east side of *Hotel Riande Continental*, C Ricardo Arias, T263-5143, T269-4569, English spoken, very helpful. *Shirley Tours*, between the *Marriott* and *Continental* hotels on C Ricardo Arias, T613-8223, F434-0428, www.panamacanal2000.com Broad range of activities including hiking and trekking the Camino Real, good for ecotourism options. *Sun Line Tours*, C Eusebio A Morales, Edif Estela, local 2, El Cangrejo, Apdo Postal 2323, Zona 9A, Panama, T269-6620/263-8451, T223-7609, for Panama Canal Transits (US$99, recommended) and trips to Contadora. *Tropic Tours*, C 53, El Cangrejo, Edif Las Margaritas PB, T269-3147, F263-4626 well-organized trips, multilingual. For *Chadwick's* and *Starlite* in Balboa, see page 1181.

Useful addresses

Conservation: Asociación Nacional de Conservación de la Naturaleza (ANCON), C Amela Dennis de Icaza, Ancón Hill, past Panama's Supreme Court, in former Quarry Heights, Casa 153, T314-0060, F314-0061, www.ancon.org, for comprehensive information on the country's natural attractions and environmental matters. They also run a chain of lodges throughout the country eg in Darién and Bocas. **Customs:** for renewal of permits and obtaining exit papers for vehicles at Paitilla airport. **Immigration:** Migración y Naturalización, Av Cuba (2 Sur) y C 29, T225-8925; visa extensions and exit permits issued Mon-Fri 0800-1530. **Ministerio de Hacienda y Tesoro:** Av Perú/C 36, T227-4879, for tax compliance certificate (*paz y salvo*) required for exit visa (*permiso de salida*) if you stay more than 30 days.

Excursions from Panama City

Panamá Viejo

A recommended short trip is to the ruins of Panamá Viejo, 6½ km northeast along the coast. A wander among the ruins still gives an idea of the site's former glory, although many of the structures have been worn by time, fungus and the sea. The narrow **King's Bridge** (1620) at the north end of the town's limits is a good starting point; it marked the beginning of the three trails across the isthmus and took seven years to build. Walking south brings the visitor to **Convento de San José**, where the Golden Altar originally stood (see page 1161); it was spared by the great fire that swept the town during Morgan's attack (which side started the fire is still debated). Several blocks further south is the main Plaza, where the square stone tower of the **cathedral** (1535-1580) is a prominent feature. In the immediate vicinity are the Cabildo, with imposing arches and columns, the remnants of **Convento de Santo Domingo**, the **Bishop's Residence**, and the **Slave Market** (or House of the Genovese), whose gaol-like structure was the hub of the American slave trade. There were about 4,000 African slaves in 1610, valued at about 300 pesos apiece. Beyond the plazas to the south, on a rocky eminence overlooking the bay, stand the **Royal Houses**, the administrative stronghold including the **Quartermaster's House**, the **Court** and **Chancellery**, the **Real Audiencia** and the **Governor's Residence**.

Further west along the Pacific strand are the dungeons, kitchens and meat market (now almost obliterated by the sea); a store and refreshment stands cluster here on the south side of the plaza, and handicrafts from the Darién are sold along the beach. Across Calle de la Carrera stands another great complex of religious convents: **La Concepción** (1598) and the **Compañía de Jesús** (1621). These too were outside the area destroyed by the 1671 fire but are today little more than rubble. Only a wall remains of the Franciscan **Hospital de San Juan de Dios**, once a huge structure encompassing wards, courtyards and a church. Another block west can be seen part of the **Convento de San Francisco** and its gardens, facing the rocky beach. About 100 m west is the beautiful **Convento de La Merced**, where Pizarro, Almagro and their men attended Mass on the morning they sailed on their final and momentous expedition to Perú. Decades later Morgan stored his plunder here until it could be counted, divided up and sent back to the Atlantic side. At the western limit of Panamá Viejo stands **La Navidad Fort** (1658). Its purpose was merely to defend the **Matadero (Slaughterhouse) Bridge** across the Río Agarroba but its 50-man garrison and half-dozen cannon were no match for the determined force of privateers; it is also known as Morgan's Bridge because it was here that the attack began.

The whole area (unfenced) is attractively landscaped, with plenty of benches to rest on, and floodlit at night. Late afternoon when the sun is low is an especially nice time to visit, although at least two hours should be allowed to appreciate the site fully. The main ruins are patrolled by police and reasonably safe. Take care, though, between the King's Bridge and the ruins; if arriving at this north entrance by taxi, it is prudent to pause at the bridge then continue in the taxi the 1 km to San José, where the main ruins begin. **Dame Margot Fonteyn**, the ballerina, is buried alongside her husband Roberto Arías Guardia in the Jardín de la Paz cemetery behind Panamá Viejo. IPAT has a handicrafts store (*Artesanía Nacional*) at the ruins, although prices are rather expensive. It also organizes free folklore events and local dance displays on Saturdays in the dry season (*verano*), which are worth seeing. The tourist office in Panama City (T226-7000) has a list of programmes and can supply professional guides if required.

■ *Free. Getting there: taxi from the city centre, US$1.80; buses from Vía España or Avenida Balboa, US$0.20. Panamá Viejo also makes a good excursion for passengers with a little time to kill at nearby Tocumen Airport; taxis can be as much as US$5 but still reasonable, especially if this is the only chance you'll have to see Panamá. Alternatively, take any bus marked Vía España, get off at Vía Cincuentenario, then take a bus to Panamá Viejo, total cost US$0.45.*

By the ruins is **Museo de Panamá Viejo**, Vía Cincuentenario, T224-2155, F224-2157, www.panamaviejo.org ■ *Mon-Sun 0900-1700, US$2.*

Panamá Viejo

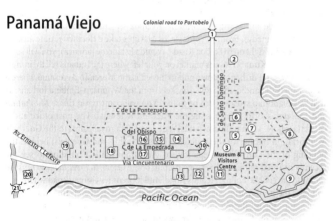

1 King's Bridge	9 Royal Houses	17 Hospital de San Juan de Dios
2 Convento de San José	10 Emperor's Bridge	18 Convento de San Francisco
3 Main Plaza	11 Dungeons	19 Convento de la Merced
4 Cathedral	12 Kitchens	20 La Navidad Fort
5 Cabildo	13 Meat Market	21 Matadero/
6 Convento de Santo Domingo	14 Convento de Compañía	Slaughterhouse Bridge
7 Bishop's Residence	de Jesús	
8 Slave's House/	15 Convento La Concepción	
House of the Genovese	16 Church of La Concepción	

Panama

Henry Morgan and the sack of 'Golden Panama'

Panamá Viejo, 6½ km east of the modern capital, was the original site of Panama City, founded by Pedro Arias de Avila (often called 'Pedrarias') on 15 August 1519, recognized as a town two years later and granted a coat of arms. It was initially a storage point for Peruvian gold until it could be loaded onto mules and transported across the Isthmus, initially to Venta de Cruces and Fort San Lorenzo, later along the Camino Real to Nombre de Dios and Portobelo for shipment to Spain.

The town became the centre of the New World; gold mines in Veraguas and Darién contributed two tons of gold a year, and many expeditions to North, Central and South America were launched from here. By 1570 a quarter of its 500 residents were extremely wealthy, and the town could boast a grand cathedral, a dozen religious institutions, a hospital, lavish public buildings, huge warehouses and a thriving slave market.

No enemy had ever penetrated as far as 'Golden Panama', not even Francis Drake, so the shock was all the greater when Henry Morgan and 1,200 men fell upon the town on 28 January 1671. After a gruelling nine-day overland trek from San Lorenzo the city was captured following a three-hour battle. They took 600 prisoners ransom, looted for three weeks and took away a fortune in gold, silver and precious stones valued at £70,000, requiring 195 mules to transport it back to the Caribbean.

With this new-found wealth Morgan bought respectability: he was knighted and appointed Governor of Jamaica, where he died in 1688. After the attack, the population of Panamá Viejo was transferred to the present-day Casco Viejo section of Panama City, which was enclosed by walls and could be defended on both landward and seaward sides.

Ancón

Take care on Ancón Hill, robberies sometimes occur

Ancón curves round the hill of the same name north and east and merges into Panama City. It has picturesque views of the palm-fringed shore. The name has also been applied to the district, including the village of Balboa, created when the area reverted to Panama.

The following walk takes in the sights of Ancón. Walk to the top of the hill in the morning for views of the city, Balboa and the Canal (toilets and water fountain at the top – you may have to climb part of the radio tower to see anything); the entrance is on Avenida de los Mártires (formerly Avenida de Julio and briefly Avenida Presidente Kennedy). From Avenida de los Mártires take a clockwise route around the hill, bearing right on to Balboa Road (Avenida Estado de Jamaica), you will soon come upon the **Kuna Artesans** market on your left where the Indians sell their multicolored *molas*. Further on down and to the left is the **Mercado Artesanal** where a wider variety of handicrafts, woven baskets from the Wounaan-Embera Indians, as well as Ecuadorian sweaters can be found. You will come upon *Chase Manhattan* and *Citibank* shortly after passing the Mercado Artesanal. The post office and a cafetería follow. Then walk down the Prado lined with royal palms to the **Goethals Memorial**, in honour of the engineer George Washington Goethals, behind the building of the Canal. The steps lead to the administration building to see the recently restored murals of the Construction of the Canal. ■ *Free. Identity must be shown to the guards.* Follow Heights Road until it becomes Gorgas Road where you will pass the headquarters of the Smithsonian Tropical Research Institute (where applications to visit Barro Colorado Island are made). A little further, among trees and flowers, is the former **Gorgas Army Community Hospital**. Named after William Crawford Gorgas, the physician who is credited with clearing the Canal Zone of the more malignant tropical diseases before construction began in the beginning of the 20th century. Gorgas Road leads back to Avenida de los Mártires, but look out for the sign to the **Museo de Arte Contemporáneo**, on Avenida de los Mártires, T262-8012, F262-3376. The entrance is on Avenida San Blas in a former Masonic Lodge (1936). The permanent exhibition of national and international modern paintings and sculptures has special exhibitions from time to time, with marquetry, silkscreen and engraving workshops, library of contemporary visual art open to students, entry free but donations welcomed (privately owned). ■ *Mon-Fri 0900-1600, Sat 0900-1200.* Next door is the **Smithsonian Tropical Research Institute**, opposite Plaza 5 de Mayo with the English language scientific research library in Panama open to the public. ■ *Mon-Fri 0900-1700, Sat 0900-1200, T212-8113, F212-8147, changyau@tivoli.si.edu café/bookshop selling English-language environmental books and nature guides, including national park maps, Mon-Fri 1000-0430.*

At the foot of Ancón Hill the **Instituto Nacional** stands on the four-lane Avenida de los Mártires.

Balboa
Colour map 8, grid B1

The town and docks of Balboa are just over 3 km west of Panama City, some 10 minutes by taxi, and stand attractively between the Canal quays and Ancón Hill. It has been described as efficient, planned and sterilized – a typical American answer to the wilfulness and riot of the tropics.

The Canal administration building (with fine murals on the ground floor) and a few other official residences are on Balboa Heights. At the foot of the Heights is the town of Balboa, with a small park, a reflecting pool and marble shaft commemorating Goethals, as well as a long palm-flanked parkway known as the Prado. At its eastern end is a theatre, a service centre building, post office and bank. Farther along Balboa Road is a large YMCA (no lodging).

Directory Banks *Chase Manhattan Bank* and *Citibank.* **Communications** Post office: Av Balboa and El Prado. Telephone: *Cable & Wireless*; *Tropical Radio & Telegraph Co* public telex booth. **Tour operators** *Argo Tours*, 808 Balboa Road, Ancón, T228-4348, F228-1234, www.big-ditch.com, with several options for trips down the Canal. A half-day transit US$90 (children US$45), full-day US$135 (children US$55), departures every 2nd Sat from Balboa, Pier 18 at 0730. *Chadwick's*, in YMCA building, T228-6244, F228-1409. *Starlite Travel*, in former Balboa railway station opposite Canal Administration building, T232-6401, F232-6448, www.starlitepanama.com, excellent, English spoken.

Fuerte Amador

Before the Puente de las Américas crosses the Panama Canal is a long peninsula into the Pacific on which is Fuerte Amador, formerly the HQ of the Panamanian Defence Force, seized by US forces in 1989 and returned to Panama in 1994. Beyond Fuerte Amador are the formerly fortified islands of Naos, Perico and Flamenco, linked by the 4-km causeway (**Calzada Amador**) built of rubble excavated from the Canal. A tourist complex was under construction here in mid-1999. To cross the causeway costs US$0.25. There are many interesting buildings in this area bearing the marks of the conflict, and some attractive lawns and parkland. The Calzada is used by joggers and cyclists (bikes for hire at the causeway entrance, US$1.50-2 per hour). It has fine views of the Puente de las Américas and the ships lined up to enter the Canal. *Mi Ranchito*, T228-4909, the charming, simple, outdoor restaurant at the far end of the Calzada, is highly recommended in the evening for seeing the skyline and passing ships, as well as good, cheap traditional food and drink. There are small charges for entry and for swimming at Solidaridad beach on **Naos** (crowded at weekends and the water is polluted – not recommended). Here there is a small marine park with local marine life on show. At Punta Culebra on Naos is the new **Marine Exhibition Center** of the Smithsonian Tropical Research Institute, interesting aquaria and exhibitions on marine fauna. ■ *Tue-Fri 1300-1700, Sat-Sun 1000-1700, T227-6022 ext 2366. US$0.50.* There are two small restaurants on the next island, **Perico**, and the promise (with luck) of a cold beer. **Flamenco**, the last of the islands, is headquarters for the National Maritime Service and is closed to the public. The causeway and islands have been declared a 'tourism zone'.

Panama

Taboga Island
All items are expensive on the island; bring cash as there is no bank

There is a launch service to Taboga Island, about 20 km offshore. The island is a favourite year-round resort, and produces lip-slurping pineapples and mangoes, and has one of the oldest churches in the Western hemisphere. Admission to beach at *Hotel Taboga* , US$10, redeemable in tokens to buy food and drink, good swimming, covered picnic huts extra. There are other good places to swim around the island, but its south side is rocky and sharks visit regularly.

The trip out to Taboga is very interesting, passing the naval installations at the Pacific end of the Canal, the great bridge linking the Americas, tuna boats and shrimp fishers in for supplies, visiting yachts from all over the world at what remains of the Balboa Yacht Club, and the Calzada Amador. Part of the route follows the channel of the Canal, with its busy traffic. Taboga itself, with a promontory rising to 488 m, is carpeted with flowers at certain times of year. There are few cars in the meandering, helter-skelter streets, and just one footpath as a road.

The first Spanish settlement on the island was in 1515, two years after Balboa's discovery of the Pacific. It was from here that Pizarro set out for Peru in 1524. For two centuries it was a stronghold of the pirates who preyed on the traffic to Panama. With deep-water and sheltered anchorage, it was used in colonial times as the terminal point for ships coming up the west coast of South America. **El Morro**, at low tide joined to Taboga, is at high tide an island; it was once owned by the Pacific Steam Navigation Company, whose ships sailed from there. For a fine view, walk through the town and up to the top of **Cerro Turco**, the hill with a cross at the summit (285 m), to the right of the radar station (there is a short cut, ask locals). When surveying the view, don't miss the pelican rookery on the back side of the island. Further south is **Cerro Vigía** (307 m), the highest point, a two-hour hike from the central plaza; wear strong shoes or boots and take mosquito repellent. Another trail runs west along the north coast, about one hour, where there are pleasant beaches. The southern coast of Taboga and all of neighbouring **Isla Uraba** are wildlife reserves; you will need a permit from ANAM, whose office is near *Hotel Taboga*.

Sleeping A *Taboga*, T264-1748, F223-5739, htaboga@sinfo.net. Apdo 550357, Paitilla, Panamá, 300 m east of wharf. A/c, TV, restaurant, café, pool, beach, tropical birds. **C** *Chu*, on main street, 200 m left of wharf, T250-2036. Wooden colonial style, thin walls, shared bath, beautiful views, own beach, terrace restaurant serving traditional fish and chicken dishes. You may be able to find locals to stay with, ask around. *Hotel California* has a good restaurant and bar.

Transport Boats Taboga is reached in 1-1½ hrs from Pier 17-18 in Balboa (check the times in advance – office T228-4348, or pier T232-5395); taxi Bella Vista – Pier 18, US$3-4 per person. There are 2 boats daily during the week (0830 and 1500 or 1700 Thu) and 3 boats on Sat, Sun and holidays (0830, 1130 and 1600). Return boats at 1000 and 1630 or 1830 – Thu; 1000, 1430 and 1700 at weekends. From Nov to Jan there are 3 boats daily. Return fare US$7. You can charter a boat for US$120 per day including fishing. Ask at the Balboa Yacht Club office.

Pearl Islands
Colour map 8, grid B2

A longer trip, 75 km southwest by launch, takes you to the Pearl Islands, visited mostly by sea anglers for the Pacific mackerel, red snapper, corvina, sailfish, marlin and the other species which abound in the waters around. High mountains rise from the sea, and there is a little fishing village on a shelf of land at the water's edge. There was much pearl fishing in colonial days. **Contadora**, one of the smallest Pearl Islands (three-hour boat trip), has become quite famous since its name became associated with a Central American peace initiative. It was also where the Shah of Iran was exiled, in a house called Puntalara, after the Iranian Revolution. Contadora is popular with Canadian, Spanish and Italian holidaymakers and is becoming crowded, built up and consequently is not as peaceful as it once was. Lack of drinking water is now harming the tourist development. There are beautiful beaches with crystal-clear water, good skin-diving and sailing, and lots of sharks.

Sleeping L *Contadora Resort*, T250-4033, F250-4000, in Panama City, T227-2335, F227-2328. Same ownership as *El Panamá*, very luxurious chalet complex, nice location on beach, but reported run down. **Eating** at *Gallo Nero*, run by German couple, Gerald and Sabine, restaurant with good seafood especially lobster, pizza and pasta, by runway, reasonable prices. *Michael's*, opposite *Gallo Nero*, good pizzas, ice-cream. *Fonda Sagitario*, nearby, café, cheap; also a supermarket and a duty-free shop.

Transport Air Return air ticket to **Contadora** from Paitilla, US$54 by *Aeroperlas*, T250-4026, (extra flights at weekends, 15 mins, crowded). **Mountain bike** hire US$5 per hr, by entrance to *Caesar Park*.

Directory Tour operators Day trip to Contadora on Sun, US$50 per person includes food and drinks. 3-day package tour, US$150 for 2. Recommended. *Argonaut Steamship Agency*, C 55 No 7-82, Panama City, T264-3459, runs launch cruises.

About 40 km north east of Panama City is Cerro Azul, a cooler highland area on the **Cerro Azul**
western limits of Parque Nacional Chagres. At 850 m, the area has been developed as a weekend cottage resort. It is best visited by private car.

Sleeping A *Hostal Casa de Campo*, T270-0018, F226-0363, www.panamacasadecampo.com Formerly private, now Panamanian-owned family residence, all rooms with bath, hot water, pool. Can provide many different activities and ways of relaxing. Recommended. **B** *Mesón Tía Toya*, at El Castillo, T232-5806. Friendly country restaurant with nice porch for dining, also has good cottages for daily rental.

The Canal, Colón and the San Blas Islands

Panama City

Whether travelling through the Canal, or just standing at its side, watching the vast ocean-going vessels rise and fall as they pass through the huge canal locks is a spectacular sight. In the middle of Lago Gatún is Parque Nacional Isla Barro Colorado, a popular destination for nature lovers and bird-watchers. From the chaotic free port of Colón, the Caribbean coast spreads out to the east, where the San Blas Islands are a cultural treasure waiting to be explored, and to the west, where the region's history of trade and commerce comes alive.

Panama

The Canal

The Panama Canal was created from the artificial, river-fed Lago Gatún, 26 m above sea-level which supplies the water for the lock-system to function. Ships sail across the lake after having been raised from sea-level by a series of locks on either the Atlantic or the Pacific approach. They are then lowered by the locks on the opposite side. As the crow flies, the distance across the isthmus is 55 km. From shore to shore the Canal is 67½ km, or 82 km (44.08 nautical miles) from deep water to deep water. It has been widened to 150 m in most places. The trip normally takes eight or nine hours for the 30 to 40 ships passing through each day. On the Atlantic side there is a normal variation of 30 cm between high and low tides, and on the Pacific of about 380 cm, rising sometimes to 640 cm. Everything that crosses the Canal pays by weight, although there are plans to introduce a flat fee. The record for the smallest sum is held by Richard Halliburton, who swam from ocean to ocean between 14 and 23 August 1928, paying US$0.36 for his 150 lbs.

Balboa Yacht Club has a noticeboard with cheap crewing trips – although preferred, no experience is necessary, but you may have to wait a while

From the Pacific, the Canal channel goes beneath the Puente de las Américas and passes the port of Balboa. The waterway has to rise 16½ m to Lago Miraflores. The first stage of the process is the Miraflores Locks, 1½ km before the lake. A taxi to the locks from the city costs US$10. At the far end of the lake, ships are raised another 9½ m by the single-step Pedro Miguel Locks, after which the 13 km Gaillard, or Culebra Cut is entered, a narrow rock defile leading to Lago Gatún. Opposite Miraflores Locks, there is a swing bridge. Gaillard Cut can be seen from Contractor's Hill, on the west side, reached by car (no buses) by turning right 3 km past Puente de las Américas, passing Cocolí, then turning as signed. The road beyond Cocolí goes on to Posa, where there are good views of the locks, the cut and former Canal Zone buildings.

On the eastern side of the canal, 2 km after Miraflores Lock, is the entrance to the **Parque Nacional Camino de Cruces** which has several designated hiking trails including the Camino de Cruces colonial gold route which continues through Parque Nacional Soberanía (see below) as far as the Chagres River.

Barro Colorado

For 37 km the Canal passes through Lago Gatún. Enough water must be accumulated in the reservoir during the rainy season to operate the locks throughout the 3-4 month dry season, since a single ship's transit can use up to 50 million gallons. (A high level reservoir, Lago Alajuela, formerly Madden Lake, feeds the lake and maintains its level; see below.) In the lake is Barro Colorado Island, to which animals fled as the basin slowly filled. It is a formally protected area called the **Barro Colorado Nature Monument** and has been a site of scientific research for over 70 years. The excursion is highly recommended for seeing wildlife, especially monkeys, and includes a walk around a guided trail with over 50 points of interest.

Panama Canal

Tours

Visitors without permits will be turned away on arrival

Daily trips can be arranged with the *Smithsonian Institute* at the Tupper Building in Ancón, US$40, T212-8026, F212-8148, visitstri@tivoli.si.edu Trips last 4-6 hrs, including boat, audio-visual display and lunch, but take water. Take a Gamboa Summit bus from next to Plaza 5 de Mayo (0600 and 0615) to the Dredging Division dock at Gamboa (US$0.65), from where the boat leaves. Make arrangements with the Institute in Ancón. Tours don't go Mon or Thu, max of 12 people Tue and Wed, 15 on Fri, 25-30 Sat and Sun – book in advance as tours often booked up well in advance, especially at weekends. Individuals may find it easier to join a tour party. For longer stays, write to the Director, Smithsonian Tropical Research Institute, Box 2072, Balboa, Panamá, www.stri.org Barro Colorado island is only seen from the water, but tourists walk a nature trail on the Gigante Peninsula, which is also part of the national park.

Gatún Locks

Continuing north, or 10 km southwest of Colón are the Gatún Locks (*Esclusas de Gatún*) with their neat, attendant town. The observation point here (open 1000-1630) is perhaps the best spot in the Canal Area for photographing the

Linehandling the Panama Canal

The best way to see the Panama Canal is by boat. If you don't have your own, it is possible to sail through as a linehandler on a yacht. Each yacht is required to have four on-board linehandlers plus the helmsman for what is normally a two-day journey. While many Panamanians work full-time as linehandlers, people with experience, or at least a modicum of common sense, may be able to get a position as a linehander and work their way through. One experienced captain in Costa Rica said the task is not difficult, but you do have to work when it is time to work – so don't expect to sunbathe all the way through.

The benefit is that while getting to see the canal from the inside the yacht's owners are required to feed linehandlers three meals a day and, if the journey takes more than one day – and for most yachts transit requires two days – accommodation.

If you are interested, go to the Panama Canal Yacht Club in Colón on the Caribbean side, or the Balboa Yacht Club on the Pacific side. The rickety old Balboa club building was burnt down in mysterious circumstances in 1999, but there is still an office above the fuel dock where linehandlers meet. Ask in the club or office for the best person to speak to. Don't expect to just turn up and get a job. Private yacht transits are seasonal and there may be competition for linehandling positions. Transit obviously has its risks, and no yacht owner will put their vessel at risk when they can use professional and experienced Panamanians. But nevertheless, with all these caveats, it is still the best way to see the canal.

passage of ships. The most magnificent of the Canal's locks, Gatún integrates all three lock 'steps' on the Atlantic side, raising or lowering ships to or from 26 m in one operation. The flights are in duplicate to allow ships to pass in opposite directions simultaneously. Passage of the locks takes about one hour.

After crossing the lock, the road forks with the left-hand branch bridging the Chagres River just downstream from the graceful Gatún Dam – the largest earth dam in the world when it was built in 1906. Opposite the power plant is the *Tarpon Club* (T443-5316), a fishing club which has a very nice restaurant, disco and bar. A short distance further south is an attractive lakeside picnic area and small boat-launching area. The partly paved road goes on down the lake to Escobal and Cuipo through lovely scenery (good birding). There are no hotels in Cuipo but plenty of buses to/from Colón (US$1.60, two hours, US$0.25 to the locks). Bus from Colón to Gatún Locks US$0.75.

Most people are surprised by the stunning beauty of the scenery around the Canal, **Canal tours** and it is also interesting to see the mechanics of the passage. Since the Panama City-Colón train is not running (except to Summit on Sunday, US$2 return), travellers should take a bus to the **Miraflores Locks** to see shipping. Try to find out when large boats, particularly cruise liners, are in transit. The viewing gallery and a brochure are free. A detailed model of the canal, formerly in the Department of Transport at Ancón, has been moved here and there is also a free eight-minute slide show given throughout the day, with explanations in Spanish and English. ■ *Open 0900-1700, best between 0900-1000 for photos and 1430-1800 for viewing only. Commentaries in English and Spanish begin every 15-20 mins.*

About 250 m past the entrance to the locks is a road (left) to the filtration plant and observatory, behind which is a picnic area and viewing point.

Transport Orange bus from Panama City to Miraflores Locks leaves from the bus station next to Plaza 5 de Mayo (direction Paraíso), 20 mins, US$0.35. Ask driver to let you off at the stop for 'Esclusas de Miraflores', from where it's a 10-min walk to the locks. Taxi to the locks, US$10 per hr. Another good way to see the Panama Canal area is to rent a car, or, if you have done well at the casinos, by air: *Aerotours*, T262-8710, fly Piper J3 Cub trips, 30 mins US$60 per person, full coast to coast, 2 hrs, US$200.

Directory **Tour operators** *Agencia Giscomes*, T/F264-0111, offers trips through the canal every 2nd and 4th Sat (or Sun) of the month, leaves at 0730. Partial boat trips are also offered on the canal, through Miraflores locks as far as Pedro Miguel locks. *Argo Tours,* T228-6069/4348, F228-1234, www.big-ditch.com, Balboa, offer half transits every Sat from pier 17, Balboa, 0730, US$45, children under 12 US$25, refreshments and snacks on sale, and once a month (usually the 2nd Sat), a full transit including breakfast, lunch, open bar, bus back from Cristóbal, US$90, children US$70 (MV *Islamorada* arrives at the Caribbean side about 1800). Highly recommended. Enquire at any travel agent.

Lago Alajuela

It is a two-hour drive through picturesque jungle to Lago Alajuela, formerly Madden Lake, east of the Canal. The lake, used to generate electricity as well as to maintain the level of Lago Gatún, covers 50 sq km and is within **Parque Nacional Chagres**. The park can be reached by bus from Panama City, first to Las Cumbres and then a second bus to Caimitillo. After that it is a 3½-4 hr walk to Nuevo Caimitillo. Dugout canoe will take you to Indian villages at Para Puru (15 min) and Embera Drua (30-40 min). The Camino Real passes through the park. There is another refuge at Cerro Azul, marking the start of a challenging three-day hike to the north coast, guide essential. Take a bus for Chepo from Panama City and get off at Vista Hermosa, then walk the 6 km to the ranger hut.

The canal drive runs from Balboa along the Gaillard Highway. Beyond Fort Clayton there is a fine view of the Miraflores and Pedro Miguel locks. Beyond Pedro Miguel town a road branches off to the left to Summit (Las Cumbres), where there are experimental gardens containing tropical plants from all over the world (closed Monday) and a good, small zoo containing native wildlife. *La Hacienda* restaurant serves native dishes. The alternative road to Lago Alajuela (37 km) crosses the Las Cruces trail (an old cannon marks the spot), and beyond is deep jungle. If walking the trail, take machete and compass. Halfway along the Las Cruces trail (1¼ hrs) a gravel track, the Plantation Road, turns left, emerging after 1¼ hours on the Gamboa highway 1½ km north of Summit. A large area of rainforest between Lago Gatún and Lago Alajuela has been set aside as **Parque Nacional Soberanía** which has many trails for walking. The park is very popular with bird-watchers with just under 400 species recorded to date, and is reputedly one of the finest observation areas for birds in the world, at one point holding the record for most birds counted in a 24-hour period. The park has two fabulous trails for wildlife observation (in particular bird-watching) and also has an aviary for harpie eagles. Plantation Trail begins right at the entrance of the road that leads to the Canopy Tower and Pipeline Road is about 17 km long in total, accessed from the Gaillard highway running along the canal, just north of Gamboa, the old American dredging port. The now abandoned coast-to-coast pipeline was built during the Second World War by the United States and hidden in the jungle as a guarantee of oil supply should the canal be sabotaged. The Park has an information centre at the Summit Garden.

Expensive accommodation in the area is offset by the benefits of nearby nature tours **Sleeping** **LL-L** *Gamboa Rainforest Resort*, on the hill above Gamboa overlooking the Chagres River, T314-9000, F314-9020, www.gamboaresort.com This looming green and white resort built on old American golf course has a reception area like a huge greenhouse, restaurant (bit soulless) and swimming pool. There is an ancient tree dividing the complex which, because it was built round rather than chopped, could be valued at US$250,000 (the additional construction expense). Cheapest rooms are in apartments formerly occupied by American dredging engineers. An **aerial tramway** runs silently through the canopy to a *mirador* with good views of the canal (at US$35 not cheap but an easy way to see monkeys, sloths and crocodiles without too much effort). Orchid, butterfly, fish and crocodile exhibits are also part of this tour which can be taken even if not resident. They also run tours to see crocodiles at night and birding trips to the Pipeline Road (see above). **LL-L** *Canopy Tower Ecolodge and Nature Observancy*, signposted from just beyond Summit Gardens on the Transisthmus Highway, T264-5720, F263-2784, www.canopytower.com A hotel and ecolodge that rises to the rainforest canopy in a converted old communications tower. 7 quirky little rooms, with private bath, price includes meals and guided walks. Some cheaper rooms available off season. Excellent for wildlife and bird-watching. Day trips and guided tours also welcome. Another interesting place to stay in the region is the **C** *Cabañas Flotantes* in the Chagres River, thatched 'floating cabins' moored between Lago Alajuela and the Canal. For further information call *Panama Paradise*, T269-9860.

Transport The trip to Summit may be made by train on Sun or buses marked Gamboa, every 1-1½ hrs, from bus station next to Plaza 5 de Mayo, US$0.45, 1½-hr journey; the Paraíso bus will also take you to the Miraflores and Pedro Miguel locks.

Colón and Cristóbal

Landfall on the Caribbean side for the passage of the Canal is made at the twin cities of Cristóbal and Colón, the one merging into the other almost imperceptibly and both built on Manzanillo Island at the entrance of the Canal in Bahía Limón. The island has now been connected with the mainland. Colón was founded in 1852 as the terminus of the railway across the isthmus; Cristóbal came into being as the port of entry for the supplies used in building the Canal.

    At Cristóbal ships usually dock at Pier No 9, five minutes from the shops of Colón. Vehicles are always waiting at the docks for those who want to visit Colón and other places.

Colour map 8, grid B1
Population: 200,172

Tourist office There is an IPAT tourist office on C 13 between Central y Domingo Días, (just before *Ley* supermarket, opp *Silenciadores Colón*), T441-4460, Mon-Fri 0830-1630, helpful. Also try Cámara de Comercio on Plaza 5 de Mayo if your tourism involves business.

Sights

Colón was originally called Aspinwall, after one of the founders of the Transisthmian Railway. The French-influenced **cathedral** at Calle 5 y Avenida Herrera has an attractive altar and good stained-glass windows. ■ *1400-1745 daily*. The *Washington Hotel*, on the seafront at the north end of the town, is the town's most historic structure and is worth a look. The original wooden hotel was built in 1850 for employees of the Railroad Company. President Taft ordered a new fireproof hotel to be built in 1912 and the old one was later razed. Although remodelled a number of times, today's building, with its broad verandas, waving palms, splendid chandelier, plush carpets and casino, still conjures up a past age, while the cafetería provides an excellent view of ships waiting to enter the Canal.

    Next door is the **Casa de Lesseps**, home of the Suez Canal's chief engineer during the 1880s (not open to the public). Across from the *Washington* is the **Old Stone Episcopal Church**, built in 1865 for the railway workers; it was then the only Protestant church in Colombia (of which Panama was a province). Running north through the centre of Colón is the palm-lined **Avenida Central**, with many statues (including one of Columbus and the Indian Girl, a gift from the Empress of France). The public market is at the corner of Calle 11 but holds little of interest. Avenida del Frente, facing the Bahía de Limón, has many old wooden buildings with wide verandas. This is the main commercial street and is quite active but has lost its past splendour: the famous Bazar Francés closed in 1990, the curio shops are not noteworthy and the railway station stands virtually deserted except for the movement of a few freight trains. Nevertheless, there is talk of declaring the whole of Colón a Free Zone, the authorities are moving to give the city new housing and employment (residential estates like 'Rainbow City' and 'Puerto Escondido' are being extended on the landward side to relocate entire neighbourhoods of slums), and the demands on Cristóbal's busy port facilities (200 million tons of cargo a year) continue to increase. It is to be hoped that, if these plans are realized, Colón may become a pleasant place again.

Panama

The main reason to come to Colón is to shop at the **Zona Libre** (Free Zone), the second-largest in the world, an extensive compound of international stores and warehouses established in 1949 and surrounded by a huge wall – pick up a free map showing who sells what from hotels or tourist office. Businessmen and tourists from all over Latin America come here to place orders for the (mostly bulk) merchandise on offer, or to arrange duty-free importation of bulk goods for re-export to neighbouring countries after packaging. Individual items can be bought at some stores, which theoretically must be mailed out of the country or sent in-bond to Tocumen Airport before you leave (allow a day for delivery and check-in two hours early to pick up the goods). Bargain hard, but most items are almost as competitively priced as in Panama City. Several banks provide exchange facilities. ■ *A passport or official ID must be shown to gain entry to the Zone, which is*

Colón

Panama

■ Sleeping			● Eating
1	Andros	7 Nuevo Washington	1 Dos Mares
2	Astor	8 Pensión Acrópolis	2 Fenix
3	Carlton	9 Pensión Anita	3 La Cabaña Avila
4	García	10 Plaza	4 Nuevo China
5	International	11 Sotelo	5 Recession
6	Meryland		6 Veteranos

N

Not to scale

open Mon-Fri 0800-1700 (a few places retail on Sat morning, but not many). If you have a car, pay a minder US$1 to watch it while in the Zone.

The 30-minute beach drive around Colón's perimeter is pleasant and cool in the evening; despite the slums at the south end there are some nice homes along the east shore of the peninsula. Permission from the Port Authority security officer is required to enter the port area, where agents for all the world's great shipping lines are located in colonial Caribbean-style buildings dating from 1914. Almost lost in a forest of containers is the **Cristóbal Yacht Club** (T441-5881), whose open-air restaurant and historically decorated bar offer very good food (seafood and Chinese). This is the place to enquire about sailing boat charters to the San Blas Islands or shorter trips aboard visiting yachts.

Excursions

A well-paved road branches off the Transisthmus Highway at Sabanitas, 14 km east of Colón, and runs northeast along the coast for 33 km to the historic Spanish garrison port of **Portobelo** (see below). The rocky **Costa Arriba** is very attractive, with a number of lovely white-sand beaches (crowded at weekends). Playa María Chiquita (14 km) has a bathing pavilion, toilets, bar and restaurant managed by the government tourist bureau. A local speciality is *sao*, Jamaican-style pig's feet pickled with lime and chillies, sold from roadside stalls. Playa Langosta, also with swimming facilities, bar and restaurant, is 3 km further on. There are plenty of small restaurants along this road serving fresh seafood. A group of people can rent a coastal boat at Puerto Pilón, close to Sabanita, (US$100-150 a day) for an adventurous ride to Portobelo, seas are often rough, take precautions. In **Buenavista**, just before entering Portobelo, a cannon marks the spot where Henry Morgan landed for his devastating 15-day sack of the town in 1668.

Security

Mugging, even in daylight, is a real threat in both Colón and Cristóbal. We have received repeated warnings of robbery in Colón, often within 5 mins of arrival. But the situation has improved now that the 2 main streets and some of the connecting ones are guarded by police officers; however, you are still strongly recommended not to stray too far from their range of sight. Keep a few dollars handy for muggers if the worst happens.

Sleeping

AL *Nuevo Washington*, Av del Frente Final, T441-7390, nwh@sinfo.net. Art deco style, guarded enclave, clean, good restaurant, good view of ships entering the canal, there is also the small *Pharaoh* casino and the 24-hours *Los Piratas* bar. **AL** *Meryland*, C 7 y Santa Isabel, T441-7055, F441-0705, new with restaurant.

B *Carlton*, C 10 y Av Meléndez, T445-0744, a good choice and one of the better hotels. **C** *Andros*, Av Herrera, between C 9 y 10, T441-0477/7923. Modern, clean, fan or a/c, bath, TV, good restaurant, cafetería. **C** *International*, Av Bolívar, y C 11, T441-8879, F441-2930, well furnished, bar, restaurant. **C** *Sotelo*, Guerrero y C 11, T441-7702, F441-5713.

D-E *Pensión Plaza*, Av Central y C 7, T441-3216. Clean and cheap, more expensive rooms have a/c and TV. **D-E** *Garcia*, C 4, 75 m east of Av Central, T441-0860 basic, but airier than some others in this category, pay a little more and get a/c. **E** *Pensión Acrópolis*, Av Amador Guerrero y C 11, opposite *Sotelo*, T441-1456. Shared bath.

E *Pensión Anita*, Amador Guerrero y C 10, dark rooms, basic. **E** *Astor*, Frente, between C 7 y C 8, big airy rooms – best at front leading on to large plant-filled balcony. Recommended.

Eating

Hotel Andros, modern, self-service, open until 2000, except Sun – check out the mirrors, news is you just have to be there. Hotels *Carlton* and *Washington* also have good restaurants. See above for *Cristóbal Yacht Club*. *Antonio*, Av Herrera y C 11, unremarkable but decent. *La Cabaña Avila*, Av Central y C 8, Caribbean food. *Dos Mares*, Av Bolívar y C 5; *Galeón de Oro*, C 10 y Santa Isabel. *Fenix*, Central y C 8, basic local fare; Nacional, esquina Guerrero y C 11, popular with locals, good for breakfast. *Nuevo China*, Av Central y C 9. *Recession*, C13 y Central, good soups, Chinese and other dishes, cheap. *Veteranos*, C 9 y Av

Panama

del Frente, T441-3563. Popular with visiting businessmen, port officials and lately with younger clientele. Several fast food outlets.

Entertainment **Cinemas** *Cine Fuerte Espinar*, just outside town. **Nightclubs** *Jungle*, popular with younger crowd. *Magia Latina*, Guerrero between C 6 y C 7.

Sports **Golf** 18-hole course at *Brazos Brook Country Club*.

Transport **Local Taxis**: tariffs vary but not expensive, US$0.75 in Colón, US$1.25 to outskirts, US$5-7 per hr, US$50-80 per day. Car rental and taxis on Av del Frente facing C 11; most drivers speak some English and can advise on 'no-go' areas.

Long distance **Air** Former US France Field AFB has replaced Colón's old airstrip as the busy local airport, on mainland east of city, taxi under US$1 but bargain. *Aeroperlas* has many flights daily Mon-Fri to Panama City; T430-1038, US$72 return. Flights are hectic with Free Zone executives, no reservation system so allow plenty of time or plan to stay the night in Colón.

Buses Bus station on Av del Frente and C 12. Express (a/c) US$2.25, and regular buses, US$1.75, daily to **Panama City** every 20 mins, less frequent at weekends, about 2 hrs. Hourly to **Portobelo** daily, US$2, 1 hr.

Train US$20, one way, US$35 return, to Panama City, leaves 1730, station on west side of town just off the centre.

Sea Shipping a vehicle: to South America, see page 1153. For San Blas try asking at Coco Solo pier, T430-7327.

Directory **Banks** *Banco Nacional de Panamá. Caja de Ahorros. Chase Manhattan Bank. Citibank. Lloyds Bank* agency in Colón Free Zone, at Av Santa Isabel y C 14, T445-2177. Open 0800-1300, Mon to Fri. **Communications** Internet *Explonet*, Frente, between C 9 y C 10, Mon-Sat 0800-2300, Sun 1300-2000, US$2.50/hr. *Dollar Rent-a-Computer*, C 11 Y Av Guerrero, above *Café Nacional*, T441-7632, entrance 3 doors down through double doors, US$2.50/hr, net phones US$0.61c/min to England. **Post office**: in Cristóbal Administration Building, on corner of Av Bolívar and C 9. **Telephone** *Cable & Wireless* in Cristóbal.

West of Colón

From Colón the Caribbean **Costa Abajo**, stretching west of the Canal, can also be visited. The road leaves Colón through new housing developments (on the left is the modern city of Margarita) and runs 10 km southwest to the Gatún Locks (see under The Canal above).

The north road branch at Gatún follows Limón Bay through a well-preserved forest reserve to Fort Sherman, running beside the remnants of the French Canal excavations (most of their work on the Atlantic side is now below the lake while the Pacific excavations were incorporated into the US construction). Fort Sherman is heavily forested military property and a guard at the gate may issue you with a pass. Since it is also the US Army's Jungle and Guerrilla Warfare Training Center it is advisable not to court any unpleasant surprises by leaving the road, which is gravel and well signposted (no public transport) for the 10 km to Fuerte San Lorenzo.

Fuerte San
Lorenzo
Colour map 8, grid B1

Perched on a cliff-top promontory overlooking the mouth of the Río Chagres with great views of the coast, Fort San Lorenzo is one of the oldest and best-preserved Spanish fortifications in the Americas. Construction had begun the year before Drake launched a 23-ship attack on the post (1596) and proceeded up the Chagres in an unsuccessful attempt to reach Panama City. The following century, Morgan fought a bloody 11-day battle to take the fort as a prelude to his decisive swoop on Panamá Viejo in 1671. Although new defences were then built, they were unable to prevent British Admiral Edward Vernon's successful attack in 1740 (one of Vernon's cannon with the 'GR' monogram can still be seen). Engineer Hernández

Exploring the Camino Real and surrounding area

Although little of the Camino Real remains, its two branches from Madden Lake/Lago Alajuela across the mountains to Nombre de Dios (30 km) and Portobelo can still be hiked. The trail starts at the old manganese mining zone (Mina 1, on the dirt road that runs from the Transístmica to a little way up the Río Boquerón). Buses run occasionally from the Transístmica to Salamanca, roughly where the Río Boquerón empties into Madden Lake. The trail follows the Río Boquerón up to the continental divide and the Río Nombre de Dios down the northern watershed to the coast near the present-day town. This historic trek is easy for anyone with reasonable fitness, as one can drive to entry and exit points. Guides are not really necessary, the rivers are beautiful (and carry little water in the dry season) and the jungle almost untouched; the trail is straightforward and rises only to 330 m at the divide. Allow about three days for the Boquerón-Nombre de Dios trek. The trail to Portobelo branches off the Boquerón trail at the Río Diablo or Río Longue. After you leave the Boquerón you will need to navigate by compass. The Diablo takes the trekker higher into the divide (700 m) than the Longue (350 m, the route the treasure-laden mules followed) and the terrain is more broken; both lead to the Río Cascajal (higher reaches are strewn with large boulders), which descends to the Caribbean. The highest point in the region, Cerro Brujo (979 m), is passed en route. There are jaguars in this forested refuge, but they are unlikely to present any danger to hikers – indeed, if you're lucky, you see one. The Cascajal reaches the road about 1 km east of Portobelo. The Boquerón-Portobelo hike is more demanding than the other and takes four days maximum, a good machete is essential, and solitude is guaranteed for at least two days.

To the south and east of the Camino Real are the rivers of the Chagres system which flow into Lago Alajuela. Some of these are now being exploited for rafting. Check with tourist agencies in Panama City, Shirley Eco Tours for example, for Camino Real treks.

then spent seven years strengthening the garrison (1760-67), but the threat to San Lorenzo gradually receded as Spanish galleons were diverted to the Cape Horn route and the era of the freebooters approached its end. The last Royalist soldiers left the fort in 1821 as Colombia declared its Independence from Spain. The earliest artillery sheds can be seen on the lower cliff level but most of the bulwarks, arched stone rooms and lines of cannon are 18th century. The site recently underwent an extensive UNESCO renovation programme and is well worth a visit. There is a picnic area and a tiny beach is accessible by a steep path down the cliff. Take insect repellent.

There is no crossing of the Chagres at San Lorenzo. To continue down the **Costa Abajo** you have to return to the Gatún Dam and take the gravel road along the west side of the river, which winds its way through pristine forest to the coastal village of Piña and its kilometre-long beach. The road runs west along a steep and rocky shore punctured by many small coves to Nuevo Chagres and Palmas Bellas, quiet fishing resorts in coconut palm groves, but with few facilities. Four-wheel drive is required to continue to Río Indio and Miguel de la Borda, where the road comes to an end. The villages beyond, including historic Río Belén where one of Columbus' ships was abandoned in 1502, remain accessible only by sea.

Portobelo and east of Colón

East of Colón along the Caribbean coastline is Portobelo, founded in 1519 on the protected bay in which **Columbus** sought shelter in 1502. Researchers believe they have now located the wreck of the Vizcaina, abandoned by Columbus, in shallow waters somewhere off the coast of Portobelo. Now little more than a large village, the 'Beautiful Port' was once the northern terminus of the **Camino Real**, where Peruvian treasure, carried on mule trains across the isthmus from Panama City, was stored in fortified warehouses. The gold moved on when the periodic arrival of the

Colour map 8, grid B1
Population: 5,850

The nearby beach of La Huerta can only be reached by boat

Panama

Spanish Armada created famed fairs where the wealth of the New World was exchanged for goods and supplies from Europe. The fair of 1637 saw so much material change hands that, according to the Englishman Thomas Gage, it took 30 days for the loading and unloading to be completed. In the **Royal Contaduría**, or Customs House, bars of gold and silver were piled up like firewood. Such riches could hardly fail to attract foreign pirates. Portobelo was one of **Francis Drake's** favourite targets but it was also his downfall; he died here of dysentery in 1596 and was buried in a lead-lined coffin in the bay off Isla Drake. Divers are currently attempting to discover the exact spot, intending to return Drake's body to his home city of Plymouth. By the beginning of the 17th century several *castillos* (Santiago, San Gerónimo and San Fernando) had been built of coral stone quarried nearby to protect the harbour. Attacks continued, however, until in 1740 the treasure fleets were rerouted around the Horn and the Portobelo Fairs ended. The fortifications were rebuilt after Vernon's attack in 1744 but they were no longer seriously challenged, leaving the fortresses visible today. The largest, the aptly named 'Iron Castle', was largely dismantled during Canal construction (its stones form the breakwaters at the north entrance to the Canal). But there are many other interesting ruined fortresses, walls, rows of cannon and remains of the town's 120 houses and public buildings still to be seen standing along the foreshore amid the present-day village. In 1980 the remains of the colonial structure, known as the **Monumental Complex**, was declared a World Cultural Heritage monument by UNESCO. The Contaduría (1630) has been restored, with similar plans for the Plaza, Hospital Chapel and the Fernández House. There is a small museum with a collection of arms. ■ *US$1, closed Sun.*

In **San Felipe Church** (1776) is the 17th-century cocobolo-wood statue of the Black Christ, about whose origin there are many legends. One tells of how it was found by fishermen floating in the sea during an epidemic of cholera in the town. It was brought ashore and immediately the epidemic began to wane. Another says that the life-size image was on its way to Cartagena when the ship put in to Portobelo to buy supplies. After being thwarted five times by rough weather to leave port, the crew decided the statue wished to remain in Panama. It was thrown overboard, floated ashore and was rescued by the locals. Services in town are limited with no bank or post office and just one minimarket.

The **Tourist office** (*IPAT*) has an office just west of the square behind the Alcadía, T448-2073, open Monday-Friday 0830-1630, and can provide guides, schedules of *Congos* and other performances, as well as comprehensive information about the many local points of interest, including the surrounding 34,846-ha **Portobelo National Park**, which has 70 km of coast line with beautiful beaches, superb scuba diving sites and boat rental to visit secluded beaches nearby.

Sleeping **B** *Cabañas el Mar*, in Buenaventura, 5 km west on road to Colón, T448-2102. With a/c, cheaper with fan, quiet location by the sea. **B** *Scubaportobelo*, also in Buenaventura, T448-2147, scuba gear available for hire. **D** *Aquatic Park*, on road towards Colón. Dormitory accommodation, expensive. In town on the main square is **E** *Hospedaje La Aduana*, with a somewhat noisy bar.

Eating *El Hostal del Rey*, corner of Parque Central, good meals and value. *La Torre*, T448-2039, in La Escucha, 3 km before the town, good food. A number of small *fondas* serving coconut rice with fresh shrimps, Caribbean food (spicy) with octopus or fish, or *fufú* (fish soup cooked with coconut milk and vegetables). *Los Cañones,* in Buenaventura, 5 km west on road to Colón, good food in a lovely setting by the water, not cheap.

Festivals The *Black Christ*'s miraculous reputation is celebrated each year on **21 Oct**, when purple-clad pilgrims come from all over the country and the statue is paraded through the town at 1800 on a flower- and candle-covered litter carried by 80 men (who take 3 steps forward and 2 steps back to musical accompaniment); feasting and dancing till dawn follow the solemn procession.

Other fiestas in the Portobelo region – for example *New Year's Eve*, *Carnival*, *Patron Saint's Day*, **20 Mar** – are opportunities to experience the *Congos*. Unlike the dance of the same name found elsewhere on the Caribbean coast, the *Congo* here is the name given both to the main, male participants and a slowly unfolding ritual which lasts from the *Día de los Reyes*, 6 Jan (Epiphany) to *Easter*. Among the various explanations of its symbolism are elements of the people's original African religions, their capture into slavery, their conversion to Catholicism and mockery of the colonial Spaniards. Members of the audience are often 'imprisoned' in a makeshift palisade and have to pay a 'ransom' to be freed.

Bus Buses from **Colón**, every hr from 0700 from the bus station on Av del Frente y C 13, 1 hr, US$1; **María Chiquita**, 40 mins, US$0.80. Portobelo can be visited from Panama City in a day without going into Colón by taking an early bus as far as the Sabanitas turn-off (US$1) and waiting for a Colón-Portobelo service (US$1).

Transport

To villages east, take buses marked 'Costa Arriba' from stop at back of square: **Nombre de Dios**, 45 mins US$1; **Palenque**, 70 mins, US$1.50; **Miramar**, 80 mins US$3, **Cuango**, 1½ hrs, US$3.50. Road paved until just beyond Nombre de Dios.

Boat Launch to **Santa Isabel** (beyond reach of Costa Arriba road), 2 hrs, to **San Blas** 3 hrs (see under Miramar for prices).

Isla Grande

A paved road continues northeast from Portobelo to Isla Grande, and another heads east to Nombre de Dios (25 km) and Palenque. Scuba diving is offered at several places along the way. It passes through Garrote and La Guaira (D *Cabañas Montecarlo*, T441-2054), from where *pangas* can be hired (US$1, although they might try and charge US$2 if you take the boat on your own) at the car park to cross to Isla Grande. The island is a favourite with international visitors and Panamanians alike because of its relaxed lifestyle, fishing, scuba diving and snorkelling, windsurfing and dazzling white palm-fringed beaches. The best beaches are in front of the two expensive hotels, enclosed, but you should be able to use them. A good, more public beach, is on a spit before *Hotel Isla Grande*. The island's 300 black inhabitants make a living from fishing and coconut cultivation, and a powerful French-built lighthouse crowns the small island's northern point, where there is a mirador, reached by steep path (slippery during the rainy season). There are a number of colourful African-tinged festivals held here throughout the year, particularly on 24 June, 16 July and the pre-Lenten Carnival with *Congos*. The part of the village to the right of the landing stage is more lively with competing salsa sounds.

Panama

LL *Bananas Village Resort*, on north side of island, usually accessed by boat but also by path over the steep hill, T263-9510, F264-7556, www.bananasresort.com Relatively discrete luxury hotel, despite the name, on the best beach on the island, with a good but expensive bar.

A-B *Sister Moon*, 500 m outside village heading anticlockwise from landing stage, T226-2257, www.hotel_sistermoon.com, nice setting, wooden cabañas of varying luxury perched on hillside, each with a hammock, bit of a walk from good beach. Good value.

B *Damaris*, 300m to right of the dock, T687-8202, Turquesa bar/restaurant, popular with Panamanians. **B** *Isla Grande*, T225-6722, F225-6721. US$45 for 4 beds, with a/c. Bungalows scattered along an excellent sandy beach. Popular with Panamanians, restaurant, pool table, ping pong, a little bit run down but good value. **B** *Villa Ensueño*, right at the landing stage, T/F448-2964, large lawns (big enough to play football) with gardens and a hammock on each balcony. **D** *Cabañas Jackson*, immediately behind main landing stage, T441-5656. Many huts/bungalows available.

Candy Rose, serves drinks with a special octopus cooked in coconut milk. *Kiosco Milly Mar*, just west of landing pier, excellent fish dishes, moderate prices.

Sleeping & eating
On holidays and dry season weekends, make reservations in advance; prices often double during high season

All hotels have bars and simple restaurants

On Sun the last bus from La Guaira back to Portobelo leaves at 1500 is always packed. Hitching with Panamanian weekenders is possible, all the way to Panama City if you're lucky!

Transport

Directory **Communications** There are 2 pay phones on the island, 150 m to the left of the landing jetty, on a small plaza, and to the right beside the basketball court.

Nombre de Dios

Colour map 8, grid B1

The beautiful, deserted mainland beaches continue as the 'road' heads east to Nombre de Dios. The historic town (1520) near the present village was once the thriving trading port which first hosted the famed Fairs, located at the end of the stone-paved Camino Real from the capital. By the 1550s more than half the trade between Spain and its colonies was passing through its lightly defended harbour, but in 1594 the decision was made to move operations to the more sheltered site of Portobelo. The Camino Real was diverted and Nombre de Dios was already dying when Drake captured and burnt it two years later, so that William Dampier could describe the site some years later as "only a name ... everything is covered by the Jungle with no sign that it was ever populated". Excavations have taken place revealing the Spanish town, parts of the Camino Real, a broken cannon and other objects, most of which are now in the National Museum. The modern village is built on either side of a freshwater channel, a footbridge links the two. The church is built on a plaza on the west side, the main square is on the east. It has few facilities, one hotel – **E** *Casa de Huéspedes* – and a restaurant the on main square, but a beautiful beach can be enjoyed by those few who get this far. A *cayuco* (US$3 per person, 12 minutes) can be taken to Playa Damas, an unusual beach where alternating patches of red and white sand resemble a chess board. The beach is owned by an amateur ecologist who has built some rustic huts and a campsite (*Costa El Oro*, T263-5955) on a small island here, he also offers expert guidance on local fishing and diving spots. Buses come into the centre en route to Portobelo or Cuango but note that while most go as far as the main square before coming back the same way, some turn round before this at the little plaza beside the police station.

The track staggers on for another 25 km linking the peaceful fishing villages of the Costa Arriba. Locals eagerly await the paved road's eventual extension through the succession of seaside villages to the Golfo de San Blas opposite El Porvenir, the capital of the Kunas' self-governed *comarca* of Kuna Yala (Kuna Earth).

Not far beyond Nombe de Dios, near Viento Frío is **C** *Diver's Haven*, recommended for its diving tours. The next village up is **Palenque**, unspoilt, with a good beach where very rudimentary huts are being built for visitors. **Miramar** is the cleanest of all the pueblitos along this coastline. The occasional smuggling boat puts in here and a few Panama City tourists come to stay in the three houses on the tiny Isla Bellavista in the cove (ask Niano at *Bohio* Miramar bar/restaurant to rent – US$70 for house with 3 double beds, no beach but can swim off jetty). **E** *Bohio* , to left of road, on beach 50 m before the quay, 2 small but light rooms with TV and fan; the restaurant at the back of the jetty rents out 2 dark rooms. Boats can take you on to **Santa Isabel** (beyond the reach of the dirt road), US$35 for the boat, or to **San Blas** US$25 per person, minimum 8 people. The village at the end of the road is **Cuango,** a bit run down and dusty between rains, with a littered beach. One basic, nameless *hospedaje*, **F** – ask for María Meneses at first house on the left on east side of square, one restaurant and store.

San Blas Islands

Colour map 8, grid B2
Population: 40,092

The Archipiélago de San Blas (or Las Mulatas) is a broad string of 365 islands ranging in size from deserted islets with just a few coconut palms to inhabited islands, about 50 in total, home to hundreds of Kuna Indians. Lying off the Caribbean coast east of Colón, the archipelago stretches along the coast for over 200 km from the Gulf of San Blas to the Colombian border. The islands' distance from the mainland ranges from 100 m to several kilometres.

La mola

You might not know what it is until you see one, but the mola – literal translation a 'blouse' – is the most brilliant and colourful artistic expression of Kuna Yala – the San Blas archipelago. A mola is a reverse appliqué, or 'cut-out', decorative textile made by Kuna women. First created in the mid-19th century it is still worn daily on the front and back of a blouse.

Usually measuring about 40 by 33 cm, molas are made out of up to seven (but on average three to four) superimposed, differently coloured materials. Each layer is cut to make up a design element constituted by the unveiled layer beneath it. The ragged hem is folded over and sewn down with concealed stitching. This careful craftwork and step by step process slowly reveals a design of a bird, aquatic creature, monster, a generic scene such as fishing or even perhaps a protecting spirit or a wild dance of colours, but always something personal to the creator's imagination.

The traditional mola, the 'serkan' design, with its small range of totemic objects, has been added to by the Kuna encounter with modern Panama and you are as likely to see a mola depicting an aeroplane, map, flag, political leanings, or an American invasion, which can be just as interesting. Another development is machine-made molas with simplistic motifs and gaudy colours.

As gifts and souvenirs, molas make great miniature wall hangings and have the advantage of being light and small, so they don't take up too much precious space in the backpack. It's worth seeking out a good quality one. Don't worry about exact symmetry, but do look for fine and even outlines, the narrower, the better, The larger pattern should come out of the top layer, often black or maroon, and the detail mainly from lower layers. Some molas have appliqué – sewed on, as opposed to cut away, motifs – and they can create additional depth and enliven the surface, but try to avoid those with fill-in – dots and triangles and small circles roughly applied to fill up space. Stitching should be even and usually hidden, never substituted with tape, and where there is decorative surface stitching it shouldn't compete with the more graphic cut-away. Check the quality of the material in the lower layers and run your hand across the surface of the mola to make sure the layers are not scrunching up.

The Kuna (Cuna, or Tule) are the most sophisticated and politically organized of the country's three major groups. They run the San Blas Territory virtually on their own terms after a rebellion in 1925, with internal autonomy and, uniquely among Panama's Indians they send their representative to the National Assembly. Each community is presided over by a *sáhila* (or chief). Land is communally owned but coconut trees may belong to individuals. The Kuna have their own language, but Spanish is widely spoken. The women wear gold nose and ear-rings, costumes with unique designs and *molas* based on local themes, geometric patterns, stylized fauna and flora, and pictorial representations of current events or political propaganda. They are outside the Panamanian tax zone and have negotiated a treaty perpetuating their long-standing trade with small craft from Colombia. Many men work on the mainland, but live on the islands.

There are about 20 airstrips in the San Blas Islands and province, but most are 'larger' than the islands or places on which they are built. They include: El Porvenir, Cartí, Río Sidra, Río Azúcar, Narganá, Corazón, Río Tigre, Playón Chico, Tupile, Tikankiki, Ailigandi, Achutupu (also known as Uaguitupu), Mamitupu, Ogobsucum, Ustupu, Mansucum, Mulatupu, Tubuala, Calidonia and Puerto Obaldía. You can be dropped off at any island or village and picked up later, subject to negotiations with the pilot, but though this may sound appealing as the islands have nice-looking beaches, it is probably not wise since there is no drinking water or food. One of the best islands to visit from the Porvenir area is **Dog Island** with a superb beach and great snorkelling on a wreck just 20 m off shore. Hotel prices usually include a trip here. A 'local' tax of US$1 per island has been introduced.

Photographers need plenty of cash, as the set price for a Kuna to pose is US$1 per photo

Panama

An alternative route to San Blas is to walk over the continental divide from Cañita to Sarti. Take a bus from Panama City towards Darién and get off at Cañita, then walk 2-3 hrs to the EcoLodge at Burbayar – there is also a lodge at Nusagrande. The following day camp on the coastal side of the Serranía de San Blas and on the third day make sure that you reach **Cartí** before 1600 when the last boat leaves for the islands – US$20-30 to El Porvenir, or US$10 (20 minutes) to Isla Naranjos. At Cartí there is a museum of Kuna culture.

Sleeping

Camping is generally discouraged on the islands but if you want to, make sure that you speak to the sáhila first

Any travel agent in Panama can book a San Blas tour. One of the agents which will handle bookings is *Chadwicks*, see page 1181. It may be possible to book direct with a hotel and it is always necessary to book somewhere for the first night. In the vicinity of El Porvenir, on **Wichub-Huala**, is **A** *Hotel Hanay Kantule* (also spelt *Anai Katule*), T220-0746, including food and lodging. For the *Hanay*, ask for Israel Fernández on arrival at El Porvenir. **C** *Cabañas Ukuptupu*, reservations T220-4781 or T299-9011. Run by the family of Juan García, has canoes for hire and has been recommended. You have to get up early for the return flight. Other hotels in the Porvenir area include **B** *Hotel San Blas*, T290-6528, on **Nalunega Island**, 10 mins by boat from the El Porvenir airstrip. Traditional cane and thatch, shared showers, price includes breakfast, lunch, lobster dinner and 2 excursions, owner Sr Burgos meets incoming flights every morning, and boats to Cartagena pick up passengers from here. Closer still to the airstrip is **B** *Hotel El Porvenir*, similar to San Blas, good for boat trips.

Hotels and lodges are being opened on the islands off the Caribbean coast. These include, from west to east: *Sugtupu Hotel*, in the Cartí-Sugtupu community (from the coast of Cartí a road runs inland to the Pan-American Highway at El Llano – see page 1224). **A** *Kuanidup*, T227-6026. 7 huts on the island, good food, lovely beaches, no electricity, bathrooms in the centre of the island. At **Narganá**, which has an airstrip, there is a basic hotel, **F**, and 1 restaurant, *El Caprichito*, good crab dishes. **L** *Kwadule*, near Corazón de Jesús and Narganá, F269-6309, has a very nice restaurant/bar over the reef, some cabins built over the water, with bath. A short canoe ride from Narganá is **Isla Tigre**, a very traditional island. Further east again, reached from Playón Chico, is the **LL** *Iskardup Ecoresort*, T269-6047, F269-1604. With cabins, bar, restaurant, solar power, package tours include trips to the mainland. Another recommended trip is to *Dolphin Lodge*, about halfway along the coast between El Porvenir and the Colombian border, T225-8435, F225-2521, owned by a Kuna Indian family on the island of Uaguitupu, US$139 including air fare, meals and overnight stay.

Festivals

IPAT lists the following fiestas in the San Blas islands: **Feb**, anniversary of the *Tule Revolution*, at Playón Chico, Tupile, Ailigandi and Ustupu. **19 Mar**, *fiesta patronal* on Narganá. **8 Jul**, anniversary of *Inakiña* on Mulatupo. **29-31 Jul**, *fiesta patronal* on Fulipe. **20 Aug**, Charles Robinson anniversary on Narganá. **3 Sep**, anniversary of Nele-Kantule on Ustupo. **11 Sep**, anniversary of Yabilikiña on Tuwala. All involve dances, games, meals and speeches and are traditional, except those on Narganá, which have a stronger Western element (but also typical dancing and food).

Shopping

Molas – see box – cost upwards of US$10 each (also obtainable in many Panama City and Colón shops). You can also try the San Blas perfume *Kantule*, similarly available in city shops.

Transport

Air Several companies fly from Panama City (Albrook) including *Aeroperlas*, (T315-7500), *Ansa* (T315-0300) *Transpasa* (T236-0842) and *Aerotaxi* (T264-8644) to San Blas and charter flights. The most popular destination is El Porvenir (other airports are listed above), on the north side of the Golfo de San Blas, where tourists are picked up by boat to go to a neighbouring island, about 20 mins. 1-way fares to the islands are US$32 to El Porvenir and US$47 to Puerto Obaldía. All other air fares are scaled in between (price includes a 5% sales tax). You must take your passport because every once in a blue moon a hijack attempt to Colombia is made. All flights leave between 0600 and 0630, Mon-Sat, returning 0800-0830. Evening and Sun flights must be booked privately. Baggage over 15 kg is charged at US$0.50 per kg, so wear your heavy stuff.

Sea There are occasional boats to the San Blas islands from Colón, but there is no scheduled service and the trip can be rough. One ship that goes from time to time is the *Almirante*, try to find the captain, Figueres Cooper, who charges US$30 for the trip. The port captain's office at Coco Solo may have information on boat departures, T441-5231 or 445-1055, although most boats are not keen to take gringos. Alternatively, go to Portobelo (see above) and try for a boat from there, 9 hrs to El Porvenir, every other day, US$17.

There are 2 sailing boats regularly taking passengers from Cartagena, **Colombia**, to San Blas and back. Frequency depends on the number of people who sign up. Journey time 2 days to reach the San Blas islands, 2 more to Porvenir for the airport and immigration, US$185 one way, safer than many cargo boats. Intermittent boats go from Cartagena to El Porvenir. For information on sailing contact *Hotel Casa Viena* (www.casaviena.com) in Cartagena for details. Or contact Sr Burgos at *Hotel San Blas*.

The 'Interior'

Cross the Puente de las Américas from Panama City and you enter the most densely populated rural quarter of the country, a Panama that is in great contrast to the cosmopolitan capital and the Canal: colonial towns, varied agriculture, traditional crafts and music, Pacific beaches and beautiful mountain landscapes with good walking. The Pan-American Highway crosses the region known as 'El Interior' (though the term can refer to any area outside the capital), en route to Costa Rica.

The Pan-American Highway, also known as the Interamericana, heads westwards along a well graded and completely paved road from Panama City through Concepción to the Costa Rican border for 489 km. Leaving Panama City, the Pan-American Highway crosses the **Puente de las Américas** over the Canal at the Pacific entrance (if on a bus, sit on the right-hand side – north – for the best views). The bridge was built between 1958 and 1962 by the USA to replace the ferry crossing. It is 1,653 m long and, with a road surface to seaway distance of 117 m, there is ample room for all ships to pass below. The bridge, which has three lanes, is the only vehicular crossing on the Pacific side of the canal. At busy times, lane changing is frequent and indication minimal. There is also a pedestrian walkway for the length of the bridge, but muggings have occurred on the bridge even in broad daylight so take care. Buses run to a *mirador* on the far side of the bridge from the city.

Panama City to Costa Rica

The first place you reach, 13 km from Panama City, is the small town of **Arraiján**. Another 21 km by four-lane highway (toll US$0.50) takes you to La Chorrera with an interesting store, *Artes de las Américas*, filled with wooden carvings. A branch road (right) leads 1½ km to **El Chorro**, the waterfall from which the town takes its name. At Km 20, among hills, is the old town of Capira (good food next to Shell station run by Chinese). Just west of Capira is a sign indicating the turn-off to Lídice, 4 km north of the highway. At the foot of Cerro Trinidad, which local tradition calls 'the end of the Andes'. The town was the home of Czech immigrants who in 1945 succeeded in having the name changed from Potero to commemorate Lídice in their homeland, which suffered heavily in the Second World War.

La Chorrera
Colour map 8,
grid B1
Population: 37,000

The highway passes through the orange groves of Campana, where a 4-km road climbs to **Altos de Campana National Park**. Created in 1966, the 4,816-ha park – the first in Panama – protects humid tropical forest growing on mountainous volcanic rock that forms picturesque cliffs ideal for walking and hiking. Trails lead through the hills where Panama's famous golden frog can be seen, along with sloths and monkeys, and there is a lookout point near the administration office of the park with fantastic views of the valleys and mountains all the way to the Pacific coastline. Rangers will advise. Lodging at ranger station is possible, 5 km up the road and there are five other refuges about the park. There are two designated camping areas. The road then twists down to Río Sajalices (bathing) and the low-level plains. Good views on the road to the

Panama

summit of Cerro Campana. Another 10 km up a side road, 2 km before the village of Chicá, is a colony of retired North Americans, who appreciate visitors.

Sleeping D *Tropical*, pink and green building on Pan-American. With fan, bath. Recommended. **D** *Hospedaje Lamas*, on side street just right of *Tropical*. A/c or fan, clean, big rooms, TV. Recommended.

San Carlos & beaches
Colour map 8, grid B1

At Bejuco, 5 km east of Chame, the road stretches down a 28 km peninsula to Punta Chame, with a white-sand beach, a few houses, and just one hotel/restaurant. At low tide the sand is alive with legions of small pink crabs. There is a splendid view northeast to Taboga Island and the entrance to the Canal in the distance. Food is prepared by the beach, there are several bars and a pick-up running between the highway and the beach costing US$1 is your link to the outside world.

Beyond Chame are two beaches: **Nueva Gorgona**, 3-4 km long, waves increasing in size from west to east, and a well-stocked grocery store. A little further along the Pan-American is **Playa Coronado**, the most popular beach in Panama, but rarely crowded. Homeowners from Playa Coronado have installed a checkpoint at the turning, unaffiliated with the police station opposite. Be polite, but do not be deterred from using the public beach.

Sleeping and eating **B** *Gorgona Hayes*, T223-7775. With pleasant pool, fountain, tennis court, restaurant, good. **B** *Cabañas de Playa Gorgona*, T269-2433. Cheaper, with kitchenettes, BBQ grills, pool, shade, hammocks, on the ocean, prices rise at weekend. Camping possible on Palmar Beach, **F**. Restaurant *El Prado*, on the beach.

Opposite the turning to Playa Coronado is a road inland to Las Lajas and beyond to the hills and **Lagunas del Valle**, about one hour from the highway. **Sleeping B** *Hostal Chiquito*, a 160-ha farm with eight guest rooms, two double rooms in separate units, meals included, riding, hiking, lake swimming, electricity evenings only, transport provided by Panama City, information T236-4632 (Panama City).

Ten kilometres beyond Playa Coronado is the town of **San Carlos**, near the sea; good river and sea-bathing (beware jelly fish and do not bathe in the estuarine lake). Not many restaurants in San Carlos, but there are plenty of food shops.

Sleeping Beyond San Carlos is the Río Mar beach, with the **A** *Río Mar*, T223-0192, which has a good seafood restaurant. **Transport Bus** Panama City-San Carlos, frequent from 0615, US$3.50, San Carlos-David, US$10.

El Valle
Gold-coloured frogs can be seen in the area, and there are trees with square trunks, near Hotel Campestre

Five kilometres on, a road (right) leads after a few kilometres to a climb through fine scenery to the summit of **Los Llanitos** (792 m), and then down 200 m to a mountain-rimmed plateau (7 by 5½ km) on which is the comparatively cool, summer resort of El Valle. Direct bus from Panama City US$3.50, or US$1 from San Carlos. Four kilometres before El Valle is a parking spot with fine views of the village and a waterfall nearby. Soapstone carvings of animals, straw birds, painted gourds (*totumas*), carved wood tableware, pottery and *molas* are sold in the famous Sunday market, which is very popular with Panamanians and tourists. There is also a colourful flower market. The orchid nursery has a small zoo and Panama's best-known petroglyphs can be seen near the town. This is one of many good walks in the vicinity (ask directions); another is to the cross in the hills to the west of town.

Beyond El Valle is Panama's only zip-wire attraction, the **Canopy Adventure**, with a series of cables and wires whizzing you through the forest. Good for all ages, the last stage swoops across the face of a waterfall. The whole experience takes about 1½ hours and includes a short hike through the forest. ■ *Open every day, 0600-1700. US$40. In El Valle T983-6547 (Spanish only), in Panama City T264-5720, F263-2784. From El Valle get a bus to El Chorro Macho or taxi getting out at La Mesa.*

Sleeping B *Hotel Campestre*, T983-6146, F226-4069, www.hotelcampestre.com Swiss-style *The town has no real* lunch dishes from US$6. B *Cabañas Las Mozas*, T983-6071. Offers Arabic food. D *El Greco Motel*, *centre; everyone cycles* C Central, T983-6149, restaurant. E *Pensión Niña Dalia*. No towels or soap; will look after bags; private houses nearby rent rooms, F with meals. Accommodation is hard to find at weekends.

Santa Clara, with its famous beach, 115 km from Panama City, is the usual target for **Santa Clara** motorists. The beach is about 20 minutes from the Pan-American Highway and has **& Antón** fishing, launches for hire, and riding. About 13 km beyond is **Antón**, which has a special local type of *manjar blanco* (a gooey fudge) and a crucifix reputed to be miraculous.

Sleeping There are cabañas to rent, the principal centre is *Cabañas Las Sirenas*, T263-8771, F263-7860, **AL** per day for 5 people, **L** for 7 (minimum 2 nights), in an attractive landscaped environment. 100 m from the highway on the north side is *XS Memories*, T993-3096. 12 full-service RV hookups in a gated compound, also 3 hotel rooms, sports bar and restaurant.

   In Antón D *Hotel Rivera*, with bath and a/c, cheaper without bath, a/c or fan, clean, Km 131, T997-2245. Across the Pan-American Highway is E *Pensión/Restaurant Panamá*, friendly, clean, safe, a/c. E *Chung*, on highway, moderately priced food.

A further 20 km is the capital of Coclé province, Penonomé, an old town even when **Penonomé** the Spaniards arrived. An advanced culture which once lived here was *Colour map 8, grid B1* overwhelmed by volcanic eruption. Objects revealed by archaeologists are now in *Population: 10,715* Panama City, in the American Museum of Natural History in New York, and in the local **Museo Conte de Penonomé**. ■ *Tue-Sat 0900-1230, 1330-1600, Sun 0830-1300*. There is a local university and the Mercado de Artesanato on the highway is worth a visit. There is a delightful central plaza with the air of a tiny provincial capital of times past. The town is frequently the lunch stop for motorists making the whole-day trip from Panama City to the western border.

Sleeping and eating C-D *Dos Continentes*, Av Juan D Arosemena, T997-9325, F997-9390. With shower, a/c, pool, restaurant. E *Pensión Dos Reales*, C Juan Vásquez. Basic, mosquitoes, noisy. E *Pensión Los Pinos*, on left of highway to Panama City. With bath and fan (D with a/c). E *Residencial El País*, C Juan Arosemena near church and Parque, no sign but look for black lanterns on wall. With bath, good value. Also, good basic restaurant, *Cielo Mar*, will let you sling a hammock free. *Mac Aro*, on Juan Arosemena, good for light meals, takeaway, English spoken.

Just under 1 km northwest of Penonomé is Balneario Las Mendozas, on a street of **Balneario** the same name, an excellent river pool for bathing in deep water. Further down the **Las Mendozas** Río Zaratí, also known as the Santa María, is La Angostura where the river dives **& Churuquita** down a canyon. The dirt access road is usually suitable for ordinary cars. There are **Grande** copper and gold mining activities in this area and further north beyond La Pintada, where a new 35-km road has been built to Coclecito on the Caribbean side of the Continental Divide. The operating mining company is also involved in conservation work including reforestation near La Angostura. Northeast of Penonomé is Churuquita Grande (camping is possible near the river with a waterfall and swimming hole). There's a *Feria de la Naranja* last weekend of January, inauguration and dancing on Saturday, big day on Sunday which includes a colourful parade and huge displays of fruit.

Sleeping Further inland, an excellent purpose-built lodge for walkers and ecotourists has been opened: **AL** *Posada del Cerro La Vieja*, Apdo 543 Estafeta 9A Carrasquilla, Panama City, local address, Chiguirí Arriba, Coclé, T223-4553, F264-4858; it offers guided treks on foot or mule, including through the mountains to El Valle, or across the isthmus to the Atlantic coast with the final stage by dugout.

El Caño is 24 km west of Penonomé, and 3½ km from the main road is the **Parque** **El Caño, El** **Arqueológico del Caño** with a small museum, some excavations (several human **Copé & Natá**

Panama

skeletons have been found in the burial site), and standing stones. ■ *Tue-Fri 0900-1600, Sat-Sun 1030-1300, closed Mon. US$1.*

From El Caño (the ruins) you can take a *chiva* up into the mountains, changing to another at Río Grande, to the village of El Copé (hut, direct buses from Panama City), which gives access to the **Parque Nacional Omar Torrijos** a protected forest of rubber trees with some good trails.

A further 7 km along the Pan-American Highway is Natá, one of the oldest towns in Panama and the Americas (1520). The early colonists fought constant Indian attacks led by Urracá. The Iglesia de Santiago Apóstol (1522) is impressive, with some interesting wood carvings. It is sadly run down now; donations gratefully received for restoration work in progress.

Aguadulce
Colour map 8, grid B1
Population: 14,800

Some 10 km beyond is Aguadulce, a prosperous supply centre (bus from Panama, US$6), with local pottery for sale and *salinas* (saltworks) nearby.

Sleeping C *El Interamericano*, on Pan-American Highway, T997-4148, F997-4975. With bath, a/c, TV, balcony, clean rooms, swimming pool. D per person *Pensión Sarita*, T997-4437, and others (it may be possible to sleep by the fire station).

Another 17 km further on, just after the large Santa Rosa sugar plantation, a road leads off right to the mountain spa of **Calobre** (31 km). The hot springs are, however, a good hour's drive away, on a very rough road, through great mountain scenery.

The Azuero Peninsula

The small town of Divisa, 61 km beyond Penonomé is the crossroads for a major paved road that branches south into the Azuero Peninsula, one of the earliest parts of Panama to be settled. Despite recent road paving in the south and east, many of the peninsula's small towns are still remote and preserve much of their 400-year-old colonial traditions, costumes and a number of white churches. In addition to its tranquillity, the region's cleanliness and prosperity are a welcome change from Panama City. Most towns of any size on the Peninsula have annual Carnivals (the four days before Ash Wednesday) but the on in Las Tablas is especially picturesque and popular with visitors. Accommodation is in short supply at this time throughout the region.

Chitré

Colour map 8, grid C1
Population: 40,000

Passing through **Parita**, with a church dating from 1556, the road reaches the cattle centre of Chitré (37 km), capital of Herrera Province and the best base for exploration. The cathedral (1578) is imposing and beautifully preserved. The small **Museo de Herrera**, on Calle Manuel Correa, has historical exhibits, a few archaeological artefacts, and some local ethnographic displays. ■ *Tue-Sat 0900-1230, 1330-1500, Sun 0900-1200, US$1.* The town is known primarily for its red clay pottery, especially roofing and floor tiles which are exported, and for its woven mats and carpets.

Excursions

There are some nice beaches close to Chitré served by local buses; for example **Playas Monagre** and **El Rompio**, busy at weekends and holidays. Take the Santa Ana bus from Chitré terminal (frequent services throughout the day, 30 minutes, US$1) to Monagre. It is a pleasant 30 minute walk south along the beach from Monagre to El Rompío, where you can catch a bus back to Chitré or continue further south at low tide for mangroves and solitude. There are a few restaurants at Monagre but no accommodation. Near El Rompío are D *Cabañas Bayano Mar*, pleasant cabins with private bath and fan, nice setting, restaurant and bar. At **Puerto Agallito**, 15 minutes by bus from Chitré, many migratory birds congregate and are studied at the

Humboldt Ecological Station. Along the swampy coast just to the north is the 8,000-ha **Sarigua National Park**, established in 1984 to preserve the distinctive tropical desert and mangrove margins of the Bahía de Parita. Ancient artefacts have been unearthed within the park's boundaries. The pre-Columbian site of **Monegrillo** is considered very significant but there is little for the non-specialist to appreciate.

La Arena, the centre for Panamanian pottery, is 2 km west of Chitré. The Christmas festivities here, 22-25 December, are worth seeing, with music, dancing, bull running in the *plaza de toros* and cock fights (popular all over Panama). Tour operators in Panama City can arrange whirlwind shopping tours to La Arena. Bus from Chitré US$0.30; taxi US$1.50.

Sleeping & eating B *Hong Kong*, Av Carmelo Espadafora, T996-4483, F996-5229. A/c, pool, restaurant. B *Versalles*, Paseo Enrique Grensier, near entrance to town, T996-4422, F996-2090. A/c, pool, restaurant. **C** *El Prado*, Av Herrera and C Correa, T996-4620, F996-6859. Clean, quiet, well run, a/c, cheaper with fan, parking, upstairs restaurant. Recommended. **C** *Rex*, C Maliton Matín by main plaza, T996-2408, F996-4310. A/c, restaurant downstairs. **D** *Pensión Central*, Av Herrera next to *El Prado*. With bath, a/c, cheaper with fan, noisy in front rooms. **D** *Pensión Colombia*, C Manuel Correa near museum (3 blocks from Plaza), T996-1856. Fan, private bath, basic. **D** *Santa Rita*, C Manuel Correa y Av Herrera, T996-4610, F996-2404. Friendly, clean, large rooms, cheaper rooms have fans and cold water, restaurant, good value. Recommended. **E** *Pensión Herrerana*, Av Centenario. Small rooms with fan, private bath, very hot, clean, parking, basic. There are many restaurants serving economical *comida corriente*, plus a few Chinese. *El Meson* in the Hotel Rex is slightly upmarket. *El Chitreano,* C Antonio Burgos, good food and large portions.

Festivals *Fiesta de San Juan Bautista*, **24 Jun** and the preceding week; the district's founding (1848) is celebrated with colourful parades and historical events each **19 Oct**.

Transport **Air** Twice-daily flights (one on Sun) to the capital with *Chitreana de Aviación* and *Aeroperlas*, US$32 – these also serve Los Santos, Guararé and Las Tablas; taxi to the small airport US$1.50 (maximum).

Buses Chitré is the transport hub of the peninsula, there is a bus terminal just outside town, take city bus *Las Arenas*. To **Panama City** (250 km), regular departures by several companies 4 hrs, US$6. To **Santiago**, frequent service, 1 hr, US$2. There is no direct service to David, change at Santiago. To **Divisa**, 30 mins, US$1.30; same fare and time to **Las Tablas** (buses leave when full). To **Tonosí**, 3 hrs, US$4.15; to **Santiago**, 1½ hrs, US$2.50.

Directory **Communications Internet** at *Econoútiles* stationary store, Av Herrera 1 block from cathedral, US$3 per hour. Also at *Abacus*, Belarmino Urriola, US$2.50 per hour. **Shopping** Many well-stocked supermarkets. Craft shop on C Meliton Martín, 1 block from cathedral, has ceramics and basketry.

Los Santos
Colour map 8, grid C1
Population: 9,000

Los Santos, only 4 km across the Río La Villa from Chitré in Los Santos province, is a charming old town with a fine 18th-century church (San Anastasio) containing many images. The first call for Independence came from here, recognized in the interesting **Museo de la Nacionalidad** on Plaza Bolívar set in a lovely house where the Declaration was signed on 10 November 1821. ■ *Tue-Sat 0900-1600, Sun 0900-1200, US$1.* The Azuero regional IPAT office is next door. ■ *Open Mon-Fri 0830-1630.* T966-8072, F966-8040.

Sleeping and eating **C** *La Villa de Los Santos*, C Alzamora Julio, T/F996-8201. A/c caravans, with swimming pool and good restaurant. **E** *Pensión Deportiva*. No single rooms, private showers. There are a few simple eating places in town.

Festivals The 4-day Feast of *Corpus Christi* (40 days after Easter) is celebrated in Los Santos with one of the country's most famous and popular festivals, medieval dances, skits and costumes galore, a glorious distillation of the Peninsula's uniquely strong Spanish roots and well

Panama

worth attending. The *Feria de Azuero* is held at the end of **Apr** (variable date). 'Little Devil' (*diablito*) and other masks featuring prominently in these *fiestas* are the local handicraft speciality and may be purchased from many stalls or workshops around town and in Parita.

Guararé   The main road continues 22 km southeast through agricultural country to the tiny town of Guararé, notable only for its folkloric museum, the **Museo Manuel Zárate** two blocks behind the church, T996-2535, where examples of Azuero's many traditional costumes, masks and crafts are exhibited in a turn-of-the-century house. There is also a wealth of traditional dance, music and singing contests during the annual National Festival of *La Mejorana* (24 September). **Sleeping C** *Residencial Mejorana*, T994-5794, F994-5796, a/c, TV, restaurant. Two other hotels: *Eida* and *Guararé*.

Las Tablas

Colour map 8, grid C1   Las Tablas (6 km further) is capital of Los Santos province and the Peninsula's sec-
Population: 22,140   ond-largest city, 67 km from the Divisa turn-off. The central **Iglesia de Santa Librada** with its gold-leaf altar and majestic carvings is one of the finest churches in this part of Panama and is now a National Historic Monument. **El Pausilipo**, former home of thrice-President Porras – known to Panamanians as 'the great man' – is in the process of being turned into a museum. **Fiesta**: Las Tablas is also widely known for its *Fiesta de Santa Librada* and incorporated *Fiesta de la Pollera*, 19-23 July. The *pollera* is a ruffled, intricately embroidered in a single colour, off-the-shoulder dress based on colonial fashions and is now the national costume of Panama; *polleras* are made in a number of villages near Las Tablas (for example La Tiza, El Cocal, San José), the most beautiful coming from Santo Domingo (5 km east). Another high-quality manufacturing centre is **La Enea**, a small village close to Guararé.

The lovely and unspoilt beach of **El Uverito** is about 10 km to the east of town but has no public transport; taxi US$4.50. A paved road runs to the port of **Mensabé**.

Sleeping &   **D** *Oria*, Vía Santo Domingo, T994-6315. Out of town. **D** *Piamonte*, Av Belisario Porras,
eating   T994-6372. A/c. **D** *Zafiro*, Av Belisario Porras, across from main plaza, T/F994-8200. Modern, a/c, TV. **E** *Pensión Mariela*, opposite. Basic, run down. **E** *Pensión Marta*. Dirty, unfriendly, noisy and overpriced. There are some eating places around the church but not a lot of variety.

Transport   **Buses** To Panama City, several daily, 4½ hrs, US$7; to Santo Domingo, 10 mins, US$0.40; to Tonosí, 2½ hrs, US$4.25. Last bus from Los Santos to Las Tablas at 1800.

South of Las Tablas

Smaller paved roads fan out from Las Tablas to the beaches along the south coast and the small villages in the hills of the peninsula. A circular tour around the eastern mountain range can be done by continuing south to **Pocrí** and **Pedasí** (42 km), then west to **Tonosí**, all with their ancient churches and lack of spectacular sights, but typical of the Azuero Peninsula. Another 57 km of paved road runs directly over the hills from Tonosí to Las Tablas, good from the small tropical village of Flores.

Pedasí   A peaceful little town, the municipal library near the church has many old volumes.
Colour map 8, grid C1   The local festival is *Patronales de San Pablo* (29 June). President Mireya Moscoso was born in Pedasí and the family figures prominently in the town's history. Beautiful empty beaches (Playa del Toro, Playa La Garita, and Playa Arena) and crystal-clear seas are 3 km away, but beware of dangerous cross-currents when swimming. There is no public transport to the beaches but it is a pleasant walk early in the morning. You can also walk along the seashore from one beach to another, best at low tide. The small local fishing craft are based at Playa Arena (also the safest for swimming) and boats can be hired for sport fishing, whale watching and visits to to **Isla Iguana**, a wildlife sanctuary 8 km offshore, protecting the island's birdlife,

reptiles (including turtles) and forest. Locally hired boats cost about US$40 for half a day. The IPAT office in Los Santos can arrange a tour with knowledgeable naturalist René Chan who lives locally.

Sleeping C *Hotel Residencial Pedasí*, at the entrance to town, T995-2322. A/c, spacious grounds. **D** *Dim's*, Av Principal, T995-2303. A/c, lovely garden with hammocks. **D** *Residencial Moscoso*, T995-2203. With shower, TV, a/c, **E** with fan, clean, good, friendly, meals arranged by owner at nearby bar. *Turístico JR's*, T995-2176. Owner was head chef at *El Panamá*, Swiss/French dishes, good quality and variety, expensive. Recommended. *Angela*, local fare, good.

Transport Buses From Las Tablas leave when full, US$2, 1 hr, bumpy trip.

About 31 km kilometres from Pedasí, and 12 kms before Cañas, a small sign points to | **Playa Venado** the black-sand beach of **Playa Venado**, a surfers' paradise. There are five cabañas for rent here (**D**, no electricity, very basic, overpriced), and plenty of idyllic camping spots (camping free, showers cost US$0.25), as well as a combined open-air restaurant. The road onwards goes to **Cañas** (no hotel), running near the Pacific coast for a short distance, with a string of lovely coves and sandy beaches accessible by rough tracks.

From Tonosí a branch road goes a few kilometres further south to **Cambutal**, west of which begins **Cerro Hoya National Park**, where sea turtles come ashore to lay their eggs from July to November. There is also a 20-km long beach at Guánico Abajo, 20 minutes drive from Tonosí, but no public transport.

Sleeping in Tonosí D *Pensión Boamy*, T995-8142. With a/c, cheaper with fan, friendly, and **D** *Pensión Roslyn*, a/c, **E** with fan, basic. There are a few other simple restaurants, a gas station, pharmacy and a few basic shops. There are cabañas for rent (**E** per person), plenty of idyllic camping spots and a small basic restaurant.

1 bus a day to **Playa Venado** from Las Tablas at 1300, about 2 hrs, US$3.20, return at 0700. | **Transport** No direct bus Pedasí-Tonosí. Pedasí-Cañas around 0700 and 1500, US$2; **Cañas-Tonosí** 1 a day. **Tonosí-Las Tablas**, 4 a day between 0700 and 1300, US$3, 1 hrs, leave when full. A milk truck leaves Tonosí at 0700 for Chitré, via Cañas, Playa Venado, Pedasí and Las Tablas, takes passengers, returns 1230. Bus **Tonosí-Chitré via Macaracas**, 4 a day before 1100, 3 hrs, US$4, mostly good, paved road. Hitching is difficult as there is little traffic.

An alternative to the main road returning to Las Tablas takes the inland road north following the Río Tonosí. Crossing a saddle between the two mountain ranges that occupy the centre of the Peninsula (picturesque views of forested Cerro Quema, 950 m), the road arrives at **Macaracas**, another attractive but unremarkable colonial town, from where two paved roads return to Los Santos and Chitré (35 km).

About 45 km west of Chitré is Ocú, an old colonial town, whose inhabitants celebrate a | **Ocú** few notable fiestas throughout the year with traditional dress, music, masks and danc- | *Population: 2,750* ing. Ocú is also known for its woven hats, which are cheaper than elsewhere in Panama.

Festivals *San Sebastián*, the district's patron saint, costumed folklore groups, **19-24 Jan**. The *Festival del Manito* at the Assumption (**15 Aug**). Straight from medieval Spain, and well-worth witnessing, are the festivities of *El Matrimonio Campesino*, *El Penitente de la Otra Vida* and *El Duelo del Tamarindo*. IPAT tourist offices (Panama City, David, Santiago, Chitré) are best informed about dates and details.

Sleeping E *Posada San Sebastián,* on the plaza. Fans, clean bathrooms, patio, charming.

Transport Ocú can be reached directly from the Pan-American Highway (19 km) by a paved turn-off south just past the Río Conaca bridge (11 km west of Divisa); *colectivos* run from here for US$0.80. Alternatively, a mostly gravel road runs west from Parita along the Río

Panama

Parita valley, giving good views of the fertile agricultural landscapes of the northern Penin-sula. Several buses a day from Chitré, 1 hr, US$1.75, and buses on to Panama City, US$7. Those with limited time can get a representative glimpse of the Peninsula and villages by taking a bus from Chitré to Pesé, Los Pozos or Las Minas, all in the foothills of the western range, and then another to Ocú; staying the night and taking another bus on to Santiago to return to the Panama City-David highway.

The central mountains effectively cut off the western side of the Pensinsula from the more developed eastern half. There is only one road down from the highway, a gruelling gravel/dirt ribbon which staggers from near Santiago down the western coastline of the Peninsula as far south as the village of Arenas (80 km) before giving up in the face of the surrounding scrubby mountain slopes. Eastward from here the Peninsula reaches its highest point at Cerro Hoya (1,559 m). No roads pene-trate either to the coast or into the mountains, ensuring solitude for the **Cerro Hoya National Park**, which protects most of the southwest tip. The 32,557-ha park protects four life zones in a region that has been devasated by agriculture, over-grazing, season burning and human population pressuse. More than 30 spe-cies of endemic plants have been recorded in the park and it is one of the last known sites to see the red macaw. One research trip in 1987 even found an endemic species of howler monkey. Turtles also use the coastal beaches for nesting from July to November. There are no refuges at the park.

Santiago

Colour map 7, grid C6
Population: 69,117

Santiago is
the mid-point
rest stop for
cross-country buses

Back on the Pan-American Highway, from the junction at Divisa the roads enters the Province of Veraguas – the only one with seaboards on both oceans – and arrives after 37 km in Santiago. Capital of the province, Santiago is one of the oldest towns in the country, in a grain-growing region that is very dry in summer. Very good and cheap *chácaras* – macramé bags adopted by male peasants from the Indians as a convenient hold all for lunch and other necessities in the fields – are sold in the market here. Head-ing north for 18 km is **San Francisco**; which has a wonderful old church with wooden images, altar pieces and pulpit. Adjacent to the church is a swimming pool.

Sleeping   **In Santiago C** *Gran David*, on Pan-American Highway, T998-4510, F998-1866. A/c, TV, **E** with fan, private bath, clean, pool, good cheap restaurant. Recommended. **D** *Piramidal* on Pan-Am Highway nearing stopping point for David-Panama buses, T998-4483, F998-5411. A/c, TV, shower, clean, quiet, good pool. Recommended. **C** *Roselas Apartotel*, Vía San Fran-cisco, T998-7269. Apartments with kitchen, a/c, hot water, clean, friendly, safe parking for motorcycles. **D** *Santiago*, C 2 near the cathedral, T998-4824. Clean, with a/c, TV and shower, cheaper with shared bath. Recommended. **Pensiones** on Av Central include: **E** *Jigoneva*, No 2038. Basic, friendly; **E** *Central*, next door. Basic, all rooms with shower, Chinese owner; *Continental*, next door. Friendly, basic, shared bath. Swimming pool near town centre.

West of Santiago Camping Some 28 km west of Santiago, off the road to Canazas, you can camp at Campana Esperanza. It's a beautiful setting on a lake with camping (**F** or **G**) and a few cabins. There is also plenty of simple accommodation in the town of **Tole**.

Transport   **Buses** from **Penonomé**, US$4; from **Aguadulce**, US$2.50. Panama City-David buses stop outside *Hotel Piramidal*. Bus to **David** from here US$7. To **Panama City** US$7.

East of Santiago is the turn-off to **La Atalaya**, site of a major pilgrimage and festival in honour of a miraculous statue of Christ, and home of the Instituto Jesús Nazareno, an important agricultural school for rural boys (open to visitors on Sunday). Further on is La Mesa (turn-off at Km 27), with a beautiful, white colonial church. The old rough road heads south through **Soná** in a deep fertile valley and rejoins the Pan-American at **Guabalá**. The direct paved highway from Santiago to Guabalá saves a couple of hours. From Guabalá to David is 94 km.

Panama

Las Lajas is 20 km west of Guabalá – take turn-off at San Félix. It has good wide beaches (no facilities, two bars, costly shade for cars, shark-infested waters and strong waves). To get there take a bus from David to the turn-off (US$2.50), then walk 3 km to the town, from where it is 10 km to the beach (taxis US$5).

A turning left, 38 km west of Las Lajas, leads to Horconcitos and 13 km beyond on a dirt road, is the tiny fishing village of Boca Chica. From there you can cross in a few minutes to the island of Boca Brava (US$1 per person) in the **Golfo de Chiriquí National Maritime Park**. On the island is *Restaurante Boca Brava*, T8731-774-3117, with **D** cabins, **E** cane huts and **F** per person camping. Lots of wildlife and interesting flora, snorkelling on the nearby rocks, German owners.

Some 80 km to the southeast is **Isla de Coiba**. A former penal colony, the limited interaction has ensured the protection of the plant, animal and marine life in the area which has been protected since 1992 as **Parque Nacional Coiba**. Tourist agencies offer chartered diving trips but, with some difficulty, you can go independently (charter a launch, US$50-60, at Santa Catalina and there is accommodation on the island at US$5 per person). The wet and dry seasons are well defined, and the consistent year-round temperatures of 26°C are certain to make this an exceptional area for research. The reef here is the oldest in Central America and you can see rare fire coral. Marine wildlife is as abundant and big as anywhere in Panama.

About 10 km east of David is the small town of **Chiriquí**. A new paved road through Gualaca leads north to the mountains and over the divide to Chiriquí Grande (see page 1218).

David

David, capital of Chiriquí Province and a hot and humid city, rich in timber, coffee, cacao, sugar, rice, bananas and cattle, is the second city of the Republic. Founded in colonial times as San José de David, it has managed to keep its traditions intact while modernizing itself.

Colour map 7, grid C5
Population: 122,000

The attractive city is safe and friendly and a gateway to the Chiriquí Highlands and the Caribbean province of Bocas del Toro. With a wide selection of hotels and restaurants, it is a good place to break the trip from Costa Rica to become acquainted with Panama and its people.

The city of Davis focuses on the fine central plaza, Parque Cervantes, which teems with birds in the early morning, providing good bird-watching from the balconies of the *Hotel Occidental* or *Iris*. The colonial-style **Iglesia de San José** is on the west side of the park. The bell tower in Barrio Bolívar was built separately as a defence against Indian attacks. The Palacio Municipal is opposite *Hotel Nacional* on Avenida and Calle Central. The **Museo José de Obaldía**, Av 8 Este, No 5067 y Calle A, Norte, four blocks from Plaza, is a museum of history and art in the house of the founder of Chiriquí province. ■ *Mon-Sat 0830-1630, US$0.25*. Major week-long international fair and **fiesta** mid-March. The **tourist office**, *IPAT*, Avenida 3 Este y Calle A Norte on Parque Cervantes, T775-4120, Monday-Friday, 0830-1630, is friendly and helpful.

David presents a significant navigational challenge to the visitor. It is perfectly flat with no prominent landmarks, the central plaza is not central, there are no street signs, some streets have two names and the locals use neither, preferring nostalgic points of reference (eg: across the street from where the old oak used to be) to genuinely useful guidance. City bus routes are circuitous and generate additional confusion. When you get hopelessly lost take a taxi – for US$0.65 it's not such a bad idea.

Excursions A few kilometres north of David on the Boquete road is *Balneario Majagua*, where you can swim in a river under a waterfall (cold drinks for sale). There is another bathing place on the right 10 km further on. Take a Dolega or Boquete bus and ask the driver to drop you off. About 2 km along the main road to the border is the *Carta Vieja* rum factory, free tour and something to take away with you. ■ *Mon-Fri 0800-1600*.

Panama

Sleeping **A** *Nacional*, Av and C Central, T775-2221, F775-7729, www.panamainfo.com/granhotelnacional Clean rooms, good restaurant, small gaming room, major renovations but still traditional and charming. **B** *Castilla*, Calle A Norte between Av 2 and 3 Este, T774-5260, F774-5246. Modern and comfortable, centrally located. **B** *Fiesta*, on Pan-American Highway, T775-5454, F774-4584. Restaurant, good pool (US$2 for non-residents). **B** *Puerto del Sol*, Av 3 Este y C Central, T774-8422, F775-1662, new, clean, well furnished, TV, a/c, internet US$1/hr. **C** *Alcalá*, Av 3 Este between Calle D and E Norte, T774-9018, F774-9021, halcala@ chiriqui.com With parking, comfortable, nice. **C** *Panamá Rey*, Av 3 Este y Calle A Sur, T775-0253, F775-7115. Modern high-rise building, restaurant.

C-D *Iris* Calle A Norte, on Parque Cervantes T775-2251, F775-7233. With bath and a/c, cheaper with fan. Friendly and clean. **D** *Avenida*, Av 3 Este between Calle D and E Norte, T774-0451, F775-7279. With bath and a/c, E with fan, parking, good value. **D** *Occidental*, Av 4 Este on Parque Cervantes, T775-4068, F775-7424. With bath and a/c, cheaper with fan, nice balcony overlooking park, good value. Recommended. **D** *Pensión Costa Rica*, Av 5 Este, Calle A Sur, T775-1241. Variety of rooms, with shower and/or a/c, basic, clean, safe, friendly and good value, but a bit run down and noisy. **D** *Pensión Saval*, Calle D Norte between Cincuentenario y Av 1 Este, across the Plaza OTEIMA, T775-3543. With bath and a/c, **E** with fan, basic, run-down but friendly. **E** *Pensión Clark*, Av Francisco Clark, T774-3452. Bath, north of bus terminal. **E** (**F** singles) *Pensión Fanita*, C5 between 5 Este y 6 Este, T775-3718, family run in an old wooden house. Most cheap hotels are on Av 5 Este.

Eating *Panadería Pinzón*, Av 5 Este, Calle A Sur, opposite *Pensión Costa Rica*. Excellent shop/café with sandwiches, cakes. *El Steak House*, Pan-American Highway west of Av Obaldía. Good Chinese, moderate prices. *Ely's*, Av 3 E y Calle A Norte, also at Plaza OTEIMA. Good bread and

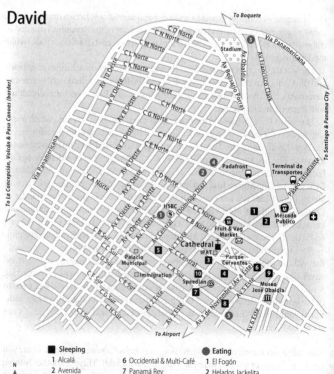

David

■ Sleeping		● Eating
1 Alcalá	6 Occidental & Multi-Café	1 El Fogón
2 Avenida	7 Panamá Rey	2 Helados Jackelita
3 Castilla	8 Pensión Costa Rica	3 La Cacerola
4 Iris	9 Pensión Fanita	4 Palacio Oriental
5 Nacional	10 Puerto del Sol	5 Panadería Pinzón

N

Not to scale

pastries. *Helados Jackelita*, Calle E Norte y Av Domingo Díaz. Very good fresh fruit ice-cream. *La Cacerola*, Av Obaldía behind Super Barú, just off Pan-American Highway. Self-service, clean, fresh Panamanian dishes all day, a/c, good value. Highly recommended. *Mariscos Daiquirí*, Av Central, Calle C Sur. Fish and seafood, not cheap, but good. *Mar del Sur*, Av Central y Calle H Norte. International food, expensive. *Multi-Café*, in *Hotel Occidental*, Av 4 Este on Parque Cervantes. Popular with locals, good quality, variety and value. *Parrillada El Portal*, Calle A Sur, Av 5 Este. Good. Many around central plaza (*Parque*, *Don Pedro*, all a/c). *El Fogón*, Av 1 Este y Calle B Norte. Good, reasonable prices. *Café Don Dicky*, Calle C Norte near Av Domingo Díaz (Central). Better than it looks. *Pizzería Mio Bello*, Calle A Sur y Av 5 Este. Good. Many good Chinese including: *El Palacio Oriental*, Av Domingo Díaz (Central) y Calle E Norte; *Nueva China*, Av Obaldía.

Discos *Brandy Wine*, Av 5 Este y C Central. *Momentos,* Av Obaldía.

Entertainment

Air *Aeroperlas*, Calle A Norte y Av 3 Este next to *Hotel Castilla*, T721-1230. F721-0852. Several flights a day from Panama City, US$57 one-way. Also to Bocas del Toro and Changuinola, both US$26 one-way (occasional seasonal offers, eg US$20). Daily service to San José, Costa Rica, US$83, one way. *Mapiex Aero*, Plaza OTEIMA, C D N between Av 1 and 2 Este, T775-0812, also flies to Panama City (3 daily), Changuinola and Bocas del Toro.

Transport

   Local Bus: urban buses US$0.20; taxis US$0.65 in city. **Car hire**: *Budget*, T775-5597; *Hertz*, T775-6828; *Mike's*, T775-4963. If wishing to rent a 4WD vehicle for Volcán Barú, do so in David.

   Buses The main bus terminal is at Av 2 Este, 1 block north of Av Obaldía. Taxi to centre US$1. All companies use this except Padafront, whose terminal is nearby at Av 2 Este y Av Obaldía. To **Panama City** regular buses US$10.60, express US$15, 6 hrs, 10 daily with Padafront, good service. To **Paso Canoas** (border with Costa Rica), US$1.50, 1½ hrs, every 15 mins 0500-1830. Direct to **San José** with *Tracopa*, 0830 daily, US$12, 8 hrs, with stop in San Isidro. Boarding *Tracopa* buses in David can be chaotic as tickets are only sold once the bus has arrived, and then people start clamouring for seats immediately. Regular bus to **Boquete** every 25 mins, 0600-2145, US$1.20 1 hr; **Volcán**, every 15 mins, 0700-1800, 1½ hrs, US$2.30; **Chiriquí Grande**, every 90 mins, 0630-1600, 3 hrs, US$7; buses to Almirante every 40 mins, 0500-1900, 4 hrs, US$7; **Cerro Punto**, 2¼ hrs, US$3.

Banks *Banistmo*, Av 2 Este y Calle A Norte, also on Av Obaldía, for Visa cash advances, changes AMEX TCs without commission. *Banco Nacional de Panamá*, 0800-1330 (generally very convenient, but officious guards have been known to turn away neatly dressed travellers wearing shorts), changes Amex TCs, 1% commission plus US$0.10 tax per cheque. *Banco General*, Av 3 Este y Calle C Norte, changes TCs, 1% commission, Visa ATM. *Caja de Ahorro* (Caja Pronto), Av 2 Este y C Central, for MasterCard and Amex TCs. **Communications** Internet: *Sinfonet*, Calle E Norte y Av Domingo Díaz, daily 0800-0000, US$1 per hr; *Speedlan*, Av 3 este y C A sur, beside *Panamá Rey* hotel, T777-2438, US$1/hr. *Instituto OTEIMA*, C D N between Av 1 and 2 Este, daily 0800-1200, 1330-2000, US$1 per hr; *Electrónica Nacional*, Av Obaldía, opposite *Domino's Pizza*, US$1.50 per hr. **Post office**: Calle C Norte y Av 3 Este. **Embassies and consulates** Costa Rica Urb El Bosque, 2 blocks west of clinic, best take a taxi, T774-1923. **Laundry** *Lavandería One*, Av Centenario Central y 1A Sur; *Lavafast*, 1 Av Obaldia. **Tour operators** *Fénix*, Edificio Erikan, Av Sur y Av 3 Este, T774-5300, F7745301. Travesías, Calle B Norte between Av 5 and 6 Este, T/F774-5352, travesias@mixmail.com Regional tours. *Servicios Turísticos*, C Central, T775-4644. Regional tours. **Useful addresses** Immigration office: Calle C Sur between Av Central and 1 Este, T775-4515, F774-1332, Mon-Fri 0800-1500. **Ministerio de Hacienda y Tesoro**: Calle C Norte, 1 block from Parque Cervantes, near the post office.

Directory

Panama

West of David

Heading towards the Costa Rican border, a dirt road turns off to the left to **Las Palmas**, a pleasant orange-growing village which welcomes tourists. Just before the village is a waterfall where a single column of water falls into a pool, delightful for swimming and camping. Ask in David for directions.

   The Pan-American Highway, now a modern divided highway, goes through cattle land for 26 km west to **La Concepción**, which also goes by the name of Bugaba, the local name for the district. It is an important agricultural shipping point, also widely known for its hand-made saddles. There are several decent hotels, but better accommodation can be found in Volcán, Cerro Punta or David. The fiesta of La Candelaria is held at the end of January. *Lee Chang Hermanos* stores is recommended for food, supplies, auto parts.

La Concepción is the gateway to the town of Volcán, the western section of the Chiriqui Highlands. From here you can travel to Río Sereno and cross the border into Costa Rica.

La Concepción to the border, Paso Canoas

Paso Canoas, the principal port of entry between Costa Rica and Panama, is 30 km west of La Concepción on the Pan-American Highways. At Jacú there is a secondary checkpoint, where most often only cars and buses heading east from the border are checked. Have passport, tourist card, vehicle permit and driver's licence handy in case they are asked for (usually hassle-free).

Paso Canoas is a busy border town, with many shops and outdoor stalls. There are also many good eating places, especially open-front restaurants opposite Costa Rican customs. Informally crossing back and forth among shops and business areas is easy, but travellers intending to leave one country for the other must submit to formalities before proceeding.

Remember Panama is one hour ahead of Costa Rica

Panamanian immigration Panamanian customs are open 24 hrs – However, the Costa Rican side is open 0500-2100 Panama time. After checking in at Entrada, buy a tourist card from the IPAT tourist office (open 0800-2300) around the corner of the building to the left. Then return to Entrada for an entry stamp. All relatively quick and painless, unless an international bus has arrived just before you. Free maps of Panama available at IPAT.

Sleeping **E** *Palace*, clean bathroom, basic. There is a reasonable restaurant at the border. Greater choice, although not necessarily better, on the Costa Rican side.

Exchange Money changers on the Panamanian side will change colones into dollars at a good rate; the Banco Nacional de Panama cashes TCs and also has Visa ATM.

Transport **Buses** to **Panama City** via La Concepción and David with Padafront, T727-6642, 10 daily every 1½-2 hrs, from terminal on northeast corner of main intersection. Reservations recommended; first leg from border to David unlikely to be full, but onward to Panama City may be booked up (they require reserved tickets to be paid for the previous day, but will hold seats for travellers arriving same day from Costa Rica; explain when reserving). Fare to Panama City, US$12; express 2300, 2400, US$17. Regular buses run to **David** for US$1.50, 1½ hrs.

Puerto Armuelles
Colour map 7, grid C4

Due south of Paso Canoas, on a good paved road, is Puerto Armuelles, the port through which all bananas grown in the area used to be exported before strikes forced producers to send their bananas by road to the Caribbean coast for shipping. Puerto Armuelles on the Pacific and Almirante and Chiriquí Grande (Bocas del Toro) are the only ports in Panama outside the Canal area at which ocean-going vessels habitually call and anchor in deep water close inshore. For information on visiting banana plantations, consult *Chiriquí Land Company* (Chirilanco), the local subsidiary of *Chiquita Brands*. Beyond the church and supermarket, opposite the golf course, in the smaller of two buildings is the management office (*gerencia*); there are no scheduled tours, but the staff will give good advice.

Sleeping **C** *Kokos Place*, T770-7049, F770-9175. **E** *Pensión Trébol*, 1 block from waterfront. Plenty of cheap eating places, eg *Club Social*, on water, ask any taxi, chicken and rice dishes. *Enrique's*, Chinese, good.

Transport **Trains** **Chiriquí Railway**: passenger service Puerto Armuelles-Progreso (half way to Paso Canoas), twice a day each way, 2 hr, US$1. There is also a 'Finca Train', 4 decrepit,

Panama

converted banana trucks, leaving at 1500 for the banana *fincas*, returning, by a different route, at 1800. No charge for passengers. Minibuses also leave all day for the *fincas*.

Buses from David via Concepción and Paso Canoas, every 15 mins, 0500-2000, 2½ hr, US$3.

Chiriquí Highlands

The Tierras Altas de Chiriquí include the highland areas around Boquete, Volcán Barú and Cerros Punta. The mingling of Atlantic and Pacific winds creates a year-round spring-like climate. The bajareque (literally 'falling down') shrouds the area in a fine mist creating cloud forests at higher altitudes.

Closer to the ground, the black volcanic soil creates highly fertile conditions. Coffee fincas and intensive farming, that produces most of the country's vegetables, are interspersed with tourist resorts, popular with Panameños seeking to escape the tropical heat during vacations (December to March). It's an ideal place to spend some time hiking, horse-riding, fishing, rafting and bird-watching.

Daytime temperatures are cool; evenings and nights chilly. Some days can be rather windy in the dry season. Mornings are especially clear and beautiful all year round. Travellers entering Panama from the north should consider a visit before pushing on to Panama City.

Boquete and the Eastern Highlands

Heading north towards Boquete in the heart of the cool Eastern Highlands, a well-paved road climbs gently from David, passing (after 10 km) a waterfall with a swimming hole, open-air restaurant/bar and space for wild camping. It passes through **Dolega** (swimming pool, one *pensión*, notable for its carnival four days before Ash Wednesday) before reaching (after 40 km) the popular mountain resort of Boquete, at 1,060 m in the valley of the Río Caldera, with the slopes of Volcán Barú to the west. It is a beautiful panorama of coffee plantations and orange groves, strawberry fields and gardens.

Colour map 7, grid B5

Good lodging and facilities make **Boquete** an excellent base for fishing, riding and hiking in the area. It is a slow-paced, predominantly wood-built town with several attractive landscaped parks, including the main plaza and the nearby Parque de las Madres. The fairground east of the river is the site for the annual *Feria de las Flores y el Café*, usually held mid-January. In April, a *Feria de las Orquídeas* is held with many varieties of local and exotic orchids, as well as other flowers. The cemetery is worth a visit, there is a small museum of *huacas* (funerary sculptures) in the centre (■ *Mon-Sat 0930-1300, 1400-1800*) and a fine panoramic view from the 'Bienvenidos a Boquete' arch at the entrance to the town. The **tourist information centre** (*CEFATI*) is at the southern entrance to town and there's a regional website at www.cometoboquete.com

AL *Cabañas La Montaña y El Valle*, Jaramillo Arriba, T/F720-2211, 2½ km from San Juan Bautista church in Boquete (pass church, turn right at fork, cross river, turn left at intersection, then follow signs), Canadian run, 3 deluxe cottages in 2½ ha (with kitchen, hot water, spacious), fine views, breakfast and dinner available, also camping (dry season only) US$10 for 2.

AL *Panamonte*, T720-1327, F720-2055, www.chiriqui.com/panamonte With bath, some with kitchen, dinner (US$13.50) is highly recommended, popular, garden boasts over 200 varieties of orchid, very attractive surroundings, built in 1919 and very well maintained, charming, run by the Collins family (Swedish/American), tours available, see below. **A** *Villa Marita*, 4 km on road to Alto Lino, T/F720-2164. Comfortable modern cottages amid coffee plantations, nice views.

Sleeping
■ *on map, page 1210*

Accommodation is difficult to find during the feria

Panama

B *Villa Lorena Cabañas*, by bridge near Panamonte. T/F720-1848. Comfortable cottages for 4 to 6 persons, overlooking the Río Caldera. **C** *Fundadores*, Av Central at south end of town, T720-1298, F720-1034, hotfundland@cwp.net.pa Restaurant, beautiful grounds with stream running through. **C** *Rebequet*, Av A Este y C 6 Sur, T720-1365. Excellent spacious rooms around a garden, with bath, TV and fridge, kitchen and eating area for guests' use, popular, friendly and helpful. Recommended. **D** *Hostal Boquete*, just off C 4 Sur to left of bridge, T720-2573, clean, TV, nice terrace and garden at back overlooking river, recommended. **D** *Pensión Topaz*, behind Texaco station at south end of town, T/F720-1005, schoeb@chiriqui.com With bath, **E** without, garden with view of Volcán Barú, small pool, good breakfasts, run by Schöb family (artist/anthropologist), tours arranged, beer garden at the family *finca* during the dry season. **D** *Hostal Palacios*, Av Central on main plaza, T720-1653. With bath and hot water, **E** without, basic, use of kitchen facilities. Friendly with good information on hiking, recommended. **E** *Pensión Marilós*, Av A Este y C 6 Sur, opposite *Rebequet*, T720-1380, with bath (1 single E without bath), hot water, English spoken, very clean and well run, motorcycle parking. Recommended. Often full but will permit sharing, tours organized, will store bags.

Eating
● *on map, page 1210*

Salvatore, Av Central at south end of town. Slightly upscale, Italian and pizza. *Pizzería La Volcánica*, on Av Central, ½ block from main plaza. Good pizzas and pasta at reasonable prices, popular. Opposite is *La Conquista*, delicious trout (but portions not too generous) and good local fare. Also on this side of the road are *Casona Mexicana*, for moderately priced Mexican food, and *Lourdes*, outside terrace, friendly, good value, recommended. *Sabrosón*, on Av Central near church, good quality and value. *Los Arcos*, C 1 Sur ½ block from Av Central. Good seafood, open 1600-0000, popular disco at night. Punto de Encuentro, near *Marilo's*, pancakes, fruit salad and juices, breakfast only. Two reasonable American-owned restaurants are *La Huaca*, near *Hotel Panamonte*, and *Santa Fe*, near the Feria ground.

There are several bakeries in town: *King's*, Av B Este near Parque a Las Madres, is particularly good. *Pastelería Alemana*, south of the arch at the entrance to town, has delicious coffee and pastries.

A 45-min walk from Boquete (past *Hotel Panamonte*) is restaurant *El Explorador*, across from La Montaña y El Valle. Beautiful location, picnic area, children's playground, hammocks, etc, entrance to area, US$1, but free to restaurant (excellent local food, breakfast and dinner), open weekends and holidays only.

Sports

River rafting *Chiriqui River Rafting*, Av Central, next to *La Conquista* restaurant, T720-1505, F720-1506, www.panama-rafting.com, open 0830-1730. Bilingual

Boquete

0 metres 50
0 yards 50

■ **Sleeping**
1 Fundadores
2 Palacios
3 Panamonte
4 Pensión Boquete
5 Pensión Marilos
6 Pensión Topaz
7 Rebequet
8 Villa Lorena Cabañas

● **Eating**
1 Casona Mexicana
2 Gringo Scooters & Internet
3 La Conquista
4 Lourdes
5 Pizzería La Volcánica

father-and-son team Héctor and Ian Sánchez, offer 4-hr Class III and IV trips with modern equipment on **Río Chiriquí**, US$75-90 per person. They can arrange lodging and logistics such as transport to starting-point or vehicle delivery to landing point. During dry season, Dec-Apr, they arrange trips on **Río Chiriquí Viejo** (Class III/IV Technical, US$90-100). Recommended. Also *Panama River Rafting*, Sr Graciano Cruz, speaks English, T774-1230. Offers shorter trips on Río Chirique, US$75 per person. **Hiking**: see below.

Buses 10 buses daily to **Panama City** via **David** with Padafront, US$11, 7 hr; terminal beside Delta petrol station next to *El Sótano* restaurant, east of Volcán intersection on Pan-American Highway, T770-4485. Local buses depart from the main plaza, called *El Parque*, old fashioned and picturesque, every 20 mins to **Volcán** (US$1.65), **David** (US$0.50), and **Paso Canoas** (US$0.75). **Bike and scooter hire** See Tour operators below. **Transport**

Banks *Global Bank*, open Mon-Fri, 0800-1500, Sat 0800-1500 changes TCs with a commission of US$1 per cheque. Same hours at *Banco Nacional* and *Banolar*, on the main street, who will both cash TCs. **Communications** Internet: *Estate Office* (see Tour operators), *Oasis Internet*, near *Pastelería Alemán*; *Kelnix*, beside Chiriquí River Rafting, T720-2803 0800-2000, Mon-Sun, US$1.80/hr. **Post office**: In the Palacio Municipal. **Laundry** *Lavomático Las Burbujas*, just south of church, very friendly, US$1 to wash. **Tour operators** *Hiking Tours*, Av A Ote on road to cemetery, T/F720-2726, owner Sr Bouttet, friendly and helpful, arranges guided tours in the area including Volcán Barú, Cerro Punta (around US$50 per day for a group of up to 3) and can give advice on where to stay overnight. Also arranges rafting. *Estate Office-Gringo's Scooter Hire*, On Av Central near park, Infomation on hiking, bike hire (US$2.50/hr, US$10/day 8 hrs), scooter hire (US$6.50/hr, US$20/day), deposits required. Good coffee shop. *Hotel Panamonte* organizes day trips to Volcán Barú, bird-watching, and coffee plantations, US$150 for a group of up to 4. **Sr Frank Glavas** at *Hotel Marilo's* organizes guides and trips throughout the area. **Directory**

Volcán Barú

The highest point in the country, Volcán Barú rises to an altitude of 3,475 m and is reached easily from Boquete, 21 km to the east, and not so easily from Volcán to the west. The summit lies within the boundaries of **Volcán Barú National Park** which covers some 14,000 ha and borders the vast La Amistad International Park, to the north, which itself spans the Panamanian-Costa Rican border covering much of the Cordillera Talamanca. Rainfall in the park ranges between 3,000 and 4,000 mm a year, and temperatures range from a subtropical 17°C to a distinctly chilly 7°C. Rich cloud forest makes ideal conditions for reptiles, amphibians and birds, with around 40 species endemic to the park.

From Boquete it is 21 km to the summit. The first 7 km is paved, but the rest of the track is rough, bumpy and steep for which four-wheel drive is necessary (there are no service stations en route). The paved road, sometimes lined with aromatic pines, goes through coffee groves, most numerous in the area during the year-end harvest season, mainly tended by Ngöbe-Buglé (Guaymí) Indians. Shortly after the end of the paved road you come to a small ANAM (National Authority for the Environment) office (seldom manned). There is also an office on the southern outskirts of town near the Colegio Franciscano, where there is some information available. The track winds up from the office through tall, impressive cloud forest, thick with hanging creepers, lichen and bromeliads. The steep cuttings are carpeted with a glorious array of ferns and colourful flowers; many birds can be seen, including bee hummingbirds, as well as wild turkeys and squirrels. The perfume from the flowers, especially in the wet season when there are many more blooms, is magnificent.

As the road rises, increasingly steeply, there are wonderful views of the Boquete valley, the Río Caldera running through a steep gorge, and the misty plain beyond stretching to the Pacific. Some 9 km from the park entrance is a sign on the right, 'La Nevera' (the ice-box). A small side-trail here leads to a cool mossy gully where there is a stream for water, but no flat ground to camp. This is the only reliable water

Panama

source during the dry season, so take plenty with you. Another sign, 2 km further on, marks several good campsites in the trees to the left but there's no water and a lot of rubbish has been left; take out what you bring in.

At the summit the cloud forest is replaced by a forest of TV and radio aerials in fenced-off enclosures. A short path leads to a small cross and a trigonometric point, from where the best views of dusty craters and the valleys of Volcán, Bambito and Cerro Punta stretch out below. The high altitude brush contrasts spectacularly with the dark green forest, wisps of mist and cloud clinging to the treetops. Occasionally horizontal rainbows can be seen in the haze, formed in the *bajareque* drizzle. There are many craters around the main summit, with dwarf vegetation, lichens and orchids. Even in the dry season, you will be lucky to have a clear view of both oceans.

In a suitable vehicle it takes about two hours to the top (depending on the weather), or 4½-6 hours hike up, three hours down, from the park office. A guide to the summit is not necessary, but Gonzalo Miranda (T637-6023) and Generoso Rodríguez (T720-1261 or leave a message with Sr Frank at *Pensión Marilós*), are a couple of guides who, although not trained, are both very knowledgeable and willing to take visitors to the summit, and other sites. Zona Urbana minibuses (US$1) go to El Salto, 4 km from Boquete and 3 km from the end of the asphalt. Vehicles which service the antenna installations often go up to the summit. Officially they are not allowed to take passengers, but drivers may give you a lift. They are also very friendly and like a chat. A taxi to the end of the paved road costs US$4 (recommended during the wet season as there is little chance of hitching and because the mountain summit usually clouds over in the afternoon making an early start your best option). Hiking from the summit all the way back to Boquete takes at least six hours. For those wishing to continue over Barú to Volcán on the mountain's west side, a trail begins 50 m before the cross, descending steeply over loose sand and scree before entering the forest; 8 to 12 hrs to Volcán, no water until you are half-way down. A challenging and rewarding hike (see page 1213).

The managers of the *Hotel Panamonte* in Boquete own *Finca Lérida*, on the slopes of Barú volcano, tours can be arranged. Ask at the hotel's front desk (see above).

Other hikes & excursions A recommended half-day walk is across the suspension bridge in Boquete, then take a right-hand fork winding steeply uphill. After about 30 minutes the paved road gives way to gravel; keep going to a crossroads (10 minutes) where you take the right-hand fork, heading due south. (For a view of the Pacific continue straight on from the crossroads for 5 minutes.) The right-hand fork continues with the river on your right and sweeping hillsides to your left. Eventually you rejoin the main road, turning right along an avenue lined with pine trees. The road winds down and across the Wilson bridge by a dam. After an exposed, flat stretch you meet the main road into Boquete from David; from here it is 30 minutes back to town.

Twenty-seven kilometres north of the Pan-American Highway (13 km south of Boquete) is a turn-off east to Caldera (14 km), from where a 25-30 minute walk leads to **Los Pozos de Caldera**, a well-known series of hot springs said to be good for rheumatism sufferers. No facilities, they are on land belonging to the Collins family (*Hotel Panamonte* in Boquete), who ask only that visitors and campers leave the area clean and litter-free, admission US$1. There are six buses a day from David to Caldera, four a day from Boquete to Caldera, and pick-ups from the main road to the village. River-rafting trips on the Chiriquí start from Caldera (see Sports, above).

Across the suspension bridge, **Conservas de Antaño** is a very friendly family-owned business that makes old-fashioned fruit preserves. ■ *T720-1539*. **Café Ruiz**, 2 km north of Boquete, a small factory known for its premium-grade roasted coffees. They welcome visitors for a free guided tour (Don José Ruiz speaks English), explaining the whole process from harvesting to hand selecting only the best beans and vacuum packing the product. ■ *T720-1392*. Next door is **Villa Marta**, a private mansion with a huge landscaped garden open to the public, and a sign: '*Mi jardín es* *su jardín'*. **Los Ladrillos**, a few kilometres further up the Caldera valley, is a small area of basalt cliffs with octagonal fingers of rock in clusters. Beyond is **Horqueta**, a picturesque hillside area of coffee groves, with a roadside waterfall and banks of pink impatiens; beautiful views to the south.

Volcán and the Western Highlands

The western section of the Tierras Altas (Highlands) de Chiriquí is bounded on the north by the Cordillera and on the west by the Costa Rican border, a prosperous and dynamic agricultural region renowned for vegetables, flowers, superb coffees, and the Brown Swiss and Holstein dairy herds that thrive in the cool highland pastures. The area is a bird-watchers' Mecca and is also popular with residents of Panama City wishing to cool off for a few days.

Heading away from La Concepción there is a very good paved road north, rising 1,200 m in 32 km to Volcán. From Cuesta de Piedra, a turning to the right will take you to the canyons of the Macho de Monte, a rather small river which has worn deep and narrow gorges. Further on, to the left, is the **Mirador Alan Her**, with good views from the purpose-built tower (US$0.10) to the sea, and on a clear day, the Punto Burica peninsula which marks the Panama-Costa Rica border. Local cheeses on sale are very good, especially the mozzarella. Near Volcán, you can get excellent wood carvings at *Artes Cruz* where Don Cruz, who speaks English, will make charming souvenirs to order and have them ready on your return trip.

La Concepción to Volcán

Volcán

Volcán sits on a broad 1,450-m high plateau formed by an ancient eruption of Volcán Barú. The pumice soil is extremely porous and dries within minutes of the frequent torrential downpours in the rainy season; in summer the area is tinder dry.

    The town is very spread out. The centre (with police station, gas station, supermarket, and bakery) clusters around the crossroads to Cerro Punta and Río Sereno. Volcán is a rapidly growing farming town, with nurseries cultivating ferns for export, the **Beneficio Café Volcán Barú** (interesting tours during October-February harvest season), and a small factory owned by the Swiss Bérard family producing excellent European-style sausages. San Benito school is noted for hardwood furniture, woodcarvings using *cocobolo* hardwood and hand-painted ceramics sold for the benefit of the school. Brother Alfred will let you browse through his warehouse full of English books from the now-closed Canal Zone libraries and you can take away what you will. **Cerámica Beija-Flor** is run by local women who market their own wares.

    Southwest of town is the **Las Lagunas de Volcán** nature reserve, with two beautiful lakes, abundant aquatic and other birdlife. High vehicles or four-wheel drives are required in the wet season. **Sitio Barriles**, 6 km from town on the road to Caizán (several buses daily, US$0.50), has interesting petroglyphs; also past Fina Palo Santo, 5 km from town on the road to Río Sereno. **La Fuente** park (signed from the main road) has playing fields and a spring-fed swimming hole (source of Río Gariché) excellent for children. ■ *US$0.25.*

    Volcán is a good jumping-off place for the ascent of **Volcán Barú**. It is possible to climb the west side in one or two days, camping about halfway by a small spring (the only reliable water in the dry season) or in a crater near the top (no water), descending the following day to Boquete on the vehicle road (see page 1211). The trail is beautiful, climbing gently at first through lush cloud forest (many birds, butterflies, and orchids), then scrambling steeply over loose volcanic sand and scree – a challenging but rewarding hike. Rubbish is a serious problem here; make sure you take yours away with you. **Tourist information** Angel Rodríguez at *Hotel Don Tavo* speaks fluent English and is very knowledgeable about the area.

Colour map 7, grid B5

Panama

Guides can be arranged in Volcán; climbers sometimes do get lost

Sleeping

Price categories shown for cottages are for 1 or 2 persons, but most accommodate larger groups for the same price or slightly more. Hotels are often fully booked during holidays

A *Cabañas Dr Esquivel*, T771-4770. Several large houses in a compound on the road behind *Supermercado Bérard*, friendly. **A** *Las Huacas*, main street at west end of town, T771-4363. Nice cottages, hot water, clubhouse, elaborate gardens, interesting aviaries, English spoken. **C** *Cabañas Las Reinas*, signed from main road, T771-4338. Self-contained units with a kitchen in lawn setting. **C** *Dos Ríos*, T771-4271. Older wooden building (upper floor rooms quieter), restaurant, bar, garden with stream, private baths, hot water unreliable. **C** *Don Tavo*, main street, T/F771-5144, volcanbaru.com/hdt/ Comfortable, nice garden, private baths, hot water, restaurant, clean, friendly. Recommended. **D** *Cabañas Señorial*, main street at entrance to town, T771-4239. Basic, caters to short stay couples. **D** *El Oasis*, behind restaurant, C La Fuente, El Valle, T771-4644. Bar can be noisy, owner also rents rooms in her home by La Fuente pool. **D** *Hotel California*, on main street, T771-4272. Friendly Croatian owner (Sr Zizic Jr) speaks English, clean private baths, hot water, parking, larger units for up to 7, restaurant, bar, quiet, good but check beds, some are very old and soft. **D** *La Nona*, C La Fuente, El Valle, T771-4284. Cabins for up to 5, friendly, good value.

Eating & nightlife

Plenty of cheap eating places. *Biga Deli*, good pizza and Italian, nice atmosphere, slightly upscale. *La Luna*, 4 km on the road to Cerro Punta in Paso Ancho. Good Chinese food. *Lizzy's*, near post office. Fast food, English spoken. *Lorena*, on the road to Río Sereno. Tables on porch. Good fish brought from coast daily, *Marisquería El Pacífico*, main road east of main intersection. Recommended. The restaurant at *Hotel Don Tavo* serves pizza and local fare. **Weekend discos** at *Eruption* and *Kalahari*, rustic, good places to meet young locals.

Festival

The *Feria de las Tierras Altas* is held in La Fuente Park on the **2nd weekend of Dec**, rodeo, dancing, crafts fair and many attractions.

Directory

Banks *Banco Nacional* and *Banco de Istmo*, Mon-Fri 0800-1500, Sat 0800-1200, both change dollar TCs. **Communications** Internet: *Sinfonet*, in *Hotel Don Tavo*, US$1 per hr, friendly and helpful.

Around Boquete

Based on Map by Ing l Ordóñez

Sleeping
1 Cabañas La Montaña y El Valle

Eating
1 Pastelería Alemana

Hardware store *Ferremax*, main road opposite police station, T771-4461, sends and receives international faxes, 0700-1200, 1400-1800, US$1.50 per page plus telephone charge, English spoken. **Laundry** *Lavamático Volcán*, main road opposite *Jardín Alegría* dancehall. Service only US$2.50, wash, dry and fold, reliable, Doña Miriam will have washing ready when promised.

Bambito

The road divides at the police station in Volcán. The right branch continues north to tiny Bambito and Cerro Punta (22 km), following the Chiriquí Viejo river valley up the northwest foothills of Volcán Barú. Cross the dry plain known as *Paso Ancho*, with coffee farms in the hill to the west. Just beyond is the moderately priced *La Hacienda Restaurant*, T771-4152, fresh trout, barbecued chicken. Recommended.

Sleeping and eating L *Bambito Camping Resort*, luxury cottages, also camping in A tents provided by the resort. **L** *Hotel Bambito*, T771-4265, F771-4207, www.chiriqui.com/bambito Luxurious, indoor pool, spa, conference room, good but expensive restaurant, with a view of a looming cliff, tennis courts, motor-scooter rental, horse-riding, mini-golf – the lot! Very good bargains can be negotiated here in the off-season. Across the road is *Truchas de Bambito*, a trout farm supplying the *Hotel Bambito* and the *Hotel Panamá* in Panama City. Visits are free, trout is US$2.65 per lb. **AL** *Cabañas Kucikas*, T771-4245, cottages in pleasant surroundings. Many roadside stands sell fresh vegetables and *chicha*, a fruit drink made from wild raspberries or fresh strawberries in season.

Cerro Punta

At the end of the road is Cerro Punta (buses from David via La Concepción and Volcán, two hours, US$2.65). Set in a beautiful valley, it is at the heart of a vegetable and flower-growing zone, and a region of dairy farms and racehorse stables. It is sometimes called 'Little Switzerland' because of its Alpine-style houses and the influence of Swiss and former-Yugoslav settlers (there is a settlement called Nueva Suiza just south of town). The countryside, full of orchids, is beautiful, though economic pressures push the potato fields ever higher up the hillsides, to the cost of the wooded areas, and sadly encourage the extensive use of agro-chemicals. There are many fine walks in the crisp mountain air. Continue through Cerro Punta to follow the main street as it curves to the left. **Haras Cerro Punta** (topiary initials clipped in the hedge) and **Haras Carinthia** (name visible on stable roof) are well-known thoroughbred farms who will usually receive visitors and show them round. Further on is the small bridge at Bajo Grande. The right fork leads to **Respingo**, where there is a small forest ranger station.

Altitude: 2,130 m

Panama

Hikes & nature trails

Camino Los Quetzales Continuing along this road is the starting point of the easy six-hour hike, mostly downhill after an initial climb, to Boquete. The track is clear in places and there are a few signs showing the direction and time to Boquete, with the last section following the Río Caldera canyon. It is easier in the dry season (December-April), but can be enjoyed throughout the year. Take food, insect repellent and rain gear. This hike is also recommended for bird-watching; quetzales and many other species may be seen. Four-wheel drive taxi from Cerro Punta to the Respingo ranger station, US$10. You can stay overnight here in the rangers' quarters (**F**) per person, clean, shared bath and kitchen. The Camino Los Quetzales leads to Bajo Mono, from which there are irregular local buses to Boquete (20 min, US$1). The walk can also be done in the opposite direction (uphill). It is possible to set out from and return to Boquete in one (very long) day.

    Parque la Amistad is another park, 7 km from the centre of Cerro Punta (sign-posted at road junction); open since 1991, with two trails, good for bird-watching, including quetzales. Nature buffs should also visit Los Quetzales reserve inside Parque La Amistad. See Sleeping. ■ *Entrance fee US$1, payable at Las Nubes.*

Sleeping

AL *Cabañas Los Quetzales*, T771-2182, F771-2226, www.losquetzales.com, at Guadalupe. A true forest hideaway, 5 self-contained cabins, baths, hot water, no electricity, on a spectacular cloud forest reserve at 2,020 m, inside Volcán Barú National Park, nearly 100 bird species, including quetzales, visible from porches, streams, trout hatchery, primeval forest, 4WD drive only, bit of a hike from parking area, but worth it. Owner Carlos Alfaro, fluent English, can arrange transport or daily cook. **B** *Hotel Cerro Punta*, T720-2020. With 9 simple rooms and a quite good restaurant, just before the turning to La Amistad. **B** *Hotel Los Quetzales*, T771-2182, F771-2226, Guadalupe. 10 basic rooms with baths, same owners as *Cabañas Los Quetzales*, sauna, restaurant, conference room, pizzería. **D** *Pensión Eterna Primavera*, in Cerro Punta town. Basic.

Volcán to the border

From the fork at the police station in Volcán, the left branch loops 48 very scenic kilometres west, climbing over the Cerro Pando, and passing through beautiful cattle country and coffee plantations on a well paved, little travelled, winding road to the Costa Rican border. **Los Pozos**, an area of small thermal pools beside a rushing river, is a good campsite, but only accessible by four-wheel drive vehicles and hard to find as the turn-off from Volcán-Río Sereno road is unmarked. Enquire at *Panadería Mollek* (good espresso, pastries), opposite police station in Volcán. Sr Juan Mollek has a farm at Los Pozos and can provide information. At **Río Colorado**, 15 km from Volcán, *Beneficio Café Durán*, a coffee processing plant whose delicious aroma of fermenting pulp and drying beans will announce its proximity from kilometres away, is hospitable to visitors. At Santa Clara, 25 km from Volcán, is the *Finca Hartmann*, 1,300-1,800 m, where the US Smithsonian Tropical Research Institute maintains a biological research station devoted to ecological studies. Enter the unmarked drive 50 m west of petrol station, next to a green house with 'Ab Santa Clara #2' sign and proceed 1 km on a dirt road. Latest bird-watching checklist compiled by researchers lists 277 species observable on the densely wooded coffee and cattle farm which borders La Amistad International Park to the north. Biologists and the Hartmann family welcome visitors and have information in Spanish and English. The Hartmanns (who are also excellent auto mechanics) have a comfortable wooden cabin available in the woods 1 km beyond the end of the dirt road (**AL** no electricity but with bath and hot water, fincahartmann@hotmail.com).

Border with Costa Rica – Río Sereno

The village of **Río Sereno** has the air of a cowboy town. The Panamanian businesses are centred around the plaza (including Banco Nacional – changes TCs), and the Costa Rican businesses along a street right on the border. Approaching the village from Volcán, abandoned installations from the era of military government are visible on the right. The bus station is just to the right of the *alto* (stop) sign. Follow the main street left along the plaza (public telephone) to where it ends at a steep road crossing diagonally. This is the border with Costa Rica, otherwise unmarked. Numerous vendors' stalls, especially Sunday during coffee harvest (October-December or January), when Indian workers and families shop. It is safe to park (and lock) your vehicle in the open area of *Almacén Universal*. Costa Rican shops selling leather goods, a few crafts, clothing, gladly accept US$ at current rates. Do not miss the upper floor of *Super Universal* and *Supermercado Xenia*. If entering Panama, sell colones here; it will be much more difficult at Volcán or David and rates will be worse in Panama City.

Sleeping and eating **D** *Hotel Los Andes*, good. Several good eating places. *Bar Universal* recommended for fried chicken with plantain chips (family atmosphere during the day, more raucous Sat pm and on pay day during the coffee harvest). *Sr Eli* has a new, unnamed restaurant at the top end of the Costa Rican street, good food, friendly and helpful.

Crossing to Costa Rica This is a minor international crossing post, recommended because the area is prettier and cooler than Paso Canoas (see page 1208), but only for those using public transport, private vehicles cannot complete formalities here, and Panamanian tourist cards are not available. Customs and immigration officials at Río Sereno are unconcerned about local pedestrians or small purchases crossing in either direction.

Panamanian immigration Immigration and customs are in the wooden police station visible on the hill north of the main Panamanian street. Departing travellers who have been in Panama for over 30 days should see Essentials, for details on exit permits. Those entering Panama with a visa, or from countries which require neither visa nor tourist card, will be admitted; those requiring a tourist card or a visa will be directed to Paso Canoas.

Costa Rican immigration The office is in a new white building at Río Sereno, open 0800-1600 Costa Rican time, Sun till 1400. Departing travellers who have overstayed their 90-day permit will be directed to Paso Canoas for the required tax payments and fines.

Transport There is a frequent bus service dawn to dusk from David to Río Sereno, 3 hr, US$4, via La Concepción, Volcán, Santa Clara; several minibuses daily Río Sereno-Paso Canoas, 2½ hr, US$2.50. On the Costa Rican side bus from San Vito via Sabalito (see page 1112) to the border.

Río Sereno to Paso Canoas

A recently paved winding road runs 50 km south along the Panama side of the border to Paso Canoas, about 2-2½ hours by bus. If questioned at the Breñón frontier station (unlikely), travellers who could not enter at Río Sereno should explain that they are en route to Paso Canoas to complete formalities, which is permissible. At Km 41 an impressive cascade over 100 m high pours over a cliff on the left of the Río Chiriquí Viejo below. For information on whitewater rafting on the Río Chiriquí Viejo from Breñón during the dry season, see Boquete, Sports, above. There is a good view of the river valley at Km 47, with Volcán Barú visible to the northeast.

Northwest Caribbean Coast

Panama's Caribbean banana-growing region has historical links with Columbus' fourth voyage and with the black slaves imported to work the plantations. Ports of varying age and activity lie on the Laguna de Chiriquí, providing an alternative land route to Costa Rica. This region is subject to heavy rainfall which may be daily afternoon downpours or violent tropical storms. Only from January to March is there much respite from the regular soakings.

Panama

From Chiriquí on the Pan-American Highway, 14 km east of David, there is a spectacular road north over the mountains to Chiriquí Grande (98 km). Beyond Gualaca the road passes the Fortuna hydroelectric plant, the Cricamola Indian Reservation and descends through virgin rainforest to the Caribbean. On the way up the hill, just north of Valle de la Mina is *Mary's*, a simple restaurant. If travelling under your own steam you can stop to admire the views across Lago Fortuna resevoir, from where the road is a tough, steep and twisting climb to the the continental divide, 62 km from the Pan-American Highway, and marked by nothing more than an altitude marker sign.

Over the continental divide to Laguna de Chiriquí

There is a 10-m waterfall 2½ km north of the divide. Going north from the continental divide to Chiriquí Grande is a cyclist's delight – good road, spectacular views, little traffic and downhill all the way, but nowhere to eat until Punta Pena, just outside Chiriquí Grande.

Sleeping On the southern side of the Fortuna Reserve is **B** *Finca La Suiza*, Quadrifoglio, T615-3774, afinis@chiriqui.com, in David, F774-4030, owned by a Swiss couple, Herbert Brüllmann and Monika Kohler, excellent for bird-watching on 20 km of forest trails, very good food, comfortable accommodation with bath and hot water, breakfast US$3.50, dinner US$8.50. To get there from Gualaca: pass the sign to Los Planes (16.4 km) and the turning to

Chiriquicito; 300 m after this junction is the sign for the Fortuna Reserve, 1 km beyond the sign is the gate to the *Finca* on the right.

The road reaches the sea at **Chiriquí Grande**, once the embarkation point for travellers catching the ferry to Almirante and beyond, but now, with the new road heading north, rarely visited.

Sleeping & eating **D** *Pensión Emperador*, with balconies overlooking the wharf, T757-9656. Clean and friendly. **E** *Buena Vista*, friendly, breakfast available, shared baths, **F** per person. Eating options include *Café*, good, *Dallys*, popular, to right of wharf .

The Banana Coast Fifty kilometres north of Chiriquí Grande one of Central America's most important banana-growing regions extends from **Almirante** northwest across the border to Costa Rica. In the 1940s and 50s, disease virtually wiped out the business and plantations were converted to *abacá* and cacao. With the development of disease resistant strains of banana, the *abacá* and cacao have been all but replaced, and banana planations once again thrive. The main players in the industry are large multi-national companies. **Cobanat** (*Cooperativa Bananera del Atlántico*), export through *Chiquirí Land Company*, a subsidiary of *Chiquita Brands* (formerly *United Fruit Company*) and **Dole**, subsidiary of *Standard Brands*, export bananas to Europe and the US from Almirante.

In April 1991 a devastating earthquake struck northwest Panama and southeast Costa Rica. An island in the bay which sank during the earthquake now shows as nothing more than a patch of shallow turquoise water.

Today **Almirante** is a small commercial port, usually just a transit point for tourists heading to or from the Bocas archipelago. The banana railway starts/ends here.

Sleeping **D-E** *San Francisco*, a/c or fan, small dark rooms, overpriced. **E** *Albergue Bahía*, T778-9211. Clean, friendly owner, will store belongings.

Transport **Bus**: to **David**, every 40 mins, 4 hrs, US$7; **Changuinola**, 30 mins, US$1; **Boat**: water taxi to **Bocas** US$3. To get to the *muelle* from bus station, cross over railway line, bear left following far side of fence across scrub land to road, head left along road 2 blocks to the quay. **Train**: see under Changuinola.

Car: the road between Chiriquí Grande and Almirante is in excellent condition for the 74 km length of the new road.

Isla Colón and Bocas del Toro

Colour map 7, grid B5 Across the bay are the rainforest, reefs and beaches of the Bocas Islands, the most important of which is Isla Colón. Formerly a major banana producer, the industry failed to revive alongside the mainland plantations and the main sources of income are now fishing and tourism. **Bocas del Toro** town, where most visitors stay, is on the southeast tip of the island. Most activity takes place around the broad main street – Calle 3 – and the leafy square. The *Fiesta del Mar* is at the end of September/early October, but for most of the rest of the year it is peaceful and quiet, although more hotels are appearing each year. English is spoken by most of the black population. The protected bay offers all forms of watersport and diving, beautiful sunrises and sunsets. All the islands harbour plenteous wildlife but especially those east of Colón where tropical birds, butterflies, red, yellow and orange frogs and a great variety of other wildlife abounds. For some, this is being called the new Galápagos, but, as in that fragile paradise, attraction and concern walk hand in hand. There is an informative permanent exhibit at the tourist office, with English translations about Columbus' landfall, indigenous peoples in the province, the fire at Bocas in 1904 and the *United Fruit Company* years.

The **tourist office** (*IPAT*) is on the seafront. ■ *Mon-Sun 0830-1630, T757-9642, F757-9857.*

Bocas del Toro AL *Bocas del Toro*, C 1 y Av C, T757-9018, F689-2684, h_bocasdel toro@hotmail.com, latest upmarket hotel in Bocas. **AL-A** *Swan's Cay*, opposite the municipal building on main street, T757-9090, F757-9027. Pricey and upscale, 2 restaurants, internet, laundry. **A** *Cocomo-on-the-Sea*, Av H y C 6, T/F757-9259, www.panamainfo.com/cocomo 4 rooms on the seafront with a/c, private bathroom, breakfast included, simple and clean, home-cooked meals, book swap, new US owners. **A-B** *Laguna*, on main street with Calle C, T757-9091, on main street with Calle C, breakfast terrace and bar.

B *Hostal Ancón*, north end of Main St, pleasant, spacious bar and terrace and communal veranda upstairs, good platform for swimming. **B-C** *Bahía*, south end of main street, T757-9626, www.panamainfo.com/hotelbahia Building formerly the HQ of the *United Fruit Company*, newly remodelled rooms with TV more expensive, some rooms without hot water, laundry and good value. **B** *Los Delfines*, Av G y C 5, T/F757-9963, hlaguna@cwp.net.pa, clean, reasonable size rooms.

C (**D** low season) *Del Parque*, seaward side of square, T757-9008, well-kept old town house with light airy rooms and good beds, hot water, free coffee and fruit all day. **C** *Dos Palmas*, Av

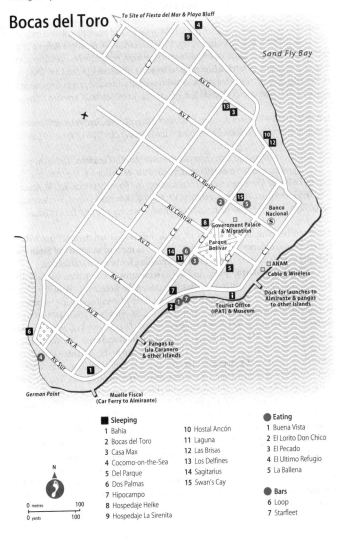

Bocas del Toro

To Site of Fiesta del Mar & Playa Bluff

Sand Fly Bay

Av G

Av E

Av L Rusel

Av Central

Banco Nacional

Government Palace & Migration

Parque Bolívar

ANAM
Cable & Wireless

Dock for launches to Almirante & pangas to other islands

Tourist Office (IPAT) & Museum

Pangas to Isla Caranero & other Islands

German Point

Muelle Fiscal (Car Ferry to Almirante)

Av D
Av C
Av B
Av A
Av Sur
C 8
C 6

0 metres 100
0 yards 100

N

Sur y C 6, T757-9906, quaint, built over water, a/c, cheaper with fan, clean, swim off platform at back, free coffee before midday. **C-D** *Hipocampo*, C1 y Av C, T/F757-9261, clean, upstairs rooms with TV and hot water, but more expensive. **C-E** *Las Brisas*, in 3 buildings with the main one on the sea at north end of the main street, (formerly *Botel Thomas*), T757-9248, F 757-9247, vendi69@yahoo.com, Apdo 5, Bocas del Toro. Wooden building on stilts, with bath and fan, restaurant, bicycle, snorkel and canoe hire, good but cockroaches and thin walls. More expensive rooms have a/c. If looking for a guide, ask for Baillo. **C-D** *Sagitarius*, 1 block from main street on Av D, T757-9578. With bath, a/c, cheaper with fan and TV. Clean and good.

D *Casa Max*, Av y C 4, T757-9120, colourful, renovated old house, hot water, free coffee and fruit in morning. **D** *La Sirenita*, Av H y C6, T757-9372, clean, family run.

E *Heike*, on main square, T757-9708, 7 rooms with a communal veranda, occasional restaurant open until 1030. Friendly and highly recommended. **G** *Mondo Taitu*, cheap surfers hostal at far end of island near *Hotel Las Brisas*.

Eating

Le Pirate bar has an information stand on the main street

Buena Vista Bar and Grill is an American-style sports bar with DirecTV, good sandwiches, brownies and mixed drinks. *El Lorito Don Chico*, on main street. Popular, cheap, cafetería-style, good dishes and cakes, bar by public dock very active, especially at weekends. *El Pecado*, on southwest corner of parque, Panamanian and international food including Lebanese, probably best restaurant in town, not too expensive. *El Ultimo Refugio* at the southern end of town. Good variety of international food. *Hostal Heike*, international cuisine, nice atmosphere. *Hotel La Laguna* great breakfast, moderately priced. *La Ballena* next to *Swan Key Hotel*. Bit pricey but delicious Italian seafood pastas and cappuccinos, good for breakfast and tables outside. *Rápido Sub*, good sandwiches. See also **Caranero** below.

Bars & nightlife

Loop Bar H, southeast corner of square, trendy spot with pool tables. *Starfleet*, near tourist office, relaxed waterfront bar, best low-key hangout in town, happy hour 1700-1900, closed Sun.

Caranero

Opposite Bocas, 200 m across the channel is the small island of **Caranero**, reached by panga either flagged down from a waterfront restaurant/bar, or boarded at the small quay just beyond **Le Pirate**. There are a number of restaurants and hotels here including **AL** *Acuario*, T757-9565, nicely situated on a pontoon, kitchen, bar, American owned. Restaurant/bar *Pargo Rojo*, T757-9649 good place to hang out while waiting for a boat back to Bocas.

Excursions

Trips can be made to the islands of the archipelago (Bastimentos – see below, **Carenero** and **Solarte** – also known as Nancy), to the bird sanctuary of **Swan Cay (Isla del Cisne)**, and the beautiful **Islas Zapatillas**, for beaches and fishing.

The **National Marine Park** on Isla Bastimentos encompasses virtually the whole island, bar the small town of Bastimentos on the western tip. Both this island and Isla Colón are turtle nesting grounds and their protection is being improved. ■ *Tours of the marine park US$15-20 per person, US$75 per boat, 0900-1600, entry to the park is US$10 extra, see below for tour organizers.* There is snorkelling and a lunch stop at Cay Crawl. Many tour boats also visit **Laguna Bocatorito** (no snorkelling), part of Isla Cristóbal, to view dolphins before going on to the Zapatillas Cays in the park. Colón also has **La Gruta del Drago**, a cave occupied by long-beaked white bats, which fly out at dusk (tour US$10 plus US$5 for lunch on beach). You can walk to the cave, a pleasant day, but ask locals for directions and advice on safety.

On Bastimentos it's a 30-minute walk to northern beaches with soft off-white sand and strong undertow; ask directions, take food and drink, or ask if anywhere is open selling meals. Red Frog Beach is the best known, but Polo's Beach (with red-and-black frog accompaniment) is also recommended – look out for sloths and monkeys. For those into frogs, Hospital Point (good snorkelling) on Cayo Nancy is the orange frog hangout. Note that many of the names relate to Columbus' landfall here on his fourth voyage in October 1502 (Carenero was where he careened his ships, Bastimentos where he took on supplies). The area has a rich buccaneering past, too.

Panama

Colón: Playa Bluff, 8-9 km northwest of Bocas (1 hr by bike – take paved road out of town past the cemetery until it runs out and then straight on following the shoreline); Playa del Drago on the northwest point reached by road across the island. **Bastimentos**: Red Frog Beach (see above), has a strong rip tide (3 drownings in recent years); Playa Larga, halfway along the north shore, is best reached by boat, as is nearby Polo's Beach.

Cayos Zapatillas: North Cay is the quieter because the tour boats do not generally stop here.

Isla Popa and **Cayo Agua**, the other main islands in the area, are sparsely settled, heavily forested and have no beaches.

Beaches
Do not go to deserted stretches of beach alone and be wary of strong ocean currents at most of them

Bastimentos village is a stilted, ramshackle, wooden affair that clings to a steep slope on the lee side of the island. Tourism seems to skirt round it which helps the place hold on to its old-style Caribbean charm.

Sleeping and Eating E *Tom e Ina*, in centre of village, T757-9831. **E** *El Limbo*, in next bay east of Bastimentos village T624-1965. **E** *Pelícano*, at east end of town, T676-2348.

Roots, just east of the centre, bar and restaurant with a nice terrace, run by Oscar who will also guide tourists to visit the lake in the middle of the island. *Calypso Club*, breakfast US$2.50, dinners from US$3.50, room and hammocks for rent, boat trips to the National Marine Park arranged. Rooms may also be arranged through Gabriel.

Diving Several places throughout the archipelago are popular for diving. On Isla Colón **AL** *Mangrove Inn Eco-Dive Resort*, T/F757-9594, manginn@pty.com, office in Bocas del Toro, C 3 (*Mangrove Roots Shop*). Several good locations near the resort for scuba diving and for snorkelling in the clear waters around Mangrove Point.

Cavern diving at Polo's Beach, but only in calm sea, Punta Vieja on northeast shore of Bastimentos and boat dives at Cayos Zapatillas.

Best **snorkelling** sites: Hospital Point on **Cayo Nancy**, **Punta Vieja**, **Islas Zapatillas**, but only outside the reef – tour boats will just drop you off at **North Cay** for snorkelling off the beach (points en route on tours are also disappointing – Cay Crawl, the lunch stop for most

Watersports in the region

Panama

Bocas del Toro Archipelago

has shallow waters and only sea grass habitat, no reef), hire a boat and guide from one of the dive shops to see the best of the reef.

Equipment hire & courses *Starfleet*, near tourist office, T/F757-9630, www.explorepanama.com/starfleet.htm, run by Canadian Joanne Gadd who has years of experience in the Bocas waters, German spoken, PADI course US$205, discounts for cash and groups, US47.50 for 2 dives for qualified divers, snorkel trips, incl gear US$15. Also in Bocas del Toro town is *Bocas Watersports*, T757-9541, www.bocaswatersports.com, C 3, with similar services, 2 dives US$40. 3 neighbouring islands are also visited. Snorkelling gear can be hired from several places (eg *Las Brisas*, *Le Pirate*), US$5 a day *J&J Boat Tours*, T/F757- 9915, next to Le Pirate Bar, offers snorkeling and diving tours.

Surfing Playa Bluff, **Playa Paunch**, both on Colón, and the northeast point of **Caranero** have the best breaks.

Transport **Cycle hire** US$7.50/day, US$1.50/hr, from *Las Brisas* and *Hotel Delfines*. On main street, Isla Colón, southwest corner of plaza. Cheapest hire is from shop on road out to cemetery, US$1 per hr but in all cases check bicycles carefully. **Moped hire**, at Bocas Property, Av G, T757-9982, near *Hotel Delfines*,on other side of road, US$5/hr, US$8/2 hrs, US$12/4 hrs, US$20/all day 0900-1900, no deposit. Can also arrange **horse-riding**.

Air Bocas del Toro (T757-9341) can be reached by *Aeroperlas* from Albrook Airport, Panama City (US$50 one-way). To **David** US$26, seasonal offers at US$20.

Boat Water taxis to and from **Almirante** daily from 0530-1830, 30 mins minimum, US$3, leave when full.

Vehicle ferry ('Palanga') Sat, Sun, Wed, Fri, between Almirante and Bocas, leaves Almirante 0900, leaves Bocas 1700, US$15 per car (more expensive for large vehicles), US$1 foot passengers.

To Bocas del Toro by canoe with outboard motor, US$10, or US$15 for 2. Hire boats or water taxis in Bocas del Toro to Bastimentos and the other islands. Boat to Bastimentos US$2 per person one-way, ask around *Le Pirate Bar* or elsewhere along waterfront. Inter-island boats also go from the water taxi *muelle*, near the tourist office. Don't forget to arrange a time to be picked up. If hiring a boat, try to arrange it the day before, US$5/hr not including petrol, 4 hrs minimum, can take 5 people. If going on to Costa Rica from Bocas, get the first water taxi for connections at Sixaola.

Directory **Banks** *Banco Nacional de Panamá*, Av F, between C 1-2, Bocas del Toro, open Mon-Fri 0800-1500, Sat 0900-1200. At Changuinola: *Banistmo*, open till 1500 weekdays, 1200 Sats, changes AMEX TCs and cash advances on Visa and MasterCard.

Communications Internet at tourist office, next to *El Lorito* restaurant, US$1/hr. **Laundry** *Lavamático*, on the right, just beyond *Hostal Ancón* at north end of town, US$3 per load, wash and dry, pick up following day. **Immigration** Migración office, at the back of the Palacio, is for visitors arriving by air or boat. Official waits at the airport to stamp passports of those arriving nationals covered by the '*convenio*' and to provide tourist cards for others (eg US citizens arriving from Costa Rica; see 'visa and immigration' in Essentials). Those requiring visas must go to the Banco Nacional to purchase the relevant documentation (US$10) and then go to the office in the Palacio. This office does not renew tourist cards or visas (done in Changuinola). **Tour operators** *Transparente Tours*, main street beside *Le Pirate*, US$20 to Laguna Bocatorito, Cayo Crawl, Zapatillas or Red Frog Beach, and sometimes snorkelling at Hospital Point. Make sure that tours last for the whole day if you pay for it, some simply return to Bocas after lunch at Cay Crawl.

Towards Costa Rica

Changuinola Between Almirante and the Costa Rica border is sprawling Changuinola, the main commercial centre in the region which, although architecturally not attractive, has an airport and lively nightlife with clubs, cinema and theatre.

Excursions can be made to Naso/Teribe Indian villages. *Wekso Ecolodge*, reached by taxi to El Silencio US$5, then launch on Río Teribe US$30 per boat, or US$5 on local boat. Organize in advance through ODESEN (National Organization for Sustainable Ecotourism Development), T620-0192, www.ecotour.org/destinations/wekso.htm

C *Alhambra*, on the main street (C 17 de Abril), T758-9819, F758-9820, large rooms, hot water TV, a/c, telephone. **C** *Semiramis*, diagonally opposite the Alhambra, T758-6006, F7586016, dark rooms with outstanding kitsch pictures, a/c, TV, restaurant serving Chinese plus standard Panamanian food. **D-E** *Carol*, T758-8731, 200 m from bus station. With bath, hot water, a/c (cheaper rooms without), TV, small dark rooms, restaurant next door same ownership. **D** *Changuinola*,T758-8681, near airport. **D** *Taliali*, 150 m from bus station, set back from C 17 de Abril, a/c, TV, hot water, smallish rooms.

El Portal, just round bend from *Hotel Carol*, friendly. *Chiquita Banana*, opposite bus station, curt service.

Air To **David** US$26, **Panama City** (Albrook) $53 with *Aeroperlas*, T758-7521.

Trains The banana railways provide links between **Guabito** on the Costa Rican border, Changuinola and **Almirante**. No passenger trains although passage can be negotiated with officials. Schedules and fares should be checked with the *Chiriquí Land Company*, Almirante T758-3215, should leave for border every day.

Buses There is a road from Changuinola to **Almirante** (buses every 30 mins till 2000, 30 mins, US$1). Bus to **San José** leaves Changuinola 1000 daily (no office – pay on bus) US$8, 6-7 hrs, one stop for refreshments in Limón, but many police checks (this bus may not always run). Bus to **David**, 4 hrs, US$7.

Bank *Bancistmo*. **Migración** Office deals with renewal of visas and tourist cards.

The border at Sixaola/Guabito is open 0800-1800 Panama time. Formalities for entry/exit for each country are performed at either end of the banana train bridge which crosses the border. Just a short walk over the bridge; onward ticket may not be asked for on the Costa Rican side.

Entering Panama If you need a visa or tourist card, best to obtain it in San José. Entry charge normally US$0.75 (receipt given) although if you already have a visa you may not be charged, 30 days given if you already have a visa, 5 days' entry card if not, US$2 (extensions at Changuinola airport immigration, opens 0830 – 5 passport photos, photographer nearby charges US$7 for 6).

Advance clocks one hour when entering Panama

Sleeping No accommodation in **Guabito**, but if seeking cheap accommodation, cross the border as early as possible in order to get as far as **Almirante** (US$1 by bus).

Transport The bus from **Changuinola** to the border and back is marked 'Las Tablas', US$0.75, 30 mins (every hour until 1700), or *colectivo* taxi, US$1.25 per person (private taxi US$10). Bus to San José, Costa Rica, at 1000, US$8, 6-7 hrs, 1 stop for refreshments, but many police checks, also to Puerto Viejo.

Directory Money exchange It is difficult to change colones to dollars in Guabito. If not returning to Costa Rica, try to use up all colones before crossing the border. Be sure to have enough small denomination US dollar bills to hand, US$50 notes are unlikely to be accepted.

Panama

Darién and the routes to Colombia

As one of the great impenetrable wildernesses of the world, crossing the Darién Gap is the dream of many, but not a trip to be undertaken lightly. By all accounts good Spanish, good guides, serious planning and lots of money are essential. If you're looking for an exciting route to Colombia, the river crossings and jungle treks of the Darién are one option; alternatively, you can use use launches and canoes to skip along the Pacific or Caribbean coastline; but neither option is cheap.

East of Chepo the Darién stretches out over a third of the area of Panama and is almost undeveloped. Most villages are accessible only by air, river or on foot. The Pan-American Highway ends at Yaviza; from there, if you want to cross by land to South America, it's on foot through the jungles of Darién.

At the end of 1992, Panama and Colombia revealed a plan to build a road through the Darién Gap, which includes environmental protection. Construction of a previous project had been halted in the 1970s by a lawsuit filed by US environmental groups who feared deforestation, soil erosion, endangerment of indigenous groups and the threat of foot-and-mouth disease reaching the USA. Even if the plan is completed, the Darién Gap road linking Panama with Colombia will not be open for many years, so the usual way of getting to Colombia is by sea or air. It is possible to go overland, but the journey is in fact more expensive than by air – and considerably more dangerous.

By land

The Pan-American Highway runs east 60 km from Panama City to the sizeable town of **Chepo**. There are no hotels or *pensiones* in Chepo, but if you are stuck there, ask at the fire station, they will be able to find a place for you. There is a document check in Chepo and at one or two other places. From Chepo the highway has been completed as far as **Yaviza** (225 km). It is gravel from Chepo until the last 30 km which are of earth (often impassable in the rainy season).

From **El Llano**, 18 km east of Chepo, a road goes north to the Caribbean coast. After 27 km it passes the *Nusagandi Nature Lodge* in the Pemansky Nature Park. The Lodge is in Kuna (Cuna) territory, in an area of mostly primary forest. The coast is reached at Cartí, 20 km from Nusagandi. From here there is access to the Archipiélago de San Blas.

Thirty-five kilometres east of Chepo the Pan-American crosses the Lago Bayano dam by bridge (the land to the north of the highway as far as Cañazas is the **Reserva Indígena del Bayano**). Lago Bayano dam supplies a significant amount of Panama's electricity, and has been a source of friction with the Kuna Indians who occupy the land around the lake and especially above in the catchment area. However, it is hoped that the new autonomous *Comarca*, created in 1996, will confirm the Indian title to the land and set up conservation measures.

The main villages (Yaviza, Púcuro, Paya and Cristales) have electricity, radios and cassette decks; canned food is available in Yaviza, Pinogana, Unión de Chocó, Púcuro and Paya (but no gasoline), only the Emberá-Wunan (also spelt Wunaan) of the Chocó and Kuna women retain traditional dress. Organized jungle tours to Kuna Indians, Emberá-Wunan Indians and the Río Bayano costing from US$65 to over US$300 can be purchased through *Argo Tours* in Balboa (see page 1181) or through *Extreme Tours* in Panama City. Two of the easiest villages to visit on your own are Mogue, 45 minutes upriver from La Palma (at high tide), US$10 (possible to see Harpie eagles in this area) and at Puerto Lara – one hour's walk from turning off the main highway just south of Santa Fe (4-person huts, US$20 per person, including meals).

Panama

The bus service from Panama City (see below) has its problems; the road is bad and may be washed out after rains. Find out before you leave how far you can get. Alternatively there is an irregular boat to Yaviza, about once a week, US$12 including meals, leaving from the harbour by the market in the old city, information from Muelle Fiscal, Calle 13 next to the Mercado Público. The only sleeping accommodation is the deck (take a hammock) and there is one primitive toilet for about 120 people. The advertised travel time is 16 hours, but it can take as long as two days.

Transport

From bus terminal in Panama City, buses leave every 2 hrs 0630-1430 for **Pacora**, US$0.80, **Chepo**, US$1.60, **Cañitas**, 4 hrs, US$3.10, **Arretí**, 6 hrs, US$9, **Metetí** and **Canglón**, 8 hrs, US$11.20. Beyond, to **Yaviza**, in the dry season only (Jan-Apr), US$15, 10 hrs minimum. Plenty of pick-ups run on the last stretch to Yaviza, eg about 3 hrs from Metetí to Yaviza.

Yaviza/El Real

Another possibility is to fly to La Palma and take the much shorter boat trip to Yaviza, or direct to El Real (three a week, US$68 return), which is about 10 km from Yaviza. There is only one hotel at **Yaviza** (**E** *Tres Américas*, pay in *Casa Indira* shop next door, take mosquito coils – nowhere to hang a net, basic, but friendly); there is a TB clinic and a hospital. Crossing the river in Yaviza costs US$0.25. From Yaviza it is an easy two-hours' walk to **Pinogana** (small and primitive), where you have to cross the Río Tuira by dugout, US$1 per person. From Pinogana you can walk on, keeping the river to your left to Vista Alegre (three hours), recross the river and walk a further 30 minutes to **Unión de Chocó** (some provisions and you can hammock overnight; you can sleep in the village hall but use a net to protect against *vinchucas* – Chagas disease). It's 1 km upriver to Yape, on the tributary of the same name, then three to four hours' walk to Boca de Cupe. Alternatively you can go by motor dugout from Pinogana to Boca de Cupe (about US$65 per boat). Or you can take a boat from Yaviza to **El Real** (US$10), where there is a very basic place to stay (**E** *El Nazareno*, T228-3673). Directly opposite there is a lady who will prepare meals if given notice. From there take a motor dugout to Boca de Cupe, about US$15-20 per person, five hours (if possible, take a banana dugout, otherwise bargain hard on boats). A boat all the way to Paya costs about US$35 per person for groups of four or five. Boats from El Real are not very frequent and may only go as far as Unión de Chocó or Pinogana. A jeep track runs from El Real to Pinogana. There are various other combinations of going on foot or by boat, prices for boat trips vary widely, so negotiate. They tend to be lower going downstream than up. It is wise to make payment always on arrival.

Boca de Cupe
Colour map 8, grid B3

Stay the night at Boca de Cupe with a family. Food and cold beer is on sale here (last chance if you are going through to Colombia), and *Restaurant Nena* (blue building near landing dock) serves meals for US$2 and is a good source of information. Lodging (**D**) in Boca de Cupe with Antonio (son of María who helped many hikers crossing Darién, but who died in 1989). Don Ramón will prepare meals for US$2 and let you sleep on his floor. You can go with Emberá-Wunan Indians to Unión de Chocó, stay one or two days with them and share some food (they won't charge for lodging). The Emberá-Wunan are very friendly and shy, better not to take pictures. In Boca de Cupe get your exit stamp (though you may be told to get it at Púcuro) and keep an eye on your luggage. From Boca de Cupe to Púcuro by dugout, US$20-50, to Paya (if river level is high enough), US$80. The section Boca de Cupe-Púcuro is possible on foot.

Púcuro

Púcuro is a Kuna Indian village and it is customary to ask the chief's permission to stay (he will ask to see your passport). Immigration here, if arriving from Colombia, can be very officious. The women wear colourful ornamented *molas* and gold rings through their noses. There is a small shop selling basic provisions, such as tinned meats and salted biscuits. Visitors usually stay in the assembly house. People show little interest in travellers. From Púcuro you can walk through lush jungle to Paya,

Panama

six hours (guide costs US$20, not really necessary, do not pay in advance), which was the capital of the Kuna Empire. From Púcuro to Paya there are four river crossings. The path is clear after the first kilometre.

Paya
Colour map 8, grid B3

In Paya you may be able to stay in the assembly house at the village, but it is usual to stay 2 km away eastwards in the barracks; US$2.50 per person, recommended. There's a passport check, baggage search and, on entry into Panama at least, all gear is treated with a chemical which eats plastic and ruins leather – wash it off as soon as possible. For US$2-2.50 you will get meals. The Kuna Indians in Paya are more friendly than in Púcuro. From Paya there are two routes.

Paya to Turbo

Route 1 From Paya, the next step is 4-6 hours' walk to **Palo de las Letras**, the frontier stone, where you enter Los Katíos, one of Colombia's national arks (see below). The path is not difficult, but is frequently blocked up to the frontier. From there you go down until you reach the left bank of the Río Tulé (3 hours, no water between these points), you follow it downstream, which involves seven crossings (at the third crossing the trail almost disappears, so walk along the river bed – if possible – to the next crossing). If any of these watercourses are dry, watch out for snakes. About 30 minutes after leaving this river you cross a small creek; 45 minutes further on is the abandoned camp of the Montadero, near where the Tulé and Pailón rivers meet to form the Río Cacarica. Cross the Cacarica and follow the trail to the MA (Ministerio del Medio Ambiente – Colombian National Parks) abandoned rangers' hut at

Darién

Cristales (7 hrs from Palo de las Letras). Guides from Paya to Cristales (they work in a rota and always go in pairs), charge US$55-200. They each carry a gun and a small bag of provisions, and travel very fast.

If you insist on walking beyond Montadero, a machete, compass and fishing gear (or extra food) are essential. The path is so overgrown that it is easier, when the river is low, to walk and swim down it (Cristales is on the left bank, so perhaps it would be better to stick to this side). Occasional dugout will take you to **Bijao** (or Viajado), two hours, for around US$120 per boat. There is no village nearby, so arrive prepared. It is possible to walk to Bijao down the right (west) bank of the Río Cacarica (heavy going). From the bend to the east of the river the path improves and it is one hour to Bijao. At Bijao ask for the ANAM station, where you can eat and sleep (floor space, or camp). At the end of 1998 guerrillas seized Bijao, killing several people and driving out others, so it is unclear what facilities are available now.

From Bijao a motor dugout used to run to **Travesía** (also called Puerto América) for US$40 per person (2-5 hours), from where motorboats go to Turbo for US$10 (in scheduled boat – if it stops; if not it'll cost you about US$250 to hire a boat). Travesía has some accommodation and provisions but has been reported as expensive and anti-gringo. Once again, there is a walking route south to Limón (2 hours) and east to La Tapa (½ hour). A cargo boat may be caught from here to Turbo. There is one *residencial* and a shop in Travesía. The last section from Travesía down the Atrato goes through an area full of birdlife including hummingbirds, kingfishers, herons, and 'screamers' which are about the size of turkeys and are believed to be endemic to the Atrato valley. The river enters the Great Atrato swamp and from there to the Bahía de Colombia. Turbo is on the opposite coast.

On arrival in Turbo, you must go to the DAS office (Security Police) at Postadero Naval, north along Carrera 13 near airport (open 0800-1630), to get your entrance stamp. If you fail to do this, you will have to wait until Cartagena, or elsewhere, and then explain yourself in great detail to DAS and quite likely you will be fined. If you arrive at the weekend and the DAS is closed, make sure you obtain a letter or document from the police in Turbo that states when you arrived in Colombia. The problems with this route are mostly on the Colombian side, where route finding is difficult, the undergrowth very hard to get through, and the terrain steep. Any rain adds greatly to the difficulties though equally, when the water is low, boats need more pole assistance and the cost increases.

If you are coming into Panama from Colombia by these routes, and you have difficulty in obtaining entry stamps at Púcuro or Boca de Cupe, obtain a document from an official en route stating when you arrived in Panama. This may be equally hard to get. When you arrive in Panama City, go to the Oficina Nacional de Migración (who may send

Cautions and general notes on crossing the Darién Gap

When planning your trip by land or along the coast to Colombia, remember there are strict rules on entry into Colombia and you must aim for either Turbo or Buenaventura to obtain your entry stamp. Failure to do this will almost certainly involve you in significant fines, accusations of illegal entry, or worse in Colombia. Also, do not enter Darién without first obtaining full details of which areas to avoid because of the activities of drug traffickers, bandits and guerrilla groups, mostly from Colombia, but operating on both sides of the border. **Warning**: latest information is that armed Colombian insurgents, hostile to travellers including tourists, regularly cross into Panamanian territory. Additional Panamanian forces have been sent into the area and the situation is dangerous. If the situation has not improved before you set out to cross Darién by land either way, you are advised not to go.

The New Tribes Mission, following the kidnap of three missionaries in 1993 who are still being held, has withdrawn its staff from the area. In December 2000 two British 'orchid collectors' were released unharmed by guerrillas after being held in the area for several months.

The best time to go is in the dry months (January-mid April); in the wet season (May-December) it is only recommended for the hardy. Even when totally covered in mosquito repellent you will get bitten and you run the risk of dengue fever. Travel with a reliable companion or two. Talk to knowledgeable locals for the best advice. Hire at least one Indian guide, but do it through the village corregidor, whose involvement may add to the reliability of the selected guides. (Budget up to US$8 per day for the guide and his food. Negotiate with the chief, but do not begrudge the cost.) Travel light and move fast. The journey described here takes about seven days to Turbo.

Maps of the Darién area can be purchased from the Ministerio de Obras Públicas, Instituto Geográfico Nacional Tommy Guardia, in Panama City (US$4, reported to contain serious mistakes). Information is also available from Asociación Nacional para de la Conservación de la Naturaleza, C Amela Dennis de Icaza, Ancón Hill, past Panama's Supreme Court, in former Quarry Heights, Casa 153, T314-0060, F314-0061, www.ancon.org.

you to the port immigration) and explain the problem. One traveller reports hearing of several arrests of travellers caught without their entry stamp. Many of these 'illegals' stay arrested for weeks. It may help to be able to prove that you have sufficient money to cover your stay in Panama.

Entry by motorized vehicle is prohibited

The **Katios National Park**, extending in Colombia to the Panamanian border, can be visited with mules from the MA headquarters in Sautatá (rangers may offer free accommodation, very friendly). In the park is the Tilupo waterfall, 125 m high, where the water cascades down a series of rock staircases, surrounded by orchids and other fantastic plants. Also in the park are the Alto de la Guillermina, a mountain behind which is a strange forest of palms called 'mil pesos', and the Ciénagas de Tumaradó, with red monkeys, waterfowl and alligators.

Route 2 The second route is a strenuous hike up the Río Paya valley through dense jungle (machete country) for about 16 hours to the last point on the Paya (fill up with water), then a further 3 hours to the continental divide where you cross into Colombia. Down through easier country (3-4 hours) brings you to **Unguía** (F *Residencias Viajero*, with bath; F *Doña Julia*, also with bath; several basic restaurants) where motor boats are available to take you down the Río Tarena, out into the Gulf of Urabá, across to Turbo. This trip should not be taken without a guide, though you may be lucky and find an Indian, or a group of Indians, making the journey and willing to take you along. They will appreciate a gift when you arrive in Unguía. Hazards include blood-sucking ticks, the inevitable mosquitoes and, if that weren't enough, thirst.

There are many other possible routes from Panama crossing the land frontier used by locals. Most involve river systems and are affected by water levels. There are few tracks and no reliable maps. We have heard of successful crossings using the Salaqui and Balsas rivers, and a land route Jaqué-Jurado-Río Sucio. Good Spanish and guides, serious planning and money are essential. See below for sea routes.

By sea

Boats leave, irregularly, from the Coco Solo wharf in Colón (minibus from Calle 12, 15 minutes, US$0.80, taxi US$4) for Puerto Obaldía, via the San Blas Islands. These are small boats and give a rough ride in bad weather, cost around US$30 per person, take your own food, water and shade; with stops, the journey takes two to four days. There are flights with *Ansa* (T226-7891/6881) and *Transpasa* (T226-0932/0843) at 0600-0630 from Panama City to Puerto Obaldía, daily except Sunday for US$44 single (book well in advance). There are also flights with *Aerotaxi*. Puerto Obaldía is a few kilometres from the Colombian border. There are *expresos* (speedboats) from Puerto Obaldía (after clearing Customs) to Capurganá, and then another on to Acandí (**F** *Hotel Central*, clean, safe; **F** *Hotel Pilar*, safe). From Acandí you can go on to Turbo, on the Gulf of Urabá, no fixed schedule (you cannot get to Turbo in the same day; take shade and drinks and be prepared for seasickness). Medellín can be reached by road from Turbo. Walk from Puerto Obaldía to Zapzurro, just beyond the border, for a dugout to Turbo, US$15, where you must get your Colombia entry stamp. It seems that most of the vessels leaving Puerto Obaldía for Colombian ports are contraband boats. One traveller obtained an unnecessary visa (free) from the Colombian consul in Puerto Obaldía which proved to be useful in Colombia where soldiers and police took it to be an entry stamp. As in other parts of Darién seek current advice concerning security. An American disappeared somewhere along this coastline in 2001.

The Carribean route via Puerto Obaldía
Arriving in Puerto Obaldía you have to pass through the military control for baggage search, immigration (proof of funds and onward ticket asked for) and malaria control

Sleeping There is a good *pensión* in Puerto Obaldía: **E** *Residencia Cande*, nice and clean, which also serves very good meals for US$1.50, order meals in advance.

Useful services In Puerto Obaldía there are shops, Colombian Consulate, Panamanian Immigration, but nowhere to change TCs until well into Colombia (not Turbo); changing cash is possible.

Alternatively you can get from Puerto Obaldía to Acandí on the Colombian side of the border, either by walking for nine hours or by hiring a dugout or a launch to Capurganá (US$8), and then another launch at 0715, which takes one hour and costs US$3. The snorkelling is good in Capurganá. There is a Panamanian consul (Roberto) that issues visas for Panama. There are *Twin Otter* flights to Medellín. To walk to Capurganá takes four hours, guide recommended (they charge US$10); first go to **La Miel** (2 hours), then to **Zapzurro** (20 minutes), where there are shops and cabins for rent, then 1-1½ hours to Capurganá. Most of the time the path follows the coast, but there are some hills to cross (hot – take drinking water). From Acandí a daily boat is scheduled to go at 0800 to Turbo (US$15, 3 hours). Take pesos, if possible, to these Colombian places, the rate of exchange for dollars is poor.

Capurganá (Colombia)

Sleeping There are several hotels in Capurganá: **B** *Calypso*, Reservations T094-250-3921 (Medellín number), **D** *Náutico*, **E** *Uvita*, clean, safe; **E** *Al Mar*. There are cheaper *pensiones* and you can camp near the beach.

Although not quick, the Pacific coastline provides another relatively straightforward route across the Darién (Spanish is essential). Take a bus from Panama City (Plaza 5 de Mayo) to **Metetí** (**D-E** *Hospedaje Feliz*, basic 'box' rooms), 50 km from Yaviza, the junction for transport to **Puerto Quimba**, where boats can be taken to La Palma.

The Pacific route

Panama

Advice for overland Darién travellers

Dr Richard Dawood, author of Travellers' Health: How to Stay Healthy Abroad, and photographer Anthony Dawton, crossed the Darién Gap at the end of the wet season (Nov). We are pleased to include Dr Dawood's health recommendations for such a journey.

Heat *Acclimatization to a hot climate usually takes around three weeks. It is more difficult in humid climates than in dry ones, since sweat cannot evaporate easily, and when high humidity persists through the night as well, the body has no respite. (In desert conditions, where the temperature falls at night, adaptation is much easier.) Requirements for salt and water increase dramatically under such conditions. We had to drink 12 litres per day to keep pace with our own fluid loss on some parts of the trip.*

We were travelling under extreme conditions, but it is important to remember that the human thirst sensation is not an accurate guide to true fluid requirements. In hot countries it is always essential to drink beyond the point of thirst quenching, and to drink sufficient water to ensure that the urine is consistently pale in colour.

Salt losses also need to be replaced. Deficiency of salt, water, or both, is referred to as heat exhaustion; lethargy, fatigue and headache are typical features, eventually leading to coma and death. Prevention is the best approach, and we used the pre-salted water regime. Salt is added to all fluids, one quarter of a level teaspoon (approximately 1 gm) per pint – to produce a solution that is just below the taste threshold. Salt tablets, however, are poorly absorbed, irritate the stomach and may cause vomiting; plenty of pre-salted fluid should be the rule for anyone spending much time outdoors in the tropics. (Salted biscuits are recommended by Darién travellers.)

Sun *Overcast conditions in the tropics can be misleading. The sun's rays can be fierce, and it is important to make sure that all exposed skin is constantly protected with a high-factor sun screen – preferably waterproof for humid conditions. This was especially important while we were travelling by canoe. A hat was also essential.*

Food and water *Diarrhoea can be annoying enough in a luxurious holiday resort with comfortable sanitary facilities. The inconvenience under jungle conditions would have been more than trivial, however, with the added problem of coping with further fluid loss and dehydration.*

Much caution was therefore needed with food hygiene. We carried our own supplies, which we prepared carefully ourselves: rather uninspiring camping fare, such as canned tuna fish, sardines, pasta, dried soup, biscuits and dried fruit. In the villages, oranges, bananas and coconuts were available. The freshly baked bread was safe, and so would have been the rice.

We purified our water with two percent tincture of iodine carried in a small plastic dropping bottle, four drops to each litre – more when the water is very turbid – wait 20 mins before drinking. This method is safe and effective, and is the only suitable technique for such conditions. (Another suggestion from Peter Ovenden is a water purifying pump based on a ceramic filter. There are several on the market, Peter used a Katadyn. It takes about a minute to purify a litre of water. When the water is cloudy, for example after rain, water pumps are less effective and harder work. Take purification tablets as back-up – Ed) It is also worth travelling with a suitable antidiarrhoeal medication such as Arret.

Malaria *Chloroquine resistant malaria is present in the Darién area, so appropriate antimalarial medication is essential. We took Paludrine, 2 tablets daily, and chloroquine, 2 tablets weekly. Free advice on antimalarial medication for all destinations is available from the Malaria Reference Laboratory, T0891-600350 in the UK. An insect repellent is also essential, and so are precautions to avoid insect bites.*

Insects *Besides malaria and yellow fever, other insect-borne diseases such as dengue fever and leishmaniasis may pose a risk. The* old-fashioned mosquito net is ideal if you have to sleep outdoors, or in a room that is not mosquito-proof. Mosquito nets for hammocks are widely available in Latin America. An insecticide spray is valuable for clearing your room of flying insects before you go to sleep, and mosquito coils that burn through the night giving off an insecticidal vapour, are also valuable.

Ticks It is said that ticks should be removed by holding a lighted cigarette close to them, and we had an opportunity to put this old remedy to the test. We duly unwrapped a pack of American duty-frees that we had preserved carefully in plastic just for such a purpose, as our Indian guides looked on in amazement, incredulous that we should use these prized items for such a lowly purpose. The British Army expedition to Darién in 1972 carried 60,000 cigarettes among its supplies, and one wonders if they were for this purpose! The cigarette method didn't work, but caused much amusement. (Further discussion with the experts indicates that the currently favoured method is to ease the tick's head gently away from the skin with tweezers.) New advice is that cigarettes are definitely a no-no since it roasts the tick but leaves the mouthpiece in the skin. In the jungle, this could lead to a dangerous tropical ulcer. Ticks breathe through small openings in the skin. Smoothing with oil or Vaseline will kill the tick and release the mouthparts. So too will alcohols. When removing, don't pull straight – the best way to break off the head – but gently and firmly twist to left or right while pulling to dislodge the barbs. Use tweezers, as close to the tiny head as possible.

Vaccinations A yellow fever vaccination certificate is required from all travellers arriving from infected areas, and vaccination is advised for personal protection. Immunization against Hepatitis A (see Health information in Essentials) and typhoid are strongly advised. Attacks by dogs are relatively common: the new rabies vaccine is safe and effective, and carrying a machete for the extra purpose of discouraging animals is advised. In addition, all travellers should be protected against tetanus, diphtheria and polio.

Supplies You can get some food along the way, but take enough for at least 5 days. Do take, though, a torch/flashlight, and a bottle of rum (or similar!) and other useful items for those who give help and information. A compass can save your life in the more remote sections if you are without a guide – getting lost is the greatest danger according to the rangers. It is highly recommended to travel in the dry season only, when there is no mud and fewer mosquitoes. A hammock can be very useful. If you have time, bargains can be found but, as pointed out above, costs of guides and water transport are steadily increasing. Buying pesos in Panama is recommended as changing dollars when you enter Colombia will be at poor rates. You will need small denomination dollar notes on the trip.

By bike or motorbike Crossing by motorcycle cannot be recommended, but crossing by bicycle has been successfully completed. Taking a motorcycle through Darién is not an endeavour to be undertaken lightly. The late Ed Culberson (who, in 1986 after two unsuccessful attempts, was the first to accomplish the feat) wrote: "Dry season passage is comparatively easy on foot and even with a bicycle. But it simply cannot be done with a standard-sized motorcycle unless helped by Indians at a heavy cost in dollars ... It is a very strenuous, dangerous adventure, often underestimated by motorcyclists, some of whom have come to untimely ends in the jungle." Culberson's account of his journey (in the October 1986 issue of Rider and in a book, Obsessions Die Hard, published 1991 by Teakwood Press, 160 Fiesta Drive, Kissimmee, Fla, USA, 34743, T407-348-7330) makes harrowing reading, not least his encounter with an emotionally unstable police official in Bijao; the 46-km 'ride' from Púcuro to Palo de las Letras took 6 days with the help of 6 Indians (at US$8 a day each). Two riders were caught in an early start of rains in 1991 and barely escaped with their machines.

Panama

Alternatively, take a bus to **Santa Fe**, which is 75 km short of Yaviza and off to the south, a rough but scenic 6-8 hours (US$8, three a day, check times). In Santa Fe it is possible to camp near the police post – one *pensión* (**E** *Guacamaya*, T299-6727). Then hitch a ride on a truck (scarce), or walk two hours to the Río Sabanas at Puerto Larda (11 km) where you must take a dugout or launch to La Palma, or hire one (US$5, 2 hours). **La Palma** is also reached by boat from Yaviza (US$3, eight hours). It is the capital of Darién – you can change cash and travellers' cheques – has one *pensión* (**F**, friendly, English-speaking owners, with cooking and laundry facilities, or see if you can stay with the *guardia*). There are two daily *Aeroperlas* flights from Panama City to La Palma, US$36, and one a day to Jaqué on the Pacific shore, US$44; also to Yaviza three days a week, but check with the airline Parsa, T226-3883. They have an office at the domestic airport in Panama City. It is not clear if you can get a plane from La Palma to Jaqué, but there are boats, US$15. En route there is an Ancón lodge at Punta Patino. Details from *Ancón Expediciones* in Panama City. **Jaqué** is on the Pacific coast, near Puerto Piña, 50 km north of the Colombian border (one hotel **B**). At **Bahía Piña** is the *Tropic Star Lodge*, T264-5549, T1-800-682-3424, www.tropicstar.com, where a luxury fishing holiday may be enjoyed on the sea and in the jungle from over US$2,580 a week. (Information from *Hotel El Panamá*.) Bahía Piña has a runway, used mainly by the expensive fishing resort. These isolated settlements on the Pacific coast are close to the **Parque Nacional Darién**, Panama's largest and wildest protected area. Cana and Cerro Pirre are at its heart but at present it is not advisable to visit because of the various armed bands that use the jungle as cover. From Jaqué you can catch a launch to Jurado in Colombia (US$25, four 'murderous' hours, take something soft to sit on). The launch continues to Bahía Solano or there are weekly cargo boats to Buenaventura (M/N Fronteras US$45 including food, 36 hours, bunks but OK), where there is a friendly DAS office where you can sort out your paperwork.

Alternatively, at the Muelle Fiscal in Panama City (next to the main waterfront market, near Calle 13), ask for a passenger boat going to Jaqué. The journey takes 18 hours, is cramped and passengers cook food themselves, but costs only US$12. Jaqué is only reached by sea or air (the airstrip is used mostly by wealthy visitors going sports fishing); there are small stores with few fruit and vegetables, a good *comedor*, one *hospedaje*, **F** *Chavela*, clean, basic, friendly (but it is easy to find accommodation with local families), and camping is possible anywhere on the beautiful 4-km beach. The guard post is open every day and gives exit stamps. Canoes from Jaqué go to Juradó (US$20, 4½ hours) or Bahía Solano (US$45, 160 km, with two overnight stops) in Chocó. The first night is spent in Jurado (where the boat's captain may put you up and the local military commander may search you out of curiosity). There are flights from Jurado to Turbo, but it is possible to get 'stuck' in Jurado for several days. Bahía Solano is a deep-sea fishing resort with an airport and *residencias*. Flights from Bahía Solano go to Quibdó, connecting to Cali, or Medellín (all flights have to be booked in advance; the town is popular with Colombian tourists). On this journey, you sail past the lush, mountainous Pacific coast of Darién and Chocó, with its beautiful coves and beaches, and you will see a great variety of marine life.

Shipping agencies do not have the authority to charge passengers. Many travellers think they can travel as crew on cargo liners, but this is not possible because Panamanian law requires all crew taken on in Panama to be Panamanian nationals

NB It is not easy to get passage to any of the larger Colombian ports as the main shipping lines rarely take passengers. Those that do are booked up well in advance. The company *Agencias Panamá*, Muelle 18, Balboa, represents *Delta Line* and accepts passengers to Buenaventura. Anyone interested in using the *Delta Line* ships should book a passage before arriving in Panama. The only easy way of getting to Colombia is to fly (see Essentials).

Colombia officially demands an exit ticket from the country. If you travel by air the tickets should be bought outside Panama and Colombia, which have taxes on all international air tickets. If you buy air tickets from IATA companies, they can be refunded. *Copa* tickets can be refunded in Cartagena (Calle Santos de Piedra 3466 – takes four days), Barranquilla (two days), Cali or Medellín. Refunds in pesos only. *Copa* office in Panama City, Avenida Justo Arosemena y Calle 39, T227-5000.

Background

History

The history of Panama is the history of its pass-route; its fate was determined on 15 September 1513 when Vasco Núñez de Balboa first glimpsed the Pacific (see page 62). Panama City was of paramount importance to the Spaniards: it was the focus of conquering expeditions both northwards and southwards along the Pacific coasts. All trade to and from these Pacific countries – including the fantastic gold of the Incas – passed across or around the isthmus. As part of Colombia and its predecessors, Panama was traditionally considered part of South America, until recent years, when it has more and more been classed as a Central American republic. The distinction has political significance as international economic integration increases in importance.

The Camino Real

Panama City was founded in 1519 after a trail had been discovered and opened up between what is now the Bay of Panama on the Pacific and the Caribbean. The Royal Road, or the *Camino Real*, ran from Panama City to Nombre de Dios until it was re-routed to Portobelo. An alternative route was used later for bulkier, less-valuable merchandise; it ran from Panama City to Las Cruces, on the Chagres River but has now been swallowed up in the Gatún Lake. It ran near to Gamboa on the Gaillard / Culebra Cut and was navigable to the Caribbean, particularly during the rainy season. Vestiges of these trails are still in existence, although much of both routes was flooded by the artificial Gatún and Madden/Alajuela lakes created to feed the Canal. It was in these early years that crossing between the Atlantic and Pacific became part of a Panamanian tradition that ultimately led to the construction of the Canal.

Intruders were quickly attracted by the wealth passing over the Camino Real. **Sir Francis Drake** attacked Nombre de Dios, and in 1573 his men penetrated inland to Vera Cruz, further up the Chagres River on the Camino Real, plundering the town. Spain countered later attacks by building strongholds and forts to protect the route: among them San Felipe at the entrances to Portobelo and San Lorenzo at the mouth of the Chagres. Spanish galleons, loaded with treasure and escorted against attack, left Portobelo once a year. They returned with European goods sold at great fairs held at Portobelo, Cartagena and Vera Cruz. Feverish activity either side of the loading and unloading of the galleons made it a favourite time for attack, especially for those with political as well as pecuniary motives. Perhaps the most famous was the attack by **Henry Morgan** in 1671. After capturing the fort of San Lorenzo, he pushed up the Chagres River to Las Cruces. From there he descended to Panama City, which he looted and burnt. A month later Morgan returned to the Caribbean with 195 mules loaded with booty. Panama City was rebuilt on a new site, at the base of Ancón Hill, and fortified. With Britain and Spain at war, attacks reached their climax with Admiral Vernon's capture of Portobelo in 1739 and the fort of San Lorenzo the following year. Spain abandoned the route in 1746 and began trading round Cape Horn. San Lorenzo was rebuilt: it is still there, and has been tidied up and landscaped.

In 1821, Gran Colombia won Independence from Spain. Panama, in an event celebrated annually on 28 November, declared its own Independence and promptly joined Bolívar's Gran Colombia federation. Though known as the 'Sovereign State' of Panama it remained, even after the federation disintegrated, a province of Colombia.

The Panama Railroad

Some 30 years after Independence, streams of men were once more moving up the Chagres and down to Panama City: the forty-niners on their way to the newly discovered gold fields of California. Many perished on this 'road to hell', as it was called, and the gold rush brought into being a railway across the isthmus. The Panama Railroad from Colón (then only two streets) to Panama City took four years to build, with great loss of life. The first train ran on 26 November 1853. The railway was an enormous financial success until the re-routing of the

Panama

Pacific Steam Navigation Company's ships round Cape Horn in 1867 and the opening of the first US transcontinental railroad in 1869 reduced its traffic. Having been out of operation for several years, a concession to operate the line was awarded to a Kansas rail company in 1998 and service is being restored; initially for freight, perhaps later for passengers.

Building of the Canal

Ferdinand de Lesseps, builder of the Suez Canal, arrived in Panama in 1881 to a hero's welcome, having decided to build a sea-level canal along the Chagres River and the Río Grande. Work started in 1882. One of the diggers in 1886 and 1887 was the painter Gauguin, aged 39. About 30 km had been dug before the Company crashed in 1893, defeated by extravagance, corruption, tropical diseases (22,000 people died, mostly of yellow fever and malaria) and by engineering difficulties inherent in the construction of a canal without lift-locks. Eventually the Colombian government authorized the Company to sell all its rights and properties to the United States, but the Colombian Senate rejected the treaty, and the inhabitants of Panama, encouraged by the United States, declared their dence on 3 November 1903. The United States intervened and, in spite of protests by Colombia, recognized the new republic. Colombia did not accept the severance until 1921.

Within two weeks of its dence, Panama, represented in Washington by the controversial Frenchman **Philippe Bunau-Varilla**, signed a treaty granting to the USA 'in perpetuity' a 16-km wide corridor across the isthmus over which the USA would exercise authority 'as if it were sovereign'. Bunau-Varilla, an official of the bankrupt French canal company, presented the revolutionary junta with the *fait accompli* of a signed treaty. The history of Panama then became that of two nations, with the Canal Zone governor, also a retired US general, responsible only to the President of the USA.

Before beginning the task of building the Canal, the United States performed one of the greatest sanitary operations in history: the clearance from the area of the more malignant tropical diseases. The name of the physician William Crawford Gorgas will always be associated with this, as will that of the engineer George Washington Goethals with the actual building of the Canal. On 15 August 1914, the first official passage was made, by the ship *Ancón*. During this period, and until the military seized power in 1968, a small commercially orientated oligarchy dominated Panamanian politics, although presidential successions were not always smooth and peaceful.

1939 Treaty with USA

As a result of bitter resentment, the USA ended Panama's protectorate status in 1939 with a treaty which limited US rights of intervention. However, the disparity in living standards continued to provoke anti-US feeling, culminating in riots that began on 9 January 1964, resulting in the death of 23 Panamanians (the day is commemorated annually as Martyrs' Day), four US marines and the suspension of diplomatic relations for some months.

In 1968 **Arnulfo Arias Madrid** was elected president for the third time, having been ousted twice previously. After only 10 days in office he was forcibly removed by the National Guard which installed a provisional junta. Brigadier General Omar Torrijos Herrera ultimately became Commander of the National Guard and principal power in the junta, dominating Panamanian politics for the next 13 years. Gradually, the theoretically civilian National Guard was converted into a full-scale army and renamed the Panama Defence Forces. Constitutional government was restored in 1972 after elections for a 505-member National Assembly of Community Representatives, which revised the 1946 constitution, elected Demetrio Basilio Lakas Bahas as president, and vested temporary extraordinary executive powers in General Torrijos for six years. Torrijos' rule was characterized by his pragmatic nationalism; he carried out limited agrarian reform and nationalized major industries, yet satisfied business interests; he had close links with left wing movements in Cuba, El Salvador and Nicaragua, yet reached agreement with the USA to restore sovereignty over the canal zone to Panama and to close the US military bases by the year 2000. In 1978 elections for a new National Assembly were held and the new representatives elected Arístedes Royo Sánchez president of the country. General Torrijos resigned as Chief of Government but retained the powerful post of Commander of the National Guard until his death in a small plane air-crash in 1981. There followed several years of rapid governmental changes as tension rose between presidents and National Guard leaders.

Following an election in May 1984, Nicolás Ardito Barletta was inaugurated in October for a six-year term, though the fairness of the elections was widely questioned. He was removed from office by military pressure in September 1985 as he attempted to assert some civilian control and was replaced by Eric Arturo Delvalle. His attempts to reduce military influence in government, by then concentrated principally in the hands of **General Manuel Antonio Noriega Moreno**, led to his own removal by General Noriega in February 1988. Manuel Solís Palma was named President in his place.

With the economy reeling and banks closed as a result of US economic sanctions, the campaign leading up to the election of May 1989 saw the growing influence of a movement called the *Civilista* Crusade, led by upper and middle-class figures. When their coalition candidate, Guillermo Endara Galimany, triumphed over Noriega's candidate, Carlos Duque Jaén, the election was annulled by the military.

General Noriega appointed Francisco Rodríguez as provisional President in September, but by December, General Noriega had formally assumed power as Head of State. These events provoked the US military invasion Operation 'Just Cause' on 20 December to overthrow him. He finally surrendered in mid-January, having first taken refuge in the Papal Nunciature on Christmas Eve. He was taken to the USA for trial on charges of drugs trafficking and other offences, and sentenced to 30 years in prison. **Guillermo Endara** was installed as President. The Panamanian Defence Forces were immediately remodelled into a new Public Force whose largest component is the civilian National Police, with a compulsory retirement after 25 years' service. More than 150 senior officers were dismissed and many were arrested. Panama has not had a regular army since.

After the overthrow of General Noriega's administration, the US Senate approved a US$1 bn aid package including US$480 mn in direct assistance to provide liquidity and get the economy moving again. A further US$540 mn aid package was requested from the USA, Japan, Taiwan and the EEC to enable Panama to help clear its US$610 mn arrears with multilateral creditors and support the Panamanian banking system, but inevitably there were delays and little progress was made until 1991. The USA put Panama under considerable pressure to sign a Treaty of Mutual Legal Assistance, which would limit bank secrecy and enable investigation into suspected drug traffickers' bank accounts. Higher levels of crime and drugs trafficking led to the Government passing a law to create the Technical Judicial Police (PTJ) to pursue criminals.

While structural, economic and legal changes impacted Panama in the early 1990s, Panama was still not without problems. Charges of corruption at the highest level were made by Panamanians and US officials. President Endara himself was weakened by allegations that his law firm had been involved with companies owned by drugs traffickers. Though the economy grew under Endara, street crime increased, social problems continued, there were isolated bombings and pro-military elements failed in a coup attempt.

Fears that violence would disrupt the 1994 elections were unfounded. In the presence of 2,000 local and international observers, polling was largely incident-free and open, receiving praise world-wide. The winner of the presidency, with less than a third of the popular vote, was **Ernesto Pérez Balladares** of the Partido Revolucionario Democrático (PRD), whose campaign harked back to the record of the party's founder, Omar Torrijos, successfully avoiding any links with its more recent leader Noriega. The PRD also won a narrow majority in the Legislative Assembly. In second place was the widow of thrice-elected and thrice-deposed president Arnulfo Arias, Mireya Moscoso de Gruber of the Partido Arnulfista, supported by Endara, and third was the lawyer, Salsa star, actor and Grammy award winner, **Rubén Blades**, whose party Papa Egoró ('Mother Earth') won six seats in the legislature on its first electoral outing. Pérez Balladares, who appointed a cabinet containing members of opposition parties as well as from the PRD, gave priority in his campaign to tackling the problems of social inequality, unemployment, deteriorating education standards and rising crime which had all characterized the end of Endara's term. In January 1995, it was announced by the government that a coup against Pérez Balladares had been foiled. All sides in the Assembly hastened to support the government and pledged their commitment to democracy.

In 1997 the ruling PRD proposed that the constitution be changed to allow President Pérez Balladares to stand for re-election, but this was defeated in a 1998 referendum.

In May 1999, Mireya Moscoso emerged victorious in presidential elections which saw a 78% voter turnout and were considered entirely free and fair by international observers. Moscoso obtained 45% of the popular vote, ahead of her closest rival Martín Torrijos (son of General Omar Torrijos) with 38%. Torrijos' incumbent PRD alliance won a majority of seats in Congress however, promising a healthy balance of power with the president-elect's Partido Arnulfista. Moscoso took office on September 1, becoming the first female president of Panama, enjoying the honour of receiving control of the Panama Canal from the US on 31 December 1999, and the prospect of presiding over the nation's centennial celebrations in 2003; both important milestones in the nation's history.

Criticisms from the international community in early 2000 suggested that Panama was 'inward looking' and that the country was suffering accordingly. Given the historically dominant role of the international community in Panamanian affairs, it would be surprising if the country displayed signs of a mature self-determining nation. Strong economic growth in 2000 was accompanied by decisions to analyze the past with an announcment by President Moscoso to investigate crimes committed while military goverments were in power between 1968 and 1989.

Two incidents in late 2000 also showed a willingness to play an internationally responsible role. Discussions between Moscoso and the Colombian president Andrés Pastrana produced agreement to strengthen security on their shared border in the Darién region, in an attempt to reduce violence by Colombian rebels and paramilitary groups and to tackle arms and drugs smuggling in region. Even allowing for greater cooperation, drug smuggling between the two countries is still a major problem. In early 2002, 1,600kg of cocaine was seized from a container ship as it headed towards Costa Rican waters.

The political crisis in Peru bought to the fore the country's reputation as number one destination for politicians seeking exile. Peru's former intelligence chief Vladimiro Montesinos fled to Panama under cover of darkness and, while the Panamanian government was keen to reject his request for political asylum, pressure from Latin American leaders, the US and the Organization of American States means he was granted temporary asylum in the interests of stability in Peru, before eventually being tracked down and arrested in Venezuela having undergone plastic surgery. While Panama wracks up political points with her neighbours, the country is keen to move away from the image of being a dumping ground for political criminals – an unenviable reputation that has seen the Shah of Iran, former Guatemalan President Jorge Serrano Elias, the Haitian military leader Raoul Cedras and the former Ecuadorean President Abdala Bucaram all seek asylum within the country.

Canal area The former Canal Zone was a ribbon of territory under US control extending 8 km on either side of the Canal, including the cities of Cristóbal and Balboa. The price paid by the United States Government to Panama for construction rights was US$10 mn. The French company received US$40 mn for its rights and properties after the first attempt at constructing a canal finally ground to a halt in 1893 and US$25 mn was given to Colombia in compensation. The total cost at completion was US$387 mn. Panama long ago rejected the perpetuity clause of the original Canal Treaty, but in April 1978 a new treaty was ratified and on 1 October 1979 the Canal Zone, now known officially as the Canal Area, including the ports of Cristóbal and Balboa, the Canal dry docks and the trans-isthmus railway, was formally restored to Panamanian sovereignty. The US Southern Command moved to Miami in 1997, and by the end of 1999 the few remaining bases had closed.

Though polls indicated that many Panamanians supported retention of US military bases, largely because of their employment of civilians and direct governmental expenditures in Panama (about US$350 mn a year in the last years of US operation), vocal minorities demanded their departure. In the run-up to the final hand-over however, there prevailed a curious mixture of national euphoria and apprehension over the country's ability to successfully manage so vital an international resource. US phasing out of the bases was achieved ahead of schedule, though the two countries agreed in 1997 to create a Multilateral Anti-drug Centre which would occupy one of the former US bases and would have some military components. In June 1999 however, the general in charge of the Southern Command declared that Panama was unable to defend its border with Colombia against insurgents from that neighbouring country, and that the US was prepared to intervene militarily in the Darién if it felt guerrillas posed a threat to the security of the Canal; remarks which proved intensely controversial in Panama.

While the doubters are still waiting for problems with the new Canal Administration, the Panamanian Canal authorities are confident they can deliver a world class service. In the first 100 days 3,700 vessels transported 61.5 mn tons of cargo through the canal, providing US$143 mn in tolls. But some small private users have noted that break-downs have increased due to a less rigorous maintenance programme.

According to 1996 figures, about 13,700 ships then passed through the Panama Canal annually, providing US$105 mn for the Panamanian government (out of total Canal revenues of US$486 mn). Some 17,000 ships pass through the canal each year providing revenue of roughly US$600 mn a year. In 2001 the French-owned cruise ship *Infitiny* became the heaviest vessel to ever travel through the canal. Weighing in at 90,000 tonnes, the ship also paid a record toll of US$200,000 for passage. For several years the possibility of widening the Canal, or even building a new one, has been under study. A report in 1993 estimated that the Canal would reach maximum shipping capacity in 2025, but re-evaluation led to a modernization programme, due for completion in 2005. This includes the widening of the Gaillard Cut, upgrading of the locks and a 20% increase in the capacity for shipping. If demand rises as quickly as expected, even the current programme will be insufficient. Immediate problems include the inability of the existing locks to handle large ships, the inadequacy of the purpose-built lakes to supply enough water for the operation of the locks (made worse by silting as a result of deforestation and, in 1998, by drought caused by El Niño), and the scale of fees charged to ships and small vessels in transit.

Government

Constitutional reforms were adopted by referendum in April 1983. Legislative power is vested in a unicameral, 72-member Legislative Assembly which is elected by universal adult suffrage for a term of five years (and whose elections are hotly contested, in part because a five-year term yields members total compensation of US$600,000 each). Executive power is held by the President, assisted by two Vice Presidents and an appointed Cabinet. Panama is divided into nine provinces and two semi-autonomous Indian reservations. Provincial governors are appointed by the central authorities. Each province is divided into *distritos* which in turn are divided into *corregimientos*. The magistrates (*alcaldes*) of the larger districts, who combine both executive and judicial functions, are elected, others are appointed. They in turn appoint subordinate authorities (*corregidores*) in the towns and villages.

Economy

Structure of production

Panama's economy has traditionally been founded on income derived from services rendered to visitors, taking advantage of its geographical position, its banking centre, Canal employees and US military personnel spending money in the Republic. However, this contribution is lessening with the departure of the US military and Canal workers, so the country is developing new sources of income including tourism, agricultural exports, industry and copper.

Apart from the Canal the other traditional mainstay of the Panamanian economy is agriculture, which contributes about 10% of GDP. The leading agricultural export crop is bananas, a large proportion of which are marketed by subsidiaries of the US multinationals Chiquita and Dole. Shrimp is another major export, having grown to about 12% of total earnings and competing strongly with Ecuador and Honduras for the US market. Raw sugar is also an important export item, while smaller quantities of pineapples, coffee and hides and skins are sold abroad.

The main industry is food processing but there are also textile and clothing concerns, cement, chemicals, plastics and other light industries. Petroleum products, made from imported crude, are the only industrial export. The lowering of import tariffs in 1993, as a part of trade liberalization measures, contributed to a decline in manufacturing output.

Vast deposits of copper have been found in Panama. The mine at Cerro Colorado, if fully developed, could be one of the largest in the world with reserves said to exceed 1 bn tonnes. A 25-year concession granted to a Canadian company is being vigorously opposed by the Ngöbe-Buglé indigenous group. Large coal, gold and silver deposits have been found. So far no oil has been discovered, but exploration is taking place. The country's mining code is being revised to speed up approval of mining concessions and to encourage foreign investment.

One of the most dynamic sectors of the economy is banking. Since 1970 offshore banks have increased from 20 in number to 115, with the establishment of liberal conditions and the abolition of currency controls. In the mid-1980s, total assets amounted to over US$40 bn, while deposits were around US$35 bn. However, in 1987-88 political uncertainties severely affected the international banking centre. By 1993, the financial sector was flourishing again, boosted by the relaxation of restrictions on financial services throughout Latin America. Although deposits were affected by the Mexican pesos crisis in 1995, declining by 13% to US$20 bn, they have risen again since then.

Recent trends

The adoption of neo-liberal economic policies in the 1990s brought rising discontent as spending cuts caused job losses. Strikes and demonstrations became commonplace and poverty increased. The economic plan announced at the outset of Pérez Balladares' term gave priority to reducing poverty by 50%, though it achieved little. According to statistics in 1997 one-third of the population lives below the poverty line and over 10% live in extreme poverty (according to the World Bank, wealth distribution is among "the most unequal in the hemisphere").

Steady inflation, the stable political situation and a growth in tourism are expected to stimulate the economy in the coming years. Panama also hopes to benefit from e-commerce setting up a world-class communications system making the country an important hub in the e-commerce world. While prospects appear to be promising, growing social unrest became apparent in 2001 when general strikes over bus prices revealed a greater disillusionment amongst Panamanians suffering from recession and increased unemployment.

Culture

People The population is mostly of mixed descent but there are communities of Indians, blacks and a few Asians. Most of the rural population live in the six provinces on the Pacific side, west of the Canal. There is only one rural population centre of any importance on the Caribbean: in Bocas del Toro, in the extreme northwest. Of the 60 Indian tribes who inhabited the isthmus at the time of the Spanish conquest, only three have survived in any number: the Kunas (also spelt Cunas particularly in Colombia) of the San Blas Islands (50,000), the Guaymíes, who prefer to be called Ngöbe-Buglé, of the western provinces (80,000), and the Emberá-Wunan, formerly known as Chocóes of Darién (10,000). These, and a few others, such as the Teribes, account for 6% of the total population. Indian opposition to the opening of copper mines at Cerro Colorado (see Economy section), and demonstrations supporting greater autonomy for Indians in the area characterized 1996, but were inconclusive. However, an administrative enclave, the Comarca, providing for some Ngöbe-Buglé home rule, has been created.

In Bocas de Toro half the population speaks Spanish, half speaks English

Numbers of African slaves escaped from their Spanish owners during the 16th century. They set up free communities in the Darién jungles and their Spanish-speaking descendants, known as *cimarrones*, still live there and in the Pearl Islands. The majority of Panama's blacks, often bilingual, are descended from English-speaking West Indians, brought in for the building of the railway in 1850, and later of the Canal. There are also a number of East Indians and Chinese, a few of whom, especially in the older generations, tend to cling to their own languages and customs.

Music & dance

Being at the crossroads of the Americas, where Central America meets South America and the Caribbean backs on to the Pacific, and being one of the smallest Latin American republics, Panama possesses an outstandingly rich and attractive musical culture. Albeit related to that of the Caribbean coast of Colombia and Venezuela, it is very different. The classic Panamanian folk dances are the *tambor* or *tamborito*, *cumbia*, *punto* and *mejorana*, largely centred on the central provinces of Coclé, and Veraguas and those of Herrera and Los Santos on the Península Azuero. Towns that are particularly noted for their musical traditions are Los Santos, Ocú, Las Tablas, Tonosí and Chorrera. The dances are for couples and groups of couples and the rhythms are lively and graceful, the man often dancing close to his partner without touching her, moving his hat in rhythmic imitation of fanning. The woman's *pollera* costume is arguably the most beautiful in Latin America and her handling of the voluminous skirt is an important element of the dance. The *tamborito* is considered to be Panama's national dance and is accompanied by three tall drums. The *cumbia*, which has a common origin with the better-known Colombian dance of the same name, has a fast variant called the *atravesado*, while the *punto* is slower and more stately. The name *mejorana* is shared by a small native guitar, a dance, a song form and a specific tune. The commonest instruments to be found today are the tall drums that provide the basic beat, the violin, the guitar and the accordion, with the last-named rapidly becoming predominant. The *tuna* is a highly rhythmic musical procession with women's chorus and massed hand-clapping.

Turning to song, there are two traditional forms, both of Spanish origin: the *copla*, sung by women and accompanying the *tamborito*, and the *mejorana*, which is a male solo preserve, with the lyrics in the form of *décimas*, a verse form used by the great Spanish poets of the Golden Age. It is accompanied by the ukulele-like guitar of the same name. Quite unique to Panama are the *salomas* and *gritos*, the latter between two or more men. The yodelling and falsetto of the *salomas* are in fact carried over into the singing style and it is this element, more than any other, that gives Panamanian folk song its unique and instantly recognizable sound. There are other traditional masked street dances of a carnavalesque nature, such as the very African *Congos*, the *Diablicos Sucios* (dirty little devils) and the *Grandiablos* (big devils). In the area of the Canal there is a significant English-speaking black population, similar to those in Nicaragua and Costa Rica, who also sing calypso, while the Guaymí (Ngöbe-Buglé) Indians in the west and the Kuna and Chocó (Emberá-Wunan) of the San Blas islands and Darién isthmus possess their own song, rituals and very attractive flute music.

When travelling in rural areas during working hours, listen for the distinctive yodelling call of Panamanian farm workers, who greet each other in the fields over long distances with the *saloma*, a cry that slides from a rumble in the throat to a falsetto and back into a rumble, usually rendered in Spanish as *¡Ajuuúa!* Folk tradition says the custom was adopted from the Indians, who are certainly among its most expert and frequent practitioners. Psychologists say letting fly with such a yelp releases the fatigue and heat-induced tension built up by long hours swinging a machete to eliminate weeds from pastures, or to prepare fields for planting. Complex *saloma*-based calls have heavily influenced Panamanian traditional song and the chanting that accompanies much dance. The *¡Ajuuúa!* can also be heard as an expression of approval at baseball games, football matches, and anywhere high spirits provide the occasion for whoops of delight.

The rise in popularity of Latin music is evident in Panama, in particular as a result of the multi-talented Rubén Blades, with his latest album *Tiempos* which, supported by the Costa Rican trio *Editus*, won a Grammy in 2000.

Education

Education is compulsory from the age of six to 15. Ninety-two percent of children attend elementary school. English is the compulsory second language in secondary schools, and many Panamanians speak a little English. There are several universities, including the

Panama

massive **Nacional**, with 55,000 students, the **Tecnológica**, with 13,000, the important Catholic **Santa María La Antigua** (5,000 students), and eight small private ones.

Religion Panama's Constitution makes Roman Catholicism the official religion of the country, but guarantees freedom of practice to all others. As with neighbouring countries, evangelical churches have been active in recent years. Mosques have been built in Panama City and David, the third city of the Republic.

Land and environment

Panama is most easily visualized as a slightly stretched, horizontal 'S', with the 767 km Caribbean coastline on the north and the 1,234 km Pacific coast on the south and lying between 7° and 10° north of the Equator. The Canal, which runs southeast-northwest, bisects the country; the mountains running along the isthmus divide the country from north to south. About one-third of the population lives in Panama City on the east side of the Canal at its southern terminus. Most of the rural population live in the quarter of the country south of the mountains and west of the Canal.

At the border with Costa Rica there are several inactive volcanic cones, the boldest of which is the Volcán Barú, 3,475 m high and the highest point in the country. The sharp-sided Cordillera de Talamanca continues southeast at a general altitude of about 900 m, but subsides suddenly southwest of Panama City. The next range, the San Blas, rises east of Colón (the city at the north end of the Canal) running parallel to the Caribbean coastline, into Colombia. Its highest peak Tacarcuna, at 1,875 m, is in the heart of the Darién. A third range rises from the Pacific littoral in the southeast, running along the Pacific coast of Colombia as the Serranía de Baudó.

Nature decreed a gap between the Talamanca and San Blas ranges in which the divide is no more than 87 m high. The ranges are so placed that the gap, through which the Canal runs, follows a line from northwest to southeast. To reach the Pacific from the Atlantic you must travel eastwards so when travelling through the canal, as in much of the country, the sun rises over the Pacific and sets over the Atlantic.

The rate of deforestation in Panama has accelerated in the 1980s and early 1990s. Although more of the country is forested than any other Central American republic except Belize, the loss of forest in 1990 was estimated at 220,000 acres, against felling of up to 154,000 acres per year between 1985 and 1989. The government reported a slowing of deforestation during 1993-95, but in early 1996 estimated it was continuing at 2,200 acres (100 ha) a year. Deforestation is affecting the pattern of rainfall upon which depend not only the birds (over 800 species), animals, insects and plants, but also the Panama Canal. A further threat to the Canal caused by deforestation is silting as a result of soil erosion.

Books and films

For the history of the Canal, see David McCullough's *The Path Between the Seas*. For the era of military rule, John Dinges, *Our Man in Panama*. Graham Greene's *Getting to Know the General* (Torrijos) is subjective and, as such, is not historically reliable, but is worth reading. John Le Carré's recent *Tailor of Panama* is a cynical but entertaining view of Panama City society, recently put on the big screen starring Pierce Brosnan. Manuel Noriega has written *America's Prisoner* (Random House).

Cinema has failed to be inspired by Panama so far. In addition to Le Carré's *Tailor of Panama*, which refreshingly takes Pierce Brosnan out of the Bonded facial expression role, the *Canal Zone*, directed by Frederick Wiseman (1977), is a triology documentary series looking at life in the Canal Zone. The critics response: "deadly boring."

For ornithologists, Robert S Ridgely's and John Gwynn's richly illustrated *Guide to the Birds of Panama*, Princeton University Press, describes 929 species and is the definitive guide.

Footnotes

11

Footnotes

Basic Spanish

Whether you have been taught the 'Castillian' pronounciation (all *z's*, and *c's* followed by *i* or *e*, are pronunounced as the *th* in *think*) or the 'American' pronounciation (they are pronounced as *s*) you will encounter little difficulty in understanding either: Spanish pronunciation varies geographically much less than English.

Pronouns   In the Americas, the plural, familiar pronoun *vosotros* (with the verb endings – *áis*, – *éis*), though much used in Spain, is never heard: two or more people, whoever they are, are always addressed as *Ustedes (Uds)*. The singular, familiar prounoun *tú* is replaced in many areas by the pronoun *vos*; when it is, the accent on the verb tends to move toward the end: instead of *tú quieres*, one hears *vos querés* (though both will be understood).

Expressions of time   Many misunderstandings about engagements stem from terminology rather than tardiness. *Ahora* is often a synonym for *hoy*, 'today', not the 'now' in the dictionary; 'now' or 'soon' are *ahorita*; 'right now' is *ahora mismo* or *enseguida*.

   While *en la tarde* could conceivably mean at 1230 or 1300 in the afternoon, it is more likely to mean 1500 or 1600, even 1730 or 1800. A polite way of pinning down a vague commitment is to ask *¿A qué hora más o menos?* ('At about what time?').

Terms of address   Almost anyone qualified to a title uses it. A physician, dentist, or vet is always addressed as *Doctor(a)*, as is any holder of a doctoral degree. Primary school teachers are always *Maestro(a)*, as are some skilled crafts people, builders, etc. Secondary school and all university teachers are always addressed as *Profesor(a)*, or, informally by their students, as *Profe*. Lawyers and university graduates in any of the arts or social sciences are addressed as *Licenciado(a)*, abbreviated *Lic*; graduate engineers, and holders of any degree in a technical field, use *Ingeniero(a)*, abbreviated *Ing*. Architects use *Arquitecto(a)*, abbreviated *Arq*. Protestant clergy are always *Reverendo(a)*, never just *Sr(a)*.

   Address male strangers over the age of 20 or so as *Señor*; younger men may be addressed as *Joven*. Address female strangers over the age of 20 or so, or younger women if they are obviousonly accompanied by (their own) children or a husband, as *Señora*. Younger women can safely be addressed as *Señorita*. Note that the terms *Señorita* and *Señora* can have implications of virginity as well as marital status (an elderly woman who has no children and has never married may well correct you if addressed as *Señora*).The terms *Don* and *Doña*, usually used to address older men and women, also enable you to use a person's first name without sounding disrespectful, as in Don Juan or Doña Josefina.

Bs and Vs   Travellers whose names include the letters *'b'* or *'v'* (pronounced the same in Spanish) should learn to distinguish between them when spelling aloud as *be larga* or *be grande* and *ve corta, ve chica* or *uve*. (Children often say *ve de vaca* and *be de burro* to distinguish between the two letters.)

Greetings & courtesies

English	Spanish
Hello/ Good morning	Hola/ Buenos días
Good afternoon/ evening/night	Buenas tardes/ noches
Goodbye	Adiós/chao
See you later	Hasta luego
How are you?	¿Cómo está/ estás?
I'm fine	Muy bien gracias
Pleased to meet you	Mucho gusto/ encantado/a
Please	Por favor
Thank you	(Muchas) gracias
Yes/no	(muchas) Sí/no
Excuse me/ I'm sorry	Con permiso Lo siento/disculpe
I don't understand	No entiendo
I don't want it	No lo quiero
Please speak slowly	Hable despacio, por favor
What's your name?	¿Cómo se llama?
I'm called_	Me llamo_
Go away!	¡Váyase!
Leave me alone	¡No me moleste!
I'm off/leaving	Me voy

Questions

Where is_?	¿Dónde está_?
I should like	Me gustaría/quisiera
How much does it cost?	¿Cuánto vale?/¿cuánto cuesta?
When?	¿Cuándo?/¿ a qué hora?
When does the bus leave/arrive?	¿A qué hora sale/llega el autobus?
Why?	¿Por qué?
How do I get to_?	¿Cómo llego a_?
Do you have_?	¿Tiene_?
Are there any rooms tonight	¿Hay cuartos para esta noche?
Bring me the bill, please	La cuenta por favor
Can I have my change, please	Deme el cambio, por favor
Can I make a phone call?	¿Puedo llamar por teléfono?

Basics

police (policeman)	la policía (el policía)/ el carabinero
hotel	el hotel (la pensión, el residencial, el hospedaje)
room	el cuarto/ la habitación
single/double	sencilla/doble
with two beds	con dos camas
bathroom/toilet	el baño
hot/cold water	el agua caliente/fría
toilet paper	el papel higiénico
restaurant	el restaurant
post office/ telephone office	el correo/el centro de llamadas
supermarket	el supermercado
market	el mercado
bank	el banco
exchange house	la casa de cambio
exchange rate	la tasa de cambio
travellers' cheques	los travelers/ los cheques de viajero
cash	el efectivo
breakfast	el desayuno
lunch	el almuerzo/la comida
dinner/supper	la cena
meal	la comida
drink	la bebida
mineral water	el agua mineral
beer	la cerveza
with/without sugar	con/sin azúcar

Getting around

on the left/right	a la izquierda/ derecha
straight on	derecho
bus station	la terminal (terrestre)
bus stop	la parada/el paradero
interurban bus	el bus/el camión
urban bus	el micro
train/(train) station	el tren/la estación (de tren)
airport	el aeropuerto
aeroplane	el avión
ticket	el boleto
ticket office	la taquilla
luggage	el equipaje
rucksack	la mochila
bag	la bolsa

Time

What time is it?	*¿Qué hora es?*
At half past two	*A las dos y media*
Ten minutes	*Diez minutos*
Five hours	*Cinco horas*
It's one o'clock	*Es la una*
It's seven o'clock	*Son las siete*
It's ten to seven	*Son las siete menos diez*
It's 6.20	*Son las seis y veinte*

Medical terms

It hurts here	*Me duele aquí*
I have a headache /stomach ache	*Tengo dolor de cabeza/de estómago*
I don't feel well	*No me siento bien*
I need a doctor	*Necesito asistencia médica*

Numbers

	Spanish		
1	*uno/una*	11	*once*
2	*dos*	12	*doce*
3	*tres*	13	*trece*
4	*cuatro*	14	*catorce*
5	*cinco*	15	*quince*
6	*seis*	16	*dieciséis*
7	*siete*	17	*diecisiete*
8	*ocho*	18	*dieciocho*
9	*nueve*	19	*diecinueve*
10	*diez*	20	*veinte*

21	*veintiuno*
30	*treinte*
40	*cuarenta*
50	*cincuenta*
60	*sesenta*
70	*setenta*
80	*ochenta*
90	*noventa*
100	*cien*
1000	*mil*

Days/months

Monday	*lunes*		March	*marzo*
Tuesday	*martes*		April	*abril*
Wednesday	*miércoles*		May	*mayo*
Thursday	*jueves*		June	*junio*
Friday	*viernes*		July	*julio*
Saturday	*sábado*		August	*agosto*
Sunday	*domingo*		September	*septiembre*
			October	*octubre*
January	*enero*		November	*noviembre*
February	*febrero*		December	*diciembre*

Key verbs

To go	***Ir***
I go	*voy*
you go	*vas*
s/he/it goes	*va*
you (formal) go	*va*
we go	*vamos*
they/you (plural) go	*van*

To be (in a permanent state)	***Ser***
I am	*soy*
you are	*eres*
s/he/it is	*es*
you (formal) are	*es*
we are	*somos*
they/you (plural) are	*son*

To have	***Tener***
I have	*tengo*
you have	*tienes*
s/he/it has	*tiene*
you (formal) have	*tiene*
we have	*tenemos*
they/you (plural) have	*tienen*

To be (positional or temporary state)	***Estar***
I am	*estoy*
you are	*estás*
s/he/it is	*está*
you (formal) are	*está*
we are	*estamos*
they/you (plural) are	*están*

Index

Map index

Footnotes

Shorts index

Advertisers' index

Footnotes

Acknowledgements

This is the third year of updates for me and it now seems to be just about under control. As ever there is so much more work that could be done than is managed given that the time required to annually update the *Central America and Mexico Handbook* is the publishing equivalent of estimating the length of a piece of string. One of the many positive experiences that come out of the enjoyable task is meeting and working with so many people who are passionately involved in the region.

Naturally readers' letters play a big part in the process pointing out errors (sometimes painfully), making suggestions and pointers to the way 'things' are going. From one-line snippets to comprehensive overviews all are much appreciated and credited on *Travellers' Letters*.

As in previous years, the *Handbook* owes a great deal to the inherited work and guiding hand of Ben Box and Sarah Cameron.

Normally saved till the end, a particular thanks to Felicity Laughton in the Footprint office who has toiled over several re-orderings, entertaining and supporting the various ideas, which hopefully make the information in the guidebook more accessible

In Mexico thanks go, as ever, to John Gibbs of Mexport UK in Mexico City, who kept on top of developments in the capital, providing a finger on the pulse that only residence provides and welcoming me to private celebrations while visiting the capital. Carolyn Bointon did a fantastic job taking in much of the country from Mexico City east to the Yucután Peninsula. Also thanks to the many people I met while travelling overland from Tijuana, through the Baja Peninsula to Mexico City at the end of 2001. Similar to the journey I first did back in 1993, it's amazing to see how some things have changed while others are exactly as I remembered.

Guatemala owes its currency to the fair hand of Claire Boobbyer, author of *Guatemala Handbook*.

Belize received updates from a number of sources – thanks as ever go out to the several who responded and the anonymous individual who coordinated the effort despite the obstacles that nature seemed determine to put in the way.

El Salvador once again received contributions from a range of sources, including a couple of trips by Andre Vltchek, and my own visit to the country. Specifically many thanks to Jo Harrington for much detail on El Salvador and useful snippets on Mexico.

Andre also visited Honduras, travelling through much of the country with supporting information provided by the watchful eye of Howard Rosenzweig and several other smaller contributions from others in the country.

After creating the *Nicaragua Handbook* Richard Leonardi kindly contributed his work, and considerable updates to the regional guide ensuring travellers to this increasingly popular country get the most up-to-date information.

Costa Rica got a once over building on the *Costa Rica Handbook* along with several useful regional updates.

Finally Panama got a thorough work over by the industrious feet, eyes and cartographic skills of Simon Harvey who not only travelled extensively through the country, but also provided useful updates, contributions and advice on Costa Rica, Honduras and Guatemala.

For specialist contributions this year, or in previous years, we would like to thank: Nigel Gallop for music and dance; John Alton for details on cargo ship cruises; Binka and Robin le Breton for motoring; Ashley Rawlings for motorcycling; Hallam Murray for cycling; Hilary Bradt for hiking and trekking; David Fishlow for language and Mark Eckstein for responsible tourism. The health section was written by Dr Charlie Easmon MBBS MRCP MSc Public Health DTM&H DoccMed, Director of *Travel Screening Services*.

The day-to-day contribution of many in the office in Bath is greatly appreciated. In particular to Rachel Fielding for the concise and pointed guidance, and agreeing to the skewed deadline for this years' *Handbook* which allowed me to complete a first descent of a little known river in southeast Bolivia. Thanks also to Footprint for their personal support for that expedition, details of which can be seen at www.coursingtheparapeti.com

Finally, thanks to the support of family and friends who may once again have experienced the familiar feeling of scratching temples and wondering where I had disappeared to this time.

Footnotes

Travellers' letters

Travelling through Central America and Mexico you're going to be bombarded with experiences – good and bad. While it's up to you to decide where you go and what you do, we've tried to provide information about some of the basics by keeping the information up to date. Many people help with the task by writing to us with information about new hotels that have opened, gone downhill, got refurbished, restaurants that provide a fresh change to the usual, new bus routes and so on.

Many thanks to the travellers who have taken the time to write to us by post or, increasingly, by email over the last year.

Imran Ahmed, UK (Gua); Christian Albaret, Saint Martin de Vinoux, France (Mex, Gua, Bel); Elin Folkesson and Lars Alberg, Sweden (Nic); Nancy Alfaro, Costa Rica (Cos); Dror Alumot, Israel (Mex); Massimo Amaducci, Italy (Nic); Gustavo Araya, Liberia, Costa Rica (Cos); Tobias Baechle, Loeffingen, Germany (Mex, Gua, Bel, El Sal, Hon); Manuel Bichsel, (Mex, Gua); Christa Bischof, Munich, Germany (Cos); Mike Boon (Mex, Gua); Christophe Bouskela (Mex); Rodney Boyd (Mex, Gua); Janey Byrne (Gua); Nicole and Pascal Burri, Italy (Mex); Robert Card, Garretson, USA (Mex, Gua); Danilo Negri & Suzanne Charkas, Victoria, Australia (Hon, Nic, Cos, Pan); Wayne Chinook, USA (Mex); Simon Dale - painfully - by email; Shazza Davies, UK (Mex); Alex de Vet, The Netherlands (Mex); Gilly Dorey, United Kingdom (Cos, Pan); Aidan Doyle, Melbourne, Australia (Mex, Gua, Hon, Cos); Noah Duguid (Hon); Philip Dundas, Sydney, Australia (Hon, Nic, Cos, Pan - sounds like a great bike ride); Charlotte Durand, UK (Mex); Markus Eberl (Mex); Corrine Ennulat, Oberwil, Switzerland (Mex); Roi Faust (Mex, Gua); Jacky Feetz, Germany (Mex, Gua, Hon); B & E Feldbrugge, Amsterdam, The Netherlands (Cos); Steve Frankham, UK (Nic); Pedro Garcia, (Pan); Nicolas Gonze, Belgium (Mex, Gua); Nicholas Good, (Mex); Michael Green, Tamworth, UK (Hon, Nic); Jan Guinovart, Barcelona, Catalonia (Gua, Nic); Malcolm and Jenny Gunter, Tewkesbury, UK (Mex); Anke Kertscher and Peter Hahn, Berlin, Germany (Mex, Gua, Bel); Jo Harrington, Portsmouth, UK (Mex, El Sal); Jan Henrik Mo, Norway (Cos); C Hertog (Mex); Judith Hill, New York (Pan); Josefin Hoenders, The Netherlands (Nic); Ursina Akermann and Markus Howald, Germany (Mex, Gua, Bel); Irene Huber, Switzerland (Mex, Gua, Pan); Ian Jackson, UK (Mex); Ryan Johnston (Mex); Raymundo Kaser, Switzerland (Nic); Yonatan Klein, Israel (Mex); Andrej Kolaja (Mex, Gua, Bel); Ruediger Arnold and Tanja Koradin, Germany (Mex); James Lakey, London, UK (Mex, Nic); Paul Larkin, Ireland (Nic); John Lewis, London, UK (Mex, Cos, Nic); Tod Lokey (Cos); William Loukides, Toronto, Canada (Mex, Gua); Paul M Mack, Warrenville, USA (Gua, Bel); Louis Mamie, Germany (Mex); Bob Makransky, Guatemala (Gua); Ole Mandrup, Denmark (Gua, Hon, Nic, Cos, Pan); Karin Mayer, Germany (Cos); Marc Monsarrat, Burnaby, Canada (Gua, Bel, Nic); Benjamin Moser, New York, USA ; Dr Martin, Mowforth Plymouth, UK (Nic); Tova Payne, Canada (Cos); Monique Peeters (Gua); Dr Jens Peglau, Germany (Mex); Lennart Poettering, Germany (Mex); Judith Polak (Mex); Matthew Price, Lanquin, Guatemala (Gua); Jeannine Rauchentstein (Gua); Jean Reagan, USA (Cos); Ralph Regenfelder, Austria (Mex); Doug Rhodes, Mexico (Mex); Jorge Rodrigues, Alajuela, Costa Rica (Cos); Hansruedi Ruchti, Switzerland (Pan); Norbert Tobaben and Esther Saavedra, Barcelona, Spain, and Hamburg, Germany (Mex); Alessandro Sacerdoti (Mex); Uwe Sacherer, Germany (Mex); Livio Sardara, Costa Rica (Cos); Liliana and Emil Schmid (Cos); Sascha Schmidt, Rüdesheim, Germany, (Nic, Cos); Judit Segarra, Spain (Cos); D Singl (Pan); Rachel Smith, Liverpool, UK (Mex, Nic); Karola Stolk, The Netherlands (Pan); Philippe Studer, Switzerland (Mex); Kaija Tittanen, Suomi, Finland (Nic); Alejandro Tomas (Mex); Esther Trachsel (Cos); Jeroen Uittenbogaard (Cos); Kurt Van de Casteele, Belgium (Gua); G & R Vereecke, Zellick, Belgium (Mex, Gua); Joerg Viereck, Norway (Mex, Gua, Hon, Cos); Margaret Wardlow, Sheffield, UK (Mex, Gua, Bel - couldn't have asked for more detail, many thanks); Toby Waterman (Mex); Vicki West, Bristol, UK (Mex, Gua); Bernard Woznik, Germany (Mex); Sarit Zadok, USA (Nic); Maria Zeledon, Esteli, Nicaragua (Nic); Christa Jongeling and Jelle Zikkenheiner Dordect, The Netherlands (Mex - thanks for the comments about kicking ass); Lani & Michael (Cos); Levi, Buenos Aires, Argentina (Pan); Melanie and Tina (Mex); Peter (Mex); Terry - Unicorn1 (Nic); Linda Nye (Gua).

Also many thanks to the hoteliers, restaurateurs, tour operators and others mentioned in the *Central America and Mexico Handbook* who have kindly taken the time to inform us when their contact details have changed. While we are unlikely to include the details of a new establishment without a specific recommendation, or, ideally, a visit, it is very useful to receive details about changes in telephone numbers, emails, addresses, services provided, prices and so on. Thanks.

Footprint feedback

We try as hard as we can to make each Footprint Handbook as up-to-date and accurate as possible but, of course, things always change. Many people email or write to us – with corrections, new information, or simply comments. If you want to let us know about your experiences and adventures – be they good, bad or ugly – then don't delay; we're dying to hear from you. And please try to include all the relevant details and juicy bits. Your help will be greatly appreciated, especially by other travellers. In return we will send you details about our special guidebook offer.

email Footprint at:
cam2003_online@footprintbooks.com

or write to:

Elizabeth Taylor
Footprint Handbooks
6 Riverside Court
Lower Bristol Road
Bath
BA2 3DZ
UK

Map symbols

Administration

⌒ International border
⌒ State/province border
□ CAPITAL CITY
○ Other town

Roads and travel

Urban

Main through route
Main street
Minor street
Pedestrianized street
→ One way street

Regional

National highway
including Pan-
American Highway
Paved road
Unpaved all-weather road
(including unpaved
sections of Pan-
American Highway)
Seasonal unpaved
road/track
Footpath
Railway with station

Sights and services

■ Sleeping
● Eating
▫ Sight
Building
🅿 Parking
Steps
Park, garden, stadium
Fortified wall
✈ Airport
🚌 Bus station
Ⓜ Metro station
✚ Hospital
Market
🏛 Museum

✠✠ Cathedral, church
✡ Synagogue
⛽ Petrol station
Ⓟ Police station
Ⓢ Bank
✉ Post office
♪ Telephone office
@ Internet
🛈 Tourist office
⤢ Bridge
⁘ Archaeological site
✾ Viewing point
♦ National park, wildlife
sanctuary
▲ Camp site
⌂ Refuge
🌴 Mangrove
🌴 Palm trees
 Detail map
Related map

Water features

River
Lake, reservoir, tank
Seasonal marshland
Sand bank, beach
Ocean
Waterfall
Ferry
⛵ Boat anchorage
Windsurfing

Topographical features

Contours (approx),
rock outcrop
△ Mountain
Volcano
Mountain pass
Gorge
Escarpment
Salt flat

Weights and measures

Weight

1 kilogram = 2.205 pounds
1 pound = 0.454 kilograms

Capacity

1 litre = 0.220 gallons
1 gallon = 4.546 litres
1 pint = 0.863 litres

Length

1 metre = 1.094 yards
1 yard = 0.914 metres

1 kilometre = 0.621 miles
1 mile = 1.609 kilometres

Your Caribbean delight set in mysterious Mayan majesty

The Caracol Village Resort is located on the Riviera Maya (Playa del Carmen), the eastern coast of the Yucatán Peninsula.

This environmentally friendly Caribbean beachfront resort lies at the edge of an exotic jungle, surrounded by mangroves and natural lagoons.

At the 4 star Caracol Village Resort vacationers enjoy the beauty of the Caribbean and the ageless wonders of the Mayan civilization. The all inclusive resort has over 366 rooms, 4 restaurants, 3 bars, 2 swimming pools and a full range of facilities and activities for a complete vacation.

Caracol Village Resort,
Carretera Cancun-Chetumal Kilometro 295,
Playa del Carmen, Quintana Roo, Mexico 77710.
Telephone (52) 998-873-4444
Fax (52) 998-873-4446
E-mail reservas@caracolvillage.com
Visit us at www.caracolvillage.com

Central America & Mexico

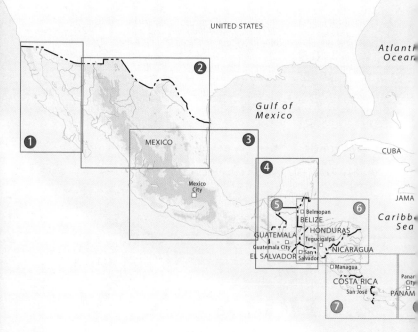

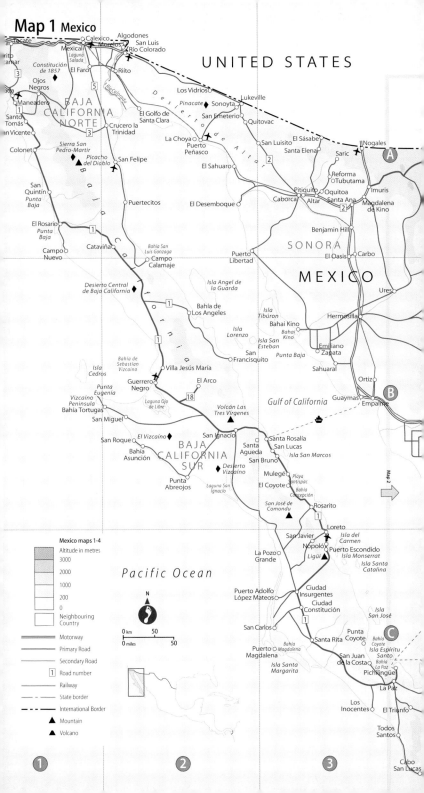

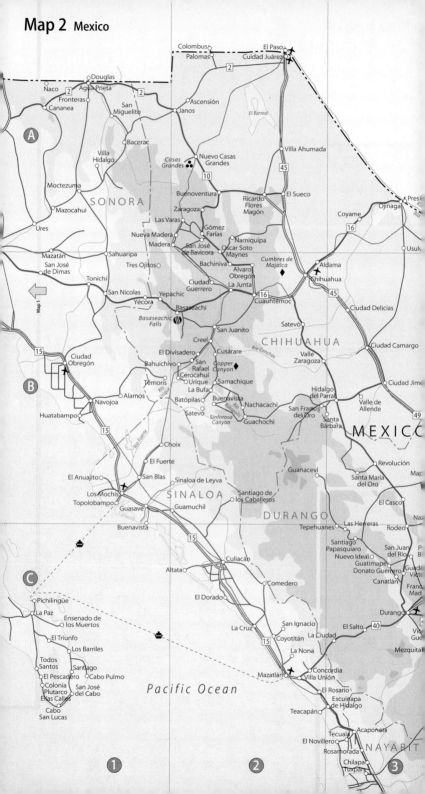

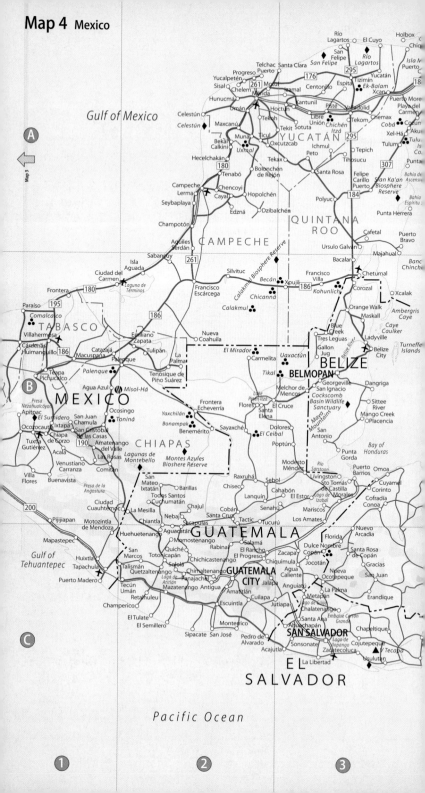

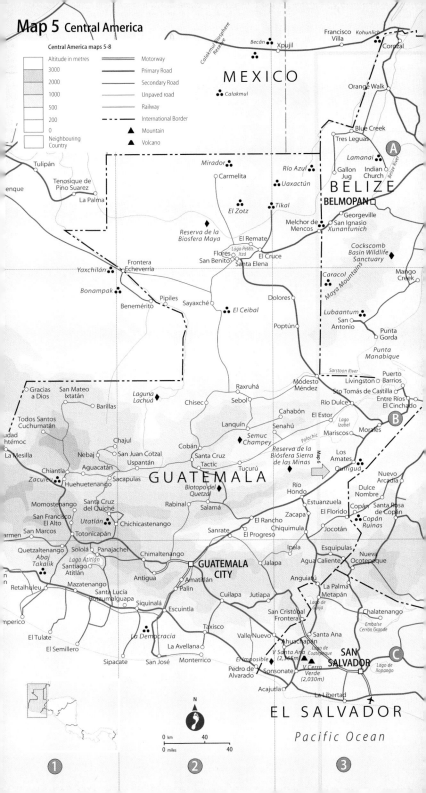

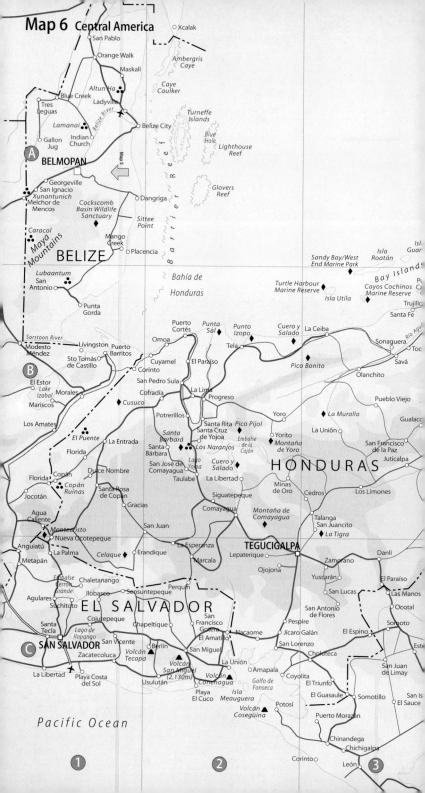

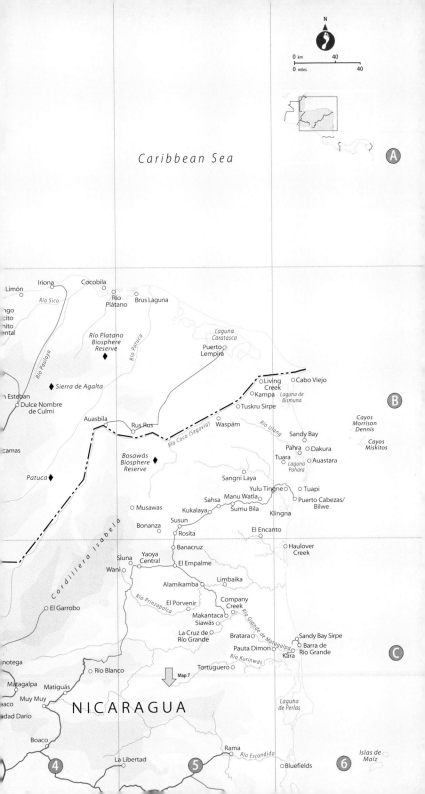

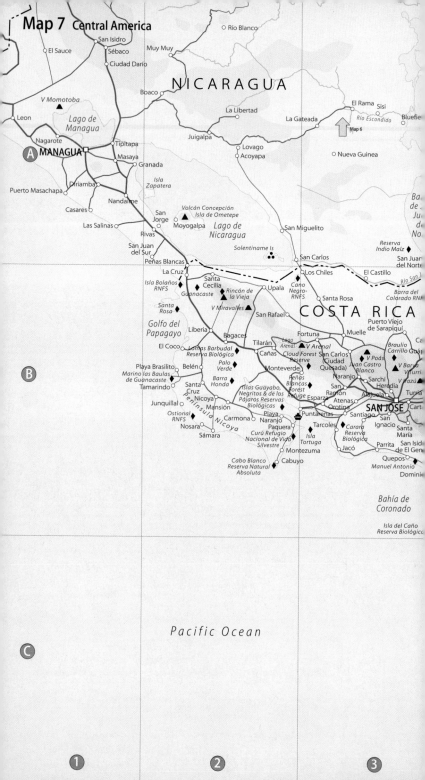

Map 8 Central America

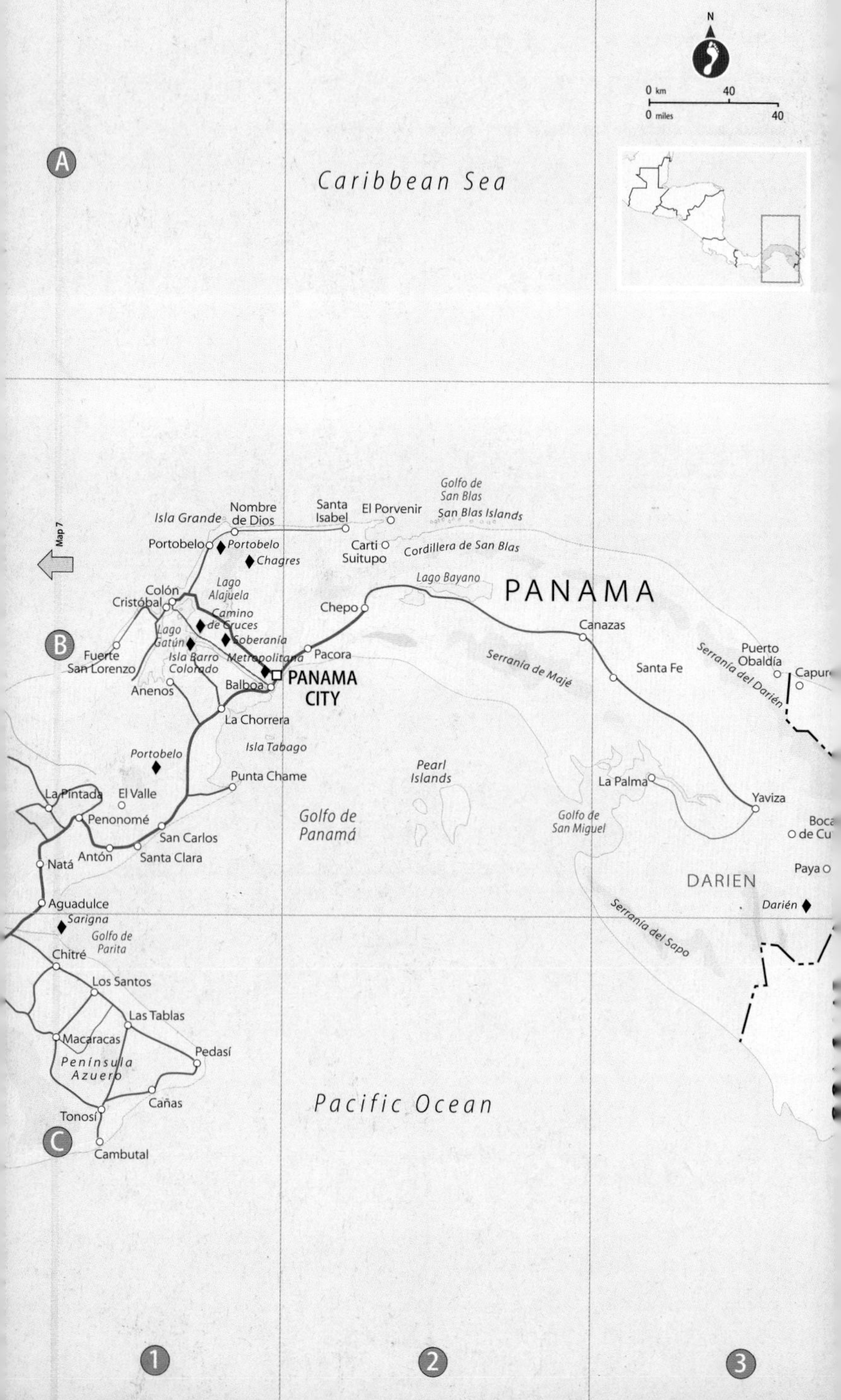

N

0 km 40
0 miles 40

Caribbean Sea

A

B

C

1 **2** **3**

Isla Grande
Nombre de Dios
Santa Isabel
El Porvenir
Golfo de San Blas
San Blas Islands
Portobelo
Portobelo
Chagres
Carti Suitupo
Cordillera de San Blas
Colón
Cristóbal
Lago Alajuela
Camino de Cruces
Chepo
Lago Bayano
PANAMA
Canazas
Puerto Obaldía
Capur
Fuerte San Lorenzo
Lago Gatún
Isla Barro Colorado
Soberania
Metropolitana
Pacora
Serranía de Majé
Santa Fe
Serranía del Darién
Anenos
Balboa
PANAMA CITY
La Chorrera
Isla Tabago
Portobelo
Punta Chame
Pearl Islands
La Palma
Yaviza
Boca de Cu
La Pintada
El Valle
Golfo de Panamá
Golfo de San Miguel
Paya
Penonomé
San Carlos
Santa Clara
DARIEN
Antón
Natá
Serranía del Sapo
Darién
Aguadulce
Sarigna
Golfo de Parita
Chitré
Los Santos
Las Tablas
Macaracas
Pedasí
Península Azuero
Pacific Ocean
Tonosí
Cañas
Cambutal

Map 7